Contemporary Authors

Contemporary Authors

A BIO-BIBLIOGRAPHICAL GUIDE TO
CURRENT AUTHORS AND THEIR WORKS

CLARE D. KINSMAN

Editor

volumes 17-20

first revision

GALE RESEARCH COMPANY • BOOK TOWER • DETROIT, MICHIGAN 48226

CONTEMPORARY AUTHORS

Published by
Gale Research Company, Book Tower, Detroit, Michigan 48226
Each Year's Volumes Are Cumulated and Revised About Five Years Later

Frederick G. Ruffner, *Publisher*   James M. Ethridge, *Editorial Director*

Clare D. Kinsman, *General Editor, Contemporary Authors*

Clare D. Kinsman, *Editor*
Christine Nasso, *Associate Editor*
Jane Bowden, Robin Farbman, Frances Carol Locher,
Larry J. Moore, Alexander James Roman, Nancy M. Rusin,
and Frank Michael Soley, *Assistant Editors*
Laura Bryant, *Operations Supervisor*
Daphne Cox, *Production Manager*

EDITORIAL ASSISTANTS

Ellen Koral, Norma Sawaya, and Shirley Seip

Copyright © 1965, 1966, 1976
GALE RESEARCH COMPANY
Library of Congress Card Number 62-52046
ISBN 0-8103-0032-X

PREFACE

VOLUME 17-20, FIRST REVISION

This volume represents a complete revision and a consolidation into one alphabet of biographical material which originally appeared in *Contemporary Authors,* volumes 17-18, published in 1967, and volumes 19-20, published in 1968. The revision is up-to-date, in most cases, through 1975.

In preparing the revision, the following are the major steps which have been taken:

1) *Every sketch has been submitted to the authors concerned,* if still living, and all changes requested which were within the scope and purpose of *Contemporary Authors* have been made.

2) *The editors have attempted to verify present address, present position, and the bibliography* if authors have failed to submit changes or to approve sketches as still correct. A symbol (†) has been used to indicate those sketches appearing in this revision which have not been personally verified by their subjects.

3) *Additional research has been done on the bibliographies of many authors,* both to pick up publications which were not included in the previous versions of their sketches and to assure that all recent works have been included.

All sketches, therefore, should be regarded as "revised," even if they contain no changes, since the material in them has been approved as currently correct, or *CA* editors have made any possible changes in the absence of word from the author.

4) *"Sidelights" have been added to many listings* for prominent authors whose sketches did not include this material previously, and *"Sidelights"* for numerous other authors have been revised substantially.

As a result of these editorial procedures, the amount of new material in this volume is substantial, and, even after the deletions described below, the revised volume contains approximately the same number of pages as the two original volumes.

Series of Permanent Volumes Established
For Retired and Deceased Authors

A series of Permanent Volumes has been established as an adjunct to *Contemporary Authors,* in order to avoid reprinting in future revisions the sketches of authors which will normally not require further change.

Therefore, the editors are omitting from this revision and from future revisions two classes of authors—first, persons now deceased, and second, persons who are approaching or who have passed normal retirement age and who have not reported in revising their listings that they have published books recently or expect to do so in the future.

Cumulative Index Should Always be Consulted

As always, the cumulative index published in alternate volumes of *CA* will continue to be the user's guide to the location of an individual author's listing. Authors not included in this revision will be indicated in the cumulative index as having appeared in specific original volumes of *CA* (for the benefit of those who do not hold Permanent Volumes), *and* as having their finally revised sketches listed in a specific Permanent Volume.

The editors believe that this revision plan will prove to be not only convenient but over the long run will be to the financial advantage of libraries, as well. Because the plan removes from the revision cycle material which no longer needs periodic review and reprinting, many expenses which would have to be reflected in selling prices will be avoided.

As always, suggestions from users on revision or any other aspect of *CA* will be welcomed.

CONTEMPORARY AUTHORS

† Indicates that author has not personally verified the entry in this edition.

ABBOTT, Anthony S. 1935-

PERSONAL: Born January 7, 1935, in San Francisco, Calif.; son of Howard Johnson and Frances (Hayden) Abbott; married Susan Dudley, August 27, 1960; children: David, Stephen, Andrew. *Education:* Princeton University, A.B. (magna cum laude), 1957; Harvard University, A.M., 1960, Ph.D., 1962. *Religion:* Episcopalian. *Home address:* Box 2136, Davidson, N.C. 28036. *Office:* Department of English, Davidson College, Davidson, N.C. 28036.

CAREER: Bates College, Lewiston, Me., instructor in English, 1961-64; Davidson College, Davidson, N.C., assistant professor of English, 1964-67, associate professor of English, 1967—. *Member:* Phi Beta Kappa. *Awards, honors:* Thomas Jefferson Award from Davidson College, 1969.

WRITINGS: Shaw and Christianity, Seabury, 1965.

WORK IN PROGRESS: Short stories, poems, and a book on North Carolina's prisons.

* * *

ABBOTT, John J(amison) 1930-

PERSONAL: Born March 17, 1930, in Boston, Mass.; son of Robert Emmet (a tobacconist) and Cathleen N. (Hoolihan) Abbott; married Rachel Rappaport (a model), July 12, 1956; children: James Connolly, Michael Collins, Nora Cathleen, Avram Stern, Mary Roberta. *Education:* Fordham University, A.B., 1951; Trinity College, Dublin, D. Phil., 1953. *Politics:* Irish Nationalist.

CAREER: Full-time professional writer. *Member:* International Nationalist Brotherhood, Clan na Gael, Anti-Partition League, League for the Restoration of Cilician Armenia, Balkan Friendship Society, Flat Earth Society, Anti-Digit-Dialing League, Ahfen Yahm (North American corresponding member).

WRITINGS: The Truth About Macedonia, Warlock Press, 1958; *Rebel's Cry!,* Barnstable, 1961; *The Holy Light of Freedom,* Barnstable, 1962; *Fell's Guide to Investing in U.S. and Foreign Coins,* Fell, 1965. Contributor to journals.

WORK IN PROGRESS: A biography of David Raziel, co-founder of the Palestinian Stern Gang, tentatively titled *With Bible and Gun.*

SIDELIGHTS: Abbott told *CA:* "With the exception of the coin investment book, my writing has been wholly political, with a focus upon small and little-known nationalist groups."†

* * *

ABEL, Alan (Irwin) 1928-
(Julius Bristol)

PERSONAL: Born August 2, 1928, in Zanesville, Ohio; son of Louis and Ida (Hamberger) Abel; married Jeanne Allgeier (a writer), September 11, 1959. *Education:* Ohio State University, B.S., 1950. *Home:* 1 Crow Hollow Lane, Westport, Conn. 06880. *Agent:* Bruce Spencer, 507 Fifth Ave., New York, N.Y. 10017.

CAREER: Writer; lecturer at 1,500 schools and colleges between 1950 and 1965; *San Francisco Chronicle,* San Francisco, Calif., weekly columnist, 1965—. *Military service:* U.S. Army Air Forces, 1943-46.

WRITINGS: The Crazy Ads, Citadel, 1960; *The Great American Hoax* (also serialized by the *New York Post*), Trident, 1966 (published in England as *Yours for Decency,* Elek, 1967); (compiler with wife, J. A. Abel) *The Button Book,* Citadel, 1967; *Confessions of a Hoaxer,* Macmillan, 1971; *The Fallacy of Creative Thinking,* McClelland & Stewart, 1972; (with J. A. Abel) *Is There Sex After Death?* (screenplay), Bantam, 1975.

WORK IN PROGRESS: A book, *Jester at Large;* a screenplay and a television series, both comedies.

SIDELIGHTS: The Great American Hoax is the story of SINA (Society for Indecency to Naked Animals), a fake organization with which Abel fooled the *Los Angeles Times,* the *San Francisco Chronicle,* the *San Francisco Examiner,* Walter Cronkite and CBS News (as well as ABC and NBC News), the *New York Times, Life* Magazine, the *Baltimore Sun,* the *Chicago Daily News,* Jack Paar, Les Crane (and dozens of other newspapers and television personalities) for nearly five years. The *Detroit Free Press* reported: "Having turned a practical joke into a minor hoax on the 'Today' show in 1959, Abel decided to see how far he could go." He hired pickets, printed leaflets, established an answering service, and invented G. Clifford Prout, whose supposed $400,000 bequest to SINA initiated the Society's campaign. Thus Abel created Mr.

Prout and his organization "to urge all good people to clothe their animals with proper covering so that vital areas will not be observed by the human naked eye." (Abel allegedly contrived the hoax after watching "the anguished reaction of a lady motorist to a scene of bovine love on the highway.")

Abel never fooled the *Insider's Newsletter, Time,* and *Newsweek,* but even as late as 1965 some journals, including the *New York Daily News,* the largest newspaper in the country, were conscientiously writing of "a weird crusade to put pants on pets."

The pseudonym Julius Bristol was used for an article in *Golf Digest* in which Abel explained his "revolutionary putting techniques." His agent notes: "Naturally, he has never been on a golf course in his life."

Alan Abel directed, wrote, produced (with his wife, Jeanne), and starred in "Is There Sex After Death." A documentary-style spoof released by Abel-Child Productions in 1971.

The Great American Hoax has been purchased for filming.

BIOGRAPHICAL/CRITICAL SOURCES: New Yorker, September 15, 1951; *Detroit Free Press,* July 3, 1966.

*   *   *

ABEL, Jeanne 1937-
(Yetta Bronstein)

PERSONAL: Born February 14, 1937, in Cincinnati, Ohio; daughter of Mark (a salesman) and Mildred (Feige) Allgeier; married Alan Abel (a writer), September 11, 1959. *Education:* University of Cincinnati, student, 1955-58. *Politics:* Democrat. *Home:* 1 Crow Hollow Lane, Westport, Conn. 06880. *Agent:* Bruce Spencer, 507 Fifth Ave., New York, N.Y. 10017.

WRITINGS: (Under pseudonym Yetta Bronstein) *The President I Almost Was,* Hawthorn, 1966; (compiler with husband, Alan Abel) *The Button Book,* Citadel, 1967; (with Alan Abel) *Is There Sex After Death?* (screenplay), Bantam, 1975. Author of "The Last Man" (screenplay), produced by Arthur Storch, 1966.

SIDELIGHTS: Jeanne Abel wrote, produced, and directed "Is There Sex After Death?" with her husband. The film a documentary-style comedy was released by Abel-Child Productions in 1971.

*   *   *

ABERNATHY, (M.) Elton 1913-

PERSONAL: Born April 4, 1913, in Brady, Tex.; son of Miles Edward (a teacher) and Millard (Woody) Abernathy; married Irene Lynn, June 1, 1940; children: Miles Lynn, Donald Allen. *Education:* Abilene Christian College, B.A., 1932; University of Iowa, M.A., 1937, Ph.D., 1940. *Politics:* Democrat. *Religion:* Church of Christ. *Home and office:* Southwest Texas State University, Marcos, Tex.

CAREER: Louisiana Polytechnic Institute, Ruston, assistant professor, 1938-46; Southwest Texas State University, San Marcos, professor of speech, 1947—. ARICANA (binational cultural center), Rosario, Argentina, director, 1964-66. *Military service:* U.S. Naval Reserve, 1944—, on active duty, 1943-46; now lieutenant commander. *Member:* Speech Association of America, Southern Speech Association (president, 1956), Texas Association of College Teachers (president, 1960).

WRITINGS: Fundamentals of Speech Communication,

W. C. Brown, 1958, 4th revision, 1975; *Advocate: A Manual of Persuasion,* McKay, 1964; *Directing Speech Activities,* University Press (Wolf, Tex.), 1970.

*   *   *

ABODAHER, David J. (Naiph) 1919-

PERSONAL: Surname is pronounced *Ab*-o-dar; born February 1, 1919, in Streator, Ill.; son of Simon George (a grocer) and Rose (Ayoub) Abodaher; married Lynda Haddad, September 16, 1945 (divorced); children: Lynda Anne, Mounir C. *Education:* Attended University of Notre Dame and University of Detroit. *Politics:* Independent (most often Democrat). *Religion:* Roman Catholic. *Home:* 24603 Walden Rd. E., Southfield, Mich. 48075.

CAREER: Program director or production manager of radio stations in Oklahoma City, Okla., 1938-40, Kalamazoo, Mich., 1940-41; radio director of advertising firms in Detroit, Mich., 1944-50; self-employed radio-television writer and producer, 1950-56; Simons-Michelson Co., Detroit, Mich., account executive and writer, 1956-59; Jam Handy Organization, Detroit, Mich., writer, 1959-61; free-lance writer, 1961-64; J. Walter Thompson Co., Detroit, Mich., writer, 1964-69; Kenyon and Eckhardt, Inc., Detroit, Mich., writer, 1969-70; A. R. Brasch Advertising, Inc., Detroit, Mich., writer, 1970-74; free-lance writer, 1974—. Radio chairman of Michigan War Finance Committee, 1944-50, and Detroit Retailers Public Service Committee, 1944-50. *Military service:* U.S. Army, Signal Corps, 1942-44; became staff sergeant.

WRITINGS: Under Three Flags: The Story of Gabriel Richard, Hawthorn, 1965; *Daniel Duluth: Explorer of the Northlands,* Kenedy, 1966; *Kosciuszko: Warrior on Two Continents,* Messner, 1968; *Casimir Pulaski: Freedom Fighter,* Messner, 1969; *Rebel on Two Continents: Thomas Meagher,* Messner, 1970; *French Explorers of North America,* Messner, 1970; *Mag Wheels and Racing Stripes,* Messner, 1973. *The Polish-Americans,* Messner, 1975; *The Compact Car Explosion,* Messner, 1975. Contributor of short stories to magazines. Wrote, produced, and directed half-hour color motion picture for Sisters of St. Joseph, Nazareth, Mich.; author of network radio features and documentaries, including "Famous Jury Trials" and "Smoke Dreams."

SIDELIGHTS: David Abodaher speaks Arabic, some French and Spanish. *Avocational interests:* Photography, sports.

*   *   *

ACHTEMEIER, Elizabeth (Rice) 1926-

PERSONAL: Born June 11, 1926, in Bartlesville, Okla; daughter of Francis Edgar (a petroleum engineer) and Ida (Schafer) Rice; married Paul John Achtemeier (a professor of New Testament), June 11, 1952; children: Paul Mark, Marie Louise. *Education:* Stephens College, A.A., 1946; Stanford University, B.A. (with great distinction), 1948; Union Theological Seminary, New York, N.Y., B.D. (summa cum laude), 1951; studied at University of Heidelberg and University of Basel, 1952-54; Columbia University, Ph.D. 1959. *Home:* 1508 Brookland Pkwy., Richmond, Va. 23227.

CAREER: Lancaster Theological Seminary of the United Church of Christ, Lancaster, Pa., visiting lecturer in Old Testament, 1959-71, adjunct professor of Old Testament, 1971-73; Union Theological Seminary in Virginia, Richmond, visiting Professor of homiletics, 1973—. Visiting professor, Gettysburg Lutheran Theological Seminary, 1968. Lecturer and preacher for church groups and conferences. *Member:* Society of Biblical Literature, Phi Beta Kappa.

WRITINGS: The Feminine Crisis in Christian Faith, Abingdon, 1965; *The Old Testament and the Proclamation of the Gospel,* Westminster, 1973; (contributor) Howard N. Bream, R. D. Heim, and C. A. Moore, editors, *A Light Unto My Path: Old Testament Studies in Honor of Jacob M. Myers,* Temple University Press, 1974.

With husband, Paul John Achtemeier: *The Old Testament Roots of our Faith,* Abingdon, 1962; *To Save All People,* United Church Press, 1967; *Proclamation-Epiphany: Aids for Interpreting the Lessons of the Church Year,* Fortress, 1973.

Contributor to *Interpreter's Dictionary of the Bible,* and to theological and biblical journals.

WORK IN PROGRESS: Research on Second Isaiah; a book on marriage and the family from a biblical perspective.

SIDELIGHTS: Elizabeth Achtemeier is competent in German and Hebrew and reads Greek.

* * *

ACHTEMEIER, Paul J(ohn) 1927-

PERSONAL: Born September 3, 1927, in Lincoln, Neb.; son of Arthur R. (a pastor) and Clara (Barnstein) Achtemeier; married Elizabeth Rice, June 11, 1952; children: Paul Mark, Marie Louise. *Education:* Elmhurst College, A.B., 1949; Union Theological Seminary, New York, N.Y., B.D., 1952, Th.D., 1958; additional study at University of Heidelberg, 1952-53, and University of Basel, 1953-54. *Politics:* Liberal Republican. *Home:* 1508 Brookland Parkway, Richmond, Va. 23227. *Office:* Union Theological Seminary, 3401 Brook Rd., Richmond, Va. 23227.

CAREER: Minister of United Church of Christ. Elmhurst College, Elmhurst, Ill., instructor in biblical literature and Greek, 1956-57; Lancaster Theological Seminary, Lancaster, Pa., assistant professor, 1957-59, associate professor, 1959-61, Kunz Professor of New Testament, 1961-73; Union Theological Seminary, Richmond, Va., professor of New Testament, 1973—. Tutor, Ecumenical Institute of World Council of Churches, 1963-64; visiting professor, Pittsburgh Theological Seminary, 1968, Lutheran Theological Seminary, Gettysburg, Pa., 1970-71 and 1971-72; Staley Distinguished Christian Scholar, Rollins College, 1972, and Northwest Christian College, 1973; Rosenstiel fellow, Notre Dame University, 1974. *Member:* American Theological Society, Catholic Biblical Society, Society of Biblical Literature (associate in council, 1972-74; chairman of synoptics section), Studiorum Novi Testamenti Societas, World Alliance of Reformed Churches (recording clerk, North American area, 1963-70), Reformed Roman Catholic Dialogue (member of world level). *Awards, honors:* Union Theological Seminary traveling fellowship, 1952.

WRITINGS—All with wife, Elizabeth R. Achtemeier, except as noted: *The Old Testament Roots of Our Faith,* Abingdon, 1962; *To Save All People,* United Church Press, 1967; *Epiphany,* Fortress, 1973; (sole author) *An Introduction to the New Hermeneutic,* Westminster Press, 1969; *Mark,* Fortress, 1975.

Contributor: Herman G. Stuempfle, editor, *Preaching in the Witnessing Community,* Fortress, 1973; *Aspects of Re-* *ligious Propaganda in Judaism and Early Christianity,* Notre Dame University Press, 1975.

Contributor to *Interpreter's Dictionary of the Bible* and to theological journals. Book review editor, *Theology and Life,* 1958-65; member of editorial board, *Interpretation* and *Journal of Biblical Literature;* member of advisory editorial board, *Religious Studies Review.*

WORK IN PROGRESS: A book for Westminster Press on hermeneutics; continuing research on the gospel of Mark, on magic and miracles in primitive Christianity and the Hellenistic world, and on problems of interpretation (hermeneutics).

SIDELIGHTS: Achtemeier is fluent in German and has reading knowledge of French and New Testament Greek, and a working knowledge of Hebrew and Latin. He has translated several theological books and articles. *Avocational interests:* Woodworking, sailing, gardening, financial affairs on national scene.

* * *

ADAIR, James R. 1923-

PERSONAL: Born February 2, 1923, in Asheville, N.C.; son of Radford Riden (a realtor) and Sue (Simkins) Adair; married Virginia George, July 4, 1959; children: Mary Sue and Martha Lou (twins). *Education:* Attended Bob Jones University and took courses at Biltmore Junior College and Northwestern University. *Religion:* Protestant. *Home:* 703 Webster St., Wheaton, Ill. 60187.

CAREER: Handyman, copy boy, and ticket agent at bus station; later, was a newspaper reporter in Asheville, N.C., 1943-45; Scripture Press Publications, Wheaton, Ill., editorial staff, 1945—, editorial director of Victor Books division, currently editing *Power for Living, Young Teen Power, Counselor,* and *FreeWay* (all Sunday school take-home papers). Scripture Press Foundation, member. *Awards, honors:* First prize in articles division, Midwestern Writers Conference, 1947, for "Ebony Samaritan."

WRITINGS: Saints Alive, Van Kampen Press, 1951; (editor) *God's Power Within,* Prentice-Hall, 1961; (editor with Ted Miller) *We Found Our Way Out,* Baker Book, 1964; (editor) *Teen With a Future,* Baker Book, 1965; (editor) *God's Power to Triumph,* Prentice-Hall, 1965; *The Old Lighthouse,* Moody, 1966; *The Man from Steamtown* (biography of F. Nelson Blount), Moody, 1967; (editor) *Tom Skinner: Top Man of the Lords and Other Stories,* Baker Book, 1967; *M. R. De Haan: The Man and His Ministry,* Zondervan, 1969; (editor) *Unhooked,* Baker Book, 1971; (editor) *Hooked on Jesus,* Baker Book, 1971; (editor) *Brothers Black,* Baker Book, 1973. Editor of *Pacific Garden Mission News.*

* * *

ADAM, Helen 1909-

PERSONAL: Born December 2, 1909, in Glasgow, Scotland; came to United States in 1939. *Education:* Educated in Scotland at Seymour Lodge, Navin Academy; attended University of Edinburgh, two years.

CAREER: Has done various odd jobs. Writer. *Awards, honors:* Ingram Merrill Award.

WRITINGS: The Queen O' Crow Castle, White Rabbit, 1958; *Ballads,* White Rabbit, 1961; *San Francisco's Burning* (play; produced at Judson Memorial Church, New York, 1966), Oannes (Berkeley), 1963; *Selected Poems and Ballads,* Helikon Press, 1974.

WORK IN PROGRESS: A musical play on a mystery theme; American folklore.

* * *

ADAMS, Charles J(oseph) 1924-

PERSONAL: Born April 24, 1924, in Houston, Tex.; son of Joseph Edward (a barber) and Viola (Terry) Adams; married Joanna Zofia Teslar, August 18, 1963. *Education:* Baylor University, B.A., 1947; University of Chicago, Ph.D., 1955. *Religion:* Protestant. *Home:* 445 Victoria Ave., Montreal, Quebec, Canada. *Office:* McGill University, Sherbrooke St., Montreal, Quebec, Canada.

CAREER: Princeton University, Princeton, N.J., instructor in the history of religions, 1953-54; McGill University, Montreal, Quebec, assistant professor, 1957-59, associate director of Institute of Islamic Studies, 1959-63, professor and director of Institute of Islamic Studies, 1963—. *Military service:* U.S. Army Air Forces, airborne radio operator, 1942-45. *Member:* American Society for the Study of Religion (vice-president), American Oriental Society, American Academy of Religion, Middle East Studies Association.

WRITINGS: (Editor) *A Reader's Guide to the Great Religions*, Free Press, 1965; (with Janet K. O'Dea and others) *Judaism, Christianity, and Islam*, Harper, 1972; (editor) *Iranian Civilization and Culture: Essays in Honor of the 2500th Anniversary of the Founding of the Persian Empire*, McGill-Queens University Press, 1973. Editor, "McGill Islamics Series."

WORK IN PROGRESS: Research on the history of Muslim India in the past two centuries.

SIDELIGHTS: Adams is proficient in Arabic, French, German, and Urdu. *Avocational interests:* Woodworking and traveling.

* * *

ADAMS, Graham, Jr. 1928-

PERSONAL: Born March 4, 1928, in New York, N.Y.; son of Graham and Jeannette K. Adams. *Education:* Williams College, B.A., 1948; Columbia University, Ph.D., 1962. *Office:* Department of History, Mount Allison University, Sackville, New Brunswick, Canada.

CAREER: King's College, University of Aberdeen, Aberdeen, Scotland, visiting lecturer, 1962-63; Barnard College, Columbia University, New York, N.Y., assistant professor of history, 1963-64; University of Missouri, Columbia, assistant professor of history, 1964-66; Wayne State University, Detroit, Mich., associate professor of history, 1966-67; Mount Allison University, Sackville, New Brunswick, professor of history, and head of department, 1967—. *Member:* American Historical Association, Canadian Historical Association, Organization of American Historians, Atlantic Association of Historians (president, 1974-75), Canadian Association for American Studies.

WRITINGS: Age of Industrial Violence, 1910-1915, Columbia University Press, 1966. Also author of series of lectures, "Elections Which Shaped Modern America," University of the Air, televised nationally in Canada. Contributor to *Dictionary of American Biography, American Historical Review, Canadian Historical Review, Canadian Journal of History, Labor History*, and *East Texas Journal of History*.

WORK IN PROGRESS: American history, 1877—, with particular interest in the Progressive period, 1900-1918, and New Deal, 1932-38; research in labor, violence, and industrial relations.

* * *

ADAMS, Harriet S(tratemeyer)
(Carolyn Keene)

PERSONAL: Born in New Jersey; daughter of Edward L. (an author) and Magdalene Stratemeyer; married Russell Vroom Adams (deceased); children: Russell Jr. (deceased), Patricia Adams Harr, Camilla Adams McClave, Edward Stratemeyer Adams. *Education:* Graduate of Wellesley College. *Office:* Stratemeyer Syndicate, 519 Main St., East Orange, N.J. 07018.

CAREER: Full-time professional writer, speaker, and seminar director. Partner in Stratemeyer Syndicate. Interests have included Sunday school teaching and writings, founding woman's club magazine, chairman of literature department, chairman of a college's fund-raising work for New Jersey, two years as Republican county committeewoman, Red Cross and Girl Scout work. *Member:* League of American Pen Women, New Jersey Woman's Press Club, New Jersey Wellesley Club (founder and first president; class treasurer), Zonta, Business and Professional Women's Club, New York Wellesley Club. *Awards, honors:* Two citations from New Jersey Institute of Technology, for "Nancy Drew" series and *Nancy Drew Cookbook*: certificate of merit from American Red Cross.

WRITINGS—Under pseudonym Carolyn Keene; published by Grosset, except as noted: "Dana Girls" series: *By the Light of the Study Lamp*, 1934; *Secret at Lone Tree Cottage*, 1934; *In the Shadow of the Tower*, 1934; *Three-Cornered Mystery*, 1935; *Secret at the Hermitage*, 1936; *Circle of Footprints*, 1937; *Mystery of the Locked Room*, 1938; *Clue in the Cobweb*, 1939; *Secret at the Gatehouse*, 1940; *Mysterious Fireplace*, 1941; *Clue of the Rusty Key*, 1942; *Portrait in the Sand*, 1943; *Secret in the Old Well*, 1944.

Clue in the Ivy, 1952; *Secret of the Jade Ring*, 1953; *Mystery at the Crossroads*, 1954; *Ghost in the Gallery*, 1955, revised edition, 1975; *Clue of the Black Flower*, 1956; *Winking Ruby Mystery*, 1957, revised edition, 1974; *Secret of the Swiss Chalet*, 1958, revised edition, 1973; *Haunted Lagoon*, 1959, revised edition, 1973; *Mystery of the Bamboo Bird*, 1960, revised edition, 1973; *Sierra Gold Mystery*, 1961, revised edition, 1973; *Secret of Lost Lake*, 1963, revised edition, 1974; *Mystery of the Stone Tiger*, 1963, revised edition, 1972; *Riddle of the Frozen Fountain*, 1964, revised edition, 1972; *Secret of the Silver Dolphin*, 1965, revised edition, 1972; *Mystery of the Wax Queen*, 1966, revised edition, 1972; *Secret of the Minstrel's Guitar*, 1967, revised edition, 1972; *Phantom Surfer*, 1968, revised edition, 1972; *The Curious Coronation*, in press.

"Nancy Drew" series: *Secret of the Old Clock*, 1930, revised edition, 1959; *Hidden Staircase*, 1930, revised edition, 1959; *Bungalow Mystery*, 1930, revised edition, 1960; *Mystery at Lilac Inn*, 1930, revised edition, 1961; *Secret of Shadow Rancho*, 1931, revised edition, 1965; *Secret of Red Gate Farm*, 1931, revised edition, 1961; *Clue in the Diary*, 1932, revised edition, 1962; *Nancy's Mysterious Letter*, 1932, revised edition, 1968; *Sign of the Twisted Candles*, 1933, revised edition, 1968; *Password to Larkspur Lane*, 1933, revised edition, 1966; *Clue of the Broken Locket*, 1934, revised edition, 1965; *Message in the Hollow Oak*, 1935, revised edition, 1972; *Mystery of the Ivory Charm*,

1936, revised edition, 1974; *Whispering Statue*, 1937, revised edition, 1970; *Haunted Bridge*, 1937, revised edition, 1972; *Clue of the Tapping Heels*, 1939, revised edition 1969; *Mystery of the Brass Bound Trunk*, 1940; *Mystery at the Moss-Covered Mansion*, 1941, revised edition, 1971; *Quest of the Missing Map*, 1942, revised edition, 1969; *Clue in the Jewel Box*, 1943, revised edition, 1972; *Secret in the Old Attic*, 1944, revised edition, 1970; *Clue in the Crumbling Wall*, 1945, revised edition, 1973; *Mystery of the Tolling Bell*, 1946, revised edition, 1973; *Clue in the Old Album*, 1947; *Ghost of Blackwood Hall*, 1948, revised edition, Low, 1967; *Clue of the Leaning Chimney*, 1949, revised edition, 1967.

Secret of the Wooden Lady, 1950, revised edition, 1967; *Clue of the Black Keys*, 1951, revised edition, 1968; *Mystery at the Ski Jump*, 1952, revised edition, 1968; *Clue of the Velvet Mask*, 1953, revised edition, 1969; *Ringmaster's Secret*, 1953, revised edition, 1974; *Scarlet Slipper Mystery*, 1954, revised edition, 1974; *Witch Tree Symbol*, 1955, revised edition, 1975; *Hidden Window Mystery*, 1956, revised edition, 1975; *Haunted Showboat*, 1957; *Secret of the Golden Pavilion*, 1959; *Clue in the Old Stagecoach*, 1960; *Mystery of the Fire Dragon*, 1961; *Clue of the Dancing Puppet*, 1962; *Moonstone Castle Mystery*, 1963; *Clue of the Whistling Bagpipes*, 1964; *Phantom of Pine Hill*, 1965; *Mystery of the 99 Steps*, 1966; *Clue in the Crossword Cipher*, 1967; *Spider Sapphire Mystery*, 1968; *Invisible Intruder*, 1969.

Mysterious Mannequin, 1970; *Crooked Banister*, 1971; *Secret of Mirror Bay*, 1972; *Double Jinx Mystery*, 1973; *Mystery of the Glowing Eye*, 1974; *Secret of the Forgotten City*, 1975; *The Sky Phantom*, in press.

Other: *Nancy Drew Cookbook: Clues to Good Cooking*, 1973.

SIDELIGHTS: Mrs. Adams has made extensive trips throughout the United States, Canada, Mexico, South America, Europe, Hawaii, the Orient and Africa, and has set many of her stories in these foreign locales.

Four films have been made from the "Nancy Drew" series, "Nancy Drew and the Hidden Staircase," "Nancy Drew, Detective," "Nancy Drew, Reporter," and "Nancy Drew, Trouble Shooter," by Warner Brothers, 1938 and 1939.

AVOCATIONAL INTERESTS: Doll collecting, running a farm, and traveling.

BIOGRAPHICAL/CRITICAL SOURCES: Saturday Review, July 10, 1971; *New York Times Book Review*, May 4, 1975; *Detroit Free Press*, October 10, 1975.

See **STRATEMEYER, Edward L.** and **SVENSON, Andrew E.**

*   *   *

ADAMS, James F(rederick) 1927-

PERSONAL: Born December 27, 1927, in Andong, Korea; son of Benjamin N. (a minister) and Phyllis (Taylor) Adams; married Maria Miranda, 1964; children: James Edward, Dorothy Lee, Robert Benjamin. *Education:* University of California, Berkeley, B.A., 1950; Temple University, Ed.M., 1951; Washington State University, Ph.D., 1959. *Politics:* Independent. *Religion:* Presbyterian. *Home:* 165 Stoneway Lane, Bala Cynwyd, Pa. 19004.

CAREER: Temple University, Philadelphia, Pa., staff member of testing bureau, department of psychology, 1951-

52; Whitworth College, Spokane, Wash., assistant professor of psychology, 1952-55; Washington State University, instructor, Evening Extension Division, Spokane, 1955-57; Miami University, Oxford, Ohio, research associate, 1957-59; Temple University, assistant professor, 1959-62, associate professor, 1962-66, professor of psychology, 1966—, chairman of counselor education and director of counseling psychology, 1969-72, chairman of department of counseling psychology, 1973—, coordinator of division of educational psychology, 1974—. University of Puerto Rico, 1963-64, Catholic University of Puerto Rico, 1971-72. *Military service:* U.S. Marine Corps, 1945-46.

MEMBER: American Psychological Association (fellow), American Personnel and Guidance Association, National Vocational Guidance Association, American Association for the Advancement of Science. Association for Counselor Education and Supervision, Eastern Psychological Association, Pennsylvania Psychological Association, Philadelphia Society for Clinical Psychologists, Psi Chi, Sigma Xi. *Awards, honors:* Bolton Fund research grants, Temple University, 1960, 1962; faculty research grants, Temple University, 1962, 1963; Commonwealth of Pennsylvania research grants, 1969-72.

WRITINGS: A Workbook to Occupations, Whitworth College, 1953; *Adams Self-Analysis Inventory*, Whitworth College, 1954; (with C. L. Davis) *The Use of the VuGraph as an Instructional Aid*, Charles Beseler Co., 1960; (with R. B. Hackman) *Adams-Hackman Test of Occupational Information*, Randolph Publishing Co., 1961; *Problems in Counseling: A Case Study Approach*, Macmillan, 1962; (editor) *Counseling and Guidance: A Summary View*, Macmillan, 1965; (editor) *Understanding Adolescence: Current Developments in Adolescent Psychology*, Allyn & Bacon, 1968, 3rd edition, in press; *Instructors Manual for Understanding Adolescence*, Allyn & Bacon, 1969; (author of introduction) J. Buchanan, *The Philosophy of Human Nature*, M & S Press (Weston, Mass.), 1970; (editor) *Human Behavior in a Changing Society*, Holbrook Press, 1973.

Contributor: V. H. Noll and R. P. Noll, editors, *Readings in Educational Psychology*, Macmillan, 1962; H. A. Estrin and D. M. Goode, editors, *College and University Teaching*, W. C. Brown, 1964; J. M. Seidman, editor, *Readings in Educational Psychology*, Houghton, 1965; D. R. Cook, editor, *A Guide to Educational Research*, Allyn & Bacon, 1965; C. E. Beck, editor, *Guidelines for Guidance: Readings in the Philosophy of Guidance*, W. C. Brown, 1966, 2nd edition, 1971; R. S. Dunlop, editor, *Professional Problems in School Counseling Practice*, International Textbook Co., 1968; R. E. Muuss, editor, *Adolescent Behavior and Society: A Book of Readings*, Random House, 1970; M. Powell and A. H. Frerichs, editors, *Readings in Adolescent Psychology*, Burgess, 1971; M. A. Kanwar, editor, *The Sociology of the Family: An Interdisciplinary Approach*, Linnet Books, 1971. Contributor to *International Encyclopedia of Neurology, Psychiatry, Psychoanalysis, and Psychology* and to professional journals.

*   *   *

ADELBERG, Roy P. 1928-

PERSONAL: Born February 28, 1928, in Union City, N.J.; son of Parker (a building contractor) and Emily (Scott) Adelberg; married Elsie Freese, June 25, 1950; children: Lisa Kristin. *Education:* Hope College, A.B. (cum laude), 1952; New Brunswick Theological Seminary, B.D., 1955. *Politics:* Independent.

CAREER: Ordained minister, Reformed Church in America, 1955; minister of churches in Stone Ridge and High Falls, N.Y., 1954-58; Reformed Church in America, New York, N.Y., national director of audio-visual education, 1958-61; free-lance writer in Mallorca, Spain, and New York, N.Y., 1961-64; Young Men's Christian Association of Metropolitan Detroit, Detroit, Mich., public relations director, beginning, 1964. National Council of Churches of Christ in the U.S.A., vice-chairman of Broadcasting and Film Commission, 1961, and member of Commission on Missionary Education. *Military service:* U.S. Army Air Forces, 1946-49.

WRITINGS: Youth Guide on New Nations, Friendship, 1964; *The Way in the World*, Friendship, 1965; *Now Hear This!*, CLC Press, 1965. Writer of about a dozen filmscripts.

WORK IN PROGRESS: A book on interfaith encounters, still untitled; a tourist handbook on conversational Mallorquin; a novel, *The Hatemaker*; revision of Boy Scouts "God and Country Program."

SIDELIGHTS: Adelberg is fluent in Spanish.†

*   *   *

ADELSON, Joseph (Bernard) 1925-

PERSONAL: Born July 25, 1925, in New York, N.Y.; son of Jacob and Clara (Prince) Adelson; married Edna Kamener (a psychologist), February 10, 1946; children: Lawrence, Edward, Paul. *Education:* City College (now City College of the City University of New York), B.S., 1945; University of California, Berkeley, M.A., 1947, Ph.D., 1950. *Politics:* Democrat. *Religion:* Jewish. *Home:* 930 Loyola Dr., Ann Arbor, Mich. 48103. *Office:* Department of Psychology, University of Michigan, Ann Arbor, Mich. 48104.

CAREER: Michigan State University, East Lansing, instructor in psychology, 1950-51; Bennington College, Bennington, Vt., faculty of social science, 1951-56; University of Michigan, Ann Arbor, assistant professor, 1956-59, professor of psychology and co-director of psychological clinic, 1956—. Executive director, Royce J. Noble Fund, 1970—. *Member:* American Psychological Association (fellow), American Sociological Association (fellow). *Awards, honors:* Ford Foundation behavioral science fellowship, 1960-61; Social Science Research Council faculty research fellowship, 1964-65; Rackham Fund faculty research fellowship, 1966-67.

WRITINGS: (With Elizabeth Douvan) *The Adolescent Experience*, Wiley, 1966. Contributor to professional journals, including *American Scholar, Journal of Abnormal and Social Psychology, Psychiatry*, and *Contemporary Psychology*. Consulting editor, *Merrill-Palmer Quarterly*, 1960—, *Journal of Personality and Social Psychology*, 1961-68, *Contemporary Psychology*, 1966-67; associate editor, *Journal of Youth and Adolescence*, 1971—.

WORK IN PROGRESS: A cross-national study of the development of political thought in adolescence.†

*   *   *

ADLER, Jacob 1913-

PERSONAL: Born March 18, 1913, in Chicago, Ill.; son of Hyman and Mollie (Hasenfratz) Adlerblum; married Thelma C. Figurski (a management analyst), September 13, 1946. *Education:* University of Chicago, B.S., 1933; Columbia University, M.S., 1956, Ph.D., 1959. *Home:* 5704

Kalanianaole Hwy., Honolulu, Hawaii. *Office:* University of Hawaii, Honolulu, Hawaii.

CAREER: Free-lance translator of medical and technical German in earlier years; U.S. Railroad Retirement Board, claims examiner, 1939-42; University of Hawaii, Honolulu, assistant professor of business, 1947-51, associate professor of economics and business, 1951-60, professor, 1960—. Certified public accountant and financial consultant, 1948—; controller, City Mill Co. Ltd., 1947-51; director, Hawaiian Imports. Member of Hawaii Governor's Economic Advisory Council; trustee, Hawaiian Historical Society. *Military service:* U.S. Army Air Forces, 1942-46; became first lieutenant. *Member:* American Institute of Certified Public Accountants, American Accounting Association, Economic History Association, Hawaiian Economic Association (past president), Phi Beta Kappa.

WRITINGS: Claus Spreckels, Sugar King of Hawaii, University of Hawaii Press, 1966; (editor) *The Journal of Prince Alexander Liholiho*, University of Hawaii Press, 1967; (editor with Gwynn W. Barrett) *The Diaries of Walter Murray Gibson: 1886-1887*, University of Hawaii Press, 1973. Contributor to history journals. Co-editor, "Professor's Notebook," *Honolulu Star-Bulletin*, 1959—.

WORK IN PROGRESS: Research in history and economic development of Hawaii and the Pacific Basin.†

*   *   *

ADLER, Sol 1925-

PERSONAL: Born January 6, 1925, in Brooklyn, N.Y.; son of George and Pauline (Mauser) Adler; married Betty Tunnell, March 26, 1953; children: Suzette, Gerald, Alisa, Deborah, Beth. *Education:* Brooklyn College (now Brooklyn College of the City University of New York), B.A., 1952, M.A., 1953; Ohio State University, Ph.D., 1956. *Religion:* Unitarian Universalist. *Home:* 4022 Towanda Trail, Knoxville, Tenn. *Office:* Department of Speech Pathology and Audiology, University of Tennessee, Knoxville, Tenn.

CAREER: Ohio State University, Columbus, research associate in psychological laboratory, 1954-56; East Tennessee State University, Johnson City, director of speech and hearing clinic, beginning 1956, professor of special education and chairman of department, beginning 1965; University of Tennessee, Knoxville, professor of audiology and speech pathology, 1967—, director of Speech and Hearing Clinic, 1967-72, director of Pediatric Language Clinic, 1972—. *Member:* American Speech and Hearing Association.

WRITINGS: The Non-Verbal Child, C. C Thomas, 1964, 2nd edition, 1975; *A Clinician's Guide to Stuttering*, C. C Thomas, 1966; *The Health and Education of the Economically Deprived Child*, Warren Green, 1967.

WORK IN PROGRESS: The Culturally-Different Child: Teaching and Treating Strategies.

*   *   *

AFRICA, Thomas Wilson 1927-

PERSONAL: Born December 24, 1927, in Portland, Ore.; son of Charles Edward (a salesman) and Leah (Wilson) Africa; married Ursula Helga Jung, January 12, 1952; children: Deborah Marlea, Thomas Charles. *Education:* University of California, Los Angeles, A.B., 1956, M.A., 1957, Ph.D., 1959. *Home:* 421 African Road, Vestal, N.Y. 13850. *Office:* State University of New York, Binghamton, N.Y. 13901.

CAREER: U.S. Army, 1945-53, advancing to master sergeant; University of California, Santa Barbara, instructor in history, 1959-60; Louisiana State University, New Orleans, assistant professor of history, 1960-61; University of Southern California, Los Angeles, assistant professor, 1961-64, associate professor, 1964-67; State University of New York, Binghamton, professor of history, 1969—. *Member:* American Historical Association, History of Science Society, Hellenic Society, Phi Beta Kappa. *Awards, honors:* American Council of Learned Societies research grant, 1960-61.

WRITINGS: Phylarchus and the Spartan Revolution, University of California Press, 1961; *Rome of the Caesars,* Wiley, 1965; *Science and the State in Greece and Rome,* Wiley, 1968; *The Ancient World,* Houghton, 1969; *The Immense Majesty,* Crowell, 1974. Contributor to learned journals.

WORK IN PROGRESS: A History of the Hellenistic World.

*   *   *

AGEE, Warren Kendall 1916-

PERSONAL: Born October 23, 1916, in Sherman, Tex.; son of Frederic Marvin (a contractor) and Minnie (Logsdon) Agee; married Edda Robbins, June 1, 1941; children: Kim Kathleen (Mrs. Michael Stimpert), Robyn Kendall. *Education:* Texas Christian University, B.A. (cum laude), 1937; University of Minnesota, M.A., 1949, Ph.D., 1955. *Politics:* Democrat. *Religion:* Protestant. *Home:* 130 Highland Dr., Athens, Ga. 30601.

CAREER: Fort Worth Star-Telegram, Fort Worth, Tex., member of editorial staff, 1937-48; Texas Christian University, Fort Worth, instructor, 1948-50, assistant professor, 1950-55, associate professor, 1955-57, professor of journalism, 1957-58, chairman of department, 1950-58; West Virginia University, Morgantown, professor and dean, School of Journalism, 1958-60; Sigma Delta Chi (professional journalism society), Chicago, Ill., national executive officer, 1960-62; Texas Christian University, professor of journalism and dean, Evening College, 1962-65; University of Kansas, Lawrence, professor and dean, William Allen White School of Journalism, 1965-69; University of Georgia, Athens, Henry W. Grady School of Journalism, professor and dean, 1969—. Gave George Polk Memorial address, New York, 1962; trustee of William Allen White Foundation. *Military service:* U.S. Coast Guard, 1942-45; became chief specialist (public relations).

MEMBER: Association for Education in Journalism (president, 1958), American Society of Journalism School Administrators (president, 1956), American Studies Association, American Council on Education for Journalism (chairman of accrediting committee), Sigma Delta Chi (president of Fort Worth professional chapter, 1954; vice-president of student chapter affairs, 1966-69), Journalism Council, Kappa Tau Alpha, Texas Gridiron Club, Rotary Club. *Awards, honors:* Outstanding news writing award, Fort Worth professional chapter, Sigma Delta Chi, 1946; Carl Towley Award from Journalism Education Association, 1969, for service to high school journalism; Outstanding Achievement Award from University of Minnesota Board of Regents, 1973.

WRITINGS: (With Edwin Emery and Phillip H. Ault) *Introduction to Mass Communications,* Dodd, 1960, 5th edition, 1976; (contributor) *Freedom and Responsibility in Broadcasting,* edited by John E. Coons, Northwestern

University Press, 1961; *The Press and the Public Interest,* Public Affairs Press, 1968; (editor) *Mass in a Free Society,* University Press of Kansas, 1969. Contributor to journalism publications. Member of editorial advisory board, *Journalism Quarterly,* 1955-60.

*   *   *

AGWANI, Mohammed Shafi 1928-

PERSONAL: Born March 2, 1928, in Udaipur, India; son of Ahmed Bakhsh Agwani (a civil servant); wife's name Fareeda; married May 19, 1959; children: Minoo (daughter), Suhail (son). *Education:* Rajasthan University, M.A., 1952; University of Utrecht, Ph.D., 1954. *Home:* F/24 West Nizamuddin, New Delhi, India. *Office:* Indian School of International Studies, Jawaharlal Nehru University, New Mehrauli Rd., New Delhi-110057, India.

CAREER: Aligarh Muslim University, Aligarh, Uttar Pradesh, India, senior research fellow, 1955-56; Indian School of International Studies, New Delhi, India, lecturer, 1957-59, reader, 1959-64, professor of West Asian studies, 1964—, dean, 1974—. Visiting scholar, Middle East Institute of Columbia University, 1968-69.

WRITINGS: The United States and the Arab World 1945-1952, Aligarh Muslim University Press, 1955; *The Lebanese Crisis, 1958,* Asia Publishing, 1965; (contributor) Meenakshi Prakashan, editor, *The West Asian Crisis,* Meerut, 1968; *Communism in the Arab East,* Asia Publishing, 1969. Contributor to learned journals.

WORK IN PROGRESS: India and West Asia and *Politics in the Gulf.*

SIDELIGHTS: Agwani is competent in Arabic, Persian, and English, and he has working knowledge of French. He has traveled extensively in the Arab world since 1958.

*   *   *

AHMAD, Nafis 1913-

PERSONAL: Born January 23, 1913; son of Abdul Wase; married Akhtar Jahan; children: Zulfia (daughter), Nadimahmad, Nawaidahmad (sons). *Education:* Aligarh Muslim University, B.A. (honors in geography), 1934, M.S. (first class honors), 1935; London School of Economics and Political Science, London, Ph.D., 1953. *Office:* Department of Geography, University of Dacca, Ramna, Dacca, Bangladesh.

CAREER: Aligarh Muslim University, Aligarh, India, lecturer in geography, 1936-39; Bengal Educational Service, professor of geography and head of department at Islamia College, Calcutta, India, 1940-47, part-time graduate lecturer in international relations, Calcutta University, Calcutta, India, 1941-47; University of Dacca, Dacca, Bangladesh, reader and head of department of geography, 1948-56, university professor and head of department of geography, beginning 1956, dean, faculty of science, 1964-66. Member of Pakistan's National Committee on Geodesy and Geophysics, 1952—; Pakistan-nominated member of geography, oceanography, and geophysics section of Pan Indian Ocean Science Association; attended twelve international geographical conferences and seminars in England, United States, Spain, Brazil, Japan, Sweden, Thailand, and Malaya, 1955-62. Conducted pilot project on land use in East Pakistan, sponsored by Cultural Affairs Council, New York, 1957-59, and land-use studies financed by Ford Foundation, 1961-62. Visiting senior scientist to U.S. Army Natick Laboratories, Natick, Mass., on appointment by U.S. National Academy of Sciences, 1966-67.

MEMBER: Royal Geographical Society (England; fellow), American Geographical Society (fellow), All Pakistan Geographical Association (vice president), East Pakistan Geographical Society (president), Indian Geographers Association (treasurer, 1947-48), Pakistan Association for the Advancement of Science (secretary of east regional branch, 1948-50; council member, 1949-51; president of section on geology and geography, 1953-54). *Awards, honors:* U.S. government fellowship to Cornell University, 1960; Tamgha-i-Imtiaz (medal of distinction), awarded by President of Pakistan for services to education, 1961.

WRITINGS: Muslim Contribution to Geography, M. Ashraf (Lahore), 1947, revised edition, 1965; *The Basis of Pakistan*, Thacker Spink (Calcutta), 1947; *An Economic Geography of East Pakistan*, Oxford University Press, 1958, revised edition, 1968; (editor) *Oxford School Atlas for Pakistan*, Oxford University Press, 1959; (with F. Karim Khan) *Land Use in Fydabad Area*, Nos. 1 and 2 (monographs), East Pakistan Geographical Society, 1959 and 1962; (with Kahn) *Milk Supply of Dacca City*, Department of Geography, University of Dacca, 1967. Contributor to *Collier's Encyclopedia*, and to *Geographical Review* (New York), *Economic Geography* (Clark University), and other geographical journals in India, Pakistan, England, Europe, and United States. Editor, *Oriental Geographer* (semiannual journal of East Pakistan Geographical Society); member of editorial board, *Calcutta Geographical Review*, 1944-47; corresponding editor, *Pakistan Geographical Review*, 1953—.

WORK IN PROGRESS: The Urban Morphology of Dacca District; Functional Aspects of Food Market in Dacca Urban Area; other research work in land use, population, and land economics.†

* * *

AKITA, George 1926-

PERSONAL: Born April 26, 1926, in Honolulu, Hawaii; son of Jukichi and Takino (Kawaguchi) Akita; married Akiko Teshirogi, December 2, 1950; children: Naomi M., Makoto A., Izumi J. *Education:* University of Hawaii, B.A., 1951; Harvard University, M.A., 1953, Ph.D., 1960. *Office:* Department of History, University of Hawaii, Honolulu, Hawaii 96822.

CAREER: U.S. Department of the Army, researcher and analyst, Tokyo, Japan, 1957-61; University of Hawaii, Honolulu, assistant professor, 1961-63, associate professor, 1963-67, professor of history, 1967—. *Military service:* U.S. Army, 1945-47. *Member:* Association for Asian Studies.

WRITINGS: Foundations of Constitutional Government in Modern Japan, 1868-1900, Harvard University Press, 1967; (contributor) Albert Craig and Donald Shively, editors, *Personality in Japanese History*, Center for Japanese and Korean Studies, University of California, Berkeley, 1970. Contributor to professional journals.

WORK IN PROGRESS: Yamagata Aritomo: His Later Years, co-editor with Samon Kimbara and contributor.

SIDELIGHTS: Akita speaks and reads Japanese.

* * *

ALBRECHT, Ruth E. 1910-

PERSONAL: Born October 27, 1910, in Wittenberg, Mo.; daughter of Frank Albert and Johanna (Bregas) Albrecht. *Education:* Washington University, St. Louis, Mo., B.A., 1934; University of Chicago, M.A., 1946, Ph.D., 1951. *Re-*

ligion: Protestant. *Home:* 1218 Northwest Sixth St., Gainesville, Fla. 32601. *Office:* 312 Peabody Hall, University of Florida, Gainesville, Fla. 32603.

CAREER: Indiana University, Bloomington, instructor, 1948-49; Alabama Polytechnic Institute (now Auburn University), Auburn, research professor of family life, 1951-57; University of Florida, Gainesville, professor of family life and head of department, 1957-60, professor of sociology, 1960—. Florida Council on Aging, trustee. *Member:* National Council on Family Relations (board of directors), Gerontological Society (chairman of psychological and social science section, 1963-65; secretary, 1960-63), American Sociological Association, American Association for the Advancement of Science, American Academy of Political and Social Science, Southern Sociological Society (chairman of problems of aging section, 1965-66; vice-president, 1973-74), Pi Lambda Theta, Alpha Kappa Delta.

WRITINGS: (With R. J. Havighurst) *Older People*, Longmans, Green, 1954; (editor) *Aging in a Changing Society*, University of Florida Press, 1962; *Encounter: Love, Marriage, and Family*, Holbrook, 1972.

Contributor: *Good Living After 50*, University of Chicago Press, 1952; *Aging: A Current Appraisal*, University of Florida Press, 1956; *The Meaning of Religion to Older People*, University of Florida Press, 1958; *Society and the Health of Older People*, University of Florida Press, 1959; *Aging: A Regional Appraisal*, University of Florida Press, 1961; *Social and Psychological Aspects of Aging*, edited by Wilma Donahue and Clark Tibbitts, Columbia University Press, 1962. Contributor of twenty articles to journals.

WORK IN PROGRESS: A revision of *Encounter*.

* * *

ALDEN, John D. 1921-

PERSONAL: Born October 23, 1921, in San Diego, Calif.; son of Harold W. and Elizabeth (Doughty) Alden; married Ann Buchholz, 1944; children: six. *Education:* Cornell University, A.B. (chemistry), 1943; Massachusetts Institute of Technology, B.S.E.E., 1949. *Residence:* Pleasantville, N.Y. 10570.

CAREER: U.S. Navy, career service, 1943-65, retiring as commander; Engineers Joint Council, New York, N.Y., director of manpower activities, 1965—. *Member:* U.S. Naval Institute, American Society of Naval Engineers, American Society for Engineering Education. *Awards, honors:* Second prize for essay, U.S. Naval Institute, 1964; Award of Merit from U.S. Naval Institute, 1973.

WRITINGS: Flush Decks and Four Pipes, U.S. Naval Institute, 1965; *The American Steel Navy*, U.S. Naval Institute, 1972. Contributor to *Naval Review*, 1964, 1965, and to periodicals, including *American Neptune, Armed Forces Management, Naval Engineers Journal*, and *Engineering Manpower Bulletin*.

WORK IN PROGRESS: General research and articles on U.S. naval history.

* * *

ALDRIDGE, A(lfred) Owen 1915-

PERSONAL: Born December 16, 1915, in Buffalo, N.Y.; son of Abel and Jane (Ette) Aldridge; married Mary Hennen Dellinger, May 18, 1941 (divorced, 1956); married Adriana Garcia Davila, June 7, 1963; children: (first marriage) Cecily Joan (Mrs. John Ward). *Education:* Indiana

University, B.S., 1937; University of Georgia, M.A., 1938; Duke University, Ph.D., 1942; Sorbonne, University of Paris, Docteur Litterature comparee, 1955. *Home:* 101 East Chalmers St., Champaign, Ill. 61820. *Office:* Department of Comparative Literature, University of Illinois, Urbana, Ill. 61801.

CAREER: North Carolina College at Raleigh, instructor, 1942; State University of New York at Buffalo, instructor, 1942-44, assistant professor, 1944-46, associate professor of English, 1946-47; University of Maryland, College Park, professor of English, 1947-58, professor of comparative literature, 1958-67, director of comparative literature program, 1960-64, head of department of comparative literature, 1964-67; University of Illinois, Urbana, professor of comparative literature, 1967—. Visiting professor at University of Southern California, 1947, New York University, 1948, Duke University, 1952, University of Toulouse, 1952, University of Clermont-Ferrand, 1953, University of Brazil, 1957, University of Colorado, 1968. *Member:* International Comparative Literature Association (advisory board member, 1970—), Institute of Ibero-American Enlightenment (vice-president, 1969-70), Modern Language Association of America, American Comparative Literature Association (advisory board member, 1968—), American Society for Eighteenth-Century Studies (advisory board member, 1970—), Society of American Historians.

WRITINGS: Shaftesbury and the Deist Manifesto, American Philosophical Society, 1951; *Benjamin Franklin and His French Contemporaries*, New York University Press, 1957; *Man of Reason: The Life of Thomas Paine*, Lippincott, 1959.

(Contributor) John A. Garraty, editor, *The Unforgettable Americans*, Channel Press, 1960; *Essai sur les personnages des "Liaisons Dangereuses" en tant que types litteraires*, (title means "Essay on the Character of 'Les Liaisons dangereuses' as Literary Types"), Les Lettres Modernes, 1960; (contributor) Charles Coleman Sellers, editor, *Early Dickinsonia*, Dickinson College Library, 1961; (contributor) Pierre Francastel, editor, *Utopia et institutions au XVIII e siecle: Le Pragmatisme des Lumieres* (title means "Utopia and Institutions of the Eighteenth Century: Pragmatism of the Enlightenment"), Mouton & Co. (Paris), 1963; *Jonathan Edwards*, Washington Square Press, 1964, 2nd edition, 1966; *Benjamin Franklin: Philosopher and Man*, Lippincott, 1965; *Benjamin Franklin and Nature's God*, Duke University Press, 1967; (contributor) Clarence Gohdes, editor, *Essays on American Literature in Honor of Jay B. Hubbell*, Duke University Press, 1967; (editor) *Comparative Literature: Matter and Method*, University of Illinois Press, 1969.

(Editor) *The Ibero-American Enlightenment*, University of Illinois Press, 1970. Contributor to the proceedings of learned congresses; also contributor to literary and scholarly journals. Editor, *Comparative Literature Studies*, 1963—.

SIDELIGHTS: Benjamin Franklin and His French Contemporaries has been translated into French, and *Man of Reason: The Life of Thomas Paine* has been translated into French, Arabic, Bengali, and Urdu.

*   *   *

ALEXANDER, Milton   1917-

PERSONAL: Born July 15, 1917, in Kielce, Poland; son of Philip and Dora (Rels) Alexander; married Edith Robbins, September 17, 1949; children: Charlotte, Marcia, Robert,

Don (deceased). *Education:* Brooklyn College (now Brooklyn College of the City University of New York), B.A. (summa cum laude), 1942; Columbia University, M.A., 1945; New York University, Ph.D., 1959. *Politics:* Independent Democrat. *Religion:* Jewish. *Home:* 44 Joan Dr., Yonkers, N.Y. 10704. *Office:* Fordham University, Bronx, N.Y. 10458.

CAREER: New York World-Telegram, New York, N.Y., staff writer and columnist on labor-management, 1945-46; *Journal of Commerce*, New York, N.Y., contributing editor, 1947-58; Fordham University, New York, N.Y., 1955—, associate professor, 1959-67, professor of marketing, 1967—. Consultant in marketing to government and industry, 1949—. Member of President's Panel on Consumer Education for People with Limited Income, 1964—; advisor on consumer affairs, National Association of Manufacturers, 1965-67. *Military service:* U.S. Army, 1942-44. *Member:* American Association for the Advancement of Science, American Economic Association, American Marketing Association, Academy of Political Science, American Association of University Professors, Alpha Beta Gamma.

WRITINGS: (With Kriesberg and Leiman) *The Use of Field Men by Voluntary Chains and Affiliated Retailers*, U.S. Department of Agriculture, 1958; (contributor) *Advancing Marketing Efficiency*, American Marketing Association, 1958; (with Edward Mazze) *Sales Management: Theory and Practice*, Pitman, 1965; (with E. Mazze) *Case Histories in Sales Management*, Pitman, 1965; (with others) *The Most for Their Money*, Consumer Advisory Council, 1965; (contributor) J. U. McNeal, editor, *Dimensions of Consumer Behavior*, Appleton, 1965, 2nd edition, 1969; (with Robert J. Franko and Jerry Schorr) *Logistics in Marketing*, Pitman, 1966; (contributor) P. R. Cateora and L. Richardson, editors, *Readings in Marketing: The Qualitative and Quantitative Areas*, Appleton, 1967; *Prospects for Price Stability in the 1970's*, General Electric Co., 1971; (contributor) *Consumer Communications With Retailers*, Liggett Myers, Inc., 1972. Also author of *Sub-Cultures Food Habits and Their Impact On American Food Marketing Here and Abroad*, Consumer Research Institute. Contributor to consumer and business journals.

WORK IN PROGRESS: A monograph on proposed new methods for collegiate teaching of business administration, completion expected in 1978.

SIDELIGHTS: Alexander became interested in marketing while working way through college as a retail grocer.

*   *   *

ALEXANDERSSON, Gunnar V(ilhelm)   1922-

PERSONAL: Born March 14, 1922, in Bergkvara, Sweden; son of Albert and Marta (Nilsson) Alexandersson; married Ingrid Schioler (now a teacher), March 30, 1947; children: Ragnhild, Gun, Sonja, John Gunnar. *Education:* Stockholm School of Economics, civilekonom, 1947, ekon. lic., 1956. *Home:* Kallforsvagen 31, Bandhagen, Sweden. *Office:* Stockholm School of Economics, Sveavagen 65, Stockholm Va, Sweden.

CAREER: Stockholm School of Economics, Stockholm, Sweden, assistant professor, 1956-60, associate professor, 1960-64, professor of international economic geography, 1964—. Research associate, University of Maryland, 1952; visiting professor, University of Nebraska, 1953-54, University of Wisconsin, 1959, 1964. *Military service:* Swedish Coast Artillery, 1942-44.

WRITINGS: The Industrial Structure of American Cities, University of Nebraska Press, 1956; (with Goran Norstrom) *World Shipping: An Economic Geography of Ports and Seaborne Trade*, Wiley, 1963; *Geography of Manufacturing*, Prentice-Hall, 1967; *Les Pays du Nord*, Presses universitaires de France, 1971; *Australien: Land, folk, naaringsliv*, Prisma, 1972; *De Nordiska laanderna: Natur, befolkniŋg, naaringsliv*, Prisma, 1972.

SIDELIGHTS: Alexandersson speaks Swedish, English, German, French, Spanish, and Russian.

* * *

ALGEO, John (Thomas) 1930-

PERSONAL: Born November 12, 1930, in St. Louis, Mo.; son of Thomas George and Julia (Wathen) Algeo; married Adele Silbereisen, September 6, 1958; children: Thomas, John, Catherine Marie. *Education:* University of Miami, Coral Gables, Fla., B.Ed., 1955; University of Florida, M.A., 1957, Ph.D., 1960. *Politics:* Democrat. *Religion:* Episcopalian. *Home:* 220 Cedar Dr., Athens, Ga. 30601. *Office:* Department of English, University of Georgia, Athens, Ga.

CAREER: Florida State University, Tallahassee, instructor, 1959-61; University of Florida, Gainesville, assistant professor, 1961-66, associate professor, 1966-69, professor of English, 1970-71, assistant dean of the graduate school, 1969-71; University of Georgia, Athens, professor of English, 1971—. *Military service:* U.S. Army, 1950-53; became sergeant. *Member:* International Phonetic Association, Modern Language Association of America, American Dialect Society, Linguistic Society of America, Early English Text Society, South Atlantic Modern Language Association, International Linguistic Association, National Council of Teachers of English, American Name Society, Phi Beta Kappa.

WRITINGS: (With Thomas Pyles) *Problems in the Origins and Development of the English Language*, Harcourt, 1966, 2nd edition, 1972; (with Pyles) *English: An Introduction to Language*, Harcourt, 1970; (with Ralph Williams and others) *Spelling: Sound to Letter*, Macmillan, 1971; *On Defining the Proper Name*, University of Florida Press, 1973; (contributor) Adam Makkai and David Lockwood, editors, *Readings in Stratificational Linguistics*, University of Alabama Press, 1973; *Exercises in Contemporary English*, Harcourt, 1974; (contributor) R. M. Brend, editor, *Advances in Tagmemics*, North Holland, 1974; (contributor) Adam Makkai and Valerie Makkai, editors, *First Lacus Forum*, Hornbeam, 1975. Contributor to linguistic and English journals. Editor of *American Speech*, 1971—.

WORK IN PROGRESS: Current Trends in the Study of American English; research in contemporary and historical English linguistics.

* * *

ALILUNAS, Leo John 1912-

PERSONAL: Born April 4, 1912, in De Kalb, Ill.; son of John J. and Marian (Kasarskis) Alilunas; married Wilma Kleive, June 17, 1939; children: John Kleive, Kristine Horne. *Education:* University of Missouri, B.J., 1933, M.A., 1938; University of Michigan, Ph.D., 1946. *Office:* State University College, Fredonia, N.Y. 14063.

CAREER: State University of New York, College at Fredonia, professor of education, 1946—. Visiting summer professor at University of Michigan, 1950, University of Vermont, 1956, Michigan State University, 1960-65. *Member:* National Council for the Social Studies, National Society of College Teachers of Education, American Association of University Professors, American Sociological Association, Phi Kappa Phi, Phi Delta Kappa. *Awards, honors:* First prize for best research article published in *Journal of Negro History* during 1940.

WRITINGS: (With J. Woodrow Sayre) *Youth Faces American Citizenship*, Lippincott, 1956, 4th edition, 1970. Contributor of more than fifty articles and reviews to *Michigan History, Journal of Negro History, Quill and Scroll*, and to education journals.

SIDELIGHTS: Alilunas speaks Lithuanian and French. *Avocational interests:* Tennis (former college tennis coach).

* * *

ALKER, Hayward R(ose), Jr. 1937-

PERSONAL: Born October 3, 1937, in New York, N.Y.; son of Hayward Rose and Dorothy (Fitzsimmons) Alker; married Ann Tickner, June 3, 1961; children: Joan Christina, Heather Jane, Gwendolyn Ann. *Education:* Massachusetts Institute of Techonology, B.S., 1959; Yale University, Ph.D., 1963. *Home:* 288 Mill St., Newtonville, Mass. 02160. *Office:* Department of Political Science, Massachusetts Institute of Technology, Cambridge, Mass. 02139.

CAREER: Yale University, New Haven, Conn., instructor in political science and staff member of Computer Center, 1963-64, assistant professor, 1964-66, associate professor of political science, 1966-68; Massachusetts Institute of Technology, Cambridge, Mass., professor of political science, 1968—. Rapporteur for Committee on Research Evaluation, Carnegie Endowment for International Peace, 1963-66; visiting professor, University of Michigan, 1968, Facultad Latinoamericana de Ciencias Sociales, 1970-71 and 1973; Mathematics and Social Sciences Board, member, 1967-70, chairman, 1970-71. First vice-president, New Haven Chorale, 1965-66. *Member:* American Political Science Association, American Association for the Advancement of Science, International Studies Association, International Peace Research Association. *Awards, honors:* Center for the Advanced Study in Behavioral Sciences fellowship, 1967-68.

WRITINGS: (With B. M. Russett, K. W. Deutsch, and H. D. Lasswell) *World Handbook of Political and Social Indicators*, Yale University Press, 1964; (with Russett) *World Politics in the General Assembly*, Yale University Press, 1965; *Mathematics and Politics*, Macmillan, 1965; (co-editor) *Mathematical Approaches To Politics*, Elsevier, 1973. Also author with Bloomfield and Choudri of *Analyzing Global Interdependence*, 1974. Contributor of more than 20 professional papers to proceedings and journals.

WORK IN PROGRESS: A book on cybernetic models of political systems.

* * *

ALLAN, Alfred K. 1930-

PERSONAL: Surname originally Katz; born November 11, 1930, in Brooklyn, N.Y.; son of Morris (a bookbinder) and Mildred (Levy) Katz. *Education:* Attended New York University, 1959, and City College (now City College of the City University of New York), 1960. *Home and office:* 2882 Nostrand Ave., Brooklyn, N.Y. 11229. *Agent:* Paul R. Reynolds, Inc., 12 East 41st St., New York, N.Y. 10017.

CAREER: Professional writer. *Member:* National Writers Club (president, New York chapter, 1964-65). *Awards, honors:* Caldwell Award for best article on patriotic theme, 1963; Catholic Press Association, Best Article award, 1974; Writers Digest article awards, 1973 and 1974.

WRITINGS: Catholics Courageous, Citadel, 1965. Contributor of more than five thousand articles to *McCalls, Mademoiselle, The Rotarian, Columbia, Today's Health*, and other publications. Contributing editor, *Partners*.

* * *

ALLEN, Donald M(erriam) 1912-

PERSONAL: Born March 26, 1912, in Muscatine, Iowa; son of Paul Edward (a doctor) and Mildred (Quinn) Allen. *Education:* University of Iowa, B.A., 1934, M.A., 1935; graduate study at University of Wisconsin, 1940-42, and University of California, Berkeley, 1947-49. *Address:* P.O. Box 159, Bolinas, Calif. 94924.

CAREER: Associated with Grove Press, 1950—, as editor in New York, 1950-60, co-editor, *Evergreen Review*, 1957-60, West Coast editor, 1960-70. *Military service:* U.S. Navy, 1942-47; became lieutenant commander; received Purple Heart and Bronze Star. *Member:* Zen Center (San Francisco).

WRITINGS: (Editor with Francisco Garcia Lorca) Federico Garcia Lorca, *Selected Poems*, New Directions, 1955; (translator) Eugene Ionesco, *Four Plays*, Grove, 1958; (editor) *The New American Poetry, 1945-60*, Grove, 1960; (editor with Robert Creeley) *New American Story*, Grove, 1965; (editor) Charles Olson, *Human Universe*, Auerhahn, 1965; (editor with Robert Creeley) *New Writing in the U.S.A.*, Penguin, 1967; (editor with Warren Tallman) *The Poetics of the New American Poetry*, Grove, 1973.

WORK IN PROGRESS: Editing the correspondence of Lew Welch and his friends, and three posthumous volumes of Frank O'Hara.

SIDELIGHTS: Allen writes: "Aside from contemporary American and European literature, I am concerned with Oriental history and religion and culture, and with the archaeology and contemporary culture of Latin America." He is competent in French. Allen has traveled in Europe, Latin America, and the Far East, living in England, China, Japan, and Mexico.

* * *

ALLEN, Harold B(yron) 1902-

PERSONAL: Born October 6, 1902, in Grand Rapids, Mich.; son of Arthur Kingsbury (a railroad auditor) and Edith (Welch) Allen; married Elizabeth Mitchell, June 19, 1934; children: Marjorie (Mrs. Alexander G. Russell), Susan Kingsbury (Mrs. David Stevenson). *Education:* Kalamazoo College, B.A., 1924; University of Michigan, M.A., 1928, Ph.D., 1941. *Politics:* Democrat-Farm-Labor. *Religion:* United Church of Christ (Congregational). *Home:* 200 Cecil St., S.E., Minneapolis, Minn. 55414. *Office:* University of Minnesota, Minneapolis, Minn. 55455.

CAREER: Shurtleff College, Alton, Ill., professor of rhetoric, 1925-34; University of Michigan, Ann Arbor, assistant editor of *Early Modern English Dictionary*, 1934-39, and *Middle English Dictionary*, 1939-40; San Diego State College, San Diego, Calif., assistant professor of English, 1940-43; University of Minnesota, Minneapolis, 1944—, started as professional lecturer, professor of English, 1958-67, professor of English and linguistics, 1967-71, professor

emeritus, 1971—. Fulbright lecturer in Egypt and consultant to Ministry of Education, Cairo, 1954-55; Smith-Mundt visiting professor in linguistics, United Arab Republic Higher Ministry of Education, 1958-59; consultant to University of Teheran, 1971 and 1973; Fulbright-Hays lecturer, Kossuth Lajos University, 1972; visiting professor, University of Victoria, summers, 1973 and 1974. Minnesota State Board of Education, chairman of Language Arts Advisory Committee.

MEMBER: National Council of Teachers of English (president, 1961; director of commission on the English language, 1965-67, 1969-72), Conference on College Composition and Communication (chairman, 1952), American Dialect Society (executive council member, 1964-67; vice-president, 1968-70; president, 1970-72), Modern Language Association of America, Linguistic Society of America, American Name Society, Speech Association of America, American Association of University Professors, Canadian Linguistic Association, Teachers of English to Speakers of Other Languages (president, 1966-67), American Friends of the Middle East, American Civil Liberties Union. *Awards, honors:* Fund for the Advancement of Education fellowship, 1951-52; National Council of Teachers of English distinguished lecturer, 1970, distinguished service award, 1971, distinguished service citation, 1971, distinguished research award, 1973.

WRITINGS: (With Thomas Dunn and Alfred Ranous) *Learning Our Language*, Ronald, 1950; (editor) *Readings in Applied English Linguistics*, Appleton, 1958, 2nd edition, 1964; *Introduction to the Sound Structure of English*, Amalgamated (Cairo), 1959; *English for Use*, Book One, Amalgamated, 1959; (editor) *Teaching English as a Second Language*, McGraw, 1965, 2nd edition, with Russell Campbell, 1972; (editor) *Linguistics and English Linguistics: A Bibliography*, Appleton, 1966; (editor with Gary Underwood) *Readings in American Dialectology*, Appleton, 1971; *The Linguistic Atlas of the Upper Midwest*, University of Minnesota Press, Volume I, 1973. Contributor of more than eighty articles to journals of speech, English, and linguistics.

WORK IN PROGRESS: Volume II of *Linguistic Atlas of the Upper Midwest*.

* * *

ALLEN, Maury 1932-

PERSONAL: Born May 2, 1932; son of Harry and Frances (Leon) Allen; married Janet Kelly, March 3, 1962. *Education:* City College (now City College of the City University of New York), B.A., 1953. *Politics:* Liberal Democrat. *Religion:* Hebrew.

CAREER: New York Post, New York, N.Y., sports writer, 1962—. *Military service:* U.S. Army, 1953-55.

WRITINGS: Ten Great Moments in Sports, Follett, 1960; (with Samuel Moody) *Reprieve from Hell*, Pageant, 1962; *Now Wait a Minute, Casey!*, Doubleday, 1965; *The Record Breakers*, Prentice-Hall, 1968; *The Incredible Mets*, Paperback Library, 1969; *Joe Namath's Sportin' Life*, Paperback Library, 1969; (editor) *Voices of Sport*, Grosset, 1971; (with Bo Belinsky) *Bo: Pitching and Wooing*, Dial, 1973; *Where Have You Gone, Joe DiMaggio?*, Dutton, 1975.

* * *

ALLEN, R(onald) R(oyce) 1930-

PERSONAL: Born December 8, 1930, in Horicon, Wis.;

son of Clayton Francis and Hazel (Whipple) Allen; married JoAnne Elizabeth Kuehl, February 2, 1957; children: John Jeffery, David Jennings. *Education:* Wisconsin State University, Eau Claire, B.S., 1952; University of Wisconsin, M.S., 1957, Ph.D., 1960. *Home:* 1809 Peacock Ct., Sun Prairie, Wis. *Office:* Department of Communication Arts, University of Wisconsin, Madison, Wis. 53706.

CAREER: Amherst College, Amherst, Mass., assistant professor, 1960-63; University of Wisconsin, Madison, 1963—, began as associate professor of speech education, became professor of communication arts. *Military service:* U.S. Naval Reserve, 1952-56; served in Far Eastern Theatre; became lieutenant. *Member:* Speech Communication Association, Central States Speech Association, Wisconsin Communication Association.

WRITINGS: (With Wil Linkugel and Richard Johannesen) *Contemporary American Speeches,* Wadsworth, 1965; (contributor) Keith Brooks, editor, *The Communicative Arts and Sciences of Speech,* C. E. Merrill, 1966; with Sharol Anderson and Jere Hough) *Speech in American Society,* C. E. Merrill, 1968; (with S. Clay Willmington) *Speech Communication in the Secondary School,* Allyn & Bacon, 1972; (with Sharol Parish and C. David Mortenser) *Communication: Interacting Through Speech,* C. E. Merrill, 1974; (with P. Judson Newcombe) *New Horizons for Teacher Education in Speech Communication,* National Textbook Co., 1974. Contributor to journals.

WORK IN PROGRESS: Speech Communication Competencies in Children, with Barbara Lieb-Brilhart, a report for the National Project on Speech Communication Competencies.

* * *

ALLEN, Robert Livingston 1916-

PERSONAL: Born March 22, 1916, in Hamadan, Iran; son of Cady Hews (a minister) and Helen (Hague) Allen; married Virginia French (a teacher), June 16, 1951; married second wife, 1968; children: four. *Education:* Hamilton College, B.A., 1938; Columbia University, M.A., 1951, Ph.D., 1962. *Politics:* Independent. *Office:* Department of Languages, Literature, Speech, and Theatre, Teachers College, Columbia University, 525 West 120th St., New York, N.Y. 10027.

CAREER: Robert College, Istanbul, Turkey, instructor, 1938-41; U.S. Legation, Tehran, clerk, 1941-42; Kabul, Afghanistan, clerk, 1942-43; Teachers Training School, Kabul, Afghanistan, instructor in English, 1943-45; Robert College, head of department of English (preparatory division), 1945-50; Teachers College, Columbia University, New York, N.Y., instructor in English as a foreign language, 1950-51, foreign student adviser, 1951-52; Fulbright lecturer in Mandalay, Burma, 1953-54; Teachers College, Columbia University, instructor, 1954-57; Caltex Pacific Oil Co., Sumatra, language consultant, 1957-59; Teachers College, Columbia University, lecturer, 1959-63, associate professor, 1963-66, professor of English, 1966—, chairman of department of languages, literature, speech, and theatre, 1965-69.

MEMBER: International Linguistic Association, National Council of Teachers of English (co-chairman of committee on teaching English as a second language, 1960-63), Linguistic Society of America, American National Theatre and Academy, American Association for the United Nations, International Reading Association, Linguistic Circle of New York, Phi Beta Kappa, Lambda Chi Alpha, Pi Delta Epsilon.

WRITINGS: Controlled English, three books, Amerikan Bord Nesriyat Dairesi (Turkey), 1948-50; (with wife, Virginia Allen) *Review Exercises,* Crowell, 1961; (with Virginia Allen) *Read Along With Me,* three books, Teachers College Press, Columbia University, 1964; (with Virginia Allen) *Listen and Guess* (text, with teacher's manual and laboratory book), McGraw, 1964; (contributor) Fred Guggenheim and C. L. Guggenheim, editors, *New Frontiers in Education,* Grune, 1966; *The Verb System of Present-Day English,* Mouton & Co., 1966; (with Virginia Allen and Margaret Shute) *English Sounds and Their Spellings: A Handbook for Teachers and Students,* Crowell, 1966; *Linguistic Approach to Writing,* Noble, 1967; *English Grammars and English Grammar,* Scribner, 1972. Author one-act play, "Of Death But Once," produced at Columbia University, 1956. Contributor to professional journals.

SIDELIGHTS: Allen spent most of boyhood in Iran and he speaks fluent Persian. *Avocational interests:* Music and the theater.†

* * *

ALLEN, William R(ichard) 1924-

PERSONAL: Born April 3, 1924, in Eldorado, Ill.; son of Oliver Boyd (a Methodist minister) and Justa Lee (Wingo) Allen; married Frances Lorraine Swoboda, August 15, 1948; children: Janet Elizabeth, Sandra Lee. *Education:* Cornell College, Mount Vernon, Iowa, B.A., 1948; Duke University, Ph.D., 1953. *Home:* 11809 Allaseba Dr., Los Angeles, Calif. 90066. *Office:* Department of Economics, University of California, Los Angeles, Calif. 90024.

CAREER: Washington University, St. Louis, Mo., instructor in economics, 1951-52; University of California, Los Angeles, lecturer, 1952-53, assistant professor, 1953-58, associate professor, 1958-63, professor of economics, 1963—. U.S. Department of Commerce, economist, summer, 1962; summer teaching posts at Northwestern University, 1952, University of Wisconsin, 1964, University of Michigan, 1965; visiting professor, Southern Illinois University, 1969, Texas A&M University, 1971-73. *Military service:* U.S. Army Air Forces, 1943-46; became first lieutenant. *Member:* American Economic Association, Southern Economic Association, Western Economic Association (president, 1970-71). *Awards, honors:* Research grants from Social Science Research Council, 1950-51, 1962, Ford Foundation, 1958-59, National Science Foundation, 1965-66, Earhart Foundation, 1972, 1974-75.

WRITINGS: (Contributor) *Isolation and Security,* Duke University Press, 1957; (editor with Clark Lee Allen) *Foreign Trade and Finance: Essays in International Economic Equilibrium and Adjustment,* Macmillan, 1959; (editor with J. J. Spengler) *Essays in Economic Thought,* Rand McNally, 1960; (with Armen A. Alchian) *University Economics,* Wadsworth, 1964; (editor) *International Trade Theory: Hume to Ohlin,* Random, 1965. Contributor to learned journals.

WORK IN PROGRESS: Research in history and policy issues of international economics, and in the late career of Irving Fisher.

* * *

ALLEY, Louis Edward 1914-

PERSONAL: Born December 9, 1914, in Drexel, Mo.; son of Ernest Calvin (a farmer) and Ona B. (Cook) Alley; married Mary Lee Brinegar, November 26, 1936; children:

Rebecca Ann, Louis William. *Education:* Central Missouri State College, B.S., 1935; University of Missouri, graduate student, 1938; University of Wisconsin, M.S., 1941; University of Iowa, Ph.D., 1949. *Home:* 1204 Ashley Dr., Iowa City, Iowa 52240.

CAREER: Teacher at public schools in Missouri, 1935-42, Kansas, 1945-46; University of Iowa, Iowa City, critic teacher and instructor at University High School, 1942-43, 1946-49, assistant professor of physical education, 1950-53, associate professor, 1953-59, professor, 1960—, head of department of physical education for men, 1960—. Fulbright professor, Union of Burma, 1949-50. *Military service:* U.S. Naval Reserve, air navigator, 1943-45; served in central Pacific; became lieutenant.

MEMBER: American Academy of Physical Education (fellow), American College of Sports Medicine (fellow), American Association for Health, Physical Education and Recreation (fellow; chairman of national committee on junior high athletics, 1959-61; chairman of National joint committee on physical education for college men and women, 1963-65; president of Iowa branch, 1957-58; president of Central District branch, 1964-65; national president, 1971-72), National Association on Standard Medical Vocabulary, National College Physical Education Association (president, 1966-67), Phi Sigma Epsilon, Phi Delta Kappa, Phi Epsilon Kappa, Phi Kappa Phi, Kiwanis International.

WRITINGS: (Contributor) *Research Methods Applied to Health, Physical Education, and Recreation,* University of Iowa, Extension Division, 1960; *Let's Have Some Fun!* (textbook in physical education for high school boys), University of Iowa, Extension Division, 1960; (chairman of editorial board, and contributor) *Standards for Junior High Athletics,* American Association for Health, Physical Education and Recreation, 1963; (with Donald R. Casady and Donald F. Mapes) *A Handbook of Physical Fitness Activities,* Macmillan, 1965; (with F. X. Cretzmeyer and Charles Tiptou) *Track and Field Athletics,* Mosley, 1974. Contributor of more than eighty articles to periodicals in America, Burma, and Japan.

WORK IN PROGRESS: A personal philosophy of physical education.

* * *

ALLRED, Gordon T. 1930-

PERSONAL: Born December 27, 1930, in Iowa City, Iowa; son of M. Thatcher (a professor) and Pearl (Oberhansley) Allred; married Sharon Wallace, October 26, 1956; children: Mark, Anthony, Kathryn, Amy, John, Robert, Christopher, Aaron, Shannon. *Education:* University of Utah, B.S., 1957, M.S., 1958, Ph.D., 1972. *Religion:* Mormon. *Home:* 2006 Polk Ave., Ogden, Utah.

CAREER: Associate editor, *Improvement Era,* 1956-58; writer for U.S. Forest Service Intermountain Region, 1959-62; Weber State College, Ogden, Utah, 1962—, became professor of creative writing and modern literature. Freelance writer. *Military service:* U.S. Army, 1954-56; served in Japan.

WRITINGS: Kamikaze, Ballantine, 1957; *If a Man Die,* Bookcraft, 1964; *Old Crackfoot,* Astor-Honor, 1965; *The Valley of Tomorrow,* Bookcraft, 1966; *Dori the Mallard,* Astor-Honor, 1968; *Lonesome Coyote,* Lantern Press, 1969; *The Hungry Journey,* Hawkes, 1973; (compiler) *Immortality,* Hawkes, 1974. Writer of articles and stories for magazines, including *True, Argosy,* and *Cavalier.*

WORK IN PROGRESS: Starfire, a novel about a crippled boy and his involvement with hummingbirds; *The Nederlander,* a novel on the life of a Dutch underground leader; *The Breath of Life: Characterization in Modern Literature.*

* * *

ALTHOUSE, LaVonne 1932-

PERSONAL: Born March 30, 1932, in Ephrata, Pa.; daughter of Harvey S. (a carpenter) and Arletta May (Fry) Althouse. *Education:* Pennsylvania State University, B.A. in Journalism, 1953; Union Theological Seminary, New York, N.Y., B.D., 1959; writing courses at New School for Social Research and New York University. *Home:* 5227 Castor, Philadelphia, Pa. 19124. *Office:* 1925 Harrison, Philadelphia, Pa. 19124.

CAREER: United Lutheran Church in America, Board of Higher Education, New York, N.Y., staff writer, 1960-62; Lutheran Church Women, Philadelphia, Pa., editor of *Lutheran Women,* 1962-74; Salem Lutheran Church, Philadelphia, Pa., pastor, 1974—. *Member:* Associated Church Press (member of board of directors), American Civil Liberties Union, League of Women Voters (Philadelphia), Mensa, Theta Sigma Phi, Pi Gamma Mu.

WRITINGS: When Jew and Christian Meet, Friendship, 1966; *The Parish and the Patriot,* Friendship, 1975.

* * *

ALTSHULER, Edward A. 1919-

PERSONAL: Born September 25, 1919, in Kansas City, Mo.; son of David and Ida (Glassman) Altshuler; married Juliette Deutsch, January 23, 1944. *Education:* Attended University of Missouri, 1937-40, University of Texas, 1940-41, University of Southern California, 1946-48; University of California, Los Angeles, special courses, 1949-65.

CAREER: Ross, Gardner & White (advertising agency), Los Angeles, Calif., public relations director, 1947-49; Kaye-Halbert (television manufacturers), Los Angeles, Calif., director of marketing, 1949-53; American Electronics Corp., Los Angeles, Calif., director of research, 1953-57; Ascon Corp. (consultants to management), Los Angeles, Calif., president, 1957—. Educational consultant to trade and business associations. *Military service:* U.S. Army Air Forces, World War II; became staff sergeant. *Member:* Association of Management Consultants (trustee), National Audio-Visual Association, National Education Association, American Society of Training and Development. *Awards, honors:* National Electronic Distributors Association award for outstanding contribution to field of management education.

WRITINGS: "NEDA: Electronic Distribution Aids," six books, National Electronic Distributors Association, 1962; *Standard Operating Procedures for Every Business,* Every Businessman's Library, 1963; *Electronic Systems for Convenience, Safety, and Enjoyment,* H. W. Sams, 1964; *EDP for Small Business,* National Electronic Distributors Association, 1967; *Power, People, and Profits,* Bobbs-Merrill, 1967; *P.L.A.N. Your Business Architecture,* National Electronic Distributors Association with Electronic Industry Show Corp., 1968; (with Katrina M. McGovern) *The Manager's Project Control Handbook,* A & M, 1969. Consulting editor, *NEDA Journal.*†

* * *

AMBIRAJAN, Srinivasa 1936-

PERSONAL: Born January 10, 1936, in Tuticorin, Madras,

India; son of Kodaganallur Ramaswami (a university professor) and Padmasani Srinivasa Iyengar; married Prabha Dorasamy, September 16, 1964; children: Amrit (son), Neela. *Education:* Andhra University, B.A., 1955, M.A., 1957, and Ph.D., 1960; University of Manchester, Ph.D., 1964. *Religion:* Hindu. *Office:* School of Economics, University of New South Wales, Kensington, New South Wales, Australia.

CAREER: University of Queensland, Brisbane, Australia, lecturer in economics, 1964-66; University of New South Wales, Kensington, Australia, senior lecturer, 1966-74, associate professor of economics, 1975—. *Member:* Royal Economic Society, Economic Society of Australia and New Zealand, American Economic Association.

WRITINGS: A Grammar of Indian Planning, Popular Book Depot (Bombay), 1959; *Malthus and Classical Economics*, Popular Book Depot, 1960; *The Taxation of Corporate Income in India*, Asia Publishing House, 1964.

WORK IN PROGRESS: The Political Economy of British Raj, a study of the influence of economic ideas on Indian economic policy; *Economic Evolution in South India 1850-1914*, a study of the economic history of Tamil districts during the Madras presidency.

SIDELIGHTS: Ambirajan has knowledge of four Indian languages: Tamil, Telugu, Kannada, and Sanskrit. *Avocational interests:* Classical music, swimming.

*   *   *

AMES, Francis H.   1900-
(Frank Watson)

PERSONAL: Born September 10, 1900, in Omaha, Neb.; son of Oakes Kay (a rancher) and Emily (Watson) Ames; married Laurel Dondono, 1933 (died, 1974); children: Emily Francis (Mrs. John MacLaine). *Education:* Attended high school in Baker, Mont. *Religion:* Christian. *Home address:* P.O. Box 411, Amity, Ore. 97101. *Agent:* August Lenniger, Lenniger Literary Agency, 437 5th Ave., New York, N.Y. 10016.

CAREER: Raised on Montana cattle ranch as cowpuncher and fur trapper; worked as mechanic and coal miner in early youth after leaving home in 1919; became salesman and sales manager in Los Angeles; was real estate broker in Oregon until 1947, when he became a full-time writer. Once worked out of Seattle on an Alaska steamer. Outdoor editor of *Trail-R-News* and *Camper Coachman. Military service:* U.S. Army, World War I. *Member:* Elks, various sportsmen's clubs. *Awards, honors:* Western Writers of America plaque, 1966, best book of northwest award, 1966, Book Sellers Award, The Grande Prix des Treize, 1974 (all for *That Callahan Spunk*).

WRITINGS: That Callahan Spunk (Literary Guild selection), Doubleday, 1965; *Fishing the Oregon Country*, Caxton, 1966; *The Callahans' Gamble*, Doubleday, 1970. Also author of several television scripts and of approximately six hundred articles, novelettes, and short fiction pieces for magazines.

WORK IN PROGRESS: Four other books, *The Age of the Hobos, Cowboy in Hollywood, Callahan Goes South*, and *The Cannonball County Feud*.

AVOCATIONAL INTERESTS: Travel, photography, fishing, hunting, boating, and research on the early West.

AMMER, Dean S.   1926-

PERSONAL: Born June 14, 1926, in Highland Park, Mich.; son of Paul and Ann (Anderson) Ammer; married Christine Parker (a writer), March 3, 1960; children: Karen, John. *Education:* Massachusetts Institute of Technology, B.S., 1948; New York University, M.B.A., 1956, Ph.D., 1959. *Politics:* Independent.

CAREER: Purchasing Magazine, New York, N.Y., executive editor, 1954-62; Northeastern University, Boston, Mass., research professor and director of Bureau of Business and Economic Research, 1962—. *Member:* American Economic Association, National Association of Purchasing Agents, American Production and Inventory Control Society, American Society for Quality Control, Academy of Management.

WRITINGS: Automation and Manpower in Gray Iron Foundries, Northeastern University Press, 1961; *Materials Management*, Irwin, 1962, revised edition, 1968; (editor) *Readings and Cases in Economics*, Ginn, 1965; *Manufacturing Management and Control*, Appleton, 1968; *Productivity, Personnel, and Problems of Hospital Clinical Laboratories*, Bureau of Business and Economic Research, Northeastern University, 1969.†

*   *   *

AMORY, Anne Reinberg   1931-

PERSONAL: Born September 2, 1931, in Montclair, N.J.; daughter of Gustave (an engineer) and Helen (Minshull) Reinberg; married Frederic Amory (a teacher), January 29, 1955 (divorced July 6, 1962); married Adam Milman Parry (an associate professor of classics), April 11, 1966. *Education:* Vassar College, A.B., 1952; Radcliffe College, A.M., 1955, Ph.D., 1957.

CAREER: Brearly School, New York, N.Y., instructor in classics, 1952-53; University of California, Berkeley, lecturer, 1957-61, assistant professor of classics, 1960-64; Center for Hellenic Studies, Washington, D.C., junior fellow, 1964-65; Yale University, New Haven, Conn., visiting lecturer in classics, 1965-66; Connecticut College, New London, Conn., part-time lecturer in classics, 1965-66, associate professor of classics, 1966—. Part-time instructor in history, Mills College, 1958-59. *Member:* American Philological Association, Philological Association of the Pacific Coast, Phi Beta Kappa.

WRITINGS: (Editor with Mason Hammond) *Aeneas to Augustus: A Beginning Latin Reader for College Students*, Harvard University Press, 1962, 2nd revised edition, 1967; (contributor) Charles H. Taylor, Jr., editor, *Essays on the Odyssey*, Indiana University Press, 1963. Contributor to "Yale Classical Studies," Volume 20, 1966.

WORK IN PROGRESS: A monograph on Homeric Epithets, for Center of Hellenic Studies; an annotated edition of *The Odyssey* in translation, for Crowell; a translation, with commentary, of Sophocles' *Trachiiviae*, for a series under the editorship of Eric A. Havelock, for Prentice-Hall.

SIDELIGHTS: Anne Amory lived in Peru, 1931-40. She reads Greek, Latin, French, German, Spanish.†

*   *   *

AMOS, William E.   1926-

PERSONAL: Born July 20, 1926, in Charleston, Ark.; married Ava Mitchell (now a speech correctionist), June,

1952; children: William E., Jr., Randy, Laura, Lisa. *Education:* Arkansas State Teachers College, B.S.E., 1949; University of Tulsa, M.A., 1950; University of Maryland, M.Ed., 1959, Ed.D., 1960. *Religion:* Methodist. *Home:* 9235 Limestone Pl., College Park, Md.

CAREER: Cabot (Ark.) public schools, superintendent, 1950-51; U.S. Secret Service, agent, 1956-58; Cedar Knoll Training School for Delinquents, Laurel, Md., superintendent, 1960-63; U.S. Department of Labor, Washington, D.C., chief, Division of Youth Employment and Guidance Services, 1963-69, member of U.S. Board of Parole, 1969—; George Washington University, professorial lecturer, 1959-72. Certified psychologist. *Military service:* U.S. Army, 1945-46, 1951-56; became major. *Member:* American Psychological Association (fellow), American Correctional Association, District of Columbia Psychological Association. *Awards, honors:* D.P.A., Culver-Stockton College.

WRITINGS: (Editor with R. L. Manella) *Readings in the Administration of Institutions for Delinquent Youth*, C. C Thomas, 1965; (with M. Southwell and R. L. Manella) *Action Programs for Delinquency Prevention*, C. C Thomas, 1965; (with R. L. Manella) *Institutional Child Care: Reception and Diagnostic Centers*, C. C Thomas, 1966; (with C. Wellford) *Juvenile Delinquency: Theory and Practice*, Prentice-Hall, 1967; *Counseling Disadvantaged Youth*, Prentice-Hall, 1967; *Managing Student Behavior*, Green, 1967; *Community Counseling*, Green, 1972; *Parole*, Federal Legal Publications, 1974.

* * *

ANDERSON, Barry (Franklin) 1935-

PERSONAL: Born September 14, 1935, in Palo Alto, Calif.; son of Harold (an attorney) and Lillian (Thompson) Anderson; married Aliki Ganiatsos, June 25, 1961; children: Delia, Erik. *Education:* Stanford University, B.A., 1957; Johns Hopkins University, Ph.D., 1963. *Home:* 3634 South East Ogden, Portland, Ore. 97202. *Office:* Department of Psychology, Portland State University, Box 751, Portland, Ore. 97207.

CAREER: University of Oregon, Eugene, assistant professor of psychology, 1963-68; Portland State University, Portland, Ore., associate professor, 1968-74, professor of psychology, 1974—. *Member:* American Psychological Association, Phi Beta Kappa, Sigma Xi.

WRITINGS: The Psychology Experiment: An Introduction to the Scientific Method, Wadsworth, 1966, 2nd edition, Breeds-Cole, 1971; *Cognitive Psychology: The Study of Knowing, Learning, and Thinking*, Academic Press, 1975.

WORK IN PROGRESS: A book on the improvement of cognitive skills; a book on inductive reasoning.

* * *

ANDERSON, Gerald H(arry) 1930-

PERSONAL: Born June 9, 1930, in New Castle, Pa.; son of E. Arthur and Dorothy (Miller) Anderson; married Joanne Pemberton (an assistant director of college records), July 9, 1960; children: Brooks Arthur, Allison Hope. *Education:* Grove City College, B.S. in Commerce, 1952; Boston University, M.Div., 1955, Ph.D., 1960; additional graduate study at University of Marburg, 1955-56, University of Geneva, 1956-57, University of Edinburgh, 1957. *Home and office:* Overseas Ministries Study Center, P.O. Box 2057, 6315 Ocean Ave., Ventnor, N.J. 08406.

CAREER: Methodist minister and educator. Trinity United Methodist Church, Providence, R.I., associate minister, 1957-60; Union Theological Seminary, Manila, Philippines, professor of church history and ecumenics, 1960-70, academic dean, 1963-66, director of graduate studies, 1968-70; Scarritt College for Christian Workers, Nashville, Tenn., professor of world Christianity and president, 1970-73; Cornell University, Ithaca, N.Y., senior research associate in Southeast Asia program, 1973-74; Overseas Ministries Study Center, Ventnor, N.J., associate director, 1974—. Visiting scholar, Union Theological Seminary, New York, N.Y., 1965-66; visiting professor, Stillman University, Philippines, summer, 1964 and 1969, Garrett Theological Seminary, summer, 1966; Beamer lecturer, DePauw University, 1971; visiting lecturer, Drew University Theological School, 1974—. Trustee, Christian Literature Society of the Philippines, 1967-70, United Board for Christian Higher Education in Asia, 1973—, Foundation for Theological Education in Southeast Asia, 1974—.

MEMBER: International Association for Mission Studies (member of executive committee, 1972—), Royal Asiatic Society (fellow), Deutsche Gesellschaft fuer Missionwissenschaft, American Academy of Religion, American Society of Church History, American Catholic History Association, American Society of Missiology (president, 1973-74), Association for Asian Studies, Iona Community (associate member), Fellowship of Reconciliation, Wider Quaker Fellowship, Omicron Delta Kappa. *Awards, honors:* Fulbright scholar, University of Marburg, Germany, 1955-56; Boston University School of Theology distinguished alumnus award, 1971.

WRITINGS: (Compiler) *A Bibliography of the Theology of Missions in the Twentieth Century*, Missionary Research Library, 1958, 3rd edition, 1966; (editor) *The Theology of the Christian Mission*, McGraw, 1961; (contributor) Peter G. Gowing, *Christianity in the Philippines Yesterday and Today*, [Philippines], 1965; (editor) *Sermons to Men of Other Faiths and Traditions*, Abingdon, 1966; *Christianity in Southeast Asia: A Bibliographical Guide*, Missionary Research Library, 1966; (editor) *Christian Mission in Theological Perspective*, Abingdon, 1967; (editor) *Studies in Philippine Church History*, Cornell University Press, 1968; (editor) *Christ and Crisis in Southeast Asia*, Friendship, 1968; (editor with Stephen Neill and John Goodwin) *Concise Dictionary of the Christian World Mission*, Abingdon, 1971; (contributor) William J. Danker and Wi Jo Kang, editors, *The Future of the World Mission*, Eerdmans, 1971; (editor) *Asian Voices in Christian Theology*, Orbis, 1976; (contributor) Fredi Chiappelli, editor, *First Images of America*, University of California Press, 1976.

Editor with Thomas F. Stransky of "Mission Trends" series, Paulist/Neuman and Eerdmans, 1974—. Guest editor, *Southeast Asia Journal of Theology*, July, 1962, *Stillman Journal*, April, 1965; editorial board member, *Southeast Asia Journal of Theology*, 1968-70, *Missiology: An International Review*, 1972—.

* * *

ANDERSON, J(ohn) K(inloch) 1924-

PERSONAL: Born January 3, 1924, in Multan, Pakistan; son of Sir James Drummond and Jean (MacPherson) Anderson; married Esperance Batham, August 10, 1954; children: Elizabeth, John, Katherine. *Education:* Oxford University, B.A., 1949, M.A., 1958. *Politics:* Conservative. *Religion:* Church of England. *Home:* 1020 Middlefield Rd.,

Berkeley, Calif. 94709. *Office:* Department of Classics, University of California, Berkeley, Calif. 94720.

CAREER: University of Otago, Dunedin, New Zealand, lecturer in classics, 1953-58; University of California, Berkeley, assistant professor, 1958-60, associate professor of classical archaeology, 1960—. *Military service:* British Army, 1942-46; became lieutenant. *Member:* Archaeological Institute of America (former president, San Francisco branch), Society of Hellenic Studies (London). *Awards, honors:* Guggenheim fellowship, 1966-67.

WRITINGS: Greek Vases in the Otago Museum, Otago Museum, 1955; *Ancient Greek Horsemanship,* University of California Press, 1961; *Military Theory and Practice in the Age of Xenophon,* University of California Press, 1971; *Xenophon,* Duckworth, 1974. Contributor of articles and reviews to scholarly journals.

WORK IN PROGRESS: A book on Pausonias, publication by Duckworth expected in 1977.

SIDELIGHTS: Anderson participated in excavations in Corinth, with the American School of Archeology in Athens, 1945, and in Greece and Turkey, with the British School of Archaeology in Athens, 1949-52. He is competent in French and Greek, knows some German, Italian, Turkish, Urdu, and reads Spanish. *Avocational interests:* Riding and nature study.

*   *   *

ANDERSON, John M(ueller)   1914-

PERSONAL: Born July 29, 1914, in Cedar Rapids, Iowa; son of Arthur G. (a professor) and Lois (Mueller) Anderson; married Mary Gale (a teacher), June 11, 1936. *Education:* University of Illinois, B.A., 1935, M.A., 1936; University of California, Berkeley, Ph.D., 1939. *Office:* Pennsylvania State University, 420 Boucke, University Park, Pa. 16802.

CAREER: Variously employed with Sears, Roebuck & Co., 1939-41, Elgin National Watch Co., 1941-42; Minneapolis-Honeywell Regulator Co., Minneapolis, Minn., senior design engineer, 1942-43, chief of special projects section, 1943-44, assistant to chief engineer, 1944-45, administrative engineer, 1945; University of Minnesota, Minneapolis, lecturer in mathematics, 1945-46; Pennsylvania State University, University Park, assistant professor of philosophy, 1946-48, associate professor, 1948-51, professor, 1951—, head of department of philosophy, 1948-49, 1952-55, director of Institute for the Arts and Humanistic Studies, 1966—. University of New Zealand, Fulbright professor, 1955; Free University of Berlin, guest professor, 1960-61. Consultant on operations research and computer design; holder of two patents in computer field. *Member:* American Mathematical Society, American Philosophical Association, Association for Symbolic Logic, Society for Phenomenology and Existential Philosophy (executive committee member, 1965-68), American Society for Aesthetics, American Association of University Professors, Western Pennsylvania Philosophical Society (president, 1963-64), Phi Beta Kappa, Sigma Xi, Pi Gamma Mu.

WRITINGS: (With Anderson and Maudeville) *Industrial Management,* Ronald, 1942; *Calhoun: Basic Documents,* Bald Eagle, 1952; (with H. W. Johnstone, Jr.) *Natural Deduction: The Logic of Axiom Systems,* Wadsworth, 1962; (translator and author of introduction with E. H. Freund) Martin Heidegger, *Discourse on Thinking,* Harper, 1966; *The Realm of Art,* Pennsylvania State Univer-

sity Press, 1967. Also author of classified books on solution of certain problems by use of analogue computers, and the use of mathematical models for evaluating performance in certain areas. Contributor of essays and articles to journals. Liberal arts editor, "Penn State Studies," 1963—.

WORK IN PROGRESS: A book on political theory, based on contemporary society; *Man and Being,* a book on metaphysics; investigations of the nature of implication in logic.

AVOCATIONAL INTERESTS: Foreign travel.†

*   *   *

ANDERSON, Robert W(illiam)   1926-

PERSONAL: Born July 2, 1926, in San Mateo, Calif.; son of Leonard R. (a sales representative) and Grace (Read) Anderson; married Blanca Cordova (a professor), August 10, 1952; children: four. *Education:* San Mateo Junior College, A.A., 1945; University of Chicago, M.A., 1948; University of California, Berkeley, Ph.D., 1960. *Home:* Padre Las Casas 205, Hato Rey, Puerto Rico. *Office:* College of Social Science, University of Puerto Rico, Rio Piedras, Puerto Rico.

CAREER: University of Puerto Rico, Rio Piedras, instructor in social science, 1948-50, instructor in political science, 1951-54, assistant professor, 1954-60, associate professor of political science, 1960-62; University of California, Berkeley, assistant professor of political science, 1962-64; University of Puerto Rico, associate professor and chairman of department of political science, 1964-66, professor of political science, 1967—, dean of College of Social Science, 1966-70. Fulbright lecturer in Peru, 1961; visiting professor, Brooklyn College of the City University of New York, 1970-72. Consultant to Puerto Rico Civil Liberties Commission, 1958, 1966, 1974-75, and to Puerto Rico Department of Education, 1966-67; member of Governor's Committee on Esthetics and Natural Resources, Puerto Rico, 1966. *Member:* American Political Science Association, International Studies Association, Latin American Studies Association.

WRITINGS: Party Politics in Puerto Rico, Stanford University Press, 1965; (with Milton Pabon) *Los derechos y los partidos en la sociedad puertorriquena,* Edil (San Juan), 1968. Contributor to *San Juan Review, Revista de Ciencias Sociales, Caribbean Review,* and *Caribbean Studies.*

WORK IN PROGRESS: A book, *Puerto Rico: A Case Study in the Problems of Decolonialization.*

AVOCATIONAL INTERESTS: Music, especially the piano.

*   *   *

ANDERSON, Vivienne   1916-

PERSONAL: Born July 28, 1916. *Education:* Temple University, B.S. in Ed., 1936, M.A. in Ed., 1939; Columbia University, Ed.D., 1955. *Agent:* Nannine Joseph, 200 West 54th St., New York, N.Y. 10019. *Office:* General Education and Curricular Services, New York State Education Department, Albany, N.Y.

CAREER: Philadelphia (Pa.) public schools, administrative work in adult education, 1936-44, junior high school teacher, 1944-47, executive assistant to associate superintendent, 1947-50; New York State Education Department, Albany, 1950—, acting chief, Bureau of Secondary Curriculum Development, 1962-63, chief, Bureau of Continuing

Education Curriculum Development, 1965-67, director, Division of the Humanities and the Arts, 1967-74, assistant commissioner, General Education and Curricular Services, 1974—. Columbia University, Teachers College, New York, N.Y., adjunct professor of administration, 1958-64, coordinator of Teachers College, Columbia University, paperback book project, 1964-66; State University of New York at Albany, adjunct lecturer in administration, 1960—. Chairperson of Citizens Planning Committee for Greater Albany, 1963—, and for New York State Alliance for Arts Education; member of National Advisory Board of the Kennedy Center; advisor to Lincoln Center for the Performing Arts, Saratoga Performing Arts Center, National Committee on Arts for the Mentally Retarded and Handicapped, and New York State Committee on Special Olympics; vice-president, New York State Citizens Council. Special consultant on arts to U.S. Education Commissioner, and other organizations. *Awards, honors:* Freedoms Foundation award; Distinguished Leadership award from the National Association of Humanities Education.

WRITINGS: (With Daniel Davies) *Patterns of Educational Leadership*, Prentice-Hall, 1956; (with Benjamin Fine) *The School Administrator and the Press*, Croft, 1956; (with Fine) *The School Administrator and His Publications*, Croft, 1957; (with Laura Shufelt) *Your America* (history text), Prentice-Hall, 1964; (editor) *Paperbacks in Education*, Teachers College, Columbia University, 1966.

Writer of filmstrip, "New Look at the Superintendent of Schools," for Kellogg Foundation and Teachers College, Columbia University. Author of more than two hundred articles, including several monthly series for *School Executive*; some 50 curriculum bulletins for New York State Education Department, and foreign travel articles for Albany newspapers. Editor of various educational periodicals, including *Schools in Action*, New York State Education Department.

* * *

ANDERSON, Wallace Ludwig 1917-

PERSONAL: Born September 9, 1917, in Hartford, Conn.; son of Ludwig Emanuel (a tool and die maker) and Greta (Askerbloom) Anderson; married Mary Elizabeth Belden (a social worker), March 10, 1943; children: Hale, Whit. *Education:* Trinity College, Hartford, Conn., B.A., 1939, M.A., 1945; Harvard University, graduate study, 1940, 1941; University of Chicago, Ph.D., 1948. *Politics:* Independent. *Religion:* Episcopalian. *Home:* 185 Lakeside Dr., Bridgewater, Mass. 02324. *Office:* Bridgewater State College, Bridgewater, Mass. 02324.

CAREER: Instructor at private schools, 1939-40, 1941-42; University of Northern Iowa, Cedar Falls, assistant professor, 1948-54, associate professor, 1954-58, professor of English, 1958-72, assistant dean of instruction, 1959-63, associate dean of instruction, 1963-65, dean of undergraduate studies, 1965-71; Bridgewater State College, Bridgewater, Mass., academic dean and professor of English, 1972—. Member of intercultural affairs committee, Education and World Affairs, 1967—. *Military service:* U.A. Army Air Forces, Air Transport Command, 1942-45; became chief warrant officer. *Member:* Modern Language Association of America, National Education Association, National Council of Teachers of English, Association of Higher Education, American Association of University Professors. *Awards, honors:* Fulbright professor in the Netherlands, 1957-58; Guggenheim fellow, 1967-68.

WRITINGS: (With N. C. Stageberg) *Poetry as Experience*, American Book Co., 1952; (editor with Stageberg) *Introductory Readings on Language*, Holt, 1962, 4th edition, 1975; (compiler with Stageberg) *Readings on Semantics*, Holt, 1967; *Edwin Arlington Robinson: A Critical Introduction*, Houghton, 1967. Contributor to *College English, American Literature* and *Saturday Review*.

WORK IN PROGRESS: Editing *The Collected Letters of Edwin Arlington Robinson*, for Harvard University Press.

* * *

ANDERSON, Warren DeWitt 1920-

PERSONAL: Born March 19, 1920, in New York, N.Y.; son of Cyril DeWitt and Susan (Olsen) Anderson; married Anne Worden, June 14, 1947; children: Claudia, Eric Worden, Peter DeWitt. *Education:* Haverford College, B.A. 1942; Harvard University, M.A., 1947, Ph.D., 1954; Oxford University, B.A., 1949. *Politics:* Democrat. *Religion:* Episcopalian. *Home:* 27 High Point Dr., Amherst, Mass. 01002. *Office:* Department of Comparative Literature, University of Massachusetts, Amherst, Mass. 01002.

CAREER: College of Wooster, Wooster, Ohio, instructor, 1950-54, assistant professor, 1954-55, associate professor, 1955-60, professor of Greek and Latin, 1960-67, head of department, 1955-67; University of Iowa, Iowa City, professor of English and comparative literature, 1967-70; University of Massachusetts, Amherst, professor of comparative literature, 1970—, chairman of department, 1971-74. Visiting professor, University of Michigan, summers, 1963 and 1965. *Military service:* U.S. Army, Intelligence, 1942-45. U.S. Army Reserve; became second lieutenant. *Member:* American Comparative Literature Association, American Musicological Society, Phi Beta Kappa. *Awards, honors:* Rhodes scholar, 1947-49.

WRITINGS: (Translator, and author of introduction and notes) Aeschylus, *Prometheus Bound*, Bobbs-Merrill, 1963; *Matthew Arnold and the Classical Tradition*, University of Michigan Press, 1965; *Ethos and Education in Greek Music: The Evidence of Poetry and Philosophy*, Harvard University Press, 1966; (editor with Thomas D. Clareson, and contributor) *Victorian Essays: A Symposium*, Kent State University Press, 1967; (translator) *Theophrastus: The Character Sketches*, Kent State University Press, 1970. Contributor of seventy-two articles to *Grove's Dictionary of Music and Musicians* and to journals.

WORK IN PROGRESS: A book on classical influences in Gerard Manley Hopkins.

SIDELIGHTS: Anderson's special fields are ancient Greek music and the classical elements in Victorian poetry.

* * *

ANDERSON, Wilton T(homas) 1916-

PERSONAL: Born November 21, 1916, in Richland, Tex.; son of William Nix and Ruth (Skipper) Anderson; married Gwendolyn Hollis, December 10, 1938; children: Kay Lynn (Mrs. Joseph S. Bowles), Wilton T., Jr. *Education:* Northwestern State College, Alva, Okla., B.S., 1938; University of Oklahoma, M.C.E., 1942; University of Colorado, Ed.D., 1953. *Home:* 1019 Osage Dr., Stillwater, Okla. 74074.

CAREER: High school teacher, Cyril, Okla., 1938-40; Northern Oklahoma Junior College, Tonkawa, associate professor of business and head of department, 1940-46; Bowling Green College of Commerce, Bowling Green,

Ky., professor and head of department of business administration, 1946-47; University of Colorado, Boulder, associate professor of accounting, 1947-57; American Institute of Certified Public Accountants, New York, N.Y., director of education, 1957-60; Oklahoma State University, Stillwater, professor of accounting and head of department, 1960—. Certified public accountant in Colorado and Oklahoma, 1954—. *Member:* American Institute of Certified Public Accountants, American Accounting Association (vice-president, 1964-65; president, 1975-76), Oklahoma Society of Certified Public Accountants (director, 1965-67), Beta Alpha Psi (national president, 1966-67). *Awards, honors:* Teacher of the Year, College of Business, Oklahoma State University, 1963, 1969, and 1970; Oklahoma State University Outstanding Teacher, 1970; American Accounting Association Outstanding Accounting Educator, 1973.

WRITINGS: (With C. A. Moyer and A. R. Watts) *Accounting: Basic Financial, Cost and Control Concepts*, Wiley, 1965. Contributor to *Rocky Mountain Law Review* and accounting journals. Editor, education and professional training section, *Journal of Accounting*, 1958-63; associate editor, *The Journal of Accountancy*, 1974.

*   *   *

ANDERSON-IMBERT, Enrique 1910-

PERSONAL: Born February 12, 1910, in Argentina; son of Jose Enrique and Honorina (Imbert) Anderson; married Margot Di Clerico (a librarian), March 30, 1935; children: Carlos, Anabel (Mrs. Jack Himelblau). *Education:* National University of Buenos Aires, Ph.D., 1946. *Home:* 20 Elizabeth Rd., Belmont, Mass. 02178. *Office:* Harvard University, Cambridge, Mass. 02138.

CAREER: Universidad de Tucuman, Tucuman, Argentina, professor of Spanish literature, 1940-47; University of Michigan, Ann Arbor, assistant professor, 1947-48, associate professor, 1948-51, professor of Spanish literature, 1951-65; Harvard University, Cambridge, Mass., Victor S. Thomas Professor of Hispanic American Literature, 1965—. Princeton University, visiting associate professor, 1950. *Member:* American Academy of Arts and Sciences, Instituto Internacional de Literatura Iberoamericana. *Awards, honors:* Buenos Aires City Hall literary prize, 1934, for manuscript of novel, *Vigilia;* Guggenheim fellowship, 1954-55.

WRITINGS: La flecha en el aire, La Vanguardia (Buenos Aires), 1937; *Tres novelas de Payro con picaros en tres miras*, Facultad de Filosofia y Letras, University of Tucuman, 1942; *Ensayos*, privately printed, 1946; *Ibsen y su tiempo*, Yerba Buena (La Plata), 1946; *Las pruebas del caos*, Yerba Buena, 1946; *El arte de la prosa en Juan Montalvo*, El Colegio de Mexico, 1948.

Estudios sobre escritores de America, Editorial Raigal (Buenos Aires), 1954; *Historia de la literatura hispanoamericana*, two volumes, Fondo de Cultura Economica (Mexico), 1954-61, 7th edition, 1974, translation of 2nd edition by J. V. Falconieri published in one volume as *Spanish-American Literature: A History*, Wayne State University Press, 1963, 2nd edition of translation revised by Elaine Mallery and published in two volumes, 1966; *La critica literaria contemporanea*, Editorial Platania (Buenos Aires), 1957; *Los grandes libros de Occidente y otros ensayos*, Ediciones de Andrea (Mexico), 1957; *Que es la prosa?*, Editorial Columba (Buenos Aires), 1958; *El cuento espanol*, Editorial Columba, 1959.

Critica interna, Editorial Taurus (Madrid), 1961; *El grimorio*, Editorial Losada (Buenos Aires), 1961, translation by Isabel Reade published as *The Other Side of the Mirror*, Southern Illinois University Press, 1966; *Vigilia [and] Fuga*, Editorial Losada, 1962, translation by Esther Whitmarsh Phillips published as *Fugue*, Coronado Press, 1967; *El gato de Cheshire*, Editorial Losada, 1965; *Los domingos del professor*, Editorial Cultura (Mexico), 1965; *La originalidad de Ruben Dario*, Centro Editor de America Latina (Buenos Aires), 1967; *Genio y figura de Sarmiento*, Editorial Universitaria (Buenos Aires), 1967; *Analisis de "Tabare,"* Centro Editor de America Latina, 1968; *Analisis de "Fausto,"* Centro Editor de America Latina, 1968; *La sandia y otros cuentos*, Editorial Galerna (Buenos Aires), 1969; *Una aventura amorosa de Sarmiento*, Editorial Losada, 1969; *Metodos de critica Literaria*, Revista de Occidente (Madrid), 1969.

(Compiler with Eugenio Florit) *Literatura hispanoamericana*, Holt, 1970; *La locura juega al ajedrez*, Siglo XXI Editores (Mexico), 1971; *La Flecha en el aire*, Editorial Gure (Buenos Aires), 1972; *Estudios sobre letras hispanicas*, Editorial Libros de Mexico, 1974; *El Arte de la prosa en Juan Montalvo*, California State University, Sacramento, 1975; *La Botella de Klein*, P.E.N. Club (Buenos Aires), 1975.

SIDELIGHTS: As a writer, Anderson-Imbert "prefers nonrealist literature." Donald A. Yates described his style as "bookish in its allusions, still whimsical at times, and openly flirtatious with fantasy." As a scholar, he "prefers to approach literature from a formalist and aesthetical point of view."

*   *   *

ANDREWES, Christopher Howard 1896-

PERSONAL: Born June 7, 1896, in London, England; son of Sir Frederick William (a pathologist) and Phyllis Mary (Hamer) Andrewes; married Kathleen Helen Lamb, May 26, 1927; children: John Frederick, Michael Robert, David Anthony. *Education:* Attended Highgate School, London, England, 1906-15; University of London, M.B., B.S., M.R.C.S., and L.R.C.P., 1921, M.D., 1922, M.R.C.P., 1923. *Politics:* Liberal. *Home:* Overchalke, Coombe Bissett, Salisbury, Wiltshire, England.

CAREER: St. Bartholomew's Hospital, London, England, house physician, 1921-23; Hospital of the Rockefeller Institute, New York, N.Y., assistant resident physician, 1923-25; St. Bartholomew's Hospital, clinical assistant, 1925-26; National Institute of Medical Research, London, England, 1926-61, began as member of scientific staff, deputy director, 1952-61. Director of Common Cold Research Unit, Medical Research Council, 1946-61, and World Influenza Centre, World Health Organization, 1948-61; Oliver-Sharpey lecturer, Royal College of Physicians, 1934. *Military service:* Royal Navy, 1918-19; became surgeon sublieutenant. *Member:* Royal Society (fellow), Royal College of Physicians (fellow), Royal Society of Medicine (honorary member of epidemiology section), Royal College of Pathologists (honorary fellow), Institute of Biology (fellow), National Academy of Sciences (foreign associate), American Philosophical Society (foreign associate). *Awards, honors:* William Julius Mickle fellowship, University of London, 1931; Bisset-Hawkins Medal, Royal College of Physicians, 1947; Stewart Prize, British Medical Association, 1952, knighted, 1961; L.L.D., University of Aberdeen, 1963; Ricketts Award, University of Chicago, 1964; M.D., University of Lund, 1968.

WRITINGS: Viruses of Vertebrates, Williams & Watkins, 1964, 3rd edition, with H. G. Pereira, 1972; *The Common Cold*, Norton, 1965; *Natural History of Viruses*, Norton, 1967; *The Lives of Wasps and Bees*, Elsevier, 1969; *Viruses and Cancer*, Weidenfeld & Nicholson, 1970; *In Pursuit of the Common Cold*, Heinemann, 1973. Contributor of over two hundred papers to scientific journals, mostly on viruses.

SIDELIGHTS: Andrewes has traveled on professional matters in United States, including Alaska, Union of Soviet Socialist Republics, most European countries, South Africa, Nigeria, Brazil, and Japan. *Avocational interests:* Natural history, especially entomology.

* * *

ANDREWS, Peter 1931-

PERSONAL: Born May 23, 1931, in New York, N.Y.; son of Bert A. (a newspaperman) and Nadine (Wright) Andrews; married Marjorie Key, January 16, 1960; children: Regan. *Education:* Attended Hamilton College, 1950-51, and American Academy of Art, 1951-52. *Home:* Todd Road, Katonah, N.Y. 10536. *Agent:* Scott Meredith Literary Agency, 580 Fifth Ave., New York, N.Y. 10036.

CAREER: United Press International, Washington, D.C., wire editor, Washington Capital News Service, 1958; Hearst Publications, national correspondent for Washington (D.C.) Bureau, 1958-63; *Newsweek*, New York, N.Y., associate editor, 1963; *Playboy*, Chicago, Ill., associate editor, 1964-66; *Reader's Digest*, Pleasantville, N.Y., senior editor, 1967-70; *Americana* magazine, editor, 1972—. Freelance writer. *Member:* Authors Guild of the Authors League of America, Society of Magazine Writers, Overseas Press Club, National Press Club (Washington, D.C.). *Awards, honors:* Gavel Award from American Bar Association, 1972.

WRITINGS: (With father, Bert Andrews) *A Tragedy of History*, Robert B. Luce, 1962; *In Honored Glory*, Putnam, 1966; *Sergeant York: Reluctant Hero*, Putnam, 1969. Writer, producer, and narrator of television documentary film, "Street Crime in the Nation's Capital," for Metro Media Television. Contributor of articles and stories to *TV Guide, Playboy, Saturday Review, American Heritage, Coronet, Horizon*, and other periodicals.†

* * *

ANGELL, Frank Joseph 1919-

PERSONAL: Surname originally Angelilli; born November 14, 1919, in Bronx, N.Y.; son of Nicholas C. (a builder) and Marietta (Emma) Angelilli; married Joan Danza, October 21, 1941; children: Marietta (Mrs. Lawrence Schiff), Peter. *Education:* New York University, B.S., 1941; City College of New York, M.B.A., 1958. *Religion:* Roman Catholic. *Home:* 142 Flamingo St., Atlantic Beach, N.Y. 11509. *Office:* New York University, College of Business and Public Administration, Department of Banking and Finance, 737 Tisch Hall, Washington Square, New York, N.Y. 10003.

CAREER: New York University, New York, N.Y., instructor, 1948-56, assistant professor, 1956-59, associate professor, 1959-64, professor of insurance and finance, 1964—. Chartered property and casualty underwriter, 1958. Consultant to National Commission on Consumer Finance, 1971. *Member:* Iota Nu Sigma, Phi Alpha Kappa, Alpha Phi Sigma, Sigma Eta Phi, Delta Sigma Pi, Arch and Square, Sphinx, Lawyer's Club.

WRITINGS: Insurance Principles and Practices, Ronald, 1959; *Health Insurance*, Ronald, 1963; *Angell's Study Manual on Insurance*, Insurance Advocate, 1966, published as *Study Manual on Insurance with Questions and Answers*, 1969. Contributor to journals.

WORK IN PROGRESS: Revision of several texts.

* * *

ANNESS, Milford E(dwin) 1918-

PERSONAL: Born February 14, 1918, in Metamora, Ind.; son of Clyde H. (hardware dealer) and Grace (Stegner) Anness; married Marie Cramer, July 8, 1939; children: Grace Suzanne (Mrs. James W. Gillum), Ronald Kent, Dennis Jay, Milford Edwin, Jr., Mark Richard, John Cramer. *Education:* Attended Ball State Teachers College (now Ball State University), 1936-37; Indiana University, A.B., 1940, LL.B., 1954. *Politics:* Republican. *Religion:* Church of Christ. *Home address:* R.R. 7, Columbus, Ind. 47201. *Office address:* P.O. Box 623, Columbus, Ind.

CAREER: Proprietor of retail hardware store in Metamora, Ind., 1941-51; Indiana state senator, 1946-62; American United Life Insurance Co., Indianapolis, Ind., legal department, 1952-55; Fayette County Circuit Court, Connersville, Ind., judge, 1955-62; attorney in private practice in Columbus, Ind., 1962—. Indiana Judicial Council, member, 1960-64; Indiana Governor's Council on Children and Youth, Fayette County representative; Indiana Sesquicentennial Advisory Committee, member. Cincinnati Bible Seminary, trustee; Alexander Christian Foundation, vice-president. *Military service:* U.S. Army, 1943-45; served in South Pacific Theater; became sergeant. *Member:* Bible Study League of America (president, Indiana chapter), American Legion, Veterans of Foreign Wars, Sons of the American Revolution (state treasurer), Lambda Chi Alpha, Sigma Delta Kappa, Kiwanis, Masons, Odd Fellows.

WRITINGS: Tippecanoe, as the Red Man Saw It and Fought It, privately printed, 1961; *Song of Metamoris*, Caxton, 1964; *Forever the Song*, Caxton, 1967; *Stars Above America*, Commercial Service Co. (Hudson, Indiana), 1968. Also author of *Golden Moment of Hoosier History*, 1969; *Metamora, Canal Town*, 1970; *Low Bridge and Locks Ahead on the Whitewater Canal*, 1972; *Sing a New Song of Glory* (book of hymns), 1973.

* * *

ANOUILH, Jean (Marie Lucien Pierre) 1910-

PERSONAL: Surname pronounced "Ahn-wee"; born June 23, 1910, in Bordeaux, France; son of Francois (a tailor) and Marie-Magdeleine (a pianist; maiden name, Soulue) Anouilh; married Monelle Valentin (an actress; divorced); married Nicole Lancon, July 30, 1953; children: (first marriage) Catherine (Mme. Francois Pages); (second marriage) Caroline, Nicolas, Marie-Colombe. *Education:* Graduated from Ecole Colbert, Bordeaux; College Chaptal, baccalaureate; Sorbonne, University of Paris, law student, 1931-32. *Home:* 3, rue Furstenberg, Paris 6, France.

CAREER: Free-lance writer of publicity scripts and comic gags for films, and advertising copy writer for Publicite Damour, Paris, France, two years; worked as secretary to Louis Jouvet's theatrical company, Comedie des Champs-Elysees, Paris, 1931-32; worked as general assistant to Georges Pitoeff, a director, in Paris; now a full-time writer. *Military service:* Served in France during 1930's. *Awards, honors:* Grand Prix du Cinema Francais, 1949, for film,

"Monsieur Vincent"; Antoinette Perry Award, and citation from the cultural division of the French Embassy, both 1955, for *Thieves' Carnival* (New York production); New York Drama Critics' Circle award for best foreign play of 1956-57, for "Waltz of the Toreadors"; First Prize for best play of the year from Syndicate of French Drama Critics, 1970, for "Cher Antoine" and "Les Poissons rouges"; Paris Critics Prize, 1971, for "Ne Reveillez pas Madame."

WRITINGS—Plays: (With Jean Aurenche) *Humulus le muet*, Editions Francaises Nouvelles, c. 1929; "L'-Hermine" (first produced in Paris at Theatre de l'Oeuvre, 1932), published in *Les Oeuvres libres*, No. 151, Fayard, 1934, translation by Miriam John published as "The Ermine," in *Plays of the Year*, Volume 13, edited by J. C. Trewin, Ungar, 1956; "Y'avait un prisonnier" (title means "There was a Prisoner"; first produced in Paris at Theatre des Ambassadeurs, 1935), published in *La Petite Illustration* (periodical), May 18, 1935; *Le Voyageur sans bagage* (first produced in Paris at Theatre des Mathurins, 1937), published in *La Petite Illustration*, April 10, 1937, included in *Pieces Norires*, Editions Balzac, 1942, translation by John Whiting published as *Traveller Without Luggage*, Methuen, 1959 (produced in London at Arts Theatre, 1959), translation by Lucienne Hill produced in New York as "Traveller Without Luggage," ANTA Theatre, 1964, French-language edition, edited by Diane Birckbichler, Ann Dube, and Walter Meiden, Holt, 1973; *La Sauvage* (first produced in Paris at Theatre des Mathurins, 1938), published in *Les Oeuvres libres*, No. 201, Fayard, 1938, translation by Lucienne Hill published as *Restless Heart*, Methuen, 1957 (produced in London at St. James Theatre, 1957), French-language edition, with essay and notes by Jean-Pierre Reynaud, Livre de Poche, 1968; *Le Bal des voleurs* (first produced in Paris at Theatre des Arts, 1938; French-language production in New York at Theatre des Quatre Saisons, 1938), published in *Les Oeuvres libres*, No. 209, Fayard, 1938, published separately by Editions Francaises Nouvelles, 1945, translation by Lucienne Hill published as *Thieves' Carnival*, Methuen, 1952, Samuel French (New York), 1952 (produced in New York at Cherry Lane Theatre, 1955).

Rendez-vous de Senlis (first produced in Paris at Theatre de l'Atelier, 1938), published in *Pieces roses*, Editions Balzac, 1942, published separately by Editions de la Table Ronde, 1958, translation by Edwin O. Marsh published as *Dinner With the Family*, Methuen, 1958 (produced in London at New Theatre, 1957, and in New York at Gramercy Arts, 1961); *Leocadia* (first produced in Paris at Theatre de l'Atelier, 1939), published in *Pieces roses*, Editions Balzac, 1942, same, edited by Bettina L. Knapp and Alba della Fazia, Appleton, 1965, translation by Patricia Moyes published as *Time Remembered*, Methuen, 1955, Coward, 1958 (produced in New York at Morosco Theater, 1957), condensed version published in *The Best Plays of 1957-58*, edited by Louis Kronenberger, Dodd, 1958; *Eurydice* (based on the Orpheus and Eurydice myth; first produced in Paris at Theatre de l'Atelier, 1941), published in *Pieces noires*, Editions Balzac, 1945, translation by Mel Ferrer produced in Hollywood at Coronet Theatre, 1948, translation by Kitty Black published as *Point of Departure*, Samuel French, 1951 (produced in London at Lyric-Hammersmith Theatre, 1950; produced in New York by Performing Group at Mannhard't Theatre Foundation, October 28, 1967), published in America as *Legend of Lovers*, Coward, 1952 (produced in New York at Plymouth

Theatre, 1951), French-language edition, with annotation by Rambert George, Bordas, 1968.

Antigone (based on the play by Sophocles; first produced in Paris at Theatre de l'Atelier, 1944), Editions de la Table Ronde, 1946, translation by Lewis Galantiere published as *Antigone*, Random House, 1946 (produced in New York at Cort Theatre, 1946), excerpts, with notes and critical material by Jacques Monfrier, published as *Antigone: Extraits*, Bordas, 1968; "Oreste" (fragment), published in *La Table Ronde*, 3rd book (periodical), 1945, included in *Jean Anouilh*, by Robert de Luppe, Editions Universitaires, 1959; "Romeo et Jeannette" (based on *Romeo and Juliet*; first produced in Paris at Theatre de l'Atelier, 1946), published in *Nouvelles pieces noires*, Editions de la Table Ronde, 1946, adaptation by Donagh MacDonagh produced under title "Fading Mansion," in London at Duchess Theatre, 1949, translation by Miriam John produced as "Jeannette," in New York at Maidman Playhouse, 1960; "Jezebel," published in *Nouvelles pieces noires*, Editions de la Table Ronde, 1946; *L'Invitation au chateau* (first produced in Paris at Theatre de l'Atelier, 1947), Editions de la Table Ronde, 1948, same, edited by D. J. Conlon, Cambridge University Press, 1962, translation by Christopher Fry published as *Ring Around the Moon*, Oxford University Press (New York), 1950 (produced in New York at Martin Beck Theatre, 1950), adaptation by Clifford Bax published in London as *The Pleasure of Your Company*; *Ardele, ou La Marguerite* (first produced, on the same bill with "Episode de la vie d'un auteur," in Paris at Comedie des Champs-Elysees, 1948), Editions de la Table Ronde, 1949, adaptation by Cecil Robson produced as "Cry of the Peacock," in New York at Mansfield Theatre, 1950, translation by Lucienne Hill published as *Ardele*, Methuen, 1951 (produced in New York at Cricket Theatre, 1958).

"Episode de la vie d'un auteur" (ten-minute curtain raiser; first produced in Paris at Comedie des Champs-Elysees, 1948), published in *Cahiers de la compagnie Madeleine Renaud—Jean-Louis Barrault*, Julliard, 1959, translation produced as "Episode in the Life of an Author," in Buffalo, N.Y. at Studio Arena Theatre, September, 1969, and later produced Off-Broadway; *Cecile, ou L'Ecole des peres* (first produced in Paris at Comedie des Champs-Elysees, 1949), published in *Pieces brillantes*, Editions de la Table Ronde, 1951, published separately by Editions de la Table Ronde, 1954, translation by Luce Klein and Arthur Klein published as "Cecile, or the School for Fathers," in *From the Modern Repertoire*, 3rd series, edited by Eric Bentley, Indiana University Press, 1958; *La Repetition, ou L'Amour puni* (first produced in Paris at Theatre Marigny, 1950; French-language production by Jean-Louis Barrault in New York at Ziegfield Theatre, 1952), La Palatine (Geneva), 1950, translation by Pamela Hansford Johnson and Kitty Black published as *The Rehearsal*, Coward, 1961 (produced in New York at Royale Theatre, 1963), French-language critical edition by Philippe Sellier, Bordas, 1970; *Colombe* (first produced in Paris at Theatre de l'Atelier, 1951), published in *Pieces brillantes*, Editions de la Table Ronde, 1951, published separately by Livre de Poche, 1963, adaptation by Denis Cannan published as *Colombe*, Coward, 1954 (produced in New York at Longacre Theatre, 1954); *Monsieur Vincent* (dialogue), Bayerisch Schuelbuch-Verlag, 1951; *La Valse des Toreadors*, Editions de la Table Ronde, 1952, translation by Lucienne Hill published as *The Waltz of the Toreadors*, Elek, 1956, Coward, 1957 (English translation produced in New York at Coronet Theatre, 1957), condensed version published in

The Best Plays of 1956-57, edited by Louis Kronenberger, Dodd, 1957, French-language edition, edited by Clifford King, Harrap, 1968; *L'Alouette* (based on the story of Joan of Arc; first produced in Paris at Theatre Montparnasse, 1953), Editions de la Table Ronde, 1953, same, edited by Merlin Thomas and Simon Lee, Methuen, 1956, Appleton, 1957, translation by Christopher Fry published as *The Lark*, Methuen, 1955, Oxford University Press (New York), 1956, translation by Lucienne Hill (originally titled "Joan"), published as *The Lark*, Random House, 1956, adaptation by Lillian Hellman produced as "The Lark," in New York at Longacre Theatre, 1955, condensed version published in *The Best Plays of 1955-56*, edited by Louis Kronenberger, Dodd, 1956; *Medee* (first produced in Paris at Theatre de l'Atelier, 1953), published in *Nouvelles pieces noires*, Editions de la Table Ronde, 1946, published separately by Editions de la Table Ronde, 1953, translation by Lothian Small published as "Medea," in *Plays of the Year, 1956*, Volume 15, Ungar, 1957.

Ornifle, ou Le Courant d'air (first produced in Paris at Comedie des Champs-Elysees, 1955), Editions de la Table Ronde, 1955, translation by Hill published as *Ornifle: A Play*, Hill & Wang, 1970; *Pauvre Bitos, ou Le Diner de tetes* (first produced in Paris at Theatre Montparnasse, 1956), Editions de la Table Ronde, 1958, same, edited by W. D. Howarth, Harrap, 1958, translation by Lucienne Hill published as *Poor Bitos*, Coward, 1964 (produced in New York by Classic Stage Co. Repertory, 1969); *L'-Hurluberlu, ou Le Reactionnaire amoureux* (first produced in Paris at Comedie des Champs-Elysees, 1959), Editions de la Table Ronde, 1959, adaptation by Lucienne Hill published as *The Fighting Cock*, Coward, 1960 (produced in New York at ANTA Theatre, 1959); *Becket, ou L'-Honneur de Dieu* (first produced in Paris at Theatre Montparnasse-Gaston Baty, 1959), Editions de la Table Ronde, 1959, translation by Lucienne Hill published as *Becket, or the Honor of God*, Coward, 1960 (produced as "Becket" in New York at St. James Theatre, 1960), French-language edition, edited by W. D. Howarth, Harrap, 1962, edition by Bettina L. Knapp and Alba della Fazia, Appleton, 1969; *Madame De . . .* (based on a story by Louise de Vilmorin; original play neither published nor produced), translation by John Whiting, Samuel French (London), ca. 1959 (produced, on the same bill with "Traveller Without Luggage," in London at Arts Theatre, 1959); (with Roland Laudenback) "La Petite Moliere" (first produced in France at Festival of Bordeaux, 1960), published in *L'Avant-Scene* (periodical), December 15, 1959.

La Grotte (first produced in Paris at Theatre Montparnasse, 1961), Editions de la Table Ronde, 1961, translation by Lucienne Hill published as *The Cavern*, Hill & Wang, 1966 (produced in Cincinnati at Playhouse in the Park, June, 1967; produced in New York by Classic Stage Co., 1968); *Le Songe du critique*, published in *L'Avant-Scene*, No. 143, 1961, published separately (French language) by Lensing (Dortmund, Germany), 1963; *La Foire d'-Empoigne* (first produced in Paris, 1962), Editions de la Table Ronde, 1961; "L'Orchestre" (first produced in Paris, 1962), published in *L'Avant-Scene*, November 15, 1962, translation produced as "The Orchestra," in Buffalo, N.Y. at Studio Arena Theatre, September, 1969, later produced Off-Broadway; *Fables*, Editions de la Table Ronde, 1962; *Cher Antoine, ou l'Amour rate* (first produced in Paris at Comedie des Champs-Elysees, October 1, 1969), Editions de la Table Ronde, 1969, translation by Lucienne Hill published as *Dear Antoine, or The Love that Failed* (produced

in England at Chichester Festival Theatre, May 19, 1971; produced in Cambridge, Mass., at Loeb Drama Center of Harvard University, July 20, 1973), Hill & Wang, 1971; *Le Boulanger, la boulangere et le petit mitron* (first produced at Comedie des Champs-Elysees, November 13, 1968), Editions de la Table Ronde, 1969, translation by Hill produced as "The Baker, the Baker's Wife, and the Baker's Boy," in Newcastle, England, at University Theatre, fall, 1972.

"Le Theatre, ou La Vie comme elle est" (title means "Theatre, or Life as It Is"), first produced at Comedie des Champs-Elysees, c.1970; *Ne reveillez pas Madame* (title means "Don't Wake Up Madame"; first produced at Comedie des Champs-Elysees, October 21, 1970), Editions de la Table Ronde, 1970; *Les Poissons rouges, ou Mon Pere, ce heros* (title translated as "The Goldfish" or "The Red Fish"; first produced in Paris at Theatre de l'Oeuvre, c.1970), Editions de la Table Ronde, 1970; *Tu etais si gentil quand tu etais petit* (title means "You Were So Nice when You Were Little"; first produced in Paris at Theatre Antoine, January 18, 1972), Editions de la Table Ronde, 1972; *Le Directeur de l'Opera*, Editions de la Table Ronde, 1972.

Unpublished plays: "Attile le magnifique," 1930; "Mandarine," produced in Paris at Theatre de l'Athenee, 1933; "Le Petit bonheur," 1935; "L'Incertain," 1938. Also author of an English television play.

Ballet: "Les Demoiselles de la nuit," score by Jean-Rene Francaix, 1948; (with Georges Neveux) *Le Loup*, score by Henri Dutilleux, Editions Ricordi, 1953.

Other writings: (Editor and translator) William Shakespeare, *Trois Comedies* [*As You Like It, Winter's Tale*, and *Twelfth Night*], Editions de la Table Ronde, 1952; (with Pierre Imbourg and Andre Warnod) *Michel-Marie Poulain*, Braun, 1953; (translator with wife, Nicole Anouilh) Graham Greene, *L'Amant complaisant* [*The Complaisant Lover*], Laffont, 1962; (adaptor) Roger Vitrac, "Victor," published in *L'Avant-Scene*, November 15, 1962; (with Leon Thoorens and others) *Le Dossier Moliere*, Gerard, 1964; (translator) Shakespeare, *Richard III* (performed in Paris at Theatre Montparnasse, 1964), Livre de Poche; (editor with Claude Vincent) Oscar Wilde, "Il est important d'etre aime" [*The Importance of Being Earnest*], published in *L'Avant-Scene*, No. 101.

Omnibus volumes—French language; all published by Editions de la Table Ronde, except as noted: *Pieces roses: Le Bal des voleurs, Le Rendez-vous de Senlis, [et] Leocadia*, Editions Balzac, 1942, 2nd edition, with addition of "Humulus le muet," Editions de la Table Ronde, 1958; *Pieces noires: L'Hermine, La Sauvage, Le Voyageur sans bagage, Eurydice*, Editions Balzac, 1942; *Nouvelles pieces noires: Jezebel, Antigone, Romeo et Jeannette, [et] Medee*, 1946; *Antigone [et] Medee*, Le Club Francais du Livre, 1948; *Pieces brillantes: L'Invitation au chateau, Colombe, La Repetition ou L'Amour puni, [et] Cecile, ou L'Ecole des peres*, 1951; *Deux Pieces brillantes: L'Invitation au chateau [et] La Repetition ou L'Amour puni*, Le Club Francais du Livre, 1953; *La Sauvage [et] Le Bal des voleurs*, Colmann-Levy, 1955; *Antigone [et] L'Alouette*, Livre Club de Libraire, 1956; *Pieces grincantes* (includes "Ardele, ou La Marguerite," "La Valse des toreadors," "Ornifle, ou Le Courant d'air," and "Pauvre Bitos, ou Le Diner de tetes"), 1956; *Une Piece rose, deux pieces noires* (includes "Le Bal des voleurs," "La Sauvage," and "Eurydice"), Club des Libraires de France, 1956; *Le Rendez-vous de Senlis [et] Leocadia*, 1958; *Le Voyageur sans bagage, Le*

Bal des voleurs, 1958; *Antigone, Becket, [et] Cecile*, 1959; *La Sauvage [et] L'Invitation au chateau*, 1960; *Pieces costumees* (includes "L'Alouette," "Becket, ou L'Honneur de Dieu," and "La Foire d'Empoigne"), 1960; *Theatre complet*, six volumes (*Pieces grincantes, Pieces costumees, Pieces brillantes, Pieces noires, Nouvelles Pieces noires, Pieces roses*), 1961-63; *Deux Pieces roses: Le Bal des voleurs [et] Le Rendezvous de Senlis*, Le Club Francais du Livre, 1963; *La Repetition, ou L'Amour puni, Leocadia, [et] Eurydice*, Club des Amis, no date; *Ardele, ou La Marguerite suivi de La Valse des toreadors*, 1970; *Nouvelles Pieces grincantes* (contains "L'Hurluberlu, ou Le Reactionnaire amoureux," "La Grotte," "L'Orchestre," "Le Boulanger, la boulangere, et le petit mitron," "Les Poissons rouges, ou Mon Pere, ce heros"), 1970; *Eurydice. Suivi de Romeo et Jeannette*, 1971.

Omnibus volumes—English language: *Antigone [and] Eurydice* (translated by Lewis Galantiere and Lothian Small, respectively), Methuen, 1951; *. . . Plays*, three volumes, Hill & Wang, Volume I published as *Five Plays* (contains "Antigone," "Eurydice," "The Ermine," "The Rehearsal," and "Romeo and Jeannette"), 1958, Volume II published as *Five Plays* (contains "Restless Heart," "Time Remembered," "Ardele," "Mademoiselle Colombe," and "The Lark"), 1959, Volume III published as *Seven Plays* (contains "Thieves' Carnival," "Medea," "Cecile, or The School for Fathers," "Traveler without Luggage," "The Orchestra," "Episode in the Life of an Author," "Catch as Catch Can"), 1967; *Ardele [and] Colombe* (translated by Lucienne Hill and Denis Cannan, respectively), Methuen, 1959; *Leocadia [and] Humulus le muet*, edited by Bernard Fielding, Harrap, 1961; *Ardele [and] Pauvre Bitos*, edited by Raymond Riva, Dell, 1965; *The Collected Plays*, Methuen, Volume I (contains "The Ermine," "Thieves' Carnival," "Restless Heart," "Traveller without Luggage," "Dinner with the Family"), 1966, Volume II (contains "Time Remembered," "Point of Departure," "Antigone," "Romeo and Jeanette," "Medea"), 1967.

Plays are represented in anthologies, including: *Contemporary Drama*, edited by E. Bradlee Watson and Benfield Pressey, Scribner, 1956; *One-Act: Eleven Short Plays of the Modern Theatre*, edited by Samuel Moon, Grove, 1961; *Joan of Arc: Fact, Legend and Literature*, by Wilfred Jewkes and Jerome B. Landfield, Harcourt, 1964; *Masterpieces of Modern French Theatre*, edited by Robert W. Corrigan, Macmillan, 1967.

Films: (Dialogue with Jean Aurenche) "Les Degourdis de la onzieme," 1936; (dialogue with Aurenche) "Vous n'avez rien a declarer," 1937; (dialogue with Aurenche) "Les Otages," 1939; (scenario with Aurenche, and author of dialogue) "Le Voyageur sans bagage," 1943 (released in U.S. with title "Identity Unknown," Republic, 1945); (adaptor and author of dialogue with J. Duvivier and G. Morgan) "Anna Karenina," 1947; (dialogue with J. Bernard-Luc, and author of scenario) "Monsieur Vincent" (released in U.S. by Lopert, 1949); (scenario with Bernard-Luc, adaptor, and author of dialogue) "Pattes Blanches," 1948; (adaptor and author of dialogue) "Un Caprice de Caroline cherie," 1950; (adaptor and author of dialogue with first wife, Monelle Valentin) "Deux sous de violettes," 1951; (adaptor and author of scenario and dialogue) "Le Rideau rouge (ce soir on joue Macbeth)," 1952; (adaptor and author of dialogue) "Le Chevalier de la nuit," 1953; (author of screenplay) "The End of Belle" (reviewed as "The Passion of Slow Fire"), Trans-Lux Distributing (United States), 1962; "Waterloo," c.1969; "Time for Loving,"

1972; "A Room in Paris." Also adapted Jean Clot's "La Grain de beaute" as a film, c.1969.

SIDELIGHTS: At the age of nine, Anouilh was already writing plays in imitation of Edmond Rostand; at sixteen he wrote his first long play, although it has been neither published nor produced. But it was not until 1944, with the production of *Antigone*, that Anouilh's popularity was established in France.

Anouilh has divided his plays into the "rosy" or pleasant plays (the *pieces roses* and the *pieces brillantes*), and the "black" or unpleasant plays (the *pieces noires* and the *pieces grincantes*). In the former, the forces of good, as represented by symbolic characters, are victorious. In the black plays, the wicked triumph without concession. The two categories, as Anouilh has defined them, roughly correspond to the formalized genres, Comedy and Tragedy. In general, the black plays, or tragedies, have enjoyed greater success than the lighter works.

Discussing Anouilh's method in the black plays, David Grossvogel writes: "Aristotle's tragic protagonist was an ideal projection but for the one, circumscribed area of his failing. His ills thus grew from him organically without disfiguring him. Anouilh's protagonist is conceived disfigured but for that clamorous pride which must shield his true being from the world and, for a while, from himself. The moment of his dramatic life is measured by the time required for the individual to destroy this shield." Grossvogel demonstrates that, since the evils depicted in Anouilh's tragic theater are "the world and its various excrescences, all symbolized by massiveness," the secondary characters emerge as "the one real presence of the stage on stage." The characters who are least important to the drama, then, "enjoy the finest delineation and all the play's color. . . ." The principals, by contrast, "remain thin, ghostly ephemerae, waiting to leave these too weighty antagonists, though hoping that their own off-stage substance will be sufficiently indicated by contrast." H. A. Smith explains: "Anouilh's characteristic method is to take the world of the theatre, with its traditions, conventions and the backstage or off-the-boards life of the theatre-folk, as an image for the world at large. The effect is to hold up the mirror, not to nature, but to a series of other mirrors, poised at a variety of angles, so that the ensuing reflections and refractions create the curiously wraith-like impression felt in a hall of mirrors." Grossvogel summarizes: ". . . Rather than black and rose, Anouilh's theater is frequently just black and white. Black and white are the terms of the conflict, black and white is the hero's elementary complexity, both terms being derived from the same harsh reality and splendid illusion which it enfolds." John Harvey adds: "The inner visions of an Anouilh character are often so intense that they blind him to outer reality. One moment he may nurture a smoldering memory, another, a mere figment, but it is always imagination, and not actuality, that runs his life."

In his preface to Christopher Fry's translation of *L'-Invitation au chateau* (published with title *Ring Around the Moon*, Oxford University Press, 1950), Peter Brook wrote: "Anouilh writes plays for performance rather than for paper. His literary quality is rather that of theatre literature the elegance of his dialogue appears when it is spoken by comedians in the rhythm of a comic scene. . . . Anouilh is in the tradition of the *Commedia dell' arte*. His plays are recorded improvisations. . . . He is a poet, but not a poet of words: he is a poet of words-acted, of scenes-set, of players performing."

L. C. Pronko writes: "Anouilh ... is interested primarily in revealing to us his view of man and man's place in the universe. His principal theme is man himself as he faces his destiny. The secondary themes of love and money are but further illustrations of this theme, as they reveal man in his aspirations and his compromises, his greatness and his baseness.... Man's condition—the central preoccupation of this theater—is presented to us in a dynamic way; painted now in realistic, now in romantic, now in classical terms; sometimes grave, sometimes amusing, always absorbing. Our interest is kept alive by characters who are not only interesting as symbols but appealing as people, or meaningful as types who possess a certain reality given to them either by their complexity, by their very passion, or by their presentation as caricatures." Wallace Fowlie, however, introduces this reservation: "[Anouilh] is certainly of his time, fully aware of the manias and the problems of his age. But in order that the public in France today may laugh with him, without shame, and for future publics in France and elsewhere to continue to laugh without shame, he will have to effect a more drastic aesthetic transposition than he has yet achieved."

Analyzing the import of Anouilh's work for modern theater in general, Pronko wrote: "... Within the framework of a theater that is largely oriented toward commercialism and pure entertainment, Anouilh continues to reflect a profound awareness of our anxious era when man, insecure in a universe that seems devoid of reason, has come to doubt the authenticity of those values he had always accepted. Anouilh has revealed to him more clearly his predicament.... Such a theater will always be of value and interest, for it helps make him aware, not only of those forces with which he must contend, but of those qualities within himself which may give him strength for the struggle."

In 1962, Anouilh directed Roger Vitrac's play, "Victor," at Theatre de l'Ambigu in Paris. Anouilh told *CA* that he wishes to emphasize this production because, he believes, Vitrac was a bitter and unrecognized man. Further, Anouilh notes that this play has been cited as an important source of Ionesco's work, as well as of contemporary theater in general.

The film "Monsoon" (United Artists, 1953) was based on "Romeo and Jeannette"; *L'Alouette* was adapted for television and presented as "The Lark," in the Hallmark "Hall of Fame" series, 1956-57; *Madame De ...* was filmed in 1959; Patricia Moyes' translation of *Leocadia* was adapted for television and presented by Compass Productions as "Time Remembered" for the Hallmark "Hall of Fame" series, 1961; *La Valse des toreadors* was filmed with the title "Waltz of the Toreadors" (based on the translation by Lucienne Hill), Continental Distributing, 1962; *Becket, ou L'Honneur de Dieu* was filmed with the title "Becket" (based on the translation by Lucienne Hill), Paramount Pictures, 1963; "Colombe" was produced as an opera at Opera Comique, Paris, c.1970; "Traveller without Luggage" was adapted for NET Playhouse in 1971; a new version of "Antigone" was produced for "Playhouse New York" series of Public Broadcasting System in 1972.

BIOGRAPHICAL/CRITICAL SOURCES: E. O. Marsh, *Jean Anouilh*, British Book Centre, 1953; David I. Grossvogel, *The Self-Conscious Stage in Modern French Drama*, Columbia University Press, 1958; Robert de Luppe, *Jean Anouilh*, Editions Universitaires, 1959; John Gassner, *Theatre at the Crossroads: Plays and Playwrights of the Mid-Century American Stage*, Holt, 1960; Wallace Fowlie, *Dionysus in Paris: A Guide to Contemporary French Theater*, World, 1960; Toby Cole, editor, *Playwrights on Playwriting*, Hill & Wang, 1961; Leonard Cabell Pronko, *The World of Jean Anouilh*, University of California Press, 1961; H. A. Smith, *Contemporary Theater*, Arnold, 1962; Phillippe Jolivet, *Le Theatre de Jean Anouilh*, Editions Michel Brient, 1963; John Harvey, *Anouilh: A Study in Theatrics*, Yale University Press, 1964; Travis Bogard and William I. Oliver, editors, *Modern Drama: Essays in Criticism*, Oxford University Press, 1965; P. M. W. Thody, *Anouilh*, Oliver & Boyd, 1968; A. M. della Fazia, *Jean Anouilh*, Twayne, 1969; K. W. Kelly, *Jean Anouilh: An Annotated Bibliography*, Scarecrow, 1973; Carolyn Riley, editor, *Contemporary Literary Criticism*, Gale, Volume I, 1973, Volume III, 1975.†

* * *

ANSELL, Jack 1925-

PERSONAL: Born November 21, 1925, in Monroe, La.; son of Jack and Sadie (Flemin) Ansell. *Education:* Attended Louisiana State University, 1942-43; University of Missouri, B.A. in journalism, 1948, M.A., 1950. *Home:* 320 East 54th St., New York, N.Y. 10022. *Agent:* Bill Berger Associates, 535 East 72nd St., New York, N.Y.

CAREER: Monroe Morning World-News Star, Monroe, La., columnist, 1950-53; KNOE-TV, Monroe, La., vicepresident in charge of sales, 1953-59; *Sponsor* Magazine, New York, N.Y., senior editor, 1959-60; ABC Television Network, New York, N.Y., supervisor of program development, 1962-71, assistant to president, 1971—. Frequent lecturer on topics concerning the portrayal of the Jew in modern American fiction, drama, and broadcasting.

WRITINGS: His Brother, the Bear, Doubleday, 1960; *The Shermans of Mannerville*, Arbor House, 1971; *Jelly*, Arbor House, 1971; *Gospel: An American Success Story*, Arbor House, 1973; *Summer* (short stories), Arbor House, 1973; *Dynasty of Air*, Arbor House, 1974.

WORK IN PROGRESS: A companion piece to *Dynasty of Air*; a novel tentatively titled *Giants in Lilliput*.

* * *

ANTHONY, Michael 1932-

PERSONAL: Born February 10, 1932, in Mayaro, Trinidad; son of Nathaniel (a farmer) and Eva (Jones) Anthony; married Yvette (a typist), February 8, 1958; children: two sons, two daughters. *Education:* "No institution of note attended and no degrees or awards gained." *Politics:* "Uncategorized." *Office:* Publications Department, Texaco Trinidad, Pointe-a-Pierre, Trinidad.

CAREER: Held a number of factory jobs after immigrating to England; Reuter News Agency, London, England, subeditor, 1964-68; lived in Brazil, 1968-70; Texaco Trinidad, Pointe-a-Pierre, Trinidad, assistant editor, 1970—.

WRITINGS: The Games Were Coming, Deutsch, 1963, Houghton, 1968; *The Year in San Fernando*, Deutsch, 1965; *Green Days by the River*, Houghton, 1967.

SIDELIGHTS: Anthony told *CA*: "I am essentially a novelist and since I hold that the novel tells a story I feel strongly that I should not use the medium to air my philosophies. However, I feel very strongly about the brotherhood of mankind, and as a consequence abominate war. One of my main hopes is that human beings will find a way to live together without friction and my feeling is that the most distressing thing in this world is the inhumanity of man to man on the grounds of race. I feel that if the racial problem is solved man will have found the key to peace on this planet. Although I am not hopeful about any immediate change in the Southern African situation I think the thousands of people who are trying to solve the problem in the United States must make a great difference to the basic situation there. Yet, though I feel this way, the books I write have nothing (on the surface) to do with race or war.''

All of his books have met with critical success. Referring to *The Games Were Coming*, McGuinness remarked that ''not one single word seemed superfluous in the entire book.'' Eve Burgess praised *Green Days by the River* for its ''freshness of impact.'' She compared it to ''the first calypsos we heard a dozen years ago; not the later commercialised espresso-bar ones, but the originals, with their mixture of innocence and bawdiness that saved them from being sentimental. It is not a very ambitious novel, but in its own way it is perfect.''

Anthony writes that he is extremely interested in space exploration ''as I sometimes find the mystery of the Universe too much to bear. I often wonder if space exploration will one day explode our present theories about God, and about the origin and formation of the matter about us. I do consider man's quest for knowledge vital and, in fact, inevitable.'' He also commented that he would ''like to see this world of rich and poor nations, powerful and weak nations, superseded by a world of one strong nation formed out of all. In other words I am advocating World Government. I sometimes think that I am merely being idealistic, but being an optimist I am not surprised.''

BIOGRAPHICAL/CRITICAL SOURCES: Punch, February 22, 1967; *London Magazine*, April, 1967, Kenneth Ramchand, *The West Indian Novel and Its Background*, Faber, 1970.†

*   *   *

ANTHONY, William G.   1934-

PERSONAL: Born September 25, 1934, in Fort Monmouth, N.J.; son of Emile Peter (an army colonel) and Martha G. (Armstrong) Anthony. *Education:* Yale University, B.A., 1958; Art Students League, New York, N.Y., graduate study, 1961. *Politics:* Democrat. *Address:* 216 Westbeth, 463 West Street, New York, N.Y. 10014.

CAREER: Artist. San Francisco Academy of Art, teacher of drawing, 1962. His work is in the collection of the Palace of the Legion of Honor (San Francisco), Art Institute of Chicago, Corcoran Gallery of Art (Washington, D.C.), Cleveland Museum of Art, Delgado Museum of Art (New Orleans), Waliraf-Richartz Museum (Cologne, Germany), Whitney Museum of American Art (New York, N.Y.), and other museums. *Military service:* U.S. Army, 1953-55.

WRITINGS: A New Approach to Figure Drawing, Crown, 1965.†

*   *   *

APPLETON, Victor II
[Collective pseudonym]

WRITINGS—''Tom Swift, Jr.'' series; published by Grosset: *Tom Swift and His Atomic Earth Blaster*, 1954; *. . . and His Giant Robot*, 1954; *. . . and His Flying Lab*, 1954; *. . . and His Jetmarine*, 1954; *. . . and His Rocket Ship*, 1954; *. . . and His Outpost in Space*, 1955; *. . . and His Diving Seacopter*, 1956; *. . . in the Caves of Nuclear Fire*, 1956; *. . . on the Phantom Satellite*, 1956; *. . . and His Ultrasonic Cycloplane*, 1957; *. . . and His Deep-Sea Hy-*

drodome, 1958; *. . . and His Space Solartron*, 1958; *. . . in the Race to the Moon*, 1958; *. . . and His Electronic Retroscope*, 1959.

Tom Swift and His Spectromarine Selector, 1960; *. . . and the Cosmic Astronauts*, 1960; *. . . and the Visitor from Planet X*, 1961; *. . . and the Electronic Hydrolung*, 1961; *. . . and His Megascope Space Prober*, 1962; *. . . and His Triphibian Atomicar*, 1962; *. . . and the Asteroid Pirates*, 1963; *. . . and His Repelatron Skyway*, 1963; *. . . and His Aquatomic Tracker*, 1964; *. . . and His 3-D Telejector*, 1964; *. . . and His Polar Ray Dynasphere*, 1965; *. . . and His Sonic Boom Trap*, 1965; *. . . and His Subocean Geotron, 1966; . . . and the Mystery Comet*, 1966; *. . . and the Captive Planetoid*, 1967; *. . . and His G-Force Inverter*, 1968; *. . . and His Dyna-4 Capsule*, 1969.

Tom Swift and His Cosmotron Express, 1970; *. . . and the Galaxy Ghosts*, 1971. Also written under this pseudonym, *Tom Swift in the Jungle of the Mayas*.

SIDELIGHTS: See **ADAMS, Harriet S., STRATEMEYER, Edward L.** and **SVENSON, Andrew E.**†

*   *   *

APPLEYARD, Reginald Thomas   1927-

PERSONAL: Born September 16, 1927, in Claremont, Western Australia; son of Albert John (a metal moulder) and Jessie (Johns) Appleyard; married Iris Evelyn Clifton, March 20, 1954; children: Wendy, Helen, Ingrid. *Education:* University of Western Australia, B.A. (honors), 1954; Duke University, M.A., 1957, Ph.D., 1962. *Home:* 14 Lentara Crescent, City Beach, 6015, West Australia. *Office:* Department of Economics, University of Western Australia, Nedlands 6009, W.A., Australia.

CAREER: Australian National University, Canberra, Australian Capital Territory, senior fellow (researcher) in demography, 1958-67, academic assistant to the director of School of Social Sciences, 1963-67; University of Western Australia, Perth, professor of economic history and chairman of department, 1967—. *Member:* Economic Society of Australia, Academy for the Social Sciences in Australia, International Population Union.

WRITINGS: British Emigration to Australia, University of Toronto Press, 1965; (editor) *Man and His Environment*, University of Western Australia, 1970.'Also author of *Low-Cost Housing and the Migrant Population,* 1963.

WORK IN PROGRESS: The First Five Years in Australia; Australia and Asia, a demographic-economic study; *Economic History of Freemantle Port.*

*   *   *

ARBINGAST, Stanley A(lan)   1910-

PERSONAL: Born September 26, 1910, in Lisbon, Iowa; son of Clarence Earle and Faye (Oxley) Arbingast. *Education:* Winona State College, B.A., 1934; University of Washington, Seattle, M.A., 1948, Ph.D., 1956. *Religion:* Episcopalian. *Home:* 3208 Duval, Austin, Tex. 78705. *Office:* Bureau of Business Research, Austin, Tex. 78712.

CAREER: Elementary school teacher and principal in Lewisville, Minn., 1929-33; teacher in Lewiston, Minn., 1934-38; Duluth (Minn.) public schools, junior high school teacher, 1938-42, high school teacher, 1945-47; University of Texas, Austin, assistant professor, 1949-53, associate professor, 1953-59, professor of marketing, 1959—, resources specialist, Bureau of Business Research, 1949—, assistant director, 1951-60, associate director, 1960-69, director, 1969—. *Military service:* U.S. Army Air Forces, 1942-45. *Member:* American Geographical Society (fellow), Association of American Geographers, American Association for the Advancement of Science, American Association of University Professors, Regional Science Association, Southwestern Social Science Association (vice-president, 1958-60; president, 1960-61), Associated University Bureaus of Business and Economic Research (secretary-treasurer, 1962-64; president, 1968; member of executive committee), Travel Research Association (member of executive committee), Texas Travel Research Association, Delta Sigma Pi, Phi Kappa Sigma, Phi Kappa Phi, Omicron Delta Kappa. *Awards, honors:* Guggenheim award, 1949; Teaching Excellence Award, Students' Association, University of Texas, 1965.

WRITINGS: (With Al E. Cudlipp, Jr. and Anne K. Schuler) *Community Relations in Texas Industry*, Bureau of Business Research, University of Texas, 1955; (with J. R. Stockton, R. C. Henshaw, and Alfred G. Dale) *Water for the Future: The Texas Economy to 1975*, four volumes, Bureau of Business Research, University of Texas, 1959; (with Lorrin G. Kennamer) *Atlas of Texas*, Bureau of Business Research, University of Texas, 1963, revised edition, 1967; (with Michael E. Bonine and others) *Atlas of Mexico*, Bureau of Business Research, University of Texas, 1970. Also author of more than eight geographic, economic, and industrial surveys of selected areas of Texas. Contributor of monographs and articles to professional publications. Editor, *Texas Industrial Expansion*, 1950—, *Texas Business Review*, 1963—.

WORK IN PROGRESS: A revision of *Atlas of Mexico*; a book, *Atlas of Central America*.

* * *

ARCHER, Sellers G. 1908-

PERSONAL: Born July 28, 1908, in Comanche, Tex.; son of Isaac Williamson and Priscilla (Hendrick) Archer; married Lorena Morris, April 26, 1930; children: Constance Louise (Mrs. Robert J. Douglas). *Education:* Attended University of Oklahoma, Southwestern State College, Weatherford, Okla., B.A. *Religion:* Baptist. *Home:* 5709 Wheaton Dr., Fort Worth, Tex. 76133.

CAREER: U.S. Department of Agriculture, Soil Conservation Service, 1935-73, serving in the field as camp foreman for Civilian Conservation Corps, as conservation aide, conservationist, and as information specialist in the South, 1958-66, head of Information and Education Unit, South Region, 1966-73. *Member:* Soil Conservation Society of America (president, South Carolina chapter, 1964, and of North Texas chapter, 1970).

WRITINGS: (With Clarence E. Bunch) *The American Grass Book*, University of Oklahoma Press, 1953; *Soil Conservation*, University of Oklahoma Press, 1955; *Rain, Rivers and Reservoirs*, Coward, 1963, revised edition, 1973; *Archers on the Frontier*, privately printed, 1975. Contributor to agriculture and other periodicals.

* * *

ARCHER, Stephen H(unt) 1928-

PERSONAL: Born November 30, 1928, in Fargo, N.D.; son of Clifford Paul (a professor) and Myrtle (Blair) Archer; married Carol Mohr, December 29, 1951 (divorced February, 1971); married Lana Jo Urban, September 23,

1972; children: Stephen P., Paul, Timothy William, David Conrad. *Education:* University of Minnesota, B.A., 1949, M.A., 1953, Ph.D., 1958. *Home:* 880 Kingswood Drive, Salem, Ore. 97304. *Office:* Graduate School of Administration, Willamette University, Salem, Ore.

CAREER: University of Washington, Seattle, assistant professor, 1956-60, associate professor, 1960-65, professor of finance and statistics, 1965-73, chairman of department, 1966-70; Williamette University, Salem, Ore., dean of Graduate School of Administration, 1973—. Hinton, Jones, & Co., investments vice-president, 1969-70; consultant to Washington Bankers Association, 1971-72. *Military service:* U.S. Navy, 1950-52; became lieutenant. *Member:* Institute of Management Sciences, American Financial Management Association (president, 1973-74), Operations Research Society, American Association of Collegiate Schools of Business, National Association of Schools of Public Affairs and Administration, American Economic Association, Western Finance Association, Phi Beta Kappa.

WRITINGS: (With R. Meier) *Introduction to Mathematics for Business Analysis*, McGraw, 1960; (with C. D'Ambrosio) *Business Finance: Theory and Management*, Macmillan, 1966, revised edition, 1972; (editor with D'Ambrosio) *The Theory of Business Finance*, Macmillan, 1967; (with Jack Clark Francis) *Portfolio Analysis*, Prentice-Hall, 1971. Contributor to professional journals. Editor, *Journal of Financial and Quantitative Analysis*, 1966-70.†

* * *

ARENDT, Hannah 1906-

PERSONAL: Born October 14, 1906, in Hannover, Germany; came to the United States, 1941, naturalized, 1950; daughter of Paul (an engineer) and Martha (Cohn) Arendt; married Heinrich Bluecher (a professor of philosophy), 1940 (died, 1970). *Education:* Koenigsberg University, B.A., 1924; attended universities at Marburg and Freiburg; Heidelberg University, studied with Karl Jaspers, awarded Ph.D. (philosophy), 1928; Notgemeinschaft der Deutschen Wissenschaft, research fellow, 1931-33. *Politics:* Independent. *Religion:* No religious affiliation. *Home:* 370 Riverside Dr., New York, N.Y. 10025. *Office:* Graduate Faculty of Political and Social Science, New School for Social Research, New York, N.Y.

CAREER: Fled Germany for Paris in 1933; did social work for Youth Aliyah, Paris, France, 1934-40; Conference on Jewish Relations, New York, N.Y., research director, 1944-46; Schocken Books, Inc., New York, N.Y., chief editor, 1946-48; Jewish Cultural Reconstruction, New York, N.Y., executive director, 1949-52; Princeton University, Princeton, N.J., visiting professor of politics (the first woman to be appointed a full professor there), 1959; University of Chicago, Chicago, Ill., professor with committee on social thought, 1963-67; New School for Social Research, Graduate Faculty of Political and Social Science, New York, N.Y., professor, 1967—. Visiting professor at University of California, Berkeley, 1955, Columbia University, 1960, and at Brooklyn College (now Brooklyn College of the City University of New York). Member of board of directors, Conference on Jewish Relations, Jewish Cultural Reconstruction, and Judah Magnes Foundation. *Member:* Institut International de Philosophie Politique, American Academy of Political and Social Science, National Institute of Arts and Letters, American Academy of Arts and Sciences (fellow), American Political Science Association,

American Society of Political and Legal Philosophy, Deutsche Akademie fuer Sprache und Dichtung (corresponding member), P.E.N. *Awards, honors:* Guggenheim fellow, 1952-53; award from National Institute of Arts and Letters, 1954; Rockefeller fellow, 1958-60 and 1969-70; Lessing Preis, Hamburg, 1959; Freud Preis from Deutsche Akademie fur Sprache und Dichtung, 1967; Emerson-Thoreau Medal from American Academy of Arts and Sciences, 1969; M. Cary Thomas Prize from Bryn Mawr College, 1971; honorary degrees from numerous colleges and universities, including Yale University, 1971, Dartmouth College, 1972, and Princeton University, 1972.

WRITINGS: Der Liebesbegriff bei Augustin, J. Springer (Berlin), 1929; *Sechs Essays,* L. Schneider (Heidelberg), 1948; (translator with M. Greenberg) Franz Kafka, *Diaries,* edited by Max Brod, Volume 2, Schocken, 1949.

The Origins of Totalitarianism, Harcourt, 1951, new edition, 1966, three volume edition, Volume I: *Totalitarianism,* Volume II: *Imperialism,* Volume III: *Anti-Semitism,* 1968, new edition with added prefaces, 1973 (published in England as *Burden of Our Time,* Secker & Warburg, 1951); (editor, and author of introduction) Hermann Broch, *Essays,* Volume I: *Dichten und Erkennen,* Volume II: *Erkennen und Handeln,* Rhein-Verlag (Zurich), 1955; *Fragwuerdige Traditionsbestaende im politischen Denken der Gegenwart: Vier Essays,* Europaeische Verlagsanstalt (Frankfurt am Main), 1957; *The Human Condition* (lectures delivered under the title "Vita Activa"), University of Chicago Press, 1958, collector's edition, 1969; *Die Krise in der Erziehung,* Angelsachsen Verlag (Bremen), 1958; *Rahen Varnhagen: The Life of a Jewess,* translation by Richard and Clara Winston, East and West Library for Leo Baeck Institute, 1958, original German text published as *Rahel Varnhagen: Lebensgeschichte einer Deutschen Juedin aus der Romantic,* Piper (Munich), 1959; *Die ungarische Revolution und der totalitaere Imperialismus,* Piper, 1958; *Wahrheit, Freiheit, und Friede: Karl Jaspers,* Piper, 1958; *Elemente totaler Herrschaft,* Europaeische Verlagsanstalt, 1958.

Von der Menschlichkeit in finsteren Zeiten: Rede ueber Lessing, Piper, 1960; *Between Past and Future: Six Exercises in Political Thought,* one essay translated by Denver Lindley, Viking, 1961, enlarged edition published as *Between Past and Future: Eight Exercises in Political Thought,* 1968; *Freedom and Revolution,* Connecticut College, 1961; (editor) Karl Jaspers, *The Great Philosophers,* translated by Ralph Manheim, Harcourt, Volume I: *The Foundations* (also published in three parts as *Kant, Plato and Augustine,* and *Socrates, Buddha, Confucius, Jesus*) 1962, Volume II: *The Original Thinkers,* 1966; *On Revolution,* Faber, 1963; *Eichmann in Jerusalem: A Report on the Banality of Evil,* Viking, 1963, revised and enlarged edition, 1964; *Men in Dark Times,* Harcourt, 1968; (editor and author of introduction) Walter Benjamin, *Illuminations: Essays and Reflections,* translated by Harry Zohn, Harcourt, 1968.

Machf und Gewalt, Piper, 1970; *On Violence,* Harcourt, 1970; *Crises of the Republic: Lying in Politics, Civil Disobedience, On Violence, Thoughts on Politics and Revolution,* Harcourt, 1972; *Wahrheit und Luege in der Politik: Zwei Essays,* Piper, 1972.

Contributor: K. S. Pinson, editor, *Essays on Antisemitism,* 2nd edition, Conference on Jewish Relations, 1946; William Ebenstein, editor, *Modern Political Thought,* Rinehart, 1954; Columbia College, *Man in Contemporary Society,*

Volume 2, Columbia University Press, 1956; Carl J. Friedrich, editor, *Authority,* Harvard University Press, 1958; Robert M. Hutchins and Mortimer J. Adler, editors, *The Great Ideas Today, 1961-1963,* Encyclopaedia Britannica, 1961-1963; Peter Demetz, editor, *Brecht,* Prentice-Hall, 1962; *Analyse d'un vertige,* Societe d'Editions et de Publications Artistiques et Litteraires, 1968; Arthur A. Cohn, editor, *Arguments and Doctrines: A Reader of Jewish Thinking in the Aftermath of the Holocaust,* Harper, 1970; Carl Saner, compiler, *Karl Jaspers in der Diskussion,* Piper, 1973. Contributor to *Contemporary Jewish Record, Review of Politics, New Yorker, New York Review of Books,* and other publications.

SIDELIGHTS: William Barrett once wrote: "Dr. Arendt's mind has always seemed to me something of an eighth wonder; an erudite and disciplined thinker, she still retains the ebullient intuition of a woman able always to come at things from a fresh and unusual angle." She is "one of the most brilliant and original of living political philosophers," wrote Irving Kristol. "There is throughout [the essays in *Between Past and Future*], a tension between an almost uncanny (and exceedingly feminine) percipience and a noble, elevated (and exceedingly masculine) architectonic of ideas.... Her essays at their best, liberate us from prejudices and preconceptions that we are not even aware we possess." Kristol considers her essay "What Is Authority?" one that scholars of the future "will very likely treasure ... as one of the remarkable intellectual achievements of our age."

Dr. Arendt's subtle, sometimes difficult, interpretations of history and ideas leave some critics bewildered, others cautious of accepting her conclusions. Peter Laslett calls her "an interesting phenomenon," and adds: "It is for her readers to decide whether they are willing to accept her bizarre declaration of her occasionally unpalatable conclusions in order to experience her extraordinary powers of insight." However much her critics may argue her methods and conclusions, they generally agree with Robert Bierstedt's comment (specifically on *The Human Condition*) that even with its minor shortcomings, such a book "must be regarded as a significant contribution to the intellectual history of our time."

Believing that revolution and war constitute the central forces of our time, Dr. Arendt's writings are in effect a continuing investigation of political and philosophical developments. Taking her background into account, the *New Yorker* sent her to Israel to report on the Eichmann trial. The resulting articles, later expanded into the book *Eichmann in Jerusalem,* caused a proliferation of emotional responses. Justice Michael A. Musmanno accused Dr. Arendt of errors of fact compounded by what he termed a display of "purely private prejudice." Norman Podhoretz, in addition to similar rebukes, chastised her for ascribing the judgment "banal" to Eichmann's personality, and discounted her report as one "riddled with paradox and ambiguity." Irving Howe feared the possibility that "hundreds of thousands of good middle-class Americans will have learned from those articles that the Jewish leadership in Europe was cowardly, inept, and even collaborationist; that the Jewish community helped the Nazis achieve their goal of racial genocide.... " Some critics even believed that Dr. Arendt defended Eichmann's participation in the Nazi slaughters. B'nai B'rith pronounced the book evil, a distortion of facts to prove a preconceived notion, the "notion" being what Dr. Arendt had termed a "total moral collapse" on the part of European Jews.

In her defense Dr. Arendt published one protest in which she reiterated that she was not implying that active resistance on the part of the Jews would have been feasible. Ideally, they should have done nothing. "And in order to do nothing," she said, "one needed only to say: I am just a simple Jew, and I have no desire to play any other role." In a not altogether favorable review Bruno Bettelheim wrote: "The issues are so vast that we do not seem able yet to cope with them intellectually, though her book is certainly a most serious and in part successful effort to do so. . . . [She] is right not to grant the murdered Jews the sainthood of martyrs, and to view them simply as men." Edwin Samuel saw the book as a valuable attempt to put the whole ghastly period into correct perspective for the ordinary reader." The *New Yorker*, replying especially to Justice Musmanno's attack, ventured to say that Dr. Arendt's condemnation of Nazi leaders "was far more withering than any that had been made before," and that "her sorrow over [the suffering of the Jews] was far more eloquent than the Justice's own. . . . He accused her of indifference to 'the screams of horror-stricken women and terrorized children as they saw the tornado of death sweeping toward them,' although an important purpose of her inquiry was to determine the causes of those screams, so that they might never be heard again."

In 1970 Hannah Arendt became the center of a dispute over Bertolt Brecht's political ideology. The occasion was the British publication of *Men in Dark Times*, which included an essay on Brecht. In question was Brecht's attitude toward Stalin, as revealed in writings during the latter part of his life, which Dr. Arendt contended indicates "there is no doubt that Brecht had high praise for Stalin."

BIOGRAPHICAL/CRITICAL SOURCES: American Sociological Review, February, 1959; *New Republic*, July 10, 1961, June 15, 1963; *Guardian*, November 3, 1961; *Atlantic*, March, 1963; *Saturday Review*, May 18, 1963; *New York Times Book Review*, May 19, 1963; *New Yorker*, July 20, 1963; *Commentary*, September, 1963, October, 1963; *Essays and Reviews From the Times Literary Supplement*, 1964, Volume 3, Oxford University Press, 1965; *New York Times*, March 28, 1970.†

* * *

ARKHURST, Joyce Cooper 1921-

PERSONAL: Born October 20, 1921, in Seattle, Wash.; daughter of Felix Bond (a dentist) and Hazel (James) Cooper; married Frederick Arkhurst (an economist), October 3, 1959; children: Cecile Nanaba. *Education:* University of Washington, Seattle, B.A., 1944; Columbia University, M.L.S., 1949. *Politics:* Democrat. *Religion:* Protestant. *Home:* 2500 Johnson Ave., Bronx, N.Y. 10463.

CAREER: Chicago Public Library, Chicago, Ill., librarian, 1967-69; Fieldston School, Riverdale, N.Y., 1970-73; writer. *Member:* American Society of African Culture, National Association for the Advancement of Colored People, Delta Sigma Theta.

WRITINGS: The Adventures of Spider—West African Folktales, Little, Brown, 1964; *More Adventures of Spider*, Scholastic, 1971; (compiler with Anne Pellowski) *Have You Seen a Comet?*, John Day, 1971.

WORK IN PROGRESS: An autobiography.

SIDELIGHTS: Joyce Arkhurst lived in Paris for nine months, and in Ghana, two years. She visited Liberia to collect folktales in 1956.

ARMSTRONG, Roger D. 1939-

PERSONAL: Born December 3, 1939, in Kansas City, Mo.; son of Housen Barr and Esther (Wolfley) Armstrong; married Janis Ann Davenport (an educator), June 17, 1960; children: David, Allen, Joy. *Education:* Vanderbilt University, B.A.; Yale University, B.D. *Politics:* Liberal Democrat.

CAREER: Currently administrator with New Haven Redevelopment Agency, New Haven, Conn.

WRITINGS: Peace Corps and Christian Mission, Friendship, 1965.†

* * *

ARMSTRONG, William A(rthur) 1915-

PERSONAL: Born December 29, 1915, in Annfield Plain, Durham, England; son of William (a mining engineer) and Edith Armstrong; married Margaret Patricia Cairns, March 24, 1951; children: William David, Jean Margaret. *Education:* University of Sheffield, B.A., 1938, M.A., 1940; Yale University, graduate study, 1940-42, Ph.D., 1943. *Religion:* Church of England. *Home:* 17 St. Mary's Rd., London S.W. 19, England. *Office:* Department of English, Birkbeck College, University of London, London, England.

CAREER: British Institute, Gozo, Malta, director, 1942-44; University College of Wales, Aberystwyth, lecturer in English, 1945-48; King's College, University of London, London, England, reader in English, 1948-65; University of Hull, Hull, England, professor of English, 1965-67; University of London, professor of English, Westfield College, 1962-74, professor of English, Birkbeck College, 1974—, chairman of university board of studies in English, 1968-70. Lecturer for British Foreign Office and British Council in Sweden, Finland, Germany, Holland, Egypt, and Malta. *Member:* English Association (honorary treasurer, 1959-63), Society for Theatre Research (executive committee, 1957-60), Standing Conference of Drama Associations (chairman, 1965-68), Malone Society (council, 1961-74). *Awards, honors:* Commonwealth Fund fellowship to Yale University, 1940-42.

WRITINGS: The Elizabethan Private Theatres: Facts and Problems, Society for Theatre Research, 1958; (editor and contributor) *Experimental Drama*, G. Bell, 1963; (editor) *Essays and Studies, 1964* (Shakespeare quarter-centenary volume), J. Murray, for English Association, 1964; *Classic Irish Drama*, Penguin, 1964; (editor) *Elizabethan History Plays*, Oxford University Press, 1965; *Marlowe's "Tamburlaine": The Image and the Stage*, University of Hull Press, 1966; *Sean O'Casey* (monograph), Longmans, Green, 1967; *Shakespeare's Typology: Miracle and Morality Motifs in "Macbeth"*, Westfield College, 1970; (compiler) *Shakespeare's Histories: An Anthology of Modern Criticism*, Penguin, 1972; (editor) Francis Bacon, *The Advancement of Learning*, Nelson, 1974. Also associate editor of *The Diary of Samuel Pepys*, eleven volumes, G. Bell, 1970-74. Contributor to literary journals. Advisory editor of *Modern Drama, Renaissance Drama*, and *Nineteenth Century Theatre Research*.

WORK IN PROGRESS: A two-volume work, *The Development of the English Theatre*; *The Indoor Theatre in the Age of Shakespeare*, both for Allen & Unwin.

SIDELIGHTS: William Armstrong is competent in French, German, and Italian.

ARMSTRONG, William H(oward) 1914-

PERSONAL: Born September 14, 1914, in Lexington, Va.; son of Howard Gratton and Ida (Morris) Armstrong; married Martha Stone Street Williams, August 24, 1942 (deceased); children: Christopher, David, Mary. *Education:* Hampden-Sydney College, A.B. (cum laude), 1936. *Home:* Kimadee Hill, Kent, Conn. 06757.

CAREER: Kent School, Kent, Conn., history master, 1945—. *Awards, honors:* National School Bell Award of National Association of School Administrators, 1963, for distinguished service in the interpretation of education; John Newbery Medal from American Library Association, 1970, Mark Twain Award from Missouri Association of School Librarians, 1972, and Nene Award from Hawaii Association of School Librarians and Hawaii Library Association, all for *Sounder.*

WRITINGS: Study is Hard Work, Harper, 1956, 2nd edition, 1967; *Through Troubled Waters*, Harper, 1957; (with Joseph W. Swain) *The Peoples of the Ancient World*, Harper, 1959; *87 Ways to Help Your Child in School*, Barron's, 1961; *Sounder*, Harper, 1969; *Sour Land*, Harper, 1971; *The MacLeod Place*, Coward, 1972; *Hadassah: Esther the Orphan Queen*, Doubleday, 1972; *Barefoot in the Grass: The Story of Grandma Moses*, Doubleday, 1972; *The Mills of God*, Doubleday, 1973; *My Animals*, Doubleday, 1973; *The Education of Abraham Lincoln*, Coward, 1974.

SIDELIGHTS: Sounder was called the best book of 1969 by the Children's Editor of the New York Times Book Review. June Meyer Jordan said of the book: "We engage a history frozen around loving people who never scream, who never cry: they search, they continue any way they can, and they wait. It seems that *Sounder* is worth reading—by young, and not so young, adults.

"The deliberate cool of its telling follows McLuhan's rule: We are urged into participation, a moral questioning and a moral wonder. When we stop reading, we want to hear the living voice, the distinctively human sound of this anonymous, black family."

A movie adapted from the book was released by Twentieth-Century Fox in 1972.

Armstrong told *CA*: "I raise purebred Corriedale sheep on a rocky hillside in Connecticut and live in a house built entirely by my own hands. I prefer stone masonry and carpentry to writing."

* * *

ARNDT, Karl John Richard 1903-

PERSONAL: Born September 17, 1903, in St. Paul, Minn.; son of Edward Louis (a professor and founder of Lutheran Church, Missouri Synod, in China) and Maria (Solomon) Arndt; married Anne Linhorst, 1933 (divorced); married Blanca Hedwig Renner, October 7, 1950; children: Karl Siegfried Norman, Carola Anne Sylvia. *Education:* Undergraduate study at St. John's College, Winfield, Kan., and under father in Hankow, China; Concordia Seminary, St. Louis, Mo., diploma, 1927; Washington University, St. Louis, Mo., A.M., 1928; graduate study at University of Marburg and University of Berlin, 1928-29; Johns Hopkins University, Ph.D., 1933. *Politics:* Conservative Independent. *Home:* 5 Hazelwood Rd., Worcester, Mass. 01610. *Office:* Department of German, Clark University, Worcester, Mass. 01610.

CAREER: Worked with U.S. Mississippi River Survey Service, 1924-25; instructor in German and Greek at Concordia College, Edmonton, Alberta, Canada, 1925-26, and in German at University of Missouri, Columbia, 1929-31, and Goucher College and Johns Hopkins University, Baltimore, Md., 1931-33; Hartwick College, Oneonta, N.Y., professor of German and Greek, 1933-35; Louisiana State University, Baton Rouge, assistant professor of Germanics, 1935-42, associate professor, 1942-45; U.S. Military Government for Germany, staff of Education and Religious Affairs Division, 1945-50; Clark University, Worcester, Mass., professor of German and head of department, 1950—. Sealsfield lecturer in Germany (at invitation of Sealsfield Gesellschaft), 1964; lecturer on German-American press history at universities in Germany, 1965.

MEMBER: Modern Language Association of America, American Association of Teachers of German, American Antiquarian Society, Sealsfield Gesellschaft (Germany), Gesellschaft fuer deutsche Presseforschung (Bremen; corresponding member), Phi Beta Kappa. *Awards, honors:* Guggenheim research fellow, 1957-58; research grants from American Philosophical Society, Social Science Research Council, Carl Schurz Foundation, Pabst Foundation, National Endowment for the Humanities, Lilly Endowment, Stiftung Volkswagenwerk, and Deutsche Forschungsgemeinschaft.

WRITINGS: Early German-American Narratives, American Book Co., 1941; (with May E. Olson) *German-American Newspapers and Periodicals, 1732-1955: History and Bibliography*, Quelle & Meyer (Heidelberg), 1961, 2nd edition, revised with appendix, Johnson Reprint, 1965; *George Rapp's Harmony Society: 1785-1847*, University of Pennsylvania Press, 1965, revised edition, Fairleigh University Press, 1972; *George Rapp's Successors and Material Heirs, 1847-1916*, Fairleigh Dickinson University Press, 1971; (editor) *Charles Sealsfields Saemtliche Werke*, nine volumes, Verlag Georg Olms, 1972-74; (with May Olson) *The German Language Press of the Americas*, Verlag Dokumentation, 1973. Contributor to *Proceedings of the American Antiquarian Society* and other proceedings, yearbooks, and learned journals. About fifty articles and reviews (many on Charles Sealsfield, George Rapp's Harmonists, and German-American relations) have been published in language and history journals in America and Germany.

WORK IN PROGRESS: Documentary History of George Rapp's Harmony Society, 1706-1916, six volumes; *A History and Bibliography of the First Hundred Years of German Printing in America*; editor of *The German P.O.W. Camp Papers in America, 1943-45*; a biography of Ernst Steigner, nineteenth century German-American publisher; a critical biography of Charles Sealsfield.

* * *

ARNOLD, Arnold (Ferdinand) 1921-

PERSONAL: Born February 6, 1921, in Germany; came to United States in 1938, naturalized in 1942; children: Francis. *Education:* Studied at St. Martin's School of Art, London, England, 1937-38, Pratt Institute, 1938-39, New York University and Columbia University, 1939-40. *Religion:* Jewish. *Home:* 14 Crystal Gade, St. Thomas, Charlotte, Amalie, Virgin Islands. *Agent:* Toni Mendez, Inc., 140 East 56th St., New York, N.Y. 10022.

CAREER: Designer for advertising agencies and publishers, 1939-40; Workshop School of Design, New York, N.Y., director, 1949-50; Arnold Arnold Design, Inc., New York, N.Y., president, 1963—; Manuscript Press, Inc.,

New York, N.Y. president, 1963—. Designer of children's play and learning material; work in this field was subject of one-man show at Museum of Modern Art, 1953, and has been exhibited throughout United States and abroad. Writer and editor. *Military service:* U.S. Army, Infantry, 1942-45; served in European theater; received Purple Heart.

WRITINGS: How to Play with Your Child, Ballantine, 1954; *Toy Soldiers* (self-illustrated), Random House, 1963; *Tongue Twisters and Double Talk* (self-illustrated), Random House, 1964; *Children's Books before 1850*, Dover, 1966; *Your Child's Play: How to Help Your Child Reap the Full Benefit of Creative Play*, Essandess, 1968; *Violence and Your Child*, Regnery, 1969; (compiler) *Pictures and Stories from Forgotten Children's Books*, Dover, 1969; *The World Book of Children's Games*, World, 1970; *Your Child and You*, Regnery, 1970; *The Yes and No Book*, Reilly & Lee, 1970; *Career Choices for the Seventies*, Crowell, 1971; *How to Teach Your Child from Birth to School Age*, Prentice-Hall, 1971. Writer of newspaper column, "Parents and Children." Consultant editor, Rutledge Books, 1962—; editor, "Look and Do Books," Rand McNally, 1963-64.†

* * *

ARNOLD, Elliott 1912-

PERSONAL: Born September 13, 1912, in New York, N.Y.; son of Jack and Gertrude (Frank) Arnold; married Helen Emmons (divorced, 1957); married Julie Kennedy, September, 1958 (divorced, January, 1961); married Jacqueline Harris Stephens, February, 1961 (divorced, 1963); married Glynis Johns (an actress), October, 1964 (divorced, 1973); children: (first marriage) Thomas Guy, Mary Jean. *Agent:* McIntosh & Otis, Inc., 18 East 41st St., New York, N.Y. 10017.

CAREER: New York World-Telegram, New York, N.Y., newspaperman, 1934-42; *American Indian*, member of editorial staff, 1948—; author. *Military service:* U.S. Army Air Forces, 1942-45; became captain; received Bronze Star. *Member:* The Players (New York). *Awards, honors:* Commonwealth Club of California Silver Medals, 1948, for *Blood Brother*, and, 1960, for *Flight from Ashiya*; William Allen White Children's Book Award for best juvenile fiction of the year, 1958, for *White Falcon*.

WRITINGS—Novels, unless otherwise indicated: *Two Loves*, Greenburg, 1934; *Personal Combat*, Greystone, 1936; *Finlandia: The Life of Sibelius* (biography), Holt, 1938; *Only the Young*, Holt, 1939; *The Commandos*, Duell, Sloan & Pearce, 1942, published as *First Comes Courage*, Triangle, 1943; (with Donald Hough) *Mediterranean Sweep* (nonfiction), Duell, Sloan & Pearce, 1944; (with Richard Thruelsen) *Big Distance* (nonfiction), Duell, Sloan & Pearce, 1945; *Tomorrow Will Sing*, Duell, Sloan & Pearce, 1945; *Blood Brother*, Duell, Sloan & Pearce, 1947; *Everybody Slept Here*, Duell, Sloan & Pearce, 1948; *Deep in My Heart* (biography of Sigmund Romberg), Duell, Sloan & Pearce, 1949.

Walk With the Devil, Knopf, 1950; *Broken Arrow* (juvenile), Duell, Sloan & Pearce, 1951; *Time of the Gringo*, Knopf, 1953; *Rescue* (nonfiction), Duell, Sloan & Pearce, 1956; *White Falcon* (juvenile), Knopf, 1958; *Flight from Ashiya*, Knopf, 1959; *Brave Jimmy Stone* (juvenile), Knopf, 1960; *A Night of Watching*, Scribner, 1967; *A Kind of Secret Weapon* (juvenile), Scribner, 1969.

Code of Conduct, Scribner, 1970; *Forests of the Night*,

Scribner, 1971; *The Spirit of Cochise*, Scribner, 1972; *Proving Ground*, Scribner, 1973; *The Camp Grant Massacre*, Simon & Schuster, in press. Short stories published in most contemporary magazines, and included in anthologies. Writer of screen and television plays.

SIDELIGHTS: Elliott Arnold writes: "I must confess that I write books for young readers for a selfish reason. I write them to improve my writing. ... I find an inclination to indulge myself in wordiness because I develop an affection for words ... and I have found ... that excesses and indulgences are total disaster if one wants to hold the interest of a young reader. You can't fake with those minds.

"A young reader has his mind and tastes and experiences untainted and he can smell a phony a mile off and you're on your guard. So, as it has come about, for me, writing for young people is a kind of purgative. It helps me shed the increments of bad taste, or most of them. It helps to restore purity and sight. Writing for young people is in its way going into a kind of artistic retreat, refinding the truths."

Fictionalizing historical events continually evokes critical response, such as that occasioned by Arnold's novel, *A Night of Watching*. While at first he considered writing a documentary about the evacuation of the Jews in Denmark, Arnold decided that "as exciting as fact may be it is very often not artistically exciting. There are two kinds of truth: factual and artistic. Fact tells you what happened. Art should tell you why it happened; it should say something permanent about experience. The historian is a journalist. The fiction writer creates characters—he plays God on paper."

Critical opinion is diverse regarding Arnold's stylistic success of treating fact in fiction. Margot Lester notes that "*A Night of Watching* ... is a fictional presentation of the magnificent concerted action of the Danish people in saving Danish Jews from Nazi extermination," but she adds that "the literary quality of the novel is poor, and inferior varnishing and garnishing cannot do justice to the factual drama on which the story is based." However, Eugene A. Dooley feels that "the story is well told in many crisp episodes," and that the characters' "personalities seem to come alive under the incisive pen of Mr. Arnold in his vivid rapid-fire prose."

A television documentary has been created based on *A Night of Watching*.

BIOGRAPHICAL/CRITICAL SOURCES: New York Times Book Review, June 16, 1967; *Time*, September 1, 1967; *Harper's*, September, 1967; *Books*, Summer, 1968; *Jewish Quarterly*, Autumn, 1968; *Variety*, November 6, 1968.

* * *

ARNTSON, Herbert E(dward) 1911-

PERSONAL: Born April 8, 1911, in Tacoma, Wash.; son of Anthony M. and Sigrid (Wingard) Arntson; married Dorothy Horine (a writer and teacher), November 8, 1946; children: Paul R., Helen, Laura. *Education:* University of Puget Sound, B.A., 1937, M.A., 1940; University of Washington, Seattle, graduate study, 1943-46, and summers, 1948, 1952. *Religion:* Congregational. *Home address:* P.O. Box 132, Stretch Island, Grapeview, Wash. 98546. *Agent:* McIntosh & Otis, Inc., 18 East 41st St., New York, N.Y. 10017.

CAREER: Grade and high school teacher in Waterville, Wash., 1941-42; Cunningham Steel Foundry, Seattle,

Wash., purchasing agent, 1942-43; Washington State University, Pullman, instructor, 1946-50, assistant professor, 1950-58, associate professor, 1958-65, professor of English and member of graduate faculty, 1965-74, professor emeritus, 1974—. *Member:* Modern Language Association of America, Oregon Historical Society, Washington Historical Society. *Awards, honors:* Franklin Watts Juvenile Fiction Award for distinguished contribution to children's literature, 1961, for *Adam Gray: Stowaway;* governor's citation, 1966.

WRITINGS: Caravan to Oregon, Binfords, 1957; *Adam Gray: Stowaway,* F. Watts, 1961; *Two Guns in Old Oregon,* F. Watts, 1964; *Frontier Boy,* Washburn, 1967; *Mountain Boy,* Washburn, 1968; *River Boy,* Washburn, 1969. Also contributor of short stories and scholarly articles to periodicals.

WORK IN PROGRESS: Adult novels, young people's novels, and short stories.

*   *   *

ARRINGTON, Leonard James   1917-

PERSONAL: Born July 2, 1917, in Twin Falls, Idaho; son of Noah Wesley (a farmer) and Edna (Corn) Arrington; married Grace Fort, April 24, 1943; children: James Wesley, Carl Wayne, Susan Grace. *Education:* University of Idaho, B.A., 1939; University of North Carolina, Ph.D., 1952. *Politics:* Independent. *Religion:* Church of Jesus Christ of Latter-day Saints. *Home:* 2236 South 2200 East, Salt Lake City, Utah 84109. *Office:* Department of History, Brigham Young University, Provo, Utah 84601; and Historical Department, Church of Jesus Christ of the Latterday Saints, 50 East North Temple, Salt Lake City, Utah 84150.

CAREER: U.S. Office of Price Administration, price analyst, 1942-43; North Carolina State College (now North Carolina State University at Raleigh), assistant professor of economics, 1946; Utah State University, Logan, associate professor, 1946-58, professor of economics, 1958-72; Brigham Young University, Provo, Utah, Lemuel Redd Professor of Western History, 1972—, director, Charles Redd Center for Western History, 1972—. Fulbright professor, University of Genoa, 1958-59; visiting professor, University of California, Los Angeles, 1966-67. Historian, Church of Jesus Christ of the Latterday Saints, 1972—. *Military service:* U. S. Army, 1943-46. *Member:* Economic History Association, American Historical Association (member of council, 1963-66), Organization of American Historians, Agricultural History Society (president, 1969-70), Western Economics Association, Western History Association (president, 1968-69), Utah Historical Association (fellow), Phi Beta Kappa. *Awards, honors:* Huntington Library fellow, 1957-58; Charles Redd Humanities Award from Utah Academy of Sciences, Arts, and Letters, 1966; David O. McKay Humanities Award from Brigham Young University, 1969.

WRITINGS: Great Basin Kingdom, Harvard University Press, 1958; *Introduzione alla storia economica degli Stati Uniti,* [Genoa], 1959; *The Changing Economic Structure of the Mountain West, 1850-1950* (monograph), Utah State University, 1963; (with Gary B. Hansen) *The Richest Hole on Earth: A History of the Bingham Copper Mine,* Utah State University Press, 1963; (with George Jensen) *The Defense Industry of Utah,* Utah State University Press, 1965; *Beet Sugar in the West,* University of Washington Press, 1966; (with George Jensen) *Impact of Defense*

Spending on the Economy of Utah, Utah State University, 1967; (with Anthony T. Cluff) *Federally Financed Industrial Plants Constructed in Utah During World War II,* Utah State University Press, 1969; (with William L. Roper) *William Spry: Man of Firmness, Governor of Utah,* Utah State University Press, 1971.

Contributor to Italian periodicals, 1958-59. Member of editorial board, *Pacific Historical Review,* 1959-62, *Dialogue, Journal of Mormon Thought,* 1966-69, and editor, *Western Historical Quarterly,* 1969-72.†

*   *   *

ARTHER, Richard O.   1928-

PERSONAL: Born May 10, 1928, in Pittsburgh, Pa.; son of William C. and Florence (Oberlin) Arther; married Mary-Esther Wuensch, September 12, 1951; children: Catherine, Linda, William III. *Education:* Michigan State University, B.S., 1951; Columbia University, M.A., 1960. *Office:* 57 West 57th St., New York, N.Y. 10019.

CAREER: Certified polygraphist by John E. Reid & Associates, 1952; president, Scientific Lie Detection, Inc., and National Training Center of Lie Detection, Inc., both New York, N.Y., 1958—. Director of Polygraph Examiners of New York State; fellow of National Training Center Academy of Certified Polygraphists. *Military service:* U.S. Army Reserve; became staff sergeant.

WRITINGS: (With R. R. Caputo) *Interrogation for Investigators,* Law & Order, 1958; *The Scientific Investigator,* C. C Thomas, 1964; *Arther's Polygraph Reference Guide,* National Training Center, 1975. Managing editor, *Journal of Polygraph Studies.*

*   *   *

ASHBY, Philip Harrison   1916-

PERSONAL: Born September 28, 1916, in Lynden, Wash.; son of Paul Hardin (a clergyman) and Tressie (Flesher) Ashby; married Mabel Kelley, August 30, 1936; children: Joan (Mrs. Llewelyn G. Pritchard), Philip Kelley. *Education:* Attended Whitman College, 1934-36, University of Washington, Seattle, 1936-37; College of Puget Sound, A.B., 1938; Pacific School of Religion, B.D., 1943; University of Chicago, Ph.D., 1950. *Home:* 478 Lake Dr., Princeton, N.J. 08540. *Office:* 79 Hall, Princeton University, Princeton, N.J. 08540.

CAREER: Ordained to Methodist ministry, 1943; Princeton University, Princeton, N.J., assistant professor, 1950-55, associate professor, 1955-65, professor of the history of religion, 1965—, William H. Danforth Professor of religion, 1972—, assistant dean of the college, 1959-62, chairman of department of religion, 1968-73, chairman of board of Wesley Foundation. Visiting lecturer at Lawrenceville School, 1951-52; visiting professor at Drew University, 1955, Southern Methodist University, 1952, Pacific School of Religion, 1964, and University of California, 1968. American Council of Learned Societies, secretary of Committee on History of Religion. *Military service:* U.S. Naval Reserve, chaplain, 1944-46; served in Southwest Pacific. *Member:* American Society for the Study of Religion (councilor, 1959-60, 1965—), National Council on Religion in Higher Education.

WRITINGS: The Conflict of Religions, Scribner, 1955; *The History and Future of Religious Thought,* Prentice-Hall, 1963; (contributor) P. Ramsey, editor, *Religion,* Prentice-Hall, 1965; *Modern Trends in Hinduism,* Columbia University Press, 1974; (contributor) R. J. Miller, editor, *Religious Ferment in Asia*, University of Kansas Press, 1974. Contributor to *Christian Century* and *Theology Today*.

WORK IN PROGRESS: Research on contemporary Hinduism.

* * *

ASHEIM, Lester E(ugene) 1914-

PERSONAL: Born January 22, 1914, in Spokane, Wash.; son of Sol (a plumber) and Bertha (Bergman) Asheim. *Education:* University of Washington, Seattle, B.A., 1936, B.A.L.S., 1937, M.A., 1941; University of Chicago, Ph.D., 1949. *Home:* 21 Banbury Lane, Chapel Hill, N.C. *Office:* School of Library Science, University of North Carolina, Chapel Hill, N.C. 27514.

CAREER: University of Washington, Seattle, junior reference assistant, 1937-41; U.S. Federal Penitentiary, McNeil Island, Wash., librarian, 1941-42; U.S. Federal Public Housing Authority, Seattle, Wash., regional librarian, 1946; University of Chicago, Graduate Library School, Chicago, Ill., assistant professor, 1948-52, associate professor and dean, 1952-61; American Library Association, Chicago, Ill., director of international realtions office, 1961-66, director of office for library education, 1966-71; University of Chicago, Graduate Library School, Chicago, Ill., professor, 1971-74; University of North Carolina, School of Library Science, Chapel Hill, William Raud Kenan, Jr. Professor of Library Science, 1974—. Visiting professor, University of Illinois, graduate school of library science, summer, 1949. *Military service:* U.S. Army, Alaska Communications System, 1942-45, *Member:* American Library Association (councilor-at-large; chairman of committee, White House Conference on Education, 1954-56), Special Libraries Association, American Association of University Professors, Illinois Library Association, Phi Beta Kappa, Beta Phi Mu. *Awards, honors:* Distinguished Alumnus Award, University of Washington, Seattle, 1966; Intellectual Freedom Award, Illinois Library Association, 1966; Scarecrow Press award for library literature, 1968, for *Librarianship in the Developing Countries;* Beta Phi Mu award for distinguised service to education for librarianship, 1973.

WRITINGS: (With Bernard Berelson) *Library's Public*, Columbia University Press, 1949; (contributor) Wilbur L. Schramm, editor, *Mass Communications*, University of Illinois Press, 1949; (contributor) Bernard Berelson and Morris Janowitz, editors, *Reader in Public Opinion and Communication*, Free Press, 1950; (editor) *Forum on the Public Library Inquiry*, Columbia University Press, 1950; (editor) *Core of Education for Librarianship*, American Library Association, 1954; (editor) *The Future of the Book*, University of Chicago Press, 1955; *New Directions in Public Library Development*, University of Chicago, Press, 1957; (with others) *The Humanities and the Library*, American Library Association, 1957; *Persistent Issues in American Librarianship*, University of Chicago Press, 1961; (with others) *Educational Television, the Next Ten Years*, Stanford University Institute for Communication Research, 1962; *Librarianship in the Developing Countries*, University of Illinois Press, 1966; (with Sara Fenwick) *Differentiating the Media*, University of Chicago Press, 1975. American Library Association, member of editorial committee, 1951-54, chairman of editorial committee, 1955-57; editor, *Library Quarterly, 1972-74.*

SIDELIGHTS: Official travels for American Library Association have taken Asheim to thirteen countries in Africa, thirteen countries in Latin America, and to seventeen countries in the Far and Middle East and Asia.

* * *

ASHLEY, Robert P(aul), Jr. 1915-

PERSONAL: Born April 15, 1915, in Baltimore, Md.; son of Robert Paul and Ethel (Rice) Ashley; married Virginia Woods, June 24, 1939; children: June (Mrs. L. M. Hager), Dianne (Mrs. C. W. Per-Lee, Jr.), Cynthia, Robert Paul III, Jacquelyn. *Education:* Bowdoin College, A.B., 1936; Harvard University, M.A., 1937, Ph.D., 1949. *Home:* 504 Watson St., Ripon, Wis. 54971. *Agent:* Howard Moorepark, 500 East 79th St., New York, N.Y. 10021. *Office:* Department of English, Ripon College, Ripon, Wis.

CAREER: Portland Junior College, Portland, Me., instructor in English and tennis coach, 1938-39; Colby Junior College, New London, N.H., instructor in English, 1939-44; Boston Quartermaster Depot, Boston, Mass., training instructor, 1944; Harvard University, Cambridge, Mass., teaching fellow and tennis coach, 1946-48; Washington and Jefferson College, Washington, Pa., assistant dean, assistant professor of English, and tennis coach, 1948-51; U.S. Military Academy, West Point, N.Y., assistant professor, 1951-55; Ripon College, Ripon, Wis., professor of English, 1955—, tennis coach, 1955-64, dean of the college, 1955-74, acting president, 1966. Distinguished visiting professor, U.S. Naval Academy, 1969. Midwest Athletic Conference, director of news and records, 1956—, vice-president, 1957-58, president, 1958-59, commissioner, 1960-66. *Military service:* U.S. Naval Reserve, 1944-46; became lieutenant junior grade; U.S. Army Reserve, 1951-55; now colonel (retired). *Member:* Modern Language Association, American Association of University Professors, Midwest Modern Language Association, Phi Beta Kappa, Zeta Psi.

WRITINGS: Wilkie Collins (biography), Roy, 1952; (editor with Edwin M. Moseley) *Elizabethan Fiction* (anthology), Rinehart, 1953; *The Stolen Train: A Story of the Andrews Raiders*, Winston, 1953; (editor with Herbert van Thal) *Tales of Suspense* (anthology), Library Publishers, 1954; *Rebel Raiders: A Story of the St. Albans Raid*, Winston, 1956; (editor with Joseph Fant) *Faulkner at West Point* (anthology), Random, 1964; (contributor) *Victorian Fiction: A Guide to Research*, edited by Lionel Stevenson, Harvard University Press, 1964; (editor) *Civil War Poetry: An Anthology*, U.S. Naval Academy, 1970; (with daughter, Diane Ashley Per-Lee) *Understanding the Novel*, J. Weston Walch, 1973. Contributor to *New England Quarterly, College English, North Central Association Quarterly, The Dickensian, Nineteenth-Century Fiction*, and *Princeton University Library Chronicle*.

AVOCATIONAL INTERESTS: Civil War history, tennis.

* * *

ASTIN, Alexander W(illiam) 1932-

PERSONAL: Born May 30, 1932, in Washington, D.C.; son of Allen V. (director, National Bureau of Standards) and Margaret (Mackenzie) Astin; married Helen Stavridou (a psychologist), February 11, 1956; children: John, Paul. *Education:* Gettysburg College, A.B., (music), 1953; University of Maryland, M.A., 1954, Ph.D., 1957. *Politics:* Independent. *Religion:* None. *Office:* University of California, Los Angeles, Calif. 90024.

CAREER: U.S. Veterans Administration, counseling psychologist in Perry Point, Md., 1954-57, assistant chief of psychology research unit at Veterans Administration Hospital, Baltimore, Md., 1959-60; National Merit Scholarship Corp., Evanston, Ill., research associate, later director of research, 1960-65; American Council on Education, Washington, D.C., director of research, 1965-73; University of California, Los Angeles, professor of education, 1973—. President, Higher Education Research Institute, 1974—; consultant, Surgeon General's Advisory Committee on Smoking and Health. *Military service:* U.S. Public Health Service, 1957-59; became lieutenant commander. *Member:* American Psychological Association, American Educational Research Association, Psychometric Society, American Association for the Advancement of Science, American Personnel and Guidance Association. *Awards, honors:* American Personnel and Guidance Association Award for outstanding research, 1965, for studies of college characteristics and college effects; fellow, Institute for Advanced Study in the Behavioral Sciences, 1967-68.

WRITINGS: Who Goes Where to College?, Science Research Associates, 1965; (contributor) C. W. Taylor, editor, *Widening Horizons in Creativity*, Wiley, 1965; *The College Environment*, American Council on Education, 1968; *The Educational and Vocational Development of College Students*, American Council on Education, 1969; *Predicting Academic Performance in College*, Free Press, 1971; (with C.B.T. Lee) *The Invisible Colleges*, McGraw, 1972; *Open Admissions at City University of New York*, Prentice-Hall, 1974. Contributor of over a hundred articles to more than twenty scientific and other professional journals.

WORK IN PROGRESS: Research on prediction of student achievement and measurement of college environments; assessing effects of college environments on student behavior; working on national research data bank for higher education.

* * *

ATCHISON, Sandra Dallas 1939-
(Sandra Dallas)

PERSONAL: Born June 11, 1939, in Washington, D.C.; daughter of Forrest E. and Harriett (Mavity) Dallas; married Robert Thomas Atchison (in public relations work), April 20, 1963; children: Dana Dallas. *Education:* University of Denver, B.A., 1960. *Home:* 444 Gilpin, Denver, Colo. 80218.

CAREER: Business Week, Denver, Colo., editorial assistant, 1961-63; University of Denver, Denver, Colo., in public relations, 1965-66. Writer. *Member:* Denver Woman's Press Club.

WRITINGS—Under name Sandra Dallas; *Gaslights and Gingerbread*, Sage Books, 1965; *Vail*, Pruett, 1969; *Cherry Creek Gothic: Victorian Architecture in Denver*, University of Oklahoma Press, 1971. Writer of travel articles for various magazines. Book reviewer, *Denver Post*, 1962—.†

* * *

ATKINS, James G. 1932-
(Jim Atkins)

PERSONAL: Born September 10, 1932, in San Francisco, Calif.; son of John Bunyon (a newspaper reporter) and Lillian (Jenkins) Atkins; married Leslie Ann Meriwether, July 17, 1959 (divorced 1971); married Marylou Richmond,

August 11, 1974; children: (first marriage) James David, Joan Leslie. *Education:* Attended Birmingham-Southern College, 1954-56; writing courses at University of Alabama, 1963, New School for Social Research, 1963-65. *Politics:* Democrat. *Religion:* Methodist. *Home:* 200-04 58th Ave., Bayside, N.Y. 11364.

CAREER: Newsman and photographer in Birmingham, for *Birmingham Post-Herald,* 1953-57, and WAPI-TV, 1957; WBRC-TV, news director, Birmingham, 1957-62; public relations work for American Federation of Labor-Congress of Industrial Organizations (AFL-CIO), New York, N.Y., and Washington, D.C., 1962-65, and American Trucking Association, Washington, D.C., 1965-66; National Milk Producers Federation, assistant director of information, Washington, D.C., 1965-66; National Features Syndicate, Washington, D.C., founder and owner, 1966-72; Exposition Press, Hoke Communications, Publishers Clearing House, promotion and copywriter, 1972-74; currently free-lance writer and consultant, 1974—. Free-lance writer and photographer, and sometime correspondent for national news services and radio and television networks, 1955—; editor of *Western Sun* (Alabama weekly), 1960-61; vice-president, Laff Book Club, New York 1966—. *Military service:* U.S. Naval Reserve, active duty, 1951-53. *Member:* Overseas Press Club, National Press Club, National Press Photographers Association. Direct Mail Advertising Association. *Awards, honors:* Third prize, Southeastern branch of National Press Photographers Association, 1962, for news film.

WRITINGS—Under name Jim Atkins: (With Leo Willette) *Shooting TV News and Documentaries*, Amphoto, 1965; *Barnabas Collings Vampire Jokes*, Paperback Library, 1967; *Encyclopedia of Howard Hughes Jokes*, Acropolis Press, 1970. Correspondent for *Tennis;* Washington correspondent for *Sick;* co-author of monthly column, "Humor Exchange," in *Author and Journalist;* free-lance work has included articles for magazines, including *Monocle* and *New Republic*, and for religious and trade journals; films used in Columbia Broadcasting System documentary, "Who Speaks for Birmingham?," and photographs in *True* and various detective magazines.

WORK IN PROGRESS: Collecting political stories and jokes for a book, *Washington Humor.*

SIDELIGHTS: Atkins and George Q. Lewis, director of the Humor Societies of America, recently founded the Laff Book Club, with a board of electors (to help select books) that includes Joey Adams, Rudy Vallee, and Harry Hershfield. Atkins did a humor column for the college newspaper at Birmingham-Southern; he also has written television skits for comic Jackie Vernon, and founded the Comic-Gagwriters Round Table in Washington.

* * *

ATKINSON, R(ichard) C(hatham) 1929-

PERSONAL: Born March 19, 1929, in Oak Park, Ill.; son of Herbert Atkinson; children: Lynn Loyd. *Education:* University of Chicago, Ph.B., 1948; Indiana University, Ph.D., 1955. *Home:* 724 Santa Ynez, Stanford, Calif. 94305. *Office:* Department of Psychology, Stanford University, 420 Jordan Hall, Stanford, Calif. 94305.

CAREER: University of California, Los Angeles, assistant professor of psychology, 1957-61; Stanford University, Stanford, Calif., professor of psychology, 1961—. Science consultant, RAND Corp. and System Development Corp. *Military service:* U.S. Army, 1953-55. *Member:* American

Academy of Arts and Sciences, American Psychological Association, Psychonomic Society, Society of Experimental Psychologists. *Awards, honors:* Distinguished Research Award, Social Science Research Council, 1962; Guggenheim Fellow, 1967-68.

WRITINGS: (With Patrick Suppes) *Markov Learning Models for Multiperson Interactions*, Stanford University Press, 1960; (editor) *Studies in Mathematical Psychology*, Stanford University Press, 1964; (with G. H. Bower and E. J. Crothers) *An Introduction to Mathematical Learning Theory*, Wiley, 1965; (with E. R. Hilgard and R. L. Atkinson) *Introduction to Psychology*, 6th edition, Harcourt, 1975; (editor) *Contemporary Psychology*, W. H. Freeman, 1971. Editor, *Journal of Mathematical Psychology*, Academic Press.

* * *

ATKINSON, Ronald Field 1928-

PERSONAL: Born February 8, 1928, in Leeds, England; son of Norman Limbert (a tailor) and Anne (Field) Atkinson; married Margaret Joan Harvey (a teacher), July 28, 1951; children: David Michael, Rosemary Frances, Katharine Amanda. *Education:* Keble College, Oxford, B.A., 1951, B.Phil., 1953. *Religion:* None. *Office:* Department of Philosophy, University of York, Heslington, York Y01 5DD, England.

CAREER: University of Keele, Keele, England, assistant lecturer in philosophy, 1953-56, lecturer, 1956-62, senior lecturer, 1962-66, reader, 1966-67; University of York, Heslington, York, England, professor of philosophy, 1967—.

WRITINGS: Sexual Morality, Hutchinson, 1965; *Conduct: An Introduction to Moral Philosophy*, Macmillan, 1969.

* * *

AUDEMARS, Pierre 1909-

PERSONAL: Born December 25, 1909, in London, England; married Joan Wood; children: Michael, Peter. *Education:* Educated in London, England. *Residence:* London, England. *Agent:* Winant Towers Ltd., 1 Furnival St., London E.C. 4, England.

CAREER: Louis Audemars & Co. (watch importers), London, England, salesman, 1928-39; Camerer Cuss & Co. (jewellers), London, manager, 1949-56; Zenith Watch Co. Ltd., London, sales manager, 1960—. Author. *Military service:* British Army, 1940-46; became lieutenant.

WRITINGS: Night without Darkness (novel), Selwyn & Blount, 1936; *Hercule and the Gods*, Pilot Press, 1944, Rinehart, 1946; *The Temptations of Hercule*, Pilot Press, 1945; *The Obligations of Hercule*, Sampson Low, Marston & Co., 1947; *Wrath of the Valley* (novel), Rockliff, 1947; *The Confessions of Hercule*, Sampson Low, Marston & Co., 1948.

The Thieves of Enchantment, W. & R. Chambers, 1956; *The Two Imposters*, John Long, 1958; *The Fire and the Clay*, John Long, 1959; *The Turns of Time*, John Long, 1960, Harper, 1961; *The Crown of Night*, John Long, 1961, Harper, 1962; *The Dream and the Dead*, John Long, 1962; *Street of Grass*, Harper, 1963 (published in England as *The Wings of Darkness*, John Long, 1963); *Fair Maids Missing*, Doubleday, 1964; *The Woven Web*, Doubleday, 1965 (published in England as *Dead with Sorrow*, John Long, 1965).

Time of Temptation, Doubleday, 1966; *A Thorn in the Dust*, John Long, 1967; *The Veins of Compassion*, John Long, 1967; *The White Leaves of Death*, John Long, 1968; *The Flame in the Mist*, John Long, 1969; *A Host for Dying*, John Long, 1970, Curtis, 1972; *Stolen Like Magic Away*, John Long, 1971. Contributor to *Chambers' Journal*, 1934-39.†

* * *

AUERBACH, Arnold M. 1912-

PERSONAL: Born May 23, 1912, in New York, N.Y.; son of Julius (a physician) and Ogla (Ehrlich) Auerbach; married Justine Rubin, December 29, 1940; children: Nina, Andrew. *Education:* Attended Columbia University, 1932-33. *Politics:* Democrat (usually). *Religion:* Jewish. *Residence:* New York, N.Y.

CAREER: Writer for radio, stage, and television; employed by Fred Allen, 1936-41, by Paramount and Warner Bros., 1941-42; writer for Frank Sinatra, Milton Berle, Phil Silvers, Jackie Gleason, and others, 1951-55. *Military service:* U.S. Army, 1943-46.

WRITINGS: Funny Men Don't Laugh, Doubleday, 1965; *Is That Your Best Offer?*, Doubleday, 1971. Contributor to *New York Sunday Times, Harper's, Saturday Review*, and other magazines. Broadway revues: "Call Me Mister," 1946, "Inside U.S.A.," 1948, and "Bless You All," 1950.

SIDELIGHTS: Auerbach told *CA* that he speaks "pretty good French, skimpy German. My aim [in writing] is to entertain and, sometimes, to deflate something that needs deflating."†

* * *

AUGELLI, John P(at) 1921-

PERSONAL: Surname is pronounced *O*-jelly; born January 30, 1921, in Italy. *Education:* Clark University, Worcester, Mass., B.A., 1943; Harvard University, M.A., 1949, Ph.D., 1951. *Home:* 2424 Brush Creek, Lawrence, Kan. 66044. *Office:* University of Kansas, Lawrence, Kan. 66045.

CAREER: University of Puerto Rico, Rio Piedras, assistant professor, later associate professor of geography, 1948-52; University of Maryland, College Park, associate professor, 1952-60, professor of geography, 1960-61; University of Kansas, Lawrence, professor of geography and director, Center of Latin America Area Studies, 1961-70; University of Illinois, Urbana, professor of geography and director of Center for Latin American Studies, 1970-71; University of Kansas, Lawrence, 1972-73. Consultant at various times to U.S. Department of State, Ford Foundation, Foreign Area Fellowship Program, and publishing firms. Social Science Research Council, member of Joint Committee on Latin American Studies, 1964-70; U.S. National Committee for International Geographical Union, secretary, 1965-70; Pan American Institute of Geography and History, U.S. member, 1965-69. *Military service:* U.S. Army Air Forces, 1943-45. U.S. Air Force Reserve, 1948-52; became lieutenant. *Member:* Association of American Geographers (chairman of Middle Atlantic division, 1960; national secretary, 1966-69), American Geographical Society, Association for Latin American Studies (president, Midwest council, 1963-64). *Awards, honors:* Research and travel grants from governments of Brazil and Puerto Rico, University of Maryland, Organization of American States, Social Science Research Council, the University of Kansas, and American

Council of Learned Societies, Board of Foreign Scholarships.

WRITINGS: (Contributor) C. F. Jones and R. Pico, editors, *Symposium on the Geography of Puerto Rico*, University of Puerto Rico Press, 1955; (geography editor) *The Great Plains States*, Fideler, 1963; (editor) *American Geography, 1960-63: Education, Employment, and Other Trends*, Association of American Geographers, 1964; (contributor) R. Thomas and D. Patton, editors, *Focus on Geographical Activity*, McGraw, 1964; *Caribbean Lands* (junior high text), Fideler, 1965; (with Robert West) *Geography of Middle America*, Prentice-Hall, 1966; *Puerto Rico*, Ginn, 1973. Author of five U.S. State Department monographs on West Indies, 1957-59. Contributor to *Encyclopaedia Britannica, American Peoples Encyclopedia, Collier's Encyclopedia*; also contributor of articles and reviews to professional journals. Consulting editor, *Annals of the Association of American Geographers*; associate editor, *Journal of Geography*, 1962-64; geography editor, *Handbook of Latin American Studies*, 1961-64.

SIDELIGHTS: John Augelli has traveled for research in Central and South America, West Indies, Europe, Oceania. He is fluent in Spanish, reads and has limited speaking knowledge of French, Portuguese, and Italian.

*   *   *

AUGUSTIN, Pius   1934-

PERSONAL: Surname is pronounced Au-gus-*teen*; born February 11, 1934, in Loretto, Tenn.; son of Edward M. (a farmer) and Magdelin (Beckman) Augustin. *Educaiton:* St. Ambrose College, B.A., 1955; Collegio Sant'Anselmo, Rome, Italy, S.T.L., 1961; Lateran University, Rome, Italy, S.T.D., 1964.

CAREER: Roman Catholic priest of Benedictine Order (O.S.B.); St. Bernard College, St. Bernard, Ala., professor of theology, beginning 1964.

WRITINGS: Religious Freedom in Church and State, Helicon, 1967.

WORK IN PROGRESS: A book on the Catholic overview of modern "radical" Protestant theologians.

SIDELIGHTS: Augustin speaks German, French, Italian, Latin, and reads Greek and Spanish. He is active in ecumenical work, and in work with college students who aid the needy.†

*   *   *

AULTMAN, Donald S.   1930-

PERSONAL: Born September 22, 1930, in Gadsden, Ala.; son of Leonard Howard (a clergyman) and Esther (Barnwell) Aultman; married Winona Cook, June 7, 1950; children: Melodie Dawn, Melissa Diane. *Education:* Attended University of Kentucky, 1948; Samford University, B.A., 1964; University of Tennessee, Ed.D., 1969. *Office:* Office of the Dean, Lee College, Cleveland, Tenn. 37311.

CAREER: Church of God, clergyman, 1950—, Church of God, state youth director in Michigan, 1954-58, Florida, 1958-60, assistant national youth director, 1960-64, national youth director of Christian education, 1964-68; Lee College, Cleveland, Tenn., vice-president, 1967-68, dean, 1968—. Member of board of directors, National Sunday School Association, 1964-68; lecturer on world tour, 1965, and in South Africa, Germany, and England, 1966. President and chairman of board, Worship Music, Inc., 1966.

Instructor, University of Tennessee, 1967-68. *Member:* American Psychological Association, National Sunday School Association (member of board of directors), Denominational Sunday School Secretaries Association (president).

WRITINGS: Learning Christian Leadership, Pathway Publications, 1958, 2nd edition, Baker Book, 1960; *Guiding Youth*, Pathway Publications, 1964; *The Ministry of Christian Teaching*, Pathway Publications, 1966; *Youth and the Church Organizing for Youth* (monograph), Moody, 1966; *A Comparison of the Word Associations of Culturally Advantaged and Disadvantaged Children and Teachers*, University of Tennessee Press, 1969. Writer of motion picture scripts, "Decision for Destiny" and "Impact."†

*   *   *

AUVIL, Kenneth W(illiam)   1925-

PERSONAL: Surname is pronounced *Aw*-vil; born December 18, 1925, in Ryderwood, Wash.; son of Daniel M. (a timber worker) and Rebecca (Justice) Auvil; married Mary Hallowell, June 11, 1955. *Education:* University of Washington, Seattle, B.A., 1950, M.F.A., 1953. *Home:* 605 Olson Rd., Santa Cruz, Calif. 95065.

CAREER: Boeing Aircraft Co., Seattle, Wash., technical illustrator, 1953-56; California State University, San Jose, 1956—, began as assistant professor, now professor of art. University of Washington, Seattle, visiting professor of art, 1961, 1970, 1973. Artist, primarily working in serigraphy; prints included in more than one hundred national and international competitions and invitational exhibitions, including Fourth Biennale, Italy, 1956, Denver Art Museum, 1959, Smithsonian Institution, 1960; works owned by Bibliotheque Nationale (Paris), Victoria and Albert Museum (London), and galleries and institutions in America. *Military service:* U.S. Army, 1950-52. *Member:* California Society of Printmakers, Phi Beta Kappa.

WRITINGS: Serigraphy—Silk Screen Techniques for the Artist, Prentice-Hall, 1965.

WORK IN PROGRESS: Photographic stencil processes, photomechanical methods for the artist.

*   *   *

AVISON, Margaret   1918-

PERSONAL: Born April 23, 1918, in Galt, Ontario, Canada; daughter of Harold Wilson (a clergyman) and Mabel (Kirkland) Avison. *Education:* University of Toronto, B.A., 1940, M.A., 1964.

CAREER: Writer. *Awards, honors:* Guggenheim fellowship, 1956; Governor General's Literary Award for poetry, 1960.

WRITINGS: Winter Sun, Routledge & Kegan Paul, 1960; *The Research Compendium*, University of Toronto Press, 1964; *The Dumbfounding*, Norton, 1966; *Silverick*, Ganglia Press, 1969; *The Cosmic Chef*, Oberon Press, 1970.

BIOGRAPHICAL/CRITICAL SOURCES: William H. New, *Twentieth Century Literature*, July, 1970; Carolyn Riley, editor, *Contemporary Literary Criticism*, Gale, Volume II, 1974, Volume IV, 1975.†

*   *   *

AWAD, Elias M.   1934-

PERSONAL: Born October 6, 1934, in Latakia, Syria; son of Michael and Naifa Awad. *Education:* Geneva College

(Beaver Falls, Pa.), B.S.B.A., 1956; University of Tulsa, M.B.A., 1958; New York University, graduate study, 1964; Northwestern University, M.A., 1968; University of Kentucky, D.B.A., 1975. *Religion:* Presbyterian. *Home:* 933 Northwoods Dr., Deerfield, Ill.

CAREER: Aleppo College, Aleppo, Syria, business manager and instructor, 1958-59; Rochester Institute of Technology, College of Business, Rochester, N.Y., assistant professor of organization theory, 1960-65; DePaul University, Graduate School of Business, Chicago, Ill., assistant professor of management, 1967-75; Ball State University, College of Business, Muncie, Ind., George A. Ball Distinguished Professor of Management, 1975—. *Member:* Academy of Management, American Economic Association, Date Processing Management Association, American Association of University Professors.

WRITINGS:—All published by Prentice-Hall, except as noted: *Business Data Processing*, 1965; *Automatic Data Processing*, 1966; *Problems and Exercises in Data Processing*, 1966; (editor) *Perspectives in Electronic Data Processing*, 1972; *Concepts in Business Data Processing*, 1975; *Issues in Business Data Processing*, 1975; *Business Data Processing Systems: Analysis, Design, Behavior*, Irwin, in press; *Automatic Data Processing*, in press.

AVOCATIONAL INTERESTS: Travel, camping, and photography.

* * *

AYERS, Donald Murray 1923-

PERSONAL: Born January 19, 1923, in Los Angeles, Calif.; son of Murray Chase (a civil engineer) and Elsie (Whittemore) Ayers; married Esther Belew, June 15, 1946; children: Thomas Murray, Barbara Louise. *Education:* Stanford University, B.A., 1943, M.A., 1947; Princeton University, Ph.D., 1950. *Politics:* Republican. *Religion:* Presbyterian. *Home:* 5222 East Third St., Tucson, Ariz. *Office:* Department of Classics, University of Arizona, Tucson, Ariz. 85721.

CAREER: Vanderbilt University, Nashville, Tenn., instructor in classics, 1950-51; University of Arizona, Tucson, instructor, 1951-54, assistant professor, 1954-59, associate professor, 1959-64, professor of classics, beginning, 1964. *Military service:* U.S. Naval Reserve, 1943-46; became lieutenant junior grade. *Member:* American Philological Association, American Classical League, American Association of University Professors, Philological Association of the Pacific Coast (chairman of classical section, 1956; member of executive committee, 1966-67), Classical Association of the Pacific States, Phi Beta Kappa, Stanford Club of Southern Arizona (vice-president, 1966-67).

WRITINGS: English Words from Latin and Greek Elements, University of Arizona Press, 1965; *Bioscientific Terminology: Words from Latin and Greek Stems*, University of Arizona Press, 1972.

WORK IN PROGRESS: Studies in Latin literature.†

* * *

BACKER, Morton 1918-

PERSONAL: Born March 24, 1918; son of Isaac and Fay (Antell) Backer; married Lucille Machlin (a teacher); children: Joan, Nancy. *Education:* Attended City College (now City College of the City University of New York), 1933-35; Boston University, B.B.A., 1939; University of Pittsburgh, M.Litt., 1954, Ph.D., 1958. *Home:* Market Hill Rd., Am-

herst, Mass. *Office:* School of Business Administration, University of Massachusetts, Amherst, Mass.

CAREER: University of Massachusetts, Amherst, professor of accounting, 1966—. Consultant to National Association of Accountants, U.S. Treasury Department, Italian Government, International Business Machines, Grace Corp., and Panama Canal Corp. *Member:* American Accounting Association, American Institute of Certified Public Accountants, National Association of Accountants, American Association of University Professors.

WRITINGS: (Editor) *Handbook of Modern Accounting Theory*, Prentice-Hall, 1956; (with Lyle Jacobsen) *Cost Accounting: A Managerial Approach*, McGraw, 1964; (editor) *Modern Accounting Theory*, Prentice-Hall, 1966; *External Reporting for Segments of a Business*, National Association of Accountants, 1968; *Financial Reporting for Security Investment and Credit Decisions*, National Association of Accountants, 1970; *Current Value Accounting*, Financial Executives Research Foundation, 1973. Contributor to professional journals.

SIDELIGHTS: Backer is competent in Spanish, French, and Italian.

BIOGRAPHICAL/CRITICAL SOURCES: Journal of Accounting, July, 1966; *Financial World*, September, 1966.†

* * *

BACKMAN, Carl W(ard) 1923-

PERSONAL: Born July 1, 1923, in Canadaigua, N.Y.; son of Carl Fritios and Edna (Ward) Backman; married Shirley L. Bennett, June 25, 1947; children: Carl, Lorraine, Elaine, Valerie, Mark. *Education:* Oberlin College, B.A., 1948; Indiana University, M.A., 1950, Ph.D., 1954. *Home:* 1225 Hoge Rd., Reno, Nev. 89503. *Office:* University of Nevada, Reno, Nev. 89507.

CAREER: University of Arkansas, Fayetteville, instructor in sociology, 1951-55; University of Nevada, Reno, assistant professor, 1955-59, associate professor of sociology, 1960-65, chairman of department, 1962-64; National Science Foundation, Washington, D.C., program director for sociology and social psychology, 1965-67; University of Nevada, Reno, professor of sociology, 1967—, chairman of department, 1967-1972. Visiting professor, University of California, Los Angeles, 1959. Consultant to U.S. Air Force, Navy, and Veterans Administration, National Science Foundation, and National Institute of Mental Health. *Military service:* U.S. Army, 1943-46. *Member:* American Sociological Association (fellow), American Psychological Association (fellow), American Association for the Advancement of Science (fellow), Society for Experimental Social Psychology, American Association for Public Opinion Research, Pacific Sociological Association (first vice-president, 1965-66), West Coast Conference for Small Group Research (past chairman). *Awards, honors:* National Institute of Mental Health grant, 1959-63; U.S. Office of Education grant, 1964-65.

WRITINGS: (With Paul F. Secord) *Social Psychology*, McGraw, 1964; (editor with Secord) *Problems of Social Psychology: Selected Readings*, McGraw, 1966; (with Secord) *A Social Psychological View of Education*, Harcourt, 1968. Editor, *Sociometry*, 1970-73. Contributor to books of others, and to professional journals.

WORK IN PROGRESS: Research on interpersonal attraction and personality theory.†

BACON, Wallace A(lger) 1914-

PERSONAL: Born January 17, 1914, in Bad Axe, Mich.; son of Russell A. and Mana E. (Wallace) Bacon. *Education:* Albion College, A.B., 1935; University of Michigan, M.A., 1936, Ph.D., 1940. *Home:* 315 Linder Ave., Northfield, Ill. 60093. *Office:* Department of Interpretation, Northwestern University, Evanston, Ill. 60201.

CAREER: University of Michigan, Ann Arbor, instructor in English, 1941-47; Northwestern University, Evanston, Ill., assistant professor, 1947-50, associate professor of English and speech, 1950-55, professor of interpretation, 1955—, chairman of department of interpretation, 1947—. Fulbright lecturer in the Philippines, 1961-62; Fulbright-Hays lecturer in the Philippines, 1964-65. *Military service:* U.S. Army, Military Intelligence, 1942-46; received Legion of Merit.

MEMBER: Speech Communication Association (second vice-president, 1975; first vice-president, 1976; president, 1977), Central States Speech Association, Malone Society (England), Phi Beta Kappa, Delta Sigma Rho, Theta Alpha Phi. *Awards, honors:* Hopwood (major) Award in drama, University of Michigan, 1936; Alfred Lloyd postdoctoral fellow, University of Michigan, 1940-41; Bishop Sheil Award from National Catholic Theater Conference, 1946, for "Savonarola"; Rockefeller Foundation fellow, 1948-49; Ford Foundation fellow, 1954-55; Golden Anniversary Prize Fund Award from Speech Association of America, 1965 and 1974, for scholarly publication; special citation from University of the Philippines and special commendation from Educational Foundation in the Philippines, 1965; Litt.D., Albion College, 1966; LL.D., Emerson College, 1975.

WRITINGS: (Editor) W. Warner, *Syrinx* (critical edition of the Elizabethan novel), Northwestern University Studies, 1950; *Savonarola* (verse play), Bookman Associates, 1950; (with Robert S. Breen) *Literature as Experience,* McGraw, 1959; (editor) with R. S. Breen) *Literature for Interpretation,* Holt, 1961; (with Natividad Crame-Rogers and Consuelo V. Fonacier) *Spoken English,* Phoenix Press (Manila), 1965; *The Art of Oral Interpretation,* Phoenix Press, 1965; *The Art of Interpretation,* Holt, 1966; 2nd edition, 1972; *Oral Interpretation and the Teaching of Literature in Secondary Schools,* Educational Resources-Information Center with Speech Communication Association 1972; (contributor) Richard Haas and David Williams, editors, *The Study of Oral Interpretation,* Bobbs-Merrill, 1975. Contributor of articles and poetry to professional journals. Associate editor, *Quarterly Journal of Speech,* 1957-59, 1963-65, 1975-77, and *Speech Monographs,* 1965-72.

WORK IN PROGRESS: A biography of Edna G. Bacon and a book on the oral performance of Shakespeare.

* * *

BAGLEY, Desmond 1923-

PERSONAL: Born October 29, 1923, in Kendal, England; son of John (a miner) and Hannah Marie (Whittle) Bagley; married Joan Margaret Brown, September 2, 1960. *Home:* Hay Hill, Totnes, Devonshire, England.

CAREER: Began free-lance writing in South Africa in early 1950's, part-time at first and then as a full-time free lance; novelist, living and writing in England, 1964—. Did radio talks on scientific subjects for Durban studio of South African Broadcasting Corp., 1951-52; edited a house magazine for Masonite (Africa) Ltd., 1953; film critic for *Rand Daily Mail,* Johannesburg, 1958-62, and contributor to *Star* (Johannesburg), and other newspapers and magazines; scenario writer for Filmlets Ltd. (subsidiary of Twentieth Century-Fox), Johannesburg, 1960-61. *Member:* Society of Authors, Crime Writers Association (both England), Mystery Writers of America, Authors Guild of the Authors League of America, Authors' Club (London).

WRITINGS–Novels; all published by Doubleday, except as noted: *The Golden Keel,* Collins, 1963, 1964; *High Citadel,* 1965; *Wyatt's Hurricane,* 1966; *Landslide,* 1967; *The Vivero Letter,* 1968; *Running Blind,* 1969; *The Spoilers,* 1970; *The Freedom Trap,* 1971; *The Tightrope Men,* 1973; (contributor) A. S. Burack, editor, *Techniques of Novel Writing,* Writer, Inc., 1973; *The Snow Tiger,* 1975. Short stories have been published in *Argosy* (England) and *Magazine of Fantasy and Science Fiction.*

WORK IN PROGRESS: Researching "at least three books which I wish to write, although that does not mean that they will be written; one of these is concerned with the Antarctic."

SIDELIGHTS: Bagley's novels, which have been published in Iceland and Australia and numerous points between, evolve spontaneously, since he makes no working notes—preferring to let the plot develop out of the actions and motivations of the characters. "My working habits are not too exceptional," he notes. "I am old-fashioned enough to believe that a story should have a beginning, a middle and an end. When on the typewriter I work strict office hours—an eight-hour day and a five-day week, ... don't rely on inspiration because nothing gets done that way. I work comparatively quickly, doing from three to five thousand words a day on the first draft. But then the whole book gets a thorough going-over and is rewritten in its entirety. I write novels of action, sometimes called adventure novels or thrillers, and I believe that in this field someone, perhaps not me, will eventually write a true work of art."

All Bagley's books are in print, both in hard and soft cover editions in nineteen languages, in large print, in Braille, and on tape. One has been filmed, *The Freedom Trap,* released as "The Mackintosh Man" by Warner Brothers.

During his years in Africa, Bagley traveled extensively from the Mediterranean to the Cape of Good Hope. This involved at one time a crossing of the Sahara Desert, an adventure that he expects to use in a book some day. In 1966 he and his wife returned to Africa to photograph animals in the wild ("the shooting of animals, except for the pot, I consider uncivilized"). He has long been interested in animal and other photography, both still and motion picture.

* * *

BAILEY, Dudley 1918-

PERSONAL: Born February 7, 1918, in Lamoni, Iowa; son of Vaughn Corless (a salesman) and Lida (Hayer) Bailey; married Sue Ogden, April 27, 1945; children: Geoffrey Ogden, Paul Fletcher, Jane Barker. *Education:* University of Kansas City (now University of Missouri at Kansas City), A.B., 1942, M.A., 1944; University of Illinois, Ph.D., 1954. *Home:* 1800 South 22nd St., Lincoln, Neb. 68502. *Office:* 212 Andrews Hall, University of Nebraska, Lincoln, Neb. 68508.

CAREER: Instructor at University of Nebraska, Lincoln, 1943-44, 1945-46, Wentworth Military Academy, Lexington, Mo., 1944-45, and University of Kansas City (now University of Missouri at Kansas City), 1946-48; University of Nebraska, assistant professor, 1954-58, associate professor, 1958-63, professor of English, 1963—, chairman of department, 1962-72. *Member:* Modern Language Association of America, National Council of Teachers of English, Conference on College Composition and Communication (chairman), American Association of Colleges for Teacher Education, National Council for Accreditation of Teacher Education. *Awards, honors:* Woods fellowship, 1962-63.

WRITINGS: (With Wallace C. and Dona W. Brown) *Form in Modern English*, Oxford University Press, 1958; (editor) *Essays on Rhetoric*, Oxford University Press, 1965; (editor) *Introductory Language Essays*, Norton, 1965. Contributor to journals.

* * *

BAILEY, J(ames) O(sler) 1903-

PERSONAL: Born August 12, 1903, in Raleigh, N.C.; son of Thomas Benjamin and Nancy Priscilla (Smith) Bailey; married Mary Ethel Misenheimer, June 12, 1938; children: Nancy Barden (Mrs. Millard R. Rich, Jr.). *Education:* University of North Carolina, A.B., 1924, M.A., 1927, Ph.D., 1934. *Politics:* Democrat. *Religion:* Baptist. *Home:* 801 Woodland Ave., Chapel Hill, N.C. 27514.

CAREER: High school teacher in North Carolina, 1924-25; Wofford College, Spartanburg, N.C., assistant professor of English, 1926-27; University of North Carolina, Chapel Hill, instructor, 1927-34, assistant professor, 1934-42, associate professor, 1942-52, professor of English, 1952—. U.S. Army, Quartermaster School, text writer, 1942-43. Lecturer at Robert College and at Istanbul University, both Turkey, 1956-57. *Member:* Modern Language Association of America, South Atlantic Modern Language Association (vice-president, 1957-58; chairman of program committee, 1958-63).

WRITINGS: Pilgrims Through Space and Time, Argus Books, 1947, reprinted, Greenwood Press, 1972; *Proper Words in Proper Places* (textbook), American Book Co., 1952; *Creative Exercises in College English* (textbook), American Book Co., 1952; *Thomas Hardy and the Cosmic Mind*, University of North Carolina Press, 1956; (annotator and reviser) E. K. Brown, *Victorian Poetry*, 2nd edition, Ronald, 1962; (author of introduction) Symmes, *Symzonia*, Scholars' Facsimiles, 1965; *British Plays of the Nineteenth Century*, Odyssey, 1966; *The Poetry of Thomas Hardy: A Handbook and Commentary*, University of North Carolina Press, 1970. Contributor to scholarly journals.

* * *

BAILEY, Thomas Andrew 1902-

PERSONAL: Born December 14, 1902, in San Jose, Calif.; son of James Andrew (an orchardist) and Annie Mary (Nelson) Bailey; married Sylvia Dean, August 28, 1928; children: Arthur Dean. *Education:* Stanford University, A.B. (with great distinction), 1924, M.A., 1925, Ph.D., 1927; University of California, Berkeley, graduate study, 1925-26. *Politics:* Independent. *Religion:* Baptist ("nonpracticing"). *Home:* 293 Santa Teresa, Stanford, Calif. 94305. *Office:* Department of History, Stanford University, Stanford, Calif. 94305.

CAREER: University of Hawaii, Honolulu, instructor, 1927-28, assistant professor of history and political science,

1928-30; Stanford University, Stanford, Calif., assistant professor, 1930-35, associate professor, 1935-40, professor of American history, 1940-68, Margaret Byrne Professor of American History, 1952-68, head of department, 1952-55, 1957-59, professor emeritus, 1968—. Visiting professor, University of Washington, summer, 1931, George Washington University, 1936-37; member of Institute of Advanced Study, 1939-40; Albert Shaw lecturer in diplomatic history, Johns Hopkins University, 1941; lecturer, Harvard University, 1943-44, Cornell University, 1950; civilian member of staff and observer in Europe, National War College, 1947; director of Stanford University Institute of American History, 1952-53.

MEMBER: American Historical Association (president, Pacific Coast branch, 1959-60), Organization of American Historians (president, 1967-68), Society for Historians of American Foreign Relations (president, 1968), Phi Beta Kappa, Delta Sigma Rho. *Awards, honors:* Rockefeller Foundation fellowship, 1939-40; Commonwealth Club of California Silver Medal, 1941, for *A Diplomatic History of the American People*, and Gold Medals, 1945, for *Woodrow Wilson and the Lost Peace*, and 1951, for *America Faces Russia*.

WRITINGS: Theodore Roosevelt and the Japanese-American Crises: An Account of the International Complications Arising from the Race Problem on the Pacific Coast, Stanford University Press, 1934; *A Diplomatic History of the American People*, Crofts, 1940, 9th edition, Appleton, 1974; *The Policy of the United States toward the Neutrals, 1917-1918*, Johns Hopkins Press, 1942; *America's Foreign Policies: Past and Present*, Foreign Policy Association, 1943, revised edition, 1945; *Woodrow Wilson and the Lost Peace*, Macmillan, 1944; *Woodrow Wilson and the Great Betrayal*, Macmillan, 1945; *Woodrow Wilson and the Peacemakers* (one-volume edition of two earlier Woodrow Wilson books), Macmillan, 1947; *The Man in the Street: The Impact of American Public Opinion on Foreign Policy*, Macmillan, 1948.

America Faces Russia: Russian-American Relations from Early Times to Our Day, Cornell University Press, 1950; *The American Pageant: A History of the Republic*, Heath, 1956, 5th edition, 1974, *Quiz Book*, 1958, 4th edition, 1971, *Guidebook*, with Hugh Ross, 1964, 4th edition, 1971; (with Allan Nevins and others) *Times of Trial*, Knopf, 1958; *Presidential Greatness: The Image and the Man from George Washington to the Present*, Appleton, 1966; *The Art of Diplomacy: The American Experience*, Appleton, 1968; *Democrats vs. Republicans: The Continuing Clash*, Meredith, 1968; *Essays Diplomatic and Undiplomatic of Thomas A. Bailey*, edited, with preface and introduction, by Alexander DeConde and Armin Rappaport, Appleton, 1969; *Probing America's Past: A Critical Examination of Major Myths and Misconceptions*, two volumes, Heath, 1973.

Editor: (With F. A. Golder and J. L. Smith) *The March of the Mormon Battalion from Council Bluffs to California: Taken from the Journal of Henry Standage*, Century, 1928; *The American Spirit: United States History as Seen by Contemporaries*, Heath, 1963, 3rd edition, 1973.

Feature writer for *Honolulu Star-Bulletin*, 1928. Contributor to professional journals. Member of board of editors, *Pacific Historical Review*, 1937-40.

WORK IN PROGRESS: Maxims for American Diplomacy.

BIOGRAPHICAL/CRITICAL SOURCES: Social Education, Volume XXIV, 1960, pages 371-374.

BAIRD, John Edward 1922-

PERSONAL: Born February 3, 1922, in Eugene, Ore.; son of William Robb (a minister) and Martha (Watson) Baird; married Eleanor Bertuleit (a teacher), June 15, 1947; children: John Edward, Jr., Barbara Ann, Donald Roy. *Education:* Northwest Christian College, B.Th., 1944; University of the Pacific, B.A., 1947, M.A., 1948; Columbia University, Ph.D., 1959. *Home:* 5255 Crane Ave., Castro Valley, Calif. 94546. *Office:* California State University, Hayward, Calif. 94542.

CAREER: University of Oregon, Eugene, instructor in speech, 1947-48; University of New Hampshire, Extension Service, Durham, assistant, 1948-51; instructor in speech at Columbia University, New York, N.Y., 1951-53, Manhattan College, Manhattan, Kan., 1953-55, Modesto Junior College, Modesto, Calif., 1955-63; Phillips University, Enid, Okla., associate professor of speech, 1963-67; California State University, Hayward, professor of speech, 1967—. *Military service:* U.S. Army, 1945-46. *Member:* Speech Association of America, American Association of University Professors.

WRITINGS: A Guide to Conducting Meetings, Abingdon, 1965; (co-author) W. R. Baird, Sr., *Funeral Meditations*, Abingdon, 1966; *Preparing for Platform and Pulpit*, Abingdon, 1968.

*   *   *

BAIRD, Russell N. 1922-

PERSONAL: Born June 14, 1922, in Joffre, Pa.; son of Robert and Annie (Seiler) Baird; married Cecilia Spencer (a secretary), November 26, 1942; children: Mary, Russell J., Margaret, Kathryn, Michael, Jane. *Education:* Attended Ohio State University, 1943; Kent State University, A.B., 1946; University of Wisconsin, M.A., 1947; Western Reserve University (now Case Western Reserve University), graduate study, 1949. *Politics:* Democrat. *Home:* 49 Madison Ave., Athens, Ohio 45701.

CAREER: Akron Beacon Journal, Akron, Ohio, reporter, 1942-43; Bowling Green State University, Bowling Green, Ohio, instructor, later assistant professor of journalism, 1947-52; Ohio University, Athens, assistant professor, 1952-56, associate professor, 1956-64, professor of journalism, 1964—. Ohio College Newspaper Association, executive secretary, 1947-57. *Military service:* U.S. Army, 1944-46; received Bronze Star Medal. *Member:* Association for Education in Journalism (chairman, graphic arts division), Sigma Delta Chi. *Awards, honors:* Baker Fund research award, Ohio University Fund, for study of the penal press, 1966.

WRITINGS: (With A. T. Turnbull) *Industrial and Business Journalism*, Chilton, 1961; (with A. T. Turnbull) *Graphics of Communication*, Holt, 1964; *The Penal Press*, Northwestern University Press, 1967; (with J. W. Click) *Magazine Editing and Production*, W. C. Brown, 1974. Assistant editor, *SPE Journal* (publication of Society of Plastics Engineers).

*   *   *

BAKER, Charlotte 1910-

PERSONAL: Born August 31, 1910, in Nacogdoches, Texas; daughter of Thomas Ellis (a banker) and Karle (a writer; maiden name Wilson) Baker; married Roger Montgomery (an attorney), October 23, 1942. *Education:* Attended Stephen F. Austin State College, 1925-26; Mills

College, B.A., 1929; University of California, Berkeley, M.A., 1930. *Religion:* Episcopal. *Home:* 1703 North St., Nacogdoches, Texas 75961. *Office:* Humane Society, Nacogdoches County, 421 Rusk St., Nacogdoches, Texas 75961.

CAREER: Kilgore Texas Public Schools, Kilgore, Tex., art teacher, 1931-34; Ball State Teachers College, Muncie, Ind., art teacher, 1934-35; Texas College of Arts and Industries, Kingsville, Tex., acting head of art department, 1940-42; Portland Art Museum, Portland, Oregon, acting director, docent, 1945-50; full-time writer-illustrator, 1950—. President, Humane Society of Nacogdoches County, 1959-62. *Member:* Texas Institute of Letters. *Awards, honors:* Texas Institute of Letters Cokesbury Awards, 1953, for *Magic for Mary M*, and 1966, for *Best of Friends*; Society for Animal Protection Poag Award as "Humanitarian of the Year," 1960-61; Humane Society of the United States certificate of appreciation, 1969; Book World Children's Spring Book Festival, first prize, University of Wisconsin Lewis Carroll Shelf Award, University of Minnesota Kerlan Collection award, and Newbury Award nomination, all 1972, for *Cockleburr Quarters*.

WRITINGS: A Sombrero for Miss Brown (novel), Dutton, 1941; *House of the Roses* (novel), Dutton, 1942; *Hope Hacienda* (juvenile; Pro Parvula Book Club selection), Crowell, 1942; *Necessary Nellie* (juvenile; Junior Literary Guild selection), Coward, 1945; *Nellie and the Mayor's Hat* (juvenile; Junior Literary Guild selection), Coward, 1947; *House on the River* (juvenile), Coward, 1948; *Kinnery Camp* (juvenile), McKay, 1951; *Sunrise Island* (juvenile), McKay, 1952; *Magic for Mary M* (juvenile), McKay, 1953; *The Venture of the Thunderbird* (juvenile), McKay, 1954; *The Return of the Thunderbird* (juvenile), McKay, 1954; *The Green Poodles* (juvenile; Junior Literary Guild selection), McKay, 1956; *Thomas, the Ship's Cat* (juvenile; *Parents Magazine* Book Club selection), McKay, 1958; *Little Brother* (juvenile), McKay, 1959; *An ABC of Dog Care for Young Owners* (juvenile), McKay, 1959; *The Best of Friends* (juvenile; Junior Literary Guild selection), McKay, 1966; *The Kittens and the Cardinals* (juvenile), McKay, 1969; *Cockleburr Quarters* (juvenile), Prentice-Hall, 1972; *Return to Eden* (play), Parameter Press, 1973. Weekly column, "Noah's Notebook," for *Nacogdoches Daily Sentinel*. Contributor of short stories and articles to *Young World* and *Child Life*.

WORK IN PROGRESS: Humane education materials.

*   *   *

BAKER, Frank S(heaffer) 1910-

PERSONAL: Born May 20, 1910, in Findlay, Ohio; son of Frank K. and Jennie (Sheaffer) Baker; married Marion Weir (now a part-time college librarian), June 25, 1935; children: Weir, Barbara, Marilyn. *Education:* College of Wooster, A.B., 1930; Ball State University, graduate study, 1932-33; Harvard University, A.M., 1943; additional study at Indiana University, summers, 1947-53, and University of Missouri, summers, 1960-61. *Politics:* Independent. *Religion:* Presbyterian. *Home address:* Box 157, Hanover, Ind. 47243. *Office:* Hanover College, Hanover, Ind. 47243.

CAREER: Junior and senior high school teacher, Anderson, Ind., 1933-46; Hanover College, Hanover, Ind., assistant professor, 1946-53, associate professor of English and journalism, 1953-66, associate professor of journalism, 1966—, director of publicity, 1946-62, director of public information, 1962-68, college editor, 1968—. Indiana Presbyterian Synod, member of executive council and chairman of board of managers of *Indiana Presbyterian*, 1955-61. *Member:* National Council of Teachers of English, National Press Photographers Association, National Council of College Publications Advisers (state chairman, 1965-66), Association for Education in Journalism, American Association of University Professors, Conference on College Composition and Communication (executive committee, 1961-63), Alpha Phi Gamma (national vice-president, 1957-58; president, 1958-59).

WRITINGS: (With Lee Miles) *A Brief Guide to Writing Term Papers*, W. C. Brown, 1955, expanded edition, under title *A Guide to Writing Term Papers*, W. C. Brown, 1959; (editor) *Christian Perspectives in Contemporary Culture*, Twayne, 1962; *History of the Hanover United Presbyterian Church, 1820-1970*, Superior, 1970; *Genealogical History of the Descendants of David Baker, 1808-82, of Lancaster County, Pa.*, privately printed, 1974. Contributor to *Indiana Magazine of History, Scholastic Editor, Presbyterian Tribune*, and other periodicals. Editor, *Proceedings of the Hanover College Workshop*, 1958, *Hanover Forum*, 1961-63, *Hanover College Alumni News*, 1966-69, *The Hanoverian*, 1969—.

WORK IN PROGRESS: Collaborating in the preparation of a sesquicentennial history of Hanover College, 1977.

* * *

BAKER, Nelson B(laisdell) 1905-

PERSONAL: Born December 24, 1905, in Manchester, Mass.; son of John Davis (a carpenter) and Huldah (Burns) Baker; married Ruth Glazier, August 23, 1930. *Education:* Tufts University, B.S. in Engineering, 1927; Eastern Baptist Theological Seminary, B.D., 1931, Th.M., 1932, Th.D., 1933; University of Southern California, Ph.D., 1951. *Politics:* Liberal Republican. *Home:* 62 Locust St., Apt. 225, Falmouth, Mass. 02540.

CAREER: Baptist minister; pastor in Philadelphia, Pa., 1930-36, Arlington, Mass., 1936-43; California Baptist Theological Seminary, Los Angeles (now American Baptist Seminary of the West, Covina campus), professor of theology, 1946-51; Eastern Baptist Theological Seminary, Philadelphia, Pa., professor of English Bible, 1951-71, professor emeritus, 1971—. Minister in interim pastorates. *Military service:* U.S. Army, chaplain, 1943-45; served in Europe twenty months; became captain.

WRITINGS: What is the World Coming To?, Westminster, 1965; *You Can Understand the Bible, by Its Unifying Themes*, A. J. Holman, 1973. Contributor, *The Zondervan Pictorial Encyclopedia of the Bible*, 1975, *The Wycliffe Bible Dictionary*, 1975, and to religious periodicals.

* * *

BAKER, Pearl Biddlecome 1907-

PERSONAL: Born August 5, 1907, in Ferron, Utah; daughter of Joe and Millie (Scharf) Biddlecome; children: Joe, Jack, Noel. *Education:* Graduated from high school in Salt Lake City, Utah. *Politics:* Republican. *Religion:* Episcopalian. *Home address:* P.O. Box 355, Green River, Utah 84525.

CAREER: Taught school at one time, and ran the trading post and post office at Hite-White Canyon on the Colorado River for years, former clerk-receptionist at the Bosque del Apache National Wildlife Refuge, San Antonio, N.M. *Member:* Western Writers of America.

WRITINGS: The Wild Bunch at Robbers Roost, Westernlore, 1965, revised and enlarged edition, Abelard-Schuman, 1971; *Trail on the Water*, Pruett Press, 1969; *Robbers Roost Recollections*, Utah State University, 1975. Also author of *Rim Flying Canyonlands*, with Hurst, published by Canyonlands Gift and Book Shop.

WORK IN PROGRESS: It's for the Birds.

BIOGRAPHICAL/CRITICAL SOURCES: Desert Magazine, May, 1963.

* * *

BAKER, Robin Campbell 1941-

PERSONAL: Born October 20, 1941, in Bristol, England; son of Auther Eric (a bookseller and publisher) and Helen (Bean) Baker. *Education:* Attended Clayesmore School in England, 1954-58. *Home:* Oakapples, Littlemead, Esher, Surrey, England. *Agent:* Winant, Towers Ltd., 1 Furnival St., London E.C. 4, England.

CAREER: Has lived and worked in Australia, New Zealand, United States, and Sweden; student of ballet and choreography with Royal Ballet, London, England, and with Royal Winnipeg Ballet. Children's Book Center Ltd., London, England, co-director with father, 1968—.

WRITINGS: Land Rovers, Scholastic Book Services, 1964 (published in England as *A Map for Giants*, Constable Young Books, 1964).

SIDELIGHTS: Robin Baker speaks fair French and Swedish. *Avocational interests:* Travel, especially in Greece, to study ancient cultures; music.

* * *

BAKWIN, Ruth Morris 1898-

PERSONAL: Born June 3, 1898, in Chicago, Ill.; daughter of Edward (a meat packer) and Helen (Swift) Morris; married Harry Bakwin (a physician), February 2, 1925; children: Edward, Patricia (Mrs. Frederick R. Selch), Barbara (Mrs. William S. Rosenthal), Michael. *Education:* Wellesley College, B.A., 1919; Cornell Medical College, M.D., 1923; studied at Universities of Vienna and Berlin, 1924-25; Columbia University, M.A. (psychology), 1929. *Home and office:* 132 East 71st St., New York, N.Y. 10021.

CAREER: Fifth Avenue Hospital, New York, N.Y., intern, 1923-24, assistant pediatrician, 1925-35; Columbia University, New York, N.Y., instructor in pediatrics, 1927-30; Bellevue Hospital, New York, N.Y., assistant pediatrician, 1927-43, visiting physician, 1943-48, associate visiting physician, Children's Medical Service, 1948-55, visiting physician, 1955—; New York University, New York, N.Y., faculty, 1927—, started as instructor, professor of clinical pediatrics, 1961—; New York Infirmary, New York, N.Y., associate pediatrician, 1929-31, director of pediatrics, 1936-54, director emeritus, 1955-66, co-director, 1966. National Association for Mental Health, member of board of directors, 1962-66; Association for Mentally Ill Children, Inc., member of board of directors. National Committee for Children and Youth, member of national advisory committee, 1965. New York Infirmary, trustee; League School, member of advisory board.

MEMBER: American Academy of Pediatrics (fellow; New York State chairman, 1965—), American Medical Association (fellow), American Medical Women's Association, Pan American Medical Women's Alliance, Women's Medical Society of New York State, Women's Medical Association of New York City, Cosmopolitan Club, Wellesley Club. *Awards, honors:* Elizabeth Blackwell Award, 1950; Alpha Phi Award, 1952; New York Infirmary Award of Merit, 1960.

WRITINGS: (With husband, Harry Bakwin) *Psychologic Care During Infancy and Childhood*, Appleton, 1942; (with Harry Bakwin) *Clinical Management of Behavior Disorders in Children*, Saunders, 1953, 3rd edition, 1966, 4th edition published as *Behavior Disorders in Children*, 1974. Author of articles relating to behavior in children.

WORK IN PROGRESS: A study of the siblings of schizophrenic children.

AVOCATIONAL INTERESTS: Art collecting, gardening, and world travel.

BIOGRAPHICAL/CRITICAL SOURCES: Alpha Phi Bulletin, Spring, 1966.

*   *   *

BALDRY, Harold (Caparne)   1907-

PERSONAL: First syllable of surname rhymes with "tall"; born March 4, 1907, in Nottingham, England; son of William and Gertrude (Caparne) Baldry; married Carina Hetley Pearson, June 29, 1934; children: Michelle, Cynthia, William. *Education:* Trinity Hall, Cambridge, M.A., 1931. *Home:* 19 Uplands Way, Southampton, England.

CAREER: Trinity Hall, Cambridge University, Cambridge, England, educational staff, 1931-34; University College of Swansea, Swansea, Wales, assistant lecturer in classics, 1934-35; University of Cape Town, Rondebosch, South Africa, lecturer in classics, 1936-48, professor, 1948-54; University of Southampton, Southampton, England, professor of classics, 1954-72, dean of Faculty of Arts, 1959-62, deputy vice-chancellor, 1963-66. *Member:* Classical Association of Great Britain, Society for Promotion of Hellenic Studies, Arts Council of Great Britain, Southern Arts Association (chairman). *Awards, honors:* Anisfield-Wolf Award, 1966, for *The Unity of Mankind in Greek Thought*.

WRITINGS: The Classics in the Modern World (lecture), Oxford University Press (Cape Town), 1949; *Greek Literature for the Modern Reader*, Cambridge University Press, 1951; *Ancient Utopias* (lecture), Southampton University Press, 1956; (with H. Schwabl and others) *Grecs et Barbares*, Fondation Hardt (Geneva), 1961; (with others) *The Birth of Western Civilization*, Thames & Hudson, 1964; *The Unity of Mankind in Greek Thought*, Cambridge University Press, 1965; *Ancient Greek Literature in Living Context*, Thames & Hudson, 1968; *The Greek Tragic Theatre*, Chatto & Windus, 1971. Contributor of articles and reviews to classical journals.

WORK IN PROGRESS: Other works on Greek literature and thought.

*   *   *

BALDWIN, David A.   1936-

PERSONAL: Born July 28, 1936, in Indianapolis, Ind.; married Marilyn Austin; children: Sarah, Rebecca, Emily. *Education:* Indiana University, A.B. (highest honors), 1958; University of Michigan, graduate student, 1958-59; Princeton University, Ph.D., 1965. *Home:* 2 Ridge Road, Hanover, N.H. *Office:* Department of Government, Dartmouth College, Hanover, N.H.

CAREER: Dartmouth College, Hanover, N.H., assistant

professor, and assistant to director of Public Affairs Center, 1965-69, associate professor of government, 1970—. *Military service:* U.S. Army, 1962-63; became first lieutenant. *Member:* Phi Beta Kappa. *Awards, honors:* Woodrow Wilson fellowship, 1958-59; Brookings Institution research fellowship, 1964-65; Dartmouth Faculty fellowship, 1969-70.

WRITINGS: Economic Development and American Foreign Policy: 1943-1962, University of Chicago Press, 1966; *Foreign Aid and American Foreign Policy: A Documentary Analysis*, Praeger, 1966. Contributor to journals.

*   *   *

BALL, F(rederick) Carlton   1911-

PERSONAL: Born April 2, 1911, in Sutter Creek, Calif.; son of Fred Arthur (an elementary school principal) and Norma E. (Werner) Ball; married Mary Ann Ellison; children: Mary Ann, Jr., Carlton Arthur. *Education:* Attended Sacramento Junior College, 1929-31; University of Southern California, A.B., 1933, M.A., 1934; also studied at University of Mexico, summer, 1931, and University of California, Berkeley, 1937-38. *Religion:* Protestant.

CAREER: California College of Arts and Crafts, Oakland, instructor, 1935-38; Sacramento High School, Sacramento, Calif., instructor in design, 1938-39; Mills College, Oakland, Calif., associate professor, 1939-40; California School of Fine Arts, San Francisco, instructor, 1943-44; University of Wisconsin, Madison, associate professor, 1950-51; Southern Illinois University, Carbondale, associate professor of fine arts, 1951-56; University of Southern California, Los Angeles, professor of fine arts, 1956—. Guest professor, University of Mississippi, 1953; lecturer in ceramics at Whittier College, 1959-61. His work in pottery, jewelry, and silversmithing has been shown in several hundred exhibitions and collections, including U.S. Information Service exhibits in many foreign countries. Lecturer, demonstrator, and jury member of art exhibitions. *Member:* American Craftsmen's Council, American Association of University Professors, Midwest Designer Craftsmen, Southern California Designer Craftsmen, American Ceramic Society, San Francisco Association of Potters (honorary member), Delta Phi Delta, Alpha Phi Omega. *Awards, honors:* Ford Foundation fellow, 1954-55; winner of first prizes in ceramics, jewelry, and silversmithing at fourteen exhibitions, including National Ceramics Exhibition, Miami, and International Ceramics Exhibition, Syracuse.

WRITINGS: (With Janice Lanoos) *Making Pottery Without a Wheel: Texture and Form in Clay*, Reinhold, 1965; *Decorating Pottery with Clay, Slip, and Glaze*, Professional Publications, 1967. Regular contributor to *Ceramics Monthly*, 1957—; contributor to *American School and University Yearbook, House Beautiful, New Yorker, Los Angeles Times*, and art journals.

WORK IN PROGRESS: Design in Nature; Design and Decorative Techniques for People Who Can't Draw; Complete Book of Pottery for Beginners.

SIDELIGHTS: A phase of ceramic work for which Ball has become well-known is the making and firing of extremely large pieces, up to six feet in height which may take as much as 150 pounds of clay.

BIOGRAPHICAL/CRITICAL SOURCES: American Artist, June, 1964.†

BALLIETT, Whitney 1926-

PERSONAL: Born April 17, 1926, in New York, N.Y.; son of Fargo and Dorothy (Lyon) Balliett; married Elizabeth Hurley King, July 21, 1951; married, Nancy Kraemer, June 4, 1965; children: (first marriage) Julia Lyon, Elizabeth Erving, Will King; (second marriage) Whitney Lyon, Jr., James Fargo. *Education:* Attended Phillips Exeter Academy; Cornell University, B.A., 1951. *Politics:* Democrat. *Agent:* Harold Ober Associates, Inc., 40 East 49th St., New York, N.Y. 10017. *Office: New Yorker,* 25 West 43rd St., New York, N.Y. 10036.

CAREER: New Yorker, New York, N.Y., proofreader, then reporter, 1951-57, staff writer, 1957—, doing column on jazz, movie and drama reviews, occasional short essays, book reviews, profiles, and other reporting. Co-advisor for Columbia Broadcasting System television show, "Sound of Jazz," 1957; writer and broadcaster of two segments of National Educational Television series, "Trio," 1962. *Military service:* U.S. Army Air Corps, 1946-47; became sergeant. *Member:* Delta Phi.

WRITINGS: The Sound of Surprise: 46 Pieces on Jazz, Dutton, 1959; *Dinosaurs in the Morning: 41 Pieces on Jazz,* Lippincott, 1962; *Such Sweet Thunder: 49 Pieces on Jazz,* Bobbs-Merrill, 1966; *Super-Drummer: A Profile of Buddy Rich,* Bobbs-Merrill, 1968; *Ecstasy at the Onion: 31 Pieces on Jazz,* Bobbs-Merrill, 1971; *Alec Wilder and His Friends,* Houghton, 1974; *New York Notes: A Journal of Jazz, 1972-74,* Houghton, 1975. Contributor of articles and reviews to *Atlantic, New Republic, Reporter;* contributor of poetry to *Saturday Review, Atlantic,* and *New Yorker.*

* * *

BALLIN, Caroline

PERSONAL: Born in Oregon City, Oregon; daughter of Philip Mayhew and Elizabeth (Collier) Collier; married. *Education:* Attended University of Alabama, New School for Social Research, Queens College (now Queens College of City University of New York), and C. W. Post College of Long Island University. *Religion:* Episcopalian. *Agent:* McIntosh & Otis, Inc., 18 East 41st St., New York, N.Y. 10017.

CAREER: Has held many jobs, from selling in Georgia tobacco markets to work as an artist and journalist. *Member:* National Association for the Advancement of Colored People, Women's International League for Peace and Freedom, Episcopal Society for Cultural and Racial Unity.

WRITINGS: Search for Freedom (novel), Citadel, 1966.

WORK IN PROGRESS: A novel, *Jeremiah.*

SIDELIGHTS: Caroline Ballin has traveled throughout the United States and in Puerto Rico, the Caribbean, South America, France, Italy, and Switzerland.†

* * *

BALLINGER, James Lawrence 1919-

PERSONAL: Born August 26, 1919, in Yakima, Wash.; son of LaPier Ballinger; married Evamarie Brown (a secretary), June 7, 1942; children: Lawrence David, Jerry Lynn, Teresa Kay. *Education:* Northwest Christian College, B.Th., 1942; Phillips University, B.A. and M.A., 1945; additional study at Syracuse University, University of Maine, and Butler University. *Politics:* Republican. *Office:* United Christian Missionary Society, 222 South Downey Ave., Indianapolis, Ind. 46207.

CAREER: Clergyman of Christian Church (Disciples of Christ). Pastor in Oregon, Oklahoma, and Washington; later area director of Christian education in Colorado, New Mexico, and Wyoming; United Christian Missionary Society, Indianapolis, Ind., national staff member, 1952—, became executive director of Christian education, camping, and conferences of Christian Education Department. Vice-chairman of Committee on Camps and Conferences, National Council of Churches of Christ in the U.S.A. Consultant to Christian Churches in England and Scotland, 1955. *Member:* American Camping Association.

WRITINGS: (Co-author) *Chi Rho Fellowship Handbook,* Christian Board of Publication, 1950; *Church Conferences for Youth and Adults,* Bethany, 1965. Writer of pamphlets on youth work; contributor to religious journals.†

* * *

BALMA, Michael J(ames) 1930-

PERSONAL: Born September 9, 1930, in Joliet, Ill.; son of Michael J. and Martha (Harris) Balma; married Janice Brethorst, June 10, 1951; children: Melinda, Michael, Martha. *Education:* Attended Joliet Junior College, 1947; Purdue University, B.S., 1952, Ph.D., 1954. *Home:* 241 West Blodgett Ave., Lake Bluff, Ill. 60044. *Office:* Abbott Laboratories, North Chicago, Ill. 60064.

CAREER: General Electric Co., Flight Propulsion Division, Cincinnati, Ohio, 1954-63, began as industrial training specialist, became manager of personnel practices; Abbott Laboratories, North Chicago, Ill., vice-president in charge of personnel, 1963—. Director and vice-president, Abbot Foundation; chairman, Police Commission. *Member:* American Psychological Association, Society for Personnel Administration, Institute of Medicine of Chicago, Urban League, Waukegan-North Chicago Chamber of Commerce, Waukegan Yacht Club, Chicago Yacht Club, Bath and Tennis Club.

WRITINGS: (With C. H. Lawshe) *Principles of Personnel Testing,* McGraw, 1966. Contributor to *Personnel Psychology, Advanced Management, Chemical Week.*

AVOCATIONAL INTERESTS: Sailing, tennis, photography, skiing.

* * *

BALTAZAR, Eulalio R. 1925-

PERSONAL: Born January 11, 1925, in the Philippines; son of Eulalio P. (a professor) and Cesaria (Rilloraza) Baltazar. *Education:* University of the Philippines, B.S., 1945; Sacred Heart Novitiate, Philippines, A.B., 1949; Berchmans College, M.A., 1952; Woodstock College, B.Th., 1959; Georgetown University, Ph.D., 1962. *Home:* 6008 Belle Ct., Hyattsville, Md. 20782. *Office:* Department of History and Philosophy, Federal City College, Washington, D.C. 20001.

CAREER: Teacher in a Jesuit high school in the Philippines, 1952-55; University of Dayton, Dayton, Ohio, instructor, 1962-64, assistant professor, 1964-67, associate professor of philosophy, 1967-69; Federal City College, Washington, D.C., professor of philosophy and theology, 1969—. Visiting professor, St. Bernard's Seminary, 1968. *Member:* American Catholic Philosophical Association, American Association of University Professors.

WRITINGS: (With others) *Contraception and Holiness,* Herder & Herder, 1964; (contributor) Martin E. Marty and Dean G. Peerman, editors, *New Theology,* Volume II,

Macmillan, 1965; *Teihard and the Supernatural*, Helicon, 1966; *God Within Process*, Paulist/Newman, 1970; *The Dark Center*, Paulist/Newman, 1973. Contributor of articles to journals.

WORK IN PROGRESS: Research on religion in public education.

* * *

BALY, (Alfred) Denis   1913-

PERSONAL: Born April 24, 1913, in Liverpool, England; son of Edward Charles Cyril (a college professor) and Ellen Agnes (Jago) Baly; married Louise Gehan, December 12, 1960. *Education:* University of Liverpool, B.A., (honors), 1935, Diploma in Education, 1936. *Religion:* Episcopalian. *Address:* Box 46, Gambier, Ohio 43022. *Office:* Department of Religion, Kenyon College, Gambier, Ohio 43022.

CAREER: Jerusalem and East Mission, teacher, 1937-54; World Council of Churches, secretary for laymen's work, 1948-49; St. George's Church, New York, N.Y., lecturer in world Christianity, 1954-56; Episcopal dioceses of Ohio and Southern Ohio, adviser on church and university, 1956-58; Kenyon College, Gambier, Ohio, visiting lecturer, 1956-58, associate professor, 1958-63, professor of religion, 1963—. Winslow Lecturer at General Theological Seminary, 1961; Beattie Lecturer, St. Luke's Seminary, 1962; Danforth Lecturer, Association of American Colleges, 1963; Sprigg Lecturer, Virginia Theological Seminary, 1971.

MEMBER: American Academy of Religion, American Association of University Professors, Association of American Geographers, Middle East Institute, Middle East Studies Association, Oriental Institute, Society for Biblical Literature, Society for Iranian Studies, Geographical Association, Royal Central Asian Society, and Palestine Exploration Society (all in Britain); American Geographical Society, American Schools of Oriental Research, American Friends of the Middle East. *Awards, honors:* Outstanding Educator of America Award, 1971.

WRITINGS: Chosen Peoples, Christian Education Press, 1956; *The Geography of the Bible*, Harper, 1957, revised edition, 1974; *Multitudes in the Valley: Church and Crisis in the Middle East*, Seabury, 1957; *Besieged City: The Church in the World*, Seabury, 1958; *Palestine and the Bible*, World Christian Books, 1960; *Academic Illusion*, Seabury, 1961; *A Geographical Companion to the Bible*, McGraw, 1963; (contributor) Frank and Reed, editors, *Translating and Understanding the Old Testament*, Abingdon, 1970; (with A. D. Tushingham) *Atlas of the Biblical World*, World Publishing, 1971. Contributor to *Encyclopaedia Britannica*, *Interpreter's Dictionary of the Bible*, and *A Companion to the Bible*.

WORK IN PROGRESS: A book in collaboration with students on the concept of God in the Old Testament for Harper.

SIDELIGHTS: Baly has language competency in Latin, Greek, French, Arabic, Hebrew, and Turkish. *Avocational interests:* Music, photography, walking.

* * *

BANGS, Carl (Oliver)   1922-

PERSONAL: Born April 5, 1922, in Seattle, Wash.; son of Carl Oliver (a builder) and Mary (Dupertuis) Bangs; married Marjorie E. Friesen (a church organist), September 6, 1942; children: Carl O. III, Jeremy D., Jeanne E. *Educa-*

tion: Pasadena College, A.B., 1945; Nazarene Theological Seminary, B.D., 1949; University of Chicago, Ph.D., 1958. *Home:* 7205 Canterbury, Prairie Village, Kan. 66208. *Office:* Saint Paul School of Theology-Methodist, Truman Rd. and Van Brunt Blvd., Kansas City, Mo. 64127.

CAREER: Methodist clergyman. Olivet Nazarene College, Kankakee, Ill., assistant professor, 1953-57, associate professor of philosophy and religion, 1957-61; Saint Paul School of Theology-Methodist, Kansas City, Mo., professor of historical theology, 1961—. Fulbright professor, University of Leiden, 1968-69. Guest lecturer at University of Leiden, University of Kansas, and Roman Catholic seminaries. Member of board, Kansas City Ecumenical Library; member of Kansas City Council for Responsible Dialogue. *Member:* American Theological Society (president, Midwest division, 1966-67), American Society of Church History (chairman of membership committee, 1964—), American Society for Reformation Research, Kansas City Society for Theological Societies (president, 1963-64). *Awards, honors:* Christian Research Foundation award for translation of Lucien Laberthonniere's *Le Realisme chretien et l'idealisme grec*, 1962; Kansas City Council on Higher Education research grant; Netherlands Organization for Pure Scientific Research, grant, 1975.

WRITINGS: German-English Theological Word List, Allenson, 1952, revised edition, 1962; *The Communist Encounter*, Beacon, 1963; *Arminius: A Study of the Dutch Reformation*, Abingdon, 1971; (contributor) John H. Bratt, editor, *The Heritage of John Calvin*, Eerdmans, 1973. Contributor to *Encyclopaedia Britannica*, religion and church history journals, and to book review section of *Kansas City Star*.

WORK IN PROGRESS: Two books, *The Kleine Geminde Mennonites*, and *The Remonstrance of 1610*.

SIDELIGHTS: Bangs has lived or traveled in Europe during four periods since 1956; competent in French, German, Dutch, Greek, Hebrew, and Latin.

AVOCATIONAL INTERESTS: Music (French horn and recorder), camping, mountaineering.

* * *

BARBER, Charles (Laurence)   1915-

PERSONAL: Born April 20, 1915, in Harold Wood, Essex, England; son of Charles Henry (a produce broker) and Agnes Maud (Pitts) Barber; married Barbara Best (a teacher), July 27, 1943; children: Elizabeth, Karin Judith, Charles Nicolas, John Andrew. *Education:* St. Catharine's College, Cambridge, B.A., 1937, M.A., 1941; Institute of Education, University of London, teacher's diploma, 1938; University of Gothenburg, Filosofie Licentiat, 1956, Filosofie Doktor, 1957. *Home:* 7 North Parade, Leeds LS16 5AY, England. *Office:* School of English, University of Leeds, Leeds LS2 9JT, England.

CAREER: Wandsworth Grammar School, London, England, assistant English master, 1938-40, 1946-47; University of Gothenburg, Gothenburg, Sweden, lecturer in English, 1947-56; The Queen's University of Belfast, Belfast, Northern Ireland, assistant lecturer in English, 1956-59; University of Leeds, Leeds, England, lecturer, 1959-62, senior lecturer, 1962-69, reader in English, 1969—. Lecturer in India, Pakistan, Lebanon, Greece, Poland, and Belgium. *Military service:* Royal Air Force, 1940-46; became flight lieutenant.

WRITINGS: The Idea of Honour in the English Drama,

Almquist & Wiksell, 1957; *The Story of Language*, Pan Books, 1964, published as *The Story of Speech and Language*, Crowell, 1965; *Linguistic Change in Present-Day English*, University of Alabama Press, 1964; (author of introduction and notes) Shakespeare, *Hamlet*, translation by F.-V. Hugo, Editions Sociales, 1964; (editor) Thomas Middleton, *A Trick to Catch the Old One*, Oliver & Boyd, 1968; (editor) Thomas Middleton, *A Chaste Maid in Cheapside*, Oliver & Boyd, 1969; (editor) Thomas Middleton, *Women Beware Women*, Oliver & Boyd, 1969; *Shakespeare's Festive Comedy*, Princeton University Press, 1972. Writer of scripts on language subjects for British Broadcasting Corp. Contributor of articles on language and literature to learned journals.

WORK IN PROGRESS: A book on the English language from 1500 to 1700.

SIDELIGHTS: Barber is competent in French and Swedish. *Avocational interests:* Music, theater, and physical sciences.

* * *

BARBOUR, Frances Martha 1895-

PERSONAL: Born March 15, 1985, in Carbondale, Ill.; daughter of George Graham (a boat manufacturer) and Grace (Munger) Barbour. *Education:* Washington University, St. Louis, Mo., A.B., 1919, A.M., 1920; graduate study at Kings College, London, 1930-31, and at University of Texas, 1938-39. *Politics:* Liberal. *Religion:* Episcopalian. *Home:* Apartment 24, Apartment Community, 9500 Route 460, Belleville, Ill. 62223.

WRITINGS: (Collector and editor) *Proverbs and Proverbial Phrases of Illinois*, Southern Illinois University Press, 1965; (editor) *A Concordance to the sayings in Franklin's Poor Richard*, Gale, 1974. Contributor to periodicals.

* * *

BARGAR, B(radley) D(uffee) 1924-

PERSONAL: "G" in surname is hard, pronounced as in "guard"; born August 17, 1924, in Jamestown, N.Y.; son of Allen E. and Deige D. (Duffee) Bargar. *Education:* Miami University, Oxford, Ohio, A.B., 1946; Ohio State University, M.A., 1947; University of Toronto, Ph.D., 1952; Exeter College, Oxford, postdoctoral research, 1952-53. *Office:* History Department, University of South Carolina, Columbia, S.C. 29208.

CAREER: State University of New York and Jamestown Community College, instructor in history, 1947-48, 1950-51; Ohio State University, Columbus, instructor in history, 1953-54; University of South Carolina, Columbia, assistant professor, 1954-61, associate professor, 1961-66, professor of history, 1966—. *Member:* African Studies Association, Southern Historical Association, South Carolina Historical Association (past president), South Carolina Association of Non-Western Scholars, Phi Beta Kappa, Phi Eta Sigma, Phi Alpha Theta. *Awards, honors:* Fulbright scholar at Oxford University, 1952-53.

WRITINGS: (Contributor) H. E. Bell and R. L. Ollard, editors, *Historical Essays, 1600-1750, Presented to David Ogg*, A. & C. Black, 1963; *Lord Dartmouth and the American Revolution*, University of South Carolina Press, 1965; *Royal South Carolina, 1719-1763*, University of South Carolina Press, 1970. Contributor of articles and reviews to historical journals.

WORK IN PROGRESS: Five Empires: Five Centuries; The Expansion of Europe to 1870.

BARKER, John W(alton, Jr.) 1933-

PERSONAL: Born October 7, 1933, in Brooklyn, N.Y.; son of John Walton (an office worker) and Evelyn (Doty) Barker; married Joan M. Sweeney (a librarian), 1958; children: Christopher Neil, Ellen Carla. *Education:* Brooklyn College (now Brooklyn College of the City University of New York), B.A., 1955; Rutgers University, M.A., 1956, Ph.D., 1961. *Office:* Department of History, University of Wisconsin, Madison, Wis. 53706.

CAREER: Brooklyn College (now Brooklyn College of the City University of New York), Brooklyn N.Y., evening class lecturer in classics department, 1958-59; University of Wisconsin, Madison, assistant professor, 1962-68, associate professor, 1968-71, professor of history, 1971—. Visiting professor, Institute of Research in Humanities, University of Wisconsin, 1964-65. *Member:* American Historical Association, American Musicological Society, Carl Nielsen Society of America (founder and executive secretary), Phi Beta Kappa. *Awards, honors:* Dumbarton Oaks visiting fellow, Harvard University, 1959-62.

WRITINGS: Justinian and the Later Roman Empire, University of Wisconsin Press, 1966; *Manuel II Palaeologus (1391-1425): A Study in Late Byzantine Statesmanship*, Rutgers University Press, 1969. Regular contributor of articles and reviews to *American Record Guide*; contributor of scholarly articles and reviews to *Byzantinische Zeitschrift, Orientalia Christiana Periodica*, and other professional journals.

WORK IN PROGRESS: A bibliographical supplement to *Justinian and the Later Roman Empire*, for publication by University of Wisconsin Press; a book on Alexius I Comnenus (1081-1118), for University of Wisconsin Press; a book giving texts, translations, and commentaries for several late Byzantine historical writings; work on music history and discography.

AVOCATIONAL INTERESTS: Music, including record collecting and singing with choral groups.†

* * *

BARKMAN, Paul Friesen 1921-

PERSONAL: Born June 1, 1921, in Hochstadt, Manitoba, Canada; son of John Reimer (director of Grace Children's Home) and Anna (Friesen) Barkman; married Frieda Ediger (a writer), December 18, 1942; children: Elizabeth Ann, John Paul Fleming. *Education:* Bethel College, North Newton, Kan., A.B., 1943; Biblical Seminary in New York, S.T.B., 1946; New York University, M.A., 1946, Ph.D., 1959. *Office:* 177 North Madison Ave., Pasadena, Calif. 91101.

CAREER: Ordained clergyman of Evangelical Mennonite Church; clinical psychologist, certified by State of California. Grace Children's Home, Henderson, Neb., superintendent and houseparent, 1946-55; pastor in Aurora, Neb., 1950-55; Taylor University, Upland, Ind., assistant professor of psychology and religion, 1956-60, associate professor and head of department of psychology, 1960-64; pastor in Marion, Ind., 1957-61; Reiss-Davis Clinic for Child Guidance, Los Angeles, Calif., fellow, 1963-64; Pacific State Hospital, Pomona, Calif., staff psychologist, 1964—; Fuller Theological Seminary, Pasadena, Calif., associate professor of psychology, 1964—. *Member:* American Psychological Association, American Scientific Affiliation (chairman of commission on psychology, 1964—), American Association of Pastoral Counselors, Society for the Scientific Study of Religion, California State Psychological Association, Los Angeles Society of Clinical Psychologists, Kappa Delta Pi, Phi Delta Kappa, Alpha Psi Omega.

WRITINGS: (With wife, Frieda Barkman) *Lad with Summer Eyes* (biography), Moody, 1958; *Man in Conflict*, Zondervan, 1965; (with Edward R. Dayton and Edward L. Gruman) *Christian Collegians and Foreign Missions*, Missions Advanced Research and Communications Center, 1969.†

*   *   *

BARLOWE, Raleigh 1914-

PERSONAL: Born November 10, 1914, in Lincoln, Idaho; son of George E. (a farmer) and Charlotte (Campbell) Barlowe; married Jeanette Topp, October 4, 1941; children: Bob Bruce. *Education:* Utah State Agricultural College (now Utah State University), B.S., 1936; American University, M.A., 1939; University of Wisconsin, Ph.D., 1946. *Politics:* Democrat. *Home:* 907 Southlawn, East Lansing, Mich. 48823. *Office:* Department of Resource Development, Michigan State University, East Lansing, Mich. 48823.

CAREER: American University, Washington, D.C., instructor in political science, 1937-38; Library of Congress, assistant, 1937-40; Southwestern Land Tenure Research Project, Fayetteville, Ark., land economist, 1942-43; U.S. Department of Agriculture, economist, Milwaukee, Wis., 1943-47; United Nations Food and Agriculture Organization, economist, Washington, D.C., 1947; Michigan State University, East Lansing, 1948—, began as lecturer, professor of agricultural economics, 1959—, chairman of resource development department, 1959-71. Consultant to University of Puerto Rico, 1958, Colombian government, 1959, University of Nigeria, 1967, Korean government, 1971-72, U.S. Agricultural Development Council, 1972—, and the Organization for European Cooperation and Development, 1973. Treasurer of Michigan Natural Resources Council, 1961-63, chairman, 1963-65, member of executive committee, 1965—. Member of Michigan governor's task force on water rights, use, and polution control, 1964-66 and U.S. delegation to Indo- U.S. Pugwash Conference, 1974.

MEMBER: American Economic Association, American Agricultural Economics Association, Economic History Association, Agricultural History Society, Soil Conservation Society of America, American Farm Economics Association, Regional Science Association.

WRITINGS: (With V. Webster Johnson) *Land Problems and Policies*, McGraw, 1954; *Land Resource Economics*, Prentice-Hall, 1958, 2nd edition, 1972; (with James Ahl and Gordon Bachman) *Land Disposal Techniques and Procedures*, Department of Resource Development, Michigan State University, 1970; *Valuation of Lands in Southcentral Iowa, 1839-1843: Royce Cession Area 262*, Clearwater Publishing, 1973; (with Conrad H. Hammar) *Valuation of Lands in Eastern Iowa: Royce Areas 175, 226, and 244, 1833-1839*, Clearwater Publishing, 1973; *Spanish Land Grants in Royce's Cession 50 in Missouri*, Clearwater Publishing, 1973; *Appraisal of Sac and Fox Lands in Portions of Royce Area 50 in Wisconsin, Illinois, and Missouri, 1805*, Clearwater Publications, 1974. Writer of more than one hundred bulletins and articles.

BARNETT, (Nicolas) Guy 1928-

PERSONAL: Surname is pronounced *Bar*-nett; born August 23, 1928, in England; son of Gordon Berthel and Elaine Mary (Black) Barnett; married Daphne Anne Hortin, 1967; children: one son, one daughter. *Education:* Oxford University, M.A. and Dip.Ed., 1953. *Politics:* Labour. *Religion:* Quaker (Society of Friends). *Home:* 32 Westcombe Park Rd., London SE3, England. *Agent:* David Higham Associates Ltd., 76 Dean St., London W.1, England.

CAREER: Teacher at Queen Elizabeth Grammar School, Wakefield, Yorkshire, England, 1953-59, and Friends School, Kamusinga, Kenya, 1960-61; Labour member of Parliament, South Dorset Division, 1962-64; Voluntary Service Overseas, London, England, staff member, 1966-69; Commonwealth Institute, London, England, chief education officer, 1969-71. *Member:* Savile Club, Royal Commonwealth Society Club.

WRITINGS: By the Lake, Cambridge University Press, 1965.

WORK IN PROGRESS: British parliamentary institutions.

AVOCATIONAL INTERESTS: Walking, music.†

*   *   *

BARNSTONE, Willis 1927-

PERSONAL: Born November 13, 1927, in Lewiston, Me.; son of Robert Carl (a businessman) and Dora (Lempert) Barnstone; married Helle Phaedra Tzapoulou (a painter), June 1, 1949; children: Aliki, Robert, Anthony. *Education:* Bowdoin College, B.A. (cum laude), 1948; graduate study at University of Paris, 1948-49, and School of Oriental and African Studies, University of London, 1952-53; Columbia University, M.A. (with high honors), 1956; Yale University, Ph.D. (with distinction), 1960. *Residence:* Heritage Woods, Bloomington, Ind. 47401.

CAREER: American Friends Service Committees, social worker in Mexico, 1945-46; Anavrita Academy, Anavrita, Greece, instructor in French and English, 1949; Les Editions Skira, Geneva, Switzerland, translator of French art texts, 1951; Wesleyan University, Middletown, Conn., instructor, 1958-59, assistant professor of Romance languages, 1959-61; Indiana University, Bloomington, associate professor of Spanish, Portuguese, and comparative literature, 1962-66, professor, 1966—. Visiting professor, University of California, Riverside, 1968-69; O'Connor professor of literature, Colgate University, 1973. *Military service:* U.S. Army, 1954-56. *Member:* Modern Language Association of America. *Awards, honors:* Danforth summer grant, 1960; nomination for Pulitzer Prize in literature, 1960, for *From This White Island*; Guggenheim fellowship, 1961-62; American Council of Learned Societies fellowship, 1969-70.

WRITINGS: Poems of Exchange, Institut Francais d'-Athenes, 1951; *Notes for a Bible* (poetry), Hermanos Hernandez (Malaga), 1952; *From This White Island*, Twayne, 1959; (translator) *Eighty Poems of Antonio Machado*, Las Americas, 1959; (translator from the Greek, with wife, Helle Barnstone) Margarita Liberaki, *The Other Alexander* (novel), Noonday, 1959.

(Editor with Hugh A. Harter) Miguel de Cervantes, *Rinconete y Cortadillo* (college text), Las Americas, 1960; (editor and translator) *Greek Lyric Poetry*, Bantam, 1962, enlarged edition, Indiana University Press, 1966; (translator, and author of introduction) Ignacio Bernal, *Mexico Before Cortez: Art, History and Legend*, Dolphin Books, 1963; (translator) *Physiologus Theobaldi Episcopi de Naturis Duodecim Animalium*, Indiana University Press, 1964; *Sappho: Lyrics in the Original Greek with Translations*, Doubleday-Anchor and New York University Press, 1965; (editor and reviser) Luis de Gongora, *Soledades*, translated by Edward Wilson, Las Americas, 1965.

(General editor) *Modern European Poetry* (anthology), Bantam, 1966; *A Sky of Days* (poems), Indiana University Fine Arts, 1967; (editor, translator, and author of introduction) *The Poems of Saint John of the Cross*, Indiana University Press, 1967; (editor and author of introduction) Edgar Lee Masters, *New Spoon River*, Macmillan, 1968; (contributor) Juan Marichal and Ivar Ivask, editors, *Luminous Reality: Critical Essays on the Poetry of Jorge Guillen*, University of Oklahoma Press, 1968; (editor with Mary Ellen Solt) *Concrete Poetry: A World View*, Indiana University Press, 1969; (editor) *Spanish Poetry From the Beginning Through the Nineteenth Century* (anthology), Oxford University Press, 1970; (translator) Shir Hashirin, *The Song of Songs*, Kedros (Athens), 1970.

A Day in the Country (poems), Harper, 1971; *Antijournal* (poems), Sono Nis Press, 1971; (editor) *Eighteen Texts: Writings by Contemporary Greek Authors*, Harvard University Press, 1972; (translator with Ko Ching-po) *The Poems of Mao Tse-tung*, Harper, 1972; *New Faces of China* (poems and photographs), Indiana University Press, 1973; (translator and author of introduction) Pedro Salinas, *My Voice Because of You*, State University of New York Press, 1975. Also author of a verse play, "The Girl and the Poison Tree."

Contributor of translations: (Greek, Latin, and Portuguese sections) *The World's Love Poetry*, edited by Michael R. Martin, Bantam, 1960; *Anthology of Spanish Poetry*, edited by Angel Flores, Anchor Books, 1961; *Concise Encyclopaedia of Modern World Literature*, edited by Geoffrey Grigson, Hawthorn, 1963; (poetry sections) Nikos Kazantzakis, *Spain*, translated by Amy Mims, Simon & Schuster, 1963; *Language of Love* (short stories), edited by Michael R. Martin, Bantam, 1964; *Genius of the Spanish Theater* (plays), edited by Robert O'Brien, Mentor Books, 1965.

Medieval Lyric Poetry, edited by W. T. H. Jackson, Bantam, 1966; Helen Hill Miller, *Bridge to Asia*, Scribners, 1967; *Adventures in World Literature*, edited by Applegate, Browne, and others, Harcourt, 1970; *Stoney Lonesome*, edited by Richard Pflum, Bloomington, Ind., 1971; *Poems of the Greek Anthology*, edited by Peter Jay, Penguin, 1973; Audrey Popping, *Dawn Wakes in the East*, Harper, 1974; *For Neruda, For Chile*, edited by Walter Lowenfels, Beacon Press, 1974. Also contributor of translations to other anthologies, books, and periodicals.

Plays in verse translation: Calderon de la Barca, "King Balshazzar's Feast," first produced at St. Leo College, St. Leo, Fla., March, 1969; Lope de Vega, "The Outrageous Saint," first produced at Dalhousie University, Nova Scotia, January, 1971; Pablo Neruda, "Rage and Death of Joaquin Murieta," 1972.

Original poems included in *New Campus Writing, Number 3*, Grove, 1959. Other original poems have been published in more than fifteen periodicals, including *New Yorker, Antioch Review, Columbia University Forum, Prairie Schooner, Nine* (London), *Points* (Paris), and *Triad*. Contributor of verse translations, and occasional prose translations and articles to *Nation, Arizona Quarterly, Tulane*

Drama Review, Evergreen Review, and other literary journals. Editor-in-chief, *Artes Hispanicas Hispanic Arts*, published jointly by Indiana University and Macmillan.

WORK IN PROGRESS: Antonio Machado, a study of the lyrical speaker in the poems, for Las Americas, and *From Sappho to Mao: Essays on Poetry*.

SIDELIGHTS: Barnstone has spent extended periods in Mexico, Spain, France, England, Greece, and China.

* * *

BARNWELL, D. Robinson 1915-

PERSONAL: Born April 16, 1915, in Pageland, S.C.; daughter of Aaron Coner and Ruby (Funderburk) Robinson; married George Shelby Barnwell (a mechanical engineer), December 21, 1940; children: Susan Jane Holmes (Mrs. Jack Anthony), Sharon Anne (deceased). *Education:* Winthrop College, A.B., 1937; Elon College, special writing courses, 1964-65. *Religion:* Methodist. *Home:* 1315 Briarcliff Rd., Burlington, N.C. *Agent:* Muriel Fuller, P.O. Box 193, Grand Central Station, New York, N.Y. 10017.

CAREER: Writer. High school teacher of English in Mineral Springs, N.C., 1937-39, of English and French in Goldsboro, N.C., 1941; teacher of social studies in Marshville, N.C., 1941-43; Walter Williams High School, Burlington, N.C., teacher of English, 1966—. *Member:* Burlington Writers Club (vice-president, 1963; president, 1964). *Awards, honors:* Seventeen first-place awards for short stories and nonfiction in local, county, and state contests.

WRITINGS: Head into the Wind (young adult novel), McKay, 1966; *Shadow on the Water* (young adult novel), McKay, 1967.

WORK IN PROGRESS: A novel, *For Love's Sake Only*.

* * *

BARON, Hans 1900-

PERSONAL: Born June 22, 1900, in Berlin, Germany; came to United States in 1938, naturalized in 1945; son of Theodor (a physician) and Marta (Mecklenburg) Baron; married Edith Alexander, March 31, 1929; children: Rinehart, Renate (Mrs. Marcel Franciscono). *Education:* Studied at Universities of Leipzig and Berlin, 1918-22; University of Berlin, Dr. Phil., 1922, postdoctoral study, 1922-24. *Home:* 28 Huron Ave., Cambridge, Mass. 02138; North Pomfret, Vt. 05053 (summer). *Office:* Hilles Library 222, Harvard University, Cambridge, Mass. 02138.

CAREER: Munich Academy of Sciences, Historical Commission, Munich, Germany, research associate, 1928-33; University of Berlin, Berlin, Germany, privatdozent in medieval and modern history, 1929-33; studied privately in Italy, 1935-36, and did research in London, England, 1936-38; Queens College, Flushing, N.Y., assistant professor of history, 1939-42; Institute for Advanced Study, Princeton, N.J., member, 1944-48; Newberry Library, Chicago, Ill., research fellow and bibliographer, 1949-65, distinguished research fellow, 1965-70; University of Chicago, Chicago, Ill., professorial lecturer in Renaissance studies, 1963-68. Visiting lecturer at Johns Hopkins University, 1946-47, at Cornell University, 1961; visiting professor at Ohio State University, 1958-59, Dartmouth College, 1964, Harvard University, 1970.

MEMBER: American Academy of Arts and Sciences (fellow emeritus), American Historical Association, Renaissance Society of America, American Society for Reformation Research (president, 1957), Mediaeval Academy of America, Society for Italian Historical Studies, Dante Society of America, Tuscan Academy of Sciences and Letters (Florence, Italy; corresponding fellow), Deputazione di Storia Patria per le Venezie (Venice, Italy; honorary fellow), British Academy (corresponding fellow).

AWARDS, HONORS: Notgemeinschaft der deutschen Wissenschaft postdoctoral traveling fellowship for studies in Italy, 1925-27; Guggenheim fellowship, 1942-43; American Philosophical Society grant, 1943-44; honorary L.H.D., Lawrence University, 1957; Rockefeller Foundation grant, 1961-63; Premio Internazionale Forte dei Marmi (auspices of Italian government and University of Pisa), in Italian history, 1965; Center for Advanced Study in the Behavioral Sciences fellowship, 1967-68; Society for Italian Historical Studies citation for distinguished achievement, 1970; Guggenheim fellowship, 1974.

WRITINGS: Calvins Staatsanschauung und das konfessionelle Zeitalter, R. Oldenbourg, 1924; *Leonardo Bruni Aretino, Humanistisch-philosophische Schriften: Herausgegeben und erlaeutert*, Teubner, 1928; *Cicero and the Roman Civic Spirit in the Middle Ages and the Early Renaissance*, Manchester University Press, 1928, revised edition included in F. L. Cheyette, editor, *Lordship and Community in Medieval Europe*, Holt, 1968; *Humanistic and Political Literature in Florence and Venice at the Beginning of the Quattrocento*, Harvard University Press, 1955, reprinted with new introduction, Russell, 1968; *The Crisis of the Early Italian Renaissance: Civic Humanism and Republican Liberty in an Age of Classicism and Tyranny*, two volumes, Princeton University Press, 1955, revised one-volume edition with an epilogue, 1966; *From Petrarch to Leonardo Bruni: Studies in Humanistic and Political Literature*, University of Chicago Press, 1968.

Editor—Ernst Troeltsch's posthumous works: *Spektator-Briefe, Aufsaetze veber die deutsche Revolution und die Weltpolitik 1918-22*, Mohr, 1924; *Aufsaetze zur Geistesgeschichte und Religionssoziologie*, Mohr, 1925; *Deutscher Geist und Westeuropa*, Mohr, 1925.

Contributor: *Kultur-und Universalgeschichte: Walter Goetz zu seinem 60. Geburtstage dargebracht*, Teubner, 1927; *Friedrich Meinecke zum 30. Oktober 1932, Historische Zeitschrift Band 147*, R. Oldenbourg, 1933; *The Quest for Political Unity in World History*, American Historical Association, 1944; *The New Cambridge Modern History*, Volume I: *The Renaissance*, Cambridge University Press, 1957; Karl H. Dannenfeldt, editor, *The Renaissance, Medieval or Modern?*, Heath, 1959; Denys Hay, editor, *The Renaissance Debate*, Holt, 1965; *Essays in History and Literature Presented by Fellows of the Newberry Library to Stanley Pargellis*, Newberry Library, 1965; P. O. Kristeller and P. P. Wiener, editors, *Renaissance Essays*, Harper, 1968; A. Buck, editor, *Zu Begriff und Problem der Renaissance*, Deutsche Buchgesellschaft, 1969; R. M. Kingdon and R. D. Linder, editors, *Calvin and Calvinism: Sources of Democracy?*, Heath, 1970; *Florilegium Historiale: Essays Presented to Wallace K. Ferguson*, University of Toronto Press, 1971.

Contributor of more than fifty articles on Humanism and on late-medieval, Renaissance, and Reformation history to scholarly journals in United States, England, Switzerland, Italy, and Germany. Co-editor, *Bibliotheque d'Humanisme et Renaissance* (Geneva), 1956—, and *Studies in Medieval and Renaissance History*, 1963-71.

WORK IN PROGRESS: Collected Papers on Civic Hu-

manism and the Renaissance, some revised, some new; another book, almost finished in manuscript, tentatively entitled *Franciscan Poverty and Civic Wealth: Spirituality and Secular Values from Petrarch to the Italian Renaissance Humanists*; a volume, *The Florentine Humanism and the Historiography of Leonardo Bruni*; various studies on Machiavelli.

BIOGRAPHICAL/CRITICAL SOURCES: Nuova Rivista Storica, Volume XXXIX, 1955; *Storia di Milano*, Volume VII, 1956; *Newberry Library Bulletin*, Volume IV, 1956; *Rivista Storica Italiana*, Volume LXIX, 1957; W. K. Ferguson, "The Interpretation of Italian Humanism: The Contribution of Hans Baron," *Journal of the History of Ideas*, Volume XIX, 1958, reprinted in Ferguson's *Renaissance Studies*, University of Western Ontario Press, 1963; A. Molho and J. A. Tedeschi, editors, *Renaissance: Studies in Honor of Hans Baron*, Northern Illinois University Press, 1971; "I miei studi" (autobiographical), *Critica Storica*, Volume IX, 1972.

*   *   *

BARRETT, George W(est)   1908-

PERSONAL: Born May 10, 1908, in Iowa City, Iowa; son of Edward Cecil and Mary (West) Barrett; married Emma Dee Hanford, October 6, 1936; married Bettina Tvede Durland, April 25, 1970; children: Myra (Mrs. Michael Casper), Richard, Margaret (Mrs. John Walls). *Education:* University of California, Los Angeles, B.A., 1930; Episcopal Theological School, Cambridge, Mass., B.D., 1933. *Home:* 128 West Arrellaga, Santa Barbara, Calif. 93101. *Office:* 322 Palm Ave., Santa Barbara, Calif. 93101.

CAREER: Clergyman of The Protestant Episcopal Church. Rector of churches in Upland, Calif., 1936-42, Monrovia, Calif., 1942-46, Los Angeles, Calif., 1947-52; Episcopal chaplain of Pomona, Scripps, and Claremont Colleges, Claremont, Calif., 1940-42; General Theological Seminary, New York, N.Y., professor of pastoral theology, 1952-55; Christ Church, Bronxville, N.Y., rector, 1955-63; Rochester (N.Y.) Diocese of Protestant Episcopal Church, bishop, 1963-70, consultant, 1970-72; Planned Parenthood of Santa Barbara, Santa Barbara, Calif., executive director, 1972—. Chairman of department of promotion, Diocese of New York, 1960-63. *Awards, honors:* D.D., Occidental College, 1952; S.T.D., General Theological Seminary and Hobart College, 1963; L.H.D., Alfred University, 1963.

WRITINGS: (With J. V. Langmead Casserley) *Dialogue on Destiny*, Seabury, 1955; *Key Words for Lent*, Seabury, 1963; *Demands on Ministry Today: The Issue of Integrity*, Seabury, 1969; *Christ's Keys to Happiness*, World Publishing, 1970.

*   *   *

BARRETT, Laurence I.   1935-

PERSONAL: Born September 6, 1935, in New York, N.Y.; son of Harold (a post office official) and Ruth (Gaier) Barrett; married Paulette Singer (a university official), March 9, 1957; children: Paul Meyer, David Allen. *Education:* New York University, B.A., 1956; Columbia University, M.S., 1957. *Politics:* Independent. *Religion:* Jewish. *Home:* 28 Tenafly Rd., Tenafly, N.J. 07670. *Agent:* McIntosh & Otis, Inc., 18 East 41st St., New York, N.Y. 10017. *Office:* Time Inc., Rockefeller Center, New York, N.Y. 10020.

CAREER: New York Herald Tribune, New York, N.Y., successively political reporter, columnist, and Washington correspondent, 1958-65; Time, New York, N.Y., contributing editor, 1965-67, associate editor, 1968-69, senior editor, national affairs section, 1970—. Military service: U.S. Army Reserve, 1957-59. Member: Phi Beta Kappa, Kappa Tau Alpha.

WRITINGS: The Mayor of New York, Doubleday, 1965. Contributor to magazines and newspapers.

WORK IN PROGRESS: Short stories, and essays on the press.

*   *   *

BARRETT, Mary Ellin 1927-

PERSONAL: Born November 25, 1927, in New York, N.Y.; daughter of Irving (composer) and Ellin (an author; maiden name, MacKay) Berlin; married Marvin Barrett (an editor), October 14, 1952; children: Elisabeth, Irving, Mary Ellin, Katherine. Education: Attended Bryn Mawr, 1945-47; Barnard College, B.A. (cum laude), 1949.

CAREER: Time Magazine, New York, N.Y., researcher, 1950-52; Glamour Magazine, New York, N.Y., literary editor, 1959-1964; Vogue Magazine, New York, N.Y., feature associate, 1965-1966. Member: Phi Beta Kappa.

WRITINGS: Castle Ugly, Dutton, 1966; An Accident of Love, Dutton, 1973. Wrote column with husband, Marvin Barrett, for Good Housekeeping, 1957-59. Contributor to Reporter, Charm, Glamour, and Ladies' Home Journal.

SIDELIGHTS: Mrs. Barrett told Library Journal that she wanted her first novel to "say something about the traps people lay for themselves when they play games with love." She writes about summer people, those she calls "the rich, spoiled kind of men and women who never grow up and whose children grow up too soon—characters who were supposed to have gone out with Scott Fitzgerald and the Second World War but are in fact all over the place today." The reviewers were impressed with Mrs. Barrett's ability to recall the 1930's and "the way things used to look," wrote Paul Zimmerman, "the marvelously pretentious wooden cathedrals by the sea, ... the breezes, footsteps, swimsuits and incidental rambles of America's summer aristocrats before the war. Her book belongs in the tradition of Gothic romance, a young girl growing up in a big house haunted by human demons."

BIOGRAPHICAL/CRITICAL SOURCES: Library Journal, October 1, 1966; Time, December 30, 1966; Saturday Review, January 7, 1967; Newsweek, January 23, 1967.†

*   *   *

BARRETT, Nathan N(oble) 1933-

PERSONAL: Born May 24, 1933, in New York, N.Y.; son of Nathaniel N. and Bertha (Blackburn) Barrett. Education: Brooklyn College (now Brooklyn College of the City University of New York), student at various periods, 1950-57.

CAREER: Full-time free-lance writer. Military service: U.S. Army, 1951-53. Member: Dramatists Guild of the Authors League of America (associate). Awards, honors: Huntington Hartford Foundation Award, 1961; John Hay Whitney Opportunity Award, 1965-66.

WRITINGS: Bars of Adamant: A Tropical Novel, Fleet, 1966. Also author of poetry collection, Floating World, 1962.

Plays produced: "Room of Roses," 1964; "Evening of Black Comedy," 1965.†

*   *   *

BARRETT, Russell H(unter) 1919-

PERSONAL: Born December 30, 1919, in Cottonwood Falls, Kan.; son of Raymond John and Mable Adele (Hunter) Barrett; married Alamada Orpha Bollier (a doctoral candidate), June 17, 1947; children: Valerie Sue, Pamela Anne. Education: University of Kansas, B.A., 1946, M.A., 1947; University of Melbourne, Ph.D., 1952. Politics: Democrat. Home: 544 North Ninth St., Oxford, Miss. 38655.

CAREER: Instructor in political science at University of Kansas, Lawrence, 1947-50, University of California, Berkeley, 1952-53, San Francisco State College, San Francisco, Calif., 1953-54; University of Mississippi, University, assistant professor, 1954-56, associate professor, 1957-60, professor of political science, 1961—. Military service: U.S. Army Air Forces, 1942-45; became technical sergeant; received five campaign stars for service in Asiatic-Pacific Theater. Member: American Political Science Association, American Association of University Professors (national council, 1964-67), Southern Political Science Association, Mississippi Council on Human Relations, Phi Beta Kappa, Phi Kappa Phi, Omicron Delta Kappa, Pi Sigma Alpha. Awards, honors: Fulbright fellowship to Australia, 1951-52; fellowship in East Asian studies, Harvard University, 1958-59; grant-in-aid, Social Science Research Council, 1964; Rockefeller Foundation grant, 1966-67.

WRITINGS: Promises and Performances in Australian Politics, Institute of Pacific Relations, 1959, revised edition, Publications Center, University of British Columbia, 1963; Integration at Ole Miss, Quadrangle, 1965. Contributor to Far Eastern Survey, Asian World, Southwestern Social Science, and University of Mississippi Quarterly.

WORK IN PROGRESS: Research on Negro voting in Mississippi, and the political ideas of William Faulkner.

*   *   *

BARRIE, Donald C(onway) 1905-

PERSONAL: Original name Donald C. Willmann, name legally changed, 1941; born May 24, 1905, in Buffalo, N.Y.; son of Leo George and Maye Virginia (Gronachan) Willmann. Education: Educated at private and public schools in America and England; studied at Theodora Irvine's School of the Theatre and Neighborhood Playhouse, both New York, N.Y. Home: 1479 Golden Glow Dr., Elmira, N.Y. 14905. Agent: Miss Toni Strassman, 130 East 18th St., New York, N.Y. 10003.

CAREER: Electrician. Former vice-president of Southwestern Producers, Inc., Texas, and president of Flame-Out Fire Protection, Inc., North Carolina. Inventor, and holder of patent on a control device for electric circuits. Member: Authors Guild, Mystery Writers of America, International Brotherhood of Electrical Workers, International Association of Radio Artists, Toastmasters International, Santa Monica Writers Club.

WRITINGS: Phoebe and the Macfairlie Mystery, Lothrop, 1961; Bible of the Undead, Chemung Books, 1971. Writer of radio and television scripts. Contributor to Albany Times Union and other newspapers.

WORK IN PROGRESS: A novel for adults and a novel for children.

AVOCATIONAL INTERESTS: Helping mentally disturbed children.†

*   *   *

BARROW, Geoffrey W(allis) S(teuart) 1924-

PERSONAL: Born November 28, 1924, in Leeds, England; son of Charles Embleton (an architect) and Marjorie (Steuart) Barrow; married Heather E. A. Lownie, July 6, 1951; children: Julia Steuart, Andrew Charles Steuart. *Education:* University of St. Andrews, M.A. (honors), 1948; Pembroke College, Oxford, B.Litt., 1950. *Religion:* Christian. *Home:* The Old Manse, Cupar, Fife, Scotland.

CAREER: University College, University of London, London, England, lecturer in history, 1950-61; University of Newcastle upon Tyne, Newcastle upon Tyne, England, professor of medieval history, 1961-74; University of St. Andrews, Scotland, professor of Scottish history, 1974—. *Military service:* Royal Navy, 1943-46. *Member:* Royal Historical Society, Scottish History Society (chairman, 1965-64; president, 1972—), Society of Antiquaries of Scotland. *Awards, honors:* Alexander Prize of Royal Historical Society for essay, 1952; Joint Senior Hume Brown Prize, 1961, for *Acts of Malcolm IV, King of Scots, 1153-1165*; Agnes Mure Mackenzie Award of Saltire Society, 1965, for *Robert Bruce and the Community of the Realm of Scotland*; D.Litt., University of St. Andrews, 1971.

WRITINGS: Feudal Britain, St. Martins, 1956; *Acts of Malcolm IV, King of Scots, 1153-1165*, Edinburgh University Press, 1960; *Robert Bruce and the Community of the Realm of Scotland*, University of California Press, 1965; *Acts of William I, King of Scots, 1165-1214*, Edinburgh University Press, 1971; *The Kingdom of the Scots*, Edward Arnold, 1973; (editor) *The Scottish Tradition: Essays in Honor of R. G. Cant*, Scottish Academic Press, 1974.

WORK IN PROGRESS: A new edition of W. D. Simpson's, *The Earldom of Mar*, completion expected in 1977.

*   *   *

BARRY, Lucy (Brown) 1934-

PERSONAL: Born January 15, 1934, in Boston, Mass.; daughter of Herbert, Jr. (a psychiatrist) and Lucy (Brown) Barry. *Education:* Radcliffe College, B.A., 1955; graduate study at New York University, 1962-63, and New School for Social Research, 1967. *Politics:* Republican. *Religion:* Episcopalian. *Home:* 350 East 52nd St., New York, N.Y. 10022. *Agent:* Lenniger Literary Agency, 437 Fifth Ave., New York, N.Y. 10016.

CAREER: Theatrical secretary and script analyst, New York, N.Y., 1955—. Secretary to authors Betty Comden, Adolph Green, and Frank Loesser, and for various productions, including "How to Succeed in Business Without Really Trying," "Bells Are Ringing," and a revival of "On the Town," and to Gene Saks, Frederick Brisson, Henry Fonda, and to William Goodhart for the production, "Generation," 1965; script analyst at various times for Brisson Productions, Elliot Martin Productions, William Morris Agency, CBS-TV, and "Kraft TV Theatre"; also secretary for "several Broadway shows that were flops." *Member:* Writers Guild of America East.

WRITINGS: Stagestruck Secretary, Morrow, 1966. Contributor to *Woman's Day*.

WORK IN PROGRESS: Three novels for young adults, one about mental retardation, one about a temporary secretary in New York, and a mystery.†

BARTEL, Roland 1919-

PERSONAL: Born February 17, 1919, in Hillsboro, Kan.; son of Peter and Anna (Schmidt) Bartel; married Betty Long, October 19, 1943; children: David Roland, Brian Leevern. *Education:* Attended Bethel College, North Newton, Kan., 1936-38, B.A., 1947; Kansas State Teachers College, Emporia, summer study, 1939, 1940; Indiana University, Ph.D., 1951. *Religion:* Mennonite. *Home:* 2660 Baker Blvd., Eugene, Ore. 97403. *Office:* Department of English, University of Oregon, Eugene, Ore. 97403.

CAREER: Teacher in Kansas public schools, 1938-41; University of Oregon, Eugene, instructor, 1951-54, assistant professor, 1955-58, associate professor, 1959-63, professor of English, 1964—. Oregon Council on Advanced Placement, director, 1960-62. *Member:* Modern Language Association of America, National Council of Teachers of English, American Association of University Professors. *Awards, honors:* Ersted Award ($1,000) for outstanding teaching, University of Oregon, 1965.

WRITINGS—Editor: *Johnson's London*, Heath, 1956; (with Edwin R. Bingham) *America Through Foreign Eyes, 1827-1842*, Heath, 1956; *London in Plague and Fire, 1665-1666*, Heath, 1957; *Liberty and Terror in England: Reactions to the French Revolution*, Heath, 1965; *The Bible in Literature*, Abingdon, 1975. General editor of Heath's "Selected Source Materials for College Research Papers" series, which includes the above volumes. Contributor of articles on eighteenth- and nineteenth-century English literature to *Huntington Library Quarterly, Papers on English Language and Literature*, and other journals.

*   *   *

BARTHOLOMEW, Paul C(harles) 1907-

PERSONAL: Born July 15, 1907, in Salem, Ohio; son of Charles Edward and Laura Frances (Doyle) Bartholomew; married Mary Agnes Carey, June 13, 1933; children: Thomas Charles, Robert Paul. *Education:* University of Notre Dame, A.B., 1929, M.A., 1931; Northwestern University, summer study, 1931-33; University of Kentucky, Ph.D., 1938. *Religion:* Roman Catholic. *Home:* 415 East Pokagon St., South Bend, Ind. 46617.

CAREER: University of Notre Dame, Notre Dame, Ind., instructor, 1930-33, assistant professor, 1933-36, associate professor, 1936-42, professor of political science, 1952—, head of department, 1943-52. Visiting professor at Northwestern University, Michigan State University, Loyola University (Chicago), University of Tennessee, University of Chicago, Southwest Texas State University, University of Texas at Austin, National University of Ireland. Consultant to Indiana State Commission on Tax and Financing Policy, U.S. House of Representatives, and U.S. Department of the Navy. *Member:* American Political Science Association, Midwest Conference of Political Scientists (executive council, 1950; vice-president, 1960-61), Indiana Academy of the Social Sciences (vice-president, 1954-55; director, 1965-67).

WRITINGS: A Manual of American Government, Burgess, 1936, 2nd edition, 1939; *A Manual of Political Science Research*, University of Notre Dame Press, 1940; (with Samuel B. Pettingill) *For Americans Only*, Nesterman, 1944; *American Government Under the Constitution*, W. C. Brown, 1947, 3rd edition, 1956; *Leading Cases on the Constitution*, Littlefield, 1954, 9th revised edition, 1974; *Public Administration*, Littlefield, 1959, 3rd revised edition, 1972; *Ruling American Constitutional Law*, two volumes,

Littlefield, 1970; *Profile of a Precinct Committeeman*, Oceana, 1968; *The Indiana Third Congressional District: A Political History*, University of Notre Dame Press, 1970. Contributor to *Encyclopedia Americana, Compton Yearbook, Encyclopaedia Britannica, Dictionary of American History*; also contributor to about twenty legal, sociological, and political science journals.

WORK IN PROGRESS: American Government, The Prophets of the Supreme Court, and *Cases on International Law*.

* * *

BARTLETT, C(hristopher) J(ohn) 1931-

PERSONAL: Born October 12, 1931, in Bournemouth, England; son of Reginald George (an officer, Royal Air Force) and Kathleen (Luther) Bartlett; married Shirley Briggs, August 7, 1958; children: Paul Anthony (deceased), Roger Neil, Nigel Keith. *Education:* University College, Exeter, B.A. (first class honors), 1953; London School of Economics and Political Science, London, Ph.D., 1956. *Home:* 5 Strathspey Pl., Broughty Ferry, Dundee DD5 1QB, Scotland. *Agent:* Shaw-Maclean, 11 Rumbold St., London SW6, England. *Office:* Department of History, The University, Dundee DD1 4HN, Scotland.

CAREER: University College, University of London, London, England, research assistant, 1956-57; University of Edinburgh, Edinburgh, Scotland, assistant lecturer, 1957-59; University of the West Indies, Kingston, Jamaica, lecturer, 1959-62; University of Dundee, Dundee, Scotland, lecturer in history, 1962-68, reader in international history, 1968—. *Member:* Historical Association, Royal Historical Society (fellow).

WRITINGS: Great Britain and Sea Power, 1815-1853, Clarendon Press, 1963; *Castlereagh* (biography), Scribner, 1966; (contributor) K. Bourne and D. C. Watt, editors, *Studies in International History*, Longmans, Green, 1967; (editor) *Britain Pre-eminent*, Macmillan, 1969; (with E. V. Goveia) *Chapters in Caribbean History*, Caribbean Universities Press, 1970; (contributor) R. Higham, editor, *A Guide to the Sources of British Military History*, University of California Press, 1971; *The Long Retreat: A Short History of British Defence Policy, 1945-70*, Macmillan, 1971; *The Rise and Fall of the Pax Americana*, Paul Elek, 1974.

WORK IN PROGRESS: British History Since 1945, for Longman, expected in 1977.

SIDELIGHTS: Bartlett told *CA*, "The British Navy was my first great interest. From that interest there has been a fairly straightforward progression into defence questions in general, great power rivalries, and so inevitably a move into contemporary history. I am fascinated by the changing character of international affairs since the late eighteenth century...."

* * *

BARTLETT, Elizabeth (Winters) 1911-

PERSONAL: Born July 20, 1911, in New York, N.Y.; married Paul Bartlett (an artist and novelist), April 19, 1943; children: Steven. *Education:* Teachers College, Columbia University, B.S., 1931, and Columbia University, extension courses. *Residence:* Comala, Colima, Mex. *Office address:* ETC, Box 2469, San Francisco, Calif. 94126.

CAREER: Southern Methodist University, Dallas, Tex., instructor in department of speech and theater, 1947-49; New School for Social Research, New York, N.Y., director of Creative Writers Association, 1955; assistant professor in department of English at San Jose State College (now University), San Jose, Calif., 1961-62, and associate in department of English at University of California, Santa Barbara, 1962-64; *ETC: A Review of General Semantics*, San Francisco, Calif., poetry editor, 1964—. Visiting lecturer at various universities in the U.S. and Canada, 1965—. Consultant at writers' conferences in California, New York, and other states. *Member:* International Society for General Semantics, Poetry Society of America. *Awards, honors:* Huntington Hartford Foundation writing fellowships, 1959, 1960; Montalve Foundation writing fellowship, 1961; grants from National Institute of Arts and Letters and PEN International; National Endowment for the Arts poetry award, 1968-70; Yaddo and MacDowell writing fellowships, 1970.

WRITINGS: Poems of Yes and No, Editorial Jus (Mexico), 1952; *Behold This Dreamer* (poems), Editorial Jus, 1959; *Poetry Concerto*, Vagrom Press, 1961; *It Takes Practice Not to Die* (poems), Van Riper & Thompson, 1964; *Threads* (poems), Unicorn Press, 1968; *Twelve-Tone Poems*, Sun Press, 1969; *Selected Poems*, Carrefour Press, 1970; *The House of Sleep* (poems), Autograph Editions, 1975. Contributor of more than four hundred poems to *Harper's, Saturday Review, New York Times, Accent*, and other literary periodicals; writer of short stories, reviews, articles, and translations.

WORK IN PROGRESS: In Search of Identity, poems; *Address in Time*, poems; *Dialogue of Dust*, a one-act play in verse; *The Secret*, a ballet script.

SIDELIGHTS: Mrs. Bartlett told *CA*: "My major interest is in the role of man as creator, as expressed in philosophy, religion, literature, art, music, and other creative efforts." She has lived in Mexico and France.

* * *

BARTLETT, Ruth

PERSONAL: Born in Chicago, Ill.; daughter of Horace Clifford (a theoretical physicist) and Alma (a painter; maiden name, Wells) Bartlett. *Education:* Studied painting with Yasuo Kuniyosh. *Agent:* Curtis Brown Ltd., 60 East 56th St., New York, N.Y. 10022.

CAREER: Writer.

WRITINGS: Insect Engineers: The Story of Ants (juvenile nonfiction), Morrow, 1957; *The Miracle of the Talking Jungle* (juvenile fiction), Van Nostrand, 1965; (illustrator) Wilhelm Matthiessen, *Folk Tales*, Grove, 1968.

WORK IN PROGRESS: Two juvenile nonfiction books, tentatively titled *Learning in the Wild* and *Growth in Nature*; an adult book on her travels in Spain.

SIDELIGHTS: Ruth Bartlett told *CA*, she believes that writers for children are endangered by "the great economic pressures placed on editors (and consequently on writers) by school teachers and librarians. Some children's books," she continues, "cannot fill more than a literary or dramatic role, whereas there is at present a tendency to insist on didactic content which, along with control of the number of pages (for economy), may cripple the literary value of the work." She speaks French and Spanish. *Avocational interests:* The theatre.†

* * *

BARZANTI, Sergio 1925-

PERSONAL: Born October 4, 1925, in Rome, Italy; came

to United States, 1955, naturalized citizen, 1961; son of
Domenico and Pierina (Casadei) Barzanti; married Jean
Margaret Gwynne, March 13, 1954; married Gabriele A.
Stormer, October 24, 1968; children: (first marriage) Simo-
netta, Paul, Mark, Lorenzo. *Education:* University of
Rome, Dr. of Law, 1947; University of Paris, graduate
study, 1959-60; New York University, M.A., 1958, Ph.D.,
1962. *Home:* 540 80th St., Brooklyn, N.Y. 11209. *Office:*
Department of Social Sciences, Fairleigh Dickinson Uni-
versity, Rutherford, N.J. 07070.

CAREER: Long Island University, Brooklyn, N.Y., instructor, 1962-63; Fairleigh Dickinson University, Rutherford, N.J., lecturer, 1963-64, associate professor, 1964-67,
associate professor of political science and history, 1967—.
Member: American Political Science Association, American Association of University Professors. *Awards, honors:*
Founders Day Award from New York University, 1963;
Fulbright scholar in Egypt, 1965.

*WRITINGS: The Underdeveloped Areas Within the
Common Market,* Princeton University Press, 1965. Contributor to encyclopedias and scholarly journals.

SIDELIGHTS: Barzanti speaks Italian, French, Spanish,
and reads Portuguese.†

*   *   *

BASCOM, William R(ussel) 1912-

PERSONAL: Born May 23, 1912, in Princeton, Ill.; son of
George Rockwell (an engineer) and Litta (Banschbach)
Bascom; married Berta Maria Montero-Sanchez (a Spanish
teacher), November 26, 1948. *Education:* University of
Wisconsin, B.A., 1933, M.A., 1936; Northwestern University, Ph.D., 1939. *Home:* 624 Beloit Ave., Berkeley, Calif.
94708. *Office:* Lowie Museum of Anthropology, University
of California, Berkeley, Calif. 94720.

CAREER: Northwestern University, Evanston, Ill., instructor, 1939-42, assistant professor, 1946-49, associate
professor, 1949-54, professor of anthropology, 1954-57,
chairman of department and acting director, program of
African studies, 1956-57; University of California, Berkeley, professor of anthropology and director of Robert H.
Lowie Museum of Anthropology, 1957—. U.S. Government service includes special assistant, Office of Strategic
Services, in Nigeria, 1942, special representative of Foreign
Economic Administration to British West Africa, 1943-45,
and ethnological research on Ponape, Caroline Islands,
with U.S. Commercial Company Survey of Micronesia,
1946. Member of advisory board, Museum of African Art,
Washington, D.C., 1964-69; member of board of directors,
Oakland Museums Association, 1963-73.

MEMBER: American Anthropological Association (fellow;
member of executive board, 1961-64), Royal Anthropological Institute (fellow), American Folklore Society (president, 1952-54; fellow), International African Institute
(member of governing board, 1947-49), Royal African Society (fellow), American Association of Museums (member
of council, 1962-67), Societe Internationale d'Ethnologie et
de Folklore, International Society for Folk-Narrative Research, International Council of Museums, Central States
Anthropological Society (president, 1950-51), Southwestern
Anthropological Association, California Folklore Society
(vice-president, 1962-68), California Academy of Sciences,
Nigerian Field Society (fellow), California League for the
American Indian (member of board of directors, 1964-65),
Kroeber Anthropological Society, Phi Beta Kappa, Sigma
Xi, Phi Eta Sigma.

AWARDS, HONORS: Social Science Research Council
fellowship for research among the Yoruba of Nigeria, 1937-
38, and grant, 1965; Wenner-Gren Foundation grant, 1948;
Fulbright grant to Nigeria, 1950-51; National Science Foundation senior postdoctoral fellowship for research on Yoruba materials at Cambridge University, 1958; Pitre International Folklore Prize, 1969, for *Ifa Divination.*

*WRITINGS: The Sociological Role of the Yoruba Cult-
Group,* American Anthropological Association, 1944; (with
Paul Gebauer) *Handbook of West African Art,* Bruce, for
Milwaukee Public Museum, 1953; (editor with M. J. Her-
skovits, and contributor) *Continuity and Change in African
Cultures,* University of Chicago Press, 1959, revised edi-
tion with new preface, 1962; *Ponape: A Pacific Economy in
Transition,* University of California Press, 1965; *African
Arts,* Robert H. Lowie Museum of Anthropology, 1967; *Ifa
Divination: Communications Between Gods and Men in
West Africa,* Indiana University Press, 1969; *The Yoruba
of Southwestern Nigeria,* Holt, 1969; *Shango in the New
World,* University of Texas, 1972; *African Art in Cultural
Perspective: An Introduction,* Norton, 1973; *African Di-
lemma Tales,* Mouton, 1975.

Contributor: *Most of the World,* edited by Ralph Linton,
Columbia University Press, 1949; *Acculturation in the
Americas,* edited by Sol Tax, University of Chicago Press,
1952; *Cultures and Societies of Africa,* edited by S. and P.
Ottenberg, Random, 1960; *Man and Society,* edited by J.
G. Manis and S. I. Clark, Macmillan, 1960; *Men and Cultures,* edited by A. F. C. Wallace, University of California
Press, 1960; *The African World: A Survey of Social Research,* edited by R. A. Lystad, Praeger, 1965; *Africa: Social Problems of Change and Conflict,* edited by P. L. van
den Berghe, Chandler Publishing, 1965; *The Study of Folklore,* edited by A. Dundes, Prentice-Hall, 1965.

Contributor of short sections to a number of other books on
anthropology and sociology, and to *Funk and Wagnalls
Standard Dictionary of Folklore, Mythology and Legend,
Collier's Encyclopedia,* and *Encyclopedia Americana.*
Author of museum booklets. Recorded "Drums of the
Yoruba of Nigeria," Ethnic Folkways Library, 1953, and
educational collaborator for film, "Life of a Primitive Peo-
ple," Coronet Instructional Films, 1957; did record notes
(with Spanish translation by his wife, Berta M. Bascom) for
"Mongo in Havana," Fantasy Records, 1961. Contributor
of about one hundred articles and reviews to professional
journals, magazines, and the press, including *Illustrated
London News, American Anthropologist, Current Anthropology, American Journal of Sociology, Africa Report,
Scientific Monthly, Esquire, Journal of American Folklore,
Natural History,* and numerous other periodicals in America, Africa, France, Belgium, New Zealand, and Ireland.

*   *   *

BASKIN, Samuel 1921-

PERSONAL: Born October 4, 1921, in Lithuania; son of
Harry (a salesman) and Ida (Benjamin) Baskin; married
Florence Esther Schwartzberg, February, 1924; children:
Robert, David. *Education:* Brooklyn College (now
Brooklyn College of the City University of New York),
B.A., 1942; New York University, M.A., 1948, Ph.D.,
1954. *Home:* 1126 Livermore St., Yellow Springs, Ohio
45387. *Office:* Union for Experimenting Colleges and Uni-
versities, Yellow Springs, Ohio 45387.

CAREER: New York University, New York, N.Y., lecturer in education, 1948-49; Stephens College, Columbia,

Mo., lecturer and counselor, 1949-51; Antioch College, Yellow Springs, Ohio, professor of guidance and psychology, 1951-65, director of office of program development and Research in Education (originally called office of educational research), 1955-65; Union for Experimenting Colleges and Universities, Yellow Springs, Ohio, president, 1965—. Consultant to U.S. Office of Education, 1960; chief consultant to Florida Atlantic University and other educational institutions. *Military service:* U.S. Army, 1942-46; became sergeant. *Member:* Association for Higher Education, American Psychological Association, American Personnel and Guidance Association, National Institutional Research Forum.

WRITINGS: Quest for Quality, U.S. Office of Education, 1961; (contributor) *A Conceptual Framework for Institutional Research*, Washington State University Press, 1964; (editor) *Higher Education: Some Newer Developments*, McGraw, 1965. Also author of *Innovations in College Teaching*. Writer or contributor to other education research reports.

* * *

BASSETT, Glenn Arthur 1930-

PERSONAL: Born December 19, 1930, in Fort Collins, Colo.; son of Glenn Willard (a music teacher) and Rosalie (Morrish) Bassett; married Mary Ellen Gregory, May 9, 1952; children: Glenna Lynn, Glenn Arthur, Jr. *Education:* University of California, Berkeley, B.A., 1954; California State College (now University), at Long Beach, M.A., 1958. *Home:* 121 Spring Valley Rd., Fairfield, Conn. 06430. *Office:* General Electric Co., Fairfield, Conn. 06431.

CAREER: State Farm Insurance Co., underwriter in Santa Ana, Calif., 1954-56; Travelers Insurance Co., Long Beach, Calif., in field claims, 1956-60; Climax Molybdenum Co., Climax, Colo., psychologist, 1960-62; General Electric Co., Daytona Beach, Fla., manager of relations program, 1962-67; General Electric Co., Fairfield, Conn., corporate employee relations consultant, 1967—. Lecturer on interviewing techniques for employer associations. *Military service:* U.S. Air Force, 1950-53. *Member:* American Psychological Association.

WRITINGS: Practical Interviewing: A Handbook for Managers, American Management Association, 1965; *Management Style in Transition*, American Management Association, 1966; *The New Face of Communication*, American Management Association, 1968; *Personnel Systems and Data Management*, American Management Association, 1971; *Communication: A Management Approach*, American Management Association, in press. Also wrote two tape cassettes produced by American Management Association, *Communicating Both Ways*, 1967, and *Interviewing the Problem Employee*, 1975. Contributor to *Personnel, California Management Review, Human Resources Management Quarterly, The Conference Board Record*.

* * *

BATES, Alan Lawrence 1923-

PERSONAL: Born June 6, 1923, in Louisville, Ky.; son of C. Roy (an electrician) and Beulah (Williams) Bates; married Rita Aschbacher, July 15, 1944; children: Patricia (Mrs. Charles O. Cooley, Jr.), Lawrence, Catherine (Mrs. Anthony G. Osborne), Barbara. *Education:* Attended public schools in Louisville, Ky. *Politics:* Changeable. *Home:* 2040 Sherwood Ave., Louisville, Ky. 40205.

CAREER: Architect in Louisville, Ky., 1953—. Dance band musician and arranger. President of Howard Steamboat Museum, 1958-62; restorer of steamboat, "Belle of Louisville," 1962-63, and mate, 1964-66; designer of steamboat "Natchez"; master licensee for Mississippi River and tributaries. *Military service:* U.S. Army, 1943-46. *Member:* National Model Railroaders Association, American Turners, Sons and Daughters of Pioneer Rivermen, Moose Club.

WRITINGS: Belle of Louisville, Howell-North, 1965; *The Western Rivers Steamboat Cyclopoedium*, Hustle Press, 1968. Regular columnist for *Ships and the Sea*, 1957-61. Contributor to *Trains* and *Railroad Model Craftsman*.

WORK IN PROGRESS: A novel about coalboat towing on the Ohio River, circa 1900-1912.

AVOCATIONAL INTERESTS: Amateur painting, model railroading.

* * *

BATES, Barbara S(nedeker) 1919-
(Stephen Cuyler, Jim Roberts)

PERSONAL: Born April 28, 1919, in Philadelphia, Pa.; daughter of R. Cuyler (a builder) and Dorothy (Roberts) Snedeker; married Frederick H. Bates (a budget analyst), January 20, 1945; children: Susan Penelope, Stephen Cuyler. *Education:* Wellesley College, B.A., 1940. *Religion:* Presbyterian. *Home:* 104 Runnymede Ave., Jenkintown, Pa. 19046.

CAREER: Westminster Press, Philadelphia, Pa., story papers editor, 1941-46, fiction editor, 1944-46, children's book editor, 1967—. Adult education teacher of creative writing in Abington, Pa., 1957-63; in Cheltenham, Pa., 1965-66, and Willow Grove, Pa., 1963-65; workshop leader at writers conferences, 1959—, including International Writers Seminar, Green Lake, Wis., 1962. *Member:* American Library Association, Authors Guild of the Authors League of America, Franklin Institute, Abington Library Association, Old York Road Symphony Society, Philadelphia Children's Reading Round Table, Peale Club of Philadelphia.

WRITINGS: The Roly Poly Puppy, Wonder Books, 1950; *The Happy Birthday Present*, Wonder Books, 1951; *The Real Book of Pets*, Garden City Books, 1952; (under pseudonym Jim Roberts) *The Real Book of Camping*, Garden City Books, 1953; *Trudy Phillips, New Girl*, Whitman Publishing Co., 1953; *Trudy Phillips, Headline Year*, Whitman Publishing Co., 1954; *New Boy Next Door*, Broadman, 1965; *Bible Festivals and Holy Days*, Broadman, 1966. Represented in anthologies. Contributor to *Jack and Jill, Child Life, The Writer's Digest, Golden Magazine, Trailblazer*.

BIOGRAPHICAL/CRITICAL SOURCES: More Parades, edited by Gray, Monroe, Artley, and Arbuthnot, Scott, 1957.

* * *

BATES, Jerome E. 1917-

PERSONAL: Born April 8, 1917, in New York, N.Y.; son of Leonard Walter (an executive) and Zillah (Genung) Bates; married Jenny Lind, September 22, 1943; children: Jacquelyn, Randall. *Education:* Long Island University, B.A., 1941; Columbia University, M.S., 1947; Wayne State University, graduate study, 1958-62; Midwest Institute of Alcohol Studies, certificate, 1961; Rutgers University

School of Alcohol Studies, diploma, 1962. *Religion:* Episcopalian.

CAREER: During his early career, held every rank in a marine engine room from fireman to chief engineer; Court of General Sessions, New York, N.Y., probation officer, 1947-48; Childrens' Center, New York, N.Y., assistant director, 1949-55; Church Youth Service, Inc., Detroit, Mich., executive director, 1956-65; American Society of Tool and Manufacturing Engineers, Dearborn, Mich., assistant director of member relations, 1965—. Lecturer, Wayne State University; member of speaker's bureau, United Foundation, Detroit, 1956-64. *Military service:* U.S. Army Air Forces, 1942-44; became staff sergeant. U.S. Maritime Service, 1944-45; became lieutenant senior grade. *Member:* American Association for Social Psychiatry (fellow; vice-president, 1966), Knights Templar.

WRITINGS: (With Edward S. Zawadzki) *Criminal Abortion: A Study in Medical Sociology*, C. C Thomas, 1964. Scriptwriter, WXYZ television program, "Youth Bureau," 1958-60. Contributor to journals.

WORK IN PROGRESS: Tanker Chief, a novel.†

*   *   *

BATES, Margaret J(ane)   1918-

PERSONAL: Born January 27, 1918, in New York, N.Y.; daughter of Herbert P. (an engineer) and Annie (Flanagan) Bates. *Education:* Hunter College (now Hunter College of the City University of New York), B.A., 1938; Columbia University, B.L.S., 1940; Catholic University of America, Ph.D., 1945. *Religion:* Roman Catholic. *Home:* 5914 Carlton Lane, Bethesda, Md. 20016. *Office:* Catholic University of America, Box 6, Washington, D.C. 20017.

CAREER: U.S. Department of State and Library of Congress, Washington, D.C., member of interdepartmental committee for the organization of libraries in Rio de Janeiro, Brazil, and Lima, Peru, 1940-44; University of Maryland, College Park, assistant professor of Spanish, 1944-45; Catholic University of America, Washington, D.C., assistant professor, 1945-55, associate professor of Spanish literature, 1956—, director of Institute of Ibero-American Studies, 1955-61. *Member:* American Association of Teachers of Spanish and Portuguese, Modern Language Association of America. *Awards, honors:* Ford faculty fellowship, 1953-54.

WRITINGS: Discrecion in the Works of Cervantes, Catholic University of America Press, 1945; (editor) *Poesias completas de Gabriela Mistral* (critical edition), Aguilar (Madrid), 1958, 2nd edition, 1962. Contributor to *Hispanic Review, Explicator, Americas*, and other journals.

WORK IN PROGRESS: Study of Valle-Inclan's *Sonatas*.

SIDELIGHTS: Margaret Bates is interested in electronic devices to measure speech.

*   *   *

BATTY, C(harles) D(avid)   1932-

PERSONAL: Born July 8, 1932, in Tynemouth, Northumberland, England; son of Charles Cecil and Lilian (Hague) Batty; married Frances Mary Cook, July 30, 1956; children: Charles Francis Philip, Miles Roger David. *Education:* University of Durham, B.A., 1954. *Home:* Tyglyneiddwen, Eglwysfach, Machynlleth, Montgomeryshire, Wales.

CAREER: City Reference Library, Birmingham, England, assistant librarian, 1957-62; Birmingham School of Librarianship, Birmingham, England, lecturer, 1962-64; College of Librarianship, Aberystwyth, Wales, head of department of information and retrieval studies, 1964—. *Member:* Library Association (fellow; vice-chairman of cataloging and indexing group, 1965—), Association of British Library Schools.

WRITINGS: An Introduction to the Dewey Decimal Classification (programmed text), Shoe String, 1965, published as *An Introduction to the Eighteenth Edition of the Dewey Decimal Classification*, Linnet Books, 1971; *An Introduction to the Colon Classification* (programmed text), Clive Bingley, 1966, Archon Books, 1967; (editor) *The Library and the Machine*, Library Association (England), 1966; (editor) *Libraries and Machines Today*, Library Association (England), 1967. Editor of series of programmed texts in librarianship for Clive Bingley. Contributor to professional journals.

WORK IN PROGRESS: A book on cataloging, for Clive Bingley; research on training of documentalists and the application of programmed learning techniques to library science.

SIDELIGHTS: Batty is competent in French and has some knowledge of German and Russian. *Avocational interests:* Medieval and early Renaissance music, building and playing musical instruments, reading, travel, talking, and wasting time.†

*   *   *

BATTY, Joyce D(orothea)   1919-

PERSONAL: Born May 25, 1919, in Australia; daughter of August Benjamin (a farmer) and Louise (Hausler) Gursansky; married Leonard W. Batty (an air conditioning consultant), October 14, 1941; children: Ian, Christopher. *Education:* Attended Technical School, Gawler, South Australia, and adult education classes in English literature at University of Adelaide, 1948-50. *Politics:* Liberal. *Religion:* Christian. *Home:* 3 Gilbertson Rd., Seacliff Park, Adelaide, South Australia.

CAREER: Writer, and photographer. *Women's Australian National Service Magazine*, Adelaide, South Australia, editor, 1950; Anglo-Swiss Trans-Australian Film Expedition, public relations officer, 1960; Messenger Press Ltd., Adelaide, South Australia, feature writer, 1966. With royalties from Namatjira biography, founded annual Namatjira Memorial Art Prize, 1964, to aid young unknown artists; director of tour for young artists through Australian heartland, 1966. Long active in Australian Red Cross Society, serving as a volunteer nurse, 1938-52. *Member:* Arts Society for Handicapped (associate), Writers World, Beta Sigma Phi (secretary, 1958), Adelaide Soaring Club (associate).

WRITINGS: Namatjira, Wanderer Between Two Worlds, Hodder & Stoughton, 1963. Writer of narrative for "The Stars of Dibah Buddeh," a record for children based on aboriginal legends set to music, 1959. Contributor of articles to *Panorama, Walkabout*, and *Australiasian Post*.

WORK IN PROGRESS: Research on histories of Simpson Desert explorations from 1845-1973, and Tanami Desert explorations from 1886 to 1975.

SIDELIGHTS: Joyce Batty has made eight tours into the Australian outback—covering some 5,000 miles by air, rail, and landrover, visiting aboriginal missions and opal fields and camping with opal gougers, and two visits to far northern Australia, interviewing and photographing station owners and outback characters. She has recently explored the Simpson and Tanami Deserts in Australia.

BIOGRAPHICAL/CRITICAL SOURCES: New Idea, July 11, 1962; *Guardian*, November 10, 1965; *Australian Woman's Day*, July, 1966; *Adelaide Advertiser*, September 20, 1969; *Australian Post*, October, 1973; *Panorama*, October, 1973.

* * *

BAUM, Allyn Z(elton) 1924-

PERSONAL: Born October 22, 1924, in Chicago, Ill.; son of Moses (an insurance broker) and Effie F. (Kaufman) Baum; married Pell Le Witt (an art historian), September 16, 1963. *Education:* Northwestern University, B.S. in Journalism, 1948. *Home:* The Barn, Box 371, East Canaan, Conn. 06024. *Office: Medical Economics*, Onadell, N.J. 07649.

CAREER: International News Photos, bureau chief in Berlin, Germany, 1948-49, general manager for Europe, Paris, France, 1949-50; United Press Photos, general manager for Germany, Berlin and Frankfurt, 1950-52; *American Daily*, London, England, photo editor and writer, 1953-55; *Coronet*, New York, N.Y., associate editor, 1955-57; *New York Times*, New York, N.Y., staff photographer, 1957-67; *Medical Economics*, Oradell, N.J., senior associate editor, 1967—. *Military service:* U.S. Army Air Forces, 1943-46; became sergeant. *Member:* Explorers Club and The Players (both New York).

WRITINGS: Antarctica, the Worst Place in the World, Macmillan, 1966. Contributor of photographs and articles to newspapers and magazines throughout the world.

SIDELIGHTS: Baum's extensive travels have included two expeditions to Antarctica. He is competent in French and German. *Avocational interests:* Eighteenth-century English furniture.

* * *

BAXTER, Eric George 1918-

PERSONAL: Born January 8, 1918, in Birmingham, England; son of Frank Cyril (a bank cashier) and Florence (Field) Baxter; married Audrey Constance Perry, October 26, 1946; children: Josephine, Christopher. *Education:* St. Peter's College, Oxford, 1936-39, M.A. *Politics and religion:* "Temperamentally non-conformist." *Home:* 28 Queens Rd., Kenilworth, Warwickshire, England. *Office:* Lanchester Polytechnic, Coventry, England.

CAREER: University of London Library, London, England, assistant, 1939-40; College for the Blind, Worcester, England, assistant master, 1940-46; Derby School, Derby, England, assistant master, 1947; Coventry Technical College, Coventry, England, librarian, 1948-60; Coventry College of Art, Coventry, librarian, 1960-70; Lanchester Polytechnic, Coventry, librarian, 1960—. *Member:* Library Association (fellow).

WRITINGS: (With D. L. Smith) *College Library Administration*, Oxford University Press, 1965; *Catalogue of the Private Papers of F. W. Lanchester in the Library of Lanchester College of Technology* (fellowship thesis), Library Association, 1966. Contributor to publications on librarianship and local history.

BAXTER, Stephen B(artow) 1929-

PERSONAL: Born March 8, 1929, in Boston, Mass.; son of James Phinney III (a historian) and Anne (Strang) Baxter; married Ann Sweeney, August 22, 1953; children: Clare, Persis, James, Nicholas, Padriac, Michael. *Education:* Harvard University, B.A., 1950; Trinity College, Cambridge, Ph.D., 1955. *Politics:* Democrat. *Home:* 608 Morgan Creek Rd., Chapel Hill, N.C. 27514. *Office:* Department of History, University of North Carolina, Chapel Hill, N.C. 27514.

CAREER: Dartmouth College, Hanover, N.H., instructor in history, 1954-57; University of Missouri, Columbia, visiting assistant professor of history, 1957-58; University of North Carolina, Chapel Hill, assistant professor, 1958-62, associate professor, 1962-66, professor of history, 1966—. *Member:* Royal Historical Society (fellow), American Historical Association, Mediaeval Academy of America, Conference on British Studies. *Awards, honors:* Fiske scholar at Trinity College, Cambridge, 1950-51; Guggenheim fellow, 1959-60 and 1973-74.

WRITINGS: The Development of the Treasury, 1660-1702, Harvard University Press, 1957; (contributor) Lewis W. Spitz and Richard W. Lyman, editors, *Major Crises in Western Civilization*, Harcourt, 1965; *William III and the Defense of European Liberty, 1650-1702*, Harcourt, 1966 (published in England as *William III*, Longmans, Green, 1966); (editor) *Basic Documents of English History*, Houghton, 1968; (contributor) Peter Gay, editor, *Eighteen-Century Studies Presented to Arthur M. Wilson*, University of New England, 1972.

SIDELIGHTS: Baxter is competent in French, German, Dutch, and Latin. *Avocational interests:* Classical music, travel.

BIOGRAPHICAL/CRITICAL SOURCES: New York Review of Books, June 29, 1967.

* * *

BAYLY, Joseph T(ate) 1920-

PERSONAL: Born April 5, 1920, in Germantown, Philadelphia, Pa.; son of Joseph Tate III and Mary (Baker) Bayly; married Mary Louise DeWalt, December 18, 1943; children: Joseph T., Deborah E., Daniel D., Timothy B., John M., David J., Nathan C. *Education:* Wheaton College, Wheaton, Ill., A.B., 1941; Columbia University and Union Theological Seminary, graduate student, 1942; Faith Theological Seminary, B.D., 1944. *Politics:* Independent. *Home:* 29W515 Orchard Lane, Bartlett, Ill. 60103. *Office:* David C. Cook Publishing Co., Elgin, Ill. 60120.

CAREER: Inter-Varsity Christian Fellowship, student worker in Boston, Mass., 1944-49, regional secretary, Philadelphia, Pa., 1949-52; Inter-Varsity Press, Chicago, Ill., director, and editor of *HIS* (magazine), 1952-60; free-lance writer and speaker, Philadelphia, Pa., 1960-63; David C. Cook Publishing Co., Elgin, Ill., managing editor, 1963-72, product and marketing vice-president, 1972—. Member of council, Latin American Mission and Inter-Varsity Christian Fellowship; member of board, National Association of Christian Schools. *Member:* Evangelical Press Association (president, 1960-62).

WRITINGS: The Gospel Blimp, Zondervan, 1960; *Meditations for Students*, David C. Cook, 1964; *Congo Crisis*, Zondervan, 1966; *The View From a Hearse*, David C. Cook, 1969; *Out of My Mind*, Tyndale, 1970; *What About Horoscopes?*, David C. Cook, 1970; *Martyred*, Zondervan,

1971; *Psalms of My Life*, Tyndale, 1971; *How Silently, How Silently*, David C. Cook, 1973. Writer of monthly column for *Eternity* (magazine); consulting editor, *HIS* and *Eternity*.

SIDELIGHTS: *The Gospel Blimp* has been produced as a color film. Some of his books have been published in England, Sweden, and Spain.

* * *

BAZELON, David T. 1923-

PERSONAL: Surname is accented on first syllable; born March 2, 1923, in Shreveport, La.; son of Jacob L. (an inventor) and Florence (Groner) Bazelon; separated from wife; children: Coleman David. *Education:* Columbia University, B.S., 1949; Yale University, LL.B., 1953. *Politics:* "Restrained radical." *Religion:* "A bit o' Jewish." *Home:* 2724 Main St., Buffalo, N.Y. 14214. *Office:* State University of New York, Buffalo, N.Y. 14214.

CAREER: Bard College, Annandale, N.Y., teacher of literature, 1949-50; admitted to New York bar, 1953; corporate attorney, Hays, Podell, Algase, Crum & Feuer, New York, N.Y., 1953-56, Paul, Weiss, Rifkind, Wharton & Garrison (legal firm), New York, N.Y., 1956-58; Institute for Policy Studies, Washington, D.C., visiting fellow, 1963-65; Rutgers University, School of Law, Newark, N.J., visiting professor, 1965-67; State University of New York at Buffalo, professor of policy sciences, 1969—. Free-lance writer and editor, 1943—. Writer-reporter for "The Mike Wallace Interview" television series; writer and editorial consultant for film "Point of Order!" Participant-consultant in conferences of Aspen Institute of Humanistic Studies, Center for Study of Democratic Institutions, Religion and Labor Council of America, American Institute of Planners, National Humanities Faculty, and American Library in Paris; participant in radio and television programs, including "Court of Reason" and "Books for Our Times." *Member:* League for Industrial Democracy, Association for Evolutionary Economics, Law and Society Association, Association of Existential Psychology and Psychiatry, Institute for Policy Studies (associate fellow), A. Philip Randolph Institute (trustee), P.E.N. *Awards, honors:* *The Paper Economy* was on American Library Association list of fifty notable books, 1963; Guggenheim fellow, 1967-68.

WRITINGS: *The Paper Economy*, Random House, 1963; *Power in America: The Politics of the New Class*, New American Library, 1967; *Nothing But a Fine Tooth Comb: Essays in Social Criticism*, Simon & Schuster, 1970. Contributor of more than a hundred articles, stories, reviews, and poems to anthologies and magazines, including *Commentary, Reporter, Partisan Review, New Republic, New Leader, Dissent*, and *Yale Law Journal*.

SIDELIGHTS: Bazelon told *CA*, "I am an eccentric social critic—not a scholar, not a journalist." He once wrote: "Like so many others, I started out writing book reviews and autobiographical fiction. But with my lawyer/accountant's mind, I soon became bogged down in self-accusatory detail—from which I have never recovered. So I began to write about other people and other things, somewhat novelistically. There is just too much fiction in life for us to write novels—or try to see life without novelistic understanding."

* * *

BEADLES, William T(homas) 1902-

PERSONAL: Born March 16, 1902, in Quincy, Ill.; son of Robert Oscar (a dentist) and Myrtella (Du Bois) Beadles; married Leta Richardson, July 4, 1926; children: Martha Elaine (Mrs. Tilio Giacobassi), William Richard. *Education:* Illinois Wesleyan University, A.B., 1923; University of Illinois, M.A., 1924; advanced study at University of Illinois and University of Pennsylvania. *Religion:* Methodist. *Home:* 409 East Kelsey, Bloomington, Ill. 61701.

CAREER: Illinois Wesleyan University, Bloomington, instructor and assistant registrar, 1924-26, assistant professor, 1926-32, professor of economics, 1932-51, dean of university, 1951-59, vice-president, 1953-59, professor of insurance, 1959-68, professor emeritus, 1968—. Member of summer faculty at Illinois State University, University of Illinois, University of Denver, and Syracuse University. Chartered life underwriter. Public panel member of War Labor Board during World War II; director, Great States Life Insurance Co.; senior educational consultant, American College of Life Underwriters, 1961—; national insurance education adviser, State Farm Insurance Companies, 1968—. *Member:* American Risk and Insurance Association (president, 1958; executive secretary, 1961—). *Awards, honors:* D.B.A., Simpson College, 1958; Teacher of the Year Award, Illinois Wesleyan University, 1960.

WRITINGS: (Contributor) *Life and Health Insurance Handbook*, Irwin, 1959, 3rd edition, 1973; (with Janice Greider) *Law and the Life Insurance Contract*, Irwin, 1960, 3rd edition, 1974; (with J. Greider) *Principles of Life Insurance*, Volume I, Irwin, 1964, revised edition, 1972. Editor, *Journal of Risk and Insurance*, 1960-74, administrative editor, 1974—.

* * *

BEARDSLEY, Monroe C(urtis) 1915-

PERSONAL: Born December 10, 1915, in Bridgeport, Conn.; son of Samuel Birdsey and Esther (Carney) Beardsley; married Elizabeth Lane (a professor), June 29, 1940; children: Philip, Mark. *Education:* Yale University, B.A., 1936, Ph.D., 1939. *Home:* 1916 Delancey Place, Philadelphia, Pa. 19103. *Office:* Department of Philosophy, Temple University, Philadelphia, Pa.

CAREER: Yale University, New Haven, Conn., instructor, 1940-44, assistant professor, 1946-47; Mount Holyoke College, South Hadley, Mass., assistant professor, 1944-46; Swarthmore College, Swarthmore, Pa., assistant professor, 1947-52, associate professor, 1952-59, professor of philosophy, 1959-69; Temple University, Philadelphia, Pa., professor of philosophy, 1969—. *Member:* American Philosophical Association, American Society for Aesthetics (past president), American Association for Legal and Political Philosophy, American Civil Liberties Union, Phi Beta Kappa.

WRITINGS: *Practical Logic*, Prentice-Hall, 1950; *Thinking Straight*, Prentice-Hall, 1950, 4th revised edition, 1975; (editor with Robert Daniel and Glenn Leggett) *Theme and Form: Introduction to Literature*, Prentice-Hall, 1956, 4th edition, 1975; *Aesthetics: Problems in the Philosophy of Criticism*, Harcourt, 1958; (editor) *The European Philosophers from Descartes to Nietzsche*, Modern Library, 1960; (with wife, Elizabeth Beardsley) *Philosophical Thinking: An Introduction*, Harcourt, 1965; *Aesthetics from Ancient Greece to the Present: A Short History*, Macmillan, 1966; (editor with Herbert Schueller) *Aesthetic Inquiry*, Dickenson, 1967; *The Possibility of Criticism*, Wayne State University Press, 1970. Editor with Elizabeth Beardsley, "Foundations of Philosophy" series, Prentice-

Hall, twenty-one volumes, 1964—. Contributor of articles on aesthetics and other branches of philosophy to journals.

WORK IN PROGRESS: A book, *The Language of History.*

* * *

BEARDSLEY, Richard K(ing) 1918-

PERSONAL: Born December 16, 1918, in Cripple Creek, Colo.; son of Earl Parson and Alice (Smith) Beardsley; married Grace Cornog, April 11, 1942; children: Elizabeth K., Kelcy A., Margaret B. *Education:* University of California, Berkeley, A.B., 1939, Ph.D., 1947. *Politics:* Democrat. *Home:* 1121 Fredone Rd., Ann Arbor, Mich. 48104. *Office:* Department of Anthropology, University of Michigan, Ann Arbor, Mich.

CAREER: University of Minnesota, Minneapolis, instructor in anthropology, 1947; University of Michigan, Ann Arbor, instructor, 1947-48; assistant professor, 1948-53, associate professor, 1954-59, professor of anthropology, 1960—, director of Center for Japanese Studies, 1961-64, 1973-74. *Military service:* U.S. Naval Reserve, 1942-46; became lieutenant. *Member:* American Association for the Advancement of Science (fellow), American Anthropological Association (fellow), Society for American Archaeology, Association for Asian Studies (director, 1961-64), Japanese Ethnological Society, Phi Beta Kappa, Sigma Xi. *Awards, honors:* Faculty fellow from Center for Japanese Studies, University of Michigan, at Library of Congress, 1948; Social Science Research Council fellow in Japan, 1950; Ford Foundation fellow in Japan, 1953-54; Guggenheim fellow in Spain, 1958-59; Carnegie Corporation Fellow in Japan, 1964-65; National Science Foundation grant for research in Japan, 1974-75.

WRITINGS: (With J. W. Hall and R. E. Ward) *Village Japan,* University of Chicago Press, 1959; (editor with R. J. Smith) *Japanese Culture,* Aldine, 1962; (with J. W. Hall) *Twelve Doors to Japan,* McGraw, 1965. Contributor to *American Antiquity, Far Eastern Quarterly,* and *American Anthropologist.*

WORK IN PROGRESS: A restudy of *Village Japan,* and field research in Japan.

SIDELIGHTS: Beardsley is competent in Japanese, Spanish, German, and French.

* * *

BECK, Barbara L. 1927-

PERSONAL: Born March 25, 1927, in Boston, Mass.; daughter of James J. (executive of a restaurant chain) and Frances Louise (Holmberg) Curry; divorced; children: Sandra L. Beck. *Education:* Monmouth College, Monmouth, Ill., B.A. *Politics:* "Unreconstructed Republican." *Religion:* Episcopalian. *Home:* 4 Rustic Dr., Cohasset, Mass. 02025.

CAREER: Free-lance journalist and advertising copywriter in Boston, Mass., 1948-52; John C. Dowd, Advertising, Boston, Mass., research director, 1953-54; self-employed insurance and real estate broker, Scituate, Mass., 1954-57; Ginn and Co. (educational publishers), Boston, Mass., assistant advertising manager, 1957—. Lecturer on books and traveling. Executive director, Massachusetts Taxpayers Association, 1954-55; member of personnel board, Town of Scituate, 1958-59; co-director, United Fund of Greater Boston, 1956.

WRITINGS—All published by F. Watts; all juvenile: *First Book of Weeds,* 1963; *First Book of Palaces,* 1964; *First Book of the Ancient Maya,* 1965; *First Book of the Incas,* 1966; *First Book of the Aztecs,* 1966; *First Book of Fruits,* 1967; *First Book of Columbia,* 1968; *First Book of Venezuela,* 1969; *First Book of Vegetables,* 1970; *The Pilgrims of Plymouth,* 1972.

SIDELIGHTS: Barbara Beck researched four of her books on travels in Mexico, Central America, and South America, studying Maya ruins in the jungles and Inca ruins in the highlands of Peru.†

* * *

BECKER, Joseph M(aria) 1908-

PERSONAL: Born February 17, 1908, in Denver, Colo.; son of John W. and Clara (Wahl) Becker. *Education:* Xavier University, Cincinnati, Ohio, A.B., 1931; St. Louis University, M.A., 1936, S.T.L., 1940; Columbia University, Ph.D., 1951. *Office:* Jesuit Center for Social Studies, Georgetown University, Washington, D.C. 20007.

CAREER: Roman Catholic priest of the Society of Jesus; Institute of Social Order (national Jesuit social science center), St. Louis, Mo., research associate, 1950-65; St. Louis University, St. Louis, Mo., professor of economics and research assistant in Institute of Social Order, 1950-65; Cambridge Center for Social Studies, Cambridge, Mass., research associate, 1966-71; Georgetown University, Jesuit Center for Social Studies, Washington, D.C., research professor of economics and research associate, 1971—. Research associate, W. E. Upjohn Institute for Employment Research; consultant, U.S. Department of Labor. *Member:* Catholic Economic Association (executive board member), American Economic Association, Association for Social Economics, International Industrial Relations Association, Industrial Relations Research Association, International Association of Personnel in Employment Security, International Society for Labor Law and Social Legislation.

WRITINGS: The Problem of Abuse in Unemployment Benefits, Columbia University Press, 1953; *Shared Government in Employment Security,* Columbia University Press, 1959; (editor) *In Aid of the Unemployed,* Johns Hopkins Press, 1965; *Supplemental Unemployment Benefits,* Cambridge Center for Social Studies, 1967; *Guaranteed Income for the Unemployed: The Story of SUB,* Johns Hopkins Press, 1968; (contributor) Sar A. Levitan, editor, *Towards Freedom From Want,* Industrial Relations Research Association, 1968; (contributor) *Hyphenated Priests: The Ministry of the Future,* Corpus Books, 1969; *Experience Rating in Unemployment Insurance: An Experiment in Competitive Socialism,* Johns Hopkins Press, 1972; *Experience Rating in Unemployment Insurance: Virtue or Vice?,* W. E. Upjohn Institute for Employment Research, 1972; *Depression: Theory and Research,* Halsted, 1974. Contributor to social science journals.

* * *

BECKER, Paula Lee 1941-

PERSONAL: Born March 29, 1941, in Denver, Colo.; daughter of Elmer LeRoy (a certified public accountant) and Beuna (Slater) Becker. *Education:* La Sierra College (now Loma Linda University), B.A., 1960; graduate study at University of Maryland, 1960, Vanderbilt University, 1964-66. *Politics:* Republican. *Religion:* Seventh-day Adventist. *Home:* 8207 Sawyer Brown Rd., Nashville, Tenn. 37221.

CAREER; Southern Publishing Association, Nashville, Tenn., assistant book editor, 1964-66, director of public relations, 1966-74. Glaser Productions (artists' management), Nashville, public relations, 1966-71; Group 3 Public Relations, Inc., Nashville, president, 1974—. Free-lance public relations and promotional work for Grand Ole Opry stars and other country music artists. *Member:* Religious Public Relations Council (secretary, 1966-67; president, 1973-75), National Academy of Recording Arts and Sciences, Public Relations Society of America.

WRITINGS: (With Warren L. Johns) *Dateline Sunday, U.S.A.,* Pacific Publishing, 1968; *Let the Song Go On* (biography), Impact, 1972. Also author of six books in the "Susan and Jimmy" series published by Southern Publishing, 1965.

AVOCATIONAL INTERESTS: Golf, travel.

*   *   *

BECKERMAN, Wilfred 1925-

PERSONAL: Born May 19, 1925, in Croydon, England; son of Morris (a tailor) and Matilda (Pavilotsky) Beckerman; married Nicole Ritter, June 22, 1952; children: Stephen Daniel, Clare Deborah, Carole Sophia. *Education:* Trinity College, Cambridge, M.A. and Ph.D., 1950. *Politics:* Independent. *Religion:* Agnostic. *Home:* 12 Chadlington Rd., Oxford, England. *Office:* Balliol College, Broad St., Oxford, England.

CAREER: University of Nottingham, Nottingham, England, lecturer in economics, 1950-52; affiliated with Organisation for European Economic Cooperation (later Organisation for European Co-operation and Development), Paris, France, 1952-61; National Institute of Economic and Social Research, London, England, director of research into long-term prospects of British economy, 1962-64; Oxford University, Oxford, England, fellow of Balliol College and tutor in economics, 1964-69; University College, University of London, professor of political economy, and head of department, 1969—. Economic consultant to British Department of Economic Affairs, 1964-65; economic advisor to Board of Trade, 1967-69. Member of Royal Commission on Environmental Pollution, 1970-73. Governor and member of executive committee of National Institute for Economic and Social Research, 1972—. *Military service:* Royal Naval Volunteer Reserve, 1943-46; became sub-lieutenant. *Member:* International Association for Research in Income and Wealth, Royal Economic Society.

WRITINGS: (With others) *The British Economy in 1975,* Cambridge University Press, 1965; *International Comparisons of Real Incomes,* Organization for Economic Co-operation and Development, 1966; (contributor) *Economic Growth in Britain,* edited by P. D. Henderson, Weidenfeld & Nicolson, 1966; *An Introduction to National Income Analysis,* Weidenfeld & Nicholson, 1968; (editor and contributor) *The Labour Government's Economic Record 1964-1970,* Duckworth, 1972; *In Defence of Economic Growth,* Cape, 1974; *Two Cheers for the Affluent Society,* St. Martin's Press, 1974. Contributor to economic journals.

WORK IN PROGRESS: Research into income maintenance policies in various countries.

*   *   *

BEE, (John) David (Ashford) 1931-

PERSONAL: Born December 1, 1931, in Simonstown, South Africa; son of Allan Gordon (a surgeon-commander in Royal Navy, and writer) and Kate Ellen (Ashford) Bee; married Sandra Logan, January 15, 1966. *Education:* University of Natal, B.A., 1954. *Religion:* Church of England. *Mailing address:* c/o Barclays Bank Ltd., West End Foreign Branch, 1 Pall Mall East, London S.W. 1, England. *Agent:* Willis Kingsley Wing, 24 East 38th St., New York, N.Y. 10016. *Office:* District Office, Auki, Malaita, British Solomon Islands Protectorate.

CAREER: British Overseas Civil Service, officer in Department of Labour, Tanganyika (now Tanzania), 1959-61, district officer in Western Pacific High Commission, stationed at Auki, British Solomon Islands Protectorate, 1965—. *Member:* East African Wildlife Society (Nairobi), Tanganyika Society.

WRITINGS: Children of Yesterday, Bles, 1961; *Our Fatal Shadows,* Bles, 1964, published as *Curse of Magira,* Harper, 1965; *The Victims,* Macmillan, 1971.

SIDELIGHTS: Bee was encouraged to take up writing by his father, who published a number of books on life in South Africa and in the Royal Navy, and who contributed regularly to *Blackwood's Magazine.* He has traveled throughout southern and eastern Africa, visited the Wadi Hadramaut in South Arabia in 1965, and the interior of Papua and New Guinea that same year. Bee speaks German, Afrikaans, and Swahili.†

*   *   *

BEHREND, Jeanne 1911-

PERSONAL: Born May 11, 1911, in Philadelphia, Pa.; daughter of Moses (a sugeon) and Clara (Rosenbaum) Behrend; married Alexander Kelberine (a pianist), 1934; married second husband, George S. MacManus (dealer in rare books), March 31, 1950. *Education:* Curtis Institute of Music, student, 1925-33. *Religion:* Jewish. *Home:* Apartment 4A, 2401 Pennsylvania Ave., Philadelphia, Pa. 19130.

CAREER: Curtis Institute of Music, Philadelphia, Pa., teacher of supplementary piano, 1936-53; Western College for Women, Oxford, Ohio, associate professor of music, 1943-45; member of the music faculty at the Juilliard School of Music, New York, N.Y., 1946-53, Philadelphia Conservatory of Music, Philadelphia, Pa., 1949-54, and Temple University, Philadelphia, Pa., 1954; Philadelphia (Pa.) Board of Education, teacher of in-service course on American music (for teachers), 1959; New School of Music, Philadelphia, Pa., teacher of piano, 1969—. Teacher of adult beginning course, Philadelphia Musical Academy, 1974—. Concert pianist and lecturer on tour in South America, 1945-46; gives lecture-recitals on Beethoven's piano sonatas and music of the Western Hemisphere. Founder and director, Philadelphia Festival of Western Hemisphere Music, 1959-60.

MEMBER: American Musicological Society, Musicians Club of America, American Society of Composers, Authors, and Publishers, American Federation of Musicians, Philadelphia Composers Forum (chairman, 1954-65), Philadelphia Record Society. *Awards, honors:* Joseph Bearns Prize, Columbia University, for piano suite and song cycle, 1936; U.S. State Department grant for tour of Brazil, 1945; Cruzeiro do Sul (Brazil), 1965.

WRITINGS: (Editor) Louis Moreau Gottschalk, *Notes of a Pianist,* Knopf, 1964. Author of pamphlets, program notes, introductions to her own music publications, and liner notes for her recordings, contributor to music journals.

Compositions for piano: "The Old Scissorsgrinder," Theo. Presser, 1923; "Quiet Piece" and "Dance into Space," Axelrod Publications, c. 1930; "From Dawn until Dusk," Elkan-Vogel, 1934. Also composer of unpublished songs and works for string quartet, viola and piano, and orchestra, 1932-59.

Editor of scores—All published by Presser: "Choral Music of the American Folk Tradition," Elkan-Vogel, "Piano Music by Louis Moreau Gottschalk," "The Unknown Foster" (seven songs by Stephen Foster).

WORK IN PROGRESS: A book for adult beginning piano.

SIDELIGHTS: "With limitations in all five," Jeanne Behrend can read Spanish, French, Portuguese, Italian, and can speak German. *Avocational interests:* Reading, walking, swimming, photography, animals, and the sea.

* * *

BEHRENS, June York 1925-

PERSONAL: Born April 25, 1925, in Maricopa, Calif.; daughter of Mark Hanna and Aline (Stafford) York; married Henry W. Behrens (a school principal), August 23, 1947; children: Terry Lynne, Denise. *Education:* University of California, Santa Barbara, B.A., 1947; University of Maryland (Overseas Program), Munich, Germany, graduate study, 1955; University of Southern California, M.A., 1961; graduate study, University of California, Los Angeles, and University of London. *Religion:* Protestant. *Home:* 3022 Hermosa Ave., Hermosa Beach, Calif. 90254.

CAREER: Elementary teacher in California, 1947-54, 1956-63, in overseas schools, 1954-56; vice-principal in Los Angeles, 1966; reading specialist in Los Angeles City Schools, 1966—. *Member:* National Education Association, American Association of University Women, California Teachers' Association.

WRITINGS—Juvenile books, all published by Elk Grove Press, except as indicated: *Soo Ling Finds a Way* (Junior Literary Guild selection), Golden Gate, 1965; *A Walk in the Neighborhood*, 1968; *Who Am I?*, 1968; *Where Am I?*, 1969; *Air Cargo*, 1970; *Look at the Zoo Animals*, 1970; *Truck Cargo*, 1970.

Earth is Home: The Pollution Story, 1971; *Look at the Farm Animals*, 1971; *Ship Cargo*, 1971; *How I Feel*, 1973; *Look at the Desert Animals*, 1973; *Look at the Forest Animals*, 1974; *Train Cargo*, 1974; *My Brown Bag Book*, J. Alden, 1974; *Feast of Thanksgiving: The First American Holiday*, 1974; *True Book of Metric Measurement*, 1975; *Look at the Sea Animals*, 1975.

SIDELIGHTS: A family of "school people," the Behrenses use vacations for travel, have gone to Alaska, Africa, Asia, Canada, Hawaii, and Europe, and often to Mexico. These travels have motivated "the desire to share experiences *with* children *about* children from another environment, related and foreign."

* * *

BELFORD, Lee A(rcher) 1913-

PERSONAL: Born October 14, 1913, in Savannah, Ga.; son of William Thomas (a wholesale grocer) and Minnie (Archer) Belford; married Cora Louise McGee (an administrator), April 12, 1939; children: Fontaine Maury, Mimi Okino. *Education:* University of the South, B.A., 1935, B.D., 1938; Union Theological Seminary, New York,

N.Y., S.T.M., 1947; Columbia University, Ph.D., 1953. *Politics:* Democrat Liberal. *Home:* 55 Bank St., New York, N.Y. 10014. *Office:* Department of Religious Education, New York University, New York, N.Y. 10003.

CAREER: Ordained Episcopalian priest, 1938; vicar in Douglas, Ga., 1938-41; rector in Brunswick, Ga., 1941-43; New York University, New York, N.Y., instructor, 1950-52, assistant professor, 1952-55, associate professor, 1955-60, professor of religious education, 1960—, chairman of department of religious education, School of Education, 1954—. Associate rector, Church of the Epiphany, New York, N.Y., 1948—. Chairman of family life section, Protestant Council, 1952-56; member of worship and fine arts section, National Council of Churches, 1960-63. *Military service:* U.S. Naval Reserve, chaplain, 1943-46; became lieutenant. *Member:* American Academy of Religion, Academy of Religion and Mental Health, Society for the Scientific Study of Religion, Religious Research Association, Delta Tau Delta, Sigma Upsilon. *Awards, honors:* U.S. State Department study grants for India, 1961-62, and Israel, 1964.

WRITINGS: Introduction to Judaism, Association Press, 1961; (editor) *Religious Dimensions in Literature*, Seabury, 1968.

Contributor: (Author of foreword) Leroy Nixon, *John Calvin's Teachings on Human Reason*, Exposition, 1963; Hugo G. Beigle, editor, *Advances in Sex Research*, Hoeber Medical Division of Harper, 1963; Sidney Hook, editor, *Philosophy and History*, New York University Press, 1963; Malcolm Boyd, editor, *On the Battle Lines*, Morehouse, 1965; *Al-Anon Faces Alcoholism*, Al-Anon, 1965; K. B. Cully, editor, *The Episcopal Church and Education*, Morehouse, 1966. Contributor to *The Westminster Dictionary of Christian Education*, 1963, *The Catholic Encyclopedia for School and Home*, *Encyclopedia Americana*. Also contributor of articles on Christian-Jewish relations, Catholic-Protestant relations, alcoholism, homosexuality, and other personality problems, to journals. Contributing editor, *Churchman*, 1958—; associate editor, *Witness*, 1961-72.†

* * *

BELL, J. Bowyer 1931-

PERSONAL: Born November 15, 1931, in New York, N.Y.; married; children: four. *Education:* Washington and Lee University, A.B., 1953; Duke University, A.M., 1954, Ph.D., 1958; University of Rome, graduate study, 1956-57. *Politics:* Democrat. *Religion:* Episcopalian. *Home:* 317 West 89th Street, New York, N.Y. 10024. *Agent:* Oliver Swan, Julian Bach, Inc., 18 East 48th Street, New York, N.Y. 10017. *Office:* Institute of War and Peace Studies, Columbia University, New York, N.Y. 10027.

CAREER: New York Institute of Technology, New York, N.Y., associate professor of history, 1963-67; Harvard University, Center for International Affairs, Cambridge, Mass., research associate, 1968-72; Massachusetts Institute of Technology, Center for International Studies, Cambridge, Mass., research associate, 1972-73; Columbia University, Institute of War and Peace Studies, New York, N.Y., research associate, 1973—. Member of Inter-University Seminar on Armed Forces and Society and Harvard-MIT Arms Control Seminar. *Member:* International Institute for Strategic Studies, American Historical Association, American Political Science Association, American Committee for Irish Studies, Middle East Institute. *Awards, honors:* Earhart fellowship, 1972; Guggenheim fellowship, 1972-73; Ford Foundation grant, 1973-75.

WRITINGS: Besieged: Seven Cities Under Attack, Chilton, 1966; *The Long War: Israel and the Arabs Since 1946*, Prentice-Hall, 1969; *The Secret Army: The IRA 1916-1970*, Blond, 1970, John Day, 1971, revised edition published as *The Secret Army: The IRA 1916-1974*, MIT Press, 1974; *The Myth of the Guerrilla: Revolutionary Theory and Malpractice*, Knopf, 1971; *Cyprus: A Greek Tragedy*, St. Martin's, 1974; *Blood and Fire: The Irgun, LEHI, and Palestine*, St. Martin's, in press; *Wars of National Liberation*, Harvard University Press, in press.

Contributor: L. P. Wallace and W. C. Askew, editors, *Power, Public Opinion and Democracy*, Duke University Press, 1959; R. O. Keohane and S. J. Nye, editors, *Transnational Relations and World Politics*, Harvard University Press, 1972; R. D. S. Higham, editor, *Civil War in the Twentieth Century*, University Press of Kentucky, 1972; *International Terrorism*, Praeger, 1975; *New Dimensions in Military History*, Presidio Press, 1975. Also writer of monographs. Contributor of articles to *International Studies Quarterly, The World Today, The Middle East Journal, Military Affairs, The Review of Politics, United Irishman*, and other journals.

* * *

BELL, Joyce Denebrink   1936-

PERSONAL: Born July 28, 1936, in Long Beach, Calif.; daughter of Francis Compton (a vice admiral, U.S. Navy) and Fanny (McCook) Denebrink; married Byron Bell (an architect), May 1, 1966. *Education:* Attended Denison University, 1954-56; Stanford University, B.A., 1958. *Home:* 136 West 15th St., New York, N.Y. 10011. *Agent:* Lynn Nesbitt, Artists Agency Corp., 1271 Avenue of the Americas, New York, N.Y. 10020.

CAREER: Wadsworth Publishing Co., San Francisco, Calif., editorial assistant, 1959-60; Batten, Barton, Durstine & Osborne, Inc., San Francisco, Calif., secretary in copy department, 1960-61; *Sports Illustrated*, New York, N.Y., assistant in promotion department, 1962; *Mademoiselle*, New York, N.Y., assistant feature editor, 1962-64; Simon & Schuster, Inc., New York, N.Y., assistant promotion director, 1966; Biow Co., New York, N.Y., editor of *Merchandise Display News*, beginning 1966. *Awards, honors:* Guest managing editor of *Mademoiselle*, 1958, as winner of College Board Contest.

WRITINGS: (Editor) *Barbed Wires: A Collection of Famous, Funny Telegrams*, Simon & Schuster, 1965; (contributor) *New York Spy*, David White, 1967.†

* * *

BELL, R(obert) C(harles)   1917-

PERSONAL: Born November 22, 1917, in Sudbury, Ontario, Canada; son of Robert Duncan (a missionary) and Violet Lydia (Clarke) Bell; married Phyllis Pearl Hunter Codling, June 28, 1941; children: Robert Graham, Geoffrey Duncan, Diana Mary. *Education:* St. Bartholomew's Hospital Medical College, London, M.R.C.S. and L.R.C.P., 1941; University of London, M.B. and B.S., 1941. *Religion:* Church of England. *Home:* 20 Linden Rd., Gosforth, Newcastle-on-Tyne 3, Northumberland NE3 4EY, England.

CAREER: Plastic surgeon on board of Newcastle Regional Hospital, 1952—. *Military service:* Royal Canadian Air Force, 1945-48. *Member:* Royal College of Surgeons (fellow), British Association of Plastic Surgeons, North of England Surgical Society, Numismatic Literary Guild (life member), Hadrianic Society (Durham; chairman, 1975—). *Awards, honors:* First outstanding award, Doctors' Hobbies Exhibitions, London, 1959, for manuscript of *Board and Table Games of Many Civilizations*.

WRITINGS: Board and Table Games of Many Civilizations, Oxford University Press, Volume I, 1960, Volume II, 1969; *Commercial Coins 1787-1084*, Corbitt & Hunter, 1963; *Copper Commercial Coins 1811-1819*, Corbitt & Hunter, 1964; *Tangram Teasers*, Corbitt & Hunter, 1965; *Tradesmen's Tickets and Private Tokens 1785-1819*, Corbitt & Hunter, 1966; *Specious Tokens and Those Struck for General Circulation, 1784-1804*, Corbitt & Hunter, 1968; *Tyneside Pottery*, Studio Vista, 1971; (with M. A. V. Gill) *The Potteries of Tyneside*, Graham, 1973; *The Use of Skin Grafts* (monograph), Oxford University Press, 1973; *Discovering Old Board Games*, Shire, 1973; *Diaries from the Days of Sail*, Holt, 1974; *Discovering Backgammon*, Shire, 1975. Regular contributor to *World Coins* and *Token Tales*.

WORK IN PROGRESS: Medalets of Kempson and Skidmore, for Graham; writing introduction and editing *Games of the World*, for Time-Life; *Unofficial Farthings 1820-1870*, for B. A. Seaby; *Political Pieces*.

* * *

BELL, Winifred   1914-

PERSONAL: Born October 10, 1914, in Detroit, Mich.; daughter of Rupert A. (a corporation lawyer) and Elizabeth (Simmons) Bell. *Education:* University of Michigan, A.B., 1936, M.S.W., 1944; Columbia University, D.S.W., 1964. *Office:* Center for Study of Income Maintainence Policies, 310 Rubin Hall, New York University, 35 Fifth Avenue, New York, N.Y. 10003.

CAREER: Michigan Child Guidance Clinic, Ann Arbor, psychiatric caseworker, 1942-43; Family Service Association of Metropolitan Detroit, Detroit, Mich., district supervisor, 1944-48; Adult Psychiatric Clinic, Detroit, casework supervisor and acting director, 1948-59; U. S. Department of Health, Education, and Welfare, Washington, D.C., Bureau of Family Services, demonstration project specialist, 1962-66; University of Maryland, Baltimore Campus, professor of social work, 1966-68; State University of New York at Albany, School of Social Welfare, professor of social policy, 1968-72; New York University, New York, N.Y., professor of social policy and co-director of Center for Study of Income Maintainence, 1972—. Member of social service reorganization task force, U.S. Department of Health, Education and Welfare, 1968-69, member of New York State Committee on Children, 1972—. Consultant to public welfare and mental health departments, and to model city programs. *Member:* National Association of Social Workers, American Public Welfare Association, American Civil Liberties Union.

WRITINGS: (With Elizabeth Wickenden) *Public Welfare: Time for a Change*, Columbia University School of Social Work, 1961; *Aid to Dependent Children*, Columbia University Press, 1965. Contributor of articles to social work journals.

WORK IN PROGRESS: The Project Approach to Poverty; and a study of the relative responsibility provisions in social welfare.

AVOCATIONAL INTERESTS: Music, reading, and travel.†

BELLMAN, Samuel Irving 1926-

PERSONAL: Born September 28, 1926, in El Paso, Tex.; son of Max (a storekeeper) and Bessie (Levenson) Bellman; married Jeanne Lisker, March 16, 1952; children: Joel Ethan, Jonathan David. *Education:* University of Texas, B.A., 1947; Wayne State University, M.A., 1951; Ohio State University, Ph.D., 1955. *Religion:* Jewish. *Office:* Department of English and Modern Languages, California State Polytechnic University, Pomona, Calif. 91768.

CAREER: Fresno State College (now California State University, Fresno), instructor in English, 1955-57; California State Polytechnic College (now California Polytechnic State University), San Luis Obispo, assistant professor of English, 1957-59; California State Polytechnic University, Pomona, assistant professor, 1959-62, associate professor, 1962-66, professor, 1966—. *Member:* American Studies Association, College English Association, Popular Culture Association, Rocky Mountain Modern Language Association, Philological Association of the Pacific Coast.

WRITINGS: (Editor) *The College Experience*, Chandler Publishing, 1962; *The "New Woman" in the Space Age*, Association of Women Deans and Vice-Principals, 1965; (editor) *Survey and Forecast*, Chandler Publishing, 1966; (contributor) Leslie Field, editors, *Bernard Malamud and the Critics*, New York University Press, 1970; *Marjorie Kinnan Rawlings* (biography), Twayne, 1974. Contributor of articles to educational and literary journals, reviews to *Saturday Review* and other periodicals, and poems to little magazines and journals.

WORK IN PROGRESS: A critical volume on Constance Rourke for Twayne's "U.S. Authors" series, completion expected in 1978; articles and reviews on contemporary literature; poetry.

*   *   *

BENCHLEY, Peter B(radford) 1940-

PERSONAL: Born May 8, 1940, in New York, N.Y.; son of Nathaniel Goddard (an author) and Marjorie (Bradford) Benchley; married Wendy Wesson, September 19, 1964. *Education:* Harvard University, A.B. (cum laude), 1961. *Home:* 35 Boudinot St., Princeton, N.J. 08540. *Agent:* Ashley Famous Agency, Inc., 1301 Avenue of the Americas, New York, N.Y. 10019.

CAREER: Washington Post, Washington, D.C., reporter, 1963; *Newsweek*, New York, N.Y., associate editor, 1964-67; The White House, Washington, D.C., staff assistant to the President, 1967-69; freelance writer and television news correspondent, 1969—. *Military service:* U.S. Marine Corps Reserve, 1962-63. *Member:* Coffee House, Spee Club, Pacific Club, Hasty Pudding Institute of 1770.

WRITINGS: Time and a Ticket, Houghton, 1964; *Jonathan Visits the White House* (juvenile), McGraw, 1964; *Jaws*, Doubleday, 1974. Contributor to *Holiday, New Yorker, Diplomat, Moderator, Vogue, New York Herald-Tribune, Time Magazine, National Geographic*, and other periodicals.

SIDELIGHTS: Benchley is the grandson of Robert Benchley. He speaks French, some Italian and Spanish. *Avocational interests:* Guitar, tennis, fishing, sharks, poker, the theater, films.

BIOGRAPHICAL/CRITICAL SOURCES: Carolyn Riley, editor, *Contemporary Literary Criticism*, Volume IV, Gale, 1975.

BENDER, James F(rederick) 1905-

PERSONAL: Born April 6, 1905, in Dayton, Ohio; son of Frederick Jacob (an engineer) and Bertha (Zimmerman) Bender; married Ann Parsons, June 25, 1925 (deceased). *Education:* Columbia University, B.S., 1928, Ph.D., 1939. *Politics:* Republican. *Religion:* Religious Society of Friends. *Home:* 44 Thornwood Lane, Roslyn Heights, N.Y. *Office:* School of Business, Adelphi University, Garden City, N.Y.

CAREER: City College, New York, N.Y., psychological examiner in personnel bureau, 1928-37; Brooklyn Polytechnical Institute, Brooklyn, N.Y., part-time lecturer and adjunct professor of psychology, 1928-40; Queens College, Flushing, N.Y., chairman of department of speech and director of Queens Speech and Hearing Center, 1937-44; National Institute for Human Relations, New York, N.Y., director, 1944-54; James F. Bender & Associates, New York, N.Y., senior partner, 1954—; Adelphi University, Garden City, N.Y., professor of business administration and dean of School of Business, 1960—, dean of Center of Banking and Money Management, 1973—. New York University, part-time lecturer, 1943-49; Columbia University, lecturer, 1950-57. Licensed psychologist, 1958—. Consultant to WPIX television, 1948-50, and to business and industrial firms, including Kimberly Clark Corp. and International Business Machine Co. Director of Lehigh Navigation Coal Sales Co., 1953—, First Multifund of America, Inc., and Tech Products. President of Enterprise Fund of Adelphi University, Inc. Trustee of Queens Council of Social Welfare, 1940-43, Queens Speech and Hearing Center, Inc., 1941—, and Friends Academy, 1957.

MEMBER: American Speech and Hearing Association (fellow), American Psychological Association, New York Academy of Sciences, New York State Psychological Association, New York Society of Clinical Psychologists, Nassau County Historical Society, Sigma Chi. *Awards, honors:* American Economic Foundation certificate for outstanding service.

WRITINGS: (With Victor M. Kleinfeld) *Speech Correction Manual*, Farrar & Rinehart, 1936; (with Kleinfeld) *Principles and Practices of Speech Correction*, Pitman, 1938; with Victor Fields) *Phonetic Readings in American Speech*, Pitman, 1939; *Personality Structure of Stuttering*, Pitman, 1939; *N.B.C. Handbook of Pronunciation*, Crowell, 1943, 3rd edition, revised by Thomas Lee Crowell, Jr., 1964; *How to Talk Well*, McGraw, 1948; *The Technique of Executive Leadership*, McGraw, 1949; *How to Sleep*, Coward, 1949; (with Fields) *Voice and Diction*, Macmillan, 1949, reprinted, 1963; (with Lee Graham) *Your Way to Popularity and Personal Power*, New American Library, 1950; *Victory Over Fear*, Coward, 1951; *Profits From Business Letters*, R. L. Polk, 1953; *How to Sell Well*, Pitman, 1961; *Make Your Business Letters Make Friends*, World Work, 1963; (with Judy T. Stark) *You*, Benjamin Co., 1973. Also author of *Salesman's Mispronunciations*; author of more than five hundred articles.

WORK IN PROGRESS: Research in interpersonal and structural communications.

*   *   *

BENEDICT, Rex 1920-

PERSONAL: Born June 27, 1920, in Jet, Okla.; son of Excel Edward (a farmer) and Violet (Lambert) Benedict; married Giusi Usai (a secretary), January 5, 1966. *Education:* Northwestern State College, B.A., 1949; Oklahoma

University, graduate study, 1949. *Home and office:* 23 West 88th St., New York, N.Y. 10024.

CAREER: Dance orchestra leader in Alva, Okla., 1939-41; translator and movie dubber in Rome, Italy, 1952-60; reader for various publishing houses in New York, N.Y., 1960—, and translator. *Military service:* U.S. Navy, 1941-45, 1951-53; served as naval aviator; became lieutenant; received Distinguished Flying Cross and three air medals.

WRITINGS: O ... Brother Juniper!, Pantheon, 1963; *Fantasano*, Corsair Press, 1967; *Good Luck Arizona Man*, Pantheon, 1972; *Goodbye to the Purple Sage*, Pantheon, 1973; *Last Stand at Goodbye Gulch*, Pantheon, 1974; *The Ballad of Cactus Jack*, Pantheon, 1975. Also author of six volumes of poetry published by Corsair Press, 1968-72.

Translator: *The Prayers of Man*, Obolensky, 1961; *Amorous Tales from the Decameron*, Fawcett, 1963; *Those Cursed Tuscans*, Ohio University Press, 1964; *One Moonless Night*, Braziller, 1964; *The Polka Dot Twins*, Braziller, 1964.

SIDELIGHTS: Benedict told *CA*, "My real interest is rather anthropological, being simply what makes an Italian an Italian, or a Japanese a Japanese? ... When not musing thusly, or playing the recorder, I listen to Mozart and Bach, trying to solve the mysteries, or read Mrs. Woolf.... Write and translate because words fascinate me. Study languages (Italian and French mainly) for the same reason."

* * *

BENJAMIN, Annette Francis 1928-

PERSONAL: Born December 12, 1928, in Waco, Tex.; daughter of Abraham S. and Selma (Saul) Levy; married Bry Benjamin (a physician), June 27, 1955; children: Alan Dean. *Education:* Studied at Sophie Newcomb College, 1945-47, and College of Music of Cincinnati, 1947-49. *Home:* 176 East 71st St., New York, N.Y. 10021. *Agent:* Gloria Safier, 667 Madison Ave., New York, N.Y. 10021.

CAREER: WOR and WOR-TV, New York, N.Y., assistant promotion manager, 1953-54; National Broadcasting Co. and NBC-TV, New York, N.Y., presentation writer, 1954-55; RKO Teleradio Pictures, New York, N.Y., copy supervisor, 1955-56; *McCall's*, New York, N.Y., promotion manager, drugs and toiletries, 1957-59; free-lance writer. *Member:* American Society of Composers, Authors and Publishers.

WRITINGS: (With husband, Bry Benjamin) *In Case of Emergency: What To Do Until the Doctor Arrives*, Doubleday, 1965, revised edition, 1970; (with Bry Benjamin) *New Facts of Life for Women*, Doubleday, 1969. Contributor to *American Home.*†

* * *

BENJAMIN, Bry 1924-

PERSONAL: Given name is pronounced Bree; born October 20, 1924, in New York, N.Y.; son of Maurice S. and Edith (Bry) Benjamin; married Annette Francis Levy (a writer), June 27, 1955; children: Alan Dean. *Education:* Yale University, B.S., 1945; Harvard University, M.D., 1947. *Home:* 176 East 71st St., New York, N.Y. 10021. *Agent:* Gloria Safier, 667 Madison Ave., New York, N.Y.10021. *Office:* 10 East 78th St., New York, N.Y. 10021.

CAREER: New York Hospital, New York, N.Y., physi-

cian to outpatients, 1955-65, assistant attending physician, 1966—; Cornell University Medical College, New York, N.Y., clinical assistant professor of medicine, 1965—. Consultant to Gracie Square College, 1964—. *Military service:* U.S. Army, 1943-47; U.S. Air Force, flight surgeon, 1951-53; became captain. *Member:* American College of Physicians (fellow), American Medical Association, American Psychosomatic Society, American Public Health Association, American Psychosomatic Society, American Public Health Association, American Association for the Advancement of Science, New York Academy of Medicine (fellow), New York State Medical Society, New York County Medical Society, New York Heart Association, Alpha Omega Alpha, Harvey Society. *Awards, honors:* Commonwealth fellow, 1950-51.

WRITINGS: (With wife, Annette Francis Benjamin) *In Case of Emergency: What To Do Until the Doctor Arrives*, Doubleday, 1965, revised edition, 1970; (with Annette Francis Benjamin) *New Facts of Life for Women*, Doubleday, 1969.

WORK IN PROGRESS: Studies in coronary heart disease.†

* * *

BENNETT, Anna Elizabeth 1914-

PERSONAL: Born July 18, 1914, in Brooklyn, N.Y.; daughter of Walter Scott (a physician) and Frances (Livermore) Bennett. *Education:* Adelphi College (now University), A.B., 1935; Pratt Institute, L.S.B., 1937; St. John's University, Jamaica, N.Y., Teacher-Librarian Certificate, 1954. *Religion:* Divine Science. *Home:* Box 334, Southampton, N.Y. 11968.

CAREER: Member of children's room staff at New York (N.Y.) Public Library, 1937-38, and Lansing (Mich.) Public Library, 1938-42; children's librarian at Morristown (N.J.) Library, 1942-43, and Newark (N.J.) Public Library, 1943-44; U.S. Army, Cambridge Hospital, Cambridge, Ohio, post librarian, 1944-46; Children's Museum, Brooklyn, N.Y., assistant children's librarian, 1946-48; Brooklyn (N.Y.) Public Library, cataloger, 1948-52; Greenburgh (N.Y.) public schools, school librarian, 1953-55; Northport (N.Y.) Public Library, children's director and librarian, 1956—. *Member:* Poetry Society of America, National Writers Club, Spiritual Frontiers' Fellowship. *Awards, honors:* Lippincotts' Helen Dean Award for *Little Witch*.

WRITINGS: Little Witch (juvenile), Lippincott, 1953; *Cantabile* (poetry), Fine Editions Press, 1954. Children's story anthologized in *Holiday Roundup* published by Macrae Smith. Poetry has appeared in *Poetry* (Chicago), *American Scholar, Lyric*, and *Commonweal*.

WORK IN PROGRESS: Occasional poems; keeping a "dream diary" (interested in psychic phenomena, particularly dreams).†

* * *

BENNETT, Kay Curley 1922-

PERSONAL: Born July 15, 1922, in Sheepsprings, N.M.; daughter of Keedah (a silversmith) and Mary (Chahiilbahi) Chischillie; married second husband, Russell C. Bennett (an engineer), April 6, 1956; children: (first marriage) two daughters. *Education:* Attended Toadlena Boarding School, Toadlena, N.M. *Home:* 6 Aida Ct., Gallup, N.M. 87301.

CAREER: File clerk at Douglas Aircraft, Long Beach,

Calif., 1942-45; dormitory attendant at Toadlena Boarding School, Toadlena, N.M., 1945-46; teacher-interpreter at Phoenix Indian School, Phoenix, Ariz., 1946-52; chronicler of Navajo history (her Indian name is Kaibah), singing their songs, and making Navajo dolls. Member of New Mexico Human Rights Commission, 1969-73. *Member:* Inter-Tribal Indian Ceremonial Association. *Awards, honors:* First prize for dolls at state fairs in Arizona and New Mexico and at Navajo Tribal Fair; New Mexico Mother of the Year, 1968.

WRITINGS: Kaibah: Recollection of a Navajo Girlhood, Westernlore, 1965; *A Navajo Saga: History 1846-1870*, Naylor, 1969.

WORK IN PROGRESS: Navajo legends.

SIDELIGHTS: Kay Bennett has lived in Afghanistan, 1958-60, and has traveled in the Far and Middle East and Europe.

* * *

BENNETT, William L. 1924-

PERSONAL: Born June 26, 1924, in Shallotte, N.C.; son of Samuel L. (a minister) and Margaret (Jenrette) Bennett; married Doris Palmer, July 19, 1952; children: William L., Jr., Philip Judson, David Palmer. *Education:* Wake Forest College, A.B. (summa cum laude), 1948; Duke University, B.D., 1950, M.A., 1953; New Orleans Baptist Theological Seminary, Th.D., 1965. *Home:* 3016 Birchfield Dr., Memphis, Tenn. *Office:* Speedway Baptist Church, 601 North Bellevue, Memphis, Tenn. 38107.

CAREER: Baptist clergyman. Pastor in Durham, N.C., 1950-54, and Greensboro, N.C., 1954-61; Speedway Terrace Baptist Church, Memphis, Tenn., pastor, 1963—. *Member:* Phi Beta Kappa.

WRITINGS: Trumpet of the Lord, Zondervan, 1959.

WORK IN PROGRESS: A book on the Holy Spirit.†

* * *

BENSON, Charles S(cott) 1922-

PERSONAL: Born May 20, 1922, in Atlanta, Ga.; son of Marion Trotti (a physician) and Sallie (Bagley) Benson; married Dorothy Merrick, June 8, 1946; children: Michele, Scott, Sally. *Education:* Princeton University, A.B. (honors), 1943; Columbia University, M.A., 1948, Ph.D., 1955. *Office:* University of California, Berkeley, Calif.

CAREER: Bowdoin College, Brunswick, Me., instructor in economics, 1950-52, assistant professor, 1952-55; Harvard University, Cambridge, Mass., assistant professor of education, 1955-57, research associate, Center for Field Studies, 1955-64, member of department of economics, 1957-59, lecturer on education, 1957-64; University of California, Berkeley, associate professor of education, 1964—, research associate, Institute of Governmental Studies, 1965—. Consultant on finance to committees and organizations, including U.S. Office of Education and Ministry of Education, Colombia. Former secretary and trustee of New England Economic Education Council. *Military service:* U.S. Navy, 1943-46; commanding officer of minesweeper in western Pacific; became lieutenant junior grade.

MEMBER: American Economic Association, American Association for the Advancement of Science, American Academy of Political and Social Science, American Association of School Administrators, Econometric Society, Regional Science Association, California Association of School Administrators, Phi Delta Kappa. *Awards, honors:* Ford Foundation grant for investigation of finance of education in England and Wales, 1962-63.

WRITINGS: Teachers' Salaries: The Process of Change in 43 Metropolitan School Systems, New England School Development Council, 1959; *The Economics of Public Education*, Houghton, 1961, 2nd edition, 1968; *Are School Debt Finances Costs Too High?*, New England School Development Council, 1962; (editor) *Perspectives on the Economics of Education*, Houghton, 1963; *State and Local Fiscal Relationships in Education in California*, State Senate (Sacramento), 1965; *The Cheerful Prospect: A Statement on the Future of American Education*, Houghton, 1965; *The School and the Economic System*, Science Research Associates, 1966; (with James W. Guthrie) *An Essay on Federal Incentives and Local and State Educational Initiative*, University of California, Berkeley, 1968; (with Peter B. Lund) *Neighborhood Distribution of Local Public Services*, University of California Institute of Governmental Studies, 1969; (with H. L. Hodgkinson) *Implementing the Learning Society*, Jossey-Bass, 1974.

Contributor: *The Internship in Administrative Preparation*, University Council for Educational Administration, Ohio State University, 1963; Jesse Burkhead, *Public School Finance*, Syracuse University Press, 1964; *Change and Challenge in American Education*, edited by S. Harris, McCutchan, 1965; *Trends in Financing Public Education*, Committee on Educational Finance, National Education Association, 1965; *Planning for Educational Reform: Financial and Social Alternatives*, Dodd, 1974. Contributor to learned journals. Member of board of editors, *Educational Administration Quarterly*.

* * *

BENSTOCK, Bernard 1930-

PERSONAL: Born March 23, 1930, in New York, N.Y.; son of Sol (a carpenter) and Lily (Garde) Benstock; married Eve Cohen, May 28, 1959; married Sharon Shivvers, May 6, 1973; children: (first marriage) Kevin, Erika (daughters). *Education:* Brooklyn College (now of the City University of New York), A.B., 1950; Columbia University, M.A., 1954; Florida State University, Ph.D., 1957. *Politics:* "Not codifiable in a word or phrase." *Religion:* None. *Home:* 615 West University Ave., Champaign, Ill. 61820. *Office:* English Department, University of Illinois, Urbana, Ill.

CAREER: Louisiana State University, Baton Rouge, 1957-65, began as instructor, became assistant professor of English; Kent State University, Kent, Ohio, associate professor, 1965-1967, professor of English, 1967-74; University of Illinois, Urbana, professor of English and comparative literature, 1974—. President, James Joyce Foundation, 1971—. University of Tabriz, Tabriz, Iran, Fulbright lecturer in American literature, 1961-62. *Military service:* U.S. Army, 1951-53; Public Information Office correspondent and editor (in Korea), 1952-53. *Member:* Modern Language Association of America, American Committee for Irish Studies, South Central Modern Language Association (chairman of comparative literature section, 1966), Midwest Modern Language Association (chairman, Modern Literature section, 1969).

WRITINGS: Joyce-again's Wake: An Analysis of Finnegan's Wake, University of Washington Press, 1965; *Sean O'Casey*, Bucknell University Press, 1971; (co-editor) *Approaches to Ulysses*, University of Pittsburgh Press, 1971; *Approaches to James Joyce's Portrait*, University of Pittsburgh Press, in press. Contributor to literary and other learned journals.

WORK IN PROGRESS: A James Joyce Directory, with wife, Sharon Benstock.

SIDELIGHTS: Benstock has lectured on James Joyce in the U.S., Canada, Ireland, France, West Germany, Belgium, Italy, and India.

* * *

BENTON, Lewis R(obert) 1920-

PERSONAL: Born July 4, 1920, in New York, N.Y.; son of Nathaniel T. (a real estate executive) and Fania (Roblon) Benton; married Frances Golden, March 17, 1948 (divorced, 1973); children: Valerie Gay, Roger Neil. *Education:* Brooklyn College (now Brooklyn College of the City University of New York), B.S., 1940; graduate study at Yale University, 1943-44, University of Michigan, 1944-45; New York University, M.A., 1948, Ph.D., 1952. *Home:* 3335 Frederick St., Oceanside, N.Y. 11572. *Agent:* Murray Benson, 8 Channel Dr., Kings Point, Great Neck, N.Y. *Office:* Hofstra University, Hemstead, N.Y. 11550.

CAREER: Management consultant, 1946-55; M. Lowenstein & Sons, Inc. (textiles), New York, N.Y., personnel director, 1956-63; self-employed management consultant, New York, N.Y., 1963—; Beaunit Corp. (textiles), New York, N.Y., personnel manager, 1965-66; Hofstra University, Hempstead, N.Y., professor of management, 1962—. Teacher of management courses at New School for Social Research, Cornell University, City College of the City University of New York, and other colleges. Trustee of *Journal of Educational Sociology*, 1952-59, and of Payne Educational Sociology Foundation. *Military service:* U.S. Army Air Forces, 1942-45; glider pilot, and Japanese military intelligence specialist; became captain. *Member:* American Management Association, Commerce and Industry Association, American Association of University Professors, Friends of the Human Relations Center (New York University), Phi Delta Kappa (vice-president, 1955-60).

WRITINGS: A Guide to Creative Personnel Management, Prentice-Hall, 1962; (editor) *Beverly Hillbilies' Book of Country Humor*, Stein & Day, 1964; (editor) Renee Verdon, *The White House Chef Cookbook*, Doubleday, 1967; *Management and Profitability*, Hofstra University, 1972; *Supervision and Management*, McGraw, 1972; *Management of Nonprofit Institutions*, Heath, 1975. Contributor of articles on management to professional journals.

SIDELIGHTS: Benton speaks Japanese, French, and Spanish.

* * *

BERARD, J(ules) Aram 1933-

PERSONAL: Born January 1, 1933, in Woonsocket, R.I.; son of Joseph Aram and Rose (Alma) Berard. *Education:* University of Montreal, Ph.B., 1957; Boston College, M.A., 1961. *Address:* Weston College, Weston, Mass. 02193.

CAREER: Ordained Roman Catholic priest, Society of Jesus of New England, 1966. Boston College High School, Boston, Mass., professor of French, 1961-63; Father Berard was reported, in 1975, to have been working in South Vietnam for the past few years and planning to remain.

WRITINGS: Preparatory Reports: Second Vatican Council, Westminster, 1965.†

* * *

BERDIE, Ralph F(reimuth) 1916-

PERSONAL: Born June 21, 1916, in Chicago, Ill.; son of Sidney S. (a merchant) and Enid (Freimuth) Berdie; married Frances Strong (an administrative assistant), August 6, 1942; children: Phyllis (Mrs. Imre Somlai), Douglas, Carl. *Education:* University of Minnesota, B.A., 1938, M.A., 1939, Ph.D., 1942. *Home:* 2208 Folwell St., St. Paul, Minn. 55108.

CAREER: University of Minnesota, Minneapolis, assistant to director of testing bureau, 1941-42, counselor and assistant professor of psychology, 1942-43; George Peabody College for Teachers, Nashville, Tenn., associate professor, 1946-47; University of Minnesota, associate professor, 1947-49, professor of psychology, 1965—, director of student life studies, 1965-71, coordinator of admissions, registration, and student records, 1971—. *Military service:* U.S. Naval Reserve, 1943-46; became lieutenant. *Member:* American Psychological Association (president, division of counseling, 1957), American Personnel and Guidance Association (member of executive council, 1963-66; president, 1970-71), American College Personnel Association (president, 1965-66), American Educational Research Association, Minnesota Psychological Association (executive secretary, 1947-50). *Awards, honors:* Fulbright scholarship, 1956-57.

WRITINGS: After High School—What?, University of Minnesota Press, 1954; (with Layton and others) *Testing in Guidance and Counseling*, McGraw, 1964; (with A. Hood) *Decisions for Tomorrow*, University of Minnesota Press, 1965; (with Bonifaco Pilapil) *Graduating Seniors' Satisfaction with the University*, University of Minnesota, 1968. Contributor of about two hundred items to professional journals.

WORK IN PROGRESS: Research on personality theory and vocational interests.

* * *

BERETTA, Lia 1934-

PERSONAL: Born August 25, 1934, in Piacenza, Italy; daughter of Elio (a farmer) and Ines (Vercesi) Beretta. *Education:* Instituto Universitario di Magistero, Genoa, Italy, Doctor's Degree, 1958. *Religion:* Roman Catholic. *Home:* Via Verdi 13, Castelsangiovanni, Piacenza, Italy.

CAREER: University of Virginia, Mary Washington College, Fredericksburg, assistant professor of Italian, 1960-63; Instituto Magistrale C. Tenca, Milan, Italy, professor of English, 1964—. *Member:* Phi Sigma Iota.

WRITINGS: (With Lee Cooper and Marion Greene) *Fun with Italian*, Little, 1964.

SIDELIGHTS: Lia Beretta speaks French and Spanish, and is currently studying Japanese.†

* * *

BERG, Darrel E. 1920-

PERSONAL: Born November 14, 1920, in Boone, Iowa; son of Elmer John (a maintenance man) and Irene (McFee) Berg; married Ruth Sanborn, January 31, 1942; children: Brenda Nelson, Lowell Sanborn, Bruce Darrel, Debbie Ann. *Education:* Attended St. Paul Bible College, 1938-41;

Nebraska Wesleyan University, B.A., 1948; Garrett Theological Seminary, B.D., 1951. *Politics:* Democrat. *Residence:* Lincoln, Neb.

CAREER: Methodist minister; served for nine years as minister in Seattle, Wash., and spent one summer as exchange minister in Japan; Minister at Trinity Methodist Church, Lincoln, Neb., beginning 1960. *Awards, honors:* D.D., Nebraska Wesleyan University, 1965.

WRITINGS: A Piece of Blue Sky, Zondervan, 1965. Contributor to religious journals.

WORK IN PROGRESS: Something Like a Star, a devotional book.†

* * *

BERG, Orley M. 1918-

PERSONAL: Born August 11, 1918, in Escondido, Calif.; son of Dave and Rachel (Nightingale) Berg; married Olive Ellen Etter (a librarian); children: David, John, Shirlee. *Education:* Attended La Sierra College; Pacific Union College, B.A.; Potomac University, M.A.; Hebrew Union College-Jewish Institute of Religion, Jerusalem, graduate study.

CAREER: Minister of Seventh-day Adventist Church. Pastoral ministry, 1945-67; ministerial secretary, Potomac Conference of Seventh-day Adventists, 1965-66; assistant secretary, Ministerial Association General Conference of Seventh-day Adventists, and executive editor, *The Ministry*, 1967—.

WRITINGS: Historical and Archeological Evidences, Taylor Publishers, 1959; *The Work of the Pastor*, Southern Publishing, 1966; *Restless Land: Israel, Its Place in History and Prophecy*, Review and Herald, 1974.

SIDELIGHTS: Berg spent summer of 1965 in explorations in the Negeb in Palestine and in excavations at Gezer, ancient fortress city of Solomon.

* * *

BERGONZI, Bernard 1929-

PERSONAL: Born April 13, 1929, in London, England; son of Charles Ernest and Louisa (Lloyd) Bergonzi; married Gabriel Wall, April 19, 1960; children: Benet, Clarissa, Lucy. *Education:* Wadham College, Oxford, B.Litt., 1961, M.A., 1962. *Religion:* Roman Catholic. *Agent:* A. D. Peters, 10 Buckingham St., Adelphi, London W.C. 2, England. *Office:* Department of English, University of Warwick, Coventry, Warwickshire, England.

CAREER: University of Manchester, Manchester, England, 1959-66, began as assistant lecturer, became lecturer in English; University of Warwick, Coventry, Warwickshire, England, senior lecturer, 1966-71, professor of English, 1971—. Visiting lecturer, Brandeis University, 1964-65; Beckman Summer Lecturer, University of California, Berkeley, 1965.

WRITINGS: Descartes and the Animals: Poems 1948-54, Platform, 1954; *The Early H. G. Wells: A Study of the Scientific Romances*, Manchester University Press, 1961; *Heroes' Twilight: A Study of the Literature of the Great War*, Constable, 1965, Coward, 1966; *The Situation of the Novel*, Macmillan, 1970; *T. S. Eliot*, Macmillan, 1972; *The Turn of a Century: Essays on Victorian and Modern English Literature*, Macmillan, 1973. Contributor to *Encounter, New Statesman*, and other periodicals.

BERNARDO, James V. 1913-

PERSONAL: Born February 22, 1913, in New Haven, Conn.; son of Dominick (a landscaper) and Florence (Mongillo) Bernardo; married Pauline E. Agner; children: Donald V., Pamela G., Bonnie L. *Education:* Duke University, B.A., 1934; Boston University, M.S., 1935. *Home:* 4222 Robertson Blvd., Alexandria, Va.

CAREER: Teacher of mathematics and science in Braggtown, N.C., 1935-36, in Plainville, Conn., 1936-42; school principal in Plainville, Conn., 1942-44; U.S. Civil Aeronautics Administration, Washington, D.C., principal educationalist, 1944-47, assistant regional administrator, New York, N.Y., 1947-57; Civil Aeronautics Administration-Federal Aeronautics Administration, Washington, D.C., assistant administrator, 1957-60; National Aeronautics and Space Administration, Washington, D.C., now director of Educational Programs Division. *Member:* National Aerospace Education Council (vice-president), Aerospace Writers Association, National Education Association, National Science Teachers Association, Wings Club. *Awards, honors:* Frank G. Brewer Trophy of National Aeronautic Association, for contributing most to development of air youth.

WRITINGS: Aviation in the Modern World, Dutton, 1960, 2nd edition published as *Aviation and Space in the Modern World*, 1968. Coordinating editor, Holt's "Space Science" series for young adults, with fourteen books published, 1966.

SIDELIGHTS: Bernardo speaks Italian, some Spanish and German.†

* * *

BERNAYS, Edward L. 1891-

PERSONAL: Born November 22, 1891, in Vienna, Austria; brought to United States in 1892; son of Ely (a grain exporter) and Anna (Freud) Bernays; married Doris Fleischman (a public relations counsel), September 16, 1922; children: Doris Fleischman (Mrs. Richard M. Held), Anne Fleischman (Mrs. Justin Kaplan). *Education:* Cornell University, B.S., 1912. *Home and office:* 7 Lowell St., Cambridge, Mass. 02138. *Agent:* Ivan Von Auw, Jr., Harold Ober Associates, Inc., 40 East 49th St., New York, N.Y. 10017.

CAREER: Newspaper writer in New York, N.Y., 1913-15; publicity director for U.S. tour of Ballet Russe, 1915-16, and for tours of Caruso and others, 1917-18; served with U.S. Committee on Public Information at Paris Peace Conference, 1918-19, and with U.S. War Department, 1919; public relations counsel in partnership with wife, Doris E. Fleischman, to government, business, and trade organizations, 1919—. New York University, first lecturer on public relations, 1923; adjunct professor of public relations, New York University, 1949-50, University of Hawaii, 1950, Boston University, 1968-69. Founder and president, Edward L. Bernays Foundation. Member of President Hoover's Emergency Committee for Unemployment, 1930-31, New York State Committee on Discrimination in Employment, 1942, national public relations committee, American Red Cross, 1942—, Massachusetts Council on Crime and Correction, 1969—, U.S. State Department Bureau of Educational and Cultural Affairs, 1970—; member of advisory council of Edward R. Murrow Center, Tufts University, and of School of General Education, Columbia University. Trustee and director of government, civic, and health and welfare institutions and organizations.

MEMBER: Society for the Psychological Study of Social Issues, American Association for Public Opinion Research, Royal Society of Arts (Benjamin Franklin fellow), Tau Mu Epsilon, and many civic organizations. *Awards, honors:* Created Officer of Public Instruction (France), 1926; King Christian X Medal (Denmark), 1946; Bronze Medallion of Southwestern Journalists Forum and Southern Methodist University, 1954; Bronze Medallion of Honor, City of New York, 1961; Dr. of Humanities, Boston University, 1966; honor award from Ohio University, 1970; honorary diploma, Art Institute of Boston, 1970.

WRITINGS: (With others) *Broadway Anthology*, Dutton, 1917; *Crystallizing Public Opinion*, Boni & Liveright, 1923; *Propoganda*, Liveright, 1928; (editor and contributor) *Outline of Careers*, George H. Doran, 1929; *Speak Up for Democracy*, Viking, 1940; *Take Your Place at the Peace Table*, Duell, Sloan & Pearce, 1945; *Public Relations: A Growing Profession*, Bellman Publishing, 1945; *Public Relations*, Oklahoma University Press, 1952; (editor and contributor) *Engineering of Consent*, University of Oklahoma Press, 1955; *Your Future in Public Relations*, Richard Rosen Press, 1961; *Biography of an Idea: Memoirs of Public Relations Counsel Edward L. Bernays*, Simon and Schuster, 1965; (editor with Burnet Hershey) *The Case for Reappraisal of U.S. Overseas Information Policies and Programs*, Praeger, 1970. Contributor to *Fortune* and other magazines.

BIOGRAPHICAL/CRITICAL SOURCES: American Mercury, Volume 19, number 74, February, 1930; *Atlantic Monthly*, Volume 149, May, 1932; *Public Relations, Edward L. Bernays and the American Scene*, Faxon; *Two Way Street—the Emergence of the Public Relations Counsel*, Bellman, 1948.

*   *   *

BERND, Joseph Laurence 1923-

PERSONAL: Surname pronounced burned; born December 8, 1923, in Macon, Ga.; son of Laurence J. (president of a wholesale firm) and Eva (Bloom) Bernd; married Ruth A. Brady, July 2, 1960; children: Alison Ruth. *Education:* Vanderbilt University, student, 1942-43; Mercer University, B.A., 1945; Emory University, graduate study, 1951; Boston University, M.A., 1953; Duke University, Ph.D., 1957. *Office:* Virginia Polytechnic Institute and State University, Blacksburg, Va. 24061.

CAREER: Worked in family firm, Macon, Ga., 1943-48; Young Peoples League for Better Government, Macon, Ga., founder, 1947; instructor at Boston University, Boston, Mass., 1952-53, and Georgia Military College, Milledgeville, 1953-54; High Point College, High Point, N.C., 1957-59, began as assistant professor, became associate professor of political science; Southern Methodist University, Dallas, Tex., 1959-65, began as assistant professor, became associate professor of political science; Virginia Polytechnic Institute and State University, Blacksburg, professor of political science, 1965—, chairman of department of political science, 1965-70. Campaign assistant to M. E. Thompson, former governor of Georgia, 1950, 1954. Consultant to U.S. Commission on Civil Rights, National Science Foundation, and to university presses.

MEMBER: American Political Science Association, Southern Political Science Association, American Association of University Professors, American Civil Liberties Union. *Awards, honors:* Social Science Research Council fellowship, 1956-57, Council of Humanities fellow, 1962-63.

WRITINGS: Grass Roots Politics in Georgia, Emory University Research Committee, 1960; (editor) *Mathematical Applications in Political Science*, Volume II, Southern Methodist University Press, 1966, University Press of Virginia, (editor) Volume III, 1967, (editor) Volume IV, 1969, (co-editor) Volume V, 1970, (co-editor) Volume VI, 1972, (co-editor) Volume VII, 1974. Contributor to *Changing Politics of the South*; *Law and Justice*. Writer of booklet on American constitutional system, 1961. Contributor to professional journals.

*   *   *

BERNSTEIN, Merton C(lay) 1923-

PERSONAL: Born March 26, 1923, in New York, N.Y.; son of Benjamin (a lawyer) and Ruth (Kleeblatt) Bernstein; married Joan Brodshaug, December 17, 1955; children: Johanna, Inga, Matthew, Rachel. *Education:* Oberlin College, A.B., 1943; Columbia University, LL.B., 1948. *Politics:* Democrat. *Religion:* Jewish. *Office:* Law School, Ohio State University, Columbus, Ohio.

CAREER: U.S. Senate, Washington, D.C., counsel for Subcommittee on Labor and Labor Management Relations, 1952; legislative assistant to Senator Wayne Morse of Oregon, Washington, D.C., 1953-56; U.S. Senate, special counsel for Subcommittee on Railroad Retirement, 1957-58, University of Nebraska, Lincoln, associate professor of law, 1958-59; Yale University, New Haven, Conn., Walter E. Meyer Research Fellow, 1959-62, lecturer at Law School, 1960-65; Ohio State University, Columbus, professor of law, 1965—. Visiting professor of law, Columbia Law School, 1967-68; member, Ohio Retirement Study Commission, 1972—. Consultant to U.S. Treasury, Department of Labor, Department of Health, Education, and Welfare, and to Twentieth Century Fund. *Military service:* U.S. Army, 1943-45.

MEMBER: International Association for Labor and Social Legislation, National Academy of Arbitrators, American Bar Association (co-chairman, committee on pension, welfare, and related plans, 1964-65, 1966-67), Industrial Relations Research Association. *Awards, honors:* Elizar Wright Award for most outstanding contribution to the literature on insurance in 1965, for *The Future of Private Pensions*.

WRITINGS: The Future of Private Pensions, Free Press, 1964; *Private Dispute Settlement: Cases and Materials on Arbitration*, Free Press, 1969. Contributor to *New Republic, Nation, Challenge*, law reviews, and other periodicals.

WORK IN PROGRESS: A book on disability in the U.S.

*   *   *

BERRILL, Jacquelyn (Batsel) 1905-

PERSONAL: Born November 5, 1905, in South Carrollton, Ky.; daughter of Edmond and Mary Batsel; married Norman John Berrill (a professor of zoology), June 3, 1939; children: Peggy, Elsilyn, Michael. *Education:* University of Toledo, A.B., 1927; attended New York University. *Home:* 410 Swarthmore Ave., Swarthmore, Pa. 19081.

CAREER: Young Women's Christian Association, Jackson, Mich., social worker, 1927-39; full-time writer, 1939—.

WRITINGS—All published by Dodd: Wonders of the Seashore, 1951, *Wonders of the Woodland*, 1953, *Wonders of Strange Nurseries*, 1954, *Wonders of the Wild*, 1955, *Albert Schweitzer: Man of Mercy*, 1956, (with N. J. Berrill) *1001 Questions Answered about the Seashore*, 1957, *Wonders of the Antarctic*, 1958, *Wonders of the Arctic*, 1959,

Wonders of the Ponds and Fields at Night, 1962, *Wonders of the Woods and Desert at Night*, 1963, *Wonders of the Monkey World*, 1967; *Wonders of Animal Nurseries*, 1968; *Wonders of the World of Wolves*, 1970.

WORK IN PROGRESS: A book about animals in danger.

AVOCATIONAL INTERESTS: Art, jewelry making, ceramics, painting, and sewing.

*   *   *

BERRILL, N(orman) J(ohn)   1903-

PERSONAL: Born April 28, 1903, in Bristol, England; son of Percy and Kate Berrill; married Jacquelyn Batsel (a writer and illustrator), June 3, 1939; children: Peggy, Elsilyn, Michael. *Education:* Bristol University, B.Sc., 1924; University of London, Ph.D., 1929, D.Sc., 1931. *Home:* 410 Swarthmore Ave., Swarthmore, Pa. 19081.

CAREER: McGill University, Montreal, Quebec, professor of zoology, 1928-65; University of Hawaii, Honolulu, Guggenheim fellow, 1964-65; Swarthmore College, Swarthmore, Pa., lecturer in zoology, 1967—. *Member:* Royal Society of London, Royal Society of Canada, American Society of Zoologists, Society for Developmental Biology. *Awards, honors:* Governor-General of Canada Gold Medal for Creative Nonfiction, 1953, 1955; LL.D., University of Windsor, 1966; D.Sc., University of British Columbia, 1972, and from McGill University, 1973.

WRITINGS: The Living Tide, Dodd, 1951; *Journey into Wonder*, Dodd, 1952; *Sex and the Nature of Things*, Dodd, 1953; *Man's Emerging Mind*, Dodd, 1955; *Origin of Vertebrates*, Oxford University Press, 1955; (with wife, Jacquelyn Berrill) *1001 Questions Answered about the Seashore*, Dodd, 1957; *You and the Universe*, Dodd, 1958; *Growth, Development and Pattern*, W. H. Freeman, 1961; *World's Without End*, Macmillan, 1964; *Inherit the Earth*, Dodd, 1966; *Biology in Action*, Dodd, 1966; *Life of the Oceans*, McGraw, 1967; *The Person in the Womb*, Dodd, 1968; (with son, Michael Berrill) *Life of the Sea Islands*, McGraw, 1969; *Developmental Biology*, McGraw, 1971. Contributor of articles to magazines and scientific journals.

WORK IN PROGRESS: Research and books on aspects of developmental biology.

SIDELIGHTS: Berrill told *CA* that he is "a biologist primarily concerned with the study of the phenomena and problems of development and also with the nature of man on earth." He is interested in "any marine coastline where there is a marine biological laboratory."

*   *   *

BERRY, Wallace Taft   1928-

PERSONAL: Born January 10, 1928, in La Crosse, Wis.; son of Edward Carl and Louise (George) Berry; married Maxine Metzner (a painter), May 11, 1954. *Education:* University of Southern California, B.Mus., 1949, Ph.D., 1956; studied at National Conservatory of Music, Paris, France, 1953-54. *Religion:* None. *Office:* School of Music, University of Michigan, Ann Arbor, Mich. 48105.

CAREER: University of Southern California, Los Angeles, lecturer in music, 1956-57; University of Michigan, Ann Arbor, instructor, 1957-60, assistant professor, 1960-63, associate professor, 1963-66, professor of music, 1966—, director of music honors program, 1960-68, chairman of department of music theory, 1968-74. Recital pianist and composer. *Military service:* U.S. Army, 1954-56. *Member:*

American Society of Composers, Authors and Publishers, American Association of University Professors. *Awards, honors:* University of Michigan Distinguished Faculty Award, 1963; American Society of Composers, Authors and Publishers Composer Award, 1966, and 1974; University of Southern California, Outstanding Music Alumnus, 1973.

WRITINGS: Form in Music, Prentice-Hall, 1966; (with E. Chudacoff) *Eighteenth Century Imitative Counterpoint: Music for Analysis*, Appleton, 1969; *Structural Functions in Music*, Prentice-Hall, 1975.

Musical works: "Duo for Violin and Piano," Carl Fischer, 1964; "Five Pieces for Small Orchestra," Carl Fischer, 1965; "Two Canons for Two Clarinets," Elkan-Vogel, 1966; "Eight 20th-Century Miniatures for Piano," Carl Fischer, 1967; "String Quartet No. 2," Elkan-Vogel, 1967; "Divertimento for Wind Quintet, Piano, and Percussion," Elkan-Vogel, 1967. Recording of "String Quartet No. 2," "Duo for Flute and Piano," "Canto Lirico for Viola and Piano," Composers Recordings, Inc., 1972.

WORK IN PROGRESS: With E. Chudacoff, *Eighteenth-Century Imitative Counterpoint: Music for Analysis*, for Appleton, 1968; *Studies in Musical Analysis*, for Prentice-Hall, completion expected in 1969.

SIDELIGHTS: Berry speaks French and Italian, some German. He has traveled extensively in Europe, 1953-54, 1960, 1963-64. *Avocational interests:* Archery, horseback riding, swimming, cooking.

*   *   *

BERTHOUD, Jacques (Alexandre)   1935-

PERSONAL: Surname is pronounced Bear-too; born March 1, 1935, in St. Imier, Switzerland; son of Alexandre Leon (a parson and missionary) and Madeleine (Bourquin) Berthoud; married Astrid Irene Titlestad (an art teacher), January 29, 1958; children: Mireille Christine, Josephine Madeleine, Tristan Alexandre. *Education:* University of the Witwatersrand, B.A., 1955; University of Johannesburg, B.A. (honors in comparative literature), 1958. *Politics:* Liberal. *Religion:* Protestant. *Office:* Department of English, University of Southampton, Southampton, England.

CAREER: Junior lecturer in English in Durban, South Africa, 1957, and Johannesburg, South Africa, 1958-59; University of Pretoria, Pretoria, South Africa, lecturer in English, 1960; University of Natal, Pietermaritzburg, lecturer in English literature, 1961-67; University of Southampton, Southampton, England, permanent lecturer in English, 1967—. Provincial examiner in English (for matriculation).

WRITINGS: (With C. van Heyningen) *Uys Krige*, Twayne, 1966; (editor) *The Sole Function*, University of Natal Press, 1969. Contributor of essays on literature and history to local periodicals.

WORK IN PROGRESS: Doctoral thesis on medieval literature in England, France, and Italy.

SIDELIGHTS: Berthoud told *CA* that he is "very much involved in opposing the racial and arbitrary government of South Africa." He acts in and directs dramatic productions, and is interested in music criticism.†

*   *   *

BERTOCCI, Peter A(nthony)   1910-

PERSONAL: Surname is pronounced Bur-to-chi; born

May 13, 1910, in Elena, Italy; son of Gaetano (a laborer) and Annunziata (Guglietta) Bertocci; married Lucy Soldani; children: Peter John, Stephen Paul, Richard Anthony. *Education:* Boston University, A.B., 1931, Ph.D., 1935; Harvard University, A.M., 1932; Cambridge University, research scholar, 1934-35. *Politics:* Democrat. *Religion:* Protestant. *Home:* 243 Park Ave., Arlington, Mass. 02174. *Office:* Department of Philosophy, Boston University, Boston, Mass.

CAREER: Bates College, Lewiston, Me., instructor, 1935-39, assistant professor of philosophy and psychology, 1939-44; Boston University, Boston, Mass., professor, 1944—, Borden Parker Bowne Professor of Philosophy, 1953—. *Member:* American Philosophical Association, Metaphysical Society of America (president, 1963-64), American Theological Society (president, 1963-64), American Psychological Association (fellow), American Academy of Religion, Philosophy of Education Society, American Association of University Professors, Phi Beta Kappa. *Awards, honors:* Fulbright research scholar in Italy, 1950-51, and India, 1960-61; Guggenheim fellowship, 1967-68.

WRITINGS: Empirical Argument for God in Late British Thought, Harvard University Press, 1938; *The Human Venture in Sex, Love, and Marriage*, Association Press, 1949; *Introduction to the Philosophy of Religion*, Prentice-Hall, 1951; *Free Will, Responsibility, and Grace*, Abingdon, 1957; *Religion as Creative Insecurity*, Greenwood, 1958; (editor with J. E. Newhall) Edgar S. Brightman, *Person and Reality*, Ronald, 1958; (with R. M. Millard) *Personality and the Good: Psychological and Ethical Perspectives*, McKay, 1963; *Sex, Love, and the Person*, Sheed, 1967; *Why Believe in God?*, Association Press, 1968; *The Person God Is*, Humanities Press, 1970; *Is God for Real?*, Nelson, 1971; (editor) *Mid-Twentieth Century American Philosophy: Personal Statements*, Humanities Press, 1974. Contributor to *Encyclopedia of Religion* and *Dictionary of Psychology*.

WORK IN PROGRESS: Three books, *Philosophy of Personality, Man, Reason, and God*, and *Philosophy of Education*.

AVOCATIONAL INTERESTS: Gardening and building.

*   *   *

BEST, John Wesley 1909-

PERSONAL: Born July 3, 1909, in Chicago, Ill.; son of John and Edith M. (Richards) Best; married Solveig Ager; children: John W., Jr. *Education:* Lawrence College, Appleton, Wis., A.B., 1932; University of Wisconsin, M.A., 1946, Ph.D., 1948. *Politics:* Democrat. *Religion:* Congregational. *Home:* 480 West Hampton Dr., Indianapolis, Ind. 46208.

CAREER: Butler University, Indianapolis, Ind., 1948—, professor of education, 1954—. Chairman of Selective Service Board 221. Member of board of Civic Ballet Society, Young Audiences, Inc., and Clowes Memorial Hall. *Military service:* U.S. Army, 1943-46; became technical sergeant. *Member:* American Educational Research Association, Comparative Education Society, Phi Delta Kappa, Sigma Phi Epsilon, Wisconsin Alumni Club (board). *Awards, honors:* Baxter Foundation Award ($500) for distinguished teaching, 1954, 1955, 1956.

WRITINGS: Research in Education, Prentice-Hall, 1959, 2nd edition, 1970. Contributor to professional journals.

WORK IN PROGRESS: Research on the religious attitudes of teachers.

SIDELIGHTS: Research in Education was published in a Far Eastern edition in New Delhi, 1963, and translated for publication in Spain. *Avocational interests:* Foreign travel, collecting antiques, photography, and tape recording.

*   *   *

BETTMANN, Otto Ludwig 1903-

PERSONAL: Born October 15, 1903, in Leipzig, Germany; came to United States, 1935; naturalized, 1939; son of Hans (an orthopedic surgeon) and Charlotte (Frank) Bettmann; married Anne Clemens Gray, March 4, 1938. *Education:* University of Leipzig, Ph.D., 1927, M.S. in L.S., 1932. *Politics:* Democrat. *Religion:* Jewish. *Home:* 2800 S. Ocean Blvd., Boca Raton, Fla. 33432. *Office:* The Bettmann Archive, Inc., 136 East 57th St., New York, N.Y. 10022.

CAREER: C. F. Peters Co. (music publishers), Leipzig, Germany, associate editor, 1927-28; Axel Juncker Publishers, Berlin, Germany, editor, 1928-30; State Art Library, Berlin, Germany, curator of rare books, 1930-33; The Bettmann Archive, Inc. (collection of more than one million prints and photographs on the history of civilization), New York, N.Y., founder and director, 1941—. Developer of picture filing systems; director of Bettmann Panopticon Exhibit, 1963. *Member:* American Federation of Arts, American Institute of Graphic Art, Special Libraries Association, French Institute.

WRITINGS: (With Bellamy Partridge) *As We Were: Family Life in America, 1850-1900*, Whittlesey House, 1946; (with John Durant) *A Pictorial History of American Sports*, A. S. Barnes, 1952; *A Pictorial History of Medicine*, C. C Thomas, 1956; (with Van Wyck Brooks) *Our Literary Heritage*, Dutton, 1956; (with Paul H. Lang) *A Pictorial History of Music*, Norton, 1960; *Bettmann Portable Archive*, Picture House Press, 1966; *The Good Old Days: They Were Terrible*, Random House, 1974. Picture editor, *The New Pictorial Encyclopedia of the World*, 1954.

SIDELIGHTS: The nucleus of Bettmann's famous picture library was a personal collection of 25,000 art, music, and medicine prints that accompanied him when he left Nazi Germany. The expanded collection, now filed under more than two thousand categories, is used as a research source by publishers, advertising agencies, television producers, and industry. *Avocational interests:* Music.

BIOGRAPHICAL/CRITICAL SOURCES: Time, May 28, 1956; *Saturday Review*, February 11, 1961; *New York World-Telegram*, March 4, 1961; *Publishers' Weekly*, September 25, 1961.

*   *   *

BHAGWATI, Jagdish N. 1934-

PERSONAL: Born July 26, 1934, in Bombay, India; son of Natwarlal H. (a judge of the Supreme Court of India) and Saraswati (Amin) Bhagwati. *Education:* Sydenham College, Bombay University, B.Com., 1954; St. John's College, Cambridge, M.A., 1956; graduate study at Massachusetts Institute of Technology, 1956-57, Ph.D., 1967; graduate study at Nuffield College, Oxford, 1957-59. *Office:* Department of Economics, Massachusetts Institute of Technology, Cambridge, Mass.

CAREER: Oxford University, Oxford, England, research fellow at Nuffield College, 1959-61; Indian Statistical Institute, Delhi, India, professor of economics, 1961-63; Delhi University, School of Economics, Delhi, India, professor of international trade, 1963-67; Massachusetts Institute of Technology, Cambridge, professor of economics, 1967—. Columbia University, New York, N.Y., visiting professor of economics, 1966-67. Ford research professor, University of California, Berkeley, 1973-74. Frank Graham lecturer, Princeton University, 1967. Consultant to Turkish State Planning Organization, 1964, and to Indian Ministry of Commerce and Ministry of Finance, at various periods, 1964—; member of expert groups on international trade, Economic Commission for Asia and the Far East, 1964, and United Nations Conference on Trade and Development, 1966.

WRITINGS: (Contributor) Roy Harrod, editor, *International Trade Theory in a Developing World*, Macmillan, 1963; (contributor) Baldwin and others, editors, *Trade, Growth and the Balance of Payments*, Rand McNally, 1965; (contributor) *Surveys in Economic Theory*, Volume III, *Growth and Development*, Macmillan, for American Economic Association and Royal Economic Society, 1965; *The Economics of Underdeveloped Countries*, McGraw, 1966; (editor) *International Trade*, Penguin, 1969; (with Padma Desai) *India: Planning for Industrialization*, Oxford University Press, 1970; *Trade, Tariffs, and Growth*, M.I.T. Press, 1971; (editor) *Economics and World Order*, Macmillan, 1972. Editor, *Journal of International Economics*. Member of editorial board, *World Development* and *Journal of Development Economics*. Contributor of lesser sections to other books.

AVOCATIONAL INTERESTS: Indian classical music.

* * *

BIDDLE, Bruce J(esse) 1928-

PERSONAL: Born December 30, 1928, in Ossining, N.Y.; son of William Wishart (an author and consultant in community development) and Loureide Jeannette (Cobb) Biddle; married Ellen Horgan (a sociologist), March 28, 1954; children: David Charles, William Jesse, Jennifer Loureide. *Education:* Antioch College, A.B., 1951; University of North Carolina, graduate study, 1950-51; University of Michigan, Ph.D., 1957. *Home:* 810 Edgewood, Columbia, Mo. *Office:* Center for Research in Social Behavior, University of Missouri, Columbia, Mo.

CAREER: Wayne State University, Detroit, Mich., research associate in education, 1953, 1956-57; University of Kentucky, Lexington, assistant professor of sociology, 1957-58; University of Kansas City (now University of Missouri at Kansas City), associate professor of education, 1958-60; University of Missouri, Columbia, associate professor of psychology and sociology, 1960-66, professor, and director of Center for Research in Social Behavior, 1966—. Visiting associate professor at University of Queensland, Brisbane, Australia, 1965. Member of Missouri Science Advisory Committee; consultant to National Opinion Research Center, U.S. Office of Education, Bank Street College of Education, and other institutions. *Military service:* U.S. Army, 1954-56. *Member:* American Psychological Association, American Sociological Association, American Educational Research Association, Society for the Psychological Study of Social Issues, Midwestern Psychological Association, Midwestern Sociological Society.

WRITINGS: (Editor with W. J. Ellena) *Contemporary Research on Teacher Effectiveness*, Holt, 1964; (editor with E. J. Thomas) *Role Theory: Concepts and Research*, Wiley, 1966; (editor with P. H. Rossi) *The New Media: Their Impact on Education and Society*, Aldine, 1966;

(with M. J. Dunkin) *The Study of Teaching*, Holt, 1974. Writer of research reports and monographs. Contributor of articles to professional journals.

WORK IN PROGRESS: A comparative study of the role of the teacher in British, Canadian, Australian, New Zealand, and American schools; a study of classroom interaction using videotapes of actual classrooms; a formal analysis of role theory concepts and propositions.

AVOCATIONAL INTERESTS: Tennis and other sports; music, particularly the cello; electronics, and flying.

* * *

BIEBER, Margarete 1879-

PERSONAL: Surname is pronounced *Bee*-ber; born July 31, 1879, in Schoenau, in Westprussia (now Poland); came to United States in 1934 "because of Hitler regime"; naturalized in 1940; daughter of Jacob (an industrialist) and Vally (Bukofzer) Bieber; children: (adopted) Ingeborg Christine (Mrs. William S. Sachs). *Education:* Berlin University, 1901-1904; Bonn University, Ph.D., 1907. *Politics:* "I vote for the best qualified person." *Religion:* "Old Catholic—Protestant Episcopal." *Home:* 605 West 113th St., Apt. 33, New York 25, N.Y.

CAREER: German Archaeological Institute, Athens, Greece, assistant, 1910; assistant in museum in Kassel, Germany, 1913; Archaeological Institute, University of Berlin, Berlin, Germany, assistant, 1914; University of Giessen, Giessen, Germany, lecturer, 1919, associate professor of archaeology, 1923-31, professor and director of seminar, 1931-33; Somerville College, Oxford, England, honorary fellow, 1933-34; Barnard College, New York, N.Y., lecturer, 1934-36; Columbia University, New York, N.Y., associate professor of fine arts and archaeology, 1936-48, retired; Princeton University, Princeton, N.J., member of department of art, 1949-51; Institute of General Studies, Columbia University, New York, N.Y., 1948-56; Associate University Seminars, department of classical civilization, 1960-74. *Member:* American Academy of Arts and Sciences (fellow), American Archaeological Society, German Archaeological Institute. *Awards, honors:* American Association of University Women, international fellowship, 1931-32; D.Litt., Columbia University, 1954; Honorary Senator, Giessen University, 1959; American Philosophical Society award; Red Cross medal; National Endowment for the Humanities fellowship, 1971.

WRITINGS: Skenika, 75., Winckelmanns-Programm, 1915; *Katalog der Skulpturen in Kassel*, Marburg, 1916; *Die Denkmaeler zum Theaterwesen im Altertum*, Walter de Gruyter, 1920; *Griechische Kleidung*, Walter de Gruyter, 1928; *Entwicklungsgeschichte der griechischen Tracht*, Gebr. Mann, 1934, revised edition, 1966; *The History of the Greek and Roman Theatre*, Princeton University Press, 1939, revised edition, 1961; *Laocoon: The Influence of the Group since Its Rediscovery*, Columbia University Press, 1942, revised edition, Wayne State University Press, 1966; (editor) *German Readings in the History and Theory of Fine Arts*, Part one, part one, H. Bittner, 1946, 3rd edition published as *A Short Survey of Greek and Roman Art for Students of German and Fine Arts*, 1958; *The Sculpture of the Hellenistic Age*, Columbia University Press, 1955, revised edition, 1961; *A Bronze Statuette in Cincinnati and its Place in the History of the Asklepios Type*, 1957; *Roman Men in Greek Himation*, Proceedings of American Philosophical Society, 1959; *The Copies of the Herculaneum Women*, American Philosophical Society, 1962; *The*

Greek and Roman Portraits of Alexander the Great, Argonaut, 1964; *Graeco-Roman Copies*, New York University Press, 1973; *Copies of Greek and Roman Art*, New York University Press, 1975; *The History of Greek, Etruscan, and Roman Clothing*, Thames and Hudson, 1975. Contributor to *American Journal of Archaeology*, *American Journal of Philology*, *Classical World*, and memorial volumes.

WORK IN PROGRESS: Contributions to the history of copying.

SIDELIGHTS: Margarete Bieber has traveled in Italy, Greece, Turkey, England, France, Germany, and the United States. Competent in English, German, French, Italian, Greek, and Latin. *Avocational interests:* Theater, clothing, and coins.

BIOGRAPHICAL/CRITICAL SOURCES: New York Times, May 22, 1971.

* * *

BIERMAN, Harold, Jr. 1924-

PERSONAL: Born June 17, 1924, in New York, N.Y.; son of Harold and Frieda (Zelezney) Bierman; married Florence Kelso, February 2, 1952; children: James Landon, Harold Scott, Donald Bruce, Jonathan David. *Education:* U. S. Naval Academy, B.S., 1945; University of Michigan, M.B.A., 1949, Ph.D., 1955. *Home:* 109 Kay St., Ithaca, N.Y. 14850. *Office:* Graduate School of Business Administration, Cornell University, Ithaca, N.Y. 14850.

CAREER: Instructor at Louisiana State University, Baton Rouge, 1950-51, and University of Michigan, Ann Arbor, 1953-55; University of Chicago, Chicago, Ill., assistant professor, 1955-56; Cornell University, Graduate School of Business Administration, Ithaca, N.Y., professor of accounting and managerial economics, 1956-69, Nicholas H. Noyes Professor of Business Administration, 1969—. Consultant to Ford Foundation. *Military service:* U.S. Navy, 1942-47, 1951-53; became lieutenant. *Member:* American Accounting Association, American Finance Association, Financial Management Association.

WRITINGS: Managerial Accounting, Macmillan, 1958, published as *Financial and Managerial Accounting*, 1963; (with Seymour Smidt) *The Capital Budgeting Decision*, Macmillan, 1960, 3rd edition, 1971; (with Lawrence Fouraker and Robert Jaedicke) *Quantitative Analysis for Business Decisions*, Irwin, 1961, 4th edition (with Charles P. Bonini and Warren H. Houseman), 1973; (with Alan K. McAdams) *Management Decisions for Cash and Marketable Securities*, Cornell University, 1962; *Topics in Cost Accounting and Decisions*, McGraw, 1962; *Financial Accounting Theory*, Macmillan, 1965.

(With Allan R. Drebin) *Financial Accounting: An Introduction*, Macmillan, 1968, 2nd edition, 1972; (with Drebin) *Managerial Accounting: An Introduction*, Macmillan, 1968, 2nd edition, 1972; (with Houseman and Richard R. West) *Financial Policy Decisions*, Macmillan, 1970; (with Thomas R. Dyckman) *Managerial Cost Accounting*, Macmillan, 1971; (with Jerome E. Hass) *An Introduction to Managerial Finance*, Norton, 1973. Contributor to professional journals.†

* * *

BIEZANEK, Anne C(ampbell) 1927-

PERSONAL: Born October 25, 1927, in London, England; daughter of Benjamin (an engineer) and Leslie (Campbell) Greene; married Jan Biezanek (a seaman), July 16, 1949; (divorced, 1972); married Frank Perree, November 9, 1972; children: (first marriage) Benedict, Nicholas, Victoria, Dominic, Stephen, Alexander, Lucy. *Education:* University of Aberdeen, B.Sc., M.B., and Ch.B., 1951. *Religion:* Roman Catholic. *Home:* "Cluny," Manor Rd., Wallasey, Cheshire, England. *Agent:* Curtis Brown Ltd., 1 Craven Hill, London W2 3EW, England.

CAREER: House surgeon at Kirkcaldy General Hospital, Kirkcaldy, Scotland, 1952, at Royal Buckinghamshire Hospital, Aylesbury, England, 1953; Stratheden Mental Hospital, Fifeshire, Scotland, senior house officer, 1953-55; Rainhill Hospital, Liverpool, England, registrar, 1955-58; Clinic St. Martin de Porres, Wallasey, Cheshire, England, medical director, 1963—; British National Health Service, general practitioner, Wallasey, Cheshire, England, 1965—.

WRITINGS: All Things New, Peter Smith, 1964.

WORK IN PROGRESS: Research on the relationship of family planning services to British National Health Service, and the use of interception in general practice.

BIOGRAPHICAL/CRITICAL SOURCES: Look, August 8, 1965.

* * *

BINGLEY, Clive (Hamilton) 1936-

PERSONAL: Born April 2, 1936, in South Africa; son of Alexander Hamilton and Stella (Hanscomb) Bingley; married Anne Chichester-Constable (a publishing director), March 16, 1963; children: Miranda, Kate, Zillah. *Education:* Oxford University, M.A. (honors), 1962. *Politics:* "Interested amateur!" *Home:* 16 Pembridge Rd., London W.11, England.

CAREER: Various executive positions in book and journal publishing, 1958-65, including period as editor of British trade journal, *Publisher*; Clive Bingley Ltd. (book publishers), London, England, founder and director, 1965—.

WRITINGS: Book Publishing Practice, Archon Books, 1966; (contributor) R. L. Collison, editor, *Progress in Library Science*, Butterworth & Co., 1966; *The Business of Book Publishing*, Pergamon, 1972. Editor, *New Library World*, 1971—. Occasional contributor to library periodicals.

SIDELIGHTS: Bingley told *CA:* "Private interests include classical music, food and wine, and a mad English game called cricket. If I confessed to an admiration for the 'image' of the U.S.A. we receive here in England it might be construed as flattery, but is nevertheless the case. Personal ambitions: health, wealth, travel."

* * *

BIRD, Caroline 1915-

PERSONAL: Born April 15, 1915, in New York, N.Y.; daughter of Hobart S. (a lawyer) and Ida (Brattrud) Bird; married Edward A. Menuez, June 8, 1934 (divorced, 1945); married John Thomas Mahoney (a writer), 1957; children: (first marriage) Carol (Mrs. John Paul Barach); (second marriage) John Thomas, Jr. *Education:* Attended Vassar College, 1931-34; University of Toledo, B.A., 1938; University of Wisconsin–Madison, M.A., 1939. *Politics:* Democrat. *Religion:* Protestant. *Home:* 31 Sunrise Lane, Poughkeepsie, N.Y. 12603; and 60 Gramercy Park, New York, N.Y. 10010.

CAREER: Newsweek, New York, N.Y., researcher, 1942-

43; *New York Journal of Commerce*, New York, N.Y., desk editor, 1943-44; *Fortune*, New York, N.Y., researcher, 1944-46; Dudley-Anderson-Yutzy (public relations firm), New York, N.Y., staff writer, 1947-68; Russell Sage College, Troy, N.Y., Froman Distinguished Professor, 1972-73. *Member:* Society of Magazine Writers (secretary, 1953), American Sociological Association, Women in Communications, Women's Equity Action League, National Organization for Women.

WRITINGS—All published by McKay: *The Invisible Scar*, 1966; (with Sara Welles Briller) *Born Female*, 1968, revised edition, 1970; *The Crowding Syndrome*, 1972; *Everything a Woman Needs to Know to Get Paid What She's Worth*, 1973; *The Case Against College*, 1975; *Enterprising Women*, W. W. Norton, in press. Contributor to *New York*, *Family Circle*, *Woman's Day*, *Esquire*, *Reader's Digest*, and other magazines.

WORK IN PROGRESS: A book, *Enterprising Women;* writing on women in education and jobs, population, and economic affairs.

SIDELIGHTS: Reviewing *Born Female*, Ann Birstein describes Caroline Bird as a commentator who is "committed and convincing, proving point by point, patiently and painstakingly, with footnotes and heavy documentation, in category after category . . . that women are indeed kept down on the job, and that such discrimination is not only inherently ridiculous but immoral." Gloria Steinem believes that "'Born Female' is enough to convince anyone literate, from male chauvinist to female Uncle Tom, that the superstition and restrictive prejudices on which our system of work is built are depriving the country of nearly half its talent. . . . Unlike most books of its kind, 'Born Female' isn't fed by some subterranean Isostatic Theory that men's position must go down as women's goes up. Her proposals for equality are meant to liberate everyone."

* * *

BIRMINGHAM, David (Bevis) 1938-

PERSONAL: Born June 6, 1938, in Dorking, England; son of Walter Barr (an economist) and Norah (Langford) Birmingham; married Elizabeth Taylor, February 17, 1962; children: Robert, Stephen. *Education:* College Henchoz, Switzerland, certificate, 1954; University of Ghana, B.A. (honors in history), 1961; University of London, Ph.D., 1964. *Politics:* Labour. *Religion:* Quaker. *Home:* 45 Westcombe Park Rd., London S.E.3, England.

CAREER: University of Ghana, Legon, Accra, lecturer in history, 1964-66; University of London, London, England, lecturer in history, 1966—.

WRITINGS: The Portuguese Conquest of Angola, Oxford University Press, 1965; *Trade and Conflict in Angola*, Clarendon, 1966; (editor with Richard Gray) *Pre-Colonial African Trade*, Oxford University Press, 1970.

WORK IN PROGRESS: Research into the pre-colonial history of Central Africa (Zaire, Angola, and Zambia), and into the late-colonial and post-colonial history of Portuguese-speaking Africa.

SIDELIGHTS: Birmingham is fluent in German, French, and Portuguese.

* * *

BIRMINGHAM, F(rederic) A(lexander) 1911-

PERSONAL: Born November 13, 1911, in New York, N.Y.; son of John Francis and Louise (Westher) Birmingham; married Frances Atherton, November 8, 1941. *Education:* Dartmouth College, B.A., 1933. *Religion:* Episcopalian. *Home:* 801 Olive St., Scranton, Pa. 18500. *Agent:* Sterling Lord Agency, 75 East 55th St., New York, N.Y. 10022. *Office: Saturday Evening Post*, 1100 Waterway Blvd., Indianapolis, Ind. 46202.

CAREER: Apparel Arts (magazine), Eastern editor, 1935-36, consulting editor, 1941—; *Time*, New York, N.Y., editorial staff, 1936-37; author of cartoon-essay feature for Bell Syndicate and North American Newspaper Alliance, 1936-37; Ogden-Watney (publishers), New York, N.Y., editor, 1938-39; *Esquire*, New York, N.Y., sales promotion manager, 1941-43, managing editor, 1946-53, editor-in-chief, 1953-57; *Gentleman's Quarterly*, New York, N.Y., executive editor, 1947-57; free-lance writer and lecturer, 1957-62; Fawcett Publications, Inc., New York, N.Y., editor, 1962-65; *Reader's Digest*, Pleasantville, N.Y., special project editor, 1966-67; Status-Diplomat Magazines, New York, N.Y., editorial director, 1967-68; editor, *Status Magazine*, 1968-71; *Saturday Evening Post*, Indianapolis, Ind., managing editor, 1971—. Senior editor, U.S. Office of War Information, 1942-43. *Military service:* U.S. Naval Reserve, 1943-46; became lieutenant commander. *Member:* Authors League, Overseas Press Club, Sigma Phi Epsilon, Alpha Iota Epsilon, Sigma Delta Phi.

WRITINGS: (Editor) *The Esquire Book of Etiquette*, Lippincott, 1953; (editor) *The Girls from Esquire*, Random House, 1953; *It Was Fun While It Lasted*, Lippincott, 1956; (editor and contributor) *The Esquire Drink Book*, Harper, 1956; (editor and contributor) *The Esquire Fashion Book*, Harper, 1957; *The Writer's Craft*, Hawthorn, 1958; *The Ivy League Today*, Crowell, 1961; *The Cookbook for Men*, Harper, 1961; *How to Succeed at Touch Football*, Harper, 1962; (with wife, Frances Birmingham) *The Wedding Book*, Harper, 1964. Contributor of articles and short stories to magazines and newspapers in United States and abroad.

AVOCATIONAL INTERESTS: Music, painting, sports.†

* * *

BIRMINGHAM, Frances A(therton) 1920-

PERSONAL: Born June 14, 1920, in Scranton, Pa.; daughter of Fred Bicknell (a broker) and Ruth (Lansing) Atherton; married Frederic A. Birmingham (an editor-author), November 8, 1941. *Education:* Attended Scranton Country Day School and Knox School, Copperstown, N.Y. *Religion:* Episcopalian. *Home:* 801 Olive Street, Scranton, Pa. 18500. *Agent:* The Sterling Lord Agency, 75 East 55th St., New York, N.Y. 10022.

CAREER: Station WTVU-TV, Scranton, Pa., woman's program director, 1953-55. Lecturer under management of W. Colston Leigh Agency, 1960-61. *Member:* Daughters of the American Revolution, Junior League (charter member, Scranton chapter; sustaining member, Westchester-on-Hudson chapter). *Awards, honors:* Cross of Aragon for nursing activities during World War II.

WRITINGS: House Within, Chevy Chase Press, 1947; *Mrs. Winterbottom's Surprise*, Cheshire, 1948; (with husband, F. A. Birmingham) *The Wedding Book*, Harper, 1964. Author of television plays and scripts.

AVOCATIONAL INTERESTS: Gardening, music, history of education.†

BIRMINGHAM, Walter (Barr) 1913-

PERSONAL: Born January 4, 1913, in Ferozepore, India; son of Walter Robert (a soldier) and Helen (Barr) Birmingham; married Maisie Jukes, December 17, 1948; children: David, Deirdre (Mrs. Paul Battersby), Duncan, Richard, Karen. *Education:* Attended Royal Liberty School, Romford, England; London School of Economics and Political Science, London, B.Sc., 1937. *Religion:* Quaker. *Office:* Department of Economics, University of Cape Coast, Cape Coast, Ghana.

CAREER: In British civil service, 1929-42; University of Wales, Cardiff, lecturer, 1943-51; University of Ghana, Legon, Accra, senior lecturer in economics, 1952-60; University of Leicester, Leicester, England, senior lecturer in economics, 1961-64; Toynbee Hall, London, England, warden, 1964-72; University of Cape Coast, Cape Coast, Ghana, professor of economics, 1972—. Visiting professor, Roosevelt University, Chicago, Ill., 1948-49, 1958.

WRITINGS: Introduction to Economics, Penguin, 1955, 2nd edition, 1962, 2nd edition, revised, published as *Economics: An Introduction*, Allen & Unwin, 1966; (editor with Alec G. Ford and contributor) *Planning and Growth in Rich and Poor Countries*, Allen & Unwin, 1966; (editor with others) *Study of Contemporary Ghana*, Allen & Unwin, Volume I, 1966, Volume II, 1967; *Poverty and Development*, University of Cape Coast, 1974.

* * *

BIRNE, Henry 1921-

PERSONAL: Born September 1, 1921, in New York, N.Y.; son of Irving and Flo (Furman) Birne; married Anne Marie Marcotte, June 15, 1950; children: Jacques, Leslie. *Education:* University of Paris, D.V.M.; Columbia University, M.P.H. *Residence:* Brooklyn, N.Y. *Agent:* McIntosh & Otis, Inc., 18 East 41st St., New York, N.Y. 10017.

CAREER: Seaman and student, 1946-50; worked as epidemiologist in Mexico, 1950-52; full-time writer, 1953—.

WRITINGS: Wait for the New Grass, St. Martins, 1961.

WORK IN PROGRESS: Journey to the King; Cricket in the Snow.

SIDELIGHTS: Birne speaks French and Spanish.†

* * *

BIRREN, James E(mmett) 1918-

PERSONAL: Born April 4, 1918, in Chicago, Ill.; son of August (a businessman) and Elisie F. (Kolkmann) Birren; married Elizabeth Solomon, December 12, 1942; children: Barbara Ann, Jeffrey Emmett, Bruce William. *Education:* Chicago Teachers College (now Chicago State University), B.Ed., 1941; Northwestern University, M.A., 1942, Ph.D., 1947. *Office:* Rossmoor-Cortese Institute, University of Southern California, Los Angeles, Calif. 90007.

CAREER: National Institutes of Health, Bethesda, Md., research psychologist, 1947-51, research psychologist, National Institute of Mental Health, 1951-53, chief of section on aging, National Institute of Mental Health, 1953-64, director of aging program, National Institute of Child Health and Human Development, 1964-65; University of Southern California, Los Angeles, director of Institute for the Study of Retirement and Aging, and professor of psychology, 1965—. *Military service:* U.S. Naval Reserve, 1943-46; became lieutenant. *Member:* American Associa-

tion for the Advancement of Science, American Educational Research Association, American Geriatrics Society, American Physiological Society, American Psychological Association (fellow), Gerontological Society (fellow). *Awards, honors:* Ciba Foundation award, 1956, for research on aging; Stratton Award, 1962; U.S. Public Health Service medal for meritorious service, 1965.

WRITINGS: (Editor) *Handbook of Aging and the Individual: Psychological and Biological Aspects*, University of Chicago Press, 1959; (editor with A. T. Welford) *The Process of Aging in the Nervous System*, C. C Thomas, 1959; (editor) *Human Aging: A Biological and Behavioral Study*, U.S. Public Health Service, 1963; *The Psychology of Aging*, Prentice-Hall, 1964; (editor) *Relations of Development and Aging*, C. C Thomas, 1964; (co-editor) *Behavior, Aging and the Nervous System*, C. C Thomas, 1964; (editor) *Decision Making and Age*, S. Karger, 1969.†

* * *

BIRSTEIN, Ann

PERSONAL: Born in New York, N.Y.; daughter of Bernard (a rabbi) and Clara (Gordon) Birstein; married Alfred Kazin (an author), June 26, 1952; children: Cathrael. *Education:* Queens College (now Queens College of the City University of New York), B.A., 1948. *Home:* 440 West End Ave., New York, N.Y. 10024. *Agent:* Lynn Nesbit, International Famous Agency, 1301 Avenue of the Americas, New York, N.Y. 10019.

CAREER: Author. Teacher for brief periods at Queens College (now Queens College of the City University of New York), and New School for Social Research, New York, N.Y. Writer-in-residence, City College of the City University of New York, 1970. Visiting professor of creative writing, University of Iowa, 1973. *Member:* Authors League of America, Authors Guild, P.E.N. (member of executive board).

WRITINGS: Star of Glass (novel), Dodd, 1950; *The Troublemaker* (novel), Dodd, 1955; (editor with husband, Alfred Kazin) *The Works of Anne Frank*, Doubleday, 1959; *The Sweet Birds of Gorham* (novel), McKay, 1966; *Summer Situations* (novellas), Coward, 1972; *Dickie's List* (novel), Coward, 1973. Contributor of short stories, articles, and book reviews to *Mademoiselle, New Yorker, Reporter*, and *Vogue*; also contributor of motion picture reviews to *Vogue*.

WORK IN PROGRESS: A biography of Rabbi Bernard Birstein, Ann Birstein's late father, and a novel about young students in a New York college in the late 1940's, both for Coward.

* * *

BISHOP, James Alonzo 1907-
(Jim Bishop)

PERSONAL: Born November 21, 1907, in Jersey City, N.J.; son of John Michael (a policeman) and Jenny Josephine (Tier) Bishop; married Elinor Dunning, June 14, 1930 (died, October, 1957); married Elizabeth Kelly Stone, May, 1961; children: (first marriage) Virginia Lee Bishop Frechette, Gayle Peggy; (second marriage) Karen, Kathleen. *Education:* Attended Drake's Secretarial College, 1923. *Religion:* Roman Catholic. *Home:* 442 Tamarind Dr., Golden Isles, Hallandale, Fla. 33009.

CAREER: New York Daily News, copy boy, 1928, cub reporter, 1929; *New York Daily Mirror*, reporter, 1930-32, assistant to Mark Hellinger, columnist, 1932-34, rewrite man, feature writer, 1934-43; *Collier's* (magazine), associate editor, 1943-44, war editor, 1944-45; executive editor, *Liberty* (magazine), 1945-47; director of literature department, Music Corporation of America, 1947-49; founding editor, Gold Medal Books, 1949-51; *Catholic Digest*, executive editor, 1954, founding editor of *Catholic Digest* Book Club, 1954-55; columnist, King Features Syndicate, 1957—. Commentator, weekly television program, "Byline—Jim Bishop," WABC-TV, 1961-62; moderator, "A Re-Examination of the Warren Commission Findings: A Minority Report," WNEW-TV, 1966. *Awards, honors:* Catholic Institute of the Press Award, 1956; National Association of Independent School Award, 1956, for *The Day Lincoln Was Shot*; D.Litt., St. Bonaventure University, 1958, Belmont Abbey College, 1968.

WRITINGS—Under name Jim Bishop: *The Glass Crutch: The Biographical Novel of William Wynne Wister*, Doubleday, 1945; *The Mark Hellinger Story: A Biography of Broadway and Hollywood*, Appleton, 1952; (with Le Roy E. McWilliams) *Parish Priest*, McGraw, 1953; *The Day Lincoln Was Shot* (Book-of-the-Month Club selection), Harper, 1955; *The Golden Ham: A Candid Biography of Jackie Gleason*, Simon & Schuster, 1956; *The Day Christ Died* (Literary Guild selection), Harper, 1957; *Go With God*, McGraw, 1958; *The Day Christ Was Born: A Reverential Reconstruction*, Harper, 1960; *Some of My Very Best*, All Saints Press, 1960; *The Murder Trial of Judge Peel*, Simon & Schuster, 1962; *Honeymoon Diary* (novel), Harper, 1963; *A Day in the Life of President Kennedy*, Random House, 1964; *Jim Bishop, Reporter*, Random House, 1966; *A Day in the Life of President Johnson*, Random House, 1967; *The Day Kennedy Was Shot*, Funk, 1968; *The Days of Martin Luther King, Jr.*, Putnam, 1971; *FDR's Last Year*, Morrow, 1974. Contributor to national magazines.

SIDELIGHTS: A television play based on *The Day Lincoln Was Shot* was broadcast on "Ford Star Jubilee." Bishop's books have appeared in multiple translations, including Italian, Spanish, German, Polish, French, Swedish, Dutch, and Danish. Research materials and manuscripts from Bishop's books, columns, and magazine articles are in the Friedsam Memorial Library, St. Bonaventure University.

BIOGRAPHICAL/CRITICAL SOURCES: New Yorker, January 29, 1955; *New York Herald Tribune Book Review*, January 30, 1955; *Atlantic*, February, 1955; Kirkus Service, March 1, 1957; *New York Times*, May 19, 1957, December 17, 1966; *Chicago Sunday Tribune*, May 19, 1957; *New Republic*, June 10, 1957; *Best Sellers*, April 1, 1964.

* * *

BISHOP, William W(arner), Jr. 1906-

PERSONAL: Born June 10, 1906, in Princeton, N.J.; son of William Warner (a librarian) and Finie Murfree (Burton) Bishop; married Mary F. Shreve, July 19, 1947; children: Elizabeth Shreve. *Education:* University of Michigan, A.B., 1928, J.D., 1931; advanced study in law at Harvard University, 1928-29, Columbia University, 1938-39. *Home:* 1612 Morton Ave., Ann Arbor, Mich. 48104. *Office:* University of Michigan Law School, Ann Arbor, Mich. 48104.

CAREER: Admitted to Michigan bar, 1931, bar of U.S. Supreme Court, 1941. University of Michigan Law School, Ann Arbor, research and teaching assistant, 1931-35; Root, Clark, Buckner & Ballantine (law firm), New York, N.Y.,

associate, 1935-36; Princeton University, Princeton, N.J., lecturer in politics, 1936-38; U.S. Department of State, Washington, D.C., assistant legal adviser, 1939-47; University of Pennsylvania Law School, Philadelphia, professor of law, 1947-48; University of Michigan Law School, professor of international law, 1948—. Visiting professor, Columbia University, 1948; lecturer, Hague Academy of International Law, 1961, 1965. Legal adviser to U.S. delegation to Council of Foreign Ministers, London, Paris, and New York, 1946-47, and to Paris Peace Conference, 1946.

MEMBER: International Law Association, Institut de Droit International, American Society of International Law (vice-president, 1961, 1965-66), American Bar Association. *Awards, honors:* University of Michigan Distinguished Faculty Achievement Award, 1965.

WRITINGS: International Law Cases and Materials, preliminary edition, Prentice-Hall, 1951, 1st edition, 1953, 3rd edition, Little, Brown, 1971. Contributor to law journals. Editor-in-chief, *American Journal of International Law*, 1953-55, 1962-70.

* * *

BIXBY, Jerome Lewis 1923-
(Jay Lewis Bixby; Jay B. Drexel, Emerson Jan, D. B. Lewis, Harry Neal, Albert Russell, J. Russell, M. St. Vivant)

PERSONAL: Born January 11, 1923, in Los Angeles, Calif.; son of Rex Vancil and Ila (Lewis) Bixby; married Linda Burman (divorced); children: Russell Albert, Jan Emerson, Leonardo Brook. *Politics:* Democrat. *Religion:* Agnostic. *Home address:* Box BB, Crestline, Calif. 92325. *Agent:* Otto Klement, 9772 Olympic Blvd., Beverly Hills, Calif.

CAREER: Writer for science fiction, adventure, and western magazines; writer for films. Exoterica (mail-order specialties), Bullhead City, Ariz., owner, 1963-64; Walden Realty Co., Bullhead City, Ariz., owner, 1964-65. Founder, Church of Reality Research.

WRITINGS: Space by the Tale (short stories), Ballantine, 1964; *Devil's Scrapbook* (short stories), Brandon House, 1964. Author of scripts for television plays, and for motion pictures, including "Curse of the Faceless Man," "It! The Terro from Beyond Space," and, with John McPartland, "The Lost Missle"; also author, under name Jay Lewis Bixby, of screen story of "Fantastic·Voyage"; has had nearly thirteen hundred short stories published, many under pseudonyms. Editor of several science fiction and western collections; at times editor of *Planet Stories, Jungle Stories, Frontier Stories*, and *Action Stories*; intermittently assistant editor of *Galaxy*, and associate editor of *Startling Stories, Thrilling Wonder Stories, Space Stories*, and *Wonder Story Annual*.

WORK IN PROGRESS: The Candidate from Space, a collection of short stories; a feature for television, tentatively entitled "Death in Circles."

SIDELIGHTS: Bixby told *CA:* "My major interest is serious musical composition; writing is merely my livelihood." *Avocational interests:* Astronomy, hi-fi design, domestic architecture.

* * *

BLACKBURN, Joyce Knight 1920-
PERSONAL: Born November 1, 1920, in Mount Vernon,

Ind.; daughter of Leroy (a minister) and Audry (an artist; maiden name, Knight) Blackburn. *Education:* Moody Institute, Chicago, graduate; attended Northwestern University, 1943, 1950, 1957, Chicago Institute of Design, 1950. *Politics:* Jeffersonian Independent. *Religion:* Christian. *Home address:* Route 4, Box 287-A, St. Simons Island, Ga. 31522.

CAREER: Radio station WMBI, Chicago, Ill., 1941-60, broadcaster and supervisor, directing dramatic programs and presenting own series, "Listening Post," "From a City Tower," and "Music-Story Lady"; Zondervan Publishing House, Grand Rapids, Mich., editorial consultant, 1961—. Sometime actress in motion pictures (educational and feature films), slide films, and in radio series, "Unshackled," WGN, Chicago. *Member:* Authors Guild, Authors League of America, Screen Actors Guild, American Federation of Television and Radio Artists, Coastal Georgia Historical Society. *Awards, honors:* Literary achievement award for non-fiction, Georgia Writers Association, 1970; Fiction Author of the Year, Dixie Council of Authors and Journalists, 1971; National Christian School Award, 1971, for *Suki and the Wonder Star.*

WRITINGS—All juveniles: *Suki and the Invisible Peacock,* Zondervan, 1965; *Wilfred Grenfell: Explorer-Doctor,* Zondervan, 1966; *Suki and the Old Umbrella,* Zondervan, 1966; *Theodore Roosevelt: Naturalist-Statesman,* Zondervan, 1967; *Martha Berry: Little Woman With a Big Dream,* Lippincott, 1968; *Suki and the Magic Sand Dollar,* Word Books, 1969; *John Adams: Farmer from Braintree,* Word Books, 1970; *James Edward Oglethorpe,* Lippincott, 1970; *Suki and the Wonder Star,* Word Books, 1971; *The Earth Is the Lord's?,* Word Books, 1972; *George Wythe,* Harper, 1975.

SIDELIGHTS: Joyce Blackburn's work is represented in the Special Collections Library of Emory University.

* * *

BLACKSTONE, William T(homas)   1931-

PERSONAL: Born December 8, 1931, in Augusta, Ga.; son of Thomas Watson and Katie (Curtis) Blackstone; married Norma Jean Tew, March 27, 1954; children: Lisa Brooks, Jeffrey. *Education:* Elon College, B.A., 1953; Duke University, M.A., 1955, Ph.D., 1957. *Home:* Barnett Shoals Rd., Athens, Ga. 30601.

CAREER: Elon College, Elon College, N.C., associate professor of philosophy, 1957-58; University of Florida, Gainesville, assistant professor of philosophy, 1958-61; University of Georgia, Athens, associate professor, 1961-63, professor of philosophy and religion and head of department, 1963—, became chairman of Division of Social Sciences. *Member:* American Philosophical Association, Southern Society for Philosophy of Religion, Southern Society for Philosophy and Psychology (executive council member, 1965-68), Southeastern Philosophy of Education Society, Georgia Philosophical Society. *Awards, honors:* Southern Society for Philosophy and Psychology annual award for 1958-59, 1959-60, 1960-61; Michael Award, University of Georgia, 1965.

WRITINGS: The Problem of Religious Knowledge, Prentice-Hall, 1963; *Francis Hutcheson and Contemporary Ethical Theory,* University of Georgia Press, 1965; *The Concept of Equality,* Burgess, 1969; *Ethics and Education,* University of Georgia Press, 1970; (editor) *Meaning and Existence,* Holt, 1971; *Political Philosophy,* Crowell, 1973; *Philosophy and Environmental Crisis,* University of Georgia Press, 1974. Contributor to philosophy journals.

WORK IN PROGRESS: Essays in the area of moral and political philosophy.

AVOCATIONAL INTERESTS: Tennis.

* * *

BLACKWELDER, Boyce W.   1913-

PERSONAL: Born February 3, 1913, in Concord, N.C.; son of Charles Black (in textile business) and Martha Alice (McInnis) Blackwelder; married Alice Lela Smith (a bookkeeper), July 19, 1943; children: Charles, Dorothea, Rhoda. *Education:* Anderson College, A.B., 1936, B.D., 1938; Butler University, M.A., 1944; Northern Baptist Theological Seminary, Th.D., 1951. *Home:* 612 Walnut St., Anderson, Ind. 46012. *Office:* Anderson College, East Fifth St., Anderson, Ind. 46011.

CAREER: Minister of Church of God; pastor in Anderson, Ind., 1933-44, Chicago, Ill., 1945-51, Connersville, Ind., 1951-53, and Erie, Pa., 1953-63; Anderson College, School of Theology, Anderson, Ind., associate professor of Bible, 1963—. *Member:* Society of Biblical Literature, Phi Kappa Phi, Theta Phi.

WRITINGS—All published by Warner Press: *Light from the Greek New Testament,* 1958; *Toward Understanding Paul,* 1961; *Toward Understanding Romans,* 1962; *Toward Understanding Thessalonians,* 1965; *Letters From Paul: An Exegetical Translation,* 1971.

* * *

BLAIKLOCK, Edward Musgrave   1903-
(Grammaticus)

PERSONAL: Born July 6, 1903, in Birmingham, England; son of Edward (an electrician) and Florence Blaiklock; married Kathleen Mitchell, November 13, 1928; children: Peter Edward, David Andrew. *Education:* University of Auckland, M.A., 1925. *Religion:* Baptist. *Home:* 47 Koromiko Rd., Titirangi, Auckland 7, New Zealand. *Office:* University of Auckland, Box 2175, Auckland, New Zealand.

CAREER: University of Auckland, Auckland, New Zealand, lecturer, 1927-37, senior lecturer in classics, 1937-47, professor of classics, 1947-68, professor emeritus. Public orator, University of Auckland, 1958-69. President, Baptist Union of New Zealand, 1971, New Zealand Bible Training Institute, and Scripture Union of New Zealand. *Member:* P.E.N. *Awards, honors:* Litt.D., University of Auckland, 1945, for *The Male Characters of Euripides;* officer, Order of the British Empire, 1974.

WRITINGS: The Seven Churches, Marshall, Morgan & Scott, 1951; *The Male Characters of Euripides: A Study in Realism,* New Zealand University Press, 1952; *Out of the Earth: The Witness of Archaeology to the New Testament,* Eerdmans, 1957, 2nd edition, 1961; *Faith Is the Victory: Studies in the First Epistle of John,* Eerdmans, 1959; *Rome in the New Testament,* Inter-Varsity Fellowship, 1959; *The Acts of the Apostles: An Historical Commentary,* Eerdmans, 1959.

The Century of the New Testament, Inter-Varsity Fellowship, 1962; (contributor) James D. Douglas, editor, *New Bible Dictionary,* Tyndale Press, 1962; (contributor) *Pictorial Bible Dictionary,* Zondervan, 1962; *Our Lord's Teaching on Prayer,* Zondervan, 1964; *From Prison in Rome: Letters to the Philippians and Philemon,* Zondervan, 1964; *Ten Pounds an Acre,* A. H. & A. W. Reed, 1965; *The Young Man Mark: Studies in Some Aspects of*

Mark and His Gospel, Paternoster Press, 1965, published as *In the Image of Peter*, Moody, 1969; *Cities of the New Testament*, Revell, 1965; *Hills of Home*, Tri-Ocean, 1966; *St. Luke*, Eerdmans, 1966; (contributor) *Dictionary of Practical Theology*, Eerdmans, 1967; *Green Shade*, A. H. & A. W. Reed, 1968; *The Way of Excellence*, Pickering & Inglis, 1968; (with David A. Blaiklock) *Is It, or Isn't It? Why We Believe in the Existence of God*, Zondervan, 1968 (published in England as *This Faith or That*, Pickering & Inglis, 1969); *Layman's Answer: An Examination of the New Theology*, Judson Press, 1968; (editor and contributor) *Pictorial Bible Atlas*, Zondervan, 1969; *Word Pictures From the Bible*, Pickering & Inglis, 1969, Zondervan, 1971.

The Archaeology of the New Testament, Zondervan, 1970; *The Psalms of the Great Rebellion*, Marshall, Morgan & Scott, 1970; *Romans*, Eerdmans, 1971; (editor and contributor) *Why I Am Still A Christian*, Zondervan, 1971; *The Pastoral Epistles*, Zondervan, 1972; (with D. A. Blaiklock) *Why Didn't They Tell Me?*, Zondervan, 1972; (contributor) *Bible Characters and Doctrines*, Eerdmans, 1971-74; *Who Was Jesus*, Moody, 1974; *The Positive Power of Prayer*, Regal Books, 1974. Also author of monographs on classical and religious subjects.

Columnist, under pseudonym Grammaticus, in *Auckland Weekly News*, 1942—. Contributor of editorials, articles, and reviews to classical journals in the United States and United Kingdom, and to New Zealand newspapers.

WORK IN PROGRESS: Dictionary of Biblical Archaeology, for Zondervan; contributing to *Pictorial Encyclopedia of the Bible*, for Zondervan; commentary on the Psalms, for Scripture Union.

* * *

BLAIR, Edward H. 1938-

PERSONAL: Born December 17, 1938, in Leadville, Colo.; surname legally changed from Smith to Blair; son of Whaite and Alberta Marie (Burkhardt) Smith; married Kay Kimery Reynolds, February 24, 1966. *Education:* Colorado State College, A.B., 1962; Western State College of Colorado, M.A., 1969. *Politics:* "Democrat of sorts." *Home:* 912 Harrison Ave., Leadville, Colo. 80461.

CAREER: During his college years was employed as reporter, freight handler, filling station operator, shoe salesman, and juvenile counselor; Frontier Service Station, Leadville, Colo., manager, 1962-63; Weld County Library, Greeley, Colo., library assistant, 1964-65; Lake County Junior High School, Leadville, Colo., head of social studies, 1966-72; now regional curator for State Historical Society of Colorado, and part-time professor of history, Colorado Mountain College, Leadville. Treasurer, Lake County School Board. Former newspaper editor in Memphis, Tenn. *Member:* State Historical Society of Colorado.

WRITINGS: (With E. Richard Churchill) *Games and Puzzles for Family Leisure*, Abingdon, 1965; (with E. R. Churchill and Linda R. Churchill) *Fun with American History*, Abingdon, 1966; (with wife, Kay K. Blair, E. R. Churchill, and L. R. Churchill) *Fun with American Literature*, Abingdon, 1968; (with E. R. Churchill) *Everybody Come to Leadville*, Timberline Books, 1972; *Palace of Ice*, Timberline Books, 1973. Also author of short stories and articles on Colorado history.

WORK IN PROGRESS: A history of Leadville, Colorado; articles on western topics.

BLAIR, George S(imms) 1924-

PERSONAL: Born May 31, 1924, in Homewood, Kan.; son of William Horace (a farmer) and Mary (Simms) Blair; married Gloria Jean Barnes, September 10, 1949; children: David Lawrence, Rebecca Lynn. *Education:* Kansas State Teachers College of Emporia, A.B. and B.S. in Ed., 1948, M.S., 1949; Northwestern University, Ph.D., 1951. *Religion:* Methodist. *Home:* 509 Bowling Green Dr., Claremont, Calif. 91711. *Office:* Claremont Graduate School, Claremont, Calif. 91711.

CAREER: University of Tennessee, Knoxville, assistant professor of political science, 1951-53, acting associate director, Bureau of Public Administration, 1952-53; University of Pennsylvania, Philadelphia, assistant professor, 1953-56, associate professor of political science, 1956-60; Claremont Graduate School, Claremont, Calif., associate professor, 1960-64, professor of government, 1964-72, Elisabeth Helm Rosecrans Professor of Social Science, 1972—. Member, Claremont City Planning Commission. *Military service:* U.S. Army, Amphibious Engineers, 1943-46. *Member:* American Political Science Association, American Society for Public Administration, American Association of University Professors, National Municipal League, Western Political Science Association, Western Governmental Research Association, Southern California Political Science Association. *Awards, honors:* Fruin-Colnon Award of National Municipal League, 1959, for *Metropolitan Analysis.*

WRITINGS: (With S. B. Sweeney) *Metropolitan Analysis*, University of Pennsylvania Press, 1958; *Cumulative Voting: An Effective Electoral Device in Illinois Politics*, University of Illinois Press, 1960; *American Local Government*, Harper, 1964; (with Houston I. Flournoy) *Legislative Bodies in California*, Dickenson, 1967; *American Legislatures: Structure and Process*, Harper, 1967. Also author of *Planning in Suburbia*, 1972. Contributor to *Book of the States, Collier's Year Book*, and to professional journals.

WORK IN PROGRESS: A revision of *American Local Government*; a study of freedom in federal systems.

AVOCATIONAL INTERESTS: Tennis, swimming, playing bridge, collecting stamps and Indian artifacts.

* * *

BLAKE, Sally Mirliss 1925-
(Sara)

PERSONAL: Born June 11, 1925, in Boston, Mass., daughter of Samuel (a cabinet-maker) and Eva (Lansman) Mirliss; married Bernard P. Blake, October 4, 1947; children: Andrew, Gail Cynthia. *Education:* Boston University, B.S. in journalism, 1945; San Francisco State College (now San Francisco State University), M.A. in creative writing, 1964. *Politics:* Democrat. *Religion:* Jewish. *Home:* 200 Julia Ave., Mill Valley, Calif. 94941. *Agent:* Robert E. Lewis, 500 Fifth Ave., New York, N.Y. 10036.

CAREER: United Press Association, Boston, Mass., reporter, 1943-45; Muriel Francis Agency, New York, N.Y., publicist, 1945-47; *Jewish Community Bulletin*, San Francisco, Calif., assistant editor, 1948-50, 1953-55, 1956-57; Promotion Programs, Inc., San Francisco, Calif., advertising copywriter, 1957-62; Jewish Welfare Federation, San Francisco, Calif., publicist, 1965-66; *Jewish Community Bulletin*, assistant editor, 1966-69; public information officer, California State International Programs, 1970-71. *Awards, honors:* O. Henry Memorial Award, 1964, for short story "So I'm Not Lady Chatterley, So Better I Should Know It Now."

WRITINGS—Under pseudonym Sara: *Where Mist Clothes Dream and Song Runs Naked*, McGraw, 1965; *A House Divided*, McGraw, 1968. Short fiction published in *New Campus Writing #4*, Grove, 1962, and *O. Henry Memorial Award Prize Stories*, Doubleday, 1964. Contributor to *Commentary*.

*   *   *

BLAUNER, Robert 1929-

PERSONAL: First syllable of surname rhymes with "clown"; born May 18, 1929, in Chicago, Ill.; son of Samuel (a lawyer and poet) and Esther (Shapiro) Blauner; married Rena Katznelson (a child psychotherapist), July 29, 1962. *Education:* University of Chicago, A.B., 1948, M.A., 1950; University of California, Berkeley, Ph.D., 1962. *Home:* 1003 Mariposa Ave., Berkeley, Calif. 94707.

CAREER: Worked five years as factory laborer; University of Chicago, Chicago, Ill., assistant professor in department of sociology, 1962-63; University of California, Berkeley, assistant professor, 1963-67, associate professor of sociology, 1967—.

WRITINGS: Alienation and Freedom: The Factory Worker and His Industry, University of Chicago Press, 1964; *Racial Oppression in America*, Harper, 1972. Contributor of book reviews to sociological journals, and articles to *Psychiatry* and *Transaction*.

*   *   *

BLEES, Robert A(rthur) 1922-

PERSONAL: Born October 12, 1922, in Stratford, Conn.; married Katie Howe, August 7, 1944; children: Robert D., Elizabeth Ann, Margaret Lynne. *Education:* Denison University, B.A., 1948; Ohio State University, M.A., 1950, completed course work for Ph.D., 1960; Andover Newton Theological School, B.D., 1962. *Office:* First Community Church, 1320 Cambridge Blvd., Columbus, Ohio 43212.

CAREER: Ordained minister at First Community Church, Columbus, Ohio, October 14, 1962. Columbus State Hospital, Columbus, Ohio, staff psychologist, 1950-56; Children's Mental Health Center, Columbus, Ohio, staff psychologist, 1956-57; First Community Church, Columbus, Ohio, minister of counseling, 1957—, director of pastoral counseling center, 1963—. *Member:* American Psychological Association, American Group Psychotherapy Association, Academy of Religion and Mental Health, American Association of Pastoral Counselors, Ohio Psychological Association, Psi Chi.

WRITINGS: Counseling with Teen-Agers, Prentice-Hall, 1965.†

*   *   *

BLESH, Rudolph Pickett 1899-
(Rudi Blesh)

PERSONAL: Born January 21, 1899, in Guthrie, Okla.; son of Abraham Lincoln (a surgeon) and Belle (Pickett) Blesh; married Editha Tuttle, February 22, 1925; married second wife, Barbara Lamont, July, 1938 (divorced); children: (first marriage) Hilary (Mrs. Peter W. Morton). *Education:* Attended Dartmouth College, 1917-20; University of California, Berkeley, A.B. (honors), 1924. *Home:* 38 East Fourth St., New York, N.Y. 10003; and Hillforge,

Gilmanton, N.H. (summer). *Agent:* Ivan von Auw, Jr., Harold Ober Associates, Inc., 40 East 49th St., New York, N.Y. 10017.

CAREER: Industrial, furniture, and architectural designer, 1924-43; abstract artist, with one-man show of paintings, New York, N.Y., 1946; lecturer on Afro-American music and jazz at Queens College of the City University of New York, 1956—, and New York University, New York, N.Y., 1957—; writer on jazz and other subjects. Writer and narrator of radio programs, "This Is Jazz," WOR-Mutual Broadcasting Co., 1947, "Our Singing Land," WYNC, 1949, "Jazz Saga," WFDR, 1950, and "Dimensions of Jazz," WYNC, 1964.

WRITINGS—All under name Rudi Blesh: *This Is Jazz*, San Francisco Museum, 1943; *Shining Trumpets: A History of Jazz*, Knopf, 1946, revised edition, 1958; (with Harriet Janis) *They All Played Ragtime*, Knopf, 1950, revised edition, Oak, 1966; *Modern Art, U.S.A.*, Knopf, 1956; *O Susanna*, Grove, 1960; *Stuart Davis*, Grove, 1960; (with Janis) *De Kooning*, Grove, 1960; (with Janis) *Collage: Personalities, Concepts, Techniques*, Chilton, 1962, revised edition, 1966; *Dimensions of Jazz*, Queens College Press, 1964; *Keaton*, Macmillan, 1966; *Combo U.S.A.*, Chilton, 1971.

WORK IN PROGRESS: A college textbook on the history of jazz.

AVOCATIONAL INTERESTS: American architecture, all periods; collecting Americana, including country antiques; collecting American and other modern art.

*   *   *

BLISHEN, Edward 1920-

PERSONAL: Born April 29, 1920, in Whetstone, Middlesex, England; son of William George (a civil servant) and Elizabeth Ann (Pye) Blishen; married Nancy Smith, November 4, 1948; children: Jonathan Edward, Nicholas Martin. *Education:* Educated in England. *Home:* 12 Bartrams Lane, Hadley Wood, Barnet, England. *Agent:* Irene Josephy, 35 Craven St., Strand, London W.C. 2, England.

CAREER: Employed in London, England, and vicinity, as journalist, 1937-41, preparatory schoolmaster, 1946-49, and teacher of English in secondary school, 1950-59; University of York, Heslington, England, part-time lecturer in department of education, 1963-65; full-time professional writer, Barnet, England, 1965—. Conductor for thirteen years of British Broadcasting Corp. overseas program directed at young African writers. *Member:* P.E.N. (member of executive committee of English Center, 1962-66), Society of Authors. *Awards, honors:* Carnegie Award, Library Association, 1971, for *The God Beneath the Sea*.

WRITINGS: Roaring Boys, Thames & Hudson, 1955; (editor) *Junior Pears Encyclopaedia*, Pelham Books, 1961, and annual revisions, 1962—; (editor) *Education Today*, BBC Publications, 1963; (editor) *Oxford Book of Poetry for Children*, Oxford University Press, 1963; *Town Story*, Anthony Blond, 1964; (editor) *Miscellany*, Oxford University Press, annually, 1964-69; (editor) *Come Reading* (anthology of prose for young readers), M. Joseph, 1968; *Hugh Lofting* (monograph), Bodley Head, 1968; (editor) *Encyclopaedia of Education*, Anthony Blond, 1969; *This Soft Lot*, Thames & Hudson, 1969; *The School That I'd Like*, Penguin, 1969; (with Leon Garfield) *The God Beneath the Sea*, Longmans, Green, 1970; *A Cackhanded War*, Thames & Hudson, 1972; (with Garfield) *The Golden Shadow*, Longman, 1973; *Uncommon Embrace*, Thames & Hudson, 1974.

WORK IN PROGRESS: A further autobiographical novel based on the experience of being trained as a teacher.

SIDELIGHTS: Blishen told *CA*, "My chief frustrated ambition is to write a series of novels that would trace the extraordinary and often deeply painful changes brought about within a single family by the educational advance of the past seventy years."

* * *

BLIVEN, Bruce, Jr. 1916-

PERSONAL: Born January 31, 1916, in Los Angeles, Calif.; son of Bruce and Rose (Emery) Bliven; married Naomi Horowitz (a book reviewer), May 26, 1950; children: Frederic Bruce. *Education:* Harvard University, A.B., 1937. *Politics:* Democrat. *Home:* 451 West End Ave., New York, N.Y. 10024. *Agent:* Theron Raines, 244 Madison Ave., New York, N.Y. 10016.

CAREER: Manchester Guardian, staff reporter, 1936, New York correspondent, 1938-42; *New York Post*, editorial writer, 1938-42; full-time writer, 1946—. Judge, *Scholastic Magazine's* Writing Awards, 1958—; lecturer, Indiana University Writer's Conference, 1955, 1966. *Military service:* U.S. Army, 1942-45; became captain; received Bronze Star with cluster. *Member:* Society of Magazine Writers, Authors Guild, P.E.N., Society of American Historians.

WRITINGS: The Wonderful Writing Machine, Random House, 1954; *The Story of D-Day, June 6, 1944* (juvenile), Random House, 1956; *Battle for Manhattan*, Holt, 1956; *The American Revolution* (juvenile), Random House, 1958; *From Pearl Harbor to Okinawa* (juvenile), Random House, 1960; *From Casablanca to Berlin* (juvenile), Random House, 1965; (with wife, Naomi Bliven) *New York: The Story of the World's Most Exciting City* (juvenile), Random House, 1969; *Under the Guns: New York 1775-1776*, Harper, 1972; *Book Traveller*, Dodd, 1974. Contributor of articles and reviews to *New Yorker* and other publications.

WORK IN PROGRESS: A book about the all-volunteer armed forces of the United States, for Reader's Digest Press, tentatively entitled *Zero Draft*.

SIDELIGHTS: "My interest in military history started in the Second World War," Bliven told *CA*. "I was a lieutenant in the field artillery and took part in the D-Day landings in Normandy, and wrote a children's book about it, a dozen years later, to find out what had happened. But five books about wars and warfare is misleading: I do not consider myself a military expert. My first book was about typewriters. My seventh was about New York City, more often at peace than at war. My eighth was a study of New York City politics on the eve of the Revolution. And my ninth was a mystery book about how to sell books."

* * *

BLOCK, Irvin 1917-

PERSONAL: Born April 1, 1917, in Pittsburgh, Pa.; son of Morris and Minnie Block; married Doris Senk, June 6, 1948; children: Jessica, Amy, Rachel, Mark. *Education:* Western Reserve University (now Case Western Reserve University), A.B. (cum laude), 1938. *Religion:* "Not particularly." *Home:* 2 Carpenter Ave., Sea Cliff, N.Y. 11579. *Office:* H. P. Publishing Co., 485 Madison Ave., New York, N.Y. 10022.

CAREER: U.S. Army, Infantry, 1939-45, leaving service as first lieutenant; free-lance writer, 1946-58; Blue Cross

Association, New York, N.Y., public relations manager, 1959-63; New York Governor's Committee on Hospital Costs, editor and researcher, 1964; Schless & Co. (public relations), New York, N.Y., vice-president, 1965; Metropolitan Life Insurance Co., New York, N.Y., editor of "Statistical Bulletin," 1966-68, *Hospital Practice*, senior editor, 1968—. *Member:* Authors Guild, American Public Health Association, Population Association of America. *Awards, honors*—Military: Purple Heart, Bronze Star with oak leaf cluster, Presidential Unit Citation.

WRITINGS: Real Book About Explorers, Garden City Books, 1952; *Real Book About the Mounties*, Garden City Books, 1952; *Real Book About Christopher Columbus*, Garden City Books, 1953; *People*, F. Watts, 1956; *Real Book About Ships*, Garden City Books, 1961; *Neighbor to the World*, Crowell, 1969; *The Lives of Pearl Buck*, Crowell, 1973. Contributor of fiction to *Saturday Evening Post, Liberty*, and *Maclean's Magazine*.

WORK IN PROGRESS: Books for young people.

AVOCATIONAL INTERESTS: "Sailing in summer and thinking about sailing in winter."

* * *

BLODGETT, Geoffrey Thomas 1931-

PERSONAL: Born October 13, 1931, in Hanover, N.H.; son of Harold William (a professor) and Dorothy (Briggs) Blodgett; married Jane Taggart, December 22, 1954; children: Lauren Elizabeth, Barbara Jane, Sally McCall. *Education:* Oberlin College, A.B., 1953; Harvard University, A.M., 1956, Ph.D., 1960. *Politics:* Democrat. *Religion:* Protestant. *Home:* 273 Oak St., Oberlin, Ohio. *Office:* Department of History, Rice Hall, Oberlin College, Oberlin, Ohio.

CAREER: Oberlin College, Oberlin, Ohio, instructor, 1960-62, assistant professor, 1962-66, associate professor, 1966-68, professor of history, 1968—. *Military service:* U.S. Navy, 1953-55; served with Pacific Fleet; became lieutenant junior grade. *Member:* American Historical Association, Organization of American Historians, Ohio Academy of Historians, Phi Beta Kappa. *Awards, honors:* Social Science Research Council fellow, 1959-60; American Council of Learned Societies fellow, 1973-74; Charles Warren fellow, 1973-74.

WRITINGS: The Gentle Reformers: Massachusetts Democrats in the Cleveland Era, Harvard University Press, 1966; (contributor) H. Wayne Morgan, editor, *The Gilded Age*, Syracuse University Press, 1970; (contributor) Edward James, editor, *Notable American Women*, Harvard University Press, 1972. Contributor to historical journals.

WORK IN PROGRESS: A study on conservative reform thought in the American urban middle class, 1870-1890.

* * *

BLOOM, Lillian D. 1920-

PERSONAL: Born July 17, 1920, in New York, N.Y.; daughter of Benjamin (an architect) and Frances (Eisenberg) Blumberg; married Edward A. Bloom (a college professor), June 17, 1947. *Education:* New York University, B.A., 1941, M.A., 1942; Yale University, Ph.D., 1946. *Home:* 82 Laurel Ave., Providence, R.I. *Office:* Rhode Island College, Providence, R.I.

CAREER: University of Illinois, Urbana, instructor in

English, 1945-46; Queens College (now Queen's College of the City University of New York), instructor in English, 1946-47; University of Rhode Island, Kingston, assistant professor of English, 1947-51; Rhode Island College, Providence, professor of English, 1956—. *Member:* Modern Language Association of America, American Association of University Professors, Phi Beta Kappa, Sigma Delta Omicron, Kappa Delta Pi. *Awards, honors:* American Council of Learned Societies grant, 1967-68.

WRITINGS—With husband, Edward A. Bloom: *Willa Cather's Gift of Sympathy*, Southern Illinois University Press, 1962; *The Variety of Fiction*, Odyssey, 1969; *Joseph Addison's Sociable Animal*, Brown University Press, 1971; *Fanny Burney's 'Camilla,'* Oxford University Press, 1972. Contributor to scholarly journals.

WORK IN PROGRESS: The Humanism of Joseph Addison's Aesthetics; The Journals and Letters of Fanny Burney; The Letters of Mrs. Piozzi.

*   *   *

BLOOM, Murray Teigh   1916-

PERSONAL: Born May 19, 1916, in New York, N.Y.; son of Louis I. (a toy manufacturer) and Anna (Teighblum) Bloom; married Sydelle Cohen (a college teacher), April 30, 1944; children: Ellen Susan (Mrs. Michael Lubell), Amy Beth. *Education:* Columbia University, B.A., 1937, M.S. in Journalism, 1938. *Politics:* Independent Democrat. *Religion:* Jewish. *Home:* 40 Hemlock Dr., Kings Point, N.Y. 11024. *Agent:* Julian Bach, Jr., 3 East 48th St., New York, N.Y. 10017.

CAREER: New York Post, New York, N.Y., reporter, 1939; free-lance writer, primarily for magazines, 1945—. Founder and former trustee, United Community Fund of Great Neck (N.Y.). *Military service:* U.S. Army, 1943-45; correspondent for *Stars and Stripes* (Paris and German editions), 1944-45; became technical sergeant. *Member:* Society of Magazine Writers (one of three founders and past president), Dramatists Guild of the Authors League of America (associate member). *Awards, honors:* Fiftieth Anniversary Award, Graduate School of Journalism, Columbia University; honorary life member, Virginia State Bar Association; first place media award, Family Service Association of America; merit award, American Bar Association.

WRITINGS: Money of Their Own, Scribner, 1957; *The Man Who Stole Portugal*, Scribner, 1966; *The Trouble with Lawyers*, Simon & Schuster, 1969; *Rogues to Riches*, Putnam, 1972. Author of three-act play, "Leonora," produced at Southern Methodist University, 1966. Contributor of more than five hundred articles to magazines, including *Harper's, Reader's Digest, McCall's, Playboy, New Republic, Esquire*, and *New York Times Magazine.*

WORK IN PROGRESS: A novel.

SIDELIGHTS: A story by Bloom was adapted as "The Girl Who Knew Too Much" and broadcast on U.S. Steel Hour, 1960. Bloom reads French and German.

*   *   *

BLOOM, Robert   1930-

PERSONAL: Born May 28, 1930, in Brooklyn, N.Y.; son of Michael (a detective) and Fannie (Hecker) Bloom; married Gloria Loebenson, August 29, 1953; children: Claudia, Madeline, Jonathan. *Education:* New York University, B.A., 1951; Columbia University, M.A., 1952; University

of Michigan, Ph.D., 1960. *Home:* 2340 Vine St., Berkeley, Calif. *Office:* Department of English, University of California, Berkeley, Calif.

CAREER: University of Michigan, Ann Arbor, instructor in English, 1958-60; University of California, Berkeley, assistant professor of English, 1960—. *Military service:* U.S. Coast Guard, 1952-54; became lieutenant junior grade. *Member:* Modern Language Association of America, Phi Beta Kappa. *Awards, honors:* Bruern fellow in American literature at University of Leeds, 1963-64; Fulbright travel grant to England, 1963.

WRITINGS: The Indeterminate World: A Study of the Novels of Joyce Cary, University of Pennsylvania Press, 1963. Contributor of essays on Irving Babbitt and Emerson, Stuart Sherman and H. L. Mencken, Allan Seager, and W. H. Auden to literary reviews.

WORK IN PROGRESS: A critical study of modern poetry.

AVOCATIONAL INTERESTS: Music (plays the piano).

*   *   *

BLOTNER, Joseph (Leo)   1923-

PERSONAL: Born June 21, 1923, in Plainfield, N.J.; son of Joseph (a businessman) and Johanna (Slattery) Blotner; married Yvonne Wright, August 24, 1946; children: Tracy, Pamela, Nancy. *Education:* Drew University, B.A., 1947; Northwestern University, M.A., 1947; University of Pennsylvania, Ph.D., 1951. *Politics:* Democrat. *Religion:* Presbyterian. *Home:* 816 Berkshire Rd., Ann Arbor, Mich. 48104. *Agent:* Brandt & Brandt, 101 Park Ave., New York, N.Y. 10017. *Office:* Department of English Language and Literature, University of Michigan, Ann Arbor, Mich. 48104.

CAREER: Radio Corp. of America Laboratories, Princeton, N.J., technical writer, 1949-53, consultant on writing, summers, 1955-56; University of Idaho, Moscow, instructor in English, 1953-55; University of Virginia, Charlottesville, assistant professor, 1955-61, associate professor of English, 1961-68, executive secretary of department, 1961-63; University of North Carolina, Chapel Hill, professor of English, 1968-71; University of Michigan, Ann Arbor, professor of English, 1972—. Fulbright lecturer in American literature, University of Copenhagen, 1958-59, 1963-64. Consultant, Encyclopaedia Britannica Educational Corp., 1975. *Military service:* U.S. Army Air Forces, 1943-45; became first lieutenant; received Air Medal. *Member:* Modern Language Association of America, Authors Guild, P.E.N., Sigma Phi, Omicron Delta Kappa, Racquet Club of Ann Arbor. *Awards, honors:* Guggenheim fellow, 1965, 1968.

WRITINGS: The Political Novel, Doubleday, 1955; (with F. L. Gwynn) *Faulkner in the University*, University Press of Virginia, 1959; (with Gwynn) *The Fiction of J. D. Salinger*, University of Pittsburgh Press, 1959; *William Faulkner's Library: A Catalogue*, University Press of Virginia, 1964; *The Modern American Political Novel: 1900-1960*, University of Texas Press, 1966; (contributor) W. R. Robinson, editor, *Man and the Movies*, Louisiana State University Press, 1967; (contributor) Ray B. Browne and Donald Pizer, editors, *Themes and Directions in American Literature*, Purdue University Studies, 1969; (contributor) *William Faulkner/ Eugene O'Neill/ John Steinbeck*, CRM Publishing, 1971; *Faulkner: A Biography*, two volumes, Random House, 1974. Contributor of articles and essays on modern American and British fiction to journals. Bibliographical editor, *Twentieth Century Literature*, 1954-58; book review editor, *College English*, 1955-58.

WORK IN PROGRESS: Editing *Selected Letters of William Faulkner*, for Random House.

* * *

BLOUNT, Charles (Harold Clavell) 1913-

PERSONAL: Surname is pronounced Blunt; born November 19, 1913, in East Farleigh, Kent, England; son of George Ronald Beddard (in Royal Navy) and Cecilia Frances (Hore) Blount; married Evelyn Derry, November 4, 1939; children: Rose Derry. *Education:* Cambridge University, B.A., 1935, M.A., 1939. *Home:* 7 Reservoir Rd., Cofton Hackett, Birmingham B45 8PJ, England. *Office:* King Edward's School, Edgbaston Park Rd., Birmingham B15 2UA, England.

CAREER: Cambridge University, Cambridge, England, member of history faculty, 1939-40; King Edward's School, Birmingham, England, senior history master (head of history department), and librarian, 1940-75. Adult education lecturer at Cambridge University, 1935-40, University of Birmingham, 1946-64. *Military service:* Royal Air Force, 1941-46; became flight lieutenant. *Member:* Historical Association (president, Birmingham branch, 1960, 1973), Birmingham History Forum (chairman, 1958-74).

WRITINGS: (With W. E. Tate) *British Institutions*, Oxford University Press, 1955; *The Last Hundred Years*, Oxford University Press, 1956; (with T. K. Derry and T. L. Jarman) *Great Britain*, Oxford University Press, 1960; *Years of Challenge*, Oxford University Press, 1972. General editor, Oxford University Press "Modern World" Series.

* * *

BOGGS, W(ilmot) Arthur 1916-

PERSONAL: Born December 4, 1916, in Los Angeles, Calif.; son of William Arthur (a salesman) and Melissa Elizabeth (Rischel) Boggs; married Alice Jean Weisenberg (a cytologist), October 8, 1942; children: Steven Allan, Warren Arthur. *Education:* Attended University of Wyoming, 1935-37; University of Southern California, B.A. (magna cum laude), 1939, M.A., 1941; University of California, Berkeley, Ph.D., 1950. *Home:* 653 D Ave., Lake Oswego, Ore. 97034. *Office:* Division of Arts and Letters, Portland State College, P.O. Box 751, Portland, Ore. 97207.

CAREER: Teacher in Montebello, Calif., 1941-42; National Brands, Inc., cost accountant, 1946-47; Portland State University, Portland, Ore., instructor, 1950-53, assistant professor, 1953-56, associate professor, 1956-65, professor of English, 1965—. *Military service:* U.S. Army, Ordnance, 1942-46; became technical sergeant. *Member:* Modern Language Association of America, National Council of Teachers of English, Linguistic Society of America, American Academy of Political and Social Science, Philological Association of the Pacific Coast, Oregon State Poetry Association (president, 1962-64; treasurer, 1964-66), Phi Beta Kappa, Phi Kappa Phi, Epsilon Phi, Phi Delta Kappa, Delta Phi Alpha.

WRITINGS: *Odysseus, and Other Poems*, Merchants Press (Taylor, Tex.), 1962; (translator with Joseph Grosz) *Hungarian Anthology* (poems), Griff (Munich), 1963, revised and expanded edition, Pannonia Books, 1966; *The*

Idol-Maker, Centro Studi e Scambi Internazionali (Rome), 1965; *Quatrains*, Merchants Press, 1966. About six hundred poems have been published in more than fifty periodicals and newspapers, including *American Weave, Yankee, Flame, Wormwood Review, Antioch Review, Canadian Poetry, American Judaism, New York Herald Tribune, Oregon Journal, Choice, Christian Century*, and *New York Times*. Also contributor of articles, a number of them on Smollett's *Humphry Clinker*, to professional journals.

WORK IN PROGRESS: Various linguistic, literary, and bibliographical problems presented by Smollett's *Humphry Clinker*.

AVOCATIONAL INTERESTS: Reading.†

* * *

BOHN, Ralph C. 1930-

PERSONAL: Born February 19, 1930, in Detroit, Mich.; son of Carl N. (a carpenter) and Bertha (Abrams) Bohn; married Adella N. Stanul, September 2, 1950; children: Cheryl Ann, Jeffrey Ralph. *Education:* Wayne State University, B.S., 1951, M.A., 1954, Ed.D., 1957. *Religion:* Lutheran. *Home:* 1874 Harris Ave., San Jose, Calif. 95124. *Office:* Continuing Education, San Jose State University, San Jose, Calif. 95192.

CAREER: Detroit (Mich.) public schools, teacher of industrial arts, 1947-51, 1953-55; San Jose State University, San Jose, Calif., director of auto, safety, and driver education programs, 1955-61, chairman of department of industrial arts, 1961-69, associate dean of educational services, 1968-70, dean of continuing education, 1970—. Director of Inservice Education Program for Industrial Teachers, sponsored by U.S. Office of Education, 1966-67; director of National Driver Education Association's Institute for Advanced Study in Industrial Arts Education, summer, 1967. Member of guest faculty, Colorado State College, summer, 1963, Arizona State University, summer, 1966. Research consultant, U.S. Office of Education. Member, California State Chamber of Commerce. *Military service:* U.S. Coast Guard, active duty, 1951-53, Inactive Reserve, 1953—; now captain.

MEMBER: American Council of Industrial Arts Teacher Education (past president), American Industrial Arts Association (past president), National Education Association, National Fluid Power Association, Association of Organizations for Teacher Education, Consortium of Professional Associations (member of board, 1967—), Western Association of Summer Session Administrators (president-elect, 1973-74), California Driver's Education Association, California State Employees Association (president, San Jose chapter, 1966-67), California Industrial Education Association, Lutheran Academy of Scholarship, Epsilon Pi Tau, Phi Delta Kappa, Rotary. *Awards, honors:* Service awards, American Vocational Association, 1966, 1967; Man-of-the-Year Award, American Council of Industrial Arts Teacher Education, 1967; SHIP's citations, California Industrial Education Association, and American Industrial Arts Association, both 1971.

WRITINGS: (With Angus McDonald) *Power: Mechanics of Energy Control*, McKnight & McKnight, 1960; (editor with Ralph Norman) *Graduate Programs in Industrial Arts*, McKnight & McKnight, 1961; (with G. Harold Silvius) *Organizing Course Materials for Industrial Education*, McKnight & McKnight, 1961; (with Marland Strasser, James Arron, and John Eales) *Fundamentals of Safety*

Education, Macmillan, 1964; (with Silvius) *Planning and Organizing Instruction*, McKnight & McKnight, 1974. Contributor of articles to *Encyclopedia of Education, Bulletin of the National Association of Secondary School Principals, Industrial Arts and Vocational Education, School Shop, Journal of Industrial Arts Education, American Vocational Journal, International Labor Journal, Theory into Practice*. Co-editor of yearbook, American Council of Industrial Arts Teacher Education, 1961; editor, *Journal of Industrial Teacher Education*, 1962-64; industrial arts editor, *American Vocational Journal*, 1963-66; newsletter editor, *Western Association of Summer Session Administrators*, 1970—.

*   *   *

BOLES, Harold W(ilson) 1915-

PERSONAL: Born July 25, 1915, in Trafalgar, Ind.; son of Forest J. (a farmer) and Audra "B" (Foster) Boles; married Esther L. Bowers, November 2, 1944; children: Sharon Kaye, Deborah Dee, David Brian, Dennis Ray. *Education:* Indiana State University, B.S., 1937; Ohio State University, M.A., 1950, Ph.D., 1957; University of Colorado, graduate study, 1951; University of Chicago, postdoctoral study, 1968. *Politics:* Independent. *Religion:* Unitarian Universalist. *Home:* 5123 Ridgebrook Dr., Kalamazoo, Mich. *Office:* Western Michigan University, Kalamazoo, Mich. 49001.

CAREER: Marion Local Schools, Columbus, Ohio, superintendent, 1952-55; Joseph Baker and Associates, Architects, Newark, Ohio, educational facilities consultant, 1955-61; Western Michigan University, Kalamazoo, associate professor, 1961-63, professor of education, 1963—, head of department of school services, 1965-68, head of department of educational leadership, 1968-71. Facilities consultant to school districts in Michigan, Kentucky, and Ohio; visiting lecturer, Arizona State University, 1963, Washington State University, 1965; visiting fellow, Western Australian Institute of Technology, 1974-75. *Military service:* U.S. Naval Reserve, 1941-46; became lieutenant. *Member:* American Association of School Administrators, National Conference of Professors of Educational Administration, Michigan Association of School Administrators, Michigan Association of Professors of Educational Administration, Phi Delta Kappa.

WRITINGS: 258 Ways to Save Money . . . , School of Graduate Studies, Western Michigan University, 1963; *Step by Step to Better School Facilities*, Holt, 1965; (contributor) Robert E. Wilson, editor, *Educational Administration*, C. E. Merrill, 1965; (with son, David B. Boles) *Some Earlier Americans: Boles and Bowers Relatives ca. 1700-1970*, privately printed, 1970; *The Three R's and the New Religion*, Pendell, 1973; (contributor) Maurice F. Seay, editor, *Community Education: A Developing Concept*, Pendell, 1974; *Exercises in Educational Leadership*, Harper, 1975; (editor) *Interdisciplinary Readings in Educational Leadership*, MSS Educational Publishing, 1975; (with J. A. Davenport) *Introduction to Educational Leadership*, Harper, 1975. Contributor to education and training journals.

AVOCATIONAL INTERESTS: Genealogical research, gardening, reading, and travel.

*   *   *

BOLLING, Richard (Walker) 1916-

PERSONAL: Born May 17, 1916, in New York, N.Y.; son of Richard Walker and Florence (Easton) Bolling; married

Jim Grant, January 13, 1964; children: Three. *Education:* University of the South, B.A., 1937, M.A., 1939; Vanderbilt University,, graduate study, 1939-40. *Politics:* Democrat. *Religion:* Episcopalian. *Home:* 307 Warrenton Dr., Silver Spring, Md. 20904. *Office:* 2465 Rayburn Office Building, Washington, D.C. 20515.

CAREER: University of Kansas City (now University of Missouri at Kansas City), director of student activities and veterans affairs, 1946-47; American Veterans Committee, national vice-chairman, 1947-48; U.S. House of Representatives, Washington, D.C., congressman representing Fifth District of Missouri, 1949—, currently member of House Rules Committee, Joint Economic Committee, and chairman of Select Committee on Committees. *Military service:* U.S. Army, 1941-46; became lieutenant colonel. *Awards, honors:* Congressional Distinguished Service Award, American Political Science Association, 1961; honorary Doctor of Civil Laws, University of the South, 1963, Kansas City College of Osteopathy and Surgery; honorary Doctor of Laws, Rockhurst College.

WRITINGS: House Out of Order, Dutton, 1965; *Power in the House: A History of the Leadership of the House of Representatives*, Dutton, 1968, revised edition, Capricorn Books, 1974.

*   *   *

BOLT, Robert (Oxton) 1924-

PERSONAL: Born August 15, 1924, in Sale, Manchester, England; son of Ralph (a shopkeeper) and Leah (a teacher; maiden name, Binnion) Bolt; married Celia Ann Roberts (a painter), November 6, 1949 (divorced, 1967); married Sarah Miles (an actress), 1967; children (first marriage) Sally Simmons, Benedict, Joanna; (second marriage) Thomas. *Education:* University of Manchester, B.A. (honours in history), 1950; University of Exeter, teaching diploma, 1950. *Politics:* Left-wing. *Agent:* Margaret Ramsay, 14a Goodwin's Court, London WC 2, England.

CAREER: Office boy with Sun Life Assurance Office, Manchester, England, 1942; in Devon, 1950-52; Millfield School, Street, Somerset, England, teacher and head of English department, 1952-58. Playwright and film director. *Military service:* Royal Air Force, 1943-44, Royal West African Frontier Force, 1944-46; became lieutenant. *Member:* Campaign for Nuclear Disarmament, Association of Cinematography and Television Technicians (president), Writers Guild of Great Britain, The Spares (Somerset; honorary life member). *Awards, honors:* Evening Standard Drama Award, 1957, for *Flowering Cherry*; New York Drama Critics Circle Award, 1962, for *A Man for All Seasons*; British Film Academy Award, and Academy of Motion Picture Arts and Sciences, Academy Award (Oscar) nomination, 1962, both for "Lawrence of Arabia"; Academy of Motion Picture Arts and Sciences, Academy Award, 1966, for "Doctor Zhivago"; New York Film Critics Award for best picture of the year, 1966, Golden Globe Press Award, 1967, and Academy of Motion Picture Arts and Sciences, Academy Award, 1967, all for film, "A Man for All Seasons"; Antoinette Perry (Tony) Award nomination, 1972, for *Vivat! Vivat Regina!*; Commander of British Empire, 1972.

WRITINGS—Plays: Flowering Cherry (produced in London, 1957, in New York, 1959), Heinemann, 1958; *A Man for All Seasons* (two-act; first draft was broadcast in England, 1954, televised on B.B.C., 1957, full-length play produced in London, 1960, in New York, 1961), Samuel

French, 1960, Random House, 1962; *The Tiger and the Horse* (three-act; produced in London, 1960), Heinemann, 1961; *Three Plays* (contains *Flowering Cherry, A Man for All Seasons*, and *The Tiger and the Horse*), Heinemann, 1963; *Gentle Jack* (produced in London, 1960), Samuel French, 1964, Random House, 1965; *The Thwarting of Baron Bolligrew* (two-act children's play; produced in London, 1966), Samuel French, 1966; *Vivat! Vivat Regina!* (two-act; first produced in Chichester, England, at the Chichester Theatre, May 20, 1970, produced in Boston at the Shubert Theatre, December 27, 1971), Random House, 1971.

Unpublished plays: "The Last of the Wine" (adaptation of his radio play), produced in London, 1956; "The Critic and the Heart," produced in Oxford, England, 1957; "Brother and Sister," produced in Brighton, England, 1967.

Screenplays: "Lawrence of Arabia," Columbia, 1962; "Doctor Zhivago," United Artists, 1966, published as *Doctor Zhivago: The Screenplay*, Random House, 1966; "A Man for All Seasons" (adaptation of own play), Columbia, 1966; "Ryan's Daughter," Metro-Goldwyn-Mayer, 1970; "Lady Caroline Lamb," United Artists, 1972.

Radio plays: "The Master," 1953; "Fifty Pigs," 1953; "Ladies and Gentlemen," 1954; "The Last of the Wine," 1955; "Mr. Sampson's Sundays," 1955; "The Window," 1958; "The Drunken Sailor," 1958; "The Banana Tree," 1961.

Work included in anthology, *The New Theatre of Europe*, Volume I, edited by Robert W. Corrigan, Dell, 1962. Contributor to *Esquire, Theatre Arts, Saturday Review*, and other periodicals.

WORK IN PROGRESS: A play on the subject of the Russian Revolution.

SIDELIGHTS: Bolt first turned to playwriting when a Nativity play was needed for the school where he was then teaching. He later left teaching to devote all his time to writing. Unlike many of his British contemporaries, he is not a startling innovator but rather, as John Russell Taylor describes him, "a good, traditional playwright." Bolt would, however, like to see drama fictionalized to the point where masks would be worn by the characters.

His portrayal of Thomas More, *A Man for All Seasons*, J. C. Trewin believes is "one of the few contemporary portrait-plays likely to last." Another observer wrote that Bolt "preserves a personal aloofness when it comes to translating life into art. He does not preach; he stands back and relates, creating his own reality in place of an aggressive naturalism." And Walter Kerr praised the play as being "as remarkable in its restraint as in its ultimate fire.... What Mr. Bolt has done is to make the human mind shine. The glare is dazzling; the experience exhilarating."

Bolt wrote about his imagery and poetry in a preface to *A Man for All Seasons*: "As a figure for the superhuman context, I took the largest, most alien, least formulated thing I know, the sea and water. The references to ships, rivers, currents, tides, navigation, and so on, are all used for this purpose. Society by contrast figures as dry land. I set out with no very well formed idea of the kind of play it was to be, except that it was not to be naturalistic.... I comfort myself with the thought that it's the nature of imagery to work, in performance at any rate, unconsciously. But if, as I think, a play is more like a poem than a straight narration, still less a demonstration or lecture, then imagery

ought to be important. It's perhaps necessary to add that by a poem I mean something tough and precise, not something dreamy." Bolt says he chose More as his protagonist because "a very few people give a tinker's cuss whether or not the sovereign of England is the supreme head of the Church of England insofar as the law of God allows.... I wanted an issue which was largely drained of its emotional content now, so that you could see it, as it were, diagramatically.... And the second reason why I was attracted to More particularly was that he was a martyr, [though] I am not attracted to martyrs in general.... [But] then there dawned the slow realization that More was very good at living as well as able to die. And running these two things in harness, reading more and more about him and thinking about his problem in general, I came very strongly to the conclusion that in a way you can't live properly until you have come to terms with your death."

Bolt's successes have been largely in the area of historical drama. Speaking of *Vivat! Vivat Regina!*, a play about the conflict between Mary, Queen of Scots and Elizabeth I, he said: "I think there is a quite narrow limit to what you may do with the known facts of history. Clearly, you're not writing a history book, but on the other hand, you must be loyal to such facts as are definitely known. Particularly such a salient fact as that these two women, whose lives were so closely intertwined, never in fact effected a meeting! They wanted to meet, but the political circumstances made it either imprudent or disadvantageous for one or the other of them, so it never came off.

"One cannot rewrite history for dramatic effect—not as it happened, but as *should* have happened. If you have a marvelous play in your mind about two queens who eventually meet and have a stand-up barney, fine. But you may not call them Elizabeth and Mary, because we know they didn't meet....

"Where the facts are not definitely knowable, the playwright is at liberty to read such evidence as is available to him and make up his own mind. But undoubtedly his decision will be colored by his desires as a playwright."

Not only working well with historical subjects, Bolt also uses historical devices, J. W. Lambert said: "Mr. Bolt is what might be called an experimental mainstream dramatist: He effortlessly incorporates the devices of effective staging from any age, including our own, and uses them as what they should be, a means to an end, never allowing them to take charge as ends in themselves. Scene flows easily into scene, scene plays against scene, passing time is covered in a snatch of dialogue, distance is annihilated in an exchange between one side of the stage and the other, naturalism gives way to symbolism, declamation to fantasy—all ... without the slightest obscurity. Here is real craftsmanship."

Some critics attribute his tremendous success in film to this same traditionalism. Clifford A. Ridly commented that "Bolt's popularity with the Hollywood Establishment should not be too surprising. Hollywood is a conservative place, and *A Man for All Seasons*—like 'Lawrence' and 'Zhivago' before it—is essentially a 'traditional' movie in its values, its conception, its direction." Others see the film success in Bolt's ability to understand the differences between the stage and the screen. Bolt has said "I understand and respect it when a man like Antonioni says that cinema is a visual medium and therefore must make its impact by visual means. I say the less dialogue in a film the better, simply because to see something is more effective than to be told it. But where I differ is that I believe that although absolutely a visual medium, cinema is also a *narrative* medium. It can't help but be simply because it exists over a period of time. I think that the visual people who say they'll make it up hanker after the status of a painter. We have a specific time. An audience sits down at 8 and leaves at 10. There is a need for connection. It need not be like the films David [Lean] and I make—[with] a logical and explicit connection. But one simply cannot juxtapose images and leave it to the imagination of audiences for that connection, or what you wind up with is deadly. When one is responsible for the creation of a film, one is responsible for the necessary connection. There is danger in a film not being explicitly thought out.'' Bolt commented elsewhere on adapting *A Man for All Seasons*: "Some things had to be sacrificed in order to bring the film in at around two hours. The Common Man, for instance—there's a definite loss there, even though we've given some of his speeches to other characters. . . . There were compensations, of course. We were able to *show* the symbolism of the water, for one thing.''

Bolt, says Trewin, is "concerned fiercely with the problems of the individual and his social conscience.'' Bolt has said: "My first intention in writing this play [*Vivat! Vivat Regina!*] was not to give a history lesson but to create an effective, entertaining, possibly disturbing—and truthful—evening in the theatre. While I hope audiences will find this an exciting narrative, I also hope anyone who thinks about it—or even those who don't—will come away with some slight uneasiness about the nature of power, and about figures who are endowed with power. Both with a certain uneasiness about what they are up to 'on our behalf' and also with a certain pity for the terrifying pressures to which they are subjected.''

Theatre Arts notes that he "owes something to such fashionable playwrights of the day as Brecht, Beckett and Tennessee Williams; something but not much. Brecht has taught him now to construct an episodic drama, Beckett and Williams have each contributed to his preoccupation with moral and metaphysical problems. But far more than they, he is a detached writer who separates his creative and intellectual life.''

Bolt was jailed briefly in 1961, after participating in a demonstration for nuclear disarmament.

AVOCATIONAL INTERESTS: Walking and sailing.

BIOGRAPHICAL/CRITICAL SOURCES: Catholic World, September, 1962; W. A. Armstrong and others, editors, *Experimental Drama*, G. Bell, 1963; *Theatre Arts*, May, 1963; *New York Times*, December 13, 1966, December 18, 1966; Ronald Hayman, *Robert Bolt*, Heinemann, 1969; *Sunday Times* (London), November 12, 1972; *Film-Makers Newsletter*, October, 1973.

* * *

BOLTON, W(hitney) F(rench) 1930-

PERSONAL: Born October 15, 1930, in New York, N.Y.; son of John Whitney (a New York drama critic and author) and Frances (Schiff) Bolton; married Margaret Gossling, July 6, 1962; children: Sarah Ruth. *Education:* Bard College, B.A., 1951; Princeton University, M.A., 1953, Ph.D., 1955. *Politics:* Socialist. *Religion:* None. *Home:* 96 Moore St., Princeton, N.J. 08540. *Office:* Department of English, Douglass College, Rutgers University, New Brunswick, N.J. 08903.

CAREER: University of California, Berkeley, instructor, 1959-60, assistant professor of English, 1960-61; University of Reading, Reading, England, lecturer, 1961-64, senior lecturer, 1964-65, professor of English, 1965-70, senior tutor, 1966-68; Douglass College, Rutgers University, New Brunswick, N.J., professor of English, 1970—, chairman of English department, 1971—. Sellers visiting professor of English, Simon Fraser University, 1968-69. Guest lecturer at many universities in Great Britain, Canada, and United States. *Member:* American Association of University Professors, Early English Text Society, English Institute, Mediaeval Academy of America, Modern Language Association of America, Philological Society, Royal Historical Society (fellow), Society of Antiquaries (fellow).

WRITINGS: (Compiler) *An Old English Anthology*, Edward Arnold, 1963, Northwestern University Press, 1966; (editor and author of introduction) Ben Jonson, *Sejanus His Fall*, Benn, 1966, Hill & Wang, 1969; (compiler) *The English Language: Essays by English and American Men of Letters, 1490-1839*, Volume I, Cambridge University Press, 1966, Volume II (with D. Crystal), Cambridge University Press, 1969; *A History of Anglo-Latin Literature, 597-1066*, Volume I, Princeton University Press, 1967; *A Short History of Literary English*, Edward Arnold, 1967, 2nd edition, 1972, Littlefield, Adams, 1973; (general editor and contributor) *The Middle Ages*, Sphere Books, 1970; (reviser) Charles Leslie Wrenn, editor, *Beowulf with the Finnesburg Fragments*, 3rd edition (Bolton was not associated with earlier editions), St. Martin's Press, 1973; (editor) Ben Jonson, *Catiline*, University of Nebraska Press, 1973. Contributor of over thirty articles and reviews to journals in America, England, Italy, and Germany.

WORK IN PROGRESS: Alcuin and Beowulf; (with C. A. Ladd) volume II of *A History of Anglo-Latin Literature, 597-1066*.

AVOCATIONAL INTERESTS: Playing, singing, and listening to music.

* * *

BONHAM, Barbara Thomas 1926-

PERSONAL: Born September 27, 1926, in Franklin, Neb.; daughter of Laroy Oscar and Ethel (Dependehner) Thomas; married Max Bonham (a grain-elevator operator), December 24, 1950. *Education:* Attended University of Nebraska. *Politics:* Independent. *Religion:* Agnostic. *Residence:* Naponee, Neb. 68960. *Agent:* Lenniger Literary Agency, 437 Fifth Ave., New York, N.Y. 10016.

CAREER: Writer. *Member:* Franklin County Historical Society.

WRITINGS: Diagnosis: Love, Monarch, 1964; *Challenge of the Prairie* (juvenile), Bobbs-Merrill, 1965; *Army Nurse*, Bouregy, 1965; *Nina Stuart, R.N.*, Bouregy, 1966; *Crisis at Fort Laramie* (juvenile), Duell, 1967; *To Secure the Blessings of Liberty* (juvenile), Hawthorn, 1970; *Willa Cather* (juvenile), Chilton, 1970; *Heroes of the Wild West* (juvenile), Whitman, 1970; *Sweet and Bitter Fancy*, Popular Library, in press. Editor of Franklin County Historical Society's county history, 1966.

WORK IN PROGRESS: An historical novel, *A Stain on Canaan*.

* * *

BOOT, John C. G. 1936-

PERSONAL: Surname is pronounced Boat; born June 10,

1936, in Semarang, Indonesia; son of Frederik R. (a banker) and Maria (den Tex) Boot; married A. M. Hinke Tuinman, May 22, 1965; children: Maren C., Mark F. A. *Education:* Netherlands School of Economics, candidate, 1956, doctoral (with highest possible distinction), 1960, Ph.D. (with highest possible distinction), 1964; Stanford University, graduate study, 1959-60. *Home:* 177 Beard Ave., Buffalo, N.Y. 14214. *Office:* Department of Management Science, Crosby Hall, State University of New York at Buffalo, Buffalo, N.Y. 14214.

CAREER: Netherlands School of Economics, Econometric Institute, Rotterdam, research associate, 1960-64; State University of New York at Buffalo, associate professor, 1964-65, professor of management science, 1965—. Visiting associate professor at U.S. Army Mathematics Research Center, 1962; guest lecturer at International Business Machines Corp. Educational Center, Blaricum, Netherlands, 1963-64; Bugas Professor, University of Wyoming, 1972. Consultant to Marine Midland Banks, 1965—. *Member:* Institute of Management Sciences.

WRITINGS: Quadratic Programming, Algorithms, Anomalies, Applications, Rand McNally, 1964; *Voorspellen en Beslissen,* Spectrum, 1964; (with Theil and Kloek) *Quantitative Economics and Operations Research,* McGraw, 1965; *Mathematical Reasoning in Economics and Management Science: Twelve Topics,* Prentice-Hall, 1967; *Statistical Analysis for Managerial Decisions,* McGraw, 1970; *Common Globe or Global Commons,* Dekker, 1974. Contributor to *DeEconomist, Banker,* and other journals in his field; also contributor of several articles to *Bridge,* on the mathematical aspects of that game. Member of editorial board, *International Journal of Systems Science.*

* * *

BOOTH, Edwin
(Don Blunt, Jack Hazard)

PERSONAL: Born in Beatrice, Neb.; son of Edwin (a clergyman) and Fay (Stewart) Booth; married Irene Sullivan, September 2, 1933. *Education:* Attended Colorado College. *Home:* 5891 Morpeth St., Oakland, Calif. 94618. *Agent:* Paul R. Reynolds, Inc., 599 Fifth Ave., New York, N.Y. 10017.

CAREER: Has been post-office clerk, guide in Colorado's Cave of the Winds, chain grocery store manager, wholesale grocery company office manager, and credit manager; now self-employed accountant and writer. *Member:* Western Writers of America (secretary treasurer, 1963-67; vice-president, 1970), Toastmasters Club (president of Oakland club, 1973).

WRITINGS: Showdown at Warbird, Ace Books, 1956; *Jinx Rider,* Ace Books, 1957; *Boot Heel Range,* Bouregy, 1957; *The Man Who Killed Tex,* Ace Books, 1957; *The Trail to Tomahawk,* Ace Books, 1958; *Wyoming Welcome,* Ace Books, 1959; *Lost Valley,* Bouregy, 1959; *Danger Trail,* Bouregy, 1959.

The Broken Window, Arcadia House, 1960; *Death on a Summer Day,* Arcadia House, 1960; *The Desperate Dude,* Ace Books, 1960; *Return to Apache Springs,* Bouregy, 1960; *Reluctant Lawman,* Ballantine, 1960; (under pseudonym Jack Hazard) *Crooked Spur,* Arcadia House, 1960; *Outlaw Town,* Ballantine, 1961; *The Troublemaker,* Ace Books, 1961; (under pseudonym Don Blunt) *Short Cut,* Bouregy, 1962; *Sidewinder,* Ballantine, 1962; *Valley of Violence,* Bouregy, 1962; *John Sutter—Californian,* Bobbs-Merrill, 1962; *Hardcase Hotel,* Berkley Books, 1962; *Dead*

Giveaway, Bouregy, 1962; *Devil's Canyon,* Bouregy, 1962; *The Dry Gulchers,* Bouregy, 1963; *The Stolen Saddle,* Bouregy, 1964; *Renegade Guns,* Bouregy, 1965; *Trouble at Tragedy Springs,* Berkley Books, 1966; *Triple Cross Trail,* Berkley Books, 1966; *Shoot Out at Twin Buttes,* Berkley Books, 1966; *No Spurs for Johnny Loop,* Berkley Books, 1967; *One Man Posse,* Berkley Books, 1967; *Stranger in Buffalo Springs,* Berkley Books, 1968; *The Backshooters,* Ballantine, 1968; *The Man From Dakota,* Berkley Books, 1968; *The Prodigal Gun,* Berkley Books, 1969; *Stage to San Felipe,* Berkley Books, 1970; *Grudge Killer,* Ballantine, 1971; *Hardesty,* Ace Books, 1971; *Bushwhack,* Ace Books, 1973; *Small Spread,* Ballantine, 1973.

AVOCATIONAL INTERESTS: Playing various musical instruments, including Hammond organ.

* * *

BORDEN, Norman E(aston), Jr. 1907-

PERSONAL: Born July 31, 1907, in Lowell, Mass.; son of Norman E. (a businessman) and Elizabeth L. (Barry) Borden; married Raby Crandall, August 9, 1960; children: Edward Barry; (stepdaughter) Suzanne Crandall (deceased). *Education:* Norwich University, student, 1926-28; New York University, B.S. in M.E., 1930. *Religion:* Protestant. *Home:* Route 4, Montpelier, Vt. 05602.

CAREER: U.S. Army Air Forces, student pilot, 1930-31, pilot, 1932-37; Douglas Aircraft Co., Santa Monica, Calif., airplane designer engineer, 1938-40; U.S. Army Air Forces (and later U.S. Air Force), pilot and maintenance officer, 1940-46, 1950-53, retired with rank of lieutenant colonel; Pratt & Whitney Aircraft, East Hartford, Conn., engineer, and writer of training manuals and operating instructions for military and commercial aircraft pilots, 1953-70. *Member:* Order of Daedalians. *Awards, honors:* Stephen Greene Award, 1974, for paper, "Aviation Comes to Vermont."

WRITINGS: Dear Sarah, Wheelwright, 1966; *Jet Engine Fundamentals,* Hayden, 1967; *Air Mail Emergency,* Wheelwright, 1968; (with Walter Cake) *Fundamentals of Aircraft Piston Engines,* Hayden, 1971. About twenty technical and historical articles have appeared in military and historical periodicals.

WORK IN PROGRESS: The Aviators, a factual account of very early American flying.

AVOCATIONAL INTERESTS: Antique cars and aircraft, aviation history.

* * *

BOREN, Henry C(harles) 1921-

PERSONAL: Born February 10, 1921, in Pike County, Ill.; son of Homer T. and Verna (Renoud) Boren; married Martha Malone, September 19, 1944; children: Annette Gail. *Education:* Southwest Missouri State College, A.B., 1948; University of Illinois, A.M., 1950, Ph.D., 1952. *Politics:* Democrat. *Religion:* Church of Christ. *Home:* 220 Flemington Rd., Chapel Hill, N.C. 27514. *Office:* Department of History, University of North Carolina, Chapel Hill, N.C. 27514.

CAREER: Illinois State Journal, Springfield, reporter, 1941-42; Southwest Missouri State College, Springfield, instructor in English and history, 1952-54; University of Nebraska, Lincoln, instructor in history, 1955; Southern Illinois University, Carbondale, assistant professor of ancient history, 1955-60; University of North Carolina,

Chapel Hill, associate professor, 1960-67, professor of ancient history, 1967—, secretary of the faculty, 1969—. *Military service:* U.S. Army, Mechanized Cavalry, 1942-46; became captain; received Silver Star and Purple Heart. *Member:* American Historical Association, American Philological Association, American Numismatic Society, Archaeological Institute of America, Classical Association of Middle West and South, Society for the Promotion of Roman Studies. *Awards, honors:* Research grants from American Numismatic Society, American Philosophical Society, National Endowment for the Humanities.

WRITINGS: The Roman Republic, Van Nostrand, 1965; *The Gracchi*, Twayne, 1968. Contributor to professional journals.

WORK IN PROGRESS: A book on Roman society; research on Roman numismatics.

*   *   *

BORGMANN, Dmitri A(lfred)   1927-
(El Uqsor, Prof. Merlin X. Houdini, Ms. Ramona J. Quincunx, Ms. Jezebel Q. Xixx)

PERSONAL: Born October 22, 1927, in Berlin, Germany; came to United States, 1936; naturalized citizen, 1943; son of Hans (a clerk) and Lisa (Kalnitzkaya) Borgmann; married Iris S. Sterling, October 27, 1962; children: Keith Alan. *Education:* University of Chicago, Ph.B., 1946. *Politics:* Independent. *Religion:* Lutheran. *Home:* 410 South 2nd St., Dayton, Wash. 99328. *Office:* 405 East Spring St., Dayton, Wash. 99328. *Mailing address:* P.O. Box 138, Dayton, Wash. 99328.

CAREER: Central Standard Life Insurance Co., Chicago, Ill., 1946-61, policy change supervisor, 1954-61; Harry S. Tressel & Associates (consulting actuaries and accountants), Chicago, Ill., actuarial assistant, 1961-65; full-time writer, 1965—; RC Research, Dayton, Wash., executive director, 1972—; Research Unlimited, Dayton, Wash., 1975—. Inventor of word games, and wordplay expert. *Member:* International 4-Cyte Champions Club, Life Office Management Association Institute.

WRITINGS: (Contributor) C. C. Bombaugh, *Oddities and Curiosities of Words and Literature*, annotated by Martin Gardner, revised edition, Dover, 1961; *Language on Vacation*, Scribner, 1965; *Beyond Language*, Scribner, 1967; *Curious Crosswords*, Scribner, 1970; (compiler with Darryl H. Francis) *The Transposal Dictionary*, Harrap, 1976.

Contributor of articles and puzzles in verse, under pseudonym El Uqsor to *Enigma*, under other pseudonyms to *Word Ways*, and word puzzles and curiosities to *Scientific American*, *Chicago Tribune* "Line o'Type or Two" column, and to syndicated feature, "Uncle Nugent's Funland." Author of "Word Row" column in *Books*, 1966, in *Puzzle Lovers Newspaper*, 1968-71; and of periodic "Word Games" department in *Chicago Tribune Magazine*, 1973—. Editor of *Word Ways*, 1968.

SIDELIGHTS: A crossword puzzle devotee as a youth, Borgmann became interested in more challenging forms of word play—palindromes, anagrams, word squares, pangrams, and transpositions. Between 1947 and 1974 he won many thousands of dollars in numerous puzzle contests, and earned about $4,000 as a successful candidate for eight weeks on a television program, "It's in the Name," WGN-TV, Chicago. *Avocational interests:* Astronomy, chess, ancient Asiatic religions.

BIOGRAPHICAL/CRITICAL SOURCES: "Life and

Leisure," *Newsweek*, November 2, 1964; *Chicago Tribune Magazine*, March 4, 1973.

*   *   *

BORGSTROM, Georg A(rne)   1912-

PERSONAL: Born April 5, 1912, in Gustav Adolf, Sweden; came to U.S., 1956, became citizen, 1962; son of Algot Georg (a vicar) and Anna Elisabet (Littorin) Borgstrom; married Greta Ingrid Stromback. *Education:* University of Lund, B.S., 1932, M.S., 1933, Dr. Sci., 1939. *Home:* 4550 Comanche Dr., Okemos, Mich. 48864. *Office:* Department of Food Science, Michigan State University, East Lansing, Mich. 48824.

CAREER: University of Lund, Lund, Sweden, associate professor of plant physiology, 1940-43; Institute of Plant Research and Food Storage, Nynashamn, Sweden, head, 1942-48; Swedish Institute of Food Preservation Research, Goteborg, Sweden, head, 1948-56; Chalmers School of Engineering, Goteborg, associate professor of food technology, 1952-56; professor of food science and human nutrition, 1953; Michigan State University, East Lansing, professor of food science, 1956—, professor of geography, 1966—, Centennial Review lecturer, 1966. *Military service:* Swedish Army, 1939-42; became captain. *Member:* World Academy of Arts and Sciences (fellow), American Institute of Nutrition (fellow), Royal Swedish Academy of Engineering Sciences (fellow), Royal Swedish Academy of Agricultural Sciences (fellow), American Association of Geographers. *Awards, honors: The Hungry Planet* was listed by American Library Association as one of fifty most important books of 1965; International Socrates Prize, 1968; Distinguished Faculty Award, Michigan State University, 1969; Literary Merit Prize, Swedish Authors Foundation, 1973; Wahlberg Gold Medal, 1974; International Award, Institute of Food Technologists, 1975.

WRITINGS: Jorden Vart Ode (title means "The Earth—Our Destiny"), Forum, 1954; (editor) *Fish as Food*, four volumes, Academic Press, 1959-62; (editor) *Atlantic Ocean Fisheries*, Heighway Publishers, 1959; *Mat for Miljarder* (title means "Food for Billions"), LT, 1962; *Japan's World Success in Fishing*, Heighway Publishers, 1963; *Granser for Var Tillvaro* (title means "The Limitations of Man's Existence"), LT, 1964; *The Hungry Planet: The Modern World at the Edge of Famine*, Macmillan, 1965, 3rd edition, 1972; *Revolution i Varldsfisket* (title means "Revolution in World Fisheries"), LT, 1966; *Principles of Food Science*, two volumes, Macmillan, 1968; *Too Many: A Study of Earth's Biological Limitations*, Macmillan, 1969, revised edition, 1971; *Focal Points*, Macmillan, 1973; *Harvesting the Earth*, Intext, 1973; *The Food and People Dilemma*, Duxbury, 1973.

SIDELIGHTS: Georg Borgstrom told *CA:* "The most critical issue facing the world is the growing discrepancy between haves and have nots, both as to countries of the world and social groups within countries. Man has failed to recognize in time the magnitude and urgency of this development. Chief reason for this state of affairs is the simplistic approach to the dynamic relationship between population and resources. Both the historical and biological dimension has been missing in analyses, education, and development programs. A disastrous piece-meal approach, often successful in detail, has failed to recognize realities and the indispensability of coordination in planning and programming.

The most crucial shortcomings are mirrored in the 'sudden'

ecology crisis, and yet this is the logical and inevitable consequence of man's failure to recognize his unchanged dependence on the creative forces of nature (photosynthesis as reflected in food, crops, and forestry) and the basic resources of soil, water, minerals, and fuel. Equally crucial is the failure of Western Man to make a complete accounting of his endeavors, merely registering the credit posts and failing to consider the debit posts. This will lead to a thorough reappraisal of our Western success stories. —But time is in short supply. Drastic countermeasures will be needed in the seventies, if we are to wage successfully the war for human survival in a world now adding one billion people in a single decade.''

Borgstrom speaks, reads, and writes five languages—Swedish, German, Spanish, French, and English; reads six other languages—Russian, Italian, Portuguese, Dutch, Norwegian, and Danish. He has traveled and lectured in Europe, the Soviet Union, Latin America, and Asia.

* * *

BORK, Alfred M. 1926-

PERSONAL: Born September 18, 1926, in Jacksonville, Fla.; son of Philip C. and Elizabeth (Baker) Bork; married Annette Vitsky (a teacher); children: Ellen, Brenda, Carol. *Education:* Georgia Institute of Technology, B.S., 1947; Brown University, Ph.D., 1953. *Home:* 4505 Sandburg Way, Irvine, Calif. 92664.

CAREER: Dublin Institute of Advanced Studies, Ireland, scholar, 1951-52; University of Alaska, College, assistant professor, 1952-55, associate professor, 1955-59, professor of physics, 1959-62; Harvard University, Cambridge, Mass., research fellow in physics, 1962-63; Reed College, Portland, Ore., associate professor of physics, 1963-66, professor, 1966-68; University of California, Irvine, professor of physics, 1968—. *Member:* American Association for the Advancement of Science, American Association of Physics Teachers, Association for Computing Machinery (director of physics computer development project). *Awards, honors:* National Science Foundation faculty fellow, 1962-63.

WRITINGS: (Editor with Arnold Arons) *Science and Ideas*, Prentice-Hall, 1964; (editor) *Science and Language*, Heath, 1966; *FORTRAN for Physics*, Addison-Wesley, 1967; *Using the IBM 1130*, Addison-Wesley, 1968; *Notions About Motion* (preliminary edition), W. H. Freeman, 1970. Contributor to professional journals.

WORK IN PROGRESS: Research on the history of physics in the last half of the nineteenth century and the beginning of the twentieth century, on interactions of the sciences and the arts, and on the use of the computer as a teaching device.

* * *

BORMANN, Ernest G(ordon) 1925-

PERSONAL: Born July 28, 1925, in Mitchell, S.D.; son of Ernest Gottlieb (a banker) and Annette (Doering) Bormann; married Nancy Curtis (a writer and teacher), September 13, 1952; children: Lisa, Ruth, Ellen, Sally. *Education:* University of South Dakota, B.A., 1949; University of Iowa, M.A., 1952, Ph.D., 1953. *Religion:* Protestant. *Home:* 1921 Irving Ave., South, Minneapolis, Minn. 55403. *Office:* University of Minnesota, Minneapolis, Minn.

CAREER: University of South Dakota, Vermillion, in-

structor, 1950; Eastern Illinois University, Charleston, assistant professor, 1953-55, associate professor, 1955-56; Florida State University, Tallahassee, associate professor, 1956-59; University of Minnesota, Minneapolis, assistant professor, 1959-62, associate professor, 1962-65, professor of speech, 1965—. Communication consultant to business and industry. *Military service:* U.S. Army, 1943-46. *Member:* International Communication Association, Speech Association of America, Central States Speech Association (president, 1971-72), Speech Communication Association.

WRITINGS: Theory and Research in the Communicative Arts, Holt, 1965; *Discussion and Group Methods*, Harper, 1969, revised edition, 1975; (with others) *Interpersonal Communication in the Modern Organization*, Prentice-Hall, 1969; (with William Howell) *Presentation Speaking for Business and the Professions*, Harper, 1971; (editor) *Forerunners of Black Power*, Prentice-Hall, 1971; (with wife, Nancy Bormann) *Speech Communication: An Interpersonal Approach*, Harper, 1972; (with Nancy Bormann) *Effective Small Group Communication*, Burgess, 1972; *Effective Committees and Groups in the Church*, Augsburg, 1973.

Author of play, "Hell, That's Politics," first produced in Minneapolis at Theatre in the Round, December 7, 1972, and other plays produced by university and children's theaters and on television. Contributor to speech journals.

WORK IN PROGRESS: Rhetorical Criticism of Religious and Reform Speaking, 1620-1860.

* * *

BOSMAJIAN, Haig Aram 1928-

PERSONAL: Surname rhymes with "contagion"; born March 26, 1928, in Fresno, Calif.; son of Aram and Aurora (Keosyan) Bosmajian; married Hamida Just (a teacher), February 27, 1957. *Education:* University of California, B.A., 1949; University of the Pacific, M.A., 1951; Stanford University, Ph.D., 1960. *Office:* Department of Speech, University of Washington, Seattle, Wash.

CAREER: University of Connecticut, Storrs, assistant professor of speech, 1961-65; University of Washington, Seattle, assistant professor of speech, 1965—. *Member:* Speech Association of America, American Association of University Professors, Western Speech Association.

WRITINGS: (Editor) *Readings in Speech*, Harper, 1965; *The Rhetoric of the Speaker*, Heath, 1967; *Readings in Parliamentary Procedure*, Harper, 1968; *The Rhetoric of the Civil Rights Movement*, Random House, 1969.

The Principles and Practice of Freedom of Speech, Houghton, 1971; *The Rhetoric of Nonverbal Communication*, Scott, Foresman, 1971; *Dissent: Symbolic Behavior and Rhetorical Strategies*, Allyn & Bacon, 1972; *This Great Argument: The Rights of Women*, Addison-Wesley, 1972; *Obscenity and Freedom of Expression*, Lenox Hill, 1974; *The Language of Oppression*, Public Affairs Press, 1974. Contributor to *Dalhousie Review*, *Christian Century*, and speech and education journals.

* * *

BOUCHARD, Robert H. 1923-

PERSONAL: Born June 26, 1923, in St. Albans, Vt.; son of Henry J. and Annette (Jarvis) Bouchard; married Ann M. Morrison; children: Catherine, David, Ellen, Margaret. *Education:* Boston Conservatory of Music, B.M., 1950;

University of Arizona, M.M.Ed., 1960. *Home:* 1060 Bonnie View Rd., Hollister, Calif. 95023.

CAREER: San Benito County Schools, Hollister, Calif., music consultant. San Benito Concert Association, president, 1964-66; Hollister Community Band, director; Fine Arts Council of San Benito County, chairman. *Military service:* U.S. Navy, 1943-46. *Member:* California Association for Supervision and Curriculum Development.

WRITINGS: Let's Play the Recorder, Humphries, 1962.

* * *

BOURNE, Frank Card 1914-

PERSONAL: Born July 17, 1914, in Wells, Me.; son of Moses Avander (a farmer) and Grace (Card) Bourne. *Education:* Princeton University, A.B., 1936, M.A., 1940, Ph.D., 1941. *Politics:* Independent. *Religion:* Protestant. *Home:* R.F.D. 1, Wells, Me. 04090. *Office:* Princeton University, 112 East Pyne Building, Princeton, N.J. 08540.

CAREER: Princeton University, Princeton, N.J., instructor, 1946-47, assistant professor, 1947-50, bicentennial perceptor, 1950-54, associate professor, 1954-66, professor of classics, 1966-71, Kennedy Professor of Latin Language and Literature, 1971—. *Military service:* U.S. Army Air Forces, 1941-45. *Member:* American Philological Association, Archaeological Institute of America, Association Internationale d'epigraphie Latine, Association Internationale Papyrologue, Vergilian Society of America (secretary-treasurer, 1951-54), Classical Association of the Atlantic States (president, 1957-58), Phi Beta Kappa.

WRITINGS: Public Works of the Julio-Claudians and Flavians, Princeton University Press, 1946; (with A. C. Johnson and P. R. Coleman-Norton) *Ancient Roman Statues*, Texas University Press, 1961; (editor) Edward Gibbon, *Decline and Fall of the Roman Empire*, Dell, 1963; *A History of the Romans*, Heath, 1966.

WORK IN PROGRESS: An exposition of Roman civil law to be used by students of Roman history.

SIDELIGHTS: Bourne told *CA:* "I am, from May till September, a dedicated Maine farmer. My desk receives some attention during that time, but the greatest attention is given to vegetable gardens, hayfields, and reclamation.

* * *

BOWDEN, Leonard (Walter) 1933-

PERSONAL: Born February 28, 1933, in Haxtun, Colo.; son of Walter Spelts (a farmer) and Eva B. (Murphy) Bowden; married Geraldine Marie Flood (a teacher), October 4, 1952; children: Jerald Dean, Melanie Rae, Jacqueline Kay. *Education:* University of Colorado, B.A., 1954, M.S., 1961; Clark University, Worcester, Mass., Ph.D., 1964. *Home:* 3642 Mt. Vernon Ave., Riverside, Calif. *Office:* Department of Earth Science, University of California, Riverside, Calif. 92502.

CAREER: Rhode Island College, Providence, instructor in geography, 1962-63; University of Southern California, Los Angeles, assistant professor of geography, 1963-64; University of California, Riverside, assistant professor, beginning 1964, now professor of geography. Office of Naval Research, Washington, D.C., consultant to head of Geography Branch, 1966. *Military service:* U.S. Air Force, navigator and intelligence officer, 1954-59; became first lieutenant. *Member:* Association of American Geographers, American Geographical Society, American Society

of Photogrammetry, American Association for the Advancement of Science, National Council for Geographic Education, Sigma Xi.

WRITINGS: Diffusion of the Decision to Irrigate, University of Chicago Press, 1965; (contributor) David Amiran and Andrew Wilson, editors, *Coastal Deserts: Their Natural and Human Environments*, University of Arizona Press, 1973. Also author of *Manual of Remote Sensing*, American Society of Photogrammetry. Contributor to *Yuma Pioneer, Professional Geographer, Science*, and *Journal of Remote Sensing*.

WORK IN PROGRESS: Research in remote sensing of the environment by spacecraft.

* * *

BOWEN, J(ean) Donald 1922-

PERSONAL: Born March 19, 1922, in Malad, Idaho; son of John David (a railroad agent) and Lillian (Larsen) Bowen; married Catherine Holley, May 27, 1948; children: David James, Douglas Ray, Dale Eugene, Christina Lee, Karen Lucy. *Education:* Brigham Young University, A.B., 1944; Columbia University, M.A., 1949; University of New Mexico, Ph.D., 1952. *Religion:* Church of Jesus Christ of Latter-day Saints. *Home:* 3055 Corda Dr., Los Angeles, Calif. 90049. *Office:* University of California, 900 Hilgard Ave., Los Angeles, Calif. 90024.

CAREER: Duke University, Durham, N.C., instructor, 1952-53; U.S. Department of State Foreign Service Institute, Washington, D.C., scientific linguist, 1953-58; Philippine Center for Language Study, Manila, co-director, 1958-63; University of California, Los Angeles, 1958—, professor of English, 1966—. Consultant to U.S. Office of Education, State of California, Agency for International Development, and Center for Applied Linguistics. *Military service:* U.S. Army, 1943-46. *Member:* Modern Language Association of America, Linguistic Society of America, Teachers of English to Speakers of Other Languages.

WRITINGS: (With Robert P. Stockwell) *Patterns of Spanish Pronunciation*, University of Chicago Press, 1960; (with others) *Modern Spanish*, Harcourt, 1960, 3rd edition, 1973; (editor) *Techniques and Procedures in Second Language Teaching*, Phoenix House, 1963; (with R. P. Stockwell) *The Sounds of English and Spanish*, University of Chicago Press, 1965; (with R. P. Stockwell and J. W. Martin) *The Grammatical Structures of English and Spanish*, University of Chicago Press, 1965; (editor) *Beginning Tagalog: A Course for Speakers of English*, University of California Press, 1965; (editor) *Basic Readers for English Teaching*, Phoenix House, 1965; (editor) *Intermediate Readings in Tagalog*, University of California Press, 1968; (co-editor) *Linguistics in Oceania*, Mouton, 1970; (editor with M. L. Bender, R. L. Cooper, and C. A. Ferguson) *Language in Ethiopia*, Oxford University Press, 1975; *Patterns of English Pronunciation*, Newbury House Publishers, 1975; (editor with J. Ornstein) *Studies in Southwest Spanish*, Newbury House Publishers, in press. Author of other texts in English and Spanish. Contributor to language journals.

WORK IN PROGRESS: A text on adaption in language teaching, with H. S. Mudsen.

* * *

BOWER, Gordon H(oward) 1932-

PERSONAL: Born December 30, 1932, in Scio, Ohio; son

of Clyde Ward (a grocer) and Mabelle (Bosart) Bower; married Sharon Anthony (a part-time college teacher), January 30, 1957; children: Lori Ann, Anthony Gordon, Julia Alice. *Education:* Western Reserve University (now Case Western Reserve University), B.A., 1954; University of Minnesota, graduate study, 1954-55; Yale University, M.S., 1956, Ph.D., 1959. *Politics:* Independent. *Religion:* Unitarian Universalist. *Office:* Department of Psychology, Stanford University, Stanford, Calif. 94305.

CAREER: Stanford University, Stanford, Calif., assistant professor, 1959-64, associate professor, 1964-66, professor of experimental psychology, 1966—. *Member:* American Psychological Association, American Association for the Advancement of Science, National Academy of Science, Society of Experimental Psychologists, Psychonomic Society, Sigma Xi.

WRITINGS: (With R. C. Atkinson and E. J. Crothers) *Introduction to Mathematical Learning Theory*, Wiley, 1965; (with E. R. Hilgard) *Theories of Learning*, 3rd edition, Appleton, 1966; *Attention on Learning*, Wiley, 1968; (with John Robert Anderson) *Human Associative Memory*, V. H. Winston, 1973. Also contributor to professional journals. Counsulting editor to five journals of psychology.

AVOCATIONAL INTERESTS: Computers, sports, literature, and drama.†

* * *

BOYD, Mildred Worthy 1921-

PERSONAL: Born April 20, 1921, in Ranger, Tex.; daughter of James Elbert and Gladys (Meek) Worthy; divorced; children: Kathleen (Mrs. Danny Paul Easly), Elizabeth (Mrs. Clark Drummond), Judy. *Education:* Attended Texas Christian University, 1954-60, University of Utah, 1960-61. *Politics:* Independent. *Home:* 3315 El Serrito Dr., Salt Lake City, Utah 84109.

CAREER: Draftsman for North American Aviation, Grand Prairie, Tex., 1943-45; designer for Convair (aircraft), Fort Worth, Tex., 1954-60, Sperry Utah (missiles), Salt Lake City, Utah, 1960-62, and Hercules Powder Co. (missiles), Magna, Utah, 1962—.

WRITINGS: History in Harness—The Story of Horses, Criterion, 1965; *Black Flags and Pieces of Eight*, Criterion, 1965; *The Silent Cities*, Criterion, 1966; *Rulers in Petticoats*, Criterion, 1967; *Man, Myth, and Magic*, Criterion, 1969.

SIDELIGHTS: Mildred Boyd told *CA*: "My dream is to visit the archaeological sites I now only read about."†

* * *

BOYD, Robin 1919-

PERSONAL: Born January 3, 1919, in Melbourne, Victoria, Australia; son of Penleigh (an artist) and Edith Susan (Anderson) Boyd; married Patricia Madder, December 27, 1947; children: Caroline (Mrs. Simon Eckersley), Penleigh, Suzy. *Education:* Attended Royal Melbourne Institute of Technology, 1935-41. *Home:* 290 Walsh St., South Yalla, Melbourne C2, Australia. *Office:* 340 Albert St., East Melbourne, Victoria, Australia.

CAREER: Royal Victorian Institute of Architects, Melbourne, Victoria, Australia, director of Home Service, 1946-53; Grounds, Romberg & Boyd (architects), Melbourne, partner, 1954-62; Romberg & Boyd (architects), Melbourne, partner, 1962—. Part-time lecturer on design

and architectural history, University of Melbourne, 1948-56; Bemis Professor of Architecture, Massachusetts Institute of Technology, 1956-57. Trustee, National Gallery of Victoria. *Military service:* Australian Army, 1941-45; became warrant officer. *Member:* Royal Australian Institute of Architects (fellow), Royal Society of Arts (England; fellow), American Institute of Architects (honorary fellow).

WRITINGS: Victorian Modern, Architectural Student's Society of the Royal Victorian Institute of Architects, 1947; *Australia's Home*, Melbourne University Press, 1952, 2nd edition, Penguin, 1968; *The Australian Ugliness*, F. W. Cheshire, 1960, 2nd edition, Penguin, 1968; *The Walls Around Us* (juvenile), F. W. Cheshire, 1962; *Kenzo Tange*, Braziller, 1962; *The Puzzle of Architecture*, Cambridge University Press, 1965; *Artificial Australia*, Australian Broadcasting Commission, 1967; *New Directions in Japanese Architecture*, Braziller, 1968; *Living in Australia*, Pergamon, 1970; *The Great Australian Dream*, Pergamon, 1972. Contributor to architectural journals in United States, Australia, and England.

WORK IN PROGRESS: A book on the Sydney Opera House.

SIDELIGHTS: Boyd told *CA* that his major interest is relating architecture and design to social development. He travels frequently to United States, Europe, Japan.

BIOGRAPHICAL/CRITICAL SOURCES: John Hetherington, *Uncommon Men*, Cheshire, 1965.†

* * *

BOYLE, Robert H. 1928-

PERSONAL: Born August 21, 1928, in Brooklyn, N.Y.; son of Robert H. (a ship's engineer) and Elizabeth (Condouris) Boyle; married Jane C. Sanger, January 7, 1956; children: Stephanie, Peter, Alexander. *Education:* Trinity College, Hartford, Conn., B.A., 1949; Yale University, M.A., 1950. *Politics:* Independent. *Religion:* Roman Catholic. *Home:* Finney Farm, Croton-on-Hudson, N.Y. 10520. *Agent:* John Cushman Associates, 24 East 38th St., New York, N.Y. 10016. *Office: Sports Illustrated*, Time-Life Building, New York, N.Y.

CAREER: With United Press, New York, N.Y., 1953-54; *Sports Illustrated*, New York, N.Y., staff writer, 1954-56; *Sports Illustrated* and *Time*, San Francisco, Calif., and Chicago, Ill., bureaus, staff correspondent, 1956-60; *Sports Illustrated*, New York, N.Y., senior editor, 1960—. *Military service:* U.S. Marine Corps, 1950-52; served as officer. *Member:* American Littoral Society (member of advisory board), Scenic Hudson Preservation Conference (vice-chairman), Hudson River Fishermen's Association (director), Sierra Club, Saw Mill River Audubon Society. *Awards, honors:* Salmo Award, of Theodore Gordon Flyfishers, for conservation articles in *Sports Illustrated*, 1965.

WRITINGS: Sport, Mirror of American Life, Little, Brown, 1963; *The Hudson River*, Norton, 1969; (with others) *The Water Hustlers*, Sierra Club, 1971. Contributor to *Commonweal, Atlantic Monthly, Garden Journal*.

WORK IN PROGRESS: A book on the natural history of the southern New England Coast and a book on the life and times of the black bass, both for Norton.

SIDELIGHTS: Boyle told *CA* he is "active in conservation work because I have no wish to see natural resources destroyed for what is mistakenly called progress." *The Hudson River*, Boyle's second book has been called a classic work in conservation and natural history. *Avoca-*

tional interests: Russian literature, fishing, fly-tying, dragon flies.

* * *

BRACK, Harold Arthur 1923-

PERSONAL: Surname is pronounced Brock; born October 8, 1923, in East Moline, Ill.; son of Willis (a service station proprietor) and Mary C. (Petrie) Brack; married Mary Lou Lundahl, August 9, 1952; children: Barbara Anne, Susan Elizabeth, Janet Lee. *Education:* Augustana College, Rock Island, Ill., B.A., 1948; Garrett Biblical Institute, B.D., 1951; Northwestern University, M.A., 1951, Ph.D., 1953. *Politics:* Registered Republican. *Home:* 57 Madison Ave., Madison, N.J. 07940. *Office:* Theological School, Drew University, Madison, N.J.

CAREER: Ordained elder in Central Illinois Conference of The Methodist Church, 1952; Drew University, Theological School, Madison, N.J., assistant professor, 1953-58, associate professor, 1958-68, professor of speech and homiletics, 1969—. Visiting professor, Immaculate Conception Seminary, Darlington, N.J. *Military service:* U.S. Army, 1943-46; became technical sergeant. *Member:* Speech Association of America.

WRITINGS: (With Kenneth G. Nance) *Public Speaking and Discussion for Religious Leaders*, Prentice-Hall, 1961; *Effective Oral Interpretation for Religious Leaders*, Prentice-Hall, 1964; (contributor) Holland DeWitte and others, editors, *Preaching in American History; Selected Issues in the American Pulpit, 1630-1967*, Abingdon, 1969. Associate editor, *Quarterly Journal of Speech*, 1963-65.

* * *

BRACKER, Jon 1936-

PERSONAL: Born October 10, 1936, in New York, N.Y.; son of Joseph Henry and Nadine (Katzenstein) Bracker; married Joan Allen, December 27, 1965 (divorced, 1973). *Education:* University of Texas, B.A., 1958, M.A., 1960. *Home:* 19 Homestead St., San Francisco, Calif. 94114.

CAREER: Humanities Research Center, University of Texas, Austin, manuscript cataloger, 1960-62; Amarillo Junior College, Amarillo, Tex., instructor, 1963-64; Midwestern University, Wichita Falls, Tex., instructor, 1965-66, assistant professor of English, 1966-68; Slippery Rock State College, Slippery Rock, Pa., assistant professor, 1968-69; Indiana State University, Terre Haute, Ind., assistant professor, 1969-73.

WRITINGS: (Editor) *Bright Cages: The Selected Poems of Christopher Morley*, University of Pennsylvania Press, 1965; *Constellations of Clover* (poems), Prickly Pear Press, 1973; *Either You Call Me Or I'll Call You* (poems), Thorpe Springs Press, in press; (with Mark Wallach) *Christopher Morley*, Twayne, in press. Founder and editor, *Penny Poems from Amarillo College*, 1963-64. Founder and editor, *Penny Poems from Midwestern University*, 1965-68.

* * *

BRADDY, Haldeen 1908-

PERSONAL: Born January 22, 1908, in Fairlie, Tex.; son of J. W. (a building contractor) and Lena M. (Roundtree) Braddy; married Virginia Bell, June, 1927. *Education:* East Texas State University, A.B., 1928; University of Texas, M.A., 1929; New York University, Ph.D., 1934. *Religion:* Christian. *Home:* 2109 Arizona Ave., El Paso, Tex. 79930.

CAREER: New York University, New York, N.Y., instructor in English, 1929-35; Sul Ross State College, Alpine, Tex., professor of English and head of department, 1935-36; Texas Christian University, Fort Worth, associate professor, 1938-40, professor of English, 1940-42; Texas Technological College, Lubbock, supervisor of military English, 1943-44; University of Kansas, Lawrence, associate professor of English, 1944-45; Texas Western College, El Paso, associate professor, 1946-50, professor of English, 1950—. Visiting lecturer at Tulane University, 1946, University of Southern California, summer, 1946, University of New Mexico, summer, 1949. *Military service:* U.S. Army Air Forces, 1942; became lieutenant.

MEMBER: Modern Language Association of America (chairman of Chaucer group, 1935, 1937, 1942-44), American Folklore Society (councillor, 1951-52), Texas Folklore Society (president, 1951-53), Rocky Mountain Modern Language Association (president, 1973; honorary president, 1974), El Paso Historical Society, Kappa Sigma. *Awards, honors:* American Council of Learned Societies, grant-in-aid, 1937, development leave, 1968; distinguished alumnus award from East Texas State University, 1972; University of Texas at El Paso faculty research award, 1973.

WRITINGS: (Contributor) *Three Chaucer Studies* (also see below), Oxford University Press, 1932; (contributor) *A Book of English Literature*, Macmillan, 1942; (with others) *Reading Around the World*, Macmillan, 1946; *Chaucer and the French Poet Graunson*, Louisiana State University Press, 1947, reprinted, Kennikat, 1968; *Glorious Incense: The Fulfillment of Edgar Allan Poe*, Scarecrow, 1953, reprinted, Kennikat, 1968; *Cock of the Walk: Legend of Pancho Villa*, University of New Mexico Press, 1955, reprinted, Kennikat, 1970; *Hamlet's Wounded Name*, Texas Western College Press, 1964, reprinted, Kennikat, 1974; *Pershing's Mission in Mexico*, Texas Western Press, 1966; *Chaucer's Parlement of Foules, In Its Relation to Contemporary Events* (enlarged edition of contribution first published in *Three Chaucer Studies*), Octagon, 1969; *Geoffrey Chaucer: Literary and Historical Studies*, Kennikat, 1971; *Mexico and the Old Southwest: People, Palaver, Places*, Kennikat, 1971; *Three Dimensional Poe*, Texas Western Press, 1973.

Also author of pamphlets on Chaucer and Mexican history. Review editor, *Journal of American Folklore*, 1945.

WORK IN PROGRESS: King Alfred, for Twayne.

SIDELIGHTS: Braddy is competent in Anglo-Saxon, French, and Spanish.

* * *

BRADFIELD, Roger 1924-
(Jolly Roger Bradfield)

PERSONAL: Born September 22, 1924, in White Bear, Minn.; son of Clarence and Marie (Martin) Bradfield; married Joan Jurgens, July 4, 1948; children: Steve, Kari, Cindy, Suzy, Heidi. *Education:* Attended Minneapolis School of Art, 1946, Academie Julian, (Paris), 1949, and Heatherly School of Art, (London), 1950. *Politics:* "Wishy-washy Republican." *Religion:* Lutheran.

CAREER: Batten, Barton, Durstine & Osborn (advertising agency), Minneapolis, Minn., layout artist, 1948; free-lance artist, specializing in package design and humorous illustration, 1951-65; author and illustrator of children's books. *Military service:* U.S. Army, 1943-46.

WRITINGS: There's an Elephant in the Bathtub, Whitman, 1964; (with wife, Joan Bradfield) *The Big Happy ABC*, Whitman, 1965; (with Joan Bradfield) *The Big Happy 123*, Whitman, 1965; *Hello Rock*, Whitman, 1965.

"Jolly Roger" series, under name Jolly Roger Bradfield: *The Flying Hockey Stick*, Rand McNally, 1966; *Giants Come in Different Sizes*, Rand McNally, 1966; *A Good Knight for Dragons*, Scott, 1967; *Benjamin Dilley's Thirsty Camel*, Rand McNally, 1967; *Pickle-Chiffon Pie*, Rand McNally, 1967; *Benjamin Dilley's Lavender Lion*, Rand McNally, 1968.

WORK IN PROGRESS: More books for Rand McNally's "Jolly Roger" series.

SIDELIGHTS: Bradfield once told *CA*: "On the outside I may be forty-some years old, but, luckily, on the inside I am only nine or ten at most. Thus it is not too hard to slip into the child's world of fantasy long enough to get something down on paper. Then the forty-some year old outside takes over and illustrates the book. What a way to make a living!" *Avocational interests:* Travel, golf.†

* * *

BRALY, Malcolm 1925-

PERSONAL: Surname is pronounced *Braw*-lee; born July 16, 1925, in Portland, Ore.; son of James W. and Catherine (Cole) Braly; married second wife, Beverly; children: (first marriage) Steven; (second marraige) Ananda. *Education:* Left high school before graduation. *Agent:* Knox Burger Associates, 39½ Washington Square South, New York, N.Y. 10012.

CAREER: Professional writer, with variable residences. *Awards, honors:* Mystery Writers of America scroll for *Felony Tank*, runner-up as best first mystery novel of 1961.

WRITINGS—Novels, except as noted: *Felony Tank*, Fawcett, 1961; *Shake Him Till He Rattles*, Fawcett, 1963; *It's Cold Out There*, Fawcett, 1966; *On the Yard*, Little, Brown, 1967; *An Underdetermined Sentence* (memoir), Little, Brown, in press; *And Into the Fire*, Playboy Press, in press; *Bad Company*, Little, Brown, in press. Contributor to periodicals.

WORK IN PROGRESS: A novel with working title *Not That, Not That.*

SIDELIGHTS: Braly told *CA*: "While I don't think of myself as a commercial novelist in the formula sense, I write for a living, and all that this implies applies."

* * *

BRAMELD, Theodore 1904-

PERSONAL: First syllable of surname is accented, pronounced to rhyme with "jam"; born January 20, 1904, in Neillsville, Wis; son of Theodore Edward (a realtor) and Minnie (Dangers) Brameld; married second wife, Midori Matsuyama; children: Katherine, Patricia, Kristin. *Education:* Ripon College, B.A., 1926; University of Chicago, Ph.D., 1931. *Politics:* Independent. *Religion:* Humanist. *Residence:* Lyme Center, N.H. 03769.

CAREER: Long Island University, Brooklyn, N.Y., instructor in philosophy, 1931-35; Adelphi University, Garden City, N.Y., assistant professor, 1935-38, associate professor of philosophy, 1938-39; University of Minnesota, Minneapolis, associate professor, 1939-44, professor of educational philosophy, 1944-47; New York University, New York, N.Y., professor of educational philosophy, 1947-58; Boston University, Boston, Mass., professor of

educational philosophy, 1958-69, professor emeritus, 1969—. Visiting professor or lecturer at Dartmouth College, University of Puerto Rico, Columbia University, Springfield College, 1969-70, University of Hawaii, 1970-72. U.S. Department of State specialist in Japan and Korea, 1962. *Member:* Philosophy of Education Society, American Philosophical Association, Council for the Study of Mankind (member of executive board, 1969—), Society for Educational Reconstruction. *Awards, honors:* Wenner-Gren Foundation grants, 1953-56, 1963-64, 1974; Fulbright research scholar in Japan, 1964-65; East West Center, senior fellow, 1971-72; Ed.D., Rhode Island College.

WRITINGS: A Philosophic Approach to Communism, University of Chicago Press, 1933; (editor and co-author) *Workers Education in the United States*, Harper, 1941; *Design for America*, Hinds, 1945; *Minority Problems in the Public Schools*, Harper, 1945; *Ends and Means in Education*, Harper, 1950; *Patterns of Educational Philosophy*, World, 1950, revised edition, Holt, 1971; *Philosophies of Education in Cultural Perspective*, Holt, 1955.

Toward a Reconstructed Philosophy of Education, Holt, 1956; *Cultural Foundations of Education*, Harper, 1957; *The Remaking of a Culture—Life and Education in Puerto Rico*, Harper, 1959; (co-editor and co-author) *Values in American Education*, Phi Delta Kappa, 1964; *Education as Power*, Holt, 1965; *Education for the Emerging Age*, Harper, 1965; *The Use of Explosive Ideas in Education*, University of Pittsburgh Press, 1965; *Japan: Culture, Education, and Change in Two Communities*, Holt, 1968; *The Climactic Decades: Mandate to Education*, Praeger, 1970; *The Teacher as World Citizen*, Kappa Delta Pi, 1974.†

* * *

BRANCH, Daniel Paulk 1931-

PERSONAL: Born March 3, 1931, in Fitzgerald, Ga.; son of Felix W. (an electrical engineer) and Mavis Branch; married Sonya Meyer, December 10, 1961; children: Thomas, Martin. *Education:* University of Florida, B.Arch., 1954; Columbia University, M.S.Arch., 1956; Architectural Association, London, England, Certificate in Tropical Architecture, 1956. *Home:* 11245 8th St. E., Treasure Island, Fla. *Office:* 2901 58th Ave. N., St. Petersburg, Fla. 33714.

CAREER: Columbia University, New York, N.Y., instructor in architecture, 1957-59; junior partner of architectural firm in Tallahassee, Fla., 1959-61; principal of architectural firm in Gainesville, Fla., beginning, 1961; University of Florida, Gainesville, 1961-73, began as assistant professor, professor of architecture, 1966-73; University of Miami, Coral Gables, Fla., professor of architecture, 1973—. Associate architect, C. R. Wedding & Associates. Consulting architect and urban planner. *Member:* American Institute of Architects, Architectural Association (London), Gainesville Fine Arts Association.

WRITINGS: Folk Architecture of the East Mediterranean, Columbia University Press, 1966. Contributor to professional journals.

WORK IN PROGRESS: Research on climatic and vernacular architecture of North and South America.

* * *

BRANDON, Dick H.

PERSONAL: Born in Amsterdam, Netherlands; son of Jack and Lynn Brandon; wife's name, Sonya; children: George Ian, Douglas Ivor, Marja Helene. *Education:* Columbia University, B.S.Eng., 1955, M.S.Eng., 1961. *Office:* Brandon Applied Systems, Inc., 1700 Broadway, New York, N.Y. 10019.

CAREER: Brandon Applied Systems, Inc. (consulting firm in New York, N.Y., Washington, D.C., and London, England), president, 1964—, Brandon Computer Services Ltd., director, 1965—; Accounting Services Ltd., director, 1970—. Columbia University, Graduate School of Business, adjunct assistant professor, 1963-73. *Member:* Data Processing Management Association.

WRITINGS: Management Standards for Data Processing, Van Nostrand, 1963; *Management Planning for Data Processing,* Brandon/Systems, 1970; (with Max Grey) *Project Control Standards,* Brandon/Systems, 1970; *Data Processing Organization and Manpower Planning,* Petrocelli Books, 1974; *Data Processing Management: Methods and Standards,* Macmillan, 1974, new edition, 1975. Contributor to professional journals.

SIDELIGHTS: Brandon speaks Dutch and French.

* * *

BRANNEN, Ted R. 1924-

PERSONAL: Born February 24, 1924, in Tulsa, Okla.; son of Ted R. and Hazel Renelle (Adams) Brannen; married Betty Mathis, June 1, 1948; children: Michael Sean, David Lance, Brooke Ellen. *Education:* University of Arkansas, B.S. in B.A., 1944, M.S., 1947; University of Texas, Ph.D., 1954. *Office:* School of Business, 800 Hoffman Hall, University of Southern California, Los Angeles, Calif. 90007.

CAREER: Member of faculty of University of Arkansas, Fayetteville, Texas A&M University, College Station, and University of Texas, Austin, 1946-51; U.S. Office of Price Stabilization, economist and chief of economic analysis branch of Southwest, 1951-53; Texaco Corp., New York, N.Y., economic analyst, 1954; Arabian-American Oil Co., Drahran, Saudi Arabia, industrial relations adviser, 1954-57; University of Florida, Gainesville, lecturer in management, 1958; University of Kansas City (now University of Missouri at Kansas City), dean of School of Business Administration, 1958-59, vice-chancellor, 1959-60; Graduate Research Center of the Southwest, Dallas, Tex., director of Institute for Graduate Education and Research, 1960-63; Oklahoma State University, Stillwater, professor of management, head of department of finance and general business, and director of graduate studies, College of Business, 1963-65; University of Houston, Houston, Tex., dean of College of Business Administration, 1965-71; University of Southern California, Los Angeles, dean of School of Business, 1971—. Consultant to Southwestern Bell Telephone Co., 1965-72, and to oil companies, 1965—. *Military service:* U.S. Navy, 1943-46; became lieutenant junior grade.

MEMBER: American Academy of Political and Social Science, Association for Evolutionary Economics, American Economic Association, American Academy of Management, Southwest Social Science Association, Southwest Management Association, Omicron Delta Epsilon (honorary member), Beta Gamma Sigma.

WRITINGS: (With F. X. Hodgson) *Overseas Management,* McGraw, 1965. Contributor to economics journals.

WORK IN PROGRESS: A book on management theory.†

* * *

BRASS, Paul Richard 1936-

PERSONAL: Born November 8, 1936, in Boston, Mass.;

married; children: two. *Education:* Boston Latin School, graduate, 1954; Harvard University, B.A. (cum laude), 1958; University of Chicago, M.A., 1959, Ph.D., 1964. *Office:* Department of Political Science, University of Washington, Seattle, Wash.

CAREER: Bryn Mawr College, Bryn Mawr, Pa., lecturer in political science, 1964-65; University of Washington, Seattle, assistant professor, 1965-74, professor of political science, 1974—. *Member:* American Political Science Association, Association for Asian Studies, American Anthropological Association. *Awards, honors:* Fellowships from Ford Foundation, 1961-63 and 1968-69, American Institute of Indian Studies, 1966-67, Guggenheim Foundation, 1972-73; grants from American Council of Learned Societies, 1966-67 and 1973-74, Social Science Research Council, 1973-74.

WRITINGS: Factional Politics in an Indian State: The Congress Party in Uttar Pradesh, University of California Press, 1965; (contributor) Myron Weiner and Rajni Kothari, editors, *Indian Voting Behavior,* Firma K. L. Mukhopadhyay, 1965; (contributor) Weiner, editor, *State Politics in India,* Princeton University Press, 1968; (contributor) Susanne Rudolph and Lloyd Rudolph, editors, *Education and Politics in India,* Harvard University Press, 1972; *Radical Politics in South Asia,* M.I.T. Press, 1973; *Language, Religion, and Politics in North India,* Cambridge University Press, 1974; (contributor) *Electoral Politics in the Indian States: Party Systems and Cleavages,* Manohar Book Service, in press. Contributor to journals.

WORK IN PROGRESS: A book, *Party Systems and Political Change in India.*

SIDELIGHTS: Brass has knowledge of French and Hindi.

* * *

BRATT, John H(arold) 1909-

PERSONAL: Born August 23, 1909, in Holland, Mich.; son of Hero (a carpenter) and Jennie (Langejans) Bratt; married Gladys Buurma, August 15, 1941; children: Marcia Lynne (Mrs. Thomas Vander Woude), Evonne Alice (Mrs. Peter J. Kok), James Stuart. *Education:* Calvin College, A.B., 1934; Calvin Theological Seminary, Th.B., 1937; Columbia Theological Seminary, Decatur, Ga., Th.M., 1938; Harvard Divinity School, S.T.M., 1939; Union Theological Seminary in Virginia, Th.D., 1955. *Home:* 2238 Hall St. S.E., Grand Rapids, Mich. 49506. *Office:* Department of Theology, Calvin College, Grand Rapids, Mich.

CAREER: Ordained to ministry of Christian Reformed Church, 1942; Christian Reformed Church, Dorr, Mich., pastor, 1942-46; Calvin College, Grand Rapids, Mich., professor of religion and theology, 1946—. *Member:* American Society of Church History, Evangelical Theological Society.

WRITINGS: New Testament Guide, Eerdmans, 1946, 2nd edition, 1958; *Life and Teachings of John Calvin,* Baker Book, 1957; (co-author) *The Rise and Development of Calvinism,* Eerdmans, 1958, 2nd edition, 1963; (editor) *The Heritage of John Calvin,* Eerdmans, 1973.

* * *

BRAUDE, Michael 1936-

PERSONAL: Born March 6, 1936, in Chicago, Ill.; son of Sheldon and Nan (Resnik) Braude; married Linda Miller (a teacher), August 20, 1961. *Education:* University of Missouri, B.S., 1957; Columbia University, M.S., 1958. *Poli-*

tics: Independent. *Religion:* Jewish. *Home:* 5319 Mission Woods Ter., Shawnee Mission, Kan. 66205. *Office:* Commerce Bank of Kansas City, 10th and Walnut, Kansas City, Mo. 64141.

CAREER: Commerce Bank of Kansas City, Kansas City, Mo., 1962—, vice-president, 1966—. Lecturer in business administration at Kansas City Extension Center, University of Kansas, and Evening Division, Rockhurst College. A director, Kansas City Civic Orchestra. *Member:* Kansas City Chamber of Commerce, Kansas City Advertising and Sales Executives Club, Beta Gamma Sigma, Alpha Pi Zeta, Omicron Delta Kappa.

WRITINGS—Children's books: *Who's Zoo?*, Prairie School Press, 1963; *Shelby Goes to Wall Street*, Denison, 1965; *Danny Graham—Banker*, Denison, 1966; *Bruce Learns About Life*, Denison, 1967; *Andy Learns About Advertising*, Denison, 1967; *Peter Enters the Jet Age*, Denison, 1967; *Chad Learns About Naval Aviation*, Denison, 1968; *Jeff Learns About the F.B.I.*, Denison, 1968; *Ray Visits the Air Force Academy*, Denison, 1968; *Ronald Learns About College Teaching*, Denison, 1968; *Tim Learns About Mutual Funds*, Denison, 1969; *Richard Learns About Railroading*, Denison, 1969; *Managing Your Money: A Guide to Personal Finance*, Management Center of Cambridge (Mass.), 1969; *Larry Learns About Computers*, Denison, 1969; *A Man and His Money: A Primer on Personal Money Management*, Denison, 1971.

* * *

BRAYNARD, Frank O. 1916-

PERSONAL: Born August 21, 1916, in Sea Cliff, Long Island, N.Y. *Education:* Duke University, A.B., 1939; Columbia University, A.M., 1940. *Home:* 98 DuBois Ave., Sea Cliff, N.Y. *Office:* South Street Seaport Museum, 16 Fulton St., New York, N.Y. 10038.

CAREER: Taught school in Poughkeepsie, N.Y., 1941-42; American Merchant Marine Institute, editor of weekly *Bulletin*, and assistant director of bureau of information, 1943-48; *New York Herald Tribune*, New York, N.Y., assistant ship news editor, 1948-52; director of bureau of information, American Merchant Marine Institute; Moran Towing, New York, N.Y., manager of public relations, and editor of *Tow Line* Magazine, 1961—. *Member:* Steamship Historical Society of America (editor of quarterly journal, *Steamboat Bill*, 1945-49; president, 1953-54).

WRITINGS: Lives of the Liners, Cornell Maritime, 1947; *Famous American Ships*, Hastings, 1957; *The Story of Ships*, Grosset, 1962; *"SS Savannah," The Elegant Steam Ship*, University of Georgia Press, 1963; *A Tugman's Sketchbook*, DeGraff, 1965; *One Square Mile: A Sea Cliff Sketchbook*, privately printed, 1967; *Fire Island to Venice*, DeGraff, 1967; *By Their Works Ye Shall Know Them: The Life of William Francis Gibbs*, privately printed, 1968; *Leviathan: The World's Greatest Ship*, South Street Seaport Museum, Volume I, 1972, Volume II, 1974.

WORK IN PROGRESS: Volume III of *Leviathan*, bringing the story of the S.S. Leviathan up to 1926.

* * *

BREIMYER, Harold F(rederick) 1914-

PERSONAL: Born April 13, 1914, in Fort Recovery, Ohio; son of Fred C. and Ella (Schulz) Breimyer; married Rachel Styles, December 13, 1941; children: Frederick S. *Education:* Ohio State University, B.S., 1934, M.S., 1935;

University of California, graduate study, 1935-36; American University, Ph.D., 1960. *Religion:* Methodist. *Home:* 1616 Princeton Dr., Columbia, Mo. 65201. *Office:* University of Missouri, Columbia, Mo. 65201.

CAREER: U.S. Department of Agriculture, Washington, D.C., agricultural economist, 1936-42, 1946-59; Council of Economic Advisers, Washington, D.C., staff economist, 1959-61; U.S. Department of Agriculture, staff economist, Agricultural Marketing Service, 1961-66; University of Missouri, Columbia, professor of agricultural economics, 1966—. U.S. Department of Agriculture Graduate School, instructor, 1956-66; University of Illinois, visiting research professor, 1963-64; Montgomery Junior College, instructor, 1965-66. Member of agricultural exchange delegation to Soviet Union, 1958; did research studies for Argentine government, 1961, 1962, for Guatemala government, 1965, and for Spanish government, 1974. Member of Montgomery County (Md.) Board of Education, 1959-62, president, 1961. *Military service:* U.S. Naval Reserve, active duty, 1942-45; now lieutenant commander (retired).

MEMBER: American Farm Economic Association, American Marketing Association. *Awards, honors:* Superior Service Award, U.S. Department of Agriculture, 1954; best article award, *Journal of Farm Economics*, 1954, 1957, 1962; Certificate of Merit, Agricultural Marketing Service, 1963.

WRITINGS: (Editor) *Challenges of the Sixties*, Graduate School Press, U.S. Department of Agriculture, 1963; *Individual Freedom and the Economic Organization of Agriculture*, University of Illinois Press, 1965. Technical articles in the agricultural press and other journals.

WORK IN PROGRESS: A textbook, *The Economics of the Product Markets of Agriculture*.

* * *

BREMSER, Ray 1934-

PERSONAL: Born February 22, 1934, in Jersey City, N.J.; son of Frank (a pianist) and Gertrude (Ferdon) Bremser; married Bonnie Frazer (a technical advisor), March 21, 1959; children: Rachel. *Education:* Two years of correspondence courses in journalism, University of Oklahoma, 1956-57. *Politics:* Democrat. *Religion:* Pagan.

CAREER: Served several prison terms, New Jersey State Prison, 1953-65, for armed robbery, parole violations, and bail jumping. Gives poetry readings in New York City. Writer. *Military service:* U.S. Air Force.

WRITINGS: Poems of Madness, Paperbook Gallery, 1965; *Angel* (prose poem; introduction by Lawrence Ferlinghetti), Tompkins Square Press, 1967; *Drive Suite*, Nova Broadcast Press, 1968. Contributor to little magazines.†

* * *

BRENNAN, Louis A(rthur) 1911-

PERSONAL: Born February 5, 1911, in Portsmouth, Ohio; son of Edward Henry (a shoemaker) and Gertrude (Scherer) Brennan; married Margaret Cecilia Pierron, April 13, 1936; children: Ann Margaret (Mrs. Henry Calam), Edward, Matthew. *Education:* University of Notre Dame, A.B., 1932. *Home:* 39 Hamilton Ave., Ossining, N.Y. 10562.

CAREER: National Youth Administration, Cincinnati (Ohio) area office, assistant area director, 1937-40; with an architectural and engineering firm, 1940-43; owner and operator of sawmill, 1946-47; free-lance writer, 1947-50; *New-castle News*, Chappaqua, N.Y., 1950-52; *Croton-Cortlandt News*, Croton-on-Hudson, N.Y., associate editor, 1956-72; Briarcliff College Museum and Laboratory for Archaeology, Briarcliff, N.Y., director, 1972—. Briarcliff College Center for Hudson Valley Archaeology and Prehistory, Briarcliff, N.Y., director, 1964-66. *Military service:* U.S. Naval Reserve, commanding officer of gunboat in Pacific service, 1944-45; became lieutenant; received Bronze Star for action in Okinawa. *Member:* Society for American Archaeology.

WRITINGS: These Items of Desire (novel), Random House, 1952; *Masque of Virtue* (novel), Random House, 1954; *More Than Flesh* (novel), Dell, 1955; *The Long Knife* (novel), Dell, 1956; *Death at Floodtide* (novel), Dell, 1957; *No Stone Unturned* (archaeology), Random House, 1959; *The Buried Treasure of Archaeology*, Random House, 1964; *Tree of Arrows* (novel), Macmillan, 1964; *American Dawn* (archaeology), Macmillan, 1970; *Beginners Guide to Archaeology*, Stackpole, 1972; *Artifacts of Stone Age America*, Stackpole, 1975. Editor of *Bulletin* (of New York State Archaeological Association), 1958—, *Archaeology of Eastern North America* (annual of Eastern States Archaeological Federation).

WORK IN PROGRESS: Research in Hudson Valley archaeology, another novel, and movie scripts.

*   *   *

BRETSCHER, Paul G(erhardt)   1921-

PERSONAL: Born November 29, 1921, in Milwaukee, Wis.; son of Paul M. (a professor) and Minnie (Spohn) Bretscher; married Marguerite Melcher, August 4, 1946; children: Prisca, Bethel, Paul, Jr., Sarah, Monica, Rachel, Joel, Seth, Nathan, Matthew. *Education:* Concordia Seminary, St. Louis, Mo., B.D., 1945, S.T.M., 1964, Th.D., 1966; Washington University, St. Louis, Mo., M.A., 1946. *Home:* 752 Dore Dr., Valparaiso, Ind. 46383.

CAREER: Ordained minister in Lutheran Church, 1945; Concordia Seminary, Springfield, Ill., instructor in mathematics and science, 1946-47; Lutheran High School, St. Louis, Mo., instructor in languages and history, 1947-48; pastor in New Orleans, La., 1948-58; Valparaiso University, Valparaiso, Ind., assistant professor of theology, 1958-66, associate professor, 1966-69. Immanuel Lutheran Church, Valparaiso, Ind., pastor, 1969—. Member of Missouri Synod Commission on Theology and Church Relations of the Lutheran Church, 1967-75. *Member:* Society of Biblical Literature, Lutheran Academy for Scholarship.

WRITINGS: The World Upside Down or Rightside Up?, Concordia, 1965; *The Holy Infection*, Concordia, 1969; *After the Purifying*, Lutheran Education Association, 1975. Contributor to *Concordia Theological Monthly, Currents in Theology and Mission*, and *Lutheran World*.

SIDELIGHTS: Has reading competence in Latin, German, Hebrew, Greek, French.

*   *   *

BREWER, Fredric (Aldwyn)   1921-
(Alfred Wynn)

PERSONAL: Born December 20, 1921, near Andrews, Ind.; son of Fred George (a grocer) and Madalyn (Swartz) Brewer; married Joan Scherer, October 20, 1956; children: Eric, Aran, Ian. *Education:* Indiana University, B.Sc. and M.Sc., 1950; Arts Students League, New York, N.Y., stu-

dent, 1958. *Politics:* Independent. *Home:* 4043 Morningside Dr., Bloomington, Ind. 47401. *Office address:* Room 204, Television Building, Indiana University, Bloomington, Ind. 47401.

CAREER: Newspaperman in Huntington, Ind., 1940-42, 1945-46, in Yakima, Wash., 1954-55, in Pawtucket, R.I., 1955-56, and in Garden Grove, Calif., 1956-57; Ithaca College, Ithaca, N.Y., chairman of radio and television department, 1950-53; Oregon State System of Higher Education, Portland, assistant professor of radio and television, 1953-54; *Parade*, New York, N.Y., staff writer, 1957-58; free-lance writer, New York, N.Y., 1958-60; Thorpe & Porter Ltd. (publishers), London, England, executive editor, 1960-62; Scholastic Magazines, Inc., New York, N.Y., associate editor, 1962-64; Indiana University, Bloomington, associate professor of writing, radio, television, and film, 1964—. Consultant, Curtis Publishing Co., 1971. *Military service:* U.S. Army, 1942-45; became first sergeant.

MEMBER: American Association for the Advancement of Science (fellow), American Association of University Professors, Society of Professional Journalists, British Astronomical Association, Astronomical Society of the Pacific, Overseas Press Club of America, Custer Battlefield Historical and Museum Association, Torch Club International. *Awards, honors:* Association for Education in Radio and Television award for best children's script; Sigma Delta Chi award for distinguished public service in journalism for children's news program broadcast by WTTS, Bloomington, Ind.

WRITINGS: (With H. J. Skornia and R. H. Lee) *Creative Broadcasting*, Prentice-Hall, 1950; *Challengers of the Unknown*, Scholastic Book Services, 1965; *The Solar System*, Wilson, 1972. Writer of educational radio and television scripts. Contributor to *Classics Illustrated, World Illustrated* (London), *Pixie Tales* (London), and to popular and corporate magazines. Editor of *Media Matters*, 1974—.

WORK IN PROGRESS: Research for a book on botany with working title, *Yellow Flower in the Grass.*

*   *   *

BRICE, Marshall Moore   1898-

PERSONAL: Born August 30, 1898, in Whiteoak, S.C.; son of Richardson Walker (a farmer) and Nancy (Mobley) Brice; married Margaret Harris, June 7, 1923 (divorced, 1947); children: Love (Mrs. Jim Morton), Elizabeth (Mrs. Armando Lendian). *Education:* Clemson University, B.S., 1917; Columbia University, graduate study, summers, 1919, 1922; University of Wisconsin, M.A., 1927; University of Virginia, Ed.D., 1956. *Politics:* Democrat. *Religion:* Presbyterian. *Home:* Woodward Apartments, Staunton, Va. 24401. *Office:* P.O. Box 276, Staunton, Va. 24401.

CAREER: Staunton Military Academy, Staunton, Va., 1920-56, became head of English department; Mary Baldwin College, Staunton, Va., professor of English, 1956-68. *Military service:* U.S. Army Reserve, 1924-56; active duty, 1941-46; now colonel (retired). *Member:* National Council of Teachers of English, Conference on College Composition and Communication, American Association of University Professors, Masons.

WRITINGS: (With Ullin W. Leavell and Virginia Hyde Kennan) *How To Study With Success and Satisfaction*, Anderson Brothers Book Store (Charlottesville, Va.), 1955; *Conquest of a Valley*, University Press of Virginia, 1965; *The Stonewall Brigade Band*, McClure Press, 1967;

Daughter of the Stars (novel), McClure Press, 1973. Contributor to several journals in field.

WORK IN PROGRESS: A collection of poems.

AVOCATIONAL INTERESTS: Genealogical research.

* * *

BRILL, Earl H(ubert) 1925-

PERSONAL: Born November 17, 1925, in Abington, Pa.; son of Joseph and Stella (Scheer) Brill; married Ruth Ball, January 26, 1952; children: Lesley, Grace, Kenneth. *Education:* University of Pennsylvania, A.B., 1951; Philadelphia Divinity School, Th.B., 1956; Princeton Theological Seminary, Th.M., 1958; American University, Ph.D., 1969. *Politics:* Democrat. *Home:* 3504 Woodley Rd. N.W., Washington, D.C. 20016. *Office:* College of Preachers, 3510 Woodley Rd. N.W., Washington, D.C. 20016.

CAREER: Philadelphia Naval Shipyard, Philadelphia, Pa., training officer, 1951-53; ordained priest of Protestant Episcopal Church, 1956; pastor in Royersford, Pa., 1956-59; University of Pennsylvania, Philadelphia, Episcopal chaplain, 1959-61; American University, Washington, D.C., Episcopal chaplain and teacher of American civilization, 1961-74. College of Preachers and Canon, Washington, D.C., director of studies, 1974—. Episcopal Diocese of Washington, chairman of social relations department. *Military service:* U.S. Army, 1944-46. *Member:* Episcopal Society for Cultural and Racial Unity (board, 1963-67), Phi Beta Kappa, Phi Kappa Phi, Phi Alpha Theta, Omicron Delta Kappa.

WRITINGS: The Creative Edge of American Protestantism, Seabury, 1966; *Sex Is Dead, and Other Postmortems*, Seabury, 1967; *The Future of the American Past*, Seabury, 1974.

AVOCATIONAL INTERESTS: Music, literature, and the arts.

* * *

BRIN, Ruth Firestone 1921-

PERSONAL: Born May 5, 1921, in St. Paul, Minn.; daughter of Milton P. and Irma (Cain) Firestone; married Howard B. Brin (a business executive), August 6, 1941; children: Judith, Arthur, David, Deborah. *Education:* Vassar College, B.A., 1941; University of Minnesota, M.A., 1972. *Religion:* Jewish. *Home:* 2861 Burnham Blvd., Minneapolis, Minn. 55416.

CAREER: Writer. *Member:* National Council of Jewish Women, Urban League, League of Women Voters, Phi Beta Kappa.

WRITINGS: A Time to Search, David, 1959; *Interpretations*, Lerner, 1965; *A Rag of Love*, Emmett Publishing Co. (Minneapolis), 1969; *Butterflies are Beautiful* (children's book), Lerner, 1974. Contributor of articles and book reviews to *Minneapolis Star and Tribune*, and *Reconstructionist*; also contributor of verse, articles, and fiction to Jewish and secular magazines.

WORK IN PROGRESS: Two children's books based on biblical themes to be published by Lerner; research into the preparation of materials for Jewish families to use at home in observing the Sabbath.

SIDELIGHTS: Interpretations, based on the weekly Bible reading, is used as a supplement to the prayer book in a number of American synagogues.

BRINKLEY, George A. (Jr.) 1931-

PERSONAL: Born April 20, 1931, in Wilmington, N.C.; son of George Arnold (a highway engineer) and Ida (West) Brinkley; married Ann Kreps, August 9, 1959; children: Heidi Ann. *Education:* Davidson College, A.B., 1953; Columbia University, M.A. and Certificate of Russian Institute, 1955, Ph.D., 1964. *Home:* 19539 Cowles Ave., South Bend, Ind. 46637. *Office:* Department of Government, University of Notre Dame, Notre Dame, Ind. 46556.

CAREER: Columbia University, New York, N.Y., instructor in international relations, 1957-58; University of Notre Dame, Notre Dame, Ind., 1959—, associate professor, 1966-70, professor of government and international studies, 1970—, director of program of Soviet and East European studies. *Member:* American Political Science Association, American Association for the Advancement of Slavic Studies, American Association of University Professors. *Awards, honors:* Inter-University Committee on Travel Grants award for research year in the Soviet Union, 1962-63; International Affairs fellow, Council on Foreign Relations, 1968-69.

WRITINGS: (Contributor) W. Laqueur and L. Labedz, editors, *The Future of Communist Society*, Praeger, 1962; (contributor) T. T. Hammond, editor, *Bibliography of Soviet Foreign Relations and World Communism*, Princeton University Press, 1965; *The Volunteer Army and Allied Intervention in South Russia, 1917-1921*, University of Notre Dame Press, 1966; (contributor) S. D. Kertesz, editor, *Nuclear Non-Proliferation*, University of Notre Dame Press, 1967; (contributor) Michael Curtis, editor, *Marxism*, Atherton, 1970; (contributor) B. Dexter, editor, *The Foreign Affairs 50-Year Bibliography*, Council on Foreign Relations, 1972. Contributor of articles to *Review of Politics, Soviet Studies*, and *Survey*.

WORK IN PROGRESS: Editing and translating a selection of readings in primary sources, *Foundations of Soviet Foreign Policy*; research on Soviet policy in the United Nations.

* * *

BRISCOE, D(avid) Stuart 1930-

PERSONAL: Born November 9, 1930, in Millom, Cumberland, England; son of Stanley (a sales representative) and Mary (Wardle) Briscoe; married Jill Pauline Ryder, June 29, 1958; children: David Stanley Campbell, Judith Margaret, Peter Alan Stuart. *Education:* Attended Millom Grammar School, Cumberland, England, 1941-47. *Religion:* Christian. *Home:* 2545 Eastwood Dr., Brookfield, Wis. 53005.

CAREER: District Bank Ltd., Spring Gardens, Manchester, England, member of inspection staff, 1955-60. Secretary of Capernwray Missionary Fellowship, and evangelist and Bible teacher in over fifty countries; pastor of Elmbrook Church, Brookfield, Wis., 1970—. *Military service:* Royal Marine Commandos, 1948-50.

WRITINGS: The Fullness of Christ, Zondervan, 1965; *Living Dangerously*, Zondervan, 1968; *Where Was the Church When the Youth Exploded?*, Zondervan, 1972; *Discovering God*, Sowers of Seed, 1972.

* * *

BRISTOW, Gwen 1903-

PERSONAL: Born September 16, 1903, in Marion, S.C.; daughter of Louis Judson (a minister) and Caroline Cornelia (Winkler) Bristow; married Bruce Manning, January 14, 1929 (deceased). *Education:* Judson College, A.B., 1924; attended Columbia University School of Journalism, 1924-25, and Anderson College. *Agent:* Brandt & Brandt, 101 Park Ave., New York, N.Y. 10017.

CAREER: Times-Picayune, New Orleans, La., reporter, 1925-34; full-time professional writer, 1934—. *Member:* Authors League of America, P.E.N. International (Los Angeles center president, 1969-71; international corresponding secretary, 1971—), Pen and Brush.

WRITINGS: (With husband, Bruce Manning) *The Invisible Host*, Mystery League, 1930; (with Manning) *Gutenberg Murders*, Mystery League, 1931; (with Manning) *Two and Two Make Twenty-Two*, Mystery League, 1932; *Deep Summer*, Crowell, 1937; *The Handsome Road*, Crowell, 1938; *This Side of Glory*, Crowell, 1940; *Tomorrow is Forever*, Crowell, 1943; *Jubilee Trail* (Literary Guild selection), Crowell, 1950; *Celia Garth* (Literary Guild selection), Crowell, 1959; *Plantation Trilogy* (includes *Deep Summer, The Handsome Road, This Side of Glory*, and additional historical material to preface each book), Crowell, 1962; *Calico Palace*, Crowell, 1970.

SIDELIGHTS: Gwen Bristow's first mystery novel, in collaboration with her husband, grew out of schemes to murder their next-door neighbor who had a "raucous radio." After three mystery collaborations, she branched into the field of historical fiction with her trilogy of Louisiana novels, taking the aristocratic Larne family and the plebeian Upjohns from pre-Revolutionary days to the World War. Discussing the last book of the trilogy, *This Side of Glory*, a *Times Literary Supplement* reviewer wrote: "It is a vigorous and thoughtful piece of work, done with an admirably firm sense of character and a loving eye for the landscape of the Mississippi valley in the neighbourhood of New Orleans. Miss Bristow is a good storyteller, as adroit in dramatic effect as she is emotionally sincere in sympathy ... Not a completely harmonious novel, but a very honest and well-written one." Along with her natural storytelling ability, she has been praised for her use of common sense. "It may all seem too unreal, too contrived," Edward Weeks wrote of *Tomorrow is Forever*, "but it is a book filled with wisdom and understanding of human problems." Regarding her novel, *Celia Garth*, A. F. Wolfe added: "Miss Bristow's fictional characters may lack depth, but they serve a veteran novelist as fresh proof that the true storyteller knows how to entertain."

The Invisible Host was dramatized by Owen Davis as "The Ninth Guest" in 1931. It was also filmed by Columbia with the latter title in 1934. *Tomorrow is Forever* was made into a motion picture by RKO in 1946, and *Jubilee Trail* was filmed by Republic in 1953. Her books have been translated into German, French, Italian, Norwegian, Danish, Swedish, Finnish, Czechoslovakian, Dutch, Spanish, and Portuguese.

BIOGRAPHICAL/CRITICAL SOURCES: Times Literary Supplement, July 13, 1940; *Atlantic Monthly*, January, 1944; *New York Times Book Review*, May 31, 1959.

*   *   *

BRITTIN, Norman A(ylsworth) 1906-

PERSONAL: Born September 9, 1906, in Syracuse, N.Y.; son of Lewis J. and Grace (Aylsworth) Brittin; married Florence Mellor, March 1, 1929 (deceased); married Ruth Lowe (a professor), June 3, 1951; children: (first marriage) Geoffrey Mellor, Anthony Norman. *Education:* Syracuse

University, A.B., 1927, A.M., 1930; University of California, Berkeley, graduate study, 1934-37; University of Washington, Seattle, Ph.D., 1947. *Politics:* "Usually Democratic." *Religion:* Unitarian Universalist. *Office:* Department of English, Auburn University, Auburn, Ala.

CAREER: University of Southern California, Los Angeles, associate in character education, 1931-34; University of Utah, Salt Lake City, instructor, 1937-45, assistant professor of English, 1947; University of Chicago, Chicago, Ill., visiting assistant professor of humanities, 1947-48; Auburn University, Auburn, Ala., associate professor, became professor of English, 1948-62; University of Puerto Rico, Rio Piedras, lecturer and professor of English, 1962-66; Auburn University, professor of English, 1966—. Fulbright lecturer, University of La Laguna (Canary Islands), 1968-69.

MEMBER: National Council of Teachers of English, American Association of University Professors (president of Auburn chapter, 1956-57), Modern Language Association of America, Shakespeare Association of America, Renaissance Society of America. *Awards, honors:* Co-winner of Warshaw Award for the Humanities, 1952; Faculty fellow of Fund for the Advancement of Education (Ford Foundation) at Columbia and Harvard Universities, 1952-53; Folger Library fellow, 1965.

WRITINGS: A Writing Apprenticeship, Holt, 1963; *Edna St. Vincent Millay*, Twayne, 1967; (editor) *A Reading Apprenticeship*, Holt, 1971; *Thomas Middleton*, Twayne, 1972. Contributor of articles and poetry to professional journals and to magazines. Acting editor, *Experiment* (poetry quarterly), 1944; co-editor, *Southern Humanities Review*, 1966—.

WORK IN PROGRESS: Research on Shakespeare and the drama of Elizabethan and Jacobean periods.

SIDELIGHTS: Brittin is competent in Spanish and French. *Avocational interests:* Oratorio and madrigal singing, recorder playing, hiking, botanizing, snorkeling, and the history of art and music.

*   *   *

BROCKWAY, Edith E. 1914-

PERSONAL: Born February 25, 1914, in Dunlap, Okla.; daughter of George and Emma (Arnold) Swain; married Charles Edward Brockway (a chemist), June 11, 1940; children: Ann (Mrs. Ian Kleiman), Joy (Mrs. Richard Price), Kay. *Education:* Studied at Kansas City Art Institute, 1934-37, Akron Art Institute, 1955, and West Valley College, 1974-75. *Politics:* Bipartisan. *Religion:* Reorganized Church of Jesus Christ of Latter Day Saints. *Home:* 5544 Copeland Lane, San Jose, Calif. 95124.

CAREER: Cartlich Advertising Co., Kansas City, Mo., traveling artist and writer, 1938-41; Fram Filter Co., Ann Arbor, Mich., artist, 1941-42; Gluck, Linn & Scruggs (dress shops), Decatur, Ill., fashion illustrator, 1957-59; *Advertiser*, Decatur, writer and artist, 1958; *Decatur Tribune*, Decatur, feature editor, 1968-70; script writer for educational film company, 1975; also free-lance writer, photographer, and artist.

WRITINGS: Range Doctor, Albert Whitman, 1964; *Land Beyond the Rivers*, Westminster, 1966; *The Golden Land*, Herald House, 1968; *Antebellum Decatur* (local history), privately printed, 1969. Writer of filmstrip on architecture. Photographs have appeared in textbooks, and drawings in religious publications; regular contributor of articles to art education magazines.

WORK IN PROGRESS: Don't Insult the Loving Tree, a novel for teens based on psychic research; a history of San Jose for bicentennial.

* * *

BRODIE, Bernard 1910-

PERSONAL: Born May 20, 1910, in Chicago, Ill.; son of Max and Esther (Bloch) Brodie; married Fawn McKay (a writer and professor), August 28, 1936; children: Richard M., Bruce R., Pamela B. *Education:* University of Chicago, Ph.B., 1932, Ph.D., 1940. *Home:* 619 Resolano Dr., Pacific Palisades, Calif. *Office:* Department of Political Science, University of California, Los Angeles, Calif.

CAREER: Institute for Advanced Study, Princeton, N.J., Carnegie fellow, 1941; Dartmouth College, Hanover, N.H., instructor, 1941-43; Yale University, New Haven, Conn., associate professor and director of graduate studies, department of international relations, 1945-51; RAND Corp., Santa Monica, Calif., senior staff member, 1951-66; University of California, Los Angeles, professorial lecturer, 1963-66, professor of political science, 1966—. Technical expert, U.S. Delegation to the United Nations, San Francisco, 1945; resident professor, National War College, 1946-47, and member of board of consultants, 1955-57; senior specialist in national defense for Legislative Reference Service, Library of Congress, 1946-49; special assistant to Chief of Staff, U.S. Air Force, 1950-51; visiting lecturer, Graduate Institute of International Studies, Geneva, 1956, 1960. *Military service:* U.S. Naval Reserve, Bureau of Ordnance, 1943-45. *Awards, honors:* Carnegie Corp. reflective year fellowship in France, 1960-61.

WRITINGS: Sea Power in the Machine Age, Princeton University Press, 1941, revised edition, 1944; *A Guide to Naval Strategy*, Princeton University Press, 1942, 5th revised edition, 1964; (editor, and co-author) *The Absolute Weapon*, Harcourt, 1946; *Strategy in the Missile Age*, Princeton University Press, 1959; (with wife, Fawn M. Brodie) *From Cross-Bow to H-Bomb*, Dell, 1962, revised edition, University of Indiana Press, 1973; (editor and co-author) *La Guerre Nucleaire*, Editions Stock, 1965; *Escalation and the Nuclear Option*, Princeton University Press, 1966; *War and Politics*, Macmillan, 1973. Contributor to *Encyclopaedia Britannica, Encyclopedia of the Social Sciences*, and to *Harper's, Reporter, World Politics, Bulletin of the Atomic Scientists*, and other journals.

SIDELIGHTS: Brodie is competent in French, German, and Italian. *Avocational interests:* Music, gardening, riding.

* * *

BRODIE, Fawn M(cKay) 1915-

PERSONAL: Born September 15, 1915, in Ogden, Utah; daughter of Thomas Evans and Fawn (Brimhall) McKay; married Bernard Brodie (a professor at University of California, Los Angeles), August 28, 1936; children: Richard M., Bruce R., Pamela B. *Education:* University of Utah, B.A., 1934; University of Chicago, M.A., 1936. *Home:* 619 Resolano Dr., Pacific Palisades, Calif. 90272.

CAREER: Writer and editor. *Member:* American Historical Association. *Awards, honors:* Alfred A. Knopf fellowship in biography, 1943; Silver Medal, Commonwealth Club of California, 1960, for *Thaddeus Stevens, Scourge of the South*.

WRITINGS: No Man Knows My History (biography of Joseph Smith, the Mormon prophet), Knopf, 1945; *Thad-*

deus Stevens: Scourge of the South, Norton, 1959; (with husband, Bernard Brodie) *From Cross-Bow to H-Bomb*, Dell, 1962; (editor) Frederick H. Piercy, *Route from Liverpool to Salt Lake City*, Harvard University Press, 1962; (editor) Richard F. Burton, *City of the Saints*, Knopf, 1963; *The Devil Drives: A Life of Sir Richard Burton*, Norton, 1967; *Thomas Jefferson: An Intimate History* (Book-of-the-Month Club selection), Norton, 1974.

SIDELIGHTS: Reviewing *The Devil Drives*, Philip Toynbee states "Mrs. Brodie has written her book from her own overt moral platform, as any serious writer must. She does not excuse Burton; she does nothing so patronising as that. She admires him, pities him and tries to understand him. She enables us to do the same by writing about him without wearing the blinkers either of the moralist or of the dispassionate observer." Nicholas Laprete, Jr. estimates that her biography of Burton ". . . is a lucid and always compelling account and is to be recommended for the wealth of information exactly presented and the caution with which that material is evaluated."

* * *

BRONER, E(sther) M(asserman)

PERSONAL: Born in Detroit, Mich.; daughter of Paul and Beatrice Masserman; married Robert Broner (an artist and assistant professor); children: Sari, Adam and Jeremy (twins), Nahama. *Education:* Wayne State University, B.A., 1950, M.A., 1962. *Home:* 18244 Parkside, Detroit, Mich. 48221. *Office:* Department of English, Wayne State University, Detroit, Mich. 48202.

CAREER: Wayne State University, Detroit, Mich., 1962—, began as instructor in creative writing, became associate professor and writer in residence. Visiting professor, Haifa University, 1972 and 1975; writer in residence workshops at Bar-Ilan University and Haifa University. Convener of Conference for a Concerned Jewish Faculty, Wayne State University. *Member:* Professors for Peace in the Mideast, American Federation of Teachers, Faculty for a Democratic Society. *Awards, honors: Esquire* Magazine writing fellowship; two Wayne State University faculty research grants for creative work; Emma Lazarus Shaver Fund grant; O. Henry Awards, second prize, 1968.

WRITINGS: Summer is a Foreign Land (play; first produced at Studio Theater, Wayne State University, 1962), Wayne State University Press, 1966; *Journal-Nocturnal and Seven Stories* (novella with stories), Harcourt, 1968; *Her Mothers* (novel), Holt, 1975. One act plays performed at Raven Reader's Theatre, Birmingham, Mich. Author of television play, "Wait Till I Swallow My Saliva," broadcast on WXYZ, Detroit, Mich., 1968, and of film script, "Dilatory Ship." Short stories in *Epoch, North American Review, Commentary, Midstream, National Jewish Monthly, Story Quarterly, New Letters, Southern Humanities Review, Florida Quarterly, Seneca Review, Nimrod*, and others.

WORK IN PROGRESS: Woman's Haggadah, a textbook on creative writing; a book about a Jewish boy's Bar Mitzvah.

BIOGRAPHICAL/CRITICAL SOURCES: Detroit News, October 23, 1975.

* * *

BROOKS, Anita 1914-

PERSONAL: Born January 7, 1914, in Forest Hills, Long

Island, N.Y.; daughter of Charles F. and Amelia (Koch) Zeltner; married Thomas Vail Brooks, 1937 (divorced, 1957); married Max Abramovitz (an architect), February 29, 1964; children: (first marriage) Antoinette (Mrs. Thomas Stucklen), Cora Vail, Henry Stanford II. *Education:* Sarah Lawrence College, B.A., 1934. *Home and office:* 418 East 50th St., New York, N.Y. 10022.

CAREER: The New Yorker, New York, N.Y., editorial assistant, 1943-46; Sarah Lawrence College, Bronxville, N.Y., editor of alumnae magazine, 1947-48, teacher of remedial reading, 1950, assistant to professor of history, 1958-60, assistant in writing for lecture courses, 1960-62, assistant to director of Paris summer school, 1963; author. *Member:* Authors Guild, League of Women Voters, American Civil Liberties Union, Village League (founding member).

WRITINGS: Winifred, Steck, 1971; "Picture Aids to World Geography" series published by John Day: *Picture Book of Fisheries*, 1961; *Picture Book of Tea and Coffee*, 1962; *Picture Book of Grains*, 1962; *Picture Book of Salt*, 1964; *Picture Book of Oil*, 1965; *Picture Book of Timber*, 1966; *A Small Bird Sang*, 1967; *Picture Book of Metals*, 1972. Contributor of children's stories and articles to periodicals.

WORK IN PROGRESS: Equality, essays; children's readers.

*   *   *

BROOKS, Cleanth   1906-

PERSONAL: Born October 16, 1906, in Murray, Ky.; son of Cleanth (a minister) and Bessie Lee (Witherspoon) Brooks; married Edith Amy Blanchard, September 12, 1934. *Education:* Vanderbilt University, B.A., 1928; Tulane University, M.A., 1929; Oxford University, Rhodes Scholar, 1929-32, B.A. (with honours), 1931, B.Litt., 1932. *Politics:* Independent Democrat. *Religion:* Episcopalian. *Home:* Forest Road, Northford, Conn. 06472. *Office:* English Department, Yale University, New Haven, Conn. 06520.

CAREER: Louisiana State University, Baton Rouge, 1932-47, began as lecturer, became professor of English; Yale University, New Haven, Conn., professor of English, 1947-60, Gray Professor of Rhetoric, 1960-75, professor emeritus, 1975—. American embassy, London, England, cultural attache, 1964-66. Library of Congress, fellow, 1953-63. Visiting professor of English at University of Texas, summer, 1941, Breadloaf School of English, 1942, 1963, University of Michigan, summer, 1942, University of Chicago, 1945-46, Kenyon School of English, summer, 1948 (fellow, 1948—), University of Southern California, 1953. *Member:* Modern Language Association of America, American Academy of Arts and Sciences, National Institute of Arts and Letters, American Philosophical Society, American Association of University Professors, Phi Beta Kappa, Yale Club (New York), Athenaeum, Savile (both London). *Awards, honors:* Guggenheim fellow, 1953, 1960; D.Litt. from Upsala College, 1963, University of Kentucky, 1963, University of Exeter, 1966, Washington and Lee University, 1968, Tulane University, 1969, and University of the South, 1975; L.H.D. from University of St. Louis, 1958, and Centenary College, 1972.

WRITINGS: The Relation of the Alabama-Georgia Dialect to the Provincial Dialects of Great Britain, Louisiana State University Press, 1935; *Modern Poetry and the Tradition*, University of North Carolina Press, 1939; *The Well Wrought Urn*, Reynal & Hitchcock, 1947, Harcourt, 1956; (with Robert Penn Warren) *Modern Rhetoric*, Harcourt, 1949, 2nd edition, 1958, abridged edition, 1961; (with Warren) *Fundamentals of Good Writing*, Harcourt, 1950; (contributor) *Humanities: An Appraisal*, University of Wisconsin Press, 1950; (with William Wimsatt) *Literary Criticism: A Short History*, Knopf, 1957; *The Hidden God: Studies in Hemingway, Faulkner, Yeats, Eliot and Warren*, Yale University Press, 1963; *William Faulkner: The Yoknapatawpha Country*, Yale University Press, 1963; *A Shaping Joy: Studies in the Writer's Craft*, Harcourt, 1972. Contributor of articles and reviews to literary journals.

Editor: (With others) *An Approach to Literature*, Louisiana State University Press, 1936, 5th edition, Prentice-Hall, 1975; (editor with Robert Penn Warren, and co-author) *Understanding Poetry*, Holt, 1938, 4th edition, 1975, transcript of tape recording to accompany 3rd edition entitled *Conversations on the Craft of Poetry: Cleanth Brooks and Robert Penn Warren, with Robert Frost, John Crowe Ransom, Robert Lowell, and Theodore Roethke*, Holt, 1961; (with Warren) *Understanding Fiction*, F. S. Crofts, 1943, 2nd edition, Appleton, 1959, abridged edition published as *The Scope of Fiction*, Appleton, 1960; (with Robert Heilman) *Understanding Drama*, Holt, 1945; *The Poems of John Milton* (1645 edition), Harcourt, 1951; *The Letters of Thomas Percy, Volume 2*, Louisiana State University Press, 1951; (with Warren) *An Anthology of Stories from the "Southern Review,"* Louisiana State University Press, 1953; *Tragic Themes in Western Literature: Seven Essays by Bernard Knox [and Others]*, Yale University Press, 1956; (with Warren and R. W. B. Lewis) *American Literature: The Makers and the Making*, two volumes, St. Martin's, 1973, paperbound edition published in four volumes, 1974. Managing editor, with Robert Penn Warren, *Southern Review*, 1935-41, editor, with Warren, 1941-42; member of advisory board, *Kenyon Review*, 1942-60.

SIDELIGHTS: Maxwell Geismar introduces Brooks as "a brilliant critic of literary technique and rhetoric, particularly in modern verse, and . . . a leading figure in the formalist school of New Critics." Considering Brooks' development as a critic, John Paul Pritchard noted that "Brooks sounded his first note for metaphor as the prime characteristic of poetry in 1935." Pritchard observed that Brooks and Robert Penn Warren, in *Understanding Poetry* (1938), asserted that "the poem . . . must be grasped as a literary object before it can be otherwise considered. . . . A poem proves itself by its effect, and its effect arises not out of the things used but from the poet's use of them. . . . Verse controls words and entices the reader's imagination by its recurrent rhythms to the willing temporary suspension of disbelief."

Central to Brooks's critical position is his contention that a poem cannot be paraphrased without essential loss. Pritchard writes: "In Brooks's eyes the basic critical ill is the tendency to confuse comment on the poem with its essential core. Critics are prone to restate the poem in a prose paraphrase as a step toward elucidating it. Such a procedure, he declares, presumes the paraphrasable part of the poem to be its essential part. But the act splits the poem, which is by nature a whole, into form and content. . . . It totally ignores the poetic function of metaphor and meter."

In a discussion of *The Well Wrought Urn* (1947), Rene Wellek wrote: "Brooks attacks [as] the "heresy of paraphrase," all attempts to reduce the poem to its prose content, and he has defended a well defined absolutism: the need of judgement against the flaccid surrender to relativism and historicism. But ... Brooks has taken special pains to demonstrate that his absolutism of values is not incompatible with a proper regard for history." Speaking of Brooks's critical approach, Wellek notes: "Brooks analyzes poems as structures of opposites, tensions, paradoxes, and ironies with unparalleled skill. Paradox and irony are terms used by him very broadly. Irony is not the opposite of an overt statement, but [according to Brooks] 'a general term for the kind of qualification which the various elements in a context receive from the context.'" In a later discussion of Brooks's approach, Wellek explains: "Irony for Brooks indicates the recognition of incongruities, the ambiguity, the reconciliation of opposites which Brooks finds in all good, that is, complex poetry. Poetry must be ironic in the sense of being able to withstand ironic contemplation."

John Crowe Ransom, poet, and himself a critic, was generally conceded to have christened Brooks and others of similar critical opinion the "New Critics." In 1955, Ransom wrote: "It seems to me that Brooks just now is probably the most forceful and influential critic of poetry that we have. But this does not imply that his authority is universally accepted, for it has turned out even better than that. Where he does not gain assent, he arouses protest and countercriticism. His tone toward other critics is that of an independent, and his tone toward scholars who are occasional critics is cool. This is why a new book by Brooks is a public service."

Ransom goes on to say: "... of course there will be readers who will go all the way with Brooks as if under a spell. I believe the peculiar fascination of his view of poetry is due to its being a kind of modern version of the ancient doctrine of divine inspiration or frenzy. For Brooks, the poem exists in its metaphors. The rest of it he does not particularly remark. He goes straight to the metaphors, thinking it is they which work the miracle that is poetry; and naturally he elects for special notice the most unlikely ones. Hence paradox and irony, of which he is so fond."

In recent years, Brooks's critical study has extended from the examination of poetry to the study of the novels of William Faulkner. James B. Meriwether wrote of Brooks's *William Faulkner: The Yoknapatawpha Country* (1963): "Brooks's emphasis is literary, not sociological; but his fine synthesis of the major elements in the culture upon which most of Faulkner's best fiction draws is a valuable corrective to studies which have distorted that fiction through a misapprehension of its social and historical background." Meriwether goes on to say that Brooks's book on Faulkner "is one of the best critical studies of any American novelist, and perhaps the most important single critical study yet made of any American novelist of this century."

BIOGRAPHICAL/CRITICAL SOURCES: Poems and Essays, Vintage, 1955; John Paul Pritchard, *Criticism in America*, University of Oklahoma Press, 1956; Murray Krieger, *The New Apologists for Poetry*, University of Minnesota Press, 1956; Rene Wellek, *Concepts of Criticism*, Yale University Press, 1963; *New York Herald Tribune Books*, July 28, 1963; *New York Review of Books*, January 9, 1964; Rene Wellek, *Discriminations*, Yale University Press, 1970; Jackson R. Bryher, editor, *Sixteen Modern American Authors*, Norton, 1973; Lewis P. Simpson, editor, *The Possibilities of Order: Cleanth Brooks and His Work*, Louisiana State University Press, 1975.

BROOKS, Keith 1923-

PERSONAL: Born May 14, 1923, in Tigerton, Wis.; son of Oscar Derby and Etta (Mierswa) Brooks; married Laquata S. Walters, December 29, 1951; children: Todd Randall, Craig William. *Education:* University of Wisconsin, B.S. and M.S., 1949; Ohio State University, Ph.D., 1955. *Home:* 3732 Romnay Rd., Columbus, Ohio 43221. *Office:* Ohio State University, Columbus, Ohio.

CAREER: Eastern Kentucky State University, Richmond, teacher of speech, 1949-53; Ohio State University, Columbus, graduate assistant, 1953-55, instructor, 1955-56, assistant professor, 1956-61, associate professor, 1961-66, professor of communications, 1966—. Visiting professor, California State University, 1970; director of International Study Research Tour, British Isles, 1972. Consultant to Shaw University, Men in Government Institutes, Eastern Railroad Presidents Conference, Management and Business Service, Ohio Funeral Directors, and communications consultant to Ohio Bell Telephone Co. and Procter & Gamble. *Military service:* U.S. Navy, 1946. *Member:* Speech Association of America, Central States Speech Association, Delta Sigma Rho.

WRITINGS: (With John E. Dietrich) *Practical Speaking for the Technical Man*, Prentice-Hall, 1958; (editor and author of introduction) *The Communicative Arts and Sciences of Speech*, C. E. Merrill, 1967; (with Eugene Bahn and Lamont Okey) *The Communicative Act of Oral Interpretation*, Allyn and Bacon, 1967; (with Bahn and Okey) *Literature for Listening*, Allyn and Bacon, 1968; (with Jack E. Douglas, Carroll C. Arnold, and Robert S. Brubaker) *Exploration in Speech Communication*, Part I, C. E. Merrill, 1973. Editor, *Central States Speech Journal*, 1958-61.

* * *

BROOKS, Stewart M. 1923-

PERSONAL: Born April 6, 1923, in Sidney, N.Y.; son of William Morris and Mabel (Elliott) Brooks; married Natalie Paynton, September 20, 1952; children: S. Marshall. *Education:* Albany College of Pharmacy, B.S. (cum laude), 1949; Philadelphia College of Pharmacy and Science, M.S., 1951. *Residence:* Waban, Mass.

CAREER: Muhlenberg Hospital School of Nursing, Plainfield, N.J., instructor in basic science, 1951-57; Lasell Junior College, Auburndale, Mass., science instructor, 1957-62; Boston City Hospital School of Nursing, Boston, Mass., instructor in basic science, 1962-65; full-time professional writer, 1965—. *Military service:* U.S. Army, Signal Corps, 1942-45; became sergeant. *Member:* American Pharmaceutical Association, Kappa Psi.

WRITINGS: Basic Facts of General Chemistry, Saunders, 1956; *Selected Experiments in General Chemistry*, Saunders, 1956; *Basic Facts of Pharmacology*, Saunders, 1957, 2nd edition, 1963; *Basic Facts of Medical Microbiology*, Saunders, 1958, 2nd edition, 1962; *Selected Experiments in Medical Microbiology*, Saunders, 1958, 2nd edition, 1962; *Body Water and Ions*, Springer, 1960, 3rd edition, 1973; *Integrated Basic Science*, Mosby, 1962, 3rd edition, 1970, laboratory manual and workbook, 1964, 2nd edition, 1971; *Our Murdered Presidents: The Medical Story*, Fell, 1966; *Civil War Medicine*, C. C Thomas, 1966; *Basic Chemistry: A Programmed Presentation*, Mosby, 1966, 2nd edition, 1971; *A Programmed Introduction to Microbiology*, Mosby, 1968, 2nd edition, 1973; *The Sea Inside Us*, Meredith, 1968; *McBurney's Point*, Barnes, 1969; *The World of the Viruses*, Barnes, 1970; *The V.D.*

Story, Barnes, 1971; *The Cancer Story*, Barnes, 1973; *Ptomaine*, Barnes, 1974; *Basic Science and the Human Body*, Mosby, 1975; *Going Metric*, Barnes, in press. Contributor to popular and professional journals.

AVOCATIONAL INTERESTS: Civil War buff; classical music, birdwatching, walking, gardening.

* * *

BROUN, Heywood Hale 1918-

PERSONAL: Surname rhymes with "croon"; born March 10, 1918; son of Heywood Campbell (a newspaperman) and Ruth (Hale) Broun; married Jane Lloyd-Jones (an actress), 1949; children: Heywood Orren. *Education:* Swarthmore College, B.A., 1940. *Home:* 35 West 81st St., New York, N.Y. 10024.

CAREER: Sportswriter and columnist for *PM* and *New York Star*, New York, N.Y., before switching to acting; stage and television actor, 1949—, appearing on Broadway in "Bird Cage," "Pink Elephant," "Bells Are Ringing," and other productions. *Military service:* U.S. Army, Field Artillery; served with 9th Army in Europe; became technical sergeant. *Member:* Actors' Equity Association, Screen Actors Guild, American Federation of Television and Radio Artists, American Newspaper Guild, Phi Beta Kappa, Coffee House, Franklin Inn.

WRITINGS: (Editor) *The Collected Edition of Heywood Broun* (writings of his father), Harcourt, 1941; *A Studied Madness*, Doubleday, 1965. Contributor to magazines.

* * *

BROWN, Anne S(eddon) K(insolving) 1906-

PERSONAL: Born March 25, 1906, in Brooklyn, N.Y.; daughter of Arthur B. (a clergyman) and Sally (Bruce) Kinsolving; married John Nicholas Brown, October 18, 1930; children: Nicholas, John Carter, Angela Bayard (Mrs. Edwin G. Fischer). *Education:* Bryn Mawr School, Baltimore, Md., graduated, 1924. *Politics:* Democrat. *Religion:* Anglican. *Home:* 357 Benefit St., Providence, R.I. 02903.

CAREER: Baltimore News, Baltimore, Md., feature writer and columnist, 1925-30, music critic, 1927-30; Providence Community Concert Association, president, 1931-36, program chairman, 1937-52. Newport Music Festival, Rhode Island Arts Foundation, Newport, vice-president, 1968, president, 1969-73, member of board of directors, 1974—. Member of visiting committee, Harvard University department of music, 1936-49, national board of U.S. Navy Relief Society, 1946-49, advisory board for Fort Ticonderoga, 1959-63, national council for Metropolitan Opera, 1960-63, Save Venice Committee, International Fund for Monuments, 1970—, and advisory board, U.S. Army Military History Research Collection, 1970—. *Member:* Company of Military Collectors and Historians (co-founder, 1949; fellow; governor, 1951—; treasurer, 1951-63; president, 1963-65), Company of Military Historians (fellow), American Military Institute, National Society of Colonial Dames of America, Society for Army Historical Research (London; life), Societe de la Sabretache (Paris), honorary member of other foreign societies; Phi Alpha Theta (honorary). *Awards, honors:* L.H.D., Brown University, 1962; Rhode Island Governor's Award for Excellence in the Arts, 1969; Chinard Prize, 1972, for leading publication in the Franco-American Field; Award of Merit, American Association for State and Local History, 1973; National Daughters of the American Revolution Medal of Honor,

1973; Certificate of Merit, State of Rhode Island Bicentennial Commission, 1973.

WRITINGS: (With Henry Lachouque) *The Anatomy of Glory: Napoleon and His Guard*, Brown University Press, 1961; (with Howard C. Rice, Jr.) *The American Campaigns of Rochambeau's Army: 1780-1783*, Princeton University Press, 1972; (compiler with R. G. Thurburn) *Index to British Military Costume Prints, 1500-1914*, Army Museums Ogilby Trust (London), 1972. Contributor to military and history periodicals.

AVOCATIONAL INTERESTS: Collecting books, prints, and documents on history of military dress; music; sailing.

* * *

BROWN, G(eorge) Neville 1932-

PERSONAL: Born April 8, 1932, in Watlington, Oxfordshire, England; son of Harold (a businessman) and Nellie (Jones) Brown; married Yu-Ying Lu, 1974. *Education:* University College, London, B.Sc., 1954; New College, Oxford, M.A., 1957. *Religion:* Anglican. *Home:* Roheki, 105 Puory Rd., London N8 8LY, England. *Agent:* A. D. Peters, 18 Adam St., London W.C. 2, England. *Office:* Faculty of Commerce and Social Science, University of Birmingham, Birmingham 15, England.

CAREER: Royal Military Academy, Sandhurst, Berkshire, England, lecturer in international relations and military history, 1960-62; research associate at Institute for Strategic Studies, 1962-64; free-lance writer, 1964-65; University of Birmingham, Birmingham, England, lecturer, 1965-70, senior lecturer in international politics, 1970—. Academic consultant, National Defence College, Latimer, England, 1972—. *Military service:* Royal Navy, Fleet Air Arm, 1957-60; became lieutenant. *Member:* Royal United Services Institute for Defence Studies (RUSI; elected to the council, 1974), Royal Meteorological Society (fellow), Fabian Society, Institute for Strategic Studies. *Awards, honors:* Trench Gascoigne Prize, Royal United Service Institution, for an essay on seapower, 1959.

WRITINGS: Strategic Mobility, Praeger, 1963; *Nuclear War—The Impending Strategic Deadlock*, Praeger, 1965; *Arms Without Empire*, Penguin, 1967; *The Geography of Conflict*, Morrow, 1967; *British Arms and Strategy, 1970-80*, Royal Institute for Defence Studies, 1969; *European Security, 1972-80*, Royal Institute for Defence studies, 1972; *The Drift to Nineteen Eighty-Four*, Hodder & Stoughton, in press. Contributor of articles on defense and foreign policy to *New Scientist, World Today, New Statesman, LeMonde Diplomatique*, and other journals.

WORK IN PROGRESS: A History of the World in the Twentieth Century, in collaboration with Frank Spencer and Donald Watt.

* * *

BROWN, Giles T(yler) 1916-

PERSONAL: Born April 21, 1916, in Marshall, Mich.; son of A. Watson (a minister) and Ettroile LeMar (Kent) Brown; married Crysta Beth Cosner (a librarian), November 21, 1951. *Education:* San Diego State College (now California State University), A.B., 1937; University of California, Berkeley, M.A., 1941; Claremont Graduate School, Ph.D., 1949; University of Edinburgh, postdoctoral study, 1949. *Religion:* Protestant. *Home:* 413 Catalina Dr., Newport Beach, Calif. 92660. *Office:* California State University, Fullerton, Calif.

CAREER: Teacher in San Diego (Calif.) city schools, 1937-46; Orange Coast College, Costa Mesa, Calif., instructor and chairman of social science department, 1948-60; California State University, Fullerton, professor of history and chairman of department, 1960-67, dean of graduate studies, 1967—. Public lecturer on international affairs, 1951; moderator for weekly Behind the Headlines Forum, sponsored by Orange Coast College; chairman, Historical Landmarks Committee of Orange County; vice-president, World Affairs Council of Orange County. *Military service:* U.S. Navy, 1942-45; became lieutenant. *Member:* American Association for the Advancement of Science, Sons of the American Revolution, International Platform Association (president, Western region, 1963), Kappa Delta Phi, Phi Delta Kappa, Phi Alpha Theta, Masonic Lodge. *Awards, honors:* Pacific History Award, Pacific Coast branch of American Historical Association, 1950; named outstanding professor, California State College, Fullerton, 1966.

WRITINGS: Ships That Sail No More, University of Kentucky Press, 1966. Author of television script, "Africa in Change." Book reviewer for *Pacific Historical Review, The Historian*, and *Western Historical Quarterly*. Contributor to *Encyclopaedia Britannica*, and education and historical journals.

* * *

BROWN, James I(saac) 1908-

PERSONAL: Born December 15, 1908, in Tarkio, Mo.; son of John Vallance (a teacher) and Ada (Moore) Brown; married Ruth Sam, September 19, 1942; children: Katherine Ada, Susan Phyllis. *Education:* Tarkio College, B.A., 1930; University of Chicago, M.A., 1933; University of Iowa, graduate study, 1943-44; University of Colorado, Ph.D., 1949. *Religion:* Methodist. *Home:* 1269 N. Cleveland, St. Paul, Minn. 55108. *Office:* Department of Rhetoric, University of Minnesota, St. Paul, Minn. 55101.

CAREER: Monmouth College, Monmouth, Ill., instructor in English, 1933-34; University of Minnesota, St. Paul, instructor, 1934-46, assistant professor, 1946-49, associate professor, 1949-54, professor of rhetoric, 1954—, acting chief of department, 1947-48. Visiting summer lecturer at University of Colorado, 1950, 1952, 1954, University of Utah, 1955, University of Minnesota at Itasca, 1957, 1958. Communications consultant to industrial and business firms. *Military service:* U.S. Army, 1943-45; served in Europe. *Member:* International Reading Association, National Council of Teachers of English, Speech Association of America, National Society for the Study of Communication (executive secretary, 1951; president, 1964), American Association of University Professors, Phi Delta Kappa. *Awards, honors:* Alumni Citation, 1962, Hall of Fame Award, 1965, both from Tarkio College; Certificate of Merit, National University Extension Association, 1972.

WRITINGS: Efficient Reading, Heath, 1952, alternate edition, 1956, revised edition, 1962, revised Form A, 1971, revised Form B, 1975; (compiler) *Explorations in College Readings*, with *Exercise Manual*, Heath, 1959; (with Rachel Salisbury) *Building a Better Vocabulary*, Ronald, 1959; (with George Sanderlin) *Effective Writing and Reading*, Heath, 1962; *Programed Vocabulary*, preliminary television edition, overhead projector edition, and college edition, Appleton, 1964, 2nd edition, New Century, 1971; *Guide to Effective Reading*, Heath, 1966; *Reading Power*, Heath, 1975.

Scriptwriter of educational television series, "Thru Eye and Ear," 1959, "Efficient Reading," 1960, "MISOTA Efficient Reading," 1961, "MISOTA Advanced Efficient Reading," 1962, "Words, Words, Words," 1964, "Putting Words to Work," 1966. Inventor of word game, "Pyramid," for Perceptual Development Laboratories, 1963. Co-author of reviser of listening comprehension test and reading test for Harcourt, 1953, and Houghton, 1958, 1972. Also co-author of *College English Placement Test*, Houghton, 1969.

WORK IN PROGRESS: A series to teach reading, using new linguistic principles and overhead projector; *Alphy's Show-and-Tell Book, Canny Cat, Betty Big-Ear*, and *Bob's Wish Cap*.

SIDELIGHTS: James Brown has traveled in Russia, France, Italy, Switzerland, and England researching background material on Tolstoy and such eighteenth century writers as Voltaire, Rousseau, and Locke. Brown told *CA:* "My major interest is communication—all areas and aspects—writing, reading, listening, and speaking. In our growingly complex world, these seem to be taking on more and more significance."

* * *

BROWN, John Arthur 1914-

PERSONAL: Born August 28, 1914, in Burlington, Wash.; son of Marcus and Bernice (Sawyer) Brown; married Mary Rae Hansen, August 19, 1939; children: Janet. *Education:* Studied at Mount Vernon Junior College, Mount Vernon, Wash., 1932-33, Seattle Pacific College, 1933-35; University of Washington, Seattle, B.A., 1938, M.A., 1942. *Home:* 1325 South Hills Dr., Wenatchee, Wash. 98801. *Office:* Wenatchee Valley College, Wenatchee, Wash.

CAREER: Wenatchee Valley College, Wenatchee, Wash., instructor in history, 1946—, dean of men, 1948-52. Chelan County Public Utility District Historical Advisory Committee, member, 1961—; City of Wenatchee Heritage Committee, member, 1965—. *Member:* National Education Association, Western Historical Association, Washington Educational Association.

WRITINGS: (With Robert H. Ruby) *Half-Sun on the Columbia*, University of Oklahoma Press, 1965; (with Ruby) *The Spokane Indians: Children of the Sun*, University of Oklahoma Press, 1970; (with Ruby) *The Cayuse Indians: Imperial Tribesman of Old Oregon*, University of Oklahoma Press, 1972; (with Ruby) *Ferryboats of the Columbia River*, Superior, 1974; *The Chinook Indians: Traders of the Lower Columbia River*, University of Oklahoma Press, in press. Contributor to educational journals.

SIDELIGHTS: John Arthur Brown speaks French. *Avocational interests:* Archaeology, particularly in the Columbia River area.

* * *

BROWN, Leslie Wilfrid 1912-

PERSONAL: Born June 10, 1912, in London, England; son of Harry (a merchant) and Maud (Brunning) Brown; married Winifred Megaw (a physician), August 15, 1939; children: Alison Mary Megaw. *Education:* London College of Divinity, University of London, A.L.C.D., 1935, B.D., 1936, M.Th., 1944, D.D., 1957. *Home:* Bishop's House, Ipswich, Suffolk, England.

CAREER: Ordained deacon, Church of England, 1935, priest, 1936; missionary of Church Missionary Society in

Kottayam, Kerala, South India, 1938-43; Downing College, Cambridge University, Cambridge, England, chaplain, 1943-44; Kerala United Theological Seminary, Trivandrum, South India, principal, 1944-52; Jesus College, Cambridge University, chaplain, 1950-51; Church of Uganda, Kampala, bishop, 1953-61, archbishop, 1961-65; Church of England, bishop of St. Edmundsbury and Ipswich, 1966—. *Awards, honors:* Commander, Order of the British Empire, 1965; D.D., Trinity College, Toronto; M.A., Cambridge University; named chaplain and subprelate, Order of St. John of Jerusalem, 1968.

WRITINGS: The Indian Christians of St. Thomas, Cambridge University Press, 1956; (with W. Brown) *The Christian Family*, World Christian Books, 1961; *God as Christians See Him*, Oxford University Press, 1963; *Relevant Liturgy*, Oxford University Press (New York), 1965.

SIDELIGHTS: Speaks Malayalam, Lugaunda, and French.

AVOCATIONAL INTERESTS: Birdwatching.

* * *

BROWN, Raymond Bryan 1923-

PERSONAL: Born November 16, 1923, in Winnfield, La.; son of George Franklin and Lovie (Phenald) Brown; married Caralie Nelson, September 2, 1946; children: B. Nancye, Helen Anne. *Education:* Louisiana State University, A.B., 1944; Yale University Divinity School, B.D., 1947, S.T.M., 1948; Southern Baptist Theological Seminary, Th.D., 1950; Tuebingen University, Tuebingen, Germany, postdoctoral study, 1972. *Home:* 3704 Shadybrook Dr., Raleigh, N.C. 27609. *Office:* Southeastern Baptist Theological Seminary, Wake Forest, N.C. 27587.

CAREER: Baptist clergyman. Pastor in Halifax, Va., 1950-52; University of Richmond, Richmond, Va., assistant professor of Bible and religion, 1952-55; pastor in Richmond, Va., 1955-60; Southern Baptist Theological Seminary, Louisville, Ky., associate professor of New Testament, 1960-64; Southeastern Baptist Theological Seminary, Wake Forest, N.C., professor of New Testament, 1964—, dean of the faculty, 1966-74, Distinguished Professor of New Testament Interpretation, 1973—.

WRITINGS: (Editor with W. Morgan Patterson) *Professor in the Pulpit*, Broadman, 1963; (with Velma Darbo) *A Study of the New Testament*, pupil's and teacher's books, Broadman, 1965. Columnist, "Know Your Bible," in *Louisville Courier-Journal*, 1963-65; contributor of articles and reviews to journals of religion.

* * *

BROWN, Richard Maxwell 1927-

PERSONAL: Born July 26, 1927, in Mobridge, S.D.; son of John Floyd and Norma Lena (McClary) Brown; married Estella Dee Cutler, January 25, 1951; children: Brooks, Laura Jean. *Education:* Reed College, B.A., 1952; Harvard University, A.M., 1955, Ph.D., 1959. *Politics:* Democrat. *Office:* Department of History, College of William and Mary, Williamsburg, Va.

CAREER: Rutgers University, New Brunswick, N.J., assistant professor, 1960-64, associate professor of history, 1964-67; College of William and Mary, Williamsburg, Va., professor of history, 1967—. Consultant to National Commission on the Causes and Prevention of Violence, 1968-69; member of council, Institute of Early American History and Culture, 1969-72. *Military service:* U.S. Army, 1946-

48; became sergeant. *Member:* American Historical Association, Organization of American Historians, American Association of University Professors, Southern Historical Association (program chairman, 1974), South Carolina Historical Society, Virginia Historical Society, Phi Beta Kappa. *Awards, honors:* Award of Merit, American Association for State and Local History, for *The South Carolina Regulators*; William and Mary Phi Beta Kappa Faculty Award for the Advancement of Scholarship, 1970.

WRITINGS: The South Carolina Regulators, Harvard University Press, 1963; (contributor) John A. Carroll, editor, *Reflections of Western Historians*, University of Arizona Press, 1969; (contributor) Hugh D. Graham and Ted R. Gurr, editors, *The History of Violence in America*, Praeger, 1969; (contributor) Thomas Rose, editor, *Violence in America*, Random House, 1970; (editor) *American Violence*, Prentice-Hall, 1970; (editor with A. G. Olson) *Anglo-American Political Relations, 1675-1775*, Rutgers University Press, 1970; (contributor) Donald Fleming and Bernard Bailyn, editors, *Law in American History*, Little, Brown, 1972; (contributor) Stephen G. Kurtz and James Hutson, editors, *Essays on the American Revolution*, University of North Carolina Press, 1973. Member of editorial board, *William amd Mary Quarterly*, 1970-71.

WORK IN PROGRESS: Books on colonial South Carolina, the prosopography of the South Carolina Regulators, and American vigilantism and violence.

* * *

BROWN, Sanborn C(onner) 1913-

PERSONAL: Born January 19, 1913, in Beirut, Lebanon, of American parents; son of Julius Arthur (a professor) and Helen (Conner) Brown; married Lois Wright, June 21, 1940; children: Peter M., Stanley W., Prudence E. *Education:* Dartmouth College, A.B., 1935, M.A., 1937; Massachusetts Institute of Technology, Ph.D., 1944. *Home:* 37 Maple St., Lexington, Mass. 02173. *Office:* Massachusetts Institute of Technology, 77 Massachusetts Ave., Cambridge, Mass. 02139.

CAREER: Massachusetts Institute of Technology, Cambridge, instructor, 1941-45, assistant professor, 1945-49, associate professor, 1949-62, professor of physics, 1962—, associate dean of Graduate School, 1963—. U.S. Office of Scientific Research and Development, staff, 1941-44. Technical adviser to U.S. delegation, United Nations International Conference on Peaceful Uses of Atomic Energy, Geneva, 1958; U.S. delegate to International Atomic Energy Agency Conference on Plasma Physics and Controlled Thermonuclear Fusion, Salzburg, 1961; member of Research Advisory Committee on Fluid Mechanics, National Aeronautics and Space Administration, 1963-65. Member of U.S. national committee, International Union of Pure and Applied Physics and president of Union's Commission on Physics Education; member of Interunion Commission on the Teaching of Science, International Council of Scientific Unions. Member of Lexington (Mass.) School Committee, 1958-64, chairman, 1961-64.

MEMBER: American Physical Society (fellow; chairman of division of electron physics, 1951-52), American Association for the Advancement of Science (fellow), American Association of Physics Teachers (treasurer, 1955-62), American Academy of Arts and Sciences (fellow; secretary, 1964—), History of Science Society, Royal Institution of Great Britain, National Science Teachers Association, Conference Board of Associated Research Councils, Phi

Beta Kappa, Sigma Xi (national lecturer, 1961). *Awards, honors:* Distinguished service citation, American Association of Physics Teachers, 1962; Guggenheim fellow, 1968-69.

WRITINGS: Basic Data of Plasma Physics, Technology Press and Wiley, 1959, revised edition, 1961, second edition published as *Basic Data of Plasma Physics 1966*, M.I.T. Press, 1967; (with Norman Clarke) *International Education in Physics*, Technology Press and Wiley, 1960; *Count Rumford, Physicist Extraordinary*, Anchor Books, 1962; (with Norman Clarke and Jayme Tiomno) *Why Teach Physics?*, M.I.T. Press, 1964; *The Education of a Physicist*, M.I.T. Press, 1966; *Introduction to Electrical Discharges in Gases*, Wiley, 1966; *Count Rumford on the Nature of Heat*, Pergamon, 1967; (editor) *Electrons, Ions and Waves: Selected Works of William Phelps Allis*, M.I.T. Press, 1967; (editor) *Collected Works of Count Rumford*, Harvard University Press, Volume I: *The Nature of Heat*, 1968, Volume II: *Practical Applications*, 1969, Volume III: *Devices and Techniques*, 1969, Volume IV: *Light and Armament*, 1970, Volume V: *Public Institutions*, 1970; (with Brian B. Schwartz) *Scientific Manpower: Dilemma for Graduate Education*, M.I.T. Press, 1971; (with F. J. Kedves and E. J. Wenham) *Teaching Physics: An Insoluble Task?*, M.I.T. Press, 1971; *Changing Careers in Science and Engineering*, M.I.T. Press, 1972; *Physics Fifty Years Later*, National Academy of Sciences, 1973; (with Leonard M. Rieser) *Natural Philosophy at Dartmouth: From Surveyors' Chains to the Pressure of Light*, University of New England, 1974. Contributor to physics journals.

SIDELIGHTS: Basic Data of Plasma Physics was published in the Soviet Union in an unauthorized translation, 1961.

* * *

BROWN, Wallace 1933-

PERSONAL: Born November 20, 1933, in Edmonton, Alberta, Canada; son of Alexander Binnie (a biologist) and Mary McF. (Wallace) Brown; married E. Charlotte Mueller, August 16, 1957 (divorced); married Paula L. Bollinger, April 28, 1971. *Education:* St. Edmund Hall, Oxford, B.A., 1957, M.A., 1962; University of Nebraska, M.A., 1959; University of California, Berkeley, Ph.D., 1964. *Politics:* Democrat. *Religion:* Agnostic. *Home:* 323 Aebert St., Frederiton, New Brunswick, Canada. *Office:* History Department, University of New Brunswick, Frederiton, New Brunswick, Canada.

CAREER: University of California, Berkeley, extension lecturer, 1961-63; University of Alberta, Edmonton, Canada, assistant professor of history, 1963-64; Brown University, Providence, R.I., assistant professor of history, 1964-67; University of New Brunswick, Frederiton, New Brunswick, professor of history, 1967—. *Military service:* British Army, Engineers, 1952-54; became sergeant. *Member:* American Historical Association, Historical Association (England). *Awards, honors:* Woodrow Wilson traveling fellow, 1963; Canada Council grant, 1964; Canada Council Leave Fellowship, 1973-76.

WRITINGS: The King's Friends, Brown University Press, 1966; *The Good Americans*, Morrow, 1969. Contributor to historical journals.

WORK IN PROGRESS: Two books, *The Loyalists After 1783*, and *The Influence of America on British History, 1715-1776*.

SIDELIGHTS: Wallace Brown reads French. *Avocational interests:* Motion picture history, the history of food and drink.

* * *

BROWNE, Malcolm W(ilde) 1931-

PERSONAL: Born April 17, 1931, in New York, N.Y.; son of Douglas G. (an architect) and Dorothy (Wilde) Browne; married Huynh thi Le Lieu, July 18, 1966. *Education:* Attended Swarthmore College, 1948-50, New York University, 1950-51. *Religion:* Atheist. *Address:* c/o Foreign News Desk, *New York Times*, 229 West 43rd St., New York, N.Y. 10036.

CAREER: Laboratory chemist for five years before switching to journalism; *Middletown Daily Record*, Middletown, N.Y., editor, 1958-60; Associated Press, reporter in Baltimore, Md., 1960-61, Vietnam correspondent, 1961-65; American Broadcasting Co., Vietnam correspondent, 1965-66; free lance writer, 1966-68; *New York Times*, correspondent in Buenos Aires, 1968-71, correspondent in Southeast Asia, 1971—. *Military service:* U.S. Army, Korea correspondent for *Pacific Stars and Stripes*, 1956-58. *Member:* Overseas Press Club of America, National Press Club, Authors Guild. *Awards, honors:* Grand prize, World Press Photo Awards (The Hague), 1963; Pulitzer Prize for international reporting, 1964; National Headliner Award, 1964; Overseas Press Club Award, 1964; Louis M. Lyons Award, 1964; George Polk Memorial Award, 1964; Sigma Delta Chi Award, 1964; Associated Press Managing Editors Award, 1964; Edward R. Murrow memorial fellowship, Council of Foreign Relations, 1966-67.

WRITINGS: The New Face of War, Bobbs-Merrill, 1965, revised edition, 1968. Contributor of monthly article to *True*, and articles to other magazines.

WORK IN PROGRESS: Research for a novel set in contemporary Vietnam.

SIDELIGHTS: Browne speaks French and German, and some Spanish, Russian, Japanese, and Vietnamese.†

* * *

BROWNE, Ray B(roadus) 1922-

PERSONAL: Born January 15, 1922, in Millport, Ala.; son of Garfield (a banker) and Anne Nola (Trull) Browne; married second wife, Alice Matthews, August 1, 1965; children: (first marriage) Glenn, Kevin, (second marriage) Alicia. *Education:* University of Alabama, A.B., 1943; Columbia University, M.A., 1947; University of California, Los Angeles, Ph.D., 1956. *Home:* 210 North Grove, Bowling Green, Ohio 43402. *Office:* Department of English, Bowling Green State University, Bowling Green, Ohio 43402.

CAREER: Instructor in English at University of Nebraska, Lincoln, 1947-50, and University of Maryland, College Park, 1956-60; Purdue University, Lafayette, Ind., assistant professor, 1960-63, associate professor of American literature, 1963-67; Bowling Green State University, Bowling Green, Ohio, professor of English, 1967—. Visiting professor, University of Maryland, 1975-76. *Military service:* U.S. Army, Field Artillery, 1943-46; became sergeant. *Member:* American Studies Association, Modern Language Association of America, American Folklore Society, Melville Society, Popular Culture Association (founder, 1970; secretary-treasurer).

WRITINGS: Folk Beliefs and Practices from Alabama,

University of California Press, 1958; (editor) *The Burke-Paine Controversy: Text and Criticism,* Harcourt, 1963; (editor with William John Roscelli and Richard Loftus) *The Celtic Cross: Studies in Irish Culture and Literature,* Purdue University Studies, 1964; *The Indian Doctor: Frontier Pharmacology,* Indiana Historical Society, 1964; (editor with Martin Light) *Critical Approaches to American Literature,* Crowell, 1965; (editor) *New Voices in American Studies,* Purdue University Studies, 1966; (editor with others) *Frontiers of American Culture,* Purdue University Studies, 1968; (editor) *Themes and Directions in American Literature,* Purdue University Studies, 1969; (editor) *Mark Twain's Quarrel with Heaven, "Captain Stormfield's Visit to Heaven" and Other Sketches,* College and University Press, 1969; (editor with Ronald J. Ambrosetti) *Popular Culture and Curricula,* Bowling Green University Popular Press, 1969, 2nd edition, 1972; (editor with others) *Challenges in American Culture,* Bowling Green University Popular Press, 1969; (editor with Marshall Fishwick) *Icons of Popular Culture,* Bowling Green University Popular Press, 1970, 2nd edition, 1972; (editor with Russel Blaine Nye) *Crises on Campus,* Bowling Green University Popular Press, 1970; (editor with B. D. Owens) *Teach In: Viability of Change,* Bowling Green University Popular Press, 1971; *Melville's Drive to Humanism,* Purdue University Popular Press, 1971; (compiler with David Madden) *The Popular Culture Explosion,* William C. Brown, 1972; (editor with Marshall Fishwick and Michael Marsden) *Heroes of Popular Culture,* Bowling Green University Popular Press, 1972; (editor) *Popular Culture and the Expanding Consciousness,* Wiley, 1973; *Lincoln Lore: Lincoln in the Contemporary Popular Mind,* Bowling Green University Popular Press, 1975. Editor, *Journal of Popular Culture.*

WORK IN PROGRESS: A Night with the Hants and Other Alabama Folk Experiences; A Research Guide to Popular Culture; The Importance of Exhibitions and Fairs in American History.

* * *

BRUCE, Donald (James) 1930-

PERSONAL: Born January 25, 1930, in London, England; son of James Bethune (an engineer) and Anne (Williams) Bruce; married Enrika Gun Ohlsson, October 10, 1959 (divorced, 1965); married Frieda Maria Anselma Panholzl, March 25, 1971; children: (second marriage) Toby Johann-Anselm, Anne Fidelia. *Education:* University College, University of London, B.A., 1953, M.A., 1959; Institute of Education, University of London, Postgraduate Certificate in Education, 1954. *Home:* 314 Tudor Dr., Kingston, Surrey, England. *Agent:* Miss S. McIlwraith, A. D. Peters & Co., 10 Buckingham St., London WC2 6BW, England. *Office:* University of London, Westfield College, London NW3, England.

CAREER: University of Stockholm Extramural Board, Stockholm, Sweden, lecturer in English, 1955-57; English master at grammar school in England, 1957-61; University of London, London, England, lecturer in education, Institute of Education, 1961-67, lecturer in English, Westfield College, 1968—. *Member:* Society for Renaissance Studies.

WRITINGS: Radical Dr. Smollett, Gollancz, 1964, revised edition, Houghton, 1965; *Topics of Restoration Comedy,* Gollancz, 1974, St. Martin's, 1975. Contributor to *Contemporary Review.*

WORK IN PROGRESS: A critical biography of the German painter, Lucas Cranach the Elder.

SIDELIGHTS: Donald Bruce is competent in French, German, Swedish, Norwegian, Welsh, and Latin. *Avocational interests:* History of art, travel, music, gardening, and swimming (swam for University of London, 1954).

* * *

BUCHANAN, Daniel C(rump) 1892-

PERSONAL: Born June 13, 1892, in Kobe, Japan; son of William C. (a clergyman) and Minnie (Crump) Buchanan; married Katharine Baetjer, June 7, 1921 (deceased); children: George C., Daniel C., Jr., Katharine (Mrs. W. Peter Sax), Margaret-Anne (Mrs. R. P. Warlick). *Education:* Fredericksburg College, B.A., 1912; Washington and Lee University, M.A., 1914; McCormick Theological Seminary, B.D., 1921; Tokyo School of Japanese Language and Culture, graduate, 1922; Hartford Seminary Foundation, Ph.D., 1934. *Politics:* Independent. *Home:* The Wee Hoose, Glebe Rd., Easton, Md. 21601.

CAREER: Teacher of English language and American culture in Japanese schools and universities, 1914-18, 1924-25, 1928-31; ordained minister of Presbyterian Church in the U.S.A., 1921; Presbyterian Church Mission, Japan, information officer and newspaper evangelism specialist, 1921-41; wartime posts with U.S. Government included chief of Japan desk, Office of War Information, 1942-43, chief of Japan-Korea desk, Secret Intelligence Section, Office of Strategic Services, 1943-45, and senior language officer with Morale Division of the Army's Strategic Bombing Survey, 1945-46; U.S. Department of State, regional specialist, Bureau of Far Eastern Affairs, 1946-52; U.S. Office of Far Eastern Programs, foreign affairs officer, 1952-53; U.S. Division of Biographic Information, senior coordinator of psychological intelligence, 1953-54; Takoma Park Presbyterian Church, Takoma Park, Md., minister for visitation and pastoral counseling, 1954-58; retired, 1958. *Military service:* U.S. Army, 1918. *Member:* Asiatic Society of Japan, American Oriental Society, American Academy of Political and Social Science, Far Eastern Association.

WRITINGS: Inari: Its Origin, Development and Nature, Asiatic Society of Japan, 1935; (contributor) *Understanding Other Cultures,* American Council of Learned Societies, 1954; *Japanese Proverbs and Sayings,* University of Oklahoma Press, 1965; (translator and compiler) *One Hundred Famous Haiku,* Japan Publications, 1973. Contributor to *Encyclopedia Americana, Japanese Christian Quarterly, Monumenta Nipponica,* and other publications.

SIDELIGHTS: During thirty-five years in the Far East, Buchanan traveled extensively in Japan, China, Korea, Manchuria, and Malaya. He is fluent in Japanese, with competency in German and French.†

* * *

BUCHANAN, R(obert) A(ngus) 1930-

PERSONAL: Born June 5, 1930, in Sheffield, England; son of Robert Graham (a businessman) and Bertha (Davis) Buchanan; married Brenda June Wade (now a teacher), August 10, 1955; children: Andrew Nassau, Thomas Claridge. *Education:* St. Catharine's College, Cambridge, B.A., 1953, M.A., 1957, Ph.D., 1957. *Politics:* Radical. *Religion:* Christian Humanist. *Office:* University of Bath, Claverton Down, Bath, England.

CAREER: Adult education officer in an East London settlement, 1956-60; University of Bath, Claverton Down, Bath, England, lecturer in social and technological history,

1960—, director of Centre for Study of History of Technology. *Military service:* British Army, Royal Ordnance Corps, 1948-50. *Member:* Newcomen Society for History of Technology, Economic History Society, British Society for the History of Science, International Committee for the History of Technology.

WRITINGS: Technology and Social Progress, Pergamon, 1965; (with Neil Cossons) *Industrial Archaeology of the Bristol Region*, David & Charles, 1969; *Industrial Archaeology in Britain*, Pelican, 1972. Editor of *Technology and Society* and *BIAS Journal*.

WORK IN PROGRESS: Material on survey of industrial monuments of the Bristol region; books on prospects of Western civilization; the history of technical education, and science and government.

* * *

BUEHNER, Andrew J(ohn) 1905-

PERSONAL: Surname is pronounced *Bew*-ner; born January 25, 1905, in Clayton, S.D.; son of George S. (a merchant) and Kathryn (Klueber) Buehner; married Pauline K. Beck, June 20, 1928; children: Allan A., Dorothy P. (Mrs. Merle G. Golnick), Phyllis E. (Mrs. Richard W. Duesenberg). *Education:* Studied at Concordia College, St. Paul, Minn., 1918-25, Concordia Seminary, St. Louis, Mo., 1925-28, 1936-37; University of Missouri, M.Ed., 1944; other study at University of Chicago, University of Adelaide, and in India. *Home:* 8100 Rockwood Dr., St. Louis, Mo. 63123. *Office:* Concordia Publishing House, 3558 South Jefferson St., St. Louis, Mo. 63118.

CAREER: Clergyman of Lutheran Church-Missouri Synod; spent over twenty years in Travancore (now Kerala), India, as evangelistic missionary, 1928-36, and education director for about fifty mission schools, 1938-44, and 1946-50; pastor in Nebraska, 1951-58, in Indiana, 1958-61; editor of *Lutheran Scholar*, 1957—; house editor, Concordia Publishing House, St. Louis, Mo., 1961—. *Member:* Lutheran Human Relations Association of America (president of St. Louis chapter, 1965-66), Phi Delta Kappa, Alpha Lambda Phi.

WRITINGS: A Syllabus for Lutheran Mission Schools, Lutheran Mission (India), circa 1939; (editor) *Colloquy on Law and Theology*, Lutheran Academy for Scholarship, 1961; (editor) *Law and Theology*, Concordia, 1965; (assistant editor) *Medical Ethics*, Aid Association for Lutherans, 1965; (editor) *The Christian in Business*, Bethany, 1966; (editor with Karl W. Linsenmann) *Collequium on Christian Medical Ethics*, Lutheran Academy for Scholarship, 1967; (editor and author of preface) *The New American Revolution*, Lutheran Academy for Scholarship, 1968; (editor and author of preface) *Operation Theology: The Layman and Current Religious Developments*, Lutheran Academy for Scholarship, 1968; (editor) *Theology and Social Welfare: Redemption and Good Works*, Lutheran Academy for Scholarship, 1968; (editor) *The Church and the Visual Arts*, Lutheran Academy for Scholarship, 1968; (editor) *The Church and the Dramatic Arts*, Lutheran Academy for Scholarship, 1969; (editor and author of preface) *Science: Demonic, Angelic, or What?*, Lutheran Academy for Scholarship, 1971. Contributor to Lutheran periodicals.

SIDELIGHTS: Buehner has varying degrees of competency in German, Latin, Greek, Hebrew, Malayalam, Sanscrit, Russian, and French. He also knows some Tamil and Hindustani. *Avocational interests:* Radio, hi-fi (design and construction), photography and audiovisual equipment, automobile maintenance and repair.†

BUKOWSKI, Charles 1920-

PERSONAL: Born August 16, 1920, in Andernach, Germany; married Barbara Fry, October, 1955 (divorced); children: Marina Louise. *Education:* Attended Los Angeles City College, 1939-41. *Politics:* None. *Religion:* None. *Home:* 5437-2/5 Carlton Way, Los Angeles, Calif. 90027.

CAREER: Unskilled laborer, beginning, 1941, whose positions include dishwasher, truckdriver and loader, mailman, guard, gas station attendant, stock boy, warehouseman, shipping clerk, post office clerk, parking lot attendant, Red Cross orderly, and elevator operator; has worked in dog biscuit factory, slaughterhouse, cake and cookie factory, and has hung posters in New York subways; currently "surviving as a professional writer." *Awards, honors:* Silver Reel award from San Francisco Festival of the Arts for documentary film; National Foundation for the Arts grant, 1963.

WRITINGS: Flower, Fist, and Bestial Wail, Hearse Press, 1959; *Longshot Pomes for Broke Players*, 7 Poets Press, 1961; *Run With the Hunted*, Midwest Poetry Chapbooks, 1962; *Poems and Drawings*, EPOS, 1962; *It Catches My Heart in Its Hands*, Loujon Press, 1963; *Cold Dogs in the Courtyard*, Chicago Literary Times, 1965; *Crucifix in a Deathhand*, Loujon Press, 1965; *Confessions of a Man Insane Enough to Live With Beasts*, Mimeo Press, 1966; *The Genius of the Crowd*, 7 Flowers Press, 1966; *All the Assholes in the World and Mine*, Mimeo Press, 1966; *Poems Written Before Jumping Out of an 8 Story Window*, Mad Virgin Press, 1968; *At Terror Street and Agony Way*, Black Sparrow Press, 1968; *Notes of a Dirty Old Man*, Essex House, 1969; *The Days Run Away Like Wild Horses Over the Hills*, Black Sparrow Press, 1969; *Fire Station*, Capricorn Press, 1970; *Post Office*, Black Sparrow Press, 1971; *Mockingbird Wish Me Luck*, Black Sparrow Press, 1972; *Erections, Ejaculations, Exhibitions, and General Tales of Ordinary Madness*, City Lights, 1972; *Me and Your Sometimes Love Poems*, Kisskill Press, 1972; *South of No North*, Black Sparrow Press, 1973; *Burning in Water, Drowning in Flame*, Black Sparrow Press, 1974.

Work represented in anthologies, including *Penguin Modern Poets: Number Thirteen*, and *Notes from the Underground*, edited by John Bryan. Also wrote one-hour documentary film, produced by KCET, public television, Los Angeles.

SIDELIGHTS: Bukowski began writing poetry at the age of 35, but he says he does not consider himself a poet but simply a writer. "To say I'm a poet puts me in the company of versifiers, neon-tasters, fools, clods, and skoundrels masquerading as wise men." He does not like "form" in poetry, calling it "a paycheck for learning to turn the same screw that has held things together." He believes that "life is a spider, we can only dance in the web so long, the thing is gonna get us. . . . I am pretty well hooked-in now, have fallen into some traps, and speak mostly from the bent bone, the flogged spirit. I've had some wild and horrible years & electric & lucky years. . . ." *Avocational interests:* Horse playing, symphony music.

BIOGRAPHICAL/CRITICAL SOURCES: Northwest Review, fall, 1963; *Americas*, February, 1964; *Today*, April, 1966; *Down Here*, Volume I, No. 1, 1966; Sanford Dorbin, *A Bibliography of Charles Bukowski*, Black Sparrow Press, 1969; Hugh Fox, *Charles Bukowski: A Critical and Bibliographical Study*, Abyss Publications, 1969; Carolyn Riley, editor, *Contemporary Literary Criticism*, Gale, Volume II, 1974, Volume V, 1976.

BULLARD, Helen 1902-

PERSONAL: Born August 15, 1902, in Elgin, Ill.; daughter of Charles Wickliffe (a construction superintendent) and Minnie (Cook) Bullard; married Lloyd Ernst Rohrke, 1924 (divorced, 1931); married Joseph Marshall Krechniak (a writer), January 30, 1932 (died Feburary 22, 1964); children: (first marriage) Ann Louise (Mrs. Ross D. Netherton), Barbara Jane (Mrs. V. Emil Gudmundson); (second marriage) Martha (deceased), Mariana (Mrs. Epifanio Medina). *Education:* University of Chicago, student, three years. *Politics:* Democrat. *Religion:* Unitarian Universalist. *Home:* Ozone, Tenn. 37842. *Agent:* Harold Ober Associates, Inc., 40 East 49th St., New York, N.Y. 10017.

CAREER: Research assistant for an industrial engineering firm, Chicago, Ill., 1920-22, and production control operator for a manufacturer, Detroit, Mich., 1922-24; director of Play Center, Crossville, Tenn., 1949-50; creator of hand-carved wooden dolls, 1949—, starting with a line sold under the label, "Holly Dolls," and adding an advanced type of originals carrying the "Helen Bullard" signature, 1954; also has done wood sculptures, 1958—. Campaign chairman, American Cancer Society drive, Cumberland County, Tenn., 1947-52. *Member:* United Federation of Doll Clubs (regional director, 1963-65), National Institute of American Doll Artists (founder; president, 1963-67, 1969-71). Southern Highland Handicraft Guild (director, 1957-59). *Awards, honors:* Ribbons and special awards at conventions of United Federation of Doll Clubs, 1950-67; other awards at craft shows and fairs.

WRITINGS: (With Joseph Marshall Krechniak) *Cumberland Country's First 100 Years*, Centennial Committee, Crossville, Tenn., 1956; *The American Doll Artist*, Volume I, Branford, 1965, Volume II, Athena Publishing Co., 1975. *A Bullard Family*, privately printed, 1966. Contributor of articles on dolls and Tennessee crafts to hobby and regional magazines. Editor, *Doll News* (publication of United Federation of Doll Clubs), 1960-61.

* * *

BULLOCK, Michael 1918-
(Michael Hale)

PERSONAL: Born April 19, 1918, in London, England; son of Herbert Stanley Billingsley (an insurance manager) and Katherine (Wortham) Bullock; married Charlotte Schneller (a novelist), January 10, 1941; children: Miriam Raya, Marcus Paul. *Education:* Attended Stowe School, Bucks, England, and Hornsey School of Art. *Home:* 3836 West 18th Avenue, Vancouver, British Columbia, Canada. *Agent:* Joan Daves, 145 East 49th St., New York 17, N.Y.

CAREER: Free-lance literary translator and writer, 1954—; University of British Columbia, associate professor of creative writing, and director of translation program, 1970—. *Member:* International P.E.N. (member of executive committee of English Centre), Translators Association (committee member, 1961-66, chairman, 1964-66), Society of Authors (member of committee of management, 1967—). *Awards, honors:* Schlegel-Tieck German Translation Prize, administered by Translators Association for the German Government, German Publishers Association, and British publishers, 1965, for *Report on Bruno* by Joseph Breitbach, and *The Thirtieth Year*, by Ingeborg Bachmann; Canada Council fellowship, 1968.

WRITINGS—Poetry: (Under pseudonym Michael Hale) *Transmutations*, Favil Press, 1938; *Sunday is a Day of*

Incest, Abelard, 1960; *World Without Beginning Amen!*, Favil and Barrie & Rockliff, 1963; *Zwei Stimmen in meinem Mund (Two Voices in My Mouth)*, (bilingual selection), Atelier Verlag, 1967; *A Savage Darkness*, Sono Nis, 1969.

Fiction: *Sixteen Stories As They Happened*, Sono Nis, 1969; *Green Beginning Black Ending*, Sono Nis, 1971; *Randolph Cranstone and the Pursuing River*, Rainbird, 1974.

Plays: "The Coats," produced on stage and radio, "Not to Hong Kong," and "The Island Abode of Bliss and Couple."

Translator: Willibald Klinke, *Kant for Everyman*, Macmillan, 1952; Wilhelm Worringer, *Abstraction and Empathy: A Contribution to the Psychology of Style*, International Universities Press, 1953; (with Ronald Gregor) Martin Buber, *Good and Evil: Two Interpretations*, Scribner, 1953; Karl Jaspers, *Origin and Goal of History*, Yale University Press, 1953; Josef Pieper, *End of Time: A Meditation on the Philosophy of History*, Pantheon, 1954; Walter Jens, *Blind Man*, Macmillan, 1954; Paul Herrmann, *Conquest by Man*, Harper, 1954; Gustav Schenk, *Book of Poisons*, Rinehart, 1955; Theodor Heuss, *Preludes to Life: Early Memoirs*, Citadel, 1955; Georges Houot and P. H. Willm, *2,000 Fathoms Down*, Dutton, 1955; Gustav von Koenigswald, *Meeting Prehistoric Man*, Thames & Hudson, 1956; Rene von Nebesky-Wojkowitz, *Where the Gods are Mountains*, Weidenfeld & Nicholson, 1956, Reynal, 1957; Alfred Metraux, *Easter Island*, Oxford University Press, 1957; Reinhard Lullies, *Greek Sculpture*, Abrams, 1957, revised edition, 1960; Walter Erben, *Marc Chagall*, Praeger, 1957, revised edition, 1966; Marcellin Boule, *Fossil Men*, Macmillan, 1957; Will Berthold, *Sinking of the Bismarck*, Longmans, Green, 1958; Alfred Andersch, *Flight to Afar*, Coward, 1958; Max Frisch, *I'm Not Stiller*, Abelard, 1958; Anton Luebke, *World of Caves*, Weidenfeld & Nicholson, 1958, Coward, 1959; Herbert Wendt, *Out of Noah's Ark*, Houghton, 1959; Zoe Oldenbourg, *Chains of Love*, Pantheon, 1959; Joachim Leithaeuser, *Inventors' Progress*, World Publishing, 1959; Walter Erben, *Joan Miro*, Lund, 1959, Braziller, 1960; Gilbert Cesbron, *Lost Children of Paris*, Abelard, 1959; Pierre Rousseau, *Man's Conquest of the Stars*, Jarrolds, 1959, Norton, 1961; Max Frisch, *Homo Faber: A Report*, Abelard, 1959; Joachim Maass, *Gouffe Case*, Barrie & Rockliff, 1960; Alfred Andersch, *The Redhead*, Heinemann, 1960; Siegfried Lenz, *The Lightship*, Hill & Wang, 1960; Will Grohmann, *Art of Henry Moore*, Abrams, 1960; (and editor, with Jerome Ch'en) *Poems of Solitude* (from the Chinese), Abelard, 1960; Eduard Trier, *The Sculpture of Marino Marini*, Praeger, 1961; (with Johanna Capra) Giovanni Mariacher, *Italian Blown Glass*, McGraw, 1961; Bernhard Bultmann, *Oskar Kokoschka*, Abrams, 1961; Ulrich Schamoni, *Their Fathers' Sons*, Barrie & Rockliff, 1962; Otto Walter, *The Mute*, Grove, 1962; (with Alisa Jaffa) Frederic Neuberg, *Ancient Glass*, Barrie & Rockliff, 1962; Max Frisch, *The Fire Raisers*, Methuen, 1962; Max Frisch, *Andorra*, Methuen, 1962, Hill & Wang, 1963; Max Frisch, *Count Oederland*, Methuen, 1962; Max Frisch, *Philipp Hotz's Fury*, Gambit, no date; Robert Neumann, *Festival*, Barrie & Rockliff, 1963; (and editor) Ernst Theodor Hoffmann, *The Tales of Hoffmann*, Ungar, 1963; Siegfried Lenz, *The Survivor*, Hill & Wang, 1963; Roger Goepper, *The Essence of Chinese Painting*, Lund, 1963, Boston Book Co., 1964; Ingeborg Bachmann, *The Thirtieth Year*, Deutsch, 1964; Joseph Breitbach, *Report on Bruno*, Knopf, 1964; (from German) Wali al-Din

Samih, *Daily Life in Ancient Egypt*, McGraw, 1964; Johan Henrik Langaard and Reidar Revold, *Edvard Munch*, McGraw, 1964; Siegfried Lenz, *Time of the Guiltless*, B.B.C., 1965; Max Frisch, *Wilderness of Mirrors*, Methuen, 1965; P. Verlet, *French Royal Furniture*, C. N. Potter, no date; Klaus Berger, *Odilon Redon: Fantasy and Colour*, McGraw, 1965; (with Jerome Ch'en) *Mao and the Chinese Revolution, with 37 Poems by Mao Tse-Tung*, Oxford University Press, 1965; (with Henry Mins) Charles DeTolnay, *Hieronymus Bosch*, Methuen, 1966; Walter August Staehelin, *The Book of Porcelain*, Macmillan, 1966; Friedrich Duerrenmatt, *The Marriage of Mr. Mississippi* (published with an essay, *Problems of the Theatre*, translated by Gerhard Nellhaus), Grove, 1966; Rolf Schneider, *Bridges and Bars*, J. Cape, 1967; Charles Chasse, *The Nabis and Their Period*, Lund Humphries, 1969; Cecile and Michel Beurdeley, *Giuseppe Castiglione, Lund Humphries*, 1969; Georges Boudaille, *Courbet*, New York Graphic Society, 1969; Karl Krolow, *Invisible Hands*, Grossman, 1969; Karl Krolow, *Foreign Bodies*, Ohio University Press, 1969; Andre Busza, *Astrologer in the Underground*, Ohio University Press, 1970; Joachim C. Fest, *Face of the Third Reich: Portraits of the Nazi Leadership*, Pantheon, 1970; Francoise Cachin, *Paul Signac*, New York Graphic Society, 1971. Also translator of eight plays by Max Frisch, "Don Juan," "Santa Cruz," "The Great Wall of China," "Now They're Singing Again," "Philip Hotz's Fury," "Count Oderland," "The Fire Raisers," and "Biography." Translator of poems by Karl Krolow, Guenter Eich, Paul Celan, Ingeborg Bachmann, Hilde Domin, Rosemarie Strebe, Paul Eluard, Guillevic, and others, published in periodicals. Translator of stories by Ugo Betti, Mario Soldati, and Guido Piovene, published in periodicals and anthologies.

WORK IN PROGRESS: A sixth book of poems, *Black Wings White Dead*, a fiction work, *The Hollow World*, and further translations.

SIDELIGHTS: Bullock writes: "Have travelled widely in Europe, India, the United States, and Canada. Am also a graphic artist and have exhibited my drawings in England and Germany as well as illustrating my own and other people's books. In my own writing and drawing, and as editor of *Prism International*, try to express and foster a view of life and literature that is imaginative and personal and opposed to mechanization and alienation of much contemporary art."

BIOGRAPHICAL/CRITICAL SOURCES: The Author, summer, 1966; *Madame* (German), January 1, 1967; *British Columbia Library Quarterly*, April, 1973.

*   *   *

BUNZEL, John H(arvey) 1924-

PERSONAL: Born April 15, 1924, in New York, N.Y.; son of Ernest Everett (a physician) and Harriet (Harvey) Bunzel; married Barbara Bovyer, May 11, 1963; children: (previous marriage) Cameron (daughter), Reed (son). *Education:* Princeton University, A.B. (magna cum laude), 1948; Columbia University, M.A., 1949; University of California, Berkeley, Ph.D., 1954. *Politics:* Democrat. *Home:* 1519 Escondido Way, Belmont, Calif. 94002. *Office:* San Jose State University, San Jose, Calif. 95114.

CAREER: Instructor at San Francisco State College (now University), San Francisco, Calif., 1953-56, and Michigan State University, East Lansing, 1956-57; Stanford University, Stanford, Calif., assistant professor of political sci-

ence, 1957-63; San Francisco State University, San Francisco, Calif., associate professor, 1963-67, professor of political science and chairman of department, 1967-70; San Jose State University, San Jose, Calif., president, 1970—. Visiting scholar, Center for Advanced Study in the Behavioral Sciences, 1969-70. Public speaker on contemporary political and social issues. Director of Michigan Citizenship Clearing House, 1956-57, and Northern California Citizenship Clearing House, 1959-62; member of California Attorney General's Advisory Committee on Constitutional Rights, 1960-61; conducted KPIX television show "The American Voter," 1964; delegate to Democratic Nation Convention, 1968. *Military service:* U.S. Army, 1943-46; became master sergeant. *Member:* American Political Science Association, Western Political Science Association, Northern California Political Science Association (president, 1962-63). *Awards, honors:* Research grants from Ford Foundation, 1958-61 and 1969-70, Rabinowitz Foundation, 1961-62, Rockefeller Foundation, 1965-66; outstanding service award from North California Political Science Association, 1969; certificate from City and County of San Francisco, 1974.

WRITINGS: The American Small Businessman, Knopf, 1962; *The California Democratic Delegation of 1960*, Prentice-Hall, 1962; (editor) *Issues of American Public Policy*, Prentice-Hall, 1964, 2nd edition, 1968; *Anti-Politics in America*, Knopf, 1967. Weekly columnist for *San Jose Mercury News*. Contributor to professional journals.

AVOCATIONAL INTERESTS: Golf, baseball, espionage novels, American humor.

*   *   *

BURGER, Ruth (Pazen) 1917-

PERSONAL: Born July 26, 1917, in Jersey City, N.J.; daughter of Joseph and Sarah (Fried) Pazen; married Irving Burger, 1944 (deceased); children: John, Arthur. *Education:* Rutgers, The State University, B.A., 1937. *Home:* 20 East 74th St., New York, N.Y. 10021. *Office:* Research Institute of America, 589 Fifth Ave., New York, N.Y. 10017.

CAREER: Research Institute of America, New York, N.Y., research assistant, 1938-40, editor of development division, 1940-44, 1956-60, director of human resources research, 1960-64, managing editor, 1964—. Free-lance writer, 1955—.

WRITINGS: (With Benjamin Balinsky) *Executive Interview: A Bridge to People*, Harper, 1959; *The Psychologist in Industry*, Research Institute of America, 1960; (contributor) Carl Heyel, editor, *The Encyclopedia of Management*, Van Nostrand, 1973. Contributor to business magazines, including *Nation's Business, Management Review*, and *Supervisory Management*. Editor of *Managing Men* (periodical for sales managers).

WORK IN PROGRESS: Research on women in industry.

*   *   *

BURGHARD, August 1901-

PERSONAL: Born August 19, 1901, in Opelika, Ala.; son of August (a dentist) and Margaret (Meadors) Burghard; married Lois Baker, June 8, 1928; children: Patricia (Mrs. Wallace A. Kennedy), Jacqueline (Mrs. Albert G. Griffith). *Education:* Attended Mercer University, 1921-25, Northwestern University, 1937-39, Emory University, 1941, and University of North Carolina, 1942-43. *Politics:*

Democrat. *Religion:* Presbyterian. *Home:* 1131 Southwest Ninth Ave. (Pinar del Rio), Fort Lauderdale, Fla. 33315. *Office:* Nova University, College Ave., Fort Lauderdale, Fla. 33314.

CAREER: Fort Lauderdale News, Fort Lauderdale, Fla., reporter, later editor, 1925-35; Chamber of Commerce, Fort Lauderdale, manager, 1935-45; August Burghard, Inc. (advertising agency), Fort Lauderdale, president, 1945-56; Campbell-Dickey Advertising, Inc., Fort Lauderdale, senior vice-president, 1957-66; member, Fort Lauderdale city commission, 1963-64; Nova University, Fort Lauderdale, executive director of Gold Key, 1966-72. Director of Everglades Bank and Lauderdale Memorial Gardens; chairman of Everglades National Park Commission and Birch State Park Advisory Board. *Member:* Historical Society of Southern Florida (director and vice-president), Audubon Society (local president), Historical Society of Fort Lauderdale (first president), Pi Kappa Alpha, Lauderdale Yacht Club, Advertising Club, Tower Club. *Awards, honors:* Silver Medal of Advertising Federation of America and *Printers' Ink*, 1959.

WRITINGS: (With Philip Weidling) *Checkered Sunshine: The History of Fort Lauderdale, 1793-1955*, University of Florida Press, 1966; *Watchie-Esta/Hutrie*, Historical Society of Fort Lauderdale, 1968; *Alligator Alley*, Lanman, 1969; *The Story of Frederick C. Peters*, Tropical Press, 1972; *America's First Family: The Savages of Virginia*, Dorrance, 1974; *Nova University: The First Ten Years*, Nova University Press, 1975. Contributor to *Yachting, Atlanta Journal, Boston Post, St. Louis Post Dispatch, Miami Herald*, and to wire services.

WORK IN PROGRESS: Ambassador of the Everglades, and *Erkins's Early Days in Florida*.

SIDELIGHTS: Has visited most of the national parks of the United States, and has traveled in Mexico, the Caribbean, and South America; speaks some Spanish.

*   *   *

BURHOE, Ralph Wendell 1911-

PERSONAL: Born June 21, 1911, in Somerville, Mass.; son of Winslow Page and Mary Trenaman (Stumbles) Burhoe; married Frances Bickford, August 4, 1931 (died August 19, 1967); married Calla C. G. Butler, April 6, 1969; children: Winslow Newton, Laura Jean, Thomas Allen, Diana May. *Education:* Studied at Harvard University, 1928-32, and Andover Newton Theological School, 1934-36. *Home:* 1524 East 59th Street, Chicago, Ill. 60637.

CAREER: Harvard University, Cambridge, Mass., observer and research assistant at Blue Hill Meteorological Observatory, 1936-47; American Academy of Arts and Sciences, Boston, Mass., executive officer, from 1947-64; Meadville Theological School, Chicago, Ill., now professor emeritus of theology and the sciences.

MEMBER: Academy of Religion and Mental Health, American Academy of Arts and Sciences (fellow; member of council), American Association for the Advancement of Science (fellow; member of council, 1965-71), Society for the Scientific Study of Religion (member of council, 1956-59, 1965-70; treasurer, 1965-70), American Academy of Religion, American Philosophical Association, American Theological Association, World Academy of Art and Science (fellow), American Meteorological Society (assistant secretary, 1936-47; treasurer, 1942-47), Institute for Religion in an Age of Science (co-founder; honorary president).

WRITINGS: (Editor with Hudson Hoagland) *Evolution and Man's Progress*, Columbia University Press, 1962; (editor and contributor) *Science and Human Values in the 21st Century*, Westminster Press, 1971; (contributor) Ervin Laszlo, editor, *The World System*, Braziller, 1973; (contributor) Allan W. Eister, editor, *Changing Perspectives in the Scientific Study of Religion*, Wiley-Interscience, 1974. Contributor of more than fifty articles and papers to social, philosophical, and religious journals. Editor, *Zygon, Journal of Religion and Science*, 1966—.

WORK IN PROGRESS: A book, *Man's Place in the Scheme of Things*; revisions of earlier papers; editing a book from contributions to *Zygon*.

*   *   *

BURI, Fritz 1907-

PERSONAL: Born November 4, 1907, in Kernenried, Bern, Switzerland; son of Fritz and Rosalie (Rutschi) Buri; married Elsa Richard, August 7, 1931; children: Ursula, Samuel, Barbara, Dorothea. *Education:* Attended Universities of Basel, Marburg, and Berlin; University of Bern, D.Th., 1934. *Religion:* Evangelical Reform. *Home:* Auf der Alp 3, Basel, Switzerland.

CAREER: Formerly assistant professor at University of Bern, Bern, Switzerland, and professor of systematic theology at University of Basel, Basel, Switzerland. Guest professor at Drew University, Madison, N.J., 1966-67, International Christian University, Tokyo, 1968-69, Syracuse University, N.Y., 1971; Dudleian Lecturer at Harvard University, 1967. Basler Cathedral, rector. *Military service:* Chaplain. *Awards, honors:* Haller medal.

WRITINGS: Die Bedeutung der neutestamentlichen Eschatologie fuer die neuere protestantische Theologie, Max Niehans, 1934; *Clemens Alexandrinus und der paulinische Freiheitsbegriff*, Max Niehans, 1939; *Gottfried Kellers Glaube*, Paul Haupt (bern), 1944; *Prometheus und Christus: Groesse uns Grenzen von Carl Spittelers religioeser Weltanschauung*, A. Francke, 1945; *Kreuz und Ring: Die Kreuzestheologie des jungen Luther und die Lehre von der ewigen Wiederkunft in Nietzsches "Zarathustra"*, Paul Haupt, 1947; *Albert Schweitzer und Karl Jaspers*, Artemis, 1950; *Christlicher Glaube in dieser Zeit*, Paul Haupt, 1952, translation by Edward Allen published as *Christian Faith in Our Time*, Macmillan, 1966; *Theologie der Existenz*, Paul Haupt, 1954, translation by Harold H. Oliver and Gerhard Onder published as *Theology of Existence*, Attic Books, 1966; *Dogmatik als Selbstverstaendnis des christlichen Glaubens*, Paul Haupt, Volume I: *Vernunft und Offenvarung*, 1956; Volume II: *Der Mensch und die Gnade*, 1962; *Die Reformation geht weiter*, Paul Haupt, 1956; *Das lebendige Wort*, Herbert Reich (Hamburg), 1957; *Unterricht im christlichen Glauben*, Paul Haupt, 1957; *Der Weg des Glaubens*, Ernst Reinhardt, 1958; *Basler Bekenntnis heute*, Evangelischer Verlag A. G. Zollikon, 1959; *Die Predigt der Saeulen*, Phoebus, 1959; *Gebot und Gebet*, Evangelischer Verlag A. G. Zollikon, 1960; *Die Bilder und das Wort am Basler Muenster*, Phoebus, 1961; *Das dreifache Heilswerk Christi und seine Aneignung im Glauben*, Herbert Reich, 1962; *Vermaechtnis der Vaeter: Die Vorsteher der Basler Kirche seit der Reformation*, Pharos (Basel), 1963; *Von Sinn des Leidens: Eine Auslegung des Liedes von leidenden Gottesknecht*, Friedrich Reinhardt, 1963; *Bildnerische Kunst und Theologie*, Basilius Presse, 1964; *Wie koennen wir heute noch verantwortlich so fort reden?*, Mohr (Guetersloh),

1967, translation published as *How Can We Speak Responsibly of God?*, Fortress, 1968; *Hoffnung, Wesen und Bewaehrung*, Herbert Reuer, 1967; *Denkender Glaube*, Haupt, 1967, translation by Harold H. Oliver published as *Thinking Faith: Steps on the Way to a Philosophical Theology*, Fortress, 1968; *Der Pantokrator: Ontologie und Eschatologie als Grundlage der Lehre von Gott*, Herbert Reich, 1969; *Gott in America*, Paul Haupt, Volume I: *Amerikanische Theologie seit 1960*, 1970, Volume II: *Religion, Theologie, und Philosophie seit 1969*, 1972; *Zur Theologie der Verantwortung*, edited by Guenther Hauff, Paul Haupt, 1971; (with others) *Die Kirche und die letzten Dinge*, Mohn, 1973.

SIDELIGHTS: Buri is competent in French, English, Italian, and Dutch.

* * *

BURLING, Robbins 1926-

PERSONAL: Born April 18, 1926, in Minneapolis, Minn.; son of Temple (a physician) and Katherine (White) Burling; married Sibyl Straub, 1951; children: Stephen, Helen, Adele. *Education:* Yale University, B.A., 1950; Harvard University, Ph.D., 1958. *Office:* Anthropology Department, University of Michigan, Ann Arbor, Mich.

CAREER: Ford Foundation anthropological research fellow in Garo Hills, Assam, India, 1954-56; University of Pennsylvania, Philadelphia, instructor, 1957-59, assistant professor of anthropology, 1959-63; University of Michigan, Ann Arbor, associate professor of anthropology, 1963-67, professor of anthropology and linguistics, 1967—. Rangoon University, Rangoon, Burma, Fulbright lecturer, 1959-60. *Military service:* U.S. Navy, 1944-46. *Member:* American Anthropological Association, Linguistic Society of America, Association for Asian Studies. *Awards, honors:* Guggenheim fellowship, 1971-72.

WRITINGS: A Garo Grammar, Deccan College (Poona, India), 1961; *Rengsanggri: Family and Kinship in a Garo Village*, University of Pennsylvania Press, 1963; *Hill Farms and Paddy Fields*, Prentice-Hall, 1965; *Man's Many Voices*, Holt, 1970; *English in Black and White*, Holt, 1973; *The Passage of Power: Studies in Political Succession*, Academic Press, 1974.

* * *

BURNETT, Joe Ray 1928-

PERSONAL: Born May 7, 1928, in Welch, W.Va.; son of James B. Weaver and Vada Christine (Watson) Burnett; married Jacquetta Hill (an assistant professor of educational anthropology), January 2, 1953 (divorced). *Education:* Bluefield Junior College, A.A., 1950; University of Tennessee, B.A., 1951, M.A., 1953; New York University, Ph.D., 1958. *Home:* 1210 West John St., Champaign, Ill. 61820. *Office:* College of Education, University of Illinois, Urbana, Ill. 61803.

CAREER: Taught at New York City Community College of Applied Arts and Sciences, New York, N.Y., 1955-56; University of Kansas City (now University of Missouri at Kansas City), 1956-57; New York University, New York, N.Y., instructor, 1957-58, assistant professor of philosophy of education, 1958-59; University of Illinois, Urbana, assistant professor, 1959-62, associate professor, 1962-66, professor of philosophy of education, 1966—, chairman of department of history and philosophy of education, 1972—. Visiting professor, University of Puerto Rico, summer,

1965; visiting lecturer, University of British Columbia, summer, 1969, 1970. *Military service:* U.S. Navy, 1946-48. *Member:* American Philosophical Association (fellow), Philosophy of Education Society (executive board member, 1963-65), Society of Education (executive board member, 1973-75), John Dewey Society (executive board member, 1963-66; president 1966-68), Midwest Philosophy of Education Society (president, 1963-65; executive board member, 1965-66).

WRITINGS: (With Harry S. Broudy and B. Othanel Smith) *Democracy and Excellence in American Secondary Education*, Rand McNally, 1964. Editor-in-chief, *Educational Theory*, 1962-65; member of editorial board, *Studies in Philosophy and Education*, 1960-65.

WORK IN PROGRESS: Research on theories of educational and social change in Latin America; research on John Dewey's educational writings, in connection with the center for Dewey studies at Southern Illinois University.

* * *

BURNHAM, Robert Ward, Jr. 1913-

PERSONAL: Born July 11, 1913, in Hornell, N.Y.; son of Robert Ward (a salesman) and Mary-Blanche (Sizeland) Burnham; married Wilma Virginia Gucker, April 18, 1942; children: Kathryn (Mrs. Peter D. Little), Christine Davis, Robert Ward III. *Education:* Attended Syracuse University, 1930-32; St. Lawrence University, B.S. (magna cum laude), 1937; University of Rochester, M.S., 1938; Rutgers College (now University), Ph.D., 1941. *Politics:* Republican.. *Home:* 307 Allen's Creek Rd., Rochester, N.Y. 14618.

CAREER: General Motors Corp., Rochester Products Division, Rochester, N.Y., personnel trainee, 1945-46; Hobart College, Geneva, N.Y., instructor in psychology, 1946-47; Eastman Kodak Co., Rochester, N.Y., research psychologist, 1947-59, systems engineer, 1959-65, senior research technologist, 1965-69, research associate, 1969—. *Military service:* U.S. Army, 1941-45; became major; received Bronze Star and European Theater Medal with five battle stars. *Member:* Gyro International, American Association for the Advancement of Science, American Psychological Association, Optical Society of America, Society of Photographic Scientists and Engineers, Society of Motion Picture and Television Engineers, Inter-Society Color Council, American Association for Information Science, Phi Beta Kappa, Sigma Xi, Phi Delta Theta. *Awards, honors:* National Microfilm Association, first award, 1967.

WRITINGS: (With R. M. Hanes and C. J. Bartleson) *Color: A Guide to Basic Facts and Concepts*, Wiley, 1963; (contributor) Walter M. Lifton, editor, *Educating for Tomorrow: The Role of Media in Career Development and Society*, Wiley, 1969. Contributor of fifty articles to psychology and science journals.

WORK IN PROGRESS: Research on technical information systems.

* * *

BURNS, E(dward) Bradford 1932-

PERSONAL: Born August 28, 1932, in Muscatine, Iowa; son of Edward Sylvester (former mayor of Muscatine) and Wanda A. (Schwandke) Burns. *Education:* University of Iowa, B.A., 1954; Tulane University, M.A., 1955; Columbia University, Ph.D., 1964; foreign study at University of San Carlos, Guatemala, 1953, University of Lisbon,

1955-56, Central University of Caracas, 1959-60. *Religion:* Episcopalian. *Office:* Department of History, University of California, Los Angeles, Calif. 90024.

CAREER: Researcher in Brazil, principally in Historical Archives of Itamaraty, 1962-63; State University of New York at Buffalo, assistant professor of history, 1963-64; University of California, Los Angeles, assistant professor of history, 1964-67; Columbia University, New York, N.Y., associate professor of history, 1967-69; University of California, Los Angeles, professor of history, 1969—. Portuguese and Spanish language consultant to Council on Foreign Relations, 1961-64; Latin America area lecturer for National Council of Churches, 1963-66; also lecturer at University of Parana and University of Brazil. *Military service:* U.S. Navy, 1956-59; became lieutenant junior grade.

MEMBER: American Historical Association, Conference on Latin American Studies, Academy of Political Science, Society for the History of Discoveries, Association of Brazilian Historians (executive secretary, 1964-65), Instituto Historico e Geographico Brasilerio, Pacific Coast Council on Latin American Studies (president, 1973-74), Phi Beta Kappa, Phi Sigma Iota. *Awards, honors:* Ford Foundation grant; Rockefeller Foundation fellowship for further research on Brazilian foreign policy (in Brazil), 1966-67; Bolton Prize for *Perspectives on Brazilian History,* 1967; Fulbright fellowship, 1974; other fellowships for study in South and Central America.

WRITINGS: A Documentary History of Brazil, Knopf, 1966; *The Unwritten Alliance, Rio-Branco and Brazilian-American Relations,* Columbia University Press, 1966; *Perspectives on Brazilian History,* Columbia University Press, 1967; *Nationalism in Brazil,* Praeger, 1967; *A History of Brazil,* Columbia University Press, 1970; *Latin America: A Concise Interpretive History,* Prentice-Hall, 1972. Contributor of articles on Latin American history to scholarly journals in United States, Panama, Brazil, and Portugal.

WORK IN PROGRESS: Yesterday's Latin America, and *A Pictorial History of Twentieth Century Latin America,* expected in 1976.

SIDELIGHTS: Burns is competent in Spanish and Portuguese; has been in Brazil on ten occasions, and has traveled throughout other Latin America countries and in Europe.

* * *

BURNS, Gerald P(hillip)   1918-

PERSONAL: Born October 1, 1918, in Winthrop, Mass.; son of Gerald John (an advertising executive) and Lillian (Griffin) Burns; married Nell Lovett (divorced); married Cecile Gayzik, June 20, 1970; children: (first marriage) Gerald P., Jr., Michael J.; (second marriage) James. *Education:* Boston University, B.S., 1941; Columbia University, M.A., 1946, Ed.D., 1948; New York University, Ph.D., 1962. *Politics:* Independent. *Religion:* Roman Catholic. *Home:* 6915 Callaghan St., Antonio, Tex. 78216.

CAREER: Brooklyn College (now Brooklyn College of the City University of New York), Brooklyn, N.Y., instructor in hygiene, 1947-48; American Camping Association, Chicago, Ill., executive director, 1948-52; New York University, New York, N.Y., assistant vice-president, 1952-55; Reed College, Portland, Ore., vice-president, 1955-58; Independent College Funds, New York, N.Y., president, 1958-67; Johns Hopkins University, Baltimore, Md., Vice-

president, 1967-69; Florida State University, Tallahassee, Fla., professor of higher education, 1969-73; Our Lady of the Lake College, San Antonio, Tex., president, 1973—. Member of Presidential Task Force on Students in Government, 1968-69; chairman of board of directors, Educational Reference and Advisory Corp. Trustee, Windham College. *Military service:* U.S. Army Air Force, 1941-45; became major. *Member:* American Association for the Advancement of Science, American Academy of Political and Social Science, Association for Higher Education, Public Relations Society of America, Phi Epsilon Kappa, Phi Delta Kappa, University Club.

WRITINGS: (Editor and contributor) *Program of the Modern Camp,* Prentice-Hall, 1950; (editor) *Administrators in Higher Education,* Harper, 1962; *Trustees in Higher Education: Their Functions and Coordination* Independent College Funds, 1966.

WORK IN PROGRESS: Death in the Air, a novel; "Ask Not," a play.

SIDELIGHTS: Burns speaks Spanish and French. *Avocational interests:* Swimming, sailing, skin diving.

* * *

BURNS, Richard Dean   1929-

PERSONAL: Born June 16, 1929, in Des Moines, Iowa; son of Richard B. (a teacher) and Luella E. Burns; married Frances Regina Sullivan, January 14, 1950; children: Richard Dean III. *Education:* University of Illinois, B.S. (honors), 1957, M.A., 1958, Ph.D., 1960. *Residence:* Arcadia, Calif. *Office:* California State University, Los Angeles, Calif. 90032.

CAREER: U.S. Army Air Forces and U.S. Air Force, 1947-56; California State University, Los Angeles, professor of history. *Member:* Phi Kappa Phi.

WRITINGS: (With Donald Dewey, Eugene Fingerhut, and Samuel McSeveney) *The Continuing Dialogue,* two volumes, Pacific Books, 1964; (editor with Walter R. Fisher) *Armament and Disarmament,* Wadsworth, 1964; (with Donald Urquidi) *Disarmament in Historical Perspective, 1919-1941,* four volumes, Government Printing Office, 1968; (compiler with Milton Leitenberg) *The Vietnam Conflict,* Clio, 1973; (editor with Edward M. Bennett) *Diplomats in Crisis, 1919-1941,* Clio, 1974. Editor of "War/Peace Bibliography Series." Contributor to political and history journals.

WORK IN PROGRESS: Two volume bibliography on arms control and disarmament, and a two volume bibliography on the Cold War, both for Clio.

* * *

BURNS, Robert Ignatius   1921-

PERSONAL: Born August 16, 1921, in San Francisco, Calif.; son of Harry (a railroad engineer) and Viola (Whearty) Burns. *Education:* Attended University of San Francisco, 1939-40, and University of Santa Clara; Gonzaga University, B.A. (with honors), 1945, M.A. (philosophy) and Phil.Lic., 1947; Fordham University, M.A. (history), 1949; Jesuit Faculty of Theology, S.Th.B. and S.Th.Lic., 1953; graduate study at Villa Machiavelli, Florence, Italy, 1953-54, Gregorian University, Rome, Italy, 1954-55, and Campion Hall, Oxford, 1955-56; Johns Hopkins University, Ph.D. (with honors), 1958; University of Fribourg, Doc. es Sc. Hist. (double summa cum laude), 1961. *Home:* Faculty Residences, University of San Francisco, San Francisco, Calif. 94117. *Office:* History Department, University of San Francisco, San Francisco, Calif. 94117.

CAREER: Entered Society of Jesus (Jesuits), 1940, ordained priest, 1952, Jesuit Historical Archives, Spokane, Wash., assistant archivist, 1946-47; University of San Francisco, San Francisco, Calif., instructor in history, 1947-48, assistant professor, 1958-63, associate professor, 1963-66; professor of history, 1967—. Visiting professor of history at College of Notre Dame, Belmont, Calif., 1963—; visiting professor, James Chair, Brown University, 1970; member, Princeton University Institute for Advanced Study, 1972; visiting lecturer at University of Santa Clara, Stanford University, Mills College, and University of California, Davis. Served briefly as civilian relief chaplain to U.S. Air Force near Casablanca, and in pastoral work during study periods in England and Italy.

MEMBER: American Historical Association, American Society of Church History (vice-president, Pacific Coast branch, 1962), American Catholic Historical Association (life member; vice-president, 1974; president, 1975), Medieval Association of the Pacific, Society for Spanish and Portuguese Historical Studies, Academy of Research Historians on Medieval Spain, Medieval Academy of America, Conference on Peace Research in History. *Awards, honors:* Guggenheim fellowship to Spain, 1963-64; John Gilmary Shea Prize, American Catholic Historical Society, 1966, 1968; D.Litt., Gonzaga University, 1968; American Council of Learned Societies fellowship, 1972; National Endowment for the Humanities award, 1971, 1973, 1974. Other grants include Ford Foundation, Guggenheim, and Robb.

WRITINGS: (Contributor) *I Lift My Lamp*, Newman Press, 1955; *The Jesuits and the Indian Wars of the Northwest*, Yale University Press, 1966; *The Crusader Kingdom of Valencia*, two volumes, Harvard University Press, 1967; *Islam Under the Crusaders: Colonialism in the Thirteenth Century Kingdom of Valencia*, Princeton University Press, 1974; *Medieval Colonialism: Postcrusade Exploitation of Islamic Valencia*, Princeton University Press, in press; (co-author) *Islam and Cultural Change in the Middle Ages*, University of California Press, in press. Other publications include more than one hundred encyclopedia articles on Spanish historical topics, about forty articles in *Speculum, Mid-America, Anuario de estudios medievales, American Historical Review*, and many other technical journals, and articles in Catholic magazines. Regular abstracter for *Historical Abstracts* and *America: History and Life*.

WORK IN PROGRESS: The Crusader-Muslim Predicament: Colonial Confrontation in the Conquered Kingdom of Valencia; Diplomatarium Regni Valentiae, Regnante Jacobo I Ejus Conquistatoris, in six volumes.

SIDELIGHTS: Burns told *CA* that the University of California, Los Angeles maintains a permanent deposit for his manuscript drafts and correspondence in the library's special collection. He has traveled extensively for research and study in Europe, Near East, and North Africa. He reads Italian, French, German, Spanish, Catalan, Latin, and Greek.

*   *   *

BURT, Nathaniel 1913-

PERSONAL: Born November 21, 1913, in Moose, Wyo.; son of Struthers (an author) and Katharine (Newlin) Burt (an author); married Margaret Clinton, August 5, 1942; children: Margery Brooke, Christopher Clinton. *Education:* Attended Princeton University, New York University, B.S. in Mus.Ed., 1939; Princeton University, M.F.A., 1949. *Politics:* Democrat. *Religion:* Episcopalian. *Home:* 20 Hibben Rd., Princeton, N.J. 08540. *Agent:* McIntosh & Otis, Inc., 18 East 41st St., New York, N.Y. 10017.

CAREER: Princeton University, Princeton, N.J., teacher in music department, 1939-41, 1950-52; Westminster Choir School, Princeton, N.J., teacher in music department, 1950-51; full-time writer, 1954—. Composer, with performed works including a ballet, "Chanson Innocente," and an orchestral overture, "The Elegy of Lycidas." Vice-president, Princeton Chamber Orchestra. *Military service:* U.S. Naval Reserve, active duty, 1942-45; served as communications officer in Pacific theater; became lieutenant. *Member:* Authors League of America, P.E.N., Princeton Historical Society, Friends of Music of Princeton University (chairman); Atheneum (trustee), Franklin Inn, and Rittenhouse Club (all Philadelphia); Coffee House Club (New York), Nassau Club (Princeton), Century Association (New York).

WRITINGS: Rooms in a House (poetry), Scribner, 1947; *Question on a Kite* (poetry), Scribner, 1950; *Scotland's Burning* (novel), Little, Brown, 1954; *Make My Bed* (novel), Little, Brown, 1957; *The Perennial Philadelphians*, Little, Brown, 1963; (co-author) *Literary Heritage of New Jersey* (Volume 20 of 300th anniversary series), 1964; *Leopards in the Garden* (novel), Little, Brown, 1968; *First Families* (nonfiction), Little, Brown, 1970. Contributor to *Musical Quarterly, Town and Country*, and other periodicals.

WORK IN PROGRESS: Pleasures and Palaces, a nonfiction book for Little, Brown.

*   *   *

BURTNESS, Paul Sidney 1923-

PERSONAL: Born June 30, 1923, in Chicago, Ill.; son of Sidney Thorander and Margaret (Johnsen) Burtness; married Jean Bordwell, December 26, 1945; children: Karen Lynn, Neil Jeffrey. *Education:* Attended University of Chattanooga, 1941-43, and Carson-Newman College, 1943-44; University of Chicago, A.M., 1947, Ph.D., 1953. *Home:* 395 Parkside Dr., Sycamore, Ill. 60178. *Office:* Zulauf Hall, Northern Illinois University, DeKalb, Ill. 60115.

CAREER: University of Kansas City (now University of Missouri at Kansas City), instructor in English, 1949-53; Northern Illinois University, DeKalb, assistant professor, 1953-57, associate professor, 1957-62, professor of English, 1962—, dean, College of Liberal Arts and Sciences, 1969—. Consultant to Motorola, Inc., and Coronet Instructional Media. Chairman of Citizens Advisory Committee, Sycamore (Ill.) Board of Education, 1961-62; member of Faculty Advisory Committee, Illinois Board of Higher Education, 1962-65. *Military service:* U.S. Naval Reserve, 1943-46; became lieutenant junior grade. *Member:* Modern Language Association of America, U.S. Naval Institute, Conference on College Composition and Communication, American Association of University Professors, American Conference of Academic Deans, Council of Colleges of Arts and Sciences, American Association of School Administrators, American Association for Higher Education, Lyric Opera Guild. *Awards, honors:* Ellis L. Phillips Foundation intern in academic administration at Stanford University and University of Michigan, 1965-66.

WRITINGS: (Editor with Warren Ober and William Seat,

Jr.) *The Enigma of Poe*, Heath, 1960; (editor with Ober and Seat) *The University Reader*, American Book Co., 1960, 2nd edition published as *The New University Reader*, 1966; (with Ober and Seat) *Close Reading of Factual Prose*, Harper, 1962; (editor with Ober) *The Puzzle of Pearl Harbor*, Harper, 1962; (editor with Ober and Seat) *Young Coleridge*, Heath, 1963; (editor) *The Contemporary University Reader*, American Book Co., 1963; (with Robert Ray Aurner) *Practical English for Colleges*, 4th edition, South-Western, 1969, 5th edition published as *Effective English for Colleges*, 1975; (with Aurner) *Effective English for Business Communication*, 6th edition, South-Western, 1970; (editor with Seat) *The Strategy of Prose: Structure, Purpose, Style*, Van Nostrand, 1970. Contributor to military and other journals.

WORK IN PROGRESS: An article, "Historical Factors Influencing Milton's Ludlow Masque."

* * *

BURTON, Ian 1935-

PERSONAL: Born June 24, 1935, in Derby, England; son of Frank (a businessman) and Elsie (Barnes) Burton. *Education:* University of Birmingham, Birmingham, England, B.A., 1956, M.A., 1957; Oberlin College, graduate study, 1957-58; University of Chicago, Ph.D., 1962. *Office:* Department of Geography, University of Toronto, Toronto 5, Ontario, Canada.

CAREER: University of Toronto, Toronto, Ontario, 1961—, started as lecturer, associate professor of geography, 1966—. Consultant to International Development Research Centre, UNESCO's Man and the Biosphere Program. *Member:* Canadian Association of American Geographers.

WRITINGS: Types of Agricultural Occupance of Flood Plains in the United States, Department of Geography, University of Chicago, 1962; (editor with Robert W. Kates) *Reading in Resource Management and Conservation*, University of Chicago Press, 1965; (with Kenneth Hewitt) *The Hazardousness of a Place*, University of Toronto Press, 1971; (with Kates and G. F. White) *The Environment as Hazard*, Oxford University Press, in press. Contributor to professional journals.

WORK IN PROGRESS: Research in environmental hazards, perception, and man-made systems.

* * *

BURY, J(ohn) P(atrick) T(uer) 1908-

PERSONAL: Surname rhymes with *fury*; born July 30, 1908, in Cambridge, England; son of Robert Gregg (a clergyman) and Eloise Ives (Lanyon) Bury; married Mary Elizabeth Russell Jones, January 28, 1944; children: Clare Susan Cunningham, Mark Edmund Piers. *Education:* Corpus Christi College, Cambridge, B.A., 1930, M.A., 1933. *Religion:* Church of England. *Home:* 71 Grange Rd., Cambridge, England. *Office:* Corpus Christi College, Cambridge, England.

CAREER: Corpus Christi College, Cambridge, England, fellow, 1933—, lecturer in history, 1937—, librarian, 1937-56, principal in ministry of supply, 1939-44, president, 1959-64, steward of estates, 1965-69, warden of Lockhampton, 1969—. *Member:* Royal Historical Society (fellow), Academie du Second Empire (associate member). *Awards, honors:* D. Litt., Cambridge University.

WRITINGS: Gambetta and the National Defence, Long-

mans, Green, 1936; (contributor) *France: A Companion to French Studies*, edited by W. R. L. Graeme Ritchie, Methuen, 1937; *France 1814-1940*, Methuen, 1949, 3rd edition, 1957; *A History of Corpus Christi College, Cambridge, from 1822 to 1952*, Cambridge University Press, 1952; (editor with J. C. Barry) Bertie Greatheed, *An Englishman in Paris*, Bles, 1953; (editor) *New Cambridge Modern History*, Volume X, Cambridge University Press, 1960; (editor with R. Butler) *Documents on British Foreign Policy 1919-1939*, Volumes X-XV, H. M. Stationery Office, 1960-67; *Napoleon III and the Second Empire*, English Universities Press, 1964; (editor) *Romilly's Cambridge Diary 1832-42*, Cambridge University Press, 1967; (contributor) *Melanges G. Jacquemyns*, Universite libre de Bruxelles, 1967; *France: The Insecure Peace*, Macdonald, 1972; *Gambetta and the Making of the Third Republic*, Longman, 1973. Editor, *Cambridge Historical Journal* (now *Historical Journal*), 1953-60. Contributor to *English Historical Review, Revue Historique, Annales de Normandie, French Historical Studies*, and other publications.

WORK IN PROGRESS: Gambetta and the Mastery of the Third Republic, 1877-82, completion expected in 1976 or 1977; a study of the Mediterranean world, 1830-1914.

SIDELIGHTS: Bury is competent in French (spoken as well as written), reads German and Italian.

* * *

BUSH, George P(ollock) 1892-

PERSONAL: Born March 3, 1892, in Seattle, Wash.; son of George S. (a lawyer) and Loue (Pollock) Bush; married Erna Olschewsky, April 18, 1914; children: George B., Richard S., Edward R., Virginia Bush Potter. *Education:* Harvard University, M.B.A., 1933; American University, M.A., 1946, Ph.D., 1949.

CAREER: U.S. Army, career service, 1912-44, rising from private to colonel; American University, Washington, D.C., lecturer, 1947-48, assistant professor, 1948-51, associate professor, 1951-55, professor of public administration, 1955-56, professor emeritus, 1956—. Consultant to U.S. Navy, 1953, U.S. Army, 1956, National Science Foundation, 1957, American University, 1961-62, and other institutions and agencies. *Member:* American Association for the Advancement of Science, American Political Science Association, Institute of Electrical and Electronics Engineers, American Documentation Institute, American Association of University Professors, History of Science Society.

WRITINGS: (Editor with L. H. Hattery) *Scientific Research: Its Administration and Organization*, American University Press, 1950; (editor with Hattery) *Teamwork in Research*, American University Press, 1953; *Bibliography on Research Administration*, University Press of Washington, D.C., 1954; (editor with Hattery) *Electronics in Management*, University Press of Washington, D.C., 1956; (editor with Hattery) *Reprography and Copyright Law*, American Institute of Biological Sciences, 1964; (editor with Hattery) *Automation and Electronics in Publishing*, Spartan Books, 1965; (editor) *Technology and Copyright: Annotated Bibliography and Source Materials*, Lomond Systems, 1972. Editor of *Biographical Directory* of American Political Science Association, 1953.†

* * *

BUSH, Ted J. 1922-

PERSONAL: Born July 27, 1922; son of J. C. and Alice

Adelia (Stearns) Bush; married Anne Acton, June 19, 1948; children: Ted, Jr., John, Anne, Allan, William, Julia. *Education:* Attended Multnomah College, 1939-41, and University of Notre Dame, 1944; University of Oregon, B.S., 1946.

CAREER: Sigma Phi Epsilon Fraternity, Richmond, Va., national field representative, 1946-48; Multnomah College, Portland, Ore., director of public relations, 1948-50; U.S. Navy, public information officer, Pacific Fleet, 1950-52, press officer, Department of Defense, Washington, D.C., 1952-54; *Norfolk Virginian-Pilot*, Norfolk, Va., military writer, 1954-57; Army Times Publishing Co., Washington, D.C., associate editor of *Navy Times*, 1957-63; U.S. Navy, Washington, D.C., public affairs officer, beginning 1963, became a commander and public affairs officer for Military Sea Transportation Service. Director of Delta Corp.

WRITINGS: (With John V. Noel) *Naval Terms Dictionary*, U.S. Naval Institute, 1966. Contributor to *Navy* and *Aerospace*.

WORK IN PROGRESS: Continuing studies in the total impact of sea transportation on the American economy; also in the communications problem posed by the proliferation of documents with acronyms.

SIDELIGHTS: Bush told *CA* he believes "file cabinets are a deterrent to progress because they encourage 'doing things like we did them last time' and stymie original thought and research." *Avocational interests:* Winter sports and travel.†

*   *   *

BUSHRUI, S(uheil) B(adi) 1929-

PERSONAL: Born September 14, 1929, in Nazareth, Palestine; now a Jordanian national; married Mary Antonia Ellul, Septmeber 19, 1954; children: Nadia. *Education:* University of Alexandria, B.A. (first class honors), 1954; University of Southampton, Ph.D., 1962. *Religion:* Bahai. *Office:* Department of English, American University of Beirut, Beirut, Lebanon.

CAREER: Khartoum Technical Institute, Khartoum, Sudan, lecturer in English, 1954-59, lecturer in English and Arabic at Secretarial College of the Institute, 1955-58; University of Ibadan, Ibadan, Nigeria, lecturer, 1962-64, senior lecturer in English and assistant dean of Faculty of Arts, 1964-66; University of Calgary, Calgary, Alberta, associate professor of English, 1966-67; York University, Toronto, Ontario, associate professor of English, 1967-68; American University of Beirut, Beirut, Lebanon, associate professor, 1968-73, professor of English, 1973—, chairman of department, 1971—. Tutor in English, and examiner, for civil service employees in England, Sudan, Nigeria, and Lebanon, 1955-72; former teacher of English in own private school. Broadcaster on English literature, Omdurman Broadcasting Service (Sudan), 1958, Western Nigeria Broadcasting Service, 1964, British Broadcasting Corporation, 1970-72. Secretary at Sudan Cultural Centre, 1955-59, and at Royal Moroccan Embassy (London, England), 1962. Organizer of exhibits and international celebrations commemorating Shakespeare, Ben Jonson, Yeats, Gibran, J. M. Synge, and James Joyce, 1965-72.

MEMBER: International Association for the Study of Anglo-Irish Literature (member of executive council, 1970-76), International Poetry Institute (life association), Association of University Teachers of English in the Arab World (founder, 1970; president, 1970-75). *Awards, honors:*

Bursary from Federal Republic of Germany, 1959, for cultural activities in Sudan; University of Southampton research grant, 1961-62; Una Ellis-Fermor Memorial Fund award from Bedford College, University of London, 1963, for *Yeat's Verse Plays: The Revisions, 1900-1910*; Bourse de Marque from French government, 1965; British Council visitorship, 1965, 1973; bursary from Cultural Relations Committee of Ireland, 1971.

WRITINGS: Yeat's Verse Plays: The Revisions, 1900-1910, Clarendon Press, 1965; (editor with D.E.S. Maxwell, and contributor) *W. B. Yeats, 1865-1965: Centenary Essays on the Art of W. B. Yeats*, Ibadan University Press, 1965; (contributor) Alexander Norman Jeffares and Kenneth Gustav Walter Cross, editors, *In Excited Reverie: A Centenary Tribute to William Butler Yeats, 1865-1939*, Macmillan, 1965; (editor) *Kahlil Gibran, 1883-1931: An Introductory Survey of His Life and His Work*, University Library, University of Ibadan, 1966; (author of introduction, and translator) *Shai 'un Min Yeats: Shi 'r, Nathr, Masrah* (title means "On Yeats: Poetry, Prose, Drama"), English Department, American University of Beirut, 1969.

(Editor) *An Introduction to Kahlil Gibran*, Dar al-Mashreq (Beirut), 1970; (editor with N.J.Q. Bratton) *The World of J. M. Synge: A Compendium and Catalogue*, English Department, American University of Beirut, 1971; *Ameen Rihani* (pamphlet), Rihani House (Beirut), 1972; *Kahlil Gibran, 1883-1931* (pamphlet), Gibran National Committee (Beirut), 1972; (editor and contributor) *A Centenary Tribute to John Millington Synge, 1871-1909: Sunshine and the Moon's Delight*, Barnes & Noble, 1972; (editor with Paul Gotch) *Gibran of Lebanon: New Papers*, Librairie du Liban (Beirut), 1975.

Editor with John Munro: *Images and Memories: A Pictorial Record of the Life and Work of W. B. Yeats*, Dar al-Mashreq, 1970; (and with Sa'id Abu'Hamdeh and Marcus Smith) *A Poet and His Country: Gibran's Lebanon*, Middle East Export Press (Beirut), 1970; *Kahlil Gibran: Essays and Introductions*, Rihani House, 1970; Ameen Rihani, *A Path of Vision*, Rihani House, 1970; Ameen Rihani, *A Chant of Mystics and Other Poems*, Rihani House, 1970. Translator into Arabic, C. Achebe, *Things Fall Apart*. Contributor of poetry and articles in English and Arabic to journals in his field, including *A Review of English Literature, Middle East Forum, Irish University Review, Voices: Aswat*, and *al-Adeeb*. Editor, with D.E.S. Maxwell, of Shakespeare edition of *Abadan*, 1964. Member of advisory council of *Yeats Studies: An International Journal*.

WORK IN PROGRESS: The Influence of the Arabian Nights on English Literature, for Pergamon; a fully annotated edition of William Beckford's *Vathek*; articles and translations.

SIDELIGHTS: Bushrui writes: "English studies are vital to a liberal education whether or not one's first language is English." He notes that "teaching at Khartoum, Southampton, Nigeria, Canada, and Beirut has helped me to compare methods appropriate to the teaching of literature to English and to non-English students. I have consequently given much thought to the problems that face the student whose mother-tongue is not English, but who is eager to understand and appreciate English literature."

*   *   *

BUTLER, George D. 1893-

PERSONAL: Born November 14, 1893, in Seymour, Conn.; son of Albert C. and Mary R. Butler; married Rebecca P. Jones, September 6, 1921; children: George D., Jr., Robert J. *Education:* Yale University, B.A., 1916. *Religion:* Protestant. *Home:* 117 Columbus Blvd., Sarasota, Fla. 33581.

CAREER: National Recreation Association, New York, N.Y., director of research, 1919-62; retired, 1962. *Awards, honors:* National Recreation & Park Association, National Literary Award, 1972; American Academy of Physical Education, special citation for whole of writing, 1974. *Military service:* U.S. Army Ambulance Service with French Army, World War I; received Croix de Guerre.

WRITINGS: Play Areas: Their Design and Equipment, A. S. Barnes, 1928; *County Parks*, Playground and Recreation Association of America, 1930; *Playgrounds: Their Administration and Operation*, A. S. Barnes, 1936, 2nd edition, 1950, 3rd edition, Ronald, 1960; *Introduction to Community Recreation*, McGraw, 1940, 5th edition, 1975; *Municipal Recreation Administration*, International City Managers Association, 1940, 2nd edition, 1950; *Recreation Areas: Design and Equipment*, A. S. Barnes, 1947, 2nd edition, Ronald, 1958; *Community Sports and Athletics*, A. S. Barnes, 1949; *Pioneers in Public Recreation*, Burgess, 1965. Author of scores of pamphlets and magazine articles. Editor, *Recreation and Park Yearbook*, 1928-61; assistant editor, *Recreation*, 1952-62.

*   *   *

BUXBAUM, Martin 1912-
(Martin David Noll)

PERSONAL: Legally took surname of stepfather, 1920; born June 27, 1912, in Richmond, Va.; son of David (a cabinetmaker) and Olive (McGuffin) Noll; married Alice Lee Lyons, September 4, 1938; children: Joan (Mrs. Robert Galope), Alice (Mrs. Daniel J. Dick), Rosemary (Mrs. Samuel D. Redding), Roberta (Mrs. Daniel Walker), Martha (Mrs. Thomas Newpher), Kathleen (Mrs. Joseph Stubbs), Martin, William. *Education:* Studied in Washington, D.C., at Columbia Technical School, 1934-38, and at Newman Sudduth School of Art, two years. *Home:* 7819 Custer Rd., Bethesda, Md. 20014. *Office:* Marriott Corporation, 5161 River Rd., Washington, D.C. 20016.

CAREER: Hechinger Co., Washington, D.C., editor, 1938-45; free-lance photographer and writer, Washington, D.C., 1945-47; Sealtest Dairies, Washington, D.C., director of communications, 1947-53; Marriott-Hot Shoppes, Inc., Bethesda, Md., director of communications, 1953—, currently editing "Table Talk" (publication for customers). *Military service:* National Guard and Guard Reserve, 1931-35. *Member:* Maryland Poetry Society, Kiwanis. *Awards, honors:* George Washington Medal of Honor of Freedoms Foundation, 1963, 1970-73; State of Maryland, poet of the year, 1967; Lizette Woodward Reese Poetry Award, 1968; Kentucky Colonel, 1971.

WRITINGS: Rivers of Thought (poetry), Books, Inc., 1958; *Bux's Scrapbook* (humor, puzzles), National Publishing, 1960; *The Underside of Heaven* (poetry), Books, Inc., 1963; *Table Talk for Family Fun* (humor, puzzles), Books, Inc., 1964; (editor) *The Unsung* (anthology), Colortone Press, Volume I, 1965, Volume II, 1966; *Whispers in the Wind* (poetry), Books, Inc., 1966; (under name Martin Noll) *What Every Young Bridegroom Should Know*, Muses Library, 1966; *Once Upon a Dream* (poetry), World, 1970; *Fifteen Years of Table Talk* (humor, puzzles), Popular Library, 1972; *The Warm World of Martin Buxbaum* (poetry), Acropolis Books, 1974; *Sing a Song of Sixpence*

(humor), Acropolis Books, 1975. Contributor to *Reader's Digest, Sunshine, Modern Maturity*, and other periodicals. Consultant to *Sunshine*, 1968—; associate editor, *Playtime*, 1970—. Contributor to *Guideposts, Sunshine*, and other publications.

SIDELIGHTS: Martin Buxbaum told *Washington Post* writer Mollee Kruger: "Poets are like artists. One works in oils or watercolors or pencil, another paints with obscenities. I use gentle things, the subtle approach. We all work differently. You can't say one paints better than the other. I couldn't write like Allen Ginsberg the best poet and he couldn't write like me." Syracuse University began a Martin Buxbaum Manuscript collection in 1958. *Avocational interests:* Gardening, mosaics (Venetian glass), woodworking.

BIOGRAPHICAL/CRITICAL SOURCES: Washington Post, August 28, 1969.

*   *   *

BYRD, Cecil Kash 1913-

PERSONAL: Born October 23, 1913, in Winchester, Ky.; son of George Madison and Eliza (Morrow) Byrd; married Ester Sample, February 25, 1938; children: Jean Scott, Claire Ann, Charles Thomas. *Education:* Anderson College, Anderson, Ind., A.B., 1937; Indiana University, A.M., 1938, Ph.D., 1942. *Politics:* Democrat. *Religion:* Methodist. *Office:* Office of the President, The American University in Cairo, 113 Kasr El Aini, Cairo, Egypt.

CAREER: Indiana University, Bloomington, curator of rare books and special collections, 1942-46, assistant director of libraries, 1946-48, associate director of libraries, 1948-64, staff member of Graduate Division, Library School, 1949-72, university librarian, 1964-72; American University in Cairo, Egypt, 1973—. Carnegie Project in Advanced Library Administration at Rutgers University, fellow, 1958; Center for Research Libraries, Indiana University representative on board of directors; National Institute of Administration, Djakarta, Indonesia, library adviser, 1961-62. Building consultant to Vincennes University, Anderson College, and Newberry Library. *Military service:* U.S. Naval Reserve, 1943-45; became lieutenant.

MEMBER: American Library Association (board on bibliography, 1955-61), Association of College and Reference Libraries (library buildings committee, 1954-57), Bibliographical Society of America, Indiana Library Association, Caxton Club (Chicago), Grolier Club (New York).

WRITINGS: A Statement of Program for an Undergraduate Library at Indiana University, Indiana University Press, 1952; (with Howard H. Peckham) *A Bibliography of Indiana Imprints, 1804-1854*, Indiana Historical Bureau, 1955; (contributor) *Studies in Library Administrative Problems*, edited by Keyes D. Metcalf, Rutgers University Press, 1960; *An Exhibit to Commemorate the One Hundred Fiftieth Anniversary of the Beginning of the War of 1812*, Indiana University Press, 1962.

A Bibliography of Illinois Imprints, 1814-1858, University of Chicago Press, 1966; *One Hundred and Fifty Years: An Exhibit Commemorating the Sesquicentennial of Indiana Statehood*, Indiana University Press, 1966; (with others) *Developmental Book Activities and Needs in Indonesia*, Agency for International Development, 1967; (with David Kaser and C. Walter Stone) *Library Development in Eight Asian Countries*, Scarecrow, 1969; *Books in Singapore: A*

Survey of Publishing, Printing, Bookselling, and Library Activity in the Republic of Singapore (Singapore), 1970; *Early Printing in the Straights Settlements* (Singapore), 1970. Also author of *Bernardo Mendel: A Short Biography*, 1973. Contributor of articles and reviews to historical and library journals. Past editor, *Indiana Quarterly for Bookmen*.

* * *

BYRON, Gilbert 1903-

PERSONAL: Born July 12, 1903, in Chestertown, Md.; son of George V. and Mary E. (Wood) Byron. *Education:* Washington College, Chestertown, Md., A.B., 1923; additional study at University of Maryland, Johns Hopkins University, University of Virginia, and University of Delaware. *Religion:* Episcopal. *Home:* Old House Cove, St. Michaels, Md. 21663.

CAREER: High school teacher of social studies and English in Maryland, Pennsylvania, and Delaware, 1923-57; full-time writer, 1957—. Talbot County Free Library, trustee, 1963-66; Poet-in-Residence for public schools of Talbot and Caroline counties, 1972—; member of Talbot County Bicentennial Committee, 1974—. *Member:* Historical Society of Talbot County (honorary member). *Awards, honors:* Scimitor and Song, best long poem award, 1972-73.

*WRITINGS—*Verse, except as indicated: *These Chesapeake Men*, Driftwind Press, 1942; *Delaware Poems*, Driftwind Press, 1943; *White Collar and Chain*, Driftwind Press, 1945; *Chesapeake Cove*, Easton Publishing, 1953; *The Lord's Oysters* (novel), Little, Brown, 1957, 2nd edition, Tradition Press, 1967; (contributor) *Shoremen: An Anthology of Eastern Shore Prose and Verse*, edited by Jopp and Ingersoll, Tidewater Publishers, 1974; *The Wind's Will*, Easton Publishing, 1961; *Chesapeake Duke* (novel), Rand McNally, 1965.

Historical studies: *Early Explorations of Chesapeake Bay*, Maryland Historical Society, 1960; *St. Michaels: The Town That Fooled the British*, St. Michaels Sesquicentennial Commission, 1963; *The War of 1812 on the Chesapeake Bay*, Maryland Historical Society, 1964; *Talbot's Libraries*, Talbot County Free Library, 1965.

Contributor of verse, articles, and short stories to *Saturday Review, Collier's, Christian Science Monitor, Ford Times, Prarie Schooner, Bulletin of the Thoreau Society, Living Wilderness, New York Times, Yachting, Motorboating, Audubon, Canadian Forum*, and other publications; some fifteen short stories about teaching appeared in *Educational Forum*, 1945-63; weekly column, "Chesapeake Cove," runs in a number of Bay newspapers, 1959—; daily newspaper column, "One Man's Meat," 1973—.

WORK IN PROGRESS: A children's novel set on the Eastern shore about a girl who trains a wild pinto pony.

* * *

CABALLERO, Ann Mallory 1928-

PERSONAL: Born April 30, 1928, in Burnet, Tex.; daughter of James Dunn and Charlotte (Chamberlain) Mallory; married O'Neal Caballero, April 15, 1952; children: Catherine, Mary Alice, Felice, Nicholas, Natalie, Patrick, John. *Politics:* Democrat. *Home:* 4282 Sierra Vista, San Diego, Calif. *Agent:* Donald MacCampbell, Inc., 12 East 41st St., New York, N.Y. 10017.

WRITINGS: Stranger in the House, Coward, 1965. Contributor to *Alfred Hitchcock's Magazine.*†

CAEFER, Raymond J(ohn) 1926-

PERSONAL: Born April 16, 1926, in Fitchburg, Mass.; son of William and Blanche (Denomme) Caefer. *Education:* Clark University, A.B., 1950; University of Grenoble, certificate, 1951; Syracuse University, M.A., 1954. *Home:* 76 Pleasant St., Wellesley, Mass. 02181.

CAREER: Syracuse University, Syracuse, N.Y., instructor in French and Spanish, 1952-55; Wellesley (Mass.) public schools, senior high school teacher of French and Spanish, 1955-60, head of schools' department of Romance languages, 1960—. National Defense Education Act Institute, University of Maine, instructor, 1962, associate director, 1964, 1965. Educational Testing Service, member of committee of examiners (college board). *Military service:* U.S. Navy, 1944-46. *Member:* American Association of Teachers of French, Modern Language Association of America, National Education Association, New England Modern Language Association (member of board of directors, 1965-68), Massachusetts Foreign Language Association, Massachusetts Teachers Association. *Awards, honors:* Fulbright grant, 1950-51.

WRITINGS: (With James Etmekjian and Frances O'Brien) *Speaking French*, Allyn & Bacon, 1963; (with Etmekjian and O'Brian) *Le Francais Courant I*, Allyn & Bacon, 1964; (with Etmekjian) *Le Francais Courant II*, Allyn & Bacon, 1963; (with Etmekjian) *Spoken and Written French in Review*, Bobbs-Merrill, 1972.

* * *

CAFFREY, John G(ordon) 1922-

PERSONAL: Born September 4, 1922, in Arlington, Mass.; son of Donald John (an entomologist) and Lois (Hersey) Caffrey; married Ann Gourley (a secretary), December 21, 1957; children: Cathleen, Morgan, Liam, Ian, Evan. *Education:* University of California, Berkeley, A.B., 1944, Ph.D., 1953; University of Washington, Seattle, M.A., 1948. *Politics:* None. *Religion:* None. *Office:* Rockland Community College, 145 College Road, Suffern, N.Y. 10901.

CAREER: High School teacher of English, Redwood City, Calif., 1946-53; Sacramento State College (now California State University, Sacramento), instructor in drama, 1947-48; Office of Los Angeles County (Calif.) Superintendent of Schools, educational statistician, 1953-55; Educational Testing Service, associate director of Los Angeles office, Los Angeles, Calif., 1955-58; Palo Alto (Calif.) Unified School District, director of research, 1958-62; Harvard University, Graduate School of Education, Cambridge, Mass., lecturer and research associate, 1962-63; System Development Corp., Santa Monica, Calif., program director for education, 1963-66; American Council on Education, Washington, D.C., director of Commission on Administrative Affairs, 1966-70; Educational Systems Research Group, Washington, D.C., president, 1970-72; Rockland Community College, Suffern, N.Y., executive vice-president, 1972—. Visiting summer instructor at Stanford University, University of California, San Jose State University and other institutions, 1955-63. Chairman of board of trustees, Educational Systems Corp., 1963—; consultant to U.S. Office of Education, 1964-70; trustee, Harvard University Institute for Educational Management, 1970—.

MEMBER: American Association for the Advancement of Science, American Association for Higher Education, Association for Educational Data Systems (president, 1963-

64), American Psychological Association, Psychometric Society, American Educational Research Association, Association for Computing Machinery, California Education Research Association (president, 1962-63), California Educational Data Processing Association (charter president, 1961).

WRITINGS: (With R. B. Clarke and A. P. Coladarci) *Statistical Reasoning and Procedures*, C. E. Merrill, 1965; (with C. J. Mosmann) *Computers on Campus: A Report to the President on Their Use and Management*, American Council on Education, 1967; (editor) *The Future Academic Community: Continuity and Change*, American Council on Education, 1969; (with H. H. Isaacs) *Estimating the Impact of a College or University on the Local Economy*, American Council on Education, 1971. Contributor of articles to education journals.

AVOCATIONAL INTERESTS: Painting, music (piano and composition), writing fiction and poetry.†

* * *

CAGAN, Phillip D(avid) 1927-

PERSONAL: Born April 30, 1927, in Seattle, Wash.; son of Herman Solomon (a businessman) and Lillian (Levinson) Cagan; married Elizabeth Quincy Wright, June, 1952 (divorced, 1968); children: John, Laird, David. *Education:* University of California, Los Angeles, A.A., 1948; University of Chicago, M.A., 1951, Ph.D., 1954. *Office:* National Bureau of Economic Research, Inc., 261 Madison Ave., New York, N.Y. 10016.

CAREER: National Bureau of Economic Research, Inc., New York, N.Y., research associate, 1953-55; University of Chicago, Chicago, Ill., assistant professor of economics, 1955-58; Brown University, Providence, R.I., associate professor of economics, 1958-61; Carnegie Institute of Technology, Pittsburgh, Pa., visiting associate professor of economics, 1961-62; Brown University, professor of economics, 1962-64; National Bureau of Economic Research, Inc., member of senior research staff, 1959—; Columbia University, New York, N.Y., professor of economics, 1966—. *Military service:* U.S. Naval Reserve, 1945-46. *Member:* American Economic Association, Phi Beta Kappa.

WRITINGS: (Contributor) *Studies in the Quantity Theory of Money*, edited by M. Friedman, University of Chicago Press, 1956; *Determinants and Effects of Changes in the Money Stock 1875-1960*, Columbia University Press, 1965; *The Effects of Pension Plans on Aggregate Saving: Evidence from a Sample Survey*, Columbia University Press, 1965; *The Channels of Monetary Effects on Interest Rates*, Columbia University Press, 1972.

WORK IN PROGRESS: Research on the behavior of prices during inflation for the National Bureau of Economic Research.

* * *

CAHEN, Alfred B. 1932-

PERSONAL: Born September 13, 1932, in Cleveland, Ohio; son of Herman S. (an engineer) and Madeline (Roser) Cahen; married Roberta Kayne, April, 1956; children: Harley Scott. *Education:* Carnegie Institute of Technology (now Carnegie-Mellon University), B.S. in mechanical engineering, 1954; Case Institute of Technology (now Case Western Reserve University), M.S. in engineering administration, 1962.

CAREER: World Publishing Co., Cleveland, Ohio, various executive capacities, 1954-66; full-time writer and editor, 1966—.

WRITINGS: House of Ice (poems), American Weave Press, 1966. Editor, *American Weave*, 1966—.†

* * *

CAIN, James M(allahan) 1892-

PERSONAL: Born July 1, 1892, in Annapolis, Md.; son of James William (former president of Washington College) and Rose Cecilia (Mallahan) Cain; married Mary Rebecca Clough, 1920 (divorced); married Elina Sjosted Tyszecka, 1927; married Aileen Pringle, 1944 (divorced); married Florence Macbeth Whitwell (an opera singer), 1947 (deceased). *Education:* Washington College, A.B., 1910, A.M., 1917. *Politics:* Democrat. *Home:* 6707 44th Ave., University Park, Hyattsville, Md. 20782.

CAREER: Baltimore American, Baltimore, Md., staff member, 1917-18; *Baltimore Sun*, Baltimore, Md., reporter, 1919-23; St. John's College, Annapolis, Md., professor of journalism, 1923-24; *New York World*, New York, N.Y., editorial writer, 1924-31; screenwriter in Hollywood, Calif., 1932-48; writer. *Military service:* American Expeditionary Forces, 1918-19; served as editor-in-chief of *Lorraine Cross*, official newspaper of the 79th Division, A.E.F.

WRITINGS: Our Government (sketches), Knopf, 1930; *The Postman Always Rings Twice*, Knopf, 1934; *Serenade*, Knopf, 1937; *Two Can Sing*, 1938 (published as "Career in C Major," in *Three of a Kind*); *Mildred Pierce*, Knopf, 1941; *Love's Lovely Counterfeit*, Knopf, 1942; *Double Indemnity*, Avon, 1943; *Three of a Kind* (includes "Career in C Major," "The Embezzler," and "Double Indemnity"), Knopf, 1943; *Cain Omnibus: The Postman Always Rings Twice, Serenade, [and] Mildred Pierce*, Sun Dial Press, 1943, published as *Three Novels: The Postman Always Rings Twice, Serenade, [and] Mildred Pierce*, World, 1946; *The Embezzler*, New Avon Library, 1944; (editor) *For Men Only* (short stories), World, 1944; *Past All Dishonor*, Knopf, 1946; *The Butterfly*, Knopf, 1947; *Sinful Woman*, Avon, 1947; *The Embezzler [and] Double Indemnity*, Triangle Books, 1948; *The Moth*, Knopf, 1948, abridged edition, New American Library, 1950; *Jealous Woman*, Avon, 1950; *Galatea*, Knopf, 1953; *Root of His Evil*, R. Hale, 1954; *Jealous Woman [and] Sinful Woman*, R. Hale, 1955; *Mignon*, Dial, 1962; *The Magician's Wife*, Dial, 1965; *The Root of His Evil*, Transworld, 1966; *Cain x 3: Three Novels (The Postman Always Rings Twice, Mildred Pierce*, and *Double Indemnity*; a Book-of-the-Month selection), introduction by Tom Wolfe, Knopf, 1969; *Three Novels by James M. Cain: Double Indemnity, The Postman Always Rings Twice, Serenade*, Bantam, 1973.

WORK IN PROGRESS: A novel.

SIDELIGHTS: One of Cain's novels, *The Postman Always Rings Twice*, has been selling for 40 years—others for almost that length of time, confirming Cain's belief that the critic most to be respected is "Posterity." Nonetheless, after the publication of *Cain x 3*, the critic, Thomas Lask, wrote of Cain's style that "the accuracy of the dialogue can be seen by noting how much was lifted intact for the movie versions of these novels. Cain's ability to tell more in fewer words is equaled by no one in the game. If you doubt it, try the first seven pages of *Postman*. The amount of information in them will make a punched computer card seem as talky as Henry James." Tom Wolfe's introduction to the book states that "Cain lets nothing get in the way of the pace . . . momentum is the thing . . . [he creates] atmosphere . . . with amazingly few details.'' Wolfe continues: "In book after book Cain puts you inside the skin of one utterly egocentric heel after another, losers who will stop at nothing—and makes you care about them. Sympathy runs along shank to flank with the horror and disgust. It's strange stuff! Perhaps he has touched the Universal Heel in everybody. . . . I don't know. . . . The sin Cain likes to play on is not murder or sadism but betrayal.''

James M. Cain told John Leonard in an interview for the *New York Times Book Review* that "A lot of novelists start late—Conrad, Pirandello, even Mark Twain. When you're young, chess is all right, and music and poetry. But novel writing is something else. It has to be learned, but it can't be taught. This bunkum and stinkum of college creative writing courses—writers make their decision to write in secret. The academics don't know that. They don't know that the only thing you can do for someone who wants to write is to buy him a typewriter. . . . Writing a novel is like working on foreign policy. There are problems to be solved. It's not all inspiration. . . . Time is the only critic. If your algebra is right, if the progression is logical but still surprising, it keeps.''

The following of Cain's works have been filmed: "The Baby in the Icebox'' (short story) was filmed as "She Made Her Bed,'' Paramount, 1934; "Career in C Major'' was filmed as "Wife, Husband, Friend,'' Twentieth Century-Fox, 1938; *The Embezzler* was filmed as "Money and the Woman,'' Warner Bros., 1940; *The Root of His Evil* was filmed as "Interlude,'' Universal, 1943; *Double Indemnity*, Paramount, 1944; *Mildred Pierce*, Warner Bros., 1945; *Serenade*, Warner Bros., 1956; *Loves' Lovely Counterfeit* was filmed as "Slightly Scarlet,'' by Benjamin Beaugeus, 1956. In 1938 an authorized version of *The Postman Always Rings Twice* was made in France by Gladiator Films, with title "Le Dernier Tourant,'' because Metro-Goldwyn-Mayer, the American owners of the film rights, decided that the film could not be released in the United States. In 1939 G. Musso of Italy released "Obsessione'' (a Cocinor-Marcean release of ICI Productions), also based on *The Postman Always Rings Twice*. M-G-M and Gladiator Films then filed a joint suit against the Italian producers, charging plagiarism. In 1946 the U.S. censorship of the film was lifted and the M-G-M production was released. Critics agreed, however, that the Italian version was superior to both the American and the French efforts.

James Cain told *CA* that his portrayal of the miners in *Past All Dishonor*, of "the dreadful life they led'' in the Virginia City of the 1860's was based on his own knowledge of that life . . . that he had worked in mines, himself, and was a member of the United Mine Workers of America, Ward (W. Va.) local.

AVOCATIONAL INTERESTS: Music.

BIOGRAPHICAL/CRITICAL SOURCES: Variety, December 28, 1949, November 4, 1959; Edmund Wilson, *Classics and Commercials*, Farrar, Straus, 1950; *Chicago Sunday Times*, May 27, 1962; *New York Times Book Review*, August 8, 1965; Granville Hicks in *Saturday Review*, August 14, 1965; *Time*, August 27, 1965; *New Yorker*, January 8, 1966; *Washington Post*, January 19, 1969; Carolyn Riley, editor, *Contemporary Literary Criticism*, Volume III, Gale, 1975.

* * *

CALDWELL, Robert Graham 1904-

PERSONAL: Born November 9, 1904, in Philadelphia, Pa.; son of Robert Graham (a businessman) and Rebecca Jane (Stewart) Caldwell; married La Merle Sutton, August 22, 1935. *Education:* University of Pennsylvania, B.S. (cum laude), 1928, M.A., 1934, Ph.D., 1939; Jackson School of Law, LL.B., 1948. *Religion:* Baptist. *Office:* Department of Sociology, University of Iowa, Iowa City, Iowa 52240.

CAREER: Bell Telephone Co., Pennsylvania, research consultant, 1928-36; University of Pennsylvania, Philadelphia, instructor in sociology, 1936-38; University of Delaware, Newark, assistant professor of sociology, 1938-43; Federal Security Agency, field representative, 1943-45; College of William and Mary, Williamsburg, Va., associate professor, 1945-47, professor of sociology, 1947-48; University of Iowa, Iowa City, professor of criminology, 1948—. Consultant in criminology to Iowa State Board of Control, 1948-58; member of Commission for commutation of Sentences of Life-Termers in Iowa, 1954-58; consultant to Iowa Probation and Parole Board, 1960-70; member of Governor's Committee on Iowa Corrections, 1966-68, and Governor's Committee on Modernization of Iowa's Criminal Code, 1968-69.

MEMBER: American Society of Criminology, American Correctional Association, International Society of Criminology, American Academy of Political and Social Sciences, National Council on Crime and Delinquency, American Sociological Society, Midwest Sociological Society, Iowa Welfare Association, Virginia Bar Association, Virginia Social Services Association, New York Academy of Sciences, Alpha Kappa Delta, Pi Gamma Mu, Mason. *Awards, honors:* Social Science Research Council grant, 1946; senior research fellow, University of Chicago Law School, 1959-60.

WRITINGS: New Castle County Workhouse, University of Delaware Press, 1940; *The Penitentiary Movement in Delaware*, Historical Society of Delaware, 1946; *Red Hannah: Delaware Whipping Post*, University of Pennsylvania Press, 1947; *Criminology* (text), Ronald, 1956, revised edition, 1965; (with James A. Black) *Juvenile Delinquency*, Ronald, 1971. Contributor of articles to professional publications.†

* * *

CALLAHAN, Sidney Cornelia 1933-

PERSONAL: Born March 6, 1933, in Washington, D.C.; daughter of George Sidney (a dentist and captain, U.S. Navy) and Lethama (Jones) de Shazo; married Daniel John Callahan (an editor and author), June 5, 1954; children: Mark, Stephen, John, Peter, Sarah, David. *Education:* Bryn Mawr College, B.A. (magna cum laude); Sarah Lawrence College, M.A., 1971. *Politics:* Democrat. *Religion:* Roman Catholic. *Home:* 84 Summit Dr., Hastings–on–Hudson, N.Y.

CAREER: Writer. Lecturer or workshop leader at Harvard University, Yale University, Michigan State University, and Syracuse Medical School. Member of board of trustees, Mercy College, Dobbs Ferry, N.Y. Member of advisory board, Kennedy Institute of Bioethics. Consultant to United Church Women, and New York Archdiocesan committee on family life. *Member:* League of Women Voters. *Awards, honors:* Doctorates from Regis College, and St. Mary's College; Catholic Press Association Award for best column, 1971.

WRITINGS: What Modern Catholics Think About Birth Control, New American Library, 1964; *The Illusion of*

Eve: Modern Woman's Quest for Identity, Sheed, 1965; *Beyond Birth Control: The Christian Experience of Sex*, Sheed, 1968, published as *Exiled to Eden: The Christian Experience of Sex*, 1969; *Christian Family Planning and Sex Education*, Ave Maria Press, 1969; *The Working Mother*, Macmillan, 1971; *Parenting: Principles and Politics of Parenthood*, Doubleday, 1973.

Contributor: J. G. Deedy, editor, *Eyes on the Modern World*, Kenedy, 1965; S. B. Doley, editor, *Women's Liberation and the Church*, Association Press, 1970; Donald L. Grummond and others, editors, *Sexuality: A Search for Perspective*, Van Nostrand, 1971; Clayton C. Barbeau, editor, *The Future of the Family*, Bruce, 1971; M. J. Taylor, editor, *Sex: Thoughts for Contemporary Christians*, Doubleday, 1972; S. Halpert and T. Murray, editors, *Witness of the Berrigans*, Doubleday, 1972. Contributor of articles to *Commonweal*, *New Republic*, *Saturday Review*, *Notre Dame Journal of Education*, *Catholic World*, and other periodicals. Writer of syndicated column, 1969-72.

AVOCATIONAL INTERESTS: Yoga and tennis.†

* * *

CALLAN, Edward T. 1917-

PERSONAL: Born December 3, 1917, in Ballina, Ireland; became U.S. citizen; son of Owen and Ellen (O'Connor) Callan; married Claire Wegner, August 6, 1955; children: Joseph Mark, Ruth Ann. *Education:* University of the Witwatersrand, B.A., 1947; Fordham University, M.A., 1954; University of South Africa, D. Litt. et Phil., 1959; Oxford University, postdoctoral study, 1960-61. *Politics:* "Generally Democratic." *Religion:* Roman Catholic. *Home:* 640 Homecrest Ave., Kalamazoo, Mich. 49001. *Office:* English Department, Western Michigan University, Kalamazoo, Mich. 49001.

CAREER: High school teacher of English in South Africa, 1947-49; lecturer for British Ministry of Information, London, England, 1950-52; instructor in English at Fordham University, New York, N.Y., 1952-54, and Loyola University, Chicago, Ill., 1954-57; Western Michigan University, Kalamazoo, assistant professor, 1957-61, associate professor, 1961-63, professor of English, 1963—. Visiting professor, Rackham School of Graduate Studies, University of Michigan, 1968; external examiner of doctoral theses, Rhodes University, 1967-70. *Military service:* South African Army, 1942-46; served in North Africa and Italy. *Member:* Modern Language Association of America, English Academy of Southern Africa, African Studies Association, Michigan Academy, Oxford Society. *Awards, honors:* Jagger Bequest Award (Johannesburg), 1947; Carnegie grant to St. Antony's College, Oxford University, 1960-61; *Choice*, outstanding academic book for *Alan Paton*, 1969-70.

WRITINGS: Annotated Checklist of W. H. Auden, A. Swallow, 1958; *Albert John Luthuli and the South African Race Conflict*, Western Michigan University Press, 1962, revised edition, 1965; (contributor) Monroe K. Spears, editor, *Auden*, Prentice-Hall, 1964; (contributor) James Boatright, editor, *A Tribute to Wystan Hugh Auden on His Sixtieth Birthday*, Washington and Lee University, 1967; *Alan Paton*, Twayne, 1968; (editor) Alan Paton, *The Long View*, Praeger, 1968; *Hamburger Bibliographien XI: Alan Paton*, Hans Christians Verlag, 1970; (contributor) James Vinson, editor, *Contemporary Poets*, St. James Press, 1974. Contributor to *Encyclopedia Americana*, *Saturday Review*, *New York Times Book Review*, *The London Magazine*, *The Dublin Magazine*, *Southern Review*, *Africana Journal*, *Twentieth Century Literature*, and other periodicals.

WORK IN PROGRESS: A critical study of W. H. Auden, completion expected in 1975; editing *A General Introduction for My Work*, by W. B. Yeats, expected completion also 1975.

SIDELIGHTS: Callan is competent in Afrikaans, Italian, French, and Gaelic. *Avocational interests:* Contemporary poetry, cricket, acting.

* * *

CALLENDER, Wesley P(ayne), Jr. 1923-

PERSONAL: Born July 9, 1923, in Brooklyn, N.Y.; son of Wesley Payne (a banker) and Adelaide E. (Morris) Callender; married Maybelle A. Carmichael, June 14, 1952; children: Wesley P. III, Kenneth Frank, Roy Bradford. *Education:* Marietta College, B.A., 1946; New York University, M.A., 1950. *Religion:* Quaker. *Home:* 129 Bella Vista St., Tuckahoe, N.Y. 10707. *Office:* Barnes & Noble, Inc., 105 Fifth Ave., New York, N.Y. 10003.

CAREER: Teacher at public high schools in Chandlersville, Ohio, 1947-48, Pleasantville, N.Y., 1952-54, and at Friends Academy, Locust Valley, N.Y., 1948-52; American Book Co., New York, N.Y., assistant managing editor, 1954-62; Scholastic Book Services, New York, N.Y., book editor, 1962-65; Barnes & Noble, Inc., New York, N.Y., editor, 1965—. American Friends Service Committee, member of foreign student committee. Tuckahoe Urban Renewal Program, member of citizens advisory committee, 1963—. *Military service:* U.S. Army, edited battalion newspaper in Japan, 1946-47. *Member:* National Association of Book Editors (founder; first president, 1962-65), National Amateur Press Association, American Amateur Press Association, Eastchester Historical Society (co-founder; trustee), Westchester Park Citizens Association (president, 1965-66), Westchester Chappel.

WRITINGS: (Author of introductions, and editor with William D. Boutwell and Robert E. Gerber) *Great Speeches from Pericles to Kennedy*, Scholastic Book Services, 1965. Author of two one-act plays; contributor to journals.

WORK IN PROGRESS: The Man Who Started the Circus, a juvenile biography of Hachaliah Bailey; a collection of speeches; a collection of American humor of the late nineteenth century; a three-act play.

SIDELIGHTS: As a hobby, Callender has operated his own private press at home since 1956. The Village Green Press has a small hand press and a larger job press.†

* * *

CALLEO, David P(atrick) 1934-

PERSONAL: Born July 19, 1934, in Binghamton, N.Y.; son of Patrick and Gertrude (Crowe) Calleo. *Education:* Yale University, B.A., 1955, M.A., 1957, Ph.D., 1959. *Office:* 1740 Massachusetts Ave., N.W., Washington, D.C. 20036.

CAREER: Brown University, Providence, R.I., instructor in political science, 1959-61; Yale University, New Haven, Conn., assistant professor of political science, 1961-67; U.S. Department of State, consultant to undersecretary for political affairs, 1967-68; Johns Hopkins School of Advanced International Studies, Washington, D.C., professor and director of European studies, 1968—, Washington Center of Foreign Policy Research, research associate, 1968-74, director, 1974—. Nuffield College, Oxford, Oxford, England, research fellow, 1966-67. *Military service:* U.S. Army Reserve, 1956-65; became captain.

WRITINGS: Europe's Future: The Grand Alternatives, Horizon, 1965; *Coleridge and the Idea of the Modern State*, Yale University Press, 1966; *Europe's Future*, Hodder & Stoughton, 1967; *Britain's Future*, Horizon, 1968; *The Atlantic Fantasy*, Johns Hopkins Press, 1970; (with Benjamin M. Rowland) *America and the World Political Economy*, Indiana University Press, 1974.

WORK IN PROGRESS: A study of British views on European unity.

* * *

CAMBON, Glauco (Gianlorenzo) 1921-

PERSONAL: Born May 7, 1921, in Pusiano, Italy; son of Glauco (a painter) and Gilda (also a painter; maiden name, Pansiotti) Cambon; first married, 1952; married Marlis Zeller, November 11, 1961; children: Gilda, Alexander, Natalie. *Education:* Lycee Berchet, Milan, Italy, Maturita classica (B.A. equivalent), 1939; University of Pavia, Ph.D., 1947; Columbia University, graduate studies, 1951-52. *Politics:* Democrat ("no formal commitment"). *Religion:* Freethinker (former Catholic). *Address:* R.R. 2, Willimantic, Conn. *Office:* Department of English, University of Connecticut, Storrs, Conn.

CAREER: Verri Institute, Milan, Italy, teacher of English, 1948-49; Scuola Interpreti, Milan, Italy, lecturer in English and American literature, 1954-57; Fermi Lycee, Arona, Italy, professor of English, 1956-58; University of Michigan, Ann Arbor, visiting lecturer in English and comparative literature, 1958-61; Rutgers University, New Brunswick, N.J., professor of comparative and Italian literature, 1961-69; University of Connecticut, Storrs, professor of comparative literature and Italian literature, 1969—. Arnoldo Mondadori (publishers), Milan, consultant and translator, 1949—; Tungsram (Milan), foreign correspondent, 1950-51. Lecturer on literary topics in Italy and United States. *Military service:* Italian Army, 1940-47.

MEMBER: Dante Society of America, National Council of Teachers of English, American Association of Teachers of Italian, Ghislieri College Alumni. *Awards, honors:* Fulbright fellowship at Columbia University, 1951-52; Del Duca Prize (Milan), for essays on American literature, 1956; fellow, Indiana School of Letters, 1960.

WRITINGS: (Translator into Italian, and author of preface) William Faulkner, *Absalom, Absalom!*, Mondadori (Milan), 1954; (translator into Italian, and author of preface) Robert Penn Warren, *World Enough and Time*, Mondadori, 1954; *Tematica e sviluppo della poesia americana*, Edizioni di Storia e Letteratura (Rome), 1956; (contributor) *The Poem Itself*, edited by S. Burnshaw, Holt, 1960; (author of preface to Italian edition) W. Y. Tindall, *James Joyce*, Bompiani (Milan), 1960; *Recent American Poetry*, University of Minnesota, 1962; *La Lotta con Proteo*, Bompiani (Milan), 1963; *The Inclusive Flame*, Indiana University Press, 1963; (editor) Eugenio Montale, *Selected Poems* (in English and Italian), New Directions, 1966; (editor) *Pirandello* (collection of critical essays), Prentice-Hall, 1967; *Dante's Craft*, Eugenio Montale, 1972.

Consultant on Italian translation of James Joyce's *Ulysses*, 1960. Verse has been published in American and Italian journals, including *Accent, Poetry* (Chicago), *Sewanee Review, Southern Review, Comparative Literature, Studi Americani*, and other periodicals. Also contributor to language journals.

WORK IN PROGRESS: Research on style in American and Italian fiction and poetry.

SIDELIGHTS: Cambon has traveled in Africa, France, Switzerland, Austria, and Canada. "Apart from literature," he says, "I am interested in philosophy and in the arts (visual and dramatic)."

* * *

CAMERON, Polly 1928-

PERSONAL: Born October 14, 1928, in Walnut Creek, Calif.; daughter of Donald (a salesman) and Dorothy (Knox) McQuiston. *Education:* Attended Phoenix College, 1947-48, and University of California, Santa Barbara, 1948-49. *Politics:* Democrat. *Home and office:* Snedens Landing, Palisades, N.Y.

CAREER: Advertising and display manager in Phoenix, Ariz., 1949-50; theater publicity director, Santa Fe, N.M., 1951; architectural draftsman in Casablanca, Morocco, 1952; free-lance graphic designer in New York, 1953—. Painter and sculptor, exhibiting in New York and Washington, D.C. Design consultant. *Awards, honors:* American Institute of Graphic Arts Award for outstanding book design, for *A Child's Book of Nonsense*; American Library Association, Notable Book Award for *"I Can't," Said the Ant*, 1961.

WRITINGS—All self-illustrated except as indicated, all published by Coward: *The Cat Who Thought He Was a Tiger*, 1956; *The Cat Who Couldn't Purr*, 1957; *The Dog Who Grew Too Much* (Junior Literary Guild Book Club selection), 1958; *The Boy Who Drew Birds*, 1959; *A Child's Book of Nonsense*, 1960; *"I Can't," Said the Ant*, 1961; *The 2 Ton Canary and Other Nonsense Riddles*, 1965; *The Green Machine* (illustrated by Consuelo Joerns), 1969; *The Polly Cameron Picture Book*, 1970; *The Secret Toy Machine*, 1972.

SIDELIGHTS: Polly Cameron lived in France, Spain, and Morocco for two years. Her classic sports car, a Morgan, was the inspiration for *The Green Machine*.

* * *

CAMP, Wesley D(ouglass) 1915-

PERSONAL: Born January 2, 1915, in Bedford Hills, N.Y.; son of Douglass Fletcher (a railroad trainman) and Edna (Westcott) Camp; married Kathleen Virginia Bamman, December 22, 1936; children: Mary Virginia (Mrs. H. Lee Smith), Wesley D., Jr. *Education:* Columbia University, B.A., 1936, M.A., 1940, Ph.D., 1957; University of Lille, diploma, 1937. *Religion:* Methodist. *Home:* 481 Dogwood Ave., West Hempstead, N.Y. 11552. *Office:* Adelphi University, Garden City, N.Y. 11530.

CAREER: Monmouth College, West Long Branch, N.J., instructor in social science, 1941-45, chairman of department, 1946-60; Signal Corps Publications Agency, Fort Monmouth, N.J., editor, 1944-46; Bibliotheque Nationale, Paris, France, independent research, 1960-61; Carnegie Institute of Technology (now Carnegie-Mellon University), Pittsburgh, Pa., associate professor of history, 1961-62; Adelphi University, Garden City, N.Y., professor of history, 1962—, chairman of department, 1962-74. Trustee of Elberon Memorial Church, Elberon, N.J., 1960-70.

Member: American Historical Association, Societe d'-Histoire Moderne, American Association of University Professors, Society for French Historical Studies.

WRITINGS: Marriage and the Family in France Since the Revolution: An Essay in the History of Population, Bookman Associates, 1961. Contributor of reviews to *American Historical Review, American Political Science Review, Historian*, and *Choice*.

WORK IN PROGRESS: A history of Paris from Julius Caesar to Charles De Gaulle; a translation of Jean Egret's *The Prerevolution, 1787-88*.

SIDELIGHTS: Camp is fluent in French and reads German, Italian, and Spanish. He resided in France, 1936-37, 1960-61, and summers, 1965 and 1970, and has travelled in Italy, Germany, Belgium, and Switzerland. *Avocational interests:* Chess, wine-tasting, sports, and history of science and art.

* * *

CAMPBELL, Don(ald Guy) 1922-

PERSONAL: Born June 27, 1922, in Brownsburg, Ind.; son of George Guy and Ella (Menefee) Campbell; married Jean Farson, October 15, 1949; children: Scott Guy, Jennifer Lee. *Education:* Indiana University, A.B., 1948. *Politics:* Republican. *Religion:* Unitarian Universalist. *Home:* 4426 East Vermont, Phoenix, Ariz. 85018.

CAREER: St. Petersburg Times, St. Petersburg, Fla., feature writer, 1948; National Safety Council, Chicago, Ill., writer, 1948-52; *Indianapolis Star*, Indianapolis, Ind., feature writer, 1952-54, business and financial editor, 1954-65; *Dow Theory Trader*, Indianapolis, chief writer, researcher, 1956-71; *Arizona Republic*, Phoenix, Ariz., executive business and financial editor, 1965-72; *New York Daily News*, New York, N.Y., financial editor, 1972-74; syndicated columnist for United Feature Syndicate, 1972—. *Military service:* U.S. Army, 1942-45; received five battle stars. *Member:* Authors Guild, Society of American Business Writers, Sigma Delta Chi.

WRITINGS: Let's Take Stock, Bobbs-Merrill, 1959; *What Does Daddy Do All Day?*, Bobbs-Merrill, 1962; *Understanding Stocks*, Doubleday, 1965; *The Handbook of Real Estate Investment*, Bobbs-Merrill, 1969.

WORK IN PROGRESS: A book for the layman on self-retirement under the provisions of the 1974 pension reform legislation.

* * *

CANDELARIA, Frederick (Henry) 1929-

PERSONAL: Born December 2, 1929, in El Paso, Tex.; son of R. O. and Margaret (Work) Candelaria; children: Philip F., Stewart S. *Education:* University of Texas, B.A., 1954; Yale University, graduate study, 1954-55; University of Missouri, Ph.D., 1959. *Politics:* Socialist. *Home:* 4588 Marineview Crescent, North Vancouver, British Columbia, Canada.

CAREER: University of Missouri, Columbia, instructor in English, 1955-59; University of Oregon, Eugene, assistant professor of English, and director of composition, 1959-65; Simon Fraser University, Burnaby, British Columbia, Canada, associate professor of English, 1965—. Free-lance consultant and editor for college English textbooks. *Military service:* U.S. Army, Intelligence, 1951-53. *Member:* Renaissance Society of America. *Awards, honors:* Leopold

Egerinsky Award for musical composition, "Symphonic Essay"; Canada Council Senior fellowship to Spain, 1967-68.

WRITINGS: (Editor with William C. Strange) *Perspectives on Epic*, Allyn & Bacon, 1965; (editor with William E. Stafford) *The Voices of Prose*, McGraw, 1966; *Dimensions* (poems), Morris, 1967; (editor) *Perspectives on Style*, Allyn & Bacon, 1968; (editor) *Robert Heath: Clarastella, 1652*, Scholars' Facimiles, 1970. Contributor of articles to professional journals; and poetry to many reviews. Editor, *West Coast Review*.

WORK IN PROGRESS: Neglected Worthies, a study of minor seventeenth-century English poets; *Death, Poetry, and Jacobean Drama*; and *Ikon and Other Poems*.

SIDELIGHTS: "I'm sceptical about manifestos, artistic absolutes, etc., but if I had to subscribe to any, I suppose I'd maintain that art and genuinely creative research are anti-establishment." Proficient in Spanish, has growing interest in Quevedo and Gongora. Composes music (his award-winning "Symphonic Essay" is for symphony orchestra), and plays chess as hobby.

* * *

CANZONERI, Robert (Wilburn) 1925-

PERSONAL: Born November 21, 1925, in San Marcos, Tex.; son of Joe (a minister) and Mabel (Barnett) Canzoneri; married Candyce Barnes. *Education:* Mississippi College, Clinton, B.A., 1948; University of Mississippi, M.A., 1951; Stanford University, Ph.D., 1965. *Office:* Department of English, Ohio State University, 164 West 17th Ave., Columbus, Ohio 43210.

CAREER: Associate professor of English at Georgetown College, Georgetown, Ky., 1955-57, Mississippi College, Clinton, 1957-61, and Louisiana College, Pineville, 1961-63; Ohio State University, Columbus, assistant professor, 1965-66, associate professor, 1966-68, professor of English, 1968—. *Awards, honors:* Danforth teacher study grants, 1960, 1963, 1964; Henry H. Bellamann Foundation Award in writing, 1965.

WRITINGS: "*I Do So Politely*": *A Voice from the South*, Houghton, 1965; *Watch Us Pass* (poems), Ohio State University Press, 1968; *Men With Little Hammers* (novel), Dial, 1969; *Barbed Wire and Other Stories*, Dial, 1970; (editor with Page Stegner) *Fiction and Analysis*, Scott, Foresman, 1970; (contributor) Foley and Burnett, editors, *Best American Short Stories*, Houghton, 1971; (contributor) Johnson and Greenberg, editors, *Best Little Magazine Fiction*, New York University Press, 1971; (contributor) Miller Williams, editors, *Contemporary Poetry in America*, Random House, 1973. Writing anthologized in *Southern Fiction of the Sixties*, Louisiana State University Press, 1966, and *Southern Poetry of the Sixties*, Louisiana State University Press, 1967. Contributor of poems, short stories, and articles to *Southern Review, McCall's, Harper's, Saturday Review, Story, Sewanee Review*, and other periodicals.

WORK IN PROGRESS: A book with working title, *A Highly Ramified Tree*, a half Sicilian's personal account.

* * *

CAPPON, Daniel 1921-

PERSONAL: Born June 6, 1921, in London, England; son of Maurice (a businessman) and Henrietta (Trubb) Cappon; married Barbara Edna Williams, June 20, 1942; children:

Ian David, Bruce Henry, Paul Scott, Mark James Anthony, Fiona Barbara. *Education:* Studied at St. Mary's Hospital Medical School, Maudsley Institute of Psychiatry, and Guy's Hospital Medical School, all University of London; received L.M.S.S.A., 1944, M.B., B.S., L.R.C.P. and M.R.C.S., 1945, doctorate and M.R.C.P., 1947. *Religion:* Anglican. *Office:* 32A York Valley Crescent, Willowdale, Ontario, Canada.

CAREER: Physician in private practice of psychiatry, Toronto, Ontario, 1958—; University of Toronto, Toronto, Ontario, assistant professor, department of psychiatry, 1958—. Professor in environmental studies, York University. *Military service:* Royal Army Medical Corps, officer, 1945-48; served in Far East. *Member:* Royal College of Physicians (England; fellow), American Psychiatric Association (fellow), Canadian Medical Association, Canadian Psychiatric Association, New York Academy of Sciences.

WRITINGS: Toward an Understanding of Homosexuality, Prentice-Hall, 1965; *Technology and Perception,* C. C Thomas, 1972; *Eating, Loving, and Dying,* University of Toronto Press, 1973. Also author of radio lecture for Canadian Broadcasting System, 1968, two plays, "The Last Loon" and "One Way; or, Don't Kick the Bucket Unless it Has Stopped Rolling." Wrote poetry for Man in His Community pavillion of Expo '67.

*　*　*

CARANO, Paul 1919-

PERSONAL: Born July 15, 1919, in Krebs, Okla.; son of John (a businessman) and Mary (Ross) Carano. *Education:* Fresno State College (now California State University at Fresno), B.A., 1943; University of New Hampshire, graduate student, 1950-51; Stanford University, M.A., 1954. *Politics:* Democrat. *Religion:* Christian. *Residence:* (Permanent address) Krebs, Okla. *Office:* College of Guam, Agana, Guam 96910.

CAREER: Hilaan School, Agana, Guam, principal, 1951-53; Territory of Guam, Agana, administrative assistant to Director of Education, 1958-62; College of Guam, Agana, associate professor, 1962-64, professor of social science, 1964—, director of Micronesian Area Research Center, 1967—. Member, Guam Parks and Historical Monuments Commission, counselor and director of youth camp, Young Men's Christian Association, Kings County, Calif. *Member:* American Association of University Professors.

WRITINGS: (With Pedro C. Sanchez) *A Complete History of Guam,* Tuttle, 1964.

WORK IN PROGRESS: Research for a book, *The Government of Guam.†*

*　*　*

CARAWAN, Carolanne M. 1939-
(Candie Carawan)

PERSONAL: Born December 27, 1939, in Los Angeles, Calif.; daughter of Howard T. (a geologist) and Lois Belle (Patterson) Anderson; married Guy H. Carawan, Jr., March 17, 1961; children: Evan. *Education:* Pomona College, B.A., 1961.

WRITINGS—Under name Candie Carawan, with husband, Guy H. Carawan, Jr.; song collections with photographs and narrative: *We Shall Overcome,* Oak, 1963; *Ain't You Got a Right to the Tree of Life—The People of Johns Island, S.C., Their Words, Faces and Songs,* Simon & Schuster, 1966; *Freedom Is a Constant Struggle,* Oak, 1967.†

CARAWAN, Guy H., Jr. 1927-

PERSONAL: Born July 28, 1927, in Santa Monica, Calif.; son of Guy H. (an insulation contractor) and Henrietta Amanda (Kelly) Carawan; married Carolanne M. Anderson, March 17, 1961; children: Evan. *Education:* Occidental College, B.A., 1949; University of California, Los Angeles, M.A., 1952.

CAREER: Highlander Research and Educational Center, Knoxville, Tenn., director of music; folk singer, collector of folk songs and folk life, and organizer of regional folk festivals. *Awards, honors:* Grants from Newport Folk Foundation, to develop regional folk festivals in the Sea Islands of South Carolina and Georgia, and to record the songs of the freedom movement in Mississippi and Georgia.

WRITINGS—With wife, Candie Carawan; song collections with photographs and narrative: *We Shall Overcome,* Oak, 1963; *Ain't You Got a Right to the Tree of Life—The People of Johns Island, S.C., Their Words, Faces and Songs,* Simon & Schuster, 1966; *Freedom Is a Constant Struggle,* Oak, 1967.†

*　*　*

CARDONE, Samuel S(teve) 1938-

PERSONAL: Born May 8, 1938, in Chicago, Ill.; son of Frank (a watchman) and Jennie (Caccamo) Cardone. *Education:* De Paul University, B.A., 1961, M.A., 1964; Illinois Institute of Technology, Ph.D., 1967. *Religion:* Catholic. *Home:* 1181 Wade, Highland Park, Ill.

CAREER: Chicago State Hospital, Chicago, Ill., psychologist, beginning 1962, head of clinical research, Read Zone Center Complex, beginning 1968; alcoholism coordinator of region two, Illinois Department of Mental Health. Instructor in child psychology at Pestalozzi-Froebel College, Chicago, 1965-66; instructor at Loyola University, Chicago. *Member:* Psi Chi (treasurer, 1965).

WRITINGS: (With Raymond J. Corsini) *Roleplaying in Psychotherapy: A Manual,* Aldine, 1966.

WORK IN PROGRESS: Writings in group psychotherapy; writings in psychotherapy with children.

*　*　*

CARLSEN, G(eorge) Robert 1917-

PERSONAL: Born April 15, 1917, in Bozeman, Mont.; son of Charles E. (an attorney) and Carolyn (Mason) Carlsen; married Ruth Christoffer (now a juvenile writer), April 5, 1941; children: Christopher, Kristin, Peter, Jane. *Education:* University of Minnesota, B.A., 1939, B.S., 1940, M.A., 1943, Ph.D., 1948. *Home:* Lake Maebride, Rt. 3, Box 342, Solon, Iowa 52333. *Office:* N104 East Hall, University of Iowa, Iowa City, Iowa 52240.

CAREER: University of Minnesota, Minneapolis, instructor in English and education, 1942-47; University of Colorado, Boulder, associate professor of English and education, 1947-52; University of Texas, Austin, associate professor of curriculum and instruction, 1952-58; University of Iowa, Iowa City, professor of English and education, 1958—. Faculty member at University of Colorado, summers, 1953, 1955, 1958, and University of Hawaii, 1957, 1970. *Member:* National Council of Teachers of English (second vice-president, 1959; first vice-president, 1961; president, 1962), Phi Beta Kappa, Phi Delta Kappa. *Awards, honors:* Award for distinguished contributions in secondary school teaching, 1957, and Distinguished Service Award, 1970, both from National Council of Teachers of English.

WRITINGS: Brown-Carlsen Test of Listening Comprehension, World Publishing, 1952; (with Richard Alm) *Social Understanding Through Literature*, National Council for Social Studies, 1954; (editor with wife, Ruth C. Carlsen) *The Great Auto Race, and Other Stories*, Scholastic Book Services, 1965; (editor with Ruth C. Carlsen) *52 Miles to Terror* (collection), Scholastic Book Services, 1966; (editor) "Themes and Writers" series, McGraw, four volumes, *American Literature*, 1966, *Encounters—Themes in Literature*, 1967, 2nd edition, 1973, *Insights—Themes in Literature*, 1967, 2nd edition, 1973, *Western Literature—Themes and Writers*, 1967, 2nd edition, 1973; *Books and the Teen Age Reader*, Harper, 1967, 2nd edition, 1971; *Focus and Perception*, McGraw, 1969, 2nd edition, 1974.

*   *   *

CARLSEN, Ruth C(hristoffer) 1918-

PERSONAL: Born February 21, 1918, in Milwaukee, Wis.; daughter of Carl Severin (a railroad official) and Lydia (Diefenthaeler) Christoffer; married George Robert Carlsen (a professor at University of Iowa), April 5, 1941; children: Christopher, Kristin, Peter, Jane. *Education:* University of Minnesota, B.A., 1939. *Religion:* Unitarian. *Home:* Lake Macbride, R.R.3, Box 342, Solon, Iowa 52333.

CAREER: Author of children's books. *Member:* Author's Guild, National P.E.N. Women's League, Athens Historical Circle, P.E.O. Sisterhood, Theta Sigma Phi.

WRITINGS: Mr. Pudgins, Houghton, 1953; (editor with husband, G. Robert Carlsen) *The Great Auto Race, and Other Stories*, Scholastic Book Services, 1965; (editor with G. Robert Carlsen) *52 Miles to Terror* (collection), Scholastic Book Services, 1966; *Henrietta Goes West*, Houghton, 1966; *Hildy and the Cuckoo Clock*, Houghton, 1966; *Monty and the Tree House*, Houghton, 1967; *Sam Bottleby*, Houghton, 1968; *Ride A Wild Horse*, Houghton, 1970; *Sometimes It's Up*, Houghton, 1971; *Half Past Tomorrow*, Houghton, 1973. Editor of book in "Themes and Writers" series, McGraw, 1967, and participating editor on three other books in the series.

WORK IN PROGRESS: I Never Said I'd Be an Angel.

AVOCATIONAL INTERESTS: Travel, refinishing antiques, quilt making.

*   *   *

CARLSON, Leland H(enry) 1908-

PERSONAL: Born March 25, 1908, in Rockford, Ill.; son of Henry J. (a painter) and Bessie (Nilson) Carlson; married LaVerne Larson, June 10, 1933; children: Timothy, Kay (Mrs. John Roberts III). *Education:* Beloit College, B.A., 1931; Chicago Theological Seminary, B.D., 1938; University of Chicago, Ph.D., 1939. *Religion:* Protestant. *Home:* 1325 North College Ave., Claremont, Calif.

CAREER: North Park College, Chicago, Ill., dean of men, 1932-42; Northwestern University, Evanston, Ill., assistant professor, then associate professor of history, 1942-54; Rockford College, Rockford, Ill., president, 1954-59; Claremont Graduate School and University Center, Claremont, Calif., professor of history, and professor of church history in School of Theology, 1959-73. *Member:* American Historical Association, Royal Historical Society (London;

fellow), Swedish Historical Society, Phi Beta Kappa, Sigma Xi. *Awards, honors:* King Gustav V Royal Sweden Medal, 1951; Folger Shakespeare Library fellow, 1953, 1958, 1960, 1973; LL.D., Beloit College, 1956; Rockefeller Foundation fellowship, 1962-63; L.H.D., Rockford College, 1972; three awards for excellence of teaching.

WRITINGS: History of North Park College, North Park College, 1941; *An Alaskan Gold Mine*, Northwestern University Press, 1951; "Elizabethan Nonconformists" series, Allen & Unwin: Volume I, *Cartwrightiana*, 1951, Volume II, *The Writings of Robert Harrison and Robert Browne*, 1953, Volume III, *The Writings of Henry Barrow, 1587-1590*, 1962, Volume IV, *The Writings of John Greenwood, 1587-1590*, 1962, Volume V, *The Writings of Henry Barrow, 1590-1591*, 1966, Volume VI, *The Writings of John Greenwood and Henry Barrow, 1591-1593*, 1970; *English Satire*, William Andrews Clark Memorial Library, 1972. Section editor, *American Historical Review*, 1949-74.

WORK IN PROGRESS: Further volumes in projected eight-volume series "Elizabethan Nonconformists." *The Writings of John Penroy*, in two volumes.

SIDELIGHTS: Carlson's interest in nonconformity and the history of thought led to his ambitious work on the forerunners of the Pilgrim Fathers, scheduled for completion in 1975. Carlson has traveled in sixty-odd countries, and circled the world three times. He is competent in Swedish, French, German, Greek, and Latin. *Avocational interests:* Reading, chess, tennis, swimming.

*   *   *

CARLTON, Robert G(oodrich) 1927-

PERSONAL: Born July 14, 1927, in Grapeland, Tex.; son of William Earl (an auto dealer) and Arlie (Goodrich) Carlton; married Doris McFarling, October 16, 1959; children: Curtis, Gina. *Education:* Attended University of Texas, 1945, and Southern Methodist University, 1950; Syracuse University, B.A. (summa cum laude), 1958; Columbia University, M.A. and Certificate of Russian Institute, 1960.

CAREER: Seismograph Service Corp., Caracas, Venezuela, surveyor and party manager, 1947-49, 1954-57; Library of Congress, Washington, D.C., librarian/bibliographer, beginning 1960. Writer. *Military service:* U.S. Air Force, language specialist, 1950-54; became staff sergeant. *Member:* American Association for the Advancement of Slavic Studies. *Awards, honors:* Ford Foundation foreign area training fellowship, 1958-60.

WRITINGS: (Compiler with P. L. Horecky) *The USSR and Eastern Europe; Periodicals in Western Languages*, U.S. Government Printing Office, 1964, 3rd edition, 1967; (editor) *Newspapers of East Central and Southeastern Europe in the Library of Congress*, U.S. Government Printing Office, 1965; (assistant editor and indexer) *Russia and the Soviet Union; A Bibliographical Guide to Western-Language Publications*, University of Chicago Press, 1965; (editor) *Latin America in Soviet Writings*, Johns Hopkins Press, 1966. Contributor of articles on Rumania and eastern Europe to *Library of Congress Quarterly Journal*.

SIDELIGHTS: Carlton is fluent in Spanish, Russian, Rumanian, and German.†

*   *   *

CARMICHAEL, Fred 1924-

PERSONAL: Born February 1, 1924, in Pelham, N.Y.;

son of Cyril and Edith (Nichols) Carmichael; married Patricia Wyn Rose (a theater director), May 31, 1952. *Education:* Educated in England and Pelham, N.Y.; attended Feagin School of Drama, New York, N.Y., 1941-43. *Home:* 307 West Fourth St., New York, N.Y. 10014. *Agent:* Samuel French, Inc., 25 West 45th St., New York, N.Y. 10036.

CAREER: Playwright, producer in summer stock, and actor. Producer at Dorset Playhouse (summer theater), Dorset, Vt., 1949—, and of Champlain Festival Pageant for Fort Edward, N.Y.; editor of ship's newspaper on Home Lines cruises plying the Caribbean and South America for two months each winter, 1952-66; actor on television and stage, appearing with two companies on U.S. tours. *Member:* Actors' Equity Association, American Federation of Television and Radio Artists, Screen Actors Guild.

WRITINGS—Three-act plays—all published by Samuel French: *More Than Meets the Eye*, 1954; *Inside Lester*, 1955; *The Night Is My Enemy*, 1956; *Petey's Choice*, 1957; *Luxury Cruise*, 1958; *The Pen Is Deadlier*, 1959; *Exit the Body*, 1961; *The Robin Hood Caper*, 1962; *Dream World*, 1963; *Any Number Can Die*, 1964; *The Best Laid Plans*, 1966; *All the Better to Kill You With*, 1967; *Surprise*, 1968; *Victoria's House*, 1969; *Done to Death*, 1971; *Mixed Doubles*, 1972; *Who Needs a Waltz*, 1973; *Hey, Naked Lady*, 1974.

One-act plays—all published by Baker Co.: *Florence Unlimited*, 1952; *Green Room Blues*, 1956; *Four for the Money*, 1960; *Dear Millie*, 1962; *There's a Fly in My Soap*, 1973.

Author of scripts for seven half-hour historical shows presented daily each summer at Old Sturbridge Village in Massachusetts; also has done material for television and radio comedians, including a record album, "The Other Side of Lee Tully."

WORK IN PROGRESS: A play, to be produced, 1975.

* * *

CARPER, Jean Elinor 1932-

PERSONAL: Born January 3, 1932, in Delaware, Ohio; daughter of Jethro C. and Natella (Boyer) Carper. *Education:* Ohio Wesleyan University, A.B., 1953; Indiana University, M.S. *Religion:* Methodist. *Agent:* Marcia Higgins, William Morris Agency, 1350 Avenue of the Americas, New York, N.Y. 10019.

CAREER: National Safety Council, Chicago, Ill., editor of *Family Safety Magazine*, 1959-65. On staff of Senator Warren G. Magnuson. Full-time writer.

WRITINGS: (With Grace Dickerson) *Little Turtle, Miami Chief*, Albert Whitman, 1959; *Wonderland of Tomorrow*, Albert Whitman, 1961; (with Elizabeth Gundry) *Stay Alive!*, Doubleday, 1965; *Bitter Greetings: The Scandal of the Military Draft*, Grossman, 1967; (with Warren Grant Magnuson) *The Dark Side of the Marketplace*, Prentice-Hall, 1968; *Not With a Gun*, Grossman, 1973; (with Jacqueline Verrett) *Eating May Be Hazardous to Your Health*, Simon & Schuster, 1974.

* * *

CARR, Raymond 1919-

PERSONAL: Born April 11, 1919, in Bath, England; son of Reginald Henry and Ethel (Graham) Carr; married Sara Strickland. *Education:* Christ Church, Oxford, B.A. (first class honors), 1941. *Politics:* Conservative. *Religion:* Church of England. *Home:* Woolhanger Manor, Parracombe, Barnstaple, Devonshire, England. *Office:* Latin American Centre, St. Antony's College, Oxford, England.

CAREER: Oxford University, Oxford, England, fellow of All Souls College, 1945-52, fellow of New College, 1952-65, St. Antony's College, Oxford, professor of Latin American history, and director of Latin American Centre, 1965-68, Warden of St. Antony's College, Oxford, 1968—. *Member:* Royal Historical Society (fellow).

WRITINGS: (Contributor) *European Nobility of the XVIII Century*, Adam Black, 1954; (contributor) M. Howard, *Soldiers and Politics*, Eyre & Spottiswoode, 1957; (contributor) *New Cambridge Modern History*, Cambridge University Press, 1965; *Spain 1808-1939*, Oxford University Press, 1966; (contributor) *Cuba and the United States*, Brookings Institution, 1968. Early articles were mainly on Sweden, later writings on Spain and Latin America; contributor to *Economic History Review* and *Observer*; reviewer for *New York Review of Books* and professional journals.

WORK IN PROGRESS: A survey of modern Spain and the Spanish Civil War.

SIDELIGHTS: Carr knows Swedish, Norwegian, Danish, Italian, Spanish, French, and German.

* * *

CARRIER, Esther Jane 1925-

PERSONAL: Born June 22, 1925, in Punxsutawney, Pa.; daughter of Gerald Burton (an insurance agent) and Mabel (Lines) Carrier. *Education:* Attended Bob Jones College (now University), 1942-44; Geneva College, A.B., 1946; Carnegie Institute of Technology, B.S. in L.S., 1947; Pennsylvania State University, M.A., 1950; University of Michigan, A.M.L.S., 1958, Ph.D., 1960. *Politics:* Republican. *Religion:* Christian and Missionary Alliance. *Home:* 410 Highland Ave., Punxsutawney, Pa. 15767. *Office:* Willard J. Houghton Library, Houghton College, Houghton, N.Y. 14744.

CAREER: Pennsylvania State University, State College, circulation and reference assistant, 1947-50; Houghton College, Houghton, N.Y., head librarian, 1950—. *Member:* American Library Association.

WRITINGS: Fiction in Public Libraries, 1876-1900, Scarecrow, 1965.

* * *

CARTER, Neil 1913-

PERSONAL: Born December 31, 1913, in New York, N.Y.; son of Louis and Eve (Lambert) Carter; married Evelyn Wagman, February 24, 1934; children: Stephen Keith. *Education:* University of Manchester, B.A., 1934. *Religion:* Jewish. *Home:* 888 Eighth Ave., New York, N.Y. 10019.

CAREER: Greater New York Mutual Insurance Co., New York, N.Y., 1956—, now assistant to general manager and manager of workmen's compensation claims department. Member of Faculty, Pohs Institute of Insurance, president of medical council, New York Medical College, 1963. *Member:* New York Claim Association (president, 1962; chairman of workmen's compensation committee, 1966), Compensation Association of New Jersey, American Opera Society, Jewish Chautauqua Society, Metropolitan Opera Guild, Museum of Modern Art.

WRITINGS: Moses (biography), privately printed, 1934; *Guide to Workmen's Compensation Investigations*, Insurance Advocate, 1961; *Guide to Workmen's Compensation Claims*, Roberts, 1965, 3rd edition, 1970. Contributor of poems and short stories to magazines, including *Saturday Review* and *Collier's*; columnist, *Real Estate News Journal*, and contributor to other insurance journals.

WORK IN PROGRESS: Glossary of Insurance Claims Terms; Glossary of Insurance Medical Terms; a novel about contemporary business life; a compilation of poems and stories.

AVOCATIONAL INTERESTS: Opera (has visited major opera houses of the world and owns collection of more than two hundred complete recordings of operas); also collects autographs, first editions of books, first issues and anniversary editions of magazines, and stamps dealing with music.†

*   *   *

CARTER, William E. 1926-

PERSONAL: Born April 29, 1926, in Dayton, Ohio; son of Homer Earl and Mabel (Martin) Carter; married Bertha V. Garcia Roca, December 26, 1954; children: Olivia Denise, Vivian Linette, Emily Jeanne. *Education:* Muskingum College, B.A., 1949; Boston University, S.T.B., 1955; Columbia University, M.A., 1958, Ph.D., 1963. *Home:* 1011 Northwest 21st St., Gainesville, Fla. *Agent:* International Creative Management, 1301 Avenue of the Americas, New York, N.Y. 10019.

CAREER: Iglesia Metodista Central, Montevideo, Uruguay, 1950-53; Aymara Boy's School, Ancoraimes, Bolivia, director, 1954; Passaic Valley Methodist Parish, Paterson, N.J., administrative director, 1955-59; National School of Social Work, Bolivia, instructor in social problems, 1960-61; University of Florida, Gainesville, assistant professor of anthropology, 1962-65; University of Washington, Seattle, associate professor of anthropology and cross-cultural studies coordinator for Peace Corps training, 1965-66; University of Florida, Gainesville, associate professor, 1967, professor of anthropology and director of Center for Latin American Studies, 1968—. Chairman of Southeast Fulbright Hays Senior Scholars Conference, 1973. Consultant to Foreign Area Fellowship Program, and Division of International Studies of U.S. Office of Education. *Member:* American Anthropological Association, Society for Applied Anthropology, Southern Anthropological Society, Southeastern Conference on Latin American Studies (president, 1969-70), Latin American Studies Association (chairman of national consortium, 1971). *Awards, honors:* National Institute of Mental Health research fellow, 1960-62; National Defense Education Act foreign area research fellow, 1965; Fulbright Hays fellow, 1965-66; National Science Foundation research fellow, 1969.

WRITINGS: The First Book of South America, F. Watts, 1961, revised edition, 1972; *The First Book of Bolivia*, F. Watts, 1963; *Aymara Communities and the Bolivian Agrarian Reform*, University of Florida Press, 1965; *New Lands and Old Traditions*, University of Florida Press, 1968; *Bolivia: A Profile*, Praeger, 1971. Contributor to *American Anthropologist, American Indigena*, and *Proceedings of the Congress of Americanists*.

WORK IN PROGRESS: A study of chronic cannabis use in San Jose, Costa Rica.

CASE, Leland D(avidson) 1900-

PERSONAL: Born May 8, 1900, in Wesley, Iowa; son of Herbert Llewelyn (a clergyman) and Mary Ellen (Grannis) Case; married Josephine Altman, July 28, 1931. *Education:* Attended Dakota Wesleyan University, 1918-20; Macalester College, B.A., 1922; Northwestern University, M.A., 1926; graduate study at University of Minnesota and University of Chicago. *Politics:* Republican. *Religion:* Methodist. *Office:* 9900 E. Broadway, Tuscon, Ariz. 85710.

CAREER: Newspaperman in Lead, S.D., 1923-25, with Paris edition of *New York Herald Tribune*, Paris, France, 1926-27; Northwestern University, Evanston, Ill., instructor in journalism, 1925-26, assistant professor, 1927-28; *Evening Star*, Hot Springs, S.D., co-publisher, 1928-34; *Rotarian* (magazine), Chicago, Ill., editor, 1930-50, field editor, 1950-52; editorial director of *Christian Advocate*, and founder and editorial director of *Together*, Chicago, Ill., 1955-63; University of the Pacific, Stockton, Calif., director of Pacific Center for Western Historical Studies, 1965-67, and editor of *Pacific Historian*. U.S. Department of State, associate consultant at United Nations Conference, San Francisco, 1945.

MEMBER: Associated Church Press (honorary life member), Society of Midland Authors, Western History Association (honorary life member), Friends of the Middle Border (Mitchell, S.D.; founder), Westerners International (co-founder and president emeritus), Rotary, Sigma Delta Chi, Pi Kappa Delta, Sigma Tau Delta. *Awards, honors:* Alumni awards from Macalester College, 1949, Northwestern University, 1951, and Dakota Wesleyan University, 1962; Litt.D., Dakota Wesleyan University, 1941, Morningside College, 1957, and Simpson College; LL.D., McKendree College, 1963.

WRITINGS: (With George C. Bastian) *Editing the Day's News*, Macmillan, 1932; (with George C. Bastian and Roland E. Wolseley) *Around the Copydesk*, Macmillan, 1933; *Guide Book to Black Hills and Badlands*, Black Hills and Badlands Association, 1949; (contributor) R. Peattie, editor, *The Black Hills*, Vanguard, 1952; (editor with E. Grannis) *New Hampshire to Minnesota: Memoirs of S. H. Grannis*, privately printed, 1962; (editor) *Reader's Choice Treasury*, Doubleday, 1965; *Our Historic Black Hills: A Guide Book*, Swallow Press, 1975.

Editor of series for Rotary International, 1942-45. Contributor to *Papers of Bibliographic Society of America, Town Journal, National Geographic*, and other magazines. Writer of filmstrip celebrating Methodist Bicentennial in America, "Live or Die, I Must Ride!", narrated by Lowell Thomas.

WORK IN PROGRESS: A bibliography, *Eighteenth-Century American Methodist-Related Imprints*.

*   *   *

CASHIN, James A. 1911-

PERSONAL: Born May 24, 1911, in Augusta, Ga.; son of James A. (a businessman) and Mary (Hennessy) Cashin; married Dorothy B. Hamburg, August 29, 1941 (deceased); married Nancy L. Barton Ripple, October 12, 1973; children: (first marriage) James A., Jr., Gary Charles. *Education:* University of Georgia, B.S., 1932; New York University, M.B.A., 1940. *Home address:* P.O. Box 139, Locust Valley, N.Y. 11560. *Office:* Hofstra University, 1000 Fulton St., Hempstead, Long Island, N.Y. 11550.

CAREER: Certified public accountant, 1942. Accountant, later industrial engineer, with manufacturing firms, 1934-39; Bristol-Myers Co., New York, N.Y., chief accountant, 1939-50; St. Regis Paper Co., New York, N.Y., chief auditor, 1950-63; Hofstra University, Hempstead, N.Y., professor of accounting, 1963—, chairman of department of accounting, 1963-72. New York University, adjunct assistant professor, 1954-59; The City University of New York, lecturer at Baruch School, 1959-63. Chairman of college proficiency examination committee in accounting, New York State Department of Education, 1966—. *Member:* American Institute of Certified Public Accountants, New York State Society of Certified Public Accountants, Authors Guild, Financial Executives Institute, Institute of Internal Auditors, American Association of University Professors, University of Georgia Alumni Society. *Awards, honors:* Hofstra Accounting Society, Man of the Year, 1968.

WRITINGS: (With Walter Kamp) *Internal Controls*, Brock & Wallston, 1947; (with V. C. Brink) *Internal Auditing*, Roland, 1958; (with G. C. Owens) *Auditing*, Ronald, 1963; *Careers and Opportunities in Accounting*, Dutton, 1965; *Management Controls*, Hofstra University, 1967; *Impact of Medicare on Hospital Costs*, Hofstra University, 1970; *Handbook for Auditors*, McGraw, 1971; (with V. C. Brink and H. Witt) *Internal Auditing*, Ronald, 1973; (with J. Lerner) *Accounting I*, McGraw, 1973; (with Lerner) *Accounting II*, McGraw, 1974. Contributor to *Accounting Education* and *Financial Executive*. Contributor to *Accountants Encyclopedia*, Prentice-Hall, 1962. Columnist, *Internal Auditor*.

WORK IN PROGRESS: Accounting series outline, six volumes, for McGraw.

* * *

CASSITY, (Allen) Turner 1929-

PERSONAL: Born January 12, 1929, in Jackson, Miss.; son of Allen Davenport and Dorothy (Turner) Cassity. *Education:* Millsaps College, B.A., 1951; Stanford University, M.A., 1952; Columbia University, M.S., 1956. *Politics:* "I am by investment, temperament, and conviction a burgher." *Home:* 510-J East Ponce de Leon Ave., Decatur, Ga. 30030. *Office:* Emory University Library, Atlanta, Ga. 30322.

CAREER: Jackson Municipal Library, Jackson, Miss., assistant librarian, 1957-58; Transvaal Provincial Library, Pretoria, South Africa, assistant librarian, 1959-61; Emory University Library, Atlanta, Ga., chief of serials and binding department, 1962—. *Military service:* U.S. Army, 1952-54. *Awards, honors:* Blumenthal-Leviton-Blonder Prize for poetry, 1966.

WRITINGS: Watchboy, What of the Night? (poetry), Wesleyan University Press, 1966; *Steeplejacks in Babel*, Godine, 1973. Contributor of poems to *Poetry, Kenyon Review*, and other publications.

SIDELIGHTS: Cassity writes: "I am a writer of colonial pastorals, in both poetry and prose. In *Watchboy, What of the Night?* the worlds of Wallace Stevens and of Rudyard Kipling will come, or will not come, to accommodation."

* * *

CASSTEVENS, Thomas W(illiam) 1937-

PERSONAL: Born February 3, 1937, in Fayette, Mo.; son of Harold Turner (a farmer) and Willa (Hargis) Casstevens; married Jeanne Isabel Savery, June 3, 1958; children: Willa Jeanne, Margot Lee. *Education:* Capitol Page School, Washington, D.C., diploma, 1955; Reed College, B.A., 1959; Michigan State University, Ph.D., 1966. *Politics:* Republican. *Office:* Department of Political Science, Oakland University, Rochester, Mich. 48063.

CAREER: University of California, Berkeley, lecturer in political science, 1963-64, assistant research political scientist and assistant specialist, Institute of Governmental Studies, 1963-66; Oakland University, Rochester, Mich., assistant professor, 1966-69, associate professor, 1969-72, professor of political science, 1972—. Visiting fellow in mathematics, Dartmouth College, Hanover, N.H., 1968-69; visiting scholar, Darwin College, University of Kent, Canterbury, England, 1973. Consultant to Republican State Central Committee of California, 1965-66, research and statistical director of Michigan Committee for the Re-election of the President, 1972. *Awards, honors:* National Science Foundation, science faculty fellowship, 1968-69.

WRITINGS: Politics, Housing and Race Relations; The Defeat of Berkeley's Fair Housing Ordinance, Institute of Governmental Studies, University of California, 1965; (contributor) *The California Governmental Process: Problems and Issues*, edited by Eugene C. Lee, Little, 1966; *Politics, Housing, and Race Relations: California's Rumford Act and Proposition 14*, Institute of Governmental Studies, University of California, 1967; (editor with Lynn W. Eley) *The Politics of Fair Housing Legislation*, Chandler, 1968. Contributor to journals, and to bulletins of the Institute of Governmental Studies, University of California.

WORK IN PROGRESS: Introduction to Mathematical Political Science.

SIDELIGHTS: Casstevens is a "science fiction aficionado and a blistered thumb gardner."

* * *

CASTOR, Henry 1909-

PERSONAL: Born July 17, 1909, in Philadelphia, Pa.; son of Harry Shoemaker (a salesman) and Carrie (Wilsey) Castor; married Gladys Crofoot (a copy editor), February 23, 1948. *Education:* University of Pennsylvania, B.S., 1930. *Politics:* Democrat. *Religion:* Unitarian Universalist. *Home:* 467 Buena Vista, E., San Francisco, Calif. 94117.

CAREER: Publishers' representative: with Doubleday & Co., 1931-47, Little, Brown & Co., 1950-60, Alfred A. Knopf, 1958-60, Houghton Mifflin Co., 1958-60, Franklin Watts, 1961-62, Healy, Castor & Morse, 1963-69. Writer. *Military service:* U.S. Army, 1943-44; became first lieutenant. *Member:* San Francisco Press Club, Sierra Club.

WRITINGS: The Spanglers, Doubleday, 1948; *The Year of the Spaniard*, Doubleday, 1950; *Teddy Roosevelt and the Rough Riders*, Random House, 1955; *America's First World War*, Random House, 1957; *The First Book of the Spanish-American West*, F. Watts, 1963; *The First Book of the War with Mexico*, F. Watts, 1964; *Fifty-four Forty or Fight!*, F. Watts, 1970; *The Tripolitan War*, 1971.

WORK IN PROGRESS: A California Almanac.

* * *

CAVAN, Sherri 1938-

PERSONAL: Born March 13, 1938, in Baldwin, N.Y.; daughter of Lester H. (a salesman) and Gloria (Bennett)

Goldberg; married Phillip Cavan, June 10, 1957 (divorced 1966); children: Adam. *Education:* University of California, Los Angeles, B.A., 1959, M.A., 1961; University of California, Berkeley, Ph.D., 1965. *Home:* 1283 Page St., San Francisco, Calif. *Office:* Department of Sociology, San Fransisco State University, San Francisco, Calif.

CAREER: San Francisco State University, San Francisco, Calif., 1965—, professor of sociology, 1974—. *Member:* American Sociological Association, Society for the Study of Social Problems, Pacific Sociological Association.

WRITINGS: Liquor License: An Ethnography of Bar Behavior, Aldine, 1966; *Hippies of the Haight*, New Critics, 1972.

AVOCATIONAL INTERESTS: Knitting, embroidery.

* * *

CAVANAUGH, Arthur   1926-

PERSONAL: Surname legally changed; born April 9, 1926, in Woodhaven, N.Y.; son of Peter F. (a businessman) and Anne (Menahan) Fuchs; married Mary Josephine Carroll; children: Maria Teresa, Francis Joseph. *Education:* Attended College of William and Mary, 1944. *Politics:* Democrat. *Religion:* Roman Catholic. *Agent:* Phyllis Jackson, Ashley Famous Agency, Inc., 1301 Avenue of the Americas, New York, N.Y. 10019. *Office:* 342 Madison Ave., Room 1070-A, New York, N.Y.

CAREER: Actor with U.S.O. overseas company of "Junior Miss" and with road company of "Life with Father." Television playwright for national networks, 1953-59; Harcourt, Brace & World, Inc. (publishers), New York, N.Y., associate editor, 1960-63; *Sign* (magazine), Union City, N.J., drama critic, 1964—; author.

WRITINGS: My Own Back Yard (autobiography), Doubleday, 1962; *The Children Are Gone* (novel), Simon & Schuster, 1966; *Leaving Home* (novel), Simon & Schuster, 1970. Short story anthologized in *Prize Short Stories, 1965: The O. Henry Awards*; stories also have appeared in *McCall's, Redbook, Ladies' Home Journal*, and other magazines.†

* * *

CAVERS, David F(arquhar)   1902-

PERSONAL: First syllable of surname rhymes with "gave"; born September 3, 1902, in Buffalo, N.Y.; son of William Watt (a dentist) and Elizabeth (Farquhar) Cavers; married Lelia Yeaman, September 8, 1931; children: David F., Jr. *Education:* University of Pennsylvania, B.S., 1923; Harvard University, LL.B., 1926. *Politics:* Democrat. *Home:* 986 Memorial Dr., Cambridge, Mass. 02138. *Office:* Harvard Law School, Cambridge, Mass. 02138.

CAREER: Admitted to bar of New York State, 1928, and bar of Massachusetts, 1958; Harvard University, Cambridge, Mass., instructor, 1929-30; West Virginia University, College of Law, Morgantown, assistant professor, 1930-31; Duke University, School of Law, Durham, N.C., assistant professor, 1931-32, professor of law, 1932-45; Harvard University Law School, professor of law, 1945-69, Fessenden Professor of Law, 1952-69, professor emeritus, 1969—, associate dean, 1951-58, chairman of Graduate Division, 1965-69. Visiting professor of law at Yale University, 1936-37, and University of Chicago, 1940-41. U.S. Office of Price Administration, assistant general counsel, 1943-45, associate general counsel, 1945-46. Meyer Research Institute of Law, president, 1958-69; president,

Council on Law Related Studies, 1969—; U.S. delegate to Hague Conference on private international law, 1971-73.

MEMBER: American Bar Association, American Association for the Comparative Study of Law, American Society of International Law, Japanese American Society for Legal Studies (director, 1964—), American Academy of Arts and Sciences, Century Association (New York). *Awards, honors:* D.J.S., Suffolk University, 1957; LL.D., Chuo University, Tokyo, 1964.

WRITINGS: (With J. R. Nelson) *Electric Power Regulation in Latin America*, Johns Hopkins Press, 1959; *The Choice-of-Law Process*, University of Michigan Press, 1965; *Contemporary Conflicts: Law in American Perspective*, Hague Academy of Private International Law, 1970. Contributor to legal periodicals, legal education, and periodicals dealing with control of nuclear energy. Editor, *Law and Contemporary Problems*, 1933-43; member of board of editors, *Journal of Legal Education*, 1948-52.

WORK IN PROGRESS: Research in history of non-traditional law-related conflict in the United States.

* * *

CAWS, Peter (James)   1931-

PERSONAL: Born May 25, 1931, in Southall, England; son of Geoffrey Tulloh (an insurance man) and Olive (Budden) Caws; married Mary Ann Rorison (a professor of French), June 2, 1956; children: Hilary, Matthew. *Education:* University of London, B.Sc., 1952; Yale University, M.A., 1954, Ph.D., 1956. *Home:* 140 East 81st St., New York, N.Y. 10028. *Office:* Hunter College of the City University of New York, 695 Park Ave., New York, N.Y. 10021.

CAREER: Michigan State University, East Lansing, instructor in natural science, 1956-57; University of Kansas, Lawrence, assistant professor of philosophy, 1957-60, associate professor, 1960-62, chairman of department, 1961-62; Carnegie Corp. of New York (educational foundation), New York, N.Y., executive associate, 1962-65, consultant, 1965-67; Hunter College of the City University of New York, professor of philosophy and chairman of department, 1965-67; City University of New York, executive officer of doctoral program in philosophy, 1967-70. Visiting professor or lecturer at Wilmington College, 1956, and University of Costa Rica, 1961; Rose Morgan Visiting Professor at University of Kansas, 1963. *Member:* American Philosophical Association (member of board, 1974—), American Association for the Advancement of Science (vice-president, 1967; fellow), Philosophy of Science Association, Society for General Systems Research (president, 1966—), Association for Symbolic Logic. *Awards, honors:* American Council of Learned Societies fellowship, 1972-73.

WRITINGS: (Contributor) *Measurement: Definition and Theories*, Wiley, 1959; (contributor) *Six Studies in Nineteenth-Century Literature and Thought*, University of Kansas Press, 1962; *The Philosophy of Science: A Systematic Account*, Van Nostrand, 1965; (translator) J. M. Bochenski, *The Methods of Contemporary Thought*, Reidel (Netherlands), 1965; (contributor) *The Little Magazine and Contemporary Literature*, Modern Language Association, 1966; *Science and the Theory of Value*, Random House, 1967; (contributor) *The Concept of Order*, University of Washington Press, 1968; (contributor) *The Arts on Campus*, New York Graphic Society, 1970; (contributor) *The Enlightened University*, Braziller, 1970; (contributor) *Philosophy and Political Action*, Oxford University Press,

1972; (contributor) *The Bankruptcy of Academic Policy*, Acropolis, 1972. Contributor to philosophy journals.

WORK IN PROGRESS: Sartre, publication by Routledge & Kegan Paul in 1976.

SIDELIGHTS: Caws has a "functional command of French, elementary of Spanish, rudimentary of German."

* * *

CELNIK, Max 1933-

PERSONAL: Born June 15, 1933, in Berlin, Germany; came to United States in 1939; son of Leib Gitla (Schnall) Celnik; married Faith Caplan, March 25, 1958; children: Eli, Gerald. *Education:* Brooklyn College (now Brooklyn College of the City University of New York), B.A., 1955; Rutgers University, M.L.S., 1956; Jewish Theological Seminary of America, B.H.L., 1957. *Religion:* Jewish. *Home:* 2186 Cruger Ave., Bronx, N.Y. 10462. *Office:* Touro College, 30 West 44th St., New York, N.Y. 10036.

CAREER: New York (N.Y.) Public Library, research librarian, 1956-57; Congregation Shearith Israel (Spanish and Portuguese synagogue), New York, N.Y., chief librarian, 1956—; Yeshiva University, New York, N.Y., college librarian and instructor in library methodology, Stern College for Women, 1957-69, instructor in library administration, Graduate School of Education, 1958-60, director of libraries for Yeshiva University high schools, 1961-69; NCR Corp., PCMI Library Information System, New York, N.Y., managing editor and library consultant, 1969-72; Touro College, New York, N.Y., director of libraries, 1971—, law librarian, Law School, 1974—. Library consultant to United Synagogues of America, 1959-60, Federation of Jewish Philanthropies of New York, 1964—, Crowell-Collier-Macmillan Charitable Donations Program, 1966-74, Maimonides School for Exceptional Children, 1966-67, Mid-Island Hospital, 1967, Microlection Publishing Co., 1972-74. Organizer of libraries for religious schools, synagogues, and community centers; worked with Peace Corps, U.S. Navy Handclasp, and similar groups, to establish libraries in disadvantaged areas in America and abroad. Creator of Celnik Judaica Classification System for libraries.

MEMBER: Jewish Librarians Association (secretary, 1958-63), Association of Jewish Libraries (secretary, 1966—), American Association of University Professors (vice-president, Yeshiva University chapter, 1961-63), American Association of Law Librarians, American Library Association, Federation of Jewish Philanthropies of New York. *Awards, honors:* Citation of Merit for distinguished service in fostering Judaica libraries in social welfare agencies, Federation of Jewish Philanthropies of New York, 1965.

WRITINGS: The Synagogue Library: Organization and Administration, United Synagogue of America, 1960, 2nd edition, 1968; *A Basic Booklist for Synagogue and School Libraries*, United Synagogue of America, (compiler with Isaac Celnik) *A Bibliography on Judaism and Jewish Christian Relations: A Selected Annotated Listing of Works on Jewish Faith and Life, and the Jewish Christian Encounter*, B'nai B'rith, 1965; (bibliographer) *Jews in American Life*, B'nai B'rith, 1967; (editor) *Physician's Book Compendium: 1969-70*, Physician's Book Compendium, 1970; *How to Organize and Administer the "Y," Camp, Hospital, and Synagogue Library*, Federation of Jewish Philanthropies of Greater New York, 1974. Contributor to scholarly journals. Author of "Library Corner," a column in *Jewish Principal*, 1961.

CENCI, Louis 1918-

PERSONAL: Surname is pronounced Chensy; born October 12, 1918, in Jersey City, N.J.; son of Joseph and Adelina (Fiorentino) Cenci; married Marie Louise Major, December 1, 1940; children: Louis Pierre, Mamise. *Education:* New York University, B.S., 1959; Hunter College (now Hunter College of the City University of New York), M.S., 1962. *Home:* 110 Lily Pond Ave., Staten Island, N.Y. 10305. *Office:* Advisory Board for Vocational Education, Board of Education, 110 Livingston St., Brooklyn, N.Y. 11201.

CAREER: Industrial electrician, 1935-47; Ford Motor Co., supervisor, 1947-49; New York (N.Y.) public schools, teacher, 1949-55; New York State Department of Education, industrial teacher trainer, 1955-65; guidance counselor, 1960-65; Board of Education, Advisory Board for Vocational Education, Brooklyn, N.Y., executive secretary, 1966—. Educational consultant to industry, 1957—. Member of advisory board, Doctors Hospital and Community National Bank (both Staten Island); trustee, Staten Island Museum. *Member:* American Society for Training and Development, American Vocational Association.

WRITINGS: (With G. G. Weaver) *Applied Teaching Techniques*, Pitman, 1960, 2nd edition, 1968; *Skill Training for the Job*, Pitman, 1966.†

* * *

CERMINARA, Gina

PERSONAL: Born in Milwaukee, Wis.; daughter of Angelo (a lawyer) and Alma (Heuel) Cerminara. *Education:* University of Wisconsin, B.A., M.A., and Ph.D., receiving doctorate in 1943. *Residence:* Virginia Beach, Va.

CAREER: Latin-American Institute, New York, N.Y., teacher of speech, psychology, and Italian, 1945-46; freelance teacher of general semantics, 1950—. Lecturer on parapsychology and general semantics in United States and abroad; writer. Member of board of directors, Animal Protection Institute of America. *Member:* International Society for General Semantics, Humane Society of the United States, Pet Pride (Los Angeles).

WRITINGS: Italian for Students of Singing, privately published, 1942; *Many Mansions*, Sloane, 1950; *The World Within*, Sloane, 1957; *Many Lives, Many Loves*, Sloane, 1963; *Insights for the Age of Aquarius*, Prentice-Hall, 1973. Author of foreword, Gladys Jones, *The Flowering Tree*, Sloane, 1965, and Richard Calore, *In Defense of Cats*, Voice of the Voiceless, 1965. Editor, *Bulletin of Association for Research and Enlightenment*, 1945-46; associate editor, *Journal of Communication*, 1959-60.

WORK IN PROGRESS: Continued research in parapsychology and general semantics.

SIDELIGHTS: Cerminara speaks Italian, Spanish, and French. *Avocational interests:* Intercultural relations, cats and animal welfare, music, comparative religion, unidentified flying objects.

* * *

CHAMBERS, Edward J(ames) 1925-

PERSONAL: Born April 18, 1925, in Vancouver, British Columbia, Canada; son of James and Anne C. (Bannan) Chambers; married Elizabeth Ross (a religious education director), October 7, 1945; children: Neil J., Paul E., R. Scott, Anne E., Justine E. *Education:* University of British

Columbia, B.Comm., 1945, B.A., 1946, M.A., 1947; University of Nebraska, Ph.D., 1953. *Religion:* Unitarian Universalist. *Office:* Department of Business Administration, University of Alberta, Alberta D0600, Canada.

CAREER: Whitman College, Walla Walla, Wash., instructor in economics, 1947-51; Canadian Department of Trade and Commerce, Ottawa, Ontario, economist, 1953-55; Rutgers University, Newark Campus, Newark, N.J., lecturer in economics, 1955-56; Prudential Insurance Co., Newark, N.J., economist, 1955-56; Montana State University, Missoula, director of Bureau of Business and Economic Research, 1956-60; University of Washington, Seattle, 1960-68 began as associate professor, became professor of business administration; University of Alberta, Edmonton, professor and dean of faculty of business administration and commerce, 1969—. Visiting professor, Markerere University, 1968-69; former president of Puget Sound Unitarian Universalist Council. *Member:* American Economic Society, Royal Economic Society, Canadian Political Science Association.

WRITINGS: Economic Fluctuations and Forecasting, Prentice-Hall, 1961; (co-author) *National Income Analysis and Forecasting,* Scott, Foresman, 1975.

*   *   *

CHAMBERS, R(aymond) J(ohn) 1917-

PERSONAL: Born November 16, 1917, in Newcastle, New South Wales, Australia; son of Joseph and Louisa (Mogg) Chambers; married Margaret Scott Brown, September 9, 1939; children: Margaret (Mrs. M. E. Kaye), Rosemary (Mrs. J. H. Pearce), Kevin. *Education:* University of Sydney, B.Ec., 1939. *Home:* 18 Amy St., Blakehurst, New South Wales, Australia. *Office:* University of Sydney, Sydney, New South Wales 2006, Australia.

CAREER: Held various commercial, industrial, and government positions until 1945; Sydney Technical College, Sydney, New South Wales, Australia, lecturer, School of Management, 1945-52; University of Sydney, Sydney, New South Wales, Australia, senior lecturer, 1953-55, associate professor, 1955-59, professor of accounting, 1960—. Director, The Nestle Company (Australia) Ltd., 1967—. Visiting professor at University of Chicago, 1962, University of California, Berkeley, 1966, University of Washington, 1967, University of Florida, 1970, University of Kansas, 1970, University of Waseda (Tokyo), 1971. University Cooperative Bookshop Ltd., chairman of board and director, 1958-65. *Member:* Australian Society of Accountants (division councillor, 1964—; general councillor, 1972—), Chartered Institute of Secretaries, American Accounting Association, Academy of the Social Sciences in Australia, Australasian Association of University Teachers of Accounting (president, 1960-61; member of executive, 1960-65). *Awards, honors:* Australian Institute of Certified Public Accountants gold medal for *Accounting Evaluation and Economic Behavior,* 1967; D.Sc.Econ., University of Sydney, 1973.

WRITINGS: Financial Management, Law Book Co. of Australasia, 1947, 3rd revised edition, 1967; *Function and Design of Company Annual Reports,* Law Book Co. of Australia, 1955; *Accounting and Action,* Law Book Co. of Australasia, 1957, revised edition, 1966; (co-editor and contributor) *The Accounting Frontier,* F. W. Cheshire, 1965; *Accounting Evaluation and Economic Behavior,* Prentice-Hall, 1966; *Accounting, Finance, and Management,* Butterworth, 1969; *Securities and Obscurities,* Gower Press,

1973. Contributor to accounting journals in Australia and abroad. Editor, *Abacus,* 1965—.

*   *   *

CHAMPION, John C(arr) 1923-

PERSONAL: Born October 13, 1923, in Denver, Colo.; son of Lee Rogers (a judge) and Alice Champion; married Madelon F. Green, January 27, 1951; children: John, Jr., Robert, Gina. *Education:* Attended Stanford University, 1941-42, 1945; additional study at Wittenburg College. *Agent:* Paul R. Reynolds, Inc., 599 Fifth Ave., New York, N.Y. 10017.

CAREER: Did some radio work and was in stock at Metro Goldwyn Mayer Studios, briefly; co-pilot for Western Airlines, 1943; writer-producer for motion pictures and television, 1946—; worked as writer and producer for Allied Artists, vice-president in charge of production for Commander Films Corp., president, Champion Pictures, Inc., and as writer and producer for Metro Goldwyn Mayer, Warner Brothers and Paramount; executive writer and producer of "Laramie," series for Universal-National Broadcasting Co., 1959-62; creator of "McHale's Navy" for Universal-American Broadcasting Co., 1963. *Military service:* U.S. Army Air Forces, Air Transport Command, 1943-45; became flight officer. *Member:* National Academy of Television Arts and Sciences, Screen Writers Guild, Screen Producers Guild, Society of Independent Motion Picture Producers, Screen Actors Guild.

WRITINGS: The Hawks of Noon (novel), McKay, 1965.

Screenplays: "Panhandle," Allied Artists, 1948; "Stampede," Allied Artists, 1949; "Hellgate," Allied Artists, 1952; "Dragonfly Squadron," Allied Artists, 1954; "Shotgun," Allied Artists, 1955; (with Arthur Hailey and Hall Bartlet) "Zero Hour," Paramount, 1958; "The Texican," Columbia, 1966; "Attack on the Iron Coast," United Artists, 1968; "Submarine X-1," United Artists, 1969; "The Last Escape," United Artists, 1970; "Brother of the Wind," Sun International, 1972.

WORK IN PROGRESS: A play.†

*   *   *

CHANDA, Asok Kumar 1902-

PERSONAL: Born October 25, 1902, in India; son of Kamini Kumar and Chandraprabha Chanda; married Monica Gupta, 1928; children: two daughters. *Education:* Educated at Calcutta University and London School of Economics and Political Science. *Home:* 54e Sujan Singh Park, New Delhi 3, India.

CAREER: Entered Indian government service, with Audit and Accounts Branch, New Delhi, 1926; deputy high commissioner for India in London, England, 1948-49; financial commissioner for railways, 1949-52; secretary, Ministry of Production, 1952-54; comptroller and auditor general of India, 1954-60; chairman of Finance Commission, 1961-62, of Central Excise Reorganization Committee, 1961-63, and of Committee on Broadcasting and Information Media, 1965—. First chairman of Hindustan Steel and Hindustan Machine Tools, 1953; chairman of Sindhri Fertilizers, 1953, Jessop & Co. Ltd. (engineers), 1960—, Bolani Ores, 1962, Industrial & Economic Consultants International Pvt. Ltd., 1963, and Modella Cottons, 1965. Director of Union Carbon India Ltd., Modella Woolens, Titaghur Paper Mills, and Bisra Stone Lime Co. Member of Lend-Lease delegation to United States, 1946, and other Indian delegations to United Kingdom and Europe. Visiting professor, Indian Institute of Public Administration, New Delhi, 1964-65. *Awards, honors:* Officer, Order of the British Empire.

WRITINGS: Indian Administration, Allen & Unwin, 1958, 2nd edition, 1967; *Aspects of Audit Control*, Asia Publishing House (Bombay), 1960; *Public Enterprises in India* (Franco Memorial Lectures), Madras University Press, 1960; *Federalism in India*, Allen & Unwin, 1965; *Under the Indian Sky*, Nachiketa Publications (Bombay), 1971. Contributor to newspapers and magazines.

AVOCATIONAL INTERESTS: Golf, swimming, and photography.†

* * *

CHANDLER, Caroline A(ugusta) 1906-

PERSONAL: Born December 7, 1906, in Ford City, Pa.; daughter of Andrew Hartupee (an executive of a plate glass company) and Lucile Isobel (Brown) Chandler. *Education:* Attended University of Pittsburgh, 1924-27; Barnard College, A.B., 1929; Yale University, M.D. (cum laude), 1933. *Religion:* Roman Catholic. *Home and office:* 4977 Battery Lane, Bethesda, Md. 20014. *Agent:* William T. Snyder, 879 Park Ave., Baltimore, Md.

CAREER: Diplomate of National Board of Medical Examiners, American Board of Pediatrics, and American Board of Preventive Medicine and Public Health. New Haven Hospital, New Haven, Conn., intern, 1933-34; Children's Hospital, Boston, Mass., assistant in Medical Service, 1934-36; Harvard University, Medical School, Boston, Mass., research fellow, 1934-36, assistant in bacteriology, 1936-39; Johns Hopkins University, Medical School, Baltimore, research fellow in pediatrics, 1939-41, instructor in preventive medicine, 1941-43; U.S. Department of Labor, Children's Bureau, Washington, D.C., specialist, 1943-44; Johns Hopkins University, assistant professor of preventive medicine and instructor in pediatrics, Medical School, 1946-53, assistant professor of pediatrics, Medical School, 1953-72, assistant professor emeritus, 1972—, instructor in mental hygiene, School of Hygiene and Public Health, 1960-72. Chief, Center for Studies of Mental Health of Children and Youth, 1954-57; medical director, Family and Children's Society, 1954-57. Maryland State Department of Health, chief, Division of Maternal and Child Health, and acting chief, Division of Mental Health, 1957-59, chief, Office of Mental Health and Child Health, 1959-61. Consultant to National Institute of Mental Health, 1961-68, Project Headstart, 1968-71, and Children's Hospital, Washington, D.C., 1968—. *Military service:* U.S. Public Health Service Reserve, 1944—; active duty as surgeon, National Institutes of Health, 1944-45; current rank, medical director.

MEMBER: American Academy of Pediatrics (fellow), Society for Pediatric Research (fellow), American Public Health Association (fellow), American College of Preventive Medicine (fellow), American Orthopsychiatric Association, Royal Society of Health (England), Maryland Psychiatric Association (associate), Maryland Association for Mental Health (member of board), Medical and Chirurgical Faculty of State of Maryland, Phi Beta Kappa, Sigma Xi. *Awards, honors:* Superior Work Performance Award from U.S. Public Health Service, 1968.

WRITINGS: Susie Stuart, M.D., Dodd, 1941; *Susie Stuart, Home Front Doctor*, Dodd, 1943; (with Marion L. Faegre) *Your Child From One to Six*, revised edition, U.S.

Government Printing Office, 1945; *Dr. Kay Winthrop, Intern*, Dodd, 1947; *Famous Men of Medicine*, Dodd, 1950; *Phenylketonuria: An Annotated Bibliography*, National Institute of Mental Health, 1961; *Famous Modern Men of Medicine*, Dodd, 1966; (contributor) Laura L. Dittmann, editor, *Early Child Care: The New Perspectives*, Atherton, 1968; (with S. H. Kempf) *Nursing as a Career*, Dodd, 1970.

Contributor to *World Book Encyclopedia*, and more than seventy articles and papers to *Current Therapy* and other medical publications. Member of editorial board, *Yale Journal of Biology and Medicine*, 1931-33, *American Journal of Orthopsychiatry*, 1966—; medical columnist, *Catholic Woman's World*, 1939-42; contributing editor, *Child Health Farm Journal*, and *Farmer's Wife*, 1946-60.

WORK IN PROGRESS: Research for *Biography of Gardner Murphy.*

AVOCATIONAL INTERESTS: Literature, music (classical and modern), art, swimming, horseback riding, and sailing.†

* * *

CHANDLER, Margaret Kueffner 1922-

PERSONAL: Born September 30, 1922, in St. Paul, Minn.; daughter of Otto Carl (a chemist) and Marie (Schaedlich) Kueffner; married Louis Chandler (a professor of physics), April 8, 1943. *Education:* University of Chicago, B.A., 1942, M.A., 1944, Ph.D., 1948. *Home:* 560 Riverside Dr., New York, N.Y. 10027. *Office:* Graduate School of Business, Columbia University, New York, N.Y. 10027.

CAREER: University of Illinois, Urbana Campus, instructor, 1948-49, assistant professor, 1949-54, associate professor, 1954-62, Chicago Division, associate professor, 1962-63, professor of sociology, 1963-65; Columbia University, New York, N.Y., professor of business, 1965—. Fulbright research professor, Keio University, Tokyo, Japan, 1963-64; visiting lecturer, McGill University, 1963, Emory University, 1966, Michigan State University, 1970, Tel Aviv University, 1971. *Member:* American Sociological Association (fellow), American Economic Association, Society for Applied Anthropology (fellow), Industrial Relations Research Association, American Statistical Association, American Arbitration Association, Phi Beta Kappa. *Awards, honors:* Postdoctoral fellowship in statistics, Yale University, 1953-54; Ford Foundation faculty research fellowship, 1960-61; associate, Center for Advanced Study, University of Illinois Graduate College, 1964-65; McKinsey Foundation Book Award for best book in the field of management, 1965, for *Management Rights and Union Interests,* Ford Foundation grant, 1967.

WRITINGS: (With W. E. Chalmers and Milton Derber) *Labor-Management Relations in Illini City*, Institute of Labor and Industrial Relations, University of Illinois, Volume I, 1953, Volume II, 1954; (editor with H. Heneman) *Employment Relations Research*, Harper, 1960; *Management Rights and Union Interests*, McGraw, 1964.; (contributor) J. T. Dunlop and N. W. Chamberlain, editors, *Frontiers of Collective Bargaining*, Harper, 1967; (with Leonard R. Sayles) *Managing Large Systems: Organizations for the Future*, Harper, 1971. Contributor of articles to professional journals. Editor-in-chief, *Columbia Journal of World Business*, 1972—.

WORK IN PROGRESS: A book on the Japanese system of subcontracting, based on field work in more than seventy large industrial firms in Japan.†

CHAPMAN, Samuel Greeley 1929-

PERSONAL: Born September 29, 1929, in Atlanta, Ga.; son of Calvin C. (a stock broker) and Jane (Greeley) Chapman; married Patricia Hepfer, June 19, 1949; children: Lynn Randall, Deborah Jane. *Education:* University of California, Berkeley, B.A., 1951, M.A., 1959. *Politics:* Republican. *Religion:* Protestant. *Office:* Department of Political Science, University of Oklahoma, Norman, Okla. 73069.

CAREER: Berkeley Police Department, Berkeley, Calif., undercover agent in Vice Division, 1950-51, patrolman, 1951-56; Public Administration Service, Chicago, Ill., police consultant, 1956-59; Michigan State University, East Lansing, assistant professor, School of Police Administration and Public Safety, 1959-63; Multnomah County Sheriff's Police Department, Portland, Ore., chief 1963-65; U.S. Department of Justice, Washington, D.C., assistant director, President's Commission on Law Enforcement and Administration of Justice, 1965-67; University of Oklahoma, Norman, professor of political science, 1967—. Member of Norman, Okla. City Council, 1972—, mayor pro-tempore, 1974. Consultant on police service, fire protection, and other matters of municipal government to more than fifty cities in United States and Canada. *Member:* International Association of Chiefs of Police, Lambda Alpha Epsilon, Alpha Delta Phi, Alpha Phi Sigma.

WRITINGS: Dogs in Police Work: A Summary of Experience in Great Britain and the United States, Public Administration Service, 1960; (contributor) *Municipal Police Administration,* 5th edition, International City Managers' Association, 1961; (with Sir Eric Johnson) *The Police Heritage in England and America,* Michigan State University, 1962; (editor) *Police Patrol Readings,* C. C Thomas, 1964, 2nd edition, 1970; (contributor) William Hewitt, *British Police Administration,* C. C Thomas, 1965; (with Donald E. Clark) *A Forward Step: Educational Backgrounds for Police,* Springfield, Ill., 1966; (with others) *Perspectives on Assaults on Police in the South Central United States,* University of Oklahoma Bureau of Government Research, 1974.

AVOCATIONAL INTERESTS: Bridge, fly fishing, and softball.

* * *

CHAPPELL, Warren 1904-

PERSONAL: Born July 9, 1904, in Richmond, Va.; son of Samuel M. (a railway clerk) and Mary L. (Hardie) Chappell; married Lydia A. Hatfield, August 28, 1928. *Education:* University of Richmond, B.A., 1926; studied art at Art Students League, New York, N.Y., 1926-28, Offenbacher Werkstatt in Germany, 1931-32, and Colorado Springs Fine Arts Center, 1935-36. *Politics:* Independent. *Religion:* Protestant. *Home:* James St., Norwalk, Conn. 06850.

CAREER: Designer, graphic artist, and illustrator. Art Students League, member of board of control, 1927-31; instructor at Art Students League, New York, N.Y., 1933-35, at Colorado Springs Fine Arts Center, Colorado Springs, Colo., 1935-36; lecturer at New York University, New York, N.Y. Consultant to Book-of-the-Month Club, 1944—. *Member:* Phi Beta Kappa. *Awards, honors:* Doctor of Fine Arts, University of Richmond, 1968; Goudy Award from Rochester Institute of Technology, 1970.

WRITINGS: The Anatomy of Lettering, Loring & Mus-

sey, 1935; *Sixty-Three Drawings by Warren Chappell,* privately printed, 1955; *They Say Stories,* Knopf, 1960; *A Short History of the Printed Word: A New York Times Book,* Knopf, 1970.

Adapter: *The Nutcracker* (music by Tchaikovsky), Knopf, 1958; *The Sleeping Beauty* (music by Tchaikovsky), Knopf, 1961; *Coppelia* (music by Delibes), Knopf, 1965.

Illustrator: *Tom Jones,* Illustrated Modern Library, 1943; *The Tragedies of Shakespeare,* Illustrated Modern Library; *The Complete Novels of Jane Austen,* two volumes, Random House, 1950; Geoffrey Household, *Prisoner of the Indies,* Little, Brown, 1968. Contributor to *Virginia Quarterly Review, Dolphin,* and other periodicals.

BIOGRAPHICAL/CRITICAL SOURCES: American Artist, October, 1944; *Sixty-Three Drawings by Warren Chappell,* privately printed, 1955; *Publisher's Weekly,* October 1, 1955.

* * *

CHARI, V. Krishna 1924-

PERSONAL: Born November 28, 1924, in Samalkot, India; son of Ramanuja V. and Krishnamma Chari; married Vasantha, 1945; children: Ranga Ramanuja (son), Pramila (daughter). *Education:* Banaras Hindu University, B.A., 1944, M.A., 1946, Ph.D., 1950. *Religion:* Hindu. *Home:* 121 Norice St., Ottawa K2G 2YI, Canada. *Office:* Department of English, Carleton University, Ottawa K1S 5B6, Canada.

CAREER: Indian Government Educational Service, Madhya Pradesh, assistant professor of English, 1950-62; Banaras Hindu University, Varanasi, India, reader in English, 1962-66; Carleton University, Ottawa, Ontario, professor of English, 1966—. Visiting professor, State University of New York College at New Paltz, 1960-61. *Member:* P.E.N. (India). *Awards, honors:* Fulbright fellowship, 1959-61; Canada Council scholarship, 1972-73.

WRITINGS: Whitman in the Light of Vedantic Mysticism, University of Nebraska Press, 1964. Contributor to *Western Humanities Review, Walt Whitman Review, Journal of Aesthetics and Art Criticism, Journal of American Studies,* and to journals in India.

WORK IN PROGRESS: A book on Sanskrit poetics from a comparative standpoint.

AVOCATIONAL INTERESTS: Classical Indian dancing, drums, Vedic recitation, and contemporary theater.

* * *

CHARTERS, Ann (Danberg) 1936-

PERSONAL: Born November 10, 1936, in Bridgeport, Conn.; daughter of Nathan (a contractor) and Kate (Schultz) Danberg; married Samuel Barclay Charters (an ethnomusicologist and writer), March 10, 1959; children: Mallay, Nora Lili. *Education:* University of California, Berkeley, B.A., 1957; Columbia University, M.A., 1959, Ph.D., 1965. *Office:* University of Connecticut, Storrs, Conn. 06268.

CAREER: Colby Junior College, New London, N.H., teacher of creative writing, 1961-63; Random House-Knopf (publishers), New York, N.Y., assistant editor, 1965; Columbia University, New York, N.Y., instructor in literature, 1965-66; New York City Community College, Brooklyn, N.Y., assistant professor of English, 1967-70; University of Connecticut, Storrs, Conn., associate professor, 1974—. Pianist featured on records, "Essay in Ragtime," issued by Folkways, and "A Scott Joplin Bouquet" and "Treemonisha: The First Negro Folk Opera," both issued by Portents. *Member:* International P.E.N., Phi Beta Kappa.

WRITINGS: The Ragtime Songbook, Oak, 1965; (editorial assistant) Perry Bradford, *Born with the Blues*, Oak, 1965; *Nobody: The Life and Times of Bert Williams*, Oak, 1966; *A Bibliography of Works by Jack Kerouac*, Phoenix Bibliographies, 1967; *Olson/Melville: A Study in Affinity*, Oyez, 1968; *Melville in the Berkshires: A Construct*, Portents, 1969; *Charles Olson: The Special View of History*, Oyez, 1970; (with Allen Ginsberg) *Scenes Along the Road*, (photographs, text, and poems), Gotham Book Mart, 1970; (editor) *Scattered Poems by Jack Kerouac*, City Lights, 1971; *Nobody: The Story of Bert Williams*, Macmillan, 1970; *Kerouac: A Biography*, Straight Arrow, 1973.

* * *

CHASE, Gilbert 1906-

PERSONAL: Born September 4, 1906, in Havana, Cuba; son of Gilbert P. (a commander, U.S. Navy) and Edelmira (Culmell) Chase; married Kathleen Barnetzen (a writer), December 27, 1929; children: Paul T., Peter G., John E. *Education:* Attended Columbia University, 1926; University of North Carolina, B.A., 1950; private study of music with Max Wald, Paris, France. *Residence:* Guilford, Conn. *Office:* Yearbook, Richardson Hall, University of Texas, Austin, Tex. 78712.

CAREER: Daily Mail, Paris, France, music critic, 1929-35; *International Cyclopedia of Music and Musicians*, New York, N.Y., associate editor, 1936-38; G. Schirmer, Inc., New York, N.Y., editor, 1939-40; U.S. Library of Congress, Washington, D.C., Latin American specialist, Music Division, 1940-43; National Broadcasting Co. music supervisor, University of the Air, 1943-48; RCA Victor, Camden, N.J., manager of education department, 1948-49; cultural attache of American Embassy, Lima, Peru, 1951-53, Buenos Aires, Argentina, 1953-55; University of Oklahoma, Norman, director of School of Music, 1955-56, acting dean of College of Fine Arts, 1956-57; American Embassy, Brussels, Belgium, cultural attache, 1958-60; Tulane University of Louisiana, New Orleans, professor of Latin American studies, 1960-66; Brooklyn College of the City University of New York, Brooklyn, New York, Institute for Studies in American Music, senior research fellow, 1972-73; State University of New York, Buffalo, visiting professor, 1973-74; University of Texas, Austin, visiting professor of comparative studies, 1975-76. Columbia University, lecturer on history of American music, 1946-48. U.S. Department of State, member of advisory committee on music, 1943-45; Pan American Union, music consultant, 1943-45; U.S. Advisory Committee on Cultural Information, member, 1957-60; Inter-American Music Council, president, 1960-64; National Music Council, member of Bicentennial committee, 1975-76. Book-of-the-Month Club, adviser and reviewer, 1938-49. *Member:* Association for Latin American Studies, American Musicological Society, Music Library Association, Society for Ethnomusicology. *Awards, honors:* D.Litt., University of Miami, 1955.

WRITINGS: Cities and Souls: Poems of Spain, Durand (Chartres), 1929; *The Music of Spain*, Norton, 1941, 2nd edition, Dover, 1959; *A Guide to the Music of Latin America*, Library of Congress, 1945, 2nd revised edition, Pan American Union, 1962; (editor) *Music in Radio Broadcast-*

ing, McGraw, 1946; *America's Music: From the Pilgrims to the Present*, McGraw, 1955, 3rd edition, University of Illinois Press, 1976; (contributor) J. J. Johnson, editor, *Continuity and Change in Latin America*, Stanford University Press, 1964; (editor) *The American Composer Speaks*, Louisiana State University Press, 1966; *A Concise Cultural History of Latin America*, Praeger, 1966; *Contemporary Art in Latin America*, Free Press, 1971; *Two Lectures in the Form of a Pair*, Brooklyn College of the City University of New York, 1973. Paris correspondent, *Musical America*, 1930-35, and *Musical Times* (London), 1931-35; music editor, *Handbook of Latin American Studies*, 1941-43, 1963-65, and *Inter-American Magazine*, 1940-43; contributing editor, *Arts in Society*, 1968—.

SIDELIGHTS: Chase speaks Spanish, French, and Italian.

* * *

CHECKLAND, S(ydney) G(eorge) 1916-

PERSONAL: Born October 9, 1916, in Ottawa, Ontario, Canada; son of Sydney Tom (a journalist) and Fanny Selina (Mason) Checkland; married Edith Olive Anthony (an extramural lecturer), September 11, 1942; children: John Anthony, Stephen Francis, Edith Deborah, Sydney Clare, Sarah Jane. *Education:* University of Birmingham, B.Comm. (first class honors), 1941, M.Comm., 1946; University of Liverpool, Ph.D., 1953; Cambridge University, M.A., 1953. *Home:* 2 Queen's Pl., Glasgow, Scotland. *Office:* Department of Economic History, University of Glasgow, Glasgow, Scotland.

CAREER: University of Liverpool, Liverpool, England, 1946-53, began as assistant lecturer, became senior lecturer in economic science; Cambridge University, Cambridge, England, university lecturer in history, 1953-57, lector in history at Trinity College, 1955-57; University of Glasgow, Glasgow, Scotland, professor of economic history, 1957—. Member of Institute for Advanced Study, Princeton, N.J., 1960, 1964. Chairman of National Register of Archives of Scotland; vice-chairman of Scottish Business Archives Council; vice-president of Scottish Labour History Committee; member of Scottish Records Advisory Council. *Military service:* British and Canadian Armies, 1942-45. *Member:* Economic History Society (council).

WRITINGS: The Rise of Industrial Society in England, 1815-1885, St. Martins, 1964; *The Mines of Tharsis: Roman, French, and British Enterprise in Spain*, Allyn & Unwin, 1967; *The Gladstones: Family Biography*, Cambridge University Press, 1971; *A Social and Economic History of England*, Longman, 1971. Also editor with wife, E. O. Checkland, *The Poor Law Report of 1834*. Contributor of articles and reviews to professional journals.

WORK IN PROGRESS: Scottish Banking: A History, 1695-1973; The Economic Context of History.

* * *

CHEN, Kenneth K(uan-) S(heng) 1907-

PERSONAL: Born September 20, 1907, in Honolulu, Hawaii; son of Hua-hsiu (a farmer) and Shih (Chu) Chen; married Chao-ying Tan, August 3, 1935 (deceased); married Man Hing Y. Mok, June 12, 1970; children: Sylvia (Mrs. Clarence Shangraw), Leighton. *Education:* University of Hawaii, B.A., 1931; Yenching University, M.A., 1934; University of California, Berkeley, graduate study, 1940-41; Harvard University, Ph.D., 1946. *Religion:* "Protestant Christianity." *Home:* 969 Hilgard Ave., Los Angeles, Calif. 90024. *Office:* Department of Oriental Languages, University of California at Los Angeles, Los Angeles, Calif. 90024.

CAREER: University of Hawaii, Honolulu, instructor in Chinese, 1936-40; Yenching University, Peking, China, professor of history, 1947-50; Harvard University, Cambridge, Mass., lecturer in Far Eastern languages, 1950-58; University of California, Los Angeles, professor of Oriental languages, 1958-61, acting chairman of department of Oriental languages, 1959-61; Princeton University, Princeton, N.J., professor of Buddhism, 1961-68, William H. Danforth Professor of Religion, 1968-71; University of California at Los Angeles, professor of Buddhism and chairman of department of Oriental languages, 1971—. Harvard Yenching Institute, assistant director, 1947-50, and concurrently executive secretary of Peking office of the Institute; Kyoto University, Fulbright research scholar and Guggenheim fellow, 1964-65. Special consultant to Rockefeller Foundation on Tibetan Studies, 1959. *Member:* Association for Asian Studies, American Oriental Society, American Society for the Study of Religion, Phi Beta Kappa. *Awards, honors:* Grant-in-aid for research, American Council of Learned Societies, 1960; Lindback Award for distinguished teaching, Princeton University, 1963; Guggenheim fellowship, 1964-65; McCosh faculty fellowship, 1970-71.

WRITINGS: Buddhism in China: A Historical Survey, Princeton University Press, 1964; *Buddhism: Light of the East*, Barron's, 1967; *The Chinese Transformation of Buddhism*, Princeton University Press, 1973. Contributor to professional journals and *Encyclopaedia Britannica*. Member of editorial board, *Yenching Journal of Chinese Studies*, 1947-50, and *Tsinghua Journal of Chinese Studies*, 1960—.

WORK IN PROGRESS: The Buddhist studies of Liang Ch'i-Ch'ao; a translation from Chinese of Ch'en Yuan, *Survey of Chinese Buddhist Literature*.

* * *

CHILES, Robert E(ugene) 1923-

PERSONAL: Born March 1, 1923, in Convoy, Ohio; son of Clarence Delmore and Alice (Smith) Chiles; children: Barbara Lynne. *Education:* Kent State University, A.B., 1944; Garrett Theological Seminary, B.D., 1947; Northwestern University, M.A., 1947; Columbia University, Ph.D., 1964. *Politics:* Independent. *Office:* Department of Religious Studies, Richmond College, Staten Island, N.Y. 10301.

CAREER: Concord Methodist Church, Dayton, Ohio, minister, 1950-60; Hunter College (now Hunter College of the City University of New York), New York, N.Y., adult education coordinator, 1960-64, assistant dean of general studies, 1964-67; Richmond College, Staten Island, N.Y., executive assistant to the president, 1967-68, associate professor of philosophy, 1968-72, professor of religious studies, 1972—, dean of students, 1968-72. *Member:* American Personnel and Guidance Association.

WRITINGS: (Editor with R. W. Burtner) *A Compend of Wesley's Theology*, Abingdon, 1954; *Theological Transition in American Methodism, 1790-1935*, Abingdon, 1964. Contributor to journals.†

CHINOY, Helen Krich 1922-

PERSONAL: Born September 25, 1922, in Newark, N.J.; daughter of Ben and Anne (Kalen) Krich; married Ely Chinoy (a professor at Smith College), June 6, 1948; children: Michael, Claire. *Education:* New York University, B.A., 1943, M.A., 1945; Columbia University, Ph.D., 1963. *Home:* 230 Crescent St., Northampton, Mass. 01060. *Office:* Smith College, Northampton, Mass. 01060.

CAREER: Instructor in English at Queens College, Flushing, N.Y., 1945-46, and at Rutgers University, Newark, N.J., 1946-48; McClelland & Stewart (publishers), Toronto, Ontario, Canada, editorial assistant, 1949-50; Smith College, Northampton, Mass., part-time instructor, 1952-55, full-time instructor, 1956-60, lecturer, 1965-68, associate professor of theatre, 1968—, head of department, 1968-71. Visiting lecturer, University of Leicester, 1963-64. *Member:* American Theatre Association, National Theatre Conference, American Society for Theatre Research, American Association of University Women, National League of Women Voters.

WRITINGS: (Editor with Toby Cole) *Actors on Acting*, Crown, 1949, revised edition, 1970; (editor with Toby Cole) *Directing the Play*, Bobbs-Merrill, 1953, revised edition (under title *Directors on Directing*), 1963; (contributor) *American Theatre: A Sum of its Parts*, Samuel French, 1971. Contributor of reviews and articles to theater periodicals and encyclopedias.

WORK IN PROGRESS: A study of the impact of the theatrical director on American plays, playwrights, and theaters, with special emphasis on Eugene O'Neill; a study of Group Theatre, background, experience and influence on American theatre.

AVOCATIONAL INTERESTS: Children's theater and puppetry.

* * *

CHODOROV, Stephan 1934-

PERSONAL: Born 1934, in Los Angeles, Calif. *Education:* Haverford College, B.A., 1956; attended University of Munich; Yale University, LL.B., 1960. *Address:* P.O. 298, New Milford, Conn.

CAREER: Staff writer for Columbia Broadcasting System weekly television program, "Camera Three," beginning, 1964; television producer, writer, director for documentary films and plays.

WRITINGS: A Criminal Case, Collier Books, 1964. Longer television documentaries and dramas written include: "The Judgement" (adaptation of Franz Kafka's story, "Das Urteil"); "In the Last Place"; "Out of the Ashes" (documentary on the history of the Jewish community of Holland); "Inspiration"; "At the Cafe Opera Buff"; "Colette By Herself" (dramatization of Collette's last work, *Le Fanal Bleu*); "Brecht on Shakespeare"; "In Search of Ezra Pound" (three-part dramatic series); "A Primer for '2001'"; "Portrait of Leni Riefenstahl"; "World of Paolo Soleri"; "The City in the Image of Man." Also author of industrial films, and of short plays for U.S. Department of Health, Education and Welfare.

* * *

CHOMSKY, A(vram) Noam 1928-

PERSONAL: Born December 7, 1928, in Philadelphia, Pa.; son of William (a teacher) and Elsie (Simonofsky)

Chomsky; married Carol Schatz, December 24, 1949; children: Aviva, Diane, Harry Alan. *Education:* University of Pennsylvania, B.A., 1949, M.A., 1951, Ph.D., 1955. *Politics:* Libertarian socialist. *Home:* 15 Suzanne Rd., Lexington, Mass. 02173. *Office:* Room 20C-128, Massachusetts Institute of Technology, Cambridge, Mass. 02139.

CAREER: Massachusetts Institute of Technology, Cambridge, assistant professor of linguistics, 1955-58, associate professor, 1958-62, professor, 1962-66, Ferrari Ward Professor of Modern Languages and Linguistics, 1966—. *Member:* National Academy of Sciences, American Academy of Arts and Sciences, Linguistic Society of America, American Philosophical Society, Association for Symbolic Logic, Academy of Political and Social Science, Aristotelian Society of Great Britain. *Awards, honors:* D.Litt., University of London, 1967; D.Hum.Litt., University of Chicago, 1967; D.Hum. Letters, Loyola University, 1970; Swarthmore College, 1970; D.Litt., Delhi University, 1972; Doc. of Hum. Letters, University of Massachusetts, 1973; Guggenheim fellowship, 1971-72.

WRITINGS: Syntactic Structures, Mouton & Co., 1957; *Current Issues in Linguistic Theory*, Mouton & Co., 1964; *Aspects of the Theory of Syntax*, M.I.T. Press, 1965; *Cartesian Linguistics*, Harper, 1966; *Topics in the Theory of Generative Grammar*, Mouton & Co., 1966; (with Morris Halle) *Sound Pattern of English*, Harper, 1968; *Language and Mind*, Harcourt, 1968; *American Power and the New Mandarins*, Pantheon, 1969; *At War With Asia*, Pantheon, 1970; *Problems of Knowledge and Freedom*, Pantheon, 1971; *Studies on Semantics in Generative Grammar*, Mouton & Co., 1972; *For Reasons of State,* Pantheon, 1973; (with Edward Herman) *Counterevolutionary Violence*, Warner Modular, Inc., 1973; *Peace in the Middle East?*, Pantheon, 1974; *Logical Structure of Linguistic Theory*, Plenum, in press. Contributor to *Ramparts, Liberation*, and to professional journals.

WORK IN PROGRESS: Essays in linguistics for various collections.

SIDELIGHTS: Aside from his revolutionary linguistic theories, Chomsky came forward in the late sixties as a spokesman against American intervention in the war in Vietnam. His collection of essays entitled *American Power and the New Mandarins* brought a wave of critical response. Martin Duberman wrote, "There is no shortage these days of critiques of American power, but Chomsky's formulation is quite special, and his tone—so free of exaggeration or misrepresentation—is all but unique. He avoids self-righteousness . . . is able to admit when a conclusion is uncertain or when the evidence allows for several possible conclusions. . . . These qualities—this integrity, gives unusual strength to Chomsky's writing."

While acknowledging Chomsky's distinction in the field of linguistics, Arthur Schlesinger, Jr., objected to Chomsky's political analysis. He wrote, "The Vietnam war drove Chomsky into the public arena; it has obviously been the formative experience in his political thought, and it provides the perspective through which he sees both the American past and the American future. He views this war not as the result of miscalculation or stupidity but as the expression of profound aggressive drives rooted in the American commercial and industrial system."

BIOGRAPHICAL/CRITICAL SOURCES: Nation, September 9, 1968; *Commentary*, May, 1969; *New Yorker*, November 11, 1969; John Lyons and Frank Kermode, *Noam Chomsky*, Viking, 1970.

CHRISTIE, Agatha (Mary Clarissa) 1890-
(Mary Westmacott)

PERSONAL: Born in 1890, in Torquay, Devon, England; daughter of Frederick Alvah and Clarissa Miller; married Archibald Christie (a colonel in Royal Air Corps), December 24, 1914 (divorced, 1928; died, 1962); married Max Edgar Lucien Mallowan (an archaeologist), September 11, 1930; children: (first marriage) Rosalind (married). *Education:* Tutored at home by her mother until age 16; later studied singing and piano in Paris. *Home:* Greenway House, Churston Ferrers, South Devon, England; and Winterbrook House, Wallingford, Oxfordshire, England; also resides intermittently in London, England. *Agent:* Hughes Massie Ltd., 69 Great Russell St., London W.C. 1, England.

CAREER: During World War I, served as Voluntary Aid Detachment (V.A.D.) nurse in a Red Cross Hospital, Torquay, South Devon, England; after divorce in 1928, traveled for several years; after marriage to Mallowan, 1930, helped him with tabulations and photography at his excavations in Iraq and Syria; during World War II, worked in dispensary for University College Hospital, London, England; during post-war 1940's helped Mallowan with excavation of Assyrian ruins. *Member:* Royal Society of Literature (fellow). *Awards, honors:* New York Drama Critics' Circle Award for best foreign play of the year, 1955, for *Witness for the Prosecution*; Commander of the British Empire, 1956, created Dame Film Daily Poll 10 Best Pictures award, 1958, for "Witness for the Prosecution"; D.Litt., University of Exeter.

WRITINGS—Novels; all published by Dodd, except as noted: *The Mysterious Affair at Styles*, Lane, 1920, Grosset, 1928; *The Secret Adversary*, 1922; *The Murder on the Links*, 1923; *The Man in the Brown Suit*, Lane, 1924, Dell, 1958; *The Secret of Chimneys*, 1925; *The Murder of Roger Ackroyd*, 1926; *The Big Four*, 1927; *Mystery of the Blue Train*, 1928; *Partners in Crime*, 1929; *The Seven Dials Mystery*, 1929; *Murder at the Vicarage*, 1930; *The Mysterious Mr. Quinn*, 1930; *The Murder at Hazelmoor*, 1931; *The Sittaford Mystery*, Collins, 1931; *Peril at End House*, 1932; *Thirteen at Dinner*, 1933 (published in England as *Lord Edgware Dies*, Collins, 1933); *Why Didn't They Ask Evans?*, Collins, 1934, published in America as *Boomerang Clue*, 1935; *Murder in the Calais Coach*, 1934 (published in England as *Murder on the Orient Express*, Collins, 1934); *Murder in Three Acts*, 1934 (published in England as *Three Act Tragedy*, Collins, 1935); *Death in the Air*, 1935 (published in England as *Death in the Clouds*, Collins, 1935); *The A.B.C. Murders*, 1936; *Cards on the Table*, Collins, 1936, 1937; *Murder in Mesopotamia*, 1936; *Death on the Nile*, Collins, 1937, 1938; *Dumb Witness*, Collins, 1937; *Poirot Loses a Client*, 1937; *Appointment With Death*, 1938; *Hercule Poirot's Christmas*, Collins, 1938, published as *Murder for Christmas*, 1939, and in paperback as *A Holiday for Murder*, New Avon Library, 1947; *Easy to Kill*, 1939 (published in England as *Murder is Easy*, Collins, 1939); *Ten Little Niggers*, Collins, 1939, published as *And Then There Were None*, 1940.

One, Two, Buckle My Shoe, Collins, 1940, published as *The Patriotic Murders*, 1941, and in paperback as *An Overdose of Death*, Dell, 1966; *Sad Cypress*, 1940; *Evil Under the Sun*, 1941; *N or M?*, 1941; *Body in the Library*, 1942; *Moving Finger*, 1942; *Murder in Retrospect*, 1942 (published in England as *Five Little Pigs*, Collins, 1943); *Death Comes as the End*, 1944; *Towards Zero*, 1944; *Remem-*

bered Death, 1945 (published in England as *Sparkling Cyanide*, Collins, 1945); *The Hollow*, 1946, published in paperback as *Murder After Hours*, Dell, 1961; *Murder Medley*, Harrap, 1948; *There is a Tide*, 1948 (published in England as *Taken at the Flood*, Collins, 1948); *Crooked House*, 1949; *A Murder is Announced*, 1950; *Blood Will Tell*, Black, 1951; *They Came to Baghdad*, 1951; *Murder With Mirrors*, 1952 (published in England as *They Do it With Mirrors*, Collins, 1952); *Mrs. McGinty's Dead*, 1952; *Funerals Are Fatal* (serialized in *Chicago Tribune* as "After the Funeral," beginning January 12, 1953), 1953 (published in England as *After the Funeral*, Collins, 1953); *Pocket Full of Rye*, Collins, 1953, 1954; *Destination Unknown*, Collins, 1954, published as *So Many Steps to Death*, 1955; *Hickory, Dickory, Death*, 1955 (published in England as *Hickory, Dickory, Dock*, Collins, 1955); *Dead Man's Folly*, 1956; *What Mrs. McGillicuddy Saw!* (serialized as "Eye Witness to Murder"), 1957 (published in England as *4:50 From Paddington*, Collins, 1957), also published as *Murder She Said*, Pocket Books, 1961; *Ordeal by Innocence*, 1958; *Cat Among the Pigeons*, 1959.

The Adventure of the Christmas Pudding, and Selection of Entrees, Collins, 1960; *The Pale Horse*, Collins, 1961, 1962; *The Mirror Crack'd from Side to Side*, Collins, 1962, published as *The Mirror Crack'd*, 1963; *The Clocks*, Collins, 1963, 1964; *A Caribbean Mystery*, Collins, 1964, 1965; *At Bertram's Hotel*, 1965; *Third Girl*, Collins, 1966, 1967; *Endless Night*, Collins, 1967, 1968; *By the Pricking of My Thumbs*, 1968; *Hallowe'en Party*, 1969; *Passenger to Frankfurt*, 1970; *Nemesis*, 1971; *Elephants Can Remember*, 1972; *Postern of Fate*, 1973; *Curtain*, 1975.

Short stories; all published by Dodd, except as noted: *Poirot Investigates*, Lane, 1924, 1925; *Thirteen Problems*, Collins, 1932, published as *Tuesday Club Murders*, 1933; *The Hound of Death, and Other Stories*, Odhams, 1933; *Mr. Parker Pyne, Detective*, 1934 (published in England as *Parker Pyne Investigates*, Collins, 1934); *The Listerdale Mystery, and Other Stories*, Collins, 1934; *Dead Man's Mirror, and Other Stories*, 1937 (published in England as *Murder in the Mews, and Other Stories*, Collins, 1937); *Regatta Mystery, and Other Stories*, 1939; *Mystery of the Blue Geranium, and Other Tuesday Club Murders* (abridged edition of stories originally published in *Tuesday Club Murders*), Bantam, 1940; *The Mystery of the Baghdad Chest*, Todd (London), 1943; *The Mystery of the Crime in Cabin 66*, Todd, 1943, reissued as *The Crime in Cabin 66*, Vallencey (London), 1944; *Poirot and the Regatta Mystery*, Todd, 1943; *Poirot on Holiday* (contains "The Regatta Mystery" and "The Crime in Cabin 66"), Todd, 1943; *Problem at Pollensa Bay [and] Christmas Adventure*, Todd, 1943; *The Veiled Lady [and] The Baghdad Chest*, Francis Hodgson, 1944; *Poirot Knows the Murderer* (contains "The Mystery of the Baghdad Chest," "The Crime in Cabin 66," and "Christmas Adventure"), [New York and London], 1946; *Poirot Lends a Hand* (contains "Problem at Pollensa Bay," "The Regatta Mystery," and "The Veiled Lady"), [New York and London], 1946; *Labors of Hercules: New Adventures in Crime by Hercule Poirot*, 1947 (published in England as *Labours of Hercules: Short Stories*, Collins, 1947); *Witness for the Prosecution, and Other Stories*, 1948; *Three Blind Mice, and Other Stories*, 1950, published in paperbacks as *The Mousetrap*, Dell, 1965; *Under Dog, and Other Stories*, 1951; *Double Sin, and Other Stories*, 1961; *13 for Luck!* (selection of stories for young readers), 1961; *Star Over Bethlehem, and Other Stories*, 1965; *Surprise! Surprise!: A Collection of*

Mystery Stories with Unexpected Endings, 1965; *13 Clues for Miss Marple*, 1966; *Selected Stories*, Progress Publishers (Moscow), 1969; *The Golden Ball, and Other Stories* (contains fifteen stories), 1971.

Plays; published by Samuel French, unless otherwise noted: *Alibi* (based on *The Murder of Roger Ackroyd*; first produced in London at Prince of Wales's Theatre, 1928), dramatized by Michael Morton, 1929; *Black Coffee* (first produced in London at St. Martin's Theatre, 1931), Baker, 1934; *Love From a Stranger* (based on the short story "Philomel Cottage"; first produced in London at Wyndham's Theatre, 1936), dramatized by Frank Vosper, Collins, 1936; *Peril at End House* (first produced in London at Vaudeville Theatre, 1940), dramatized by Arnold Ridley, 1945; *Ten Little Niggers* (Miss Christie's dramatization of her novel of the same title [published as *And Then There Were None*]; first produced in London at Wimbledon Theatre, 1943), 1945, revised edition (based on *And Then There Were None*; first produced in New York at Broadhurst Theatre, 1944), published as *Ten Little Indians*, 1946; *Appointment With Death* (Miss Christie's dramatization of her novel; first produced in London at Piccadilly Theatre, 1945), 1945; *Murder on the Nile* (Miss Christie's dramatization of her novel *Death on the Nile*; first produced in London at Ambassadors' Theatre, 1946, then in New York under title "Hidden Horizon," at Plymouth Theatre, 1946), 1948; *Murder at the Vicarage* (first produced in London at Playhouse Theatre, 1949), dramatized by Moie Charles and Barbara Toy, 1950; *The Hollow* (Miss Christie's dramatization of her novel; first produced in London at Fortune Theatre, 1951), 1951; *The Mousetrap* (a radio play, originally titled "Three Blind Mice," written at the request of Queen Mary; first produced in London for BBC; Miss Christie's adaptation for stage first produced in London at Ambassadors' Theatre, November 25, 1952, now in 23rd year of continuous production at St. Martin's Theatre; produced in New York at Maidman Playhouse, 1960), 1954; *Witness for the Prosecution* (Miss Christie's dramatization of her short story; first produced in London at Winter Garden Theatre, 1953, then in New York at Henry Miller's Theatre, 1954), 1954; *Towards Zero* (first produced in New York at St. James' Theatre, 1956), dramatized by Gerald Verner, 1956; *The Spider's Web* (first produced in London at Savoy Theatre, 1954), 1957; "The Unexpected Guest," first produced in London at Duchess Theatre, 1958, unpublished; "Verdict," first produced in London at Strand Theatre, 1958, unpublished; *Go Back for Murder* (Miss Christie's dramatization of her novel *Five Little Pigs*; first produced in London at Duchess Theatre, 1960), 1960; *Rule of Three* (contains "Afternoon at the Seaside," "The Patient," and "The Rats," all one-act), 1963; "Fiddlers Five; first produced in Southsea, England at Kings Theatre, June 7, 1971; *Akhnaton* (three-act), Dodd, 1973.

Poetry: *The Road of Dreams*, G. Bles, 1925; *Poems*, Dodd, 1973.

Nonfiction: *Come, Tell Me How You Live* (humorous accounts of archaeological expeditions with her husband, Mallowan), Dodd, 1946.

Omnibus volumes; published by Dodd, except as noted: *Agatha Christie Omnibus* (contains *The Mysterious Affair at Styles, The Murder on the Links and Poirot Investigates*), Lane, 1931; *The Agatha Christie Omnibus of Crime* (contains *The Sittaford Mystery, The Seven Dials Mystery, The Mystery of the Blue Train*, and *The Murder of Roger Ackroyd*), Collins, 1932; *Hercule Poirot, Master Detective* (contains *The Murder of Roger Ackroyd, Murder in the*

Calais Coach, and *Thirteen at Dinner*), 1936, same three novels published together as *Three Christie Crimes*, Grosset, 1937; *Two Detective Stories in One Volume: The Mysterious Affair at Styles [and] The Murder on the Links*, 1940; *Triple Threat: Exploits of Three Famous Detectives, Hercule Poirot, Harley Quin and Tuppence* (contains *Poirot Investigates, The Mysterious Mr. Quin*, and *Partners in Crime*), 1943; *Crime Reader* (contains selections from *Poirot Investigates, The Mysterious Mr. Quin*, and *Partners in Crime*), World, 1944; *Perilous Journeys of Hercule Poirot* (contains *The Mystery of the Blue Train, Death on the Nile*, and *Murder in Mesopotamia*), 1954; *Surprise Ending by Hercule Poirot* (contains *The A.B.C. Murders, Murder in Three Acts*, and *Cards on the Table*), 1956; *Christie Classics* (contains *The Murder of Roger Ackroyd, And Then There Were None, The Witness for the Prosecution, Philomel Cottage*, and *Three Blind Mice*), 1957; *Murder Preferred* (contains *The Patriotic Murders, A Murder is Announced*, and *Murder in Retrospect*), 1960; *Make Mine Murder!* (contains *Appointment with Death, Peril at End House*, and *Sad Cypress*), 1962; *A Holiday for Murder*, Bantam, 1962; *Murder International* (contains *So Many Steps to Death, Death Comes as the End*, and *Evil Under the Sun*), 1965; *Murder in Our Midst* (contains *The Body in the Library, Murder at the Vicarage, The Moving Finger*), 1967; *Spies among Us* (contains *They Came to Baghdad, N or M?, Murder in Mesopotamia*), 1968; *The Nursery Rhyme Murders* (contains *A Pocket Full of Rye, Hickory, Dickory, Death, The Crooked House*), 1970; *Murder-Go-Round* (contains *Thirteen at Dinner, The A.B.C. Murders, Funerals are Fatal*), 1972; *Murder on Board* (contains *Death in the Air, The Mystery of the Blue Train, What Mrs. McGillicudy Saw!*), 1974.

Contributor: *The Under Dog [and] Blackman's Wool* (the latter by E. Phillips Oppenheim), Readers Library Publishing (London), 1929, reissued as *Two Thrillers*, Daily Express Fiction Library, 1936; *The Body in the Library, Double or Quits, [and] The Rio Casino Intrigue* (the second by A. A. Fair, pseudonym of Erle Stanley Gardner, the third by Van Wyck Mason), Detective Book Club, 1942; *Funerals Are Fatal, The Black Iris, [and] Death of an Intruder* (the second by Constance and Gwenyth Little, the third by Nedra Tyre), Black, 1953; *So Many Steps to Death, Maigret in New York, [and] Death in Lilac Time* (the second by Georges Simenon, the third by Frances Crane), 1956(?); *Dead Man's Folly, What Crime Is It?, [and] The Man in the Net* (the second by Dorothy Gardiner, the third by Patrick Quentin), Black, 1956(?); *Ordeal by Innocence, The Fatal Amateur, [and] Where There's Smoke* (the second by D. L. Mathews, the third by C. B. Kelland), Black, 1959; *The Pale Horse, The Well-Dressed Skeleton, [and] The Lady Finger* (the second by Brad Williams, the third by George Malcolm-Smith), Black, 1962; *The Clocks, Counterstroke, [and] Ax* (the second by Patrick Wayland, the third by Ed McBain, pseudonym of Evan Hunter), Black, 1964; *A Treasury of Modern Mysteries*, two volumes, Doubleday, 1973.

Films: "The Passing of Mr. Quin," [London], c. 1928; "Black Coffee," Twickenham Films, 1931; "Love From a Stranger" (based on the play by Frank Vosper), United Artists, 1937, re-filmed by Eagle-Lion Films, 1947; "And Then There Were None," 20th Century-Fox, 1945, remade and released as "Ten Little Indians" in 1965 and again in 1974. "Witness for the Prosecution," United Artists, 1957; "Murder She Said" (based on *What Mrs. McGillicuddy Saw!*), adaptation by David Osborn, M-G-M, 1962;

"Murder at the Gallop" (based on *Funerals Are Fatal*), M-G-M, 1963; "Murder Most Foul" (based on *Mrs. McGinty's Dead*), M-G-M, 1964; "The Alphabet Murders" (based on *The ABC Murders*), M-G-M, 1965.

Under pseudonym Mary Westmacott: *Giants' Bread*, Doubleday, 1930; *Unfinished Portrait*, Doubleday, 1934; *Absent in Spring*, Farrar & Rinehart, 1944; *The Rose and the Yew Tree* , Rinehart 1948; *A Daughter's a Daughter*, Heinemann, 1952; *The Burden*, Heinemann, 1956.

Editor, with others, *The Times of London Anthology of Detective Stories*, John Day, 1973.

WORK IN PROGRESS: Publishers' Weekly reports that "Miss Christie told Francis Wyndham that she was at work on her autobiography, which is only to be published after her death, adding 'if anybody writes about my life in the future, I'd rather they got the facts right.'"

SIDELIGHTS: Agatha Christie has been writing novels, short stories, and plays for over fifty-five years. More than 350 million copies of her books have been sold and she is the author of the longest-running play in British stage history. Critics continue to praise her stories, but now, after so many years, they seem to be at a loss for further specific commendations. One *New Yorker* reviewer wrote simply: ". . . As always when we read a book by Agatha Christie, we think, What on earth would we do without this talented, vigorous lady?" And Miss Christie does not intend to so deprive her fans. It has been reported that she wants to retire, but she told *CA* that this is "quite untrue!" Stephanie Nettell, however, notes that "in an interview with Julian Symons in *The Sunday Times* a few years ago, she sounded wistful and almost depressed about her work. 'I don't enjoy writing detective stories,' [she said]. 'I enjoy thinking of a detective story, planning it, but when the time comes to write it, it is like going to work every day, like having a job.'" Miss Christie has said that in past years she planned her stories while sitting in her bathtub munching apples. The actual writing of a novel takes about six to twelve weeks.

The *Times Literary Supplement* writer offered an explanation for Miss Christie's tremendous popularity: "It is not for feats of detection that we turn to [Agatha Christie], nor even, since her early *tours de force*, for the criminological ingenuity of her plots, workmanlike though they are. Her cardinal virtue is simpler and more subtle. It is sheer readability; her books can be gulped down like cream.... The story holds unflaggingly, and holds with a grip which is gentle as well as firm." Anthony Boucher, a Christie fan for many years, cited the "smooth, deft storytelling that the public loves and the faultless intricacy of plotting that makes her the marvel of her colleagues...." Edmund Wilson, however, is a notable exception among the many critics who have discussed her work. A consistently captious judge of popular detective fiction, Wilson includes Miss Christie in his long list of inept mystery writers. ". . . Her writing is of a mawkishness and banality which seem to me literally impossible to read," he remarked. "You cannot *read* such a book, you run through it to see the problem worked out; and you cannot become interested in the characters, because they never can be allowed an existence of their own even in a flat two dimensions but have always to be contrived so that they can seem either reliable or sinister, depending on which quarter, at the moment, is to be baited for the reader's suspicion."

Regardless of Wilson's testy remarks, Miss Christie is in

little danger of losing her large and devoted audience. The *Times Literary Supplement* said of her 1965 novel, *At Bertram's Hotel:* "Agatha Christie is really astonishing. She is an old lady now, and her gentlewoman detective, Miss Marple, an older one; but, unlike too many of her contemporaries, she capitalizes instead of concealing the facts. . . . Miss Christie has lost none of her toughness. Almost alone among nice English detective writers she has never excluded any characters from possible revelation as murderers, not the sweet young girl, the charming youth, the wise old man, not even the dear old lady. And neither does she here."

Miss Christie's famous play, *The Mousetrap*, passed its 9,000th London performance in late ·1974 (the former British record holder, *Chu Chin Chow*, ran for 2,238 performances), and is now in its twenty-third year of continuous production. An Associated Press reporter discovered that only two of the critics present on opening night were still writing as of 1967 and eight of the newspapers that originally reviewed it were defunct. Peter Saunders, the producer, had predicted a six-month run; he recently told *Time*: "Just about everybody in England has seen it except the Queen, and she thinks she's seen it." Miss Christie hasn't granted an interview to discuss the play since 1961; she explains that she has nothing more to say about it.

Despite her success in several genres, Miss Christie's reputation as a novelist of particular distinction is most firmly established. Boucher writes: "I strongly suspect that future scholars of the simon-pure detective novel will hold that its greatest practitioner, outranking even Ellery Queen and John Dickson Carr in their best periods, has been Agatha Christie—not only for her incomparable plot construction, but for her extraordinary ability to limn character and era with so few (and such skilled) strokes. . . . Christie, at 76, is virtually as good as ever."

G. R. McRae's novelization of the filmscript "The Passing of Mr. Quin" was published under that title by London Book Co., 1929; *The Murder of Roger Ackroyd* was adapted for young readers by George F. Wear and published under that title by Oxford University Press, 1948; during the 1950's, *A Murder is Announced* was adapted for television by William Templeton and produced for "Goodyear Playhouse"; the film "Murder Ahoy" (M-G-M, 1964) was made from an original screenplay by David Pursall and Jack Seddon based on their interpretation of Miss Christie's character, Miss Marple; "Endless Night" was filmed by British Lion, c. 1969; "Murder on the Orient Express" was filmed in 1974. Her work has also been adapted for BBC radio.

Miss Christie's work has been translated into almost every modern language, including Japanese.

AVOCATIONAL INTERESTS: Miss Christie has said that her hobby was buying, remodeling, and decorating houses, which she sold after living in them for a short time. She also enjoys sun, sea, flowers, traveling, trying strange food, cooking, swimming, tennis, playing the piano, theatre, concerts, reading, and embroidery.

BIOGRAPHICAL/CRITICAL SOURCES: Edmund Wilson, *Classics and Commercials*, Farrar, Straus, 1950; *New York Times Book Review*, October 4, 1964, September 25, 1966; *Books and Bookmen*, September, 1965; *Times Literary Supplement*, December 2, 1965; *Publishers' Weekly*, April 11, 1966; *New York Times*, October 27, 1966; G. C. Ramsey, *Agatha Christie: Mistress of Mystery*, Dodd, 1967; *McCalls*, February, 1969; *Washington Post*, September 15, 1970; *Writer*, June, 1972; Carolyn Riley, editor, *Contemporary Literary Criticism*, Volume I, Gale, 1973.

*   *   *

CHRISTIE, Milton 1921-

PERSONAL: Born June 12, 1921, in Wilmington, N.C.; son of Christopher (an editor) and Rebecca (Jutter) Christie; married second wife, Marian Jensby; children: (first marraige) Peter, Theodore. *Education:* Queens College (now Queens College of the City University of New York), B.A., 1943; New York University, M.A., 1950. *Home:* 9342 Harvey Rd., Silver Spring, Md. 20910. *Office:* Kiplingers Washington Editors, 1729 H St., N.W., Washington D.C. 20006.

CAREER: Journal of Commerce, New York, N.Y., financial reporter, 1946-48; Biddle Purchasing Co., New York, N.Y., associate editor of *Biddle Survey* (newsletter), 1948-50; Kiplinger Washington Editors (newsletters), Washington, D.C., senior editor, 1950—. *Military service:* U.S. Army, 1943-45. *Member:* National Press Club, National Economists Club, International Club.

WRITINGS: You and Your Taxes, Kiplinger Washington Editors, 1964, new edition, 1965; (with John W. Hazard) *The Investment Business*, Harper, 1964.

*   *   *

CHRISTMAN, Don(ald) R. 1919-

PERSONAL: Born January 19, 1919, in Mount Vernon, Ohio; son of Harry Krum (a minister) and Ruth (Robbins) Christman; married Dorothy Daniel (a teacher), May 31, 1943; children: Kenneth Daniel, Robert Harry, Ronald Murrell, Gerald David. *Education:* Attended Columbia Union College. *Residence:* Lima, Peru.

CAREER: Seventh-day Adventist missionary.

WRITINGS: Savage Fire, Review & Herald, 1961; (with Bob Thrower) *About Face*, Review & Herald, 1972. Contributor to denominational periodicals.

SIDELIGHTS: All of the Christmans play in a family orchestra composed of four violins, one cello, and piano. Their recording, "The Green Cathedral," was issued by Chapel Records, 1965.†

*   *   *

CHURCHILL, E(lmer) Richard 1937-

PERSONAL: Born May 25, 1937, in Greeley, Colo.; son of Emery Roy and Olive (Whitteker) Churchill; married Linda Ruler (a junior high school teacher), August 18, 1961; children: Eric Richard, Robert Sean. *Education:* Colorado State College, A.B., 1959, M.A., 1962. *Home address:* Rt. 1, Box 329B, Kersey, Colo. 80644.

CAREER: Part-time and sometime full-time public library employee in Greeley, Colo., for total of ten years; Park Elementary School, Greeley, Colo., fifth grade teacher, 1959—. *Military service:* Colorado Air National Guard, 1961-67.

WRITINGS: (With Edward H. Blair) *Games and Puzzles for Family Leisure*, Abingdon, 1965; (with wife, Linda R. Churchill and Edward H. Blair) *Fun with American History*, Abingdon, 1966; (with Linda R. Churchill) *Fun With American Literature*, Abingdon, 1968; *Short Lessons in World History*, Walch, 1971; *Everybody Came to Leadville*, Timberline, 1971; *Puzzle it Out*, Scholastic, 1971; *How Our Nation Became Great*, Walch, 1972; *The Mc-*

Cartys, Timberline, 1972; *Casebook on Community Civics*, Walch, 1973; *Enriched Social Studies Teaching*, Fearon, 1973; *Colorado Quiz Bag*, Timberline, 1973; *United States History Activity Reader*, Walch, 1974; *World History Activity Reader*, Walch, 1974; *Puzzles and Quizzes*, Scholastic, 1974; *Doc Holliday, Bat Masterson, and Wyatt Earp: Their Colorado Careers*, Timberline, 1974.

WORK IN PROGRESS: Marriage and Family Casebook and *Family Health Casebook*, both for Walch; *Rascals in the Rockies* for Timberline; two series of educational duplicator masters for Allyn & Bacon, and Walch.

*   *   *

CHURCHILL, Samuel 1911-

PERSONAL: Born December 6, 1911, in Astoria, Ore.; son of Samuel Job (a logger) and Caroline M. (Snow) Churchill; married Dorothy Louise Sheller (a bookkeeper); children: Susan (Mrs. Ronald Holman), Alan, Samuel James. *Education:* Attended Santa Ana Junior College, 1932-34, and University of Oregon, 1934-35. *Politics:* Democrat ("vote independent"). *Religion:* Methodist. *Home:* 1576 Irving Ave., Apt. 11, Astoria, Ore. 97103.

CAREER: Logger in Oregon, 1937-39, purchasing agent for mining company, 1939-40, and cashier and bookkeeper for utility firm, 1940-42; Station KREW, Sunnyside, Wash., radio newsman, 1948-50; Republic Publishing Co., Yakima, Wash., farm editor of *Yakima Morning Herald* and *Yakima Daily Republic*, beginning 1951. *Military service:* U.S. Navy, 1942-45; became chief radio technician. *Member:* Pacific Northwest Writers Conference, Masons, American Legion. *Awards, honors:* Award for distinctive reporting from Washington State Press Club, and later from Washington Newspaper Editors Association.

WRITINGS: Big Sam, Doubleday, 1965. Contributor to *Reader's Digest, American Forests, Rotarian*.

WORK IN PROGRESS: Historical research for a second book on the Pacific Northwest with working title, *Don't Call Me Ma*, for Doubleday; completion expected late in 1975.

AVOCATIONAL INTERESTS: Photography, travel, outdoor recreation (hiking, fishing, and camping), steam locomotives, and old logging railroads.

*   *   *

CHWALEK, Henryka C. 1918-

PERSONAL: Surname is pronounced *Shwall*-ek; born January 4, 1918, in Cudahy, Wis.; daughter of Vincent Stanley and Josephine (Dryja) Chwalek. *Education:* University of Wisconsin, Milwaukee, B.S., 1938, M.Ed., 1953; graduate study at Marquette University, 1957-58, Milwaukee Institute of Technology, 1965-66, University of Iowa, 1966, University of Wisconsin, Madison, 1969-70. *Politics:* No affiliation. *Religion:* Roman Catholic. *Home:* 5510 Bonnie Lane, Hales Corners, Wis. 53130. *Office:* Pulaski High School, 2500 West Oklahoma Ave., Milwaukee, Wis.

CAREER: Milwaukee (Wis.) public schools, primary teacher, 1938-45, teacher of social studies in Milwaukee (Wis.) secondary schools, 1945—, currently at Pulaski High School, 1970—. Participant in National Defense Education Act institutes. *Member:* National Education Association, Wisconsin Education Association, Milwaukee Teachers Association, Tuckaway Country Club.

WRITINGS: Exploring Vocations, Milwaukee Public

Schools, 1953; (with Dunwiddie and Kussow) *Productivity and Automation*, edited by J. J. Jehring, Center for Productivity Motivation, School of Commerce, University of Wisconsin, 1965.

*   *   *

CIOFFARI, Vincenzo 1905-

PERSONAL: Born February 24, 1905, in Calitri, Italy; son of Costantino and Antonietta (Armiento) Cioffari; married Angelina Grimaldi (a professor), December 27, 1937; children: Vincent G. *Education:* Cornell University, A.B., 1927, A.M., 1928; Columbia University, Ph.D., 1935. *Religion:* Roman Catholic. *Home:* 45 Amherst Rd., Waban, Mass. 02168. *Office:* Boston University, 718 Commonwealth Ave., Boston, Mass. 02115.

CAREER: Lecturer at College of New Rochelle, New Rochelle, N.Y., 1931-35, Hunter College, New York, N.Y., 1938-42, 1945; State University of Iowa (now University of Iowa), Iowa City, associate professor, 1943-44; special consultant to editorial staff of U.S. Armed Forces Institute, Washington, D.C., 1943, and to War Department, New York, N.Y., 1944-45; D. C. Heath and Co., Boston, Mass., head of modern language department, 1946-67; Boston University, Boston, Mass., visiting professor of romance languages, 1967-71, scholar-in-residence, 1971—. Joint Brazil-U.S. Commission, Rio de Janeiro, member, 1945; Dante Centenary, national chairman, 1965. Lecturer on Italian literature and the teaching of modern languages in United States and Canada.

MEMBER: Modern Language Association of America, Dante Society of America (member of council; president, 1967-73), Mediaeval Academy of America, Societa Dantesca (honorary life member), Renaissance Society of America, Dante Alighieri Society (honorary life member), Linguistic Society of America, American Association of Teachers of Italian (council; vice-president), American Association of Teachers of Spanish and Portuguese, Phi Beta Kappa, Phi Kappa Phi, Phi Sigma Iota. *Awards, honors:* National Achievement Award, National Federation of Modern Language Teachers Associations.

WRITINGS: Fortune and Fate from Democritus to St. Thomas Aquinas, privately printed, 1935; (contributor of translation) Spiers and Barry, *Pascal's Physical Treatise*, Columbia University Press, 1937; *Italian Review Grammar and Composition*, Heath, 1937, 3rd edition, 1969; *The Conception of Fortune and Fate in the Works of Dante*, Harvard University Press, for Dante Society, 1940; *Spoken Italian* (with teacher's manual), Heath, 1944; *Fortune in Dante's Fourteenth Century Commentators*, Dante Society of Cambridge (Mass.), 1944; (with Reno and Hall) *Spoken Portuguese* (with teacher's manual), Heath, 1946; (with Gonzales) *Spanish Review Grammar*, Heath, 1957, 3rd edition, 1972; *Beginning Italian Grammar*, Heath, 1958, revised edition, 1965; *Guido da Pisa's Commentary on Dante's Inferno*, State University of New York Press, 1974. Contributor to *Scribner's Dictionary of the History of Ideas*, 1974.

"Heath-Chicago Italian Series," published by Heath, all with John Van Horne: *Amici di Scuola*, 1938; *Raccontini*, 1940; *Giulietta e Romeo*, 1941; Massimo d'Azeglio, *I Miei Ricordi*, 1943; Goldoni, *Il Ventaglio*, 1948: Books 1-5 published in one volume as *Letture Varie*, 1949, revised edition, 1961.

Editor: (With De Luca) Guareschi, *Corrierino delle Famiglie*, Heath, 1962; (with A. Grimaldi) Silone, *Il Segreto di*

Luca, Heath, 1964; (with C. Ross) Calvino, *La Nuvola di Smog*, Heath, 1967. Directed writing of five manuals for U.S. War Department, 1944-45. Contributor of articles, reviews, and short plays to *Speculum, Modern Language Journal, Hispania*, and other journals. Associate editor, *Italica*.

WORK IN PROGRESS: Fourth edition of *Spanish Review Grammar*; third edition of *Beginning Italian Grammar*; continuation of work on Guido da Pisa and Fortune and Fate.

SIDELIGHTS: Cioffari is competent in Italian, French, Spanish, Portuguese, German, Latin, and Provencal. *Avocational interests:* Music, playing the mandolin.

* * *

CLARK, Ann L(ivezey) 1913-

PERSONAL: Born November 27, 1913, in Baltimore, Md.; daughter of Jacob O. and Florence (Everitt) Livesey. *Education:* Maryland General Hospital School of Nursing, diploma, 1935; Seton Hall University, B.S., 1953; New York University, M.A., 1957. *Religion:* Episcopalian. *Home and office:* 1777 A1A Moana, No. 1536, Honolulu, Hawaii 96815.

CAREER: Former associate professor of maternal and child nursing and chairman of department at Rutgers University, Newark, N.J.; currently professor at University of Hawaii, Honolulu. Free-lance writer, researcher, and Consultant; former Consultant on expectant parent classes, Elizabeth General Hospital. Past visiting professor, Arizona State University. *Member:* American Nurses Association, National League for Nursing (vice-president, council of maternal and child nursing, Newark chapter), Sigma Theta Tau.

WRITINGS: Leadership Technique in Expectant Parent Education, Springer, 1962, 2nd edition, 1973; (with Hella Hakerem, Stephanie Basara, and Diane Walano) *Patient Studies in Maternal and Child Nursing*, Lippincott, 1966; (contributor) *Parent-Child Relationships: The Role of the Nurse*, Rutgers University, 1968; (with Dyanne Affonso) *Childbearing: A Nursing Perspective*, F. A. Davis, in press. Contributor to nursing journals.

* * *

CLARK, David Ridgley 1920-

PERSONAL: Born September 17, 1920, in Seymour, Conn.; son of Ridgley Colfax (a superintendent of schools) and Idella May (Hill) Clark; married Mary Adele Matthieu, July 10, 1948; children: Rosalind Elizabeth, John Bradford, Matthew Ridgley, Mary Frances. *Education:* Wesleyan University, Middletown, Conn., B.A., 1947; Yale University, M.A., 1950, Ph.D., 1955; also studied at Reed College, 1940-41, Indiana University, 1948-50, and Kenyon College, 1949. *Politics:* Independent. *Religion:* Society of Friends. *Home:* 330 Market Hill Rd., Amherst, Mass. 01002. *Office:* Department of English, University of Massachusetts, Amherst, Mass. 01002.

CAREER: Instructor in English at Mohawk College, Utica, N.Y., 1947, and University of Massachusetts, Amherst, 1951-56; Smith College, Northampton, Mass., lecturer in English, 1956-57; University of Massachusetts, Amherst, assistant professor, 1958, associate professor, 1958-65, professor of English, 1965—. Fulbright Lecturer at University of Iceland, Reykjavik, 1960-61, and University College, Dublin, Ireland, 1965-66; lecturer at Yeats Inter-

national Summer School, Ireland, 1960; visiting associate professor, University of Michigan, summer, 1966; visiting professor at Syracuse University, 1968; University of Victoria, 1971-72; Sir George Williams University, 1972. *Wartime service:* Civilian Public Service as conscientious objector. *Member:* Modern Language Association of America, American Committee for Irish Studies, Canada Association for Irish Studies. *Awards, honors:* Bollingen Foundation fellowship, 1957, 1961, 1962, 1963; Eugene Saxton and American Philosophical Society fellowships, 1957; American Council of Learned Societies grant-in-aid, 1958, 1965; Modern Language Association of America grant, 1958; National Endowment for the Humanities grant, 1969.

WRITINGS: (With Stanley Koehler, Leon Barron, and Robert Tucker) *A Curious Quire* (poems), University of Massachusetts Press, 1962; *W. B. Yeats and the Theatre of Desolate Reality*, Dufour, 1965; (editor with Robin Skelton) *Irish Renaissance*, Dolmen Press (Dublin), 1965; (editor with Robin Skelton) *Irish Renaissance*, Dolmen, 1965; *Dry Tree* (poems), Dolmen, 1965; (with Fred B. Millett and Arthur W. Hoffman) *Reading Poetry*, Harper, 1968; *John Millington Synge, Riders to the Sea*, Merrill, 1970; *Studies in the Bridge*, Merrill, 1970; (editor) *Twentieth Century Interpretations of Murder in the Cathedral*, Prentice-Hall, 1971; (with George R. Mayhew) *A Tower of Polished Black Stones*, Dolmen, 1971; (with Mayhew and Michael J. Sidnell) *Druid Craft: The Writing of the Shadowy Waters*, University of Massachusetts Press, 1971; *Lyric Resonances*, University of Massachusetts Press, 1972. Also general editor of *Manuscripts of W. B. Yeats*, Northern Illinois University Press. Poetry has appeared in *Kenyon Review, Poetry, Folio, Voices, Transatlantic Review, Dublin Magazine*, and other publications; contributor of more than thirty articles to literary journals. Contributing editor, *Massachusetts Review*.

WORK IN PROGRESS: Studies on W. B. Yeats and Thomas Kinsella.

* * *

CLARK, Francis 1919-

PERSONAL: Born February 2, 1919, in Cape of Good Hope, Union of South Africa; son of George Frederick Headington (a schoolmaster) and Bertha (Pearce) Clark; married Pauline Mannion, 1968; children: three. *Education:* Attended Cardinal Vaughan School; Heythrop College, Lic. Ph., 1950, S.T.L., 1955; Pontifical Gregorian University, Rome, Italy, D.D. (summa cum laude), 1959. *Home:* 5 Alexander Godley Close, Ashtead, Surrey KT21 1DF, England. *Office:* Faculty of Arts, Open University, Milton Keynes MK7 6AA, England.

CAREER: Entered Society of Jesus, 1945, ordained Roman Catholic priest, 1954; Heythrop College, Oxfordshire, England, professor of theology, 1959-67; Pontifical Gregorian University, Rome, Italy, associate professor of theology, 1963-67; Fordham University, New York, N.Y., visiting professor of theology, 1969-70; Open University, Milton Keynes, England, senior lecturer in history of religion, 1970-72, reader in religious studies, 1972—. Chairman, board of examiners for history syllabus of Ordination Examination for Church of England. *Member:* London Society for the Study of Religion (honorary secretary). *Military service:* British Army, Royal Fusiliers, 1939-44; served in Iraq, Palestine, Egypt, Libya, Tunisia, and in Italy, where he was seriously wounded in the Salerno landing; became captain.

WRITINGS: Anglican Orders and Defect of Intention, Longmans, Green, 1956; *Eucharistic Sacrifice and the Reformation*, Newman, 1960, 2nd edition, Blackwell, 1967; (contributor) *Christian Unity*, edited by K. McNamara, Furrow Trust (Maynooth, Ireland), 1962; *A New Theology of the Real Presence?*, Catholic Truth Society, 1967; *Origins of the Reformation*, Open University Press, 1972; *Luther and Lutherism*, Open University Press, 1972; *Calvin and Other Reformers*, Open University Press, 1972; *The Catholic Reformation*, Open University Press, 1972; *Religion in Two Worlds*, Open University Press, 1973; *The Rise of Christianity*, Open University Press, 1974. Writer of three Latin textbooks issued for the use of Gregorian University students, 1963-66. Contributor to *The Journal of Theological Studies, The Clergy Review, Gregorianum, The Heythrop Journal, Irish Theological Quarterly, Unitas* (Rome), *The Catholic Mind*, and other journals. Also contributor to *The New Catholic Encyclopedia*.

WORK IN PROGRESS: Studies in reformation doctrine and history, and a course project on man's religious quest, for Open University.

SIDELIGHTS; Clark is competent in the main European languages.

* * *

CLARK, John G(arretson) 1932-

PERSONAL: Born May 26, 1932, in Somerville, N.J.; son of Emmett S. (a mechanic) and Elizabeth (McLaughlin) Clark; married Lois Elaine Meisinger, January 30, 1954; children: Garry David, Steven McLaughlin, Larisa. *Education:* Park College, A.B., 1954; University of Kansas, A.M., 1960; Stanford University, Ph.D., 1963. *Politics:* Independent. *Religion:* Unitarian Universalist. *Home:* 1732 Louisiana, Lawrence, Kan. *Office:* Department of History, University of Kansas, Lawrence, Kan.

CAREER: Mercantile Stores Co., Inc., buyer in New York, N.Y., Duluth, Minn., and Fargo, N.D., 1956-58; University of Kansas, Lawrence, assistant professor, 1963-67, associate professor, 1967-71, professor of history, 1971—, assistant dean of faculties, research administration, 1969-70, associate chairman, department of history, 1973—. Visiting assistant professor, Louisiana State University, Baton Rouge, 1966-67; research associate, State Geological Survey of Kansas, 1969-72. *Military service:* U.S. Army, 1954-56. *Member:* American Historical Association, Organization of American Historians. *Awards, honors:* Agricultural History Society Prize for *The Grain Trade in the Old Northwest*, 1965; National Endowment for the Humanities Fellowship, 1968; American Philosophical Society grant, 1970-71; Council on Economic History grant, 1970-71.

WRITINGS: The Grain Trade in the Old Northwest, University of Illinois Press, 1965; *New Orleans, 1718-1812: An Economic History*, Louisiana State University Press, 1970; *Towns and Minerals in Southeastern Kansas: A Study of Regional Industrialization*, State Geological Survey of Kansas, 1970; (editor) *The Frontier Challenge: Responses to the Transmississippi West*, University of Kansas Press, 1971. Contributor to scholarly journals.

WORK IN PROGRESS: Research for a book on the economic history of New Orleans, 1815-1880; comparative study of capital formation in French Atlantic ports; a study of families and Communities in twentieth century U.S.

CLARK, Patricia Finrow 1929-

PERSONAL: Born January 3, 1929, in Walla Walla, Wash.; daughter of Vernon Hyatt (a salesman) and Alys (Olson) Finrow; married William Emmer Clark (a religious camp director), July 27, 1957; children: William E., Jr., Michelle, Christopher, Pamela Monica. *Education:* Prairie Bible Institute, Alberta, Canada, diploma, 1950; Aoyama Gakuin, Tokyo, Japan, student, 1954-55; Seattle Pacific College, B.A. in Ed., 1958. *Religion:* Interdenominational. *Home:* 7329 12th N.E., Seattle, Wash.

CAREER: Evangelical Alliance Mission, Chicago, Ill., missionary to Japan, 1951-56; Oriental Bible Camp Association, Seattle, Wash., missionary to Japan, 1957-64; Island Lake Bible Camp, Poulsbo, Wash., 1964-72; Worldwide Dental Health, missionary to Liberia, West Africa, 1972—. Japan Christian College, dean of women, 1955-56.

WRITINGS: Jan Ken Pon (true stories about Japanese children), Moody, 1961; (with husband, William E. Clark) *Children of the Sun*, Tuttle, 1965; *Bobby in Japan*, New Life Press, 1969.

WORK IN PROGRESS: Fly, Liberia, Fly.

* * *

CLARK, Romane Lewis 1925-

PERSONAL: Born December 3, 1925, in Waverly, Iowa; son of Fred G., Jr. and Mildred (Cole) Clark; married Marilyn Cash, August 8, 1948; children: Ronald, Carol, Kathleen, John. *Education:* University of Iowa, B.A., 1949, M.A., 1950, Ph.D., 1952. *Home:* R3, Inverness Woods Rd., Bloomington, Ind. 47401. *Office:* Department of Philosophy, Sycamore Hall, Indiana University, Bloomington, Ind. 47401.

CAREER: University of Iowa, Iowa City, instructor in philosophy, 1952; Duke University, Durham, N.C., instructor, 1953, assistant professor, 1954-60, associate professor, 1960-64, professor of philosophy, 1964-70; Indiana University, Bloomington, professor of philosophy, 1970—. Visiting professor, University of Western Ontario, 1968-69. *Military service:* U.S. Army Air Forces, 1944-45. *Member:* American Philosophical Association.

WRITINGS: (With Paul Welsh) *Introduction to Logic*, Van Nostrand, 1962. Contributor to *Philosophy Quarterly*.

* * *

CLARKE, David E(gerton) 1920-

PERSONAL: Born February 16, 1920, in Leicester, England; son of William Oswald (a teacher) and Marguerite (Branson) Clarke. *Education:* Institution of Civil Engineers, London, England, A.M., 1945; Trinity College, Cambridge, B.A., 1952, M.A., 1957; Stanford University, Ph.D., 1964. *Politics:* Democrat. *Religion:* Unitarian Universalist. *Home:* 816 16th St., Bellingham, Wash. 98225. *Office:* Department of Political Science, Western Washington State College, Bellingham, Wash. 98225.

CAREER: London and North Eastern Railway, England, civil engineer, 1936-45; Ministry of Town and Country Planning, England, town planner, 1945-47; Cambridge County Council, Cambridge, England, town planner, 1947-49; Albert Schweitzer College, Switzerland, co-founder and secretary, later tutor and lecturer, 1952-58; University of Alaska, College, professor of political science, 1965-66; Western Washington State College, Bellingham, professor of political science, 1966—. Held various offices in International Religious Fellowship, 1947-52; radio commentator and lecturer for Pacifica Foundation, 1964-65. *Military service:* Royal Engineers, 1941-42. *Member:* American Political Science Association, American Association for the Advancement of Science, Western Political Science Association.

WRITINGS: (With Jon Bridgman) *German Africa: A Select Annotated Bibliography*, Hoover Institution, 1965; (contributor) Eleanore Bushnell, editor, *Impact of Reapportionment on the Thirteen Western States*, University of Utah Press, 1970.

* * *

CLARKE, Kenneth W(endell) 1917-

PERSONAL: Born January 6, 1917, in Spokane, Wash.; son of Ralph Walter (a railroad agent) and Mary (Harrah) Clarke; married Mary Louise Washington (now a professor), August 20, 1960; children: (prior marriage) Suzanne Elizabeth Clarke Ellis. *Education:* Washington State University, B.A., 1948, M.A., 1949; Indiana University, Ph.D., 1957. *Politics:* Democrat. *Religion:* Unitarian Universalist. *Home:* Route 5, Box 71, Bowling Green, Ky. 42101. *Office:* Western Kentucky University, Bowling Green, Ky. 42101.

CAREER: Washington State University, Pullman, instructor in English, 1950-53; Chico State College, Chico, Calif., associate professor of English, 1955-60; University of Nevada, Reno, director of Off-campus Center, 1960-62; Indiana University, Bloomington, assistant director of Jeffersonville Campus, 1962-64; Western Kentucky University, Bowling Green, professor of folklore and English, 1964-74, professor of folk studies, 1974—. Urban renewal commissioner, Jeffersonville, Ind., 1963, 1964. *Military service:* U.S. Naval Reserve, 1941-45. *Member:* American Folklore Society, American Association of University Professors, Phi Beta Kappa, Phi Kappa Phi.

WRITINGS: (With wife, Mary Clarke) *Introducing Folklore*, Holt, 1963; (with Mary Clarke) *A Folklore Reader*, A. S. Barnes, 1965; (with Mary Clarke) *A Concise Dictionary of Folklore*, Kentucky Folklore Society, 1965, revised edition, 1971; *Uncle Bud Long: The Birth of a Kentucky Folk Legend*, University Press of Kentucky, 1973; *The Harvest and the Reapers: Oral Traditions of Kentucky*, University Press of Kentucky, 1974. Co-editor, *Kentucky Folklore Record*, 1965-70.

WORK IN PROGRESS: Theoretical Folklore, a survey of the field in light of modern theory; *Hewers and Carvers: Kentucky Traditional Craftsmen*, with illustrations by Ira Kohn; a revised and expanded edition of *Introducing Folklore*, with Mary Clarke.

* * *

CLAY, James 1924-
   (Jim Clay)

PERSONAL: Born February 13, 1924, in Crewe, Va.; son of Charles Richard (an engineer) and Kate Augusta (Redford) Clay; married Phyllis Laughlin, October 26, 1963. *Education:* Attended University of Richmond and University of Rochester. *Politics:* Independent. *Religion:* Protestant. *Home:* 1605 17th Pl. S.E., Washington, D.C.

CAREER: "Between World War II and Korean War, I floundered around in business, very frustrated and very unhappy. Following Korean War, I worked as salesman, but got into politics where I began writing a great deal—mainly my own speeches. I ran for Congress in 1956—as a Republican in a heavily Democratic district in Virginia (if the Byrd machine had been Republican, I would have been a Democrat). My speeches got attention in Washington, and in 1957 I was invited to become a press secretary for a member of Congress. Later I was employed as a speech writer by the Senate Republican Policy Committee. Later worked as press secretary and legislative assistant to a senator. During this period I ghosted two books which were published with the by-lines of senators. I began free lancing in October, 1963." *Military service:* U.S. Air Force pilot during World War II and Korean War.

WRITINGS: (under name Jim Clay) *Hoffa, Ten Angels Swearing*, Beaverdam Books, 1965.

WORK IN PROGRESS: A biography of Senator Robert F. Kennedy.

BIOGRAPHICAL/CRITICAL SOURCES: Richmond Times-Dispatch, Richmond, Va., May 2, 1966.†

* * *

CLEARY, James W(illiam) 1927-

PERSONAL: Born April 16, 1927, in Milwaukee, Wis.; son of James W. and Mary (Plautz) Cleary; married Mary Augustyne, 1950; children: Colleen Mary, Patricia Ann, Janet Ellen. *Education:* Marquette University, Ph.B., 1950, A.M., 1951; University of Wisconsin, Ph.D., 1956. *Home:* 19855 Septo St., Chatsworth, Calif. 91311. *Office:* Office of the President, California State University, Northridge, Northridge, Calif. 91324.

CAREER: Notre Dame High School, Milwaukee, Wis., director of forensics, 1949-51; Marquette University, Milwaukee, Wis., instructor and head coach of debate, 1951-53; University of Wisconsin, Madison, instructor, 1956-57, assistant professor, 1957-61, associate professor, 1961-63, professor of speech, 1963-69, assistant chancellor, 1965-66, vice-chancellor for academic affairs, 1966-69; California State University, Northridge, president and professor of speech communication, 1969—. Lecturer-critic at adult educational institutes, 1957-62; visiting professor at University of California, Los Angeles, under grant from Ellis L. Phillips Foundation, 1963-64. *Military service:* U.S. Army, Infantry, 1945-47; became second lieutenant.

MEMBER: Speech Association of America (chairman of bibliography committee; delegate-at-large to legislative assembly, 1963-65), Central States Speech Association (chairman of rhetoric and public address, 1959, 1962, 1963), Delta Sigma Rho, Alpha Sigma Nu, Phi Kappa Phi. *Awards, honors:* Outstanding Teaching Award, Central States Speech Association, 1959; Alumnus Award for College Teaching, Marquette University, 1960; research grants, University of Wisconsin, 1961-62, 1964; William H. Kiekhofer Memorial Award for Excellence in Teaching ($1,000), University of Wisconsin.

WRITINGS: (Editor with Frederick W. Haberman) *Rhetoric and Public Address: A Bibliography*, University of Wisconsin Press, 1964. Contributor of articles and reviews to speech journals. Associate editor, *Central States Speech Association Journal*, 1958-61; (with Mrs. S. Robert) *Robert's Rules of Order, Newly Revised*, Scott, Foresman, 1970; (editor and author of introduction and notes) *John Bulwer's Chirologia Chironomia, 1644: A Critical Edition*, Southern Illinois University Press, 1974. Contributing editor, *Speech Monographs*, 1957—.

CLEAVER, Dale G. 1928-

PERSONAL: Born June 24, 1928, in Lafayette, Ind.; son of Harry Morris (an agricultural economist) and Pearl (Fegley) Cleaver. *Education:* Willamette University, B.A., 1950; University of Chicago, M.A., 1952, Ph.D., 1955. *Office:* Department of Art, University of Tennessee, Knoxville, Tenn.

CAREER: University of Tennessee, Knoxville, assistant professor, 1958-63, associate professor, 1963-66, professor of art history, 1966—. *Military service:* U.S. Army, 1955-58. *Member:* College Art Association of America, American Association of University Professors, Southeastern College Art Association. *Awards, honors:* Fulbright grant to Belgium, 1952-53; Outstanding Teacher Award, University of Tennessee, 1966.

WRITINGS: Art, An Introduction, Harcourt, 1966. Play translation included in *Chicago Review Anthology*, edited by David Ray, University of Chicago Press, 1959. Contributor to art journals.

WORK IN PROGRESS: Research on nineteenth- and early twentieth-century painting and sculpture in France and Belgium.

* * *

CLELLAND, Richard C(ook) 1921-

PERSONAL: Born August 23, 1921, in Camden, N.Y.; son of Ford John (a civil engineer) and Beryl (Cook) Clelland; married Anne Buel. *Education:* Hamilton College, B.A., 1944; Columbia University, A.M., 1949; University of Pennsylvania, Ph.D., 1956. *Home:* 530 Hilaire Rd., St. Davids, Pa. 19087. *Office:* E 239 Dietrich Hall, University of Pennsylvania, Philadelphia, Pa. 19174.

CAREER: Instructor in mathematics at Hamilton College, Clinton, N.Y., 1943-44, 1950-53, and Utica College, Utica, N.Y., 1946-47; University of Pennsylvania, Philadelphia, assistant professor, 1956-61, associate professor, 1961-66, professor of statistics and operations research, 1966—, chairman of department, 1966-71, acting dean, The Wharton School, 1971-72. *Military service:* U.S. Army, Signal Corps, 1944-46; became master sergeant. *Member:* American Statistical Association, Mathematical Association of America, Operations Research Society of America, Institute of Mathematical Statistics, American Association of University Professors.

WRITINGS: (With M. W. Tate) *Nonparametric and Shortcut Statistics*, Interstate, 1957; (with J. B. O'Hara) *Effective Use of Statistics in Accounting*, Holt, 1964; (with J. S. de Cani, F. E. Brown, J. P. Bursk, and D. S. Murray) *Basic Statistics with Business Applications*, Wiley, 1966, 2nd edition (with Cani and Brown), 1973.

* * *

CLEMENS, Walter C., Jr. 1933-

PERSONAL: Born April 6, 1933, in Cincinnati, Ohio; son of Walter C. (a salesman) and Ellen (White) Clemens; married Diane Shaver (a historian), September 5, 1960; children: Iolani Lenore. *Education:* Student at Xavier University, Cincinnati, Ohio, 1951-52, University of Vienna, 1952-53; University of Notre Dame, A.B. (magna cum laude), 1955; University of Moscow, graduate study, 1958-59; Columbia University, Certificate of Russian Institute, and M.A., 1957, Ph.D., 1961. *Home:* 11 Rumford Rd., Lexington, Mass. 02173. *Office:* Department of Government, Boston University, 236 Bay State Rd., Boston, Mass.

CAREER: Iolani School, Honolulu, Hawaii, chairman of language department, 1960-61; University of California, Santa Barbara, assistant professor of political science, 1961-63; Massachusetts Institute of Technology, Cambridge, assistant professor of political science and research associate, Center for International Studies, 1963-66; Boston University, Boston, Mass., professor of political science. Harvard University associate of Russian Research Center, 1963—; Salzburg Seminar in American Studies, Salzburg, Austria, member of faculty, 1965. Consultant to Special Operations Research Office, The American University, 1960-61, Technical Military Planning Operation, General Electric Co., 1961-63, and Washington Center of Foreign Policy Research, Johns Hopkins University, 1965-66, Arthur D. Little, Inc., 1966-68. Member of disarmament committee, World Peace Through Law Center, 1965—; executive officer, Arms Control and Disarmament Committee, U.S. National Citizens Commission, International Cooperation Year, 1965.

MEMBER: American Political Science Association, American Association for the Advancement of Slavic Studies, International Institute for Strategic Studies, American Historical Association, International Studies Association (president, New England region, 1972-73). *Awards, honors:* Faculty fellowship, Institute of International Studies, University of California, 1962, 1963; NATO fellowship, 1970-71; *Military Review*, outstanding achievement award, 1970.

WRITINGS: Soviet Disarmament Policy, 1917-1963: An Annotated Bibliography of Soviet and Western Sources, Hoover Institution, 1965; (editor, and author of introduction) *World Perspectives on International Politics*, Little, 1965; (editor, and author of introduction) *Toward a Strategy of Peace* (foreword by Robert F. Kennedy), Rand McNally, 1965; (with Franklyn Griffiths and Lincoln P. Bloomfield) *Khrushchev and the Arms Race*, M.I.T. Press, 1966; *Arms Control and Outer Space*, M.I.T. Center for Space Research, 1966; *The Arms Race and Sino-Soviet Relations*, Hoover Institution Press, 1968; *The Superpowers and Arms Control*, Lexington Books, 1973.

Contributor: Alexander Dallin, editor, *The Soviet Union and Disarmament*, Praeger, 1965; Thomas T. Hammond, editor, *Soviet Foreign Relations and World Communism*, Princeton University Press, 1965; H. M. Halperin, editor, *Sino-Soviet Relations and Arms Control*, M.I.T. Press, 1967; William Coplin, editor, *Simulation in The Study of Politics*, Markham, 1968; Thomas E. Cronin and Sanford D. Greenberg, editors, *The Presidential Advisory System*, Harper, 1969; Robert E. Osgood, editor, *Alliances and American Foreign Policy*, Johns Hopkins Press, 1969; Abdul A. Said, editor, *America's World Role in the 70's*, Prentice-Hall, 1970; W. Raymond Duncan, editor, *Soviet Policy in Developing Countries*, Ginn, 1970; Roman Kolkowicz and others, editors, *The Soviet Union and Arms Control: A Superpower Dilemma*, Johns Hopkins Press, 1970.

Contributor to *Science and Human Survival* (proceedings of Second National Conference of Scientists on Survival, 1963); *Challenges from the Future* (proceedings of International Future Research Conference, 1971). Also contributor to *World Book Encyclopedia*. Contributor of articles and reviews to *One World, China Quarterly, New York Herald Tribune, Orbis, Military Review, Journal of International Affairs, American Political Science Review*, and other periodicals.

WORK IN PROGRESS: Several books and more articles on world politics.

SIDELIGHTS: Clemens is competent in German, Russian, and French. He also has some command of Italian, Spanish, Serbo-Croat, Czech, and Slovak. He has traveled widely in Western and Eastern Europe, and has visited Australia, New Zealand, and the Far East.

* * *

CLENDENIN, John C(ameron) 1903-

PERSONAL: Born May 2, 1903, in Sparta, Ill.; son of Harry O. (a florist) and Mabel (Ritchie) Clendenin; married Fietta Wilkin, February 20, 1928. *Education:* University of Illinois, B.S., 1925; University of California, M.S., 1927; University of Iowa, Ph.D., 1935. *Home:* Sparta, Ill. 62286.

CAREER: University of California, Los Angeles, professor of finance, 1936-64, professor emeritus, 1964—. Research consultant, Pacific Coast Stock Exchange, 1949-64. *Military service:* U.S. Army Air Forces, 1943-45; became captain. *Member:* American Economic Association, American Finance Association.

WRITINGS: Introduction to Investments, McGraw, 1950, 6th edition, with George A. Christy, 1974. Contributor to *Barron's* and other periodicals.

* * *

CLIFFORD, John W(illiam) 1918-

PERSONAL: Born October 19, 1918, in Springfield, Ill.; son of John Bernard (an office manager) and Rose (Collins) Clifford; married Carol Cline, April 3, 1943; children: Christine, John. *Education:* Emporia State College, B.S., 1952. *Home:* 801 Mississippi, Lawrence, Kan. 66044.

CAREER: Topeka Daily Capital, Topeka, Kan., copy editor, 1953-55; Harry Turner Advertising, Topeka, Kan., copywriter, 1955-60; Centron Corp. (motion picture producers), Lawrence, Kan., script writer, 1960—. *Military service:* U.S. Army, 1941-45. *Member:* American Society of Composers, Authors and Publishers.

WRITINGS: The Shooting of Storey James, Doubleday, 1962.

Plays: "Wild Bill," 1972; "Return of the Swordfighter," 1973; "Riffraff at the Rubaiyat," 1974. Also author of a feature length film, "Carnival of Souls," 1963; and scripts for more than one hundred motion pictures in the educational and industrial fields.

* * *

CLINE, Catherine Ann 1927-

PERSONAL: Born July 27, 1927, in West Springfield, Mass.; daughter of Daniel E. (an engineer) and Agnes (Howard) Cline. *Education:* Smith College, A.B., 1948; Columbia University, M.A., 1950; Bryn Mawr College, Ph.D., 1957. *Politics:* Democrat. *Religion:* Catholic. *Home:* 3801 Connecticut Ave., N.W., Washington, D.C. 20008. *Office:* Department of History, Catholic University of America, Washington, D.C. 20017.

CAREER: Smith College, Northampton, Mass., assistant in history department, 1952-53; St. Marys' College, South Bend, Ind., instructor in history, 1953-54; Notre Dame College of Staten Island, Staten Island, N.Y., assistant professor, 1954-57, associate professor, 1958-60, professor of history, 1961-68; Catholic University of America, Washington, D.C., associate professor, 1968-73, professor of history, 1973—. *Member:* American Historical Association, American Catholic Historical Society, American Associa-

tion of University Professors, Conference on British Studies, Society of Labour History (England).

WRITINGS: Recruits to Labour: The British Labour Party, 1914-31, Syracuse University Press, 1963; (contributor) A. J. H. Morris, editor, *Edwardian Radicalism*, Routledge & Kegan Paul, 1974. Contributor to periodicals, including *Commonweal, Journal of Modern History, Church History*, and *American Catholic Historical Review.*

WORK IN PROGRESS: A biographical study of E. D. Morel.

* * *

CLOSE, Reginald Arthur 1909-

PERSONAL: Born February 3, 1909, in London, England; son of Harry Maynard (a businessman) and Edith (Tidman) Close; married Eleanor Darroch, December 22, 1934; children: Anthony John, David Henry, Peter Maynard. *Education:* King's College, London, B.A. (honors), 1931. *Religion:* Protestant. *Home:* 8 Highgate Close, London N.6, England.

CAREER: Went to Hongkong to teach English, 1933, then became head of modern languages department in a public school, Shanghai, China, until 1938; with British Council, 1938-68, as lecturer at Institute of English Studies, Athens, Greece, 1939-41, headmaster of St. John's School, Concepcion, Chile, 1941-43, posts in Santiago, Chile, and in Belgium, Czechoslovakia, Japan, and London, England, 1943-59, and representative in Greece, 1959-68; University College, London, England, honorary research fellow, 1968—. Lecturer at University of Chile, University of Prague, and Keio University; external examiner in English as a foreign language, University of London. *Menber:* International Association of Teachers of English as a Foreign Language, British Association of Applied Linguistics, Anglo-Hellenic League (honorary secretary), Japan Society of London (vice-president), Modern Humanities Research Association. *Awards, honors:* M.Litt., University of Chile; Commander, Order of the British Empire, 1967.

WRITINGS: The English We Use, Longmans, Green, 1961, second edition, 1971; *English as a Foreign Language*, Harvard University Press, 1962; *The New English Grammar: Lessons in English as a Foreign Language*, Parts I and II, Harvard University Press, 1964; *The English We Use for Science*, Longmans, Green, 1965; *English Conversation*, Allen & Unwin, 1965; *The New English Grammar: More Lessons in English as a Foreign Language*, Harvard University Press, 1968; *A Reference Grammar for Students of English*, Longman, 1975. Contributor of articles on travel, education, and English teaching to *Times, Listener*, and other periodicals. Former member of editorial board, *English Language Teaching.*

WORK IN PROGRESS: A new edition of *English as a Foreign Language.*

SIDELIGHTS: Close is fluent in French, Spanish, and modern Greek. He has some knowledge of Czech, Chinese, and Japanese.

* * *

CLOUDSLEY-THOMPSON, J(ohn) L(eonard) 1921-

PERSONAL: Born May 23, 1921, in Murree, India; son of A. G. G. (a medical doctor) and M. E. (Griffiths) Thompson; married J. Anne Cloudsley (a physiotherapist), 1944; children: John Hugh, Timothy, Peter Leslie. *Education:* Pembroke College, Cambridge, B.A., 1946, M.A.,

1948, Ph.D., 1950. *Religion:* Church of England. *Home:* 4 Craven Hill, London W2 3D5, England. *Office:* Department of Zoology, Birkbeck College, University of London, Malet St., London WC1E 7HX, England.

CAREER: King's College, University of London, London, England, lecturer in zoology, 1950-60; University of Khartoum, Khartoum, Sudan, professor of zoology and keeper of Sudan Natural History Museum, 1960-71. Member of expeditions to Iceland, 1947, southern Tunisia, 1954, and various parts of central Africa, 1960—. Delegate to twelve international congresses on entomology, zoology, biological rhythm, and bioclimatology. Honorary captain, Freeman of the City of London; liveryman, Worshipful Company of Skinners. *Military service:* British Army, 1940-44; wounded, 1942, but rejoined regiment for D-Day offensive in Normandy; became captain. *Member:* World Academy of Art and Science (fellow), Institute of Biology (fellow), Linnean Society (fellow), Royal Entomological Society (London; fellow), Zoological Society (London; fellow). *Awards, honors:* D.Sc., University of London, 1960; Royal African Society Medal, 1969.

WRITINGS: (Editor) *Biology of Deserts*, Institute of Biology, 1954; *Spiders, Scorpions, Centipedes, and Mites*, Pergamon Press, 1958; *Animal Behaviour*, Oliver & Boyd, 1960; (with John Sankey) *Land Invertebrates*, Methuen, 1961; *Rhythmic Activity in Animal Physiology and Behaviour*, Academic Press, 1961; (with M. J. Chadwick) *Life in Deserts*, Dufour, 1964; *Animal Conflict and Adaptation*, Dufour, 1965; *Desert Life*, Pergamon, 1965; *Animal Twilight: Man and Game in Eastern Africa*, Dufour, 1967; *Microecology*, St. Martin's, 1967; *The Zoology of Tropical Africa*, Norton, 1969; (with F. T. Abushama) *A Guide to the Physiology of Terrestrial Arthropoda*, Khartoum University Press, 1970; *Animals of the Desert*, McGraw, 1971; *The Temperature and Water Relations of Reptiles*, Merrow, 1971; *Desert Life*, Aldus, 1974; *Terrestrial Environments*, Croom Helm, 1975; *Man and the Biology of Arid Zones*, E. J. Arnold, 1975; *Insects and History*, Weidenfeld & Nicolson, in press. Also author of monographs and children's books. Contributor to science journals. Former member of editorial board, Royal Entomological Society and *Entomologist*; member of publications committee, Zoological Society of London.

WORK IN PROGRESS: Ecology, Adaptation, and Biological Rhythm, for publication by Braziller; research on the ecology and physiology of desert animals, thermal physiology, and rhythms.

AVOCATIONAL INTERESTS: Music, particularly opera; travel, and photography.

BIOGRAPHICAL/CRITICAL SOURCES: The Voices of Time, Braziller, 1966.

* * *

CLOUGH, Wilson O(ber) 1894-

PERSONAL: Surname rhymes with "now"; born January 7, 1894, in New Brunswick, N.J.; son of Clinton Wilson and Mary (Ober) Clough; married Laura Lee Bowman, 1921 (died April 26, 1961); children: Mary Cecelia (Mrs. Ralph E. Schmiedeskamp), Francis Bowman, David Van Wormer. *Education:* Union College and University, A.B., 1917; University of Colorado, A.M., 1925; also studied at University of Montpellier (France), 1919, University of Chicago, 1929, University of Wisconsin, 1930-31. *Politics:* Independent. *Home:* 1415 Custer St., Laramie, Wyo. 82070. *Office:* c/o American Studies, University of Wyoming, Laramie, Wyo. 82070.

CAREER: High school teacher of Latin, English, and French, 1917, 1919-24; University of Wyoming, Laramie, 1924—, started as instructor in English, professor, 1939-56, Coe Professor of American Studies, 1956-61,. professor emeritus, 1961—, chairman of department of English, 1946-49. Visiting summer professor at University of New Mexico, 1926, Lehigh University, 1939, New York University, 1949, College of Idaho, 1962. *Military service:* American Expeditionary Forces, Field Artillery, 1917-18. *Member:* Modern Language Association of America, American Studies Association (council, 1965-68), American Association of University Professors, Phi Beta Kappa, Phi Sigma Iota, Psi Chi, Phi Kappa Phi. *Awards, honors:* Fellow, University of Wisconsin, 1930-31; honorary Litt.D., Union College and University, 1957; LL.D., University of Wyoming, 1961.

WRITINGS: History of University of Wyoming, 1887-1937, Laramie Printing Co., 1937; *Grammar of English Communication*, Lippincott, 1949; *Brief Oasis* (poems), A. Swallow, 1954; (editor) *Our Long Heritage: Pages from the Books Our Founding Fathers Read*, University of Minnesota Press, 1955, 2nd edition published as *Intellectual Origins of American National Thought*, Citadel, 1961; *The Necessary Earth: Nature and Solitude in American Literature*, University of Texas Press, 1964; (translator from the French) Arthur Honegger, *I Am a Composer*, St. Martins, 1965; (translator) Louis Simonin, *The Rocky Mountain West in 1867*, University of Nebraska Press, 1965; *Academic and Otherwise* (selected papers), University of Wyoming Press, 1969; *Past's Persisting* (collected poems), University of Wyoming Press, 1971; (translator) Charles Moraze, *The Logic of History*, Mouton, 1975. Writer of short stories and poems; contributor of reviews and articles to professional journals. Book review editor, *Laramie Republican-Boomerang*, 1926-36; member of editorial board, *Western Humanities Review*, 1952-70.

SIDELIGHTS: Our Long Heritage was translated into Korean for a two-volume paperback edition, 1964. *The Necessary Earth* was translated into Japanese, 1974.

* * *

COCKSHUT, A(nthony) O(liver) J(ohn) 1927-

PERSONAL: Born May 8, 1927; son of Rowland William (a doctor) and Gertrude (Chrimes) Cockshut; married Gillian Avery (an author), August 25, 1952; children: Ursula. *Education:* Attended Winchester College, 1940-45; New College, Oxford, B.A. (first class honors), 1948. *Religion:* Roman Catholic. *Home:* 32 charlbury Rd., Oxford, England.

CAREER: Balliol College, Oxford, England, research fellow, 1950-54; Manchester Grammar School, Manchester, England, assistant master, 1954-64; Oxford University, lecturer in nineteenth-century literature, 1965—, fellow of Hertford College, 1966—.

WRITINGS: Anthony Trollope: A Critical Study, Collins, 1955, New York University Press, 1968; *Anglican Attitudes: A Study of Victorian Religious Controversies*, Collins, 1959; *The Imagination of Charles Dickens*, Collins, 1961, New York University Press, 1962; *The Unbelievers: English Agnostic Thought, 1840-1890*, Collins, 1964, New York University Press, 1966; (editor) *Religious Controversies of the Nineteenth Century*, University of Nebraska, 1966; *Middlemarch* (study guide to the novel by George Eliot), Barnes & Noble, 1966; *The Achievement of Walter Scott*, New York University Press, 1969; *Truth to Life:*

The Art of Biography in the Nineteenth Century, Harcourt, 1974.

WORK IN PROGRESS: Man and Woman: A Study of Sexual Conduct and Morality in the English World.

*   *   *

COGGAN, (Frederick) Donald 1909-

PERSONAL: Born October 9, 1909, in London, England; son of Cornish Arthur and Fannie Sarah (Chubb) Coggan; married Jean Braithwaite Strain, October 17, 1935; children: Dorothy Ann, Ruth Evelyn. *Education:* Attended Merchant Taylors' School, London, England, and St. John's College, Cambridge, 1928; Wycliffe Hall, Oxford, England, M.A., 1935, B.D., 1941. *Home:* Lambeth Palace, London SE1 7JV, England and Old Palace, Canterbury, Kent CT1 2EE, England.

CAREER: Clergyman, Church of England. University of Manchester, Manchester, England, assistant lecturer in Semitic languages and literature, 1931-34; curate at St. Mary, Islington, England, 1934-37; Wycliffe College, Toronto, Ontario, Canada, professor of New Testament, 1937-44; London College of Divinity, London, England, principal, 1944-56; examining chaplain to Bishop of Lincoln, 1946-56, Bishop of Manchester, 1951, Bishop of Southwark, 1954-56, Bishop of Chester, 1955-56; proctor in convocation, London, England, 1950-56; Bishop of Bradford, 1956-61; Archbishop of York, 1961-75; Archbishop of Canterbury, 1975—. Order of St. John of Jerusalem, chaplain and sub-prelate, 1960; University of Oxford, select preacher, 1961. Chairman of Liturgical Commission, 1960-63.

MEMBER: Athenaeum Club. *Awards, honors:* D.D., Wycliffe College, 1944, Lambeth, 1957, University of Leeds, 1958, Cambridge University, 1962, University of Hull, 1963, University of Aberdeen, 1963, Huron College, 1963, University of Saskatoon, 1963, and University of Tokyo, 1963; honorary fellow, St. John's College, Cambridge University, 1961.

WRITINGS: A People's Heritage, Morehouse, 1944; *The Ministry of the Word,* Canterbury Press, 1945; *The Glory of God,* 1950; *Stewards of Grace,* Hodder & Stoughton, 1958; *Five Makers of the New Testament,* Hodder & Stoughton, 1962; *Christian Priorities,* Harper, 1963; *The Prayers of the New Testament,* Hodder & Stoughton, 1967; *Sinews of Faith,* Hodder & Stoughton, 1969; *Word and World,* Hodder & Stoughton, 1971. Contributor to *Theology* and other journals.

AVOCATIONAL INTERESTS: Gardening, motoring, music.

*   *   *

COGHLAN, Brian (Laurence Dillon) 1926-

PERSONAL: Born February 26, 1926, in Birmingham, England; son of Herbert George (a headmaster) and Nora Elizabeth (Dillon) Coghlan; married Sybil Elizabeth May, February 3, 1953; children: Adrian Mark May, Martin Richard May, Justin Laurence May, Julian Francis May. *Education:* University of Birmingham, B.A. (honors), 1949, Ph.D., 1957. *Religion:* Catholic. *Office:* University of Adelaide, Adelaide, South Australia.

CAREER: University of Birmingham, Birmingham, England, assistant lecturer, 1950-53; University of Adelaide, Adelaide, South Australia, lecturer, 1953-56, senior lecturer, 1956-59; University of New England, Armidale, New

South Wales, Australia, Foundation Professor of German Language and Literature, 1959-62; University of Adelaide, professor of German, 1962—. Lecturer at University of Mainz, University of Innsbruck, University of Jena, University of Pennsylvania, Princeton University, and University of Texas. Drama adviser, Adelaide Festival of Arts. *Member:* Australasian Universities Language and Literature Association (Adelaide representative, 1963—), Goethe Society in South Australia (president, 1962—), Modern Language Teachers' Association of South Australia (president, 1964-66), Theodor Storm Gesellschaft.

WRITINGS: (Contributor) *Stil-und. Formprobleme in der Literatur,* Carl Winter, 1959; *Poets, Prophets. Preceptors,* University of New England Press, 1962; *Hofmansthal's Festival Dramas,* Cambridge University Press, 1964; (contributor) J. M. Ritchie, editor, *Periods in German Literature,* Wolff, 1966. Contributor to *Proceedings of English Goethe Society.*

WORK IN PROGRESS: Hofmansthal's Comedies and Literary Essays; the later stories (from *Draussen im Heiderdorf,* 1871) of Theodor Storm.

SIDELIGHTS: Brian Coghlan speaks German, French, Italian. He traveled in United States under auspices of Carnegie Corp. of New York, 1957-58, and has studied at various periods in Innsbruck, Goettingen, Cologne, and Zurich. *Avocational interests:* The theater, opera, music, swimming, cricket, rugby football (former university coach).†

*   *   *

COHEN, Morris 1912-
(Mike Cohen)

PERSONAL: Born July 16, 1912, in Boston, Mass.; son of Richard (a furniture manufacturer) and Ethel (Okon) Cohen; married Katherine Phelps, December 1, 1945; children: Michael, Katherine. *Education:* Colby College, B.S., 1935. *Politics:* Middle-of-the-road. *Religion:* Unitarian Universalist. *Home:* The Mill House, Bedford Village, N.Y. 10506.

CAREER: Burlington Industries, Inc. (textiles), New York, N.Y., sales manager, 1949—. *Military service:* U.S. Army, 1942-46; became first.lieutenant; received Bronze Star medal with oak leaf cluster, Purple Heart.

WRITINGS: (Under name Mike Cohen) *The Bright Young Man* (novel), Lippincott, 1966.

WORK IN PROGRESS: Uncle Tom's Office, a novel.

SIDELIGHTS: Cohen said: "The American businessman has been catching hell from cliche writers who portray him as a totally immoral buck-chaser. . . . The businessman is a creature struggling between appetite and conscience. His substantial success in satisfying his appetite has made him a sitting duck for buckshot critics. *The Bright Young Man* tries to answer the scoffers by showing that the businessman's conscience, too, has its occasional successes."

*   *   *

COHEN, William Howard 1927-

PERSONAL: Born August 13, 1927, in Jacksonville, Fla.; son of Isaac (a railroad telegrapher) and Sarah (Diamond) Cohen; married Dolores Brooke (a music teacher), April 12, 1952. *Education:* University of Florida, B.A., 1950, M.A., 1954; University of Chicago, graduate study, 1950-51; Emory University, graduate study, 1954-56, 1960-62;

Southern Illinois University, Ph.D., 1970. *Politics:* Liberal Democrat. *Religion:* Jewish. *Home:* 138 King St., St. Augustine, Fla. *Office:* Kent Campus, Florida Junior College, Jacksonville, Fla. 32205.

CAREER: Georgia State College (now University), Atlanta, instructor in English and world literature, 1956; Southern Illinois University, Carbondale, lecturer on world literature, 1956-60; Oglethorpe College (now University), Atlanta, Ga., assistant professor of English and humanities, 1960-63; Alice Lloyd College, Pippa Passes, Ky., assistant professor, 1963-70, professor of English and humanities, 1970-71, poet in residence, 1963-71; free-lance writer and lecturer, 1971-72; Florida Junior College, Jacksonville, visiting lecturer, 1973—. Visiting professor, Winston-Salem State University, spring, 1973. *Military service:* U.S. Army, 1946-47; became sergeant. *Member:* National Council of Teachers of English, Poetry Society of America, Association for Higher Education, National Education Association, American Association of University Professors, Kentucky Education Association, Poetry Society of Kentucky. *Awards, honors:* Named U.S. Olympic Poet for 1968.

WRITINGS: A House in the Country (verse), privately printed, 1962; *The Hill Way Home* (verse), Alice Lloyd College Press, 1965; *Mexico 68: The New World of Man* (verse), Southern Illinois University International Education Office, 1971; *To Walk in Seasons: An Introduction to Haiku*, Tuttle, 1972. Poetry has appeared in *Southern Humanities Review, Modern Haiku, American Haiku, Literature East and West, Poet Lore, American Bard*, and other publications.

WORK IN PROGRESS: Poems for Meditators; *Poems of a Chinese Jew*; translations of Rilke.

*   *   *

COLDWELL, David F(rederick) C(larke)   1923-

PERSONAL: Born December 31, 1923, in Hantsport, Nova Scotia, Canada; now U.S. citizen; son of Lewis Henry and Helen (Clarke) Coldwell; married Patricia Carothers (a college teacher) June 4, 1947; children: Catherine Blake, David Lewis. *Education:* Dalhousie University, B.A. (honors), 1944, M.A., 1945; Yale University, Ph.D., 1947; University of Edinburgh, postdoctoral study, 1950-52. *Politics:* Democrat. *Home:* 3106 Beverly Dr., Dallas, Tex. 75205. *Office:* Southern Methodist University, Dallas, Tex. 75222.

CAREER: Yale University, New Haven, Conn., instructor in English, 1947-48; Elmira College, Elmira, N.Y., assistant professor, 1948-50; University of Edinburgh, Edinburgh, Scotland, lecturer, 1951-52; Southern Methodist University, Dallas, Tex., assistant professor, 1952-56, associate professor, 1956-65, professor of comparative literature, 1965—. Consultant on communication theory and research, Southwestern Graduate School of Banking, 1959—. *Member:* Modern Language Association of America, American Association of University Professors, Scottish Text Society. *Awards, honors:* Danforth fellow, 1963-64

WRITINGS: (Editor) Virgil, *Aeneid*, translated by Gavin Douglas, four volumes, Scottish Text Society, 1958-62; (editor) *Selections from Gavin Douglas*, Clarendon Press, 1964. Author of pamphlets; contributor to periodicals.

WORK IN PROGRESS: Studies in Scottish history and literature.

SIDELIGHTS: Coldwell writes: "I have a less esoteric interest in business history and improved business communication, reflected in many business reports I have rewritten. Direct, simple English is almost a foreign language for many business writers."†

*   *   *

COLE, William Earle   1904-

PERSONAL: Born July 23, 1904, in Shady Valley, Tenn.; son of William S. Cole (a farmer); married Beulah Atchley (a sales manager); children: Glenda Mateel (Mrs. John Bogert), William E. *Education:* University of Tennessee, B.S.A., 1926; Cornell University, A.M., 1928, Ph.D., 1930. *Religion:* Presbyterian. *Home:* 6508 Sherwood Dr., Knoxville, Tenn.

CAREER: University of Tennessee, Knoxville, assistant professor of education, 1930-33, associate professor of sociology, 1933-36, professor of sociology, beginning, 1936, head of department, 1936-65, Phi Kappa Phi Lecturer, 1958-59. Visiting summer professor at Peabody College for Teachers, Cornell University, and University of North Carolina. Chief of program review and analysis staff, Tennessee Valley Authority, 1942-47; chairman of advisory committee, Tennessee Department of Welfare, 1950-57; chairman of Tennessee Council for the Community Development Foundation, 1961—; member of Tennessee Governor's Commission on Aging, 1962-70.

MEMBER: American Sociological Association (fellow; chairman of urban sections, 1965), American Association of University Professors, Southern Sociological Society (cofounder; past president), Tennessee Conference of Social Work (president), Tennessee Education Association, Phi Kappa Phi, Omicron Delta Kappa, Phi Delta Kappa, Alpha Phi Epsilon, Alpha Delta Kappa. *Awards, honors:* Award from Knoxville Council of Community Services for distinguished service, 1957.

WRITINGS: Teaching of Biology, Appleton, 1934; (with Hugh Price Crowe) *Recent Trends in Rural Planning*, Prentice-Hall, 1937; (with C. S. Montgomery) *School Sociology*, Allyn & Bacon, 1937, 3rd revised edition, 1964; (with William H. Combs) *Tennessee: A Political Study*, University of Tennessee Press, 1940.

(With Clyde B. Moore) *Sociology in Educational Practice*, Houghton, 1952; (editor and co-author) *Dynamic Urban Sociology*, Stackpole, 1954; *Urban Society*, Houghton, 1958; (with Rubye Johnson) *The Tennessee Citizen*, Harlow Publishing, 1958, revised edition, 1963; (with Montgomery) *High School Sociology*, Allyn & Bacon, 1959, 2nd edition, 1963; (with Roy L. Cox) *Southern Citizenship Problems*, Harlow Publishing, 1960; *Introductory Sociology*, McKay, 1962; (contributor) Thomas R. Ford, editor, *The Southern Appalachian Region*, University of Kentucky Press, 1962; (with Charles H. Miller) *Social Problems: A Sociological Interpretation*, McKay, 1965; (contributor) John Michaelis and A. M. Johnson, editors, *The Social Sciences*, Allyn & Bacon, 1965; (with Roy L. Cox) *Social Foundations of Education*, Appleton, 1968; (editor with Diana K. Harris) *Readings in Social Gerontology*, Xerox Corp., 1975; (with Harris) *Aging in American Society*, Allyn & Bacon, 1975. Contributor to "Florida Institute of Gerontology Series," *Dictionary of Education, Encyclopedia of Relevant Knowledge, Encyclopedia of Criminology*, and to journals. Guest issue editor, *Educational Sociology*.

WORK IN PROGRESS: Two books, *Tales From a Country Ledger* and *Urban Society*.

COLE, William Graham 1917-

PERSONAL: Born March 7, 1917, in Jamaica, N.Y.; son of John D. (in advertising) and Helen (Graham) Cole; married Doris E. Williams, December 20, 1941 (divorced September, 1969); married Sally Kint Sarver, July 18, 1970; children: (first marriage) William Graham, Edward M., Stephen S. *Education:* Columbia University, B.A., 1940, Ph.D., 1954; Union Theological Seminary, New York, N.Y., M.Div., 1943. *Home:* 2360 Sheridan Rd., Highland Park, Ill. 60035.

CAREER: Ordained to Presbyterian ministry, 1942, demitted ministry, 1970; assistant minister in Cleveland, Ohio, 1943-46; Western Reserve University (now Case-Western Reserve University), Cleveland, chaplain and lecturer, 1943-46; Stanford University, Stanford, Calif., visiting chaplain, 1946; Columbia University, New York, N.Y., counselor to Protestant students, 1946-48; Smith College, Northampton, Mass., chaplain and assistant professor of religion, 1948-52; Williams College, Williamstown, Mass., Cluett Professor of Religion and dean of freshmen, 1952-60; Lake Forest College, Lake Forest, Ill, president, 1960-69; Chicago Council on Foreign Relations, director, 1964-69, executive director, 1969-71; Chicago State University, Chicago, Ill., vice-president of academic affairs, 1971—. Illinois Commission on Human Relations, chairman 1962—; National Merit Scholarship Corp., director.

MEMBER: Society for Religion in Higher Education, Phi Beta Kappa. *Awards, honors:* LL.D., Grinnell College, 1961; Brotherhood Award of National Council of Christians and Jews, 1962; D.D., Colgate University, 1963.

WRITINGS: Sex in Christianity and Psychoanalysis, Oxford University Press, 1956; *Sex and Love in the Bible,* Association Press, 1959; *The Restless Quest of Modern Man,* Oxford University Press, 1966; *Sex and Selfhood,* Westminster Press, 1968.†

* * *

COLEGATE, Isabel 1931-

PERSONAL: Born September 10, 1931, in London, England; daughter of Sir Arthur Colegate (a member of Parliament) and Lady Colegate Worsley; married Michael Briggs (director of an engineering firm), September 12, 1953; children: Emily, Barnaby, Joshua. *Education:* Attended three boarding schools in England. *Home:* Midford Castle, Bath, Somersetshire, England. *Agent:* Harold Matson Co., Inc., 30 Rockefeller Plaza, New York, N.Y. 10020.

CAREER: Novelist and critic.

WRITINGS—Novels: The Blackmailer, Anthony Blond, 1958; *A Man of Power,* Anthony Blond, 1960; *The Great Occasion,* Anthony Blond, 1962; *Statues in a Garden,* Bodley Head, 1964, Knopf, 1966; *Orlando King,* Knopf, 1968; *Orlando at the Brazen Threshold,* Bodley Head, 1971; *Agatha,* Bodley Head, 1974. Contributor to literary journals.

WORK IN PROGRESS: An eighth novel.

* * *

COLEMAN, Elliott 1906-

PERSONAL: Born September 26, 1906, in Binghamton, N.Y.; son of Benjamin Archibald and Jennie (Galbraith) Coleman. *Education:* Wheaton College, Wheaton, Ill., B.A., 1928; graduate study at Princeton Theological Seminary, at St. Stephen's House, Oxford, England, and General Theological Seminary, New York, N.Y. *Politics:* Democrat. *Home:* 3501 St. Paul Street, Baltimore, Md. *Office:* Johns Hopkins University, Baltimore, Md. 21218.

CAREER: Ordained to diaconate of Episcopal Church; Johns Hopkins University, Baltimore, Md., professor of English writing and director of writing seminars, 1945—. *Member:* American Association of University Professors, Phi Beta Kappa (honorary member).

WRITINGS: Poems, Dutton, 1936; *An American in Augustland,* University of North Carolina Press, 1940; *Pearl Harbor,* privately printed, 1942; *Twenty-seven Night Sonnets,* New Directions, 1949; (editor) *Lectures in Criticism,* Pantheon, 1949; *A Glass Darkly,* Contemporary Poetry, 1952; *The Golden Angel: Papers on Proust,* Coley Taylor & Co. and Academy Library Guild, 1954; *Thirty-three Night Sonnets,* Contemporary Poetry, 1955; *Mockingbirds at Fort McHenry,* Atlantis Editions (Spain), 1963; *Broken Death,* Linden Press, 1964; (editor) *Poems of Byron, Keats, and Shelley,* Doubleday, 1968; *100 Poems,* Tinker Press, 1972; *The Tangerine Birds,* Harbor House, 1973; *In the Canyon,* Bay Press, 1974.

Translations from the French: (In collaboration with the author, Georges Poulet) *Studies in Human Time,* Johns Hopkins Press, 1956; Pierre Emmanuel, *The Mad Poet* (unrhymed sections), Contemporary Poetry, 1956; (in collaboration with the author, Georges Poulet) *The Interior Distance,* Johns Hopkins Press, 1959; (in collaboration with the author, Alfredo Rizzardi) *Towns of This World,* Contemporary Poetry, 1962; (in collaboration with Carley Dawson, and the author, Georges Poulet) *The Metamorphoses of the Circle,* Johns Hopkins Press, 1967.

* * *

COLEMAN, Marion (Reeves) Moore 1900-

PERSONAL: Born March 10, 1900, in Brooklyn, N.Y.; daughter of David Halsey (a bookkeeper) and Elizabeth Shaw (Merrill) Moore; married Arthur Prudden Coleman (president of Alliance College), 1922. *Education:* State University of New York at Albany, B.A., 1920. *Politics:* Democrat. *Religion:* Congregational. *Home and office:* 202 Highland Ave., Cheshire, Conn. 06410.

CAREER: Writer. Alliance College, Alliance, Pa., lecturer in comparative cultures, 1950-62. *Awards, honors:* Chevalier of Polonia Restituta, 1963; Polish PEN of Warsaw award, 1973.

WRITINGS: (With husband, Arthur Prudden Coleman) *The Polish Insurrection of 1863,* Bayard Press, 1934; (editor) *The Polish Land,* Columbia University Press, 1943; (editor) *The Wayside Willow,* Columbia University Press, 1945; *Young Mickiewicz,* Alliance College Press, 1956; (compiler) *Polish Literature in English Translation, 960-1960, A Bibliography,* Cherry Hill, 1963; (with Arthur Prudden Coleman) *Wanderers Twain, Modjeska and Sienkiewicz: A View from California,* Cherry Hill, 1964; *A World Remembered,* Cherry Hill, 1965; *Mazeppa on the American Stage,* Cherry Hill, 1966; *Fair Rosalind: The American Career of Helena Modjeska,* Cherry Hill, 1969; *The Man on the Moon: The Story of Pan Twardowski,* Cherry Hill, 1971; *A Brigand, Two Queens, and a Prankster,* Cherry Hill, 1972; *Vistula Voyage: A Journey Down the Polish Mother of Waters,* Cherry Hill, 1974; (compiler) *The Polish Land,* Cherry Hill, 1974. Contributor to journals. Editor, American Association of Teachers of Slavic and East European Languages, 1943-48, *Alliance Journal* (Alliance College), 1951-60, *Polish Folklore,* 1956-62.

WORK IN PROGRESS: The American Influence on Henryk Sienkiewicz.

SIDELIGHTS: Mrs. Coleman became interested in the Slavs, especially the Poles after her marriage to Dr. Coleman. Since then, she learned to read Polish, and has made several trips to Poland and Eastern Europe besides visiting Slavic settlements in the U.S.

* * *

COLINA, Tessa Patterson 1915-

PERSONAL: Surname pronounced Co-lye-nah; born November 10, 1915, in Williamstown, Ky.; daughter of George W. (a minister and farmer) and Nancy (Mullins) Patterson; married Edward J. Colina (with printing firm), October 12, 1951; children: Jean (Mrs. Robert Shannon), Dale, Deborah. Education: Studied at Cincinnati Bible Seminary, two years, and at University of Cincinnati. Politics: Republican. Religion: Christian.

CAREER: Standard Publishing Co., Cincinnati, Ohio, assistant editor, 1946-47, elementary editor, 1948-51, vacation Bible school editor, 1951-57; free-lance writer. Member: National League of American Pen Women. Awards, honors: Author of the year, Cincinnati chapter, League of American Pen Women.

WRITINGS: Bible Stories about Jesus, Standard Publishing, 1954; Nursery Life of Jesus, Standard Publishing, 1954; How to Conduct a Vacation Bible School, Standard Publishing, 1954; Ark Full of Animals, Standard Publishing, 1955; A Year of Programs for Children's Church, Standard Publishing, 1962; God, We Thank You, David Cook, 1964; As We Saw It, David Cook, 1965; Tested Ideas for the Presession, David Cook, 1965; The Beatitudes, David Cook, 1965; God Cares for You, David Cook, 1965; Stories from Daniel, Standard Publishing, 1965; Pict-O-Lessons, Standard Publishing, 1965, 1966, and 1967; Children in Bible Lands, Standard Publishing, 1966; Noah and the Animals, Standard Publishing, 1966. Contributor of articles, stories, and poems to Christian journals; author of Sunday school manuals.†

* * *

COLLIER, (Alan) Graham 1923-

PERSONAL: Born September 12, 1923, in Farnsworth, Lancashire, England; son of Stanley (a hotelier) and Ann (Millier) Collier; married Mary Clacy (a concert singer), March 18, 1944 (divorced, 1970); married Helena Wessler (a painter), 1970; children: Mary Wendy, Ruth Cecelia, Andrew Graham. Education: Studied in England at Lincoln School of Art, 1940-43, and Newark School of Art, 1943-44; University of London, study at Slade School of Fine Art, 1944-45, and Institute of Education, 1947-49, receiving N.R.D. (national registered designer; awarded by Council of Industrial Design, London), and M. Coll. H. (member of College of Handicrafts); also studied two summers at University of Perugia in Italy. Religion: Agnostic. Office: Department of Art, University of Georgia, Athens, Ga. 30601.

CAREER: Painter, designer, and teacher of art. Richmond School of Art, London, England, head of department of design, 1946-47; St. Peter's College, Yorkshire, England, director of art, 1949-54; Lancing College, Sussex, England, director of art, 1954-60; former associate professor of art at Western Washington State College, and University of Connecticut; now with University of Georgia, Athens, as pro-

fessor of art. Part-time lecturer in art education, University of London, 1954-60. Paintings exhibited at one-man shows in England and Canada, and in group exhibitions at Royal Academy, London, and elsewhere; commissioned portraits include Sir John Barbirolli, Sir Reginald Thatcher, Earl of Harewood, Hugo Rignold, and others; also has done advertising design for British corporations, and wallpaper and textile designing. Adviser on art books to Prentice-Hall, Inc., 1961—. Member: Royal Drawing Society of London.

WRITINGS: Form, Space and Vision (text), Prentice-Hall, 1963, 3rd edition, 1972; Art and the Creative Consciousness, Prentice-Hall, 1972. Art correspondent, Yorkshire Evening Press, 1947-52.

WORK IN PROGRESS: WOMBAT, an account of RAF bomber command in World War II.

SIDELIGHTS: Collier painted and drew in France, Netherlands, Germany, Austria, Italy, and Spain between 1948-59. He studied art training in liberal arts colleges of the East on U.S. tour, 1956. Avocational interests: Philosophy and Jungian psychology.

* * *

COLLINS, Carvel 1912-

PERSONAL: First name rhymes with marvel; born June 14, 1912, in West Union, Ohio; son of John Edgar (a professor) and Ina (Treber) Collins; married Mary Brewster, November 17, 1939 (divorced, 1956); married Ann Green, October 1, 1960; children: (first marriage) Lucy Collins. Education: Miami University, Oxford, Ohio, B.S., 1933; University of Chicago, M.A., 1937, Ph.D., 1944. Home: 52606 Highlands Dr., South Bend, Ind. 46635. Office: University of Notre Dame, Notre Dame, Ind. 46556.

CAREER: Instructor in English at Colorado State College, Fort Collins, 1938-39, Stephens College, Columbia, Mo., 1939-40, Harvard University, Cambridge, Mass., 1942-45; assistant professor of English at Swarthmore College, Swarthmore, Pa., 1945-46, Harvard University, 1946-50; Massachusetts Institute of Technology, Cambridge, associate professor, 1950-56, professor of English, 1956-67; University of Notre Dame, Notre Dame, Ind., professor of English, 1967—. Visiting professor at University of California, Berkeley, 1949, Salzburg Seminar in American Studies, 1955, University of Aix-Marseille, 1955, and University of Tokyo, 1961-62. Military service: U.S. Naval Reserve, 1942; became lieutenant junior grade.

MEMBER: Modern Language Association of America, College English Association, American Studies Association, National Council of Teachers of English, Modern Humanities Research Association. Awards, honors: Fidelis Foundation research grant, 1963; Bolligen Foundation fellowship, 1964-65; O'Brien Fund grant, 1970.

WRITINGS: The American Sporting Gallery, Harvard University Press, 1949; Sam Ward in the Gold Rush, Stanford University Press, 1949; (editor and author of introduction) Frank Norris, McTeague, Rinehart, 1950, new edition, Holt, 1968; (with others) Trends in Research in American Literature, Modern Language Association, 1951; (with others) Literature in the Modern World, George Peabody College Press, 1954; (editor and author of introduction) William Faulkner, New Orleans Sketches, Rutgers University Press, 1958, revised and expanded edition, Random House, 1968; (author of introduction) William Faulkner, The Unvanquished, Signet Books, 1959; (editor and author of introduction) Erskine Caldwell, Men and

Women, Little, Brown, 1961; (editor and author of introduction) *William Faulkner's University Pieces*, Kendyusha Press, 1962; (editor and author of introduction) William Faulkner, *Early Prose and Poetry*, Atlantic-Little, Brown, 1962.

Contributor: *English Institute Essays, 1952*, Columbia University Press, 1954; Malcolm Cowley, editor, *Writers at Work*, Viking, 1958; K. Hunt and P. Stoakes, editors, *Our Living Language*, Houghton, 1961; Irving Malin, editor, *Psychoanalysis and American Fiction*, Dutton, 1965; Wallace Stegner, editor, *The American Novel from James Fenimore Cooper to William Faulkner*, Basic Books, 1965; Charles F. Madden, editor, *Talks With Authors*, Southern Illinois University Press, 1968; Michael Cowan, editor, *Twentieth-Century Interpretations of "The Sound and the Fury,"* Prentice-Hall, 1968; Harrison Hayford and Hershel Parker, editors, *"Moby-Dick" as Doubloon: Essays and Extracts, 1851-1969*, Norton, 1970; James Meriwether, editor, *Studies in "The Sound and the Fury,"* C. E. Merrill, 1970; Jay Martin, editor, *Twentieth-Century Views of Nathanael West*, Prentice-Hall, 1971.

WORK IN PROGRESS: A biographical-critical volume on William Faulkner for Farrar, Straus.

*   *   *

COLLINS, Henry   1917-

PERSONAL: Born July 7, 1917, in Newcastle-on-Tyne, England; son of Abraham and Ida (Hamburger) Collins; married Edith Kirkman, April 1, 1960. *Education:* Queen's College, Oxford, B.A., 1939, M.A., 1943, D.Phil, 1959. *Politics:* Labour party. *Home:* 5 Furze Hill Court, Hove 2, Sussex, England.

CAREER: Oxford University, Oxford, England, staff tutor in social studies, department of extramural studies, 1947—. Labour candidate for Parliament from North Lewisham in 1964 general election. *Military service:* British Army, 1939-46; served in Nigeria and France; became sergeant. *Member:* Society for the Study of Labour History (honorary secretary, 1961-64), Association of Tutors in Adult Education (honorary treasurer, 1956-59).

WRITINGS: Trade Unions Today, Muller, 1950; (contributor) Basil Davidson and A. Ademola, editors, *The New West Africa*, Allen & Unwin, 1953; (with H. J. Fyrth) *The Foundry Workers: A Trade Union History*, Amalgamated Union of Foundry Workers, 1959; (with C. Abramsky) *Karl Marx and the British Labour Movement*, St. Martin's, 1965. Writer of regular column on economic affairs for *Tribune* (weekly); contributor to *Economic History Review*. Member of editorial board, *Views* (quarterly).

WORK IN PROGRESS: Karl Marx, a biography, in collaboration with C. Abramsky.†

*   *   *

COLORADO CAPELLA, Antonio Julio   1903-
(Antonio J. Colorado)

PERSONAL: Born February 13, 1903, in San Juan, Puerto Rico; son of Rafael D'Assoy Colorado (a photographer) and Lorenza Capella Colorado Martinez; married Isabel Laguna Matienzo (a social worker), 1939; children: Antonio, Isabelita, Rafael. *Education:* University of Puerto Rico, B.A., 1932; Clark University, M.A., 1933; Universidad Central, Madrid, Spain, Ph.D., 1934. *Politics:* Popular Democratic Party. *Religion:* Roman Catholic. *Home:* Vesta St. 821, Rio Piedras, Puerto Rico.

CAREER: U.S. Department of State, writer, 1942-43; University of Puerto Rico, dean of social science, 1943-46, director of university press, 1946-48; Department of Education of Puerto Rico, director of department press, 1948-55; Labor Relations Board of Puerto Rico, president, 1962—. Member of Board of directors, Metropolitan Bus Authority, Puerto Rico. *Member:* World Federalism (Puerto Rico; vice-president), Academia Puertorriquena de la Lengua Espanola (secretary), Academia de Artes y Ciencias (Puerto Rico.)

WRITINGS—Under name Antonio J. Colorado: (Colaborator) *New World Guides to Latin America Republics*, Duell, Sloan & Pearce, 1943; *Puerto Rico y Tu*, Prentice-Hall, 1948; (with Cruz Monclova) *Noticia y Pulso del Movimiento Politico Puertorriqueno*, 1955; *Luis Pales Matos, el Hombre y el Poeta*, Rodadero, 1964; *The First Book of Puerto Rico*, Watts, 1964. Also author of *Puerto Rico: La Tierra y otros ensayos*, 1972. Editor, *Diario de Puerto Rico*, 1948-50.

Translations: *Historia de los Estados Unidos*, Ginn & Co., 1953; *La Cancion Verde*, Troutman, 1956; *Nuestro Mundo a Traves de las Edades*, Prentice-Hall, 1959; *America de Todos*, Rand McNally, 1963; *El Arbol de la Violeta*, Troutman, 1964.

WORK IN PROGRESS: Biografias Varias; Ensayos y conferencias; critica literaria.

SIDELIGHTS: Colorado Capella is interested in journalism, labor relations, political science and sociology. He has traveled through Central and northern South America, Spain, France, Santo Domingo, Caribbean Islands, Cuba, United States, and Canada.

*   *   *

COLTHARP, Lurline H(ughes)   1913-

PERSONAL: Born May 9, 1913, in Bridgeport, Tex.; daughter of Frank Alexis (a civil engineer) and Mary (Fisher) Hughes; first married, 1935; married second husband, J. Robert Coltharp (now an associate professor of engineering), October 9, 1963; children: (first marriage) Mary Lurline Douglas, Robert E. Douglas. *Education:* Texas Western College, student, 1929-31; University of Texas, B.A., 1935, M.A., 1951, Ph.D., 1964. *Religion:* Presbyterian. *Home:* 4263 Ridgecrest, El Paso, Tex. 79902. *Office:* University of Texas, El Paso, Tex. 79968.

CAREER: Elementary teacher, 1932-34, and high school teacher of English, 1945-47, 1949-50, 1952-53, Ysleta, Tex.; University of Texas, Texas Western College, El Paso, 1954—, associate professor, 1965-70, professor of English, 1970—. *Member:* Modern Language Association of America, Linguistic Society of America, Teachers of English to Speakers of Other Languages (charter member), American Dialect Society, American Name Society, American Association of University Women (president of El Paso branch, 1953-54), American Association of University Professors, PEO Sisterhood (chapter president, 1958), Zeta Tau Alpha Alumnae, Phi Kappa Phi, Pi Lambda Theta, Delta Kappa Gamma, Woman's Club of El Paso. *Awards, honors:* Two Ford Foundation grants.

WRITINGS: The Tongue of the Tirilones: A Linguistic Study of a Criminal Argot, University of Alabama Press, 1965; (contributor) Glenn Gilbert, editor, *Texas Studies in Bilingualism*, Walter Gruyter and Co., 1970; (contributor) Paul Turner, editor, *Bilingualism in the Southwest*, University of Arizona Press, 1972. Contributor to journals.

WORK IN PROGRESS: Dialect study and place name studies.

SIDELIGHTS: Coltharp has produced lecture tapes which are used worldwide.

*   *   *

COMBS, A(rthur) W(right) 1912-

PERSONAL: Born June 3, 1912, in Newark, N.J.; son of Arthur Wright (a veterinarian) and Charlotte (Vyse) Combs; married Mildred Mitchell (now a teacher), September 23, 1934 (divorced); children: Carol Andrea Hole, Peter Arthur. *Education:* Cornell University, student, 1930-33; The Ohio State University, B.S. in Ed., 1935, M.A., 1941, Ph.D., 1945. *Home:* 2904 Southwest Second Court, Gainesville, Fla. 32601. *Office:* 285 Norman Hall, University of Florida, Gainesville, Fla. 32601.

CAREER: Diplomate, American Board of Examiners in Professional Psychology. Teacher and school psychologist, Alliance, Ohio, 1935-41; Syracuse University, Syracuse, N.Y., instructor, 1942-44, assistant professor, 1944-48, associate professor of psychology and head of personal counseling service, 1948-53; University of Florida, Gainesville, professor of education, 1953—. Consulting psychologist to other schools. Chairman of Joint Council of New York State Psychologists, 1952. *Member:* Association for Supervision and Curriculum Development (president, 1966), American Psychological Association (fellow), American Personnel and Guidance Association, Society for the Psychological Study of Social Issues, National Education Association, Southeastern Psychological Association, Florida Association of School Psychologists (president, 1960), Florida Psychological Association, Florida Education Association, Sigma Xi, Phi Delta Kappa.

WRITINGS: (With Snyder and others) *Casebook of Non-Directive Counseling*, Houghton, 1947; (with D. Snygg) *Individual Behavior: A New Frame of Reference for Psychology*, Harper, 1949, revised edition, 1959; (with others) *Instructor's Handbook for NCO Human Relations Course*, U.S. Air Force, 1954; (editor) *Personality Theory and Counseling Practice*, University of Florida, 1961; (with D. W. Soper) *The Relationship of Child Perceptions to Achievement and Behavior in the Early School Years*, U.S. Office of Education and University of Florida, 1963; *The Professional Education of Teachers*, Allyn & Bacon, 1965; (with others) *Florida Studies in the Helping Professions*, University of Florida Press, 1969; (with D. L. Avila and W. W. Purkey) *Helping Relationships: Basic Concepts for the Helping Professions*, Allyn & Bacon, 1971; (with Avila and Purkey) *Helping Relationships Sourcebook*, Allyn & Bacon, 1971; *Educational Accountability: Beyond Behavioral Objectives*, Association for Supervision and Curriculum Development, 1972; (with others) *The Professional Education of Teachers: A Humanistic Approach to Teacher Preparation*, Allyn & Bacon, 1974.

Contributor: D. C. McClelland, editor, *Studies in Motivation*, Appleton, 1955; Fullager and others, editors, *Readings in Educational Psychology*, Crowell, 1956, 2nd edition, 1964; E. L. Hartley and R. E. Hartley, editors, *Outside Readings in Psychology*, Crowell, 1957; Dalaney and others, *Contributions to Modern Psychology*, Oxford University Press, 1958; Farwall and Peters, editors, *Guidance Readings for Counselors*, Rand McNally, 1960; W. C. Resnick and D. H. Heller, *On Your Own in College*, C. E. Merrill, 1963; D. E. Hamachek, *The Self in Growth, Teaching, and Learning*, Prentice-Hall, 1965; J. J. Fry-

mier, *Handbook of Research on Human Motivation*, Ohio State University, 1971; Alexander Schuller, editor, *Lehrerrole im Wandel*, Beltz, 1971.

Editor, *Yearbook* of Association for Supervision and Curriculum Development, 1962. Contributor to annals and proceedings of other organizations and more than 100 articles to psychology, social science, and education journals.

WORK IN PROGRESS: Research on the nature of the helping professions, teacher education, and perceptual psychology.

*   *   *

CONANT, Howard (Somers) 1921-

PERSONAL: Surname is pronounced *Co*-nunt; born May 5, 1921, in Beloit, Wis.; son of Rufus P. (a typewriter dealer) and Edith (Somers) Conant; children: Judith Lynne, Jeffrey Scott. *Education:* University of Wisconsin, Milwaukee, B.S., 1946; University of Wisconsin, Madison, M.S., 1947; State University of New York at Buffalo, Ed.D., 1950; also studied at Art Students League, New York, N.Y., 1944-45. *Home:* 139 Thompson St., New York, N.Y. 10012. *Office:* New York University, Washington Sq., New York, N.Y. 10003.

CAREER: University of Wisconsin, Madison, instructor in art, 1946-47; State University of New York at Buffalo, assistant professor, 1947-50, professor of art, 1950-55; New York University, New York, N.Y., professor of art education, chairman of department, and chairman of art collection, 1955—. Artist, exhibiting at one-man shows in Washington, D.C., New York, Buffalo, Milwaukee, and in group shows. Moderator of art programs on WBEN-TV, Buffalo, 1951-55; consultant to, and participant in, Girl Scouts of America-NBC television and film series on hand arts, 1958-59; lecturer in India on modern American art under auspices of U.S. Department of State, 1964; director of Seminar on Education in Visual Arts, U.S. Office of Education, 1964-65. *Military service:* U.S. Army Air Forces, 1943-46; became first lieutenant.

MEMBER: National Committee on Art Education (council, 1951-65; chairman, 1962-63), National Art Education Association (council, 1961-65), Institute for the Study of Art in Education (president, 1965—), Eastern Arts Association, New York State Art Teachers Association, Washington Square Torch Club (president, 1964-65).

WRITINGS: Art Workshop Leaders Planning Guide, Davis Publications, 1958; (with Arne Randall) *Art in Education*, Bennett, 1959, 2nd edition, 1964; (editor) *Masterpieces of the Arts*, Volume IV of "Cultural Library," Parents Institute, 1959, 2nd revised edition, 1964; *Art Education*, Center for Applied Research in Education, 1964; *Seminar on Elementary and Secondary Education in the Visual Arts*, New York University, 1965; (contributor) Gregory Battcock, editor, *Ideas in Art Education*, Dutton, 1973; (contributor) *Festschrift*, Syracuse University Press, 1974. Also author of evaluation reports for Guggenheim Museum and New York University Center for Educational Research. Author of seven volumes and editor of two for Lincoln Library of the Arts. Contributor to *Saturday Review, Art News*, and to journals of art and art education.

*   *   *

CONDEE, Ralph Waterbury 1916-

PERSONAL: Born January 11, 1916, in Chicago, Ill.; son of Ralph Waterbury (a lawyer) and Ruth (Hanecy) Condee;

married Norma Faricy, October 10, 1942; children: Ralph, Nancy, William. *Education:* University of Illinois, B.A., 1937, Ph.D., 1949; University of Chicago, A.M., 1939. *Home:* 443 East Waring Ave., State College, Pa. 16801. *Office:* Pennsylvania State University, University Park, Pa. 16802.

CAREER: Pennsylvania State University, University Park, instructor in English literature, 1949-51, assistant professor, 1951-56, associate professor, 1956-58, professor of English literature and humanities, 1958—. *Military service:* U.S. Navy, 1942-46; became lieutenant. *Member:* Modern Language Association of America, Milton Society of America, National Trust for Scotland.

WRITINGS: (With F. L. Gwynn and A. O. Lewis) *The Case for Poetry*, Prentice-Hall, 1954, 2nd edition, 1965; (editor with Luther Harshbarger, Benjamin Kahn, and John Mourant) *Exploring Religious Ideas*, Center for Continuing Liberal Education, 1959; (with Deborah Austin and Chadwick Hansen) *Modern Fiction*, Center for Continuing Liberal Education, 1959; (editor) *Great Modern Short Stories*, Center for Continuing Liberal Education, 1960; (contributor) J.W. Binns, editor, *The Latin Poetry of English Poets*, Routledge & Kegan Paul, 1974; *Structure in Milton's Poetry*, Pennsylvania State University Press, 1974. Contributor to *Encyclopaedia Britannica Book of the Year*, 1942; contributor of articles and reviews to *Reporter, Explicator*, and learned periodicals.

* * *

CONE, John F(rederick) 1926-

PERSONAL: Born October 10, 1926, in Salem, Ohio; son of Stephen F. (a florist) and Nina J. (Bean) Cone. *Education:* Rutgers University. A.B., 1948, A.M., 1953; University of Florence, graduate study, 1959; New York University, Ph.D., 1964. *Residence:* Winston-Salem, N.C.

CAREER: Teacher of English at Montclair Academy, Montclair, N.J., 1949-52, Hackley School, Tarrytown, N.Y., 1957-58, and Scarsdale High School, Scarsdale, N.Y., 1952-66; North Carolina School of the Arts, Winston-Salem, dean of academic studies, beginning, 1966. Assistant to opera director, Chautauqua Opera Co., 1948; member of summer stock companies. *Awards, honors:* Founders Day Award, New York University; Miriam and Ira D. Wallach Foundation grant.

WRITINGS: Oscar Hammerstein's Manhattan Opera Company, University of Oklahoma Press, 1966. Contributor to two anthologies, *The World's Love Poetry*, Bantam, 1960, and *A Treasury of Civil War Humor*, Yoseloff, 1964.

WORK IN PROGRESS: Early Years of the Metropolitan Opera Company.

SIDELIGHTS: Cone possesses some competence in French, German, Italian, and Spanish.†

* * *

CONGDON, William Grosvenor 1912-

PERSONAL: Born April 15, 1912, in Providence, R.I.; son of Gilbert Maurice (an industrialist) and Caroline (Grosvenor) Congdon. *Education:* Yale University. B.A., 1934; studied at Demetrious School of Sculpture, 1935, 1939, and Pennsylvania Academy of Fine Arts, 1935. *Religion:* Roman Catholic. *Home:* Monastery Beato Lorenzo, Subiaco, Italy. *Agent:* (Art) Betty Parsons Gallery, 24 West 57th St., New York, N.Y. 10019.

CAREER: Painter, living and working in Italy for twenty-four years, with occasional periods of residence in other countries. Exhibitor at one-man shows in New York, Washington, D.C., Santa Barbara, Chicago, Iowa, Boston, Venice, Italy, and others, 1949-64; also exhibitor in shows at Carnegie Institute, Whitney Museum of American Art, Museum of Modern Art, Rhode Island Museum, and other museums and galleries in America, Italy, England, and Japan. Works owned by private collectors and Metropolitan Museum of Art, Whitney Museum of American Art, Detroit Institute of Arts, New York Museum of Modern Art, and a number of other museums, galleries, and universities. *Wartime service:* American Field Service, attached to British 8th Army in Middle East and Europe, 1942-45. *Awards, honors:* Temple Gold Medal, Pennsylvania Academy of Fine Arts, 1951; purchase award, University of Illinois, 1952; W. A. Clark Award, Corcoran Gallery of Art, 1953; first International Sacred Art Award, Trieste, Italy, 1961.

WRITINGS: In My Disc of Gold, Reynal, 1962; *Esistenza/Viaggio: di pittore americano diario*, Jaca Books, 1975. Contributor to *Atlantic Monthly, Botteghe Oscure, Critic, America*.

SIDELIGHTS: Congdon speaks French, Italian, Spanish, and Greek. His foreign residence, in addition to Italy, includes periods of painting in Greece, Mexico, India, Egypt, France, Spain, and North Africa.

* * *

CONLIN, David A. 1897-

PERSONAL: Born June 23, 1897, in Long Island City, N.Y.; son of Alexander H. (a stonemason) and Martha (Bruder) Conlin; married Jane McKillion, October 1, 1921; children: David A., Jr., Robert D., Donald E. *Education:* Syracuse University, A.B., 1920; Yale University, Ph.D., 1933. *Politics:* Democrat.

CAREER: New York State College for Teachers (now State University of New York at Albany), assistant professor, 1940-41; U.S. Department of Interior, War Relocation Authority, Poston, Ariz., director of adult education, 1942-45; Arizona State University, Tempe, professor of English education, beginning 1948. *Military service:* U.S. Army, 1918-19. *Member:* National Council of Teachers of English (associate chairman of committee on preparation and certification of teachers), Conference on College Composition and Communication, Modern Language Association of America, Phi Kappa Phi, Pi Mu Epsilon.

WRITINGS: Grammar for Written English, Houghton, 1961; (with George Herman) *Modern Grammar and Composition*, Books 1-3, American Book Co., 1965; (with Herman) *Resources for Modern Grammar and Composition*, American Book Co., 1965; *A Modern Approach to English*, American Book Co., 1968; (with Herman and Jerome Martin) *Gains in Our Language Today*, American Book Co., 1971; (with A. Renee LeRoy) *Asking About Our Language Today*, American Book Co., 1971. Contributor to *English Journal*. Member of editorial board, *Arizona English Bulletin*.†

* * *

CONNELLY, Owen (Sergeson, Jr.) 1924-

PERSONAL: Born January 29, 1924, in Morganton, N.C.; son of Owen Sergeson and Mary L. (Earle) Connelly; married. *Education:* Wake Forest College, B.S., 1948, M.A.,

1949; University of North Carolina, Ph.D., 1960. *Home:* Hunting Creek Farms, Columbia, S.C. 29061. *Office:* 202 Carrell, University of South Carolina, Columbia, S.C. 29208.

CAREER: In U.S. Army Air Forces, 1943-46, and Air Force and Army (Rangers), 1950-56, served in Europe, 1945, and in Korea and Japan, 1950-52; instructor in history at University of North Carolina, Chapel Hill, 1956-60, and Duke University, Durham, N.C., 1960-61; University of North Carolina at Greensboro, assistant professor, 1961-65, associate professor of modern European history, 1965-67; University of South Carolina, Columbia, professor, 1967-69; University of Kentucky, Lexington, professor, 1969-70; University of South Carolina, Columbia, professor of modern European history, 1970—. *Member:* American Historical Association, Society for French Historical Studies, Societe d'Histoire Moderne, Institut Napoleon, U.S. Commission on Military History.

WRITINGS: Napoleon's Satellite Kingdoms, Free Press, 1965; *The Gentle Bonaparte* (biography of Joseph Bonaparte), Macmillan, 1968; *Epoch of Napoleon,* Holt, 1972. Contributor of articles and reviews to journals.

*   *   *

CONNELLY, Thomas L(awrence) 1938-

PERSONAL: Born February 14, 1938, in Nashville, Tenn.; son of Fred Marlin (a certified public accountant) and Mildred Inez Connelly; married Sally Eaves (a free-lance editor). *Education:* David Lipscomb College, B.A., 1959; Rice University, M.A., 1961, Ph.D., 1963. *Office:* Department of History, University of South Carolina, Columbia, S.C. 20208.

CAREER: Presbyterian College, Clinton, S.C., professor of history and head of department, 1963-64; Mississippi State University, State College, assistant professor, 1964-66, associate professor of history, 1966-69; University of South Carolina, Columbia, 1969—, professor of history, 1971—. *Member:* American Historical Association, Organization of American Historians, American Association for State and Local History, Southern Historical Association, Tennessee Historical Society, East Tennessee Historical Society, Phi Alpha Theta, Phi Kappa Phi, Pi Kappa Delta, Cumberland Mountain Hiking Club (president). *Awards, honors:* John Gardner Award, Rice University, 1963; John T. Moore Award, Tennessee Historical Society, 1964; American Philosophical Society research grant, 1965; Mississippi State University Development Foundation research grants, 1965-66, 1967; Jules Landry Award, Louisiana State University Press, 1971; Jefferson Davis Award, 1971; Fletcher Pratt Award, New York City Civil War Roundtable, 1972.

WRITINGS: Historic Sites of Middle Tennessee, privately printed, 1957; *Will Success Spoil Jeff Davis?* McGraw, 1963; *Army of the Heartland: The Army of Tennessee, 1861-1862,* Louisiana State University Press, 1967; *Discovering the Appalachians,* Stackpole, 1968; *Autumn of Glory: The Army of Tennessee, 1862-1865,* Louisiana State University Press, 1971; *The Politics of Command: Factions and Ideas in Confederate Strategy,* Louisiana State University Press, 1973. Contributor to historical journals.

AVOCATIONAL INTERESTS: Collecting weapons, Americana (discovered long-lost papers of General Don Carlos Buell, U.S. Army of the Ohio, 1961), and Indian relics; writing folk songs, hiking, photography, trout fishing, raft expeditions on white water rivers.

BIOGRAPHICAL/CRITICAL SOURCES: Nashville Tennessean Sunday Magazine, May 5, 1957; *Houston Post,* October 8, 1961; *State and Columbia Record,* December 8, 1963.†

*   *   *

CONNER, Paul Willard 1937-

PERSONAL: Born April 16, 1937, in Oak Park, Ill.; son of Nevelle Allan (a Chicago fire chief) and Lucy Madelyn (Brooks) Conner. *Education:* San Bernardino Valley College (now California State College at San Bernardino), A.A., 1957; University of California, Riverside, B.A. (magna cum laude), 1959; Princeton University, M.A., 1961, Ph.D., 1963. *Home:* 163 Pacific St., Brooklyn, N.Y. 11201. *Office:* Inter Future, 535 Fifth Ave., New York, N.Y. 10017.

CAREER: George Washington University, Washington, D.C., assistant professor of political science, 1962-63; Princeton University, Princeton, N.J.,lecturer, 1964-65, assistant professor of politics, 1965-67; Pace University, New York, N.Y., associate professor of social-sciences, 1967-72; Inter Future, New York, N.Y., president, 1972—. Director of International Honors Program, 1965-67. *Member:* American Political Science Association, American Civil Liberties Union. *Awards, honors:* Received Wilson, Heartshorne, and Danforth fellowships, Princeton University.

WRITINGS: Poor Richard's Politicks: Benjamin Franklin and His New American Order, Oxford University Press, 1965. Also editor of *Inter Future Reports 1971-74,* 1975. Contributor to *American Quarterly.*

WORK IN PROGRESS: Demons, Blacks, and Radicals: Forbodings of Granville Sharp, a selection from the notes and letters of the English abolitionist, 1735-1814.

*   *   *

CONRAD, David Eugene 1928-

PERSONAL: Born August 22, 1928, in Marietta, Okla.; son of David E. (a Civil Service employee) and Lurlyn (Herrin) Conrad; married Beverly Anne Lester, February 27, 1952; children: Cynthia, Edward. *Religion:* Methodist. *Education:* Attended Baylor University, 1947-48; University of Oklahoma, B.A., 1952, M.A., 1955, Ph.D., 1962. *Office:* Department of History, Southern Illinois University, Carbondale, Ill. 62901.

CAREER: Southwest Texas State College (now University), San Marcos, instructor, 1957-61, assistant professor, 1961-63, associate professor of history, 1963-67; Southern Illinois University, Carbondale, associate professor of history, 1967—. Fulbright visiting professor, Universidad de Concepcion, 1965; visiting professor, University of Oklahoma, summer, 1967. *Military service:* U.S. Army, 1946-47, 1952-53; served in Japan and Korea; became captain; received Commendation Medal. *Member:* Organization of American Historians, Economic History Association, Agricultural History Society, Great Plains Historical Association, Western Historical Association, Rotary International. *Awards, honors:* Book Award of Agricultural History Society, 1964.

WRITINGS: The Forgotten Farmers: The Story of Sharecroppers in the New Deal, University of Illinois Press, 1965; (with William C. Pool and Emmie Craddock) *Lyndon B. Johnson: The Formative Years,* Southwest Texas State College Press, 1965. Contributor to *Great Plains Journal,* and other periodicals.

WORK IN PROGRESS: Theodore Roosevelt and the Great West.

AVOCATIONAL INTERESTS: Conservation, travel writing, photography.†

*   *   *

CONRON, (Alfred) Brandon   1919-

PERSONAL: Born November 29, 1919, in St. John, New Brunswick, Canada; son of Matthew English (a clergyman) and Rose H. (Bradley) Conron; married Caroline L. Spencer, May 28, 1949; children: Caroline Ross, Augusta L., Alexander B. *Education:* University of Western Ontario, B.A., 1941, M.A., 1947; Harvard University, A.M., 1948, Ph.D., 1951. *Religion:* United Church of Canada. *Home:* 605 Windermere Rd., London, Ontario, Canada. *Office:* University of Western Ontario, London, Ontario, Canada.

CAREER: University of Western Ontario, London, lecturer in English, 1946-47, assistant professor, 1949-52, associate professor, 1952-56, professor of English and head of department, 1956-58, principal of Middlesex College, 1958-61, professor of English, 1961—. United Community Services, London, director, 1958-61; London Boy Scout Executive, member, 1956—. *Military service:* Canadian Army, Armoured Corps, 1941-46; became major; received Distinguished Service Order, French Croix de Guerre. Canada Militia, lieutenant colonel and commanding officer of First Hussars, 1950-52. *Member:* Modern Language Association of America, Humanities Association of Canada, Association of University Teachers of English, London Hunt and Country Club (director, 1965—).

WRITINGS: (Assistant Latin editor) *The Literary Works of Matthew Prior,* edited by H. B. Wright and Monroe Spears, Oxford University Press, 1959; (editor with Guy Sylvestre and Carl F. Klinck) *Canadian Writers,* Ryerson, 1964; (contributor) *The Literary History of Canada,* University of Toronto Press, 1964; *Morley Callaghan,* Twayne, 1966. Contributor of articles and reviews to Canadian periodicals.

WORK IN PROGRESS: Morley Callaghan for McGraw's "Critical Views of Canadian Writers" series.

*   *   *

COOMBS, Philip H(all)   1915-

PERSONAL: Born August 15, 1915, in Holyoke, Mass.; son of Charles Gilmore and Nellie (Hall) Coombs; married Helena Brooks, October 18, 1941; children: Peter Brooks, Helena Hall. *Education:* Amherst College, B.A., 1937; graduate study at University of Chicago, 1937-39, and Brookings Institution, 1939-40. *Politics:* Democrat. *Home address:* River Road, Essex, Conn. 06426. *Office address:* International Council for Educational Development, P.O. Box 217, Essex, Conn. 06426.

CAREER: Williams College, Williamstown, Mass., instructor in economics, 1939, 1940-41; U.S. government, Washington, D.C., economist, Office of Price Administration, 1941-42, economic adviser, Office of Economic Stabilization, 1945-46; Amherst College, Amherst, Mass., professor of economics, 1947-49; President's Materials Policy Commission (Paley Commission), Washington, D.C., executive director, 1950-52; Ford Foundation, New York, N.Y., program director for education, and director of research, Fund for the Advancement of Education, 1952-60; U.S. Department of State, Washington, D.C., assistant secretary of state for international educational and cultural

affairs, 1961-62; International Institute for Educational Planning, Paris, France, director, 1963-68, director of research, 1969-70; International Council for Educational Development, Essex, Conn., vice-chairman, 1970—. Chairman of U.S. delegation to UNESCO Conferences on Economic Growth and Educational Development in Addis Ababa, 1961, and Santiago, 1962; chairman of Organization for Economic Co-operation and Development Conference on Educational Investment and Economic Growth, Washington, D.C., 1962. Consultant on education and economic planning to governments of India, 1953-55, Turkey, 1957, and Spain, 1967-71. Visiting lecturer, Harvard University, Graduate School of Education, 1969; visiting professor, Yale University, Institute of Social Science, 1970-71. Co-founder, Center for Educational Enquiry, 1970. *Military service:* U.S. Army, Office of Strategic Services, 1943-45; received Legion of Merit.

MEMBER: International Society for Public Administration, American Economic Association, Council on Foreign Relations, Phi Beta Kappa, Century Association (New York). *Awards, honors:* L.H.D., Amherst College, 1962; LL.D., Brandeis University and Monmouth College, 1962; Council on Foreign Relations, fellowship, 1962-63; Brookings Institution guest fellow, 1963.

WRITINGS: The Fourth Dimension of Foreign Policy—Educational and Cultural Affairs, Council on Foreign Relations and Harper, 1964; *Education and Foreign Aid,* Harvard University Press, 1965; *The New Media: Memo to Educational Planners,* UNESCO, 1967; *The World Educational Crisis: A Systems Analysis,* Oxford University Press, 1968; *What is Educational Planning,* UNESCO, 1970; (editor) *Psychological Aspects of Medical Training,* C. C Thomas, 1971; *Managing Educational Costs,* Oxford University Press, 1972; *New Paths to Learning for Rural Children and Youth,* International Council for Educational Development, 1973: *Attacking Rural Poverty: How Nonformal Education Can Help,* Johns Hopkins Press, 1974; (editor) *Education for Rural Development: Case Studies for Planners,* Praeger, 1975. Contributor to collections and journals in area of cultural affairs, education, economics and planning.

AVOCATIONAL INTERESTS: Sailing, fishing, swimming, touring, reading, house repairs, community service.

*   *   *

COONEY, David M(artin)   1930-

PERSONAL: Born August 5, 1930, in Los Angeles, Calif.; son of Arthur Byron (a teacher) and Margaret (Metcalf) Cooney; married Beverly Satchwell, February 22, 1952; children: Kathleen, David M., Jr., Karen, Kacy. *Education:* University of Southern California, A.B., 1951; George Washington University, M.A., 1965; U.S. Naval War College, diplomate, 1965. *Religion:* Protestant. *Address:* Staff, Commander, Sixth Fleet, F.P.O. New York, N.Y. 09501; 215 North Valencia St., Alhambra, Calif.

CAREER: U.S. Navy, regular officer, with duty in Far East, Pacific, Arctic, Mediterranean, and Europe, 1951—, public affairs officer, Sixth Fleet, 1965—, with rank of commander.

WRITINGS: The Navy Man Speaks, U.S. Navy, 1959; *A Chronology of the U.S. Navy 1775-1965,* F. Watts, 1965; *The Role of the Naval Commander in Psychological Warfare in the Cold War,* U.S. Navy, 1965. Articles include travel stories and encyclopedia entries on seapower, naval history, and military insignia. Editor, Comsixth Fleet *Newsletter* (official-use-only publication).

WORK IN PROGRESS: Researching biographical material on early naval leaders who served in the Mediterranean; studying other phases of naval history, especially the influence of seapower on U.S. development.†

* * *

COONS, Frederica Bertha (Safley) 1910-

PERSONAL: Born March 27, 1910, in Drain, Ore.; daughter of John Houston (a merchant) and Katherine (Sagaberd) Safley; married Loyd Lewis Coons (an electrician), June 30, 1928; children: Larry Ronald, Lynn Houston. *Education:* Oregon College of Education, graduate, 1936; University of Oregon, B.S. in Ed., 1950, M.A., 1951. *Religion:* Methodist. *Home:* 1800 Lakewood Ct., Eugene, Ore. 97402. *Office:* District 4, Lane County, 275 East Seventh, Eugene, Ore. 97401.

CAREER: Elementary and junior high school teacher in Oregon, 1927-72. Member of board of directors, Friends of the University of Oregon Library. *Member:* National Education Association, American Association of University Women, National League of American Pen Women, Oregon Education Association, Oregon Historical Society, Pi Lambda Theta. *Awards, honors:* Ford Foundation grant for travel and research in Northwest history, 1953.

WRITINGS: The Trail to Oregon, Binfords, 1954; *The Early History of Eugene*, D. D. Printing Co., 1956; (with John Prater) *Trails to Freedom*, Ginn, 1965, revised edition published as *Many Peoples, One Country*, 1971.

WORK IN PROGRESS: Textbook material.

BIOGRAPHICAL/CRITICAL SOURCES: Eugene Register-Guard, May 23, 1964.†

* * *

COOPER, Arnold Cook 1933-

PERSONAL: Born March 9, 1933, in Chicago, Ill.; son of Millard and Ellen (Cook) Cooper; married Jean Lord, September 12, 1959; children: Katherine Lord, David Andrew. *Education:* Purdue University, B.S., 1955, M.S., 1957; Harvard University, D.B.A., 1962. *Religion:* Methodist. *Home:* 605 Ridgewood Dr., West Lafayette, Ind.

CAREER: Harvard Graduate School of Business Administration, Boston, Mass., assistant professor, 1961-63; Purdue University, West Lafayette, Ind., 1963—, began as associate professor, became professor of industrial management. Visiting professor, Stanford University, 1967-68, Manchester Business School, 1972. *Military service:* U.S. Army, 1956; became first lieutenant.

WRITINGS: (With W. Arnold Hosmer and Frank L. Tucker) *Small Business Management: A Casebook*, Irwin, 1966; *The Founding of Technologically Based Firms*, Center for Venture Management, 1971; (editor with John Komives) *Technical Entrepreneurship: A Symposium*, Center for Venture Management, 1972.

* * *

COOPER, Joseph Bonar 1912-

PERSONAL: Born December 10, 1912, in Indianapolis, Ind.; son of William Hand (a broker) and Eva (Bonar) Cooper; married Hazel L. Gasch, November 16, 1949; children: Barbara, Gretchen, Gwendolyn, Mary. *Education:* University of California, Los Angeles, B.A., 1936, Ph.D., 1940. *Home:* 14036 Saratoga Hills Rd., Saratoga, Calif. 95070. *Office:* San Jose State University, San Jose, Calif. 95192.

CAREER: San Jose State College, San Jose, Calif., instructor, 1940-42, assistant professor, 1946-48, associate professor, 1948-51, professor of psychology, 1951—. *Military service:* U.S. Naval Reserve, active duty, 1942-46; became lieutenant. U.S. Public Health Service, 1958—; now senior scientist. *Member:* American Association for the Advancement of Science (fellow), American Psychological Association (fellow).

WRITINGS: (With James L. McGaugh) *Integrating Principles of Social Psychology*, Schenkman, 1963; *Comparative Psychology*, Ronald, 1972. Contributor of more than thirty articles to professional journals.

WORK IN PROGRESS: Studies related to the role of emotion in prejudicial attitudes; a book on human behavioral adaptation.

* * *

COOPER, Mae (Klein)
(Nina Cooper-Klein, Nina Farewell)

PERSONAL: Born in New York, N.Y.; daughter of Louis (an accountant) and Anna (Moskovitz) Klein; married David Cooper (a technical consultant); children: Anita (Mrs. Allan Miller). *Education:* Attended Cooper Union Day Art School, 1936-40, The Dramatic Workshop under Erwin Piscator, 1940-42, Brooklyn College, 1964-66. *Religion:* Jewish. *Residence:* Brooklyn, N.Y.

CAREER: Actress, 1941-50; Dramatic Workshop, New York, N.Y., teacher of acting, 1946-48; now full-time professional writer. *Member:* Actors' Equity Association (senior member).

*WRITINGS—*Under name Mae Cooper: *Lily Henry*, Dutton, 1948.

Author under own name, Mae Cooper, with sister, the late Grace Klein, of stage adaptation of *Lily Henry* (closed in rehearsal, 1950), and of "The Bride Cried," play produced on television, 1951.

With Grace Klein, under joint pseudonym Nina Farewell: *The Unfair Sex*, Simon and Schuster, 1953; *Someone to Love*, Messner, 1959; *Every Girl is Entitled to a Husband*, McGraw, 1963; *Here Comes the Bride*, Muller, 1965.

Sole author under pseudonym Nina Farewell: *Boy and the Square Uncle* (two short novels), Crown, 1967.

With Grace Klein, under joint pseudonym Nina Cooper-Klein: *Daughter of Ishtar* (historical-Biblical novel), Arthur Barker, 1962.

Also wrote, with Grace Klein, "The Bride Cried," television play, produced on U.S. Steel Hour, August 17, 1955.

WORK IN PROGRESS: The Gabriel Crusade, a novel.

SIDELIGHTS: Mrs. Cooper's sister-collaborator, Grace Klein, died in 1965, but Mae continues to write as Nina Farewell, one of the pseudonyms they shared. Their joint books have had foreign editions in nine countries, including Israel, Japan, and Brazil and *The Unfair Sex* had twenty-two printings in England. Mrs. Cooper wrote to *CA*: "No aptitude for foreign languages, orally speaking—but read Italian and French fairly well. Love traditional opera (dislike most modern ones). Probably a good play in me, but I can't bear the conflicts of a Broadway production. Writing books is so peaceful—and the finished product is your own!" *Avocational interests:* Archaeology, ancient history, photography, tennis, and bicycling.

COPPEL, Alfred 1921-
(Robert Cham Gilman, A. C. Marin)

PERSONAL: Born November 9, 1921, in Oakland, Calif.; son of Alfredo Jose de Marini and Ana Roumalda (de Arana) y Coppel; married Elisabeth Schorr, March 10, 1943; children: Elisabeth Ann, Alfred III. *Education:* Attended Stanford University, 1943. *Politics:* Independent. *Home:* 270 Tennyson St., Palo Alto, Calif. 94801. *Agent:* Robert Lescher, 155 East 71st St., New York, N.Y. 10021.

CAREER: Writer, 1947—; *San Francisco Chronicle*, San Francisco, Calif., critic, 1969—. *Military service:* U.S. Army Air Forces, fighter pilot, 1942-45; became first lieutenant.

WRITINGS—All published by Harcourt, except as indicated: *Hero Driver*, Crown, 1954; *Night of Fire and Snow*, Simon & Schuster, 1957; *Dark December*, Fawcett, 1960; *A Certainty of Love*, 1966; *The Gate of Hell*, 1967; *Order of Battle*, 1968; *A Little Time for Laughter*, 1969; *Between the Thunder and the Sun*, 1971; *Landlocked Man*, 1972; *Thirty-Four East*, 1974; *The Boyar Conspiracy*, in press.

Under pseudonym Robert Cham Gilman: *The Rebel of Rhada*, 1968; *The Navigator of Rhada*, 1969; *The Starkahan of Rhada*, 1970.

Under pseudonym A. C. Marin: *The Clash of Distant Thunder*, 1968; *Rise With the Wind*, 1969; *A Storm of Spears*, 1970. Contributor to *Playboy, Galaxy, Analog, Auto*, and other magazines.

*   *   *

CORBETT, Edward P(atrick) J(oseph) 1919-

PERSONAL: Born October 29, 1919, in Jamestown, N.D.; son of John T. (a maintenance man) and Adrienne (Beaupre) Corbett; married Sylvia M. Mikkelsen, November 4, 1944; children: Mary Elizabeth, James, John, Catherine and Maureen (twins), Peter, Thomas. *Education:* Venard College, Clark Summit, Pa., student, 1938-42; University of Chicago, M.A., 1948; Loyola University, Chicago, Ill., Ph.D., 1956. *Politics:* Democrat. *Religion:* Roman Catholic. *Office:* Department of English, Ohio State University, Columbus, Ohio 43210.

CAREER: Instructor in English at Creighton University, Omaha, Neb., 1948-50, and Loyola University, Chicago, Ill., 1952-53; Creighton University, assistant professor, 1953-56, associate professor, 1956-61, professor of English, 1961-66; Ohio State University, Columbus, professor of English and director of freshman English, 1966-71; *Quarterly Journal of Speech*, associate editor, 1972-74; *College Composition and Communication*, editor, 1974—. Does television and radio commercials for network use, and acts in community theater roles. Trustee of St. John Vianney Seminary, Elkhorn, Neb., 1960-66. *Military service:* U.S. Marine Corps, 1944-46; became staff sergeant. *Member:* Modern Language Association of America, National Council of Teachers of English, Conference on College Composition and Communication, Rhetoric Society of America (chairman, 1973—), Speech Association of America, American Association of University Professors.

WRITINGS: Classical Rhetoric for the Modern Student, Oxford University Press, 1965, 2nd edition, 1971; (editor with Gary Tate) *Teaching Freshman Composition*, Oxford University Press, 1967; (editor with James Golden) *The Rhetoric of Blair, Campbell, and Whately*, Holt, 1968; *Rhetorical Analyses of Literary Works*, Oxford University Press, 1969; (editor with Tate) *Teaching High School*

Composition, Oxford University Press, 1970; (editor with Virginia Burke) *The New Century Composition-Rhetoric*, Appleton, 1971; *The Little English Handbook: Choices and Conventions*, Wiley, 1973; *The Essay: Subject and Stances*, Prentice-Hall, 1974.

Contributor to *Commonweal, America*, and professional journals. Member of editorial board, *Philosophy and Rhetoric*, 1973—.

*   *   *

CORBETT, (John) Patrick 1916-

PERSONAL: Born March 5, 1916, in Surrey, England; son of Eric and Katherine (Dracopoli) Corbett; married Nina Angeloni, January 27, 1940; married Janet Mary Adams, April 1, 1969; children: (first marriage) Simon, Charles; (second marriage) Katherine, Victoria. *Education:* Attended Royal Naval College, Dartmouth, 1929-33, and Magdalen College, Oxford, 1934-37. *Politics:* Labour. *Office:* University of Bradford, Bradford, Yorkshire, England.

CAREER: Balliol College, Oxford University, Oxford, England, fellow and tutor, 1945-61; University of Sussex, Brighton, Sussex, England, professor of philosophy and senior tutor, 1961-72; University of Bradford, Bradford, England, professor of philosophy, 1972—. Yale University, visiting lecturer, 1958. *Military service:* British Army, 1939-45; prisoner of war in Germany, 1940-45; became lieutenant. *Awards, honors:* Council of Europe fellow, 1957; North Atlantic Treaty Organization fellow, 1960.

WRITINGS: Europe and the Social Order, Sijthoft, 1959; *Ideologies*, Hutchinson, 1966.

WORK IN PROGRESS: Study of the literature of Muth in religion and morality.

*   *   *

CORDER, Jim(my Wayne) 1929-

PERSONAL: Born September 25, 1929, in Jayton, Tex.; son of Nolan J. (a millwright) and Ruth (Durham) Corder; married Patsy Akey, April 1, 1951; children: David, Catherine, Melinda. *Education:* Texas Christian University, B.A. and M.A., 1954; University of Oklahoma, Ph.D., 1958. *Religion:* Presbyterian. *Home:* 3137 Stadium Dr., Fort Worth, Tex.

CAREER: Texas Christian University, Fort Worth, assistant professor, 1958-62, associate professor, 1962-66, professor of English, 1966—. *Military service:* U.S. Army, 1950-52. *Member:* Modern Language Association of America, National Council of Teachers of English, College English Association, South Central Modern Language Association, Texas Council of Teachers of English.

WRITINGS: (With L. H. Kendall) *A College Rhetoric*, Random, 1962; *Rhetoric: A Reader*, Random, 1965; (reviser) *A Handbook of Current English*, Scott, Foresman, 3rd edition, 1968, 4th edition, 1975; *Uses of Rhetoric*, Lippincott, 1971; *Finding A Voice*, Scott, Foresman, 1973.

WORK IN PROGRESS: A Guide to College Writing, for Scott, Foresman.

*   *   *

CORNILLON, John Raymond Koppleman 1941-

PERSONAL: Surname pronounced Kor-nee-yohn; born April 7, 1941, in Cannes, France; son of Jacques Marie (an aeronautical engineer) and Elizabeth (Johnson) Cornillon;

married Susan Huddis Koppelman (a writer), September 1, 1962. *Education:* Columbia College, A.B., 1963; B.D., 1969; Bowling Green State University, M.A., 1974. *Residence:* Twin Willows, Point Pleasant, Pa.

CAREER: Has worked as farm hand, camp counsellor, car delivery man, comicbook writer for "Classics Illustrated," medical research subject, insurance investigator, factory worker, teacher of English and art, production manager for industrial magazine, post office clerk, library assistant, magazine and encyclopedia salesman, reader for a blind student, and handyman; editor and publisher of *Gooseberry*, Point Pleasant, Pa., and Somerville, Mass., 1964—.

WRITINGS: Falling Blocks, and Other Poems, Hufnagle Press, 1957. Work represented in anthologies, including *Cleveland, 365, Moonstones*, and *Tribute to Jim Lowell*. Wrote "Male Consciousness Raising" column for *Crystal City News*. Contributor to *Wormwood Review, Input, El Cornu Emplumado, Ole, Angels, Free Lance, Marijuana Quarterly, Poets at the Gate, Blacklist*, and other publications.

WORK IN PROGRESS: A biography of Flora Tristan and translating her work into English.

SIDELIGHTS: Cornillon writes: "Was greatly influenced by Beat Generation, i.e. Kerouac, Ginsberg. Have passed through the subsequent beat-inspired, hood-scene, drug-scene, political-scene, religious-activists scene, mystical trip, and radical politics. I then became and continue to be very involved in the feminist movement. I enjoy nature, gardening, and foraging; and I believe we should make restitution to the American Indian for treaties the U.S. government has violated."

* * *

CORNISH, Dudley T(aylor) 1915-

PERSONAL: Born January 11, 1915, in Carmel, N.Y.; son of Stanley Dyckman (a druggist) and Jane (Taylor) Cornish; married Maxine Fisher, September 10, 1946; children: Dudley Taylor, Jr. *Education:* University of Rochester, A.B., 1938; University of Colorado, A.M., 1947, Ph.D., 1949. *Politics:* Liberal Democrat. *Religion:* Protestant. *Home:* 112 West Potlitzer, Pittsbury, Kan. 66762. *Office:* Kansas State College of Pittsburg, Pittsburg, Kan. 66762.

CAREER: Kansas State College of Pittsburg, assistant professor of social science, 1949-56, associate professor of social science, 1956-58, professor of history, 1958—, chairman of department of social science, 1959-61, chairman of department of history, 1966—. Summer visiting professor, Vanderbilt University, 1962. Technical adviser to Fort Scott Historic Site Committees, 1960-65; secretary of Crawford County (Kan.) Democratic Central Committee, 1956-58; member of Kansas American Revolution Bicentennial Commission, 1974—; honorary fellow of Truman Library Institute, 1974—. *Military service:* U.S. Army, 1942-46; became captain. *Member:* American Historical Association, American Studies Association (executive committee member of Midcontinent chapter, 1960-63), Organization of American Historians, Southern Historical Association, Kansas Association of Teachers of History (president), Kansas State Historical Society (president, 1973-74), Kappa Alpha Psi, Omicron Delta Kappa, Alpha Delta Phi, Phi Alpha Theta.

WRITINGS: The Sable Arm: Negro Troops in the Union Army, 1861-1865, Longmans, Green, 1956, Norton, 1966; (compiler of section on the Negro) *Civil War Books: A Critical Bibliography*, Volume I, Louisiana State University Press, 1967. Contributor to historical journals. Editor-in-chief, *Midwest Quarterly* (publication of Kansas State College), 1959-67.

WORK IN PROGRESS: Continuing research in the American Civil War, with special reference to Rear Admiral S. Phillips Lee.

* * *

CORNUELLE, Richard C. 1927-

PERSONAL: Surname is pronounced Core-nell; born April 10, 1927, in Elwood, Ind.; son of Herbert Cumming (a minister) and Gertrude (Schleitzer) Cornuelle; married Sydney Walton, September 10, 1954 (divorced, 1967); children: Suzanne, Peter, Jenny. *Education:* Occidental College, A.B., 1948; New York University, graduate study, 1948-49. *Politics:* Independent. *Home:* 327 E. 10th St., New York, N.Y. *Agent:* Brandt & Brandt, 101 Park Ave., New York, N.Y. 10017.

CAREER: National Industrial Conference Board, New York, N.Y., assistant editor, *American Affairs*, 1949-50; Foundation for Economic Education, Irvington-on-Hudson, N.Y., consulting economist, 1950-51; Small Business Economic Foundation, Evanston, Ill., research director, 1951-52; William Volker Fund, Burlingame, Calif., liaison officer, 1952-56; Princeton Panel, Inc., Princeton, N.J., vice-president, 1957-58; Center for Independent Action, Belmont, Calif., director, 1958-65 (also concurrently director of United Student Aid Funds, 1958-63); National Association of Manufacturers, New York, N.Y., executive vice-president, 1966-69; free-lance writer and consultant, 1969—. *Military service:* U.S. Naval Reserve, 1944-45. *Member:* Mount Pelerin Society, Phi Beta Kappa. *Awards, honors:* LL.D., Rockford College; Hoover Institution on War, Revolution, and Peace research fellowship.

WRITINGS: Reclaiming the American Dream, Random, 1965; *Self-Management: Why Management Doesn't Work and What Does*, Random House, 1975.

BIOGRAPHICAL/CRITICAL SOURCES: Look, December 29, 1964.

* * *

CORSA, Helen Storm 1915-

PERSONAL: Born September 27, 1915, in Amherst, Mass.; daughter of John and Mary (Thomas) Corsa. *Education:* Eastman School of Music, student, 1933-35; Mount Holyoke College, B.A., 1938; Bryn Mawr College, M.A., 1939, Ph.D., 1942. *Politics:* Democrat. *Religion:* Roman Catholic. *Home:* 6 Richland Rd., Wellesley, Mass. 02181. *Office:* Wellesley College, Wellesley, Mass. 02181.

CAREER: Hartwick College, Oneonta, N.Y., instructor in English, 1942-43; Russell Sage College, Troy, N.Y., instructor, later assistant professor of English, 1943-48; Wellesley College, Wellesley, Mass., began as assistant professor, became professor of English, 1948-70, Martha Hale Shackford Professor of English, 1970—, chairman of department, 1972-75.

WRITINGS: Chaucer: Poet of Mirth and Morality, University of Notre Dame Press, 1964. Contributor to *Literature and Psychology, Hartford Studies in Literature, American Imago, Journal of Geriatric Psychiatry*.

WORK IN PROGRESS: Editing an edition of "The Physicians Tale" for *Chaucer Variorum* to be published by the University of Oklahoma Press.

AVOCATIONAL INTERESTS: Music (opera and piano), English history, biography, gardening, travel.

* * *

CORWIN, Ronald Gary 1932-

PERSONAL: Born June 14, 1932, in Waterloo, Iowa; son of Leonard John and Beuhlah (Morris) Corwin; married Bonnie Titus, June 20, 1954; children: Cheryl, Marcia, Blair. *Education:* State College of Iowa (now University of Northern Iowa), B.A. (with high honors), 1954; University of Iowa, graduate study, 1956; University of Minnesota, M.A., 1958, Ph.D., 1960. *Home:* 2006 Collingswood Rd., Columbus, Ohio. *Office:* Department of Sociology, Ohio State University, Columbus, Ohio.

CAREER: University of Minnesota, Minneapolis, instructor in sociology and research associate, 1959-60, assistant professor of education and research associate, 1960-61; Ohio State University, Columbus, assistant professor, 1961-65; associate professor , 1965-69, professor of sociology, 1969—. Visiting summer lecturer, Columbia University, 1965. Acting branch chief, Bureau of Research, U.S. Office of Education, 1967. *Military service:* U.S. Army, 1954-56; became sergeant. *Member:* American Educational Research Association (vice-president, 1969-71), American Sociological Association.

WRITINGS: A Sociology of Education, Appleton, 1965; (with Willard Lane) *A Sociology of School Administration: Bureaucracy in Public Education,* Macmillon, 1967; *Militant Professionalism: A Study of Conflict in High Schools,* Appleton, 1970; *Reform and Organizational Survival: The Teacher Corps As An Instrument of Educational Change,* Wiley, 1973; *Education in Crisis: A Sociological Analysis of Schools and Universities in Transition,* Wiley, 1974.

Contributor: Donald Hansen, editor, *Counseling in Society,* Houghton, 1966; Donald Hansen and Joel Gerst, editors, *On Education: Sociological Perspectives,* Wiley, 1967; Saad Nagi and Ronald Corwin, editors, *The Social Contexts of Research,* Wiley, 1972; John Carroll, editor, *Review of Research in Education: 1974,* F. T. Peacock, 1974. Contributor of about twenty articles and reviews to professional journals.

* * *

COSSMAN, E(li) Joseph 1918-

PERSONAL: Born April 13, 1918, in Pittsburgh, Pa.; son of Theodore H. (a merchant) and Bess (Soltz) Cossman; married Pearl Levine, October 10, 1940; children: Ronna Dale (Mrs. Evan Binn), Howard Lee. *Education:* Attended public schools in Pennsylvania. *Home:* 1838 Barona Rd., Palm Springs, Calif. 92262. *Office:* Cossman International, Inc., Smoketree Village, Suite 108, 1729 East Palm Canyon Dr., Palm Springs, Calif. 92262.

CAREER: Door-to-door salesman, 1936-41; E. Joseph Cossman & Co. (mail order firm), Los Angeles, Calif., president, 1947—; Cossman & Levine, Inc., Los Angeles, Calif., vice-president, 1954-62, president, 1962—; presently head of Cossman International, Inc., Palm Springs, Calif. Mail Order Institute of America, founder, 1951. *Military service:* U.S. Army, 1941-45. *Member:* Masons, Los Angeles Chamber of Commerce. *Awards, honors:* Sales promotion man of the year, Los Angeles chapter of Sales Promotion Executives Association, 1965.

WRITINGS: How I Made $1,000,000 in Mail Order, Prentice-Hall, 1964; *How to Get $50,000 Worth of Services*

Free Each Year from the U.S. Government, Fell, 1965, revised edition published as *How to Get $100,000 Worth of Services Free Each Year from the U.S. Government,* 1975; *The Virile Male,* Farnsworth Publishing, 1975. Contributor to magazines.

* * *

COSTELLO, Donald P(aul) 1931-

PERSONAL: Born August 4, 1931, in Chicago, Ill.; son of Ben J. (a clerk) and Marie (Huntsha) Costello; married Christine Kane, March 22, 1952; children: Christopher, Maria, Monica, Paul, Matthew, John. *Education:* De Paul University, A.B. (summa cum laude), 1955; University of Chicago, M.A., 1956, Ph.D., 1962. *Religion:* Roman Catholic. *Home:* 209 Wakewa, South Bend, Ind. *Office:* Department of English, University of Notre Dame, Notre Dame, Ind. 46566.

CAREER: Roosevelt University, Chicago, Ill., instructor in English, 1957-60; Chicago City Junior College, Chicago, Ill., instructor, 1958-59; University of Notre Dame, Notre Dame, Ind., assistant professor, 1960-66, associate professor, 1966-70, professor of English, 1971—. Director of Notre Dame's foreign studies program in Innsbruck, Austria, 1973-75. *Military service:* U.S. Navy, 1951-52. *Member:* American Association of University Professors. *Awards, honors:* Woodrow Wilson fellowship, 1955.

WRITINGS: (Contributor) *Generation of the Third Eye,* Sheed, 1965; *The Serpent's Eye: Shaw and the Cinema,* University of Notre Dame Press, 1965. Contributor to scholarly journals, including *Renascence, Modern Drama, American Speech,* and *Modern Language Notes.* Motion picture editor of *Today* for six years.

* * *

COSTIKYAN, Edward N. 1924-

PERSONAL: Surname is pronounced Cos-*tik*-yan; born September 14, 1924, in Weehawken, N.J.; son of Mihran Nazar (a rug merchant) and Berthe (Muller) Costikyan; children: Gregory John, Emilie Berthe. *Education:* Columbia University, A.B., 1947, LL.B., 1949. *Politics:* Democrat. *Religion:* Unitarian Universalist. *Home:* 310 East 50th St., New York, N.Y. *Office:* 345 Park Ave., New York, N.Y.

CAREER: Admitted to New York bar, 1949, bars of U.S. District Court and U.S. Court of Appeals, 1950, and U.S. Supreme Court, 1963; law secretary to Judge Harold R. Medina, New York, N.Y., 1949-51; Paul, Weiss, Rifkind, Wharton, and Garrison (attorneys), New York, N.Y., associate, 1951-60, partner, 1960—, specializing in civil trials and civil and criminal appeals. Lecturer at Practising Law Institute, 1955-56. Leader Democratic County Committee of New York County (Tammany Hall), 1962-64. *Military service:* U.S. Army, Infantry, 1943-46; became first lieutenant. *Member:* Bar Association of the City of New York.

WRITINGS: Behind Closed Doors: Politics in the Public Interest (autobiographical), Harcourt, 1966; (with Maxwell Lehman) *Restructuring the Government of New York City,* Praeger, 1972; *New Strategies for Regional Cooperation,* Praeger, 1973. Writer of legal and political articles. Editor, *Columbia Law Review,* 1949.

WORK IN PROGRESS: Cities in Crisis: Alternatives to Bankruptcy.

AVOCATIONAL INTERESTS: Amateur conducting for music groups; skiing, and gardening.

BIOGRAPHICAL/CRITICAL SOURCES: New York *Times*, March 3, 1962.

* * *

COUDERT, Jo 1923-

PERSONAL: Surname is pronounced Coo-dare; born March 14, 1923, in Williamsport, Pa.; daughter of John (with U.S. Navy) and Jane (Krouse) Coudert; divorced. *Education:* Attended Dean Academy and Smith College. *Politics:* Liberal. *Residence:* New York, N.Y. 10014.

CAREER: L. W. Frohlich Co. (advertising agency), New York, N.Y., editor and copywriter, 1953-56; Grune & Stratton, Inc., (publishers), New York, N.Y., editor of psychiatric and medical books, 1956-60; *International Journal of Group Psychotherapy*, New York, N.Y., managing editor, 1960—.

WRITINGS: The I Never Cooked Before Cookbook, Stein & Day, 1963; *Advice from a Failure*, Stein & Day, 1965; *The Alcoholic in Your Life*, Stein & Day, 1972; *Gowell—The Story of a House*, Stein & Day, 1974. Contributor of articles to *Readers' Digest, Ladies' Home Journal*, and *Parents Magazine*.

WORK IN PROGRESS: "Knightsbridge," a play.

AVOCATIONAL INTERESTS: Sculpture, gardening, golf, tennis.

* * *

COULOUMBIS, Theodore A. 1935-

PERSONAL: Born June 25, 1935, in Athens, Greece; came to United States in 1952; son of Alexandros T. (an army officer) and Angela (Tasfos) Couloumbis; married Zoe Papadopoulou (a professor of pediatrics); children: Alexander, Angelike. *Education:* Attended Athens College, Athens, Greece, and Chicheley Hall, Buckinghamshire, England; University of Connecticut, B.A. (honors), 1956, M.A., 1958; Georgetown University, graduate study, 1956-57; American University, Ph.D., 1965. *Home:* 8148 Inverness Ridge Rd., Potomac, Md. 20854. *Office:* School of International Service, American University, Washington, D.C. 20016.

CAREER: U.S. Department of the Navy, Washington, D.C., personnel research analyst, 1960-64, operations research analyst, 1964-65; American University, Washington, D.C., assistant professor, 1965-68, associate professor, 1968-72, professor of international relations, 1973—, associate dean for graduate studies, School of International Service, 1968-70. *Military service:* U.S. Army, Artillery, 1958-60. U.S. Army Reserve, 1960-65; became first lieutenant. *Member:* International Studies Association (Washington chapter, vice-president, 1972-73, president, 1973-74), American Political Science Association, American Society of International Law, American Association of University Professors, Modern Greek Studies Association, Center for Mediterranean Studies (vice-president for planning, 1972—).

Contributor: A. A. Said, editor, *Theory of International Relations: The Crisis of Relevance*, Prentice-Hall, 1970; Said, editor, *America's World Role in the 70's*, Prentice-Hall, 1971; Said, editor, *Protagonists of Change*, Prentice-Hall, 1971; (with Elias Georgiades) Said, editor, *The New Sovereigns*, Prentice-Hall, 1974; (with M'Kean Tredway) Robin Higham, editor, *Intervention or Abstention: The Dilemma of U.S. Foreign Policy*, University of Kentucky Press, 1975; (with John Nicolopoulos) Said, editor, *Neoethnicism in World Politics*, Transaction Books, 1975.

Author of papers for professional conferences. Contributor of articles and reviews, in Greek and English, to journals and newspapers, including *World Affairs, Midwest Quarterly, Polity, Perspective*, and *Ethnikos Kyrix*. Associate editor for international affairs, *Intellect*, 1973—.

WORK IN PROGRESS: A textbook on international politics, *Cosmopolitics: The Study of International Conflict, Cooperation and Coexistence*, for Prentice-Hall.

* * *

COUSE, Harold C. 1925-

PERSONAL: Surname rhymes with "house"; born November 16, 1925, in San Jose, Calif.; son of Harry C. (a horseman) and Phebe (Eicher) Couse; married Edna Van Orthwick (a high school teacher of homemaking), April 6, 1952; children: Scott Van Orthwick, Harry Clinton. *Education:* San Jose State College (now University), B.A., 1947; Stanford University, M.A., 1951. *Politics:* Democrat. *Religion:* Protestant. *Home:* 75 Mary Lane, Red Bluff, Calif. 96080. *Office:* Red Bluff Union High School, Douglas St., Red Bluff, Calif. 96080.

CAREER: Social studies teacher at junior high school in Santa Cruz, Calif., 1949-52, at high school in Santa Barbara, Calif., 1952-53; Red Bluff Union High School, Red Bluff, Calif., counselor and teacher, 1953—. *Military service:* U.S. Navy, 1943-45; became lieutenant junior grade. *Member* National Education Association, Northern California Guidance Association, California Teachers Association. *Awards, honors:* Named teacher of the year, Red Bluff High School District, 1960.

WRITINGS: (With Marvin Koller) *Modern Sociology*, Holt, 1965.†

* * *

COUSINS, Norman 1912-

PERSONAL: Born June 24, 1912, in Union Hill, N.J.; son of Samuel and Sara Barry (Miller) Cousins; married Ellen Kopf, June 23, 1939; children: Andrea, Amy, Candis, Sara Kit. *Education:* Teachers College, Columbia University, graduated, 1933. *Home:* 160 Silvermine Rd., New Canaan, Conn. *Office: Saturday Review*, 488 Madison Ave., New York, N.Y. 10022.

CAREER: New York Evening Post, New York, N.Y., educational editor, 1934-35; *Current History*, New York, N.Y., 1935-40, began as book critic, became literary editor and managing editor; *Saturday Review of Literature* (now *Saturday Review*), New York, N.Y., executive editor, 1940-42, editor, 1942-71; *World*, New York, N.Y., editor, 1972-73; *Saturday Review/World*, New York, N.Y., editor, 1973-74; *Saturday Review*, New York, N.Y., editor, 1975—. *U.S.A.*, editor, 1943-45; McCall's Corp., New York, N.Y., vice-president and director, 1961—. Office of War Information, Overseas Bureau, member of editorial board, 1943-45; co-chairman of national campaign board of 1943 Victory Book Campaign. U.S. Government lecturer in India, Pakistan, and Ceylon, 1951; Japan-America exchange lecturer, Japan, 1953. Chairman of board of directors of National Educational Television, 1969-70; member of Commission to Study Organized Peace; member of board of directors of Freedom House and Willkie Memorial Foundation; member of board of directors of Columbia University Conference on Science, Philosophy, and Religion. Chairman of Connecticut Fact Finding Commission on Education, 1948-52; founder and president of United

World Federalists, 1952-54, honorary president, 1955—; co-chairman of National Committee for a Sane Nuclear Policy, 1958—. *Member:* Council of Learned Societies (member-at-large), National Planning Association, United Nations Association (director of U.S. Division), World Association of World Federalists, Council on Foreign Relations, National Press Club, Overseas Press Club (member of board of governors), P.E.N. (vice-president of American Center, 1952-55), Century Club, Coffee House (New York).

AWARDS, HONORS: Litt.D., American University, 1948; L.H.D., Boston University and Colby College, 1953; L.H.D., Dennison University, 1954; LL.D., Washington and Jefferson College, 1956; LL.D., Syracuse University and Albright College, 1957; L.H.D., Colgate University, 1958; Doctor of Letters or Litt.D., Elmira College, Ripon College, Wilmington College, University of Vermont, 1957, Newark State College, 1958; Ed.D., Rhode Island College of Education, 1958; Litt.D., Western Michigan University; Thomas Jefferson Award for the Advancement of Democracy in Journalism, 1948; Tuition Plan Award for Outstanding Service to American Education, 1951; Benjamin Franklin citation in magazine journalism, 1956; Wayne State University award for national service to education, 1958; New York State Citizens Education Commission Award, 1959; John Dewey Award for Education, 1959.

WRITINGS: The Good Inheritance: The Democratic Chance, Coward, 1942; (editor) *A Treasury of Democracy,* Coward, 1942; *Modern Man is Obsolete,* Viking, 1945; (editor with William Rose Benet) *An Anthology of the Poetry of Liberty,* Modern Library, 1945; (editor) *Writing for Love or Money: Thirty-Five Essays Reprinted From the Saturday Review of Literature,* Longmans, Green, 1949, reprinted, Books for Libraries Press, 1970; (contributor) John W. Chase, editor, *Years of the Modern,* Longmans, Green, 1949; (with Jawaharlal Nehru) *Talks With Nehru,* Day, 1951; *Who Speaks for Man?,* Macmillan, 1953; *Amy Loveman, 1881-1955: A Eulogy* (pamphlet), Overbrook Press, 1956; *The Religious Beliefs of the Founding Fathers, 1958; (editor) In God We Trust, Harper, 1958; (editor) Francis March, Thesaurus Dictionary, Doubleday, 1958;* The Rejection of Nothingness *(pamphlet), Pacific School of Religion, 1959.*

Dr. Schweitzer of Lambarene, Harper, 1960; *The Last Defense in a Nuclear Age,* 1960; *In Place of Folly,* Harper, 1961, revised edition, Washington Square Press, 1962; *Can Cultures Co-Exist?* (symposium), Ministry of Scientific Research & Cultural Affairs (New Delhi), 1963; (with others) *"... Therefore Choose Life, That Thou Mayest Live, Thou and Thy Seed,"* Center for the Study of Democratic Institutions, 1965; (editor) *Profiles of Nehru: America Remembers a World Leader,* Indian Book Co., 1966; (editor) *Great American Essays,* Dell, 1967; *Present Tense: A American Editor's Oddessey,* McGraw, 1967; (with others) *Issues: 1968,* University Press of Kansas, 1968; *Profiles of Gandhi: America Remembers a World Leader,* Indian Book Co., 1969; *The Improbable Triumvirate: John F. Kennedy, Pope Paul, Nikita Khruschev, an Asterisk to the History of a Hopeful Year, 1962-1963,* Norton, 1972; *The Celebration of Life,* Harper, 1974; *The Quest for Immortality,* Harper, 1974; (editor with Mary L. Dimond) *Memoirs of a Man: Grenville Clark,* Norton, 1975. Member of board of editors, *Encyclopaedia Britannica.*

BIOGRAPHICAL/CRITICAL SOURCES: New York Times, June 22, 1972.†

COWAN, G(eorge) H(amilton) 1917-

PERSONAL: Born August 14, 1917, in Kilmarnock, Scotland; son of William (a weaver) and Catherine (Aitken) Cowan; married Hilda Bryant, November 27, 1943; children: Peter, Christine. *Education:* University of Glasgow, M.A., (first class honors in classics), 1939; Queen's College, Oxford, B.A., 1945, M.A., 1964. *Home:* 4 Honister Gardens, Stanmore, Middlesex, England.

CAREER: Mercer's School, assistant classics master, 1947-58; King Edward VII, Sheffield, England, senior classics master, 1958-64; Harrow County School for Boys, Harrow, Middlesex, England, deputy head master, 1964—. *Military service:* Royal Artillery, 1940-46; became captain.

WRITINGS: Latin Translations: Principle to Practice, Macmillan, 1964.

WORK IN PROGRESS: Three books, *Beginners' Latin Course, Latin Prose Composition,* and *Latin Prose Idiom and Practice.*†

*   *   *

COWDREY, A(lbert) E(dward) 1933-

PERSONAL: Born December 8, 1933, in New Orleans, La.; son of Albert Edward (an auditor) and Jane (Lucas) Cowdrey. *Education:* Tulane University of Louisiana, B.A., 1956; Johns Hopkins University, M.A., 1957. *Agent:* Scott Meredith Literary Agency, Inc., 580 Fifth Ave., New York, N.Y. 10036.

CAREER: Tulane University of Louisiana, New Orleans, lecturer in history, 1960-64; Louisiana State University, New Orleans, lecturer in history, 1965-66; writer. *Military service:* U.S. Army, 1957-59. U.S. Army Reserve, 1960-63. *Member:* Authors Guild, Phi Beta Kappa, Johns Hopkins Club.

WRITINGS: Elixir of Life, Doubleday, 1965; *The Delta Engineers: A History of the Army Corps of Engineers in the New Orleans District* (New Orleans), 1971.

WORK IN PROGRESS: Two novels; two plays.

SIDELIGHTS: Cowdrey told *CA:* "I am a slow and laborious writer, atypical, apolitical, and so far a-successful. My favorite recreations are eating and drinking, though I also paint and, when I have the money, travel. For reading I like mysteries, histories, Oriental poetry, and fantasy of all types from Apuleius to Scheherazade. I like *Lolita* and hate crisis journalism and significant novels, which I never read."†

*   *   *

COX, Alva Irwin, Jr. 1925-

PERSONAL: Born April 27, 1925, in Cleveland, Ohio; son of Alva I. and Helen (Roe) Cox; married Patricia Garth, June 21, 1947; children: Catherine Anne, David Garth, Deborah Sue, Daniel Wesley. *Education:* Baldwin-Wallace College, A.B., 1945; Garrett Theological Seminary, B.D., 1948; Yale Divinity School, S.T.M., 1951. *Address:* Box 254 Cos Cob, Conn. 06807. *Office:* Synesthetics, Inc., 5510 16th St. N.W., Washington, D.C. 20011.

CAREER: Ordained to Methodist ministry, 1949; Grace Methodist Church, Waterville, Conn., pastor, 1948-51; National Council of Churches of Christ in the U.S.A., New York, N.Y., associate director of Educational Evangelism, 1951-57; director of Educational Media, 1957-67; Communication Trends, Inc., Cos Cob, Conn., vice-president, 1967-69; Synesthetics, Inc., Washington, D.C., president, 1969—. Free-lance writer for CBS news, 1967—.

WRITINGS: (Editor) *The Delinquent, The Hipster, and The Square, and Other Plays,* Bethany, 1962; (editor) *Christian Education in the Church Today,* Graded Press, 1965.

* * *

COX, Bertha Mae (Hill) 1901-

PERSONAL: Born March 10, 1901, in Kosse, Tex.; daughter of M. Victor (a physician) and Ollie E. (Phifer) Hill; married Willis L. Cox, June 8, 1924. *Education:* Attended Southwest Texas State Normal School (now Southwest Texas State University), 1922, and Baylor University, 1923-24; North Texas State Teachers College (now North Texas State University), B.S., 1935, M.S., 1950; extension study at Southern Methodist University. *Politics:* Democrat. *Religion:* Methodist. *Home:* 1130 North Winnetka, Dallas, Tex. 75208.

CAREER: Teacher and principal in Kosse, Tex., 1918-24; acting postmaster of Kosse, Tex.; teacher in Dallas County, Tex., 1924-28, and in Dallas city schools, 1928-64; director of day school, Kessler Park Methodist Church, Dallas, Tex., 1964-72. *Member:* National Education Association (life member), Association for Childhood Education, Texas State Teachers' Association (life member), Texas Congress of Parents and Teachers (honorary life member), Women's Society of Christian Service (Methodist Church; honorary life member), Delta Kappa Gamma, Delta Pi. *Awards, honors:* Teacher of the year award, *Dallas Times Herald,* 1950.

WRITINGS: (Editor) A. W. Johnson, *Tell Us About Texas,* Turner Co., 1947; *True Tales of Texas,* Turner Co., 1949; (with Robert H. McKay) *Susan's Happy Year,* Banks Upshaw, 1957; *Let's Read About Texas,* with teacher's manual, workbook, and tests, Turner Co., 1963; *Our Texas,* with teacher's manual, Turner Co., 1965; (with Charles Beamer and Joe B. Frantz) *The Texans: Tejas to Today,* Graphic Ideas, 1972; (with others) *Play a Story,* Graphic Ideas, 1973; (with others) *Imagine That,* Graphic Ideas, 1973. Author of church school literature. Consulting editor, "Graphic Ideas Readers" series.

WORK IN PROGRESS: Several books for children.

BIOGRAPHICAL/CRITICAL SOURCES: Mildred P. Harrington, editor, *The Southwest Children's Books,* Louisiana State University Press, 1952.

* * *

CRAGG, (Albert) Kenneth 1913-

PERSONAL: Born March 8, 1913, in Blackpool, England; son of Albert (a merchant) and Emily (Hides) Cragg; married Melita Arnold, December 31, 1940; children John Theodore, Arnold George Francis, Christopher Temple. *Education:* Oxford University, B.A., 1934, M.A., 1938, D.Phil., 1950. *Home and office:* 174 Osbourne Rd., University of Sussex, Brighton, Sussex, England.

CAREER: Ordained deacon, Church of England, 1936; priest, 1937; curate in Birkenhead, England, 1936-39; chaplain in Beirut, Lebanon, 1939-47; warden of St. Justin's House, and assistant professor of philosophy at American University of Beirut, Beirut, Lebanon, 1942-47; rector of Longworth, Berkshire, England, 1947-51; Hartford Seminary Foundation, Hartford, Conn., professor of Arabic and Islamics, 1951-56; St. George's Collegiate Church, Jerusalem, canon, 1956-61; St. Augustine's College, Canterbury, England, fellow, 1959-60, warden, 1961-67; Cambridge University, Cambridge, England, Bye-Fellow of Gonville and Caius College, 1968-73; University of Sussex, Brighton, England, reader in religious studies, 1973—. Near East Council of Churches, traveling director of study program in Islamics, 1956-59; assistant bishop in Jerusalem, 1970-74, in Chichester, England, 1973—. Visiting professor, Union Theological Seminary, New York, N.Y., 1965-66, University of Ibadan, 1968. *Awards, honors:* Rockefeller traveling fellowship for Islamic studies, 1954.

WRITINGS: The Call of the Minaret, Oxford University Press, 1956; *Sandals at the Mosque,* Oxford University Press, 1959; (translator) *City of Wrong,* Bles, 1959; *The Dome and the Rock,* Seabury, 1964; *Counsels in Contemporary Islam,* Edinburgh University Press, 1965; (translator) *The Theology of Unity,* Allen & Unwin, 1966; *Christianity in World Perspective,* Lutterworth, 1968; *The Privilege of Man,* Athlone Press, 1968; *Alive to God,* Oxford University Press, 1970; *The Event of the Qur'an,* Allen & Unwin, 1970; *The Mind of the Qur'an,* Allen & Unwin, 1973. Editor, *Muslim World Quarterly,* 1952-60.

WORK IN PROGRESS: Quranic studies.

* * *

CRAIG, Robert C(harles) 1921-

PERSONAL: Born March 9, 1921, in Sault Sainte Marie, Mich.; son of Frank Lyle (a teacher) and Syla (Crowell) Craig; married Rosalie DeBoer (a nurse), September 2, 1950; children: Bruce, Stephen (deceased), Jeffrey, Barbara Anne. *Education:* Michigan State University, B.S., 1943, M.A., 1948; Columbia University, Ph.D., 1952. *Home:* 185 Maplewood, East Lansing, Mich. 48823. *Office:* 443 Erickson, Michigan State University, East Lansing, Mich. 48823.

CAREER: State University of Washington, Pullman, assistant professor of education, 1952-55; American Institute for Research, Pittsburgh, Pa., research scientist, 1955-58; Marquette University, Milwaukee, Wis., associate professor of education, 1958-65; Michigan State University, East Lansing, professor of educational psychology and director of consultative services in Advanced School of Education, 1966-67, chairman of department of counseling, personnel services, and educational psychology, 1967—. University of Pittsburgh, lecturer, 1956-57. Consultant to American Institute for Research, 1958—, and Bel-Mort Films, 1960—. *Military service:* U.S. Naval Reserve, 1943-46; became lieutenant junior grade. *Member:* American Educational Research Association, American Psychological Association (fellow), American Statistical Association (president of Milwaukee chapter, 1963-64), American Association for the Advancement of Science (fellow), National Council on Measurements Used in Education, National Society for the Study of Education, Sigma Xi, Phi Kappa Phi, Phi Delta Kappa.

WRITINGS: Transfer Value of Guided Learning, Teachers College, Columbia University, 1953; (with Adrian M. Dupuis) *American Education,* Bruce, 1963; *Psychology of Learning in the Classroom,* Macmillan, 1966; (with H. Clarizio and W. Mehrens) *Contemporary Issues in Educational Psychology,* Allyn & Bacon, 1970, 2nd edition, 1975; (with Clarizio and Mehrens) *Contemporary Educational Psychology,* Wiley, 1975. Contributor to *Catholic Encyclopedia of Education* and to educational journals.

WORK IN PROGRESS: Experimental studies on vicarious discovery of concepts and principles, and on automation of classrooms.

CRANE, (Lauren) Edgar 1917-

PERSONAL: Born December 3, 1917, in Hastings, Minn.; married Lois Mary Bernadine Hilgeman (a clinical psychologist), 1955; children: Richard, Margaret, Lauren Edgar, Jr. *Education:* University of Minnesota, B.A., 1939; Iowa State University of Science and Technology, M.S., 1946; Stanford University, Ph.D., 1961. *Politics:* Democrat. *Religion:* Unitarian Universalist. *Home:* 13507 Kingside, Houston, Tex. 77024. *Office:* Department of Business Administration, University of Houston, 3801 Cullen Blvd., Houston, Tex. 77004.

CAREER: Minneapolis Tribune, Minneapolis, Minn., reporter, 1946-53; University of Iowa, Iowa City, instructor in journalism, 1955-56; University of North Carolina, Chapel Hill, lecturer in journalism, 1957-58; Michigan State University, East Lansing, assistant professor, 1958-61; University of Notre Dame, Notre Dame, Ind., associate professor of marketing, 1961-67; University of Houston, Houston, Tex., professor of marketing, 1967—. Visiting professor, Norwegian School of Economics and Business Administration, 1973-74. *Member:* American Psychological Association, Academy of International Business, American Marketing Association, Association for Education in Journalism, Phi Beta Kappa.

WRITINGS: Marketing Communications, Wiley, 1965. Contributor to *Journalism Quarterly, AV Communications Review,* and *Journal of Broadcasting.*

*   *   *

CRAZ, Albert G. 1926-

PERSONAL: Born June 26, 1926, in New York, N.Y.; son of Albert G. and Louise (Gottlock) Craz; married Joan-Carol McMunn, September 10, 1949; children: Lynda Constance, Peter Bruce. *Education:* Middlebury College, A.B., 1950, A.M., 1955; additional study at Columbia University, Cornell University, Boston University, and other schools. *Politics:* Democrat. *Religion:* Protestant.

CAREER: Teacher in Boston and New York, 1950-57 and 1959-66, in Army schools in Germany, 1957-59; Patchogue-Medford (N.Y.) public schools, supervisor of English, 1966—. Semi-professional singer (bass) for past ten years. Chairman of English council, Columbia Teachers College Metropolitan School Study Council, 1964-66. *Military service:* U.S. Army Air Forces, 1944-46. *Member:* Westchester English Council (vice-president, 1964-66), Teachers Association of Tarrytown (president, 1964-66).

WRITINGS: Getting to Know Liberia, Coward, 1958; *Getting to Know Italy,* Coward, 1961; (editor) *Lord Jim,* and *Teacher's Manual,* Macmillan, 1962; *Getting to Know the Mississippi River,* Coward, 1965; *A Study of Drama,* and *Teacher's Manual,* McCormick-Mathers, 1965; *A Study of Nonfiction,* and *Teacher's Manual,* McCormick-Mathers, 1965; (contributor) *English Literature, I-V,* five volumes, McCormick-Mathers, 1967. Contributor to *New York Herald Tribune* and to journals.

WORK IN PROGRESS: A twelfth-grade English textbook, covering the period from John Donne to Oliver Goldsmith.†

*   *   *

CREAGER, Alfred L(eon) 1910-

PERSONAL: Surname is pronounced to rhyme with "meager"; born December 14, 1910, in York, Pa.; son of Chester W. (a storekeeper) and Emma A. (Grandemann) Creager; married Grace Williams, June 13, 1936; children: Sarah (Mrs. Jack Scott), Martha R., Philip A., Mary C. *Education:* Ursinus College, B.S., 1933; Lancaster Theological Seminary, B.D., 1936; Temple University, graduate study, 1944-46. *Home:* 139 Seventh Ave., Collegeville, Pa. 19426.

CAREER: Clergyman, United Church of Christ. Trinity United Church of Christ, Collegeville, Pa., minister, 1946; Ursinus College, Collegeville, Pa., lecturer in philosophy of religion, 1947-49, associate professor, 1949—, chaplain, 1948-68. United Church of Christ, member of Council on Higher Education, 1958-68. *Awards, honors:* D.D., Ursinus College, 1955

WRITINGS: Old Testament Heritage, Pilgrim Press, 1955, revised edition, United Church, 1962; *The Church: The Faith Community,* two volumes, Christian Education Press and Pilgrim Press, 1962; (contributor) Charles L. Wallis, editor, *The Minister's Manual,* Harper, 1974. Author of devotional booklets and teacher's guides; contributor of poetry to magazines, and articles to religious journals.

WORK IN PROGRESS: Small-town personalities in free verse (no plans for publication).

*   *   *

CRESSWELL, Helen 1936-

PERSONAL: Born July 11, 1936, in Nottinghamshire, England; daughter of J. E. (an electrical engineer) and A. E. (Clarke) Cresswell; married Brian Rowe (in textiles), April 14, 1962; children: Caroline Jane. *Education:* Kings College, University of London, B.A. (honors), 1955. *Religion:* Church of England. *Home:* Hunters' Green, 130 Cotgrave Lane, Tollerton, Nottinghamshire, England. *Agent:* A. M. Heath & Co. Ltd., 35 Dover St., London W.1, England.

CAREER: Career up to marriage was varied, including periods as literary assistant to a foreign author, fashion buyer, and teacher, and television work for British Broadcasting Corp.; writer, mainly for children, 1961—. *Member:* Society of Authors. *Awards, honors:* Nottingham Poetry Society Award for best poem submitted in annual competition, 1950.

WRITINGS: Sonya-by-the-Shore, Dent, 1961; *Jumbo Spencer,* Brockhampton Press, 1963, Lippincott, 1966; *The White Sea Horse,* Oliver & Boyd, 1964, Lippincott, 1965; *Jumbo Back to Nature,* Brockhampton Press, 1965; *Pietro and the Mule,* Oliver & Boyd, 1965, Bobbs-Merrill, 1970, *Jumbo Afloat,* Brockhampton Press, 1966; *Where the Wind Blows,* Faber, 1966, Funk, 1968; *The Piemakers,* Faber, 1967, Lippincott, 1968; *A Day on Big O,* Benn, 1967, Follett, 1968; *A Tide for the Captain,* Chatto & Windus, 1967; *The Signposters,* Faber, 1968; *The Sea Piper,* Chatto & Windus, 1968; *Jumbo and the Big Dig,* Brockhampton Press, 1968; *Rug is a Bear,* Benn, 1968; *Rug Plays Tricks,* Benn, 1968; *The Night-Watchmen,* Faber, 1969, Macmillan, 1970; *A Game of Catch,* Chatto & Windus, 1969; *A Gift from Winklesea,* Brockhampton Press, 1969; *A House for Jones,* Benn, 1969; *Rug Plays Ball,* Benn, 1969; *Rug and a Picnic,* Benn, 1969.

The Outlanders, Faber, 1970; *The Wilkses,* B.B.C. Publications, 1970; *Rainbow Pavement,* Benn, 1970; *John's First Fish,* Macmillan, 1970; *Up the Pier,* Macmillan, 1971; *The Weather Cat,* Benn, 1971; *The Bird Fancier,* Benn, 1971; *At the Stroke of Midnight,* Collins, 1971; *The Beachcombers,* Macmillan, 1972; *Jane's Policeman,* Benn, 1972;

The Long Day, Benn, 1972; *Short Back and Sides*, Benn, 1972; *Blue Birds Over Pit Row*, Benn, 1972; *Roof Fall*, Benn, 1972; *Lizzie Dripping*, B.B.C. Publications, 1972; *The White Sea Horse and Other Tales*, Chatto & Windus, 1972; *The Bongleweed*, Macmillan, 1973; *The Bower Bird*, Benn, 1973; *The Key*, Benn, 1973; *The Trap*, Benn, 1973; *The Beetle Hunt*, Longman, 1973; *More Lizzie Dripping*, B.B.C. Publications, 1974; *The Two Hoots*, Benn, 1974; *The Two Hoots by the Sea*, Benn, 1974; *Cheap Day Return*, Benn, 1974; *The Shady Deal*, Benn, 1974.

Contributor: A. D. Maclean, editor, *Winters Tales*, Macmillan, 1969; *World Book of Ballet*, Collins, 1970; Eileen Colwell, editor, *Bad Boys*, Puffin, 1972; *Authors' Choice*, Hamish Hamilton, Number 2, 1973; Garfield, editor, *Bakers Dozen*, Ward, Lock, 1973; Richard Church and others, *My England*, Heinemann, 1973; Noel Streatfeild, *Christmas Holiday Book*, Dent, 1973; Noel Streatfeild, *Summer Holiday Book*, Dent, 1973; Noel Streatfeild, *Birthday Book*, Dent, 1975.

WORK IN PROGRESS: The Winter of the Birds.

SIDELIGHTS: Helen Cresswell told *CA* her motto is, "When you don't know where a road leads, it sure as hell will take you there (Leo Rosten)." *Avocational interests:* Philosophy, walking, gardening, and collecting coincidences.

* * *

CRIBBET, John E(dward) 1918-

PERSONAL: Born February 21, 1918, in Findlay, Ill.; son of Howard H. and Ruth (Wright) Cribbet; married Betty Smith, December 24, 1941; children: Pamela (Mrs. Thomas Steward), Carol Ann (Mrs. Michael Bell). *Education:* Illinois Wesleyan University, A.B., 1940; University of Illinois, J.D., 1947 (converted to LL.D., 1972). *Religion:* Methodist. *Home:* 1412 Waverly Dr., Champaign, Ill. 61821.

CAREER: Private practice of law, Bloomington, Ill., 1947; University of Illinois, College of Law, Urbana, assistant professor, 1947-51, associate professor, 1951-53, professor of law, 1953—, dean, 1967—. President of Champaign County United Fund, 1962-63; member of Champaign City Planning Commission, 1965—. *Military service:* U.S. Army, 1941-45; became major; received Bronze Star and Croix de Guerre. *Member:* American Bar Association, American Judicature Society, Illinois Bar Association, Rotary Club (Urbana).

WRITINGS: Cases and Materials on Judicial Remedies, West Publishing, 1954; (with Fritz and Johson) *Cases and Materials on Property*, Foundation Press, 1960, 3rd edition, 1972; *Principles of Law of Property*, Foundation Press, 1962, 2nd edition, 1975. Faculty editor, University of Illinois *Law Forum*, 1949-55.

WORK IN PROGRESS: Articles on property and land-use planning.

* * *

CRICHTON, John 1916-

PERSONAL: Surname is pronounced *Cra*-ton; born October 16, 1916, in Crichton, La.; son of Tom Jack (owner of a cotton plantation) and Mary (Boyleston) Crichton; married Marilyn Berry, December 6, 1952; children: Anne, Catherine. *Education:* Texas A&M College (now University), B.S., 1937, Professional Degree in Petroleum Engineering, 1953; Massachusetts Institute of Technology,

M.S., 1938; additional study at Southern Methodist University. *Politics:* Republican. *Religion:* Presbyterian. *Office:* Crichton & Co., 1100 Vaughan Building, Dallas, Tex.

CAREER: Registered professional engineer in Texas, Louisiana, and California. Union Producing Company, Houston, Tex., and Shreveport, La., geologist, 1938-41; vice-president of DeGoyler and MacNaughton (consulting geologists and engineers), Dallas, Tex., 1946-51, and San Juan Oil Co., Dallas, 1951-53; president of Oil and Gas Management Property, Inc., Dallas, Tex., 1953-59, Natco Oil & Gas Co., Inc., Dallas, 1959-63, Dallas Resources, Inc., 1963—, and Crichton & Co. (petroleum consultants), Dallas, 1963—. Director of Dorchester Corp. and McWood Corp. Negotiated oil concession in Yemen, 1955; member of U.S. delegation studying Rumanian oil industry, 1963. Republican candidate for governor of Texas, 1964.

MILITARY SERVICE: U.S. Army, Intelligence, 1941-45; became major; received Air Medal, Bronze Star, European theater ribbon with five battle stars. U.S. Army Reserve, current rank, colonel. *Member:* American Institute of Mining Engineers, Young Presidents Organization (past director), Engineers Club of Dallas (past president), Petroleum Engineers Club of Dallas (past president), Texas A&M Alumni Association (president).

WRITINGS: (With John Jacobs and Alfred M. Leeston) *The Dynamic Natural Gas Industry*, University of Oklahoma Press, 1963.

WORK IN PROGRESS: Foreign oil activity.†

* * *

CRICHTON, Robert 1925-

PERSONAL: Surname pronounced *Cry*-ton; born January 29, 1925, in Albuquerque, N.M.; son of Kyle S. (a writer) and Mary (Collier) Crichton; married Judy Feiner (a TV producer), July 16, 1966; children: Sarah, Rob, Jennifer, Susan. *Education:* Harvard University, B.A., 1950.

CAREER: Former chicken farmer and magazine editor; now full-time writer. *Military service:* U.S. Army, 1943-46; became sergeant; awarded Bronze Star, Purple Heart, and Presidential Unit Citation.

WRITINGS: The Great Impostor, Random House, 1959; *The Rascal and the Road*, Random House, 1961; *The Secret of Santa Vittoria*, Simon & Schuster, 1966; *The Camerons*, Knopf, 1972. Contributor of articles to periodicals.

WORK IN PROGRESS: A novel about World War II, to be titled *The Poor Miserable Rotten Stinking Infantry.*

SIDELIGHTS: Crichton told *CA:* "I continue to maintain that telling a story to convey feeling and experience is, despite all efforts to disown it, as natural to man and as vital to man, and as intuitive and ageless, as is the urge to laugh or cry, as to embrace when in love and to flee when in fear. Some form of the novel will always exist because there is no other way to convey certain things in life that are precious or fearful to us." His novels, *The Great Impostor* and *The Secret of Santa Vittoria* were adapted and filmed.

BIOGRAPHICAL/CRITICAL SOURCES: Time, June 29, 1959, December 16, 1966; *Saturday Review*, August 27, 1966, December 31, 1966; *New York Times Book Review*, August 28, 1966; *Life*, September 2, 1966. *Biography News*, Gale, March, 1974.†

CRISTOL, Vivian

PERSONAL: Born in Dublin, Ireland; daughter of Meyer (a dentist) and Mollie (Khan) Cristol. *Education:* Moravian College, graduated, 1938; special courses at New York University and Columbia University. *Residence:* New York, N.Y.

CAREER: Has worked in New York, N.Y., as secretary, editor, promotion writer, and in fund-raising campaigns with the late Dr. Thomas A. Dooley and others; with Dudley-Anderson-Yutzy (public relations firm), New York, N.Y., beginning, 1963. Operator of own tape and transcript business service.

WRITINGS: Good-Time Charlie: A Real Greenwich Village Cat, Harper, 1965.

WORK IN PROGRESS: A cat book for children; a naughty cat book for adults; a somewhat autobiographical book.

SIDELIGHTS: Miss Cristol writes: "I do not consider *Charlie* intrinsically a cat book, but a personal commentary tied to a cat tale. I think of myself as a writer who happened to have a cat, not a cat-owner who happened to write a book."†

*   *   *

CRISWELL, W(allie) A(mos)   1909-

PERSONAL: Born December 19, 1909, in Eldorado, Okla.; married Bessie Marie Harris, February 14, 1937; children: Mabel Ann (Mrs. Kenneth Jackson). *Education:* Baylor University, B.A., 1931, D.D., 1945; Southern Baptist Theological Seminary, M.Th., 1934, Ph.D., 1937. *Home:* 5901 Swiss, Dallas, Tex. 75214. *Office:* First Baptist Church, Dallas, Tex. 75201.

CAREER: Ordained Baptist minister, August 28, 1928; pastor in Chickasha, Okla., 1937-41, in Muskogee, Okla., 1941-44; First Baptist Church, Dallas, Tex., pastor, 1944—. Conducted preaching mission in Japan, 1950; speaker throughout America. Former president of Southern Baptist Convention. *Member:* Sigma Tau Delta. *Awards, honors:* D.D., Baylor University, 1945.

WRITINGS—All published by Zondervan, except as noted: *The Gospel According to Moses*, Boardman, 1950; (with Duke K. McCall) *Passport to the World*, Boardman, 1951; *These Issues We Must Face*, 1953; *Did Man Just Happen?*, 1957; *Five Great Questions of the Bible*, 1958; *Five Great Affirmations of the Bible*, 1959; *Expository Notes on the Gospel of Matthew*, 1961; *Expository Sermons on Revelation*, Volume I, 1962; Volume II, 1963, Volume III, 1964, Volume IV, 1965, Volume V, 1966, published in one volume, 1966; *The Bible for Today's World*, 1965; *The Holy Spirit in Today's World*, 1966; (contributor) Erwin L. McDonald, editor, *The Church Proclaiming and Witnessing*, Baker Book, 1966; *In Defense of the Faith*, 1967; *Expository Sermons on the Book of Daniel*, four volumes, 1968-72; *Why I Preach the Bible is Literally True*, Broadman, 1969; (with George Truett) *Fifty Years of Preaching at the Palace*, 1969; *Look Up, Brother! The Buoyant Assertion of What's Right With Us*, Broadman, 1970; *The Scarlet Thread Through the Bible*, Broadman, 1970; *Christ and Contemporary Crises*, Crescendo, 1972; *The Baptism, Filling, and Gift of the Holy Spirit*, 1973; *Expository Sermons on Galatians*, 1973; *Ephesians: An Exposition*, 1974. Contributor to religious journals.

BIOGRAPHICAL/CRITICAL SOURCES: Billy Keith, *W. A. Criswell: The Authorized Biography*, Revell, 1973.

CROCKER, Walter Russell   1902-

PERSONAL: Born March 25, 1902, Parnaroo, South Australia; son of Robert (a farmer) and Alma (Bray) Crocker; married Claire Ward Gooden, August 7, 1951 (divorced, 1968); children: Christopher, Robert. *Education:* University of Adelaide, B.A., 1925; Oxford University, B.A., 1927, M.A., 1928; Stanford University, graduate student, 1928-30. *Politics:* Independent ("non-party"). *Religion:* Anglican. *Home:* Peak Farm, Tarlee, South Australia. *Office:* Government House, Adelaide, South Australia.

CAREER: Served with British Colonial Service in Nigeria, 1930-34, with League of Nations, 1934-40; farmed at Parnaroo, South Australia, 1946; United Nations Secretariat, chief of Africa Section, 1946-49; Australian National University, Canberra, professor of international relations, 1949-52, acting vice-chancellor, 1951; High Commissioner for Australia to India, 1952-55; Ambassador to Indonesia, 1955-57; High Commissioner of Australia in Canada, 1957-58; High Commissioner of Australia in India, and Ambassador to Nepal, 1958-62; Ambassador to Netherlands, 1962-65; Ambassador to Ethiopia, and High Commissioner to Uganda and Kenya, 1965-67; Ambassador to Italy, 1967-70; Lieutenant-governor of South Australia, 1973—. *Military service:* British Army, 1940-46; became lieutenant colonel; received Croix de Guerre with palm, Ordre royal du Lion (Belgium). *Member:* Advertising Enquiry Council (London), Pedestrian Protection Association, Hakluyt Society, Oxford and Cambridge Club, Reform Club, Adelaide Club. *Awards, honors:* Commander of Order of the British Empire, 1955; Knight of Italy, 1970.

WRITINGS: The Japanese Population Problem, Allen & Unwin, 1931; *Nigeria: Critique of British Colonial Administration*, Allen & Unwin, 1936; *On Governing Colonies*, Allen & Unwin, 1946; *Self-Government for the Colonies*, Allen & Unwin, 1949; *The Racial Factor in International Relations* (pamphlet), Australian National University, 1956; *Nehru*, Allen & Unwin, 1966; *Australian Ambassador: International Relations at First Hand*, Melbourne University Press, 1971. Also author of *Can the U.N. Succeed?*, 1951.

WORK IN PROGRESS: Australia during Menzies' Prime Ministership and *The Cultural Decline*.

SIDELIGHTS: Crocker speaks French, Italian, Hausa. *Avocational interests:* Ornithology, travel.

*   *   *

CROMWELL, Harvey   1907-

PERSONAL: Born August 16, 1907, in Wanette, Okla.; son of Sheldon W. (a grocer) and Mattie (Hibbard) Cromwell; married Mattie Lou Patterson, June 10, 1931 (deceased); children: Harvey, Jr., Betty Jane Cromwell Lawrence. *Education:* East Central State College, Ada, Okla., B.S., 1930; State University of Iowa (now University of Iowa), graduate student, 1937-38; University of Oklahoma, M.A., 1940; Purdue University, Ph.D., 1949. *Politics:* Democrat. *Religion:* Baptist. *Home:* 310 North 12th St., Number 5, Columbus, Miss. 39701. *Office:* Mississippi University for Women, Columbus, Miss. 39701.

CAREER: High school teacher and sometime insurance salesman in Oklahoma, 1929-40; McMurry College, Abilene, Tex., head of department of speech, 1940-42; U.S. Army Air Forces Technical Center, Sheppard Field, Tex., civilian coordinator of instructor training, 1942-44; Purdue University, Lafayette, Ind., member of speech faculty and coach of varsity debating team, 1944-49; Mississippi University for Women, Columbus, professor and head of department of speech, 1949—, director of program for superior students, 1961-64, dean of Graduate School, 1965—, director of research, 1969—. Member of President's Committee on Employment of the Handicapped, 1967, of board of directors, University Press of Mississippi, 1969.

MEMBER: Speech Association of America (legislative assembly, 1959-61; chairman of national discussion and debate questions committee, 1960-61), American Forensic Association, National Forensic League, Southern Speech Association (director of debate, 1963; director of oratory, 1964), Mississippi Speech Association (president, 1951; council, 1952-64; secretary-treasurer, 1964), Pi Kappa Delta (national president, 1959-61; chairman of national convention, 1963), Phi Kappa Phi, Tau Kappa Alpha. *Awards, honors:* Special Distinction Service Award from Pi Kappa Delta, 1963.

WRITINGS: (With A. H. Monroe and L. S. Winch) *Interview Problems*, Tri-State Offset Co. (Cincinnati), 1946, 3rd edition, 1957; *Working for More Effective Speech*, Scott, 1955, 2nd edition, 1964; (editorial adviser) Monroe, *Principles and Types of Speech*, Scott, revised edition, 1955; *Suggestions for the Beginning Courses in Speech*, Scott, 1956, 2nd edition, 1964; *United States Armed Forces Institute Instructor's Guide for Speech I and Speech II*, Scott, 1956; *United States Armed Forces Institute Student Guide for Speech I and II*, Scott, 1956, 2nd edition, 1965; (contributor) *An Introduction to Speaking*, edited by Gilman, Aly, and White, Macmillan, 1962; *The Compact Guide to Parliamentary Procedure*, Hawthorn, 1966; (with R. Van Dusen) *An Oral Approach to Phonetics*, C. E. Merrill, 1969. Contributor to professional journals and newspapers.

WORK IN PROGRESS: Mississippi Orators; a cookbook; short stories and essays.

* * *

CROSBY, Alfred W., Jr. 1931-

PERSONAL: Born January 15, 1931, in Boston, Mass.; son of Alfred W. (a commercial artist) and Ruth (Coleman) Crosby; married second wife, Barbara Stevens, June 27, 1964; children: (first marriage) Kevin R.; (second marriage) Carolyn J. *Education:* Harvard University, A.B., 1952, A.M.T., 1956; Boston University, Ph.D., 1961. *Home:* 1853 23rd Ave., San Francisco, Calif. 94122. *Office:* History Department, Washington State University, Pullman, Wash. 99163.

CAREER: Albion College, Albion, Mich., instructor in history, 1960-61; Ohio State University, Columbus, instructor in history, 1961-65; San Fernando Valley State College (now California State University, Northridge), assistant professor of history, 1965-66; Washington State University, Pullman, associate professor of history, 1966—. Fellow, National Institutes of Health, 1971-73; fellow, Humanities Institute, 1975-76. *Military service:* U.S. Army, 1952-55; became sergeant. *Member:* American Historical Association.

WRITINGS: America, Russia, Hemp and Napoleon, Ohio State University Press, 1965; *The Columbian Exchange: Biological and Cultural Consequences of 1492*, Greenwood Press, 1972; *The Purple Death: The Pandemic of 1918 and the Ending of World War I*, Greenwood Press, in press. Contributor to *American Neptune, Pennsylvania Magazine of History and Biography, Hispanic American Review, Sexual Behavior*, and *American Anthropologist*.

CROSBY, John F. 1931-

PERSONAL: Born September 28, 1931, in Youngstown, Ohio; son of F. MacCalmont (a Blue Cross employee) and Blanche (Fulling) Crosby; married Marjorie Eastwick (a nurse), June 18, 1955; children: Richard Alan, Andrew Robert, Scott David. *Education:* Denison University, B.A., 1953; Princeton Theological Seminary, B.D., 1956; Syracuse University, graduate study.

CAREER: Ordained minister of Presbyterian Church, 1956; associate minister of Congregational church in Saginaw, Mich., 1956-58; organizing pastor of Presbyterian church in Battle Creek, Mich., 1958-62; pastor of First Presbyterian Church, Baldwinsville, N.Y., beginning 1962.

WRITINGS: Witness for Christ, Westminster, 1965; *From Religion to Grace: The Doctrine of Justification by Grace through Faith*, Abingdon, 1967; *Illusion and Disillusion: The Self in Love and Marriage*, Wadsworth, 1973.†

* * *

CROSBY, Michael 1940-
(Jeremiah Crosby)

PERSONAL: Born February 16, 1940, in Fond du Lac, Wis.; son of Hugh John (an insurance man) and Blanche (Bouser) Crosby. *Education:* St. Lawrence College, Mount Calvary, Wis., student, one year; Capuchin Seminary of St. Mary, Crown Point, Ind., B.A., 1963. *Home:* St. Anthony Friary, Marathon, Wis. 54448.

CAREER: Ordained Roman Catholic priest of Capuchin order (O.F.M.Cap.), 1966.

WRITINGS: (Under pseudonym Jeremiah Crosby) *Bearing Witness: The Place of the Franciscan Family in the Church*, Franciscan Herald, 1966; *The Call and the Answer*, Franciscan Herald, 1969. Contributor to *New Catholic Encyclopedia, America, Emmanuel, Bible Today*, and other periodicals. Past editor, *Round Table of Franciscan Research*.

WORK IN PROGRESS: A book developing a theology of vocation.

SIDELIGHTS: Crosby is competent in Latin; knows some Italian and Spanish.†

* * *

CROSBY, Muriel (Estelle) 1908-

PERSONAL: Born March 1, 1908, in Washington, D.C.; daughter of George W. and Mary (Granville) Crosby. *Education:* Wilson Teachers College (now District of Columbia Teachers College), B.S., 1936; University of Maryland, M.A., 1942, D.Ed., 1951. *Home:* 1627 North Franklin St., Wilmington, Del. 19806. *Office:* Board of Education, 1400 Washington St., Wilmington, Del. 19899.

CAREER: Washington (D.C.) public schools, teacher, 1928-33, supervisor, 1933-47; Silver Burdett Co. (publishers), New York, N.Y., director of Research Curriculum Division, 1947-49; Adelphi College, Garden City, N.Y., associate professor of education, 1949-51; Wilmington (Del.) public schools, assistant superintendent in charge of elementary education, 1951-65, assistant superintendent for educational programs, 1965-67, acting superintendent, 1967-68; associate superintendent, 1968. Consultant on urban education, 1968—; member of board of directors, Girls Clubs of America, 1965-67; member of advisory board, Grolier Publishing Co., 1968-69; Distinguished Lecturer, National Council of Teachers of English, 1970. *Member:*

National Council of Teachers of English (president, 1966), National Education Association (adviser, educational policies commission, 1965-69), Association for Supervision and Curriculum Development (member of board of directors, 1963-67; president 1968-69), Phi Kappa Phi, Kappa Delta Pi. *Awards, honors:* Pacemaker Award, National Conference of Christians and Jews, 1965; American Association of University Women award, 1965; Delaware Federation of Business and Professional Women's Club award, 1966; National Council of Teachers of English, distinguished service award, 1969.

WRITINGS: Supervision as Cooperative Action, Appleton, 1957; *Curriculum Development for Elementary Schools in a Changing Society*, Heath, 1963; (editor) *Reading Ladders for Human Relations*, American Council on Education, 1963; 5th edition, 1972; *An Adventure in Human Relations*, Follett, 1965; (co-chairman) *Programs for the Disadvantaged*, National Council of Teachers of English, 1966; (contributor) W. A. VanTil, editor, *Curriculum: Quest for Relevance*, Houghton, 1971; (general editor) "The World of Language" series, Follett, 1974. Contributor to education journals. Member of publications advisory committee, National Education Association's Department of Elementary School Principals.†

* * *

CROWE, Charles 1928-

PERSONAL: Born January 6, 1928, in Harriman, Tenn.; son of Thomas E. and Bonnie Wright (Seiler) Crowe; married Joyce Slocumb, January 30, 1949; children: Lisa, Charles Thaddeus. *Education:* College of William and Mary, A.B., 1950; Brown University, A.M., 1951, Ph.D., 1955. *Politics:* Democrat. *Home:* 445 Ponderosa Dr., Athens, Ga. 30601 (winter); 725 South Atlantic Ave., Virginia Beach, Va. (summer). *Agent:* Gerard F. McCauley, Curtis Brown Ltd., 60 East 56th St., New York, N.Y. 10022.

CAREER: Assistant professor of history at Virginia Polytechnic Institute, Blacksburg, 1955-56, College of William and Mary, Norfolk and Williamsburg, Va., 1956-58, and Michigan State University, 1958-60; George Washington University, Washington, D.C., assistant professor of American studies, 1961-63; Western Reserve University (now Case Western Reserve University), Cleveland, Ohio, assistant professor of history, 1963-65; University of Georgia, Athens, associate professor, 1965-74, professor of history, 1974—. University of Kiel, Fulbright lecturer, 1960-61; University of Manchester, lecturer, 1961; Free University of Berlin, guest professon, American Institute, 1962-63. Georgia Council on Human Relations, member. *Military service:* U.S. Army, 1946-47. *Member:* American Historical Association, American Association of University Professors, National Association for the Advancement of Colored People, Association for the Study of Negro Life and History, Southern Historical Association. *Awards, honors:* Grants from American Philosophical Society, 1959, 1962-63, and 1968, Colonial Williamsburg, 1960, 1962, and National Institutes of Health, 1962-63.

WRITINGS: (Co-author) *A Picture History of the Modern World*, Little, 1961; *A Documentary History of American Life and Thought*, Allyn & Bacon, 1965; *The Age of Civil War and Reconstruction*, Dorsey, 1966, 2nd edition, 1975. Contributor to *Journal of the History of Ideas, Church History, Archiv fuer Neuren Sprachen und Literaturen, Il Politico, Journal of Southern History, Journal of Negro History.* Member of board of editors, *Journal of Negro History*, 1968-73.

WORK IN PROGRESS: Four books, *Explaining American History: Essays in Historiography, Racial Conflict and Violence in 1906, A Social History of America, 1848-1880, Feminism and Black History, 1836-70.*

SIDELIGHTS: Crowe is competent in German and French. He has traveled in Europe, Morocco, China, and Japan.

* * *

CROWN, Paul 1928-

PERSONAL: Born June 19, 1928, in Braddock, Pa.; son of Harry (a retailer) and Dora (Schwartz) Crown; married Joanne Newman (now a teacher), December 23, 1951; children: Nancy, Valerie. *Education:* University of Pittsburgh, B.B.A., 1952; New York University, M.S., 1962. *Home:* 12 Chance St., Hicksville, N.Y. 11801.

CAREER: National Bellas Hess (mail-order catalog firm), New York, N.Y., merchandise manager, 1954-67; Haber-Klein, Inc. (shoe sales firm), New York, N.Y., principal and merchandise manager, 1967—. Formerly lecturer at Brooklyn College; lecturer at Fashion Institute of Technology. *Military service:* U.S. Army, 1952-54; became second lieutenant.

WRITINGS: Legal Protection for the Consumer, Oceana, 1963; *What You Should Know about Retail Merchandising*, Oceana, 1966; *What You Should Know About Building Your Mailing Lists*, Oceana, 1973. Business editor, Oceana's "Business Almanac Series."

* * *

CRYSTAL, David 1941-

PERSONAL: Born July 6, 1941, in Lisburn, County Antrim, Northern Ireland; son of Samuel Cyril and Mary (Morris) Crystal; married Molly Stack, April 1, 1964; children: Steven David, Susan Mary, Timothy Joseph, Lucy Alexandra. *Education:* University College, University of London, B.A., 1962, Ph.D., 1966. *Politics:* None. *Religion:* Roman Catholic. *Home:* 67 Westwood Rd., Tilehurst, Berkshire, England. *Office:* Department of Linguistic Science, University of Reading, Reading, Berkshire, England.

CAREER: University College, University of London, London, England, research assistant, 1962-63; University College of North Wales, University of Wales, Bangor, assistant lecturer in linguistics, 1963-65; University of Reading, Reading, England, lecturer in linguistics, 1965-69, reader in linguistics, 1969—. *Member:* Linguistic Association of Great Britain, International Phonetic Association, British Association of Applied Linguistics, Philological Society, Linguistic Society of America.

WRITINGS: (With R. Quirk) *Systems of Prosodic and Paralinguistic Features*, Mouton & Co., 1964; *Linguistics, Language and Religion*, Hawthorn, 1965; *What is Linguistics?*, Edward Arnold, 1968; (with D. Davy) *Investigating English Style*, Longmans, Green, 1969; *Prosadic Systems and Intonation in English*, Cambridge University Press, 1969; (editor with W. Bolton) *The English Language*, Cambridge University Press, 1969; *Linguistics*, Penguin, 1971; *The English Tone of Voice*, Edward Arnold, 1975; (with Davy) *Advanced Conversational English*, Longman, 1975; (with P. Fletcher and M. Garman) *The Grammatical Analysis of Language Disability*, Edward Arnold, 1975; (with J. Bevington) *Skylarks*, Nelson, 1975. Editor of *Journal of Child Languages.*

WORK IN PROGRESS: Language acquisition; the application of linguistics to problems of language disability and the study of language in education; general research into English structure and style.

AVOCATIONAL INTERESTS: Music, in all forms; book collecting.

* * *

CUA, Antonio S. 1932-

PERSONAL: Born July 23, 1932, in Manila, Philippines; son of Oh (a merchant) and Chio (So) Cua, came to U.S. in 1953, naturalized citizen, 1971; married Shoke-Hwee Khaw, June 11, 1956; children: Athene Khaw. Education: Far Eastern University, Manila, Philippines, B.A., 1952; University of California, Berkeley, M.A., 1954, Ph.D., 1958. Home: 7525 Cayuga Avenue, Bethesda, Md. 20034. Office: Department of Philosophy, Catholic University of America, Washington, D.C. 20034.

CAREER: Ohio University, Athens, instructor, 1958-61, assistant professor of philosophy, 1961-62; State University of New York College at Oswego, professor of philosophy and chairman of department, 1962-69; Catholic University of America, Washington, D.C., professor of philosophy, 1969—. Visiting professor, University of Missouri, Columbia, 1975. Member: American Philosophical Association, Mind Association, Society for Asian and Comparative Philosophy, American Catholic Philosophical Association, Metaphysical Society of America, American Association of University Professors. Awards, honors: Research award from State University of New York, 1966.

WRITINGS: Reason and Virtue: A Study in the Ethics of Richard Price, Ohio University Press, 1966. Contributor to American Philosophical Quarterly, New Scholasticism, Inquiry, and other journals. Co-editor, Journal of Chinese Philosophy, 1973—; member of editorial board, American Philosophical Quarterly, 1973—.

WORK IN PROGRESS: Paradigms, Principles and Ideals.

SIDELIGHTS: Cua writes and speaks Mandarin and Amoy dialect.

* * *

CULLER, A(rthur) Dwight 1917-

PERSONAL: Born July 25, 1917, in McPherson, Kan.; son of Arthur Jerome (a clergyman) and Mary (Stover) Culler; married Helen Lucille Simpson (a teacher), September 14, 1941; children: Jonathan Dwight, Helen Elizabeth. Education: Oberlin College, B.A., 1938; Yale University, Ph.D., 1941. Home: 80 Tokeneke Dr., Hamden, Conn. 06518. Office: 108 Linsly-Chittenden Hall, Yale University, New Haven, Conn. 06518.

CAREER: Cornell University, Ithaca, N.Y., instructor in English, 1941-42; Yale University, New Haven, Conn., instructor, 1946-49, assistant professor of English, 1949-55; University of Illinois, Urbana, associate professor of English, 1955-58; Yale University, professor of English, 1958—. Wartime service: Civilian Public Service, 1943-46. Member: Modern Language Association of America (member of advisory committee, 1971-74), Phi Beta Kappa. Awards, honors: Fulbright research fellow in England, 1950-51; Guggenheim fellow, 1961-62; D.Litt., Merrimack College, 1972.

WRITINGS: The Imperial Intellect: A Study of New-

man's Educational Ideal, Yale University Press, 1955; (editor) John Henry Newman, Apologia pro vita sua, Houghton, 1956; (editor with George P. Clark) Student and Society, Row, Peterson & Co., 1958; (editor) Poetry and Criticism of Matthew Arnold, Houghton, 1961; Imaginative Reason: The Poetry of Matthew Arnold, Yale University Press, 1966.

WORK IN PROGRESS: The poetry of Tennyson.

* * *

CULP, Delos Poe 1911-

PERSONAL: Born July 26, 1911, in Clanton, Ala.; son of Joseph D. and Lela (Popwell) Culp; married Martha Street, December 23, 1934; children: Martha Jean (Mrs. W. M. Flanigan), James David, John Stephen. Education: Jacksonville State College (now University), Jacksonville, Ala., diploma, 1934; Alabama Polytechnic Institute (now Auburn University), B.S., 1937, M.S., 1940; Columbia University, Ed.D., 1949. Politics: Democrat. Religion: Methodist. Home: President's Home, East Tennessee State University, Johnson City, Tenn. 37601. Office: East Tennessee State University, Johnson City, Tenn. 37601.

CAREER: Teacher and principal, Chilton and Butler county schools, Ala., 1935-42; Chilton County (Ala.) public schools, superintendent, 1941-46; Alabama State Department of Education, Montgomery, division director, 1946-51; Auburn University, Auburn, Ala., professor of education, 1951-54; Livingston State College, Livingston, Ala., president, 1954-63; Alabama College (now University of Montevallo), Montevallo, president, 1963-68; East Tennessee State University, Johnson City, president, 1968—. Director of Alabama Education Commission, 1957-59; member of U.S. special education mission to Philippines, 1959-60; special consultant to American Association of Colleges for Teacher Education, 1960-61; chairman of National Commission on Safety Education, 1965—; member of special study commission of Alabama Department of Education, 1967-68. Director of First Peoples Bank, Johnson City, 1968—. Member: American Association of School Administrators, Alabama Association of School Administrators (president, 1960), Alabama Education Association (chairman of policies commission, 1960-62, 1965—), Kappa Delta Pi, Phi Delta Kappa, Rotary International.

WRITINGS: Administrators Handbook of Pupil Transportation, Alabama State Board of Education, 1949; Pupil Transportation, Rural Department, National Education Association, 1953; (with others) School Business Administration, Ronald, 1956; (with E. Glenn Featherston) Pupil Transportation: State and Local Systems, Harper, 1965. Contributor to The Encyclopedia of Education, Macmillan, 1971.

* * *

CUMBERLAND, William Henry 1929-

PERSONAL: Born June 14, 1929, in Vinton, Iowa; son of Roscoe Lawrence (a farmer) and Clida (Hawley) Cumberland; married Ingrid Wagner, July 31, 1959, in Giessen, Germany. Education: University of Dubuque, B.A., 1950; University of Iowa, M.A., 1953, Ph.D., 1958. Politics: Democrat. Religion: Presbyterian. Home: 812 Pleasantview Dr., Storm Lake, Iowa 50588. Office: Buena Vista College, Fourth and College, Storm Lake, Iowa 50588.

CAREER: Buena Vista College, Storm Lake, Iowa, professor of history, 1958—, chairman of Social Science Division, 1964—, chairman of faculty senate, 1966-67 and 1968-69. *Member:* American Historical Association, Organization of American Historians, American Association of University Professors.

WRITINGS: History of Buena Vista College, Iowa State University Press, 1966.

WORK IN PROGRESS: Research in American social and intellectual history in the period, 1890-1920.

* * *

CUNNINGHAM, Lyda Sue Martin 1938-

PERSONAL: Born March 16, 1938, in New York, N.Y.; daughter of James Edward (a newspaperman) and Suzanne (Kokus) Martin; married Neil Russell Cunningham (in data processing), March 24, 1962. *Education:* Duke University, B.S., 1959; Columbia University, M.A., 1967.

CAREER: Columbia-Presbyterian Medical Center, New York, N.Y., successively staff nurse, head nurse, instructor in nursing, and administrative assistant, 1960-66; Mount Sinai Hospital, New York, N.Y., former assistant director of nursing. Writer. *Member:* American Nurses Association, National League for Nursing.

WRITINGS: How to Become a Nurse, Macfadden, 1963; (editor) *Readings in Basic Medical-Surgical Nursing*, W. C. Brown, 1966; (editor) *Readings in Advanced Medical-Surgical Nursing*, W. C. Brown, 1966; *A Layman's Guide to First Aid*, Macfadden, 1966. Contributor to nursing journals. Editor, *Tomorrow in Nursing* (nationwide monthly newsletter).†

* * *

CURRAN, Francis X. 1914-

PERSONAL: Born February 6, 1914, in New York, N.Y., son of Francis and Catherine (Reilly) Curran. *Education:* Georgetown University, B.A., 1938; Weston College, S.T.L., 1946; Columbia University, Ph.D., 1951. *Home and office:* Fordham University, Bronx, N.Y. 10458.

CAREER: Roman Catholic priest of Jesuit order (S.J.); Regis High School, New York, N.Y., instructor, 1939-42; Loyola Seminary, Shrub Oak, N.Y., assistant professor of history, 1955-62; Fordham University, New York, N.Y., associate professor, 1962-66, professor of history, 1966—. Ateneo de Manila University, visiting professor of history, 1964-65. New York Province of Society of Jesus, historian, 1951—. *Member:* American Historical Association, American Catholic Historical Association, American Society of Church History, United States Catholic Historical Society.

WRITINGS: Major Trends in American Church History, America Press, 1946; *The Churches and Schools*, Loyola University Press (Chicago), 1954; *Catholics in Colonial Law*, Loyola University Press (Chicago), 1963; *The Return of the Jesuits*, Loyola University Press (Chicago), 1966. Contributor to encyclopedias, and to *America, Thought, Catholic Historical Review, Mid-America*, and other periodicals.

WORK IN PROGRESS: Research in the history of the Christian churches in the United States.

* * *

CURRENT-GARCIA, Eugene 1908-

PERSONAL: Born July 8, 1908, in New Orleans, La.; son of Joseph Robustiano and Bertha (Ehrhardt) Current-Garcia; married Alva Garrett (a university teacher), June

18, 1935; children: William J., Alison E., Adele. *Education:* Tulane University, A.B., 1930, M.A., 1932; Harvard University, A.M., 1942, Ph.D., 1947. *Politics:* Democrat. *Home:* 510 E. Samford Ave., Auburn, Ala. 36830. *Office:* Department of English, Auburn University, Auburn, Ala.

CAREER: Instructor in English at University of Nebraska, Lincoln, 1936-39, Suffolk University, Boston, Mass., 1939-42, and Louisiana State University, Baton Rouge, 1944-47; Auburn University, Auburn, Ala., 1947—, started as assistant professor, professor of American literature, 1952—. University of Salonika, Fulbright lecturer, 1956-58; lecturer in Latin America, 1961. *Member:* American Studies Association, American Association of University Professors, South Atlantic Modern Language Association, Southern Humanities Conference (secretary, 1961-63), Society for Study of Southern Literature (executive committee member, 1972-75), Southeastern American Studies Association (secretary, later president, 1958-62), Alabama Education Association, Alabama Historical Association, Phi Beta Kappa, Phi Kappa Phi. *Awards, honors:* Elected first Phi Kappa Phi American Scholar, 1974.

WRITINGS: (With W. R. Patrick) *American Short Stories*, Scott, 1952, 3rd edition, 1975; (with W. R. Patrick) *What Is the Short Story?*, Scott, 1961, 2nd edition, 1974; (with W. R. Patrick) *Realism and Romanticism in Fiction*, Scott, 1962; *O. Henry: A Critical Study*, Twayne, 1965; (contributor) Louis D. Rubin, Jr., editor, *A Bibliographical Guide to the Study of Southern Literature*, Louisiana State University Press, 1969; (editor with Dorothy B. Hatfield) *Shem, Ham, and Japheth: The Papers of W. O. Tuggle*, University of Georgia Press, 1973. Contributor to journals. Co-editor, *Southern Humanities Review*, 1967.

WORK IN PROGRESS: The Short Story in America, Volume I; and *Josephine Preston Peabody and Her Circle*, both for Twayne.

SIDELIGHTS: Current-Garcia speaks Spanish.

* * *

CURRY, Jane L(ouise) 1932-

PERSONAL: Born September 24, 1932, in East Liverpool, Ohio; daughter of William Jack, Jr. and Helen (Willis) Curry. *Education:* Pennsylvania State University, student, 1950-51; Indiana State College (now Indiana University of Pennsylvania), Indiana, Pa., B.S. (art education), 1954; attended University of California at Los Angeles, 1957-59; University of London, graduate studies, 1961-62, 1965-66; Stanford University, M.A., 1962, Ph.D., 1969. *Residence:* Los Angeles, Calif.

CAREER: Art teacher in Los Angeles (Calif.) city schools, 1955-59; Stanford University, Stanford, Calif., teaching assistant, 1964-65, acting instructor in English literature, 1967-68. Paintings shown in London at exhibitions of Royal Society of British Artists and other groups, 1962. *Member:* Mediaeval Academy of America, International Arthurian Society, London Mediaeval Association, Authors Guild, Medieval Association of the Pacific. *Awards, honors:* Fulbright grant, 1961-62, and Stanford-Leverhulme fellowship, 1965-66, for study in London; Book World Spring Children's Book Festival, honor book award, and Southern California Council on Literature for Children and Young People, outstanding book by a southern California author award, 1970, for *The Daybreakers*.

WRITINGS—All juveniles: *Down from the Lonely Mountain*, Harcourt, 1965, self-illustrated edition, Dobson, 1967;

Beneath the Hill, Harcourt, 1967; *The Sleepers*, Harcourt, 1968; *The Change-Child*, Harcourt, 1969; *The Daybreakers*, Harcourt, 1970; *Mindy's Mysterious Miniature*, Harcourt, 1970; *Over the Sea's Edge*, Harcourt, 1971; *The Ice Ghosts Mystery*, Atheneum, 1972; *The Lost Farm*, Atheneum, 1974; *Parsley Sage, Rosemary, and Time*, Atheneum, 1975; *The Watchers*, Atheneum, 1975.

WORK IN PROGRESS: The Wonderful Cakebread Cupboard, juvenile; *The Bassumthyte Treasure*, juvenile; and *Poor Tom's Ghost*.

AVOCATIONAL INTERESTS: Cooking, gardening, painting, travel, reading mysteries.

* * *

CURRY, Kenneth 1910-

PERSONAL: Born October 24, 1910, in Orlando, Fla.; son of W. K. and Corinne (Sias) Curry. *Education:* Rollins College, A.B., 1932; Yale University, Ph.D., 1935. *Religion:* Episcopalian. *Office:* University of Tennessee, Knoxville, Tenn. 37916.

CAREER: University of Tennessee, Knoxville, instructor, later assistant professor, 1935-46, associate professor, 1946-60, professor of English, 1960—. *Member:* International Association of University Professors of English, Modern Language Association of America, Modern Humanities Research Association.

WRITINGS: (Editor) *New Letters of Robert Southey*, two volumes, Columbia University Press, 1965; *Southey*, Routledge & Kegan Paul, 1975. Contributor to learned journals.

WORK IN PROGRESS: A book on Scott's *Edinburgh Annual Register*.

* * *

CURTIN, James R(udd) 1922-

PERSONAL: Born February 25, 1922, in Milwaukee, Wis.; son of Francis L. (a fireman) and Frances (Rudd) Curtin; married Mary Anne Rausch, May 28, 1948; children: Julie, Ellen, Jane, Anne. *Education:* University of Wisconsin-Milwaukee, B.S., 1946; University of Iowa, M.A., 1950, Ph.D., 1954. *Politics:* Independent. *Religion:* Roman Catholic.

CAREER: Oregon College of Education, Monmouth, assistant professor of elementary education, 1952-55; University of Minnesota, Minneapolis, 1955—, started as assistant professor, professor of elementary education, 1963—. *Member:* Association for the Evaluation of Elementary Schools (past president), National Education Association, Minnesota Elementary School Principals Association (past president).

WRITINGS: Supervision in Today's Elementary Schools, Macmillan, 1964; *Pressures on the Principal*, Minnesota Association for Supervision and Curriculum Development, 1964; *The Changing Role of the Elementary School Principal* (monograph), Minnesota Elementary Principal's Association, 1965. Contributor to elementary education journals.

WORK IN PROGRESS: Introduction to Elementary Education (tentative title), for Macmillan; *Elementary School Administration* (tentative title), for Rand McNally.†

* * *

CURTO, Josephine J. 1927-

PERSONAL: Born July 27, 1927, in Brevard, N.C.; daughter of Joseph and Lelia (Sexton) Curto. *Education:* Attended Brevard Junior College, 1944-45; Western Carolina College (now University), B.S. (cum laude), 1947; George Peabody College for Teachers, M.A., 1951; Florida State University, Ph.D., 1969. *Politics:* Democrat. *Religion:* Protestant. *Home:* 2109 Croydon Dr., Tallahassee, Fla. 32303.

CAREER: English teacher, department chairman, and librarian at high schools in North Carolina and Florida, 1945-46, 1948-63; Miami-Dade Junior College, Miami, Fla., associate professor of English and chairman of writing department, 1963-67; Tallahassee Community College, Tallahassee, Fla., professor of children's and American literature, 1967—. Visiting assistant professor of English, Western Carolina College (now University), 1966-67. *Member:* National Council of Teachers of English, National Education Association, Children's Literature Association, National Writers Club, American Association of University Professors, American Association of University Women.

WRITINGS: (With Frances MacLoed) *Reading Forward*, Wadsworth, 1965; *Writing With Understanding*, C. E. Merrill, 1966; (with MacLoed) *Ladder of Language*, Scott, Foresman, 1967; (with Jean English) *Handbook for Readers and Writers*, C. E. Merrill, 1968; *Biography of an Alligator*, Putnam, 1974. Book reviewer for "Children's Bookshelf" in *Tallahassee Democrat*, 1970—, and for *The United Teacher*, 1975—. Contributor of articles to educational journals.

WORK IN PROGRESS: Two books, *We Get Our Comeuppance* and *Faulkner: A New Look at the Humorist*; and a trilogy, *Fury in the Blood*.

SIDELIGHTS: Josephine Curto is proficient in French. *Avocational interests:* Art, gardening, and swimming.

* * *

DABBS, Jack Autrey 1914-

PERSONAL: Born January 31, 1914, in Mercury, Tex.; son of John Franklin (a farmer) and Florence Susan (Boyd) Dabbs; married Anna V. Johnson, May 25, 1940; children: Danielle Elizabeth. *Education:* University of Texas, B.A., 1935, M.A., 1936, Ph.D., 1950. *Religion:* Protestant. *Home:* 1011 Edgewood, Bryan, Tex. 77801.

CAREER: High school teacher in Texas, 1937-38; St. Edward's University, Austin, Tex., instructor, 1938-40, 1948-50; Texas A&M University, College Station, assistant professor, 1950-53, associate professor of modern languages, 1953-57; American Language Institute, Baghdad, Iraq, director, 1957-58; Texas A&M University, professor of modern languages, 1958—. *Military service:* National Guard, 1929-40. U.S. Army, active duty, 1940-48; served in Iran, Korea, and Germany. U.S. Army Reserve, 1948-60; became major. *Member:* Société de Linguistique de Paris, American Name Society (president, 1962). *Awards, honors:* Ford Foundation grant, 1960; Faculty Distinguished Service Award for Research, Texas A&M University, 1974.

WRITINGS: (Contributor) *Handbook of Latin American Studies*, Harvard University Press, 1940; (with C. E. Castaneda) *Guide to the Latin American Manuscripts in the University of Texas Library*, Harvard University Press, 1940; (with C. E. Castaneda) *Calendar of the Manuel E. Gondra Manuscript Collection*, Editorial Jus (Mexico City), 1952; (with Castaneda) *Independent Mexico in Documents*, Editorial Jus, 1954; (contributor) *Studies in Mexican History*, University of Texas Press, 1958; *A Short*

Bengali-English, English-Bengali Dictionary, Department of Modern Languages, Texas A&M University, 1962, 3rd edition, 1971; *History of the Discovery and Exploration of Chinese Turkestan*, Mouton & Co. (The Hague), 1963; *The French Army in Mexico: A Study in Military Government*, Mouton & Co., 1963; *Dei Gratia in Royal Titles*, Mouton & Co., 1971; (compiler) *The Mariano Riva Palacio Archives*, three volumes, Editorial Jus, 1967-72. Contributor of articles and reviews to *Names, Mid-America, Southwestern Journal of Anthropology, Military Review, Language*, and other journals. Editor, *Bulletin of the Texas Foreign Language Association*, 1954-56.

WORK IN PROGRESS: Biographies of Spanish officials in New Spain toward the end of the colonial period.

*   *   *

D'AGOSTINO, Angelo 1926-

PERSONAL: Born January 26, 1926, in Providence, R.I.; son of Luigi and Julia (lonardo) D'Agostino. *Education:* St. Michael's College, Winooski, Vt., B.S., 1945; Tufts University, M.D., 1949, M.S. (surgery), 1953. *Home:* Georgetown University, Washington, D.C. 20007.

CAREER: Roman Catholic priest of Jesuit order (S.J.); licensed to practice psychiatry in District of Columbia, Maryland, Massachusetts, Pennsylvania, and Rhode Island; diplomate, National Board of Medical Examiners, 1950; resident in psychiatry at D.C. General Hospital, 1959-60, and Georgetown Hospital, 1960-62; psychiatrist in private practice, beginning 1962; Georgetown Medical School, Washington, D.C., instructor in department of psychiatry, beginning 1962; ordained to priesthood, 1966; George Washington University, Medical Center, Washington, D.C., clinical associate professor, department of psychiatry, 1969—. Director, Center for Religion and Psychiatry; adjunct professor, Washington Theological Coalition. Lecturer and panelist on medical and theological topics at more than thirty seminars and professional meetings.

MEMBER: American Medical Association, American Psychiatric Association, National Medical Association, Association for Clinical Pastoral Education, Association for the Sociology of Religion, National Association of Catholic Chaplains, National Council on Family Relations, Society for the Scientific Study of Religion, Academy of Pastoral Counselors, American-Italian Historical Association, Medical Society of the District of Columbia, Rhode Island Medical Association, Washington Psychiatric Society, Italian Cultural Society of Washington, Alpha Omega Alpha, Cosmos Club. *Awards, honors:* Grand Knight, Order of Merit of the Italian Government, 1972.

WRITINGS: (Editor) *Family, Church and Community*, Kenedy, 1965. Also compiler with Loughlan Scofield of *Directory of Counseling Centers for Priests and Religious*. Contributor of articles to medical journals.

WORK IN PROGRESS: Research in theology and psychiatry; pastoral training of clergy in the area of group counseling methods.

*   *   *

DAHLSTROM, Earl C(arl) 1914-

PERSONAL: Born January 31, 1914, in Rockford, Ill.; son of Emil N. (a mechanic) and Nannie (Lundstrom) Dahlstrom; married Rosalie Madeline Jones, September 12, 1942; children: Konrad P., Karl J. *Education:* North Park Col-

lege, A.A., 1936; University of Chicago, A.B., 1939; North Park Theological Seminary, diploma, 1940; Kennedy School of Missions, M.A., 1949; Hartford Seminary Foundation, Ph.D., 1950; Boston University School of Theology, visiting scholar, 1961-62. *Home:* 5340 North Sawyer, Chicago, Ill. *Office:* North Park Seminary, Chicago, Ill. 60625.

CAREER: Clergyman of Evangelical Covenant Church of America. Pastor in Hartford, Conn., 1942-46, Chicago, Ill., 1950-54. Missionary-teacher in China, 1940-42, 1946-48. North Park Theological Seminary, Chicago, Ill., professor of pastoral studies, 1954—. President of Church Federation of Greater Chicago, 1964-65; member of board of directors, Chicago Conference on Religion and Race, 1964—. *Member:* Academy of Religion and Mental Health, Association for Clinical Pastoral Education, Association for Professional Education for Ministry (president, 1974—), Association of Theological Field Education (chairman, 1962-64), City Club (Chicago).

WRITINGS: History of the Covenant Missionary Society in China, Hartford Seminary Foundation, 1950; *The Christian Church*, Covenant Press, 1959; (with E. G. Hawkinson and H. M. Carlson) *A Book of Worship for Covenant Churches*, Covenant Press, 1964; *Helping Human Beings*, Public Affairs, 1964. Member of editorial committee of *Covenant Quarterly*; editor of *Biennial Report* of Association for Professional Education for Ministry, 1960-64.

WORK IN PROGRESS: A new *Book of Worship* with J. R. Hawkinson and G. J. Uriberg for Covenant Press, and *The Developing Role of the National Pastors of the Younger Churches of the World.*

*   *   *

DALBOR, John B(ronislaw) 1929-

PERSONAL: Born August 26, 1929, in Erie, Pa.; son of Bronislaw (a lithographer) and Bessie (Johnson) Dalbor; married Dorothy Green, September 1, 1951; children: Steven, Michael. *Education:* Pennsylvania State University, B.A., 1951, M.A., 1953; University of Michigan, Ph.D., 1961. *Politics:* Democrat. *Home:* 512 Hillside Ave., State College, Pa. 16801. *Office:* N-344 Burrowes, Pennsylvania State University, University Park, Pa. 16802.

CAREER: Pennsylvania State University, University Park, instructor, 1958-61, assistant professor, 1961-66, associate professor, 1966-72, professor of Spanish and linguistics, 1972—. *Military service:* U.S. Army, 1953-55. *Member:* Modern Language Association of America, American Association of Teachers of Spanish and Portuguese, Linguistic Society of America, American Council on the Teaching of Foreign Languages.

WRITINGS: (Editor with Donald A. Yates) *Imaginacion y Fantasia*, Holt, 1960, revised edition, 1968; (with Tracy Sturcken) *Oral Spanish Review*, Holt, 1965; *Spanish Pronunciation*, Holt, 1969; *Beginning College Spanish*, Random House, 1972. Contributor of articles and book reviews to professional journals.

AVOCATIONAL INTERESTS: Sports.

*   *   *

d'ALELIO, Ellen F. 1938-

PERSONAL: Born November 30, 1938, in Boston, Mass.; daughter of G. Francis (a professor) and Josephine (McCarthy) d'Alelio. *Education:* St. Mary's College, Notre Dame, Ind., B.A., 1960; University of Caen, graduate student, 1960-61; New York University, M.A., 1962, doctoral candidate; summer study at Trinity College, University of Dublin. *Home:* 2 Washington Square Village, New York, N.Y. 10012. *Office:* Department of Romance Languages, New York University, New York, N.Y. 10003.

CAREER: New York University, New York, N.Y., instructor in French language and literature, 1961—. *Member:* Modern Language Association of America, American Association of University Professors. *Awards, honors:* Fulbright grant for study in France, 1960-61.

WRITINGS: (With Micheline Dufau) *Poetry for Explication*, Harcourt, 1966; (with Dufau) *En Avant: A Progressive Review of French*, Harcourt, 1972.

WORK IN PROGRESS: Medieval French Recits.

SIDELIGHTS: Ellen d'Alelio speaks French and Italian. *Avocational interests:* Piano, harpsichord.†

* * *

DALY, Sister Mary Virginia 1925-
(Sister Mary Virgene Daly)

PERSONAL: Born July 25, 1925, in Omaha, Neb.; daughter of Arthur and Catherine (Rowley) Daly. *Education:* Creighton University, A.B., 1945, M.A., 1960; St. Louis University, currently Ph.D. candidate. *Politics:* Democrat. *Office:* Mercy High School, 1501 South 48th, Omaha, Neb.

CAREER: Roman Catholic nun, member of Religious Sisters of Mercy. College of St. Mary, Ohama, Neb., assistant professor of English, 1963-65; Mercy High School, Omaha, Neb., principal, 1972—. *Member:* Sigma Tau Delta.

WRITINGS: (With Lowrie J. Daly; under name Sister Mary Virgene Daly) *Meditations for Educators*, Sheed, 1965.

WORK IN PROGRESS: With Lowrie J. Daly, a four-volume work on meditation.

* * *

DAMERST, William A. 1923-

PERSONAL: Born August 21, 1923, in Pelham, Mass.; son of Steven M. and Clara (Peterson) Damerst; married Dorothy Blackburn February 16, 1946; children: Jeffrey, Laura, Gail. *Education:* Attended Amherst College, 1941-43, 1945-46; University of Illinois, B.S., 1946; University of Massachusetts, M.A., 1955. *Politics:* Independent voter. *Religion:* Episcopalian. *Home:* 248 East Waring Ave., State College, Pa. 16801. *Office:* S-222 Burrowes Building, Pennsylvania State University, University Park, Pa. 16802.

CAREER: Wellworth Pharmacy, Inc., Amherst, Mass., president, 1946-55; Pennsylvania State University, University Park, 1955—, began as instructor, associate professor, 1965-72, professor of English, 1972—. Consultant to industry on technical and business writing. *Military service:* U.S. Army Air Forces, 1943-45; received Air Medal with five oak leaf clusters. *Member:* American Business Communication Association (fellow; president, 1972), Society for Technical Communication, Centre Hills Country Club, Elks. *Awards, honors:* Gulf Oil Corp. aid-to-education grants, 1959, 1960.

WRITINGS: Good Gulf Letters and Reports, Gulf Oil Corp., 1959; *Resourceful Business Communication*, Harcourt, 1966; *Clear Technical Reports*, Harcourt, 1972.

WORK IN PROGRESS: A novel, completion expected in 1975.

DANA, Barbara 1940-

PERSONAL: Born December 28, 1940, in New York, N.Y.; daughter of Richard Anderson (a writer and advertising agency executive) and Mildred (Ferry) Dana; married Alan Arkin (an actor), June 16, 1964; children: Anthony. *Education:* Quintano's School for Young Professionals, high school diploma. *Agent:* Phyllis Wender, Wender & Associates, 30 East 60th St., New York, N.Y. 10022.

CAREER: Stage and television actress. Broadway appearances include roles in "Who's Afraid of Virginia Woolf?," "Where's Daddy?," and "Enter Laughing"; on television has appeared in "Daughter of the Mind," an original movie for television, "As the World Turns," "New York Television Theatre," "N.E.T. Playhouse," and over 100 network shows.

WRITINGS: Spencer and His Friends (juvenile), Atheneum, 1966; *Rutgers and the Water-Snouts* (juvenile), Harper, 1969; *Zuchini, The Ninety-Second Street Ferret* (juvenile), Harper, in press.

WORK IN PROGRESS: A book for children, *Leonard, The Viking Troll*; a two-act play.

* * *

DANCE, Stanley (Frank) 1910-

PERSONAL: Born September 15, 1910, in Braintree, England; son of Frank Albert (in tobacco trade) and Violet Mary (Shead) Dance; married Helen Oakley, January 29, 1947; children: Teresa Mary Violet, Rupert Stanley Frank, Francis John Edward, Cynthia Maria Paula. *Education:* Attended Framlingham College, 1925-28. *Religion:* Roman Catholic. *Home:* 12 Oakleigh Ct., Rowayton, Conn. 06853.

CAREER: F. A. Dance Ltd. (wholesale tobacconists), Braintree, England, director, 1928-58; now free-lance writer specializing in jazz. Member of board of trustees, New York Jazz Museum, 1972—; director, New York Jazz Repertory Company, 1974—. *Military service:* Royal Observer Corps, 1935-45. *Member:* National Academy of Recording Arts and Sciences. *Awards, honors:* Grammy Award for best liner notes, National Academy of Recording Arts and Sciences, 1963, for "The Ellington Era."

WRITINGS: (Editor) *The Jazz Era*, MacGibbon & Kee, 1961; *The World of Duke Ellington*, Scribner, 1970; (with Dicky Wells) *The Night People*, Crescendo, 1971; *The World of Swing*, Scribner, 1974. Regular columnist, *Music Journal, Jazz Journal* (London). Writer of narrative for CBS-TV Special, "Alley Celebrates Ellington," 1974.

WORK IN PROGRESS: Volumes II and III of *The World of Swing*; biography of Duke Ellington with Mercer Ellington.

SIDELIGHTS: Stanley Dance told *CA:* "Interest in medieval history has only been pushed into the background by the necessity to make a living."

* * *

DANIELS, Harold R(obert) 1919-

PERSONAL: Born November 3, 1919, in Winchendon, Mass.; son of Alan Joseph and Margaret (Hurley) Daniels; married Dorothy Helen Theresa Mahoney, May 19, 1942; children: Michael Robert, Dean Joseph, Brian Austin. *Education:* Graduated from high school in Milford, Conn. *Politics:* Republican. *Religion:* Roman Catholic. *Home and office:* West Main Rd., Little Compton, R.I. *Agent:* Jay Sanford, Ashley Famous Agency, Inc., 1301 Avenue of the Americas, New York, N.Y. 10019.

CAREER: Worked in earlier years as laborer, master mechanic, public relations officer, and plant superintendent; free-lance writer, 1948-58; *Metalworking* (magazine), Boston, Mass., senior editor (associate), 1958-72; now freelance writer. Consultant on metals accounts to public relations firms. *Military service:* U.S. Army and U.S. Air Force, 1941-48; became major; received Bronze Star. *Member:* American Metal Stamping Association (technical research and standards committee), American Legion. *Awards, honors:* Edgar Allan Poe Award ("Edgar") of Mystery Writers of America, 1956, for *In His Blood*; Industrial Marketing Award, 1965, for best technical article of the year.

WRITINGS: In His Blood, Dell, 1956; *The Girl in 304*, Dell, 1958; *The Accused*, Dell, 1959; *The Snatch*, Dell, 1961; *For the Asking*, Fawcett, 1962; *Press Brake and Shear Handbook*, Cahners, 1965, revised edition, 1975; *The House on Greenapple Road*, Random House, 1966; (editor) *Mechanical Press Handbook*, 3rd edition (Daniels was not associated with earlier editions), Cahners, 1969. Contributor to anthologies; regular contributor to *Ellery Queen's Mystery Magazine*. Consulting editor of *Metal Stamping*.

WORK IN PROGRESS: A contemporary novel (not a mystery); a play.

SIDELIGHTS: Harold Daniels speaks French. *Avocational interests:* Reading history.

* * *

DANTO, Arthur C(oleman) 1924-

PERSONAL: Born January 1, 1924, in Ann Arbor, Mich.; son of Samuel Budd (a dentist) and Sylvia (Gittleman) Danto; married Shirley Rovetch, August 9, 1946; children: Elizabeth Ann, Jane Nicole. *Education:* Wayne State University, B.A., 1948; Columbia University, M.A., 1949, Ph.D., 1952; University of Paris, post-graduate study, 1949-50. *Politics:* Democrat. *Religion:* Jewish. *Home:* 420 Riverside Dr., New York, N.Y. 10025.

CAREER: University of Colorado, Boulder, instructor, 1950-51; Columbia University, New York, N.Y., instructor, 1951-54, assistant professor, 1954-59, associate professor 1959-66, professor of philosophy, 1966—. Visiting lecturer at Princeton University and University of California, Santa Barbara, 1965; visiting professor, Catholic University of America, 1972, University of California, San Diego, 1973; resident scholar at Rockefeller Study Center, 1974. Artist, with works in public collections. *Military service:* U.S. Army, 1942-45. *Awards, honors:* Fulbright fellowship in France, 1949-50; fellow, American Council of Learned Societies, 1962, 1969; Guggenheim fellow, 1970.

WRITINGS: (Editor with Sidney Morgenbesser) *Philosophy of Science*, Meridian, 1961; *Nietzsche as Philosopher*, Macmillan, 1965; *Analytical Philosophy of History*, Cambridge University Press, 1965; *Analytical Philosophy of Knowledge*, Cambridge University Press, 1968; *What Philosophy Is*, Harper, 1968; *Mysticism and Morality: Oriental Thought and Moral Philosophy*, Basic Books, 1972; *Analytical Philosophy of Action*, Cambridge University Press, 1973; *Jean Paul Sartre*, Viking, in press. Contributor to philosophical periodicals. Editor, *Journal of Philosophy*, 1964—.

WORK IN PROGRESS: A book on philosophy of art.

SIDELIGHTS: Danto has lived in Paris, Provence, and Rome.

DAPPER, Gloria 1922-

PERSONAL: Born September 18, 1922, in Faribault, Minn.; daughter of George C. and Ethyl (Shields) Dapper. *Education:* University of Minnesota, B.A., 1944. *Politics:* Democrat.

CAREER: WCCO-CBS, Minneapolis, Minn., news writer, 1944-46; American Forces Network, Germany, director of continuity, 1946-49; National Citizens Commission for the Public Schools, New York, N.Y., public relations director, 1950-59; Glick & Lorwin, Inc., New York, N.Y., vice-president, 1960-62; Free Lance Associates, New York, N.Y., president, 1962—. *Member:* Education Writers Association, Overseas Press Club of America, Women's City Club (New York).

WRITINGS: Public Relations for Educators, Macmillan, 1964; (with Barbara Carter) *A Guide for School Board Members*, Follett, 1966; (with Carl B. Smith and Carter) *Conquering Reading Problems*, International Reading Association, 1970; (with Smith and Carter) *Treating Reading Difficulties: The Role of the Principal, Teacher, Specialist, [and] Administrator*, National Center for Educational Communication, 1970; (with Carter) *School Volunteers: What They Do, How They Do It*, Citation, 1972. Author with Smith and Carter of educational study pamphlets. Contributor of articles to *Saturday Review* and education journals.†

* * *

DARBY, Ray(mond) 1912-

PERSONAL: Born March 9, 1912, in Edmonton, Alberta, Canada; son of Charles Edgar (a salesman) and Julala M. (Hopkins) Darby; married Patricia Paulsen, October 26, 1954; children: Glen, Jessica, Grant, Raymond, Jr.; stepchildren: Edward, Rebecca. *Education:* Attended Kelvin Technical High School, Winnipeg, Canada. *Politics:* Republican. *Religion:* Episcopalian. *Home:* 2527 Hereford Rd., Thousand Oaks, Calif. *Agent:* August Lenniger, Lenniger Literary Agency, 11 West 42nd St., New York, N.Y. 10036.

CAREER: Full-time professional writer, chiefly free lance; has been employed at periods as motion picture writer by U.S. Navy, U.S. Air Force, and Walt Disney Productions. Film, "The Chuting Stars" accepted at Versailles and Edinburgh film festivals, 1963. *Member:* American Society of Composers, Authors and Publishers, Writers Guild of America (West), Conejo Valley Historical Society (board of directors). *Awards, honors:* Christopher Award for Disney film series, 1957; CHRIS Award for Air Force Film, "The U.S. Air Force in Southeast Asia."

WRITINGS: Oomah, Contemporary Publishers, 1946; *Sky-Diving, the Space Age Sport* (Junior Literary Guild selection), Messner, 1964; *Your Career in Physical Therapy* (Junior Literary Guild selection), Messner, 1967; *Conquering the Deep Sea Frontier*, (Junior Literary guild selection), McKay, 1970. Author of about one hundred motion picture documentaries. Contributor to *Reader's Digest, This Week, True, Cavalier, Good Housekeeping, Coronet*, and other magazines.

WORK IN PROGRESS: A series of Junior books for backward readers.

AVOCATIONAL INTERESTS: Fishing.

* * *

D'ARCY, Paul F(rancis) 1921-

PERSONAL: Born August 9, 1921, in New York, N.Y.;

son of James Joseph (owner of a furniture-moving business) and Ida (Etzel) D'Arcy. *Education:* Attended Maryknoll Apostolic College, Clarks Summit, Pa., 1937-41, and Maryknoll Seminary, 1942-46; Catholic University of America, M.A., 1948, Ph.D., 1954. *Home and office:* Maryknoll Fathers, Maryknoll, N.Y. 10545.

CAREER: Ordained Roman Catholic priest of Maryknoll order, 1946; instructor at Catholic University of America, Washington, D.C., 1947-48, at Maryknoll seminaries, 1948-60; U.S. Veterans Administration Hospital, Downey, Ill., postdoctoral trainee, 1960-61; Maryknoll Fathers, Maryknoll, N.Y., director of education, 1961—, and professor of pastoral counseling at Maryknoll Seminary, 1961—. Iona College, New Rochelle, N.Y., staff member, graduate division of pastoral counseling, 1962—. Member, National Institute of Mental Health.

MEMBER: American Catholic Psychological Association (president), American Psychological Association, Association for Counselor Education and Supervision, American Personnel and Guidance Association, Society for Scientific Study of Religion, Religious Research Association, Academy of Religion and Mental Health, Religious Education Association, National Catholic Education Association, Society for Asian Studies, Psychologists Interested in Advancement of Psychotherapy of Religion, New York State Psychological Association.

WRITINGS: Constancy of Interest Factor Patterns within the Specific Vocation of Foreign Missioner, Catholic University of America Press, 1954; (with V. V. Herr, M. G. Arnold, and C. A. Weisgerber) *Screening Candidates for the Priesthood and Religious Life*, Loyola University Press (Chicago), 1962; (with Eugene C. Kennedy) *The Genius of the Apostolate*, Sheed, 1965.†

* * *

DARLING, Frank Clayton 1925-

PERSONAL: Born May 8, 1925, in Chicago, Ill.; son of Frank D. and Nora (Pomeroy) Darling; married Ann Bardwell, June 10, 1952; children: Diane Heather. *Education:* Principia College, B.A., 1951; University of Chicago, M.A., 1957; American University, Ph.D., 1960. *Politics:* Independent. *Religion:* Christian Science. *Residence:* Greencastle, Ind.

CAREER: Lecturer at Chulalongkorn University and Thammasat University, Bangkok, Thailand, 1954-56; U.S. Government, Washington, D.C., research analyst, 1952-53, 1957-60; University of Colorado, Boulder, began as acting assistant professor, 1960, associate professor of political science, 1965-67; DePauw University, Greencastle, Ind., professor and head, department of political science, 1967—. Fulbright professor in the Philippines, 1965-66. *Military service:* U.S. Navy, 1943-46; received five campaign bars and three battle stars. *Member:* American Political Science Association, Association for Asian Studies, and other professional organizations.

WRITINGS: Thailand and the United States, Public Affairs, 1965. Also author of *Thailand: The Modern Kingdom*, 1971. Contributor to professional journals.

WORK IN PROGRESS: Comparative Political History: An Analytical Framework Applied to Asian Societies.

SIDELIGHTS: Frank Clayton Darling speaks and some German and Thai.

DAUER, Victor Paul 1909-

PERSONAL: Born April 14, 1909, in Hammond, Ind.; son of Theodore Henry and Hulda (Heinemann) Dauer; married Alice L. Lange, June 7, 1941; children: Theodore E., Thomas O. *Education:* Indiana University, B.S. (with distinction), 1932, M.S., 1941; University of Michigan, Ph.D., 1951.

CAREER: High school teacher and coach, Cannelton (Ind.) High School, 1932-36, Muncie (Ind.) School System, 1936-37, Wabash (Ind.) High School, 1937-41; Valparaiso University, Valparaiso, Ind., professor of physical education and athletic director, 1941-42; University of Michigan, Ann Arbor, assistant, 1946-47; Springfield College, Springfield, Mass., assistant professor, 1947-49; Washington State University, Pullman, assistant professor, 1949-52, associate professor, 1952-57, professor of physical education, 1957—. *Military service:* U.S. Army, Coast Artillery, 1943-46; became first lieutenant. *Member:* American Association for Health, Physical Education, and Recreation, National College Physical Education Association, Washington Association for Health, Physical Education, and Recreation (president, 1955), Phi Delta Kappa, Phi Epsilon Kappa, Kiwanis Club. *Awards, honors:* U.S. Office of Education grants, 1967-70 and summer, 1970; honor awards from health associations, 1966, 1968, and 1970.

WRITINGS: Fitness for Elementary School Children Through Physical Education, Burgess, 1962, 4th edition published as *Dynamic Physical Education for Elementary School Children*, 1971; *Essential Movement Experiences for Preschool and Primary Children*, Burgess, 1972. Also editor of research papers on physical education and recreation.

WORK IN PROGRESS: A book on methods in physical education; research in physical fitness testing.

SIDELIGHTS: Dauer visited twenty-seven European countries during 1965-66 to study physical education, mostly on the elementary level. *Avocational interests:* Hunting, fishing, camping, skiing.†

* * *

DAUGERT, Stanley M(atthew) 1918-

PERSONAL: First syllable of surname is pronounced as "dog"; born June 10, 1918, in Wilkes-Barre, Pa.; son of Lawrence Fabian and Elizabeth (White) Daugert; married Barbara Bredin (a school psychologist), October 4, 1944; children: Lawrence, Stephen, Frederic, Elizabeth. *Education:* Bucknell Junior College (now Wilkes College), student, 1936-38; Columbia University, B.A., 1940, M.A., 1942, Ph.D., 1949. *Politics:* Democrat. *Religion:* Unitarian Universalist. *Home:* 1881 N. Shore Rd., Bellingham, Wash. 98225. *Office:* Department of Philosophy, Western Washington State College, Bellingham, Wash. 98225.

CAREER: Oglethorpe College, Atlanta, Ga., faculty, 1947-62, began as instructor, and became professor of philosophy, chairman of Division of Human Understanding, 1955-57, 1959-61; Western Washington State College, Bellingham, professor of philosophy and chairman of department, 1962—. Part-time lecturer in philosophy at Emory University, 1949-50, and Atlanta Division, University of Georgia, 1950-51; lecturer at Pacific Philosophy Institute, 1965. Programs associate, Southern Regional Education Board, 1955-56. Vice-president, Human Relations Commission, Bellingham, 1964; Great Books leader, Bellingham, 1964-74. President, Bellingham Unitarian Fellowship, 1966-

67. *Military service:* U.S. Army, 1942-46; served in South Pacific, Philippines, and Korea; became first lieutenant. *Member:* American Philosophical Association, American Association of University Professors, Northwest Philosophy Association, American Civil Liberties Union. *Awards, honors:* Rockefeller Foundation grant to study the Oglethorpe College program, 1950-51.

WRITINGS: (Assistant editor) P. O. Kristeller, *The Philosophy of Marsilio Ficino*, Columbia University Press, 1943; *The Philosophy of Thorstein Veblen*, King's Crown Press, 1950; (reviser and editor) *Ethical Philosophies of India*, Johnsen, 1965; (editor and reviser) Ishwar Chandra Sharma, *India's Democracy and the Communist Challenge*, Johnsen, 1967. Contributor to *Main Currents in Modern Thought, Personalist, Pacific Philosophy Forum*, and *Educational Forum*.

* * *

DAUGHTREY, Anne Scott 1920-

PERSONAL: Surname is pronounced *Daw*-tree; born January 12, 1920, in Radford, Va.; daughter of Joppa Beebe and Minnie Virginia (Hutton) Scott; married Greyson Daughtrey (director of health and physical education, Norfolk public schools), November 22, 1945. *Education:* Radford College, B.S., 1941; University of South Dakota, M.A., 1957, D.Ed., 1967. *Religion:* Methodist. *Home:* 4816 Gosnold Ave., Norfolk, Va. 23508. *Office:* School of Business, Old Dominion University, Norfolk, Va.

CAREER: Teacher of business education at schools in South Norfolk, Va., 1941-46, and in Norfolk, Va., 1946-59; Old Dominion University, Norfolk, Va., 1959—, began as associate professor, now professor of business education. College of William and Mary, adult education teacher, 1951-52. Accrediting Commission for Business Schools, member, 1964—; Tidewater Area Advisory Council for Business and Education, co-chairman, 1956-58. *Member:* National Business Education Association, Society for Automation in Business Education, American Business Writing Association, Administrative Management Society (former vice-president), American Association of University Professors, Virginia Business Education Association (former officer), Eastern Business Teachers Association, Virginia Education Association, South Norfolk Education Association (former officer), Norfolk Society of Arts, Tau Kappa Alpha, Kappa Delta Pi.

WRITINGS: Methods of Basic Business and Economic Education (textbook), South-Western Publishing, 1965, revised edition, 1974. Also co-author of *Methods and Resources for General Business*, 1973. Contributor to education journals and yearbooks.

AVOCATIONAL INTERESTS: Travel, reading (history, mystery, and business).

* * *

DAVENTRY, Leonard John 1915-

PERSONAL: Born March 7, 1915, in Brixton, London, England; son of Leonard (an army captain) and Dorothy (Davies) Daventry; married Margaret Alexander (a business partner), 1941; children: Anna Betsy, Martin Leonard. *Education:* Mostly self-educated. *Politics:* "Nil." *Religion:* "Nil."

CAREER: Left school at thirteen and worked as errand boy until seventeen; joined British Army in 1932, went on Reserve in 1939, was recalled and promoted to sergeant in 1940; after discharge in 1941 was long-distance lorry driver, market porter, and hearse driver; in 1957 he and his wife became vegetable suppliers to caterers, a business they still operate. *Awards, honors:* Atlantic Literary Award, 1946.

WRITINGS: A Man of Double Deed, Doubleday, 1965; *Reflections in a Mirage* [and] *The Ticking is in Your Head*, Doubleday, 1969; *Twenty-One Billionth Paradox*, Doubleday, 1971. Author of short stories published in England and America, 1943-47.

SIDELIGHTS: Daventry told *CA:* [I] "am an enemy of divisionary aspects of Man: Religion, politics, classes, flag waving cults, clubs, uniforms, etc. Having had to struggle against bias, ignorance, anger, and insanity in myself for fifty years, I consider these to be the major evils of man.... H. G. Wells made me want to think. Macaulay and E. M. Forster to write."†

* * *

DAVIDSON, H(ilda) R(oderick) Ellis 1914-
(Hilda Roderick Ellis)

PERSONAL: Born October 1, 1914, in Bebington, Cheshire, England; daughter of Henry Roderick (a stationer) and Millie (Cheesman) Ellis; married Richard Robertson Davidson (a research scientist), December 27, 1943; children: Hilary, Richard Neil Roderick. *Education:* Newnham College, Cambridge, M.A., 1939, Ph.D., 1940. *Politics:* Liberal. *Religion:* Church of England.

CAREER: University of London, London, England, assistant lecturer in English, Royal Holloway College, 1939-44, part-time lecturer in English, Birkbeck College, 1945-54, lecturer in extramural department, 1942-54; Cambridge University, Lucy Cavendish College, Cambridge, England, research fellow, 1968-71, lecturer, 1971—. *Member:* Society of Antiquaries of London (fellow), Folklore Society (council member). *Awards, honors:* Leverhulme research award for work in Soviet Union, 1964.

WRITINGS: (Under name Hilda Roderick Ellis) *The Road to Hel: A Study of the Conception of the Dead in Old Norse Literature*, Cambridge University Press, 1943, reprinted, Greenwood Press, 1968; *The Golden Age of Northumbria*, Longmans, Green, 1958; *The Sword in Anglo-Saxon England*, Clarendon Press, 1961; *Gods and Myths of Northern Europe*, Pelican Books, 1965; (contributor) Joan Cadogan Lancaster, *Godiva of Coventry*, Coventry Corp., 1967; *Pagan Scandinavia*, Praeger, 1967; (with G. N. Garmonsway and Jacqueline Simpson) *Beowulf and Its Analogues*, Dent, 1968; *Scandinavian Mythology*, Hamlyn, 1969; (with Peter Gelling) *The Chariot of the Sun*, Praeger, 1969. Contributor to *Encyclopaedia Britannica*, and to *Antiquity, Folklore, Arms and Armour*, and other journals.

SIDELIGHTS: Mrs. Davidson has reading knowledge of Anglo-Saxon, early Norse, Norwegian, Swedish, Danish, Icelandic, Russian, Latin, and German.†

* * *

DAVIDSON, Herbert A(lan) 1932-

PERSONAL: Born May 25, 1932, in Boston, Mass.; son of Louis N. and Ettabelle (Baker) Davidson; married Kinneret Bernstein, 1958; children: Rachel. *Education:* Harvard University, B.A., 1953, Ph.D., 1959. *Office:* University of California, Los Angeles, Calif. 90024.

CAREER: Harvard University, Cambridge, Mass., lecturer in Hebrew, 1960-61; University of California, Los Angeles, assistant professor of Hebrew, 1961-66, associate professor, 1966-72, professor of Hebrew, 1972—. *Member:*

Mediaeval Academy of America, American Oriental Society, American Academy for Jewish Research.

WRITINGS: The Philosophy of Abraham Shalom, University of California Press, 1964; (editor and translator) Averrois Cordubensis Commentarium Medium in Porphyrii Isagogen et Aristoelis Categorias, Mediaeval Academy of America, 1969, translation published as Middle Commentary on Porphyry's Isagoge, Translated from the Hebrew and Latin Versions, and on Aristotle's Categoriae, Translated from the Original Arabic and the Hebrew and Latin Versions. Also author of introduction, Judah hal Levi's Liber Cosri, 1971, and Almosnino's Pirque Moshe, 1972. Contributor to Grollier's Encyclopedia, Encyclopaedia Judaica, Dictionary of Scientific Biography, and to professional journals.

*   *   *

DAVIDSON, Sol M.   1924-

PERSONAL: Born December 13, 1924, in Newark, N.J.; son of Isidore (a merchant) and Helen (Black) Davidson; married Hermia Goldfinger (onetime art teacher), June 19, 1949; children: Cliff Ian, Ron Hunter, Brian Howard. Education: Louisiana State University, B.A., 1946; New York University, M.A., 1950, Ph.D., 1959. Politics: Independent. Religion: Jewish. Home: 5200 Shriver Ave., Des Moines, Iowa 50312. Office: Northwestern Bell Telephone Co., 909 High St., Des Moines, Iowa.

CAREER: Baton Rouge Morning Advocate, Baton Rouge, La., assistant sports editor, 1945; Beneficial Finance Co., Morristown, N.J., educational director, 1948-59; DIAL Finance Co., Des Moines, Iowa, director of personnel, 1959-66, director of operations, 1967-73; Northwestern Bell Telephone Co., Des Moines, Iowa, executive assistant, 1974—. Maplewood-South Orange (N.J.) Department of Adult Education, instructor, 1957; Adult Education Advisory Council of Des Moines Public Schools, chairman, 1962; Des Moines Board of International Education, president; Des Moines Human Rights Commission, chairman. Military service: U.S. Navy, 1945-47; managing editor of Ships' Editorial Association (Navy syndicate). Awards, honors: Named outstanding Jaycee of the year, Des Moines, 1960-61.

WRITINGS: The Cultivation of Imperfection, Fell, 1965; The Value of Friction, Fell, in press. Writer of weekly newspaper column, "City Limits," for South Des Moines Messenger. Contributor of articles on business, comic strips, and other subjects to magazines, including Discovery, Our Navy, and Management Magazine.

WORK IN PROGRESS: A comic strip, "Philbert the Flea"; a novel, Ours is the Earth.

*   *   *

DAVIDSON, William Robert   1919-

PERSONAL: Born July 19, 1919, in Gove County, Kan.; son of William Bryan (a retailer) and Clara (Wecker) Davidson; married Anne Elizabeth Anderson, October 16, 1945; children: Joyce West, Judith Anne. Education: College of Emporia, A.B., 1940; Washington University, St. Louis, Mo., M.S.B.A., 1947; Ohio State University, Ph.D., 1950. Religion: Episcopalian. Home: 247 Preston Rd., Columbus, Ohio 43209. Office: Management Horizons, Inc., 1651 Northwest Professional Plaza, Columbia, Ohio 43220.

CAREER: F. W. Woolworth Co., Emporia and McPherson, Kan., assistant store manager, 1940-41; G. Myron Gwinner Associates, St. Louis, Mo., research analyst, 1946-47; Ohio State University, Columbus, faculty member, 1947-72, professor of marketing, 1959-72, chairman of marketing faculty, 1969-71; Management Horizons, Inc., Columbus, Ohio, co-founder, chairman of board, and chief executive officer, 1968—. Visiting professor, Stanford University, Graduate School of Business, 1958-59; Harvard University, 1974. Gilbert Shoe Stores, Inc., director; Management and Business Services, Columbus, Ohio, senior associated consultant, 1960-68. Columbus School for Girls, trustee. Military service: U.S. Naval Reserve, naval aviator, 1941-45; became lieutenant; received Distinguished Flying Cross and Purple Heart. Member: American Marketing Association (president, 1963-64), American Academy of Political and Social Science, Newcomen Society, Ohio State University Faculty Club, Columbus Country Club, Rotary International. Awards, honors: Marketing man of the year, Central Ohio chapter, American Marketing Association, 1961; elected to Hall of Fame in Distribution, Boston Conference on Distribution, 1964.

WRITINGS: Retailing—Principles and Practices, Ronald, 1953, 3rd edition, with Alton F. Doody and Daniel Sweeney, published as Retailing Management, 1966, 4th edition, 1975; The Wholesale Wine Trade in Ohio, Ohio State University Bureau of Business Research, 1955; (with Theodore N. Beckman and Harold H. Maynard) Principles of Marketing, 6th edition, Ronald, 1957, 8th edition, with Beckman and J. F. Engel, published as Marketing, 1967, 9th edition with Beckman and Wayne Tolaryzk, 1973; (contributing editor) The Marketing Handbook, Ronald, 1965.

Contributor: The Frontiers of Marketing Thought and Science, edited by Frank M. Bass, American Marketing Association, 1958; Toward Scientific Marketing, edited by Stephen A. Greyser, American Marketing Association, 1964. Contributor of articles to professional journals and business magazines.

*   *   *

DAVIES, A(lfred) Mervyn   1899-

PERSONAL: Born November 20, 1899, in Liverpool, England; son of Sir Alfred Thomas (a lawyer and educator) and Lady Mary (Colton) Davies; married Monica Borglum, October 31, 1925; children: Harold Borglum, Alfred Thomas, Gwyneth Mary (Mrs. John Beverley Kelley). Education: Jesus College, Oxford, B.A., 1922, M.A., 1925. Politics: Independent Democrat. Religion: Protestant. Home: 89 Borglum Rd., Wilton, Conn. 06897.

CAREER: British Library of Information, New York, N.Y., assistant, 1924-25; authors' representative, New York, N.Y., 1925-37; British Information Services, New York, N.Y., staff writer and reporter, 1939-42; St. Louis Post-Dispatch, St. Louis, Mo., secretary to publisher and book review editor, 1942-62; full-time free-lance writer, 1962—. Military service: Royal Air Force, Meteorological Branch, 1918-19; became pilot officer. Member: American Historical Association, Presbyterian Historical Society.

WRITINGS: George III and the Constitution, Oxford University Press, 1922; Strange Destiny: A Biography of Warren Hastings, Putnam, 1935 (published in England as Warren Hastings: Maker of British India, Nicholson & Watson, 1935); Clive of Plassey, Scribner, 1939; Foundation of American Freedom, Abingdon, 1955; Presbyterian Heritage, John Knox, 1965; Solon H. Borglum: A Biography, Pequot, 1974. Occasional contributor of articles to St. Louis Post-Dispatch and other newspapers.

WORK IN PROGRESS: A memoir of my father.

DAVIES, R(onald) E. G.   1921-

PERSONAL: Born July 3, 1921, in Mottingham, Kent, England; son of William George (in Royal Navy) and Gertrude (Jacobs) Davies; married Marjorie Emily Chapman, October 9, 1948; children: Jacqueline, Annette. *Education:* Attended Shaftesbury Grammar School, 1931-38. *Religion:* Church of England. *Home:* 777 Avocado Ave., Apartment B42, Corona del Mar, Calif. 92625.

CAREER: Ministry of Civil Aviation, London; England, clerk, Economics and Intelligence Department, 1946-49; British European Airways, London, England, economic research officer, 1949-56; Bristol Aircraft Co. Ltd., Bristol, England, market research manager, 1956-59; Hawker Siddeley Aviation Ltd. (formerly deHavilland Aircraft Co. Ltd.), Hatfield, England, chief market research analyst, 1959-68; Douglas Aircraft Co., Long Beach, Calif., manager of market research, 1968—. Sometime owner of small record company, and lecturer on music. *Military service:* British Army, volunteer reserve, called to active duty, 1939-46. *Member:* Royal Aeronautical Society (associate), Institute of Transport (associate), Industrial Market Research Association, Pacific Area Travel Association (former research council chairman).

WRITINGS: A History of the World's Airlines, Oxford University Press, 1964; *Airlines of the United States Since 1914*, Putnam, 1972. Author of monograph on British Air Transport published in *Royal Aeronautical Society Journal* Centenary issue, 1966, and of numerous research papers published by Douglas Aircraft Co. Contributor to *Air Pictorial, Flight* (England), *Flight* (United States), and other aviation journals.

WORK IN PROGRESS: Certain revisions for *A History of the World's Airlines*; continuing research in air transport history.

SIDELIGHTS: Davies is competent in French. *Avocational interests:* Music (all kinds, including traditional jazz), do-it-yourself carpentry and woodcraft, ancient English history, and cartography.

*   *   *

DAVIES, Richard O.   1937-

PERSONAL: Born October 26, 1937, in Hamilton, Ohio; son of Robert O. (a teacher) and Ruth (Klein) Davies; married Sharon Kay Dye (a nurse), June 15, 1962; children: Jennifer Lynne, Robert Oakley. *Education:* Marietta College, B.A., 1959; Ohio University, M.A., 1960; University of Missouri, Ph.D., 1963. *Home:* 3240 South Troxler Cr., Flagstaff, Ariz. 86001.

CAREER: Reporter on newspapers in Marietta, Ohio, 1959, and Middletown, Ohio, 1960; University of Missouri, Columbia, instructor in history, 1960-63; Northern Arizona University, Flagstaff, assistant professor, 1963-65, associate professor of history, 1965-68; Memphis State University, Memphis, Tenn., associate professor of history, 1968-69; Northern Arizona University, Flagstaff, associate professor, 1969-70, professor of history, 1970—, director of honors program, 1968-72, chairman of faculty senate, 1972-73, director of Center for Integrated Studies, 1972—, dean of College of Public and Environmental Service, 1974—. Visiting professor, University of Southern California, summer, 1971. *Member:* American Historical Association, Organization of American Historians, Southern Historical Association, Urban History Group, Phi Kappa Phi. *Awards, honors:* Grant for research at Harry S Truman

Library, 1961; National Endowment for the Humanities fellowship for younger scholars, 1967-68.

WRITINGS: Housing Reform During the Truman Administration, University of Missouri Press, 1966; (contributor) Richard S. Kirkendall, editor, *The Truman Administration as a Research Field*, University of Missouri Press, 1967; (editor with Franklin D. Mitchell) *America's Recent Past*, Wiley, 1969; *The Age of Asphalt: The Freeway, the Automobile, and the Condition of Urban American*, Lippincott, in press; *A History of Urban America, 1930-70*, Schenkman, in press.

*   *   *

DAVIS, Clive E(dward)   1914-

PERSONAL: Born October 19, 1914, in South New Berlin, N.Y.; son of Clyde Seymour (a civil engineer) and Eva (Bird) Davis; married Maxine Peterson (a secretary); children: Douglas Michael, Bruce Edward. *Education:* Syracuse University, student, 1932-36. *Politics:* Democratic. *Religion:* Episcopalian. *Home:* 3309 Bristol Rd., Sacramento 25, Calif. 95825.

CAREER: Announcer and program assistant at radio stations in Philadelphia, Pa., Worchester, Mass., New York, N.Y., Great Falls, Mont., and Sacramento, Calif., 1937-62; free-lance writer. Licensed commercial pilot, 1947—. *Military service:* U.S. Army Air Forces, World War II; served in Asia, Africa, Europe, and with armies of occupation in Italy and Philippines; became first lieutenant; received Silver Star, Bronze Star (twice), Distinguished Unit Citation with oak leaf cluster. U.S. Air Force Reserve; now lieutenant colonel (retired). *Member:* Air Force Association. *Awards, honors:* Air Force Association Medal of Merit, 1956, and citations, 1957 and 1958; Arts and Letters Award of California wing of Air Force Association.

WRITINGS—All published by Dodd: The Junior Airman's Book of Airplanes, 1958; *The Book of Missiles*, 1959; *Man and Space*, 1960, *Message From Space*, 1961; *The Book of Air Force Airplanes and Helicopters*, 1967.

*   *   *

DAVIS, D(onald) Evan   1923-

PERSONAL: Born March 13, 1923, in Los Angeles, Calif.; son of Robert Author and A. Loreen (Crawford) Davis; married Clara Janice, June 23, 1947; children: Janet, Britton, Dawn, Curtis, Ewan. *Education:* University of California, Los Angeles, B.A., 1946; University of Southern California, graduate study, 1946-47; Northwestern University, M.Mus., 1948; University of Oregon, D.Ed., 1953; Vienna State Academy of Music, postdoctoral study, 1961. *Religion:* Church of Jesus Christ of Latter-day Saints. *Home:* 2585 North 650 East, Provo, Utah 84601.

CAREER: Assistant professor of music at Northern Arizona University, Flagstaff, 1953-55, and Oregon State University, Corvallis, 1955-58; University of British Columbia, Vancouver, Canada, associate professor of music, 1958-65; Brigham Young University, College of Fine Arts, Provo, Utah, professor of music, 1965—. Church of Jesus Christ of Latter-day Saints, former president of Vancouver stake. *Military service:* U.S. Army, Infantry, 1942-43; U.S. Army Air Forces, bombardier-navigator, 1943-45; became second lieutenant. *Member:* Music Educators National Conference, National Association of Teachers of Singing. *Awards, honors:* Postdoctoral fellowship, Canada Council for the Arts, 1961, for research in comparative music education; grants from Koerner Foundation, 1962-64, and U.S. Office of Education, 1969.

WRITINGS: (With others) *Music Education in Oregon Public Schools*, Oregon State Department of Education, 1958; *Self-Evaluative Criteria for Music*, British Columbia Department of Education, 1964; (with L. Slind) *Bringing Music to Children*, Harper, 1965. Composer of *Rise We from Death*, published by Rock Canyon Press, *Sing With Me*, published by Deseret Books, and a choral anthem published by Waterloo Music Co. Contributor to music and education journals.

WORK IN PROGRESS: Six compositions for women's chorus.

* * *

DAVIS, David Brion 1927-

PERSONAL: Born February 16, 1927, in Denver, Colo.; son of Clyde Brion (a writer) and Martha (Wirt) Davis; married Frances Warner (a teacher), October 22, 1948 (divorced, 1971); married Toni Hahn (a psychiatric social worker), September 9, 1971; children: (first marriage) Jeremiah, Martha, Sarah; (second marriage) Adam. *Education:* Dartmouth College, A.B., 1950; Harvard University, A.M., 1953, Ph.D., 1956. *Politics:* Democrat. *Home:* 733 Lambert Rd., Orange, Conn. 06477. *Office:* 226 Hall of Graduate Studies, Yale University, New Haven, Conn. 06520.

CAREER: Dartmouth College, Hanover, N.H., instructor in history and Fund for the Advancement of Education intern, 1953-54; Cornell University, Ithaca, N.Y., assistant professor, 1955-58, associate professor, 1958-63, Ernest I. White Professor of History, 1963-69; Yale University, New Haven, Conn., professor of history, 1969-72, Farnham Professor of History, 1972—. Fulbright lecturer in India, 1967; Harold Vyvyan Harmsworth Professor of American History, Oxford University, 1969-70; fellow of Center for Advanced Study in Behavioral Sciences, 1972-73. *Military service:* U.S. Army, 1945-46. *Member:* American Historical Association (member of Pulitzer and Beveridge Prize committees), Organization of American Historians, Phi Beta Kappa. *Awards, honors:* Guggenheim fellowship, 1958-59; Anisfield-Wolf Award, 1967; Pulitzer Prize, 1967, for *The Problem of Slavery in Western Culture*; National Mass Media Award from National Conference of Christians and Jews, 1967. M.A. from Oxford University, 1969, and Yale University, 1970.

WRITINGS: Homicide in American Fiction, Cornell University Press, 1957; *The Problem of Slavery in Western Culture*, Cornell University Press, 1967; (editor) *Ante-Bellum Reform*, Harper, 1967; *The Slave Power Conspiracy and the Paranoid Style*, Louisiana State University Press, 1969; *Was Thomas Jefferson an Authentic Enemy of Slavery?*, Clarendon Press, 1970; (editor) *The Fear of Conspiracy: Images of Un-American Subversion from the Revolution to the Present*, Cornell University Press, 1971; *The Problem of Slavery in the Age of Revolution, 1770-1823*, Cornell University Press, 1974.

Contributor: Alfred Kazin and Charles Shapiro, editors, *The Stature of Theodore Dreiser*, Indiana University Press, 1955; Shapiro, editor, *Twelve Original Essays on Great American Novels*, Wayne State University Press, 1958; Martin Duberman, editor, *The Antislavery Vanguard*, Princeton University Press, 1965; C. Vann Woodward, editor, *The Comparability of American History*, Basic Books, 1967; Samuel Klausner, editor, *Why Man*

Takes Chances, Anchor Books, 1968; Richard Blum, editor, *Surveillance and Espionage in a Free Society*, Praeger, 1972.

Contributor to historical and other learned journals.

WORK IN PROGRESS: The Struggle Against Slavery in the New World, for Oxford University Press.

* * *

DAVIS, Jed H(orace, Jr.) 1921-

PERSONAL: Born July 31, 1921, in Stillwater, Minn.; son of Jed Horace (a bookkeeper) and Meda Margarita (Culver) Davis; married Betty Jane Crosby, August 4, 1945; children: John C., Brian T., Julie K. *Education:* University of Minnesota, B.A., 1947, M.A., 1949, Ph.D., 1958. *Politics:* Democrat. *Religion:* Presbyterian. *Home:* 2602 Louisiana St., Lawrence, Kan. 66044. *Office:* University Theatre, University of Kansas, Lawrence, Kan. 66045.

CAREER: Macalester College, St. Paul, Minn., instructor, 1947-50, assistant professor of speech and theater, and director of children's theater, 1950-53; Michigan State University, East Lansing, assistant professor of speech and drama, and director of children's theater, 1953-60; University of Kansas, Lawrence, assistant professor, 1960-62, associate professor, 1962-65, professor of speech and drama, 1965—, director of children's theater, 1960—, director of university theatre, 1967—. Children's Theatre Foundation, trustee and treasurer, 1956—. *Military service:* U.S. Army, Signal Corps, 1942-46.

MEMBER: American Theatre Association (fellow; assistant executive secretary, 1959-60; board member, 1959-61, 1963-65; executive committee member, 1963-65; 2nd vice-president, 1970; 1st vice-president, 1971; president, 1972), Children's Theatre Conference (board member, 1955-58, 1961-66; director, 1963-65), International Association of Theatres for Children and Young People (board member, U.S. center member, 1965—), National Collegiate Players, American Association of University Professors, National Theatre Conference, Association of Kansas Theatre, American Community Theatre Association, Secondary School Theatre Association, University and College Theatre Association.

WRITINGS: (With Mary Jane Larson Watkins) *Children's Theatre Play Production for the Child Audience*, text and trade editions, Harper, 1960; (contributor) *Children's Theatre and Creative Dramatics*, edited by Geraldine B. Siks and Hazel B. Dunnington, University of Washington Press, 1961 (compiler and editor) *A Directory of Children's Theatres in the United States*, American Educational Theatre Association, 1968. Contributor to *Encyclopedia Americana*, and of articles and reviews, primarily on children's theater topics, to journals. Children's theater editor, *Players*, 1962-66, *Speech Teacher*, 1968-72.

WORK IN PROGRESS: Theatre for Young Audiences, with Mary Jane Evans, completion expected in 1976.

SIDELIGHTS: Davis wrote, produced, and acted in barn-show plays beginning at the age of seven, but had no formal training in this direction until late in high school. This, he notes, "is much too late in life for schools to show interest in children's dramatic development!"

BIOGRAPHICAL/CRITICAL SOURCES: Michigan Education Journal, Volume XXVIII, Number 6, November 1, 1959; *Kansas Teacher*, Volume LXIX, Number 9, May, 1961.

DAVIS, Kenneth R(exton) 1921-

PERSONAL: Born August 15, 1921, in Glendive, Mont.; son of Robert T. and Edith M. (Root) Davis; married Mary Elizabeth Gunn, December 29, 1945; children: Jane Claire, John Gunn. *Education:* University of Wisconsin, Ph.B., 1946, M.B.A., 1947; University of Chicago, Ph.D., 1955. *Home:* 10 Kingsford Rd., Hanover, N.H. 03755.

CAREER: University of Wisconsin, Madison, instructor, 1947-49; University of North Carolina, Chapel Hill, assistant professor, 1949-53; Dartmouth College, Amos Tuck School of Business Administration, Hanover, N.H., assistant professor, 1953-57, professor of marketing, 1957—. Management consultant. *Military service:* U.S. Army Air Forces, 1943-47; became captain. *Member:* American Marketing Association, American Association of University Professors, Delta Upsilon, Beta Gamma Sigma.

WRITINGS: Furniture Marketing, University of North Carolina Press, 1957; (with Albert W. Frey) *The Advertising Industry,* Association of National Advertisers, 1958; *Marketing Management,* Ronald, 1961, 3rd edition, 1972; *Sales Force Management,* Ronald, 1968; (with F. E. Webster) *Readings in Sales Management,* Ronald, 1968.

*   *   *

DAVIS, (Benton) Vincent (Jr.) 1930-

PERSONAL: Born May 3, 1930, in Chattanooga, Tenn.; son of Benton Vincent (a businessman) and Mildred Elizabeth (Jackson) Davis; married Anne DePierri, March 16, 1957; children: Gail Borden, Benton Vincent III, Jackson Beecher. *Education:* Vanderbilt University, B.A. (cum laude), 1952; Princeton University, M.P.A., 1959, M.A., 1960, Ph.D., 1961. *Home:* 3533 Gloucester Dr., Westmorland, Lexington, Ky. 40504. *Office:* Patterson Tower 1665, University of Kentucky, Lexington, Ky. 40506.

CAREER: Princeton University, Princeton, N.J., instructor in political science and research assistant, Center of International Studies, 1959-61; Dartmouth College, Hanover, N.H., assistant professor of government, 1961-62; University of Denver, Denver, Colo., associate professor in Graduate School of International Studies and research associate of Social Science Foundation, 1962-69; Princeton University, Princeton, N.J., Center of International Studies, visiting research professor, 1969-70; U.S. Naval War College, Newport, R.I., Nimitz Professor of Foreign Affairs, 1969-70; University of Kentucky, Lexington, Patterson Professor of International Studies and director of Patterson School of Diplomacy and International Commerce, 1971—. International Studies Association, part-time executive director, 1964-70. Littleton Council for Human Relations, president, 1965-66. *Military service:* U.S. Naval Reserve, active duty, 1952-56, primarily as dive-bomber with carrier squadrons in Caribbean and Mediterranean. *Member:* International Institute of Strategic Studies (London), American Political Science Association, International Studies Association, U.S. Naval Institute, Naval Historical Foundation, Southern Political Science Association.

WRITINGS: Postwar Defense Policy and the U.S. Navy, 1943-46, University of North Carolina Press, 1966; *The Admirals Lobby,* University of North Carolina Press, 1967; *The Politics of Innovation: Patterns in Navy Cases,* University of Denver Graduate School of International Studies "Monograph Series in World Affairs," 1967. Contributor to professional journals.

WORK IN PROGRESS: A book on the role of U.S. Defense Department in making U.S. foreign policy; a book on the impact of scientific and technological advances in shaping the nature of the international political environment.

*   *   *

DAVISSON, William I. 1929-

PERSONAL: Born January 27, 1929, in Tacoma, Wash.; son of Ralph F. and Florence (Davis) Davisson; married Deloris Jungert, June, 1955; children: Michael C., Margaret A., Sandra D., Joanna L. *Education:* College of Puget Sound, B.A., 1953, M.A., 1954; Cornell University, Ph.D., 1961. *Office:* University of Notre Dame, Notre Dame, Ind.

CAREER: Eastern Montana College of Education, Billings, assistant professor of economics, 1957-59; Whittier College, Whittier, Calif., assistant professor of economics, 1959-60; Sacramento State College, Sacramento, Calif., associate professor of economics, 1960-66; University of Notre Dame, Notre Dame, Ind., professor of economics, 1966—. Consultant to State of California and to industry. *Military service:* U.S. Army, 1951-53; served in Japan.

WRITINGS: (With John G. Ranlett) *An Introduction to Microeconomic Theory,* Harcourt, 1965; *Information Processing: Applications in the Social Behavioral Sciences,* Plenum, 1970; (with James E. Harper) *European Economic History,* Appleton, 1972. Author of monographs; contributor to professional journals.

WORK IN PROGRESS: Research in computer programming and computer application to economic growth and development.

*   *   *

DAWSON, Grace S(trickler) 1891-

PERSONAL: Born November 30, 1891, in Keokuk, Iowa; daughter of Henry and Mary Bell (Stafford) Strickler; married Robert E. Dawson, 1915; children: Robert S., Donald E. *Education:* Northwestern University, B.A., 1913. *Home:* 1150 North Holliston, Pasadena, Calif.

CAREER: Writer.

WRITINGS: The Nuggets of Singing Creek, Doubleday, 1938; *California: Story of Our Southwest Corner,* Macmillan, 1939; *The Butterfly Shawl,* Doubleday, 1940; *Your World and Mine* (social studies), Ginn, 1951, 3rd edition, 1965; *For a Deeper Life,* Abingdon, 1963; *Our World: Inquiring and Learning,* Ginn, in press. Contributor of verse to magazines.

WORK IN PROGRESS: Two other books.

*   *   *

DAWSON, Mildred A. 1897-

PERSONAL: Born June 4, 1897; daughter of Henry and Emma Margaret (Fuller) Dawson. *Education:* State College of Iowa, B.A. and Critic Teacher Diploma, 1922; University of Chicago, M.A., 1928; New York University, Ed.D., 1936. *Home:* 5232 Piner Ct., Kelseyville, Calif. 95451.

CAREER: Teacher in Sumner, Iowa, 1916-19, 1924-25; critic teacher at Indiana State College, Indiana, Pa., 1922-24, State College of Iowa, Cedar Falls, 1925-27; head of elementary education department at University of Wyoming, Laramie, 1929-35, University of Georgia, Athens,

1936-37, University of Tennessee, Knoxville, 1937-45; books editor of F. A. Owen Publishing Co., Dansville, N.Y., 1945-47; director of elementary education, Kingston, N.Y., 1947-49; professor of education at State University of New York College at Fredonia, 1949-52, Appalachian State Teachers College (now Appalachian State University), Boone, N.C., 1952-54, Sacramento State University, Sacramento, Calif., 1954-65; writer on educational subjects, 1965—.

MEMBER: International Reading Association (president), National Council of Teachers of English (past chairman of elementary section), National Conference on Research in English (past president), National Society for the Study of Education, American Association of University Women, League of Women Voters, Delta Kappa Gamma (past state president), Pi Lambda Theta, Kappa Delta Pi.

WRITINGS: (With F. H. Dingee) *Directing Learning in the Language Arts*, Burgess, 1942, revised edition, 1948; (with J. M. Miller and others) *Language for Daily Use*, Grades 3-6, World Book, 1948; *Language Teaching in Grades 1 and 2*, World Book, 1949, revised edition, 1957; (with J. M. Miller and others) *Language for Daily Use*, Grades 7-8, World Book, 1949-50; *Teaching Language in the Grades*, World Book, 1951; (with Bonnie Scales) *Language for Daily Use*, Grade 2, World Book, 1952; (with Marian Zollinger) *Guiding Language Learning*, World Book, 1957, 2nd edition (with Marian Zollinger and Ardell Elwell), Harcourt, 1963; (with H. A. Bamman) *Fundamentals of Basic Reading Instruction*, Longmans, Green, 1959, 2nd edition, McKay, 1963; (with F. H. Dingee) *Children Learn the Language Arts*, Burgess, 1959; (editor with M. A. Choate) *How to Help a Child Appreciate Poetry: 100 Poems to Express with Voice and Action*, Fearon, 1960; (with H. A. Bamman and R. J. Whitehead) *Oral Interpretation of Children's Literature*, Brown, 1964; (editor) *Children, Books, and Reading*, International Reading Association, 1964; *Let's Talk and Write*, Harcourt, 1965; (with G. Newman) *Language Teaching in Kindergarten and the Early Primary Grades*, Harcourt, 1966; (with others) *Adventures in Reading*, Benefic, 1967; (with Newman) *Oral Reading and Linguistics*, Benefic, 1969; (with others) *Kaleidoscope Readers*, Addison-Wesley, 1969; (with others) *Cornerstone Readers*, Addison-Wesley, 1970.

Also author, with H. Bamman, of "Target" reading cassette series, Addison-Wesley, 1972.

Editor, *Teacher Education in English Language Arts*, Part I, National Council of Teachers of English, 1960. Author of pamphlet on reading skills, and editor of a series of instructor pamphlets published by F. A. Owen, 1946-47. Also author of research bulletins; contributor to education publications.

AVOCATIONAL INTERESTS: Gardening, bird lore, palmistry, reading, bridge, spectator sports, fishing.

* * *

DAY, Alice Taylor 1928-

PERSONAL: Born June 20, 1928, in New York, N.Y.; daughter of Howard Canning (a physician) and Caroline (Colgate) Taylor; married Lincoln H. Day (an associate professor of sociology and public health at Yale University), November 26, 1952; children: Thomas Hills, Caroline Wolfe. *Education:* Brearley School, graduate, 1946; Smith College, B.A. (magna cum laude), 1950; Columbia University, M.A., 1952. *Religion:* Agnostic. *Home:* 158 Kent St., Hughes, A.C.T., Australia. *Office:* Department of Sociol-

ogy, Research School of Social Studies, Australian National University, Canberra, A.C.T., Australia.

CAREER: Columbia University, Bureau of Applied Social Research, New York, N.Y., research assistant, 1952; Mount Holyoke College, South Hadley, Mass., instructor in sociology, 1953; American Institute of Public Opinion, Princeton, N.J., research assistant, 1954; University of Massachusetts, Amherst, part-time instructor in sociology, 1958; Yale University, New Haven, Conn., research associate in sociology, 1966-70, lecturer, 1970-73; Australian National University, Research School of Social Sciences, Canberra, research scholar in sociology, 1973—. Adjunct associate professor, Albertus Magnus College, 1970-73. *Member:* American Sociological Association, Population Association of America.

WRITINGS: (With husband, Lincoln H. Day) *Too Many Americans*, Houghton, 1964; (with Lincoln Day) *Family Size and Society*, Allyn & Bacon, 1972. Contributor to journals.

WORK IN PROGRESS: Ph.D. thesis, *Changing Roles of Women in Australia Since World War II.*

* * *

DAY, John A(rthur) 1913-

PERSONAL: Born May 24, 1913; son of Arthur Cutler and Elnora (Wilson) Day; married Mary Hyatt, November 3, 1937; children: Patricia Anne (Mrs. Leslie Pierce), Carolyn Gail (Mrs. Ronald Materna), John Whitman, Janice Hyatt (Mrs. Alan Pearson), Christy Elaine (Mrs. Bill Bailey). *Education:* Colorado College, Colorado Springs, B.A., 1936; Boeing School of Aeronautics, Certificate in Meteorology, 1937; Oregon State University, M.S., 1952, Ph.D., 1956. *Politics:* Republican. *Religion:* United Methodist. *Home:* 609 North Cowls, McMinnville, Ore. 97128. *Office:* Linfield College, McMinnville, Ore. 97128.

CAREER: Pan American World Airways, San Francisco, Calif., division meteorologist, 1937-46; Oregon State University, Corvallis, instructor in physics, 1946-56; University of Redlands, Redlands, Calif., visiting associate professor of physics, 1956-58; Linfield College, McMinnville, Ore., professor of physics, 1958—. *Military service:* U.S. Naval Reserve, 1942-46; became lieutenant. *Member:* American Meteorological Society, American Association of University Professors. *Awards, honors:* National Science Foundation faculty fellow in London, England, 1962-63.

WRITINGS: (With F. W. Decker) *Rudiments of Weather*, Oregon State University Co-op Press, 1958; (with K. S. Davis) *Water, the Mirror of Science*, Anchor Books, 1961; *Science, Change and the Christian*, Abingdon, 1965; *The Science of Weather*, Addison-Wesley, 1966; (with G. S. Stearnes) *Climate and Weather*, Addison-Wesley, 1970; (with F. Frost and P. Rose) *Dimensions of the Environmental Crisis*, Wiley, 1971; (with E. Loomis and S. Paulson) *Healing for Everyone: Medicine of the Whole Man*, Hawthorn, 1975.

WORK IN PROGRESS: *Peterson's Field Guide to the Atmosphere*, with V. J. Schaefer, publication by Houghton expected in 1976.

* * *

DAY, Lincoln H(ubert) 1928-

PERSONAL: Born January 7, 1928, in Ames, Iowa; son of John Armstrong and Vera (Hills) Day; married C. Alice

Taylor (a research scholar), November 26, 1952; children: Thomas Hills, Caroline Wolfe. *Education:* Yale University, B.A. (honors), 1949; Columbia University, M.A., 1951, Ph.D., 1957. *Religion:* Agnostic. *Home:* 158 Kent St., Hughes, A.C.T., Australia. *Office:* Department of Demography, Australian National University, Canberra, A.C.T., Australia.

CAREER: United Nations, New York, N.Y., statistical clerk, 1951, 1952; Mount Holyoke College, South Hadley, Mass., instructor, 1952-53, 1955-56, assistant professor of sociology, 1957-58; Princeton University, Princeton, N.J., assistant professor, 1958-59; Columbia University, New York, N.Y., research associate, Bureau of Applied Social Research, 1959-64; Harvard University, Cambridge, Mass., research associate, 1964-65; Yale University, New Haven, Conn., associate professor of sociology and public health, 1965-70; United Nations, New York, N.Y., chief of demographic and social statistics branch, 1970-73; Australian National University, Institute of Advanced Studies, Canberra, senior fellow in demography, 1973—. Australian National University, visiting fellow, 1962-64. *Military service:* U.S. Army, 1953-55. *Member:* American Sociological Association, Population Association of America, International Population Union, Sociological Association of Australia and New Zealand. *Awards, honors:* Fulbright fellow, 1968.

WRITINGS: (With wife, Alice Taylor Day) *Too Many Americans*, Houghton, 1964; (with A. J. Jaffe and Walter Adams) *Disabled Workers in the Labor Market*, Bedminster, 1964; (with Alice Day) *Family Size and Society*, Allyn & Bacon, 1972. Contributor to journals and symposia.

WORK IN PROGRESS: Context of low natality in industrialized countries; differential natality in Australia.

SIDELIGHTS: Day and his wife have frequently worked together on demographic research—carried out thus far in America, Australia, New Zealand, the Scandinavian countries (1966), and other parts of Europe.

* * *

DAY J(ames) Edward 1914-

PERSONAL: Born October 11, 1914, in Jacksonville, Ill.; son of James Allmond and Frances (Wilmot) Day; married Mary Louise Burgess, July 2, 1941; children: Geraldine, Mary Louise, James Edward. *Education:* University of Chicago, A.B., 1935; Harvard University, LL.B. (cum laude), 1938. *Home:* 5804 Brookside Dr., Chevy Chase, Md. 20015. *Office:* 21 Dupont Cr., N.W., Washington, D.C. 20036.

CAREER: Admitted to Illinois, Maryland, and District of Columbia bar; Sidley, Austin, Burgess & Harper, Chicago, Ill., attorney, 1939-40, 1945-49; office of Governor Adlai Stevenson, Springfield, Ill., legal and legislative assistant, 1949-50; state of Illinois, Springfield, commissioner of insurance, 1950-53; Prudential Insurance Co. of America, Newark, N.J., associate general solicitor, 1953-56, associate general counsel, 1956, senior vice-president in charge of Western operations, Los Angeles, Calif., 1957-60; Postmaster General of United States, Washington, D.C., 1961-63; Sidley & Austin, Washington, D.C., partner, 1963-73; Cox, Langford & Brown, Washington, D.C., partner, 1973—. Delegate to Democratic National Convention, 1960. Vice-chairman of California Governor's Committee on Metropolitan Area Problems and member of Governor's Business Advisory Council, 1959-61. *Military service:* U.S. Naval Reserve, 1941-45; became lieutenant. *Member:*

American Bar Association, Federal Bar Association, District of Columbia Bar Association, Washington Urban League, Citizen's Research Foundation, and clubs. *Awards, honors:* LL.D., Illinois College (Jacksonville), and University of Nevada.

WRITINGS: Bartholf Street (novel), Dorrance, 1946; *My Appointed Round: 929 Days as Postmaster General*, Holt, 1965; *Humor in Public Speaking*, Prentice-Hall, 1965. Editor, *Harvard Law Review*, 1936-37.

* * *

DEAN, Dwight G(antz) 1918-

PERSONAL: Born December 9, 1918, in Granville, Ohio; son of Edgar B. (a minister) and Della May (Gantz) Dean; married Ruth Jean Fennell (a public school teacher), April 22, 1949; children: Philip Leslie, Robert Wesley. *Education:* Capital University, A.B., 1943; Garrett Seminary, M.Div., 1946; Northwestern University, M.A., 1947; Ohio State University, Ph.D., 1956. *Religion:* Methodist. *Home:* 211 Clark St., Ames, Iowa 50010. *Office:* Department of Sociology, Iowa State University, Ames, Iowa 50010.

CAREER: Chicago City Junior College, Chicago, Ill., instructor, 1949-51; Capital University, Columbus, Ohio, 1953-59, began as instructor, became assistant professor; Denison University, Granville, Ohio, assistant professor, 1959-62, associate professor, 1962-68, professor of sociology, 1968—, head of department, 1965-68. *Member:* American Sociological Association (fellow), National Council on Family Relations, North Central Sociological Association (formerly Ohio Valley Sociological Association; president, 1969-70; member of executive council, 1970-72), Ohio Council on Family Relations (president, 1964), Ohio Academy of Science (fellow; vice-president, 1964-65), Iowa Council on Family Relations (president, 1972-74), Phi Kappa Phi, Alpha Kappa Delta. *Awards, honors:* American Association for Middle East Studies fellowship for study in Israel, 1965.

WRITINGS: (With Donald M. Valdes) *Experiments in Sociology*, Appleton, 1963, 3rd edition, 1975; (editor with Valdes) *Sociology in Use*, Macmillan, 1965; (editor) *Dynamic Social Psychology*, Random House, 1969. Author of papers for professional conferences. Contributor of articles and reviews to numerous sociological journals, including *Social Forces, American Sociological Review, Marriage and Family Living, Journal of Marriage and the Family, Sociological Quarterly*, and *Sociological Focus*.

WORK IN PROGRESS: A revision of *Dynamic Social Psychology*; projects on roles, and on marital prediction.

* * *

DEAN, Edwin R(obinson) 1933-

PERSONAL: Born July 25, 1933, in South Bend, Ind.; son of William Stover (a business executive) and Eleanor (Hatcher) Dean; married Emily Finlay (a teacher), February 2, 1963. *Education:* Yale University, B.A., 1955; Gokhale Institute of Politics and Economics, Poona, India, graduate study, 1955-56; Columbia University, Ph.D., 1963. *Home and office:* Nigerian Institute of Social and Economic Research, University of Ibadan, Ibadan, Nigeria.

CAREER: Columbia University, New York, N.Y., lecturer, later preceptor, then instructor, 1960-64, assistant professor of economics, 1964-66; Nigerian Institute of Social and Economic Research, University of Ibadan, Ibadan,

Nigeria, research fellow, 1965—. *Member:* American Economic Association, Royal Economic Society, African Studies Association.

WRITINGS: (Editor) *The Controversy over the Quantity Theory of Money*, Heath, 1965; *The Supply Responses of African Farmers: Theory and Measurement in Malawi*, North-Holland Publishing Co., 1966. Contributor to *Journal of Farm Economics, Economic Development and Cultural Change, Nigerian Journal of Economic and Social Studies*, and other journals.

SIDELIGHTS: Dean is competent in French.†

* * *

de BOIS, Wilhelmina J. E. 1923-
(Helma de Bois)

PERSONAL: Born May 1, 1923, in Amsterdam, Netherlands; daughter of Willem Johannes and Martha (Boll) de Bois; divorced. *Education:* Attended schools in Amsterdam, 1929-41. *Agent:* Barthold Fles Literary Agency, 507 Fifth Ave., New York, N.Y. 10017. *Office:* United Nations, Palais des Nations, Geneva, Switzerland.

CAREER: United Nations Office, Geneva, Switzerland, personal assistant to director-general, 1955—.

WRITINGS—Under name Helma de Bois: *The Incorruptible*, Crown, 1965.

WORK IN PROGRESS: A sequel to *The Incorruptible*, with the main figure Bonaparte.

SIDELIGHTS: Wilhelmina de Bois speaks Dutch, English, French, and German and has traveled in Middle East in connection with United Nations work, and in Canada and America.†

* * *

DeCECCO, John Paul 1925-

PERSONAL: Surname is pronounced Dee-*check*-oh; born April 18, 1925, in Erie, Pa.; son of John (a restaurateur) and Rose (Lombardozzi) DeCecco. *Education:* Allegheny College, B.S., 1946; University of Pennsylvania, M.A., 1949, Ph.D., 1953; Michigan State University, postdoctoral study, 1956-59. *Politics:* Independent. *Religion:* None. *Home:* 829 Ashbury St., San Francisco, Calif. 94117. *Office:* Department of Psychology, San Francisco State University, San Francisco, Calif. 94132.

CAREER: University of Detroit, Detroit, Mich., instructor, 1953-55; Michigan State University, East Lansing, 1955-60, started as instructor, became assistant professor; San Francisco State University, San Francisco, Calif., associate professor of psychology and education, 1960—. Research consultant. *Member:* American Educational Research Association, American Psychological Association, Western Psychological Association, Phi Delta Kappa.

WRITINGS: Human Learning in the School, Holt, 1963; *Educational Technology*, Holt, 1964; *Psychology of Language, Thought, and Instruction*, Holt, 1967; (with William R. Crawford) *Psychology of Learning and Instruction*, Prentice-Hall, 1968, 2nd edition, 1974; (with Arlene K. Richards) *Growing Pains: Uses of School Conflict*, Aberdeen Press, 1974.

WORK IN PROGRESS: A book on school negotiation; research on use of negotiation in interpersonal conflict.

DEEMER, Bill 1945-

PERSONAL: Born March 4, 1945, in Norfolk, Va.; son of Charles Robert (retired from U.S. Navy) and Florence (Lear) Deemer; married Toby Murray, 1966. *Education:* Formal education ended in tenth grade. *Home:* 4246 River Rd., Junction City, Ore. 97448.

CAREER: Poet. *Awards, honors:* National Endowment for the Arts award, 1968.

WRITINGS: Poems, Auerhahn Press, 1964; *Diana*, Coyote Books, 1966; *The King's Bounty*, privately printed, 1968; *A Few for Lew*, Tenth Muse Corp., 1972; *A Few for Lew and Other Poems*, Christopher Books, 1974; *All Wet*, Blackberry, 1975.

WORK IN PROGRESS: An autobiography, *Flames and Phlegm*; a book of drawings, *With One Hand Behind My Back*; poems.

SIDELIGHTS: Deemer told *CA:* "Transformation in 1972: *Comic Romantic*. Catalysts: the disappearance of Lew Welch; and discovering Gulley Jimson. Ideal: to restore the word *silly* to its original meaning (happy, blessed, prosperous). Forerunners: Issa, Klee, James Broughton and Gregory Corso."

* * *

DEENER, David R(ussell) 1920-

PERSONAL: Born January 8, 1920, in Weverton, Md.; son of Russell M. (a contractor) and Josephine (Main) Deener; married Helen Buchner, January 30, 1943; children: Karen Lee, Helen Jane. *Education:* University of Pittsburgh, B.A., 1941, M.A., 1948; Duke University, Ph.D., 1951. *Politics:* Democrat. *Religion:* Church of the Brethren. *Home:* 7733 St. Charles Ave., New Orleans, La. 70118. *Office:* Tulane University, New Orleans, La. 70118.

CAREER: University of Pittsburgh, Pittsburgh, Pa., instructor, 1946; Duke University, Durham, N.C., part-time instructor, 1948-50, research associate, 1951-52; Tulane University of Louisiana, New Orleans, associate professor, 1952-57, professor of political science, 1957—, professor at Newcomb College, 1960—, acting dean of Newcomb College, 1965-66, dean of university's Graduate School, 1966—, provost, 1967—. Consultant to Brookings Institution 1951, and Institute of Public Administration, 1961; researcher in Australia, England, Africa, Pakistan, Malaysia, and other areas. *Military service:* U.S. Navy, 1942-46; became lieutenant. *Member:* American Society of International Law (vice-president, 1964-65), American Political Science Association, Southern Political Science Association, Cosmos Club (Washington, D.C.).

WRITINGS: (Co-author) *Presidential Politics in Louisiana, 1952*, Tulane University Press, 1954, *United States Attorneys General and International Law*, Nijhoff, 1957; (co-author) *Mental Health in Metropolitan Areas*, Institute of Public Administration, 1961; (editor and contributor) *Canada-United States Treaty Relations*, Duke University Press, 1963; (editor and contributor) *de Lege Pactorum*, Duke University Press, 1970. Also editor of and contributor to *International Law of Environment*, 1974. Contributor to journals. Editorial consultant, Hauser Press.

WORK IN PROGRESS: Treaty-Making in Canada; Judicial Review in the Commonwealth.

* * *

DEER, Irving 1924-

PERSONAL: Born August 15, 1924, in Chicago, Ill.; son

of William (a building contractor) and Ethel (Godinger) Deer; married Harriet A. Hall (a college instructor), August 21, 1954; children: Daniel Nathan, Jonathan Michael, Joseph Hugh, Helen Elizabeth. *Education:* University of Michigan, B.S., 1947; University of Minnesota, M.A., 1951, Ph.D., 1956. *Home:* 303 Brentwood Dr., Temple Terrace, Fla. *Office:* University of South Florida, Tampa, Fla.

CAREER: University of Minnesota, Minneapolis, instructor in English and humanities, 1952-56; University of California, Santa Barbara, assistant professor, 1956-58; State Teachers College, (now Mayville State College), Mayville, N.D., professor of English and drama, 1958-59; Lock Haven State College, Lock Haven, Pa., professor of English, 1959-64; Dickinson State Teachers College (now Dickinson State College), Dickinson, N.D., professor of English, and chairman of Division of Literature and Language, 1964-66; University of South Florida, Tampa, professor of English, 1966—, associate dean of language and literature, 1966-71. *Military service:* U.S. Army Air Forces, 1942-46; became first lieutenant. *Member:* Modern Language Association of America, American Society for Aesthetics, South Atlantic Modern Language Association. *Awards, honors:* Robert Gordon Sproul faculty writing fellowship, University of California, 1956; National Defense Education Act English Institute grants, 1965 and 1966; University of South Florida research council awards, 1972 and 1974.

WRITINGS: (Editor with wife, Harriet A. Deer) *Languages of the Mass Media*, Heath, 1965; (contributor) Herbert Goldstone, editor, *Chekhov's "The Cherry Orchard,"* Allyn & Bacon, 1965; (contributor) Rolf Fjelde, editor, *Ibsen: A Collection of Critical Essays*, Prentice-Hall, 1965; (with Harriet Deer) *Popular Arts*, Scribner, 1967; *Person to Person*, Holt, 1973; (editor with Harriet Deer) *Selves: Drama in Perspective*, Harcourt, in press. Contributor of articles and reviews to drama, English and other professional journals. Editor, *Lock Haven Review*, 1960-64.

WORK IN PROGRESS: A book on critical perspectives on the popular arts.

* * *

DEFFNER, Donald L(ouis) 1924-

PERSONAL: Born March 12, 1924, in Wichita, Kan.; son of Louis H. (a clergyman) and Rose Mae (Kreitzer) Deffner; married Corinne C. Clasen, January 30, 1949; children: David Louis, Deborah Kathleen, Carol Rose, Christina Corinne. *Education:* Concordia Seminary, St. Louis, Mo., B.A., 1945, B.D., 1947; University of Michigan, M.A., 1946; University of California, Berkeley, Ph.D., 1957; Pacific Lutheran Theological Seminary, Th.M., 1962. *Home:* 2770 Marin, Berkeley, Calif. 94708.

CAREER: Ordained minister of Lutheran Church-Missouri Synod, 1947; University of California, Berkeley, campus pastor, 1947-59; Concordia Theological Seminary, St. Louis, Mo., professor of religious education and chairman of department of practical theology, 1959-69; Pacific Lutheran Theological Seminary, Berkeley, Calif., professor of Christian education and homiletics, 1969—. Religion-in-Life Week speaker on college campuses in West and Midwest. Lutheran Church-Missouri Synod, chairman of Commission on College and University work and of Concordia Leadership Training Committee. *Member:* Lutheran Academy for Scholarship, Association of Seminary Profes-

sors in Practical Fields, Lutheran Education Association, Religious Education Association, Lutheran Society for Worship, Music and the Arts, Gamma Delta (honorary).

WRITINGS: (With W. H. Fields, Ronald Goerss, and Edward Wessling) *Meditations for College Students*, Concordia, 1961; (editor, and author with H. G. Coiner, Roland Seboldt, and Warren Schmidt) *Toward Adult Christian Education: A Symposium*, Lutheran Education Association, 1962; *Christ on Campus: Meditations for College Life*, Concordia, 1965; *Bold Ones on Campus: A Call for Christian Committment*, Concordia, 1973; *The Possible Years: Thoughts After Thirty Years on Christian Adulthood*, Concordia, 1973; *God, I'm Depressed: Coping With Adulthood*, Abingdon, in press. Contributor of articles and discussion guides to *Campus Pastor's Workbook* and other periodicals. Editor of California and Nevada edition of *Lutheran Witness*, 1951-54, and of *Lutheran Education Association Yearbook on Adult Education*, 1962.

WORK IN PROGRESS: Studies in inter-disciplinary relationships between theology and modern literature.

* * *

DEHONEY, W(illiam) Wayne 1918-

PERSONAL: Born August 22, 1918, in New Raymer, Colo.; son of William Warren (a schoolteacher) and Harriet (Northup) Dehoney; married Lealice Bishop, August 24, 1944; children: Rebecca Ann Dehoney Richardson, Katherine Elaine, William Wayne. *Education:* Attended Baylor University, 1938-39; Vanderbilt University, A.B., 1941; Southern Baptist Theological Seminary, B.D., 1946. *Politics:* Democrat. *Home:* 2103 High Ridge Rd., Louisville, Ky. 40207. *Office:* Walnut Street Baptist Church, 221 West St. Catherine, Louisville, Ky. 40203.

CAREER: Ordained to the Baptist ministry, 1940; minister in rural Tennessee, 1940-43, Rogersville, Tenn., 1943-45, Pineville, Ky., 1945-48, Paducah, Ky., 1948-50, Birmingham, Ala., 1950-57, Jackson, Tenn., 1957-67, Walnut Street Baptist Church, Louisville, Ky., 1967—. Billy Graham Evangelism Professor, Southern Baptist Theological Seminary, 1969-70; visiting professor, Midwestern Baptist Seminary, 1973. Southern Baptist Convention, member of executive committee, 1959-66, president, 1964-66; Executive committee member, Baptist World Alliance, 1965-75, Kentucky Baptist Convention, 1973—, and President Johnson's Community Relations Committee; North American coordinator, Crusade of Americas, 1965-75; member, Govenor's Human Rights Commission. Trustee, Union University, Jackson, Tenn., Southern Baptist Theological Seminary, 1968—, and Campbellsburg College, 1972—. Preacher on missions to Cuba, 1951, Mexico, 1953, Hawaii, 1958; director of evangelistic crusades in Europe, 1963, 1964, Bahama Islands and Africa, 1965, Far East, 1967; regular speaker on Baptist television and radio programs. *Member:* Rotary. *Awards, honors:* D.D., Union University, 1964; LL.D., Atlanta Law School, 1965.

WRITINGS—All published by Broadman, except as noted: *Challenges to the Cross*, 1962; *Homemade Happiness*, 1963; *African Diary*, 1966; *Disciples in Uniform*, 1967; *Baptist's See Black*, Word Books, 1969; *Set the Church Afire*, 1970; *An Evangelical's Guide to the Holy Land*, 1973; *Preaching to Change Lives*, 1974. Contributor to religious publications.

WORK IN PROGRESS: A book on contemporary issues facing Protestantism completion expected in 1976; the story of the evangelical faith in Eastern Europe, 1976.

AVOCATIONAL INTERESTS: Photography, hunting, fishing.

* * *

DEINZER, Harvey T. 1908-

PERSONAL: Born December 24, 1908, in Monroe, Mich.; son of Edwin T. (a cabinetmaker) and Emily (Meissner) Deinzer; married Margaret E. Reed, June 18, 1934. *Education:* University of Michigan, A.B., 1932, M.B.A., 1933, Ph.D., 1947; University of Florida, LL.B. (converted to J.D., 1967), 1955. *Home:* 928 Northwest 21st Ter., Gainesville, Fla. 32603.

CAREER: Ernst & Ernst (certified public accountants), Detroit, Mich., accountant, 1933-37; F. E. Ross & Co. (certified public accountants), Ann Arbor, Mich., accountant, 1937-38; Public Administration Service, Chicago, Ill., staff consultant, 1938-39; U.S. Government, Washington, D.C., fiscal analyst and business economist, 1942-43; University of Florida, Gainesville, associate professor of accounting, 1947-49, professor, 1949-73, professor emeritus, 1973—. *Military service:* U.S. Army, 1943-46; became first lieutenant. *Member:* American Accounting Association, American Economic Association, Phi Delta Phi, Beta Gamma Sigma, Order of the Coif.

WRITINGS: (Contributor) W. A. Paton, editor, *Accountants' Handbook*, Ronald, 1943; *The American Accounting Association-Sponsored Statements of Standards for Corporate Financial Reports: A Perspective*, College of Business Administration, University of Florida, 1964; *Development of Accounting Thought*, Holt, 1965; *Methodological Presuppositions in Financial Accounting Models*, College of Business Administration, University of Florida, 1968; (contributor) Willard E. Stone, editor, *Foundations of Accounting Theory*, College of Business Administration, University of Florida, 1971. Contributor to accounting journals.

* * *

DEKLE, Bernard 1905-

PERSONAL: Born June 23, 1905, in McRae, Ga.; son of DeRoy (an optometrist) and Levietta Dekle; married Kimiko Hirata (a Japanese flower arranger), December 4, 1972; children: Donne, Robert, William. *Education:* Oglethorpe University, B.A., 1927; special courses at New York Institute of Banking, 1929, and New York University, 1953. *Politics:* Democrat. *Religion:* Protestant. *Home:* Route One, Register, Ga. 30452. *Agent:* A.L. Fierst, 630 Ninth Ave., New York, N.Y.

CAREER: Oglethorpe University, Atlanta, Ga., instructor in English, 1927; First National City Bank of New York, Osaka, Japan, junior officer, 1929-30; *North Carolina Morning Herald*, Durham, reporter, later city editor, 1930-41; *Charlotte Observer*, Charlotte, N.C., staff writer, 1941-42; U.S. Office of War Information, editor in New York, Cairo, Rome, and Vienna, 1942-46; Headquarters, Supreme Commander of the Allied Powers in Japan, Tokyo, economic affairs information officer, 1947-52; Voice of America, chief writer for Japanese Service in New York and Washington, D.C., 1952-56; U.S. Information Agency, director of American cultural centers in Matsuyama, Japan, 1956-58, and Kobe, Japan, 1958-61; U.S. Department of Defense, editor of *Freedom* (magazine), published in Tokyo, Japan, for distribution in South Korea, 1961-68. Freelance writer, 1968—. Onetime correspondent for *Time* and Fairchild Publications.

WRITINGS: Night Angel Street (novel), Tuttle, 1965; *Profiles of Modern American Authors*, Tuttle, 1969; *Fighters for Freedom* (biography), Seibido, 1970.

WORK IN PROGRESS: Never Call Me Darling, a novel, and *Little Girls Love Pretty Kimonos*, Short stories, both about Japan.

SIDELIGHTS: Dekle is competent in French and speaks fair German. *Avocational interests:* Fishing and growing vegetables.

BIOGRAPHICAL/CRITICAL SOURCES: Mainichi Daily News, Tokyo, Japan, August 17, 1965.

* * *

de KUN, Nicolas 1923-

PERSONAL: Born October 10, 1923, in Budapest, Hungary; son of Nicolas and Bianca (Muller) de Kun. *Education:* Palatine Joseph University, Hungary, M.Sc., 1947; Bergakademie, Clausthal, West Germany, D.Eng., 1958. *Religion:* Presbyterian. *Office:* c/o Seminar on Industrial Development, Columbia University, New York, N.Y.

CAREER: Explorer of mineral resources and developer of mineral-based industries in Africa, mainly in the Congo, 1948-61, and director of Cobelmin, Bukavu, Zaire, 1948—; Columbia University, New York, N.Y., adjunct professor, 1961-64, co-chairman of Seminar on Industrial Development, 1966—. Consultant to corporations, governments, and United Nations on industrial and mineral development, New York, N.Y., 1963-66. *Member:* Society for International Development (director of New York chapter, 1965), Geological Society of America, American Institute of Mining, Metallurgical, and Petroleum Engineers, African Studies Association, and geological societies of central Africa, Belgium, and Germany.

WRITINGS: Les gisements de cassiterite et de columbotantalite du Nord Lugulu, Societe Geologique de Belgique, 1959; *The Mineral Resources of Africa*, Elsevier Publishing Co., 1964. Contributor of numerous scientific papers in English, French, and German, to scholarly journals. Member of board of editors, *Chemical Geology*.

WORK IN PROGRESS: Co-editing *International Development*, for Oceana; *Niobium (Columbium) and Tantalum*, for Elsevier Publishing Co.; *L'art Lega*, for Royal Museum of Central Africa, Tervuren.

SIDELIGHTS: De Kun has lived or traveled in sixty countries of Africa, Asia, Oceania, the Americas, and Europe. He is fluent in English, French, German, Hungarian, and Swahili and has reading knowledge of Dutch, Spanish, Portuguese, and Italian.†

* * *

DELANEY, Shelagh 1939-

PERSONAL: First name is pronounced *She*-la; born 1939, in Salford, Lancashire, England; daughter of a transport worker and Elsie Delaney. *Education:* Attended Broughton Secondary School. *Residence:* Salford, Lancashire, England.

CAREER: Salesgirl, milk depot clerk, usherette; Metro-Vickers, research photography department, assistant; now director, Granada Television Network, Ltd. *Awards, honors:* Charles Henry Foyle New Play Award, 1958, Arts Council Bursary, and New York Drama Critics Award, 1961, all for the play, *A Taste of Honey*; British Film Academy Award, 1961, Robert Flaherty Award, both for screenplay, "A Taste of Honey"; Writer Guild Award for best screenplay, 1968, for "Charlie Bubbles."

WRITINGS: Sweetly Sings the Donkey (short stories), Putnam, 1963. Contributor of articles to *New York Times Magazine* and *Cosmopolitan.*

Plays: *A Taste of Honey* (first produced in London by Joan Littlewood at Theatre Royal, Stratford, May 27, 1958; produced on Broadway at Lyceum Theatre, October 4, 1960), Grove, 1959; *The Lion in Love* (first produced in Coventry at the Belgrade Theatre, September 5, 1960; produced in New York at One Sheridan Square, April 25, 1963), Grove, 1961.

Screenplays: (With Tony Richardson) "A Taste of Honey," Continental Film Corp., 1962; "Charlie Bubbles," produced by Michael Medwin, 1968; "Did Your Nanny Come From Bergen?," BBC Television, 1970; "The Raging Moon," Associated British Films, 1970.

SIDELIGHTS: While working as an usherette, Miss Delaney became disgusted with the type of plays being presented under the guise of modern drama. Terence Rattigan's "Variations on a Theme," which she disliked intensely, finally impelled her to "try it herself." One of the characters in *A Taste of Honey* echoes her complaint: "The cinema has become more and more like the theatre, it's all mauling and muttering, can't hear what they're saying half the time and when you do it's not worth listening to." Upon completion of the script she sent it to Joan Littlewood, director of the Theatre Workshop, for criticism. The play went into rehearsal within two weeks. It concerns a mother and daughter who cannot relate to each other, a typical avant garde theme of alienation. The daughter has an affair with a Black sailor and is helped through pregnancy by a young homosexual. "Told thus baldly there sounds to be little to the play," wrote John Russell Taylor, "and indeed in conventional terms there is little: it has no 'ideas' which can be isolated and considered as such apart from their dramatic context, and if one tries to read the play away from the theatre . . . it is virtually non-existent. . . . And yet in the theatre the whole thing works, and works almost infallibly—it has the unique power of holding us simply as a tale that is told, and the words the characters are given to speak take on, when spoken, a strange independent life of their own. . . . It has . . . the disturbing ring of truth about it . . . ." Graham Greene described it as having the freshness of John Osborne's "Look Back in Anger" and a greater maturity. "Many who have seen or read the play," commented Eric Gillett, "have been struck by the deep insight shown by the author in her portrayal of the mother-daughter relationship. . . ."

Many critics want to label the Lancashire playwright as the "Angry Young Woman," but a program note for the premiere of *A Taste of Honey* maintained that she "is the antithesis of London's 'Angry Young Men.' She knows what she is angry about." The characters in the play, wrote Taylor, "accept their life and go on living, without making any too serious complaint about their lot; unlike Jimmy Porter ["Look Back in Anger"] and his followers, Jo [the daughter] is not angry, nor does she rail savagely and ineffectually against the others—authority, the Establishment, fate. In practice, she recognizes that her fate is in her own hands, and takes responsibility for the running of her own life without a second's thought—indeed, in almost every way the action might be taking place before the Welfare State was invented." Miss Delaney is more easily classified as a regional realist portraying industrial Northern England.

Miss Delaney has been active in British movements advocating nuclear disarmament and on September 17, 1961, she and John Osborne were arrested with other demonstrators for the Committee of 100, at a sit-down staged in London's Trafalgar Square. Her favorite authors include Chaucer, Brecht, O'Neill, Chekhov, and Beckett, as well as the Elizabethan and Greek Classical authors.

BIOGRAPHICAL/CRITICAL SOURCES: John Russell Taylor, *Anger and After*, Methuen, 1962; W. A. Armstrong, editor, *Experimental Drama*, G. Bell, 1963; George Wellwarth, *Theatre of Protest and Paradox*, New York University Press, 1964.*†

* * *

DELBANCO, Nicholas (Franklin) 1942-

PERSONAL: Born August 27, 1942, in London, England; son of Kurt (a businessman) and Barbara (Bernstein) Delbanco. *Education:* Harvard University, B.A., 1963; Columbia University, M.A., 1966. *Home:* Spraguetown Rd., Greenwich, N.Y. *Agent:* Paul Reynolds, Inc., 599 Fifth Ave., New York, N.Y. 10017.

CAREER: Bennington College, Bennington, Vt., member, department of language and literature, 1966—. *Member:* P.E.N., Authors Guild, Signet Society, Phi Beta Kappa. *Awards, honors:* Woodrow Wilson fellowship, Edward John Noble fellowship, National Endowment for the Arts creative writing award, 1973.

WRITINGS—All novels: *The Martlet's Tale*, Lippincott, 1966; *Grasse, 3/23/66*, Lippincott, 1968; *Consider Sappho Burning*, Morrow, 1969; *News*, Morrow, 1970; *In the Middle Distance*, Morrow, 1971; *Fathering*, Morrow, 1973; *Small Rain*, edited by James Landis, Morrow, 1975. Adapted *The Martlet's Tale* for film.

* * *

**del BARCO, Lucy Salamanca
    (Lucy Salamanca)**

PERSONAL: Born in London, England; daughter of Joseph J. (a writer) and Anne (Robinson) Nuttall; second husband, Marquis de Colonnetta, Count del Barco; children: (first marriage) J. R. Salamanca, Raoul Joseph Salamanca (deceased). *Education:* Educated in many parts of the world, including schools in Colombia, Italy, France, and England. *Religion:* Episcopalian. *Agent:* Elizabeth McKee, McIntosh, McKee & Dodds, Inc., 22 East 40th, New York, N.Y. 10016.

CAREER: Writer and painter; instructor in creative writing at Barry College, Miami, Fla., 1956—; instructor in creative writing and art appreciation at Miami-Dade Junior College, Miami, Fla., 1958—. During World War II, was appointed chief research counsel, head of Inquiry and Research Section of Legislative Reference Service, Library of Congress. Had own television program, "Our Written Heritage," Miami, beginning 1955. *Member:* Authors League of America, Poetry Society of America.

WRITINGS: Fortress of Freedom (foreword by Archibald MacLeish), Lippincott, 1942; *How to Write a Short Story*, Universal Press (Miami), 1952; *Audubon in the Florida Keys*, Volume I of "Illustrated Library of the Natural Sciences," Simon & Schuster, 1958; *Tommy Tiger of the Seminoles* (juvenile), F. Watts, 1961. Short stories and articles have appeared in *Saturday Evening Post, Natural History, Collier's*, and other magazines.

WORK IN PROGRESS: An adult novel; research on the Florida Everglades.

SIDELIGHTS: Lucy del Barco is fluent in Spanish; has lived for extended periods in Europe and South America.†

* * *

DELIUS, Anthony Ronald St. Martin 1916-

PERSONAL: Born June 11, 1916, in Simonstown, South Africa; son of Edwin St. Martin (an officer, Royal Navy) and Mignonne (Elliott) Delius; married Christina Truter, August, 1941; children: Christonie (daughter), Peter Nicholas. *Education:* Rhodes University, B.A., 1938. *Home:* Midway, Bertram Crescent, Rondebosch, Cape Province, South Africa. *Office: Cape Times*, Cape Town, South Africa.

CAREER: Saturday Post (now *Evening Post*), Port Elizabeth, Cape Province, South Africa, co-founder, 1947, editor and political correspondent, 1947-50; *Cape Times*, Cape Town, South Africa, parliamentary note- and leader-writer, 1951-54, 1958—. *Military service:* South African Directorate of Military Intelligence, 1940-45; became captain. *Awards, honors:* South African Poetry Prize, 1960.

WRITINGS: Young Traveller in South Africa, Phoenix House, 1947; *The Unknown Border* (poems), Balkema, 1954; *The Long Way Round* (travel), Timmins, 1956; *The Last Division* (satirical verse), Human & Rousseau, 1959; *The Fall* (play), Human & Rousseau, 1960; *A Corner of the World* (verse), Human & Rousseau, 1962; *The Day Natal Took Off* (prose satire), Human & Rousseau, 1963. Contributor to *New Yorker, Reporter, Think, Washington Post, Encounter, Guardian*, and other magazines and newspapers. Member of editorial boards of *Standpunte* and *Contrast*.

WORK IN PROGRESS: Verse and prose.

SIDELIGHTS: Delius studied and reported on politics in most of the African countries, with special interest in Ethiopia and Liberia.†

* * *

DENNIS, Wayne 1905-

PERSONAL: Born September 1, 1905, in Washington County, Ohio; son of Samuel R. (a merchant) and Mary V. (Fox) Dennis; married Marsena Anne Galbreath, March 19, 1928 (died July, 1965); married Margaret Wallihan Hudson (an educator and author), March 18, 1970; children: (first marriage) Mary (Mrs. Geoffrey Ravenhall), Anne (Mrs. Ivan Jankovic), James Gill. *Education:* Marietta College, B.A., 1926; Clark University, M.A., 1928, Ph.D., 1930; Yale University, postdoctoral study, 1936-37. *Home address:* Box 180, Rt. 1, Doswell, Virginia. *Office:* Brooklyn College, Brooklyn, N.Y.

CAREER: University of Virginia, Charlottesville, assistant professor of psychology, 1930-42; Louisiana State University, Baton Rouge, professor of psychology and head of department, 1942-43; University of Pittsburgh, Pittsburgh, Pa., professor of psychology and head of department, 1945-51; Brooklyn College of the City University of New York, professor of psychology, 1951-70, professor emeritus, 1970—. Visiting professor at Clark University, 1937-38, and American University of Beirut, 1955-56, 1958-59. *Military service:* U.S. Navy, 1943-45; became lieutenant. *Member:* American Psychological Association (fellow), Society for Research in Child Development (fellow), Gerontological Society (fellow), Phi Beta Kappa, Sigma Xi. *Awards, honors:* Social Science Research Council fellowship, Yale University, 1936-37.

WRITINGS: The Hopi Child, Appleton, 1940; *Group Values Through Children's Drawings*, Wiley, 1966.

Editor: *Current Trends in Psychology*, University of Pittsburgh Press, 1947; *Current Trends in Social Psychology*, University of Pittsburgh Press, 1948; *Readings in the History of Psychology*, Appleton, 1948; *Current Trends in Industrial Psychology*, University of Pittsburgh Press, 1949; *Readings in General Psychology*, Prentice-Hall, 1949; *Current Trends in the Relation of Psychology to Medicine*, University of Pittsburgh Press, 1950; *Current Trends in Psychological Theory*, University of Pittsburgh Press, 1951; *Readings in Child Psychology*, Prentice-Hall, 1951, revised edition, 1963; (with Ihsan Al-Issa) *Cross-Cultural Studies of Behavior*, Holt, 1970; *Historical Readings in Developmental Psychology*, Appleton, 1972. Editor, *Psychological Bulletin*, 1953-58.

Contributor of numerous articles to psychological journals.

WORK IN PROGRESS: The Content of Free Associations.

SIDELIGHTS: Dennis has traveled widely for research on psychological aspects of different ethnic groups and cultures.

* * *

de ROPP, Robert S(ylvester) 1913-

PERSONAL: Born February 1, 1913, in London, England; son of Wilhelm S. and Ruth (Fisher) De Ropp; married Elizabeth Knowlman, June, 1948; children: James, Susan Huntsman, Sally, Jeffrey. *Education:* University of London, Ph.D., 1939. *Religion:* Buddhist. *Home:* 6412 Sonoma Mountain Rd., Santa Rosa, Calif. 95404.

CAREER: Agricultural Research Council, research associate, 1941-45; with Rockefeller Institute, 1945-46; New York Botanical Garden, New York, N.Y., assistant curator, 1945-50; American Cyanamid Co., senior research scientist, 1950-61; University of San Francisco, San Francisco, Calif., research biochemist, beginning, 1961, now retired.

WRITINGS: If I Forget Thee (fiction), St. Martins, 1956; *Drugs and the Mind*, St. Martins, 1957; *Man Against Aging*, St. Martins, 1960; *Science and Salvation*, St. Martins, 1962; *The Master Game*, Delacorte, 1968; *Sex Energy*, Delacorte, 1970; *Church of the Earth*, Delacorte, 1974; *Eco-Tech*, Delacorte, in press. Contributor of more than forty papers to scientific journals and proceedings.

AVOCATIONAL INTERESTS: Painting, gardening, and fishing.

* * *

DESBARATS, Peter 1933-

PERSONAL: Surname is pronounced *Deb-ah-rah*; born July 2, 1933, in Montreal, Quebec, Canada; son of Hullett John and Margaret (Rettie) Desbarats; married Marjorie Rogers, September 1, 1955; children: Michelle, Gabrielle, Lissa Dean, Sharon Nicolle, Catherine Heather Brynne, Shasta. *Education:* Attended Loyola College, Montreal, Quebec, Canada. *Agent:* Willis Kingsley Wing, 24 East 38th St., New York, N.Y. 10016. *Office: Parallel*, 1110 Sherbrooke St., W., Montreal, Quebec, Canada.

CAREER: Writer for *Montreal Gazette*, Montreal, Quebec, Canada, 1952-55, Reuters, London, England, 1955; *Winnipeg Tribune*, Winnipeg, Manitoba, Canada, political reporter, 1956-60; *Montreal Star*, Montreal, Quebec, Canada, staff writer, 1960-66; *Parallel* (magazine), Montreal, Quebec, Canada, editor, 1966—. Writer, commentator, and radio and television interviewer for Canadian Broadcasting Corp. *Member:* Association of Canadian Television and Radio Artists, Montreal Men's Press Club.

WRITINGS: The State of Quebec: A Journalist's View of the Quiet Revolution, McClelland & Stewart, 1965; *Halibut York* [and] *The Night the City Sang* (poems), privately printed, 1964; *Halibut York and More* (verse for children), privately printed, 1965; *Gabriell and Selena*, Harcourt, 1968; (editor and author of introduction) *What They Used to Tell About: Indian Legends from Labrador*, McClelland & Stewart, 1969. Writer of scripts for National Film Board of Canada, British Broadcasting Corp., and other outlets. Canadian correspondent, *National Observer*, Washington, D.C.; also contributor to *Weekend, Maclean's Magazine, Canadian Forum*, and *Canadian Commentator*. Selected and introduced, commemorative portfolio of *Canadian Illustrated News*, November, 1970.

WORK IN PROGRESS: A biography of Joseph Cohen, Montreal criminal lawyer, under contract to McClelland & Stewart.

SIDELIGHTS: In recent years Desbarats has written for *National Observer* and various Canadian newspapers from Europe (including Iron Curtain countries), Japan, Australia, Pakistan, and Israel. He has fair knowledge of French. *Avocational interests:* Motorcycles.†

*   *   *

DE TARR, Francis 1926-

PERSONAL: Born March 15, 1926, in Berkeley, Calif.; son of Adraith and Elizabeth (Henry) De Tarr; married Geraldine Dallas, 1951; children: Claire, Anne, Charles, Christine. *Education:* Yale University, B.A., 1949, M.A., 1953, Ph.D., 1958; studied at University of Geneva, 1947-49, Sorbonne, University of Paris, 1948, 1949-51, and National War College, 1970-71. *Home:* 409 Vermont Ave., Berkeley, Calif. *Office:* c/o U.S. Department of State, Washington, D.C.

CAREER: U.S. Army Engineers, Skagway, Alaska, civilian dock representative, 1943-44; Lycee Paul Langevin, Suresnes, France, teacher, 1949-50; Sorbonne, University of Paris, Paris, France, instructor, 1950-51; Foreign Policy Association, New York, N.Y., consultant, 1952-53; Yale University Library, New Haven, Conn., curator, 1954-57; U.S. Department of State, vice-consul in Florence, Italy, 1958-60, research specialist in Washington, D.C., second secretary at American Embassy, Paris, France, 1961-66, second, later first secretary, Saigon, Vietnam, 1966-68; first secretary and chief of internal political unit, Paris, France, 1968-70; counselor for political affairs, 1971-74; diplomat-in-residence at Brown University, Providence, R.I., Providence College, Providence, R.I., and University of Rhode Island, Kingston, 1974—. *Military service:* U.S. Army Air Forces, 1944-45. *Member:* International Political Science Association, American Political Science Association.

WRITINGS: The French Radical Party from Herriot to Mendes-France (with foreword by Pierre Mendes-France), Oxford University Press, 1961.

*   *   *

DEVANEY, John 1926-

PERSONAL: Born March 15, 1926, in New York, N.Y.;

son of John (an engineer) and Delia Devaney; married Barbara Masciocchi (an artist), April 16, 1955. *Education:* New York University, B.S., 1949. *Politics:* Democrat. *Religion:* Roman Catholic. *Residence:* New York, N.Y.

CAREER: Science Illustrated, New York, N.Y., writer, 1948-50; *Quick*, New York, N.Y., Medical editor, 1952-54; *Parade*, New York, N.Y., sports editor, 1955-61; freelance writer, 1961—. *Military service:* U.S. Army, 1944-46.

WRITINGS: Bob Cousy, Putnam, 1965; *The Pro Quarterbacks*, Putnam, 1966; *The Great Olympic Champions*, Putnam, 1967; *Bart Starr*, Scholastic Magazine, 1967; *The Greatest Cardinals of Them All*, Putnam, 1968; *Baseball's Youngest Big Leaguers*, Holt, 1969; *The Baseball Life of Mickey Mantle*, Scholastic, 1970; *Juan Marichal: Mister Strike*, Putnam, 1970; *Super Bowl!*, Random House, 1971; *Star Pass Receivers of the NFL*, Random House, 1972; (with Burt Goldblatt) *The World Series: A Complete Pictorial History*, Rand McNally, 1972; *The Complete Handbook of Pro Football*, Lancer, 1972, 1973; *Gil Hodges: Baseball Miracle Man*, Putnam, 1973; *The Bobby Orr Story*, Random House, 1973; *Joe Namath*, Scholastic, 1973; (with Goldblatt) *The Stanley Cup: An Illustrated History*, Rand McNally, 1974; *Tom Seaver*, Popular Library, 1974; *O. J. Simpson: Football's Greatest Runner*, Paperback Library, 1974; *The Baseball Life of Johnny Bench*, Scholastic, 1974. Contributor of articles to *Saturday Evening Post, Redbook, Parade, This Week, Sport, Pageant, American Legion, Boys' Life*, and *Catholic Digest*.†

*   *   *

D'EVELYN, Katherine E(dith) 1899-

PERSONAL: Born December 2, 1899, Madelia, Minn.; daughter of Dudley Gamble (a realtor) and Viola E. (Gunter) D'Evelyn. *Education:* Columbia University, B.S., 1927, M.A., 1936, Ed.D., 1944. *Home:* 205 Whitehall Blvd., Garden City, N.Y. 11530.

CAREER: Teacher in Garden City, N.Y., 1931-43; Elmont (N.Y.) public schools, director of guidance, 1944-49; Great Neck (N.Y.) Board of Education, director of psychological services, beginning 1949. Visiting instructor at Teachers College, Columbia University, and State University of New York College at Oneonta. Member of board of directors, Community Mental Health Board of Nassau County, 1956-62, Nassau County Mental Health Association, and Nassau County Council of Social Agencies. *Member:* American Psychological Association (fellow; past president of division 16), National Education Association, New York State Psychological Association, Nassau County Psychological Association (president, 1955). *Awards, honors:* Named Woman of the Year in Education, 1956; Dorothy N. Hughes Award, New York University. 1962.

WRITINGS: Individual Parent-Teacher Conferences, Teachers College, Columbia University, 1954, revised edition, 1963; *Meeting Children's Emotional Needs*, Prentice-Hall, 1957; (with others) *Developing Mentally Healthy Children*, National Education Association, 1970. Writer of brochures and articles. Editor, *Newsletter*, Division of School Psychologists, American Psychological Association, 1957-58.†

*   *   *

de VINCK, (Baron) Jose M. G. A. 1912-

PERSONAL: Born March 31, 1912, in Brussels, Belgium; came to United States in 1948; son of Baron Marcel A. and

Emma (de Wouters d'Oplinter) de Vinck; married Marie-Louise Albertine Kestens, February 1, 1945; children: Bruno, Oliver, Anne-Catherine, Christopher, Jose, Jr., Maria. *Education:* College St. Michel, Brussels, Belgium, Certificate of Greco-Latin Humanities, 1929; Institut St. Louis, Brussels, Licence in Philosophy and Letters, 1931; University of Louvain, Docteur en Droit, 1935. *Religion:* Roman Catholic. *Home address:* Box 103, Allendale, N.J. 07401. *Office:* Sunday Publications, 88 Clinton Rd., Fairfield, N.J. 07006.

CAREER: Seton Hall University, South Orange, N.J., professor of philosophy, 1950-54; St. Anthony Guild Press, Paterson, N.J., editor and translator, 1955-70; Sunday Publications, Fairfield, N.J., associate editor, 1974—. Owner of Alleluia Press. Lecturer. *Military service:* Belgian Army; received Regimental Citation, 1945. *Awards, honors:* Highest poetry award, Belgian Royal Academy of Literature, 1944, for *Le Cantique de la Vie.*

WRITINGS: Images (poetry in French and English), [Brussels], 1940; (with Etienne du Bus de Warnaffe) *Le Cantique de la Vie* (poetry), [Brussels], 1944; *The Virtue of Sex*, Hawthorn, 1966; (with John T. Catoir) *The Challenge of Love*, Hawthorn, 1969; *The Yes Book: An Answer to Life*, Alleluia Press, 1972.

Translator: (From the French and Greek, with J. Raya) *Byzantine Missal for Sundays and Feast Days*, privately printed, 1958; (from the Latin) "The Works of Bonaventure," St. Anthony Guild Press, Volume I: *Mystical Opuscula*, 1960, Volume II: *The Breviloquim*, 1963, Volume III: *Opuscula, Second Series*, 1966, Volume IV: *Defense of the Mendicants*, 1966, Volume V: *Collations on the Six Days*, 1970; (from the French) Guy Bougerol, *Introduction to the Works of St. Bonaventure*, St. Anthony Guild Press, 1964; *Byzantine Daily Worship*, Alleluia Press, 1969.

WORK IN PROGRESS: A Book of Reassurance: Theology for Today.

* * *

DEVINE, Thomas G. 1928-

PERSONAL: Born January 1, 1928, in Somerville, Mass.; son of Thomas J. and Anna G. (Whitham) Devine; married Claire T. Lawlor, November 17, 1956; children: Thomas J. *Education:* Boston University, A.B., 1950, A.M., 1952, Ed.D., 1961. *Politics:* Democrat. *Religion:* Roman Catholic. *Home:* 8 Rambler Rd., Jamaica Plain, Mass. 02130. *Office:* Boston University, Boston, Mass.

CAREER: Rhode Island College, Providence, assistant professor of English, 1961-65; Boston University, Boston, Mass., associate professor of English education, 1965—. Visiting lecturer, Clark University, 1961, Syracuse University, 1964, Claflin College, 1965. *Member:* National Council of Teachers of English (director), National Society for the Study of Education, International Reading Association, New England Association of Teachers of English.

WRITINGS: (With David Russell, Agnella Gunn, and Ralph Staiger) *Exploration Through Reading*, Ginn, 1964; (with D. Russell, A. Gunn, and Paul Roswell) *Achievement Through Reading*, Ginn, 1965; *Workbook for Reading Skills*, Ginn, 1965; (with Howard Evans) *Reading in the Secondary Schools*, Kendall/Hunt, 1971. Contributor to professional journals.

* * *

DE VRIES, Peter 1910-

PERSONAL: Born February 27, 1910, in Chicago, Ill.; son

of Joost (a furniture warehouse owner) and Henrietta (Eldersveld) De Vries; married Katinka Loeser (a writer), October 16, 1943; children: Jan, Peter Jon, Emily, Derek. *Education:* Calvin College, A.B., 1931; Northwestern University, summer student, 1931. *Politics:* Democrat. *Home:* 170 Cross Highway, Westport, Conn. *Office:* The New Yorker, 25 West 43rd St., New York, N.Y.

CAREER: Editor of community newspapers, Chicago, Ill., 1931; worked as operator of candy-vending machines, taffy apple peddler, and radio actor, 1931-38; free-lance writer, 1931—; *Poetry* magazine, associate editor, 1938-42, co-editor, 1942-44; *New Yorker* magazine, member of editorial staff, 1944—. *Member:* National Institute of Arts and Letters. *Awards, honors:* American Academy of Arts and Letters grant, 1946.

WRITINGS—All published by Little, Brown, except as indicated: *But Who Wakes the Bugler?*, Houghton, 1940; *The Handsome Heart*, Coward, 1943; *Angels Can't Do Better*, Coward, 1944; *No But I Saw the Movie* (stories), 1952; *The Tunnel of Love* (Atlantic Book Club selection), 1954; *Comfort Me With Apples*, 1956; (with Joseph Fields) *The Tunnel of Love* (dramatization of the novel; produced on Broadway by Theatre Guild, 1957), 1957; *The Mackerel Plaza*, 1958; *The Tents of Wickedness* (sequel to *Comfort Me With Apples*; Book-of-the-Month Club selection), 1959; *Through the Fields of Clover*, 1961; *The Blood of the Lamb*, 1962; *Reuben, Reuben*, 1964 (adapted by Herman Shumlin, play titled "Spofford", produced on Broadway ANTA Theatre, December 12, 1967); *Let Me Count the Ways*, 1965; *The Vale of Laughter*, 1967; *The Cat's Pajamas and Witch's Milk*, 1968; *Mrs. Wallop*, 1970; *Into Your Tent I'll Creep*, 1971; *Without a Stitch in Time* (stories), 1972; *Forever Panting*, 1973; *The Glory of the Hummingbird*, 1974.

SIDELIGHTS: W. J. Smith calls De Vries "the greatest living American comic novelist.... And beyond any doubt the greatest punster the world has ever known...." Richard P. Brickner writes: "Our literature's most accomplished cliche-duster and word-restorer is Peter De Vries. In [*Let Me Count the Ways*] he again gives the sheen they deserve to five important and much-abused adjectives. We have long since come to expect books labeled 'irreverent, outrageous, witty, wise and warm' to be dinky family reminiscences or giddy farces, their irreverence cute, their outrageousness sophomoric, their wit flabby, wisdom hackneyed and warmth suffocating. But in De Vries's world there is nothing too sacred for profanation, and nothing too ludicrous for serious treatment.... De Vries's achievement, in terms of productivity and a sustained high level, is unmatched by any other comic writer currently at work, possibly excepting Evelyn Waugh [now deceased]."

J. E. Bruns said of *The Blood of the Lamb*: "A masterpiece of realism and literary craftsmanship. It tells a poignant story without relying on sentiment or sacrificing humor; it asks serious questions about life and religion without intruding wooden characters and pretentious dialogue. Yet for all that, it remains, in many ways, a strange book...." William Hogan added: "I don't know what makes De Vries funny. I think it is mostly a genius for keeping tongue firmly in cheek while documenting contemporary American life. To a lesser degree it is his dialogue.... All in all, he seems to write with a Fourth of July sparkler dipped in sulphuric acid."

The Tunnel of Love was filmed by M-G-M in 1958; *Let Me Count the Ways*, adapted by Freeman and Karl Tunberg, filmed by ABC Pictures Corp. as "How Do I Love Thee?", 1970; *Witch's Milk* was adapted by Julius J. Epstein, filmed by Universal as "Pete 'n' Tillie", 1972.

BIOGRAPHICAL/CRITICAL SOURCES: San Francisco Chronicle, March 9, 1958; *Commonweal*, February 10, 1961; *Saturday Review*, March 24, 1962; *Catholic World*, April, 1962; *Newsweek*, February 17, 1964; *Life*, August 6, 1965; *Harper's*, September, 1965; Roderick Jellema, *Peter De Vries: A Critical Essay*, Eerdmans, 1966; *New York Times*, January 27, 1969; Carolyn Riley, editor, *Contemporary Literary Criticism*, Gale, Volume I, 1973, Volume II, 1974, Volume III, 1975.

*   *   *

DEWALD, Paul A.   1920-

PERSONAL: Born March 12, 1920, in New York, N.Y.; son of Jacob F. and Elsie W. Dewald; married Eleanor Whitman, September 1, 1961; children: Jonathan S., Ellen F. *Education:* Swarthmore College, A.B., 1942; University of Rochester, M.D., 1945. *Home:* 60 Conway Lane, St. Louis, Mo. 63124. *Office:* 4524 Forest Park, St. Louis, Mo. 63108.

CAREER: Diplomate, National Board of Medical Examiners and American Board of Psychiatry and Neurology; certified in psychoanalysis, division of psychoanalytic education, State University of New York, 1960. Strong Memorial-Rochester Municipal Hospitals, Rochester, N.Y., chief resident in psychiatry, 1951-52, assistant psychiatrist, 1952-57, associate psychiatrist, 1957-61; University of Rochester School of Medicine, Rochester, N.Y., instructor, 1952-57, assistant professor of psychiatry, 1957-61; Washington University School of Medicine, St. Louis, Mo., assistant professor of clinical psychiatry, 1961-65; St. Louis University School of Medicine, St. Louis, Mo., associate professor, 1965-69, professor of clinical psychiatry, 1969—. Institute for Psychoanalysis, Chicago, Ill., lecturer, 1961—, training and supervising analyst, 1965—; St. Louis Psychoanalytic Institute, medical director, 1972—. Psychoanalytic Foundation, St. Louis, director of low-cost treatment service; Mental Health Association, St. Louis, member of medical advisory committee. *Military service:* U.S. Army, Medical Corps, 1946-48.

MEMBER: American Psychiatric Association (fellow), American Psychoanalytic Association, Mid-Continent Psychiatric Society, Missouri State Medical Society, St. Louis Psychoanalytic Society, Chicago Psychoanalytic Society, Sigma Xi (associate), Alpha Omega Alpha. *Awards, honors:* U.S. Public Health Service fellow, 1949-52, career teacher in psychiatry, 1955-57; American Fund for Psychiatry fellow, 1957-58.

WRITINGS: Psychotherapy: A Dynamic Approach, Basic Books, 1964, 2nd edition, 1969; *The Psychoanalytic Process: A Case Illustration*, Basic Books, 1972. Contributor to professional journals.

*   *   *

DIBBLE, J(ames) Birney   1925-

PERSONAL: Born December 8, 1925, in Madras, India; son of Paul Gladstone (a minister) and Marie Bjerno (Larsen) Dibble; married Edna Baird, June 21, 1949; children: Eric David, Barbara Jean. *Education:* Attended Duke University (during naval service), 1943-45; University of Illinois, M.D., 1949. *Religion:* Methodist. *Home:* Route 4, Box 222, Eau Claire, Wis. 54701. *Office:* 1030 Oakridge Dr., Eau Claire, Wis. 54701.

CAREER: Diplomate, American Board of Surgery. Cook County Hospital, Chicago, Ill., resident in surgery, 1953-57; surgeon in private practice, Eau Claire, Wis., 1957-68; Luther Memorial Hospital, Eau Claire, Wis., chief of surgery, 1970-72; Sacred Heart Hospital, Eau Claire, Wis., chief of surgery, 1975—. Temporary emergency service, Kiomboi Lutheran Mission Hospital; Tanzania, Tanganyika, 1962-63 and 1968-69. Co-founder of Chippewa Valley Ethological Society and WYNOT Alcholic Rehabilitation Center. *Military service:* U.S. Navy, enlisted service, 1943-45, medical officer with Marines in Korea, 1951-53; became lieutenant; received Bronze Star and commendation ribbon. *Member:* American Medical Association, Wisconsin State Medical Association, Eau Claire County Medical Association.

WRITINGS: In This Land of Eve, Abingdon, 1965; *The Plains Brood Alone,* Zondervan, 1974.

SIDELIGHTS: Dibble studied cultural anthropology of African tribes while doing medical work in Tanganyika and acquired fair conversational knowledge of Swahili. *Avocational interests:* Hunting and fishing (Dibble has done both in Alaska, Africa, and locally).

*   *   *

DICHTER, Ernest   1907-

PERSONAL: Born August 14, 1907, in Vienna, Austria; son of Wilhelm and Mathilde (Kurz) Dichter; married Hedy Langfelder (a pianist and builder); children: Thomas W., Susan J. (Mrs. Joel Diemond). *Education:* Sorbonne, University of Paris, Licencee, 1931; University of Vienna, Ph.D., 1934. *Home:* Albany Post Rd., Croton-on-Hudson, N.Y. 10520. *Office:* Ernest Dichter Associates International, Ltd., Croton-on-Hudson, N.Y. 10520.

CAREER: J. Sterling Getchell, Inc., director of motivational research, 1938-43; Columbia Broadcasting System, New York, N.Y., consulting psychologist, 1943-46; Institute for Motivational Research, Croton-on-Hudson, N.Y., president, beginning 1946; Motivational Publications, Inc., Croton-on-Hudson, N.Y., president and publisher, beginning 1956; now president of Ernest Dichter Associates International, Ltd. *Member:* American Psychological Association, American Marketing Association, American Sociological Association, Authors League of America.

WRITINGS: The Psychology of Everyday Living, Barnes & Noble, 1947; *The Strategy of Desire*, Doubleday, 1960; *Handbook of Consumer Motivations*, McGraw, 1964; *Motivating Human Behavior*, McGraw, 1971; *The Naked Manager*, Cahners Publications, 1974. Contributor to *Harvard Business Review* and other publications.

*   *   *

DICKERSON, F(rederick) Reed   1909-

PERSONAL: Born November 11, 1909, in Chicago, Ill.; son of Fred George (an inventor and manufacturer), and Rena Marian (Reed) Dickerson; married Jane Morrison, June 14, 1939; children: Elizabeth Ann (Mrs. David D. Brown), John Scott, Martha Reed. *Education:* Williams College, A.B., 1931; Harvard University, LL.B., 1934; Columbia University, LL.M., 1939, J.S.D., 1950. *Religion:* Presbyterian. *Home:* 870 Woodscrest Dr., Bloomington, Ind. 47401. *Office:* School of Law, Indiana University, Bloomington, Ind. 47401.

CAREER: Lawyer with Goodwin, Procter & Hoar, Boston, Mass., 1934-35, and McNab, Holmes & Long, Chicago, Ill., 1936-38; assistant professor of law, Washington University, St. Louis, Mo., 1939-40, and University of Pittsburgh, Pittsburgh, Pa., 1940-42; U.S. Government, Washington, D.C., attorney with Office of Price Administration, 1942-47, assistant legislative counsel, House of Representatives, 1947-49, and attorney with Department of Defense (chairman, Committee on Codification of Military Laws), 1949-58; Indiana University, Bloomington, professor of law, 1958—, associate dean for bar relations, 1971-75. President, F. G. Dickerson Co. (milk fillers), Chicago, Ill., 1949—. Consultant to U.S. Department of Defense, 1959 and 1966, Federal Aviation Agency, 1960-65, U.S. Department of Transportation, 1967-69, President's Committee on Consumer's Interests, 1967-68, Commission on Government Procurement, 1971-72, U.S. Government Accounting Office, 1973—. Commissioner for Indiana, National Conference of Commissioners on Uniform State Laws; chairman of Indiana Commission on Uniform State Laws, 1969—. *Member:* American Bar Association, Federal Bar Association, American Law Institute, National Legislative Conference. *Awards, honors:* Distinguished Civilian Service Award, U.S. Department of Defense, 1957; Ford Foundation faculty fellowship, Harvard University, 1961-62.

WRITINGS: Products Liability and the Food Consumer, Little, Brown, 1951; *Legislative Drafting,* Little, Brown, 1954; (editor) *Legal Problems Affecting Private Swimming Pools,* Hoffman, Harris, 1961; *The Fundamentals of Legal Drafting,* Little, Brown, 1965; (editor) *Product Safety in Household Goods,* Bobbs-Merrill, 1968; (co-editor) *Cases and Materials on Legislation,* West Publishing, 1969; (editor) *Professionalizing Legislation Drafting: The Federal Experience,* American Bar Association, 1973; *The Interpretation and Application of Statutes,* Little, Brown, 1975. Contributor to *Encyclopedia Americana,* and to *Harper's Magazine* and *Esquire.* Member of editorial board, *Modern Uses of Logic in Law,* quarterly, published by American Bar Association.

* * *

DIEHL, W(illiam) W(ells) 1916-
(Duncan Clay)

PERSONAL: Born October 14, 1916, in Newark, Ohio; son of Grover Louis and Ruby (Wells) Diehl; married Betty Creusere (executive director of social services department of Holy Cross Hospital), June 25, 1948. *Education:* Kent State University, student, 1936-37. *Politics:* Democrat. *Religion:* Congregational. *Home and office:* 757 Covington Dr., Detroit, Mich. 48203.

CAREER: Reporter and photographer on newspapers in Ashtabula, Ohio, 1939-40, and Newark, Ohio, 1940-48; *Providence Journal,* Providence, R.I., picture editor, 1948-49; *Toledo Blade,* Toledo, Ohio, assistant Sunday editor, 1949-50; Hamilton Wright Organization, New York, N.Y., manager of public relations accounts for Puerto Rico and Haiti, 1950-51; Mutual Broadcasting System, New York, N.Y., administrative assistant, press information, 1951-53; *TV Guide* (magazine), editor, Detroit (Mich.) edition, 1953-54; *TV Today* (magazine), Detroit, Mich., editor and publisher, 1955-59; Prince & Co., Inc. (advertising and publishing agency), Detroit, Mich., account executive and editor of *Dodge News* (magazine), 1959-62; full-time freelance writer and editorial consultant, 1962—. *Member:* National Headliners Club. *Awards, honors:* Eleven top awards for photography, Associated Press Editors of Ohio, 1941-

48; National Headliners Club Medal for newspaper series on bad conditions in Veterans Administration hospitals, 1946; Freedoms Foundation George Washington Honor Medals, 1950, 1952, 1961; Leader's Award, Direct Mail Advertising Association, for best external publication in nationwide competition, 1960.

WRITINGS: (With Barbara Powers, former wife of U-2 pilot, Gary Powers) *Spy Wife,* Pyramid Books, 1965. Writer of syndicated column, "Up Town—Down Town: New York Vignettes," 1952-53; columnist, "Detroit Dateline" in *TV Guide,* 1953-54, and "Motor City Channels" in *TV Today,* 1955. Articles and features have appeared in *American Mercury, Everybody's Digest, Sports Extra, Motor News, Detroit Free Press Sunday Magazine,* and other periodicals and newspapers.

* * *

DIERENFIELD, Richard B(ruce) 1922-

PERSONAL: Born October 15, 1922, in Aberdeen, S.D.; son of Herbert E. (a minister) and Elizabeth (Brown) Dierenfield; married Yvonne Fahlgren, August 19, 1950; children: Bruce Jonathan, David Roger. *Education:* Macalester College, B.A., 1948, M.Ed., 1951; University of Bristol, graduate student, 1951-52; University of Colorado, Ed.D., 1958. *Politics:* Republican. *Religion:* Presbyterian. *Home:* 1566 Red Cedar Rd., St. Paul, Minn. 55111. *Office:* Macalester College, St. Paul, Minn. 55101.

CAREER: Macalester College, St. Paul, Minn., 1951—, associate professor of education, 1958—. *Military service:* U.S. Army Air Forces, 1943-46. *Member:* National Education Association, Association for Student Teaching, American Association of University Professors, Minnesota Education Association, Phi Delta Kappa, Kappa Delta Pi.

WRITINGS: Religion in American Schools, Public Affairs, 1962; (contributor) *The High School Curriculum,* Ronald, 1964; *The Cinderella Subject: Religion in the County Secondary Schools of England,* Macalester Press, 1965; (co-author) *The Sociology of Religion,* Appleton, 1967.

WORK IN PROGRESS: The "House System" in English Comprehensive Schools—A Way to Personalize Education.

* * *

DIETRICH, John E(rb) 1913-

PERSONAL: Born November 13, 1913, in Spokane, Wash.; son of John Hassler and Louise Ernestine (Erb) Dietrich; married Lois Gernhardt, April 13, 1949; children: Lisa, John. *Education:* University of Wisconsin, B.A., 1937, M.A., 1941, Ph.D., 1945. *Office:* Michigan State University, East Lansing, Mich. 48823.

CAREER: Purdue University, LaFayette, Ind., instructor and associate director of university theater, 1937-41; University of Wisconsin, Madison, lecturer, 1942-45, assistant professor, 1945-47, associate professor, 1947-52, professor of speech, 1952-55, associate director of university theater, 1942-54, director of production, WHA-TV, 1954; Ohio State University, Columbus, professor of speech and director of university theater, 1955-59; Michigan State University, East Lansing, professor of speech and chairman of department, 1959-64, assistant provost, and director of educational development program, 1964—. Delegate, American Council on Education, 1957-59, White House Conference on Children and Youth, 1960. Trustee, Milton College. *Member:* American Educational Theatre Association (member of board of research, 1954-57; executive committee member, 1955-58), Speech Communication Association (second vice-president, 1957; first vice-president, 1958; president, 1959), American National Theatre and Academy (member of board of directors, 1960-63), Central States Speech Association (president, 1953), Speech Association of Eastern States, Phi Eta Sigma, Delta Sigma Rho, Pi Epsilon Delta.

WRITINGS: Play Direction, Prentice-Hall, 1953; *Practical Speaking for the Technical Man*, Prentice-Hall, 1958. Contributor to professional journals. Associate editor, *Players Magazine*, 1948-52; member of editorial board, *Speech Monographs*, 1950-53.†

*   *   *

DILLENBERGER, Jane 1916-

PERSONAL: Born February 27, 1916, in Hartford, Wis.; daughter of John Minot Daggett (an automotive sales representative); married John Dillenberger (a professor of historical theology at Graduate Theological Union, Berkeley), July 19, 1962. *Education:* Attended University of Wisconsin, one year, and University of Iowa, one year; University of Chicago, B.A., 1940; Radcliffe College, M.A., 1944; Drew University, postgraduate study, 1958-59. *Home:* 1536 Le Roy, Berkeley, Calif. 94708. *Office:* Graduate Theological Union, Berkeley, Calif.

CAREER: Art Institute of Chicago, Chicago, Ill., curatorial assistant, department of prints and drawings, 1940-41; Boston Athenaeum, Boston, Mass., head of art department, 1944-45; Newark Museum, Newark, N.J., docent and staff member, 1945-46; Drew Theological Seminary, Madison, N.J., lecturer in Christianity and art, 1950-62; San Francisco Theological Seminary, San Francisco, Calif., lecturer, 1963-65, associate professor of Christianity and the arts, 1965—. University of California Extension Division, lecturer in art history, 1963—; San Francisco Museum of Art, special researcher in charge of catalogue of collection, 1963—; Graduate Theological Union, Berkeley, Calif., associate professor, 1969—. Adjunct associate professor, Jesuit School of Theology, Berkeley, 1974—. Director of exhibition "The Hand and the Spirit: Religious Art in America, 1700-1900," shown at University Art Museum, Berkeley, National Collection of Fine Arts, Washington, Indianapolis Museum of Art, and Dallas Museum of Art, 1972-73. *Member:* College Art Association, Liturgical Arts Association, Society for Contemporary Arts, Religion, and Culture. *Awards, honors:* Rockefeller grant to study modern religious art in Europe, 1961; National Endowment for the Humanities grant for research in American art, 1973-74; National Endowment for the Arts grant for research in twentieth century American art, 1974-76.

WRITINGS: Style and Content in Christian Art, Abingdon, 1965; *Secular Art with Sacred Themes*, Abingdon, 1969. Contributor of articles and reviews to journals.

*   *   *

DILLON, Richard H(ugh) 1924-

PERSONAL: Born January 16, 1924, in Sausalito, Calif.; son of William Tarleton and Alice Mabel (Burke) Dillon; married Barbara A. Sutherland, June, 1950; children: Brian, David, Ross. *Education:* University of California, Berkeley, A.B., 1948, A.M., 1949, B.L.S., 1950. *Politics:* Independent. *Religion:* Independent. *Office:* Sutro Library, 2130 Fulton St., San Francisco, Calif. 94117.

CAREER: Sutro Library, San Francisco, Calif., assistant librarian, 1950-53, librarian, 1953—. California History Commission, member, 1964—. *Military service:* U.S. Army, 1943-46; received Purple Heart. *Member:* Western History Association, California Historical Society, California Library Association, California Writers Club, Phi Beta Kappa, Phi Alpha Theta, Roxburghe Club. *Awards, honors:* James D. Phelan Award in literature, 1960, for *Embarcadero*; Gold Medal of Commonwealth Club of California for best nonfiction book of 1965 by a Californian, for *Meriwether Lewis*; Silver Medal of Commonwealth Club of California for best nonfiction book by a Californian, 1967, for *Fool's Gold*; Spur Award, Western Writers of America for best nonfiction book in Western America, 1973, for *Burnt-Out Fires*.

WRITINGS: Embarcadero, Coward, 1959; (editor) W. H. Boyle, *Personal Observations on the Conduct of the Modoc War*, Dawsons, 1959; (editor) Benjamin B. Harris, *The Gila Trail*, University of Oklahoma Press, 1960; *Shanghaiing Days*, Coward, 1961; (editor) C. C. Loveland, *California Trail Herd*, Talisman, 1961; *The Hatchet Men*, Coward, 1962; *Meriwether Lewis* (biography), Coward, 1965; *J. Ross Browne*, University of Oklahoma Press, 1965; *The Legend of Grizzly Adams*, Coward, 1966; *Fool's Gold: The Biography of John Sutter*, Coward, 1967; *Wells, Fargo Detective*, Coward, 1969; *Humbugs and Heroes: A Gallery of California Pioneers*, Doubleday, 1970; *Burnt-Out Fires*, Prentice-Hall, 1973; *Exploring the Mother Lode Country*, Ward Ritchie, 1974. Contributor of articles and reviews to popular and scholarly journals.

WORK IN PROGRESS: Siskiyou Trail, the Hudson's Bay Co. Trappers in California, for McGraw.

*   *   *

DIMMITT, Richard Bertrand 1925-

PERSONAL: Born August 22, 1925, in Los Angeles, Calif.; son of Ralph Bertrand (a general and building contractor) and Jennie (Lambert) Dimmitt. *Education:* California State College (now University), Long Beach, A.B., 1952; additional study at San Jose State College (now San Jose State University), and Immaculate Heart College, Los Angeles, Calif., received state special secondary credential in library science, 1954. *Politics:* Registered Republican. *Religion:* Episcopalian. *Home:* 223 via Nia, Lido Isle, Newport Beach, Calif.; 178 Birkirkar Rd., St. Jullians, Maltese Islands.

CAREER: Buena Park (Calif.) Library District, children's librarian, 1954-57; Marquard Corp., Van Nuys, Calif., head cataloger in engineering library, 1957; Los Angeles County (Calif.) Library, branch film and reference librarian, 1963; Orange County (Calif.) Library, special projects librarian, 1968—. Writer and researcher in Italy, Switzerland, and Malta, 1964—. *Military service:* U.S. Army, 1944-46, 1950; served in Europe, World War II, and Korean conflict; received Purple Heart. *Member:* Friends of the Library (University of California, Irvine), Villa Montalvo Association.

WRITINGS—Compiler: The Title Guide to the Talkies (listing of 16,000 feature-length films, 1927-63), Scarecrow, 1965; *An Actor Guide to the Talkies: A Comprehensive Listing of 8,000 Feature-Length Films from January, 1949 until December, 1964*, Scarecrow, 1968.

*   *   *

DIMONT, Max I. 1912-

PERSONAL: Born August 12, 1912, in Kaunas, Lithuania;

came to United States, 1929; son of Hyman (a Hebrew teacher) and Hannah (Podgur) Dimont; married Ethel Kurzfeld (an office manager), November, 1945; children: Karen (Mrs. Charles Clark), Gail (Mrs. Michael Goldey). *Education:* Attended high schools in Helsinki, Finland, and Cleveland, Ohio. *Politics:* "Mostly Democratic party." *Religion:* Hebraic. *Home:* 228 Gay Ave., Clayton, Mo. *Office:* Edison Brothers Stores, Inc., 400 Washington St., St. Louis, Mo.

CAREER: Edison Brothers Stores, Inc., St. Louis, Mo., publicity and editorial work, 1946—. Lecturer at Weizmann Institute, Israel, and in United States. *Military service:* U.S. Army, Intelligence, World War II; served in Europe; became sergeant. *Member:* Authors Guild.

WRITINGS: Jews, God, and History, Simon & Schuster, 1962; *The Indestructible Jews: Is There a Manifest Destiny in Jewish History?*, World Publishing, 1971.

WORK IN PROGRESS: Love and Loot, a book of short stories: *The Wonderful Adventures and Fortunes of the Jewish People*, a book for juveniles on Jewish civilization.

SIDELIGHTS: Dimont speaks seven languages, including Finnish, German, and Scandinavian.†

* * *

Di PIETRO, Robert Joseph 1932-

PERSONAL: Born July 18, 1932, in Endicott, N.Y.; son of Americo and Mary (Di Pietro) Di Pietro; married Vincenzina A. Giallo, September 5, 1953; children: Angela Maria, Mark Andrew. *Education:* Harpur College, B.A. (cum laude), 1954; Harvard University, M.A., 1955; Cornell University, Ph.D., 1960. *Home:* 1706 Woodman Dr., McLean, Va. 22101. *Office:* Georgetown University, Washington, D.C. 20057.

CAREER: Cornell University, Ithaca, N.Y., instructor in French and Italian, 1956-60; project linguist, Center for Applied Linguistics, Washington, D.C., and during same time Fulbright lecturer in English, University of Rome, Rome, Italy, 1960-61; Georgetown University, Washington, D.C., assistant professor, 1961-63, associate professor, 1964-68, professor of linguistics, 1968—. Fulbright professor, University of Madrid, 1963-64. *Member:* Linguistic Society of America, Modern Language Association of America, American Association of Teachers of Italian, American Anthropological Association. *Awards, honors:* U.S. Department of State specialist grant to Spain, 1964; elected one of Outstanding Young Men of America by U.S. Junior Chamber of Commerce, 1965; American Council of Learned Societies travel grant to Spain, 1965, to Italy, 1972.

WRITINGS: (Editor) *Languages and Linguistics* (monograph), Georgetown University Press, 1963; (with F. B. Agard) *The Sounds of English and Italian*, University of Chicago Press, 1965; (with Agard) *The Grammatical Structures of English and Italian*, University of Chicago Press, 1965; (contributor) T. A. Sebeok, editor, *Current Trends in Linguistics*, Indiana University Press, 1966; *Language Structures in Contrast*, Newbury House, 1971. Contributor to English, Spanish, and Italian language journals. Book review editor for *Modern Language Journal*, and for Italian publications.

WORK IN PROGRESS: A textbook on verbal strategies, and a textbook on creativity in languages.

SIDELIGHTS: Di Pietro speaks Italian, French, Spanish, German, and Portuguese; he reads Rumanian. *Avocational*

interests: Music (plays piano, guitar, and mandolin), gardening.

* * *

di PRIMA, Diane 1934-

PERSONAL: Born August 6, 1934, in New York, N.Y.; daughter of Francis and Emma (Mallozzi) de Prima; married Alan S. Marlowe (a printer and publisher), November 30, 1962; children: Jeanne, Dominique, Alexander. *Education:* Attended Swarthmore College, 1951-52. *Politics:* Anarchist. *Religion:* Buddhist. *Residence:* New York, N.Y.

CAREER: Co-editor with LeRoi Jones (Imamu Amiri Baraka) of *The Floating Bear*, 1961-63; contributing editor, *Kulchur* (now defunct), 1960-61; associate editor, *Signal Magazine*, 1963—; The Poets Press, New York, N.Y., publisher and editor, 1964—. Free-lance editor and writer. *Awards, honors:* Grant from National Institute of Arts and Letters, 1965.

WRITINGS: This Kind of Bird Flies Backward, Totem Press, 1959; (editor) *Various Fables from Various Places*, Putnam, 1960; *Dinners and Nightmares* (fiction), Corinth, 1961; *The New Handbook of Heaven*, Auerhahn, 1963; (translator) *Seven Love Poems from Middle Latin*, Poets Press, 1965; *The Calculus of Variation* (autobiographical novel), Poets Press, 1966; *Spring and Autumn Annals* (novel), Frontier Press, 1966; *Poems for Freddie*, Poets Press, 1966; *Some Haiku*, Seagull Press, 1966; *Earthsong: Poems 1957-1959*, Poets Press, 1968; (editor) *War Poems*, Poets Press, 1968; *Hotel Albert Poems*, Kriya Press for Poets Press, 1968; *L. A. Odyssey*, Poets Press, 1969; *Memoirs of a Beatnik*, Traveller's Companion, 1969; *The Book of Hours*, Brownstone Press, 1970; *Kerhonkson Journal: 1966*, Oyez, 1971; *Revolutionary Letters*, City Lights, 1971; *Loba: Part One*, Capra Press, 1973.

Plays: "Murder Cake," produced by Living Theatre, 1960, Judson Poets Theatre, 1963, and New York Poets Theatre, 1964; "Paideuma," produced by Living Theatre, 1960; "Like," produced by New York Poets Theatre, 1964; "Monuments," produced at Caffe Cino, New York, N.Y., 1968.

SIDELIGHTS: Diane di Prima told *CA* that she had been influenced by her "beautiful anarchist atheist grandfather mystic (in childhood); John Keats (early teens); Ezra Pound (college years and early twenties); eastern and mystical writing, especially Tibetan Buddhism and Tantric Hinduism (present)."†

* * *

DISHMAN, Pat(ricia L.) 1939-

PERSONAL: Born October 20, 1939, in Fort Worth, Tex.; daughter of Hubert Clinton (a bookkeeper) and Ophelia (Wood) Dishman. *Education:* Hardin-Simmons University, B.S., 1962; graduate courses at Southwest Baptist Theological Seminary, 1963, and Springfield College, 1966; University of Oklahoma, M.A., 1969. *Religion:* Southern Baptist. *Home:* 3001 West Ohio #26, Midland, Tex. 79701. *Office:* Midland Memorial Hospital, 2200 West Illinois, Midland, Tex. 79701.

CAREER: Southern Baptist Radio-Television Commission, Fort Worth, Tex., editorial assistant on *Beam* (monthly magazine), 1962-63; Young Men's Christian Association, Midland, Tex., secretary to department heads, 1964-65, director of adult program and public relations, 1965-68; Midland Memorial Hospital, Midland, Tex., director of public relations and development, 1969—; Concept Copy-writers (public relations firm), partner, 1971—. *Member:* National Association for Hospital Development, American Society of Hospital Public Relations, Public Relations Society of America, Texas Society for Hospital Public Relations (president elect, 1974), Texas Press Women.

WRITINGS: Ten Who Overcame (nonfiction), Broadman, 1966. Also author of *Hospitals.* Contributor to *Beam, Window, YMCA Forum,* and *Baptist Standard.*

WORK IN PROGRESS: A novel set in a present day hospital.

SIDELIGHTS: Selections from *Ten Who Overcame* have been recorded for "Talking Book Magazine" (long-playing records). *Avocational interests:* Photography.

* * *

DITZEN, Lowell Russell 1913-

PERSONAL: Born February 16, 1913, in Kansas City, Kan.; son of Paul H. (a lawyer) and Emma (a musician; maiden name, Brenner) Ditzen; married Virginia Stuart, August 19, 1933 (divorced, 1965); married Eleanor Davies, December 19, 1966; children: (first marriage) Lowell Stuart, Deborah Stuart. *Education:* Attended Park College, 1929-31; William Jewell College, B.A., 1933; McCormick Theological Seminary, B.D., 1936; graduate study at University of Chicago, 1936-38, and Union Theological Seminary, New York, N.Y., 1942. *Home:* 2474 Tracy Pl. N.W., Washington, D.C. 20008.

CAREER: Ordained minister, Presbyterian Church in the U.S.A., 1936; minister in Chicago, Ill., 1934-42, New York, N.Y., 1942-43, Utica, N.Y., 1943-50, and Bronxville, N.Y., 1950-62; National Presbyterian Center, Washington, D.C., director, 1963-75, director emeritus, 1975—. Pinehurst Village Chapel, Pinehurst, N.C., preacher in charge, 1965-66. Lecturer at American University and Wesley Theological Seminary, Washington, D.C., 1964—; exchange preacher to England, Scotland, and France, 1948; lecturer at major universities and colleges in India, 1957; preacher in other countries, at U.S. universities, and on television and radio series. Commissioner to General Council of the Presbyterian-Reformed World Alliance, 1948-60; vice-president, American Committee on Interchange of Preachers, 1958-62. Member of board of directors, Society of Crippled Children and Adults, 1954-63; trustee of Finch College, 1956-64.

MEMBER: Newcomen Society (England), Phi Gamma Delta, Sigma Tau Delta, Pi Kappa Delta, Chevy Chase Club, Cosmos Club (both Washington, D.C.). *Awards, honors:* D.D., Park College, 1943; LL.D., Central College, 1957; Litt.D., William Jewell College, 1961; L.H.D., Hope College, 1961. Ten national awards, Freedoms Foundation of Valley Forge, 1951-62; citation for outstanding service to America, Daughters of the American Revolution, 1957.

WRITINGS: (Assistant editor) N. E. Richardson, *Toward a More Efficient Church,* Presbyterian Theological Seminary, 1940; *Personal Security Through Faith,* Holt, 1954; *You Are Never Alone,* Holt, 1958; *Secrets of Self-Mastery,* Holt, 1958; *The Storm and the Rainbow,* Holt, 1959; *Handbook of Church Administration,* Macmillan, 1962; *Jesus and Our Human Needs,* Crowell, 1963; *Handbook for the Church Secretary,* Prentice-Hall, 1963; *Benjamin Goodall Symon, Jr.* (biography), Amherst College Press, 1964; *The Minister's Deskbook,* Prentice-Hall, 1965.

Sermons anthologized in *Sermons of Goodwill,* Association Press, 1948, and *Best Sermons,* Volume IV, Macmillan, 1953, and Volume V, McGraw, 1955; orations published in volumes by Northwestern University Press and Noble. Writer of *Today* (monthly devotional), 1945-49, and contributor of articles and sermons to *Parade, Reader's Digest, Christian Century, Think, Kiwanian,* and other periodicals.

AVOCATIONAL INTERESTS: Golf and philately.

* * *

DIXON, Franklin W.
[Collective pseudonym]

WRITINGS—All published by Grosset: "Hardy Boys" series: *The Secret of the Old Mill,* 1927, revised edition, 1962; *The Shore Road Mystery,* 1928, revised edition, 1964; *Hunting for Hidden Gold,* 1928, revised edition, 1963; *The Missing Chums,* 1928, revised edition, 1962; *The Mystery of Cabin Island,* 1929, revised edition, 1966; *The Secret of the Caves,* 1929, revised edition 1964.

The Great Airport Mystery, 1930, revised edition, 1965; *What Happened at Midnight,* 1931, revised edition, 1967; *While the Clock Ticked,* 1932, revised edition, 1962; *Footprints Under the Window,* 1933, revised edition, 1965; *The Mark on the Door,* 1934, revised edition, 1967; *The Hidden Harbor Mystery,* 1935, revised edition, 1961; *The Sinister Sign Post,* 1936, revised edition, 1968; *A Figure in Hiding,* 1937, revised edition, 1965; *The Secret Warning,* 1938, revised edition, 1966; *The Twisted Claw,* 1939, revised edition, 1969.

The Disappearing Floor, 1940, revised edition, 1964; *The Mystery of the Flying Express,* 1941, revised edition, 1970; *The Clue of the Broken Blade,* 1942, revised edition, 1970; *The Flickering Torch Mystery,* 1943, revised edition, 1971; *The Melted Coins,* 1944, revised edition, 1970; *The Short-Wave Mystery,* 1945; *The Secret Panel,* 1946, revised edition, 1969; *The Phantom Freighter,* 1947, revised edition, 1970; *The Secret of Skull Mountain,* 1948, revised edition, 1966; *The Sign of the Crooked Arrow,* 1949, revised edition, 1970.

The Secret of the Lost Tunnel, 1950, revised edition, 1968; *The Wailing Siren Mystery,* 1951, revised edition, 1968; *The Secret of Wildcat Swamp,* 1952, revised edition, 1969; *The Yellow Feather Mystery,* 1953, revised edition, 1971; *The Crisscross Shadow,* 1953, revised edition, 1969; *The Hooded Hawk Mystery,* 1954, revised edition, 1971; *The Clue in the Embers,* 1955, revised edition, 1972; *The Secret of Pirate's Hill,* 1956, revised edition, 1972; *The Ghost at Skeleton Rock,* 1957; (with D. A. Spina) *The Hardy Boy's Detective Handbook,* 1959, revised edition (with William F. Flynn), 1972: *The House on the Cliff,* 1959; *The Mystery at Devil's Paw,* 1959; *The Tower Treasure,* 1959.

The Mystery of the Chinese Junk, 1960; *The Mystery of the Desert Giant,* 1961; *The Clue of the Screeching Owl,* 1962; *The Viking Symbol Mystery,* 1963; *The Mystery of the Aztec Warrior,* 1964; *The Haunted Fort,* 1965; *The Mystery of the Spiral Bridge,* 1966; *The Secret Agent on Flight 101,* 1967; *Mystery of the Whale Tattoo,* 1968; *The Arctic Patrol Mystery,* 1969.

The Bombay Boomerang, 1970; *Danger on Vampire Trail,* 1971; *The Masked Monkey,* 1972; *The Shattered Helmet,* 1973; *The Clue of the Hissing Serpent,* 1974; *The Mysterious Caravan,* 1975. Some of the "Hardy Boys" series were adapted for television and produced by Walt Disney, and for an animated series by ABC-TV in 1969.

"Ted Scott Flying Stories" series: *Rescued in the Clouds; or, Ted Scott, Hero of the Air*, 1927; *Over the Rockies with the Air Mail; or, Ted Scott Lost in the Wilderness*, 1927; *Over the Ocean to Paris; or, Ted Scott's Daring Long-Distance Flight*, 1927; *First Stop Honolulu; or, Ted Scott over the Pacific*, 1927; *Across the Pacific; or, Ted Scott's Hop to Australia*, 1928; *The Search for the Lost Flyers; or, Ted Scott over the West Indies*, 1928; *South of the Rio Grande; or, Ted Scott on a Secret Mission*, 1928; *Flying Against Time; or, Ted Scott Breaking the Ocean to Ocean Record*, 1929; *The Lone Eagle of the Border; or, Ted Scott and the Diamond Smugglers*, 1929; *Over the Jungle Trails; or, Ted Scott and the Missing Explorers*, 1929.

Lost at the South Pole; or, Ted Scott in Blizzard Land, 1930; *Through the Air to Alaska; or, Ted Scott's Search in Nugget Valley*, 1930; *Flying to the Rescue; or, Ted Scott and the Big Dirigible*, 1930; *Danger Trails of the Sky; or, Ted Scott's Great Mountain Climb*, 1931; *Following the Sun Shadow; or, Ted Scott and the Great Eclipse*, 1932; *Battling the Wind; or, Ted Scott Flying Around Cape Horn*, 1933; *Brushing the Mountain Top; or, Aiding the Lost Traveler*, 1934; *Castaways of the Stratosphere; or, Hunting the Vanished Balloonists*, 1935; *Hunting the Sky Spies; or, Testing the Invisible Plane*, 1941; *The Pursuit Patrol; or, Chasing the Platinum Pirates*, 1943.

SIDELIGHTS: See **ADAMS, Harriet S.**, **STRATEMEYER, Edward L.**, and **SVENSON, Andrew E.**†

*   *   *

DIZARD, Wilson P(aul) 1922-

PERSONAL: Born March 6, 1922, in New York, N.Y.; son of Wilson Paul and Helen Marie (Oliver) Dizard; married Lynn Margaret Wood, March 11, 1944; children: John William, Stephen Wood, Wilson Paul III, Mark Christopher. *Education:* Fordham University, B.S., 1947; Columbia University, graduate student, 1947-49. *Home:* 2811 28th St., N.W., Washington, D.C. 20008. *Office:* Office of Policy, U.S. Information Agency, 1750 Pennsylvania Ave., Washington, D.C. 20547.

CAREER: Time Inc., New York, N.Y., writer-editor, 1947-51; U.S. Department of State, Foreign Service officer, 1951-53, serving as vice-consul in Istanbul, Turkey, 1951-52, policy and program officer, Washington, D.C., 1952-53; U.S. Information Agency, 1953—, information officer, U.S. Embassy, Athens, Greece, 1955-60, public affairs officer, then consul, Dacca, East Pakistan, 1960-62, policy officer, Washington, D.C., 1963-64, special assistant to deputy director, Washington, D.C., 1964-65, Agency Planning Officer, 1965-66, Assistant Deputy Director of Agency, 1966—, chief of Agency operations, American Embassy, Warsaw, Poland, 1968-70, assistant director, public affairs office, U.S. Embassy, Saigon, 1970-71, chief, operational plans and policy, 1973—. Massachusetts Institute of Technology, research associate, Center for International Studies, 1962-63. *Military service:* U.S. Army, 1943-46. *Member:* International Club (Washington, D.C.). *Awards, honors:* Encaenia Award, Fordham University, 1962.

WRITINGS: The Strategy of Truth, Public Affairs, 1961; *Television: A World View*, Syracuse University Press, 1966. Writer of monographs, pamphlets, and articles.

DOLE, Jeremy H(askell) 1932-

PERSONAL: Born December 26, 1932, in Winchester, Mass.; son of Harold Sanford and Thalia (Smith) Dole; married Claudia Frost, June 10, 1961; children: Elizabeth Sanford, Sarah Howard, Gwendolyn Frost. *Education:* Middlesex School, student, 1947-51; Yale University, B.A., 1955. *Home:* 12 Wood End Lane, Bronxville, N.Y. *Agent:* McIntosh & Otis, Inc., 18 East 41st St., New York, N.Y. 10017. *Office: Reader's Digest*, Pleasantville, N.Y. 10570.

CAREER: Free-lance writer, 1959-61; *Playboy*, Chicago, Ill., associate editor, 1961-63; *Ladies' Home Journal*, New York, N.Y., senior editor, 1964; *Reader's Digest*, Pleasantville, N.Y., associate editor, 1965-68, senior editor, 1968-70, senior staff editor, 1970-74, assistant managing editor, 1974—. *Military service:* U.S. Navy, 1955-59; instructor in French at U.S. Naval Academy, 1957-59; became lieutenant junior grade.

WRITINGS: Venus Disarmed (novel), Crown, 1966. Short stories published in *McCall's, Argosy, Playboy*, and other magazines.

*   *   *

DOLIM, Mary N(uzum) 1925-

PERSONAL: Born August 15, 1925, in Timberhill, Kan.; daughter of Alonzo L. (a realtor) and Lula (Radford) Nuzum; married Abel L. Dolim (a real estate broker), January 11, 1946; children: Patricia, Robert. *Education:* Mound Park School of Nursing, R.N., 1946. *Politics:* Democrat. *Home:* 20555 Western Blvd., Hayward, Calif. 94541. *Agent:* Barthold Fles Literary Agency, 507 Fifth Ave., New York, N.Y. 10017.

CAREER: Professional writer; nurse. *Member:* California Writers Club.

WRITINGS: The Bishop Pattern, Morrow, 1963; *Miss Mac* (juvenile), Van Nostrand, 1963; (with Gen Kakacek) *Four Hands for Mercy* (juvenile), Van Nostrand, 1965; *The Omen*, Morrow, 1967.

WORK IN PROGRESS: Nonfiction, *Stroke: A Family Crisis*, completion expected in 1975.

*   *   *

DOMANSKA, Janina

PERSONAL: Born in Warsaw, Poland; came to U.S. in 1952, naturalized citizen, 1964; daughter of Wladyslaw (an engineer) and Jadwiga (a writer, maiden name, Muszynska) Domanski; married Jerzy Laskowski (a writer), December 22, 1953. *Education:* Academy of Fine Arts, Warsaw, Poland, diploma, 1939. *Home and office:* 3 Sweetcake Mountain Road, New Fairfield, Conn.

CAREER: Artist and illustrator. Lived in Italy, 1946-51, teaching at Academy of Fine Arts, Rome, and exhibiting at Roman Foundation of Fine Ats Show and at the International Exposition in Genoa; came to United States in 1952, and exhibited at one-man shows in the New York area, 1957, 1959. Paintings owned by Warsaw's Museum of Modern Art and private galleries in Rome, Italy. *Awards, honors: The Golden Seed* was exhibited in the American Institute of Graphic Arts Children's Book Show, 1962, and received first place certificate from the Printing Industries of Metropolitan New York, 1963; *The Coconut Thieves* was a prize book in the *New York Herald Tribune* Children's Book Festival, 1964, was listed as a notable children's book of 1964 by the American Library Association, and was exhibited in the American Institute of Graphic Arts Children's Book Show, 1964; *If All the Seas Were One Sea*, was listed as a notable children's book of 1971, by the American Library Association, and was an Honor Book for the Caldecott Medal, 1972.

WRITINGS—All self-illustrated: (Translator from the Polish) Maria Konopnicka, *The Golden Seed*, adapted by Catharine Fournier, Scribner, 1962; (translator from the Polish) *The Coconut Thieves*, adapted by Catharine Fournier, Scribner, 1964; (adapter) *Why So Much Noise?*, Harper, 1964; *Palmiero and the Orge*, MacMillan, 1967; *Look, There is a Turtle Flying*, Macmillan, 1968; (adapter) *The Turnip*, Macmillan, 1969; *Marilka*, Macmillan, 1970; *If All the Seas Were One Sea*, Macmillan, 1971; *I Saw a Ship A-Sailing* (Junior Literary Guild Selection), Macmillan, 1972; (adapter) *Little Red Hen*, Macmillan, 1973; *What Do You See?*, Macmillan, 1974.

Illustrator: Alma R. Reck, *Clocks Tell the Time*, Scribner, 1960; Dorothy Kunhardt, *Gas Station Gus*, Harper, 1961; Natalie Savage Carlson, *Song of the Lop-Eared Mule*, Harper, 1961; Astrid Lindgren, *Mischevious Meg*, Viking, 1962; Aileen Fisher, *I Like Weather*, Crowell, 1963; Mara Kay, *In Place of Katia*, Scribner, 1963; Sally P. Johnson, *Harper Book of Prince's*, Harper, 1964; Ruth Tooze, *Nikkos of the Pink Pelican*, Viking, 1964; Babette Deutsch and Avram Yarmolinsky, editors, *More Tales of Faraway Folk*, Harper, 1964; Deutsch and Yarmolinsky, *Steel Flea*, Harper, 1964; Bernice Kohn, *Light*, Coward, 1965; Dorothy Hogue, *The Black Heart of Indri*, Scribner, 1966; Eric P. Kelly, *Trumpeter of Krakow*, Macmillan, 1966; Jerzy Laskowski, *The Dragon Liked Smoked Fish*, Seabury, 1967; Laskowski, *Master of the Royal Cats*, Seabury, 1967; Elizabeth Coatsworth, *Under the Green Willow*, Macmillan, 1971; Edward Lear, *Whizz!*, Macmillan, 1973. Drawings have appeared in *Harper's*, *Reporter*, and other magazines.†

* * *

DOMMERMUTH, William P. 1925-

PERSONAL: Surname is pronounced *Dah*-mer-myooth; born June 29, 1925, in Chicago, Ill.; son of Peter R. (an office manager) and Gertrude (Schnell) Dommermuth; married Joan Hasty, June 6, 1959; children: Karin, Margaret, Jean. *Education:* University of Iowa, B.A., 1948; Northwestern University, Ph.D., 1964. *Politics:* Democrat. *Religion:* Roman Catholic. *Office:* Department of Marketing, Southern Illinois University, Carbondale, Ill. 62901.

CAREER: Sears, Roebuck & Co., Chicago, Ill., copywriter, 1949-51, sales manager, 1951-58; Syracuse University, Syracuse, N.Y., director of special programs, 1958-59; University of Texas, Austin, assistant professor, 1961-66, associate professor of marketing, 1966-67; University of Iowa, Iowa City, associate professor of business administration, 1967-68; Southern Illinois University, Carbondale, professor of marketing, 1968—, chairman of department, 1972—. *Member:* American Marketing Association, Phi Beta Kappa.

WRITINGS: The Road to the Top, Bureau of Business Research, University of Texas, 1965; (with Jerome B. Kernan) *Promotion: An Introductory Analysis*, McGraw, 1970; (compiler with R. Clifton Andersen) *Distribution Systems*, Appleton, 1972; (co-author) *Modern Marketing*, Random House, 1975; *The Use of Sampling in Marketing Research*, American Marketing Association, 1975. Contributor to professional journals.

DONAGAN, Barbara (Galley) 1927-

PERSONAL: Born October 28, 1927, in Adelaide, Australia; daughter of William Hubert (an engineer) and Doris (Stappard) Galley; married Alan Donagan (a professor of philosophy), August 18, 1951. *Education:* University of Melbourne, B.A., 1948; University of Minnesota, M.A., 1961.

WRITINGS: (Editor with husband, Alan Donagan) *Philosophy of History*, Macmillan, 1965.†

* * *

DONAHOE, Bernard (Frances) 1932-

PERSONAL: Born March 16, 1932, in Madison, Wis.; son of John Stephen (a chain store employee) and May (Sullivan) Donahoe. *Education:* University of Notre Dame, A.B., 1955, M.A., 1958, Ph.D., 1965. *Home:* Columba Hall, Notre Dame, Ind. 46556.

CAREER: Roman Catholic religious, member of Brothers of Holy Cross (C.S.C.). Cathedral High School, Indianapolis, Ind., teacher and director of studies, 1957-61; St. Joseph Novitiate, Rolling Prairie, Ind., master of novices, 1964-68; St. Mary's College and Holy Cross Junior College, South Bend, Ind., professor of history, 1968—. University of Notre Dame, South Bend, Ind., visiting lecturer, 1966, 1971-72. *Member:* American Historical Association, Association of American Historians.

WRITINGS: Public Plans and Private Dangers: The Story of F.D.R.'s Third Nomination, University of Notre Dame Press, 1966.

Juvenile biographies; all published by Dujarie Press: *Where Roams the River*, 1958; *Patriot in Purple*, 1959; *Stars on My Shoulder*, 1960; *Fold It Gently*, 1960; *Up From the Streets*, 1960; *The Voice that Shook the Windows*, 1960. Contributor to *Review of Politics*.

WORK IN PROGRESS: Research on the intellectual evolution of American Catholicism in the twentieth century.

* * *

DONAHUE, Francis J. 1917-

PERSONAL: Born November 21, 1917, in Chicago, Ill.; son of Frank J. and Agnes (Danaher) Donahue; married Cecilia Osta (a librarian), August 20, 1947; children: Teresita. *Education:* University of Omaha, B.A., 1941; University of Wisconsin, M.A., 1942; Columbia University, graduate study, 1946-48; University of Southern California, Ph.D., 1965. *Office:* California State University, Long Beach, Calif.

CAREER: City College (now City College of the City University of New York), New York, N.Y., instructor, 1947-48; U.S. Merchant Marine Academy, Kings Point, N.Y., assistant professor, 1948-54; U.S. Information Agency, cultural attache in Havana, Cuba, and Caracas, Venezuela, 1954-60; California State University, Long Beach, professor of Spanish and Latin American literature, 1960—. *Military service:* U.S. Navy, Intelligence, 1942-46. *Member:* Academia Cubana de la Lengua (Havana; corresponding member), Phi Beta Kappa. *Awards, honors:* Commendable Service Award, 1956, and Meritorious Service Award, 1959, both from U.S. Information Agency.

WRITINGS: Washington Irving (in Spanish), Embajada de los Estados Unidos de America (Havana), 1958; *The Dramatic World of Tennessee Williams*, Ungar, 1964; *Diez Figuras Illustres de la Literatura Norteamericana*, Estades

(Madrid), 1965; *Leandro Fernandez de Moratin: El Si de las Ninas*, Plus Ultra (Buenos Aires), 1967; (contributor) Alexander De Conde, editor, *Student Activism*, Scribner, 1971; *Alfonso Sastre: Dramaturgo y Preceptista*, Plus Vetra (Buenos Aires), 1973. Contributor to *Antioch Review*, *Books Abroad*, *Western Humanities Review*, and Spanish language periodicals.

WORK IN PROGRESS: A book on contemporary theater, in Spanish.

* * *

DONAHUE, George T. 1911-

PERSONAL: Born February 22, 1911, in Jersey City, N.J.; son of Robert Frederick and Anna (Egar) Donahue; married Anna E. Nead; children: Sharon. *Education:* Seton Hall College (now University), B.A., 1932; New Jersey State Teachers College (now Kean College of New Jersey), M.A., 1934; Hofstra University, graduate study, 1959; New York University, Ed.D., 1963. *Office:* 207 East Buffalo St., Milwaukee, Wis. 53202.

CAREER: High school teacher, then guidance director, 1941-43; New York State Education Department, Albany, supervisor, Bureau of Guidance, 1943-51; Brooklyn Community College, Brooklyn, N.Y., assistant director, 1951-54; Elmont (N.Y.) public schools, junior high school principal, 1954-66, assistant superintendent of Union Free School District 16, 1966; New Rochelle (N.Y.) City School District, assistant superintendent, 1966—. New York State Education Department, member of advisory board, Division of Pupil Personnel Services. National Hadassah, member of advisory board on youth services; West Nassau Mental Health Clinic, president of advisory board, 1963-64. *Military service:* U.S. Navy; became lieutenant commander. *Member:* National Education Association, New York State Teachers Association. *Awards, honors:* Research grants from National Institute of Mental Health.

WRITINGS: (With Sol Nichtern) *Teaching the Troubled Child*, Free Press, 1965. Author or co-author of research reports on childhood schizophrenics and other emotionally disturbed children.†

* * *

DONELSON, Irene W(itmer) 1913-

PERSONAL: Born March 5, 1913, in Placerville, Calif.; daughter of John H. (a pharmacist) and Emma (Frechette) Witmer; married Kenneth W. Donelson (an attorney), July 25, 1937; children: Carol Ann, Richard Kenneth. *Education:* University of California, Berkeley, A.A., 1932; studied at Sacramento Junior College (now Sacramento City College), 1933-34, McGeorge College of Law (now McGeorge School of Law, University of the Pacific), 1949-51. *Politics:* Republican. *Religion:* Protestant. *Home:* 2525 H St., Sacramento, Calif. 95816. *Office:* Suite 814, Forum Building, Sacramento, Calif. 95814.

CAREER: Hale's (department store), Sacramento, Calif., advertising copywriter, 1934-37; free-lance radio scriptwriter, 1934-37; Breuner's (home furnishings), Sacramento, Calif., advertising copywriter, 1939-41; Kenneth W. Donelson (attorney), Sacramento, Calif., legal secretary, 1950-55, law clerk and office manager, 1955—. Free-lance writer. *Member:* Authors League of America, Authors Guild, Society of Magazine Writers, American Humane Association (children's division), League of Women Voters, California Writers' Club (president of Sacramento branch, 1962-63;

director of Berkeley branch, 1962-63, and Sacramento branch, 1963-64), California Historical Society, Commonwealth Club of California (San Francisco), Sacramento County Historical Society, Sacramento Book Collectors Club. *Awards, honors:* "A Woman with a View" Award, *Sacramento Union*, 1972.

WRITINGS: (With husband, Kenneth W. Donelson) *When You Need A Lawyer*, Doubleday, 1964; (with K. W. Donelson) *How to Handle Your Legal Problems*, Doubleday, 1965; (with K. W. Donelson) *Married Today, Single Tomorrow: Marriage Breakup and the Law*, Doubleday, 1969; (with K. W. Donelson) *Your Child and the Law*, Doubleday, 1975. Contributor of more than fifty articles to magazines, some authored with husband.

WORK IN PROGRESS: A nonfiction book in collaboration with husband.

SIDELIGHTS: When You Need A Lawyer was syndicated for publication in New York, Los Angeles, and other cities. *Avocational interests:* Public speaking, early California history, music, and collecting rare books.

* * *

DONELSON, Kenneth W(ilber) 1910-

PERSONAL: Born August 5, 1910, in Portland, Ore.; son of Daniel August (a salesman, broker, and promoter) and Charlotte (Wilber) Donelson; married Irene Witmer (a writer and office manager), July 25, 1937; children: Carol Ann, Richard Kenneth. *Education:* Oregon State University, B.S., 1933; McGeorge College of Law (now McGeorge School of Law, University of the Pacific), LL.B. (with distinction), 1940. *Politics:* Republican. *Religion:* Protestant. *Home:* 2525 H St., Sacramento, Calif. 95816. *Office:* Suite 814, Forum Building, Sacramento, Calif. 95814.

CAREER: State of California, Sacramento, supervising auditor, Board of Equalization, 1935-43, referee, Personnel Board, 1943-45; admitted to California bar, 1940; general practice of law, Sacramento, Calif., 1945—. Free-lance writer in collaboration with wife, 1960—. Director of Sacramento Estate Planning Council, 1959. *Member:* American Bar Association, Toastmasters International, American Judicature Society, Association of Trial Lawyers of America, National Council of Juvenile Court Judges (associate member), California Bar Association, Society of California Accountants, California Writers' Club (president of Sacramento branch, 1966-67), Sacramento Book Collectors Club (president, 1958), Sacramento County Historical Society (vice-president, 1959), Sigma Nu, Commonwealth Club of California, Sacramento Torch Club, Elks Club.

WRITINGS: (With wife, Irene Donelson) *When You Need A Lawyer*, Doubleday, 1964; (with Irene Donelson) *How to Handle Your Legal Problems*, Doubleday, 1965; (with Irene Donelson) *Married Today, Single Tomorrow: Marriage Breakup and the Law*, Doubleday, 1969; *Your Child and the Law*, Doubleday, 1975. Author of magazine articles in collaboration with wife.

WORK IN PROGRESS: A nonfiction book.

AVOCATIONAL INTERESTS: Music, photography, rare-book collecting, public speaking, parliamentary procedure, communication theory and history.

* * *

DONNITHORNE, Audrey 1922-

PERSONAL: Born November 27, 1922, in Santai Sze-chuan, China; daughter of Vyvyan Henry (an Anglican clergyman) and Gladys (Ingram) Donnithorne. *Education:* West China Union University, student, 1941-42; Somerville College, Oxford, B.A., 1948, M.A., 1951. *Religion:* Catholic. *Office:* Research School of Pacific Studies, Australian National University, Canberra A.C.T. 2600, Australia.

CAREER: University College, University of London, London, England, lecturer in department of political economy, 1951-66, reader in Chinese economic studies, 1966-68; Australian National University, Canberra, professorial fellow, 1969——.

WRITINGS: (With G. C. Allen) *Western Enterprise in Far Eastern Economic Enterprise: China and Japan*, Allen & Unwin, 1954; (with G. C. Allen) *Western Enterprise in Indonesia and Malaya*, Allen & Unwin, 1957; *British Rubber Manufacturing*, Duckworth, 1958; *China's Economic System*, Praeger, 1967. Contributor to *Pacific Affairs, World Today, China Quarterly, Soviet Studies*, and other journals.

SIDELIGHTS: Ms. Donnithorne speaks and reads Chinese.

*   *   *

DONOGHUE, Denis 1928-

PERSONAL: Born December 1, 1928, in Tullow, Ireland; son of Denis (a policeman) and Johanna (O'Neill) Donoghue; married Frances P. Rutledge, December 1, 1951; children: David, Helen, Celia, Hugh, Mark, Barbara, Stella, Emma. *Education:* National University of Ireland, B.A., 1950, M.A., 1953, Ph.D., 1956. *Religion:* Roman Catholic. *Home and office:* University College, Dublin, Ireland.

CAREER: Irish government, Department of Finance, Dublin, administrative officer, 1950-54; National University of Ireland, Dublin, college lecturer, 1954-65; Cambridge University, Cambridge, England, fellow of King's College, 1965; University College, Dublin, Ireland, professor of English and American literature, 1966——. Visiting scholar, University of Pennsylvania, 1963-64; teacher of courses at Harvard University, University of California, Los Angeles, and University of Edinburgh; director of Yeats International Summer School, 1960. Member of board of Abbey Theatre, Dublin. *Awards, honors:* American Council of Learned Societies fellowship, 1963-64.

WRITINGS: The Third Voice, Princeton University Press, 1959; (editor) *The Integrity of Yeats*, Mercier Press, 1964; *Connoisseurs of Chaos*, Macmillan, 1965; (editor with J. R. Mulryne) *An Honoured Guest*, Edward Arnold, 1965; *Jonathan Swift: A Critical Introduction*, Cambridge University Press, 1967; *The Ordinary Universe*, Macmillan, 1969; (editor and transcriber) *Memoirs: W. B. Yeats*, Macmillan, 1972; *Thieves of Fire*, Oxford University Press, 1974. Music critic, *Irish Times*, 1957. Contributor to *New Statesman, Hudson Review, Sewanee Review*, and other journals in America, England, and Ireland.

WORK IN PROGRESS: A study of imagination in literary theory and practice.

SIDELIGHTS: Donoghue told *CA:* "Primarily interested, as a literary critic, in the involvement of attitudes and values in the otherwise 'pure' world of literature."

*   *   *

DONOUGHUE, Bernard 1934-

PERSONAL: Born September 8, 1934, in Northampton-shire, England; son of T. J. Donoughue; married Carol Goodman (a television writer), 1959. *Education:* Lincoln College, Oxford, B.A. (first class honors), 1957, D.Phil., 1960. *Politics:* Democratic Socialist. *Religion:* Agnostic. *Home:* 7 Brookfield Park, London N.W. 5, England.

CAREER: Economist, London, England, editorial writer, 1957-60; *Sunday Times*, London, news reporter, 1960; *Sunday Telegraph*, London, editorial writer, 1960-62; Political and Economic Planning, London, senior research officer, 1961-63; London School of Economics and Political Science, University of London, senior lecturer in politics, 1963-74, senior policy advisor to the Prime Minister, 1974——. United Kingdom Sports Council, member, 1964——. *Member:* Political Studies Association, Fabian Society (executive, 1964——). *Awards, honors:* Henry Fellow at Harvard University, 1958-59.

WRITINGS: (Editor) *Oxford Poetry, 1956*, Fantasy Press, 1956; *Trade Unions in a Changing Society*, Political and Economic Planning, 1963; *British Politics and the American Revolution*, Macmillan (London), 1964, St. Martin's, 1965; (with W. T. Rodgers) *The People into Parliament*, Viking, 1966; *Herbert Morrison: Portrait of a Politician*, Weidenfeld & Nicolson, 1974.

WORK IN PROGRESS: British Politics from Churchill to Wilson, 1940-70, completion expected in 1978.

*   *   *

DONOVAN, Robert Alan 1921-

PERSONAL: Born September 27, 1921, in Chicago, Ill.; son of John E. (a banker) and Dorothy (Dickey) Donovan; married Hope Taussig, September 15, 1942; children: Faith, Peter, Brian. *Education:* University of Chicago, Ph.B., 1948, M.A., 1950; Washington University, St. Louis, Mo., Ph.D., 1953. *Home:* El Retiro, State Farm Rd., Guilderland, N.Y. *Office:* State University of New York, Albany, Albany, N.Y.

CAREER: Cornell University, Ithaca, N.Y., instructor, 1953-57, assistant professor of English, 1957-62; State University of New York, Albany, professor of English, 1962——. *Military service:* U.S. Army, 1942-46; served in England, France, and Germany; became sergeant. *Member:* Modern Language Association of America, American Association of University Professors, Phi Beta Kappa. *Awards, honors:* State University of New York Research Foundation grant, 1964, 1966, and 1972.

WRITINGS: The Shaping Vision: Imagination in the English Novel from Defoe to Dickens, Cornell University Press, 1966. Contributor of articles and reviews to literary and historical journals.

WORK IN PROGRESS: A study of the image of the hero in Victorian literature.

SIDELIGHTS: Most of Donovan's serious writing is done in a one-room cabin on an island in Georgian Bay, without benefit of electricity, plumbing, or telephone.

*   *   *

DOREY, T(homas) A(lan) 1921-

PERSONAL: Born March 23, 1921, in London, England, son of Edgar Alex (a judge) and Olive Kathleen (Giffard) Dorey; married Joan Ailsa Price, December 21, 1944; children: Richard Philippe, Caroline Julia. *Education:* Attended Victoria College, Jersey, Channel Islands, 1930-38; University of Exeter, 1938-39; Merton College, Oxford,

B.A., and M.A., 1946. *Politics:* Conservative. *Religion:* Anglican. *Home:* La Maison Brulee, St. John, Jersey, Channel Islands. *Office:* Judicial Greffe, Royal Court, Jersey, Channel Islands.

CAREER: Cardiff High School for Boys, Cardiff, Wales, assistant master, 1948-51; lecturer in Latin at University College of the West Indies, Kingston, Jamaica, and inspector of schools, Jamaica, 1952-54; University of Sheffield, Sheffield, England, lecturer in Latin, 1954-57; University of Birmingham, Birmingham, England, senior lecturer in Latin, 1957-69. Barrister at law, Gray's Inn, 1958; Royal Court of Jersey, advocate, 1958, judicial greffier, 1972—. Member of Leamington Borough Council, 1959-69. Mayor of Royal Leamington Spa, 1965-66. *Military service:* Royal Air Force, staff navigation instructor, 1940-46; became flying officer. *Member:* Society for Promotion of Roman Studies (council, 1964-67), Leamington Conservative Association (chairman, 1959-62). *Awards, honors:* Ph.D., University of Birmingham, 1959.

WRITINGS: (Editor) *Studies in Latin Literature: Cicero*, Routledge & Kegan Paul, 1964, published as *Cicero*, Basic Books, 1965; (compiler with Allison Leon) *The Norman Kings* (medieval Latin reader), Mason Publications, 1964; (editor and contributor) *Latin Historians*, Basic Books, 1966—; (editor and contributor) *Latin Biography*, Basic Books, 1967; (editor) Titus Livius, *Livy XXIX*, Kenneth Mason, 1968; (editor and contributor) *Tacitus*, Basic Books, 1969; (editor and contributor) *Erasmus*, University of New Mexico Press, 1970; (editor) *Livy XXI-XXII*, Teubner, 1971; (editor) *Livy*, Routledge & Kegan Paul, 1971; (with D. R. Dudley) *Rome Against Carthage*, Secker & Warburg, 1971, Doubleday, 1972; (editor) *Livy XXXIII*, University Tutorial Press, 1972; *Empire and Aftermath*, Routledge & Kegan Paul, 1975. Contributor to *Penguin Companion to Classical, Oriental, and African Literature* and to classical and other learned journals.

WORK IN PROGRESS: Editing an edition of *Livy XXIII-XXV* for Teubner.

*　　*　　*

DORFMAN, Robert 1916-

PERSONAL: Born October 27, 1916, in New York, N.Y.; son of Samuel Maurice (a businessman) and Mina (Gordon) Dorfman; married Nancy Schelling (an economist), November 6, 1949; children: Peter J., Anne E. *Education:* Columbia University, B.A., 1936, M.A., 1937; University of California, Berkeley, Ph.D., 1950. *Home:* 81 Kilburn Rd., Belmont, Mass. 02178. *Office:* Littauer Center 325, Harvard University, Cambridge, Mass. 02138.

CAREER: U.S. Government, Washington, D.C., statistician, Bureau of Labor Statistics, 1939-41, economist, Office of Price Administration, 1941-43, operations analyst, Department of the Air Force, 1943-46, 1949-50; University of California, Berkeley, associate professor of economics, 1950-55; Harvard University, Cambridge, Mass., professor of economics, 1955—. Consultant to RAND Corp., 1950—, Executive Office of the President, 1961-62, and to International Bank for Reconstruction and Development, Agency for International Development, and Brookings Institution.

MEMBER: American Economic Association (member of council, 1969-72), Royal Economic Society, Econometric Society (council, 1961-64), American Association for the Advancement of Science (fellow), Institute of Management Sciences (chairman of council, 1966), Institute of Mathematical Statistics, Operations Research Society of America

(council, 1959-62), American Statistical Association. *Awards, honors:* Fellow, Center for Advanced Study in the Behavioral Sciences, 1960-61; Ford Foundation faculty research fellow, University of California, 1966; Guggenheim prize fellow, 1970-71.

WRITINGS: Linear Programming and the Theory of the Firm, University of California Press, 1951; (with P. O. Steiner) *Economic Status of the Aged*, University of California Press, 1956; (with P. Samuelson and R. Solow) *Linear Programming and Economic Analysis*, McGraw, 1958; (with A. Maass and others) *Design of Water Resources Systems*, Harvard University Press, 1960; *The Price System*, Prentice-Hall, 1964; *Price and Markets*, Prentice-Hall, 1967; (with H. D. Jacoby and others) *Models for Managing Regional Water Quality*, Harvard University Press, 1972; (with wife, Nancy S. Dorfman) *Economics of the Environment: Selected Readings*, Norton, 1972. Contributor of scholarly papers to journals.

*　　*　　*

DORIAN, Marguerite

PERSONAL: Born in Bucharest, Rumania; came to United States, 1952; married Hugo Taussig. *Education:* Attended University of Bucharest and the Sorbonne, University of Paris; Brown University, M.Sc. *Residence:* Providence, R.I.

CAREER: Lived in Paris, France, for several years. Writer and illustrator. *Member:* Sigma Xi. *Awards, honors:* Fellowship to Bread Loaf Writers' Conference, 1965; associate scholar, Radcliffe Institute for Independent Study, 1966-68.

WRITINGS: Ierbar (poems), Forum (Bucharest), 1946; *Le roi qui ne pouvait pas eternuer* (juvenile), Flammarion (Paris), 1954; self-illustrated) *When the Snow Is Blue* (juvenile), Lothrop, 1960; (self-illustrated) *The Alligator's Toothache* (juvenile), Lothrop, 1965; *A Ride on the Milky Way* (novel), Crown, 1967; *The Waterbearer* (novel) Macmillan, in press; *The Seasons*, Macmillan, in press. Contributor of short fiction to the *New Yorker*.

*　　*　　*

DORPALEN, Andreas 1911-

PERSONAL: Surname is pronounced Dor-*pay*-len; born May 2, 1911, in Berlin, Germany; now U.S. citizen; son of Georg and Alice (Kuczynski) Dorpalen; married Rose-Marie Mietusch, December 12, 1942; children: Peter, Bruce. *Education:* Attended University of Freiburg, 1929-30, and University of Munich, 1930; University of Bonn, Dr.jur., 1933. *Home:* 2040 Tremont Rd., Columbus, Ohio 43221. *Office:* Department of History, Ohio State University, Columbus, Ohio 43210.

CAREER: Columbia Encyclopedia, New York, N.Y., editorial assistant, 1938-42; Kenyon College, Gambier, Ohio, visiting assistant professor, 1943-44; St. Lawrence University, Canton, N.Y., visiting lecturer, 1944-46, associate professor, 1946-48, professor of history, 1948-58; Ohio State University, Columbus, professor of history, 1958—. *Member:* American Historical Association, American Association of University Professors, Conference Group on Central European History (chairman, 1972), Ohio Academy of History. *Awards, honors:* Guggenheim fellow, 1953-54; Institute for Advanced Study, Princeton, N.J., visiting member, 1953-54, 1969; Social Science Research Council and American Philosophical Society grants; honorable mention, Herbert Baxter Adams Prize of American

Historical Association, 1958, for *Heinrich von Treitschke*; honorable mention, Higby Prize of *Journal of Modern History*, 1962, for article on Gerhard Ritter.

WRITINGS: Heinrich von Treitschke, Yale University Press, 1957, reprinted, Kennikat, 1973; *Hindenburg and the Weimar Republic*, Princeton University Press, 1964; *Europe in the Twentieth Century*, Macmillan, 1968; (contributor) Theodore Schieder, editor, *Gesellshaft und Revolution*, Herder Verlag, 1973; (contributor) Bernd Faulenbach, editor, *Geschichtswissenshaft in Deutschland*, Beck Verlag, 1974. Contributor to historical journals. Editor, *Central European History*, 1974-76.

WORK IN PROGRESS: Marxism and History: East German Interpretations of German History, completion expected in 1977.

* * *

DOTY, Brant Lee 1921-

PERSONAL: Born October 23, 1921, in Bridgeport, Ill.; son of Corydon Lee (a minister) and Lula Bruce (MacRoberts) Doty; married Ruth Lois James (an accounting clerk), September 14, 1943; children: Elizabeth Joan, Sally Joice, Margaret Louise, Brant Lee, Jr., Timothy Lloyd. *Education:* Cincinnati Bible Seminary, A.B., 1943, M.A., 1951; graduate study at Alma College and University of Detroit; Michigan State University, Ph.D., 1969. *Politics:* "Uncommitted." *Home:* 6212 West Willow, Lansing, Mich. 48917. *Office:* Great Lakes Bible College, 6211 West Willow, Lansing, Mich. 48917.

CAREER: Clergyman of Church of Christ; Memorial Christian Church, Detroit, Mich., minister, 1944-53; Great Lakes Bible College, Lansing, Mich., dean and professor, 1953—. Member Lansing Citizens School Committee, 1965-66. *Member:* North American Christian Convention (member of executive committee), Mission Services Association (member of board of directors), Delta Alpha Tau.

WRITINGS: The Apostle Paul, Standard Publishing, 1964; *Numbers*, College & University Press, 1973. Contributor to religious journals.

SIDELIGHTS: Doty has a working knowledge of Greek, Hebrew, Latin, French, Old and Middle English, and Gothic. *Avocational interests:* Woodcarving, oil painting, flower gardening.

* * *

DOW, Neal 1906-

PERSONAL: Born April 23, 1906, in Exeter, N.H.; son of Albert N. (a forester) and Florence (Griffin) Dow; married Marie-Therese Liniere (a professor). *Education:* Kenyon College, A.B., 1928; Sorbonne, University of Paris, graduate study, 1926-27; University of Pennsylvania, A.M., 1933, Ph.D., 1938. *Religion:* Roman Catholic. *Home:* 2252 Cranford Rd., Durham, N.C. 27706. *Office:* Department of Languages, Duke University, Durham, N.C. 27706.

CAREER: Phillips Exeter Academy, Exeter, N.H., instructor in French, 1928-30; University of Pennsylvania, Philadelphia, instructor in Romance languages, 1930-32; Duke University, Durham, N.C., 1934—, started as instructor, professor of Romance languages, 1959-71, professor emeritus, 1971—. *Member:* American Association of Teachers of French (president, North Carolina chapter, 1964-65), Modern Language Association of America, American Association of University Professors, South Atlantic Modern Language Association.

WRITINGS: The Concept and Term: Nature in Montaigne's Essays, privately printed, 1940; (with Gifford Davis) *French in Review*, Holt, 1940; *Review in French*, Holt, 1956, revised edition with *Workbook*, 1965; (with Patrick Vincent) *Contes a Lire et a Raconter*, Ronald, 1960; (with Anne-Marie Despres Bryan) *A la decouverte de la France, Themes de conversations vivantes*, Van Nostrand, 1970.

* * *

DOWD, Laurence P(hillips) 1914-

PERSONAL: Born October 21, 1914, at Fort Monroe, Va.; son of William S. (an army officer and diplomat) and Julia M. (Phillips) Dowd; married Juliet I. Rudolph, September 7, 1938; children: William L. (deceased), Richard S., Judith I. *Education:* University of Washington, Seattle, B.A. (magna cum laude), 1938; University of Hawaii, M.A., 1940; University of Michigan, Ph.D., 1954. *Religion:* Protestant. *Home:* 3047 Hillside Dr., Burlingame, Calif. 94010. *Office:* San Francisco State University, San Francisco, Calif. 94132.

CAREER: University of Michigan, Ann Arbor, instructor in economics, 1946-50; University of Washington, Seattle, associate professor of international business, 1950-55; Kobe University, Kobe, Japan, Fulbright lecturer on business administration, 1955-57; University of Michigan, Ann Arbor, lecturer in School of Business Administration, 1957-60; San Francisco State University, San Francisco, Calif., professor of world business and director of Center for World Business, 1960—. Visiting professor at University of Oregon, 1969-70, Kinki University, Osaka, Japan, spring, 1974. Consultant on trade promotion activities in Far East to Port of Seattle; member of San Francisco Regional Export Expansion Council, 1962-74. Director of programs, Association Internationale des Etudiants en Sciences Economiques et Commerciales, Japan, and University of Stockholm Institute of Physics, Stockholm, Sweden, 1972-74. *Military service:* U.S. Army, Military Intelligence, 1941-45; became major.

MEMBER: American Economic Association, American Marketing Association (board of Northern California chapter, 1962—), World Affairs Council of Northern California, World Trade Association of San Francisco, Phi Beta Kappa, Pan Xenia, Beta Gamma Sigma, Phi Kappa Phi. *Awards, honors:* Meritorious Award 'from Pan American Airways for furtherance of trade expansion among nations of the world.

WRITINGS: (With Toro) *The St. Lawrence Seaway, Practical Aspects for Michigan Industry*, Bureau of Business Research, University of Michigan, 1961; (editor) *The European Economic Community: Implications for Michigan Business*, Bureau of Business Research, University of Michigan, 1961; (contributor) *Comparative Marketing: Wholesaling in Fifteen Countries*, Robert Bartels, editor, Irwin, 1963; *Principles of World Business*, Allyn & Bacon, 1965; (contributor) *Marketing Manager's Handbook*, Steuart H. Britt, editor, Dartnell, 1973. Consulting editor, *Journal of Marketing*, 1958-74.

WORK IN PROGRESS: A study on the impact of international trade on the economy of northern California; research for a book on philosophies and methods of European business management; study of opportunities and problems in international joint ventures for medium-size firms.

SIDELIGHTS: Dowd lived in Tokyo, 1931-34, 1955-57, spring, 1974. He is competent in Japanese.

DOWNEY, Lawrence William (Lorne) 1921-

PERSONAL: Born December 7, 1921, in Saskatchewan, Canada. *Education:* University of British Columbia, B.A., 1947; University of Washington, Seattle, graduate study, 1955-56; University of Chicago, Ph.D., 1959. *Office:* Human Resources Research Council, 11507 74th Avenue, Edmonton, Alberta, Canada.

CAREER: Teacher, principal, and supervising principal in British Columbia, 1946-54, 1956-57; University of Chicago, Chicago, Ill., assistant professor, 1959-60; University of Alberta, Edmonton, associate professor, 1960-62, professor of educational administration and head of department of secondary education, 1962-65; University of British Columbia, Vancouver, professor of educational administration and chairman of department, beginning, 1965; Human Resources Research Council, Edmonton, Alberta, director, 1968—. Visiting summer professor, University of California, Berkeley, 1963; academic consultant, West Kootenay Regional College, 1964-65. Consultant to Canadian Education Association, superintendents, 1960-65, Studies of Research Organizations, and Canadian Department of Labour; project director, Alberta School Trustees Association Secondary School Study, 1964-65.

WRITINGS: The Task of Public Education, Midwest Administration Center, 1960; *Leadership Training for Educational Administrators,* University of Alberta Press, 1961; (editor) *The Social Sciences and Educational Administration,* University Council for Educational Administration and University of Alberta, 1962; (editor and contributor) *The Canadian Secondary School—An Appraisal and a Forecast,* Macmillan (Canada), 1963; (contributor) Donald Leu, editor, *Common and Specialized Learnings for Different Administrative Positions,* University of Michigan Press, 1963; (contributor) John Wormsbecker, editor, *Symposium on Canadian Education,* Epsilon Delta Chapter of Phi Delta Kappa, 1963; (contributor) *Evaluation: A Function of Administration,* Department of Educational Administration, University of Alberta, 1964; *The Secondary Phase of Education,* Blaisdell, 1965; *The Small High School,* Alberta School Trustees Association, 1965; *Alberta, 1971: Toward a Social Audit,* Human Resources Research Council, 1972. Contributor to the proceedings of professional societies and to scholarly journals.†

*   *   *

DOWNIE, N(orville) M(organ) 1910-

PERSONAL: Born December 13, 1910, in Troy, N.Y.; son of James N. (a businessman) and Elizabeth (Morgan) Downie; married Johanna C. Munson, April 2, 1942; children: Elizabeth, Johanna (deceased), James, Paul. *Education:* St. Lawrence University, B.S., 1932, M.A., 1933; Syracuse University, Ph.D., 1948. *Politics:* Democrat. *Home:* 505 Lingle Ter., Lafayette, Ind. 47901. *Office:* Department of Psychological Sciences, Purdue University, Lafayette, Ind. 47907.

CAREER: Robert College, Istanbul, Turkey, instructor in biology, 1936-39; high school teacher, New York State, 1939-42; Syracuse University, Syracuse, N.Y., instructor in psychology, 1946-48; Washington State University, Pullman, assistant professor, later associate professor of psychology, 1948-51; Purdue University, Lafayette, Ind., associate professor, 1951-59, professor of psychology, 1959—, associate head of department, 1971—. Consultant to U.S. Veterans Administration. *Military service:* U.S. Army Air Forces, 1942-45; became technical sergeant. *Member:*

American Association for the Advancement of Science (fellow), American Psychological Association (fellow), Midwestern Psychological Association, Phi Beta Kappa, Sigma Xi.

WRITINGS: Fundamentals of Measurement: Techniques and Practices, Oxford University Press, 1958, 2nd edition, 1967; (with R. W. Heath) *Basic Statistical Methods,* Harper, 1959, 4th edition, 1974; (with E. C. Cottle) *Procedures and Preparation for Counseling,* Prentice-Hall, 1960, 2nd edition, 1970; *Types of Test Scores,* Houghton, 1968. Contributor to education and psychology journals.

*   *   *

DRACHKOVITCH, Milorad M. 1921-

PERSONAL: Surname is pronounced Drash-ko-vich; born November 8, 1921, in Belgrade, Yugoslavia; came to U.S., 1958; naturalized U.S. citizen, 1965; son of Milorad Timotije (a statesman) and Jovanka (Milanovich) Drachkovitch; married Jelena Dzigurski, August 5, 1956 (divorced, 1972); children: Radoye (son), Alexandra. *Education:* University of Geneva, B.A., 1949, Ph.D., 1953; College of Europe, Bruges, Belgium, Diploma in Higher European Studies, 1952. *Home:* 724 Arrastradero Rd., Palo Alto, Calif. 94306. *Office:* The Hoover Institution, Stanford University, Stanford, Calif. 94305.

CAREER: College of Europe, Bruges, Belgium, director of studies, 1956-58; University of California, Berkeley, visiting assistant professor of political science, 1959-60; Harvard University, Cambridge, Mass., fellow of Russian Research Center, 1960-61; Stanford University, Stanford, Calif., lecturer in department of political science, 1961-69, senior fellow and director of archives of the Hoover Institution on War, Revolution and Peace, 1961—. Consultant to International Security Agency of U.S. Department of Defense, Washington, D.C., 1970—. Member of foreign policy advisory group to Republican presidential candidate, 1968. *Member:* American Political Science Association, American Association for the Advancement of Slavic Studies.

WRITINGS: Les Socialismes francais et allemand et le probleme de la guerre, 1870-1914, E. Droz, 1953; *De Karl Marx a Leon Blum: La Crise de la social-democratie,* E. Droz, 1954; *United States Aid to Yugoslavia and Poland: Analysis of a Controversy,* American Enterprise Institute for Public Policy Research, 1963; (editor) *Marxism in the Modern World,* Stanford University Press, for the Hoover Institution, 1965; (editor and contributor) *The Revolutionary Internationals: 1864-1943,* Stanford University Press, for the Hoover Institution, 1966; (editor) *Marxist Ideology in the Contemporary World: Its Appeals and Paradoxes,* Praeger, for the Hoover Institution, 1966; (editor with Branko Lazitch) *The Comintern: Historical Highlights,* Praeger, 1966; (editor) *Yearbook of International Communist Affairs,* Stanford University Press, 1966; (editor, and author of introduction) *Fifty Years of Communism in Russia,* Pennsylvania State University Press, 1968; (with Lazitch) *Lenin and the Comintern,* volume I, Hoover Institution Press, 1972. Contributor to *Encyclopedia Americana Annual,* and of about forty articles to periodicals.

WORK IN PROGRESS: Two books, *History of the Communist Party of Yugoslavia,* completion expected in 1976, and Volume II of the book with Lazitch, *Lenin and the Comintern.*

SIDELIGHTS: Drachkovitch told *CA:* "As a historian and political scientist I have always been fascinated by the discrepancy of revolutionary promises and performances, particularly in our century. Although many books have been written on this or a similar topic, I hope to be able to make a significant contribution to the never-ending elucidation of that crucial issue of our time." He added: "I am a kidney transplantee [of 1970]. To witness the ending of my natural life, and to continue to live and work quasi-normally owing to the miracle of modern medical science, is certainly the most extraordinary event in my existence."

*   *   *

DRAKE, Frank D(onald)   1930-

PERSONAL: Born May 28, 1930, in Chicago, Ill.; son of Richard Carvel (a chemical engineer) and Winifred Pearl (Thompson) Drake; married Elizabeth Buckner Bell, March 7, 1953; children: Stephen D., Richard P., Paul R. *Education:* Cornell University, B.E.P., 1952; Harvard University, M.A., 1956, Ph.D., 1958. *Home:* 121 Pine Tree Rd., Ithaca, N.Y. 14850. *Office:* Space Sciences Building, Cornell University, Ithaca, N.Y. 14850.

CAREER: Director of astronomical research group, Ewen-Knight, Corp., 1958; National Radio Astronomy Observatory, Green Bank, W.Va., scientist, 1958-63; Jet Propulsion Laboratory, Pasadena, Calif., chief of lunar and planetary sciences section, 1963-64; Cornell University, Ithaca, N.Y., associate professor, 1964-66, professor of astronomy, 1966—, chairman of department, 1968-71, associate director of Center for Radio Physics and Space Research, 1965—, director of Arecibo Ionosphere Observatory, 1966-68, director of National Astronomy and Ionosphere Center, 1971—. Consultant, Ryan Aeronautical Co., 1964—. *Military service:* U.S. Navy, 1952-55. *Member:* American Astronomical Society, International Astronomical Union, National Academy of Sciences, American Academy of Arts and Sciences (vice-president, 1972-73), Sigma Xi, Tau Beta Pi.

WRITINGS: Intelligent Life in Space, Macmillan, 1963. Contributor to *Astrophysical Journal, Science, Nature*, and other scientific publications.

*   *   *

DRAKE, Robert (Young, Jr.)   1930-

PERSONAL: Born October 20, 1930, in Ripley, Tenn.; son of Robert Young (a merchant and farmer) and Lillian (Wood) Drake. *Education:* Vanderbilt University, B.A., 1952, M.A., 1953; Yale University, M.A., 1954, Ph.D., 1955. *Religion:* Episcopalian. *Address:* Box 273, Ripley, Tenn. 38063. *Office:* Department of English, University of Tennessee, Knoxville, Tenn. 37916.

CAREER: University of Michigan, Ann Arbor, instructor in English, 1955-58; Northwestern University, Evanston, Ill., instructor in English, 1958-61; University of Texas, Austin, assistant professor of English, 1961-65; University of Tennessee, Knoxville, associate professor, 1965-73, professor of English, 1973—. *Member:* Modern Language Association of America, College English Association, Society for the Study of Southern Literature, South Atlantic Modern Language Association, Tennessee Folklore Society, Phi Beta Kappa. *Awards, honors:* Fiction award Annual Texas Writers Roundup, 1965 for *Amazing Grace*; research grants from Bollingen Foundation, Northwestern University, University of Tennessee, and Institute for Philosophical and Historical Studies.

WRITINGS: Amazing Grace (short stories), Chilton,

1965; *Flannery O'Connor*, Eerdmans, 1966; *The Writer and His Tradition*, University of Tennessee Publications Service Bureau, 1969; *The Single Heart* (short stories), Aurora Publications, 1971. Contributor of essays and reviews to literary and language journals.

WORK IN PROGRESS: More short stories and critical essays.

SIDELIGHTS: Drake told *CA:* "Never expected to write fiction. . . . Nobody could have been more surprised than I. My greatest experience [abroad] has been getting to know England, which I've been visiting every summer for some years."

*   *   *

DRAPER, Cena C(hristopher)   1907-

PERSONAL: Born October 17, 1907, in Warrensburg, Mo.; daughter of Marion Jackson and Tacy (Baile) Christopher; married Mont Clayton Draper, Jr.; children: Mont Clayton III. *Education:* Central Missouri State College (now University), student, two years; University of Missouri, B.A., 1931. *Address:* Stuart Yacht and Country Club, Stuart, Fla. 33494.

CAREER: Writer, mainly for children. Trails Regional Library, board member, 1957-66. *Member:* Missouri Press Women, Kappa Kappa Gamma. *Awards, honors:* First prize of Missouri Press Women for *Rim of the Ridge*; first prize in Kansas City Children's Playwriting Contest; Women's Centennial Honor Award, University of Missouri, 1968; Central Missouri State University Award for outstanding children's literature, 1969.

WRITINGS: Plays of Fancy, Row Peterson & Co., 1948; *Deep in the Dingel Dell*, Row Peterson & Co., 1951; *Ridge Willoughby*, Steck, 1952; *Papa Says* (adult novel), Liveright, 1956; *Children's Plays from Favorite Stories*, Plays, 1960; *Mother, the Overseer*, privately printed, 1962; *Rim of the Ridge*, Criterion, 1965; *Dandy and the Mystery of the Locked Room*, Independence Press, 1974. Author of shorter plays for children, five of them produced by Kansas City Children's Community Theatre.

*   *   *

DRAPER, (Ellinor) Elizabeth (Nancy)   1915-

PERSONAL: Born February 17, 1915, in Oundle, England; daughter of Ernest I. (a scientist, schoolmaster, and writer) and Ellinor Susannah (Edmonds) Lewis; married John Dalziel Wyndham Pearce (a medical practitioner), March 21, 1964; children: (previous marriage) Marie Elizabeth Jane Irving Draper. *Education:* Studied at University of Munich, 1932, and University of Hamburg, 1933. *Politics:* Eclectic. *Religion:* Roman Catholic. *Home:* 4 Hampstead Sq., London N.W. 3, England.

CAREER: Association of Special Libraries and Information Bureaux, London, England, assistant secretary, 1934; administrative posts in advertising and market research, London, England, 1935-40, and with Kent Education Committee, Maidstone, Kent, England, 1941-42; National Association for Mental Health, London, England, administrative officer in psychiatric after-care, in social services department, and finally assistant general secretary, 1942-47; Institute for the Study and Treatment of Delinquency, London, England, general secretary, 1947-52; Family Planning Association, London, England, researcher, 1960-63; Committee on Voluntary Workers in the Social Services, secretary, 1966-68. Assistant secretary, National Federation of Consumer Groups. *Member:* International Union for Child Welfare, Howard League for Penal Reform, International Planned Parenthood Federation, Consumer's Association, British-Italian Society (former secretary; honorary member), Caledonian Club (London).

WRITINGS: (Contributor) *Family Planning in the Sixties,* Family Planning Association (London), 1963; *Birth Control in the Modern World,* Penguin, 1965; (contributor) *Family Planning,* M. Pollock, editor, Bailliere, Tindall & Cassell, 1966. Contributor to *Focus* and *Times* (London).

SIDELIGHTS: Ms. Draper speaks French and German. *Avocational interests:* Art and architecture.

* * *

DRAPER, Hal 1914-

PERSONAL: Born September 19, 1914, in Brooklyn, N.Y.; married Anne Draper, July 7, 1939 (died March, 1973). *Education:* Brooklyn College, B.A., 1934. *Politics:* Socialist. *Religion:* None. *Home:* 846 Solano Ave., Albany, Calif. 94706.

CAREER: Editor, *The New International,* 1948-49, *Labor Action,* 1949-57; University of California, Berkeley, part-time librarian, 1960—. Independent Socialist Committee, Berkeley, Calif., chairman. *Awards, honors:* M.L.S., University of California, Berkeley, 1960.

WRITINGS: Introduction to Independent Socialism, Independent Socialist Press, 1963, 2nd edition, 1970; *Berkeley: The New Student Revolt,* Grove, 1965; *The Two Souls of Socialism,* Independent Socialist Press, 1966; (editor) *Karl Marx & Friedrich Engels: Articles in the New American Encyclopaedia,* Independent Socialist Press, 1969; (editor) *Marx and Engels: Writings on the Paris Commune,* Monthly Review Press, 1971. Member of editorial board, *New Politics* (quarterly), 1960-74.

* * *

DROWNE, Tatiana B(alkoff) 1913-

PERSONAL: Born November 19, 1913, in St. Petersburg (now Leningrad), Russia; daughter of Peter Serge (an engineer) and Zenaida (Bosniatskaia) Balkoff; married H. Russell Drowne, Jr., January 4, 1940 (died, 1967); married Charles Joseph Lipscomb, December 16, 1972; children: Tatiana Gillette Infante; stepchildren: H. Russell III, Bradley C., Lorraine Lipscomb (Mrs. Philip R. Roberts), C. Christopher Lipscomb. *Education:* Attended schools in New York, N.Y. *Politics:* Republican. *Religion:* Greek Orthodox. *Home:* 825 Fifth Ave., New York, N.Y. 10021. *Agent:* McIntosh & Otis, Inc., 18 East 41st St., New York, N.Y. 10017.

CAREER: Came to America with her father, who was attached to the last White Russian Embassy here. Projects for many years have been linked with the arts—writing and translating, including librettos for operas performed by Metropolitan Opera Co., and lyrics for popular songs; reviewing French, Russian, and other cultural films as a member of a special committee of National Board of Review of Motion Pictures, 1950—; translating; and lecturing on censorship in mass media. Trustee and governor of Goldovsky Opera Institute, 1964—. *Member:* Authors League of America, Colony Club (New York). *Awards, honors: New York Herald Tribune* Children's Spring Book Festival Honor Book Award, 1947, for *Treasure Trove of the Sun;* Boys' Clubs of America Junior Book Award, 1961, for *But Charlie Wasn't Listening.*

WRITINGS: (Translator) P. P. Ershov, *Little Magic Horse,* Macmillan, 1942; (translator) M. M. Prishvin, *Treasure Trove of the Sun,* Viking, 1947; (translator) O. Zhigalova, *Across the Green Past,* Regnery, 1952; *But Charlie Wasn't Listening,* Pantheon, 1960; *I Am From Siam,* Pantheon, 1961; *Take Wing,* Viking, 1963; (translator) V. Yurasov, *Parallax,* Norton, 1966.

Opera librettos: "Coq d'Or," 1942, "Fidelio," 1947, "Khovanschina," 1947 (all performed by Metropolitan Opera Co. and on radio); "Eugene Onegin," 1943, performed by New England Opera Co. and on radio.

* * *

DROZE, Wilmon Henry 1924-

PERSONAL: Surname rhymes with "hose"; born April 25, 1924, in Charleston, S.C.; son of Henry Stevens (a farmer) and Julia (Bluminburg) Droze; married Carolyn Jung, November 24, 1951; children: William Middleton, Wesley Rutledge. *Education:* North Texas State University, B.S., 1949, M.S., 1950; Vanderbilt University, Ph.D., 1960. *Politics:* Democrat. *Religion:* Presbyterian. *Home:* 1900 Hollyhill Lane, Denton, Tex. 76201. *Office:* Office of the Provost, University General Divisions, Texas Women's University, Box 22627, TWU Station, Denton, Tex. 76204.

CAREER: East Central State College, Ada, Okla., associate professor of history, 1957-61; assistant professor of history at East Carolina College, Greenville, N.C., 1961-62, and McNeese State College, Lake Charles, La., 1962-65; University of Texas, Arlington State College, Arlington, assistant professor of history, 1965-69; state librarian and archivist, Nashville, Tenn., 1969-71; Texas Women's University, Denton, associate professor of history and provost, 1971—. *Military service:* U.S. Army, 1943-46. *Member:* Organization of American Historians, American Historical Association, Agricultural History Association, Forest History Society, Western Historical Association, Southern Historical Association, Texas Historical Society, Texas Association of College Teachers.

WRITINGS: High Dams and Slack Waters: TVA Rebuilds a River, Louisiana State University Press, 1965; (with George Wolfskill and William E. Leuchtenberg) *Essays on the New Deal,* University of Texas Press, 1969. Contributor to historical journals.

WORK IN PROGRESS: A history of the afforestation of the American prairies and Great Plains, entitled *The Afforestation of the Great Plains.*

SIDELIGHTS: High Dams and Slack Waters was translated by the U.S. Information Agency for publication in Brazil and Mexico. Droze is competent in German and French. *Avocational interests:* Gardening, shop work, collecting books.

* * *

DRUMMOND, Kenneth H(erbert) 1922-

PERSONAL: Born January 19, 1922, in Riverside, Calif., son of Finlay Mackay (president of a manufacturing company) and Mary (Holland) Drummond; married Marion Emily Deane, May 14, 1955; children: Laurie Lynn, Finlay Bruce, Carter Holland. *Education:* Bates College, student, 1941-43; University of Arizona, B.S., 1949; Texas A&M University, graduate study, 1950-57. *Home:* 9104 Santayana Dr., Fairfax, Va. 22030. *Office:* Suite 910, 1875 Connecticut Ave., N.W., Washington, D.C. 20009.

CAREER: Scripps Institution of Oceanography, La Jolla, Calif., marine technician, 1949-50; Texas A&M University Research Foundation, College Station, senior scientist, oceanographic projects, 1950-52, 1953-57; U.S. Naval Oceanographic Office, senior scientist aboard "USS Sheldrake," 1952-53; Smithsonian Astrophysical Observatory, Cambridge, Mass., executive officer, Satellite Tracking Program, 1957-58, administrator in charge, Satellite Tracking Program, 1958-59, assistant director of observatory, 1959-60; University of California, San Diego, assistant to the chancellor, 1960-62; Texas Instruments, Inc., Science Services Division, Washington (D.C.) representative, 1962—. *Military service:* U.S. Naval Reserve, 1943; served in Pacific theater, 1944-46; became lieutenant commander.

MEMBER: American Association for the Advancement of Science (fellow), American Geophysical Union, American Astronomical Society, American Geochemical Society, American Society of Photogrammetry, American Astronautical Society, American Ordnance Association, National Ocean Industries Association (treasurer; member of board of directors), Explorers Club (fellow), Marine Technology Society (chairman of arrangements committee), National Space Club, Texas Academy of Sciences (fellow).

WRITINGS: (Editor with Charles A. Whitten) *Contemporary Geodesy*, National Academy of Sciences-National Research Council, 1959; (with Eloise Engle) *Sky Rangers*, Day, 1965. Co-author of classified reports on oceanography surveys, 1955.

WORK IN PROGRESS: Research on oceanography.

SIDELIGHTS: Drummond's travels cover much of the globe—Europe, South America, Mexico, southern Asia, West Indies, Europe, and most recently, a three month tour of the South Pacific. *Avocational interests:* Tennis (fourth ranking player in Southwest during college days), sailing, swimming, golf, music, and bridge.

*   *   *

DuBAY, William H.   1934-

PERSONAL: Born December 24, 1934, in Long Beach, Calif.; son of John Lewis (a sign painter) and Viola (Gauger) DuBay; married Mary Ellen Wall (a headmistress), August 10, 1968 (divorced, 1971). *Education:* Los Angeles College Junior Seminary, A.A., 1954; St. John's Seminary, Camarillo, Calif., B.A., 1960. *Politics:* Democrat. *Religion:* Humanist. *Address:* General Delivery, Ninilchik, Alaska 99639.

CAREER: Ordained Roman Catholic priest, 1960; served with six parishes in the Archdiocese of Los Angeles, 1960-66; consultant to Synanon House (a rehabilitation center for drug addicts), Santa Monica, Calif., 1966; Volunteers in Service to America (VISTA), Los Angeles, Calif., director of training program, 1967-71; Stonewall Inc., Seattle, Wash., co-founder and co-director, 1971-72; farmer and writer in Alaska, 1975—. Lecturer.

WRITINGS: The Human Church, Doubleday, 1966; (contributor) Claude A. Frazier, editor, *What Faith Has Meant to Me*, Westminster Press, 1975. Regular contributor to *Advocate*; contributor of articles to *Commonweal, Saturday Evening Post, McCalls, Christian Century, Changing Education*, and other periodicals.

WORK IN PROGRESS: An Autobiography for Random House, *Handbook for Ex-Catholics*, and *Reflections on Gay Liberation*.

SIDELIGHTS: Father DuBay was suspended from his duties in the Archdiocese of Los Angeles on February 25, 1966, after he refused to submit all future manuscripts to the censorship of James Francis Cardinal McIntyre. His book, published without the usual imprimatur, proposes formation of a labor union for priests.

BIOGRAPHICAL/CRITICAL SOURCES: Life, June 26, 1964; *Newsweek*, June 29, 1964; *Commonweal*, July 10, 1964; *New York Times*, March 4, 1966; *Catholic World*, June, 1966; *Saturday Review*, June 4, 1966; *Christian Century*, June 15, 1966; *Parade*, June 19, 1966; *Life*, June 24, 1966; *Time*, August 19, 1966.

*   *   *

DuBRUCK, Edelgard (Conradt)   1925-

PERSONAL: Born November 1, 1925, in Breslau, Germany; now U.S. citizen; daughter of Willy Arthur (a merchant) and Edelgard (Callenius) Conradt; married Alfred DuBruck (a professor), June 15, 1957; children: Alfred John. *Education:* Kant Academy, Germany, A.B. equivalent, 1947; University of Freiburg, student, 1949-52; University of Michigan, M.A., 1955, Ph.D., 1962. *Religion:* Lutheran. *Home:* 2045 South Hammond Lake Dr., West Bloomfield, Mich. 48033. *Agent:* Mouton Publishers, The Hague, Netherlands. *Office:* Marygrove College, Detroit, Mich. 48221.

CAREER: Marygrove College, Detroit, Mich., professor of French, 1965—. Visiting lecturer in German at Kalamazoo College, 1961, and lecturer in French at Oakland University, 1962-65. *Member:* Modern Language Association of America, Michigan Academy, Phi Beta Kappa, Phi Kappa Phi, Sigma Delta Pi, Pi Delta Phi.

WRITINGS: The Theme of Death in French Poetry of the Middle Ages and the Renaissance, Mouton & Co., 1964. Contributor to journals and periodicals including *Romania, Romanic Review, Esprit Createur, Neophilologus, Modern Language Notes*, and *Modern Language Journal*.

WORK IN PROGRESS: Analysis of humoristic elements in early French literature; French baroque literature; stylistic analyses of selected French authors; a revised edition of P. Riviere's *Ship of Fools*, in French.

SIDELIGHTS: DuBruck is competent in French, German, and Spanish. *Avocational interests:* Travel; baroque, prebaroque, and Renaissance music (owns a one-manual harpsichord).

*   *   *

DUERRENMATT, Friedrich   1921-

PERSONAL: Born January 5, 1921, in Konolfingen, Bern, Switzerland; son of Reinhold (a parson) and Hulda (Zimmermann) Duerrenmatt; married Lotti Geissler (a former actress), 1946; children: Peter, Barbara, Ruth. *Education:* Attended Universitaet Bern and Universitaet Zuerich. *Home:* Pertuis-du-Sault 34, Neuchatel, Switzerland.

CAREER: Playwright, author, and painter. Former drama critic for *Die Weltwoche*, Zurich, Switzerland. *Member:* Modern Language Association of America (honorary fellow). *Awards, honors:* Zurich Literature Prize, 1947, for "Es steht Geschrieben"; Hoerspielpreis der Kriegsblinden (Germany), 1956, for "Die Panne"; Schiller Prize of Mannheim, Germany, 1960; Italian Radio-Television Prize, 1958, for "Abendstunde im Spaetherbst"; New York Drama Critics Award, 1959, for "The Visit" as best foreign play of the season; Bern Literature Prize, 1960, for

Das Versprechen; Groesser Schillerpreis, 1960; D.Litt, Temple University, 1969.

WRITINGS—Full-length plays: *Es steht Geschrieben: Ein Drama* (title means "It Is Written"; first produced in Zurich at Schauspielhaus, April 19, 1947), Verlag der Arche (Zurich), 1959, revised and rewritten version published as *Der Wiedertaeufer: Ein Komoedie in Zwei Teilen* (title means "The Anna-baptists"; produced in Zurich, 1967), 1967; *Der Blinde: Ein Drama* (title means "The Blind Man"; produced in Basel, 1948), Verlag der Arche, 1960, new edition, 1965; *Romulus der Grosse* (produced in Basel, 1949), Reiss Buehnenvertrieb, 1956, German language edition edited by H. F. Garten, Houghton, 1962, new version, Verlag der Arche, 1964, 2nd edition, 1968, adaptation by Gore Vidal (produced in New York, 1962) published as *Romulus*, Dramatists Play Service, 1962, translation by Gerhard Nellhaus published in *An Angel Comes to Babylon and Romulus the Great*, Grove, 1964.

Die Ehe des Herrn Mississippi (produced in Munich, 1952), Oprecht (Zurich), 1952, second version, 1957, third version, Verlag der Arche, 1966, German language edition edited by Reinhold Grimm and Helene Scher, Holt, 1973, adaptation by Maximilian Slater produced in New York as "Fools Are Passing Through," 1958, translation by E. Peters and R. Schnorr produced in London as "The Marriage of Mr. Mississippi," 1959, translation by Michael Bullock published in *Problems of the Theatre: An Essay and the Marriage of Mr. Mississippi: A Play*, Grove, 1966; "Die Arche," produced in Zurich, 1952; *Ein Engel kommt nach Babylon: Eine fragmentarische Komoedie in drei Akten* (produced in Munich, 1953), Verlag der Arche, 1954, new version, 1958, 2nd edition, 1960, translation by George White (produced at University of California, 1962) published as *An Angel Comes to Babylon*, K. Hellmer, c.1962, translation by William McElwee published in *An Angel Comes to Babylon and Romulus the Great*, Grove, 1964; *Der Besuch der Alten Dame* (produced in Zurich, 1956), Verlag der Arche, 1956, 11th edition, 1968, German language edition edited by Paul K. Ackermann, Houghton, 1960, adaptation by Maurice Valency and the author (produced in New York, 1958) published as *The Visit*, Random House, 1958, translation by Patrick Bowles published as *The Visit: A Tragi-Comedy*, Grove, 1962; *Frank der Fuenfte: Oper einer Privatbank* (satirical comedy with music by Paul Burkhard; title means "Frank the Fifth: Opera of a Private Bank"; produced in Zurich, 1959), Verlag der Arche, 1960.

Die Physiker (produced in Zurich, 1962), Verlag der Arche, 1962, German language edition edited by Robert E. Helbling, Oxford University Press, 1965, translation by James Kirkup (produced in New York, 1963) published as *The Physicists*, Samuel French, 1963, Grove, 1964; *Herkules und der Stall des Augias* (expanded version of radio play; also see below), Verlag der Arche, 1963, translation by Agnes Hamilton published as *Hercules and the Augean Stables*, Dramatic Publishing, 1963; *The Meteor* (first produced in Zurich at Schauspielhaus, January 20, 1966), Verlag der Arche, 1966, adaptation produced under same title in Philadelphia, 1969, translation by James Kirkup published under the same title, J. Cape, 1973, Grove, 1974; *Koenig Johann: Nach Shakespeare*, Verlag der Arche, 1968; *Monstervortrag ueber Gerechtigkeit und Recht nebst einem helvetischen Zwischenspiel*, Verlag der Arche, 1969; *Play Strindberg: Totentanz nach August Strindberg*, Verlag der Arche, 1969, translation by James Kirkup (produced in New York at Repertory Theatre of Lincoln Center, 1971)

published as *Play Strindberg: "The Dance of Death" Choreographed*, Dramatic Publishing, 1970.

Titus Andronicus: Eine Komoedie nach Shakespeare, Verlag der Arche, 1970; *Portraet eines Planeten* (produced in Dusseldorf, 1970), Verlag der Arche, 1971; *Der Mitmacher*, Verlag der Arche, 1973. Plays represented in many anthologies, including *The Modern Theatre*, edited by R. W. Corrigan, Macmillan, 1964; *The Best Plays of 1964-65*, edited by O. L. Guernsey, Jr., Dodd, 1965; *Forms of Drama*, edited by James L. Calderwood and Harold E. Toliver, Prentice-Hall, 1969.

Radio plays: *Herkules und der Stall des Augias* (expanded into full-length play in 1963; also see above), Verlag der Arche, 1954, 2nd edition, 1959; *Naechtliches Gespraech mit einem verachteten Menschen* (title means "A Nocturnal Conversation With a Despised Man"), Verlag der Arche, 1957, 5th edition, 1967; *Das Unternehmen der Wega* (title means "The Vega Enterprise"; broadcast, 1954), Verlag der Arche, 1958; *Der Prozess um des Esels Schatten* (title means "The Trial of the Asses' Shadow"), Verlad der Arche, 1959; *Stranitzky and der Nationalheld* (title means "Stranitzky and the National Hero"), Verlag der Arche, 1959; *Abendstunde im Spaetherbst*, Verlag der Arche, 1959, translation by Gabriel Karminski published as *Episode on an Autumn Evening*, Dramatic Publishing, 1959; *Der Doppelgaenger*, Verlag der Arche, 1960; *Die Panne* (also a novel: see below), Verlag der Arche, 1961. Radio plays anthologized in *Drei Hoerspiele*, compiled by A. Engles, J. B. Wolters (Groningen, Netherlands), 1967; *Drei Hoerspiele*, compiled by Leonard R. P. McGlashan, Harrap, 1966.

Novels; except as noted: *Pilatus*, Vereinigung Oltner Buecherfreunde, 1949; *Der Nihilist*, Holunderpresse (Zurich), 1950; *Der Richter und sein Henker*, Benziger (Zurich), 1952, 6th edition, 1962, German language edition edited by William Gillis and J. J. Neumaier, Houghton, 1961, translation by Therese Pol published as *The Judge and His Hangman*, Harper, 1955, translation by Cyrus Brooks published under same title, Four Square Books, 1961; *Die Stadt: Prosa I-IV* (stories; title means "The City"), Verlag der Arche, 1952, new edition, 1959; *Die Fall* (story), Verlag der Arche, 1952; *Der Verdacht*, Benziger, 1953, 4th edition, 1961, German language edition edited by William Gillis, Houghton, 1964, translation by Eva H. Morreale published as the *The Quarry*, Grove, 1961; *Grieche sucht Griechin*, Verlag der Arche, 1955, new edition, 1966, translation by Richard Winston and Clara Winston published as *Once a Greek . . .*, Knopf, 1965; *Das Versprechen: Requiem auf den Kriminalroman*, Verlag der Arche, 1958, 5th edition, 1966, translation by Richard Winston and Clara Winston published as *The Pledge*, Knopf, 1959.

Die Panne: Ein noch moegliche Geschichte (title means "The Breakdown"; radio play published under same title; see above), Verlag der Arche, 1960, translation by Richard Winston and Clara Winston published as *Traps*, Knopf, 1960 (published in England as *A Dangerous Game*, J. Cape, 1960), stage adaptation by James Yaffe (produced in New York, 1966) published as *The Deadly Game*, Dramatists Play Service, 1966; *Die Heimat im Plakat: Ein Buch fuer Schweizer Kinder* (juvenile), Diogenes Verlag (Zurich), 1963; *Der Tunnel* (story), Verlag der Arche, 1964; *Das Bild des Sisyphos*, Verlag der Arche, 1968; *Der Sturz*, Verlag der Arche, 1971; (contributor) *Die besten klassischen und modernen Hundegeschichten* (stories), Diogenes Verlag, 1973. Short stories represented in many anthologies, including *Erzaehlungen: Stories* (both in

German and English), edited by Klaus Zobel, Hueber (Munich), 1964.

Nonfiction: *Theaterprobleme*, Verlag der Arche, 1955, new edition, 1963, translation by Gerhard Nellhaus published in *Problems of the Theatre: An Essay and the Marriage of Mr. Mississippi: A Play*, Grove, 1966; *Friedrich Schiller: Eine Rede* (speech), Verlag der Arche, 1960; (with Werner Weber) *Der Rest ist Dank* (speeches), Verlag der Arche, 1961; *Theater: Schriften und Reden* (essays and speeches), edited by Elisabeth Brock-Sulzer, Verlag der Arche, Volume I, 1966, Volume II, 1972; (author of introduction) Willy Guggenheim, *Varlin*, Basel Kunsthalle, 1967; *Saetze aus Amerika* (travel), Verlag der Arche, 1970.

Omnibus volumes: *Komoedien* (collected comedies), Verlag der Arche, Volume I, 1957, Volume II, 1963, Volume III, 1970; *Gesammelte Hoerspiele* (collected radio plays), Verlag der Arche, 1961; *Four Plays, 1957-62* (includes "Romulus the Great," "The Marriage of Mr. Mississippi," "An Angel Comes to Babylon," and "The Physicists"), translated by Gerhard Nellhaus and others, J. Cape, 1964, published as *Four Plays*, Grove, 1965; *Drei Hoerspiele* (radio plays; includes "Abendstunde im Spaetherbst," "Der Doppelgaenger," and "Die Panne"), edited by Henry Regensteiner, Holt, 1965; *Romulus: The Broadway Adaptation and the Original Romulus the Great*, adaptation by Gore Vidal, translation by Gerhard Nellhaus, Grove, 1966; *Vier Hoerspiele* (four radio plays), Volk & Welt (Berlin), 1967; *Die Panne and Der Tunnel*, edited by F. J. Alexander, Oxford University Press, 1967; *Der Richter und sein Henker* [and] *Die Panne*, Volk & Welt, 1969.

Screen plays: "It Happened in Broad Daylight," Continental, 1960 (a version of *The Pledge*).

Recordings: "Friedrich Duerrenmatt Liest: 'Herkules und der Stall des Augias,' 'Eine Kurzfassung der Komoedie,'" Deutsche Grammophon Gesellschaft, 1957; "Naechtliches Gespraech," Platern Club, 1963.

SIDELIGHTS:". . . I would ask you not to look upon me as the spokesman of some specific movement in the theatre or of a certain dramatic technique, nor to believe that I knock at your door as the traveling salesman of one of the philosophies current on our stages today, whether as existentialist, nihilist, expressionist, or satirist, or any other label put on the compote dished up by literary criticism. For me, the stage is not a battlefield for theories, philosophies, and manifestos, but rather an instrument whose possibilities I seek to know by playing with it. . . . My plays are not for what people have to say: what is said is there because my plays deal with people, and thinking and believing and philosophizing are all, to some extent at least, a part of human behavior."

So Duerrenmatt summarizes his approach to the theatre. For him, the playwright's task is to present a new, fantastic, even grotesque and bizarre world upon a stage by using everything at his command: language, irony, ideas, and what Adolf D. Klarmann calls "theatrical pyro-technics." Klarmann cites a few of these from Duerrenmatt's work: "Figures appear out of trap doors, enter through windows and clocks, scenery flies up and down in full view, torture wheels are outlined against the sky, moon dances are performed on roofs, angels alight on chandeliers, chickens run across the stage, in short, every conceivable trick of the trade of the theatre, of the cabaret, the burlesque, and the movies is applied with a lusty abandon." Duerrenmatt's avowed objective is to leave the audience frightened. "That," he says, "is the modern form of empathy."

Believing that true tragedy is impossible to create in a world without form, he calls his dramatic pieces comedies, though the comedy to be found therein is no more merry than gallows humor. He writes: ". . . the task of art, insofar as art can have a task at all, and hence also the task of drama today, is to create something concrete, something that has form. This can be accomplished best by comedy. . . . [But] we can achieve the tragic out of comedy. We can bring it forth as a frightening moment, as an abyss that opens suddenly. . . . [The conceit employed by comedy] easily transforms the crowd of theatregoers into a mass which can be attacked, deceived, outsmarted into listening to things it would otherwise not so readily listen to. Comedy is a mousetrap in which the public is easily caught and in which it will get caught over and over again. Tragedy on the other hand, predicates a true community, a kind of community whose existence in our day is but an embarrassing fiction."

"Duerrenmatt is a disillusioned analyst of the human character," writes George Wellwarth. "Even the plays with political themes are ultimately about the human beings rather that the issues. Like Ionesco, like Beckett, like all the writers of the dramatic avant-gardé in fact, Duerrenmatt feels deep down in himself that the problems of humanity are insoluble. And so he takes refuge from this knowledge in a mordantly sardonic portrayal of life." Duerrenmatt's recurring themes, according to Wellwarth, are "the effect of the possession of power on the human soul," and the senselessness of death, which "renders human acts trivial." But, Wellwarth contends, "Duerrenmatt always implies that events must be resisted. Nothing is inevitable and determined in Duerrenmatt. The fact that things are insignificant from a cosmic viewpoint does not alter the fact that they are significant in the immediate present: it merely argues that they are finally insoluble and will always repeat themselves." Duerrenmatt writes: "The universal escapes my grasp. I refuse to find the universal in a doctrine. The universal for me is chaos. The world (hence the stage which represents this world) is for me something monstrous, a riddle of misfortunes which must be accepted but before which one must not capitulate." Duerrenmatt admires Kafka, Brecht, Ionesco, Samuel Beckett, and Kierkegaard.

Ten years ago he was virtually unknown and earned less than a thousand dollars a year. He and his family were assisted by an anonymous sympathizer who sent a food package each month. Now he is perhaps the most important and most frequently-performed living, German-language dramatist. *The Visit* is often called Duerrenmatts finest play. Frederick Lumley wrote: [*The Visit*] raises Duerrenmatt to the level of the leading playwright of our times. Not only is it a good play in itself, it is one of the most forceful statements ever made on the corruption of the power of money, a radical indictment of the values of our society and the hypocrisy on which it is built."

Duerrenmatt believes Switzerland is ideal for a writer because "one is close enough to observe events in the surrounding countries and yet, at the same time, by a virtue of neutrality, removed from them." He writes slowly, rewrites a great deal, always working at night, finishing perhaps one page per night. He says he likes to arrive at his plays "from the unique, the sudden idea or conceit, rather than from some general concept or plan. Speaking for myself, I need to write off into the blue, as I like to put it so that I might give critics a catchword to hang onto."

He lists his avocational interests as astronomy and painting. He illustrates some of his own books, and claims he had founded a new "truly capitalist art form," one which incorporates banknotes into canvases. "That way," he says, "the painting is sure to have at least some intrinsic value."

A dramatization of *The Judge and His Hangman* was televised in the United States, 1956 and an adaptation of "The Deadly Game" was televised in the United States, 1957. Many of Duerrenmatt's works have been adapted for the screen. *The Visit* was filmed by Twentieth Century-Fox in 1964, *The Marriage of Mr. Mississippi* was filmed as "Fools are Passing Through" in 1961, and Sergeo Amidei adapted a short story for an Italian film in 1972. *The Visit* was also made into an opera by Gottfried von Einem.

BIOGRAPHICAL/CRITICAL SOURCES: H. M. Block and H. Salinger, editors, *Creative Vision*, Evergreen, 1960; *Nation*, January 9, 1960, May 4, 1963; *Tulane Drama Review*, May, 1960; Kenneth Tynan, *Curtains*, Atheneum, 1961; *Esquire*, May, 1961; Toby Cole, editor, *Playwrights on Playwriting*, Hill & Wang, 1961; *Times Literary Supplement*, January 11, 1963, October 27, 1972; *New York Times*, October 18, 1964; *Christian Century*, October 28, 1964; George Wellwarth, *The Theater of Protest and Paradox*, New York University Press, 1964; Travis Bogard and William I. Oliver, editors, *Modern Drama*, Oxford University Press, 1965; *Books Abroad*, autumn, 1967; Frederich Lumley, *New Trends in Twentieth Century Drama*, Oxford University Press, 1967; M. B. Peppard, *Friedrich Duerrenmatt*, Twayne, 1969; U. Jenny, *Duerrenmatt: A Study of His Plays*, Methuen, 1971; A. Arnold, *Friedrich Duerrenmatt*, Ungar, 1972; J. K. Fickert, *To Heaven and Back*, University Press of Kentucky, 1972; Carolyn Riley, editor, *Contemporary Literary Criticism*, Gale, Volume I, 1973, Volume IV, 1975.

* * *

DUFFY, Helene (Krainovich) 1926-

PERSONAL: Born February 9, 1926, in Chicago, Ill.; daughter of Isaac and Violet (Jerich) Krainovich; married Robert J. Duffy (a financial reporter), November 25, 1946; children: Robert F. *Education:* University of Illinois, B.A., 1947. *Home:* 321 Avenue C, Apartment 3F, New York, N.Y. 10017.

CAREER: American Bankers Association, New York, N.Y., assistant director of banking education committee, 1961—. Queens College (now Queens College of the City University of New York), Flushing, N.Y., lecturer in money and banking and basic economics, 1965—. *Member:* National Association of Industry-Education Cooperation (New York chapter secretary), American Economic Association, National Council of Teachers of Mathematics.

WRITINGS: (With D. H. McKinley and M. G. Lee) *Forecasting Business Conditions*, American Bankers Association, 1965. Columnist, *Banking Magazine*.

SIDELIGHTS: Helene Duffy speaks Yugoslav (Serbian).†

* * *

DUFFY, John 1915-

PERSONAL: Born March 27, 1915, in Barrow in Furness, England; son of James (a ship-plater) and Ethel (Hough) Duffy; married Florence Corinne Cook, June 13, 1942; children: James Norman, John, Jr. *Education:* Louisiana State Normal College (now Northwestern State University of Louisiana), B.A., 1941; Louisiana State University, M.A., 1943; University of California, Los Angeles, Ph.D.,

1946. *Politics:* Democrat. *Home:* 4401 College Heights Dr., Hyattsville, Md. 20782. *Office:* Priscilla Alden Burke Professor of History, University of Maryland, College Park, Md. 20740.

CAREER: Northwestern State College of Louisiana, Natchitoches, assistant professor of history, 1946-47; Southeastern Louisiana College, Hammond, associate professor of history, 1947-49; Northwestern State College of Louisiana, associate professor of history, 1949-53; Louisiana State University, Baton Rouge, associate professor, 1953-60; University of Pittsburgh, Graduate School of Public Health, Pittsburgh, Pa., associate professor, 1960-64, professor of public health history, 1965; Tulane University of Louisiana, New Orleans, professor of history of medicine, with dual appointment in Medical School and history department, 1965-72; University of Maryland, College Park, Priscilla Alden Burke Professor of History, 1972—. Consultant to New York City Health Department.

MEMBER: American Association for the History of Medicine (executive council, 1963-66; vice-president, 1974-76), American Historical Association, Organization of American Historians, American Association of University Professors, Southern Historical Association (executive council, 1962-65), Louisiana Historical Association, Maryland Historical Society. *Awards, honors:* Ford Foundation fellow, 1951-52; Louisiana Library Association Literary Award, 1958, for Volume I of Matas work.

WRITINGS: Epidemics in Colonial America, Louisiana State University Press, 1953; (editor) *Parson Clapp of the Strangers' Church of New Orleans*, Louisiana State University Studies, 1957; (editor) Rudolph Matas, *History of Medicine in Louisiana*, Louisiana State University Press, Volume I, 1958, Volume II, 1962; *Sword of Pestilence: The New Orleans Yellow Fever Epidemic of 1853*, Louisiana State University Press, 1966; *A History of Public Health in New York City, 1625-1866*, Russell Sage, 1968; *A History of Public Health in New York City, 1866-1966*, Russell Sage, 1974; *A History of American Medicine*, McGraw, 1975. Contributor to *Mississippi Valley Historical Review, Bulletin of the History of Medicine, Historian, Journal of the American Medical Association*, and other professional journals.

* * *

DUGGAN, George Henry 1912-

PERSONAL: Born July 3, 1912, in Runanga, New Zealand; son of George (an inspector of mines) and Teresa (Rasmussen) Duggan. *Education:* Attended St. Bede's College, Christchurch, New Zealand, 1924-28, and Marist Seminary, Greenmeadows, New Zealand, 1929-33; Angelicum University, Rome, Italy, S.T.D., 1937. *Office:* St. Mary's Seminary, Greenmeadows, New Zealand.

CAREER: Roman Catholic priest, member of Society of Mary (Marist). Marist Seminary, Greenmeadows, New Zealand, teacher of philosophy, 1938-54; University of Canterbury, Christchurch, New Zealand, rector of Rochester Hall (hostel for Catholic men), 1956-64; Maryknoll, Greenmeadows, New Zealand, rector of second novitiate, 1965-71; St. Mary's Seminary, Greenmeadows, New Zealand, member of staff, 1971—.

WRITINGS: Evolution and Philosophy, A. H. & A. W. Reed, 1949; *Hans Kueng and Reunion*, Mercier Press, 1964, Newman, 1965. Contributor to *New Scholasticism, New Zealand Tablet, Zealandia, Australasian Catholic Record*, and *The Priest*.

WORK IN PROGRESS: A paper on natural theology, to be published in Proceedings of Thomistic Congress, Rome.

SIDELIGHTS: Duggan has reading competence in Latin, French, Italian; some knowledge of German.

*   *   *

DUKE, Donald Norman   1929-
   (Roger Valentine)

PERSONAL: Born April 1, 1929, in Los Angeles, Calif.; son of Roger Valentine Duke. *Education:* Colorado College, Colorado Springs, B.S. (business administration) and B.A. (educational psychology), 1951. *Politics:* Republican. *Religion:* Presbyterian. *Home:* 2304 Melville Dr., San Marino, Calif. 91108. *Office:* Golden West Books, 525 North Electric, Alhambra, Calif. 91801.

CAREER: Mobil Oil Co., sales promotion manager in Los Angeles, Calif., 1955-63; Golden West Books, San Marino, Calif., publisher, 1963—. Athletic Press, publisher, 1972—. Atchison, Topeka & Santa Fe Railway, public relations consultant. *Member:* PEN International, Railway and Locomotive Historical Society, Newcomen Society of North America, The Westerners, Western Writers of America, California Writers Guild, California Book Publishers Association, Kappa Sigma.

WRITINGS: All published by Golden West: *Southern Pacific Steam Locomotives*, 1955; *The Pacific Electric Railway*, 1958; *Night Train*, 1961; *Santa Fe . . . Steel Rails Through California*, 1963; *George Westinghouse & Electric Traction*, 1967. Contributor to *Arizona Highways, American Heritage, Sunset*, and railroad magazines. Editor, *Pacific Railway Journal*, 1954-61, and *American Railway Journal*, 1965—, *The Westerners* (quarterly); book review editor, Kappa Sigma's *Caduceus*.

SIDELIGHTS: Duke's travels have spanned North America, southern Central America, South America, Europe, and West Indies. *Avocational interests:* Photography, was one of the U.S. photographers at the Olympic Games, Munich, Germany, 1972.

*   *   *

DUNAS, Joseph C.   1900-

PERSONAL: Born February 8, 1900, in Chicago, Ill.; son of Cassell (a designer) and Tillie (Kurtzon) Dunas; married Beatrice Sanders; children: Casselle Dunas Rotter, Ronald, Barbara Dunas Meyer. *Education:* Attended University of Chicago, two years. *Residence:* Los Angeles, Calif.

CAREER: Owner of real estate development firm in Los Angeles, Calif., 1937—. *Military service:* U.S. Navy, World War I.

WRITINGS: Joy for Daily Living, Fell, 1966; *The Great Search*, Fell, in press.

*   *   *

DUNCAN, Charles T(homas)   1914-

PERSONAL: Born May 20, 1914, in Marietta, Minn.; son of Henry (a physician) and Clara B. (Olson) Duncan; married Gretchen L. Altermatt, November 8, 1940; children: Thomas Scott, Diana Lynn, Jean Marie. *Education:* University of Minnesota, A.B., 1936, M.A., 1946; University of Washington, Seattle, graduate study, 1941. *Politics:* Democrat. *Religion:* Protestant. *Office:* Department of Journalism, University of Oregon, Eugene, Ore. 97403.

CAREER: Newspaper reporter and editor, 1936-40; Uni-

versity of Nevada, Reno, instructor in journalism, 1940-42; University of Nebraska, Lincoln, assistant professor of journalism, 1946-47; University of Minnesota, Minneapolis, associate professor of journalism, 1947-50; University of Oregon, Eugene, professor of journalism, 1950-65, dean of School of Journalism, 1956-62; University of Colorado, Boulder, dean of School of Journalism, 1962-65; University of Oregon, associate dean and dean of faculties, 1965-71, professor of journalism, 1971—. Consultant on journalism education, Ford Foundation, 1964-65. Member of Oregon Corrections Division Advisory Committee, 1965, Eugene Renewal Agency, 1966-69, and Oregon Educational Council, 1974—. *Military service:* U.S. Naval Reserve, 1942-45; became lieutenant. *Member:* Association for Education in Journalism (president, 1961), American Association of University Professors, American Civil Liberties Union. *Awards, honors:* Travel grant for six months study in Europe, Newspaper Fund, 1960.

WRITINGS: (With Alfred Blaustein and Charles O. Porter) *The American Lawyer*, University of Chicago Press, 1952; (editor and author of introduction and notes) Horace Greeley, *An Overland Journey from New York to San Francisco in the Summer of 1859*, Knopf, 1964. Contributor to *Journalism Quarterly*.

*   *   *

DUNCAN, Clyde H.   1903-

PERSONAL: Born July 27, 1903, in Lake City, Ark.; son of Thomas and Cordelia (Lumsden) Duncan; wife deceased. *Education:* University of Missouri, B.S., 1926, M.A., 1957. *Politics:* Independent. *Address:* P.O. Box 85, Ironton, Mo. 63650. *Agent:* The Cambridge Company, Hollywood, Calif.

CAREER: Arkansas Farmer, Little Rock, Ark., field editor, 1926-28; United Press, night bureau manager in Kansas City and St. Louis, Mo., 1929; advertising copywriter, St. Louis, 1930-33; *Madison County Press*, Fredricktown, Mo., editor, 1933-41; advertising copywriter in Seattle, Wash., and Charles City, Iowa, 1946-47; farm editor of newspapers in Laurel, Miss., 1948, Camden, Ark., 1948-50, and Tulsa, Okla., 1950-55; University of Missouri, Columbia, associate professor and associate agricultural editor, 1955-66, professor emeritus, 1966—. Agricultural College Magazines Associated, past president and national adviser. *Military service:* U.S. Navy, World War II. *Member:* Future Farmers of America (honorary member), Gamma Sigma Delta, Kappa Tau Alpha, Lambda Chi Alpha. *Awards, honors:* Fellowships from Kellogg Fund, 1937, Huntington Hartford Foundation, 1962, Villa Montalvo, 1963, and Bellamann Foundation, 1965.

WRITINGS: Straight Furrows: A Story of 4-H Club Work, University of New Mexico Press, 1954; *Find a Career in Agriculture*, Putnam, 1961; *Big Men, Big Jobs*, University of Missouri Press, 1964; *Fifty Years of 4-H in Missouri, 1914-1964*, University of Missouri Press, 1970; *History of McAlester Boys Club*, McAlester (Okla.) Democrat Publisher, 1970.

WORK IN PROGRESS: Three books, *Jonathan Turner: Yankee Schoolmaster, Under the Arctic's Rim*, and *One Man's Alcan*.

*   *   *

DUNHAM, Montrew Goetz   1919-

PERSONAL: Born September 19, 1919, in Indianapolis,

Ind.; daughter of Albert Howard (an insurance agent) and Idella (Darling) Goetz; married Robert E. Dunham (an industrial relations director), August 29, 1942; children: Charles Reynolds, Diane Palmer, Denise Darling, James Mitchell. *Education:* Butler University, A.B., 1941; Northwestern University, M.A., 1966. *Religion:* Congregationalist. *Residence:* Downers Grove, Ill.

CAREER: U.S. Employment Service, Chicago, Ill., senior interviewer and vocational counselor, 1941-46.

WRITINGS: Oliver Wendell Holmes, Jr.: Boy of Justice, Bobbs-Merrill, 1961; *George Westinghouse: Young Inventor*, Bobbs-Merrill, 1963; *Abner Doubleday: Young Baseball Pioneer*, Bobbs-Merrill, 1965; *Anne Bradstreet: Young Puritan Poet*, Bobbs-Merrill, 1969; *Langston Hughes: Young Black Poet*, Bobbs-Merrill, 1972; *Mahalia Jackson: Young Gospel Singer*, Bobbs-Merrill, 1974.†

* * *

DUNLOP, Richard 1921-

PERSONAL: Born June 20, 1921, in Chicago, Ill.; son of Delbert James (an engineer) and Grace (Blew) Dunlop; married Joan Titus, April 16, 1949; children: Nancy, Richard, Jr., James, Jeffrey. *Education:* Northwestern University, B.S. (in absentia), 1945. *Politics:* Democrat. *Religion:* Presbyterian. *Home:* 1115 Mayfair Rd., Arlington Heights, Ill. 60004. *Agent:* 425 East 51st St., New York, N.Y. 10022.

CAREER: Richard B. Dunlop, Inc. (export-import), New York, N.Y., president, 1948-50; National College of Education, Evanston, Ill., assistant to president, 1950-52; *Chicago* (magazine), Chicago, Ill., contributing editor, 1954-55; *Home & Highway* (magazine), Skokie, Ill., associate editor, 1955-56; full-time free-lance writer, 1956—. *Military service:* U.S. Army, 1943-45; with Office of Strategic Services in China-India-Burma theater; became sergeant. *Member:* Society of American Travel Writers (past president), Authors League, Society of Magazine Writers, Westerners (deputy sheriff, 1958—), Society of Midland Authors, Cliff Dwellers Club (Chicago).

WRITINGS: (Contributor) *This Is the West*, Rand McNally, 1957; *St. Louis*, Doubleday, 1958; *Burma*, Doubleday, 1959; *The Mississippi River*, Doubleday, 1959; *The Young David*, Doubleday, 1960; (contributor) *This Is the South*, Rand McNally, 1961; *Rand McNally Vacation Guide*, Rand McNally, annually, 1964-67; *Doctors of the American Frontier*, Doubleday, 1965; *Great Trails of the West*, Abingdon, 1971; *Outdoor Recreation Guide*, Rand McNally, 1974. Compiler of *Texaco Touring Atlas*, Rand McNally, 1965-66, and *Sinclair Tour Guide*, Rand McNally, 1966. Contributor of articles on travel and history, and poetry and short stories to magazines, including *Saturday Evening Post, Reader's Digest, Today's Health*, and *Popular Mechanics*.

* * *

DURGNAT, Raymond (Eric) 1932-
(O. O. Green)

PERSONAL: Born September 1, 1932, in London, England; son of Louis Albert (a draper) and Yvonne Marie (Colliard) Durgnat. *Education:* Pembroke College, Cambridge, B.A. (honours), 1957. *Home:* 84 St. Thomas's Rd., London N.4., England.

CAREER: Associated British Picture Corp., Borehamwood, Herts, England, staff writer, 1957-60; Film University College, Postgraduate Research Department of Film, London, England, researcher, 1960-61; free-lance film scripts and journalism, 1961—; St. Martin's School of Art, London, lecturer, 1964-73; Queen's University, Kingston, Ontario, associate professor, department of film, 1973-74; Columbia University, New York, N.Y., visiting professor, department of film, 1974-75. Member of lecture panel, British Film Institute, 1961-73. *Military service:* Royal Army Education Corps, 1952-54; became sergeant. *Member:* British Society of Aesthetics, British Film Institute.

WRITINGS: Nouvelle Vague: The First Decade, Motion (Essex, England), 1963; *Sexus Eros Kino*, Carl Schunemann-City Books (Bremen and Munich), 1964, published in England as *Eros in the Cinema*, Calder & Boyars, 1966; *Greta Garbo*, Studio Vista, 1965; *The Marx Brothers*, Oesterreich Filmuseum (Vienna), 1966; *Films and Feelings*, M.I.T. Press, 1967; *Luis Bunuel*, Studio Vista, 1967, University of California Press, 1968; *Franju*, University of California Press, 1968; *The Crazy Mirror*, Faber, 1969, Horizon Press, 1970; *A Mirror for England*, Praeger, 1971; *Sexual Alienation in the Cinema*, Studio Vista, 1974; *The Strange Case of Alfred Hitchcock*, M.I.T. Press, 1974; *The Films of Jean Renoir*, University of California Press, 1974; *Durgnat on Film*, Faber, 1975. Editor, with Ian Johnson, *Motion*, numbers 4-6, 1962-64. Regular contributor to *Film Comment*, and *Midi-Minuit Fantastique* and poems and articles elsewhere.

WORK IN PROGRESS: Aesthetics of the mass media, and aesthetics and avant-garde.

SIDELIGHTS: Durgnat writes: "Alternate between the mass media and the academic world in a Cloister-and-the-Hearth (not to say Jekyll-and-Hyde) fashion and for the last few years have been interested in building up a 'unified field' aesthetic applying to artworks of all levels of sophistication and diverse media. After finishing the projects outlined above will revert to creative writing. [Believe] art ought to be an extension of human experience and feelings, not examination-fodder.

"Owing to wartime conditions I went to 15 different schools (and was born into a Swiss family living in London anyway), ranging from the roughest to (even!) an upper-middle-class girls' boarding school; so I don't take local myths on trust."

* * *

DURRELL, Donald D(e Witt) 1903-

PERSONAL: Born December 18, 1903, in Fergus Falls, Minn.; son of William Benmore and Fanny (Richardson) Durrell; married Katharine Moore, August 20, 1929; children: Suzanne, Elizabeth. *Education:* University of Iowa, A.B., 1926, A.M., 1927; Harvard University, Ed.D., 1930. *Politics:* Republican. *Religion:* Unitarian Universalist. *Home:* 19 Orchard Dr., Durham, N.H. 03824.

CAREER: Harvard University, Cambridge, Mass., instructor, 1927-30; Boston University, Boston, Mass., assistant professor, 1930-33, associate professor, 1933-35, professor of education, 1935-69, professor emeritus, 1969—, dean of School of Education, 1942-52, U.S. Air Force, director of operations analysis, Third Air Force, 1945-46. Adjunct professor, University of New Hampshire, 1973—. U.S. Office of Education, member of Research Advisory Council, 1962-65; consultant on current national study of first-grade reading. *Member:* International Reading Association, American Educational Research Association,

American Association for the Advancement of Science (vice-president, 1952), National Society for the Study of Education. *Awards, honors:* L.H.D., Boston University, 1969; Citation of Merit, International Reading Association, 1970.

WRITINGS: Improving Reading Instruction, Harcourt, 1956; *Durrell Reading Analysis*, Harcourt, 1957; (with Helen A. Murphy) *Speech-to-Print Phonics*, Harcourt, 1964; (editor with B. Alice Crossley) *Favorite Plays for Classroom Reading*, Plays, 1965, new edition, 1971; (editor with Crossley) *Thirty Plays for Classroom Reading*, Plays, 1966, 2nd edition, 1968; *Phonics Practice Program*, Harcourt, 1969; *Plays for Echo Reading*, Harcourt, 1970; (compiler) *Teen-Age Plays for Classroom Reading*, Plays, 1971; *Learning Letter Sounds*, Borg-Wagner, 1972; *Beginning Language Concepts*, Borg-Wagner, 1974; *Learning Letters Through Sounds*, Borg-Wagner, 1974; *Vocabulary Improvement Program*, Harcourt, 1974. Also author of more than one hundred articles on reading and elementary education.

WORK IN PROGRESS: Sound Start in Reading; pre-reading skills instruction; learning programs to improve reading skills.

* * *

DUVALL, W(illiam) Clyde (Jr.) 1917-

PERSONAL: Born February 4, 1917, in Farmville, Va.; son of William Clyde (a merchant) and Harriet King (Bugg) Duvall; married Ruth Elizabeth Jones, September 30, 1939; children: William Clyde III, George Drummond, Charles Montgomery, Elizabeth Leigh, Thomas King. *Education:* Attended Hampden-Sydney College, 1934-36; Washington Musical Institute, 1936-38. *Politics:* Democrat. *Religion:* Episcopalian. *Home:* 4714 River Shore Rd., Portsmouth, Va. 23703. *Office:* Chesapeake Public Schools, 300 Cedar Rd., Chesapeake, Va. 23320.

CAREER: Band director at high schools in Charlotte County, Va., 1939-43, and Norfolk County, Va., 1946-55; Norfolk County (Va.) public schools, director of music, 1951-55, director of music and teaching materials, 1955-63; Chesapeake (Va.) public schools, director of music and teaching materials, 1963-72, director of teaching materials, 1972—. *Military service:* U.S. Navy, 1943-45. *Member:* Virginia Music Educators Association (vice-president, 1953-55), Virginia Band and Orchestra Directors Association (president, 1953-55).

WRITINGS: The High School Band Director's Handbook, Prentice-Hall, 1960. Contributor to music journals and newspapers.

* * *

DWIGGINS, Don 1913-

PERSONAL: Born November 15, 1913, in Plainfield, N.J.; son of Clare Victor (a cartoonist) and Betsey (Lindsay) Dwiggins; married Olga Arabsky; children: Don Lindsay, Toni Kay. *Education:* Los Angeles Junior College, student, 1932-33. *Home:* 3816 Paseo Hidalgo, Malibu, Calif. *Agent:* Lenninger Literary Agency, 437 Fifth Ave., New York, N.Y. 10016.

CAREER: Former commercial pilot; aviation editor of *Los Angeles Daily News*, Los Angeles, Calif., 1947-54, and *Los Angeles Mirror News*, 1956-62 (both newspapers defunct); space technology consultant, Lockheed Aircraft Co., Burbank, Calif., 1964; news writer, KTTV, Los Angeles,

Calif., 1964; editor of "Mickey Mouse Newsreel," Disney Studios, Burbank, Calif., 1965; *Plane & Pilot* (magazine), senior editor, 1974; free-lance writer for magazines and television. *Military service:* U.S. Army Air Forces, 1942-43; became master sergeant. *Member:* Aviation Aerospace Writers Association, Screen Actors Guild, Writers Guild of America (West), Motion Picture Pilots Association, Sheriff's Aero Squadron (Los Angeles). *Awards, honors:* Award for best California news story of 1960 for coverage of Chessman execution; Aviation Aerospace Writers Association award for best aviation feature in metropolitan newspaper, 1961.

WRITINGS: "Frankie" (Frank Sinatra), Paperback Library, 1961; *The S. O. Bees*, New American Library, 1963; *They Flew the Bendix Race*, Lippincott, 1965; *The Air Devils*, Lippincott, 1966; *Hollywood Pilot*, Doubleday, 1967; *The SST: Here It Comes, Ready or Not*, Doubleday, 1968; *The Barnstormers*, Grosset & Dunlap, 1968; *Space and the Weather*, Golden Gate, 1968; *Bailout*, Crowell, 1969; *Famous Flyers and the Ships They Flew*, Grosset & Dunlap, 1969; *Voices in the Sky*, Golden Gate, 1969; *On Silent Wings*, Grosset & Dunlap, 1970; *Eagle has Landed*, Golden Gate, 1970; *Spaceship Earth*, Golden Gate, 1970; *Into the Unknown*, Golden Gate, 1971; *Robots in the Sky*, Golden Gate, 1972; *The Sky is Yours*, Childrens Press, 1973; *Riders of the Winds*, Hawthorn Books, 1973; *The Search for Energy*, Childrens Press, 1974; *Build Your Own Sports Plane*, Hawthorn Books, 1974. Writer of more than 1,000 articles, appearing in *Saturday Evening Post, Reader's Digest, Collier's, True, Argosy, This Week, Parade*, and other magazines; former writer for television.

WORK IN PROGRESS: The Next Ten Years in Space, for Childrens Press.

* * *

DYER, Frederick C. 1918-

PERSONAL: Born February 17, 1918, in St. Louis, Mo.; son of George L. (an insurance executive) and Katherine M. (Dobson) Dyer; married Lucrecia E. Herrera, July 21, 1946; children: John R., Michael G., Elisa M. *Education:* College of the Holy Cross, A.B., 1938; Dartmouth College, M.B.A., 1948. *Home:* 4509 Cumberland Ave., Chevy Chase, Md. 20015.

CAREER: U.S. Department of the Navy, Washington, D.C., educational specialist, Training Publications Section, 1948-58, advisor in leadership, Bureau of Naval Personnel, 1958-64; special assistant to Under Secretary of the Navy, 1964-66; Office of Civilian Manpower Management, assistant for special projects, 1966-68; Navy Publications and Printing Service, Program Analysis Division, director, 1968-74. George Washington University, professorial lecturer, 1956-60; Drexel Institute of Technology, adjunct professor of communications, 1962-67; American University, professorial lecturer, 1967-71. Town of Somerset, Md., councilman, 1962-64. Trinity College, Washington, D.C., lay trustee, 1958-62. *Military service:* U.S. Naval Reserve, active duty, World War II and Korean War; now Commander (retired).

MEMBER: Federal Professional Association, Authors Guild, National Press Club, University Club, Army and Navy Country Club, Cosmos Club, Columbia Country Club, Sycamore Island Club. *Awards, honors:* Navy League Writing Award, 1959; Superior Civilian Service Award, U.S. Department of the Navy, 1961; Clover International Poetry Award, 1974.

WRITINGS: (With Harley F. Cope) *The Petty Officer's Guide* Stackpole, 1952, 6th edition, 1966; (with Ross Evans and Dale Lovell) *Putting Yourself Over in Business*, Prentice-Hall, 1957; *Executive's Guide to Handling People*, Prentice-Hall, 1958; *Executive's Guide to Effective Speaking and Writing*, Prentice-Hall, 1962; (with brother, John M. Dyer) *Export Financing: Modern U.S. Methods*, University of Miami Press, 1964; *Blueprint for Executive Success*, three volumes, Prentice-Hall, 1964; (with J. M. Dyer) *Bureaucracy vs. Creativity*, University of Miami Press, 1965; (with Charles A. Dailey) *How to Make Decisions about People*, Parker Publishing, 1966; (with J. M. Dyer) *The Enjoyment of Management*, Dow Jones-Irwin, 1971.

Chief author or editor of ten books for U.S. Navy, and writer of Navy film scripts. Contributor of articles to general magazines, and to business and military journals. Contributing editor, *The Pope Speaks* Magazine, 1954—; editor, *Naval Training Bulletin*, 1956-58.

WORK IN PROGRESS: A book on books; two novels; a collection of short stories; and a book of poems.

SIDELIGHTS: Dyer's books have had editions in Mexico, England, and India.

*   *   *

DYKES, Archie R(eese)   1931-

PERSONAL: Born January 20, 1931, in Rogersville, Tenn.; son of Claude R. (a farmer) and Rose (Quillen) Dykes; married Nancy Haun; children: John Reece, Thomas Mack. *Education:* East Tennessee State University, B.S., 1952, M.A., 1956; University of Tennessee, Ed.D., 1959. *Home:* 1532 Lilac Lane, Lawrence, Kan. 66044.

CAREER: High school teacher of social studies in Church Hill, Tenn., 1952-55, supervising principal, 1955-58; superintendent of schools in Greeneville, Tenn., 1959-62; University of Tennessee, Memphis, 1962-71, professor of education, 1964-66, chancellor, 1967-71; University of Tennessee, Knoxville, chancellor, 1971-73; University of Kansas, Lawrence, chancellor, 1973—. *Member:* American Association of School Administrators, National Association of State Universities and Land Grant Colleges (member of council on presidents), National Conference of Professors of Education Administration, Tennessee College Association (president, 1969-70), Phi Kappa Phi, Phi Delta Kappa, Exchange Club (Memphis; vice-president, 1962), Ruritan Club (president, 1958). *Awards, honors:* Ford Foundation fellow, 1957-59; American Council on Education fellowship in academic administration at University of Illinois, 1966-67; named Outstanding Alumnus, East Tennessee State University, 1970.

WRITINGS: School Board and Superintendent, Interstate, 1965; (with J. M. Godard and D. R. Coker) *College Administration: Concepts and Techniques*, Institute of Higher Education, University of Georgia, 1971. Contributor to educational periodicals.

*   *   *

EARLE, Peter G.   1923-

PERSONAL: Born May 31, 1923, in Yonkers, N.Y.; son of Victor M. (a real estate agent) and Helen (Moore) Earle; married Rebeca Orozco, September 3, 1949; children: Peter G., Jr., Rebeca Susan, Thomas Harriman. *Education:* Columbia University, student, 1946-48; Mexico City Col-

lege, B.A., 1949, M.A., 1951; University of Kansas, Ph.D., 1959. *Home:* 543 Hampshire Rd., Drexel Hill, Pa. 19026. *Office:* University of Pennsylvania, Philadelphia, Pa. 19174.

CAREER: Princeton University, Princeton, N.J., instructor in Spanish, 1956-59; Wesleyan University, Middletown, Conn., assistant professor of Spanish, 1959-63; University of Pennsylvania, Philadelphia, associate professor, 1963-69, professor of Spanish, 1969—. President, Instituto Internacional de Literatura Iberoamericana, 1973-75. *Military service:* U.S. Army Air Forces, 1942-45; became first lieutenant; received Distinguished Flying Cross and Air Medal. *Member:* Modern Language Association of America, Modern Humanities Research Association, American Association of Teachers of Spanish and Portuguese. *Awards, honors:* Danforth Foundation grant, 1960; second prize in Concurso de Critica Bibliografica for review of Antonello Gerbi's *Disputa del Nuevo Mundo* in *La Gaceta* (Mexico City), 1964.

WRITINGS: Unamuno and English Literature, Hispanic Institute in the United States, 1960; (translator) Samuel Ramos, *Profile of Man and Culture in Mexico*, University of Texas Press, 1962; (editor) *Voces Hispanoamericanas*, Harcourt, 1966; *Prophet in the Wilderness: The Works of Ezequiel Martinez Estrada*, University of Texas Press, 1971; (with Robert G. Mead) *Historia del ensayo hispanoamericana*, Ediciones de Andrea, 1973. Contributor of articles to *World Book Encyclopedia*, and professional journals in America, Argentina, and Mexico. Editor, *Hispanic Review*; advisory editor, *Latin American Literary Review*.

WORK IN PROGRESS: A book on literary criticism in Hispanic America; a biography of Miguel de Unamuno.

SIDELIGHTS: Peter Earle is competent in Spanish, French, Portuguese and Italian.

*   *   *

EAST, Charles   1924-

PERSONAL: Born December 11, 1924, in Shelby, Miss.; son of Elmo Montan and Mabel (Gradolph) East; married Sarah Simmons, September 30, 1948; children: Charles, Jr. *Education:* Louisiana State University, B.A., 1948, M.A., 1962. *Home:* 1455 Knollwood Dr., Baton Rouge, La. 70808. *Agent:* Elizabeth McKee, Harold Matson Co., 22 East 40th St., New York, N.Y. 10016. *Office:* Louisiana State University Press, Baton Rouge, La. 70803.

CAREER: Collier's, New York, N.Y., editorial assistant, 1948-49; *Morning Advocate*, Baton Rouge, La., reporter, then Sunday magazine editor, 1949-55; *State-Times*, Baton Rouge, La., feature writer, then assistant city editor, 1955-62; Louisiana State University Press, Baton Rouge, assistant director and editor, 1962-70, director, 1970—. *Military service:* U.S. Navy, 1944-46. *Member:* Louisiana Genealogical and Historical Society (co-founder, 1953).

WRITINGS: Where the Music Was (short stories), Harcourt, 1965, (with Elemore Morgan) *The Face of Louisiana*, Louisiana State University Press, 1969. Short stories have appeared in *Virginia Quarterly Review, New Mexico Quarterly, Mademoiselle, Yale Review, Red Clay Reader, Antioch Review*, and other literary quarterlies. Co-founder and first editor, *Delta* (Louisiana State University student literary magazine); former editor, *Genealogical Register* (journal of Louisiana Genealogical and Historical Society).

WORK IN PROGRESS: A novel, as yet untitled.

EAST, John Porter 1931-

PERSONAL: Born May 5, 1931, in Springfield, Ill.; son of Laurence John and Virginia (Porter) East; married Priscilla Sherk; children: Kathryn, Martha. *Education:* Earlham College, B.A., 1953; University of Illinois, LL.B., 1959; University of Florida, M.A., 1962, Ph.D., 1964. *Politics:* Republican. *Religion:* Presbyterian. *Home:* 212 Longmeadow Rd., Greenville, N.C. 27834.

CAREER: Practising attorney, 1959-61; East Carolina University, Greenville, N.C., assistant professor, 1964-66, associate professor, 1966-71, professor of political science, 1971—. *Military service:* U.S. Marine Corps, 1953-55. *Member:* Phi Beta Kappa.

WRITINGS: Council-Manager Government: The Political Thought of Its Founder, Richard S. Childs, University of North Carolina Press, 1965. Contributor of articles to professional journals in his field. Member of advisory editorial board, *The Political Science Reviewer,* and *Modern Age.*

* * *

EASTMAN, Richard M(orse) 1916-

PERSONAL: Born August 20, 1916, in Oyster Bay, N.Y.; son of Fred and Lilla Frances (Morse) Eastman; married Vivian Clare Bolger, November 14, 1942; children: Patricia Clare, Julie Ann, Susan Jill. *Education:* Oberlin College, B.A., 1937; Yale University, graduate study, 1937-39; University of Chicago, M.A., 1949, Ph.D. (with honors), 1952. *Home:* 961 Porter Ave., Naperville, Ill. 60540. *Office:* North Central College, Naperville, Ill. 60540.

CAREER: North Central College, Naperville, Ill., 1946—, began as instructor, professor of English, 1955—, department chairman, 1952-70, director of Summer School, 1961-67, chairman of Humanities Division, 1961-70, dean of faculty and vice-president for academic affairs, 1970—. *Military service:* U.S. Army, 1941-46; became major. *Member:* American Conference of Academic Deans, American Association of University Professors.

WRITINGS: A Guide to the Novel, Chandler Publishing, 1965; *Style: Writing as the Discovery of Outlook,* Oxford University Press, 1970. Contributor of articles on modern drama, the novel, and critical theory to *College English, Modern Drama,* and *Novel.*

* * *

EBERHART, (Wilfred) Perry 1924-

PERSONAL: Born August 5, 1924, in Yankton, S.D.; stepson of Carl Howard Haberl and son of Lucille (Bennett) Eberhart Haberl; married Helen Barbara Tecklin (in personnel work), November 12, 1949; children: Daniel, Peter, Medley Ann, Eve Marie. *Education:* University of Colorado, B.A., 1949; Sorbonne, University of Paris, Certificate of Foreign Study, 1952. *Politics:* Democrat. *Address:* 1160 Niver Ave., North Glenn, Colorado 80221.

CAREER: Social worker for Denver Bureau of Public Welfare, 1950-51; *Denver Post,* Denver, Colo., reporter, 1954-55; International News Service, Denver, wire reporter, 1955-58; Denver Board of Education, Denver, high school teacher of history and journalism, 1959-60; National Farmers Union, Denver, editor of publications, 1960-63; U.S. Soil Conservation Service, Denver, information specialist, 1963-65; Mayor's Platte River Development Study, Denver, writer and editor, 1965-66; South Platte Area Redevelopment Council, Denver, executive director, 1967-71, member of executive committee, 1971—; State Historical

Society of Colorado, Denver, research associate, 1971-73; Colorado. Bicentennial-Centennial Commission, Denver, deputy director and historical coordinator, 1973-74; freelance writer, 1974—. Member of board of directors, Regional Transportation District. *Military service:* U.S. Naval Reserve, 1943-46. *Member:* State Historical Society of Colorado, Colorado Citizens Committee on Environmental Planning, Colorado Authors League (former vice-chairman), Denver Posse of Westerners. *Awards, honors:* Award of merit, Farmers Union Press Association, 1963.

WRITINGS: Guide to Colorado Ghost Towns and Mining Camps, Sage Books, 1959, 4th revised edition, 1970; *Treasure Tales of the Rockies,* Sage Books, 1962, 3rd revised edition, 1968; (with C. E. Huff) *The Friend of the Family Farmer: History of National Farmers Union,* National Farmers Union, 1963; (with Philip Schmuck) *The Fourteeners: Colorado's Great Mountains,* Sage Books, 1970. Contributor to *Yearbook of Westerners,* 1974; contributor of historical and conservation articles, and book reviews, to periodicals.

AVOCATIONAL INTERESTS: Riding river rapids, exploring caves, gardening, painting, photography.

* * *

ECKBLAD, Edith Berven 1923-

PERSONAL: Born April 14, 1923, in Baltic, S.D.; daughter of Leander G. (a teacher) and Louise (Simonson) Berven; married Marshall D. Eckblad (a company president), June 9, 1943; children: Mark, Jonathan, James, Nancy, Peter. *Education:* Wheaton College, Wheaton, Ill., student, 1941-42. *Home:* 5224 Spring St., Racine, Wis. 53406.

CAREER: Free-lance writer, and instructor in creative writing. Member of board of directors, council for Wisconsin writers. *Member:* National League of American Pen Women, Wisconsin Regional Writers Association, Racine Writers (co-chairman). *Awards, honors:* Midwest Writers' Conference award for juvenile nonfiction.

WRITINGS: Living with Jesus, Augsburg, 1955; *Something for Jesus,* Augsburg, 1959; *Danny's Straw Hat,* Augsburg, 1962; *Kindness Is a Lot of Things,* C. R. Gibson, 1966; *A Smile Is to Give,* Rand McNally, 1969; *Danny's Orange Christmas Camel,* Augsburg, 1970; *Soft As the Wind,* Augsburg, 1974. Contributor of verse, short stories, and features to religious and family-type magazines.

WORK IN PROGRESS: A conversational style cookbook, *Recipes from Meadowlane,* juvenile mystery books.

AVOCATIONAL INTERESTS: Foreign travel, family entertaining, books, music, the out-of-doors, herb-gardening, and "my two small grand-daughters!"

* * *

EDDY, Roger (Whittlesey) 1920-

PERSONAL: Born March 29, 1920, in Newington, Conn.; son of E. W. Eddy; married Deborah Bankart; children: Heidi B., Lucy L. *Education:* Yale University, B.A., 1942. *Politics:* Republican. *Religion:* Protestant. *Agent:* A. Watkins, Inc., 77 Park Ave., New York, N.Y. 10016.

CAREER: Inventor and Manufacturer of the Audubon Birdcall; operator of a dairy farm and a truck farm. Writer. *Military service:* U.S. Army, Infantry, 1942-46.

WRITINGS: The Rimless Wheel, Macmillan, 1948; *The Bulls and the Bees,* Crowell, 1958; *A Family Affair,* Crowell, 1959; *Best by Far*, Doubleday, 1966; *Never Trust a President of the United States: So Said Jefferson, So Said Lincoln*, Vantage Press, 1969. Contributor to *Saturday Evening Post*.†

* * *

EDELSON, Edward 1932-

PERSONAL: Born September 19, 1932, in New York, N.Y.; son of Saul (a restaurateur) and Sarah (Sunshine) Edelson; married Phyllis Kaplan, October 26, 1957; children: Noah, Daniel, Anne. *Education:* New York University, B.S., 1953; Columbia University, student in advanced science writing program, 1963-64. *Home:* 170-29 Henley Rd., Jamaica, N.Y. 11432. *Office:* 220 East 42nd St., New York, N.Y. 10017.

CAREER: Times-Herald Record, Middletown, N.Y., telegraph editor and city editor, 1959-62; reporter and science editor, *New York World Telegram*, 1962-66; science editor, *New York World Journal Tribune*, 1966-67; WNDT-TV, New York, N.Y., 1968-70; *Family Health*, New York, N.Y., senior staff writer, 1968-71, contributing editor, 1971—; *New York News*, New York, N.Y., science writer, 1971—. *Military service:* U.S. Army, 1954-55. *Member:* National Association of Science Writers. *Awards, honors:* New York Citizens for Clean Air award, 1965; writing award certificate of merit, American Medical Association, 1970; science writing award, American Dental Association, 1970.

WRITINGS: Parents' Guide to Science, Crowell, 1966; (with Fred Warshofsky) *Poisons in the Air*, Pocket Books, 1966; *Healers in Uniform*, Doubleday, 1971; *Help for Your Headache*, Grosset, 1971; *Great Monsters of the Movies*, Doubleday, 1973; *The Book of Prophecy*, Doubleday, 1974; *Visions of Tomorrow*, Doubleday, 1975. Contributor of articles to *Smithsonian Magazine, Saturday Review/World, Popular Science*, and other journals.

* * *

EDMUNDS, Simeon 1917-

PERSONAL: Born April 13, 1917, in St. Helens, Isle of Wight; son of Douglas John Perry and Elsie Kate (Moreton) Edmunds; divorced. *Education:* "Not for publication." *Politics:* Liberal. *Religion:* Humanist.

CAREER: Author, journalist, parapsychologist, hypnotist, and lecturer. *Member:* Society for Psychical Research, British Humanist Association, Society of Authors, National Union of Journalists (honorary membership secretary, London free-lance branch, 1966).

WRITINGS: Hypnotism and the Supernormal, Aquarian Press, 1961; *Miracles of the Mind: An Introduction to Parapsychology*, C. C Thomas, 1965; *'Spirit' Photography*, Society for Psychical Research (London), 1965; *Spiritualism: A Critical Study*, Aquarian Press, 1966; *Hypnosis: Key to Psychic Powers*, Aquarian Press, 1968; *Hypnotism and the Supernormal*, Wilshire, 1968. Contributor of articles on psychical research to periodicals.

WORK IN PROGRESS: The Slick and the Dead.

SIDELIGHTS: Edmunds says he is anti-religion, almost life-long vegetarian, and against color discrimination. *Avocational interests:* Drinking ("but not an alcoholic"), sailing, dogs, and travel.†

EDWARDS, Charles Edward 1930-

PERSONAL: Born July 19, 1930, in Charleston, S.C.; son of Edward (an automobile dealer) and Elizabeth (Orr) Edwards; married Carol Little, April 28, 1951; children: Mary Lynn, Charles E., Jr., Betty Ann, John Orr. *Education:* Georgia Institute of Technology, B.S., 1952, M.A., 1953; University of North Carolina, Ph.D., 1961. *Politics:* Independent. *Religion:* Presbyterian. *Home:* 4615 Limestone Rd., Columbia, S.C. 29206. *Office:* College of Business Administration, University of South Carolina, Columbia, S.C. 29208.

CAREER: University of South Carolina, Columbia, assistant professor, 1959-63, associate professor, 1963-68, professor of business administration, 1968—. *Military service:* U.S. Air Force, 1953-55; became first lieutenant. *Member:* American Economic Association, American Finance Association, American Association of University Professors, Southern Economic Association, Southern Finance Association (secretary-treasurer, 1971-73; president, 1973-74). *Awards, honors:* Ford Foundation faculty follow for regional seminar in economics, University of Virginia, 1962.

WRITINGS: Industrial Markets Survey: Estimated Annual Materials Consumption of South Carolina Manufacturing Establishments, Bureau of Business and Economic Research, University of South Carolina, 1963; *Dynamics of the United States Automobile Industry*, University of South Carolina Press, 1965. Contributor to professional journals in his field.

WORK IN PROGRESS: Studies of financial markets, of depreciation policies, and of variations in automobile sales.

* * *

EDWARDS, Corwin D. 1901-

PERSONAL: Born November 1, 1901, in Nevada, Mo.; son of Granville Dennis (a preacher and teacher) and Ida (Moore) Edwards; married Janet Morris Ward, 1924; married Gertrude Greig (a research associate), February 15, 1948; children: (first marriage) Ward Edwards, Corinne (Mrs. Gerald Greenwald). *Education:* University of Missouri, A.B., 1920, B.J., 1921; Oxford University (Rhodes scholar), B.Litt., 1924; Cornell University, Ph.D., 1928. *Politics:* Democrat. *Home and office:* 11 New Jersey Ave., Lewes, Del. 19958.

CAREER: Cornell University, Ithaca, N.Y., instructor in economics, 1924-26; New York University, New York, N.Y., 1926-33, began as instructor, became associate professor of economics; National Recovery Administration, Washington, D.C., 1933-36, began as economist, became chief of Trade Practices Section, Division of Review; Federal Trade Commission, Washington, D.C., economist, later assistant chief economist, 1937-39; U.S. Department of Justice, Antitrust Division, Washington, D.C., economist, then chairman of policy board, 1939-44; Northwestern University, Evanston, Ill., professor of economics, 1944-48; Federal Trade Commission, chief economist, 1948-53; Cambridge University, Cambridge, England, Pitt Professor of American Institutions, 1953-54; University of Virginia, Charlottesville, professor of economics, 1954-55; University of Chicago, Chicago, Ill., professor of government and business, 1955-63; University of Oregon, Eugene, professor of economics, 1964-71. Lecturer at American University, 1937-38, 1940-41, Columbia University, 1939-40, Harvard University, 1941-1942. American technical mission to Brazil, chief of staff, 1942; U.S. Department of State, consultant on cartels, 1944-48; head of U.S. Mission on Japanese

Combines, 1946; United Nations Economic and Social Council, U.S. representative on Ad Hoc Committee on Restrictive Practices, 1951-52. *Member:* American Economic Association (vice-president, 1951), Phi Beta Kappa.

WRITINGS: Economic and Political Aspects of International Cartels, Government Printing Office, 1944; *Maintaining Competition*, McGraw, 1949; *Big Business and the Policy of Competition*, Western Reserve Press, 1955; *The Price Discrimination Law*, Brookings Institution, 1959; *Cartelization in Western Europe*, U.S. Department of State, 1964; *Trade Regulations Overseas*, Oceana, 1966; *Control of Cartels and Monopolies: An International Comparison*, Oceana, 1967.

Contributor: *The Economics of Modern Life*, Fisher, 1928; *American Labor Dynamics*, Harcourt, 1928; *Economic Behavior*, Houghton, 1931; *Economic Problems in a Changing World*, Farrar & Rinehart, 1939; *Readings in the Social Control of Industry*, Blakiston, 1942; *Economic Problems of Latin America*, McGraw, 1944; *A Cartel Policy for the United Nations*, Columbia University Press, 1945; *Report of Mission on Japanese Combines*, U.S. Department of State, 1946; *The Structure of American Industry*, Macmillan, 1950; *Business Concentration and Price Policy*, Princeton University Press, 1955; *National Standards in a Modern Economy*, Harper, 1956; *Economic Consequences of the Size of Nations*, Macmillan, 1960; *Legal Problems in International Trade and Investment*, World Community Association, 1962; *Industrial Organization and Public Policy—Selected Readings*, Houghton, 1967; *Das Unternehmen in der Rechtsordnung*, C. F. Mueller, 1967; *World Business: Promise and Problems*, Macmillan, 1970; *Die Konzentration in der Wirtschaft*, Dunckler & Humblot, 1971; *The United States and International Markets*, Heath, 1972. Contributor to legal and economics journals.

* * *

EHRLICH, Howard J. 1932-

PERSONAL: Born September 14, 1932, in Brooklyn, N.Y.; son of Herbert (a retailer) and Dorothy (Block) Ehrlich; married Carol Nagel, April 30, 1961; children: Linda J. *Education:* Ohio State University, B.A., 1953, M.A., 1955; Michigan State University, Ph.D., 1959. *Address:* 2743 Maryland Ave., Baltimore, Md. 21218.

CAREER: Michigan State University, East Lansing, instructor, 1956-57; Ohio State University, Columbus, instructor, 1959-62, assistant professor, 1960-62; Columbus Psychiatric Institute and Hospital, Columbus, Ohio, independent researcher, 1959-62; National Institute of Mental Health, Mental Health Study Center, Bethesda, Md., project director, 1962-64; University of Iowa, Iowa City, professor of sociology and director of program in social psychology, 1965-71; executive co-ordinator of Research Group One, 1971—. Co-producer, "The Great Atlantic Radio Conspiracy", 1972—. *Member:* American Sociological Association (fellow), American Psychological Association, Society for the Study of Social Problems, Union of Radical American Social Scientists, Midwestern Sociological Society.

WRITINGS: (Editor with William V. D'Antonio, and contributor) *Power and Democracy in America*, University of Notre Dame Press, 1961; (with Jack J. Preiss) *An Examination of Role Theory: The Case of the State Police*, University of Nebraska Press, 1966; *The Social Psychology of Prejudice*, Wiley, 1973. Contributor of about fifty articles to sociology and psychology journals.

WORK IN PROGRESS: A book, *Preface to an Anarchist Manifesto: Essays of an Impossible Person.*

* * *

EICHER, (Ethel) Elizabeth
(Edna Temple Crane [a house name]; Emily Paul, William Paul)

PERSONAL: Surname is pronounced *I*-ker; born in Miamisburg, Ohio; daughter of Charles A. (a bank cashier) and Minne (Stupp) Eicher. *Education:* Attended Miami University, Oxford, Ohio, 1934-35; Ohio State University, A.B., 1939, M.A., 1940. *Politics:* Democrat. *Religion:* Lutheran. *Home:* 817 South Blvd., Lakeland, Fla. 33801.

CAREER: Franklin (Ohio) public schools, teacher of English, 1940-42; teacher of psychology in private junior college in Virginia, 1942-43; Patterson Field, Dayton, Ohio, head of civilian personnel testing, 1943-46; full-time writer, 1946—.

WRITINGS: (Under pseudonym Edna Temple Crane, a house name) *New Girl at Merrywhether*, Dell, 1963; *Penny Takes the Stage*, Dell, 1964. Contributor of approximately six hundred short stories, under own name, to teen-age, juvenile, and adult periodicals, including *Calling All Girls, American Girl, Ingenue, Scholastic*, and *Progressive Farmer*; also occasionally writes for magazines under pseudonyms Emily Paul and William Paul.

WORK IN PROGRESS: A Vote for Penny; short stories.

AVOCATIONAL INTERESTS: Music, collecting records, books (especially travel, archeology, and suspense fiction), touring southern United States searching for examples of Greek Revival architecture.†

* * *

EISENSON, Jon 1907-

PERSONAL: Born December 17, 1907, in New York, N.Y.; son of Abraham Eli and Sarah (Eisenson) Eisenson; married Freda Francke, June 28, 1931; children: Elinore Ruth (Mrs. Lawrence B. Lurie), Arthur Michael. *Education:* City College (now City College of the City University of New York), B.S.S., 1928; Columbia University, M.A., 1930, Ph.D., 1935. *Office:* San Francisco State University, 1600 Holloway, San Francisco, Calif. 94137.

CAREER: City University of New York, New York, N.Y., began as instructor, became assistant professor of speech at Brooklyn College, 1935-42, associate professor at Queens College, 1946-58, then professor of speech and director of Speech and Hearing Center at Queens College, until 1962; Stanford University, School of Medicine, Palo Alto, Calif., professor of speech pathology and audiology, and director of Institute for Childhood Aphasia, 1962-73; San Francisco State University, professor of speech, 1973—. Columbia University, College of Physicians and Surgeons, part-time lecturer in otolaryngology, 1947-60; visiting professor at University of Queensland, 1969, and Tel Aviv Medical School, 1970; guest lecturer at University of Wisconsin, Northwestern University, University of Michigan, and eighteen other American universities. Diplomate in clinical psychology, American Board of Examiners in Professional Psychology. Consultant to U.S. Veterans Administration and National Institutes of Health. President of American Speech and Hearing Foundation; chairman of special education advisory committee, member of medical and scientific committee, United Cerebral Palsy Association. *Military service:* U.S. Army, 1942-46; assistant chief clinical psychologist, War Department, 1944-45; became major.

MEMBER: American Speech and Hearing Association (fellow; council, 1953-56; president, 1958-59), American Psychological Association (fellow), Speech Association of America, American Association for the Advancement of Science (fellow), Phi Beta Kappa. *Awards, honors:* National Institute of Neurological Diseases and Blindness research grant, 1959-60.

WRITINGS: The Psychology of Speech, Crofts, 1938; (with Pintner and Stanton) *The Psychology of the Physically Handicapped*, Crofts, 1940; (with Berry) *The Defective in Speech*, Crofts, 1942; *Examining for Aphasia*, Psychological Corp., 1946, revised edition, 1954; *Basic Speech*, Macmillan, 1950, 2nd edition (with Paul Boase), 1964; (with Berry) *Speech Disorders*, Appleton, 1956; *Improvement of Voice and Diction*, Macmillan, 1957, 3rd edition published as *Voice and Diction: A Program for Improvement*, 1973; (with Mardel Oglivie) *Speech Correction for the Schools*, Macmillan, 1957, 3rd editon, revised, 1971; (editor and contributor) *Stuttering: A Symposium*, Harper, 1958; (with J. J. Auer and J. Irwin) *Psychology of Communication*, Appleton, 1963; *Aphasia in Children*, Harper, 1972; *Adult Aphasia*, Prentice-Hall, 1973.

Contributor: A. Wiener, editor, *Towards Medical Psychology*, Ronald, 1953; William Cruikshank, editor, *Psychology of Exceptional Children and Youth*, Prentice-Hall, 1955; L. E. Travis, editor, *Handbook of Speech Pathology*, Appleton, 1957; B. Wolman, editor, *Handbook of Clinical Psychology*, McGraw, 1965; *Planning for Better Living*, Heinemann Medical Books, 1969; L. E. Travis, editor, *Handbook of Speech Pathology and Audiology*, Appleton, 1971. Contributor to other symposia, and author of about fifty articles for speech and medical journals.

WORK IN PROGRESS: Research on brain damage and its effects on language and intellect in children.

AVOCATIONAL INTERESTS: Gardening, writing "terse verse."

*   *   *

EKOLA, Giles C(hester) 1927-

PERSONAL: Surname is accented on first syllable; born March 28, 1927, in Crystal Falls, Mich.; son of August A. (a farmer) and Hilja (Hoikka) Ekola; married Sally Ann Soderberg, August 2, 1952; children: Susan, Guy, Olynden, Lindberg, Eva. *Education:* Attended Suomi College, 1949; Augustana College, Rock Island, Ill., B.A., 1953; additional study at Lutheran School of Theology, Chicago, Ill., and Garrett Biblical Institute. *Home address:* Route 1, Box 18, Garfield, Minn. 56332. *Office:* Calvary Lutheran Church, 605 Douglas St., Alexandria, Minn. 56308.

CAREER: Lutheran Church-Suomi Synod, ordained minister, 1953; pastor in New York Mills, Minn., 1953-56; Suomi College, Hancock, Mich., director of admissions, 1956-59, director of development, 1959-61; National Lutheran Council, Division of American Missions, Chicago, Ill., associate secretary, church in town and country, 1961-67; assistant secretary for church development, Board of American missions of Lutheran Church in America, 1967-69; Calvary Lutheran Church, Alexandria, Minn., senior pastor, 1969—. Member of advisory board, Lutheran Welfare Society of Minnesota, 1954-56. *Member:* American Country Life Association. *Awards, honors:* Educational awards, Minnesota chapter of Soil Conservation Society of Amer-

ica, 1973, Minnesota Association of Soil and Water Conservation Districts, 1974.

WRITINGS: (Editor with E. W. Mueller) *The Silent Struggle for Mid-America*, Augsburg, 1963; (editor with Mueller) *Mission in the American Outdoors*, Concordia, 1966; *Town and Country America*, Concordia, 1967; *Big Country*, Red River Valley Synod, Lutheran Church in America, 1970. Author of pamphlets. Correspondent, Religious News Service; former feature and book review editor, *Lutheran Counselor*.

*   *   *

ELBRECHT, Paul G. 1921-

PERSONAL: Born September 30, 1921, in Cleveland, Ohio; son of Fred William (an engineer) and Emelie (Eckert) Elbrecht; married Marie L. Sperduto, August 11, 1944; children: Paula, George, Kathy, Mark, Lynn, Chris, Tim. *Education:* Texas Technological College (now Texas Tech University), B.A., 1958; Concordia Theological Seminary, B.D., 1963; University of Illinois, M.A., 1963. *Office:* Alabama Lutheran Academy and College, 1804 Green St., Selma, Ala.

CAREER: Lutheran clergyman. Pastor, 1954-58; Concordia Theological Seminary, Springfield, Ill., professor, 1958-66; Alabama Lutheran Academy and College, Selma, president, beginning 1966. Former supervisor. Sangamon (Ill.) County. *Member:* American Speech and Hearing Association, Speech Association of America, Lutheran Academy for Scholarship.

WRITINGS: Politics and Government, Concordia, 1965.†

*   *   *

ELIOSEFF, Lee Andrew 1933-

PERSONAL: Born August 28, 1933, in Brooklyn, N.Y.; son of Alex (a teacher) and Claire (Linder) Elioseff; married Jane Woodward (an account executive), June 21, 1963. *Education:* University of Rochester, B.A., 1955; Johns Hopkins University, graduate study, 1955-56; New York University, M.A., 1957, Ph.D., 1960. *Politics:* Independent Democrat. *Religion:* "Heterodox Jew." *Office:* Department of English, University of Kentucky, Lexington, Ky. 40506.

CAREER: University of Texas, Austin, instructor, 1959-62, assistant professor of English, 1962-66; Tufts University, Medford, Mass., associate professor of English, 1966-70; University of Massachusetts, Boston, lecturer, 1970-71; University of Kentucky, Lexington, associate professor of English, 1971—. *Member:* Modern Language Association of America, American Society for Eighteenth-Century studies, Linguistic Society of America, Comparative Literature Association, Mediaeval Academy of America, American Society for Aesthetics. *Awards, honors:* Center for Advanced Study in the Behavioral Sciences and American Council of Learned Societies fellowships, 1963-64.

WRITINGS: The Cultural Milieu of Addison's Literary Criticism, University of Texas Press, 1963. Contributor to *Journal of Aesthetics and Art Criticism*.

WORK IN PROGRESS: Contemporary Theories of Literature; The 'Tragic' Vision of Lemuel Gulliver.

SIDELIGHTS: Elioseff told *CA*: "... Concerned with the problem of the writer: his use of his art for self-analysis and self-therapy. In this last ... influenced by Eissler's *Goethe: A Psychoanalytic Study* and a number of books by Erik

Erikson. . . . Fairly competent in French and German, less so in Latin and Italian."†

* * *

ELLIOTT, Raymond Pruitt   1904-

PERSONAL: Born October 27, 1904, in Cleburne, Tex.; son of Alfred Samuel and Annie Earl (Myres) Elliott; married Helen Gould Sidenfaden, September 8, 1932; children: Roberta Annette (Mrs. Hershel Lindly), Phyllis Rae (Mrs. James Metze). *Education:* North Texas State University, student, 1925; University of Kansas, B.M., 1929, M.A., 1936; postgraduate study at New York University, Christiansen Choral School, and Williamson Choral School. *Politics:* Independent. *Religion:* Baptist. *Home:* Glen Rose Star Rt., Gleburne, Tex. 76031.

CAREER: Teacher of music in elementary and secondary schools, Troy, Kan., 1929-30, at St. Joseph Junior College, St. Joseph, Mo., 1930-46; Texas College of Arts and Industries, Kingsville, assistant professor of music, 1946-50; Texas Tech University, Lubbock, associate professor of music, 1950-60, professor of music, 1960-69, professor emeritus, 1969—, chairman of department of music education, 1960-69. *Member:* Music Educators National Conference, Texas Music Educators Association, Texas Association of Classroom Teachers, Phi Mu Alpha, Tau Beta Sigma, Kappa Kappa Psi, Scottish Rite Mason.

WRITINGS: Fundamentals of Music, Prentice-Hall, 1955, 3rd edition, 1971; *Learning Music*, C. E. Merrill, 1960, 2nd edition, 1966; *Teaching Music*, C. E. Merrill, 1960, 2nd edition, 1966; (contributor) *Music Education in Action*, Allyn & Bacon, 1960; *A Sprig of Grass*, privately printed, 1971; *Only Believe*, privately printed, 1973. Choral number, "Fisherman Luck," published by Southern Music Co.; other songs included in collections for school use. Contributor to music and education journals.

* * *

ELLSWORTH, P(aul) T(heodore)   1897-

PERSONAL: Born November 20, 1897, in Rutland, Vt.; son of Jesse Abram (a salesman) and Lilian (Butts) Ellsworth; married Adelaide Fairbanks, June 10, 1926; married second wife, Viola DeBerrienne Engel, August 5, 1944; children: (adopted) Eileen Patricia, Barry Ian. *Education:* University of Washington, Seattle, B.A., 1920; Oxford University, Rhodes scholar, 1922-25, B.A., 1924; Harvard University, M.A., 1930, Ph.D., 1932. *Home:* 5375 Penny Pl., San Diego, Calif. 92115.

CAREER: Dartmouth College, Hanover, N.H., instructor in economics, 1925-26; Reed College, Portland, Ore., assistant professor of economics, 1926-27; Harvard University, Cambridge, Mass., instructor and tutor in economics, 1928-32; University of Cincinnati, Cincinnati, Ohio, associate professor of economics, 1932-41; U.S. government, Washington, D.C., senior economist, Treasury Department, 1935-36, division chief, Board of Economic Warfare, 1942-43, assistant chief of research, Department of State, 1943-44; University of Wisconsin, Madison, professor of economics, 1944-67; professor emeritus, 1967—. Visiting professor at University of California, Berkeley, 1949-50, University of Hawaii, Honolulu, 1963-64. International Bank for Reconstruction and Development (World Bank), economic adviser, Washington, D.C., 1951-52, chief of Economic Survey Mission, Bangkok, Thailand, 1957-58; National Planning Board, United Nations technical expert, Quito, Ecuador, 1964-65. Consultant to United Nations,

1960, and Pan-American Union, 1962. *Military service:* U.S. Army, Coast Artillery Corps, 1918-19; became second lieutenant. *Member:* American Economic Association (vice-president, 1953), Royal Economic Society, Phi Beta Kappa, Delta Kappa Epsilon. *Awards, honors:* Rhodes scholar, 1922-25; Guggenheim fellowship, 1941-42.

WRITINGS: International Economics, Macmillan, 1938; *Chile: An Economy in Transition*, Macmillan, 1945; *The International Economy*, Macmillan, 1950, 5th edition, 1975. Contributor to economic journals.

* * *

ELMAN, Richard   1934-
(Eric Pearl)

PERSONAL: Born April 23, 1934, in Brooklyn, N.Y.; son of Edward (an attorney) and Pearl (Beckerman) Elman; married Emily Schorr (an artist), June 16, 1956; children: Margaret Ruth. *Education:* Syracuse University, B.A., 1955; Stanford University, M.A., 1957; *Politics:* Socialist. *Residence:* New York, N.Y. *Agent:* Roberta Pryor, International Famous Agency, 1301 Avenue of the Americas, New York, N.Y. 10019.

CAREER: Professional writer. Pacifica Foundation, WBAI-FM, New York, N.Y., public affairs director, 1961-64; Columbia University, School of Social Work Research Center, New York, N.Y., research associate, 1965; Hunter College, New York, N.Y., lecturer in English, 1966; Bennington College, Bennington, Vt., visiting writer, 1966-67; Columbia University, New York, N.Y., adjunct professor of writing, 1968—.

WRITINGS: A Coat for the Tsar (novel), University of Texas Press, 1959; *The Poorhouse State: The American Way of Life on Public Assistance* (reportage), Pantheon, 1966; *The 28th Day of Elul* (novel), Scribner, 1967; *Ill-at-Ease in Compton* (reportage), Pantheon, 1967; *The Reckoning* (novel), Scribner, 1968; (editor and compiler with Albert Fried) *Charles Booth's London*, Pantheon, 1968; *An Education in Blood* (novel), Scribner, 1970; *Fridi and Shirl and the Kids* (novel), Scribner, 1971; *Crossing Over and other Tales* (short stories), Scribner, 1973; *Uptight with the Rolling Stones* (reportage), Scribner, 1973. Occasional writer for radio and television. Contributor of articles, stories, reviews, and poetry—sometimes under the pseudonym Eric Pearl—to magazines, including *Nation, New Republic, Commonweal, Paris Review, Evergreen Review, New York Times Book Review*, and *Book Week.*

WORK IN PROGRESS: Poetry; a novel, *The Man Who Liked Strangers.*

SIDELIGHTS: Elman told *CA*: "[I] travel and read as much as I can but that is really quite little. Mostly I depend upon being provoked by events—whether real or imagined—which forces me to attempt to muster the curiosity to put myself in somebody else's shoes. All my life I have admired writers who have evinced a rage against personal injustice. Not that I believe writers must all exhibit the same dreary consciences. . . . In my case, I would not know how to write of a [nonfictional] subject if I were not deeply moved by it—through rage, or compassion, or, perhaps, amazement and a sense of wonder."

Elman spent two years interviewing people on relief in New York's Lower East Side for *The Poorhouse State*. James J. Graham wrote of the book: "With much compassion, objectivity and insight, Elman has managed to write an exciting treatise on a very unpopular subject. His book should destroy both liberal and conservative myths about the welfare poor and those who service and oppress them. The only villain in this book is the Poorhouse State itself, which Elman describes as a 'system of inadequate payments, grudging services, petty rules tyrannies, and surveillance mechanism that, though always regarded as a temporary arrangement, has preserved all in their deprivations'."

Betty Kronsky notes: "If this book is read as a pilgrim's progress into "the other America," it rewards us with its honest record of one man's commitment to hunting down the truth, often at the expense of his own dignity and with his nerves exposed."

The 28th Day of Elul "comes off as an unequivocally honest book," writes Joel Lieber, "in the way that most recent novels are not honest books. . . . Primed by an ironic, stinging intelligence, sections in *Elul* are nothing short of masterly. It is among the few novels that one could read five years from now and still be moved and instructed by it."

BIOGRAPHICAL/CRITICAL SOURCES: Commonweal, January 6, 1967; *Village Voice*, March 2, 1967; *Saturday Review*, April 15, 1967; *Commentary*, August, 1967; *Observer Review*, February 16, 1969; *New York Times Book Review*, September 14, 1969; *Life*, June 25, 1971.

*   *   *

EL-MELIGI, A(bdel) Moneim 1923-

PERSONAL: Born November 2, 1923, in Egypt; came to United States in 1961; son of Abdel-Aziz El-Meligi (an accountant) and Zahiya (El-Zehery) Seleem; married Ninon Agogue, November 13, 1954; children: Nadia (duaghter), Nohman, Karim (sons). *Education:* University of Alexandria, B.A., 1943; Ain-Shams University, Dip.Ed., 1945; University of Cairo, M.A. (first class honors), 1951; University of London, Ph.D., 1954.

CAREER: Teacher at secondary school in Cairo, Egypt, 1945-49; Ain-Shams University, College of Education, Cairo, assistant lecturer in psychology, 1949-51; Runwell Hospital, Essex, England, intern in clinical psychology, 1954; Ain-Shams University, Cairo, lecturer, 1955-60, associate professor of clinical psychology, 1960-61; State University of New York College at New Paltz, associate professor of psychology, 1961-62; New Jersey Neuro-Psychiatric Institute, Princeton, N.J., associate director of psychology service and research center, 1962-66, research scientist, 1967—. Rutgers University, New Brunswick, N.J., part-time lecturer in psychology, 1963-65, supervisor of training in school psychology, 1964—, visiting professor of psychology, 1965—; director of psychology, Pinehaven Sanitarium, Bayville, N.J., 1966-67. Consultant psychologist and staff clinical psychologist at hospitals and clinics in Egypt and United States.

MEMBER: International Council of Psychologists (fellow), International Society of General Semantics, American Psychological Association, Egyptian Association of Psychological Studies (founding member), British Psychological Society, British Rorschach Forum (associate), American Association of University Professors, Eastern Psychological Association, New Jersey Academy of Science (chairman of psychology section, 1965-66), New Jersey Psychological Association. *Awards, honors:* Grant from Bureau of Research in Neurology and Psychiatry to develop diagnostic tests of schizophrenia.

WRITINGS: Ways of Thinking (in Arabic), Nahdat Misr Bookshop, 1949; *Psychological Development* (in Arabic), Misr Press, 1949; *Development of Religious Feeling in Childhood and Adolescence* (in Arabic), Al-Maaref, 1955; *Psychological Experts* (in Arabic), Misr Press, 1956; (translator into Arabic, with M. Ziwar) Sigmund Freud, *Autobiographical Study*, Al-Maaref, 1956; *Recent Scientific Developments in Egypt*, National Commission for UNESCO, 1957; (translator into Arabic) Sibylle Escalona, *Understanding Hostility in Children*, co-published by Franklin Publications and Renaissance Bookshop, 1957; (contributor of section translated from the French) Cyril M. Franks, editor, *Conditioning Techniques in Clinical Practice and Research*, Springer, 1964; (with Humphry Osmond) *Manual for the Experiential World Inventory*, University Books, 1966; *Crises in Our Lives* (in Arabic), Al-Maaref. Contributor to professional journals in Egypt and America, and to Egyptian and Sudanese magazines and newspapers.

SIDELIGHTS: El-Meligi is proficient in English, Arabic, and French, and has some knowledge of Latin. He appeared in a film titled, "Schizophrenia: A Shattered Mirror," financed by National Institutes of Health, and shown on educational television. *Avocational interests:* Sculpture.†

*   *   *

ELVIN, Anne Katharine Stevenson 1933-
(Anne Stevenson)

PERSONAL: Born January 3, 1933, in Cambridge, England; daughter of Charles Leslie (a philosopher) and Louise (Destler) Stevenson; married second husband, John Mark Dutton Elvin (a lecturer in Chinese at Cambridge University), November, 1962; children: (first marriage) Caroline Margaret Hitchcock. *Education:* University of Michigan, B.A., 1954, M.A., 1962. *Politics:* Democrat.

CAREER: Writer. Part-time teacher of cello in Cambridge, England; cellist in string orchestra connected with Cambridge University. *Member:* Phi Beta Kappa. *Awards, honors:* Avery and Jule Hopwood awards at University of Michigan, 1950, 1952, and major prize in poetry, 1954.

WRITINGS—Under name Anne Stevenson: *Living in America* (poetry), Generation, 1965; *Elizabeth Bishop* (criticism), Twayne, 1966; *Ralph Dacre* (novel) Collins, 1967; *Reversals*, Wesleyan University Press, 1969; *A Relative Stranger* (novel), Putnam, 1970; *A Game of Statues*, Putnam, 1972; *French Inheritance*, Putnam, 1974; *Correspondences*, Wesleyan University Press, 1974. Contributor to American periodicals.

WORK IN PROGRESS: Writing stories and poems.

AVOCATIONAL INTERESTS: Music, traveling.†

*   *   *

EMERSON, James G(ordon), Jr. 1926-

PERSONAL: Born June 4, 1926, in Palo Alto, Calif.; son of James Gordon and Edith (Willman) Emerson; married Margaret Bonnell, September 18, 1952; children: John Bonnell, Lynne Edith, James Edward. *Education:* Stanford University, A.B., 1946; Princeton Theological Seminary, B.D., 1949; University of Chicago, Ph.D., 1959. *Home:* 3250 S. Detroit St., Denver, Colo. 80210. *Office:* Central Presbyterian Church, 1660 Sherman St., Denver, Colo. 80203.

CAREER: Presbyterian clergyman, serving as minister in Forest Hills, N.Y., 1955-59, and Bloomfield, N.J., 1959-65; Larchmont Avenue Church, Larchmont, N.Y., minister,

1965-69; now affiliated with Central Presbyterian Church, Denver, Colo. Princeton Theological Seminary, Princeton, N.J., visiting lecturer in pastoral theology, beginning 1964; general director, Community Service Society, beginning 1969. Presbyterian Church in the U.S.A., member of advisory committee on vocational counseling. Bloomfield College, member of board of directors. *Member:* Bloomfield Ministerial Association, University Club of New York, Denver Rotary Club.

WRITINGS: Divorce, the Church, and Remarriage, Westminster, 1961; *The Dynamics of Forgiveness*, Westminster, 1964. Contributor to *Pastoral Psychology.*

WORK IN PROGRESS: Research on the dynamics of administrative work; a book on mysticism.

*   *   *

EMPSON, William   1906-

PERSONAL: Born September 27, 1906, in Yorkshire, England; son of A. R. and Laura (Micklethwait) Empson; married Hester Henrietta Crouse, 1941; children: William Hendrick Mogador, Jacobus Arthur Calais. *Education:* Winchester College, 1920-25; Magdalen College, Cambridge, B.A. in mathematics, 1929. *Home:* Studio House, 1 Hampstead Hill Gardens, London N.W. 3, England.

CAREER: Bunrika Daigaku, Tokyo, Japan, chair of English literature, 1931-34; Peking National University (then part of South-Western Combined Universities), Peking, China, professor of English literature, 1937-39; British Broadcasting Co., London, England, editor in monitoring department, 1940-41, Chinese editor, 1941-46; Peking National University, Peking, China, professor of English, 1947-52; Sheffield University, Sheffield, England, professor of English literature, 1953-71, became professor emeritus. *Awards, honors:* Ingram Merrill Foundation Award for Literature, 1968; D.Litt., from University of East Anglia, 1968, and University of Bristol, 1971.

WRITINGS: Seven Types of Ambiguity (criticism), Chatto & Windus, 1930, 3rd edition, 1953, Meridan, 1957; *Some Versions of Pastoral*, Chatto & Windus, 1935, New Directions, 1950, reissued as *English Pastoral Poetry*, Norton, 1938, reprinted, Books for Libraries, 1972. *Poems*, Chatto & Windus, 1935; (translator from technical into basic English) John Haldane, *Outlook of Science*, Routledge & Kegan Paul, 1935; (translator from technical into basic English) Haldane, *Science and Well-Being*, Routledge & Kegan Paul, 1935; (with George Garrett) *Shakespeare Survey*, Brendin Publishing Co., 1937; *The Gathering Storm* (poems), Faber, 1940; *Collected Poems*, Harcourt, 1949, enlarged edition, 1961; *The Structure of Complex Words*, New Directions, 1951, 2nd edition, Chatto & Windus, 1964, University of Michigan Press, 1967; *Milton's God*, Chatto & Windus, 1961, New Directions, 1962, enlarged edition, Chatto & Windus, 1965; (author of introduction) John R. Harrison, *The Reactionaries: Yeats, Lewis, Pound, Eliot, Lawrence*, Schoken, 1967; (editor with David Pirie) *Coleridge's Verse: A Selection*, Faber, 1972, Schoken, 1973. Also author of introduction for a Signet edition of Shakespeare's *Poems*, 1968.

SIDELIGHTS: Seven Types of Ambiguity is now regarded as one of the most important contributions to the formalist school of New Criticism. Hugh Kenner writes: "In 1930 William Empson published a book of criticism which had the unique distinction of reducing the passivity before poetry of hundreds of readers without imposing—or proposing—a single critical judgment of any salience. *Seven*

Types of Ambiguity neither altered the genealogy of sensibility, . . . nor renovated criteria of technique, . . . nor suspended familiar works from new terminological pegs. . . .''

Empson's definition of ambiguity is a broad one: "An ambiguity, in ordinary speech, means something very pronounced, and as a rule witty or deceitful. I propose to use the word in an extended sense, and shall think relevant to my subject any verbal nuance, however slight, which gives room for alternative reactions to the same piece of language" (*Seven Types of Ambiguity*, 2nd edition). Empson's seven types are briefly defined in the table of contents: "First-type ambiguities arise when a detail is effective in several ways at once. . . . In second-type ambiguities two or more alternative meanings are fully resolved into one. . . . The condition for third type ambiguity is that two apparently unconnected meanings are given simultaneously. . . . In the fourth type the alternative meanings combine to make clear a complicated state of mind in the author. . . . The fifth type is a fortunate confusion, as when the author is discovering his idea in the act of writing . . . or not holding it all in mind at once. . . . In the sixth type what is said is contradictory or irrelevant and the reader is forced to invent interpretations. . . . The seventh type is that of full contradiction, marking a division in the author's mind. . . .'' Kenner notes: "The motive behind such criticism as is contained in *Seven Types of Ambiguity* is not the enlightenment of the reader but the satisfaction of the author: "The object of life, after all,' [Empson] tells us late in *Ambiguity*, 'is not to understand things, but to maintain one's defenses and equilibrium and live as well as one can; it is not only maiden aunts who are placed like this'.'' Roger Sale, however, believes that the book has been too harshly judged by many critics. He writes: "Most discussions have picked on its least interesting aspects, its use of the word 'ambiguity' and its ranging of the 'types' along a scale of 'advancing logical disorder.' But these matters are really minor. . . . The book, [Empson] says, is not philosophical but literary, and its aim is to examine lines Empson finds beautiful and haunting. The seven types are only pegs and 'ambiguity' is a kind of hatrack. . . . But in at least fifteen places Empson shows that the aim of analysis is not so much understanding lines as uncovering whole tracts of the mind, and the book is studded with the right things said about a poet or an historical period.'' Sale believes that *Some Versions of Pastoral* is Empson's best book, although it too has been misjudged as a literary work and misused as a critical tool. Sale notes that "in [this book] he can move from the work at hand to his vision with almost no shoving of the evidence, so even though his prose and organization may seem difficult on first reading, he turns with almost indescribable grace from the smallest particular to the largest generalization and back to various middle grounds. When one becomes used to the book and begins to hear the massive chords of its orchestrations supporting even the most irrelevant aside, the effect is one only the greatest books can produce—it envelopes and controls such large areas of the imagination that for a while one is willing to admit it is the only book ever written. As a modern work of persuasion it is unrivaled.''

Although Empson is best known for his criticism, John Wain writes: ". . . . It may well be that criticism will be read and remembered while poetry is forgotten, for criticism breeds fresh criticism more easily than poetry breeds fresh poetry; but in Empson's case it would be a pity if he were known simply as the 'ambiguity' man, and not as a poet.'' A. Alvarez writes: "The poetry of William Empson has been more used than that of any other English poet of our time.... Empson's verse was read with an overwhelming sense of relief after the brash and embarrassed incoherence of wartime and post-war poetry.'' Explaining that Empson's poetry was ''used'' by his readers, even if with ''undergraduate delight,'' Alvarez notes that ''there is something in his work which encourages other writers to use it for their own ends. It has, I think, an *essential* objectivity. This is not to say that it has an unmistakable, individual tone, or that a great deal of personal trouble may not have gone into its making. But in the later poems what goes in as strong personal feeling comes out as something more general; whilst in the earlier work all the personal energy goes into a particularly impersonal business.''

Alvarez believes that Empson's poetry depends on his control over a large range of ideas: ''[Empson] is less interested in saying his own say than in the agility and skill and variety with which he juggles his ideas. So it is a personal poem only at a remove: the subject is impersonal; the involvement is all in his effort to make as much as he can out of the subject, and in the accomplishment with which he relates his manifold themes so elegantly together. Empson's, in short, is a poetry of wit in the most traditional sense.... And, like most wit, the pleasure it gives is largely in the immaculate performance, which is a rare pleasure but a limited one.''

In tracing the development of Empson's poetry, Alvarez says of the early poems: ''In his sardonic way, Empson made his polish and inventiveness seem like a personal claim for sanity, as though he saw everything in a fourth and horrifying dimension but was too well-mannered to say so. Hence the wry despair and vigorous stylishness seemed not at all contradictory.'' He notes that ''what the [later] poems have gained in general truth they have lost in stylish and enquiring originality. And it is as a stylist of poetry and ideas that, I think, Empson is most important. He took over all [T. S.] Eliot's hints about what was most significant in the English tradition, and he put them into practice without any of the techniques Eliot had derived from the French and Italians. And so his poetry shows powerfully and with great purity the perennial vitality of the English tradition; and in showing this it also expresses the vitality and excitement of the extraordinarily creative moment when Empson began writing.''

BIOGRAPHICAL/CRITICAL SOURCES: Hugh Kenner, *Gnomon: Essays on Contemporary Literature*, McDowell, 1951; John Wain, *Preliminary Essays*, Macmillan (London), 1957; A. Alvarez, *Stewards of Excellence*, Scribner, 1958 (published in England as *The Shaping Spirit*, Chatto & Windus, 1958); *Times Literary Supplement*, *Yale Review*, June 1962; *Time*, August 10, 1962; *Criticism*, fall, 1966; Roger Sale in *Hudson Review*, autumn, 1966.

* * *

ENELOW, Allen J(ay) 1922-

PERSONAL: Born January 15, 1922, in Pittsburgh, Pa.; son of Isadore M. (a businessman) and Rose (Kasdan) Enelow; married 2nd wife, Sheila Kearns, October 1, 1966; children: David, James, Susan, Margaret, Lauren, Lisa, Patience, Abigail. *Education:* West Virginia University, A.B., 1942; University of Louisville, M.D., 1944.

CAREER: In private practice of psychiatry and psychoanalysis, Los Angeles, Calif., 1952-60; University of Southern California, School of Medicine, Los Angeles, associate professor, 1960-64, professor of psychiatry, 1964-

67; Michigan State University, East Lansing, professor and chairman of department of psychiatry, 1967-72; University of the Pacific, Stockton, Calif., professor of psychiatry, 1972—; Pacific Medical Center, San Francisco, Calif., chairman of department of psychiatry, 1972—. *Military service:* U.S. Army, Medical Corps, 1945-47; became captain. *Member:* American Medical Association (assistant secretary of nervous and mental disease section, 1967-68), American Psychiatric Association (fellow), American Psychoanalytic Association, American Psychosomatic Society, American College of Physicians (fellow).

WRITINGS: (With M. Wexler) *Psychiatry in the Practice of Medicine*, Oxford University Press, 1966; (editor) *Depression in Medical Practice*, Merck Sharp & Dohme, 1970; (editor with D. G. Langsley, and J. F. McDermott, Jr.) *Mental Health Education in the New Medical Schools*, Jossey-Bass, 1973. Contributor of more than thirty articles to medical and psychiatric journals.†

* * *

ENGEL, Pauline Newton 1918-

PERSONAL: Born January 10, 1918, in Chicago, Ill.; daughter of Leonard Victor (a consulting engineer) and Mabel (Dennis) Newton; children: Diane (Mrs. James F. Johnson IV). *Education:* Attended University of Illinois, 1935-36, University of California, 1936-39. *Office:* Famous Artists Schools, Inc., 54 Wilton Rd., Westport, Conn. 06881.

CAREER: Famous Artists Schools, Inc., Westport, Conn., associate editor of *Famous Artists* (magazine), 1953-55, editor, 1958—, assistant to president, 1955-64, assistant vice-president, 1964-65, assistant secretary, 1965—. Westport Public Library, trustee, 1965—; Mid-Fairfield County Youth Museum, trustee, 1965—; secretary, 1966.

WRITINGS: Executive Secretary's Handbook, Prentice-Hall, 1965.†

* * *

ENSLIN, Morton S(cott) 1897-

PERSONAL: Born March 8, 1897, in Somerville, Mass.; son of Theodore V. (a merchant) and Ada (Scott) Enslin; married Ruth Tuttle, June 21, 1922; children: Theodore V. II, Priscilla (Mrs. James R. Marsh). *Education:* Harvard University, A.B., 1919, Th.D., 1924; Newton Theological Institution, B.D., 1922. *Politics:* Republican. *Religion:* Christian. *Home:* 708 Argyle Rd., Wynnewood, Pa. 19096. *Office:* Department of Literature, Dropsie University, Philadelphia, Pa. 19132.

CAREER: Crozer Theological Seminary, Chester, Pa., professor of New Testament, 1924-54; University of Pennsylvania, Philadelphia, lecturer in patristics, 1925-54; St. Lawrence University, Theological School, Canton, N.Y., Craig Professor of Biblical Languages and Literature, 1955-65; Bryn Mawr College, Bryn Mawr, Pa., visiting lecturer and chairman of department of history of religion, 1965-68; Dropsie University, Philadelphia, Pa., professor of early Christian history, 1968—. Visiting professor at University of Chicago, summer, 1929, Drew Theological Seminary, 1953-54, Iliff School of Theology, summer, 1956. Member of managing committee, American School of Classical Studies, Athens, 1942—. *Military service:* U.S. Naval Reserve Force, 1918-22; active duty, 1918-19; became ensign. *Member:* American Theological Society (treasurer, 1927-55; president, 1952), Society of Biblical Literature (president, 1945), American Oriental Society, Philadelphia Classical Club, Phi Beta Kappa, Phi Gamma Mu. *Awards, honors:* D.D., Colby College, 1945; D.H.L., Hebrew Union College, 1964.

WRITINGS: The Ethics of Paul, Harper, 1930, reissued, Abingdon, 1962; *Christian Beginnings*, Harper, 1938; *The Prophet from Nazareth*, McGraw, 1961; *Letters to the Churches*, Lutterworth, 1963; *From Jesus to Christianity*, Beacon, 1964; *The Book of Judith*, Brill, 1972; *Reapproaching Paul*, Westminster Press, 1972. Contributor to professional journals and encyclopedias. Editor of *Crozer Quarterly*, 1941-52, and *Journal of Biblical Literature*, 1960-69.

* * *

EPP, Eldon Jay 1930-

PERSONAL: Born November 1, 1930, in Mountain Lake, Minn.; son of Jacob Jay (a merchant) and Louise (Kintzi) Epp; married ElDoris Balzer, June 13, 1951; children: Gregory Thomas, Jennifer Elizabeth. *Education:* Wheaton College, Wheaton, Ill., A.B. (magna cum laude), 1952; Fuller Theological Seminary, B.D. (magna cum laude), 1955; Harvard University, S.T.M., 1956, Ph.D., 1961. *Home:* 19051 Fairmount Blvd., Shaker Heights, Ohio 44118. *Office:* Department of Religion, Case Western Reserve University, Cleveland, Ohio 44106.

CAREER: Princeton Theological Seminary, Princeton, N.J., special research assistant, 1961-62; University of Southern California, Graduate School of Religion, Los Angeles, assistant professor, 1962-65, associate professor of religion, 1965-67, associate professor of classics, 1966-68; Case Western Reserve University, Cleveland, Ohio, associate professor, 1968-71, professor of religion, 1971—, Harkness Professor of Biblical Literature, 1971—. Member of board of managers, St. Paul's Cathedral-Episcopal, Los Angeles, 1964-68; member of executive committee, International Greek New Testament Project, 1968—. *Member:* American Academy of Religion (vice-president of Pacific Coast section, 1964-65; president, Pacific Coast section, 1965-66; national executive council, 1965), New Testament Colloquium, Society of Biblical Literature (chairman of Textual Criticism Seminar, 1966, 1971—), Catholic Biblical Association, Institute for Antiquity and Christianity Studiorum Novi Testamenti Societas. *Awards, honors:* Rockefeller Doctoral Fellow in Religion, 1959-60; Guggenheim Fellow, 1974-75.

WRITINGS: The Theological Tendency of Codex Bazae Cantabrigiensis in Acts, Cambridge University Press, 1966; (contributor) B. L. Daniels and M. J. Suggs, *Studies in the History and Text of the New Testament in Honor of Kenneth Willis Clark*, University of Utah, 1967; (contributor) H. D. Betz, editor, *Christology and a Modern Pilgrimage: A Discussion with Norman Perrin*, New Testament Colloquium, 1971; (contributor) G. G. Hawthorne, editor, *Current Issues in Biblical and Patristic Interpretation*, Eerdmans, 1975.

Associate editor, *Journal of Biblical Literature*, 1971—; member of editorial board: *Heremeneia: A Critical and Historical Commentary on the Bible*, Fortress Press, 1966—; *Society of Biblical Literature Monograph Series*, 1969-72; *Studies and Documents*, 1971—.

WORK IN PROGRESS: Research in New Testament manuscript studies and textual criticism, particularly text-critical method, including the preparation of an introduction to textual criticism and a history of textual criticism in America.

EPPS, Robert L(ee) 1932-

PERSONAL: Born March 23, 1932, in Fort Worth, Tex.; son of Robert Jay (an oil driller) and Gurley (Milliken) Epps; married Richie Lane, June 12, 1955; children: Thomas Lane, Elise Claire. *Education:* McMurry College, B.A., 1954; Yale University, B.D., 1957, S.T.M., 1958; graduate study at University of Missouri at Kansas City, University of Kansas, and Washington University, St. Louis, Mo. *Politics:* Independent. *Home:* 1537 Swallow Dr., Brentwood, Mo. 63144. *Office:* 600 East 22nd St., Kansas City, Mo.

CAREER: Methodist clergyman, 1957—. National College, Kansas City, Mo., assistant professor, 1958-59; Central Methodist Church, Kansas City, associate minister, 1959-61; Greater Kansas City Mental Health Foundation, Kansas City, Mo., research associate, 1964—. Director, Wesley Foundation; staff member of Experimental Campus Ministry, St. Louis; member of board, Kansas City Social Health Society, 1960-64, Children and Family Services, 1965.

WRITINGS: (With Lee D. Hanes) *Day Care of Psychiatric Patients*, C. C Thomas, 1964; (with Robert H. Barnes and Thomas S. McPartland) *A Community Concern: The Management of Major Mental Illness in the Community*, C. C Thomas, 1965.

WORK IN PROGRESS: Research on the structure, philosophy, and theology of the church in relation to urban institutions and urbanization.†

* * *

EPSTEIN, Edward Jay 1935-

PERSONAL: Born December 6, 1935, in New York, N.Y.; son of Louis J. (an executive) and Betty (Opolinsky) Epstein. *Education:* Cornell University, A.B., 1957, M.A., 1966; Harvard University, Ph.D. candidate. *Religion:* Jewish.

CAREER: Assistant professor of government, Massachusetts Institute of Technology, Cambridge, Mass.; tutor in sociology, Harvard University, Cambridge. Reporter-at-large, *New Yorker*. *Military service:* U.S. Army Reserves.

WRITINGS: Inquest: The Warren Commission and the Establishment of Truth, Viking, 1966 (also serialized in *True* Magazine, November, 1966); *Counterplot*, Viking, 1969; *News from Nowhere: Television and the News*, Random House, 1973. Contributor of articles and reviews to *Esquire, Commentary, New Yorker*, and *New York Times*.

WORK IN PROGRESS: A study on the establishment of truth in a political environment.

SIDELIGHTS: Epstein is competent in French and Spanish.

BIOGRAPHICAL/CRITICAL SOURCES: Look, June 29, 1966, July 12, 1966; *New York Herald Tribune*, Paris edition, October 5, 1966.†

* * *

ERICKSON, Marion J. 1913-

PERSONAL: Born November 10, 1913, in Centuria, Wis.; daughter of William A. (a farmer) and Mabel A. (Ten Eyck) Ihrig; married Ernst Walfred Erickson (a librarian), July 2, 1938; children: Karen C. (Mrs. James Spaulding), Susan E. (Mrs. Vernon Fahle), David S. *Education:* State Teachers College (now University of Wisconsin), Superior, B.S.,

1938; Eastern Michigan University, M.A., 1958; University of Michigan, graduate study, 1958. *Office:* Ypsilanti Public Schools, Ypsilanti, Mich.

CAREER: Elementary teacher in Clear Lake, Wis., 1935-37, Escanaba, Mich., 1937-38, LaGrande, Ore., 1948-50, Urbana, Ill., 1950-52; Ypsilanti (Mich.) public schools, teacher of regular classes and of the mentally retarded, 1956—, research associate, 1966. Educational adviser to Nepal under Smith-Mundt grant, U.S. Department of State, 1958-59. *Member:* Council for Exceptional Children, Michigan Education Association, Ypsilanti Education Association.

WRITINGS: (Contributor) J. F. Magary and J. R. Eichorn, editors, *The Exceptional Child*, Holt, 1960; (contributor) Victor H. Noll and Rachel P. Noll, editors, *Readings in Educational Psychology*, Macmillan, 1962, 2nd edition, 1968; *The Mentally Retarded Child in the Classroom*, Macmillan, 1965; *A Program to Prepare Disadvantaged High School Students for Employment as Preschool and Kindergarten Aides*, Ypsilanti Public Schools, 1966.†

* * *

ESCARPENTER, Claudio 1922-

PERSONAL: Born October 23, 1922, in Havana, Cuba; son of Claudio (a merchant) and Rosa (Fargas) Escarpenter; married Maria-Teresa Ferran, July 1, 1955; children: Maria-Teresa, Juan-Claudio, Alfredo, Andres, Rosa-Maria, Nuria-Caridad. *Education:* Fordham University and George Washington University, M.A.; Havana National University, LL.D.; University of Barcelona, Licenciado of Laws and Licenciado in History. *Religion:* Roman Catholic. *Home:* Rafael Salgado No. 3, Madrid, Spain. *Office:* Harris Bosch Aymerich, S.A., Avda. Generalisimo 20, Madrid, Spain.

CAREER: Central Bank of Cuba, Havana, Chief of National Incomes and Sugar Division, 1948-56; Havana Catholic University, Havana, Cuba, professor of economics and dean of School of Economics, 1948-60; Ward-Garcia Steamship Line, Havana, vice-president, 1956-59; Cuba's Bank for Foreign Trade, Havana, general manager, 1959-60; Organization of American States, Washington, D.C., chief of Transportation Unit, 1960-63; Harris Bosch Aymerich, S.A., Madrid, Spain, general manager, 1963—. Member, Catholic Universities International Secretariat, 1946-50.

WRITINGS: La Economia del Trafico Maritimo Internacional de Cuba, Echevarria, 1958, translation by Enrique Ierdau and Federico Lerdau published as *The Economics of International ocean Transport*, University of Wisconsin Press, 1965; *General Problems of Transportation in Latin America*, Pan American Union, 1962; *La Empresa Transportista y la estructura de los mercados del transporte*, Ministry of Public Works (Spain), 1965. Contributor to journals.

WORK IN PROGRESS: Writing on the origin and development of the old Banco de la Habana during Cuba's colonial history.

SIDELIGHTS: Escarpenter said, "Circumstances out of my control, mainly political, have diverted me from what is my deepest vocation: university life." He speaks Catalan, English, French, Italian, and some Latin, Arabic, and German.†

ESFANDIARY, F(ereidoun) M. 1930-

PERSONAL: Born October 15, 1930, in Teheran, Iran; son of A. H. Sadigh (a diplomat) and Mohtaram Esfandiary. *Education:* Attended schools in the Middle East, Europe, and the United States. *Agent:* Curtis Brown Ltd., 60 East 56th St., New York, N.Y. 10022. *Office address:* P.O. Box 61, Village Station, New York, N.Y. 10014.

CAREER: United Nations, member of Conciliation Commission for Palestine, 1952-54; did research on social problems in Iran, 1961-62; writer, 1954—. Worked at various times as counselor in camps for children in New York and California. Instructor in futurist philosophy, New School for Social Research, Smithsonian Institution, and elsewhere. *Awards, honors:* Farfield Foundation grant, 1965; fellowship to Bread Loaf Writers Conference, 1966; Rockefeller Foundation grant, 1966.

WRITINGS: Day of Sacrifice (novel), Obolensky, 1959; *The Beggar* (novel), Obolensky, 1965; *Identity Card*, (novel), Grove, 1966; *Optimism One* (nonfiction), Norton, 1970; *Up-Wingers* (nonfiction), John Day, 1973. Work represented in anthologies, including *Essays Today*, edited by William Moynihan, Harcourt, 1968; *Dimensions of the Future*, edited by Maxwell Norman, Holt, 1974; *Woman Year 2000*, edited by Maggie Tripp and others, Arbor House, 1974. Contributor to *Nation, New York Times Sunday Magazine, Saturday Review, New York Times*, and other periodicals.

WORK IN PROGRESS: Telespheres.

SIDELIGHTS: Esfandiary's first novel, according to the critics, achieves a double success: "He tells an engrossing tale and he proves his point." His point is that backward societies and governments are beset by many internal problems which must be analyzed and studied in an effort to achieve workable solutions. Hal Lehrman wrote: "His excellent first novel contains—in addition to a full cup of sex, intrigue, and murder—some masterful insights into the mysterious follies of the mad Middle East.... [It] is a whopping good yarn plus a deliciously penetrating commentary on the lunatic inner workings of an important area in our foreign news headlines.... Mr. Esfandiary sounds a strange but refreshing note among the confused alarums of his own angry generation. His bold and sparkling analysis deserves wide reading."

When Esfandiary mailed the manuscript of his third novel, *Identity Card*, to his agent in New York, it was confiscated by the Teheran postal authorities. American friends helped Esfandiary to send the second typed copy abroad. H. T. Anderson observed that the novel is "basically the story of a man who has outgrown his own country." The protagonist, a young Iranian, becomes restless and leaves the country to travel. When he does return to Iran, it is as the "modern man who has become an alien in his own land," noted Anderson. But in order to leave the country again, he must obtain a passport, and he finds that he has lost his identity card, which he must have to prove that he is Iranian. "... So the absurd, circuitous bureaucratic waltz begins," wrote Anderson. "He must apply for another one and he finds himself committed to an insane attempt at getting it that for months takes him through bewilderment and frustration reminiscent of Kafka's [The] Trial. The end is success and ironic tragedy.... Mr. Esfandiary makes it clear what happens when ritual becomes more important than truth, when the system becomes more important than the man." Thomas Lask commented: "The book is severe not only on government service but on the entire structure of Iranian life and values: the greed and irresponsibility of the rich; the cynicism of the politicians; the venality of officials; the slavishness of the poor; the rigidity of the parent-child relationship; the cloud-cuckoo land of the intellectuals who substitute the vaporings of poets in the style of Kahlil Gibran for rigorous thought, and the compliance of the average citizen, who is willing to go along with the system. . . . The fury in the book derives from a complex love of country and a frustration in not being able to change it.''

Esfandiary's purpose was not the creation of satire. He wrote in the foreword to *Identity Card*: ''For those who don't know the Middle East, it will be well to mention that *Identity Card* is not a work of satire.'' He told *CA*: ''My writings are committed to the struggle against the major problems of our times: Hunger, political and social oppression, ignorance.''

Esfandiary has travelled extensively in the Middle East, North Africa, Europe, and the United States. He speaks Arabic, English, and French, as well as Iranian.

AVOCATIONAL INTERESTS: World politics, United Nations global planning, normative philosophy, post-industrial world, space, physical immortality, the future.

BIOGRAPHICAL/CRITICAL SOURCES: New York Herald Tribune Book Review, August 30, 1959; *New Yorker*, September 12, 1959, *New York Times Book Review*, November 14, 1965; *Time*, December 24, 1965; *New York Times*, July 24, 1966, August 31, 1966, November 8, 1966; *Publishers' Weekly*, September 26, 1966; *Best Sellers*, October 15, 1966.

*   *   *

ESTERGREEN, Marian Morgan 1917-
(M. Morgan Estergreen)

PERSONAL: Born January 27, 1917, in Albuquerque, N.M.; daughter of Francis Marion and Glennie (Holland) Morgan; married Paul Henry Estergreen, May 31, 1931 (deceased); children: Lee. *Education:* University of New Mexico, B.A., M.A.; University of Wisconsin, extension student, 1945-46. *Religion:* Presbyterian.

CAREER: Taos (N.M.) Chamber of Commerce, executive secretary, 1947-49; editor and proofreader for twelve university presses; reader for University of Oklahoma Press; free-lance writer. Kit Carson Memorial Park, chairman of advisory board, 1951—; Ranchos de Taos Library, librarian, 1958. *Member:* National League of American Pen Women (charter president of Taos chapter), Taos Historical Society (charter president, 1954), Taos Garden Club (vice-president; program chairman), Taos Opera Guild, Taos Artists Association. *Awards, honors:* First award of honor for article, and third for research, National League of American Pen Women's national contest, 1960; first prize in American Poet Laureate Search, 1962.

WRITINGS—Under name M. Morgan Estergreen: *Kit Carson: A Portrait in Courage*, University of Oklahoma Press, 1962. Contributor since 1936 of articles and verse to *New Mexico Magazine, Desert Magazine, Southwest Courier*, and other publications. Weekly columnist, *Health City Sun*, Albuquerque, N.M., 1939-46; editor, *Taos Guide and Art Directory*, 1950—. Author and editor of historical booklets.

WORK IN PROGRESS: Biographies of Governor Charles Bent, and Lucien Bonapart Maxwell, one time owner of two million acres of land in Northern New Mexico and Southern Colorado.

SIDELIGHTS: Marian Estergreen speaks Spanish and French. She has traveled through Mexico and Hawaii. *Avocational interests:* youth psychology and recreation; Indians of the Southwest.

*   *   *

ESTEROW, Milton 1928-

PERSONAL: Born July 28, 1928, in Brooklyn, N.Y.; son of Bernard and Yetta (Barash) Esterow; married Jacqueline Levine, January 6, 1951; children: Judith, Deborah. *Education:* Attended Brooklyn College (now Brooklyn College of the City University of New York), New York, N.Y.

CAREER: New York Times, New York, N.Y., general news reporter, 1948-61, cultural reporter, 1961-63, assistant to cultural news director, 1963-68; Kennedy Galleries, New York, N.Y., associate director, 1968-72; *Art News*, New York, N.Y., editor and publisher, 1972—.

WRITINGS: The Art Stealers, Macmillan, 1966. Contributor to *New York Times Magazine, Harper's, Saturday Evening Post.†

*   *   *

ESTRADA, Doris (Perkins) 1923-

PERSONAL: Surname is pronounced Es-*trah*-duh; born December 13, 1923, in Fanshawe, Okla.; daughter of William Newton (a merchant) and Nettie (Goss) Perkins; married Frank Estrada (in plumbing business), October 20, 1946; children: Denise, William, Alan. *Education:* Graceland College, A.A., 1944; College of the Pacific, B.A., 1946. *Politics:* ''I do not vote a straight party ticket.'' *Religion:* Reorganized Church of Jesus Christ of Latter-day Saints. *Residence:* Stockton, Calif.

CAREER: Children's librarian in Stockton, Calif., 1966—. Drama director, Sacramento District of Reorganized Church of Jesus Christ of Latter-day Saints. *Member:* California Library Association.

WRITINGS: Three on a Bench (one-act play), Row, Peterson & Co., 1953, included in *Plays for Players*, Row, Peterson & Co., 1957; *Periwinkle Jones*, Doubleday, 1965. Contributor of children's stories to religious journals.†

*   *   *

ESTRIN, Herman A. 1915-

PERSONAL: Born June 2, 1915, in North Plainfield, N.J.; son of Morris I. (a tailor) and Ida Ruth (Bender) Estrin; married Pearl Simon (a teacher), June 26, 1949; children: Robert Keith, Karen Ruth. *Education:* Drew University, A.B., 1937; Columbia University, A.M., 1942, Ed.D., 1954. *Home:* 315 Henry St., Scotch Plains, N.J. 07076. *Office:* Newark College of Engineering, 323 High St., Newark, N.J. 07102.

CAREER: Junior high school instructor in social studies, South Plainfield, N.J., 1938-42; Newark College of Engineering, Newark, N.J., 1946—, began as assistant professor, professor of English, 1948—. Consultant in technical communications for Western Electric, and New York Port Authority. *Military service:* U.S. Army, Adjutant General's Department, 1942-46; became captain. *Member:* American Society for Engineering Education, National Council of Teachers of English, Conference on College Composition and Communication, National Council of College Publications Advisers (president, 1963-65), New Jersey Collegiate Press Association (founder; executive secretary,

1951—), Greater New York Regional College English Association (president), New Jersey Council of Teachers of English (president, 1966-70), Tau Delta Phi, Sigma Delta Chi, Alpha Phi Omega, Phi Eta Sigma, Pi Delta Epsilon (president, 1959-65), Phi Delta Kappa, Kappa Delta Pi, Sigma Tau Delta, Omicron Delta Kappa. *Awards, honors:* Named outstanding alumnus, Drew University, 1957; Gold Key Award, Columbia Scholastic Press; Medal of Merit, Pi Delta Epsilon, Robert W. Van Houten Award for Teaching Excellence, NCE Alumni Association, 1970; awards for contributions made to the field of collegiate journalism from New Jersey Collegiate Press Association, Council of College Publications Advisers, and *The Wall Street Journal*, all 1970; Western Electric Fund Award for Excellence in Instruction of Engineering Students, 1971; Eugene Best Memorial Award for the Distinguished Teaching of English, New Jersey Council of Teachers of English, 1973.

WRITINGS: (Editor with P. Obler) *The New Scientist: Essays and Values of Science*, Doubleday, 1962; (editor) *Higher Education in Engineering and Science*, McGraw, 1963; (editor) *Technical and Professional Writing: A Practical Anthology*, Harcourt, 1963; *Teaching of College English to Scientific and Technical Students*, National Council of Teachers of English, 1963; (editor with D. Goode) *College and University Teaching*, W. C. Brown, 1964; (editor) *Freedom and Censorship of College Press*, W. C. Brown, 1966; (with Esther Lloyd-Jones) *The American Student and His College*, Houghton, 1967; (compiler with Lloyd-Jones) *How Many Roads? ... The 70's*, Glencoe Press, 1970; (with Donald V. Mahus) *The American Language in the 70's*, Boyd & Fraser, 1974. Contributor to education and other professional journals. Member of editorial board, *Journal of Technical Writing and Communications, Improving College and University Teaching,* and *Journal of Composition and Communication.*

WORK IN PROGRESS: A textbook for students in technical writing courses, *A Handbook for Technical Reporting*; with Edward Monahan; *The Techniques of Technical Communications: A Practical Anthology*; editor with Louis Calazzo, *From Ape to Civilization: Readings in Science and Technology*; editor with Donald Cunningham, *Teaching Technical Writing*; editor with Frank Deaver, *The College Press.*

* * *

ETHRIDGE, Willie Snow 1900-

PERSONAL: Born December 10, 1900, in Savannah, Ga.; daughter of William Aaron and Georgia (Cubbedge) Snow; married Mark Foster Ethridge (with the University of North Carolina), October 12, 1921; children: Mary Snow (Mrs. Frank Abbott), Mark, Jr., Georgia (Mrs. Marc Schneider), William Davidson. *Education:* Wesleyan College, Macon, Ga., A.B., 1920. *Politics:* Democrat. *Home:* Route 1, Moncourse, N.C. *Agent:* Maurice Crain, Inc., 18 East 41st St., New York, N.Y. 10017.

CAREER: Macon Telegraph, Macon, Ga., reporter, 1920. Writer and lecturer. Trustee, Wesleyan College, Macon, Ga., and Lincoln Institute, Pleasant Ridge, Ky. *Awards, honors:* Carl Schurz Foundation fellow, 1933; Litt.D., University of Kentucky, 1942, Ohio Wesleyan University, 1962, and Morris-Harvey College; Minerva Award, University of Louisville, 1963; LL.D., Mercer University, 1973.

WRITINGS: As I Live and Breathe, Stokes, 1936; *Mingled Yarn* (novel), Macmillan, 1938; *I'll Sing One Song*,

Macmillan, 1941; *This Little Pig Stayed Home*, Vanguard, 1944; *It's Greek to Me*, Vanguard, 1948; *Going to Jerusalem*, Vanguard, 1950; *Let's Talk Turkey*, Vanguard, 1952; *Nila*, Simon & Schuster, 1956; *Summer Thunder* (novel), Coward, 1958; *Russian Duet*, Simon & Schuster, 1959; *There's Yeast in the Middle East*, Vanguard, 1962; *I Just Happen to Have Some Pictures*, Vanguard, 1964; *You Can't Hardly Get There from Here*, Vanguard, 1965; *Strange Fires: The True Story of John Wesley's Love Affair in Georgia*, Vanguard, 1971; *Side by Each*, Vanguard, 1973. Contributor to newspapers and magazines.

AVOCATIONAL INTERESTS: Gardening.†

* * *

ETTER, Dave 1928-

PERSONAL: Born March 18, 1928, in Huntington Park, Calif.; son of Harold Pearson and Judith (Goodenow) Etter; married Margaret Cochran, August 8, 1959; children: Emily Louise, George Goodenow. *Education:* University of Iowa, B.A., 1953. *Politics:* Independent. *Home:* 416 South First St., Geneva, Ill. 60134. *Office:* Northern Illinois University Press, De Kalb, Ill.

CAREER: Before 1961, did odd jobs in Iowa, Indiana, Illinois, Massachusetts, and California; Northwestern University Press, Evanston, Ill., editor, 1961-63; *Encyclopaedia Britannica*, Chicago, Ill., editor and writer, 1964-73; Northern Illinois University Press, De Kalb, Ill., editor, 1974—. *Military service:* U.S. Army, 1953-55. *Member:* Illinois State Historical Society. *Awards, honors:* Midland Poetry Award, 1967, and Friends of Literature poetry award, 1967, both for *Go Read the River*; Illinois Sesquicentennial Poetry Prize, 1968, for *The Last Train to Prophetstown*; Theodore Roethke Poetry Prize, 1971.

*WRITINGS—*Poetry: *Go Read the River*, University of Nebraska Press, 1966; *The Last Train to Prophetstown*, University of Nebraska Press, 1968; *Strawberries*, Juniper Press, 1970; *Voyages to the Inland Sea* (poetry and prose), University of Wisconsin, 1971; *Crabtree's Woman*, Book Mark Press, 1972. Work represented in more than forty anthologies and textbooks including *Heartlands: Poets of the Midwest*, edited by Lucien Stryk, Northern Illinois University Press, 1967; *31 New American Poets*, edited by R. Schreiber, Hill & Wang, 1969; and *Contemporary Poetry in America*, compiled by M. Williams, Random House, 1973. Contributor to more than one hundred literary magazines including *Prairie Schooner, Massachusetts Review, Midwest Choice, Poetry Northwest, Beloit Poetry Journal, Saturday Review, Chicago Review,* and *Kansas Quarterly.*

WORK IN PROGRESS: A book of poems, *Whistle Cross, Illinois.*

SIDELIGHTS: Dave Etter told *CA:* "I am particularly interested in the Middle West with emphasis on Iowa, Illinois, and Indiana. The Mississippi River is my great passion. Authors that have influenced me the most include Mark Twain, Richard Bissell, Carl Sandburg, Sherwood Anderson, and Vachel Lindsay. *Raintree County* by Ross Lockridge, Jr. is one of the most important and significant books I have ever read."

Reviewing *The Last Train to Prophetstown* Lisel Mueller writes: "His poems arise from a deep-seated love-hate; they reveal a complex temperament. There is loneliness and much anger. There is also much love: for the landscape, the long sunny silences in the fields, the sound of trains, ... the great humanists the Midwest has produced, Lincoln, Darrow, Altgeld, Stevenson."

BIOGRAPHICAL/CRITICAL SOURCES: Panorama (Chicago Daily News), July 16, 1966; *Poetry*, February, 1967; *Chicagoland*, November, 1968, March, 1969; *Poetry*, February, 1971.

*   *   *

EUBANKS, Ralph T(ravis) 1920-

PERSONAL: Born October 22, 1920, in Cecil, Ark.; son of James Claude (a teacher) and Mamie C. (Meeks) Eubanks; married Betty Carty, October 31, 1943; children: Linda Cheryl, Ralph Carty. *Education:* University of Arkansas, B.S.E., 1949; University of Florida, M.A., 1950, Ph.D., 1957. *Politics:* Conservative. *Religion:* Presbyterian. *Home:* 8922 Scenic Hills Dr., Pensacola, Fla. 32504. *Office:* Department of Communication Arts, University of West Florida, Pensacola, Fla. 32504.

CAREER: University of Arkansas, Fayetteville, instructor and director of forensics, 1950-54, assistant professor, 1954-57, associate professor, 1957-64, professor of public address, 1964-67, supervisor of graduate studies in speech, 1957-67; University of West Florida, Pensacola, professor of communication arts, and chairman of communication arts department, 1967—. *Military service:* U.S. Marine Corps, 1942-46; became captain. *Member:* Speech Association of America (committee of fifty), Rhetoric Society of America, Southern Speech Communication Association, Florida Speech Communication Association, Northwest Florida Speech and Hearing Association (member of board of directors), Arkansas Speech Association (president, 1958), Phi Beta Kappa, Omicron Delta Kappa, Tau Kappa Alpha. *Awards, honors:* Southern Regional Fellowship Fund graduate award, 1957.

WRITINGS: (contributor) David Potter, editor, *Argumentation and Debate*, Dryden Press, 1954; (contributor) Joseph Schwartz and John A. Rycenga, editors, *The Province of Rhetoric*, Ronald, 1965; (contributor) Wil A. Linkugel and R. R. Allen, and Richard L. Johannesen, *Contemporary American Speeches: A Sourcebook of Speech Forms and Principles*, Wadsworth, 1965; (with Virgil L. Baker) *Speech in Personal and Public Affairs*, McKay, 1965; (editor with R. Johannesen and R. Strickland) *Language is Sermonic: Richard Weaver on the Nature of Rhetoric*, Louisiana State University Press, 1970. Contributor of articles, reviews, and bibliographies to professional journals. Editor, *Southern Speech Communication Journal*.

AVOCATIONAL INTERESTS: Onomastics, American word coinages, collecting rare works on elocution.

*   *   *

EURICH, Alvin C(hristian) 1902-

PERSONAL: Surname is pronounced Ur-ik; born June 14, 1902, in Bay City, Mich.; son of Christian Henry (a shoe merchant) and Hulda (Steinke) Eurich; married second wife, Nell P. Hutchinson (an educator), March 15, 1953; children: Juliet Ann, Donald Alan. *Education:* North Central College, Naperville, Ill., B.A!, 1924; University of Maine, M.A., 1926; University of Minnesota, Ph.D., 1929. *Religion:* Protestant. *Home:* Sherman, Conn. 06784. *Office:* Academy for Educational Development, 680 Fifth Ave., New York, N.Y. 10019.

CAREER: University of Minnesota, Minneapolis, 1929-37, began as assistant professor, professor of educational psychology, 1936-37, assistant to the president, 1935-36, assistant dean of College of Education, 1936-37; Northwestern University, Evanston, Ill., professor of education, 1937-38; Stanford University, Stanford, Calif., professor of education, 1938-44 (on leave, 1942-44), academic vice-president, 1944-45, vice-president, 1945-48, acting president, 1948; State University of New York, Albany, first president, 1949-51; Ford Foundation, New York, N.Y., vice-president of Fund for the Advancement of Education, 1951-64, director, 1952—, executive director of Education Division, 1958-64; Academy for Educational Development, New York, N.Y., president, 1963—. President of Aspen Institute of Humanistic Studies, 1963-67. Visiting fellow, Clare College, University of Cambridge, 1967; visiting professor at various universities. U.S. government posts include director of Consumer Division, Office of Price Administration, 1942; member of President Truman's Commission on Higher Education, Personnel Policy Committee of the Hoover Commission, President Kennedy's Task Force on Education, National Committee on Libraries, and Committee on International Exchange of Persons. Chairman of U.S. delegation to UNESCO (General Conference, Paris, 1968, and of U.S. National Commission for UNESCO; chairman of advisory committee, Haile Selaissee University (Ethiopia); planning adviser to University of Patras (Greece); educational adviser to Libya; Consultant to Office of the Surgeon General, National Aeronautics and Space Administration, Agency for International Development, and Peace Corps. Vice-chairman of board of Educational Facilities Laboratories. Trustee of Lovelace Foundation for Medical Education and Penn Mutual Life Insurance Co. *Military service:* U.S. Naval Reserve, director of Standard and Curriculum Division, Bureau of Naval Personnel, 1942-44; became commander.

MEMBER: American Association for the Advancement of Science (fellow; member of council, 1941-45), American Psychological Association (fellow), American Educational Research Association (vice-president, 1944; president, 1945), Sigma Xi, Phi Delta Kappa, Cosmos Club (Washington, D.C.), Century Association and University Club (both New York), Bohemian Club (San Francisco), Cactus Club (Denver), Athenaeum (London).

AWARDS, HONORS: Distinguished Achievement Award, University of Minnesota, 1951; New York Academy of Public Education Annual Award, 1963. Honorary degrees from Hamline University, 1944, North Central College, 1949, Alfred University, 1949, Clarke University, 1950, Miami University 1951, New School for Social Research, 1952, University of Florida, 1953, Yeshiva University, 1954, University of Redlands, 1960, Akron University, 1960, University of Maine, 1965, Albion College, 1965, University of Miami (Fla.), 1968, Fairfield University, 1971.

WRITINGS: The Reading Abilities of College Students: An Experimental Study, University of Minnesota Press, 1931; (editor) *The Changing Educational World*, University of Minnesota Press, 1931; (with Howard A. Carroll) *Educational Psychology*, Heath, 1935; (with James E. Wert) *Applications for Federal Aid at Minnesota Colleges*, University of Minnesota, 1937; (with Eric C. Wilson) *In 1936* (news summary of the year), Holt, 1937; (with Wilson) *In 1937*, Holt, 1938; (with C. Robert Pace) *Follow-up Study of Minnesota Graduates from 1928-1936*, Commission of Educational Research, University of Minnesota, 1938; (editor) *General Education in the American College*, University of Chicago Press, 1939; (with J. Paul Leonard) *An Evaluation of Modern Education*, Appleton, 1942; *Looking Ahead to Better Education in Missouri: A Report on Or-*

ganization, Structure, and Financing of Schools and Junior Colleges (field study), Academy for Educational Development (New York), 1966; (editor) *Campus 1980: The Shape of the Future in American Higher Education*, Delacorte, 1968; (with Lucien B. Kinney and Sidney G. Tickton) *The Expansion of Graduate and Professional Education During the Period 1966 to 1980: A Summary of Findings and Conclusions*, Academy for Educational Development, 1969; *Reforming American Education: The Innovative Approach to Improving Our Schools and Colleges*, Harper, 1969; (editor) *High School 1980: The Shape of the Future in American Secondary Education*, Pitman, 1970. Also author, with Melvin E. Haggerty, of *Minnesota Reading Examination for College Students*, University of Minnesota Press.

Contributor: *Studies in College Examinations*, University of Minnesota Press, 1934; *The General College Curriculum as Revealed by Examinations*, University of Minnesota Press, 1937; *Federal Aid to College Students*, University of Minnesota Press, 1937; *Guidance in Education Institutions*, Public School Publishing, 1938; *General Education in the American College*, Public School Publishing, 1939; *Social Education*, Macmillan, 1939; *The Improvement of College Instruction*, University of Chicago Press, 1940; *Encyclopedia of Educational Research*, Macmillan, 1941.

Editor of Farrar and Rinehart "Series in Education." Originator and compiler with Wilson of tri-annual "Current Affairs Test" for *Time*, 1935-55, and "Contemporary Affairs Test" for American Council on Education. Contributor of more than three hundred articles to *Atlantic Monthly, Saturday Review, Nation, Vital Speeches*, and other periodicals.

WORK IN PROGRESS: Vitae Teaching and Learning.

*   *   *

EVANS, Geoffrey (Charles) 1901-

PERSONAL: Born March 13, 1901, in Aldershot, England; son of C. R. (a colonel) Evans; married Ida Louise Sidney. *Education:* Attended Aldenham School and Royal Military College, Sandhurst. *Home:* 11 Wellington Sq., London S.W. 3, England.

CAREER: British Army, commissioned second lieutenant, Royal Warwickshire Regiment, 1920, retired as lieutenant general, 1957. Commandant of Staff College, Quetta, India, 1942; brigade commander in Burma, 1943, and division commander in Burma and United Kingdom, 1944-47; commander of general allied land forces in Thailand, 1945-46; director of military training, War Office, London, England, 1948-49; temporary commander of British Forces, Hong Kong, 1951; assistant chief of staff for organization and training, Supreme Headquarters, Allied Powers, Europe, 1952-53; commanding general, Northern Command, United Kingdom, 1953-57. Chairman, London and Middlesex Playing Fields Association, 1959-70; and Anglo/Thai Society, 1967-71, commissioner, Royal Hospital, Chelsea, London, 1968—; deputy lieutenant, greater London, 1970—. *Awards, honors*—For military service: Distinguished Service Order, 1941, and two bars; Companion of the Bath, 1946; knight commander, Order of the British Empire, 1954.

WRITINGS: The Desert and the Jungle, Kimber & Co., 1959; (with A. Brett-James) *Imphal*, Macmillan, 1962; *The Johnnies*, Cassell, 1964; *Slim as Military Commander*, Batsford, 1968; *Tannenberg 1410:1914*, Hamish Hamilton, 1970; *Kensington*, Hamish Hamilton, 1975; (contributor) *The Decisive Battles of the 20th Century*, Sidgwick & Jack-

son, 1975; (contributor) *The War Lords*, Weidenfeld & Nicolson, 1975. Contributor to numerous magazines and historical journals.

*   *   *

EVANS, Luther Harris 1902-

PERSONAL: Born October 13, 1902, in Sayers, Tex.; son of George Washington (a railway section foreman) and Lillie (Johnson) Evans; married Helen Murphy, September 12, 1925; children: Gill Cofer. *Education:* University of Texas, A.B., 1923, A.M., 1924; Stanford University, Ph.D., 1927. *Politics:* Democrat. *Religion:* Methodist. *Home:* 25 Claremont Ave., New York, N.Y. 10027.

CAREER: Instructor at Stanford University, Stanford, Calif., 1924-27, New York University, New York, N.Y., 1927-28, Dartmouth College, Hanover, N.H., 1928-30; Princeton University, Princeton, N.J.; assistant professor of politics, 1930-35; U.S. Works Progress Administration, Washington, D.C., national director of Historical Records Survey, 1935-39; Library of Congress, Washington, D.C., director of Legislative Reference Service, 1939-40, chief assistant librarian, 1940-45, Librarian of Congress, 1945-53; UNESCO, member of U.S. National Commission, 1946-52, 1959-63, director-general, Paris, France, 1953-58; Brookings Institution, Washington, D.C., director of survey of federal departmental libraries, 1959-61; National Education Association, Washington, D.C., director of project on the educational implications of automation, 1961-62; Columbia University, New York, N.Y., director of international and legal collections, 1962-71. Fisk University, trustee, 1951-53; member of national board, American Civil Liberties Union, 1963-69, and American Association for the United Nations.

MEMBER: American Library Association, American Documentation Institute (president, 1951-52), American Political Science Association, World Federalists U.S.A. (president, 1971—), Society for International Development, American Society of the French Legion of Honor, Archons of Colophon. *Awards, honors:* Honorary degrees from twelve universities, including Columbia University, Yale University, Brown University, Dartmouth College, University of British Columbia, and National University of Nicaragua; decorated by governments of Brazil, France, Japan, Lebanon, and Peru.

WRITINGS: The Virgin Islands from Naval Base to New Deal, Edwards, 1945; (joint editor) *Automation and the Challenge to Education*, National Education Association, 1962; (principal author) *Federal Departmental Libraries*, Brookings, 1963; *Background Book, Tenth National Conference of U.S. National Commission for UNESCO*, and *Supplement*, U.S. National Commission for UNESCO, 1965, revised edition published as *The Decade of Development: Problems and Issues*, Oceana, 1966; *The United States and UNESCO*, Oceana, 1971. Contributor to *Saturday Review* and professional journals. Editor, *American Documentation* (quarterly), 1961.

WORK IN PROGRESS: An autobiography.

*   *   *

EVANS, Oliver 1915-

PERSONAL: Born March 19, 1915, in New Orleans, La.; son of Linson R. (a government official) and Olive (White) Evans. *Education:* Louisiana State University, B.A., 1935, graduate study at Royal University of Milan, 1935-36, and

Oxford University, summer, 1937; University of Tennessee, M.A., 1941; further study at Ohio State University, 1941-42, and Vanderbilt University, 1942-43. *Home:* 1504 Northwest 21st Ave., Gainesville, Fla. 32603. *Agent:* Gunther Stuhlman, 65 Irving Pl., New York, N.Y. 10003. *Office:* English Department, San Fernando Valley State College, Northridge, Calif. 91324.

CAREER: Athens College, Athens, Greece, instructor in English, 1936-37; University of Nebraska, Lincoln, instructor in English, 1947-50; City College (now City College of the City University of New York), New York, N.Y., lecturer, 1950-51; University of Illinois, Urbana, instructor, 1957-59, assistant professor of English, 1959-62; California State University (formerly San Fernando Valley State College), Northridge, assistant professor, 1962-66, became professor of English, now professor emeritus. Fulbright professor, Chulalongkorn University, Bangkok, Thailand, 1966-67. *Military service:* U.S. Army Air Forces, 1943-45. *Awards, honors:* Grants totaling $3,000, Authors League of America, 1949; award for best unpublished poem of the year, American Literary Association, 1951; co-winner of Reynolds Lyric Award of Poetry Society of America, 1952; Yaddo fellowship, 1952; faculty fellowship, University of Illinois, 1960.

WRITINGS: Young Man With a Screwdriver (poetry), University of Nebraska Press, 1950; *New Orleans*, Macmillan, 1959; (translator from the Italian) Niccolo Machiavelli, *La Clizia*, Barron's, 1962; (translator from the Italian) "La Calandria," in *Genius of the Italian Theater*, edited by Eric Bentley, New American Library, 1964; *Carson McCullers: Her Life and Work*, P. Owen, 1965, published as *The Ballad of Carson McCullers*, Coward, 1966; *E. M. Forster's A Passage to India: A Critical Commentary*, American R.D.M., 1967; *Anais Nin*, preface by Harry T. Moore, Southern Illinois University Press, 1968; (editor and author of introduction with Harry Finestone) *The World of the Short Story: Archetypes in Action*, Knopf, 1970. Editor of modern poetry section of *Americana Literary Scholarship* (annual), Duke University Press.

WORK IN PROGRESS: A historical novel of nineteenth-century New Orleans.

SIDELIGHTS: "I am obsessed with the atmosphere of places. [Have] fluent reading and speaking acquaintance with Italian, Spanish, and French, gained from five trips to Europe and a total of four years' residence there. Also extensive travel in North Africa, Mexico, Central America, Canary Islands, and West Indies."

*   *   *

EVANS, Robert, Jr.   1932-

PERSONAL: Born March 20, 1932, in Sterling, Colo.; son of Robert (a salesman) and Louise (Paridice) Evans; married Lois Ellen Herr, November 6, 1955; children: Karen E., Robert III, Janet K., Thomas W., Linda, Laura E. *Education:* Massachusetts Institute of Technology, S.B., 1954; University of Chicago, Ph.D., 1959. *Religion:* Congregational. *Home:* 43 High St., South Acton, Mass. 01771.

CAREER: Faculty member, Massachusetts Institute of Technology, Cambridge, 1959-65; Brandeis University, Waltham, Mass., assoc. professor of economics, 1965-71, professor, 1971—, Clinton S. Darling Professor of economics, 1971—, chairman of economics department, 1970-72, 1973—. With Keio-Illinois Exchange Program in Industrial Relations, Cambridge, Mass., and Tokyo, Japan, 1965-67; visiting professor, Institute of Management and Labor

Studies, Keio University, 1972-73. Massachusetts Advisory Committee for Manpower Development and Retraining, member, 1963-64. *Military service:* U.S. Army, 1955-57; became lieutenant. *Member:* American Economic Association, Industrial Relations Research Association.

WRITINGS: Public Policy Toward Labor, Harper, 1965; *The Labor Economics of Japan and the United States*, Praeger, 1971; *Developing Policies for Public Security and Criminal Justice*, Information Canada, 1973.

WORK IN PROGRESS: Research in the role of computer-assisted placement in the Public Employment Service, and in Japanese labor markets.

SIDELIGHTS: Robert Evans, Jr. is competent in Japanese.

*   *   *

EVERSON, Dale Millar   1928-

PERSONAL: Born April 12, 1928, in Vallejo, Calif.; daughter of Edwin Alexander (an employee of Mare Island Naval Yard) and Jeanne (Hahn) Millar; married Stanley G. Everson (a junior executive in a wholesale sporting goods firm); children: Jeffrey, Jennifer, Leslye. *Education:* University of California, Berkeley, B.A., 1949. *Politics:* Republican. *Religion:* Protestant.

CAREER: Former elementary teacher; writer for children.

WRITINGS: The Different Dog, Morrow, 1960; *Mrs. Popover Goes to the Zoo*, Morrow, 1963.

WORK IN PROGRESS: Picture books for five- to-eight-year-old group.

AVOCATIONAL INTERESTS: "Do it yourself" decorating, gardening, entertaining, bridge, tennis, swimming, dancing.†

*   *   *

EVERSON, R(onald) G(ilmour)   1903-

PERSONAL: Born November 18, 1903, in Oshawa, Ontario, Canada; son of Thomas Henry (a financier) and Mary Elizabeth (Farwell) Everson; married Lorna Jean Austin, April 15, 1931. *Education:* University of Toronto, B.A., 1927; Upper Canada Law School, called to bar, 1930. *Religion:* Protestant. *Home:* Apartment 608, 4855 Cote St. Luc Rd., Montreal 29, Quebec, Canada. *Office:* 212 King St. West, Toronto, Ontario, Canada.

CAREER: Johnston, Everson & Charlesworth, Ltd. (public relations), Toronto, Ontario, and Montreal, Quebec, president, 1958—; Communications-6, Inc., Montreal, Quebec, and Toronto, Ontario, chairman, 1964-72.

WRITINGS—All poetry: *Three Dozen Poems*, Cambridge Press (Montreal), 1957; *A Lattice for Momos*, Contact Press, 1958; *Blind Man's Holiday*, Ryerson, 1963; *Four Poems*, American Letter Press, 1964; *Wrestle With an Angel*, Delta Canada, 1965; *Incident at Cote Des Neiges*, Green Knight Press, 1966; *Raby Head*, Green Knight Press, 1967; *The Dark Is Not So Dark*, Delta Canada, 1969; *Selected Poems (1920-70)*, Delta Canada, 1970; (contributor) *How Do I Love Thee: Sixty Poets of Canada (and Quebec) Select and Introduce Their Favourite Poems from Their Own Work*, edited by John Robert Colombo, M. G. Hurtig, 1970. Contributor to periodicals, including *Atlantic Monthly, Canadian Forum, Poetry*, and *Saturday Review*.

SIDELIGHTS: Reviewing *The Dark Is not So Dark*, Carl Ballstadt writes: "...Everson exercises an historical perspective and his volume contains many poems based on personal reminiscence and the changing face of Canada. . . . His fertile imagination yields poems which are progressions of images illuminating and intensifying one another."

BIOGRAPHICAL/CRITICAL SOURCES: Guy Sylvestre, Brandon Conron, and Carl F. Klinck, editors, *Canadian Writers*, Ryerson Press, 1964; *Canadian Forum*, September, 1970.

* * *

EWART, Andrew 1911-

PERSONAL: Born January 30, 1911, in Scotland; son of John and Marion (McLeod) Ewart; married Catherine Dunlop, June 10, 1939; children: Vian. *Education:* University of Glasgow, M.A., 1933. *Home:* 167 Mortlake Rd., London, England. *Office:* Associated Newspapers, New Carmelite House, London, England.

CAREER: Journalist, 1933—, in Scotland, England, and Switzerland, with editorial posts on *Sunday Express* in Scotland, 1954-56, and *Daily Express*, London, 1956-58; *Sunday Graphic*, London, editor, 1960-61; *Sunday Times*, London, assistant editor, 1961-62; *Weekly Tribune*, Geneva, editor-in-chief, 1962-63; also Geneva correspondent for *London Observer* and regular contributor to syndicated Observer Foreign News Service, 1962-63; *Daily Sketch*, London, assistant editor, 1963—. *Military service:* Royal Air Force, 1940-45; became flight lieutenant; mentioned in dispatches. *Member:* Press Club and New Arts Theatre Club (both London).

WRITINGS: The World's Wickedest Men, Odhams, 1963, Taplinger, 1965; *The World's Wickedest Women*, Odhams, 1964, Taplinger, 1965; (contributor) J. Canning, editor, *One Hundred Great Modern Lives*, Odhams, 1965; *The World's Greatest Love Affairs*, Odhams, 1968, published as *The Great Lovers*, Hart Publishing, 1968. Author of five radio plays broadcast by British Broadcasting Corp., 1950-51, and of short stories and newspaper features.

WORK IN PROGRESS: Contributing to *One Hundred Great Books.*†

* * *

EWERS, John C(anfield) 1909-

PERSONAL: Surname sounds like "yours"; born July 21, 1909, in Cleveland, Ohio; son of John Ray (a minister) and Mary Alice (Canfield) Ewers; married Margaret Elizabeth Dumville, September 6, 1934; children: Jane (Mrs. Richard Robinson), Diane (Mrs. Paul Peterson). *Education:* Dartmouth College, A.M., 1931; Arts Students League of New York, student, 1931-32; Yale University, M.A. (honors), 1934. *Home:* 4432 26th Rd., N., Arlington, Va. 22207. *Office:* Smithsonian Institution, Washington, D.C. 20025.

CAREER: National Park Service, field curator in Morristown, N.J., Berkeley, Calif., and Macon, Ga., 1935-40; Museum of the Plains Indian, Browning, Mont., curator, 1941-44; Smithsonian Institution, Washington, D.C., associate curator of ethnology, 1946-56, Museum of History and Technology, planning officer, 1956-59, assistant director, then director, 1959-65, senior research anthropologist, 1965—. Museum planning consultant to National Park Service, Montana Historical Society, and U.S. Bureau of Indian Affairs; trustee, Museum of the American Indian, Hayes Foundation, 1972—. *Military service:* U.S. Naval Reserve, 1944-46; served in Pacific; became lieutenant. *Member:* American Anthropological Association (fellow), American Indian Ethnological Conference (president, 1960-

61), American Association of Museums, Western History Association (member of council, 1970-73), Washington Academy of Sciences (fellow), Sigma Xi (District of Columbia chapter president, 1965-66). *Awards, honors:* First Exceptional Service Award of Smithsonian Institution, 1965; LL.D., University of Montana, 1966; Sci.D., Dartmouth College, 1968.

WRITINGS: Plains Indian Painting, Stanford University Press, 1939; *The Story of the Blackfeet*, privately printed, 1944; *Blackfeet Crafts*, privately printed, 1945; *Gustavus Sohon's Portraits of Flathead and Pend d'Oreille Indians, 1854*, Smithsonian Institution, 1948; *The Horse in Blackfoot Indian Culture, With Comparative Material From Other Western Tribes*, Bureau of American Ethnology, 1955; *George Caitlin: Painter of Indians and the West*, privately printed, 1955; *The Blackfeet: Raiders on the Northwestern Plains*, University of Oklahoma Press, 1958; (with William Wildschut) *Crow Indian Beadwork: A Descriptive and Historical Study*, Heye Foundation, 1959; *Artists of the Old West*, Doubleday, 1965, 2nd edition, revised and enlarged, 1973; *Indian Life on the Upper Missouri*, University of Oklahoma Press, 1967.

Editor: (And author of introduction) *Adventures of Zenas Leonard, Fur Trader*, University of Oklahoma Press, 1959; (and author of concluding chapter) William Wildschut, *Crow Indian Medicine Bundles*, Heye Foundation, 1960; (and author of introduction) Edwin T. Denig, *Five Indian Tribes of the Upper Missouri*, University of Oklahoma Press, 1961; (and author of introduction) George Caitlin, *O-Kee-Pa: A Religious Ceremony and Other Customs of the Mandans*, Yale University Press, 1967; *Jean Louis Barlandior's Indians of Texas in 1830* (History Book Club Selection), Smithsonian Institution, 1969; Jose Francisco Ruiz, *Report on the Indian Tribes of Texas in 1828*, Yale University Library, 1972.

Contributor: G. A. Campbell and J. E. Moseley, editors, *My Dad: Preacher, Pastor, Person*, privately printed, 1939; Joseph Kinsey Howard, editor, *Montana Margins: A State Anthology*, Yale University Press, 1946; *Great Western Indian Fights*, Doubleday, 1960; *Probing the American West*, Museum of New Mexico Press, 1962; Michael S. Kennedy, editor, *The Red Man's West*, Hastings, 1965; Paul Bohannan, editor, *Law and Warfare: Studies in the Anthropology of Conflict*, Natural History Press, 1967; Walter Muir Whitehill, editor, *A Cabinet of Curiosities: Five Essays on the Evolution of the Museum in America*, University of Virginia Press, 1967; John Francis McDermott, editor, *The Frontier Re-Examined*, University of Illinois Press, 1967; Joseph P. Donnelly, editor, *Wilderness Kingdom: The Journals and Paintings Father Nicholas Point, 1839-1847*, Holt, 1967; Jean Lipman, editor, *The Artist Speaks*, Norton, 1967; John Francis McDermott, editor, *Travelers on the Western Frontier*, University of Illinois Press, 1970; Deward E. Walker, Jr., editor, *The Emergent Americans: A Reader in Culture Contrast*, Little, Brown, 1972; Charles Jones, editor, *Look to the Mountain Top*, Gousha, 1972; Malvina Bolus, editor, *People and Pelts: Selected Papers of the Second North American Fur Trade Conference*, Peguis, 1972; John Francis McDermott, editor, *The Spanish in the Mississippi Valley, 1762-1804*, University of Illinois Press, 1974; *The World of the American Indian*, National Geographic Society, 1974; *Art of the Western Frontier*, Boston Museum of Art, in press.

Contributor of about one hundred articles to historical and anthropological journals; contributor of about seventy-five book reviews to *New York Times, Saturday Review, Sci-*

ence, and other publications. Member of editorial board, *American West*, 1965—, consultant in ethnology, *Montana Magazine of Western History*, 1968—.

WORK IN PROGRESS: Studies in the ethnology, ethnohistory, arts, and crafts of Indian tribes of the Great Plains.

SIDELIGHTS: John Ewers has spent more than six years in anthropological field work among Plains Indian tribes, including residence among the Blackfeet for three and a half years. In recent years he has traveled widely in this country and abroad studying American Indian artifacts in public and private collections.

*   *   *

FABER, Doris (Greenberg)   1924-

PERSONAL: Born January 29, 1924, in New York, N.Y.; daughter of Harry (a clothing manufacturer) and Florence (Greenwald) Greenberg; married Harold Faber (a correspondent for *New York Times*), June 21, 1951; children: Alice, Marjorie. *Education:* Attended Goucher College, 1940-42; New York University, B.A., 1943. *Home:* R.D.1, Ancram, N.Y. 12502.

CAREER: New York Times, New York, N.Y., reporter, 1943-51; writer for young people.

WRITINGS: Elaine Stinson: Campus Reporter, Knopf, 1955; *The Wonderful Tumble of Timothy Smith*, Knopf, 1958; *Printer's Devil to Publisher: Adolph S. Ochs of the New York Times* (Junior Literary Guild selection), Messner, 1963; *Luther Burbank: Partner of Nature*, Garrard, 1963; *The Life of Pocahontas*, Prentice-Hall, 1963; *Behind the Headlines: The Story of Newspapers*, Pantheon, 1963; *The Miracle of Vitamins*, Putnam, 1964; *Horace Greeley: The People's Editor*, Prentice-Hall, 1964; *Robert Frost: America's Poet* (Junior Literary Guild selection), Prentice-Hall, 1964.

Clarence Darrow: Defender of the People, Prentice-Hall, 1965; *Captive Rivers: The Story of Big Dams*, Putnam, 1966; *Enrico Fermi: Atomic Pioneer*, Prentice-Hall, 1966; *John Jay*, Putnam, 1967; *Rose Greenhow: Spy for the Confederacy*, Putnam, 1967; *Petticoat Politics: How American Women Won the Right to Vote*, Lothrop, 1967; (with husband, Harold Faber) *American Heroes of the 20th Century*, Random House, 1967; *The Mothers of American Presidents*, New American Library, 1968; *Anne Hutchinson*, Garrard, 1970; *I Will Be Heard: The Life of William Lloyd Garrison*, Lothrop, 1970; *Lucretia Mott*, Garrard, 1971; *Enough! The Revolt of the American Consumer*, Farrar, Straus, 1972; *Harry Truman*, Abelard-Schuman, 1972; *Oh, Lizzie! The Life of Elizabeth Cady Stanton*, Lothrop, 1972; *Nationalism*, Harper & Row, 1973; *The Perfect Life: The Shakers in America*, Farrar, Straus, 1974; *Franklin Roosevelt*, Abelard Schuman, 1975. Contributor of occasional feature stories to newspapers, 1951—.

WORK IN PROGRESS: Several biographical and historical books.

*   *   *

FACKRE, Gabriel Joseph   1926-

PERSONAL: Born January 25, 1926, in Jersey City, N.J.; son of Toufick (an Arabic newspaper editor) and Mary (Comstock) Fackre; married Dorothy Ashman, September 22, 1945; children: Bonnie, Gabrielle, Judith, Skye, Kirk. *Education:* Attended Bucknell University, 1942-44; University of Chicago Divinity School, B.D., 1948, Ph.D., 1962. *Politics:* Democrat.

CAREER: Clergyman of United Church of Christ; pastor in Chicago, Ill., 1949-50, Duquesne and West Mifflin, Pa., 1951-60; Lancaster Theological Seminary, Lancaster, Pa., assistant professor, 1961-62, associate professor, 1963-65, professor of theology and culture, 1965-70; Andover Newton Theological School, Newton, Mass., professor of theology, 1971—. Visiting professor at University of Hawaii, 1970, and San Francisco Theological Seminar, 1972; visiting scholar, Cambridge University, 1974-75. United Church of Christ, chairman of Ethics Task Force and member of Council for Christian Social Action. *Awards, honors:* Research fellow, Oxford University, 1967-68.

WRITINGS: (With wife, Dorothy A. Fackre) *Under the Steeple*, Abingdon, 1957; *The Purpose and Work of the Ministry*, Christian Education Press, 1959; *The Baptismal Encounter*, Lancaster Theological Seminary Press, 1962; *The Pastor and the World*, United Church Press, 1964; *Conversation in Faith*, United Church Press, 1968; *Secular Impact*, United Church Press, 1968; *Second Fronts in Metropolitan Mission*, Eerdmans, 1968; *The Rainbow Sign*, Epworth, 1968, Eerdmans, 1969; *Humiliation and Celebration*, Sheed & Ward, 1969; *The Promise of Reinhold Niebuhr*, Lippincott, 1970; *Liberation in Middle America*, Pilgrim Press, 1971; *Do and Tell*, Eerdmans, 1973; *Word in Deed*, Eerdmans, 1975.

Contributor: *Voluntary Associations: Essays in Honor of James Luther Adams*, John Knox, 1966; Martin Marty and Dean Peerman, editors, *New Theology No. 4*, Macmillan, 1967; *Storm Over Ethics*, United Church Press, 1967; David Marshall, editor, *Creative Ministries*, United Church Press, 1967; Herman Ahrens, editor, *Tune In*, Pilgrim Press, 1968; Paul Jersild and Dale Johnson, editors, *Moral Issues and Christian Response*, Holt, 1971; Claude Frazier, editor, *Should Doctors Play God?*, Broadman Press, 1971; John Florer and William Baker, editors, *Class and Group Behavior: A Book of Readings on Protest and Pressure in American Society*, Kendall/Hunt, 1971; Paul Crow, Jr. and William Boney, editors, *Church Union at Mid-Point*, Association Press, 1972; *Leisure and the Quality of Life*, AAHPER Press, 1972; Ian Barbour, editor, *Western Man and Environmental Ethics*, Addison Wesley, 1973. Contributor to *Christian Century, Theology Today, Religion in Life*, and other journals.

WORK IN PROGRESS: Multi-volume work on systematic theology, publication expected by Eerdmans.

BIOGRAPHICAL/CRITICAL SOURCES: New York Times, December 6, 1965; *Christian Century*, March 5, 1969, May 13, 1970; *Commonweal*, February 27, 1970.

*   *   *

FAGEN, Richard R.   1933-

PERSONAL: Born March 1, 1933, in Chicago, Ill.; son of Abel E. (a salesman) and Mildred (Rees) Fagen; married Patricia Weiss, June 3, 1970; children: (previous marriage) Sharon, Ruth, Elizabeth. *Education:* Yale University, B.A., 1954; Stanford University, M.A., 1959, Ph.D., 1962. *Office:* Department of Political Science, Stanford University, Stanford, Calif. 94305.

CAREER: Stanford University, Stanford, Calif., 1962—, began as assistant professor, professor of political science, 1970—, acting chairman of department, 1967-69. Visiting professor at El Colegio de Mexico City, 1966, and Latin American Faculty of the Social Sciences, Santiago, Chile, 1972-73; resident consultant, Ford Foundation, Santiago, Chile, 1972-73. *Military service:* U.S. Army, 1954-56.

Member: American Political Science Association, Latin American Studies Association (member of executive council, 1970—; vice-president, 1974; president, 1975), American Association for Public Opinion Research. *Awards, honors:* Social Science Research Council fellowship, 1964; Ford Foundation fellowship, 1965-67; fellow, Center for Advanced Study in the Behavioral Sciences, 1970-71.

WRITINGS: Cuba: The Political Content of Adult Education, Hoover Institution, 1964; *Politics and Communication,* Little, Brown, 1966; (with David Finlay and Ole Holsti) *Enemies in Politics,* Rand McNally, 1967; (with Richard Brody and Thomas O'Leary) *Cuban in Exile: Disaffection and the Revolution,* Stanford University Press, 1968; (with Wayne Cornelius) *Political Power in Latin America,* Prentice-Hall, 1969; *The Transformation of Political Culture in Cuba,* Stanford University Press, 1969; (with William Tuohy) *Politics and Privilege in a Mexican City,* Stanford University Press, 1972; (editor with Julio Cotler, and contributor) *Latin America and the United States: The Changing Political Realities,* Stanford University Press, 1974. Contributor of articles to political science journals.

WORK IN PROGRESS: A book on United States foreign policy and the future of the Third World, with special emphasis on Latin America.

*　　*　　*

FAINLIGHT, Ruth (Esther) 1931-

PERSONAL: Born May 2, 1931, in New York, N.Y.; daughter of Leslie Alexander and Fanny (Nimhauser) Fainlight; married Alan Sillitoe (an authOr), November 19, 1959; children: David N. *Education:* Attended schools in United States and England until sixteen; then studied two years at Birmingham and Brighton Colleges of Arts and Crafts, England. *Religion:* Jewish. *Residence:* London, England. *Agent:* Olwen Hughes, 100 Chetwynd Rd., London NW5 1DH, England.

CAREER: Poet.

WRITINGS—Poetry: *A Forecast, A Fable,* Outposts Publications, 1958; *Cages,* St. Martin's, 1966; *18 Poems from 1966,* Turret Books, 1967; *To See the Matter Clearly,* Macmillan (London), 1968, Dufour, 1969; (with husband, Alan Sillitoe, and Ted Hughes) *Poems,* Rainbow Press, 1971; *The Region's Violence,* Hutchinson, 1973; *21 Poems,* Turret Books, 1973; *Another Full Moon,* Hutchinson, in press.

Short stories: *Daylife and Nightlife,* Deutsch, 1971. Work also included in *Penguin Modern Stories,* edited by Judith Burnley, Volume IX, Penguin, 1971.

Translations: (With husband, Alan Sillitoe) Lope de Vega, *All Citizens Are Soldiers* (first produced as "Fuente Ovejuna" in London, 1967), Macmillan (London), 1969, Dufour, 1970; various translations of Spanish poetry.

WORK IN PROGRESS: Writing poetry.

SIDELIGHTS: Ruth Fainlight told *CA:* "I enjoy slow travel, by which I mean going somewhere and living there a while. So far I have only done this in France, Spain, Morocco, and England.... My main interests apart from literature are in the fields of sociology, psychology, anthropology, religion, history, animal behaviour, and certain other sciences."

FALCON, William D(yche) 1932-

PERSONAL: Born February 18, 1932, in Chicago, Ill.; married Eleanor (a public relations manager, Metropolitan Museum of Art), July 29, 1961. *Education:* Wesleyan University, B.A., 1954. *Office:* American Management Association, 135 West 50th St., New York, N.Y. 10020.

CAREER: Harvard Business School, Boston, Mass., editor and business manager of *Executive* (monthly magazine), 1960-64; American Management Association, New York, N.Y., book acquisitions and planning editor, 1964—. Has advised on magazine subscription fulfillment. *Military service:* U.S. Navy, 1954-56; became lieutenant junior grade.

WRITINGS: (With Lawrence Creedon) *United for Separation,* Bruce, 1959; (editor) *Value Analysis/Value Engineering,* American Management Association, 1964; (editor) *Reporting Financial Data to Management,* American Management Association, 1965; (editor) *Financing International Operations,* American Management Association, 1965. Editor of eight booklets on business topics published by American Management Association, 1964-65.

WORK IN PROGRESS: Several books on management topics.†

*　　*　　*

FARBEROW, Norman L(ouis) 1918-

PERSONAL: Born February 12, 1918, in Pittsburgh, Pa.; son of Louis (a tailor) and Minnie (Cohen) Farberow; married Pearl Ross, March 16, 1947; children: Lori (son), Hilary (daughter). *Education:* University of Pittsburgh, A.B., 1938, M.Sc., 1940; University of California, Los Angeles, Ph.D., 1950. *Politics:* Democrat. *Religion:* Jewish. *Office:* Central Research Unit, U.S. Veterans Administration, Wadsworth Hospital Center, Los Angeles, Calif.

CAREER: Diplomate, American Board of Examiners in Professional Psychology. U.S. Veterans Administration, Wadsworth Hospital Center, Los Angeles, Calif., clinical psychologist, Mental Hygiene Clinic, 1949-58, principal investigator, Central Research Center, and co-director of Suicide Prevention Center, 1958—. University of California Extension, Los Angeles, instructor, 1950—; University of Southern California, Los Angeles, clinical professor of psychology, 1958—. Consultant to various agencies on problems involving suicidal activity. *Military service:* U.S. Air Force, 1941-45; became captain.

MEMBER: International Society for Suicide Prevention (president, 1973-75), American Psychological Association (fellow; president of division of clinical psychology, 1971-72; president of division of psychologists in government service, 1974-75), Society for Personality Assessment (president, 1971-72), American Group Psychotherapy Association, Western Psychological Association, California State Psychological Association, Southern California Psychological Association, Los Angeles County Psychological Association, Sigma Xi, Psi Chi, Pi Gamma Mu.

WRITINGS: (Editor with Edwin S. Shneidman) *Clues to Suicide,* McGraw, 1957; (editor with Shneidman) *The Cry for Help,* McGraw, 1961; (editor) *Taboo Topics,* Atherton, 1963; (compiler with Shneidman and Robert E. Litman) *Psychology of Suicide,* Science House, 1970.

Contributor: G. S. Welsh and W. G. Dahlstrom, editors, *Basic Readings on the MMPI in Psychology and Medicine,* University of Minnesota Press, 1956; (with Shneidman)

Georgene Seward, editor, *Clinical Studies in Culture Conflict*, Ronald, 1958; (with Shneidman) Herman Feifel, editor, *The Meaning of Death*, McGraw, 1959; (with Shneidman) H. P. David, editor, *Perspectives in Personality Research*, Basic Books, 1960; E. S. Shneidman, editor, *Essays in Self-Destruction*, Science House, 1967; (contributor of two chapters, one of which is with Shneidman) H. L. P. Resnik, editor, *Suicidal Behavior: Diagnosis and Management*, Little, Brown, 1968.

Writer with others of medical bulletins for Veterans Administration. Contributor of thirty articles to periodicals. Associate editor, *Journal of Personality Assessment*, 1958—; consulting editor, *Professional Psychologist*; consulting editor in psychology to Jossey-Bass Publishing Co., 1966—.

WORK IN PROGRESS: A book, *Suicide in Different Cultures.*

*　　*　　*

FARER, Tom J. 1935-

PERSONAL: Born July 28, 1935, in New York, N.Y.; son of Louis and Lola (Garfink) Farer; married Mika Ignatieff (a social worker), December 26, 1964. *Education:* Princeton University, A.B. (magna cum laude), 1957; University of Glasgow, graduate study, 1957-58; Harvard University, LL.B. (magna cum laude), 1961. *Home:* 420 East Main St., Moorestown, N.J. 08056. *Office:* Rutgers Law School, Camden, N.J. 08102.

CAREER: Agency for International Development, Washington, D.C., program officer, 1962; U.S. Department of Defense, Washington, D.C., special assistant to general counsel, 1962-63; Somali Police Force, Republic of Somalia, legal adviser, 1963-64; Massachusetts Institute of Technology, Cambridge, research associate, 1964-65; Davis, Polk, Wardwell, Sunderland, and Kiendl (law firm), New York, N.Y., attorney, 1965-66; Columbia University, New York, N.Y., assistant professor 1966-69, associate professor of law, 1969-71; Rutgers Law School, Camden, N.J., professor of law, 1971—. Lecturer, Naval War College, 1971. New York University, lecturer in constitutional law, 1966. Temporary Committee for Revision of New York Constitution, assistant counsel, 1966. *Member:* American Bar Association, American Society of International Law (member of board of review and development, 1971—), American Academy of Political and Social Science, Association for International Development, Bar Association of City of New York, Metropolitan Museum of Art, Phi Beta Kappa. *Awards, honors:* Fulbright scholar to University of Glasgow.

WRITINGS: (Editor) *Financing African Development*, M.I.T. Press, 1965; (with Jack B. Weinstein) *State Credit Card Crime Act*, [New York], 1966; *The Laws of War 25 years After Nuremberg*, Carnegie Endowment for International Peace, 1971. Contributor to *Harvard Law Review* and *Africa Today.*†

*　　*　　*

FARIS, Robert E. L(ee) 1907-

PERSONAL: Surname rhymes with "Paris"; born February 2, 1907, in Waco, Tex.; son of Ellsworth (a professor) and Elizabeth (Homan) Faris; married Claire Guignard, August 18, 1931; children: William Guignard, John Homan, Roger Stuart. *Education:* University of Chicago, Ph.B., 1928, M.A., 1930, Ph.D., 1931. *Home:* 19 Ginger Tree Lane, Coronado, Calif. 92118.

CAREER: Brown University, Providence, R.I., instructor, later assistant professor of sociology, 1931-38; McGill University, Montreal, Quebec, Canada, assistant professor of sociology, 1938-40; Bryn Mawr College, Bryn Mawr, Pa., associate professor of sociology, 1940-43; Syracuse University, Syracuse, N.Y., associate professor, later professor of sociology, 1943-48; University of Washington, Seattle, professor of sociology, 1948-72, professor emeritus, 1972—, executive officer of department, 1953-66. *Member:* American Sociological Association (president, 1961), Sociological Research Association (president, 1959), Pacific Sociological Society (president, 1956), Seattle Yacht Club, Coronado Cays Yacht Club. *Awards, honors:* Prizes for oil painting, annually for four years, Syracuse, N.Y.

WRITINGS: (With H. W. Dunham) *Mental Disorders in Urban Areas*, University of Chicago Press, 1939; *Social Disorganization*, Ronald, 1948; *Social Psychology*, Ronald, 1952; (editor) *Handbook of Modern Sociology*, Rand McNally, 1964; *Chicago Sociology: 1920-1932*, Chandler, 1966. Contributor to professional journals. Editor, *American Sociological Review*, 1953-56.

WORK IN PROGRESS: *History of American Sociology*, completion expected in 1979.

AVOCATIONAL INTERESTS: Oil painting, playing violin, sailboat racing; travel in Europe, especially Italy.

*　　*　　*

FARLEY, Walter 1915-

PERSONAL: Born June 26, 1915, in Syracuse, N.Y.; son of Walter and Isabelle (Vermilyea) Farley; married Rosemary Lutz, 1945; children: Pamela, Alice, Steve, Tim. *Education:* Attended Mercersburg Academy and Columbia University. *Residence:* Earlville, Pa.; and Florida.

CAREER: New York advertising agency, copy and radio writer, 1941; breeds and races trotters; fulltime professional writer. *Military service:* U.S. Army, 1942-46; reporter for *Yank*, an army publication.

WRITINGS—All published by Random House: *Black Stallion* (Junior Literary Guild selection), 1941 (adapted as *Big Black Horse* under supervision of Josette Frank, 1953); *Larry and the Underseas Raider*, 1942; *Black Stallion Returns* (Junior Literary Guild selection), 1945; *Son of the Black Stallion* (Junior Literary Guild selection), 1947; *Island Stallion* (Junior Literary Guild selection), 1948; *Black Stallion and Satan* (Junior Literary Guild selection), 1949; *Blood Bay Colt*, 1950; *Island Stallion's Fury*, 1951; *Black Stallion's Filly*, 1952; *Black Stallion Revolts* (Junior Literary Guild selection), 1953; *Black Stallion's Sulky Colt*, 1954; *Island Stallion Races*, 1955; *Black Stallion's Courage*, 1956; *Black Stallion Mystery*, 1957; *Horse-tamer*, 1959; *Black Stallion and Flame*, 1960; *Little Black, a Pony*, 1961; *Man o' War*, 1962; *Little Black Goes to the Circus*, 1963; *The Black Stallion Challenged!*, 1964; *The Horse That Swam Away*, 1965; *The Great Dane, Thor*, 1966; *The Little Black Pony Races*, 1968; *The Black Stallion's Ghost*, 1969; *The Black Stallion and the Girl*, 1971.

SIDELIGHTS: "My great love was, and still is, horses," wrote Walter Farley. "I wanted a pony as much as any boy or girl could possibly want anything—but I never owned one. I tried selling subscriptions to win a pony, which was offered as a prize to the kid who sold the most subscriptions. Then my uncle with a flock of show horses and jumpers moved from the West Coast to Syracuse, and I was deliriously happy. I was at the stables every chance I could get."

Farley's now-famous children's book, *Black Stallion*, "did not emerge all of a sudden, over a single evening and bottle of beer," wrote LewIs Nichols. "... He began it as a student at Erasmus High, wrote another version while a student at Mercersburg, ... wrote other versions as class assignments at Columbia. His first editor told him he never could make a living writing children's books, which was one of the misstatements of the age.... Sales of the books have gone over the 5 million copy mark in the United States alone, and all are in print in 14 other countries."

Farley's *The Great Dane, Thor*, "atypically, ... is not a boy-animal love affair, as so many children's books about horses and dogs tend to be," commented Taliaferro Boatwright. "Lars Newton, its 15-year-old hero, does not like his father's Great Dane, Thor, and is happy when their new colt outwits the dog.... It's an exciting climax, but it's a little too pat for belief.... Nevertheless, the knowledge and the love of nature that permeate the book and the understanding of a boy's behavior and wellsprings, as well as those of horses and dogs, make it well worth while."

BIOGRAPHICAL/CRITICAL SOURCES: Young Wings, September, 1945; *New York Times Book Review*, November 6, 1966; *Book Week*, April 30, 1967.†

* * *

FARMER, Richard Neil 1928-

PERSONAL: Born August 19, 1928, in California; son of George A. and Alice (Mellin) Farmer; married Barbara Jean Flaherty, September 18, 1951; children: Christine, Geoffrey, Sarah, Daniel. *Education:* University of California, Berkeley, B.A., 1950, M.A., 1951, Ph.D., 1957. *Home:* 1115 East Wylie, Bloomington, Ind. *Office:* Indiana University, Bloomington, Ind.

CAREER: American University of Beirut, Beirut, Lebanon, assistant professor of business, 1957-59; General Contracting Co., Al Khobar, Saudi Arabia, general manager, 1959-61; University of California, Davis, lecturer in economics, 1961-62; University of California, Los Angeles, assistant professor of business, 1962-64; Indiana University, Bloomington, professor of international business administration, 1964—. *Military service:* U.S. Army, 1951-53; became sergeant. *Member:* American Economic Association, Society for International Development, Association for Education in International Business.

WRITINGS: Technical Studies in Transportation: Cost Finding (booklet), Department of Engineering, University of California, Los Angeles, 1963; (with Barry M. Richman) *Comparative Management and Economic Progress*, Irwin, 1965, revised edition, Cedarwood, 1970; (with Richman and William G. Ryan) *Incidents in Applying Management Theory*, Wadsworth, 1966; (with Richman) *International Business: An Operational Theory*, Irwin, 1966; *Management in the Future*, Wadsworth, 1967; *Incidents in International Business*, Irwin, 1967, revised edition, Cedarwood Press, 1972; *International Management*, Dickenson, 1968; (editor with John D. Long and George J. Stolnitz) *World Population: The View Ahead*, Bureau of Business Research, Indiana University, 1968; *New Directions in Management Information Transfer*, Gottlieb Duttweiler Institute for Economic and Social Studies, 1968; *Incidents for Introduction to Business*, Wadsworth, 1969; (with Richman and Ryan) *Incidents for Studying Management and Organization*, Wadsworth, 1970; *Introduction to Business: Systems and Environment*, Random House, 1972; (compiler with Robert W. Stevens and Hans Schoellhammer) *Read-*

ings in International Business, Dickenson, 1972; *Benevolent Aggression*, McKay, 1972; *Farmer's Law: Junk in the World of Affluence*, Stein & Day, 1973; *The Real World of 1984*, McKay, 1973; (with W. Dickerson Hogue) *Corporate Social Responsibility*, Science Research Associates, 1973. Contributor of more than fifty articles to professional journals.

* * *

FAULKNOR, Cliff(ord Vernon) 1913-
(Pete Williams)

PERSONAL: Born March 3, 1913, in Vancouver, British Columbia, Canada; son of George Henry and Rhoda Anne Faulknor; married Elizabeth Harriette Sloan, August 21, 1943; children: Stephen Edward Vernon, Noreen Elizabeth. *Education:* University of British Columbia, B.S.A. (honors), 1949. *Politics:* "I travel the center lane. It gives you a broader view of the road." *Religion:* Protestant. *Home:* 2919 14th Ave., N.W., Calgary, Alberta, Canada. *Office:* Public Press Ltd., 1962 14th Ave., N.W., Calgary, Alberta, Canada.

CAREER: Went to work for Royal Bank of Canada in 1929, later worked with coast lumber companies, and as an assistant ranger for British Columbia Forest Service; British Columbia Department of Lands and Forests, Land Utilization Research and Survey Division, Victoria, land inspector, 1949-54; *Country Guide* (national farm monthly), Winnipeg, Manitoba, member of staff, 1954—, currently associate editor, based in Calgary, Alberta. *Military service:* Canadian Army, water transport, 1939-45; became sergeant. *Member:* Agricultural Institute of Canada, Canadian Farm Writers' Federation, Alberta Farm Writers' Association (past president). *Awards, honors:* Editorial Award of Canadian Farm Writers' Federation, 1962; Canadian Children's Book Award ($1,000) of Little, Brown & Co., 1964, for *The White Calf*.

WRITINGS: The White Calf (juvenile), Little, Brown, 1965; *The White Peril* (juvenile), Little, Brown, 1966; *The In-Betweener*, Little, Brown, 1967; *The Smoke Horse*, McClelland, 1968. Also author of *The Romance of Beef*, 1967. Short magazine fiction includes boys' adventure stories published in Canada, Britain, and United States; contributor of nonfiction to *Toronto Star Weekly, Liberty, Atlantic Advocate, Vancouver Sun*, and other newspapers. Writes national rural column, under pseudonym Pete Williams, for *Country Guide*; former free-lance columnist, *Victoria Times*.

WORK IN PROGRESS: Two books, *West to Cattle Country*, and *Johnny Eagleclaw*.

SIDELIGHTS: Faulknor told *CA:* "My ambition is to become a full-time pleasure fisherman. My real vacation (which I perform free of charge) is trying out spoons and plugs for a well-known fishing lure manufacturer." In 1966 Faulknor visited several South American countries.

* * *

FAVRET, Andrew G. 1925-

PERSONAL: Born May 9, 1925, in Cincinnati, Ohio; son of James Raymond (a certified public accountant) and Helen (Gilligan) Favret; married Loretta Moore, September 10, 1949; children: Andrew A., Peter J., Michael J., Patrick J., Thomas R., Mary A., James V., Loretta M., Martin A., John D., Anne M. *Education:* U.S. Military Academy, B.S., 1945; University of Pennsylvania,

M.S.E.E., 1950; Catholic University of America, D.Eng., 1964. *Religion:* Roman Catholic. *Home:* 2105 Gatewood Pl., Silver Spring, Md. 20903. *Office:* Electrical Engineering Department, Catholic University of America, Washington, D.C. 20017.

CAREER: Served in U.S. Army, 1945-54, attaining rank of captain; Massachusetts Institute of Technology, Lincoln Laboratory, Lexington, staff member, 1954-55; American Machine & Foundry Co., Alexandria, Va., department manager, 1955-59; U.S. Department of the Army, Washington, D.C., senior scientific adviser to chief of Army Intelligence, 1959-63; Catholic University of America, Washington, D.C., professor of electrical engineering, 1963—. Consultant to U.S. Department of Defense and to industry. *Member:* Institute of Electrical and Electronic Engineers (senior member), Association for Computing Machinery, Sigma Xi.

WRITINGS: Introduction to Digital Computer Applications, Reinhold, 1965; *Digital Computer Principles and Applications*, Van Nostrand, 1972. Contributor to *Review of Scientific Instruments, Obstetrics and Gynecology*, and physics and electronics journals.

*   *   *

FEDER, Karah (Tal)   1920-

PERSONAL: Born May 3, 1920, in The Hague, Holland; daughter of Baruch Chaim and Sophia (de Jongh) Tal; married Ard Feder (a theatre director), January 16, 1951; children: Margaliet, Jon, Anat. *Education:* Attended University of Amsterdam, one year, and a teachers' seminary, two years. *Religion:* "Jewish but not religious." *Home:* Shoshanat Hacarmelstreet 18, Haifa, Israel. *Agent:* Robert Harben, 3 Church Vale, London N.2, England.

CAREER: Alternately Full-time writer and teacher of English at the secondary school and college in Kibbutz Jifat, Israel.

WRITINGS: Laten wij vrede sluiten, Uitgeverij Ploegsma (Amsterdam), 1958, published as *The Stone of Peace*, Abelard, 1961; *Waar bleef de Ring*, Uitgeverij Ploegsma, 1962, published as *The Ring*, Abelard, 1965. Also author of *Andrea and Michael,* published by Massadah (Ramt Gan, Israel). Translated *The Way of the Four Winds*, by Yrjo Kokko, into Dutch. Contributor of stories to *World Over.*

WORK IN PROGRESS: A book of stories about the Jewish feasts; *The Diary of a Stupid Girl*; *Mr. Apple*, for small children.

SIDELIGHTS: Karah Feder told *CA*: "I was born in Holland, finished the gymnasium and had one year of university, studied history and philosophy, prepared myself for life in Israel by working on a farm and learning all aspects of farm life. I speak Dutch, English, Hebrew, German and a little French. My subject is in general children's life in Israel, and life in a country which operates as a smeltingpot." *The Stone of Peace* and *The Ring* have been translated and published in Israel, Germany, Norway, Denmark, England, and America. Some of her stories were read for Dutch radio broadcasts.†

*   *   *

FEDERMAN, Raymond   1928-

PERSONAL: Born May 15, 1928, in Paris, France; came to United States, 1951; son of Simon (a painter) and Marguerite (Epstein) Federman; married Erica Hubscher, September 14, 1960; children: Simone Juliette. *Education:* Co-

lumbia University, B.A. (cum laude), 1957; University of California, Los Angeles, M.A., 1959, Ph.D., 1963. *Home:* 227 Depew Ave., Buffalo, N.Y. 14214. *Office:* State University of New York, Buffalo, N.Y. 14214.

CAREER: University of California, Santa Barbara, assistant professor, 1962-64; State University of New York at Buffalo, associate professor of English literature and comparative literature, 1964—. *Military service:* U.S. Army, 82nd Airborne Division, 1951-54; served in Korea, 1952. *Member:* Modern Language Association of America, American Association of Teachers of French, American Comparative Literature Association, Modern Humanities Research Association, American Association for the Studies of Dada and Surrealist Movements, American Association of University Professors, Phi Beta Kappa. *Awards, honors:* Grant from State University of New York Research Grant Foundation for research in France on contemporary French poetry; Guggenheim fellowship, 1966-67.

WRITINGS: Journey to Chaos: Samuel Beckett's Early Fiction, University of California Press, 1965; (editor and translator) Yvonne Caroutch, *Temporary Landscapes* (bilingual edition), Stamperia di Venizia, 1965; (with John Fletcher) *Samuel Beckett: His Works and His Critics*, University of California Press, 1970; *Double or Nothing* (novel), Swallow Press, 1971; *Amer Eldorado* (novel, written in French), Editions Stock, 1974; (editor) *Surfiction* (essays), Swallow Press, 1975. Contributor of articles to *French Review, Modern Drama, Film Quarterly, Comparative Literature Studies*; also contributor of poetry and translations to poetry magazines. Co-editor of *MICA* (poetry magazine), 1960-63; chairman of publication committee, American Association for the Studies of Dada and Surrealist Movements.

SIDELIGHTS: Federman is bilingual in French and English. He also has good knowledge of German and Spanish. *Avocational interests:* Cinema and the theater.

*   *   *

FEIFFER, Jules   1929-

PERSONAL: Born January 26, 1929, in Bronx, New York; son of David (who held a variety of jobs from dental technician to salesman) and Rhoda (a' fashion designer; maiden name, Davis) Feiffer; married Judith Sheftel (a production executive with Warner Bros.), September 17, 1961; children: Kate. *Education:* Attended Art Students League, New York, N.Y., 1946, Pratt Institute, 1947-48, 1949-51. *Agent:* Robert Lantz, 114 West 54th St., New York, N.Y. 10019. *Office:* c/o Publishers-Hall Syndicate, 30 East 42nd St., New York, N.Y. 10017.

CAREER: Assistant to Will Eisner (cartoonist), 1946-51; ghost-scripted "The Spirit," 1949-51; drew syndicated cartoon, "Clifford," 1949-51; held various art jobs, 1953-56, including a job making slide films, a job as writer for Terrytoons, and one designing booklets for an art firm; cartoons published in *Village Voice*, 1956—, published weekly in London *Observer*, 1958-66, 1972—, and regularly in *Playboy* magazine, 1959—; cartoons now syndicated by Publishers-Hall Syndicate and distributed to over 100 newspapers in the United States and abroad. *Military service:* U.S. Army, Signal Corps, 1951-53; worked in a cartoon animation unit. *Member:* Authors League of America, Dramatists Guild (member of council), P.E.N., Writers Guild of America, East. *Awards, honors:* Special George Polk Memorial Award, 1962; named most promising playwright of 1966-67 season by New York drama critics, for

"Little Murders"; London critics named "Little Murders" the best foreign play of the year, 1967; Outer Critics Circle Award, and Obie Award of *Village Voice*, both 1969, for "Little Murders"; Outer Critics Circle Award, 1970, for "The White House Murder Case."

WRITINGS—All cartoons, unless otherwise noted: *Sick, Sick, Sick*, McGraw, 1958, published with introduction by Kenneth Tynan, Collins, 1959; *Passionella, and Other Stories*, McGraw, 1959; *The Explainers*, McGraw, 1960; *Boy, Girl, Boy, Girl*, Random House, 1961; *Feiffer's Album*, Random House, 1963; *Harry, the Rat with Women* (novel), McGraw, 1963; *Hold Me!*, Random House, 1963; (editor and annotater) *The Great Comic Book Heroes*, Dial, 1965; *The Unexpurgated Memoirs of Bernard Mergendeiler*, Random House, 1965; *The Penguin Feiffer*, Penguin, 1966; *Feiffer's Marriage Manual*, Random House, 1967; *Feiffer on Civil Rights*, Anti-Defamation League, 1967; *Feiffer's People: Sketches and Observations*, Dramatists Play Service, 1969; *Pictures at a Prosecution: Drawings and Text from the Chicago Conspiracy Trial*, Grove, 1971; *Feiffer on Nixon: The Cartoon Presidency*, Random House, 1974.

Plays: "The Explainers" (satirical review), produced in Chicago, Ill., at Playwrights Cabaret Theater, 1961; *Crawling Arnold* (one-act; first produced in Spoleto, Italy, at Gian-Carlo Menotti's Festival of Two Worlds, 1961, later produced in United States), Dramatists Play Service, 1963; *Little Murders* (two-act comedy; first produced in Broadway at Broadhurst Theatre, April 25, 1967 [closed after seven performances]; first American play produced by Royal Shakespeare Co. in London at Aldwych Theatre, 1967; revived Off-Broadway at Circle in the Square, January 5, 1969), Random House, 1968; "The Unexpurgated Memoirs of Bernard Mergendeiler," first produced with other plays under title "Collision Course" Off-Broadway at Cafe au Go Go, May 8, 1968, published in *Collision Course*, edited by Edward Parone, Random House, 1968; "God Bless," first produced in New Haven, Conn., by Yale Repertory Theatre Co., October 10, 1968; produced by Royal Shakespeare Co. at Aldwych Theatre, 1968; "Dick and Jane" (one-act), first produced in New York at Eden Theatre as part of "Oh! Calcutta!," devised by Kenneth Tynan, June, 1969, published in *Oh! Calcutta!*, edited by Tynan, Grove, 1969 [also see below]; *The White House Murder Case: A Play in Two Acts* [and] *Dick and Jane: A One-Act Play* ("The White House Murder Case" first produced at Circle in the Square, February 19, 1970), Grove, 1970; "Knock-Knock," 1975.

Screenplays: *Carnal Knowledge* (released by Avco Embassy, 1971), Farrar, Straus, 1971; "Little Murders," Twentieth Century-Fox, 1971.

Illustrator: Robert Mines, *My Mind Went All to Pieces*, Dial, 1959; Norton Juster, *The Phantom Tollbooth*, Random House, 1961.

Has contributed sketches to productions of DMZ Cabaret, New York; contributor to *Ramparts*.

SIDELIGHTS: Kenneth Tynan once called Feiffer "the best writer now cartooning," an accurate compliment, as the captions Feiffer appends are more important than the line drawings. His work may at first look like a comic strip, but instead of gags and preposterous situations it offers what David Segal referred to as "comic nightmares," biting vignettes of contemporary life as it is experienced and explained away by sensitive adults, beatniks, precocious children, and politicians. The introspective adults are by far the most frequently portrayed, they who, according to *News-*

week, have "rationalized Hostile Group attitudes," and are trying to find themselves. Segal believes that "ultimately Feiffer may do more to popularize anxiety than Norman Vincent Peale has done to popularize tranquility."

Feiffer's strips, writes Russell Lynes, "are intended to wound rather than to amuse, though the blood they draw is in droplets. Feiffer is a compassionate satirist, and he uses his needle with a bedside manner ('I'm sorry, but this is going to hurt a little'), though he hopes to expose the basic ills of society and do what he can to cure them. He is at war with complacency, with the cliche mongers who provide society with meaningless slogans to live by, with the pomposity of officialdom, and with the carefully cultivated dullness of our carefully protected daily lives. But he wages his war by needling at the flanks."

Always cautious of classification, he once said: "I'm probably with most of the people in the cartoons—urban, middle-class. But I'm not a spokesman for any group. I'm a spokesman for myself. Once you start representing people, you have to be responsible, and I want to retain the right to be irresponsible."

Segal speaks of the bomb as being, for Feiffer, "both a representative symbol and an appalling apotheosis." Feiffer has said that he is "against the misuse of power of all kinds. I'm against people who use their views and authority as a ploy against others." His political strips, he feels, have not been particularly effective because "they still aren't doing things my way. . . . I always write the cartoons in a terrible mood of frustration, and I guess the mood is partly self-pity. The self-pity being: "My God, we've gone through this so many times, why can't we have it right just once?" Everybody knows what's happening. It seems so little to ask that things go right." He added: "I always feel terribly shy politically. I've lent my name to groups like SANE, but I don't really believe in these organizations. I'm just not a group man and there's no group activity, no political organization, no parties, probably nothing in my life—beyond *one*—which I can truly believe in."

He draws his cartoons easily, but he sometimes rewrites his captions 15 times. Once he has completed the strip, his contract specifies that no one can tamper with his words. He maintains he has no trouble finding new material each week for the *Voice*: "There really is no deliberate search for material," he told *Mademoiselle*, "because once I start doing *that* I separate myself from what I'm doing. Really the strips are a normal outgrowth of how I feel from time to time. This doesn't mean I don't sit down and worry about what I'm going to do this week. But what comes up, I discover looking back later, always had something directly to do with what I was feeling about some particular situation at that particular moment . . . week after week doing this strip for the *Voice* puts me in a position of having directly to compete with myself—not saying the same things over. . . . The strip forces me to move on, whether I want to or not." Beginning in the 1960's, Feiffer's cartoons concentrated increasingly on political themes such as civil rights, Vietnam, and the presidency.

Feiffer believes that he has been influenced to a greater degree by writers rather than by cartoonists. Among cartoonists, he most admires Saul Steinberg. "The drawing style has been most influenced by a combination of people," he says, "from William Steig to Robert Osborn to Andre Francois. The writing began, I guess, being patterned after Benchley." Then he read *Notes from the Underground* and realized that he had "always hoped to get in terms of humor *some* of the feeling that Dostoevski got about his man, ... to show within the space of the strip first how a man views himself and then show what the outside sees him as. And the two have absolutely no connection." He is interested in the breakdown of communication, not only between people but with oneself, the latter being "more basic. Because if somebody can't even talk to himself, how can he be expected to meet with, talk to and evaluate others?"

Though he continues his cartoons, he regularly works in other forms. His only novel, *Harry: The Rat With Women*, received kind reviews, although Saul Maloff called it "vintage Feiffer cartoons, unillustrated." When he decided to write a full-length play, he reports, "friends warned that while I was skilled at my usual profession of drawing one anti-American cartoon a week, if I ventured into the field of anti-American plays I'd be in danger of spreading myself thin. My reply was that I'd be hardly an artist and less than a man if I didn't say, in whatever form necessary, what I felt had to be said. ... Floundering helplessly for a theme, I sought as refuge the first piece of advice given to all young writers by all old writers: Write about what you know. So I chose random violence.... Since I am city bred, it has always been an issue with me, and I cannot remember a time since childhood when I did not expect to be struck down momentarily by Nazis, Japs, Bigger Kids, Smaller Kids, Teachers, or Parents.... What a relief, then, to see that what I often suspected to be private paranoia has today been institutionalized as national paranoia." "Little Murders" was the result.

Feiffer's film, "Carnal Knowledge," released in 1971, became the focus of obscenity prosecutions when it was banned by the state supreme court of Georgia. The film was used by the motion picture industry as a test case on obscenity laws and was appealed before the U.S. supreme court in 1974; the court ruled 8-0 in its favor.

An animated cartoon, "Munro," based on a Feiffer story, was filmed by Rembrandt Films, 1961, and won an Oscar as the best short-subject cartoon; "The Feiffer Film," a recreation of some of his cartoons, was released in 1965; "The Apple Tree," a musical by Jerry Bock and Sheldon Harnick, produced in 1966, consists of three playlets, one based on Feiffer's "Passionella." *Harry: The Rat With Women* was made into a play and first produced at Institute of Arts, Detroit, 1966; a take-off on Feiffer's cartoons, "What Are We Saying?," was produced in Rome.

Feiffer's books have been translated into German, Swedish, Italian, Dutch, French, and Japanese.

A portrait of Feiffer was produced for the "Artists in America" series of Public Broadcasting System, 1971.

BIOGRAPHICAL/CRITICAL SOURCES: Time, February 9, 1959, May 26, 1961, June 28, 1963; *New Republic*, June 6, 1960; *Mademoiselle*, January, 1961; *Horizon*, November, 1961; *Commentary*, November, 1961; *Newsweek*, November 13, 1961, May 8, 1967; *New York Times Book Review*, June 30, 1963; *Life*, July 17, 1965; *Village Voice*, April 13, 1967, May 4, 1967; *New York Times*, April 23, 1967, April 27, 1967, January 26, 1969; *Evergreen Review*, February, 1969; *Transatlantic Review*, summer, 1969; Carolyn Riley, editor, *Contemporary Literary Criticism*, Volume II, Gale, 1974.

*   *   *

FEINBERG, Joel 1926-

PERSONAL: Born October 19, 1926, in Detroit, Mich.; son of Abraham Joel (in advertising) and Marion (Tahl) Feinberg; married Betty Sowers, May 29, 1955; children: Melissa, Benjamin. *Education:* University of Michigan, B.A., 1949, M.A., 1951, Ph.D., 1957. *Home:* 48 Edgewood Ave., Larchmont, N.Y. 10538. *Office:* Department of Philosophy, Rockefeller University, New York, N.Y. 10021.

CAREER: Brown University, Providence, R.I., instructor, 1956-57, assistant professor of philosophy, 1957-62; Princeton University, Princeton, N.J., assistant professor, 1962-64, associate professor of philosophy, 1964-66; University of California, Los Angeles, professor of philosophy, 1966-67; Rockefeller University, New York, N.Y., professor of philosophy, 1967—. Director, and vice-president, Public Studies Corp. *Military service:* U.S. Army, 1944-46. *Member:* American Philosophical Association, American Society for Political and Legal Philosophy (chairman of program committee, 1965; secretary-treasurer, 1959-60, 1971-72), Conference for the Study of Political Thought. *Awards, honors:* Fellow, Center for Advanced Study in the Behavioral Sciences, 1960-61; liberal arts fellow, Harvard Law School, 1963-64; Guggenheim fellow, 1974-75.

WRITINGS: (Editor and author of section introductions) *Reason and Responsibility*, Dickenson, 1965, 3rd edition, 1975; (editor) *Moral Concepts*, Oxford University Press, 1970; *Doing and Deserving*, Princeton University Press, 1970; *Social Philosophy*, Prentice-Hall, 1973; (editor) *The Problem of Abortion*, Wadsworth, 1973; (editor) *Readings in Moral Philosophy*, Allyn & Bacon, in press; (editor) *Philosophy of Law*, Dickenson, in press. Editor, "Foundations of Philosophy" series, Prentice-Hall, 1963—. Contributor of articles to *Nation, Yale Law Review, Philosophical Review, Journal of Philosophy, American Philosophical Quarterly, Ethics*, and numerous other journals. Editorial consultant, Dickenson Publishing Co.

WORK IN PROGRESS: A book, *Justice and Truth*; co-authoring a book on the problem of victimless crimes, for Viking; contributing to *Encyclopedia of Bioethics*.

*   *   *

FEINGOLD, Eugene (Neil) 1931-

PERSONAL: Born March 21, 1931, in Brooklyn, N.Y.; son of Paul (a furrier) and Rose Elaine (Brook) Feingold; married Marcia Louise Goldberg (a computer programmer), March 26, 1960; children: Eleanor, Ruth Paula. *Education:* Cornell University, A.B., 1952; Syracuse University, graduate study, 1952-53; Princeton University, M.A., 1958, Ph.D., 1960. *Home:* 352 Hilldale Dr., Ann Arbor, Mich. *Office:* Department of Medical Care Organization, University of Michigan, Ann Arbor, Mich.

CAREER: Brookings Institution, Washington, D.C., research fellow, 1959-60; University of Michigan, Ann Arbor, instructor in political science, 1960-63, part-time assistant professor of community health services, 1963-64, assistant professor, 1963-66, associate professor, 1966-71, professor of medical care organization, and chairman of department, 1971—. Visiting professor, St. Thomas's Hospital Medical School, University of London, 1970-71. Consultant to local and federal governmental committees and agencies. *Military service:* U.S. Army, 1953-55. *Member:* American Political Science Association, American Public Health Association, Law and Society Association, Medical Committee for Human Rights, Planners for Equal Opportunity. *Awards, honors:* Grants from Walter E. Meyer Research Institute of Law, New World Foundation, and University of Michigan, 1964-65, U.S. Public Health Service, and Brookings Institution, 1968-70; research fellowship, National Center for Health Services and Development, 1970-71.

WRITINGS: Medicare: Policy and Politics, Chandler Publishing, 1966; (contributor) Edwin A. Bock, editor, *Government Regulation of Business: A Casebook*, Prentice-Hall, 1965; (contributor) Roy Penchansky, compiler, *Health Services Administration: Policy Cases and the Case Method*, Harvard University Press, 1968; (contributor) *The Social Welfare Forum 1972*, Columbia University Press, 1972; (contributor) Robert M. Hollister and Seymour S. Bellin, *Neighborhood Health Centers*, Lexington Books, 1974; (contributor) *The Citizenry and the Hospital*, Duke University, 1974. Also author of monographs on governmental subjects. Contributor to *New Republic, New University Thought, Journal of Conflict Resolution, American Federationist, American Journal of Public Health, Medical Care, Wisconsin Law Review*, and other journals. Member of editorial board, *Poverty and Human Resources*, 1966-70, *Medical Care Review*.

WORK IN PROGRESS: A study of the operation of state and local laws prohibiting ethnic discrimination in housing; a study of the administrative implementation of the Medicaid program.

* * *

FEIWEL, George R(ichard) 1929-

PERSONAL: Born July 4, 1929, in Cracow, Poland; son of Herman (a lawyer) and Reisa (Wang) Feiwel; married Ida Rieger (a research assistant), May 19, 1957. *Education:* McGill University, B.Com., 1955, M.A., 1961, Ph.D., 1963; University of California, Berkeley, graduate study, 1961-62. *Home:* 5507 Holston Hills Rd., Knoxville, Tenn. 37914. *Office:* Department of Economics, University of Tennessee, Knoxville, Tenn.

CAREER: University of Alberta, Edmonton, Alberta, associate professor of economics, 1962-66; University of Tennessee, Knoxville, professor of economics, 1966—. Visiting faculty member, Cambridge University, 1965, 1969, 1972; associate, Harvard University, 1966, 1967, 1971, 1975; visiting professor, Instituto di Studi per lo Sviluppo Economico, 1969, 1970, University of Stockholm, 1973. *Member:* American Economic Association, Association for the Study of Soviet-Type Economics, Canadian Institute of Chartered Accountants, Quebec Institute of Chartered Accountants.

AWARDS, HONORS: Guggenheim fellow, 1969-70; fellowships and grants from American Council of Learned Societies, Social Science Research Council, American Philosophical Society, Canada Council, and National Science Foundation.

WRITINGS: The Economics of a Socialist Enterprise, Praeger, 1965; *The Soviet Quest for Economic Efficiency*, Praeger, 1967; *New Economic Patterns in Czechoslovakia*, Praeger, 1968; (compiler) *New Currents in Soviet-Type Economies*, International Textbook Co., 1968; (contributor) G. Franco, editor, *Studi sulle politiche monetarie le creditizie per lo sviluppo economico*, Edizioni Cedam, 1970; *Industrialization and Planning under Polish Socialism*, two volumes, Praeger, 1971; *Recent Developments in the Polish Financial System*, Arms Control and Disarmament Agency, 1971; (aumhor of introduction) Michal Kalecki, *The Last Phase in the Transformation of Capitalism*, Monthly Review Press, 1972; *Essays on Planning in Eastern Europe*, Instituto di Studi per lo Sviluppo Econom-

ico, 1973; *The Intellectual Capital of Michal Kalecki: A Study in Economic Theory and Policy*, University of Tennessee Press, 1975. Also author of booklet on the meanings of cost. Contributor of articles to *Collier's Encyclopedia, New Currents in Soviet-Type Economies, Economia Internazionale, Ricerche Economiche, Indian Economic Journal, Rendiconti, Keio Economic Studies, Soviet Studies, Osteuropa Wirtschaft, Scientia*, and numerous other journals.

WORK IN PROGRESS: Research on industrialization policy and central planning in Bulgaria, and the politics and economics of full employment and inflation; contributing to a book on growth performance and economic gains in Eastern Europe.

SIDELIGHTS: Feiwel has traveled extensively in Europe during the summers of 1964 and 1965 for research into the operation of economic systems under various institutional arrangements. He is competent in Russian and German.

* * *

FELSHER, Howard D. 1927-

PERSONAL: Born October 18, 1927, in Perth Amboy, N.J.; son of Elbert Aaron (a merchant) and Augusta (Fogel) Felsher; married Elaine Vejans (a researcher), November 30, 1950; children: Andrew Evan. *Education:* New York University, B.A., 1947. *Politics:* Independent. *Religion:* "No affiliation, but born Jewish." *Agent:* Lurton Blassingame, 60 East 43rd St., New York, N.Y. 10017.

CAREER: General Programs, Inc., New York, N.Y., producer, 1954-60; Screen Gems, New York, N.Y., producer, 1960-62; Tele-Column, Inc., New York, N.Y., owner-publisher, 1962.—. Free-lance writer and producer for national educational television; consultant to Canadian Television Network and Granada Television, England. *Member:* United World Federalists, American Civil Liberties Union.

WRITINGS: (With Michael Rosen) *The Press in the Jury Box*, Macmillan, 1966, published as *Justice U.S.A.?*, Collier Books, 1967.

WORK IN PROGRESS: Sisyphus Sleeps with Me, a novel, for Macmillan.†

* * *

FERGUSON, C(harles) E(lmo) 1928-

PERSONAL: Born September 7, 1928, in Nashville, Ark.; son of Charles Elmo (an editor) and Fern (Reese) Ferguson; married Anna Bess McClellan (a research chemist), December 23, 1951; children: Charles Elmo, Jr. *Education:* Hendrix College, A.B. (summa cum laude), 1949; University of North Carolina, M.A., 1951, Ph D., 1957. *Politics:* Republican. *Home:* 1708 Cahill Dr., East Lansing, Mich. *Office:* Department of Economics, Michigan State University, East Lansing, Mich.

CAREER: Duke University, Durham, N.C., assistant professor, 1957-60, associate professor, 1960-62, professor of economics, 1962-67; Michigan State University, East Lansing, professor of economics, 1967—. *Military service:* U.S. Army, 1952-54. *Member:* American Economic Association, American Statistical Association, Royal Economic Society, Econometric Society, Southern Economic Association (executive committee member, 1961-63; vice president, 1966-67). *Awards, honors:* Fellowships from Ford Foundation, 1961-62, Social Science Research Council, National Science Foundation, and Inter-Universities Committee for Research.

WRITINGS: (With J. M. Kreps) *Principles of Economics*, Holt, 1962, 2nd edition, 1965; *Macroeconomic Theory of Workable Competition*, Duke University Press, 1964; *Microeconomic Theory*, Irwin, 1966, 3rd edition, 1972; *The Neoclassical Theory of Production and Distribution*, Cambridge University Press, 1969; (with S. Charles Maurice) *Economic Analysis*, Irwin, 1970. Contributor or more than fifty articles to journals of economics, statistics, mathematics, and sociology.

WORK IN PROGRESS: Research in areas of theory of production, technological progress, and economic growth.†

* * *

FERGUSON, Robert D(ouglas) 1921-

PERSONAL: Born June 23, 1921, in Peterborough, Ontario, Canada; son of William Lauder and Mary (Hannah) Ferguson; married Martha Donau, February 18, 1958; children: Robert, Lisa. *Education:* University of Toronto, B.A. (honors), 1943, B.Ed., 1964. *Home:* 21 Bernick Rd., Willowdale, Ontario, Canada. *Office:* Toronto Board of Education, 155 College St., Toronto, Ontario, Canada.

CAREER: Wingham District High School, Wingham, Ontario, teacher of English, 1946-54; Canadian Broadcasting Corp., Toronto, Ontario, program planner for school broadcasts, 1954-63; Toronto Board of Education, Toronto, publications director, 1963—. *Member:* Educational Press Association of America (regional director, 1965-66), Ontario Secondary School Teachers Federation. *Awards, honors:* Citations of excellence, from *School Management* (magazine), and Rutgers University, for school board publications; award of excellence, Educational Press Association.

WRITINGS: Man From St. Malo (biography of Jacques Cartier), Macmillan, 1959; *Fur Trader* (biography of Alexander Henry), Macmillan), 1961. Author of radio and television dramas and documentaries for Canadian Broadcasting Corp. Contributor of articles on education to periodicals. Editor, *Toronto Educational Quarterly*.

* * *

FERRY, Anne Davidson 1930-

PERSONAL: Born November 17, 1930, in New York, N.Y.; daughter of J. Edward (a businessman) and Bernice R. Davidson; married David Russell Ferry (a college professor), March 22, 1958; children: Stephen Edward, Elizabeth Emma. *Education:* Vassar College, A.B., 1951; Columbia University, M.A., 1952, Ph.D., 1956; Girton College, Cambridge, graduate study, 1955-56. *Home:* 8 Ellery St., Cambridge, Mass. *Office:* Department of English, Boston College, Chestnut Hill, Mass. 02167.

CAREER: Hunter College (now Hunter College of the City University of New York) New York, N.Y., lecturer in English, 1953-55; Wellesley College, Wellesley, Mass., instructor in English, 1956-58; Harvard University, Cambridge, Mass., lecturer in English, 1958-66; Boston College, Newton, Mass., assistant professor 1966-67, associate professor of English, 1967—. *Awards, honors:* Fulbright fellow, Cambridge University, 1955-56; American Association of University Women Sabin fellow, 1966-67.

WRITINGS: Milton's Epic Voice, Harvard University Press, 1963; (editor) *Seventeenth-Century English Minor Poets*, Dell, 1964; (editor with R. A. Brower and David Kalstone) *Beginning with Poems: An Anthology*, Norton, 1966; (editor) *Religious Prose of Seventeenth-Century Eng-*

gland, Knopf, 1966; *Milton and the Miltonic Dryden*, Harvard University Press, 1968.

Contributor: J. Mazzeo, editor, *Reason and Imagination*, Columbia University Press, 1962; R. Braver and R. Poirier, editors, *In Defense of Reading*, Dutton, 1963.†

* * *

FESSENDEN, Seth A(rthur) 1903-

PERSONAL: Born September 29, 1903, in Onawa, Iowa; son of Ralph Seth and Mary (Douglas) Fessenden; married Margaret Henrikson, August 19, 1937 (died November 19, 1969); children: John, Judith Fessenden Scholtz, Janet, Harley. *Education:* Attended University of Texas, 1925-27, University of California, Los Angeles, 1929-30; University of Illinois, B.S., 1931, M.S., 1933; New York University, Ph.D., 1941; post-doctoral study at University of Iowa, 1945, University of Southern California, 1954. *Home:* 226 Patrician Lane, Placentia, Calif. *Office:* California State University, Fullerton, Calif. 92634.

CAREER: High school teacher in Illinois, 1935-37; Eastern Illinois University, Charleston, assistant professor of speech, 1938-41; West Texas State College (now University) Canyon, professor of speech, 1941-43; Cornell College, Mount Vernon, Iowa, professor of speech, 1943-49; University of Denver, Denver, Colo., director of graduate program in speech, 1949-54; Montana State University, Missoula, professor of speech, 1954-57; Toastmasters International, Santa Ana, Calif., consultant, 1957-59; California State University at Fullerton, professor of speech, 1959-73; professor emeritus, 1973—. Director of speech training institutes for public and private groups. Guest lecturer at colleges and universities. *Member:* Speech Association of America, National Society for the Study of Communication, Western Speech Association, Society for General Semantics, Kappa Delta Pi, Tau Kappa Alpha, Phi Delta Kappa. *Awards, honors:* Danforth scholar, 1954; Certificate of Merit, California State University at Fullerton, 1965, for distinguished teaching.

WRITINGS: The Speech Inventory, Psychological Corp., 1943; *Speech and the Teacher*, Longmans, Green, 1946; (with W. N. Thompson) *Basic Experiences in Speech*, Prentice-Hall, 1951, 2nd edition, 1958; *Designed for Listening*, W. C. Brown, 1951; *The Teacher Speaks*, Prentice-Hall, 1954; *Bonney-Fessenden Sociograph*, California Test Bureau, 1955; *Helping the Bible Speak*, Association Press, 1956; *Understanding and Being Understood*, Longmans, Green, 1957; *How to Read the Bible Aloud*, Beacon, 1961; *Laereren Jaler*, Nyt Nordisk (Copenhagen), 1963; *Speech for Today*, McGraw, 1964; *Speech for the Creative Teacher*, W. C. Brown, 1968, 2nd edition, 1973; (editor) *Personally Speaking: Writings of R. C. Smedley*, Toastmasters International, 1968; (with Johnnye Akin and others) *Language Behavior: A Book of Readings in Communication*, Mouton & Co., 1970. Contributor to journals. Editor, *Education* (speech education edition), October, 1956; associate editor, *Journal of Communication*.

WORK IN PROGRESS: A Guide to Listening and Evaluation, for Wadsworth; *Significant Research in Listening*, for Rodopi; *How to Learn How to Listen*.

* * *

FEUERLICHT, Roberta Strauss 1931-

PERSONAL: Born November 23, 1931, in New York, N.Y.; daughter of Isaac and Lena (Wesler) Strauss; married Herbert Alan Feuerlicht (a sculptor), December 14, 1958; children: Ira Mannes. *Education:* Hunter College, B.A., 1952. *Home:* 711 Amsterdam Ave., New York, N.Y. 10025. *Agent:* Anita Diamant, 51 East 42nd St., New York, N.Y. 10017.

CAREER: Glen Oaks News, New York, N.Y., associate editor, 1952-53; Gilberton Co., Inc., New York, N.Y., editor, 1953-61; *This Month* (magazine), New York, N.Y., editorial director, 1961-62; free-lance writer and editor, 1962—. *Member:* Authors Guild.

WRITINGS: Andrews' Raiders, Collier, 1963; *Let's Go to a World's Fair,* Putna, 1964; *Oliver Wendell Holmes,* American R.D.M., 1965; *Gandhi,* American R.D.M., 1965; *Madame Curie,* American R.D.M., 1965; *Theodore Roosevelt,* American R.D.M., 1966; *Martin Luther King, Jr.,* American R.D.M., 1966; *Paul Bunyan,* Collier, 1966; *The Desperate Act,* McGraw, 1968; *A Free People,* Messner, 1969; *Henry VIII,* Collier, 1970; *In Search of Peace,* Messner, 1970; *America's Reign of Terror,* Random House, 1971; *Zhivko of Yugoslovia,* Messner, 1971; *Joe McCarthy and McCarthyism,* McGraw, 1972. Editor of a series on revolutions and a series of biographies for American R.D.M. Contributor to *Reporter, Ms., New York Times, Natural History, Saturday Evening Post.*

WORK IN PROGRESS: Collaboration on a book on personal campaigning; books on St. Nicholas and Sacco & Vanzetti.

AVOCATIONAL INTERESTS: History, politics, and folklore.

* * *

FEY, Harold E(dward) 1898-

PERSONAL: Born October 10, 1898, in Elwood, Ind.; son of Edward Henry (a farmer) and Eva (Gant) Fey; married Golda Conwell, July 20, 1922; children: Russell Conwell, Gordon Edward (deceased), Constance Fey Thullen. *Education:* Cotner College, B.A., 1922; Yale University Divinity School, B.D., 1927. *Politics:* Democrat. *Home:* 5360 North Kenwood Ave., Indianapolis, Ind. 46208. *Office:* Christian Theological Seminary, Indianapolis, Ind. 46208.

CAREER: Ordained minister of Disciples of Christ, 1923; pastor in Lincoln, Neb., 1925-26, Hastings, Neb., 1927-29; Union Theological Seminary, Manila, Philippine Islands, professor of sociology, 1929-31; *World Call* (international magazine of Disciples of Christ), Indianapolis, Ind., editor, 1932-35; Fellowship of Reconciliation, New York, N.Y., executive secretary, and founding editor of *Fellowship,* 1935-40; *Christian Century,* Chicago, Ill., associate editor, 1940-47, managing editor, 1947-52, executive editor, 1952-55, editor, 1956-64; Christian Theological Seminary, Indianapolis, Ind., professor of social ethics, 1964-68, professor emeritus. Accredited correspondent to United Nations forces in Japan and Korea, 1951, to World Assemblies of Churches in Amsterdam, 1948, Evanston, 1954, and Uppsala, 1968, and to Second Vatican Council, 1962. President of Associated Church Press, 1950-51; former president of Christian Century Foundation. *Military service:* U.S. Army, 1918.

MEMBER: American Association of University Professors, Sigma Delta Chi, Theta Phi. *Awards, honors:* D.D., Chicago Theological Seminary, 1948; distinguished service citation from National Congress of American Indians, for service to the Indians, 1956; Litt.D., Park College, 1961; distinguished service award, Illinois chapter of American

Civil Liberties Union; HH.D., Culver-Stockton College, 1963; journalism award, Christian Church, 1969.

WRITINGS: The Lord's Supper: Seven Meanings, Harper, 1948; (with D'Arcy McNickle) *Indians and Other Americans,* Harper, 1959, revised edition, 1971; *Cooperation in Compassion,* Friendship, 1966; (editor) *History of Ecumenical Movement,* Volume II, Westminster, 1970; *With Solemn Reverence,* Roger Williams Press, 1974. Editor, *In Common* (newsletter).

WORK IN PROGRESS: Writing memoirs.

* * *

FICHTER, George S. 1922-
(Matt Warner)

PERSONAL: Born September 17, 1922, in Hamilton, Ohio; married Nadine K. Warner, February 10, 1945; children: Susan Kay, Thomas Matt, Jane Ann. *Education:* Miami University, Ohio, B.A., 1947; North Carolina State College, M.Sc., 1948; graduate study at University of North Carolina. *Address:* P.O. Box 1368, Homestead, Fla. 33030.

CAREER: Miami University, Oxford, Ohio, instructor in zoology, 1948-50; vice-president and editor, *Fisherman* (magazine), 1950-55; Sport Fishing Institute, Washington, D.C., assistant executive vice-president, 1956-57; free-lance writer and editor of natural history books, primarily for young people, 1957—; Western Publishing Co., editor of Golden Guides, 1963-67, director of Golden Guides, 1967-68, managing editor of *Golden Encyclopedia of Natural Sciences,* and *Golden Bookshelf of Natural History. Military service:* U.S. Air Force, 1942-46. *Member:* American Entomological Society, American Littoral Society, Sigma Xi, Phi Kappa Phi.

WRITINGS—All published by Golden Press, except as indicated: (With Reuben W. Eschmeyer) *Good Fishing,* Harper, 1959; *Reptiles and Their Way of Life,* 1960; *Flying Animals,* 1961; *Fishes and How They Live,* 1961; *Fishes,* 1963; (with Phil Francis) *A Guide to Fresh and Salt-Water Fishing,* 1965; *Insect Pests,* 1966 (published in England as *Insect Pests: A Guide to Pests of Houses, Gardens, Farms and Pets,* Hamlyn, 1967); *The Animal Kingdom: An Introduction to the Major Groups of Animals,* 1968; *Snakes and Other Reptiles,* 1968; (contributor) *Exploring Biology,* 1970; (contributor) *Exploring with a Microscope,* 1970; (under pseudonym Matt Warner) *Your World, Your Survival* (Junior Literary Guild selection), Abelard, 1970; *Birds of Florida,* E. A. Seemann, 1971; (contributor) *Earth and Ecology,* 1972; (with Keith Kingbay) *Bicycling,* 1972; *Cats,* 1973; *Animals: Mammals from All Over the World,* 1973; (with Alexander R. Taylor) *Ecology,* 1973; (compiler) *The Florida Cookbook,* E. A. Seemann, 1973; (under pseudonym Matt Warner) *Reptiles and Amphibians: A Close Look at Two Fascinating Groups of Animals,* 1974.

Contributor to *Golden Encyclopedia of Natural History, World Book Encyclopedia, American People's Encyclopedia Yearbook,* and numerous other natural history books; also contributor of technical articles to professional and scientific journals, and of more than three hundred articles to *Reader's Digest, Coronet, Pageant, Science Digest, National Wildlife, Boys' Life,* and numerous other magazines.

WORK IN PROGRESS: Fruits and Vegetables of the World, Reptiles and Amphibians, Insects, The Human Body, Tree, Fruits and Garden Plants, Exploring the

Oceans, and *Changing Worlds for Wildlife,* all for Golden Press; *Fishes of the World; Fishes of Florida; Underwater Farming.*

SIDELIGHTS: Some of Fichter's books have been translated into French. *Avocational interests:* Nature study, bicycling.

* * *

FIEDLER, Lois (Wagner) 1928-

PERSONAL: Born December 6, 1928, in Homer, Ohio; divorced; children: Lou (son), Kurt. *Education:* Kent State University, B.S., 1950. *Politics:* Independent. *Religion:* Protestant. *Office:* Spring Valley Methodist Church, 7700 Spring Valley Rd., Dallas, Tex. 75240.

CAREER: First Presbyterian Church, Dallas, Tex., secretary, 1963-65; Spring Valley Methodist Church, Dallas, Tex., secretary and administrative assistant, 1965—. *Awards, honors:* Matrix Award in field of communication, Dallas chapter of Theta Sigma Phi, 1965.

WRITINGS: The Sound of Silence, Revell, 1965; *The Many Faces of Love,* Revell, 1968.†

* * *

FIELD, Gordon Lawrence 1939-

PERSONAL: Born February 13, 1939, in Hitchin, Hertfordshire, England; son of Cecil Frederick (a nurse) and Margaret (Andrews) Field. *Education:* Attended College of Education, Bognor Regis, Sussex, England, 1958-60. *Politics:* "No fixed views." *Religion:* "None." *Home:* 20 House Lane, Arlesey, Bedfordshire, England.

CAREER: Assistant master at Tamworth, Staffordshire, England, 1960-62, at Felixstowe, Suffolk, England, 1963-65, at Downham Market, Norfolk, England, 1965-66; full-time writer of school history books, 1966-69; life assurance representative, Prudential Insurance Co. Ltd., 1969-73; freelance writer, 1973—.

WRITINGS: The Minoans of Ancient Crete, Wheaton & Co., 1964; *The First World War,* Wheaton & Co., 1965; *The Growth of Civilization,* Macmillan, 1966; *The Growth of Europe,* Macmillan, 1968.

WORK IN PROGRESS: A television play.

AVOCATIONAL INTERESTS: Numismatics, classical music, foreign travel, growing citrus fruit trees.

* * *

FIELDING, Raymond E. 1931-

PERSONAL: Born January 3, 1931, in Brockton, Mass.; son of Walter Howard (an engineer) and Irma (Nelson) Fielding; married Carole Behrens, October 11, 1964. *Education:* University of California, Los Angeles, B.A., 1953, M.A., 1956; University of Southern California, Ph.D., 1961. *Home:* 1105 Clark Rd., Wyndmoor, Pa. 19118. *Office:* School of Communications, Temple University, Philadelphia, Pa. 19122.

CAREER: University of California, Los Angeles, lecturer, 1957-61, assistant professor, 1961-65, associate professor of theater arts, 1965-66, founder, and curator of Theater Arts Film Archive, 1958-65; University of Iowa, Iowa City, associate professor of speech and dramatic arts, 1966-69; Temple University, Philadelphia, Pa., professor of radio-television-film, 1969—. University of Southern California, visiting lecturer, summer, 1960, visiting assistant professor, summer, 1961; visiting associate professor, and director of

motion picture workshop, New York University, summer, 1965. Vice-president, International Congress of Schools of Cinema and Television, 1967-70. Birmingham Educational Film Festival, judge, 1972-73, member of advisory board, 1972—, consultant, 1973-74. Consultant, National Aeronautics and Space Administration, 1966-67, National Endowment for the Humanities, 1973-74, Los Angeles Civil Service Commission, and various corporations. *Military service:* U.S. Air Force Reserve, 1955-63.

MEMBER: American Film Institute (trustee, 1973—), Information Film Producers of America (formerly Industry Film Producers Association; president, 1961-62), University Film Foundation (trustee, 1967—), University Film Association (president, 1967-68), University Film Producers Association (member of board, 1964—), Society for Cinema Studies (president, 1972-74; member of council, 1974-78), Society of Motion Picture and Television Engineers, Society for Film History Research, American Historical Association, Society of American Archivists. *Awards, honors:* University of California research grants, 1961-62, 1964-65, for research in the history of the motion picture newsreel, 1962-63, for research in special cinematographic techniques; University of California faculty fellowship, summer, 1962; Lion of St. Marc, Venice International Film Festival, 1968, for *A Technological History of Motion Pictures and Television;* Frank Luther Mott Research Award Citation, 1973.

WRITINGS: (Editor) *The Wills of the Presidents,* Oceana, 1958; *The Technique of Special Effects Cinematography,* Hastings House, 1965, revised edition, 1972; (editor) *A Technological History of Motion Pictures and Television,* University of California Press, 1967; (author of introduction) Kemp R. Niver, *Motion Pictures from the Library of Congress Paper Print Collection, 1894-1912,* University of California Press, 1967; *The American Newsreel, 1911-1967,* University of Oklahoma Press, 1972; (contributor) Ronald Gottesman and Harry Geduld, editors, *Guidebook to Film,* Holt, 1972; (contributor) *The American Cinema,* United States Information Agency, 1974. Author of papers for film symposiums and conferences; also author, and director, of film, "The Honorable Mountain," produced 1953, and author of film, "The American Newsreel," produced 1974. Contributor of articles to *Focal Encyclopedia of Film and Television Techniques, Encyclopaedia Britannica, Smithsonian Journal of History, Western Political Quarterly, American Archivist, Journal of the University Film Association, Journal of the University Film Producers Association,* and other film and television journals. Member of advisory editorial board, American Film Institute.

* * *

FINE, I(sadore) V. 1918-

PERSONAL: Born May 23, 1918, in Columbia, Mo.; son of Solomon and Ida (Corenbaum) Fine; married Selma Lightman (a teacher), October 14, 1945; children: Stephen R., Debra G. *Education:* University of Rhode Island, B.S., 1942; Columbia University, M.S., 1947, Ph.D., 1952. *Politics:* Democrat. *Religion:* Jewish. *Home:* 826 South Midvale, Madison, Wis. *Office:* School of Commerce, University of Wisconsin, Madison, Wis.

CAREER: Brooklyn College (now Brooklyn College of the City University of New York), instructor, 1947; University of Wisconsin, Madison, 1947—, professor of marketing, 1958—. Board member, Hillel Foundation of Madison, 1960—; board member, Madison Welfare Council, 1961—.

Military service: U.S. Army Air Forces, 1942-46; became lieutenant colonel. *Member:* American Marketing Association, National Association of Purchasing Agents, Alpha Epsilon Pi, Phi Kappa Phi.

WRITINGS: Studies in Wisconsin Retailing, Bureau of Business Research and Service, University of Wisconsin, 1951; *Retail Trade Area Analysis,* Bureau of Business Research and Service, University of Wisconsin, 1954; (editor with John H. Westing and others) *Industrial Purchasing,* Wiley, 1955, 2nd edition, 1961, 3rd edition published as *Purchasing Management,* 1969; *Industrial Development Corporations in Wisconsin,* Bureau of Business Research and Service, University of Wisconsin, 1958; *The Effect of Industrialization on Small Cities,* Bureau of Business Research and Service, University of Wisconsin, 1959; (editor) *Purchasing as a Career,* National Association of Purchasing Agents, 1961; (with E. E. Werner) *Tourist-Vacation Industry in Wisconsin,* Wisconsin Department of Resource Development, 1961; (with Ralph B. Hovid and Philip H. Lewis, Jr.) *The Lake Superior Region Recreational Potential,* Wisconsin Department of Resource Development, 1962; (with Roy E. Tuttle) *The Tourist Overnight Accommodation Industry in Wisconsin,* Bureau of Business Research and Service, University of Wisconsin, 1963; (editor) *State Recreation Plan,* Wisconsin Department of Resource Development, 1963; *Recreation Potential—Lake Superior,* Wisconsin Department of Resource Development, 1964; *Apostle Islands,* Bureau of Business Research and Service, University of Wisconsin, 1965; (with Tuttle) *Commercial Enterprises Providing Tourist and Travel Overnight Accommodations,* Wisconsin Department of Resource Development, 1966; (with Tuttle) *Private Seasonal Housing in Wisconsin,* Wisconsin Department of Resource Development, 1966; *Wisconsin and the Vacationer,* Wisconsin Department of Resource Development, 1966. Contributor to journals.

WORK IN PROGRESS: A fourth edition of *Industrial Purchasing;* research on the economics of tourism.

*   *   *

FINE, Reuben 1914-

PERSONAL: Born October 11, 1914, in New York, N.Y.; son of Jacob (a businessman) and Bertha (Nedner) Fine; married Charlotte Margoshes (a psychologist), September 1, 1937; children: Benjamin, Ellyn June. *Education:* City College of New York (now City College of the City University of New York), B.S., 1933, M.S., 1939; University of Southern California, Ph.D., 1948. *Home:* 225 West 86th St., New York, N.Y. 10024.

CAREER: City College (now City College of the City University of New York), New York, N.Y., instructor in psychology, 1948-53; Veterans Administration, New York, N.Y., clinical psychologist, 1948—; private practice as psychologist and psychoanalyst, New York, N.Y., 1953—; Elmhurst General Hospital, Queens, N.Y., attending psychologist and supervisor of psychotherapy, Psychiatric Division, 1961—. Director of Center for Creative Living, 1963—, Center for Psychoanalytical Training, 1972—, Foundation for Formation of Psychoanalytic Universities, 1972—. Visiting professor at City College of the City University of New York, 1953-61, University of Amsterdam, 1961, Lowell Institute of Technology, 1967-69, University of Florence, 1968, Adelphi University, 1969—. President of Institute for Psychoanalytic Training and Research. Consultant to U.S. Navy. Chess master, 1933-50, co-world

champion, 1946-48. *Member:* American Psychological Association (fellow), Society for Projective Techniques (fellow), National Psychological Association for Psychoanalysis (vice-president).

WRITINGS—On chess: (Editor with Fred Reinfeld) *A. Alekhine vs. E. D. Bogoljubow: World's Chess Championship,* McKay, 1934; (editor with Reinfeld) *Dr. Lasker's Chess Career,* Black Knight Press, 1935; (reviser) Larry Evans, *Modern Chess Openings,* 6th edition, McKay, 1939; *Basic Chess Endings,* McKay, 1941; (editor) Emanuel Lasker, *Manual of Chess,* revised edition, Dutton, 1942; *Chess the Easy Way,* McKay, 1942; *The Ideas Behind the Chess Openings,* McKay, 1943, revised edition, 1949; *Chess Marches On!,* Chess Review, 1945, published as *Fifty Chess Lessons from Modern Master Play,* Capricorn, 1963; *Practical Chess Openings,* McKay, 1948; *The World's a Chessboard,* McKay, 1948, published as *Great Moments in Modern Chess,* Dover, 1965.

(Editor) *World's Great Chess Games,* Crown, 1951; *The Middle Game in Chess,* McKay, 1952; *Lessons from My Games: A Passion for Chess,* McKay, 1958; (editor with Reinfeld) *Lasker's Greatest Chess Games, 1889-1914,* Dover, 1963; (with son, Benjamin Fine) *The Teenage Chess Book,* McKay, 1965; *Psychology of the Chess Player,* Dover, 1965, with new appendix, 1967.

(Author of comments and annotations) *The Final Candidates Match, Buenos Aires, 1971: Fischer versus Petrosian,* Hostel Chess Association, 1971; *Bobby Fischer's Conquest of the World's Chess Championship: The Psychology and Tactics of the Title Match,* McKay, 1973.

Other: *Freud: A Critical Re-Evaluation of His Theories,* McKay, 1962, revised edition published as *The Development of Freud's Thought: From the Beginnings (1886-1900) Through Id Psychology (1900-1914) To Ego Psychology (1914-1939),* Jason Aronson, 1973; *The Healing of the Mind: The Technique of Psycoanalytic Psychotherapy,* McKay, 1971.†

*   *   *

FINLEY, Harold M(arshall) 1916-

PERSONAL: Born February 24, 1916, in McConnelsville, Ohio; son of Harry M. (a judge) and Kate (Cotton) Finley; married Jean Rowley, September 19, 1943; children: Robert. *Education:* Northwestern University, B.S. (cum laude), 1933; Chicago Theological Seminary, B.D. (cum laude), 1944; University of Chicago, graduate study, 1949. *Home:* 630 East 12th, Lockport, Ill. 60441.

CAREER: Lamson Bros. & Co. (stockbrokers), Chicago, Ill., customers' man, 1933-42; ordained to Congregational ministry, 1944; served as minister in Lockport, Ill., 1942-44, 1948-53; *Market Direction* (advisory service), Chicago, Ill., editor, 1946-48; Chicago Title and Trust Co., Chicago, Ill., investment analyst, 1950-54, investment officer, 1954-59; H. M. Byllesby & Co., Chicago, assistant to chairman of board, 1959-62; Supervised Investors Services, Inc., Chicago, senior analyst, 1962-63; H. M. Byllesby & Co., vice-president, 1963—; chartered financial analyst. Minister, Naperville Congregational Church, 1965-66. Member, Will County (Ill.) Board of Education, 1961-64. *Member:* Investment Analysts Society of Chicago (secretary, 1959-60; governor, 1963-66), Transportation Securities Club of Chicago (president, 1962-64), Phi Beta Kappa, Delta Sigma Pi, Rotary Club, Mid-Day Club, Antique Automobile Club of America (Illinois region treasurer and director, 1959-63).

WRITINGS: Everybody's Guide to the Stock Market, Regnery, 1956, 3rd edition, 1965; *The Logical Approach to Successful Investing*, Regnery, 1971. Regular columnist, "Market Trends," *Chicago's American*, 1961—; contributor to *Chicago Tribune Sunday Magazine*.

* * *

FINNIGAN, Joan 1925-
(Michelle Bedard)

PERSONAL: Born November 23, 1925, in Ottawa, Ontario, Canada; daughter of Frank (a former National Hockey League player; a hotel keeper) and Maye (Horner) Finnigan; married Grant MacKenzie (a psychiatrist), May 23, 1949 (died August, 1965); children: Jonathan Alexander, Christopher Roderick, Martha Ruth. *Education:* Queen's University, B.A. *Politics:* Conservative. *Religion:* "Homegrown." *Home:* 17 Parkwood Pl., Kingston, Ontario, Canada.

AWARDS' HONORS: Centennial Prize for Poetry, 1967; President's Prize for Poetry from University of Western Ontario, 1969; Canadian Film Award for best screenplay, 1969, for "The Best Damn Fiddler from Calabogie to Kaladar"; six Canada Council grants in past ten years, including Senior Canada Council grant, 1973-74.

WRITINGS—Poetry: *Through the Glass, Darkly*, Ryerson, 1957; *A Dream of Lilies*, University of New Brunswick Press, 1965; *Entrance to the Greenhouse*, Ryerson, 1968; *It Was Warm and Sunny When We Set Out*, Ryerson, 1970; *In the Brown Cottage on Loughborough Lake*, Herzig Somerville for C.B.C. Learning Systems, 1970.

Prose: (Under pseudonym Michelle Bedard) *Canada in Bed*, Pagurian Press, 1969; *Celebrate This City*, McClelland & Stewart, 1975. Author of screenplay for film, "Best Damn Fiddler from Calabogie to Kaladar," shown on Canadian television. Contributor to magazines.

WORK IN PROGRESS: A book on the Ottawa Valley, *I Come from the Valley*, for McClelland & Stewart; a new collection of poetry, *Living Together*, for Macmillan; a screenplay, *Godsend*, with Ted Kotcheff in Hollywood; commissioned C.B.C. scripts on Great Lakes mariners and on the history of hockey.

* * *

FIORE, Silvestro 1921-

PERSONAL: Born January 12, 1921, in Susa, Tunisia; son of Angelo and Rosa (Pavia) Fiore; married Edith Witte, December 25, 1951; children: Angelica, Patrick, Fabiola. *Education:* College Ste-Marie, Tunis, Tunisia, B.A., 1939; Collegio Italiano, Tunis, B.A., 1940; University of Cologne, Ph.D. (magna cum laude), 1956. *Religion:* Roman Catholic. *Home:* 13 John St., Providence, R.I. 02906. *Office:* Brown University, Box E, Providence, R.I. 02912.

CAREER: Collegio Italiano, Tunis, Tunisia, instructor in French and Latin, 1940-41; Dolmetscher-Institut, Dusseldorf, Germany, lecturer in French and Arabic, 1952-53; University of Rome, Rome, Italy, part-time instructor in French, 1953-54; University of Lyons, Lyons, France, part-time lecturer in Arabic, 1956-57; University of Florida, Gainesville, assistant professor of Romance languages and Arabic, 1959-60, associate professor of Romance languages and director of Ph.D. theses, 1962-65; Brown University, Providence, R.I., associate professor of Romance languages and comparative literature, 1965—. Convener of conference in comparative literature, College Alaoui,

Tunis, Tunisia, 1958—; research appointee, University of California, Los Angeles, Graduate School, 1965. *Member:* International Comparative Literature Association, Mediaeval Academy of America, American Oriental Society, Modern Language Association of America. *Awards, honors:* Ford Foundation fellow at University of California, Los Angeles and Berkeley, 1961; grant from Princeton University, 1963; M.S., Brown University, 1966.

WRITINGS: Uber die Beziehungen zwischen der arabischen und der fruhitalienischen Lyrik, University of Cologne, 1956; *Voices from the Clay: Development of Assyro-Bablonian Literature*, University of Oklahoma Press, 1965. Contributor to journals in Europe and the United States.

WORK IN PROGRESS: Research on pre-Islamic oriental traditions that have survived into medieval Spanish folklore and popular poetry; research on the connection of Greco-Roman Mithras liturgy with the ceremonies of medieval chivalry, and on the mythical background of Provencal poetry.

SIDELIGHTS: Fiore is extremely fluent in French, Italian, Spanish, and German. He has fair knowledge of Arabic and Portuguese, as well as, some knowledge of Persian, Russian, and the ancient languages, Latin, Greek, Akkadian, and Hebrew. *Avocational interests:* Collecting Near Eastern art objects.†

* * *

FISCHER, Carl H(ahn) 1903-

PERSONAL: Born August 22, 1903, in Newark, N.J.; son of Carl H. H. and Minnie (Hahn) Fischer; married Kathleen Kirkpatrick, September 25, 1925; children: Patrick Carl, Michael John. *Education:* Washington University, St. Louis, Mo., B.S., 1923; University of Iowa, M.S., 1930, Ph.D., 1932. *Politics:* Republican. *Religion:* Methodist. *Home:* 1706 Morton Ave., Ann Arbor, Mich. 48104.

CAREER: Engineer for American Steel Foundries, 1923-26; Beloit College, Beloit, Wis., instructor in mathematics, 1926-29; University of Minnesota, Minneapolis, instructor in mathematics, 1932-33; Northwestern National Life Insurance Co., Minneapolis, Minn., actuarial researcher, 1933-34; Wayne State University, Detroit, Mich., instructor, 1934-37, assistant professor of mathematics, 1937-41; University of Michigan, Ann Arbor, assistant professor, 1941-45, associate professor, 1945-50, professor of insurance and actuarial mathematics, 1950-74, professor emeritus, 1974—. Director of Gerber Products Co., 1972—. Visiting professor, University of California, Berkeley, 1951, University of Hawaii, 1955, Hebrew University, Jerusalem, State of Israel, 1965, 1967, Netherlands School of Economics, 1966. Social security consultant to Philippines, 1956, 1962; member of Advisory Council on Social Security Financing, U.S. Government, 1957-58; chairman of study committee on military retirement, U.S. Senate Committee on Armed Services, 1960-61; actuarial consultant to teacher retirement systems and to private pension plans. Trustee of City of Ann Arbor Retirement System, 1948-73, and Ann Arbor Board of Education, 1957-60.

MEMBER: Society of Actuaries (fellow), Fraternal Actuarial Association, Conference of Actuaries in Public Practice (fellow), American Academy of Actuaries, American Statistical Association, Mathematical Association of America, American Risk and Insurance Association, Acacia, Sigma Xi, Beta Gamma Sigma, Mason.

WRITINGS: (With Paul R. Rider) *Mathematics of Investment*, Rinehart, 1951; (with Walter O. Menge) *Mathematics of Life Insurance*, Macmillan, 1965, 2nd edition, Ulrich's Books, 1965; *Vesting and Termination Provisions in Private Pension Plans*, American Enterprise Institute for Public Policy Research, 1970. Contributor of about forty articles to professional journals.

* * *

FISCHER, David Hackett 1935-

PERSONAL: Born December 2, 1935, in Baltimore, Md.; son of John Henry and Norman (Frederick) Fischer; married Judith Hummel, 1960; children: Susan F., Anne W. *Education:* Princeton University, A.B., 1958; Johns Hopkins University, Ph.D., 1962. *Politics:* Democrat. *Religion:* Lutheran. *Home:* 36 Rich Valley Rd., Wayland, Mass.

CAREER: Brandeis University, Waltham, Mass., assistant professor, 1962-65, associate professor, 1965-70, professor, 1970-72, Warren Professor of History, 1972—. Visiting lecturer, Harvard University, 1964-65; visiting professor, University of Washington, Seattle, 1975. *Member:* American Historical Association, American Antiquarian Society, Institute of Early American History and Culture, Hakluyt Society.

WRITINGS: *The Revolution of American Conservatism*, Harper, 1965; *Historians' Fallacies: Toward a Logic of Historical Thought*, Harper, 1970.

WORK IN PROGRESS: *America: A Social History*.

* * *

FISCHER, J(ohn) L(yle) 1923-

PERSONAL: Born July 9, 1923, in Kewanee, Ill.; son of G. Lyle (a banker) and Ann (Clark) Fischer; married Ann Kindrick (an associate professor of anthropology), July 9, 1949 (died April 20, 1971); married Simonne Cholin Sanzenbach (an associate professor of French), July 30, 1973; children: (first marriage) Madeleine, Mary Anne. *Education:* Harvard University, B.A., 1946, M.A., 1949, Ph.D., 1955. *Office:* Department of Anthropology, Tulane University of Louisiana, New Orleans, La. 70118.

CAREER: U.S. Trust Territory of the Pacific Islands, district anthropologist on the Caroline Islands of Ponape and Truk, 1949-51, international affairs officer, Ponape, 1951-53; Harvard University, Graduate School of Education, Cambridge, Mass., instructor in education, 1955-58; Tulane University of Louisiana, New Orleans, assistant professor, 1958-60, associate professor, 1960-63, professor of anthropology, 1963—. Member of behavioral sciences fellowship review committee, National Institutes of Health, 1963-67. Did anthropological field work in Japan, 1961-62. *Military service:* U.S. Naval Reserve and U.S. Marine Corps Reserve, active duty, 1942-46; became first lieutenant. *Member:* American Anthropological Association, American Sociological Association, Linguistic Society of America, American Association for the Advancement of Science, American Folklore Society, American Ethnological Society.

WRITINGS: *The Eastern Carolines*, Human Relations Area File Press, 1957; (with wife, Ann Fischer) *The New Englanders of Orchard Town, U.S.A.*, Wiley, 1966; (editor with Allan Smith) *Anthropology*, Prentice-Hall, 1970.

WORK IN PROGRESS: Research on micronesian mythology, ethnography of communication, social stress and cultural changes, and the poetry of Ponape.

SIDELIGHTS: Fischer speaks Ponapean, Trukese, and Japanese; he reads French.

* * *

FISCHER, LeRoy H(enry) 1917-

PERSONAL: Born May 19, 1917, in Hoffman, Ill.; son of Andrew Leroy (a physician) and Effie (Risby) Fischer; married Martha Gwendolyn Anderson, June 20, 1948; children: Barbara Ann, James LeRoy, John Andrew. *Education:* University of Illinois, B.A., 1939, M.A., 1940, Ph.D., 1943; additional summer study at Columbia University, 1941, and Oxford University and Cambridge University, 1945. *Religion:* Methodist. *Home:* 1010 West Cantwell Ave., Stillwater, Okla. 74074. *Office:* Department of History, Oklahoma State University, Stillwater, Okla. 74074.

CAREER: Ithaca College, Ithaca, N.Y., assistant professor of history, 1946; Oklahoma State University, Stillwater, assistant professor, 1946-49, associate professor, 1949-60, professor of history, 1960-72, Oppenheim Regents Professor of History, 1973—, executive director of honors program, College of Arts and Science, 1959-61. Member, Oklahoma Civil War Centennial Commission, 1958-65, Oklahoma Chisholm Trail Centennial Commission, 1966-67. *Military service:* U.S. Army, Signal Corps, 1943-45. *Member:* American Historical Association, American Association of University Professors, Organization of American Historians, Western History Association, Southern Historical Association, Oklahoma Historical Society (member of board of directors), Illinois State Historical Society, Oklahoma Westerners, Oklahoma City Civil War Round Table (past president), Faculty Club (past president), Phi Alpha Theta (past president), Pi Gamma Mu (past president), Omicron Delta Kappa. *Awards, honors:* Literary Award of Loyal Legion of the United States for best book-length study on the Civil War, 1963, for manuscript of *Lincoln's Gadfly, Adam Gurowski*.

WRITINGS: *Lincoln's Gadfly, Adam Gurowski*, University of Oklahoma Press, 1964; *The Civil War Era in Indian Territory*, Morrison, 1974; *United States Indian Agents to the Five Civilized Tribes*, Oklahoma Historical Society, 1974. Contributor to *Dictionary of American Biography* and *Encyclopaedia Britannica*; articles on Civil War and Reconstruction history have appeared in *Chronicles of Oklahoma, Civil War History, Journal of American History*, and a number of other history journals.

WORK IN PROGRESS: A book and articles on the Civil War and Reconstruction.

AVOCATIONAL INTERESTS: Gardening, hiking, travel.

* * *

FISHER, Franklin M(arvin) 1934-

PERSONAL: Born December 13, 1934, in New York, N.Y.; son of Mitchell Salem and Esther (Oshiver) Fisher; married Ellen Paradise, June 22, 1958; children: Abraham, Abigail. *Education:* Harvard University, A.B. (summa cum laude), 1956, M.A., 1957, Ph.D., 1960. *Home:* 28 Holden Wood Rd., Concord, Mass. 01742. *Office:* Department of Economics, Massachusetts Institute of Technology, Cambridge, Mass. 02139.

CAREER: University of Chicago, Chicago, Ill., assistant professor of economics, 1959-60; Massachusetts Institute of Technology, Cambridge, assistant professor, 1960-62, associate professor, 1962-65, professor of economics, 1965—.

Visiting professor of economics, Hebrew University, 1973, University of Tel-Aviv, 1973. Member of project on econometric models, Social Science Research Council, 1960—; member of advisory committee, Brookings Institution, 1967-70. Consultant to Institute of Naval Studies, 1965-66, Federal Power Commission, 1965-69, Federal Reserve Board, 1965-69, General Services Administration, 1966-67, President's Task Force on Communications Policy, 1968, and various corporations. *Member:* American Economic Association, Econometric Society (fellow; member of council), American Academy of Arts and Sciences (fellow), Phi Beta Kappa. *Awards, honors:* National Science Foundation fellowship, 1962-63; Ford Foundation faculty research fellow in economics, 1966-67; Operations Research Society of America Prize, 1967; John Bates Clark Award, American Economic Association, 1973.

WRITINGS: A Priori Information and Time Series Analysis: Essays in Economic Theory and Measurement, North-Holland Publishing, 1962; (with Carl Kaysen) *A Study in Econometrics: The Demand for Electricity in the United States,* North-Holland Publishing, 1962; (with Albert Ando and Herbert A. Simon) *Essays on the Structure of Social Science Models,* M.I.T. Press, 1963; *Supply and Costs in the United States Petroleum Industry: Two Econometric Studies,* Johns Hopkins Press, 1964; (contributor) Donald S. Watson, editor, *Price Theory in Action,* Houghton, 1965; (contributor) James Duesenberry, G. Fromm, E. Kuh, and L. Klein, editors, *The Brookings Quarterly Econometric Model of the United States,* Rand McNally, 1965; *The Identification Problem in Econometrics,* McGraw, 1966; (contributor with Karl Shell) James N. Wolfe, editor, *Value, Capital and Growth,* University of Edinburgh Press, 1968; (contributor) Norman A. B. Wilson, editor, *Manpower Research,* English Universities Press, 1969; (contributor) John Erickson and Wolfe, editors, *The Armed Services and Society,* Aldine, 1970; (contributor) Gary Fromm, editor, *Tax Incentives and Capital Spending,* North-Holland Publishing, 1971; (with Shell) *The Economic Theory of Price Indices,* Academic Press, 1972. Contributor of more than seventy articles and reviews to professional journals. Associate editor, *Journal of the American Statistical Association,* 1965-68; American editor, *Review of Economic Studies,* 1965-68; editor, *Econometrica,* 1968—.

WORK IN PROGRESS: Contributing to *Essays in the Petroleum Industry,* edited by E. Erickson.

* * *

FISHER, Lawrence V. 1923-

PERSONAL: Born November 20, 1923, in Vinton, Iowa; son of Joseph Oscar (a machinist) and Lucy (Hitchcock) Fisher; married Dayna Laverne Larason (a university music teacher); children: Lorna, Kimberly. *Education:* University of Rochester, B.Mus., 1949, M.Mus., 1950; attended courses in journalism and writing at University of Oklahoma, 1954-59. *Residence:* Edmonton, Alberta, Canada.

CAREER: University of Iowa, Iowa City, instructor in violin, 1950-51; Northwestern State College of Louisiana, Natchitoches, assistant professor of music, 1951; University of Southern Mississippi, Hattiesburg, assistant professor of music, 1952-54; Oklahoma City Symphony Orchestra, Oklahoma City, Okla., assistant concertmaster, 1954-67; Oklahoma City University, Oklahoma City, Okla., instructor in violin, 1963-67 and second violinist of

quartet in residence; Interlochen Arts Academy, Interlochen, Mich., teacher of creative writing and violin, 1967-69; University of Alberta, Edmonton, professor of violin and chamber music, 1969—. *Military service:* U.S. Army, Signal Corps, 1943-46.

WRITINGS: Death by the Day, Berkeley Books, 1961; *Die a Little Every Day,* Random, 1963. Contributor of short stories to mystery, slick, and men's magazines. Writer of filmscripts and film scores.

WORK IN PROGRESS: A suspense novel; short stories.

SIDELIGHTS: Die a Little Every Day has been published in England, and issued in Spanish, Dutch, and German editions. Fisher says that he tries to write "of people with human dimensions, in very real human situations.... Supermen as heroes, single-dimensional types, bore me." He has some knowledge ("very small") of French, Italian, and Spanish.

AVOCATIONAL INTERESTS: Photography.

* * *

FISHER, Margaret B(arrow) 1918-

PERSONAL: Born July 18, 1918, in Lockhart, Tex.; daughter of Thomas A. (an educational administrator) and Lula V. (Barrow) Fisher. *Education:* University of Texas, B.A., 1939; Columbia University, M.A., 1941, Ph.D., 1953. *Politics:* Democrat. *Religion:* United Church of Christ (Congregationalist). *Home:* 6703 32nd St., Tampa, Fla. 33610. *Office:* University of South Florida, Tampa, Fla. 33620.

CAREER: Young Women's Christian Association, member of staff in San Francisco, Calif., 1941-44, and Beaumont, Tex., 1944-45, executive director at University of Oklahoma, 1945-47, Southwest regional director of student branch, 1947-50; State University of New York, Buffalo, director of student affairs, 1953-55; Mills College, Oakland, Calif., professor of education and dean of students, 1955-58; Hampton Institute, Hampton, Va., assistant to the president and coordinator of student personnel service, 1958-60; University of South Florida, Tampa, associate professor, 1960-68, professor of behavior sciences, 1968—, director of student personnel, 1960-63, dean of women, 1963-71, assistant to vice-president for student affairs, 1971-75. U.S. Office of Education, member of advisory committee on graduate education, 1966-67, on special services to disadvantaged students, 1970-71, on advanced developing institutions, 1973-75.

MEMBER: American Personnel and Guidance Association (chairman of women's section, National Vocational Guidance Association, 1957), National Association of Women Deans and Counselors, National League of American Pen Women, American Association of University Women, League of Women Voters (vice-president, Tampa, 1961-65), Zonta International, Florida Society for Prevention of Blindness, Florida Voluntary Health Association, Tampa Urban League (member of board of directors), Phi Beta Kappa.

WRITINGS: Leadership and Intelligence, Teachers Press, Teachers College, Columbia University, 1954; (with Jeanne Noble) *College Education as Personal Development,* Prentice-Hall, 1960; (with Leslie F. Malpass) *A Comparison of Programmed and Standard Textbooks,* Cooperative Research Program, U.S. Office of Education, 1964. Contributor of reviews, poems, articles, and line drawings to professional journals.

WORK IN PROGRESS: Research in factors affecting academic achievement, on Josiah Royce and American idealism; on organization and systems theory, and on institutional models and planning methods.

* * *

FISHER, Richard 1936-

PERSONAL: Born June 12, 1936, in New York, N.Y.; son of Steve (a writer) and Edythe (Seims) Fisher; married Mary Louise Ochoa, September 16, 1961; children: Monica Allison, Brendan Robert. *Education:* Attended high schools in Los Angeles, Calif. *Religion:* Roman Catholic. *Home:* 13903 Morrison St., Sherman Oaks, Calif. *Agent:* Paul R. Reynolds, Inc., 599 Fifth Ave., New York, N.Y. 10017.

CAREER: Writer. Has worked in public relations, journalism, television, and as a writer of documentaries for U.S. Information Agency; lived and wrote in Puerto Rico, 1961-64. *Military service:* U.S. Army, 1958. *Member:* Writers Guild of America, West.

WRITINGS: The Very First Time (novel), Doubleday, 1959; *Judgment in July* (novel), Doubleday, 1962.

WORK IN PROGRESS: A suspense novel centered on the West coast.

* * *

FISHMAN, Leo 1914-

PERSONAL: Born February 16, 1914, in New York, N.Y.; son of Max and Rebecca (Honig) Fishman; married Betty Goldstein (an economist), November, 1947; children: Margaret Ellen, Robert Michael. *Education:* New York University, B.A., 1937, M.A., 1938, Ph.D., 1945; University of Washington, Seattle, graduate study, 1938-39. *Home:* 101 Kendall Ridge, Morgantown, W.Va. *Office:* College of Commerce, West Virginia University, Morgantown, W.Va. 26505.

CAREER: Economist with U.S. Department of Commerce, U.S. War Production Board, and U.S. War Assets Administration, Washington, D.C., 1941-47; West Virginia University, Morgantown, associate professor, 1947-52, professor of economics and finance, 1952—, chairman of department of economics, 1971—. Financial adviser to government of El Salvador, 1962-63. Chairman, Council of Economic Advisers to the Governor of West Virginia, 1961-62. *Member:* American Economic Association, American Association for the Advancement of Science, Regional Science Association. *Awards, honors:* Ford Foundation research fellowships, 1953-54, 1961-62.

WRITINGS: (Co-author and co-editor) *The American Economy,* Van Nostrand, 1962; (editor) *Poverty Amid Affluence,* Yale University Press, 1966. Contributor to professional and business journals.

WORK IN PROGRESS: Research in postwar employment and unemployment changes in the United States, monetary policy, and regional and urban problems.

AVOCATIONAL INTERESTS: Latin America.

* * *

FISK, E(rnest) K(elvin) 1917-

PERSONAL: Born October 19, 1917, in Sydney, Australia; son of Ernest (an engineer) and Florence (Chudleigh) Fisk; married Jane Ferguson, April, 1958; children: Peter, Rosemary. *Education:* University of Sydney, student, 1936-39; Oxford University, B.A., 1947, M.A., 1952. *Home:* 1 Dugan St., Deakin, Australian Capital Territory, Australia. *Office:* Australian National University, Canberra, Australian Capital Territory, Australia.

CAREER: With Malayan Civil Service, 1947-58; Colombo Plan, economist, 1958-60; Australian National University, Canberra, Australian Capital Territory, professorial fellow in economics, 1960—, executive director of Development Studies Centre. *Military service:* Australian Imperial Force, 1939-45; became lieutenant colonel.

WRITINGS: The Economics of the Handloom Industry of the East Coast of Malaya, Malayan Branch, Royal Asiatic Society, 1959; (with D. G. Bettison and others) *The Independence of Papua,* Angus & Robertson, 1962; (co-editor) *The Political Economy of Independent Malaya,* University of California Press, 1964; *Studies in the Rural Economy of South East Asia,* University of London Press, 1964; (editor and contributor) *New Guinea on the Threshold,* Australian National University Press, 1966; *The Political Economy of Independent Fiji,* Australian National University Press, 1971. Contributor to *Developing Economics, Economic Record, Journal of Farm Economics, Malayan Economic Review, New Guinea,* and other journals in his field.

WORK IN PROGRESS: Economic Theory of the Earlier Stages of Development; Transition from Subsistence to Market Economics; Subsistence Component in National Income Accounts; and *The Torres Strait Islanders.*

SIDELIGHTS: Fisk is competent in Malay and Chinese (Cantonese dialect). *Avocational interests:* Raising livestock.

* * *

FITZGERALD, C(harles) P(atrick) 1902-

PERSONAL: Born March 5, 1902, in London, England; son of Johannes (a medical doctor) and Cecilia (Fitz-Patrick) Sauer; married Pamela Sara Knollys, February 15, 1941; children: Nicola (Mrs. Jonathan Dawson), Mirabel (Mrs. Mark Ward), Anthea. *Education:* Attended School of Oriental and African Studies, University of London, 1927-30. *Politics:* "Not a member of any party." *Home:* 45 Cleveland Square, W.2., Odalengo Piccolo, 15020, Alessandria, Italy.

CAREER: Lived in China most of the time from 1923 to 1939, and then again from 1946-50 as representative of the British Council in northern China; Australian National University, Canberra, Australian Capital Territory, professor of Far Eastern history, 1953-67, now professor emeritus, visiting fellow, department of international relations, 1968-69. *Member:* Savile Club (London). *Awards, honors:* Leverhulme fellowship for anthropological research in China, 1936-39; D.Litt., Australian National University, 1968.

WRITINGS: Son of Heaven, Cambridge University Press, 1933, reprinted, AMS Press, 1971; *China: A Short Cultural History,* Cresset, 1935, 3rd edition, revised, Cresset, 1961, Praeger, 1965; *The Tower of Five Glories,* Cresset, 1941; (with George Yeh) *Introducing China,* Pitman, 1948; *Revolution in China,* Cresset, 1952, revised edition published as *The Birth of Communist China,* Praeger, 1966; *The Empress Wu,* F. W. Cheshire, 1955, 2nd edition, Cresset, 1968; *Flood Tide in China,* Cresset, 1958; *Finding Out About Imperial China,* Muller, 1961; *The Chinese View of Their Place in the World,* Oxford University Press, 1964; *The Third China: The Chinese Communities in South-East*

Asia, F. W. Cheshire, 1965; *Barbarian Beds: The Origin of the Chair in China*, Cresset, 1965, A. S. Barnes, 1966; *A Concise History of East Asia*, Praeger, 1966; *The China Giant: Perspective on Communist China*, Scott, Foresman, 1967; *The Horizon History of China*, edited by Norman Kotker and others, American Heritage Publishing, 1969; *China's Revolution Twenty Years After*, D. B. Young, 1969; *Communism Takes China: How the Revolution Went Red*, American Heritage Press, 1971; *The Southern Expansion of the Chinese People*, Praeger, 1972; *China: A World So Changed*, Thomas Nelson, 1972; *China and Southeast Asia Since 1945*, Longman, 1974.

WORK IN PROGRESS: Mao Tse-tung and China for Hodder & Stoughton.

* * *

FitzGERALD, Robert D(avid)   1902-

PERSONAL: Born February 22, 1902, in Hunters Hill, New South Wales, Australia; son of Robert David and Ida (LeGay Brereton) FitzGerald; married Marjorie-Claire Harris, March 11, 1931; children: Jennifer Kerry (Mrs. John Francis Lovering), Rosaleen Moyra (Mrs. Roby Earnshaw Tidswell), Robert Desmond, Phyllida Mary FitzGerald Ives. *Education:* Attended Sydney Grammar School, 1915-19, and University of Sydney, 1920-21. *Politics:* "Floating vote." *Home:* 4 Prince Edward Pde., Hunters Hill, New South Wales, Australia.

CAREER: Land surveyor in Australia, 1923-31; Native Lands Commission, Fiji, surveyor, 1931-36; municipal surveyor in Manly and Ryde, New South Wales, 1937-39; Department of Interior, New South Wales, surveyor, 1940-65; now retired. Poet. University of Texas, visiting lecturer in modern poetry, 1963. *Member:* Institution of Surveyors (Australia; fellow), Institution of Surveyors (New South Wales; honorary secretary, 1947-49). *Awards, honors:* Australian Sesqui-Centenary Celebrations Poetry Prize, 1937; Gold Medal of Australian Literature Society, 1938, for *Moonlight Acre*; Officer, Order of the British Empire, for services to Australian literature, 1951; Grace Leven Memorial Prize for poetry, 1952, 1959, 1962; *Encyclopaedia Britannica* Award for Literature, 1965.

WRITINGS—Poetry, except as indicated: The Greater Apollo, privately printed, 1927, republished as part of *To Meet the Sun*, below; *To Meet the Sun*, Angus & Robertson, 1929; *Moonlight Acre*, Melbourne University Press, 1938; (editor) *Australian Poetry 1942*, Angus & Robertson, 1942; *Helmskerck Shoals*, Mountainside Press, 1951; *Between Two Tides*, Angus & Robertson, 1952; *This Night's Orbit*, Melbourne University Press, 1953; *The Wind at Your Door*, Talkarra Press, 1959; *South-most Twelve*, Angus & Robertson, 1962; *Selected Verse*, Angus & Robertson, 1963; *Of Some Country*, University of Texas Press, 1963; *The Elements of Poetry* (lectures), Queensland University Press, 1963; *Forty Years Poems*, Angus & Robertson, 1965; (editor) Hugh McCrae, *The Letters of Hugh McCrae*, Angus & Robertson, 1970; *R. D. FitzGerald Reads from His Own Work* (phonorecord with booklet), University of Queensland Press, 1971.

WORK IN PROGRESS: Product: Later Verses and *Cinderella and Others*, selected prose items.

BIOGRAPHICAL/CRITICAL SOURCES: T. Inglis Moore, *Six Australian Poets*, Robertson & Mullens, 1942; H. M. Green, *A History of Australian Literature*, Angus & Robertson, 1961; Geoffrey Dutton, editor, *The Literature of Australia*, Penguin, 1964; A. Grove Day, *Robert D. FitzGerald*, Twayne, 1974.

FITZPATRICK, Joseph P(atrick)   1913-

PERSONAL: Born February 22, 1913, in Bayonne, N.J.; son of Patrick Joseph and Anna V. (Burnell) Fitzpatrick. *Education:* Woodstock College, A.B., 1936, S.T.L., 1944; Fordham University, M.A., 1941; Harvard University, Ph.D., 1949. *Politics:* Democrat. *Home and office:* Fordham University, Bronx, N.Y. 10458.

CAREER: Roman Catholic priest, member of Society of Jesus (S.J.); Xavier Labor School, New York, N.Y., director, 1938-40; Fordham University, Bronx, N.Y., associate professor, 1949-65, professor of sociology and industrial relations, 1965—, chairman of department of sociology and anthropology, 1960-65. Summer lecturer at Catholic University of Puerto Rico, 1957-72, and Center of Intercultural Formation, Cuernavaca, Mexico, and Petropolis, Brazil, 1961-63; director of workshop on social change and its impact on education in Latin America, Cuernavaca, Mexico, 1964. Chaplain of U.S. Coast Guard and U.S. Marine hospitals, 1943-44. Vice-president of Puerto Rican Family Institute; member of board of directors, Puerto Rican Legal and Educational Defense Fund; chairman of board of trustees, LeMoyne College. *Member:* American Sociological Association, Association for the Sociology of Religion (formerly American Catholic Sociological Society; president, 1953), Population Association of America, American Association of University Professors.

WRITINGS: (Contributor) *The Social Sciences in Catholic College Programs*, edited by Roy J. Deferrari, Catholic University of America Press, 1954; (contributor) *Patterns of Ethics*, edited by F. Ernest Johnson, Harper, 1960; (contributor) *Helping the Family in Urban Society*, edited by Fred Delliquadri, Columbia University Press, 1963; (with John M. Martin) *Delinquent Behavior: A Redefinition of the Problem*, Random, 1964; (with John M. Martin and Robert Gould) *The Analysis of Delinquent Behavior: A Structural Approach*, Random House, 1969; *Puerto Rican American: The Meaning of Migration to the Mainland*, Prentice-Hall, 1971. Contributor to *Thought, America, Commonweal, American Catholic Sociological Review.*

WORK IN PROGRESS: Puerto Rican Addicts and Non-Addicts: A Comparison.

SIDELIGHTS: Has played an extensive role in preparing the people of New York City for an understanding of Puerto Rican newcomers. He has traveled extensively in Central and South America, and is fluent in Spanish.

* * *

FJELDE, Rolf (Gerhard)   1926-

PERSONAL: Surname pronounced Fee-yell-dee; born March 15, 1926, in Brooklyn, N.Y.; son of Paul (a sculptor and longtime professor of art at Pratt Institute) and Amy (Nordstrom) Fjelde; married Christel Mueller (a legal secretary), September 1, 1964; children: Michele, Eric, Christopher. *Education:* Yale University, B.A., 1946; Columbia University, M.A., 1947; studied at Pratt Institute (evening classes in art), 1949-50, University of Copenhagen, 1952-53, University of Heidelberg, 1953, University of Oslo, 1965. *Politics:* Independent. *Religion:* Protestant. *Home:* 261 Chatterton Parkway, White Plains, N.Y. 10606. *Office:* Department of English, Pratt Institute, Brooklyn, N.Y. 11205.

CAREER: J. M. Hickerson Advertising, Inc., New York, N.Y., copywriter, 1948-50; *Popular Science* and *Outdoor Life* Publishing Co., New York, N.Y., senior copywriter and editorial assistant in book department, 1950-52; Pratt Institute, Brooklyn, N.Y., part-time instructor, 1954-56, instructor, 1956-58, assistant professor, 1958-65, associate professor, 1965-69, professor of English and drama, 1969—. Playwright-in-residence, Eugene O'Neill Memorial Theater Foundation, 1966, 1967, and 1970; member of academic faculty, Juilliard School, 1973—. Guest lecturer on drama. *Member:* Dramatists Guild, Authors League of America, American Theatre Association, Society for the Advancement of Scandinavian Studies, American-Scandinavian Foundation, Elizabethan Club (Yale University). *Awards, honors:* American-Scandinavian Foundation fellowship, 1952; Yaddo fellowships in creative writing, 1952, 1954; Ford Foundation National Translation Center fellowship, 1967-68.

WRITINGS: Washington (poem), Caliban Press, 1955; *The Imaged Word* (poems), Pratt Adlib Press, 1962; (translator and author of critical introduction) Henrik Ibsen, *Peer Gynt*, New American Library, 1964; (translator and author of critical introduction) Henrik Ibsen, *Four Major Plays*, New American Library, Volume I, 1965, Volume II, 1970; (editor and author of introduction) *Ibsen: Twentieth Century Views*, Prentice-Hall, 1965.

Writer of original one-act and full-length plays, along with Ibsen play translations, widely produced in England, Norway, Canada, and throughout the United States. Contributor of poetry, short stories, articles, reviews, and translations to *Drama Review, Modern Drama, New Republic, New York Times, Paris Review, Hudson Review*, and other periodicals. Founding editor, *Yale Poetry Review*, 1945-49; founding editor, *Poetry New York*, 1949-51; contributing editor, *McGraw-Hill Encyclopedia of World Drama.*

WORK IN PROGRESS: Further Ibsen translations; original poetry, plays, and literary criticism.

SIDELIGHTS: Fjelde told *CA:* "What fascinates me in dramatic literature is how, in certain writers, the poet's intensive world of image, metaphor, symbol, of highly wrought and charged language, fuses with the playwright's extensive world of human character, projected into settings and sustained actions that show, as Hamlet put it, 'the very age and body of the time his form and pressure.' Within this general absorption in the possibilities open to the poet in and of the theatre, my interests are concentrated on trying to understand more fully the specifics of the art—through the great works of the dramatic tradition, from the Greeks on, that I teach; through the plays of Ibsen, with their masterful embodiment of these elements, which I've had the good fortune of studying closely through the discipline of translation; and through my own ongoing experiments in writing for the theater out of a background in poetry."

AVOCATIONAL INTERESTS: City and country walks, folk and square dancing, travel in Europe, United States, and the Caribbean.

BIOGRAPHICAL/CRITICAL SOURCES: Pratt Alumnus, summer, 1964.

* * *

FLACK, Elmer Ellsworth 1894-

PERSONAL: Born October 3, 1894, in Mendon, Ill.; son of Edward Everett (a farmer) and Sarah Elizabeth (Wright) Flack; married Erna Adelheit Dorow, June 18, 1916; children: Ruth Louise (Mrs. D. A. Flesner), Marie Elizabeth (deceased), Esther Erna (deceased). *Education:* Carthage College, student, 1912-15; Wittenberg University, A.B.,

1916, B.D., 1921, S.T.M., 1924; University of Chicago, M.A, 1923; Augustana Theological Seminary, Th.D., 1926; postdoctoral study at Universities of Chicago, Berlin, and Goettingen. *Politics:* Republican. *Home:* 5440 Cumberland Rd., Minneapolis, Minn. 55410. *Office:* Northwestern Lutheran Seminary, 1501 Fulham St., St. Paul, Minn., 55103.

CAREER: Ordained minister of Lutheran Church, 1918; pastor in Chicago, Ill., 1918-23; Wittenberg University, Hamma School of Theology, Springfield, Ohio, assistant professor, 1923-26, associate professor, 1926-28, professor of exegetical theology, 1928-63, dean, 1940-60, dean emeritus, 1960—, professor emeritus, 1963—; Northwestern Lutheran Theological Seminary, St. Paul, Minn., visiting professor of Biblical theology, 1963-69. Visiting professor at other theological seminaries. Lecturer at universities in Germany, 1937; Lutheran World Federation lecturer, 1956. United Lutheran Church in America, delegate to World Conference on Faith and Order, Edinburgh, Scotland, 1937, member of advisory board for Revised Standard Version of the Bible, 1937-52, delegate to Assembly of World Council of Churches, 1954, and delegate to Assembly of Lutheran World Federation, 1957.

MEMBER: Society of Biblical Literature, Luther Gesellschaft, American Schools of Oriental Research, Young Men's Literary Club. *Awards, honors:* D.D., Midland College, 1936; LL.D., Carthage College, 1953; L.H.D., Wilberforce University, 1956.

WRITINGS: The Book of Revelation (volume in *New Testament Commentary*), Muhlenberg Press, 1936; (contributor) Fendt, editor, *What Lutherans Are Thinking*, Wartburg Press, 1947; (editor with Alleman) *Old Testament Commentary*, Muhlenberg Press, 1948; (editor, department of Old Testament) *Twentieth Century Encyclopedia of Religious Knowledge*, two volumes, Baker Book, 1955; (editor with Bruce Metzger and others) *Text, Canon, and Principal Versions of the Bible*, Baker Book, 1956; (contributor) J. M. Myers and others, editors, *Biblical Studies in Memory of H. C. Alleman*, [Locust Valley, N.Y.], 1960; (editor with L. J. Satre) *Melanchthon: Selected Writings*, translated by C. L. Hill, Augsburg, 1962; *Leaves from the Dean's Jokebook*, C. S. S. Publishing Co., 1971; *The Witness of Jesus*, C. S. S. Publishing Co., 1973. Also author of *On This Rock*, 1973. Contributor to volumes of sermons, and to theological journals. Editor, *Hamma Digest*, 1938-62.

WORK IN PROGRESS: Studies in Christology.

SIDELIGHTS: Competent in German.

BIOGRAPHICAL/CRITICAL SOURCES: Wittenberg Bulletin, May, 1963.

* * *

FLAMMONDE, Paris
(M. M. Delfano)

PERSONAL: Born in Richmond, Va.; married Marcia Sadagursky, February 8, 1964. *Education:* Attended University of Chicago for two years, and Art Institute of Chicago, one year. *Politics:* "Iconoclast." *Religion:* "Mystic." *Address:* c/o Donald McCampbell, Inc., 12 East 41st Street, New York, N.Y. 10017.

CAREER: Variously columnist, art director, painter, and song writer during 1950's; created the Paris Flammonde Symposium—a presentation of poetry, music, painting, and other art forms—in a Greenwich Village coffee house, 1954, the prototype for the later rash of coffee houses throughout the country; producer, writer, and panelist for "Long John Nebel" radio and television shows, WOR, New York, N.Y., 1959-63, and guest and panelist on other radio and television programs, 1964-75; writer. *Member:* Poetry Society of America, Authors Guild, Committee to Investigate Assassinations (co-founder; member of board of directors, 1969—), United States Chess Federation, American Contract Bridge League.

WRITINGS: The Grey Man, Contemporary Classics, 1966; *The Kennedy Conspiracy: An Uncommissioned Report on the Jim Garrison Investigation*, Meredith Press, 1969; *The Age of Flying Saucers*, Hawthorn, 1971; *The Mystic Healers*, Stein & Day, 1974; *UFO's Exist*, Putnam, 1975.

Under pseudonym M. M. Delfano: *The Living Prophets*, Dell, 1972; *The Living Psychics*, Dell, 1973. Ghost writer of two other books. Contributor of poetry and articles, and music, art, and literary criticism to *Village Voice, East, Georgia Review, Bluestone, Worlds of Fantasy*, and other publications.

WORK IN PROGRESS: Assassinations, a book about political murders in the U.S.; *The Coffee House*; a study of the poetry of Loker Raley; a trilogy of novels entitled *Wild Plum*.

AVOCATIONAL INTERESTS: Contemplation, music (Mozart, Vivaldi), "many poets, all deceased", chess, "good scotch and cognac, and better wine."

* * *

FLANAGAN, John T(heodore)   1906-

PERSONAL: Born January 15, 1906, in St. Paul, Minn.; son of John J. (a banker) and Emma (Hamm) Flanagan; married Virginia H. McGuigan, July 24, 1929; children: Sheila (Mrs. Richard H. Paulsen), Moira (Mrs. L. J. Harris), Cathleen. *Education:* University of Minnesota, B.A., 1927, M.A., 1928, Ph.D., 1935. *Politics:* Republican. *Home:* 705 West Michigan, Urbana, Ill. 61801. *Office:* 102c English Building, University of Illinois, Urbana, Il. 61801.

CAREER: University of North Dakota, Grand Forks, instructor in English, 1928-29; University of Minnesota, Minneapolis, instructor, 1929-38, assistant professor of English, 1938-45; Southern Methodist University, Dallas, Tex., professor of English, 1945-46; University of Illinois, Urbana, associate professor, 1946-49, professor of English, 1949—. Lecturer at Kyoto University, 1952; Fulbright lecturer at University of Bordeaux, 1952-53, at Universities of Liege, Ghent, and Brussels, 1960-61; lecturer at University of Moscow and University of Leningrad, spring, 1963. *Member:* American Folklore Society, Modern Language Association of America, American Association of University Professors, Minnesota Historical Society (life member), Illinois State Historical Society (life member), Phi Beta Kappa, Caxton Club (Chicago), Dial Club (Urbana). *Awards, honors:* Newberry Library and Guggenheim fellowships, 1943-44.

WRITINGS: (Author of introduction) William J. Snelling, *Tales of the Northwest*, University of Minnesota Press, 1936; *James Hall, Literary Pioneer of the Ohio Valley*, University of Minnesota Press, 1941; (editor) *America Is West*, University of Minnesota Press, 1945; *The American Way*, J. B. Wolters (Groningen), 1953; (author of introduction) Joseph Kirkland, *Zury: The Meanest Man Spring County*, University of Illinois Press, 1956; (editor with A. P. Hudson) *Folklore in American Literature*, Row, Pe-

terson & Co., 1958; (editor with C. A. Brown) *American Literature: A College Survey*, McGraw, 1961; (contributor of introduction) James Hall, *Letters from the West*, Scholars' Facsimiles, 1967; (author of introduction) William D. Gallagher, *Selections from the Poetical Literature of the West*, Scholars' Facsimiles & Reprints, 1968; (editor) *Profile of Vachel Lindsey*, C. E. Merrill, 1970; *Edgar Lee Masters: Spoon River and His Critics*, Scarecrow, 1974. Contributor to *American Literary Scholarship: An Annual*, Duke University Press, 1967-74; reviewer for *Chicago Sun Book Week*, 1944-47; contributor to more than thirty history and literature journals.

* * *

FLANAGAN, Neal M.   1920-

PERSONAL: Born January 28, 1920, in Chicago, Ill.; son of Patrick Joseph (a secretary) and Loretta (Sullivan) Flanagan. *Education:* Loyola University, Chicago, Ill., B.S. 1942; Angelicum, Rome, S.T.D., 1948; Instituto Biblico, Rome, S.S.L., 1953; Ecole Biblique, Jerusalem, Eleve Titulaire, 1954. *Home:* San Marcello at Corso, 5, Rome, Italy.

CAREER: Roman Catholic priest of Order of Servants of Mary; teacher of theology and biblical studies in Lake Bluff, Ill., 1948-51, 1954-61, and 1964-65; teacher of scripture and biblical Greek, Benburb, Ireland, 1961-64; teacher of cathechetics at missions in Zululand, South Africa, 1962 and 1965; assistant to the father general of Order of Servants of Mary, Rome, Italy, 1965-71. Occasional instructor at Loyola University, Rome, Italy.

WRITINGS: (Author of introduction and commentary) *Acts of the Apostles*, Liturgical Press, 1960, 2nd edition, 1964; *Salvation History*, Sheed, 1964; (author of introduction and commentary) *The Books of Amos, Hosea, Micah*, Liturgical Press, 1966. Writer of pamphlets for Paulist Press; contributor to *Catholic Biblical Quarterly, Worship, Furrow* (Ireland), and other religion periodicals.†

* * *

FLANDERS, Robert Bruce   1930-

PERSONAL: Born January 31, 1930, in Independence, Mo.; son of Roland Osborne (a management consultant) and Lillian (Williams) Flanders; married Sally Harding (now a professor of English), June 27, 1953; children: Stephanie Anne, Todd Rittenhouse. *Education:* Graceland College, student, 1947-49; University of Wisconsin, B.A., 1951, M.A., 1954, Ph.D., 1964. *Religion:* Reorganized Church of Jesus Christ of Latter Day Saints. *Home:* Rt. 9, Box 15, Springfield, Mo.

CAREER: Graceland College, Lamoni, Iowa, associate professor of history and chairman of Division of Social Sciences, 1955-66; Ohio State University, Mansfield, associate professor of history, 1966-68; Southwest Missouri State University, Springfield, professor of history and head of department, 1968—. *Member:* Organization of American Historians, American Historical Association, Western Historical Association, John Whitmer Historical Association, Mormon History Association, Phi Alpha Theta.

WRITINGS: Nauvoo: Kingdom on the Mississippi, University of Illinois Press, 1965.

* * *

FLAVELL, John H(urley)   1928-

PERSONAL: Born August 9, 1928, in Rockland, Mass.;

son of Paul I. (an engineer) and Anne (O'Brien) Flavell; married Eleanor R. Wood, July 24, 1954; children: Elizabeth, James. *Education:* Northeastern University, A.B., 1951; Clark University, M.A., 1952, Ph.D., 1955; graduate study at the Sorbonne, Paris, 1963-64. *Home:* 2829 Drew Ave. So., Minneapolis, Minn. 55416. *Office:* Institute of Child Development, University of Minnesota, Minneapolis, Minn. 55455.

CAREER: University of Rochester, Rochester, N.Y., clinical associate, 1955-56, assistant professor, 1956-60, associate professor of psychology, 1960-65; University of Minnesota, Minneapolis, professor of psychology, Institute of Child Development, 1965—. *Military service:* U.S. Army, 1946-47. *Member:* American Psychological Association, Society for Research in Child Development.

WRITINGS: The Developmental Psychology of Jean Piaget, Van Nostrand, 1963; *The Development of Role-Taking and Communication Skills in Children*, Wiley, 1968; (editor with David Elkind) *Studies in Cognitive Development: Essays in Honor of Jean Piaget*, Oxford University Press, 1969. Contributor to developmental psychology journals.

WORK IN PROGRESS: An introductory textbook on cognitive development, publication by Prentice-Hall expected 1976.

SIDELIGHTS: Speaks and reads French fairly well. *Avocational interests:* Golf, bicycle riding, and travel in general.

* * *

FLEECE, Jeffrey (Atkinson) 1920-

PERSONAL: Born August 1, 1920, in Princeton, N.J.; son of Charles Leslie (a chemistry professor) and Marian (Atkinson) Fleece; married Marianne Mikes (now concertmistress of Honolulu Symphony), June 9, 1949; children: Julie, Larry. *Education:* Central Methodist College, A.B., 1941; Vanderbilt University, M.A., 1942; University of Iowa, Ph.D., 1952. *Home:* 4623 Kilauea Ave., Honolulu, Hawaii 96816. *Office:* University of Hawaii, Honolulu, Hawaii 96822.

CAREER: Instructor in English at Westminster College, Fulton, Mo., 1946-48, and University of Iowa, Iowa City, 1949-51; Western State College of Colorado, Gunnison, assistant professor of English, 1951-52; University of Hawaii, College of Continuing Education, assistant dean, 1955—. *Military service:* U.S. Army, 1942-46; became captain. *Member:* Dramatists Guild of the Authors League of America. *Awards, honors:* First prize in University of Hawaii one-act play competition for "Teatime," 1956, "Quandary in Space," 1960, and "Forgive and Remember," 1961; first prize, Honolulu Theatre for Youth, for "Kalau and the Magic Numbers," 1960, and "Manjiro's Journey," 1962.

WRITINGS: (Contributor) *Essays in Honor of Walter Clyde Curry*, Vanderbilt University Press, 1955; (with J. Gerber and D. Wylder) *Toward Better Writing*, Prentice-Hall, 1958; *The First Oyster* (one-act play), Baker Co., 1960.

In addition to one-act plays, also wrote (with L. Krause) a musical comedy, "Marry an American," produced in Honolulu, 1960, and a television play, "A Good Night's Rest," produced as episode on "Bonanza," National Broadcasting Co., 1965. Contributor of articles to *Saturday Review, Woman's Day, American Speech, College English,* and other periodicals.

FLEMING, Harold (Lee) 1927-

PERSONAL: Born June 16, 1927, in Clymer, Pa.; son of Roy (a miner; deceased) and Viola (Wyke) Fleming; married Nancy Jean Sickenberger, December 29, 1948; children: Harold Lee, Jr., Lance Roy. *Education:* Indiana State College, Indiana, Pa., B.S., 1950; Breadloaf School of English, Middlebury College, M.A., 1960. *Politics:* Republican. *Religion:* Methodist. *Home:* Sunset Ave. R.D. 3, Norristown, Pa. 19401.

CAREER: Penns Manor School, Clymer, Pa., teacher, 1950-60; Abington High School (South Campus), Abington, Pa., teacher, 1960-68; Montgomery County Community College, Blue Bell, Pa., associate professor of English, 1969—. *Military service:* U.S. Naval Reserve, 1945-46. *Awards, honors:* Bread Loaf fellowship, 1959.

WRITINGS—Textbooks, except as noted: (With Allan A. Glatthorn) *Composition: Models and Exercises, 10,* Harcourt, 1965; (with Glatthorn) *Composition: Models and Exercises, 11,* Harcourt, 1965; (contributor) *Warriner's English Grammar and Composition, 10,* Harcourt, 1965; (contributor) *Warriner's English Grammar and Composition, 11,* Harcourt, 1965; *Elizabeth Newt* (novel), Red Dust, 1967.

Contributor of poetry to *Accent, Kenyon Review, Massachusetts Review, New Orleans Poetry Journal, New York Herald Tribune, New York Times, Paris Review, Perspective, Poetry, Poetry Northwest, Prairie Schooner, Quarterly Review of Literature, Western Review, Wormwood Review,* and other periodicals.

WORK IN PROGRESS: Three novels, *A Time Made Simple, The Marriage of Becky,* and *The Sons of Orrin;* three poetry collections, *After the First Fall, In This Fleshmill,* and *Poets and Lovers in Parked Cars.*

SIDELIGHTS: Fleming told *CA:* "My major interest is the writing of poetry and fiction. . . . Teaching has always been a secondary interest. My textbook work has been done to give me the time, eventually, to devote all my time to my poems, novels, and stories." In an interview for the *Alumni News Bulletin* of Indiana State College, Fleming said that "writing is a form of breathing, but, as with breathing, the intake differs from the output. The writer needn't inhale a rarer air, but he does take something from his surroundings which, in due time, comes out in his art. I always have a couple of novels in various stages of completion. My poems come out in big batches. And I never go very long without taking time out to work on a short story." When asked his opinion of the poet's purpose, Fleming said that the poet must "write a poem that will be read and understood. He doesn't keep hours or open a shop. He courts a capricious Muse who doesn't like to be wooed."

BIOGRAPHICAL/CRITICAL SOURCES: Alumni News Bulletin, Indiana State College, June, 1960.

* * *

FLEMING, William (Coleman) 1909-

PERSONAL: Born August 3, 1909, in Pomona, Calif.; son of William Thomas and Theodora (Loney) Fleming. *Education:* Studied music in New York with Paolo Gallico, 1927-30, Leopold Mannes, 1928-30, and in Germany with Arthur Schnabel, 1930-34; Claremont Graduate School, M.A., 1939, Ph.D., 1942. *Home:* 112 Hillcrest Rd., Syracuse, N.Y. 13224. *Office:* Department of Fine Arts, College of Arts and Sciences, Syracuse University, Syracuse, N.Y. 13210.

CAREER: Concert pianist in Germany, Czechoslovakia, France, England, and United States, 1932-40; made Carnegie Hall debut, 1937; Pomona Junior College, Pomona, Calif., instructor in music and philosophy, 1939-45; Syracuse University, Syracuse, N.Y., associate professor, 1945-47, professor of fine arts and chairman of department, 1947-69, Centennial Professor of Fine Arts, 1969—. *Syracuse Post-Standard*, columnist and music critic, 1952—. *Member:* Royal Society of Arts (fellow), American Society for Aesthetics, American Musicological Society, College Art Association, College Music Association, American Association of University Professors, English-Speaking Union. *Awards, honors:* Ford Foundation faculty fellow, 1953-54; honorary D.F.A., Monmouth College, 1959.

WRITINGS: Arts and Ideas, Holt, 1955, 5th edition, 1974; (with Abraham Veinus) *Understanding Music*, Holt, 1958; *Art, Music, and Ideas*, Holt, 1970. Contributor of sections on art to *Encyclopaedia Britannica*, and biographies of composers to *World Book Encyclopedia*; also contributor to musicology journals.

WORK IN PROGRESS: Baroque Art: A Synthesis.

SIDELIGHTS: Residence abroad includes three years in Berlin, two in Florence, one in Paris, and one in London; spends a month or more in Europe annually for research and writing.

* * *

FLETCHER, Arnold Charles 1917-

PERSONAL: Born November 17, 1917, in Chicago, Ill.; son of Arnold (a physician) and Matilde (Behm) Fletcher; married Fern Mary Brittain (a teacher), January 7, 1948. *Education:* Linfield College, B.A., 1937; University of Southern California, M.A., and Ph.D., 1948. *Politics:* Democrat. *Home:* 13156 Hartsook St., Sherman Oaks, Calif. *Office:* Los Angeles Valley College, Van Nuys, Calif.

CAREER: Employed by government of Afghanistan for three years; Los Angeles Valley College, Van Nuys, Calif., associate professor of history, 1953—. University of California, Los Angeles, visiting professor, 1965. Los Angeles Police Commission, hearing examiner, 1961—. *Member:* American Historical Association, Academy of Political Science, Asian Society (Afghanistan council member).

WRITINGS: (With T. W. Wallbank) *Living World History*, Scott, 1959; *Afghanistan: Highway of Conquest* Cornell University Press, 1965; (with Charles Harold King) *A History of Civilization*, Scribner, 1969. Contributor to professional journals.

WORK IN PROGRESS: Three Books, *Ahmed Shah Durrani, The Hazara People*, and *Explorer Before Ericson*.

SIDELIGHTS: Fletcher has made three research trips to central Asia.†

* * *

FLINN, M(ichael) W(alter) 1917-

PERSONAL: Born October 22, 1917, in Manchester, England; son of Walter Leonard (a businessman) and Phyllis (Bell) Flinn; married Grace Davenport (now a musician), June 6, 1943; children: Mark Richard, Hugh Michael. *Education:* Attended Hulme Grammar School, 1927-35; University of Manchester, B.A., 1950, M.A., 1952; University of Edinburgh, D.Litt., 1965. *Home:* 5 Grosvenor Cres., Edinburgh, 12, Scotland.

CAREER: Worked as clerk in cotton industry, Manchester, England, 1935-39, 1946-47; schoolteacher in Stockton-on-Tees, England, and London, England, 1951-59; University of Edinburgh, Edinburgh, Scotland, lecturer, 1959-65, reader in economic history, 1965-1967, professor of social history, 1967—. Lecturer at Scandinavian universities, 1964, 1966. *Military service:* British Army, 1939-46; became captain.

WRITINGS: An Economic and Social History of Britain 1066-1939, Macmillan, 1961; *Men of Iron*, Edinburgh University Press, 1962; (editor) *Readings in Economic and Social History*, Macmillan, 1964; (editor) Edwin Chadwick, *Sanitary Condition of the Labouring Population of Great Britain*, Edinburgh University Press, 1965; *The Origins of the Industrial Revolution*, Longmans, Green, 1966; *British Population Growth, 1700-1850*, Macmillan, 1970. Contributor of articles and reviews to learned journals. Member of editorial board, *Scandinavian Economic History Review*.

WORK IN PROGRESS: A study of Scottish population history, 1600-1939.

SIDELIGHTS: Flinn has reading and/or speaking ability in French, German, Spanish, and Swedish.

* * *

FLOAN, Howard R(ussell) 1918-

PERSONAL: Born November 22, 1918, in Spokane, Wash.; son of Olaf S. and Amalia (Kjosness) Floan; married Maxine Margaret Harwaldt, December 26, 1941. *Education:* Gonzaga University, Ph.B., 1940; University of Washington, Seattle, M.A., 1941; Columbia University, Ph.D., 1954. *Home:* 2 Louisiana Ave., Bronxville, N.Y. 10708. *Office:* English Department, Manhattan College, New York, N.Y.

CAREER: Manhattan College, New York, N.Y., instructor, later assistant professor of humanities, 1947-53, associate professor of world literature, 1954-62, professor of English and world literature, 1962—, head of department, 1954-63. University of Zaragoza, Spain, visiting professor of American literature, 1958-59; University of Zaragoza and University of Valencia, Spain, Fulbright professor, 1966-67. *Military service:* U.S. Army Air Forces, 1942-46; became major. U.S. Air Force Reserve, 1946—; now lieutenant colonel. *Member:* American Studies Association, Modern Language Association of America.

WRITINGS: The South in Northern Eyes, University of Texas Press, 1958; *William Saroyan*, Twayne, 1966. Contributor to literary periodicals, including *Sewanee Review, Thought, Prairie Schooner, American Quarterly*, and a Madrid publication, *Arbor*.

WORK IN PROGRESS: A short story cycle.

AVOCATIONAL INTERESTS: Music, bridge, golf, and tennis.

* * *

FLORES, Ivan 1923-

PERSONAL: Born January 3, 1923, in New York, N.Y.; son of Angel (a professor) and Ruth (Blumauer) Flores; married Helen Rosenberg, March 5, 1955 (divorced, 1967); children: Pamm, Glenn. *Education:* Brooklyn College, B.A., 1948; Columbia University, M.A., 1949; New York University, Ph.D., 1955. *Politics:* None. *Religion:* None. *Home:* 108 Eighth Ave., Brooklyn, N.Y. 11215.

CAREER: Project engineer and supervisor of computer

design projects for Dunlap & Associates, Univac, and other organizations, 1951-60; conducting his own computer design consulting business, 1960—; Stevens Institute, Hoboken, N.J., professor of electrical engineering, 1965-67; Bernard M. Baruch College of the City University of New York, N.Y., professor of statistics, 1967—. Consultant to United Nations Development Program and U.S. Army Scientific Advisory Panel. *Member:* Association for Computing Machinery, Institute of Electrical and Electronic Engineers, British Computer Society, Sigma Xi.

WRITINGS—Textbooks; all published by Prentice-Hall, except as indicated: *Computer Logic*, 1960; *Logic of Computer Arithmetic*, 1963; *Computer Software*, 1965; *Computer Programming*, 1966; *Computer Design*, 1967; *Computer Sorting*, 1969; *Computer Organization*, 1969; *Data Structure and Management*, 1970; *BAL and Assemblers*, 1971; *JCL and File Definition*, 1971; *Computer Programming, S360*, 1971; *The BAL Machine*, Allyn & Bacon, 1972; *OS/MVT*, Allyn & Bacon, 1973; *Peripheral Devices*, 1973. Contributor of over forty-five papers to journals; contributor to *Encyclopedia Americana, Encyclopedia of Computer Sciences*. Editor, *Journal of Association for Computing Machinery, Modern Data*, and *Journal of Computer Languages*.

WORK IN PROGRESS: Data Organization and Use, for Prentice-Hall.

* * *

FLORIN, Lambert 1905-

PERSONAL: Born July 15, 1905, in Ranier, Ore.; son of Carl Hjalmar and Nanny Maria Florin; married, 1940 (wife deceased); children: Barbara. *Education:* Attended high schools in Portland, Ore. and Vancouver, Wash. *Politics:* Republican. *Religion:* No affiliation. *Home:* 5527 Southeast Tolman, Portland, Ore. 97206.

CAREER: Florist designer until early 1960's; full time writer and illustrator (with photographs) of books on ghost towns since then. During World War II served with Portland Fire Department. *Member:* Mazamas (Portland mountaineers club).

WRITINGS—Photographs and text; all published by Superior Publishing Co.: *Western Ghost Towns*, 1961; *Ghost Town Album*, 1962; *Ghost Town Trails*, 1963; *Ghost Town Shadows*, 1964; *Ghost Town Treasures*, 1965; *Boot Hill: Historic Graves of the West*, 1966; *Western Churches*, 1970; *Western Wagon Wheels*, 1972; *Backyard Classic*, in press. Articles and photographs appear regularly in *Desert Magazine*; also has contributed illustrated articles to *True West, Frontier Times*, and *Alaska Sportsman*.

* * *

FLYNN, John Joseph 1936-

PERSONAL: Born April 10, 1936, in Chelmsford, Mass.; son of George Ryan (a teacher) and Mary B. (Woodhead) Flynn; married Sheila Ann Horgan, December 27, 1961; children: John, Jr. Siobham Marie, Timothy Ryan. *Education:* Boston College, B.S., 1958; Georgetown University, LL.B., 1961; University of Michigan, graduate study in law, 1961-63. *Home:* 647 Elizabeth St., Salt Lake City, Utah 84102. *Office:* College of Law, University of Utah, Salt Lake City, Utah 84112

CAREER: Admitted to bar, 1961; University of Michigan, Law School, Ann Arbor, legislative analyst, 1961-63, visiting professor, 1966; University of Utah, Salt Lake City,

member of department of law, 1963—. Big Brothers of Utah, member of board of directors. *Member:* American Bar Association, Boston Bar Association, American Civil Liberties Union (member of board of directors and legal director, Utah branch), Order of the Coif.

WRITINGS: Federalism and State Antitrust Regulation, University of Michigan Law School, 1964. Contributor to legal journals. Editor of *Georgetown Law Journal*, 1960-61.

WORK IN PROGRESS: Federal and State Antitrust Remedies.†

* * *

FOGEL, Ruby

PERSONAL: Born in Georgetown, S.C.; daughter of Harry (a merchant) and Clara (Hepler) Fogel; married Jack I. Levkoff (a financial analyst); children: Lizabeth, Mary. *Education:* Duke University, A.B. *Residence:* Miami Beach, Fla.

CAREER: Poet. University of Miami, Coral Gables, Fla., leader of modern poetry discussion group, 1965. Member of Florida board, National Association for the Prevention of Blindness; member, Greater Miami Philharmonic Society. *Member:* Chi Delta Phi, Alpha Epsilon Phi. *Awards, honors:* Cummins Memorial Award of Lyric Foundation for poem, "The Last of Light," 1965; James Joyce Award of Poetry Society of America, 1968.

WRITINGS: Of Apes and Angels (poetry), A. Swallow, 1966. Poetry anthologized in *Southern Poetry Today*, and published in *Southwest Review, Lyric, Voices, Ladies' Home Journal*, and other periodicals.†

* * *

FOKKEMA, D(ouwe) W(essel) 1931-

PERSONAL: Born May 4, 1931, in Utrecht, Netherlands; son of Dirk and Gijsbertha (Van der Meulen) Fokkema; married Margo Herfst, March 4, 1958; children: Aleide, Diederik. *Education:* University of Amsterdam, M.A., 1956; State University of Leyden, Chinese studies, 1953-56, Litt.D., 1965; University of California, Berkeley, Chinese studies, 1963-64. *Office:* Institute of Comparative Literature, Ramstraat 31, Utrecht, Netherlands.

CAREER: Netherlands Ministry of Foreign Affairs, 1959-68, head of East Asia desk, The Hague, 1965-66, Netherlands Charge d'Affairs, in Peking, China, 1966-68; University of Utrecht, Netherlands, 1968—, associate professor of comparative literature, 1971—. *Military service:* Netherlands Air Force, 1956-58; became first lieutenant. *Awards, honors:* Commonwealth Fund Harkness fellowship, 1963-64; Fulbright grant, summer, 1973.

WRITINGS: Rivieren (poetry, in Dutch), Boucher, 1957; *Literary Doctrine in China and Soviet Influence 1956-60* (with foreword by S. H. Chen), Mouton & Co., 1965; *Report from Peking: Observations of a Western Diplomat on the Cultural Revolution*, C. Hurst, 1971; *Het Chinese Alternatief in Literatuur en Ideologie*, Arbeiderspers, 1972; (editor with E. Zuercher) *Balans van de Culturele Revolutie*, Arbeiderspers, 1973.

WORK IN PROGRESS: Study of Chinese literature since 1960 and on twentieth-century theories of literature.

* * *

FOLEJEWSKI, Zbigniew 1910-

PERSONAL: Surname sounds like Foley-*ef*ski; born October 18, 1910, in Wilno, Poland; son of Joseph (a lawyer) and Bronisława (Hajkowska) Folejewski; married Ulla K. Lindberg, January 6, 1945; children: Peter, Anna, Vanda, Christina, Louise, *Education:* University of Wilno, M.A., 1934; University of Uppsala, Ph.D., 1949. *Home:* 4103 West 11th Ave., Vancouver, British Columbia, Canada. *Office:* University of British Columbia, Vancouver 8, British Columbia, Canada.

CAREER: University of Stockholm, Stockholm, Sweden, lecturer, 1937-47; University of Uppsala, Uppsala, Sweden, lecturer, 1947-49, docent, 1949-50; University of Wisconsin, Madison, instructor, 1951-52, assistant professor, 1952-56, associate professor, 1956-60, professor of Slavic languages, 1960-65, chairman of department, 1960-62; University of Illinois, Urbana, visiting professor, 1965-66; University of British Columbia, Vancouver, professor of comparative literature and chairman of department, 1967—. Visiting professor at University of California, 1956, University of Toronto, 1962-63, Pennsylvania State University, 1963-64. Canadian representative of International Committee of Slavists, 1968—. *Member:* Modern Language Association of America (member of bibiography committee, 1957-67), American Association of Teachers of Slavic Languages (national president, 1957), American Comparative Literature Association (advisory board member), Canadian Association of Slavists (president, 1974-75). *Awards, honors:* Kumlien grant for work in England and France, 1951, and other research and travel grants; honorary degree from University of Warsaw, 1973.

WRITINGS: La Fonction des elements dialectaux dans les oeuvres litteraires, Slavic Institute (Uppsala), 1949; *Studies in Modern Slavic Poetry*, Slavic Institute (Uppsala), 1955; (with E. Zawacki) *Intermediate Russian*, Prentice-Hall, 1960; (editor) *Studies in Russian and Polish Literature*, Mouton & Co., 1962; (with S. Birkenmayer) *Introduction to Modern Polish*, Kosciuszko Foundation, 1965; *Maria Dabrowska*, Twayne, 1967; (editor) *Canadian Contributions to the Seventh International Congress of Slavists*, Mouton & Co., 1973. Two volumes of original poetry were published in Poland in the 1930s. Contributor of more than two hundred articles and reviews to journals. Associate editor, *Slavic and East European Journal, Books Abroad;* member of editorial board, *PMLA*, 1958-68, *Gezmano Slavica*, 1973—; chairman of editorial board, *Canadian Slavonic Papers*, 1969-74.

WORK IN PROGRESS: Futurism and Its Place in Modern Poetry.

SIDELIGHTS: Folejewski has traveled extensively in the Far East, Europe, and Soviet Union for cultural and literary studies.

* * *

FOLLMANN, J(oseph) F., Jr. 1908-

PERSONAL: Born February 24, 1908, in Philadelphia, Pa.; son of Joseph Francis (a printer) and Amelia Follmann; married Judith Brooks (now on staff of American Civil Liberties Union), June 9, 1955; children: Jeffrey, Amy. *Education:* University of Pennsylvania, B.S., 1930. *Politics:* Independent. *Religion:* Protestant. *Home:* 139 East 63rd St., New York, N.Y.

CAREER: With State of Pennsylvania Insurance Department, Harrisburg, 1930-36, 1939-45; Bureau of Accident and Health Underwriters, New York, N.Y., manager, 1945-50, general manager, 1950-56; Health Insurance Association of America, New York, N.Y., director of informa-

tion and research, later vice-president, 1956-74. Lecturer at a number of American universities. Consultant to U.S. Department of Labor, President's Committee on Migratory Labor, National Institute of Alcoholism, Rand Corp., American Health Foundation, American Medical Association, and other agencies and organizations. *Member:* American Public Health Association (fellow), American Academy of Political Science, Gerontological Society, Insurance Society of New York.

WRITINGS: Medical Care and Health Insurance, Irwin, 1963; *Insurance Coverage for Mental Illness*, American Management Association, 1970; *Health Insurance and Preventive Medicine*, American Health Foundation, 1974. Also author of monographs and contributor of articles to journals.

* * *

FONSECA, John R. 1925-

PERSONAL: Born March 13, 1925, in New Bedford, Mass.; son of Joseph R. and Mary (Vicente) Fonseca; married Joan Fagan, August 27, 1949; children: Kathleen, Patricia, Gwendolyn. *Education:* Harvard University, A.B. (cum laude), 1949, LL.B., 1952. *Home:* 26 Tamarack Lane, Clifton Knolls, Elnora, N.Y. 12065.

CAREER: Attorney and counsellor at law, New York and Massachusetts; insurance broker, New York State. Dun & Bradstreet, financial analyst, Boston, Mass., and Brazil, 1952-53; Chase Manhattan Bank, New York, N.Y., editor and trust and estate administrator, 1953-56; State University of New York at Utica, head of department of banking and insurance, 1956-65; Hamilton Research Associates, New Hartford, N.Y., president, 1965; Syracuse University, Utica College, Utica, N.Y., professor of law, 1966-68; State University of New York, Albany, professor of law and banking, 1968—. *Military service:* U.S. Army, 1943-46; served on Okinawa and in Korea; became staff sergeant; received battle star. *Member:* American Bar Association, New York Bar Association, Authors League of America, Authors Guild, American Risk and Insurance Association, American Business Law Association, Harvard Faculty Club.

WRITINGS: (Editor) *Bank Operations Manual*, three volumes, Chase Manhattan Bank, 1955; *Law of Contracts*, Addison-Wesley, 1965; *Fire Insurance*, Addison-Wesley, 1966; *Law of Sales* (Uniform Commercial Code), Addison-Wesley, 1967; *Law of Commercial Paper* (Uniform Commercial Code), Addison-Wesley, 1967; *Law of Business Organizations* (casebook), two volumes, State University of New York, 1971; *Law and Society* (casebook), three volumes, State University of New York, 1972; (with Barkley Clark) *Handling Consumer Credit Cases*, Bancroft-Whitney, 1972; *Environmental Law* (casebook), State University of New York, 1972; (reviser with Alphonse Squillante) Samuel Williston, *Williston on the Law of Sales*, 4th edition, Bancroft-Whitney, 1974.

Contributor to annual supplements of *Law of Modern Commercial Practices, Proof of Cases in Massachusetts,* and *New York Evidence: Proof of Cases,* all published by Lawyers Co-Operative Publishing Co.

Editor-in-chief of *Uniform Commercial Code Law Journal,* 1968-72; editor of *Banking Law Journal,* 1967-72, *Banking Law Journal Digest,* supplements, 1967-72, *Encyclopedia of Commercial Laws,* supplements, 1968-71, *Encyclopedia of Banking Law,* supplements, 1968-71, *Brady on Bank Checks,* supplements, 1968 and 1969; associate editor, *Criminal Law Bulletin,* 1969-71.

WORK IN PROGRESS: Automobile Insurance and No-Fault Law, co-author; On Consumer Credit, Manual and Management Training in Financial Institutions; and Property and Casualty Insurance Law; all for Lawyer Co-Operative Publishing Co. and Bancroft-Whitney.

* * *

FONTANA, Bernard L(ee) 1931-

PERSONAL: Born January 7, 1931, in Oakland, Calif.; son of Bernard Campion and Hope (Smith) Fontana; married Hazel McFeely, June 27, 1954; children: Geoffrey Earl Francis, Nicholas Anthony, Francesca Ann. Education: University of California, Berkeley, A.B., 1953; University of Arizona, Ph.D., 1960. Politics: Democrat. Religion: Protestant. Home: 7710 South Mission Rd., Tucson, Ariz. 85706. Office: Arizona State Museum, University of Arizona, Tucson, Ariz. 85721.

CAREER: University of Arizona, Arizona State Museum, Tucson, field historian, 1960-62, ethnologist, 1962—. National Park Service, Western Regional Advisory Committee member. Military service: U.S. Army, 1953-55; became sergeant. Member: American Anthropological Association, Society for American Archaeology, Society for Applied Anthropology, Society for Historical Archaeology, Society for the History of Discoveries, American Society for Ethnohistory (former president), Southwestern Mission Research Center (president), Arizona Archaeological and Historical Society (former president), Arizona Academy of Sciences, Arizona Historical Society.

WRITINGS: (With William J. Robinson, Charles W. Cormack, and Ernest E. Leavitt, Jr.) Papago Indian Pottery, University of Washington Press, 1962; (co-author and co-editor) Look to the Mountain Top, Gousha, 1972; (co-author) Indians of Arizona: A Contemporary Perspective, University of Arizona Press, 1974. Contributor to Arizona and the West, Arizona Highways, American West, Indian Historian, and to professional journals. Editor of Kiva (journal of Arizona Archaeological and Historical Society), 1957-60, Ethnohistory (journal of American Society for Ethnohistory), 1969-72.

WORK IN PROGRESS: A book on Papago Indians, preparing 1894-95 field diaries of anthropologist W. J. McGee for publication, and a book on Mission San Xavier del Bac.

* * *

FOOT, Paul Mackintosh 1937-

PERSONAL: Born November 8, 1937, in Haifa, Palestine; son of Sir Hugh Mackintosh (Lord Caradon; British diplomat and United Kingdom representative to United Nations) and Florence Sylvia (Todd) Foot; married Monica Beckinsale (a journalist), June 22, 1962; children: John Mackintosh. Education: University College, Oxford, B.A. (second class honors), 1961. Politics: Socialist. Religion: Atheist. Home: 6/120 Haverstock Hill, London N.W. 3, England. Agent: Irene Josephy, 35 Craven St., London W.C. 2, England.

CAREER: Sunday Telegraph, London, England, journalist, 1961—. Military service: British Army, Jamaica Regiment, 1956-58; became second lieutenant.

WRITINGS: Immigration and Race in British Politics, Penguin, 1965; The Politics of Harold Wilson, Penguin, 1968; The Rise of Enoch Powell: An Examination of Enoch Powell's Attitude to Immigration and Race, Penguin, 1969; Who Killed Hanratty?, J. Cape, 1971. Contributor to Scottish Daily Record, Scotsman, and British newspapers.

WORK IN PROGRESS: A book on British dockers.

SIDELIGHTS: Foot's book on the trial and hanging of James Hanratty resulted in a parliamentary motion for a public investigation.†

* * *

FORD, Daniel (Francis) 1931-

PERSONAL: Born November 2, 1931, in Arlington, Mass.; son of Patrick Joseph (a carpenter) and Anne (Crowley) Ford; married Sarah Lansing Paine (an editor), 1967; children: Katherine. Education: University of New Hampshire, B.A. (summa cum laude), 1954; University of Manchester, Manchester, England, graduate study, 1954-55. Home and office: Shankhassick Farm, Durham, N.H. 03824.

CAREER: Overseas Weekly, Frankfurt, Germany, reporter, 1958; free-lance writer and editor, 1959—. Military service: U.S. Army, Psychological Warfare, 1956-57; served overseas in France. Awards, honors: Fulbright scholar in England, 1954-55; Stern magazine writer's grant to visit South Vietnam and write series for Nation, 1964.

WRITINGS: Now Comes Theodora (novel), Doubleday, 1965; Incident at Muc Wa (novel), Doubleday, 1967; (editor) Carter's Coast of New England (travel), New Hampshire Publishing, 1969; The High Country Illuminator (novel), Doubleday, 1971. Contributor of articles to Nation, New Republic, Backpacker, Skiing, and Country Journal.

SIDELIGHTS: Ford told CA his "main source of income is editorial work for government and other agencies" but his "main interest is writing novels and magazine articles." Incident at Muc Wa was published in England and Holland and "has a seemingly-perpetual movie option." Avocational interests: Wilderness travel (especially on skis), working on his house and farm.

* * *

FORD, Franklin L(ewis) 1920-

PERSONAL: Born December 26, 1920, in Waukegan, Ill.; son of Frank Leland (a businessman) and Dorothy Elsey (Lewis) Ford; married Eleanor Rose Hamm, January 8, 1944; children: Stephen Joseph, John Franklin. Education: University of Minnesota, B.A., 1942; Harvard University, A.M., 1948, Ph.D., 1950. Home: 12 Clifton St., Belmont, Mass. 02178. Office: Harvard University, Cambridge, Mass. 02138.

CAREER: Bennington College, Bennington, Vt., member of faculty, 1949-52; Harvard University, Cambridge, Mass., assistant professor, 1953-56, associate professor, 1956-58, professor of European history, 1958-68, McLean Professor of Ancient and Modern History, 1968—, dean of Faculty of Arts and Sciences, 1962-70. Member of Institute for Advanced Study, 1974. Trustee of Bennington College, Browne and Nichols School, and Institute of International Education. Military service: U.S. Army, 1943-46; became first lieutenant. Member: American Academy of Arts and Sciences (fellow), American Historical Association (chairman of modern European section, 1972), American Philosophical Society, Massachusetts Historical Society (member of council, 1969-72), Signet Society (Cambridge), Mill Reef Club (Antigua). Awards, honors: Fulbright research fellow in France, 1952-53; Guggenheim fellow in Germany, 1955-56; Faculty Prize of Harvard University Press for Strasbourg in Transition, 1958; fellow, Center for

Advanced Study in the Behavioral Sciences, 1961-62, D.H.L., Suffolk University, 1972.

WRITINGS: (Contributor) Gordon A. Craig and Felix Gilbert, editor, *The Diplomats*, Princeton University Press, 1953; *Robe and Sword*, Harvard University Press, 1953; *Strasbourg in Transition*, Harvard University Press, 1958; (contributing editor) Jack Hexter, editor-in-chief, *Traditions of Western Civilization*, Rand, 1966; *Europe, 1780-1830*, Holt, 1969. Contributor to historical journals.

* * *

FORD, Herbert Paul 1927-

PERSONAL: Born August 27, 1927, in San Benito, Tex.; son of Jack and Bertha (Graybill) Ford; married Anita Alice Cavagnaro, September 7, 1952; children: Jana Marie, Cynthia Rae, Alyssa Ann. *Education:* Pacific Union College, B.A., 1954. *Home:* 531 Sunset Dr., Angwin, Calif. 94508. *Office:* Department of Communications, Pacific Union College, Angwin, Calif. 94508.

CAREER: Seventh-Day Adventist Church, Glendale, Calif., director of mass communications of western headquarters, 1954-63; Pacific Union Conference, public relations director, 1963-69; Voice of Prophecy (radio broadcasters), Glendale, Calif., public relations director and editor of *Voice of Prophecy News*, 1969-74; Pacific Union College, Angwin, Calif., assistant professor of journalism, 1974—. Ordained minister of Seventh-Day Adventist Church, 1967. Board member of Adventist Church State Council and of "Voice of Prophecy" (international radio program). *Military service:* U.S. Air Force, 1946-49, 1950-51; became technical sergeant. *Member:* Religious Public Relations Council, Sigma Delta Chi, Kappa Tau Alpha.

WRITINGS: Wind High, Sand Deep, Southern Publishing, 1965; *Flee the Captor*, Southern Publishing, 1966; *No Guns on Their Shoulders*, Southern Publishing, 1968; *Crimson Coats and Kimonos*, Pacific Press Publishing Association, 1968; *Rudo: The Reckless Russian*, Pacific Press Publishing Association, 1970; *For the Love of China*, Pacific Press Publishing Association, 1971; *Pitcairn*, El Camino Press, 1972. Author of radio and television scripts; contributor to religious and secular magazines.

* * *

FORD, Leighton F. S. 1931-

PERSONAL: Born October 22, 1931, in Toronto, Ontario, Canada; son of Charles (a jeweler) and Olive Ford; married Jean Coffee Graham, December 19, 1953; children: Deborah Jean, Leighton F. S., Jr., Kevin Graham. *Education:* Wheaton College, Wheaton, Ill., A.B., 1952; Columbia Theological Seminary, Decatur, Ga., B.D., 1955. *Home:* 2901 Coltsgate Rd., Charlotte, N.C. 28211.

CAREER: Presbyterian clergyman; Billy Graham Evangelistic Association, Minneapolis, Minn., evangelist, 1955—, and vice-president, 1958—. *Awards, honors:* D.D., Houghton College, 1962.

WRITINGS: The Christian Persuader, Harper, 1966; *One Way to Change the World*, Harper, 1970; *New Man ... New World*, Word Books, 1972.†

* * *

FOSS, William O(tto) 1918-

PERSONAL: Born October 2, 1918, in Boston, Mass.; son of Hans (a carpenter) and Alma Josephine (Sandstrom) Foss; married Dulcie E. Daffer, November 1, 1941. *Education:* Educated in Norway and Milton, Mass. *Politics:* Democrat. *Religion:* Protestant. *Home:* 813 Queen Elizabeth Dr., Virginia Beach, Va. 23452.

CAREER: U.S. Navy, 1937-48, becoming chief yeoman; U.S. Central Intelligence Agency, Washington, D.C., translator-researcher, 1948-51; *Navy Times*, Washington, D.C., associate editor, 1951-62; U.S. Department of Commerce, Information Division, Washington, D.C., writer-editor, 1962-67; U.S. Army R.O.T.C. Directorate, Fort Monroe, Va., public information specialist, 1967-73; free-lance writer, 1973—.

WRITINGS—With Erik Bergaust, except as indicated: *Coast Guard in Action*, Putnam, 1962; *Helicopters in Action*, Putnam, 1962; (sole author) *Here Is Your Hobby: Skiing*, Putnam, 1964; *Marines in Action*, Putnam, 1965; *Skin Divers in Action*, Putnam, 1965; *Oceanographers in Action*, Putnam, 1968. Monthly columnist, "With the U.S. Coast Guard," in *National Fisherman*; contributor of articles to national magazines.

SIDELIGHTS: Foss lived in Norway from 1920 to 1933. He speaks and writes Norwegian, Swedish, and Danish.

* * *

FOSTER, Charles Howell 1913-

PERSONAL: Born August 3, 1913, in Elizabeth, N.J.; son of Raymond (a businessman) and Alice (Adriance) Foster; married Doris E. VanDenbergh, 1934; children: John W., Thomas H., Mary A., David A. *Education:* Peddie School, graduate, 1932; Amherst College, B.A., 1936; University of Iowa, M.A., 1937, Ph.D., 1939. *Home and office:* Route 1, Box 220, Luray, Va. 22835.

CAREER: University of Iowa, Iowa City, instructor in English, 1939-41, assistant professor, 1941-43; University of Colorado, Boulder, associate professor of English, 1943-47; Grinnell College, Grinnell, Iowa, professor of English and chairman of department of language and literature, 1947-58; University of Minnesota, Minneapolis, professor of English, 1958-74, director of graduate studies in English, 1961-64. Bowdoin College, visiting professor of English, 1964-65. *Member:* Modern Language Association of America, American Association of University Professors, Society of American Historians, Thoreau Society, Phi Beta Kappa. *Awards, honors:* American Council of Learned Societies fellowship to study New England intellectual history, 1951-52.

WRITINGS: Emerson's Theory of Poetry, Midland Books, 1939; *The Rungless Ladder: Harriet Beecher Stowe and New England Puritanism*, Duke University Press, 1954; (editor, and author of critical introduction) *Beyond Concord: Selected Writings of David A. Wasson*, Indiana University Press, 1965. Contributor to journals. Member of board of editors, *New England Quarterly*, 1958-73.

WORK IN PROGRESS: Editing the journals of Benjamin Browne Foster, written in Maine between 1847 and 1855, for University of Maine Press.

AVOCATIONAL INTERESTS: Collecting rare books and periodicals in the field of New England intellectual and literary history, 1800-1890; collection is especially strong in Transcendentalism.

* * *

FOSTER, Laura Louise (James) 1918-

PERSONAL: Born January 25, 1918, in Chillicothe, Ohio;

daughter of Ellery Sedgewick (a banker) and Louise (Hoadley) James; married H. Lincoln Foster (a landscape designer and writer), December 23, 1948; children: Ellery Westwood Sinclair, John Sheldon Sinclair; (stepchildren) H. Rebecca (Mrs. Robert J. Light), Benjamin. *Education:* Attended Chapin School and Bennington College. *Politics:* "Vacillating Republican." *Religion:* Episcopalian. *Home:* Under Mountain Rd., Falls Village, Conn. 06031.

CAREER: Wartime office worker, 1942-46; assistant to husband, teacher of natural history at Vassar Summer Institute, 1949-51; *Lakeville Journal*, Lakeville, Conn., assistant editor, 1952-60. Falls Village Board of Education, chairman, 1954-58; assisted husband as landscape designer, 1964-73; lecturer, 1970—.

WRITINGS: Keer-loo: The True Story of a Young Wood Duck, Naturegraph, 1965; (self-illustrated) *Keeping the Plants You Pick*, Crowell, 1970.

Illustrator: Boughton Cobb, *A Field Guide to the Ferns*, Houghton, 1965; H. Lincoln Foster, *Rock Gardening*, Bonanza Books, 1968; Florence H. Pettit, *How to Make Whirligigs and Whimmy Diddles and Other American Folk-craft Objects*, Crowell, 1972.

SIDELIGHTS: Laura Foster does wood carvings of birds (in miniature) as well as botanical drawings. The Fosters have carried on botanical research in the mountains of eastern and western America, France, Switzerland, and Great Britain. Her botanical illustrations are in the permanent collection of the Hunt Botanical Library of Carnegie-Mellon University.

* * *

FOTHERGILL, (Arthur) Brian 1921-

PERSONAL: Born April 3, 1921, in Lytham-St. Annes, England; son of John Smirthwaite and Kathleen (Entwisle) Fothergill. *Education:* Attended Wycliffe College, Stonehouse, England, 1931-37; King's College, University of London, A.K.C., 1942; Westcott House, Cambridge, England, theological study, 1942-44. *Religion:* Roman Catholic.

CAREER: St. Philip's School, South Kensington, London, England, assistant master, 1949-56; now full-time professional writer. *Military service:* British Army, Intelligence Corps, 1944-47; served in India and Malaya. *Member:* Royal Society of Literature (fellow), Society of Antiquaries (fellow), P.E.N., Society of Authors, Reform Club. *Awards, honors:* P.E.N. Silver Pen biography award, 1970, for *Mr. William Hamilton.*

WRITINGS: The Cardinal King, Faber, 1958; *Nicholas Wiseman*, Doubleday, 1963; *Mrs. Jordan: Portrait of an Actress*, Faber, 1965; (contributor) Cecil Woolf and Brocard Sewell, editors, *New Quests for Corvo*, Icon Books, 1965; *Sir William Hamilton: Envoy Extraordinary*, Harcourt, 1969; *The Mitred Earl*, Faber, 1974. Contributor to *Encyclopaedia Britannica, Collier's Encyclopedia*, and *New Catholic Encyclopedia.*

WORK IN PROGRESS: A life of William Beckford, for Faber.

* * *

FOX, E(dward) Inman 1933-

PERSONAL: Born August 22, 1933, in Nashville, Tenn.; son of Herbert Franklin and Ladye (Inman) Fox. *Education:* Vanderbilt University, B.A., 1954, M.A., 1958; University of Montpelier, graduate student, 1956-57; Princeton University, A.M., 1959, Ph.D., 1960. *Religion:* Protestant. *Office:* Knox College, Galesburg, Ill. 61401.

CAREER: Vanderbilt University, Nashville, Tenn., assistant professor of Spanish, 1960-64, director of admissions, 1960-61, associate professor of Spanish, 1964-66; University of Massachusetts, Amherst, associate professor of Spanish, 1966-67; Vassar College, Poughkeepsie, N.Y., John Guy Vassar Professor of Modern Languages, 1967-74, acting dean of faculty, 1971-72; Knox College, Galesburg, Ill., president and professor of modern languages, 1974—. *Military service:* U.S. Navy, 1954-56. U.S. Naval Reserve, 1956—; now captain. *Member:* International Association of Hispanists, Modern Language Association of America (secretary, Spanish V, 1967), The American Association of University Professors, Phi Beta Kappa (chapter president, 1964-65), Omicron Delta Kappa. *Awards, honors:* Fulbright grants to France and Spain; American Philosophical Society research grant, 1963.

WRITINGS: Azorin as a Literary Critic, Hispanic Institute in the United States, 1962; (editor with German Bleiberg) *Spanish Thought and Letters in the Twentieth Century*, Vanderbilt University Press, 1966; (editor) *La voluntad*, Castalia, 1969, 2nd edition, 1973; (editor) *Antonio Azorin*, Labor, 1971; *Pensamiento y literaturas del 98*, Cuadernos para il Dialogo, 1975; *Articulos de Ramiro de Marztes*, Castalia, 1975.

SIDELIGHTS: Fox is proficient in Spanish and French and knows some Italian and German. He writes poetry in both English and Spanish—but not for publication. Fox is a former basketball coach and scout, and nationally ranked tennis player, winning local net title six times, and state and southern titles.

* * *

FOX, Karl A(ugust) 1917-

PERSONAL: Born July 14, 1917, in Salt Lake City, Utah; son of Feramorz Young and Anna Teresa (Wilcken) Fox; married Sylvia Olive Cate (a social worker), July 29, 1940; children: Karl Richard, Karen Anne. *Education:* University of Utah, B.A., 1937, M.A., 1938; University of California, Berkeley, Ph.D., 1954. *Home:* 3610 Woodland, Ames, Iowa 50001. *Office:* 207 East Hall, Iowa State University of Science and Technology, Ames, Iowa.

CAREER: U.S. War Food Administration, San Francisco, Calif., program analyst, 1942-44; U.S. Department of Agriculture, Bureau of Agricultural Economy, economist in Berkeley, Calif., 1944-45, in Washington, D.C., 1945-54; U.S. Council of Advisers, Washington, D.C., economist, 1954-55; Iowa State University of Science and Technology, Ames, professor of economics, 1955-68, Distinguished Professor of Sciences and Humanities, 1968—, head of department of economics and sociology, 1955-72. Technical Consultant to Committee for Economic Development, 1955, National Planning Association, 1955-56, U.S. Department of Agriculture, 1961, 1963, 1965, United Nations Food and Agriculture Organization, 1965, Environmental Sciences Administration, 1967. Member of Committee on Economic Stability, 1962-66, Research Advisory Committee of U.S. Department of Commerce, 1963-65; member of board of directors, Social Science Research Council, 1963-67; member, Committee on Prices and Price Measurement of Federal Reserve Board, 1965—, ad hoc Advisory Panel on Basic Economic Research, 1971. Visiting professor, Harvard University, 1960-61, University of California, Santa

Barbara 1971-72; visiting scholar, University of California, Berkeley, 1972-73.

MEMBER: Econometric Society (fellow), American Statistical Association (fellow), American Economic Association, American Agricultural Economics Association (vice-president, 1955-56), American Association for the Advancement of Science, American Educational Research Association, Operations Research Society of America, Regional Science Association, Phi Beta Kappa, Phi Kappa Phi. *Awards, honors:* U.S. Department of Agriculture Superior Service Award, 1948; American Farm Economic Association Awards, 1952, 1954, 1957, for outstanding published research.

WRITINGS: (Contributor) *Policies to Combat Depression: A Report of the National Bureau of Economic Research*, Princeton University Press, 1956; *Econometric Analysis for Public Policy*, Iowa State University Press, 1958; (editor with Mordecai Ezekiel) *Methods of Correlation and Regression Analysis*, 3rd edition (Fox was not associated with earlier editions), Wiley, 1959; (contributor) *Problems and Policies of American Agriculture*, Iowa State University Press, 1959; *Farming, Farmers, and Market for Farm Goods*, Committee for Economic Development, 1962; (contributor) Alan S. Manne and Harry M. Markowitz, editors, *Studies in Process Analysis: Economy-Wide Production Capabilities*, Wiley, 1963; (contributor) T. Barna, editor, *Structural Interdependence and Economic Development*, Macmillan, 1963; (contributor) J. S. Duesenbery, G. Fromm, and others, editors, *The Brookings Quarterly Econometric Model of the United States*, Rand McNally, 1965; (contributor) Wilbur R. Maki and Brian J. L. Berry, editors, *Research and Education for Regional and Area Development*, Iowa State University, 1966; (with Jati K. Sengupta and Erik Thorbecke) *The Theory of Quantitative Economic Policy: With Applications to Economic Growth and Stabilization*, Rand McNally, 1966, revised edition, North-Holland, 1973; (contributor) William J. Gore and Leroy C. Hodapp, editors, *Change in the Small Community: An Interdisciplinary Study*, Friendship Press, 1967; (contributor) Robert Kuenne, editor, *Monopolistic Competition Theory: Studies in Economic Impact, Essays in Honor of Edward H. Chamberlin*, Wiley, 1967; *Intermediate Statistics*, Wiley, 1968.

(Editor with D. Gale Johnson) *Readings in the Economics of Agriculture*, Irwin, 1969; (with Jati K. Sengupta) *Economic Analysis and Operations Research: Optimization Techniques in Quantitative Economic Models*, North-Holland, 1969; (editor with Sengupta and G.V.L. Narasimham) *Economic Models, Estimation and Risk Programming: Essays in Honor of Gerhard Tinter*, Springer-Verlag, 1969; (contributor) Ugo Papi and Charles Nunn, editors, *Economic Problems of Agriculture in Industrial Societies*, St. Martin's Press, 1969; (with William C. Merrill) *Introduction to Economic Statistics*, Wiley, 1970; (contributor) Charles L. Leven, J. B. Leger, and P. Shapiro, editors, *An Analytical Framework for Regional Development Policy*, M.I.T. Press, 1970; (editor) *Economic Analysis for Regional Planning: Resource Allocation in Nonmarket Systems*, Johns Hopkins Press, 1972; (contributor) Willy Sellekaerts, editor, *Essays in Honor of Jan Tinbergen*, Macmillan, 1972; (contributor) Hector Correa, editor, *Analytical Models for University Planning*, North-Holland, 1972. Contributor of articles to professional journals and conference volumes. Also contributor to *International Encyclopedia of the Social Sciences*, 1968.

FOX, William Lloyd 1921-

PERSONAL: Born June 26, 1921, in Cleveland, Ohio; son of William Lyman and Corinne (Jones) Fox; married Lynn G. Waters (now an office manager), August 26, 1952; children: William Lloyd, Jr., David L., Deborah L. *Education:* Ohio Wesleyan University, student, 1939-41; Western Reserve University, B.A. (cum laude), 1943, M.A., 1945; George Washington University, Ph.D., 1960. *Politics:* Democrat. *Religion:* Unitarian Universalist. *Home:* 7905 Takoma Ave., Silver Spring, Md. 20910. *Office:* Montgomery Junior College, Takoma Park, Md. 20012.

CAREER: University School, Shaker Heights, Ohio, English and history master, 1943-45; Lake Forest Academy, Lake Forest, Ill., history master, 1945-47; Montgomery Junior College, Takoma Park, Md., professor of history, 1947—, chairman of department of history and political science, 1961-67. George Washington University, summer lecturer in history, 1951, 1956, 1957; University of Maryland, adjunct associate professor of history, 1960—. Takoma Park (Md.) Public Library, president of board of trustees, 1962-63. *Military service:* U.S. Army, 1943. *Member:* American Historical Association, American Association for the History of Medicine (branch president, Washington, D.C., 1964-65), American Studies Association, Organization of American Historians, Maryland Historical Society, Southern Historical Association.

WRITINGS: (Editor with Ruth Anna Fisher) *J. Franklin Jameson: A Tribute*, Catholic University of America Press, 1965. Also author of *Montgomery College: Maryland's First Community College, 1946-1970*. Contributor to historical and academic journals. Editor, *List of Doctoral Dissertations in History*, for American Historical Association, 1961.

WORK IN PROGRESS: A biography of Walter E. Dandy, M.D. (1886-1946) and editing *Maryland: A History, 1632-1974*, with Richard Walsh.

AVOCATIONAL INTERESTS: Music, reading, athletics.

*　　　*　　　*

FOX, William Price, Jr. 1926-

PERSONAL: Born April 9, 1926, in Waukegan, Ill. *Education:* University of South Carolina, B.A., 1950. *Residence:* Hollywood, Calif. *Agent:* Lynn Nesbit, International Creative Management, 1301 Avenue of Americas, New York, N.Y. 10019.

CAREER: Full-time writer. Teacher at Writers Workshop, University of Iowa. *Military service:* U.S. Army Air Forces, 1943-46; became lieutenant.

WRITINGS: Southern Fried (stories), Gold Medal Books, 1962; *Dr. Golf*, Lippincott, 1963; *Moonshine Light, Moonshine Bright*, Lippincott, 1967; *Southern Fried Plus Six* (contains "Southern Fried" and other stories), Lippincott, 1968; *Ruby Red*, Lippincott, 1971. Wrote television pilot, "Off We Go," 1965, and two screenplays, "Cold Turkey" and "The Great Southern Amusement Company." Contributor of stories and articles to *Saturday Evening Post, Holiday, Sports Illustrated, Harper's,* and *West Magazine* of *Los Angeles Times*.

WORK IN PROGRESS: A novel, *Bibleland, Georgia;* articles for *Travel and Leisure.*

*　　　*　　　*

FRACKENPOHL, Arthur R(oland) 1924-

PERSONAL: Born April 23, 1924, in Irvington, N.J.; son

of Alex J. (an insurance agent) and Erna A. (Semner) Frackenpohl; married Mary Ellen Walkley, August 15, 1954; children: James, Steven, David, Thomas. *Education:* University of Rochester, B.A., 1947, M.A., 1949; McGill University, Mus.Doc., 1957. *Politics:* Independent. *Religion:* Presbyterian. *Home:* 13 Hillcrest Dr., Potsdam, N.Y. 13676. *Office:* Crane School of Music, State University of New York, Potsdam, N.Y. 13676.

CAREER: State University of New York, College at Potsdam, 1949—, professor of music, 1960—. Composer and arranger, with more than a hundred published works. *Military service:* U.S. Army, 1943-46. *Member:* American Society of Composers, Authors and Publishers, Music Educators National Conference, New York State School Music Association, National Association of Jazz Educators. *Awards, honors:* First prize in composition, Fontainebleau, France, 1950; Ford Foundation grant, 1959-60; several other awards and commissions.

WRITINGS: Harmonization at the Piano, W. C. Brown, 1962.

* * *

FRAM, Eugene Harry 1929-

PERSONAL: Born July 20, 1929, in Johnstown, Pa.; son of Benjamin (a merchant) and Bessie (Bricker) Fram; married Elinore Milstein, November 27, 1958; children: Bruce, Steven. *Education:* University of Pittsburgh, B.S., 1951, M.Litt., 1952; State University of New York at Buffalo, Ed.D., 1964. *Politics:* Non-partisan. *Religion:* Jewish. *Office:* Rochester Institute of Technology, Rochester, N.Y.

CAREER: Associated Merchandising Corp., New York, N.Y., assistant research director, 1954-57; Rochester Institute of Technology, Rochester, N.Y., 1957—, began as instructor, now professor of marketing and director of Center for Management Study. Lecturer, Brooklyn College (now Brooklyn College of the City University of New York), 1956-57. Associated with family business, Bricker's Economy Store, Windber, Pa., 1946—; outside director and chairman of audit committee, Neisnen Brothers, Inc.; director and treasurer, Business Resources Corp. *Military service:* U.S. Army, 1952-54. *Member:* American Marketing Association (Rochester chapter, vice-president, 1967-68, president, 1968-69), American Association of University Professors, B'nai B'rith.

WRITINGS: Small Business Credit and Finance, Oceana, 1966; *Small Business Marketing,* Oceana, 1968; (editor with J. Peter Vernon) *Readings in Consumer Behavior: A Student's Choice,* MSS Information Corp., 1973. Contributor to business and marketing journals.

* * *

FRAME, Donald M(urdoch) 1911-

PERSONAL: Born December 14, 1911, in New York, N.Y.; son of James Everett (a teacher) and Jean H. (Loomis) Frame; married Katharine M. Wygant, June 7, 1941 (died June 14, 1972); children: James W., Donald Murdoch, Jr. *Education:* Harvard University, A.B., 1932; Columbia University, A.M., 1935, Ph.D., 1941. *Politics:* Democrat. *Religion:* Agnostic. *Home:* 401 West 118th St., New York, N.Y. 10027. *Office:* Columbia University, New York, N.Y. 10027.

CAREER: Loomis School, Windsor, Conn., teacher of Latin, 1932-34; Columbia University, New York, N.Y., instructor, 1938-46, assistant professor, 1946-50, associate

professor, 1950-58, professor of French, 1958—. Teacher of courses at New York University, 1961, University of Pennsylvania, 1964-66, Fordham University, 1968, Rutgers University, 1969-70; visiting scholar, Phi Beta Kappa, 1967-68. *Military service:* U.S. Navy, 1943-46; became lieutenant. *Member:* Modern Language Association of America, American Association of Teachers of French, Renaissance Society of America, Societe des Amis de Montaigne, Century Association (New York).

WRITINGS: Montaigne in France, 1812-1852, Columbia University Press, 1940; *Montaigne's Discovery of Man,* Columbia University Press, 1955; (translator) *Montaigne: The Complete Works,* Stanford University Press, 1957; (translator) *Voltaire: Candide, Zadig and Selected Stories,* New American Library, 1961; (translator) *Prevost: Manon Lescaut,* New American Library, 1961; *Montaigne: A Biography,* Harcourt, 1965; (translator) *Moliere: Tartuffe and Other Plays,* New American Library, 1967; (translator) *The Misanthrope and Other Plays,* New American Library, 1968; *Montaigne's Essais: A Study,* Prentice-Hall, 1969. Contributor and member of editorial board, *Romanic Review;* member of editorial committee, *PMLA,* 1958-68.

WORK IN PROGRESS: Francois Rabelais, for Harcourt.

* * *

FRANCIS, Philip S(heridan) 1918-

PERSONAL: Born December 17, 1918, in Philadelphia, Pa.; son of George Faunce (an architect) and Ivy (Corlies) Francis; married Betty Ann Fitzpatrick, June 28, 1960; children: Philip Sheridan, Jr. *Education:* College of William and Mary, B.S., 1941. *Politics:* Independent. *Religion:* Unitarian Universalist. *Residence:* Clewiston, Fla.

CAREER: U.S. Sugar Corp., Clewiston, Fla., research chemist, 1947—; Dade County, Fla., pollution control inspector, 1971—. Photographer. *Member:* Outdoor Writers Association of America (member of board of directors, 1969-72). *Awards, honors:* Florida Outdoor Writers Association Award, 1957, for best magazine article of the year; International Spin Fishing Association Award, 1962, for outstanding catch of the year.

WRITINGS: Florida Fish and Fishing, Macmillan, 1955; *Salt Water Fishing from Maine to Texas,* Macmillan, 1963; (with George S. Fichter) *Fishing,* Golden Press, 1965. Contributor of over two hundred articles to magazines. Fishing editor, *Florida Wildlife,* 1951-53; regional editor, *Fisherman,* 1954-59.

WORK IN PROGRESS: Research for books on freshwater and salt-water fishing.

AVOCATIONAL INTERESTS: Fishing, sports cars, the theater, skin diving.

* * *

FRANCOIS, Pierre 1932-

PERSONAL: Born July 26, 1932, in Nancy, France; son of Georges (a civil engineer) and Therese (Fourcaulx) Francois; married Jacqueline Com (a professor), August 20, 1960; children: Michele Suzanne, Jean-Pierre. *Education:* Universite de Nancy, graduate, 1952, received License, 1958; Fordham University, M.A., 1961; Columbia University, Ph.D., 1967. *Religion:* Roman Catholic. *Home:* Wittenburg Rd., Bearsville, N.Y. 12409.

CAREER: Fordham University, Bronx, N.Y., instructor in French, 1961-65; State University of New York, New

Paltz, assistant professor of French, 1966—. *Military service:* French Army, 1958. *Member:* Societe des Professeurs Francais en Amerique (secretaire general, 1962-64; member of council), Modern Language Association of America, American Association of University Professors, L'-Association Vosgienne.

WRITINGS: (With Rudolph J. Mondelli) *Conversational French One*, American Book Co., 1963, 2nd edition, 1965; *French Conversational Review Grammar*, American Book Co., 1965, 3rd edition, Van Nostrand, 1972; (with Georges R. Decote and Bernard Lescot) *Voix et langage*, American Book Co., 1969.

AVOCATIONAL INTERESTS: History of cultures and civilizations; music, piano, and organ.†

*   *   *

FRANK, Helmut J(ack) 1922-

PERSONAL: Born June 6, 1922, in Coblence, Germany; became U.S. citizen; son of Arthur A. (a physician) and Anna T. (Sternberg) Frank; married Annemarie Bartknecht, December 30, 1961 (divorced, 1967); children: Thomas Peter. *Education:* Columbia University, B.S., 1948, M.A., 1950, Ph.D., 1961. *Politics:* Democrat. *Religion:* Roman Catholic. *Home:* 7218 East Camino Valle Verde, Tucson, Ariz. 85715. *Office:* Business and Public Administration College, University of Arizona, Tucson, Ariz. 85721.

CAREER: National Bureau of Economic Research, New York, N.Y., research assistant, 1949-50; W. J. Levy, Inc. (petroleum consultants), New York, N.Y., economist, 1950-56; Princeton University, Princeton, N.J., instructor, 1958-59; W. J. Levy, S.A., Paris, France, director of research, 1960-61; University of Arizona, Tucson, assistant professor, 1961-63, associate professor, 1963-67, professor of economics, 1967—. Lecturer, City College (now City College of the City University of New York), New York, N.Y., 1958; research economist, University of Denver Research Institute, 1967-68. Consultant to Gas Requirements Committee, Electric Power Research Institute. *Military service:* U.S. Army, 1943-45; became sergeant. *Member:* American Economic Association, Western Economic Association, Phi Kappa Phi.

WRITINGS: Crude Oil Prices in the Middle East, Praeger, 1966; (contributor) Schurr and Homan, editors, *Middle Eastern Oil and the Western World*, Elsevier, 1971; (with J. E. Weber) *Energy Consumption by States*, University of Arizona, 1972; (contributor) K. Brown, editor, *Regulation of the Natural Gas Producing Industry*, Johns Hopkins Press, 1972; (contributor) R. Lawrence, editor, *The Energy Crisis: Reality or Myth*, American Academy of Political and Social Science, 1973; *Arizona Energy Inventory*, Arizona State Fuel and Energy Office, 1975. Contributor to economic journals.

WORK IN PROGRESS: Future role of electric power in U.S. energy supplies; U.S. and Canadian energy trade; petroleum industry investment behavior.

SIDELIGHTS: Frank speaks French and German. *Avocational interests:* Music (amateur musician).

*   *   *

FRANKENA, William K(laas) 1908-

PERSONAL: Surname is accented on first syllable; born June 21, 1908, in Manhattan, Mont.; son of Nicholas A. (a farmer) and Gertie (VanderSchaaf) Frankena; married

Sadie G. Roelofs, June 23, 1934; children: Karl R., Mark W. *Education:* Calvin College, A.B., 1930; University of Michigan, A.M., 1931; Harvard University, Ph.D., 1937. *Home:* 1 Hillside Ct., Ann Arbor, Mich. 48104. *Office:* Department of Philosophy, University of Michigan, Ann Arbor, Mich.

CAREER: University of Michigan, Ann Arbor, instructor, 1937-40, assistant professor, 1940-46, associate professor, 1946-47, professor of philosophy, 1947—, chairman of department, 1947-61. Visiting professor at Columbia University, 1953, University of Tokyo, 1954, Harvard University, 1955, 1962-63, Princeton University, 1960, Chatham College, trustee, 1961—. Carns Lecturer, American Philosophical Association, 1974. *Member:* American Philosophical Association (chairman of board of officers, 1963-65; president, Western division, 1965-66), National Academy of Education, Phi Beta Kappa. *Awards, honors:* Guggenheim fellow, 1948-49; National Endowment for the Humanities senior fellow, 1972-73.

WRITINGS: Ethics, Prentice-Hall, 1963; (editor) *Philosophy of Education*, Macmillan, 1965; *Three Historical Philosophies of Education*, Scott, 1965.

Contributor: P. A. Schilpp, editor, *The Philosophy of G. E. Moore*, Northwestern University, 1942; M. Black, editor, *Philosophical Analysis*, Cornell University Press, 1950; A. I. Melden, editor, *Essays in Moral Philosophy*, University of Washington Press, 1958; P. Henle, editor, *Language Thought and Culture*, University of Michigan Press, 1958; E. A. Walter, editor, *Religion and the State University*, University of Michigan Press, 1958; Richard B. Brandt, editor, *Social Justice*, Prentice-Hall, 1962; C. L. Carter, editor, *Skepticism and Moral Principles*, New University Press, 1973; P. P. Wiener, editor, *Dictionary of the History of Ideas*, Scribners, 1973.

Contributor to professional journals. Member of board of editors, *Monist*.

WORK IN PROGRESS: Further writing on moral philosophy and on philosophy of education.

*   *   *

FRASCONA, Joseph Lohengrin 1910-

PERSONAL: Born November 11, 1910, in New York, N.Y.; son of Anthony (an opera singer) and Mathilde (Ullrich) Frascona; married Jean Helen Ezard, February 5, 1944; children: Oliver Ezard, Olivia Ezard, Rosalind Ezard. *Education:* City University of New York, B.S.S., 1932; Harvard University, LL.B. (converted to J.D.), 1935; U.S. Army Command and General Staff College, graduate, 1961. *Politics:* Republican. *Religion:* Episcopalian. *Home:* 420 Ponderosa Dr., Boulder, Colo. 80303. *Office:* College of Business and Administration, University of Colorado, Boulder, Colo. 80302.

CAREER: Member of New York, Colorado, and Federal Bars. Walton, Bannister and Stitt (law firm), New York, N.Y., lawyer, 1937-40; Office of U.S. Attorney General, Washington, D.C., associate attorney, 1942; U.S. Department of State, Washington, D.C., general counsel, 1945-46; University of Colorado, Boulder, instructor, 1946, assistant professor, 1947-48, associate professor, 1948-55, professor of business law, 1955—, head of Division of Business Law, 1963-65. Colorado School of Banking, Boulder, faculty member, 1954—, director, 1959—; American Industrial Bankers Association, faculty member of National Installment Bankers School, 1959—; visiting summer professor at

University of California, Los Angeles, 1949, University of Miami, Coral Gables, 1956. Member of National advisory board, Young Americans for Freedom. *Military service:* U.S. Army, 1942-46. U.S. Army Reserve, 1946-66; retired with rank of colonel.

MEMBER: Federal Bar Association, American Business Law Association (past president), Reserve Officers Association, Colorado Bar Association, New York Bar Association, Boulder County Bar Association, Delta Sigma Pi, Beta Gamma Sigma, Chi Psi.

WRITINGS: Visit, Search and Seizure on the High Seas: A Proposed Convention of International Law on the Regulation of This Belligerent Right, privately printed, 1938; *C.P.A. Law Review*, Irwin, 1950, 4th edition published as *C.P.A. Law Review, Under the Uniform Commercial Code, as Amended*, 1972; (with Walter B. Franklin) *Statutory Materials for the Study of Commercial Law*, Foundation Press, 1951; *Business Law*, Irwin, 1954; *Agency*, Prentice-Hall, 1964. Contributor to *Encyclopedia Americana*. Contributor of articles and reviews to journals.

WORK IN PROGRESS: A fifth edition of *C.P.A. Law Review, Under Uniform Commercial Code, as Amended.*

*   *   *

FRASIER, James E(dwin) 1923-

PERSONAL: Born January 18, 1923, in Gothenburg, Neb.; son of Clifford R. and Ruby (Delahunty) Frasier; married Jean Morrill, August 12, 1945; children: Janet, Douglas, Curtis, Thomas. *Education:* Colorado State College (now University of Northern Colorado), Greeley, A.B., 1945, Ed.D., 1954; University of Michigan, M.A., 1947. *Religion:* Episcopalian. *Home:* 311 Encanto Dr., Tempe, Ariz. 85281.

CAREER: Teacher of biology in Fort Morgan, Colo., 1945, of general science in Grosse Pointe, Mich., 1945-47; Nebraska State Teachers College (now Peru State College), Peru, Neb., assistant professor of education (concurrently junior high school principal), 1947-50; Omaha (Neb.) public schools, supervisor of junior high school education, 1950-55; Oklahoma State University, Stillwater, assistant professor, later associate professor of education, 1955-63; Arizona State University, Tempe, professor of education, 1963—. *Member:* National Education Association, Association for Higher Education, National Association of Secondary-School Principals, Arizona Education Association, Arizona Association of Secondary-School Principals, Phi Delta Kappa.

WRITINGS: (Editor and principal author) *A Manual of Evaluation for a Junior High School*, Oklahoma State Department of Education, 1958; *An Introduction to the Study of Education*, 3rd edition (Frasier was not affiliated with earlier editions), Harper, 1965; *A Taxonomy of Subject Matter Presentation*, Arizona State University, College of Education, 1971. Contributor to education journals. Former member of editorial advisory board, *Clearing House.*

*   *   *

FRAUTSCHI, R(ichard) L(ane) 1926-

PERSONAL: Born November 14, 1926, in Rockford, Ill.; son of Irving F. (in retail furniture business) and Gertrude (Lane) Frautschi; married Judith Springer Guild, December 22, 1954 (divorced February, 1971); married Lucy Brooke Woods, November 17, 1973; children: Mark, Anne,

Scott, Tyler. *Education:* University of Wisconsin, B.A., 1949; Harvard University, M.A., 1953, Ph.D., 1958. *Home address:* "Pantops," R.D. 1, Port Matilda, Pa. 16870. *Office:* Department of French, Pennsylvania State University, University Park, Pa. 16802.

CAREER: Smith College, Northampton, Mass., instructor in French, 1954-58; University of North Carolina, Chapel Hill, assistant professor, 1958-62, associate professor, 1962-67, professor of French, 1967-70; Pennsylvania State University, University Park, professor of French, and head of department, 1970—. St. Augustine's College, Raleigh, N.C., visiting professor, 1961-64; University of North Carolina Year-at-Lyon, director, 1964-65. *Military service:* U.S. Navy, 1944-46. *Member:* Modern Language Association of America, American Association of Teachers of French, American Association of University Professors.

WRITINGS: (Editor) Pierre Gringore, *Les Fantasies de Mere Sote*, University of North Carolina Press, 1962; *Voltaire: Candide*, Barron, 1968; (with Claude Bouygues) *Pour et Contre: Manuelde conversations graduees*, Dodd, 1973. Contributor of articles and reviews to language journals in America, England, and France.

WORK IN PROGRESS: Authorship study of Diderot's *Encyclopedia*, using a computer; with Angus Martin and Vivienne Mylne, a bibliography of French prose fiction, 1751-1815.

AVOCATIONAL INTERESTS: Railroads, architecture, travel.

*   *   *

FRAZER, Robert W(alter) 1911-

PERSONAL: Born December 19, 1911, in Sacramento, Calif.; son of Walter and Orilla (Stanfield) Frazer. *Education:* University of California, Los Angeles, B.A., 1936, M.A., 1940, Ph.D., 1941. *Home:* 350 Peralta Ave., Long Beach, Calif. 90814. *Office:* California State University, Long Beach, Calif.

CAREER: Adams State College, Alamosa, Colo., assistant professor of history, 1940-42; Northrop Aircraft, Inc., Hawthorne, Calif., service engineer, 1942-46; University of Wichita, Wichita, Kan., professor of history, 1946-64, chairman of department, 1956-64; California State College at Long Beach, professor of history, 1965—. University of California, Los Angeles, visiting professor of history, 1961-62. *Member:* Organization of American Historians, Western History Association, Council on Abandoned Military Posts, New Mexico Historical Society.

WRITINGS: (Editor) *Mansfield on the Condition of the Western Forts, 1853-54*, University of Oklahoma Press, 1963; *Forts of the West*, University of Oklahoma Press, 1965; *New Mexico in 1850*, University of Oklahoma Press, 1968. Contributor of articles and reviews to historical journals.

WORK IN PROGRESS: Handbook of United States Indian Agencies.

*   *   *

FRAZER, William J(ohnson), Jr. 1924-

PERSONAL: Born October 15, 1924, in Greenville, Ala.; son of William Johnson and Margaret (Thompson) Frazer; married Mary Ann Burford, 1949; children: William Johnson III. *Education:* Huntingdon College, A.B., 1950; graduate study at University of Texas, 1950-51, and American University, 1951-52; Columbia University, M.A., 1953, Ph.D., 1968. *Office:* College of Business Administration, University of Florida, Gainesville, Fla. 32601.

CAREER: Instructor in economics at Pratt Institute, Brooklyn, N.Y., 1953-54, and Rensselaer Polytechnic Institute, Troy, N.Y., 1954-56; Federal Reserve Bank of New York, New York, N.Y., economist, 1956-57; University of Florida, Gainesville, assistant professor, 1957-65, associate professor of economics and finance, 1965-66; Federal Reserve Bank of Chicago, Chicago, Ill., senior financial economist, 1966-67; University of Florida, Gainesville, professor of economics, 1968—. Visiting professor, University of Kentucky, 1967-68. *Military service:* U.S. Navy, 1943-46; became second class petty officer. *Member:* American Economic Association, American Finance Association, Southern Economic Association (executive committee member, 1973-75), Southern Finance Association. *Awards, honors:* Ford Foundation faculty fellow at Harvard University, 1959-60; National Science Foundation faculty fellow at University of Pennsylvania, 1964-65.

WRITINGS: The Liquidity Structure of Firms and Monetary Economics, University of Florida Press, 1965; (with William P. Yohe) *Introduction to the Analytics and Institutions of Money and Banking,* Van Nostrand, 1965; *The Demand for Money,* World Publishing, 1967; *Crisis in Economic Theory,* University of Florida Press, 1974. Contributor to economics journals.

*   *   *

FREDRICKSON, George M(arsh)   1934-

PERSONAL: Born July 16, 1934, in Bristol, Conn.; son of George (a merchant) and Gertrude (Marsh) Fredrickson; married Helene Osouf, October 16, 1956; children: Anne Hope, Laurel, Thomas, Caroline. *Education:* Harvard University, B.A., 1956, Ph.D., 1964; University of Oslo, graduate study, 1956-57. *Home:* 1215 Judson Ave., Evanston, Ill. 60202. *Office:* Department of History, Northwestern University, Evanston, Ill.

CAREER: Harvard University, Cambridge, Mass., instructor in history, 1963-66; Northwestern University, Evanston, Ill., associate professor, 1966-71, professor of history, 1971—. *Military service:* U.S. Navy, 1957-60; became lieutenant junior grade. *Member:* American Historical Association, Southern Historical Society, Organization of American Historians. *Awards, honors:* Annisfield Wolf Award in race relations for *Black Image in the White Mind,* 1972.

WRITINGS: The Inner Civil War: Northern Intellectuals and the Crisis of the Union, Harper, 1965; (editor) Albion Tourgee, *A Fool's Errand,* Torchbooks, 1966; (editor) Hinton R. Halper, *The Impending Crisis of the South,* Harvard University Press, 1968; (editor) *William Lloyd Garrison,* Prentice-Hall, 1968; *The Black Image in the White Mind,* Harper, 1971; (contributor) Huggins, Kilson, and Fox, editors, *Key Issues in the Afro-American Experience,* Harcourt, 1971. Contributor to *American Historical Review, Journal of Southern History, Civil War History, New York Review of Books,* and other periodicals.

WORK IN PROGRESS: A book on the comparative history of race relations in the U.S. and South Africa for Oxford University Press, expected in 1977.

SIDELIGHTS: Fredrickson has some competence in French, Dutch, and Afrikaans.

FREEDMAN, Russell (Bruce)   1929-

PERSONAL: Born October 11, 1929, in San Francisco, Calif.; son of Louis N. (a publishers' representative) and Irene (Gordon) Freedman. *Education:* Attended San Jose State College (now University), 1947-49; University of California, Berkeley, B.A., 1951. *Home and office:* 280 Riverside Dr., New York, N.Y. 10025.

CAREER: Associated Press, San Francisco, Calif., newsman, 1953-56; J. Walter Thompson Co. (advertising agency), New York, N.Y., television publicity writer, 1956-60; Columbia University Press, New York, N.Y., associate staff member, *Columbia Encyclopedia,* 1961-63; Crowell-Collier Educational Corp., New York, N.Y., editor, 1964-65; New School for Social Research, New York, N.Y., instructor of writing workshops, 1969—; free-lance writer, particularly for young people. *Military service:* U.S. Army, Counter Intelligence Corps, 1951-53. *Member:* Authors League of America, American Civil Liberties Union.

WRITINGS—Books for young people; all published by Holiday House, except as noted: *Teenagers Who Made History,* 1961; *2000 Years of Space Travel,* 1963; *Jules Verne: Portrait of a Prophet,* 1965; *Thomas Alva Edison,* Study-Master, 1966; *Scouting With Baden-Powell,* 1967; (with James E. Morriss) *How Animals Learn,* 1969; (with Morriss) *Animal Instincts,* 1970; *Animal Architects,* 1971; (with Morriss) *The Brains of Animals and Man,* 1972; *The First Days of Life,* 1974; *Growing Up Wild,* 1975. Contributor to *Columbia Encyclopedia,* 3rd edition, and Scholastic Magazines.

*   *   *

FREEDMAN, Warren   1921-

PERSONAL: Born May 2, 1921, in Scranton, Pa.; son of Samuel N. and Sarah (Spitz) Freedman; married Esther Rosenbluth (a psychiatric social worker), May 3, 1944; children: Deborah, Douglas, Miriam. *Education:* Attended Cornell University, 1942-43, Yale University, 1943-44; Rutgers University, A.B., 1943; Columbia University, LL.B., 1949. *Politics:* Democrat. *Religion:* Hebrew. *Home:* 81 Stratford Rd., New Rochelle, N.Y. *Office:* 630 Fifth Ave., New York, N.Y.

CAREER: Admitted to New York Bar, 1949; counsel for Bristol Myers Co., 1953—. New School for Social Research, New York, N.Y., professor of sociology, 1958—. Member of legislative committee, Drug, Chemical and Allied Trades Association. *Military service:* U.S. Army Air Forces, Judge Advocate General's Department, 1944-47; became captain. *Member:* American Bar Association, New York County Lawyers Association, Association of the Bar of the City of New York, B'nai B'rith.

WRITINGS: (Editor) George Richards, *Richards on Insurance,* four volumes, Baker Voorhis, 1952—; *Freedman on Allergy and Products Liability,* Central Book, 1963; *Society on Trial,* C. C Thomas, 1964; *Societal Behavior,* C. C Thomas, 1965; *Sociology and the Law,* C. C Thomas, 1972; *The Selective Guide for the Jewish Traveler,* Macmillan, 1972. Contributor of articles on insurance, taxation, products liability, and other subjects, to legal journals and other periodicals.

AVOCATIONAL INTERESTS: Sports, travel.

*   *   *

FREEMAN, James Dillet   1912-
(D. J. Mann)

PERSONAL: Legal surname Freedman; born March 20,

1912, in Wilmington, Del.; son of Jacob (a pressman) and Sarah (Elberson) Freedman; married Billie Ray (a writer), March 23, 1951. *Education:* University of Missouri, Columbia, A.B., 1932, and graduate study one year; further graduate study at University of Missouri at Kansas City, 1938, and Columbia University, 1943. *Politics:* Democrat. *Religion:* Unity. *Home:* 500 O'Brien Rd., Lee's Summit, Mo. 64063. *Office:* Unity School of Christianity, Unity Village, Mo. 64065.

CAREER: Unity School of Christianity, Unity Village, Mo., 1934—, writer, teacher, lecturer, member of worldwide prayer ministry, organizer of school for ministers, director of spiritual research.

WRITINGS: Household of Faith, Unity, 1952; *Story of Unity*, Unity, 1954; *Be!*, Unity, 1955; *Happiness Can Be a Habit*, Doubleday, 1966; *Prayer: The Master Key*, Doubleday, 1967; *Look With the Eyes of Love*, Doubleday, 1969; *The Case for Optimism*, Harper, 1971; *A Case for Believing*, Doubleday, 1972; *What God is Like*, Unity, 1973; *Love, Loved, Loving*, Doubleday, 1974. Poems anthologized in collections, and published in magazines and newspapers, including *Scientific Monthly, Saturday Review, New Yorker, Christian Herald, Good Housekeeping*, and *McCall's*; also writer of verse for Hallmark and other greeting card companies.

WORK IN PROGRESS: A book on metaphysics, for Doubleday.

SIDELIGHTS: Freeman has some competence in French, German, and Spanish.

* * *

FREMGEN, James Morgan 1933-

PERSONAL: Surname originally Froembgen; born December 5, 1933, in Chicago, Ill.; son of William H. (an attorney) and Marguerite (Morgan) Froembgen; married Eleanor Slicko, May 12, 1956; children: James Paul, Stephen John. *Education:* University of Notre Dame, B.S.C., 1954; Indiana University, M.B.A., 1955, D.B.A., 1961. *Office:* U.S. Naval Postgraduate School, Monterey, Calif. 93940.

CAREER: Certified public accountant, state of Indiana, 1962. Indiana University, Bloomington, lecturer in accounting, 1959-61; University of Notre Dame, Notre Dame, Ind., 1961-65, began as assistant professor, became associate professor of accountancy; U.S. Naval Postgraduate School, Monterey, Calif., (civilian) associate professor, 1965-69, professor of accounting, 1969—. *Military service:* U.S. Coast Guard, 1955-58; became lieutenant. *Member:* American Accounting Association, American Institute of Certified Public Accountants, National Association of Accountants, Beta Alpha Psi, Beta Gamma Sigma.

WRITINGS: Managerial Cost Analysis, Irwin, 1966, revised edition published as *Accounting for Managerial Analysis*, 1972. Contributor to professional journals.

WORK IN PROGRESS: Accounting for the cost of capital.

* * *

FRESCHET, Berniece (Louise Speck) 1927-

PERSONAL: Born August 4, 1927, in Miles City, Mont.; daughter of Paul Vernon and Rose (Zigele) Speck; married Ferruccio Freschet (a high school dean of boys and assistant principal), January 26, 1952; children: Leslie Ann,

Gina Marie, Dinah Sue, Maria Theresa, Frankie Paul. *Education:* Attended University of Montana, 1946-48.

WRITINGS: Young Eagle, Scribner, 1965; *Kangaroo Red*, Scribner, 1966; *The Little Woodcock*, Scribner, 1966; *The Old Bullfrog*, Scribner, 1968; *The Owl and the Prairie Dog*, Scribner, 1969; *Beaver on the Sawtooth*, Crowell, 1969; *The Flight of the Snow Goose*, Crown, 1970; *The Jumping Mouse*, Crowell, 1970; *Turtle Pond*, Scribner, 1971; *The Web in the Grass*, Scribner, 1972; *The Ants Go Marching*, Scribner, 1973; *Bear Mouse*, Scribner, 1973; *Pronghorn on the Powder River*, Crowell, 1973; *Skunk Baby*, Crowell, 1973.

SIDELIGHTS: Bernice Freschet told *CA*: [I] "began writing because after ten straight years of diapers and dishes I needed a new outlook. My husband encouraged me . . . and with a great deal of luck and help, I finally had a book accepted." *Avocational interests:* Music, reading, camping, and traveling.†

* * *

FRIEDERICHSEN, Kathleen (Hockman) 1910-

PERSONAL: Surname is pronounced *Free*-drick-sen; born June 16, 1910, in China; daughter of William H. (a missionary and teacher) and Katie (Rogers) Hockman; married Paul D. Friederichsen (a missionary and minister), May 2, 1932; children: Douglas, Robert. *Politics:* Republican. *Religion:* Baptist (Fundamental). *Home:* 19 Rousseau St., Hayward, Calif. 94544.

CAREER: With her husband, was a missionary to the Philippines for eleven years; interned in a Japanese concentration camp for three years; now a teacher of community Bible classes in from nine to twelve towns weekly.

WRITINGS: God's Word Made Plain, Moody, 1961; *God's Will Made Clear*, Moody, 1963; *God's Truth Made Simple*, Moody, 1966; *God's Way Made Easy*, Moody, 1971; *Like Them That Dream*, privately printed, 1973; *God's Relief for Burdens*, Moody, 1974.

SIDELIGHTS: She told *CA* that her books are "Bible doctrine and exposition, illustrated by sketches, diagrams and cartoons done by myself to make difficult truths more comprehensible."

* * *

FRIEDLANDER, Stanley Lawrence 1938-

PERSONAL: Born September 5, 1938; son of Joseph (a painter) and Anita Friedlander; married Naomi Ruth Braverman (an elementary teacher), August 22, 1959. *Education:* City College (now City College of the City University of New York), B.A., 1959; University of Illinois, M.A., 1960; Massachusetts Institute of Technology, Ph.D., 1964. *Home:* 46 Tarryhill Rd., Tarrytown, N.Y. 10591. *Office:* City College of the City University of New York, New York, N.Y. 10031.

CAREER: City College of the City University of New York, New York, N.Y., assistant professor, 1964-69, associate professor, 1969-74, professor of economics, 1975—, Senior staff economist, President's Council of Economic Advisers, 1966-67, and consultant; president, Economica Inc., 1967-75; vice-chairman, National Manpower Task Force Associates, 1968-73; executive director, North Atlantic Regional Manpower Advisory Committee, 1969-74; chairman, Planning Board, Tarrytown, N.Y., 1972-76. Consultant to U.S. Budget Bureau, U.S. Department of Health, Education, and Welfare, U.S. Department of Labor, New York City Council, and Puerto Rico Planning Board. *Member:* Industrial Relations Research Association, American Economic Association, Regional Plan Association.

WRITINGS: Labor Migration and Economic Growth: A Case Study of Puerto Rico, M.I.T. Press, 1965; *Unemployment in the Urban Core: An Analysis of Thirty Cities with Policy Recommendations*, Praeger, 1972; (contributor) Eli Ginzberg, editor, *New York City Is Very Much Alive: A Manpower View*, McGraw, 1973. Contributor to *Demography*.

WORK IN PROGRESS: Studies of the determinants of fertility behavior, of the affects of education on economic growth, and of wage determination of government employees.

AVOCATIONAL INTERESTS: Travel, music, politics, psychology, athletics, and reading.

*   *   *

FRIEDMAN, Roslyn Berger   1924-

PERSONAL: Born August 8, 1924, in Chicago, Ill.; daughter of Leo Arthur and Esther (Rand) Berger; married Robert L. Friedman (an architect), December 17, 1944; children: James Mark, Jane Ellen. *Education:* Attended Northwestern University, 1941-44; University of Illinois, B.S., 1946, M.S., 1949. *Home:* 1149 Sheridan Rd., Highland Park, Ill. 60035.

CAREER: Cub reporter on *Chicago American*, Chicago, Ill., during college days; substitute high school teacher of English and journalism, 1960—. *Member:* Theta Sigma Phi.

WRITINGS: Abroad on Her Own, Doubleday, 1966. Contributor of articles to *Chicago Tribune Magazine;* also has written children's stories for Science Research Associates.

WORK IN PROGRESS: A second book on travel.

SIDELIGHTS: Roslyn Friedman told *CA*: [I] "would love to write fiction, but the minute I hit the typewriter a 'how to . . .' article comes out."†

*   *   *

FRIIS-BAASTAD, Babbis Ellinor   1921-
(Babbis Friis Baastad, Eleanor Babbis, Babbis Friis)

PERSONAL: Born August 27, 1921, in Bergen, Norway; daughter of Carl H. and Edel J. (Moenness) Blauenfeldt; married Kaare Friis-Baastad (an airline operations manager), June 17, 1942; children: Anne (Mrs. Arvid Henriksen), Winnie, Beth, Wilhelm. *Education:* Attended Oslo University, 1941-42, received degree, 1948. *Home:* Trosterudveien, Oslo 3, Norway.

CAREER: Had to leave school during the war; subsequently lived as a refugee in Sweden. Writer. *Member:* Norwegian Association of Writers for Young People (member of board). *Awards, honors:* Damm Prize, 1959, for *Aeresord*, and 1962, for *Kjersti;* H. C. Andersen prize, 1964; Ministry of Education, 2nd prize, 1960, 3rd prize, 1963, 1st prize, 1965, for *Ikke ta Bamse;* has won prizes for radio plays.

WRITINGS: (Under name Eleanor Babbis) *Aresord*, N. W. Damm, 1959, published as *Word of Honour*, Clarke, Irwin, 1960; *Hvorfor det?*, N. W. Damm, 1960; *Tulutta og Makronelle*, N. W. Damm, 1960; *Kjertsi*, N. W. Damm, 1962, published under name Babbis Friis Baastad as *Kristy's Courage*, Harcourt, 1965 (published in England as

Kersti, Hart-Davies, 1966); *Ikke ta Bamse*, N. W. Damm, 1964, published as *Don't Take Teddy*, Scribner, 1967; *Du maa Vaakne Tor!*, N. W. Damm, 1967; *Hest paa Oenskelisten*, N. W. Damm, 1968, published as *Wanted! A Horse!*, Harcourt, 1972; *Hest i Sentrum*, N. W. Damm, 1969. Writer of scripts for radio and TV.

WORK IN PROGRESS: An experimental book for retarded readers.

SIDELIGHTS: Mrs. Friis-Baastad writes: "Being surrounded by doctors, both in family and neighbourhood, has pressed the handicapped child's problem on me and made me feel it a vocation to write so that others too can understand some more about it." She is competent in English and German, to a lesser degree in French and Spanish.†

*   *   *

FRINGS, Manfred S.   1925-

PERSONAL: Surname rhymes with "rings"; born February 27, 1925, in Cologne, Germany; son of Gottfried (a teacher) and Maria (Over) Frings; married Emma J. Broussard, February 13, 1935. *Education:* University of Cologne, Ph.D., 1953, and staatsexamen in English and Philosophy, State Teacher Training Diploma, postdoctoral student, 1953-55. *Religion:* Roman Catholic. *Office:* Department of Philosophy, DePaul University, Chicago, Ill.

CAREER: University of Detroit, Detroit, Mich., assistant professor of philosophy, 1958-61; Gymnasium of Monchen-Gladbach, Monchen-Gladbach, Germany, school master, 1961-63; Duquesne University, Pittsburgh, Pa., associate professor of philosophy, 1963-66; DePaul University, Chicago, Ill., professor of philosophy, 1966—. *Member:* American Philosophical Society, American Metaphysical Society, American Association of University Professors, Heidegger Circle.

WRITINGS: (Editor) *Readings in the Philosophy of Science*, University of Detroit Press, 1960; *Max Scheler: a Concise Introduction into the World of a Great Thinker*, Duquesne University Press, 1965. Contributor to many philosophical journals in America and Germany.

SIDELIGHTS: Frings speaks German, French, and Italian. *Avocational interests:* Art, painting, playing piano and violin.

*   *   *

FRITZ, Henry E(ugene)   1927-

PERSONAL: Born June 20, 1927, in Garrison, Kan.; son of Frank Alfred (a farmer) and Esther (Anderson) Fritz; married Dolores Moeller, September 3, 1950; children: Esther Anne, Malin Eugenia, Marie Louise. *Education:* Attended University of Kansas, 1946-47; Bradley University, B.S., 1950, M.A., 1952; University of Minnesota, Ph.D., 1957. *Politics:* Independent. *Religion:* Lutheran. *Home address:* R.R. #1, Northfield, Minn. 55057. *Office:* St. Olaf College, Northfield, Minn. 55057.

CAREER: University of Wisconsin, Milwaukee, instructor in American history, 1956-58; St. Olaf College, Northfield, Minn., assistant professor, 1958-62, associate professor, 1962-68; professor of American history, 1968—, chairman of department, 1969—, director, American Minorities program, 1970-72. *Military service:* U.S. Army, 1945-46. U.S. Army Reserve, 1948-58; became first lieutenant. *Member:* American Historical Association, Organization of American Historians, Western Historical Association. *Awards, honors:* Newberry Library fellowship, 1968-69.

WRITINGS: The Movement for Indian Assimilation, 1860-1890, University of Pennsylvania Press, 1963. Contributor to *Mid-America, Arizona and the West*, and *Kansas Quarterly.*

WORK IN PROGRESS: Territorial Expansion in the American Press, 1843-1848.

* * *

FROMM, Gary 1933-

PERSONAL: Born December 27, 1933, in Dorthund, Germany; son of Walter and Kate (Goldberg) Fromm; married Sandra M. Berkman, December 11, 1960; children: Allison Wallis, Elizabeth Jean. *Education:* Cornell University, B.M.E., 1956; Massachusetts Institute of Technology, M.S., 1958; Harvard University, A.M., 1959, Ph.D., 1960. *Home:* 4801 Dexter Ter., N.W., Washington, D.C. 20036.

CAREER: Engineer with General Electric Co., 1952-55, General Motors Corp., 1956; Harvard University, Cambridge, Mass., lecturer in economics, 1960-63; United Research, Inc., Cambridge, Mass., director of economic research, 1961-62; Brookings Institution, Washington, D.C., senior fellow, 1963—. Consultant to U.S. Joint Economic Committee, Federal Aviation Agency, Department of Commerce, and Bureau of the Budget. *Member:* American Economic Association, American Statistical Association, Financial Analysts Federation, Econometric Society, Academy of Political Science.

WRITINGS: Economic Criteria for Federal Aviation Agency Expenditures, Federal Aviation Agency, 1962; (editor) *Transport Investment and Economic Development*, Brookings, 1965; (editor with J. S. Dusenbury, L. R. Klein, and E. Kuh) *The Brookings Quarterly Econometric Model of the United States*, Rand McNally, 1965; (with P. Taubman) *Policy Simulations with an Econometric Model*, Brookings, 1968; (editor with Duesenbury, Klein, and Kuh) *The Brookings Model: Some Further Results*, Rand McNally, 1968. Contributor to professional journals.†

* * *

FROSTIC, Gwen 1906-

PERSONAL: Born April 26, 1906, in Sandusky, Mich.; daughter of Fred W. (an educator) and Sara (Alexander) Frostic. *Education:* Eastern Michigan University, life certificate, 1926; attended Western Michigan University, 1927-29. *Home and office:* River Rd., Benzonia, Mich. 49616.

CAREER: Was formerly owner of Metalcraft, Wyandotte, Mich., where she taught and made art pieces in copper. Also worked as tool designer for Ford Motor Co., Willow Run, Mich., and as art teacher at Salina School, Dearborn, Mich. President of Presscraft Papers, Inc., Benzonia, Mich., 1955—. *Member:* Northwestern Artists and Business and Professional Women's Club, Michigan Botanical Club (honorary). *Awards, honors:* LL.D., Eastern Michigan University, 1965; distinguished alumnus, Western Michigan University, 1966.

WRITINGS—All privately printed: *My Michigan*, 1956; *A Walk With Me*, 1958; *These Things Are Ours*, 1960; *A Place on Earth*, 1962; *To Those Who See*, 1964; *Wingborne*, 1967; *Wisps of Mist*, 1969; *Beyond Time*, 1971; *Contemplate*, 1973.

SIDELIGHTS: Miss Frostic told *CA*: "I hope to create a book which, as a great symphony, will carry the reader along—from pages of a word or two—a single line on a blank page—to pages full of volume—high in color and thought—such a book would give the reader room to dream and interweave his thoughts into the pages and thereby become part of it."

Miss Frostic makes notepaper, full-size stationery, and books—all with original block prints which she creates from her own drawings. She produces these for sale in her own pressroom, which contains fifteen Original Heidelberg presses and about thirty employees. In 1966, she sold 64,000 copies of her books. Jean Sharley wrote: "Miss Frostic's reoccurring credo, in both her poetry and superb block prints, is that everything in nature has a meaning and a place: 'As each thing ever fosters the thing that fosters it . . . and in return must ever give as much as it receives'." Miss Frostic sketches directly from nature and will not draw a flower if it has been picked. "Whatever she sees she draws," reports Miss Sharley. Most of her sketching is done on her own property—"200 acres of marsh marigolds, cedars, raccoons and chickadees."

In 1966 Miss Frostic spoke before forty-two groups, mostly women's clubs in Michigan, Ohio, and Kentucky. She enjoys visiting the city occasionally but added "Last year when I went, I missed the birth of the swans."

BIOGRAPHICAL/CRITICAL SOURCES: Christian Science Monitor, June 14, 1964; *Tecumseh Herald*, June 9, 1966; *Detroit*, magazine of the *Detroit Free Press*, February 26, 1967.

* * *

FRY, Christopher 1907-

PERSONAL: Name originally Christopher Fry Harris; born December 18, 1907, in Bristol, England; son of Charles John (an architect and later a church lay reader) and Emma Marguerite Fry (Hammond) Harris; married Phyllis Marjorie Hart (a journalist), December 3, 1936; children: one son. *Education:* Attended Bedford Modern School, Bedford, England, 1918-26. *Religion:* Church of England. *Home:* The Toft, East Dean, Chichester, Sussex, England.

CAREER: Master of a Froebel school and tutor, 1926-27; actor at Citizen House, Bath, England, 1927; schoolmaster at Hazelwood Preparatory School, Limpsfield, Surrey, England, 1928-31; director of Tunbridge Wells Repertory Players, 1932-35; director of Oxford Repertory Players, 1940 and 1944-46; Arts Theatre, London, England, director, 1945, staff dramatist, 1947. Playwright and translator. *Military service:* Pioneer Corps, 1940-44. *Member:* Dramatists Guild, Royal Society of Literature (fellow). *Awards, honors:* Shaw Prize Fund award, 1948, for *The Lady's Not for Burning*; William Foyle Poetry Prize, 1951, for *Venus Observed*; New York Drama Critics Circle Award, 1951, for *The Lady's Not for Burning*, 1952, for *Venus Observed*, and 1956, for *Tiger at the Gates*; Queen's Gold Medal for Poetry, 1962; Heinemann Award for Literature, 1962, for *Curtmantle*; Writers Guild Best British Television Dramatization award nomination, 1971, for "Tenant of Wildfell Hall."

WRITINGS—Plays: (Author of script) *Thursday's Child* (first produced in London, 1939), music by Martin Shaw, Girl's Friendly Press (London), 1939; *The Boy With a Cart: Cuthman, Saint of Sussex* (first produced in Coleman's Hatch, Sussex, England, 1937; produced in New York, 1953), Oxford University Press, 1939, 2nd edition, Muller, 1956; *A Phoenix Too Frequent* (comedy; first produced in London at Mercury Theatre, 1946; produced in Cambridge, Mass., 1948), Hollis & Carter, 1946, Oxford

University Press, 1949; *The Firstborn* (tragedy; first produced at Edinburgh Festival, Scotland, 1948; produced in New York, 1958), Cambridge University Press, 1946, Oxford University Press, 1950, 3rd edition, Oxford University Press, 1958; *The Lady's Not for Burning* (spring comedy; first produced in London at Arts Theatre, 1948; produced in New York, 1950), Oxford University Press, 1949, 2nd edition, 1950; *Thor, with Angels* (first produced at Canterbury Festival, England, 1948; produced in Washington, D.C., 1950), Oxford University Press, 1949.

Venus Observed (autumn comedy; first produced in London at St. James Theatre, 1950; produced in New York, 1952), Oxford University Press, 1950; *A Sleep of Prisoners* (first produced in London at St. James Church, 1951; produced in New York, 1951), Oxford University Press, 1951; *The Dark is Light Enough: A Winter Comedy* (first produced in London at Aldwych Theatre, 1954; produced in New York, 1955), Oxford University Press, 1954; *Curtmantle* (first produced in Tilburg, Holland, 1961), Oxford University Press, 1961, 2nd edition, 1965; *A Yard of Sun: A Summer Comedy* (first produced at Nottingham Festival, England, July 11, 1970; produced in Cleveland, Ohio, at Cleveland Playhouse, October 13, 1972), Oxford University Press, 1970.

Unpublished plays: "Open Door," first produced in London, 1936; "The Tower," (pageant), first produced at Tewkesbury Festival, England, 1939. Also author of radio plays for "Children's Hour" series, 1939-40, and of television plays, "The Canary," 1950, "The Tenant of Wildfell Hall," 1968, and "The Brontes of Haworth" (four plays), 1973.

Translator: Jean Anouilh, *Ring Around the Moon* (first produced in London at Globe Theatre, 1950), Oxford University Press, 1950; Jean Giraudoux, *Tiger at the Gates*, (first produced in London at Apollo Theatre, 1955), Oxford University Press, 1955, 2nd edition, Methuen, 1961; Anouilh, *The Lark* (first produced in London at Lyric Theatre, 1955), Methuen, 1955, Oxford University Press, 1956; Giraudoux, *Duel of Angels* (first produced in London at Apollo Theatre, 1958), Methuen, 1958, Oxford University Press, 1959; Giraudoux, *Judith* (first produced in London at Her Majesty's Theatre, 1962, Methuen, 1962; Sidonie Gabrielle Colette, *The Boy and the Magic*, Dobson, 1964, Putnam, 1965; Henrik Ibsen, *Peer Gynt*, Oxford University Press, 1970.

Other writings: (With W. A. Darlington and others) *An Experience of Critics and the Approach to Dramatic Criticism*, Perpetua, 1952, Oxford University Press, 1953; *The Boat that Mooed* (juvenile), Macmillan, 1965.

Omnibus volumes: *Three Plays: The Firstborn; Thor, with Angels; A Sleep of Prisoners*, Oxford University Press, 1960; (translator) Jean Giraudoux, *Plays* (contains *Judith, Tiger at the Gates*, and *Duel of Angels*), Methuen, 1963; *Plays* (contains *Thor, with Angels* and *The Lady's Not for Burning*), Oxford University Press, 1969; *Plays* (contains *The Boy with a Cart, The Firstborn*, and *Venus Observed*), Oxford University Press, 1970; *Plays* (contains *A Sleep of Prisoners, The Dark is Light Enough*, and *Curtmantle*), Oxford University Press, 1971.

Filmscripts: "A Queen is Crowned," Universal, 1953; "The Beggar's Opera," Warner Brothers, 1953; "Ben Hur," Metro-Goldwyn-Mayer, 1959; "Barabbas," Dino de Laurenti Productions, 1961; "The Bible: In the Beginning," Twentieth Century-Fox, 1966, published as *The Bible: An Original Screenplay*, Pocket Books, 1966.

Work included in anthologies, including *Representative Modern Plays: Ibsen to Tennessee Williams*, edited by Robert Warnock, Scott, Foresman, 1964; *The Modern Theatre*, edited by Robert W. Corrigan, Macmillan, 1964; *The Drama Bedside Book*, edited by H. F. Rubinstein, Atheneum, 1966.

SIDELIGHTS: Fry continually strives for what he calls "a theatre at full pressure" and achieves it through coordinating his special feeling for drama and for speech, being at the same time playwright and poet. As a dramatist he revels in what Derek Stanford calls "the properties of the sensational," believing "that he can transmute their obviousness into art." He is fond of attractive costumes, original settings, and brisk openings. Stanford believes all of Fry's plays are interrelated and comprise an organic whole. "His plays are possessed of a powerful reagent that works directly on our vision of things." His richness is "the richness of synthesis." Also, writes Stanford, "talent after talent, which exist apart in the work of other dramatists, combine in his. Humour and tragedy keep house together; wit and fantasy live here side by side; metaphysics rubs shoulders with fooling; and poetry and drama go hand in hand." Fry "subjects us to an artistic experience of the most charged and potent order; to the impact of a genius contemporary to us."

Robert Gittings describes Fry as "an original major poetic talent." Some believe the stage has not heard such munificence of diction since the days of Elizabeth I. Geoffrey Bullough notes that Fry's aim is "to restore the poetic vision of life," to renew our wonder. His words are not merely ornamental. Fry admits that sometimes in the comedies the words are "an ornament on the meaning and not the meaning itself"; but "almost as often I have meant the ornament to be, dramatically or comedically, an essential part of the meaning." He believes that "reality is incredible, reality is a whirlwind." And "what we *call* reality is a false god, the dull eye of custom.... If you accept my proposition that reality is altogether different from our stale view of it, we can say that poetry is the language of reality." He adds: "What I am trying to say is that a spade is never so merely a spade as the word spade would imply. I am asking for the sudden dramatic appearance of a spade in time and space, but I am equally asking for a spade which I can dig with. I am asking ... for both kinds of realism at once."

Fry realizes that there are many people who consider verse in the theatre pretentious and boring and question the legitimacy of such a theatre in our time. Fry answers: "I suggest we forget the questions, and go on as though verse plays, like wasps, are apparently with us for some reason which they don't reveal. I only ask you to allow me to suppose an organic discipline, pattern, or proportion in the universe, evident in all that we see, which is a government uniting the greatest with the least, form with behavior, natural event with historic event, which stamps its mark through us and through our preceptions...." He believes that poetry in the theatre is the action of listening, ... for sound itself, pure sound, has logic, as we know in music.... If it wakens harmony, modulation, and the resolving of discord in us, we are nearer to our proper natures.... It is no good asking poetry to tell us what it says; it simply *is* what it says. In the theatre it must have a direct surface meaning, an immediate impact of sense, but half its work should be going on below that meaning, drawing the ear, consciously or unconsciously, into a certain experience of being.... The truth of poetry deepens under your eye. It is never absolute. There is no moment when we can trumpet it abroad as finally understood.''

Critics of this method view the general effect of Fry's poetry as merely decorative, comparable to ''beaded bubbles winking at the brim of a cup of cocoa.'' Gerald Weales rebuts such a statement by saying that ''a word, too, is an image and Fry gathers up words, as he gathers up nature and human behavior, as sign-posts to lead him down the way of affirmation.'' Fry once said that ''the theatre we should always be trying to achieve is one where the persons and events have the recognisable ring of an old truth, and yet seem to occur in a lightning spasm of discovery. That, again, is the province of poetry. It is a province of large extent; I see it ranging from tragedy, through comedy of action and comedy of mood, even down to the playground of farce.'' In addition to attempting to achieve truth, Fry reaches for joy: ''Joy (of a kind) has been all on the devil's side, and one of the necessities of our times is to redeem it,'' he once wrote.

Fry's plays, like those of T. S. Eliot, are often religious, at least implicitly so. Weales writes that ''Fry's view of the world is reflection of his view of God.'' He harks back to the origins of both drama and verse, both emanating from religious ritual. For Fry, the world is not black or white, good or evil, but an eternal mystery. ''Poetry,'' he says, ''is the language in which man explores his own amazement. It is the language in which he says heaven and earth in one word.'' Stanford notes that ''to his person there belongs a certain aura of active cheerful tranquility, whilst in his work we discover the mobility of a divine discontent. . . . To understand Fry one must learn to understand the final paradoxical nature of truth.'' Fry once said: ''The inescapable dramatic situation for us all is that we have no idea of what our situation is. We may be mortal. What then? We may be immortal. What then?'' For *The Listener* he wrote: ''Every other form of life has a completeness, but in every human relationship, even the most perfect, there is a space of the heart, or the mind, unsatisfied, and through this space men are always reaching towards something that will complete them.

Fry's comedies, Stanford suggests, ''might best be termed serio-comedies.'' Laughter ''is not regarded with distrust. Humour, equally with the tragic, attends the cosmic ritual.'' Comedy, writes Fry, ''is an escape, not from truth but from despair, a narrow escape into faith.'' While tragedy ''is the demonstration of the human dilemma,'' comedy is a comment upon it. Fry wrote in an essay on comedy: ''The bridge by which we cross from tragedy to comedy and back again is precarious and narrow. We find ourselves in one or the other by the turn of a thought. . . . I know that when I set about writing a comedy the idea presents itself to me first of all as tragedy. The characters press on to the theme with all their divisions and perplexities heavy about them; they are already entered for the race to doom, and good and evil are an infernal tangle skinning the fingers that try to unravel them. If the characters were not qualified for tragedy there would be no comedy, and to some extent I have to cross the one before I can light on the other. . . . Somehow the characters have to unmortify themselves: to affirm life and assimilate death and persevere in joy. Their hearts must be as determined as the phoenix; what burns must also light and renew; not by a vulnerable optimism, but by the intuition of comedy, an active patience declaring the solvency of good.''

Among his contemporaries Fry stands alone. He seems to have been influenced by Shakespeare and, due to their mutual interest in verse drama and religious themes, he is frequently mentioned in connection with T. S. Eliot. But Bullough writes: ''Fry has had no rival in the particular direction of his dramatic wit, and he came nearer than anyone else to acclimatising poetic drama in the popular theatre.''

His plays have been translated into French, German, Spanish, Dutch, Norwegian, Finnish, Italian, Swedish, Danish, Greek, Serbo-Croat, Hungarian, Tamil, Portuguese, Flemish, Czech, and Polish.

BIOGRAPHICAL/CRITICAL SOURCES: Derek Stanford, *Christopher Fry: An Appreciation*, Nevill, 1951; R. A. Scott-James, *Fifty Years of English Literature, 1900-1950*, Longmans, Green, 1951; Derek Stanford, *Christopher Fry Album*, Nevill, 1952; Frederick Lumley, *Trends in Twentieth Century Drama*, Barrie & Rockliff, 1956, 3rd edition published as *New Trends in Twentieth Century Drama*, Oxford University Press, 1967; Toby Cole, editor, *Playwrights on Playwriting*, Hill & Wang, 1961; Gerald Weales, *Religion in Modern English Drama*, University of Pennsylvania Press, 1961; Kenneth Muir, *Contemporary Theatre*, Edward Arnold, 1962; William A. Armstrong, editor, *Experimental Drama*, G. Bell, 1963; Nelson Vos, *The Drama of Comedy: Victim and Victor*, John Knox Press, 1965; W. M. Merchant, *Creed and Drama*, S.P.C.K., 1965; William V. Spanos, *The Christian Tradition in Modern Verse Drama*, Rutgers University Press, 1967; Stanley M. Wiersma, *Christopher Fry: A Critical Essay*, Eerdmans, 1970; Carolyn Riley, editor, *Contemporary Literary Criticism*, Volume II, Gale, 1974.

*　　*　　*

FRY, Hilary G. 1922-

PERSONAL: Born August 11, 1922, in Aylesworth, Okla.; son of Hilary Nathan (a farmer) and Ethyl (Daniel) Fry; married Mary Amelia Roberts (an interviewing historian), December 27, 1947; children: Gary Glen, Randal Britton, Hilary Byron. *Education:* University of Illinois, B.S., 1948; University of Chicago, M.A., 1951, Ph.D., 1957. *Politics:* Democrat. *Religion:* Unitarian Universalist. *Home:* 22322 Center St., Castro Valley, Calif. 94546. *Office:* California State University at Hayward, Hayward, Calif.

CAREER: Hiram College, Hiram, Ohio, dean of students and acting dean of college, 1952-56; American Hospital Association, Chicago, Ill., director of research, 1956-58; University of California, Berkeley, administrative analyst in office of president, 1958-59, lecturer in public health, 1959-60; California State College at Hayward, professor of social science and public administration, 1960—. Director, National Drug Abuse Training Center, Hayward, Calif., consultant to Social Action Research Center, Berkeley, Calif. *Military service:* U.S. Navy, 1943-46; became lieutenant junior grade. *Member:* American Society for Public Administration, American Public Health Association, American Association for the Advancement of Science.

WRITINGS: The Operation of State Hospital Planning and Licensing Programs, American Hospital Association, 1965; *Education and Manpower in Community Health*, University of Pittsburgh Press, 1967. Contributor to *American Journal of Public Health, Public Health Reports*, and *Clinical Pediatrics*.

*　　*　　*

FRYMIER, Jack R(immel) 1925-

PERSONAL: Born March 15, 1925, in Albion, Ind.; son of

Gerald A. (a businessman) and Edith (Rimmel) Frymier; married Maxine Clouse, August 24, 1948; children: Jill, Kay, Mark. *Education:* University of Miami, Coral Gables, Fla., B.Ed., 1949, M.Ed., 1950; University of Florida, Ed.D., 1957. *Home address:* Rt. 2, London, Ohio 43140.

CAREER: University of Miami, Coral Gables, Fla., instructor in education, 1950-54; Temple University, Philadelphia, Pa., assistant professor of education, 1957-59; Auburn University, Auburn, Ala., associate professor of education, 1959-60; Orange County Board of Public Instruction, Orlando, Fla., director of instruction, 1960-62; Ohio State University, Columbus, professor of education, 1962—. *Military service:* U.S. Army, 1943-46, 1951-52; became first lieutenant. *Member:* Alliance of Associations for the Advancement of Education (president, 1972-73), American Association for the Advancement of Science, Association for Supervision and Curriculum Development (member of assessment council, 1965-68; president, 1972-73).

WRITINGS: The Nature of Educational Method, C. E. Merrill, 1965; *Fostering Educational Change*, C. E. Merrill, 1969; *Curriculum Improvement for Better Schools*, C. A. Jones, 1970; *A School for Tomorrow*, McCutchan, 1973. Contributor of over one hundred articles to professional journals. Editor, *Theory and Practice*, 1966-74; and *The Educational Forum*, 1973—.

WORK IN PROGRESS: A study of oppressive practices in schools.

* * *

FULL, Harold 1919-

PERSONAL: Born April 18, 1919, in Parkersburg, W.Va. *Education:* Marietta College, A.B., 1944; Harvard University, A.M., 1945; Columbia University, Ed.D., 1957. *Politics:* Democrat. *Religion:* Episcopalian. *Office:* Queens College of the City University of New York, Flushing, N.Y. 11367.

CAREER: High school teacher of English, Parkersburg, W.Va., 1945-47; West Virginia University, Morgantown, instructor in education, 1947-55; Queens College of the City University of New York, Flushing, N.Y., assistant professor of education, 1957—. Visiting assistant professor of education, New York University, 1963-65. *Member:* National Education Association (life member), Association for Supervision and Curriculum Development, History of Education Society, American Association of University Professors, New York State Teachers Association, Kappa Delta Pi.

WRITINGS: (Editor with Stan Dropkin and Ernest Schwarcz) *Contemporary American Education: An Anthology of Problems, Challenges, Issues*, Macmillan, 1965, 2nd edition, 1970; (editor) *Controversy in American Education: An Anthology of Crucial Issues*, Macmillan, 1967, 2nd edition, 1972.†

* * *

FULLERTON, Alexander 1924-

PERSONAL: Born September 20, 1924, in Suffolk, England; son of John Skipwith Fullerton; married Priscilla Mary Edelston, 1956; children: John, Simon, Giles. *Education:* Attended Royal Naval College, Dartmouth, England, 1938-41. *Home:* Elm Cottage, Herstmonceux, Sussex, England.

CAREER: Royal Navy, regular officer in Submarine Service and Russian interpreter, 1942-49, becoming lieutenant; Peter Davies Ltd. (publishers), London, England, editorial director; Arrow Books Ltd. (paperback division of Hutchinson & Co. Ltd.), London, England, editorial director; author. *Awards, honors*—Military: Mentioned in dispatches, Far East, 1945.

WRITINGS: Surface!, P. Davies, 1953; *Bury the Past*, P. Davies, 1954; *Old Moke*, P. Davies, 1954; *No Man's Mistress*, P. Davies, 1955; *A Wren Called Smith*, P. Davies, 1957; *The White Men Sang*, P. Davies, 1958; *The Yellow Ford*, P. Davies, 1959; *The Waiting Game*, Ives Washburn, 1961; *Soldier from the Sea*, P. Davies, 1962; *The Thunder and the Flame*, Hodder & Stoughton, 1964; *Lionheart*, Norton, 1965.

The Executive, Putnam, 1970; *The Publisher*, Putnam, 1971; *Store*, Cassell, 1971; *The Escapists*, Cassell, 1972; *Other Men's Lives*, Cassell, 1973; *Piper's Leave*, Cassell, 1974.

WORK IN PROGRESS: A novel.

* * *

FUNDERBURK, Thomas R(ay) 1928-

PERSONAL: Born November 8, 1928, in Hammond, Ind.; son of E. Ray (a steam engineer) and Alma Jane (Gay) Funderburk; married Anne Jane Crane (a textile designer), July 4, 1953; children: Alexandria Nelle. *Education:* Indiana University, B.A., 1952.

CAREER: Held "various and uninteresting" jobs, 1953-61; Bantam Books, Inc., New York, N.Y., assistant art director, 1961-66; now free-lance artist, writer, and designer. *Military service:* U.S. Marine Corps, 1946-48. *Member:* Society for the Promotion of Roman Studies, Monumental Brass Society, Society of World War I Aero Historians (also known as Cross & Cockade).

WRITINGS: The Fighters: The Men and Machines of the First Air War, Grosset, 1965; (ghost writer) Joseph A. Phelan, *Heroes and Aeroplanes of the Great War 1914-18*, Grosset, 1966; *The Early Birds of War: the Daring Pilots and Fighter Airplanes of World War I*, Grosset, 1968; (illustrator) Alexander I. Nazaroff, *Picture Map Geography of the U.S.S.R.*, Lippincott, 1969.

SIDELIGHTS: Funderburk speaks French. *Avocational interests:* Roman and medieval architecture, history.

* * *

FURTADO, Celso 1920-

PERSONAL: Born July 26, 1920, in Pombal, Paraiba, Brazil; son of Mauricio Medeiros and Maria Alice (Monteiro) Furtado; married Lucia Tosi (a chemist), September 15, 1948; children: Mario, Andre. *Education:* University of Brazil, M.A., 1944; University of Paris, Ph.D., 1948; Cambridge University, postdoctoral study, 1957-58. *Home:* 4 rue d'Anjou, 94, Chevilly Larue, France. *Office:* Universite Pantheon, Sorbonne, Paris, France.

CAREER: United Nations Economic Commission for Latin America, economist, 1949-57; Development Bank of Brazil, director, 1959-60; Superintendency for the Development of the Northeast of Brazil, executive head, 1959-64; Brazilian government, minister of planning, 1962-63; Yale university, New Haven, Conn., research fellow, 1964-65; Universite Pantheon, Sorbonne, Paris, professor of economics, 1965—. Visiting professor, American University, Washington, D.C., 1972; Cambridge University, 1973-74.

WRITINGS: The Economic Growth of Brazil, University of California Press, 1963; *Development and Underdevelopment*, University of California Press, 1964; *Diagnosis of the Brazilian Crisis*, University of California Press, 1965; *Economic Development of Latin America*, Cambridge University Press, 1970; *Obstacles to Development in Latin America*, Doubleday, 1970; *Analise do Modelo brasileiro*, Civilizacao Brasileira, 1972; *O Mito do Desenvolvimento Economico*, Paz e Terra, 1974.

* * *

FUSSELL, Paul 1924-

PERSONAL: Surname rhymes with "bustle"; born March 22, 1924, in Pasadena, Calif.; son of Paul (an attorney) and Wilhma (Sill) Fussell; married Betty Harper, June, 1949; children: Rosalind, Martin. *Education:* Pomona College, A.B., 1947; Harvard University, M.A., 1949, Ph.D., 1952. *Home:* 26 Lilac Lane, Princeton, N.J. 08540. *Office:* Department of English, Rutgers University, New Brunswick, N.J. 08903.

CAREER: Connecticut College, New London, instructor in English, 1951-54; Rutgers, The State University, New Brunswick, N.J., assistant professor, 1955-59, associate professor, 1959-64, professor of English, 1964—. University of Heidelberg, Fulbright lecturer, 1957-58. Woodrow Wilson National Fellowship Foundation, regional chairman, 1962-64. Random House, Inc., consulting editor, 1964-65. *Member:* English Institute (secretary, 1964-70). *Military service:* U.S. Army, Infantry, 1943-47; became first lieutenant; received Bronze Star and two Purple Hearts. *Awards, honors:* James D. Phelan Award in nonfictional prose, 1965; Lindsack Foundation Award; National Endowment for the Humanities, senior fellowship, 1973-74.

WRITINGS: Theory of Prosody in Eighteenth-century England, Connecticut College Press, 1954; (co-author) *The Presence of Walt Whitman*, Columbia University Press, 1962; *The Rhetorical World of Augustan Humanism*, Oxford University Press, 1965; *Poetic Meter and Poetic Form*, Random House, 1965; *Samuel Johnson and the Life of Writing*, Harcourt, 1971; *The Great War and Modern Memory*, Oxford University Press, 1975. Contributor of reviews to *Encounter, Saturday Review*, and other periodicals.

SIDELIGHTS: Fussell has lived in England, Germany, Spain, Greece, and France; speaks German and French.

BIOGRAPHICAL/CRITICAL SOURCES: Criticism, winter, 1967.

* * *

FYSH, Wilmot Hudson 1895-

PERSONAL: Born January 7, 1895, in Launceston, Tasmania, Australia; son of Wilmot (a farmer) and Mary (Reed) Fysh; married Eleanor Dove, December 5, 1924; children: John Hudson, Wendy Elizabeth Fysh Miles. *Education:* Attended Geelong Church of England Grammar School. *Religion:* Church of England. *Home:* Rosemount Ave., Sydney, New South Wales, Australia. *Office:* A.N.Z. Bank, Pitt and Hunter, Sydney, New South Wales, Australia.

CAREER: Jackeroo and wool classer after leaving school; Queensland and Northern Territory Aerial Services, began as a two plane operation, now known as Quantas Empire Airways Ltd., co-founder and pilot, 1920-30, managing director, 1923-55, chairman of the board, beginning 1947, currently serves in an advisory capacity. Member, board of directors, Tasman Empire Airways Ltd.; chairman, Kenmaster Holdings Ltd. Inaugural British Commonwealth and Empire lecturer, Royal Aeronautical Society, London, 1945. *Military service:* Australian Army, Cavalry and Flying Corps, 1914-18; became lieutenant; received Distinguished Flying Cross.

MEMBER: Royal Aeronautical Society (fellow), Institute of Transportation, Royal Geographical Society of Australia (fellow), International Air Transport Association (president, 1961-62; member of executive committee), Australian National Travel Association (deputy chairman), Rotary International (Sydney), Queensland Club, Australian Club, Royal Air Force Club, Royal New South Wales Aero Club. *Awards, honors:* Knighted, 1953.

WRITINGS: Log of the "Astraea," 1933; *Taming the North*, Angus & Robertson, 1933; *Quantas Rising*, Angus & Robertson, 1965; *Quantas at War*, Angus & Robertson, 1968; *Round the Bend in the Stream*, Angus & Robertson, 1968; *Wings to the World: The Story of Quantas, 1945-1966*, Angus & Robertson, 1970. Contributor to *Field*.

AVOCATIONAL INTERESTS: Country pursuits.†

* * *

GAA, Charles J(ohn) 1911-

PERSONAL: Surname is pronounced as "gay"; born December 29, 1911, in Chicago, Ill.; son of Charles C. and Elizabeth (O'Malley) Gaa; married Jean Powers, July 19, 1941; children: John, Charles, James, Thomas. *Education:* University of Illinois, B.S., 1932, M.S., 1936, Ph.D., 1940. *Home:* 2022 Navaho Trail, Okemos, Mich.

CAREER: Public accountant with Price, Waterhouse & Co. and George Rossetter & Co., Chicago, Ill., 1932, 1935, 1936-67; certified public accountant, state of Illinois, 1938; Dartmouth College, Hanover, N.H., assistant professor of accounting, 1941-42; U.S. Office of Price Administration, chief accountant, Chicago (Ill.) metropolitan area, 1942-43, branch chief in Accounting Department, Washington, D.C., 1945-46; University of Illinois, Urbana, 1935-41, and 1946-54, became professor of accounting; University of Michigan, Ann Arbor, professor of accounting, 1954-58, assistant dean, School of Business Administration, 1956-58; Michigan State University, East Lansing, professor of accounting, 1958—. Lecturer in accounting at American University, 1944-46, and U.S. Department of Agriculture Graduate School, 1945-46; director of Advanced Training Center, U.S. Internal Revenue Service, 1954-56. Consultant to U.S. Office of Contract Settlement, 1946-47, U.S. Atomic Energy Commission, 1951-52, and U.S. General Accounting Office, 1960-65. Member of selections committee, Ohio State Accounting Hall of Fame, 1959-65. *Military service:* U.S. Army, finance officer, 1943-45; became captain.

MEMBER: American Accounting Association (secretary-treasurer, 1950-53; vice-president, 1954; president, 1960; executive committee, 1950-54, 1960-63), American Institute of Certified Public Accountants (member of board of managers, Professional Development Program, 1960-65), Tax Institute of America (advisory council, 1962-64), Michigan Association of Certified Public Accountants, Beta Gamma Sigma, Beta Alpha Psi.

WRITINGS: Effect of Inventory Methods on Calculation of Profits and Income Taxes (monograph), Bureau of Business Research, University of Illinois, 1943; *Taxation of Corporate Income*, University of Illinois Press, 1944; *Outline of Fundamentals of Federal Income Taxation*, University of Illinois Press, 1949; *Federal Taxation—Fundamental Questions, Problems and Cases*, two volumes, McGraw, 1965; (editor) *Contemporary Thought on Federal Income Taxation*, Dickenson, 1969.

Contributor: *Taxes Interpreted*, Alexander Hamilton Institute, 1964—; *Income Tax Techniques*, Bender, 1965, and annual revisions. Also contributor to *Encyclopedia of Tax Procedures*, Prentice-Hall, *World Book Encyclopedia*, and to accounting journals. Book review editor, *Accounting Review*, 1949-50.

WORK IN PROGRESS: Co-authoring a book on estate planning.

*   *   *

GABOR, Dennis   1900-

PERSONAL: Born June 5, 1900, in Budapest, Hungary; son of Berthold and Ady (Jacobovits) Gabor; married Marjorie Louise Butler, August 8, 1936. *Education:* Technical University, Budapest, Hungary, student, 1918-20; Technische Hochschule Berlin-Charlottenburg, Diplom Ingenieur, 1924, Doctor Ingenieur, 1927. *Politics:* "Liberal, but not engaged with any party." *Religion:* Protestant. *Home:* 91 Vicarage Court, Kensington Church St., London W8, England (winter); and LaMargioretta, 00040 Anzio, Lavinio, Viale Dei Gigli, Italy (summer). *Office:* Imperial College of Science and Technology, London S.W. 7, England.

CAREER: Research engineer for Siemens & Halske A.G., Berlin-Siemensstadt, Germany, 1927-33, and British Thomson-Houston Co., Rugby, England, 1934-48; University of London, Imperial College of Science and Technology, London, England, reader in electronics, 1949-58, professor of applied electron physics, 1958-67, senior research fellow and professor emeritus, 1967—. Columbia Broadcasting System Laboratories, Stamford, Conn., staff scientist, 1957—. Research physicist and inventor, best known for invention of lensless photography (holography), 1948, and for flat television tube, predictor, and speech compression. *Member:* Royal Society (fellow), Institute of Physics (fellow), Institution of Electrical Engineers, Television Society (fellow), Hungarian Academy of Sciences, Athenaeum Club (London). *Awards, honors:* Duddell Premium, Institution of Electrical Engineers, 1945; D.Sc., University of London, 1964; Thomas Young Medal and Prize, 1967; Christoforo Colombo Prize, 1967; Rumford Medal from the Royal Society, 1968; Micheson Medal of the Franklin Institute, 1968; Semmelweiss Medal from American Hungarian Medical Association, 1970; D.Sc., University of Southampton, 1970; Commander of the British Empire, 1970; Holweek Prize from French Physical Society, 1971; D.Sc., Delft University of Technology, 1971; Nobel Prize for Physics, 1971.

WRITINGS: The Electron Microscope, Hulton Press, 1945, Chemical Publishing Co., 1948; *Inventing the Future*, Secker & Warburg, 1963, Knopf, 1964; *Innovations: Scientific, Technological and Social*, Oxford University Press, 1970; *Mature Society*, Secker & Warburg, 1972; *Proper Priorities of Science and Technology*, University of Southampton, 1972. Writer of about one hundred scientific papers on electronics, physical optics, and other subjects.

SIDELIGHTS: Gabor's books have been published in French, Dutch, and German translations, with Italian translations in preparation. He is competent in French,

German, Italian, Hungarian. *Avocational interests:* Swimming; writing on social problems.

*   *   *

GADDIS, William   1922-

PERSONAL: Born 1922, in New York, N.Y.; children: two. *Education:* Attended Harvard College. *Agent:* Candida Donadio and Associates, 111 West 57th St., New York, N.Y. 10019.

CAREER: Has earned his living at various kinds of writing, including corporate and film work, and has done brief magazine and teaching stints. *Awards, honors:* National Institute of Arts and Letters grant, 1963; grant from National Endowment for the Arts, 1967.

WRITINGS: The Recognitions (novel), Harcourt, 1955; *J. R.* (novel), Knopf, 1975.

WORK IN PROGRESS: Once at Antietam, a novel.

SIDELIGHTS: "The precision of William Gaddis' style is most unusual in his generation of writers," says Robert Graves. "And I am astonished that one who shows himself so familiar and up-to-date with the mountain of filth, perversion, falsity, and boredom revealed in *The Recognitions*, should have managed to keep his head clear and his heart warm, and his report readable." Charles J. Rolo writes: "Gaddis' Manner . . . brings to mind the phantasmagorical canvases of Hieronymus Bosch. There is a similar sense of pervasive damnation; a similar combination of surrealistically imagined monstrosities and meticulous concern with detail; a similar comic grotesquerie."

Most critics, finding a novel so immense and unique, either qualified their praise or were altogether baffled. The *Time* magazine reviewer called it "irritatingly opaque in plot and character, . . . one of those eruptions of personal vision that will be argued about without being argued away." Milton Rugoff wrote: "Like a poem it coheres only in spirit, and this it does by exemplifying throughout half a million words man's degeneration to a point where he can no longer recognize the genuine, no less create it. . . . [Gaddis'] style is protean, a stream of fantasy and realism swollen with quotations, echoes and parodies. The resulting mixture—for it is never a fusion—is unique and indescribable."

BIOGRAPHICAL/CRITICAL SOURCES: Saturday Review, March 12, 1955; *New York Times Book Review*, March 13, 1955; *New York Herald Tribune Book Review*, March 13, 1955; *Time*, March 14, 1955; *Newsweek*, March 14, 1955; *Atlantic*, April, 1955; *New Yorker*, April 9, 1955; *Commonweal*, April 15, 1955; *Nation*, April 30, 1955; *United States Quarterly Book Review*, June, 1955; *Western Review*, winter, 1956; John W. Aldridge, *In Search of Heresy*, McGraw, 1956; *Berkeley Gazette*, March 16, 1962; *Queen's Quarterly*, summer, 1962; *Observer Weekend Review*, September 9, 1962; *Village Voice*, November 1, 1962; *Critique*, winter, 1962-63; *Scotsman*, April 10, 1965; *Wisconsin Studies in Contemporary Literature*, summer, 1965; David Madden, *Rediscoveries*, Crown, 1971; Tony Tanner, *City of Words*, Cape, 1971; Carolyn Riley, editor, *Contemporary Literary Criticism*, Gale, Volume I, 1973, Volume III, 1975.

*   *   *

GALFO, Armand J.   1924-

PERSONAL: Born November 16, 1924, in Buffalo, N.Y.; son of Joseph (a florist) and Marian (Sabella) Galfo; married Mary Faust (now a science teacher), August 19, 1950.

Education: University of Buffalo, B.A., 1949, Ed.M., 1953, Ed.D., 1956; Oregon Teaching Research Division, fellow, 1966-67. *Politics:* Republican. *Religion:* Roman Catholic. *Home:* 108 Overlook Dr., Williamsburg, Va. *Office:* College of William and Mary, Williamsburg, Va.

CAREER: West Seneca School System, Buffalo, N.Y., chairman of science department and chemistry teacher, 1949-56; Dade County (Fla.) public schools, chemistry teacher, 1957-58; College of William and Mary, Williamsburg, Va., 1958—, began as assistant professor, now professor of School of Education. *Military service:* U.S. Army Air Forces, World War II; received Air Medal with two oak leaf clusters. U.S. Air Force Reserve; currently colonel and research consultant to National War College. *Member:* National Education Association, Virginia Education Association, Kappa Delta Pi, Phi Delta Kappa. *Awards, honors:* U.S. Office of Education research fellowship, 1966-67.

WRITINGS: (With Earl Miller) *Interpreting Education Research*, W. C. Brown, 1965, 3rd edition, 1975. Contributor to education journals.

AVOCATIONAL INTERESTS: Tennis, golf, fishing; current events and politics.

* * *

GALLAGHER, John F(redrick) 1936-

PERSONAL: Born February 11, 1936, in Pasadena, Calif.; son of James Alexander (a gardener) and Brita (Hermannson) Gallagher. *Education:* University of California, Los Angeles, A.B., 1957, M.P.A., 1959, Ph.D., 1964. *Politics:* Democrat. *Religion:* None. *Office:* Department of Political Science, St. Martin's College, Olympia, Wash. 98501.

CAREER: Los Angeles (Calif.) City School Districts, personnel trainee and aide, 1956-59; University of California, Davis, assistant professor of political science, 1961-66, research assistant, Institute of Governmental Affairs, 1962-66; City College, Baruch School of Business and Public Administration (now Bernard M. Baruch College of the City University of New York), New York, N.Y., assistant professor of political science, 1966; New York University, New York, N.Y., associate professor of politics, 1967-68; Ohio Legislative Service Commission, Columbus, Ohio, chief general researcher, beginning 1968; St. Martin's College, Olympia, Wash., currently on faculty of political science department. Director of Local Government Research Study, New York State Temporary Commission on the Constitutional Convention, 1967; consultant to Local Government Committee, New York State Constitutional Convention, 1967. *Member:* American Political Science Association, American Society for Public Administration, American Association of University Professors.

WRITINGS: (With Clyde E. Jacobs) *California Government: One Among Fifty*, Macmillan, 1966; (with C. E. Jacobs) *The 1948 Selective Service Act: A Case Study in American Public Policy*, Dodd, 1967. Author of five monographs published by Institute of Governmental Affairs, University of California, 1963-66. Contributor of articles and reviews to social science publications.

SIDELIGHTS: Gallagher has a good reading competence and fair writing and speaking competence in Spanish.†

GALLAGHER, Sister Mary Dominic 1917-
(Sister Mary Dominic)

PERSONAL: Born August 1, 1917, in Alberta, Canada; daughter of Dominic Joseph (a school principal) and Terese (Pryce) Gallagher. *Education:* College of St. Thomas, St. Paul, Minn., B.A. (summa cum laude), 1947; Seattle University, M.A., 1953; summer study at University of Washington, Seattle, 1953, and Creighton University, 1965, 1966. *Politics:* Democrat.

CAREER: Roman Catholic nun of Good Shepherd order (R.G.S.), 1939—; teacher of English and psychology at schools within Good Shepherd order in Omaha, Neb., St. Paul, Minn., Denver, Colo., Seattle and Spokane, Wash., and Helena, Mont., 1948-66; also caseworker in Helena, Mont., 1959-62; principal of school for juvenile delinquent girls, Omaha, Neb., 1966—. Photographer. *Member:* American Psychological Association, Nebraska Counselors Association, Nebraska Writers Guild.

WRITINGS: (Under name Sister Mary Dominic) *Little Nellie of Holy God*, Bruce, 1961; (under name Sister Mary Dominic) *Shepherdess for Christ*, Catechetical Guild, 1964. Regular columnist, *Family Digest*, for four years; contributor of articles and picture stories, using various pseudonyms at times, to magazines and educational journals. Abstractor, *Psychological Abstracts*. Editor and photographer, *Girls' Town* (newsletter).

WORK IN PROGRESS: Picture stories for magazines and newspapers.

SIDELIGHTS: Sister Mary Dominic told *CA* her major interest is "anyone who is down and out." Her major ambition is to visit all of the 450 Good Shepherd Homes throughout the world, taking pictures and writing about the needs of the persons sheltered in the homes.

* * *

GARBO, Norman 1919-

PERSONAL: Born February 15, 1919, in New York, N.Y.; son of Maximillian W. and Fannie (Deitz) Garbo; married Rhoda Locke, April 15, 1942; children: Mickey. *Education:* Studied at City College of New York, 1935-37, at New York Academy of Fine Art, 1937-41. *Residence:* Manhasset, Long Island, N.Y.

CAREER: Portrait painter, 1941—; writer, lecturer. *Military service:* U.S. Army Air Forces, 1941-45; became lieutenant.

WRITINGS: Pull Up an Easel, A. S. Barnes, 1955; (with Howard Goodkind) *Confrontation*, Harper, 1966; *The Movement* (novel), Morrow, 1969. Author of syndicated column, "Pull Up an Easel," for *Chicago Tribune* and New York News Syndicate, 1953-60; contributor of short stories to *Saturday Evening Post* and other periodicals.

WORK IN PROGRESS: Two novels, *Duvid* and *Chai*.

* * *

GARDNER, Jeanne LeMonnier 1925-

PERSONAL: Born May 24, 1925, in Chicago, Ill.; daughter of George A. and Jean (Cusack) LeMonnier; married Richard B. Gardner (an advertising salesman), September 11, 1948; children: Susan R., James B. *Education:* Denison University, student, 1943-46. *Home and office:* Harriman Rd., Irvington-on-Hudson, N.Y. 10533.

CAREER: Operations agent for Trans World Airlines during World War II; stewardess for Pan American World

Airways on flights to Central America, Caribbean, and South America, 1946-48; *Daily Register-Mail,* Galesburg, Ill., reporter, 1948-51; editorial assistant to professional poet and historian, Carl Carmen, 1958-70; Harvey House, Inc. (publishers), New York, N.Y., editor-in-chief, 1970—. Free-lance editor, 1967-70.

WRITINGS: Sky Pioneers: The Story of Wilbur and Orville Wright, Harcourt, 1963; *Mary Jemison: Seneca Captive,* Harcourt, 1966.

WORK IN PROGRESS: Research on French and Indian War period, on American Indians (especially Iroquois, Shawnee, and Delaware tribes), and on pioneer aviation.

*   *   *

GARDNER, John E(dward) 1917-

PERSONAL: Born February 2, 1917, in Sharon, Tenn.; son of Jesse O. (a farmer) and Lester (Allen) Gardner; married Amna Bailey; children: John Edward, Jr., Mary Ann, James Bailey. *Education:* Bethel College, McKenzie, Tenn., B.A., 1939; Cumberland Presbyterian Theological Seminary, B.D., 1943; McCormick Theological Seminary, Th.M., 1945; Union Theological Seminary, Richmond, Va., Th.D., 1955. *Politics:* Democrat. *Home:* 3628 Oakley Ave., Memphis, Tenn. *Office:* Memphis Theological Seminary, 168 East Parkway South, Memphis, Tenn.

CAREER: Ordained to ministry of Cumberland Presbyterian Church, 1938; Memphis Theological Seminary, Memphis, Tenn., professor of homiletics and Christian education, 1945—.

WRITINGS: A Handbook for the Committee on the Ministry, Frontier Press, 1965; *Personal Religious Disciplines,* Eerdmans, 1966.

*   *   *

GARFIELD, Leon 1921-

PERSONAL: Born July 14, 1921, in Brighton, Sussex, England; son of David Kalman (a businessman) and Rose (Blaustein) Garfield; married Vivien Dolores Alcock, October 23, 1948; children: Jane Angela. *Education:* Attended grammar school in Brighton, England. *Politics:* "Somewhere between Labour and Liberal." *Religion:* Jewish. *Home:* 59 Wood Lane, Highgate, London N.6, England. *Agent:* Monica McCall, Inc., 667 Madison Ave., New York, N.Y. 10021; Winant, Towers Ltd., Furnival St., London, England.

CAREER: Whittington Hospital, London, England, biochemical technician, 1946-66; part-time biochemical technician in various hospital laboratories in London, 1966-69; now free-lance writer. *Military service:* British Army, Medical Corps, 1940-46; served in Belgium and Germany. *Member:* International P.E.N. *Awards, honors:* Gold medal from Boys Clubs of America.

WRITINGS: Jack Holborn, Constable, 1964, Pantheon, 1965; *Devil-in-the-Fog,* Pantheon, 1966; *Smith,* Pantheon, 1967; *Mister Corbett's Ghost,* Pantheon, 1968; *Black Jack,* Longmans, Green, 1968, Pantheon, 1969; *The Restless Ghost: Three Stories,* Pantheon, 1969; *Mr. Corbett's Ghost and Other Stories,* Longman, 1969; *The Drummer Boy,* Pantheon, 1969; *The Boy and the Monkey,* F. Watts, 1969; *The God Beneath the Sea,* Longman, 1970, Pantheon, 1971; *The Ghost Downstairs,* Longman, 1970, Pantheon, 1972; *The Strange Affair of Adelaide Harris,* Pantheon, 1971; *Child o' War: The True Story of a Boy Sailor in Nelson's Navy,* Holt, 1972; *The Golden Shadow,* Long-

man, 1973. Short story included in *Oxford Miscellany,* 1965.

SIDELIGHTS: Leon Garfiled writes: "God knows why I write, except that I feel restless when I don't. If anything stirs me particularly, it is injustice; most of all when I am the victim!. . . . The writers I admire most are: Jane Austen, Fielding, Dickens, Hugo, Melville, and Thomas Mann. *Avocational interests:* Eighteenth-century music, collecting paintings and china, films, and the theater (mainly Shakespeare).†

*   *   *

GARIS, Robert (Erwin) 1925-

PERSONAL: Born May 17, 1925, in Hawley, Pa.; son of Philip Louis (a civil engineer) and Catherine (McKellin) Garis. *Education:* Muhlenberg College, B.A., 1945; Harvard University, M.A., 1946, Ph.D., 1956; University of London, graduate study, 1950-51. *Politics:* Democratic. *Religion:* "None." *Office:* English Department, Wellesley College, Wellesley, Mass. 02181.

CAREER: Wellesley College, Wellesley, Mass., instructor, 1951-56, assistant professor, 1956-62, associate professor, 1962-68, professor of English, 1968—. *Awards, honors:* Fulbright fellow at University of London, 1950-51.

WRITINGS: The Dickens Theatre, Clarendon Press, 1965; *Writing About Oneself,* Heath, 1965; (contributor) B. C. Southam, editor, *Critical Essays on Jane Austen,* Routledge & Kegan Paul, 1968. Articles and reviews published in *Nation, Victorian Studies, Hudson Review, Partisan Review, Commentary,* and other journals.

WORK IN PROGRESS: Studies on Ibsen, Shakespeare, and Donne.

BIOGRAPHICAL/CRITICAL SOURCES: Times Literary Supplement, February 10, 1966.

*   *   *

GARNER, Harry Hyman 1910-

PERSONAL: Born January 19, 1910, in Chicago, Ill.; son of Louis and Clara (Barasch) Garner; married Eleanore E. Hetherington, April 5, 1940; children: Edward A., Larry B. *Education:* University of Illinois, B.S., 1932, M.D., 1934; additional study at Illinois Neuropsychiatric Institute, 1936-41. *Religion:* Judaic. *Home:* 433 West Roscoe, Chicago, Ill. 60657. *Office:* 2720 West 15th St., Chicago, Ill. 60608.

CAREER: Diplomate of American Board of Psychiatry and American Board of Neurology, with medical posts in Chicago, Ill., 1936-41, 1946—. Chicago State Hospital, resident, 1936-39, clinic director, 1939-41; Cook County Hospital, attending neurologist, 1946-52, attending psychiatrist, 1956—; University of Illinois Medical School, assistant professor of psychiatry, 1947-48; Chicago Medical School, professor and chairman of department of psychiatry and neurology, 1948-70, professor and chairman of department of psychiatry and behavioral sciences, 1970—; Mount Sinai Hospital, attending psychiatrist, and chairman of department, 1952-70; Medical Center, chairman of department of psychiatry and behavioral sciences, 1970—. Oak Forest Infirmary, consulting neurologist and psychiatrist, 1945—; U.S. Veterans Administration West Side Hospital, consulting physician in psychiatry, 1953—. Member, State of Illinois Psychiatric Advisory Council, 1950—. *Military service:* U.S. Army, Medical Corps Reserve, 1936-41. U.S. Army, Medical Corps, 1941-46; became lieutenant colonel; received Bronze Star with oak leaf cluster.

MEMBER: American Psychiatric Society (fellow), American Academy of Neurology, Academy of Psychoanalysis, American Medical Association, Association for the Advancement of Psychotherapy, American Academy of Forensic Sciences, Board of Legal Medicine, Central Neuropsychiatric Association, Illinois Psychiatric Society (past president), Chicago Neurological Society.

WRITINGS: (Editor with A. Abrams and J. E. P. Toman) *Unfinished Tasks in the Behavioral Sciences*, Williams & Wilkins, 1964; *Psychosomatic Management of the Patient with Malignancy*, C. C Thomas, 1966; *Psychotherapy: Confrontation Problem-Solving Technique*, W. H. Green, 1970. Papers included in five other books, 1955-63. Contributor to medical journals.†

* * *

GARRETSON, Robert L. 1920-

PERSONAL: Born June 26, 1920, in Superior, Neb.; son of Charles Wesley (a jeweler) and Helen F. (Bishop) Garretson; married Aretha Ledford; children: Nancy Jo, Jean Robert. *Education:* Colorado State College (now University of Northern Colorado), Greeley, A.B., 1943, A.M., 1948; Columbia University, Ed.D., 1955. *Religion:* Protestant. *Office:* University of Cincinnati, Cincinnati, Ohio 45221.

CAREER: Director of music in Chase County (Neb.) public schools, 1946-47, and Reno (Nev.) public schools, 1947-50; University of Illinois, Urbana, music extension staff, 1951-53; University of New Hampshire, Durham, instructor in music education, 1953-56; University of Cincinnati, Cincinnati, Ohio, associate professor of music education, 1956—. *Member:* Phi Mu Alpha, Pi Kappa Lambda, Kappa Kappa Psi, Phi Delta Kappa, Kappa Delta Pi.

WRITINGS: (With Ralph L. Pounds) *Principles of Modern Education*, Macmillan, 1962; *Conducting Choral Music*, 3rd edition, Allyn & Bacon, 1970; *Music in Childhood Education*, Appleton, 1966.†

* * *

GARRETT, Leonard J(oseph) 1926-

PERSONAL: Born November 22, 1926, in Philadelphia, Pa.; son of Rolfe (a journalist) and Fanny (Berman) Garrett; married Judith Resnick, December 22, 1957; children: Robert Glenn, Susan Beth. *Education:* U.S. Military Academy, B.S., 1950; University of Pennsylvania, M.B.A., 1957, Ph.D., 1960. *Home:* 1967 Audubon Dr., Dresher, Pa. 19025.

CAREER: U.S. Army, regular officer, 1945-53, becoming captain; University of Pennsylvania, Philadelphia, assistant professor of management, 1961-65; Temple University, Philadelphia, Pa., director of University computer activities, and associate professor of management, 1965-68, professor of computer and information sciences and chairman of department, 1968—.

WRITINGS: (With Adrian M. McDonough) *Management Systems*, Irwin, 1965; (with Milton Silver) *Production Management*, Harcourt, 1966; *Production Management Case Book*, Harcourt, 1966, 2nd edition published as *Production Management Analysis*, 1974; *Information Systems*, Harcourt, in press.

* * *

GARRETT, Leslie 1931-

PERSONAL: Born July 5, 1931, in Philadelphia, Pa.; son

of Herbert Henry Garrett (a businessman) and Thelma Florence Bradley; married Jean Deloras Collier, June 4, 1949 (divorced); children: Dawne Deloras. *Education:* Left school at fifteen.

CAREER: Estimates he has had about seventy jobs in twenty years, "from sales manager to . . . you name it"; has been abroad since 1964, traveling in Europe and North Africa, and spending a year in Paris; now full-time writer, with residence on the island of Ibiza, Spain. *Military service:* U.S. Navy, journalist, 1948-50. *Awards, honors:* Maxwell E. Perkins Commemorative Novel Award (given by Charles Scribner's Sons), for *The Beasts*.

WRITINGS: *The Beasts* (novel), Scribner, 1966. Fiction has been published in *New World Writing*, *Nugget*, *Four Quarters*, *Escapade*, and *Climax*.

WORK IN PROGRESS: A second novel and a volume of short stories.

BIOGRAPHICAL/CRITICAL SOURCES: *Majorca Daily Bulletin*, Majorca, Spain, November 18, 1966; *Chicago Review*, June, 1967.†

* * *

GARTLAND, Robert Aldrich 1927-

PERSONAL: Born May 17, 1927, in Mount Vernon, N.Y.; son of Walter Zepp (an accountant) and Margaret (Feldmann) Gartland. *Education:* Attended New York University, 1946-47, State University of New York Agricultural and Technical College at Cobleskill, 1947-49, and Art Students League, New York, N.Y., 1951-53. *Politics:* Independent. *Home and Office:* 58 Macri Ave., White Plains, N.Y. 10604. *Agent:* McIntosh & Otis, Inc., 18 East 41st St., New York, N.Y. 10017.

CAREER: American Museum of Natural History, New York, N.Y., artist, 1952-62; self-employed fine and commercial artist, 1962—. Exhibitor of watercolors in United States, Spain, and Mexico; illustrator for *Life* and *Natural History*, and for children's books. *Military service:* U.S. Navy, 1945-46. *Member:* American Watercolor Society.

WRITINGS—Self-illustrated juveniles: (With Eunice Holsaert) *A Book to Begin on Dinosaurs*, Holt, 1959; *Cowboys and Cattle*, Coward, 1962.

SIDELIGHTS: Gartland has traveled and painted in United States, Canada, Cuba, and Colombia, and has lived in a small fishing village on the northern coast of Spain.†

* * *

GARTMAN, Louise 1920-

PERSONAL: Born May 18, 1920, in Goldthwaite, Tex.; daughter of Lewis Jackson (a merchant) and Jewel (Paxton) Gartman; married Charles C. Smith (an engineer), June 26, 1941; children: Evelyn Louise, Susan Christie, Laura Charles. *Education:* University of Texas, B.J., 1941. *Religion:* Presbyterian. *Home:* 6846 Gaston Ave., Dallas, Tex. 75214. *Office:* Department 703 SW, Sears, Roebuck & Co., 1000 Belleview St., Dallas, Tex. 75295.

CAREER: Has done public relations, secretarial, and newspaper work; also taught school; Sears, Roebuck & Co., Dallas, Tex., advertising and copywriter, 1961-65, in public relations, 1965—. Editor of two Sears publications, *FYI* (fashion magazine), and *The Southwesterner* (territorial employee newspaper). *Member:* Theta Sigma Phi.

WRITINGS: *Kensil Takes Over*, Westminster, 1964; *First-Time Parents' Handbook*, C. E. Saegert, 1973.

WORK IN PROGRESS: A book on quilting; collaborating on a book on salesmanship; a book about very young children.

SIDELIGHTS: Ms. Gartman speaks Spanish and travels to Mexico several times a year.

*   *   *

GASKELL, Thomas F.   1916-

PERSONAL: Born January 26, 1916, in Bolton, England; son of Harold (a dentist) and Dorothy (Frohock) Gaskell; married Joyce Kenyon, March 28, 1952; children: Anthony Horatio, Joanna Mary. *Education:* Attended Worksop College, 1928-34; Trinity College, Cambridge, M.A. (first class honors), 1937, Ph.D., 1940. *Religion:* Church of England. *Home:* 96 Belle Hill, Bexhill-on-Sea, England. *Agent:* Peter Janson-Smith Ltd., 31 Newington Green, London N16, England. *Office:* Premier Consolidated Oilfields Ltd., 23 Lower Belgrave St., London SW1, England.

CAREER: British Admiralty, London, England, scientific work connected with anti-submarine, beach reconnaissance, and wave forecasting, 1939-46; Anglo-Iranian Oil Co., chief petroleum physicist in Iran, 1946-49; British Petroleum Co. Ltd., London, England, scientific adviser to information department, 1962-73; Premier Consolidated Oilfields Ltd., London, director, 1973—. Chief scientist on "H.M.S. Challenger" Oceanographic Expedition, on leave of absence from Anglo-Iranian Oil Co., 1949-51. Consultant to and director of oil related companies.

WRITINGS: Under the Deep Oceans, Eyre & Spottiswoode, 1960; *World Beneath the Oceans,* Doubleday, 1965; (with Bryan Cooper) *North Sea Oil: The Great Gamble,* Bobbs-Merrill, 1966; (editor) *Earth's Mantle,* Academic Press, 1967; (editor with A. H. Cook) *Earth in Space,* Blackwell, 1968; *Physics of the Earth,* Thames & Hudson, 1970; (editor) *Using the Oceans,* Queen Anne, 1970; *The Gulf Stream,* Cassell, 1972. Writer of general science scripts for British Broadcasting Corp. television and radio. Contributor to scientific journals. Editor of *Geophysical Journal,* 1957-72.

WORK IN PROGRESS: Rewriting *North Sea Oil: The Great Gamble* with Bryan Cooper, to be published as *North Sea Oil: Success,* by Heinemann.

SIDELIGHTS: World Beneath the Oceans has been published in several foreign translations.

*   *   *

GASS, William H(oward)   1924-

PERSONAL: Born July 30, 1924, in Fargo, N.D.; son of William Bernard and Claire (Sorensen) Gass; married Mary Patricia O'Kelly, June 17, 1952; married Mary Alice Henderson, September 13, 1969; children: (first marriage) Richard G., Robert W., Susan H.; (second marriage) Elizabeth, Catherine. *Education:* Kenyon College, A.B., 1947; Cornell University, Ph.D., 1954. *Home:* 6304 Westminster Pl., St. Louis, Mo. 63130. *Agent:* Lynn Nesbit, International Creative Management, 40 West 57th St., New York, N.Y. 10019. *Office:* Department of Philosophy, Washington University, St. Louis, Mo. 63130.

CAREER: College of Wooster, Wooster, Ohio, instructor in philosophy, 1950-54; Purdue University, Lafayette, Ind., assistant professor, 1954-60, associate professor, 1960-66, professor of philosophy, 1966-69; Washington University, St. Louis, Mo., professor of philosophy, 1969—. Visiting lecturer in English and philosophy, University of Illinois,

1958-59. Spent 1966 in England and 1970 in Portugal. *Military service:* U.S. Navy, 1943-46; served in China and Japan; became ensign. *Member:* American Philosophical Association. *Awards, honors:* Longview Foundation Award in fiction, 1959, for "The Triumph of Israbestis Tott"; Rockefeller Foundation grant for fiction, 1965-66; Hovde Prize for good teaching, 1967; Guggenheim fellowship, 1969-70; D.Litt., Kenyon College, 1974; National Institute for Arts and Letters prize for literature, 1975.

WRITINGS: Omensetter's Luck (novel), New American Library, 1966; *In the Heart of the Heart of the Country* (short stories), Harper, 1968; *Fiction and the Figures of Life* (essays), Knopf, 1970; *Willie Masters' Lonesome Wife* (novella), Knopf, 1971; (author of introduction) *The Geographical History of America,* Random House, 1973; *On Being Blue* (essay), David R. Godine, 1975. Contributor to *Nation, South Atlantic Quarterly, Accent, Perspective, Location, Book Week, New York Times Book Review, New American Review,* and to philosophical journals.

WORK IN PROGRESS: A story for children, *Nail Soup,* completion expected in 1975; a play, *The Cost of Everything,* 1976; a novel, *The Tunnel,* 1978.

SIDELIGHTS: "*Omensetter's Luck* is a vast, vigorous, and deliberately dishevelled novel whose action falls into place only in retrospect or on second reading," writes Roger Shattuck, who compares Gass to Joyce because both seem to "submerge beneath the landscape of sheer style" most "distinctions of character and act and attitude." Both are masters in the "plastic use of language." Shattuck goes on to say that Gass "reaches beyond character and beyond event to something I can only call history. Time in his novel flows massively like the Ohio that surrounds it on every side. Without wars, kings, or voyages, *Omensetter's Luck* takes shape as a species of historical novel."

Newsweek called it "a dense, provoking, vastly rewarding and very beautiful first novel. In prose that rolls along the tongue even in silent reading, William H. Gass has set out to explore those thickets of the mind where the outside world impinges on the soul.... By that most hackneyed of literary devices, the story observed through a series of eyes, Gass achieves a masterpiece of definition, a complex and intricate creation of level within level, where the theme of Omensetter's luck becomes an intense debate on the nature of life, love, good and evil, and finally, of death.... [It] is a story of life and death in the little countries of men's hearts."

Reviewing *In the Heart of the Heart of the Country,* Eliot Fremont-Smith comments that Gass's stories "seem to contain the mainstream heritage of American literature, from Twain to Faulkner to the current absurdists.... Yet his voice is independent of these, authentic, not subservient, new, its own a presence." Robert Martin Adams finds Gass's style equally deserving of praise, noting that the stories "deal with violent feelings and blind conflicts but without baggy language of excess gestures.... The techniques, which are various and imaginative, are always in the service of vision and feeling. Mr. Gass's stories are strict and beautiful pieces of writing without waste or falsity or indulgence." And Walter Percy sums them up as "a superb union of matter and form, a dreamlike action yielding up meanings at several levels, the whole wrought in a poet's prose."

Willian Gass's manuscripts have been collected in the Washington University Library.

BIOGRAPHICAL/CRITICAL SOURCES: New York

Times Book Review, April 17, 1966; *Newsweek*, April 18, 1966; *Nation*, May 9, 1966; *New York Review of Books*, June 23, 1966; *Partisan Review*, summer, 1966; Carolyn Riley, editor, *Contemporary Literary Criticism*, Gale, Volume I, 1973, Volume II, 1974; Joe David Bellamy, editor, *The New Fiction. Interviews with Innovative American Writers*, University of Illinois Press, 1974.

* * *

GASSERT, Robert G(eorge) 1921-

PERSONAL: Born July 6, 1921, in Milwaukee, Wis.; son of Joseph (a construction superintendent) and Emily (Bier) Gassert. *Education:* St. Louis University, B.A., 1945, M.A. and Ph.L., 1948; St. Mary's College, St. Marys, Kan., S.T.L., 1955; Gregorian University, Rome, Italy, S.T.D., 1958. *Home and office:* Marquette University, 1217 West Wisconsin Ave., Milwaukee, Wis. 53233.

CAREER: Roman Catholic priest, member of Society of Jesus (S.J.); Campion High School, Prairie du Chien, Wis., teacher of Latin and Greek, 1949-51; Marquette University, Milwaukee, Wis., instructor, 1958-60, assistant professor, 1961-66, associate professor, 1966-75, professor of theology, 1975—, dean of College of Liberal Arts, 1963—. *Member:* Association for Higher Education, Association of American Colleges, Association of Jesuit Colleges and Universities, National Catholic Education Association, Phi Beta Kappa. *Awards, honors:* Postdoctoral fellowship to Menninger Foundation, 1962-63.

WRITINGS: (With Bernard H. Hall) *Psychiatry and Religious Faith*, Viking, 1964.

WORK IN PROGRESS: A study of Cardinal Newman's views on Christian higher education.

* * *

GATEWOOD, Willard B., Jr. 1931-

PERSONAL: Born February 23, 1931, in Pelham, N.C.; son of Willard B. (a farmer) and Bessie (Pryor) Gatewood; married Lu Brown; children: Willard B. III, Elizabeth Ellis. *Education:* Duke University, A.B., 1953, M.A., 1954, Ph.D., 1957. *Religion:* Presbyterian. *Home:* 1651 West Cleveland St., Fayetteville, Ark. 72701.

CAREER: Assistant professor of history at East Tennessee State University, Johnson City, 1957-58, and East Carolina College (now University), Greenville, N.C., 1958-60; North Carolina Wesleyan College, Rocky Mount, associate professor of history, 1960-64; University of Georgia, Athens, associate professor of history, 1964-70; University of Arkansas, Fayetteville, Alumni Distinguished Professor of History, 1970—. *Member:* American Historical Association, Organization of American Historians, Southern Historical Association (executive council member, 1974-77), Phi Beta Kappa, Phi Alpha Theta. *Awards, honors:* American Academy of Arts and Sciences research grants, 1961 and 1962; American Philosophical Association grants, 1962 and 1963; Truman Library research fellowship, 1962; M. G. Michael research award, 1966; Joseph Parks Excellence in Teaching Award from University of Georgia, 1970.

WRITINGS: Eugene Clyde Brooks: Educator and Public Servant, Duke University Press, 1960; *Preachers, Pedagogues and Politicians: Evolution Controversy in North Carolina*, University of North Carolina Press, 1966; (editor) *Controversy in the Twenties: Modernism, Fundamentalism, and Evolution*, Vanderbilt University Press, 1969; *Theodore Roosevelt and the Art of Controversy*, Louisiana

State University Press, 1970; *"Smoked Yankees" and the Struggle for Empire: Letters from Negro Soldiers, 1898-1902*, University of Illinois Press, 1971; *Black Americans and the White Man's Burden, 1898-1903*, University of Illinois Press, 1975. Contributor to history and regional journals. Member of editorial board, *Georgia Review*, 1967-70, *Journal of Negro History*, 1971—.

WORK IN PROGRESS: Black Aristocracy in America.

* * *

GAULDEN, Ray 1914-
(Wesley Ray)

PERSONAL: Born June 27, 1914, in Fort Worth, Tex.; son of Herman Alan (a peace officer) and Jessie (Maddin) Gaulden; married Thelma Fells, May 3, 1940; children: Marsha (Mrs. John F. Messner). *Politics:* Independent. *Religion:* Baptist. *Home:* 1699 South Zenobia Way, Denver, Colo. 80219. *Agent:* August Lenniger, Lenniger Literary Agency, 11 West 42nd St., New York, N.Y. 10036.

CAREER: During his early career was a sign painter, hotel clerk, hospital admittance clerk, and parts expediter in a munitions factory; free-lance writer. *Member:* Western Writers of America, Colorado Authors' League. *Awards, honors:* Colorado Authors' League Top-hand Award for best western short story.

WRITINGS: Shadow of the Rope, Pocket Books, 1957; *The Vengeful Men*, Pocket Books, 1958; (under pseudonym Wesley Ray) *Damaron's Gun*, New American Library, 1958; *High Country Showdown*, Monarch Books, 1961; *Action at Alameda*, Avalon, 1962; *The Devil's Deputy*, Avalon, 1963; *McVey's Valley*, Doubleday, 1965; (under pseudonym Wesley Ray) *Long Day in Latigo*, Paperback Library, 1965; *Lawless Land*, Berkley, 1968; *Five Card Stud*, Berkley, 1968; *Time to Ride*, Ballantine, 1969; *Shoot To Kill*, Ballantine, 1970; *Rage at Red Butte*, Berkley, 1971; *Wicked Women of Lobo Wells*, Belmont, 1971; *Deputy Sheriff*, Ballantine, 1972. Contributor of over two hundred short stories to magazines.

SIDELIGHTS: Gaulden's novels, *Five Card Stud* and *Glory Gulch* were adopted for films.†

* * *

GEFFEN, Roger 1919-

PERSONAL: Born April 11, 1919, in New York, N.Y.; son of Maxwell M. and Pauline (Felix) Geffen; married Johanna Franciena Dercksen, January 22, 1953; children: Leendert Paul, Christiana Reino, Anne-Marie, Mark David. *Education:* Princeton University, B.A., 1940; General Theological Seminary, graduate, 1944, M.Div., 1950. *Home:* 71 Moore Road, Wayland, Mass. 01778.

CAREER: Episcopal priest; medical missionary (government medical officer), Bahama Islands, 1944-45; Religious Book Club, Manhasset, N.Y., associate editor, 1944-64; Church of the Good Shepherd, Wakefield, New York, N.Y., rector, 1953-60. Free-lance publishers' scout, editor, rewrite man, translator from the French and Dutch, and teacher of yoga. Has had one-man shows of his photographs in New York, N.Y., and elsewhere. *Military service:* U.S. Naval Reserve, 1940-41. *Member:* Sumi-e Society of America (past president), Japan Society, Holland Sporting Club.

WRITINGS: (Compiler) *The Handbook of Public Prayer*, Macmillan, 1963. Contributor to *Living Church*, 1940—; managing editor, *New Start*, 1943-44.

WORK IN PROGRESS: Studies of energy conservation and waste disposal systems.

SIDELIGHTS: Geffen is fluent in French, German, and Dutch, and has some knowledge of Italian and the Scandinavian languages. *Avocational interests:* Electronics, automobiles, travel, photography.

*   *   *

GEHMAN, Betsy Holland 1932-
(Anne Klainikite)

PERSONAL: Surname is pronounced *Gay*-min; born June 6, 1932, in Chicago, Ill.; married; children: Pleasant, Charles, Meghan and Amy (twins). *Education:* Attended Columbia University and Wesleyan University. *Residence:* Middletown, Conn.

CAREER: Former editorial writer for *Hartford Courant*, Hartford, Conn.; free-lance writer and educational consultant in theater and women's studies.

WRITINGS: Twins: Twice the Trouble, Twice the Fun, Lippincott, 1965. Also co-editor of *Encyclopedia of the American Woman*, McGraw. Columnist, *Putnam County Courier*. Associate editor, *Promenade* (magazine).

WORK IN PROGRESS: Five, a novel.

SIDELIGHTS: Her pseudonym is used for "celebrity profiling."

*   *   *

GEIST, Harold 1916-

PERSONAL: Surname rhymes with "right"; born July 22, 1916, in Pittsburgh, Pa.; son of Alexander (an engineer) and Edna (Liebhaber) Geist. *Education:* Cornell University, A.B. (with honors), 1936; Columbia University, A.M., 1937; Stanford University, Ph.D., 1951. *Home:* 2255 Hearst Ave., Berkeley, Calif. 94709. *Office:* 2614 Telegraph Ave., Berkeley, Calif. 94704.

CAREER: Community Service Center, Paterson, N.J., educational and vocational adviser, 1946; Veterans Administration, Washington, D.C., associate advisement and guidance officer, 1946-47; Vallejo Junior College, Vallejo, Calif., part-time chief of guidance center, 1947-48; Mare Island Naval Hospital, Mare Island, Calif., chief of guidance center, 1947-48, chief clinical psychologist, 1951-53; University of California, Berkeley, psychology staff, 1951—; private practice in clinical psychology, Walnut Creek, Calif., and Berkeley, Calif., 1953—. Visiting summer professor at University of Puerto Rico, 1955-58. Consultant to school systems in California, 1952—. Principal investigator of Picture Interest Research Project for the Deaf, on grant from U.S. Department of Health, Education, and Welfare, 1959-61. *Military service:* U.S. Army, Medical Service Corps, 1942-46; served in France, Philippines, and Japan.

MEMBER: Interamerican Society of Psychology, American Psychological Association, American Association for the Advancement of Science, American Personnel and Guidance Association, National Vocational Guidance Association, National Rehabilitation Association, California State Psychological Association, Bay Area Psychologists in Private Practice (chairman), Phi Sigma Delta. *Awards, honors:* National Rehabilitation Association, best paper by behavioral scientist award, 1962; Travel Award, National Institute of Mental Health, to International Congress in Peru, 1966.

WRITINGS: The Etiology of Idiopathic Epilepsy, Exposition, 1962; *The Psychological Aspects of Diabetes*, C. C Thomas, 1964; *A Child Goes to the Hospital*, C. C Thomas, 1965; *The Psychological Aspects of Rheumatoid Arthritis*, C. C Thomas, 1966; *Psychological Aspects of Retirement*, C. C Thomas, 1968; *The Psychological Aspects of the Aging Process*, Warren Green, 1968; *From Eminently Disadvantaged to Eminence*, Warren Green, 1973. Deviser of "Picture Interest Inventory," a psychological test published by Western Psychological Services. Contributor of about thirty articles to journals.

WORK IN PROGRESS: A book on the emotional aspects of heart disease; and *Tennis Psychology*.

SIDELIGHTS: Geist's picture test to assess vocational interests has been adapted for use in eight foreign countries by altering the pictures to suit the culture of the land. It was first adapted for Puerto Rico public schools, later for Japanese, Iranian, Italian, Belgium, and schools in other countries. Geist speaks Spanish and German. *Avocational interests:* Tennis.

*   *   *

GELPI, Donald L. 1934-

PERSONAL: Surname is pronounced with soft "g"; born May 30, 1934, in New Orleans, La.; son of Albert Joseph and Alice (Delaup) Gelpi. *Education:* Attended St. Charles College, Grand Coteau, La., 1951-55; St. Louis University, M.A. and Ph.L., 1958; College St. Albert, Louvain, Belgium, theological study, 1961-63; St. Mary's College, St. Mary's, Kan., Th.L., 1965; Fordham University, candidate for Ph.D.

CAREER: Roman Catholic priest of Society of Jesus.

WRITINGS: Life and Light: A Guide to the Theology of Karl Rahner, Sheed, 1966; *Functional Asceticism: A Guideline for American Religious*, Sheed, 1966; *Discerning the Spirit: Foundations and Futures of Religious Life*, Sheed & Ward, 1970; *Pentecostalism: A Theological Viewpoint*, Paulist Press, 1971; *Pentecostal Piety*, Paulist Press, 1972. Contributor of articles on philosophy and theology to *Thought*, *Current*, and *Modern Schoolman*.

SIDELIGHTS: Gelpi speaks French, German, Latin, and some Spanish. He reads Italian and classical Greek. *Avocational interests:* Playing the recorder and ukulele.†

*   *   *

GENNE, William H. 1910-

PERSONAL: Surname is pronounced Jen-nay; born June 8, 1910, in Philadelphia, Pa.; son of William and Rose (Belser) Genne; married Elizabeth E. Steel, March 28, 1937; children: Mrs. Ronald A. Baker III, W. Thomas, Margaret Rose, Susan Steel. *Education:* Bucknell University, A.B., 1931; Yale University, B.D., 1934, M.A., 1936. *Politics:* Democrat. *Home:* 37 Essex Ave., Montclair, N.J. 07042.

CAREER: Clergyman, United Church of Christ, Michigan State University, East Lansing, director of religious activities, 1936-40; Alfred University, Alfred, N.Y., chaplain, 1940-44; Young Men's Christian Associations of the U.S.A., college secretary, Portland, Ore., 1944-47; Pacific University, Forest Grove, Ore., chaplain, 1947-51; Clara Elizabeth Fund, Flint, Mich., teacher-counselor, 1951-57; National Council of Churches of Christ in the U.S.A., New York, N.Y., director of Commission on Marriage and Family Life, 1957—. Secretary, Interfaith Commission on

Marriage and Family Life. *Member:* Sex Information and Education Council of the United States (member of board). National Council on Family Relations. *Awards, honors:* Bucknell University Alumni Award, 1961.

WRITINGS: Husbands and Pregnancy, Association Press, 1956; (with wife, Elizabeth S. Genne) *Christians and the Crisis in Sex Morality*, Association Press, 1962; (with E. S. Genne) *Church Family Camps and Conferences*, United Church, 1962; *Foundations for Christian Family Policy*, National Council of Churches, 1962; *The Ministry of Parents*, Upper Room, 1964; (editor with Mordecai Brill and Raban Hawthorne) *Marriage: An Interfaith Guide for All Couples*, Association Press, 1970; (with E. S. Genne) *First of All, Persons*, Friendship Press, 1973. Writer of filmstrip script for "Christian Parents Kit." Editor, "Marriage and Family Life Newsletter," National Council of Churches; member of editorial board, *International Journal of Religious Education*.

WORK IN PROGRESS: Research on the family, including preparation for marriage and parenthood, sex ethics, and sex education.

AVOCATIONAL INTERESTS: Camping (tenting and travel-trailer camping).

* * *

GERBER, Albert B(enjamin) 1913-

PERSONAL: Born July 10, 1913, in Philadelphia, Pa.; son of Jacob and Jennie (Suffrin) Gerber; married Rhona C. Posner, November 22, 1939; children: Jack Jay, Gail, Lynne. *Education:* University of Pennsylvania, B.S., 1934, LL.B., 1937, LL.M., 1942; George Washington University, M.A., 1941. *Politics:* Democrat. *Religion:* Hebrew (Reform).

CAREER: Admitted to Pennsylvania State Bar, 1937; University of Pennsylvania Law School, Philadelphia, member of faculty, 1937-38; attorney with Rural Electrification Administration, 1938-40, U.S. Department of Agriculture, 1940-42; private practice of law, Philadelphia, beginning 1946; partner of Gerber, Galfand & Berger, beginning 1947; writer. Corporate secretary and member of board of directors of Electronics Training Center, Allentown, Pa., Commonwealth Financial Corp., Philadelphia, and United National Insurance Co., Philadelphia, Pa. *Military service:* U.S.Army, 1942-45; served in Asiatic-Pacific theater; became sergeant. *Member:* American Bar Association, American Civil Liberties Union, Philadelphia Bar Association.

WRITINGS: The Life of Adolph Hitler, Mercury Books, 1961; *Sex, Pornography and Justice*, Lyle Stuart, 1966; *Bashful Billionaire,* Lyle Stuart, 1967; *The Lawyer*, World, 1972. Monthly columnist in *Independent* and *Petal Paper*; contributor to *Saturday Evening Post, Blue Book*, and other magazines, legal journals, and newspapers.

WORK IN PROGRESS: Two books with tentative titles of *The Homosexual, the Law, and Justice* and *A Handbook for Insurance Investigators.*†

* * *

GEROLD, William 1932-

PERSONAL: Surname is pronounced *Jer*-old; born December 24, 1932, in Bayside, N.Y.; son of William Howard (an assessor) and Veronica (Huebner) Gerold; married Carol Ashenden, June 11, 1960; children: Anna Melaina, Hansi Maria, Amy, Molly. *Education:* Attended Providence College, Providence, R.I., 1950-52. *Religion:* Christian. *Home:* Elbow Rock Rd., Chepachet, R.I. 02814.

CAREER: Photographer and artist; sometime farmer, and naturalist. *Military service:* U.S. Navy, 1952-56; served in Korean and European Theaters.

WRITINGS: College Hill (with introduction by Carl Bridenbaugh), Brown University Press, 1965.

WORK IN PROGRESS: A photographic documentary of the F. L. Ames gate lodge in North Easton, Mass., with accompanying essay by Jan Wampler.

* * *

GERSON, Louis Leib 1921-

PERSONAL: Born November 10, 1921, in Poland; son of Morris and Ann (Berger) Gerson; married Elizabeth M. Shanley, June 24, 1950; children: Elliot Francis, William Thomas, Ann Katherine. *Education:* University of Connecticut, B.A. (with highest distinction), 1948; Yale University, M.A., 1950, Ph.D., 1952. *Home:* Ball Hill Rd., Storrs, Conn. *Office:* University of Connecticut, Storrs, Conn.

CAREER: University of Connecticut, Storrs, instructor, 1950-54, assistant professor, 1954-59, associate professor, 1959-63, professor of political science, 1963—, head of department, 1967—. Yale University, research fellow, 1953-54; Columbia University, research associate, Institute of War and Peace, 1964—. Visiting research professor, Taiwan National University, 1973-74. Institute of Mediterranean Studies, trustee, 1957-60. *Member:* American Historical Association, American Political Science Association, Phi Beta Kappa, Pi Sigma Alpha, Phi Alpha Theta. *Awards, honors:* Ford Foundation fellowship, 1952-53; Guggenheim fellowship, 1956-57; Rockefeller Foundation fellowship, 1963-64; Fulbright scholar in India, 1966-67.

WRITINGS: Woodrow Wilson and the Rebirth of Poland, Yale University Press, 1953, published with a new introduction as *Woodrow Wilson und die Wiedergeburg Polens*, Holzner Verlag, 1956; *The Hyphenates in Recent American Politics and Diplomacy*, University of Kansas Press, 1964; *John Foster Dulles* (diplomatic biography), Cooper Square, 1967.

Contributor: *Issues and Conflicts*, edited by G. Anderson, Kansas University Press, 1957; *Woodrow Wilson and American Immigrants*, edited by J. P. O'Grady, University of Kentucky Press, 1967. Contributor of articles and reviews to *Issues and Conflicts, Modern Age*, and other journals.

WORK IN PROGRESS: The Foreign Policy of Dwight D. Eisenhower, completion expected in 1975.

SIDELIGHTS: Gerson participated in a symposium on U.S. foreign policy at Wiesbaden, Germany, in 1963, and traveled in nearby countries. He returned to Europe the following year to interview heads of six nations in connection with Princeton University's John Foster Dulles Oral History Project.

* * *

GESNER, Elsie Miller 1919-

PERSONAL: Born December 8, 1919, in Guilford, Conn.; daughter of William and Katherine (Fortner) Miller; married Lewis G. Gesner, Jr. (a Baptist minister), July 5, 1947; children: Joybelle, Lewis III. *Education:* Attended Barrington College, 1944-47. *Religion:* Baptist. *Residence:* Tenants Harbor, Me. 04860.

CAREER: Legal secretary.

WRITINGS: The Lumber Camp Kids, Vantage, 1957; *In the Stillness of the Storm*, Zondervan, 1963. Contributor of articles and short stories to religious journals.

* * *

GHERITY, James Arthur 1929-

PERSONAL: Born December 19, 1929, in Highland Park, Mich.; son of James Arthur (a manufacturer's representative) and Florence (Van Winkle) Gherity; married Ermadell M. Borsky, June 18, 1955; children: Christopher William, Shawn Patrick. *Education:* Wayne State University, B.A., 1951; University of Michigan, M.A., 1952; University of Illinois, Ph.D., 1958. *Home:* Lavander Hill, Route 2, #1, Kingston, Ill.

CAREER: Michigan State University, East Lansing, assistant professor of economics, 1955-61; State University of New York at Buffalo, assistant professor of economics, 1961-64; Northern Illinois University, De Kalb, associate professor, 1964-68, professor of economics, 1968—, chairman of department, 1973—. *Member:* American Economic Association, Royal Economic Society, Scottish Economic Society, Midwest Economic Association.

WRITINGS: (Editor) *Economic Thought: A Historical Anthology*, Random House, 1965. Contributor to economics journals.

* * *

GIBB, Jack R(ex) 1914-

PERSONAL: Born December 20, 1914, in Magrath, Alberta, Canada; became U.S. citizen; son of John Lye (a merchant) and Ada (Dyer) Gibb; married Lorraine F. Miller (a management consultant), December 29, 1951; children: Lawrence, Blair, Randolph. *Education:* Brigham Young University, A.B., 1936, M.A., 1937; University of Chicago, graduate study, 1937; Stanford University, Ph.D., 1943. *Politics:* Democrat. *Religion:* Church of Jesus Christ of Latter-day Saints. *Home and office:* 8475 La Jolla Scenic Dr., La Jolla, Calif. 92037.

CAREER: Brigham Young University, Provo, Utah, 1937-46, began as instructor, became associate professor of psychology; Michigan State University, East Lansing, assistant professor, 1946-47, associate professor of psychology, 1947-49; University of Colorado, Boulder, associate professor, 1949-55, professor of psychology, 1955-56; Fels Group Dynamics Center, Neward, Del., research professor, 1956-59; National Training Laboratories, Washington, D.C., director of research, 1957-60; research psychologist in private practice and management consultant, 1960—; Western Behavioral Sciences Institute, La Jolla, Calif., resident fellow, 1964-1967; private practice, 1967—. Consultant at various times to U.S. Department of State, The Methodist Church, Young Men's Christian Associations of the U.S.A., General Motors Corp., Dow Chemical Co., and other corporations.

MEMBER: American Association for Humanistic Psychology (past president), American Psychological Association, American Sociological Association, National Society for the Study of Communication, Sigma Xi, Theta Alpha Phi. *Awards, honors:* Fund for Advancement of Education faculty fellowship, 1953-54; Sigma Xi research award.

WRITINGS: (With Platts and Miller) *Dynamics of Participative Groups*, Swift, 1951; (editor with Bradford and Benne) *T-Group Theory and Laboratory Method*, Wiley, 1964. Associate editor, *Adult Leadership*.

WORK IN PROGRESS: The Emergent Group; The Development of Trust and Freedom; Living Tori; Organizational Flaw.

* * *

GIBBONS, Helen Bay 1921-

PERSONAL: Born November 4, 1921, in Junction, Utah; daughter of H. Earl (a realtor) and Iola (Maxwell) Bay; married Francis M. Gibbons (an attorney), June 7, 1945; children: Suzanne, Mark, Ruth, Daniel. *Education:* Attended public schools in Piute County, Utah, and business college. *Politics:* Usually Republican. *Religion:* Church of Jesus Christ of Latter-day Saints. *Home:* 1784 Yale Ave., Salt Lake City, Utah 84108.

CAREER: Supervisor of stenographic pool for government agency, Salt Lake City, Utah, 1942-43; Mormon missionary, Atlanta, Ga., 1943-45; secretary at University of Utah, Salt Lake City, 1946-47, Children's Service Society, Salt Lake City, 1947, and U.S. Veterans Administration Hospital, Palo Alto, Calif., 1948-50. Chairman of Salt Lake Council of Women's Industrial Development Committee, 1960-61. Member of general board, Deseret Sunday School Union, 1970-71, and Mutual Improvement Association, 1972—. *Member:* National League of American Pen Women (branch historian, 1966-67), League of Utah Writers (member of board, 1963-65; vice-president, Salt Lake City chapter, 1968-70), Salt Lake City Lady Lions Club (president, 1961-62). *Awards, honors:* First award, League of Utah Writers, for article, "Chief Tuba," 1963; First book award, National League of American Pen Women (Utah), 1967.

WRITINGS: On Your Way, Deseret, 1964; *Saint and Savage*, Deseret, 1965; (contributor) *How Glorious is Youth*, Deseret, 1968; (contributor) *In His Footsteps Today*, Deseret, 1970; (contributor) *Scriptures of the Church*, Deseret, 1971; *Letters to Mary*, privately printed, 1972. Contributor of articles, fiction, and verse to Mormon and other Utah periodicals.

WORK IN PROGRESS: Women Who Made a Difference, brief biographies of Latter Day Saints women; *Land of Space Enough*; and an article on small town life in turn of the century Utah for *Utah Historical Quarterly*.

* * *

GIBBS, A(twood) James 1922-

PERSONAL: Born January 17, 1922, in Seattle, Wash.; son of James Atwood and Vera (Smith) Gibbs; married Cherie L. Norman, May 26, 1950; children: Debbie Ann. *Education:* University of Washington, Seattle, student, one year. *Politics:* Non-partisan. *Religion:* Baptist. *Home and office:* 107 Halelo St., Lahaina, Maui, Hawaii 96761.

CAREER: Marine Digest (trade journal), Seattle, Wash., assistant editor, 1947-52; building contractor in Seattle, Wash., 1953-55; *Marine Digest*, editor, 1957-72. *Military service:* U.S. Coast Guard, World War II. *Member:* Maritime Press Association, Puget Sound Maritime Historical Society (charter member; past president). *Awards, honors:* Port of Seattle Anchor Award for outstanding journalism (eleven times); Seattle Historical Society book award.

WRITINGS: Pacific Graveyard, Binfords, 1951, 3rd edition, 1964; *Tillamook Light*, Binfords, 1953; *Sentinels of the North Pacific*, Binfords, 1955; *Shipwrecks of the Pacific Coast*, Binfords, 1957, 2nd edition, 1963; *Shipwrecks Off Juan de Fuca*, Binfords, 1967; *West Coast Windjam-*

mers, Superior, 1968; *Pacific Squareriggers*, Superior, 1969; *Disaster Log of Ships*, Superior, 1971; *Unusual Side of the Sea*, Windward, 1971; *West Coast Lighthouses*, Superior, 1974.

WORK IN PROGRESS: Shipwreck Hawaii, an informal marine history of the Hawaiian Islands; *Is Jonah Your Middle Name*.

* * *

GIBSON, Maralee G. 1924-
(Maralee G. Davis)

PERSONAL: Born January 9, 1924, in Springfield, Mass.; daughter of Frank C. (an apartment building contractor) and Beatrice G. (Tait) Gagnier; married Francis Charles Davis, July 18, 1942 (divorced); married David Joel Thibault, November 9, 1964 (divorced); married William Carter Gibson, January 21, 1970; children: (first marriage) Beverly Tait Davis Clarke, Susan Olds Davis English, Maralee Ruth Dana Chris. *Education:* Attended Bay Path Junior College. *Politics:* Republican. *Religion:* Protestant. *Home:* Juggler Meadow Rd., Leverett, Mass.; and Stuart, Fla. *Agent:* Bertha Klausner International Literary Agency, Inc., 71 Park Ave., New York, N.Y. 19916.

CAREER: Co-owner of dairy farm, Amherst, Mass., 1951-60; in radio continuity and programming, Northampton, Springfield, and Amherst, Mass., intermittently, 1955-73; owner of real estate business, Amherst, Mass., 1956-58; *Greenfield Recorder*, Greenfield, Mass., reporter and feature writer, 1958-62; *Sportsman's News*, Northampton, Mass., assistant editor, 1963-64; free-lance advertising, writing, and radio services, intermittently, 1963-73; secretary, *Collegian* (University of Massachusetts student newspaper), 1964-65; co-owner, president, and treasurer of employment service, Amherst, Mass., 1968-69; Heiser Real Estate, Northampton, Mass., associate, 1973-74. Breeder and exhibitor of Great Pyrenees dogs, 1948-58. Treasurer, Hillcrest Cemetary Marker Service, 1972—. *Member:* World Poetry Society, Poetry Society of New Hampshire, Arizona State Poetry Society, Florida State Poetry Society, Virginia State Poetry Society, Georgia State Poetry Society, Western Massachusetts Writers' Guild (founder; honorary member). *Awards, honors:* Honorable mentions, National Federation of State Poetry Societies, 1969, for *Valley of the Self*.

WRITINGS—Under name Maralee G. Davis: *Soliloquy's Virgin* (poems), Golden Quill, 1964; *The Valley of Self* (poems), NBS Co., 1969. Poetry represented in anthologies, including: *Ballet on the Wind*, Arizona State Poetry Society, 1969; *Naked Spirit, Sing*, Arizona State Poetry Society, 1970; *Echoes of the West Virginia Poetry Society*, West Virginia Poetry Society, 1970; *From the Hills*, Morris Harvey College Publications, 1970-72.

WORK IN PROGRESS: Three books of poetry, *Diary of a Courtship, My Face in Cobwebs*, and *Christmas: A Season of Heart*; a collection of poetry about Emily Dickinson, *Collage of Emily*; a novel, *To Each a Tempest; Adult Education: The Art and Humor of James H. Rinker*.

AVOCATIONAL INTERESTS: Music, sculpting, swimming, golfing, motorbiking, stock car racing, gardening.

BIOGRAPHICAL/CRITICAL SOURCES: Royal Gazette, July 24, 1969; *Daily Hampshire Gazette*, October 22, 1969, January 31, 1971.

GIBSON, William Carleton 1913-

PERSONAL: Born September 4, 1913, in Ottawa, Ontario, Canada; son of John W. (a teacher) and Belle (Crawford) Gibson; married Barbara Baird (a librarian), December 30, 1946; children: David, Ian, Kate. *Education:* University of British Columbia, B.A., 1933; McGill University, M.Sc., 1936, M.D. and C.M., 1941; Oxford University, Ph.D., 1938. *Religion:* United Church of Canada. *Home:* 4582 West Fifth Ave., Vancouver V6R1ST, British Columbia, Canada. *Office:* University of British Columbia, Vancouver V6T 1W5, British Columbia, Canada.

CAREER: Montreal Neurological Institute, Montreal, Quebec, research fellow, 1934-35; Oxford University, Oxford, England, demonstrator in physiology laboratory, 1935-38; University of Sydney, Sydney, Australia, lecturer in neuropathology, 1948-49; University of British Columbia, Vancouver, professor of history of medicine and science, head of the department, and Kinsmen Professor of Neurological Research, 1949-59, assistant to president, 1962—. Chairman of scientific advisory board, Muscular Dystrophy Associations of America; governor of Vancouver Botanical Gardens; Alderman of City of Vancouver, 1973-74; Parks Commissioner, 1974-75; member Bethune Memorial Commission of Canada. *Military service:* Royal Canadian Air Force, Medical Corps, 1941-45; consultant in neuropsychiatry, 1949-59. *Member:* Electroencephalography and Clinical Neurophysiology Society, American Electroencephalographic Society, Canadian Medical Association, American Association of History of Medicine, Canadian Neurological Society.

WRITINGS: Young Endeavour: Contributions to Science by Medical Students of the Past Four Centuries, C. C Thomas, 1959; *Creative Minds in Medicine: Scientific, Humanistic, and Cultural Contributions by Physicians*, C. C Thomas 1963; (With Edward Horne Craigie) *The World of Raymon y Cajal: With Selections from His Non-scientific Writings*, C. C Thomas, 1968; (With Ladislao Reti) *Some Aspects of Seventeenth Century Medicine and Science*, University of California, Los Angeles, 1969; (editor) *British Contributions to Medical Science*, Wellcome Institute of History of Medicine, 1971. Also author of *President Westbrook*, 1972 and writer of over 100 scientific papers.

WORK IN PROGRESS: Two books, *The World of Sir Charles Sherrington*; a translation of Raymony Cajal's, *Histologie Du Systeme Nerveux*.

SIDELIGHTS: William Gibson is competent in French and Spanish. *Avocational interests:* Conservation, music.

* * *

GIFFORD, (Charles) Henry 1913-

PERSONAL: Born June 17, 1913, in London, England; son of Walter Stanley (a consulting engineer) and Lena (Henry) Gifford; married Rosamond Van Ingen, July 29, 1938; children: Nicholas, Anthea. *Education:* Attended Harrow School, 1927-32; Christ Church, Oxford, B.A., 1936, M.A., 1946. *Politics:* Center. *Religion:* Agnostic. *Home:* 10 Hyland Grove, Westbury on Trym, Bristol, England. *Office:* University of Bristol, Bristol, England.

CAREER: University of Bristol, Bristol, England, assistant lecturer, 1946-49, lecturer, 1949-55, senior lecturer, 1955-63, professor of modern English literature, 1963-67, Winterstroke professor of English, 1967—. *Military service:* British Army, 1940-46; became captain. *Member:* Association of University Teachers.

WRITINGS: The Hero of His Time: A Theme in Russian Literature, Edward Arnold, 1950; (translator with Charles Tomlinson) *Versions from Fyodor Tyutchev, 1803-1873*, Oxford University Press, 1960; (translator with Charles Tomlinson) *Castilian Ilexes: Versions from Antonio Machado, 1875-1939*, Oxford University Press, 1963; *The Novel in Russia: From Pushkin to Pasternak*, Hutchinson, 1964; *Comparative Literature*, Routledge & Kegan Paul, 1969; *Tolstoy: A Critical Anthology*, Penguin, 1970.

WORK IN PROGRESS: Boris Pasternak, for Cambridge University Press.

SIDELIGHTS: Gifford is competent in Russian, Spanish, Latin, Greek.

*   *   *

GILB, Corinne Lathrop 1925-

PERSONAL: Born February 19, 1925, in Lethbridge, Alberta, Canada; daughter of Glen H. (a federal administrator) and Vera (Passey) Lathrop; married Tyrell T. Gilb (a manufacturing company vice-president), August 18, 1945; children: Lesley and Tyra (daughters). *Education:* University of Washington, Seattle, B.A., 1946, graduate study, 1946-47; University of California, Berkeley, M.A., 1951, law study, 1951-53; Radcliffe College, Ph.D., 1957. *Politics:* Democrat. *Religion:* Presbyterian. *Office:* Department of History, Wayne State University, Detroit, Mich. 48202.

CAREER: University of California, Berkeley, head of regional cultural history project, 1953-57, junior and later assistant research political scientist, Institute of Industrial Relations, 1956-59, research political scientist, Center for the Study of Law and Society, 1961-65; Mills College, Oakland, Calif., instructor in humanities, 1957-59, lecturer, 1959-61; San Francisco State College (now University), San Francisco, Calif., acting associate professor, 1962, lecturer, 1964-65, professor of humanities, 1965-68; Wayne State University, Detroit, Mich., professor of history, 1968—. California State Legislature, special consultant on income tax, 1963-64. Member of American Political Science Association World Tour Seminar, 1963, and Wenner-Gren Foundation for Anthropological Research seminars, 1964-65. Active in California political conferences, committees, and campaigns, 1959-64. *Member:* International Association for Philosophy of Law and Social Philosophy, American Historical Association, American Society for Political and Legal Philosophy, Organization of American Historians, American Political Science Association, American Studies Association (president, northern California chapter, 1959-61), Phi Beta Kappa, Phi Alpha Theta, Alpha Delta Pi. *Awards, honors:* Social Science Research Council grant, 1958-59; MillsCollege faculty fellowship, summer, 1960; Guggenheim fellowship, 1967-68.

WRITINGS: Conformity of State Personal Income Tax to Federal Income Tax, California Legislature, 1964; *Hidden Hierarchies: The Professions and Government*, Harper, 1966. Articles in history, political science, and law journals.

WORK IN PROGRESS: American Values, for Knopf; *Space and Time* for Harper; *The Changing Space of Power.*

SIDELIGHTS: Corinne Gilb is competent in French, German, Mandarin, and Ukrainian.

*   *   *

GILBERT, Arthur 1926-

PERSONAL: Born June 4, 1926, in Philadelphia, Pa.; son of Harry Robert (a textile manufacturer) and Esther (Glaser) Gilbert; married Jean Kroeze (a sportswear buyer), November 6, 1959; children: Karen, Amy, Lisa, Hillary. *Education:* New York University, B.A., 1947; Jewish Institute of Religion, M.H.L. and Rabbi, 1951; National Psychological Association for Psychoanalysis, certification, 1953. *Office:* 43 West 57th St., New York, N.Y. 10019.

CAREER: Anti-Defamation League of B'nai B'rith, New York, N.Y., director of Department of Inter-religious Cooperation, 1954-61; National Conference of Christians and Jews, director of Religious Freedom and Public Affairs Project, 1961-65; Anti-Defamation League of B'nai B'rith, director of Department of Religious Curriculum Research, 1965—; Jewish Reconstructionist Foundation, assistant to president, 1967—; Reconstructionist Rabbinical College, Philadelphia, Pa., dean, 1968—. Temple Adas Israel, Sag Harbor, Long Island, N.Y., rabbi. *Member:* Central Conference of American Rabbis, National Association of Intergroup Relations Officials, Religious Education Association (vice-president, New York chapter, 1966), American Civil Liberties Union, National Association for the Advancement of Colored People, New York Board of Rabbis (executive board, 1964-66). *Awards, honors:* Award from Catholic Press Association for best nonfiction article, 1961; D.D., Iowa Wesleyan College, 1967; Mass Media Brotherhood Award of the National Conference of Christians and Jews, 1969, for *The Vatican Council and the Jews.*

WRITINGS: (With Oscar Tarcov) *Your Neighbor Celebrates*, Friendly House, 1957; (contributor) Philip Scharper, editor, *American Catholics: A Protestant-Jewish Viewpoint*, Sheed & Ward, 1960; *Meet the American Jew*, Broadman, 1961; *Religion and the Public Order*, University of Chicago Press, 1964; *Currents and Trends in Contemporary Jewish Thought*, Ktav, 1965; *A Jew in Christian America*, Sheed, 1966; (contributor) *Torah and Gospel*, Sheed, 1966; (contributor) *The Star and the Cross*, Bruce, 1966; *Religion and Public Education: Resources and Reactions*, Anti-Defamation League of B'nai B'rith, 1967; *The Vatican Council and the Jews*, World Publishing, 1968; (compiler with W. M. Abbott, R. L. Hunt, and J. C. Swain) *The Bible Reader: An Interfaith Interpretation*, Bruce, 1969; *Prime Time: Children's Early Learning Years*, School Book Service, 1973. Editor of "Background Reports," a series of studies issued by National Conference of Christians and Jews, 1961-65; editor of Central Conference of American Rabbis *Journal*, 1960-65, and *Reconstructionist*, 1960—; member of editorial board, *Journal of Ecumenical Studies*, 1966—.†

*   *   *

GILBERT, Benjamin Franklin 1918-

PERSONAL: Born February 3, 1918, in San Francisco, Calif.; son of Joseph Beverley (a businessman) and Cheltza (Funk) Gilbert; married Donna A. Bornman, August 21, 1955; children: Charlene. *Education:* University of California, Berkeley, A.B., 1939, M.A., 1940, Ph.D., 1951. *Home:* 736 Cambrian Dr., Campbell, Calif. 95008. *Office:* Department of History, San Jose State University, San Jose, Calif. 95192.

CAREER: Teacher in Oakland and San Francisco, Calif., 1945-48; University of California, Berkeley, teaching fellow, 1948-50; San Jose State University, San Jose, Calif., instructor, 1950-52, assistant professor, 1952-55, associate professor, 1955-58, professor of history, 1958—. Historical writer, National Park Service, 1957, 1960-61, 1963-64. Member, Historic Landmarks Commission, San Jose, 1954-62; consultant to Oakland Museum, 1965-67, and to Attorney General of State of California, 1972—. Trustee, Sourisseau Academy for California State and Local History. *Military service:* U.S. Navy, 1942-45. *Member:* Palo Alto Historical Association. *Awards, honors:* Distinguished Public Service Medal, City of San Jose, 1960; research grants from San Jose State University, 1962, 1964, 1965, 1971, 1973, and Sourisseau Academy, 1972, 1974.

WRITINGS: Pioneers for One Hundred Years: San Jose State College, 1857-1957, San Jose State College, 1957; (with H. Brett Melendy) *The Governors of California,* Talisman, 1965; *Teachers Manual: Problems in American History,* Prentice-Hall, 1966; (contributor) Morgan B. Sherwood, editor, *Alaska and Its History,* University of Washington Press, 1967; (contributor) Robert G. Ferris, editor, *Prospector, Cowhand, and Sodbuster,* National Park Service, 1967; (author of introduction) William B. Ide, *Who Conquered California?,* Rio Grande Press, 1967; (contributor) Royce D. Delmatier, editor, *The Rumble of California Politics, 1848-1970,* Wiley, 1970; *The State of California,* Grossman, 1974. Writer of three book-length reports on the mining frontier, Alaska history, and scientific discoveries and inventions in America, 1600-1913, for internal use of National Park Service. Contributor to journals of western history, *American Neptune,* and *Civil War History.* Associate editor, *Journal of the West,* 1962—.

WORK IN PROGRESS: Research on bibliography of Santa Clara County, (Calif.) history.

BIOGRAPHICAL/CRITICAL SOURCES: California Historical Society Quarterly, Volume XXVI, March, 1947; *Quarterly News Letter* of the Book Club of California, Volume XXX, summer, 1965.

*   *   *

GILBERT, Doris Wilcox

PERSONAL: Born in Helena, Mont.; daughter of Arthur Richard (a businessman) and Marian (Parsons) Wilcox; married Luther C. Gilbert (a professor), August 21, 1926; children: Alison (Mrs. Mancur Olson). *Education:* University of Pennsylvania, B.S., 1920, M.A., 1921; graduate study at Columbia University, 1925, University of Chicago, 1927-29. *Politics:* Republican. *Religion:* Protestant. *Home:* 1044 Euclid Ave., Berkeley, Calif. 94708.

CAREER: University of Pennsylvania, Philadelphia, psychologist in Witmer Clinic, 1920-21; Norfolk (Va.) public schools, psychologist and director of special classes, 1921-26; laboratory researcher in educational psychology, 1935-40; University of California, Berkeley, director of reading improvement program, University Extension, 1940—. Visiting summer teacher at William and Mary College, 1923, 1924, University of Virginia, 1926; visiting professor at University of Melbourne, Melbourne, Australia, 1962. *Member:* International Reading Association, National Society for the Study of Education.

WRITINGS: Training for Speed and Accuracy of Visual Perception in Learning to Spell, University of California Press, 1942; *Power and Speed in Reading,* Prentice-Hall, 1954; *Breaking the Reading Barrier,* Prentice-Hall, 1959; *Study in Depth,* Prentice-Hall, 1966; *The Turning Point in Reading,* Prentice-Hall, 1969; *Breaking the Word Barrier,* Prentice-Hall, 1972. Writer of monographs and articles on the psychology of learning in spelling and reading.

WORK IN PROGRESS: A manual on reading improvement for junior college students and others.

*   *   *

GILDER, George F. 1939-

PERSONAL: Born November 29, 1939, in New York, N.Y.; son of Richard Watson and Anne (Alsop) Gilder. *Education:* Harvard University, A.B., 1962. *Politics:* Republican. *Home:* Sky Hill Farm, Tyringham, Mass.

CAREER: Advance Magazine, editor and co-founder while undergraduate at Harvard, 1961-62, and in Washington, D.C., 1962-64; Council on Foreign Relations, junior fellow, 1964-65; *New Leader,* associate editor, 1965—. Speech writer for Nelson D. Rockefeller, 1964; for Richard M. Nixon, 1968; Legislative assistant to Senator Charles McC. Mathias, 1968-70. *Military service:* U.S. Marine Corps Reserve, 1958-64. *Awards, honors:* Harvard University, Kennedy Institute of Politics fellowship, 1970-71.

WRITINGS: The Party That Lost Its Head, Knopf, 1966; *Sexual Suicide,* Quadrangle, 1973; *Naked Nomads: Unmarried Men in America,* Quadrangle, 1974; *Love and Money,* Quadrangle, 1975. Contributor to *Playboy, Harper's, True, National Review,* and other periodicals. Editor, *Ripon Forum,* 1970-71.

AVOCATIONAL INTERESTS: Track and field sports, especially long distance running.

*   *   *

GILFORD, C(harles) B(ernard) 1920-
(Donald Campbell, Douglas Farr, Elizabeth Gregory)

PERSONAL: Born November 10, 1920, in Kansas City, Mo.; son of Harry A. and Frances (Meehan) Gilford; married Martha Patricia Campbell (a teacher), August 16, 1947; children: Pamela, Robb, Stasia, Kevin. *Education:* Rockhurst College, B.S., 1942; Catholic University, M.A., 1947; University of Denver, Ph.D., 1952. *Home:* 8115 Sagamore St., Leawood, Kan. 66206. *Agent:* Scott Meredith Literary Agency, 580 Fifth Ave., New York, N.Y. 10036.

CAREER: Rockhurst College, Kansas City, Mo., instructor in speech and English, 1947-51; St. Louis University, St. Louis, Mo., associate professor of drama, 1952-59; University of Missouri, Kansas City, lecturer in theatre, 1959-69; Johnson County Community College, instructor in creative writing, 1970—. *Military service:* U.S. Army Air Forces, 1942-45; served as navigator.

WRITINGS: Quest for Innocence, Putnam, 1961; *Dead Man Out,* Caravelle, 1967; *The Liquid Man,* Lancer, 1969; *The Crooked Shamrock,* Doubleday, 1969. Author of 200 short stories, fifty of which have been anthologized, seven adapted for television, and three for film.

Plays all published by The Play House (now Baker & Ço.): *Bull in a China Shop; Lost Flight; Jury Room; Who Dunit?; Halfway to Heaven; Black Sheep, Black Sheep; Girl from Outer Space; Any Body for Tea?; Guest for Breakfast;* (under pseudonym Donald Campbell) *My Favorite Haunts;* (under pseudonym Donald Campbell) *O Men, Amen;* (under pseudonym Douglas Farr) *Beyond the Door;* (under pseudonym Douglas Farr) *The Lady Lingers;* (co-author under pseudonym Elizabeth Gregory) *Hope Springs Eternal.* Adaptor with Elizabeth Gibson, *Blackboard Jungle,* by Evan Hunter.

WORK IN PROGRESS: Four novels, three in collaboration with others.

SIDELIGHTS: Gilford writes to *CA*: "Playwriting is first love, but sad state of the theatre makes this an unrewarding affection, though I have profited well from amateur royalties. Theatre remains an engrossing hobby and avocation. Quite some experience in amateur and semi-pro acting. Enjoy writing novels and short stories, but they seem to be harder work, more words have to be gotten on paper. I have no great messages to communicate; just believe in a well-plotted story. . . ." Many of Gilford's writings have been translated for European and Japanese publications, radio and television.

* * *

GILKEY, Langdon (Brown) 1919-

PERSONAL: Born February 9, 1919, in Chicago, Ill.; son of Charles W. Gilkey; married Sonja Weber (a sculptor), January 26, 1963; children: Mark Whitney, Amos Welcome, Frouwkje Tjakien. *Education:* Harvard University, A.B., 1940; Cambridge University, Fulbright scholar, 1950-51; Columbia University, Ph.D., 1954. *Politics:* Democrat. *Home:* 5713 Harper Ave., Chicago, Ill. 60637. *Office:* Divinity School, University of Chicago, Chicago, Ill.

CAREER: Teacher at Yenching University, near Peking, China, 1940-41; interned by Japanese, first at Yenching University, later at internment camp near Weihsien, Shantung Province, where he served successively on the quarters committee, as helper to the camp mason, cook, and kitchens administrator, 1941-45; Union Theological Seminary, New York, N.Y., instructor in philosophy of religion, 1949-50; Vassar College, Poughkeepsie, N.Y., lecturer in religion, 1951-54; Vanderbilt University Divinity School, Nashville, Tenn., professor of theology, 1954-63; University of Chicago Divinity School, Chicago, Ill., professor of theology, 1963—. Fulbright visiting professor, Koyoto University (Japan), 1975. *Member:* Society for the Promotion of Science (fellow). *Awards, honors:* Guggenheim fellowship to Germany, 1960-61, 1965.

WRITINGS: Maker of Heaven and Earth, Doubleday, 1959; *How the Church Can Minister to the World Without Losing Itself*, Harper, 1964; *Shantung Compound*, Harper, 1966; *Naming the Whirlwind: The Renewal of God Language*, Bobbs-Merrill, 1969; *Religion and the Scientific Future*, Harper, 1970; *Catholicism Confronts Modernity*, Seabury, 1974.

* * *

GILLESPIE, John E. 1921-

PERSONAL: Born January 2, 1921, in Terre Haute, Ind.; son of Reverdy (a dentist) and Martha (Greiner) Gillespie; married Anna Penney, February 10, 1958; children: Frances Penney, John Willis. *Education:* DePauw University, A.B., 1941, B.M., 1942; University of Southern California, M.A., 1948, M.M., 1949, Ph.D., 1951. *Religion:* Episcopalian. *Home:* 1191 Las Alturas Rd., Santa Barbara, Calif.

CAREER: Centre Universitaire Americain, Paris, France, director of music studies, 1945-46; University of Southern California, Los Angeles, teacher of music, 1950-51; University of California, Santa Barbara, teacher of music, 1951-62, professor of music, 1962—. Has given recitals on piano and harpsichord, and made five recordings of harpsichord music; church organist. *Member:* American Musicological Association, Music Library Association, Phi Beta Kappa, Pi Kappa Lambda, Pi Beta Phi. *Awards, honors:* Fulbright grant, 1949-50; American Council of Learned Societies grant for research in Coptic music, 1965-66.

WRITINGS: Five Centuries of Keyboard Music, Wadsworth, 1965; *The Musical Experience*, Wadsworth, 1968, 2nd edition, 1972.

SIDELIGHTS: Gillespie speaks French, German, some Italian and Spanish. He has studied Arabic and is now learning Coptic.†

* * *

GILLMAN, Richard 1929-

PERSONAL: Born January 14, 1929, in Northampton, Mass.; son of Butler Walbridge (a musician) and Evelyn (Damon) Gillman; married Margot Martindale; children: Margot, Julia. *Education:* Attended Columbia University, 1965. *Home:* Barney Rd., Elnora, N.Y. *Office:* Office of University Affairs, State University of New York, 99 Washington Ave., Albany, N.Y.

CAREER: Daily Hampshire Gazette, Northampton, Mass., news writer, 1947-50, 1958-61; Brandeis University, Waltham, Mass., public affairs director, 1961-70; State University of New York, Central Administration, Albany, N.Y., assistant vice-chancellor for university affairs, 1970—. *Member:* Education Writers Association, Council for Advancement and Support of Education.

WRITINGS: Too Much Alone (poems), A. Swallow, 1965. Poetry published in *Saturday Review, Poetry, Beloit Poetry Journal, Transatlantic Review*, and other publications.

WORK IN PROGRESS: A second book of poems.

AVOCATIONAL INTERESTS: Journalism and entomology.

* * *

GILMAN, William H(enry) 1911-

PERSONAL: Born August 9, 1911, in Boston, Mass.; son of William L. F. and Frances L. (Marden) Gilman; married Barbara Benson, July 27, 1938 (deceased); married Margaret Cox Reilly, June 26, 1943; children: (first marriage) Barbara (Mrs. Ronald P. Simpson); (second marriage) Christopher, Margaret, Kathleen, Lucia, Stephen. *Education:* Harvard University, B.A., 1933; George Washington University, M.A., 1943; Yale University, Ph.D., 1948. *Politics:* Democrat. *Religion:* Roman Catholic.

CAREER: Georgetown University, School of Foreign Service, Washington, D.C., lecturer in English, 1941-44; University of Rochester, Rochester, N.Y., assistant professor, 1947-52, associate professor, 1952-58, professor of English, 1958-66, Roswell S. Burrows Professor of English, 1966—. Visiting professor, Stanford University, 1959. President, Catholic Interracial Council of Rochester, 1965-66; member of executive council, Friends of FIGHT. *Member:* Modern Language Association of America, Melville Society, Emerson Society, American Association of University Professors, American Civil Liberties Union, Elizabethan Club. *Awards, honors:* Fund for the Advancement of Education fellow, 1953-54; Guggenheim fellow, 1960-61, 1964-65.

WRITINGS: (Editor with Margaret Denny) *The American Writer and the European Tradition*, University of Minnesota Press, 1950; *Melville's Early Life and "Redburn,"* New York University Press, 1951; (editor with Merrell R. Davis) Melville, *Letters*, Yale University Press, 1960; (editor with J. E. Parsons) Ralph Waldo Emerson, *The Journals and Miscellaneous Notebooks*, Harvard University Press, Volume I, 1960, Volume II, 1961, Volume III, 1963, Volume IV, 1965, Volume V, 1966, Volume VI, 1967,

Volume VII, 1968, Volume VIII, 1969; (editor) *Selected Writings of Ralph Waldo Emerson*, New American Library, 1965; (contributor) M. LaFrance, editor, *Patterns of Commitment in American Literature*, University of Toronto Press, 1967. Writer of articles and reviews on Melville and Emerson.

AVOCATIONAL INTERESTS: Fishing, photography; football, basketball, baseball, and other spectator sports.

BIOGRAPHICAL/CRITICAL SOURCES: The Class of 1932 (25th-year directory), Harvard University Press, 1957.†

* * *

GILSON, Goodwin Woodrow 1918-

PERSONAL: Born November 1, 1918, in Orange, N.J.; son of Joseph (a merchant) and Flora (Blankfield) Gilson; married Ruth Margolin, September 7, 1940 (deceased). *Education:* City College (now of the City University of New York), New York, N.Y., B.B.A., 1939, M.S. in Ed., 1943. *Politics:* Democrat. *Religion:* Judaism. *Home:* 53 Brighton 2 Path, Brooklyn, N.Y. 11235. *Office:* Central Commercial High School, 214 East 42nd St., New York, N.Y.

CAREER: Brooklyn College (now of the City University of New York), Brooklyn, N.Y., lecturer, 1959-69; Borough of Manhattan Community College, New York, N.Y., adjunct lecturer, 1969—; Bernard M. Baruch School of Business and Public Administration, New York, N.Y., adjunct lecturer, 1973—. Central Commercial High School, New York, N.Y., chairman of secretarial studies department, 1954—. *Military service:* U.S. Maritime Service, 1943-46; became lieutenant junior grade. *Member:* Pitman Commercial Teachers Association (executive board).

WRITINGS—Textbooks: *Medical Dictation Course*, Speedwriting Co., 1960; *Dictation Patterns*, Pitman, 1961; (with Morris Mellinger) *Developing Shorthand Skills*, Pitman, 1965.

* * *

GIMPEL, Herbert J. 1915-

PERSONAL: Born March 17, 1915, in Cleveland, Ohio; son of Julius and Agatha (Witt) Gimpel; married Ruth Eleanor Rosenberg (typist and copy editor for husband), August 10, 1946. *Education:* Western Reserve University (now Case Western Reserve University), B.A., 1939. *Religion:* Protestant. *Home:* 101 Alma St. Apt. 1102, Palo Alto, Calif. 94301.

CAREER: U.S. Navy, career service, 1947-63, retiring as commander; full-time writer, 1964—. During World War II served aboard carrier, "USS Bataan," participating in Okinawa and Japan campaigns; later assigned as public information officer with Destroyer Force Atlantic, and to other posts in Naples, Pearl Harbor, San Diego, and Washington, D.C.; information officer for Project Mercury Recovery Force in Hawaii, 1962, and for First Fleet Exercises for President Kennedy, 1963. *Member:* Navy League, Armed Forces Writer's League. *Awards, honors*—Military: Asiatic-Pacific Medal with two battle stars.

WRITINGS: (With Chambliss and Rush) *The Complete Book of Submarines*, World Publishing, 1958; (with Steele) *Nuclear Submarine Skippers and What They Do*, F. Watts, 1962; *Navy Men and What They Do*, F. Watts, 1963; *The United States Nuclear Navy*, F. Watts, 1965; *Lord Nelson*, F. Watts, 1966; *Napoleon: Man of Destiny*, F. Watts,

1968; *Beethoven: Master Composer*, F. Watts, 1970; *In the Wake of Science: A 50-year History of the Naval Research Laboratory*, Government Printing Office, in press.

SIDELIGHTS: Gimpel is competent in German.

* * *

GINGER, Helen 1916-

PERSONAL: Born July 19, 1916, in Coeur d'Alene, Idaho; daughter of Oscar W. and Victoria (Petterson) Swanson; married Frank C. Ginger (a railroad checkman), October 21, 1944; children: Kay. *Education:* Kinman Business University, Spokane, Wash., secretarial course, 1935. *Politics:* "Republican most of the time." *Religion:* Christian Church. *Home:* 1919 47th Ave., S.W., Seattle, Wash. 98116.

WRITINGS: God Still Answers Prayer, Standard Publishing, 1964. Contributor to *KEY Magazine*.

* * *

GINGLEND, David R. 1913-

PERSONAL: Born September 18, 1913, in Philadelphia, Pa.; son of David A. and Mary K. (McGovern) Ginglend. *Education:* Temple University, B.S. in Ed. and M.S. in Ed., 1954; graduate study at Columbia University, Rutgers University, and Newark State College, 1956-59. *Politics:* Democrat. *Religion:* Episcopalian.

CAREER: Plainfield (N.J.) public schools, teacher of trainable mentally retarded, 1955—; Newark State College, Union, N.J., instructor in Extension Division, 1961—. *Military service:* U.S. Army Air Forces, 1942-45; became staff sergeant. *Member:* American Association on Mental Deficiency (fellow), National Association for Retarded Children (chairman of recreation sub-committee), National Education Association, New Jersey Association for Retarded Children, New Jersey Education Association, Kappa Phi Kappa.

WRITINGS: (With Bernice Wells Carlson) *Play Activities for the Retarded Child*, Abingdon, 1961; (with K. Gould) *Day Camping for the Mentally Retarded*, National Association for Retarded Children, 1962; (with Winifred E. Stiles) *Music Activities for Retarded Children*, Abingdon, 1965; *The Expressive Arts for the Mentally Retarded*, National Association for Retarded Children, 1967; (with Carlson) *Recreation for Retarded Teen-agers and Young Adults*, Abingdon, 1968. Contributor to professional journals.†

* * *

GINSBURG, Mirra

PERSONAL: Born in Russia; daughter of Joseph and Bronia (Geier) Ginsburg. *Education:* Attended schools in Russia, Latvia, Canada, and United States. *Home:* 150 West 96th St., New York, N.Y. 10025. *Agent:* Gunther Stuhlmann, 65 Irving Pl., New York, N.Y. 10003.

CAREER: Free-lance editor, and translator from Russian and Yiddish. *Member:* P.E.N. *Awards, honors:* Lewis Carroll Shelf Award, 1972, for *The Diary of Nina Kosterina*; Mildred L. Batchelder nomination, 1973, for *The Kaha Bird*, and 1974, for *The White Ship*; Children's Book Showcase Title, 1973, for *The Chick and the Duckling*.

WRITINGS—Editor and translator: *The Fatal Eggs and Other Soviet Satire*, Macmillan, 1965; *The Dragon: Fifteen Stories by Yevgeny Zamyatin*, Random House, 1966; *The*

Last Door to Ayia: Anthology of Soviet Science Fiction, S. G. Phillips, 1968; *A Soviet Heretic: Essays by Yevgeny Zamyatin*, University of Chicago Press, 1970; *The Ultimate Threshold: Anthology of Soviet Science Fiction*, Holt, 1970.

Translator: Roman Goul, *Azef*, Doubleday, 1962; Vera Alexandrova, *A History of Soviet Literature*, Doubleday, 1963; Mikhail Bulgakov, *The Master and Margarita*, Grove, 1967; Mikhail Bulgakov, *Heart of a Dog*, Grove, 1968; Mikhail Bulgakov, *Flight* (play), Grove, 1969; Nikhail Bulgakov, *The Life of Monsieur de Moliere*, Funk, 1970; Yevgeny Zamyatin, *We* (novel), Viking, 1972; Chingiz Aitmatov, *The White Ship*, Crown, 1972; Fyodor Dostoyevsky, *Notes From Underground*, Bantam, 1974; Andrey Platanov, *The Foundation Pit*, Dutton, 1975.

Children's books: (editor, adaptor, and translator) *The Diary of Nina Kosterina* (young adult; translated only), Crown, 1968; *The Fox and the Hare* (picture book), Crown, 1969; *The Master of the Winds: Folk Tales from Siberia*, Crown, 1970; *Three Rolls and One Doughnut: Fables from Russia*, Dial, 1970; *The Kaha Bird: Tales from Central Asia*, Crown, 1971; *One Trick Too Many: Tales About Foxes*, Dial, 1972; *The Chick and the Duckling* (picture book), Macmillan, 1972; *What Kind of Bird is That!* (picture book), Crown, 1972; *Three Kittens*, Crown, 1973; *The Lazies: Tales of The Peoples of Russia*, Macmillan, 1973; *How Wilka Went to Sea: Folk Tales from West of the Urals*, Crown, 1974; *Mushroom in the Rain* (picture book), Macmillan, 1974; (translator only) Lydia Obukhova, *Daughter of Night* (science fiction), Macmillan, 1974; *The Proud Maiden, Tungak, and the Sun* (picture book), Macmillan, 1974.

Other translations include stories by Isaac Bashevis Singer, Alexey Remizov, Isaac Babel, and Zoshchenko, for various anthologies, collections and periodicals; co-translator of Isaac Babel's play, "Sunset," produced in 1966 and 1972.

SIDELIGHTS: Ms. Ginsburg wrote, "I have loved folktales since childhood, and have gone on collecting them and delighting in them ever since. I place folktales among the greatest works of literature. To me they are a distillation of man's deepest experience into poetry, wisdom, truth, sadness, and laughter." *Avocational interests:* Fiction, especially fantastic and satirical, poetry, cats (big and little), birds, early music, early and primitive art.

* * *

GLASER, Milton 1929-
(Max Catz)

PERSONAL: Born June 26, 1929, in New York, N.Y.; son of Eugene and Eleanor (Bergman) Glaser; married Shirley Girton (an art gallery director), August 13, 1957. *Education:* Cooper Union, graduate, 1951; also studied at Academy of Fine Arts, Bologna, Italy. *Religion:* Hebrew. *Home:* 54 St. Mark's Pl., New York, N.Y. *Office:* Push Pin Studios, Inc., 207 East 32nd St., New York, N.Y. 10016.

CAREER: Artist and illustrator; Push-Pin Studios, Inc., New York, N.Y., founder and partner, 1954—; *New York* magazine, New York, N.Y., design director, 1968—. Member of faculty, School of Visual Arts. *Member:* American Institute of Graphic Arts (vice-president), Alliance Graphique International. *Awards, honors:* Fulbright scholarship to Bologna, Italy; Gold Medal from Society of Illus-

trators; Gold Medal from Art Directors Club; Medal Award from American Institute of Graphic Arts, 1972.

WRITINGS: (With wife, Shirley Glaser) *If Apples Had Teeth*, Knopf, 1960; (with Jerome Snyder) *The Underground Gourmet*, Simon & Schuster, 1968, revised edition, 1970.

Illustrator: Alvin Tresselt, *The Smallest Elephant in the World*, Knopf, 1959; Conrad Aiken, *Cats and Bats and Things with Wings* (poetry), Atheneum, 1965; Gian Carlo Menotti, *Help, Help, The Gobolinks*, adapted by Leigh Dean, McGraw, 1970; George Mendoza, *Fish in the Sky*, Doubleday, 1971; (with Seymour Chwast and Barry Zaid) Ormonde DeKay, Jr., translator, *Rimes de la Mere Ole*, Little, Brown, 1971.

WORK IN PROGRESS: The Underground Gourmet; and Mirror of Your Mind.

BIOGRAPHICAL/CRITICAL SOURCES: Graphis, Number 92, July, 1962; *Industrial Design*, July, 1962; *Idea*, October, 1964.†

* * *

GLASER, Robert 1921-

PERSONAL: Born January 18, 1921, in Providence, R.I.; son of Abraham (a furrier) and Rose (Klein) Glaser; married Sylvia Lotman (a clinical psychologist), March 4, 1945; children: Ellen, Karen. *Education:* City College (now City College of the City University of New York), B.S., 1942; Indiana University, M.A., 1947, Ph.D., 1949. *Home:* 5860 Marlborough Ave., Pittsburgh, Pa. 15217. *Office:* Learning Research and Development Center, 205 Mineral Industries Building, University of Pittsburgh, Pittsburgh, Pa. 15213.

CAREER: University of Kentucky, Lexington, assistant professor of psychology, 1949-51; University of Illinois, Urbana, research assistant professor of education, 1951-52; University of Pittsburgh, Pittsburgh, Pa., lecturer, 1952-56, associate professor, 1956-60, professor of psychology, 1960-71, professor of education, 1964-71, University Professor of Psychology and Education, 1971—, Learning Research and Development Center, director of research, 1964-65, director of Center, 1965—. American Institutes for Research, Pittsburgh, Pa., program director, 1952-56, research adviser, 1964-70; member of educational sub-panel, President's Scientific Advisory Committee, 1962-64; member of project advisory committee, Institute for Educational Development, 1966—. *Military service:* U.S. Army Air Forces, aviation psychologist, 1943-45. *Member:* American Association for the Advancement of Science, American Psychological Association (council representative), American Educational Research Association, (vice-president, 1966-68), Human Factors Society, Psychonomic Society, Psychometric Society, Sigma Xi. *Awards, honors:* Fulbright award, 1950; article on instructional technology included in 1965 World's Fair Time Capsule.

WRITINGS: (Editor with A. A. Lumsdaine) *Teaching Machines and Programmed Learning*, two volumes, National Education Association, 1960; (editor and contributor) *Training Research and Education*, University of Pittsburgh Press, 1962; (with A. G. Holzman and H. H. Schaefer) *Matrices and Mathematical Bases for Management Decision Making*, three volumes, Encyclopaedia Britannica, 1962; (editor and contributor) *Teaching Machines and Programmed Learning II, Data and Directions*, National Education Association, 1965; (with J. I. Taber and Schaefer) *Learning and Programmed Instruction*, Addison-Wesley,

1965; (with William W. Ramage and Joseph I. Lipson) *The Interface Between Student and Subject Matter*, Learning Research and Development Center, University of Pittsburgh, 1968; (editor) *The Nature of Reinforcement*, Academic Press, 1971.

Contributor: *Symposium on Electronics Maintenance*, U.S. Government Printing Office, 1955; *Current Trends in the Description and Analysis of Behavior*, University of Pittsburgh Press, 1958; H. H. Gilmer, editor, *Industrial Psychology*, McGraw, 1961; J. P. Lysaught, editor, *Programmed Learning: Evolving Principles and Industrial Applications*, Foundation for Research on Human Behavior, 1961; *Newer Educational Media*, Pennsylvania State University Press, 1961; R. Gagne, editor, *Psychological Principles in System Development*, Holt, 1961; J. E. Coulson, editor, *Programmed Learning and Computer-Based Instruction*, Wiley, 1962; C. M. Lindvall, editor, *Defining Educational Objectives*, University of Pittsburgh Press, 1963; R. T. Filep, editor, *Prospectives in Programming*, Macmillan, 1963; D. L. Cleland, editor, *New Dimensions in Reading*, University of Pittsburgh Press, 1963; W. Corell, editor, *Programmiertes Lernen und Lehrmaschinen*, George Westermann Verlag, 1965; L. S. Shulman and E. R. Keislar, editors, *Learning by Discovery*, Rand McNally, 1966; R. Gagne, editor, *Learning and Individual Differences*, C. E. Merrill, 1970. Contributor to 1964 and 1966 yearbooks of National Society for the Study of Education. Also contributor to *Encyclopedia of Education Research*, 4th edition, Macmillan, 1969.

Co-author of studies published by American Institutes for Research, 1952-66, many of them for U.S. Office of Naval Research; co-author of other studies for U.S. Air Force. Contributor to psychology and education journals. Member of editorial board, *AERA Journal* (publication of American Education Research Association), *Journal of Human Performance*, and *Journal of Communication*.†

*   *   *

GLAZE, Andrew (Louis III) 1920-

PERSONAL: Born April 21, 1920, in Nashville, Tenn.; son of Andrew Louis, Jr. (a physician) and Mildred (Ezell) Glaze; married Dorothy Elliott; married second wife, Adriana Keathley (a dancer), August 12, 1962; children: (first marriage) Betsy, Peter. *Education:* Harvard College, A.B. (cum laude), 1942; Stanford University, student, 1946. *Politics:* Independent. *Religion:* None. *Home:* 803 Ninth Ave., New York, N.Y. 10019. *Agent:* Jay Garon-Brooks, 415 Central Park West, New York, N.Y. 10025.

CAREER: Birmingham Post-Herald, Birmingham, Ala., reporter, 1949-56; British Travel Association, New York, N.Y., writer, 1958—. *Military service:* U.S. Army Air Forces, ground communications, 1942-46; became first lieutenant. *Awards, honors:* Eunice Tietjens Award, *Poetry* Magazine, 1951; American Library Association, Notable Books List, 1966, for *Damned Ugly Children*.

WRITINGS: Lines, privately printed by Editions Heraclita, 1964; *Damned Ugly Children* (poems), Trident, 1966; (contributor) *New Yorker Book of Poems*, Viking, 1969; (contributor) *New Directions 26*, New Directions, 1973; *Masque of Surgery*, Menard Press, 1974.

Plays: "Who Stole the Lollipop," 1961; "Miss Pete," 1962 (produced by American Place Theatre, 1966); "The Subman," 1962; "We Are All Liars," 1964; "The Wimmidge Group," 1965; "Decisions," 1970; "Kleinhoff Demonstrates Tonight," 1971 (produced at University of Texas,

1971); "Most Engaged Girl," 1971 (musical); "The Man Tree," 1973 (produced by Public Theatre); "St. Jermyn," 1973; "Love is Nothing to Laugh About," 1974.

WORK IN PROGRESS: A book of poems and a play.

SIDELIGHTS: Glaze told *CA*: "All poets who have written for the theatre in this country have gone down the wrong track. I am beginning to succeed in proving it. I speak, write, read, and translate French, I study ballet, my major interests are in anthropology, philosophy, psychology and music."

*   *   *

GLAZENER, Mary U(nderwood) 1921-

PERSONAL: Born October 14, 1921, in Atlanta, Ga.; daughter of John LaFayette (a minister) and Eunice (Upshaw) Underwood; married O. W. Glazener (a warehouse superintendent), April 2, 1944; children: Janet Olivia, Charles Upshaw, Vivian Joy. *Education:* Attended Mars Hill College and Brevard College; Clemson University, B.A., 1975. *Politics:* Democrat. *Religion:* Baptist. *Home address:* Route 3, Box 76A, Central, S.C.

CAREER: Legal secretary in Asheville, N.C., 1942-44; WLOS-TV, Asheville, N.C., producer and performer on children's television program, "Tot Town," 1956-57; Howard Johnson Motor Lodge, Asheville, N.C., secretary and housekeeper, 1966-69; American Enka Co., Central, S.C., secretary, 1969-73. Leader of conferences on church drama for Sunday School Board of Southern Baptist Convention, Nashville, Tenn.; local producer of church drama.

WRITINGS—Plays: The Stumbling Block, Broadman, 1961; *The Slave Girl*, Broadman, 1966.

WORK IN PROGRESS: A three-act biblical play based on the Joseph story, for Broadman.

AVOCATIONAL INTERESTS: Music, sewing, gardening.

*   *   *

GLEISSER, Marcus D(avid) 1923-

PERSONAL: Born February 14, 1923, in Buenos Aires, Argentina; son of Ben (merchant) and Riva (Kogan) Gleisser; married Helga Rothschild, October 23, 1955; children: Brian S., Julia L., Hannah T., Ellyn R. *Education:* Western Reserve University, B.A., 1945, M.A., 1949; Cleveland-Marshall Law School, LL.B., 1957. *Politics:* Independent. *Religion:* Jewish. *Home:* 575 Hemlock Dr., Euclid, Ohio 44132. *Office: Cleveland Plain Dealer*, 1801 Superior Ave., Cleveland, Ohio 44114.

CAREER: Cleveland Press, Cleveland, Ohio, copy editor, 1944-47; McDonough-Lewy Advertising Agency, Cleveland, Ohio, copywriter, 1947-50; *Cleveland Plain Dealer*, Cleveland, Ohio, writer, 1950—; attorney, 1957—, admitted to practice before U.S. Supreme Court, 1962. *Member:* Ohio State Bar Association, The Newspaper Guild, Society of Professional Journalists.

AWARDS, HONORS: American Newspaper Publishers Association Bronze Medal, 1944; Ohio Bar Association writing awards, 1957-62; American Bar Association Silver Gavel Award for writing, 1958; Cleveland Newspaper Guild Award, 1959; National Legal Aid and Defender Association Bronze Medal for newspaper writing, 1963; National Association of Real Estate Editors award for feature series, 1965, 71, 72, 73; G. M. Loeb Special Award, University of Connecticut, for excellence in business and financial writing, 1966; National Headliners Club silver medal, 1969; Press Club of Cleveland award, 1969; Cleveland State University, J.D., 1969.

WRITINGS: The World of Cyrus Eaton, A. S. Barnes, 1965; *Juries and Justice*, A. S. Barnes, 1968.Writer of weekly column in *Cleveland Plain Dealer*, 1963—. Editor-in-chief, *Cleveland-Marshall Law Review*, 1956-57.

WORK IN PROGRESS: A nostalgic novel describing Cleveland in 1945 entitled *Through Eden*; *The Prologue*, a study of Cleveland's black ghetto.

SIDELIGHTS: Gleisser told *CA* that he travels coast to coast annually "to get the thinking of people," and that he seeks to overcome provincialism.

*   *   *

GLENN, Norval Dwight   1933-

PERSONAL: Born August 13, 1933, in Roswell, N.M.; son of William N. (a cattle rancher) and Mary Edna (Cochrain) Glenn. *Education:* New Mexico State University, B.A., 1954; University of Texas, Ph.D., 1962. *Politics:* Independent. *Office:* Department of Sociology, University of Texas, Austin, Tex. 78712.

CAREER: Miami University, Oxford, Ohio, instructor in sociology, 1960-61; University of Illinois, Urbana, instructor, 1961-63, assistant professor of sociology, 1963-64; University of Texas, Austin, assistant professor, 1964-65, associate professor, 1965-70, professor of sociology, 1970—. *Military service:* U.S. Army, Adjutant General's Corps, 1954-56; became first lieutenant. *Member:* American Sociological Association.

WRITINGS: (With Leonard Broom) *Transformation of the Negro American*, Harper, 1965; (with Jon Alston and David Weiner) *Social Stratification*, Glendessary, 1970; (with Charles Bonjean) *Blacks in the United States*, Chandler, 1969. Also contributed 18 chapters to scholarly books. Contributor to professional journals.

WORK IN PROGRESS: Research on aging and conservatism and on the social mobility of females for journal articles and book chapters.

*   *   *

GLENNY, Lyman A.   1918-

PERSONAL: Born January 26, 1918, in Trent, S.D.; son of Walter and Anna (Henning) Glenny; married Carolyn Joy Ballou, December 19, 1942; children: Terence Alan, Celia Joy, Colleen Marie. *Education:* University of Minnesota, Duluth, B.S., 1947; University of Colorado, M.A., 1948; University of Iowa, Ph.D., 1950. *Office:* Center for Research and Development in Higher Education, University of California, Berkeley, Calif.

CAREER: Sacramento State College, 1950-62, started as assistant professor, became professor of government; Illinois Board of Higher Education, Springfield, associate director, 1962-65, executive director, 1965-69; University of California, Berkeley, professor of higher education, 1969—; director, Center for Research and Development in Higher Education, 1972—. Coordinator, Signal Corps Schools of U.S. Army, 1951-52; consultant to Carnegie research project on higher education and co-organizer of Center for the Study of Higher Education, University of California, Berkeley, 1956-57; director of Nebraska study on higher education, 1960. *Member:* American Academy of Political and Social Science, American Society for Public Adminis-

tration, Association for Higher Education, Association for Institutional Research, American Association of University Professors, Western Political Science Association, Western Governmental Research Association. *Awards, honors:* Carnegie grant, 1956; Northern Illinois University, Humanist Award, 1970; Grants from Office of Education, 1969-72; National Institute for Education, 1973; Ford Foundation, 1973.

WRITINGS: (Contributor) *Facing the Critical Decade*, Western Interstate Commission on Higher Education, 1957; *Autonomy of Public Colleges: The Challenge of Coordination*, McGraw, 1959; *Nebraska Study of Higher Education*, Legislative Council, State of Nebraska, 1961; (with Richard G. Browne) *Master Plan for Higher Education in Illinois*, Illinois Board of Higher Education, 1964; (co-author) *Growth and Government in Sacramento*, Indiana University Press, 1965; (contributor) *Emerging Patterns in American Higher Education*, edited by Logan Wilson, American Council on Education, 1965; (contributor) *Campus and Capitol*, Western Interstate Commission on Higher Education, 1966; (contributor) *Seven Crucial Issues in Education*, Education Commission of the States, 1967.

(Contributor) G. K. Smith, editor, *The Troubled Campus*, Jossey-Bass, 1970; (contributor) *Effective Use of Resources in State Higher Education*, Southern Regional Education Board, 1970; *Coordinating Higher Education for the 70's*, Center for Research and Development in Higher Education, 1971; (contributor) W. Godwin and B. P. Mann, editors, *Higher Education, Myths, Realities, and Possibilities*, Southern Regional Education Board, 1972; (contributor) R. Millard, K. Sweeney, and N. Ecklund, editors, *Planning and Management Practices in Higher Education*, Education Commission of the United States, 1972; (with T. K. Dalglish) *The University as an Organization*, Carnegie Commission on Higher Education, 1973; (with Dalglish) *Public Universities, State Agencies, and the Law: Constitutional Autonomy in Decline*, Center for Research and Development in Higher Education, 1973; (with J. R. Kidder) *State Tax Support of Higher Education: Revenue Appropriation Trends and Patterns, 1963-73*, Center for Research and Development in Higher Education, 1973; (contributor) E. Gleazer and R. Yarrington, editors, *Coordinating State Systems*, Jossey-Bass, 1974. Contributor to *Encyclopedia of Educational Research*, Macmillan, 1960, and to professional journals.

*   *   *

GLESER, Goldine C(ohnberg)   1915-

PERSONAL: Born June 15, 1915, in St. Louis, Mo.; daughter of Julius (a merchant) and Lena (Goldberg) Cohnberg; married Sol M. Gleser (an engineer), June 4, 1936; children: Leon J., Malcolm A., Judith A. *Education:* Washington University, St. Louis, Mo., A.B., 1935, M.S. 1936, Ph.D., 1950. *Politics:* Independent. *Religion:* Jewish. *Home:* 3604 Lansdowne Ave., Cincinnati, Ohio 45236. *Office:* Department of Psychiatry, University of Cincinnati Medical Center, Cincinnati, Ohio 45267.

CAREER: Washington University, St. Louis, Mo., instructor in mathematics, 1947-49, research assistant in anatomy and neuropsychiatry, 1950-51, research assistant, later research associate in neuropsychiatry, 1952-54; University of Cincinnati, Cincinnati, Ohio, assistant professor, 1956-58, associate professor, 1958-64, professor of psychology, 1964—, director of psychology division, department of psychiatry, 1967—. University of Illinois, Urbana, research assistant professor, department of education, 1957-58, research associate professor, 1958-63.

MEMBER: American Psychological Association (fellow), Psychometric Society, American Association for the Advancement of Science (fellow), Society of Multivariate Experimental Psychology, American Statistical Association (fellow), American College of Neuropsychopharmacology (fellow), Midwest Psychological Association, Ohio Psychological Association (fellow), New York Academy of Sciences, Cincinnati Psychological Association (president, 1957-58, 1965-66), American Civil Liberties Union, Phi Beta Kappa, Sigma Xi. *Awards, honors:* Foundations Fund for Research in Psychiatry interdisciplinary teaching grant, 1959-66.

WRITINGS: (With L. J. Cronbach) *Psychological Tests and Personnel Decisions,* University of Illinois Press, 1957, 2nd edition, 1965; (with L. A. Gottschalk) *The Measurement of Psychological States Through the Content Analysis of Verbal Behavior,* University of California Press, 1969; (with Gottschalk and C. N. Winget) *A Manual for Using the Gottschalk-Gleser Content Analysis Scales,* University of California Press, 1969; (with Cronbach, H. Nanda, and N. Rajaratnam) *The Dependability of Behavioral Measurements: Theory of Generalizability for Scores and Profiles,* Wiley, 1972. Contributor to *Encyclopedia of Educational Research,* Macmillan, 1960, *Annual Review of Psychology 14,* 1963, and to professional journals.

SIDELIGHTS: Goldine Gleser is "fairly" fluent in Spanish. *Avocational interests:* Travel, fishing, water sports, tennis, and needlecraft.

BIOGRAPHICAL/CRITICAL SOURCES: Cincinnati Post, June 6, 1958.

*   *   *

GLOVER, Janice 1919-

PERSONAL: Born April 25, 1919, in Brockton, Mass.; daughter of Theodore (retired director of Barnstable Vocational High School) and Lorna (Chandler) Glover. *Education:* Attended public schools in Massachusetts, and studied harp under Artiss deVolt in Boston. *Politics:* Independent. *Religion:* Unitarian Universalist. *Home:* 50 Stetson St., Hyannis, Mass. 02601.

CAREER: Various library posts in Hyannis, Mass., 1938-48, Bourne, Mass., 1948-51, Bennington, Vt., 1951, Jacksonville, Fla., 1951-54, Columbus, Ohio, 1955; Hyannis Public Library, Hyannis, Mass., part-time assistant at intervals, 1957—. Summer librarian at Bridgewater State College, Hyannis, Mass., 1957-60. Harpist with Jacksonville Symphony Orchestra, Jacksonville, Fla., 1951-54. *Member:* Massachusetts Library Association, New England Library Association, Cape Cod Library Club (past secretary). *Awards, honors:* Prize for short story in *True Experience,* 1958.

WRITINGS: Sense and Sensibility for Single Women, Doubleday, 1963; (editor) *A Cape Cod Sampler: An Anthology by the Twelve O'Clock Scholars,* William S. Sullwold, 1971; *Lighter Side of the Library,* William S. Sullwold, 1974. Contributor to magazines.

WORK IN PROGRESS: A novel not yet titled.

SIDELIGHTS: Janice Glover told *CA:* "Perhaps my deepest need to write springs from an almost greedy desire to live fully, to be more than one person, to know numerous situations, solve various dilemmas. Unless and until reincarnation becomes more of a certainty than it presently appears, multiple selfhood can most nearly be experienced by an actor or author. Lacking the talent for memorizing lines (I had to be content with the role of prompter in our school play), I choose to inhabit many lives as a writer."

*   *   *

GLOVER, Michael 1922-

PERSONAL: Born May 20, 1922, in London, England; son of James Alison (a physician) and Katharine (Merriam) Glover; married Daphne Bowring, September 1, 1945; children: Stephanie. *Education:* St. John's College, Cambridge, M.A., 1947. *Religion:* Church of England. *Address:* Bidcombe, France Lynch near Stroud, Glostershire, England.

CAREER: British Council, London, England, director of educational aids department, 1947—. *Military service:* British Army, Sherwood Foresters, 1941-46; served in North Africa and Italy; taken prisoner of war. Reserve service with London Rifle Brigade Rangers, 1948-63; became major. *Member:* Society for Army Historical Research, Royal United Service Institution.

WRITINGS: Wellington's Peninsular Victories, Macmillan, 1963; *Wellington as Military Commander,* Van Nostrand, 1968; *Britannia Sickens: Sir Arthur Wellesley and the Convention of Cintra,* Leo Cooper, 1970; *Legacy of Glory: The Bonaparte Kingdom of Spain,* Scribner, 1971; *1815,* Cardinal, 1973; *Assemblage of Indian Army Soldiers and Uniforms from the Paintings by the Late Chater Paul Chater,* P. Perpetua, 1973. Author of radio scripts, "Wellington—a Portrait" and "A Damned Serious Business." Contributor of articles to *History Today* and *Journal of the Society of Army Historical Research.*†

*   *   *

GODDARD, Donald 1934-

PERSONAL: Born April 16, 1934, in Cortland, N.Y.; son of Don Gay (a newspaperman) and Adele (Letcher) Goddard. *Education:* Princeton University, A.B., 1956. *Politics:* Independent.

CAREER: American Archives of World Art, New York, N.Y., editor, 1858-65; full-time writer on art, 1965—.

WRITINGS: (Editor) *American Library Compendium and Index of World Art,* American Archives, 1961; *Lecture Notes for the Study of Art History,* American Archives, 1961—; *Tschacbasov,* American Archives, 1964. Contributor to McGraw's *Encyclopedia of World Art,* 1968.

WORK IN PROGRESS: Writing on the American painter, Adolph Gottlieb, and the French painter, Nicolas de Stael.†

*   *   *

GOEDICKE, Victor (Alfred) 1912-

PERSONAL: Born September 25, 1912, in Holt, Wyo.; son of Ernest Paul and Florence (Walker) Goedicke; married Elizabeth Borchard, August 16, 1970. *Education:* University of Michigan, A.B., 1935, M.S., 1936, Ph.D., 1938; Cambridge University, research fellow, 1939-40. *Politics:* Liberal. *Religion:* None. *Home:* 5 Boyd St., Athens, Ohio.

CAREER: Yale University, New Haven, Conn., instructor, 1940-44, assistant professor of astronomy, 1944-46; Ohio University, Athens, associate professor, 1946-53, professor of mathematics and astronomy, 1953—. U.S. Army civilian with Information and Education branch, Florence, Italy, 1945. *Member:* American Astronomical Society, New York Academy of Sciences, Sigma Xi.

WRITINGS: Introduction to the Theory of Statistics, Harper, 1953; (with Carl Denbow) *Foundations of Mathematics,* Harper, 1959; (contributor) *Vocabularies in Special Fields,* Funk. Writer of annual reviews for *Funk & Wagnalls International Yearbook,* and research articles for astronomy journals.

AVOCATIONAL INTERESTS: Sculpture, civil rights.

* * *

GOFF, Frederick Richmond 1916-

PERSONAL: Born April 23, 1916, in Newport, R.I.; son of Francis Shubael (an insurance executive) and Amelia (Seabury) Goff. *Education:* Brown University, A.B., 1937, M.A., 1939. *Politics:* Independent. *Religion:* Unitarian Universalist. *Home:* 5034 Sherrier Pl., N.W., Washington, D.C. 20016. *Office:* Rare Book Division, Library of Congress, Washington, D.C. 20540.

CAREER: Incunabula in American Libraries, assistant to editor of *Second Census,* 1936-40; Library of Congress, Washington, D.C., assistant to curator of Rare Book Division, 1940-41, assistant chief, Rare Book Division, 1941-45, chief, 1945-72, honorary consultant in early printed book, 1972—. Member of visiting committee of Hunt Library, Carnegie Institute of Technology, of committee of management, Annmary Brown Memorial, Brown University, of honorary committee, Gennadius Library, Athens, Greece, and of consultative committee, Centro Italiano de Bibliofilia G. B. Bodoni, Parma, Italy. *Member:* Bibliographical Society of America (secretary, 1961-63; president, 1969-71), American Antiquarian Society, Bibliographical Society (London), Bibliographical Society of the University of Virginia, American Library Association (chairman, rare books section, 1961), Baltimore Bibliophiles, Grolier Club, Phi Beta Kappa, Theta Delta Chi. *Awards, honors:* Litt.D., Brown University, 1965; Sir Thomas More Medal, University of San Francisco, 1974.

WRITINGS—Published by Library of Congress, except as noted: *The Jefferson Bicentennial, 1743-1943: A Catalogue of the Exhibitions in the Library of Congress,* 1943; *A Catalogue of Important Recent Additions to the Lessing J. Rosenwald Collection Selected for Exhibition at the Library of Congress, June, 1947,* 1947.

Fifteenth Century Books in the Library of Congress, 1950; *The Rare Book Division: A Guide to Its Collections and Services,* 1950, revised edition, 1965; (editor and contributor) *Essays Honoring Lawrence C. Wroth,* privately printed, 1951; *The Rosenwald Collection: A Catalogue of Illustrated Books, and Manuscripts, of Books from Celebrated Presses, and of Bindings and Maps, 1150-1950,* 1954; *Catalog of the Jean Hersholt Collection of Hans Christian Andersen,* 1954; (author of preface) *Bishop White Kennett and His Bibliothecae Americanae Primordia,* Pan-American Union, 1959.

(Compiler and editor) *Incunabula in American Libraries, A Third Census,* Bibliographical Society of America, 1964 (with Supplement, 1972). Contributor to *Library of Congress Quarterly Journal,* 1943—; many other articles in *New Colophon, Gutenberg Jahrbuch, Library Trends,* and other journals, and festschrifts.

WORK IN PROGRESS: The Delights of a Rare Book Librarian, for the Boston Public Library.

GOLD, Milton J. 1917-

PERSONAL: Born August 9, 1917; son of Samuel and Esther (Dunkelman) Gold; married Esther Glicker (a statistician), August 25, 1945; children: Bonnie, Deborah, Janice Anne. *Education:* City College (now City College of the City University of New York), New York, N.Y., B.A., 1937; Columbia University, M.A., 1939, Ed.D., 1948. *Home:* 711 Amsterdam Ave., New York, N.Y. 10025. *Office:* Dean of Education, Hunter College, 695 Park Ave., New York, N.Y. 10021.

CAREER: New York (N.Y.) public schools, high school teacher of English, 1938-48; New York University, New York, N.Y., instructor in English, 1946-48; Office of State Superintendent of Public Instruction, Olympia, Wash., director of curriculum, 1948-56; Hunter College of the City University of New York, New York, N.Y., associate professor, 1957-63, professor of education, 1964—, coordinator of campus schools, 1957-63, deputy to director of teacher education, 1962-66, director of teacher education, 1966-68, dean of programs in education, 1968—. Visiting lecturer at Washington State University, summer, 1955, Columbia University, 1957-59, and Miami University (Ohio), summer, 1957. *Military service:* U.S. Army, Antiaircraft Artillery, 1942-46; became first lieutenant. *Member:* Association for Supervision and Curriculum Development, National Education Association, National Council of Teachers of English, American Association of University Professors, Metropolitan Association for Study of the Gifted.

WRITINGS: Working to Learn, Teachers College, Columbia University, 1951; (with Herbert Schueler and Herbert E. Mitzel) *Improvement of Student Teaching,* Hunter College Press, 1962; *Education of the Intellectually Gifted,* C. E. Merrill, 1965. Contributor to education journals. Editor, *Washington State Curriculum Journal,* 1948-56.

WORK IN PROGRESS: Investigations of measures of teacher effectiveness; research in education of the gifted.†

* * *

GOLDEN, Leon 1930-

PERSONAL: Born December 25, 1930, in Jersey City, N.J.; son of Nathan and Regina (Okun) Golden. *Education:* University of Chicago, B.A. (honors), 1950, M.A., 1953, Ph.D., 1958. *Religion:* Jewish. *Home:* 2731 Blair Stone Rd., Tallahassee, Fla. 32301. *Office:* Florida State University, Tallahassee, Fla. 32306.

CAREER: College of William and Mary, Williamsburg, Va., instructor, 1958-61, assistant professor of classics, 1961-65; Florida State University, Tallahassee, associate professor, 1965-1968, professor of classics, 1968—. *Military service:* U.S. Army, Signal Corps, 1953-55. *Member:* American Philological Association, Classical Association of the Middle West and South (president of Southern section, 1972-74), Phi Beta Kappa. *Awards, honors:* University of North Carolina and Duke University Cooperative Program in Humanities, fellow, 1964-65; Society for Religion in Higher Education, fellow, 1971-72.

WRITINGS: In Praise of Prometheus: Humanism and Rationalism in Aeschylean Thought, University of North Carolina Press, 1966; (with O. B. Hardison, Jr.), *Aristotle's Poetics: A Translation and Commentary for Students of Literature,* Prentice-Hall, 1968. Contributor of articles and reviews to classical journals.

WORK IN PROGRESS: Articles on the theory of tragedy.

SIDELIGHTS: Golden speaks German, reads French.

GOLDENTHAL, Allan Benarria 1920-
(Allan Benarria)

PERSONAL: Born June 6, 1920, in New York, N.Y.; son of Leon (a dentist and writer) and Rose (Rosenfeld) Goldenthal; married second wife, Glen Kristi (a fashion designer), June, 1963; children: (first marriage) Joel Andrea; (second marriage) Lisa. *Education:* Attended University of North Carolina, 1938-40; Fordham University, B.S. in Pharmacy, 1943; also received certificates as aerial navigation instructor from New York University, in Chinese language from Cornell University, and marketing from Rutgers University. *Religion:* Jewish.

CAREER: Registered pharmacist in state of New York; Hampton Pharmacy, Inc., New York, N.Y., president, 1946-54; Goldenthal Agency (advertising), New York, N.Y., president, 1954-57; U.S. Tele-Service (television monitoring), New York, N.Y., vice-president, 1958-61; Europe West Corp. (international news), New York, N.Y., president and editor, 1962-65; Interpublic Corp. (communications), New York, N.Y., former managing editor; writer. Onetime aerial navigation instructor for Civil Air Patrol. *Military service:* U.S. Army, Signal Intelligence Service, 1943-46; cryptanalyst in Chinese and Japanese, and later traffic analyst (enemy code); become staff sergeant.

WRITINGS: (Under name Allan Benarria) *Carole Christmas Jones*, Think Center Publishing, 1960; *The Standard Resume Guide*, Argyle Publishing, 1965; *Your Career Retirement Guide*, Regents Publishing, 1967; *Teenage Employment Guide*, Regents Publishing, 1967; *Your Career Selection Guide*, Regents Publishing, 1967; *Handbook of U.S. Markets and Industrial Growth Areas*, Volume I, Regents Publishing, 1969.†

* * *

GOLDIN, Augusta 1906-

PERSONAL: Born October 28, 1906, in New York, N.Y.; daughter of Jack and Fanny (Harris) Reider; married Oscar Goldin, October 25, 1933; children: Kenneth, Valerie Roma. *Education:* Hunter College, B.A., 1927; City College, New York, N.Y., M.S., 1929; Columbia University, Ed.D., 1947. *Home:* 590 Bard Ave., Staten Island, New York, N.Y. *Agent:* Curtis Brown Ltd., 60 East 56th St., New York, N.Y.

CAREER: New York (N.Y.) public schools, elementary teacher, 1928-39, junior high school teacher of geography and science, 1941-42, teacher-in-charge, 1942-44, elementary school principal, 1944-71; St. John's University, Staten Island, N.Y., assistant professor of education, 1971—. Writer for children. *Member:* Administrative Women in Education (vice-president), New York City Elementary Principals Association.

WRITINGS: My Toys, Rand McNally, 1955; *Spider Silk*, Crowell, 1965; *Ducks Don't Get Wet*, Crowell, 1965; *Salt*, Crowell, 1966; *Straight Hair-Curly Hair*, Crowell, 1966; *The Bottom of the Sea*, Crowell, 1967; *The Sunlit Sea*, Crowell, 1968; *Where Does Your Garden Grow*, Crowell, 1969; *How to Release the Learning Power in Children*, Parker, 1970; *Let's Go to Build a Skyscraper*, Putnam, 1974; *The Shape of Water*, Doubleday, 1975. Writer of newspaper column "Helping Your Child" in the *Staten Island Advance*. Contributor of short stories to magazines. Associate editor, *New York Supervisor*.

WORK IN PROGRESS: Grass for a Hungry Planet, for Nelson.

AVOCATIONAL INTERESTS: Gardening, cooking.

GOLDMAN, Albert 1927-

PERSONAL: Born April 15, 1927, in Dormont, Pa.; son of Harry Benjamin and Marie (Levenson) Goldman. *Education:* Attended Carnegie Institute of Technology (now Carnegie-Mellon University), 1944-45, 1946-47; University of Chicago, A.M., 1950; Columbia University, Ph.D., 1961. *Office:* 3 East 82nd St., New York, N.Y. 10028.

CAREER: Columbia University, New York, N.Y., associate professor of English, 1963-72. Moderator and writer of "Wednesday Review," weekly television cultural program, WNDT, New York. Pop music critic, *Life Magazine*, 1970-73. *Military service:* U.S. Navy, 1945-46. *Member:* P.E.N., Author's Guild, Phi Beta Kappa.

WRITINGS: (Editor with Everet Sprinchorn) *Wagner on Music and Drama*, Dutton, 1964; *The Mine and the Mint: Sources for the Writings of Thomas De Quincey*, Southern Illinois University Press, 1965; *Freakshow: The Rocksoulbluesjazzsickjewblackhumorsexpoppsych Gig and Other Scenes from the Counter—Culture*, Atheneum, 1971; *Ladies and Gentlemen—Lenny Bruce!!*, Random House, 1974. Editor-in-chief, *Cultural Affairs*.

WORK IN PROGRESS: Professor Goldman, an account of the author's teaching career for Charterhouse.

* * *

GOLDMAN, Arnold (Melvyn) 1936-

PERSONAL: Born July 19, 1936, in Lynn, Mass.; son of Michael (a business executive) and Eva (Lewis) Goldman; married Dorothy Shelton (a part-time university lecturer), March 22, 1963; children: Nicholas. *Education:* Harvard University, A.B., 1957; University of Manchester, Manchester, England, graduate study, 1957-58; Yale University, M.A., 1959, Ph.D., 1964. *Office:* Department of American Studies, University of Keele, Keele, North Staffordshire, England.

CAREER: Lecturer in English literature at University of Manchester, Manchester, England, 1961-65, Smith College, Northampton, Mass., 1965-66, University of Sussex, Falmer, England, began as lecturer, became reader in English and American studies, 1966-74; University of Keele, Keele, England, professor of American studies, 1975—. Visiting professor, State University of New York, Buffalo, 1973; visiting professor and acting director of the Changing American Culture, Vassar College, 1974-73. *Member:* British Association for American Studies (member of executive committee), Phi Beta Kappa. *Awards, honors:* Fulbright scholar, 1957-58.

WRITINGS: The Joyce Paradox, Northwestern University Press, 1966; *James Joyce*, Humanities Press, 1968; (editor) *Twentieth Century Interpretations of Absalom, Absalom*, Prentice-Hall, 1971; (editor with J. S. Whitley) Charles Dickens, *American Notes for General Circulation*, Penguin, 1972. Contributor to *Stratford Upon Avon Studies* X, XIII, and XV. Also contributor to *Judaism, James Joyce Quarterly, New Literary History, Minnesota Review*, and other periodicals.

WORK IN PROGRESS: Stanislaus James and the Politics of the Family; A Remnant to Escape: The American Writer and Minority Culture; a study of W. B. Yeats and spiritualism; a script for BBC radio.

* * *

GOLDMAN, Michael (Paul) 1936-

PERSONAL: Born May 11, 1936, in New York, N.Y.; son

of Julius David (a dentist) and Rose (Pollens) Goldman; married Eleanor Bergstein (a writer), January 17, 1965. *Education:* Columbia University, A.B., 1956; Clare College, Cambridge, B.A., 1958; Princeton University, M.A., 1960, Ph.D., 1962. *Office:* Department of English, Queens College of the City University of New York, New York, N.Y.

CAREER: Princeton University, Princeton, N.J., instructor in English, 1961-63; Columbia University, New York, N.Y., instructor, 1965-66, assistant professor of English, 1966-72; Queens College of the City University of New York, Flushing, N.Y., associate professor of English, 1972—. *Member:* Phi Beta Kappa. *Awards, honors:* Jennie Tane Prize in Poetry.

WRITINGS: First Poems, Macmillan, 1965; (contributor) Ned O'Gorman, editor, *Prophetic Voices*, Random House, 1969; *At the Edge* (poems), Macmillan, 1969; *Shakespeare and the Energies of Drama*, Princeton University Press, 1972. Poems anthologized in *Of Poetry and Power*, edited by E. A. Gilkes and P. Schwaber, Princeton University Press, 1964. Contributor to *Nation, Massachusetts Review, New Yorker, Kenyon Review*, and *Poetry*. Poetry editor, *Nation*, 1965-68.

BIOGRAPHICAL/CRITICAL SOURCES: Commonweal, September 24, 1965; *Saturday Review*, December 25, 1965.†

*   *   *

GOLDSTEIN, David 1933-

PERSONAL: Born January 31, 1933, in London, England; son of Nathan (a textile manager) and Sarah (Malwartz) Goldstein; married Berenice Phillips, August 26, 1956; children: Joshua, Daniel, Benjamin. *Education:* St. Edmund Hall, Oxford, B.A. (honors in English), 1956; University College, University of London, B.A. (honors in Hebrew), 1959, M.A., 1962, Ph.D., 1967. *Home:* 56 Creighton Ave., London N.10, England. *Office:* Liberal Jewish Synagogue, 28 St. John's Wood Rd., London N.W. 8, England.

CAREER: South London Liberal Jewish Synagogue, London, England, rabbi, 1959-64; Liberal Jewish Synagogue, London, England, associate rabbi, 1964—; Leo Baeck College, London, lecturer, 1966—. *Member:* Jewish Historical Society, Society for Jewish Study, Eurasia Society.

WRITINGS: (Editor and translator) *Hebrew Poems from Spain*, Routledge & Kegan Paul, 1965, Schocken, 1966; (editor and translator) *The Jewish Poets of Spain*, Penguin, 1971; (contributor) E. G. Parrinder, editor, *Man and His Gods: Encyclopedia of the World's Religions*, Hamlyn, 1971; (contributor) H. A. Guy, editor, *Our Religions*, Dent, 1973.

WORK IN PROGRESS: Editing *Commentary to the Pentateuch*, by Immanuel ben Solomon of Rome; translating *Anthology of the Zohar*, and *Biblical Hebrew Poetry*.

SIDELIGHTS: Goldstein is competent in French, Hebrew, Italian, classical Latin and Greek. *Avocational interests:* Cricket, music, reading poetry, philately.

*   *   *

GOLDSTEIN, Joseph 1923-

PERSONAL: Born May 7, 1923, in Springfield, Mass.; son of Nathan E. and Anna (Ginsberg) Goldstein; married Sonja Lambek (a lawyer), August 3, 1947; children: Joshua, Anne, Jeremiah, Daniel. *Education:* Dartmouth College,

A.B., 1943; London School of Economics and Political Science, University of London, Ph.D., 1950; Yale University, LL.B., 1952. *Home:* Overhill Rd., Woodbridge, Conn.

CAREER: U.S. Court of Appeals, Washington, D.C., law clerk, 1952-53; Stanford University, Stanford, Calif., acting assistant professor of law, 1954-56; Yale University, New Haven, Conn., associate professor, 1956-59, professor of law, 1959—. Harvard University, Russell Sage resident and visiting scholar, 1955-56. Consultant to committee on law and psychiatry, Group for the Advancement of Psychiatry, 1961-64, and to U.S. Office of Economic Opportunity, 1965—. Executive secretary and research director of Connecticut Governor's Prison Study Committee, 1956-57; member of U.S. Attorney General's Committee on Poverty and Administration of Criminal Justice, 1962-63, and of Consultative Panel on Mental Health, Southern Regional Education Board, 1962; consultant to New Haven (Conn.) Legal Assistance Association, 1964—; member of board of directors, Vera Institute of Justice. *Military service:* U.S. Army, 1943-46; became second lieutenant. *Member:* Virginia Bar Association, New Haven County Bar Association, American Civil Liberties Union, Elizabethan Club. *Awards, honors:* M.A. from Yale University, 1959.

WRITINGS: The Government of a British Trade Union, Free Press of Glencoe, 1952, 2nd edition, 1953; (with Richard C. Donnelly and Richard D. Schwartz) *Criminal Law*, Free Press of Glencoe, 1962; (with Jay Katz) *The Family and the Law*, Free Press of Glencoe, 1965; (with Jay Katz and Alan M. Dershowitz) *Psychoanalysis, Psychiatry and Law*, Free Press of Glencoe, 1967; (with A. S. Goldstein) *Crime Law and Society*, Free Press of New York, 1971; (with Anna Freud and A. J. Solnit) *Beyond the Best Interests of the Child*, Free Press of New York, 1973; (with A. Dershowitz and Richard D. Schwartz) *Criminal Law Theory and Process*, Free Press of New York, 1974. Contributor to legal journals.

*   *   *

GOLDSTON, Robert Conroy 1927-
(Robert Conroy, James Stark)

PERSONAL: Born July 9, 1927, in New York, N.Y.; son of Philip Henry (a salesman) and Josephine (Conroy) Goldston; married Marguerite Garvey, January 3, 1956; children: Rebecca, Gabrielle, Sarah, Francesca, Maximilian, Theresa. *Education:* Attended Columbia University, 1946-53. *Politics:* Unaffiliated socialist. *Religion:* None. *Home and office:* Lista de Correos, Santa Eulalia del Rio, Ibiza, Balearic Islands, Spain. *Agent:* Collins-Knowlton-Wing, Inc., 60 East 56th St., New York, N.Y. 10022.

CAREER: Professional writer, living abroad most of the time since 1953—ten years in Spain, and two in France and England. *Military service:* U.S. Army, 1945-46; became sergeant. *Awards, honors:* Guggenheim fellowship in fiction, 1957-58.

WRITINGS—Juvenile; all published by Bobbs-Merrill, except as indicated: (Adapter) *Tales of the Alhambra*, 1962; *The Legend of the Cid*, 1963; (adapter with wife, Marguerite Goldston) *The Song of Roland*, 1965; *The Russian Revolution*, 1966; *The Civil War in Spain*, 1966; *The Life and Death of Nazi Germany*, 1967; *Spain*, Macmillan, 1967; *The Rise of Red China*, 1967; *The Great Depression: The United States in the Thirties*, 1968; (under pseudonym Robert Conroy) *The Battle of Manila Bay: The Spanish-American War in the Philippines*, Macmillan, 1968; (under pseudonym Robert Conroy) *The Battle of Bataan: Ameri-*

ca's Greatest Defeat, Macmillan, 1969; *Barcelona: The Civic Stage*, Macmillan, 1969; *London: The Civic Spirit*, Macmillan, 1969; *The Battles of the Constitution: Old Ironsides and the Freedom of the Seas*, Macmillan, 1969.

New York: Civic Exploitation, Macmillan, 1970; *Suburbia: Civic Denial*, Macmillan, 1970; *The Cuban Revolution*, 1970; *The Coming of the Cold War*, Macmillan, 1970; *The Fall of the Winter Palace*, F. Watts, 1971; *The Long March*, F. Watts, 1971; *Communism: A Narrative History*, Fawcett, 1972; *The Vietnamese Revolution*, 1972; *The Coming of the Civil War*, Macmillan, 1972; *The Siege of the Alcazar*, F. Watts, 1972; *Pearl Harbor!*, F. Watts, 1972; *The Death of Gandhi*, F. Watts, 1973; *The American Nightmare: Senator Joseph R. McCarthy and the Politics of Hate*, 1973.

Novels: *The Eighth Day*, Rinehart, 1956; *The Catafalque*, Rinehart, 1958; *The Shore Dimly Seen*, Random House, 1963; *The Last of Lazarus*, Random House, 1966.

Other: (Under pseudonym James Stark) *The Greek Virgin*, Avon, 1959; *Satan's Disciples*, Ballantine, 1962; *The Soviets: A Pictorial History of Communist Russia*, Bantam, 1967; *The Negro Revolution*, Macmillan, 1968.

Author of television documentary films, "Sunday in Barcelona," 1958, "The Bull Fight," 1960, "Bjorn's Inferno," 1964, and "Running Away Backwards," 1965, for Canadian Broadcasting Corp.

SIDELIGHTS: Goldston observes that the "shocking and growing mindlessness and desperation of American society is a vital, if depressing interest." *Avocational interests:* Bird watching, hiking, mountain climbing.

BIOGRAPHICAL/CRITICAL SOURCES: Upptak (Stockholm magazine), spring, 1958.†

*   *   *

GOMBERG, Adeline Wishengrad 1915-

PERSONAL: Born May 28, 1915, in New York, N.Y.; daughter of Morris Charles and Pauline (Adelson) Wishengrad; married William Gomberg (a professor of industry), September 24, 1939; children: David (deceased), Paula Abigail (Mrs. Christopher Ian Higgins). *Education:* Brooklyn College (now of the City University of New York), B.A., 1938; Columbia University, M.A., 1939, Ed.D., 1960. *Home:* 392 Montgomery Ave., Wynnewood, Pa. 19096.

CAREER: Beaver College, Glenside, Pa., associate professor, 1961-70, professor of education, 1970—, acting head of department of education, 1961—, director of reading clinic, 1961—. University of Pennsylvania, Graduate School of Education, visiting lecturer, 1965—. Citizens Committee on Public Education in Philadelphia, director of reading for Summer Lighthouse Camp, 1964-65; All India Fine Arts Society, New Delhi, consultant, 1966. *Member:* National Education Association, International Reading Association (Pennsylvania state chairman, 1972-74), National Association for the Education of Young Children, Delaware Valley Reading Association, Kappa Delta Phi. *Awards, honors:* Lindbach Award for distinguished teaching, 1966.

WRITINGS: (Contributor) *Blue-Collar World*, Prentice-Hall, 1964; *A "Reading" Activities Manual to Aid the Disadvantaged*, Interstate, 1966; *Manual of Basic Reading Skills: A Guide for Teachers In Helping to Prevent Reading Problems*, Delaware Valley Reading Association, 1968, 2nd edition, 1969. Also writer of the Gomberg Diagnostic and Comprehension Reading Tests.

GOMBERG, William 1911-

PERSONAL: Born September 6, 1911, in Brooklyn, N.Y.; son of Alexander and Marie (Shuloff) Gomberg; married Adeline Wishengrad (a lecturer in education), September 24, 1939; children: Paula. *Education:* City College (now of the City University of New York), B.S., 1933; New York University, M.S., 1941; Columbia University, Ph.D., 1947. *Home:* 392 Montgomery Ave., Wynnewood, Pa. 19096. *Office:* Wharton School of Finance and Commerce, University of Pennsylvania, Philadelphia, Pa. 19104.

CAREER: Registered professional engineer. International Ladies Garment Workers' Union, New York, N.Y., collective bargaining representative, 1934-41, director of management engineering department, 1941-56; Columbia University, New York, N.Y., adjunct professor of engineering, 1941-56; Washington University, St. Louis, Mo., professor of industrial engineering, 1956-57; Columbia University, Graduate School of Business Administration, visiting professor, 1958-59; University of Pennsylvania, Wharton School of Finance and Commerce, Philadelphia, professor of industry, 1959—. Summer visiting professor at University of Wisconsin, 1941-56, University of California, 1957-58, Stanford University, 1959-65; visiting lecturer at University of Wisconsin Industrial Management Institute, 1954-57. Consultant, 1950-60, to U.S. government agencies and departments, labor unions, industry, and to National Academy of Sciences. Arbitrator in steel, automobile, electrical goods, textile, and transportation industries, 1949—. Member of board of directors, Aspen Institute for Humanistic Study.

MEMBER: American Arbitration Association, American Society of Mechanical Engineers, American Institute of Industrial Engineers, Institute of Mathematical Statistics, National Association of Cost Accountants, National Academy of Arbitrators, Sigma Xi, Tau Beta Pi, Alpha Pi Mu.

WRITINGS: A Labor Union Manual on Job Evaluation, Roosevelt College Press, 1947; *A Trade Union Analysis of Time Study*, Science Research Associates, for Industrial Relations Center, University of Chicago, 1948, 2nd edition, Prentice-Hall, 1955; (with Joy Leland) *We Want to Be Shown*, U.S. Bureau of Indian Affairs, 1962; (with Arthur Shostak) *Blue Collar World*, Prentice-Hall, 1964; (with Arthur Shostak) *New Perspectives on Poverty*, Prentice-Hall, 1965; *Entrepreneurial Lessons from the Hard Core Unemployed*, University of Pennsylvania Press.

Contributor: *New York University First Annual Conference on Labor*, edited by E. Stein, Bender, 1948; *Small Plant Management*, edited by E. H. Hempel, McGraw, 1950; *The House of Labor*, edited by J. B. S. Hardman and M. F. Neufeld, Prentice-Hall, 1951; *Handbook of Industrial Engineering and Management*, edited by Grant and Ireson, Prentice-Hall, 1955; *Critical Issues in Labor Arbitration*, edited by Jean McKelvy, Bureau of National Affairs, 1957; *Frontiers of Managerial Psychology*, edited by Fisk, Harper, 1964; *Expanding American Markets* (Freedom Forum lectures), 1964. Contributor of articles and reviews to *Nation, Current*, and professional journals in fields of labor management, applied psychology, industrial engineering, and business.

WORK IN PROGRESS: Treatise on Managerial Theory, for Irwin; *Uncertain Utopians*, with Arthur Shostak, for Knopf; *Problems in Escalation of Conflict*, for Management Science Center, University of Pennsylvania.

GOOD, Edwin M(arshall) 1928-

PERSONAL: Born April 23, 1928, in Bibia, Cameroun, West Africa; son of Albert Irwin (a missionary) and Mary (Middlemiss) Good; married Janice Sundquist, July 26, 1952; children: Brian Christopher, Lawrence Marshall, John Alexander. *Education:* Westminster College, New Wilmington, Pa., B.A., 1949; Princeton Theological Seminary, 1949-51; attended Union Theological Seminary, New York, N.Y., M.Div., 1953; Columbia University, Ph.D., 1958; Stanford University, M.A., 1974. *Politics:* Democratic. *Home:* 827 Sonoma Ter., Stanford, Calif. 94305. *Office:* Stanford University, Stanford, Calif. 94305.

CAREER: Princeton University, Princeton, N.J., part-time instructor in Old Testament, 1954-55; Union Theological Seminary, New York, N.Y., instructor in Old Testament, 1955-56; Stanford University, Stanford, Calif., assistant professor of religion and Hebrew, 1956-61, associate professor, 1970, professor of religious studies, 1970—. *Member:* Society for Religion in Higher Education, Society of Biblical Literature, Uppsala Exegetical Society (Sweden), American Academy of Religion, American Association of University Professors.

WRITINGS: You Shall Be My People: Books of Covenant and Law, Westminster, 1959; *Irony in the Old Testament*, Westminster, 1965. Editor "Westminster Guides to the Bible" series. Contributor to *Interpreter's Dictionary of the Bible, Annotated New English Bible*, and to religion and education journals.

WORK IN PROGRESS: General research on Old Testament literary forms and usages.

SIDELIGHTS: Good is competent in German and Swedish, apart from languages professionally necessary. *Avocational interests:* Music, especially piano and recorder.

* * *

GOODE, Richard (Benjamin) 1916-

PERSONAL: Surname is pronounced Good; born July 31, 1916, in Fort Worth, Tex.; son of Flavius M. and Laura Nell (Carson) Goode; married Liesel Gottscho, June 23, 1943. *Education:* Baylor University, A.B., 1937; University of Kentucky, M.A., 1939; University of Wisconsin, Ph.D., 1947. *Office:* International Monetary Fund, Washington, D.C. 20431.

CAREER: U.S. Bureau of the Budget, Washington, D.C., economist, 1941-45; U.S. Treasury Department, Washington, D.C., economist, 1945-47; University of Chicago, Chicago, Ill., assistant professor of economics, 1947-51; International Monetary Fund, Washington, D.C., assistant chief, later chief of Finance Division, 1951-59; Brookings Institution, Washington, D.C., senior staff, 1959-65; International Monetary Fund, director of Fiscal Affairs Department, 1965—. Consultant to World Bank, 1964. *Member:* American Economic Association, American Finance Association (board of directors, 1962-63), National Tax Association (executive committee, 1951-54), Royal Economic Society (England), Society for International Development.

WRITINGS: The Corporation Income Tax, Wiley, 1951; *The Individual Income Tax*, Brookings, 1964. Contributor to professional journals. Editor, *National Tax Journal*, 1948-51; member of editorial board, American Economic Association, 1955-57.

WORK IN PROGRESS: Revising *The Individual Income Tax*.

GOODMAN, David Michael 1936-

PERSONAL: Born October 13, 1936, in Cambridge, Mass.; son of Herman (owner and president of janitorial supply company) and Shirley (Kneller) Goodman. *Education:* University of Arizona, B.A., 1958, M.A., 1963; Texas Christian University, Ph.D., 1968. *Politics:* Democrat. *Home:* 302 Nelson Ave., Saratoga, N.Y. *Office:* Department of History, State University of New York, Albany, New York.

CAREER: Junior high and high school teacher of English and history in Sunland, Calif., 1960-61, Seattle, Wash., 1961-65. Arizona Historical Foundation, research fellow, 1964-66; State University of New York, Albany, professor of history, 1967—. *Member:* Western History Association, Fort Worth Corral of the Westerners, Phi Alpha Theta.

WRITINGS: A Western Panorama, 1849-1875: The Travels, Writings, and Influence of J. Ross Browne, Arthur Clark, 1966; *Arizona Odyssey: Bibliographic Adventures in 19th Century Magazines*, Arizona Historical Foundation, 1969.

WORK IN PROGRESS: A history of the Apache exiles (1886-1913); an annotated bibliography of magazine literature concerning Arizona written before 1900, for Arizona Historical Foundation, 1967.

SIDELIGHTS: Goodman is competent in French and Spanish.

BIOGRAPHICAL/CRITICAL SOURCES: Fort Worth Press, May 8, 1966; *Branding Iron* (Los Angeles Corral of the Westerners), June 1966; *Arizona Daily Star*, July 31, 1966, pages B4 and C8.

* * *

GOODY, Joan Edelman 1935-

PERSONAL: Born December 1, 1935, in New York, N.Y.; daughter of Beril and Sylvia (Feldman) Edelman; married Marvin E. Goody (an architect), December 18, 1960. *Education:* Attended University of Paris, 1954-55; Cornell University, B.A., 1956; Harvard University, M.Arch., 1960. *Religion:* Jewish. *Office:* 136 Boylston St., Boston, Mass.

CAREER: Marvin E. Goody & John M. Clancy Architects, Inc., Boston, Mass., architect, 1961—; Boston Architectural Center, Boston, Mass., teacher, 1961-66; Harvard University, Graduate School of Design, Cambridge, Mass., assistant professor, 1973—.

WRITINGS: New Architecture in Boston, M.I.T. Press, 1965.

* * *

GORDON, Donald Craigie 1911-

PERSONAL: Born August 18, 1911, in Melbourne, Australia; son of C. M. (a clergyman) and Jean (Craigie) Gordon; married Norma Slatoff (a librarian), June 18, 1941; children: Ellen, Victoria. *Education:* College of William and Mary, B.A., 1934; Columbia University, M.A., 1938, Ph.D., 1947. *Home:* 4201 Woodberry St., University Park, Hyattsville, Md. *Office:* Department of History, University of Maryland, College Park, Md.

CAREER: College of William and Mary, Norfolk Division, Norfolk, Va., 1938-45, began as instructor, became assistant professor; University of Maryland, College Park, assistant professor, 1946-53, associate professor, 1953-62, professor of history, 1962—. *Member:* American Historical

Association, American Association of University Professors, Phi Beta Kappa. *Awards, honors:* Fulbright senior research scholar in Australia, 1957-58; American Philosophical Society grant, 1960, 1968.

WRITINGS: The Australian Frontier in New Guinea: 1877-1885, Columbia University Press, 1951; (contributor) *Some Modern Historians of Britain*, Dryden Press, 1951; (editor with Gewehr, Sparks, and Stromberg, and contributor) *American Civilization: A History of the U.S.*, McGraw, 1957, 2nd edition (under title *The United States: History of a Democracy*), 1960; *The Dominion Partnership in Imperial Defense, 1870-1914*, Johns Hopkins Press, 1965; *The Moment of Power: Britain's Imperial Epoch*, Prentice-Hall, 1970; (contributor) Robin Higham, editor, *A Guide to the Sources of British Military History*, University of California Press, 1971. Contributor of articles and reviews to professional journals; also contributor of reviews to *Baltimore Sunday Sun* and *Washington Post*.

WORK IN PROGRESS: A study of Winston Churchill's attitudes toward, and policies on Britain's Imperial role.

SIDELIGHTS: Gordon has spent three sabbatical leaves in England for research at British Museum and Public Record Office.

* * *

GORDON, Edwin 1927-

PERSONAL: Born September 14, 1927, in Stamford, Conn.; son of Martin and Carrie (Stamer) Gordon; married Frances Slack, April 18, 1949; children: Jaimeson Beth, Pamela Anne, Carrie Alison. *Education:* Eastman School of Music, B.M., 1952, M.M., 1953; Ohio University M.Ed., 1954; University of Iowa, Ph.D., 1958. *Home:* 25 Brookfield Dr., Iowa City, Iowa 52240.

CAREER: University of Iowa, Iowa City, associate professor of music education, 1958—. *Military service:* U.S. Army, 1945-47; became sergeant.

WRITINGS: Musical Aptitude Profile, Houghton, 1965; *A Three-Year Longitudinal Predictive Validity Study of the Musical Aptitude Profile*, University of Iowa Press, 1967; *Iowa Tests of Musical Literacy Manual*, Bureau of Educational Research and Service, University of Iowa, 1970; (editor) *Experimental Research in the Psychology of Music*, University of Iowa Press, Volume VI, 1970, Volume VII, 1971, Volume VIII, 1972, Volume IX, 1974; *The Psychology of Music Teaching*, Prentice-Hall, 1971. Also author of *How Children Learn When They Learn Music*, 1968.†

* * *

GORDON, Noah 1926-

PERSONAL: Born November 11, 1926, in Worcester, Mass.; son of Robert and Rose (Melnikoff) Gordon; married Claire Lorraine Seay, August 25, 1951; children: Lise Ann, Jamie Beth, Michael Seay. *Education:* Boston University, B.Sc. (journalism), 1950, M.A., 1951. *Politics:* Democrat. *Religion:* Jewish. *Home:* 23 Savoy Rd., Framingham, Mass. 01701. *Agent:* Particia Schartle, McIntosh & Otis, Inc., 18 East 41st St., New York, N.Y. 10017. *Office:* 39 Cochituate Rd., Framingham, Mass. 01701.

CAREER: Avon Book, Inc., New York, N.Y., assistant editor, 1951-53; Magazine Management, Inc., New York, N.Y., associate editor, later managing editor, 1953-56; *Worcester Telegram*, Worcester, Mass., reporter, 1957-59; *Boston Herald*, Boston, Mass., science editor, 1959-63;

Opinion Publications, Inc., Framingham, Mass., publisher of *Psychiatric Opinion*, 1964—, editor, 1964-66, 1968—, president and later director of company, 1966—. Writer, 1964—. Member of national advisory board, Center for Psychological Studies on Death, Dying and Lethal Behavior, 1970; member of board of directors, Framingham Writers Workshop; vice-chairman of board of trustees, Framingham Public Libraries. *Military service:* U.S. Army, 1945-46. *Member:* National Association of Science Writers, Authors Guild, Authors League of America, American Association for the Advancement of Science, B'nai B'rith, Massachusetts Library Trustees Association, Sigma Delta Chi, Sudbury River Tennis Club. *Awards, honors:* Distinguished Achievement Award, Boston University School of Public Communication, 1966.

WRITINGS: The Rabbi (novel), McGraw, 1965; *The Death Committee* (novel), McGraw, 1969. Contributor of fiction and articles to *Saturday Evening Post, Redbook, Reporter, Ladies' Home Journal, Saturday Review*, and other magazines. Member of editorial board, *Omega*, 1970.

WORK IN PROGRESS: A long novel.

SIDELIGHTS: Gordon expects to continue working in scientific journalism (along with work on other novels) because he believes it is a vitally important field.†

* * *

GORDON, Theodore J. 1930-

PERSONAL: Born June 30, 1930, in New York, N.Y.; son of Robert L. Gordon; married Ann Jason; children: Katherine, Tom, Lisa, Michael. *Education:* Louisiana State University, B.S.A.E., 1950; Georgia Institute of Technology, M.S.A.E., 1951. *Residence:* Glastonbury, Conn. *Office:* The Futures Group, Glastonbury, Conn.

CAREER: Douglas Aircraft Co., Huntington Beach, Calif., director of Advanced Saturn Project, 1964-68; Institute for the Future, Menlo Park, Calif., vice-president, 1968-71; The Futures Group, Glastonbury, Conn., president, 1971—. Consultant. Regent's Professor, University of California, Los Angeles, 1968; lecturer, Columbia University. *Member:* World Future Society.

WRITINGS: (With J. Scheer) *First into Outer Space*, St. Martin's, 1958; *The Future*, St. Martin's, 1965; (contributor) O. Helmer, *Social Technology*, Basic Books, 1966; *Ideas in Conflict*, St. Martin's, 1966; (contributor) Albert H. Teich, editor, *Technology and Man's Future*, St. Martin's, 1972; (contributor) Alvin Toffler, editor, *The Futurists*, Random House, 1972; (with H. Harrison) *Ahead of Time*, Doubleday, 1972; (contributor) Walter A. Hahn and Kenneth F. Gordon, editors, *Assessing the Future and Policy Planning*, Gordon & Breach, 1973.

BIOGRAPHICAL/CRITICAL SOURCES: Life, September 14, 1962; L. Silver, *Profiles in Success*, Fountainhead, 1965.

* * *

GORDON, Wendell (Chaffee) 1916-

PERSONAL: Born October 9, 1916, in Birmingham, Ala.; son of Dugald (a geologist) and Gertrude (Mills) Gordon. *Education:* Rice Institute (now Rice University), B.A., 1937; American University, M.A., 1938; New York University, Ph.D., 1940; graduate study at National University of Mexico, 1939; postdoctoral study at University of Havana, 1946, Sorbonne, University of Paris, 1952. *Office:* Department of Economics, University of Texas, Austin, Tex. 78712.

CAREER: University of Texas, Austin, 1940—, began as instructor, professor of economics, 1958—. *Military service:* U.S. Army, 1942-45.

WRITINGS: Expropriation of Foreign-Owned Property in Mexico, American Council on Public Affairs, 1941; *International Trade: Goods, People and Ideas*, Knopf, 1958; *Political Economy of Latin America*, Columbia University Press, 1965.

* * *

GOSSMAN, Lionel 1929-

PERSONAL: Born May 31, 1929, in Glasgow, Scotland; son of Norman and Sarah (Gold) Gossman; married Eva Reinitz (a professor of philosophy), March 7, 1963; children: Janice Naomi. *Education:* University of Glasgow, M.A., 1951; University of Paris, Diplome d'Etudes superieures, 1952; St. Antony's College, Oxford, D.Phil., 1957. *Home:* 34 Over-ridge Ct., Baltimore, Md. 21210. *Office:* Johns Hopkins University, Baltimore, Md. 21218.

CAREER: University of Glasgow, Glasgow, Scotland, assistant lecturer in French, 1957-58; Johns Hopkins University, Baltimore, Md., assistant professor, 1958-62, associate professor, 1962-66, professor of French, 1966—. *Military service:* Royal Navy, 1952-54. *Awards, honors:* American Council of Learned Societies, study fellow, 1969-70.

WRITINGS: (Contributor) *Cabeen Bibliography of French Literature: Seventeenth Century*, edited by J. Brody and N. Edelman, Syracuse University Press, 1961; *Men and Masks: A Study of Moliere*, Johns Hopkins Press, 1963; *Medievalism and the Ideologies of the Enlightenment*, Johns Hopkins Press, 1968; *French Society and Culture: Background for Eighteenth Century Literature*, Prentice-Hall, 1972. Contributor to scholarly journals.

WORK IN PROGRESS: A study of liberal ideologies and the practice of historiography in early 19th century France.

* * *

GOTTLIEB, Lois Davidson 1926-

PERSONAL: Born November 13, 1926, in San Francisco, Calif.; daughter of George A. (an executive) and Manya (Sadicoff) Davidson; married Robert S. Gottlieb (a musician); children: Karen, Mark. *Education:* Stanford University, B.A., 1947; apprenticed to Frank Lloyd Wright (Taliesin fellowship), 1948-49; Harvard University, graduate study in deisgn, 1949-50. *Home:* 4342 Sunset Beach Dr., N.W., Olympia, Wash. 98502.

CAREER: Self-employed designer in Olympia, Wash. Lecturer on design at College of Holy Names, Oakland, Calif., 1962, Alameda State College (now California State University, Hayward), 1963, University of California, Riverside, 1965-73, Olympia Vocational Technical Institute, 1974-75. *Awards, honors:* Fulbright grant to India, 1967-68.

WRITINGS: Environment and Design in Housing, Macmillan, 1965.

* * *

GOULDEN, Joseph C. (Jr.) 1934-

PERSONAL: Surname is pronounced Golden; born May 23, 1934, in Marshall, Tex.; son of Joseph C. (a book dealer) and Lecta Mahon (Everett) Goulden; married Jody Corns, July 15, 1961; children: Joseph III, James Craig. *Education:* Attended University of Texas, 1952-56. *Residence:* Willingboro, N.J. *Agent:* Carl Brandt, Brandt &

Brandt, 101 Park Ave., New York, N.Y. 10017. *Office: Philadelphia Inquirer*, 400 North Broad St., Philadelphia, Pa.

CAREER: Molybdenum miner in Colorado, 1953; reporter for newspapers in Marshall, Tex., 1956, Dallas, Tex., 1958-61, and *Philadelphia Inquirer*, Philadelphia, Pa., beginning, 1961. Free-lance writer. Other jobs have included fry cook, male nurse, press agent for diaper service association, and stringer for Time-Life, Inc. *Military service:* U.S. Army, 1956-58. *Awards, honors:* Reporting awards from State Bar of Texas, 1960, Pennsylvania and Philadelphia Press Associations, 1964.

WRITINGS: The Curtis Caper, Putnam, 1965; *Monopoly*, Putnam, 1968; *Truth Is the First Casualty: The Gulf of Tonkin Affair, Illusion and Reality*, Rand McNally, 1969; *The Money Givers*, Random House, 1971; *Meany*, Atheneum, 1972; *The Super-Lawyers: The Small and Powerful World of the Great Washington Law Firms*, Weybright, 1972; *The Benchwarmers: The Small and Powerful World of the Great Federal Judges*, Weybright, 1974. Contributor to *Texas Observer*.

SIDELIGHTS: Goulden's first book, *The Curtis Caper*, was an outgrowth of a series of articles that Goulden did for the *Philadelphia Inquirer* on the *Saturday Evening Post* and other facets of the Curtis publishing empire. His third book, *Truth Is the First Casualty*, was described by Richard J. Walton as being "of the first importance.... Goulden has made a real contribution. He has given us vital facts about one of the crucial events, or nonevents, in American history. Future historians will be grateful."†

* * *

GOUREVITCH, Doris-Jeanne

PERSONAL: Surname is pronounced Goo-*ray*-vitch; born in Philadelphia, Pa.; daughter of Samuel and Ida Alice (Sperling) Zack; married Jacques Gourevitch (now an executive), March 29, 1956. *Education:* Hunter College, B.A. and M.A.; Columbia University, Ph.D., 1951. *Home:* 440 Riverside Dr., New York, N.Y. 10027.

CAREER: Instructor at Oberlin College, Oberlin, Ohio, 1944-45, and Columbia University, New York, N.Y., 1946-53; Chatham College, Pittsburgh, Pa., assistant professor of French and chairman of department of modern languages, 1953-54; Juilliard School of Music, Academic College, New York, N.Y., associate professor of French, 1954-59; Rutgers, The State University, Douglass College, New Brunswick, N.Y., professor of French, 1959-64; City University of New York, Borough of Manhattan Community College, New York, N.Y., professor of French and associate dean of faculty, 1964—. *Member:* American Association of Teachers of French (former vice-president; member of board of directors), Modern Language Association of America, American Association of University Professors, French Graduate Union of Columbia University. *Awards, honors:* Rutgers research grant, 1963.

WRITINGS: (With Eve Maria Stadler) *Premiers Textes Litteraires*, Blaisdell/Ginn, 1966, revised edition, 1974; (translator) *Paul Verlaine: Selected Verse*, Blaisdell, 1970. Contributor to professional periodicals. Former associate editor, *French Review*.

WORK IN PROGRESS: Verlaine: A Critical Study, Columbia University Press.

GOWEN, James A(nthony) 1928-

PERSONAL: Born October 24, 1928, in Chuquicamata, Chile; son of Joseph Lofton (an oil company executive) and Mary (Dotson) Gowen; married Marianne Porter, July 2, 1960; children: Paul Anthony, Anne Marie, Maureen Teresa, Matthew Francis. *Education:* University of San Francisco, B.A., 1956; Stanford University, Ph.D., 1966. *Politics:* Liberal. *Office:* Department of English, University of Kansas, Lawrence, Kan. 66045.

CAREER: University of Kansas, Lawrence, assistant professor, 1964-68, as sociate professor of English, 1968—. McGraw-Hill Book Co., Inc., consulting editor. *Member:* Modern Language Association of America, National Council of Teachers of English, Conference on College Composition and Communication, American Association of University Professors.

WRITINGS: English Review Manual, McGraw, 1965; *Progress in Writing*, McGraw, 1973.

* * *

GRAHAM, Angus (Charles) 1919-

PERSONAL: Born July 8, 1919, in Penarth, Wales; son of Charles Harold (a rubber planter) and Mabelle (Booker) Graham; married Der Pao Chang (an importer of oriental jewelry), March 17, 1955; children: Dawn Jee-Ying. *Education:* Corpus Christi College, Oxford, B.A., 1940, M.A., 1958; School of Oriental and African Studies, London, B.A. (honors), 1949, Ph.D., 1953. *Politics:* Labour. *Religion:* Atheist. *Home:* Hilbre, Alan Dr., Barnet, Hertfordshire, England. *Office:* Far East Department, School of Oriental and African Studies, University of London, London, England.

CAREER: School of Oriental and African Studies, University of London, London, England, lecturer in classical Chinese, 1950-66, reader in classical Chinese, 1966-71, professor of classical Chinese, 1971—. Visiting fellow, Hongkong University, 1954-55; Senior Fellow, Society of Humanities, Cornell University, 1972-73. Visiting professor of Chinese, Yale University, 1966-67, University of Michigan, 1970. *Military service:* Royal Air Force, 1940-46; served in Siam and Malaya, 1945-46; became flying officer.

WRITINGS: Two Chinese Philosophers: Ch'eng Ming-Tao and Ch'eng Yi-Ch'uan, Lund, Humphries, 1958; (translator) *The Book of Lieh-Tzu*, J. Murray, 1960; *The Problem of Value*, Hutchinson, 1961; (translator, editor, and author of introduction) *Poems of the Late T'ang*, Penguin, 1965; *The Sun Beneath the Coral* (poems), Doldrum Press, 1969. Contributor to *Anthology of Chinese Literature, Concise Encyclopedia of Living Faiths, Foundations of Language*, and to Orientalist journals. Consulting editor, *Foundations of Language*, 1965—.

WORK IN PROGRESS: Research in philosophy and in Chinese studies.

SIDELIGHTS: Graham has traveled on study leaves to Hong Kong and Japan, 1954-55, 1960-61. He reads Greek, Latin, French, German, Arabic, Chinese, and Japanese, with varying degrees of proficiency.†

* * *

GRAHAM, (Maude Fitzgerald) Susan 1912-
(Susan)

PERSONAL: Born November 12, 1912, in Cromwell, New Zealand; daughter of Guy Norman and Maude Emily (Cox) Morris; married John Campbell Graham (a journalist), December 4, 1935; children: Alan Campbell. *Education:* University of Auckland, M.A. (first class honors) and Diploma of Journalism, 1933. *Religion:* Christian. *Home:* 15 Cotter Ave., Remuera, Auckland, New Zealand.

CAREER: Journalist, writing in New Zealand for *New Zealand Herald* and *Weekly News*, and in London, England, for New Zealand publications; covered British royal tours in United States and New Zealand; weekly syndicated columnist, under by-line of Susan, for four New Zealand morning newspapers, and monthly columnist for *Family Doctor* and *Economist and Taxpayer*, both New Zealand. Lecturer. *Member:* P.E.N., Federation of University Women, English-Speaking Union, Travel Club, Ruapehu Ski Club.

WRITINGS: Susan's Book, Wilson & Horton, 1956; *Susan on Saturday*, A. H. & A. W. Reed, 1959; *Susan in Springtime* (autobiography), A. H. & A. W. Reed, 1960; *This Land I Love*, Wellington Books, 1962; *The Tender Traveller*, A. H. & A. W. Reed, 1963; *Away North, Away South*, A. H. & A. W. Reed, 1965; *Pearls and Dragons*, A. H. & A. W. Reed, 1968; *Continental Dishes Made Easy*, Hamlyn, 1970; *Quick Simple Meals*, Hamlyn, 1970.

BIOGRAPHICAL/CRITICAL SOURCES: Susan Graham, *Susan in Springtime*, A. H. & A. W. Reed, 1960.†

* * *

GRAMBS, Jean D(resden) 1919-

PERSONAL: Born April 6, 1919, in Pigeon Point, Calif.; married Harold Grambs (an employee of U.S. Department of Agriculture), June, 1945; children: Marya, Sarah, Peter. *Education:* Reed College, A.B., 1940; Stanford University, M.A., 1941, Ed.D., 1948. *Office:* College of Education, University of Maryland, College Park, Md.

CAREER: High school teacher in California, 1941-43; National Education Association, Educational Policies Commission, research assistant, 1943-44; Palo Alto Youth Council, Palo Alto, Calif., research director of study of recreational interests, 1944-45; Stanford University, School of Education, Stanford, Calif., instructor, 1948-49, assistant professor of education, 1949-53; University of Maryland, College of Education, College Park, lecturer, 1955-61, associate professor, 1961-67, professor of education, 1967—, coordinator interdisciplinary programs, Division of Human and Community Resources, 1973—. Visiting lecturer at several universities and director of workshops. Supervisor of adult education, Prince George's County, Md., 1955-58. *Member:* National Council for the Social Studies (board of directors, 1966-68), National Education Association, American Education Studies Association (member of board, 1970-73), American Historical Society, American Educational Research Association, Association for Supervision and Curriculum Development, Society for the Psychological Study of Social Issues, Phi Beta Kappa. *Awards, honors:* Ford Foundation faculty fellowship, 1952-53; University of Maryland research grant, 1963, 1964.

WRITINGS: (With W. J. Iverson) *Modern Methods in Secondary Education*, Holt, 1952, revised edition (with Iverson and F. Patterson), 1958, 3rd revised edition (with John C. Carr and Robert M. Fitch), 1970; (editor with Arthur Foff) *Readings in Education*, Harper, 1956, revised edition, in press; (with C. W. Hunnicutt and others) "Singer Social Studies Series," eleven books for elementary grades, Singer-Random House, 1957-63; (contributor) Franklin Patterson, editor, *The Adolescent Citizen*, Free

Press of Glencoe, 1960; (with L. M. McClure) *Foundation of Teaching: An Introduction to Modern Education*, Holt, 1964; *Schools, Scholars, and Society*, Prentice-Hall, 1965; (with James D. Raths) *Society and Education*, Prentice-Hall, 1965; (with Kvarceus and others) *Negro Self-Concept: Implications for School and Community*, McGraw, 1965.

(Editor with William Amos) *Guidance and Counseling the Culturally Disadvantaged Adolescent*, Prentice-Hall, 1968; *Methods and Materials in Intergroup Education*, Prentice-Hall, 1968; (editor with John C. Carr) *Black Image: Education Copes with Color*, W. C. Brown, 1971; (editor with James Banks) *Black Self-Concept*, McGraw, 1972; (editor with Carr and E. G. Campbell) *Education and the World Today*, Addison-Wesley, 1972; (with Walter B. Waetjen) *Sex: Does it Make a Difference?*, Duxbury Press, 1975; (with Albert B. Branca) *Psychology: The Science of Behavior* (a high school text), Allyn & Bacon, 1975.

Contributor of chapters to yearbooks of John Dewey Society and National Council for the Social Studies. Author of eleven pamphlets on education, reading, school integration, and allied subjects; play and discussion scripts; and about forty articles in professional journals.

* * *

GRANT, Nigel (Duncan Cameron) 1932-

PERSONAL: Born June 8, 1932, in Glasgow, Scotland; son of Alastair Cameron (a journalist) and Anne (Blythe) Grant; married Valerie Evans, August 5, 1957; children: Alison Margaret Cameron, David Alastair Cameron. *Education:* University of Glasgow, M.A., 1954, M.Ed., 1959, Ph.D., 1969; Jordanhill College of Education, teaching certificate, 1955. *Home:* 25 Ormidale Ter., Edinburgh 12, Scotland. *Office:* Department of Educational Studies, University of Edinburgh, Edinburgh, Scotland.

CAREER: Cranhill Secondary School, Glasgow, Scotland, teacher of English, 1957-60; Jordanhill College of Education, Glasgow, Scotland, lecturer in education, 1960-65; University of Edinburgh, Edinburgh, Scotland, lecturer, 1965-72; reader in educational studies, 1972—. Visiting professor, University of Michigan, 1968, 1972, 1974; visiting lecturer, University College, Dublin, 1974. *Military service:* British Army, Royal Artillery, 1955-57. *Member:* Comparative Education Society in Europe (chairman British section, 1973—), Scottish University Council for Studies in Education (chairman, 1972—), Glasgow University Institute of Soviet and East European Studies, and local political, natural, and historical organizations.

WRITINGS: Soviet Education, University of London Press, 1965; *Society, Schools, and Progress in Eastern Europe*, Pergammon, 1969; (with G. Lowe and T. D. Williams) *Education and Nation—Building in the Third World*, Scottish Academic Press, 1971; (with R. E. Bell) *A Mythology of British Education*, Panther, 1974.

Contributor: O. Anweiler, editor, *Bildungsreformen in Osteuropa*, Kohlhammer, 1971; M. Scotford Archer, editor, *Students Universities and Society*, Routledge & Kegan Paul, 1972; R. E. Bull and A. Youngson, editors, *Present and Future in Higher Education*, Edinburgh University Press, 1974; G. Goldbach and others, editors, *Paedagogiske-Problemer i Komparativ Belysning*, Gjellerup, 1974. Contributor to newspapers and educational journals.

WORK IN PROGRESS: With R. E. Bell, *Education in Britain and Ireland*, for Allen & Unwin; research on problems of continuing education and of education of national minorities.

SIDELIGHTS: Grant is competent in Spanish and Italian; knows some German and Russian, modern Greek, Serbo-Croat, French, Czech, Polish, Danish, Swedish, Dutch, Gaelic, Arabic, and Rumanian; minimal knowledge of Chinese, school Latin and Greek. *Avocational interests:* Reading, theater, poetry, current affairs, painting, natural history, linguistics, travel, archaeology.

* * *

GRANT, Vernon W(esley) 1904-

PERSONAL: Born September 6, 1904, in Cleveland, Ohio; son of Charles E. (an entertainer) and Laura (Baker) Grant; married Cleone Jenkins, October 2, 1943. *Education:* University of Chicago, Ph.B., 1927; Columbia University, M.A., 1929; Northwestern University, Ph.D., 1941. *Home address:* R.D. #2, Lafayette, Tenn. 37083.

CAREER: St. Lawrence University, Canton, N.Y., instructor in psychology, 1929-32; Northern Illinois College of Optometry, Chicago, Ill., professor of psychology, 1934-42; University of Rochester, Rochester, N.Y., assistant professor of psychology, 1944-45; Adelphi University, Garden City, N.Y., associate professor of psychology, 1946-48; Hawthornden State Hospital, Macedonia, Ohio, chief psychologist, 1949-57; Summit County Mental Hygiene Clinic, Akron, Ohio, chief psychologist, 1957—. Private practice as marriage counselor. *Military service:* U.S. Army Air Forces, 1942-43. *Member:* American Psychological Association, American Association of Marriage Counselors, Ohio Psychological Association, Cleveland Psychological Association.

WRITINGS: The Psychology of Sexual Emotion, Longmans, Green, 1957; *This is Mental Illness*, Beacon, 1963; *Great Abnormals*, Hawthorn, 1968; *Roots of Religious Doubt*, Seabury, 1974. Contributor of articles to professional journals and magazines.

WORK IN PROGRESS: Research in psychopathic personalities; psychology and history.

SIDELIGHTS: Grant has reading knowledge of French and German. *Avocational interests:* History, classical music.

* * *

GRANT, W(illiam) Leonard 1914-

PERSONAL: Born September 13, 1914, in Balmoral, Scotland; son of William Bremner (a mason) and Christina Essel (Donald) Grant; married Ella Kathleen Allen (a university lecturer), July 28, 1948; children: John Hugo Alexander. *Education:* University of British Columbia, B.A., 1936; Harvard University, A.M., 1938; University of Toronto, Ph.D., 1942. *Politics:* Liberal. *Religion:* Anglican.

CAREER: University of British Columbia, Vancouver, lecturer, 1945-47; Trinity College, University of Toronto, Toronto, Ontario, assistant professor, 1947-48; University of British Columbia, associate professor, 1948-53, professor of classics, beginning 1953. *Military service:* Royal Canadian Navy, 1942-45; became lieutenant. *Member:* Renaissance Society of America, Classical Association of Canada. *Awards, honors:* Nuffield postdoctoral research fellowship to Oxford University, 1951-52; Canadian Humanities Research Council award, 1955.

WRITINGS: *Neo-Latin Literature and the Pastoral*, University of North Carolina Press, 1965. Contributor to classical and other learned journals, and to magazines.

SIDELIGHTS: Grant is competent in Latin, Greek, German, French, Italian, Spanish, and Polish. *Avocational interests:* Baroque music.†

* * *

GRAVES, Allen W(illis) 1915-

PERSONAL: Born January 20, 1915, in Rector, Ark.; son of James Henry (a farmer and coal miner) and Joyce (Keaster) Graves; married Helen Cannan, June 1, 1937; children: Joyce (Mrs. Carl Olney), John R., Dorothy (Mrs. William Dinwiddie), David Allen, Virginia Ruth (Mrs. John Weisz), Thomas Henry. *Education:* Southern Illinois University, B.Ed., 1935; Southern Baptist Theological Seminary, Th.M., 1939, Th.D., 1942. *Politics:* Democrat. *Home:* 328 South Birchwood, Louisville, Ky. 40206. *Office:* 2825 Lexington Rd., Louisville, Ky. 40206.

CAREER: Ordained to Baptist ministry, 1935; pastor in Illinois and Kentucky, 1935-41; Baptist Sunday School Board, Nashville, Tenn., director of Baptist Young People's Union work, 1941-43; pastor in Fort Pierce, Fla., 1943-45, Charlottesville, Va., 1945-50, Tulsa, Okla., 1950-55; Southern Baptist Theological Seminary, Louisville, Ky., dean of School of Religious Education, 1955-69, administrative dean, 1969-72; Boyce Bible School, Louisville, Ky., executive director, 1973—. *Member:* Society for the Advancement of Continuing Education for Ministry, Southern Baptist Religious Education Association (president, 1962-63), Southeastern Baptist Religious Education Association (president, 1966-67).

WRITINGS: *Christ in My Career*, Convention Press, 1958; *Church Committee Manual*, Convention Press, 1958; *Using and Maintaining Church Property*, Prentice-Hall, 1965; *A Church at Work*, Convention Press, 1972; *Principles of Administration for a Baptist Association*, Home Mission Board, 1974. Regular writer of curriculum material for Baptist Sunday School Board.

* * *

GRAY, Alfred O(rren) 1914-

PERSONAL: Born September 8, 1914, in Sun Prairie, Wis.; son of Charles Orren and Amelia Katherine (Schadel) Gray; married Nicolin J. Plank (a biology professor), September 5, 1947; children: Robin, Richard. *Education:* University of Wisconsin, B.A., 1939, M.A., 1941. *Religion:* Presbyterian. *Home:* W 304 Hoerner, Spokane, Wash. 99218. *Office:* Whitworth College, Spokane, Wash. 99251.

CAREER: Did news writing, public relations work, and journalism research, 1938-42; Whitworth College, Spokane, Wash., professor of journalism, head of department, and adviser to student publications, 1946—, director of Whitworth News Bureau, 1952-58, chairman of business and communications arts division, 1958-66. Co-founder and director, Inland Empire High School Publications Clinic, 1959—. Free-lance writer and writing consultant. Vice-moderator of Synod of Washington and Alaska, United Presbyterian Church in the U.S.A., 1966-67. *Military service:* U.S. Army, 1942-46; historical editor and chief writer, Office of the Chief Ordnance Officer, European Theater of Operations, Paris and Frankfurt, 1944-46; became warrant officer junior grade; received Bronze Star Medal. *Member:* Association for Education in Journalism, National Council

of College Publications Advisers, American Association of University Professors, World Future Society, Eastern Washington Genealogical Society, Wisconsin Alumni Association, Phi Beta Kappa, Sigma Delta Chi, Phi Eta Sigma. *Awards, honors:* Named Wisconsin Scholar in Journalism, 1941; National Council of College Publication Advisors Citation, 1967; Whitworth College Alumni Association, award for excellence in teaching journalism, 1972.

WRITINGS: *Not By Might: The Story of Whitworth College, 1890-1965*, Whitworth College Press, 1965; (contributor) *Public Understanding of Education as a Field of Study*, Project Public Information, 1968. Writer of pamphlets on church communications and on careers in journalism, and contributor to periodicals. Editor, *Synod Story*, 1951-52.

WORK IN PROGRESS: A comparative study of publication ethics in the U.S. and Great Britain; *The Descendants of Karl Friedrich Moessner*.

SIDELIGHTS: Gray has conducted several nation-wide surveys and studies in religious journalism.

BIOGRAPHICAL/CRITICAL SOURCES: *Spokane Spokesman-Review*, September 15, 1946; *Whitworth College Bulletin*, October, 1946; *Spokane Daily Chronicle*, February 5, 1965; *Whitwords*, April, 1966.

* * *

GRAY, Charles A(ugustus) 1938-

PERSONAL: Born October 15, 1938, in Washington, D.C.; son of Joseph Alexander (a production analyst) and Merriam (Chandler) Gray; foster son of uncle, Augustus Clagett Gray; married Rachel Ann Davis, May 22, 1965. *Education:* Cornell University, B.Ch.E., 1961; Massachusetts Institute of Technology, Ph.D., 1966. *Religion:* Protestant. *Residence:* Princeton, N.J. *Office:* F.M.C. Corp., 500 Roosevelt Ave., Carteret, N.J.

CAREER: F.M.C. Corp., Chemicals Central Research, Princeton, N.J., research engineer, 1965-68, inorganic chemistry research and development, Carteret, N.J., 1968-71, manager, engineering research, Charleston, W.Va., 1971-74, project manager, Carteret, N.J., 1974. *Member:* American Chemical Society, American Institute of Chemical Engineers. *Awards, honors:* Thomas Alva Edison Foundation Mass Media Award for best science book for youth, 1965, for *Explorations in Chemistry*.

WRITINGS: *Explorations in Chemistry*, Dutton, 1965.

* * *

GRAY, George Hugh 1922-
(Tony Gray)

PERSONAL: Born August 23, 1922, in Dublin, Ireland; son of George (a radiographer) and Gertrude (McKee) Gray; married Patricia Mary Walters, October 1, 1946; children: Michael John, Victoria Mary. *Education:* Attended St. Andrews College, Dublin, Ireland, 1935-39. *Religion:* "None—ex-Protestant." *Home and office:* 3 Broomfield Rd., Kew Gardens, Richmond, Surrey, England. *Agent:* Toby Eady Associates, 313 Fulham Rd., London S.W. 10, England.

CAREER: *Irish Times*, Dublin, Ireland, writer, editor, 1940-59; *Daily Mirror*, London, England, features editor, 1959-62; Rediffusion (television network), London, England, script writer and programs editor, 1962-64; full-time free-lance writer, 1964—.

WRITINGS—All under name Tony Gray: *Starting from Tomorrow* (novel), Little, Brown, 1965; *The Irish Answer* (social history), Little, Brown, 1966; *The Real Professionals* (novel), Heinemann, 1966; *Gone the Time* (novel), Heinemann, 1967; *Interlude* (novel; based on an original screenplay by Lee Langely and Hugh Leonard), Dell, 1968; *The Record Breakers: The Story of the Record-Breaking Campbells*, Hamlyn, 1970; *Psalms and Slaughter: A Study in Religious Bigotry*, Heinemann, 1972; *The Orange Order* (history), Bodley Head, 1972; *The Last Laugh* (novel), Heinemann, 1972; (with Henry Ward) *Buller* (biography), Hodder & Stoughton, 1974; *No Surrender: A New History of the Siege of Londonderry 1689-1690*, MacDonald, 1975. Also author of film, television and radio scripts, in addition to articles for *Holiday, Punch, Nova*, and other periodicals.

WORK IN PROGRESS: An unofficial biography of Enoch Powell; a three-part novel set in France, and tracing changing attitudes to war and morals during the period between 1913 and 1963.

*   *   *

GRAY, John W(ylie)   1935-

PERSONAL: Born December 8, 1935, in Fordyce, Ark.; son of John McConnel (an engineer) and Aylean (Crous) Gray; married Pauline Manees (a teacher), August 18, 1957; children: Gretchen Alean, Gwendolyn Paulie. *Education:* Ouachita Baptist University, B.A., 1957; University of Arkansas, M.A., 1958; Louisiana State University, Ph.D., 1970. *Politics:* Democrat. *Religion:* Baptist. *Office:* Speech Department, Auburn University, Auburn, Ala. 36830.

CAREER: Auburn University, Auburn, Ala., assistant professor of speech and director of oral interpretation, beginning, 1959. Consultant on parliamentary procedure to business and industry. *Military service:* U.S. Army Reserve, 1959-65; became captain. *Member:* Special Association of America, Southern Speech Association (chairman of interpretation group), Alabama Speech Association (first vice-president), Alpha Psi Omega, Tau Kappa Alpha.

WRITINGS: Parliamentary Procedure: A Programmed Introduction, Scott, Foresman, 1962; (editor) *Perspectives on Oral Interpretation: Essays and Readings*, Burgess, 1968; *Communication and Leadership*, National Association of Secondary School Principals, 1973. Contributor to speech journals.†

*   *   *

GRAY, Robert F(red)   1912-

PERSONAL: Born April 28, 1912, in Marshall, Minn.; son of Frank Davis (a physician) and Nettie (Urbach) Gray; married Betty Batcup, January 19, 1955; children: Victoria. *Education:* Attended University of Minnesota, 1931-34; Northwestern University, M.D., 1939; Mackerere College, Uganda, Africa, graduate study, 1950-51; University of Chicago, Ph.D. (anthropology), 1958. *Home:* 5070 Lockehaven Dr., Victoria, British Columbia, Canada. *Office:* Department of Anthropology, University of Victoria, Victoria, British Columbia, Canada.

CAREER: Private practice of medicine in Minnesota, 1940-41; Mackerere College, Uganda, Fulbright fellow, 1950-51; Ford Foundation fellow in Africa, 1954-56; Human Relations Area Files, Inc., New Haven, Conn., research associate, 1958-59; University of Illinois, Urbana, associate professor of anthropology, 1959-61; Tulane University of

Louisiana, New Orleans, associate professor, 1961-65, professor of anthropology, 1965-72; University of Victoria, Victoria, British Columbia, professor of anthropology, 1972—. *Military service:* British Army, Medical Corps, 1941-45; became captain. U.S. Army, Medical Corps, 1943-45; became captain. *Member:* American Anthropological Association, Canadian African Studies Association.

WRITINGS: Human Burden Carrying in Tropical Africa: A Survey and Analysis, U.S. Quartermaster Corps, 1960; *The Sonjo of Tanganyika*, Oxford University Press, 1963; (editor with P. H. Gullivar, author of introduction, and contributor) *The Family Estate in Africa*, Routledge & Kegan Paul, 1964. Writer of twenty-five newsletters, dealing with anthropological and medical problems of East Africa, distributed by Institute of Current World Affairs.

Contributor: P. Bohannan and G. Dalton, editors, *Markets in Africa*, Northwestern University Press, 1962, abridged edition, Museum of Natural Hisotry, 1964; *Witchcraft and Sorcery*, Routledge & Kegan Paul, 1963; H. Fortes and G. Dieterien, editors, *African Systems of Thought*, Oxford University Press, 1965; R. A. Lystad, editor, *The African World*, Praeger for African Studies Association, 1965; J. Beattie and J. Middleton, editors, *Spirit Mediumship and Society in Africa*, Routledge & Kegan Paul, 1969. Contributor to *Encyclopaedia Britannica*, and scholarly journals.

WORK IN PROGRESS: Editing a book on primitive medicine.

*   *   *

GRAY, Ronald (Douglas)   1919-

PERSONAL: Born November 1, 1919, in London, England. *Education:* Emmanuel College, Cambridge, B.A., 1946, Ph.D., 1949. *Home:* 224 Milton Rd., Cambridge, England.

CAREER: University of Basel, Basel, Switzerland, lector, 1948-49; Cambridge University, Cambridge, England, lecturer in German, 1949—, fellow of Emmanuel College, 1958—, domestic bursar of Emmanuel College, 1964—. *Military service:* British Army, Royal Artillery, 1939-45; became captain. *Member:* Marlowe Dramatic Society (Cambridge University; senior treasurer, 1962—).

WRITINGS: Goethe the Alchemist, Cambridge University Press, 1952; *Kafka's Castle*, Cambridge University Press, 1956; *Brecht*, Oliver & Boyd, 1961, revised edition, Cambridge University Press, 1975; (editor) *Kafka: Twentieth Century Views*, Prentice-Hall, 1962; *An Introduction to German Poetry*, Cambridge University Press, 1965; *The German Tradition in Literature 1871-1945*, Cambridge University Press, 1965; (editor) *Poems of Goethe*, Cambridge University Press, 1966; *Goethe: A Critical Introduction*, Cambridge University Press, 1967; *Franz Kafka*, Cambridge University Press, 1973. Contributor to *Listener, Daily Telegraph, Cambridge Quarterly*, and other periodicals.

WORK IN PROGRESS: A rewriting of book on Brecht, publication by Cambridge University Press; a critical study of Henrik Ibsen, completion expected in 1976; further research on European drama in the nineteenth and twentieth centuries.

*   *   *

GRAYBEAL, David M(cConnell)   1921-

PERSONAL: Born June 17, 1921, in Radford, Va.; son of Henry Clay and June (McConnell) Graybeal; married Marjorie Patterson, November 6, 1948; children: Jean, Lee Anne, Clay Thomas. *Education:* Emory and Henry College, B.A., 1941; Yale University, B.D., 1949, Ph.D., 1952. *Politics:* Democrat. *Home:* 5 Grove St., Madison, N.J. 07940. *Office:* Drew University, Madison, N.J. 07940.

CAREER: Ordained Methodist minister, 1949; pastor in Wallingford, Conn., 1949-52; Emory and Henry College, Emory, Va., chaplain, 1952-56; Drew University, School of Theology, Madison, N.J., assistant professor, 1956-58, professor of church and society, 1958—. *Military service:* U.S. Naval Reserve, 1942-46; became lieutenant. *Member:* American Sociological Association, American Economic Association, American Society of Christian Ethics.

WRITINGS: The Christian Family and Its Money, Methodist Church, 1963; *Can't We All Be Rich?*, Friendship, 1966.

*   *   *

GRAYSON, Cary Travers, Jr. 1919-

PERSONAL: Born March 21, 1919, in Washington, D.C.; son of Cary Travers (an admiral and medical officer, U.S. Navy) and Alice Gertrude (Gordon) Grayson; married Priscilla Alden Roessle, September 7, 1956; children: Leslie, Carinthia, Alicia, Theodosia, *Education:* Yale University, B.A., 1942; Stanford University, M.A., 1949; Graduate Institute of International Studies, Geneva, Switzerland, Ph.D., 1953. *Politics:* Democrat. *Home:* Blue Ridge Farm, Upperville, Va. 22176. *Office address:* Potomac Books, Inc., P.O. Box 40604, Palisades Station, Washington, D.C.

CAREER: Carnegie Corp. of New York, New York, N.Y., director of special projects, 1954-57; U.S. Department of State, Washington, D.C., special assistant, Bureau of Education and Cultural Affairs, 1957-61, with Division of Private Organizations, Peace Corps, 1961-63; Potomac Books, Inc. (publishers), Washington, D.C., president, 1964—. Woodrow Wilson House Council, vice-chairman, 1964-66, chairman, 1966-72. *Military service:* U.S. Marine Corps, 1942-46; became captain.

WRITINGS: Austria's International Position, Dorz, 1953; (contributor) *American Panorama*, New York University Press, 1958; (editor) Cary Travers Grayson, Sr., *Woodrow Wilson: An Intimate Memoir*, Holt, 1960; (editor) *Washington '68*, Potomac, 1968; *The 91st Congress*, Potomac, 1969; *United States Government: The Nixon Administration*, Potomac, 1970; (editor with Susan Lukowski) *The 93rd Congress*, Potomac, 1973; *State Information and Federal Region Book*, Potomac, 1974; *The Impeachment Congress*, Potomac, 1974; *Washington IV: A Comprehensive Directory of the Nation's Capital*, Potomac, 1975. Contributor to *American Heritage*.

WORK IN PROGRESS: Editing *Woodrow Wilson at the Paris Peace Conference*, by Admiral Gary T. Grayson, completion expected in 1976.

*   *   *

GREEN, James L(eroy) 1919-

PERSONAL: Born November 5, 1919, in Centralia, Wash.; married Evelyn Joyce Hathcoat, May 25, 1950; children: Marvin Dale, James Scott. *Education:* Washington State University, B.A. (with honors), 1941; University of Minnesota, M.A., 1948, Ph.D., 1950; postdoctoral study, University of Virginia, University of Georgia. *Home:* 200 Colonial Dr., Athens, Ga. 30601.

CAREER: University of Idaho, Moscow, instructor, 1946-47; Southern Methodist University, Dallas, Tex., assistant professor of industrial relations, 1949-51; Griffenhagen & Associates, Chicago, Ill., associate economic and management consultant, 1951-52; independent business consultant, and sometime teacher at Michigan College of Mining and Technology (now Michigan Technological University), Houghton, and University of Oklahoma, Norman, 1953-56; adviser to Minister of Finance, government of Colombia, 1956-57; U.S. Air Force Institute of Technology, Graduate School of Business, Wright-Patterson Air Force Base, Ohio, professor of economics and chairman of department, 1957-60; University of Georgia, Athens, professor of economics, 1960—. Member, National Committee on Urban and Regional Affairs; consultant or advisor to Continuing Committee on Economic Development, Dekalb County Board of Commissioners, Georgia Power Company, Atlanta Regional Commission. *Military service:* U.S. Army Air Forces, pilot, 1941-46; served in Europe and Far East; became major.

MEMBER: American Association for the Advancement of Science, American Academy of Arts and Sciences, National Association of Business Economists, International Platform Association, American Society for Personnel Administration, Regional Science Association, World Future Society, Institute for Latin Studies, American Economic Association, American Society for Public Administration, Southern Economic Association, Beta Gamma Sigma, Phi Kappa Phi, Alpha Kappa Psi.

WRITINGS: Metropolitan Economic Republics, A Case Study of Regional Economic Growth, University of Georgia Press, 1965; *Economic Ecology*, University of Georgia Press, 1969; (contributor) *The Ideal City*, Georgia State University Press, 1970; (contributor) *Essays on Taxation*, University of Wisconsin Press, 1974. Writer of five annual reports to Leadership Seminar of Savannah, 1964-68. Contributor to *Personnel Journal, Commercial and Financial Chronicle, Atlanta Economic Review*, and other professional publications. Weekly editorial columnist for *Atlanta Journal-Constitution*, 1973—. Writer of monographs, and of articles for professional journals.

*   *   *

GREEN, Martin 1927-

PERSONAL: Born September 21, 1927, in London, England; son of Joseph William Elias (a shopkeeper) and Hilda (Brewster) Green; married Carol Elizabeth Hurd, 1967; children: Martin Michael, Miriam. *Education:* St. John's College, Cambridge, B.A. (English honours), 1948, M.A., 1952; King's College, University of London, teachers' diploma, 1951; Sorbonne, University of Paris, Certificat d'Etudes Francaises, 1952; University of Michigan, Ph.D., 1957. *Politics:* Labour. *Religion:* Roman Catholic. *Home:* Audenshaw, Weston, Lullingfield, Shropshire, England. *Office:* Department of English, Tufts University, Medford, Mass. 02155.

CAREER: Taught at College Moderne, Fourmies, France, 1951-52, and at Konya Koleji, Konya, Turkey, 1955-56; Wellesley College, Wellesley, Mass., instructor in modern literature, 1957-61; Tufts University, Medford, Mass., assistant professor of American literature, 1963-65; University of Birmingham, Birmingham, England, lecturer in American literature, 1965-68; Tufts University, Medford, Mass., professor of English, 1968—. *Military service:* Royal Air Force, 1948-50; became sergeant. *Awards, honors:* Three major Avery and Jule Hopwood Creative writing awards, University of Michigan, 1954.

WRITINGS: Mirror for Anglo-Saxons, Harper, 1960; *Reappraisals*, Hugh Evelyn, 1963, Norton, 1965; *Science and the Shabby Curate of Poetry*, Norton, 1965; *The Problem of Boston*, Norton, 1966; *Yeat's Blessings on von Hugel: Essays in Literature and Religion*, Norton, 1967; *Cities of Light and Sons of the Morning*, Little, Brown, 1972; *The von Richthoffen Sisters*, Basic Books, 1974; *England's Children of the Sun*, Basic Books, 1975; *Transatlantic Patterns*, Basic Books, 1975. Also author of a television play for the B.B.C. Contributor to *The Guardian* and *The Observer.*

WORK IN PROGRESS: Study of the German romantics and the English eighteenth century.

*   *   *

GREENE, James H. 1915-

PERSONAL: Born March 12, 1915, in Elmwood, Neb.; son of Ralph W. (a druggist) and Inez (Harnsberger) Greene; married Barbara Holt, August 18, 1942; children: Robin Elisabeth, Timothy James. *Education:* University of Iowa, B.S.M.E., 1947, M.S.M.E., 1948, Ph.D., 1957. *Religion:* Methodist. *Home:* 712 Sugar Hill Rd., West Lafayette, Ind. 47906.

CAREER: Purdue University, Lafayette, Ind., 1948—, professor of industrial engineering, 1961—. Finland Institute of Technology, Helsinki, Fulbright lecturer, 1960-61; European Productivity Agency, consultant, 1961, conducting seminars in England, Ireland, Denmark, and Germany. *Military service:* U.S. Army, Field Artillery, 1942-46; served in European theater. *Member:* American Society for Engineering Education, American Institute of Industrial Engineers, American Academy of Management, American Production and Inventory Control Society, Sigma Xi, Alpha Pi Mu, Pi Tau Sigma.

WRITINGS: Production and Inventory Control, Systems and Decisions, Irwin, 1965, revised edition, 1974; *Operation, Planning and Control*, Irwin, 1967; (editor) *Production Control Handbook*, McGraw, 1970. Contributor to *Grolier Encyclopedia*, and about forty articles to management and engineering journals.

*   *   *

GREENLEE, J(acob) Harold 1918-

PERSONAL: Born May 12, 1918, in Charleston, W.Va.; son of Jacob Andrew (a bookkeeper) and Ethel (Jarrett) Greenlee; married Ruth Olney, December 10, 1949; children: Dorothy Edith, Lois Jean, David Harold. *Education:* Asbury College, A.B., 1939; Asbury Theological Seminary, B.D., 1943; University of Kentucky, M.A., 1944; Harvard University, Ph.D., 1947; postdoctoral study at Oxford University, 1950-51, and University of Oklahoma, 1960. *Politics:* Republican. *Home:* 715 Kennedy Ave., Duncanville, Tex. 75116. *Office:* OMS International, Box A, Greenwood, Ind. 46142.

CAREER: Ordained to Methodist ministry, 1944; Asbury Theological Seminary, Wilmore, Ky., professor of New Testament Greek, 1944-65; Oral Roberts University, Graduate School of Theology, Tulsa, Okla., professor of New Testament Greek, 1965-69; Seminario Biblico, Medellin, Colombia, professor, 1965, 1970-74; University of Texas, Arlington, adjunct professor of linguistics, 1974—. Research associate, American Bible Society, 1955-65; mis-

sionary, OMS International, 1969—; translation consultant, Wycliffe Bible Translators, 1971—. *Member:* Society of Biblical Literature, Theta Phi. *Awards, honors:* Senior Fulbright fellowship to Oxford University, 1950-51; Christian Research Foundation prize, 1961, for manuscript of *Introduction to New Testament Textual Criticism.*

WRITINGS: A Concise Exegetical Grammar of New Testament Greek, privately printed, 1948, 3rd edition, Eerdmans, 1963; *The Gospel Text of Cyril of Jerusalem*, Ejnar Munksgaard (Copenhagen), 1955; *Introduction to New Testament Textual Criticism*, Eerdmans, 1964; (with T. M. Anderson) *How to Build Expository Sermons*, Beacon Hill, 1965; *Nine Greek Uncial Manuscripts of the New Testament*, Ejnar Munksgaard, 1969. Contributor to *Zondervan's Pictorial Bible Dictionary, Christian Minister, Bible Translator, Zondervan's Pictorial Encyclopedia of the Bible, Biblica*, and other religious periodicals.

WORK IN PROGRESS: A Greek New Testament morpheme lexicon; a book of Greek New Testament word studies.

*   *   *

GREGG, Davis W(einert) 1918-

PERSONAL: Born March 12, 1918, in Austin, Tex.; son of Davis Alexander (a lawyer) and Lorene (Murff) Gregg; married Mildred Grace McDaniel, May 15, 1942; children: Mary Cynthia, Davis William. *Education:* University of Texas, B.B.A., 1939; University of Pennsylvania, M.B.A., 1940, Ph.D., 1948. *Home:* 820 Castlepinn Lane, Bryn Mawr, Pa. 19010. *Office:* American College of Life Underwriters, 270 Bryn Mawr Ave., Bryn Mawr, Pa. 19010.

CAREER: Aetna Casualty & Surety Co., Hartford, Conn., underwriter, 1940-41; Ohio State University, Columbus, assistant professor of insurance, 1948-49; American College of Life Underwriters, Bryn Mawr, Pa., assistant dean, 1949-51, trustee, 1951-75, life trustee, 1975—, dean, 1951-54, president, 1954—. Visiting professor, Stanford University, 1949; co-director, First International Insurance Conference, 1957; pensions board vice-chairman, United Presbyterian Church; chairman, David McCahan Foundation; trustee, Charles W. Griffith Memorial Foundation for Insurance; lecturer in United States and abroad. *Military service:* U.S. Navy, 1941-46; became lieutenant. *Member:* American Risk and Insurance Association (president, 1961), American Academy of Political and Social Science, American Society of Chartered Life Underwriters (director), American Economic Association, Beta Gamma Sigma.

WRITINGS: Group Life Insurance, Irwin, 1950, 3rd edition, 1964; (editor with Vane B. Lucas) *Life and Health Insurance Handbook*, Irwin, 1959, 3rd edition, 1973; (editor with John D. Long) *Property and Liability Insurance Handbook*, Irwin, 1965. Editor, "Irwin Series in Risk and Insurance," 1949—, with thirty volumes published, 1949-75. Contributor to insurance journals.

WORK IN PROGRESS: Economic Security of Man, for McCahan Foundation for Basic Research in Security, Risk, and Insurance.

*   *   *

GREGORY, Richard Langton 1923-

PERSONAL: Born July 24, 1923, in London, England; son of Christopher Clive Langton and Patricia Helen (Gibson) Gregory; married Margaret Pattison-Muir, 1955 (divorced,

1966); married second wife, Freja Mary Balchin, 1967; children: Mark Foss Langton, Caroline Langton. *Education:* Attended Downing College, Cambridge, 1947-50. *Religion:* Agnostic. *Office:* Brain and Perception Laboratory, Department of Anatomy, The Medical School, University Walk, Briston B58 1TD, England.

CAREER: Cambridge University, Cambridge, England, began as lecturer, head of perception laboratory, department of psychology, 1953-67, fellow of Corpus Christi College, 1962-67; University of Edinburgh, Edinburgh, Scotland, professor of bionics, 1967-70, chairman of department, 1968-70; University of Bristol, England, professor of neuropsychology and director of Brain and Perception Laboratory, 1970—. Visiting professor at University of California, Los Angeles, 1963, Massachusetts Institute of Technology, 1964, and New York University, 1966. Consultant to British Ministry of Defence. Holder of about twenty-five patents on optical instruments; deviser of method for avoiding atmospheric disturbance of telescope images. *Military service:* Royal Air Force, 1939-45. *Member:* Royal Microscopical Society (fellow), Zoological Society (fellow), Royal Society of Arts (fellow), Biological Engineering Society, Experimental Psychology Society, and other scientific associations. *Awards, honors:* CIBA Foundation research prize, 1956; St. John's College, Cambridge University, Craik prize for physiological psychology, 1958; Waverly Gold Medal for invention of solid image microscope; senior visiting fellow, National Science Foundation, 1966.

WRITINGS: (With Jean G. Wallace) *Recovery from Early Blindness,* Heffer, 1963; *Eye and Brain,* McGraw, 1966, 2nd edition, 1973; *The Intelligent Eye,* McGraw, 1970; *Visual Perception,* Oxford University Press, 1973. Contributor of about sixty research articles to scientific journals. Founder, editor, *Perception* magazine.

SIDELIGHTS: Gregory has done research work in Naples on the eyes of microscopic animals. He told *CA:* "Am very poor at languages which I hate learning. It is difficult enough to think and write clearly in one language!"†

*　　*　　*

GRESSLEY, Gene M(aurice) 1931-

PERSONAL: Born June 20, 1931, in Frankfort, Ind.; son of Minor McKinley (a minister) and Lela (Hause) Gressley; married Joyce Elinor Burrous, June 13, 1952; children: Deborah Ellyn, David Randolph. *Education:* Manchester College, B.S., 1952; Indiana University, M.A., 1956; University of Oregon, Ph.D., 1964. *Politics:* Independent. *Religion:* Congregational. *Home:* 1054 Colina Dr., Laramie, Wyo. 82070. *Office:* Box 3334, University Station, Laramie, Wyo. 82070.

CAREER: Colorado State Historical Society, Denver, assistant state historian, 1952-54; University of Wyoming, Laramie, archivist, 1956—, director of Petroleum History and Research Center, 1958—, director of Western History Research Center, 1960—, research professor of American studies, 1963—, director of American Studies, 1969—. *Member:* American Historical Association (Pacific Coast branch; member of branch council, 1969-72), Organization of American Historians, Agricultural History Society (member of executive committee; member of council, 1966-69), Western Historical Association, Business History Foundation, Champlain Society, Hudson's Bay Record Society, Colorado State Historical Society, Wyoming State Historical Society, Albany County Historical Society (vice-

president, 1959). *Awards, honors:* Everett Eugene Edwards Award of Agricultural History Society, 1958, for article in *Agricultural History;* National Endownment for Humanities fellow, 1966-67; Pelzer Award, Organization of American Historians, 1973.

WRITINGS: Bankers and Cattlemen, Knopf, 1966; (editor) *The American West: A Reorientation,* University of Wyoming Press, 1966; (editor) *Bostonians and Bullion,* University of Nebraska Press, 1968; *West by East: The American West in the Gilded Age,* Brigham Young University Press, 1972. Contributor to history journals. Member of editorial board, *Western Historical Quarterly,* 1973.†

*　　*　　*

GREY, Vivian (Hoffman)

PERSONAL: Born in Newark, N.J.; daughter of Harry and Ray Dorothy (Friedlander) Hoffman; married Jerry Grey (a professor), June 27, 1948; married Ted Miller, November 24, 1973; children: (first marriage) Leslie Ann, Jacquelyn Eve. *Education:* Cornell University, B.S., 1948; Columbia University, M.A., 1956; graduate study at Columbia University. *Residence:* Philadelphia, Pa. *Agent:* McIntosh & Otis, Inc., 18 East 41st St., New York, N.Y. 10017. *Office:* 2410 Pine St., Philadelphia, Pa.

CAREER: Borden Co., New York, N.Y., in charge of women's radio and television, consumer services, 1948-50; Oxarardt and Steffner (later Wayne Steffner Productions), Hollywood, Calif., director of publicity, 1950-51; Dancer-Fitzgerald-Sample, Inc., New York, N.Y., writer of "Betty Crocker Show," 1952; Rutgers, The State University, University College, New Brunswick, N.J., lecturer in English composition, 1964-65; Mercer County Community College, Trenton, N.J., professor of English, 1968-70; Colgate-Palmolive Co., Philadelphia, Pa., research and development division, 1973-74; The Delaware Fund Co., Philadelphia, Pa., investments consultant, 1973-74. Consultant to Creative Playthings, Inc., and Educational Testing Service, both Princeton, N.J., and to New Jersey Council on the Arts. Member, Rutgers University advisory council on juvenile literature. *Member:* National Council of Teachers of English, Womens National Book Association, American Home Economics Association, Authors League of America, Kappa Delta Pi, Pi Lambda Theta, Cornell Club of Princeton, Princeton University League.

WRITINGS: The First Book of Astronomy, Watts, 1959; (co-editor) *Space Flight Report to the Nation,* Basic Books, 1962; *The Secret of the Mysterious Rays: The Discovery of Nuclear Energy,* Basic Books, 1966; *The Invisible Giants,* Little, Brown, 1969; *Roentgen's Revolution,* Little, Brown, 1972; *The Feminist Movement* (young adult), Four Winds Press, 1975. Writer and commentator, television series "The Energy Crisis."

*　　*　　*

GRIEG, Michael 1922-

PERSONAL: Surname rhymes with "league"; born February 2, 1922, in London, England; son of Maurice (a billiard player) and Henrietta (Hoffman) Grieg; married Sally Stein, February 4, 1944; children: Joi, Bart. *Education:* Attended City College (now City College of the City University of New York). *Home:* 959 Kansas St., San Francisco, Calif. 94107. *Agent:* Paul R. Reynolds, Inc., 599 Fifth Ave., New York, N.Y. 10017. *Office: San Francisco Chronicle,* Fifth and Mission, San Francisco, Calif.

CAREER: San Francisco Examiner, San Francisco, Calif., successively book critic, writer, and Sunday editor, 1959-63; *San Francisco Chronicle*, San Francisco, Calif., writer, 1963—. Book critic for educational television station KQED, and radio station KPFA. *Member:* American Newspaper Guild.

WRITINGS: (Editor, and author of introduction) Randolph Bourne, *The State*, Resistance Press, 1947; *A Guide to the City*, Black Hand Press, 1959; *A Fire in His Hand*, Doubleday, 1963. Co-writer of film, "The Bridge."

AVOCATIONAL INTERESTS: "Acting, drinking, loving, horseplay."†

*   *   *

GRIFFIN, Charles Henry 1922-

PERSONAL: Born July 3, 1922, in Blooming Grove, Tex.; son of Lindsay Ira (a farm manager) and Dorothy Fay (Pruitt) Griffin. *Education:* University of Texas, B.B.A., 1942, M.B.A., 1948, Ph.D., 1953. *Religion:* Methodist. *Home:* 1801 Lavaca, Austin, Tex. 78701. *Office:* BEB 309, University of Texas, Austin, Tex. 78712.

CAREER: Certified public accountant. Peat, Marwick, Mitchell & Co., Dallas, Tex., staff accountant, 1949-50; University of Texas, Austin, instructor and lecturer in accounting, 1950-53; University of Cincinnati, Cincinnati, Ohio, assistant professor, 1953-54, associate professor of accounting, 1954-57; University of Illinois, Urbana, associate professor, 1957-60, professor of accounting, 1960-62; University of Texas, Austin, professor of accounting, 1962—. Visiting professor, University of Birmingham (England), spring, 1972; visiting Arthur Young Distinguished Professor, University of Illinois, 1972-73. *Military service:* U.S. Naval Reserve, 1942-46. *Member:* American Institute of Certified Public Accountants, American Accounting Association, National Association of Accountants, Texas Society of Certified Public Accountants, Illinois Society of Certified Public Accountants, Beta Alpha Psi, Beta Gamma Sigma, Delta Sigma Phi, Phi Kappa Psi.

WRITINGS: (With T. H. Williams) *The Mathematical Dimension of Accountancy*, South-Western Publishing, 1964; (with T. H. Williams and G. A. Welsch) *Advanced Accounting*, Irwin, 1966, revised edition (with Williams and K. D. Larson), 1971; (with T. H. Williams) *Management Information: A Quantitative Accent*, 1967. Contributing editor, *Journal of Accountancy*, 1960-66; book review editor, *Accounting Review*, 1966-67, editor-in-chief, 1968-70.

*   *   *

GRIFFIN, Mary Claire 1924-

PERSONAL: Born April 22, 1924, in Lynchburg, S.C.; daughter of Simon and Mary Sue (Kirby) Griffin. *Education:* Winthrop College, B.S., 1945; University of Tennessee, M.S., 1948; Ohio State University, Ph.D., 1961. *Religion:* Methodist.

CAREER: Brevard College, Brevard, N.C., instructor, 1945-47; Georgia State College, (now University), Atlanta, assistant professor, 1947-48; University of Alabama, University, 1949-59, 1961-62, began as instructor, became associate professor of business education; University of Illinois, Urbana, associate professor of business education, 1962-63; Clemson University, Clemson, S.C., assistant professor of industrial management, 1963-64; Bowling Green State University, Bowling Green, Ohio, assistant professor of business administration; currently at Radford College, Radford,

Va., member of faculty in department of business. *Member:* American Academy of Management, American Association of University Women, American Association of University Professors, Phi Kappa Phi, Pi Gamma Mu, Delta Pi Epsilon, National Federation of Professional and Business Women's Clubs (Bowling Green chapter).

WRITINGS: Records Management–A Modern Tool for Business, Allyn & Bacon, 1964, and *Instructor's Manual*, Allyn & Bacon, 1965.†

*   *   *

GRIFFITH, Lucille B(lanche) 1905-

PERSONAL: Born October 25, 1905, in Bessville, Mo.; daughter of Laurence Clinton and Carolina (Mabuce) Griffith. *Education:* Belhaven College, A.B., 1929; Tulane University, M.A., 1942; Brown University, Ph.D., 1957. *Politics:* Democrat. *Religion:* Presbyterian. *Home:* 201 Plowman St., Montevallo, Ala. 35115.

CAREER: High school teacher in Mississippi, 1929-42; East Mississippi Junior College, Scooba, head of department of history, 1942-46; Alabama College (now University of Montevallo), Montevallo, instructor, 1946-48, assistant professor, 1948-54, associate professor, 1954-57, professor of history, 1957-73, head of department of social science, 1966-73. Montevallo Library Board, chairman, 1957—. *Member:* American Historical Association, Society of American Historians, American Association of University Professors, American Association of University Women (second vice-president, 1959-61; president of Alabama division, 1962-64), Southern Historical Association, Alabama Historical Association, Virginia Historical Association. *Awards, honors:* Colonial Williamsburg grant-in-aid, 1955, 1969; Southern Fellowship Fund summer grants, 1956, 1958; grant from American Association for State and Local History, 1965; Alabama Consortium for the Development of Higher Education, grant, 1973.

WRITINGS: Yours Till Death: The Civil War Letters of John W. Cotton, University of Alabama Press, 1951; *History of Alabama, 1540-1900*, Colonial Press, 1963; *Virginia House of Burgesses, 1750-1777*, Colonial Press, 1964, 2nd edition, University of Alabama Press, 1970; *History of Alabama College, 1896-1969*, privately printed, 1969; *Anne Royall's Letters from Alabama*, University of Alabama Press, 1972; *Alabama: A Documentary History to 1900*, University of Alabama Press, 1972; *I Always Wore My Topi: The Burma Letters of Ethel Mabuce, 1916-1921*, University of Alabama Press, 1974. Contributor of articles and reviews to historical journals.

WORK IN PROGRESS: Virginia's William Lee: Tobacco Merchant, London Official, and American Diplomat, a biography.

*   *   *

GRIFFITHS, Helen 1939-

PERSONAL: Born May 8, 1939, in London, England; daughter of Mary Christine (Selwood) Griffiths; married Pedro Santos de la Cal (a hotel manager), October 17, 1959 (died June 21, 1973); children: Elena, Christina, Sara. *Education:* Balham and Tooting College of Commerce, London, England, student, 1953-56. *Agent:* A. P. Watt & Son, 26-28 Bedford Row, London WC1R 4HL, England.

CAREER: Cowgirl on farm in Bedfordshire, England, 1956; Blackstock Engineering, London, England, secretary; 1956-58; Selfridges (department store), London, England, employee in record section, 1958-59; Oliver & Boyd Ltd. (publishers), London, England, secretary, 1959-60; teacher of English as a foreign language, 1973—; free-lance writer. *Member:* Society of Authors. *Awards, honors:* Carnegie Medal Award, 1966, for *The Wild Horse of Santander.*

WRITINGS—All juveniles, except as indicated: *Horse in the Clouds*, Hutchinson, 1957, Holt, 1958; *Wild and Free*, Hutchinson, 1958; *Moonlight*, Hutchinson, 1959; *Africano*, Hutchinson, 1961; *The Wild Heart*, Hutchinson, 1963, Doubleday, 1965; *The Greyhound*, Hutchinson, 1964, Doubleday, 1966; *The Dark Swallows* (adult) Hutchinson, 1966, Knopf, 1967; *The Wild Horse of Santander*, Hutchinson, 1966, Doubleday, 1967; *Leon*, Doubleday, 1967; *Stallion of the Sands* (Child Study Association book list), Lothrop, 1968; *Moshie Cat*, Holiday House, 1969; *Patch*, Hutchinson, 1970; *Federico*, Hutchinson, 1971; *Russian Blue*, Holiday House, 1973; *Just a Dog*, Holiday House, 1974; *Witch Fear*, Holiday House, 1975.

WORK IN PROGRESS: A story about wolves in Spain.

SIDELIGHTS: Ms. Griffiths has lived in Switzerland and Spain, and is fluent in Spanish.

* * *

GRIFFITHS, Richard M(athias) 1935-

PERSONAL: Born June 21, 1935, in Barry, Glamorganshire, Wales; son of William Thomas (a solicitor) and Evelyn (Hill) Griffiths; married Patricia Youles, 1971; children: one son, one daughter. *Education:* Attended Lancing College, 1948-53; King's College, Cambridge, B.A., 1957, M.A. and Ph.D., 1961. *Politics:* Conservative. *Religion:* Anglican. *Office:* Department of French, University College, Cardiff, Wales.

CAREER: Cambridge University, Cambridge, England, fellow in modern languages, Selwyn College, 1960-66; Oxford University, Oxford, England, fellow in modern languages, Brasenose College, 1966-74, lecturer at The Queen's College, 1966-71; University College, Cardiff, Wales, professor of French, 1974—. Corporation of St. Mary and St. Nicholas (Woodard Schools), fellow, 1962—; Lancing College, member of council, 1962—. *Member:* Society for French Studies, Honourable Society of Cymmrodorion, Societe Huysmans, Coningsby Club, Carlton Club, Athenaeum.

WRITINGS: (Translator, and author of introduction and notes) *Parisian Sketches* (translation of Huysmans' *Croquis Parisiens*), Fortune Press, 1961; *The Reactionary Revolution: The Catholic Revival in French Literature, 1870-1914*, Constable, 1966; (editor) *Claudel: A Reappraisal*, Rapp & Whiting, 1968; *Marshal Petain*, Constable, 1970; *The Dramatic Technique of Antoine de Montchrestien*, Clarendon, 1970. Contributor to learned journals. Editor, *Cambridge Review*, 1962-63.

WORK IN PROGRESS: Fellow-Travellers of the Right; an edition of Monthedant's *Port-Royal*; and research for a book on French Renaissance tragedy.

AVOCATIONAL INTERESTS: Conservative politics, music, jazz, lawn bowls, wine, food, and conversation.

* * *

GRISPINO, Joseph Aloysius 1922-

PERSONAL: Born November 24, 1922, in Westerly, R.I.; son of Joseph (a barber) and Angelina (DiCicco) Grispino. *Education:* University of Paris, diploma, 1948; Pontifical Angelicum Athenaeum, Rome, Italy, S.T.L., 1950; Pontifical Biblical Institute, Rome, Italy, S.S.B., 1952, S.S.L., 1953; Boston College, M.Ed., 1960; University of Southern California, M.A., 1974. *Home:* 16 Bali Lane, Pacific Palisades, Calif. 90272.

CAREER: Marist College, Framingham Center, Mass., professor of Sacred Scripture, 1950-51, 1953-57; Marist College, Washington, D.C., professor of Sacred Scripture, 1957-69; Loyola University of Los Angeles, Los Angeles, Calif., assistant professor of religious studies, 1969-70; California State University, Northridge, assistant professor of religious studies, 1970-75; Santa Ana College, Santa Ana, Calif., instructor in philosophy, 1975—. Catholic University of America, Washington, D.C., lecturer on the Gospels, School of Sacred Theology, 1958-59, 1961-62, assistant professor of New Testament studies, 1962-63. *Member:* International Society of New Testament Studies, Catholic Biblical Association of America, American Schools of Oriental Research, Society of Biblical Literature, American Oriental Society, American Academy of Religion, Chicago Society of Biblical Research.

WRITINGS: (Editor and translator) *Foundations of Biblical Spirituality*, Alba, 1965; (author of introductions and commentaries) *The Old Testament of the Holy Bible*, Guild, 1965; *The Bible Now!*, Fides, 1971. Also editor of *The New Testament of the Holy Bible*, with introductions and commentaries. Abstractor, *New Testament Abstracts*, 1957-62; reviewer for *Catholic Biblical Quarterly*, 1957—; editor and contributor, *Current Scripture Notes*, 1960-68; contributor to scholarly and popular periodicals.

WORK IN PROGRESS: Books and popular and learned articles on the Bible.

SIDELIGHTS: Grispino is competent in French, Italian, Spanish, German, Latin, and biblical Greek and Hebrew. *Avocational interests:* Opera, art history.

* * *

GROSS, Suzanne 1933-

PERSONAL: Born January 11, 1933, in Janesville, Wis.; daughter of John W. (a lawyer) and Jessica (George) Gross; married Paul E. Reed, 1967; children: one. *Education:* Attended University of Pittsburgh, 1951-52; Beloit College, B.A., 1955; graduate study at University of Wisconsin and St. Joseph College, Albuquerque, N.M. *Politics:* Independent. *Religion:* Catholic. *Home:* 3917 East 24th St. N., Wichita, Kan. 67220. *Office:* Department of Music, Wichita State University, Wichita, Kan.

CAREER: U.S. Department of Agriculture, Research Service, claims clerk, later Forest Service engineering clerk-typist, Albuquerque, N.M., 1956-60; U.S. Department of Agriculture, Forest Service, personnel clerk and information writer, Milwaukee, Wis., 1960-61, Forest Products Lab., Madison, Wis., information writer, 1962-63; St. Norbert College, De Pere, Wis., poet-in-residence, 1963-67; Wichita State University, music department faculty, 1967—. *Awards, honors:* First prize in *Choice* (magazine) competition, 1961; citation from Council for Wisconsin Writers, 1966.

WRITINGS: Sand Verbena (poems), University of Notre Dame Press, 1962; *Tern's Bone and Other Poems* (chapbook), Beloit Poetry Journal, 1965. Writer of continuity and script for U.S. Forest Service film, "Patterns of the Wild."

WORK IN PROGRESS: Deepwater Wife, a collection of DePere poems; *Preludes*, a sequence of twenty-five poems for music; *Shalako*, a collection of new poems.

GROSSMAN, Herbert 1934-

PERSONAL: Born February 19, 1934, in New York, N.Y.; son of Samuel (a mover) and Ella (Friedman) Grossman; married Marilyn Horowitz (a teacher), November 22, 1956; children: Bill Jordan. *Education:* Harvard University, A.B., 1955; Fordham University, M.S., 1959. *Home:* 435 West 238th St., Bronx, N.Y.

CAREER: Hawthorn Cedarknolls School (residential treatment center for emotionally disturbed children), Hawthorne, N.Y., teacher, later curriculum coordinator, 1957-63; Phoenix School (experimental day treatment center), New York, N.Y., director, 1965-68. *Member:* Council for Exceptional Children, Council for Children with Behavioral Disorders, National Education Association, Phi Delta Kappa, Kappa Delta Pi.

WRITINGS: Teaching the Emotionally Disturbed: A Casebook, Holt, 1965.

WORK IN PROGRESS: A book on assessment and remediation of learning difficulties.

AVOCATIONAL INTERESTS: Acting in community theater.

*   *   *

GRUEN, John 1926-

PERSONAL: Born September 12, 1926, in Enghien-les-Bains, France; married Jane Wilson (now a painter), March 28, 1948; children: Julia. *Education:* City College (now City College of the City University of New York), student, 1944-45; State University of Iowa, B.A., 1948, M.A., 1949. *Home:* 317 West 83rd St., New York, N.Y. 10024.

CAREER: Brentano's Bookstore, New York, N.Y., assistant book buyer, 1950-54; Grove Press, New York, N.Y., publicity director, 1955-56; Rapho-Guillumette Pictures, New York, N.Y., agent for photographers, 1956-59; director of Martha Jackson Gallery, New York, N.Y., 1960; *New York Herald Tribune*, New York, N.Y., associate critic of music and art, 1960-66; *New York World Journal Tribune*, New York, N.Y., chief art critic, 1966-69; *New York Magazine*, New York, N.Y., art critic, 1969-71; free-lance writer, 1971—.

WRITINGS: The New Bohemia: The Combine Generation, Shorecrest, 1966; *Close-Up*, Viking, 1968; *The Private World of Leonard Bernstein*, Viking, 1968; *The Party's Over Now*, Viking, 1972; *The Private World of Ballet*, Viking, 1974.

Author of play, "Never Tell Isabel," first produced in New York at La Mama Experimental Theatre Club, January 22, 1969. Composer of art songs, and film and theater music. Contributing editor, *Dance Magazine*, 1974-75; art critic, *Soho Weekly News*, 1974-75.

WORK IN PROGRESS: Menotti: A Biography, publication by Macmillan expected in 1976.

*   *   *

GUBSER, Nicholas J. 1938-

PERSONAL: Born September 14, 1938, in Tulsa, Okla.; son of Eugene Herbert (a lawyer) and Mary (Douglass) Gubser; married Margaret Blackwell (a teacher of French), June 15, 1966. *Education:* Yale University, B.A. (summa cum laude), 1962; Oxford University, B.Litt., 1964. *Politics:* Democratic. *Religion:* Methodist.

CAREER: Studied and wrote in Paris, France, 1964-66.

Military service: U.S. Army, beginning 1966. *Member:* Phi Beta Kappa. *Awards, honors:* Rhodes scholar at Magdalen College, Oxford University, 1962-64.

WRITINGS: The Nunamiut Eskimos: Hunters of Caribou, Yale University Press, 1965.

SIDELIGHTS: Gubser has wandered from northern Alaska to India. At eighteen he bicycled through Europe for six months, spent another six months in Pakistan, India, and Japan. The next three summers he made a canoe trip from the source of the Mississippi to the Gulf of Mexico (1958), was archaeological field assistant in the central Brooks Range of Alaska (1959), and did ethnographic research on the Nunamiut Eskimos at Anaktuvuk Pass in northern Alaska, 1960-61. Summer 1963, was spent living with a French family near Tours; summer, 1964, in Florence, Italy; and summer, 1965, in travel through the Balkans, Middle East, and Ethiopia. He told *CA* that he is: "Reasonably fluent in French, once fluent in Eskimo, moderately fluent in Italian, poor in Spanish and German."†

*   *   *

GUDER, Eileen (Likens) 1919-

PERSONAL: Born March 28, 1919, in Ventura, Calif.; daughter of George Hiram and Myrtle (Russell) Likens; married Russell O. Guder (a certified public accountant), December 29, 1938 (died, 1966); married William M. Triplett (a professor of music), 1970; children: Darrell L., Carole Ann (deceased), Donna Gail (Mrs. Michael Lee Barnes). *Education:* Ventura Junior College, A.S., 1938. *Politics:* Republican. *Religion:* Protestant. *Residence:* Hollywood, Calif.

WRITINGS: What Happened After, Zondervan, 1962; *We're Never Alone*, Zondervan, 1965; *To Live in Love*, Zondervan, 1967; *Living in Both Worlds*, Zondervan, 1968; *The Many Faces of Friendship*, Word Books, 1970; *The Naked I*, Word Books, 1971; *God, But I'm Bored*, Doubleday, 1971; *God Wants You to Smile*, Doubleday, 1974.

WORK IN PROGRESS: Deliver Us From Fear, for Word Books, publication expected in 1976.

*   *   *

GUERIN, Wilfred L(ouis) 1929-

PERSONAL: Born July 10, 1929, in New Orleans, La.; son of Wilfred Louis (a realtor) and Carmel (Cali) Guerin; married Wilda Belson, July 21, 1951; children: Wilfred Thomas, Glenn, Geoffrey, Eleanor, Gregory, Julia. *Education:* Tulane University of Louisiana, B.A. (with honors in English), 1951, M.A., 1953, Ph.D., 1958. *Politics:* Democrat. *Religion:* Roman Catholic. *Home:* 259 Atlantic Ave., Shreveport, La. 71105.

CAREER: Holy Cross High School, New Orleans, La., instructor, 1952-53; Centenary College of Louisiana, Shreveport, instructor, 1953-58, assistant professor of English, 1958-62; University of Southern Louisiana, Lafayette, associate professor of English, 1962-63; Centenary College of Louisiana, professor of English, 1963-1974; Louisiana State University, Shreveport, professor of English, 1974—. Visiting faculty audit program, Harvard University, 1970; visiting faculty, British studies program, University College, Oxford University, summer, 1974. *Member:* National Council of Teachers of English, Modern Language Association of America, American Association of University Professors, South Central Modern Language

Association, Louisiana Council of Teachers of English, Conference of College Composition and Communication, South Central Renaissance Society, Phi Beta Kappa, Phi Sigma Iota, Kappa Delta Pi. *Awards, honors:* Fellow, Southeastern Institute for Medieval and Renaissance Studies, 1966.

WRITINGS: (Contributor) *Malory's Originality: A Critical Study of "Le Morte d'Arthur,"* edited by R. M. Lumiansky, Johns Hopkins Press, 1964; (with Earle Labor, Lee Morgan, and John Willingham) *A Handbook of Critical Approaches to Literature*, Harper, 1966; (with Labor, Morgan, and Willingham) *Mandala: Literature for Critical Analysis*, Harper, 1970. Contributor to *Renascence, Explicator, America*, and *Victorian Poetry, Faculty Forum, South Central Bulletin*.

WORK IN PROGRESS: An interdisciplinary topic that involves interrelationship between poetry, literary criticism, and theology and religious practice, with special attention to Teilhard de Chardin.

SIDELIGHTS: "People and the existential present are my concern . . . though my primary field of training and study is the Middle Ages. . . . When I call up something of religious concern to me, some echo of man's past, some hope for the future, I want to be understood and want others to understand the relevance of all to the present moment, or the present person." Guerin reads French and Italian.

*   *   *

GUFFIN, Gilbert L.   1906-

PERSONAL: Born August 5, 1906, near Marietta, Ga.; son of William Thomas and Nora (Eubanks) Guffin; married Lorene Parrish, August 23, 1930; children: Gilbert Truett, Orville Thomas. *Education:* Mercer University, A.B., 1930; Eastern Baptist Theological Seminary, B.D., 1935, Th.M., 1938; Th.D., 1941. *Home:* 2832 Vestavia Forest Place, Birmingham, Ala. 35216.

CAREER: Ordained minister of Baptist Church, 1927; junior high school principal in Mableton, Ga., 1927-28, in Marietta, Ga., 1930-33; pastor in Marietta, Ga., and area, 1928-33, in Merchantville, N.J., 1935-42, in Jasper, Ala., 1942-47; Walker College, Jasper, Ala., dean of Baptist seminar, 1942-47; Howard College, Birmingham, Ala., founding director of Extension Division, 1947-49; The Eastern Baptist Theological Seminary, Philadelphia, Pa., president, 1950-61; Eastern College, Philadelphia, Pa., founding president, 1952-61; Samford University, Birmingham, Ala., dean of religion, 1961-71, dean emeritus, 1971—. Trustee of The Eastern Baptist Theological Seminary and Eastern Baptist College, 1961—. Director, Watchman-Examiner Foundation. *Member:* Omicron Delta Kappa, Masons, Rotary Club. *Awards, honors:* LL.D., Atlanta Law School, 1951; D.D., Mercer University, 1955; Freedoms Foundation Awards, 1960, 1961; L.H.D., Eastern College, 1972.

WRITINGS: Called of God, Revell, 1951; *Pastor and Church*, Broadman, 1955; (editor and contributor) *What God Hath Wrought*, Judson, 1960; (contributor) *Eighty-eight Evangelistic Sermons*, Harper, 1964; *The Gospel in Isaiah*, Convention, 1968; *The Bible: God's Missionary Message to Man*, Women's Missionary Union, Volume I, 1973, Volume II, 1974. Contributor to religious journals.

WORK IN PROGRESS: Two books, *Christian Higher Education at the Cross-Roads*, and *The Gospel of Judgment*.

GUINAGH, Kevin (Joseph)   1897-

PERSONAL: Born June 3, 1897, in New Castle, Pa.; son of Robert and Catherine (Sullivan) Guinagh; married Marie Thomas, 1931; children: Barry. *Education:* St. Vincent College, A.B., 1919, A.M., 1921; Catholic University of America, S.T.B., 1923; University of Pittsburgh, Ph.D., 1931. *Home and office:* 424 Dunedin Circle, Temple Ter., Fla. 33617. *Agent:* Walter Kahoe, Box 166, Moylan, Pa. 19065.

CAREER: Antioch College, Yellow Springs, Ohio, instructor, 1930-31; Eastern Illinois University, Charleston, 1931-64, began as instructor, professor of foreign languages, 1934-64, head of department, 1934-62, professor emeritus, 1964—; University of Puerto Rico, Mayaguez, professor of humanities, 1946-68; University of South Florida, Tampa, lecturer in humanities, 1968-69. Visiting professor, University of Illinois, summers, 1940 and 1950, University of Nebraska, summer, 1941, Antioch College, 1947-48, Ohio State University, summer, 1949. *Member:* American Philological Association, American Association of Teachers of Spanish and Portuguese, National Federation of Modern Language Teachers Association, American Association of University Professors, Classical Association of the Middle West and South.

WRITINGS: Inspired Amateurs, Longmans, Green, 1937; (editor with A. P. Dorjahn) *Latin Literature in Translation*, Longmans, Green, 1942, 2nd edition, 1952; *Search for Glory*, Longmans, Green, 1946; (with C. T. Murphy and W. J. Oates) *Greek and Roman Classics in Translation*, Longmans, Green, 1947; (translator and author of introduction) *Aeneid of Vergil*, Rinehart, 1953, revised edition, Holt, 1970; (compiler with Guy R. Lyle) *I Am Happy to Present: A Book of Introductions*, H. W. Wilson, 1953, 2nd edition, 1968; (contributor) Clarence Forbes, editor, *The Teaching of Classical Subjects in English*, American Classic League, 1958; (author of introduction) Guy Lyle, *The President, the Professor, and the College Library;* H. W. Wilson Co., 1963; (compiler and translator) *Dictionary of Foreign Phrases and Abbreviations*, H. W. Wilson, 1965, 2nd edition, 1972. Contributor of articles and reviews to classical journals, and humorous material to other journals.

*   *   *

GUION, Robert M(organ)   1924-

PERSONAL: Surname rhymes with "lion"; born September 14, 1924, in Indianapolis, Ind.; son of Leroy Herbert (an insurance salesman) and Carolyn (Morgan) Guion; married Emily Firestone, June 8, 1947; children: David, Diana, Keith, Pamela, Judith. *Education:* University of Iowa, B.A., 1948; Purdue University, M.S., 1950, Ph.D., 1952. *Religion:* Methodist. *Home:* 632 Haskins Rd., Bowling Green, Ohio 43402. *Office:* Department of Psychology, Bowling Green State University, Bowling Green, Ohio 43403.

CAREER: Purdue University, Lafayette, Ind., vocational counselor, Schools of Engineering, 1948-51, research assistant, 1951-52; Bowling Green State University, Bowling Green, Ohio, assistant professor, 1952-55, associate professor, 1955-64, professor of psychology, 1964—, department chairman, 1966-71. Visiting associate professor, University of California, Berkeley, 1963-64; visiting professor, University of New Mexico, summer, 1965; advisor, Department of Personnel Services, State of Hawaii, summer, 1970; visiting research psychologist, Educational Testing Service,

1971-72. Psychologist in private consulting practice. *Military service:* U.S. Army, 1943-46. *Member:* International Association of Applied Psychology, American Psychological Association (president, Division of Industrial and Organizational Psychology, 1972-73), Midwestern Psychological Association. *Awards, honors:* James McKeen Cattell Award of division of industrial psychology, American Psychological Association, 1965, for scientific merit of research proposal.

WRITINGS: Personnel Testing, McGraw, 1965; (contributor) H. L. Fromkin and J. J. Sherwood, editors, *Integrating the Organization,* Free Press, 1974; (contributor) M. D. Dunnette, editor, *Handbook of Industrial and Organizational Psychology,* Rand McNally, in press. Contributor to professional journals. Member of board of editors, *Organizational Behavior and Human Performance.*

WORK IN PROGRESS: Research on fair employment practices; research on validity generalization principles.

AVOCATIONAL INTERESTS: Carpentry (of sorts), travel (mountains and ocean areas preferred), music.

*   *   *

GUNN, Sister Agnes Marie   1928-

PERSONAL: Born May 18, 1928, in Philadelphia, Pa.; daughter of Ernest Francis and Agnes (Culliney) Gunn. *Education:* Chestnut Hill College, Temple University, Teacher Certificate, 1949; University of Pennsylvania, M.A., 1956, Ph.D., 1969. *Politics:* Democrat. *Home:* Mt. St. Joseph Convent, Philadelphia, Pa. 19118.

CAREER: Roman Catholic nun of Sisters of St. Joseph (S.S.J.). Teacher of English in Philadelphia, Pa., at Hallahan High School, 1953-58, West Philadelphia Catholic High School, 1958-60, Hallahan High School, 1960-67, Chestnut Hill College, 1967-72; teacher of English, St. Rose High School, Belmar, N.J., 1972-74; Sisters of St. Joseph, Philadelphia, director of education, 1974—. Catholic Archdiocese of Philadelphia, member of Syllabus Revision Committee. *Member:* Delta Epsilon Sigma.

WRITINGS: A Book of Plays, Macmillan, 1960, revised edition, 1963; (compiler) *Modern American Drama,* Macmillan, 1960, revised edition, 1963. Contributor to *Friar, Today, America,* and *Catholic School Journal.*

*   *   *

GUNN, Thom(son William)   1929-

PERSONAL: Born August 29, 1929, in Gravesend, England; son of Herbert Smith (a journalist) and Ann Charlotte (Thomson) Gunn. *Education:* Trinity College, Cambridge, B.A., 1953, M.A., 1958; studied at Stanford University, 1954-55, 1956-58. *Religion:* Atheist. *Residence:* 1216 Cole St., San Francisco, Calif. 94117.

CAREER: University of California, Berkeley, 1958-66, began as lecturer, became associate professor of English. Full-time writer, 1966—. *Military service:* British Army, National Service, 1948-50. *Awards, honors:* Levinson Prize, 1955; Somerset Maugham Award, 1959; American Institute of Arts and Letters grant, 1964; Guggenheim Award, 1971.

WRITINGS: (Editor) *Poetry from Cambridge,* Fortune Press, 1953; *Fighting Terms,* Fantasy Press, 1954, revised edition, Faber, 1962; *The Sense of Movement,* Faber, 1957, University of Chicago Press, 1959; *My Sad Captains,* University of Chicago Press, 1961; (with Ted Hughes) *Selected Poems,* Faber, 1962; (editor with Ted Hughes) *Five American Poets: Edgar Bowers, Howard Nemerov, Hyam Plutzik, Louis Simpson, and William Stafford,* Faber, 1963; *A Geography,* Stone Wall Press, 1966; (with Ander Gunn) *Positives,* Faber, 1966, University of Chicago Press, 1967; *Touch,* Faber, 1967, University of Chicago Press, 1968; *The Garden of the Gods,* Pym-Randall Press, 1968; (editor and author of introduction) Fulke Greville Brooke, *Selected Poems of Fulke Greville,* University of Chicago Press, 1968; *Poems, 1950-1966: A Selection,* Faber, 1969; *The Explorers,* R. Gilbertson, 1969; *The Fair in the Woods,* Sycamore Press, 1969; *Sunlight,* Albondocani Press, 1969; *Moly,* Faber, 1971, Farrar, Straus, 1973; *To the Air,* Godine, 1974.

Work represented in many anthologies, including *Springtime,* edited by G. S. Fraser and I. Fletcher, Peter Owen, 1953; *Mark in Time,* edited by R. Johnson and N. Harvey, Glide Publications, 1971. Poetry reviewer, *Yale Review,* 1958-64. Contributor to *Encounter, New Statesman, Poetry,* and other publications.

SIDELIGHTS: Has lived in Paris, 1950, Cambridge, 1950-53, Rome, 1953-54, San Antonio, Tex., 1955-56, California, 1954-55, 1957—. *Avocational Interests:* Reading, films, drinking.

BIOGRAPHICAL/CRITICAL SOURCES: Carolyn Riley, editor, *Contemporary Literary Criticism,* Volume III, Gale, 1975.

*   *   *

GUSS, Donald L(eroy)   1929-

PERSONAL: Born July 21, 1929, in Brooklyn, N.Y.; son of Sidney R. (in management) and Eva (Halperson) Guss; married Joanne C. Randel, November 17, 1959; children: Amy Jo, Sean Robert. *Education:* City College (now City College of the City University of New York), B.S.S., 1950; Columbia University, M.A., 1952; University of Wisconsin, Ph.D., 1961. *Politics:* Independent. *Religion:* None. *Office:* Department of English, University of California, Santa Barbara, Calif.

CAREER: City College (now City College of the City University of New York), lecturer, 1950-52; Boston College, Boston, Mass., instructor, 1958-59; Colby College, Waterville, Me., instructor in English, 1959-60; Rutgers University, New Brunswick, N.J., instructor, 1960-63, research grantee, 1962-63; Wayne State University, Detroit, Mich., assistant professor of English, 1963-65, associate professor of English, beginning 1965; currently at University of California, Santa Barbara, Calif., member of faculty in department of English. *Military service:* U.S. Army, 1952-54. *Member:* Modern Language Association of America, Renaissance Society of America, American Association of University Professors, American Association of Teachers of Italian, Michigan College English Association, Phi Beta Kappa. *Awards, honors:* Fulbright fellowship, University of Rome, 1957-58; Huntington Library fellowship, 1963; Folger Library fellowship, 1964.

WRITINGS: John Donne, Petrarchist: Italianate Conceits and Love Theory in the Songs and Sonnets, Wayne State University Press, 1966. Book review editor of *Criticism;* contributor of articles to *PMLA, Journal of English and Germanic Philology, Notes and Queries, Huntington Library Quarterly,* and other publications.

SIDELIGHTS: Guss is competent in Italian and French. *Avocational interests:* Chess.†

GUSTAFSON, Richard F(olke) 1934-

PERSONAL: Born June 17, 1934, in Hartford, Conn.; son of Folke Helmer (a sales representative) and Mary E. (Gliniak) Gustafson. Education: Yale University, A.B., 1956; Columbia University, Ph.D., 1963. Office: Department of Russian, Barnard College, Columbia University, New York, N.Y. 10027.

CAREER: Brown University, Providence, R.I., instructor in Russian, 1960-62; Yale University, New Haven, Conn., assistant professor of Russian, 1962-65; Columbia University, Barnard College, New York, N.Y., associate professor, 1965-72, professor of Russian, 1972—, chairman of department, 1965—. Member: Modern Language Association of America, American Association for Advancement of Slavic Studies, American Association of Teachers of Slavic and Eastern European Languages.

WRITINGS: The Imaginations of Spring: The Poetry of Afanasey Fet, Yale University Press, 1966. Contributor to PMLA, Slavic and East European Languages Journal, and other journals.

WORK IN PROGRESS: Nineteenth-century Russian poetry, especially the work of Baratynsky; the nineteenth-century novel in relation to the Russian novel.

SIDELIGHTS: Gustafson reads Russian, French, German, and some Latin. He is studying Greek.†

* * *

GUSTAVSON, Carl G(ustav) 1915-

PERSONAL: Born August 3, 1915, in Vinton, Iowa; son of Carl Linus and Edla (Gustafson) Gustavson; married Caryl Jennings, June 30, 1943; children: Carl, Eric, Martha. Education: Augustana College, Rock Island, Ill., A.B., 1937; University of Illinois, A.M., 1938; Cornell University, Ph.D., 1942. Religion: Episcopalian. Home: 14 Utah Pl., Athens, Ohio; (summer) General Delivery, Kenora, Ontario, Canada.

CAREER: Lake Forest College, Lake Forest, Ill., instructor in history, 1942-43; Miami University, Oxford, Ohio, acting assistant professor, 1943-45; Ohio University, Athens, assistant professor, 1945-48, associate professor, 1948-56, professor, 1956-71, distinguished professor of history, 1971—, acting chairman of department, 1955-56, chairman, 1961-65. Visiting professor at Emory University, 1949, Cornell University, 1950, Wayne State University, 1955, University of Illinois, 1961, University of Cincinnati, 1964, Western Reserve University (now Case Western Reserve University), 1965, University of Georgia, 1968, University of the Pacific, 1969.

MEMBER: American Historical Association, French Historical Society, Societe d'Histoire Moderne (Paris), Ohio Academy of History (vice-president, 1963-64; president, 1964-65), Phi Beta Kappa, Phi Alpha Theta, Swedish Club (Chicago). Awards, honors: Ford Foundation fellowship, 1953-54; American Philosophical Society grant, 1956; annual award of Ohio Academy of History for The Preface to History, 1956; Baker research award, 1965; Fulbright fellowship for study in Sweden, 1970.

WRITINGS: The Preface to History, McGraw, 1955; The Institutional Drive, Ohio University Press, 1966; Europe in the World Community Since 1939, Allyn & Bacon, 1971. Contributor to learned journals.

WORK IN PROGRESS: The Mansion of History.

SIDELIGHTS: Gustavson has lived, for purposes of research, in Munich, 1960, and Spain and Vienna, 1966, Sweden, 1970, Switzerland, 1972-73, and has traveled in most European countries and the Soviet Union. He is competent in Swedish and German; has reading knowledge of several other languages.

* * *

GUTZKE, Manford G(eorge) 1896-

PERSONAL: Surname is pronounced "Good-ski"; born July 20, 1896, in Clifford, Ontario, Canada; son of Henry Sebastian (a farmer) and Ann (Immel) Gutzke; married Sarah Bernstein, June 20, 1924; children: Miriam (Mrs. Albert C. Burke), Mark E., John H., Elizabeth (Mrs. Francis C. Grier), Peter (deceased). Education: Attended University of Manitoba, 1925-27; Southern Methodist University, B.A., 1931, M.A., 1939; Columbia University, Ph.D., 1954. Office: The Bible For You, Inc., Box 15007, Atlanta, Ga. 30333.

CAREER: Presbyterian clergyman. Pastor in Dallas, Tex., 1930-36; Austin College, Sherman, Tex., professor of Bible, 1936-39; Columbia Theological Seminary, Decatur, Ga., professor of Christian education, 1939-66, professor emeritus, 1966—. The Bible For You, Inc., Atlanta, Ga., president and broadcaster, 1961—. Military service: Canadian Army, 1917-19. Awards, honors: D.D., Austin College, 1935.

WRITINGS: John Dewey's Thought and Its Implications for Christian Education, King's Crown Press, 1955; Plain Talk About Christian Words, Royal Publishers (Nashville), 1964; Plain Talk On Acts, Zondervan, 1966; Plain Talk On Matthew, Zondervan, 1966; Plain Talk On Luke, Zondervan, 1966; Plain Talk on John, Zondervan, 1968; Go Gospel: Daily Devotions and Bible Studies in the Gospel of Mark, Regal Books, 1968; Division, Despair, and Hope: Daily Devotions and Bible Studies, Regal Books, 1969; A Look at the Book: Daily Devotions and Studies in the Bible and What It Says About Itself, Regal Books, 1969; Plain Talk on James, Zondervan, 1969; Wanderers, Slaves, and Kings: Daily Devotions and Bible Studies, Regal Books, 1969; Plain Talk on Galatians, Baker Book, 1972; Plain Talk on Ephesians, Zondervan, 1973.†

* * *

GUY, Harold A. 1904-

PERSONAL: Born July 5, 1904, in London, England; son of Frederick Bingley (a maker of scientific instruments) and Gertrude (Fisher) Guy; children: Ian N., Clifford M. Education: Richmond College, London, B.D., 1930, B.A., 1933; Cambridge University, Certificate in Education. Home: 7 Camden Way, Dorchester, Dorset, England.

CAREER: The King's School, Macclesfield, Cheshire, England, master in charge of divinity, 1941-45; Taunton School, Southampton, England, assistant master in classics, 1945-67; Alice Ottley School, Worchester, England, part time teacher, 1970-75. Lecturer in extramural department, University of Southampton, 1954-56, University of Birmingham, 1970-71; tutor at University of Ibadan, Nigeria, 1963 and 1965, University of Legon, Ghana, 1970. Examiner at Handsworth College, Birmingham, England, 1938-40, and later, for general certificate of education, University of London and Cambridge University, 1943—.

WRITINGS: New Testament Prophecy, Epworth, 1947; The New Testament Doctrine of the Last Things, Oxford University Press, 1948; Landmarks in the Story of Christi-

anity, Macmillan, 1949; *The Life of Christ*, Macmillan, 1951; *The Study of the Gospels*, Macmillan, 1952; *The Acts of the Apostles*, Macmillan, 1952; *The Origin of the Gospel of Mark*, Hodder & Stoughton, 1955; *A Critical Introduction to the Gospels*, Macmillan, 1955; *The Synoptic Gospels*, Macmillan, 1960; *The Gospel and Letters of John*, Macmillan, 1963; *Who's Who in the Gospels*, Macmillan, 1966; *The Gospel of Mark*, Macmillan, 1968; *The Church in the New Testament*, Macmillan, 1969; *The Gospel of Matthew*, Macmillan, 1971; *The Gospel of Luke*, Macmillan, 1972; *The Fourth Gospel: An Introduction*, Macmillan, 1972; (editor) *Our Religions*, Dent, 1972; *The Story of Jesus of Nazareth*, Dent, 1972; *The Story of the Hebrews*, Dent, 1972.

* * *

GUY, Rosa (Cuthbert) 1928-

PERSONAL: Born September 1, 1928, in Trinidad, West Indies; came to U.S. in 1932; daughter of Henry and Audrey (Gonzales) Cuthbert; married Warner Guy (deceased); children: Warner. *Agent:* McIntosh & Otis, Inc., 18 East 41st St., New York, N.Y. 10017.

CAREER: Writer. *Member:* Harlem Writer's Guild (president).

WRITINGS: Bird at My Window (novel), Lippincott, 1966; (editor) *Children of Longing* (anthology), Holt, 1971; *The Friends* (novel), Holt, 1973. Author of one-act play, "Venetian Blinds," 1954. Also author of a novel, *Ruby*. Contributor to *Cosmopolitan* and *Freedomways*.

WORK IN PROGRESS: A book, *Alexander Hamilton: The Enigma*; *Benidine*, a novel dealing with a Trinidadian family in New York; research in African languages.

SIDELIGHTS: Rosa Guy told *CA:* "[I am] interested in the historical and cultural aspects of all peoples of African descent. Have been to Haiti and back to Trinidad to study the ways, customs, and languages retained over the years from Africa; hope to visit Africa in the near future." She speaks French and Creole.

* * *

GUYTON, Arthur C(lifton) 1919-

PERSONAL: Born September 8, 1919, in Oxford, Miss.; son of Billy (a physician) and Mary Katherine (Smallwood) Guyton; married Ruth Alice Weigle, June 12, 1943; children: David, Robert, John, Steven, Catherine, Jean, Douglas, James, Thomas, Gregg. *Education:* University of Mississippi, B.A. (with special distinction), 1939; Harvard Medical School, M.D., 1943. *Office:* University of Mississippi Medical Center, Jackson, Miss.

CAREER: Massachusetts General Hospital, Boston, surgical intern, 1943-44, assistant resident, 1946-47; Hood College, Frederick, Md., special instructor in physics, 1946; University of Tennessee Medical School, Memphis, acting associate professor of physiology (part-time), 1947; University of Mississippi, Jackson Campus, associate professor of pharmacology, 1947-48, professor of physiology and biophysics and chairman of department, 1948—. Oak Ridge Institute of Nuclear Studies Teletherapy Evaluation Board, member of executive committee, 1952-53; National Board of Medical Examiners, chairman of physiology test committee, 1959-61; National Institutes of Health, chairman of physiology training committee, 1961-64. Developer of medical research equipment and other devices, including patient hoist for the paralyzed, electrically-operated chair for one-finger operation, and automatic knee-locking brace; holder of amateur radio license, 1936—, and commercial licenses in radiotelephone and radiotelegraph, 1937-40. *Military service:* U.S. Navy, 1944-46; received Army Commendation Citation for research in bacterial warfare.

MEMBER: American Association for the Advancement of Science (fellow), American College of Cardiology (fellow), American Physiological Society (president, 1974-75), Biophysical Society, American Federation for Clinical Research, American Heart Association (member of board of directors, 1961—), American Association of University Professors, Southern Society for Clinical Research (president, 1956-57), Mississippi Heart Association (vice-president, 1952-54; president, 1955-56), Mississippi Academy of Science (member of board of directors, 1961—; president, 1964-65), Sigma Xi, Alpha Omega Alpha, Omicron Delta Kappa. *Awards, honors:* Named one of ten outstanding young men of America, U.S. Junior Chamber of Commerce, 1951; Presidential Citation for development of aids for the handicapped, 1956; Gould Award of American Association for the Advancement of Science for cardiovascular research, 1959; Wiggers Award; McIntyre Award; Gould Award.

WRITINGS: Textbook of Medical Physiology, Saunders, 1956, 4th edition, 1971; *Function of the Human Body*, Saunders, 1959, 4th edition, 1974; *Circulatory Physiology: Cardiac Output and Its Regulation*, Saunders, 1963, 2nd edition, 1973. Author of over three hundred articles and research papers, mostly on the circulatory system. Member of editorial board, *Annual Review of Physiology*, 1966-71, and *American Journal of Physiology, Journal of Applied Physiology, American Journal of Cardiology, Excerpta Medica, Circulation Research, Medical Hypothesis*. Editor of physiology series, MTP *International Review of Sciences*.

AVOCATIONAL INTERESTS: Sailing.

* * *

GWILLIAM, Kenneth M(ason) 1937-

PERSONAL: Born June 27, 1937, in Wigan, Lancashire, England; son of John Gwilliam (a railwayman); married Jennifer Mary Bell, September 16, 1961; children: David Richard. *Education:* Attended Oxford University, 1957-60. *Home:* 533 Earlham Rd., Norwich, England. *Office:* University of East Anglia, Norwich, England.

CAREER: University of Nottingham, Nottingham, England, lecturer in economics, 1961-65; University of East Anglia, Norwich, England, lecturer in economics, 1965—.

WRITINGS: Transport and Public Policy, Allen & Unwin, 1964. Contributor to economics journals.

WORK IN PROGRESS: Research on regulation of air transport and on regional economic planning in the United Kingdom.†

* * *

HABEL, Norman C. 1932-

PERSONAL: Born September 7, 1932, in Hamilton, Queensland, Australia; son of Edwin Albert Rupert (a grazier) and Sylvia (Huf) Habel; married Barbara Kretschmer, August 12, 1956; children: Simon, Fern, Robyn. *Education:* Concordia Seminary, Adelaide, South Australia, diploma, 1955; Concordia Seminary, St. Louis, Mo., B.D., 1956, S.T.M., 1957, Th.D., 1962. *Home:* 26 Yurilla Dr., Bellevue Heights, S.A., Australia 5050. *Office:* Adelaide

College of Advanced Education, Kintore Ave., Adelaide, S.A., Australia 5000.

CAREER: Lutheran minister, 1956—; Trinity Church, Brooklyn, N.Y., pastor in charge, 1957-60; Concordia Seminary, St. Louis, Mo., professor of Old Testament, 1960-73; Adelaide College of Advanced Education, Adelaide, Australia, head of religious studies, 1974—. *Member:* Society of Biblical Literature, Lutheran Society for Worship, Music and the Arts. *Awards, honors:* Post-doctoral scholarship, New York University; second prize for drama, California Western University.

WRITINGS—Old Testament technical studies: *Yahweh Versus Baal,* Book Associates, 1964; *The Form and Meaning of the Fall Narrative,* Concordia Seminary Press, 1965; *Jeremiah,* Concordia, 1967; *Literary Criticism of the Old Testament,* Fortress Press, 1971; *Job,* Cambridge University Press, 1975.

Other: *The Visit of God* (a Christmas presentation for children), Concordia Seminary Print Shop, 1964; *Wait a Minute, Moses,* Concordia Publishing House, 1965; *Are You Joking, Jeremiah?* (poems), Concordia Publishing House, 1967; *Create in Me* (a folk Eucharist), Concordia Seminary Print Shop, 1967; *For Mature Adults Only* (booklet and recording for youth), Fortress Press, 1968; *Interrobang,* Fortress Press, 1969; (editor and contributor) *What Are We Going to Do With All these Rotting Fish?,* Fortress Press, 1970; *Hi, Have a Nice Day,* Fortress Press, 1972; *Birthquakes* (giftbook), Fortress Press, 1974.

Also author of *Invitation,* a jazz Eucharist booklet and recording, published by Concordia Seminary Print Shop, and of Concordia's "Purple Puzzle Tree Series," thirty-six titles with six recordings, 1971—.

WORK IN PROGRESS: Research in the relationship between Old Testament and world religions; development of a religious education program for Australian public schools.

*   *   *

HACKER, Louis M(orton) 1899-

PERSONAL: Born March 17, 1899, in New York, N.Y.; son of Morris (a shopkeeper) and Celia (Waxelbaum) Hacker; married Lillian Lewis, June 26, 1921 (died, 1952); married Beatrice Larson Brennan, June 17, 1953; children: (first marriage) Andrew, Betsy (Mrs. Roy Dexheimer). *Education:* Columbia University, A.B., 1922 (class of 1920), M.A., 1923. *Politics:* Republican. *Religion:* Jewish. *Home:* 430 West 116th St., New York, N.Y. 10027. *Office:* Columbia University, New York, N.Y. 10027.

CAREER: Assistant editor of *New International Encyclopedia,* New York, N.Y., 1923-24, 1928-29, of *Encyclopedia of Social Sciences,* New York, N.Y., 1932-34; free-lance writer at other periods prior to 1935; Columbia University, New York, N.Y., lecturer in economics, 1935-42, assistant professor, 1942-44, associate professor, 1944-48, professor of economic history, 1948—, director of School of General Studies, 1949-52, dean of School of General Studies, 1952-58. Oxford University, Harmsworth Professor of American History and fellow of The Queen's College, 1948-49; The Pennsylvania State University, Distinguished Visiting Professor, 1959-60. Lecturer at New School for Social Research, 1940, 1943-48, American Institute of Banking, 1940-43, Fulbright Conference on American Studies at Cambridge University, 1952, Army War College, 1952-54, 1958, 1961, Yeshiva University, 1958-59. The Ohio State Univer-

sity, 1960; Distinguished Visiting Professor, Fairleigh Dickinson University, 1967-68; summer lecturer at other colleges and universities during period, 1937-53. Consultant on adult education, academic freedom, and American capitalist system. Was foreman (1958-59) of the New York Grand Jury that exposed the television quiz scandals.

MEMBER: American Economic Association, American Historical Association, Economic History Association, American Association for Middle East Studies (director), Royal Society of Arts (England), American Civil Liberties Union (director), Mount Pelerin Society, P.E.N., Author's League, Pilgrims of the United States, Phi Beta Kappa, Athenaeum Club (London). *Awards, honors:* M.A., Oxford University, 1948; LL.D., University of Hawaii, 1953; Guggenheim fellow, 1949, 1958-59; Benjamin Franklin Fellow, Royal Society of Arts, 1961; L.H.D., Columbia University, 1972.

WRITINGS: (With B. B. Kendrick) *United States Since 1865,* Crofts, 1932, 4th edition, 1949; *The Farmer Is Doomed,* Day, 1933; *A Short History of the New Deal,* Crofts, 1934; *The United States: A Graphic History,* Random, 1937; *American Problems of Today,* Crofts, 1939; *The Triumph of American Capitalism,* Simon and Schuster, 1940; (with others) *The United States in World Affairs,* Heath, 1943; *The Shaping of the American Tradition,* Columbia University Press, 1948; *England and America: The Ties That Bind,* Oxford University Press, 1948; (with others) *The New Industrial Relations,* Cornell University Press, 1948.

(With H. S. Zahler) *The United States in the Twentieth Century,* Crofts, 1952; (with others) *Government Assistance to Universities in Great Britain,* Columbia University Press, 1952; (with others) *Capitalism and the Historians,* University of Chicago Press, 1953; *Alexander Hamilton in the American Tradition,* McGraw, 1957; *American Capitalism,* Van Nostrand, 1957; *The Larger View of the University,* Ohio State University Press, 1961; *Documents in American Economic History,* two volumes, Van Nostrand, 1961; *The World of Andrew Carnegie, 1865-1901,* Lippincott, 1968; *The Course of American Economic Growth and Development,* Wiley, 1970.

Author of introductions to other books. Editor of "American Century" series and "Modern Age" series; co-editor of "American Economic History" series.

Contributor to encyclopedias, magazines, Sunday newspaper supplements, and professional journals for more than fifty years.

WORK IN PROGRESS: Work and Wealth.

SIDELIGHTS: In connection with his work with the New York Grand Jury, Hacker wrote a report, seeking to distinguish between the corrupters, who misused and abused the confidence of the listening public, and the corruptible people, who were their victims. He writes: "It was the latter who paid a heavy price for being exposed; the corrupters got off scot-free. The court suppressed the report—and nothing has been done."

The Triumph of American Capitalism has been translated into Spanish and Japanese, *American Capitalism* into Spanish, Japanese, Portuguese, Urdu, Vietnamese, Hindi, Arabic, and Korean, and *The World of Andrew Carnegie* into Japanese. Hacker reads French and German. *Avocational interests:* Bridge and travel.

BIOGRAPHICAL/CRITICAL SOURCES: Time, February 4, 1952; *Fortune,* April, 1952.

HACKETT, John W. 1924-

PERSONAL: Born January 21, 1924, in Taunton, England; son of Albert and Bertha (Wilkings) Hackett; married Anne-Marie Lebrun (conseiller referendaire at French Cour de Comptes), August 14, 1952. *Education:* London School of Economics and Political Science, University of London, B.Sc., 1950; Institut d'Etudes politiques, Paris, France, graduate, 1952; University of Paris, Docteur d'Etat es Sciences economiques, 1956. *Office:* Organization for Economic Co-operation and Development, Paris, France.

CAREER: Institut de Science Economique appliquee, Paris, France, research officer, 1954-58; Organization for Economic Co-operation and Development, Paris, France, counselor, 1958—. Lecturer at Institut d'Etudes politiques, 1956—. *Member:* Societe d'Economie Politique, Association des Docteurs es Sciences Economiques (both Paris).

WRITINGS: (With wife, Anne-Marie Hackett) *Economic Planning in France*, Allen & Unwin, 1963; *Economic Planning in France in Relation to the Policies of the Developed Countries of Western Europe*, Council for Economic Education (Bombay), 1965; (with Anne-Marie Hackett) *L'Economie britannique—problemes et perspectives*, Foundation Nationale des Sciences Politiques, 1966; English edition, revised and augmented, published as *The British Economy: Problems and Prospects*, Allen & Unwin, 1967; (with Anne-Marie Hackett) *La Vie Economique en Grande Bretange*, A. Colin, 1969. Contributor to *Encyclopaedia Britannica*, 1965 and 1970, *Encyclopaedie Universalis*, 1972.

*　　*　　*

HACKETT, Laura Lyman 1916-

PERSONAL: Born April 19, 1916, in Oberlin, Ohio; daughter of Eugene William (professor of philosophy and religion) and Mary (professor of English Bible; maiden name, Ely) Lyman; married second husband, Frederick K. Hackett (a lawyer), June 22, 1959; children: (with first husband) Eugene L. Boutilier, Julia Boutilier Hernandez, Sybil L. Boutilier. *Education:* Smith College, B.A., 1936; Occidental College, M.A., 1955. *Residence:* Stony Brook, N.Y. 11790.

CAREER: Santa Barbara City College, Santa Barbara, Calif., instructor in English, 1950-59; Farmingdale High School, Farmingdale, Long Island, N.Y., English teacher, 1959-60; Suffolk County Community College, Selden, Long Island, N.Y., professor of English and chairman of humanities division, 1960-74, Western Campus, dean of instruction, 1974—.

WRITINGS—With Richard Williamson: *Anatomy of Reading*, McGraw, 1965; *Design for a Composition*, Harcourt, 1966. Also writer of poetry.

*　　*　　*

HADDAD, George M. 1910-

PERSONAL: Born August 7, 1910, in Homs, Syria; son of Meri T. (a merchant) and Zahiye (Iskander) Haddad; married Fresia Garcia, November 28, 1951; children: Lillian Meri George, Linda. *Education:* American University of Beirut, B.A., 1929; Sorbonne, University of Paris, License es Lettres, 1934; School of Oriental Languages, Paris, Diploma, 1934; University of Chicago, Ph.D., 1949. *Religion:* Greek Orthodox. *Home:* 23 East Pueblo St., Santa Barbara, Calif. 93105. *Office:* University of California, Santa Barbara, Calif. 93106.

CAREER: Instructor at American Friends Boys' School, Ramallah, Palestine, 1929-32, in public schools of Aleppo and Damascus, Syria, 1935-46; Syrian State University, Damascus, professor, 1949-59; University of California, Santa Barbara, associate professor, 1960—, now professor of Middle Eastern history. Visiting professor or lecturer at Bowdoin College and Thiel College, 1957-58, University of Michigan, 1959-60. Member of board of directors, Department of Antiquities, Syria, 1949-59; Syrian delegate to Conference on Cultural Cooperation among Mediterranean Countries, Palermo, Italy, 1954. *Member:* American Oriental Society, Middle East Institute, Council on Foreign Relations. *Awards, honors:* Commander of the Order of Sts. Peter and Paul (Greek Orthodox Patriarchate of Antioch).

WRITINGS: Fath al-'Arab lil-Sham (title means "The Arab Conquest of Damascus, 635 A.D."), al-Adabiyah Press (Beirut), 1931; *Tarikh al-Hadara al-'Arabiyya* (title means "History of Arab Civilization"), [Damascus], 1944; *Aspects of Social Life in Antioch in the Hellenistic-Roman Period*, Hafner, 1949; *Fifty Years of Modern Syria and Lebanon* (in English), Dar al-Hayat (Beirut), 1950; *al-Madkhal ila Tarikh al-Hadara* (title means "History of Civilization in the Middle East"), three volumes, Syrian State University Press, 1953-57; *Revolutions and Military Rule in the Middle East: The Northern Tier and the Arab Countries*, three volumes, Speller, 1965-73. Author of a series of history textbooks for Syrian secondary schools, Damascus, 1935-43. Contributor to *Muslim World, Middle East Forum, Bibliotheca Orientalis*, and other publications.

WORK IN PROGRESS: A monograph on the Egyptian revolution of 1952 and Nasserism.

SIDELIGHTS: Haddad speaks and writes Arabic, French, and a little German and Spanish.

*　　*　　*

HAFLEY, James 1928-

PERSONAL: Born June 2, 1928, in San Francisco, Calif.; son of William Aubry and Mae (Newberry) Hafley. *Education:* University of California, Berkeley, A.A., 1946, B.A., 1948, M.A., 1949, Ph.D., 1952. *Politics:* Democratic. *Home:* 166-33 89th Ave., Jamaica, N.Y. 11432. *Office:* Department of English, St. John's University, Jamaica, N.Y. 11439.

CAREER: Catholic University of America, Washington, D.C., instructor, 1952-55, assistant professor, 1955-58, associate professor of English, 1958-65; St. John's University, Jamaica, N.Y., professor of English, 1965—. Visiting professor, Columbia University, 1969 and 1971; lecturer throughout America. *Member:* Modern Language Association of America, Scottish Texts Society, Poe Studies Association.

WRITINGS: The Glass Roof: Virginia Woolf as Novelist, University of California Press, 1954. Contributor of critical essays to *Accent, New Republic, Modern Fiction Studies*, and many other journals.

WORK IN PROGRESS: Research in American poetry, Victorian critical theory, and the theory of fiction.

SIDELIGHTS: As a critic, Hafley labels himself "inductive neo-functionalist." He is competent in French and German. *Avocational interests:* Music, modern art, the theater, animals, and California ("by which I mean the San Francisco Bay area").

HAGER, Henry B. 1926-

PERSONAL: Born September 12, 1926, in Ashland, Ky.; son of John F. and Henryetta (Brandebury) Hager; married Laura Lee Price, April 26, 1958; children: John Price, Jenny Ellen Brandebury. *Education:* Yale University, B.A., 1951. *Politics:* Democrat. *Religion:* Episcopalian. *Home:* 5841 Wing Lake Rd., Birmingham, Mich. 48010. *Agent:* Helen Harvey Associates, Inc., 1697 Broadway, New York, N.Y. 10019. *Office:* Young & Rubicam International, Inc., 1800 Detroit Bank and Trust Building, Detroit, Mich. 48226.

CAREER: Campbell-Ewald Co., Detroit, Mich., 1952-60, became advertising copy supervisor; advertising copywriter at MacManus, John & Adams, 1961, and Batten, Barton, Durstine & Osborn, 1961-63, both Detroit, Mich.; Campbell-Ewald Co., advertising copy supervisor, 1964-69; Comac Co., Birmingham, Mich., historian and writer-in-residence, 1969-71; Young & Rubicam International, Inc., Detroit, Mich., creative supervisor, 1971—. Wayne State University, teacher of creative writing, 1955, instructor in English, 1956-57, instructor in writing and advertising at University Center for Adult Education, 1973-74. *Military service:* U.S. Army Air Forces, World War II; served on *Stars and Stripes* in Pacific; became sergeant. *Member:* Authors Guild, Yale Alumni Association of Michigan (publicity director, 1956-60), Creative Club of Detroit.

WRITINGS: (Contributor) *Study of a Generation in Transition* (collection of essays by Yale graduates), Yale Daily News, 1953; *Fireball* (novel), Doubleday, 1963. Writer of column for *Yale Alumni Magazine.*

WORK IN PROGRESS: A novel on racial conflicts with the setting at the time of the Detroit riot in 1967.

AVOCATIONAL INTERESTS: Conservation.

* * *

HAGSTRUM, Jean (Howard) 1913-

PERSONAL: Born March 26, 1913, in St. Paul, Minn.; son of Andrew and Sadie Gertrude (Fryckberg) Hagstrum; married Ruth Pritchett, June 29, 1941; children: Katherine Jeanne, Phyllis Ann. *Education:* University of Minnesota, B.A. (summa cum laude), 1933; Northwestern University, M.A., 1938; Yale University, Ph.D., 1941. *Politics:* Democratic. *Religion:* Episcopalian. *Home:* 819 Michigan Ave., Evanston, Ill. 60202. *Office:* Department of English, Northwestern University, Evanston, Ill. 60201.

CAREER: North Park College, Chicago, Ill., instructor in English and speech, 1933-38; Northwestern University, Evanston, Ill., instructor in English, 1940-42; U.S. Office of Censorship, Washington, D.C. director of Allocation Section, 1942-44; Northwestern University, assistant professor, 1946-52, associate professor, 1952-57, professor of English, 1957—, chairman of department, 1958-64 and 1973-74, co-director of Curriculum Center, 1962—. Lecturer at Universities of Copenhagen, Lund, Stockholm, Uppsala, and Gothenburg, aix-en-Provence, and Delhi. Public lecturer on France and Italy. Trustee of Newberry Library, Chicago; advisor to Yale Center for Literature, History, and the Arts. *Military service:* U.S. Army, 1944-46.

MEMBER: Modern Language Association of America, Swedish Pioneer Historical Society, Phi Beta Kappa, Delta Sigma Rho. *Awards, honors:* American Philosophical Society grants, 1952, 1959; Fulbright research fellowship to Italy, 1953-54, and to India, 1972; Newberry Library fellow, 1953, 1957; Melville Cane Award of Poetry Society of

America, 1964, for *William Blake, Poet-Painter*; Clark Library senior fellow, 1970; Huntington Library fellow, 1974; Guggenheim fellowship, 1974-75.

WRITINGS: Samuel Johnson's Literary Criticism, University of Minnesota, 1952; *The Sister Arts*, University of Chicago Press, 1958; *William Blake, Poet-Painter*, University of Chicago Press, 1963. Also writer of articles and essays on English literature and composition.

WORK IN PROGRESS: An edition of Samuel Johnson's sermons; a study of love and passion in literature and art; a dictionary of Blake symbols.

AVOCATIONAL INTERESTS: Photography, music (piano).

* * *

HAINES, John (Meade) 1924-

PERSONAL: Born June 29, 1924, in Norfolk, Va.; son of John Meade (a naval officer) and Helen M. (Donaldson) Haines; married Jo Ella Hussey (an artist), October 10, 1960; married Jane McWhorter (a teacher), November 23, 1970; children: Blair, Anne, Karen, Peter (stepson). *Education:* Attended National Art School, Washington, D.C., 1946-47, American University, Washington, D.C., 1948-49, and Hans Hoffmann School of Fine Art, 1950-52. *Politics:* Liberal Democrat. *Home:* 1219 South 6th Street West, Missoula, Mont. 59801. *Office:* Department of English, University of Montana, Missoula, Mont.

CAREER: Has worked as housepainter, carpenter; employed briefly as clerk in U.S. Department of the Navy, Washington, D.C.; since 1946, has worked as hunter, gardener, fisherman, trapper, and writer; homesteader in Alaska, 1954-69; freelance lecturer and writer, 1969-72; University of Alaska, Anchorage, poet-in-residence, 1972-73; University of Washington, Seattle, visiting professor of English, 1974; University of Montana, Missoula, visiting lecturer in English, 1974—. Visiting lecturer at University of Michigan, Guggenheim Museum, Oberlin College, Idaho State University, New York City Public High Schools, and other institutions. Member of Pacific Grove (Calif.) Library Board, 1972; program director, Alaska Humanites Forum, 1972-73. *Member:* National Audubon Society, Sierra Club, Alaska Conservation Society. *Awards, honors:* Sculpture prize from Corcoran Galley, 1948; Jennie Tane Award for poetry from *Massachusetts Review*, 1964; Guggenheim fellowship, 1965-66; National Endowment for the Humanites grant, 1967-68. *Military service:* U.S. Navy, 1943-46; received several battle stars.

WRITINGS—Poetry: Winter News, Wesleyan University Press, 1966; *The Mirror*, Unicorn Press, 1970; *The Stone Harp*, Wesleyan University Press, 1971; *Twenty Poems*, Unicorn Press, 1971; *Leaves and Ashes*, Kayak Press, 1975. Contributor of poems and translations to *The Critic, Epoch, Michigan Quarterly Review, Nation, Southern Poetry Review, Hudson Review, Kayak, San Francisco Review, Choice*, and other magazines. Contributor of articles to *Dragonfly, Field, Kayak*, and other periodicals.

WORK IN PROGRESS: A book of poems, and several prose items.

SIDELIGHTS: Richard Tillinghast once wrote that Haines is clearly a follower of Robert Bly, and his poems have the faults of the poems published in *The Sixties* and *Kayak*. "Aiming for simplicity, he sometimes achieves only flatness and prosiness. Sometimes a poem of his will sound, with the lack of grace in its language, like an uninspired translation from a foreign language. . . . But Haines is much better than that. He has a real tone of voice that builds up throughout *Winter News,* and a presence that gains in force the more one reads him. Above all, he has the gift of writing poems that are believable, with the utter simplicity of 'The stories they told us were true,/we should have believed them.' For me, the most interesting thing about Haines is the way he balances a concrete, knowable world with an approach that can only be called surrealistic.''

Paul Zweig wrote that he believes the quietness of the poems in their strength. ''The news that John Haines brings us is of deep winter indeed. His poems describe a world that is limitless and vastly empty, where all the sounds have been stifled, and where those movements that still resemble life are accomplished with a slowness that is familiar to us, perhaps, only in dreams. It is the massive winter of Alaska. . . . [Haines is] on the other side of life, where the events of winter are a constant illumination: 'As if Death were a voice made visible.' At their best, his poems *are* that voice.''

Fifteen poems from *Winter News* have been translated into native Alaskan languages.

BIOGRAPHICAL/CRITICAL SOURCES: Poetry, November, 1966; *Nation,* November 27, 1967.

* * *

HALASZ, Nicholas 1895-

PERSONAL: Born December 12, 1895, in Roznava, Czechoslovakia; son of Maurice and Rose (Ferder) Halasz; married Piroska Szenes (a writer), October 28, 1926; children: Michael, Robert. *Education:* University of Budapest, student, 1914-15, 1918-19; University of Bratislava, Dr. rer. pol., 1920. *Home:* 423 West 120th St., New York, N.Y. 10027. *Agent:* Max Becker, 115 East 82nd St., New York, N.Y. 10021.

CAREER: Lawyer in Czechoslovakia, 1927-37; author. New School for Social Research, New York, N.Y., lecturer in history, 1960-62. *Military service:* Austro-Hungarian Army, 1915-18; became second lieutenant.

WRITINGS: Captain Dreyfus, Simon and Schuster, 1955; *In the Shadow of Russia,* Ronald, 1959; *Nobel, A Biography,* Orion, 1960; *Roosevelt Through Foreign Eyes,* Van Nostrand, 1961; *The Rattling Chains,* McKay, 1966; (with son, Robert Halasz) *Assassins of Pure Heart,* Kossuth (Budapest), 1973. Editorial board member of *Szazadunk* (Budapest), 1926-38, *Uezenet* (Paris), 1940, and *Magyar Forum* (New York), 1943-44.

WORK IN PROGRESS: Guest on Earth, an autobiography.

* * *

HALCROW, Harold Graham 1911-

PERSONAL: Born October 11, 1911, in Bowesmont, N.D.; son of John (a farmer) and Winifred (McIntosh) Halcrow; married Eleanor Fearn, June 14, 1941; children: Meribel, Stephen, Beth, Ronald, Gayle. *Education:* North Dakota State University, B.S., 1937; Montana State University, M.S., 1938; University of Chicago, Ph.D., 1948. *Home:* 1101 Mayfair Rd., Champaign, Ill. 61820.

CAREER: Montana State University, Bozeman, 1938-41, 1946-49, started as instructor, became professor of agricultural economics; University of Connecticut, Storrs, professor of agricultural economics, 1949-57; University of Illi-

nois, Urbana, professor of agricultural economics and head of department, 1957—. National Bureau of Economic Research, member of board of directors, 1956—. *Military service:* U.S. Naval Reserve, active duty, 1942-46; became lieutenant. *Member:* American Economic Association, American Farm Economic Association, Canadian Agricultural Economics Society, Western Farm Economic Association, Urbana Rotary Club. *Awards, honors:* Award for best article published in *Journal of Farm Economics* in 1949.

WRITINGS: Agricultural Policy of the United States, Prentice-Hall, 1953; (editor) *Contemporary Readings in Agricultural Economics,* Prentice-Hall, 1955; *Federal Lending and Loan Insurance,* Princeton University Press, for National Bureau of Economic Research, 1958; (editor) *Modern Land Policy,* University of Illinois Press, 1960. Editor, *Journal of Farm Economics,* 1954-57.

WORK IN PROGRESS: World Food and Agricultural Policy, and *Food Policy for America.*

* * *

HALE, Leon 1921-

PERSONAL: Born May 30, 1921, in Stephenville, Tex.; son of Fred D. (a salesman) and May Hale; married Mary Helen Vick, April 17, 1948; children: Mark, Rebecca Ann. *Education:* Texas Technological College (now Texas Tech University), B.A., 1946. *Politics:* Independent. *Religion:* Protestant. *Home:* 2105 Elmwood Dr., Bryan, Tex. 77801. *Office address:* Drawer H, Bryan, Tex. 77801.

CAREER: Texas A&M University, College Station, assistant editor, Extension Service, 1946-48; *Houston Post,* Houston, Tex., farm editor, 1948-53; Humble Co., Houston, magazine writer, 1953-55; *Houston Post,* daily columnist, 1956—; Sam Houston State University, Huntsville, Tex., instructor in journalism, 1964—. *Military service:* U.S. Army Air Forces, aerial gunner, 1942-45; flew fifty missions with 15th Air Force in Italy; became technical sergeant. *Member:* Houston Press Club.

WRITINGS: Turn South at the Second Bridge, Doubleday, 1965; *Bonney's Place,* Doubleday, 1972.†

* * *

HALL, Arlene Stevens 1923-

PERSONAL: Born November 7, 1923; daughter of M. G. and Edna Stevens; married Kenneth Franklin Hall (an editor), September 18, 1949; children: David Eric, Kenneth Douglas. *Education:* West Liberty State College, student, 1941-43; Anderson College, Anderson, Ind., B.S., 1945; Scarritt College for Christian Workers, M.A., 1949. *Politics:* Independent. *Home:* 712 Maplewood Dr., Anderson, Ind.

CAREER: Church of God, Board of Christian Education, Anderson, Ind., associate director of children's work, 1945-48; Warner Press, Inc., Anderson, Ind., children's editor, 1949-52; *Pathways to God* (quarterly), Anderson, Ind., editor, 1959-69; Park Place Church of God, Anderson, Ind., director of Christian education, 1965—.

WRITINGS—All published by Gospel Trumpet, except as noted: Teaching Children in Your Church, 1951, *Worship Programs for Juniors,* 1954, (reviser) Egermeier, *Bible Story Book,* 1954, *Your Vacation Church School,* 1956, *So You Work with Juniors,* 1959; (reviser) Elsie Egermeier, *Egermeier's Picture-Story Life of Jesus,* Warner Press, 1965; *Toward Effective Teaching—Elementary Children,*

Christian Board of Publication, 1969; *Picture Story Bible ABC Book*, Warner Press, 1973.

*   *   *

HALL, Kenneth F(ranklin)   1926-

PERSONAL: Born December 13, 1926, in Columbiana, Ohio; son of Herbert David and Martha (Starbuck) Hall; married Arlene Stevens (now a director of Christian education), September 18, 1949; children: David Eric, Kenneth Douglas. *Education:* Anderson College, A.B., 1948; Butler University, B.D., 1954; Christian Theological Seminary, D.Min., 1973. *Home:* 712 Maplewood Ave., Anderson, Ind. 46012. *Office:* Warner Press, Inc., Anderson, Ind. 46011.

CAREER: Warner Press, Inc. (publication board of Church of God), Anderson, Ind., news editor, 1948—, editor of youth publications, 1951-55, book editor, 1955-67, director of curriculum development, 1965—. *Member:* Theta Phi, Sigma Tau Delta, Alpha Phi Gamma, Kiwanis Club (Anderson).

WRITINGS: They Stand Tall, Warner, 1953; *What Do You Believe?*, Warner, 1958; *So You Work with Senior High Youth*, Warner, 1959; (with Charles M. Schulz) *Two-by-Fours*, Warner, 1965; *On the Trail of a Twin*, Friendship, 1966; *How I Became the World's Strongest 96½ Pound Weakling*, Friendship, 1968; *On Bumping Into God*, Warner, 1972. Contributor to about thirty church-related journals.

SIDELIGHTS: Hall directed an international church work camp in Trinidad in 1961. *Avocational interests:* Camping and photography.

*   *   *

HALL, Penelope C(oker)   1933-
(Penelope Coker Wilson)

PERSONAL: Born March 19, 1933, in Charlotte, N.C.; daughter of James Lide (a manufacturer) and Elizabeth (a novelist; maiden name Boatwright) Coker; married William Parmenter Wilson (a television producer), July 18, 1963 (divorced, 1972); married Mortimer W. Hall (a radio station president, and treasurer of New York Post), December 8, 1972; children: Eliza Wilson. *Education:* Attended Sarah Lawrence College, 1950-53. *Religion:* Episcopalian. *Home:* 355 East 72nd Street, New York, N.Y. 10021. *Agent:* Curtis Brown Ltd. 60 East 56th Street, New York, N.Y. 10022.

CAREER: Researcher and writer for Cleveland Amory, New York, N.Y., 1955-60; senior editor, *Celebrity Register*, 1959—; National Broadcasting Co., television hostess on "Wrap Up," New York, N.Y., 1960, "Ten Around Town," Philadelphia, Pa., 1964, "The New Yorkers Program," New York, N.Y., 1967-68; WNEW-TV, New York, N.Y., reporter on "Ten O'Clock News," 1969-70. Member of board of directors, Veterans Hospital Television and Radio Guild. *Member:* Authors Guild, Actors Equity Association, Screen Actors Guild, American Federation of Television and Radio Artists, Piping Rock Club (Locust Valley, N.Y.), Goldin's Bridge Hunt Club (North Salem, N.Y.).

WRITINGS—Under name Penelope Coker Wilson: *Fancy and the Cement Patch*, Reilly & Lee, 1964; *The Wish Bottle Story*, Reilly & Lee, 1965. Writer of television scripts.

WORK IN PROGRESS: A novel.†

HALL, Peter (Geoffrey)   1932-

PERSONAL: Born March 19, 1932, in London, England; son of Arthur Vickers and Bertha (Keefe) Hall. *Education:* Attended St. Catharine's College, Cambridge. *Politics:* Labour. *Home:* 5 Bedford Rd., London W4 1JD, England. *Office:* Department of Geography, University of Reading, Whiteknights, Reading, Berks RG6 2AB, England.

CAREER: University of London, London, England, assistant lecturer in geography, Birkbeck College, 1957-60, lecturer in geography, Birkbeck College, 1960-65, reader in geography with special reference to regional planning, London School of Economics and Political Science, 1966-67; University of Reading, Reading, England, professor of geography and head of department, 1968—. Economics Associates Ltd., London, associate. Chairman of research group, South East Regional Economic Planning Council; member of executive committee, Regional Studies Association; chairman of integration committee, Plan Europe 2000. *Member:* Royal Geographical Society.

WRITINGS: The Industries of London, Hutchinson, 1962; *London 2000*, Faber, 1963, revised edition, 1969; (editor) *Labour's New Frontiers*, Deutsch, 1964; (editor) *Land Values*, Sweet & Maxwell, 1965; *The World Cities*, World University, 1966; (editor) J. H. von Thuenen, *Isolated State*, Pergamon, 1966; (with others) *An Advanced Geography of North-West Europe*, Hulten, 1967; *Theory and Practice of Regional Planning*, Pemberton Publishing, 1970; (with others) *Containment of Urban England*, two volumes, Allen & Unwin, 1973; (with others) *Planning and Urban Growth: An Anglo-American Comparison*, Johns Hopkins Press, 1973; *Urban and Regional Planning: An Introduction*, Penguin, 1974. Regular contributor to *New Society* (London). Editor, *Regional Studies* (periodical).

WORK IN PROGRESS: Editing *Europe 2000*, the final report of the integration committee of the Plan Europe 2000 project, and *Forecasts and Decisions*, studies in planning theory and practice, both expected to be completed in 1976.

*   *   *

HALL, Richard   1925-

PERSONAL: Born July 22, 1925, in Margate, Kent, England; son of Douglas Beecroft and Gladys (Alcock) Hall; married Barbara Taylor (a journalist), July 10, 1947; children: Robin, Nicolas, Simon, Crispin, Jeremy. *Education:* Keble College, Oxford, B.A. (honors), 1948. *Politics:* "Radical but non-party." *Religion:* Agnostic. *Home:* 23 Lanchester Rd., Ndola, Zambia. *Agent:* John Farquharson Ltd., 15 Red Lion Sq., London W.C. 1, England.

CAREER: Daily Mail, London, England, sub-editor, 1948-50, 1955-56; *Illustrated*, London, sub-editor, 1950-54; *Mufulira Magazine*, Mufulira, Zambia, editor, 1956-58; Government Information Services, Zambia, managing editor, 1958-60; *African Mail*, Lusaka, Zambia, managing editor, 1960-65; *Times of Zambia*, Ndola, Zambia, editor-in-chief, 1965—. Correspondent for *Newsweek, Observer* (London), and *Daily Mail* (London). Trustee of Zambia Arts Council. *Military service:* British Navy, 1943-45. *Member:* International Press Institute (Zurich).

WRITINGS: Kaunda, Founder of Zambia, Longmans, Green, 1964; *Zambia*, Pall Mall, 1965, Praeger, 1966; *The High Price of Principles: Kaunda and the White South*, Hodder & Stoughton, 1969, African Publishing, 1970; *Discovery of Africa*, Grosset, 1970. Contributor to *Africa Report* and other journals on Africa.

AVOCATIONAL INTERESTS: Archaeology.†

HALL, Robert E. 1924-

PERSONAL: Born October 27, 1924, in Pittsburgh, Pa.; son of Charles Springer (a banker) and Rachel (Donovan) Hall; married Natalie W. Watson (an artist and writer), October 7, 1950 (divorced); children: Suzette, Rachel, Anthony, Timothy. *Education:* Harvard University, student, 1942-43; Columbia University, M.D., 1947. *Religion:* Protestant. *Home:* 185 West End Ave., New York, N.Y. 10023.

CAREER: Physician in private practice of obstetrics and gynecology, New York, N.Y., 1955-73; Presbyterian Hospital, New York, N.Y., associate attending physician, 1965-73, and director of Birth Control Clinic; Columbia University, College of Physicians and Surgeons, New York, N.Y., associate professor of clinical obstetrics and gynecology, 1965-73; St. Luke's Hospital, New York, N.Y., resident in psychiatry, 1973—. Lecturer on abortion law reform and birth control in United States, England, Italy, Tunisia, and Mexico. *Military service:* U.S. Army, 1943-46. U.S. Air Force, Medical Corps, 1950-54; became captain. *Member:* American Medical Association, American College of Obstetricians and Gynecologists, American College of Surgeons, Association for the Study of Abortion (president, 1964—), New York Obstetrical Society, New York Academy of Medicine, New York State Medical Society, New York County Medical Society.

WRITINGS: Nine Month's Reading: A Medical Guide for Pregnant Women, Doubleday, 1963; *A Doctor's Guide to Having An Abortion*, New American Library, 1971; *Sex—An Advanced Primer*, Doubleday, 1974. Ghost-writer of two books on contract bridge. Associate editor, *American Journal of Obstetrics and Gynecology*, 1955-70. Contributor to *Nation, New York Times, Columbia University Forum, Playboy*, and to textbooks.

* * *

HALLET, Jean-Pierre 1927-

PERSONAL: Born August 4, 1927, in Louvan, Belgium; son of Andre (a painter) and Berthe (Rosseels) Hallet. *Education:* Attended University of Brussells, Belgium, 1945-46, and Sorbonne, University of Paris, 1947-48. *Home:* 5630 West 79th St., Los Angeles, Calif. 90045.

CAREER: Agronomist, sociologist, and naturalist for Belgian Colonial Government in former Belgian Congo, 1948-58; Central Africa Curio Shop, Gisenyi, Rwanda, owner and operator, 1958-60; came to United States, 1960; lecturer, 1961—; free-lance writer, 1963—; organizer and guide of Congo safaris, summers, 1969—. Founder of Congoland U.S.A., 1960; consultant Africanist and special curator, University of California, Los Angeles, 1963. *Wartime service:* Belgian Resistance Movement, 1942-43; Belgian Army, 2nd Infantry Brigade, 1944-45; received Palmes 1940-45, 1946, Volunteer's Medal with golden palms, 1947, Commemorative Medal with bronze crown, 1947, Silver Star of Service (Belgium), 1960. *Member:* Bwame Secret Society, Honolulu Adventurers' Club (honorary member). *Awards, honors:* Initiated blood-brother, Lega, 1950, Masai, 1951, Tutsi, 1955, and Nande, 1957; Gold Medal of Royal Order of Lion, 1959, presented by King Baudouin in recognition of work in Congo; American Library Association best book award, 1966.

WRITINGS: Congo Kitabu (Reader's Digest Book Club selection, Book of the Month Club alternate selection), Random House, 1966; *Animal Kitabu*, Random House,

1967; *Pygmy Kitabu*, Random House, 1973. Contributor of over thirty articles to periodicals.

WORK IN PROGRESS: About ten more kitabus, including several for children; collaborating on a movie script of *Congo Kitabu*.

SIDELIGHTS: While Hallet lived and worked with 650,000 natives of seventeen different tribes in the Congo: He lost his right hand in a dynamite explosion helping a famine-stricken tribe in 1955; he killed a lion with a spear for Masai initiation; he saved a Bantu tribesman by leaping weaponless on a leopard, which he killed only after catching a knife thrown to him; and he underwent Pygmy surgery for a poisoned arrow wound.

Not only an adventurer, Hallet produced and directed the documentary film "Pygmies," in 1973 and he is compiler of the largest private collection of African art, now housed in the University of California Art Museum.

AVOCATIONAL INTERESTS: Travel, sports, outdoors, wild animals (as conservationist, not hunter). He added: "Very special interests: Life, love, truth, justice, and peace."

BIOGRAPHICAL/CRITICAL SOURCES: William Parker, editor, *Men of Courage*, Playboy Press, 1972; Robert Gannon, *Great Survival Adventures*, Random House, 1973.

* * *

HALMOS, Paul 1911-

PERSONAL: Born December 19, 1911, in Budapest, Hungary; son of Maurice (a civil servant) and Ethel (Soos) Halmos; married Edith Molnar, July 18, 1937; married Ena Edwards, February 18, 1972; children: (first marriage) Anthony Michael. *Education:* University of Budapest, Doctor Juris, 1935; University of London, B.A. (honors), 1945; London School of Economics and Political Science, University of London, Ph.D., 1950. *Office:* Open University, P.O. Box 77, Bletchley, Bucks, U.K.

CAREER: Master at various grammar schools in Britain, 1941-47, and lecturer at technical college, 1947-56; University of Keele, Keele, Staffordshire, England, senior lecturer and tutor in charge of social studies, 1956-65; University College of South Wales and Monmouthshire, University of Wales, Cardiff, professor of sociology, 1965-74; Open University, Bletchley, England, professor of sociology, 1974—. Editorial adviser to Constable & Co. Ltd. *Member:* British Sociological Association.

WRITINGS: Solitude and Privacy, Routledge & Kegan Paul, 1952, Philosophical Library, 1953; *Towards a Measure of Man*, Humanities, 1957; *The Faith of the Counsellors*, Constable, 1965, Schocken, 1966; *The Personal Service Society*, Constable, 1970, Schocken, 1971. Monograph editor of *Sociological Review*, with twenty monographs published, 1958-73; member of editorial board of same journal.

WORK IN PROGRESS: The Personal and the Political.

* * *

HALPERN, A(braham) M(eyer) 1914-

PERSONAL: Born February 20, 1914, in Boston, Mass.; son of Solomon Leo and Fannie (Epstein) Halpern; married Mary Fujii, March 30, 1941; children: Alexander, Paul F. *Education:* Harvard University, A.B., 1933; University of California, Berkeley, graduate study, 1934-37; University of Chicago, Ph.D., 1947. *Home:* 4100 W. St. N.W., Washington, D.C. 20007.

CAREER: University of Chicago, Chicago, Ill., instructor, later assistant professor of anthropology, 1941-46; Supreme Commander of the Allied Powers, Education Division, Tokyo, Japan, adviser on language revision, 1946-48; RAND Corp., Santa Monica, Calif., senior staff member, 1949-62; Council on Foreign Relations, New York, N.Y., research fellow, China Project, 1963-65; Harvard University, Cambridge, Mass., research associate, Center for International Affairs, 1965-68; Center for Naval Analysis, Arlington, Va., senior professor staff member, 1968-72; Johns Hopkins University, School of Advanced International Studies, Baltimore, Md., lecturer, 1970, 1972-73, professor of Asian studies, 1973—. Carnegie Institution of Washington, research associate, 1941-46; University of Michigan, visiting associate professor, 1950; University of California, Los Angeles, lecturer, 1952; University of California, Berkeley, lecturer, 1962-63; American Academy of Arts and Science, Japanese-American Seminar on National Security, vice-chairman of committee, 1967-70. *Member:* Association for Asian Studies, American Political Science Association, American Anthropological Association.

WRITINGS: (Editor) *Policies Toward China: Views from Six Continents,* McGraw, 1965. Author of numerous monographs for RAND Corp., 1949-62. Author of "Yuma," a grammar run serially in *International Journal of American Linguistics,* 1946-47; contributor to *China Quarterly, World Politics, Asian Survey,* and other journals.

WORK IN PROGRESS: Research in Far Eastern international relations, especially as related to contemporary China and Japan.

SIDELIGHTS: Halpern's travel has been concentrated in Asia; he has good command of Japanese and French, a fair command of German and Spanish. *Avocational interests:* Photography.†

* * *

HALPIN, Andrew W(illiams) 1911-

PERSONAL: Born September 27, 1911, in New York, N.Y. *Education:* Columbia University, B.S., 1931, M.A., 1932; Cornell University, Ph.D., 1949. *Home:* 6370 Orange Tree Drive, Tucson, Ariz. 85704.

CAREER: Certificated as school psychologist by New York State Department of Education, as psychologist by New York State Department of Mental Hygiene. Columbia University, Teachers College, New York, N.Y., psychologist, Remedial Reading Project, 1934-37; Westchester County (N.Y.) public schools, psychologist, 1937-42; New York State Youth Commission, Albany, associate education supervisor, 1946-47; lecturer in psychology at Ithaca College, Ithaca, N.Y., 1947-48, and Cornell University, Ithaca, 1948-49; University of Tennessee, Knoxville, associate professor of educational psychology, 1949-51; Ohio State University, Columbus, research associate, 1951-55; Montana State University, Missoula, professor of education, 1955-57; University of Chicago, Chicago, Ill., associate professor of education, 1957-59; University of Utah, Salt Lake City, professor of educational administration and director of Bureau of Educational Research, 1959-62; Washington University, Graduate Institute of Education, St. Louis, Mo., professor of education and psychology, 1962-66; Claremont Graduate School, Claremont, Calif., professor of education and psychology, 1966-67; University of Georgia, Athens, research professor in College of Edu-

cation, 1967-74. Visiting summer professor at State University of New York College at New Paltz, 1952, University of British Columbia, 1964, Cornell University, 1965, and University of Toronto, 1966. Consultant to U.S. Veterans Administration, 1954-55, and Pillsbury Mills, 1954. *Military service:* U.S. Army, psychologist, 1942-46; became major. *Member:* American Psychological Association, American Educational Research Association, Sigma Xi, Phi Kappa Phi.

WRITINGS: The Leadership Behavior of School Superintendents, Ohio State University Press, 1956, 2nd edition, Midwest Administration Center, University of Chicago, 1959; (editor) *Administrative Theory in Education,* Midwest Administration Center, University of Chicago, 1958, 2nd edition, Macmillan, 1967; (with Don B. Croft) *The Organizational Climate of Schools,* Midwest Administration Center, University of Chicago, 1963; *Theory and Research in Administration,* Macmillan, 1966.

Contributor: *Leader Behavior: Its Description and Measurement,* edited by R. M. Stodgill and A. E. Coons, Bureau of Business Research, Ohio State University, 1957; *Administrative Theory as a Guide to Action,* edited by R. F. Campbell and J. M. Lipham, Midwest Administration Center, University of Chicago, 1960; *Dissemination and Implementation,* edited by Stanley Elam and Keith Goldhammer, Phi Delta Kappa, 1962; *Educational Administration: Selected Readings,* edited by A. Culbertson and Stephen P. Hencley, Interstate, 1963; *Educational Administration: Selected Readings,* edited by Walter G. Hack, John A. Ramseyer, and William J. Gephart, Allyn & Bacon, 1965; *Leituras de Administracao Escolar,* edited by Carlos Correa Mascaro and Moyses Brejon, Editora da Universidade de Sao Paulo, 1966. Contributor of more than thirty articles and reviews to education and psychology journals; book review editor, *Autonomous Groups Bulletin,* 1953-57.

WORK IN PROGRESS: A book, *The Prudent Retiree.*

* * *

HALSBAND, Robert 1914-

PERSONAL: Born March 22, 1914, in New York, N.Y.; son of Max (a contractor) and Bertha (Locker) Halsband; married Ruth Alice Norman Weil, December 30, 1954 (died, 1971). *Education:* New York University, B.S., 1934; Columbia University, M.A., 1936; Northwestern University, Ph.D., 1948. *Religion:* "Non-observing Jewish." *Home:* 1309 Brighton Dr., Urbana, Ill. 61801. *Agent:* A. P. Watt & Son, 26/28 Bedford Row, London WC1R 4HL, England.

CAREER: New York (N.Y.) public schools, high school teacher, 1938-43; Northwestern University, Evanston, Ill., instructor in English, 1944-47; Hunter College, New York, N.Y., assistant professor, 1949-57, associate professor of English, 1958-60; Columbia University, New York, N.Y., adjunct professor of English, 1963-71; University of California, Riverside, professor of English, 1971-73; University of Illinois, Urbana, professor of English, 1973—. National Book Awards judge, 1972. *Member:* Century Association, P.E.N. (vice-president, American branch, 1966-67, president, 1967-69), Morgan Library (council member, 1965-68), Phi Beta Kappa, Grolier Club (council member, 1962-67). *Awards, honors:* Guggenheim fellowship, 1968-69.

WRITINGS: (Editor) *The Nonsense of Common-Sense 1737-38,* Northwestern University Press, 1947; *The Life of Lady Mary Wortley Montagu,* Oxford University Press,

1956; (editor) *The Complete Letters of Lady Mary Wortley Montagu*, Oxford University Press, Volume I, 1965, Volume II, 1966, Volume III, 1967; (editor) *Selected Letters of Lady Mary Wortley Montagu*, Longman, 1970, St. Martin's, 1971; *Lord Hervey: Eighteenth-Century Courtier*, Oxford University Press, 1974.

WORK IN PROGRESS: Eighteenth-century biographical studies.

* * *

HALSEY, A(lbert) H(enry) 1923-

PERSONAL: Born April 13, 1923, in London, England; son of William Thomas and Ada (Draper) Halsey; married Gertrude Margaret Littler, April 12, 1949; children: Ruth, Robert, Lisa, David. *Education:* London School of Economics and Political Science, University of London, B.Sc., 1950, Ph.D., 1954. *Politics:* Socialist. *Home:* New Barnett House, 28 Little Clarendon St., Oxford OX1 2ER, England.

CAREER: University of Birmingham, Birmingham, England, senior lecturer in sociology, 1954-62; Oxford University, Oxford, England, professor and fellow of Nuffield College, and head of Department of Social and Administrative Studies, 1962—. Adviser to Secretary of State for Education, 1965-68; consultant to Organization for Economic Co-operation and Development.

WRITINGS: (Editor with J. Floud and C. Arnold Anderson) *Education, Economy and Society*, Free Press of Glencoe, 1965; (with G. N. Ostergaard) *Power in Co-operatives*, Basil Blackwell, 1965; (with Ivor Crewe) *Social Survey of the Civil Service*, H.M.S.O., 1969; (with Martin Trow) *The British Academics*, Harvard University Press, 1971; (editor) *Trends in British Society Since 1900*, Macmillan, 1971; *Education and Social Change*, UNESCO, 1972; (editor) *Educational Priority*, H.M.S.O., 1972; (with George Smith and Teresa Smith) *Early Years at School*, B.B.C. Publications, 1973. General editor of Faber series, "Society Today and Tomorrow." Contributor of numerous articles to journals.

* * *

HALTER, Carl 1915-

PERSONAL: Born October 10, 1915, in Cleveland, Ohio; son of George A. and Clara (Nehrenz) Halter; married Miriam Luecke, June 30, 1946; children: Matthew, Dale, Timothy, Claire, Amy. *Education:* Concordia Teachers College, River Forest, Ill., student, 1933-36; Baldwin-Wallace College, B.Mus., 1941; Northwestern University, M.Mus., 1945; University of Chicago, graduate study. *Religion:* Lutheran Church-Missouri Synod. *Home:* 1304 Forest Park Ave., Valparaiso, Ind. 46383.

CAREER: Concordia Teachers College, River Forest, Ill., assistant in music, 1936-37; Trinity Lutheran Church, Houston, Tex., parish teacher and musician, 1937-43; Grace Lutheran Church, River Forest, Ill., principal of school and parish musician, 1943-48; Concordia Teachers College, River Forest, Ill., professor of music, 1948—, chairman of Division of Music, 1953-55, dean of students, 1955-64, assistant to the president and executive vice-president, 1964-65, acting president, 1965-66, executive vice-president, 1966-68, director of public relations and continuing education, 1971-72, acting president, 1972-73; Valparaiso University, Valparaiso, Ind., director of Office of Continuing Education, 1974—. Consultant for teacher edu-

cation in Hong Kong, 1969-71. *Member:* American Guild of Organists, Lutheran Education Association. *Awards, honors:* Litt.D., Concordia Teachers College, Seward, Neb., 1964.

WRITINGS: The Practice of Sacred Music, Concordia, 1955; *The Christian Choir Member*, Concordia, 1959; *God and Man in Music*, Concordia, 1963. Composer of religious songs, including eight compositions published by Concordia, 1952-63. Contributor to *Christian Century, This Day, Journal of Church Music*, and Lutheran periodicals.

WORK IN PROGRESS: The Handbook of Church Music, publication by Concordia expected in 1976.

* * *

HAMACHEK, Don E. 1933-

PERSONAL: Born May 6, 1933, in Milwaukee, Wis.; son of Evans O. (a store manager) and Marvis (Borgeson) Hamachek. *Education:* University of Michigan, A.B., 1955, M.S.W., 1957, Ph.D., 1960. *Politics:* Republican. *Religion:* Protestant. *Office:* Michigan State University, 463 Erickson, East Lansing, Mich. 48823.

CAREER: Certified as consulting psychologist in Michigan. Michigan State University, East Lansing, 1960—, associate professor of educational psychology and child development, 1965—. Producer-moderator of "Dilemma," on WJIM-TV, Lansing, Mich., and broadcaster of weekday radio program exploring educational issues and childrearing, WITL, Lansing. *Member:* American Psychological Association, American Educational Research Association, Society for Research in Child Development, American Personnel and Guidance Association, Michigan Psychological Association.

WRITINGS: (Editor) *The Self in Growth, Teaching, and Learning*, Prentice-Hall, 1965; (editor) *Human Dynamics in Psychology and Education*, Allyn & Bacon, 1968; *Encounters With the Self*, Holt, 1971; *Behavior Dynamics in Teaching Learning and Growth*, Allyn & Bacon, 1975. Contributor to educational journals.

WORK IN PROGRESS: Research projects investigating relationships between self-concept and school achievement and the influence of teacher behavior on classroom performance.

* * *

HAMILTON, Kenneth (Morrison) 1917-

PERSONAL: Born August 10, 1917, in Worthing, Sussex, England; son of Edward Charles Hamilton (a doctor); married Alice Blanche Lewis (a professor of English), July 13, 1943; children: David Alexander, Kenneth Gavin Andrew, Margaret Mary Frances. *Education:* University College, University of London, B.A. (honors), 1938; New College, University of London, B.D., 1942; Dalhousie University, M.A., 1953; Pine Hill Divinity Hall, Th.M., 1957; Emmanuel College, Victoria University, Th.D., 1965. *Home:* 246 Harvard Ave., Winnipeg 9, Manitoba, Canada. *Office:* University of Winnipeg, 515 Portage Ave., Winnipeg, Manitoba R3B 2EG, Canada.

CAREER: Ordained to ministry, Congregational Union of England and Wales, 1943; pastor in Sherwood, Nottingham, England, 1943-48, in Wallington, Surrey, England, 1948-51; United Church of Canada pastor in Elmsdale, Nova Scotia, Canada, 1951-58; United College, Winnipeg, Manitoba, Canada, assistant professor, 1958-65, associate professor, 1965-68, professor of systematic theology,

1968—. External examiner, Paton College, Nottingham, England, 1944-48; guest lecturer, University of Nottingham, 1946, Dalhousie University, 1952, Elmhurst College, 1966, and at theological seminaries; Distinguished Visiting Professor, Fuller Theological Seminary, 1971; ecumenical visitor, New College, London, 1975. *Member:* Canadian Theological Society, Canadian Society for the Study of Religion, Canadian Association of University Teachers.

WRITINGS: The Protestant Way, Essential Books, 1956; *The System and the Gospel: A Critique of Paul Tillich*, Macmillan, 1963; *Revolt Against Heaven*, Eerdmans, 1965; *God Is Dead: The Anatomy of a Slogan*, Eerdmans, 1966; *In Search of Contemporary Man*, Eerdmans, 1967; *J. D. Salinger: A Critical Essay*, Eerdmans, 1967; (with Alice Hamilton) *John Updike: A Critical Essay*, Eerdmans, 1967; *What's New in Religion?*, Eerdmans, 1968; *Life in One's Stride: A Short Study in Dietrich Bonhoeffer*, Eerdmans, 1968; *The Promise of Kierkegaard*, Lippincott, 1969; (with Alice Hamilton) *The Elements of John Updike*, Eerdmans, 1970; *Words and the Word*, Eerdmans, 1971; (with Alice Hamilton) *To Be A Man—To Be A Woman*, United Methodist Publishing House, 1972; *To Turn from Idols*, Eerdmans, 1973.

Contributor: Philip E. Hughes, editor, *Creative Minds in Contemporary Theology*, Eerdmans, 1966, 2nd edition, 1969; Martin E. Marty and Dean Peerman, editors, *New Theology*, Volume III, Macmillan, 1966; Peerman, editor, *Frontline Theology*, John Knox, 1967; Jerry H. Gill, editor, *Essays in Kierkegaard*, Burgess, 1969; Allen O. Miller, editor, *Reconciliation in Today's World*, Eerdmans, 1969; Carl E. Henry, editor, *Baker's Dictionary of Christian Ethics*, Baker Book, 1974.

Writer of ninety-minute program in Canadian Broadcasting Corp. series, "The Human Condition." Contributor of about sixty articles and one hundred reviews to academic and religious journals in Canada, United States, and England.

WORK IN PROGRESS: A book on Samuel Beckett (with Alice Hamilton) for Eerdmans; a book on John Updike's writings since *Couples* (with Alice Hamilton); research for a manuscript on the biblical doctrine of Creation and its historical development in theological and philosophical thought.

SIDELIGHTS: Hamilton told *CA:* "While I am a theologian, by profession and by personal concern, my early training was in literature and philosophy, and my theological work has always been open to these frontiers. So I see theology as an integrating center for all of life, and as a key to human culture, past and present." *Avocational interests:* Painting, calligraphy.

* * *

HAMILTON, Seena M. 1926-

PERSONAL: Born February 8, 1926, in New York, N.Y.; daughter of Leonard (a tax consultant) and Helen Hamilton; married S. K. Fineberg (a physician, specializing in internal medicine), August 18, 1950; children: Bryan Scott. *Education:* Attended College of William and Mary, 1945. *Home:* 450 East 63rd St., New York, N.Y., 10021. *Office:* 1161 York Avenue, New York, N.Y. 10021.

CAREER: Apartment Life, senior editor, 1951-53; *Today's Family*, New York, N.Y., associate editor, 1953-54; *Hotel Gazette* (hotel and travel trade journal), New York, N.Y.,

editor and publisher, 1954-59; Gulliver's Trails, Inc. (children's tours and convention hospitality service), New York, N.Y., president, 1961. Lecturer and consultant in travel field; free-lance writer for trade and consumer magazines. Member of League in Aid of Crippled Children, New York. *Member:* U.S. Lawn Tennis Association, Chi Delta Phi, Armonk Tennis Club.

WRITINGS: New York on the Family Plan, Random House, 1965. Columnist on family life, *Ladies' Home Journal*, 1965-66; contributor of articles on travel, records, films, and family problems to other periodicals.

BIOGRAPHICAL/CRITICAL SOURCES: Saturday Evening Post, June 16, 1962; *Travel Weekly*, August 18, 1964; *New York World Telegram*, June 3, 1965.†

* * *

HAMMOND, Guyton B(owers) 1930-

PERSONAL: Born November 7, 1930, in Birmingham, Ala.; son of Joseph L. (in real estate) and Fanny (Bowers) Hammond; married Jean Love, June 27, 1959; children: Bruce Guyton, Mitchell Love. *Education:* Washington and Lee University, B.A., 1951; studied at University of Utrecht, 1951-52, and Southern Baptist Theological Seminary, 1952-53; Yale University, B.D., 1955; Vanderbilt University, Ph.D., 1962. *Politics:* Democrat. *Home:* 848 Hutcheson Lane, Blacksburg, Va. 24060. *Office:* Department of Philosophy and Religion, Virginia Polytechnic Institute, Blacksburg, Va. 24061.

CAREER: Virginia Polytechnic Institute, Blacksburg, instructor, 1957-58, assistant professor, 1958-62, associate professor, 1962-67, professor of philosophy and religion, 1967—, president of university-faculty senate, 1971-72 and 1975-76. Montgomery County Council on Human Relations, chairman, 1963-64. *Member:* American Academy of Religion, American Association of University Professors, Virginia Philosophical Association. *Awards, honors:* Fulbright scholarship to University of Utrecht, 1951-52.

WRITINGS: Man in Estrangement, Vanderbilt University Press, 1965; *The Power of Self-Transcendence: An Introduction to the Philosophical Theology of Paul Tillich*, Bethany, 1966.

* * *

HAMMOND, Mac (Sawyer) 1926-

PERSONAL: Born February 8, 1926, in Des Moines, Iowa; son of Mott Sawyer and Esther (McMullen) Hammond; married Katka Houdek, June 6, 1960; children: Anna Elizabeth, Ross Davenport Sawyer. *Education:* University of the South, B.A., 1948; Harvard University, M.A., 1950, Ph.D., 1962. *Home:* 314 Highland Ave., Buffalo, N.Y. 14222.

CAREER: University of Virginia, Charlottesville, instructor in English, 1956-58; Western Reserve University, Cleveland, Ohio, instructor, 1960-62, assistant professor of English, 1962-63; State University of New York at Buffalo, professor of English, 1963—. Massachusetts Institute of Technology, research associate, Center for Communications Sciences, 1960. *Military service:* U.S. Naval Reserve, 1949-60; now lieutenant junior grade (retired). *Awards, honors:* Sewanee Review fellow in poetry, 1955-56.

WRITINGS: The Horse Opera, and Other Poems, Ohio State University Press, 1966; *Cold Turkey* (poems), Swallow Press, 1969.

BIOGRAPHICAL/CRITICAL SOURCES: Poetry, December, 1966.

* * *

HAMMOND, Phillip E(verett) 1931-

PERSONAL: Born February 14, 1931, in Salem, Ore.; son of Percy Malcolm (a clergyman) and Hildred (Mohr) Hammond; married Sandra Noll (now a ballet dancer and teacher), August 21, 1957; children: Jared M., Dana M. *Education:* Willamette University, B.A., 1952, M.A., 1954; Columbia University, M.A., 1957, Ph.D., 1960. *Home:* 4950 Via Entrada, Tucson, Ariz. 85718. *Office:* Department of Sociology, University of Arizona, Tucson, Ariz. 85721.

CAREER: Yale University, New Haven, Conn., assistant professor of sociology, 1960-65; University of Wisconsin, Madison, associate professor of sociology, 1965-70; University of Arizona, Tucson, professor of sociology, 1970—. *Member:* American Sociological Association, Society for Scientific Study of Religion, Religious Research Association, American Association of University Professors, American Civil Liberties Union, Pacific Sociological Association. *Awards, honors:* Postdoctoral fellowship, Danforth Foundation.

WRITINGS: (Editor) *Sociologists at Work*, Basic Books, 1964; *The Campus Clergyman*, Basic Books, 1966; (with N. J. Demerath III) *Religion in Social Context*, Random House, 1968; (editor with Benton Johnson) *American Mosaic*, Random House, 1970; (with Kenneth Dolbeare) *The School Prayer Decisions*, University of Chicago Press, 1971; (editor with Charles Glock) *Beyond the Classics?*, Harper, 1973; (with others) *The Structure of Human Society*, Heath, 1975. Contributor to sociology, education, and public opinion journals.

* * *

HAMP, Eric P(ratt) 1920-

PERSONAL: Born November 16, 1920, in London, England; son of William Pratt and Edith (McConkey) Hamp; came to U.S. in 1925, naturalized citizen, 1947; married Margot Faust, September 29, 1951; children: Juliana, Alexander. *Education:* Amherst College, B.A., 1942; Harvard University, M.A., 1948, Ph.D., 1954. *Home:* 5200 South Greenwood Ave., Chicago, Ill. 60615. *Office:* Department of Linguistics, University of Chicago, Chicago, Ill. 60637.

CAREER: Chief of lend-lease, government of South Africa, 1942-46; University of Chicago, Chicago, Ill., instructor, 1950-53, assistant professor, 1953-58, associate professor, 1958-62, professor, of linguistics, 1962—, Robert Maynard Hutchins Distinguished Service Professor, 1972—, director of Center for Balkan and Slavic Studies, 1965—, chairman of department of linguistics, 1966-69. Visiting summer professor or lecturer at University of Michigan, 1953, University of Texas, 1960, University of Washington, Seattle, 1962, University of Indiana, 1964, University of Beograd, 1964, 1967, University of Copenhagen, 1966-67; U.S. cultural exchange lecturer in Romania, 1966 and Soviet Union, 1975; visiting scholar, Pennsylvania State University, 1969; First Vernon Hall Lecturer in Celtic Studies, Harvard University, 1971. Member of staff, Gaelic Dialect Survey, Edinburgh, 1956-58; secretary of Committee on Language Programs, American Council of Learned Societies, 1959-63, chairman, 1963-69. Member, Committee on Automatic Language Processing, National Academy of Sciences-National Research

Council, 1964—, Committee on Linguistic Information, Center for Applied Linguistics, 1964-68, committee on history and theory of linguistics, Indiana University Press, 1965-73, Illinois Place-Name Survey, 1966—, committee on language and linguistics, Center for Neo-Hellenistic Study, 1967—, U.S. National Commission for UNESCO, 1972—. Consultant to U.S. Office of Education, 1966-72 and Harper & Row Publishers, Inc., 1971—. *Military service:* U.S. Army, 1946-47.

MEMBER: International Phonetics Society, American Association for the Advancement of Science (fellow), American Anthropological Association (fellow), Linguistic Society of America (member of executive committee, 1954-56; vice-president, 1963, 1970; president, 1971), Modern Language Association of America (chairman of Celtic section, 1956; chairman of general linguistic section, 1970), Philological Society (London), Scottish Gaelic Texts Society, Acoustical Society of America, Societe de linguistique de Paris, American Names Society (member of board of managers, 1967-72), Association for the Advancement of Baltic Studies, Association for South Slavic Studies, Bulgarian Studies Group, Roumanian Studies Group (member of board of directors), Midwest Modern Language Association, Phi Beta Kappa. *Awards, honors:* Fulbright senior research scholar in Greece, 1955-56; Social Science Research Council-American Council of Learned Societies research grant for Albanian dialectology, 1960-61; Fulbright-Hayes fellowship, 1966-67; L.H.D. from Amherst College, 1972; Guggenheim fellowship, 1973-74.

WRITINGS: A Glossary of American Technical Linguistic Usage, 1925-50, Spectrum, 1957, 3rd revised edition, 1966; (editor) *Readings in Linguistics II*, University of Chicago Press, 1966; (editor) *Languages and Areas: Studies Presented to George V. Bobrinskoy*, University of Chicago, 1967; (editor) *Themes in Linguistics: The 70's*, Mouton, 1973.

Contributor of numerous articles to journals in North America, Europe, Japan, and India. Advisory editor, *Foundations of Language*, 1964—, *Papers on Language and Literature*, 1966—, *Encyclopaedia Brtiannica*, 1969—, *Journal of Linguistics*, 1971—, *Journal of Indo-European Studies*, 1972—; associate editor, *General Linguistics*, 1966—, *International Journal of America Linguistics*, 1969—.

* * *

HAN, Suyin 1917-

PERSONAL: Maiden name, Elizabeth Chou; born September 12, 1917, in Sinyang, China; daughter of Y. T. and Marguerite (Denis) Chou; married P. H. Tang, 1938 (died, 1947); married L. F. Comber (a publisher), February 1, 1952; children: (first marriage) Mei. *Education:* Attended Yenching University; University of Brussels, B.Sc.; London University, M.B., B.S. (honours), 1948.

CAREER: Medical practioner (general practice) and novelist. Nanyang University, Singapore, formerly lecturer in contemporary Asian literature, language, and psychology. Consultant and lecturer at various conferences.

WRITINGS: (With the assistance of an anonymous American woman missionary) *Destination Chungking* (autobiographical fiction), Little, Brown, 1942, new edition, J. Cape, 1953; *A Many-Splendoured Thing*, Little, Brown, 1952; *From One China to the Other*, Universe Books, 1956; *... And the Rain My Drink*, Little, Brown, 1956; *The Mountain is Young*, Putnam, 1958, *Two Loves* (novellas),

Putnam, 1962 (published in England as *Cast But One Shadow* [and] *Winter Love*, J. Cape, 1962); *The Four Faces*, Putnam, 1963; *The Crippled Tree*, Putnam, 1965; *A Mortal Flower*, Putnam, 1966; *China in the Year 2001*, Basic Books, 1967; *Birdless Summer*, Putnam, 1968; *Asia Today: Two Outlooks*, McGill-Queens University Press, 1969; *The Morning Deluge: Mao Tse Tung and the Chinese Revolution, 1893-1954*, Little, Brown, 1972. Contributor to *Life, New Yorker, Holiday, Far East Economic Review* and *Eastern Horizon*.

WORK IN PROGRESS: A five-volume work on China (part autobiography, part history and part biography) which will bear the over-all title of *My House Has Two Doors*.

SIDELIGHTS: Dr. Han is extremely sympathetic with the government of Mao Tse Tung and the problems of the Chinese people. She has said: "I write as an Asian, with all the pent-up emotions of my people. What I say will annoy many people who prefer the more conventional myths brought back by writers on the Orient. All I can say is that I try to tell the truth. Truth, like surgery, may hurt, but it cures."

Literary critics have been angered by her outspoken views and disgust for Western values. Martin Levin wrote: "Han Suyin has recently ceased the practice of medicine, according to her publishers, but she still knows how to prescribe a sugar-coated pill for her readers. In *The Four Faces* the pill has a bitter center of anti-Westernism, and the coating is a rigamarole of dope-peddling, double-dealing and intrigue in Camboida, where East is best and West is worst.... Determined one-sidedness makes her novel tough going even for a reader who is willing to believe, as Dr. Han does, that there is pie in the Asian sky for the uncommitted nations." Edward Weeks noted: "I have come to think of Han Suyin as a novelist who draws more transparently upon her emotions than on her intellect. In *A Many-Splendored Thing,* her best book, she was outgiving; the love story she proclaimed and celebrated was evocative, full-hearted and poignant. *Two Lovers* is a smaller performance—two novellas, each of which seems to have been composed in a resentful mood."

If her books have been deplored by some for their partisanship, they have been praised by others for the same reason. David Dodge wrote: "Because she is so honestly partisan [*The Crippled Tree*] is of greater interest and value than it might have been if written more objectively. It gives the Chinese side of a story that we in America know only from our own side.... *The Crippled Tree* is written by a woman who does not like and admire us as we want to be liked and admired. But it explains in its way why we are not liked and admired, and any explanation of China today is better than none. Futhermore, Han Suyin writes with elegance and style. Even when she is ripping into Americans"

Han Suyin (the pseudonym means "the Chinese gamble"—with the phrase "for liberty" implied) met with war and revolution at a very early age. She is Eurasian and has presented the problem of mixed parentage in her writing, most notably in *A Many-Splendoured Thing*. The book is about her love affair with a British newspaper correspondent who was subsequently killed in Korea. Set against war and social conflict, it was regarded as an objective report of conditions in Asia. The story was called "Love is a Many-Splendored Thing" by Twentieth Century-Fox and filmed in 1955; the movie was chosen as one of the ten best pictures of the year by the *Film Daily* Poll. A daily CBS-TV series titled "Love is a Many-Splendored Thing" and based on the novel, premiered in September, 1967.

AVOCATIONAL INTERESTS: Botany, riding, swimming, lecturing.

BIOGRAPHICAL/CRITICAL SOURCES: New York Times Book Review, September 6, 1959, October 13, 1963; *Times Literary Supplement,* October 26, 1962; *Atlantic Monthly,* December, 1962; *Saturday Review,* February 16, 1963, October 23, 1965.†

* * *

HANEY, William V. 1925-

PERSONAL: Born April 11, 1925, in Blue Island, Ill.; son of Paul L. (a railroad rate analyst) and Lillian (Smith) Haney; married Arlene Rassenfoss, June 14, 1952; children: Thomas J., Michael J., John P., Jeanne A., Ellen M. *Education:* Iowa State University of Science and Technology, student, 1946-47; Northwestern University, B.S. (with distinction), 1949, M.A., 1950, Ph.D., 1953. *Office:* Management Seminars, 2453 Cardinal Lane, Wilmette, Del. 60091.

CAREER: Beloit College, Beloit, Wis., instructor in speech, 1950-51; DePaul University, Chicago, Ill., assistant professor of speech and industrial psychology, 1953-57; Northwestern University, Evanston, Ill., assistant professor of business administration, 1957-61, associate professor, 1961-65, professor, 1965-69; Management Seminars, Wilmette, Del., president, 1969—. Director of Standard Alliance Industries, Inc., 1965-68. Consultant on communication and organization behavior to business, governmental, military, educational, and other organizations; keynote speaker for President's Program on Public-Government Communications, 1965; conductor of management development programs in Europe, Africa, and South America. *Military service:* U.S. Army, 1943-46. *Member:* International Society for General Semantics (director), Academy of Management, American Business Writing Association, International Communication Association (vice-president, 1960-62), Institute of General Semantics, American Association of University Professors, Beta Gamma Sigma.

WRITINGS: Communication: Patterns and Incidents, Irwin, 1960, revised edition published as *Communication and Organizational Behavior,* 1967, 3rd edition, 1973; (contributor) *Concepts and Issues in Administrative Behavior,* edited by Mailick and Van Ness, Prentice-Hall, 1962; (with G. L. Bergen) *Organizational Relations and Management Action,* McGraw, 1966. Also wrote film script, "The Uncalculated Risk," Roundtable Films, 1971. Contributor to *Nation's Business,* and management and semantics journals. Editorial consultant to Institute of General Semantics, 1957—, Academy of Management, 1966-69.

* * *

HANSEN, Al(fred Earl) 1927-

PERSONAL: Born October 5, 1927, in Queens, N.Y.; married; children: Bibbe Anne. *Education:* Studied at Brooklyn College (now Brooklyn College of the City University of New York), Art Students League, New York University, University of Miami (Coral Gables), Tulane University, and Hans Hoffman School of Art, during period, 1948-51, and at Pratt Institute, 1958-63.

CAREER: Commercial artist, New York, N.Y., 1955-58; co-founder of Audio-Visual Group, 1958, doing films and projections; founder of Third Rail Gallery of Current Art I in Brooklyn's Hall St., 1962, and proprietor of Third Rail Galleries (II-V) at other locations in New York metropolitan area, 1962—. Director of Bianchini Gallery, New York, 1965. His "happenings" (plastic monsters and guns, Hershey-bar wrapper collages, and rockets and kites in stretched canvas) have had one-man showings in New York and Provincetown, group showings in New Orleans, Montreal, San Francisco, Dallas, Boston, and elsewhere; works are owned by Museum of Modern Art, Chrysler Museum, and by private collectors. *Military service:* U.S. Army, 1946-48. U.S. Air Force, 1951-55.

WRITINGS: A Primer of Happenings and Time/Space Art, Something Else Press, 1965. Columnist, *Prattler* (Pratt Institute Newspaper), 1962-64.†

*   *   *

HANSEN, Mary Lewis (Patterson)   1933-

PERSONAL: Born July 19, 1933, in Pineville, Ky.; daughter of Moss and Mary J. (Solomon) Patterson; married Theodore L. Hansen, Jr. (a personnel manager), June 13, 1957; children: Theodore Moss, Andrew Corbin. *Education:* University of Kentucky, A.B., 1954; Stanford University, M.A., 1959. *Politics:* Democrat.

CAREER: Instructor in English Stanford University, Palo Alto, Calif., 1955-57, Boston University, Boston, Mass., 1962-63; writer. *Member:* League of Women Voters (Pasadena, Calif.), Phi Beta Kappa.

WRITINGS: The Towboat Summer, Allyn & Bacon, 1964; *Black Bear Adventures*, Allyn & Bacon, 1965; (with Richard E. Drdek) *Fields and Fences*, Allyn & Bacon, 1968; (with Drdek) *Town and Country*, Allyn & Bacon, 1968. Contributor of short stories to Allyn & Bacon's "Sheldon Basic Reading Series."†

*   *   *

HAPGOOD, Charles Hutchins   1904-

PERSONAL: Born May 17, 1904, in New York, N.Y.; son of Hutchins and Neith (Boyce) Hapgood; divorced; children: Frederick, William. *Education:* Harvard University, A.B., 1929, M.A., 1931; also attended University of Freiburg. *Home:* R.F.D. 3, Winchester, N.H.

CAREER: Keene State College, Keene, N.H., associate professor, 1956-66; New England College, Henniker, N.H., professor of history, 1966-67; now retired. *Member:* Royal Geographical Society.

WRITINGS: Earth's Shifting Crust, Pantheon, 1958; *Great Mysteries of the Earth* (juvenile), Putnam, 1960; *Maps of the Ancient Sea Kings*, Chilton, 1966; *The Path of the Pole*, Chilton, 1970; *Mystery in Acambaro*, Griswold Press, 1972; *Voices of Spirit*, Delacorte, 1975. Contributor of articles to *Saturday Evening Post, Coronet, Electronics*, and other periodicals.

WORK IN PROGRESS: The Testament of Vishnu Christ Conversations.

SIDELIGHTS: Earth's Shifting Crust has been published in Spanish, French, and Italian and *Great Mysteries of the Earth*, in Arabic, for distribution by U.S. Information Agency.

*   *   *

HARCAVE, Sidney S(amuel)   1916-

PERSONAL: Born September 12, 1916, in Washington, D.C.; son of Leon (a teacher) and Rose (Rozansky) Harcave; married Norah Boone, December 23, 1947. *Education:* City College, New York, N.Y., B.S., 1937; Univer-

sity of Chicago, Ph.D., 1943. *Home:* 20 Fuller Hollow Rd., Binghamton, N.Y. 13903. *Office:* State University of New York, Binghamton, N.Y. 13901.

CAREER: U.S. government, Washington, D.C., research analyst in Office of Strategic Services, 1944-45, and Department of State, 1945-46; University of Wyoming, Laramie, instructor in history, 1946-47; State University of New York College at Plattsburg (then Champlain College), assistant professor of history, 1947-50, 1951-53; Harvard University, Cambridge, Mass., research associate, 1950-51; State University of New York at Binghamton, assistant professor, 1953-55, associate professor, 1955-57, professor of history, 1957—, chairman of Division of Social Science, 1956-59. Visiting professor at University of Michigan, 1962, and University of Vermont. Consultant to Ford Foundation, 1956-59, and to Center for International Studies, Massachusetts Institute of Technology. Member of final selection committee for Soviet exchange programs, Inter-University Committee on Travel Grants, 1962-65.

MEMBER: American Historical Association, American Association for Advancement of Slavic Studies, New York State Association of European Historians. *Awards, honors:* Social Science Research Council fellowship, 1946, grant-in-aid, 1957; honorary fellow, Yale University, 1946; grants from Inter-University Committee on Travel Grants, 1957, and American Council of Learned Societies.

WRITINGS: Russia: A History, Lippincott, 1952, 6th edition, 1968; (editor) *Readings in Russian History*, Crowell, 1962; *First Blood*, Macmillan, 1964; *The Years of the Golden Cockerel*, Macmillan, 1968. Contributor to *Collier's Encyclopedia, McGraw-Hill Encyclopedia of Biography*, and *Encyclopaedia Britannica*; also contributor to *Russian Review* and *Slavic Review*.

WORK IN PROGRESS: Research on the Russian peasant movement.

SIDELIGHTS: Harcave has traveled extensively in Russia and other European countries. He is competent in Russian, German, and French.

*   *   *

HARCLEROAD, Fred F(arley)   1918-

PERSONAL: First syllable of surname rhymes with "lark"; born November 22, 1918, in Cheyenne, Wyo.; son of Fred F. and Ina Mary (Livermore) Harcleroad; married Moyne Payne, December 20, 1942; children: Patricia Irene, Fred Douglass. *Education:* Colorado State College (now University of Northern Colorado), B.A., 1939, M.A., 1942; Stanford University, Ph.D., 1948. *Home:* 840 Via Linterna, Tucson, Ariz. 85718.

CAREER: High school and junior college teacher and coach, 1939-46; San Diego State College (now University), San Diego, Calif., 1946-52, started as assistant professor, professor of education, 1951-52, director of audio-visual service, 1947-50, director of secondary education, 1949-51, chairman of Division of Education, 1951-52; San Jose State College (now California State University, San Jose), dean of instruction, 1952-57, dean of the college, 1957-59; California State College at Hayward, president, 1959-67; American College Testing Program, Iowa City, Iowa, president, 1967-74; University of Arizona, Tucson, Ariz., Center for the Study of Higher Education, director and professor, 1974—. Consultant to U.S. Office of Education and to American Association of Colleges for Teacher Education; audio-visual consultant to McGraw-Hill Book Co., Inc.

Member: American Association of Colleges for Teacher Education, Association of State Colleges and Universities (president-elect, 1967), Association of Professors of Higher Education (member of executive committee, 1973-76; president, 1974-75).

WRITINGS: Audio-Visual Administration, W. C. Brown, 1951; (with James W. Brown and Richard B. Lewis) *Audio-Visual Instruction, Materials and Methods,* McGraw, 1959, 3rd revised edition and *Teacher's Guide,* 1973; (contributor) *Audio-Visual Instructional Materials Manual,* McGraw, 1959; (editor) *Learning Resources in Colleges and Universities,* U.S. Office of Education, 1964; (with Alfred Kilmartin) *International Education in the Developing State Colleges and Universities,* 1966; *Issues of the Seventies,* Jossey-Bass, 1970; *Comprehensive Information Systems for Statewide Planning in Higher Education,* American College Testing Program, 1971; (editor with Jean H. Cornell) *Assessment of Colleges and Universities,* American College Testing Program, 1971; *Planning for State Systems of Postsecondary Education,* American College Testing Program, 1973. Audio-visual editor of *California Journal of Secondary Education,* 1952-55; member of editorial board, *Audio-Visual Communication Review.*

* * *

HARDIN, Garrett James 1915-

PERSONAL: Born April 21, 1915, in Dallas, Tex.; son of Hugh (a businessman) and Agnes (Garrett) Hardin; married Jane Swanson, September 7, 1941; children: Hyla, Peter, Sharon, David. *Education:* University of Chicago, Sc.B., 1936; Stanford University, Ph.D., 1941. *Politics:* Republican. *Religion:* Unitarian Universalist. *Home:* 399 Arboleda Rd., Santa Barbara, Calif.

CAREER: Carnegie Institution of Washington, staff member in Division of Plant Biology, Stanford, Calif., 1942-46; University of California, Santa Barbara, assistant professor, 1946-50, associate professor of biology, 1950-56, professor of human ecology, 1956—. *Member:* American Association for the Advancement of Science, American Philosophical Society, American Academy of Arts and Sciences, Sigma Xi.

WRITINGS: Nature and Man's Fate, Holt, 1959; *Biology: Its Principles and Implications,* Freeman, 1961; (editor) *Population, Evolution and Birth Control,* Freeman, 1964; *Birth Control,* Bobbs-Merrill, 1970; *Exploring New Ethics for Survival,* Viking, 1972; *Stalking the Wild Taboo,* Kaufmann, 1973; *Mandatory Motherhood,* Beacon Press, 1974.

AVOCATIONAL INTERESTS: Music (playing violin in string quartet).

* * *

HARMON, R(obert) Bartlett 1932-

PERSONAL: Born November 29, 1932, in Helper, Utah; son of John Harold (a salesman) and Winnie Ethlynn (Bartlett) Harmon; married Merlynn Swensen, August 18, 1961; children: Marriner John, Jane Anne, David Wright, James Bartlett, Nancy Louise. *Education:* Brigham Young University, B.A., 1958, M.A., 1960; Rutgers, The State University, M.L.S., 1962. *Politics:* Republican (liberal). *Religion:* Church of Jesus Christ of Latter-day Saints (Mormon). *Home:* 2570 Sue Ave., San Jose, Calif. 95111.

CAREER: San Jose State University, San Jose, Calif., librarian II, 1962-65; senior assistant librarian and head of acquisitions department, 1969—, Graduate School of Librarianship lecturer. *Member:* American Library Association (founder and director of Bibliographic Information Center for the Study of Political Science, 1970—), American Political Science Association.

WRITINGS: The Cole Family: A Bibliography, privately printed, 1964; *A Preliminary Checklist of Materials on Harman-Harmon Genealogy,* privately printed, 1964; *Political Science: A Bibliographical Guide to the Literature,* four volumes, Scarecrow, 1965-74; (with John Ray Harmon) *Descendants of Charles Claymore Bartlett and Annie Katrine Jensen,* Harmonart, 1965; *Sources and Problems of Bibliography in Political Science,* Dibco Press, 1966; *Suggestions for a Basic Political Science Library,* Bibliographic Information Center for the Study of Political Science, 1970; *Art and Practice of Diplomacy,* Scarecrow, 1971; *Elementary Cataloging Manual for Small Libraries,* Dibco, 1972; *Political Science Bibliographies,* Scarecrow, 1973.

WORK IN PROGRESS: Books of guides to comparative government, politics, and political thought.

SIDELIGHTS: Fair reading competency in French and German.

* * *

HARMS, John 1900-

PERSONAL: Born August 22, 1900, in Hamburg, Germany; brought to United States in 1901; son of August and Gretchen (Wolf) Harms. *Education:* University of Chicago, Ph.B., 1922. *Residence:* Phoenix, Ariz.

CAREER: Newspaperman in Chicago, Ill., and New York, N.Y., 1925-30; free-lance journalist on world tour, 1930-31; writer on Works Progress Administration Federal Writing Project, New York, N.Y., 1937-40; various jobs while studying and writing, 1940-60, including editing a trade magazine.

WRITINGS: Our Floundering Fair Trade, Exposition, 1956; *Romance and Truth in the Canaries,* Acorn, 1965; *The Ideological Illusion: A Guide to International Relations and World Development,* Acorn, 1965; *The Crisis in American Democracy: A Candid Look at Ourselves and the Challenge Ahead,* Acorn, 1968; *Up From Agony: A Novel of Americanization,* Acorn, 1969; *Plays and a Preface,* Acorn, 1970.†

* * *

HARPER, Howard 1904-

PERSONAL: Born June 1, 1904, in Kenton, Ohio; son of Earl Vincent (a railroad superintendent) and Grace (Howard) Harper; married Elizabeth Lane, December 2, 1935 (died, 1968); married Josephine Montgomery Williams, June 7, 1969. *Education:* Kenyon College, Ph.B., 1927, B.D., 1930. *Politics:* Republican. *Home:* 859 Robin Ct., Marco Island, Fla. *Agent:* David Scott, 225 East 57th St., New York, N.Y. 10022.

CAREER: Ordained Episcopal priest, 1930; clergyman in Cleveland, Ohio, 1931-33, Hudson, Ohio, 1933-35, Waycross, Ga., 1935-40, The Plains, Va., 1940-42, Jackson, Mich., 1942-52; assistant to bishop of Michigan, Detroit, Mich., 1952-53; canon of St. Paul's Cathedral, Detroit, Mich., 1953; Protestant Episcopal Church, National Office, New York, N.Y., director of laymen's work, 1953-67; St. Mark's Church, Marco Island, Fla., vicar, 1967-68. Founder and first president of National Diocesan Press,

1938. Member of religious advisory council, National Safety Council; director of North Conway (N.H.) Institute (for alcohol studies), 1960-67. *Awards, honors:* D.D. from Kenyon College, 1953.

WRITINGS: Days and Customs of All Faiths, Fleet, 1957; (with Lavinia Dobler) *Holidays Around the World*, Fleet, 1961; *The Vestryman's Manual*, Seabury, 1965; *Profiles of Protestant Saints*, Fleet, 1967; *The Episcopalian's Dictionary*, Seabury, 1974. Writer of weekly column, "Days of All Faiths," 1952—, and feature articles. Associate editor of *Southern Churchman*, 1940-42.

* * *

HARPER, Robert A(lexander) 1924-

PERSONAL: Born April 16, 1924, in Chicago, Ill.; son of Robert Haskell (a lawyer and credit manager) and May Isabell (Wilsdon) Harper; married Sarah Ann Lofgren, September 28, 1944; children: Carol Leslie (Mrs. Robert Green), Judith Lynn (Mrs. Ronald Hendrickson), Robert Willard. *Education:* DePauw University, student, 1941-42; University of Chicago, Ph.B., 1946, S.B., 1947, S.M., 1948, Ph.D., 1950. *Religion:* Methodist. *Home:* 13705 Creekside Dr., Silverspring, Md. 20904. *Office:* Department of Geography, University of Maryland, College Park, Md. 20742.

CAREER: Southern Illinois University, Carbondale, assistant professor, 1950-54, associate professor, 1954-59, professor of geography and chairman of department, 1959-67; University of Maryland, College Park, professor of geography and chairman of department, 1967—. Visiting lecturer, University of Manchester, 1961-62; visiting professor, University of Sidney, 1972, University of Hull, 1975. Encyclopaedia Britannica Films, consultant. *Military service:* U.S. Army Air Forces, 1943-45; became second lieutenant; received Air Medal with oak leaf cluster. *Member:* Association of American Geographers, National Council for Geographical Education (president, 1970-71), National Council for the Social Studies, American Association of University Professors, Sigma Xi, Phi Gamma Delta. *Awards, honors:* Best content article award from Journal of Geography, 1966; professional achievement award from University of Chicago, 1971.

WRITINGS: (With C. W. Sorenson) *Europe and North America*, Silver Burdett, 1953; (with C. W. Sorenson) *Economic Geography*, Silver Burdett, 1953; (with C. W. Sorenson and Raymond Crist) *Learning about Latin America*, Silver Burdett, 1961, 2nd revised edition, 1969; (editor with Jean Gottmann) *Metropolis On the Move*, Wiley, 1966; *Regions Around Us*, Burdette, 1972; (with Theodore H. Schmudde) *Between Two Worlds*, Houghton, 1973.

WORK IN PROGRESS: A high school geography text; a volume on cities as transactional centers with Jean Gottmann.

* * *

HARRER, Heinrich 1912-

PERSONAL: Born July 6, 1912, in Carinthia, Austria; son of Joseph (a postal officer) and Johanna (Penker) Harrer; married Charlotte Wegener, 1938 (divorced, 1942); married Margaretta Truxa, 1953 (divorced, 1958); married Katharina Haarhaus (in public relations), August 10, 1962; children: (first marriage) Peter. *Education:* University of Graz, graduated in geography, 1938. *Religion:* Protestant. *Home:* Schaan 491, Liechtenstein; and Kitzbuehl, Austria.

CAREER: Explorer, 1938—. Member of expedition in first ascent of north wall of Eiger, Switzerland, 1938, of expeditions to Himalaya, 1939, 1951, Andes-Amazon, 1953, Alaska, 1955, Ruwenzori, Africa, 1957, West New Guinea, 1961-62, Nepal, 1965, Surinam, 1966, Sudan, 1970, North Borneo, 1971, and Brazil. Interned in India, 1939-44, and in Tibet, 1944-51. Tutor to Dalai Lama, Lhasa, Tibet, 1944-51. *Member:* National Geographic Society (United States), Himalayan Club, Explorers Club, Austrian Alpine Club, Kitzbuehl Golf Club (president), Austrian Golf Association (president, 1964). *Awards, honors:* Awarded title of Professor by the president of the Republic of Austria, 1964.

WRITINGS: Sieben Jahre in Tibet, Ullstein, 1952, translation by Richard Graves published as *Seven Years in Tibet*, Hart-Davis, 1953, Dutton, 1954; *Meine Tibet Bilder*, Heering, 1953; *Die weisse Spinne*, Ullstein, 1958, translation by Hugh Merrick published as *The White Spider*, Dutton, 1960, revised edition (with Kurt Maix), Hart-Davis, 1965; (with Thubten Jigme Norbu) *Tibet, verlorene Heimat* (biography), Ullstein, 1960, translation by Edward Fitzgerald published as *Tibet Is My Country*, Hart-Davis, 1960, Dutton, 1961; (editor) *Das Kleine Buch der stillen Freuden*, Seemann, c. 1960; (author of foreword) *Die Leiden eines Volkes*, Veritas, 1961, 3rd revised edition, Tibethilfe-Verlag, 1962; *Ich komme aus Steinzeit*, Ullstein, 1963, translation by Edward Fitzgerald published as *I Come from the Stone Age*, Hart-Davis, 1964, Dutton, 1965; (compiler) *Tibetausstellung*, Giestel, 1966; (editor) Sven Anders Hedin, *Reissen mit Sven Hedin*, F. A. Brockhaus, 1967; *Huka-Huka*, Ullstein, 1968; *Die Goetter sollen siegen*, Ullstein, 1968; (compiler with Heinrich Pleticha) *Entdeckungsgeschichte aus erster Hand*, Arena, 1968; *Geister und Daemonen*, Ullstein, 1969.

SIDELIGHTS: Seven Years in Tibet has been translated into forty languages and was made into a motion picture shown at international film festivals at Cannes and Edinburgh. Harrer has made several television appearances.†

* * *

HARRINGTON, Michael 1928-

PERSONAL: Born February 24, 1928, in St. Louis, Mo.; son of Edward Michael (a patent attorney) and Catherine (Fitzgibbon) Harrington; married Stephanie Gervis, May 30, 1963. *Education:* Holy Cross College, A.B., 1947; attended Yale Law School, 1947-48; University of Chicago, M.A., 1949. *Politics:* Socialist. *Office:* Department of Political Science, Queens College of the City University of New York, Flushing, N.Y.

CAREER: Worked as a welfare worker in St. Louis, Mo.; associate editor, *Catholic Worker*, 1951-52; Workers Defense League, organization secretary, 1953; researcher and counsel for the Fund for the Republic, 1954—; editor, *New America*, 1961-62; Queens College of the City University of New York, Flushing, N.Y., professor of political science, 1972—. Writer; lecturer. Delegate, executive committee, International Union of Socialist Youth, Berlin, 1959; organizer of the March on the Conventions Movement, 1960; delegate to Congress Socialist International, Amsterdam, 1963; chairman of the board, League for Industrial Democracy, 1964—; Socialist Party, member of national executive board, 1960-68, chairman and co-chairman, 1968-72; chairman, Democratic Socialist organizing committee, 1973—; paid consultant (on the poverty program) to U.S. Government. Member, A. Philip Randolph Institute. *Wartime activity:* Conscientious objector, Korean War. *Member:*

American Civil Liberties Union (member of board), Workers Defense League (member of board). *Awards, honors:* George Polk award, 1963; Sidney Hillman award, 1963; Riordan award, Washington (D.C.) Newspaper Guild, 1964; D.H.L., Bard College, 1966; Eugene V. Debs Foundation award, 1973.

WRITINGS: (Editor with Paul Jacobs) *Labor in a Free Society,* University of California Press, 1959; *The Other America: Poverty in the United States,* Macmillan, 1962, revised edition, 1969; *The Retail Clerks,* Wiley, 1962; (contributor) Irwin Isenberg, editor, *The Drive Against Illiteracy,* H. W. Wilson, 1964; *Conference on Poverty-in-Plenty: The Poor in Our Affluent Society,* Georgetown University, 1964; *The Accidental Century,* Macmillan, 1965; (author of introduction) Jack Newfield, *A Prophetic Minority,* New American Library, 1966; *American Power in the Twentieth Century,* League for Industrial Democracy, 1967; (author of introduction) Irving Howe, editor, *The Radical Imagination,* New American Library, 1967; *Toward A Democratic Left: A Radical Program for a New Majority,* Macmillan, 1968; (author of introduction) George Charney, *A Long Journey,* Quadrangle, 1968; *Why We Need Socialism in America,* [New York?], 1970; *Socialism,* Saturday Review Press, 1972; (compiler with Irving Howe) *The Seventies: Problems and Proposals,* Harper, 1972; *Fragments of the Century,* Saturday Review Press, 1974; (with T. F. Lindsay) *The Conservative Party, 1918-1970,* St. Martin's, 1974. Writer of pamphlets, speeches and papers. Contributor to *New Republic, Commentary, Harper's, Atlantic, Nation, Reporter, Commonweal,* and other publications. Editor, *Democratic Left* (newsletter), 1973—; member of editorial board, *Dissent.*

SIDELIGHTS: David McReynolds considered Harrington to be "the closest thing the democratic socialist movement in this country has to a public spokesman, aside from Norman Thomas." This would seem to indicate that Harrington's advocates in the United States are few, and these something less than respectable. But this is hardly the case. President Kennedy borrowed Harrington's phrase "the invisible poor" for his speeches, and Harrington served as an advisor to the government on its poverty program planning, the federal government being, he feels, the only institution "capable of acting to abolish poverty," though the "actual implementation can be carried out through myriad institutions, and the closer they are to the specific local area, the better the results."

Harrington believes that slum living results in "a personality of poverty.... To be poor is to enter a fatal, futile universe, an America within America, with a twisted spirit." His point of departure, he says, is a sense of outrage which, according to some critics, leads him to overstate his case. A. H. Raskin wrote of *The Other America:* "[Harrington] writes with sensitivity and perception as well as indignation. The Council of Economic Advisers might say, with justice, that he has overdrawn his case as to both the size and intractability of the problem. That is no indictment. The chroniclers and celebrants of America's upward movement are plentiful; it is good to be reminded that we are still a long way from the stars."

His next major work, *The Accidental Century,* is what *Newsweek* called "an attempt to measure the dangers and possibilities of the technological revolution." Emile Capouya considered the book "as original a work as *The Other America,* much broader in scope, far more ambitious intellectually." Other critics call Harrington naive, Utopian, and his arguments labored. McReynolds early pre-

dicted that this would not be a popular book because it is "a defence of democratic socialism, and a penetrating attack on capitalism.... It does not merely rivet our attention on a problem, but on a system. This is a book which will confound both the ultra-leftists who had been so eager to write Harrington off as a member of the establishment, and those members of the establishment who thought they had tamed this Irish Catholic turned Marxist."

Milton Viorst wrote: [Harrington] is a man rich in imagination, and in *Toward a Democratic Left* he is at his best when he is most indignant at the inequities of our system ... Harrington does not succumb to the temptation of indifference and chronicles our faults in great breadth. No matter how predisposed one may be to accept his arguments, one cannot read him without a fresh sense of indignation.

"But, alas, Harrington's book is a disappointment. He fails to carry out his promise of a program to give our oppressive civilization a new start. Perhaps the promise couldn't be kept."

When writing of *Socialism,* a *New York Times* reviewer said: "What is astonishing is the imprint of the steady worker—the inexhaustible determination not to lapse into solopsistic ideology or simplicities full of the promise of violence, but to take each fragment of reality around us and fit it into a coherent whole. It is because of this determination that one is willing, at least for a moment, to share Mr. Harrington's vision ...."

BIOGRAPHICAL/CRITICAL SOURCES: New York Times Book Review, April 8, 1962; *Time,* February 7, 1964; *Village Voice,* August 26, 1965; *Newsweek,* August 30, 1965; *Saturday Review,* September 11, 1965; *Commonweal,* September 17, 1965; *Virginia Quarterly Review,* autumn, 1965; *New York Post,* August 30, 1968; *New York,* September 24, 1973.†

*   *   *

HARRIS, Gene Gray 1929-

PERSONAL: Born February 15, 1929, in Plymouth, N.C.; son of Fletcher Rudolph (a businessman) and Vonnie Mae (Blount) Harris. *Education:* Attended public schools in Plymouth, N.C. *Religion:* Episcopalian. *Home:* 304 Winesett Circle, Plymouth, N.C.

CAREER: Drug store clerk, 1949-59, free-lance artist, 1959-63, and cosmetologist, 1963—, all in Plymouth, N.C. *Military service:* U.S. Navy, 1947.

WRITINGS: Smoke on Old Thunderhead, Blair, 1962.

WORK IN PROGRESS: A book of juvenile fiction on Blackbeard, the pirate; a second juvenile set in western North Carolina.

AVOCATIONAL INTERESTS: Arts (painting and sculpture), archeology, sealore, folklore.

*   *   *

HARRIS, Louise 1903-

PERSONAL: Born September 28, 1903, in Pawtuxet (now Warwick), R.I.; daughter of Samuel P. (a machinist, printer, and manufacturer) and Faustine M. (Borden) Harris. *Education:* Brown University, A.B., 1926; studied pipe organ under T. Tertius Noble, organist of St. Thomas Church, New York, N.Y. *Politics:* Republican. *Religion:* Protestant. *Address:* Box 1926, Brown University, Providence, R.I. 02912.

CAREER: One-time teacher of organ and piano; later genealogical researcher; originator of C. A. Stephens Collection at Brown University, Providence, R.I., and continuing researcher, 1961—. *Member:* Intercontinental Biographical Association (fellow), International Platform Association, National Trust for Historic Preservation, National Historical Society, American Heritage Society, Smithsonian Associates, National Wildlife Federation, American Guild of Organists (charter member, Rhode Island chapter; treasurer, 1935-38), Hymn Society of America; Society of Stukely Westcott Descendants of America (national registrar, 1963—), Roger Williams Family Association, Audubon Society of Rhode Island, Rhode Island Hospital Guild, Rhode Island Short Story Club.

WRITINGS—All published by C. A. Stephens Collection, Brown University: *A Comprehensive Bibliography of C. A. Stephens,* 1965; *None But the Best, A Chuckle and a Laugh,* 1967; *The Star of the Youth's Companion,* 1969; (editor) C. A. Stephens, *Molly's Baby: A Little Heroine of the Seas,* 1969; (compiler) Stephens, *Under the Sea in the Salvador,* 1969; (compiler) *C. A. Stephens Looks at Norway,* 1970; *The Flag over the Schoolhouse,* 1971; (compiler) *Charles Adams Tales,* 1973.

WORK IN PROGRESS: Four books; *Our Great Story-Teller; Around Lake Peunesseeuassee, Kit Carson, Jr.; Little Big Heart;* and a compilation of C. A. Stephens stories.

*   *   *

HARRIS, Philip Robert 1926-

PERSONAL: Born January 22, 1926, in Brooklyn, N.Y.; son of Gordon Rodger and Esther E. (Delahanty) Harris; married Dorothy Lipp (chairperson of Division of Communication, U.S. International University), July 3, 1965. *Education:* St. John's University, Jamaica, N.Y., B.B.A., 1949; Fordham University, M.S., 1952, Ph.D., 1956; special courses at St. Francis College, Brooklyn, N.Y., Syracuse University, New York University, Catholic University of America, and University of Notre Dame. *Politics:* Independent. *Religion:* Christian. *Home:* 2702 Costebelle Dr., La Jolla, Calif. 92037.

CAREER: Licensed psychologist, State of New York, 1959. St. Francis College, Brooklyn, N.Y., 1956-63, became regent and vice-president; Association for Human Emergence, Inc., State College, Pa., executive director, 1964-66; Pennsylvania State University, College of Education, University Park, lecturer in counselor education, 1965-66; Leadership Resources, Inc., Washington, D.C., senior associate, 1966-69; Copely International Corp., San Diego, Calif., vice-president, 1970-71; Management and Organization Development, Inc., La Jolla, Calif., 1971—. Fulbright lecturer in India, 1962-63; consultant to Fe Y Algeria School System, Caracas, Venezuela, 1960-69; delegate to UNESCO Conference, Paris, 1962; consultant and visiting professor, Temple University, 1967-69; visiting professor, University of North Colorado, 1973-74, Pepperdine University, 1975, University of California, San Diego, 1971—. Lecturer and conductor of human and management relations and leadership institutes throughout North America.

MEMBER: American Psychological Association, American Association of Humanistic Psychology, American Personnel and Guidance Association, American Society for Training and Development. *Awards, honors:* Named Young Man of the Year, New York City Junior Chamber

of Commerce, 1959; mental health grant, U.S. Department of Health, Education, and Welfare, 1959; National Training Laboratories scholarship, National Education Association, 1965; Office of Naval Research grant, 1972-74.

WRITINGS: (Co-author) "Insight Series," four books and teacher's handbooks, Harcourt, 1957-65, with volume titles of *It's Your Life, It's Your Education, It's Your Personality,* and *It's Your Future* (Asian edition published as "Challenge Series" by Paulist Publications in Allahabad, India, 1963, Tokyo, Japan, 1964); (editor) *Regents Studyguide to Scholarship Examinations,* Republic Book Co., 1958; (editor) *NCWC Guide to Catholic Educational Institutions,* National Catholic Welfare Conference, 1959; *Organizational Dynamics,* Tam's Books, 1974. Editor of *Readings for Catholic Counselors,* 1958 and 1960. Contributor of more than a hundred articles to educational journals. Editor, *Catholic Counselor,* 1955-59.

WORK IN PROGRESS: "Increasing Managerial Effectiveness" series, an audio-written programmed learning system, for Westinghouse Learning Corp.

SIDELIGHTS: Harris has traveled extensively on five continents. *Avocational interests:* Reading, golf.

*   *   *

HARRISON, Raymond H. 1911-

PERSONAL: Born June 30, 1911, in Cheyenne, Okla.; son of William Henry and Minnie L. (McCaskill) Harrison; married Ruth I. Long (a teacher), November 10, 1933; children: Raymond Alan, Marian Faye, Patricia Eileen. *Education:* Central State College, Edmond, Okla., B.S., 1939; Oklahoma State University, M.S., 1941; University of Denver, Ed.D., 1955. *Politics:* Democrat. *Religion:* Methodist. *Home:* 5615 North Fourth St., Fresno, Calif.

CAREER: Superintendent of schools in Elkhart, Kan., 1945-53; University of Denver, Denver, Colo., instructor in secondary education, 1953-55; Fresno State University, Fresno, Calif., professor of school administration, 1955—, and coordinator of graduate studies in education. Educational consultant to Republic of Sudan, 1961-63, and to Fresno County and other California school districts. Member of evaluation team of Harrison, Nixon, & Associates.

WRITINGS: (With L. E. Gowin) *The Elementary Teacher in Action,* Wadsworth, 1958; *Personnel Appraisal and Development Handbook,* privately printed, 1966; *Supervisory Leadership in Education,* American Book Co., 1968; *Autumn is a Good Time* (poetry), Young Publications, 1969; *Selection, Orientation, and Use of Teacher Aides,* G W School Supply Specialists, 1971; *Moonflower* (poetry), Pioneer Publishing, 1973. Contributor to education journals.

WORK IN PROGRESS: Two books, *Whispers in the Wind* and *Constructive School Discipline;* and a revision of *Personnel Appraisal and Development Handbook.*

*   *   *

HARRISON, Royden John 1927-

PERSONAL: Born March 3, 1927, in London, England; son of James Madden (an executive) and Jessie Adam (Baird) Harrison; married Pauline May Cowan (now a biochemist), December 29, 1954; children: Fiona, Sheila. *Education:* St. Catherine's College, Oxford, B.A. (honors), 1951, M.A. and D.Phil., 1955. *Home:* 4 Wilton Pl., Sheffield, England. *Office:* University of Warwick, Coventry, England.

CAREER: University of Sheffield, Sheffield, England, 1955-70, senior lecturer in political science and industrial studies, 1963-69, reader in political theory and institutions, 1969; University of Warwick, Coventry, England, professor of social history, 1970—. University of Wisconsin, visiting professor of modern British and European history, 1964. Sheffield Trades and Labour Council, delegate, 1961—. *Military service:* British Army, 1945-48. *Member:* Political Studies Association, Society for the Study of Labour History.

WRITINGS: (Contributor) A. Briggs and J. Saville, editors, *Essays in Labour History*, Macmillan, Volume I, 1960, Volume II, 1972; *Before the Socialists: Studies in Labour and Politics, 1861-1881*, University of Toronto Press, 1965; (editor) *The English Defense of the Commune, 1871*, Merlin Press, 1972; *Labor and Politics in England, 1860-1970: Selected Essays*, Future Press, 1972. Contributor to *Science and Society, Labor History, Victorian Studies*, and other journals in United States and Europe. Co-editor, *Bulletin of Society for the Study of Labour History*; member of editorial board, *Political Quarterly*, 1968—.

WORK IN PROGRESS: The Webbs: The Lives and Times of Sidney and Beatrice Webb, Lord and Lady Passfield; Warwick Guide to Labour Periodicals, 1790-1970, completion expected in 1976; and editing *The Coal Miners*, completion expected 1976.

SIDELIGHTS: Harrison has lived in Australia, Canada, and the United States.

* * *

HARRISON, William 1933-

PERSONAL: Born October 29, 1933, in Dallas, Tex.; son of Samuel Scott and Mary Etta (Cook) Harrison; married Merlee Kimsey, February 2, 1957; children: Laurie, Sean, Quentin. *Education:* Texas Christian University, B.A., 1955; Vanderbilt University, M.A., 1959; University of Iowa, graduate study, 1962. *Agent:* Owen Laster, William Morris Agency, 1350 Avenue of the Americas, New York, N.Y. 10017. *Office:* University of Arkansas, Fayetteville, Ark.

CAREER: University of Arkansas, Fayetteville, member of English department, 1964—. *Member:* American Association of University Professors. *Awards, honors:* Guggenheim fellowship, 1973-74; Pulitzer Prize nomination, 1974.

WRITINGS: The Theologian (novel), Harper, 1965; *In A Wild Sanctuary* (novel), Morrow, 1969; *Lessons In Paradise* (novel), Morrow, 1971; *Roller Ball Murder and Other Stories*, Morrow, 1974. Also wrote "Rollerball" screenplay, Norman Jewison Production for United Artists, 1974-75. Work represented in many anthologies.

WORK IN PROGRESS: A novel, *Pack of Dogs*; and an original screenplay, "Arsons of Desire."

* * *

HARSS, Luis 1936-

PERSONAL: Born July 23, 1936, in Valparaiso, Chile; son of Benjamin Cohen (a diplomat-civil servant) and Chita (Arguello) Harss. *Education:* Attended English high school in Argentina; University of Notre Dame, student, 1953-54; Stanford University, B.A., 1958, M.A., 1959. *Politics:* None. *Religion:* None. *Home:* Larrea 1223, Buenos Aires, Argentina.

CAREER: Novelist; journalist; lecturer. Senior fellow, St.

Antony's College, Oxford, England; lecturer in Spanish, West Virginia University.

WRITINGS: The Blind (novel), Atheneum, 1963; *The Little Men* (novel), Atheneum, 1964; *Los Nuestros*, Sudamericana, 1966; translation, with Barbara Dohmann, published as *Into the Mainstream: Conversations with Latin American Authors*, Harper, 1967; *La otra Sara* (novel), Sudamericana, 1968. Literary editor, *Primera Plana* (Argentine news magazine), 1966.

WORK IN PROGRESS: A novel, *Los Rocha*, first part of a trilogy on a wandering musician; a critical study of Argentine novelist Julio Cortazar.

* * *

HARTFORD, (George) Huntington II 1911-

PERSONAL: Born April 18, 1911, in New York, N.Y.; son of Edward Vassalo (an inventor) and Henrietta (Guerard) Hartford; married Mary Lee Epling, April 18, 1931 (divorced, 1939); married Marjorie Steele (an actress), September 10, 1949 (divorced, 1961); married Diane Brown, October 6, 1962 (divorced, 1970); children: (second marriage) Catherine, John; (third marriage) Cynara Juliet. *Education:* Harvard University, A.B., 1934; Columbia University, graduate study, 1957-62. *Religion:* Episcopalian. *Home:* One Beekman Place, New York, N.Y. 10022. *Agent:* Mrs. Carlton Cole, Waldorf Towers, 50th St. & Park Ave., New York, N.Y. 10022. *Office:* Huntington Hartford Enterprises, 866 United Nations Plaza, Room 531, New York, N.Y. 10017.

CAREER: Financier and patron of the arts. Worked as a clerk in an A & P food store, 1935-36, as a reporter for *PM* newspaper, New York, N.Y., 1940, and for Harvell Die Casting Co. of California; founded Hartford Model Agency, New York and Hollywood, 1947, and Huntington Hartford Foundation (retreat for artists, composers, and writers), near Los Angeles, 1949; began producing movies, 1950, releasing first film, "Face to Face," 1953; financed several Broadway shows; opened Huntington Hartford Theatre, Hollywood, 1954, with "What Every Woman Knows" starring Helen Hayes; founder and president, The Handwriting Institute, Inc., 1956—; owner and developer of Paradise Island, Nassau, Bahamas, 1959—; co-chairman of the board, Oil Shale Corp., New York, 1961—; founder of *Show* magazine, and editor-in-chief, 1961-64, 1970—; founded Gallery of Modern Art (now New York Cultural Center, of Fairleigh Dickinson University), New York, 1964, trustee, 1969—; opened Show Magazine Clubs in Nassau, Bahamas, and 1972, in New York. Research associate in neurology, Columbia University, 1956-62. Member of advisory committee, John F. Kennedy Center for the Performing Arts, 1960—; patron of Lincoln Center for the Performing Arts, 1961—; chairman, American Committee to Preserve Abu Simbel, 1964-69; advisor on cultural affairs to president of Borough of Manhattan, 1967, 1968; member of advisory council, department of art history and archaeology, Columbia University, 1968—. Member of board of directors, U.S. Committee for the United Nations, 1960—, U.S. Committee for Refugees, 1960—; member of U.S. National Commission for UNESCO, 1964-67, of national council of U.S. People's Fund for the Support of the United Nations, 1969—. *Military service:* U.S. Coast Guard Reserve, 1942-45; served on Greenland Patrol and in South Pacific; became lieutenant.

MEMBER: National Council on the Arts, National Arts Club, National Sculpture Society (honorary fellow),

Friends of the Whitney Museum of American Art, Harvard Club, River Club. *Awards, honors:* Awards from National Arts Club, American Artists Professional League, and Salmagundi Club, all 1956, for article, "The Public Be Damned?"; citation of merit from National Association for American Composers and Conductors, 1961, in recognition of Huntington Hartford Foundation; named Broadway Association "Man of the Year," 1964; award from Organization of American States, 1966, and Dyer Post Award of Veterans of Foreign Wars, 1967, both for cultural contributions; cultural award from Women's Division of Anti-Defamation League, 1967.

WRITINGS: "Jane Eyre" (play adaptation of Charlotte Bronte's novel), first produced on Broadway in 1958; *Art or Anarchy?*, Doubleday, 1964; *You Are What You Write*, Macmillan, 1973. Contributor to *Esquire, American Mercury*, and other publications.

SIDELIGHTS: Hartford is the namesake of his grandfather, and heir to the Great Atlantic & Pacific Tea Company fortune, established by his grandfather. Hartford's father, inventor of the shock absorber, accumulated a personal fortune in his own right. Hartford has invented an indoor-outdoor tennis game called "Double-Up."

BIOGRAPHICAL/CRITICAL SOURCES: Playbill, November 16, 1959; *Esquire*, April, 1962; *Town and Country*, May, 1962; *New York Herald Tribune Sunday Magazine*, February 23, 1964; *Ladies' Home Journal*, May, 1965; Thomas B. Morgan, *Self-Creations*, Holt, 1965.

* * *

HARVEY, James O. 1926-

PERSONAL: Born September 9, 1926, in Charleston, S.C.; son of Charles Walter (an officer, U.S. Navy) and Erma Alice (Brown) Harvey; married Alva Jean Maloney, June 2, 1956; children: Gwendolyn Gail, Laurie Ann, Jared Blaine. *Education:* Long Beach City College, A.A., 1948; University of Oklahoma, B.A., 1950. *Home:* 426 Estancia, N.W., Albuquerque, N.M. 87105. *Agent:* Collins-Knowlton-Wing, Inc., 60 East 56th St., New York, N.Y. 10022. *Office:* Information Office, Kirtland Air Force Base, N.M.

CAREER: Radio station program director, Barstow, Calif., 1950-54; dishwasher in a cafe, Glenwood Springs, Colo., and Bureau of Indian Affairs clerk, Window Rock, Ariz., 1954-56; Kirtland Air Force Base, Albuquerque, N.M., public information officer (civilian), 1956—. *Military service:* U.S. Navy, 1944-46. *Member:* Albuquerque Press Club.

WRITINGS: Beyond the Gorge of Shadows, Lothrop, 1965. Story included in *Teen-Age Frontier Stories*, edited by A. L. Furman, Lantern, 1958.

WORK IN PROGRESS: A boys' adventure story (book), set in northeastern Arizona in 900 A.D.

SIDELIGHTS: Long-time friend of Thomas Duncan, the novelist and poet, whom he calls his mentor and motivation. *Avocational interests:* Taking color motion pictures of Arizona and New Mexico.

* * *

HASS, C(harles) Glen 1915-

PERSONAL: Born March 7, 1915, in Mansfield, Ohio; married Margaret Mary Walters (a public school curriculum specialist), June 12, 1940; children: Rolland Glen. *Education-*

tion: University of Denver, B.A., 1937; Stanford University, M.A., 1946; Columbia University, Ed.D., 1953. *Home:* 1116 Northwest 61st Ter., Gainesville, Fla. 32601. *Office:* College of Education, University of Florida, Gainesville, Fla. 32601.

CAREER: Junior high school teacher, Denver, Colo., 1937-42; Columbia University, New York, N.Y., research assistant, Horace Mann-Lincoln Institute, 1947-48; Battle Creek (Mich.) public schools, elementary principal, 1949-50; Arlington County (Va.) public schools, associate superintendent, 1950-58; University of Florida, College of Education, Gainesville, professor of education, 1958—, chairman of graduate curricula, curriculum theory and research, 1965—. Visiting professor at New York University, University of Utah, Colorado State University, and Florida State University. Member of board of educators, United Educators, Inc., Lake Bluff, Ill. *Military service:* U.S. Army, Adjutant General's Department, 1942-46; became captain. *Member:* Association for Supervision and Curriculum Development (national executive committee and board of directors, 1960-64), John Dewey Society (national board of directors; chairman, commission on meetings, 1960—; national president, 1968-70), Society of Professors of Education (national president, 1971), National Education Association (life), Florida Education Association (life).

WRITINGS: (Editor) *Leadership for Improving Instruction*, Association for Supervision and Curriculum Development, 1960; (editor with Kimball Wiles) *Readings in Curriculum*, Allyn & Bacon, 1965; *Curriculum Planning: A New Approach*, Allyn & Bacon, 1974. Author of traffic safety curriculum guides and materials for American Automobile Association, Washington, D.C., 1953-58. Contributor of about thirty articles to education journals.

WORK IN PROGRESS: Curriculum Theory and *Educational Leadership Theory*.

* * *

HASTINGS, Adrian 1929-

PERSONAL: Born June 23, 1929, in Kuala Lumpur, Malaya; son of William George (a barrister) and Hazel Mary (Davnais) Hastings. *Education:* Attended Douai Abbey School, Berkshire, England, 1943-46; Oxford University, B.A., 1949, M.A., 1953; Propaganda Fide, Rome, Italy, D.D., 1958; Cambridge University, postgraduate certificate of education, 1958. *Politics:* Liberal. *Home:* St. Edmund's House, Cambridge, England.

CAREER: Ordained Roman Catholic priest, Rome, Italy, 1955; worked in Africa, principally Uganda, Tanzania, and Zambia, 1958-72; School of Oriental and African Studies, London, England, research officer and fellow of St. Edmond's House, 1972—. University of Lovanium in Leopoldville, visiting professor of theology, 1963-64.

WRITINGS: Prophet and Witness in Jerusalem, Helicon, 1958; (editor) *The Church and the Nations*, Sheed, 1959; *One and Apostolic*, Sheed, 1963; *The World Mission of the Church*, Paulist Press, 1964; *Church and Mission in Modern Africa*, Fordham University Press, 1967; *A Guide to Vatican II*, two volumes, Darton, Longman, and Todd, 1968-69; *Mission and Ministry*, Sheed, 1971; *Church and Ministry*, Gaba, 1972; *Christian Marriage in Africa*, S.P.C.K., 1973; *Wiriyamu*, Orbis, 1974.

WORK IN PROGRESS: Research on African Christianity in the post-independence period.

HATTERY, Lowell H(arold) 1916-

PERSONAL: Born May 26, 1916, in Van Wert, Ohio; son of Harold (a teacher) and Alta (Stephenson) Hattery; married Molly Kasson, July 27, 1947; children: Maxine L., Thomas H. *Education:* Ohio University, Athens, A.B., 1936; Syracuse University, graduate student, 1936-38; American University, Ph.D., 1951. *Religion:* Unitarian Universalist. *Home:* R.D. #4, Mt. Airy, Md. 21771. *Office:* School of Government and Public Administration, American University, Washington, D.C. 20016.

CAREER: U.S. Department of Agriculture, Washington, D.C., economist and statistician, 1939-41; National Research Council, Office of Scientific Personnel, Washington, D.C., research associate, 1946-48; American University, School of Government and Public Administration, Washington, D.C., assistant professor, 1948-50, associate professor, 1950-53, professor of management and public administration, 1953—, Center for Technology and Administration, director, 1958-64, director of science/technology policy and administration program, 1973—. Technical University, Berlin, Germany, guest professor of automatic data processing, 1964; lecturer at other institutions in Netherlands, 1955, Japan, 1960, and United Arab Republic, 1962. Consultant to government and industry, 1946—. *Military service:* U.S. Naval Reserve, active duty, 1941-46.

MEMBER: Society for Advancement of Management (fellow), American Association for the Advancement of Science (fellow), American Society for Public Administration, American Society for Industrial Security, American Society for Information Science, Institute for Electrical and Electronics Engineers, International Association of Chiefs of Police.

WRITINGS: Practices in Collection and Maintenance of Information on Highly Trained and Specialized Personnel in the United States, National Research Council, 1947; *Four-Council Cooperative Higher Education Survey,* National Research Council, 1948; *Scientific Research: Its Administration and Organization,* American University Press, 1950; (with others) *Regional District Government, Prince George's County,* American University Press, 1954; *Executive Control and Data Processing,* Anderson Kramer Associates, 1959; *Information and Communication in Biological Science,* Center for Technology and Administration, American University, 1961.

Editor: (With George P. Bush) *Teamwork in Research,* American University Press, 1953; (with G. P. Bush) *Electronics in Management,* University Press of Washington, D.C., 1956; (with Edward M. McCormick) *Information Retrieval Management,* Automatic Data Processing, Inc., 1963; (with G. P. Bush) *Reprography and Copyright Law,* American Institute of Biological Sciences, 1965; (with G. P. Bush) *Electronics and Automation in Publishing,* Spartan Books, 1965.

Contributor: *Local Government in the United States of America,* Nijhoff, for International Union of Local Authorities, 1961; Fred R. Brown, editor, *Management: Concepts and Practice,* Industrial College of the Armed Forces, 1962; Paul W. Howerton, editor, *Information Handling: First Principles,* Spartan Books, 1962. Contributor of some twenty articles to statistical, administration, and social science journals.

Editor, *Newsletter on Information Retrieval and Library Automation,* 1965—, Newsletter on *Systems, Technology, and Science for Law Enforcement and Security,* 1969—, *R and D* and *Management Digest,* 1971—.

WORK IN PROGRESS: Effects of technological change, especially automation, and the revolution in information technology.

SIDELIGHTS: Hattery's travels include extensive visits worldwide.

* * *

HAUGEN, Edmund Bennett 1913-

PERSONAL: Born March 23, 1913, in Keene, N.D.; son of Ole O. and Ella (Swenson) Haugen; married Edna L. Peper, May 10, 1941; children: Ellen E. *Education:* Washington State University, B.S., 1941, B.Ed., 1947, M.S., 1951. *Religion:* Lutheran. *Address:* P.O. Box 147, Warden, Wash. 98857.

CAREER: Vocational agricultural instructor at high schools in Milan, Wash., 1941-43, Reardan, Wash., 1943-44, Asotin, Wash., 1945-46, Clarkston, Wash., 1946-64; Woodland High School, Woodland, Wash., vocational agricultural instructor, 1964—. *Military service:* U.S. Navy, 1944-45. *Member:* American Vocational Association, National Vocational Agricultural Teachers' Association, Adult Education Association of the U.S.A., National Education Association, National Association of Parliamentarians, Washington Vocational Association, Washington Education Association, Phi Delta Kappa, Alpha Tau Alpha, Washington State Grange (deputy master).

WRITINGS: Mister/Madam Chairman: Parliamentary Procedure Explained, Augsburg, 1963.†

* * *

HAUSER, Phillip M(orris) 1909-

PERSONAL: Born September 27, 1909, in Chicago, Ill.; son of Morris and Ann (Diamond) Hauser; married Zelda B. Abrams, November 27, 1935; children: William Barry, Martha Ann. *Education:* University of Chicago, Ph.B., 1929, M.A., 1933, Ph.D., 1938. *Politics:* Independent. *Home:* 5729 South Kimbark Ave., Chicago, Ill. 60637. *Office:* University of Chicago, Population Research Center, 1413 East 60th St., Chicago, Ill. 60637.

CAREER: U.S. Department of Commerce, Washington, D.C., Bureau of the Census, assistant chief statistician for population, 1938-42, assistant director, 1942-46, deputy director, 1946-49, acting director, 1949-50, assistant to Secretary of Commerce and director, Office of Program Planning, 1945-47; University of Chicago, Chicago, Ill., professor of sociology, and director of Population Research and Training Center and Chicago Community Inventory, 1947—, chairman of department of sociology, 1956-65. Walker-Ames professor, University of Washington, 1958; Ford visiting professor, Indiana University; visiting professor or lecturer at University of Washington, Seattle, at Princeton University, University of Notre Dame, and other universities. Member of board of directors, Selected American Shares and Aldine Publishing Co. U.S. representative to Population Commission, United Nations, 1947-51; chairman of U.S. National Committee for Vital and Health Statistics, U.S. Public Health Service and World Health Organization, 1948-59; statistical adviser to Union of Burma, 1951-52, to Thailand, 1955-56; chairman of technical advisory committee to Bureau of the Census for the 1960 and 1970 Population Census; member of board, United Nations Institute for Research on Social Development, 1966-73; consultant, President's Committee on Population, 1968-69; president, National Conference on Social

Welfare, 1973-74. Member of policy and advisory committees, Bureau of the Budget and U.S. Health Service. Chairman of advisory panel on integration of public schools, Chicago Board of Education; member of board of governors, Metropolitan Housing and Planning Council, Chicago; consultant to other city departments and commissions, Chicago.

MEMBER: American Statistical Association (fellow; president, 1962), American Association of University Professors, Population Association of America (president, 1950), Sociological Research Association (president, 1962), American Association for the Advancement of Science (fellow; vice-president of social and economic sciences section, 1959), American Sociological Association (president, 1967-68), Institute of Mathematical Statistics, International Union for Scientific Study of Population Problems, International Statistical Institute, American Association for Public Opinion Research, Phi Beta Kappa, Alpha Kappa Delta, Pi Gamma Mu, Lambda Alpha. *Awards, honors:* L.H.D., Roosevelt University, 1967; L.L.D. Loyola University, Chicago, 1969.

WRITINGS: (With Herbert Blumer) *Movies, Delinquency and Crime,* Macmillan, 1933, reprinted, Arno, 1970; *Workers on Relief in the U.S.,* two volumes, 1939; (editor with W. R. Leonard) *Government Statistics for Business Use,* Wiley, 1946, revised edition, 1956; (editor) *Population and World Politics,* Free Press, 1958; (editor) *Urbanization in Asia and the Far East,* UNESCO, 1958; (editor with O. Dudley Duncan) *The Study of Population: An Inventory and Appraisal,* University of Chicago Press, 1959; (with Beverly D. Duncan) *Housing a Metropolis—Chicago,* Free Press of Glencoe, 1960; (editor) *Urbanization in Latin America,* UNESCO, 1961; *Population Perspectives,* Rutgers University Press, 1961; (editor) *The Population Dilemma,* Prentice-Hall, 1963, 2nd edition, 1970; (editor with Leo F. Schnore) *The Study of Urbanization,* Wiley, 1965; (editor) *Handbook for Social Research in Urban Areas,* UNESCO, 1965; (with Patricia Leavy Hodge) *The Challenge of America's Metropolitan Population Outlook: 1960 to 1985,* Praeger, 1968; (with Evelyn M. Kitagawa) *Differential Morality in the United States: A Study in Socio-Economic Epidemiology,* Harvard University Press, 1973. Contributor to about four hundred articles to professional journals. Associate editor, *Journal of the American Statistical Association,* 1945-49.

SIDELIGHTS: Hauser has traveled extensively on five continents. *Avocational interests:* Photography, sailing.

BIOGRAPHICAL/CRITICAL SOURCES: Theodore Berland, *The Scientific Life,* Coward, 1962; *Christian Science Monitor,* April 15, 1964.

* * *

HAUSMAN, Warren H. 1939-

PERSONAL: Born September 12, 1939, in Hartford, Conn.; son of Herbert F. (an insurance executive) and Elizabeth F. (Lorenson) Hausman; married Joan L. Rascoe, June 22, 1963. *Education:* Yale University, B.A., 1961; Massachusetts Institute of Technology, Ph.D., 1966.

CAREER: Cornell University, Graduate School of Business and Public Administration, Ithaca, N.Y., assistant professor of production and quantitative analysis, beginning, 1965. Private consultant on production management, operations research, and managerial economics. *Member:* Institute of Management Sciences, American Economic Association, Operations Research Society of America (associate).

WRITINGS: (Editor) *Managing Economic Development in Africa,* M.I.T. Press, 1963; (with Harold Bierman) *Quantitative Analysis for Business Decisions,* 3rd edition, Irwin, 1969, 4th edition, 1973; (with Shayle R. Searle) *Matrix Algebra for Business and Economics,* Wiley, 1970.†

* * *

HAVEMAN, Robert H. 1936-

PERSONAL: Born July 22, 1936, in Grand Rapids, Mich.; son of Henry (a salesman) and Jeanne (Walkotten) Haveman; married Sally Anne Ruster, May 25, 1957. *Education:* Calvin College, B.A., 1958; Vanderbilt University, Ph.D., 1962. *Religion:* Congregational. *Home:* 3410 Lake Mendota Dr., Madison, Wis. 53705. *Office:* Department of Economics, 3412 Social Science Building, University of Wisconsin, Madison, Wis. 53706.

CAREER: Vanderbilt University, Nashville, Tenn., instructor in economics, 1962-63; Grinnell College, Grinnell, Iowa, instructor, 1962-63, assistant professor, 1963-66, associate professor, 1966-69, professor of economics, 1969-70, chairman of department, 1966-68; University of Wisconsin, Madison, professor of economics, 1970—, director of Institute for Research on Poverty, 1971—. Research professor, Brookings Institution, 1965-66. Senior economist of subcommittee, Joint Economic Committee, U.S. Congress, 1968-69. Resources Future, Inc., member of fellowship advisory committee, 1968-69, research associate, 1969-70. Member, Iowa State Board of Regents, 1968; member of advisory panel on economics, National Science Foundation, 1969-70. *Member:* American Economic Association.

WRITINGS: Water Resource Investment and the Public Interest, Vanderbilt University Press, 1965; (with Kenyon Knopf) *The Market System,* Wiley, 1966; *Unemployment, Idle Capacity and the Evaluation of Public Expenditures,* Johns Hopkins Press, 1968; *The Economic Performance of Public Investments,* Johns Hopkins Press, 1972. Contributor to *American Economic Review* and *Quarterly Journal of Economics.*

WORK IN PROGRESS: Research on regional employment and output impacts of income transfer programs, with Fredrick Golladay; research on earnings capacity and the target efficiency of alternative income transfer programs, with Irwin Garfinkel.

* * *

HAVERKAMP-BEGEMANN, Egbert 1923-

PERSONAL: Born March 6, 1923, in Naarden, The Netherlands. *Education:* University of Amsterdam, M.A., 1947, M. Phil., 1949; University of Utrecht, Ph.D., 1958. *Office:* Department of History of Art, Yale University, Box 2009, New Haven, Conn.

CAREER: Museum Boymans-van Beuningen, Rotterdam, Netherlands, curator, 1950-58; Harvard University, Cambridge, Mass., lecturer, 1959-60; Yale University, New Haven, Conn., assistant professor, 1960-65, associate professor, 1965—, curator of prints, 1960-64, curator of drawings and prints, 1964—.

WRITINGS: William Buytewech, Hertzberger (Amsterdam), 1959; (with Standish D. Lawder and Charles W. Talbot) *Drawings from the Clark Art Institute,* two volumes, Yale University Press, 1964; *Hercules Seghers* (booklet), J. M. Meulenhoff (Amsterdam), 1968; (author of introduction) *Rembrandt in the National Gallery of Art, Washington, D.C.,* H. K. Press, 1969; *Rembrandt after*

Three Hundred Years, Art Institute of Chicago, 1969; (with Madzy Rood-De Boer) *Kinderbescherming en gezondheidszorg*, Nationale Federatie voor Kinderbescherming (The Hague), 1969; (with Anne-Marie Logan) *European Drawings and Watercolors in the Yale University Art Gallery: 1500-1900*, two volumes, Yale University Press, 1970. Also author of catalog, with John Gordon, *Gabor Peterdi*, 1964. Co-editor, *Master Drawings*, 1963—; member of editorial board, *Art Bulletin*, 1965—.†

* * *

HAVILAND, Virginia 1911-

PERSONAL: Born May 21, 1911, in Rochester, N.Y.; daughter of William J. and Bertha (Esten) Haviland. *Education:* Cornell University, B.A., 1933. *Politics:* Democrat. *Home:* 103 G St. S.W., Washington, D.C. 20024.

CAREER: Boston (Mass.) Public Library, began 1934, children's librarian, 1941-48, branch librarian, 1948-52, reader's adviser for children, 1952-63; Library of Congress, Washington, D.C., head of Children's Book Section, 1963—. *Horn Book* (magazine), associate editor, 1952-63, reviewer, 1952—; lecturer, Simmons College, School of Library Science, 1957-62. Chairman, Newbery-Caldecott Award Committee (American Library Association), 1953-54; judge, *New York Herald Tribune* Children's Spring Book Festival Awards, 1955-57; member of jury, International Hans Christian Andersen Award, 1959—. Representative of American Library Association at European conferences of International Board on Books for Children and International Federation of Library Associations. Hewins Lecturer at New England Library Association.

MEMBER: International Board on Books for Children (member of executive board), International Federation of Library Associations, American Library Association (chairman of Children's Library Association, 1954-55), Society of Women Geographers, District of Columbia Library Association, Washington Children's Book Guild, Pi Lambda Theta.

WRITINGS: Travelogue Storybook of the Nineteenth Century, Horn Book, 1950; *William Penn, Founder and Friend*, Abingdon, 1952; "Favorite Fariy Tales" series, Little Brown, 1959—, comprising *Favorite Fairy Tales Told in England*, 1959, . . . *in France*, 1959, . . . *in Germany*, 1959, . . . *in Ireland*, 1961, . . . *in Norway*, 1961, . . . *in Russia*, 1961, . . . *in Scotland*, 1963, . . . *in Spain*, 1963, . . . *in Poland*, 1963, . . . *in Italy*, 1965, . . . *in Sweden*, 1966, . . . *in Czechoslovakia*, 1966, . . . *in Japan*, 1967, . . . *in Greece*, 1970, . . . *in Denmark*, 1971, . . . *in India*, 1973; *Ruth Sawyer*, Walck, 1965; (editor) Louise S. Bechtel, *Books in Search of Children: Essays and Speeches*, Macmillan, 1969; (editor) *The Fairy Tale Treasury*, Coward, 1972; *Childrens' Books of International Interest*, American Library Association, 1972; *Children and Literature: Views and Reviews*, Scott, Foresman, 1973; (author of introduction) *Yankee Doodle's Literary Sampler of Prose, Poetry, and Pictures*, Crowell, 1974. Contributor to *Horn Book*, *Wilson Library Bulletin*, and other library journals.

WORK IN PROGRESS: Publishing program of Children's Book Section, Library of Congress.

* * *

HAWKES, Glenn R(ogers) 1919-

PERSONAL: Born April 29, 1919, in Preston, Idaho; son of William, Jr. and Anna (Rogers) Hawkes; married

Yvonne Merrill, December 18, 1941; children: Kristen, William Ray, Gregory Merrill, Laura. *Education:* Utah State University, B.S., 1947, M.S., 1948; Cornell University, Ph.D., 1950. *Office:* Department of Applied Behavioral Sciences, University of California, Davis, Calif. 95616.

CAREER: Iowa State University of Science and Technology, Ames, 1950-66, began as assistant professor, professor of psychology and head of department of child development, 1952-66; University of California, Davis, professor of child development, 1966—. Educational consultant, Project Head Start. *Military service:* U.S. Army, 1941-45; became master sergeant. *Member:* American Psychological Association, National Association for the Education of Young Children (past president), Society for Research in Child Development.

WRITINGS: (With Damaris Pease) *Behavior and Development from 5 to 12*, Harper, 1962; (editor with Joe L. Frost) *The Disadvantaged Child*, Houghton, 1966, 2nd edition, 1970; (contributor) Frost, editor, *Early Childhood Education Revisited*, Holt, 1968.

WORK IN PROGRESS: A book, *Socialization in Human Development*, with V. A. Christopherson, for Brooks-Cole.

* * *

HAWKES, Terence 1932-

PERSONAL: Born May 13, 1932, in Birmingham, England; married Ann Roberts; children: David Timothy, Stephen Gareth. *Education:* University of Wales, B.A., 1955, M.A., 1958, Ph.D., 1964. *Home:* 39 Stanwell Rd., Penarth, Glamorganshire, Wales. *Office:* English Department, University College, University of Wales, Cardiff, Wales.

CAREER: State University of New York at Buffalo, 1957-59, began as instructor, became assistant professor of English; University of Wales, University College, Cardiff, Wales, lecturer in English, 159-60, 1961—.

WRITINGS: (With E. L. Epstein) *Linguistics and English Prosody* (monograph), Studies in Linguistics, State University of New York at Buffalo, 1959; (editor) *Coleridge's Writing on Shakespeare*, Putnam, 1959, Penguin, 1969; *Shakespeare and the Reason*, Routledge & Kegan Paul, 1964, Humanities, 1965; *Metaphor*, Methuen, 1972, Barnes & Noble, 1973; *Shakespeare's Talking Animals*, Edward Arnold, 1973, Rowman & Littlefield, 1974. Contributor to British Broadcasting Corp. radio and television and to learned journals.

WORK IN PROGRESS: A study of structuralism and semiotics.

* * *

HAWKINS, Gerald S(tanley) 1928-

PERSONAL: Born April 20, 1928, in Great Yarmouth, England; came to United States in 1954, naturalized in 1964; son of Frederick A. (a chartered accountant) and Annie L. (Nichols) Hawkins; married Dorothy Z. Willacy-Barnes, July 15, 1955; children: Lisette Carole, Carina Geraldine. *Education:* University of London, B.Sc. (second class honors), 1949; University of Manchester, Ph.D., 1952, D.Sc., 1963. *Home:* 16 Garden Rd., Wellesley Hills, Mass. 02181. *Office:* Air Force Cambridge Research Laboratories, Bedford, Mass. 01730.

CAREER: Ferranti Bros. Ltd., Wythenshaw, England, research and development work (classified), 1952-54; Harvard University, Cambridge, Mass., scientist in charge of radio meteor program at Harvard College Observatory, 1954, research associate and lecturer in radio astronomy, 1957—; Boston University, Boston, Mass., director of observatory, 1957—, assistant professor, 1957-61, associate professor, 1961-64, professor of astronomy, 1964-69, chairman of department, 1966-69; Smithsonian Astrophysical Observatory, Cambridge, Mass., astronomer, 1962—, coordinator of radio meteor program, 1965-67; now affiliated with Air Force Cambridge Research Laboratories, Bedford, Mass. Participant in Columbia Broadcasting System television special, "The Mystery of Stonehenge."

MEMBER: British Astronomical Association (member of council, 1951-52), American Astronomical Association, Meteoritical Society of America (fellow), International Astronomical Union (general member), American Geophysical Union, American Association for the Advancement of Science, Archaeological Institute of America, Sigma Xi, Harvard Club. *Awards, honors:* Smithsonian Institution, special award for exceptional service, 1964, certificate of achievement, 1966; Shell Faculty Award, Boston University, 1965; Arthur S. Flemming Award, Junior Chamber of Commerce, Washington, D.C., 1966.

WRITINGS: Splendor in the Sky, Harper, 1961; *Meteors, Comets, Meteorites*, McGraw, 1964; (with John B. White) *Stonehenge Decoded*, Doubleday, 1965; (with others) *Earth and Space Sciences*, Heath, 1966; *The Life of a Star*, Holt, 1965; *Beyond Stonehenge*, Harper, 1973. Contributor of more than sixty papers on interplanetary material, tektites, and cosmology to science journals. Consultant editor, McGraw's "Undergraduate Series in Astronomy."

* * *

HAWKINS, (Helena Ann) Quail 1905-

PERSONAL: Born March 29, 1905, in Spokane, Wash.; daughter of Heinrich Gutherz (a fruit broker) and Helen Rich (Lyon) Hawkins. *Education:* Attended University of California, Berkeley, 1927. *Politics:* Democrat. *Religion:* Episcopalian. *Home:* 1404 Glendale Ave., Berkeley, Calif. 94708.

CAREER: Bookseller in Spokane, Wash., 1923-26, and Berkeley, Calif., 1926-29; *Publisher's Weekly*, New York, N.Y., staff, 1929-30; Sather Gate Bookshop, Berkeley, Calif., sales staff, 1931-34, head of children's department, 1934-54, head of adult and juvenile departments, 1952-54; University of California Press, Berkeley, assistant sales and promotion manager, 1954-61; Sather Gate Bookshop, consultant on library services and book fairs, 1961-70. Literary agent briefly in 1940's. Lecturer to teachers, librarians, and writers on children's books; former story lady, reading from children's books over KPFA-FM, for a year.

WRITINGS: (With V. W. von Hagen) *Quetzal Quest*, Harcourt, 1939; (with von Hagen) *The Treasure of the Tortoise Islands*, Harcourt, 1940; (compiler) *Prayers and Graces for Little Children*, Grosset, 1941, revised edition published as *A Little Book of Prayers and Graces*, Doubleday, 1952; *Who Wants an Apple?*, Holiday, 1942; *A Puppy for Keeps*, Holiday, 1943; *Don't Run, Apple!*, Holiday, 1944; *Too Many Dogs*, Holiday, 1946; *Mark, Mark, Shut the Door*, Holiday, 1947; *The Best Birthday*, Doubleday, 1954; *Mountain Courage*, Doubleday, 1957; *The Aunt-Sitter*, Holiday, 1958; *Androcles and the Lion* (retold), Coward, 1970.

Contributor to *Encyclopaedia Britannica*, 1963. Also contributor to *Publisher's Weekly, Woman's Home Companion, Elementary English*.

SIDELIGHTS: Quail Hawkins wrote: "Have only a small creative talent, but I have worked hard to make each book as good as I possibly could. . . . If an idea strikes me as good I'll work on it off and on until it is publishable—sometimes years later. *Who Wants an Apple?* was written first in 1929 and published in 1942."

* * *

HAWLEY, Ellis W. 1929-

PERSONAL: Born June 2, 1929, in Cambridge, Kan.; son of Pearl W. (a farmer) and Gladys (Logsdon) Hawley; married Sofia Koltun, September 2, 1953; children: Christine J., Arnold J., Agnes F. *Education:* University of Wichita, B.A., 1950; University of Kansas, M.A., 1951; University of Wisconsin, Ph.D., 1959. *Politics:* Democrat. *Home:* 2524 Washington, Iowa City, Iowa. *Office:* Department of History, University of Iowa, Iowa City, Iowa.

CAREER: North Texas State University, Denton, instructor, 1957-58, assistant professor, 1958-63, associate professor, 1963-66, professor of history, 1966-68; Ohio State University, Columbus, professor of history, 1968-69; University of Iowa, Iowa City, professor of history, 1969—. *Military service:* U.S. Army, 1951-53; became first lieutenant. *Member:* American Historical Association, Organization of American Historians, American Association of University Professors.

WRITINGS: The New Deal and the Problem of Monopoly, Princeton University Press, 1966; (with Murray N. Rothbard, Robert F. Himmelberg, and Gerald D. Nash) *Herbert Hoover and the Crisis of American Capitalism*, Schenkman, 1973; (contributor) Heinrich A. Winkler, editor, *Die grosse Krise in Amerika*, Vandenhoeck & Ruprecht, 1973; (contributor) Martin Fausold, editor, *The Hoover Presidency*, State University of New York Press, 1974. Contributor to historical journals.

WORK IN PROGRESS: A book on Herbert Hoover and the movement for industrial self-government, 1917-1933.

SIDELIGHTS: Hawley has reading competence in German and French.

* * *

HAYDEN, Howard K. 1930-

PERSONAL: Born June 19, 1930, in Brooklyn, N.Y.; son of John Howard (a businessman) and Henrietta (Kothe) Hayden; married first wife, Lois M. Hyland, September 30, 1956 (deceased); married second wife, Ann E. Knight, August 18, 1973; children: Laurie Elizabeth, Mindy Irene. *Education:* Attended Washington College, Chestertown, Md., 1948; Rutgers University, B.A., 1952; Monmouth College, West Long Branch, N.J., graduate courses, 1958-64. *Politics:* Republican. *Religion:* Episcopalian. *Home:* 304 Overlook Ave., Elberon, N.J. 07741. *Office:* Hayden's Liquors, 278 Broadway, Long Branch, N.J. 07740.

CAREER: Owner-operator of retail liquor store, Long Branch, N.J., 1954—. Long Branch Historical Museum, historian and secretary; Long Branch Tercentenary Committee, chairman, 1963-65. *Military service:* U.S. Army Reserve, 1951-52, active duty, 1952-54; served in Korea; received Bronze Star, three battle stars, and Presidential Unit Citation. *Member:* Company of Military Historians (fellow), National Rifle Association of America, Forks of the Delaware Collecting Association, Veterans of Foreign Wars, American Legion; and various Republican and fraternal organizations. *Awards, honors:* New Jersey Tercentenary Medallion, 1964.

WRITINGS: Billy Yank—Soldier of the North (youth book), Drum Press, 1965. Contributor of articles on local historical sites to newspapers.

WORK IN PROGRESS: Research for other juvenile books dealing with the enlisted soldier of America's wars, in a series begun with *Billy Yank;* research on the U.S. Life Saving Service for juvenile fiction and adult history.

AVOCATIONAL INTERESTS: Collecting historical artifacts.

* * *

HAYES, Joseph 1918-
(Joseph H. Arnold)

PERSONAL: Born August 2, 1918, in Indianapolis, Ind.; son of Harold Joseph and Pearl M. (Arnold) Hayes; married Marrijane Johnson (a free-lance writer); children: Gregory, Jason, Daniel. *Education:* Indiana University, student, 1938-41. *Home:* 1168 Westway Dr., Sarasota, Fla. 33577. *Agent:* James Oliver Brown, James Brown Associates, Inc., 22 East 60th St., New York, N.Y. 10022.

CAREER: Full-time professional playwright and novelist; occasional producer of Broadway plays as partner in Erskine and Hayes Productions. Chairman of Open Spaces Program, Brookfield, Conn., and of theater building project, Fine Arts Council, Sarasota, Fla. *Member:* Dramatists Guild of the Authors League of America, Society of Stage Directors and Choreographers, Writers Guild of America (West), American Civil Liberties Union (chairman of Sarasota chapter). *Awards, honors:* Charles H. Sergel Drama Prize, awarded by University of Chicago, 1948; Indiana Authors' Day Award in fiction for *The Desperate Hours,* 1955; Antoinette Perry ("Tony") Award of American Theatre Wing as author and co-producer of play, "The Desperate Hours," 1956; Edgar Allen Poe ("Edgar") Award of Mystery Writers of America for best mystery screenplay, "The Desperate Hours," 1965; Doctor of Humane Letters, Indiana University, 1971.

WRITINGS—Novels: The Desperate Hours (Literary Guild selection), Random House, 1954; (with wife, Marrijane Hayes) *Bon Voyage,* Random House, 1957; *The Hours After Midnight,* Random House, 1958; *Don't Go Away Mad,* Random House, 1962; *The Third Day,* McGraw, 1964; *The Deep End,* Viking, 1967; *Like Any Other Fugitive,* Dial, 1972; *The Long Dark Night,* Putnam, 1974.

Plays: *The Thompsons,* Samuel French, 1944; *A Woman's Privilege,* Samuel French, 1945; *The Bridegroom Waits,* Samuel French, 1946; *Home for Christmas,* Samuel French, 1946; *Too Young, Too Old,* Baker Co., 1948; *The Desperate Hours* (adapted from own novel; produced on Broadway, 1955), Samuel French, 1956; *Calculated Risk* (produced on Broadway, 1962), Samuel French, 1962.

Under pseudonym, Joseph H. Arnold: *Sneak Date,* Row, Peterson & Co., 1944; *Where's Laurie?,* Row, Peterson & Co., 1946.

With wife, Marrijane Hayes, for amateur production; all published by Samuel French: *And Came the Spring,* 1944; *Too Many Dates,* 1944; *Ask for Me Tomorrow,* 1945; *Quiet Summer,* 1945; *Come Rain, Come Shine,* 1945; *Change of Heart,* 1945; *Come Over to Our House,* 1946; *Life of the Party,* 1949; *June Wedding,* 1949; *Curtain Going Up,* 1950;

Once in Every Family, 1951; *Penny,* 1951; *Mister Peepers,* 1952; *Head in the Clouds,* 1952.

Unpublished plays: "Leaf and Bough," produced on Broadway, 1949; "The Deep End" (adapted from own novel), produced on Broadway, 1969; "Is Anyone Listening?," produced in Tallahassee at Florida State University Theatre, February, 1971. Also author of screenplay, "The Young Doctors," 1962, and "The Desperate Hours" (from own novel).

WORK IN PROGRESS: A novel in collaboration with Marrijane Hayes, set in India and the Far East.

SIDELIGHTS: An author who hit the jackpot with his first novel—a best-selling book, play, and movie—Hayes is an exponent of the positive. Believes that "those who claim only negative values in the world and then spend time and talent writing to convince that all is a void . . . deny their negative philosophy by the very creative act of writing." He adds: "The trend, in uncertain times, toward nihilism, in society and literature, seems destructive, the one feeding on the other. When have times ever been certain? How did all this whining start and where will it end? If one does not like the world as it is (and who could?), then his job is to change it—by criticism, protest, politics—and not to sit and wallow in his own sour juices."

The film, "Terror After Midnight," was based on Hayes' novel *The Hours After Midnight.*

* * *

HAYMAN, David 1927-

PERSONAL: Born January 7, 1927, in New York, N.Y.; son of Nathan (a salesman) and Beth Zena (Feinberg) Hayman; married Loni Goldschmidt, June 28, 1951; children: Denise, Leslie Ann. *Education:* New York University, B.A., 1948; Sorbonne, University of Paris, Doctorat d'Universite, 1955. *Residence:* Madison, Wisconsin. *Office:* Department of Comparative Literature, University of Wisconsin, Madison, Wis. 53706.

CAREER: University of Texas, Austin, instructor, 1955-57, assistant professor, 1957-59, associate professor of English, 1959-65; University of Iowa, Iowa City, professor of English and comparative literature, 1965-73; University of Wisconsin, Madison, professor of comparative literature, and chairman of department, 1973—. *Military service:* U.S. Navy, 1945-46. *Member:* Modern Language Association of America, Modern Humanities Research Association, Comparative Literature Association. *Awards, honors:* Guggenheim fellowship, 1958-59.

WRITINGS: Joyce et Mallarme, two volumes, Lettres Modernes (Paris), 1956; (editor) James Joyce, *First-Draft Version of Finnegans Wake,* University of Texas Press, 1963; *Ulysses: The Mechanics of Meaning,* Prentice-Hall, 1970; (editor with Clive Hart) *James Joyce's Ulysses: Critical Essays,* University of California Press, 1974; (with Eric S. Rabkin) *Form in Fiction,* St. Martin's, 1974. Author of pamphlet on Celine. Contributor to *Nation, Books Abroad, PMLA, English Literary History, Poetique, Change,* and other journals. Member of editorial staff, *Texas Quarterly,* 1957-59, *James Joyce Quarterly,* 1963—, *Iowa Review,* 1971—, and *Contemporary Literature,* 1974—.

WORK IN PROGRESS: The Wake as Process, a study of the evolution of *Finnegans Wake; Finnegans Wake: The Mechanics of Meaning; Studies in the Mechanics of Mode.*

SIDELIGHTS: Hayman speaks French; he has knowledge of Spanish and German.

HAYMAN, Max 1908-

PERSONAL: Born December 19, 1908, in Winnipeg, Manitoba; became U.S. citizen in 1944; son of Michael and Leba (Lichtenstein) Hayman; children: Lorraine (Mrs. C. Helms), Martin. *Education:* University of Manitoba, B.Sc., 1929, M.D., 1935; advanced study at Phipps Psychiatric Clinic, Johns Hopkins Hospital, 1938, and New York State Psychiatric Institute, Columbia University Medical Center, 1939. *Religion:* Jewish. *Home:* 1423 San Lorenzo Dr., Palm Springs, Calif. 92262. *Office:* 160 Luring Dr., Palm Springs, Calif. 92262.

CAREER: Diplomate, American Board of Psychiatry and Neurology. Resident at Neurological Institute of New York and Vanderbilt Clinic, Columbia University Medical Center, New York, N.Y., 1939-40; Institute of Living, Hartford, Conn., fellow in psychiatry, 1940-41; Compton Foundation Hospital, Compton, Calif., psychiatrist, 1941-43; Los Angeles Institute for Psychoanalysis, Los Angeles, Calif., psychoanalyst, 1946-50; Westerly Psychiatric Hospital, Culver City, Calif., medical director, 1951-53; Compton Foundation Hospital, clinical director and president of board of directors, 1955-58, director of education and research, 1963—; University of California, School of Medicine, Los Angeles, began as clinical assistant professor, associate professor, 1956-66, clinical professor of psychiatry, 1967-74, research psychiatrist, 1966—; Desert Alcoholism Coalition, Palm Springs, Calif., president and medical director, 1974-75. Psychiatrist and psychoanalyst in private practice, Los Angeles, Calif., 1942-68; emeritus staff member at Mount Sinai Hospital; member of attending staff at Westwood Hospital, 1959—. *Military service:* U.S. Army Air Forces, Medical Corps, 1943-46; became captain.

MEMBER: American Psychiatric Association (fellow), American Psychoanalytic Association, American Medical Association, Southern California Psychiatric Society, Los Angeles Psychoanalytic Institute and Society, Sigma Xi.

WRITINGS: Alcoholism: Mechanism and Management, C. C Thomas, 1966; (contributor) W. G. Clarke and J. del Giudice, editors, *Principles of Psychopharmacology,* Academic Press, 1970. Also contributor to *Masked Depression,* edited by S. Lesse, 1975. Contributor of more than forty articles to medical journals, a number of them on alcoholism.

*   *   *

HAYWOOD, John Alfred 1913-

PERSONAL: Born April 20, 1913, in England; son of Frank (proprietor of a printing business) and Elizabeth (Walker) Haywood; married Elizabeth Grace Francis, May 12, 1948. *Education:* University of Sheffield, B.A., 1935, M.A., 1936; University of Durham, B.Mus., 1936. *Religion:* Church of England. *Home:* Ruda, Blaidwood Dr., Farewell Hall, Durham, England. *Office:* School of Oriental Studies, University of Durham, Elvet Hill, Durham, England.

CAREER: Sudan Government service, inspector of history teaching, 1946-50, education adviser in Kordofan and Darfur provinces, Western Sudan, 1950-53, chief inspector, Sudan Ministry of Education, Khartoum, 1953-55; University of Durham, Durham, England, lecturer in Arabic, 1955-64, senior lecturer, 1964-67, reader, 1967—, director of Centre for Middle Eastern and Islamic Studies, 1965-69. Lecturer on music at adult education schools. *Military service:* Territorial Army, commissioned, 1938; on active duty

with Indian Army, 1942-46; became major. Territorial Army Reserve, 1946-63. *Member:* Association of University Teachers, Royal Asiatic Society (fellow), British Society for Middle Eastern Studies, Asiatic Society of Bangladesh.

WRITINGS: Arabic Lexicography: Its History, and Its Place in the General History of Lexicography, E. J. Brill, 1960, revised and enlarged edition, 1965; (with H. M. Nahmad) *A New Arabic Grammar of the Written Language,* Harvard University Press, 1962, revised and enlarged edition, 1966; *Modern Arabic Literature,* St. Martin's, 1971. Author of history texts and handbooks in Arabic. Composer of musical work, "Helen of Krikconnell," published by Boosey & Hawkes, 1960. Regular contributor to *Encyclopaedia Britannica* and to journals in the Oriental field.

WORK IN PROGRESS: Research in Arab music, both medieval and modern, and in Urdu literature.

SIDELIGHTS: Haywood travels widely in countries related to his main career as Orientalist; he works actively in Arabic, Urdu, French, and Persian, and has some knowledge of other Indian, Semitic, and European language. Son of two musicians, he plays the piano, French horn, and organ, and accompanies singers.

*   *   *

HAZARD, Leland 1893-

PERSONAL: Born July 7, 1893, in Kansas City, Mo.; son of Henry E. and Lucinda (Holderbaum) Hazard; married Mary Chorn, December 22, 1923. *Education:* Attended William Jewell College, 1911-12; University of Missouri, A.B., 1916; Harvard University, law studies, 1919-20; University of Chicago, graduate study, 1926. *Home:* Park Mansions, 5023 Frew Ave., Pittsburgh, Pa. 15213. *Office:* Pittsburgh Plate Glass Co., One Gateway Center, Pittsburgh, Pa. 15222.

CAREER: Admitted to Missouri bar, 1920, Pennsylvania bar, 1940; lawyer in private practice, Kansas City, Mo., 1920-38; Pittsburgh Plate Glass Co., Pittsburgh, Pa., general counsel, vice-president, and director, 1939-58, director and consultant, 1959-65, consultant, 1965-68. Carnegie Institute of Technology (now Carnegie-Mellon University), Graduate School of Industrial Administration, Pittsburgh, Pa., professor of industrial administration and law, 1959-61, professor emeritus and lecturer, 1961—. Director, National Educational Television, 1954-62, Pittsburgh Urban Transit Council, 1967—. Consultant, Ford Foundation, Government of India, 1963-65. Pittsburgh Educational Television station WQED, president, 1953-57, chairman, 1957-63, honorary chairman, 1963—. Pittsburgh Symphony Society, director, 1945-60, honorary director, 1960—. Vice-president, and member of executive committee, Allegheny Conference on Community Development, 1950-60. Chairman, Rapid Transit Committee, Port Authority of Allegheny County, 1963—, Governor's Committee for Transportation (Pennsylvania), 1966-70. Board member, Council for Public Schools, 1962-67, Pittsburgh Regional Industrial Development Corporation, 1962-73, Pittsburgh Planned Parenthood Center, 1963—. Member, Commonwealth Priorities Commission (Pennsylvania), 1968—. *Military service:* U.S. Army, Adjutant General's Department, World War I; served in France and Germany; became major.

MEMBER: American Bar Association, American Arbitration Association (member of board, 1965-73), National Planning Association (chairman of business committee,

1959-67; trustee, 1959-67), Archaeological Institute of America (trustee, 1966—), Pennsylvania Bar Association, Missouri Bar Association, Allegheny County Bar Association, Sigma Nu, Phi Alpha Delta, Omicron Delta Kappa, American Legion, Century Association (New York); Duquesne Club, University Club (both Pittsburgh); Rolling Rock Club (Ligonier, Pa.), River Club (Kansas City, Mo.).

WRITINGS: (Contributor) *The Manual of Corporate Giving*, National Planning Association, 1952; (contributor) George W. Taylor and Frank C. Pierson, editors, *New Concepts in Wage Determination*, McGraw, 1957; *Empire Revisited*, Irwin, 1965; (contributor) Kurt Baiser and Nicholas Rescher, editors, *Values and the Future*, Free Press, 1969; *Law and the Changing Environment*, Holden-Day, 1971; *Attorney for the Situation*, Columbia University Press, 1974. Also author of report on transportation. Contributor to *Atlantic Monthly, Saturday Review, Harvard Business Review*.

* * *

HEADY, Earl O(rel) 1916-

PERSONAL: Born January 25, 1916, in Imperial, Neb.; son of Orel C. (a farmer) and Jessie (Banks) Heady; married Marian R. Hoppert, March 1, 1941; children: Marilyn (Mrs. Timothy Kling), Stephen, Barbara. *Education:* University of Nebraska, B.Sc., 1939, M.Sc., 1940; Iowa State University of Science and Technology, Ph.D., 1945. *Politics:* Independent. *Home:* 919 Gaskill, Ames, Iowa 50010. *Office:* Iowa State University of Science and Technology, Ames, Iowa 50010.

CAREER: Iowa State University of Science and Technology, Ames, instructor, 1940-43, assistant professor, 1944-46, associate professor, 1946-49, professor of economics, 1949—, Curtis Distinguished Professor of Economics, 1956—, executive director, Center for Agricultural and Economic Development, 1958—, director of planning project in Thailand, 1972—. Visiting professor at North Carolina State University, 1952, Harvard University, 1956; lecturer at universities and research academies in United States and abroad. Consultant to governments of Greece, India, Thailand, Mexico, and Ethiopia, President's Commission on Food and Fiber, Organization for European Cooperation and Development, U.S. Department of Agriculture, Tennessee Valley Authority, and Ford Foundation; chairman, East-West seminar on econometric models, 1968—; member, White House Advisory Group on Domestic Affairs, 1964—, Agency for International Development committee, 1971, United Nations Food and Agricultural Organization, 1971—, National Water Commission, 1971-72.

MEMBER: Econometric Society (fellow), American Economic Association, American Farm Economic Association (fellow; vice-president, 1954), International Economic Association, American Agricultural Economics Association (fellow), Canadian Agricultural Economics Society (vice-president, 1957), American Association for the Advancement of Science (fellow), American Statistical Association (fellow), Hungarian Academy of Science (honorary member), Royal Swedish Academy of Science (honorary member), Alpha Zeta, Phi Kappa Phi, Gamma Sigma Delta.

AWARDS, HONORS: American Farm Economic Association awards, 1949, 1953, 1956, 1959, 1973, 1974, for outstanding research, and, 1953, for *Economics of Agricultural Production and Resource Use*; Social Science Research Council faculty award, 1950-53; fellow, Center for Advanced Study in the Behavioral Sciences, 1960-61; Gamma Sigma Delta Distinguished Service Award, 1962, for outstanding contributions to agriculture; American Agricultural Editors Association National Award, 1965, for services to American agriculture; D.Sc., University of Nebraska, 1960, and University of Uppsala and Agricultural College of Sweden, 1965.

WRITINGS—All published by Iowa State University Press, except as indicated: (With John A. Hopkins) *Farm Records*, Iowa State College Press, 1949, 5th edition published as *Farm Records and Accounts*, 1962; *Economics of Agricultural Production and Resource Use*, Prentice-Hall, 1952; (with Harold R. Jensen) *Farm Management Economics*, Prentice-Hall, 1954; (editor with Glenn L. Johnson and Lowell S. Hardin) *Resource Productivity, Returns to Scale, and Farm Size*, Iowa State College Press, 1956; (editor with others) *Agricultural Adjustment Problems in a Growing Economy*, Iowa State College Press, 1958; (with Wilfred Chandler) *Linear Programming Methods*, Iowa State College Press, 1958; (with John L. Dillon) *Agricultural Production Functions*, 1961; (with Alvin C. Egbert) *Regional Adjustments in Grain Production*, U.S. Government Printing Office, 1961; (editor with others) *Agricultural Supply Functions*, 1961; *Agricultural Policy Under Economic Development*, 1962; (with Luther G. Tweeten) *Resource Demand and Structure of the Agricultural Industry*, 1963; (with others) *Roots of the Farm Problem*, 1965; *Problems and Policies of Agriculture in Developed Countries*, [Norway], 1967; *A Primer on Food, Agriculture and Public Policy*, Random House, 1967; (editor) *Economic Models and Quantitative Methods for the Transformation of AGriculture*, 1971; (with Ramesh C. Agrawal) *Operations Research Methods for Agricultural Decisions*, 1972; (with others) *Future Farm Programs*, 1972; (with Alan R. Ball) *Size, Structure, and Future of Farms*, 1972; *World Food Production, Demand and Trade*, 1973; *Spatial Sector Programming Models for Agricultural Policy and Land Use*, 1974; *Use of Food Aid in Economic Development*, 1974.

Contributor: Hughes and others, editors, *Forages*, Iowa State College Press, 1950; Harold G. Halcrow, editor, *Contemporary Readings in Agricultural Economics*, Prentice-Hall, 1955; C. R. Hoglund, editor, *Nutritional and Economic Aspects of Feed Utilization on Dairy Cows*, Iowa State University Press, 1959; S. May, editor, *Mechanization of Agriculture*, North-Holland Publishing, 1961; A. S. Mahne and H. M. Markowitz, editors, *Studies in Process Analysis: Economy Wide Production Capabilities*, Wiley, 1963. Contributor of sections to more than twenty other Iowa State University Press books on agriculture and economics, and more than seven hundred articles to journals.

WORK IN PROGRESS: Research on econometric analysis, on national agricultural policy, and on the structure of the farm industry.

SIDELIGHTS: Economics of Agricultural Production and Resource Use has been issued in five languages, and three other books in eight languages. Heady has traveled in thirty-odd countries, largely in Southeast Asia, the Middle East, and Europe.

* * *

HEALD, Edward Thornton 1885-

PERSONAL: Born September 20, 1885, in Portland, Ore.; son of Charles Prescott and Mary (Penfield) Heald; married Emily Ainsworth, 1910; children: Charles William.

Education: Oberlin College, A.B., 1907; Western Reserve University (now Case Western Reserve University), M.A., 1942. *Politics:* Republican. *Religion:* Presbyterian. *Office:* Stark County Historical Society, 2677 Cleveland, N.W., Canton, Ohio.

CAREER: Office and factory worker in Peoria, Ill., 1907-08; Young Men's Christian Associations, student secretary at Colorado College, Colorado Springs, 1909-1910, and Kansas State College (now University), Manhattan, 1910-1911, membership secretary in Toledo, Ohio, 1911-14, general secretary in Davenport, Iowa, 1914-16, international representative in Russia and Siberia, 1916-19, general secretary in Davenport, 1919-22, Troy, N.Y., 1922-29, and Canton, Ohio, 1929-45; Stark County Historical Society, Canton, secretary-treasurer, 1946-54, historian, 1954—. Weekly broadcaster on own program, "The Stark County Story," WHBC, Canton, 1947—. Director of Canton Civic Opera Association; patron of Canton Symphony Orchestra.

MEMBER: American Historical Association, Organization of American Historians, American Association for State and Local History, Ohio Historical Society (honorary life member), Ohioana Library Association, Masons. *Awards, honors:* War Cross of Czecho-Slovakian Republic for service to troops in Siberia, 1919; American Association for State and Local History-Stark County Award of Merit, 1947; honorable mention, 1949, for *The Stark County Story,* Volume 1, American Association for State and Local History; citations from Ohio Historical Society, 1956, and Ohioana Library Association, 1961.

WRITINGS: Taconic Trails, J. B. Lyons Co., 1929; *Bezaleel Wells: Founder of Canton and Steubenville, Ohio,* Groshan Press, 1948; *The Stark County Story,* four volumes, Stoneman Press, 1949-59, abridged edition, Stark County Historical Society, 1963; *The William McKinley Story,* Stark County Historical Society, 1964, abridged edition, 1964; *Witness to Revolution: Letters from Russia, 1916-1919,* edited by James B. Gidney, Kent State University Press, 1972.

BIOGRAPHICAL/CRITICAL SOURCES: Canton Repository, March 10, 1957, October 29, 1961; *Cleveland Plain Dealer,* May 30, 1961, October 30, 1961; *Oberlin Alumni Magazine,* March, 1962.†

*   *   *

HEALY, David F(rank)   1926-

PERSONAL: Born October 21, 1926, in River Falls, Wis.; son of Manley Burdette (a fireman) and Florence (Moll) Healy; married Ann Erickson, October 17, 1959; children: Matthew David, Ellen Louise, Jonathan Joseph. *Education:* University of Wisconsin, B.A., 1951, M.A., 1957, Ph.D., 1960. *Home:* 2515 East Menlo Blvd., Milwaukee, Wis. 53211. *Office:* Department of History, University of Wisconsin, Milwaukee, Wis.

CAREER: Served with U.S. Merchant Marine, 1945-46; Illinois College, Jacksonville, assistant professor of history, 1960-64; University of Delaware, Newark, assistant professor of history, 1964-66; University of Wisconsin-Milwaukee, associate professor, 1966-71, professor of history, 1971—. *Military service:* U.S. Navy, 1951-55. *Member:* American Historical Association, Organization of American Historians, Phi Beta Kappa. *Awards, honors:* American Council of Learned Societies research grant, 1972.

WRITINGS: The United States in Cuba, 1898-1902, University of Wisconsin Press, 1963; *Modern Imperialism*

(pamphlet), American Historical Association, 1967; *U.S. Expansionism: Imperialist Urge in the 1890s,* University of Wisconsin Press, 1970.

WORK IN PROGRESS: A study of Admiral William B. Caperton of the U.S. Navy and Caribbean intervention, 1915-1917.

*   *   *

HEALY, George Robert   1923-

PERSONAL: Born May 31, 1923; son of Russell Kerfoot (an educator) and Elmina (Hogdson) Healy; married Dorothy Kohli, August 14, 1948; children: David, Thomas, Roger. *Education:* Oberlin College, B.A., 1948; University of Minnesota, M.A., 1950, Ph.D., 1956. *Home:* Archibald Blair House, Williamsburg, Va. 23185. *Office:* College of William and Mary, Williamsburg, Va. 23185.

CAREER: University of Minnesota, Minneapolis, instructor in history, 1951-52; Massachusetts Institute of Technology, Cambridge, instructor in history, 1952-57; Bates College, Lewiston, Me., associate professor of cultural heritage and history, 1957-62, chairman of department of cultural heritage, 1958-62, dean of faculty, 1962-71, provost, 1970-71; College of William and Mary, Williamsburg, Va., academic vice-president, 1971—. *Military service:* U.S. Army Air Forces, 1943-46. *Member:* American Historical Association, Society for French Historical Studies, Rotary Club.

WRITINGS: (Editor and translator) Montesquieu, *Persian Letters,* Bobbs, 1965. Writer of articles and book reviews.

*   *   *

HEALY, Paul F(rancis)   1915-

PERSONAL: Born March 1, 1915, in Chicago, Ill.; son of Waldo W. and Julia (Henzie) Healy; married Constance Maas, January 2, 1943 (divorced); children: Kevin, Julie, Monica, Jane, Kathleen. *Education:* Loyola University, Chicago, Ill., Ph.B., 1938. *Religion:* Roman Catholic. *Home:* 4000 Tunlaw Rd. N.W., Apartment 608, Washington, D.C. 20007. *Office:* 1272 National Press Building, Washington, D.C. 20004.

CAREER: Chicago Tribune, Chicago, Ill., reporter, 1938-43; *Popular Mechanics,* Chicago, associate editor, 1943-45; Time-Life, Inc., reporter, Chicago bureau, 1945 (civilian information officer, U.S. War Department, later that year); *New York Daily News,* New York, N.Y., Washington correspondent, 1945—. Regular participant in radio program, "Washington Correspondent," KMOX, St. Louis, 1964-65. *Member:* National Press Club.

WRITINGS: (Contributor) Leon I. Salomon, editor, *The Supreme Court,* Wilson, 1961; (with Burton K. Wheeler) *Yankee from the West,* Doubleday, 1962; *Cissy* (biography of Eleanor M. Patterson), Doubleday, 1966. Contributor of articles to magazines, including *Esquire, Saturday Evening Post, Coronet, Sign,* and *Catholic Digest.*

*   *   *

HEARD, (George) Alexander   1917-

PERSONAL: Born March 14, 1917, in Savannah, Ga.; son of Richard Willis and Virginia Lord (Nisbet) Heard; married Laura Jean Keller, June 17, 1949; children: Stephen Keller, Christopher Cadek, Francis Muir, Cornelia Lord. *Education:* University of North Carolina, A.B., 1938; Columbia University, M.A., 1948, Ph.D., 1951. *Office:* Vanderbilt University, Nashville, Tenn. 37240.

CAREER: U.S. government posts, 1938-43, as editor, Historical Records Survey, Works Progress Administration of Georgia, 1938-39, researcher and administrative assistant in Indian Service, New Mexico, 1939-41, personnel research assistant, Office of Secretary of War, Washington, D.C., 1941, American vice-consul, Quito, Ecuador, 1941-43, and Department of State, Washington, D.C., 1943; University of Alabama, University, research associate in Bureau of Public Administration, 1946-49; University of North Carolina, Chapel Hill, associate professor, 1950-51, professor of political science, 1952-63, dean of Graduate School, 1958-63; Vanderbilt University, Nashville, Tenn., professor of political science and chancellor, 1963—. Chairman of President Kennedy's special bipartisan Commission on Campaign Costs, 1961-62; member by presidential appointment to numerous committees, including U.S. Advisory Commission on Governmental Relations, 1967-69. Director, Time, Inc., 1968—. Ford Foundation, trustee, 1967, chairman, 1972—. *Military service:* U.S. Navy, 1943-46; became lieutenant.

MEMBER: American Political Science Association (member of council, 1956-58; vice-president, 1962-63), Council of Graduate Schools in the United States (chairman-elect, 1961-62), Southern Political Science Association (member of executive council, 1951-54; president, 1961-62), American Academy of Arts and Sciences, Phi Beta Kappa. *Awards, honors:* Honorary degrees.

WRITINGS: (Editor and compiler with Donald S. Strong) *Southern Primaries and Elections, 1920-49*, University of Alabama Press, 1950; *A Two-Party South?*, University of North Carolina Press, 1952; *The Costs of Democracy*, University of North Carolina Press, 1960, revised edition, Anchor books, 1962; (editor and contributor) *State Legislatures in American Politics*, Prentice-Hall, 1966.

Author of foreword or introduction: John Van Doren, *Big Money in Little Sums*, Institute for Research in Social Science, University of North Carolina, 1956; Richard H. McCleery, *Policy Change in Prison Management*, Governmental Research Bureau, Michigan State University, 1957; Wilma Dykeman and James Stokely, *Seeds of Change—The Life of Will Alexander*, University of Chicago Press, 1962; Avery Leiserson, *The American South in the 1960's*, Praeger, 1964.

Writer of study, "The Lost Years in Graduate Education," Southern Regional Education Board, 1963, and several other published booklets. Contributor to *Encyclopaedia Britannica*, 1960, *Collier's Encyclopedia*, 1961, *International Encyclopedia of Social Sciences*, 1964, and to *Nation, New Republic, Economist, U.S. News and World Report, New York Times Magazine, American Political Science Review, Journal of Politics*, and other magazines and professional journals.

*   *   *

HEATH, Douglas H(amilton)   1925-

PERSONAL: Born October 1, 1925, in Woodbury, N.J.; son of Russell and Eleanor (Conrow) Heath; married Harriet Frye, 1952; children: Russell, Wendilee, Anne Marie. *Education:* Attended Swarthmore College, 1940-41; Amherst College, B.A., 1949; Harvard University, M.A., 1951, Ph.D., 1954; University of Michigan, postdoctoral study, 1957-58. *Home:* 21 Matlack Lane, Villanova, Pa. *Office:* Department of Psychology, Haverford College, Haverford, Pa. 19041.

CAREER: Haverford College, Haverford, Pa., assistant

professor, 1954-58, associate professor, 1959-65, professor of psychology, 1966—, chairman of department, 1959-65, 1967-68. Research consultant, Academy of Religion and Mental Health, 1966-71; consultant, Friends Council on Education, and National Association of Independent Schools, 1968—. Lecturer at colleges. *Military service:* U.S. Army, 1941-44. *Member:* American Psychological Association, Phi Beta Kappa. *Awards, honors:* National Science Foundation faculty fellowship; grants from Social Science Research Council, National Institute of Mental Health, Stone Foundation, Spencer Foundation.

WRITINGS: Explorations of Maturity, Appleton, 1965; *Growing Up in College*, Jossey-Bass, 1968; *Humanizing Schools*, Hayden, 1971. Contributor to professional journals.

WORK IN PROGRESS: A book, *Maturity, Competence and Maturity*; longitudinal studies of male maturation from age seventeen to thirty-one.

*   *   *

HEATH, Dwight B(raley)   1930-

PERSONAL: Born November 19, 1930, in Hartford, Conn.; son of Percy L. (an automobile mechanic) and Luise (Hosp) Heath; children: David B. *Education:* Harvard University, A.B., 1952; Yale University, Ph.D., 1959. *Politics:* Independent. *Religion:* None. *Home:* 47 Barnes St., Providence, R.I. 02906. *Office:* Department of Anthropology, Brown University, Providence, R.I. 02912.

CAREER: Yale University, New Haven, Conn., reader in anthropology, 1958-59; Brown University, Providence, R.I., instructor, 1959-60, assistant professor, 1960-62, associate professor, 1963-70, professor of anthropology, 1970—. Visiting summer associate professor and director of Land Tenure Center, Bolivian research team, University of Wisconsin, 1963; research associate, Research Institute for the Study of Man, 1964-65. Consulting anthropologist, U.S. Peace Corps, 1961-63, Special Operations Research Office, 1962-63, and World Health Organization, 1973-74. Has done field work among the Indians of Southwestern United States, Mexico, Guatemala, Costa Rica, and Bolivia. *Military service:* U.S. Army, Intelligence, 1952-54.

MEMBER: American Anthropological Association (fellow), American Association for the Advancement of Science (fellow), American Ethnological Society, American Society for Ethnohistory (formerly American Indian Ethnohistory Conference; member of executive board, 1960-61), Associates in Current Anthropology, Association for Latin American Studies, Latin American Studies Association, Conference on Anthropology and Education, Society for the Anthropology of Visual Communication, Society for Applied Anthropology, Society for Study of Social Problems, Sociedad Boliviana de Sociologia. *Awards, honors:* Henry L. and Grace Doherty Charitable Foundation fellowship for advanced study in Latin America, 1956-57; Brown University faculty research grant, 1961, and stipends for summer research, 1962-64, 1966; other research grants from Haffenreffer Museum, 1961, and Land Tenure Center, 1963; travel grants from Wenner-Gren Foundation, 1964, National Science Foundation, 1966, and National Academy of Sciences, 1974.

WRITINGS: (Contributor) David J. Pittman and Charles R. Snyder, editors, *Society, Culture, and Drinking Patterns*, Wiley, 1962; (editor) *Mourt's Relation: A Journal of the Pilgrims at Plymouth*, Corinth Books, 1962; (with Richard N. Adams) *Contemporary Cultures and Societies of Latin America*, Random House, 1965, revised edition, 1973; (with Charles J. Erasmus and Hans C. Buechler) *Land Reform and Social Revolution in Bolivia*, Praeger, 1972; *Historical Dictionary of Bolivia*, Scarecrow, 1972. Contributor to research reports, proceedings of learned societies, and about fifty articles to professional journals in United States, Latin America, Russia, and Japan.

WORK IN PROGRESS: Two books, *Illicit Distilling in Costa Rica*, and *Illicit Traffic in Antiquities*.

* * *

HEATH, (Ernest) James 1920-

PERSONAL: Born February 26, 1920, in Walsall, Staffordshire, England; son of John Swift (a businessman) and Gwladys (Owen-Jones) Heath; married Marjorie Miller, September 5, 1955; children: Robin John Swift, Timothy James Swift. *Education:* New College, Oxford, B.A., 1941, M.A., 1946, B.C.L., 1947. *Politics:* Sceptic. *Religion:* Unitarian. *Home:* Croft House, The Oval, Benton, Newcastle upon Tyne, England. *Office:* Department of Law, University of Newcastle, Newcastle upon Tyne, England.

CAREER: Called to English bar by Lincoln's Inn, 1947; practiced law in Middle Temple, 1948-49; City of Liverpool College of Commerce, Liverpool, England, senior assistant in law, 1949-50; University of Newcastle, Newcastle upon Tyne, England, lecturer in law, 1950—. *Military service:* Royal Air Force, 1941-45; became radar technical officer. *Member:* Association of University Teachers, Society of Public Teachers of Law.

WRITINGS: Constitutional Law in a Nutshell, Sweet & Maxwell, 1950; *Eighteenth-Century Penal Theory*, Oxford University Press, 1963.

WORK IN PROGRESS: Interrogatory Torture Under Roman Law; and *Interrogatory Torture*, with principal reference to English law and practice.†

* * *

HEBSON, Ann (Hellebusch) 1925-

PERSONAL: Born December 25, 1925, in Montgomery, Ala.; daughter of Charles Merle (an auditor) and Lucille (Atherton) Hellebusch; married William J. Hebson (a manufacturer's representative), June 8, 1947 (divorced, 1968); children: William, Jr., Annie Laurie, Andrew Campbell. *Education:* Attended University of Louisville, 1941-43; Grinnell College, B.A. (with honors), 1947. *Religion:* Episcopalian.

CAREER: Social worker, Iowa State Department of Welfare, 1947-48; *Parkersburg News*, Parkersburg, W.Va., author of column, 1950-53; University of Miami, Coral Gables, Fla., writer in public relations office and news bureau, 1967-69; National Business College, Roanoke, Va., instructor in literature and public relations director, 1968-69; Mary Baldwin College, Staunton, Va., director of information services, and radio producer, 1969-70; Kentucky Educational Television, Lexington, Ky., staff writer, and production assistant, 1970-71. Novelist. Member of advisory council, Grinnell College. Patron of Roanoke Fine Arts Center; member of Roanoke Symphony Society. *Member:* Authors Guild, P.E.N., Education Writers Association, Phi Beta Kappa, Theta Sigma Phi. *Awards, honors:* Macmillan Fiction Prize ($7,500), 1961, for *The Lattimer Legend*.

WRITINGS: A Fine and Private Place (novel), Macmillan, 1958; *The Lattimer Legend* (novel), Macmillan, 1961.

Also author of six art education programs for National Instructional Television series, "Images and Things"; author of scripts for programs for state agencies. Contributor to journals.

WORK IN PROGRESS: A novel, *Forests of the Night;* research on Cassius Marcellus Clay, nineteenth-century Kentucky abolitionist.

SIDELIGHTS: Ann Hebson told *CA:* "My major motivation in writing is to reflect the human predicament. It beats baking cookies for the P.T.A. . . . Like to paint and read and cook, with a little gardening and sewing thrown in by necessity." She is conversant in Spanish and French.†

* * *

HECHT, Roger 1926-

PERSONAL: Born October 22, 1926, in New York, N.Y.; son of Melvyn Hahlo (a retired businessman) and Dorothea (Holzman) Hecht. *Education:* Attended Bard College, 1945-47, Kenyon College, 1951-52. *Home:* 163 East 81st St., New York, N.Y. 10028.

CAREER: Full-time writer. *Member:* Poetry Society of America.

WRITINGS: 27 Poems, Alan Swallow, 1966; *Signposts*, Swallow Press, 1970. Work represented in anthologies. Contributor of book reviews to *Sewanee Review* and *Poetry*, 1962-64; also contributor of poems to numerous journals.

WORK IN PROGRESS: Two books of poetry, *A Parade of Ghosts*, and *38 Poems*; contributing to a volume in memory of Alan Swallow, edited by William F. Claire, for University of New Mexico Press.

SIDELIGHTS: Hecht, brother of Anthony Hecht, a poet, told *CA:* "I am chiefly concerned to write well, therefore I keep trying to learn how to write: not a simple procedure." His favorite authors are Shakespeare, Tacitus, Cervantes, Tolstoy, and Suetonius; his favorite fictional figures are Anna Karenina and the two chief characters in *Les Liaisons dangereuses*. He admires intelligence, humor, and sympathy, and despises cant, fakery, pretention to lying, and almost all military acts. He says he would most enjoy writing history in the nineteenth century.

BIOGRAPHICAL/CRITICAL SOURCES: New York Times Book Review, February 5, 1967.

* * *

HEIMSATH, Charles H. 1928-

PERSONAL: Born July 19, 1928; son of Charles H. and Star (McDaniel) Heimsath; married Surjit Mansingh; children: Charles, Peter, Arjun, Kabir. *Education:* Yale University, B.A., 1950, Ph.D., 1957; Columbia University, Master of International Affairs, 1952. *Home:* 1408 Manchester Lane N.W., Washington, D.C. 20011. *Office:* American University, Washington, D.C.

CAREER: With Yale University, New Haven, Conn., 1956-59; American University, Washington, D.C., 1959—, began as assistant professor, became professor of South Asian Studies. Director and fellow, Educational Resources Center, New Delhi, 1971-73.

WRITINGS: Indian Nationalism and Hindu Social Reform, Princeton University Press, 1964; (with wife, Surjit Mansingh) *A Diplomatic History of Modern India*, Allied Publishers (New Delhi), 1971.

WORK IN PROGRESS: Investigation of the images of

India in the United States and their influence on foreign policy; research on social reform movements in Travancore, South India, since the end of the nineteenth century.

* * *

HELITZER, Florence (Saperstein) 1928-

PERSONAL: Born April 22, 1928, in New York, N.Y.; daughter of Joseph (a painting contractor) and Sylvia (Lerner) Saperstein; married Morrie S. Helitzer (a publisher), May 29, 1955; children: Jonathan A., Cynthia A. *Education:* Queens College (now Queen's College of the City University of New York), B.A., 1950. *Religion:* Jewish. *Residence:* Washington, D.C.

WRITINGS: Hans, Who Goes There? (novel), Harper, 1964.

WORK IN PROGRESS: A second novel.

SIDELIGHTS: Mrs. Helitzer lived abroad for four years and has traveled extensively. She is competent in German.†

* * *

HELLMAN, Robert 1919-

PERSONAL: Born July 11, 1919, in New York, N.Y.; son of Simon (a tailor) and Yetta (Pitchert) Hellman; married Helen Kalin (a teacher), July 5, 1944. *Education:* New York University, B.A., 1948; University of Paris, graduate study, 1949-50; University of Iowa, M.F.A., 1955. *Politics:* Anarchist. *Religion:* None. *Home:* 10 Mill Lane, Rockport, Mass.

CAREER: Former teacher of English at City College of the City University of New York, New York, N.Y., and Juilliard School of Music, New York, N.Y. Writer. *Military service:* U.S. Army, World War II ("very bad soldier").

WRITINGS: (Translator with R. O'Gorman) *Fabliaux,* Crowell, 1964. Also author of a play, "Kling," produced at Phoenix Theatre, New York. Contributor of short stories to periodicals, including *Western Review, Folder, Black Mountain Review, Commentary.*

WORK IN PROGRESS: A play, stories, and poems.

SIDELIGHTS: Hellman has lived in France and Spain and traveled in Australia. He speaks French, Spanish, Yiddish, and reads German.†

* * *

HELLYER, David Tirrell 1913-

PERSONAL: Born October 19, 1913, in Kobe, Japan; son of Harold Jesse (partner, Hellyer & Co., a tea firm) and Dorothy (Maclean) Hellyer; married Constance Hopkins, June 20, 1936; children: Constance (Mrs. Peter Corning), Dorothy (Mrs. Douglas K. Babbitt), Tirrell (Mrs. Richard Kimball). *Education:* Privately tutored in Lausanne, Switzerland, 1920-24; attended boarding school in Surrey, England, 1924-26, and Cate School, Carpinteria, Calif., 1926-32; Yale University, A.B., 1936; University of Chicago, M.D., 1944. *Politics:* Republican. *Religion:* Episcopalian. *Home:* 7814 John Dower Rd., Tacoma, Wash. *Office:* 722 South K St., Tacoma, Wash.

CAREER: Worked for a lumber firm in Tacoma, Wash., 1936-38; co-founder of company manufacturing and installing ski lifts in the Cascade Mountains, 1938-41; University of Chicago, Chicago, Ill., resident in pediatrics, 1946-48; pediatrician in private practice, Tacoma, Wash., 1948—. Diplomate of American Board of Pediatrics.

Owner of cattle ranch and tree farm in Eatonville, Wash., 1937—. Director, Southwest Washington Muscular Dystrophy Association. Resident naturalist, Northwest Trek American Wildlife Park. *Military service:* U.S. Navy, 1942-46; became lieutenant junior grade. U.S. Army, Medical Corps, 1954-55; became captain. *Member:* American Medical Association, and North Pacific, Washington State, and Pierce County medical associations; Academy of Pediatrics (life member), Federal Union, Inc., Tacoma Zoological Society.

WRITINGS: Your Child and You, Delacorte, 1966. Contributor to medical journals.

AVOCATIONAL INTERESTS: Natural history, wood carving, horses, camping, designing and building cabins.

* * *

HELM, Robert Meredith 1917-

PERSONAL: Born February 19, 1917, in Winston-Salem, N.C.; son of Robert Meredith (a railroad employee) and Mary Alma (Jones) Helm. *Education:* Wake Forest College (now Wake Forest University), B.A., 1939; Duke University, M.A., 1940, Ph.D., 1950. *Politics:* Democrat. *Address:* P.O. Box 7252, Winston-Salem, N.C. 27106. *Office:* Wake Forest University, Winston-Salem, N.C. 27106.

CAREER: Wake Forest University, Winston-Salem, N.C., instructor, 1940-41, assistant professor, 1947-55, associate professor of philosophy and psychology, 1955-58, associate professor of philosophy, 1958-62, professor of philosophy, 1962—. Associate professor of philosophy, Salem College, 1958-60; member of faculty, North Carolina School of the Arts, 1967-69. James W. Denmark Loan fund, member of board of trustees, president, 1972—. *Military service:* U.S. Army, 1941-45; served in European theater; became major. U.S. Army Reserve; became lieutenant colonel. *Member:* American Philosophical Association, American Association of University Professors, North Carolina Philosophical Society, Phi Beta Kappa, Omicron Delta Kappa, Delta Sigma Rho-Tau Kappa Alpha, Sigma Pi.

WRITINGS: The Gloomy Dean: The Thought of William Ralph Inge, Blair, 1962; (editor with James C. O'Flaherty and Timothy J. Sellner, and contributor) *Studies in Nietzsche and the Classical Tradition,* University of North Carolina Press, in press.

WORK IN PROGRESS: Meaning and Value in Western Thought, with J. William Angell.

AVOCATIONAL INTERESTS: Painting, sculpture, singing, mountain climbing, architecture, photography, travel.

* * *

HENDERSON, Dan Fenno 1921-

PERSONAL: Born May 24, 1921, in Chelan, Wash.; married Carol Hardin, 1957; children: Louis Dea, Karen Drake, Gail Hardin, Jay Fenno. *Education:* Whitman College, A.B. (political science), 1944; University of Michigan, A.B. (Oriental studies), 1945; Harvard University, J.D., 1949; University of California, Berkeley, Ph.D., 1955. *Office:* School of Law, University of Washington, Seattle, Wash. 98195.

CAREER: Admitted to bar of state of Washington, 1949, Japan, 1954, Korea, 1954, and California, 1955. U.S. Department of Defense, Japan, radio broadcast censor, 1946-47; Little, LeSourd, Palmer, Scott & Slemmons (law firm), Seattle, Wash., attorney, 1950-51; University of California,

Berkeley, instructor in political science, 1951-55; Graham, James & Rolph (law firm), San Francisco, Calif., associate, 1955-57, Tokyo partner, 1957-61; University of Washington, Seattle, professor of law and director of Asian Law Program, 1962—. Visiting professor, Harvard Law School, 1968-69. Member of board of directors and secretary, American Chamber of Commerce in Japan, 1960-61. Consultant, Asia Foundation, San Francisco, 1965—, Batelle Institute, 1965—. President, Asian Art Council. Trustee, Seattle Art Museum. *Military service:* U.S. Army, Military Intelligence, 1943-46; became second lieutenant.

MEMBER: American Bar Association (chairman, Far Eastern law committee, 1963—), American Academy of Political and Social Science, American Political Science Association, American Society of International Law, Asiatic Society of Japan, Association for Asian Studies, Japanese American Society for Legal Studies (director, 1966—), Washington State Bar Association, California Bar Association, Daiichi Tokyo Bengoshikai (Tokyo bar association), Rainier Club (Seattle), Seattle Tennis Club, Berkeley Tennis Club, Tokyo Lawn Tennis Club, American Club of Tokyo. *Awards, honors:* Investment fellow, American Society of International Law, 1962-65.

WRITINGS: Conciliation and Japanese Law—Tokugawa and Modern, two volumes, University of Washington Press, 1965; *The Constitution of Japan: Its First Twenty Years,* University of Washington Press, 1969; *Foreign Enterprise in Japan: Laws and Policies,* University of North Carolina Press, 1973. Contributor of articles and book reviews to *American Anthropologist, Far Eastern Quarterly,* and law journals. Editor, *Law in Japan* (an annual), 1965—.

* * *

HENDERSON, William III   1922-

PERSONAL: Born October 9, 1922, in New York, N.Y.; son of James Alexander and Charlotte Henriette (Fischer) Henderson; married Maxine O. Book, April 10, 1948; children: William IV, Meredith. *Education:* Hamilton College, B.A., 1942; University of Colorado, graduate study, 1943-44; Columbia University, M.A., 1948, Ph.D., 1972. *Religion:* Episcopalian. *Home:* 606 West 116th St., New York, N.Y. 10027. *Office:* William Henderson Consultants, Inc., 88 Morningside Dr., New York, N.Y. 10027.

CAREER: U.S. Office of Alien Property Custodian, Washington, D.C., and New York, N.Y., economist, 1942-43, 1946; Adelphi College, Garden City, N.Y., faculty of department of history and government, 1948-49; Barnard College, New York, N.Y., faculty of department of government, 1949-53; Council on Foreign Relations, New York, N.Y., 1952-62, became associate executive director; Mobil Oil Corp., New York, N.Y., 1962-67, manager of international government relations, 1965-67; China Institute in America, New York, N.Y., executive director, 1967-68, consultant, 1968-69; William Henderson Consultants, Inc., New York, N.Y., founder and president, 1969—. Columbia University, associate and member of seminar on southern Asia, 1965—, senior lecturer on international relations, 1967-68; professor of Asian studies, Seton Hall University, 1968—; lecturer in political science, City University of New York, 1969-70. *Military service:* U.S. Naval Reserve, active duty, 1943-46; served in Pacific theater; received Commendation Ribbon with pendant; now lieutenant commander (retired).

MEMBER: Association for Asian Studies, Council on Foreign Relations, American Friends of Vietnam,

American-Asian Educational Exchange, Bronx County Historical Society, Phi Beta Kappa, Delta Sigma Rho.

WRITINGS: Pacific Settlement of Disputes: The Indonesian Question, 1946-49, Woodrow Wilson Foundation, 1954; *New Nations of Southeast Asia,* Foreign Policy Association, 1955; (contributor) R. W. Lindholm, editor, *Viet-Nam: The First Five Years,* Michigan State University Press, 1959; (contributor) Wesley R. Fishel, editor, *Problems of Freedom: South Vietnam Since Independence,* Free Press of Glencoe, 1962; (editor and contributor) *Southeast Asia: Problems of United States Policy,* M. I. T. Press, 1964; *Communist China, 1949-1969: A Twenty-Year Appraisal,* New York University Press, 1970; *West New Guinea: The Dispote and Its Settlement,* Seton Hall University Press, 1973. Contributor of section on southern Asia to *Information Please Almanac,* 1958; contributor of articles and reviews to *New Leader, Foreign Affairs, Virginia Quarterly Review,* and other journals. Editor, *Southeast Asian Perspectives* (formerly *Vietnam Perspectives;* quarterly journal of American Friends of Vietnam), 1966—, *Asian Affairs: An American Review,* 1973—; editor with Frank W. Trager, monograph series in Asian affairs, 1969; also editor of strategy papers, 1970—, agenda papers, 1974—.

SIDELIGHTS: Henderson speaks Japanese and French.

* * *

HENKE, E(merson) Overbeck   1916-

PERSONAL: Born February 20, 1916, in Stendal, Ind.; son of George Arthur and Sarah (Overbeck) Henke; married Beatrice Arney, June 6, 1939; children: Michael, Pamela (Mrs. Mark Bailes). *Education:* Evansville College, B.S., 1937; Indiana University, M.S., 1939, D.B.A., 1953. *Religion:* Presbyterian. *Home:* 3317 Lake Shore Dr., Waco, Tex. 76708.

CAREER: Accountant with industrial firms, Evansville, Ind., 1937-40; Evansville College, Evansville, Ind., teacher of accounting, 1940-48; Baylor University, Waco, Tex., professor of accounting and chairman of department, 1948-67, dean of Hankamer Business School, 1967—. Visiting professor at University of Miami, Coral Gables, Fla., summer, 1946, and University of Texas, spring, 1966; distinguished visiting professor, University of Denver, 1971-72. *Member:* American Institute of Certified Public Accountants, American Accounting Association, Texas Society of Certified Public Accountants (director, 1960-61), Central Chapter of Certified Public Accountants (president, 1960-61).

WRITINGS: Accounting for Non-Profit Organizations—An Exploratory Study, Bureau of Business Research, Indiana University, 1965; *Accounting for Non-Profit Organizations,* Wadsworth, 1966; (with Walstein Smith) *CPA Review Outline,* Prentice-Hall, 1969; (contributor) Sidney Davidson, editor, *Handbook of Modern Accounting,* McGraw, 1970; *Introduction to Accounting: A Conceptual Approach,* Petrocelli Books, 1974.

AVOCATIONAL INTERESTS: Fishing, water skiing, snow skiing, ballroom dancing, square dancing, tennis, and other sports.

* * *

HENLEY, Norman   1915-

PERSONAL: Born November 7, 1915, in Auburndale, Mass.; son of Elijah Forrest and Laura (Schnare) Henley;

Married Nancy Main, July 10, 1954; children: Christopher Lee. *Education:* Boston University, A.B., 1938; attended Andover Newton Theological School, 1938-40; Pacific School of Religion, B.D., 1942; University of Lausanne, graduate study, 1947-48; University of Paris, Diploma in Russian, 1949; Harvard University, M.A., 1959, Ph.D., 1967. *Office:* Department of Russian, Johns Hopkins University, Baltimore, Md. 21218.

CAREER: Pastor of Congregational churches in St. Helens, Ore., 1941-42, and North Troy, Vt., 1943-44; Raytheon Manufacturing Co., Waltham, Mass., inspector, 1944-45; Mayflower Hotel, Washington, D.C., secretary to chef, 1951-52; Library of Congress, Washington, D.C., cataloger and translator, 1952-55, 1956-59; Indiana University, Bloomington, teacher of Serbo-Croation, 1955-56; Johns Hopkins University, Baltimore, Md., lecturer in Russian, 1959—. *Military service:* U.S. Army, 1945-47; became sergeant. *Member:* American Association of Teachers of Slavic and East European Languages, American Association for the Advancement of Slavic Studies, Modern Language Association of America, American Association of University Professors.

WRITINGS: (Editor) *Russian Prose Reader*, Van Nostrand, 1963; (editor) A. N. Ostrovsky, *Groza*, Bradda Books, 1963; (editor) A. S. Pushkin, *Povesti Belkina*, Bradda Books, 1965.

WORK IN PROGRESS: Translation from the Russian of plays by Ostrovsky, Sukhovo-Kobylin, and Saltykov-Shchedrin for use in Russian drama classes.†

* * *

HENNING, Edward B. 1922-

PERSONAL: Born October 23, 1922, in Cleveland, Ohio; son of Harold Wagner and Marguerite (Burk) Henning; married Margaret Revacko (assistant to director of Case Western Reserve University Press), December 31, 1942; children: Eric, Lisa, Geoffrey. *Education:* Cleveland Institute of Art, student, 1946-49; Western Reserve University (now Case Western Reserve University), B.S. (magna cum laude), 1949, M.A., 1952; studied at Academie Julian, Paris, France, 1949-50. *Office:* Cleveland Museum of Art, 11150 East Blvd., Cleveland, Ohio 44106.

CAREER: Cleveland Museum of Art, Cleveland, Ohio, assistant curator of education, 1954-55, associate curator of education, 1955-58, assistant to director, 1958—, curator of contemporary art, 1960—. Case Western Reserve University, guest professor of art history; Cleveland Institute of Art, teacher of aesthetics. *Military service:* U.S. Army, 1942-46; served in European theater. *Member:* American Museum Association, College Art Association, American Association for Aesthetics.

WRITINGS: Paths of Abstract Art, Cleveland Museum of Art, 1960; *Fifty Years of Modern Art*, Cleveland Museum of Art, 1966. Contributor to professional publications, including *Dialectica, La Biennale di Venezia*, and *Art International*. Editorial assistant, *Journal of Aesthetics and Art Criticism*, 1955-63.

WORK IN PROGRESS: Problems of Evaluation of Modern Art, completion expected in 1976; a textbook on the history of modern art.

AVOCATIONAL INTERESTS: Contemporary American and French literature and philosophy.

HENRY, Joanne Landers 1927-

PERSONAL: Born February 24, 1927, in Indianapolis, Ind.; daughter of Delver Harold (an electrical engineer) and Octavia (Greene) Landers; married Earl Henry (a market gardener), October 11, 1958; children: David, Katherine. *Education:* University of Rochester, B.A., 1948. *Religion:* Protestant. *Residence:* Eden, N.Y.

CAREER: Bobbs-Merrill Co., Inc. (publishers), Indianapolis, Ind., editorial assistant, 1951-55; Oxford University Press, New York, N.Y., school and library consultant, 1955-58; Bobbs-Merrill Co., Inc., children's book editor, 1958; free-lance writer for children, 1958—. Vice-president, Eden Free Library Board, 1965-66.

WRITINGS: George Eastman: Young Photographer, Bobbs-Merrill, 1959; *Elizabeth Blackwell: Girl Doctor*, Bobbs-Merrill, 1961; *Andrew Carnegie: Young Steelmaker*, Bobbs-Merrill, 1966; *Marie Curie: Discoverer of Radium*, Macmillan, 1966; *Bernard Baruch: Boy from South Carolina*, Bobbs-Merrill, 1971; *Robert Fulton*, Garrard, in press.

AVOCATIONAL INTERESTS: Playing chamber music (cello), gardening, and working as a volunteer in the local school library.

* * *

HENRY, Marguerite

CAREER: Full-time professional writer. *Awards, honors:* Junior Scholastic Gold Seal Award and Award of the Friends of Literature, 1948, for *Justin Morgan Had a Horse*; Newbery Medal, 1949, for *King of the Wind*; William Allen White Award, 1956, for *Brighty of the Grand Canyon*; Sequoyah Children's Book Award, 1959, for *Black Gold*, 1969, for *Mustang: Wild Spirit of the West*; Society of Midland Author's Clara Ingram Judson Award, 1961, for *Gaudenzia: Pride of the Palio*, 1973, for *San Domingo: The Medicine Hat Stallion*; Western Heritage Award, 1967, for *Mustang: Wild Spirit of the West*.

WRITINGS: Auno and Tauno: A Story of Finland, Albert Whitman, 1940; *Dilly Dally Sally*, Saalfield, 1940; *Birds at Home*, Donohue, 1942, revised edition, Hubbard Press, 1972; *Geraldine Belinda*, Platt, 1942; (with Barbara True) *Their First Igloo on Baffin Island*, Albert Whitman, 1943; *Boy and a Dog*, Follett, 1944; *Justin Morgan Had a Horse*, Follett, 1945, revised edition, Rand McNally, 1954; *Little Fellow* (Junior Literary Guild selection), Winston, 1945; *Robert Fulton: Boy Craftsman*, Bobbs-Merrill, 1945; *Misty of Chincoteague* (Junior Literary Guild selection), Rand McNally, 1947; *Always Reddy*, McGraw, 1947; *Benjamin West and His Cat, Grimalkin*, Bobbs-Merrill, 1947; *King of the Wind*, Rand McNally, 1948; *Little-or-Nothing from Nottingham*, McGraw, 1949; *Sea Star: Orphan of Chincoteague*, Rand McNally, 1949.

Born to Trot, Rand McNally, 1950; *Album of Horses* (Junior Literary Guild selection), Rand McNally, 1951; (with Wesley Dennis) *Portfolio of Horses* (taken from *Album of Horses*), Rand McNally, 1952; *Brighty of the Grand Canyon*, Rand McNally, 1953; *Wagging Tails: An Album of Dogs*, Rand McNally, 1955; *Cinnabar: The One O'Clock Fox*, Rand McNally, 1956; *Black Gold*, Rand McNally, 1957; *Muley-Ears, Nobody's Dog* (Junior Literary Guild selection), Rand McNally, 1959.

Gaudenzia: Pride of the Palio, Rand McNally, 1960; *Misty, the Wonder Pony, by Misty, Herself*, Rand McNally, 1961; *All About Horses*, Random House, 1962; *Five*

O'Clock Charlie, Rand McNally, 1962; *Stormy, Misty's Foal*, Rand McNally, 1963; *White Stallion of Lipizza*, Rand McNally, 1964; (with Dennis) *Portfolio of Horse Paintings*, Rand McNally, 1964; *Mustang: Wild Spirit of the West*, Rand McNally, 1966; *Dear Readers and Riders*, Rand McNally, 1969; *San Domingo: The Medicine Hat Stallion*, Rand McNally, 1972.

"Pictured Geographies" series, published by Albert Whitman: *Alaska in Story and Pictures*, 1941, 2nd edition, 1942; *Argentina ...*, 1941, 2nd edition, 1942; *Brazil ...*, 1941, 2nd edition, 1942; *Canada ...*, 1941, 2nd edition, 1942; *Chile ...*, 1941, 2nd edition, 1942; *Mexico ...*, 1941, 2nd edition, 1942; *Panama ...*, 1941, 2nd edition, 1942; *West Indies ...*, 1941, 2nd edition, 1942; *Australia ...*, 1946; *Bahamas ...*, 1946; *Bermuda ...*, 1946; *British Honduras ...*, 1946; *Dominican Republic ...*, 1946; *Hawaii ...*, 1946; *New Zealand ...*, 1946; *Virgin Islands ...*, 1946. Contributor of articles to magazines including *Nations' Business*, *Saturday Evening Post*, *Reader's Digest*, and *Forum*. Contributor to *World Book Encyclopedia*.

SIDELIGHTS: Marguerite Henry relates that in 1945 she received a letter "concerning the legend of the Spanish moor ponies that were washed into the sea, centuries ago, when a Spanish galleon was wrecked on a hidden reef." She read "how the ponies swam, unhurt, for the nearest shore, which happened to be Assateague Island off the coasts of Virginia and Maryland. Today, descendants of these ponies still run wild on that island. One day a year, called Pony Penning Day, oystermen and clam diggers from Chincoteague Island nearby turn cowboy. They round up the wild ponies, drive them into the sea, swim them over to their own island, and sell the colts in a big auction." With the illustrator, Wesley Dennis, Mrs. Henry went to Pony Penning Day in search of a story. She returned with the story and a colt named Misty. This was the beginning of *Misty of Chincoteague* and of what M. B. King called "one of the finest horse stories you'll find for the eight- to 12-year olds." It strengthened Mrs. Henry's already fine reputation as an outstanding author in this field.

She has proved, also, that she is adept in other areas. Her two books for Bobbs-Merrill's "Childhood of Famous Americans" Series, *Robert Fulton* and *Benjamin West and His Cat, Grimalkin*, were well received. "In adding the story of Robert Fulton to [this] series," wrote a *Book Week* reviewer, "Marguerite Henry had to match her skill against that of a number of illustrious predecessors who have contributed to the list. It is delightful to find that she has made good to the extent of writing one of the best of the series." Her writing has been deemed enchanting and rich in human values. "Miss Henry is frequently, unabashedly sentimental," wrote E. L. Buell, "but I have never known a horse-lover to object to that."

Misty of Chincoteague was made into the film "Misty" by 20th Century-Fox in 1961; *Brighty of Grand Canyon* was filmed by Stephen F. Booth in 1966; *Justin Morgan Had a Horse* was filmed by Walt Disney Productions in 1972.

BIOGRAPHICAL/CRITICAL SOURCES: Book Week, November 11, 1945; *Chicago Sun Book Week*, October 18, 1947; *Young Wings*, December, 1947; *New York Times*, December 22, 1957.

*   *   *

HENRY, W. P. 1929-

PERSONAL: Born April 4, 1929, in Long Island, N.Y.; son of William Patrick and Mildred (Ely) Henry; married

Sophia Panayotides-Djaferis, August 17, 1960; children: Daphne, Ariadne. *Education:* University of Florida, B.A., 1953, Emory University, M.A., 1954; University of Chicago, Ph.D., 1963. *Home:* 2446 Huidekoper Pl., N.W., Washington, D.C. 20007.

CAREER: University of Chicago, Chicago, Ill., instructor in classics, 1961-65; Hamilton College, Clinton, N.Y., assistant professor of classics, 1965-66; Georgetown University, Washington, D.C., associate professor of classics, 1966—. *Awards, honors:* Fulbright fellowship to Greece, 1959-60.

WRITINGS: Greek Historical Writing, Argonaut, 1966.

*   *   *

HEPWORTH, (Charles) Philip 1912-

PERSONAL: Born June 12, 1912, in Leicester, England; married Blanche Mildred Bowers, October 12, 1940. *Education:* Attended University College, Leicester (now University of Leicester); University of London, M.A., 1935. *Religion:* Anglican. *Home:* 13 Kingston Sq., Norwich, Norfolk, England. *Office:* Central Library, Bethel St., Norwich, Norfolk, England.

CAREER: Borough librarian and curator, Stafford, England, 1946-51; city librarian, then divisional librarian, Norwich, Norfolk, England, 1951—. *Military service:* British Army, Royal Signals, World War II. *Member:* Library Association (member of council, 1953-58, 1963—), British Records Association (member of council, 1969-74), Historical Association (branch vice-president), Norfolk and Norwich Archaeological Society (member of council), Rotary Club (Norwich; past president).

WRITINGS: Primer of Assistance to Readers, Association of Assistant Librarians, 1951, 2nd edition, 1956; (with Mary Alexander) *City of Norwich Libraries: History and Treasures*, Jarrolds, 1957, 2nd edition published as *Norwich Public Libraries: Norfolk and Norwich Record Office*, Norwich Libraries Committee, 1965; *Archives and Manuscripts in Libraries*, Library Association, 1958, 2nd edition, 1964; *How to Find Out in History*, Pergamon, 1966; (editor) *Select Biographical Sources*, Library Association, 1971; *Victorian and Edwardian Norfolk*, Batsford, 1972; *Norwich as It Was*, Hendon, 1974; *Sandringham*, Wensum Books, in press. Contributor to *East Anglian Magazine*, *Norfolk Fair*, and to professional journals.

*   *   *

HERBERT, Jean (Daniel Fernand) 1897-

PERSONAL: Born July 27, 1897, in Paris, France; son of Fernand and Laurence (Mury) Herbert; married May Anbuhl, 1920; married second wife, Josette Perelli, February 18, 1964; children: (first marriage) Janine Yates, Yvette Renoux. *Education:* University of Paris, M.A., 1914, LL.B., 1920. *Religion:* Christian. *Home:* La Luciole, 1253 Vandoeuvres, Geneva, Switzerland.

CAREER: Albin Michel (publishers), Paris, France, editor-in-chief of *Spiritualities vivantes*, 1944—; United Nations, New York, N.Y., chief interpreter, 1945-49; Derain (publishers), Lyon, France, editor-in-chief of *Dieux hindous*, and *Les Trois Lotus*, 1950—; University of Geneva, Geneva, Switzerland, privat-docent, 1955—; Elsevier Publishing Co., Amsterdam, Netherlands, editor-in-chief of *Glossaria Interpretum*, and *Lexica*, 1956—. Chairman of the boards of examiners in schools for interpreters, Universities of Paris and Trieste, 1955—; adviser on interpretation to many international organizations. *Military service:* French Army, reserve officer, active duty in World Wars I and II; awarded Croix de Guerre. *Member:* Societe des Gens de Lettres (Paris), International Association of Conference Interpreters (Paris, president), Societe Mexicaine d'Archeologie et de Statistique (honorary member). *Awards, honors:* Corona d'Italia, 1920; Laureat de l'Academie Francaise, 1965; gold medal of the Royal Linguists' Society (London), 1971.

WRITINGS: Lexique francais-anglais-americain des termes d'artillerie et de balistique, Ministere de la Guere, 1918; (with Georges Mathieu) *La Grande-Bretagne au travail*, Roger, 1919; (with P. G. Wilson) *Through French Eyes* (senior level), Pitman, 1933; *Through French Eyes: Questions and Answers*, Pitman, 1934; (with P. G. Wilson) *Through French Eyes* (intermediate level), Pitman, 1934; (with P. G. Wilson and Fernand Herbert) *La Vie commerciale*, Pitman, 1934; *La Sabiduria hindu*, Ercilla, 1939; *Bibliographie de l'oeuvre de Swami Vivekananda dans les langues europeennes*, Adrien-Maisonneuve, 1939; *Etudes sur Ramana Maharshi*, Adrien-Maisonneuve, 1940; *L'Enseignement de Ramakrishna*, Adrien-Maisonneuve, 1941, 10th edition, 1962; *Vedantisme et vie pratique*, Adrien-Maisonneuve, 1942; (with Lizelle Reymond) *Etudes et Portraits*, Adrien-Maisonneuve, 1943; *Comment se preparer a la meditation*, Derain, 1943; *La Notion de la vie future dans l'hindouisme*, Adrien-Maisonneuve, 1944, new edition, Albin Michel, 1945; *Lexique Ramakrishna-Vivekananda*, Ophrys, 1945; *Spiritualite hindoue*, Albin Michel, 1947, reprinted, 1972; *Les yogas hindous*, Adyar, 1950; *Le Message de la mythologie hindoue*, Derain, 1950; *Le Yoga de Shri Aurobindo*, Derain, 1951; *Wege zum Hinduismus*, Rascher, 1951; *Manuel de l'Interprete*, Georg, 1952 English language edition, *The Interpreter's Handbook*, Georg, 1952, 2nd English language edition, revised and enlarged, published as *The Interpreter's Handbook: How to Become a Conference Interpreter*, Librairie de l'Universite (Geneva), 1968; *La Mythologie Hindoue: son message*, Albin Michel, 1953; *Indischer Mythos als geistige Realitaet*, Barth, 1953; (with H. Ghaffar) *Premier album de mythologie hindoue*, Derain, 1955; (with others) *Conference Terminology*, Elsevier, 1957, new augmented edition, 1962; *Asie*, Migros, 1957, new edition, Albin Michel, 1958; *L'Enseignement de Shivananda*, Albin Michel, 1958; (with Huguette Herbert) *Dans l'Inde: L'Accueil des dieux*, Aubier, 1959; *Asien, Denken und Lebensformen der oestilichen Welt*, Piper Verlag, 1959; *Introduction a l'Asie*, Albin Michel, 1960, translation published as *An Introduction to Asia*, Oxford University Press, 1965; *Aux sources du Japon: Le Shinto*, Albin Michel, 1964, *Les Dieux nationaux du Japon*, Albin Michel, 1965; *Dieux et sectes populaires du Japon*, Albin Michel, 1966; *Shinto: At the Fountainhead of Japan*, Stein & Day, 1967; *Bibliographie du Shinto et des sectes shintoistes*, Brill, 1968; *Ce que Gandhi a vraiment dit*, Stock, 1969; *Le Yoga de l'amour*, Albin Michel, 1973; *Le Bouddhisme en Asie au XXe siecle*, de Tartas, 1974; *Les grands courants spirituels modernes dans l'Hinduoisme*, de Tartas, 1974; *L'Hindouisme vivant*, Laffont, 1975; *Cosmogonie japonaise*, CIRCA, 1975.

Translator: (With Ester Levy) Edwyn Bevan, *Histoire des Lagides*, Payot, 1934; (and author of preface) Mahatma Gandhi, *Lettres a l'ashram*, Albin Michel, 1937; (with others) Shri Ramakrishna, *Les Paroles du maitre*, Adrien-Maisonneuve, 1937; (with Pierre Sauvageot) Adams Beck, *A la decouverte du yoga*, Attinger, 1938; (author of preface, translator with Sauvageot) Adams Beck, *Zenn*, Attinger,

1938; (and author of preface) Rabindranath Tagore, *Sadhana*, Albin Michel, 1940; (author of preface, translator with Alice Prudhomme) Swami Vijoyananda, *Ainsi parlait Christ*, Jeheber, 1940; (with Camille Rao) *Bhagavad-Gita*, Adrien-Maisonneuve, 1941; (author of preface, translator with Rao) *La Bhagavad-Gita interpretee par Shri Aurobindo*, Adrien-Maisonneuve, 1942, new edition, Albin Michel, 1947; (author of preface, translator with Odette de Saussure) Swami Brahmananda, *Disciplines monastiques*, Adrien-Maisonneuve, 1943; (with Prudhomme) Swami Ramdas, *Carnet de pelerinage* Volume I, Ophrys, 1943, new edition including Volume II, Albin Michel, 1953; (and author of preface) Ananda Moyi, *Aux sources de la joie*, Ophrys, 1943; (and author of preface and notes) Shankara-charya, *Hymnes a Shiva*, Derain, 1944; Swami Yatiswarananda, *Commentaries sur la discipline monastique de Swami Brahmananda*, Derain, 1949; (and author of preface) Swami Sivananda, *La Pratique de la meditation*, Albin Michel, 1950; (with Rose Rigaud) Nivedita, *Vivekananda tel que je l'ai vu*, Albin Michel, 1952; (author of preface, translator with H. Ghaffar) S. V. Yesudian and E. Haich, *Sport et Yoga*, Santoza, 1953; (with others) D. T. Suzuki, *Essais sur le Bouddhisme Zen*, Albin Michel, Volume I, 1954, Volume II, 1956, Volume III, 1958; (with others) Swami Ramdas, *Presence de Ram*, Albin Michel, 1956; (with Huguette Herbert) Mulk Raj Anand, *Kama-kala*, Nagel, 1958; (with Charles Andrieu) Lama Anagarika Govinda, *Les Fondements de la mystique tibetaine*, Albin Michel, 1960; Dalai-lama, *Introduction au Bouddhisme tibetain*, Dervy-livres, 1972.

Translator of works by Swami Vivekananda: (And author of preface) *Mon maitre*, Adrien-Maisonneuve, 1935; (and author of preface) *Jnana-Yoga*, Adrien-Maisonneuve, 1936; (and author of preface) *Le Yoga de la connaissance*, Adrien-Maisonneuve, 1936; (and author of preface) *Karma-Yoga*, Adrien-Maisonneuve, 1937; (and author of preface) *Entretiens inspires*, Adrien-Maisonneuve, 1937; (author of preface, translator with Lizelle Reymond) *Bhakti-Yoga*, Adrien-Maisonneuve, 1937; *Commentaires sur les aphorismes de Patanjali*, Adrien-Maisonneuve, 1938; (author of preface, translator with Reymond) *Conferences sur Bhakti-Yoga*, Adrien-Maisonneuve, 1939; *Au coeur des choses*, Adrien-Maisonneuve, 1940; (author of preface, translator with others) *Les Yogas pratiques*, Albin Michel, 1950.

Translator of works by Shri Aurobindo: (Author of preface, translator with Reymond) *Lumieres sur le yoga*, Adrien-Maisonneuve, 1938; *L'Isha Upanishad*, Adrien-Maisonneuve, 1939; (with Rene Daumal and Rao) *La Kena Upanishad*, Adrien-Maisonneuve, 1944; (with others) *La Vie divine*, Albin Michel, Volume I, 1949, Volume II, 1956, Volume III, 1958, Volume IV, 1959; (with others) *Trois Upanishads*, Albin Michel, 1949; *Lettres*, Adyar, Volume I, 1950, Volume II, 1952, Volume III, 1958; (with D. Bonarjee) *Heraclite*, Derain, 1951; (author of preface, translator with others) *Guide du Yoga*, Albin Michel, 1951.

WORK IN PROGRESS: Three books, *Ganesha, Le metaphysique et la psychologie de Shri Aurobindo*, and *Benares*, for Albin Michel; *Cosmogonie hindoue*; *Cosmogonie japonaise*.

SIDELIGHTS: Herbert's books, *Manuel de l'Interprete* and *Conference Terminology*, have both been published in six other languages.

*   *   *

HERBERT, Kevin (Barry John) 1921-

PERSONAL: Born November 18, 1921, in Chicago, Ill.;

son of William Patrick (an executive) and Margaret (Lomasney) Herbert; married Margaret Lambin, December 28, 1946; children: John, Catherine. *Education:* Loyola University, Chicago, Ill., B.A., 1946; Harvard University, M.A., 1949, Ph.D., 1954. *Politics:* Independent. *Religion:* Roman Catholic. *Home:* 1124 Basswood Lane, Olivette, Mo. 63132.

CAREER: Instructor in classics at Marquette University, Milwaukee, Wis., 1948-52, Indiana University, Bloomington, 1952-54, and St. Paul's School, Concord, N.H., 1954-55; Bowdoin College, Brunswick, Me., assistant professor of classics, 1955-62; Washington University, St. Louis, Mo., associate professor, 1962-67, professor of classics, 1967—. Fellow, Brooklyn Museum, 1967. *Military service:* U.S. Army Air Forces, 1942-45; became staff sergeant (gunner); received Distinguished Flying Cross, Air Medal with two oak leaf clusters, four battle stars, Presidential Unit Citation. *Member:* American Philological Association, Archaeological Institute of America, Classical Association of the Middle West and South. *Awards, honors:* Four grants, National Endowment for the Humanities, 1971-74.

WRITINGS: (Translator) Hugo of St. Victor, *Soliloquy on the Earnest Money of the Soul*, Marquette University Press, 1956; *Ancient Art in Bowdoin College*, Harvard University Press, 1964; *Greek and Latin Inscriptions in the Brooklyn Museum*, Brooklyn Museum, 1972; (contributor) Frank N. Magill, editor, *Great Events from History*, 2 volumes, Salem Press, 1972; (editor) *Ancient Collections in Washington University*, Washington University, 1973. Contributor to learned journals.

WORK IN PROGRESS: A book on ancient and modern versions of Greek myth, completion expected in 1976.

AVOCATIONAL INTERESTS: Travel to museums and sites of the classical world, photography of ancient art and sites, reading histories, novels, and about current events.

* * *

HERMANN, Edward J(ulius) 1919-

PERSONAL: Born May 4, 1919, in Council Bluffs, Iowa; son of Edward Christian and Anna (Schultze) Hermann; married Lillian Loeck, June 26, 1943; children: Carol Jean, Susan Kathryn, James Edward. *Education:* University of Chicago, M.A., 1942; Columbia University, Ed.D., 1953. *Religion:* Episcopalian. *Home:* 454 Elizabeth St., Baton Rouge, La. 70815. *Office:* School of Music, Louisiana State University, Baton Rouge, La. 70803.

CAREER: Caddo Parish Schools, Shreveport, La., director of music, 1946-55; Louisiana State Department of Education, Baton Rouge, supervisor of music, 1956-57, coordinator of fine arts, 1957-63; Louisiana State University, Baton Rouge, associate professor of music, 1963—, assistant to the director, 1965—. Visiting lecturer at University of Wisconsin, 1957. Member of board of directors of Shreveport Symphony, 1949-54, Baton Rouge Symphony, 1954-55. *Military service:* U.S. Naval Reserve, active duty, 1942-45; retired as lieutenant commander, 1963. *Member:* Music Educators National Conference (member of public relations committee; vice-president of Southern Division, 1967-69), Music Teachers National Association, Louisiana Music Educators Association (president, 1953-55), Kappa Lambda, Phi Mu Alpha-Sinfonia, Rotary International. *Awards, honors:* Composition award, Illinois Male Chorus Association for ''Brothers in Song'' (performed in Orchestra Hall, Chicago).

WRITINGS: *The Music Teacher and Public Relations*, Music Educators National Conference, 1958; (with Harry R. Wilson, Walter Ehret, Alice Snyder, and Albert Renna) ''Growing with Music'' (basic textbook series, including teachers manuals, recordings, and audio-visual aids), Prentice-Hall, 1963-65; *Supervising Music in the Elementary School*, Prentice-Hall, 1965.

WORK IN PROGRESS: Two college textbooks with tentative titles of *Guiding Musical Growth* and *Supervising Music in the Secondary School.*†

* * *

HERRICK, Bruce Hale 1936-

PERSONAL: Born May 29, 1936, in Minneapolis, Minn.; son of Wallace Dunbar and Ruth (Hale) Herrick; married Dianne Walkup, June 22, 1958; children: Robert Wallace, Susan Joan, Andrew Hale. *Education:* Carleton College, A.B., 1958; Massachusetts Institute of Technology, Ph.D., 1964. *Office:* Department of Economics, University of California, Los Angeles, Calif. 90024.

CAREER: University of California, Los Angeles, assistant professor, 1964-70, associate professor of economics, 1970—, vice-chairman of department, 1971-74. Economic consultant, 1966—.

WRITINGS: *Urban Migration and Economic Development in Chile*, M.I.T. Press, 1965; *An Analysis of Venezuelan National Income Statistics: Sources and Methods*, Rand Corp., 1968; (contributor) Francine F. Rabinowitz and Felicity M. Trueblood, editors, *Latin American Urban Research*, Sage Publications, 1971; (contributor) John C. Pool and Norris Clement, editors, *Economia: Enfoque America Latina*, Libros McGraw-Hill de Mexico, 1972.

* * *

HERRING, Reuben 1922-

PERSONAL: Born July 14, 1922, in Tifton, Ga.; son of John G. (an editor) and Ruby (Hewitt) Herring; married Dorothy L. McCorvey, December 2, 1942; children: Carey, Mike, Dan, Mark, Tiria Elizabeth. *Education:* University of Georgia, A.B., 1942; studied at Southern Baptist Theological Seminary, 1961, and George Peabody College for Teachers, 1965. *Home:* 1612 Tammany Dr., Nashville, Tenn. 37206. *Office:* Baptist Sunday School Board, 127 Ninth Ave. N., Nashville, Tenn. 37203.

CAREER: Dothan Eagle, Dothan, Ala., sports editor, 1946-52; Baptist Sunday School Board, Nashville, Tenn., editorial supervisor, 1953—. *Military service:* U.S. Army, 1942-45; served in Pacific theater.

WRITINGS: 17th and 18th Century Baptist Press, Southern Baptist Historical Commission, 1959; *Two Shall Be One*, Broadman, 1964; *Men Are Like That*, Broadman, 1967; (contributor) John Ishee, *When Trouble Comes*, Broadman, 1970; (contributor) George Knight, compiler, *The Christian Home in the 70's*, Broadman, 1974; *Planning Church Work*, Seminary Extension, 1974; *Building a Better Marriage*, Convention, 1975. Also contributor to *Altar Fires*, published by Broadman. Contributor to Southern Baptist periodicals.

WORK IN PROGRESS: Two books, one with working title, *A Popular History of Baptists*, publication by Broadman expected in 1976, and *Fire in the Canebrake*, a historical novel.

HERRIOTT, Robert E. 1929-

PERSONAL: Born December 25, 1929, in New York, N.Y.; son of David Paul (a clergyman) and Gertrude (Kern) Herriott; married Joy Ahrendt, August 16, 1952; children: Scott, Nancy. *Education:* University of Vermont, A.B., 1951; Harvard University, A.M., 1955, Ed.D., 1961. *Home:* 85 Jennie Dugan Rd., Concord, Mass. 01742. *Office:* Abt Associates, Inc., 55 Wheeler St., Cambridge, Mass. 02138.

CAREER: Harvard University, Cambridge, Mass., assistant professor of education, 1961-64; Florida State University, Tallahassee, associate professor, 1964-68, professor of sociology, 1968-72; Abt Associates, Inc., Cambridge, Mass., senior social scientist, 1972—. *Military service:* U.S. Army, 1951-54. *Member:* American Sociological Association, American Educational Research Association. *Awards, honors:* Outstanding Research Award of American Personnel and Guidance Association, 1964, for "Some Social Determinants of Educational Aspiration," published in *Harvard Education Review*.

WRITINGS: (With Neal Gross) *Staff Leadership in Public Schools*, Wiley, 1965; (with Nancy St. John) *Social Class and the Urban School*, Wiley, 1966; (with Benjamin J. Hodgkins) *The Environment of Schooling*, Prentice-Hall, 1973.

* * *

HERSEY, John (Richard) 1914-

PERSONAL: Born June 17, 1914, in Tientsin, China; son of American citizens Roscoe Monroe (a Y.M.C.A. secretary in China) and Grace (a missionary; maiden name Baird) Hersey; married Frances Ann Cannon, April 27, 1940 (divorced February, 1958); married Barbara Day Addams Kaufman, June 2, 1958; children: (first marriage) Martin, John, Ann, Baird; (second marriage) Brook (daughter). *Education:* Yale University, B.A., 1936; attended Clare College, Cambridge, 1936-37. *Politics:* Democrat. *Home:* 420 Humphrey St., New Haven, Conn. 06511.

CAREER: Private secretary, driver, and factotum for Sinclair Lewis, summer, 1937; writer, editor, and correspondent, *Time* magazine, 1937-44, correspondent in China and Japan, 1939, covered South Pacific warfare, 1942, correspondent in Mediterranean theater, including Sicilian campaign, 1943, and in Moscow, 1944-45; editor and correspondent for *Life* magazine, 1944-45; writer for *New Yorker* and other magazines, off and on, 1945—; made trip to China and Japan for *Life* and *New Yorker*, 1945-46; fellow, Berkeley College, Yale University, 1950-65; master, Pierson College, Yale University, 1965-70, fellow, 1965—; writer-in-residence, American Academy in Rome, 1970-71; lecturer, Yale University, 1971—. Chairman, Connecticut Volunteers for Stevenson, 1952; member of Adlai Stevenson's campaign staff, 1956. Editor and director of writers' co-operative magazine, '47. Member of Westport (Conn.) School Study Council, 1945-50, of Westport Board of Education, 1950-52, of Yale University Council Committee on the Humanities, 1951-56, of Fairfield (Conn.) Citizens School Study Council, 1952-56, of National Citizens' Commission for the Public Schools, 1954-56; consultant, Fund for the Advancement of Education, 1954-56; chairman, Connecticut Committee for the Gifted, 1954-57; member of Board of Trustees, Putney School, 1953-56; delegate to White House Conference on Education, 1955; trustee, National Citizens' Council for the Public Schools, 1956-58; member, visiting committee, Harvard Graduate School of Education, 1960-65; member, Yale University Council Committee on Yale College, 1959—; trustee, National Committee for Support of the Public Schools, 1962-68.

MEMBER: National Institute of Arts and Letters, American Academy of Arts and Letters (secretary, 1961—), Authors League of America (member of council, 1946-70; vice-president, 1949-55), Authors Guild (member of council, 1946—), P.E.N. *Awards, honors:* Pulitzer Prize, 1945, for *A Bell for Adano*; Anisfield-Wolf Award, 1950, for *The Wall*; Daroff Memorial Fiction Award, Jewish Book Council of America, 1950, for *The Wall*; Sidney Hillman Foundation Award, 1951, for *The Wall*; Howland Medal, Yale University, 1952; National Association of Independent Schools Award, 1957, for *A Single Pebble*; Tuition Plan Award, 1961; Sarah Josepha Hale Award, 1963; named honorary fellow of Clare College, Cambridge University, 1967. Honorary degrees: M.A., Yale University, 1947; LL.D., Washington and Jefferson College, 1950; D.H.L., Dropsie College, 1950; Litt.D., Wesleyan University, 1954, Clarkson College of Technology, 1972.

WRITINGS—All published by Knopf, unless otherwise noted: *Men on Bataan*, 1942; *Into the Valley: A Skirmish of the Marines*, 1943; *A Bell for Adano*, 1944, with new foreword by Hersey, Modern Library, 1946; *Hiroshima* (first published in *New Yorker*, August 31, 1946), Knopf, 1946, school edition, Oxford Book Co., 1948; *The Wall*, 1950; *The Marmot Drive*, 1953; *A Single Pebble*, 1956; *The War Lover*, 1959; *The Child Buyer*, 1960; *Here to Stay: Studies on Human Tenacity*, Hamish Hamilton, 1962, Knopf, 1963; *White Lotus*, 1965; *Too Far to Walk*, 1966; *Under the Eye of the Storm*, 1967; *The Algiers Motel Incident*, 1968; *Letter to the Alumni*, 1970; *The Conspiracy*, 1972; (editor) *The Writer's Craft*, 1974; *My Petition for More Space*, 1974; (editor) *Ralph Ellison*, Prentice-Hall, 1974.

SIDELIGHTS: In his article, "The Novel of Contemporary History" for the *Atlantic Monthly* in 1949, Hersey stated: "Truth is said to be stranger than fiction; fiction can be stronger than truth.

"Palpable 'facts' are mortal. Like certain moths and flying ants, they lay their eggs and die overnight. The important 'flashes' and 'bulletins' are already forgotten by the time yesterday morning's paper is used to line the trash can.... The things we remember for longer periods are emotions and impressions and illusions and images and characters: the elements of fiction....

"Fiction is a clarifying agent. It makes truth plausible. Who had even a tenable theory about the Soviet purge trials until he had read Koestler's *Darkness at Noon?* Who understood the impact of Italian Fascism upon peasants, on the one hand, and upon thinking men, on the other, until he had read Silone's *Fontamara* and *Bread and Wine?*... What is argued here is only this much: among all the means of communication now available, imaginative literature comes closer than any other to being able to give an *impression* of the truth....

"What should be the aims of a writer who undertakes a novel of contemporary history?... Above all, this kind of novel should make anyone who reads it better able to meet life in his generation—whenever that generation may be.... The task of this kind of novel, however, is not to illuminate events: it is to illuminate the human beings who are caught up in the events.... Journalism allows its readers to witness history; fiction gives its readers an opportunity to live it.... Much nonsense has been written about 'journalistic' novels. The novel of contemporary history is an established form. It has dignity, purpose, and separateness.''

His earlier journalistic approaches emphasize these views. Lewis Gannett, in the *New York Herald Tribune Book Review*, said of *Hiroshima*: "John Hersey is a great reporter. He doesn't generalize and he doesn't write editorials. He knows that when headlines say a hundred thousand people are killed, whether in battle, by earthquake, flood or atom bomb, the human mind refuses to react to mathematics. The heart of the story—of any story—is the individual.'' *The New Yorker* devoted the entire editorial content of one issue to the publication of *Hiroshima* before it appeared in book form.

In a later article in the *Herald Tribune*, Milton Rugoff maintained that "clarity, authority and shining honesty ... distinguish [Hersey's] work. We feel: this is the truth purged, as much as it can be, of bias and wish—and we believe. A quality that contributes such effects can hardly be dismissed. ...''

Webster Schott summarized the import of Hersey's novels when he wrote: "His testings of the social possibilities of fiction run through eight novels. [Hersey has since written additional novels.] Good, bad, or indifferent, none covers the same territory, and all shout the ministerial exhortation: Shape up! For Hersey cares what humanity does to itself.''

A Bell for Adano was adapted as a stage play, and was made into a film in 1945; *The Wall* was dramatized by Millard Lampell in 1961; *The War Lover* was made into a film in 1962; *The Child Buyer* was adapted as a stage play by Paul Shyre in 1964.

AVOCATIONAL INTERESTS: Sailing, gardening, bowling, reading.

BIOGRAPHICAL/CRITICAL SOURCES: New York Times Book Review, February 6, 1944, February 26, 1950, June 10, 1956, September 25, 1960, January 19, 1965, February 28, 1966; *New York Herald Tribune Book Review*, August 29, 1946, March 5, 1950, August 20, 1950, June 3, 1956, September 25, 1960, *Saturday Review*, November 2, 1946, March 4, 1950, June 2, 1956, January 23, 1965; *Times Literary Supplement*, December 7, 1946; *Atlantic Monthly*, November, 1949, April, 1966; *Time*, June 4, 1956, January 29, 1965, March 25, 1966; *Newsweek*, January 25, 1965, June 7, 1965; *National Observer*, February 8, 1965; *Commonweal*, March 5, 1965; *Book Week*, September 26, 1965; *Life*, March 18, 1966; Carolyn Riley, editor, *Contemporary Literary Criticism*, Gale, Volume I, 1973, Volume II, 1974.

* * *

HERSKOWITZ, Herbert Bennett 1925-

PERSONAL: Born July 24, 1925, in Bridgeport, Conn.; married Harriet Kunin (a teacher), June 25, 1950; children: Jane, Lynn. *Education:* University of Connecticut, B.A., 1950; Fairfield University, M.A., 1960; attended Stanford University, 1963, Williams College, 1966.

CAREER: Teacher of history in public schools in Storrs, Conn., beginning 1960. *Military service:* U.S. Navy, 1943-46. *Member:* National Education Association, National Council for the Social Studies, Organization of American Historians, Connecticut Education Association.

WRITINGS: (With Bernard Marlin) *Guide to Reading in American History*, New American Library, 1966.†

HERTZBERG, Arthur 1921-

PERSONAL: Born June 9, 1921, in Lubaczow, Poland; son of Zvi Elimelech (a rabbi) and Anna (Altstadt) Hertzberg; married Phyllis Cannon, March 19, 1950; children: Linda, Susan. *Education:* Johns Hopkins University, A.B., 1940; Jewish Theological Seminary, Rabbi and M.H.L., 1943; Columbia University, Ph.D., 1966. *Home:* 83 Glenwood Rd., Englewood, N.J. 07631. *Office:* Temple Emanu-El, 147 Tenafly Rd., Englewood, N.J. 07631.

CAREER: Smith College, Northampton, Mass., Hillel director, 1943-44; rabbi in Philadelphia, Pa., 1944-47, and Nashville, Tenn., 1947-56; Temple Emanu-El, Englewood, N.J., rabbi, 1956—. Lecturer, Columbia University, New York, N.Y., 1962-66, Princeton University, 1968-69; visiting professor, Rutgers University, 1966-68, Hebrew University, Jerusalem, 1970-71. President, Conference on Jewish Social Studies, 1967-72, American Jewish Congress, 1972—; member of Jewish Agency for Israel, 1969—. *Military service:* U.S. Air Force, 1952-53; deputy staff chaplain in England. *Awards, honors:* Amram Award from Jewish Publication Society, 1967, for *The French Enlightenment and the Jews*; D.D., Lafayette College, 1970.

WRITINGS: (Editor with Joseph L. Blau) *Essays in Jewish Life and Thought*, Columbia University Press, 1959; *The Zionist Idea*, Doubleday, 1959; *Judaism*, Braziller, 1961; (with Martin Marty and Joseph L. Moody) *The Outburst that Awaits Us*, Macmillan, 1963; *The French Enlightenment and the Jews*, Columbia University Press, 1967. Regular columnist, *National Catholic Reporter*; contributor to *Commentary*. Editor, *Midstream*, 1965—, and of *Journal on Jewish Social Studies*; consulting editor, *Encyclopaedia Judaica*.

WORK IN PROGRESS: The Condition of the American Jew.

* * *

HERZOG, Arthur (III) 1927-

PERSONAL: Born April 6, 1927, in New York, N.Y.; son of Arthur, Jr. and Elizabeth (Dayton) Herzog; divorced; children: Matthew. *Education:* Attended University of Arizona, 1946; Stanford University, B.A., 1950; Columbia University, M.A., 1956. *Politics:* Democrat. *Religion:* None. *Home:* 230 East 50th St., New York, N.Y. 10022. *Agent:* Candid Donadio, 111 West 57th St., New York, N.Y. 10017.

CAREER: Fawcett Publications, Greenwich, Conn., editor, 1954-57; full-time free-lance writer, 1957—. *Military service:* U.S. Navy, 1945-46.

WRITINGS: (Co-author) *Smoking and the Public Interest*, Consumers Union, 1963; *The War-Peace Establishment*, Harper, 1965; *The Church Trap*, Macmillan, 1968; *McCarthy for President*, Viking, 1969; *The B.S. Factor*, Simon & Schuster, 1973; *The Swarm*, Simon & Schuster, 1974; *Earthsound*, Simon & Schuster, 1975. Contributor of articles to *Harper's, Esquire, New York Times*, and other publications.

WORK IN PROGRESS: A novel on climate change, publication expected by Simon & Schuster.

SIDELIGHTS: Arthur Herzog speaks French.

* * *

HESS, Stephen 1933-

PERSONAL: Born April 20, 1933, in New York, N.Y.;

son of Charles and Florence (Morse) Hess; married Elena Shayne, August 23, 1959; children: Charles, James. *Education:* University of Chicago, student, 1951-52; Johns Hopkins University, A.B., 1953, graduate study, 1953-55. *Home:* 3705 Porter St., N.W., Washington, D.C. 20016. *Agent:* Elizabeth McKee, Harold Matson Co., Inc., 22 East 40th St., New York, N.Y. 10016. *Office:* Brookings Institution, 1775 Massachusetts Ave., N.W., Washington, D.C. 20036.

CAREER: White House, Washington, D.C., staff assistant to the President, 1959-61; U.S. Senate, Washington, D.C., assistant to the minority whip, 1961; BIDCO (sale of factories in underdeveloped countries), Washington, D.C., secretary-treasurer, 1962-65; Institute for Policy Studies, Washington, D.C., associate fellow, 1965; fellow, Institute of Politics, John F. Kennedy School of Government, Harvard University, Cambridge, Mass., 1967-68; White House, Washington, D.C., deputy assistant to the President for urban affairs, 1969; national chairman of Conference on Children and Youth, 1969-71; Brookings Institution, Washington, D.C., senior fellow, 1972—. Member of District of Columbia Board of Higher Education, 1973—. *Military service:* U.S. Army, 1956-58. *Member:* Phi Beta Kappa, Johns Hopkins Club of Washington (vice-president, 1960-62).

WRITINGS: (With Malcolm Moos) *Hats in the Ring: The Making of Presidential Candidates*, Random House, 1960; *America's Political Dynasties: From Adams to Kennedy*, Doubleday, 1966; (with David S. Broder) *The Republican Establishment: The Present and Future of the G.O.P.*, Harper, 1967; (with Milton Kaplan) *The Ungentlemanly Art: A History of American Political Cartoons*, Macmillan, 1968; (with Earl Mazo) *Nixon: A Political Portrait*, Harper, 1968, revised edition, 1969; (contributor) Robert P. Wolff, *Styles of Political Action in America*, Random House, 1971; *The Presidential Campaign: The Leadership Selection Progress After Watergate*, Brookings Institution, 1974. Author of documentaries for educational television. Contributor to *Grolier's Encyclopedia Yearbook* and of articles to journals.

WORK IN PROGRESS: Organizing the Presidency for Brookings Institution.

BIOGRAPHICAL/CRITICAL SOURCES: New York Times, December 14, 1970; *Washington Post/Potomac*, August 23, 1970; *Time*, July 15, 1974.

*   *   *

HESSE, Mary (Brenda)   1924-

PERSONAL: Surname rhymes with "dressy"; born October 15, 1924, in Reigate, England; daughter of Ethelbert Thomas (as accountant) and Brenda Nellie (Pelling) Hesse. *Education:* Imperial College of Science and Technology, London, B.Sc., 1947, Ph.D., 1948; University College, London, M.Sc., 1949. *Religion:* Presbyterian. *Home:* 78, Highsett, Hills Rd., Cambridge, England. *Office:* Whipple Museum, Cambridge University, Free School Lane, Cambridge, England.

CAREER: University of Leeds, Leeds, England, lecturer in mathematics, 1951-55; University of London, University College, London, England, lecturer in history and philosophy of science, 1955-59; Cambridge University, Cambridge, England, lecturer, 1960-68, university reader in Philosophy of Science, 1968—, member of council of senate, 1962-66. Visiting professor at Yale University, 1962-63, University of Minnesota, 1966, University of Chicago, 1968. *Member:* British Society for the Philosophy of Sci-

ence (secretary, 1956-60), British Society for the History of Science (former council member).

WRITINGS: Science and the Human Imagination, S.C.M. Press, 1953; *Forces and Fields*, Littlefield, 1961; *Models and Analogies in Science*, Sheed, 1963, enlarged edition, University of Notre Dame Press, 1966. Contributor to professional journals. Editor, *British Journal for the Philosophy of Science*, 1965-69.

WORK IN PROGRESS: Research in induction and confirmation theory, and in structure of scientific theories.

AVOCATIONAL INTERESTS: Walking, talking.†

*   *   *

HETTLINGER, Richard F(rederick)   1920-

PERSONAL: Surname is pronounced with hard "g"; born April 11, 1920, in Buckinghamshire, England; son of Frederick (a businessman) and Rosina (Grimes) Hettlinger; married Mary Allnutt, August 17, 1946; children: Stephen Robert, Sarah Ann, Karen Jane, Graham Paul. *Education:* Jesus College, Cambridge, B.A., 1942, M.A., 1947; Ridley Hall, Cambridge, theological study, 1942-43; Yale University Divinity School, graduate study, 1959-60. *Politics:* Democrat. *Office:* Kenyon College, Gambier, Ohio 43022.

CAREER: Clergyman, Church of England (Episcopal). Wycliffe College, Toronto, Ontario, professor of systematic theology, 1946-53; St. Augustine's College, Canterbury, England, fellow, 1953-59; Kenyon College, Gambier, Ohio, chaplain and associate professor of religion, 1960-64, professor, 1964—. Graduate School of Ecumenical Studies, Bossey, Switzerland, visiting lecturer on Anglicanism, 1953. Active in ecumenical affairs, 1946-53, serving as secretary of Commission on Faith and Order, Canadian Council of Churches, 1951-53, representative of Anglican Church of Canada at International Conference on Faith and Order, Lund, Sweden, 1952, and member of ecumenical delegation to Finland, 1953. *Member:* American Academy of Religion, Society for the Study of Theology (England). *Awards, honors:* Lilley fellowship at Yale University, 1959-60; Church Society fellow, 1959-60.

WRITINGS: Living with Sex: The Student's Dilemma, Seabury, 1966; *Sexual Maturity*, Wadsworth, 1970; *Growing Up with Sex*, Seabury, 1971; *Sex Isn't That Simple*, Seabury, 1974.

WORK IN PROGRESS: A text edition of *Sex Isn't That Simple* with selected readings to be published by Wadsworth.

*   *   *

HEWITT, William Henry   1936-

PERSONAL: Born June 20, 1936, in Dunkirk, N.Y.; son of H. Louis and Mary A. (Fera) Hewitt; married Barbara J. Firman, April 20, 1956; children: four sons. *Education:* Michigan State University, B.S., 1961; Kent State University, M.A., 1964; New York University, candidate for Ph.D. *Office:* State University of New York, Farmingdale, N.Y. 11735.

CAREER: Sears, Roebuck & Co., security director for state of Ohio, 1961-63; Kent State University, Kent, Ohio, director of School of Law Enforcement Administration and Public Safety, 1963-65; State University of New York College at Farmingdale, associate professor of political science and chairman of department, 1965—. Member of President's Committee on Law Enforcement and Administration of Justice; author of Law Enforcement Minimum Standards and Training Bill passed by Ohio Legislature, 1965. *Military service:* U.S. Army, Military Police, 1955-57. U.S. Army Reserve, special agent, Intelligence, 1962—. *Member:* International Association of Police Professors (member of executive board), International Association of Chiefs of Police, Reserve Officers Association of the United States, Alpha Phi Sigma, Pi Sigma Alpha. *Awards, honors:* Greater Cleveland Association Foundation grant, 1965.

WRITINGS: (Principal author) *British Police Administration*, C. C Thomas, 1965; *A Bibliography on Police Administration, Public Safety, and Criminology*, C. C Thomas, 1967; (editor) *Administration of Criminal Justice in New York: A Manual for Law Enforcement Officers*, Aqueduct Books, 1967; *Police Records Administration*, Aqueduct Books, 1968; (compiler with Charles L. Newman) *Police-Community Relations: An Anthology and Bibliography*, Foundation Press, 1970. Also co-author of police service studies. Contributor to police administration journals. Consulting editor, *Police.†*

* * *

HEYEL, Carl 1908-

PERSONAL: Born February 16, 1908, in Cincinnati, Ohio; son of Otto (an electroplater) and Magdelina (Thoman) Heyel; married Miriam Elizabeth Rollman, September 2, 1933; children: Barbara Ann (Mrs. Robert Paul Kromrey), Sheila Kay (Mrs. James Wang). *Education:* University of Cincinnati, E.E., 1931; New York University, graduate study in business, 1931-32. *Religion:* Protestant. *Home:* 39 Papermill Rd., Manhasset, N.Y. 11030.

CAREER: Licensed professional engineer, state of New York. McGraw-Hill Book Co., Inc., New York, N.Y., member of editorial and business staffs, 1931-37; American Management Association, New York, N.Y., director of conference planning, 1937-41; Union Bag & Paper Co., New York, N.Y., member of management research staff, 1941-43; Lehn & Fink Products Corp., New York, N.Y., assistant to the president, 1943-50; management consultant, New York, N.Y., 1950-55; Mergenthaler Linotype Co., Brooklyn, N.Y., director of planning, 1955-57; self-employed management counsel, writer, and lecturer, Manhasset, N.Y., 1957—. New York University, lecturer at Graduate School of Business, 1946-47, 1947-48; Polytechnic Institute of Brooklyn, adjunct professor, later associate professor, at Graduate School (evenings), 1958-63.

MEMBER: American Management Association, Society for the Advancement of Management (president, New York chapter, 1949-51; chapter board of directors, 1951-52), National Association of Accountants, Eta Kappa Nu, Tau Beta Pi.

WRITINGS: Human Relations Manual for Executives, McGraw, 1939; *How to Create Job Enthusiasm*, McGraw, 1942; *Standard Business-Conference Technique*, Funk, 1948; *Appraising Executive Performance*, American Management Association, 1958; *Organizing Your Job in Management*, American Management Association, 1960; *Management for Modern Supervisors*, American Management Association, 1962; *The Supervisor's Basic Management Guide—An A-Z Manual on Supervisory Effectiveness*, McGraw, 1965; *How to Communicate Better with Workers*, Clemprint, 1967, revised edition, 1975.

Editor and contributor: *The Foreman's Handbook*, McGraw, 1942, 4th edition, 1967; *Reading Course in Executive Technique*, forty-two books, Funk, 1948; "Standard Management Practice Series," National Foreman's Institute, 1951; *Handbook of Industrial Research Management*, Reinhold, 1959, revised edition, 1968; *The Encyclopedia of Management*, Reinhold, 1963, revised edition, Van Nostrand, 1973; *Computers, Office Machines, and New Information Technology*, Macmillan, 1968; (with Victor P. Buell) *Handbook of Modern Marketing*, McGraw, 1970; *Handbook of Modern Office Management and Administrative Services*, McGraw, 1972.

Writer of comprehensive supplements to *Dun's Review and Modern Industry*. Contributor to business periodicals. Editor, *Administrative Officer* (management bi-weekly letter), 1964-74; *Management Service Alert*, 1974—, and *The Better-Work Supervisor.*

* * *

HIBBERT, Eleanor Burford 1906-
(Eleanor Burford; pseudonyms: Philippa Carr, Elbur Ford, Victoria Holt, Kathleen Kellow, Jean Plaidy, Ellalice Tate)

PERSONAL: Born 1906, in London, England; daughter of Joseph and Alice (Tate) Burford; married G. P. Hibbert. *Education:* Privately educated. *Agent:* A. M. Heath & Co., Ltd., 35 Dover St., London W. 1, England.

CAREER: Full-time writer.

WRITINGS—Under name Eleanor Burford: *House at Cupid's Cross*, Jenkins, 1949; *Passionate Witness*, Jenkins, 1949; *Believe the Heart*, Jenkins, 1950; *Love Child*, Jenkins, 1950; *Saint or Sinner?*, Jenkins, 1951; *Dear Delusion*, Jenkins, 1952; *Bright Tomorrow*, Jenkins, 1952; *Leave Me My Love*, Jenkins, 1953; *When We Are Married*, Jenkins, 1953; *Castles in Spain*, Jenkins, 1954; *Heart's Afire*, Jenkins, 1954; *When Other Hearts*, Jenkins, 1955; *Two Loves in Her Life*, Jenkins, 1955; *Begin to Live*, Mills & Boon, 1956; *Married in Haste*, Mills & Boon, 1956; *To Meet a Stranger*, Mills & Boon, 1957; *Pride of the Morning*, Mills & Boon, 1958; *Dawn Chorus*, Mills & Boon, 1959; *Red Sky at Night*, Mills & Boon, 1959; *Blaze of Noon*, Mills & Boon, 1960; *Night of the Stars*, Mills & Boon, 1960; *Now That April's Gone*, Mills & Boon, 1961; *Who's Calling?*, Mills & Boon, 1962.

Under pseudonym Philippa Carr: *The Miracle at St. Bruno's*, Putnam, 1972; *The Lion Triumphant*, Putnam, 1973; *The Witch from the Sea*, Putnam, 1975.

Under pseudonym Elbur Ford: *Poison in Pimlico*, Laurie, 1950; *Flesh and the Devil*, Laurie, 1950; *Bed Disturbed*, Laurie, 1952; *Such Bitter Business*, Heinemann, 1953, published as *Evil in the House*, Morrow, 1954.

Under pseudonym Victoria Holt; all published by Doubleday, except as indicated: *Mistress of Mellya*, 1960; *Kirkland Revels*, 1962; *Bride of Pendorric*, 1963, included in *Three Great Romantic Stories*, Collins, 1972; *The Legend of the Seventh Virgin*, 1965; *Menfreya in the Morning*, 1966 (published in England as *Menfreya*, Collins, 1966); *The King of the Castle*, 1967; *Queen's Confession: A Biography of Marie Antoinette*, 1968, published as *The Queen's Confession*, Fawcett, 1974; *The Shivering Sands*, 1969; *The Secret Woman*, 1970; *The Shadow of the Lynx*, 1971; *On the Night of the Seventh Moon*, 1972; *The Curse of the Kings*, 1973; *The House of a Thousand Lanterns*, 1974.

Under pseudonym Kathleen Kellow; all published by R. Hale: *Danse Macabre*, 1952; *Rooms at Mrs. Olivers'*, 1953; *Lilith*, 1954; *It Began in Vauxhall Gardens*, 1955;

Call of the Blood, 1956; *Rochester, The Mad Earl*, 1957; *Milady Charlotte*, 1959; *The World's A Stage*, 1960.

Under pseudonym Jean Plaidy; all published by R. Hale, except as indicated: *Beyond the Blue Mountains*, Appleton, 1947, new edition, R. Hale, 1964; *Murder Most Royal*, 1949, Putnam, 1972, published as *Kings Pleasure*, Appleton, 1949.

The Goldsmith's Wife, Appleton, 1950; *Madame Serpent*, Appleton, 1951; *Italian Woman*, 1952; *Daughter of Satan*, 1952, Putnam, 1973; *Queen Jezebel*, Appleton, 1953; *The Spanish Bridegroom*, 1953, Macrae Smith, 1956; *St. Thomas's Eve*, 1954, Putnam, 1970; *The Sixth Wife*, 1954, Putnam, 1969; *Gay Lord Robert*, 1955, Putnam, 1972; *Royal Road to Fotheringay*, 1955, Fawcett, 1972, published as *Royal Road to Fotheringay: A Novel of Mary, Queen of Scots*, Putnam, 1968; *The Wandering Prince*, 1956, Putnam, 1971; *Health Unto His Majesty*, 1956, published as *A Health Unto His Majesty*, Putnam, 1972; *Flaunting, Extravagant Queen*, 1957; *Here Lies Our Sovereign Lord*, 1957, Putnam, 1973; *Madonna of the Seven Hills*, 1958, Putnam, 1974; *Triptych of Poisoners*, 1958; *Light on Lucrezia*, 1958; *Louis, the Well-Beloved*, 1959; *Rise of the Spanish Inquisition*, 1959; *Road to Compiegne*, 1959.

Castile for Isabella, 1960; *Growth of the Spanish Inquisition*, 1960; *Spain for the Sovereigns*, 1960; *Daughters of Spain*, 1961; *The Young Elizabeth*, Roy, 1961; *Meg Roper: Daughter of Sir Thomas More*, Constable, 1961, Roy, 1964; *The End of the Spanish Inquisition*, 1961; *Katharine, the Virgin Widow*, 1961; *The Kings Secret Matter*, 1962; *The Young Mary, Queen of Scots*, Parrish, 1962, Roy, 1963; *The Shadow of the Pomegranate*, 1962; *The Captive Queen of Scots*, 1963, Putnam, 1970; *The Thistle and the Rose*, 1963, Putnam, 1973; *Mary, Queen of France*, 1964; *The Murder in the Tower*, 1964, Putnam, 1974; *Evergreen Gallant*, 1965, Putnam, 1973; *The Three Crowns*, 1965; *The Haunted Sisters*, 1966; *The Queen's Favourites*, 1966; *Lilith* (originally published under pseudonym Kathleen Kellow), 1967; *Queen in Waiting*, 1967; *The Princess of Celle*, 1967; *The Prince and the Quakeress*, 1968; *Caroline, the Queen*, 1968; *It Began in Vauxhall Gardens* (originally published under pseudonym Kathleen Kellow), 1968; *The Scarlet Cloak* (originally published under pseudonym Ellalice Tate), 1969; *The Third George*, 1969; *Perdita's Prince*, 1969.

Sweet Lass of Richmond Hill, 1970; *Indiscretions of the Queen*, 1970; *The Regent's Daughter*, 1971; *Goddess of the Green Room*, 1971; *The Captive of Kensington Palace*, 1972; *Victoria in the Wings*, 1972; *The Queen's Husband*, 1973; *The Queen and Lord M*, 1973; *The Widow of Windsor*, 1974; *The King's Mistress*, Pyramid Publications, 1974.

Trilogies—Under pseudonym Jean Plaidy: *The Spanish Inquisition: Its Rise, Growth, and End* (includes *The Rise of the Spanish Inquisition, The Growth of the Spanish Inquisition*, and *The End of the Spanish Inquisition*), Citadel, 1967; *Katharine of Aragon* (includes *Katharine, the Virgin Widow, The Shadow of the Pomegranate*, and *The King's Secret Matter*), R. Hale, 1968; *Catherine de Medici* (includes *Madame Serpent, The Italian Woman*, and *Queen Jezebel*), R. Hale, 1969; *Isabella and Ferdinand* (includes *Castile for Isabella, Spain for the Sovereigns*, and *Daughters of Spain*), R. Hale, 1970; *Charles II* (includes *The Wandering Prince, Health Unto His Majesty*, and *Here Lies Our Sovereign Lord*), R. Hale, 1972.

Under pseudonym Ellalice Tate; all published by Hodder & Stoughton: *Defenders of the Faith*, 1956; *Scarlet Cloak*, 1957; *Queen of Diamonds*, 1958; *Madame du Barry*, 1959; *This Was a Man*, 1961.

Contributor to newspapers and magazines, at times under a number of undisclosed pseudonyms.

SIDELIGHTS: Mrs. Hibbert, who reportedly earns $300,000 a book, told the Woman's News Service: "I don't care about the critics. I write for the public. It's nicer to be read than to get nice reviews. I don't say my books are profound, they're pure entertainment.

"I think people want a good story and this I give them," she told *CA*. "They like something which is readable and you can't really beat the traditional for this. I write with great feeling and excitement and I think this comes over to the reader."

Doubleday has kept the Victoria Holt pseudonym a well-guarded secret since it first appeared. Many believed that Victoria Holt was in reality Daphne du Maurier. "I have heard her name mentioned in connection with mine," Mrs. Hibbert told *CA*, "and I think it is because we have both lived in Cornwall and have written about this place. *Rebecca* is the atmospheric suspense type of book which mine are but I don't think there is much similarity between her others and mine." In a Woman's News Service release she said: "My American publishers got the idea of making me into a mystery woman with the new name of Victoria Holt. People began to ask, 'Who is she?' but they wouldn't say."

The critics have been generous to the Gothic tales bearing the Holt name. Genevieve Casey said of *Kirkland Revels* in the *Chicago Sunday Tribune*: "Murder, intrigue, threats of insanity, family skeletons rattling in closets and ghosts who walk in the moonlight keep the reader credulous and turning pages fast in this absorbing story." While reviewing *The Legend of the Seventh Virgin* for *Best Sellers*, Miss Casey wrote: "Among the clamour of novels by angry young men, among the probings and circumlocution of psychological novels, the works of Victoria Holt stand out, unpretentious, sunny, astringent, diverting."

In the *New York Times Book Review*, Anthony Boucher said of *Manfreya in the Morning*: "It's hard to say objectively, just why ... [this] is so intensely readable and enjoyable.... It is Holt's weakest and slightest plot to date, and equally certainly nothing much happens in the way of either action or character development for long stretches. But somehow the magic ... is still there...."

"Dickens, Zola, Brontes (particularly), and nearly all the Victorians" have influenced her writings, she says. "I write regularly every day. I think this is important. As in everything else, practice helps to make perfect. Research is just a matter of reading old records, letters, etc., in fact everything connected with the period one is researching. I can only say that I love writing more than anything else. I find it stimulating and I never cease to be excited about it."

Mrs. Hibbert has traveled widely. She has been around the world and plans to go to Australia and the Pacific islands.

Mistress of Mellyn, Hibbert's first novel under her pseudonym Victoria Holt, was adapted for the stage by Mildred C. Kuner and *Daughter of Satan*, written under pseudonym of Jean Plaidy, is being filmed.

BIOGRAPHICAL/CRITICAL SOURCES: *Chicago Sunday Tribune*, January 14, 1962; *Best Sellers*, February 1, 1965; *New York Times Book Review*, April 17, 1966; *Atlanta Journal-Constitution*, July 4, 1966.

344

HIEBERT, D(avid) Edmond 1910-

PERSONAL: Born July 21, 1910, in Corn, Okla.; son of D. K. (a farmer) and Kathie (Warkentin) Hiebert; married Ruth Kopper, 1935; children: Larry Dean, Dorothy Jean, Alice Faye. *Education:* John Fletcher College, A.B., 1935; Southern Baptist Theological Seminary, Th.M., 1939, Th.D., 1942. *Home:* 4864 East Townsend, Fresno, Calif. 93702. *Office:* 4824 East Butler, Fresno, Calif. 93702.

CAREER: Ordained minister, Mennonite Brethren. Tabor College, Hillsboro, Kan., professor of New Testament, 1942-55; Mennonite Brethren Biblical Seminary, Fresno, Calif., professor of New Testament, 1955—. *Member:* Evangelical Theological Society.

WRITINGS: Working by Prayer, Mennonite Brethren Publishing House, 1953; *An Introduction to the Pauline Epistles*, Moody, 1954; *Titus-Philemon*, Moody, 1957; *First Timothy*, Moody, 1957; *Second Timothy*, Moody, 1958; *An Introduction to the Non-Pauline Epistles*, Moody, 1962; (contributor) *Zondervan Pictorial Bible Dictionary*, Zondervan, 1967; (contributor) *The New Testament from 26 Translations*, Zondervan, 1967; *The Thessalonian Epistles*, Moody, 1971; *Wayside Wells for the Tested and Tried*, Moody, 1972; *Personalities Around Paul*, Moody, 1973; *Mark: A Portrait of the Servant*, Moody, 1974; (contributor) Merrill C. Tenney, editor, *Zondervan Pictorial Bible Encyclopedia*, five volumes, Zondervan, 1974; *An Introduction to the Gospel and Acts*, Moody, 1975.

* * *

HIEBERT, Ray Eldon 1932-

PERSONAL: Born May 21, 1932, in Freeman, S.D.; son of Peter Nicholas and Helen (Kunkel) Hiebert; married Roselyn Lucille Peyser (a researcher and writer), January 30, 1955; children: David, Steven, Emily, Douglas. *Education:* Stanford University, B.A., 1954; Columbia University, M.S., 1957; University of Maryland, M.A., 1961, Ph.D., 1962. *Office:* College of Journalism, University of Maryland, College Park, Md. 20742.

CAREER: Newspaper reporter and copy editor in New York, N.Y., and vicinity, 1956-57; University of Minnesota, Duluth Campus, instructor in English and journalism, 1957-58; The American University, Washington, D.C., assistant professor, 1958-62, associate professor, 1962-65, chairman of journalism, public relations, and broadcasting department, 1962-67; director of Washington Journalism Center, 1966-68; University of Maryland, College Park, professor of journalism and chairman of department, 1968-72, dean of College of Journalism, 1973—. Consultant to U.S. Civil Service Commission, Department of Labor, Department of Housing and Urban Development, and to other government agencies; trustee of Foundation for Public Relations Research and Education. *Military service:* U.S. Army, Signal Corps, 1954-56. *Member:* American Studies Association, Association for Education in Journalism, American Society of Journalism School Administrators, Public Relations Society of America, American Association of Schools and Departments of Journalism (member of executive committee), Sigma Delta Chi, Kappa Tau Alpha, Pi Delta Epsilon.

WRITINGS: (Editor) *Books in Human Development*, Agency for International Development, 1965; *Courtier to the Crowd*, Iowa State University Press, 1966; (editor) *The Press in Washington*, Dodd, 1966; (editor with Carlton E. Spitzer) *The Voice of Government*, Wiley, 1968; (with wife, Roselyn Hiebert) *Franklin Delano Roosevelt: President for the People*, F. Watts, 1968; (with Roselyn Hiebert) *Thomas Edison: American Inventor*, F. Watts, 1969; (with Roselyn Hiebert) *The Stock Market Crash, 1929*, F. Watts, 1970; (with Roselyn Hiebert) *Atomic Pioneers*, Atomic Energy Commission, Volume I, 1970, Volume II, 1971, Volume III, 1973; *Trends in Public Relations Education*, Foundation for Public Relations Education and Research, 1971; (editor) *The Political Image Merchants: Strategies in the New Politics*, Acropolis Books, 1971, 2nd edition, 1974; (with others) *Mass Media: An Introduction to Modern Communication*, McKay, 1974.

Editor of Wiley's "Government and Communications" series and editorial board member of Acropolis Books' "Contemporary Issues in Journalism" series. Contributing editor, *Public Relations Journal*, 1962-68; editor, *RTNDA Communicator*, 1971—, *Public Relations Review*, 1975—.

* * *

HIGGINBOTHAM, R(obert) Don 1931-

PERSONAL: Born May 22, 1931, in Fresno, Calif.; son of E. B. (a banker) and Maude (Myers) Higginbotham; married Mary Stone, December 22, 1958 (deceased); married Mary L. Bates, November 22, 1969; children: (first marriage) Robert, Lawrence, David; (second marriage) James, Lea. *Education:* Missouri Valley College, student, 1950-52; Washington University, St. Louis, Mo., A.B. and M.A., 1954; University of Nebraska, post-graduate student, 1954-55; Duke University, Ph.D., 1958. *Home:* 236 Flemington, Chapel Hill, N.C. 27514. *Office:* Department of History, University of North Carolina, Chapel Hill, N.C. 27514.

CAREER: Duke University, Durham, N.C., instructor in history, 1957-58; College of William and Mary, Williamsburg, Va., assistant professor of history, 1958-59; Longwood College, Farmville, Va., assistant professor of history, 1959-60; Louisiana State University, Baton Rouge, assistant professor, 1960-63, associate professor, 1963-67; University of North Carolina, Chapel Hill, associate professor, 1967-70, professor of history, 1970—.

WRITINGS: Daniel Morgan: Revolutionary Rifleman, University of North Carolina Press, 1961; (contributor) *George Washington's Generals*, edited by George A. Billias, Morrow, 1964; *The War of American Independence*, Macmillan, 1971; *The Atlas of the American Revolution*, Rand McNally, 1974; (editor) *The Papers of James Iredell*, two volumes, North Carolina Division of Archives and History, 1975.

WORK IN PROGRESS: A study of George Washington, for Harcourt's "Revolution Series."

* * *

HIGGINS, Trumbull 1919-

PERSONAL: Born September 27, 1919, in New York, N.Y.; son of Charles Houchin (an architect) and Clare (Van Lenned) Higgins; married Barbara Guest Pinson (a poet and art critic), August, 1954. *Education:* Princeton University, A.B., 1942, M.A., 1946, Ph.D., 1951. *Home:* 148 Fifth Ave., New York, N.Y. 10028.

CAREER: Brooklyn College (now Brooklyn College of the City University of New York), Brooklyn, N.Y., lecturer in history, 1951-53; Hofstra College, Hempstead, N.Y., assistant professor, 1953-59; National War College, Washington, D.C., visiting professor, 1959-60; Adelphi University, Garden City, N.Y., associate professor of history, 1960-61; Institute for Defense Analysis, Washington, D.C., senior staff member, diplomatic research, 1961-62; Hunter College (now Hunter College of the City University of New York), associate professor of history, 1962-63; Historical Evaluation and Research Organization, Washington, D.C., senior staff member, 1963-66; Drexel Institute, Philadelphia, Pa., associate professor of history and government, 1966-68; John Jay College of Criminal Justice of the City University of New York, professor, 1969-75. Military lecturer at NATO Defense College, Royal United Service Institute, Yale University, New York University, and West Point. *Member:* American Historical Association, American Military Institute, American Political Science Association. *Awards, honors:* Social Science Research Council fellow, 1959-60.

WRITINGS: Winston Churchill and the Second Front, Oxford University Press, 1957; *Korea and the Fall of MacArthur,* Oxford University Press, 1960; *Winston Churchill and the Dardanelles,* Macmillan, 1963; *Hitler and Russia: The Third Reich in a Two-Front War,* Macmillan, 1966; *Soft Underbelly: The Anglo-American Controversy Over the Italian Campaign, 1939-45,* Macmillan, 1968. Author of articles; regular reviewer for *Washington Post* and *American Historical Review.*

WORK IN PROGRESS: Pluto and Vulture.

SIDELIGHTS: Higgins has made thirty-five trips to Europe and Asia for research and travel, including a National War College NATO tour to Moscow. He knows French and Spanish.

* * *

HILDEBRAND, George H(erbert) 1913-

PERSONAL: Born July 7, 1913, in Oakland, Calif.; son of George Herbert and Irene (Colegrove) Hildebrand; married Margaret Boardman, August 28, 1937; children: George C., Richard W., Stephen B. *Education:* University of California, Berkeley, B.A. (with honors), 1935; Harvard University, M.A., 1941; Cornell University, Ph:D., 1942. *Religion:* Congregationalist. *Office:* Department of Economics, Cornell University, 258 Ives, Ithaca, N.Y. 14850.

CAREER: University of Texas, Austin, assistant professor of economics, 1941-43; National War Labor Board, Washington, D.C., principal economist, 1943-44; Regional War Labor Board, Colorado, director of Wage Stabilization Division, 1944-45; University of California, Berkeley, assistant professor of social institutions, 1945-47; University of California, Los Angeles, assistant professor, 1947-49, associate professor, 1949-54, professor of economics, 1954-60, and director of Institute of Industrial Relations, 1956-60; Cornell University, Ithaca, N.Y., professor of economics and industrial and labor relations, 1960-70, Maxwell M. Upson Professor of Economics and Labor Relations, 1970—. Visiting professor at University of California, Berkeley, 1959-60, Massachusetts Institute of Technology, 1964-65. Consultant to Office of Strategic Services, 1942, Department of Labor, 1959-60, Department of Health, Education, and Welfare, 1961-62. Labor arbitrator, 1951—; member of board of directors, Social Science Research Council, 1961—; member of foreign service board, U.S. Department of State, 1969—; deputy undersecretary of labor for international affairs, U.S. Department of Labor, 1969-70.

MEMBER: American Economic Association, National Academy of Arbitrators, Industrial Relations Research Association (member of executive board, 1964-67; president, 1971), Phi Beta Kappa. *Awards, honors:* Fulbright

fellowship to Italy, 1952-53; Guggenheim fellowships, 1952-53, 1957-58; Ford Foundation research professorship, 1962-63.

WRITINGS: (Author of introduction) F. J. Teggart, *The Idea of Progress,* revised edition, University of California Press, 1949; (co-author) *Pacific Coast Maritime Shipping Industry, 1930-1948,* two volumes, University of California Press, 1952, 1954; *Growth and Structure in the Economy of Modern Italy,* Harvard University Press, 1965; (with Ta-Chung Liu) *Manufacturing Production Functions in the United States, 1957: An Inter-Industry and Interstate Comparison of Productivity,* School of Industrial and Labor Relations, Cornell University, 1965; *Growth and Structure in the Economy of Modern Italy,* Harvard University Press, 1965; *Poverty, Income Maintainence, and the Negative Income Tax,* Cornell University, 1967.

Contributor: Neil W. Chamberlain and others, editors, *A Decade of Industrial Relations Research, 1946-56,* Harper, 1958; Joseph Shister and others, editors, *Public Policy and Collective Bargaining,* Harper, 1962; J. L. Meij, editor, *Internal Wage Structure,* North-Holland Publishing Co., 1963; Jack Stieber, editor, *Employment Problems of Automation and Advanced Technology: An International Perspective,* St. Martins, 1966; Robert Aaron Gordon and Margaret S. Gordon, editors, *Prosperity and Unemployment,* Wiley, 1966. Also author of *Postwar Italy: A Study in Economic Contrasts,* University of California. Contributor to proceedings and professional journals. Member of board of editors, *American Economic Research,* 1954-57, and publications committee, 1961—.

SIDELIGHTS: Hildebrand reads and speaks Italian and reads French and German. *Avocational interests:* Railroads and western U.S. history.†

* * *

HILL, David Charles 1936-
(Dave Hill)

PERSONAL: Born October 6, 1936, in Minneapolis, Minn.; son of Charles W. (a wanderer) and Joyce (Hansen) Hill. *Education:* Attended about thirty elementary schools in Minnesota, Oregon, and Washington; earned high school diploma and some college credits by correspondence. *Politics:* "Apathetic—no choice, as I see it." *Religion:* Christian Existentialist. *Home:* 2924 36th Ave. South, Minneapolis, Minn. 55406.

CAREER: Full-time free-lance writer. *Member:* Minneapolis Writers Workshop.

WRITINGS: Juvenile books, except as indicated; all published under name Dave Hill, except as indicated: *Big Bible Puzzle Book,* Bethany, 1965; *Ramon's World,* Herald, 1965; *Welfare Kid,* Herald, 1966; *Secret of the Star* (picture book), Concordia, 1966; (under name David Charles Hill) *They Met the Master* (adult), Augsburg, 1967; *The Boy Who Gave His Lunch Away,* Concordia, 1967; *The Walls Came Tumbling Down,* Concordia, 1967; *The Most Wonderful King,* Concordia, 1968; (under name David Charles Hill) *Messengers of the King,* Augsburg, 1968; (under name David Charles Hill) *The Gospel of Matthew,* Attic Press, 1972. Stories included in teen-age anthologies. Regular contributor to denominational magazines.

SIDELIGHTS: Hill told *CA:* "I write for money, have no other interest, skill, or abilities. [I] have spent large part of my life in various jails for criminal activity of a trivial nature. [I] do have some knowledge of Chippewa Indian language." Hill calls himself an expert on the world of small-time criminals.†

* * *

HILL, Elizabeth Starr 1925-

PERSONAL: Born November 4, 1925, in Lynn Haven, Fla.; daughter of Raymond King Cummings (a writer, known professionally as Ray Cummings) and Gabrielle (Wilson) Cummings; married Russell Gibson Hill (a chemical engineer), May 28, 1949; children: Andrea van Waldron, Bradford Wray. *Education:* Attended Finch Junior College, New York, N.Y.; currently attending Columbia University. *Religion:* Episcopalian. *Residence:* Bronxville, N.Y. *Agent:* Brandt & Brandt, 101 Park Ave., New York, N.Y. 10017.

CAREER: Free-lance writer since early years; actress in radio and summer stock productions.

WRITINGS: The Wonderful Visit to Miss Liberty, Holt, 1961; *The Window Tulip*, Warne, 1964; *Evan's Corner*, Holt, 1967; *Master Mike and the Miracle Maid*, Holt, 1967; *Pardon My Fangs*, Holt, 1969; *Bells: A Book to Begin On*, Holt, 1970. Contributor of stories and articles to *New Yorker, Reader's Digest, Harper's Bazaar, Seventeen, Woman's Day, Woman's Home Companion, Collier's, New World Writing, Faith Today*, and other magazines in America, Britain, and France.

WORK IN PROGRESS: Expanding her journal of several weeks spent in Red China in the spring of 1974.

AVOCATIONAL INTERESTS: Acting, painting, and Oriental studies.

* * *

HILL, L(eroy) Draper (Jr.) 1935-

PERSONAL: Born July 1, 1935, in Boston, Mass.; son of Leroy Draper (an investment banker) and Jean (Thompson) Hill; married Sarah Adams, April 22, 1967; children: Jennifer. *Education:* Harvard University, B.A. (magna cum laude), 1957; University College, University of London, graduate study, 1960-63. *Home:* 261 West Chickasaw Pkwy., Memphis, Tenn. 38111. *Office: The Commercial Appeal*, 495 Union Ave., Memphis, Tenn. 38101.

CAREER: Quincy Patriot Ledger, Quincy, Mass., reporter and cartoonist, 1957-60, 1963-64; *Worcester Telegram* and *Evening Gazette*, Worcester, Mass., editorial cartoonist, 1964-71; *The Commercial Appeal*, Memphis, Tenn., editorial cartoonist, 1971—. One-man shows at Originals Only, 1973, Brooks Memorial Art Gallery, 1975. *Member:* Association of American Editorial Cartoonists (first vice-president, 1974-75), Club of Odd Volumes (Boston), Signet Society (Harvard). *Awards, honors:* Fulbright scholar in England, 1960-62.

WRITINGS: The Crane Library, trustees of Thomas Crane Public Library (Quincy, Mass.), 1962; *Cartoon and Caricature from Hogarth to Hoffnung*, Arts Council of Great Britain, 1962; *Mr. Gillray: The Caricaturist*, Phaidon, 1965; (editor) *Fashionable Contrasts: 100 Caricatures by James Gillray*, Phaidon, 1966; *Illingworth On Target*, Boston Public Library, 1970; (with James Roper) *The Decline and Fall of the Gibbon*, Inadvertent Press, 1974; (author of introduction) *I Feel I Should Warn You*, Preservation Press, 1975.

WORK IN PROGRESS: A Gillray Gallery, tentative title, 100 plates with introduction and commentaries, publication by Dover expected in 1976.

HILL, Samuel E(rvin) 1913-

PERSONAL: Born August 23, 1913, in New Rochelle, N.Y.; son of Ernest W. (a business executive) and Gertrude (Ervin) Hill; married Edith Nary Foster, July, 1939; married Betty Bell, November 28, 1953; children: (first marriage) Susanna (Mrs. James Shanahan), Stephen; (second marriage) William, Robert. *Education:* Ohio Wesleyan University, A.B., 1935; Harvard University, M.A., 1938, Ph.D., 1940. *Home:* R.D. 1, West Redding, Conn.

CAREER: Economist for American Federation of Labor, 1940-41, for U.S. Government, 1941-53; Princeton University, Princeton, N.J., research associate in industrial relations, 1956-59, 1961-64; self-employed labor arbitrator, 1964—. Redding Conservation Commission, chairman, 1964—. *Member:* American Economic Association, Industrial Relations Research Association, Phi Beta Kappa, Sigma Alpha Epsilon.

WRITINGS: Teamsters and Transportation, American Council on Public Affairs, 1942; (with Frederick Harbison) *Manpower and Innovation in American Industry*, Industrial Relations Section, Princeton University, 1959; (with Paul H. Norgren) *Toward Fair Employment*, Columbia University Press, 1964.

WORK IN PROGRESS: Occupational Status of Negroes.

* * *

HILLSON, Maurie 1925-

PERSONAL: Born September 20, 1925, in Stoneham, Mass.; son of David (a manufacturer) and Bessie (Levine) Hillson; married Lillian Esther Rossyn, June 5, 1947; children: Jonathan Havis, Edward Alpert. *Education:* Syracuse University, A.B., 1949; Boston University, Ed.M., 1952; Harvard University, Certificate of Advanced Study, 1956, Ed.D., 1958. *Home:* 1208 Emerson Ave., Teaneck, N.J. 07666.

CAREER: Elementary teacher in Malden, Mass., 1951-52, West Hartford, Conn., 1952-55; State University of New York at Cortland, assistant professor of education, then associate professor, 1956-59; Bucknell University, Lewisburg, Pa., associate professor of education, 1959-63; Fairleigh Dickinson University, Teaneck, N.J., professor of education and project director, School and University Relationship for Educational Development (SURED), beginning, 1963, acting dean of College of Education and executive director of SURED, beginning, 1964; Rutgers University, New Brunswick, N.J., currently professor of education. Member of Panel on Educational Research and Development, reporting to U.S. Commissioner of Education, director of National Science Foundation, and special assistant to the President for science and technology. Consultant to Office of Economic Opportunity, Kilmer Job Corps Center, and more than twenty school systems. *Military service:* U.S. Army, Infantry, 1943-45; held prisoner of war in Germany; received Purple Heart and three battle stars.

MEMBER: National Society for the Study of Education, Association for Student Teaching, Association for Supervision and Curriculum Development, Association for Higher Education, American Association of University Professors, National Education Association, International Reading Association, Rho Delta Phi, Kappa Delta Pi. *Awards, honors:* Zucker Memorial Award, Fairleigh Dickinson University.

WRITINGS: A Reading Levels Accomplishment Program

for *Shamokin, Pennsylvania*, Shamokin Public Schools, 1961; (with Joseph Del Popolo) *Teaching in the Elementary Schools: The Unit Concept* (monograph), 1963; *Change and Innovation in Elementary School Organization*, Holt, 1965, 2nd edition, with Ronald T. Hyman, 1971; (contributor) *New Frontiers in Education*, Grune, 1965; (contributor) *Nongraded Schools in Action: Bold New Venture*, Indiana University Press, 1965; *Readings in Collaborative and Team Approaches to Teaching and Learning*, Selected Academic Reading, Inc., 1965; *Elementary Education: Current Issues and Research*, Free Press, 1967; (with Frank Cordasco and Francis P. Purcell) *Education and the Urban Community: Schools and the Crisis of the Cities*, American Book Co., 1969; (author of introduction, with Cordasco) Elmer Ellsworth Brown, *The Making of our Middle Schools*, Littlefield, 1970; (with Cordasco and Henry A. Bullock) *The School in the Social Order: A Sociological Introduction to Educational Understanding*, International Textbook Co., 1970; (with Joseph Bongo) *Continuous Progress Education: A Practical Approach*, Science Research Associates, 1971.

Writer of pamphlets and bulletins on education; contributor of reviews and articles to professional journals.

* * *

HIMMELHEBER, Diana Martin 1938-

PERSONAL: Born January 25, 1938, in St. Louis, Mo.; daughter of Chesley Brooks (a salesman) and Marcella Agnes (Naumann) Martin; married Melvin Earl Himmelheber (a minister of Christian education), August 24, 1961; children: Karen Dineen. *Education:* Culver-Stockton College, B.A., 1960; Lexington Theological Seminary, M.R.E., 1963. *Home:* 2055 Center Ave., Alliance, Ohio 44601.

CAREER: Director of Christian education or youth work at Christian Churches (Disciples of Christ) in Canton, Mo., 1960, Covington, Ky., 1961-62, and Danville, Ky., 1963. *Member:* United Church Women, Christian Women's Fellowship (worship chairman, 1966-67), American Association of University Women, Young Women's Christian Association, Chi Omega.

WRITINGS: On Paths Unknown (novel for teen-agers), Bethany, 1964.†

* * *

HINDUS, Milton Henry 1916-

PERSONAL: Born August 26, 1916, in New York, N.Y.; son of Meyer (a manufacturer) and Minnie (Slutsky) Hindus; married Eva Tenenbaum (a librarian), August 30, 1942; children: Myra Gladys. *Education:* City College (now City College of the City University of New York), B.A., 1936, M.S., 1938; graduate study at Columbia University, 1938-39, University of Chicago, 1947-48. *Religion:* Jewish. *Home:* 24 Stiles Ter., Newton Centre, Mass. 02159.

CAREER: Lecturer in English at Hunter College, New York, N.Y., 1943-46, and New School for Social Research, New York, N.Y., 1944-46; University of Chicago, Chicago, Ill., assistant professor of humanities, 1946-48; Brandeis University, Waltham, Mass., associate professor, 1948-62, professor, 1962—, Wolkenstein Professor of English, 1964—. *Member:* Modern Language Association of America, College English Association, American Association of University Professors, Boston Jewish Historical

Society (member of board of trustees). *Awards, honors:* Walt Whitman Prize of Poetry Society of America for *Leaves of Grass: One Hundred Years After*, 1959.

WRITINGS: The Crippled Giant, Boar's Head Books, 1950; *The Proustian Vision*, Columbia University Press, 1954; (editor) *"Leaves of Grass": One Hundred Years After*, Stanford University Press, 1955; *A Reader's Guide to Marcel Proust*, Farrar, Straus, 1962; *F. Scott Fitzgerald: An Introduction and Interpretation*, Holt, 1967; *The Old East Side*, Jewish Publication, 1969; *Walt Whitman: The Critical Heritage*, Barnes & Noble, 1971; *A World At Twilight*, Macmillan, 1971; (author of introduction) Maurice Hindus, *A Traveller in Two Worlds*, Doubleday, 1971. Contributor of articles and reviews to *New York Times Book Review, Atlantic Monthly, New Leader, Virginia Quarterly Review, Kenyon Review*, and other periodicals. U.S. editor, *Encyclopaedia Judaica*, 1971; member of board of publications, Jewish Publication.

AVOCATIONAL INTERESTS: Chess.

* * *

HINSLEY, F(rancis) H(arry) 1918-

PERSONAL: Born November 26, 1918, in Walsall, Staffordshire, England; son of Thomas Henry (a waggoner) and Emma (Adey) Hinsley; married Hilary Brett-Smith, April 6, 1946; children: Charles, Hugh, Clarissa. *Education:* Attended St. John's College, Cambridge, 1937-39, M.A., 1946. *Home:* St. John's College, Cambridge University, Cambridge, England.

CAREER: British Foreign Office, war service, 1939-46; Cambridge University, Cambridge, England, fellow of St. John's College, 1944—, lecturer in history, 1949-65, reader in history of international relations, 1965-69, professor of history of international relations, 1969—. *Awards, honors:* Order of the British Empire, 1946, for war service in the British Foreign Office.

WRITINGS: Command of the Sea, Christophers (London), 1950; *Hitler's Strategy*, Cambridge University Press, 1951; (with Geoffrey Callender) *The Naval Side of British History*, Christophers, 1952; (editor) *The New Cambridge Modern History*, Volume XI, Cambridge University Press, 1962; *Power and the Pursuit of Peace*, Cambridge University Press, 1963; *Sovereignty*, C. A. Watts, 1966; *Nationalism and the International System*, Hodder & Stoughton, 1973. Editor, *Historical Journal*, 1960-72.

WORK IN PROGRESS: History of the international system and international law, and of British foreign policy; a history of Europe, 1878-1919, for Collins.

* * *

HINTON, Harold C(lendenin) 1924-

PERSONAL: Born October 26, 1924, in Neuilly-sur-Seine, France; son of Harold Boaz (a journalist) and Eva (Robertson) Hinton; married Virginia Stodder, December 28, 1946; children: Mary Page, John Robertson. *Education:* Harvard University, A.B. (cum laude), 1946, M.A., 1948, Ph.D., 1951. *Home:* 3401 Newark St., N.W., Washington, D.C. 20016. *Office:* Institute for Sino-Soviet Studies, George Washington University, Washington, D.C. 20006.

CAREER: Georgetown University, Washington, D.C., assistant professor of history, 1950-57; U.S. Department of State, Foreign Service Institute, Washington, D.C., training officer, 1957-60; Trinity College, Washington, D.C., associate professor of history, 1960-64; George

Washington University, Washington, D.C., associate professor of international affairs, 1964-67, professor of international affairs, 1967—. Columbia University, visiting lecturer in public law and government, 1960-61; Institute for Defense Analyses, senior staff member, 1960—. *Military service:* U.S. Army, Field Artillery, 1943-46; became first lieutenant; received Army Commendation Ribbon. *Member:* American Political Science Association, American Historical Association, Association for Asian Studies, Institute for Strategic Studies, American Association of University Professors, Phi Beta Kappa. *Awards, honors:* Fulbright senior research scholar in England, 1952-53.

WRITINGS: Leaders of Red China, RAND Corp., 1956; *China's Relations with Burma and Vietnam*, Institute of Pacific Relations, 1958; (contributor) *Major Governments of Asia*, edited by George M. Kahin, Cornell University Press, 1958, revised edition, 1963; *Communist China in World Politics*, Houghton, 1966; *China's Turbulent Quest*, Macmillan, 1970; *An Introduction to Chinese Politics*, Praeger, 1973.

WORK IN PROGRESS: Politics, and foreign and military policies of Communist China.

SIDELIGHTS: Hinton has reading knowledge of French, German, and Chinese. *Avocational interests:* Music, the outdoors, travel.

* * *

HIRSCH, Lester M. 1925-

PERSONAL: Born July 5, 1925, in New York, N.Y.; son of Max and Bella (Brill) Hirsch; married Miriam Freeman (now a college professor), June 19, 1949; children: George Robert, Diane Elizabeth. *Education:* City College, New York, N.Y., B.S., 1948; New York University, M.A., 1949, Ph.D., 1953. *Politics:* Democrat. *Religion:* Jewish. *Home:* 281 Newton Rd., Springfield, Mass. 01118. *Office:* Western New England College, 1215 Wilbraham Rd., Springfield, Mass. 01118.

CAREER: Assistant professor of English at Auburn University, Auburn, Ala., 1953-55, American International College, Springfield, Mass., 1955-59; Western New England College, Springfield, Mass., professor of English, 1959—, former chairman of department. *Military service:* U.S. Army, 1944-46. *Member:* Modern Language Association of America, College English Association, American Association of University Professors.

WRITINGS: (With others) *Modern Business Communications*, Pitman, 1963; (editor) *Man and Space*, Pitman, 1966; *All Those Voices*, Macmillan, 1971.

WORK IN PROGRESS: Articles on New England figures.

AVOCATIONAL INTERESTS: Fishing and reading.

* * *

HIRSCH, Werner Z. 1920-

PERSONAL: Born June 10, 1920, in Linz, Germany; naturalized U.S. citizen; son of Waldemar and Toni (Morgenstern) Hirsch; married Hilde E. Zwirn (associate research neurologist), 1945; children: Dan, Joel, Ilona. *Education:* University of California, Berkeley, B.S., 1947, Ph.D., 1949. *Religion:* Jewish. *Home:* 11601 Bellagio Rd., Los Angeles, Calif. 90024. *Office:* Department of Economics, University of California, Los Angeles, Calif. 90024.

CAREER: University of California, Berkeley, instructor in economics, 1949-51; United Nations, Fiscal Division, New York, N.Y., economic affairs officer, 1951-52; Brookings Institution, Washington, D.C., economist, 1952-53; Washington University, St. Louis, Mo., assistant professor, 1953-55, associate professor, 1956-58, professor of economics, 1959-63, director of Institute of Urban and Regional Studies, 1961-63; University of California, Los Angeles, professor of economics and director of Institute of Government and Public Affairs, 1963—. Assistant research director and chief economist, Ford Foundation-sponsored St. Louis Metropolitan Survey, 1956-57. Consultant to RAND Corp., 1958—, Joint Economics Committee of Congress, 1959, Internal Revenue Service, 1960-62, National Science Foundation, 1961-63, National Aeronautics and Space Administration, 1961-66, Bureau of the Budget, 1965—, U.S. Senate Committee on Public Works and California Select Senate Committee on Education, 1973—. Trustee of Midwest Research Institute, 1966—; member of board, Grunwald Center for Graphic Arts and California Council for Environmental and Economic Balance, 1973—.

MEMBER: American Economic Association, American Statistical Association (former vice-president), Regional Science Association, Midwest Economic Association (vice-president), American Farm Economic Association, Western Economic Association, Phi Beta Kappa, Sigma Xi.

WRITINGS: Introduction to Modern Statistics, Macmillan, 1957; (with others) *Exploring the Metropolitan Community*, University of California Press, 1961; (editor and contributor) *Urban Life and Form*, Holt, 1963; (with Elbert Segelhorst) *Spillover of Public Education Costs and Benefits*, Institute of Government and Public Affairs, University of California, 1964; (editor) *Elements of Regional Accounts*, Resources for the Future, 1964; *Regional Accounts for Public Decisions*, Resources for the Future, 1966; *Inventing Education for the Future*, Chandler, 1967; *The Economics of State and Local Government*, McGraw, 1970; (with Sidney Sonenblum) *Selecting Regional Information for Government Planning and Decision Making*, Praeger, 1971; *Fiscal Pressures on the Central City*, Praeger, 1971; *Program Budgeting for Primary and Secondary Public Education*, Institute of Government and Public Affairs, University of California, 1972; (editor with Sonenblum) *Governing Urban America in the 1970's*, Praeger, 1973; *Urban Economic Analysis*, McGraw, 1973.

* * *

HOBSON, Laura Z(ametkin) 1900-

PERSONAL: Born 1900, in New York, N.Y.; daughter of Michael (an editor; labor organizer) and Adella (Kean) Zametkin; married Thayer Hobson, July 23, 1930 (divorced, 1935); children: (adopted) Michael, Christopher. *Education:* Cornell University, A.B. *Religion:* "My ancestors were Jews; I am an agnostic as were my parents." *Agent:* International Famous Agency, 1301 Avenue of the Americas, New York, N.Y. 10019.

CAREER: Advertising copywriter until 1934; spent one year with *New York Evening Post* as reporter; *Time, Life*, and *Fortune* magazines, New York, N.Y., promotion writer, 1934-40, becoming promotion director of *Time* magazine. Consultant, *Time, Fortune*, and *Sports Illustrated*, 1956-62; editorial consultant, *Saturday Review*, 1960—. *Member:* Authors League of America (council member, 1970-73), P.E.N., Americans for Democratic Action, American Civil Liberties Union, Regency Whist.

WRITINGS: A Dog of His Own (juvenile), Viking, 1941; The Trespassers, Simon & Schuster, 1943; Gentleman's Agreement, Simon & Schuster, 1947; The Other Father, Simon & Schuster, 1950; The Celebrity, Simon & Schuster, 1951; First Papers (Literary Guild selection), Random, 1964; I'm Going to Have a Baby (juvenile), Day, 1967; The Tenth Month, Simon & Schuster, 1971. Columnist for International News Service, "Assignment America", 1953-54, Good Housekeeping (book page), 1953-56, Saturday Review, "Trade Winds", summers, 1952, 1953, 1956. Contributor of short stories, novelettes, and articles to national magazines.

WORK IN PROGRESS: A novel for Doubleday.

SIDELIGHTS: Mrs. Hobson is best known for her novel, Gentleman's Agreement, which dealt with anti-Semitism. Written at a time when this bigotry was widespread, the author had been warned by friends that a study of this nature would not be well received by the American public. The novel sold more than 2,000,000 copies in the United States and was translated into a dozen foreign languages. In the novel, an American journalist is assigned to write a series of articles on anti-Semitism in the United States. In order to gather material, he poses as a Jew and therein lies the plot. The chief characters are mainly those liberals who think they are free of prejudice while helping it along in subtle ways. Mrs. Hobson commented: "I had in mind decent people, who, never having probed their own prejudices, profess disgust for anti-Semitism, castigate the Bilbos and the Rankins, but let it go at that." The critics were solidly behind the message of the book, but disagreed when discussing its literary merits. "Unfortunately the story is not as good as the sermon," wrote E. R. Embree. "The English is tense, stylized, overwritten. Every situation is overcharged.... In spite of stilted writing, the sharpness of the hurt of anti-Semitism stands out and remains." Rex Stout, however, thought that the message was overshadowing the fact that it was a good job of story telling. "Mrs. Hobson had to choose her characters by types—that is inevitable in a propaganda novel—but, having picked them, she put something much more human than synthetic sawdust inside their skins and pumped real blood." The book was filmed by 20th Century-Fox and received the New York Film Critics Award and the Academy Award for best motion picture of 1947.

First Papers is concerned with a Russian immigrant who becomes completely immersed in his Americanism. When he receives his "first Papers" (naturalization papers), he feels that "a lifetime might go toward validating those papers and being worthy of them." The book has been labeled a slow-starter that only quickens its pace in the second half. "[It] is rich in details that evoke the early years of this century," wrote Felicia Lamport, "but the movement of the story is hobbled by a kind of pleated technique that consists of describing an episode from one point of view and then doubling back to recapitulate it from another. The pace is slowed further by taking the reader into the thoughts of each character in turn, and by the almost flat-footed simplicity of a style in which every detail is spelled out, every nuance explored, explained, and occasionally even reiterated. This is a pity because so much of the material speaks beautifully for itself." Life said, "Her most autobiographical and therefore best novel.... Stefan Ivarin is the storm center of the brightest and warmest family to appear in a book in years."

BIOGRAPHICAL/CRITICAL SOURCES: Chicago Sun Book Week, March 2, 1947; New York Herald Tribune Book Week, March 9, 1947, November 8, 1964; Time, May 29, 1950, November 9, 1953; Life, wnovember 27, 1964; Saturday Review, February 27, 1965.

*   *   *

HOCHWALD, Werner   1910-

PERSONAL: Born January 21, 1910, in Berlin, Germany; son of Moritz and Elsa (Stahl) Hochwald; married Hilde Landenberger, January 28, 1938 (died June, 1958); children: Miriam Ruth, Eve Fay. Education: University of Berlin, LL.B., 1932; Washington University, St. Louis, Mo., B.S., B.A., 1940, A.M., 1942, Ph.D., 1944. Home: 6910 Cornell, St. Louis, Mo. 63130. Office: Washington University, St. Louis, Mo. 63130.

CAREER: Committee on Aid and Reconstruction, counsel, 1933-38; Washington University, St. Louis, Mo., instructor, 1945-47, assistant professor, 1947-49, associate professor, 1949-50, professor of economics, 1950—, chairman of department, 1950-63. Federal Reserve Bank of St. Louis, consultant, 1947-58; National Planning Association, project director, 1955-58; National Academy of Sciences, member of research board, 1961-64. Member: International Association for Research in Income and Wealth, National Conference on Research in Income and Wealth, American Statistical Association (council, 1952-54), Economic History Association, Econometric Society, Southern Economic Association (president, 1966), Regional Science Association, Midwest Economics Association (vice-president, 1951), Phi Beta Kappa.

WRITINGS: (Contributor) Twentieth Century Economic Thought, Philosophical Library, 1950; (contributor) Regional Income, Princeton University Press, 1957; (co-author) Local Impact of Foreign Trade, National Planning Association, 1960; (editor) Design of Regional Accounts, Johns Hopkins Press, 1961; (contributor) Essays in Southern Economic Development, University of North Carolina Press, 1964. Also author of An Economist's Image of History, 1968, and The Idea of Progress, 1973. Contributor of articles and book reviews to economic and statistical journals. Member of publications committee, Washington University, 1950-55, 1960-65.

*   *   *

HOCKETT, Charles F(rancis)   1916-

PERSONAL: Born January 17, 1916, in Columbus, Ohio; son of Homer Carey (a professor) and Amy (Francisco) Hockett; married Shirley Orlinoff (a professor), April 25, 1942; children: Alpha (daughter), Asher Orlinoff (son), Amy Roberta, Rachel, Carey Beth. Education: Ohio State University, B.A. and M.A., 1936; Yale University, Ph.D., 1939; post-doctoral study at University of Chicago and University of Michigan. Religion: "Lapsed Unitarian." Home: 145 North Sunset Dr., Ithaca, N.Y. 14850. Office: Department of Anthropology, McGraw Hall, Cornell University, Ithaca, N.Y. 14850.

CAREER: Cornell University, Ithaca, N.Y., assistant professor of linguistics, 1946-49, associate professor, 1949-53, professor of linguistics, 1953-57, professor of linguistics and anthropology, 1957-70, Goldwin Smith Professor, 1970—. Center for Advanced Study in the Behavioral Sciences, fellow, 1955-56; University of Hawaii, visiting professor, 1960-61; visiting summer professor at Indiana University, 1952, University of Chicago, 1955, Canadian Summer School of Linguistics, 1960, University of Michigan, 1967. Consultant to RAND Corp., 1961—. Military service: U.S.

Army, 1942-46; became captain; received Army Commendation Medal. *Member:* American Academy of Arts and Sciences, National Academy of Science, Linguistic Society of America (president, 1964), American Anthropological Association (fellow), American Association for the Advancement of Science (fellow).

WRITINGS: A Manual of Phonology, Indiana University Press, 1955; *A Course in Modern Linguistics*, Macmillan, 1958; (with R. E. Pittenger and J. J. Danehy) *The First Five Minutes*, Martineau, 1960; *The State of Art*, Mouton, 1968; *Man's Place in Nature*, McGraw, 1973. Composer of opera, "Dona Rosita," first produced in Ithaca, N.Y., April, 1973. Contributor of articles and reviews to *Language, Current Anthropology, American Scientist*, and other journals.

WORK IN PROGRESS: Fijian Grammar.

AVOCATIONAL INTERESTS: Musical composition.

* * *

HODGES, Harold Mellor 1922-

PERSONAL: Born April 9, 1922, in Beverly Hills, Calif.; son of Harold M. and Grace Inez (Smith) Hodges; married Betty Cassidy, August 21, 1954; children: Scott Cameron, Kenneth Eliot. *Education:* Stanford University, student, 1940-43; University of Southern California, B.A., 1947, M.A., 1952, Ph.D., 1954. *Home:* 19875 Park Dr., Saratoga, Calif.

CAREER: Wisconsin State University, River Falls, assistant professor of sociology, 1955-57; San Jose State University, San Jose, Calif., 1957—, became professor. Visiting professor, University of California, Santa Barbara, 1960, Yale University, 1969-70. *Military service:* U.S. Army, 1942-46. *Member:* American Sociological Association (fellow), Society for the Study of Social Problems, Pacific Sociological Association.

WRITINGS: Peninsula People, Spartan Books, 1960; (editor with W. W. Kallenbach) *Education and Society*, C. E. Merrill, 1963; *Social Stratification: Class in America*, Schenkman, 1964, new edition, 1971; *Conflict and Consensus: An Introduction to Sociology*, Harper, 1971, 2nd revised edition, 1974; *Conflict and Consensus: Readings Toward a Sociological Perspective*, Harper, 1973; *Search for Self: The Sociology of Consciousness*, Spartan Books, 1974; *Underdogs, Middle Americans, and Elites*, General Learning Press, 1975. Contributor of articles, reviews, and a few poems to periodicals.

WORK IN PROGRESS: The New Consciousness, with Frieda Porat, 1975.

* * *

HOFF, Marilyn 1942-

PERSONAL: Born March 3, 1942, in Iowa Falls, Iowa; daughter of Jean C. (a salesman) and Gayle E. (Howe) Hoff. *Education:* Macalester College, B.A. (summa cum laude), 1964; Syracuse University, M.A., 1968. *Politics:* Radical Feminist. *Residence:* Portland, Oregon.

CAREER: Full time professional writer, 1964-70; songwriter, singer; Portland State University, Portland, Ore., lecturer in English, 1973-74. *Awards, honors:* McKnight Award in Humanities, 1964; *Saturday Review* list of best books, 1969, for *Rose*; Yaddo residency grants, 1967, 1968, and 1969; Helen Wurlitzer Foundation residency grants, 1967, 1969, and 1970-71.

WRITINGS: Dink's Blues (novel), Harcourt, 1966.

SIDELIGHTS: Of *Dink's Blues*, Maggie Rennert wrote: "[Marilyn Hoff] has . . . the witchcraft of talent, and she took me over completely. . . . Without realizing it was happening to me, I lost my anthropological distance and began to care. And I wasn't laughing, though I don't know why: Miss Hoff's twists of event, her elaborate plaiting of reality and sham, of lies and lies about lies, ought to have been laughable. . . . Surely there is no such young woman in all the wide world as Dink—is there? But I believe. And so will you." Daniel Stern summarized: "Now that her 'student' phase is over, Miss Hoff is, I would guess, going to produce some excellent work. In the meantime, she has written a book of some callowness and some originality."

BIOGRAPHICAL/CRITICAL SOURCES: Book Week, February 20, 1966; *Saturday Review*, February 26, 1966.

* * *

HOGAN, John Charles 1919-

PERSONAL: Born November 13, 1919, in Pilot Point, Tex.; son of W. C. and Ethel (Taylor) Hogan; married Nancy S., October 27, 1951; children: Cynthia Ann. *Education:* University of California, Los Angeles, A.B., 1942, M.A., 1948, Standard Teaching Credential, 1965, Ph.D., 1972. *Home:* 840 Twelfth St., Santa Monica, Calif. 90403. *Agent:* Ms. Ilse Lahn, Paul Kohner Agency, 9169 Sunset Blvd., Hollywood, Calif. 90069. *Office:* The RAND Corp., 1700 Main St., Santa Monica, Calif. 90406.

CAREER: The RAND Corp., Santa Monica, Calif., legal administrator, 1950—. Visiting professor, California Lutheran College, 1972-74; professor, Woodbury University, 1973—; lecturer, University of California, Los Angeles, 1974. *Military service:* U.S. Army, 1942-43. *Member:* American Society for Legal History (board, 1959-62; vice-president, Pacific Coast branch, 1964; president, 1966), American Association of University Professors, Societe d'Histoire du Droit (France); Royal Institute of Philosophy, Seldon Society, Classical Association, and Sherlock Holmes Society (all England); Stair Society (Scotland), Scribes (honorary), Baker Street Irregulars, Civil War Round Table of Southern California (board, 1956-57; vice-president, 1955-56), Phi Delta Phi, Pi Sigma Alpha, Sigma Alpha Epsilon, Phi Delta Kappa.

WRITINGS: The Wills of the Justices, Oceana, 1956; (with Mortimer Schwartz) *Joseph Story*, Oceana, 1959; (with Saul Cohen) *An Author's Guide to Scholarly Publishing and Law*, Prentice-Hall, 1965; *Programmed Statistics*, Holt, 1970; *The Courts, the Schools, and the Public Interest*, Heath, 1974.

Contributor to *Encyclopaedia Britannica*; writer of pamphlets for RAND Corp.; contributor of some fifty articles to *Air Force and Space Digest, Baker Street Journal*, and legal and political science journals. Author of Sherlock Holmes stories for the *Hong Kong Standard* (newspaper), 1969.

WORK IN PROGRESS: The Supreme Court and Business and *The Legal Bases of Education in the United States,* completion of both expected in 1976; contributing to *Directory of Eminent American Educators.*

SIDELIGHTS: Hogan has "Dictionary reading competence" in Latin, Greek, French, German, Spanish, and Russian. He discovered the original records of the U.S. Supreme Court in the basement of the Court Building in Washington, 1954 and has contributed to the revival of interest in Supreme Court Justice Joseph Story by publication of his previously unidentified articles.

HOLCK, Manfred, Jr. 1930-

PERSONAL: Born November 24, 1930, in Austin, Tex.; son of Manfred (a certified public accountant) and Bertha (Bohn) Holck; married Lois Albers, April 15, 1951; children: Susan Elaine, Carol Beth, Timothy Manfred, Peter Scott. *Education:* University of Texas, B.B.A., 1952, law student, 1952-53; Hamma School of Theology, B.D., 1956; Austin Presbyterian Seminary, Th.M., 1960. *Home:* 47 Hampton Dr. East, Seguin, Texas 78155. *Office:* Texas Lutheran College, Seguin, Texas 78155.

CAREER: Certified public accountant, state of Texas, 1955, and state of Ohio, 1965; ordained minister of Lutheran Church in America, 1956. Pastor in Houston, Texas., 1956-64, and Fayette County, Tex., 1964-65; Wittenberg University, Springfield, Ohio, assistant to the president, 1965-67, business manager, 1967-70, vice-president for business affairs; free-lance author, 1972-74; Texas Lutheran College, Seguin, assistant professor of business administration, 1974—.

WRITINGS: Accounting Methods for the Small Church, Augsburg, 1961; *Money Management for Ministers*, Augsburg, 1966; *Making It on a Pastor's Pay*, Abington, 1974; *Money and Your Church*, Keats, 1974; *How to Pay Your Pastor*, Religious Publishing Co., 1975; *Handbook on Church Accounting*, Prentice-Hall, 1976. Contributor to *Your Church, Church Management, The Lutheran, Organic Gardening, Horticulture, Christian Ministry*. Editor, *Church and Clergy Finance*.

*   *   *

HOLLAND, Cecelia (Anastasia) 1943-

PERSONAL: Born December 31, 1943, in Henderson, Nev.; daughter of William Dean (an executive) and Katharine (Schenck) Holland. *Education:* Pennsylvania State University, student, 1961-62; Connecticut College, B.A., 1965. *Politics:* Anarchist. *Religion:* Atheist. *Residence:* Pasadena, Calif.

CAREER: Writer.

WRITINGS—Adult historical novels: *The Firedrake*, Atheneum, 1966; *RaKossy*, Atheneum, 1967; *The Kings in Winter*, Atheneum, 1968; *Until the Sun Falls*, Atheneum, 1969; *Antichrist*, Atheneum, 1970; *The Earl*, Knopf, 1971; *The Death of Attila*, Knopf, 1973; *Great Maria*, Knopf, 1974.

Juveniles: *Ghost on the Steppe*, Atheneum, 1970; *The King's Road*, Atheneum, 1971.

WORK IN PROGRESS: Research into the Reign of King William Rufus; research into the reigns of Pharaoh Akhenaton and Pharoah Tutankhamen of the New Kingdom of Egypt (XVIII dynasty).

SIDELIGHTS: Cecelia Holland's historical novels have met wide critical acclaim. Richard Freedman said, reviewing *Until the Sun Falls*: "Her industry and breadth of historical research are staggering. She is also a serious and austere writer, leagues above the average purveyor of Hollywood historicism. In all the vast length of *Until the Sun Falls* there is no grating anachronism of thought or speech. She is never guilty of the fatuity which plagues most historical fiction: she never nudges the reader into agreeing that folks way back then were really just like you and me, only they bathed less often." Interestingly in contrast, while having problems writing that same book, Cecelia Holland said: "Why? Because my book really isn't about Mongols at all. It's about this world, this century, my own people;

I'd unconsciously used another time and another name as an allegory—a framework within which I could isolate certain attitudes and discuss them. This book isn't a historical novel at all."

*   *   *

HOLLAND, Laurence B(edwell) 1920-

PERSONAL: Born October 21, 1920, in Lincoln, Neb.; son of Eugene (a business executive) and Louise (Bedwell) Holland; married Faith Mackey (now a researcher), September 2, 1950; children: Mary Sarah, Eugene William, Kate Louise. *Education:* Princeton University, B.A., 1942; Harvard University, M.A., 1950, Ph.D., 1965. *Politics:* Democrat. *Home:* 10 West Highfield Rd., Baltimore, Md. 21218. *Office:* Department of English, Johns Hopkins University, Baltimore, Md. 21218.

CAREER: Princeton University, Princeton, N.J., instructor, 1950-56, lecturer, 1956-58, assistant professor, 1958-63, lecturer, 1963-66, associate professor of English, 1966—, chairman of Program in American Civilization, 1963-70; Johns Hopkins University, Baltimore, Md., professor of English, 1970—. Visiting professor, Haverford College, 1962-63; faculty member, Bread Loaf School of English, 1966—; visiting professor, Yale University, 1968; senior research fellow, Institute of United States Studies, University of London, 1969-70; Princeton Township Board of Education, member, 1965—. *Member:* English Institute (supervising committee, 1965-67). *Military service:* U.S. Army Air Forces, 1942-46; became captain.

WRITINGS: The Expense of Vision: Essays on the Craft of Henry James, Princeton University Press, 1964; (with A. Walton Litz and Nathaniel Burt) *The Literary History of New Jersey*, Van Nostrand, 1965; (editor) *Who Designs America?*, Anchor Books, 1966; (with James M. McPherson and others) *Blacks in America: Bibliographical Essays*, Doubleday, 1971.

*   *   *

HOLLAND, Norman N(orwood) 1927-

PERSONAL: Born September 19, 1927, in New York, N.Y.; son of Norman Norwood (a lawyer) and Harriette (Breder) Holland; married Jane Kelley (an editor), December 17, 1954; children: Katherine, John. *Education:* Massachusetts Institute of Technology, B.S., 1947; Harvard University, LL.B., 1950, Ph.D., 1956. *Politics:* Liberal-Left. *Home:* 131 High Park Blvd., Buffalo, N.Y. 14226. *Agent:* Sterling Lord Agency, 660 Madison Ave., New York, N.Y. 10021. *Office:* Department of English, State University of New York, Buffalo, N.Y. 14214.

CAREER: Massachusetts Institute of Technology, Cambridge, instructor, 1955-56, assistant professor, 1956-63, associate professor of English, 1963-66; State University of New York, Buffalo, professor of English, 1966—, chairman of department, 1966-68; director of Center for the Psychological Study of the Arts, 1970—. Visiting professor, Stanford University, summer, 1965, University of Paris, 1971-72; consultant to President's Commission on Obscenity and Pornography, Ted Bates Advertising Agency, and to publishers. *Member:* Modern Language Association of America (chairman of literature and psychology section, 1966-67), English Institute (supervising committee, 1962-65), Boston Psychoanalytic Society (affiliate), Group for Applied Psychoanalysis, Signet Society.

WRITINGS: The First Modern Comedies, Harvard University Press, 1959; *The Shakespearean Imagination*, Macmillan, 1964; *Psychoanalysis and Shakespeare*, McGraw, 1966; *The Dynamics of Literary Response*, Oxford University Press, 1968; *Poems in Persons*, Norton, 1973; *Five Readers Reading*, Yale University Press, 1975. Editor of editions of *Hamlet*, for Harcourt, and *Henry IV*, for Signet Books. Contributor to *PMLA*, *Atlantic Monthly*, *Show*, *Hudson Review*, *Nation*, *Literature and Psychology*, and *Comparative Literature*. Editor, *Journal of the Society of Cinematologists*, 1963; member of editorial board, *Literature and Psychology*, 1963, *Hartford Studies in Literature*, 1969—.

WORK IN PROGRESS: A study of the psychological bases for Shakespeare's ability to "please many and please long"; a textbook synthesizing contemporary psychoanalytic psychology.

SIDELIGHTS: Holland is competent in French, German, Italian. *Avocational interests:* Travel, photography, films, water.

* * *

HOLLISTER, Charles A(mmon) 1918-

PERSONAL: Born June 15, 1918; son of Grover Clarence (a restaurateur) and Clara Belle (Ammon) Hollister; married Mary Jane Marsteller (a biology researcher), May 31, 1947; children: Robdon Dean, Michaela Jean (Mrs. Stephen K. Johnson). *Education:* Nebraska State Teachers College, Chadron, B.A., 1940; University of Arizona, M.A., 1946; University of Pennsylvania, Ph.D., 1957. *Politics:* Democratic. *Religion:* Lutheran. *Home:* 2515 South 4th St., Charleston, Ill. 61920. *Office:* Eastern Illinois University, Charleston, Ill. 61920.

CAREER: Muhlenberg College, Allentown, Pa., instructor in history and political science, 1946-50; Bucknell University, Lewisburg, Pa., assistant professor, 1950-57, associate professor, 1957-66, professor of political science, 1966-67; Eastern Illinois University, Charleston, prelegal advisor and professor of public law, 1967—. Commonwealth of Pennsylvania, assistant director of Bureau of Municipal Affairs, Department of Internal Affairs, 1947-50, research associate, Department of Internal Affairs, 1959-67, chairman of Air Pollution Control Commission, 1960-63. Research director, A Modern Constitution for Pennsylvania (private organization), 1962-67; chairman of Union County Democratic Committee, 1965-67; Democratic candidate for Pennsylvania General Assembly, 1964, for state Senate, 1966. *Member:* American Political Science Association, American Economic Association, Pennsylvania Political Science and Public Administration Association, Sigma Tau Delta, Pi Sigma Alpha, Phi Alpha Theta, Lambda Chi Alpha.

WRITINGS: Pennsylvania's Bureau of Municipal Affairs, Commonwealth of Pennsylvania, 1960; *State Issues: Papers and Problems on Pennsylvania Government*, Pennsylvania State University Press, 1962; (reviser) *Adjusting Municipal Boundaries: The Law and Practice in 48 States*, American Municipal Association, 1963-64; *Toward A More Realistic Comprehension of Some Political Matters*, Bucknell University Press, 1965. Writer of three public law manuals; contributor to legal publications.

* * *

HOLLOWAY, Teresa (Bragunier) 1906-
(Elizabeth Beatty, Margaret Vail McLeod)

PERSONAL: Born January 17, 1906, in Apalachicola, Fla.; daughter of Ralph (an electrical engineer) and Mordina (a writer; maiden name, Floyd) Bragunier; married John C. Holloway. *Education:* Florida State College for Women, graduate, 1925. *Religion:* Roman Catholic. *Home:* 4349 Irvington Ave., Jacksonville, Fla. 32210. *Agent:* Scott Meredith, 580 Fifth Ave., New York, N.Y. 10036.

CAREER: Herring Ginger Ale Co., Jacksonville, Fla., owner, 1939-43; Chamber of Commerce, Apalachicola, Fla., manager, 1947-50; Florida Senate, Tallahassee, administrative assistant every biennium, 1947-67; author of novels for young adults. WFGA-TV, Jacksonville, staff correspondent. Taught creative writing at Florida Junior College, Jacksonville, 1966-67 and 1973-74, Jacksonville University, 1971-72. *Member:* National League of American Pen Women (past president, Jacksonville branch; Editor of southeast region, 1964-68), Authors League, Mystery Writers of America, Womens Club of Jacksonville. *Awards, honors:* Sears Foundation Award for outdoor writing; national award, National League of American Pen Women, for young adult novels, and twenty-eight Pen Women awards at state and local level; other awards from Puerto Rican government, 1933, Florida Junior College, 1966, Jacksonville University, 1972, and Florida Publishing Co., 1972.

WRITINGS—All published by Bouregy, except as indicated: *Heart's Haven*, 1955; *Rosemary King, Government Girl*, 1957; *Terry's Television Career*, 1957; *Lynn Daly, Newspaper Girl*, 1959; *Nurse Farley's Decision*, 1959; *Option to Love*, 1960; *Cry Nurse*, 1961; *Governor's Girl*, 1961; *Hoosier Doctor*, 1962; *Lady Lawyer*, 1964; *Katy's Inheritance*, 1965; *Highway to Romance*, 1966; *Girl in Studio B*, 1967; *River Nurse*, 1969; *Roses for Paula*, 1969; *Nurse on Dark Island*, Ace Books, 1969; *Nurse to Remember*, Ace Books, 1970; *Campaign for Pam*, 1970; *Nurse Transplanted*, Ace Books, 1971; *Nurse Paige's Triumph*, 1972; *Tomorrow's Nurse*, 1973; *Nurse for the Fishermen*, 1974; *Unwilling Witness*, 1974.

Under pseudonym Elizabeth Beatty—All published by Bouregy: *River in the Sun*, 1958; *Doorway to Romance*, 1959; *Jupiter Missile Mystery*, 1960; *Murder at Auction*, 1961; *Orchard House*, 1961; *Girl in Green*, 1962; also author of *Betty Pritchard, Train Hostess*, 1963.

Under pseudonym Margaret Vail McLeod—All published by Bouregy: *Captain June*, 1959; *Captain Janes' Island Rendezvous*, 1960; *River Rescue*, 1961; *The Loving Cup*, 1962; *Space Secretary*, 1963.

Scripted and filmed three television documentaries for WFGA-TV, Jacksonville, Fla. Contributor to *Alfred Hitchcock, Mystery Magazine*, *Saturday Evening Post*, *Ford Times*, *Progressive Farmer*, *Ave Maria*, and other periodicals and newspapers.

WORK IN PROGRESS: Nurse in Green, for Bouregy.

* * *

HOLM, (Else) Anne (Lise) 1922-

PERSONAL: Born September 10, 1922, in Aal, Jutland, Denmark; daughter of Viggo Marius and Elvira (Jensen) Rahbek; married Johan Christian Holm (a numismatist), June 27, 1949; children: Rudi Benedek. *Education:* "Went to school in the normal Danish way; do not know the American equivalent of my degree; ... we get it here at seventeen." *Politics:* "No secret about it—I am all for king and parliament, and against dictatorships. In this country I count as 'conservative'." *Religion:* Protestant. *Home:* Strandvejen 661, Klampenborg, Denmark.

CAREER: "After finishing school I started training as a journalist—but I have been married nearly all my life." Author. *Member:* Danish Authors' Society. *Awards, honors:* Scandinavian First prize for *David*, 1963.

WRITINGS: Dina fra Apotekergaarden, Jespersen & Pio, 1956; *Familien i Apotekergaarden*, Jespersen & Pio, 1958; *Komtessen fra Baekkeholm*, Jespersen & Pio, 1959; *David*, Gyldendal, 1963, published as *North to Freedom*, Harcourt, 1965; *Peter*, Gyldendal, 1965, Harcourt, 1968; *Adam og de voksne*, Gyldendal, 1967. Contributor to TV and young people's magazines.

SIDELIGHTS: Mrs. Holm told *CA:* "I wrote *David* because it seemed to me that children, who can love a book more passionately than any grown-up person, got such a lot of harmless entertainment, and not nearly enough of real, valuable literature."

"Have seen all countries of Western Europe, except Portugal and Finland. I speak a reasonably decent English, for a foreigner. My German is fairly awful. My Italian a little better, but certainly not much. And what I can do to the French language, our French friends shudder even to *think* about." *Avocational interests:* Traveling, theatre, cooking, books, antiquities, history, peace and quiet.

* * *

HOLM, Marilyn D. (Franzen) 1944-

PERSONAL: Born March 31, 1944 in Frederick, Okla.; daughter of Robert C. (a banker) and Ethel (Kallberg) Franzen; married Steven A. Holm, September 4, 1965. *Education:* Northern State College, Aberdeen, S.D., student, 1962-64; Augsburg College, B.A. (cum laude), 1966. *Religion:* Lutheran. *Office:* Department of English, Alexander Ramsey High School, 1261 West Highway 36, St. Paul, Minn.

CAREER: Alexander Ramsey High School, St. Paul, Minn., teacher of English, 1966—.

WRITINGS: Capital Capsules, Rushmore, 1963.†

* * *

HOLMVIK, Oyvind 1914-
(Oy-vik, Paprika, Sepia)

PERSONAL: Born February 17, 1914, in Eidsvoll, Norway; son of Ole Holt and Jonette (Langbakken) Holmvik; married Margot Walle, April 5, 1952; children: Geir, Unni, Stein. *Education:* Attended high school and Oslo Sprogskole (language school) in Norway. *Religion:* Protestant. *Home:* Fagertunveien 23, Bekkestua, Norway. *Office:* NBF, Bogstadvaegan 46, Oslo, Norway.

CAREER: Editor of monthly newspaper, *Bilbransjen/Bilteknisk Fagblad*, Oslo, Norway.

WRITINGS: Slik trener du, Nilsen, 1947; *Farlig Dykk*, Gyldendal, 1962 (English translation published as *Crack of Doom*, Harcourt, 1966); *Baten som sank*, Gyldendal, 1963 (English translation published as *Dive to Danger*, Harcourt, 1964).

SIDELIGHTS: Holmvik is competent in English, German, Swedish, and Danish. *Avocational interests:* Automobile testing and traveling.†

* * *

HOLSINGER, Jane Lumley

PERSONAL: Born in Woodstock, Ill.; daughter of Vincent S. (lawyer) and Neva (Bunker) Lumley; married Arthur Holsinger, March 31, 1945; children: Frances Marie. *Education:* Attended St. Mary's High School; writing courses at Indiana University and University of California. *Politics:* Independent. *Home:* Stone Hill, Wonder Lake, Ill. 60097. *Agent:* Scott Meredith, 580 Fifth Ave., New York, N.Y. 10036.

CAREER: Newspaper work for Fort Sheridan post newspaper, 1944, and "short shifts as telephone operator, inventory assistant in a shoe store, and three weeks as dental assistant—until the dentist ran out of teeth and patience." Currently doing lay research in natural and organic foods and health, and helping to raise two young grandsons.

WRITINGS: The Secret of Indian Ridge, Bobbs-Merrill, 1963. Earlier publications were syndicated mystery serials for the *Chicago Daily News* and the Associated Press. Contributor to *Toronto Star, Flying Cadet, Everyweek*, and *Datebook*. Wrote script for film, "The Flying Trancarsoarubus," Imperial Learning Corp., 1973.

WORK IN PROGRESS: Two books, *The Ghost of Apple Blossom Island*, and *The Purple Witch of Boston Hill*, about Colonial life in Revolutionary period.

SIDELIGHTS: Mrs. Holsinger told *CA:* "Friends ask you why you write. And on a rainy day shut away from the world in your workshop, or on a sunshiny morning when the garden calls and you cannot answer . . . I ask myself the same question. And as every writer understands, there is one single reply. I have to write. . . .

"Writing, for a writer, is part of living. I believe in children and their books, I want to share that joy with them. And, I believe that shining through today's shadows there is the sunlight of the past, and the future. I want to say to the young that each generation must work—always believing."

* * *

HOLT, Margaret 1937-

PERSONAL: Born August 22, 1937, in Buffalo, N.Y.; daughter of Edward Henry (a contractor) and Estella (Bulkley) Holt; married Tat Parish (an attorney), May 30, 1965 (divorced, 1970); children: Amy Randall, Tat David. *Education:* Elmira College, B.A., 1958; Simmons College, M.L.A., 1964; Michigan State University, Ph.D., 1975. *Politics:* Democrat. *Religion:* Episcopalian. *Office:* English Department, Miami University, Oxford, Ohio.

CAREER: Boston (Mass.) Public Library, children's assistant and librarian, 1961-65; Niles (Mich.) Public Library, children's librarian, 1965-66; Lake Michigan College, Benton Harbor, Mich., teacher of children's literature, 1966-71; Miami University, Oxford, Ohio, postdoctoral fellow teaching children's literature and composition, 1975—. *Member:* American Library Association, American Association of University Women, Michigan Library Association.

WRITINGS: David McCheever's 29 Dogs, Houghton, 1963.

WORK IN PROGRESS: Journal articles on contemporary realistic fiction for children.

* * *

HONIG, Donald 1931-

PERSONAL: Born August 17, 1931, in Maspeth, Long Island, N.Y.; son of George and Mildred (Elson) Honig; married Sandra Schindlinger (an M.B.A. candidate and marketing professional), July 11, 1965; children: Catherine Rose. *Residence:* Cromwell, Conn. *Agent:* Theron Raines, 244 Madison Ave., New York, N.Y.

CAREER: Professional writer. *Member:* Dramatists Guild, Authors League. *Awards, honors:* New York State Council of the Arts grant, 1972; Connecticut Commission on the Arts grant, 1974.

WRITINGS: Sidewalk Caesar (novel), Pyramid Books, 1958; *Walk Like A Man* (novel), Morrow, 1961; *Divide the Night* (novel), Regency Books, 1961; (editor) *Blue and Gray: Great Writings of the Civil War*, Avon, 1961; *No Song to Sing* (novel), Morrow, 1962; (editor) *Short Stories of Stephen Crane*, Avon, 1962, McGraw, 1967; *The Adventures of Jed McLane*, McGraw, 1967; *Jed McLane and the Stranger*, McGraw, 1969.

In ·the Days of the Cowboy, Random House, 1970; *Up from the Minor Leagues*, Cowles, 1970; *Dynamite*, Putnam, 1971; *Johnny Lee*, McCall Publishing, 1971; *Judgment Night*, Belmont Books, 1971; *The Journal of One Davey Wyatt*, F. Watts, 1972; *The Love Thief*, Belmont Books, 1972; *An End of Innocence*, Putnam, 1972; *Way to Go Teddy*, F. Watts, 1973; *The Severith Style*, Scribner, 1972; *Illusions*, Doubleday, 1974; *Playing for Keeps*, F. Watts, 1974; *Breaking In*, F. Watts, 1974; *The Professional*, F. Watts, 1974; *Coming Back*, F. Watts, 1974; *Fury On Skates*, Four Winds Press, 1974; *With the Consent of the Governed: Conversations with Eight U.S. Senators*, Dell, 1975; *Baseball: When the Grass Was Real*, Coward, 1975.

Author with Leon Arden of play, "The Midnight Ride of Alvin Blumm," first produced in 1966. Contributor of one hundred and sixty stories and articles to various trade publications.

* * *

HOOGASIAN-VILLA, Susie 1921-

PERSONAL: Born December 22, 1921, in Detroit, Mich.; daughter of Kazar and Hripsima (Nahkusian) Hoogasian; married John J. Villa (a metalurgical manager of operations); children: John K., Nancy E., James. *Education:* Wayne (now Wayne State) University, B.S., 1944, M.A., 1948, graduate study, 1961-62; Merrill-Palmer Institute, graduate study, 1961-62. *Religion:* Episcopalian. *Home:* 32550 Plumwood Lane, Birmingham, Mich. 48010.

CAREER: Public school teacher in Clawson, Mich., 1944-47, Detroit, Mich., 1948-61; Wayne State University, College of Education, Detroit, Mich., part-time instructor in family life education, 1965-69; Oakland Community College, Bloomfield Hills, Mich., associate professor of English, 1969—. *Member:* American Folklore Society, Michigan Folklore Society, Women of Wayne, Detroit Armenian Women's Club, Detroit Ethnic Group (member of board of directors).

WRITINGS: 100 Armenian Tales and Their Folkloristic Relevance, Wayne State University Press, 1966. Contributor to *Journal of American Folklore*.

WORK IN PROGRESS: Study of family life patterns in Turkish Armenia prior to World War I.

* * *

HOOLE, W(illiam) Stanley 1903-

PERSONAL: Born May 16, 1903, in Darlington, S.C.; son of William Brunson (a pharmacist) and Mary (Powers) Hoole; married Martha Ann Sanders, August 7, 1931 (died May 14, 1960); married Addie S. Coleman, May 31, 1970; children: Martha DuBose (Mrs. Eugene S. Taylor), Elizabeth Stanley (Mrs. Charles E. Beard). *Education:* Wofford College, A.B., 1924, A.M., 1931; Duke University, Ph.D., 1934; North Texas State University, A.M. in L.S., 1943; also studied at University of Chicago, Columbia University, and University of South Carolina. *Home:* 39 University Circle, Tuscaloosa, Ala. *Office:* University of Alabama Library, Tuscaloosa, Ala.

CAREER: High school teacher of English in Spartanburg, S.C., 1924-25, Darlington, S.C., 1927-31; Birmingham-Southern College, Birmingham, Ala., assistant professor of English, 1934-35, librarian, 1935-37; Baylor University, Waco, Tex., librarian, 1937-39; North Texas State University, Denton, director of libraries, 1939-44; University of Alabama, Tuscaloosa, librarian, 1944-69, dean of libraries, 1969-73, dean emeritus of libraries, 1973—. Consultant to U.S. House of Representatives committees, 1957-58, 1962-63, U.S. Office of Education, 1959-60. *Member:* American Library Association, Alabama Library Association, Alabama Historical Association, Newcomen Society, Phi Beta Kappa, Phi Alpha Theta, Pi Tau Chi, Kappa Phi Kappa, Pi Kappa Phi. *Awards, honors:* Litt.D., Wofford College, 1954; Fulbright research scholarship to United Kingdom, 1956-57; Alabama Library Association literary award, 1958.

WRITINGS: Check-List and Finding-List of Charleston Periodicals, 1732-1864, Duke University, 1936; *Sam Slick in Texas*, Naylor, 1945; *The Ante-Bellum Charleston Theatre*, University of Alabama Press, 1946; *Alias Simon Suggs: The Life and Times of Johnson Jones Hooper*, University of Alabama Press, 1952; *Vizetelly Covers the Confederacy*, Confederate, 1957; *Alabama Tories, 1862-1865*, Confederate, 1960; *Lawley Covers the Confederacy*, Confederate, 1964; *Four Years in the Confederate Navy: The Career of Captain John Low*, University of Georgia Press, 1964; *According to Hoole: The Collected Essays and Tales of a Scholar-Librarian and Literary Maverick*, University of Alabama Press, 1973.

Editor: *Classified List of Reference Books and Periodicals for College Libraries*, Southern Association of Colleges and Secondary Schools, 1947, revised edition, 1955; John L. Hunnicutt, *Reconstruction in West Alabama*, Confederate, 1959; Charles Girard, *A Visit to the Confederate States of America in 1863*, Confederate, 1962; Paul Pecquet du Bellet, *The Diplomacy of the Confederate Cabinet of Richmond and Its Agents Abroad*, Confederate, 1963; *Foreign Newspapers in Southeastern Libraries*, Southeastern Library Association, 1963; *And Still We Conquer: The Diary of a Nazi Unteroffizier in the German Africa Corps*, Confederate, 1968; *The Logs of the C. S. S. Alabama and the C. S. S. Tuscaloosa, 1862-1863*, Confederate, 1972; *Florida Territory in 1844: The Diary of Master Edward C. Anderson, U.S.N.*, University of Alabama Press, 1974.

Editor-in-chief, "Confederate Centennial Studies," 1956-65. Contributor to *Encyclopaedia Britannica, Grolier's Encyclopedia, Texas History Handbook*, and to professional journals and popular magazines. Editor, *Alabama Review*, 1948-67, *Southeastern Librarian*, 1951-52; associate editor, *South Atlantic Modern Language Association Bulletin*, 1947-52.

* * *

HOOPER, Walter (McGehee) 1931-

PERSONAL: Born March 27, 1931, in Reidsville, N.C.;

son of Arch Boyd (an engineer) and Madge (Kemp) Hooper. *Education:* University of North Carolina, B.A., 1954, M.A., 1957; St. Stephen's House, Oxford, England, Diploma in Theology, 1964; Wadham College, Oxford, study toward B.Litt., 1965—. *Home and office:* 19 Beaumont St., Oxford, England. *Agent:* Curtis Brown Ltd., 1 Craven Hill, London W2 3EW, England.

CAREER: Anglican priest. University of Kentucky, Lexington, instructor in English literature, 1960-62; private secretary to C. S. Lewis, Oxford, England, 1963; Oxford University, Oxford, England, chaplain of Wadham College, 1965-67, assistant chaplain of Jesus College, 1967-70; editorial trustee of the estate of C. S. Lewis, 1970—. *Military service:* U.S. Army, 1954-56.

WRITINGS: (Editor) C. S. Lewis, *Poems*, Bles, 1964, Harcourt, 1965; (contributor) *Light on C. S. Lewis*, Bles, 1965, Harcourt, 1966; (collector) C. S. Lewis, *Studies in Medieval and Renaissance Literature*, Cambridge University Press, 1966; (editor) C. S. Lewis, *Of Other Worlds: Essays and Stories*, Bles, 1966; *Of Other Worlds: Essays and Stories*, Harcourt, 1966; (editor) C. S. Lewis, *Christian Reflections*, Eerdmans, 1967; (editor) C. S. Lewis, *Narrative Poems*, Bles, 1969, Harcourt, 1972; (editor) C. S. Lewis, *Selected Literary Essays*, Cambridge University Press, 1969; (editor) C. S. Lewis, *God in the Dark*, Eerdmans, 1970 (published in England as *Undeceptions*, Bles, 1971); (contributor) Carolyn Keefe, editor, *C. S. Lewis: Speaker and Teacher*, Zondervan, 1971, Hodder & Stoughton, 1974; (contributor) C. A. Huttar, editor, *Imagination and the Spirit*, Eerdmans, 1971; (with R. L. Green) *C. S. Lewis: A Biography*, Harcourt, 1974; (editor) C. S. Lewis, *Fern-Seed and Elephants*, Collins, 1975.

WORK IN PROGRESS: Editing a collection of stories by C. S. Lewis for publication by Collins.

*   *   *

HOOPES, Ned E(dward)   1932-

PERSONAL: Born May 22, 1932, in Safford, Ariz.; son of Cloyde M. and Pearl (Greenhalgh) Hoopes. *Education:* Brigham Young University, B.A., 1956, M.A., 1957; Northwestern University, M.A., 1958, Ph.D., 1967. *Home:* 205 Third Ave., 10G, New York, N.Y. 10003.

CAREER: Special lecturer, Evanston Township High School, 1959-62; Hofstra University, Hempstead, N.Y., instructor, 1962-63; Hunter College, New York, N.Y., lecturer in School of General Studies, and instructor, Hunter College High School, 1963-68; Pace University, New York, N.Y., associate professor of English, 1968—. Master teacher, Master of Arts Program, Harvard University, summer, 1962, Yale University, summer, 1963. Television host for "The Reading Room," Columbia Broadcasting System network show for children; narrator of poetry records for Macmillan, and children's stories records for Weston Studios. Former member of editorial board, Laurel Leaf and Mayflower libraries, Dell Publishing Co. *Member:* National Council of Teachers of English (board of directors).

WRITINGS: (Editor with Diane W. Wilbur) *The Lighter Side*, Scholastic Book Services, 1964; (editor with Richard S. Beal) *Search for Perspective*, Holt, 1965; (editor) *Harte of the West: 17 Stories by Bret Harte*, Dell, 1966; (editor with Richard Corbin) *Incredible Tales by Saki*, Dell, 1966; (editor with R. Corbin) *Surprises: 20 Stories by O. Henry*, Dell, 1966; (editor) *The Wonderful World of Horses*, Dell, 1966; (editor) *Edge of Awareness: 25 Contemporary Es-*

says, Laurel, 1966; (editor) *Famous Devil Stories*, Laurel, 1967; (retelling of *Arabian Night*), *Alibi and the Thieves, and Other Stories*, Mayflower Book, 1967; (with Bernard Evslin) *Heroes and Monsters of Greek Myth*, Scholastic Book Services, 1967; (editor) *Stories to Enjoy*, Macmillan, 1967, new edition, 1974; (editor) *Ideas in Motion*, Holt, 1969; (editor) *Who Am I?*, Dell, 1969; (editor) *Great Television Plays*, Laurel, Volume I, 1969, Volume II (with Pat Gordon), 1975. Contributor to *Britannica Junior Encyclopaedia for Boys and Girls*. Former issue editor *Scholastic Teacher*. Television editor, *Media and Methods* (formerly *School Paperback Journal*). Former book editor, *Ingenue* Magazine.

WORK IN PROGRESS: A biography of Charles Laughton; novel about modern Mormon life.

*   *   *

HOOS, Ida Russakoff   1912-

PERSONAL: Born October 9, 1912, in Skowhegan, Me.; daughter of Susman (a jeweler) and Manya (Simkin) Russakoff; married Sidney S. Hoos (now a university dean and professor), June 13, 1942; children: Phyllis (Mrs. Richard E. DeLeon), Judy. *Education:* Radcliffe College, A.B., 1933, part-time graduate study, 1938-42; University of California, Ph.D., 1959. *Office:* Space Sciences Laboratory, University of California, Berkeley, Calif.

CAREER: University of California, Berkeley, research sociologist, 1961—. Consultant to U.S. Civil Service Commission, U.S. Department of Health, Education, and Welfare, and California Personnel Board.

WRITINGS: *Automation in the Office*, Public Affairs, 1961; *Retraining the Work Force*, University of California Press, 1967; *Systems Analysis in Social Policy*, Transatlantic, 1970; *Systems Analysis in Public Policy: A Critique*, University of California Press, 1972.

*   *   *

HOOSON, David J. M.   1926-

PERSONAL: Born April 25, 1926, in England; son of George (a farmer) and Kathleen (Mahler) Hooson; married Alison Nicol, July 27, 1950; children: Roger, Clare. *Education:* Oxford University, B.A., 1948, M.A., 1950; University of London, Ph.D., 1955. *Home:* 523 Cragmont Ave., Berkeley, Calif. 94708. *Office:* University of California, Berkeley, Calif. 94720.

CAREER: Schoolteacher in England, 1949-53; University of Glasgow, Glasgow, Scotland, lecturer, 1954-56; University of Maryland, College Park, assistant professor of geography, 1956-60; University of British Columbia, Vancouver, professor of geography, 1960-66; University of California, Berkeley, professor of geography, 1966—. *Military service:* Royal Navy, 1944-46. *Member:* American Geographical Society, Association of American Geographers, American Association for the Advancement of Slavic Studies.

WRITINGS: *A New Soviet Heartland?*, Van Nostrand, 1964; *The Soviet Union: People and Regions*, Wadsworth, 1966 (published in England as *The Soviet Union: A Systematic Regional Geography*, University of London Press, 1966).

WORK IN PROGRESS: A study of the history of Russian geographical thought.†

HOPE, Laura Lee
[Collective pseudonym]

WRITINGS—All published by Grosset, except as indicated: "Blythe Girls" series: *Helen, Margy and Rose; or, Facing the Great World,* 1925; *Margy's Queer Inheritance; or, The Worth of a Name,* 1925; *Rose's Great Problem; or, Face to Face With a Crisis,* 1925; *The Disappearance of Helen; or, The Art Shop Mystery,* 1928; *Snowbound in Camp; or, The Mystery at Elk Lodge,* 1929; *Margy's Mysterious Visitor; or, Guarding the Pepper Fortune,* 1930; *Rose's Hidden Talent,* 1931; *Helen's Wonderful Mistake; or, The Mysterious Necklace,* 1932.

"Bobbsey Twins" series: *The Bobbsey Twins; or, Merry Days Indoors and Out,* Mershon, 1904; *The Bobbsey Twins in the Country,* 1907, revised edition published as *The Bobbsey Twins' Adventure in the Country,* 1961; *The Bobbsey Twins at the Seashore,* Chatterton-Peck, 1907, revised edition published as *The Bobbsey Twins: The Secret at the Seashore,* Grosset, 1962; *... at School,* 1913, revised edition published as *The Bobbsey Twins' Mystery at School,* 1962; *The Bobbsey Twins on a Houseboat,* 1915; *... Keeping House,* 1925; *... and Their Schoolmates,* 1928; *... Treasure Hunting,* 1929.

The Bobbsey Twins at Spruce Lake, 1930; *The Bobbsey Twins' Wonderful Secret,* 1931; *The Bobbsey Twins at the Circus,* 1932; *... on an Airplane Trip,* 1933; *... Solve a Mystery,* 1934; *... on a Ranch,* 1935; *... in Eskimo Land,* 1936; *... in a Radio Play,* 1937; *... in Washington,* 1938, revised edition published as *The Bobbsey Twins' Adventure in Washington,* 1963; *The Bobbsey Twins at Windmill Cottage,* 1938; *... at Lighthouse Point,* 1939.

The Bobbsey Twins at Indian Hollow, 1940; *... at the Ice Carnival,* 1941; *... in the Land of Cotton,* 1942; *... in Echo Valley,* 1943; *... on the Pony Trail,* 1944; *... at Sugar Maple Hill,* 1946; *... in Mexico,* 1947; *... in Tulip Land,* 1949.

The Bobbsey Twins, 1950; *... in Rainbow Valley,* 1950; *The Bobbsey Twins' Own Little Railroad,* 1951; *The Bobbsey Twins at Whitesail Harbor,* 1952; *... and the Horseshoe Riddle,* 1953; *... at Big Bear Pond,* 1953; *Meet the Bobbsey Twins,* Wonder Books, 1954; *The Bobbsey Twins on a Bicycle Trip,* 1954; *... Camping Out,* 1955; *The Bobbsey Twins' Own Little Ferryboat,* 1956; *The Bobbsey Twins at Pilgrim Rock,* 1956; *The Bobbsey Twins' Forest Adventure,* 1957; *The Bobbsey Twins at London Tower,* 1959; *... on Blueberry Island,* 1959.

The Bobbsey Twins' Search in the Great City, 1960; *The Bobbsey Twins and the Mystery at Snow Lodge,* 1960; *The Bobbsey Twins' Big Adventure at Home,* 1960; *The Bobbsey Twins in the Mystery Cave,* 1960; *... and the Circus Surprise,* 1960; *... and the County Fair Mystery,* 1960; *... of Lakeport,* 1961; *... in Volcano Land,* 1961; *... and the Goldfish Mystery,* 1962; *The Bobbsey Twins' Mystery at Meadowbrook,* 1963; *The Bobbsey Twins and the Big River Mystery,* 1963; *... and the Greek Hat Mystery,* 1964; *The Bobbsey Twins' Search for the Green Rooster,* 1965; *... Mystery on the Deep Blue Sea,* 1965; *The Bobbsey Twins and Their Camel Adventure,* 1966; *The Bobbsey Twins' Visit to the Great West,* 1966; *... Mystery of the King's Puppet,* 1967; *The Bobbsey Twins and the Cedar Camp Mystery,* 1967; *The Bobbsey Twins' Adventures with Baby May,* 1968; *The Bobbsey Twins and the Four-Leaf Clover Mystery,* 1968; *... and the Secret of Candy Castle,* 1968; *... and the Play House Secret,* 1968; *... and the Doodlebug Mystery,* 1969.

The Bobbsey Twins and the Talking Fox Mystery, 1970; *The Red, White, and Blue Mystery,* 1971; *The Bobbsey Twins and the Tagalong Giraffe,* 1973; *... The Mystery at Cherry Corners,* 1971; *... on the Sun Moon Cruise,* 1975.

"Bunny Brown" series: *Bunny Brown and His Sister Sue on the Rolling Ocean,* 1925; *... and His Sister Sue at Shore Acres,* 1928; *... and His Sister Sue at Berry Hill,* 1929; *... and His Sister Sue at Sky Top,* 1930; *... and His Sister Sue at the Summer Carnival,* 1931; *... and His Sister Sue in the Big Woods,* 1971.

"Make Believe Stories" series: *The Story of a Bold Tin Soldier,* 1920; *... of a Calico Clown,* 1920; *... of a Candy Rabbit,* 1920; *... of a Lamb on Wheels,* 1920; *... of a Monkey on a Stick,* 1920; *... of a Sawdust Doll,* 1920; *... of a White Rocking Horse,* 1920.

"Outdoor Girls" series: *The Outdoor Girls in a Motor Car; or, the Haunted Mansion of Shadow Valley,* 1913; *... at Foaming Falls; or Robina of Red Kennels,* 1925; *... at New Moon Ranch; or, Riding with the Cowboys,* 1928; *... on a Hike; or, The Mystery of the Deserted Airplane,* 1929; *... on a Canoe Trip; or, The Secret of the Brown Mill,* 1930; *... at Cedar Ridge; or, The Mystery of the Old Windmill,* 1931; *... in the Air; or, Saving the Stolen Invention,* 1932; *... in Desert Valley; or, Strange Happenings in a Cowboy Camp,* 1933.

"Six Little Bunkers" series: *Six Little Bunkers at Grandpa Ford's,* 1918; *... at Cowboy Jack's,* 1921; *... at Indian John's,* 1925; *... at Happy Jim's,* 1928; *... at Skipper Bob's,* 1929; *... at Lighthouse Nell's,* 1930.

SIDELIGHTS: See **ADAMS, Harriet S., STRATEMEYER, Edward L.,** and **SVENSON, Andrew E.**†

*   *   *

HOPF, Alice L(ightner) 1904-
(A. M. Lightner)

PERSONAL: Born October 11, 1904, in Detroit, Mich.; daughter of Clarence Ashley (a lawyer) and Frances (McGraw) Lightner; married Ernest J. Hopf (an artist), April 29, 1935; children: Christopher. *Education:* Vassar College, B.A., 1927. *Home:* 136 West 16th St., New York, N.Y. 10011. *Agent:* Larry Sternig, 2407 North 44th St., Milwaukee, Wis. 53210.

CAREER: Grey Advertising, Inc., New York, N.Y., editorial secretary. Free-lance writer. *Member:* Authors Guild, Xerxes Society, Science Fiction Writers of America, New York Entomological Society.

WRITINGS—Nonfiction and nature: *Monarch Butterflies,* Crowell, 1965; *Wild Traveler: The Story of a Coyote,* Norton, 1967; *Earth's Bug-Eyed Monsters,* Norton, 1968; *Butterfly and Moth,* Putnam, 1969; *Carab, the Trap-Door Spider,* Putnam, 1970; *Biography of an Octopus,* Putnam, 1971; *Biography of a Rhino,* Putnam, 1972; *Wild Cousins of the Dog,* Putnam, 1973; *Misunderstood Animals,* McGraw, 1973; *Biography of an Ant,* Putnam, 1974; *Biography of an Ostrich,* Putnam, 1974, new edition, 1975; *Biography of an Armadillo,* Putnam, 1975; *Wild Cousins of the Cat,* Putnam, 1975.

Under name A. M. Lightner—Fiction and science fiction: *The Pillar and the Flame* (poem), H. Vinal, 1928; *The Rock of Three Planets,* Putnam, 1963; *The Planet Poachers,* Putnam, 1965; *Doctor to the Galaxy,* Norton, 1965; *The Galactic Troubadours,* Norton, 1965; *The Space Plague,* Norton, 1966; *The Space Olympics,* Norton, 1967; *The Space Arc,* Putnam, 1968; *The Walking Zoo of Darwin*

Dingle, Putnam, 1969; *The Day of the Drones*, Norton, 1969; *The Thursday Toads*, McGraw, 1971; *Star Dog*, McGraw, 1973; *Gods of Demons*, Four Winds, 1973; *The Space Gypsies*, McGraw, 1974.

WORK IN PROGRESS: Two books.

* * *

HOPKINSON, Henry Thomas 1905-

PERSONAL: Born April 19, 1905, in Manchester, England; son of John Henry (an archdeacon, Church of England) and Evelyn Mary (Fountaine) Hopkinson; married Dorothy Vernon, March 21, 1953; children: (previous marriages) Lyndall Hopkinson Passerini, Nicolette Hopkinson Roeske, Amanda Hopkinson Binns. *Education:* Pembroke College, Oxford, B.A., 1927, M.A., 1932. *Home:* 6 Marine Parade, Penarth, Wales. *Agent:* Richard Scott Simon Ltd., 36 Wellington St., London WC2E 7BD, England.

CAREER: Worked in advertising and as free-lance journalist in London, England, in early 1930's; assistant editor of *Clarion*, 1934, and *Weekly Illustrated*, 1934-38; helped found *Picture Post*, London, 1938, and was its editor, 1940-50, concurrently editing another London publication, *Lilliput*, 1941-46; features editor of *News Chronicle*, London, 1954-56; editor of *Drum* (magazine), Johannesburg, South Africa, 1958-61; director for International Press Institute of center founded to train African journalists, Nairobi, Kenya, 1963-66; University of Sussex, Sussex, England, senior fellow in press studies, 1967-69; University College, Cardiff, Wales, director of Centre of Journalism Studies, 1970-75. Visiting professor, University of Minnesota, 1968-69. *Member:* Savile Club (London). *Awards, honors:* Commander of British Empire, 1967, for work in Africa.

WRITINGS: Novels, except as noted: *A Wise Man Foolish*, Chapman & Hall, 1930; *A Strong Hand at the Helm* (political satire), Gollancz, 1933; *The Man Below*, Hogarth, 1939; *Mist in the Tagus*, Little, Brown, 1946; *The Transitory Venus* (short stories), Horizon Magazine, 1948; *Down the Long Slide*, Hogarth, 1949.

Love's Apprentice, J. Cape, 1953; *George Orwell* (short biography), British Council, 1953; *The Lady and the Cut-Throat* (short stories), J. Cape, 1958; *In the Fiery Continent*, Gollancz, 1962, Doubleday, 1963; *South Africa* (nonfiction), Time-Life Books, 1964; (editor and author of introduction *Picture Post, 1938-50* (nonfiction), Penguin, 1970; (with wife, Dorothy Hopkinson) *Much Silence: The Life and Work of Meher Baba*, Gollancz, 1974. Contributor of short stories and articles to *Holiday, Saturday Evening Post, London Magazine*, and other periodicals in England, America, and Africa.

SIDELIGHTS: Hopkinson was in the Congo at the time of the 1960 upheavals, and made an extensive tour of the country some months later to record the changes that followed the revolution. He has traveled extensively in other parts of Africa, particularly in South Africa, Kenya, Tanzania, Nigeria, Uganda and Ghana.

* * *

HOPPER, John 1934-

PERSONAL: Born November 21, 1934, in Philadelphia, Pa.; son of John Lewis and Virginia (Poulson) Hopper. *Education:* Muhlenberg College, Allentown, Pa., A.B., 1956.

CAREER: From 1959-61, Hopper travelled in Europe, working as a dubber in films, a publisher's reader in France, a foreign correspondent for *Metronome* magazine, an instructor in English, a translator (English-French), and a free-lance writer for French newspapers and magazines. Worked in government service, San Francisco, Calif., 1961-62; *Time* magazine, New York, N.Y., reporting house-organ editor, 1963-64. Currently working as a free-lance writer and commercial artist in New York, N.Y. *Military service:* U.S. Army, 1957-59.

WRITINGS: Miscellany: Collected Poems, 1956-1961, Visa Editions, 1962. Author of "Year of the Census," produced off-Broadway, 1964, and of a film treatment for Louis de Rochemont Associates, 1964. Contributor of articles and interviews to *Downbeat* and *Metronome*.

WORK IN PROGRESS: A book of poems, as yet untitled.

SIDELIGHTS: Hopper once told *CA:* "My chief writing interest in the past few years has been the developing of a voice in poetry. Motivating themes derived from the personal and public paranoia caused by the alienation of modern man from his fellows and his government. My work, at least in poetry, reflects this anxiety. The avant-garde, as it now exists, is expressing dead issues in either too blatant or too silly a voice to be taken seriously by any but a few devotees. Robt. Lowell, as much as I admire his work, is only a restless lull in a traditional and basically unexciting form. The artist as society's antenna must go beyond introspection into the true impulses of our age."†

* * *

HORELICK, Arnold L(awrence) 1928-

PERSONAL: Born March 24, 1928, in New York, N.Y.; son of David and Celia (Schneiderman) Horelick; children: Lisa Joy, Andrew Louis. *Education:* Rutgers University, B.A., 1948; Columbia University, graduate study, 1948; Harvard University, M.A., 1950. *Home:* 11983 Walnut Lane, Los Angeles, Calif. 90064. *Office:* RAND Corp., 1700 Main St., Santa Monica, Calif.

CAREER: U.S. Government, Washington, D.C., political affairs analyst, Foreign Broadcast Information Service, 1951-52, 1954-58; RAND Corp., Santa Monica, Calif., senior staff member, social science department, 1958—. Vice-president of Transport-A-Child Foundation, Los Angeles, Calif. *Military service:* U.S. Army, 1952-54. *Member:* American Political Science Association, American Association for the Advancement of Slavic Studies, American Institute of Aeronautics and Astronautics, Phi Beta Kappa.

WRITINGS: (Contributor) Joseph M. Goldsen, editor, *Outer Space and World Politics*, Praeger, 1963; (contributor) Bernard Brodie, editor, *La Guerre Nucleaire*, Editions Stock, 1965; (with Myron Rush) *Strategic Power and Soviet Foreign Policy*, University of Chicago Press, 1966; (contributor) Samuel Merlin, editor, *The Big Powers and the Present Crisis in the Middle East*, Fairleigh Dickinson University Press, 1968; (contributor) R. V. Burks, editor, *The Future of Communism in Europe*, Wayne State University Press, 1968.

(Contributor) E. P. Hoffman and F. J. Fleron, editors, *The Conduct of Soviet Foreign Policy*, Aldine, 1971; (contributor) P. Y. Hammond and S. S. Alexander, editors, *Political Dynamics in the Middle East*, Elsevier, 1972; (contributor) F. N. Trager and P. S. Kronenburg, editors, *National Security and American Society*, University of Kansas Press, 1973; (contributor) B. Horton, editor, *Comparative*

Defense Policy, Johns Hopkins Press, 1974. Contributor to *Saturday Evening Post, World Politics, Air Force and Space Digest, Survey, Pacific Affairs, Policy Sciences*, and other journals.

WORK IN PROGRESS: Research on the changing roles of the Party in Soviet-style societies.

SIDELIGHTS: Horelick is competent in Russian, he reads French and German.

* * *

HORNER, Dave 1934-

PERSONAL: Born December 13, 1934, in Lynchburg, Va.; son of L. David, Jr. (a banker) and Katherine (Byers) Horner; married Jayne Bond, September 10, 1955; children: Valerie Jayne, Victoria Lynn, Julie Bond. *Education:* University of Virginia, student, 1952-56; Rutgers University, graduate study. *Politics:* Conservative Republican. *Religion:* Methodist. *Residence:* Richmond, Va. *Office address:* Bank of Virginia, P.O. Box 25339, Richmond, Va. 23260.

CAREER: Banker; former president of Bank of Central Virginia, Lynchburg; The Bank of Virginia, Richmond, executive vice-president, 1969—. Consultant to Maritime Explorations Ltd. (professional diving equipment), Virginia Beach. Has been diving for twenty years in the North Atlantic, Mediterranean, and Caribbean; certified SCUBA instructor; underwater photographer, doing commercial work as well as photographs used in own lectures on diving and treasure hunting. *Military service:* U.S. Navy, 1956-58.

WRITINGS: Key to Good Diving, Maritime Explorations, 1963; *Shipwrecks, Skin Divers and Sunken Gold*, Dodd, 1965; *Better SCUBA Diving for Boys*, Dodd, 1966; *The Blockade-Runners: True Tales of Running the Yankee Blockade of the Confederate Coast*, Dodd, 1968; *The Treasure Galleons: Clues to Millions in Sunken Gold and Silver*, Dodd, 1971. Contributor to *Commonwealth* and to skin-diving journals.

SIDELIGHTS: Horner once told *CA:* [I] "am actively engaged in underwater exploration and salvage of historical shipwrecks, such as vessels of Cornwallis' fleet sunk by General Washington and the French at Yorktown in 1781, Civil War vessels including the "Monitor" off Cape Hatteras, some forty blockade runners off Cape Fear, and a Spanish galleon. My goal is to accumulate enough underwater historical items, treasure, relics to build a museum of sunken treasure."†

* * *

HORNUNG, Clarence Pearson 1899-

PERSONAL: Born June 12, 1899, in New York, N.Y.; son of Jules S. (a candy merchant) and Caroline (Pfaelzer) Hornung; married Sara Stoff, June 3, 1923; children: Richard Sanford, Donald Gilbert. *Education:* City College (now City College of the City University of New York), B.A., 1920; studied art at Cooper Union, 1921, and advertising design at New York University, 1921-22. *Home:* 12 Glen Rd., West Hempstead, N.Y. 11552.

CAREER: Industrial designer and illustrator, specializing in trademarks, packaging, and product identification; Collectors' Prints, Inc. (publishers of prints in limited editions), New York, N.Y., president, 1964-72. Founder and co-publisher of *Automobile Quarterly*, 1961-62. *Military service:* U.S. Army, Infantry, 1918-19; became second lieutenant. *Member:* American Institute of Graphic Arts, Typophiles.

WRITINGS: Bookplates of Harold Nelson, Caxton Press (New York), 1929; *Trade-Marks*, Caxton Press (New York), 1930; *Handbook of Designs and Devices*, Harper, 1932, 2nd edition, Dover, 1946; *Lettering From A to Z*, Ziff-Davis Publishing, 1946, 2nd edition, William Penn Publishing, 1954; *Handbook of Early Advertising Art*, two volumes, Dover, 1947, 3rd revised edition, 1956; *Wheels Across America*, A. S. Barnes, 1959; *Pictorial Archives of American Business and Industry*, Dover, 1959; (art editor) *Book of the American West*, Messner, 1963; *Gallery of the American Automobile*, Collectors' Prints, 1965; *Portrait Gallery of Early Automobiles*, Abrams, 1968; *Antiques and Jewelry Designs*, Braziller, 1968; *An Old Fashioned Christmas in Illustration and Decoration*, Dover, 1970; *Antique Automobile Coloring Book*, Dover, 1971; *Treasury of American Design*, two volumes, Abrams, 1972; *Will Bradley: His Graphic Work*, Dover, 1974; *Allover Patterns for Designers and Craftsmen*, Dover, 1975; *Oldtime Automobile Advertisements*, Dover, 1975; *Two Hundred Years of American Graphic Art*, Braziller, 1975; *American Antiques, Arts, and Crafts*, Abrams, 1975. Contributor to *New York Times* and to trade publications.

WORK IN PROGRESS: Treasury of Steuben Glass, for Abrams; *The American Eagle and the Arts*; and *The Beauty of the Butterfly*.

SIDELIGHTS: Hornung told *CA:* He is "an avid collector of books, posters, and printed ephemera (that overflow his garage, basement, and attic). With limited lebensraum, his constant problem is where to put incoming acquisitions. Research is a full-time project. He estimates he has spent fifteen years in preparation of his *Gallery of the American Automobile*, four solid years on the production of his *Treasury of American Design*, and almost a lifetime on his studies for the volume on the American eagle. He sketches and paints in watercolor as a hobby on frequent trips to Europe and the Orient. A recent exhibition called "Around the World in 80 Watercolors" has been shown in a number of libraries, as well as his exhibit of 100 antique automobile prints which have been exhibited in over fifty museums and libraries, coast to coast."

* * *

HORVATH, Betty 1927-

PERSONAL: Born May 20, 1927, in Jefferson City, Mo.; daughter of Brans Bolton (a railroader) and Augusta (Kapell) Ferguson; married John Anthony Horvath (a teacher), March 11, 1954; children: Sally, Polly, Jay. *Education:* Attended Jefferson City Junior College, and Phillips University. *Religion:* Episcopalian. *Home:* 2340 Waite Ave., Kalamazoo, Mich. 49008.

CAREER: Continuity writer for radio station KWOS in Jefferson City, Mo., 1946-48, and KCRC in Enid, Okla., 1948-49, with radio station WIL, St. Louis, Mo., 1949-50, and Palan Advertising Co., St. Louis, 1950-52; Camp Nebagamon for Boys, Lake Nebagamon, Wis., secretary, 1952-54; now writer for children.

WRITINGS: Hooray for Jasper, F. Watts, 1966; *Jasper Makes Music*, F. Watts, 1967; *Will the Real Tommy Wilson Please Stand Up*, F. Watts, 1969; *The Cheerful Quiet*, F. Watts, 1969; *Be Nice To Josephine*, F. Watts, 1970; *Not Enough Indians*, F. Watts, 1971; *Small Paul and the Bally of Morgan Court*, Ginn, 1971.

AVOCATIONAL INTERESTS: Reading and listening to music, particularly the violin. "Ambition: To walk the Appalachian Trail."

HOUSTON, Joan 1928-

PERSONAL: Born May 11, 1928, in New York, N.Y.; daughter of Robert Lockhart (a businessman) and Margaret (Graydon) Houston; married Andrew Carruth McCulloch (a financial analyst), June 15, 1957; children: Andrew Houston, Cynthia Graydon. *Education:* Barnard College, A.B., 1950.

CAREER: Writer. *Member:* Authors League of America, Women's National Book Association.

WRITINGS: Jump-Shy, Crowell, 1956; *Horse Show Hurdles,* Crowell, 1957; *Crofton Meadows,* Crowell, 1961.†

* * *

HOUTHAKKER, Hendrik S(amuel) 1924-

PERSONAL: First syllable in surname rhymes with "out"; born December 31, 1924, in Amsterdam, Netherlands; came to United States in 1951; naturalized, 1966; son of Bernard (an art dealer) and Marion (Lichtenstein) Houthakker; married Anna-Teresa Tymieniecka (an author), September 8, 1955; children: Louis, Isabella, Jan Nicolas. *Education:* University of Amsterdam, Doctorandus, 1949. *Politics:* Republican. *Home:* 348 Payson Rd., Belmont, Mass. 02178. *Office:* 209 Littauer Center, Harvard University, Cambridge, Mass. 02138.

CAREER: Cambridge University, Cambridge, England, economic research staff, 1949-51; University of Chicago, Chicago, Ill., assistant professor of economics on research staff of Cowles, Commission, 1952-53, visiting associate professor, 1953; Stanford University, Stanford, Calif., acting associate professor, 1954-55, associate professor, 1955-57, professor of economics, 1957-60; Harvard University, Cambridge, Mass., professor of economics, 1960—. Visiting professor at University of Tokyo, 1955, Massachusetts Institute of Technlogoy, 1957-58. Senior staff economist, Council of Economic Advisors, 1967-68, member of council, 1969-71. *Member:* International Statistical Institute, National Academy of Sciences, American Economic Association (vice-president, 1972), American Statistical Association (fellow), Econometric Society (council, 1960-63; vice-president, 1966; president, 1967). *Awards, honors:* John Bates Clark Medal, American Economic Association, 1963; honorary doctorate from University of Amsterdam, 1972, University of Fribourg, 1974.

WRITINGS: (With S. J. Prais) *The Analysis of Family Budgets,* Cambridge University Press, 1955; (with John Haldi) *Household Investment in Automobiles,* Department of Economics, Stanford University, 1959; (with Lester D. Taylor) *Consumer Demand in the U.S.,* Harvard University Press, 1966, 2nd edition, 1970; *Economic Policy for the Farm Sector,* American Enterprise Institute for Public Policy Research, 1967. Contributor to professional journals. Associate editor, *Econometrica,* 1953-60; acting editor, *Review of Economics and Statistics,* 1966-67, editor, 1971—.

WORK IN PROGRESS: Research on consumption, commodity markets, and international trade.

* * *

HOWARD, Charles Frederick 1904-

PERSONAL: Born May 28, 1904, in Manitoba, Canada; son of Charles William and Ella Louise (Julyan) Howard; married Gordena Elsie Mosher, June, 1934. *Education:* University of Saskatchewan, B.A., 1935, B.Ed., 1938; University of California, Berkeley, M.A., 1940, Ph.D.,

1947. *Religion:* United Church. *Home:* 55 Sandburg Dr., Sacramento, Calif.

CAREER: Elementary and secondary teacher, Saskatchewan, in Wishart School District, Touchwood, 1924-26, Swanson School District, Swanson, 1926-29, Saskatoon School District, Saskatoon, 1929-40; University of California, Berkeley, lecturer, 1947; Sacramento State College, Sacramento, Calif., associate professor, 1948-52, professor of education, 1952—. *Military service:* Canadian Army, Intelligence Corps, World War II; became captain. *Member:* National Council of Teachers of Mathematics, California Mathematics Council, California Teachers Association, Phi Delta Kappa.

WRITINGS: Arithmetic Charts Handbook, Fearon, 1960; *Basic Procedures in Teaching Arithmetic,* Heath, 1963; *Teaching Contemporary Mathematics in the Elementary School,* Harper, 1966; *Charts for the New Math,* Fearon, 1966; (co-author) *New Dimensions in Mathematics,* Harper, 1970; (co-author) *Mathematics Course I,* Harper, 1973; (co-author) *Mathematics Course II,* Harper, 1973.

* * *

HOWARD, Patricia (Lowe) 1937-

PERSONAL: Born October 18, 1937, in Birmingham, England; daughter of Harold (a director) and Edna M. (Homer) Lowe; married David Louis Howard (a teacher of management), July 28, 1960; children: Lucy, Charlotte Polly. *Education:* Lady Margaret Hall, Oxford, B.A. (first class honors), 1959, M.A., 1963; University of Surrey, Ph.D., 1974. *Religion:* Anglican. *Home:* Stepping Stones, Gomshall, Surrey, England.

CAREER: Holton Park Grammar School, Oxford, England, director of music, 1959-60; Open University, tutor in humanities. Music contributor, *Times Educational Supplement;* conductor of Rugby Ladies' Choir; composer. *Member:* Royal Musical Association.

WRITINGS: Gluck and the Birth of Modern Opera, Barrie & Rockliff, 1963; *The Operas of Benjamin Britten: An Introduction,* Barrie & Rockliff, 1969. Contributor to *Musical Times* and *Music Magazine.*

WORK IN PROGRESS: The Operas of Jean-Baptiste Lully.

SIDELIGHTS: Mrs. Howard is competent in Latin, French, German, and Russian.

* * *

HOWE, Charles L. 1932-

PERSONAL: Born September 16, 1932; son of Lawrence Leslie and Patricia (Morin) Howe; married Ruth Macchiarini, December 20, 1957; children: Travis Charles, Carla Brigida. *Education:* University of California, Berkeley, B.Sc. (in criminology). *Politics:* "Anarcho-Tory (but I vote Democrat)." *Religion:* "None." *Home:* 366 Pennsylvania Ave., San Francisco, Calif. 94107. *Agent:* Reece Halsey, 8733 Sunset Blvd., Los Angeles, Calif. 90069. *Office:* San Francisco Chronicle, Fifth and Mission Sts., San Francisco, Calif.

CAREER: Security Services West (detective agency), Mill Valley, Calif., owner, 1957-58; self-employed writer, Mill Valley, Calif., 1958-60; Bancroft-Whitney Co., San Francisco, Calif., legal editor, 1960-63; American School of Technical Intelligence, San Francisco, Calif., director, 1963; *San Francisco Chronicle,* San Francisco, Calif., military correspondent, 1964—. Radio commentator for "Books and People" program on KPFA-FM, Berkeley, Calif. *Military service:* U.S. Marine Corps, 1948-53; became gunnery sergeant. *Member:* Marines Memorial Association, Press Club of San Francisco.

WRITINGS: Valley of Fire, Dell, 1964; (ghostwriter) J. W. Ehrlich, *A Reasonable Doubt,* World Publishing, 1964. Writer (and director), "Veteran's Theatre of the Air" program, KVSM-AM radio.†

* * *

HOY, David 1930-

PERSONAL: Born July 31, 1930, in Evansville, Ind.; son of Clarence A. (an insuranceman and minister) and Margaret (Etter) Hoy; married Shirley A. Croslin, June 6, 1953; children: Jonathan, Kimberly, Van Andrew. *Education:* Bob Jones University, B.A., 1953; Southern Baptist Theological Seminary, B.D., 1959. *Politics:* Republican.

CAREER: Baptist minister, 1951-60; went into radio news, 1960, and then into nightclubs, 1964, with an act based on extrasensory perception; also has appeared on "Mike Douglas Show," "To Tell the Truth," and other television programs. Has presented numerous college lectures on ESP. Psychic Associates, Boston, Mass., vice-president, 1965—.

WRITINGS: Psychic and Other ESP Party Games, Doubleday, 1965; *The Meaning of Tarot,* Aurora, 1971.

BIOGRAPHICAL/CRITICAL SOURCES: Atlanta Journal, September 10, 1965; *Playboy's VIP Magazine,* summer. 1966.†

* * *

HSU, Cho-yun 1930-

PERSONAL: Born July 10, 1930, in China; son of Fengtsao and Ying (Tsang) Hsu; married Man-Li; children: Leo Lo-pung Hsu (son). *Education:* National Taiwan University, B.A., 1953, M.A., 1956; University of Chicago, Ph.D., 1961. *Home:* 5427 Hobart St., Pittsburgh, Pa. 15217.

CAREER: National Taiwan University, Taipei, Taiwan (Formosa), China, associate professor and professor of history of ancient China, 1963-70, chairman of department of history, 1965-70; University of Pittsburgh, Pittsburgh, Pa., professor of history, 1970—. Academia Sinica, Taipei, Taiwan, research fellow, Institute of History and Philology. *Member:* Chinese Historians Association, Ethnological Society of China, American Historical Society, Association for Asian Studies, American Sociological Association. *Awards, honors:* Named one of ten outstanding young men of China, 1964.

WRITINGS: The Journey Within (in Chinese), Book World Press (Taipei), 1964; *Ancient China in Transition: A Study of Social Mobility, 722-222 B.C.,* Stanford University Press, 1965; *Introduction to Historical Studies* (in Chinese), Commercial Press (Taipei), 1966. Contributor to *Comparative Studies of History and Society* and *Bulletin of the Institute of History and Philology.*

WORK IN PROGRESS: An Economic History of the Han Dynasty, Agriculture and Husbandry; Migration in Nineteenth-Century China; editing a series of monographs on the history of ancient China.

HUACO, George A. 1927-

PERSONAL: Born December 21, 1927, in Oakland, Calif.; son of Sergio A. (an engineer) and Carmen (Menendez) Huaco; married Marcia Brown, January 30, 1960; children: Miriam S., Valerie D. *Education:* University of California, Berkeley, B.A., 1954, Ph.D., 1963; University of California, Los Angeles, M.A., 1959. *Politics:* Socialist. *Religion:* None. *Office:* Department of Sociology, University of New Mexico, Albuquerque, N.M. 87106.

CAREER: Yale University, New Haven, Conn., instructor, 1963-64, assistant professor of sociology, 1964-69; State University of New York, Buffalo, associate professor of sociology and director of graduate studies, 1969-71; University of New Mexico, Albuquerque, professor of sociology, 1971—. *Military service:* U.S. Army, Quartermaster Corps, 1954-56. *Member:* American Sociological Association, American Association of University Professors.

WRITINGS: The Sociology of Film Art, Basic Books, 1965. Contributor of articles to *American Sociological Review, New Literary History,* and other periodicals.

SIDELIGHTS: Huaco is fluent in Spanish and competent in French.†

* * *

HUBBELL, Patricia 1928-

PERSONAL: Born July 10, 1928, in Bridgeport, Conn.; daughter of Franklin H. and Helen (Osborn) Hubbell; married Harold Hornstein (a newspaper editor), March 10, 1954; children: Jeffrey, Deborah. *Education:* University of Connecticut, B.S., 1950. *Politics:* Independent. *Religion:* Unitarian Universalist. *Home:* R.F.D. 1, Westport, Conn.

CAREER: Reporter for *Newtown Bee,* Newtown, Conn., 1950-51, and *Westport Town Crier,* Westport, Conn., 1951-54; free lance writer, specializing in gardening and nature.

WRITINGS: The Apple Vendor's Fair, Atheneum, 1963; *8 a.m. Shadows,* Atheneum, 1965; *Catch Me A Wind,* Atheneum, 1968.

* * *

HUBER, Morton Wesley 1923-

PERSONAL: Born July 12, 1923, in Baltimore, Md.; son of George John and Grace E. (Touchton) Huber; married Kyoko Ushio (a private piano instructor), August 20, 1962. *Education:* Johns Hopkins University, A.B., 1947, M.A., 1948; study at Cornell University, 1948-49, New York-Phoenix School of Design, 1958, Maryland Institute of Art, 1958-59. *Religion:* Methodist.

CAREER: Johns Hopkins University, Baltimore, Md., full-time research in organic chemistry and biochemistry, 1950-52; Albright College, Reading, Pa., assistant professor of chemistry, 1952-54; Emory and Henry College, Emory, Va., associate professor of chemistry, 1954-61, chairman of department of art, 1958-61; York Academy of Arts, York, Pa., member of staff, 1961-63; Huber Co. (photographic studio), Baltimore, Md., director, beginning, 1963; Morgan State College, Baltimore, Md., assistant professor of chemistry, beginning 1964. Part-time member of faculty, Maryland Institute of Arts, Baltimore, 1958-59. *Military service:* U.S. Naval Reserve, 1942-45; became ensign. *Member:* American Chemical Society, Baltimore Watercolor Club, Sigma Xi. *Awards, honors:* Awards for paintings from Baltimore Watercolor Club and Virginia Highlands Festival.

WRITINGS: (Self-illustrated) *Vanishing Japan,* Chilton, 1965.

WORK IN PROGRESS: A book on present-day descendants of Mayan Indians (an art book like *Vanishing Japan,* with photographic, drawn, and painted illustrations); research in porphyrin chemistry and the structure of hemoglobin.

SIDELIGHTS: Huber once said of his book subjects: "In a restless, and sometimes hostile world, I am interested in producing something of beauty and quality that will endure. . . . [I] feel I can achieve this best in the artists' media." He has a "fair" knowledge of Japanese.†

* * *

HUDSON, Randolph H(oyt)   1927-

PERSONAL: Born April 12, 1927, in Cleveland, Ohio; son of Hoyt Hopewell and Margaret (Dille) Hudson. *Education:* Stanford University, B.A., 1950, Ph.D., 1962; Cornell University, M.A., 1953; University of Paris, Certificate, 1949. *Politics:* Pacifist. *Office:* Dean, College of Arts and Sciences, Northwestern Illinois University, Chicago, Ill. 60625.

CAREER: Humboldt State College, Arcata, Calif., assistant professor of English literature, 1959-62; University of Colorado, Boulder, assistant professor, 1962-64, associate professor of English literature, 1964-67; Central State University, Wilberforce, Ohio, chairman of English department, 1967-69; Northwestern Illinois University, Chicago, dean of college of arts and sciences, 1969—. Colorado Language Arts Society, executive secretary, 1965-67. Consultant for various publishing firms. *Military service:* U.S. Navy, 1945-46. U.S. Army, Counterintelligence, 1953-55. *Member:* Modern Language Association of America, Conference on College Composition and Communication, National Council of Teachers of English, American Association of University Professors.

WRITINGS: A Modern Handbook of American English, Science Research Associates, 1966; *Technology, Culture, and Language,* Heath, 1966. Member of editorial board, *College Composition and Communication* (quarterly), 1964-66; editor, *Statement* (journal of Colorado Language Arts Society), 1964-67.

WORK IN PROGRESS: A history of the American short story; studies in English Gothicism.

* * *

HUGHES, Arthur Joseph   1928-

PERSONAL: Born November 21, 1928, in Brooklyn, N.Y.; son of James P. and Alice (Rhatigan) Hughes; married Irene K. McGoldrick, November 7, 1953; children: James, John, Jeanne, Joseph, Jerome, Julie. *Education:* St. John's University, Jamaica, N.Y., A.B., 1950; Niagara University, M.A., 1951; Columbia University, Ph.D., 1970. *Religion:* Roman Catholic. *Home:* 30-07 73rd St., Jackson Heights, N.Y. 11370.

CAREER: High school teacher of history, Brooklyn, N.Y., 1955-60, of social studies, Hicksville, N.Y., 1960-61; St. Francis College, Brooklyn, N.Y., professor of history and government and chairman of department, 1961—; adjunct teaching at St. Joseph's College, Fordham University, City University of New York, State University of New York, and Iona College. *Military service:* U.S. Army, 1951-53. *Member:* American Historical Association, Catholic Metropolitan Conference on History and Political Science, Knights of Columbua, Ancient Order of Hibernians.

WRITINGS: Man in Time: An Exploration of World His-

tory (10th grade text), Allyn & Bacon, 1964; *American Government* (text), Glencoe, 1969, revised edition, 1974; *Richard M. Nixon,* Dodd, 1972.

WORK IN PROGRESS: Three books on American political institutions: the presidency, the Congress, and the judiciary.

* * *

HUGHES, C(hristopher) J(ohn)   1918-

PERSONAL: Born March 6, 1918, in England; son of Geoffrey Wallace Grainger (a lieutenant colonel) and Caroline Emily Rosamund (Goodwin) Hughes; married Dorothea Lacy Addison (children's officer, Church of England Children's Society), September 11, 1957. *Education:* Attended Wellington College; University College, Oxford, B.A. and M.A., 1939, B.Phil., 1948. *Religion:* Church of England. *Home:* Cedar Lodge, Saddington, Leicestershire, England LE80QT. *Office:* Department of Politics, University of Leicester, Leicester, England.

CAREER: University of Glasgow, Glasgow, Scotland, assistant lecturer, 1949-53; British Foreign Office, German Section, 1954-56; University of Leicester, Leicester, England, 1957—, began as lecturer, professor of politics, 1962—. Visiting professor, Swiss Federal Institute of Technology, Zurich, Switzerland, 1972. *Military service:* Indian Infantry, 1939-45; became lieutenant. *Member:* British and Swiss political science associations, Swiss Historical Association, Royal Institute of International Affairs, United Services Club (London).

WRITINGS: The Federal Constitution of Switzerland: Text and Commentary, Clarendon Press, 1954; *The British Statute Book,* Rinehart, 1957; *The Parliament of Switzerland,* Oxford University Press, 1962; *Confederacies: Inaugural Lecture,* Leicester University Press, 1963; *Switzerland,* Benn, 1975. Contributor to *Festschrift, Die Moderne Demoknatie una ihr Recht,* and *Buch der Freunde.*

WORK IN PROGRESS: Swiss society and politics; *Canton Valais,* a study in development; conservative political philosophy; federalism.

* * *

HUGHES, Charles L(loyd)   1933-

PERSONAL: Born December 18, 1933, in Dallas, Tex.; son of Charles Lloyd (an auditor) and Euna (Hogan) Hughes; married Kayren Frahm, July 10, 1954; children: Michelle, Patrice, Scott. *Education:* Southern Methodist University, A.B., 1955, M.A., 1956; University of Houston, Ph.D., 1959. *Address:* Mail Station 217, Texas Instruments Inc., P.O. Box 5474, Dallas, Tex. 75222.

CAREER: Member of management development staff, International Business Machines Corp., New York, N.Y., 1959-64; industrial psychologist for Texas Instruments, Inc., Dallas, and instructor at Southern Methodist University, Dallas, 1964-67, components group personnel director, 1967-69, director of corporation industrial relations, 1969-71, director of corporation personnel, 1971-72, director of personnel and organization development, 1972—. Instructor of psychology, Southern Methodist University, Dallas, Tex., 1964-67. *Member:* American Psychological Association, Dallas Psychological Association (president). *Awards, honors:* McKinsey Award, McKinsey Foundation & Academy Management, 1965.

WRITINGS: Goal Setting—Key to Individual and Organizational Effectiveness, American Management Association, 1965. Contributor to personnel journals.

WORK IN PROGRESS: New Styles of Supervision.†

*   *   *

HUGHES, Nathaniel Cheairs, Jr.   1930-

PERSONAL: Born December 21, 1930, in Chattanooga, Tenn.; son of Nat C. (in insurance) and Celeste (Jacoway) Hughes; married Buckner Latimore, November 26, 1954; children: Frank, David L., Sam B. *Education:* Yale University, B.A., 1953; University of North Carolina, M.A., 1956, Ph.D., 1959. *Religion:* Episcopal. *Home:* 107 McFarland Ave., Chattanooga, Tenn. 37405. *Office:* Girls Preparatory School, P.O. Box 4736, Chattanooga, Tenn. 37405.

CAREER: Webb School, Bell Buckle, Tenn., teacher, 1959-62; St. Mary's Episcopal School, Memphis, Tenn., headmaster, 1962-73; Girls Preparatory School, Chattanooga, Tenn., headmaster, 1973—. Memphis State University, instructor, 1963-66. *Military service:* U.S. Marine Corps, 1952-65; became captain. *Member:* Southern Historical Association, Tennessee Historical Association.

WRITINGS: General William J. Hardee, Louisiana State University Press, 1965; *The Instruction Manual Prohibits Expressly Painting Over Portholes,* South and West, 1973. Also author of *The Civil War Comes to Dade County,* 1975.

WORK IN PROGRESS: Editing the memoirs of a Confederate general and a Kentucky newspaper editor.

*   *   *

HULL, William E(dward)   1930-

PERSONAL: Born May 28, 1930, in Birmingham, Ala.; son of William E. and Margaret J. Hull; married Julia Wylodine Hester, July 26, 1952; children: David William, Susan Virginia. *Education:* University of Alabama, student, 1948-50; Howard College (now Samford University), B.A., 1951; Southern Baptist Theological Seminary, B.D., 1954, Th.D., 1960; University of Goettingen, post-doctoral study, 1962-63. *Office:* First Baptist Church, Ockley Dr. and Highland Ave., Shreveport, La. 71106.

CAREER: Ordained Baptist minister, 1950; pastor in Wetumpka, Ala., 1950-51, Owenton, Ky., 1952-53, New Castle, Ky., 1953-58; Southern Baptist Theological Seminary, Louisville, Ky., instructor, 1955-58, assistant professor, 1958-61, associate professor, 1961-67, professor of New Testament interpretation, 1967-75, chairman of department of New Testament, 1963-68, director of graduate studies of School of Theology, 1968-70, dean of School of Theology, 1969-75, provost, 1972-75; First Baptist Church, Shreveport, La., pastor, 1975—. Guest professor at Baptist Theological Seminary, Ruschlikon-Zurich, Switzerland, 1963; speaker on Baptist missions in Europe and Middle East. *Member:* American Academy of Religion, Society of Biblical Literature, American Schools of Oriental Research. *Awards, honors:* Denominational service award, Samford University, 1974.

WRITINGS: Christ and the Modern Mood, 1960; (contributor) *Professor in the Pulpit,* Broadman, 1963; *The Gospel of John,* Broadman, 1964; (contributor) *I Dedicate Myself,* Women's Missionary Union, 1964; (contributor) *Messages on Evangelism,* Golden Rule Press, 1964; (contributor) Josef Nordenhaug, editor, *The Truth That Makes Men Free,* Broadman, 1966; Clifton J. Allen, *Broadman Bible Commentary,* Volume IX, Broadman, 1970; *The Bible,* Covenant Press, 1974. Writer of curriculum materials for

Baptist Sunday School Board. Contributor to religion periodicals.

*   *   *

HUMMEL, Charles E.   1923-

PERSONAL: Born August 8, 1923, in Minneapolis, Minn.; son of Rufus J. (an accountant) and Maria (Brandt) Hummel; married Anne Childs; children: Elizabeth Hummel Reaux, Charles Edward, Richard Austin, James Brandt. *Education:* Yale University, B.S., 1943; Massachusetts Institute of Technology, M.S., 1949; Wheaton College, Wheaton, Ill., M.A., 1962. *Politics:* Republican. *Religion:* Protestant. *Home:* 33 Adelaide Ave., Barrington, R.I. 02806. *Office:* Barrington College, Middle Hwy., Barrington, R.I. 02806.

CAREER: E. I. duPont de Nemours & Co., Grasseli, N.J., technologist, 1943-44; U.S. Army, civilian laboratory inspector at General Headquarters, Tokyo, Japan, 1946-47; Standard Oil Company of New Jersey (Esso), Bayway, chemical engineer, 1949-50; Inter-Varsity Christian Fellowship, field representative in Boston, Mass., 1950-51, regional director in Fanwood, N.J., 1952-56, executive director in Chicago, Ill., 1956-65; Barrington College, Barrington, R.I., president, 1965—. *Sunday School Times,* director. *Military service:* U.S. Army, Infantry, 1944-46; became first lieutenant; received Special Commendation Medal. *Member:* American Scientific Affiliation (fellow), Evangelical Theological Society, University Club (Providence, R.I.). *Awards, honors:* L.H.D. from Geneva College, 1965.

WRITINGS: Campus Christian Witness, Inter-Varsity, 1958; *Contemporary Christian Thought,* Inter-Varsity, 1960; *The Search,* Inter-Varsity, 1964, 3rd edition, 1974. Also author of pamphlets. Consulting editor, *His* (magazine).†

*   *   *

HUNDLEY, Norris (Cecil), Jr.   1935-

PERSONAL: Born October 26, 1935, in Houston, Tex.; son of Norris Cecil (an engineer) and Helen (Mundine) Hundley; married Carol Marie Beckquist, June 8, 1957; children: Wendy, Jacqueline. *Education:* Mount San Antonio College, A.A., 1956; Whittier College, A.B., 1958; University of California, Los Angeles, Ph.D., 1963. *Home:* 745 Alma Real Dr., Pacific Palisades, Calif. 90272. *Office:* History Department, University of California, Los Angeles, Calif. 90024.

CAREER: University of Houston, Houston, Tex., instructor in American history, 1963-64; University of California, Los Angeles, assistant professor, 1964-69, associate professor, 1969-73, professor of American history, 1973—. Whittier College, visiting assistant professor, summer, 1964. *Member:* American Historical Association, Organization of American Historians, Western History Association.

WRITINGS: John Walton Caughey, Dawson's, 1961; *Dividing the Waters: A Century of Controversy between the United States and Mexico,* University of California Press, 1966; *The American West: Frontier and Region,* Ward Ritchie, 1969; *Water and the West: The Colorado River Compact and the Politics of Water in the American West,* University of California Press, 1975. Contributor to *Notable American Women, Foreign Affairs, Pacific Historical Review, Western Historical Quarterly, California Historical Quarterly,* and other periodicals.

HUNT, Ignatius 1920-

PERSONAL: Born June 27, 1920, in Spokane, Wash.; son of Joseph Frederick (a title insurance agent) and Olga (Petersen) Hunt. Education: Attended Gonzaga University and Mount Angel College, 1938-42, B.A., 1942; University of Ottawa, S.T.L., 1948, S.T.D., 1950; Pontifical Biblical Institute, Rome, Italy, S.S.B.; Pontifical Biblical Commission, S.S.L., 1962; Ecole Biblique et Archeologique, Jerusalem, additional study, 1962-63. Home and office: Conception Abbey, Conception, Mo. 64433.

CAREER: Roman Catholic priest of Order of St. Benedict (Benedictine monk). Seminary of Christ the King, Vancouver, British Columbia, Canada, professor of Old Testament and biblical language, 1950-58; Immaculate Conception Seminary, Conception, Mo., professor of Old Testament and biblical language, 1958-61, 1963—. Lecturer on Sacred Scripture at summer institutes at St. Louis University, University of San Francisco, and other Catholic colleges. Member: Catholic Biblical Association of America (member of board of trustees), American Benedictine Academy, Society of Biblical Literature, Kansas City Theological Association.

WRITINGS: The Book of Genesis, Paulist Press, 1960; Understanding the Bible, Sheed, 1962; Joshua-Judges, Liturgical Press, 1965; World of the Patriarchs, Prentice-Hall, 1967.

Contributor: John L. McKenzie, editor, The Bible in Current Catholic Thought, Herder, 1962; R. E. Murphy, R. E. Brown, and J. F. Fitzmyer, editors, Jerome Commentary on Sacred Scripture, in press. Contributor to Catholic Youth Encyclopedia. Also contributor to more than fifteen periodicals. Associate editor, American Benedictine Review, 1956—.

SIDELIGHTS: Hunt has spent two extended periods in the Near East, covering all countries of biblical interest. He speaks, reads, and writes Latin, German, French, Spanish, and Italian, and can work in Hebrew, Arabic, Ugaritic, Aramaic, Dutch, Portuguese, Catalan, and Danish.†

* * *

HUNT, Irene 1907-

PERSONAL: Born May 18, 1907, in Newton, Ill.; daughter of Franklin Pierce and Sarah (Land) Hunt. Education: University of Illinois, A.B., 1939; University of Minnesota, M.A., 1946.

CAREER: Oak Park, Ill. public schools, teacher of French and English, 1930-45; University of South Dakota, instructor in psychology, 1946-50; Cicero Illinois public schools, teacher, 1950-65, began as consultant, became director of language arts, 1965—. Awards, honors: Charles W. Follett Award, 1964, American Notable Book Award and sole runner-up for the Newbery Medal, both 1965, both for Across Five Aprils; Newbery Medal, 1967, for Up a Road Slowly.

WRITINGS: Across Five Aprils, Follett, 1964; Up a Road Slowly, Follett, 1966; Trail of Apple Blossoms, Follett, 1968; No Promises in the Wind, Follett, 1970.

SIDELIGHTS: Up a Road Slowly chronicles ten years in the lifetime of a young girl who suffers the loss of her mother and goes to live with a spinster aunt. "[The novel] had its beginnings in an experience that has remained vivid in the author's memory throughout her life," wrote Esther Meeks. "This was the death of [Miss Hunt's] father when she was a small child. It was her first acquaintance with death; she had never even dreamed of a world without her parents."

The Newbery-Caldecott committee commented: "Up a Road Slowly is a work of poignant fiction which concerns itself with the timeless problems of all young people groping for independence and maturity. The young heroine, Julia, sent to live with a high-minded and compassionate aunt, is susceptible to a whole range of influences. . . . The many diverse characters who shape her life and emotional growth are beautifully realized with great perception and sensitivity and a happy absence of sentimentality."

D. M. Broderick praised her book for similar reasons: "Miss Hunt demonstrates that she is a writer of the first rank. . . . The adult who chooses to write a first-person novel about the child he once was faces two serious problems: the danger of over-sentimentalizing his material, and the difficulty of sustaining a young reader's interest in a past-tense narrative. The author has surmounted both obstacles triumphantly. . . . Those who follow Julie's growth—from a tantrum-throwing 7-year old to a gracious young woman of 17—will find this book has added a new dimension to their lives."

Referring to her first book, Across Five Aprils, Miss Hunt said: "I didn't plan my first book for a certain age group. I don't want to aim at a special age of reader. I write when I have something to say, and I hope to say it as well and as gracefully as I can." In discussing the qualifications of a children's writer, Miss Hunt noted that his first ability to write for children involves "a close affinity with his own childhood, and if he has this, it follows that he will have that same affinity for childhood in general. He must remember! He must remember the anxieties and uncertainties, he must remember the loneliness of being teased or misunderstood. . . . He must remember his reaction to tastes, to smell, to colors; his love of a kind hand, his fear of a harsh mouth. He must remember the imaginary companions, the wonderful secret places where he could be alone, the hoarding of nondescript material in an old box—guarding it, rearranging it, caring greatly for it without quite knowing why."

BIOGRAPHICAL/CRITICAL SOURCES: New York Times Book Review, November 6, 1966, March 19, 1967, April 14, 1968; Publisher's Weekly, March 13, 1967; G. Robert Carlsen, Books and the Teenage Reader, Harper, 1967; Commonweal, May 24, 1968; Young Readers' Review, June, 1968; New Yorker, December 14, 1968; Nancy Larrick, A Parent's Guide to Children's Reading, 3rd edition, Doubleday, 1969; The Writer, March, 1970; Horn Book, June, 1970.†

* * *

HUNTER, Beatrice Trum 1918-

PERSONAL: Born December 16, 1918, in New York, N.Y.; daughter of Gabriel (a foreman) and Martha (Engle) Trum; married John Frank Hunter (a craftsman in pewter and wood), August 2, 1943. Education: Brooklyn College (now of the City University of New York), B.A., 1940, Columbia University, M.A., 1943; graduate study at State University of New York at Buffalo, Harvard University, and New York University. Politics: Independent. Religion: Nondenominational. Home: R.F.D. 1, Hillsboro, N.H. 03244.

CAREER: Teacher of visually handicapped children in Belleville, N.J., 1940-42, Newark, N.J., 1942-45, New York, N.Y., 1945-55; lecturer and free-lance writer,

1955—. Columbia University, summer demonstration teacher, 1942, 1943. Delivered the fourteenth and fifteenth annual Martha R. Jones Lectureship in Nutrition, Asbury Theological Seminary, 1973, 1974. *Member:* Natural Food Associates (director of New Hampshire chapter), Federation of Homemakers (honorary vice-president), American Academy of Applied Nutrition (honorary vice-president), Price-Pottenger Nutrition Foundation (honorary member), Land Fellowship (Canada), Soil Association (England). *Awards, honors:* Award from Friends of Nature for public education on pesticides, 1961; Tastemaker's Award, 1973, for *The Natural Foods Primer.*

WRITINGS: The Natural Foods Cookbook, Simon and Schuster, 1961; *Gardening Without Poisons*, Houghton, 1964; *Consumer Beware!*, Simon and Schuster, 1971; *The Natural Foods Primer*, Simon and Schuster, 1972; *The Whole-Grain Baking Sampler*, Keats, 1972; *Food Additives and Your Health*, Keats, 1972; *Yogurt, Kefir, and Other Milk Cultures*, Keats, 1972; *Fermented Foods and Beverages*, Keats, 1972; *Beatrice Trum Hunter's Favorite Natural Foods*, Simon and Schuster, 1974. Contributor to *Herald of Health, Modern Nutrition* (now defunct), *Consumer Bulletin, Consumer's Research Magazine, Handbook of Buying*, and other magazines.

SIDELIGHTS: Mrs. Hunter understands French, Spanish, and German.

* * *

HURD, John C(oolidge), Jr.   1928-

PERSONAL: Born March 26, 1928, in Boston, Mass.; son of John Coolidge (a life underwriter) and Mary Knap (Hough) Hurd; married Helen Porter, December 20, 1948; children: Elisabeth, Louisa, Lyman Porter. *Education:* Harvard University, B.S., 1949; Episcopal Theological School, Cambridge, Mass., B.D., 1952; Yale University, M.A., 1957, Ph.D., 1961. *Politics:* Democrat. *Office:* Trinity College, Toronto, Ontario M5S 1H8, Canada.

CAREER: Clergyman of The Protestant Episcopal Church; Christ Church, Bethany, Conn., priest in charge, 1954-57; Princeton University, Princeton, N.J., instructor in religion, 1958-60; Episcopal Theological Seminary of the Southwest, Austin, Tex., assistant professor, 1960-62, associate professor, 1962-65, professor of New Testament, 1965-67; Trinity College, Toronto, Ontario, professor of New Testament, 1967—. *Member:* Studiorum Novi Testamenti Societas, Society of Biblical Literature, American Academy of Religion, American Association of University Professors, American Civil Liberties Union (board member, Austin, 1966). *Awards, honors:* Christian Research Foundation Award, 1964, for *The Origin of 1 Corinthians*; American Association of Theological Schools faculty fellow, 1964-65.

WRITINGS: The Origin of 1 Corinthians, Seabury, 1965; *A Bibliography of New Testament Bibliographies*, Seabury, 1966; (contributor) W. R. Farmer and others, editors, *Christian History and Interpretation: Studies Presented to John Knox*, Cambridge University Press, 1967. Also contributor to *The New English Bible*, annotated edition, Oxford University Press, 1975. Editor, *Anglican Theological Review*, 1966-69; abstractor, *New Testament Abstracts*, 1958-69.

WORK IN PROGRESS: The Origin of 1 and 2 Thessalonians.

AVOCATIONAL INTERESTS: Mountaineering, scuba diving.†

HUTCHINS, Carleen Maley   1911-

PERSONAL: Born May 24, 1911, in Springfield, Mass.; daughter of Thomas William (an accountant) and Grace (Fletcher) Maley; married Morton Aldrich Hutchins (a chemist), June 6, 1943; children: William Aldrich, Caroline. *Education:* Cornell University, B.A. (science), 1933; New York University, M.A., 1942. *Home:* 112 Essex Ave., Montclair, N.J. 07042; (summer) Box 1, Mirror Lake, N.H. 03853.

CAREER: Woodward School, Brooklyn, N.Y., teacher of science and woodworking, 1933-37; Brearley School, New York, N.Y., teacher of science, 1937-49; All Day Neighborhood Schools, New York, N.Y., assistant director, 1943-45; self-employed in violin research, development, and construction, 1947—. Science consultant to Coward-McCann, Inc., 1956-65, Girl Scouts of America, 1957-65, National Recreation Association, 1962-65. *Member:* International Violin Makers Association, Viola da gamba Society of America, Acoustical Society of America (fellow), Audio Engineering Society, Catgut Acoustical Society (secretary, 1963—), Southern California Violin Maker's Association, Sigma Xi. *Awards, honors:* Gugenheim fellowships for research in violin acoustics and development of new violin family, 1959, 1961; research grant, Martha Baird Rockefeller Fund for Music, 1966 and 1968; American Philosophical Society grant, 1968; New Jersey Symphony arts award, 1970; National Science Foundation travel grant, 1971 and 1974.

WRITINGS: Life's Key, DNA: A Biological Adventure into the Unknown, Coward, 1961; (science consultant) Warren Goodrich, *Science Through Recreation*, Holt, 1964; *Moon Moth*, Coward, 1965; *Who Will Drown the Sound*, Coward, 1972. Contributor of articles and papers on violin acoustics to *Scientific American, Journal of the Acoustical Society of America, Strad* (London), and journals for musicians.

WORK IN PROGRESS: Several other life-history books on the order of *Moon Moth.*

SIDELIGHTS: Because friends complained that her trumpet was too loud for their chamber music sessions, she bought an inexpensive viola, "dreamed" of making a better one, spent two years (1947-49) producing the better instrument, and has since made some eighty violins, violas, and cellos—all experimental in some respect. The experimental features stem from fifteen years of work in violin acoustics with the late Frederick A. Saunders of Harvard, who pioneered violin research in America. The group that worked with Saunders forms the nucleus of the Catgut Acoustical Society, Inc., an international organization sponsoring research and development of stringed instruments. There are 600 members from seventeen countries.

BIOGRAPHICAL/CRITICAL SOURCES: Scientific American, November, 1962; *Life*, November 29, 1963; *American String Teacher*, spring, 1965.

* * *

HUTCHINSON, H(ugh) Lester   1904-

PERSONAL: Born December 13, 1904, in Bury, Lancashire, England; son of Richard (a director) and Mary (Lester) Hutchinson; married Elizabeth Morgan (a teacher); children: Carolyn, Mark, Shane. *Education:* University of Neuchatel, D.es.L., 1925; University of Edinburgh, graduate study, 1925-27. *Politics:* "Cynicism." *Religion:* "Scepticism." *Home:* 4 The Close, Lichfield, Staffordshire, England.

CAREER: Journalist in Berlin, Germany, 1927-28, in India, 1928-33; journalism and adult education work in London, England, 1933-39; temporary civil servant, 1940-42, 1944-45; master at Junior School, Cheltenham College, Cheltenham, England, 1944-45; member of Parliament, 1945-50; schoolmaster, 1950-66. *Military service:* Royal Navy, 1942-44; became lieutenant; injured on antisubmarine duty in the Mediterranean and invalided out, 1944; received African Star.

WRITINGS: Conspiracy at Meerut, Allen & Unwin, 1935; *Empire of the Nabobs*, Allen & Unwin, 1938; *The Rise of Capitalism*, National Council of Labour Colleges Publishers, 1938; *European Freebooters in Mughul India*, Asia Publishing House (Bombay), 1964; *Conspiracy of Catiline*, Anthony Blond, 1966; (author of notes and introduction) Karl Marx, *Secret Diplomatic History of the Eighteenth Century*, World Books, 1968; *Murders at Larinum*, Blond & Briggs, in press. Also author of notes and introduction, *Chronique Scandalendo*.

* * *

HUTCHINSON, Michael E.   1925-

PERSONAL: Born September 14, 1925, in Barrow, Lancashire, England; son of Francis E. and Marjorie (Sewell) Hutchinson. *Education:* Trinity Hall, Cambridge, M.A. (honors in history), 1950. *Politics:* Radical Conservative. *Home:* Flat 21, Beech Park, Sandforth Rd., Liverpool, England.

CAREER: City of London School, London, England, teacher, 1953-61; Middlebury College, Middlebury, Vt., lecturer in European history, 1956-57; Ministry of Education, Western Nigeria, director of publications, 1961-62; Ruffwood Comprehensive School, Kirkby, near Liverpool, England, teacher, 1963—. *Military service:* British Army, Royal Armoured Corps, 1943-47; received Belt of Honour at Royal Military Academy, Sandhurst. *Member:* European Teachers Association, Historical Association, Royal Commonwealth Society, Assistant Masters Association, Student Christian Movement, London and Middlesex Rifle Association, Oxford and Cambridge Club.

WRITINGS: (With Christopher Young) *Educating the Intelligent*, Penguin, 1962; *Education in Britain*, Hamish Hamilton, 1966. Regular contributor to *Times Educational Supplement, Teacher, Countryman*.

WORK IN PROGRESS: A life of Ernest Bevin, for Oxford University Press "Clarendon" Series.

AVOCATIONAL INTERESTS: Travel (Europe, United States, Africa), writings, photography (preferably in mountain areas), painting.†

* * *

HUXLEY-BLYTHE, Peter J(ames)   1925-

PERSONAL: Born November 16, 1925, in Mansfield, Nottinghamshire, England; son of Joseph Henry (a consultant hypnotist) and Annie (Huxley) Blythe; married Maxine McElhinney, April 10, 1947; children: Peter Maximillian, Maxine Ita. *Education:* Attended schools in England until fourteen. *Religion:* Church of England.

CAREER: World Survey (newsletter), Fleetwood, Lancashire, England, editor, 1953-58; *Free Russia*, Fleetwood, Lancashire, England, editor, 1959-62; Peter Blythe & Associates (psychological consultants to management). Blackpool, Lancashire, England, director, beginning 1963. Director, Successful Sales & Business Ltd. *Military service:*

Royal Navy, 1940-47; received Atlantic Star, North Africa Star and rosette, Burma Star and Pacific rosette. *Member:* Institute of Ethical Hypnosis (founding member), Lions International. *Awards, honors:* Gold badge and certificate of Russian Revolutionary Forces, 1958; Knight Commander of the Sovereign Order of St. John of Jerusalem.

WRITINGS: Betrayal—The Story of Russian Anti-Communism, Friends of National Russia, 1956; *The Paid Wreckers*, Fronis, 1957; *The Healing Sleep*, Diamond Press, 1963; *East Came West*, Caxton, 1964. Contributor of articles to newspapers and magazines in Europe, North and South America, South Africa, and other parts of the free world.

WORK IN PROGRESS: A Trail of Treachery, the story of the betrayal of Hungarian anti-Communists in 1945-47 and 1956-57; *The Psychology of Treason*, about the motives that lead to treason and support for Communism.†

* * *

HYAMS, Joseph   1923-
(Joe Hyams)

PERSONAL: Born June 6, 1923, in Cambridge, Mass.; son of Joseph (a salesman) and Charlotte (Strauss) Hyams; married Elke Sommer (an actress), November 19, 1964. *Education:* New York University, B.S., 1948, M.A., 1949. *Religion:* Jewish. *Home:* 530 North Beverly Glen Blvd., West Los Angeles, Calif. 90024.

CAREER: New York Herald Tribune, Los Angeles, Calif., Hollywood columnist and bureau chief, 1951-64; full-time professional writer, 1964—. Instructor in journalism, University of California, Los Angeles, 1963-64. *Military service:* U.S. Army, Infantry, 1942-46; became master sergeant. *Member:* Authors Guild, American Newspaper Guild, Overseas Press Club.

WRITINGS—All under name Joe Hyams except as indicated: (With Major Riddle) *Weekend Gambler's Handbook*, Random House, 1964; (with Walter Wanger) *My Life with Cleopatra*, Bantam, 1964; (with Peter Sellers) *Sellers Market*, Prentice-Hall, 1965; (with Edith Head) *How to Dress for Success*, Random House, 1966; *Bogie*, New American Library, 1966; (under name Joseph Hyams) *A Field of Buttercups* (biography), Prentice-Hall, 1968; (with Thomas Murton) *Accomplices to the Crime: The Arkansas Prison Scandal* (non-fiction), Grove, 1969; (with Tony Trabert) *Winning Tactics for Weekend Tennis*, Holt, 1972; *Mislaid in Hollywood*, Peter H. Wyden, 1973; (with Pancho Gonzales) *Winning Tactics for Singles*, Holt, 1973; (editor of new edition) Billie Jean King, *Billie Jean King's Secret of Winning Tennis*, Holt, 1974.

Contributor to *McCall's, Ladies Home Journal, Cosmopolitan, Red Book, Reader's Digest*, and *Playboy*. Motion picture editor for *This Week* and *Woman's Home Companion*.

SIDELIGHTS: A Field of Buttercups was adapted for TV and produced by NBC, November 23, 1969. The film rights to *Accomplices to the Crime* were sold, April, 1970. Hyams speaks German and French. *Avocational interests:* Karate and judo (holds brown belt in both).†

* * *

HYDE, Laurence   1914-

PERSONAL: Born June 6, 1914, in London, England; son of Sydney Augustus (a musician) and Lillian (Snelling) Hyde; married Elizabeth Bainbridge (a teacher), October 7,

1939; children: Anthony, Christopher. *Education:* Attended public school and technical high school in Canada. *Politics:* Liberal. *Religion:* Protestant. *Home:* Apartment A, 1050 Graham Blvd., Montreal, Quebec, Canada. *Office:* National Film Board of Canada, Cote de Liesse Rd., Montreal, Quebec, Canada.

CAREER: National Film Board of Canada, Montreal, Quebec, writer, film director, and producer, 1942—. Author, principally of juvenile books, and artist. *Member:* Canadian Society of Film Makers.

WRITINGS: Southern Cross (adult), Ward Ritchie, 1951; *Brave Davy Coon* (juvenile), Harper, 1955; *Under the Pirate Flag* (juvenile), Houghton, 1965; *Captain Deadlock* (juvenile novel), Houghton, 1968.

WORK IN PROGRESS: An adult novel.

SIDELIGHTS: Hyde aims, in his children's books, for fast-action adventure in the tradition of Stevenson and Defoe, the two writers who have most influenced his work.

He also is an artist and works in such mediums as wood-engraving, oil, and water-color.†

*   *   *

HYLTON, Delmer P(aul) 1920-

PERSONAL: Surname is pronounced Hilton; born October 18, 1920, in Indianapolis, Ind.; son of Delmer Dick (an auditor) and Abbie (Manville) Hylton; married Helen Lois Eastwood, June 5, 1948; children: Deborah Anne, James Austin, Paula Lois. *Education:* Indiana University, B.S., 1942, M.B.A., 1949. *Religion:* Baptist. *Home:* 1856 Faculty Dr., Winston-Salem, N.C. 27106. *Office:* Wake Forest University, P.O. Box 7285, Winston-Salem, N.C. 27109.

CAREER: Public accountant, 1946-48; Internal Revenue Service, special agent, 1948-49; Wake Forest College (now University), Winston-Salem, N.C., assistant professor, 1949-51, associate professor, 1952-54, professor of accounting, 1954—. Consultant to chairman of Department of International Business Administration, American College of Switzerland, 1973-74. *Military service:* U.S. Army, 1942-45. *Member:* American Institute of Certified Public Accountants, American Accounting Association, North Carolina Association of Certified Public Accountants (past education chairman), Alpha Kappa Psi, Beta Gamma Sigma.

WRITINGS: Principles and Procedures of Modern Accounting Practice, Prentice-Hall, 1965. Contributor to professional journals.

WORK IN PROGRESS: Auditing text.

*   *   *

HYMA, Albert 1893-

PERSONAL: Born March 18, 1893, in Groningen, Netherlands; came to the United States, 1910, naturalized citizen, 1927; son of Abe and Dieuwke (Brouwer) Hijma; married Vera Alberta Nodine, August 20, 1927; children: Albert, Jr., David, Beata Maria (Mrs. Paul Timmermann). *Education:* Attended Calvin College, Grand Rapids, Mich., 1913-14; University of Michigan, A.B., 1915, A.M., 1916, Ph.D., 1922. *Politics:* Republican. *Religion:* Reformed Church in America. *Home:* 615 West 30th St., Holland, Mich. 49423.

CAREER: Knox College, Galesburg, Ill., instructor in German, 1916-17; University of North Dakota, Grand Forks, instructor in history, 1922-23, assistant professor,

1923-24; University of Michigan, Ann Arbor, member of faculty, 1924-26, assistant professor, 1926-29, associate professor, 1929-36, professor, 1936-63, professor emeritus, 1963—. Aquinas College, Grand Rapids, Mich., professor of history, 1962-63, director of historical research for City of Grand Rapids, Mich., 1962-63; professor of history, Western Kentucky University, 1971; professor of history, Christian Heritage College (San Diego), 1971-72. Has also taught at the University of Chicago, and has lectured at six foreign universities. *Member:* Renaissance Society of America, Royal Historical Society (fellow). *Awards, honors:* Henry Russell Award, University of Michigan, 1926; Guggenheim fellowship, 1928-29; knighted by the Dutch Government, 1936.

WRITINGS: The Christian Renaissance (first three chapters published as *Devotio Moderna* [doctoral dissertation], University of Michigan, 1922), Reformed Press, 1924, 2nd edition, Shoe String, 1965; *A Short History of Europe, 1500-1855*, F. S. Crofts, 1928; *Luther's Theological Development from Erfurt to Augsburg*, F. S. Crofts, 1928; *The Youth of Erasmus*, University of Michigan Press, 1930, 2nd edition, 1968; *Europe from the Renaissance to 1815*, F. S. Crofts, 1931; (with John A. Rickard) *An Outline of Ancient, Medieval and Modern History*, Barnes & Noble, 1933, 12th edition, 1957; *Christianity, Capitalism, and Communism*, privately printed, 1937; *An Outline of the Growth of Western Civilization*, Ann Arbor Press, 1938; *Christianity and Politics*, Lippincott, 1938, revised edition, Brant, 1960; (with A. E. Boak and P. W. Slosson) *Growth of European Civilization* (originally published as *The Growth of Western Civilization*), two volumes, F. S. Crofts, 1938; *Eternal Life: A Historical Analysis of the Relation Between Christianity and Spiritualism*, Craft Press, 1939; *An Outline of Ancient History*, Barnes & Noble, 1940; *The Dutch in the Far East: A History of the Dutch Commercial and Colonial Empire*, G. Wahr, 1942, revised edition published as *A History of the Dutch in the Far East*, 1953; *World History: A Christian Interpretation*, Eerdmans, 1942; *The Life of John Calvin*, Eerdmans, 1943; *An Outline of the Growth of Far Eastern Civilization*, Longs College Book Co., 1946; *Albertus C. Van Raalte and His Dutch Settlements in the United States*, Eerdmans, 1947; *How We Become Good Citizens*, Ann Arbor Press, 1949; *The Brethren of the Common Life*, Eerdmans, 1950; *Dynamic Citizenship*, Long Publishing, 1950; *Renaissance to Reformation*, Eerdmans, 1951; *Sir Henry Clinton and the American Revolution*, [Ann Arbor], 1957; *Martin Luther and the Luther Film of 1953*, Wahr, 1957, published as *New Light on Martin Luther*, Eerdmans, 1958; (with Frank Bury Woodford) *Gabriel Richard: Frontier Ambassador* (Literary Guild selection), Wayne State University Press, 1958; *The Religious Views of Benjamin Franklin*, 1958; *World Civilization*, Braun-Brumfield, Volume I: *A Survey of Ancient Civilization*, 1959, Volume II: *A Survey of Medieval Civilization*, 1960, Volume III: *A Survey of Early Modern Civilization*, 1960, Volume IV: *A Survey of Modern Civilization to 1870*, 1961, Volume V: *A Survey of Modern Civilization After 1870*, 1961, Volumes IV and V published by Brant Publishing, revised edition, with Robert Woznicki, published as *History of World Civilization*, Roadrunner Technical Publications (Tucson), Volume I, 1965, Volume II, 1966; *The Life of Desiderius Erasmus*, Tassen, Van Gorcum, 1972. Contributor of over 200 articles to six encyclopedias and eleven magazines.

Editor: Thomas a Kempis, *The Imitation of Christ*, Century, 1927; *Erasmus and the Humanists*, F. S. Crofts,

1930; (with J. F. Scott and Arthur Noyes) *Readings in Medieval History*, Crofts, 1933; (and translator) Abe Brouwer, *The Golden Whip*, Zondervan, 1947; (and translator) Gerald Zerbolt of Zutphen (teacher of Thomas a Kempis), *Imitation of Christ*, Eerdmans, 1950. Editor of two of the ten departments producing the *Twentieth Century Encyclopedia of Religious Knowledge*.

The Brederode Chronicle, Edited by George A. Hoar (University Microfilms, 1955), is a comparison of a manuscript by Hyma and Manuscript No. 5 E 23 of the University Library in Utrecht, Netherlands.

WORK IN PROGRESS: New editions of *The Imitation of Christ*; *Dynamic Christianity*; *The Christian Interpretation of History*; *Christianity and Slavery in the United States*; *Crusader Frank Murphy*; *Dutch Contributions to American Civilization*; *The Growth of Far Eastern Civilizations*; *The Inspired Word*; *The Life of Hugo Grotius*.

SIDELIGHTS: Hyma told *CA*: "Have undertaken seven research trips to Europe, reviewed 96 books in seven languages, have lectured abroad in three languages: English, German, and Dutch. . . ."

BIOGRAPHICAL/CRITICAL SOURCES: K. A. Strand, editor, *The Dawn of Modern Civilization*, Edwards Letter Shop (Ann Arbor), 1962, revised edition, 1964.

* * *

HYMAN, Dick 1904-

PERSONAL: Born March 12, 1904, in New York, N.Y.; son of Michael and Selina (Kirschbaum) Hyman; married Margaret Louise Phillips, March 11, 1938; stepchildren: Clark Phillips. *Education:* Attended Columbia University, 1927. *Politics:* Republican. *Religion:* Episcopalian. *Home:* 2 Tudor City Pl., New York, N.Y. 10017.

CAREER: Brazilian American Magazine, Rio de Janeiro, Brazil, co-editor, 1924-25; *Providence Journal*, Providence, R.I., reporter, 1928; Robert L. Ripley ("Believe It Or Not"), New York, N.Y., publicity director, 1929-33; King Features Syndicate and International News Service, New York, N.Y., publicity director, 1933-43; *Look*, New York, N.Y., special events director, 1944-46; free-lance public relations work, 1946—. *Military service:* U.S. Marine Corps Reserve; became captain. *Member:* Overseas Press Club, National Press Club, London Press Club, Sigma Delta Chi, Silvarians, Banshees.

WRITINGS: It's the Law, Doubleday, 1935; *Marine Comedy*, Mohawk, 1944; *Of All Fool Things*, Duell, Sloane & Pearce, 1948; *Nonsense; U.S.A.*, Dutton, 1953; *It's Still the Law*, McKay, 1961; *Baseball Wit and Wisdom*, McKay, 1962; *Stop the Presses*, Hawthorn, 1966; *Now, See Here Judge*, Hawthorn, 1967; *Football Wit and Humor*, Grosset, 1970; *Cockeyed Americana*, Stephen Greene Press, 1972.

* * *

HYMOFF, Edward 1924-

PERSONAL: Born October 12, 1924, in Boston, Mass.; son of Gustave and Gertrude (Kravetsky) Hymoff; children: Yves Kurt, Jennifer Toby. *Education:* Attended Northeastern University, 1946-47; Boston University, B.S. in Journalism, 1949; Columbia University, M.A. in Political Science, 1950. *Address:* P.O. Box 92, Centuck Station, Yonkers, N.Y. 10710. *Agent:* William Morris Agency, 1350 Avenue of the Americas, New York, N.Y. 10019.

CAREER: New York World-Telegram and Sun, New York, N.Y., city desk assistant, 1950-51; free-lance correspondent in Japan and Korea for fifteen New England dailies, *Newsweek*, and other magazines, 1951-52; International News Service, bureau chief in Korea, then news editor on Tokyo desk, 1952-54; National Broadcasting Co., New York, N.Y., news desk supervisor, 1954-58; free-lance reporter and magazine writer, 1958-59, traveling and reporting from Soviet Union and other East European countries, 1958; Radio Station WMGM, New York, N.Y., director of news and special events, 1959; Carl Byoir and Associates (public relations), New York, N.Y., account representative, specializing in aerospace and science, 1959-63; self-employed writer, and free-lance producer for National Educational Television, 1963—; V.M.H. Publishing Co. (in Vietnam), associate editor, 1966-69; *Think* magazine, IBM Corp., New York, N.Y., associate editor, 1969-71; NBC News, New York, N.Y., executive editor of New York television news, 1974. Consultant in propaganda dissemination to U.S. Information Agency and Department of Defense; public relations consultant to aerospace companies. Licensed pilot, 1948—. *Military service:* U.S. Army, 1943-45; served in Africa, Italy, and Balkans; became sergeant. *Member:* International Institute for Strategic Studies, Aviation/Space Writers Association, Authors Guild, Writers Guild of America, Company of Military Historians, American Institute of Aeronautics and Astronautics, Society of Magazine Writers, National Press Club, Overseas Press Club, New York Press Club, Sigma Delta Chi. *Awards, honors:* Aviation/Space Writers Association award, 1965, for *The Mission*; Distinguished Alumni Achievement Award from Boston University, 1966; Apollo Achievement Award from National Aeronautics and Space Administration (NASA), 1971.

WRITINGS: (With Martin Caidin) *The Mission*, Lippincott, 1964; (contributor) *I Can Tell It Now* (Overseas Press Club anthology), Dutton, 1964; *Guidance and Control of Spacecraft*, Holt, 1965; *Stig Von Bayer: International Troubleshooter for Peace*, James Heineman, 1965; (with Phil Hirsch) *The Kennedy Courage*, Pyramid, 1965; *First Marine Division: Vietnam*, M. W. Lads, 1967; *The First Air Cavalry Division: Vietnam*, M. W. Lads, 1967; *Fourth Infantry Division: Vietnam*, M. W. Lads, 1968; *First Marine Aircraft Wing: Vietnam*, M. W. Lads, 1969; *The OSS in World War II*, Ballantine, 1972. Contributor to *Reader's Digest, Reporter, Pageant, Coronet, True, Argosy, Popular Mechanics, Flying, Boy's Life, Newsweek*, and other magazines, and to Sunday newspaper supplements.

WORK IN PROGRESS: A book on organized crime for Holt.

* * *

IANNIELLO, Lynne Young 1925-

PERSONAL: Surname is pronounced *Eye*-ann-ello; born October 27, 1925, in New York, N.Y.; daughter of Joseph G. (a merchant) and Gertrude (Goodman) Young; married Paul J. Ianniello (a merchant), November 21, 1948; children: Geoffry Dean, Richard Gary. *Education:* New York University, B.S., 1946. *Politics:* Independent. *Religion:* Jewish. *Home:* 21 South Kensington Ave., Rockville Centre, N.Y. 11570.

CAREER: Colonial Airlines, New York, N.Y., editor of passenger magazine, 1946-47; Macy's, Inc., New York, N.Y., assistant publications editor, 1947-49; *Long Island*

Press, Jamaica, N.Y., reporter and feature writer, 1949-51; free-lance writer, Rockville Centre, N.Y., 1951-61; Oceanside (N.Y.) schools, public relations director, 1961-62; Anti-Defamation League, New York, N.Y., assistant to public relations director and editor of national publication, 1962-72, director of public relations, 1972—.

WRITINGS: (Edtior) Mary Anne Raywid, *The Ax-Grinders*, Macmillan, 1962; *Milestones along the March*, Praeger, 1965. Contributor to periodicals.

WORK IN PROGRESS: Research in human relations (interreligious and interracial), and extremist groups.

* * *

ICOLARI, Daniel Leonardo 1942-

PERSONAL: Born December 13, 1942, in New York, N.Y.; son of Vincent James (a sculptor) and Ann (Cravet) Icolari; married Ellen Norton, December 19, 1963; children: Evan. *Education:* Attended City College of the City University of New York, 1962, Hunter College of the City University of New York, 1963-64. *Politics:* "Liberal, in the 19th-century sense of the word." *Office:* 104 Fifth Ave., New York, N.Y. 10011.

CAREER: General Features Corp., New York, N.Y., proofreader and copy editor, 1962-64; B. Klein & Co. (publishers), New York, N.Y., editor, 1964—. *Member:* American Montessori Society.

WRITINGS—Editor: *Guide to American Directories*, 6th edition, McGraw, 1965; *Guide to American Educational Directories*, McGraw, 1965; *Encyclopedia of the American Indian*, Klein, 1966.

WORK IN PROGRESS: Research on historical biography; poetry.

SIDELIGHTS: Icolari told *CA*: "Interested in the introduction of reason into contemporary thought (philosophy), and politics, and, in my own writing, the successful projection of the romantic hero as a realistic character."†

* * *

IKEJIANI, Okechukwu 1917-

PERSONAL: Born December 19, 1917, in Nigeria; son of Jeremiah Ekemezie (a priest) and Elfrida Ikejiani; married Francisca Onyia, 1959; married second wife Patricia Duncan (a secretary-typist); children: Miriam, Ndidi, Uchenna, Okechukwu, Jr., Chioma, Okechukwu, Jr. III. *Education:* Attended Lincoln University, Lincoln University, Pa., 1938-40; University of New Brunswick, B.Sc., 1942; University of Chicago, M.Sc., 1943; University of Toronto, M.D. and L.M.C.C., 1948; College of Pathologists, London, England, F.C. Path., 1962. *Home and office:* 96 Apapa Rd., Ebute Metta, Nigeria.

CAREER: University of Ibadan, Ibadan, Nigeria, lecturer in Medical School, 1948-50, member of University Council, 1953—, pro-chancellor and chairman of Council, 1962—. Consultant pathologist. Chairman, Nigerian Railway Corp., 1960-65; director of many companies, including hospitals, rubber tire retreading, insurance, and electro-medical firms. Member of council, University of Nigeria, 1960—; governor of Lagos City College, 1960—. *Member:* Nigeria Medical Association (president, 1963—), Nigeria Medical Council, British Medical Association, College of Pathologists. *Awards, honors:* Sc.D., Lincoln University.

WRITINGS: (With J. W. Hanson, P. U. Okeke, and J. O. Anowi) *Nigerian Education*, Longmans, Green, 1964, pub-

lished as *Education in Nigeria*, Praeger, 1965. Member of editorial board, *West African Medical Journal* and *Journal of Nigerian Medical Association*. Contributor to journals.

WORK IN PROGRESS: Clinical Microbiology; and a novel on conflict of cultures and the educated African.

SIDELIGHTS: Ikejiani reads French and German.

* * *

ILLICK, Joseph E. 1934-

PERSONAL: Born November 15, 1934, in Bethlehem, Pa.; son of Joseph E., Jr. (a building contractor) and Margaret (Flexer) Illick; married Shirley Anthony, June 4, 1956; children: Joseph Edward IV. *Education:* Princeton University, B.S.E., 1956; University of Pennsylvania, A.M., 1957, Ph.D., 1961. *Politics:* Liberal. *Office:* Department of History, San Francisco State University, San Francisco, Calif. 94132.

CAREER: Kalamazoo College, Kalamazoo, Mich., instructor, 1961-62; Lafayette College, Easton, Pa., instructor, 1962-63; San Francisco State College (now San Francisco State University), San Francisco, Calif., assistant professor, 1963-67, associate professor, 1967-71, professor of history, 1971—. Visiting summer lecturer at Lehigh University, 1964, New York University, 1965, 1966; visiting associate professor, University of California, Berkeley, fall, 1968. *Member:* American Historical Association, Friends of Student Non-Violent Coordinating Committee.

WRITINGS: William Penn the Politician, Cornell University Press, 1965; (contributor) Alison Gilbert Olson and Richard Maxwell Brown, editors, *Anglo-American Political Relations, 1675-1775*, Rutgers University Press, 1970; (editor) *America & England, 1558-1776*, Appleton, 1970. Contributor to *San Francisco Chronicle* and *Examiner* and to historical and popular publications.

WORK IN PROGRESS: Children's books; and a study of Black nationalism in America.†

* * *

INGALLS, Daniel H(enry) H(olmes) 1916-

PERSONAL: Born May 4, 1916, in New York, N.Y.; son of Fay (a lawyer and corporation president) and Rachel (Holmes) Ingalls; married Phyllis Day; children: Sarah (Mrs. Gary Daughn), Rachel Holmes, Daniel H. H., Jr. *Education:* Harvard University, A.B., 1936, M.A., 1938; further study at Sanskrit Research Institute, Calcutta, India, 1941-42. *Home:* The Yard, Hot Springs, Va. 24445. *Office:* Widener 273, Harvard University, Cambridge, Mass. 02138.

CAREER: Harvard University, Cambridge, Mass., Society of Fellows, junior fellow, 1938-42, 1946-48, assistant professor, 1949-54, associate professor of Sanskrit and Indian studies, 1954-56, Wales Professor of Sanskrit and chairman of department of Sanskrit and Indian studies, 1956—, curator of Sanskrit manuscripts. Chairman of board, Virginia Hot Springs, Inc., Hot Springs, Va., 1963—. Trustee, Harvard-Yenching Institute, 1948—. *Military service:* U.S. Army, ·1944-46; became captain. *Member:* American Oriental Society (president, 1958), Association for Asian Studies, Societe Asiatique.

WRITINGS: Materials for the Study of Navya-Nyaya Logic, Harvard University Press, 1951; (translator) *An Anthology of Sanskrit Court Poetry: Vidyakara's Subhasitaratnakosa*, Harvard University Press, 1965; (translator)

Sanskrit Poetry from Vidyakara's "Treasury," Harvard University Press, 1969. Editor, "Harvard Oriental Series."

WORK IN PROGRESS: A description of Sanskrit epic style.

* * *

INGE, M(ilton) Thomas 1936-

PERSONAL: Surname rhymes with "fringe"; born March 18, 1936, in Newport News, Va.; son of Clyde Elmo and Bernice Lucille (Jackson) Inge; married Betty Jean Meredith, December 27, 1958; children: Scott Thomas. *Education:* Randolph-Macon College, B.A., 1959; Vanderbilt University, M.A., 1960, Ph.D., 1964. *Home:* 8624 Waxford Rd., Richmond, Va. 23235. *Office:* Department of English, Virginia Commonwealth University, 901 West Franklin St., Richmond, Va. 23284.

CAREER: Irby Studio, Richmond, Va., free-lance commercial artist, 1953-55; Virginia State Department of Highways, Richmond, traffic technician, (summers) 1956-58; Vanderbilt University, Nashville, Tenn., instructor in English, 1962-64; Michigan State University, East Lansing, assistant professor of American thought and language, became associate professor, 1964-69; Virginia Commonwealth University, Richmond, associate professor of English, 1969-74, chairman of department, 1974—. Fulbright lecturer in American literature, University of Salamanca, Spain, 1967-68, Buenos Aires, Argentina, 1971. *Member:* American Studies Association, Modern Language Association of America, American Association of University Professors, South Atlantic Modern Language Association, Society for the Study of Southern Literature, Popular Culture Association, Society for the Study of Midwestern Literature, The Melville Society, Associates of the James Branch Cabell Library, Friends of the Richmond Public Library, Phi Beta Kappa, Omicron Delta Kappa, Pi Delta Epsilon, Lambda Chi Alpha.

WRITINGS: (Contributor) *Concise American Composition and Rhetoric*, edited by Donald Davidson, Scribner, 1964; (with Thomas Daniel Young) *Donald Davidson: An Essay and a Bibliography*, Vanderbilt University Press, 1965; (editor) George Washington Harris, *Sut Lovingood's Yarns*, College and University Press, 1966; *Publications of the Faculty of the University College: A Bibliography*, Michigan State University, 1966; (editor) George Washington Harris, *High Times and Hard Times, Sketches and Tales*, Vanderbilt University Press, 1967; (editor) *Agrarianism in American Literature*, Odyssey Press, 1969; (editor) John Donald Wade, *Augustus Baldwin Longstreet: A Study of the Development of Culture in the South*, University of Georgia Press, 1969; (editor) *Honors College Essays 1967-68*, Michigan State University Honors College, 1969; (editor with others) *The Black Experience: Readings in Afro-American History and Culture from Colonial Times through the Nineteenth Century*, Michigan State University Press, 1969; (editor) *Faulkner: A Rose for Emily*, C. E. Merrill, 1970; (editor) Richmond Croom Beatty, *William Byrd of Westover*, Archon Books, 1970; (editor) *Studies in Light in August*, C. E. Merrill, 1971; (with Thomas Daniel Young) *Donald Davidson*, Twayne, 1971; (editor) *Virginia Commonwealth University Self-Study*, Virginia Commonwealth University, 1972; (editor) *Ellen Glasgow: Centennial Essays*, University Press of Virginia, 1975.

Contributor: *The Lovingood Papers, 1963, 1964, 1965*, edited by Ben Harris McClary, University of Tennessee Press; *American Literary Scholarship: An Annual, 1970,* *1971, 1972, 1973*, edited by J. Albert Robbins, Duke University Press.

Contributor of essays, articles, and reviews to *American Literature, American Quarterly, Mississippi Quarterly, Georgia Review, Encounter, Hispania, Journal of Ethnic Studies, Tennessee Studies in Literature*, and other journals. Regular reviewer, *Nashville Tennessean, Richmond Times-Dispatch, Menomonee Falls Gazette*, and *Choice.* Founding editor (with Maurice Duke and Jackson Bryer), *Resources for American Literary Study*, 1971—; general editor, "American Critical Tradition" series, David Lewis, 1973—; founding editor (with Lawrence E. Mintz), *American Humor: An Interdisciplinary Newsletter*, 1974—; general editor, research and study guide series, St. Martin's, 1975—.

WORK IN PROGRESS: Bartleby the Inscrubable, a collection of critical essays, scheduled for publication by Everett-Edwards in 1976; *American Humor and Humorists*, a biographical guide for Gale; *Classic American Comic Artists*, a collection of biographical-critical essays for Bowling Green University Popular Press; *William Faulkner: The Critical Reception*, an anthology of contemporary reviews of Faulkner's books for David Lewis; *The Frontier Humorists: Critical Views*, a collection of essays; *A Nineteenth Century American Reader*, an anthology of literary and historical documents; a biography of comic artist George Herriman.

* * *

INGLIS, Brian (St. John) 1916-

PERSONAL: Born July 31, 1916, in Dublin, Ireland; son of Sir Claud Cavendish (an engineer) and Vera (Blood) Inglis; married Ruth Langdon (a journalist), December 23, 1958; children: Diana Eleanor, Neil Langdon. *Education:* Magdalen College, Oxford, B.A. (honors), 1939; University of Dublin, Ph.D., 1950. *Home:* Garden Flat, 23 Lambolle Rd., London N.W. 3, England. *Agent:* Curtis Brown Ltd., 1 Craven Hill, London W2, England. *Office:* 7 Bulstrode St., London, England.

CAREER: Irish Times, Dublin, Ireland, columnist, 1946-48, Parliamentary correspondent, 1950-53; Trinity College, University of Dublin, Dublin, Ireland, assistant to professor of modern history, 1949-53, lecturer in economics, 1951-53; *Spectator*, London, England, assistant editor, 1954-59, editor, 1959-62, director, 1962—. Television commentator, with programs including "What the Papers Say," 1956—, and "All Our Yesterdays," 1961-73. *Military service:* Royal Air Force, 1940-46; became squadron leader; mentioned in dispatches.

WRITINGS: The Freedom of the Press in Ireland, Faber, 1954; *The Story of Ireland*, Faber, 1956; *Emotional Stress and Your Health*, Criterion, 1958 (published in England as *Revolution in Medicine*, Hutchinson, 1958); *West Briton*, Faber, 1962; *The Case for Unorthodox Medicine*, Putnam, 1964 (published in England as *Fringe Medicine*, Faber, 1964); *Private Conscience, Public Morality*, Deutsch, 1964; *A History of Medicine*, Weidenfeld & Nicolson, 1965; *Doctors, Drugs and Disease*, Deutsch, 1965; *Abdication*, Macmillan, 1966; *Men of Conscience*, Macmillan, 1971 (published in England as *Poverty and the Industrial Revolution*, Hodder and Stoughton, 1971); *Roger Casement*, Harcourt, 1974.

WORK IN PROGRESS: The Forbidden Game, a social history of drugs; *The Opium Wars.*

INMAN, Robert (Anthony) 1931-

PERSONAL: Born June 13, 1931, in San Francisco, Calif.; son of Verne Thomson (a surgeon and university executive) and Irene (Cootey) Inman; married Joan Marshall, June 18, 1958; children: Jeffrey, Michael. Education: Stanford University, A.B. (with great distinction), 1952; graduate study at University of Graz, 1952-53, University of Vienna, 1953-54, Free University of Berlin, 1956-57; University of Washington, Seattle, M.A., 1959. Home: 1386 Masonic Ave., San Francisco, Calif. 94117.

CAREER: University of Washington, Seattle, instructor in German, 1957-59, editor of Washington Alumnus, and administrative assistant, 1960-62; National Jewish Hospital, Denver, Colo., public relations, 1963; Denver Post, Denver, Colo., head librarian, 1964—. Military service: U.S. Army, 1954-56; served in Germany. Member: Special Libraries Association, Phi Beta Kappa. Awards, honors: Fulbright grant for study in Austria, 1952-54.

WRITINGS: The Torturer's Horse (novel), Bobbs-Merrill, 1965. Book reviewer for Denver Post.

WORK IN PROGRESS: Delphi Zero, a novel; also, short stories.

SIDELIGHTS: Inman traveled extensively in Austria, Germany, Italy, and Spain, 1952-57 and also visited a number of other countries in Europe. He is fluent in German, less so in French and Spanish.

* * *

IPCAR, Dahlov (Zorach) 1917-

PERSONAL: Born November 12, 1917, in Windsor, Vt.; daughter of William and Marguerite (Thompson) Zorach (both artists); married Adolph Ipcar (a dairy farmer, now retired), September 29, 1936; children: Robert William, Charles. Education: Oberlin College, student, 1933-34. Home and office: Robinhood Farm, Star Route 2, Bath, Me. 04530. Agent: McIntosh & Otis, Inc., 18 East 41st St., New York, N.Y. 10017.

CAREER: Self-taught animal artist, who began painting in earliest childhood, and author and illustrator of children's books. Had first one-man show, 1939, in Museum of Modern Art's Young People's Gallery; since then her oils, collages, and cloth sculptures have been exhibited at more than a dozen one-man shows, six of them in New York City, and included in group shows at Corcoran Gallery of Art, Carnegie Institute, Boston Art Festival, and elsewhere; oils are in the permanent collections of Metropolitan Museum, Whitney Museum, Newark Museum, Colby College, University of Maine, Westbrook Junior College, and other private and public collections; work also includes two murals for U.S. Treasury Department, Washington, D.C. Awards, honors: Clara A. Haas Award of Silvermine Guild, 1957; popular prize at Portland (Me.) Art Festival, 1959, for "Shore of Night"; Maine State Award, Maine Commission of Arts and Humanities, 1972; Junior Merit Award, Bridgeton, Me., 1973.

WRITINGS—All children's books; all self-illustrated except as noted: Animal Hide and Seek, Scott, 1947; One Horse Farm, Doubleday, 1950; World Full of Horses, Doubleday, 1955; The Wonderful Egg, Doubleday, 1958; Ten Big Farms, Knopf, 1958; Brown Cow Farm, Doubleday, 1959; I Like Animals, Knopf, 1960; Stripes and Spots, Doubleday, 1961; Deep Sea Farm, Knopf, 1961; Wild and Tame Animals, Doubleday, 1962; Lobsterman, Knopf, 1962; Black and White, Knopf, 1963; I Love My Anteater with an A, Knopf, 1964; Horses of Long Ago, Doubleday, 1965; Calico Jungle, Knopf, 1965; Bright Barnyard, Knopf, 1966; The Song of the Day Birds and the Night Birds, Doubleday, 1967; Whisperings and Other Things, Knopf, 1967; General Felice, illustrated by Kenneth Zongtemps, McGraw, 1967; Wild Whirlwind, Knopf, 1968; The Cat at Night, Doubleday, 1969; The Marvelous Merry-go-round, Doubleday, 1970; Sir Addlepate and the Unicorn, Doubleday, 1971; The Cat Came Back, Knopf, 1971; The Biggest Fish in the Sea, Viking, 1972; A Flood of Creatures, Holiday House, 1973; The Land of Flowers, Viking, 1974.

Illustrator: Margaret Wise Brown, The Little Fisherman, Scott, 1945; Evelyn Beyer, Just Like You, Scott, 1946; John G. McCullough, Good Work, Scott, 1948.

Adult short stories have been published in Texas Quarterly, Yankee, and Argosy; also contributor to Hornbook.

WORK IN PROGRESS: Children's books, for Holiday House and Doubleday.

SIDELIGHTS: Almost all the Ipcar books derive from her lifelong interest in animals. Her illustrations treat animal form with imagination but with deep respect. She feels that art for children "should be beautiful, colorful, imaginative, and not mere cartoons." Although her parents were artists, Mrs. Ipcar was never sent to art school or instructed by them; they wanted her talent to develop naturally without academic training. Some of her picture books revolve around animal life on the Maine farm where the artist-writer and her husband have lived since 1937. Her teen-age novels and adult short stories often reflect her interest in folksongs and fantasy.

BIOGRAPHICAL/CRITICAL SOURCES: Young Readers' Review, March, 1968; Lee Bennett Hopkins, Books Are By People, Citation Press, 1969.

* * *

IRWIN, Grace (Lilian) 1907-

PERSONAL: Born July 14, 1907, in Toronto, Ontario, Canada; daughter of John and Martha (Fortune) Irwin. Education: Parkdale Collegiate Institute, diploma, 1925; University of Toronto, B.A., 1929, M.A., 1932. Politics: Independent. Religion: Protestant. Home: 33 Glenwood Ave., Toronto, Ontario, Canada.

CAREER: Humberside Collegiate Institute, Toronto, Ontario, teacher of Latin, English, ancient history, 1931-42, head of classics department, 1942-69. Lecturer in literature, classics, religion. Book Society of Canada, director. Member: Canadian Classical Association, Canadian Authors Association, Ontario Secondary School Teachers Association, Toronto Classical Club. Awards, honors: Canadian centennial medal.

WRITINGS—Novels: Least of All Saints, McClelland & Stewart, 1952; Andrew Connington, McClelland & Stewart, 1954; In Little Place, Eerdmans, 1959; Servant of Slaves (biographical novel), Eerdmans, 1961; Contend with Horses, Eerdmans, 1968. Poems published in Little Songs for Little People and in magazines.

WORK IN PROGRESS: The Seventh Earl, a dramatized biography.

SIDELIGHTS: Three of her four books were published in Great Britain, in Germany, and in East Berlin; one also came out in Norwegian, Swedish, and Chinese translations.

ISAAC, Paul E(dward) 1926-

PERSONAL: Born January 3, 1926, in Bartlett, Tex.; son of Jacob (an insurance man) and Ollie (Shoemaker) Isaac; married Nancy Carter, August 26, 1960; children: Paul Carter, Sarah Elizabeth. *Education:* Pepperdine College, B.A., 1947; University of Texas, M.A., 1951, Ph.D., 1961. *Politics:* Democrat. *Religion:* Church of Christ. *Home:* 1518 Pipkin, Beaumont, Tex. 77705. *Office:* Lamar University, Beaumont, Tex. 77705.

CAREER: Assistant professor of history at Harding College, Searcy, Ark., 1952-54, and David Lipscomb College, Nashville, Tenn., 1955-60; Lamar State College of Technology (now Lamar University), Beaumont, Tex., assistant professor, 1960-61, associate professor, 1962-65, professor of history, 1966—. *Member:* Organization of American Historians, Western Historical Association, Tennessee Historical Society, Texas Association of College Teachers, Texas Gulf Coast Historical Association. *Awards, honors:* Award of Merit, American Association for State and Local History, 1967, for *Prohibition and Politics*.

WRITINGS: Prohibition and Politics: Turbulent Decades in Tennessee, 1885-1920, University of Tennessee Press and Tennessee Historical Commission, 1965; *A History of the Charters of Beaumont, Texas, 1858-1947*, Center for Urban Affairs, Lamar University, 1970. Contributor to *East Texas Historical Journal, Tennessee Historical Quarterly*, and *Southwestern Historical Quarterly*.

WORK IN PROGRESS: Research in three areas—history of the Republican party in Tennessee during the Progressive Era, Progressive Era politics in Southeast Texas, and prohibitionism and temperance in the South; articles for *Encyclopedia of Southern History*.

* * *

ISAAC, Rael Jean (Isaacs) 1933-

PERSONAL: Born June 17, 1933, in New York, N.Y.; daughter of Judah M. and Fannie (Shapiro) Isaacs; married Erich Isaac (a geographer), June 17, 1956; children: Gamaliel, Gideon, Noah. *Education:* Barnard College, B.A., 1954; Johns Hopkins University, M.A., 1956. *Religion:* Jewish.

CAREER: Various writing and editorial work in Washington, D.C., and New York, N.Y.; Pennsylvania State University, Ogontz Center, instructor in English, 1958-59; City College (now City College of the City University of New York), New York, N.Y., publications editor, 1962-64. Adoptive Parents Committee, legislative chairman, 1963-65; National Council of Adoptive Parents Organizations, member of advisory board. *Member:* Phi Beta Kappa. *Awards, honors:* Fulbright fellowship.

WRITINGS: Adopting a Child Today, Harper, 1965. Contributor to *Atlantic Monthly, Commentary, Colorado Quarterly, Judaism*, and *National Adoptalk*.

WORK IN PROGRESS: Research on sociology of the social work profession and on family planning.†

* * *

ISAACSON, Robert L. 1928-

PERSONAL: Born September 26, 1928, in Detroit, Mich.; son of E. A. and Evelyn (Johnson) Isaacson; divorced; children: Gunnar, Lars, Mary Ingrid. *Education:* University of Michigan, B.A., 1950, M.A., 1954, Ph.D., 1958. *Office:* Department of Psychology, University of Florida, Gainesville, Fla. 32611.

CAREER: University of Michigan, Ann Arbor, 1957—, started as instructor, associate professor, 1963-67, professor of psychology, 1967-68; University of Florida, Gainesville, Fla., professor of psychology, 1968—. *Military service:* U.S. Navy, 1950-53; became lieutenant junior grade. *Member:* American Association of Arts and Sciences, American Psychological Association (fellow), American Association for the Advancement of Science (fellow), Psychonomic Society, Michigan Academy of Science, Arts, and Letters, New York Academy of Sciences, Sigma Xi, Phi Sigma.

WRITINGS: (Editor) *Basic Readings in Neuropsychology*, Harper, 1964; (with M. L. Hutt and M. L. Blum) *Psychology: Science of Behavior*, Harper, 1965, 2nd edition (with Hutt), 1972, *Student Workbook* (with Sachio Ashida), 1966; (with Hutt and Blum) *Psychology: Science of Interpersonal Behavior*, Harper, 1966; *The Retarded Child: A Guide for Parents and Friends*, Argus, 1974; *The Limbic System*, Plenum, 1974; (editor with K. H. Pribram) *The Hippocampus*, Plenum, 1975.

WORK IN PROGRESS: Research in the behavioral effects of brain damage in animals and the differential effects of brain lesions made early or late in life.

* * *

ISENBERG, Irwin M. 1931-

PERSONAL: Born September 30, 1931, in Boston, Mass.; son of Harry (a salesman) and Emma (Slate) Isenberg; married Milda Rutelionis (a social worker), March 20, 1956; children: Errol, Brenda. *Education:* Boston University, A.B., 1953; Harvard University, A.M., 1955. *Home:* 129 West 94th St., New York, N.Y. 10025. *Office:* United Nations Development Programme, 866 United Nations Plaza, New York, N.Y. 10017.

CAREER: Scholastic Magazines, New York, N.Y., writer, 1959-62; Foreign Policy Association, New York, N.Y., senior editor, 1962-66; United Nations, New York, N.Y., special assistant, 1966—.

WRITINGS: (Editor) *Drive on Illiteracy*, H. W. Wilson, 1963; (co-author) *Understanding Foreign Aid*, Foreign Policy Association, 1963; *Eastern Europe*, Scholastic Book Services, 1963; *Caesar*, American Heritage, 1964; (co-author) *Making Foreign Policy in a Nuclear Age*, Foreign Policy Association, 1965; (editor) *Ferment in Eastern Europe*, H. W. Wilson, 1965; (editor) *The Russian-Chinese Rift: Impact on World Affairs*, H. W. Wilson, 1966; (editor) *France Under De Gaulle*, H. W. Wilson, 1967; (editor) *The City in Crisis*, H. W. Wilson, 1968; (editor) *The Developing Nations*, H. W. Wilson, 1969; (editor) *The Outlook for Western Europe*, H. W. Wilson, 1970; (editor) *Japan*, H. W. Wilson, 1971; (editor) *Japan*, H. W. Wilson, 1972; *Indian Subcontinent*, Scholastic Book Services, 1972; (editor) *Nations of the Indian Subcontinent*, H. W. Wilson, 1972.

* * *

ISHINO, Iwao 1921-

PERSONAL: Born March 10, 1921, in San Diego, Calif.; son of Tomota and Tei (Yoshizuka) Ishino; married Mary Kobayashi, 1944; children: Marilyn (Mrs. William G. Tanner), Catherine, Ellen Susan, Tomi Ruth. *Education:* San Diego State College (now San Diego State University), student, 1939-42; Harvard University, A.M., 1953, Ph.D., 1954. *Religion:* Congregational. *Home:* 1736 Ann St., East

Lansing, Mich. 48823. *Office:* Department of Anthropology, Michigan State University, East Lansing, Mich. 48823.

CAREER: U.S. Government, social science analyst, Office of War Information, 1944-45, research analyst in Japan, 1949-51; National Research Council, Pacific Science Board, field associate, 1951; Ohio State University, Columbus, research associate in sociology and anthropology, 1951-54, assistant professor of anthropology, 1954-56; Michigan State University, East Lansing, assistant professor, 1956-58, associate professor, 1958-62, professor of sociology and anthropology, 1962—, chairman of department, 1969—. University of Tokyo, Fulbright lecturer, 1958-59; visiting professor, University of Ryukyus, Okinawa, 1963-65. *Military service:* U.S. Army, 1946-47. *Member:* American Anthropological Association (fellow), American Association for the Advancement of Science, Association for Asian Studies, Central States Anthropological Society.

WRITINGS: (Contributor) *Japanese Culture,* Aldine, 1962; (with John W. Bennett) *Paternalism in the Japanese Economy,* University of Minnesota Press, 1963; (with Russell Dynes, Alfred Clarke, and Simon Dinitz) *Social Problems: Dissensus and Deviation in an Industrial Society,* Oxford University Press, 1964; (with others) *Seven Articles on Village Conditions,* Asian Studies Center, Michigan State University, 1966. Contributor to *American Anthropologist* and *Human Organization.*†

*   *   *

ISRAEL, Fred L.   1934-

PERSONAL: Born February 8, 1934, in New York, N.Y.; son of Jack C. (a teacher) and Evelyn (Wallach) Israel. *Education:* City College, New York, N.Y., B.S., 1955; Columbia University, M.A., 1956, Ph.D., 1959. *Home:* 330 East 58th St., New York, N.Y. 10022. *Office:* City College of the City University of New York, New York, N.Y. 10031.

CAREER: City College (now of the City University of New York), instructor, 1956-63, assistant professor, 1963-67, associate professor, 1967-74, professor of American history, 1974—. *Member:* American Historical Association, Organization of American Historians. *Awards, honors:* Louis Knott Koontz Award, Pacific Coast Branch of American Historical Association, 1962; Scribes Award of the American Bar Association, 1970.

WRITINGS: (Contributing editor) *Guide to Historical Literature,* Macmillan, 1961; *Nevada's Key Pittman,* University of Nebraska Press, 1963; (editor, and author of commentary) *The Chief Executive: Inaugural Addresses of the Presidents from Washington to Johnson,* Crown, 1965; *The War Diary of Breckinridge Long,* University of Nebraska Press, 1966; (editor) *The State of the Union Messages from Washington to Johnson,* Chelsea House, 1966; (editor) *Major Peace Treaties of Modern History, 1648-1967,* Chelsea House-McGraw, 1967; (editor with Leon Friedman) *The Justices of the United States Supreme Court,* Chelsea House, 1969; (editor with A. M. Schlesinger) *History of American Presidential Elections, 1789-1968,* Chelsea House-McGraw, 1971.

*   *   *

IWATA, Masakazu   1917-

PERSONAL: Born October 21, 1917, in Los Angeles, Calif.; son of Yasujiro and Tatsuye (Nakatani) Iwata; mar-

ried Doreen F. Hasegawa, July 5, 1952. *Education:* University of California, Los Angeles, A.B. (highest honors in history), 1954, M.A., 1956, Ph.D., 1960. *Religion:* Free Methodist. *Home:* 879 North Vail Ave., Montebello, Calif. 90640.

CAREER: Radio Press, Inc., Tokyo, Japan, member of board of directors, 1945-46; University of California, Los Angeles, instructor in history, summer, 1960, consultant, Japanese American Research Project, 1963—; Biola College, La Mirada, Calif., assistant professor, 1961-64, associate professor, 1964-67, professor of history, 1967—, chairman of history department, 1968. Missionary Strategy Agency, member of board of directors, 1964—. *Member:* American Historical Association, Association for Asian Studies, Phi Beta Kappa, Pi Gamma Mu.

WRITINGS: Okubo Toshimichi, Bismarck of Japan, University of California Press, 1964; (contributor) *Promises to Keep,* Bruce A. Glasrud and Alan M. Smith, editors, Rand McNally, 1972. Contributor to *Agricultural History.*

WORK IN PROGRESS: A monograph on the history of the Japanese in U.S. agriculture, completion expected in 1976.

SIDELIGHTS: Iwata speaks, reads, and writes Japanese; reads French and German.

*   *   *

IYENGAR, S. Kesava   1894-

PERSONAL: Born October 21, 1894, in Malur, Mysore, India; son of S. Venkatarama (a headmaster) and Antamma Iyengar; married S. K. Anasuya Devi, March 16, 1954. *Education:* Madras University, M.A., 1918. *Religion:* Hindu.

CAREER: Government economic survey officer, Mysore, India, 1925; professor of economics at Nizam's College, Hyderabad, India, 1926-28; special officer for economic investigations in Hyderabad State, 1929-30; special officer for Cooperative Department, Hyderabad State, 1931-36; professor of economics at Nizam's College, 1938-45; economic adviser to Chamber of Princes, New Delhi, India, 1946-47, to Hyderabad Government, 1947-51; director of Indian Institute of Economics, Hyderabad, 1953-59; director and professor of economic research, Indian Academy of Economics, Mysore, 1959—. President of All-India Economic Conference, 1953.

WRITINGS: Studies in Indian Rural Economics, P. S. King & Co. (London), 1926; (with Mahomed Mir Khan) *The A.B.C. of Central Banking,* Bangalore Printing and Publishing, 1946; *Economists at Home and Abroad,* Indian Institute of Economics, 1953; *A Decade of Planned Economy: A Critical Examination of Indian Plans,* Indian Academy of Economics, 1961; *Fifteen Years of Democratic Planning,* Volume I: *The Indian Outline,* Asia Publishing House, 1963, Volume II: *Sectoral Developments,* 1965; *Devaluation and After: Vicissitudes of the Fourth Plan,* Asia Publishing House, 1970.

Survey reports: *Economic Investigations in the Hyderabad State,* five volumes, Hyderabad Government, 1931, and three other economic studies published by the Hyderabad Government, 1951; *A Survey of Agricultural Tenancy Conditions in the Hyderabad State,* seven volumes, Hyderabad Economic Association, 1952, and three other reports published by the Hyderabad Economic Association, 1951-52; five reports published by Indian Institute of Economics, 1954-59.†

JACKER, Corinne L(itvin) 1933-

PERSONAL: Born June 29, 1933, in Chicago, Ill.; daughter of Thomas Henry (a plumbing contractor) and Theresa (Bellak) Litvin; married Richard Jacker, July 1, 1956 (divorced, 1958). *Education:* Stanford University, student, 1950-52; Northwestern University, B.S., 1954, M.A., 1956. *Home:* 110 West 86th St., New York, N.Y. 10024. *Agent:* Lois Berman, 530 East 72nd St., New York, N.Y. 10017.

CAREER: Macmillan Co., New York, N.Y., associate editor, 1950-63; Charles Scribner's Sons, New York, N.Y., assistant editor, 1963-65; full-time free-lance writer, 1965-70; WNET, story editor, reader, 1970-73; CBS Playhouse 90, story editor, 1973-74; CBS "Bicentennial Minutes," head writer/script editor, 1974—. *Awards, honors:* Mac-Dowell Colony fellowship, 1959; New York Emmy Citation, 1970; Cine Golden Eagle, 1970; Eugene O'Neill Theatre Center Playwrights Conference, 1971, 1974.

WRITINGS: Man, Memory, and Machines: An Introduction to Cybernetics, Macmillan, 1964; *Window on the Unknown—A History of the Microscope*, Scribner, 1967; "Inspirations of Modern Science," five pamphlets, Portal Press-Wiley, 1967; *The Black Flag of Anarchy: Antistatism in America*, Scribner, 1968; *The Biological Revolution*, Parents Press, 1971. Poems published in *Mutiny, Carleton Miscellany, Fiddlehead, Spectrum*, and other magazines.

Plays produced: "Pale Horse, Pale Rider," Off Broadway, 1958; "A Happy Ending," Off Broadway, 1959; "A Picture of Love" (television play), Columbia Broadcasting System, 1959; "Seditious Acts," Off-Off Broadway, 1969; "The Scientific Method," Stratford, Conn., Shakespeare Festival, 1970; "Project Omega: Lillian" (musical), O'Neill Theatre Center, 1971; "Bits and Pieces," 1973; "Night Thoughts," 1973; "Takine Care of Harry," 1974; "Travellers" (musical), 1974.

Television: "When This You See, Remember Me," NET, 1969; "A Singular Man," NET, 1969; "John Donne," NET, 1969; "Brewsie and Willie," *The Last G.I.s*, 1971; "The Moment Whole," NET, 1971.

WORK IN PROGRESS: A full-length play; a musical; a novel.

* * *

JACKSON, Donald (Dean) 1919-

PERSONAL: Born June 10, 1919, in Glenwood, Iowa; son of Dean (a farmer) and Eula (Woods) Jackson; married Mary Catherine Mayberry, October 6, 1943; children: Robert, Mark. *Education:* Iowa State University of Science and Technology, B.S., 1942; University of Iowa, M.A., 1947, Ph.D., 1948. *Home:* 105 Melissa Pl., Charlottesville, Va. 22901.

CAREER: University of Illinois Press, Urbana, editor, 1948-68; University of Virginia, Charlottesville, professor of history, 1968—. *Military service:* U.S. Naval Reserve, 1942-46; became lieutenant junior grade. *Member:* American Historical Association, Organization of American Historians, Western History Association. *Awards, honors:* Missouri Historical Society award, 1965, for *Letters of the Lewis and Clark Expedition*; Western Heritage Center award, 1966, for "How Lost Was Zebulon Pike?," published in *American Heritage*; Lewis and Clark Trail Heritage Foundation award of merit, 1974.

WRITINGS: Archer Pilgrim, Dodd, 1942; (editor) *Black Hawk: An Autobiography*, University of Illinois Press, 1955; (editor) *Letters of the Lewis and Clark Expedition*, University of Illinois Press, 1962; (editor) *The Journals of Zebulon Montgomery Pike*, University of Oklahoma Press, 1966; *Custer's Gold: The U.S. Cavalry Expedition of 1874*, Yale University Press, 1966; (with Mary Lee Spence) *The Expeditions of John Charles Fremont*, University of Illinois Press, volume I, 1970, volume II, 1973. Contributor of articles on trans-Mississippi exploration to journals. Editor, *Papers of George Washington*, University of Virginia, 1968—.

* * *

JACOBS, Pepita Jimenez 1932-

PERSONAL: Born November 24, 1932, in Balanga, Bataan, Philippine Islands; daughter of Jose Coronel (a high school principal) and Pacita (Gonzales) Jimenez; married D. Robert Jacobs, June 16, 1963; children: J. Albert. *Education:* Philippine Normal College, E.T.C., 1951, B.S.E., 1955; University of Michigan, A.M., 1958; Pennsylvania State University, Ph.D., 1963. *Religion:* Roman Catholic.

CAREER: Elementary schoolteacher in Balanga, Bataan, Philippine Islands, 1951-54; instructor in education at Far Eastern University, Manila, Philippine Islands, 1954-55, Philippine Normal College, Manila, 1955-60; University of the East, Manila, instructor in psychology, 1959-60; Laurelton State School and Hospital, Laurelton, Pa., clinical psychology trainee, 1960, 1963; Marygrove College, Detroit, Mich., assistant professor of psychology, beginning 1963. *Member:* Society for Research in Child Development, American Association of University Professors, Fulbright Scholars Association (Philippine).

WRITINGS: (With George M. Guthrie) *Child Rearing and Personality Development in the Philippines*, Pennsylvania State University Press, 1966. Contributor to *Child Development Abstracts and Bibliography*, and other professional journals.

WORK IN PROGRESS: A cross-cultural study of education, as background to the cultural foundations of Philippine education; a study of values, specifically developing an instrument for the assessment and description of value systems.†

* * *

JACOBS, Walter Darnell 1922-
(Peter Oboe)

PERSONAL: Born March 11, 1922, in Hobart, Okla.; son of John Clayton (a banker) and Patience (Goodlander) Jacobs. *Education:* Columbia University, B.S., 1955, M.A. and Certificate of Russian Institute, 1956, Ph.D., 1961. *Home address:* P.O. Box 450, College Park, Md. 20740. *Office:* Department of Government and Politics, University of Maryland, College Park, Md. 20742.

CAREER: American University, Special Operations Research Office, Washington, D.C., research scientist, 1959-61; University of Maryland, College Park, assistant professor, 1961-65, associate professor, 1965-67, professor of political science, 1967—. Consultant to Institute for Defense Analyses. *Military service:* U.S. Army, 1942-53. U.S. Army Reserve, Infantry, 1953-74; now colonel. *Member:* American Political Science Association, American Association for the Advancement of Slavic Studies, American Military Institute, American-African Affairs Association, Free Society Association, Southern Political Science Association, District of Columbia Political Science Association (council), Delta Kappa Epsilon. *Awards, honors:* Regent's Award for excellence in teaching, University of Maryland.

WRITINGS: (With Harold Zink) *Modern Governments*, Van Nostrand, 3rd edition, 1966; *Frunze*, Nijhoff, 1969. Contributor to encyclopedias, and to professional journals in United States and Europe.

WORK IN PROGRESS: Studies on terrorism in Africa and Latin America, and the National Security policy.

SIDELIGHTS: Jacobs has knowledge of Russian, German, Uzbek, and some French. *Avocational interests:* Chess, crossword puzzle construction.

* * *

JAMES, Joseph B. 1912-

PERSONAL: Born July 17, 1912, in Clearwater, Fla.; son of L. P. (a farmer) and Ilah (Miles) James; married Jacquelyn McWhite (a high school counselor), June 8, 1937; children: Glenn J., William B. *Education:* University of Florida, B.A.E., 1934, M.A., 1935; University of Illinois, Ph.D., 1939. *Religion:* Methodist. *Home:* 3450 Osborne Pl., Macon, Ga. 31204. *Office:* Wesleyan College, Macon, Ga. 31201.

CAREER: Union College, Barbourville, Ky., head of department of social studies, 1940-42; William Woods College, Fulton, Mo., dean of faculty, 1942-45; Mississippi State College for Women, Columbia, head of department of social sciences, 1945-58; Wesleyan College, Macon, Ga., dean of the college, 1958—. Visiting summer professor at University of Florida, University of Mississippi, Middle Tennessee University, and George Peabody College for Teachers. *Member:* American Academy of Political Scientists, Association of College Honor Societies (secretary-treasurer; chairman of admissions committee), Southern Historical Association, Southern Political Science Association, Phi Beta Kappa, Phi Kappa Phi (president of Wellesley College chapter), Kappa Delta Pi, Pi Gamma Mu (national president emeritus; trustee at large), Kappa Phi Kappa.

WRITINGS: The Framing of the Fourteenth Amendment, University of Illinois Press, 1956. Contributor to historical journals. State editor for Mississippi, *Municipal Yearbook*, 1945-58.

WORK IN PROGRESS: Development of the Fourteenth Amendment through Ratification.

SIDELIGHTS: James speaks Spanish; reads French and German.

* * *

JAMES, Robert (Vidal) Rhodes 1933-

PERSONAL: Born April 10, 1933, in Murree, India; son of William Rhodes (a lieutenant colonel, Indian Army) and Violet (Swinhoe) James; married Angela Margaret Robertson, August 18, 1956; children: Lucy Victoria Margaret, Emma Jenneffee, Charlotte Elizabeth, Katherine, Alexandra Stirling. *Education:* Worchester College, Oxford, M.A., 1955. *Religion:* Church of England. *Home:* Dale Cottage, West Burton, near Pulborough, Sussex, England. *Agent:* Julian Bach, 3 East 48th St., New York, N.Y. 10017. *Office:* c/o United Nations, Box 20, Grand Central Post Office, New York, N.Y. 10017.

CAREER: House of Commons, London, England, assistant clerk, 1955-61, senior clerk, 1961-64; All Souls College, Oxford University, Oxford, England, fellow, 1965-68; Stan-

ford University, Stanford, Calif., Kratter Professor of European History, 1968; Institute for Study of International Organisation, University of Sussex, Sussex, England, director, 1969-73; Executive Office of the Secretary General of the United Nations, New York, N.Y., principal officer, 1973—. Consultant to United Nations Conference of Human Environment, 1971-72; United Kingdom participant in United Nations Sub-committee on Prevention of Discrimination and Protection of Minorities, 1972-73. Historian. Study of Parliament Group, founder member, 1964. Lecturer on military history at Royal Military Academy, Sandhurst, 1965, Imperial Staff College, 1966, and Royal United Service Institute, 1966. *Member:* United Nations Association, Royal Society of Literature (fellow), Committee on Atlantic Studies. *Awards, honors:* John Llewellyn Rhys Memorial Prize, 1962, for *An Introduction to the House of Commons*; Royal Society of Literature Award, 1964, for *Rosebery*; North Atlantic Treaty Organization fellowship, 1965-66.

WRITINGS: Lord Randolph Churchill, Weidenfeld & Nicolson, 1959, A. S. Barnes, 1960; *An Introduction to the House of Commons*, Collins, 1961; *Rosebery*, Weidenfeld & Nicolson, 1963, Macmillan, 1964; *Gallipoli*, Macmillan, 1965; *Standardization and Production of Military Equipment in NATO*, Institute for Strategic Study, 1967; (contributor) Anthony Moncrieff, editor, *Suez Ten Years After*, British Broadcasting Corporation, 1967; (with A. J. P. Taylor, J. H. Plumb, Basil Lidell Hart, and Anthony Storr) *Churchill Revised: A Critical Assessment*, Dial, 1969; (compiler) *The United Nations*, Jackdaw Publications, 1970; *Churchill: A Study in Failure, 1900-1939*, Weidenfeld & Nicolson, 1970; *Britain's Role in the United Nations*, United Nations Association, 1971; *The Constitutional Year Book, 1885*, Harvester Press, 1971; *Staffing the United Nations Secretariat*, Institute for the Study of International Organisation, University of Sussex, 1971; *Ambitions and Realities: British Politics, 1964-1970*, Harper, 1972.

Editor: Henry Channon, *The Diaries of Sir Henry Channon*, Weidenfeld & Nicolson, 1967; J. C. C. Davidson, *Memoirs of a Conservative: J. C. C. Davidson's Memoirs and Papers, 1910-1937*, Weidenfeld & Nicolson, 1969; *The Czechoslovak Crisis, 1968*, Weidenfeld & Nicolson, 1969; *Winston S. Churchill: His Complete Speeches, 1897-1963*, eight volumes, Bowker, 1974.

Contributor to *History Today, Spectator, New Statesman, Observer, Daily Telegraph*, and other periodicals and newspapers.

WORK IN PROGRESS: The British Empire, 1860-1960; Lord Swinton; British Politics, 1880-1939.

SIDELIGHTS: James visited the United States in 1965 to study defense procedures; he worked in the Middle East (principally Turkey), 1962. *Avocational interests:* Sailing, cricket, the theatre, literature.

* * *

JAMESON, Vic(tor Loyd) 1924-

PERSONAL: Born September 4, 1924, in Clayton, N.M.; son of Earl Percy (a gasoline wholesaler) and Juna (Kephart) Jameson; married Barbara Oswald, July 13, 1947; children: Ronald Wallace, Michael Loyd. *Education:* Eastern New Mexico University, B.A., 1949. *Politics:* Democrat. *Religion:* United Presbyterian. *Home:* 210 Varsity Ave., Princeton, N.J. 08540. *Office:* 475 Riverside Dr., New York, N.Y. 10027.

CAREER: Portales Tribune, Portales, N.M., reporter, 1947-49; school teacher in Hobbs, N.M., 1949-51; *Hobbs News-Sun*, Hobbs, N.M., editorial staff, 1951-64, became city editor; Presbyterian Office of Information, New York, N.Y., associate director, 1964-73, director, 1973—. *Military service:* U.S. Army, Office of Strategic Services, 1943-46; became sergeant. *Member:* Sigma Delta Chi. *Awards, honors:* E. H. Shaffer Award for newspaper writing, New Mexico Press Association, 1955.

WRITINGS: (With Don Westfall) *Bull at a New Gate* (satire), Fortress, 1965; *What Does God Require of Us Now?*, Abingdon, 1970; (editor) *The Main Trail*, Neylor, 1971. Contributor to United Presbyterian Church magazines.

* * *

JANIS, Irving L(ester) 1918-

PERSONAL: Born May 26, 1918, in Buffalo, N.Y.; son of M. Martin and Etta (Goldstein) Janis; married Marjorie Graham (a research associate in child psychology), September 5, 1939; children: Cathy, Charlotte. *Education:* University of Chicago, B.S., 1939, graduate study, 1939-40; Columbia University, Ph.D., 1948; New York Psychoanalytic Institute, postdoctoral study, 1948-53. *Home:* 1205 Race Brook Rd., Woodbridge, Conn. 06525. *Office:* Department of Psychology, Yale University, 333 Cedar St., New Haven, Conn. 06510.

CAREER: Library of Congress, Washington, D.C., research assistant, 1941; U.S. Department of Justice, Washington, D.C., senior social science analyst, 1941-43; Social Science Research Council, research associate, 1945-46, research fellow, 1946-47; Yale University, New Haven, Conn., assistant professor, 1947-51, associate professor, 1951-60, professor of psychology, 1960—. RAND Corp., research consultant, 1948—. National Science Foundation, member of panel on social psychological research, 1965-66. *Military service:* U.S. Army, Research Branch, 1943-45.

MEMBER: American Psychological Association (fellow; chairman of committee on psychology in national and international affairs, 1965-66), American Association for the Advancement of Science (representative on council, 1965-70). *Awards, honors:* Ford Foundation research grant, 1956; Fulbright research award to University of Oslo, 1957-58; Hofheimer Prize of American Psychiatric Association for outstanding contribution in field of psychiatry and mental hygiene, 1959; faculty fellowships from Yale University and Social Science Research Council for research at Tavistock Clinic and Institute, London, England, 1961-62, 1966-67, and from Social Science Research Council for research at La Jolla, Calif., 1966-67; Guggenheim fellow, 1973.

WRITINGS: Air War and Emotional Stress, McGraw, 1951; (with C. I. Hovland and H. H. Kelley) *Communication and Persuasion*, Yale University Press, 1953; *Psychological Stress*, Wiley, 1958; (editor with C. I. Hovland) *Personality and Persuasibility*, Yale University Press, 1959; (editor) *Personality: Dynamics, Development, and Assessment*, Harcourt, 1969; *Stress and Frustration*, Harcourt, 1971; *Victims of Groupthink: A Psychological Study of Foreign Policy Decisions and Fiascoes*, Houghton, 1972.

Contributor of chapters: *The American Soldier: Combat and Its Aftermath*, edited by S. Stouffer and others, Princeton University Press, 1949; *Language of Politics: Studies in Quantitative Semantics*, edited by H. D. Lasswell and N. C. Leites, George W. Stewart, 1949.

Public Opinion and Propaganda: A Book of Readings, edited by D. Katz and others, Dryden Press, 1954; *The Order of Presentation in Persuasion*, edited by C. I. Hovland, Yale University Press, 1957; *Readings in Social Psychology*, edited by E. E. Maccoby, T. M. Newcomb, and E. L. Hartley, 3rd edition, Holt, 1958; *Psychoanalysis and the Social Sciences*, Volume V, edited by W. Muensterberger and S. Axelrad, International Universities, 1958; *Assessment of Human Motives*, edited by G. Lindzey, Rinehart, 1958; *Nebraska Symposium on Motivation*, edited by M. R. Jones, University of Nebraska Press, 1959.

Man and Society in Disaster, edited by D. Chapman and G. Baker, Basic Books, 1962; *The Science of Human Communication*, edited by W. Schramm, Basic Books, 1963; *Changing Food Habits*, edited by J. Yudkin and J. McKenzie, MacGibbon & Kee, 1964; *Handbook of Clinical Psychology*, edited by B. Wolman, McGraw, 1965; *International Behavior*, edited by H. Kelman, Holt, 1965; *Self-Control Under Stress*, edited by S. Klausner, Free Press of Glencoe, 1965; *Handbook of Personality Theory and Research*, edited by E. Borgatta and W. Lambert, Rand McNally, 1967; *Advances in Experimental Social Psychology*, edited by L. Berkowitz, Academic Press, 1967.

Writer of seven government reports on social psychological surveys. Contributor of about forty research papers to psychology and medical journals. Associate editor, *Sociometry*, 1955-58; consulting editor, *Journal of Abnormal and Social Psychology*, 1955-65, and *Journal of Experimental Social Psychology*.†

* * *

JANSSON, Tove Marika 1914-

PERSONAL: Born August 9, 1914, in Helsinki, Finland; daughter of Viktor (a sculptor) and Signe (a designer; maiden name, Hammarsten) Jansson. *Education:* Studied at art schools in Stockholm and Helsinki, and Paris. *Home:* Helsinki, Finland.

CAREER: Finnish artist and illustrator, whose oil paintings have been shown at seven exhibitions in Helsinki; creator of the "Moomins," appearing in her books for children and, earlier, in cartoon strips. Works at her studio in Helsinki in the winter, and at a cabin-retreat on a small island off the Finnish coast about five months a year; writes in Swedish (member of the Swedish-speaking minority in Finland), but all of her books for children have also been published in English.

MEMBER: Painter's Society (Helsinki), Author's Club (Helsinki). *Awards, honors:* Stockholm Award for best children's book, 1952, and Selma Lagerlof Medal, 1953, both for *The Book About Moomin, Mymble and Little My*; *Moomin Summer Madness* was nominated by the Swedish section of the International Board on Books for Young People for the International Hans Christian Andersen Award, 1956; an award by the Academy (Finland), the Hans Christian Andersen Diploma of the International Council of Youth (Florence), the Elsa Beskow Award (Malmo), and the Rudolf Koivu plaquette (Finland), all for *Moominland Mid-Winter*, 1958; Hans Christian Andersen diploma of International Council of Youth, 1962, for *Who Will Comfort Toffle?*, and 1964, for *Tales From Moomin Valley*; Anni Swan Prize (Finland), 1964, for *Tales From Moomin Valley*; Swedish Culture prize, 1963; Langman's prize, 1965; Hans Christian Andersen medal, 1966; *Expressen* (Stockholm's daily paper) Winnie-the-Pooh Prize,

1970; *The Prize of the Finnish State*, 1971; Selma Lajerlof Prize, 1972; Bonniers Publishing House, Sweden, Scholarship award, 1972; Prize of the Swedish Academy, 1972; Werner Soderstrom Publishing House and Grafia Society (Finland), scholarship and medal for illustration, 1973.

WRITINGS—Juveniles, all self-illustrated: *Mumintrollet och Kometen*, Soderstroms, 1946 (published in London as *Comet in Moominland*, Benn, 1951), Walck, 1967; *Trollkarlens Hatt*, Schildt, 1949 (published in England as *Finn Family Moomintroll*, Benn, 1950; published as *The Happy Moomins*, Bobbs, 1951); *Muminpappans Bravader*, Schildt, 1950 (published in England as *The Exploits of Moomin Pappa*, Benn, 1952), Walck, 1966; *Hur Gick det Sen?*, Schildt, 1952 (published in England as *The Book About Moomin, Mymble and Little My*, Benn, 1953); *Farlig Midsommar*, Schildt, 1954, published as *Moomin Summer Madness*, Walck, 1961; *Trollvinter*, Schildt, 1957 (published in England as *Moominland Mid-Winter*, Benn, 1958), Walck, 1962; *Vem Ska Trosta Knyttet?*, Schildt, 1960 (published in England as *Who Will Comfort Toffle?*, Benn, 1961); *Det Osynliga Barnet*, Schildt, 1962, published as *Tales From Moomin Valley*, Walck, 1964; *Pappan och Havet*, Schildt, 1965 (published in English as *Moomin Pappa at Sea*, Benn, 1966, Walck, 1967); *Bildhuggarens Dotter* (autobiographical), Schildt, 1968 (published in England as *Sculptor's Daughter*, Benn, 1969); *Sent i November*, Schildt, 1970, published as *Moominvalley in November*, Walck, 1971; *Lyssnerskan* (adult short stories), Schildt, 1971; *Sommarboken* (adult fiction), Schildt, 1972; *Solstader* (adult fiction), Schildt, 1974. Writer of two plays for children; writer of strip-cartoon, "Moomin," *The Evening News*, London, 1953-60.

SIDELIGHTS: Mrs. Jansson's books for children have also been translated into German, Italian, Norwegian, Danish, Polish, Hebrew, Japanese, Spanish, Finnish, Icelandic, Dutch, French, Yugoslavian, Czech, Russian, Ukranian, in the Faroe Islands, Persian, Portuguese, and Lithuanian.

* * *

JEFFERSON, Carter (Alfred) 1927-

PERSONAL: Born July 12, 1927, in Dallas, Tex.; son of B. C. (a newspaper editor) and Kathryn (Manner) Jefferson; married Lucy Brundrett, January 6, 1955; children: Laura. *Education:* Attended Texas A&M University, 1943-45, and U.S. Naval Academy, 1945-47; George Washington University, B.A., 1949; Southern Methodist University, M.A., 1955; University of Chicago, Ph.D., 1959. *Home:* 6 Cazenove St., Boston, Mass. 02116. *Office:* Department of History, University of Massachusetts, Boston, Mass. 02125.

CAREER: United Press staff correspondent in Colorado, Mexico, and Texas, 1949-51; *Fort Worth Press*, Fort Worth, Tex., assistant news editor, 1952-53; Wayne State University, Detroit, Mich., instructor in history, 1957-58; University of Michigan, Ann Arbor, instructor in history, 1959-62; Rutgers, The State University, New Brunswick, N.J., assistant professor of history, 1962-65, associate professor, 1965-69; University of Massachusetts, Boston, professor of history, 1969—. *Military service:* U.S. Naval Reserve, 1950-51; became lieutenant junior grade. *Member:* American Historical Association, Society for French Historical Studies, Association for Humanistic Psychology, History of Education Society, American Association of University Professors, National Audubon Society. *Awards, honors:* M.Ed., Northeastern University, 1974.

WRITINGS: Anatole France: The Politics of Skepticism, Rutgers University Press, 1965. Contributor to professional journals.

WORK IN PROGRESS: Studies on social history of intellectuals, the history of education, and emotional development of college students.

SIDELIGHTS: Jefferson reads French, German, and Spanish. *Avocational interests:* Conservation, organic gardening, and landscaping.

* * *

JEFFRIES, Roderic (Graeme) 1926-
(Jeffrey Ashford, Hastings Draper, Roderic Graeme, Graham Hastings)

PERSONAL: Born October 21, 1926, in London, England; son of Graham Montague (an author) and Lorna (Louch) Jeffries; married Rosemary Powyss Woodhouse, March 13, 1958; children: Xanthe Kathleen, Crispin John. *Education:* University of Southampton, navigation studies, 1942-43; Gray's Inn, Barrister-at-Law, 1953. *Home:* Bourne Farm, Aldington Frith, near Ashford, Kent, England. *Agent:* Mrs. G. Hughes, 68 Girdwood Rd., London S.W. 18, England; and Georges Borchardt Inc., 145 East 52nd St., New York, N.Y. 10022.

CAREER: British Merchant Navy, 1943-49, went to sea as apprentice, became second mate; began part-time writing and study of law, 1950; practiced law, 1953-54; full-time author, 1954—. Former part-time dairy farmer. *Member:* Crime Writers Association, Paternosters.

WRITINGS: Evidence of the Accused, Collins, 1961, British Book Center, 1963; *Exhibit No. Thirteen*, Collins for the Crime Club, 1962; *Police and Detection*, Brockhampton Press, 1962, published as *Against Time!*, Harper, 1963; *The Benefits of Death*, Collins for the Crime Club, 1963, Dodd, 1964; *An Embarrassing Death*, Collins for the Crime Club, 1964, Dodd, 1965; *Dead Against the Lawyers*, Dodd, 1965; *Police Dog*, Harper, 1965; *Death in the Coverts*, Collins for the Crime Club, 1966; *A Deadly Marriage*, Collins, 1967; *Police Car*, Brockhampton Press, 1967, published as *Patrol Car*, Harper, 1967; *A Traitor's Crime*, Collins for the Crime Club, 1968; *River Patrol*, Harper, 1969; *Dead Man's Bluff*, Collins, 1970; *Police Patrol Bout*, Brockhampton Press, 1971; *Trapped*, Harper, 1972; *Mistakenly in Mallorca*, Collins for the Crime Club, 1974.

Under pseudonym Jeffrey Ashford: *Counsel for the Defence*, John Long, 1960, Harper, 1961; *Investigations Are Proceeding*, John Long, 1961, published as *The D.I.*, Harper, 1962; *The Burden of Proof*, Harper, 1962; *Will Anyone Who Saw the Accident ...*, Harper, 1963; *Enquiries Are Continuing*, John Long, 1964; *The Superintendent's Room*, John Long, 1964, Harper, 1965; *The Hands of Innocence*, John Long, 1965, Walker & Co., 1966; *Consider the Evidence*, Walker & Co., 1966; *Hit and Run*, Arrow Books, 1966; *Forget What You Saw*, Walker & Co., 1967; *Grand Prix Monaco*, Putnam, 1968; *Prisoner at the Bar*, Walker & Co., 1969; *Grand Prix Germany*, Putnam, 1970; *To Protect the Guilty*, Walker & Co., 1970; *Bent Copper*, Walker & Co., 1971; *Grand Prix United States*, Putnam, 1971; *A Man Will Be Kidnapped Tomorrow*, Walker & Co., 1972; *Grand Prix Britain*, Putnam, 1973; *The Double Run*, Walker & Co., 1973; *Dick Knox At Le Mans*, Putnam, 1974; *The Color of Violence*, Walker & Co., 1974; *Three Layers of Guilt*, John Long, in press.

Under pseudonym Hastings Draper: *Wiggery Pokery*, W.

H. Allen, 1956; *Wigged and Gowned*, W. H. Allen, 1958; *Brief Help*, W. H. Allen, 1961.

Under pseudonym Roderic Graeme: *Brandy Ahoy!*, Hutchinson, 1951; *Concerning Blackshirt*, Hutchinson, 1952; *Where's Brandy?*, Hutchinson, 1953; *Blackshirt Wins the Trick*, Hutchinson, 1953; *Blackshirt Passes By*, Hutchinson, 1953; *Salute to Blackshirt*, Hutchinson, 1954; *Brandy Goes a Cruising*, Hutchinson, 1954; *Blackshirt Meets the Lady*, Hutchinson, 1956; *Paging Blackshirt*, John Long, 1957; *Blackshirt Helps Himself*, John Long, 1958; *Double for Blackshirt*, John Long, 1958; *Blackshirt Sets the Pace*, John Long, 1959; *Blackshirt Sees It Through*, John Long, 1960; *Blackshirt Finds Trouble*, John Long, 1961; *Blackshirt Takes the Trail*, John Long, 1962; *Blackshirt On the Spot*, John Long, 1963; *Call for Blackshirt*, John Long, 1963; *Blackshirt Saves the Day*, John Long, 1964; *Danger for Blackshirt*, John Long, 1965; *Blackshirt At Large*, John Long, 1966; *Blackshirt In Peril*, John Long, 1967; *Blackshirt Stirs Things Up*, John Long, 1969.

Under pseudonym Graham Hastings: *Twice Checked*, R. Hale, 1959; *Deadly Game*, R. Hale, 1961.

AVOCATIONAL INTERESTS: Shooting, training gun dogs, vintage Bentleys (Jeffries rebuilds 1924 three-litre Bentleys), travel.

* * *

JENISON, Don P. 1897-

PERSONAL: Born May 4, 1897, in Colorado Springs, Colo.; married Mary Crawford, August 12, 1922; children: Charles Leslie. *Education:* Educated in public schools of Colorado. *Politics:* Democrat. *Religion:* Protestant. *Home:* 3681 Georgia St., San Diego, Calif. 92103.

CAREER: Book and job printer for forty-seven years, specializing in intricate rule forms; began to write as a retirement hobby. Shrine bandsman for fifty years. *Military service:* U.S. Army, musician in Field Artillery regimental bands, World War I. *Member:* Masons.

WRITINGS: Man From the Yellowstone, Arcadia House, 1965; *Rails Above the Plains*, Arcadia House, 1965; *Gold In A Tin Cup*, Arcadia House, 1966; *The Silver Concho*, Ace Books, 1968; *Zero Hour at Black Butte*, Ace Books, 1969; *South to New Range*, Ace Books, 1970; *Broken Shoe*, Greenleaf Classics, 1971; *Trouble on Diamond Seven*, Ace Books, 1972; *The Man from Bozemon*, Ace Books, 1974; *Nightmare Ranch*, Ace Books, 1974.

WORK IN PROGRESS: Two books, *The Golden Meadow*, and *Sagebrush Kingdom*.

SIDELIGHTS: As a youth Jenison saw the last of the homestead rush, helped clean sagebrush land, and grew up with hardbitten old cattlemen. Now he finds it "discouraging to create prototype characters [of early westerners] and then have some sweet young thing who calls herself an editor, whittle them down to Rover Boys at an ice cream social."

* * *

JENKINS, Holt M. 1920-

PERSONAL: Born February 24, 1920, in Baltimore, Md.; son of George W. (in insurance) and Emma (Waggner) Jenkins; married Mary Louise Lenker, April 21, 1951; children: Mark, John, Mary Margaret. *Education:* Johns Hopkins University, B.S., 1942; General Theological Seminary, S.T.B., 1949. *Politics:* Democrat. *Home:* 10 South Chelsea Ave., Atlantic City, N.J. 08401.

CAREER: Clergyman of Protestant Episcopal Church; served at St. Anne's Church, Annapolis, Md., 1949-54, St. Mark's Church, Alexandria, Va., 1954-59, and Christ Church, Alexandria, Va., 1959-66; All Saints' Church, Atlantic City, N.J., clergyman, 1966—. President, Alexandria City Poverty Program, 1965-66. *Military service:* U.S. Naval Reserve, 1942-45. *Member:* Gustav Weigel Society, Kiwanis Club (Atlantic City).

WRITINGS: A Haunted House, Morehouse, 1967.

WORK IN PROGRESS: A children's book on Washington during the Civil War; a section for a commemorative volume on Gustav Weigel.†

* * *

JENNINGS, Richard (Wormington) 1907-

PERSONAL: Born October 19, 1907, in Bois D'Arc, Mo.; son of William Thomas (a banker) and Hattie Florence (Wormington) Jennings; married Elizabeth Robison, August 10, 1935; children: Susan Elizabeth (Mrs. Bruce E. Stangeland), Margaret Anne, William Thomas. *Education:* Park College, A.B., 1927; University of Pennsylvania, A.M., 1934; University of California, Berkeley, J.D., 1939. *Religion:* Presbyterian. *Home:* 425 Vassar Ave., Berkeley, Calif. *Office:* School of Law, University of California, Berkeley, Calif. 94720.

CAREER: High school teacher in Pinckneyville, Ill., 1927-30, Camden, N.J., 1930-33; admitted to California bar, 1939; Jesse H. Steinhart (law firm), San Francisco, Calif., associate, 1939-45, member of firm, 1945-47; University of California, Berkeley, lecturer in law, 1940-42, professor of law, 1947-55, Coffroth Professor of Law, 1955—. Fulbright visiting professor of law at University of Tokyo, 1961, University of Cologne, 1972, Salzburg Seminar of American Studies, summer, 1972. Consultant to U.S. Securities and Exchange Commission, 1962. President of International Institute of San Francisco, 1949-51; chairman of advisory board, San Francisco United Crusade, 1953-54, 1955-56. *Member:* American Bar Association, San Francisco Bar Association.

WRITINGS: (Editor with Ballantine and Lattin) *Cases and Materials on Corporations*, 2nd edition, 1953, 3rd edition (with Lattin), Callaghan & Co., 1959, 4th edition (with Lattin and Buxbaum), 1968, supplement, 1972; (with Marsh) *Securities Regulation—Cases and Materials*, Foundation Press, 1963, 3rd edition, 1972, supplement, 1974; *Selected Statutes: Rules and Forms under the Federal Securities Laws*, Foundation Press, 1974.

* * *

JENSEN, Clayne R. 1930-

PERSONAL: Born March 17, 1930, in Gunnison, Utah; son of Altan H. (a stockman) and Arvilla (Roylance) Jensen; married Eloise Henrie, March 4, 1962; children: Craig, Michael, Blake, Chris. *Education:* University of Utah, B.S., 1952, M.S., 1956; Indiana University, Ph.D., 1962. *Religion:* Church of Jesus Christ of Latter-day Saints. *Home:* 1900 Oak Lane, Provo, Utah 84601. *Office:* Brigham Young University, Provo, Utah 84601.

CAREER: Professor at Brigham Young University, Provo, Utah. Chairman of National Conference on Inter-Agency Planning for Recreation and Parks, 1963-64; member of advisory committee, National Conference of State and Federal Inter-Agency Committees for Recreation, 1965. Executive secretary of Utah Recreation and Parks Association, 1958-63, and Utah Inter-Agency Committee for Recreation, 1962-65. *Military service:* U.S. Marine Corps, 1952-55; became captain. *Member:* National Recreation Association (chairman of advisory board, Southwest district, 1965-66; member of board of governors, 1965-69), American Association for Health, Physical Education and Recreation (vice-president, Southwest district, 1965-66), Utah Association for Health, Physical Education and Recreation (vice-president, 1959-60; president, 1966-67), Western College Men's Physical Education Society. *Awards, honors:* Annual award for outstanding contribution to recreation and park development in Utah, 1964.

WRITINGS: (With Mary Bee Jensen) *Square Dancing*, Wadsworth, 1965; (with M. B. Jensen) *Folk Dancing*, Wadsworth, 1965; (with Vernon Barney and Cynthia Hirst) *Conditioning Exercises—Exercises to Improve Body Form and Function*, Mosby, 1965, 3rd edition, 1972; (with Karl Tucker) *Skiing*, 2nd edition, W. C. Brown, 1967; (with Arthur Wilcox) *Outdoor Recreation in America—Trends and Problems*, Burgess, 1968, 2nd edition, 1973; (with Gordon Schultz) *Applied Kinesiology*, McGraw, 1970; (with Garth Fisher) *Scientific Basis of Athletic Conditioning*, Lea & Febiger, 1972; (with N. P. Nielsen) *Measurement and Statistics in Physical Education*, Wadsworth, 1972; (with Clark Thorstenson) *Issues in Outdoor Recreation*, Burgess, 1972; (with Clarence Robison) *Modern Track and Field Coaching Technique*, Lea & Febiger, 1974. Writer of three Utah State University Extension pamphlets on recreation. Contributor to athletic and physical education periodicals. Editor, *Utah Journal of Health, Physical Education and Recreation*, 1970-72.

AVOCATIONAL INTERESTS: Conservation, and development of outdoor recreation resources, travel.

* * *

JENSEN, Irving L. 1920-

PERSONAL: Born September 28, 1920, in New York, N.Y.; son of Ole and Frances (Hoydal) Jensen; married Charlotte Christiansen, August 29, 1953; children: Donna Lea, Karen Elaine, Robert Warren. *Education:* Wagner College, student, 1939-42, A.B. (magna cum laude), 1944; Biblical Seminary in New York, S.T.B., 1949; Northwestern Theological Seminary, Th.D., 1954. *Home:* Evergreen Dr., Dayton, Tenn. 37321. *Office:* Bryan College, Dayton, Tenn. 37321.

CAREER: Mutual Life Insurance Co. of New York, New York, N.Y., actuarial writer, 1937-39; ordained to ministry of Evangelical Free Church of America, 1949; Southland Bible Institute, Pikeville, Ky., instructor in Bible, 1949-51; Bryan College, Dayton, Tenn., professor of Bible and chairman of department, 1954—. *Military service:* U.S. Army Air Forces, meteorological officer, 1942-46, serving overseas, 1943-46; became captain. *Member:* Evangelical Theological Society.

WRITINGS: Independent Bible Study, Moody, 1963; *Numbers, Journey to God's Rest-land*, Moody, 1964; *Jeremiah, Prophet of Judgment*, Moody, 1966; *Joshua, Restland Won*, Moody, 1966; *Acts: An Independent Study*, Moody, 1968; *Enjoy Your Bible*, Moody, 1969. Also author of self-study guides in New and Old Testament books, Moody, 1968—.

Editor of revised editions of books by Grace Saxe, all published by Moody: *Studies in Genesis*, 1967; *... in Exodus*, 1967; *... in Leviticus*, 1967; *... in Numbers and Deuteronomy*, 1967; *... in Joshua*, 1967; *... in Judges-Ruth*, 1967; *... in Samuel*, 1967; *... in I Kings*, 1967; *... in II Kings*, 1967; *... in Psalms*, 1967.

WORK IN PROGRESS: Old Testament Survey Guide and *Bible Charts*, both to be published by Moody.

* * *

JENSEN, Lawrence N(eil) 1924-

PERSONAL: Born February 5, 1924, in Orange, N.J.; son of Lawrence Neil (an engineer) and Dorothy (Whitmore) Jensen; children: David Whitmore, Lawrence Neil. *Education:* Columbia University, B.S., 1953, M.A., 1957, Ed.D., 1962. *Religion:* None. *Home:* Castleton, Vt.

CAREER: Commercial artist in New York, N.Y., 1946-56; William Floyd School, Shirley, Long Island, N.Y., art supervisor, 1956-57; Swain School of Design, New Bedford, Mass., instructor in design, 1957-59; State University of New York at Farmingdale, assistant professor of art, 1959-62; Castleton State College, Castleton, Vt., associate professor of art, 1962-65, professor, 1966—, chairman of department, 1962—. Southern Connecticut State College, New Haven, chairman of department of art (on leave from regular post), 1965-66; College of the Virgin Islands, professor of art (on leave from regular post), 1971-72. Paintings exhibited in more than 100 national exhibitions; work in permanent collections of U.S. Coast Guard Academy and several museums. *Military service:* U.S. Coast Guard, 1942-46; combat artist, 1944-46.

MEMBER: American Watercolor Society, American Federation of Teachers (Vermont state secretary). *Awards, honors:* Eighteen painting awards in National Exhibitions.

WRITINGS: Synthetic Painting Media, Prentice-Hall, 1964. Contributor to *American Artist*.

SIDELIGHTS: Owned and lived aboard a fifty-foot schooner during the 1950's, sailing to southern waters in winter; now owns a ketch and sails to New England in summer on sketching and painting tours.

BIOGRAPHICAL/CRITICAL SOURCES: Prize-Winning Watercolors, Book III, Allied, 1965.

* * *

JENSEN, Paul K. 1916-

PERSONAL: Born April 6, 1916, in Humboldt, Saskatchewan, Canada; son of John and Mary (Pedersen) Jensen; married Roberta Adams, August, 1942; children: Paul K. II, Karen. *Education:* Attended University of Cincinnati, 1936-37, Cincinnati Art Academy, 1938-39. *Home:* 19 Yarmouth Rd., Rowayton, Conn. 06853. *Office:* Time/Life Books, New York, N.Y. 10020.

CAREER: With Simon and Schuster, Inc., New York, N.Y., 1949-51; National Geographic Society, Washington, D.C., book designer, 1956-61; Time/Life Books, New York, N.Y., book designer. Photographer specializing in natural history subjects. *Military service:* U.S. Army Air Forces, fighter pilot, 1942-45; received Distinguished Flying Cross.

WRITINGS: (Editor) *Fireside Book of Flying Stories* (anthology), Simon and Schuster, 1951; *Golden Book of Airplanes*, Simon and Schuster, 1951; *National Parks*, Golden Press, 1964.

AVOCATIONAL INTERESTS: National parks, camping, wilderness.†

JOEDICKE, Juergen 1925-

PERSONAL: Born June 26, 1925, in Erfurt, Germany; son of Arthur (a businessman) and Frieda (Nitzschke) Joedicke; married Rosemarie Rapp, January 1, 1950; children: Jochen, Ingrid. *Education:* Hochschule fuer Architektur und bild. Kuenste, Weimar, East Germany, Dipl. Engineer, Arch., 1950; Technische Hochschule, Stuttgart, Germany, Promotion Dr.-Ing., 1953. *Office:* Technische Hochschule, Keplerstrasse 11, Stuttgart, West Germany.

CAREER: Technische Hochschule, Stuttgart, Germany, professor of theory and lines of development of modern architecture. Practicing architect. *Member:* Bund Deutscher Architekten, Deutscher Werkbund, Freier Architekt, Architektenkammer Baden-Wuerttemberg.

WRITINGS: Geschichte der Modernen Architektur, Hatje, 1958, 2nd edition, Arthur Niggli, 1971, translation by James C. Palm published as *History of Modern Architecture,* Praeger, 1959; (editor) *Sportanlagen, Hallenbaeder, Freibaeder,* Karl Kraemer, 1958; (editor) *Die international Theaterwettbewerbe Duesseldorf und Essen,* Karl Kraemer, 1960; *Buerobauten,* Hatje, 1959, translation by C. V. Amerongen published as *Office Buildings,* Praeger, 1962; *Schalenbau: Konstruktion und Gestaltung,* Karl Kraemer, 1962, published as *Shell Architecture,* Reinhold Publishing, 1963; *Architektur and Staedtebau: Das Werk van den Broek und Bakema,* Karl Kraemer, 1963; (editor) *Hugo Haering: Schriften, Entwuerfe, Bauten,* Karl Kraemer, 1965; (editor) *Fuer eine lebendige Baukunst,* Karl Kraemer, 1965; (editor) *Candilis-Josic-Woods: A Decade of Architecture and Urban Design,* translated by Palmes, A. Tiranti (London), 1968; (with Christian Plath) *Die Weissen hofsiedlung,* Karl Kraemer, 1968; *Moderne Architektur: Stroemungen und Tendenzen,* Karl Kraemer, 1968, translation by Palmes published as *Architecture Since 1945: Sources and Directions,* Praeger, 1969; (contributor) *Bewertungsprobleme in der Bauplanung,* Karl Kraemer, 1969. Chief editor, *Bauen & Wohnen.* Contributed several articles to German, French, English, Japanese, Hungarian, and other architectural journals.

SIDELIGHTS: Joedicke has lectured at German and foreign universities and to professional societies.†

* * *

JOHANNESEN, Richard L(ee) 1937-

PERSONAL: Born August 14, 1937, in Davenport, Iowa; son of Richard Tharp (a sales expediter) and Irene (Oetzmann) Johannesen; married Deedra Runyan, June 1, 1969; children: two. *Education:* Augustana College, Rock Island, Ill., A.B., 1959; University of Kansas, A.M., 1960, Ph.D., 1964. *Home:* 117 Mattek Ave., DeKalb, Ill. 60115. *Office:* Department of Speech Communication, Northern Illinois University, DeKalb, Ill. 60115.

CAREER: University of Kansas, Lawrence, instructor in speech, 1961-62; Indiana University, Bloomington, instructor, 1964-66, assistant professor of speech, 1966-71; Northern Illinois University, associate professor and coordinator of graduate studies in speech communication, 1971—. *Member:* International Communication Association, Speech Communication Association, Rhetoric Society of America, Central States Speech Association.

WRITINGS: (With W. A. Linkugel and R. R. Allen) *Contemporary American Speeches,* Wadsworth, 1965, 3rd edition, 1972; (with E. C. Buehler) *Building the Contest Oration,* Wilson, 1965; (editor) *Ethics and Persuasion,* Random House, 1967; (editor with Rennard Strickland and Ralph T. Eubanks) *Language is Sermonic: Richard M. Weaver on the Nature of Rhetoric,* Louisiana State University Press, 1970; (editor) *Contemporary Theories of Rhetoric,* Harper, 1971; (contributor) *Essays on Teaching Speech in the High School,* J. Jeffrey Auer and Edward Jenkinson, editors, Indiana University Press, 1971; (contributor) *Principles and Types of Speech Communication,* Alan H. Monroe and Douglas Ehninger, editors, 7th edition, Scott, Foresman, 1974; *Perspectives on Ethics in Human Communication,* C. E. Merrill, 1975. Contributor to *Persuasion: Reflection and Responsibility,* Charles U. Larson, editor, Wadsworth.

Contributor of articles to *Quarterly Journal of Speech, SpeechTeacher, Central States Speech Journal, Western Speech, Southern Speech Journal,* and other speech journals.

* * *

JOHNS, Richard A(lton) 1929-

PERSONAL: Born July 17, 1929, in Tyler, Tex.; son of Richard Alton (in advertising) and Annie (Hill) Johns; married Joan Turner, November 8, 1958; children: Richard Andrew, Janis. *Education:* Tyler Junior College, A.A., 1948; North Texas State University, B.A., 1950. *Religion:* Presbyterian. *Home:* 912 West Camellia, Tyler, Tex. 75701.

CAREER: General Dynamics, Fort Worth, Tex., illustrator and editor, 1951-61; *Tyler Star* (publishing company), Tyler, Tex., writer and artist, 1961. Formerly free-lance illustrator for radio and television stations in Fort Worth. *Military service:* U.S. Army, Field Artillery, 1950-51.

WRITINGS: Thirteenth Apostle, Broadman, 1966; *Garden of the Okapi,* Zondervan, 1968; *Return to Heroism,* Broadman, 1969; *Everyday Five Minutes with God,* Broadman, 1969. Author of teleplay, "The Legacy," presented on National Broadcasting Co. network.

WORK IN PROGRESS: I, Tertius, a novel.

* * *

JOHNSON, Alan P(ackard) 1929-

PERSONAL: Born January 13, 1929, in Provo, Utah; son of Clair W. (a music professor) and Alice (Packard) Johnson; married Patsy Pollard, March 17, 1952; children: Shauna Renee, Jo Ellen, Justin Richard, Brenda Ann, B. Doran, Maria. *Education:* Brigham Young University, B.A., 1954, M.A., 1960; Indiana University, M.B.A., 1955; University of Illinois, doctoral study. *Politics:* Independent. *Religion:* Church of Jesus Christ of Latter-day Saints. *Home:* 1755 25th St., Ogden, Utah.

CAREER: Brigham Young University, Provo, Utah, instructor in accountancy, 1955-57; Arthur Andersen & Co., San Francisco, Calif., public accountant, 1957-62; University of California, Berkeley, special lecturer, 1959-62; Abadan Institute of Technology, Abadan, Iran, professor of accountancy, 1962-66. *Member:* American Institute of Certified Public Accountants, American Accounting Association.

WRITINGS: (With Lillian E. Harmon) *An Introduction and Guide to the Samoan Language for Missionaries of the Church of Jesus Christ of Latter-day Saints,* Church of Jesus Christ of Latter-Day Saints, 1962; (compiler) *Castle of Zion,* Deseret, 1963; *Fasting—The Second Step to Eternal Life,* Deseret, 1963; *The Sacrament of the Lord's Supper,* Deseret, 1965.

WORK IN PROGRESS: A book on the subject of justice.†

* * *

JOHNSON, D(avid) Gale 1916-

PERSONAL: Born July 10, 1916, in Vinton, Iowa; son of Albert D. and Myra Jane (Reed) Johnson; married Helen Wallace, August 10, 1938; children: David Wallace, Kay Anne. *Education:* Iowa State College, B.S., 1938, Ph.D., 1945; University of Wisconsin, M.S., 1939; University of Chicago, graduate student, 1939-41. *Politics:* Independent. *Religion:* Baptist. *Home:* 5617 South Kenwood Ave., Chicago, Ill. 60637. *Office:* Department of Economics, University of Chicago, 1126 East 59th St., Chicago, Ill. 60637.

CAREER: Iowa State College (now University) of Science and Technology, Ames, research associate, 1941-42, assistant professor of agricultural economics, 1942-44; University of Chicago, Chicago, Ill., 1944—, began as economics research associate, professor of economics, 1954—, associate dean of Division of the Social Sciences, 1957-60, dean, 1960-70, chairman of economics department, 1971—. President of National Opinion Research Center, 1962—. Consultant to RAND Corp. and Tennessee Valley Authority, 1962—. *Member:* Social Science Research Council (director, 1954-57), American Economic Association, American Farm Economic Association (president, 1964-65), Phi Kappa Phi, Alpha Zeta.

WRITINGS: Forward Prices for Agriculture, University of Chicago Press, 1947; *Trade and Agriculture*, Wiley, 1950; (with Robert L. Gustafson) *Grain Yields and the American Food Supply*, University of Chicago Press, 1962; *World Agriculture in Disarray*, Macmillan, 1973; *Farm Commodity Programs: An Opportunity for Change*, American Enterprise Institute, 1973; *The Sugar Program: Large Costs and Small Benefits*, American Enterprise Institute, 1974. Contributor of over one hundred papers to journals and other publications.

* * *

JOHNSON, Falk S(immons) 1913-

PERSONAL: Born October 17, 1913, in Wake Forest, N.C.; son of Walter Nathan (a minister) and Eva (Coppedge) Johnson; married Laura Stark (an English teacher), June 11, 1940; children: Mark Hartman, Bruce Walter, Martha Frances, Craig Falk. *Education:* Wake Forest College (now Wake Forest University), B.A., 1935, M.A., 1936; Northwestern University, summer graduate study, 1938-40; University of Chicago, Ph.D., 1956. *Politics:* Independent. *Religion:* Protestant. *Home:* 7624 Maple St., Morton Grove, Ill. 60053. *Office:* University of Illinois at Chicago Circle, Chicago, Ill. 60680.

CAREER: Member of English faculty at Campbell College, Buies Creek, N.C., 1936-37, Mars Hill College, Mars Hill, N.C., 1938-40, Northwestern University, Evanston, Ill., 1945-49; University of Illinois, Chicago, instructor, 1949-56, assistant professor, 1956-60, associate professor, 1960-66, professor of English, 1966—, chairman of rhetoric courses, 1950-65. Teacher of composition on educational television, Chicago, Ill., summers, 1958-60. *Military service:* U.S. Army, 1941-45; signal intelligence officer in Europe; became first lieutenant; received Presidential Unit Citation, five battle stars. *Member:* College English Association, National Council of Teachers of English, College Conference on Composition and Communication (secretary, 1959-60), Linguistic Society of America, American Association of University Professors.

WRITINGS: A Spelling Guide and Workbook, Rinehart, 1959; *How to Organize What You Write*, Houghton, 1964; *Improving What You Write*, Houghton, 1965; *A Self-Improvement Guide to Spelling*, Holt, 1965. Three of his *American Mercury* articles, "How We Got Our Dialects," "English as a World Language," and "Should Spelling be Streamlined?" have been reprinted in a total of eight books; contributor to professional journals. Writer of filmstrip series, "Organizing Your Writing," produced by Encyclopaedia Britannica Films.

* * *

JOHNSON, Paul (Bede) 1928-

PERSONAL: Born November 2, 1928, in England; son of William Aloysius and Anne Johnson; married Marigold Hunt (a book reviewer), 1957; children: Daniel, Cosmo, Luke, Sophie. *Education:* Attended Stonyhurst College; Magdalen College, Oxford, B.A. (honors in history), 1950. *Politics:* Labour. *Religion:* Roman Catholic. *Home:* Copthall, Iver, Buckinghamshire, England. *Office:* New Statesman, 10 Great Turnstile, London W.C. 1, England.

CAREER: Realities, Paris, France, assistant executive editor, 1952-55; *New Statesman*, London, England, assistant editor, 1955-65, editor, 1965-70, New Statesman & Nation Publishing Co., London, director, 1965-70. Has done extensive television work, mainly in the field of current affairs broadcasts. Chairman, Iver Village Labour Party, 1966. *Member:* National Union of Journalists.

WRITINGS: The Suez War, MacGibbon & Kee, 1957; *Journey into Chaos*, MacGibbon & Kee, 1958; *Left of Centre*, MacGibbon & Kee, 1960; *Merrie England*, Macmillan, 1964; *Statesmen and Nations*, Sidgwick & Jackson, 1971; *The Offshore Islanders: England's People from Roman Occupation to the Present*, Holt, 1972; (with George Gale) *The Highland Jaunt*, Collins, 1973; *The Life and Times of Edward III*, Weidenfeld & Nicolson, 1973; *Elizabeth I: A Study in Power and Intellect*, Holt, 1974; *A Place in History*, Weidenfeld & Nicolson, 1974, Drake, 1975.

SIDELIGHTS: Paul Johnson speaks and writes French fluently; travels have been practically world-wide. *Avocational interests:* Collecting books and paintings, with emphasis on eighteenth-century paintings; painting, mountaineering.†

* * *

JOHNSON, Ray(mond Edward) 1927-

PERSONAL: Born October 16, 1927, in Detroit, Mich. *Education:* Attended Black Mountain College, 1947-50. *Address:* c/o Feigen Gallery, 27 East 79th St., New York, N.Y. 10021.

CAREER: Artist; active in American Abstract Artists, 1950-53, most prolific in collage, 1953—; founder and operator of New York Correspondence School of Art, 1962—. Works included in collection of Museum of Modern Art, New York, National Gallery, Washington, De Cordova Museum, Lincoln, Mass., as well as in other collections. Has founded and operated several art galleries, including Robin, 1963, and Woodpecker, 1965. Exhibited one-man shows in Chicago and New York; exhibited work in group shows in cities throughout the U.S. *Awards, honors:* National Institute of Arts and Letters award, 1966.

WRITINGS: Book of the Month, privately printed, 1957; *A Book About Death: Mary Crehan, 4, Choked to Death on a Peanut Butter Sandwich Last Night*, B. Porter, 1963; *The Paper Snake*, Something Else Press, 1965; (with Michael Morris) *Concrete Poetry*, [Vancouver], 1969; *Ray Johnson dal 5 al aprile 1972 alla Galleria Schwarz, Milano*, Wittenborn, 1972. Contributor to *Village Voice, Location, Yam*, and other publications.

BIOGRAPHICAL/CRITICAL SOURCES: Collage (Palermo, Sicily), Spring, 1966.†

* * *

JOHNSON, Robert W(illard) 1921-

PERSONAL: Born December 23, 1921, in Denver, Colo.; son of Ernest A. (a college president) and Edith (Glassford) Johnson; married Mary McCormack, January 7, 1945; children: Judith L., Cynthia L. *Education:* Student at Lake Forest Academy, 1935-39, and Oberlin College, 1939-42; Harvard University, M.B.A., 1946; Northwestern University, Ph.D., 1952. *Religion:* Presbyterian. *Home:* 1001 Digby Dr., Lafayette, Ind. 47905.

CAREER: Southwestern at Memphis, Memphis, Tenn., assistant professor, 1948-50; University of Buffalo (now State University of New York at Buffalo), 1950-59, began as assistant professor, became professor of finance; Michigan State University, East Lansing, professor of financial administration, 1959-64; Purdue University, Lafayette, Ind., professor of industrial administration, 1964—, director, Credit Research Center, 1974—. Federal Reserve Board, economist, 1956-57. Economic consultant to National Conference of Commissioners on Uniform State Laws; member, National Commission on Consumer Finance, 1969-72. *Military service:* U.S. Navy, 1943-46; became lieutenant commander. *Member:* American Finance Association, Financial Management Association, Institute of Management Science. *Awards, honors:* Fellow, Institute of Basic Mathematics for Application to Business, Harvard University, 1959-60.

WRITINGS: Financial Management, Allyn & Bacon, 1959, 4th edition, 1971; *Methods of Stating Consumer Finance Charges*, Graduate School of Business, Columbia University, 1961; (with Roland I. Robinson) *Self-Correcting Problems in Finance*, Allyn & Bacon, 1965, 3rd edition, 1975; *Capital Budgeting*, Wadsworth, 1970. Editor with Myron J. Gordon of Irwin's "Finance Series."

WORK IN PROGRESS: Fifth edition of *Financial Management*.

AVOCATIONAL INTERESTS: Gardening and travel.

* * *

JOHNSON, Samuel A(ugustus) 1895-

PERSONAL: Born August 27, 1895, in Kansas City, Mo.; son of Hubert B. (a railway executive) and Cornelia (Morgan) Johnson; married Winifred Feder, 1920. *Education:* University of Kansas, A.B., 1916, M.A., 1928; University of Iowa, graduate study, summers, 1922-24; University of Wisconsin, Ph.D., 1936. *Religion:* Unitarian Universalist. *Home and office:* Dove Cottage, Mountain View Dr., Peterborough, N.H. 03458.

CAREER: University of Kansas, Lawrence, instructor in history, 1926-28; Kansas State Teachers College, Emporia, associate professor of history and political science, 1928-36; Harris Teachers College, St. Louis, Mo., professor of history and political science, 1936-63; retired, 1963. Lecturer at St. Louis University, 1938-49, and Washington University, St. Louis, 1951-63; news analyst, KMOX, St. Louis,

1941-49. Executive director, St. Louis Council on World Affairs, 1949-51. *Military service:* U.S. Army, 1917-19; became sergeant. *Member:* Missouri Political Science Association.

WRITINGS: These Americas (history of the Western hemisphere), Webster Publishing Co., 1946; *The Battle Cry of Freedom*, University of Kansas Press, 1954; *Essentials of Comparative Government*, Barron's, 1963, revised edition, 1973; *Essentials of Political Science*, Barron's, 1966; *Interpretation of American History*, Barron's, 1968; *Essentials of Political Parties*, Barron's, 1973. More than twenty articles included in *Dictionary of American History*; also contributor to *World Book Encyclopedia*. Wrote weekly newspaper column on world affairs for nine years.

WORK IN PROGRESS: Interpretation of American History, for Barron's.

SIDELIGHTS: The Battle Cry of Freedom, a study of the New England Emigrant Aid Company in the Kansas conflict, was published in connection with the centennial of Kansas Territory and the founding of the Republican party.

* * *

JOHNSON, Stanley L(ewis) 1920-

PERSONAL: Born October 6, 1920, in Garland, Utah; son of E. Lewis (a farmer) and Ida (Hansen) Johnson. *Education:* University of Utah, B.A., 1942; University of Southern California, Ph.D., 1955. *Politics:* Democrat. *Home:* 2222 Northwest Johnson St., Portland, Ore. 97210.

CAREER: Portland State College, Portland, Ore., 1950—, began as instructor, assistant professor, 1955-70, associate professor of English, 1970—. *Military service:* U.S. Army, 1942-45. *Member:* American Association of University Professors, American Civil Liberties Union, Philological Association of the Pacific Coast, Bruckner Society.

WRITINGS: (Editor with Judah Bierman and James Hart) *The Dramatic Experience*, Prentice-Hall, 1958; (editor with Judah Bierman and James Hart) *The Play and the Reader*, Prentice-Hall, 1966, alternate edition, 1971; *Discovery and Response: The Strategies of Fiction*, Winthrop, 1972. Contributor of reviews to *Salt Lake Tribune, Northwest Magazine*, and other newspapers.

WORK IN PROGRESS: Study of twentieth-century war fiction.

AVOCATIONAL INTERESTS: Travel, archaeology, and music.

* * *

JOHNSON, Virginia W(eisel) 1910-

PERSONAL: Born November 13, 1910, in Missoula, Mont.; daughter of George Ferdinand and Thula (Toole) Weisel; married Walter Morris Johnson (an Army officer, now retired), October 7, 1933; children: Thula V., Linda. *Education:* Studied at University of Montana. *Religion:* Protestant. *Home:* Route 3, Pattee Canyon, Missoula, Mont. *Agent:* Russell & Volkening, Inc., 551 Fifth Ave., Room 1517, New York, N.Y. 10017.

CAREER: Writer. Bitterroot Competitive Trail Ride, secretary. *Member:* Authors League, League of Women Voters, Friends of the University of Montana Library (secretary).

WRITINGS: The Unregimented General, Houghton, 1961; *The Long, Long Trail*, Houghton, 1966; *Lady in Arms*, Houghton, 1967; *Cedars of Carlo*, Morrow, 1969;

High Country: The Rocky Mountain West, Walker, 1970. Contributor to *U.S. Lady* and *New York Times*.

WORK IN PROGRESS: For U.S. News and World Report, a chapter on Rocky Mountain West for "American People."

SIDELIGHTS: As an Army wife, Mrs. Johnson lived in England, Germany, the Philippines, Okinawa; speaks some German and a little French; once headed the V Corps Women's Club in Frankfurt, Germany, and served as a board member for the Girl Scouts in the Far East. *Avocational interests:* Horseback riding, fishing, hunting.

*   *   *

JOHNSON, William R.

PERSONAL: Born in Minneapolis, Minn.; son of Carl A. and Anna M. (Anderson) Johnson; married Pauline Doten; children: William R., Jr., Jill Anne. *Education:* Attended Dartmouth College and Jean Morgan School of Art, New York, N.Y. *Religion:* Lutheran. *Home:* 10656 Riverview Pl., Coon Rapids, Minn. 55433.

CAREER: Free-lance artist, cartoonist, and writer in New York, N.Y., 1957-65, Coon Rapids, Minn., 1965—; Trend Enterprises, Inc., St. Paul, Minn., art director and artist, 1971—. Former member of board of directors and baseball manager, Levittown (N.Y.) Boys Club. *Military service:* U.S. Naval Reserve, active duty, 1942-46. *Awards, honors:* Freedoms Foundation honor certificate for editorial cartoon.

WRITINGS: (Self-illustrated) *Holiday Funtime*, Doubleday, 1964; (illustrator) P. Werner, *How Many Angels in the Sky?*, Augsburg, 1965. Sports cartoon columnist, "Letter from the Twins," *St. Paul Dispatch*.

*   *   *

JOHNSON, William Weber 1909-

PERSONAL: Born December 18, 1909, in Mattoon, Ill.; son of Finis Ewing (a railroadman) and Jessie (Weber) Johnson; married second wife, Elizabeth Ann McMurray, October 7, 1951; children: (first marriage) Peter W., Jane (Mrs. Ronald Jones); stepchildren: Richard Ellegood. *Education:* De Pauw University, B.A., 1932; University of Illinois, M.A., 1933. *Politics:* Democratic. *Religion:* Unitarian Universalist. *Address:* Box 3056, Warner Springs, Calif. 92086. *Office:* Department of Journalism, University of California, Los Angeles, Calif. 90024.

CAREER: Newspaper reporter in Decatur, Ill., 1933-34; reporter and city editor, Urbana and Decatur, Ill., 1934-37; Associated Press, reporter, Detroit, Mich., 1937-39; N. W. Ayer, Inc., writer and public relations adviser, Chicago, Ill., and New York, N.Y., 1939-40; Time, Inc., New York, N.Y., contributing editor, 1940-43, war correspondent in Europe, 1944-45, bureau chief (sometimes of combined *Life* and *Time* bureaus), in Mexico City, 1945-47, Buenos Aires, 1947-48, Dallas, 1948-53, Boston, 1954-57, correspondent, Beverly Hills, Calif., 1958-61; University of California, Los Angeles, professor of journalism, 1961-71, professor emeritus, 1971—, chairman of department, 1968-71. *Awards, honors:* Mentioned in (British) dispatches twice while war correspondent; Guggenheim fellowship to write *Kelly Blue*, 1959; Commonwealth Club (San Francisco) gold medal for non-fiction, 1969, for *Heroic Mexico*.

WRITINGS: Sam Houston, the Tallest Texan (juvenile), Random, 1953; *The Birth of Texas* (juvenile), Houghton, 1960; *Captain Cortes Conquers Mexico* (juvenile), Ran-

dom, 1960; *Kelly Blue* (biography), Doubleday, 1960; *Mexico*, Time/Life Books, 1961; *The Andean Republics*, Time/Life Books, 1965; *Heroic Mexico*, Doubleday, 1968; *Baja California*, Time/Life Books, 1972; *The Story of Sea Otters*, Random House, 1973; *The Forty Niners*, Time/Life Books, 1974. Contributor to periodicals, including *Holiday, Saturday Evening Post, Life en Espanol, New York Times Book Review*.

WORK IN PROGRESS: A biography of Hernan Cortes, publication by Little, Brown, expected in 1976; a history of the Spanish-American West, publication by Time/Life Books, expected in 1976.

*   *   *

JOHNSTON, Bernard 1934-

PERSONAL: Born November 19, 1934, in Taft, Calif.; son of Bernard Lowe (a dentist) and Georgia V. (Fox) Johnston; married Judith Ann Sutherland, June 20, 1965; children: Sheldon, Dierdre, Kyle. *Education:* San Francisco State College (now University), B.A., 1957, M.A., 1958; Syracuse University, graduate study, 1964-65.

CAREER: Instructor in humanities at San Francisco State College (now University), San Francisco, Calif., 1958, and Contra Costa College, San Pablo, Calif., 1958-63; full-time writer. Lecturer in humanities, San Francisco State University, 1967.

WRITINGS: (Editor) *Issues in Education: An Anthology of Controversy*, Houghton, 1964; (editor and author of notes and commentary) *The Literature of Learning: A Teacher's Anthology*, Holt, 1971.

WORK IN PROGRESS: A novel; a book of criticism concerned with five New England artists—Jonathan Edwards, Horatio Greenough, Herman Melville, Charles Ives, and Wallace Stevens.

SIDELIGHTS: Bernard Johnston is competent in Latin and French. *Avocational interests:* Mountain climbing and back-pack trips into North American wilderness areas; collecting eighteenth- and twentieth-century recordings, especially chamber music.†

*   *   *

JONES, Charles O(scar) 1931-

PERSONAL: Born October 28, 1931, in Worthing, S.D.; son of Llewellyn F. (a minister) and Marjorie (Tye) Jones; married Vera Mire, June 6, 1959; children: Joseph Benjamin, Daniel Charles. *Education:* University of South Dakota, B.A., 1953; University of Wisconsin, M.S., 1956, Ph.D., 1959; London School of Economics and Political Science, graduate study, 1956-57. *Politics:* Republican. *Religion:* Unitarian Universalist. *Home:* 340 Guys Run Rd., Cheswick, Pa. 15024. *Office:* Department of Political Science, University of Pittsburgh, Pittsburgh, Pa. 15260.

CAREER: Wellesley College, Wellesley, Mass., instructor, 1959-61, assistant professor of political science, 1961-62; National Center for Education in Politics, New York, N.Y., associate director, 1962-63; University of Arizona, Tucson, associate professor, 1963-66, professor of political science, 1966-69; University of Pittsburgh, Pittsburgh, Pa., Maurice Falk Professor of Politics, 1969—. Elections analyst for National Broadcasting Co., 1964, 1966. Member, Commission on Political Activity of Government Personnel, 1966-67. *Military service:* U.S. Army, 1953-55; became first lieutenant. *Member:* American Political Science Association (treasurer, 1972-74), Midwest Political Science Association, Southern Political Science Association, Phi Beta Kappa.

WRITINGS: Party and Policy-Making, Rutgers University Press, 1964; *The Republican Party in American Politics*, Macmillan, 1965; (with Randall B. Ripley) *The Role of Political Parties in Congress* (monograph), University of Arizona Press, 1966; *"Every Second Year": Congressional Behavior and the Two-Year Term*, Brookings Institute, 1967; *The Urban Crisis in America*, National Press, 1969; *The Minority Party in Congress*, Little, Brown, 1970; *An Introduction to the Study of Public Policy*, Duxbury, 1970; *Clean Air: The Policies and Politics of Pollution Control*, University of Pittsburgh Press, 1975. Contributor of articles to professional journals. Member, board of editors, *Western Political Quarterly*, 1967-70, and *Journal of Politics*, 1969-75.

WORK IN PROGRESS: Study of policy relationships between elected representatives and professionals, technicians, experts, etc.

* * *

JONES, Clifford M(erton) 1902-

PERSONAL: Born June 14, 1902, in Wakefield, England; son of William Frederick (a miner) and Sarah Varena (Rowbotham) Jones; married Winifred May Lawrence, August 11, 1926; children: Margaret Merton, Helen Irene. *Education:* University of Leeds, B.Sc., 1924, M.Sc., 1925, Diploma in Education, 1925, Diploma in Theology, 1946, M.A., 1956. *Religion:* Methodist. *Home:* 35 West Park St., Dewsbury, Yorkshire, England.

CAREER: High school master in Leeds, England, 1925-31; Wheelright Grammar School, Dewsbury, Yorkshire, England, senior chemistry master, 1932-48; City of Leeds Training College, Leeds, England, senior lecturer in religious education, 1948-53; University of Leeds, Leeds, England, senior lecturer in religious education, Institute of Education, 1954-67, director of schools council project, 1969-72.

WRITINGS: A Beginner's Chemistry, J. Murray, 1933; *Chemical Calculations*, J. Murray, 1937; *The Methods of Christian Education*, S.C.M. Press, 1950; *Bible Study Exercises*, S.C.M. Press, 1956; *Teaching the Bible Today*, S.C.M. Press, 1963, published as *The Bible Today*, Fortress, 1964; *New Testament Illustrations*, Cambridge University Press, 1966; *Old Testament Illustrations*, Cambridge University Press, 1971; *Religious Education in Primary Schools*, Methuen, 1972. Editor, *Institute of Education Bulletin*, 1954-63, *Religion in Education*, 1957-61.

* * *

JONES, Daisy (Marvel) 1906-

PERSONAL: Born April 22, 1906, in Brownsburg, Ind.; daughter of Harlen H. and Nannie (Mark) Marvel; married Vivian L. Jones, August 3, 1927. *Education:* Attended Central Normal College, Danville, Ind., 1924-25, 1926-27; Indiana State University, B.S., 1931, M.S., 1933; Indiana University, Ed.D., 1947. *Religion:* Christian. *Home:* 928 Terrace Rd., 102, Tempe, Ariz. 85281. *Office:* Arizona State University, Tempe, Ariz. 85281.

CAREER: Marion County schools, Indianapolis, Ind., teacher, 1925-36; Central Normal College, Danville, Ind., assistant professor of education and director of student teaching, 1936-42; Muncie (Ind.) public schools, assistant supervisor, 1942-46; Richmond (Ind.) community schools,

director of elementary education, 1946-63; Arizona State University, Tempe, professor of education, 1963-73, professor emeritus, 1973—. Has conducted summer sessions and workshops for Butler University, University of Chicago, and other institutions. Member of board of directors, Child Guidance Clinic, Richmond, Ind., 1958-62.

MEMBER: Association for Supervision and Curriculum Development (member at large of board of directors, 1969-73), National Education Association (life member), International Reading Association, National Council of Teachers of English, Association for Higher Education, American Association of University Women, Delta Kappa Gamma, Pi Lambda Theta, Kappa Delta Pi. *Awards, honors:* Distinguished Alumni Award of Indiana State University, 1963; Pike High School (Indiana) Alumni award, 1974, for distinguished service to education.

WRITINGS: Richmond, Eastern Gateway to Indiana, Board of Education (Richmond, Ind.), 1959; *Building Better English*, Book 2, Harper, 1961; (with J. Louis Cooper) *From Actors to Astronauts*, Harper, 1964; (with Cooper) *From Coins to Kings*, with workbook, Harper, 1964; *Teaching Children to Read*, Harper, 1971; *From Falcons to Forests*, Harper, 1973; *From Lions to Legends*, Harper, 1973. Also author of workbooks for graded readers by Edonna Evertts and Byron VanRoekel, *Coming to Crossroads, Spanning the Seven Seas*, and *Traveling the Trade Winds*, all Harper, 1972. Contributor to education journals. Reviewer of language arts books, Curriculum Advisory Service; member of editorial board, *Child Life* and *Childhood Education*.

WORK IN PROGRESS: Curriculum Targets, for Prentice-Hall, completion expected in 1976; a language program for grades 1-6, for Benziger, 1977; a reading program for grades 4-6, for Benziger.

SIDELIGHTS: Daisy Jones's travels have spanned all fifty states, including Canada, Mexico, Central and South America, and Africa; she went around the world, 1956, to Australia and the South Pacific Islands, 1962, and has made two trips each to Europe and the Orient.

* * *

JONES, Donald (Lawrence) 1938-

PERSONAL: Born February 11, 1938, in Kimball, Neb.; son of Lawrence Roswell (a bank teller and civic servant) and Hazel (Stemen) Jones; married Joan Eunice Morton, October 4, 1958 (divorced, 1971); married Candice Elaine Marcellus, 1971. *Education:* University of Northern Colorado, B.A., 1960; Johns Hopkins University, M.A., 1961; University of Nebraska at Lincoln, graduate study, 1962-66, with coursework for Ph.D. completed. *Politics:* Democratic Socialist. *Religion:* Tolstoyan. *Office:* P.O. Box 35, Longmont, Colo. 80501.

CAREER: Medical caseworker for Department of Public Welfare, Baltimore, Md., and part-time instructor in English at Trinitarian College, Baltimore, 1961-62; University of Nebraska, Lincoln, instructor in English, 1963-64; Hastings College, Hastings, Neb., instructor in English, 1966-67, writer in residence, 1967-68; Carlton College, instructor in English, 1968-69, lecturer, 1969-70; U.S. Postal Service, Northfield, Minn., clerk-carrier, 1970; St. Olaf College, poet in residence, 1971; U.S. Postal Service, Longmont, Colo., clerk, 1972—. Speaker, American Poets Series, Kansas City, 1968. *Awards, honors:* Academy of American Poets Prize, University of Nebraska, 1963; Vreeland Award in creative writing ($300), University of Nebraska, 1965.

WRITINGS: Medical Aid, and Other Poems, University of Nebraska Press, 1967; *Miss Liberty, Meet Crazy Horse*, Swallow Press, 1972. Also author of *9 Postal Poems*, 1971. Poems published in *Prairie Schooner, Poet and Critic, Penny Poems, Massachusetts Review, Southern Poetry Review, Steppenwolf, Asparagus, Spectrum, Salt Creek Reader, AAVP Bulletin*, and other periodicals. Occasional reviewer of contemporary verse for *Prairie Schooner*.

SIDELIGHTS: Jones writes: "I have eleven poems ready for publication to be called *Rounding Out*. These eleven should 'round out' my double signature MS. of 77 'collected poems,' since they are probably the last poems ever to be given me to write. When Vachel Lindsay's cry no longer *merely* 'survives compassionate in the high school anthology,' my poems will reach their intended width of audience."

*   *   *

JONES, Edward E(llsworth) 1926-

PERSONAL: Born August 11, 1926, in Buffalo, N.Y.; son of Edward Safford (a professor) and Frances (Jeffery) Jones; married Virginia Sweetnam, April 5, 1947; children: Sarah E., Caroline A., Todd E., Amelia G., Jason L., Janet P. *Education:* Swarthmore College, student, 1943-44; Harvard University, A.B., 1949, Ph.D., 1953. *Home:* 2738 Sevier St., Durham, N.C. 27705.

CAREER: Duke University, Durham, N.C., assistant professor, 1953-58, associate professor, 1958-61, professor of psychology, 1961—, chairman of department, 1970-73. National Science Foundation, member of social psychology and sociology advisory panel, 1961-63; National Institute of Mental Health, member of behavioral sciences study section, 1965-67; Social Science Research Council, member of board of directors, 1973—. *Military service:* U.S. Army, 1944-47. *Member:* American Psychological Association (fellow). *Awards, honors:* Century Psychology Series Award given by publishers of his book, *Ingratiation*.

WRITINGS: Ingratiation, Appleton, 1964; (with Harold B. Gerard) *Foundations of Social Psychology* (textbook), Wiley, 1967; (with others) *Attribution*, General Learning, 1972. Contributor to psychology journals. Executive editor, *Journal of Personality*, 1954-56, editor, 1956-62; consulting editor, *Journal of Experimental Social Psychology, Contemporary Psychology*.

*   *   *

JONES, Emrys 1920-

PERSONAL: Born August 17, 1920, in Aberdare, Wales; son of Samuel Garfield and Annie (Williams) Jones; married Iona Vivien Hughes (now a teacher), August 7, 1948; children: Catrin, Rhianon (daughters). *Education:* University College of Wales, Aberystwyth, B.Sc. (first class honors), 1941, M.Sc., 1945, Ph.D., 1947. *Religion:* "Welsh Calvinistic Methodist." *Home:* 4 Apple Orchard, Hemel Hempstead, Hertfordshire, England. *Office:* London School of Economics and Political Science, Houghton St., Aldwych, London W.C. 2, England.

CAREER: University College, University of London, London, England, assistant lecturer, 1947-50; The Queen's University of Belfast, Belfast, Northern Ireland, lecturer, 1950-58, senior lecturer, 1958-60; London School of Economics and Political Science, University of London, professor of geography, 1960—. Sometime consultant on urbanization to United Nations. *Member:* World Society of

Eristics, Royal Geographical Society (fellow; member of council, 1973—), Institute of British Geographers (council, 1958-60), Regional Studies Association (chairman, 1968-70). *Awards, honors:* Rockefeller Foundation fellowship, 1949-50.

WRITINGS: (Editor) *Belfast in its Regional Settings*, British Association for the Advancement of Science, 1953; (co-author) *Welsh Rural Communities*, University of Wales Press, 1960; *A Social Geography of Belfast*, Oxford University Press, 1960; *Human Geography*, Chatto & Windus, 1964; *Towns and Cities*, Oxford University Press, 1966; *Atlas of London*, Pergamon, 1969; (joint editor) *Man and his Habitat*, Routledge, 1971; (with E. Van Zandt) *The City*, Aldus, 1974; *Readings in Social Geography*, Oxford University Press, in press. Contributor to *Annals* of Association of American Geographers, *Sociological Review, Town Planning Review*, and to geographical journals in England and Scotland.

AVOCATIONAL INTERESTS: Music, books.

*   *   *

JONES, Gary M(artin) 1925-

PERSONAL: Born August 22, 1925, in Bargoed, Wales; son of Hugh David and Ellen (Martin) Jones; married Joan Creason, June 9, 1952; children: David C., Gwen E. *Education:* Arkansas College, Batesville, A.B., 1950; Union Theological Seminary, Richmond, Va., B.D., 1954, Th.M., 1956. *Politics:* Republican. *Home and office:* The Webb School, Bell Buckle, Tenn. 37020.

CAREER: Clergyman, Presbyterian Church in the U.S.; minister in Tunstall, Va., 1953-56, Odessa, Tex., 1956-57, Conroe, Tex., 1957-61, and Houston, Tex., 1961-64; First Presbyterian Church, El Dorado, Ark., minister, 1964—. Trustee of Arkansas College and Dale Miller Fund for Kidney Research, 1964-69; lecturer, Vanderbilt Divinity School, Vanderbilt University, 1972-73; alternate delegate for Presbyterian Church, U.S. World Alliance of Reformed Churches, 1975. Member of board, Child-Family Guidance Center, Union County Red Cross, and Union County Tuberculosis Association (all El Dorado). *Wartime service:* British Merchant Marine, 1939-46; became first officer; received Atlantic, Mediterranean, and Pacific stars. *Awards, honors:* Americana Medal, Daughters of the American Revolution, 1963; Doctor of Ministry, Vanderbilt University, 1972.

WRITINGS: A Time for Boldness, Broadman, 1966; (contributor) *Experimental Preaching*, John Killinger, editor, Abingdon, 1973.

WORK IN PROGRESS: A Pattern for Boldness; and *Dealing with Death*, an analysis of the adjustment process; also *Encounter*, a series of essays dealing with the possibilities of meeting the Divine.

AVOCATIONAL INTERESTS: Golf, art, reading.

*   *   *

JONES, Mary Alice

PERSONAL: Born in Dallas, Tex.; daughter of Paul and Mamie (Henderson) Jones. *Education:* University of Texas, B.A., 1918; Northwestern University, M.A., 1922; Yale University, Ph.D., 1932; University of Edinburgh postdoctoral study, 1955. *Politics:* Independent. *Religion:* Methodist. *Home:* Apartment 908, 3415 West End Ave., Nashville, Tenn. 37203. *Office:* Rand McNally & Co., Box 3700, Chicago, Ill. 60680.

CAREER: The Methodist Church, Nashville, Tenn., editor of children's publications, 1922-25; also free-lance writer of church school curriculum materials, 1923-45; International Council of Religious Education (now National Council of Churches), Chicago, Ill., director of children's work, 1930-45; Rand McNally & Co., Chicago, Ill., editor of children's books, 1945-51; The Methodist Church, Board of Education, Nashville, Tenn., director of children's work, 1951-64; Rand McNally & Co., consulting religious book editor, 1964—. Visiting professor at Northwestern University, Yale Divinity School, Duke University, Iliff School of Theology, Garrett Theological Seminary, and other seminaries; special lecturer at Duke University, McMurry College, Southern Methodist University, and elsewhere; member of faculty at summer schools of religious education. Member of White House Conference on Children, 1940, 1950, 1960, and of White House Conference on Education, 1955. Church posts include membership on General Assembly of National Council of Churches and on executive board of United Council of Church Women. Member: Authors League of America, League of Women Voters, American Association of University Women, Wesleyan Service Guild, Beta Sigma Phi, Pi Beta Phi.

WRITINGS—Adult: Training Juniors in Worship, Methodist Episcopal Church, South, 1925; The Church and the Children, Cokesbury Press, 1932; The Faith of Our Children, Abingdon, 1935; Guiding Children to Christian Growth, Abingdon, 1949; The Pastor and Christian Education of Children, Division of the Local Church, General Board of Education of the Methodist Church, 1963; The Christian Faith Speaks to Children, Abingdon, 1965; Parents, Children, and the Christian Faith, Collins, 1967.

Juveniles—All published by Rand McNally, except as noted: (Editor) Winter is Coming and Other Stories, Cokesbury Press, 1925; Robert and the Rainbow, Cokesbury Press, 1926; Young America Makes Friends, Friendship Press, 1933; (editor) My Own Book of Prayers: For Boys and Girls, 1938; Old Testament Stories, 1939; Stories of the Christ Child, 1940; Jesus and His Friends, 1940; Bible Stories of the Creation, 1941; (editor) Prayers for Little Children, 1942, abridged edition, 1964; Tell Me About God, 1943, revised edition, 1967; Tell Me About Jesus, 1944, revised edition, 1967; Tell Me About the Bible, 1945; Tell Me About Prayer, 1948; Friends of Jesus, 1948; Bible Stories for Little Children, 1949.

His Name Was Jesus, 1950; Bible Stories, 1952; Tell Me About Heaven, 1952; My First Book About Jesus, 1953; Bible Stories: Old Testament, 1954; Stories of the Christ Child, 1954; Prayers and Graces for a Small Child, 1955; (with Kate Smallwood) God Is Good, 1955; Tell Me About Christmas, 1958; (editor) Ten Commandments for Children, 1958; God Speaks to Me (poems), 1961; The Baby Jesus, 1961; God Loves Me, 1961; Jesus and the Children, 1961; The Rand McNally Book of Favorite Bible Stories and Verses, 1963; The Twenty-Third Psalm, 1964; Jesus Who Helped People, 1964; God's Plan for Growing Things, 1964; The Lord's Prayer: Comments, 1964; Me, Myself, and God, 1965; Tell Me About God's Plan for Me, 1965; God's Church Is Everywhere, Friendship Press, 1965; Know Your Bible, 1965; The Story of Joseph, 1965; The Bible Story of the Creation, 1967; Friends Are for Loving, 1968.

Bible Stories: God at Work With Man, Abingdon, 1973.

Writer of curriculum materials for Presbyterian, Methodist, and Congregational church schools. Contributor to a dozen periodicals, among them Child Study, Parents' Magazine, Christian Century, and Baptist Leader.

SIDELIGHTS: Twenty-two million copies of Mary Alice Jones's children's books have been sold, with translations in eight languages. Avocational interests: Reading mystery stories ("the ones with refined, cultivated murderers—not gangsters").

BIOGRAPHICAL/CRITICAL SOURCES: Hearthstone, November, 1958; International Journal of Religious Education, December, 1963.

*   *   *

JONES, Oakah, L., Jr. 1930-

PERSONAL: Born June 20, 1930, in Providence, R.I.; son of Oakah L. (president of Consumer's Natural Gas Co.) and Dorothy (Wilson) Jones; married Nancy Aline Andre, June 14, 1953; children: Marcia Aline, Kathleen Ann, Christopher Andre. Education: Studied at University of Tulsa, 1947-48, University of Arkansas, 1948-49; U.S. Naval Academy, B.S., 1953; University of Oklahoma, M.A., 1960, Ph.D., 1964. Religion: Episcopalian. Home: Box 1545, APO, New York, N.Y. 09825. Office: Inter-American Air Forces Academy, Albrook Air Force Station, Canal Zone.

CAREER: Regular officer, U.S. Air Force, 1953—, with current rank of lieutenant colonel; U.S. Air Force Academy, Colo., instructor, 1960-62, assistant professor, 1962-63, associate professor, 1964-65, tenure associate professor and professor of Latin American history, 1965-73; Florida State University, Canal Zone Branch, adjunct professor of Latin American history, 1973—. University of Colorado, Extension Division, lecturer on Latin American history, 1964-69. Member: Conference on Latin American History, Western History Association, Rocky Mountain Council for Latin American Studies, Historical Society of New Mexico.

WRITINGS: Pueblo Warriors and Spanish Conquest, University of Oklahoma Press, 1966; Santa Anna, Twayne, 1968; My Adventures in Zuni, West Publishing, 1970; Federal Control of the Western Apaches, 1848-1886, University of New Mexico, 1970; (editor) The Spanish Borderlands: A First Reader, Lorrin L. Morrison, 1974. Contributor of articles and reviews to history journals. Regional editor, Journal of the West.

WORK IN PROGRESS: Los Paisanos: Civil Settlers on the Northern Frontier of New Spain for University of Oklahoma Press.

SIDELIGHTS: Jones is competent in Spanish. Avocational interests: Baseball, tennis, American Indians.

*   *   *

JONES, Weyman (B.) 1928-

PERSONAL: Born February 6, 1928, in Lima, Ohio; son of Paul W. and Jewel (Beckett) Jones; married Marilyn Ann Blasio, February 6, 1954; children: Lynn, Paula. Education: Harvard University, A.B. (cum laude), 1950. Home: 3211 Rolling Rd., Chevy Chase, Md. 20015. Agent: Collins-Knowlton-Wing, Inc., 60 East 56th St., New York, N.Y. 10022. Office: International Business Machines Corp., Gaithersburg, Md.

CAREER: International Business Machines Corp., salesman in St. Louis, Mo., and Washington, D.C., 1955-59, manager of information services, Federal Systems Division, Gaithersburg, Md., 1959-63, director of communications, Federal Systems Division, 1963—. *Military service:* U.S. Navy, 1950-54; became lieutenant junior grade. *Awards, honors:* Western Heritage Award for outstanding western juvenile novel, 1969, for *The Edge of Two Worlds.*

WRITINGS: The Talking Leaf, Dial, 1965; *Edge of Two Worlds*, Dial, 1968; *Computer: The Mind Stretcher*, Dial, 1969. Contributor of fiction to magazines.

SIDELIGHTS: Jones inherited an interest in the Cherokee as a descendent of early settlers in Oklahoma; his undergraduate honors thesis at Harvard was largely researched in his grandfather's library of Indian history and law.†

*   *   *

JOSEPHSON, Clifford A. 1922-

PERSONAL: Born July 23, 1922, in New York, N.Y.; son of Eskil (an engineer) and Jennie (Zingone) Josephson; married Claudette Pomerantz, November, 1957; children: Jennifer, Joshua. *Education:* Franklin and Marshall College, B.S., 1944; Columbia University, M.A., 1950, Ph.D., 1955; Cambridge University, graduate study, 1953-54. *Home:* 136 Terrace Ave., Kentfield, Calif. *Office:* Department of English, San Francisco State University, 1600 Holloway, San Francisco, Calif. 94132.

CAREER: Instructor in English at City College (now City College of the City University of New York), New York, N.Y., 1955-58, and Hunter College, New York, 1958-59; San Francisco State College (now San Francisco State University), San Francisco, Calif., assistant professor, 1959-63, associate professor, 1963-68, professor of English, 1968—, vice-chairman of English department, 1973—. Salzburg Seminar in American Studies, Salzburg, Austria, assistant director, 1964-65; Law Research Services, area director, 1966—. American Civil Liberties Union, member of board of directors, Marin chapter. *Member:* American Association of University Professors, American Federation of Teachers. *Awards, honors:* Fulbright scholarship to England, 1953-54.

WRITINGS: (With Caroline Shrodes and James Wilson) *Reading for Rhetoric*, Macmillan, 1962, 3rd edition, 1974.†

*   *   *

JOSEPHY, Alvin M., Jr. 1915-

PERSONAL: Surname is accented on second syllable, Joseph-y; born May 18, 1915, in Woodmere, N.Y.; son of Alvin M. (a businessman) and Sophia C. (Knopf) Josephy; married Elizabeth C. Peet, March 13, 1948; children: Diane, Alvin M. III, Allison, Katherine. *Education:* Harvard University, student, 1932-34. *Politics:* Democrat. *Home:* 4 Kinsman Lane, Greenwich, Conn. 06830. *Office:* American Heritage Publishing Co., 1221 Ave. of the Americas, New York, N.Y. 10020.

CAREER: New York Herald-Tribune, New York, N.Y., reporter and correspondent, 1937-38; WOR-Mutual, New York, N.Y., director of news and special features, 1938-42; Office of War Information, Washington, D.C., chief of special events, Radio Bureau, 1942-43; Metro-Goldwyn-Mayer Studios, Culver City, Calif., screenwriter, 1945-51; *Time*, New York, N.Y., associate editor, 1951-60; American Heritage Publishing Co., New York, N.Y., vice-president and senior editor of American Heritage Books, 1960—. Consultant to Secretary of the Interior, 1963, and to National Congress of American Indians, 1958-65; commissioner, Indian Arts and Crafts Board, Department of

the Interior, 1966-70; author of Report on Indian Affairs for President Nixon, 1969; consultant to Public Land Law Review Commission, 1970; member, National Advisory Committee on Indian Work, Executive Council, Episcopal Church; member of executive committee, Association on American Indian Affairs. Democratic state central committeeman, Connecticut, 1956-60; Democratic candidate for Connecticut Legislature, 1958, 1960; member of Connecticut Small Business Advisory Committee, 1961-63. *Military service:* U.S. Marine Corps, combat correspondent, 1943-45; became master sergeant; received Bronze Star (action at Guam).

MEMBER: Society of American Historians (member of executive committee, 1971—), Western History Association, New York Westerners, Third Marine Division Association; Overseas Press Club, Harvard Club, Coffee House, and The Players (all New York). *Awards, honors:* Awards from National Cowboy Hall of Fame and Western Heritage Center for best books on the American West, 1961 and 1965; Western Writers of America Golden Spur and Golden Saddleman awards, 1965; New York Westerners Buffalo Award for best books on the American West, 1965 and 1968; American Association for State and Local History national award of merit, 1966; Guggenheim fellowship, 1966-67; National Book award nominee for history, 1968.

WRITINGS: (Co-author) *The U.S. Marine on Iwo Jima*, Dial, 1945; (contributor) *My Favorite War Story*, Whittlesey House, 1946; *The Long and the Short and the Tall*, Knopf, 1946; (co-author) *Uncommon Valor*, Infantry Journal Press, 1946; (contributor) *Semper Fidelis*, Sloane, 1947; (co-author) *The American Heritage Book of the Pioneer Spirit*, American Heritage Publishing Co., 1959; *The Patriot Chiefs*, Viking, 1961; *Chief Joseph's People and Their War*, Yellowstone Library and Museum Association, 1964; *The Nez Perce Indians and the Opening of the Northwest*, Yale University Press, 1965; (contributor) *The Red Man's West*, Hastings House, 1965; (co-author) *The American Heritage Pictorial Atlas of United States History*, American Heritage Publishing Co., 1966; (contributor) *The Mountain Men*, Volume III, Arthur H. Clark, 1966; (editor) *RFK: His Life and Death*, Dell, 1968; *The Indian Heritage of America*, Knopf, 1968; (contributor) *Great Adventures of the Old West*, American Heritage Press, 1969; (contributor) *The United States Marine Corps in World War II*, Random House, 1969; *The Artist Was a Young Man*, Amon Carter Museum, 1970; *Red Power*, American Heritage Press, 1971; (reviser) Oliver LaFarge, *The Pictorial History of the American Indian*, Crown, 1974; *History of the Congress of the United States*, McGraw, 1975. Contributor to *Collier's Encyclopedia, Brand Book*, and other publications.

Editor; all published by American Heritage Press: *The American Heritage Book of Indians*, 1961; *The American Heritage History of Flight*, 1962; *The American Heritage Book of Natural Wonders*, 1962; *The American Heritage History of World War I*, 1964; *The American Heritage History of the Great West*, 1965; *The Horizon History of Africa*, 1971; *American Heritage History of Business and Industry*, 1972; *The Horizon History of Vanishing Primitive Man*, 1973; *The Law in America*, 1974.

WORK IN PROGRESS: A general book on Indians of the Americas; a book on the present-day status and character of American Indians.

JUMPER, Andrew Albert 1927-

PERSONAL: Born September 11, 1927, in Marks, Miss.; son of Irma (Nason) Jumper Owings and stepson of Laurence B. Owings (a grocer); married Elizabeth Anne Sharpe, August 14, 1948 (died December 28, 1973); children: Mark Andrew, Peter Sharpe, Kathryn Elizabeth, Carol Anne. *Education:* University of Mississippi, B.A., 1951; Austin Presbyterian Theological Seminary, B.D., 1954, Th.M., 1960, currently doctoral candidate. *Home:* 22 Williamsburg Rd., St. Louis, Mo. 63141. *Office:* Central Presbyterian Church, 7700 Davis Dr., St. Louis, Mo. 63105.

CAREER: Minister in the Presbyterian Church in the U.S., 1954—. Christ Presbyterian Church, Houston, Tex., pastor, 1954-58; West Shore Presbyterian Church, Dallas, Tex., pastor, 1958-62; First Presbyterian Church, Lubbock, Tex., senior pastor, 1962-70; Central Presbyterian Church, St. Louis, Mo., senior pastor, 1970—. Member, Board of Annuities and Relief and General Council, Presbyterian Church in the U.S.; President and chairman of board, Government Fellowship of Presbyterians; board member of Lubbock United Fund, Red Cross, Boy Scouts, and other organizations. Has participated in several evangelistic congresses. *Military service:* U.S. Coast Guard, 1945-48; became second class petty officer. *Member:* West Texas Tuberculosis Association (president), Omicron Delta Kappa. *Awards, honors:* D.D., King's College, and Belhaven College, 1971.

WRITINGS: Chosen to Serve, John Knox, 1961; *The Noble Task*, John Knox, 1961. Associate editor, *Open Letter.*

WORK IN PROGRESS: Theology for Beginners.

* * *

JUNG, John A. 1937-

PERSONAL: Born April 2, 1937, in Macon, Ga.; son of Frank and Grace (Shee) Jung; married Phyllis Lickver, June 4, 1968; children: Jeffrey. *Education:* University of California, Berkeley, B.A. (with honors), 1959; Northwestern University, M.S., 1960, Ph.D., 1962. *Office:* California State University, Long Beach, Calif.

CAREER: Experimental psychologist. California State University, Long Beach, assistant professor of psychology, 1962-65; York University, Toronto, Ontario, assistant professor, 1965-68, associate professor of psychology, 1968-70; California State University, Long Beach, professor of psychology and chairman of department, 1970—. *Member:* American Psychological Association.

WRITINGS: (With Joan H. Bailey) *Contemporary Psychology Experiments: Adaptations for Laboratory*, Wiley, 1966, revised edition, 1975; *Verbal Learning*, Holt, 1968; *The Experimenter's Dilemma*, Harper, 1971. Contributor to professional journals.

WORK IN PROGRESS: A Question of Motives.

* * *

JURGENSEN, Barbara (Bitting) 1928-

PERSONAL: Born November 22, 1928, in Excelsior, Minn.; daughter of William Harold (an accountant) and Ethel (Nesbitt) Bitting; married Laverne Richard Jurgensen (a campus pastor and former state senator), August 28, 1949; children: Janet, Marie, Peter. *Education:* St. Olaf College, B.A., 1950; University of Chicago, M.A., 1975. *Religion:* Lutheran. *Home:* 5135 South Kimbark, Chicago, Ill. 60615.

CAREER: High school teacher of English, 1958-63; Wurlitzer Co., Chicago, Ill., editor and copywriter, 1969-73.

WRITINGS: Leaping Upon the Mountains, Augsburg, 1960; *All the Bandits of China*, Augsburg, 1965; *Oh Please . . . Not Bethlehem!*, Augsburg, 1966; *Men Who Dared*, Zondervan, 1967; *Parents . . . Ugh!*, Zondervan, 1968; *Quit Bugging Me*, Zondervan, 1968; *The Lord Is My Shepherd, But*, Zondervan, 1969; *You're Out of Date, God*, Zondervan, 1971; *Don't Bug Me, Preacher*, Zondervan, 1972; *Some Day We've Got to Get Organized*, Carlton, 1972; *God Probably Doesn't Know I Exist*, Zondervan, 1973; *How to Live Better on Less*, Augsburg, 1974; *A Polluter's Garden of Verses*, Keats, 1975. Contributor of over three hundred stories, articles, and poems to more than forty magazines.

* * *

KAELBLING, Rudolf 1928-

PERSONAL: Born July 19, 1928, in Ulm, Germany. *Education:* University of Tuebingen College of Medicine, M.D., 1954; Ohio State University, M.Sc., 1959. *Office:* Department of Psychiatry, Ohio State University, Columbus, Ohio.

CAREER: Licensed to practice medicine in Germany, Virginia, and Ohio; certified by Educational Council for Foreign Medical Graduates, 1959; certified in psychiatry by American Board of Psychiatry and Neurology, 1961. Intern at hospitals in Bremen, Germany, 1955, and Toledo, Ohio, 1955-56; Ohio State University, Columbus, resident in psychiatry at University Hospital, 1956-59, attending staff psychiatrist, 1959—, instructor in department of psychiatry, College of Medicine, 1959-62, assistant professor, 1962-66, associate professor, 1966-69, professor, 1969—, instructor, later assistant professor in department of anatomy, College of Medicine, 1959-66. U.S. Veterans Administration, psychiatric consultant, 1960—.

MEMBER: American Medical Association, American Psychiatric Association, American Association for the Advancement of Science, American Association of University Professors, Association for the Physiological Study of Sleep, Society of Biological Psychiatry, Central Neuro-Psychiatric Association, Central Ohio Neuro-Psychiatric Society, Ohio Psychiatric Association, Ohio State Medical Association.

WRITINGS: (With R. M. Patterson) *Eclectic Psychiatry*, C. C Thomas, 1966; (contributor) *The Book of Popular Science*, Grolier, 1967. Contributor to *Proceedings* of World Congresses of Psychiatry and about twenty articles to medical journals.

* * *

KAHL, Ann Hammel 1929-

PERSONAL: Born August 3, 1929, in Washington, D.C.; daughter of Louis J. and Mabel (Weber) Hammel; married Norman A. Kahl (an editorial assistant), April 23, 1960; children: Christopher Hammel. *Education:* Skidmore College, B.S., 1951.

CAREER: Teacher at private schools in Washington, D.C., 1951-52, Spring Lake, N.J., 1952-54; McIver Art, Washington, D.C., commercial artist, 1954-57; Hammel's Restaurant, Washington, D.C., manager, 1957-60; Station WTOP, Washington, D.C., artist, 1961-63; free-lance designer and illustrator, Washington, D.C., 1963—. *Member:* American Institute of Graphic Arts, Art Directors Club of

Metropolitan Washington. *Awards, honors:* Guest editor, *Mademoiselle*, 1949; merit awards for illustrations, Art Directors Club of Metropolitan Washington, 1964, 1966.

WRITINGS—Juveniles, self-illustrated: *Francis Discovers the World*, Robert B. Luce, 1962; *Trouble is a Çat*, Robert B. Luce, 1963.

WORK IN PROGRESS: Another children's book:†

* * *

KAHN, Robert L(ouis) 1918-

PERSONAL: Born March 28, 1918, in Detroit, Mich.; son of George Arthur and Mabel (Sufinsky) Kahn; married Beatrice Goldstein, August 25, 1940; children: Judith M., Marcia M., Janet R. *Education:* University of Michigan, B.A., 1939, M.A., 1940, Ph.D., 1952. *Home:* 2211 Avalon Pl., Ann Arbor, Mich. *Office:* Survey Research Center, University of Michigan, Ann Arbor, Mich. 48104.

CAREER: Detroit (Mich.) public schools, secondary school teacher, 1940-42; U.S. Bureau of the Census, 1942-48, began as state supervisor, became acting chief of Field Division; University of Michigan, Ann Arbor, lecturer, 1948-54, associate professor, 1954-60, professor of psychology, 1960—, Survey Research Center, 1948—, became director, 1970—. Visiting professor at Massachusetts Institute of Technology, 1965-66, and at Cambridge University, 1969-70. National Conference of Christians and Jews, member of Ann Arbor executive board, 1961—. *Member:* American Psychological Association (chairman of committee on participation, 1954-56), Society for the Psychological Study of Social Issues (secretary/treasurer, 1955-58; president, 1970-71), American Statistical Association. Industrial Relations Research Association, National Training Laboratories, American Association of University Professors, Michigan Psychological Association, Phi Beta Kappa, Sigma Xi, Phi Kappa Phi, Phi Delta Kappa, Quadrangle Club. *Awards, honors:* Hamilton Award, American College of Hospital Administrators, 1968.

WRITINGS: (With Charles Cannell) *The Dynamics of Interviewing: Theory, Techniques, and Cases*, Wiley, 1957; (with A. S. Tannenbaum), *Participation in Union Locals*, Row, Peterson & Co., 1958; (contributor) *Human Relations and Modern Management*, North-Holland Publishing, 1958; (editor with Elsie Boulding) *Power and Conflict in Organizations*, Basic Books, 1964; (editor with Elsie Boulding) *Organizational Stress*, Philosophical Library, 1964; *The Social Psychology of Organizations*, Wiley, 1966; (co-author) *Justifying Violence: Attitudes of American Men*, Institute of Social Research, 1971. Contributor of articles and reviews to labor, sociology, psychology, and business journals. Joint editor of individual issues, *Journal of Social Issues.*†

* * *

KAKAPO, Leilani 1939-

PERSONAL: Born August 11, 1939, in Kalano, Hawaii; daughter of Caldwell and Martha (Loki) Kiilehau; married Arnold Kakapo (a migrant worker), June 24, 1961 (divorced, 1964); children: Carter, Semantha, Arnold, Jr. *Education:* Attended Kalano Junior College, 1957-58; extension courses at Zug Island University, 1960; Michigan State University, B.A., 1972. *Politics:* Reaganist. *Home:* 20497 Van Antwerp, Harper Woods, Mich. 48225.

CAREER: Free-lance writer and "busy little housewife." *Member:* Ethnic Writers of America. *Awards, honors:* Homecoming Queen, Kalano High School, 1957; certificate of merit, 1965, for *Uki-Buki-Wuki*; gold medal, Northeast Kalano Library Association, 1966.

WRITINGS: Kowa Bengay, Sandwich Islands Press, 1959; *The Pagans of Porter Bay*, Sandwich Islands Press, 1960; *The Revolt of Kamana Kow*, Vishlag Press, 1962; *Hang Twelve*, Anton, 1963; *Meeska Mooska Mousketeer*, Sandwich Islands Press, 1964; *Uki-Buki-Wuki*, Vishlag Press, 1965; *How Uki-Buki-Wukis Are Made*, Vishlag Press, 1965; *From Here to Michigan*, Anton, 1966; *Art and Archeology of Hawaiian Tikis*, Sandwich Islands Press, 1969; (editor) Nan Russini, *My Hawaiian Vacation*, Pineapple Press, 1975. Contributor to numerous periodicals.

WORK IN PROGRESS: A teenage novel, *Honoluee Luau*; an autobiography, *Pineapple Juice in Michigan*.

SIDELIGHTS: Mrs. Kakapo's books have received mixed reviews. Reginald Tipton, in the *Kalano Post Advertiser*, wrote: "[She] has a definite flair for writing. *Kowa Bengay* is a thoroughly engrossing novel and should be read by anyone interested in this enthralling topic. . . . It is the best in its field."

Gordon Holifield, however, was more critical. In an article in the *Milani Times Register*, he said: "I am curious to know where Mrs. Kakapo does her research. She must keep a stack of old newspapers in her basement. Surely she could not have obtained her information from a public library. . . . *Hang Twelve* is undoubtedly the worst book on surfing I have ever read."

Mrs. Kakapo has toured most of the world with her family and "fell in love with Michigan weather and decided to live there permanently." She says of her writings: "When I write, I am oblivious to the world. I generally spend about ten hours a day writing."

BIOGRAPHICAL/CRITICAL SOURCES: Kalano Post Advertiser, November 12, 1959; *Milani Times Register*, May 1, 1963.†

* * *

KALISHER, Simpson 1926-

PERSONAL: Born July 27, 1926, in New York, N.Y.; son of Ben and Sheva (Roskalenko) Kalisher; married Colby Harris, 1968; children: (prior marriage) Jesse; (present marriage) Amy Simpson, David Colby, Allon Brownell. *Education:* Indiana University, B.A., 1948. *Home and office:* Worth St., Roxbury, Conn. 06783.

CAREER: Free-lance photographer, New York, N.Y., 1948—, professional work centers on magazines, advertising agencies, industrial and corporate publications. Photographs exhibited at Museum of Modern Art, Image Gallery, George Eastman House, Art Institute of Chicago, Albright Knox Gallery, Poses Institute of Fine Arts, Whitney Museum of American Art, and others. *Military service:* U.S. Army, Infantry, World War II; served in European Theater; received Combat Infantryman's Badge. *Member:* American Society of Magazine Photographers (alternate secretary, 1962-63), Committee for a Sane Nuclear Policy. *Awards, honors: Railroad Men* was designated as one of fifty best books of 1961 by American Institute of Graphic Arts, and also received the Institute's Design and Printing for Commerce Award, 1961; New York State Council on the Arts grants, 1968-73.

WRITINGS: Railroad Men, Clarke & Way, 1961.

WORK IN PROGRESS: Propaganda, and Other Photographs.

KALLAS, James (Gus) 1928-

PERSONAL: Born December 15, 1928, in Chicago, Ill.; son of James Gus and Lillian (Pulaski) Kallas; married Darlean Quernemoen, June 3, 1950; children: James, Paris, Jacqueline, Kingsley (each born in a different country). Education: St. Olaf College, B.A. (cum laude), 1950; Luther Theological Seminary, St. Paul, Minn., B.Th., 1955; additional study at University of Paris, 1955-56, 1957-58, and at University of Durham, 1956-57, 1960-61. Home and office: California Lutheran College, Thousand Oaks, Calif. 91360.

CAREER: University of Oregon, Eugene, Lutheran chaplain, 1953-54; American Lutheran Church Foreign Mission, French Cameroun, West Africa, director of mission schools, 1958-60; California Lutheran College, Thousand Oaks, associate professor of theology and chairman of division of theology and philosophy, 1961—. Professional football player, working out with Chicago Cardinals, 1950, and Chicago Bears, 1954. Guest lecturer at colleges in United States and at U.S. Army Retreat Center in Germany. Military service: U.S. Navy, 1943 (enlisted at fourteen). Member: Phi Beta Kappa. Awards, honors: Fulbright scholar to England.

WRITINGS: The Significance of the Synoptic Miracles, S.P.C.K., 1961; The Satanward View—A Study in Pauline Theology, Westminster, 1966; The Story of Paul, Augsburg, 1966; Revelation—God and Satan in the Apocalypse, Augsburg, 1973. Writer of film scripts for Cathedral Films. Contributor of articles to New Testament Studies, Dialog, and other periodicals.

SIDELIGHTS: James Kallas has covered all European countries in his travels, and most of west and north Africa.

*   *   *

KANNER, Leo 1894-

PERSONAL: Born June 13, 1894, in Klekotow, Austria; came to United States in 1924, naturalized in 1930; son of Abraham (a merchant) and Clara (Reisfeld) Kanner; married June Lewin, February 11, 1921; children: Anita (Mrs. Theodore Gilbert; deceased), Albert (a physician). Education: University of Berlin, M.D., 1921. Home and office: 4000 North Charles St., Baltimore, Md. 21218.

CAREER: Private practice of medicine, Berlin, Germany, 1920-23; State Hospital, Yankton, S.D., senior assistant physician, 1924-28; Johns Hopkins University, Baltimore, Md., Commonwealth Fund fellow in psychiatry, 1928-30, director of Children's Psychiatric Service, Johns Hopkins Hospital, 1930-59, associate professor of psychiatry, 1933-57, associate professor of pediatrics, 1948-57, professor of child psychiatry, 1957-59, professor emeritus, and honorary consultant, Johns Hopkins Hospital, 1959—. Kemper Knapp Distinguished Visiting Professor, University of Wisconsin, 1956; visiting professor at University of Minnesota, 1959-60, Stanford University, 1961; visiting lecturer at other universities in America and Canada; also has lectured before groups throughout America, and in Mexico, South America, England, and continental Europe. Psychiatric consultant to Juvenile Court of Baltimore, 1930-41, Maryland State Hospital, Spring Grove, 1962-63, and Children's Guild of Baltimore, 1962-70; lecturer and consultant, University of Maryland School of Nursing, 1962. Member of advisory board of schools for exceptional children in Pennsylvania and Wisconsin; member of scientific advisory committee, National Association for Retarded Children; member of board of directors, Jewish Family and Children's society and National Organization for Mentally Ill Children. Honorary president, Fourth International Congress of Child Psychiatry, Lisbon, 1958.

MEMBER: American Psychiatric Association (chairman of child psychiatry section, 1942-43; life fellow), American Association on Mental Deficiency (fellow), American Orthopsychiatric Association (life fellow), American Academy of Child Psychiatry (life fellow), American Association for the Advancement of Science (fellow), American Academy of Pediatrics (associate fellow), History of Science Society, American Association for the History of Medicine, American Epilepsy Society, American Association of University Professors, Maryland Psychiatric Society (president, 1957-58), and other Maryland and Baltimore Societies, Phi Beta Kappa.

AWARDS, HONORS: Association for the Help of Retarded Children award for outstanding contribution in the field of medicine, 1954; first annual award, National Organization for Mentally Ill Children, 1960; Gutheil Memorial Medal, American Association for the Advancement of Psychotherapy, 1962; Fund for the Behavioral Sciences award for basic research accomplishments in the behavioral sciences, 1965; the following have been named in honor of Kanner: School for Emotionally Disturbed Children at the University of Leiden, Holland, division of Devereux Schools, Devon, Pa., Instituto Infanto-Juvenil, Porto Alegre, Brazil, Speech and Hearing Center at Rosewood Hospital Center, Oxings Mill, Md., Home for Autistic Adolescents, Arnhem, Holland.

WRITINGS: Folklore of the Teeth, Macmillan, 1928; Judging Emotions from Facial Expressions, Princeton Monographs, 1931; Child Psychiatry, C. C Thomas, 1935, 4th edition, 1972; In Defense of Mothers, Dodd, 1941; A Miniature Textbook of Feeblemindedness, Child Care Publications, 1949; A Word to Parents About Mental Hygiene, University of Wisconsin Press, 1957; History of the Care and Study of the Mentally Retarded, C. C Thomas, 1964; Childhood Psychosis: Initial Studies and New Insights, Winston, 1973. Contributor of chapters to other books, and more than 250 articles on psychiatry, psychology, pediatrics, and the history and folklore of medicine to scientific and popular journals.

Member of editorial board, American Journal of Psychiatry, 1949-65, Nervous Child, Journal of Child Psychiatry, Quarterly Journal of Child Behavior, Journal of Clinical and Experimental Psycho-Pathology, Archives of Criminal Psychodynamics, Journal of Child Psychiatry and Psychology (London), Acta Paedopsychiatrica, and Psychiatry Digest.

WORK IN PROGRESS: Freedom is Within, an autobiography.

SIDELIGHTS: Child Psychiatry has been published in Spanish and Japanese editions.

*   *   *

KAPLAN, Harold 1916-

PERSONAL: Born January 3, 1916, in Chicago, Ill.; son of Elia and Hayah (Meyer) Kaplan; married Isabelle Ollier (a college teacher), July 31, 1962; children: Anne, Gabriel, Claire. Education: University of Chicago, A.B., 1937, A.M., 1939. Office: Department of English, Northwestern University, Evanston, Ill.

CAREER: Rutgers University, New Brunswick, N.J., member of department of English, 1946-49; Bennington

College, Bennington, Vt., member of department of English, 1949-72; Northwestern University, Evanston, Ill., professor of English, 1972—. Fulbright professor in Italy, 1956-57, and France, 1960-61, 1967-68. *Military service:* U.S. Army Air Forces, 1942-46; became captain. *Member:* American Association of University Professors.

WRITINGS: The Passive Voice, Ohio University Press, 1966; *Democratic Humanism and American Literature*, University of Chicago Press, 1972. Contributor of criticism and verse to *Commentary, The New Leader, Salmagundi, Partisan Review, Hudson Review, Nation*, and other periodicals.

WORK IN PROGRESS: A study of American literary naturalism and the ethics of determinism; *The Literature of Power and Process.*

*   *   *

KAPLAN, Justin 1925-

PERSONAL: Born September 5, 1925, in New York, N.Y.; son of Tobias D. (a manufacturer) and Anna (Rudman) Kaplan; married Anne Bernays (a writer), July 29, 1954; children: Susanna Bernays, Hester Margaret, Polly Anne. *Education:* Harvard University, B.S., 1945. *Politics:* Democrat. *Religion:* Jewish. *Home:* 16 Francis Ave., Cambridge, Mass. 02138.

CAREER: Free-lance work for various New York publishers, 1946-54; Simon & Schuster, Inc., New York, N.Y., editor, 1954-59; full-time professional writer, 1959—. Lecturer at Harvard University, 1969, 1973. *Member:* Phi Beta Kappa. *Awards, honors:* National Book Award and Pulitzer Prize, 1967, both for *Mr. Clemens and Mark Twain.*

WRITINGS: (Editor) *Dialogues of Plato*, Pocket Books, 1950; (editor) *With Malice Toward Women*, Dodd, 1952; (editor) *The Pocket Aristotle*, Pocket Books, 1958; (editor) *Mark Twain, The Gilded Age*, Trident, 1964; *Mr. Clemens and Mark Twain*, Simon & Schuster, 1966; (editor) *Great Short Works of Mark Twain*, Harper, 1967; *Mark Twain: A Profile*, Hill & Wang, 1967; *Lincoln Steffens, A Biography*, Simon & Schuster, 1974; *Mark Twain and His World*, Simon & Schuster, 1974.

WORK IN PROGRESS: A biography of Walt Whitman.

SIDELIGHTS: In the prize-winning biography, *Mr. Clemens and Mark Twain*, "the conflict," wrote A. G. Day, "is the battle between 'Mark Twain'—. . . the exploder of sham—and the success-hunting Samuel Clemens, victim of the 'Gilded Age' that he himself named and satirized. Nowhere does Mr. Kaplan use the word 'schizophrenia,' but his book examines almost clinically the growing gap between the man and his mask." Although there have been many biographies on the man from Hannibal, this book, commented *Newsweek*, "came from the presses unmistakably destined for classic status in its field." The reasons cited were Kaplan's superb documentation and powerful insight into Twain, the man, as opposed to Twain, the legend. "Kaplan," said Malcolm Bradbury, "gives us a better and deeper Mark Twain than we ever had, a Twain who carried the tensions of the age he lived in and felt his way into the possibilities, and the crudities, of his culture. The place of a mind in a culture is superbly caught, and the narrative remains throughout human and sympathetic while catching it. It redeems a writer who has been as badly served by excessive claims about his 'wisdom' or intelligence as by false claims about his 'primitivism.' It is altogether an admirable and important book."

"The biographer," said Kaplan, "dealing with this funny, noble, enigmatic, over-reading man, who moved effortlessly from laughter to remorse, and from anger to nostalgia, has to come to special terms with his subject. . . . The purpose was not only to explore the mystery of this man but also to respect it. . . . Two currents flowed through his life. One flowed away from Hannibal, Missouri, toward the world of wealth, fame and materialities. The other flowed back to Hannibal again. Out of the opposition of these currents, out of the turbulent dark waters, came one of the great styles and dazzling personalities of our literature, one of its undisputed masterpieces, and half a dozen of its major books." In his National Book Award acceptance speech, Kaplan added: "Mark Twain said he hated the past because it was so 'damned humiliating,' hated prying, hated to read over old letters—they 'make my flesh creep,' he said. His biographer is inevitably his enemy, and there were nights during the writing of this book when punishment from beyond the grave seemed perfectly possible. There were also, when this book was finished and its subject laid to rest once again, weeks of a very powerful emotion which I finally recognized as grief."

AVOCATIONAL INTERESTS: Walking, swimming, Cape Cod, and talk.

BIOGRAPHICAL/CRITICAL SOURCES: Saturday Review, June 18, 1966; *Punch*, March 1, 1967; *Detroit Free Press*, March 12, 1967; *Newsweek*, March 20, 1967; *Library Journal*, April 1, 1967; *New York Times*, May 2, 1967.

*   *   *

KAPLOW, Jeffry 1937-

PERSONAL: Born September 7, 1937, in Newark, N.J.; son of Abraham and Reva (Bayer) Kaplow; married Susan Cohen, March 20, 1964. *Education:* University of Wisconsin, B.A., 1956; Princeton University, M.A., 1958, Ph.D., 1963; Sorbonne, University of Paris, postgraduate study, 1959-61. *Office:* 809 Hamilton Hall, Columbia University, New York, N.Y. 10027.

CAREER: Hunter College (now Hunter College of the City University of New York), New York, N.Y., lecturer in history, 1961-62; New York University, New York, N.Y., instructor in history, 1962-64; Columbia University, New York, N.Y., assistant professor of history, 1965—. Visiting assistant professor, University of Iowa, Iowa City, summer, 1964. *Member:* American Historical Association, Past and Present Society, Societe d'Histoire Moderne, Societe des Etudes Robespierrieres.

WRITINGS: Elbeuf during the Revolutionary Period: History and Social Structure, Johns Hopkins Press, 1964; *New Perspectives on the French Revolution*, Wiley, 1965; (editor and author of preface) Arthur Young, *Travels in France During the Years 1787, 1788, and 1789*, Doubleday, 1969; *France on the Eve of Revolution: A Book of Readings*, Wiley, 1971; *The Names of Kings: The Parisian Laboring Poor in the Eighteen Century*, Basic Books, 1972; *Western Civilization: Mainstream Readings and Radical Critiques*, Knopf, 1973. Contributor to *Nation, Saturday Review, New York Times Book Review*, and *American Historical Review.*

SIDELIGHTS: Kaplow is competent in French, German, and Russian.†

*   *   *

KARDOUCHE, G(eorge) Khalil 1935-

PERSONAL: Born September 25, 1935, in Port Said,

United Arab Republic; son of Khalil Mikhail (a banker) and Olga (Choueri) Kardouche. *Education:* London School of Economics and Political Science, B.A., 1957; Clark University, M.A., 1959; Brown University, Ph.D., 1965. *Religion:* Greek Orthodox.

CAREER: City College (now City College of the City University of New York), New York, N.Y., lecturer in economics, 1962-65; National Industrial Conference Board, New York, N.Y., economist, 1965—. *Member:* American Economic Association, Society for International Development.

WRITINGS: The U.A.R. in Development: A Study in Expansionary Finance, Praeger, 1966. Author of economic research reports published by National Industrial Conference Board.†

*   *   *

KAREN, Ruth   1922-

PERSONAL: Born February 18, 1922, in Germany; daughter of David (an attorney) and Paula (Freudenthal) Karpf; married S. Alexander Hagai (a management sciences consultant), March, 1962. *Education:* Studied at Hebrew University of Jerusalem and University of London; New School for Social Research, graduate. *Politics:* Democrat. *Home:* 360 East 55th St., PHC, New York, N.Y. 10022. *Agent:* Curtis Brown Ltd., 60 East 56th St., New York, N.Y. 10022.

CAREER: War, foreign, and United Nations correspondent for *Reporter, Toronto Star,* and World Wide Press, 1947-62; full-time writer, 1962-66; Business International Corp., New York, N.Y., assistant editor of Latin America division, 1966-71, senior editor of Asia/Africa division, 1972—. *Wartime service:* War correspondent with British Army, with assimilated rank of lieutenant colonel, 1947-48, and with U.S. Army, with assimilated rank of major, 1952-53. *Member:* Overseas Press Club of America.

WRITINGS: The Land and People of Central America, Lippincott, 1965; *Neighbors in a New World: The Organization of American States,* World Publishing, 1966; *The Seven Worlds of Peru,* Funk, 1968; *Hello Guatemala,* Norton, 1970; *Song of the Quail: The Wondrous World of the Maya,* Four Winds Press, 1972; *Brazil Today: A Case Study in Developmental Economics that Worked,* Getulio Vargas Foundation, 1974; *Kingdom of the Sun: The Inca, Empire Builders of the Americas,* Four Winds Press, 1975; *Feathered Serpent, the Rise and Fall of the Aztecs,* Four Winds Press, in press. Writer of radio scripts for Voice of America and Radio Free Europe. Contributor of articles to *New York Times Magazine, This Week, Collier's, Business Abroad,* and other periodicals.

*   *   *

KARGER, Delmar William   1913-

PERSONAL: Born May 9, 1913, in Cape Girardeau, Mo.; son of Ernest John (a foreman) and Clara M. (Hellewege) Karger; married Paula Miller, July 5, 1935 (died November, 1958); married Edith Kennedy, January 11, 1962 (died August 31, 1969); married Ruth Lounsberry, October 31, 1970; children: (first marriage) Bonnie E. (Mrs. Lloyd McCormack), Karin R. (Mrs. Douglas Van Slyke), Joyce P. *Education:* Valparaiso University, B.S. in E.E., 1935; University of Pittsburgh, M.S. in Gen.Eng., 1947. *Religion:* Presbyterian. *Home:* 5 Whitman' Ct., Troy, N.Y. 12180. *Office:* Rensselaer Polytechnic Institute, Troy, N.Y. 12181.

CAREER: International Harvester Co., Fort Wayne, Ind., assistant chief electrician, 1935-41, assistant plant engineer, 1941-42; Westinghouse Electric Corp., Pittsburgh, Pa., head manufacturing engineer, 1942-45, manager of cooperative education, 1945-47; Pennsylvania Electric Coil Corp., Pittsburgh, Pa., plant manager, 1947-48; Radio Corp. of America, Camden, N.J., manager of organization and systems, 1948-49, chief industrial engineer of RCA Service Co., 1949-51; Magnavox Corp., Fort Wayne, Ind., chief plant and industrial engineer, 1951-56, manager of new product development, 1956-59; Rensselaer Polytechnic Institute, Troy, N.Y., professor and head of department of management engineering, 1959-63, dean of School of Management, 1963-70, Ford Foundation professor of management, 1970—. Management consultant, 1959—. Director of Fiber Glass Industries, 1961—, Wellington Technical Industries, 1963—, Wellington Computer Graphics, 1969—, and Bunker Ramo Corp., 1974—. American Cancer Society, chapter president, 1963-64, director, 1964—; New York State Finance Committee, member, 1964-68, state director, 1965-72.

MEMBER: American Institute of Industrial Engineers (fellow; national vice-president, 1958-59), American Institute of Plant Engineers, American Society for Engineering Education, Council for International Progress in Management (board of directors, 1962-65), Methods Time Measurement Association for Standards and Research (president, 1958-60; chairman of research committee, 1962-70), Society for the Advancement of Management (fellow), Institute of Management Sciences, International University Contact for Management Education, American Association of University Professors, Academy of Management, American Association for the Advancement of Science (fellow), International Platform Association, De Funiak Springs Country Club, Santa Rosa Beach and Golf Club.

WRITINGS: (With Franklin H. Bayha) *Engineered Work Measurement,* Industrial Press, 1957, 2nd edition, 1966; *The New Product,* Industrial Press, 1960; (with Robert G. Murdick) *Managing Engineering and Research,* Industrial Press, 1963; (with A. B. Jack) *Problems of Small Business in Developing and Exploiting New Products,* Rensselaer Polytechnic Institute and U.S. Small Business Administration, 1963; (with Murdick) *New Product Venture Management,* Gordon & Breach, 1973; (with Bayha) *Advanced Investment Decision-Making: The Science and Art of Professional Investing,* Investors Intelligence, in press.

SIDELIGHTS: Karger's books have been published in French and Dutch.

*   *   *

KARK, Nina Mary (Mabey)   1925-
(Nina Bawden)

PERSONAL: Born January 19, 1925, in London, England; daughter of Charles Mabey and Ellalaine Ursula May (Cushing) Mabey; married Austen Steven Kark (an executive in Overseas Department of British Broadcasting Corp.), 1954; children: (prior marriage) Nicholas Bawden, Robert Humphrey Felix Bawden; (present marriage) Perdita Emily Helena Kark. *Education:* Somerville College, Oxford, B.A., 1946, M.A., 1951; Salzburg Seminar in American Studies, student, 1960. *Home:* 30 Hanger Hill, Weybridge, Surrey, England. *Agent:* Curtis Brown Ltd., 60 East 56th St., New York, N.Y. 10022.

CAREER: Writer. Assistant, Town and Country Planning Associates, 1946-47; Justice of the Peace, Surrey, 1968.

Member: P.E.N., Royal Society of Literature (fellow), British Ski Club.

WRITINGS—All under name Nina Bawden; adult novels: *Eyes of Green*, Morrow, 1953 (published in England as *Who Calls the Tune*, Collins, 1953); *The Odd Flamingo*, Collins, 1955; *The Solitary Child*, Collins, 1956; *Devil by the Sea*, Collins, 1957, Lippincott, 1959; *Change Here for Babylon*, Collins, 1957; *Just Like a Lady*, Longmans, Green, 1960, published as *Glass Slippers Always Pinch*, Lippincott, 1960; *In Honour Bound*, Longmans, Green, 1961; *Tortoise By Candlelight*, Harper, 1963; *Under the Skin*, Harper, 1964; *A Little Love, A Little Learning*, Harper, 1966; *A Woman of My Age*, Harper, 1967; *The Grain of Truth*, Harper, 1968; *The Birds on the Trees*, Harper, 1970; *Anna Apparent*, Harper, 1972; *George Beneath a Paper Moon*, Harper, 1974.

Juveniles: *Secret Passage*, Gollancz, 1963, published as *The House of Secrets*, Lippincott, 1964; *On the Run*, Gollancz, 1964, published as *Three on the Run*, Lippincott, 1965; *The White Horse Gang*, Lippincott, 1966; *The Witch's Daughter*, Lippincott, 1966; *A Handful of Thieves*, Lippincott, 1967; *The Runaway Summer*, Lippincott, 1969; *Squib*, Lippincott, 1971; *Carrie's War*, Lippincott, 1973; *The Peppermint Pig*, Lippincott, 1975. contributor to *Evening Standard, Daily Telegraph,* and *London Mystery.*

SIDELIGHTS: Mary Stoltz said: "If [*The Runaway Summer*] is a sample of Nina Bawden's books for young readers, she should be as much valued by children as she is by her adult audience." Anne Francis finds her writing highly complex, also subtle," and Anne Keeham refers to her "fine etchings of the human experience." Calling *The Grain of Truth* "a minor classic," John Greenya points out that it is "one of those books that can force the reader to seek his own grain of truth."

* * *

KARLAN, Richard　1919-

PERSONAL: Born April 24, 1919, in Brooklyn, N.Y.; son of David (a grocer) and Anna Karlan; married Patricia Helene Banfield. *Education:* Attended Brooklyn College (now Brooklyn College of the City University of New York), 1937. *Residence:* Hollywood, Calif. *Agent:* Collins-Knowlton-Wing, Inc., 60 East 56th St., New York, N.Y. 10022.

CAREER: Actor on Broadway in eleven plays, including "Johnny on a Spot," with Keenan Wynn, and "The Song of Bernadette"; producer of "Comes the Revelation," starring Wendell Corey; performer in shows on all radio networks, including "Jack Pearl Radio Show," for National Broadcasting Co.; featured actor in Hollywood films, "Rhubarb," "Union Station," "Wait Till the Sun Shines, Nellie," "The Racket," "Abbot and Costello Meet the Mummy," "Blowing Wild," "Pocketful of Miracles"; television pioneer and featured actor in "Medic," "Get Smart," "Favorite Story," "Matinee Theatre," "Westinghouse Playhouse," "Hank," "Rawhide," "Ben Casey," "Twilight Zone," and "The Untouchables." *Member:* American Federation of Radio and Television Artists, Authors Guild, Screen Actors Guild, Actors Equity Association, Academy of Motion Picture Arts and Sciences. *Awards, honors:* Richard Karlan Collection was established at Boston University, 1966.

WRITINGS: A Circle of Sand (novel), Bobbs-Merrill, 1966; *Pageant Faded* (novel), Bobbs-Merrill, 1972. Television scripts produced on "Four Star Playhouse" and "Screen Directors Playhouse."

WORK IN PROGRESS: A novel.

SIDELIGHTS: Richard Karlan has some knowledge of German and a traveler's vocabulary in French and Spanish.

* * *

KAROLEVITZ, Robert F.　1922-
(Bob Karolevitz)

PERSONAL: Surname is pronounced Kar-*le*-vitz; born April 26, 1922, in Yankton, S.D.; son of Frank Bernard and Martha (Rathjen) Karolevitz; married Phyllis J. Gunderson, January 4, 1951; children: Jan Marie, Martha Jill. *Education:* South Dakota State University, B.S., 1948; University of Oregon, M.S., 1950. *Religion:* Roman Catholic. *Home and office:* Cedar Crest Farm, Mission Hill, S.D. 57046.

CAREER: Did public relations work for Curtiss Candy Co., Chicago, Ill., 1948-49; taught typography at University of Minnesota, Minneapolis, summer, 1950; sold printing in Seattle, Wash., 1953-54; decided he had a grudge against steady jobs and turned to free-lance writing. Member of board of trustees, Sacred Heart Hospital; member of board of directors, South Dakota Advisory Council for Comprehensive Health Planning, Regional Medical Program, and South Dakota State University Alumni Association. *Military service:* U.S. Army, Infantry, 1943-46, serving in Philippines and Japan; recalled, 1951-52, for duty in Korea; became captain; received Army Commendation Medal with cluster. *Member:* South Dakota State Historical Society (member of executive board), American Legion, Elks Club, Veterans of Foreign Wars, Sigma Delta Chi. *Awards, honors:* Wrangler Award from National Cowboy Hall of Fame, 1970, for *Where Your Heart Is.*

WRITINGS: The 25th Infantry Division and World War II, Army-Navy Publishing Co., 1946; *Newspapering in the Old West*, Superior, 1965; *This Was Trucking*, Superior, 1966; *Doctors of the Old West*, Superior, 1967; *E. G.: Inventor by Necessity*, North Plains Press, 1968; *This Was Pioneer Motoring*, Superior, 1968; *The Prairie Is My Garden*, North Plains Press, 1969; *Old-Time Agriculture in the Ads*, North Plains Press, 1970; *Where Your Heart Is*, North Plains Press, 1970; *Pioneer Church in a Pioneer City*, North Plains Press, 1971; *Everything's Green But My Thumb*, North Plains Press, 1972; *Yankton: A Pioneer Past*, North Plains Press, 1972; *Old Time Autos in the Ads*, Homestead Publishers, 1973; *Flight of Eagles*, Brevet Press, 1974; *Challenge! The South Dakota Story*, Brevet Press, 1975. More than a thousand articles on subjects ranging from space travel to dogfish have appeared in over one hundred magazines and newspapers.

WORK IN PROGRESS: Half a dozen books in various stages of completion.

SIDELIGHTS: Karolevitz, in addition to books and magazine articles, does advertising copy, public relations work, and ghost writing.

BIOGRAPHICAL/CRITICAL SOURCES: Enterprise, Lynnwood, Wash., January 15, 1964.

* * *

KARP, Ivan C.　1926-

PERSONAL: Born June 4, 1926, in New York, N.Y.; son of Sam and Ada (Epstein) Karp; married Marilynn Gelfman-Pereira (a sculptor and university instructor), March 11, 1964; children: (prior marriage) Ethan. *Educa-*

tion: Attended public schools in New York, N.Y. *Politics:* Democrat-Socialist. *Religion:* Jewish. *Home:* 380 West Broadway, New York, N.Y. *Office:* O. K. Harris Gallery, 383 West Broadway, New York, N.Y.

CAREER: Leo Castelli Gallery (contemporary fine arts), New York, N.Y., director, beginning 1959; O. K. Harris Gallery, president and director, 1969—. Lecturer in fine arts on radio, TV, and at many universities. *Military service:* U.S. Army Air Forces, 1944-47. *Member:* Anonymous Arts Recovery Society (founding president, 1956—), Municipal Arts Society.

WRITINGS: Doobie Doo, Doubleday, 1966. Also author of essays, art criticism, and short stories.

WORK IN PROGRESS: The Pleasing Prospect Ticket, a novel on the decay of American urban landscape and small city political life.

SIDELIGHTS: As the discoverer of Andy Warhol, Roy Lichtenstein, James Rosenquist, John Chamberlain, and other pop art masters, and as the author of one of the first pop art novels, Karp has been called the "father of pop art." He also founded the Anonymous Arts Recovery Society to rescue architectural sculptures and other ornaments from buildings being demolished or remodeled. Karp and his wife spend their Sundays driving around New York "in a beat-up jeep, furtively slipping into half-demolished brownstones and kicking around in rubble heaps," searching for gargoyles, "columns, capitals and cornices, gods and giants, nymphs and satyrs" (*New York Herald Tribune*). But the Karps' major interest, reports Emy Thomas, "is in preserving the 'genre portraiture' that is uniquely local. It seems that 19th century immigrant stone carvers, who learned their trade in Italy and Germany, sometimes departed from the neo-classical style they were hired to execute and instead carved portraits of each other—warts, missing teeth and all. Two of the Karps' favorite examples of these 'eccentricities' are now preserved in their home.... Both of these heads, found on a Pitt Street apartment building, are swathed in bandages."

About fifteen hundred selected pieces from the collection of the Anonymous Arts Recovery Society were shown at the Brooklyn Museum in the spring of 1966—some purchased by the Society, others solicited from demolition contractors. While the Society concentrates strictly on American buildings, constructed between 1875 and 1910, Karp is also interested in early medieval architecture, archaeology, and late Roman history. He has traveled extensively in Europe, North Africa, the Near East, and Mexico.

BIOGRAPHICAL/CRITICAL SOURCES: New Yorker, November 14, 1964; *New York Times*, June 26, 1965; *New York Herald Tribune*, March 20, 1966.

* * *

KASER, David 1924-

PERSONAL: Born March 12, 1924, in Mishawaka, Ind.; son of Arthur LeRoy (an author) and Loah (Stelle) Kaser; married Jane Ann Jewell, September 1, 1950; children: John Andrew, Kathleen Jewell. *Education:* Houghton College, A.B., 1949; University of Notre Dame, M.A., 1950; University of Michigan, A.M.L.S., 1952, Ph.D., 1956.

CAREER: Ball State College Library, Muncie, Ind., serials librarian, 1952-54; University of Michigan Libraries, Ann Arbor, exchange assistant, 1954-56; Washington University Libraries, St. Louis, Mo., chief of acquisitions, 1956-59, assistant director, 1959-60; Joint University Li-

braries (Peabody College, Scarritt College, and Vanderbilt University), director, 1960-68; Cornell University Libraries, Ithaca, N.Y., director, 1968-73; Indiana University, Bloomington, professor, Graduate Library School, 1973—. *Military service:* U.S. Army, 1943-47; served in Alaskan and European Theaters. *Member:* American Library Association (chairman, universities section, 1963-64), Bibliographical Society of America (regional advisory board, 1958-63), Association of College and Research Libraries (president, 1968-69), American Antiquarian Society, Phi Beta Kappa. *Awards, honors:* Guggenheim fellow, 1967.

WRITINGS: Messrs. Carey & Lea of Philadelphia, University of Pennsylvania Press, 1957; *Directory of the St. Louis Book and Printing Trades*, New York Public Library, 1961; *Joseph Charless, Printer in the Western Country*, University of Pennsylvania Press, 1963; (editor) *The Cost Book of Carey and Lea, 1825-1838*, University of Pennsylvania Press, 1963; *Directory of the Book and Printing Industries in Ante-Bellum Nashville*, New York Public Library, 1966; (editor) *Books in America's Past*, University Press of Virginia, 1966; *Book Pirating in Taiwan*, University of Pennsylvania Press, 1969; *Library Development in Eight Asian Countries*, Scarecrow Press, 1969. Editor, *Missouri Library Association Quarterly*, 1958-60, *College and Research Libraries*, 1963-69.

BIOGRAPHICAL/CRITICAL SOURCES: Library Quarterly, January, 1956; *College and Research Libraries*, May, 1960; *Southeastern Librarian*, spring, 1964.

* * *

KASER, Michael (Charles) 1926-

PERSONAL: Born May 2, 1926, in London, England; son of Charles Joseph (a bank official) and Mabel (Blunden) Kaser; married Elizabeth Piggford, May 13, 1954; children: Gregory, Matthew, Benet, Thomas, Lucy. *Education:* King's College, Cambridge, B.A., 1946, M.A., 1950. *Religion:* Roman Catholic. *Home:* 7 Chadlington Rd., Oxford, England. *Office:* St. Antony's College, Oxford, England.

CAREER: British Foreign Office, London, England, economist, 1947-51; United Nations, Geneva, Switzerland, economist, 1951-63; Oxford University, Oxford, England, reader in Soviet economics and professorial fellow of St. Antony's College, 1963-72, reader in economics, 1972—. Visiting professor of economics, University of Michigan, 1966. Missions for research in Eastern European countries include nine in the Soviet Union, and others in Albania, Bulgaria, Czechoslovakia, German Democratic Republic, Hungary, Poland, and Romania. Convener of Conference of Teachers and Research Workers on the U.S.S.R., England, 1965-73. *Member:* International Economic Society, American Economic Association, Association for Comparative Economic Studies (United States), Reform Club (London).

WRITINGS: COMECON—Integration Problems of the Planned Economies, Oxford University Press, 1965; 2nd edition, 1967; *Soviet Economics*, McGraw, 1970; (with J. Zielinski) *Planning in East Europe*, Bodley Head, 1970.

WORK IN PROGRESS: Third edition of *COMECON*; editing the first two volumes of *Economic History of Eastern Europe Since 1919*.

* * *

KASSEBAUM, Gene G(irard) 1929-

PERSONAL: Born June 24, 1929, in St. Louis, Mo.; son of

John George (a toolmaker) and Flora (Girard) Kassebaum; married Gayathri Rajapur, 1960. *Education:* University of Missouri, A.B., 1951; Harvard University, A.M., 1956, Ph.D., 1958.

CAREER: Cornell University, Medical College, New York, N.Y., research associate, 1957-60; University of California, School of Public Health, Los Angeles, research associate and associate director of study of correctional effectiveness, 1960-65; American University in Cairo, Cairo, Egypt, associate professor of sociology, 1965-67. *Military service:* U.S. Army, 1951-53. *Member:* American Sociological Association, Phi Beta Kappa.

WRITINGS: (With David Ward) *Women's Prison: Sex and Social Structure,* Aldine, 1965; (editor with Daniel Wilner) *Narcotics,* McGraw, 1965; (with others) *Prison Treatment and Parole Survival: An Empirical Assessment,* Wiley, 1971; *Delinquency and Social Policy,* Prentice-Hall, 1974. Author of prison research surveys. Contributor of about twenty articles to journals.

WORK IN PROGRESS: Research on Egyptian villages.†

*   *   *

KATES, Robert W. 1929-

PERSONAL: Born January 31, 1929, in Brooklyn, N.Y.; son of Simon Jack and Helen Gordon (Brener) Kates; married Eleanor Clare Hackman, February 9, 1948; children: Kathy Ann, Jonathan Simon, Barbara Ellen. *Education:* Attended New York University, 1946-48, Indiana University, 1957; University of Chicago, M.A., 1960, Ph.D., 1962. *Office:* Graduate School of Geography, Clark University, Worcester, Mass. 01610.

CAREER: Clark University, Graduate School of Geography, Worcester, Mass., assistant professor, 1962-65, associate professor, 1965-67, professor of geography, 1968—, university professor, 1974—. Staff member of summer geography institute for small southern colleges, 1966; lecturer, N.S.F. summer institute in introductory college geography, 1966; University of Dar es Salaam, Tanzania, lecturer, 1967-68, honorary research professor, 1970-71. Consultant to UNESCO Interdisciplinary Symposium on Man's Role in Changing the Environment, 1970, and Natural Hazard Research Assessment, Institute of Behavioral Science, 1972-74; senior consultant to Scientific Committee on Problems of the Environment, 1974—; member of Energy Task Force, City of Worcester, 1974—. *Member:* American Geographical Society, Association of American Geographers, American Geophysical Union, American Association for the Advancement of Science, American Association of University Professors (president of Clark Chapter, 1966-67).

WRITINGS: (Editor with Ian Burton) *Readings in Resource Management and Conservation,* University of Chicago Press, 1965; (with Clifford S. Russell and David Arney) *Drought and Water Supply: Implication of the Massachusetts Experience for Municipal Planning,* Johns Hopkins Press, 1970; (with Burton and Gilbert F. White) *The Environment as Hazard,* Oxford University Press, 1975. Author of monographs on flood problems published by Department of Geography, and University of Chicago, 1962, 1965, 1969. Contributor of more than forty articles and reviews to journals. Assistant editor, *Economic Geography,* 1963-64.

KAUDER, Emil 1901-

PERSONAL: Surname rhymes with "chowder"; born June 23, 1901, in Berlin, Germany; son of Hugo (an architect) and Ernestine (von Feilen) Kauder; married Helene Riegner (a teacher), July 11, 1943; children: Eunice, Hugh. *Education:* University of Berlin, Ph.D., 1924. *Politics:* Republican. *Religion:* Episcopalian. *Home:* 6761 22nd Way South, St. Petersburg, Fla. 33712.

CAREER: Head of private school in Germany, 1926-28; researcher at New York University, New York, N.Y., 1938-39; teacher at private preparatory schools in New Jersey and Michigan, 1938-47; University of Wyoming, Laramie, assistant professor of economics, 1947-52; Illinois Wesleyan University, Bloomington, professor of economics and head of department, 1952-60; Hitotsubashi University, Kunitachi, Tokyo, Japan, research professor, 1960-61; Florida Presbyterian College, St. Petersburg, professor of economics and head of department, 1961-68; University of South Florida, Tampa, distinguished lecturer in economics, 1968-74, professor emeritus, 1974—. *Member:* American Economic Association.

WRITINGS: Repetitorium der theoretischen Nationaloekonomie (title means "Outlines of Economic Theory"), Springer, 1932; (with J. Jastrow) *Die Prinzipienfragen in den Aufwertungsdebatten,* Rudolf M. Rohrer Brno, 1937; (editor) *Carl Menger's Zusaetze zu "Grundsaeze der Volkswirthschaftslehre"* (unpublished manuscripts concerning Menger's principles), Hitotsubashi University, 1961; (editor) *Carl Menger's Erster Entwurf zu seinem Hauptwerk "Grundsaetze"* (Menger's first draft of his principles), Hitotsubashi University, 1963; *The History of Marginal Utility Theory,* Princeton University Press, 1965.

Contributor to *Collier's Encyclopedia* and *Encyclopedia of Social Sciences.* Monographs and other studies, several of them on Keynes and the Keynesian system, have been published in yearbooks and journals in America, Germany, Austria, and Japan.

WORK IN PROGRESS: A book, *Economics for the Layman.*

SIDELIGHTS: Kauder is fluent in German and French, and "fair" in Spanish; he reads Italian. *Avocational interests:* Collecting books on Japanese art and on nineteenth-century European firearms.

*   *   *

KAUFFMAN, Dorotha S(trayer) 1925-

PERSONAL: Born January 8, 1925, in Zanesfield, Ohio; daughter of Forrest Bernard (an auctioneer) and Helen Marie (Hildreth) Strayer; married Glen Kauffman (a factory worker and mechanic), September 9, 1962; children: Sue, Glenna Lee, Garold James. *Education:* Studied music at Marion College, Marion, Ind., 1946, 1947, and Bible at Moody Bible Institute, 1949-51.

CAREER: Zanesfield Auction, Zanesfield, Ohio, co-manager and clerk, part-time, 1946-51, full-time, 1951-65; Strayer Manufacturing Co. (rope manufacturer), Bellefontaine, Ohio, owner, 1965—.

WRITINGS: The Singing Pen, Greenwich, 1955; *Dark Side of Nowhere,* Zondervan, 1965. Author of radio scripts, poetry, and short articles.

WORK IN PROGRESS: With Willis H. Liggitt, *High Flies the Eagle,* a novel dealing with Ohio history; *Tears on the Roses,* a Civil War novel; *Twenty Feet from the Cross,* a Biblical novel.†

KAUFFMAN, George B(ernard) 1930-

PERSONAL: Born September 4, 1930, in Philadelphia, Pa.; son of Philip Jack (a broker) and Laura (Fisher) Kauffman; married Inge Salomon, June 5, 1952 (divorced December 16, 1969); married Laurie Marks Papazian (a teacher), December 21, 1969; children: (first marriage) Ruth Deborah, Judith Miriam. Education: University of Pennsylvania, B.A. (honors in chemistry), 1951; University of Florida, Ph.D., 1956. Religion: Jewish. Home: 3881 East Pico Ave., Fresno, Calif. 93726. Office: Department of Chemistry, California State University, Fresno, Calif. 93740.

CAREER: University of Texas, Austin, instructor in chemistry, 1955-56; California State University, Fresno, assistant professor, 1956-61, associate professor, 1961-66, professor of chemistry, 1966—. Research chemist with Humble Oil and Refining Co. summer, 1956, and General Electric Co., summers, 1957, 1959.

MEMBER: American Chemical Society, American Association for the Advancement of Science, American Association of University Professors, History of Science Society, United Professors of California, Society for the History of Alchemy and Chemistry, Pacific Lazzaroni: West Coast History of Science Society, Association of University of Pennsylvania Chemists, Sigma Xi, Phi Kappa Phi, Gamma Sigma Epsilon, Phi Lambda Upsilon, Alpha Chi Sigma. Awards, honors: Second place winner for city of Philadelphia, Science Talent Search, 1948; research grants from Research Corp., 1957-59, 1959-61, 1969, National Science Foundation, 1960-61, 1967-69, American Chemical Society Petroleum Research Fund, 1962-64, 1965-68, and from National Science Foundation and American Philosophical Society, 1963-64, 1969-70; Guggenheim fellowship, 1972-73.

WRITINGS: Alfred Werner—Founder of Coordination Chemistry, Springer, 1966; Classics in Coordination Chemistry, Dover, Part I: The Selected Papers of Alfred Werner, 1968, Part II, in press; (editor) Teaching the History of Chemistry, Adler, 1968; The Constitution and Configuration of Coordination Compounds, Reidel, in press; Coordination Chemistry: Its History through the Time of Werner, American Chemical Society, in press; Creators of American Chemistry, Dekker, in press. Also chairman of Werner Centennial, proceedings of symposium published by American Chemical Society, 1967. Contributor of more than two hundred articles and reviews to American Scientist and chemistry journals.

WORK IN PROGRESS: Blomstrand and Joergensen: Their Correspondence from 1870 to 1897; An Introduction to the Art of Scientific Research: A Personal View.

*   *   *

KAUFFMANN, Lane 1921-

PERSONAL: Born July 24, 1921, in Washington, D.C.; son of Philip Christopher and Nancy (Lane) Kauffmann; married Faith Diana Lilien, October 17, 1959; children: Christopher Lane, Jill Suzanne. Education: Attended Princeton University, 1939-41. Agent: Phyllis Jackson, International Famous Agency, 1301 Avenue of the Americas, New York, N.Y. 10019.

CAREER: Professional writer and editor, including writing for Metro-Goldwyn-Mayer International, ghost writing and titling for foreign films. Story analyst for Columbia Broadcasting System Television, New York, N.Y. 1951-54.

WRITINGS—Novels; all published by Lippincott: The Perfectionist, 1954; Six Weeks in March, 1956; A Lesser Lion, 1957; Waldo, 1960; An Honorable Estate, 1964; Another Helen, 1968; A Plot of Grass, 1970; The Villain of the Piece, 1973.

Translator: Vicente Silva, Libros Escogidos, 1947.

WORK IN PROGRESS: A novel.

SIDELIGHTS: Kauffman lived in France, 1960-66, and in South America at earlier periods. He is competent in French and Spanish. Avocational interests: History, foreign affairs, classic murder cases, chess, bridge, reading, and bricolage ("which is badly translated as puttering about the house").

*   *   *

KAUFMAN, Robert 1931-

PERSONAL: Born March 22, 1931; son of Leo (a pharmacist) and Estelle (Mandel) Kaufman; married Judith Pokempner, June 28, 1954; children: Richard, Melissa, Robin, Christopher. Education: Attended Columbia University, 1948-51. Politics: Progressive Democrat. Religion: Jewish-American-Agnostic. Home: 17039 Cotter Pl., Encino, Calif. Agent: William Morris Agency, 151 El Camino, Beverly Hills, Calif.

CAREER: Hitchhiked from San Diego, Calif., to Bangor, Me., and from Paris to Copenhagen, 1951-54; publicist in New York, N.Y., 1954-57; comedy writer in New York, 1957-59; writer for "Bob Newhart Show," 1960-61; full-time writer-producer, of films and motion pictures, California, 1959—. Member: Writers Guild of America (West). Awards, honors: Emmy Award, 1960-61, and Peabody Award, 1960-61, both for "Bob Newhart Show"; Academy Award nomination, 1967, for "Divorce, American Style."

WRITINGS: (With Louis Manheim) Isolation Booth, Gold Medal, 1960; (with Peter Barry) The Right People, Gold Medal, 1963; In Training. Do Not Talk to Me, Bantam, 1966.

Films: "Dr. Goldfoot and the Bikini Machine," 1965; "Ski Party," 1965; "A Hot Time in the Old Town Tonight," 1966; "The Cool Ones," 1966; "Divorce, American Style," 1966; "Getting Straight," 1969; "I Love My Wife," 1970.

Scriptwriter and story consultant of ABC television series, "Here We Go Again," 1973.

SIDELIGHTS: Kaufman told CA: "I am basically a satirist—and since satire today is black comedy, I guess I am to be identified in the Kubrick, Tony Richardson, Terry Southern school of angry but well paid young men. It seems that people are willing to finally admit that they're victims, fools, masochists, and liars. This catharsis makes them feel better. It also unfortunately allows them to continue to be victims, fools, etc. The anti-heroes that I and my fellow thumb-suckers create are such charmingly attractive but cruel villains that Adolph Hitler himself would feel nervous and a little self-righteous about having any one of them to the house for dinner."†

*   *   *

KAUSLER, Donald H(arvey) 1927-

PERSONAL: Born July 16, 1927, in St. Louis, Mo.; son of Charles Richard (a merchant) and Pauline (Svejkousky) Kausler; married Martha Roeper, October 25, 1952; children: Rene, Donald Harvey, Jr., Jill, Barry. Education:

Washington University, St. Louis, Mo., A.B., 1947, Ph.D., 1951. *Office:* University of Missouri, Columbia, Mo.

CAREER: U.S. Air Force, Mather Air Force Base, Calif., research psychologist, 1951-55 (as civilian, 1951-53; as member of the military, with rank of first lieutenant, 1953-55); University of Arkansas, Fayetteville, assistant professor, 1955-58, associate professor of psychology, 1958-60; St. Louis University, St. Louis, Mo., associate professor, 1960-62, professor of psychology, 1962-71, chairman of department, 1963-71; University of Missouri, Columbia, professor of psychology, 1971—. *Member:* American Psychological Association, American Association for the Advancement of Science, American Association of University Professors, Phi Beta Kappa, Sigma Xi.

WRITINGS: (Editor) *Readings in Verbal Learning: Contemporary Theory and Research*, Wiley, 1966; *Psychology of Verbal Learning and Memory*, Academic Press, 1974. Contributor to *Journal of Verbal Learning and Verbal Behavior* and psychology journals.

WORK IN PROGRESS: Studies on verbal learning in children and elderly subjects.

* * *

KAVESH, Robert A(llyn) 1927-

PERSONAL: Born September 12, 1927, in New York, N.Y.; son of Samuel (in electronics) and Pearl (Berlin) Kavesh; married Ruth Freidson, June 24, 1951; children: Richard, Laura, Andrew, Joseph. *Education:* New York University, B.S., 1949; Harvard University, A.M., 1950, Ph.D., 1954. *Religion:* Jewish. *Home:* 390 Highland Ave., Upper Montclair, N.J. 07043. *Office:* New York University, 100 Trinity Pl., New York, N.Y. 10006.

CAREER: Dartmouth College, Hanover, N.H., assistant professor of economics, 1953-56; Chase Manhattan Bank, New York, N.Y., business economist, 1956-58; New York University, New York, N.Y., associate professor, 1958-62, professor of economics and finance, 1962—. *Military service:* U.S. Navy, 1945-46. *Member:* American Finance Association (secretary-treasurer, 1961—), American Economic Association.

WRITINGS: Businessmen in Fiction, Dartmouth College Press, 1955; (editor with W. F. Butler) *How Business Economists Forecast*, Prentice-Hall, 1966; *Methods and Techniques of Business Forecasting*, Prentice-Hall, 1974.

WORK IN PROGRESS: Further research in economic and financial forecasting.

* * *

KAY, Terence 1918-
(Terry Kay)

PERSONAL: Born June 16, 1918, in Barrow-in-Furness, England; son of Ian F. (a railroadman) and Constance (Fergusson) Kay; married Dorothy Hanson, August, 1938; children: Ronald. *Education:* Attended public schools in Tracy, Minn.

CAREER: San Francisco Naval Shipyard, San Francisco, Calif., electrician, 1950-55, assistant editor of shipyard paper, 1955-63, editor, 1963-66; full-time free-lance writer, 1966—. *Military service:* U.S. Army, paratrooper, 1944-46. *Member:* Authors Guild of the Authors League of America.

WRITINGS: Space Volunteers, Harper, 1960; *Target:*

Moon, Bobbs-Merrill, 1965. Stories and articles, under name Terry Kay, have appeared in *Flying, American Weekly, Saga*, and other magazines, and some three hundred in Sunday school papers.

WORK IN PROGRESS: The Sea Invaders, a nonfiction juvenile on man's upcoming conquest of the sea; *Jed Smith: Master of the Wilderness*, a biography; *Mystery of the Spying Squid*, juvenile fiction.†

* * *

KAYIRA, Legson Didimu c. 1940-

PERSONAL: Surname is pronounced Kaw-*yee*-ra; born "in the year of the harvest," in Karonga, Nyasaland (now Malawi), Africa; son of Timothy and Ziya (Nakawonga) Kayira; married Carol Lawson. *Education:* Skagit Valley College, A.A., 1963; University of Washington, B.A., 1965; Cambridge University, graduate study, 1965-66. *Religion:* Presbyterian. *Home:* 26 Goldstone Way, Hove 4, Sussex, England. *Agent:* Harold Matson, Inc., 30 Rockefeller Plaza, New York, N.Y. 10020.

CAREER: Writer.

WRITINGS: I Will Try (autobiography), Doubleday, 1965; *The Looming Shadow* (novel), Doubleday, 1967; *Jingala* (novel), Doubleday, 1969; *Things Black and Beautiful* (novel), Doubleday, 1970; *The Civil Servant* (novel), Longman, 1971.

SIDELIGHTS: Soon after Kayira's birth, his mother threw him into the Didimu River because she felt she could not feed and care for him. After he was rescued and returned to her, he was given his middle name, Didimu. While he was in school, he decided to add an English-sounding name and coined Legson. After attending school in Nyasaland for eleven years, Kayira decided: "We have 3,000,000 people in Nyasaland and only 22 university graduates. Nobody has ever earned a degree from an American college. I want to be the first" (*Time*). In 1958 he began a journey, on foot, to the United States. Subsisting on a diet of bananas, which he bought with money earned doing chores for a few cents a day, "he traveled in dry season and wet, in blinding dust and miasmic jungle, through friendly villages and hostile. He tried to learn three words in each tongue: *food, water, job*" (*Reader's Digest*).

In January, 1960, he reached Kampala, Uganda. At the United States Information Service free library there, he stumbled on a directory of American colleges and universities. The first entry he saw was Skagit Valley Junior College at Mount Vernon, Washington. He wrote to Skagit Valley and received a letter informing him that his application had been favorably received, that he might apply for a scholarship, and that the school would find a job for him. While Kayira studied algebra at the USIS library in Khartoum, the students at Skagit Valley raised $1700 to bring him to the United States.

On December 16, 1960, Kayira arrived at Skagit Valley to a standing ovation from students. He had completed a journey of two years and 12,000 miles; 2500 miles had been accomplished on foot. Of his future plans, Kayira told *Time*: "When I go back to Nyasaland, I will be a teacher. Then I enter politics. When I get defeated, I go back to teaching. You can always trust education."

AVOCATIONAL INTERESTS: Travel, reading, bicycling, classical music, photography.

BIOGRAPHICAL/CRITICAL SOURCES: Time, December 19, 1960; *Reader's Digest*, February, 1962; *Guide-*

posts, April, 1964; Legson Kayira, *I Will Try*, Doubleday, 1965.†

* * *

KAYSEN, Carl 1920-

PERSONAL: Born March 5, 1920, in Philadelphia, Pa.; son of Samuel and Elizabeth Kaysen; married Annette Neutra, September 13, 1940; children: Susanna Neutra, Laura Neutra. *Education:* University of Pennsylvania, A.B. (with highest honors in economics), 1940; Columbia University, graduate study, 1940-42; Harvard University, M.A., 1947, Ph.D., 1954. *Home:* 97 Olden Lane, Princeton, N.J. 08540. *Office:* Institute for Advanced Study, Princeton, N.J. 08540.

CAREER: National Bureau of Economic Research, New York, N.Y., financial research project staff, 1940-42; U.S. Office of Strategic Services, Washington, D.C., economist, 1942-43; Harvard University, Cambridge, Mass., assistant professor, 1950-55, associate professor, 1955-57, professor of economics, 1957-66, Lucius N. Littauer Professor of Political Economy, 1964-66, associate dean, Graduate School of Public Administration, 1960-66; Institute for Advanced Study, Princeton, N.J., director, 1966—. Deputy special assistant to the President for national security affairs, 1961-63; special consultant to the President, 1963—; chairman of President's Task Force on Foreign Economic Policy, 1964. *Military service:* U.S. Army Air Forces, Intelligence, 1943-45; served in European theater; became captain.

MEMBER: American Economic Association, American Academy of Arts and Sciences, American Philosophical Society, Econometric Society, Phi Beta Kappa. *Awards, honors:* Fulbright research scholar, London School of Economics and Political Science, University of London, 1955-56; Guggenheim fellowship, 1955-56.

WRITINGS: United States versus United Shoe Machinery Corporation: An Economic Analysis of an Anti-Trust Case, Harvard University Press, 1956; (with F. K. Sutton, W. E. Harris, and J. Tobin) *The American Business Creed*, Harvard University Press, 1956; (with Franklin M. Fisher) *The Demand for Electricity in the United States*, North-Holland Publishing Co., 1962; *The Higher Learning: The Universities and the Public*, Princeton University Press, 1969; *Content and Context*, McGraw, 1973.

Contributor: E. S. Mason, editor, *The Corporation in the Modern Economy*, Harvard University Press, 1960; H. Arndt, editor, *Die Konzentration in der Wirtschaft*, Dunker and Humboldt, 1960; Seymour E. Harris, editor, *Higher Education in the United States*, Harvard University Press, 1960. Contributor of articles and book reviews to *World Politics, New Republic*, and other scholarly journals in America and abroad.

* * *

KAZAMIAS, Andreas M. 1927-

PERSONAL: Born November 6, 1927, in Cyprus; married Valerie Poulos, November 11, 1956; children: Michael. *Education:* University of Bristol, B.A., 1948; Fort Hays Kansas State College, S.M., 1954; Harvard University, Ed.D., 1958. *Home:* 2453 Fontaine Circle, Madison, Wis. *Office:* 206 Education Building, University of Wisconsin, Madison, Wis.

CAREER: Secondary school teacher in Cyprus, 1948-53; Oberlin College, Oberlin, Ohio, assistant professor of education, 1958-61; University of Chicago, Chicago, Ill., assis-

tant professor of education, 1961-64; University of Wisconsin, Madison, professor of educational policy studies, 1964—. Consultant, Agency for International Development. *Member:* History of Education Society, Comparative Education Society (member of board of directors), American Association of University Professors, Phi Delta Kappa. *Awards, honors:* Kappa Delta Pi fellowship in international education for field research in Greece and Turkey, 1962-63.

WRITINGS: (Editor with B. G. Massialas) *Crucial Issues in the Teaching of Social Studies*, Prentice-Hall, 1964; (editor with P. Nash and H. J. Perkinson) *The Educated Man*, Wiley, 1965; (with B. G. Massialas) *Tradition and Change in Education: A Comparative Study*, Prentice-Hall, 1965; (editor) *Herbert Spencer on Education*, Teachers College, Columbia University, 1966; *Politics, Society, and Secondary Education in England*, University of Pennsylvania Press, 1966; *Education and the Quest for Modernity in Turkey*, University of Chicago Press, 1966; (editor with Erwin H. Epstein) *Schools in Transition: Essays in Comparative Education*, Allyn & Beacon, 1968. Author of research reports. Editor of "Comparative and International Education" series, Addison-Wesley, 1966—.

WORK IN PROGRESS: Two books, *Education and the Welfare State* and *Education and Society in Greece*; research on education and modern values in the eastern Mediterranean, with special reference to the work of schools in social and political development.†

* * *

KEARNS, Lionel 1937-

PERSONAL: Born February 16, 1937, in Nelson, British Columbia, Canada; son of Frank (a game warden and writer) and Dorothy (Welch) Kearns; married Dolly Revati Maharaj (a teacher), June, 1960; children: Frank, Shakuntala, Liam. *Education:* University of British Columbia, B.A., 1961, M.A., 1964; additional study at School of Oriental and African Studies, University of London, 1964-65. *Home:* 4505 Mountain Highway N., Vancouver, British Columbia, Canada. *Office:* Simon Fraser University, Burnaby, British Columbia, Canada.

CAREER: Prior to 1961, worked as waiter, laborer, peatworker, truck driver, and at other jobs; University of British Columbia, Vancouver, teaching assistant and lecturer in English, 1961-64; Simon Fraser University, Burnaby, British Columbia, assistant professor, 1966—. *Awards, honors:* Several poetry prizes while still a student; Canada Council fellowship, 1964-65, 1965-66; Canada Council Arts Award, 1973.

WRITINGS: Songs of Circumstance (poems in stacked verse), Tish Press, 1963; *Pointing*, Ryerson Press, 1967; *By the Light of the Silvery McLune: Media Parables, Poems, Signs, Gestures and other Assaults on the Interface*, Daylight Press, 1969; *About Time*, Prince George, 1974. Creator with Gordan Payne, of animated film/poems, "The Birth of God," 1973; "Negotiating a New Canadian Constitution," National Film Board of Canada, 1974. Work represented in anthology, *How Do I Love Thee: Sixty Poets of Canada (and Quebec) Select and Introduce Their Favourite Poems from Their Own Work*, edited by John Robert Colombo, M. G. Hurtig, 1970.

WORK IN PROGRESS: A series of poems, plays, stories and film-scripts dealing with the history of the northwest coast of North America.

SIDELIGHTS: George Bowering calls Kearns "the best young poet in Vancouver, and possibly the best in Canada." Jack Kerouac called him "absolutely brilliant." Bowering writes: "Kearns is a student of poetry, in the sense that the artist should be a student of his art. He examines the possibilities of his media, and their relation with what he wants to say. He seldom leaves a poem alone after it has been written, even after it has been published." Reviewing *Pointing*, Allen Barry Cameron writes: "Many of Kearns poems convey a sense of immediacy and a reluctance to fix a poem to something outside itself; but a few poems . . . clearly point to social issues beyond the poet's immediate sensuous grasp of experience."

Kearns believes his principal influences are Norbert Weiner, Buckminster Fuller, Kenneth Boulding, and Stafford Beer. He has traveled and lived in Mexico, Great Britain, and the West Indies, and considers that his principal occupation is "being human."

BIOGRAPHICAL/CRITICAL SOURCES: Delta, number 19, October, 1962, number 25, November, 1965; *Canadian Literature*, spring, 1964; *Kulchur*, number 15, autumn, 1964, number 20, winter, 1965-66; *Poetry* (Chicago), September, 1964; *Quarry*, spring, 1966; *Parallel*, March-April, 1966; *Canadian Forum*, January, 1969.

*   *   *

KEDZIE, Daniel Peter 1930-

PERSONAL: Born April 30, 1930, in Milwaukee, Wis.; son of Edmund H. (a machinist-mechanic) and Tillie (Lassa) Kedzierski; married Patricia Jakubicz, September 13, 1952; children: Daniel, Kathleen, Timothy, Thomas. *Education:* University of Wisconsin, B.B.A., 1952, M.B.A., 1953, Ph.D., 1956. *Politics:* Republican. *Religion:* Roman Catholic. *Home:* 425 North Park Blvd., Glen Ellyn, Ill. 60137.

CAREER: University of Wisconsin, Madison, acting instructor, 1953-56; Wisconsin State Insurance Department, Madison, insurance examiner, 1953-56; Marquette University, Milwaukee, Wis., assistant professor of insurance and finance, 1956-57; Continental Casualty Co., Chicago, Ill., director of education and training, 1957-60; American College of Life Underwriters, Bryn Mawr, Pa., director of management education, 1960-62; Continental-National-American Group (insurance), Chicago, Ill., assistant vice-president, 1962-65, special assistant to chairman of boards, 1965-67, vice-president of corporate planning, of Continental Assurance Co., 1967-68, executive assistant and vice-president of CNA Financial Corp., 1968; Management Programs, Inc., Chicago, Ill., executive vice-president and director, 1969—. *Member:* American Society of Chartered Property and Casualty Underwriters, American Society for Training and Development, American Risk and Insurance Association.

WRITINGS: Consumer Credit Insurance, Irwin, 1957; (with A. Sommer) *Your Future in Insurance*, Rosen, 1965; (consulting editor) *Property and Liability Insurance Handbook*, edited by J. D. Long and D. W. Gregg, Irwin, 1965. Author of monthly column, "Management Today," in *Best's Insurance Review*, 1969-73. Contributor to insurance journals.

WORK IN PROGRESS: A text on management principles.

KEENAN, Boyd R(aymond) 1928-

PERSONAL: Born June 29, 1928, in Parkersburg, W. Va.; son of Claude J. (a machine operator) and Lillie (Sayre) Keenan; married Donna Booth, June 9, 1951; children: Kevin, Karen. *Education:* University of Kentucky, A.B., 1949, M.A., 1957; University of Illinois, Ph.D., 1960. *Office:* Department of Political Science, University of Illinois at Chicago Circle, Box 4348, Chicago, Ill. 60680.

CAREER: Lexington Herald, Lexington, Ky., state editor, 1950-52; University of Kentucky, Lexington, news editor, 1952-56, director of news bureau, 1956-57; Committee on Institutional Cooperation (Big Ten project), assistant to director, Lafayette, Ind., 1959-60; Marshall University, Huntington, W. Va., assistant professor of political science, 1960-62; Purdue University, Lafayette, Ind., visiting professor, 1962-64, professor of political science and head of department, 1964-67; University of Illinois at Chicago Circle, Chicato, professor of political science, 1967—. Director, Illinois Board of Higher Education, 1970-71; Science advisor to Governor of Illinois, 1971-72. *Member:* American Political Science Association, American Society for Public Administration, Midwest Conference of Political Scientists.

WRITINGS: (Editor and contributor) *Science and the University*, Columbia University Press, 1966. Contributor to *Public Administration Review, Journal of Higher Education, Christian Science*, and *American Political Science Review*.

*   *   *

KEITH, Agnes Newton 1901-

PERSONAL: Born July 6, 1901, in Oak Park, Ill.; daughter of Joseph Gilbert (a businessman) and Grace (Goodwillie) Newton; married Henry George Keith (in Commonwealth government service in Asia), July 23, 1934; children: Jean Alison (Mrs. Harold Knappett), Henry George Newton. *Education:* University of California, Berkeley, B.A., 1924. *Religion:* Protestant. *Home:* 785 Island Rd., Oak Bay, Victoria, British Columbia V8S 2TH, Canada.

CAREER: Hired as reporter by *San Francisco Examiner*, San Francisco, Calif., 1924, but had worked only briefly when she was attacked with an iron bar by a crazed drug addict outside the *Examiner* office and severely injured; eventually lost use of her eyes for several years, and didn't return to writing until much later in Borneo, where she went as a bride in 1934; the Keiths remained in Borneo until 1952; went to Philippines with Food and Agriculture Organization (United Nations), 1952; went to Libya in 1955 and stayed until 1964. *Member:* Society of Woman Geographers (honorary), Theta Sigma Phi, Alpha Gamma Delta. *Awards, honors: Atlantic Monthly* non-fiction award, 1939, for *Land Below the Wind*; Alpha Gamma Delta Distinguished Citizen Award, 1959.

WRITINGS—All self-illustrated with sketches; all published by Little, Brown: *Land Below the Wind*, 1939; *Three Came Home*, 1947; *White Man Returns*, 1951; *Bare Feet in the Palace*, 1955; *Children of Allah*, 1966; *Beloved Exiles*, 1972. Contributor to *Book of Knowledge* and *Atlantic Monthly*.

WORK IN PROGRESS: A non-fiction book about Japan.

SIDELIGHTS: Agnes Keith told *CA*: "I have special interests in Asia and Africa and the peoples of these continents. I believe that basically people are people regardless of geography, but it is our differences which charm, delight and frighten us."

KEITH, W(illiam) J(ohn) 1934-

PERSONAL: Born May 9, 1934, in London, England; son of William Henry (a clerk) and Elna Mary (Harpham) Keith; married Hiroko Teresa Sato, December 3, 1965. *Education:* Cambridge University, B.A., 1958; University of Toronto, M.A., 1959, Ph.D., 1961. *Home:* 50 Cambridge Ave., Apartment 1111, Toronto, Ontario, Canada.

CAREER: McMaster University, Hamilton, Ontario, lecturer, 1961-62, assistant professor of English, 1962-66; University of Toronto, Toronto, Ontario, associate professor of English, 1966—.

WRITINGS: Richard Jefferies: A Critical Study, University of Toronto Press, 1965; *Charles G. D. Roberts*, Copp Clark, 1969; *Rural Tradition: A Study of the Nonfiction Prose Writers of the English Country Side*, University of Toronto, 1974.†

*　*　*

KELLING, Furn L. 1914-

PERSONAL: Born September 1, 1914, in Shawnee, Okla.; daughter of William E. (a railroad engineer) and Grace L. (Craig) Kelling. *Education:* Southwestern Baptist Theological Seminary, Certificate in Elementary Education, 1949; also studied at George Peabody College for Teachers, 1949-50. *Politics:* "Vote for the best man." *Home:* 768 Holcomb Ave., Reno, Nev. 89502.

CAREER: Owner and operator of beauty shops, St. Louis, Mo., 1933-47; Knoxville (Tenn.) public schools, kindergarten teacher, 1950-52; director of children's work at Baptist church in Birmingham, Ala., 1952-55; Arizona Southern Baptist Convention, Phoenix, director of children's work, 1955-57; Southern Baptist Convention of California, director of children's activities, 1957-60; director of children's work in Oklahoma, California, and Alabama; currently with University of Nevada, Reno. *Member:* National Association for Nursery Education, National Education Association. *Awards, honors: Listen to the Night* was included in U.S. cultural exhibit in Moscow, 1958.

WRITINGS: Listen to the Night (picture book for children), Broadman, 1957; *This is My Family* (picture book for children), Broadman, 1963. Contributor of articles to Southern Baptist periodicals.

WORK IN PROGRESS: Recreation for Young Children, Parents and Teachers; and *Little Ones*.

AVOCATIONAL INTERESTS: Music, baseball, traveling.†

*　*　*

KELLY, Balmer H(ancock) 1914-

PERSONAL: Born June 12, 1914, in Wytheville, Va.; son of James Montgomery and Caroline (Hancock) Kelly; married Ann Franklin Wood; children: Ruth Wood, Caroline Ann, Franklin Wood. *Education:* King College, A.B., 1934; Union Theological Seminary, Richmond, Va., B.D., 1939, Th.M., 1940; Princeton Theological Seminary, Ph.D., 1946. *Home:* 1224 Rennie Ave., Richmond, Va. 23227. *Office:* Union Theological Seminary, 3401 Brook Rd., Richmond, Va. 23227.

CAREER: Ordained to ministry of Presbyterian Church in the United States, 1940; King College, Bristol, Tenn., professor of Bible, 1940-41; Union Theological Seminary, Richmond, Va., associate professor of New Testament,

1943-47, Aubrey Lee Brooks Professor of Biblical Theology, 1947—, dean of seminary, 1965-73. *Member:* Society of Biblical Literature.

WRITINGS: "Layman's Bible Commentary," editor of twenty-five volume series, John Knox, 1959-65, and author of Volume VIII, *Ezra, Nehemiah, Esther, Job*, 1964. Editor, *Interpretation: A Journal of Bible and Theology* (publication of Union Theological Seminary, Richmond), 1947-65.

*　*　*

KELLY, George A. 1916-

PERSONAL: Born September 17, 1916, in New York, N.Y. *Education:* Catholic University of America, M.A., 1943, Ph.D., 1946. *Office:* St. John's University, Grand Central and Utopia Parkways, Jamaica, N.Y. 11439.

CAREER: Ordained Roman Catholic priest, 1942, elevated to right reverend monsignor, 1964. Parish priest, 1945-59; Archdiocese of New York, New York, N.Y., director of Family Life Bureau, 1955, secretary for education, 1966-70; St. John's University, Jamaica, N.Y., John A. Flynn professor of contemporary Catholic problems, 1970—. Member of Papal Birth Control Commission, 1965. Lecturer at St. Joseph's Seminary, Yonkers, N.Y., 1946-49, Catholic University of America, 1952. Associate chaplain for Catholic Trade Unionists Association, 1942-52; conductor of Family Life Institutes, U.S. Army and U.S. Air Force, 1960-61; member of advisory board, National Catholic Welfare Conference, 1965. *Member:* American Association of University Professors, American Sociological Association, Association for the Sociology of Religion, American Catholic Historical Association, American Catholic Theological Society, American Catholic Sociological Society, National Catholic Education Association.

WRITINGS: Catholics and the Practice of Faith, 1946; *Primer on the Taft-Hartley Act*, Christopher, 1948; *The Story of St. Monica's Parish*, Monica Press, 1954; *Catholic Marriage Manual*, Random House, 1958; *Catholic Family Handbook*, Random House, 1959; *Catholic Youth's Guide to Life and Love*, Random House, 1960; *Overpopulation—A Catholic View*, Paulist Press, 1960; *Catholic Guide to Expectant Motherhood*, Random House, 1961; *Dating for Young Catholics*, Doubleday, 1963; *Birth Control and Catholics*, Doubleday, 1963; *Your Child and Sex*, Random House, 1964. *Who Is My Neighbor?*, Random House, 1966; *The Christian Role in Today's Society*, Random House, 1966; *Catholics and the Practice of the Faith*, St. John's University Press, Volume I: *Catholic Youth*, 1967, Volume II: *Catholic Parents*, 1971.

(Editor) *Government Aid to Nonpublic Schools: Yes or No?*, St. John's University Press, 1972; *The Parish*, St. John's University Press, 1973. Contributor to *Catholic Digest, Homiletic & Pastoral Review*, and other periodicals.

*　*　*

KELLY, Robert 1935-

PERSONAL: Born September 24, 1935, in Brooklyn, N.Y.; son of Samuel Jason and Margaret (Kane) Kelly; married Joan Lasker (a librarian), August 27, 1955 (divorced); married Helen Belinky, April 17, 1969. *Education:* City College (now City College of the City University of New York), A.B., 1955; attended Columbia University, 1955-58. *Politics:* "Radical (to nurture the radix)." *Reli-*

gion: "Xtian." *Office:* Bard College, Annandale-on-Hudson, N.Y. 12504.

CAREER: Continental Translation Service, New York, N.Y., treasurer, 1955-58; Wagner College, New York, N.Y., lecturer in English, 1960-61; Bard College, Annandale-on-Hudson, N.Y., assistant professor of English, 1961-68; California Institute of Technology, Pasadena, poet-in-residence, 1971-72; Bard College, professor of English, 1974—. State University of New York at Buffalo, Buffalo, N.Y., assistant professor of English, 1964. Tufts University, Medford, Mass., visiting lecturer in modern poetry, 1966; New York City Writers Conference, Staten Island, conducted fiction workshop, summer, 1967.

*WRITINGS—*Poetry: *Armed Descent*, Hawk's Well Press, 1961; *Her Body Against Time* (English and Spanish edition), Ediciones El Corno Emplumado, 1963; *Tabula*, Dialogue Press, 1964; *Round Dances*, Trobar, 1964; (with Jerome Rothenberg) *Lunes* [and] *Sightings* (the later by Rothenberg) Hawk's Well Press, 1964; *Lectiones*, Duende, 1965; *Weeks*, Ediciones El Corno Emplumado, 1966; *Devotions*, Salitter, 1967; *Twenty Poems*, Matter, 1967; *Axon Dendron Tree* (long poem), Matter, 1967; *Song XXIV*, Pym-Randall Press, 1967; *A Joining: A Sequence for H.D.*, Graham Mackintosh for Black Sparrow Press, 1967; *Alpha*, J. Fisher, 1967; *From the Common Shore, Book V*, Minkoff, 1968; *Songs I-XXX*, Pym-Randall Press, 1968; *Statement*, Black Sparrow Press, 1968; *Sonnets, 1967*, Black Sparrow Press, 1968; *Finding the Measure*, Black Sparrow Press, 1968; *The Common Shore, Books I-V: A Long Poem About America*, Black Sparrow Press, 1969; *A California Journal*, Big Venus, 1969.

Kali Yuga, Grossman, 1970; *Flesh, Dream, Book*, Black Sparrow Press, 1971; *In Time*, Frontier Press, 1971; *Ralegh*, Black Sparrow Press, 1972; *The Pastorals*, Black Sparrow Press, 1973; *The Tears of Edmund Burke*, Helen in Annandale, 1973; *The Mill of Particulars*, Black Sparrow Press, 1973; *The Loom*, Black Sparrow Press, 1975.

Prose: *The Scorpions* (novel), Doubleday, 1967; *Cities*, Frontier Press, 1972; *A Line of Sight*, Black Sparrow Press, 1974.

Editor: (With Paris Leary and contributor) *A Controversy of Poets: An Anthology of Contemporary American Poetry*, Doubleday-Anchor, 1965; Paul Blackburn, *The Journals*, Black Sparrow Press, 1975.

WORK IN PROGRESS: Parsifal, a novel; *Kaligrams*, an introduction to Tantric stenography.

SIDELIGHTS: Kelly told *CA:* "My life's concern is to be instrumentality of utterance, that is, to be of the everlasting human maker—with the sense of continuous song or declaration. I am consequently concerned with all forms of transmutation & the sciences that compel them: linguistics, theology, magic, alchemy, politics, biology, cinema, painting, dance, music, medicine, archeology, geology, anthropology. There is no history."

In an interview with David Ossman, Kelly explained his conception of the "poetry of images": ". . . if you want to divide all the ways of going into the poem, all the quanta and quotients of poetry, I think the division of powers that Ezra Pound made long ago, into three, is best." Pound called the three aspects *logos*—the word, *melos*—the musical aspect, and *phanos*—the image. ". . . *Phanos*," Kelly continued, "literally 'brightness,' . . . [equaled], for Pound, 'throwing the image onto the mind.' . . . You might call word the mystical hypostasis of all poetry, of all literary art. At the same time, music (*melos*) is the space-time of poetry—its line, extent, duration. . . . The third, *phanos*, the image, has gotten rather slighting attention. . . . The image poetry that I'm talking about is not what Pound nowadays means when he speaks of the poetry *des Amygistes*. When I speak of Image Poetry, I'm speaking both of a way of looking at all poetry, and also, in our own time, of a particular stance of the poet as regards his material; that stand generates a kind of poetry not necessarily dominated by the images which form the dominant movement of the poem. . . . I will say that all great poetry generates its images, both the Final Emergent Image of the work of art . . . and more so, the image as prime generated material of the poem—the primal image—which can be expressed as it normally is—in the word—but must also be expressed, must cohere in, SOUND. . . . And I feel, rightly or wrongly, that the poetry of Images (stress on Poetry; it's not a technique) is essentially a mode of Vision. . . . The poetic Image is not a thing. It is a process and a discovered identity. It discovers its being in its function. . . . Image is the rhythm of poetry."

Kelly's fourth book, *Lunes*, introduces and defines a new poetic form, the lune, of his own invention. In the foreword to *Lunes*, he writes: "Lunes are small poems that spend half their lives in darkness & half in light. Each lune has thirteen syllables one for each month of the moon's year. Along about the middle, the dark of the moon comes. The full moon is the approximate splendor of the whole lune, provided the clouds do not fall too heavily on that poem. The lune is a form. Each lune is a separate poem." A. R. Ammons says of these poems: "The method for . . . Kelly . . . is to make minimal means reverberate to the maximum. This can seem like straining both ways. But in enough cases the reverberations asked for are generated."

Kelly's novel, *The Scorpions*, seemed to thoroughly mystify critics. They compared both style and content to the works of other writers (Andersen, Grimm, J. R. R. Tolkien, C. S. Lewis, William Golding, Carl Jung, J. P. Donleavy, Ray Bradbury, and Vladimir Nabokov are mentioned in Eliot Fremont-Smith's review in the *New York Times*), but all agree that Kelly's work cannot effectively be defined by comparisons. A reviewer for Kirkus writes: "If the late Shirley Jackson and Ian Fleming had paired under the direction of the Marquis de Sade and between them a book begat, the result might have been this strange but elegant spoof." Fremont-Smith adds: "I suppose it should be noted, too, that the author, a teacher and a poet, makes frequent reference to the fact that scorpions attack in reverse, as it were, over their backs; so perhaps we are supposed to read backwards from the closing page. Or something."

BIOGRAPHICAL/CRITICAL SOURCES: Virginia Kirkus Service, November 1, 1960, November 1, 1966; *New York Times Book Review*, January 8, 1961; *Atlantic*, February, 1961; *Saturday Review*, February 4, 1961; *Kulchur*, autumn, 1962; David Ossman, *The Sullen Art*, Corinth, 1963; *Poetry*, June, 1966, September, 1966; *New York Times*, January 11, 1967.

*   *   *

KENDALL, Elaine (Becker) 1929-

PERSONAL: Born June 29, 1929, in New York, N.Y.; daughter of Herman W. (a banker) and Rhoda (Wolfe) Becker; married Herbert Kendall (a builder), June 28, 1950;

children: Richard, Nancy. *Education:* Mount Holyoke College, B.A., 1949. *Residence:* Santa Ana, Calif. *Agent:* Betty Ann Clark, I.C.M., Time-Life Bldg., New York, N.Y. 10022.

CAREER: Full-time professional writer. *Member:* Authors League of America.

WRITINGS: The Upper Hand, Little, Brown, 1965; *The Happy Mediocrity*, Putnam, 1971; *Peculiar Institutions*, Putnam, 1975. Contributor of articles on various aspects of the current American scene, travel, and the arts, to *Holiday, Saturday Evening Post, New York Times Magazine, Harper's, Saturday Review, Mademoiselle, Reporter, Show, Venture*, and other magazines.

WORK IN PROGRESS: A variety of magazine and newspaper pieces.

SIDELIGHTS: Elaine Kendall wrote *The Upper Hand*, a book about American men, in answer to the rash of books on American women. She speaks French and Spanish and has traveled widely in Europe, South America, and the Middle and Far East. *Avocational interests:* Modern painting, sculpture, the theater.

* * *

KENDALL, Lyle H(arris), Jr. 1919-

PERSONAL: Born February 3, 1919, in Kingsville, Tex.; son of Lyle Harris (an engineer) and Ollie (Gibson) Kendall; married Aubyn Townsend, April 25, 1941; children: Susan, Peter Townsend. *Education:* University of Texas, B.A., 1947, M.A., 1948, Ph.D., 1952. *Politics:* Democrat. *Religion:* Episcopalian. *Residence:* Glen Rose, Tex. 76043. *Office:* Department of English, University of Texas, Arlington, Tex. 76019.

CAREER: University of Texas, Austin, instructor in English, 1949-52; U.S. Naval Academy, Annapolis, Md., assistant professor of English, 1952-56; Texas Christian University, Fort Worth, assistant professor, 1956-58, associate professor, 1958-62, professor of English, 1962-66; University of Texas, Arlington, professor of English, 1966—. American Council on Education, consultant to Committee on Accreditation of Service Experience; Tarrant Literacy Association, member of board, 1963—. *Military service:* U.S. Army Air Forces, 1943-46; became sergeant. U.S. Naval Air Reserve, 1949-60; became lieutenant. *Member:* Bibliographical Society of America, Bibliographical Society (British), Oxford Bibliographical Society. *Awards, honors:* Research fellow, Folger Shakespeare Library, 1955.

WRITINGS: (With Jim W. Corder) *A College Rhetoric*, Random House, 1962; *Exercises for College Writers*, Random House, 1963; (with Thomas P. Harrison and others) *Shakespeare 1964*, Texas Christian University Press, 1965; (contributor) Thomas E. Kakonis and James C. Wilcox, editors, *Forms of Rhetoric*, McGraw, 1969; (contributor) Thomas Woodson, editor, *Twentieth-Century Interpretations of "The Fall of the House of Usher,"* Prentice-Hall, 1969; (with James T. Bratcher) *A Suppressed Critique of Wise's Swinburne Translations*, University of Texas Press, 1970; *A Descriptive Catalogue of the W. L. Lewis Collection*, Volume I, Texas Christian University Press, 1970. Contributor to *Papers of the Bibliographical Society of America, Library, Keats-Shelley Journal, Nineteenth-Century Fiction, Book Collector*, and other journals. Associate editor, *American Literary Realism*, 1967—.

WORK IN PROGRESS: An edition of Frederick Locker's

poetry, with James T. Batcher; *Owen Wister in Mesquite; A Bibliography of Works about Thomas J. Wise.*

AVOCATIONAL INTERESTS: Portrait photography.

* * *

KENDLER, Howard H(arvard) 1919-

PERSONAL: Born June 9, 1919, in New York, N.Y.; son of Harry H. and Sylvia (Rosenberg) Kendler; married Tracy Seedman (a professor of psychology), September 20, 1941; children: Kenneth Seedman, Joel Harlan. *Education:* Brooklyn College (now of the City University of New York), B.A., 1940; University of Iowa, M.A., 1941, Ph.D., 1943. *Home:* 4596 Camino Molinero, Santa Barbara, Calif. 93105. *Office:* University of California, Santa Barbara, Calif. 93106.

CAREER: University of Iowa, Iowa City, instructor, 1943-44; University of Colorado, Boulder, assistant professor of psychology, 1946-48; New York University, New York, N.Y., associate professor, 1948-51, professor of psychology, 1951-63; University of California, Santa Barbara, professor of psychology and chairman of department, 1963—. University of California, Berkeley, visiting professor, 1960-61. National Institutes of Health, consultant to National Institute of Child Health and Human Development, 1963—. *Military service:* U.S. Army, chief clinical psychologist, Walter Reed General Hospital, 1944-46; became first lieutenant. *Member:* Society of Experimental Psychologists, American Psychological Association, American Association for the Advancement of Science, Psychonomic Society, Western Psychological Association (president, 1970-71), Sigma Xi. *Awards, honors:* National Science Foundation grants.

WRITINGS: (Contributor) *Current Trends in Psychology*, University of Pittsburgh Press, 1960; *Basic Psychology*, Appleton, 1963, (with wife, Tracy S. Kendler), brief edition, 1971, 3rd edition, 1974; (contributor) A. W. Melton, editor, *Categories of Human Learning*, Academic Press, 1964; (contributor) D. Levine, editor, *Nebraska Symposium on Motivation*, University of Nebraska Press, 1965; (contributor) T. R. Dixon and H. L. Horton, editors, *Verbal Behavior and General Behavior Theory*, Prentice-Hall, 1968; (contributor and editor with J. T. Spence) *Essays in Neobehaviorism: A Memorial Volume to Kenneth W. Spence*, Appleton, 1971; (contributor) T. S. Krawiec, editor, *The Psychologists*, Oxford University Press, 1974. Associate editor, *Journal of Experimental Psychology*, 1963-65.

* * *

KENNEY, John Paul 1920-

PERSONAL: Born April 6, 1920, in Morristown, S.D.; son of Charles Franklin and Maud (Davis) Kenney; married Dorothy Hamilton; children: Richard H., Ronald D., Roger L., Diane M. *Education:* University of California, Berkeley, A.B., 1944; University of Southern California, M.S. in P.A., 1952; University of California, Los Angeles, Ph.D., 1963. *Home:* 1530 Anita Lane, Newport Beach, Calif. 92660. *Office:* Department of Criminal Justice, California State University, Long Beach, Calif. 90840.

CAREER: Policeman in Berkeley, Calif., 1942-47; College of the Sequoias, Visalia, Calif., director of police training program, 1947; California Youth Authority, San Francisco, consultant on juvenile control, 1947-50; University of Southern California, Los Angeles, professor of public administration, 1950-64; California Department of Justice, Sacramento, deputy director, Division of Law Enforcement, 1964-66; California State University, Long Beach, professor of criminal justice, 1966—. Consultant to U.S. Children's Bureau, 1953, Office of Public Safety, Agency for International Development, 1957-67, U.S. Air Force, 1960-63. President of Los Angeles Board of Police Commissioners, 1961-64. *Military service:* U.S. Navy, 1944-46; served in Pacific Theater; became lieutenant junior grade.

MEMBER: American Academy of Criminal Justice, American Society of Criminology (president, 1957 and 1958), American Society for Public Administration, National Council on Crime and Delinquency (chairman, committee on automatic data processing), Peace Officers Association of California, Pi Sigma Alpha.

WRITINGS: (With Dan G. Pursuit) *Police Work with Juveniles and the Administration of Juvenile Justice*, C. C Thomas, 1954, 5th edition, 1975; (with E. Caroline Gabard) *Police Writing*, C. C Thomas, 1958; *Police Management Planning*, C. C Thomas, 1959; (with John B. Williams) *Police Operations: Policies and Procedures*, C. C Thomas, 1960; *The California Police*, C. C Thomas, 1964; *Police Administration*, C. C Thomas, 1972, revised edition, 1975. Author of four monographs on juvenile control and other law enforcement topics; contributor to journals.

* * *

KENNY, John P. 1909-

PERSONAL: Born December 17, 1909, in Providence, R.I.; son of Florance Joseph (a letter carrier) and Grace Dorothy (Maloney) Kenny. *Education:* Providence College, A.B., 1931; Catholic University of America, M.A., 1941; Pontifical Faculty of St. Thomas Aquinas, River Forest, Ill., Ph.L., 1946, Ph.D., 1947. *Politics:* Independent. *Home and office:* Providence College, Providence, R.I.

CAREER: Ordained Roman Catholic priest, Order of Preachers (Dominicans), 1938; University of Dayton, Dayton, Ohio, associate professor, 1940-45; College of Notre Dame of Maryland, Baltimore, and Xaverian College, Silver Spring, Md., professor of philosophy, 1947-50; Emmanuel College, Boston, Mass., professor of theology, 1950-52; Providence College, Providence, R.I., professor and chairman of philosophy department, 1952—. *Member:* National Catholic Educational Association, Alpha Epsilon Delta, Delta Epsilon Sigma, Phi Sigma Tau, Knights of Columbus, Friendly Sons of St. Patrick.

WRITINGS: Moral Aspects of Nuremberg, Thomist, 1949; *Principles of Medical Ethics*, Newman, 1952, 2nd edition, 1962; *A Workbook in Medical Ethics*, Newman, 1953; *Greek and Medieval Philosophy: Contributions to the Development of Western Civilization*, Providence College Press, 1974. Contributor to *New Catholic Encyclopedia* and to *Thomist.*

AVOCATIONAL INTERESTS: Golf, skiing, and photography.

* * *

KENT, Donald P. 1916-

PERSONAL: Born June 4, 1916, in Philadelphia, Pa.; son of Ralph (a printer) and Ida (Peterson) Kent; married Marrion H. Clime, August 30, 1941; children: Marrion H., Martha H. *Education:* West Chester State College, West Chester, Pa., B.A., 1940; Temple University, M.A., 1945;

University of Pennsylvania, Ph.D., 1950. *Home:* 926 Outer Dr., State College, Pa. 16802. *Office:* Pennsylvania State University, University Park, Pa. 16802.

CAREER: University of Connecticut, Storrs, director of Institute of Gerontology, 1950-61; U.S. Office of Aging, Washington, D.C., director, 1961-65; Pennsylvania State University, University Park, professor of sociology and chairman of department of sociology and anthropology, 1965—. Visiting professor or lecturer at University of Pennsylvania, Duke University, and University of Southern California, Chairman of Connecticut Commission on Services for Elderly Persons, 1957-61. *Member:* American Sociological Society (fellow), Gerontological Society (fellow; former president of psychological and sociological science section), American Association of University Professors, Alpha Kappa Delta. *Awards, honors:* Distinguished Service Award, New School for Social Research, for services and work in gerontology.

WRITINGS: The Refugee Intellectual, Columbia University Press, 1953; (editor with Robert Kastenbaum and Sylvia Sherwood) *Research Planning and Action for the Elderly: The Power and Potential of Social Science*, Behavioral Publications, 1972. Author of research papers and reports dealing with aging. Contributor of more than forty articles to professional journals. Editor, *Gerontologist.*

WORK IN PROGRESS: Co-editing two books, *Attitudes and Attitude Change*, for Wiley, and *Social Gerontology Research and Programs*, for University of Southern California Press; principal contributor, *Social Policy and Social Research*, for Appleton.†

* * *

KEPPLER, C(arl) F(rancis) 1909-

PERSONAL: Born December 17, 1909, in Hillside, N.J.; son of Carl Richard (a surgeon) and Elizabeth Mary (O'Neill) Keppler; married Katherine Hastings, January 30, 1936. *Education:* Princeton University, B.A., 1930; University of Arizona, M.A., 1951; University of Michigan, Ph.D., 1956. *Politics:* Democrat. *Religion:* Protestant. *Home:* 4025 West Ironwood Hills Dr., Tucson, Ariz. 85705. *Office:* English Department, University of Arizona, Tucson, Ariz.

CAREER: University of Arizona, Tucson, instructor, 1949-58, assistant professor, 1958-65, associate professor, 1965-70, professor of English, 1970—. *Member:* American Association of University Professors, Phi Beta Kappa, Phi Kappa Phi.

WRITINGS: The Other, Houghton, 1964; *The Literature of the Second Self*, University of Arizona Press, 1970. Contributor of short stories, articles, and reviews to periodicals.

WORK IN PROGRESS: A book on the reconciliation of opposites in English romantic literature.

* * *

KERR, James Stolee 1928-

PERSONAL: Born February 28, 1928, in Camrose, Alberta, Canada; son of Thomas Allison (an electrician) and Agnes (Stolee) Kerr; married Anne Corrigan, February 16, 1949; children: Joyce, Christine, Timothy, Robert, Katherine, Paul. *Politics:* Independent. *Religion:* Lutheran. *Home:* R.D. 2, Greenville, Pa. 16125.

CAREER: Christian Youth Publications, Minneapolis,

Minn., associate editor, 1957-60; free-lance writer, Minneapolis, Minn., 1960-63; Thiel College, Greenville, Pa., director of publications, 1963—. Anlo Publishers, Greenville, Pa., part-owner. Filmstrip and motion picture consultant to Rusten Film Associates, 1960-63; symbol designer. Director of Mercer County (Pa.) Tourist Promotion Agency, and Northern Region District Boy Scouts of America. *Member:* National Council of College Publications Advisers, Lutheran Society for Worship, Music and the Arts, Pi Delta Epsilon, Alpha Psi Omega. *Awards, honors:* Blue Ribbon Award nomination for "This is Thiel," American Film Festival, 1966.

WRITINGS: Dandy the Dime, Denison, 1960; *Billy's Lost Smile*, Augsburg, 1960; *Tommy Had a Quarter*, Augsburg, 1960; *Missionary Mike*, Augsburg, 1960; *Sorry Sally*, Augsburg, 1961; *Susie's Time*, Augsburg, 1961; *Come and See the Symbols of My Church*, Augsburg, 1961; *Whose Zoo?*, Augsburg, 1963; *The Key to Good Church Drama*, Augsburg, 1964; *The Little Liturgy: A Children's Introduction to Lutheran Worship*, Augsburg, 1965; *That's the Way the Christian Crumbles*, Anlo, 1965; *A Clutch of Clergy*, Anlo, 1965; (with Charles Lutz) *A Christian's Dictionary: 1,600 Names, Words, and Phrases*, Fortress, 1969.

Author of "The Back Seat of Bus 29," a high school musical comedy, produced, 1966.

Writer for filmstrips, slides, and motion pictures; also writer of religious plays and historical pageants, including those for Minnesota Centennial Lutheran Pageant and Camrose Lutheran College Golden Anniversary Pageant, and of texts for church choir anthems.

WORK IN PROGRESS: The Christian Vocabulary, a glossary of terminology of the Christian Church interpreted for the layman; a series of juvenile novels; "Bang! Said the Capgun," a musical comedy.†

*   *   *

KESSLER, Jascha (Frederick) 1929-

PERSONAL: Born November 27, 1929, in New York, N.Y.; son of Hyman (a furrier) and Rosella (Bronsweig) Kessler; married Julia Braun (a free-lance editor and writer), July 17, 1950; children: Margot Lucia Braun, Adam Theodore Braun, William Alessandro Braun. *Education:* New York University, A.B., 1950; University of Michigan, M.A., 1951, Ph.D., 1955. *Politics:* Independent. *Home:* 218 Sixteenth Street, Santa Monica, Calif. 90402. *Office:* English Department, University of California, Los Angeles, Calif. 90024.

CAREER: Instructor in English at New York University, 1954-56, and Hunter College (now of the City University of New York), both New York, N.Y., 1955-56; Harcourt, Brace & Co., New York, N.Y., educational research director, 1956-57; Hamilton College, Clinton, N.Y., assistant professor of English, 1957-61; University of California, Los Angeles, assistant professor, 1961-64, associate professor, 1964-70, professor of English, 1970—. Lecturer in Israel, 1964. *Awards, honors:* Avery and Jule Hopwood Award (major) in poetry, University of Michigan, 1952; Danforth Foundation writing fellowship, 1960; D. H. Lawrence fellow, University of New Mexico, 1961; Wurlitzer Foundation fellow, 1961; Fulbright research scholar in Italy, 1963-64; Institute of Creative Arts fellowship, University of California, 1963-64, 1968, 1974; American Place Theatre, fellowship, 1967; Academy Award Nomination, 1971, for "A Long Way from Nowhere"; National Endowment for the Arts, fellowship, 1974-75.

WRITINGS: (Editor) *American Poems: A Contemporary Collection*, Southern Illinois University Press, 1964; (contributor of translations) David Ray, editor, *From the Hungarian Revolt* (poems), Cornell University Press, 1966; *An Egyptian Bondage and other Stories*, Harper, 1967; *Whatever Love Declares* (poems), Plantin Press, 1969; *After the Armies Have Passed*, New York University Press, 1970.

Plays: "Perfect Days" and "The Dummy" (one-acts), first produced at University of California at Los Angeles, August, 1965; "Crane, Crane, Montrose and Crane" (one-act), first produced in New York at American Place Theatre, December, 1968. Also author of "The Cave" (libretto for an opera in two acts), 1963. "Perfect Days" is anthologized in *Modern Occasions*, edited by Philip Rahv, Farrar, Strauss, 1966.

Films: "Autistic Children" (teaching film), 1968; "Reaching Them with Reward-Punishment Therapy" (teaching film), 1969; "The Tender Power" (documentary), 1969; "A Long Way From Nowhere" (documentary), 1970; "An American Family" (documentary), 1971; "The Fire of the Gods" (teaching film), 1974.

Contributor of poetry to *Encounter, Poetry, Kayak, Midstream, The Centennial Review, West Coast Poetry Review, The Southwest Review*, and other periodicals. Contributor of articles and reviews to *The Emerson Review, Los Angeles Times, Saturday Review, Parnassus: Poetry in Review*, and other periodicals. Contributor of translations to *The Hungarian Pen, Mundis Artium, The New Hungarian Quarterly*, and *Modern Poetry in Translation*.

WORK IN PROGRESS: Poetry; plays; a novel.

SIDELIGHTS: Some of Kessler's poetry has been recorded for broadcast and for the National Poetry Archives. His work has been translated into Italian and Hungarian. Kessler is competent in Italian, French, Hungarian and German.

BIOGRAPHICAL/CRITICAL SOURCES: Carolyn Riley, editor, *Contemporary Literary Criticism*, Volume IV, Gale, 1975.

*   *   *

KEYES, Daniel 1927-

PERSONAL: Born August 9, 1927, in Brooklyn, N.Y.; son of William and Betty (Alicke) Keyes; married Aurea Vazquez (a fashion stylist), October 14, 1952; children: Hillary Ann, Leslie Joan. *Education:* Brooklyn College (now of the City University of New York), A.B., 1950, A.M., 1961. *Residence:* Athens, Ohio. *Agent:* Robert P. Mills, 156 East 52nd St., New York, N.Y. 10022. *Office:* Department of English, Ohio University, Athens, Ohio.

CAREER: Stadium Publishing Co., New York, N.Y., associate editor, 1951-52; Fenko & Keyes Photography, Inc., New York, N.Y., co-owner, 1953; high school teacher of English, Brooklyn, N.Y., 1954-55, 1957-62; Wayne State University, Detroit, Mich., instructor in English, 1962-66; Ohio University, Athens, lecturer, 1966-72, professor of English, 1972—, director of creative writing center, 1971-73. *Wartime service:* U.S. Maritime Service, senior assistant purser, 1945-47. *Member:* Modern Language Association of America, P.E.N. *Awards, honors:* Science Fiction Writers of America Hugo Award, 1959, for "Flowers for Algernon" (short story); Nebula Award, 1966, for *Flowers for Algernon* (novel).

WRITINGS: Flowers for Algernon (novel), Harcourt, 1966; *The Touch* (novel), Harcourt, 1968.

WORK IN PROGRESS: A novel.

SIDELIGHTS: Flowers for Algernon was filmed as "Charly." Cliff Robertson won an Oscar for his performance in the title role.

* * *

KEYES, Kenneth S(cofield), Jr. 1921-

PERSONAL: Surname rhymes with "eyes"; born January 19, 1921, in Atlanta, Ga.; son of Kenneth S. (in real estate) and Lucille (Thomas) Keyes; children: Kenneth S. III, Clara Lucille. *Education:* Duke University, student, 1938-40; University of Miami, Coral Gables, Fla., A.B., 1953. *Home:* Living Love Center, 1730 La Loma Ave., Berkeley, Calif. 94709.

CAREER: In real estate business, 1953-64; Keyes Realty International, Inc., Miami, Fla., vice-president, 1964-68; Keyes National Investors, Miami, Fla., president, 1968-71; Living Love Center, Berkeley, Calif., founder, 1973—. *Military service:* U.S. Navy, 1941-45; became chief petty officer.

WRITINGS: How to Develop Your Thinking Ability, McGraw, 1951; *How to Live Longer-Stronger-Slimmer,* Fell, 1966; (with Jacque Fresco) *Looking Forward,* A. S. Barnes, 1969; *Handbook to Higher Consciousness,* Living Love Center, 1973; (with Tolly Burkan) *How to Make Your Life Happy; or, Why Aren't You Happy?,* Living Love Center, 1974.

AVOCATIONAL INTERESTS: Yachting, general semantics, classical music.

* * *

KHAZZOOM, J. Daniel 1932-

PERSONAL: First syllable of surname is accented, *Kazz-um;* born January 6, 1932, in Baghdad, Iraq; immigrated to Israel, 1951; came to United States, 1958, became citizen; son of Abraham K. (an attorney) and Loulou (Raby) Khazzoom; married Edythe J. Hicks; children: Aziza-Shoshana Loolwa. *Education:* University of Tel-Aviv, B.Sc., 1957; Harvard University, M.A., Ph.D., 1962. *Office:* Department of Economics, McGill University, Montreal Quebec, Canada.

CAREER: Union of Co-operative Consumers' Societies, Tel-Aviv, Israel, economist, 1957-58; Cornell University, Ithaca, N.Y., assistant professor of economics, 1963-65; New York University, New York, N.Y., assistant professor of economics, 1965-67; McGill University, Montreal, Quebec, assistant professor, 1967-68, associate professor of economics, 1968—. Consultant to W. P. Gace & Co., 1966-67; Federal Power Commission, consultant, 1967, chief econometrician, 1967-71; visiting faculty member, Stanford University, 1974-76. *Military service:* Israeli Air Force, 1951-53. *Member:* American Economic Association, American Statistical Association, American Farm Economic Association, Econometric Society, Omicron Delta Epsilon.

WRITINGS: The Currency Ratio in Developing Countries, Praeger, 1966; *An Econometric Model of Natural Gas Supply in the U.S.,* Federal Power Commission, 1970. Contributor of articles on energy problems to journals and reports.

WORK IN PROGRESS: An integrated econometric linear programming model of the energy industry in a national setting.

AVOCATIONAL INTERESTS: Sociological problems of immigration; Judaism and the history of the Jewish people.†

* * *

KIANG, Ying-cheng

EDUCATION: Columbia University, Ph.D., 1955. *Office:* Department of Geography, Northeastern Illinois University, Chicago, Ill.

CAREER: Professor of geography at Northeastern Illinois University, Chicago.

WRITINGS: Urban Geography (textbook), privately printed, 1964, W. C. Brown, 1966; *Cities in Maps,* Adams, 1964; *Chicago,* Adams, 1968.

* * *

KIDD, Aline H(alstead) 1922-

PERSONAL: Born November 28, 1922, in Munich, Germany; daughter of Albert (a salesman) and Agnes (Carpenter) Halstead; married Robert McMahan Kidd (an Episcopal priest), December 13, 1948; children: R. Geoffrey, Elizabeth R., Kathleen C. *Education:* University of Michigan, B.S., 1944, M. Cl. Psychol., 1945; University of Arizona, Ph.D., 1960. *Religion:* Episcopalian. *Home:* 3951 Lynoak Dr., Claremont, Calif. 91712. *Agent:* Harold Kant, 9465 Wilshire Blvd., Los Angeles, Calif. 90212. *Office:* Department of Psychology, Mills College, Oakland, Calif.

CAREER: Institute for Human Adjustment, Ann Arbor, Mich., intern, 1945; Illinois Institute of Technology, Chicago, chief of psychometrics, 1946-47; private practice as clinical psychologist, Tucson, Ariz., 1954-60; Agnews State Hospital, San Jose, Calif., clinical psychologist, 1960-62; assistant professor of psychology at Mills College, Oakland, Calif., 1962-63, and Pomona College, Claremont, Calif., 1963-65; California State College (now University), at Los Angeles, assistant professor of psychology, 1965-67; Mills College, associate professor of clinical psychology, 1967—. Clinical psychologist, Summit Psychiatric Center, 1969—. Consultant to Tri-city Mental Health Authority, Pomona, and Headstart Program, San Gabriel Valley. *Member:* American Psychological Association, Sigma Xi, Phi Sigma, Phi Kappa Phi, Psi Chi.

WRITINGS: (Editor with J. L. Rivoire) *Perceptual Development in Children,* International Universities, 1966. Contributor to psychology journals.

WORK IN PROGRESS: Adolescent Psychology, with husband, R. M. Kidd.

* * *

KILBURN, Robert E(dward) 1931-

PERSONAL: Born April 2, 1931, in Erie, Pa.; son of Corttis Raymond (a manufacturing engineer) and Mildred (Whitesmith) Kilburn; married Irmeli Ahomaki, June 6, 1955; children: Eric, Daniel, Kristina, William. *Education:* Grove City College, B.S., 1953; University of Pittsburgh, M.S., 1955; Syracuse University, Ph.D., 1972. *Religion:* Unitarian Universalist. *Residence:* Needham, Mass.

CAREER: General Electric Research Laboratory, Schenectady, N.Y., research biophysicist, 1955-57, junior high school science teacher in Burnt Hills, N.Y., 1957-59, Liverpool, N.Y., 1959-62, Fayetteville, N.Y., 1962-66; Newton (Mass.) public schools science teacher and coordinator, 1966—. *Member:* National Science Teachers Association, American Association for the Advancement of Science, National Science Supervisors Association, Association for the Education of Teachers in Science, Phi Delta Kappa.

WRITINGS—With W. A. Thurber: *Exploring Science*, Grades 7-8, Allyn & Bacon, 1965, Grade 9, 1966; *Exploring Earth Science*, Allyn & Bacon, 1965, 3rd edition (with Peter Howell), 1975; *Exploring Life Science*, Allyn & Bacon, 1966, 3rd edition (with Peter Howell), 1975; *Exploring Physical Science*, Allyn & Bacon, 1966, 3rd edition (with Peter Howell), in press.

* * *

KILLION, Katheryn L. 1936-

PERSONAL: Born June 5, 1936, in Centralia, Ill.; daughter of Ivan Kirkwood and Doreather (Thompson) Killion; married Delbert M. Patterson (a welder), November 16, 1952; children: Karen Denise, Delbert II, Stephen, Brian. *Education:* Attended public schools in Centralia, Ill., returning to high school to graduate in 1959. *Residence:* Canton, Ill. 61520.

CAREER: Young Men's Christian Association, Canton, Ill., receptionist and clerk, 1964—. Member of Fulton County (Ill.) Association for the Handicapped and Retarded; recording secretary of Illinois Childrens Hospital School, 1965-66. *Awards, honors:* Royal Knights of Chicago plaque for *No Time for Tears.*

WRITINGS: No Time for Tears, John H. Johnson Publishing, 1965.

WORK IN PROGRESS: Research on large midwestern farm family as subject for novel.

SIDELIGHTS: Katheryn Killion told *CA:* "I wrote the book [*No Time For Tears*] with the hope of informing some and consoling others in this society on the trials of the handicapped and the immediate family.... I have the dream of someday heading a coast to coast organization of parents of hydrocephalics."

BIOGRAPHICAL/CRITICAL SOURCES: Jet, August, 1961; *Ebony*, April, 1965.†

* * *

KILMARTIN, Edward J(ohn) 1923-

PERSONAL: Born August 31, 1923, in Portland, Me.; son of Patrick Joseph and Elizabeth (Sullivan) Kilmartin. *Education:* Boston College, A.B., 1947, M.A., 1948; College of the Holy Cross, M.S., 1950; Weston College, S.T.L., 1955; Gregorian University, Rome, Italy, S.T.D., 1958. *Home:* 1627 Massachusetts Ave., Cambridge, Mass. 02138. *Office:* Weston College School of Theology, 3 Phillips Place, Cambridge, Mass. 02138.

CAREER: Entered Roman Catholic order, Society of Jesus (S.J.), 1941, ordained priest, 1954. Fairfield Preparatory School, Fairfield, Conn., teacher of chemistry, 1950-51; Weston College School of Theology, Cambridge, Mass., professor of dogmatic theology, 1958—; Boston College, Chestnut Hill, Mass., associate professor, 1962-67, professor of thoelogy, 1967—. *Member:* Catholic Biblical Association of America, North American Patristic Society, Catholic Theological Society of America.

WRITINGS: The Eucharist in the Primitive Church, Prentice-Hall, 1965. Contributor to theological journals in United States and Europe. Assistant editor, *New Testament Abstracts*, 1959-67; *Theological Studies*, 1968—.

WORK IN PROGRESS: A historical study of the eucha-

ristic faith and practice in the Patristic period up to and including Eusebius of Caesarea (A.D. 340), completion expected in 1975.

SIDELIGHTS: Kilmartin reads German, French, Italian, Spanish, Dutch, Latin, and Greek.

* * *

KIM, Yong-ik 1920-

PERSONAL: Born May 15, 1920, in Korea. *Education:* Aoyama Gakuin University, Tokyo, Japan, B.A., 1942; Florida Southern College, B.A., 1951; University of Kentucky, M.A., 1952; University of Iowa, graduate study, 1952-56. *Home:* 420 East Jackson St., Macomb, Ill. *Agent:* McIntosh & Otis, Inc., 18 East 41st St., New York, N.Y. 10017. *Office:* Western Illinois University, Macomb, Ill.

CAREER: Pusan National University, Pusan, South Korea, member of department of literature, 1946-48; Korea University, Seoul, member of department of literature, 1954-57; Western Illinois University, Macomb, teacher of creative writing, 1957—. *Awards, honors:* Residence fellowships from Yaddo, Edward MacDowell Association, and Huntington Hartford Foundation.

WRITINGS: Moons of Korea, Korea Information Service, 1960; *The Happy Days*, Little, Brown, 1960 (published in England as *The Days of Happiness*, Hutchinson, 1962); *The Diving Gourd*, Knopf, 1962; *Love in Winter*, Korea University Press, 1963, Doubleday, 1969; *Blue in the Seed*, Little, Brown, 1964; *The Shoes From Yan San Valley*, Doubleday, 1970.

WORK IN PROGRESS: A novel.

BIOGRAPHICAL/CRITICAL SOURCES: Writer, October, 1965.†

* * *

KIMBALL, Stanley B(uchholz) 1926-

PERSONAL: Born November 25, 1926, in Farmington, Utah; son of Richard H. and Vontella (Hess) Kimball; married Violet Tew, June 27, 1953; children: Chase, Hope, Vontella Kay, April. *Education:* University of Denver, B.A., 1948, M.A., 1952; Columbia University, Ph.D. and Certificate, Program on East Central Europe, 1959. *Religion:* Mormon. *Home:* 745 Saddle Dr., Florissant, Mo. 63033. *Office:* Southern Illinois University, Edwardsville, Ill. 62025.

CAREER: Worker for Mormon Church in Prague, Czechoslovakia, 1948-50; Arts Council, Inc., Winston-Salem, N.C., director, 1952-55; City College, New York, N.Y., instructor, 1956-59; Columbia University, New York, N.Y., instructor, 1958-59; Southern Illinois University, Edwardsville Campus, assistant professor, 1959-64, associate professor, 1964-69, professor of European history, 1969—. *Military service:* U.S. Army Air Forces, 1945. *Member:* American Historical Association, American Association for the Advancement of Slavic Studies, Society of Mormon Historians, Conference for Central European Affairs.

WRITINGS: Czech Nationalism: A Study of the National Theatre Movement, 1845-1883, University of Illinois Press, 1964; *The Sources of Mormon History in Illinois, 1839-1848: An Annotated Catalogue of the Microfilm Collection at Southern Illinois University*, Southern Illinois University Press, 1964, revised edition, 1966; *The Travelers' Guide to Historic Mormon America*, Bookcraft Co., 1965; *The*

Austro-Slav Revival, American Philosophical Society, 1973. Contributor to journals. Member of board of editors, *Dialogue: A Journal of Mormon Thought*, 1966-70.

WORK IN PROGRESS: Slavic Civilization: A Book of Readings.

SIDELIGHTS: Kimball speaks French and German; can do research in most of the Slavic tongues. He has traveled behind the Iron Curtain in Russia, Poland, East Germany, Czechoslovakia, Hungary, and Yugoslavia.

* * *

KIMBROUGH, Emily 1899-

PERSONAL: Born October 23, 1899, in Muncie, Ind.; daughter of Hal Curry (a manufacturer) and Charlotte (Wiles) Kimbrough; married John Wrench, December 31, 1926 (divorced); children: Alis Emily (Mrs. Richard B. McCurdy), Margaret Achsah (Mrs. R. Parker Kuhn, Jr.). *Education:* Bryn Mawr College, B.A., 1921. *Politics:* Democrat. *Religion:* Episcopal. *Home:* 11 East 73rd St., New York, N.Y. 10021.

CAREER: "Fashions of the Hour," editor, 1922-26; *Ladies' Home Journal*, New York, N.Y., fashion editor, 1926, managing editor, 1927-29; writer, lecturer.

WRITINGS: (With Cornelia Otis Skinner) *Our Hearts Were Young and Gay* (Book-of-the-Month Club selection), Dodd, 1942; *We Followed Our Hearts to Hollywood*, Dodd, 1943; *How Dear to My Heart*, Dodd, 1944; *It Gives Me Great Pleasure*, Dodd, 1948, new edition, 1958; *The Innocents from Indiana*, Harper, 1950 (published in England as *Hand in Hand: The Innocents from Indiana*, Constable, 1951); *Through Charley's Door*, Harper, 1952; *Forty Plus and Fancy Free*, Harper, 1954; *So Near and Yet So Far*, Harper, 1955; *Water, Water Everywhere*, Harper, 1956; *And a Right Good Crew*, Harper, 1958 (published in England as *Right Good Crew*, Heinemann, 1959); *Pleasure by the Busload*, Harper, 1961; *Forever Old, Forever New*, Harper, 1964; *Floating Island*, Harper, 1968; *Now and Then*, Harper, 1972; *Time Enough*, Harper, 1974. Contributor to magazines. Author of film scripts for television and motion pictures.

SIDELIGHTS: Emily Kimbrough's popular first book, *Our Hearts Were Young and Gay*, is a light-hearted reminiscence of a pre-war trip to Europe. Despite the fact that the book describes a bout with measles on shipboard and a recurring battle with European bed bugs, it is, wrote Rose Feld, "a joyous chronicle from beginning to end."

Cornelia Otis Skinner once wrote of her friend: "To know Emily Kimbrough is to enhance one's days with gaity, charm, and occasional terror. She attracts incident as serge attracts lint. The fact that she once set forth to visit me in my modest apartment and arrived by mistake at the mansion of Mr. J. P. Morgan gives one a rough idea of what to expect." Miss Kimbrough enjoys travel ("more times to Greece than other countries"), music, and theater.

BIOGRAPHICAL/CRITICAL SOURCES: Books, November 15, 1942; *New York Times Book Review*, November 22, 1942.

* * *

KING, Anthony (Stephen) 1934-

PERSONAL: Born November 17, 1934, in Toronto, Ontario, Canada; son of Harold Stark (a teacher) and Marjorie (James) King; married Vera Korte, August 28, 1965 (died

October 12, 1971). *Education:* Queen's University, Kingston, Ontario, B.A., 1956; Oxford University, B.A., 1958, D.Phil., 1962; Columbia University, postdoctoral study, 1962-63. *Home:* The Mill House, Middle Green, Wakes Colne, near Colchester, Essex, England. *Office:* Department of Government, University of Essex, Colchester, Essex, England.

CAREER: Magdalen College, Oxford University, Oxford, England, fellow, 1961-65; University of Essex, Colchester, England, senior lecturer, 1966-68, professor of government, 1968—. *Member:* American Political Science Association, Political Studies Association of United Kingdom. *Awards, honors:* American Council of Learned Societies fellow, 1962-63.

WRITINGS: (With D. E. Butler) *The British General Election of 1964*, St. Martins, 1965; (contributor) *European Politics*, Volume I, edited by William G. Andrews, Van Nostrand, 1966; (editor) *British Politics: People, Parties, and Parliament*, Heath, 1966; (with D. E. Butler) *The British General Election of 1966*, St. Martins, 1966; (editor) *The British Prime Minister*, Humanities Press, 1969; (with Anne Sloman) *Westminster and Beyond*, Macmillan, 1973; *British Members of Parliament: A Self-Portrait*, Macmillan, 1974; (contributor) Fred I. Greenstein and Nelson W. Polsby, editors, *Handbook of Political Science*, Volume IV, Addison-Wesley, 1975. Contributor to *Observer* and *New Society*.

WORK IN PROGRESS: Politicians, Civil Servants and Party Government: The British Experience Explored; Politics and Policy: The Process of Government in Britain, completion expected in 1976.

* * *

KING, Clyde S(tuart) 1919-

PERSONAL: Born December 23, 1919, in Terre Haute, Ind.; son of Zora Jay and Mabel (Sale) King; married Ruth Elizabeth Schaffer (a library clerk), April 16, 1946; children: John S., David C., Thomas S., Nancy S. *Education:* Attended Kansas State College of Pittsburg, 1937-40; George Washington University, A.B., 1948; Kutztown State Teachers College (now Kutztown State College), Certificate in Library Science, 1951; Columbia University, M.S.L.S., 1961. *Politics:* "Accidental Republican." *Religion:* Methodist. *Home:* 4670 Tibbett Ave., Bronx, N.Y. 10471.

CAREER: Librarian in Flemington, N.J., 1951-53, and Mays Landing, N.J., 1953-57; Horace Mann School, Bronx, N.Y., librarian, 1957—. Sometime book indexer. High school track meet official. *Wartime service:* U.S. Merchant Marine, 1942-45; became second mate. *Member:* New York Historical Society, Hudson Valley Library Association.

WRITINGS: (With Harry H. Williams) *Bibliographic Guide for Advanced Placement: Chemistry*, New York State Education Department, 1965; *Horace Mann, 1796-1859: A Bibliography*, Oceana, 1966. Occasional contributor to newspapers and magazines.

WORK IN PROGRESS: A biography of William Yost Lenhart, American mathematician.

AVOCATIONAL INTERESTS: Collecting stereo recordings of classical and other music.†

* * *

KING, Robert Charles 1928-

PERSONAL: Born June 3, 1928, in New York, N.Y.; son

of Charles J. (a pianist) and Amanda (McCutchen) King; married Violet Mejia de Leon, February 20, 1953; children: Donald, Archie, Amanda. *Education:* Yale University, B.S., 1949, Ph.D., 1952. *Office:* Department of Biology, Northwestern University, Evanston, Ill.

CAREER: Brookhaven National Laboratory, Upton, N.Y., scientist, 1951-55; Northwestern University, Evanston, Ill., assistant professor, 1956-59, associate professor, 1959-64, professor of biology, 1964—, acting chairman of department, 1964-65. Rockefeller Institute, visiting investigator and fellow, 1959. *Member:* American Society for Cell Biology, American Society of Zoologists, Histochemical Society, Genetics Society of America, Society for the Study of Development and Growth, Sigma Xi. *Awards, honors:* National Science Foundation senior postdoctoral fellowships to University of Edinburgh, 1958-59, and to Commonwealth Scientific and Industrial Research Organization, Canberra, Australia, 1963.

WRITINGS: Genetics, Oxford University Press, 1962, 2nd edition, 1965; *Dictionary of Genetics,* Oxford University Press, 1968, 2nd edition, 1972; *Ovarian Development in Drosophila Melanogaster,* Academic Press, 1970; *Handbook of Genetics,* Plenum, 1974. Contributor of some eighty articles to scientific journals.

* * *

KING, Terry Johnson 1929-

PERSONAL: Born May 29, 1929, in Clearwater, Fla.; daughter of Timothy Augustin (a banker) and Ruth Johnson; married Blake I. King July 10, 1948 (divorced); children: Cecilia Wolcott, Mary Kinnier. *Education:* University of Miami, Miami, Fla., B.A., 1950, M.S., 1956. *Politics:* Democrat. *Religion:* None. *Home:* 2121 North Bayshore Dr., Apt. 616, Miami Fla. 33137. *Agent:* McIntosh & Otis, Inc., 18 East 41st St., New York, N.Y. 10017. *Office: Miami News,* #1 Herald Plaza, Miami, Fla. 33132.

CAREER: Village Post, Miami, Fla., travel editor, 1963-66; *Miami Daily News,* Miami, Fla., music editor, 1966-71; lifestyle editor, 1971—. *Member:* Society of American Travel Writers, Coconut Grove Sailing Club, Sigma Delta Chi.

WRITINGS: The Neutron Beam Murder, Abelard, 1965; *The Noose of Red Beads,* Abelard, 1969.

WORK IN PROGRESS: The Indians of Los Micas, Colombia; and a novel, *The Gemini.*

SIDELIGHTS: Ms. King is fluent in Spanish. *Avocational interests:* Sailing and sailboat racing.

BIOGRAPHICAL/CRITICAL SOURCES: Clearwater Sun, September 12, 1965, *Miami News,* November, 1971.

* * *

KINSELLA, Thomas 1928-

PERSONAL: Surname accented on first syllable; born May 4, 1928, in Dublin, Ireland; son of John Paul and Agnes (Casserly) Kinsella; married Eleanor Walsh, December 28, 1955; children: Sara, John, Mary. *Education:* Attended University College, Dublin. *Home:* 47 Percy Pl., Dublin 4, Ireland. *Office:* English Department, Temple University, Philadelphia, Pa. 19103.

CAREER: Associated with Irish Civil Service, Dublin, Ireland, 1946-65, becoming assistant principal officer in Department of Finance. Director, Dolmen Press Ltd. and

Cuala Press Ltd., Dublin, Ireland. Artistic director, Lyric Players Theatre, Belfast, Ireland. Poet. Southern Illinois University, Carbondale, Ill., artist-in-residence and professor of English, 1967-70; Temple University, Philadelphia, Pa., professor of English, 1970—. Founded Peppercanister, a small publishing company, Dublin, Ireland, 1972. *Member:* Irish Academy of Letters. *Awards, honors:* Guinness Poetry Award, 1958; Irish Arts Council Triennial Book Award, 1961, for *Poems and Translations;* Denis Devlin Memorial Award, 1964-66, for *Wormwood,* and 1967-69, for *Nightwalker and Other Poems;* Guggenheim fellowship, 1968-69 and 1971-72.

WRITINGS: Poems, Dolmen, 1956; *Another September* (Poetry Book Society choice), Dolmen and Oxford University Press, 1958; *Moralities,* Dolmen, 1960; *Poems and Translations,* Atheneum, 1961; (with John Montague and Richard Murphy) *Three Irish Poets,* [Dublin], 1961; *Downstream* (Poetry Book Society choice), Dolmen and Oxford University Press, 1962; *Wormwood,* Dolmen, 1966; *Nightwalker,* Dolmen, 1967; *Nightwalker and Other Poems,* Dolmen and Oxford University Press, 1968, Knopf, 1969; (translator) *The Tain* (eighth-century Irish prose epic, *Tain Bo Cuailgne*), Dolmen, 1969, Oxford University Press, 1970; *Finistere,* Dolmen, 1971; *Notes from the Land of the Dead,* Cuala Press, 1971; *Butcher's Dozen* and *A Selected Life,* Peppercanister, 1972; *Vertical Man* and *The Good Fight,* Peppercanister, 1973; *New Poems, 1973,* Dolmen and Oxford University Press, 1973; *Selected Poems, 1916-1968,* Dolmen and Oxford University Press, 1973; *One,* Peppercanister, 1974; *A Technical Supplement* (poems), Peppercanister, 1975.

WORK IN PROGRESS: An edition of Austin Clarke's *Selected Poems;* an anthology of Irish poems; another book of poems.

SIDELIGHTS: Kinsella told *CA:* "Poems since 1956—almost entirely lyrical—have dealt with love, death and the artistic act; with persons and relationships, places and objects, seen against the world's processes of growth, maturing and extinction. Now more and more concerned—in longer poem—with questions of value and order, seeing the human function (in so far as it is not simply to survive the ignominies of existence) as the eliciting of order from experience—the detection of the significant substance of the individual and common past and its translation imaginatively, scientifically, bodily, into an increasingly coherent and capacious entity; or the attempt to do this, to the point of failure. These matters are dealt with, more or less, in *Nightwalker and Other Poems.* The poetry after 1968 and continuing, turned downward into the psyche toward origin and myth, and is set toward some kind of individuation.''

BIOGRAPHICAL/CRITICAL SOURCES: Carolyn Riley, editor, *Contemporary Literary Criticism,* Volume IV, Gale, 1975.

* * *

KINSEY, Barry Allan 1931-

PERSONAL: Born February 20, 1931, in Cartersville, Okla.; son of Jess (a farmer) and Gladys Kinsey; married Carmen Ward, December 30, 1953; children: Joni Louise, Brian Thomas. *Education:* Oklahoma State University, A.B., 1953; University of Nebraska, M.A., 1957, Ph.D., 1961. *Office:* Department of Sociology, University of Tulsa, Tulsa, Okla. 74104.

CAREER: University of North Dakota, Grand Forks, instructor in sociology, 1958-59; Gustavus Adolphus College,

St. Peter, Minn., assistant professor of sociology, 1959-62; Oklahoma State University, Stillwater, associate professor, 1962-65, professor of sociology, 1965-67, associate director of Research Foundation, 1966-67; University of Tulsa, Tulsa, Okla., professor of sociology and anthropology, and department head, 1967—. Consultant to Bureau of Indian Affairs, 1968-72, and National Drug Education Center, 1971-72; member, State (Okla.) Technical Planning Committee, 1968—. *Military service:* U.S. Army Reserve, 1953-55; became first lieutenant. *Member:* American Society of Criminology, American Sociological Association, American Association of University Professors, Midwest Sociological Society, Southwest Sociological Association.

WRITINGS: The Female Alcoholic: A Social Psychological Study, C. C Thomas, 1966. Contributor of articles to journals in his field.†

*   *   *

KIPARSKY, Valentin (Julius Alexander) 1904-

PERSONAL: Born July 4, 1904, in St. Petersburg, Russia; son of Rene Carl Victor and Hedwig (von Sturtzel) von Kiparsky; married Dagmar Jaatinen, January 24, 1940; children: Paul. *Education:* Finnish Commercial School, B.A., 1926; Helsinki University, M.A., 1929, Ph.D., 1934; attended Prague University, 1930-32. *Religion:* Lutheran. *Home:* Maurinkatu 8-12 C 37, Helsinki, Finland. *Office:* Helsinki University, Helsinki, Finland.

CAREER: Helsinki University, Helsinki, Finland, junior lecturer, 1933-35, senior lecturer, 1938-45, acting professor, 1946, professor, 1947-58; Freie Universitaet, West Berlin, Germany, professor and director of Osteuropa-Institut, 1958-63; Helsinki University, professor, 1964-74. Visiting professor, Indiana University, 1952, University of Birmingham, 1952-55, and University of Minnesota, 1961-62. Translator and interpreter to Finnish Government, 1942-44; director of Finnish Governmental Institute for Studies of U.S.S.R., 1948-50. *Wartime service:* Finnish Army, 1939-42; became lieutenant. *Member:* Societas Scientiarum Fennica, Academia Scientiarum Fennica, Akademie der Wissenschaften und Literatur (corresponding member). *Awards, honors:* Commander of the Finnish Lion, 1955; Dr. honoris causa (Poznan, Poland), 1973.

WRITINGS: Die gemeinslavischen Lehnwoerter aus dem Germanischen, Academia Scientiarum Fennica, 1934; *Fremdes im Baltendeutsch*, Societe Neophilologique, 1936; *Die Kurenfrage*, Academia Scientiarum Fennica, 1939; *Suomi Venajan kirjallisuudessa*, Suomen Kirja, 1943, revised edition, 1945; *Norden i den ryska skonlitteratura*, Kooperativa, 1947; *Der Wortakzent der Russischen Schriftsprache*, Winter, 1962; *Russische historische Grammatik*, Winter, Volume I, 1963, Volume II, 1967, Volume III, 1974; *English and American Characters in Russian Fiction*, Harrassowitz, 1964. Co-editor, *Erasmus*, 1949-52. Co-editor, *Slavistische Veroeffentilchungen*, 1953-65.

SIDELIGHTS: Kiparsky knows Finnish, German, Swedish, Russian, French, English, Estonian, Lettish, Italian, Polish, Rumanian and Czech.

*   *   *

KIRK, H. David 1918-

PERSONAL: Born March 15, 1918, in Dusseldorf, Germany; son of Simon (a manufacturer) and Anna C. (Simson) Kirk; married Ruth Vail (a psychologist), August 30, 1942; children: Peter, Frances, Deborah, William. *Edu-*

cation: City College (now City College of the City University of New York), B.S. (cum laude), 1948; Cornell University, M.A., 1950, Ph.D., 1953. *Office:* University of Waterloo, Waterloo, Ontario, Canada.

CAREER: State University of New York, College at Cortland, assistant professor of sociology, 1953-54; McGill University, Montreal, Quebec, associate professor of sociology, 1954-64; University of Waterloo, Waterloo, Ontario, professor of sociology, 1964—. Visiting professor at Whittier College, 1959-61, and Los Angeles State College (now California State University, Los Angeles), 1961; summer visiting professor at Allegheny College, and faculty research fellow, Community Studies, Inc., Kansas City, Mo., 1961. Consultant to Mental Hygiene Institute of Montreal. *Member:* American Sociological Association, National Council on Family Relations, Canadian Association of Anthropology and Sociology, Canadian Peace Research and Education Association, Eastern Sociological Association.

WRITINGS: Shared Fate: A Theory of Adoption and Mental Health, Collier-Macmillan, 1964. Contributor of papers on child adoption, formal organization, and social change to learned journals.†

*   *   *

KLAPPER, Marvin 1922-

PERSONAL: Born September 5, 1922, in New York, N.Y.; son of Herbert (a salesman) and Alma (Brodsky) Klapper; married Blanche Lauber (an educational secretary), October 3, 1941; children: Sherry Ann. *Education:* New York University, B.A., 1946. *Home:* 3444 Knight St., Oceanside, N.Y.

CAREER: Fairchild Publications, New York, N.Y., editor of *Home Furnishings Daily. Military service:* U.S. Army, 78th Infantry Division, 1942-45; served in European theater.

WRITINGS: Fabric Almanac, Fairchild, 1966, 2nd edition, 1971.

AVOCATIONAL INTERESTS: Fishing.†

*   *   *

KLAUSNER, Samuel Z(undel) 1923-

PERSONAL: Born December 19, 1923, in New York, N.Y.; son of Edward S. (an engineer) and Bertha (Adler) Klausner; married second wife Madeleine Suringar, February 20, 1964; children: Rina Ellen, Jonathan David, Daphne, Tamar. *Education:* New York University, B.S., 1947; Columbia University, M.A., 1950, Ed.D., 1951, Ph.D., 1963. *Religion:* Jewish. *Home:* 2324 Bryn Mawr Ave., Philadelphia, Pa. 19131. *Office:* 4025 Chestnut St., Philadelphia, Pa. 19104.

CAREER: City College (now City College of the City University of New York), New York, N.Y., lecturer in education, 1951-52, 1955-57; The Hebrew University, Jerusalem, Israel, coordinator, department of psychology, 1952-53; Government Mental Hospital, Jerusalem, Israel, clinical psychologist, 1954-55; Columbia University, New York, N.Y., project director, Bureau of Applied Social Research, 1955-60, lecturer in religion, 1958-60; Bureau of Social Science Research, Washington, D.C., senior research associate, 1960-67; University of Pennsylvania, Philadelphia, professor of sociology, 1967—, acting director of Albert M. Greenfield Center for Human Relations, 1968-69, member of the academic advisory board of Monell

Chemical Senses Center, 1972. Union Theological Seminary, New York, N.Y., lecturer in religion and psychiatry, 1959-61. Director and president, Center for Research on Acts of Man, 1967; associate, National Center for Energy Management and Power, 1971—; member of Panel on Solar Energy, Office of Science and Technology, 1972; chairman of Panel on Social and Political Impacts, Bay Area Rapid Transit, 1972—. *Military service:* U.S. Army Air Forces, 1943-45; became second lieutenant; received Air Medal; Israeli Air Force, 1948. *Member:* Society for the Scientific Study of Religion (executive secretary, 1964-70, vice-president, 1971-73), National Academy of Sciences, National Academy of Engineering, American Academy of Religion, American Sociological Association, American Psychological Association, American Association for the Advancement of Science (council, 1965-67), Institute of Religion and Health. *Awards, honors:* Ford Foundation research fellow, Middle East, 1953-54.

WRITINGS: Psychiatry and Religion, Free Press of Glencoe, 1964; (editor and contributor) *The Quest for Self Control: Classical Philosophies and Scientific Research*, Free Press of Glencoe, 1965; (editor and author of introduction) *The Study of Total Societies*, Anchor Books, 1967; (editor) *Why Man Takes Chances: Studies in Stress-seeking*, Anchor Books, 1968; (editor) *Society and its Physical Environment*, Jossey-Bass, 1971. Contributor to *The Encyclopedia of Sexual Behavior*, 1961. Contributor to professional journals. Editor, *Journal for the Scientific Study of Religion*.

WORK IN PROGRESS: Research reports on social influences on conceptualization in science and on the control of fear among sport parachutists and air commandos.

SIDELIGHTS: Samuel Klausner speaks Hebrew, French, Spanish, Arabic, Dutch, and Yiddish.

BIOGRAPHICAL/CRITICAL SOURCES: Lily Silver, *Profiles in Success*, Fountainhead, 1965.†

*   *   *

KLEIN, Bernard 1921-

PERSONAL: Born September 20, 1921, in Bronx, N.Y.; son of Joseph (designer patentee) and Anna (Wolfe) Klein; married Betty Stecher, February 17, 1946; children: Cheryl Rona, Barry Todd, Cindy Ann. *Education:* 3150 Holiday Springs Blvd., Margate, Fla. 33063. *Office:* B. Klein Publications, Inc., P.O. Box 8503, Coral Springs, Fla. 33065.

CAREER: U.S. List Co., Inc., president, 1946—; B. Klein Publications, Inc., president, 1953—. *Military service:* U.S. Army, 1943-45; became sergeant. *Member:* Direct Mail Advertising Association, Masons, B'nai B'rith.

WRITINGS—Editor: *Guide to American Directories*, McGraw, 1954, 9th edition, Klein, 1975; *Mail Order Business Directory*, Klein, 1955, 10th edition, 1975; *Directory of Mailing List Houses*, Klein, 1958, 9th edition, in press; *Directory of College Stores*, Klein, 1958, 9th edition, in press; Directory of College Media, *Klein, 1958;* Directory of American Automobile Dealers, *Klein, 1958, 2nd edition, 1959;* Guide to American Educational Directories, *Klein, 1963, 3rd edition, 1970;* Encyclopedia of the American Indian, *Klein, 1966.*

WORK IN PROGRESS: Research for historical biography, and other reference books.

SIDELIGHTS: Klein is interested in "the research and development of useful and marketable reference books."

KLEIN, John J(acob) 1929-

PERSONAL: Born August 30, 1929, in Chicago, Ill.; son of John (a transportation supervisor) and Mathilda (Keller) Klein; married Sylvia Knauss, November 25, 1953; children: Leslie (daughter). *Education:* Northwestern University, B.A. (with distinction), 1950; University of Chicago, M.A., 1952, Ph.D., 1955. *Home:* Plaza Towers, 2575 Peachtree Rd. N.E., Atlanta, Ga. 30305. *Office:* University Plaza, Georgia State University, Atlanta, Ga. 30303.

CAREER: University of Maryland, College Park, instructor in Far East program, 1956-57; Oklahoma State University of Agriculture and Applied Science, Stillwater, assistant professor, 1957-60; Fordham University, New York, N.Y., began as associate professor, became professor of economics, 1960-67; Georgia State University, Atlanta, professor of economics, 1967—. *Military service:* U.S. Army, 1955-57; became sergeant. *Member:* American Economic Association, Phi Beta Kappa, Pi Mu Epsilon.

WRITINGS: (With R. Selden, M. Friedman, P. Cagan, and E. Lerner) *Studies in the Quantity Theory of Money*, University of Chicago Press, 1956; (with R. Poole, R. Leftwich, and R. Trenton) *The Oklahoma Economy*, Oklahoma State University Press, 1963; *Money and the Economy*, Harcourt, 1965, 3rd edition, 1974. Contributor to *Journal of Political Economy, Economic Notes*, and *Revista Internazionale di Science Economicke e Commerceal*.

WORK IN PROGRESS: Articles on non-member bank earnings; the comparative statistics of monetary policy targets.

*   *   *

KLEIN, Philip A(lexander) 1927-

PERSONAL: Born October 8, 1927, in Austin, Tex.; son of David Ballin (a professor of psychology) and Rose (Schaffer) Klein; married Margaret McCormack (a librarian), May 20, 1961; children: Kathleen, Alan. *Education:* University of Texas, B.A., 1948, M.A., 1949; University of California, Berkeley, Ph.D., 1955. *Home:* 719 South Sparks St., State College, Pa. 16801.

CAREER: Carleton College, Northfield, Minn., instructor, 1955; Pennsylvania State University, University Park, associate professor of economics, 1955—; National Bureau of Economic Research, New York, N.Y., member of research staff, 1956—. Visiting professor, San Francisco State College (now University), 1962; faculty member; European Institute of Business Administration, 1963-64; vice-president, Citizens Committee for the College Area Schools. *Military service:* U.S. Army, Medical Corps, 1946-47. *Member:* American Economic Association, American Association of University Professors, Phi Beta Kappa, Beta Gamma Sigma, Artus. *Awards, honors:* Fulbright fellow in France, 1963-64; Fulbright fellow in Yugoslavia, 1970.

WRITINGS: Financial Adjustments to Unemployment, Columbia University Press, for National Bureau of Economic Research, 1965; (with G. H. Moore) *The Quality of Consumer Installment Credit*, Columbia University Press, 1968; *Pennsylvania Market Region*, two volumes, Pennsylvania Department of Commerce, 1969; *Cyclical Timing of Consumer Credit*, Columbia University Press, 1971; (with R. L. Gordon) *The Cyclical Impact of Activity in the Steel Industry*, Pennsylvania State University, 1971. Contributor to economics journals.

WORK IN PROGRESS: International Economic Activities, for the National Bureau of Economic Research.

SIDELIGHTS: Klein speaks French. *Avocational interests:* Music, art.

* * *

KLEINFELD, Vincent A. 1907-

PERSONAL: Born February 10, 1907; son of Isaac and Anna (Rothfeld) Kleinfeld; married Elise Moritz, May 29, 1934; children: Lawrence, Jane. *Education:* City College (now City College of the City University of New York), student, 1923-27; Columbia University, LL.B., 1929.

CAREER: U.S. Government, Washington, D.C., attorney, 1935-53, with Office of Solicitor, Department of Agriculture, 1936-41, legal adviser and coordinator of government films, 1941, head attorney, Board of Economic Warfare, 1942, and special assistant to Attorney General, Criminal Division, Department of Justice, 1943-53; private practice of law, Washington, D.C., 1953—. Adjunct associate professor of law at New York University, 1949—, and George Washington University, 1953—. *Member:* American Bar Association, Federal Bar Association, New York State Bar Association, District of Columbia Bar Association.

WRITINGS: (With Dunn) *Federal Food, Drug, and Cosmetic Act*, Commerce, 1949, 6th revised edition, 1973; (with others) *Food, Drug, and Cosmetic Industry*, Practising Law Institute, 1972.†

* * *

KLIMISCH, Sister Mary Jane 1920-

PERSONAL: Born August 22, 1920, in Yankton, S.D.; daughter of A. and Mary (Block) Klimisch. *Education:* St. Mary-of-the-Woods College, B.A., 1943; American Conservatory of Music, Chicago, Ill., M.Mus., 1951; Washington University, St. Louis, Ph.D., 1971. *Home:* Sacred Heart Convent, Yankton, S.D. 57078. *Office:* Mount Marty College, Yankton, S.D. 57078.

CAREER: Roman Catholic nun of Benedictine order (O.S.B.). Mount Marty College, Yankton, S.D., faculty member, 1943—, professor of music, 1971—, director of Sacred Music Resource Center, 1971—, vice-president for academic affairs, 1974—. Composer. *Member:* American Benedictine Academy, National Catholic Music Educators Association, American Guild of Organists, Delta Kappa Gamma. *Awards, honors:* Three time recipient of James Faculty Award, Mount Marty College, for publications.

WRITINGS: (With Sister Claudia Duratscheck) *Travellers on the Way of Peace*, Brown & Saenger, 1955; *The One Bride*, Sheed, 1965. Composer of music published by World Library of Sacred Music. Contributor to musical and religious journals.

WORK IN PROGRESS: Compositions of music for English liturgy; a cumulative index of Gregorian Chant sources; research on liberal arts concept in higher education.

* * *

KLINCK, Carl Frederick 1908-

PERSONAL: Born March 24, 1908, in Elmira, Ontario, Canada; son of John (a merchant) and Anna (Milhausen) Klinck; married Margaret Elizabeth Witzel, February 27, 1934; children: David Michael. *Education:* University of Western Ontario, B.A., 1927; Columbia University, M.A., 1929, Ph.D., 1943. *Religion:* Anglican. *Home:* 8 Grosvenor St., London, Ontario, Canada. *Office:* University College, University of Western Ontario, London, Ontario, Canada.

CAREER: Waterloo College, Waterloo, Ontario, 1928-47, began as instructor, became professor of English, served as dean of arts, 1942-47; University of Western Ontario, London, Ontario, University College, associate professor, 1947-48, professor and head of Department of English, 1948-55, professor of Canadian literature, 1955-63, Middlesex College, senior professor, 1963-73, professor emeritus, 1973—. Visiting lecturer in Canadian literature, University of Leeds, 1965. *Member:* Royal Society of Canada (fellow), Modern Language Association, Association of Commonwealth Literature and Language Studies, Canadian Association for American Studies. *Awards, honors:* Officer of the Order of Canada, 1973; D.Litt., University of Western Ontario, 1974.

WRITINGS: Wilfred Campbell: A Study in Late Provincial Victorianism, Ryerson, 1942; (with H. G. Wells) *Edwin J. Pratt: The Man and His Poetry*, Ryerson, 1947; (editor with R. E. Watters) *Canadian Anthology*, Gage, 1955, revised edition, 1974; (editor, and author of introduction) *Major Richardson's "Kensington Gardens in 1830,"* Bibliographical Society of Canada, 1957; (editor, and author of introductions and notes) *William "Tiger" Dunlop, "Blackwoodian Blackwoodsman,"* Ryerson, 1958; (editor, and author of introductions and notes) *Tecumseh: Fact and Fiction in Early Records*, Prentice-Hall, 1961; (editor with Guy Sylvestre and Brandon Conron) *Canadian Writers/Ecrivains Canadiens*, Ryerson, 1964; (general editor) *Literary History of Canada*, University of Toronto Press, 1965, revised edition, 1975; (editor with J. J. Talman) *The Journal of Major John Norton 1816*, Champlain Society, 1970.

WORK IN PROGRESS: Articles on early Canadian literature in the context of the United Kingdom and the United States; the biography of Robert W. Service.

* * *

KLINE, George L(ouis) 1921-

PERSONAL: Born March 3, 1921, in Galesburg, Ill.; son of Allen Sides and Wahneta (Burner) Kline; married Virginia Hardy (a registration coordinator at Villanova University), April 17, 1943; children: Brenda Marie, Jeffrey Allen, Christina Hardy. *Education:* Boston University, student, 1938-41; Columbia University, A.B. (honors), 1947, M.A., 1948, Ph.D., 1950. *Home:* 632 Valley View Rd., Ardmore, Pa. 19003. *Office:* Thomas Library, Bryn Mawr College, Bryn Mawr, Pa. 19010.

CAREER: Columbia University, New York, N.Y., instructor in philosophy, 1950-52; University of Chicago, Chicago, Ill., visiting assistant professor of philosophy, 1952-53; Columbia University, instructor, 1953-54, assistant professor of philosophy, 1954-59; Bryn Mawr College, Bryn Mawr, Pa., lecturer in philosophy and Russian, 1959-60, associate professor, 1960-66, professor of philosophy, 1966—. Consultant, U.S.S.R. research program, 1952-55, Foreign Area fellowship program, 1959-64, National Endowment for the Humanities, 1972—. Visiting professor, University of Puerto Rico, summer, 1957, Johns Hopkins University, 1968-69. *Military service:* U.S. Army Air Forces, 1942-45; became first lieutenant; received Distinguished Flying Cross. *Member:* American Philosophical Association, Society for Ancient Greek Philosophy, Society for Phenomenology and Existential Philosophy, Metaphysical Society of America (councillor, 1969-71), American Association for the Advancement of Slavic Studies (member of board of directors, 1972-75), Philosophy Education Society (member of board of directors, 1966—), Hegel Society of America (councillor, 1968-70, 1974-76; vice-president, 1971-73), Phi Beta Kappa. *Awards, honors:* Cutting fellowship for study in Paris, and Fulbright fellowship, 1949-50; Ford Foundation fellowship to Paris, 1954-55; Rockefeller fellowship to Soviet Union and other East European countries, 1960; Emerson Prize nomination, 1969, for *Religious and Anti-Religious Thought in Russia;* National Endowment for the Humanities senior fellowship, 1970-71; other grants for study in Europe and Soviet Union.

WRITINGS: Spinoza in Soviet Philosophy, Humanities, 1952; (editor) *Soviet Education*, Columbia University Press, 1957; (editor) *Alfred North Whitehead: Essays on His Philosophy*, Prentice-Hall, 1963; (contributor) W. Reese and E. Freeman, editors, *Process and Divinity: The Hartshorne Festschrift*, Open Court, 1964; (editor and contributor) *European Philosophy Today*, Quadrangle, 1965; (editor with James M. Edie, James P. Scanlan, and Mary-Barbara Zeldin, and contributor) *Russian Philosophy*, three volumes, Quadrangle, 1965, revised edition, 1969; (contributor) E. N. Lee and M. Mandelbaum, editors, *Phenomenology and Existentialism*, Johns Hopkins Press, 1967, revised edition, 1969; *Religious and Anti-Religious Thought in Russia*, University of Chicago Press, 1968; (contributor) Mary Warnock, editor, *Sartre: A Collection of Critical Essays*, Anchor Books, 1971; (contributor) Rudolf Tokes, editor, *Dissent in the U.S.S.R.: Politics,` Ideology, and People*, Johns Hopkins Press, 1975.

Translator: V. V. Zenkovsky, *A History of Russian Philosophy*, two volumes, Columbia University Press, 1953; *Boris Pasternak: Seven Poems*, Unicorn Press, 1969, 2nd edition, 1972; *Joseph Brodsky: Selected Poems*, Penguin, 1973.

Contributor of translations: P. A. Schilpp, editor, *The Philosophy of Karl Jaspers*, Tudor, 1957; Ernest J. Simmons, editor, *Leo Tolstoy: Short Stories*, Modern Library, 1964; Peter Spackman and Lee Ambrose, editors, *Forum Anthology*, Atheneum, 1968; Leopold Tyrmand, editor, *Explorations in Freedom: Prose, Narrative, and Poetry from Kultura*, Free Press with State University of New York, Albany, 1970; Daniel Weissbort, editor, *Post-War Russian Poetry*, Penguin, 1974; Donald Junkins, editor, *The Contemporary World Poets*, Harcourt, 1976.

Contributor to *Dictionary of Russian Literature, Encyclopedia of Morals, Encyclopedia of Russia and the Soviet Union*, and *The Encyclopedia of Philosophy*. Contributor of articles and short essays and translations to books and periodicals. Editor of philosophy section, *American Bibliography of Slavic Studies*, 1957-67; *Journal of Philosophy*, co-editor, 1959-64, consulting editor, 1964—; consulting editor, *Current Digest of the Soviet Press*, 1961-64, *Studies in Soviet Thought*, 1962—, *Journal of Value Inquiry*, 1967—, *Process Studies*, 1970—, *Soviet Union*, 1975—; member of editorial board, *Encyclopedia of Philosophy*, 1962—.

WORK IN PROGRESS: Further studies of Russian philosophy, especially ethics and social theory.

SIDELIGHTS: Kline reads Russian, German, Spanish, Italian and French. He made seven study trips to Eastern Europe, 1950-67, and six to Soviet Union, 1956-68. Kline told *CA:* "The number of trips I've made to (Western) Europe is much higher, probably between twenty and twenty-five; I've lost count."

KLINGER, Kurt 1914-

PERSONAL: Born May 2, 1914, in Berlin, Germany; son of Karl (a merchant) and Anna (von Loebardt) Klinger; married Marianne Sikorski (a portrait artist), November 5, 1925. *Education:* Oberrealschule Berlin, Bachelor's degree. *Religion:* Evangelical-Lutheran. *Agent:* Heinrich Scheffler, Grueneburgweg 151, Frankfurt am Main, Germany. *Residence:* Rio de Janeiro, Brazil.

CAREER: Deutsche Presse-Agentur, Bonn and Hamburg, correspondent in Italy, 1949-63, correspondent to the Holy See, 1949-63, director for Brazil, beginning 1964. *Member:* Foreign Press Club (Rio de Janeiro; vice-president), Foreign Press Association (Rome; president, 1959), Deutscher Journalisten-Verband (Frankfurt am Main). *Awards, honors:* Vatican Silvercross of the Holy Year, 1950; medal of the City of New York for journalistic services; Commendatore Cross of the Italian Republic.

WRITINGS: Ein Papst lacht, Heinrich Scheffler, 1963, translation by Sally McDevitt Cunneen published as *A Pope Laughs*, Holt, 1964; *Studien im Sueden*, Kulturamt der Stadt Linz, 1965.

WORK IN PROGRESS: Brasilien, verhinderte Weltmacht (title means "Brazil, Prevented World-power"); *Deutschland 1975.*

SIDELIGHTS: A Pope Laughs was on the best-seller list for eight months in West Germany. Klinger speaks English, French, Italian, and Portuguese. *Avocational interests:* Travel, history, church-history, and modern political developments.†

* * *

KLOSE, Norma Cline 1936-

PERSONAL: Born November 23, 1936, in Flint, Mich.; daughter of Howard Dallas (a lawyer) and Ila (Wood) Cline; married Peter E. Klose (a teacher), August 27, 1960. *Education:* Attended University of Michigan, 1954-55, and Miami University, Oxford, Ohio, 1957; Stephens College, A.A., 1956. *Religion:* Protestant.

CAREER: Full-time secretary. Horse trainer and teacher of horseback riding.

WRITINGS: Benny—The Biography of a Horse, Lothrop, 1965; *Grey Cloud* (juvenile), Lothrop, in press.

BIOGRAPHICAL SOURCES: Flint Journal, Flint, Mich., August 25, 1963, December 4, 1965, January 9, 1966; *Grand Blanc News*, September 12, 1963; *Detroit News*, December 8, 1965.†

* * *

KNELLER, John W(illiam) 1916-

PERSONAL: Born October 15, 1916, in Oldham, England; son of John William and Margaret (Truslove) Kneller; married Alice Bowerman Hart, April 30, 1943; children: Linda. *Education:* Clark University, Worcester, Mass., A.B., 1938; Yale University, M.A., 1948, Ph.D., 1950; University of Paris, graduate study, 1949-50. *Home:* 115 Westminster Rd., Brooklyn, N.Y. 11218. *Office:* Brooklyn College of the City University of New York, Brooklyn, N.Y. 11210.

CAREER: Oberlin College, Oberlin, Ohio, instructor, 1950-52, assistant professor, 1952-55, associate professor, 1955-59, professor of French and chairman of department of Romance languages, 1959-65, provost, 1965-69; Brooklyn College of the City University of New York, Brooklyn,

N.Y., president, 1969—. Member of New York State Education Commission Advisory Council on Higher Education; member of board of trustees, Clark University, Downtown Brooklyn Development Association, South Brooklyn Savings Bank; member of board of directors, G. F. Kneller Foundation, Brooklyn Institute of Arts and Sciences, Brooklyn Chamber of Commerce. *Military service:* U.S. Army, 1942-46. *Member:* Modern Language Association of America (executive council, 1966-69), American Association of Teachers of French, American Association of University Professors, Rembrandt Club, Yale Club of New York, Brooklyn Club, Kappa Delta Pi, Alpha Sigma Lambda. *Awards, honors:* Fulbright and French government fellowships, 1949-50; doctor of letters, Clark University, 1970; Chevalier of the Ordre des Palmes Academiques (France), 1972.

WRITINGS: (With Henry A. Grubbs) *Introduction a la poesie francaise*, Ginn, 1962; (with Grubbs and Simon Barenbaum) *Initiation au francais*, Macmillan, 1963. Contributor to *PMLA* and *Yale French Studies*. Managing editor, *French Review*, 1962-65, editor, 1965—.

WORK IN PROGRESS: A study of the poetry of Gerard De Nerval.

*   *   *

KNIGHT, Karl F.   1930-

PERSONAL: Born July 3, 1930, in Statesville, N.C.; son of Hill (a factory worker) and Jessie (Eagle) Knight; married Jean Walker, December 20, 1959; children: Margaret, Charles. *Education:* University of North Carolina, A.B., 1956, M.A., 1957; Emory University, Ph.D., 1962. *Politics:* Democrat. *Religion:* Episcopalian. *Home:* 1420 Mallory Ct., Norfolk, Va. *Office:* Old Dominion University, Norfolk, Va.

CAREER: Berry College, Mount Berry, Ga., instructor in English, 1957-58; University of Alabama, Tuscaloosa, instructor in English, 1960-62; Old Dominion University, Norfolk, Va., professor of English, 1962—, chairman of department of English, 1969-74. University of North Carolina, in residence doing research on Herman Melville, 1965-66. *Military service:* U.S. Air Force, 1950-54; became staff sergeant. *Member:* Modern Language Association of America, American Association of University Professors, South Atlantic Modern Language Association, Phi Beta Kappa. *Awards, honors:* Humanities fellowship, Duke University-University of North Carolina Cooperative Program in the Humanities.

WRITINGS: The Poetry of John Crowe Ransom, Mouton & Co., 1964; (editor with Floyd C. Watkins) *Writer to Writer: Readings on the Craft of Writing*, Houghton, 1966; (with L. Hugh Moore) *A Concise Handbook of English Composition*, Prentice-Hall, 1972.

*   *   *

KNIGHT, Thomas S(tanley, Jr.)   1921-

PERSONAL: Born December 21, 1921, in Sharon, Pa.; son of Thomas S. and Mary (McCarthy) Knight; married Betty A. Roller (an applications engineer), April 18, 1942; children: Thomas S. III, Irvin R. *Education:* West Liberty State College, A.B., 1951; Syracuse University, M.A., 1953, Ph.D., 1956. *Politics:* Democrat. *Religion:* None. *Office:* Department of Philosophy and Religion, Adelphi University, Garden City, N.Y.

CAREER: Russell Sage College, Troy, N.Y., assistant professor of philosophy, 1953-58; Syracuse University, Utica College, Utica, N.Y., associate professor of philosophy, 1958-65; Adelphi University, Garden City, N.Y., professor of philosophy, 1965—, chairman of philosophy and religion department, 1967—. *Military service:* U.S. Army, 1942-45. *Member:* American Philosophical Association, American Association of University Professors.

WRITINGS: Charles Peirce, Washington Square Press, 1965. Editor with Arthur W. Brown, "American Thinkers" Series, Washington Square. Contributor of reviews and articles on metaphysics, philosophy, and phenomenological research to professional journals.

WORK IN PROGRESS: A book, *Philosophy of Continuity*; a novel.

SIDELIGHTS: Knight reads German and French. *Avocational interests:* Golf, poker, and fishing.†

*   *   *

KNOWLES, Alison   1933-

PERSONAL: Born April 29, 1933, in New York, N.Y.; daughter of Edwin B. (a professor) and Helen Lois (Beckwith) Knowles; married James Ericson, 1955; married second husband, Richard C. (Dick) Higgins (a writer; manager of Something Else Press), May 31, 1960; children: Hannah and Jessica (twins). *Education:* Attended Middlebury College, 1950-52; Pratt Institute, A.B., 1955. *Politics:* Liberal. *Religion:* "?" *Residence:* New York, N.Y.

CAREER: Free-lance silk screen work (both technical and artistic), New York, N.Y., 1959—. Had one-woman shows in New York at Nonagon Gallery, 1958, and Judson Gallery, 1962; also exhibitor in group shows in New York, Los Angeles, Chicago, and Germany. Performer in Fluxus Festivals in New York and abroad, 1962-64, Yam Festival in New York, 1963, other happenings and festivals, and in works by Dick Higgins, Allan Kaprow, Nam June Paik, Oscar Emmett Williams, Al Hansen, and others.

WRITINGS: Alison Knowles Bean Rolls, Fluxus, 1964; (contributor) *The Four Suits*, Something Else Press, 1965; *By Alison Knowles*, Something Else Press, 1965; *The Big Book*, Something Else Press, 1967. Also author of *Alison Knowles*. Contributor to *Yam, Fluxus, CC V TRE, V TRE, and other magazines.*

WORK IN PROGRESS: New Pieces, for Something Else Press.

SIDELIGHTS: Alison Knowles' *The Big Book* is an eight-foot tall, one-ton reading structure equipped with a telephone, toilet, hot plate, art gallery, graffiti wall, and a four-foot sleeping tunnel lined with artificial grass. Her earlier book, *Alison Knowles Bean Rolls*, is a tin can full of bean recipes and lore written on scrolls.†

*   *   *

KNOWLES, John   1926-

PERSONAL: Born September 16, 1926, in Fairmont, W.Va.; son of James Myron and Mary Beatrice (Shea) Knowles. *Education:* Graduate of Phillips Exeter Academy, 1945; Yale University, B.A., 1949. *Residence:* New York, N.Y.

CAREER: Hartford Courant, Hartford, Conn., reporter, 1950-52; free-lance writer, 1952-56; *Holiday*, associate editor, 1956-60; full-time writer, 1960—. *Awards, honors:* Rosenthal award from National Institute of Arts and Letters, and William Faulkner Foundation award, both 1960, for *A Separate Peace.*

WRITINGS: A Separate Peace (novel), Macmillan, 1960; *Morning in Antibes* (novel), Macmillan, 1962; *Double Vision: American Thoughts Abroad* (travel), Macmillan, 1964; *Indian Summer* (novel), Random House, 1966; *Phineas* (short stories), Random House, 1968; *The Paragon* (novel), Random House, 1971; *Spreading Fires* (novel), Random House, 1974.

SIDELIGHTS: The Times Literary Supplement called *A Separate Peace* "a novel of altogether exceptional power and distinction." *The Manchester Guardian* noted that Knowles "draws with tenderness and restraint the pure joy of affection between the boys, their laconic, conscientiously fantastic language, and the extra tension of the summer—1942—when they see their youth curtailed by war."

His later novels have received mixed reviews, but critics all agree on the quality of Knowles work. Reviewing *The Paragon*, the *New Republic* asserted: "Mr. Knowles remains a writer of very real importance. In this new book he seems to be engaged in his own artistic struggle, something no one has yet invented a way to bypass."

A film version of *A Separate Peace* was released by Paramount Pictures in 1972.

BIOGRAPHICAL/CRITICAL SOURCES: Manchester Guardian, May 1, 1959; *Times Literary Supplement*, May 1, 1959; *New Statesman*, May 2, 1959; *New York Times Book Review*, February 7, 1960, August 14, 1966; *Commonweal*, December 9, 1960; *Harper's*, July, 1966; *Book Week*, July 24, 1966; *Life*, August 5, 1966; *Saturday Review*, August 13, 1966; *English Journal*, April, 1969, December, 1969; *Clearing House*, September, 1973; Carolyn Riley, editor, *Contemporary Literary Criticism*, Gale, Volume I, 1973, Volume IV, 1975.

* * *

KNOWLTON, William H. 1927-

PERSONAL: Born December 31, 1927, in Akron, Ohio; son of William Hardy (a lawyer) and Louise (Hagelbarger) Knowlton; married Louise Short, June 30, 1951; children: William, Douglas, Mark. *Education:* Oberlin College, A.B., 1949, M.A., 1951; Harvard University, M.Ed., 1957. *Home:* 63 Piper Pali, Honolulu, Hawaii 96822. *Agent:* Harold Ober Associates, Inc., 40 East 49th St., New York, N.Y. 10017. *Office:* Punahou School, Honolulu, Hawaii 96822.

CAREER: Punahou School, Honolulu, Hawaii, teacher, 1950—. *Military service:* U.S. Navy, 1945-46.

WRITINGS: Let's Explore Beneath the Sea, Knopf, 1957; *Sea Monsters*, Knopf, 1959; *Hawaii: Pacific Wonderland*, Dodd, 1962; *Beneath Hawaiian Seas*, Knopf, 1962; *The Boastful Fisherman*, Knopf, 1970.

WORK IN PROGRESS: Children's books.

AVOCATIONAL INTERESTS: The ocean; diving for seashells.

* * *

KOCH, Hans-Gerhard 1913-

PERSONAL: Born May 3, 1913, in Magdeburg, Germany; son of Friedrich (Oberkonsistorialrat, a high official in Lutheran Church) and Elisabeth (von Schneidemesser) Koch; married Gertrud Buerkner, April 6, 1940; children: Sabine, Hans-Ulrich, Irene. *Education:* Attended University of Berlin, 1931-32; University of Erlangen, 1932-36; University of Koenigsberg, summer, 1935; Evangelisches Konsistorium Magdeburg, degree in theology, 1939; University of Halle, Ph.D., 1950. *Religion:* Presbyterian. *Home:* Erftstrasse 106, 404 Neuss, Federal Republic of Germany. *Office:* Schwann-Gymnasium, Platz am Niedertor, 404 Neuss, Federal Republic of Germany.

CAREER: Ordained minister, 1939. Freyburg, Magdeburg, and Halle, Germany, assistant minister, 1936-39; Halle an der Saale, German Democratic Republic, minister, 1950-60; Schwann-Gymnasium, Neuss, Germany, minister, and teacher of religion and philosophy, 1960—, Studienrat, 1965-69, Studiendirektor, 1969—. City Council, Neuss, Germany, councillor, 1964-69, expert consultant to City Council, 1969—. Chairman of public school commission and member of culture council, Neuss, Germany, 1969—. *Wartime service:* German Army, 1939-45; became first lieutenant; awarded Kriegsverdienstkreuz mit Schwerten, second and first class. Russian prisoner of war, 1945-50. *Member:* Philologenverband Nordrhein-Westfalen, Studentenverbindung Uttenruthia (Erlangen).

WRITINGS: Die Stadtkirche zu Freyburg in Geschichte und Gegenwart, Sieling, 1938; (contributor) *Das Bildnis des Evangelisten Meuschen*, Evangelische Verlagsanstalt, 1955; *Abschaffung Gottes?*, Quell-Verlag, 1961, translation published as *The Abolition of God*, Fortress, 1963; *Neue Erde ohne Himmel*, Quell-Verlag, 1963; (contributor) Hermann Friedrich Gertz, editor, *Der Konipf gegen Religion und Kirche in der S.B.Z.*, Quell-Verlag, 1966; *Luther's Reformation in Kommunistischer Sicht*, Quell-Verlag, 1967; *Heinrich Heine und die Religion*, Zeitwende, 1967; *Das sozialistische Menschenbild*, Zeitwende, 1969. Editor of parish newspaper, Halle, Germany, 1950-55; Neuss, Germany, 1964—.

WORK IN PROGRESS: Ohme Kirche? Zinn Verhaltnis von Staat ima Kirche in der D.D.R. von 1945 bis 1974, completion expected by 1980.

SIDELIGHTS: Dr. Koch told *CA*: "My literary activity on the opposition of Christian belief and dialectic materialism . . . is connected with the fact that I was in the German Democratic Republic (the East Zone) from 1950 to 1960 and was not allowed by the government to publish. Therefore, in 1960 I fled with my family to West Germany, where I am now a teacher of religion. I collect all publications of the communist sphere against Christianity, analyze them, and try to refute them. Communism, materialism, and atheism attack Christianity, and therefore I am concerned with the defense of Christianity against these attacks. . . . I became well acquainted with communist theory and practice, but I can see in its atheistic principles no truth and no blessing for mankind."

* * *

KOCH, Thomas Walter 1933-

PERSONAL: Born August 22, 1933, in Rochester, N.Y.; son of Walter Arthur and Clair (Burns) Koch; married Ann G. Runzo (a teacher), December 14, 1963. *Education:* University of Rochester, A.B., 1955, A.M., 1958; Stanford University, graduate study, 1965. *Politics:* Democrat. *Religion:* No affiliation. *Home:* 94 Bellevue Dr., Rochester, N.Y. 14620.

CAREER: Taught general science in New York, 1958-59; Franklin High School, Rochester, N.Y., teacher of American history, 1958-65; Edison Technical and Industrial High School, Rochester, N.Y., head of History Department, 1966—. *Member:* American Federation of Teachers.

Awards, honors: Coe fellowship in American History, summer, 1965.

WRITINGS: (With Raymond S. Iman) *Labor in American Society*, Scott, 1965.

* * *

KOCH, William H., Jr. 1923-

PERSONAL: Born July 10, 1923, in New Rochelle, N.Y.; son of William H. and Natalie (Fitzpatrick) Koch; married Rebecca Nace (a teacher), August 28, 1951; children: Susan K., John A., Emily J., Theodore W., Sarah L. *Education:* Attended Columbia University, 1943-47; Springfield College, Springfield, Mass., B.S., 1951, M.S., 1955; University of Chicago, graduate study. *Politics:* "Usually independent voter." *Religion:* United Church of Christ. *Home:* 2103 Rowley Ave., Madison, Wis. *Office:* Department of Social Work, University of Wisconsin Extension, 606 State St., Madison, Wis.

CAREER: Springfield College, Springfield, Mass., instructor in recreation and community leadership, 1953-54; National Council of Churches, director of Arizona migrant ministry, Phoenix, 1954-57, Migrant Citizenship Education Project, Chicago, Ill., 1957-60, and community development, Division of Home Missions, New York, N.Y., 1961-63; North Carolina Fund, Durham, director of community development, 1964-65; U.S. Office of Economic Opportunity, Washington, D.C., consultant for War on Poverty, 1966; University of Wisconsin Extension, Madison, lecturer in social work, beginning 1966. Secretary of Arizona Governor's Committee on Seasonal Farm Labor, 1956-57. *Member:* National Association of Social Workers, Adult Education Association of the U.S.A., Phi Delta Kappa. *Awards, honors:* Essay award in national competition of Foundation for Voluntary Welfare, 1957, published in *Grass Roots Private Welfare*.

WRITINGS: (Contributor) *Grass Roots Private Welfare*, New York University Press, 1957; *Dignity of Their Own*, Friendship, 1966. Contributor of articles on community development to house and church periodicals.†

* * *

KOH, Byung Chul 1936-

PERSONAL: Born April 6, 1936, in Seoul, Korea; son of Young Whan and Yongsun (Ho) Koh. *Education:* Seoul National University, LL.B., 1959; Miami University, Oxford, Ohio, M.A., 1960; Cornell University, M.P.A., 1962, Ph.D., 1963. *Home:* 4207 Woodland Ave., Western Springs, Ill. 60558. *Office:* Department of Political Science, University of Illinois, Chicago, Ill. 60680.

CAREER: Korean Republic (English-language daily newspaper), Seoul, Korea, reporter, 1959; Louisiana State University, Baton Rouge, assistant professor of government, 1963-65; University of Illinois, Chicago Campus, assistant professor, 1965-68, associate professor, 1968-72, professor of political science, 1972—. *Military service:* Republic of Korea Air Force, 1957-59; became second lieutenant.

WRITINGS: The United Nations Administrative Tribunal, Louisiana State University Press, 1966; *The Foreign Policy of North Korea*, Praeger, 1969. Contributor of articles and reviews to professional journals.

WORK IN PROGRESS: A book on a comparative study of the foreign policies of North and South Korea.

SIDELIGHTS: Koh is competent in Japanese and Mandarin Chinese, and reads French.

KOH, Sung Jae 1917-

PERSONAL: Born February 5, 1917, in Seoul, Korea; came to United States in 1960; son of Ui Song and Hong Sun (Yang) Koh; married Zung Nye Kim, October 1, 1942; children: Soon Ja, Soo Il, Soo Sam, Soon Sim, Soon Sen. *Education:* Rykkyo University, B.A., 1941; Seoul National University, Ph.D., 1960. *Religion:* Presbyterian. *Home:* 128-12 Pill-Dong, Chung-Ku, Seoul, Korea.

CAREER: Research associate at Yamasaki Asian Economic Research Institute and the Oriental Economic Research Institute, both Tokyo, Japan, 1942-44; professor of economics, Yonsei University, Seoul, Korea, and Korea University, Seoul, 1944-52; Seoul National University, Seoul, Korea, professor of economics, 1953-61; Columbia University, New York, N.Y., senior research associate, 1961-63; University of Pennsylvania, Philadelphia, research scholar, 1963-65; University of Chicago, Chicago, Ill., research associate at Research Center in Economic Development and Cultural Change, 1965-67; executive member of President's Council of Economic and Scientific Advisers, 1967-68; now lecturer in Asian economic history, Seoul National University. *Member:* American Economic Association, Association for Asian Studies, Economic History Association, National Academy of Sciences (Republic of Korea), Philadelphia Oriental Club. *Awards, honors:* National Academy Prize, 1969, for *Stages of Industrial Development in Asia*.

WRITINGS: Industrial History of Modern Korea (in Korean), Taidong Cultural Publishing Co. (Seoul), 1959; *Stages of Industrial Development in Asia*, University of Pennsylvania Press, 1966; *History of the Colonial Banking Policies in Korea* (in Japanese), Ochanomizu Publishing Co. (Tokyo), 1972; *History of the Minorities in Hawaii, Japan, Manchuria and East Russia* (in Korean), Jangmmonkak Publishing Co. (Seoul), 1973. Contributor to journals in his field.

WORK IN PROGRESS: History of the village system in Korea, to be published in Korean and Japanese.†

* * *

KOINER, Richard B. 1929-

PERSONAL: Born January 28, 1929, in Atlantic City, N.J.; son of Betty Banks (Jamison) Koiner; divorced; children: Karen T., Richard B. II, Stacey Jean, Eric B., Kyle B. *Education:* Studied music privately for four years; attended Cartoonist and Illustrators School, New York, N.Y., and American Institute of Banking. *Politics:* Democrat. *Religion:* Catholic.

CAREER: Onetime professional cartoonist; now free-lance writer and clerk-typist. *Military service:* U.S. Army, 1945-47. U.S. Air Force, 1950-53; received Korean Citation, two bronze stars, and Syngman Rhee Unit Citation. *Awards, honors:* Bread Loaf Writers' Conference fellowship for novel, *Jack Be Quick*, 1966.

WRITINGS: Jack Be Quick, Lyle Stuart, 1966.

WORK IN PROGRESS: A novel, tentatively titled *A Place to Write Home From*.

SIDELIGHTS: Koiner told *CA:* "Though I have struck out in many (I repeat, many) directions, the idea of being a professional writer has never been far from practice. For years I was a cartoonist, successfully published nationally, but aside from whatever monetary reward I got, art gave me no esthetic pleasure whatsoever. Vocational interest? Writing. Writing. Writing. Writing."†

KOLINSKI, Charles J(ames) 1916-

PERSONAL: Born July 17, 1916, in Milwaukee, Wis.; son of Peter C. and Grace (Ramsey) Kolinski; married Margaret Magee, September 9, 1944; children: Carol Jane, Jean. *Education:* Attended Lake Forest College, 1934-35; George Washington University, B.A., 1940; University of Florida, M.A., 1961, Ph.D., 1963. *Home:* 1198 Southwest 14th St., Boca Raton, Fla., 33432. *Office:* Florida Atlantic University, Boca Raton, Fla. 33432.

CAREER: U.S. Department of State, Foreign Service officer, 1940-60, as second secretary and consul in Portugal, Scotland, Portuguese West Africa, Brazil, Ecuador, and Paraguay; Rollins College, Winter Park, Fla., assistant professor of Latin American history and culture, 1963-64; Florida Atlantic University, Boca Raton, 1964—, began as associate professor, now professor of Latin American history and culture. Marymount College, Boca Raton, consultant and professor of United States history and Latin American history and culture, 1966-68. *Military service:* U.S. Naval Reserve, 1944-46; served in European theater; became lieutenant junior grade. *Member:* Southeastern Conference on Latin American History, Latin American Studies Association, Florida Historical Society. Phi Kappa Phi, Pi Gamma Mu, Phi Alpha Theta.

WRITINGS: Independence or Death: The Story of the Paraguayan War, University of Florida Press, 1965; *The Historical Dictionary of Paraguay,* Scarecrow, 1973. Regular contributor to *Foreign Commerce Weekly,* 1948-60; also contributor to *Historian, American Historical Review,* and *Hispanic American Historical Review.*

WORK IN PROGRESS: Several works on River Plate republics of South America.

*   *   *

KOLJEVIC, Svetozar 1930-

PERSONAL: Surname is pronounced Kohl-*yeh*-vich; born September 9, 1930, in Banja Luka, Yugoslavia; son of Doko Stojan (a merchant) and Kosara (Simic) Koljevic; married Ksenija Medic (a teacher), September 28, 1957; children: Svetlana, Radovan. *Education:* University of Belgrade, B.A., 1954; Cambridge University, M.Litt., 1957; University of Zagreb, Ph.D., 1959. *Home:* 9, Visnjik, Sarajevo, Yugoslavia.

CAREER: University of Sarajevo, Faculty of Philosophy, Sarajevo, Yugoslavia, professor of English literature, 1958—. Indiana University, Bloomington, Ind., visiting assistant professor of English and Yugoslav literature, 1963-64; visiting fellow, All Souls College, Oxford, 1975-76. *Member:* Association of Literary Translators (Sarajevo), Writer's Association (Sarajevo), P.E.N. (Belgrade center). *Awards, honors:* City of Sarajevo Award for *Humor i mit,* 1968.

WRITINGS: Trijumf inteligencije, Prosveta, 1963; (editor and translator) *Yugoslav Short Stories,* Oxford University Press, 1966; *Humor i mit,* Nolit, 1967; *Nas junackiep,* Nolit, 1974. Contributor to Yugoslav journals.

WORK IN PROGRESS: Chapters on twentieth century British literature for *A History of English Literature,* edited by Veselin Kostic; an English edition of book on Yugoslav epic poetry.

*   *   *

KOLSTOE, Oliver P(aul) 1920-

PERSONAL: Born February 28, 1920, in Canton, S.D.; son of Soren Olaf and Inger (Hertsgaard) Kolstoe; married to second wife, Betty J.; children: Lee Paul, Kathleen Jane, Bradley Louis, Nancy Annette, Janice Green. *Education:* Valley City State Teachers College (now Valley City State College), B.A. in Ed., 1941; University of North Dakota, M.S., 1948; University of Iowa, Ph.D., 1952. *Home:* 1618 Lakeside Drive, Greeley, Colo. *Office:* School of Special Education, University of Northern Colorado, Greeley, Colo.

CAREER: High school teacher, high school principal, and superintendent of public schools in North Dakota towns, 1945-48; State College of Iowa (now University of Northern Iowa), Cedar Falls, instructor in education, 1948-50; University of Iowa, Iowa City, principal of Perkins School in Childrens Hospital, 1950-52; University of Illinois, Urbana, associate professor, Institute for Research on Exceptional Children, 1952-56; Southern Illinois University, Carbondale, professor of special education and chairman of department, 1956-65, executive officer for advanced graduate study in education, 1963-65; University of Northern Colorado, Greeley, professor of special education and chairman of department of special education, 1965—. Children's Hospital School, Chicago, member of advisory committee, 1960-65; Illinois Governor's Committee on Mental Retardation, member, 1964-65. District 165 School Board, Carbondale, member, 1963-65; National Advisory Council on Vocational Education, member, 1969-70; Colorado Advisory Council on Special Education, member, 1972—. *Military service:* U.S. Army Air Forces, 1941-45; became first lieutenant; received Air Medal with three oak leaf clusters, Distinguished Flying Cross, European Theater ribbon with three battle stars.

MEMBER: American Association on Mental Deficiency (fellow), Council for Exceptional Children, Phi Delta Kappa.

WRITINGS: (Contributor) *Modern Methods of Elementary Education,* edited by Merle M. Ohlsen, Dryden Press, 1959; (contributor) *Educational Psychology,* edited by Charles E. Skinner, Prentice-Hall, 1959; (contributor) *Mental Retardation: Readings and Resources,* edited by Jerome Rothstein, Holt, 1961; (with Roger M. Frey) *A High School Work Study Program for the Mentally Subnormal Student,* Southern Illinois University Press, 1965; (contributor) *Perspectives in Mental Retardation,* edited by Thomas E. Jordan, Southern Illinois University Press, 1966.

Teaching Educable Mentally Retarded Children, Holt, 1970; *Mental Retardation: An Educational Viewpoint,* Holt, 1972; *College Professoring: Through Academia with Gun and Camera,* Southern Illinois University Press, 1975; (contributor) James Kaufman and James Payne, editors, *Personal Perspectives in Mental Retardation,* Charles E. Merrill, 1975. Contributor to *World Book Encyclopedia* and education journals.

WORK IN PROGRESS: Research on standards and strategies of the mentally retarded, a ten-year project investigating the learning theory of Miller, Galanter, and Pribram; continuing study of the operation of sheltered workshops for the handicapped; preparing a manual on career education for the Bureau of Education for the Handicapped.

AVOCATIONAL INTERESTS: Skiing, golfing, swimming.

KOOP, Katherine C. 1923-
(Katherine C. LaMancusa)

PERSONAL: Born January 9, 1923, in Richmond, Calif.; daughter of Joseph (a potter) and Catherine (DeGregorio) LaMancusa; divorced. *Education:* San Francisco State College (now San Francisco State University), A.B., 1945, M.A., 1956; Stanford University, graduate study, 1962. *Politics:* Democrat. *Religion:* Roman Catholic. *Residence:* Pacifica, Calif.

CAREER: Elementary and secondary teacher and art supervisor, 1945-55; Frederic Burk Laboratory Demonstration School, teacher, 1955-59, vice-principal, 1962-63, principal (summer session), 1960-63; San Francisco State College (now San Francisco State University), San Francisco, Calif., assistant professor of art, 1959-65, professor of art education, beginning 1965. *Member:* Alpha Phi Gamma, Phi Lambda Theta.

WRITINGS—Under name Katherine C. LaMancusa: *Source Book for Art Teachers*, International Textbook, 1965; *We Do Not Throw Rocks at the Teacher*, International Textbook, 1966.

WORK IN PROGRESS: Art for the Visually Handicapped.†

*   *   *

KORNRICH, Milton 1933-

PERSONAL: Born August 14, 1933, in Brooklyn, N.Y.; son of Max and Rose Kornrich; married Linda Kramer (a teacher), December 17, 1955; children: William Jon, Jason Marc, Evan Kennedy. *Education:* City College (now City College of the City University of New York), B.S., 1955, M.S., 1956; Adelphi University, Ph.D., 1960. *Politics:* Democrat. *Religion:* Jewish. *Home:* 139-15 83rd Ave., Kew Gardens, N.Y. 11435. *Office:* Long Beach School System, Long Beach, N.Y. 11561.

CAREER: Intern in clinical psychology at U.S. Veterans Administration Hospitals, 1958-61; Massapequa (N.Y.) School System, psychologist, 1961-64; North Shore Child Guidance Center, Manhasset, N.Y., supervising clinical psychologist, 1964-66; Long Beach (N.Y.) School System, psychologist, 1966—; private practice of psychology, 1963—. Clinical psychologist, Brooklyn Community Counseling Center, 1961-62; psychotherapist, Bleuler Center for Psychotherapy, 1961-63, 1966—. Lecturer in psychology at Hunter College of the City University of New York. Consultant, Early Childhood Center of Queens College of the City University of New York, 1965-67. *Member:* American Psychological Association, American Academy of Psychotherapists, American Association for the Advancement of Science, Society for Personality Assessment, Association for Applied Psychoanalysis, Eastern Psychological Association, New York Psychological Association, Psi Chi. *Awards, honors:* Fellow, Postgraduate Center for Mental Health, 1963-66.

WRITINGS: (Editor and compiler) *Underachievement*, C. C Thomas, 1965; (editor and compiler) *Psychological Test Modifications*, C. C Thomas, 1965. Contributor of book reviews and articles to professional journals.

WORK IN PROGRESS: A book on "school phobia."

AVOCATIONAL INTERESTS: Music, particularly chamber music.†

KOSINSKI, Jerzy (Nikodem) 1933-
(Joseph Novak)

PERSONAL: Born June 14, 1933, in Lodz, Poland; came to United States, 1957; became U.S. citizen, 1965; only child of Mieczyslaw and Elzbieta (Liniecka) Kosinski; married Mary Hayward Weir, 1962 (died, 1968). *Education:* University of Lodz, M.A. (history), 1953, M.A. (political science), 1955; researcher at Polish Academy of Arts and Sciences, 1955-57, and at Lomonosov University, 1957; Columbia University, Ph.D. candidate in sociology, 1958-66; New School for Social Research, graduate study, 1962-66. *Office:* c/o Scientia-Factum, Inc., Hemisphere House, 60 West 57th St., New York, N.Y. 10019.

CAREER: Was a ski instructor in Zakopane, Poland, winters, 1950-56; Polish Academy of Arts and Sciences, Institute of the History of Culture, Warsaw, Poland, assistant professor of sociology, 1955-57; knew no English when he arrived in America, and worked as a paint scraper on excursion-line boats, a truck driver, chauffeur, and photographer; Wesleyan Univeristy, Center for Advanced Study, Middletown, Conn., professor of English, 1967-68; Princeton University, Princeton, N.J., visiting lecturer in English and senior fellow of the Council of the Humanities, 1969-70; Yale University, School of Drama, New Haven, Conn., professor of English prose and criticism, and fellow of Davenport College, 1970—.

MEMBER: P.E.N. (president, 1973—), National Writers Club (member of board, 1970—), Authors League, American Association of University Professors, American Translators Association, International League for the Rights of Man (director, 1973—), Amnesty International, American Civil Liberties Union, Inter-American Association for Democracy and Freedom, American Federation of Television and Radio Artists. *Awards, honors:* Ford Foundation fellowship, 1958-60; Prix du Meilleur Livre Etranger (France), 1966, for *The Painted Bird*; Guggenheim fellowship in creative writing, 1967-68; National Book Award, 1969, for *Steps*; National Institute of Arts and Letters and the American Academy of Arts and Letters award in literature, 1970; John Golden fellowship in playwriting, 1970-72; Brith Sholom Humanitarian Freedom Award, 1974.

WRITINGS—Fiction: *The Painted Bird*, abridged edition, Houghton, 1965, complete edition, Modern Library, 1970; *Steps*, Random House, 1968; *Being There*, Harcourt, 1971; *The Devil Tree*, Harcourt, 1973; *Cockpit*, Houghton, 1975.

Nonfiction: (Under pseudonym Joseph Novak) *The Future is Ours, Comrade: Conversations with the Russians*, Doubleday, 1960; (under pseudonym Joseph Novak) *No Third Path: A Study of Collective Behavior*, Doubleday, 1962; (editor) *Socjologia Amerykanska: Wybor Prac, 1950-1960* (title means "American Sociology: Selected Works, 1950-1960"), Polish Institute of Arts and Sciences (New York), 1962; *Notes of the Author on "The Painted Bird,"* Scientia-Factum, 1965; *The Art of the Self: Essays a propos "Steps,"* Scientia-Factum, 1968. Contributor to *The American Scholar* and *The New York Times*. Contributing editor, *The American Pen: International Quarterly*.

SIDELIGHTS: Arthur Miller wrote to Kosinski: "The surrealistic quality of [*The Painted Bird*] is a powerful blow on the mind because it is so carefully kept within the margins of probability and fact. To me, the Nazi experience is the key one of this century—they merely carried to the final extreme what otherwise lies within so-called normal social existence and normal man. You have made the normality of it all apparent, and this is a very important and difficult thing to have done. It is hard to speak of beauty in relation to this subject, yet you have created it through the gradual and shifting content of the central image. I hope your work will be recognized for its uniqueness in this respect. ... ''

In *Notes of the Author* Kosinski writes: "We fit experiences into molds which simplify, shape and give them an acceptable emotional clarity. *The remembered event becomes a fiction, a structure made to accomodate certain feelings.* If there were not these structures, art would be too personal for the artist to create, much less for the audience to grasp. *There is no art which is reality; rather, art is the using of symbols by which an otherwise unstateable subjective reality is made manifest....* Whether involved with nonfiction or fiction, the actively creating mind edits out what is unimportant or non-communicable and directs itself toward the fictive situations. One cannot say that memory is either literal or exact; if memories have a truth, it is more an emotional than actual one. It can be said that we transmute our experiences into little films.''

Kosinski, in *The New York Times*, also states: "Today, the attempt to define 'Who am I?' is often replaced in each of our minds by the question, 'Who do they want me to be?' or 'With whom ought I to be?' Thus the knowledge we form of ourselves is nothing but a collective image which, like ubiquitous television, engulfs us. One image is interchangeable with another. But what about the self? I am convinced, and I see it manifested in almost every phase of modern living, from the corporate to the Woodstock ends of the spectrum, from the hardhat executive to the professional revolutionary, that we are a culture of the denial of the self.

"In its increasing collectivization, modern society offers every conceivable escape from the realization of self. Participation in the collective rites, such as mass-spectator sports, rock and pop festivals is a stage in the loss of self which has assiduously been rubbed off from earliest childhood by the collective-conformist eraser.

"What the collective offers is the hypnotic notion that just as others are, and always will be, so one is and will continue to be; that one cannot fail because only individuals, setting standards for themselves, fail. The collective, at worst, only underachieves. As if betraying a profound guilt, the collective jargon sometimes tries to rescue a single face from the blur of the crowd. The phrase 'doing one's own thing' is really no more than a mockery uttered by people whose own thing is to be part of an amorphous supergang.... Some of us claim to have the courage to give our lives if the need arises. Few of us have the courage to face it as it comes to us day to day.''

"With Kosinski," Lary Swindell remarks that "style becomes distillation itself. Every syllable functions toward a rhythm and cadence that stimulates reading; and the imagery is so vivid as to purge any possible ambiguity. Yet the heartbeat of Kosinski's fiction is not style but substance. I suspect Kosinski finds little fascination for conventionality or the best-seller list. He is a vital, committed social critic; and if he believes the world is stuck with a pretty sorry human race, he may also believe that society itself is salvageable. But only possibly.''

"*Steps*," notes Kosinski, in *The Art of the Self*, about his National Book Award winning novel, "has no plot in the Aristotelian sense. In Aristotle's terms for the revelation of the action, the end fulfills the beginning and the middle determines the end. But the aim of *Steps* precludes such an ordering of time. The relationship of the characters exists in the fissure between past and present. And it is precisely between the past and present of the incidents of *Steps* that the projected struggle takes place. The incidents are interludes in the contest, and, as in Greek drama, they are the vehicle of its lyric and thematic sense: the incident is the symbol, the enactment of the struggle.''

According to the citation from the judges of the National Book Award in Fiction: " ... [Kosinski] is already close to being a master of English prose: he writes with brilliant lucidity and vividness. At a time when our culture is plagued with exhibitionism and wanton display, Mr. Kosinski recalls the tradition of high art as a mode of imaginative order." From the citation by the American Academy of Arts and Letters and the National Institute of Arts and Letters award in literature, the judges state that "His art has dealt with the fangs and colors of dream and of daily life among the violations of the spirit and body of human beings. The presence of beauty, the possibility of kindness are suggested, but in a context which has left many with nothing but silence.''

Jonathan Baumbach says of *Cockpit* and Kosinski's other works of fiction: " ... all of Kosinski's novels are extremely similar in method and impulse and extend into one another as if they were one long, fantastic autobiographical nightmare, manipulations in slightly varied forms of the same obsessive materials.... he moves through the void of a self-created world changing roles as the seasons of vengeance or survival demand." Continuing the survival theme, Ross Wetzsteon comments that "He [Kosinski] is fated to become a writer in order to survive. To admit his past is real would be to allow it to cripple him; to admit his fiction is autobiographical would be to allow himself to be devastated by the horror of its experiences. 'I am not the person who experienced those horrors,' Kosinski is saying, but rather, 'I am the one who *conquered* them'.''

Kosinski's motto, taken from Descartes, is "Larvatus prodeo." He says that he would most like to live in New York or London, and that his ideal of earthly happiness is to remain free and non-regimented. The summit of misery for him would be the lack of freedom and privacy. He notes that prejudice and intolerance are the faults for which he has the greatest tolerance; he most admires integrity and directness in a man, as in a woman; and he most appreciates integrity in his friends. Kosinski says that writing is the occupation most enjoyable for him, and, when asked what person he would like to be he replied: "A simple one." He considers inflexibility to be his principal character trait, and accuses himself of egocentrism and fear of entrapment as his principal faults. He chose Julien Sorel as his favorite fictional figure; Anais Nin as his favorite living woman; Tatiana (from Pushkin's *Evgeny Onegin*) as his favorite fictional woman; Hieronymus Bosch, painter; Beethoven, musician; Kuprin, Malaparte, Faulkner, prose authors; Pushkin, W. H. Auden, poets; and Socrates as his favorite hero in history. He names Andrei Vishinsky (Stalin's public prosecutor) as the historical character whom he most despises. He added that he admired no military action and most admires self-imposed reform. Kosinski says that brown is his favorite color, the owl his favorite bird. Of the fits of nature he would choose quiescence and imperturbability for himself. He would like to die "not in nature's time but in my own." and considers his present state of mind to be "inconstant (as always).''

Kosinski's first non-fiction books were published pseudonymously in order to prevent the author from becoming involved in controversies which might have led to the interruption of his academic work at Columbia. In order to learn to write in English, Kosinski enlisted the aid of the telephone company. He would dial the operator, he told the *New York Times Book Review*, and ask her to explain difficult sentences. He says he "dialed zero, an endless series of zeroes, and zero was most helpful." Three years after his arrival in the United States he published his first book, in English. His swift and sure familiarization with the English language makes him reminiscent of another Pole, Joseph Conrad. *The Painted Bird* has been translated into thirty-eight languages, *Steps*, twenty-six, *Being There*, nineteen, *The Devil Tree*, eighteen, and *Cockpit*, eighteen. Kosinski recorded "Selected Readings from *The Painted Bird*," for CMS Records in 1967. Scenes from *Steps* were performed on television show "Critique," 1969. Kosinski is competent in Polish, French, and Russian; he reads Italian, Spanish, Portuguese, Ukranian, Ruthenian, and Esperanto. He travels at least six or seven months a year. *Avocational interests:* Skiing and photography.

BIOGRAPHICAL/CRITICAL SOURCES—Books: Carolyn Riley, editor, *Contemporary Literary Criticism*, Gale, Volume I, 1972, Volume II, 1974, Volume III, 1975; John Watson Aldridge, editor, *The Devil in the Fire: Retrospective Essays on American Literature and Culture, 1951-71*, Harper's Magazine Press, 1972; Joe D. Bellamy, editor, *The New Fiction: Interviews with Innovative American Writers*, University of Illinois Press, 1974; Jerome Klinkowitz, *Literary Disruptions: The Making of a Post-Contemporary American Fiction*, University of Illinois Press, 1975; Lawrence L. Langer, *Holocaust and the Literary Imagination*, Yale University Press, 1975.

Periodicals: *New York Times Book Review*, May 22, 1960, October 31, 1965, October 20, 1968, August 10, 1975; *Manchester Guardian*, October 21, 1960; *New Statesman*, October 22, 1960; *Harper's*, October, 1965, March, 1969; *Saturday Review*, November 13, 1965, April 17, 1971, April 24, 1971, March 11, 1972; *Book Week*, November 14, 1965; *Nation*, November 29, 1965; *National Review*, February 8, 1966; *Times Literary Supplement*, May 19, 1966; *Commentary*, June, 1966; *Commonweal*, July 1, 1966; *New York Times*, December 12, 1966; *New Leader*, October, 1968; *Time*, October 18, 1968, April 26, 1971; *New Republic*, October 26, 1968, June 26, 1971; *New York Review of Books*, February 27, 1969; *Listener*, May 8, 1969; *Denver Quarterly*, Autumn, 1969, Spring, 1971, Winter, 1973; *New York Post*, August 21, 1969, February 19, 1973; *Newsweek*, April 26, 1971, February 19, 1973; *Publishers Weekly*, April 26, 1971; *Washington Post*, August 30, 1971, March 25, 1973; *Paris Review*, Summer, 1972; *Centennial Review*, Winter, 1972; *Denver Post*, February 11, 1973; *Philadelphia Inquirer*, February 18, 1973; *North American Review*, Spring, 1973; *Los Angeles Times Calendar Magazine*, April 22, 1973; *Guardian*, June 25, 1973; *Fiction International*, Fall, 1973; *Media & Methods*, April, 1975; *Village Voice*, August 11, 1975.

* * *

KOSTKA, Edmund Karl 1915-

PERSONAL: Born October 1, 1915, in Rossberg, Germany; son of Karl (a miner) and Albina (Bannek) Kostka; married Bona de Panizza (a teacher), September 2, 1946; children: Victor, Carlo. *Education:* Attended University of Rome, 1945-47, and University of Kansas, 1947-48; Columbia University, M.A., 1951, Ph.D., 1961. *Home:* 838 Riverside Dr., New York, N.Y., 10032. *Office:* College of St. Elizabeth, Convent Station, N.J. 07961.

CAREER: Adelphi Academy, Brooklyn, N.Y., teacher of German and history, 1948-51; College of St. Elizabeth, Convent Station, N.J., 1951—, associate professor, 1961-68, professor of modern languages and comparative literature, 1968—. *Military service:* British Army, Artillery, 1942-47; became cadet officer; received Monte Cassino Cross and Star of Italy. *Member:* Modern Language Association of America, American Association of Teachers of German, Societe des Professeurs Francais en Amerique, Deutsches Theater.

WRITINGS: Schiller in Russian Literature, University of Pennsylvania Press, 1965; *Glimpses of Germanic-Slavic Relations: From Pushkin to Heinrich Mann*, Bucknell University Press, 1974. Contributor to literary journals in United States and abroad.

WORK IN PROGRESS: A book on Italian-German literary relations, proposed title, *Schiller in Italy*, completion expected in 1976.

SIDELIGHTS: As a native of a tri-lingual border region, Kostka developed an early interest in foreign languages, traditions, and customs, and a desire to understand the mentality of other nations. Kostka is competent in German, Russian, Italian, Polish, French, and Dutch.

* * *

KOTSCHEVAR, Lendal H(enry) 1908-

PERSONAL: Born June 12, 1908, in Noonan, N.D.; son of Henry Jacob and Anna (Belangue) Kotschevar; married Margaret Scoles, 1934; children: Julia Anne. *Education:* University of Washington, Seattle, B.A., 1934, B.S., 1946, M.A., 1948; Columbia University, Ph.D., 1954. *Home:* 3570 Villa Knolls Dr. N., Las Vegas; Nev. *Office:* College of Hotel Administration, University of Nevada, Las Vegas, Nev.

CAREER: Michigan State University, East Lansing, faculty member, 1958-68; United Nations, New York, N.Y., consultant in mass feeding, 1968-72; University of Nevada, Las Vegas, faculty member, 1972—. *Military service:* U.S. Naval Reserve, 1941-64; now commander (retired). *Member:* American Dietetic Association.

WRITINGS: Quantity Food Purchasing, Wiley, 1961; (with Margaret Terrell) *Food Service Planning*, Wiley, 1961; *Quantity Food Production*, McCutchan, 1964, 2nd edition, 1966; (with Donald Lundberg) *Understanding Cooking*, Gazette Publishing (Amherst, Mass.), 1965; (with Margaret Williams) *Understanding Foods*, Wiley, 1967; *Menu Management*, National Institute for the Foodservice Industry, 1975. Contributing and consulting editor, *Drive-In Management*; contributing editor, *Canadian Food Journal*.

WORK IN PROGRESS: Energy Concepts for the Foodservice Industry; Nutrition for Foodservice Workers; Wine and Beverage Management, with Gary Hotchkin; a second edtion, with Margaret Terrell, of *Food Service Planning*.

* * *

KOUSOULAS, D(imitrios) George 1923-

PERSONAL: Surname is pronounced *Koo*-soo-lass; born December 22, 1923, in Khalkis, Greece; son of George D. (a professional officer in Greek Army) and Barbara (Lachnidakis) Kousoulas; married Mary Katris, January 17, 1952; children: George. *Education:* University of Athens, LL.B., 1948; Syracuse University, M.A., 1953, Ph.D., 1956.

Home: 6252 Clearwood Rd., Bethesda, Md. 20034. *Office:* Department of Government, Howard University, Washington, D.C.

CAREER: Writer for U.S. Information Agency International Broadcasting Service, Washington, D.C., 1955-60; Howard University, Washington, D.C., assistant professor, 1960-64, associate professor, 1964-66, professor of government, 1967—, department chairman, 1967-70. Professorial lecturer on Soviet affairs at National War College and George Washington University, 1961-72. President of American Committee for Cyprus Self-determination, 1964-66. *Military service:* National Greek Army, 1948-50. *Member:* American Academy of Political and Social Science, Academy of Political Science, American Political Science Association. *Awards, honors:* Knight of the Gold Cross of the Royal Order of Phoenix; nominated for award of Academy of Athens for *The Price of Freedom*, 1955.

WRITINGS: The Price of Freedom: Greece in World Affairs, 1939-1953, Syracuse University Press, 1953; *Key to Economic Progress*, Ballantine, 1958; *Revolution and Defeat: The Story of the Greek Communist Party*, Oxford University Press, 1965; *On Government: A Comparative Analysis*, Wadsworth, 1968; *On Government and Politics*, Duxbury, 1971; *Modern Greece: Profile of a Nation*, Scribner, 1974. Writer of weekly column, "Letters from Washington," for *Athinaik* (Athens daily), 1955-59. Contributor to *Washington Post*.

SIDELIGHTS: Kousoulas is competent in French and Russian. *Key to Economic Progress* has been translated and published in twenty-one European, Asiatic, and African languages.

*   *   *

KOVEL, Ralph 1920-

PERSONAL: Surname is pronounced Cove-*el*; born August 20, 1920, in Milwaukee, Wis.; son of Lester (a clothing manufacturer) and Dorothy (Bernstein) Kovel; married Terry Horvitz (a writer), June 27, 1950; children: Lee Ralph, Kim (daughter). *Education:* Attended Ohio State University, 1939. *Home:* 22000 Shaker Blvd., Shaker Heights, Ohio 44122.

CAREER: Ralph M. Kovel and Associates (food brokers), Cleveland, Ohio, president, 1958—. Writer on antiques (with wife), 1952—, and joint columnist, "Know Your Antiques," Register and Tribune Syndicate, Des Moines, Iowa, 1954—. Also writer with wife of monthly newsletter, "Ralph and Terry Kovel on Antiques," 1974—. Short course instructor in American decorative arts, Western Reserve University (now Case Western Reserve University), 1958-63. President, East End Neighborhood House, Cleveland, Ohio, 1962-63. *Member:* Oakwood Club, Whitehill Club. *Awards, honors:* Cleveland Area Television Academy Award, 1971; National Antiques Show Annual Award, 1974.

WRITINGS—With wife, Terry Kovel, all published by Crown: *Dictionary of Marks: Pottery and Porcelain*, 1953; *Directory of American Silver Pewter and Silver Plate*, 1961; *American Country Furniture*, 1965; *Know Your Antiques*, 1967, revised edition, 1973; *Kovel's Complete Antiques Price List*, 1968-74; *The Official bottle Price List*, 1971, 1973; *The Kovel Collector's Guide to Limited Editions*, 1974; *The Kovel Book of American Art Pottery*, 1974. Also collaborator with wife in magazine articles on antiques.

KOVEL, Terry 1928-

PERSONAL: Surname is pronounced Cove-*el*; born October 27, 1928, in Cleveland, Ohio; daughter of Isadore (a publisher) and Rix (Osteryoung) Horvitz; married Ralph Kovel (a writer), June 27, 1950; children: Lee, Kim (daughter). *Education:* Wellesley College, B.A., 1950; University of Illinois, graduate study, 1961. *Home:* 22000 Shaker Blvd., Shaker Heights, Ohio 44122.

CAREER: Teacher in Lyndhurst, Ohio, 1959-72, writer on antiques, in collaboration with husband, 1952—, and joint columnist, "Know Your Antiques," Register and Tribune Syndicate, Des Moines, Iowa, 1954—. Cleveland College, Western Reserve University, Cleveland, Ohio, short course instructor in American decorative arts, 1958-63. Writer with husband of monthly newsletter, "Ralph and Terry Kovel on Antiques," 1974—. *Member:* Ohio Newspaper Womens Association.

WRITINGS—With husband, Ralph Kovel, all published by Crown: *Dictionary of Marks: Pottery and Porcelain*, 1953; *Directory of American Silver Pewter and Silver Plate*, 1961; *American Country Furniture*, 1965; *Know Your Antiques*, 1967, revised edition, 1973; *Kovel's Complete Antiques Price List*, 1968-74; *The Official Bottle Price List*, 1971, 1973; *The Kovel Collector's Guide to Limited Editions*, 1974; *The Kovel Book of American Art Pottery*, 1974. Contributor to magazines.

*   *   *

KRANIDAS, Kathleen Collins 1931-

PERSONAL: Surname is pronounced Kra-*nee*-das; born January 30, 1931, in Seattle, Wash.; daughter of Edward D. and Myrtle (Munson) Collins; married Thomas Kranidas (a professor), October 5, 1951 (divorced, 1974); children: Stephen Bruce, Thomas Theodore, Anne Frederica, Mary Caroline. *Education:* Barnard College, B.A., 1952; State University of New York, Stony Brook, M.A., 1974. *Politics:* Democrat. *Religion:* "Non-affiliated." *Agent:* Patricia Schartle, McIntosh & Otis, Inc., 18 East 41st St., New York, N.Y. 10017. *Office:* Northport High School, Northport, N.Y.

CAREER: Northport High School, Northport, N.Y., teacher of writing.

WRITINGS: One Year in Autumn, Lippincott, 1965.

WORK IN PROGRESS: A novel; a group of stories set in Athens; a guidebook for teaching the writing of poetry to children.

SIDELIGHTS: Ms. Kranidas lived for a year in Athens, Greece.

*   *   *

KRAUSS, Robert M. 1931-

PERSONAL; Born August 19, 1931, in Newark, N.J.; son of Milton B. (a salesman) and May (Temkin) Krauss; married Iseli Koenig, September 1, 1957 (divorced, July 7, 1970); children: Pamela, Erika. *Education:* New York University, B.A., 1955, Ph.D., 1964. *Home:* 560 Riverside Drive, New York, N.Y. 10027. *Office:* Department of Psychology, Columbia University, New York, N.Y.

CAREER: Bell Telephone Laboratories, Murray Hill, N.J., social psychologist on technical staff, 1958-65; Princeton University, Princeton, N.J., assistant professor of psychology, 1966-67; Harvard University, Cambridge, Mass., visiting lecturer in department of social relations,

1967-68; Rutgers University, New Brunswick, N.J., associate professor of psychology, 1968-70; Columbia University, New York, N.Y., professor of psychology, 1970—. Visiting scientist, Bell Telephone Laboratories, Inc., 1974. *Member:* American Association for the Advancement of Science, American Psychological Association, Eastern Psychological Association. *Awards, honors:* Winner with Morton Deutsch of meritorious essay award in socio-psychological inquiry, American Association for the Advancement of Science, 1961, for "Studies in Interpersonal Bargaining."

WRITINGS: (With Morton Deutsch) *Theories in Social Psychology*, Basic Books, 1965. Editor, *Journal of Experimental Social Psychology*, 1970-75. Senior consultant, Time-Life Books series on human behavior, 1972—.

WORK IN PROGRESS: A book with working title, *The Social Psychology of Communication.*

*   *   *

KRAVIS, Irving B(ernard) 1916-

PERSONAL: Born August 30, 1916, in Philadelphia, Pa.; son of Nathan and Ethel (Gelgood) Kravis; married Lillian Panzer (a physician), June 22, 1941; children: Robert, Marcia, Ellen, Nathan. *Education:* University of Pennsylvania, B.S., 1938, A.M., 1940, Ph.D., 1947. *Home:* 438 Warick Rd., Wynnewood, Pa. 19096. *Office:* Department of Economics, University of Pennsylvania, Philadelphia, Pa. 19104.

CAREER: U.S. Department of Labor, economist, 1946-48; University of Massachusetts, Amherst, associate professor of economics, 1948-49; University of Pennsylvania, Philadelphia, assistant professor of economics, 1949-53, associate professor, 1953-56, professor, 1956—, chairman of department of economics, 1955-58, 1962-67, associate dean, Wharton School of Finance and Commerce, 1958-60. Summer professor at University of Southern California and Harvard University. Member of senior staff, National Bureau of Economic Research, 1962—; consultant to Department of State, and other government departments, and to the United Nations. *Military service:* U.S. Army Air Forces, 1942-46; became lieutenant; received Bronze Star.

MEMBER: American Economic Association, Royal Economic Society (England). *Awards, honors:* Ford Foundation faculty research fellowship, 1960-61; grant from Social Science Research Council, 1961; Guggenheim fellowship, 1967-68.

WRITINGS: (Co-author) *An International Comparison of National Products and the Purchasing Power of Currencies*, Organization for European Economic Cooperation, 1954; *The Structure of Income: Some Quantitative Essays*, University of Pennsylvania Consumer Expenditures Study, 1962; *Domestic Interests and International Obligations: A Study of Trade Safeguards*, University of Pennsylvania Press, 1963; (co-author) *Price Competitiveness in World Trade*, National Bureau of Economic Research, 1971.

Contributor: *Manpower in the United States*, edited by I. Haber and others, Harper, 1954; *Income and Wealth*, edited by M. Gilbert and R. Stone, International Association for Research in Income and Wealth (London), 1954; *Consumer Behavior*, edited by L. N. Clark, Harper, 1958. Contributor to *Encyclopaedia Britannica* and professional journals.

KREINDLER, Lee (Stanley) 1924-

PERSONAL: Born March 11, 1924, in New York, N.Y.; son of Harry E. (a lawyer) and Doris (Barsky) Kreindler; married Ruth Bilgrei, September 1, 1952; children: James Paul, Laurie Jane. *Education:* Dartmouth College, A.B., 1947; Harvard University, LL.B., 1949. *Politics:* Democrat. *Religion:* Jewish. *Home:* 25 McKesson Hill Rd., Chappaqua, N.Y. *Office:* 99 Park Ave., New York, N.Y. 10016.

CAREER: Admitted to New York Bar, 1949, and to practice before U.S. Supreme Court and U.S. Court of Appeals; Kreindler & Kreindler (attorneys), New York, N.Y., partner, 1949—, specializing in aviation crash law and litigation growing out of airline, military, and private plane accidents. Lecturer on air law at universities and to legal groups. Member of national panel, American Arbitration Association. *Military service:* U.S. Army, 1942-45. *Member:* International Academy of Trial Lawyers (fellow), American Bar Association, American Trial Lawyers Association, American Institute of Aeronautics and Astronautics, Federal Bar Association, New York State Bar Association, New York County Lawyers Association (vice-chairman, aeronautical law committee), and bar and trial lawyers associations of New York City.

WRITINGS: Aviation Accident Law, two volumes, Bender, 1963, revised edition, 1973; (editor with others) *The Belgrade Spaceship Trial*, World Peace Through Law Center, 1972. Contributor of articles on air and tort law to legal journals.

*   *   *

KRIEGER, Leonard 1918-

PERSONAL: Born August 28, 1918, in Newark, N.J.; son of Isidore (a builder) and Jennie (Glinn) Krieger; married Esther Smith, August 13, 1949; children: Alan Davis, David Jonathan, Nathaniel Richard. *Education:* Rutgers University, B.A., 1938; Yale University, M.A., 1942, Ph.D., 1949. *Office:* University of Chicago, 1126 East 59th St., Chicago, Ill. 60637.

CAREER: U.S. Department of State, Washington, D.C., political analyst, 1946; Yale University, New Haven, Conn., instructor in history, 1948-50, assistant professor, 1950-55, associate professor, 1955-61, professor of history, 1961-62; University of Chicago, Chicago, Ill., professor of history, 1962-69; Columbia University, New York, N.Y., professor of history, 1969-72; University of Chicago, Chicago, Ill., University professor of history, 1972—. Fellow, Center for Advanced Study in the Behavioral Sciences, 1956-57; member, Institute for Advanced Study, 1963, 1969-70. Visiting lecturer at Northwestern University, 1950, Brandeis University, 1958, Columbia University, 1960-61, Stanford University, 1968. *Military service:* U.S. Army, 1942-46; became first lieutenant. *Member:* American Historical Association (chairman of program committee, 1960; chairman of committee on research needs, 1963-64), American Society for Political and Legal Philosophy, International Society for the History of Ideas.

WRITINGS: The German Idea of Freedom, Beacon, 1957; *The Politics of Discretion*, University of Chicago Press, 1965; (with John Higham and Felix Gilbert) *History*, Prentice-Hall, 1965; (editor with Fritz Stern) *The Responsibility of Power*, Doubleday, 1967; *Kings and Philosophers, 1689-1789*, Norton, 1970; *Essay on the Theory of Enlightened Despotism*, University of Chicago Press, 1975. Contributor to *American Historical Review, Journal of the His-*

tory of Ideas, Journal of Modern History, Political Science Quarterly, and *Public Policy*. Consulting editor, "Great Ages of Man" series, Time/Life Books, 1964—.

WORK IN PROGRESS: Ranke: An Historiographical Essay; History of the Modern State; Ideas and Events.

SIDELIGHTS: Kreiger told *CA*, "I write and teach on the basis of two related beliefs; that history should be studied to illuminate universal problems still with us; and that because history provides one of the fundamental perspectives upon human reality it can illuminate universal problems still with us."

* * *

KRIMERMAN, Leonard Isaiah 1934-

PERSONAL: Born September 27, 1934; in New York, N.Y.; son of Samuel (a businessman) and Mina (Fields) Krimerman; married Eleano Jones (a medical student), June 15, 1962. *Education:* Cornell University, A.B., 1955, Ph.D., 1964. *Office:* Department of Philosophy, University of Connecticut, Storrs, Conn. 06268.

CAREER: Louisiana State University, New Orleans, instructor, 1961-64, assistant professor of philosophy, 1965-68; University of Connecticut, Storrs, associate professor of philosophy, 1968—. Coordinator, Free School of New Orleans. Member, Carnegie Foundation Summer Institute in Philosophy, 1966. *Military service:* U.S. Army, Quartermaster Corps, 1955-57; became first lieutenant. *Member:* Southwestern Philosophical Association, Southern Society for Philosophy and Psychology, Phi Beta Kappa. *Awards, honors:* American Philosophical Society grant, 1965-66.

WRITINGS: (Editor with Lewis Perry) *Patterns of Anarchy*, Anchor Books, 1966; (editor) *The Nature and Scope of Social Science: A Critical Anthology*, Appleton, 1969; (compiler with Harry S. Broudy) *Philosophy of Educational Research*, Wiley, 1973. Contributor to philosophy journals.

WORK IN PROGRESS: A three-volume work, *A Programmed Introduction to Logic*, for Chandler Publishing; *A Bakunin Reader*, with original essays on anarchism and the New Left.†

* * *

KRIPKE, Dorothy Karp

PERSONAL: Born in Highland Falls, N.Y.; daughter of Max Samuel (a rabbi) and Goldie (Mereminsky) Karp; married Myer S. Kripke (a rabbi), June 13, 1937; children: Saul A., Madeline F., Netta E. *Education:* Hunter College (now of the City University of New York), B.A., 1932; Columbia University, M.A., 1935; Jewish Theological Seminary of America, B.H.L., 1935. *Religion:* Jewish. *Home:* 119 North Happy Hollow Blvd., Omaha, Neb. 68132.

CAREER: High School English teacher in New York, N.Y., 1936-37. Hebrew and religion teacher. Lecturer. *Member:* National Women's League of the United Synagogue of America (past vice-president).

WRITINGS: Rhymes to Play, Bloch Publishing, 1952; *Rhymes to Pray*, Bloch Publishing, 1952; *Let's Talk About God*, Behrman, 1953; *Let's Talk About Right and Wrong*, Behrman, 1955; *Let's Talk About Judaism*, Behrman, 1957; *Debbie in Dreamland*, National Women's League, 1960; (with Meyer Levin) *God and the Story of Judaism*, Behrman, 1962; *Children's Books: A Bibliography*, American Jewish Historical Society, 1962; *Let's Talk About the*

Jewish Holidays, Jonathan David, 1970. Writer of scripts for National Women's League and United Synagogue of America. Contributor to *Jewish Book Annual*, 1960 and 1961. Also contributor to *Outlook* and *The Jewish Child*.

* * *

KROETSCH, Robert 1927-

PERSONAL: Born June 26, 1927, in Heisler, Alberta, Canada; son of Paul (a farmer) and Hilda (Weller) Kroetsch; married Mary Jane Lewis, January 13, 1956; children: Laura Caroline, Margaret Ann. *Education:* University of Alberta, B.A., 1948; McGill University, graduate study, 1954-55; Middlebury College, M.A., 1956; University of Iowa, Ph.D., 1961. *Home:* 48 Lathrop Ave., Binghamton, N.Y. 13905. *Agent:* Raines & Raines, 244 Madison Ave., New York, N.Y. 10016. *Office:* State University of New York, Binghamton, N.Y.

CAREER: Yellowknife Transportation Co. (riverboats), Northwest Territories, Canada, laborer and purser, 1948-50; U.S. Air Force, Goose Bay, Labrador, information and education specialist (as civilian), 1951-54; State University of New York at Binghamton, assistant professor, 1961-65, associate professor, 1965-68, professor of English, 1968—. *Member:* Modern Language Association of America, American Association of University Professors. *Awards, honors:* Fellowship to Bread Loaf Writers' Conference, 1966; Governor General's Award for fiction, 1969.

WRITINGS: But We Are Exiles (novel), St. Martin's, 1966; *The Words of My Roaring* (novel), St. Martin's, 1966; *The Studhorse Man* (novel), Simon & Schuster, 1970; *Gone Indian* (novel), New Press, 1973.

WORK IN PROGRESS: A fifth novel.

BIOGRAPHICAL/CRITICAL SOURCES: Carolyn Riley, editor, *Contemporary Literary Criticism*, Volume V, Gale, 1976.

* * *

KROSNEY, Mary Stewart 1939-

PERSONAL: Born August 19, 1939, in Shreveport, La.; daughter of Philip Dewitt (a petroleum engineer) and Mary (Calder) Baker; married Herbert Krosney (a writer and television producer); children: Ellen Calder, Andrew Bernard. *Education:* Attended Wheaton College, Norton, Mass., 1957-59; University of North Carolina, B.A., 1961. *Politics:* Registered Democrat. *Religion:* "Reared Episcopalian, now maintain a Jewish home."

CAREER: Formerly, reporter for *Shreveport Times*, Shreveport, La., and guide at United Nations Headquarters, New York, N.Y.; teacher of English.

WRITINGS: (With husband, Herbert Krosney) *Careers and Opportunities in International Service*, Dutton, 1965.†

* * *

KRULIK, Stephen 1933-

PERSONAL: Born May 1, 1933, in Brooklyn, N.Y.; son of Max and Sadie Krulik; married Gladys Olshan, December, 1959; children: Nancy, Jeffry. *Education:* Brooklyn College (now Brooklyn College of the City University of New York), B.A., 1954; Columbia University, M.A., 1955, Ed.D., 1961.

CAREER: New York (N.Y.) Board of Education, teacher, 1954—. Educational consultant to Anti-Poverty Program. *Member:* Phi Delta Kappa, Kappa Delta Pi, Pi Mu Epsilon.

WRITINGS: (With Irwin Kaufman) *Multi-Sensory Techniques in Mathematics Teaching*, Prentice-Hall, 1963; (with Kaufman) *High School Geometry Review Notes*, Monarch, 1964; (with Kaufman and Jerome Shostak) *The Handbook of College Entrance Examinations*, Pocket Books, 1965; (with Kaufman) *Elementary Algebra: High School Level*, Monarch, 1965; (with Kaufman) *How to Use the Overhead Projector in Mathematics Education* (booklet), National Council of Teachers of Mathematics, 1966; (with Kaufman and Shostak) *The Civil Service Examination Handbook*, New American Library, 1970; *A Handbook of Aids for Teaching Junior-Senior High School Mathematics*, Saunders, 1971; *A Mathematics Laboratory Handbook for Secondary Schools*, Saunders, 1972; (with Ingrid B. Weise) *Teaching Secondary School Mathematics*, Saunders, 1975. Contributor to journals.†

* * *

KRYTHE, Maymie Richardson

PERSONAL: Born in Springfield, Ohio; daughter of William Schillinger (a mechanic) and Jane Isabel (Young) Richardson; married Gerard Krythe; children: Martha Elteen (Mrs. Albert J. Kirschbaum). *Education:* Wittenberg University, A.B.; graduate study at University of Jena, University of Berlin, University of Chicago, and also at other American universities; University of Southern California, A.M. *Politics:* Democrat. *Religion:* Methodist.

CAREER: High school teacher of English and German in Springfield, Ohio, in Alamosa, Colo., and in Long Beach, Calif., until 1948; full-time writer. *Member:* Authors Guild of the Authors League of America, California Historical Society, California Writers Guild, Historical Society of Southern California, Long Beach Historical Society, Delta Kappa Gamma, Long Beach Writers Club. *Awards, honors:* Golden Apple Award, 1965.

WRITINGS: All About Christmas, Harper, 1954; *The Port Admiral: Phineas Banning*, California Historical Society, 1957; *All About American Holidays*, Harper, 1962; *All About the Months*, Harper, 1966; *What So Proudly We Hail: All About Our American Flag*, Harper, 1968; *Sampler of American Songs*, Harper, 1969. Contributor of more than seven hundred articles to magazines.

AVOCATIONAL INTERESTS: Art, photography, music, theater, travel.†

* * *

KUBECK, James (Ernest) 1920-

PERSONAL: Surname is pronounced *Cue*-beck; born March 14, 1920, in Sioux Falls, S.D.; son of Ernest J. (an attorney) and Nannie Mae (Huguley) Kubeck; married Marinette Durgin, July 12, 1947; children: Evan James. *Education:* University of California, Los Angeles, A.B., 1948, M.S., 1952. *Home:* 20674 Rockpoint Rd., Malibu, Calif. 90265.

CAREER: University of California Press, Los Angeles, 1952—, senior editor, 1961-66, managing editor, 1966-73, sponsoring editor, 1973—. *Wartime service:* U.S. Merchant Marine, 1943-46. *Member:* Kappa Tau Alpha.

WRITINGS: The Calendar Epic (novel), Putnam, 1956; *The Monument* (novel), McNally & Loftin, 1965.

AVOCATIONAL INTERESTS: Art, music, and travel (has traveled in Central and South America, West Indies, China, Korea, Japan, Southeast Asia, Canada, Australia, Europe and islands of the North and South Pacific).

BIOGRAPHICAL/CRITICAL SOURCES: This World, September 16, 1956.

* * *

KUEHL, Warren F(rederick) 1924-

PERSONAL: Surname is pronounced Keel; born June 14, 1924, in Bettendorf, Iowa; son of Gustav F. and Elsie I. (Dobler) Kuehl; married Olga Llano (a pianist), September 7, 1950; children: Marshall Reed, Paul Bennett. *Education:* Rollins College, B.A., 1949; Northwestern University, M.A., 1951, Ph.D., 1954. *Home:* 590 Rotunda Ave., Akron, Ohio 44313.

CAREER: Ohio University, Athens, instructor in history, 1955; Rockford College, Rockford, Ill., assistant professor of history, 1955-58; Mississippi State University, State College, associate professor, 1958-61, professor of history, 1961-64; University of Akron, Akron, Ohio, professor of history, 1964—, chairman of department, 1964-71, director, Center for Peace Studies, 1970—. Visiting summer professor at Northwestern University, 1963, Duke University, 1964, University of North Carolina, 1965, Case Western Reserve University, 1968. *Member:* American Historical Association, Society for Historians of American Foreign Policy (joint executive secretary-treasurer, 1974—), Organization of American Historians, Southern Historical Association, Phi Kappa Phi. *Awards, honors:* Ohio Academy of History Award, 1969; L.H.D., Rollins College, 1970.

WRITINGS: (Editor) *Blow the Man Down!*, Dutton, 1959; *Hamilton Holt: Journalist, Internationalist, Educator*, University of Florida Press, 1960; *Dissertations in History, 1873-1960*, University of Kentucky Press, 1965; *Seeking World Order: The United States and International Organization to 1920*, Vanderbilt University Press, 1969; *Dissertations in History, 1961-1970*, University Press of Kentucky, 1972. Contributor to *Notable American Women*, Harvard University Press, 1972; *Dictionary of the History of Ideas, III*, Scribner, 1973; *Dictionary of American Biography*, Scribner, 1973.

WORK IN PROGRESS: A second volume of *The United States and International Organization* to cover 1920-1941; *Man's Quest for Peace*; general editor, *Library of World Peace Studies*, for Clearwater Publishing; *Internationalism: Its History and Development*, for Clio.

* * *

KUENZLI, Alfred E(ugene) 1923-

PERSONAL: Surname is pronounced Kinzli; born July 24, 1923, in Springfield, Ohio; son of Irvin R. and Esther Kuenzli; married Corinne DeLuca (a research associate), June 12, 1951; children: John, Linda, Grant. *Education:* Ohio University, A.B. and M.A., 1951; Indiana University, Ed.D., 1953. *Politics:* Democrat. *Religion:* Unitarian Universalist. *Home:* 512 North Main St., Edwardsville, Ill. 62025. *Office:* Southern Illinois University, Edwardsville, Ill. 62025.

CAREER: Harvard University, Cambridge, Mass., visiting fellow in social relations, 1953-54; State University of New York at Albany, assistant professor of psychology, 1954-56; Wisconsin State University, River Falls, associate professor of psychology, 1956-58; Southern Illinois University, Edwardsville Campus, 1958—, began as associate professor, professor of psychology, 1962—. Visiting professor, University of Puerto Rico, 1966-67. Consultant on anti-poverty programs in Illinois and Mississippi, 1965-66. *Mili-*

tary service: U.S. Marine Corps, 1942-44. *Member:* American Psychological Association (fellow), American Humanist Association (board, 1961), American Association of University Professors, Society for the Psychological Study of Social Issues, American Civil Liberties Union, Committee for World Development and World Disarmament, Congress of Racial Equality, National Association for the Advancement of Colored People, Phi Delta Kappa.

WRITINGS: The Phenomenological Problem, Harper, 1959; *Reconstruction in Religion*, Beacon, 1961. Contributor to *Psychological Abstracts*, 1952-62, and to proceedings of American Psychological Association, American Sociological Association, and National Society of College Teachers of Education; contributor of more than forty articles and reviews to magazines and journals. Editor, *Technical Data Digest*, 1948-49; associate editor, *Journal of Conflict Resolution*, 1957-62; contributing editor, *Humanist*, 1961-62.

WORK IN PROGRESS: A book on perceptual psychology.

SIDELIGHTS: Kuenzli is competent in Spanish. He lived in Puerto Rico, 1965-66.†

* * *

KUHLMAN, John M(elville) 1923-

PERSONAL: Born June 25, 1923, in Lamont, Wash.; son of Oscar W. and Amy (Melville) Kuhlman; married Mary Ann Sigley, 1950; children: Ann, Kay, John, Jr. *Education:* Washington State University, B.A., 1948; University of Wisconsin, M.S., 1949, Ph.D., 1953. *Home:* 205 Bittersweet Ct., Columbia, Mo. 65201.

CAREER: University of Wisconsin, Wausau, instructor in economics, 1951-53; University of Richmond, Richmond, Va., assistant professor of economics, 1953-55; University of Cincinnati, Cincinnati, Ohio, assistant professor, 1955-59, associate professor of economics, 1959-61; University of Missouri, Columbia, professor of economics, 1961—. Consultant to business and government organizations. *Military service:* U.S. Army, 1943-46. *Member:* American Economic Association, Midwest Economic Association, Southern Economic Association, Southwestern Social Science Association. *Awards, honors:* Ford Foundation fellowship, Stanford University, 1959-60.

WRITINGS: (With Gordon S. Skinner) *The Economic System*, Irwin, 1959, 2nd edition, 1964; (compiler) *Economic Problems and Policies*, Goodyear Publishing, 1969, 2nd edition, 1973; *Studying Economics*, Goodyear Publishing, 1972; (editor with Louis J. Mensonides) *The Future of Inter-Bloc Relations in Europe*, Praeger, 1974. Contributor of articles to professional journals.†

* * *

KURTZ, Harold 1913-

PERSONAL: Born September 2, 1913, in Stuttgart, Germany; son of Hermann (a publisher) and Marguerite (Don-Wauchope) Kurtz. *Education:* Attended schools in Germany, and University of Geneva, 1935-36. *Politics:* Liberal. *Religion:* Protestant. *Home:* 19 Holywell, Oxford, England. *Agent:* John Johnson, 79 Davies St., London W.C. 1, England.

CAREER: Full-time writer.

WRITINGS: The Trial of Marshal Newy, Knopf, 1957; *The Empress Eugenie*, Houghton, 1964; (translator) Vic-

tor De Pange, editor, *Unpublished Correspondence of Madame De Staal and the Duke of Wellington*, Fernhill, 1968; *The Second Reich: Kaiser Wilhelm II and his Germany*, American Heritage Press, 1970. Writer of radio scripts; contributor of articles and reviews to *History Today* and other journals.

WORK IN PROGRESS: Fouche.†

* * *

KURZWEG, Bernhard F. 1926-

PERSONAL: Surname is pronounced Kurts-weg; born December 28, 1926, in Rollingstone, Minn.; son of Carl Frederick (a minister) and Flora C. (Wienke) Kurzweg; married Barbara Faye Reinhardt, April 8, 1953; children: David Michael, John Philip, Steven Paul, Ann Marie. *Education:* Concordia College, St. Paul, Minn., A.A., 1945; Concordia Lutheran Seminary, St. Louis, Mo., B.D., 1951, S.T.M., 1952; also studied at University of Texas, 1949-50, Valparaiso University, 1951, San Francisco State College (now University), 1958, Pacific Lutheran Seminary, 1959, Union Theological Seminary, New York, N.Y., 1961-63. *Home:* 3130 Cabot Rd., Tallahassee, Fla. 32303. *Office:* Epiphany Lutheran Church, 3208 Thomasville Rd., Tallahassee, Fla. 32303.

CAREER: Ordained Lutheran minister, 1951. Concordia College, Austin, Tex., teacher of music and Greek, 1948-50; pastor in New Orleans, La., 1952-56, San Francisco, Calif., 1956-61; Concordia Theological Seminary, Springfield, Ill., assistant professor of homiletics, 1961-65; pastor in Richmond, Va., 1965-74, and Tallahassee, Fla., 1974—.

WRITINGS: The World That Is, Concordia, 1965.

WORK IN PROGRESS: "Aspects of Biblical Interpretation in Missouri Synod Lutheran Preaching," for Union Theological Seminary, New York.

AVOCATIONAL INTERESTS: Choral work.

* * *

KWAN, Kian M(oon) 1929-

PERSONAL: Born June 15, 1929, in Canton, China; son of J. C. and Tak Q. (Mar) Kawn; married Grace Lo, 1961; children: Joseph Homen, Gregory Lipmen, Christine Faye. *Education:* Far Eastern University, Manila, Philippines, B.A. (magna cum laude), 1952; University of California, Berkeley, M.A., 1954, Ph.D., 1958. *Religion:* Roman Catholic. *Home:* 8512 Chimineas Ave., Northridge, Calif. 91324. *Office:* Department of Sociology, California State University, Northridge, Calif. 91324.

CAREER: Ohio University, Athens, instructor, 1958-61, assistant professor of sociology, 1961-65, chairman of department of sociology and anthropology, 1963-65; California State University Northridge, associate professor, 1965-69, professor of sociology, 1969—, chairman of department, 1969-71. Visiting professor, University of Hawaii, 1972-73. *Member:* American Sociological Association (fellow).

WRITINGS: (With Tamotsu Shibutani) *Ethnic Stratification: A Comparative Approach*, Macmillan, 1965. Contributor to professional journals.

WORK IN PROGRESS: Sojourners and Citizens: The Chinese in American Society.

* * *

LACE, O(live) Jessie 1906-

PERSONAL: Born May 24, 1906, in Sheffield, Yorkshire,

England; daughter of Oswald Herbert (a schoolmaster) and Alice Mary (Field) Lace. *Education:* St. Hugh's College, Oxford, M.A., 1928; University of Manchester, B.D., 1948. *Home:* 4 Brookside, Hook Norton, Banbury OX15 5NS, England.

CAREER: Teacher of mathematics at St. Catherine's School, Bramley, Surrey, England, 1929-36, and St. Margaret's School, Bushey, Hertfordshire, England, 1936-40; Langdale Hall, Manchester, England, warden, 1941-47; William Temple College, Rugby, Warwickshire, England, lecturer and tutor in Biblical studies, 1948-53, senior lecturer and tutor, 1954-68. *Member:* Society for Old Testament Study.

WRITINGS: Why Do We Teach Christianity?, S.P.C.K., 1957; *Teaching the Old Testament*, Seabury, 1960; *Teaching the New Testament*, Seabury, 1961; (editor) *Understanding the New Testament*, Cambridge University Press, 1965; (editor) *Understanding the Old Testament*, Cambridge University Press, 1972.

* * *

LACY, Eric Russell 1933-

PERSONAL: Born October 2, 1933, in Johnson City, Tenn.; son of Leland Ernest (a clothier) and Beatrice (Russell) Lacy; married Barbara Fields, July 3, 1961; children: Eric Russell, Jr., Joseph Flinn. *Education:* East Tennessee State University, B.S., 1955, M.A., 1960; University of Georgia, Ph.D., 1963. *Office:* Department of History, East Tennessee State University, Johnson City, Tenn. 37601.

CAREER: Senier Theatre Corp., Johnson City, Tenn., manager, 1950-53; junior high school teacher, later assistant principal, Kingsport, Tenn., 1957-61; Tennessee Wesleyan College, Athens, associate professor of history, 1963-64; East Tennessee State University, Johnson City, assistant professor of history, 1964-65; University of Georgia, Athens, assistant professor of history, 1965-68; East Tennessee State University, Johnson City, Associate professor, 1968-70, professor of history, 1970—, director of American Studies Program, 1970-72. Lecturer at University of Georgia, 1967 and 1968. *Military service:* U.S. Army, Adjutant General's Corps, 1955-57; became first lieutenant. *Awards, honors:* Moore Award for best article in *Tennessee Historical Quarterly*, 1964.

WRITINGS: Vanquished Volunteers: East Tennessee Sectionalism from Statehood to Secession, East Tennessee State University Press, 1965; (editor) *Readings on Historical Method*, MSS Educational Publishing, 1969; (compiler) *Antebellum Tennessee: A Documentary History*, McCuthan, 1969.

WORK IN PROGRESS: A book on race relations in Tennessee, 1870-1900.†

* * *

LACY, Mary Lou (Pannill) 1914-

PERSONAL: Born November 4, 1914, in Mayodan, N.C.; daughter of William Letcher (a textile manufacturer) and Adele (Dillard) Pannill; married Frank McCormick Lacy (president of Lacy Manufacturing Co.), September 11, 1937; children: Margaret Adele (Mrs. Francis Marshall James), Mary Lou (Mrs. Richard Whitt Critz), Frank M., Jr. *Education:* Randolph-Macon Woman's College, A.B., 1935; University of North Carolina, graduate study, 1935. *Religion:* Presbyterian. *Home:* 1234 Sam Lions Trail, Martinsville, Va. 24112.

CAREER: Lacy Manufacturing Co. (textiles), Martinsville, Va., secretary, 1950—. Active in women's work of Presbyterian Church and speaker to other denominations.

WRITINGS: The Pullers of the Star, John Knox, 1954; *A Woman Wants God*, John Knox, 1959; *And God Wants People*, John Knox, 1962; *Springboard to Discovery*, John Knox, 1965. ƒWriter of musical plays for local community theater; contributor to *Presbyterian Survey.*†

* * *

LADENSON, Alex 1907-

PERSONAL: Born September 25, 1907, in Russia; son of Nathan and Bertha (Schoenheit) Ladenson; married Inez Sher (a teacher), August 14, 1938; children: Mark, Robert. *Education:* Northwestern University, B.S., 1929, J.D., 1932; University of Chicago, M.A., 1935, Ph.D., 1938. *Religion:* Jewish. *Home:* 6517 North Artesian Ave., Chicago, Ill. 60645. *Office:* Chicago Public Library, 78 East Washington St., Chicago, Ill. 60602.

CAREER: Admitted to Illinois Bar, 1929. Chicago Public Library, Chicago, Ill., executive assistant, 1943-44, assistant librarian, acquisitions and preparations department, 1944-67, acting chief librarian, 1967-70, chief librarian, 1970—. Rosary College, River Forest, Ill., lecturer in department of library science. Illinois State Library, chairman of advisory committee. *Member:* American Library Association (chairman of constitution and bylaws committee, 1953-54), Illinois Library Association (president, 1959-60), Chicago Library Club (president, 1950-51). *Awards, honors:* Librarian Citation Award, Illinois Library Association, 1965; Doctor of Letters, Rosary College, 1968.

WRITINGS: (With others) *Subject Analysis of Library Materials*, School of Library Service, Columbia University, 1953; (editor) *American Library Laws*, 4th edition, American Library Association, 1973, *Supplement*, 1965, 1967, 1969, 1971; (with others) *The Library Trustee*, Bowker, 1969.

WORK IN PROGRESS: A book on library government and legislation.

* * *

LAKEY, George (Russell) 1937-

PERSONAL: Born November 2, 1937, in Bangor, Pa.; son of Russell George (a slate-splitter) and Dora (Shook) Lakey; married Berit Mathiesen, June 27, 1959; children: Esther Christina, Peter George, Liv Ingrid. *Education:* Attended West Chester State College, 1955-58, University of Oslo, 1959-60; Cheyney State College, B.S. in Ed., 1961; University of Pennsylvania, M.A., 1963. *Politics:* "Democratic nonviolent radical." *Religion:* Society of Friends. *Home:* 4719 Springfield Ave., Philadelphia, Pa. 19143. *Office:* Friends Peace Committee, 1515 Cherry St., Philadelphia, Pa. 19102.

CAREER: Part-time work with American Friends Service Committee, Philadelphia, Pa., 1958-59, 1960-61; high school teacher of English and music in Oslo, Norway, 1959-60; Friends Peace Committee, Philadelphia, Pa., executive director, 1963-65; Upland Institute, Chester, Pa., instructor in sociology, 1965-69; lecturer in Great Britain, 1969-70; A Quaker Action Group, Philadelphia, Pa., executive director, 1970-71; lecturer in U.S. and abroad, 1971-73; Friends Peace Committee, Philadelphia, Pa., peace conversion coordinator, 1973—. *Member:* Fellowship of Reconciliation, War Resisters League, Friends Peace Committee, Movement for a New Society.

WRITINGS: (With Martin Oppenheimer) *A Manual for Direct Action*, Quadrangle, 1965; (co-author) *In Place of War*, Grossman, 1967; *The Sociological Mechanisms of Nonviolent Action*, Canadian Peace Research Institute, 1968; *Strategy for a Living Revolution*, Grossman, 1973; (co-author) *Moving Toward a New Society*, New Society Press, 1974. Contributor to *Friends Journal, Win Magazine*.

WORK IN PROGRESS: Research in cultural aspects of nonviolent movements.

SIDELIGHTS: Lakey is a member of working party "producting strategic plan for nonviolent defense of the nation."

* * *

LAMAR, Howard R(oberts) 1923-

PERSONAL: Born November 18, 1923, in Tuskegee, Ala.; son of John Howard (a planter) and Elma (Roberts) Lamar; married Shirley White, September 3, 1959; children: Susan Kent, Sarah Howard. *Education:* Emory University, B.A., 1944; Yale University, M.A., 1945, Ph.D., 1951. *Religion:* Protestant. *Office:* 237 Hall of Graduate Studies, Yale University, New Haven, Conn.

CAREER: Instructor in history at University of Massachusetts, Amherst, 1945-46, and Wesleyan University, Middletown, Conn., 1948-49; Yale University, New Haven, Conn., instructor, 1949-54, assistant professor, 1954-57, associate professor, 1957-64, professor of American history, 1964—, chairman of department, 1962-63, 1967-70, director of graduate studies in history, 1964-67, director of humanities division, 1972-74. City of New Haven, alderman, 1951-53. *Member:* Organization of American Historians, Western History Association (president, 1972), New Haven Colony Historical Society. *Awards, honors:* American Council of Learned Societies fellowship, 1959-60; Social Science Research Council fellowship, 1960-61.

WRITINGS: *Dakota Territory, 1861-1889: A Study of Frontier Politics*, Yale University Press, 1956; (editor) Joseph Downey, *The Cruise of the Portsmouth, 1845-47*, Yale University Press, 1958; (editor) D. M. Potter, *Party Politics and Public Action, 1877-1917*, Holt, 1960; *The Far Southwest, 1846-1912: A Territorial History*, Yale University Press, 1966; (editor) *Reader's Encyclopedia of the American West*, Crowell, 1975. Member of board of editors, "Yale Western American Series."

AVOCATIONAL INTERESTS: Contemporary theater.

* * *

LAMIRANDE, Emilien 1926-

PERSONAL: Born May 22, 1926, in Saint-Georges de Windsor, Quebec; son of Armand and Valentine (Boucher) Lamirande. *Education:* University of Ottawa, B.A., 1949, L.Ph., 1950, M.A., 1951, L.Th., 1955; Leopold-Franens Universitaet, D.Th., 1960; Union Theological Seminary, S.T.M., 1965. *Home:* 60 Cartier, Apt. 602, Ottawa, Ontario, Canada. *Office:* Department of Religious Studies, University of Ottawa, Ottawa, Ontario, Canada.

CAREER: University of Ottawa, Ottawa, Ontario, lecturer in theology, 1954-58, associate professor, 1960-64, titular professor, 1964-65; Saint Paul University (federated with the University of Ottawa), titular professor of theology, 1970, dean of the faculty of theology, 1967-69; University of Ottawa, titular professor of religious studies, 1970—, chairman of department, 1972—. Member of the Academic Senate of the University of Ottawa, 1965-69. *Member:* Catholic Theological Society of America, Societe Canadienne de Theologie, Societe Canadienne de l'Histoire de l'Eglise Catholique.

WRITINGS: *La Communion des Saints*, Fayard, 1962, published as *The Communion of Saints*, Hawthorne, 1963; *Un siecle et demi d'etudes sur l'ecclesiologie de Saint Augustin* (bibliographical essay), Etudes Augustiniennes (Paris), 1962; *L'Eglise Celeste Selon Saint Augustin*, Etudes Augustiniennes, 1963; (introduction and notes) *Oeuvres de Saint Augustin*, Volume 32, Desclee de Brouwer, 1965; *Dieu chez les hommes: La signification du pavillon chretien de l'Expo 67*, Montreal, 1967; *Etudes sur l'ecclesiologie de saint Augustin*, Editions de l'Universite, 1969; *La situation ecclesiologique des Donatistes selon Saint Augustin*, Editions de l'Universite, 1972. Contributor of articles to theological journals in Europe and America.

WORK IN PROGRESS: Research on the history of the African Church, Augustine, and ecclesiology.

SIDELIGHTS: Besides French, Lamirande has a "reading knowledge of English, German, Spanish, Italian, Portuguese, etc."

* * *

LAMM, Maurice 1930-

PERSONAL: Born March 20, 1930, in Bronx, N.Y.; son of Samuel and Pearl (Baumol) Lamm; married Shirley Friedman, June 19, 1955; children: David Jay, Janet Lynne, Dodi Lee. *Education:* Yeshiva University, B.A., 1951, graduate study, 1958-63; Rabbi Isaac Elchanan Theological Seminary, Rabbi, 1954. *Politics:* Independent Democrat. *Home:* 1889 Sedgewick Ave., N.Y. and 1835 University Ave., Bronx, N.Y.

CAREER: Rabbi of Jewish centers in San Juan, Puerto Rico, 1956-57, and Floral Park, N.Y., 1957-65; Hebrew Institute of University Heights, Bronx, N.Y., rabbi, 1965—. National Jewish Welfare Board, director of Jewish Chaplaincy Experimental Program, 1961, member of Commission on Jewish Chaplaincy, 1964—. Dean, Akiba Hebrew Academy. Long Island Commission of Rabbis, vice-president, 1959; New York Board of Rabbis, member of executive committee, 1963—; Chaplaincy Committee of Yeshiva University, chairman, 1963—; Yeshiva University Rabbinic Alumni, first vice-president, 1966; Rabbinical Council of America, member of executive committee, 1966. *Military service:* U.S. Army, chaplain, 1954-56; became first lieutenant. *Awards, honors:* B'nai B'rith Award, 1965.

WRITINGS: *I Shall Glorify Him*, Bloch & Co., 1963; *The Jewish Way of Death*, David, 1966; *The Jewish Way in Death and Mourning*, David, 1969. Contributor to *Jewish Digest* and *Journal of Religion and Mental Health*. Editor, *Chavrusa*, 1963—; member of editorial board, *Tradition*, 1966.

WORK IN PROGRESS: *Social Violence*, a study in Biblical attempts to curb it, and their applicability to contemporary concerns, first presented as a series of televised lectures, 1965; doctoral thesis on "The Just War."†

* * *

LAMONT, Lansing 1930-

PERSONAL: Born March 13, 1930, in New York, N.Y.; son of Thomas Stilwell (a banker) and Elinor (Miner) Lamont; married Ada Jung, September 18, 1954; children: Douglas, Elisabeth, Virginia, Thomas S. II. *Education:*

Milton Academy, Diploma, 1948; Harvard University, A.B., 1952; Columbia University, M.S. (honors), 1958. *Politics:* Republican. *Religion:* Episcopal. *Home:* 133 East 80th St., New York, N.Y. *Office:* Time/Life Bldg., Rockefeller Center, New York, N.Y.

CAREER: Washington Star, Washington, D.C., reporter, 1958-59; Congressional correspondent for *Worcester Gazette*, Worcester, Mass., and other New England dailies, 1959-60; *Time*, New York, N.Y., congressional and national correspondent with Washington bureau, 1961-68, deputy chief of London bureau, 1969-71, chief Canadian correspondent and Ottawa bureau chief, 1971-73, United Nations bureau chief and world affairs writer, 1973-74. *Military service:* U.S. Army, 1954-57; became first lieutenant. *Member:* National Press Club. *Awards, honors: Day of Trinity* was among 250 best American books, 1961-65, chosen by American Booksellers Association for presentation to White House library.

WRITINGS: Day of Trinity (Literary Guild alternate selection), Atheneum, 1965.

SIDELIGHTS: Foreign publishing rights to *Day of Trinity* have been sold in France, England, Spain, and Germany; hardback sales in America have totaled more than 50,000 copies and paperback sales have reached 100,000 copies.

*   *   *

LANDAU, Jacob M.   1924-

PERSONAL: Born March 20, 1924, in Chisinau, Rumania; taken to Palestine in 1935; son of Michel and Maria (Abeles) Landau; married Zipora Marcus (a teacher), July 29, 1947; children: Ronnit (daughter), Iddo (son). *Education:* Hebrew University of Jerusalem, M.A., 1946; School of Oriental and African Studies, London, Ph.D., 1949. *Religion:* Jewish. *Home:* 5 Mishael St., Jerusalem, Israel. *Office:* Hebrew University, Jerusalem, Israel.

CAREER: Hebrew University of Jerusalem, Jerusalem, Israel, lecturer in Near and Middle Eastern political systems, faculty of social sciences, 1959—, professor of social sciences, 1974—. Brandeis University, Waltham, Mass., visiting lecturer in Near Eastern studies, 1955-56; University of Tel Aviv, Tel Aviv, Israel, lecturer on modern Middle East, 1956-59; visiting associate professor, University of California, Los Angeles, 1963-64; visiting professor at Wayne State University, 1968-69, Columbia University, 1969, University of Ankara, 1974, University of Texas, Austin, 1975. *Member:* Academy of Political Science (New York), Israel Oriental Society, American Oriental Society, Middle East Studies Association of North America. *Awards, honors:* Fulbright travel grant, 1963; President Ben Zvi Memorial Award, 1968; Itzhak Grunbaum Scholarly Award, 1974.

WRITINGS: Parliaments and Parties in Egypt, Praeger, 1954; *Studies in the Arab Theater and Cinema*, University of Pennsylvania Press, 1958; *A Word Count of Modern Arabic Prose*, American Council of Learned Societies, 1958; (editor) *Teaching of Arabic as a Foreign Language* (in Hebrew), School of Education, Hebrew University, 1961; (editor) *Der Staat Israel*, Glock and Lutz (Nuernberg), 1964; (with M. M. Czudnowski) *The Israel Communist Party and the Elections for the Fifth Knesset, 1961*, Hoover Institution, 1965; *ha-Yehudim be-Mitsrayim bame'ah hatesha'-' esreh*, Ben Zvi Institute, Hebrew University, 1967, revised edition translated and published as *Jews in Nineteenth-Century Egypt*, New York University Press, 1969; *The Arabs in Israel: A Political Study*, Oxford Uni-

versity Press, for the Royal Institute of International Affairs, 1969; *The Hejaf Railway and the Muslim Pilgrimage: A Case of Ottoman Political Propaganda*, Wayne State University Press, 1971; (editor) *Man, State and Society in the Contemporary Middle East*, Praeger, 1972; *Middle Eastern Themes: Papers in History and Politics*, Cass, 1973; *Radical Politics in Modern Turkey*, Brill, 1974. Contributor to specialized journals, including *Middle Eastern Studies* (London), *Journal of Modern History* (Chicago), *Oriente Moderno* (Rome), and *Western Political Quarterly* (Salt Lake City).

WORK IN PROGRESS: A study on politics in contemporary Turkey.

SIDELIGHTS: Landau reads ten languages fluently—Hebrew, Arabic, Turkish, English, French, German, Italian, Spanish, Romanian, and Russian.

*   *   *

LANDSBERG, Hans H.   1913-

PERSONAL: Born September 9, 1913, in Posen, Germany; became U.S. citizen, in 1942; son of Max (a physician) and Clara (Kantorowicz) Landsberg; married Gianna Giannetti, September 18, 1945; children: Ann. *Education:* London School of Economics and Political Science, B.Sc., 1936; Columbia University, M.A., 1941. *Office:* Resources for the Future, Inc., 1755 Massachusetts Ave., N.W., Washington, D.C. 20036.

CAREER: Economist with Works Progress Administration, 1936-39, National Bureau of Economic Research, 1939-42, Office of Strategic Services, 1942-45, United Nations Relief and Rehabilitation Administration, Italy, 1946, and with United Nations Food and Agriculture Organization, Italian Technical Delegation, and U.S. Department of Commerce, all Washington, D.C., in period, 1947-49; Office of the Economic Adviser to the Israel Government, Washington, D.C., economist, 1950-55; Gass, Bell, and Associates (consulting economists), Washington, D.C., economist, 1956-59; Resources for the Future, Inc., Washington, D.C., director of resource appraisal program, 1960-73, director of energy and minerals program, 1974—. *Military service:* U.S. Army, Office of Strategic Services, 1944-46; became first lieutenant. *Member:* American Economic Association, American Association for the Advancement of Science, American Academy of Arts and Sciences (fellow).

WRITINGS: (With Harold Barger) *Output, Employment and Productivity in American Agriculture, 1899-1939*, National Bureau of Economic Research, 1941; (with George Perazich) *Report on Nuclear Power and Economic Development in Israel*, National Planning Association, 1957; (contributor) *Energy in the American Economy, 1850-1975*, Johns Hopkins Press, 1960; (with Bruce C. Netschert) *The Future Supply of the Major Metals*, Resources for the Future, 1961; (contributor) *Technological Planning on the Corporate Level*, Harvard University Graduate School of Business Administration, 1962; (with Leonard L. Fischman and Joseph L. Fisher) *Resources in America's Future: Patterns of Requirements and Availabilities, 1960-2000*, Johns Hopkins Press, 1963; *Natural Resources for U.S. Growth*, Johns Hopkins Press, 1964; (contributor) *Readings in Resource Management and Conservation*, University of Chicago Press, 1965; (contributor) *America—1980*, Graduate School, U.S. Department of Agriculture, 1965; (contributor) *New Horizons for Resources Research*, University of Colorado Press, 1965.

(Contributor) *World Population: The View Ahead*, Indiana University Press, 1968; (with Sam Schurr) *Energy in the United States: Sources Uses and Policy Issues*, Random House, 1968; (editor with Roger Revelle) *America's Changing Environment*, Houghton, 1970; (with Marion Clawson and Lyle T. Alexander) *The Agricultural Potential of the Middle-East*, Elsevier, 1971; (editor with Clawson) *Desalting Seawater*, Gordon & Breach, 1972; (contributor) *Population, Resources and the Environment*, U.S. Commission on Population Growth and the American Future, 1972. Contributor to *Reporter*, 1950-70.

SIDELIGHTS: Landsberg is competent in German, Italian, French, and Spanish.

* * *

LANG, Allen Kim 1928-

PERSONAL: Born July 31, 1928, in Fort Wayne, Ind.; son of Frank J. and Ona J. (Allen) Lang; married Alberta R. Miller (a draftsman). *Education:* Attended Indiana University and Roosevelt University. *Politics:* Left-Democrat. *Religion:* Unitarian Universalist. *Home:* 5476 South Everett Ave., Chicago, Ill. 60615.

CAREER: Formerly chief technician, American Red Cross Blood Center, Fort Wayne, Ind.; Michael Reese Research Foundation, Blood Center, Chicago, Ill., blood bank supervisor, 1956—. Moderately active pacifist and propagandist as member of Fellowship of Reconciliation, and supporter of Catholic Worker, student Peace Union, and similar organizations and movements. *Military service:* U.S. Army, Infantry and Air Forces, 1946-54. *Member:* American Association of Blood Banks, Mystery Writers of America, Science Fiction Writers of America, Fellowship of Reconciliation.

WRITINGS: Wild and Outside, Chilton, 1966. Contributor of short stories to *Alfred Hitchcock's Mystery Magazine* and to other mystery and science-fiction magazines.

WORK IN PROGRESS: A mystery novel, a science fiction novel, and short stories.

AVOCATIONAL INTERESTS: Germany (Germanophile, before 1932 and after 1945), amateur microscopy.

* * *

LANGE, (Leo) Joseph (Jr.) 1932-

PERSONAL: Born December 12, 1932, in Wilmington, Del.; son of Leo Joseph (in insurance) and Helen (Seiler) Lange. *Education:* Niagara University, B.S. (summa cum laude), 1956; Catholic University of America, M.S., 1958; Loyola University, M.A., 1966; University of Chicago, graduate study, 1965-68. *Address:* P.O. Box 1452, Wilmington, Del. 19899.

CAREER: Roman Catholic priest of Oblate Fathers of St. Francis of Sales (O.S.F.S.). Northeast Catholic High School, Philadelphia, Pa., chemistry teacher, 1960-61; Cathedral Preparatory School, Erie, Pa., chemistry teacher, 1961-62; Salesianum School, Wilmington, Del., television science teacher, 1963-65, program director of educational television studio, 1964-65; Allentown College, Allentown, Pa., lecturer in philosophy, 1968-71; Center for Renewal, Allentown, Pa., director, 1970—. *Member:* Sigma Xi.

WRITINGS: A Christian Understanding of Existence, Newman, 1965; *Friendship with Jesus*, Dove Publications, 1974. Contributor to *Journal of Physical Chemistry* and religious journals.

WORK IN PROGRESS: Three more volumes in a series of which *Friendship with Jesus* is the first volume.

* * *

LANIER, Alison Raymond 1917-
(G. Alison Raymond)

PERSONAL: Born April 1, 1917, in New York, N.Y.; daughter of Edward H. (a physician) and Isabel (Ashwell) Raymond. *Education:* Bryn Mawr College, A.B. (cum laude), 1938. *Home:* 230 East 50th St., New York, N.Y. 10022.

CAREER: Proxy Parents, New York, N.Y., owner and director, 1938-40; Bryn Mawr College, Bryn Mawr, Pa., assistant director of public relations and director of residence hall, 1940-42; International Child Welfare Union, Geneva, Switzerland, co-director (in New York Office) of overseas schools, 1946-50; Pennsylvania Civil Defense Organization, Harrisburg, deputy for eastern area, 1950-54; Committee of Correspondence, New York, N.Y., executive director, 1954-61; Carnegie Endowment for International Peace, New York, N.Y., director of Hospitality Information Services, 1961—. Instructor at New School for Social Research, New York, and U.S. Department of State Foreign Service Institute, Washington, D.C.; director of orientation and seminars (at intervals) for Council on Student Travel. Chairman of overseas selection, Girl Scouts of America. *Military service:* U.S. Navy, Women's Reserve, 1942—; active duty, 1942-46; now commander. *Member:* American Association of University Women (board).

WRITINGS: (Under name G. Alison Raymond) *Half the World's People*, Appleton, 1965; *Living in Europe*, Scribner, 1973; *Living in the U.S.A.*, Scribner, 1973. Writer of feature stories for U.S. Information Service "Women's Packets," distributed abroad; contributor to magazines.

SIDELIGHTS: About 900 wives of U.S. officials going abroad have passed through Alison Raymond Lanier's Foreign Service Institute course, learning about the countries for which they are bound. In New York, she reverses the orientation—supplying information about this country to members of United Nations missions and editing a monthly directory on New York resources for them. In her earlier post with the Committee of Correspondence, she traveled and organized seminars in 37 countries in Europe, Latin America, the Middle East, Africa, and Asia, working primarily with women on community development planning.†

* * *

LANKFORD, John (Errett) 1934-

PERSONAL: Born July 31, 1934, in Washington, D.C.; son of Jesse William (director of accident analysis, Civil Aeronautics Board) and Gladys (Webb) Lankford; married Nancy Zank, March 8, 1965. *Education:* Oberlin College, A.B., 1956; University of Wisconsin, M.S., 1957, Ph.D., 1962. *Agent:* Gerard McCauley, P.O. Box 456, Cranbury, N.J. 08512. *Office:* Department of History, University of Missouri, Columbia, Mo. 65201.

CAREER: Wisconsin State University, River Falls, instructor, 1961-62, assistant professor of history, 1962-65; Manhattanville College, Purchase, N.Y., assistant professor of history, 1965-66; University of Missouri, Columbia, associate professor, 1966-71, professor of American social history, 1971—. Summer research assistant to Congressman Richard W. Bolling, 1956-1957. *Member:* American Historical Association, Organization of American Historians, American Society for Church History, Society for Religion in Higher Education (fellow), American Association of University Professors, Society for the Scientific Study of Religion, State Historical Society of Wisconsin. *Awards, honors:* Society for Religion in Higher Education postdoctoral fellowship at Union Theological Seminary, New York, N.Y., 1964-65.

WRITINGS: Congress and the Foundations in the Twentieth Century, Wisconsin State University Press, 1964; (editor) *Captain John Smith's America; Selections from His Writings,* Torchbook, 1967; (member of editorial board, and contributor) Walker D. Wyman, editor, *Centennial History of the Wisconsin State University System,* edited by Walker D. Wyman, Wisconsin State University Press, 1968; (editor with David Reimers) *Essays in American Social History,* Holt, 1970.

WORK IN PROGRESS: The Historical Imagination, an essay on the philosophical and sociological nature of history and the history profession today.

SIDELIGHTS: Lankford told *CA,* "Clio is in trouble and the future of the past looks grim. My commitment is to a fundamental paradigm change which will revitalize historical studies and allow history to take its place with other disciplines interested in the study of human behavior—in the past, the present, and the future."

*   *   *

LANNING, Edward P(utnam) 1930-

PERSONAL: Born September 21, 1930, in Northville, Mich.; son of Floyd Robert and Marjorie (Hansy) Lanning; married second wife, Ruth Eileen Martinez (a student), March 25, 1966; children: (first marriage) Zaida Elaine, Edward Hansy. *Education:* Attended University of Michigan, 1948-51; University of California, Berkeley, A.B., 1953, Ph.D., 1960. *Office:* Department of Anthropology, Columbia University, New York, N.Y. 10027.

CAREER: University of San Marcos, Lima, Peru, lecturer, 1958; Sacramento State College (now California State University, Sacramento), instructor in anthropology, 1959-60; University of California, Berkeley, senior museum anthropologist, 1960-61; University of San Marcos, Fulbright lecturer, 1961-63; Columbia University, New York, N.Y., assistant professor, 1963-65, associate professor, 1965-70, professor of anthropology, 1970—. Visiting professor, Yale University, 1967-68, State University of New York at Stony Brook, 1972-73. Field researcher on human paleocology in Peru, 1956-58, 1961-63, Ecuador, 1964, Chile, 1966-73. *Member:* Society for American Archaeology, Institute of Andean Studies (vice-president, 1961), Kroeber Anthropological Society (president, 1955-56), Phi Beta Kappa.

WRITINGS: A Ceramic Sequence for the Piura and Chira Coast, North Peru, University of California Press, 1963; *Archaeology of the Rose Spring Site, Iny-372,* University of California Press, 1963; *Peru before the Incas,* Prentice-Hall, 1967. Editor, publications of Kroeber Anthropological Society, 1954-55; assistant editor, publications of Society for American Archaeology, 1962-64.

WORK IN PROGRESS: Study of early man in the Andean area, with resulting publications.

SIDELIGHTS: Edward Lanning is fluent in Spanish, and reads several other languages.†

LAPIN, Howard S(idney) 1922-

PERSONAL: Born October 13, 1922, in Los Angeles, Calif. *Education:* Yale University, B.S. (honors), 1947; University of California, Berkeley, M.Eng., 1960; Catholic University of America, Ph.D., 1969. *Home:* 300 M St., S.W., Washington, D.C. 20024. *Office:* Robert R. Nathan Associates, 1200 18th St., N.W., Washington, D.C. 20036.

CAREER: Planning, development, and transport consultant, 1950-64; U.S. Agency for International Development, Washington, D.C., transport planning officer, Bureau for Latin America, 1965-66; U.S. Department of Transportation, Washington, D.C., Division of International Affairs, chief of technical assistance, 1967-72; Robert R. Nathan Associates, Washington, D.C., director of transportation and urban studies, 1972—. *Military service:* U.S. Army Air Forces, 1942-45; became first lieutenant; received Air Medal with five oak leaf clusters. Distinguished Flying Cross, Purple Heart, and five battle stars. *Member:* American Institute of Planners, Institute of Traffic Engineers, American Economic Association, Regional Science Association, American Association for the United Nations (founder and first chairman of Greater Boston chapter, 1962-63), Sigma Xi, Tau Beta Pi.

WRITINGS: Structuring the Journey to Work, University of Pennsylvania Press, 1964. Contributor of a dozen articles to technical journals.

WORK IN PROGRESS: Transportation Planning for Underdeveloped Areas.†

*   *   *

LARSEN, Beverly (Namen) 1929-

PERSONAL: Born March 2, 1929, in Fort Dodge, Iowa; married Edwin F. Larsen (a farm operator and owner); children: Stephen, Christie, Rachel. *Education:* Dana College, B.S., 1963. *Religion:* Lutheran. *Home:* Route 2, Exira, Iowa 50076.

CAREER: Elementary teacher in Iowa, 1963-74. Full-time writer, 1974—.

WRITINGS: Jesus Has Many Names, Augsburg, 1964; *Damsel from Afar,* Augsburg, 1965; *The Brave Ones: Early Iowa Pioneer Women,* Pioneer Press, 1971. Writer of weekly column, "Farm Flavor," for *Audubon Iowa News-Advocate.* Contributor to religious periodicals.

*   *   *

LARSEN, William E(dward) 1936-

PERSONAL: Born December 7, 1936, in Waynesboro, Va.; son of William Eugene and Tursell Mildred (Childs) Larsen. *Education:* Brigham Young University, B.A., 1957; University of Virginia, M.A., 1958, Ph.D., 1961. *Residence:* Childress, Va. *Office:* Department of History, Radford College, Radford, Va.

CAREER: University of Missouri, Columbia, instructor in English, 1958-59; University of Maine, Orono, instructor in history, 1961-63; University of Cincinnati, Cincinnati, Ohio, assistant professor of history, 1963-64; Radford College, Radford, Va., associate professor of history, 1964-66, professor, 1966—. Summer professor of history at Louisiana State University, Baton Rouge, 1964, and Lewis and Clark College, 1966. *Military service:* U.S. Army, 1959. U.S. Army Reserve, 1959—; now captain. *Member:* Organization of American Historians, Southern Historical Association, Virginia Historical Society, Phi Beta Kappa.

WRITINGS: Montague of Virginia: The Making of a Southern Progressive, Louisiana State University Press, 1965. Contributor to *Americana Annual*.

* * *

LARSON, Esther Elisabeth

PERSONAL: Born in Williamsport, Pa.; daughter of Gustav Severin (a minister) and Selma (Christiansen) Larson. *Education:* West Chester State College, B.S., 1931; Columbia University, M.A., 1945; New York University, Ph.D., 1959. *Religion:* Lutheran. *Home:* 584 East Broad St., East Stroudsburg, Pa. 18301.

CAREER: High school teacher, Jamestown, N.Y., 1934-44; lecturer or instructor in English at Columbia University, New York, N.Y., 1952-54, Bennett College, Millbrook, N.Y., 1954-56, New York University, New York, N.Y., 1957; East Stroudsburg State College, East Stroudsburg, Pa., associate professor, 1959-60, professor of English, 1960-74, head of department, 1960-69. Free-lance writer, 1974—.

MEMBER: Modern Language Association of America, National Council of Teachers of English, College English Association, American Association of University Women, American-Scandinavian Foundation, Swedish Pioneer Historical Society, Soroptimist International (president, Monroe branch, 1973-74), Monroe County Historical Society, Kappa Delta Pi, Pi Lambda Theta, Women's Club of Stroudsburg, Woman's Graduate Club (Columbia University; vice-president, 1950-52). *Awards, honors:* American-Scandinavian Foundation fellowship, 1949-50, New York University Founders Day Award, 1959.

WRITINGS: Swedish Commentators on America, 1638-1865, New York Public Library, 1963. Contributor to Swedish and U.S. publications.

WORK IN PROGRESS: Research on American-Scandinavian relations.

AVOCATIONAL INTERESTS: Music (has sung as soloist in choral groups).

* * *

LASH, Joseph P. 1909-

PERSONAL: Born December 2, 1909, in New York, N.Y.; son of Samuel (a storekeeper) and Mary (Avchin) Lash; married Trude Wenzel (a director of Citizens Committee for Children), November 8, 1944; children: Jonathan. *Education:* City College (now City College of the City University of New York), A.B., 1931; Columbia University, M.A., 1932. *Politics:* Democrat. *Religion:* Jewish. *Home:* Skyline Dr., Oakland, N.J. 07436.

CAREER: Americans for Democratic Action, New York, N.Y., director, 1946-49; *New York Post*, New York, N.Y., United Nations correspondent, 1950-61, assistant editor of editorial page, 1961-66; free-lance writer, 1966—. *Military service:* U.S. Army, World War II; became second lieutenant; received Air Medal. *Awards, honors:* Pulitzer Prize and National Book Award for biography, 1972, for *Eleanor and Franklin.*

WRITINGS: Dag Hammarskjold: Custodian of the Brushfire Peace, Doubleday, 1961; *Eleanor Roosevelt: A Friend's Memoir*, Doubleday, 1965; *Eleanor and Franklin*, Norton, 1971; *Eleanor: The Years Alone*, Norton, 1972; *From the Diaries of Felix Frankfurter*, Norton, 1975; *Roosevelt and Churchill: A Study of Their Relationship*, Norton, in press.

BIOGRAPHICAL/CRITICAL SOURCES: New York Post, March 31, 1966.

* * *

LASLEY, John Wayne III 1925-
(Jack Lasley)

PERSONAL: Born June 23, 1925, in Chapel Hill, N.C.; son of John Wayne and Edna (Millikan) Lasley; married Mary Jones, August 30, 1949; children: Mary Ann, John, James, Elizabeth. *Education:* University of North Carolina, B.S., 1949, LL.B., 1952. *Politics:* Democrat. *Home:* 523 East Rosemary, Chapel Hill, N.C.

CAREER: Private law practice, Chapel Hill, N.C., 1956—. Institute for International Studies, Chapel Hill, N.C., director, 1963—. *Member:* World Law Center (Geneva), American Bar Association, American Society of International Law.

WRITINGS—All under name Jack Lasley: *World Law: The Consensus of Athens—A Universal Challenge*, Institute for International Studies (Chapel Hill), 1963; *The War System and You*, Institute for International Studies, 1965, 2nd edition, 1965; *My Country—Right or Wrong?*, 1966; (compiler) *In Quest of Freedom: Abolish the Draft*, 2nd edition, Institute for International Studies, 1969. Writer of articles in field of international law and foreign affairs.

WORK IN PROGRESS: International law, with respect to the relationship of national governments to the individual citizen.†

* * *

LASSERS, Willard J. 1919-

PERSONAL: Born August 24, 1919, in Kankakee, Ill.; son of Henry and Sylvia Lassers; married Elisabeth Stern; children: Deborah. *Education:* University of Chicago, A.B., 1940, J.D., 1942. *Home:* 1509 East 56th St., Chicago, Ill. *Office:* Elson, Lassers and Wolff, 11 South LaSalle St., Chicago, Ill. 60603.

CAREER: Elson, Lassers and Wolff (law firm), Chicago, Ill., partner, 1960—.

WRITINGS: (With Alex Elson and Aaron S. Wolff) *Civil Practice Forms Annotated, Illinois and Federal*, Bobbs-Merrill, 1952, 2nd revised edition, 1965; *Scapegoat Justice: Lloyd Miller and the Failure of the American Legal System*, Indiana University Press, 1973.

* * *

LASSWELL, Thomas Ely 1919-

PERSONAL: Born October 29, 1919, in St. Louis, Mo.; son of Gus and Miriam (Ely) Lasswell; married Marcia Lee Eck (a psychologist), May 29, 1950; children: Marcia Jane, Thomas Ely, Jr., Julia Lee. *Education:* Attended Westminster College, Fulton, Mo., 1936-38; Arkansas College, Batesville, A.B., 1940; University of Southern California, M.S., 1947, Ph.D., 1953. *Politics:* Democrat. *Religion:* Congregational. *Home:* 875 Hillcrest Dr., Pomona, Calif. 91768. *Office:* Department of Sociology, University of Southern California, Los Angeles, Calif. 90007.

CAREER: Assistant professor of sociology in extension divisions, University of Southern California and Pepperdine College, Los Angeles, 1950-54; Grinnell College, Grinnell, Iowa, 1954-59, began as associate professor, became professor of sociology; University of Southern California, associate professor, 1959-63, professor of sociology,

1963—, chairman of department of sociology and anthropology, 1965-66, coordinating director, marriage and counseling center, 1970-71, director of graduate studies in sociology, 1971—. Visiting professor of sociology and acting head of department, Pamona College, 1967-68, and at Revelle College, University of California, San Diego, 1967-68. Visiting summer professor, Austin State College, 1950, 1956, 1958; Whittier College, 1957; Northwestern University, 1960. Consultant, Deasy and Bolling Architects, 1965—. Member of board of directors, Hacker Foundation, 1970—. *Military service:* U.S. Naval Reserve, active duty, 1942-46; became lieutenant. *Member:* American Sociological Association (fellow), International Congress for Social Welfare, International Sociological Association, National Council on Family Relations, Pacific Sociological Association, Phi Kappa Phi, Alpha Kappa Delta.

WRITINGS: (With E. C. McDonagh) *Sociology: An Introduction*, Lucas Brothers, 1953, 2nd edition (with Jon E. Simpson), 1963, 3rd edition (with Simpson and Sharon Y. Moriwaki), 1971; (contributor) Gilbert Geis and others, editors, *The Role of the Institutional Teacher*, Youth Studies Center, 1964; (with John H. Burma and Sidney H. Aronson) *Life in Society*, Scott, Foresman, 1965, 2nd edition, 1970; *Class and Stratum: An Introduction to Concepts and Research*, Houghton, 1965; (contributor) Melvin M. Tumin, editor, *Readings on Social Stratification*, Prentice-Hall, 1970; (contributor) Holger R. Stub, editor, *Status Communities in Modern Society: Alternatives to Class Analysis*, Oryden Press, 1972; (with wife, Marcia E. Lasswell) *Love, Marriage, Family: A Developmental Approach*, Scott, Foresman, 1973; (with Jerry G. Bode) *Sociology in Context: Scientific and Humanistic*, General Learning Press, 1974; (editor) C. M. Deasy, *Design for Human Affairs*, Halstead Press, 1974; (contributor) Arthur B. Shostak, editor, *Putting Sociology to Work*, McKay, 1974. Contributor to *American Sociological Review, Sociology and Social Research*, and other professional publications. Series editor, "Schenkman Series in Stratification" and "General Learning Press Instructional System Series." Associate editor, *Sociology and Social Research*.

WORK IN PROGRESS: Growth to Love, with Marcia E. Lasswell, for Scott, Foresman; research in marriage and the family; research in social psychological aspects of architectural programming.

* * *

LAUERMAN, David A(nthony) 1931-

PERSONAL: Born June 13, 1931, in Hammond, Ind.; son of Frank A. and Mary E. (Dimond) Lauerman; married Kathleen Hanna, December 31, 1955; children: David, John, Mary Caitlin, Patrick, Margaret, Rosemary, Lucian. *Education:* University of Notre Dame, B.S., 1953, M.A., 1958; Indiana University, Ph.D., 1972. *Religion:* Roman Catholic. *Home:* 25 Woodward Ave., Buffalo, N.Y. 14214. *Office:* Department of English, Canisius College, Buffalo, N.Y. 14208.

CAREER: Northern Illinois University, DeKalb, instructor in English, 1960-62; Canisius College, Buffalo, N.Y., assistant professor, 1962-72, associate professor of English, 1972—. *Military service:* U.S. Army, 1953-56. *Member:* National Council of Teachers of English, American Association of University Professors, Modern Language Association of America.

WRITINGS: (With Louis Glorfeld and Norman Stageberg) *A Concise Guide for Student Writers*, Holt, 1963, revised edition published as *A Concise Guide for Writers*, 1974.

LAUFE, Abe 1906-

PERSONAL: Born May 25, 1906, in Pittsburgh, Pa.; son of Louis and Lea (Malachofsky) Laufe. *Education:* University of Pittsburgh, B.A., 1928, M.A., 1935, Ph.D., 1952. *Home:* 4614 Fifth Ave., Pittsburgh, Pa. 15213. *Agent:* Julian Bach, Jr., 249 East 48th St., New York, N.Y. 10017.

CAREER: Arnold (Pa.) public schools, teacher of English, 1928-42; *Editorial Management*, New York, N.Y., editor, 1945-47; University of Pittsburgh, Pittsburgh, Pa., lecturer, 1947-49, instructor, 1949-53, assistant professor, 1953-56, associate professor, 1956-66, professor of English, 1966-72, professor emeritus, 1972—. Radio speaker and public lecturer on the theater, musical comedy, and Hollywood music, giving most of the programs with piano illustrations. *Military service:* U.S. Army, Special Services, 1942-45; became master sergeant; received Legion of Merit, 1946.

WRITINGS: (Editor) *An Army Doctor's Wife on the Frontier: Letters from Alaska and the Far West*, University of Pittsburgh Press, 1962; *Anatomy of a Hit*, Hawthorn, 1966; *Broadway's Greatest Musicals*, Funk, 1969, 3rd edition, 1973. Contributor of about sixty articles to women's magazines and professional journals, 1937-42.

WORK IN PROGRESS: The Wicked Stage, a history and encyclopedia of musical productions adapted from plays, films, books, or stories.

* * *

LAUNE, Paul Sidney 1899-

PERSONAL: Surname is pronounced Lawn; born May 5, 1899, in Milford, Neb.; son of Sidney Benton (a lawyer) and Seigniora (Russell) Laune; married second wife, Irene Wilson (a film editor); children: Sidney (Mrs. Colin E. Unsworth), Paul Wilson. *Education:* Attended University of Oklahoma, 1918, and University of Nebraska, 1919. *Politics:* Republican. *Religion:* Protestant. *Home:* 130 Height's Dr., Yonkers, N.Y. 10710.

CAREER: Free-lance artist and illustrator, Lincoln, Neb., 1919-25; *New York Sun*, New York, N.Y., head of art department, 1927-30; free-lance artist and illustrator, beginning 1930. *Member:* Society of Illustrators.

WRITINGS—Self-illustrated: The Thirsty Pony, Grossett, 1941; *Mustang Roundup*, Holt, 1964; *America's Quarter Horses*, Doubleday, 1973.

SIDELIGHTS: Laune's lifelong interest in horses began when he herded cattle and moved herds of mustangs to widely separated pastures in Nebraska. Other interests: Art history and history generally.†

* * *

LAURENCE, Dan H. 1920-

PERSONAL: Born March 28, 1920, in New York, N.Y. *Education:* Hofstra University, B.A., 1946; New York University, M.A., 1950. *Office:* c/o Dodd, Mead & Co., 79 Madison Ave., New York, N.Y. 10016.

CAREER: Hofstra University, Hempstead, N.Y., instructor in English, 1953-58; New York University, New York, N.Y., associate professor, 1962-67, professor of English, 1967-70. Visiting professor, University of Texas at Austin, 1974-75. *Military service:* U.S. Army Air Forces, 1942-45. *Awards, honors:* Guggenheim fellow, 1960, 1961, 1972.

WRITINGS: (With Leon Edel) *A Bibliography of Henry James*, Hart-Davis, 1957, revised edition, 1961; *Robert*

Nathan: A Bibliography, Yale University Library, 1960; (editor) *Uncollected Writings of Bernard Shaw*, Hill & Wang, Volume I: *How to Become a Musical Critic*, 1961, Volume II: *Platform & Pulpit*, 1961, Volume III: (with David Greene) *The Matter with Ireland*, 1962; (editor) *Collected Letters of Bernard Shaw*, Dodd, Volume I, 1965, Volume II, 1972; (editor) *Bodley-Head Shaw: Collected Plays*, seven volumes, Reinhardt, 1970-74.

WORK IN PROGRESS: Editing Volumes III and IV of *Collected Letters of Bernard Shaw*, for Dodd; a Shaw bibliography, for Oxford University Press, and a study of Shaw and the American theatre.

*   *   *

LAURIE, Edward James 1925-

PERSONAL: Born November 21, 1925, in Sparks, Nev.; son of Albert Edward (a railroad conductor) and Margaret (Fraser) Laurie; married Patricia Jean Johnson, March 31, 1962; children: Katherine Louise, Margaret Dee, Elizabeth Ann. *Education:* University of California, Los Angeles, B.S., 1946, M.B.A., 1950, Ed.D., 1959. *Home:* 1287 Pampas Dr., San Jose, Calif. 95120.

CAREER: San Jose State College (now University), San Jose, Calif., assistant professor, 1956-59, associate professor, 1959-63, professor of management, 1964-70, professor of marketing, 1971—, chairman of department, 1972—. Faculty research fellow, International Business Machines, Systems Research Institute, 1962-63. *Military service:* U.S. Naval Reserve, active duty, 1943-45; became lieutenant junior grade. *Member:* Association for Computing Machinery, American Marketing Association, American Association of University Professors, American Academy of Political and Social Sciences, Association of California State College Professors, Phi Delta Kappa, Pi Omega Pi.

WRITINGS: Computer Applications in the U.S., South-Western Publishing, 1960; *Computers and How They Work and Study Guide*, South-Western Publishing, 1963; *Computers and Computer Languages* and *Study Guide*, South-Western Publishing, 1966; *Modern Computer Concepts*, South-Western Publishing, 1970. Contributor to professional journals.

WORK IN PROGRESS: Basic EDP (text and workbooks).

AVOCATIONAL INTERESTS: General history, Egyptology, history of science, astronomy.

*   *   *

LAWRENCE, J(ames) D(uncan) 1918-

PERSONAL: Born October 22, 1918, in Detroit, Mich.; son of Charles Wilbert (a salesman) and Pearl Susan (Best) Lawrence; married Marie Catherine Blum, December 30, 1939; children: Sherry, Liane, James D., Jr., John William, Vivian, Gillian. *Education:* Attended U.S. Naval Academy; Wayne State University, B.A. in Ed., 1939; Detroit Institute of Technology, B.S. in Mechanical Engineering, 1939. *Home:* 63 Tall Oaks Dr., Summit, N.J. 07901. *Office:* Stratemeyer Syndicate, 519 Main St., East Orange, N.J.

CAREER: Stratemeyer Syndicate (creators of juvenile books), East Orange, N.J., writer-editor, 1962—.

WRITINGS: Davy Crockett and the Indian Secret: Adventures of a Boy Pioneer, Books, Inc., 1955; *Barnaby's Bells*, Macmillan, 1965; *Binky Brothers: Detectives*, Harper,

1968; *Binky Brothers and the Fearless Four*, Harper, 1970. Writer of numerous juvenile fiction books under undisclosed pseudonyms. Also has done commercial and educational film scripts, radio drama scripts, magazine articles, and comic strips.†

*   *   *

LAWSON, Richard H(enry) 1919-

PERSONAL: Born January 11, 1919, in San Francisco, Calif.; son of Henry Porter and Alice (Hanchett) Lawson; married Eldene Laura Balcom, August 26, 1950. *Education:* Attended Multnomah School of the Bible (now Multnomah College), 1937-39; University of Oregon, B.A., 1941, M.A., 1948; University of California, Los Angeles, Ph.D., 1956. *Politics:* Democrat. *Home:* 6228 Anvil Lake Ave., San Diego, California 92119. *Office:* Department of German and Slavic Languages and Literature, San Diego State University, San Diego, Calif. 92115.

CAREER: Washington State University, Pullman, instructor in German, 1953-57; San Diego State University, San Diego, Calif., assistant professor, 1957-62, associate professor, 1962-66, professor of German, 1966—, chairman of department of foreign languages, 1965, and department of German and Russian, 1966-68, chairman of division of humanities, 1968-69, acting associate or assistant dean of graduate studies, 1970—. Consultant on etymologies, *Webster's New International Dictionary*, 1955-57. *Military service:* U.S. Army Air Forces, 1941-46; became first lieutenant; received Air Medal. U.S. Air Force Reserve, 1946—; became major. *Member:* Modern Language Association of America, Linguistic Society of America, American Committee for the Study of Austrian Literature, Internationale Vereinigung fuer Germanische Sprach-und Literaturforschung, American Association of Teachers of German, International Arthur Schnitzler Research Association, Philological Association of the Pacific Coast.

WRITINGS: (With others) *Studies in Arthur Schnitzler*, University of North Carolina Press, 1963; (editor) *Novellen aus Wien*, Scribner, 1964; (with others) *Encyclopedia of World Literature in the Twentieth Century*, Ungar, 1969; (with others) *Dichtung, Sprache, Gesellschaft*, Athenaeun Verlag, 1971; *Edith Wharton and German Literature*, Bouvier Verlag, 1974; *Edith Wharton*, Ungar, 1975. Contributor to language and other professional journals. Editor, current bibliography committee, *Twentieth Century Literature*.

WORK IN PROGRESS: Studies on linguistics in Old High German.

SIDELIGHTS: Lawson is competent in German, Spanish, Russian, French, Italian, Latin, and classical Greek.

*   *   *

LAYTON, William (Isaac) 1913-

PERSONAL: Born September 26, 1913, in Cameron, Mo.; son of Joseph Evening (a teacher) and Mary (Leighton) Layton; married Eva Wade, March 28, 1941; children: Mary Elizabeth, Gay Wade. *Education:* University of South Carolina, B.S. (Cum Laude), 1934, M.S., 1935; graduate study at University of Chicago, 1936-37, and Duke University, 1938; George Peabody College for Teachers, Ph.D., 1948. *Religion:* Presbyterian. *Home:* 3519 Old Lufkin Rd., Nacogdoches, Tex. 75961. *Office:* Stephen F. Austin State University, Nacogdoches, Tex. 75961.

CAREER: High school teacher of mathematics in Greer,

S.C., 1935-36, Rome, Ga., 1937-39, and Albany, Ga., 1939-40; Amarillo Junior College, Amarillo, Tex., instructor in mathematics and engineering, 1941-42, head of mathematics department, 1942-46; Austin Peay State College, Clarksville, Tenn., professor of mathematics and head óf department, 1946-48; Auburn University, Auburn, Ala., associate professor of mathematics, 1948-49; Frostburg State College, Frostburg, Md., dean of instruction, 1949-50; Stephen F. Austin State University, Nacogdoches, Tex., professor of mathematics and head of department, 1950—, coordinator of data processing center, 1963-68.

MEMBER: Mathematical Association of America (president of Texas section, 1961-62), American Mathematical Society, National Council of Teachers of Mathematics, Texas Council of Mathematics Teachers, East Texas Council of Mathematics Teachers (president, 1964-66), Phi Beta Kappa, Sigma Xi, Kappa Phi Kappa, Gamma Alpha, Phi Delta Kappa, Pi Mu Epsilon.

WRITINGS: An Analysis of Certification Requirements for Teachers of Mathematics, Bureau of Publications, George Peabody College, 1949; (co-author) *College Algebra*, Pitman, 1956; (co-author) *Mathematics of Finance*, Pitman, 1958; *College Arithmetic*, Wiley, 1959, 2nd edition, 1971; *Essential Business Mathematics*, Wiley, 1965. Contributor to mathematics journals.

WORK IN PROGRESS: Text in trigonometry; research in numerical analysis.

AVOCATIONAL INTERESTS: Horseback riding, music.

*   *   *

LAZARUS, Mell   1927-

PERSONAL: Born May 3, 1927, in New York, N.Y.; son of Sidney and Frances (Mushkin) Lazarus; married Hortense Israel, June 19, 1949; children: Marjorie, Susan, Catherine. *Education:* Educated in public schools, New York, N.Y. *Office:* Publishers-Hall Syndicate, 401 North Wabash Avenue, Chicago, Ill. 60611.

CAREER: Cartoonist ("Miss Peach" and "Momma" comic strips) with Publishers-Hall Syndicate, Chicago, Ill. *Military service:* U.S. Navy, 1945. *Member:* National Cartoonists Society (chairman of membership committee, 1965), Newspaper Comics Council, Writers Guild of America, Overseas Press Club, President's People-to-People Committee.

WRITINGS: Miss Peach, Prentice-Hall, 1960; *Miss Peach, Are These Your Children?*, Dial, 1964; *The Boss is Crazy, Too: The Story of a Boy and His Dog of a Boss* (novel), Dial, 1964; *Dear Mr. ASPCA*, Taplinger, 1965; *Please Pass the P's and Q's*, World, 1967; (with B. Hazen) *Please Protect the Porcupine*, World, 1967; *Momma*, Dell, 1972.

Plays: "Everybody into the Lake," "Elliman's Fly," "Lifetime Eggeream," 1969-70.†

*   *   *

LEACH, Douglas Edward   1920-

PERSONAL: Born May 27, 1920, in Providence, R.I.; son of Arthur Edward (a manufacturing jeweler) and Saidee (Raybold) Leach; married Brenda Mason, June 24, 1950; children: Carol Brenda, Bradford Raybold. *Education:* Brown University, A.B., 1942; Harvard University, M.A., 1947, Ph.D., 1952. *Religion:* Disciples of Christ. *Home:* 1805 Graybar Lane, Nashville, Tenn. 37215. *Office:* De-

partment of History, Vanderbilt University, Nashville, Tenn.

CAREER: Bates College, Lewiston, Me., instructor, 1950-52, assistant professor of history, 1952-56; Vanderbilt University, Nashville, Tenn., assistant professor, 1956-59, became associate professor, 1959, now professor of history. Fulbright lecturer, University of Liverpool, 1959-60; University of Aukland, 1967. Visiting professor, University of Leeds, 1974-75. *Military service:* U.S. Navy, 1942-46; became lieutenant. *Member:* American Historical Association, Organization of American Historians, American Association of University Professors, Colonial Society of Massachusetts, Phi Beta Kappa.

WRITINGS: Flintlock and Tomahawk: New England in King Philip's War, Macmillan, 1958; (editor) *A Rhode Islander Reports on King Philip's War: The Second William Harris Letter of August, 1676*, Rhode Island Historical Society, 1963; *The Northern Colonial Frontier, 1607-1763*, Holt, 1966; *Arms for Empire: A Military History of the British Colonies in North America, 1607-1763*, Macmillan, 1973.

*   *   *

LEARY, Paris   1931-

PERSONAL: Born January 7, 1931, in Shreveport, La.; son of Graham (an insurance agent) and Helen (Cox) Leary. *Education:* Centenary College, B.A., 1949; St. Edmund Hall, Oxford, D.Phil., 1958. *Politics:* Catholic Egalitarian. *Religion:* Anglican ("Frightfully High"). *Home:* 3a Albert Rd., Stoneygate, Leicestershire, England. *Agent:* Robert P. Mills, 20 East 53rd St., New York, N.Y. 10022.

CAREER: Taught in Department of English and Philosophy at State University College (now State University of New York College at New Paltz), New Paltz, N.Y. University of Leicester, Fulbright Lecturer in English Literature, 1964-65, lecturer in American literature, 1965—. *Awards, honors:* Yaddo fellowship, 1963; Bread Loaf Poetry fellowship, 1963.

WRITINGS: Views of the Oxford Colleges, and Other Poems, Scribner, 1960; *The Innocent Curate* (novel), Doubleday, 1963; *Jack Sprat Cookbook*, Doubleday, 1965; (editor with Robert Kelly) *A Controversy of Poets*, Doubleday, 1965; *The Snake at Saffron Walden* (poems), Carcanet Press, 1975. Author of three-act play, "A Rushing of Wings," produced by Laboratory Theatre, University of Kentucky, 1960. Anthologized in *Best Poems of 1957* and *Best Poems of 1963*, Stanford University Press, and in *Oxford Poetry 1958*, Fantasy Press.

BIOGRAPHICAL/CRITICAL SOURCES: Approach, summer, 1960.

*   *   *

LEE, James Michael   1931-

PERSONAL: Born September 29, 1931, in New York, N.Y.; son of James (a certified public accountant) and Emma (Brenner) Lee. *Education:* St. John's University, New York, N.Y., A.B., 1955; Columbia University, A.M., 1956, Ed.D., 1958. *Politics:* Democrat. *Religion:* Roman Catholic. *Home:* 52088 Harvest Dr., South Bend, Ind. *Office:* Department of Education, University of Notre Dame, Notre Dame, Ind. 46556.

CAREER: Lecturer at Seton Hall University, South Orange, N.J., and Hunter College (now of the City University of New York), 1959-60; St. Joseph College, West Hartford, Conn., instructor, 1959-60, assistant professor of education, 1960-62; University of Notre Dame, Notre Dame, Ind., assistant professor, 1962-65, associate professor, 1965-68, professor of education, 1968—, chairman of department, 1966-71, chairman of department of education, 1966—. Neighborhood Study Help Program, South Bend, Ind., vice-president, and principal investigator of Office of Economic Opportunity study. *Member:* American Educational Research Association, Association of Professors and Researchers in Religious Education, Religious Education Association, Society for the Study of Religion, National Education Association.

WRITINGS: Principles and Methods of Secondary Education, McGraw, 1963; (senior editor and contributor) *Seminary Education in a Time of Change*, Fides, 1965; (with Nathaniel J. Pallore) *Guidance and Counseling in Schools*, McGraw, 1966; (senior editor and contributor) *Readings in Guidance and Counseling*, Sheed, 1966; (editor and contributor) *Catholic Education in the Western World*, University of Notre Dame Press, 1967; *The Purpose of Catholic Schooling*, Pflaum, 1968; (editor and contributor) *Toward a Future for Religious Education*, Pflaum, 1970; *The Shape of Religious Instruction*, Religious Education Press, 1971; *The Flow of Religious Instruction*, Religious Education Press, 1973; *Forward Together! A Training Program for Religious Educators*, Thomas More Association, 1973.

SIDELIGHTS: Seminary Education in a Time of Change has been translated into French.

BIOGRAPHICAL/CRITICAL SOURCES: Newsweek, Religion Section, May 3, 1965.

* * *

LEE, Lamar, Jr. 1911-

PERSONAL: Born March 21, 1911, in Philadelphia, Pa.; son of Lamar and Edna (Walsh) Lee; married Peggy Pitman, June 1, 1935; children: John Walter. *Education:* U.S. Naval Academy, B.S., 1933; Attended National War College, 1953-54; Stanford University, M.B.A., 1958. *Religion:* Presbyterian. *Office:* Stanford University, Stanford, Calif.

CAREER: U.S. Navy, regular officer, Supply Corps, 1933-57, retired as rear admiral; Stanford University, Stanford, Calif., associate professor and director of purchasing, 1957—. Periodic consultant to Lockheed Aircraft, U.S. Navy, Consolidated Freightways, and Microwave Electronics. *Member:* American Management Association, National Industrial Conference Board. *Awards, honors*—Military: Legion of Merit, Navy Commendation Medal.

WRITINGS: Manual of Naval Standard for Inventory Control, U.S. Government Printing Office, 1948; (with D. W. Dobler) *Purchasing and Materials Management*, McGraw, 1965, 2nd edition, 1971. Contributing editor and regular columnist, *Purchasing Week.*

AVOCATIONAL INTERESTS: Hiking, camping, traveling.†

* * *

LEED, Jacob R. 1924-

PERSONAL: Born September 26, 1924, in Lititz, Pa.; son of Jacob MacHugh (a businessman) and Ada (Leaman) Leed; married Mary Snider (employed in a book store), February 6, 1952; children: Phoebe, Coby. *Education:*

Harvard University, A.B., 1946; University of Iowa, M.F.A., 1952; University of Chicago, Ph.D., 1958. *Home:* 410 Stow, Kent, Ohio 44240.

CAREER: Pennsylvania State University, University Park, instructor in English composition, 1952-55; Northwestern University, Evanston, Ill., instructor in English, 1958-63; Kent State University, Kent, Ohio, assistant professor, 1963-70, professor of English, 1970—. *Member:* Modern Language Association of America, Association for Machine Translation and Computational Linguistics, American Association of University Professors.

WRITINGS: (Editor) *The Computer and Literary Style: Introductory Essays and Studies*, Kent State University Press, 1966; *Poems*, 7 Flowers Press, 1966; *Poet-Painter*, Press Here, 1967. Contributor of poetry to *Poetry, Nation, Black Mountain Review, Chicago Review, 10, Poetry Review*, and other journals and magazines.

WORK IN PROGRESS: A volume of poetry.

SIDELIGHTS: Leed has acted in three films by Richard Myers; "Akran," 1969, "Deathstyles," 1971, and "37-73," 1974.

* * *

LEEDS, Anthony 1925-

PERSONAL: Born January 26, 1925, in New York, N.Y.; son of Arthur S. (a lawyer) and Polly (a psychoanalyst; maiden name, Cahn) Leeds; married Jo Alice Lowrey (a professor of art), November 24, 1948; married second wife Elizabeth Plotkin (a social welfare research associate), January 28, 1967; children: (first marriage) Madeleine, John Christopher, Anne Lowrey. *Education:* Columbia University, B.A. (with honors), 1949, Ph.D., 1957. *Politics:* Independent. *Religion:* None. *Home:* 62 River Place, Dedham, Mass. 02026. *Office:* Department of Anthropology, Boston University, Boston, Mass.

CAREER: Instructor at Baldwin School (for emotionally disturbed children), New York, N.Y., 1954-56, and Hofstra University, Hempstead, Long Island, N.Y., 1956-59; City College (now of the City University of New York) New York, N.Y., assistant professor, 1959-61; Pan American Union, Washington, D.C., research specialist in anthropology, 1961-63; University of Texas, Austin, associate professor, 1963-67, professor, 1967-72, and research associate, Institute of Latin American Studies; Boston University, Boston, Mass., professor of anthropology, 1972—. Visiting professor at Latin American Centers of University of London, and Oxford University, 1972-73. Part-time lecturer or instructor at City College (now of the City University of New York), 1956-59, Columbia University, 1959-60, and American University, 1962-63.

MEMBER: American Ethnological Society, Society for the History of Technology, Society for American Archaeology, Royal Anthropological Society, American Association for the Advancement of Science, Phi Beta Kappa, Sigma Xi. *Awards, honors:* Exchange scholarships, Brazilian Government, 1951-52; travel and research grants from Columbia University, 1951-52, 1959, Social Science Research Council, 1958, American Philosophical Society, 1960, Research Institute for the Study of Man, 1960, American Anthropological Association, 1960, Wenner-Gren Foundation, 1960, 1964, 1965, Instituto Nacional de Estudos Pedagogicos, Rio de Janeiro, 1962, and Ford Foundation-Social Science Research Council, 1965-66; Fulbright fellowship, 1969, 1972-73.

WRITINGS: (Contributor) J. Masserman, editor, Science and Psychoanalysis, Volume VI, Violence and War, with Clinical Studies, Grune, 1963; (editor with A. P. Vayda, co-author of preface, and contributor) Man, Culture, and Animals: The Place of Animals in Human Ecological Adjustment, American Association for the Advancement of Science, 1965; (contributor) R. N. Adams and D. W. Meath, editors, Contemporary Societies and Cultures of Latin America, Random House, 1965; (editor, author of preface and introduction, and contributor) Social Structure and Social Mobility, with Special Reference to Latin America, Pan American Union, 1967; (contributor) E. M. Eddy, editor, Urban Anthropology, University of Georgia Press, 1968.

Contributor: A. J. Field, editor, City and Country in the Third World, Schenkman, 1970; E. B. Leacock, editor, The Culture of Poverty: A Critique, Simon & Schuster, 1971; (with E. Leeds) Brazil in the 1960s: Favelas and Polity, the Continuity of the Structure of Social Control, Institute of Latin American Studies, 1972; A. Southall, editor, Urban Anthropology, Oxford University Press, 1973; F. Rabinovitz and F. Trueblood, editors, Latin American Urban Research, Volume III, Sage, 1973; F. Trueblood and W. Cornelius, editors, Latin American Urban Research, Volume IV, Sage, 1974; M. A. Nettleship, editor, War: Its Causes and Correlates, Mouton, 1974; R. J. Seeger and R. S. Cohen, editors, Boston Studies in the Philosophy of Science, Volume XI, Philosophical Foundations of Science, Reidel, 1974; T. Glick, editor, The Comparative Acceptance of Darwin, University of Texas Press, in press. Contributor to American Oxford Encyclopedia and to symposia and professional journals. Consulting editor to Sage publications on Africa, Urban Anthropology, and Studies in Comparative International Development.

WORK IN PROGRESS: Studying a Metropolis: Field Work in Rio de Janeiro and other Cities: Rio's Favelas, for the Institute of Latin American Studies.

SIDELIGHTS: Leeds has done research in Brazil, Venezuela, Peru, and Texas. His language competency in order of proficiency is—Portuguese, German, Spanish, French, Italian, and Dutch.

*   *   *

LEER, Norman Robert   1937-

PERSONAL: Born February 25, 1937, in Chicago, Ill.; son of Andrew (a public accountant) and Lillian (Farkas) Leer. Education: Grinnell College, A.B., 1958; Indiana University, M.A., 1960, Ph.D., 1964. Politics: Liberal. Religion: Jewish. Office: Department of English, Roosevelt University, Chicago, Ill. 60605.

CAREER: State University of New York at Stony Brook, instructor in English, 1963-65; Beloit College, Beloit, Wis., assistant professor of English, 1965-67; Roosevelt University, Chicago, Ill., associate professor of English, 1967—. Member of academic advisory board, St. Mary's Center for Learning, 1968—; member of board, Urban Life Center, 1972—. Member: Modern Language Association of America, American Association for Humanistic Psychology, Phi Beta Kappa.

WRITINGS: The Limited Hero in the Novels of Ford Madox Ford, Michigan State University Press, 1966. Contributor of articles and poems to journals in his field.

WORK IN PROGRESS: A book of poems, tentatively titled Monologues and Dialogues.†

LEFEVRE, Helen (Elveback)

PERSONAL: Born in Grand Forks, N.D.; married Carl A. Lefevre. Education: University of Minnesota, Ph.D., 1946. Office: Community College of Philadelphia, 34 South 11th St., Philadelphia, Pa. 19107.

CAREER: Chicago City Junior College, Wright branch, Chicago, Ill., professor of English, 1956-66; Community College of Philadelphia, Philadelphia, Pa., 1966—, began as associate professor, became professor of English. Consultant on applied English linguistics. Member: National Council of Teachers of English, Conference on College Composition and Communication, International Reading Association.

WRITINGS: (With husband, Carl A. Lefevre) Writing by Patterns, Knopf, 1965; English Writing Patterns, Grades 2-5, 4 volumes, L. W. Singer, 1967; English Writing Patterns, Grades 6-12, L. W. Singer, 1968; Oral/Written Practice, Knopf, 1970.

WORK IN PROGRESS: College Prep Reader, for Prentice-Hall.

*   *   *

LEFKOWITZ, Annette S(ara)   1922-

PERSONAL: Surname is accented on first syllable, Lef-kowitz; born October 3, 1922, in Shenandoah, Pa.; daughter of Martin A. and Libbie (Horowitz) Lefkowitz. Education: Cornell Medical Center-New York Hospital, R.N., 1941; Pennsylvania State University, B.A. 1949; Columbia University, M.A., 1954, Ed.D., 1958. Religion: Hebrew. Office: Northern Illinois University, DeKalb, Ill.

CAREER: Lock Haven Hospital, Lock Haven, Pa., instructor in nursing, 1949-50, director of nursing service education, 1950-53; Idaho State University, Pocatello, chairman of department of nursing, 1954-57; Northern Illinois University, DeKalb, professor of nursing and director of School of Nursing, 1958—. Consultant to Peace Corps; advisor to DeKalb County Nursing Home. Member of Committee For Nursing and Nursing Education, and Illinois State Board of Nurse Examiners. Military service: U.S. Army, Nurse Corps, 1942-46. Member: American Nurses Association, American Diabetes Association (member of advisory committee), Illinois Nurses Association, Illinois League for Nursing, Kappa Delta Pi, Pi Lambda Theta.

WRITINGS: (With C. B. Vedder) Problems of the Aged, C. C Thomas, 1965. Contributor to Forum and other journals.

*   *   *

LEHR, Delores   1920-

PERSONAL: Surname is pronounced Leer; born December 22, 1920, in Dallas, Tex.; daughter of Robert Powers and LaNette (Mims) Lehr. Education: Attended Southern Methodist University, 1944-45. Politics: Republican. Religion: Presbyterian. Home: 3017 Mahunna Springs Drive, Dallas, Tex. 75235.

CAREER: Farm and Ranch (magazine), youth editor, 1945-50; Wyatt Advertising Agency, San Antonio, Tex., radio-television director, 1951-56; Monte Rosenwald & Associates (advertising agency), Amarillo, Tex., account executive, 1956-60; Wyatt Advertising Agency, radio-television director, 1960-68; Dallas Market Center, Dallas, Tex., director of public relations, 1968-73, vice-president of public relations and advertising, 1973—. *Member:* National Multiple Sclerosis Society, Texas Teenage Library Association (honorary), Women in Communications (San Antonio chapter president, 1951, 1961); Public Relations Society of America (Dallas chapter), Press Club of Dallas (member of board of directors). *Awards, honors:* Headliner Award, Theta Sigma Phi (San Antonio), 1964; Dallas Chapter, Women in Communications, Matrix Award in journalism, 1973.

WRITINGS: The Tender Age, Lothrop, 1961; *Turnabout Summer*, Doubleday, 1964. Contributor of about 125 teenage short stories to magazines, including *Ingenue, American Girl, Catholic Miss, Co-ed, Venture*, and many other denominational teenage magazines.

WORK IN PROGRESS: A third teen-age novel; short stories.

AVOCATIONAL INTERESTS: Swimming, reading, and travel.

* * *

LEHRER, Keith 1936-

PERSONAL: Born January 10, 1936, in Minneapolis, Minn.; son of Abraham I. (a salesman) and Estelle (Mayrick) Lehrer; married Adrienne Kroman (a linguist), 1957; children: Mark Alan, David Russell. *Education:* University of Minnesota, B.A., 1957; Brown University, A.M., 1959, Ph.D., 1960. *Office:* Department of Philosophy, University of Arizona, Tucson, Ariz. 85721.

CAREER: Wayne State University, Detroit, Mich., instructor 1960-62, assistant professor of philosophy, 1962-63; University of Rochester, Rochester, N.Y., assistant professor, 1963-65, associate professor, and professor of philosophy, 1965-73; University of Arizona, Tucson, professor of philosophy, 1974—. Visiting associate professor, University of Calgary, summer, 1966; visiting lecturer in Scotland, summer, 1967; visiting professor, Vanderbilt University, 1970. *Member:* American Philosophical Association, Philosophy of Science Association, Centro Superiore Di Logica e Scienze Comparate (associate member), American Association for the Advancement of Science, Phi Beta Kappa. *Awards and honors:* National Science Foundation senior postdoctoral fellowship, 1966-67; American Council of Learned Societies fellowship, 1973; Center for Advanced Study in the Behavioral Sciences fellowship, 1973-74.

WRITINGS: (Editor and contributor) *Freedom and Determinism*, Random House, 1966; (contributor) Hector Casteneda, editor, *Intentionality, Minds, and Perception*, Wayne State University Press, 1966; (with James Cornman) *Philosophical Problems and Arguments: An Introduction*, Macmillan, 1968, revised edition, 1974; (editor with Adrienne Lehrer) *Theory and Meaning*, Prentice-Hall, 1970; (contributor) Robert Swartz and Roderick Chisholm, editors, *Empirical Knowledge*, Prentice-Hall, 1971; (editor with Herbert Feigland and Wilfrid Sellars) *New Readings in Philosophical Analysis*, Appleton, 1972; (contributor) R. Maynard and G. Pearce, editors, *Conceptual Change*, Reidel, 1973; *Knowledge*, Clarendon, 1974; (editor with Ronald Beanblossom) *Reid's Inquiry and Essays*, Bobbs-Merrill, 1975; (editor and contributor) *Analysis and Metaphysics: Essays in Honor of R. M. Chisholm*, Reidel, 1975. Also author of a teaching module, *The Philosophy of Skepticism*, 1973. Contributor to *Journal of Philosophy, Metaphilosophy, The Philosophical Review, The Philosophical Forum*, and other philosophy journals. Editor-in-chief, *Philosophical Studies*; member of editorial board, *Amer-*

ican Philosophical Quarterly, and *Grazer Philosophischen Studien*; member of editorial advisory board, *Philosophical Forum*.

* * *

LEIBOWITZ, Herschel W. 1925-

PERSONAL: Born February 21, 1925, in York, Pa.; son of Lewis (a salesman) and Nettie (Wolfson) Leibowitz; married Eileen Wirtshafter, June 12, 1949; children: Marjorie, Michael. *Education:* Attended University of Paris, 1945-46; University of Pennsylvania, B.A., 1948; Columbia University, M.A., 1950, Ph.D., 1951. *Religion:* Jewish. *Home:* 500 Glenn Rd., State College, Pa. 16801. *Office:* Department of Psychology, Pennsylvania State University, University Park, Pa. 16802.

CAREER: University of Wisconsin, Madison, 1951-61, started as instructor in psychology, professor, 1960-61, research associate, School of Medicine, 1953-56; Pennsylvania State University, University Park, professor of psychology, 1962—. Visiting lecturer at University of Maryland, 1960-62; visiting summer professor at University of Michigan, 1962, Massachusetts Institute of Technology, 1963, Florida State University, 1972; visiting scientist in Japan, 1965. Advisory psychologist, International Business Machines Corp., 1960-62, research consultant, 1964—; consultant to Veterans Administration, 1959—, Institute for Defense Analysis, 1964—, U.S. Department of the Interior, 1965-67, U.S. Department of Defense, 1967—, Institute of Environmental Medicine, 1971—. Member of psychobiology review panel, National Science Foundation, 1962-65; member of National Academy of Sciences-National Research Council Armed Forces Vision Committee, 1963—. Member of advisory board, Applied Research Laboratory, 1973—. *Military service:* U.S. Army, 1943-46; served in Europe with 75th Infantry Division. *Member:* American Psychological Association (fellow), American Association for the Advancement of Science (fellow), American Academy of Optometry (fellow), Optical Society of America, Human Factors Society, Psychonomic Society. *Awards, honors:* Guggenheim fellowship, 1957; Heineman stipend, 1967.

WRITINGS: (Contributor) M. Marx, *Some Trends in Perceptual Theory*, 2nd edition, Macmillan, 1963; *Visual Perception*, Macmillan, 1965. Contributor of over eighty articles to professional journals. Member of editorial advisory board, *International Journal of Vision Research*, 1959-64, 1970—, *Psychologische Forschung*, 1965—, *Perception and Psychophysics*, 1969—; consulting editor, *Journal of Experimental Psychology*, 1960—, *Psychological Bulletin*, 1964-68, *Behavioral Research and Instrumentation*, 1970, *Contemporary Psychology*, 1973—.†

* * *

LEMAY, J(oseph) A(lberic) Leo 1935-

PERSONAL: Born January 7, 1935, in Bristow, Va.; son of Joseph Albert (a steelworker) and Valencia L. (Winslow) Lemay; married Muriel Ann Clarke, August 11, 1965. *Education:* University of Maryland, A.B., 1957, A.M., 1962; University of Pennsylvania, Ph.D., 1964. *Politics:* Democrat. *Religion:* Unitarian Universalist. *Home:* 501 21st Pl., Santa Monica, Calif. 90402. *Office:* Department of English, University of California, Los Angeles, Calif. 90024.

CAREER: George Washington University, Washington, D.C., assistant professor of English, 1963-65; University of California, Los Angeles, assistant professor, 1965-70, associate professor, 1970-75, professor of English, 1975—. *Military service:* U.S. Army, 1957-59. *Member:* Modern Language Association of America, American Studies Association, American Antiquarian Society, Maryland Historical Society, Pennsylvania Historical Society, Virginia Historical Society, Hakluyt Society. *Awards, honors:* Grants from American Philosophical Society and Colonial Wiliamsburg; Guggenheim fellowship.

WRITINGS: Ebenezer Kinnersley: Franklin's Friend, University of Pennsylvania Press, 1964; *Men of Letters in Colonial Maryland*, University of Tennessee Press, 1972; *A Calendar of American Poetry in Colonial Newspapers and Magazines through 1765*, American Antiquarian Society, 1972.

WORK IN PROGRESS: The Ideology of Early American Humor.

* * *

LEMON, Lee T(homas) 1931-

PERSONAL: Born January 9, 1931, in Kansas City, Kan.; son of Theodore G. and Margaret (Baldwin) Lemon; married Maria Mullinaux, May 5, 1973; children: (previous marriage) Kristina Lynn, Geoffrey Williams, Katherine Renee, Gregory Badgley. *Education:* St. Louis University, B.S., 1951; Southern Illinois University, M.A., 1952; University of Illinois, Ph.D., 1961. *Politics:* Independent. *Religion:* "Doubtful." *Home:* 7201 Eastborough Lane, Lincoln, Neb. 68502. *Office:* 218 Andrews Hall, University of Nebraska, Lincoln, Neb. 68508.

CAREER: University of Nebraska, Lincoln, 1961—, began as assistant professor, professor of literature 1965—. *Military service:* U.S. Army, 1952-54. *Member:* Modern Language Association of America, National Council of Teachers of English, Midwest Modern Language Association, American Association of University Professors. *Awards, honors:* Woods fellowship, 1965; Maud Hammond Fling award, 1974.

WRITINGS: The Partial Critics, Oxford University Press, 1965; (translator and editor with Marion J. Reis) *The Russian Formalist Critics: Four Essays*, University of Nebraska Press, 1965; *Approaches to Literature*, Oxford University Press, 1969; *A Glossary for the Study of English*, Oxford University Press, 1971. Contributor to literary journals. Advisory editor, *Prairie Schooner.*

WORK IN PROGRESS: A book on unusual forms of fiction; a study of symbolist theories of language; studies of Eastern aesthetics.

SIDELIGHTS: Lemon has some competence in French, Russian, and German.

* * *

LENTZ, Donald A. 1910-

PERSONAL: Born January 24, 1910, in South Dakota; son of Elmer Anthony (a dentist) and Margaret (Gamble) Lentz; married Velma Gildemeister (a pianist). *Education:* South Dakota State College (now University), B.S., 1930; University of South Dakota, M.F.A., 1935; private study in flute, composition, and conducting with George Barrere, Albert Stoessel, Vladimir Bakaleinikoff, and Virgil Thomson. *Office:* University of Nebraska, Lincoln, Neb. 68505.

CAREER: Vermillion (S.D.) public schools, director of music, 1932; University of Nebraska, Lincoln, 1937—, as-

sociate professor, 1939-53, professor of music, 1953—, professor of ethnomusicology, 1973—, director of bands, 1937-73. Summer instructor at University of Idaho, University of Wyoming, National Music Camp, and elsewhere. Former flutist with New York Symphony Orchestra and Sousa Band; conductor of music festivals throughout United States. *Member:* American Bandmasters Association, College Band Directors National Association, American Association of University Professors, Asia Society, Nebraska Music Educators Conference, Pi Kappa Lambda, Phi Beta Mu. *Awards, honors:* Woods Foundation research grants to India and Ceylon, 1957, and Indonesia and Malaya, 1962; university research grant, Central Asia, 1968.

WRITINGS: Lentz Bassoon Method, Book I, Belwin, 1940, Book II, 1942; *Clef Transposition*, Paul A. Schmitt Co., 1948; *Tones and Intervals of Hindu Classical Music*, University of Nebraska Press, 1961; *The Gamelan Music of Java and Bali*, University of Nebraska Press, 1962. Composer of music for band, flute, and piano, published by Lavell, Belwin, Witmark, Tempo, and Carl Fischer, 1941-73; works also include five filmstrips on woodwinds, 1950-53. Contributor to *Inmusica* (Calcutta), and *Chinese Music Journal.* Reviewer of band music, *Nebraska Music Educators Journal*, 1958—.

WORK IN PROGRESS: Research on tonal systems of Sumatra, Malaya, and some Burmese cultures.

* * *

LEONARD, George K., Jr. 1915-

PERSONAL: Born January 12, 1915, in Lincoln, Neb.; son of George K. (a civil engineer) and Charlotte (Calder) Leonard; married Ellouise White, October 3, 1945; children: George III, Thomas, James, Ernest. *Education:* Studied at University of Nebraska, 1932-34, Northwestern University, 1934-35; University of Alabama, B.A., 1936. *Religion:* Episcopalian. *Home:* 3818 Hilldale Dr., Nashville, Tenn. 37215. *Office: Nashville Banner*, 1100 Broad, Nashville, Tenn. 37202.

CAREER: Nashville Banner, Nashville, Tenn., sports writer, 1936-40, 1946—; Associated Press, Lincoln, Neb., 1941; *Chattanooga Times*, Cahttanooga, Tenn., reporter, 1941-42. *Military service:* U.S. Navy, 1942-46; became lieutenant. *Member:* Football Writers Association of America. *Awards, honors:* Dutton Sports Story Award for best news sports story, 1964; Tennessee Sports Writer of the Year Award, 1968.

WRITINGS: (With Fred Russell) *Big Bowl Football*, Ronald, 1963. Story included in *Best Sports Stories*, Dutton, 1961, 1964, 1969.

* * *

LEONDES, Cornelius Thomas 1927-

PERSONAL: Born July 27, 1927, in Philadelphia, Pa.; son of Themistocles and Calypso (Bezzerides) Leondes; married Nancy Lyle Rinehart, 1952; children: Gregory Philip. *Education:* University of Pennsylvania, B.S., 1949, M.S., 1951, Ph.D., 1954. *Home:* 175 Ashdal Pl., Los Angeles, Calif. 90049. *Office:* Department of Engineering, University of California, Los Angeles, Calif. 90024.

CAREER: Engineer at Naval Air Development Center, Johnsville, Pa., 1949, at Burroughs Corp., Paoli, Pa., 1950, and at University of Pennsylvania, Philadelphia, 1950-55; University of California, Los Angeles, U.S. Air Force Scientific Advisory Board, consultant to guidance and control panel. *Member:* Institute of Radio Engineers (fellow), American Institute of Electrical Engineers, American Rocket Society, American Astronautical Society (senior member), American Association of University Professors, Sigma Xi, Tau Beta Pi, Sigma Tau, Eta Kappa Nu, Pi Mu Epsilon. *Awards, honors:* Baiter Prize, 1970; Barry Carlton Award, 1973.

WRITINGS: (Editor) Llewellyn M. K. Boelter and others, *Computer Control Systems Technology*, McGraw, 1961; *Guidance and Control of Aerospace Vehicles*, McGraw, 1963; (editor) *Advances in Control System Theory and Application*, Volumes I-XII, Academic Press, 1964; (editor with R. W. Vance) M. S. Agbabian and others, *Lunar Missions and Exploration*, Wiley, 1964.

* * *

LERNER, Eugene Max 1928-

PERSONAL: Born October 9, 1928, in Milwaukee, Wis.; son of Hyman (a businessman) and Dorothy (Buchler) Lerner; married Janet Ruth Weiss (a professor), July 1, 1951; children: Susan, Laura, Dean. *Education:* University of Wisconsin, B.A., 1949, M.A., 1950; University of Chicago, Ph.D., 1954. *Religion:* Jewish. *Home:* 823 Ingleside, Evanston, Ill. *Office:* Department of Finance, Northwestern University, Evanston, Ill. 60201.

CAREER: Elmhurst College, Elmhurst, Ill., instructor, 1952-54; University of Idaho, Moscow, assistant professor, 1954-55; National Bureau of Economic Research, research associate, 1955; Federal Reserve Bank of Chicago, Chicago, Ill., senior economist, 1957-59; Northwestern University, Evanston, Ill., assistant professor, and research economist, Transportation Center, 1958-59; City College (now City College of the City University of New York), New York, N.Y., assistant professor of economics, 1959-62; New York University, New York, N.Y., associate professor, 1962-66; Northwestern University, professor of finance, 1966—. Economist, New York State Joint Legislative Committee to Revise Banking Law, 1962-66, and Banking and Currency Committee, U.S. House of Representatives, 1965. *Member:* American Economic Association, American Finance Association.

WRITINGS: Economic Value of American Merchant Marine, Northwestern University Press, 1960; (editor) *Readings in Financial Analysis and Investment Management*, Irwin, 1964; (with W. T. Carleton) *Theory of Financial Analysis*, Harcourt, 1966; (with Alfred Rappaport) *A Framework for Financial Reporting by Diversified Companies*, National Association of Accountants, 1969; *Managerial Finance: A Systems Approach*, Harcourt, 1971; (with Rappaport) *Segment Reporting for Managers and Investors*, National Association of Accountants, 1972.†

* * *

LeSHAN, Lawrence L(ee) 1920-
(Edward Grendon)

PERSONAL: Born September 8, 1920, in New York, N.Y.; son of Julius (a scientist) and Rose (Adelson) LeShan; married Edna Grossman (a parent education specialist and writer), 1944; children: Wendy. *Education:* College of William and Mary, B.A., 1942; University of Nebraska, M.S., 1943; University of Chicago, Ph.D., 1954. *Office:* 29 West 75th St., New York, N.Y. 10023.

CAREER: Roosevelt University, Chicago, Ill., instructor,

later assistant professor of psychology, 1948-51; Worthington Associates, Inc., associate psychologist, 1950-51; Foundation for Human Research, research associate, 1952-54; Institute of Applied Biology, New York, N.Y., chief of department of psychology, 1954-64; Ayer Foundation, Inc., New York, N.Y., research associate, 1954-70. Union Theological Seminary Program in Psychiatry and Religion, research psychologist. *Military service:* U.S. Army, 1943-46, 1950-52; became second lieutenant. *Member:* American Psychological Association, Federation of American Scientists, American Psychical Research.

WRITINGS: (With Bowers, Jackson, and Knight) *Counselling the Dying*, Nelson, 1964; (editor with Kissen) *Psychosomatic Aspects of Neoplastic Disease*, Lippincott, 1964; *How to Meditate: A Guide to Self-Discovery*, Little, Brown, 1974. Also author of *The Medium, the Mystic, and the Physicist: Toward a General Theory of the Paranormal*, 1974. Contributor of fifty articles to psychological and psychiatric journals, four short stories to science fiction magazines.

WORK IN PROGRESS: Research in parapsychology.

* * *

LESKO, George 1932-

PERSONAL: Born February 22, 1932, in McKeesport, Pa.; son of George and Ann (Barno) Lesko; married Ruth Garland (a television writer and producer), August 25, 1957; children: Tanya, Hud. *Education:* New York University, B.A., 1962.

CAREER: Palmer, Willson & Worden, Inc. (advertising and public relations agency), New York, N.Y., manager of Pittsburgh (Pa.) office, 1962—. Photographer. *Military service:* U.S. Army, Signal Corps, 1953-55. *Member:* Public Relations Society of America, Association of Industrial Advertisers, Pittsburgh Press Club.

WRITINGS: You and Your Boat, Lothrop, 1964.

SIDELIGHTS: Lesko is competent in Russian, German, and Spanish.†

* * *

LESLIE, Cecilie 1914-
(Eve MacAdam)

PERSONAL: Born July 18, 1914, in Motihari, India; daughter of Kenneth Marshall Murray (a solicitor) and Dorothy May (Issard) Leslie; married Arthur Coulton Hartley (in British Ministry of Defence); children: Folla Leslie (Mrs. L. J. Quine), John Murray Leslie. *Education:* Educated in Darjeeling, India, Worchestershire, England and at Sorbonne, University of Paris. *Politics:* Liberal. *Home:* Stream Mill, Chiddingly (Lewes), Sussex, England. *Agent:* John Green, Hughes Massie, Ltd., 18 Southampton Pl., London W.C. 1, England; Maurice Crain, Inc., 18 East 41st St., New York, N.Y. 10017.

CAREER: Former staff writer on *Evening Standard, Daily Mirror*, and *Daily Sketch*, all London, England; later associate editor, *Woman's Own* (magazine); editor-in-chief of government publications and information officer of Indian Ministry of Information during World War II.

WRITINGS: The Viennese Hat, Methuen, 1935; *Goat to Kali*, Cassell, 1948; *Award of Custody*, Cassell, 1949; *Blue Devils*, Cassell, 1951; *Rope Bridge* (about country of Sikkim), Doubleday, 1964; *The Golden Stairs*, Doubleday, 1966. Contributor to periodicals, including *Playbill* and

Television Times; critic for *Catholic Herald*, under pseudonym Eve MacAdam.

SIDELIGHTS: Cecile Leslie told *CA* that she was born into a family which has had business and administrative connections in India and Burma for 250 years, and was married to a long-time civil servant in India. She spent her childhood and much of her adult life there.†

*   *   *

LESLIE, F(rederic) Andrew   1927-

PERSONAL: Born February 20, 1927, in Mahwah, N.J.; son of Harold D. and Margaret (Schmucker) Leslie; married Constance Clement, June 30, 1956; children: Alison, Duncan. *Education:* Colgate University, B.A., 1950; New York University, M.A., 1964. *Home:* Apartment 11B, 21 Stuyvesant Oval, New York, N.Y. 10009. *Office:* Dramatists Play Service, Inc., 440 Park Ave. South, New York, N.Y. 10016.

CAREER: National Concert and Artists Corp., New York, N.Y., artists representative, 1953-57; William Morris Agency, Inc., New York, agent, 1957-59; Maurice Evans Productions, Inc., New York, director of sales, 1959-60; Dramatists Play Service, Inc., New York, executive director and secretary-treasurer, 1960—. *Military service:* U.S. Navy, Naval Aviation, 1944-46.

WRITINGS—Stage adaptations of novels and screenplays by others; all published by Dramatists Play Service: *The Bachelor and the Bobby-Soxer*, 1961; *The Boy With the Green Hair*, 1961; *The Farmer's Daughter*, 1962; *The Spiral Staircase*, 1962; *Mr. Hobb's Vacation*, 1963; *The Haunting of Hill House*, 1964; *Splendor in the Grass*, 1966; *The Wheeler Dealers*, 1966; *The Lilies of the Field*, 1967. Also author of unpublished stage adaptations.

*   *   *

LESLIE, Gerald R(onnell)   1925-

PERSONAL: Born April 16, 1925, in Columbus, Ohio; son of Robert Miles and Nellie (Wittkugle) Leslie; married Elizabeth McLaughlin. *Education:* Ohio State University, B.A., 1948, M.A., 1949, Ph.D., 1951. *Home:* 2015 North West 27 St., Gainesville, Fla. 32604. *Office:* Department of Sociology, University of Florida, Gainesville, Fla. 32601.

CAREER: Purdue University, Lafayette, Ind., instructor, 1950-52, assistant professor, 1952-53, associate professor, 1955-56, professor of sociology, 1956-63; Oklahoma State University, Stillwater, professor of sociology, and head of department, 1963-67; University of Florida, Gainesville, professor of sociology, and head of department, 1967—. Visiting professor at University of North Carolina, 1953-54, Columbia University, 1956-57, University of California, Berkeley, 1959. *Military service:* U.S. Army, 1943-46. *Member:* American Sociological Association, American Association of Marriage Counselors (president, 1966-67), American Association of University Professors, National Council on Family Relations, (president, 1970-71), Phi Beta Kappa.

WRITINGS: (With Paul B. Horton) *The Sociology of Social Problems*, 3rd edition, Appleton, 1965, 5th edition, Prentice-Hall, 1974; *The Family in Social Context*, Oxford University Press, 1967, 2nd edition, 1973; (editor with Horton) *Studies in the Sociology of Social Problems*, Appleton, 1970, 2nd edition, Prentice-Hall, 1975; (with Richard F. Larson and Benjamin L. Gorman) *Order and Change*, Oxford University Press, 1973. Contributor to journals in field.

LESSMANN, Paul G.   1919-

PERSONAL: Born June 16, 1919, in Milwaukee, Wis.; son of Ernest H. and Marie (Krienitz) Lessmann; married Ruth Brauer, October 20, 1944; children: Ronald, Gary. *Education:* Attended Concordia College, Milwaukee, Wis., 1937-39; Concordia Seminary, St. Louis, Mo., A.B., 1941, B.D., 1944; Johns Hopkins University, M.Ed., 1956. *Politics:* Republican. *Home and office:* Concordia Seminary in Exile, 306 N. Grand St., St. Louis, Mo. 63103.

CAREER: Ordained minister of Lutheran Church, Missouri Synod, 1944; minister in Towson, Md., 1944-56, and Peoria, Ill., 1956-65; Concordia Seminary, St. Louis, Mo., director of field education and assistant professor, beginning 1965, became associate professor of practical theology. Pastoral counselor of International Lutheran Women's Missionary League, 1961-65. *Member:* Phi Delta Kappa.

WRITINGS: The Lord's Prayer and the Lord's Passion, Concordia, 1965; *An Advent Alphabet*, Concordia, 1968; *The New You*, Concordia, 1969. Contributor to books of sermons and to Lutheran periodicals.

SIDELIGHTS: Lessmann is competent in German, Latin, Greek, Hebrew, and Spanish.

*   *   *

LESTER, Julius B.   1939-

PERSONAL: Born January 27, 1939, in St. Louis, Mo.; son of W. D. (a minister) and Julia (Smith) Lester; married Joan Steinau (a researcher), December 22, 1962; children: Jody Simone. *Education:* Fisk University, B.A., 1960.

CAREER: Professional musician and singer, recording with Vanguard Records; folklorist and writer on Black culture. Newport Folk Festival, director, 1966-68. *Member:* American Folklore Society, Student Non-violent Coordinating Committee.

WRITINGS: (With Pete Seeger) *The 12-String Guitar as Played by Leadbelly*, Oak, 1965; *Look Out Whitey! Black Power's Gon' Get Your Mama!*, Dial, 1968; *To Be a Slave*, Dial, 1969; *Black Folktales*, Baron, 1969; *Search for the New Land: History as Subjective Experience*, Dial, 1969; *Revolutionary Notes*, Baron, 1969; (editor) *The Seventh Son: The Thoughts and Writings of W.E.B. DuBois*, two volumes, Random House, 1971; (compiler with Rae Pace Alexander) *Young and Black in America*, Random House, 1971; *The Long Journey Home: Stories from Black History*, Dial, 1972; *The Knee High Man and Other Tales*, Dial, 1972; *Two Love Stories*, Dial, 1972; (editor) Stanley Couch, *Ain't No Ambulances for No Nigguhs Tonight* (poems), Baron, 1972; *Who Am I?* (poems), Dial, 1974.

Associate editor, *Sing Out*, 1964—; contributing editor, *Broadside of New York*, 1964—; contributor to *Sounds & Fury, Village Voice*, and other periodicals.

BIOGRAPHICAL/CRITICAL SOURCES: Nation, June 22, 1970.†

*   *   *

LETTAU, Reinhard   1929-

PERSONAL: Born September 10, 1929, in Erfurt, Germany; son of Reinhard F. and Gertrude (Felsberg) Lettau; married Mary Gene Carter, September 4, 1954; children: Karen, Kevyn, Catherine. *Education:* Harvard University, Ph.D., 1960; attended University of Heidelberg. *Home:* 1150 Cuchara Dr., Del Mar, Calif. *Office:* Department of Literature, San Diego State University, P.O. Box 109, La Jolla, Calif. 92037.

CAREER: Harvard University, Cambridge, Mass., teaching fellow, 1955-57; Smith College, Northampton, Mass., instructor, 1957-59, assistant professor, 1959-63, associate professor of German literature and language, 1963-67; San Diego State University, La Jolla, Calif., professor of German literature and creative writing, 1967—. Guest lecturer at University of Massachusetts, 1958, and Mt. Holyoke College, 1960; Hanser Verlag, Munich, Germany, scout, 1965—. *Member:* Modern Language Association, Group 47.

WRITINGS: Schwierigkeiten beim Haeuserbauen (short stories), Hanser Verlag, 1962; *Auftritt Manigs* (short prose), Hanser Verlag, 1963; (editor) *Lachen mit Thurber*, Rowohlt, 1963; *Obstacles* (short stories), Pantheon, 1965; *Gedichte*, Colloquium, 1967; *Handbuch der Gruppe 47*, Luehterhand, 1967; *Feinde*, Hanser Verlag, 1968 (published in England as *Enemies*, Calder Boyars, 1973); *Taglicher Faschismus*, Hanser Verlag, 1971; *Immer kurzer Werdende Gesihichten*, Hanser Verlag, 1973.

WORK IN PROGRESS: Breakfast Conversations in Miami (prose).

SIDELIGHTS: Translations of Dr. Lettau's books have appeared in France, England, Spain, Italy, Poland, Sweden, Denmark, Norway, and Finland.

* * *

LETWIN, Shirley Robin 1924-

PERSONAL: Born February 17, 1924, in Chicago, Ill.; daughter of Morris H. and Mary (Beitch) Robin; married William Letwin, January 4, 1944; children: Oliver. *Education:* University of Chicago, M.A., 1944, Ph.D., 1951. *Home:* 3 Kent Terrace, London N.W. 1, England.

CAREER: Teacher of political theory and history at University of Chicago, Brandeis University, and Harvard University, 1951-64; London School of Economics and Political Science, London, England, lecturer in philosophy, 1969-72; Cambridge University, Peterhouse College, Cambridge, England, member of faculty of philosophy, 1972—. Fellow, Radcliffe Institute, Cambridge, Mass., 1961-63.

WRITINGS: Pursuit of Certainty, Cambridge University Press, 1965. Contributor to *Dictionary of the History of Ideas*, and *The Great Ideas Today*. Also contributor of articles to *Review of Politics, Cambridge Journal, Encounter, Historical Journal, The Human World, Spectator*, and other periodicals.

WORK IN PROGRESS: Trollope's Gentleman: An English Morality; History of the Philosophy of Law.

* * *

LEVER, Katherine 1916-

PERSONAL: Born February 15, 1916, in St. Louis, Mo.; daughter of John H. and Cora (Medbury) Lever. *Education:* Swarthmore College, A.B., 1936. Bryn Mawr College, M.A., 1937, Ph.D., 1943. *Politics:* Independent. *Religion:* Episcopalian. *Office:* Department of English, Wellesley College, Wellesley, Mass. 02181.

CAREER: University of Rochester, Rochester, N.Y., instructor in English, 1939-41; Wellesley College, Wellesley, Mass., professor of English, 1942—, chairman of department, 1959-62. *Member:* Modern Language Association of America, American Philological Association, Phi Beta Kappa. *Awards, honors:* Folger Shakespeare Library fellow.

WRITINGS: The Art of Greek Comedy, Methuen, 1956; *The Novel and the Reader*, Appleton, 1961; *The Perfect Teacher*, Seabury, 1964. Contributor to professional journals.

* * *

LEVI, Lennart 1930-

PERSONAL: Born May 20, 1930, in Riga, Latvia; son of Sam (a merchant) and Debora (Lowenstein) Levi; married Isabella Weitman, August 16, 1957; children: Jan Richard, George Ragnar. *Education:* Attended University of Stockholm, one year; Karolinska Institute, M.D., 1959. *Home:* Solangsvagen 35, S-19154 Sollentuna, Sweden. *Office:* Laboratory for Clinical Stress Research, Fack, S-10401 Stockholm, Sweden.

CAREER: State Rehabilitation Clinic, Stockholm, Sweden, physician, 1956-58; Karolinska Hospital, Stockholm, research physician in departments of medicine and psychiatry, 1959—, and director of Laboratory for Clinical Stress Research and World Health Organization Psychosocial Centre; industrial physician (part-time), Swedish AEG Concern. *Military service:* Swedish Army, surgeon, 1965—. *Member:* Swedish Medical Association, American Psychosomatic Society, Society for Psychophysiological Research, International Society of Psychoneuroendocrinology, International College of Psychosomatic Medicine.

WRITINGS: Stress-Korper, Seele und Krankheit, Musterschmidt-Verlag, 1964 (English translation published as *Stress: Sources, Management and Prevention*, Liveright, 1967); *Fran sjuksang till arbetsbank* (title means "From Sick-bed to Work-Table"), Swedish Personnel Administration Council, 1966; (editor) *Emotional Stress: Physiological and Psychological: Reactions—Medical, Industrial, and Military Implications*, American Elsevier, 1967; (with Kurt Bronner) *The Stress of Everyday Work*, Personnel Administration Council, 1967; *Psycho-Physiological Reactions During Emotional Stress*, American Elsevier, 1967.

(Editor) *Society, Stress and Disease: The Psychosocial Environment and Psychosomatic Diseases*, Oxford University Press, 1971; *Stress and Disease in Response to Psychosocial Stimuli*, Pergamon, 1972; (with Lars Andersson) *Psychosocial Stress: Population, Environment, and Quality of Life*, Spectrum, 1975; (editor) *Emotions: Their Parameters and Measurement*, Raven Press, 1975; (editor) *Society, Stress and Disease: Childhood and Adolescence*, Oxford University Press, 1975.

Contributor: W. Raab, editor, *Preventive Cardiology*, C. C Thomas, 1966; E. Bajusz, editor, *An Introduction to Clinical Neuro-endocrinology*, S. Karger, 1967. Contributor of research papers to medical journals in United States and Sweden.

* * *

LEVINE, David 1928-

PERSONAL: Born July 14, 1928, in New York, N.Y.; son of Max and Esther (Trager) Levine; married June Perry (an instructor in English), June, 1949; children: Katha, Jane, Adam, Emily. *Education:* Attended City College (now City College of the City University of New York), 1944-46; University of Michigan, B.S., 1949; New York University, Ph.D., 1953. *Residence:* Lincoln, Neb. *Office:* Department of Psychology, University of Nebraska, Lincoln, Neb.

CAREER: Diplomate, American Board of Examiners in Professional Psychology. U.S. Veterans Administration, clinical psychologist, 1953-57, consultant, 1958—; University of Nebraska, Lincoln, associate professor of psychology, 1958-63, professor, 1963—, chairman of department, 1968-74. Visiting fellow, Cambridge University Institute of Criminology, 1974-75. *Member:* American Psychological Association, American Association for the Advancement of Science, Society for the Study of Social Issues, American Psychology of Law Society, Judicature Society.

WRITINGS: (With James Clifton) *Klamath Personalities*, University of Oregon Press, 1961; (editor) *Nebraska Symposium on Motivation*, University of Nebraska Press, 1964, 1965; (contributor) Maly and Harshberger, editors, *Behavioral Analysis & Systems Analysis: An Integrative Approach to Mental Health Programs*, Behaviordelia, 1974.

WORK IN PROGRESS: Contribution to a collection entitled *Socialization and the Law.*

* * *

LEVINE, Mortimer 1922-

PERSONAL: Born December 19, 1922, in Brooklyn, N.Y.; son of Jacob and Anna (Schiller) Levine. *Education:* New York University, B.A., 1948; University of Pennsylvania, M.A., 1949, Ph.D., 1954. *Home:* 529 Woodhaven Dr., Morgantown, W.Va. 26505. *Office:* West Virginia University, Morgantown, W.Va. 26506.

CAREER: Brooklyn College (now of the City University of New York), Brooklyn, N.Y., lecturer in history, 1955; West Virginia University, Morgantown, instructor, 1955-57, assistant professor, 1957-61, associate professor, 1961-67, professor of history, 1967—. *Military service:* U.S. Coast Guard, radioman, 1942-46. *Member:* American Historical Association, Conference on British Studies, Renaissance Society of America, Royal Historical Society (fellow).

WRITINGS: The Early Elizabethan Succession Question, 1558-1568, Stanford University Press, 1966; *Tudor England, 1485-1603*, Cambridge University Press, 1968; (contributor) Arthur J. Slavin, editor, *Tudor Men and Institutions*, Louisiana State University Press, 1972; *Tudor Dynastic Problems, 1460-1571*, Barnes & Noble, 1973. Coeditor, "Archives of British History and Culture," annual documentary series published by Conference on British Studies at West Virginia University. Contributor to *Speculum, American Journal of Legal History, Huntington Library Quarterly, Historical Journal* (Cambridge), and *Historian.*

WORK IN PROGRESS: Queen Anne Boleyn, for Stanford University Press, completion expected in 1976.

* * *

LEVINE, Stuart (George) 1932-

PERSONAL: Born May 25, 1932, in New York, N.Y.; son of Max and Jean (Berens) Levine; married Susan Matthews, June, 1963; children: Rebecca Marian, Aaron Daniel, Allen Joel. *Education:* Harvard University, A.B., 1954; Brown University, M.A., 1956, Ph.D., 1958. *Politics:* Democrat. *Religion:* Jewish. *Home:* 1313 Massachusetts St., Lawrence, Kan. 66044. *Office:* American Studies Program, University of Kansas, 1135 Maine St., Lawrence, Kan. 66045.

CAREER: University of Kansas, Lawrence, instructor, 1958-61, assistant professor, 1961-63, associate professor of

American studies, 1964—, chairman of American studies department, 1965-71. Fulbright lecturer at University of La Plata, 1962, at University of Costa Rica, 1965, 1967, and at National Autonomous University of Mexico, 1972. Guest professor at Kansas State University, 1965, University of Missouri at Kansas City, 1966, 1974; visiting professor, California State University, 1969, 1971; scholar-in-residence, University of Arizona, 1971-72. Regional chairman, Harvard College Fund. *Member:* American Studies Association, Modern Language Association of America, Mid-continent American Studies Association (member of executive board), Midwest Modern Language Association, Phi Beta Kappa. *Awards, honors:* Research grants from University of Kansas Graduate School, 1958-63, and Carnegie Foundation; Anisfield-Wolf Award in Race Relations, 1968.

WRITINGS: Materials for Technical Writing, Allyn & Bacon, 1963; (contributor) *American Culture in the Sixties*, H. W. Wilson, 1964; *The American Indian Today*, Everett Edwards, 1967, revised edition, Penguin, 1970; (editor and author of biographical and critical study) Charles Caffin, *The Story of American Painting*, Johnson, 1970; *Edgar Poe: Seer and Craftsman*, Everett Edwards, 1972. Contributor of articles and reviews to *American Quarterly* and other journals. Editor, *American Studies*, 1959—, including booklength issue on the "Indian Today," 1965.

WORK IN PROGRESS: With wife, Susan Levine, *The Short Fiction of Edgar Allan Poe: An Annotated Edition*, for Bobbs-Merrill.

SIDELIGHTS: Levine speaks Spanish. *Avocational interests:* Painting, music (former concert music commentator; plays French horn and banjo).

* * *

LEVY, Howard S(eymour) 1923-

PERSONAL: Born April 5, 1923, in Brooklyn, N.Y.; son of Isidore and Pauline (Hoffman) Levy; married second wife, Henriette Liu, October 15, 1961; children: (first marriage) Ian Hideo, Raoul Nelson; (second marriage) Lincoln Isidore; (adopted) Nina Marie. *Education:* Brooklyn College (now Brooklyn College of the City University of New York), B.A., 1943; University of Michigan, M.A., 1947; University of California, Ph.D., 1951. *Address:* Foreign Service Institute Field School, FPO San Francisco, Calif. 98761.

CAREER: Instructor in Oriental languages at University of Denver Community Center, Denver, Colo., 1952-56, and University of Colorado Extension, Denver, 1954-56; U.S. Department of State, Foreign Service Institute, director of Chinese Language School, Taiwan, 1957-61, director of Japanese Language School, Tokyo, Japan, 1961-69, linguist in Washington, D.C., 1969-74, linguist at Japanese Language and Area Training Center, Yokohama, Japan, 1974—. *Military service:* U.S. Army, 1943-46. *Member:* Association for Asian Studies, International Conversation Society (Yokohama), Japan America Society, Sinologica.

WRITINGS: (Editor) *Selections of Modern Chinese Literature*, [Denver], 1954; *The Career of Yang Kuei-fei*, R. J. Brill, 1957; *Harem Favorites of an Illustrious Celestial* (essays), Lin Yun-p'eng (Taiwan), 1958; (with Ryoji Susaki) *Unsung Hero: The Late Nagao Ryuzo Conversation*, Paragon, 1967; *Chinese Footbinding: The History of a Curious Erotic Custom*, Twayne, 1966; (with Akira Ishihara) *Tao of Sex*, [Yokohama], 1968, Harper, 1970; *Sex, Love, and the Japanese*, Warm Soft Village Press, 1971, published as *Oriental Sex Manners*, New England Library, 1972.

Translator: (And editor) Hsiu Ou-yang, *Biography of Huang Ch'ao*, University of California Press, 1955, 2nd edition, revised and enlarged, 1961; *Biography of An Lushan*, University of California Press, 1960; *The Illusory Flame: Chinese Love Stories*, Warm Soft Village Press, 1962; (and editor) Po Chu-i, *Lament Everlasting: The Death of Yang Kuei-fei*, Paragon, 1962; *Warm-Soft Village: Chinese Essays on Love*, Paragon, 1964; Cho Chang, *The Dwelling of Playful Goddesses*, Paragon, 1965; Huai Yu, *Feast of Mist and Flower*, Paragon, 1966; Chang Ching-Sheng, *Sex Histories: China's Earliest Modern Treatise on Sex Education*, Paragon, 1967, 3rd edition, Warm Soft Village Press, 1970; *Translations from Po Chu-i's Collected Works*, Volume I: *The Old Style Poems*, Volume II: *The Regular Poems*, Paragon, 1971; (with R. F. Yang) *Monks and Nuns in a Sea of Sins*, Warm Soft Village Press, 1971, also published as *Chinese Monks and Nuns in a Sea of Sins*, 1971; (and compiler) *Korean Sex Jokes in Traditional Times*, Warm Soft Village Press, 1972; (and compiler) *Japanese Sex Jokes in Traditional Times*, Warm Soft Village Press, 1973; (and compiler) *Chinese Sex Jokes in Traditional Times*, Warm Soft Village Press, 1973; (and compiler) *China's Dirtiest Trickster: Folklore About Hsu Wen-ch'ang*, Paragon, 1974.

Editor, Twayne's "Chinese Literature" series, 1964-68; Chief editor, *Journal of China Society*, 1961.

WORK IN PROGRESS: Translations from Po Chu-i, Volumes 3 and 4; *Japanese Sex Crimes in Modern Times*, for Warm Soft Village Press.

* * *

LEVY, Lillian (Berliner) 1918-

PERSONAL: Born March 16, 1918, in Chicago, Ill.; daughter of Morris Abraham (a textile merchant) and Clara (Youkelson) Berliner; married Aaron Levy (director, Division of Corporate Regulation, U.S. Securities and Exchange Commission), December 31, 1940; children: Esther Tekla, Steven Abraham. *Education:* Attended Birmingham-Southern College, 1936-37, and University of Chicago, 1937-39. *Religion:* Jewish. *Home:* 4609 Norwood Dr., Chevy Chase, Md. 20015. *Agent:* Ruth Aley, Maxwell Aley Associates, 145 East 35th St., New York, N.Y. 10016. *Office:* National Aeronautics and Space Administration, Washington, D.C. 20546.

CAREER: National Jewish Post, Indianapolis, Ind., Washington Bureau chief, 1956-64; Science Service, Inc., Washington, D.C., capitol correspondent, covering White House, Capitol Hill, and various government departments, 1960-63; National Aeronautics and Space Administration, Washington, D.C., consultant, 1963-64, reporter in residence and senior science writer, 1964—; free-lance writer. *Member:* Hadassah (chapter president, Silver Spring, Md., 1951-53; regional vice-president, 1959-60), National Press Club, Washington Press Club, Alpha Lambda Delta.

WRITINGS: (Contributing editor) *Space: Its Impact on Man and Society*, Norton, 1965; (editor) *Science News Yearbook, 1969-1970*, Scribner, 1969. Writer of scripts for Voice of America and commercial radio and television. Contributor to *Harper's Encyclopedia of Science* (section on International Geophysical Year), and to *Saturday Review, Washington Evening Star, London Jewish Chronicle*, and other publications in America and abroad. Editor of Women's National Press Club *Newsletter*, 1959-61.

WORK IN PROGRESS: The Search for Cold, for Crowell-Collier.

SIDELIGHTS: Ms. Levy was a participant in presidential news conferences in three administrations and the only woman selected for a pool position to report on a manned space flight. She was also the first reporter to travel on a commercial flight behind the Iron Curtain, accompanying the "Ravensbruck Lapins" (Polish women survivors of experiments performed by the Nazis during World War II) on their return to Poland after medical treatment in the United States.

* * *

LEWANSKI, Richard C(asimir) 1918-

PERSONAL: Born November 24, 1918, in Warsaw, Poland; son of Rudolf (a civil engineer) and Marcela (Schoenwald) Lewanski; married Lucia Panzavolta, November 24, 1948; children: Rudolf John. *Education:* Attended University of Warsaw, 1937-39; University of Bologna, Dottore in Lettere, 1948; Polish University College, London, England, M.Ph., 1952; University of California, Berkeley, M.L.S., 1958. *Home:* Via Borghi Mamo 7, Bologna, Italy. *Office:* European Center, Johns Hopkins University, via Belmeloro 11, Bologna, Italy.

CAREER: U.S. Department of Defense Language School, Monterey, Calif., senior instructor, 1951-57; University of California, Berkeley, language instructor, 1957-58; New York (N.Y.) Public Library, first assistant, later acting chief of Slavonic Division, 1958-60; Johns Hopkins University, European Center, Bologna, Italy, head librarian, 1961—; University of Pisa, professore incaricato, of Polish language and literature, 1973—. *Military service:* Polish Army, public relations officer, 1941-47; served in Russia, Middle East, Italy, and Great Britain. *Member:* Accademia di Storia e Letteratura Polacca e Slava "Adamo Mickiewicz."

WRITINGS: (With Edward Wechsler) *Polish-English-Italian Dictionary*, three volumes, Tipografia Compositori (Bologna), 1946; *Storia delle relazioni fra la Polonia e Bologna*, Zuffi (Bologna), 1951; *A Bibliography of Slavic Dictionaries*, three volumes, New York Public Library, 1959-63, 2nd edition, 1973-74; *A Guide to the Libraries of Bologna*, Patron, 1964; *Subject Collections in European Libraries*, Bowker, 1965, 2nd edition, in press; *A Bibliography of Slavic Literatures in English Translation (to 1960)*, New York Public Library, 1967; *European Library Directory*, Olschki (Florence), 1967; *Literatures of the World in English Translation*, 2 volumes, Ungar, 1967. *The Slavonic Division of the New York Public Library* (festschrift for Professor Stummvoll), National Library of Austria; *Guide to Polish Libraries and Archives*, Columbia University Press, in press. Also author of library directories and library science dictionaries.

WORK IN PROGRESS: Manuscript sources to Polish history in Italian libraries and archives.

SIDELIGHTS: Lewanski is proficient in Italian, Polish, Russian, German, and French. He has traveled in Western Europe, Central Asia, European Russia and most other Iron Curtain countries, the Middle East, Canada, and Mexico.

* * *

LEWIN, Leonard C(ase) 1916-
(L. L. Case)

PERSONAL: Born October 2, 1916, in New York, N.Y.; son of M. G. and Eva (Case) Lewin; married Eve Merriam (a writer), August 1, 1963; children: Michael Z., Julie E. *Education:* Harvard University, A.B., 1936. *Home:* 10 Water St., Stonington, Conn. 06378. *Agent:* Lois Wallace, 118 East 61st St., New York, N.Y. 10021.

CAREER: Full-time professional writer and editor.

WRITINGS: (Editor) *A Treasury of American Political Humor*, Delacorte, 1964; *Report from Iron Mountain on the Possibility and Desirability of Peace*, Dial, 1967; *Triage*, Dial, 1972. Contributor to various periodicals.

WORK IN PROGRESS: A book of fiction.

* * *

LEWIS, (William) Arthur 1915-

PERSONAL: Born January 23, 1915, in St. Lucia, West Indies; son of George Ferdinand (a civil servant) and Ida (Barton) Lewis; married Gladys Isabel Jacobs, May 8, 1947; children: Elizabeth, Barbara. *Education:* London School of Economics and Political Science, B.Com., 1937, Ph.D., 1940. *Home:* 172 Prospect Avenue, Princeton, N.J. 08540.

CAREER: University of London, London, England, lecturer in London School of Economics and Political Science, 1938-47, university reader in colonial economics, 1947; University of Manchester, Manchester, England, Stanley Jevons Professor of Political Economy, 1948-58; University of the West Indies, Mona, Kingston, Jamaica, principal of University College, 1959-62, vice-chancellor of university, 1962-63; Princeton University, Princeton, N.J., professor of economics, 1963—. Member of United Nations group of experts on underdeveloped countries, 1951, consultant to Economic Commission for Asia and Far East, 1952, economic adviser to Prime Minister of Ghana, 1957-58, deputy managing director of United Nations Special Fund, 1959-60. Consultant to Caribbean Commonwealth, 1949, to Gold Coast government, 1953, and to Western Nigeria, 1955. Temporary principal of British Board of Trade, 1943, and of British Colonial Office, 1944.

MEMBER: American Economic Association (vice-president, 1965), American Philosophical Society, American Academy of Arts and Sciences (honorary foreign member). *Awards, honors:* Knighted; honorary L.H.D. from Columbia University, 1954; LL.D. from Williams College, 1960, Rutgers University, 1965, University of Toronto, University of Wales, University of Bristol, University of Dakar, and University of Leicester; Lit.D. from University of the West Indies, 1966; honorary fellow, London School of Economics and Political Science.

WRITINGS: Economic Survey, 1919-38, Blakiston, 1949; *Overhead Costs*, Allen & Unwin, 1949; *The Principles of Economic Planning*, Allen & Unwin, 1949; *The Theory of Economic Growth*, Irwin, 1955; *Politics in West Africa*, Oxford University Press, 1965; *Development Planning*, Harper, 1966. Contributor to *Observer*, *Reporter*, and to technical and economic journals.

WORK IN PROGRESS: Study of economic policy in underdeveloped countries.

* * *

LEWIS, Herbert S(amuel) 1934-

PERSONAL: Born May 8, 1934, in Jersey City, N.J.; son of Frederic and Estelle (Sachs) Lewis; married Marcia Barbash, June 23, 1957; children: Tamar Anne, Paula Miriam, Joshua Daniel. *Education:* Brandeis University, A.B.

(cum laude), 1955; Columbia University, Ph.D., 1963. *Religion:* Jewish. *Office:* Department of Anthropology, University of Wisconsin, Madison, Wis. 53706.

CAREER: American Museum of Natural History, New York, N.Y., instructor in anthropology, 1957; Columbia University, New York, N.Y., lecturer in anthropology, School of General Studies, 1961; Northwestern University, Evanston, Ill., instructor in anthropology and political science, 1961-63; University of Wisconsin, Madison, assistant professor, 1963-67, associate professor, 1967-73, professor of anthropology, 1973—. Field work in Ethiopia, 1958-60, 1965-66, West Indies, and Israel. *Member:* American Anthropological Association (fellow), African Studies Association (fellow), American Ethnological Society, Royal Anthropological Institute (fellow), International African Institute. *Awards, honors:* Ford Foundation grants for research in Ethiopia, 1958-60; National Science Foundation grant for research in Ethiopia, 1965-66; National Institute of Mental Health grant for research in Israel.

WRITINGS: A Galla Monarchy: Jimma Abba Jifar, 1830-1932, University of Wisconsin Press, 1965; *Leaders and Followers: Some Anthropological Perspectives*, Addison-Wesley, in press. Articles published in *Journal of African History*, *Cahiers d'Etudes Africaines*, *Journal of Semitic Studies*, *Annals* of New York Academy of Sciences, and elsewhere.

WORK IN PROGRESS: Correlating results of research in western Ethiopian Galla leadership and community organization; research on ethnicity and culture change in Israel.

SIDELIGHTS: Lewis speaks French, Italian, Amharic, some Galla and Hebrew.

* * *

LEXAU, Joan M.
(Joan L. Nodset)

PERSONAL: Surname is pronounced Lex-o; born in St. Paul, Minn., daughter of Ole H. and Anne (Haas) Lexau. *Education:* Took special courses at College of St. Thomas and College of St. Catherine in St. Paul, Minn., and at New School for Social Research. *Politics:* Independent Democrat. *Religion:* Roman Catholic. *Residence:* New York, N.Y.

CAREER: Worked for short periods as department store saleswoman, library clerk, bookkeeper, and kitchen girl in a Montana resort; *Catholic Digest*, St. Paul, Minn., editorial secretary, 1953-55; *Glass Packer* (trade magazine), New York, N.Y., advertising production manager, 1955-56; *Catholic News*, New York, N.Y., reporter, 1956-57; Religious News Service, New York, N.Y., free-lance correspondent, 1957; Harper & Row, Publishers, Inc., New York, N.Y., production-liaison work on children's books, 1957-61; full-time free-lance writer, mostly for young people, 1961—. *Member:* Authors Guild of the Authors League of America. *Awards, honors:* Child Study Association of America Children's Book Award for *The Trouble with Terry*, 1962.

WRITINGS—All for young people, except as noted: *Cathy Is Company*, Dial, 1961; *Olaf Reads*, Dial, 1961, Initial Teaching Alphabet edition published as *Oelaf Reedz*, Scholastic Book Services, 1965; *Millicent's Ghost*, Dial, 1962; *The Trouble with Terry*, Dial, 1962; *Olaf Is Late*, Dial, 1963; *That's Good, That's Bad*, Dial, 1963; *Jose's Christmas Secret*, Dial, 1963; *Benjie*, Dial, 1964; *Maria*, Dial, 1964; (editor) *Convent Life* (adult anthology),

Dial, 1964; *I Should Have Stayed in Bed*, Harper, 1965; *More Beautiful than Flowers*, Lippincott, 1966; *The Homework Caper*, Harper, 1966; *Kite Over Tenth Avenue*, Doubleday, 1967; *Finders Keepers, Losers Weepers*, Lippincott, 1967; *Every Day a Dragon*, Harper, 1967; *Three Wishes for Abner*, Ginn, 1967; *Striped Ice Cream*, Lippincott, 1968; *The Rooftop Mystery*, Harper, 1968; *A House So Big*, Harper, 1968; *Archimedes Takes a Bath*, Crowell, 1969; *Crocidile and Hen*, Harper, 1969; *It All Began With a Drip, Drip, Drip*, McCall, 1970; *Benjie on His Own*, Dial, 1970; *Me Day*, Dial, 1971; *T for Tommy*, Garrard, 1971; *That's Just Fine and Who-o-o Did It?*, Garrard, 1971; *Emily and the Klunky Baby and the Next-Door Dog*, Dial, 1972; *The Christmas Secret*, School Book Service, 1973.

Under pseudonym Joan L. Nodset: *Who Took the Farmer's Hat?*, Harper, 1963; *Go Away, Dog*, Harper, 1963; *Where Do You Go When You Run Away?*, Bobbs-Merrill, 1964; *Come Here, Cat*, Harper, 1973.

Author of other stories for children's textbooks, and articles about children's books and poetry for adult periodicals.

SIDELIGHTS: Joan Lexau told *CA* that she plans to live for a time in a small Southern town and in the Appalachians to meet the children of those areas and write for them. *Avocational interests:* Indoor gardening (miniature tomatoes and flowers), photography, swimming.

BIOGRAPHICAL/CRITICAL SOURCES: Lee Bennett Hopkins, *Books Are By People*, Citation Press, 1969.†

* * *

LI, C(hing) C(hun) 1912-

PERSONAL: Surname is pronounced Lee; born October 27, 1912, in Tientsin, China; son of Jui Li (a businessman); married Clara A. Lem (an associate editor), September 20, 1941; children: Carol, Steven. *Education:* Nanking University, B.S., 1936; Cornell University, Ph.D., 1940; postdoctoral study at University of Chicago, summer, 1940, Columbia University, 1940-41, and North Carolina State College, summer, 1941. *Home:* 1360 Terrace Dr., Pittsburgh, Pa. 15228. *Office:* University of Pittsburgh, Pittsburgh, Pa. 15261.

CAREER: National Kwangsi University, Agriculture College, China, assistant professor, 1942-43; Nanking University, Agriculture College, Nanking, China, professor of genetics, 1943-46; National Peking University, Peking, China, professor of biometry and genetics and chairman of department of agronomy, 1946-50; University of Pittsburgh, Graduate School of Public Health, Pittsburgh, Pa., 1951—, began as research fellow, became professor of biometry, 1960—, chairman of department of biostatistics, 1969—. *Member:* American Society of Human Genetics (president, 1960-61), American Genetic Association, American Statistical Association (fellow), Biometric Society, Genetics Society of America, Society for the Study of Evolution, American Society of Naturalists, Population Reference Bureau (fellow), American Association for the Advancement of Science (fellow), Academia Sinica.

WRITINGS: An Introduction to Population Genetics (in English), National Peking University Press, 1948; *Population Genetics*, University of Chicago Press, 1955; *Numbers from Experiments: A Basic Analysis of Variation*, Boxwood, 1959; *Human Genetics: Principles and Methods*, McGraw, 1961; *Introduction to Experimental Statistics*, McGraw, 1964; *A Primer of Path Analysis*, Boxwood, 1975.

Translations into the Chinese: T. D. Lysenko, *Heredity and Its Variability*, New China Book Co., 1949; Julian Huxley, *Soviet Genetics and World Science*, Chinese Cultural Publishing Committee, 1953. Associate editor, *American Journal of Human Genetics* and *American Naturalist*.

BIOGRAPHICAL/CRITICAL SOURCES: Mathematics, Life Science Library, 1963.

* * *

LICHTBLAU, Myron Ivor 1925-

PERSONAL: Born October 10, 1925, in New York, N.Y.; son of Samuel (a salesman) and Sadonia (Weinberg) Lichtblau; married Bernice Glanz (a social worker), June 23, 1956; children: Anita, Eric. *Education:* City College (now of the City University of New York), B.A., 1947; National University of Mexico, M.A., 1948; Columbia University, Ph.D., 1957. *Religion:* Jewish. *Home:* 111 Saybrook Lane, Dewitt, N.Y. 13214. *Office:* Department of Foreign Languages and Literature, Syracuse University, Syracuse, N.Y.

CAREER: Secondary school teacher of Spanish, New York, N.Y., 1948-57; Indiana University, Bloomington, instructor in Spanish, 1957-59; Syracuse University, Syracuse, N.Y., assistant professor, 1959-63, associate professor, 1963-68, professor of Romance languages, 1968—, chairman of department of Romance languages, 1968-74. Coordinator, Peru Peace Corps training program, Syracuse University, summer, 1966. *Military service:* U.S. Army, 1944-46. *Member:* American Association of Teachers of Spanish and Portuguese, Modern Language Association of America, American Association of University Professors, Instituto Internacional de Literatura Iberoamericana (executive secretary, 1959-63), Sigma Delta Pi, Phi Sigma Iota. *Awards, honors:* Honorary diploma, Centro de Estudios Humanisticos de la Universidad de Nuevo Leon (Mexico), for series of articles on Latin-American literature in *Humanitas*, 1964.

WRITINGS: The Argentine Novel in the Nineteenth Century, Hispanic Institute in the United States, 1959; (editor, and author of introduction, footnotes, exercises, and vocabulary) *Las dos vidas del pobre Napoleon* (college edition), Scribner, 1963; *El arte estilistico de Eduardo Mallea*, Editorial Goyanarte, 1967; *Manuel Galvez*, Twayne, 1972. Writer of some twenty-five articles on Latin American literature for language journals. Review editor, *Symposium*, and acting editor, 1966-67.

WORK IN PROGRESS: Studies in the ironic mode in Latin American fiction, completion expected in 1976.

SIDELIGHTS: Lichtblau lived in Mexico, 1947-48, and five months in 1963; also spent time in Argentina, 1952, in Guatemala in 1964, Columbia, 1969, and Spain, 1974, with shorter stays in Cuba, Italy, and France.

* * *

LICHTENSTEIN, Aharon 1933-

PERSONAL: Born May 23, 1933, in Paris, France; son of Jechiel (a teacher) and Bluma (Schwartz) Lichtenstein; married Tovah Soloveitchik (a teacher), January 26, 1960; children: Mosheh Yitzchak Abba, Mayer Eliyahv, Esther Gruna. *Education:* Yeshiva University, B.A., 1953, Rabbi, 1959; Harvard University, M.A., 1954, Ph.D., 1957. *Politics:* Independent Democrat.

CAREER: Rabbi and professor. Yeshiva University, New York, N.Y., instructor, later assistant professor of English at Stern College for Women, 1957-63; professor of Jewish law at Rabbi Isaac Elchanan Theological Seminary, beginning 1963; currently at Yeshiva University, New York, N.Y., professor of English. Member of national advisory board, Yavneh-National Religious Jewish Students Association. *Member:* Modern Language Association of America, Rabbinical Council of America.

WRITINGS: Henry More: The Rational Theology of a Cambridge Platonist, Harvard University Press, 1962. Contributor to Jewish periodicals. Member of editorial board, *Hadarom*.

SIDELIGHTS: Lichtenstein told *CA* that he feels strongly about the need to integrate traditional Judaism and aspects of general culture at a profound level. He has "reasonable competence" in Hebrew, Aramaic, French, Yiddish, and German, and a "limited knowledge" of Greek and Latin.†

* * *

LIEBERMAN, Joseph I. 1942-

PERSONAL: Born February 24, 1942, in Stamford, Conn.; son of Henry (a merchant and realtor) and Marcia (Manger) Lieberman; married Elizabeth Haas (an urban redevelopment executive), December 20, 1965; children: Matthew, Rebecca. *Education:* Yale University, B.A., 1964, LL.B., 1967. *Religion:* Jewish. *Home:* 69 Colony Rd., New Haven, Conn. 06511.

CAREER: Assistant to Senator Abraham Ribicoff of Connecticut, 1963, and to John M. Bailey, chairman of Democratic National Committee, 1964; Wiggin and Dana (law firm), New Haven, Conn., attorney, 1967-69; Connecticut State Senator from 10th district, 1970—, majority leader, 1975—; Baldwin, Lieberman, and Segaloff (law firm), New Haven, Conn., partner, 1972—. *Member:* Phi Beta Kappa.

WRITINGS: The Power Broker, Houghton, 1966; *The Scorpion and the Tarantula: The Struggle to Control Atomic Weapons, 1945-1949*, Houghton, 1970. Chairman of editorial board, *Yale Daily News*, 1964.

* * *

LIEBERMAN, Laurence J(ames) 1935-

PERSONAL: Born February 16, 1935, in Detroit, Mich.; son of Nathan (a businessman) and Anita (Cohen) Lieberman; married Bernice Braun (an editor), June 16, 1956; children: Carla, Deborah, Isaac. *Education:* University of Michigan, B.A., 1956, M.A., 1958; University of California, Berkeley, graduate study, 1958-60. *Home:* 108 West Florida Ave., Urbana, Ill. 61801. *Office:* Department of English, University of Illinois, Urbana, Ill. 61801.

CAREER: Orange Coast College, Costa Mesa, Calif., instructor, 1960-64; College of the Virgin Islands, St. Thomas, assistant professor, 1964-66, associate professor of English, 1966-68; University of Illinois, Urbana, associate professor, 1968-70, professor of English and creative writing, 1970—. *Awards, honors:* University of Michigan, Hopwood Award in Poetry, 1958; Yaddo fellowship, 1963 and 1967; Huntington Hartford Foundation fellowship, 1964; National Endowment for Arts award, 1969, for poem "Tarpon"; University of Illinois Center for Advanced Study grant to write poetry in Japan, 1971-72.

WRITINGS: (Contributor) *New Campus Writing #4*, edited by Nolan Miller and Judson Jerome, Grove, 1962; (contributor) *A Controversy of Poets*, edited by Paris Leary and Robert Kelly, Doubleday, 1965; *The Unblinding* (poems), Macmillan, 1968; *The Achievement of James*

Dickey, Scott, Foresman, 1969; *The Osprey Suicides* (poems), Macmillan, 1973; *The Blind Dancers: Ten Years of American Poetry* (criticism), University of Illinois Press, 1976. Contributor of poems to *New Yorker, Atlantic Monthly, Paris Review, Hudson Review, New Republic, Saturday Review, Poetry, Harper's, Quarterly Review, Audience*, and other periodicals. Contributor of poetry chronicles and critical articles to *Antioch Review* and *Hudson Review*. Poetry editor and contributing editor, *Orange County Illustrated*, 1964-65; poetry editor, *Orange County Sun*, 1965—; editor, Poetry Books Program, University of Illinois Press, 1970—; regular poetry reviewer, *Yale Review*, 1971—.

WORK IN PROGRESS: A third book of poems involving the year of travels in Japan, 1971-72.

BIOGRAPHICAL/CRITICAL SOURCES: Carolyn Riley, *Contemporary Literary Criticism*, Volume IV, Gale, 1975.

* * *

LIEBERMAN, Samuel 1911-

PERSONAL: Born December 11, 1911, in New York, N.Y.; son of Harry (a tailor) and Anna (Zlatkin) Lieberman; married Bertha Scholnik (a junior high school teacher), March 12, 1938; children: Nathaniel Harold. *Education:* City College (now of the City University of New York), B.A. (magna cum laude), 1932, M.S., 1935; Columbia Univeristy, Ph.D., 1953. *Religion:* Jewish. *Office:* Queens College of the City University of New York, Flushing, N.Y. 11367.

CAREER: New York (N.Y.) public schools, high school teacher, 1934-43; City College (now of the City University of New York), New York, N.Y., lecturer in Latin, 1939-41; Queens College (now of the City University of New York), 1947—, professor of classical languages, 1964—. *Military service:* U.S. Army, 1943-46; served in China-Burma-India Theater and Pacific area; became first lieutenant. *Member:* American Philological Association, American Oriental Society, American Association of University Professors, American Classical League, American Council on the Teaching of Foreign Languages, Classical Association of the Atlantic States, Joint National Committee for Languages, New York Classical Club, Ancient Civilization Group (New York), Phi Beta Kappa.

WRITINGS: Roman Drama, Bantam, 1964. Contributor of articles and reviews to classical journals. Associate editor, *Classical World*, 1953—.

WORK IN PROGRESS: Analysis and translation of the Roman poet, Propertius; continued research in field of contact between Ancient Rome and China.

AVOCATIONAL INTERESTS: The theater, arts, listening to music, writing poetry.

* * *

LIEBMAN, Seymour B. 1907-

PERSONAL: Born March 12, 1907, in New York, N.Y.; son of Henry (an insurance man) and Fannie (Abend) Liebman; married Malvina Weiss (a professor of education), June 25, 1950; children: (previous marriage) Charles. *Education:* St. Lawrence University, LL.B., 1929; attended Seminary School of Jewish Studies, 1942-44; University of the Americas, M.A. (magna cum laude), 1963, graduate study, 1963-66. *Politics:* Democrat. *Religion:* Jewish. *Home:* 8119 South West 82 Place, Miami, Fla. 33143.

CAREER: Member of Bars of New York and Florida. Private practice of law, 1929-60. State of Israel, counsel for Florida, 1951-57; Bank of Miami Beach, counsel and vice-chairman of board of directors, 1955-58; State of Florida, special assistant attorney general, 1956-57; University of the Americas, Mexico City, Mexico, instructor in history, 1963-66; Miami-Dade Junior College, Miami, Fla., instructor in history, 1966—. Israel Development Corp., member of board of governors, 1951-59; Zionist Organization of America, member of national executive committee, 1954-60, president of Southeast region, 1955-57. Boy Scouts of America, commissioner, 1941-45; Dade County Community Chest, co-chairman, 1949-50; Miami Beach Taxpayers Association, vice-president, 1958-59. Director or officer of other Jewish educational bodies and of civic organizations. Member: American Historical Association, American Jewish Historical Society, Jewish Historical Society of England, Miami Beach Bar Association (director, 1958-60). Awards, honors: Grants from Memorial Foundation for Jewish Culture, 1966-67, American Philosophical Society, 1968, National Foundation for Jewish Culture, 1969, Henry E. Huntington Library, 1969.

WRITINGS: Guide to Jewish References in Mexican Colonial Era, University of Pennsylvania Press, 1964; The Enlightened, University of Miami Press, 1967; Jews in New Spain, University of Miami Press, 1970; The Inquisitors and the Jews in the New World, University of Miami Press, 1974; The Great Auto de Fe of 1649, Coronado Press, 1974; The Middle East: A Return to Facts, American Zion Federation, 1974. Contributor of articles to Hispanic American Historical Review, Jewish Quarterly (London), Historia Mexicana, Journal of Inter-American Studies, and other periodicals.

WORK IN PROGRESS: A two-volume History of American Jewry; a monograph on Latin American personality and Alliance for Progress problems.

SIDELIGHTS: Liebman told CA, "I love to teach and regret that too many people with Ph.D.s are regarded as qualified university instructors while they have no sympathy or rapport with students, and those who are extremely well-qualified to teach at the university level are denied to the students because they do not have a Ph.D. Research and writing are my preoccupations."

*   *   *

LIEDTKE, Kurt E(rnst) H(einrich)   1919-

PERSONAL: Born September 14, 1919, in Elbing, Germany; now U.S. citizen; son of Kurt F. W. (a sculptor) and Emma (Koch) Liedtke; married Helen Greenwood, March 19, 1955; children: Barbara, Erika, Karl. Education: University of Erlangen, Referendar, 1950, Assessor, 1951, Ph.D., 1954; Michigan State University, M.A., 1952. Home: 2475 Trenton Dr., San Bruno, Calif. 94066. Office: San Francisco State University, San Francisco, Calif. 94132.

CAREER: Studienreferendar in German, English, and French at gymnasium in Erlangen, Germany, 1950-51; studienrat at gymnasium in Nurnberg, Germany, 1952-54; instructor in German at U.S. Army Language School, Monterey, Calif., 1955, and Monterey Peninsula College and U.S. Naval Post-Graduate School, both Monterey, 1956; Southeastern Louisiana College, Hammond, assistant professor of German and French, 1956-57; San Francisco State University, San Francisco, Calif., 1957—, began as associate professor, became professor of German. Middlebury

College, assistant professor, summer, 1957; director of studies at Middlebury Graduate School of German in Germany, University of Mainz, 1966. Member: Modern Language Association of America, American Association of Teachers of German (chapter president, 1959-60), Foreign Language Association of Northern California (vice-president, 1959-60).

WRITINGS: (With Stanley Sharp and Henry Blauth) A Solid Foundation in German, Blaisdell/Ginn, 1965. Contributor to language journals in United States and Germany.

WORK IN PROGRESS: Picture of America as reflected in works of nineteenth-century German authors; experimental textbook material.

*   *   *

LIFFRING, Joan Louise   1929-

PERSONAL: Born February 20, 1929, in Iowa City, Iowa; daughter of Lawrence Edward (a lawyer) and Esther (a college professor; maiden name, Lang) Liffring; children: Artie, David, Heusinkveld. Education: Attended University of Iowa, 1945-48. Politics: Independent. Religion: Episcopalian.

CAREER: Cedar Rapids Gazette, Cedar Rapids, Iowa, photographer-writer, 1948-51; free-lance photographer for Des Moines Register, and Iowan (magazine), and other magazines and newspapers, 1951—. Creator of note cards which are sold commercially.

WRITINGS—Children's books, self-illustrated: Ray and Stevie on a Corn Belt Farm, Follett, 1956; Dee and Curtis on a Dairy Farm, Follett, 1957; Jim and Alan on a Cotton Farm, Follett, 1959; Mike and Dick on a Washington Apple Farm, Follett, 1962. Contributor to Book of Knowledge. Portfolios of photographs have been published in Photographic Methods for Industry and Infinity.

WORK IN PROGRESS: A collection of photographs on people and things.†

*   *   *

LIFTON, Robert Jay   1926-

PERSONAL: Born May 16, 1926, in Brooklyn, N.Y.; son of Harold A. (a businessman) and Ciel (Roth) Lifton; married Betty Jean Kirschner (a writer for children), March 1, 1952; children: Kenneth Jay, Karen. Education: Cornell University, student, 1942-44; New York Medical College, M.D., 1948. Home: 300 Central Park W., New York, N.Y. 10024. Office: Department of Psychiatry, Yale University School of Medicine, 34 Park St., New Haven, Conn. 06519.

CAREER: Washington School of Psychiatry, Washington, D.C., member of faculty, 1954-55; Harvard University, Cambridge, Mass., research associate in psychiatry, 1956-61; Yale University, New Haven, Conn., Foundation Fund for Research in Psychiatry Associate Professor of Psychiatry, 1961-67, Professor, 1967—. Consultant, Columbia seminars on modern Japan and Oriental thought and religion, 1965—; has also served as consultant to National Institutes of Mental Health and New York State Bar Association. Military service: U.S. Air Force, 1951-53; became captain.

MEMBER: American Psychiatric Association, Group for the Advancement of Psychiatry, Association for Asian Studies, American Anthropological Association, American Association for the Advancement of Science, American

Academy of Arts and Sciences (fellow), Group for the Study of Psychohistorical Process, American Academy of Psychoanalysis, Physicans for Social Responsibility, Medical Committee for Human Rights. *Awards, honors:* National Book Award in the sciences and Van Wyck Brooks Award for nonfiction, both 1969, for *Death in Life: Survivors of Hiroshima*; D.Sc. from Lawrence University, 1971, from Merrimack College, 1973; Karen Horney Lecture Award of Association for the Advancement of Psychoanalysis, 1972; distinguished service award of Society for Adolescent Psychology, 1972; Mount Airy Foundation Gold Medal for excellence in psychiatry, 1973.

WRITINGS: Thought Reform and the Psychology of Totalism: A Study of "Brainwashing" in China, Norton, 1961; *Death in Life: Survivors of Hiroshima*, Random House, 1968; *Revolutionary Immortality: Mao Tse-Tung and the Chinese Cultural Revolution*, Random House, 1968; *Birds* (cartoons), Random House, 1969; *History and Human Survival: Essays on the Young and the Old, Survivors and the Dead, Peace and War, and on Contemporary Psychohistory*, Random House, 1970; *Boundaries: Psychological Man in Revolution*, Random House, 1970; *Home from the War: Vietnam Veterans—Neither Victims nor Executioners*, Simon & Schuster, 1973; (with Eric Olson) *Living and Dying*, Praeger, 1974.

Editor: *The Woman in America*, Houghton, 1965; *America and the Asian Revolutions*, Trans-Action Books, 1970; (with Richard A. Falk and Gabriel Kolko) *Crimes of War*, Random House, 1971; (with Eric Olson) *Explorations in Psychohistory: The Wellfleet Papers of Erik Erikson, Robert Jay Lifton, and Kenneth Kenniston*, Simon & Schuster, 1975.

Contributor to *New York Review of Books, Daedalus, American Scholar, New Republic, Partisan Review*, and to *American Journal of Psychiatry, Psychiatry*, and other professional journals in the fields of psychiatry, psychology, history, and Asian studies.

WORK IN PROGRESS: Continued study of the survivor theme, of the psychological paradigm of death and continuity and the relationship between death imagery and violence, especially in American society, and of new psychological and social forms in innovative young professionals.

SIDELIGHTS: In a review of *Death in Life*, Lifton's award-winning study of the survivors of Hiroshima's bombing, Robert Coles noted: "I believe that Robert Lifton's work is extremely important, and valuable in its own right. In addition, as a thinker and an investigator he offers us significant evidence that at least one young American psychiatrist can use psychoanalytic insight without worshipping psychoanalytic tenets; can observe the mind's life without turning all life into a subdivision of psychology; and, perhaps most important of all, can be both a doctor and a student of history and politics." Lifton has some knowledge of Japanese.

AVOCATIONAL INTERESTS: Tennis, films.

* * *

LIKENESS, George C(lark) 1927-

PERSONAL: Born May 19, 1927, in Soda Springs, Idaho; son of George Michael and Mary (Clark) Likeness. *Education:* Northwestern University, B.S. in Journalism, 1950, M.S., 1951. *Politics:* "Generally Republican." *Religion:* Methodist. *Home:* 201 Seventh St., Mendota, Ill. 61342. *Office:* Wayside Press, 1501 Washington Road, Mendota, Ill. 61342.

CAREER: Newspaper reporter, Twin Falls, Idaho, 1948-50; Butler Graphic Design (publication layout and counseling), Mendota, Ill., executive director, 1951—; K.B.B.& A. (advertising), Mendota, Ill., layout artist, 1958—. *Yankee* (magazine), Dublin, N.H., layout consultant. Mendota Community Theatre, co-founder, 1953, director, 1953—, president, 1955-56. *Military service:* U.S. Naval Reserve, 1945-46. *Member:* Elks, Kiwanis Club, Theta Xi.

WRITINGS: (Editor and co-author) *Magnificent Whistle Stop: The 100 Year History of Mendota, Illinois*, Wayside Press, 1953; *The Oscar People*, Wayside Press, 1966.

With Kenneth B. Butler; all published by Butler Clinic: *101 Usable Publication Layouts*, 1954; *Practical Handbook on Double-Spreads in Publication Layout*, 1956; *Ken Butler's Layout Scrapbook*, 1958; *Practical Handbook on Display Typefaces*, 1959; *Practical Handbook on Back-of-the-Book Publication Layout Problems*, 1960; *Practical Handbook on Borders, Ornamentation, and Boxes in Publication Layout*, 1960.

Author of three plays produced locally by amateur players' groups.

* * *

LIMENTANI, Uberto 1913-

PERSONAL: Born December 15, 1913, in Milan, Italy; son of Umberto (a professor) and Elisa (Levi) Limentani; married Barbara Hoban, March 25, 1946; children: Julian David, Alexander Esmond, Rupert Nicholas. *Education:* University of Milan, Dr. in Giurispr., 1935, Dr. in Lettere, 1939; University of London, Ph.D., 1946. *Home:* 17 St. Barnabas Rd., Cambridge, England. *Office:* Magdalene College, Cambridge University, Cambridge, England; and Faculty of Modern Languages, Sidgwick Ave., Cambridge, England.

CAREER: British Broadcasting Corp., London, England, commentator and scriptwriter, Italian section of European Service, 1939-45; Cambridge University, Cambridge, England, lector, 1945-48, assistant lecturer, 1948-52, lecturer, 1952-62, professor of Italian, 1962—, fellow of Magdalene College. *Member:* Accademia Letteraria (corresponding member), Italiana dell' Arcadia.

WRITINGS: Stillistica e Metrica, A. Vallardi (Milan), 1936; *Poesie e Lettere Inedite di Salvator Rosa*, Olschki (Florence), 1950; *L'attivita letteraria di Giuseppe Mazzini*, Il Pensiero Mazziniano (Turin), 1950; (translator) E. R. Vincent, *Ugo Foscolo Esule fra gli Inglesi*, F. Le Monnier (Florence), 1954; *La satira nel Seicento*, Ricciardi (Milan), 1961; *The Fortunes of Dante in 17th Century Italy*, Cambridge University Press, 1964; (editor) *The Mind of Dante*, Cambridge University Press, 1965. Co-editor, *Studi Secenteschi* (yearly review), published by Olschki; member of editorial board, *Italian Studies*. Contributor to *Encyclopaedia Britannica, Cassell's Encyclopaedia of Literature*, and English and Italian journals.

WORK IN PROGRESS: Volume XII of *The Edizione Nazionale delle Opere di Ugo Foscolo*.

AVOCATIONAL INTERESTS: Fencing, photography, mountain walking.

* * *

LIN, San-su C(hen) 1916-

PERSONAL: Born June 3, 1916, in Hong Kong; came to United States, 1949, naturalized, 1966; daughter of L. O. (a merchant) and Nelly (Wong) Chen; married Paul J. Lin (a college teacher), October 7, 1939; children: Elizabeth, Jean. *Education:* National Peking University, B.A., 1939; Columbia University, M.A., 1950, Ed.D., 1953. *Office:* Department of English, Southern University, Baton Rouge, La.

CAREER: Teacher of English at middle schools in China, 1944, 1946-47, and at Provincial Teachers College, Taipei, Taiwan, China, 1948-49; Claflin College, Orangeburg, S.C., professor of English, 1955-64, head of department, 1957-64, director of research, 1961-64; Southern University, Baton Rouge, La., professor of English, 1964—, director of freshman English, 1970—. Director, National Defense Education Act Institute in English, 1966, 1967, 1968, and 1969-70. *Member:* National Council of Teachers of English (member of special task force to study English programs for disadvantaged students, 1965; member of college section committee, 1972-75), American Dialect Society.

WRITINGS: Pattern Practice in the Teaching of Standard English to Students with a Nonstandard Dialect, Teachers College, Columbia University, 1965; (contributor) Roger Shuy, editor, *Social Dialects and Language Learning*, National Council of Teachers of English, 1965. Contributor to *Young Sun* (magazine), in Hong Kong, and to professional journals in America.

SIDELIGHTS: Mrs. Lin is fluent in Chinese (Cantonese, Mandarin, and Amoy).

*   *   *

LINAMEN, Harold Frederick   1921-

PERSONAL: Born December 3, 1921, in Hill City, Pa.; son of John Wallace and Eyla (Farringer) Linamen; married Maxine Line, June 17, 1950; children: Christopher Eugene, Larry Harold. *Education:* Indiana State Teachers College (now Indiana State University of Pennsylvania), B.S., 1943; Columbia University, M.S., 1948, Ed.D., 1956; University of California, graduate study, 1948-49. *Religion:* Church of God. *Home:* 914 Myers Ave., Anderson, Ind. 46012. *Office:* Anderson College, Anderson, Ind. 46012.

CAREER: Anderson College, Anderson, Ind., 1949—, began as instructor, professor of economics, 1964—, chairman of department of business and economics, 1965—. Partner, Falls & Linamen (accountants), Anderson, Ind., 1953-62. Research associate, Indiana Commission on State Tax and Financing Policy. Accountant and consultant, Church of God Board of Pensions. Associate, Danforth Foundation, 1958-62. *Military service:* U.S. Army, 1943-46. *Member:* American Economic Association, Midwest Economic Association, Indiana Academy of Social Sciences, Optimist Club. *Awards, honors:* Ford Foundation fellow, summer, 1959; Marathon Oil Co. fellow, 1962; Case Institute of Technology "Economics-in-Action" fellow, 1966; Anderson College Alumni Service Award, 1972.

WRITINGS: Business Handbook for Churches, Warner, 1957, revised edition, 1965; *Letter Writing for Churches*, Warner, 1958; *The Church Says, Welcome!*, Warner, 1960; *Success in Money Matters*, Warner, 1961. Writer of research studies for Indiana Commission on State Tax and Financing Policy. Contributor to tax and religious journals.

WORK IN PROGRESS: Revising *Success in Money Matters*.

*   *   *

LINDBERGH, Anne Morrow (Spencer)   1906-

PERSONAL: Born 1906, in Englewood, N.J.; daughter of Dwight Whitney (formerly U.S. Ambassador to Mexico) and Elizabeth Reeve (Cutter) Morrow; married Charles Augustus Lindbergh (aviator, first pilot to fly N.Y. to Paris, May, 1927; deceased); children: Charles Augustus, Jr. (deceased), Jon Morrow, Land Morrow, Anne, Spencer, Reeve, Scott. *Education:* Smith College, B.A., 1927. *Home:* Scott's Cove, Darien, Conn.

CAREER: Writer. *Awards, honors:* Hubbard Medal of the National Geographic Society, 1934; M.A., Smith College, 1935; LL.D., Amherst College, 1939; LL.D., University of Rochester, 1939.

WRITINGS: North to the Orient, Harcourt, 1935; *Listen, the Wind*, Harcourt, 1938; *The Wave of the Future*, Harcourt, 1940; *The Steep Ascent*, Harcourt, 1944; *Gift from the Sea*, Pantheon, 1955; *Unicorn and Other Poems, 1935-1955*, Pantheon, 1956; *Dearly Beloved*, Harcourt, 1962; *Selections from Gift From the Sea*, Hallmark Editions, 1967; *Earth Shine*, Harcourt, 1969; *Christmas in Mexico: 1927*, Harcourt, 1971; *Bring Me a Unicorn: Diaries and Letters of Anne Morrow Lindbergh*, Harcourt, 1972; *Hour of Gold, Hour of Lead: Diaries and Letters of Anne Morrow Lindbergh, 1929-1932*, Harcourt, 1973; *Locked Rooms and Open Doors: The Diaries and Letters of Anne Morrow Lindbergh, 1932-1935*, G. K. Hall, 1974.

SIDELIGHTS: Mrs. Lindbergh's popularity with the American reading public was put on trial when John Ciardi condemned *Unicorn and Other Poems* in *The Saturday Review*. Norman Cousins reported that the review "produced the biggest storm of reader protest in the thirty-three-year history of *The Saturday Review*. Hundreds of readers hastened to tell us of their pointed disapproval of Mr. Ciardi's review; four [wrote] in his support. . . .

"There are few living authors who are using the English language more sensitively or with more genuine appeal [than Mrs. Lindbergh]." Cousins continued: "There is in her books a respect for human responses to beauty and for the great connections between humankind and nature that gives her work rare distinction and that earns her the gratitude and loyalty of her readers. . . ." One letter, representing public thinking, asked, "Why take a baseball bat to club a butterfly?"

Her books have been well received, not as works of art but as a "gift to all women who hope for individual expression while they make peanut-butter sandwiches, iron clothes and dream." (*Woman's Home Companion*) Following her husband's interests, Mrs. Lindbergh acquired her pilot's and radio operator's licenses and accompanied him on many expeditions.

BIOGRAPHICAL/CRITICAL SOURCES: Saturday Review, April 21, 1955, February 16, 1957, June 9, 1962; *Newsweek*, April 11, 1955; *Woman's Home Companion*, January, 1956; *Time*, September 17, 1956, June 8, 1962; *McCall's*, October, 1956; *New York Herald Tribune Books*, June 10, 1962; *New York Times Book Week*, June 10, 1962; *New York Times*, October 12, 1969, February 21, 1970; *Bring Me a Unicorn*, Harcourt, 1972; *Hour of Gold, Hour of Lead*, Harcourt, 1973; *Locked Rooms and Open Doors*, G. K. Hall, 1974.†

*   *   *

LINDGREN, Alvin J.   1917-

PERSONAL: Born April 17, 1917, in Roxbury, Kan.; son of Charles T. (a banker) and Isla (Tinsley) Lindgren; married Alma Huebscher, July 16, 1945; children: Patricia, Judith (Mrs. Richard Fasteson), James, John, Diane. *Education:* McPherson College, B.A., 1937; Garrett Theological Seminary, B.D., 1940. *Home:* 2285 Landwehr Rd., Northbrook, Ill. 60062. *Office:* Garrett Theological Seminary, 2121 Sheridan Rd., Evanston, Ill. 60201.

CAREER: Ordained Methodist minister, 1940; minister of Methodist churches in Manawa, Green Bay, and Oshkosh, Wis., 1941-53; East Wisconsin Conference, The Methodist Church, 1953-57; Garrett Theological Seminary, Evanston, Ill., professor of church administration and director of field education, 1957—. *Awards, honors:* Swift fellowship, 1940-41; honorary D.D., McPherson College, 1958.

WRITINGS: Field Education Manual, Garrett Theological Seminary, 1963; *Foundations for Purposeful Church Administration,* Abingdon, 1965.

* * *

LING, Cyril Curtis   1936-

PERSONAL: Born January 28, 1936, in Detroit, Mich.; son of Robert Harold (a business executive) and Marie M. (Guilloz) Ling; married Beatrice Elaine Panizzoli, January 25, 1957; children: Robin Kyle, Renee Hollis, Roslyn Elaine. *Education:* Wayne State University, B.S., 1957, M.B.A., 1958; Indiana University, D.B.A., 1962. *Politics:* Republican. *Religion:* Protestant. *Office:* Management Center, University of Richmond, 601 North Lombardy St., Richmond, Va. 23220.

CAREER: Indiana University, Bloomington, faculty lecturer in management, 1959-60; University of Cincinnati, Cincinnati, Ohio, assistant professor, 1960-63, associate professor of management, 1963-66; University of Richmond, Richmond, Va., director of Management Center and associate professor of business administration, beginning 1966. Consultant and trainer, City of Cincinnati, University of Cincinnati Executive Management Program, U.S. Veterans Administration Hospital (Cincinnati), Virginia Department of Agriculture and Immigration, Virginia State Technical Services Agency, and U.S. Civil Service Commission. *Member:* Academy of Management, Society for Advancement of Management, Sigma Iota Epsilon, Psi Chi, Omicron Delta Kappa, Beta Gamma Sigma.

WRITINGS: The Management of Personnel Relations: History and Origins, Irwin, 1965.

Editor—all published by American Association of Collegiate Schools of Business: *Image and Impact of Education for Business,* 1967; *The Next Half Century in Higher Education for Business,* 1968; *A Seminar for New Deans,* 1968, 2nd edition, 1970; *Entrepreneurship and the Dynamics of the Educational Process,* 1969; *The Business Schools in the 70's: Preparing the Leaders of the 80's and 90's,* 1970; *Designing a Blueprint for Progress,* 1971. Co-author of eight study reports for Indiana State Chamber of Commerce, 1958-59.

AVOCATIONAL INTERESTS: Boating, woodwork, auto racing.†

* * *

LINGEMAN, Richard R(oberts)   1931-
   (Niles Chignon; William Randolph Hirsch, a joint pseudonym)

PERSONAL: Born January 2, 1931, in Crawfordsville, Ind.; son of Byron Newton and Vera (Spencer) Lingeman; married Anthea Nicholson (a graphic designer), April 3, 1965. *Education:* Harverford College, B.A., 1953; also

studied law at Yale University, and did graduate work at Columbia University.

CAREER: Monocle (magazine), New York, N.Y., cofounder and executive editor, beginning 1962. Public relations consultant to Peace Corps. *Military service:* U.S. Army, 1953-56.

WRITINGS: (Editor with Victor Navasky) *The Monocle Peep Show,* Bantam, 1965; (under pseudonym Niles Chignon) *The Camp Follower's Guide,* Avon, 1965; (with Marvin Kitman and Navasky, under joint pseudonym William Randolph Hirsch) *The Red Chinese Air Force Diet, Exercise, and Sex Book,* Stein & Day, 1967; *Drugs from A to Z,* McGraw, 1969; *Don't You Know There's a War On: The American Home Front, 1941-45,* Putnam, 1970. Contributor to *New York Times Book Review, Der Spiegel, Negro Digest, Realist, Nugget, Mademoiselle,* and other magazines. Editor, *Outsider's Newsletter.*†

* * *

LINK, John R(einhardt)   1907-

PERSONAL: Born April 15, 1907, in Lincolnton, N.C.; son of John Robert (a farmer) and Lecky (Lawing) Link; married Clarice Pritchard (a school music teacher), August 31, 1937; children: Jane Elizabeth (Mrs. W. L. Fleming, Jr.), John Pritchard. *Education:* Wake Forest College (now University), A.B. (cum laude), 1931; Crozer Theological Seminary, B.D., 1935; Duke University, graduate study, 1938-40; Southeastern Baptist Theological Seminary, Th.M., 1967. *Home:* 221 Second St., Spring Hope, N.C. 27882.

CAREER: Ordained Baptist minister, 1935. Pastor in Elizabeth City, N.C., 1935-37, and Apex, N.C., 1938-44; Mars Hill College, Mars Hill, N.C., instructor in Bible, 1945-46, campus pastor, 1946-50; pastor in Mount Gilead, N.C., 1951-55, Warrenton, N.C., 1956-58; First Baptist Church, Spring Hope, N.C., pastor, 1968-73; teacher of biblical interpretation of seminary extension, 1973—. *Member:* Lions Club, Civitan Club, Masons.

WRITINGS: You Can Understand the Bible, Judson, 1966; *Help in Understanding the Bible,* Judson, 1974; *Anecdotes about the Mountain People,* Judson, in press. Writer of column, "Youth Asks," in *Warren Record;* contributor to religion journals.

AVOCATIONAL INTERESTS: Gardening, poultry, and bird study.

* * *

LINKUGEL, Wilmer A(lbert)   1929-

PERSONAL: Born January 12, 1929, in Bremen, Kan.; son of Otto (a farmer) and Louise (Knabe) Linkugel; married Helen Motyka (a speech therapist), June 21, 1958; children: LeAnn Margaret, Kristin Sue. *Education:* University of Nebraska, B.S. in Ed. (with distinction), 1953, M.A., 1954; University of Wisconsin, Ph.D., 1960. *Politics:* Democrat. *Religion:* Lutheran. *Home:* 2456 Jasu Dr., Lawrence, Kan. *Office:* University of Kansas, Lawrence, Kan.

CAREER: University of Kansas, Lawrence, instructor in speech, 1956-58, assistant professor, 1959-63, associate professor of speech communication, 1963-68, professor of speech communication and human relations, 1968—. *Member:* Speech Association of America, American Association of University Professors, Central States Speech Association.

WRITINGS: (With E. C. Buehler) *Speech: A First Course*, Harper, 1962, 3rd edition, 1975; (editor with R. R. Allen and Richard L. Johannesen) *Contemporary American Speeches*, Wadsworth, 1965, 3rd edition, 1972. Contributor to speech journals.

WORK IN PROGRESS: With Carl W. Downs and David M. Berg, *Personal Communication in Organizations.*

* * *

LIPPINCOTT, Sarah Lee 1920-

PERSONAL: Born October 26, 1920, in Philadelphia, Pa.; daughter of George E. and Sarah (Evans) Lippincott. *Education:* University of Pennsylvania, B.A., 1942; Swarthmore College, M.A., 1950. *Office:* Sproul Observatory, Swarthmore College, Swarthmore, Pa.

CAREER: Swarthmore College, Swarthmore, Pa., research associate at Sproul Observatory, 1951-72, director, 1972—, lecturer, 1960—. Fulbright fellow at Paris Observatory, Meudon, France, 1953-54; member of French Solar Eclipse Expedition to Oland, Sweden, and researcher at Pic du Midi Observatory in French Pyrenees, 1954; summer researcher at High Altitude Observatory, Sunspot, N.M., 1955; participant in General Assembly of Astronomical Union, Moscow, 1958, in North Atlantic Treaty Organization-sponsored course in problems on galactic structure, Netherlands, 1960, and in visiting professors in astronomy program of American Astronomical Society, 1961—. *Member:* International Astronomical Union, American Astronomical Society, Rittenhouse Astronomical Society, Commission 26 (president, 1973—), Societ de Bienfaisance de Philadelphie (board), Sigma Xi (president of Swarthmore chapter, 1959-60), Kappa Kappa Gamma. *Awards, honors:* D.Sc. from Villanova University, 1973.

WRITINGS: (With Joseph M. Joseph) *Point to the Stars*, McGraw, 1963, 2nd edition, 1972; (with Laurence Lafore) *Philadelphia: The Unexpected City*, Doubleday, 1965. Contributor of scientific research papers to journals in United States, Canada, France, and Netherlands, and popular articles to magazines.

* * *

LIPSYTE, Robert 1938-

PERSONAL: Born January 16, 1938, in New York, N.Y.; son of Sidney I. and Fanny (Finston) Lipsyte; married Marjorie L. Rubin, 1966. *Education:* Columbia University, B.A., 1957, M.S., 1959. *Agent:* Lynn Nesbit, International Creative Management, 1301 Avenue of Americas, New York, N.Y. 10019. *Office: New York Times*, New York, N.Y.

CAREER: New York Times, New York, N.Y., columnist, 1957-71. Author. *Military service:* U.S. Army, 1961. *Awards, honors:* Mike Berger Award for distinguished reporting, 1966; best novel of year award from Child Study Association of America, 1967, for *The Contender.*

WRITINGS: (With Dick Gregory) *Nigger*, Dutton, 1964; *The Masculine Mystique*, New American Library, 1966; *The Contender*, Harper, 1967; *Assignment: Sports*, Harper, 1970; (with Steve Cady) *Something Going*, Dutton, 1973; *Liberty Two*, Simon & Schuster, 1974; *Sports World: An American Dreamland*, Quadrangle, 1975.

* * *

LISTON, Robert A. 1927-

PERSONAL: Born August 23, 1927, in Youngstown, Ohio;

son of Benjamin Furman and Lola (Carder) Liston; married Jean Altman, September 8, 1950; children: Cynthia Kay, Stephen Ward, Felicia Kay. *Education:* Hiram College, A.B., 1949. *Home:* 23 Twitchgrass Rd., Trumbull, Conn. 06611. *Agent:* Curtis Brown Ltd., 60 East 56th St., New York, N.Y. 10022.

CAREER: Former newspaperman in Marion, Ohio, 1954, Mansfield, Ohio, 1954-56, and on *Baltimore News American*, Baltimore, Md., 1956-64; now full-time free-lance writer. *Military service:* U.S. Army, Infantry, 1952-53; served in Korea.

WRITINGS: Sargent Shriver: A Candid Portrait, Farrar, Straus, 1964; *Your Career in Law Enforcement*, Messner, 1965, revised edition, 1973; *Your Career in Civil Service*, Messner, 1966; *Your Career in Transportation*, Messner, 1966; *Great Detectives*, Platt, 1966; *Tides of Justice*, Delacorte, 1966; *On the Job Training and Where to Get It*, Messner, 1967, revised edition, 1973; *Your Career in Selling*, Messner, 1967; *The Dangerous World of Spies and Spying*, Platt, 1967; (with Robert M. N. Crosby) *The Waysiders*, Delacorte, 1968 (published in England as *Reading and the Dyslexic Child*, Souvenir Press, 1969); *Downtown: Our Challenging Urban Problems*, Delacorte, 1968; *Politics from Precinct to President*, Delacorte, 1968; *What You Should Know about Pills*, Pocket Books, 1968; (with Surrey Marshe) *The Girl in the Centerfold*, Dell, 1969.

Slavery in America: History of Slavery, McGraw, 1970; *The American Poor*, Delacorte, 1970; *Greetings, You Are Hereby Ordered for Induction: The Story of the Draft*, McGraw, 1970; *The Limits of Defiance: Strikes, Rights and Government*, F. Watts, 1971; *Young Americans Abroad*, Messner, 1971; *Dissent in America*, McGraw, 1971; *Edge of Madness: Prisons and Prison Reform in America*, F. Watts, 1972; *Slavery in America: The Heritage of Slavery*, McGraw, 1972; *Who Shall Pay?: Taxes and Tax Reform in America*, Messner, 1972; *When Reason Fails: Psychotherapy in America*, Macrae, 1972; *Presidential Power: How Much is Too Much*, McGraw, 1972; *The American Political System*, Parents Magazine Press, 1972; *The Right to Know: Censorship in America*, F. Watts, 1973; *The United States and the Soviet Union*, Parents Magazine Press, 1973; *The Ugly Palaces: Housing in America*, F. Watts, 1974; *Violence in America*, Messner, 1974; *Healing the Mind*, Praeger, 1974; *Who Really Runs America?*, Doubleday, 1974; *Who Stole the Sunset?: Dilemmas in Morality*, Thomas Nelson, 1974; *Defense Against Tyranny*, Messner, 1975; *We, the People?: Congressional Power*, McGraw, 1975; *Promise or Peril?: The Role of Technology in Society*, Thomas Nelson, in press; *How to Get in Touch with Government*, Messner, in press; *Some Call It Madness*, F. Watts, in press. Contributor to national magazines.

SIDELIGHTS: Liston writes: "I am heavily committed to writing books for teen-agers, a field I never considered when I began to write. . . . The secret of it is to write *up* to teen-agers, for they know more than adults."

* * *

LITTLE, Kenneth L(indsay) 1908-

PERSONAL: Born September 19, 1908, in Liverpool, England; son of Harold M. (a shipbroker) and Anne (Kellett) Little; married Iris Cadogan (a public health nurse), June, 1956; children: (previous marriage) Johann Lindsay, Kathrine Anne Lindsay. *Education:* Cambridge University, B.A., 1941, M.A., 1943; University of London, Ph.D.,

1945. *Office:* African Urban Studies, University of Edinburgh, Edinburgh, Scotland.

CAREER: London School of Economics and Political Science, London, England, lecturer in anthropology, 1946-50; University of Edinburgh, Edinburgh, Scotland, 1950—, began as reader, became professor of social anthropology and head of department, professor of African urban studies, 1971—. Visiting professor, University of California, Los Angeles, 1956, Khartoum University, 1957, New York University, 1965, University of Washington, 1969.

WRITINGS: Negroes in Britain, Routledge & Kegan Paul, 1947; *The Mende of Sierra Leone*, Routledge & Kegan Paul, 1951; *Race and Society*, UNESCO, 1952; *West African Urbanization*, Cambridge University Press, 1965; *African Women in Towns*, Cambridge University Press, 1973; *Urbanization as a Social Process*, Routledge & Kegan Paul, 1974.

WORK IN PROGRESS: Studies of the changing status of women in West Africa.

SIDELIGHTS: Little has traveled in most countries of western Europe and western Africa, the United States, and the West Indies.

*   *   *

LITTLE, Paul H.   1915-
   (Paula Little)

PERSONAL: Born February 5, 1915, in Chicago, Ill.; son of Israel Isaac (a linen merchant) and Ida Marie (Demont) Litwinsky; married Helen Mary McGrew (a teacher and designer, Hull House weaver), April 3, 1941. *Education:* Northwestern University, B.S., 1937. *Politics:* Democrat. *Religion:* Episcopalian. *Home:* 5485 Hyde Park Blvd., Chicago, Ill. 60615. *Agent:* A. C. Fierst, 630 Ninth Ave., New York, N.Y. 10036.

CAREER: Sometime radio announcer in San Francisco, Calif., advertising manager for two food chains, and assistant advertising manager of Armour & Co., 1944-46; full-time professional writer, 1964—.

WRITINGS: Paul Morphy Memorial Chess Tourney, McKay, 1937; *Sweet Torment*, Domino, 1964; *Sins of Tonia*, Domino, 1964; *From Torment to Rapture*, Lancer, 1964; *Deliver Her to Evil*, Domino, 1964; *Secret Melody*, Lancer, 1964; *We Love in Shadow*, Domino, 1964; *No Barriers*, Domino, 1964, reissued as *Their Aching Hunger*, 1965; *The Procurer*, Lancer, 1964; *Punishment for Passion*, Domino, 1964; *The Burning Flesh*, Domino, 1964; *Engraved in Evil*, Lancer, 1964; *Obey Me, My Love*, Domino, 1965; *Rapture for Three*, Domino, 1965; *The Smashers*, Lancer, 1965; *Hand of the Imposter*, Lancer, 1965; *The Agony of Desire*, Domino, 1965; (under pseudonym Paula Little) *One True Love*, Paperback Library, 1965; *Orphan of the Shadows*, Lancer, 1965; *Love in Style*, Paperback Library, 1966; *Playgirl for Hire*, Domino, 1966; *Thunder Over the Reef*, Lancer, 1966; *The Juvenile Delinquent*, Macfadden, 1971; *Codominium*, Brandon Books, 1974; *Famous Last Round Chess*, Sutton Coldfield, 1975.

Contributor to chess periodicals and to hotel and restaurant trade publications.

WORK IN PROGRESS: A Tutress Taught for Carlyle Communications.

*   *   *

LITVINOFF, Barnet   1917-

PERSONAL: Born November 23, 1917, in London, England; son of Mark and Rose (Michaelson) Litvinoff; married Sylvia Roytman (now a library researcher), December 17, 1940; children: Adrian and Miles (sons). *Education:* Attended British state schools. *Religion:* Jewish. *Address:* 28 Hollycroft Ave., London N.W. 3, England.

CAREER: Free-lance journalist in England, 1947-49; director of public relations for Jewish National Fund and Joint Palestine Appeal, Great Britain and Ireland, 1950-60; managing director of Barnet Litvinoff Associates Ltd. (public relations consultants), London, England, 1960-66; full-time writer, 1966—. *Military service:* British Army, 1940-47; served at Dunkirk, 1940, in Middle East, 1941-42; prisoner of war in Italy and Germany, 1942-45; became sergeant.

WRITINGS: Ben-Gurion of Israel, Weidenfeld & Nicolson, 1954, Praeger, 1955; *David Ben-Gurion* (for young people), Oceana, 1957; *To the House of Their Fathers*, Praeger, 1965 (published in England as *Road to Jerusalem*, Weidenfeld & Nicolson, 1966); *A Peculiar People*, Weybright, 1969; *Another Time, Another Voice* (novel), W. H. Allen, 1971; (editor) Chaim Weizmann, *The Weizmann Letters and Papers*, Volumes II-VI, Oxford University Press, 1971-75; *Israel: A Chronology and Fact Book*, Oceana, 1974.

*   *   *

LIVINGOOD, James W(eston)   1910-

PERSONAL: Born July 5, 1910, in Birdsboro, Pa.; son of Howard Manwiller and Minnie (Potts) Livingood; married Alma Lawshe, June 19, 1937; children: James Weston, Jr., Richard Shafto. *Education:* Gettysburg College, B.S., 1932; Princeton University, M.A., 1934, Ph.D., 1937. *Religion:* Episcopalian. *Home:* 395 Shallowford Rd., Chattanooga, Tenn. 37411. *Office:* University of Chattanooga, McCallie Ave., Chattanooga, Tenn. 37403.

CAREER: Princeton University, Princeton, N.J., instructor in history, 1935-36; University of Tennessee at Chattanooga, faculty member, 1937—, professor of history, 1951—, Guerry Professor of History, 1962—, chairman of Division of Social Sciences, 1951-52, dean of College of Arts and Sciences, 1957-66, dean of the university, 1966-69. *Member:* American Historical Association, Southern Historical Association, Tennessee Historical Society, East Tennessee Historical Society, Tennessee College Association (president), Chattanooga Area Historical Society (charter member; past president), Phi Beta Kappa, Pi Gamma Mu, Phi Delta Theta.

WRITINGS: Philadelphia-Baltimore Trade Rivalry, 1780-1860, Pennsylvania Historical and Museum Commission, 1947, reprinted, Arno, 1970; (with Gilbert E. Govan) *The University of Chattanooga: Sixty Years*, University of Chattanooga Press, 1947; (with Govan) *The Chattanooga Country: From Tomahawks to T.V.A.*, Dutton, 1952, revised edition, University of North Carolina Press, 1963; (with Govan) *A Different Valor: The Story of General Joseph E. Johnston, C.S.A.*, Bobbs-Merrill, 1956, reprinted, Greenwood Press, 1974; (editor with Govan) *The Haskell Memoirs*, Putnam, 1960; (with Govan) *Chronology: University of Chattanooga 1872-1961*, University of Chattanooga Press; (contributor) *Landmarks of Tennessee History*, Tennessee Historical Society and Tennessee Historical Commission, 1965; (with J. Leonard Raulston) *Sequatchie: A Story of the Southern Cumberlands*, University of Tennessee Press, 1974. Contributor to *Collier's Encyclopedia, Encyclopedia Americana*, and *Encyclopaedia Britannica*;

contributor of articles and reviews to *Saturday Review, Chattanooga Times*, and historical journals.

* * *

LIVINGSTON, A(lfred) D(elano) 1932-

PERSONAL: Born November 8, 1932, in Headland, Ala.; son of Aaron Gordon (a farmer) and Beatrice (DuPere) Livingston. *Education:* Studied at Auburn University, 1954-57, University of Alabama, 1957-60. *Address:* Drawer 8, Belleview, Fla.

CAREER: Radio Corporation of America, Huntsville, Ala., editor, beginning 1955. Free-lance writer and photographer.

WRITINGS: The Sky's the Limit, Lippincott, 1966; *Poker Strategy and Winning Play*, Lippincott, 1971; *Dealing With Cheats*, Lippincott, 1973. Editor, *Space Information Digest* (National Aeronautics and Space Administration weekly).†

* * *

LOADES, David Michael 1934-

PERSONAL: Born January 19, 1934, in Cambridge, England; married Ann Glover (a university lecturer), Dec. 18, 1965. *Education:* Emmanuel College, Cambridge, B.A., 1958, M.A. and Ph.D., 1961. *Office:* University of Durham, Durham, England.

CAREER: University of St. Andrews, St. Andrews, Scotland, lecturer in political science, 1961-63; University of Durham, Durham, England, lecturer, 1963-71, senior lecturer in modern history, 1971—. *Member:* Royal Historical Society (fellow), Historical Association, Ecclesiastical History Society, Surtees Society. *Awards, honors:* Prince Consort Prize and Seeley Medal from Cambridge University, 1962, for an essay on the rebellion of Sir Thomas Wyatt.

WRITINGS: Two Tudor Conspiracies, Cambridge University Press, 1965; (editor) *The Papers of George Wyatt Esquire*, Royal Historical Society, 1969; *The Oxford Martyrs*, Batsford, 1970, Stein & Day, 1971; *Politics and the Nation: 1450-1660*, Fontana, 1974.

WORK IN PROGRESS: A study of the reign of Mary Tudor.

* * *

LOCKARD, (Walter) Duane 1921-

PERSONAL: Born November 26, 1921, in West Virginia; son of Clyde (a coal miner) and Virgie (Walters) Lockard; married Beverly White, July 6, 1942; children: Linda, Janet, Leslie. *Education:* Attended Fairmont State College and West Virginia University; Yale University, B.A., 1947, M.A., 1948, Ph.D., 1952. *Politics:* Democrat. *Home:* 120 FitzRandolph Rd., Princeton, N.J. *Office:* Department of Politics, Princeton University, Princeton, N.J. 08540.

CAREER: Wesleyan University, Middletown, Conn., instructor, 1950-51; Connecticut College, New London, assistant professor of political science, 1951-61; Princeton University, Princeton, N.J., associate professor, 1961-65, professor of political science, 1965—, chairman of department of politics, 1969-72. Fulbright professor in England, 1972-73. State senator, Connecticut, 1955-57; delegate to New Jersey Constitutional Convention, 1966. *Military service:* U.S. Army Air Forces, pilot, 1942-46; became captain. *Member:* American Political Science Association. *Awards, honors:* Ford Foundation fellowship, 1954-55.

WRITINGS: New England State Politics, Princeton University Press, 1959; *The Politics of State and Local Government*, Macmillan, 1963; *The New Jersey Governor*, Van Nostrand, 1964; *Toward Equal Opportunity*, Macmillan, 1968; *The Perverted Priorities of American Politics*, Macmillan, 1971.

* * *

LOCKYER, Roger 1927-
(Philip Francis)

PERSONAL: Born November 26, 1927, in London, England; son of Walter (a businessman) and May-Florence (Cook) Lockyer. *Education:* Pembroke College, Cambridge, B.A. (first class honors in history), 1950, M.A., 1955. *Politics:* Liberal. *Residence:* London W. 1, England.

CAREER: Lycee Louis-le-Grand, Paris, France, assistant in English, 1951-52; Haileybury and Imperial Service College, Hertford, England, head of history department, 1952-53; Ernest Benn Ltd. (publishers), London, England, assistant editor, "Blue Guides," 1953-54; Lancing College, Sussex, England, head of history department, 1954-61; University of London, London, temporary lecturer in history at Royal Holloway College, Englefield Green, Surrey, 1961-63, lecturer in history at Goldsmiths' College, 1963-64, lecturer in history at Royal Holloway College, 1964—. *Military service:* Royal Navy, instructor, 1946-48; became lieutenant. *Member:* Economic History Society, Historical Association, Past and Present Society, Victorian Society, National Trust, London Library.

WRITINGS: (Editor) *The Trial of Charles I*, Folio Society, 1959; (with John Thorn and David Smith) *History of England*, Benn, 1961; (editor, and author of introduction) *Cavendish's Life of Wolsey*, Folio Society, 1962; (under pseudonym Philip Francis; editor, and author of introduction) *John Evelyn's Diary*, Folio Society, 1963; *Tudor and Stuart Britain, 1471-1741*, Longmans, Green, 1964; *The Monarchy*, Blond Educational, 1965; (editor) Richard Hyde Clarendon, *The History of the Great Rebellion*, Oxford University Press, 1967; (translator and adapter with John Thorn and D. Smith) Therese Henrot, *Histoire de l'Angleterre*, Gerard, 1968; *Henry VII*, Longmans, Green, 1968; Harper, 1971; (editor) Francis Bacon, *The History of the Reign of King Henry the Seventh*, Folio Society, 1971.

SIDELIGHTS: Lockyer is fluent in French. *Avocational interests:* Looking at buildings, reading novels and poetry, theater-going, cooking and eating.†

* * *

LODGE, David 1935-

PERSONAL: Born January 28, 1935, in England; son of William Frederick and Rosalie (Murphy) Lodge; married Mary Frances Jacob, May 16, 1959; children: Julia, Stephen, Christopher. *Education:* University College, London, B.A. (first class honours), 1955, M.A., 1959; University of Birmingham, Ph.D., 1967. *Religion:* Roman Catholic. *Agent:* Curtis Brown Ltd., 1 Craven Hill, London W2 3EP, England. *Office:* Department of English, University of Birmingham, Birmingham B15 2TT, England.

CAREER: British Council, London, England, assistant, 1959-60; University of Birmingham, Birmingham, England, lecturer, 1960-71, senior lecturer in English, 1971—. Visiting associate professor, University of California at Berkeley, 1969. *Military service:* British Army, 1955-57. *Awards, honors:* Harkness Commonwealth fellowship, 1964-65, for study and travel in United States.

WRITINGS: The Picturegoers (novel), MacGibbon & Kee, 1960; Ginger, You're Barmy (novel), MacGibbon & Kee, 1962, Doubleday, 1965; The British Museum Is Falling Down (novel), MacGibbon & Kee, 1965, Holt, 1967; Language of Fiction (criticism), Columbia University Press, 1966; Graham Greene, Columbia University Press, 1966; (editor) Jane Austen's "Emma": A Casebook, Macmillan, 1968; Out of the Shelter (novel), Macmillan, 1970; (editor) Jane Austen, Emma, Oxford University Press, 1971; Evelyn Waugh, Columbia University Press, 1971; The Novelists at the Crossroads and Other Essays (criticism), Cornell University Press, 1971; (editor) Twentieth Century Literary Criticism, Longman, 1972.

Plays: (With Malcolm Bradbury and James Duckett) "Between These Four Walls," produced in Birmingham, 1963; (with others) "Slap in the Middle," produced in Birmingham, 1965.

Contributor of articles and reviews to Critical Quarterly, Spectator, Tablet, Novel, Encounter, and other journals.

BIOGRAPHICAL/CRITICAL SOURCES: Month, February, 1970.

*　*　*

LODGE, George Cabot 1927-

PERSONAL: Born July 7, 1927, in Boston, Mass.; son of Henry Cabot (statesman and ambassador) and Emily (Sears) Lodge; married Nancy Kunhardt, April 23, 1949; children: Nancy, Emily, Dorothy, Henry Cabot, George Cabot, David. Education: Harvard University, A.B., 1950. Politics: Republican. Religion: Protestant. Home: 275 Hale St., Beverly, Mass. Office: Harvard Business School, Soldiers Field, Boston, Mass. 02163.

CAREER: Boston Herald, Boston, Mass., political reporter, 1950-54; U.S. Department of Labor, Washington, D.C., director of information, 1954-58, assistant Secretary of Labor for International Affairs, 1958-61; Harvard Business School, Boston, Mass., lecturer, 1963-68, associate professor, 1968-70, professor of business administration, 1970—. Military service: U.S. Navy, 1945-46. Member: American Arbitration Association, American Association for the United Nations, Council on Foreign Relations, Federal City Club (Washington, D.C.). Awards, honors: Named one of ten outstanding young men in the country by United States Junior Chamber of Commerce, 1960; Arthur S. Fleming Award; Distinguished Service Award, U.S. Department of Labor.

WRITINGS: Spearheads of Democracy, Harper, 1962; Engines of Change, Knopf, 1970.

*　*　*

LOESER, Katinka 1913-

PERSONAL: Born July 2, 1913, in Ottumwa, Iowa; daughter of Louis and Eva (Hardy) Loeser; married Peter De Vries (an author and editor), October 16, 1943; children: Jan, Peter Jon, Derek. Education: Attended Mount Holyoke College, 1930-31; University of Chicago, A.B., 1936. Politics: Democrat. Religion: Protestant. Home: 170 Cross Hwy., Westport, Conn., 06880. Agent: A. Watkins, Inc., 77 Park Ave., New York, N.Y. 10016.

CAREER: Writer. Awards, honors: Young Poet's Prize of Poetry (magazine), 1943.

WRITINGS: Tomorrow Will Be Monday (fiction), Atheneum, 1964; The Archers at Home (fiction), Atheneum,

1968. Story anthologized in Best American Short Stories, 1963; contributor of short stories to New Yorker, McCall's, Redbook, Ladies' Home Journal; contributor of poetry to Poetry and New Yorker. Associate editor, Poetry, 1942-43.

*　*　*

LOH, Pichon P(ei) Y(ung) 1928-

PERSONAL: Born May 30, 1928, in Shanghai, China; son of K. Z. and Ying-sze (Hsu) Loh; married Vivien S. Lee (an M.D.), June 19, 1955; children: Karl I-hua, Karen Chi-hua, Kristine. Education: Attended St. John's University, Shanghai, China, 1946-48; Phillips University, Enid, Okla., B.A., 1950; University of Chicago, M.A., 1951, Ph.D., 1955. Religion: Methodist. Home: 15 Evergreen Pl., Tenafly, N.J. 07670. Office: Upsala College, East Orange, N.J.

CAREER: Anderson College, Anderson, Ind., visiting assistant professor of history, 1953-54; American People's Encyclopedia, Chicago, Ill., editor, 1955-56; Anderson College, assistant professor of history and political science, 1956-59, associate professor, 1959-63, professor, 1963-65, chairman of department, 1958-63; Upsala College, East Orange, N.J., associate professor, 1965-67, professor of political science and East Asian History, 1967—. Visiting associate professor, Drew University, 1966-67; Columbia University, associate, 1966—, research associate, East Asian Institute, 1967-68. Member: Association for Asian Studies, American Political Science Association, American Historical Association, American Academy of Political and Social Science, New Jersey Academy of Social Science. Awards, honors: Carnegie Corp. senior fellow at Columbia University, 1961-62; faculty fellowship, Upsala College, 1967-68; research award, Social Science Research Council and American Council of Learned Societies, 1974-75.

WRITINGS: (Contributor) Robert Byrnes, editor, The Non-Western Areas in Undergraduate Education in Indiana, Indiana University Press, 1959; The Kuomintang Debacle of 1949: Conquest or Collapse, Heath, 1965; The Early Chiang Kaishek: A Study of His Personality and Politics, 1887-1924, Columbia University Press, 1970. Contributor to Proceedings of the Indiana Academy of Social Sciences, 1957, 1964, and to Journal of Asian Studies, and Modern Asian Studies.

WORK IN PROGRESS: Research in twentieth-century Chinese politics, and Chiang Kai-shek.

*　*　*

LOH, Robert 1924-

PERSONAL: Born November 3, 1924, in Shanghai, China; son of Don M. (a businessman) and Wei (Sheng) Loh. Education: University of Shanghai, B.A., 1946; University of Wisconsin, M.A., 1949. Home: 3801 Connecticut Ave. N.W., Washington, D.C. 20008.

CAREER: University of Shanghai, Shanghai, China, associate professor, 1944-51; Foo Sing Flour Mills, Shanghai, China, manager, 1952-57; China Can Co., Hong Kong, assistant to president, 1958-59; U.S. Government, Army Research and Translation Group, Washington, D.C., researcher, beginning 1960. Lecturer in Marxism-Leninism at Socialist Institution in Shanghai, China. Awards, honors: Award, 1960, for The Rainbow Chaser.

WRITINGS: The Rainbow Chaser, Union Press (Hong Kong), 1959; Businessmen in China, China Viewpoints (Hong Kong), 1960; (consultant) U.S. Congress, House Committee on Un-American Activities, How the Chinese

Reds Hoodwink Visiting Foreigners, U.S. Government Printing Office, 1960; (with Humphrey Evans) *Escape from Red China*, Coward, 1962. Contributor to *Atlantic Monthly*.

WORK IN PROGRESS: Research on Communist China.

SIDELIGHTS: Loh traveled widely in the Soviet Union as member of a Chinese Communist "tourist group" in late 1956 and early 1957.

BIOGRAPHICAL/CRITICAL SOURCES: Escape from Red China, Coward, 1962.†

* * *

LOHRER, M(ary) Alice 1907-

PERSONAL: Born January 29, 1907, in Chicago, Ill.; daughter of Richard Hugo (an engineer) and Mary (Nyman) Schultz. *Education:* University of Chicago, Ph.B., 1928, A.M., 1945; University of Illinois, B.S. in L.S., 1937. *Politics:* Democrat. *Religion:* Congregationalist. *Home:* 1905 North Melanie Lane, Champaign, Ill. 61820.

CAREER: Assistant high school librarian in Oak Park, Ill., 1928-38; high school librarian in Hinsdale, Ill., 1938-41; University of Illinois, Graduate School of Library Science, Urbana, assistant professor, 1941-59, associate professor, 1959-67, professor of library science, 1967-74, professor emeritus, 1974—. Tehran International College, Tehran, Iran, professor, 1974-76. Chulalongkorn University, Bangkok, Thailand, Fulbright lecturer, 1955-56; Japan Library School, Keio University, Tokyo, Japan, visiting professor, 1959. Summer teacher at Purdue University, 1939-42, West Virginia University, 1952, University of Southern California, 1953, University of Wisconsin, 1960, University of Denver, 1964, 1966. Library consultant, Fulbright lecturer, University of Tehran, 1966-67. Member of teams surveying libraries in Europe, 1947, Indianapolis school libraries, 1953-54, Missouri libraries, 1960-61; director of research study on school libraries as materials centers, under U.S. Office of Education grant, 1961-62. Consultant to Coronet Educational Films and to school libraries in a number of states.

MEMBER: American Library Association (member of council), American Association of School Libraries, National Education Association, American Association of University Professors, American Association of University Women, Illinois Association of High School Librarians (president, 1940-41), Illinois Library Association (president, 1946-47), Illinois Association of School Librarians, Delta Kappa Gamma, Beta Phi Mu, Phi Kappa Phi. *Awards, honors:* Rockefeller Foundation grant to Japan; U.S. Office of Education grant.

WRITINGS: (With Frances Henne and Ersted) *Planning Guide for the High School Library Program*, American Library Association, 1951; (editor) *The School Library Materials Center: Its Resources and Their Utilization*, Allerton Institute, University of Illinois, 1964; *The Identification and Role of School Libraries that Function as Instructional Materials Centers, and Implications for Library Education in the United States*, Graduate School of Library Science, University of Illinois, 1970; (contributor) Harold S. Davis, editor, *Instructional Media Center*, Indiana University Press, 1971; (contributor) Jean Lowrie, editor, *Libraries: International Developments*, Scarecrow, 1972. Contributor of reviews to *Saturday Review* and articles to library periodicals. Issue editor of *Library Trends*, University of Illinois Library School, January 1, 1953, October, 1973.

LONG, Father Valentine W. 1902-

PERSONAL: Secular name, William George Long; born October 28, 1902, in Cumberland, Md.; son of George Louis (a salesman) and Agnes Catherine (Lippold) Long. *Education:* St. Bonaventure University, B.A., 1925, M.A., 1927. *Home and office:* Mount Alverno Novitiate, Warwick, N.Y. 10990.

CAREER: Ordained Roman Catholic priest of Franciscan order (O.F.M.), 1921; professor of English at St. Joseph's Seminary, Callicoon, N.Y., 1928-29, Aquinas Institute, Rochester, N.Y., 1929-30, and St. Bonaventure University, St. Bonaventure, N.Y., 1930-40; parish priest in New York, N.Y., 1940-45; Siena College, Loudonville, N.Y., professor of English, 1945-57; Mount Alverno Novitiate, Warwick, N.Y., chaplain and professor, 1957—. Radio lecturer.

WRITINGS—All published by Lumen Christi Press: Not On Bread Alone, 1934; *They Have Seen His Star*, 1938; *Magnificent Man*, 1948; *Fountain of Living Waters*, 1957; *Bernadette and Her Lady of Glory*, 1958; *Whatever Comes to Mind*, 1966; *The Angels in Religion and Art*, 1970. Contributor to magazines.

* * *

LONG, John D(ouglas) 1920-

PERSONAL: Born July 21, 1920, in Earlington, Ky.; son of John B. and Effie (Yates) Long; married Hazel E. Schnyder, July 12, 1952; children: Douglas P.; Martha S. and Elinor J. (twins). *Education:* University of Kentucky, B.S., 1942; Harvard University, M.B.A., 1947; Indiana University, D.B.A., 1954. *Politics:* Republican. *Religion:* Evangelical. *Home:* 2008 Windsor Dr., Bloomington, Ind. *Office:* Graduate School of Business, Indiana University, Bloomington, Ind. 47401.

CAREER: DePauw University, Greencastle, Ind., instructor, 1947; Indiana University, Bloomington, instructor in business, 1947-51, assistant professor, 1954-55, associate professor, 1956-59, professor of insurance, Graduate School of Business, 1959—. *Military service:* U.S. Army, 1943-46, 1951-52; served in General Staff Corps; became captain; received Bronze Star. *Member:* Society of Chartered Property and Casualty Underwriters, American Risk and Insurance Association (past president), American Finance Association.

WRITINGS: Methods of Agency Continuation, Bureau of Business Research, Indiana University, 1955; (with Arthur M. Weimer) *Business Administration: An Introductory Management Approach*, with workbook, Irwin, 1959, 5th edition, 1974; (editor with Davis W. Gregg) *Property and Liability Insurance Handbook*, Irwin, 1965; *Ethics, Morality, and Insurance: A Long Range Outlook*, Bureau of Business Research, Indiana University, 1971. Also author of research reports and editor of conference proceedings.

* * *

LOOMIS, Robert D.

PERSONAL: Born in Conneaut, Ohio; son of Kline (a mayor) and Louise (Chapman) Loomis; married Gloria Colliani, 1956; children: Diana. *Education:* Duke University, B.A., 1950. *Office:* Random House, Inc., 201 East 50th St., New York, N.Y. 10022.

CAREER: Random House, Inc., New York, N.Y., senior editor.

WRITINGS: (Editor) *William March Omnibus*, Rinehart, 1956; *The Story of the United States Air Force*, Random House, 1959; *Great American Fighter Pilots of World War II*, Random House, 1961; *All About Aviation*, Random House, 1964.

* * *

LORD, Francis A. 1911-

PERSONAL: Born December 8, 1911, in Los Angeles, Calif.; son of Edward Brown and Alice (Buffum) Lord; married Marjorie Terracall, November 19, 1941; children: Terry Gail, Francis Buffum, Frederick Allan. *Education:* University of Massachusetts, B.S., 1936; Michigan State University, M.A., 1939; University of Michigan, Ph.D., 1948. *Religion:* Episcopalian. *Office:* University of South Carolina Museum, Columbia, S.C. 29208.

CAREER: Lawrence Institute of Technology, Detroit, Mich., instructor in history, 1940-41; Mississippi College, Clinton, professor of history, 1948-51; Central Intelligence Agency, Washington, D.C., research analyst, 1951-65; University of South Carolina, Columbia, director of Lancaster Campus, 1965-72, curator of University Museum, 1972—, lecturer in history, 1972—. Guest lecturer, Georgetown University, University of Maryland. *Military service:* U.S. Army, Infantry, 1929-31, Cavalry, 1936-37, Intelligence, 1941-46; served in Europe, World War II; became major; received Commendation Medal. U.S. Army Reserve, 1946-54; became lieutenant colonel. *Member:* American Historical Association, Society of Military Historians (fellow), Rotary.

WRITINGS: They Fought for the Union, Stackpole, 1960; *Civil War Collector's Encyclopedia*, Stackpole, 1963; *Civil War Bands and Drummer Boys*, A. S. Barnes, 1966; *Civil War Sutlers and Their Wares*, Thomas Yoseloff, 1969; *Lincoln's Railroad Man: Herman Haupt*, Fairleigh Dickinson University Press, 1969; *Uniforms of the Civil War*, Thomas Yoseloff, 1970. Contributor to military journals. Former consulting editor, *Civil War Times Illustrated*.

WORK IN PROGRESS: Volume II of *Civil War Collector's Encyclopedia*.

SIDELIGHTS: Lord speaks German and French.

* * *

LORIA, Jeffrey H. 1940-

PERSONAL: Born November 20, 1940, in New York, N.Y.; son of Walter J. (an attorney) and Ruth O. Loria. *Education:* Yale University, B.A., 1962; Columbia University, Graduate School of Business, received degree, 1967. *Agent:* Harold Ober Associates, Inc., 40 East 49th St., New York, N.Y. 10017.

CAREER: Sears, Roebuck & Co., New York, N.Y., art buyer, associated with Vincent Price Collection, beginning 1962. Art Consultant.

WRITINGS: Collecting Original Art (forward by Vincent Price), Harper, 1965; (with Pat K. Lynch and Susan Newman) *What's It All About Charlie Brown?*, Holt, 1968. Contributor to *House Beautiful* and *Philadelphia Inquirer*.†

* * *

LOTT, Milton 1919-

PERSONAL: Born January 14, 1919, in Menan, Idaho; son of John Smile (a farmer) and Otilda (Johnson) Lott; married Vivian Chabrier (a teacher), September 28, 1940; children:

Lauren, Camas, Jory, Jacqueline. *Education:* University of California, Berkeley, A.B., 1940. *Home:* 1212 Soda Canyon Rd., Napa, Calif. 94558.

CAREER: Welder in West Coast shipyard, 1940-44, and millwright for aggregates firm, 1948-54; novelist. *Military service:* U.S. Navy, 1944-46. *Awards, honors:* Houghton Mifflin literary fellowship ($5000), 1954, for manuscript of *The Last Hunt*, and Albert M. Bender Award of California Arts Association for the same book; National Institute of Arts and Letters grant in literature, 1955.

WRITINGS: The Last Hunt, Houghton, 1954; *Dance Back the Buffalo*, Houghton, 1959; *Backtrack*, Houghton, 1965.

WORK IN PROGRESS: A modern novel set in Africa, *A Beast in View*.

SIDELIGHTS: Lott told *CA*: "At the moment I am interested in viewing man as an animal, as a member of this planet's life, rather than as a superior being—or as a thinking machine. On the whole, I believe man uses thought mainly to disguise from himself his deeper animal meanings."

The Last Hunt was made into a film, script adaptation by Richard Brooks, 1956.

* * *

LOTTICH, Kenneth V(erne) 1904-
(Kenneth Conrad)

PERSONAL: Born March 13, 1904, in Danville, Ind.; son of Clyde Roy (an attorney and judge) and Ida Pearl (Shuck) Lottich; married Margaret Lois Moon, February 1, 1929; children: Sylvia Jane (Mrs. Charles Oscar Tindall). *Education:* Attended University of Louisville, 1925-27; Hanover College, A.B., 1928; Ohio State University, M.A., 1933; Columbia University, graduate study, 1944-46; Harvard University, D.Ed., 1951. *Politics:* Independent. *Religion:* Independent. *Home:* 7658 East Medlock Dr., Scottsdale, Ariz. 85253. *Office:* 4205 Winfield Scott Plaza, Scottsdale, Ariz. 85251.

CAREER: Orlando Junior College, Orlando, Fla., instructor in history and geography, 1941-43; Elon College, Elon, N.C., associate professor of history and geography, 1943-44; State University of New York College at Fredonia, assistant professor of social studies, 1944-48; Willamette University, Salem, Ore., associate professor of education, 1948-56; Boise College, Boise, Idaho, department head, 1956-57; University of Montana, Missoula, associate professor, 1957-62, professor of history and philosophy of education, 1962-69, professor emeritus, 1969—. Visiting professor, University of Hawaii, 1966, University of California at Davis, 1967-68, and Portland State University, 1971. *Member:* American Historical Association, History of Education Society, Comparative Education Association, Philosophy of Education Society, American Association of University Professors, Northwest Philosophy of Education Society (president, 1965-66), Delta Tau Kappa (vice-president, 1966), Kappa Phi Kappa. *Awards, honors:* Delta Tau Kappa Award of Merit, 1964; citation from Association of European Captive Nations, 1965, for *Behind the Iron Curtain*.

WRITINGS: (With Elmer H. Wilds) *Foundations of Modern Education*, Holt, 1961, 4th edition, 1970; *Poland*, International Institute of Arts and Letters, 1963; *Cardinal Concepts in the History and Philosophy of Education*, University of Montana, 1963; *New England Transplanted*,

Royal Publishers, 1964; (with Joseph S. Roucek) *Behind the Iron Curtain*, Caxton, 1964; (with Hugh C. Black) *The Great Educators*, Nelson-Hall, 1972.

Contributor: Richard E. Gross, editor, *The Heritage of American Education*, Allyn & Bacon, 1962; J. S. Roucek, editor, *The Difficult Child*, Philosophical Library, 1964; *Programmed Teaching*, Philosophical Library, 1965. Poetry represented in *Anthology of American Poetry*, Royal Publishers, 1964-68. Contributor to *Social Science, Social Forces, Comparative Education Review, History of Education Quarterly, School and Society*, and other publications.

WORK IN PROGRESS: A book, *A Pageant of American Education; Essentials of Sociology*, with Joseph S. Roucek, for Littlefield; *Social Issues and Education in Urban and Suburban Society*, with Kent Pillsbury and Donald S. Seckinger, for Nelson-Hall; *American Heritage*, for Bicentennial Commission.

SIDELIGHTS: Lottich's travels over much of the world include visits to Iron Curtain countries of east central Europe, U.S.S.R., and Siberia.

* * *

LOUCH, A(lfred) R(ichard) 1927-

PERSONAL: Born February 14, 1927, in Fresno, Calif.; son of Clarence William (a railroad clerk) and Frances (Gould) Louch; married Janet Haight; married Brenda Schweig; children: Julia Elizabeth, Martin Edward, Sophia Katherine, Peter Charles, John Owen, Hugh William. *Education:* Univeristy of California, Berkeley, B.A., 1949, M.A., 1951; Cambridge University, Ph.D., 1956. *Politics:* Democrat. *Religion:* Episcopalian. *Home:* 224 West Seventh St., Claremont, Calif. 91711.

CAREER: Oberlin College, Oberlin, Ohio, instructor in philosophy, 1957-59; Syracuse University, Syracuse, N.Y., assistant professor, later associate professor of philosophy, 1959-65; Claremont Graduate School, Claremont, Calif., associate professor, 1965-67, professor of philosophy, 1967—. Visiting associate professor, University of California, Los Angeles, 1963-64.

WRITINGS: Explanation and Human Action, University of California Press, 1966. Book review editor, *Journal of the History of Philosophy*.

WORK IN PROGRESS: Papers on explanation, the history of philosophy, and the philosophy of law.

* * *

LOUKES, Harold 1912-

PERSONAL: First three letters of surname are pronounced to rhyme with "now"; born March 1, 1912, in England; son of William (a cutlery manufacturer) and Annie (Atkins) Loukes; married Mary Linsell, August 28, 1937; children: Anthony Michael, Christopher D., N. Peter, S. Mary. *Education:* Jesus College, Oxford, M.A. and Diploma in Education, 1934. *Politics:* Labour. *Religion:* Quaker. *Home:* 2 Lynch Farm, Wytham, Oxford, England. *Office:* Department of Education, Oxford University, 15 Norham Gardens, Oxford, England.

CAREER: Delhi University, Delhi, India, reader in English, 1934-40; New School, Darjeeling, India, headmaster, 1940-45; English specialist at Oundle School, Peterborough, England, 1945-46, Leighton Park School, Reading, England, 1946-47, Thorne Grammar School, Yorkshire, England, 1947-49; Oxford University, Oxford, England, lec-

turer, 1949-51, reader in education, 1951—, fellow of Jesus College, 1966—. Justice of the peace.

WRITINGS: Friends Face Reality, Harrap, 1954; *Secondary Modern*, Harrap, 1956; *Friends and Their Children*, Harrap, 1958; *Castle and the Field*, Humanities, 1959; *The Discovery of Quakerism*, Harrap, 1960; *Teenage Religion*, S. C. M. Press, 1961; *Readiness for Religion*, Pendle Hill, 1963; *The Quaker Contribution*, S. C. M. Press, 1965; *New Ground in Christian Education*, Macmillan, 1965; *Teenage Morality*, S. C. M. Press, 1973. Editor, *Learning for Living*, 1962-64.

WORK IN PROGRESS: A book, *Personal Relationships in School*.

* * *

LOWE, Victor (Augustus) 1907-

PERSONAL: Born August 29, 1907, in Cleveland, Ohio; son of Henry A. (a manufacturer) and Katherine (Heiser) Lowe; married Victoria Lincoln (an author), April 3, 1934; children: Penelope Thayer (Mrs. Paul Williams; stepdaughter), Thomas Cobb, Louise Lincoln (Mrs. Robert B. Kittredge). *Education:* Case School of Applied Science (now Case Western Reserve University), B.S. in E.E., 1928; Harvard University, M.A., 1931, Ph.D., 1935. *Politics:* Independent (registered Democrat). *Home:* 3947 Cloverhill Rd., Baltimore, Md. 21218. *Office:* Department of Philosophy, Johns Hopkins University, Baltimore, Md. 21218.

CAREER: Harvard University, Cambridge, Mass., assistant in philosophy, 1937-39; Syracuse University, Syracuse, N.Y., instructor in philosophy, 1941-42; Ohio State University, Columbus, Ohio, instructor, later assistant professor of philosophy, 1942-47; Johns Hopkins University, Baltimore, Md., associate professor, 1947-61, professor of philosophy, 1961-73, professor emeritus, 1973—. Visiting professor of philosophy, McGill University, 1963-64. *Member:* American Philosophical Association (member of executive committee, Eastern division, 1954-57), Phi Beta Kappa, Sigma Xi, Tau Beta Pi. *Awards, honors:* Senior fellow, National Endowment for the Humanities, 1968-69; honorary research fellow, University College, University of London, 1967-68, 1970, 1972.

WRITINGS: (Contributor) P. A. Schlipp, editor, *The Philosophy of Alfred North Whitehead*, Northwestern University Press, 1941; (contributor) *In Commemoration of William James: 1842-1942*, Columbia University Press, 1942; (with Charles Hartshorne and A. H. Johnson) *Whitehead and the Modern World*, Beacon, 1950; (contributor) Max H. Fisch, editor, *Classic American Philosophers*, Appleton, 1951; *Understanding Whitehead*, Johns Hopkins Press, 1962; (contributor) Edward C. Moore and Richard S. Robin, editors, *Studies in the Philosophy of Charles Sanders Peirce*, 2nd series, University of Massachusetts Press, 1964; (contributor) Schlipp, editor, *The Philosophy of C. I. Lewis*, Open Court, 1968. Contributor to *Encyclopedia of Education, Encyclopaedia Britannica*, and to philosophy journals.

WORK IN PROGRESS: A book, *Alfred North Whitehead: The Man and His Work*.

SIDELIGHTS: Lowe told *CA*, "I discovered philosophy only as I was taking my degree in engineering (which I never practiced)."

* * *

LOWEN, Alexander 1910-

PERSONAL: Born December 23, 1910, New York, N.Y.;

son of Nathan and Esther Lowen; married Rowfreta Leslie Walker; children: Fredric L. *Education:* City College (now City College of the City University of New York), B.S., 1930; Brooklyn Law School, LL.B., 1934, J.S.D., 1936; University of Geneva, M.D., 1951. *Religion:* Protestant. *Home:* Puddin Hill Rd., New Canaan, Conn. *Office:* 144 East 36th St., New York, N.Y. 10016.

CAREER: Admitted to the Bar of New York State, 1934. Psychiatrist, 1953—. Institute for Bio-Energetic Analysis, New York, N.Y., executive director, 1954—. *Member:* Society for Scientific Study of Sex, American Academy of Psychotherapists.

WRITINGS: Physical Dynamics of Character Structure, Grune, 1958, published as *The Language of the Body,* Collier, 1971; *Love and Orgasm,* Macmillan, 1967; *The Betrayal of the Body,* Macmillan, 1967; *Pleasure: A Creative Approach to Life,* Coward, 1970; *Depression and the Body,* Coward, 1972; *Bioenergetics,* Coward, 1975. Also author of numerous papers on the body. Contributor to *Encyclopedia of Sexual Behavior.*

* * *

LOWENFELD, Berthold 1901-

PERSONAL: Born November 2, 1901, in Linz, Austria; came to United States, 1938, naturalized, 1944; son of Markus (a businessman) and Emilie (Reinisch) Lowenfeld; married Greta Platzko (a teacher), September 11, 1930. *Education:* University of Vienna, Ph.D., 1927. *Home:* 2928 Avalon Ave., Berkeley, Calif. 94705.

CAREER: School for the Blind, Vienna, Austria, head teacher, 1922-33; Children's Institute, Austria, Vienna, director, 1933-38; American Foundation for the Blind, New York, N.Y., director of educational research, 1939-49; Columbia University, Teachers College, New York, N.Y., instructor, 1944-49; California School for the Blind, Berkeley, superintendent, 1949-64; San Francisco State College (now University), San Francisco, Calif., research professor, Frederic Burk Foundation for Education, 1964-67. Visiting summer professor at University of Washington, Seattle, 1944-49; member of summer graduate faculty, Institute of Social Work, University of Michigan, 1945-49. U.S. Vocational Rehabilitation Administration, member of sensory study section, 1961-66, of national advisory council, 1966-70. Introduced talking books as an educational tool in schools for the blind, 1939; organized first national conference on blind preschool children, 1947.

MEMBER: American Psychological Association (fellow), American Association of Workers for the Blind, American Association of Instructors of the Blind, Council for Exceptional Children, National Rehabilitation Association, City Commons Club (Berkeley). *Awards, honors:* Rockefeller research fellowship in United States, 1930-31; Ambrose M. Shotwell Award for distinguished services, American Association of Workers for the Blind, 1965; Migel Medal for Outstanding Service to the Blind, American Foundation for the Blind, 1968; National Accreditation Council Award, 1972.

WRITINGS: Teachers of the Blind, American Foundation for the Blind, 1941; *Braille and Talking Book Reading,* American Foundation for the Blind, 1945; (editor) *The Blind Preschool Child,* American Foundation for the Blind, 1947; *Our Blind Children,* C. C Thomas, 1956, 3rd edition, 1971; *Blind Children Learn to Read,* C. C Thomas, 1969; *The Visually Handicapped Child in School,* John Day Co., 1973; *The Changing Status of the Blind: From Separation*

to Integration, C. C Thomas, 1975. Associate editor, *Exceptional Children,* 1945—.

Contributor: W. Donahue and D. Dabelstein, editors, *Psychological Diagnosis and Counseling of the Adult Blind,* American Foundation for the Blind, 1950; P. Zahl, editor, *Blindness,* Princeton University Press, 1950; W. M. Cruickshank, editor, *Psychology of Exceptional Children and Youth,* Prentice-Hall, 1955, 3rd edition, 1971; M. G. and G. B. Gottsegen, editors, *Professional School Psychology,* Grove & Stratton, 1963; J. F. Garrett, editor, *Psychological Aspects of Physical Disability,* U.S. Government Printing Office. Also contributor to 49th *Yearbook* of the National Society for the Study of Education, 1950 and to *Childcraft,* Volume 12, 1954.

AVOCATIONAL INTERESTS: Playing violin in string quartets.

* * *

LOWENS, Irving 1916-

PERSONAL: First syllable of surname rhymes with "row"; born August 19, 1916, in New York, N.Y.; son of Harry and Hedwig (Abramovich) Lowens; married Violet Elen Halper (a music librarian), July 30, 1939. *Education:* Columbia University, B.S. in Music, 1939; University of Maryland, M.A., 1957, graduate study, 1957-59. *Home:* 503 Heron House, Reston, Va. 22090 *Office: Washington Star,* 225 Virginia Ave., S.E., Washington, D.C. 20003.

CAREER: Washington Star, Washington, D.C., contributing music critic, 1953-61, principal music critic, 1961—; Library of Congress, Music Division, Washington, D.C., reference librarian for sound recordings, 1959-61, assistant head of reference section, 1962-66. Lecturer in music, Dunbarton College, 1958-59; public lecturer at Yale University, University of Michigan, Ohio State University, University of Southern California, and other universities and schools. Member of advisory board, Inter-American Institute for Musical Research, Tulane University, 1961—; consultant to Juilliard Repertory Project, 1965, and to Moravian Music Foundation; trustee, Robert D. Lehman Foundation, 1964-66; acting chairman of organizational committee, Musical Arts Research and Development Institute, 1965; member of board of directors, American Music Center, 1966-72.

MEMBER: International Musicological Society, International Association of Music Libraries, American Musicological Society (member of national council; member-at-large, executive board, 1965), Music Library Association (president, 1965), Music Critics Association (treasurer), Society for Ethnomusicology, American Studies Association, Inter-American Association of Music Critics (vice-president, 1973—), American Antiquarian Society (fellow), American Folklore Society, Bibliographical Society of America, Sonneck Society, Cosmos Club (Washington, D.C.).

AWARDS, HONORS: First recipient of Moramus Award from Moravian Music Foundation, 1960, for distinguished service to American music; American Council of Learned Societies and Rockefeller Foundation travel grants to International Musicological Congresses in Germany, 1962, Austria, 1964, Romania, 1967; U.S. Department of State travel grant, Venezuela, 1968, Greece and Cyprus, 1970; American Council of Learned Societies grant to complete *A Bibliography of American Songsters Published Before 1821;* American Society of Composers, Authors and Publishers Deems Taylor Award, 1973, for newspaper articles on music.

WRITINGS: The Hartford Harmony: A Selection of American Hymns from the Late 18th and Early 19th Centuries, Hartford Seminary Foundation, 1953; (editor) John Tufts, *Introduction to the Singing of Psalm-Tunes* (facsimile edition), Musical Americana, 1954; (with Vincent Silliman) *We Sing of Life: Songs for Children, Young People, Adults*, Starr King Press, 1955; (editor) Benjamin Carr, *Federal Overture* (facsimile edition), Musical Americana, 1957; (editor) John Wyeth, *Repository of Sacred Music, Part Second* (facsimile edition), Da Capo Press, 1964; (editor) O. G. Sonneck and W. T. Upton, *A Bibliography of Early Secular American Music* (facsimile edition), Da Capo Press, 1964; *Music and Musicians of Early America*, Norton, 1964; *A Bibliography of American Songsters Published Before 1821*, American Antiquitarian Society, 1964; *Critical and Historical Essays*, Da Capo Press, 1969. Also author of *Opera and Sonic Collage*, and *Beatrix Cenci*. Contributor of more than thirty articles and reviews to music journals and other publications.

Recordings: Editor, "The American Harmony," Washington Records, 1961. Original songs and choruses published by G. Schirmer and Willis Music Co., and in *Musicology*; compiler of editions of early American music published by E. B. Marks Music Corp. and G. Schirmer.

WORK IN PROGRESS: Music in America, for Doubleday-Anchor; *Source Readings in American Music History*, for Macmillan; *A History of American Music*.

SIDELIGHTS: Lowens is fluent in German; competent in French, Italian, Spanish; has reading knowledge of Romanian.

AVOCATIONAL INTERESTS: Collecting musical Americana and stamps about music, chess, and subminiature photography.

* * *

LOWENSTEIN, Ralph Lynn   1930-

PERSONAL: Born March 8, 1930, in Danville, Va.; son of Henry (a jeweler) and Rachel (Berman) Lowenstein; married Bronia Levenson, February 6, 1955; children: Joan Holly, Henry Alan. *Education:* Columbia University, B.A., 1951; M.S. in Journalism, 1952; University of Missouri, Ph.D., 1967. *Home:* 1408 Bradford Dr., Columbia, Mo. 65201.

CAREER: Reporter in Danville, Va., 1952, for *El Paso Times*, El Paso, Tex., 1954-57; Texas Western College, El Paso, assistant professor, 1956-62, associate professor of journalism, 1962-65; University of Missouri, Columbia, publications editor of Freedom of Information Center's *FOI Digest*, 1965-67, associate professor and later professor of journalism, 1968—, chairman of news-editorial department of School of Journalism, 1975—. Visiting professor and head of journalistic studies, Tel Aviv University, 1967-68. *Military service:* Israeli Army, 1948-49. U.S. Army, Signal Corps, 1952-54. *Member:* Association for Education in Journalism, Society of Professional Journalists, Kappa Tau Alpha. *Awards, honors:* Austin Headliners Club Award (first place), 1956; Columbia School of Journalism Alumni Award for distinguished service to journalism, 1957; Pall Mall "Big Story" Award, 1957; Sigma Delta Chi distinguished service award for research about journalism, 1971.

WRITINGS: Bring My Sons From Far (novel), World Publishing, 1966; (editor with Paul Fisher) *Race and the News Media*, Praeger, 1967; (with John C. Merrill) *Media, Messages, and Men*, McKay, 1971.

LOWREY, Sara   1897-

PERSONAL: Born November 14, 1897, in Blue Mountain, Miss.; daughter of William Tyndale (a college president) and Theodosia (Searcy) Lowrey. *Education:* Blue Mountain College, B.L., 1917; Columbia College of Expression, Chicago, Ill., diploma, 1919; Baylor University, M.A., 1923; summer study at other schools, including Central School of Speech, London, England. *Politics:* "Democrat or Independent." *Religion:* Baptist. *Home:* 23 West Hillcrest Dr., Greenville, S.C. 29609.

CAREER: Teacher of expression at Ouachita College, Arkadelphia, Ark., 1919-20, Blue Mountain College, Blue Mountain, Miss., 1921-22; Baylor University, Waco, Tex., professor of speech, 1923-48, chairman of speech department, 1924-48, radio supervisor, 1937-44; Furman University, Greenville, S.C., chairman of speech department, 1949-63. Visiting professor at University of California, Berkeley, 1948, Northwestern University, 1950, University of Florida, 1953, University of Utah, 1965. Broadcaster of educational television program, "How Do You Say It?," WFBC-TV, 1958-61 SCE-TV, 1962—. Member, Greenville Human Relations Council. *Member:* American Association of University Professors, Speech Association of America, Southern Speech Association, Texas and South Carolina Speech Associations, League of Women Voters (president of Greenville branch), Council on Aging (first chairman), Citizens Advisory Committee for Public Transportation (mayor's appointee, 1973-75), Beta Sigma Phi (honorary).

WRITINGS: Interpretative Reading, Appleton, 1949, revised edition, 1953; *How Do You Say It?*, Furman University Press, 1960; *Theodosia, Gift of God*, Carlton Press, 1972. Writer of *How Do You Say It?*, South Carolina Educational Television Center, 1959-69. Contributor to professional journals.

* * *

LOWRY, Ritchie P(eter)   1926-

PERSONAL: Born April 13, 1926, in Meriden, Conn.; son of George Maus (a rear admiral, U.S. Navy) and Caroline (Coleman) Lowry; married Betty Trishman (a writer-poet), September 5, 1948; children: Peter R., Robin E. *Education:* University of California, Berkeley, A.B., 1952, M.A., 1954, Ph.D., 1962. *Politics:* Democrat. *Religion:* Protestant. *Home:* 79 Moore Rd., Wayland, Mass. 01778. *Office:* Department of Sociology, Boston College, Chestnut Hill, Mass. 02167.

CAREER: In import-export business in San Francisco, Calif., later assistant to manager in Tokyo, Japan, 1947-50; Chico State College (now California State University at Chico), 1955-64, began as instructor, became associate professor of sociology; American University, Special Operations Research Office, Washington, D.C., senior research scientist and associate professor in research, 1964-66, acting chairman of basic studies division, 1964-65, professorial lecturer in sociology; Boston College, Boston, Mass., professor of sociology, 1966—, chairman of department, 1967-70. Visiting professor, Andover-Newton Theological School, 1968-69; visiting research professor, Institute for the Study of War, Free University of Brussels, 1972; visiting professor of sociology, University of Essex, 1972. Advisory editor in sociology, Charles Scribner's Sons, 1968—; member of academic advisory board, Dushkin Publishing Group, 1973—. Member of Inter-University Seminar on Armed Forces and Society, University of Chicago, 1964—. Member of board of directors, Chico (Calif.)

Community Council, 1961-63, and New Boston Athletic Association, 1967-70; commissioner, Butte County (Calif.) Housing Authority, 1956-64. *Military service:* U.S. Navy, 1944-46. U.S. Naval Reserve, 1951-65; retired with rank of lieutenant.

MEMBER: International Sociological Society, American Sociological Association, American Association of University Professors, American Civil Liberties Union, Federation of American Scientists, National Geographic Society, World Future Society, Authors Guild, Eastern Sociological Society, Massachusetts Sociological Society, Boston Authors Club.

WRITINGS: Who's Running This Town?: Community Leadership and Social Change, Harper, 1965; (editor) *Problems of Studying Military Roles in Other Cultures*, Center for Research in Social Systems, American University, 1967; (with Robert P. Rankin) *Sociology: The Science of Society*, Scribner, 1969, 2nd edition published as *Sociology: Social Science and Social Concern*, 1972; *Social Problems: A Critical Analysis of Theory and Public Policy*, Heath, 1974; *War and the Military*, C. E. Merrill, 1975.

Contributor: Alvin Gouldner and S. M. Miller, editors, *Applied Sociology: Opportunities and Problems*, Free Press, 1965; Arthur B. Shostak, editor, *Sociology in Action*, Dorsey, 1966; James G. Nutsch, editor, *Readings in Contemporary Problems, Issues, and Values*, MSS Information Corp., 1973; Walter D. Burnham, editor, *American Government*, Transaction, 1973; Clarence C. Clendenen, editor, *The Bull in the China Shop: The Political Role of the Military in the Post World War Era*, University of Kentucky Press, 1974; Elise Boulding, editor, *Sociology of World Conflicts*, American Sociological Association, 1975.

Also author of sociological papers and reports. Contributor of more than twenty-five articles and reviews to newspapers and sociological journals. Contributing editor, Comparative International Development Board, Social Science Institute, Rutgers University, 1965—; member of editorial board, *Urban and Social Change Review*, 1969—.

WORK IN PROGRESS: A book, *Secrecy in Contemporary Society.*

SIDELIGHTS: Lowry has traveled extensively in Europe, North America, Asia, and the Pacific.

* * *

LOWY, George 1924-

PERSONAL: Born May 17, 1924, in Budapest, Hungary; son of David and Margaret (Weisz) Lowy; married Livia Gyepes (a statistician), July 23, 1955; children: Gabriel. *Education:* University of Economic Sciences, Budapest, Hungary, B.A., 1952; Columbia University, M.S. in L.S., 1961, Ph.D., 1970. *Home:* 110-26 68th Rd., Forest Hills, N.Y. 11375. *Office:* Columbia University Libraries, 420 West 118 St., New York, N.Y. 10027.

CAREER: University of Economic Sciences, Budapest, Hungary, researcher, then assistant professor, 1952-56; Columbia University Libraries, New York, N.Y., searcher, 1958-61, bibliographer, 1961-64; *International Encyclopedia of the Social Sciences*, New York, N.Y., bibliographic editor, 1964-67; Macmillan Publishing Co., Inc., New York, N.Y., director of bibliographic and indexing services, 1967-68; Columbia University, New York, N.Y., director of International Affairs Library, 1969-73, chief of social science center, Universities Libraries, 1974—. *Member:* American Library Association, Special Library Association.

WRITINGS: A Searcher's Manual, Shoe String, 1965. Also author of *Guide to Russian Reprints and Microforms*, 1973.

SIDELIGHTS: Lowy speaks Russian and German.

* * *

LUCAS, Carol 1929-

PERSONAL: Born July 11, 1929, in Hewlett, Long Island, N.Y.; daughter of Irving William (a dentist) and Julia (Cutler) Lucas. *Education:* College of William and Mary, B.S., 1949; Columbia University, M.A., 1951, Ed.D., 1953. *Home:* 141 Woodmere Blvd., Woodmere, N.Y. 11598. *Office:* Town Hall, Hempstead, N.Y. 11550.

CAREER: Greater New York (N.Y.) Council of Girl Scouts, field director, 1949-51; Neponsit Beach Hospital (tuberculosis hospital), Neponsit Beach, N.Y., recreation director, 1951-53; National Council of Jewish Women, New York, N.Y., consultant, 1954-55; West San Gabriel Valley-Los Angeles County Heart Association, area coordinator, 1955-56; rehabilitation consultant, City of Hope (medical center for cardiovascular diseases), Duarte, Calif., 1956-57, and Los Angeles Tuberculosis and Health Association, Los Angeles, Calif., 1957-58; Federation of Protestant Welfare Agencies, New York, N.Y., recreation consultant, 1958-60; Columbia University, Teachers College, New York, N.Y., instructor, 1960-64, concurrently directing pilot study in gerontology; Five Towns Golden Age Club, Inc. (education and recreation center for oldsters), Woodmere, N.Y., executive director, 1964-66; Senior Center of Uniondale (N.Y.), supervisor of Administration on Aging Project, 1966—; president, New York State Conference for the Aging; co-chairman, White House Conference for the Aging (Region II).

MEMBER: Academy of Certified Social Workers, National Association of Social Workers, National Association of Public School Adult Educators, National Recreations and Parks Association (fellow), American Recreation Society, Royal Society of Health (London), Kappa Delta Pi, Delta Psi Omega. *Awards, honors:* Award of Royal Society of Health (London) for outstanding contribution in field of geriatrics; certificate of merit for Distinguished Services in International Geriatrics.

WRITINGS: (With Josephine L. Rathbone) *Recreation in Total Rehabilitation*, C. C Thomas, 1958; *Recreation Activity Development in Nursing Homes: Homes for the Aging and Hospitals*, C. C Thomas, 1962; *Recreation in Gerontology*, C. C Thomas, 1963; (with Josephine L. Rathbone) *Recreation in Total Rehabilitation*, C. C Thomas, 1970; *Recreational Activity Development for the Aging in Homes, Hospitals, and Nursing Homes*, C. C Thomas, 1974. Contributor to journals.

* * *

LUCHINS, Edith H(irsch) 1921-

PERSONAL: Surname is pronounced *Loo*-kins; born December 21, 1921, in Poland; daughter of Max (a businessman, writer, and actor) and Leath (Kravetsky) Hirsch; married Abraham S. Luchins (a professor of psychology), October 10, 1942; children: David, Daniel, Jeremy, Anne, Joseph. *Education:* Brooklyn College (now Brooklyn College of the City University of New York), B.A. (cum laude), 1942; New York University, M.S., 1944, further study, 1944-46; University of Oregon, Ph.D., 1957. *Religion:* Hebrew. *Residence:* Albany, N.Y. *Office:* Department of Mathematics, Rensselaer Polytechnic Institute, Troy, N.Y. 12180.

CAREER: Sperry Gyroscope Co., Long Island, N.Y., government inspector, 1942-43; Brooklyn College (now Brooklyn College of the City University of New York), instructor in mathematics, 1944-46, 1948-49; University of Miami, Coral Gables, Fla., research associate and associate professor, department of mathematics, 1959-62; Rensselaer Polytechnic Institute, Troy, N.Y., associate professor, 1962-70, professor of mathematics, 1970—. *Member:* American Mathematical Society, Mathematical Association of America, American Association for the Advancement of Science, American Association of University Professors, Sigma Xi, Pi Mu Epsilon. *Awards, honors:* New York State fellowship, American Association of University Women, 1958-59, for research in mathematics.

WRITINGS: (With husband, Abraham S. Luchins) *Rigidity of Behavior*, University of Oregon Press. 1959: (with Abratham S. Luchins) *Logical Foundations of Mathematics for Behavorial Scientists*, Holt, 1965. Contributor of more than a score of articles and book reviews to mathematics and psychology journals.

WORK IN PROGRESS: A joint psychology-mathematic project, undertaken with her husband, Abraham S. Luchins, with the aim of producing books on logic and thinking.

* * *

LUDWIG, Richard M(ilton) 1920-

PERSONAL: Born November 24, 1920, in Reading, Pa.; son of Ralph O. and Millie M. (Smeltzer) Ludwig. *Education:* University of Michigan, A.B., 1942; Harvard University, A.M., 1943, Ph.D., 1950. *Politics:* Democratic. *Religion:* Lutheran. *Home:* 143 Hartley Ave., Princeton, N.J. *Office:* Department of English, Princeton University, Princeton, N.J. 08540.

CAREER: Princeton University, Princeton, N.J., instructor, 1950-53, assistant professor, 1953-59, associate professor, 1959-68, professor of English, 1968—, Jonathan Edwards preceptor, 1954-57, assistant university librarian for rare books, 1974—. *Military service:* U.S. Army, Cavalry, 1944-46; became staff sergeant. *Member:* Modern Language Association of America, National Council of Teachers of English, American Studies Association, American Association of University Professors. *Awards, honors:* McCosh faculty fellow, Princeton University, 1967-68.

WRITINGS: (With Howard Mumford Jones) *Guide to American Literature and Its Backgrounds Since 1890*, 3rd edition, Harvard University Press, 1964, 4th edition, 1972.

Editor: (With Howard Mumford Jones and Ernest E. Leisy) *Major American Writers*, 3rd edition, Harcourt, 1952; (with Marvin B. Perry, Jr.) *Nine Short Novels*, Heath, 1952, 2nd edition, 1964; *Aspects of American Poetry: Essays Presented to Howard Mumford Jones*, Ohio State University Press, 1963; *Letters of Ford Madox Ford*, Princeton University Press, 1965; (with Robert E. Spiller and others) *Literary History of the United States*, 4th edition, two volumes, Macmillan, 1974; *Dr. Panofsky and Mr. Tarkington*, Princeton University Library, 1974.

WORK IN PROGRESS: Studies in American poetry.

* * *

LUEKER, Erwin L(ouis) 1914-

PERSONAL: Born December 15, 1914, near Dover, Ark;

son of Charles H. (a farmer) and Louise (Harms) Lueker; married Anna Marie Schick, May 2, 1942; children: Erwin, Jr., Lisette, George, Jonathan. *Education:* Attended St. Paul's College, Concordia, Mo., 1933-35; Concordia Seminary, St. Louis, Mo., B.D., 1939; Washington University, St. Louis, Mo., M.A., 1940, Ph.D, 1942. *Home:* 7049 Camden Ct., University City, Mo. 63130. *Office:* Concordia Seminary in Exile, 306 North Grand, St. Louis, Mo. 63103.

CAREER: Ordained Lutheran minister, 1939; pastor in Richmond Heights, Mo., 1943-46; Concordia Seminary, St. Louis, Mo., instructor, 1945-46; St. Paul's College, Concordia, Mo., associate professor of languages and humanities, 1946-55; Concordia Seminary, professor of theology and philosophy, 1955-74, director of Correspondence School, 1957-69, acing director of graduate studies, 1965-66; Concordia Seminary in Exile, St. Louis, Mo., instructor, 1974—. Adjunct professor, St. Louis University and Eden Seminary, 1974—. *Member:* American Philological Association.

WRITINGS: (Editor) *Lutheran Cyclopedia*, Concordia, 1954; (with O. E. Feucht, P. Hansen, and F. Kramer) *Engagement and Marriage*, Concordia, 1959; *The Concordia Bible Dictionary*, Concordia, 1963; (with Carl S. Meyer and others) *Moving Frontiers*, Concordia, 1964; (with Richard Caemmerer) *Church and Ministry in Transition*, Concordia, 1964; *Structured Musings of EL*, privately printed, 1968; *Change and the Church*, Concordia, 1969. Also author of numerous essays on religious subjects. Writer of poetry and of articles for reference works and journals. Former member of editorial board, *Lutheran Witness*.

WORK IN PROGRESS: A revision of *Lutheran Cyclopedia*.

* * *

LUND, Doris Herold 1919-

PERSONAL: Born January 14, 1919, in Indianapolis, Ind.; daughter of Don (a writer, humorist, and cartoonist) and Katherine (Brown) Herold; married Sidney C. Lund (an industrial writer), January 6, 1945; children: Meredith (Mrs. James Cohen), Eric (died February, 1972), Mark, Lisa. *Education:* Attended Wellesley College, 1935-37; Swarthmore College, B.A. (high honors), 1939. *Home:* 9 Sunwich Rd., Rowayton, Conn

CAREER: Young & Rubicam, Inc. (advertising agency), New York, N.Y., copywriter, 1940-46; William Esty, Inc. (advertising agency), New York, N.Y., copywriter, 1946-47; free-lance copywriter and layout artist; cartoonist and illustrator. *Member:* Authors Guild.

WRITINGS: Did You Ever?, Parents' Magazine Press, 1965; *Attic of the Wind* (verse), Parents' Magazine Press, 1966; (self-illustrated) *Hello Baby!*, C. R. Gibson, 1968; *Did You Ever Dream?*, (juvenile), Parents' Magazine Press, 1969; *I Wonder What's Under* (juvenile), Parents' Magazine Press, 1972; *The Paint-Box Sea* (juvenile), McGraw, 1973; *You Ought to See Herbert's House*, F. Watts, 1974; *Eric*, Lippincott, 1974. Contributor of poems, series verse, and cartoons to *Ladies' Home Journal*, *Look*, and *Advertising Age*; also contributor of articles to *Good Housekeeping*, *Reader's Digest*, and *Parents' Magazine*.

WORK IN PROGRESS: A non-fiction book, for Lippincott.

LUPER, Harold L(ee) 1924-

PERSONAL: Born December 21, 1924, in Oporto, Portugal, became U.S. citizen; son of Albert Ward and Fannie (Hawkins) Luper; married Mary Leatherwood, January 24, 1944; children: John Stephen, Robert Louis, Sally Ann. *Education:* Western Michigan College (now University), A.B., 1949; Ohio State University, M.A., 1950, Ph.D., 1954. *Politics:* Independent. *Religion:* Protestant. *Home:* 7705 Sabre Dr., Knoxville, Tenn. 37919. *Office:* University of Tennessee, Knoxville, Tenn. 37916.

CAREER: Central Michigan College (now University), Mount Pleasant, assistant professor of speech, 1950-51; Ohio State University, Columbus, instructor in speech pathology, 1951-54; University of Georgia, Athens, assistant professor, 1954-59, associate professor of speech correction, 1959-63; University of Tennessee, Knoxville, professor of audiology and speech pathology and head of department, 1963—, director of Hearing and Speech Center, 1966-72. Georgia Federation Council for Exceptional Children, member, 1956-63, president, 1961-62; consultant and member of professional advisory board, Knoxville Cerebral Palsy Center, 1963—; consultant to Daniel Arthur Rehabilitation Center, Oak Ridge, Tenn., 1964-65. *Military service:* U.S. Army Air Forces, 1943-46.

MEMBER: American Speech and Hearing Association (vice-president of administration, 1971-73; fellow), Speech Association of America, Southern Speech Association (chairman of committee on speech and hearing disorders, 1958-59), Tennessee Speech and Hearing Association (president, 1966-67).

WRITINGS: (Assistant editor and contributor) *Stuttering and its Treatment*, Speech Foundation of America, 1960; (contributor) *Stuttering: Its Prevention*, Speech Foundation of America, 1963; (with Robert Mulder) *Stuttering: Therapy for Children*, Prentice-Hall, 1964; (contributor) *Stuttering: Treatment of the Young Stutterer in the School*, Speech Foundation of America, 1965. Contributor to professional journals. Associate editor, *Exceptional Children*.

WORK IN PROGRESS: Evaluation of stuttering; studies on the difficulty of auditory discrimination items.†

*   *   *

LUYBEN, Helen L. 1932-

PERSONAL: First syllable of surname rhymes with "buy"; born July 26, 1932, in Omaha, Neb.; daughter of August Michael and Beatrice (Landes) Luyben. *Education:* Pennsylvania State University, B.A., 1954; Indiana University, M.A., 1957; University of Pennsylvania, Ph.D., 1961. *Residence:* New York, N.Y. *Office:* Department of English, St. John's University, Jamaica, N.Y. 11432.

CAREER: Purdue University, Lafayette, Ind., assistant professor of English, 1961-63; St. John's University, Jamaica, N.Y., assistant professor, 1964-68, associate professor of English, 1968—. *Member:* Modern Language Association of America, American Association of University Professors. *Awards, honors:* Purdue Research Foundation grant for research for *James Bridie: Clown and Philosopher*; St. John's University grant for research.

WRITINGS: James Bridie: Clown and Philosopher, University of Pennsylvania Press, 1965. Contributor to drama journals. Advisory editor, *Drama and Theatre*, 1964—.†

*   *   *

LYNCH, W(illiam) E(dward) 1930-

PERSONAL: Born May 17, 1930, in Chicago, Ill.; son of William E. and Mable (Kessel) Lynch. *Education:* St. Mary's of the Barrens, Perryville, Mo., B.A., 1952, and theology study, 1956; Angelicum, Rome, Italy, S.T.L., 1958; Biblicum, Rome, S.S.L., 1960. *Home:* 3016 West French Pl., San Antonio, Tex. 78228.

CAREER: Entered Roman Catholic order of Congregation of the Mission (Vincentians), 1947, ordained priest, 1956; St. Mary's Seminary, Perryville, Mo., professor of Bible and theology, 1956-57; St. Mary's University of San Antonio, San Antonio, Tex., professor of Greek, Bible, and theology, 1960—; Assumption Seminary, San Antonio, Tex., professor of Greek, Bible, and theology, 1960—, dean of students, 1961—.

WRITINGS: Word Dwells Among Us, Bruce, 1965; *Jesus in the Synoptic Gospels*, Bruce, 1967. Contributor to *New Catholic Encyclopedia* and *Bible Today*.

SIDELIGHTS: Lynch traveled widely in Europe during three years of study in Rome. He is competent in Latin, Greek, Hebrew, Spanish, Italian, German, and French.†

*   *   *

LYNN, Robert A(than) 1930-

PERSONAL: Born November 11, 1930, in Oak Park, Ill.; son of Harvey Leroy (a business executive) and Mabel (Brian) Lynn; married Naomi Burgos, August 28, 1854; children: Mary Louise, Nancy Ruth, Judith Mae, Joan Ellen. *Education:* Maryville College, Maryville Tenn., B.S., 1951; University of Tennessee, M.S., 1955; University of Illinois, Ph.D., 1958. *Politics:* Democrat. *Home:* 1324 North Eighth St., Manhattan, Kan. 66502. *Office:* College of Business Administration, Kansas State University, Manhattan, Kan. 66506.

CAREER: Maryville College, Maryville, Tenn., instructor, 1955-58, associate professor 1958-62, professor of economics and business, 1962-64; University of Missouri, Columbia, 1964-68, began as associate professor, became professor of business administration; Kansas State University, Manhattan dean of College of Business Administration, 1968—. Consultant, Station KSEW, Sitka, Alaska, 1961. *Military service:* U.S. Army, 1952-53; served in Korea; became sergeant first class. *Member:* American Marketing Association, American Economic Association, Southern Economic Association, Missouri Economics Association.

WRITINGS: Basic Economic Principles, with instructor's manual and student workbook, McGraw, 1965, 3rd edition, 1974; *Price Policies and Marketing Management*, Irwin, 1967; *Marketing Principles and Marketing Management*, McGraw, 1969. Contributor to *Journal of Marketing and Business History Review*.

WORK IN PROGRESS: Research on changing consumer actions and their effects on markets.

AVOCATIONAL INTERESTS: Hiking, playing piano.

BIOGRAPHICAL/CRITICAL SOURCES: Technical Education News, June, 1965.

*   *   *

MACARTNEY, (Carlile) Aylmer 1895-

PERSONAL: Born January 24, 1895, in Kent, England; son of Carlile Henry Hayes and Louisa (Gardiner) Macartney; married Nedella Mamarchev. *Education:* Attended Winchester College, 1908-14, Trinity College, Cambridge, 1914-19. *Home:* Hornbeams, Boars Hill, near Oxford, England.

CAREER: H.M. vice-consul (acting), Vienna, Austria, 1919-25; *Encyclopaedia Britannica*, London, England, staff member, 1926-28; League of Nations Union, London, England, intelligence department, 1928-36; All Souls College, Oxford University, Oxford, England, research fellow, 1936-65; University of Edinburgh, Edinburgh, Scotland, Montagu Burton Professor of International Relations, 1949-56. Historian. Head of Hungarian Section, British Foreign Office Research Department, 1939-46; regular broadcaster to Hungary, 1940-43; frequent broadcaster later from London and Radio Free Europe, Munich. *Military service:* British Army, Hampshire Regiment, 1914-16; Royal Artillery, 1916-19; wounded in action. *Member:* British Academy (fellow), British-Hungarian Fellowship (president), Donau Institut (Vienna). *Awards, honors:* M.A. and D.Litt., Oxford University; freeman of the city of Cleveland, Ohio.

WRITINGS: Poems, Erskine Macdonald, 1915; *The Social Revolution in Austria*, Cambridge University Press, 1926; *The Magyars in the Ninth Century*, Cambridge University Press, 1930; *National States and National Minorities*, Oxford University Press, 1934; *Hungary*, Benn, 1934; *Hungary and Her Successors: The Treaty of Trianon and Its Consequences, 1919-1937*, Oxford University Press, 1937, 2nd edition, 1965; *Studies in the Earliest Hungarian Historical Sources*, four volumes, [Budapest], 1938, Volumes VI, VII, Basil Blackwell, 1952.

Problems of the Danube Basin, Cambridge University Press, 1942; *The Mediaeval Hungarian Historians*, Cambridge University Press, 1953; *October 15th*, Edinburgh University Press, 1957, 2nd edition, 1963, published as *A History of Hungary 1929-1944*, Praeger, 1957; *Hungary: A Short History*, Aldine, 1962; (with A. W. Palmer) *Independent Eastern Europe*, Macmillan, 1962; *The Hapsburg Empire, 1790-1918*, Weidenfeld & Nicolson, 1969, 2nd edition, 1971; *Maria Theresa and the House of Austria*, Verry, 1969; (editor) *Hapsburg and Hohenzollern Dynasties in the Seventeenth and Eighteenth Centuries*, Macmillan, 1969. Contributor to *Encyclopaedia Britannica, Chamber's Encyclopaedia, Encyclopedia Americana*, and to British and central European periodicals.†

*   *   *

MacBRIDE, Robert O(liver) 1926-

PERSONAL: Born December 24, 1926, in Springfield, Mo.; son of Herbert Leslie (an engineer) and Dorothy (Harper) MacBride; married Laidily Sloan (a psychologist), October 3, 1964. *Education:* Attended Philadelphia Museum College of Art, 1946-49, and McCoy College, 1954. *Home and office:* 41 Glen Byron Ave., Nyack, N.Y. 10960. *Agent:* Oliver G. Swan, Paul R. Reynolds, Inc., 599 Fifth Ave., New York, N.Y. 10017.

CAREER: Royer and Roger, Inc. (technical publications), New York, N.Y., art director, 1953-59; General Electric Co., Philadelphia, Pa., art director, military systems design, 1959-61; Ewing Technical Design (technical publications), Philadelphia, Pa., graphics manager, 1961-62; Auerbach Corp. (computer consultants), Philadelphia, Pa., art director, 1963-66; free-lance art director, illustrator, and writer, 1966—. *Military service:* U.S. Navy, 1944-46.

WRITINGS: Civil War Iron-Clads: The Dawn of Naval Armor (self-illustrated), Chilton, 1963; *The Automated State: Computer Systems as a New Force in Society*, Chilton, 1967.

WORK IN PROGRESS: A survey of recent developments and future trends in computer-assisted graphic and display techniques; science fiction.

SIDELIGHTS: MacBride speaks French. *Avocational interests:* History of technology, archaeology; "future history"—probable technical, social, and economic developments in the next twenty to thirty years.†

*   *   *

MacCORKLE, Stuart A(lexander) 1903-

PERSONAL: Born September 1, 1903, in Lexington, Va.; son of John Gold and Mattie Ella (Swink) MacCorkle; married L. Lucile Emerson, September 26, 1942. *Education:* Washington and Lee University, A.B., 1924; University of Virginia, M.A., 1928; Johns Hopkins University, Ph.D., 1931. *Religion:* Presbyterian. *Home:* 3719 Gilbert St., Austin, Tex. 78703.

CAREER: University of Texas, Austin, instructor in government, 1930-31; Southwestern College, Memphis, Tenn., associate professor of government, 1931-32; University of Texas, instructor, 1932-34, assistant professor, 1934-37, associate professor of government, 1937-41, professor, 1941—, director of Bureau of Municipal Research, 1937-50, director of Institute of Public Affairs, 1950-67. Educational counselor, National Institute of Public Affairs, Washington, D.C., 1941-42; special consultant to U.S. Army Air Forces, 1942; executive director of Texas Economy Commission, 1951-52; adviser in public administration, Seoul National University, Seoul, Korea, 1958-60; visiting lecturer, National University of Mexico, summer, 1944 and 1968; Fulbright-Hayes lecturer, College of Europe, Bruges, Belgium, 1964. Civilian mobilization adviser, Office of Civlian Defense, 1942-43. Member of Austin City Council, 1949-53; Major Pro-Tem of Austin, 1951-53 and 1969-70. Member of board of directors, Western Republic Life Insurance Co., 1953-67.

MEMBER: American Political Science Association, American Society for Public Administration, International City Managers Association (honorary), National Municipal League, Southwestern Social Science Association (secretary-treasurer, 1934-37), Phi Beta Kappa, Pi Sigma Alpha, Kappa Sigma, Rotary, University Club (Washington, D.C.), Headliners Club (Austin). *Awards, honors:* LL.D., Washington and Lee University, 1964.

WRITINGS: The American Recognition Policy Toward Mexico, Johns Hopkins Press, 1933; *Police and Allied Power of Municipalities in Texas*, University of Texas Press, 1938; *Municipal Administration*, Prentice-Hall, 1942; *American Municipal Government and Administration*, Heath, 1948; (with Wilfred D. Webb) *Forms of Local Government*, University of Texas Press, 1948; (with Dick Smith) *Texas Government*, McGraw, 1949, 7th edition, 1974; (with D. Smith and Thomas P. Yoakum) *Texas Civics*, Banks Upshaw & Co., 1955; *Handbook for Councilmen in Council-Manager Cities*, International City Managers Association, 1955; (contributor) *Lectures on Local Government*, Rice University Press, 1958; *Austin's Three Forms of Government*, Naylor, 1973; *Cities From Scratch*, Naylor, 1974.

Publications include booklets on problems of municipal government, articles in *World Book Encyclopedia* and *Handbook of Texas*, and articles in public administration and legal journals. Member of editorial board, *Public Administration Review*, 1942-44.

MACDONALD, Coll 1924-

PERSONAL: Born January 21, 1924, in Westcliff-on-Sea, Essex, England; son of Coll and Elizabeth (Murray) Macdonald; married Hilary Constance Mowle, August 25, 1955; children: Coll, Murray. *Education:* Christ's College, Cambridge, B.A. (honors), 1948, M.A., 1952. *Home:* Uppingham School, Uppingham, Leicestershire LE15 9QU, England.

CAREER: University of Sydney, Sydney, Australia, Woodhouse fellow at St. Andrew's College, and lecturer in Greek, 1949; University of Otago, Dunedin, New Zealand, lecturer in classics, 1950-51; assistant master at Bradfield College, Berkshire, England, 1952-55, and Sherborne School, Dorsetshire, England, 1955-60; headmaster at Maidenhead Grammar School, Berkshire, England, 1960-65, Portsmouth Grammar School, Portsmouth, Hampshire, England, 1965-75, Uppingham School, Uppingham, England, 1975—. Justice of the peace, county of Berkshire, 1964-65, City of Portsmouth, 1967-75; Loeb Fellow in Classical Philology, Harvard University, 1972-73. *Military service:* Royal Air Force Volunteer Reserve, pilot, 1943-46; became flight lieutenant. *Member:* Classical Association, Society for the Promotion of Roman Studies.

WRITINGS: (With Sutherland and Warman) *From Pericles to Cleophon*, Rivingtons, 1954; (with Hawthorn) *Roman Politics 80-44 B.C.*, Macmillan, 1960; (editor) *Cicero, De Imperio Cn. Pompei, ad quirites oratio*, Macmillan, 1966; (editor) Cicero, *Pro Murena*, Macmillan, 1969; (editor) Cicero, *De provinciis consularibus*, Macmillan, 1971. Contributor of articles to *Classical Review* and *Greece and Rome*, of reviews to *Times Educational Supplement* (London).

WORK IN PROGRESS: Editions of Cicero's *In Catilinam I-IV, Pro Murena, Pro Sulla, Pro Flacco*, for Loeb Classical Library, and *Pro Sestio* for Macmillan; research on political history of the last century of the Roman Republic.

* * *

MACDONALD, H(enry) Malcolm 1914-

PERSONAL: Born May 21, 1914, in San Francisco, Calif; son of George Childs (a physician) and Helena (Zaun) Macdonald. *Education:* University of San Francisco, B.A. (summa cum laude), 1935; Harvard University, M.A., 1937, Ph.D., 1939. *Politics:* Democrat. *Religion:* Episcopalian. *Home:* 3518 Lakeland Dr., Austin, Tex. 78731. *Office:* Department of Government, University of Texas, Austin, Tex. 78712.

CAREER: University of Texas, Austin, instructor, 1938-41, assistant professor, 1941-47, associated professor, 1947-53, professor of government, 1953—, chairman of department, 1957-70. Instructor at U.S. Naval Academy, 1945-46; Johnson Visiting Professor at Pomona College and Claremont Graduate Center, 1966; summer visiting professor at other universities. Director of Clan Donald Educational Trust. *Military service:* U.S. Navy, 1941-45; became lieutenant commander. U.S. Naval Reserve, 1946—; now captain.

MEMBER: American Political Science Association, American Association for Political and Legal Philosophy, Royal Economic Society (fellow), Southwestern Social Science Association, Southwestern Political Science Association, Southern Politial Science Association, U.S. Naval Institute, Phi Sigma Alpha, Phi Kappa Phi, Alpha Tau Omega,

Harvard Club (Boston), Headliners Club (Austin), Army and Navy Club (Washington, D.C.). *Awards, honors:* St. Mary's University of San Antonio annual award for contribution to the study of international politics, 1966.

WRITINGS: (Editor, with others) *Outside Readings in American Government*, Crowell, 1949, 4th edition published as *Readings in American Government*, 1963; *A Christian View of Political Man*, National Council of the Episcopal Church, 1957; (contributor) Kenneth J. Carey, editor, *Making the World of Tomorrow*, International Relations Institute, St. Mary's University, 1958; (contributor) Arthur L. Harding, editor, *The Rule of Law*, Southern Methodist School of Law, 1961; (editor with W. O. Webb, Edward Lewis, and W. A. Strauss) *Readings in American National Government*, Crowell, 1964; (editor, and author of introductory chapter) *The Intellectual in Politics*, University of Texas Press, 1966; (contributor) *Communism and Nationalism*, St. Mary's University Graduate School, 1967. Book review editor, *Southwestern Social Science Quarterly*, 1947—. Contributor to professional journals.

WORK IN PROGRESS: Evolution of Western Political Theory.

SIDELIGHTS: MacDonald has traveled in eastern and western Europe, including the Soviet Union and Balkans, in the Near East, Southeast Asia, Mexico, and Canada.

* * *

MACDONALD, Julie 1926-

PERSONAL: Born February 14, 1926, in Los Angeles, Calif.; daughter of Alexander and Aileen (McCarthy) Macdonald; married William H. Hood; children: (previous marriage) Judith Alexander, Alexander Macdonald II. *Education:* Attended Stanford University, 1944-45, and Jepson Art Institute, 1948-50. *Politics:* Democrat. *Home and office:* 485 Maylin St., Pasadena, Calif. 91105. *Agent:* Paul R. Reynolds, Inc., 599 Fifth Ave., New York, N.Y. 10017.

CAREER: Sculptor. *Awards, honors:* San Francisco Museum, California State Fair, and Allied Artists of America awards for sculpture.

WRITINGS: *Almost Human: The Baboon Wild and Tame—In Fact and in Legend*, Chilton, 1965.

WORK IN PROGRESS: A book about the hyena.

* * *

MACDONALD, Robert W. 1922-

PERSONAL: Born December 18, 1922, in Wantagh, N.Y.; son of William DeForest (a business executive) and Alma (Geib) Macdonald; married Joan Marie Farrell, 1966. *Education:* Attended Oberlin College, 1941-42, Worcester Polytechnic Institute, 1946-47; Clark University, Worcester, Mass., B.A. (with honor), 1948; Brown University, M.A., 1949; State University of New York at Albany, graduate study, 1950-51; Georgetown University, Ph.D., 1962. *Office:* U.S. Information Agency, Washington, D.C. 20547.

CAREER: U.S. Army, enlisted service with 10th Mountain Division, 1943-45; instructor and staff officer, Chemical Corps, 1951-60; now lieutenant colonel, U.S. Army Reserve. Teacher of social studies, Schoharie, N.Y., 1950-51; Middle East Research Associates (MERA), Washington, D.C., owner, 1960-63, editor of "Trend" (series of reports on the contemporary Middle East), 1960-62; U.S. Information Agency, communications researcher, 1963-67, with headquarters in Beirut, Lebanon, 1964-67; American Embassy, Kabul, Afghanistan, cultural attache, 1968-71; U.S. Department of State, Washington, D.C., chief of Near East programs, Bureau of Educational and Cultural Affairs; U.S. Information Agency, Motion Picture Service, Washington, D.C., film evaluation officer, 1974—. Consultant to Macdonald Associates, Inc. (engineers), Corvallis, Ore., 1960-64. Member of board of directors of Middle East Research Associates International Services, Inc., and Magnus Middle East Ltd. *Member:* American Political Science Association, World Association for Public Opinion Research, Middle East Institute (Washington, D.C.), Sigma Xi, Pi Sigma Alpha, Honorary Society of Kentucky Colonels. *Awards, honors*—Military: Bronze Star, World War II.

WRITINGS: (Editor) *Inside the Arab Mind* (annotated bibliography), Middle East Research Associates, 1960; *Morocco: A Politico-Economic Study*, Middle East Research Associates, 1961; (editor and contributor) *A Forest Industry Processing and Marketing Complex for Eastern Kentucky*, U.S. Government Printing Office, 1963; *The League of Arab States: A Study in The Dynamics of Regional Organization*, Princeton University Press, 1965; (contributor) Francis A. Beer, editor, *Alliances*, Holt, 1970.

AVOCATIONAL INTERESTS: Photography, mountaineering, skiing.

* * *

MacDOUGALL, Ruth Doan   1939-

PERSONAL: Born March 19, 1939, in Laconia, N.H.; daughter of Daniel (a writer) and Ernestine (Crone) Doan; married Donald K. MacDougall, October 9, 1957. *Education:* Bennington College, student, 1957-59; Keene State College, Keene, N.H., B.Ed., 1961. *Agent:* Russell & Volkening, Inc., 551 Fifth Ave., New York, N.Y. 10017.

WRITINGS: The Lilting House, Bobbs-Merrill, 1965; *The Cost of Living*, Putnam, 1971; *One Minus One*, Putnam, 1971; *The Cheerleader*, Putnam, 1973.

WORK IN PROGRESS: A novel.

* * *

Mac HORTON, Ian D(uncan)   1923-

PERSONAL: Born April 13, 1923, in Maidstone, Kent, England; son of William and Valentine E. (Rose) MacHorton; married Mary G. Fisher, November 10, 1945; children: Sheena Mary, John Graeme Barrie. *Education:* Attended Indian Military Academy, Dehra Dun, India, 1941-42, and University of London, 1953-54. *Politics:* Conservative. *Religion:* Presbyterian. *Home:* Strathnairn, 55 Mospey Crescent, Epsom, Surrey, England. *Agent:* H. R. Maule, 39 Bath Rd., Reading, Berkshire, England. *Office:* The Polytechnic School of Management Studies, 309 Regent St., London W. 1, England.

CAREER: Joined Indian Army as officer in 8th Gurkha Rifles, serving in India and Burma, 1942-46; transferred to Cameronians (Scottish Rifles), regular British Army, after recovering from severe wounds received at Irrawaddy bridgehead, 1945; invalided out with rank of major (honorary lieutenant colonel), 1957; began new career in marketing and public relations, and subsequently as designer and organizer of management courses for British companies; senior lecturer and director of short courses in general management at The Polytechnic, London, England, 1964—. *Member:* Ifield Tennis Club (founder-member and past chairman), Airborne Club.

WRITINGS: Safer Than a Known Way, Odhams, 1958, published as *One Hundred Days of Lt. MacHorton*, Mackay, 1960; *How to Get a Better Job in Management*, Cahners, 1971. Contributor of articles on business management to journals in England.

WORK IN PROGRESS: Introduction to Business Management; a book dealing with war experiences, 1944-45.

SIDELIGHTS: MacHorton's family had soldiered in India since the days of "John Company," including one ancestor who was a colonel under Clive. MacHorton's war experiences have been portrayed on several radio and television programs in England, including "Forgotten Heroes," Independent Television, and "Chance in a Million," British Broadcasting Corp.†

* * *

MACKIE, Alastair   1925-

PERSONAL: Surname rhymes with "away"; born August 10, 1925, in Aberdeen, Scotland; son of Frank and Anne (Ross) Mackie; married Elizabeth Law, August 11, 1951; children: Frances Law, Kathryn Elizabeth. *Education:* Attended Robert Gordon's College, Aberdeen, Scotland, 1937-43; University of Aberdeen, M.A. (first class honors in English language and literature), 1950. *Politics:* Scottish Nationalist. *Home:* 13 St. Adrian's Pl., Anstruther, Fife, Scotland.

CAREER: Stromness Academy, Orkney, Scotland, teacher of English, 1951-59; Waid Academy, Anstruther, Fife, Scotland, teacher of English, 1959—. *Military service:* Royal Air Force and Royal Navy, 1943-46 ("regard these years as contributing nothing of any value to me as a person. My real life was contained in a private notebook, stolen on an Italian destroyer in the Mediterranean, 1945. Some total stranger owes me three years.").

WRITINGS: Soundings (poems), Akros Publications (Preston, England), 1966; *Clytach: Twenty-Eight Scots Poems*, Arkros Publications, 1972; *At the Heich Kirkyaird: A Hielant Sequence*, Arkros Publications, 1975. Work represented in many anthologies, including *Contemporary Scottish Verse, 1959-69*, edited by Norman MacCaig and Alexander Scott, Calder & Boyars, 1969; *Scottish Poetry 5* and *Scottish Poetry 6*, both edited by George Bruce, Maurice Lindsay, and Edwin Morgan, Edinburgh University Press, 1972; poems also are to appear in *Scottish Poetry 7*, edited by Alex Scott, Rory Watson, and Maurice Lindsay.

WORK IN PROGRESS: Short stories entirely in Scots.

SIDELIGHTS: Mackie told *CA:* "I live against the sea and this gets into my work. Two seminal books for me: in Scots, being lent MacDiarmid's *Sangschaw* in 1954, the first major publication for understanding modern Scots poetry. In English: 1962, Robert Lowell's *Imitations*, [Lowell being] the poet I most like to read, of those writing in English. I am interested in the genre of translation as a separate mode of expression. I want Lowell to have a go at the *Aeneid*. Started learning Italian to do Leopardi lyrics in Scots and hope to gather these one day into a small collection. Have done some Propertius in English—too Poundian in retrospect."

About his short stories, Mackie said: "I commenced writing my first short stories entirely in Scots, summer, 1974. I have completed three . . . and intend to explore now for Scots can be extended in this genre."

MacLEISH, Andrew 1923-

PERSONAL: Born August 30, 1923, in Philadelphia, Pa.; son of Norman Hillard (an artist) and Lenore (McCall) MacLeish; married Ann Pullen, June 17, 1950 (died, 1971); children: Andrew, Eve, Geoffrey. *Education:* Roosevelt University, A.B., 1950; University of Chicago, M.A., 1951; University of Wisconsin, Ph.D., 1961. *Office:* University of Minnesota, Minneapolis, Minn.

CAREER: Instructor in English at Valparaiso University, Valparaiso, Ind., 1951-53, and Rockford College, Rockford, Ill., 1956-58; Northern Illinois University, DeKalb, assistant professor, 1958-62, associate professor of English, 1962-70; University of Minnesota, Minneapolis, professor, 1970—. State College of Iowa (now University of Northern Iowa), summer visiting associate professor, 1963. Hawaii State Office of Education, consultant in linguistics on Pidgin English Project. *Military service:* U.S. Naval Reserve, 1942-46. *Member:* Linguistic Society of America, National Council of Teachers of English, Midwest Modern Language Association.

WRITINGS: (With Martin Kallich) *The American Revolution Through British Eyes*, Harper, 1962; (with Martin Kallich and Gertrude Schoenbohm) *Oedipus: Myth and Drama*, Odyssey, 1968; *The Middle English Subject-Verb Cluster*, Mouton & Co., 1969; (with Louise E. Glorfeld) *The Dictionary and Usage*, Holt, 1969; (with Arnold Lazarus and H. Wendell Smith) *Modern English*, Grosset, 1971. Also author of *The Pronunciation of English in Sabah*, 1969.

WORK IN PROGRESS: A computer-assisted study of middle English syntax.

*   *   *

MACLEOD, Donald 1914-

PERSONAL: Born 1914, in Nova Scotia, Canada; son of Donald A. and Anne (MacKenzie) Macleod; married Norma E. Harper, 1948; children: John Fraser, David, Anne, Leslie. *Education:* Dalhousie University, A.B., 1934, M.A., 1935; Pine Hill Divinity Hall, B.D., 1938; Emmanuel College, University of Toronto, Th.D., 1947. *Home:* 48 Mercer St., Princeton, N.J. *Office:* Princeton Theological Seminary, Princeton, N.J.

CAREER: First United Presbyterian Church, Louisburg, Nova Scotia, minister, 1938-41; Bloor Street Presbyterian Church, Toronto, Ontario, associate minister, 1941-45; Princeton Theological Seminary, Princeton, N.J., teaching fellow, 1946-47, assistant professor, 1947-53, associate professor, 1953-61, professor of homiletics and liturgics, 1961—. Member of Presbytery of New Brunswick, N.J.; chairman of Captital Church Committee, Synod of New Jersey. Frequent guest lecturer at seminaries and theological institutes. *Member:* American Association of Theological Professors in the Practical Fields (executive board member, 1955-57), Church Service Society of America (vice-president, 1957-59), National Council of Churches (member of committee on worship and arts). *Awards, honors:* American Association of Theological Schools fellowship, 1958-59; Freedoms Foundation Award, 1974, for sermon.

WRITINGS: Here Is My Method (Pulpit Book Club selection), Revell, 1952; *Word and Sacrament*, Prentice-Hall, 1960; *Presbyterian Worship*, John Knox, 1965; (translator) R. Paquier, *Dynamics of Worship*, Fortress, 1967; *Higher Reaches*, Epworth Press, 1972; (with J. T. Forestell) *Pro-*

clamation: *Pentecost 2*, Fortress, 1975. American correspondent, United Church *Observer*, 1947-56; member of editorial board and circulation secretary, *Theology Today*, 1948—; editor, *Princeton Seminary Bulletin*, 1956—; New Jersey correspondent, *Christian Century*, 1957—. Contributor of articles and book reviews to professional periodicals.

*   *   *

MACMAHON, Arthur W(hittier) 1890-

PERSONAL: Born May 29, 1890, in Brooklyn, N.Y.; son of Benjamin (an importer) and Abbie J. (Duke) Macmahon; married Edna Cers (a professor of economics at Vassar College), August 14, 1929; children: Gail (Mrs. Christoph Cornaro), Alan. *Education:* Columbia University, B.A., 1912, M.A., 1913, Ph.D., 1923. *Politics:* Democrat. *Religion:* Unitarian Universalist. *Home:* 26 Thelberg Rd., Poughkeepsie, N.Y. 12603.

CAREER: Columbia University, New York, N.Y., instructor in government, 1913-17; U.S. Council of National Defense, Washington, D.C., staff member, 1917-19; Columbia University, instructor, 1920-23, assistant professor, 1923-27, associate professor, 1927-31, professor of government, 1931-45, Eaton Professor of Public Administration, 1945-58, director of university self-survey, 1956-58, professor emeritus, 1958—. Visiting professor at Brookings Graduate School, 1926-27, Stanford University, 1931, Yale University, 1939, 1955-56, Princeton University, 1950, College of Europe, 1954, Salzburg Seminar in American Studies, 1954, 1965, University of Istanbul, 1959, Indian Institute of Public Administration, 1960, University of Buenos Aires, 1962, and University of East Africa, 1963. Member of staff of President's Committee on Administrative Management, 1936-37, Commission on Intergovernmental Relations, 1955, and Committee on Foreign Affairs Personnel, 1962; consultant on administration to U.S. Department of State, 1941-45; member of Loyalty Review Board, U.S. Civil Service Commission, 1947-50. *Member:* American Political Science Association (president, 1947), American Academy of Arts and Letters (fellow), Phi Beta Kappa, Cosmos Club (Washington, D.C.), Century Association (New York).

WRITINGS: Statutory Sources of New York City Government, New York City Charter Commission, 1923; *Department Management*, 1937; (with J. D. Millet) *Federal Administrators: A Biographical Approach to the Problem of Departmental Management*, Columbia University Press, 1939, reprinted, AMS Press, 1967; (with W. R. Dittmar) *Autonomous Public Enterprise: The German Railways*, Academy of Political Science, 1940; (with J. D. Millet and Gladys Ogden) *The Administration of Federal Work Relief*, Public Administration Service, 1941, reprinted, Da Capo Press, 1971; *Memorandum on the Postwar International Information Program of the United States*, U.S. Department of State, 1945, reprinted, Arno, 1972; *Administration of Foreign Affairs*, University of Alabama Press, 1953; (editor and co-author) *Federalism, Mature and Emergent*, Doubleday, 1955; *Administration and Foreign Policy*, Institute of Government and Public Affairs, 1957; *Delegation and Autonomy*, Asia Publishing House, 1961; *Administrating Federalism in a Democracy*, Oxford University Press, 1972. Contributor to *Encyclopedia of Social Science* and professional journals.

WORK IN PROGRESS: Revising manuscript on "cumulative consensus" in American public policy, involving the relations of government to the economic interests and collaboration among the interests.

SIDELIGHTS: Macmahon has conducted interviews in thirty-eight countries including several behind the Iron curtain, but mostly those with mixed or developing economies. He uses German and French as research tools.†

* * *

MACQUEEN, James G(alloway) 1932-

PERSONAL: Born January 7, 1932, in Glasgow, Scotland; son of William Lochhead and Grace Palmer (Galloway) MacQueen; married Sandra Hall (a potter, sculptor, and illustrator), September 26, 1959; children: Three sons and two daughters. *Education:* University of St. Andrews, M.A. study, 1955-57. *Politics:* Liberal. *Home:* 120 Cotham Brow, Bristol 6, England. *Office:* University of Bristol, Bristol 8, England.

CAREER: British Institute of Archaeology, Ankara, Turkey, institute scholar, 1957; University of Bristol, Bristol, England, lecturer in classics, 1959—. *Military service:* Royal Engineers, 1957-59; became second lieutenant. *Member:* British Institute of Archaeology at Ankara.

WRITINGS: Babylon, R. Hale, 1964, Praeger, 1965. Contributor to *Chambers's Encyclopaedia, Oxford Classical Dictionary,* and *Anatolian Studies.*

WORK IN PROGRESS: The Hittites and Luvians, for Thames & Hudson; *Assur and Nineveh,* for R. Hale; research on Anatolia in the Second Millenium B.C.†

* * *

MacQUITTY, William

PERSONAL: Born in Belfast, Ireland; son of James (managing director of *Belfast Telegraph*) and Henrietta Jane MacQuitty; married to Betty Bastin (an economist), September 15, 1951; children: Jonathan, Jane, Miranda. *Education:* Educated at Campbell College, Belfast, Ireland. *Home:* Mote Mount, Mill Hill, London N.W. 7, England.

CAREER: Was a banker in India, Thailand, Malaya, Ceylon, and India, and an underwriter for Lloyds, London, England; Ulster Television, Northern Ireland, managing director, 1959-60, deputy chairman, 1961—. Motion picture producer, with films including "A Night to Remember," "The Informers," "The Black Tent," "Above Us the Waves," "Beachcomber," and "The Way We Live"; photographer, exhibiting at five one-man exhibitions in London, England, in recent years, and represented in Royal Photographic Society's international exhibitions. *Military service:* Punjab Light Horse, five years. *Member:* Royal Geographical Society (fellow), Royal Photographical Society (fellow). *Awards, honors:* "A Night to Remember" received a number of awards, among them the Christopher Award, Golden Globe Award, U.S. National Board of Review citations, and other honors in America; M.A., Queen's University, Belfast.

WRITINGS—All self-illustrated with photographs: *Abu Simbel,* Putnam, 1965; *Buddha,* Viking, 1969; *Great Botanical Gardens of the World,* Macmillan, 1969; *Persia, The Immortal Kingdom,* New York Graphic Society, 1971; *Tutankhamun, The Last Journey,* T. Nelson & Sons, 1972; *Princes of Jade,* T. Nelson & Sons, 1973; *World in Focus,* Bartholomew & Son, 1974; *The Island of Isis,* Macdonald & Co., 1975.

Photographer: Edward Hyams, *Irish Gardens,* Macmillan, 1967.

SIDELIGHTS: Abu Simbel is the last illustrated record of the Temples of Ramses the Great in their ancient site; the temples were moved (by international effort) to save them from the waters of the Nile when the Aswan Dam was built. In addition to his book, MacQuitty did several television films on Abu Simbel, including one for Columbia Broadcasting System, 1966. *Persia, The Immortal Kingdom* was specially commissioned by the Shah of Iran to commemorate the twenty-fifth hundred anniversary of his country.

The MacQuitty collection contains more than 150,000 photographs, some of which have been used by the British Museum, *Encyclopaedia Britannica, National Geographic,* and other magazines, and by publishers.

* * *

MACURA, Paul 1924-

PERSONAL: Born September 18, 1924, in Goleszow, Poland; son of Jan (a businessman) and Anna (Marosz) Macura; married Irene M. Pyrghes, January 1, 1959; children: Rene M. *Education:* University of Washington, Seattle, M.A., 1959. *Religion:* Lutheran. *Home:* 812 University Ter., Reno, Nev. 89507. *Office:* University of Nevada, Reno, Nev.

CAREER: High school teacher of Russian in Tuscon, Ariz., 1960-61; University of Arizona, Tucson, instructor in Russian, 1961-63; University of Nevada, Reno, lecturer in Russian and German, 1963—. *Member:* American Association of Teachers of Slavic and East European Languages.

WRITINGS: (Editor with J. Malik) *A Supplementary Russian Reader,* University of Arizona Press, 1965; (compiler) *Russian-English Dictionary of Electrotechnology and Allied Sciences,* Wiley, 1971.

WORK IN PROGRESS: Russian Reference Grammar; Russian-English Standard Dictionary.

* * *

MACVEY, John W(ishart) 1923-

PERSONAL: Born January 19, 1923, in Kelso, Scotland, son of Robert Wishart (a civil engineer) and Elise (Moffat) Macvey; married Ellen Ronald (a teacher), April 26, 1952; children: Anne Shiela, Karen Isobel. *Education:* University of Strathclyde, Diploma in Applied Chemistry, 1951. *Politics:* Conservative. *Religion:* Presbyterian (Church of Scotland). *Home:* 15 Adair Ave., Saltcoats, Ayrshire, Scotland.

CAREER: Imperial Chemical Industries Ltd., Nobel Division, Ardeer, Scotland, experimental research chemist, 1956-70; Nobel's Explosives Co., Ardeer, Scotland, technical information officer, 1970—. Amateur astronomer, 1938—; has own observatory, with two telescopes for study of variable stars. *Military service:* Royal Air Force, radio operator, 1942-47; served with South East Asia Air Forces, 1943-46. *Member:* Royal Astronomical Society (fellow), British Astronomical Association, British Interplanetary Society (fellow), Astronomical Society of the Pacific (San Francisco), Radio Society of Great Britain.

WRITINGS: (Contributor) *Speaking of Space,* Little, Brown, 1962; *Alone in the Universe?,* Macmillan, 1963; *Journey to Alpha Centauri,* Macmillan, 1965; *How We Will Reach the Stars,* Collier, 1969; *Whispers from Space,* Macmillan, 1973; *Earth Visited,* Macmillan, in press. Regular contributor of articles, features, and reviews to *Spacef-*

light, 1960—; also contributor to *U.S. Air Force Magazine* and *Space Digest*.

AVOCATIONAL INTERESTS: Classical music, radio communication, geology, and science fiction.

* * *

MADAN, T(riloki) N(ath) 1931-

PERSONAL: Born September 12, 1931, in Srinagar, Kashmir, India; married Uma Chaturvedi, May 31, 1957; children: Vibha (son), Vandana (daughter). *Education:* A. S. College, Srinagar, India, B.A., 1949; Lucknow University, M.A., 1951; Australian National University, Ph.D., 1960. *Office:* Institute of Economic Growth, Delhi-7, India.

CAREER: Delhi University, Institute of Economic Growth, Delhi, India, doing research and research guidance and teaching. *Member:* Association of Social Anthropologists (Great Britain; fellow), Indian Sociological Society.

WRITINGS: (With D. N. Majumdar) *An Introduction to Social Anthropology*, Asia Publishing House (New York), 1956; (editor with G. Sarana) *Indian Anthropology: Essays in Memory of D. N. Majumdar*, Asia Publishing House, 1962; *Family and Kinship: A Study of the Pandits of Rural Kashmir*, Asia Publishing House, 1965; (editor with A. Beteille) *Encounter and Experience: Some Personal Accounts of Fieldwork*, Asia Publishing House, 1974. Indian editor, *Ethnology*, 1965—; editor, *Contributions to Indian Sociology*, 1967—.

WORK IN PROGRESS: Organized medical practice in an Indian city (New Delhi).

* * *

MADDISON, Carol Hopkins 1923-

PERSONAL: Born December 20, 1923, in Ottawa, Ontario, Canada; daughter of Warren G. (a civil servant) and Evelyn (Bunnell) Hopkins; married Angus Maddison (an economist), April 2, 1953; children: Charles, George. *Education:* Queen's University, Kingston, Ontario, B.A. (honors), 1946; Johns Hopkins University, M.A., 1952, Ph.D., 1957. *Home:* 20 Rue de Longchamp, Paris 16e, France. *Office:* American College in Paris, 31 av. Bosquet, 75007 Paris, France.

CAREER: University of New Brunswick, Fredericton, assistant professor of classics, 1946-49; American College in Paris, Paris, France, professor of English, 1963—, dean of the faculty, 1966—.

WRITINGS: Apollo and the Nine, Johns Hopkins Press, 1960; *Marcantonio Flaminio*, University of North Carolina Press, 1965. Occasional contributor to American scholarly journals.

SIDELIGHTS: Maddison speaks French, Spanish, and Italian. *Avocational interests:* Archaeology, travel, skiing.

* * *

MADDOX, George L(amar), Jr. 1925-

PERSONAL: Born July 2, 1925, in McComb, Miss.; son of George Lamar (a textile engineer) and Dimple (McEwen) Maddox; married Evelyn Godbold, June 9, 1946; children: Patricia Alise, George David. *Education:* Millsaps College, B.A., 1949; Boston University, M.A. and S.T.B., 1952; Michigan State University, Ph.D., 1956. *Politics:* Democrat. *Religion:* Methodist. *Home:* 2750 McDowell, Durham, N.C. 27705. *Office:* Duke University, Durham, N.C. 27706.

CAREER: Millsaps College, Jackson, Miss., assistant professor, 1952-54, associate professor, 1956-58, professor of sociology, 1958-60; Duke University, Durham, N.C., visiting associate professor and Russell Sage fellow, Medical School, 1960-61, associate professor of sociology and medical sociology, 1961-63, professor, 1964—, director of Center for the Study of Aging and Human Development, 1972—. Consultant to Danforth Foundation, National Institute of Mental Health, and Research Triangle Institute, Durham. *Military service:* U.S. Army, Infantry, 1943-45; became first sergeant. *Member:* American Association for the Advancement of Science, American Sociological Association (fellow), Gerontological Society (fellow), Southern Sociological Society.

WRITINGS: (Contributor) D. Pittman and C. Snyder, editors, *Society, Culture, and Drinking Patterns*, Wiley, 1962; (with B. C. McCall) *Drinking Among Teenagers*, Rutgers Center of Alcohol Studies and College and University Press, 1964; (contributor) R. McCarthy, editor, *Alcohol Education for Classroom and Community*, McGraw, 1965; (contributor) J. McKinney and F. DeVyver, editors, *Aging and Social Policy*, Prentice-Hall, 1966; (editor) *The Domesticated Drug*, College and University Press, 1970; (editor) *The Future of Aging and the Aged*, Southern Newspaper Publishers Association Foundation, 1971; (co-author) *Behavioral Science: A Selective View*, Little, Brown, 1972; (editor) *Drug Issues in Geropsychiatry*, Williams & Wilkins, 1974.

* * *

MADDOX, Jerrold (Warren) 1932-

PERSONAL: Born March 6, 1932; son of Warren B. (a Young Men's Christian Association secretary) and Vira (Austin) Maddox; married Julia Hessel (an art teacher), March 6, 1966; children: Melissa. *Education:* Indiana University, B.S., 1954, M.F.A., 1959.

CAREER: Wayne State University, Detroit, Mich., assistant professor of humanistic studies, 1960-63; University of Kentucky, Lexington, assistant professor of painting, 1964-66; Amherst College, Amherst, Mass., assistant professor of art, 1966—. Painter, exhibiting at one-man shows and in museums and galleries, including New York Museum of Modern Art. *Military service:* U.S. Army, 1954-56. *Member:* College Art Association.

WRITINGS: (With R. M. Capers) *Images and Imagination: An Introduction to Art*, Ronald, 1965.†

* * *

MADLEE, Dorothy (Haynes) 1917-
(Anne Haynes, Wade Rogers)

PERSONAL: Born February 1, 1917, in Springfield, Mo.; daughter of Robert Calhoun (a poet and newspaperman) and Grace (Lapsley) Haynes; married Alain Madle (deceased). *Education:* Attended public schools in Marion, Ky., and high school in Lima, Ohio; additional study at Ohio Northern University and University of Wisconsin. *Politics:* Democrat. *Religion:* Unitarian Universalist. *Home:* 345 Ponce de Leon Pl., Orlando, Fla. 32801. *Agent:* Larry Sternig, 2407 North 44th St., Milwaukee, Wis. 53210.

CAREER: Milwaukee Sentinel, Milwaukee, Wis., reporter, 1942-1961, art editor, 1961-62; full-time free-lance writer, 1962-65; *Boston Record American-Sunday Advertiser*, Boston, Mass., reporter and feature writer, 1965-70; *Orlando Sentinel Star*, Orlando, Fla., reporter and feature writer,

1970—. *Member:* National Association for the Advancement of Colored People, Spiritual Frontiers Fellowship, Florida Press Club, Orlando Press Club. *Awards, honors:* William Pohl Award for humorous writing, Milwaukee Press Club, 1960; Orlando Press Club award for environmental writing, 1973.

WRITINGS: Miss Lindlow's Leopard, Norton, 1965. Contributor of short stories and articles to *Mike Shayne Mystery Magazine, Pageant, Fantastic Universe, Wisconsin Tales and Trails, Better Camping, Florida Magazine*, and other periodicals.

WORK IN PROGRESS: Impy, a book about cats; *Skin Deep*, science fiction.

SIDELIGHTS: Miss Madlee writes: "As a layman interested in depth psychology, [I] have researched in the subconscious roots of racial prejudice, for use in fiction. For personal interest my reading includes mysticism, especially Hindu religion and Zen Buddhism, parapsychology, fantasy, science fiction, contemporary poetry and fiction."

AVOCATIONAL INTERESTS: Travel, fun conversation, cats, wild creatures, and plants.

*   *   *

MAGGS, Peter B(lount)   1936-

PERSONAL: Born July 24, 1936, in Durham, N.C.; son of Douglas B. (a professor of law) and Dorothy (Mackay) Maggs; married Barbara Widenor, February 27, 1959; children: Bruce, Gregory. *Education:* Harvard University, A.B., 1957, LL.B., 1961; Leningrad State University, exchange student, 1961-62. *Politics:* Democrat. *Home:* 2011 Silver Ct. East, Urbana, Ill. 61801.

CAREER: Harvard University, Law School, Cambridge, Mass., research associate in law, 1963-64; University of Illinois, College of Law, Champaign, assistant professor of law, 1964—. *Military service:* U.S. Army Reserve, active duty, 1957. *Member:* American Bar Association, American Association for the Advancement of Slavic Studies. *Awards, honors:* Medal of Merit, U.S. Information Agency, 1959, for services at American Exhibition in Moscow.

WRITINGS: (With Harold J. Berman) *Disarmament Inspection Under Soviet Law*, Oceana, 1967; (with John Hazard and Issac Shapiro) *The Soviet Legal System*, Oceana, 1969.

WORK IN PROGRESS: Research on computer application to law; *Soviet Economic Law.*

SIDELIGHTS: In addition to his stay in Soviet Union, 1961-62, Maggs spent his first six months of 1967 in legal research in Yugoslavia, with further legal research in Bulgaria.

*   *   *

MAGNER, James Edmund, Jr.   1928-

PERSONAL: Born March 16, 1928, in New York, N.Y.; son of James Edmund and Lilian (Campbell) Magner; married Mary Ann Dick, July, 1957 (divorced, 1969); children: James III, Maureen, Gregory, David. *Education:* Attended Roman Catholic seminaries of Passionist Order, 1951-56; Duquesne University, B.A., 1957; University of Pittsburgh, M.A., 1961, Ph.D., 1966. *Politics:* Independent. *Religion:* Independent. *Home:* 3307 Chadbourne Rd., Cleveland, Ohio 44120. *Office:* John Carroll University, Cleveland, Ohio 44118.

CAREER: Teacher of English at parochial high school, Pittsburgh, Pa., 1957-61; Allegheny County Workhouse, Pittsburgh, Pa., educational social worker, 1959-61; John Carroll University, Cleveland, Ohio, instructor; 1962-65, assistant professor, 1965-68, associate professor, 1968-74, professor of English, 1974—. *Military service:* U.S. Army, Infantry, 1948-51; served in Korea; received Purple Heart, Combat Infantry Badge, and three battle stars. *Member:* National Council of Teachers of English, Modern Language Association of America, American Association of University Professors, *Awards, honors: Toiler of the Sea, Although There is the Night,* and *The Dark Is Closest to the Moon,* all were nominated for Pulitzer Prize in poetry; George E. Grawel Memorial Fellowship, 1965.

WRITINGS: Toiler of the Sea (poems), Golden Quill, 1965; *Although There is the Night* (poems), Golden Quill, 1968; *John Crowe Ransom: Critical Principles and Preoccupations,* Mouton & Co., 1971; *The Dark Is Closest to the Moon* (poems), Ryer Press, 1973. Also author of long poem, *Gethsemane,* 1969. Work represented in many anthologies, including *The Strong Voice* and *The Strong Voice: Two,* both edited by R. McGovern and R. Snyder, Ashland Poetry. Contributor of essays, poems, and reviews to journals.

WORK IN PROGRESS: The Women of the Golden Horn, poems; *Till No Light Leaps,* poems; *Music Into Night,* poems; *The Dancer and the Dance,* criticism; and *Ariance,* a play.

SIDELIGHTS: Magner has traveled in the U.S., Canada, the West Indies, Venezuela, Colombia, Panama, Ecuador, Chile, Japan, and Korea.

*   *   *

MAGNER, Thomas F(reeman)   1918-

PERSONAL: Born October 8, 1918, in Buffalo, N.Y.; son of William James (a carpenter) and Mary (Carney) Magner; married Irma Ellen Estes, April 4, 1944; children: Kathryn Ann, Mary Frances, Timothy Noel. *Education:* Niagara University, B.A., 1940; Fordham University, M.A., 1942; Yale University, Ph.D., 1950. *Religion:* Roman Catholic. *Home:* 280 Osmond St., State College, Pa. 16801. *Office:* Pennsylvania State University, University Park, Pa. 16802.

CAREER: University of Minnesota, Minneapolis, assistant professor of linguistics and Russian, 1950-56, associate professor of Slavic linguistics, 1956-59, chairman of department of Slavic and Oriental languages, 1957-59; Pennsylvania State University, University Park, professor of Slavic languages, 1959—, chairman of department, 1960—, associate dean for research and graduate study, 1966—. Official observer for American Teachers Exchange, University of Moscow, 1963. *Military service:* U.S. Army, 1942-46; became captain; received Bronze Star and three battle stars. *Member:* American Association of Teachers of Slavic and East European Languages, American Association for the Advancement of Slavic Studies, Linguistic Society of America, American Association of University Professors. *Awards, honors:* Fulbright research fellowship to Yugoslavia, 1956-66; travel-study grant to People's Republic of China, 1974.

WRITINGS: Introduction to the Serbo-Croatian Language, [Minneapolis], 1956, 3rd edition, Singidunum Press, 1972; *Manual of Scientific Russian,* Burgess, 1958; (editor) *Russian Tales,* W.C. Brown, 1960; *Applied Linguistics: Russian,* Heath, 1961; *Russian Scientific and Technical Readings,* Singidunum Press, 1965; *A Zagreb Kajkavian*

Dialect (monograph), Pennsylvania State University Press, 1966; (editor with W. R. Schmalsteig) *Baltic Linguistics*, Pennsylvania State University Press, 1970; *The Student's Dictionary of Serbo-Croatian*, Singidunum Press, 1970; (with L. Matejka) *Word Accent in Modern Serbo-Croatian*, Pennsylvania State University Press, 1971. Contributor to learned journals. Associate editor, *General Linguistics*.

WORK IN PROGRESS: A book on the dialect of the city of Split, Yugoslavia.

SIDELIGHTS: Magner, of Irish descent, speaks Russian and Serbo-Croatian.

* * *

MAGRATH, C(laude) Peter 1933-

PERSONAL: Born April 23, 1933, in New York, N.Y.; son of Laurence W. (a transportation executive) and Giulia Maria (Dentice) Magrath; married Sandra Hughes (a copy editor), June 18, 1955; children: Valerie Ruth. *Education:* University of New Hampshire, B.A. (summa cum laude), 1955; Cornell University, Ph.D., 1962. *Politics:* Independent. *Religion:* Episcopalian. *Home:* 946 Vestal Ave., Binghamton, N.Y. 13903. *Office:* State University of New York at Binghamton, Binghamton, N.Y. 13901.

CAREER: Brown University, Providence, R.I., instructor, 1961-62, assistant professor, 1962-64, associate professor, 1964-67, professor of political science, 1967-68, associate dean of Graduate School, 1965-66; University of Nebraska, Lincoln, professor of political science, 1968-72, dean of College of Arts and Sciences, 1968-69, dean of faculties, 1969-72, vice-chancellor for academic affairs, 1972; State University of New York at Binghamton, professor of political science, and president, 1972—. Member of board of directors, Saint Elizabeth Community Health Center, Lincoln, 1971-72, Roberson Center for Arts and Sciences, Binghamton, 1973—. *Military service:* U.S. Army, Artillery, 1955-57; became first lieutenant. *Member:* American Political Science Association, Organization of American Historians, American Association of University Professors, Midwest Political Science Association, Phi Beta Kappa, Phi Kappa Phi, Pi Gamma Mu, Pi Sigma Alpha.

WRITINGS: Morrison R. Waite: The Triumph of Character, Macmillan, 1963; *Yazoo: Law and Politics in the New Republic*, Brown University Press, 1966; *Constitutionalism and Politics: Conflict and Consensus*, Scott, Foresman, 1968; (with Elmer E. Cornwell, Jr., and Jay S. Goodman) *The American Democracy*, Macmillan, 1969, 2nd edition, 1973.

Contributor: John A. Garraty, editor, *Quarrels That Have Shaped the Constitution*, Harper, 1964; Andrew M. Scott and Earle Wallace, editors, *Politics: U.S.A.*, Macmillan, 1965; Richard Frost and Rocco J. Tresolini, editors, *Cases in American National Government*, Prentice-Hall, 1965; Elmer E. Cornwell, *The American Presidency: Vital Center*, Scott, Foresman, 1966; Philip B. Kurland, editor, *Supreme Court Review 1966*, University of Chicago Press, 1966; Murray S. Stedman, Jr., editor, *Modernizing American Government: The Demands of Social Change*, Prentice-Hall, 1968; John Caffrey, editor, *The Future Academic Community: Continuity and Change*, American Council on Education, 1969; Gene H. Budig, editor, *Perceptions in Public Higher Education*, University of Nebraska Press, 1970; Joseph C. Palamountain and Martin M. Shapiro, editors, *Issues and Perspectives in American Government*, Scott, Foresman, 1971. Contributor of articles and reviews to *Encyclopedia International, Commen-*

tary, American Heritage, Yale Review, Vanderbilt Law Review, and other professional journals.

WORK IN PROGRESS: Research for a book on the Supreme Court and the Granger cases.†

* * *

MAHER, John E. 1925-

PERSONAL: Surname is pronounced Mar; born December 26, 1925, in Utica, N.Y.; son of William Roscoe and Isabel (Knight) Maher: married Naomi Berg, January 30, 1947; children: Howard, David, Sean. *Education:* Harvard University, A.B., 1948, Ph.D., 1955; University of Wisconsin, M.S., 1949. *Religion:* Episcopalian. *Home:* 112 Chatterton Way, Hamden, Conn. *Office:* South Connecticut State College, New Haven, Conn.

CAREER: DePauw University, Greencastle, Ind., assistant professor of economics, 1954-57; Wesleyan University, Middletown, Conn., assistant professor of economics, 1957-61; Oakland University, Rochester, Mich., associate professor of economics, 1961-64; Joint Council on Economic Education, New York, N.Y., senior economist and director of developmental economic education program in thirty major school systems, 1964-70; South Connecticut State College, New Haven, professor of economics and chairman of department, 1970—. Director of research in taxes and expenditures, Connecticut Governor's Economic Planning and Development Committee, 1960-61. *Military service:* U.S. Navy, 1943-46, 1951-53; became chief engineer. *Member:* American Economic Association.

WRITINGS: (Contributor) Stauss and Knopf, editors, *The Teaching of Elementary Economics*, Rinehart, 1960; *Labor and the Economy*, Allyn & Bacon, 1965; *What Is Economics?*, Wiley, 1969. Contributor to economics and statistical journals.

* * *

MAHER, Robert F. 1922-

PERSONAL: Born July 14, 1922, in Eldora, Iowa; son of John Ralph (a civil engineer) and Alice (Anderson) Maher; married Lisa Lellep, January 6, 1957; children: Kevin, Mark, Michael, Eve. *Education:* University of Wisconsin, B.S., 1948, M.S., 1950, Ph.D., 1958. *Home:* 3315 West Michigan Ave., Kalamazoo, Mich. 49001. *Office:* Western Michigan University, Kalamazoo, Mich. 49001.

CAREER: Western Michigan University, Kalamazoo, 1957—, began as assistant professor, professor of anthropology, 1966—, chairman of department, 1967-71 and 1973-74. *Military service:* U.S. Army, 1942-46. *Member:* American Anthropological Association, Society for American Archaeology, American Ethnological Society, Michigan Archaeological Society, Michigan Academy of Science, Arts, and Letters, Wisconsin Archaeological Society. *Awards, honors:* Genevieve Gorst Herfurth Award for *New Men of Papua*.

WRITINGS: New Men of Papua, University of Wisconsin Press, 1961; (contributor) Shiro Saito, editor, *Philippine Ethnography: A Critically Annotated and Selected Bibliography*, University of Hawaii Press, 1972; (with Claude L. Phillips, Jr.) *The Cultural Evolution of Asia and North Africa*, Western Michigan University, 1973. Contributor to anthropology journals.

WORK IN PROGRESS: Archeology of Ifugao Province, Philippines; and *Koriki Cultural Evolution* of Papua Gulf district, New Guinea.

MAHON, John K(eith) 1912-

PERSONAL: Surname is pronounced *May*-on; born February 8, 1912, in Ottumwa, Iowa; son of John Keith and Ellen (Stoltz) Mahon; married Enid Pasek, February 29, 1948; children: John Keith III. *Education:* Swarthmore College, B.A., 1934; University of California, Los Angeles, Ph.D., 1950. *Politics:* Democrat. *Home:* 4129 Southwest Second Ave., Gainesville, Fla. 32601. *Office:* Department of History, University of Florida, Gainesville, Fla.

CAREER: Instructor in history at Colorado State University, Fort Collins, 1950, and University of California, Los Angeles, 1951; U.S. Department of the Army, Office of the Chief of Military History, Washington, D.C., civilian historian, 1951-54; University of Florida, Gainesville, assistant professor, 1954-59, associate professor of history, 1959-66, professor of history, 1966—, department chairman, 1965-73. President, Citizen's Housing Association of Gainesville, 1962; treasurer of Alachua County Council for Good Government, 1965—; director of Doris Duke Foundation Southeastern Indian oral history program. *Military service:* U.S. Army, Field Artillery, 1942-46; became captain. *Member:* American Military Institute (trustee, 1954-56 and 1971-74), Organization of American Historians, American Association of University Professors, Florida Historical Society (director, 1973—), Phi Beta Kappa. *Awards, honors:* Grants from American Philosophical Society, 1957 and 1963; Doris Duke Foundation, 1971-74; University of Florida, 1973-74.

WRITINGS: History of the Organization of United States Infantry, U.S. Government Printing Office, 1953; *International Tensions and Security Organizations,* Air Force Reserve Officer Training Corps, 1957; (author of introduction) John T. Sprague, *Origin, Progress and Conclusion of the Florida War* (facsimile reproduction of 1848 edition), University of Florida Press, 1964; (editor) John Bemrose, *Reminiscences of the Second Seminole War,* University of Florida Press, 1966; *History of the Second Seminole War,* University of Florida Press, 1965; *The War of 1812,* University of Florida Press, 1972. Contributor to *Encyclopaedia Britannica,* 1958—; contributor of about twenty-six articles to *Current History, Military Affairs,* and regional history journals. Associate editor, *Military Affairs,* 1952-54, member of editorial board, 1951-56, member of special editorial panel, 1958—; member of editorial board, *Florida Historical Quarterly,* 1963—.

WORK IN PROGRESS: The United State's attitude toward war as an instrument of policy, 1789-1860.

*   *   *

MAINPRIZE, Don 1930-
(Richard Rock)

PERSONAL: Born August 28, 1930, in Coleman, Mich.; son of James Raymond and Ople Belle Mainprize; married Doris Olive Humphrey, July 27, 1952. children: Daniel Andrew, Debra Ann, Susan Lynn, Edward Raymond. *Education:* Studied at Michigan College of Mining and Technology (now Lake Superior College), 1948-50, Grand Rapids School of the Bible and Music, 1950-53, and Dallas Theological Seminary, 1956-57; University of Oklahoma, B.A. (journalism), 1960; Central Michigan University, M.A. (English), 1968. *Home:* 145 Marquette, Houghton Lake, Mich. 48629.

CAREER: Pastor (lists religion as "undenominational") at Dildine Community Church, Ionia, Mich., 1953-56, and

First Presbyterian Church, Minco, Okla., 1958-60; Scripture Press Publications, Wheaton, Ill., associate editor of *Power* and *Counselor* (Sunday school papers), 1960-63, managing editor of *Counselor,* 1963-64; free-lance writer, Houghton Lake, Mich., 1964-65; teacher in public schools, Houghton Lake, Mich., 1965-66; Central Michigan University, Mt. Pleasant, instructor in journalism, 1967; middle school teacher, Houghton Lake, Mich., 1967-74. Part-time creative writing instructor, Mid-Michigan Community College, 1968-72. *Member:* National Education Association, National Council of Teachers of English, Michigan Educational Association, Michigan Council of Teachers of English, Poetry Society of Michigan. *Awards, honors:* Two first prizes from Poetry Society of Michigan, 1972.

WRITINGS: Christian Heroes of Today, Baker Book, 1964; *How to Enjoy the Christian Life,* Zondervan, 1966, published as *Enjoy the Christian Life,* Key Publishing Co., 1971; (contributor) *Minute Prayers,* Zondervan, 1970; *Good Morning, Lord: Meditations for Teachers,* Baker Book, 1974; *ABC's for Educators,* J. Weston Walch, 1975; *Happy Anniversary,* Baker Book, 1975. About eighty articles have appeared in Sunday school and other religious periodicals.

WORK IN PROGRESS: Two poetry collections, *Stonesville, U.S.A.* and *Fragments of Faith and Failure, Book I;* a sequel to *How to Enjoy the Christian Life,* entitled *The Anatomy of Christian Joy.*

*   *   *

MAISON, Margaret M(ary Bowles) 1920-
(Margaret Clare)

PERSONAL: Surname is pronounced in the French manner; born November 22, 1920, in Beaconsfield, England; daughter of Clare Treacher and Florence (Baker) Bowles; married Lucien Maison (a schoolmaster); children: Priscilla, Paul, Louis-Philippe. *Education:* King's College, London, B.A. (honors), 1942; Oxford University, Dip.Ed. (with distinction), 1943, M.A., 1952, Ph.D., 1955. *Politics:* "Radical Christian pacifist." *Religion:* Roman Catholic.

CAREER: Newport County Grammar School, Isle of Wight, England, senior English mistress, 1943-44; Davies's School of English, London, England, tutor, 1949-56; Highwood School, London, England, principal, 1956-60; author, journalist, and examiner in English for General Certificate of Education, Associated Examining Board, 1960—. Broadcaster on literary figures, British Broadcasting Corp. Third Programme, and television speaker. *Member:* Pax (vice-chairman, 1962).

WRITINGS: Guide to Good English, [Bombay], 1960; (under pseudonym Margaret Clare) *Confessions of a Headmaster's Wife,* Hammond, Hammond, 1961; *Search Your Soul, Eustace,* Sheed (London), 1961, published as *The Victorian Vision,* Sheed (New York), 1962; *Examine Your English,* Orient Longmans (Calcutta), 1964.

Editor: *Thelma,* Longmans, Green, 1962; James Fenimore Cooper, *The Last of the Mohicans,* Longmans, Green, 1963; Charles Dickens, *Oliver Twist,* Longmans, Green, 1966; Geoffrey Household, *Watcher in the Shadows,* Longmans, 1969.

Contributor of articles and reviews to *Times Educational Supplement, English, Search, Listener, Tablet, Irish Ecclesiastical Record,* and other publications in Great Britain.

WORK IN PROGRESS: A biography of John Oliver Hobbes (Mrs. Pearl Cragie); a humorous book on teenagers; another English text; researching on female sensation novelists.

SIDELIGHTS: Margaret Maison is a non-joiner and pacifist, who says that she "appreciates *silence*, its value and beauty; enjoys domesticity but is very messy, living in happy slum style; dislikes neurotic scrub-and-polish housewives whose homes are spotless and tasteless; and enjoys being just a scribbling mama." She is interested in most aspects of English language and literature, children, poetry, painting, pets, collecting books, and travel (especially in Germany).†

* * *

MALCOM, Robert E. 1933-

PERSONAL: Born April 29, 1933, in Hamilton, Ohio; son of Edward E. (a teacher) and Pauline (Finlay) Malcom; married Ellen Mae McAllister, August 28, 1960; children: Dorothy Lynne, William Blair III, Lucinda Johanna. *Education:* Miami University, Oxford, Ohio, B.S., 1955; Ohio State University, M.B.A., 1958, Ph.D., 1962. *Office:* Business Administration Building, University Park, Pa. 16802.

CAREER: Accountant with private firm for one year; Ohio State University, Columbus, instructor in accountancy, 1960-61; Pennsylvania State University, University Park, 1962—, began as associate professor, became professor of accountancy. *Member:* American Accounting Association, American Institute of Certified Public Accountants, National Association of Accountants.

WRITINGS: (With John J. Willingham) *Accounting in Action: A Simulation,* McGraw, 1965; (with Malcolm H. Gotterer) *Computers in Business: A Fortran Introduction,* International Textbook, 1967; (with Gotterer and Frank Luh) *Computers in Administration,* Intext Educational, 1973.

* * *

MALCOSKEY, Edna Walker

PERSONAL: Born in Rapides Parish, La.; daughter of Joseph Marien and Lillie Welles (Walker) Malcoskey. *Education:* Educated by tutors abroad, and at Convent of Sisters of Divine Providence, Rapides Parish, La. *Religion:* Roman Catholic. *Agent:* Nat Lorman, 16 Park Ave., New York, N.Y.

CAREER: Writer.

WRITINGS: Eternal Variant, Dial, 1953; *Not Now, My Love,* Putnam, 1956; *The Virgin and the Priestess,* Fell, 1961; *Songs of Greener Pastures,* Fell, 1962. Contributor to *Catholic World* and *Messenger.*

WORK IN PROGRESS: These Were the Songs She Sang.

SIDELIGHTS: Edna Malcoskey speaks French. *Avocational interests:* Mythology, early Greek and Roman history.†

* * *

MALET, B(aldwyn) Hugh G(renville) 1928-

PERSONAL: Born February 13, 1928, in Salisbury, England; son of G. E. Grenville (a colonel; first registrar, National Register of Archives) and Leir (Gibbon) Malet; married Kathleen Morris, July 25, 1958; children: Phoebe Jane Grenville, Durand David Grenville. *Education:* Attended Wellington College, 1939-44, and King's College, Cambridge, 1947-50. *Religion:* Church of England. *Address:* c/o Southill House, Ditcheat, Shepton Mallet, Somersetshire, England.

CAREER: Sudan Political Service, district commissioner, 1950-56, passing Sudan government higher Arabic examination and law examination, 1954; Shell Petroleum Co. Ltd., Egypt, industrial relations, 1957-59; free-lance writer and broadcaster, 1959-61; *National Christian News,* London, England, editor, 1961-62; Brasted Place Theological Training College, Westerham, Kent, England, director of studies and lecturer in philosophy, 1962-73; University of Salford, Salford, England, lecturer in local history, 1973—. *Military serivce:* British Army, Royal Armoured Corps, 1945-47; served in Italy and Middle East.

WRITINGS: Voyage in a Bowler Hat, Hutchinson, 1960; *The Canal Duke,* David & Charles, 1961; *In the Wake of the Gods: On the Waterways of Ireland,* Chatto & Windus, 1972. Contributor to *A Cambridge Anthology,* Fortune Press, circa 1948. Contributor to publication of the Royal Society for the International Geophysical Year. Articles on general and scientific subjects have been published in England and abroad.

WORK IN PROGRESS: A second edition of *The Canal Duke* for David & Charles; *A History of the Malet Family.*

* * *

MALKOFF, Karl 1938-

PERSONAL: Born July 27, 1938, in Bronx, N.Y.; son of Murray Bernard (a commercial artist) and Rose (Klutchnick) Malkoff; divorced; children: Jason, Scott. *Education:* Columbia University, A.B., 1959, A.M., 1963, Ph.D., 1965. *Home:* 345 West 85th St., New York, N.Y. 10024.

CAREER: Long Island University, C. W. Post Campus, Brookville, N.Y., instructor in English, 1965-66; City College of the City University of New York, New York, N.Y., instructor, 1966-67, assistant professor, 1967-71, associate professor of English, 1972—. Judge in poetry, National Book Award, 1975. *Member:* Modern Language Association of America, Phi Beta Kappa. *Awards, honors:* Henry Evans traveling fellowship in Europe, Columbia University.

WRITINGS: Theodore Roethke: An Introduction to the Poetry, Columbia University Press, 1966; (contributor) Irving Malin, editor, *Critical Views of Issac Bashevis Singer,* New York University Press, 1969; (contributor) I. Malin and M. J. Friedman, editors, *William Styron's Confessions of Nat Turner,* Wadsworth, 1970; (contributor) I. Malin, editor, *Contemporary Jewish Literature,* Indiana University Press, 1973; (editor) *Crowell's Handbook of Contemporary American Poets,* Crowell, 1973. Contributor of reviews to literary journals.

WORK IN PROGRESS: The Escape From the Self: A Study in Modern Poetics.

SIDELIGHTS: Malkoff makes frequent trips to Europe; he speaks French, Spanish, and some Italian; reads German, Provencal, Latin, and Greek. *Avocational interests:* Playing guitar.

* * *

MALLIN, Jay 1927-

PERSONAL: Born December 10, 1927, in New York, N.Y.; son of Albert Milton and Cecilia (Jaffe) Mallin; married Caroll Driftmeyer, January 31, 1959; children: Jay, Linda Anne. *Education:* Ruston Academy, Havana, Cuba, student, 1941-45; Florida Southern College, A.B., 1949. *Home:* 406 Savona, Coral Gables, Fla. 33146.

CAREER: *Havana Herald*, Havana, Cuba, news editor, 1950-53; variously correspondent in Cuba for *Time, Miami News, Chicago Tribune, Wall Street Journal*, and other publications, 1954-61; stringer correspondent in Miami for *Time*, 1961—, covering Florida and Cuban affairs, Caribbean, and Central America; Copley News Service, Maimi, Fla., columnist, 1972—. Research scientist, Center for Advanced International Studies, University of Florida, 1967-70; consultant to private and governmental agencies, 1970—.

WRITINGS: *Fortress Cuba*, Regnery, 1965; *Caribbean Crisis*, Doubleday, 1965; *Terror in Viet Nam*, Van Nostrand, 1966; *"Che" Guevara on Revolution*, University of Miami Press, 1969; *Strategy for Conquest*, University of Miami Press, 1970; *Terror and Urban Guerrillas*, University of Miami Press, 1971; *Ernesto "Che" Guevara*, SamHar Press, 1973; *General Vo Nguyen Giap*, SamHar Press, 1973; *Fulgencio Batista*, SamHar Press, 1974; *The Great Managua Earthquake*, SamHar Press, 1974.

WORK IN PROGRESS: Two books, *General Giap on War* for University of Miami Press and *Salvador Allende* for SamHar Press.

SIDELIGHTS: Mallin lived in Cuba until 1961, and covered Castro guerrilla campaign and Communist take-over. He has covered the war in Viet Nam, the Dominican uprising of 1965, the Guevara campaign in Bolivia, Tupamaros in Uruguay, Salvador-Honduras War, and the Managua earthquake.

BIOGRAPHICAL/CRITICAL SOURCES: *VIP*, November, 1965.

* * *

MALM, F(inn) T(heodore) 1919-

PERSONAL: Surname rhymes with "calm"; born November 2, 1919, in Santa Cruz, Calif; son of Finn (a master mariner) and Louise (Courage) Malm; married Virginia Ferguson, June 3, 1943; children: Karen, Sandra. *Education:* University of California, Berkeley, B.S., 1941; Massachusetts Institute of Technology, Ph.D., 1946. *Office:* School of Business Administration, 350 Barrows Hall, University of California, Berkeley, Calif. 94720.

CAREER: Massachusetts Institute of Technology, Cambridge, fellow and instructor, 1942-46; University of California, Berkeley, 1946—, started as instructor, associate professor of business administration, 1956—, research fellow and research associate in Institute of Industrial Relations, 1947-55, assistant dean, School of Business Administration, 1957-62, admissions officer of undergraduate studies, 1964-66. Visiting scholar, London School of Economics and Political Science, 1965; consultant, Organization for European Economic Cooperation, European Productivity Agency, Paris, 1956-57.

MEMBER: Industrial Relations Research Association, American Economic Association, Institute of Personnel Management (London), International University Contact for Management Education (Delft), British Association for Commercial and Industrial Education, Western Economic Association, Phi Beta Kappa, Beta Gamma Sigma, Sierra Club.

WRITINGS: (Editor with Jack D. Rogers) *Production Organization and Management*, California Book, 1961; (contributor) Lee Preston, editor, *Managing the Independent Business*, Prentice-Hall, 1962; (editor with Paul Pigors and Charles A. Myers) *Management of Human Resources*, McGraw, 1964, 3rd edition, 1973. Contributor to *Encyclopaedia Britannica*, and to professional journals in America, England, Italy, Germany, and Norway.

WORK IN PROGRESS: Research in management education and executive development in the United Kingdom, the Industrial Training Act in the United Kingdom, and university admissions in the United Kingdom.

SIDELIGHTS: Malm was a resident of Hong Kong, 1923-29. *Avocational interests:* Photography, skiing.†

* * *

MALPASS, Leslie F(rederick) 1922-

PERSONAL: Born May 16, 1922, in Hartford, Conn.; son of John Fred and Lilly (Elmslie) Malpass; married Winona Cassin, May 17, 1946; children: Susan, Peter, Jennifer, Michael. *Education:* Attended University of Cincinnati, 1940-42; Syracuse University, B.A., 1947, M.A., 1949, Ph.D., 1952. *Home:* 1416 Highland Circle, Blacksburg, Va. 24060. *Office:* Virginia Polytechnic Institute and State University, Blacksburg, Va. 24061.

CAREER: Onondaga County (N.Y.) Child Guidance Center, psychologist, 1948-52; lecturer at Syracuse University, Syracuse, N.Y. and University of Buffalo (now State University of New York at Buffalo), Buffalo, N.Y., 1949-52; Southern Illinois University, Carbondale, assistant professor, 1952-55, associate professor of psychology, 1955-60; University of South Florida, Tampa, professor of psychology and chairman of Division of Behavioral Sciences, 1960-65; Virginia Polytechnic Institute and State University, Blacksburg, professor and dean of College of Arts and Sciences, 1965-68, vice-president of university, 1968—. Visiting professor, University of Florida, 1959-60. Certified as diplomate, American Board of Professional Psychology. Consultant to Peace Corps, National Science Foundation, and U.S. Office of Education. Director, First National Exchange Bank of Virginia, 1966—; member of board of directors, Showalter Memorial Hospital, 1966—. *Military service:* U.S. Army, Medical Corps, 1945-46. *Member:* American Association for the Advancement of Science, American Psychological Association (fellow), American Association of University Professors, American Association for Higher Education, American Council on Education, National Education Association, Sigma Chi, Psi Chi, Theta Chi Beta, Omicron Delta Kappa, Beta Gamma Sigma. *Awards, honors:* Phillips Foundation fellow, 1962-63.

WRITINGS: (With Chester J. Atkinson and Israel Goldiamon) *Perceptual and Response Abilities of Mentally Retarded Children*, Southern Illinois University, c.1960; (contributor) Norman R. Ellis, editor, *Handbook of Mental Deficiency*, McGraw, 1963; (with Margaret B. Fisher) *A Comparison of Programed and Standard Textbooks in College Instruction*, University of South Florida, 1963; (with others) *Comparison of Two Automated Procedures for Retarded Children*, University of South Florida, 1963; (editor and contributor) *Human Behavior: A Program for Self-Instruction*, McGraw, 1965; (with Charles F. Williams and Alden S. Gilmore) *Programmed Reading Instruction for Culturally Deprived Slow Learners* (booklet), MacDonald Training Center Foundation (Tampa), 1966; (contributor) J. S. Roucek, editor, *Programmed Teaching*, Philosophical Library, 1966; (editor) Vernon H. Edmonds and others, *Social Behavior: A Program for Self-Instruction*, McGraw, 1967. Contributor to professional journals.

WORK IN PROGRESS: Research in programmed instruction for U.S. Office of Education; chapter in *Appraisal of Mental Deficiency*, being edited by W. Hawkins.†

* * *

MAND, Ewald 1906-
(Evald Maend; pseudonym, Ain Kalmus)

PERSONAL: Born June 8, 1906, in Estonia; son of Priidu and Maria (Turu) Mand; married Elli E. Jams, December 21, 1939; children: Merike Vaike, Tahti, Marje, Elmet. *Education:* Attended schools in Estonia; Andover Newton Theological School, B.D., 1934, S.T.M., 1935, D.Min., 1974. *Home:* January Hills, Amherst, Mass. 01002.

CAREER: Pastor, editor, and teacher in Tallinn, Estonia, 1935-44; seized by German Gestapo, then escaped to Sweden, 1944; Baptist Mission, Stockholm, Sweden, secretary for refugees, 1944-46; Andover Newton Theological School, Newton Center, Mass., lecturer, 1946; pastor in Rockport, Mass., 1947-54, and Amherst, Mass., 1954-75.

WRITINGS: The World is My Home (novel), Friendship, 1952, 2nd edition, 1953; *Men of Tomorrow: Bible Stories for the Youth of Today*, Westminster, 1958.

Under name Evald Maend: *Kungens Gaester* (novella; title means "King's Visitors"), Ungas Foerlag (Stockholm), 1946; *Tarkade Teekond* (sermons; title means "The Journey of the Wise"), Eesti Usklike Uehiskirjastus (Toronto), 1954; *Igaviku Aknad* (sermons; title means "Windows Towards Eternity"), Toronto Allianskomitee, 1964.

Under pseudonym Ain Kalmus; novels, except as indicated: *Soolased Tuuled* (title means "Salty Winds"), Eesti Kirjastus (Tallinn, U.S.S.R.), 1944, 2nd edition, Orto (Vadstena, Sweden), 1946; *Oeoe Tuli Liiga Vara* (title means "Night Came Too Soon"), Orto, 1945 (Swedish, Norwegian, and Danish editions under name Evald Maend), 2nd edition, 1946; *Kaarnakuenka* (title means "Raven Hill"), Eesti Teataja (Stockholm), 1946; *Kodusadama Tuled* (title means "Lights of Home Harbor"), Orto, 1947; *Hingemaa* (title means "Private Soil"), Orto, 1948; *Prohvet*, Orto, 1950, translation published as *The Unfaithful*, Muhlenberg Press, 1954; *Tulised Vakrid I and II* (title means "Fiery Chariots"), Eesti Kirjanike Kooperatiiv (Lund), 1953; *Juudas* (title means "Judas"), Eesti Kirjanike Kooperatiiv, 1969; *Kadunud Saar* (memoirs; title means "The Lost Island"), Eesti Kirjanike Kooperatiiv, 1973; *Ajastute Vahetusel* (memoirs; title means "At Changing Times"), Eesti Kirjanike Kooperatiiv, 1975.

Trilogy; under pseudonym Ain Kalmus; published by Eesti Kirjanike Kooperatiiv: *Jumalad Lahkuvad Maalt* (title means "Gods Leave the Country"), 1956; *Toone Tuuled Uele Maa* (title means "Winds of Doom"), 1958; *Koju Enne Ohtut* (title means "Home Before the Evening"), 1964.

* * *

MANDELBAUM, Seymour J. 1936-

PERSONAL: Born January 13, 1936, in Chicago, Ill.; son of Albert N. (a rabbi) and Leah (Gordon) Mandelbaum; married Dorothy Rosenthal, August 19, 1956; children: David, Judah, Betsy. *Education:* Columbia University, B.A., 1956; Princeton University, M.A., 1958, Ph.D., 1962. *Politics:* Democratic. *Religion:* Jewish. *Office:* Department of City and Regional Planning, University of Pennsylvania, Philadelphia, Pa. 19174.

CAREER: Carnegie Institute of Technology (now Carnegie-Mellon University), Pittsburgh, Pa., instructor,

later assistant professor of history, 1959-65; University of Pennsylvania, Philadelphia, assistant professor of communications and history, 1965-67, associate professor of city and regional planning and history, 1967—. *Member:* American Historical Association, Organization of American Historians. *Awards, honors:* Guggenheim fellowship; Center for Advanced Study in the Behavioral Sciences, fellowship, 1965-66; National Endowment for the Humanities fellowship, 1969-70.

WRITINGS: (Editor) *The Social Setting of Intolerance: The Know-Nothings, the Red Scare, and McCarthyism*, Scott, 1964; *Boss Tweed's New York*, Wiley, 1965; *Community and Communications*, Norton, 1972.†

* * *

MANELLA, Raymond L(awrence) 1917-

PERSONAL: Born June 19, 1917; son of Frank and Mary Manella; wife's name, Evelyn (a social worker), married August 23, 1943; children: Mary Evelyn, Roberta Ann. *Education:* University of Pittsburgh, B.A., 1938; Western Reserve University (now Case Western Reserve University), M.S.S.W., 1939. *Religion:* Roman Catholic. *Home:* 1324 Burleigh Rd., Lutherville, Md.

CAREER: U.S. Government, Washington, D.C., consultant, 1961—. Lecturer at College of Notre Dame of Maryland, Loyola College, and Mount St. Agnes College. *Military service:* U.S. Naval Reserve, 1943-46.

WRITINGS: (Editor with William E. Amos) *Readings in the Administration of Institutions for Delinquent Youth*, C. C Thomas, 1964; (editor with Amos) *Action Programs for Delinquency Prevention*, C. C Thomas, 1965; (editor with Amos) *Delinquent Children in Correctional Institutions*, C. C Thomas, 1966; *Post Institutional Services for Delinquent Youth*, U.S. Children's Bureau, 1967.†

* * *

MANN, Harold W(ilson) 1925-

PERSONAL: Born August 10, 1925, in Columbus, Ga.; son of David G. (a minister) and Gertrude (Clark) Mann; married Frances Elizabeth Parks, February 3, 1956; children: Harold W., Jr., Martha Blair, Janet Parks. *Education:* Biarritz American University, student, 1946; Emory University, A.B., 1949, M.A., 1950; University of Wisconsin, graduate study, 1950-51; Duke University, Ph.D., 1962. *Politics:* Liberal Democrat. *Religion:* "Peripheral Protestant." *Home:* 1202 Milton Lane, Radford, Va. 24141. *Office address:* Box 5895, Radford College, Radford, Va. 24141.

CAREER: Emory University, Emory-at-Oxford, Oxford, Ga., instructor in social studies, 1951-59, assistant professor, 1959-63, chairman of Division of Social Studies, 1956-63; Radford College, Radford, Va., associate professor, 1963-66, professor of American history, 1966—. *Military service:* U.S. Army, 1943-46; received three battle stars in European campaigns. *Member:* National Education Association, New River Historical Society (vice-president), Pioneer America Society.

WRITINGS: Atticus Greene Haygood: Methodist Bishop, Editor, and Educator, University of Georgia Press, 1965.

WORK IN PROGRESS: History and the Social Sciences.

AVOCATIONAL INTERESTS: Choral singing, piano and organ playing.

MANOLSON, Frank 1925-

PERSONAL: Born November 16, 1925, in Calgary, Alberta, Canada; son of M. F. (a cattleman) and Fanny (Kline) Manolson; married second wife, Margaret Knott; children: two. *Education:* University of Toronto, D.V.M., 1948. *Home:* Cheldene, Loodsend, Aldboure, Wiltshire, United Kingdom.

CAREER: Did veterinary work for British, American, and Canadian governments in British Honduras, New York, Alberta, and Sicily, 1948-58; worked with Danilo Dolci, Partinico, Palermo, Sicily, 1959-60; veterinary surgeon in London, 1960-62; in private practice at Battersea Veterinary Hospital, London, England, 1960—. Founder and director of Battersea Drug Co. Ltd. Director of Kings Road Property Preservation Commission Society. *Member:* Royal College of Veterinary Surgeons, British Veterinary Association, Royal Court Association, Alberta Veterinary Association, Ontario Veterinary College Alumni Association, Aldbourne Society of Authors and Poets, Ogbourne St. George Union.

WRITINGS: D is for Dog, Studio-Vista, 1964, Basic Books, 1965; *C is for Cat,* Studio-Vista, 1965, Basic Books, 1966; *My Cat's in Love,* St. Martin's, 1971. Columnist of "The People's Vet" in *People* and "Our Pets" in *New Reveille.* Contributor to *The Observer* (London).

WORK IN PROGRESS: 600,000 word pet encyclopedia for Readers Digest International.

* * *

MANSFIELD, Harold H. 1912-

PERSONAL: Born April 18, 1912, in White Salmon, Wash.; son of Edward Arthur and Lucie (Fields) Mansfield; married Eileen Gormley, August 4, 1935; children: Kathleen (Mrs. James Reinhardt), Vicki (Mrs. Pepe De Chiazza). *Education:* University of Washington, Seattle, B.A. in Journalism (cum laude), 1935. *Religion:* Christian Science.

CAREER: Seattle Post-Intelligencer, Seattle, Wash., reporter, 1933-36; Boeing Co., Seattle, Wash., publicity manager and editor, 1936-39, manager of public relations and advertising, 1939-47, director of public relations and advertising, 1947-60, special assistant to president, 1960-64, director of management and employment communication, 1964—. *Member:* Sigma Delta Chi, Pi Kappa Alpha. *Awards, honors:* Special award for distinguished industrial journalism, Pacific Northwest Industrial Editors Association, 1959.

WRITINGS: Vision, the Story of Boeing: A Saga of the Sky and the New Horizons of Space, Duell, Sloan & Pearce, 1956, revised and enlarged edition, 1966; *How Wide We Stray,* Ballantine, 1960; *Space Needle, U.S.A.,* Craftsman, 1962; *Billion Dollar Battle: The Story Behind the "Impossible" 727 Project,* McKay, 1965. Writer of newspaper series, "Our Red Rivals," later published as booklet, and of a booklet on Seattle.

WORK IN PROGRESS: A novel concerning underdeveloped nations, researched in United States and India, 1964-65.

SIDELIGHTS: Mansfield speaks some Russian and German. *Avocational interests:* Mountaineering and hiking.†

MARDOCK, Robert W(inston) 1921-

PERSONAL: Born June 20, 1921, in Gaylord, Tex.; son of Lester Elkanah (an insurance agent) and Viola (Winters) Mardock; married Martha Vincent, March 17, 1945; children: James Allan, Steven Lee, Gary Arlen, Robert Lynn. *Education:* Wichita State University, science and engineering courses; Friends University, B.A., 1954; University of Colorado, M.A., 1955, Ph.D., 1958. *Politics:* Republican. *Religion:* Presbyterian. *Home:* 2290 Kenwood Ct., Decatur, Ill. 62526.

CAREER: Tool designer for eight years before preparing for an academic career; Kansas State Teachers College, Emporia, assistant professor of history, 1958-60; University of Colorado, Boulder, visiting lecturer in history, 1960-61; College of Emporia, Emporia, Kan., chairman of Social Science Division, 1961-62; Washburn University of Topeka, Topeka, Kan., associate professor of history, 1962-67; Millikin University, Decatur, Ill., chairman of history department, 1967—. *Member:* Organization of American Historians, American Historical Association, Western History Association, Illinois State Historical Society, Montana State Historical Society.

WRITINGS: (Editor with R. W. Richmond) *A Nation Moving West,* University of Nebraska Press, 1965; *The Reformers and the American Indian,* University of Missouri Press, 1971; *History of Indian Rights,* Smithsonian Institution, in press. Contributor to *Western Humanities Review, Montana Magazine, Nebraska Historical Journal,* and other regional journals.

WORK IN PROGRESS: Westward Migration, 1865-1885.

SIDELIGHTS: Mardock is competent in Spanish and French. In the past decade he has done research on Americana in Library of Congress, National Archives, Harvard University, Boston and New York Public Libraries, and in western collections. *Avocational interests:* Photography.

* * *

MARDOR, Munya Meir 1913-

PERSONAL: Born November 21, 1913, in Kowel, Russia; son of Abraham Izhak and Genia (Klein) Mardor; married Lea Spector, July 3, 1947; children: Rami (son), Gonny (daughter). *Education:* Educated at gymnasium in Kowel, Russia. *Religion:* Jewish. *Home:* 40 Hashoftim St., Tel-Aviv, Israel. *Agent:* John Smith, Christy & Moore Ltd., 52 Floral St., Covent Garden, London W. C. 2, England. *Office:* Ministry of Defence, Hakirya, Tel-Aviv, Israel.

CAREER: Permanent staff member of Haganah (illegal underground defense organization), Palestine, 1934-1948; Ministry of Defence, Tel-Aviv, Israel, director general of Aviation, 1949-50, director general of Weapons Research and Development Authority, beginning 1950. *Military service:* Israeli Air Force, commanding officer, Air Transport Command, 1948-49, with rank of colonel.

WRITINGS: Strictly Illegal (foreword by David Ben Gurion), R. Hale, 1964, published as *Haganah,* edited by D. R. Elston, New American Library, 1966.

AVOCATIONAL INTERESTS: Archaeology.†

* * *

MARIN, Diego 1914-

PERSONAL: Born March 23, 1914, in Spain; son of Diego (a veterinarian) and Laura (Molina) Marin; married Frances M. Richardson, December 23, 1959; children: Ann, Francisca, Richard. *Education:* University of Madrid, Lic. en Derecho, 1936; University of London, B.A., 1943; University of Toronto, M.A., 1953, Ph.D., 1956. *Home:* 54 Elm Ave., Toronto, Ontario, Canada. *Office:* Department of Hispanic Studies, University of Toronto, Toronto, Ontario, Canada.

CAREER: Went to France, then England, as exile from Spanish Civil War; University of Birmingham, Birmingham, England, assistant lecturer in Spanish, 1941-48; University of Western Ontario, London, instructor in Spanish, 1949-51; University of Toronto, Toronto, Ontario, lecturer, 1951-56, assistant professor, 1956-60, associate professor, 1961-64, professor of Spanish, 1964—. *Member:* Modern Language Association of America, American Association of Teachers of Spanish and Portuguese (president of Southern Ontario chapter, 1960-61). *Awards, honors:* Canada Council research award, 1965-66.

WRITINGS: (Editor, and author of critical notes) *Articulos escogidos de Larra,* G. Bell, 1948; *La vida espanola,* G. Bell, 1949, revised edition, Appleton, 1955; *Poesia espanola: Estudios y testos (siglos XV-XX),* Studium (Mexico), 1958, revised edition, Hispanofila, 1971; *La intriga secundaria en el teatro de Lope de Vega,* University of Toronto Press, 1958; *La civilizacion espanola: Panorama historico,* Holt, 1961, revised edition, 1969; *Uso y funcion de la versificacion dramatica en Lope de Vega,* Castalia (Spain), 1962; (with Angel del Rio) *Breve historia de la literatura espanola,* Holt, 1966.

WORK IN PROGRESS: Nature in contemporary Spanish poetry.

SIDELIGHTS: Marin speaks French and Italian.

* * *

MARING, Norman H(ill) 1914-

PERSONAL: Born December 1, 1914, in Chester, Pa.; son of Waldo Earle (a minister) and Emily (Hill) Maring; married Sara J., 1935; children: Donald Edward, Helen Maring Livingston, L. Ruth Leavens. *Education:* Attended Furman University, 1933-35; Eastern Baptist Theological Seminary, A.B. and Th.B., 1941; University of Maryland, M.A., 1943, Ph.D., 1948. *Politics:* Democrat. *Home:* 6355 Lancaster Ave., Philadelphia, Pa. 19151. *Office:* Eastern Baptist Theological Seminary, Lancaster and City Aves., Philadelphia, Pa. 19151.

CAREER: Eastern Baptist Theological Seminary, Philadelphia, Pa., assistant professor, 1948-52, professor of church history, 1952—, dean of faculty, 1972—. *Member:* American Society of Church History, American Historical Association, Society for the Scientific Study of Religion, American Baptist Historical Society (president, 1965—).

WRITINGS: (Contributor) Winthrop S. Hudson, editor, *Baptist Concepts of the Church,* Judson, 1959; (with Hudson) *A Baptist Manual of Polity and Practice,* Judson, 1963, 2nd edition published as *A Short Baptist Manual of Polity and Practice,* 1966; *Baptists in New Jersey: A Study in Transition,* Judson, 1964; *The Christian Calandar in the Free Churches,* Judson, 1967; *American Baptists: Whence and Whither,* Judson, 1968. Contributor to encyclopedias and religious journals. Member of editorial board, *Foundations: A Baptist Journal of History and Theology.*

* * *

MARK, Pauline (Dahlin) 1913-
(Polly Mark)

PERSONAL: Born August 11, 1913, in Mayville, N.Y.; daughter of Charles John and Nettie (Dearing) Dahlin; married Herman John Mark (a teacher), April 16, 1934; children: Charles B., Kathleen A. *Education:* Clifton Springs Sanitarium and Clinic, R.N., 1934; additional study at University of Rochester, Syracuse University, and three colleges of the State University of New York. *Politics:* Republican. *Religion:* Protestant. *Agent:* Toni Strassman, 130 East 18th St., 7-D, New York, N.Y. 10003.

CAREER: Served with her husband, under Methodist Board of Missions, in Singapore and Sarawak, 1950-55, teaching at a jungle mission school in Sarawak and conducting a small clinic for mothers and children; Chautauqua (N.Y.) Board of Education, school nurse and teacher, 1956-58; Penfield (N.Y.) Board of Education, junior high school nurse and teacher, beginning 1958, now retired. *Member:* New York State Teachers Association, Penfield Education Association (secretary, 1965-66).

WRITINGS—All under name Polly Mark: *Tani,* McKay, 1964; *The Way of the Wind,* McKay, 1965.

SIDELIGHTS: Around fifty native children lived with the Marks at the mission school at Kapit, Sarawak. The "small clinic" that Mrs. Mark once held there has grown into the modern institution, Christ Hospital.

* * *

MARK, Steven Joseph 1913-

PERSONAL: Born October 19, 1913, in Europe; married Ann (a teacher), 1938; children: Gene, Donald, Janice. *Education:* Oberlin College, A.B., 1938; Ohio State University, M.A., 1944; Pennsylvania State University, Ed.D., 1958. *Home:* 464 Miller, Kent, Ohio.

CAREER: Science teacher and supervisor in public schools, 1938-56; Kent State University, Kent, Ohio, professor of science education, 1956—. Science consultant in Tanzania, summer, 1964; studied comparative science education in twelve European countries, summer, 1966. *Member:* American Association of University Professors, National Science Teachers Association, National Association for Research in Science Teaching, National Education Association, Ohio Education Association, Ohio Academy of Science.

WRITINGS: Essentials of Chemistry, Kent State University Press, 1954; *Science Experiments for Grades K-7,* Commercial Press, 1964; *A Physics Lab of Your Own,* Houghton, 1964; *Science for Elementary School Teachers,* Commercial Press, 1966; *Teaching Science through Investigations,* C. E. Merrill, 1966; *Source Book of Science Experiments for Elementary Grades,* Vantage, 1970; *Teaching Science through Experiments,* Benefic Press, in press. Contributor to journals.

* * *

MARKE, Julius J(ay) 1913-

PERSONAL: Born January 12, 1913, in New York, N.Y.; son of Isadore and Ann (Taylor) Marke; married Sylvia Bolotin, December 15, 1949; children: Elisa Hope. *Education:* City College of New York (now City College of the City University of New York), B.S.S., 1934; New York University, LL.B., 1937; Columbia University, B.S. in L.S., 1942. *Home:* 4 Peter Cooper Rd., New York, N.Y. 10010.

CAREER: New York Public Library, New York, N.Y., reference assistant, 1937-42; admitted to New York bar, 1938; private law practice, New York, N.Y., 1939-41; New

York University, School of Law, New York, N.Y., 1949—, professor of law and law librarian, specializing in data computers and information retrieval systems, legal history, legal research, and writing, 1954—. Lecturer, Columbia University School of Library Service, 1962—. Ford Foundation consultant on government public domain policy; library consultant and lecturer, graduate college orientation program in American law, consultant to World Peace Through Law, Washington, D.C. Chairman, International Working Committee on Copyright, 1973-74; member, Conference on Resolution of Copyright Issues. *Military service:* U.S. Army, 1943-45; served in European Theater; became sergeant; received Bronze Star and four battle stars. *Member:* American Association of Law Libraries (president, 1962-63; chairman of Copyright Committee, 1968—), Order of the Coif (president of New York chapter, 1968—), New York University Faculty Club (president, 1964-66), Phi Delta Phi.

WRITINGS: (Editor) *A Catalogue of the Law Collection at New York University, with Selected Annotations,* New York University Law Center, 1953; (editor) *The Holmes Reader,* Oceana, 1955, 2nd edition, 1964; (compiler) *Dean's List of Recommended Reading for Pre-Law and Law Students,* Oceana, 1958; (editor) *Bender's Legal Business Forms,* four volumes, Edward Thompson Co., 1961; (editor with John Lexa) *International Seminar on Constitutional Review,* New York University Law School, 1963; *Vignettes of Legal History,* Rothman, 1965; *Copyright and Intellectual Property,* Fund for the Advancement of Education, 1967; *Commercial Law: A Guide to Information Sources,* Gale, 1970. Editor, "Docket Series." Columnist on legal research for *New York Law Journal.* Contributor to library and legal journals.

WORK IN PROGRESS: A revision of *Dean's List of Recommended Reading for Pre-Law and Law Students;* a book on popularization of legal history.

SIDELIGHTS: Julius Marke is proficient in French.

*   *   *

MARKOV, Vladimir   1920-

PERSONAL: Born February 24, 1920, in Leningrad, Russia; now U.S. citizen; son of Fyodor (a scientist) and Ustinya (Filippova) Markov; married Lydia Yakovleva (an actress), February 19, 1947. *Education:* University of Leningrad, student, 1936-41; University of California, Berkeley, Ph.D., 1958. *Religion:* Russian Orthodox. *Office:* Department of Slavic Languages and Literatures, University of California, Los Angeles, Calif.

CAREER: University of California, Los Angeles, acting assistant professor, 1957-58, assistant professor, 1958-61, associate professor, 1961-63, professor of Russian literature, 1963—. *Member:* Modern Language Association of America, American Association for Advancement of Slavic Studies, American Association of Teachers of Slavic and East European Languages, Phi Beta Kappa. *Awards, honors:* Guggenheim fellowship, 1964; senior fellow, National Foundation for the Arts and the Humanities, 1967-68; P.E.N. Translation Award, 1968, for *Modern Russian Poetry.*

WRITINGS: Stikhi, Echo Publishing, 1947; (editor) *Priglushennye golosa,* Chekhov Publishing House, 1952; *Gurilevskie romansy,* Rifma (Paris), 1960; *The Longer Poems of Velimir Khlebnikov,* University of California Press, 1962; (editor and translator with Merrill Sparks) *Modern Russian Poetry,* MacGibbon & Kee, 1966; *Russian Futurism: A*

History, University of California Press, 1968. Contributor of articles and essays to *Novyi Zhurnal, Grani, Vozdushnye Puti, Slavic Review,* and other professional journals.

WORK IN PROGRESS: Research in modern Russian poetry, Russian poetry, and poetics in general.

*   *   *

MARKS, Barry A(lan)   1926-

PERSONAL: Born February 1, 1926, in New York, N.Y.; son of Eric H. (a hotel owner) and Beatrice (Hecht) Marks; married Gale Holman, September 18, 1948; children: Stephen, Pamela, Dana. *Education:* Dartmouth College, A.B., 1947; University of Minnesota, M.A., 1949, Ph.D., 1957. *Politics:* Republican. *Religion:* Protestant. *Home:* 6348 Dahlonega Rd., Washington, D.C. 20016. *Office:* Department of Literature, American University, Washington, D.C. 20016.

CAREER: Dartmouth College, Hanover, N.H., assistant to dean, 1948; University of Minnesota, Minneapolis, instructor in general studies, 1949-53; Dartmouth College, instructor in great issues and government, 1953-55; Brown University, Providence, R.I., instructor, 1955-58, assistant professor, 1958-63, associate professor of English, 1963-68; American University, Washington, D.C., professor of literature, and chairman of department, 1968—. University of Lille, Fulbright lecturer, 1963-64. U.S. Commission on Civil Rights, Rhode Island advisory committee, member, 1958-65, chairman, 1960-63; Rhode Island Commission on Human Rights, chairman, 1965-68; Rhode Island Republican State Central Committee, member of executive committee, 1965-68. *Military service:* U.S. Marine Corps, 1943-45. *Member:* National Council of Teachers of English, Modern Language Association of America, American Association of University Professors, New England Association for American Studies (president, 1962-63). *Awards, honors:* A.M., Brown University, 1963.

WRITINGS: (Editor) *Mark Twain's 'Huckleberry Finn,'* Heath, 1959; *E. E. Cummings,* Twayne, 1964. Contributor to journals.

WORK IN PROGRESS: Research on nineteenth-century American romanticism—Thoreau, Whitman, Melville, Mark Twain.

AVOCATIONAL INTERESTS: Civil rights, Republican politics, France.†

*   *   *

MARKS, Edith Bobroff   1924-
(Edith Bobroff)

PERSONAL: Born June 20, 1924, in Maynard, Mass.; daughter of Samuel and Rebecca (Weber) Swartz; married Martin Bobroff, 1946 (died, 1959); married Jason Marks (a professor and writer), 1962. *Education:* Brooklyn College (now Brooklyn College of the City University of New York), B.A., 1966; Columbia University, M.A., 1969. *Religion:* Jewish. *Home:* 35 West 90th St., New York, N.Y. 10024. *Agent:* Bertha Klausner International Literary Agency, Inc., 71 Park Ave., New York, N.Y. 10016. *Office:* 400 First Ave., New York, N.Y.

CAREER: Placement manager of a New York (N.Y.) employment agency, 1957-69; New York City Board of Education, New York, N.Y., teacher, 1969—. Democratic county committeewoman, 1961-62. *Member:* New York State Association for Exceptional Children, Alpha Sigma Lambda.

WRITINGS: (Under name Edith Bobroff, with Adele Lewis) *College to Career*, Bobbs, Merrill, 1963; (under name Edith Bobroff, with Lewis) *Kitchen to Career*, Bobbs, Merrill, 1964. Contributor to *Personnel Management, Slow Learning Child, Bardic Echoes, Lyrics of Love.* Editor, Council for Exceptional Children newsletter.

WORK IN PROGRESS: A book, *Conceptual Development: A Language Oriented Approach to Reading.*

* * *

MARKS, Elaine 1930-

PERSONAL: Born November 13, 1930, in New York, N.Y.; daughter of Harry and Ruth (Elin) Marks. *Education:* Bryn Mawr, A.B., 1952; University of Pennsylvania, M.A., 1953; New York University, Ph.D., 1958. *Home:* 2202 Martin St., Madison, Wisconsin 53713.

CAREER: New York University, New York, N.Y., graduate assistant, 1953-56, instructor, 1957-59, assistant professor, 1959-62, associate professor of French, 1962-63; University of Wisconsin—Milwaukee, associate professor of French, 1963-65; University of Massachusetts, professor of French, 1965-66; University of Wisconsin—Madison, professor of French, 1966-68; University of Massachusetts, professor of French, 1972-73. University of Wisconsin—Madison, Herbert F. Johnson Postdoctoral Fellow at the Institute for Research in the Humanities, 1962-63. *Member:* Modern Library Association, American Association of University Professors. *Awards, honors:* Fulbright fellowship, Paris, 1956-57.

WRITINGS: Colette (a critical study of the French author), Rutgers University Press, 1960; (editor with Richard Tedeschi) Andre Gide, *L'Immoraliste*, Macmillan, 1963; (editor) *French Poetry From Baudelaire to the Present*, Dell, 1962; (editor with Charles Carlut) *Recits de nos jours*, Macmillan, 1964; *Simone de Beauvoir: Encounters with Death*, Rutgers University Press, 1973. Contributor of book reviews to *French Revue* and *New York Times Book Review.*

* * *

MARKS, James R(obert) 1932-

PERSONAL: Born March 9, 1932, in Syracuse, N.Y.; son of Seymour I. Marks (a jeweler); married Shirley Rotter (an educator), August 7, 1953; children: Diana, Glenn, Bruce, Gary, Deborah. *Education:* Los Angeles City College, A.A., 1952; University of California, Los Angeles, A.A., 1953, B.A., 1954; California State College at Los Angeles (now California State University, Los Angeles), graduate study, 1956-57; University of Southern California, M.S., 1958, M.Ed., 1961, Ed.D., 1962, postdoctoral study, 1964. *Office:* West Los Angeles College, 4800 Freshman Dr., Culver City, Calif. 90230.

CAREER: Brentwood Neuropsychiatric Hospital, Brentwood, Calif., educational therapist, 1951-54; Los Angeles (Calif.) Unified School District, elementary and high school teacher, later supervising master teacher and acting principal, 1954-65; University of Hawaii, Honolulu, associate professor of educational administration, 1965-66; West Los Angeles College, Culver City, Calif., professor of psychology, 1969—, president of academic senate, 1971—, chief protocol, 1970—. Advisor of post-doctoral studies, University of Southern California, 1962-68; coordinator of teacher preparation, California State Polytechnic College (now University), 1963-64; professor of administration, personnel

psychology, University of British Columbia, 1964; professor of psychology and education, University of British Columbia, 1964-65; lecturer, Los Angeles Metropolitan College, 1965-66; visiting professor, Idaho State University, 1968-69. Lecturer on family relations and child guidance, 1963—; certified (Calif.) family relations and child counseling specialist. *Member:* National Education Association, Association for Childhood Education, National Council on Family Relations, American Association of University Professors, Phi Delta Kappa, Delta Epsilon, Sigma Tau Sigma, Trojan Club. *Awards, honors:* Ph.D., University of London, 1974; Sc.D. in Ed., International Free Protestant Episcopal University, 1974.

WRITINGS: Speaking and Living, L. W. Singer, 1965; (with Emery Stoops) *Elementary School Supervision: Practices and Trends*, Allyn & Bacon, 1965; (with others) *Handbook of Educational Supervision*, Allyn & Bacon, 1971. Contributor to Educational journals.

WORK IN PROGRESS: Methods and Techniques in Elementary School Teaching, for Allyn & Bacon; *Helping Children Succeed in School* and *Classroom Testing*, both for Economy Press; a revised edition of *Handbook of Educational Supervision.*

SIDELIGHTS: Marks speaks Spanish.

* * *

MARKS, John H(enry) 1923-

PERSONAL: Born August 6, 1923, in Denver, Colo.; son of Ira and Clara (Dralle) Marks; married Aminta Willis, 1951; children: Peter, Fleur, John. *Education:* University of Denver, B.A., 1946; Princeton Theological Seminary, B.D., 1949; University of Basel, Th.D., 1953. *Home:* 107 Moore St., Princeton, N.J. *Office:* Princeton University, Princeton, N.J.

CAREER: Ordained Presbyterian minister, 1949; Princeton Theological Seminary, Princeton, N.J., instructor in speech, 1953-54; Princeton University, Princeton N.J., instructor in Oriental studies, 1954-55, assistant professor, 1955-61, associate professor, 1961—. *Military service:* U.S. Army, 1943-45. *Member:* Society of Biblical Literature, American Oriental Society, American Association of University Professors, Phi Beta Kappa.

WRITINGS: Der textkritische Wert des Psalterium Hieronymi iuxta Hebraeos, P. G. Keller (Switzerland), 1956; (with V. M. Rogers) *Beginner's Handbook to Biblical Hebrew*, Abingdon, 1958; (translator) Von Rad, *Genesis*, Westminster, 1961.

* * *

MARLAND, Edward Allen 1912-

PERSONAL: Born April 21, 1912, in England; son of John and Esther (Wilson) Marland; children: Heather Leslie, Peter Brian. *Education:* University College, Nottingham (now University of Nottingham), B.Sc., 1933; University College, London, M.Sc., 1958, Ph.D., 1966. *Office:* The Polytechnic, 309, Regent St., London W. 1, England.

CAREER: Marconi's Wireless Telegraph Co. Ltd., Chelmsford, England, 1935-40; Department of Anti-Submarine Warfare, Admiralty, Bath, England, 1940-46; Westminster Technical College, London, England, lecturer in engineering, 1947-67; with The Polytechnic, London, England, 1967—. *Member:* Institute of Electrical Engineers, Hampstead Scientific Society.

WRITINGS: Early Electrical Communication, Abelard, 1964.

AVOCATIONAL INTERESTS: Swimming, photography, and astronomy.†

* * *

MARLOWE, Derek 1938-

PERSONAL: Born May 21, 1938, in London, England; son of Frederick William (an electrician) and Helene (Alexandroupolos) Marlow. *Education:* Attended Cardinal Vaughan School, 1949-57, London University, 1957-60. *Politics:* Socialist. *Religion:* Humanist. *Home:* 8 Holland Park Rd., London W. 14, England. *Agent:* Christy & Moore, 52 Floral St., London W.C. 2, England.

CAREER: Full-time writer. *Awards, honors:* Foyle Award, best play of 1961-62, for "The Scarecrow."

WRITINGS: A Dandy in Aspic, Putnam, 1966; *Memoirs of a Venus Lackey*, Viking, 1968; *A Single Summer With L.B.: The Summer of 1816*, J. Cape, 1969, published as *A Single Summer With Lord B.*, Viking, 1970; *Echoes of Celandine*, Viking, 1970; *Do You Remember England?*, Viking, 1972.

Wrote play, "The Scarecrow," which was produced at the Royal Court Theatre, 1961. Author of screenplay for "A Dandy in Aspic," which was filmed in 1967 and of television script, "The Search for the Nile," six hours, broadcast January 25, February 1, 15, 22, and 29, 1972, by National Broadcasting Corp.

SIDELIGHTS: Marlowe told *CA* that he is "concerned with the tragedy of the individual in society—the seeds of destruction of his own personal liberty (mental and physical) either by his own personal liberty (mental and physical) either by his own weakness, or more important by the strength of conformity as a vice—as represented by politics, class, or worse—fear of being an outsider."

His first novel, *A Dandy in Aspic*, is comparable to the writings of John Le Carre, in that the role of the double agent is not as glamorous as it is usually treated. The book concerns a Russian agent who wants to quit but is not allowed to do so.

Most of the reviewers liked the novel. "The spy novel has reached its rococo period, and hypertrophy with backward tail feather and forward toe leads the dance," commented Guy Davenport. "But Mr. Marlowe is an accomplished master of the trade, and before one is halfway through his Byzantine plot anything at all has become plausible.... Only the most serious duties will keep a reader from going all the way to the end once he's hooked around page 3."

BIOGRAPHICAL/CRITICAL SOURCES: National Review, October 4, 1966; *Book Week*, October 30, 1966.†

* * *

MARQUIS, G(eorge) Welton 1916-

PERSONAL: Born March 4, 1916, in Walla Walla, Wash.; son of George Bruce and Agnes (Houck) Marquis; married Greta Jeidel, September 11, 1942 (died June 16, 1966). *Education:* Whitman College, A.B., 1936, A.M., 1942; University of Southern California, Ph.D., 1950. *Home:* 60-303 Williams Road, Richmond, British Columbia, Canada. *Office:* University of British Columbia, Vancouver, British Columbia, Canada.

CAREER: Arranger, composer, and conductor in Hollywood, Calif., 1937-41; Northern Illinois University, De-

Kalb, head of department of music, 1951-54; University of North Carolina, Woman's College, Greensboro, dean of School of Music, 1954-58; University of British Columbia, Vancouver, professor of music and head of department, 1958—. Fulbright professor, University of Oslo, 1957-58. Member of board of Vancouver Symphony Society, 1958-65, and Vancouver Festival, 1958-62; member of Vancouver Community Arts Council, 1958—. *Military service:* U.S. Army Air Forces, 1942-46. *Member:* American Musicological Society (chairman of Northwestern chapter, 1965-66), College Music Society (member of national board, 1965), Canadian Association of University Schools of Music (vice-president, 1965-69; president, 1969-71).

WRITINGS: Twentieth-Century Music Idioms, Prentice-Hall, 1964; *Yes, Sir, That's My Wolfgang*, Prentice-Hall, 1967.

WORK IN PROGRESS: A history of music from Greece to the present, tentatively titled *Music and Civilization*.

AVOCATIONAL INTERESTS: Political-social history, history of fine arts, tennis, fishing.

* * *

MARSH, Robert (Harrison) 1926-

PERSONAL: Born September 17, 1926, in San Diego, Calif.; son of Lawrence Isaac (a theatrical producer) and Mildred (Fry) Marsh; married Joanne Biesecker, 1953 (divorced); married Emilia Field Cresswell, 1969; children: Cynthia Suzan, Elizabeth Anne. *Education:* San Diego State College (now University), A.B., 1950; University of Oregon, M.S., 1951; Florida State University, graduate study, 1951-52; Johns Hopkins University, Ph.D., 1955. *Home:* 1136 East 48th Street, Chicago, Ill. 60615. *Office:* Department of English, University of Chicago, Chicago, Ill. 60637.

CAREER: State University College for Teachers (now State University of New York at Albany), Albany, N.Y., instructor in English, 1953-55; Harpur College (now State University of New York at Binghamton), instructor, 1955-56, assistant professor of English, 1956-59; University of California, Santa Barbara, assistant professor of English, 1959-61; State University of New York at Stony Brook, associate professor of English, 1961-66; University of Chicago, Chicago, Ill., professor of English, 1966—. Catholic University of America, visiting professor, 1965-66. *Military service:* U.S. Army Air Forces, 1945-47. *Member:* Modern Language Association of America.

WRITINGS: Four Dialectical Theories of Poetry: An Aspect of English Neoclassical Criticism, University of Chicago Press, 1965; (contributor) *Literary Criticism and Historical Understanding*, Columbia University Press, 1967. Contributor to *Encyclopedia of Poetry and Poetics*, and to literary and other scholarly journals.†

* * *

MARSHALL, (Sarah) Catherine 1914-

PERSONAL: Born September 27, 1914, in Johnson City, Tenn.; daughter of John Ambrose (a minister) and Leonara (Whitaker) Wood; married Peter Marshall (a minister), November 4, 1936 (died, January, 1949); married Leonard Earle LeSourd, November 14, 1959; children: (first marriage) Peter John. *Education:* Agnes Scott College, B.A., 1936. *Religion:* Presbyterian.

CAREER: Full-time writer. National Cathedral School for Girls, Washington, D.C., member of faculty, 1949-50.

Trustee, Agnes Scott College. *Member:* National League of American Pen Women, Phi Beta Kappa. *Awards, honors:* "Woman of the Year" in the field of literature, Women's National Press Club Award, 1953; D.Litt., Cedar Crest College, 1954.

WRITINGS: A Man Called Peter: The Story of Peter Marshall, McGraw, 1951; *To Live Again,* McGraw, 1957; *Christy,* McGraw, 1967; *Something More,* McGraw, 1974.

Editor—All collections of sermons and prayers by Peter Marshall: *Mr. Jones, Meet the Master,* Revell, 1949, revised edition, 1950; (with Peter Marshall) *God Loves You,* McGraw, 1953; (author of introduction) *Let's Keep Christmas,* McGraw, 1953; (author of introduction) *Prayers of Peter Marshall,* McGraw, 1954; (author of introduction) *Heart of Peter Marshall's Faith* (excerpt from *Mr. Jones, Meet the Master),* Revell, 1956; *Friends with God: Stories and Prayers of the Marshall Family,* McGraw, 1956; (author of introduction) *First Easter,* McGraw, 1959; *Beyond Our Selves,* McGraw, 1961; (author of introduction) *John Doe, Disciple: Sermons for the Young in Spirit,* McGraw, 1963. Woman's editor, *Christian Herald* magazine, 1958-60; roving editor, *Guideposts* magazine, 1960—. Contributor to *Reader's Digest* and other periodicals.

SIDELIGHTS: When seven Russian journalists visited the United States in 1955, one of them claimed that he didn't believe that Catherine Marshall existed. He had been so impressed by the story of her life that he thought she was the creation of American propaganda. Since the publication of *A Man Called Peter,* Mrs. Marshall has received letters from the world over praising the inspirational qualities of the book which made the non-fiction best-seller list ten days after its appearance. While writing this biography of her husband, Peter Marshall, who was chaplain of the U.S. Senate from 1947 until his death in 1949, Mrs. Marshall encountered some difficult moments. "Life as you and I know it is of the heart as well as the head," she wrote in *McCall's.* "Literature, if it is accurately to reflect life, must at times reach past the reader's intellect to the emotional level. In order to achieve that the writer has to *feel* something as he writes. There were times during the writing of *A Man Called Peter* when reliving the drama of my life with Peter was almost too much for me. That was particularly true during the week I wrote the chapter on Peter's death. Not only did I have to re-experience every vivid detail in order to transfer it to paper, but there was the necessity of holding that emotion in check. I am convinced that real communication in writing always has to be disciplined. It is never achieved either by sticky sentimentality or by careless diffusiveness. Trying to attain anything approaching this ideal was like attempting to rein in a pair of runaway horses—exhausting at best." *Library Journal* praised her objectivity while A. P. Davies dismissed its importance. "It can scarcely be claimed," he wrote, "that any man's wife is well equipped to be his most objective biographer." But Davies added: "In the present case this does not matter, since objectivity is not essential in portraying a beloved person for a multitude of others who also loved him. Catherine Marshall writes extremely well. Those who do not accept her religious viewpoint will nevertheless admit that she presents it with grace and charm." This book seems to have fulfilled the author's desire to "make a contribution to my time and generation."

A Man Called Peter was filmed by 20th Century-Fox in 1955 and *Christy* is scheduled for filming by MGM.

BIOGRAPHICAL/CRITICAL SOURCES: Library Jour-

nal, September 1, 1951; *New York Times Book Review,* October 7, 1951; *McCall's,* August, 1953; *Look,* March 6, 1956.*

* * *

MARSHALL, F. Ray 1928-

PERSONAL: Born August 22, 1928, in Oak Grove, La.; son of Thomas Jefferson (a farmer) and Virginia (Foster) Marshall; married Patricia Williams, November 27, 1946; children: Jill Ann, Susan Ray, John Thomas, Christopher Dow, Sarah Lee. *Education:* Hinds Junior College, student, 1946-48; Millsaps College, B.A., 1949; Louisiana State University, M.A., 1950; University of California, Berkeley, Ph.D., 1955. *Politics:* Democrat. *Religion:* Presbyterian. *Home:* 4214 Tallowood, Austin, Tex. 78712.

CAREER: Instructor in economics at Louisiana State University, Baton Rouge, 1950-51, and San Francisco State College, San Francisco, Calif., 1953; University of Mississippi, Oxford, 1953-57, began as assistant professor, became associate professor of economics; Louisiana State University, professor of economics, 1957-62; University of Texas, Austin, professor of economics, 1962-67; University of Kentucky, Lexington, Alumni Professor of Economics and chairman of department, 1967-69; University of Texas, Austin, professor of economics, 1969—, director of Center for the Study of Human Resources, 1969—, chairman of department, 1970-72. University of Helsinki, Fulbright research scholar, 1955-56. Chairman, Federal Committee on Apprenticeship, 1974—; director, consultant, and member of state, national, and private agencies, committees, and commissions. Labor arbitrator. *Military service:* U.S. Navy, 1944-46. U.S. Naval Reserve, 1946—; now lieutenant commander.

MEMBER: American Economic Association, Industrial Relations Research Association (member of board of directors, 1969-72), National Institute of Labor Education (board member, 1960—), American Association of University Professors (president, Texas chapter, 1966-67), American Arbitration Association, Association for Evolutionary Economics, Southern Economic Association (executive committee member, 1969-71; president, 1973-74), Texas Association of College Teachers, Beta Gamma Sigma, Omicron Delta Kappa, Phi Kappa Phi.

WRITINGS: (With Paul Norgren and Samuel Hill) *Toward Fair Employment,* Columbia University Press, 1964; *The Negro and Organized Labor,* Wiley, 1965; (with Allan M. Cartter) *Labor Economics: Wages, Employment and Trade Unionism,* Irwin, 1966, revised edition, 1972; *Labor in the South,* Harvard University Press, 1967; *Negro and Apprenticeship,* Johns Hopkins Press, 1967; *The Negro Worker,* Random House, 1967; (with Vernon M. Briggs, Jr.) *The Negro and Apprenticeship,* Johns Hopkins Press, 1967; *Labor in the South,* Harvard University Press, 1967; (with Briggs) *Equal Apprenticeship Opportunities: The Nature of the Issue and the New York Experience,* National Manpower Policy Task Force and Institute of Industrial Relations, University of Michigan-Wayne State University, 1968.

(With Lamond Godwin) *Cooperatives and Rural Poverty in the South,* Johns Hopkins Press, 1971; (with Sar Levitan and Garth Mangum) *Human Resources and Labor Markets,* Harper, 1972; (with Robert W. Glover) *Compensation of Texas State Employees,* Texas Public Employees Association, 1972; (with Richard Perlman) *An Anthology of Labor Economics,* Wiley, 1972; (with William S. Franklin and Glover) *Training and Entry into Union Construction*, U.S. Government Printing Office, 1974; *Rural Workers and Rural Labor Markets*, Olympus Publishing Co., 1974; (with R. Lynn Rittenoure and James Walker) *Human Resources Development in Rural Texas*, Center for the Study of Human Resources and Bureau of Business Research, University of Texas, 1974; (with Virgil Christian) *The Employment of Southern Blacks*, Olympus Publishing Co., 1974.

Contributor: Michael Moskow, editor, *Collective Bargaining in the Public Sector*, Prentice-Hall, 1971; Harold L. Sheppard, Bennett Harrison, and William J. Spring, *The Political Economy of Public Service Employment*, Heath, 1972; Seymour L. Wolfbein, editor, *Manpower Policy: Perspectives and Prospects*, Temple University, 1973; Collette Moser, editor, *Manpower Planning for Jobs in Rural America*, Center for Rural Manpower and Public Affairs, Michigan State University, 1973; Donald C. Huffman and Garnett L. Bradford, editors, *Structure and Control of Southern Agriculture*, Southern Farm Management Research Committee, 1973.

Contributor of about sixty articles to labor journals. Member of board of editors, *Southern Economic Journal*, 1967-70, *Poverty and Human Resources*, 1971—; contributing editor, *Southern Voices*, 1974—.

* * *

MARSHALL, George O(ctavius), Jr. 1922-

PERSONAL: Born February 27, 1922, in Americus, Ga., son of George Octavius, and Martha (Pryor) Marshall; married, 1956 (wife deceased); married Charlotte Thomas, 1967. *Education:* University of Georgia, A.B.J., 1942, M.A., 1951; University of Texas, Ph.D., 1955. *Politics:* Democrat. *Religion:* Baptist. *Home:* 402 Riverview Rd., Athens, Ga. 30601. *Office:* Department of English, University of Georgia, Athens, Ga. 30601.

CAREER: University of Texas, Austin, instructor in English, 1954-55; University of Georgia, Athens, instructor, 1955-56, assistant professor, 1956-61, associate professor, 1961-66, professor of English, 1966—. Hope Haven School for Mentally Retarded, member of board, 1965—. *Military service:* U.S. Army, 1943-45; became staff sergeant; received Bronze Star. *Member:* Modern Language Association of America, South Atlantic Modern Language Association, Athens Historical Society (president, 1966).

WRITINGS: (Editor) *Creativity and the Arts*, Center for Continuing Education, University of Georgia, 1961; *A Tennyson Handbook*, Twayne, 1963. Contributor to *Abstracts of English Studies*. Associate editor, *South Atlantic Bulletin*.

* * *

MARSHALL, Max Lawrence 1922-

PERSONAL: Born July 4, 1922, in Cleveland, Ohio; son of Charles Marshall; married Constance Beyer, August 1, 1950; children: Terry Allen, Constance Benita. *Education:* U.S. Military Academy, B.S., 1944; University of Missouri, M.A., 1953, Ph.D., 1968. U.S. Army Command and General Staff College, graduate, 1960. *Home:* 503 Parkade Blvd., Columbia, Mo. 65201. *Agent:* August Lenniger, Lenniger Literary Agency, 437 Fifth Ave., New York, N.Y. 10016.

CAREER: U.S. Army, 1944-64, retiring as lieutenant colonel; Texas Western College, El Paso, assistant pro-

fessor of journalism and radio-television, 1964-66; University of Missouri, Columbia, instructor, beginning 1968. Associate editor of *U.S. Army Information Digest*, 1953-56; assigned to U.S. Army Pictorial Center, Long Island City, N.Y., 1957-60, became chief of editorial branch and executive film producer; assistant executive for public relations, Office of the Chief of Communications-Electronics, Washington, D.C., 1961-64. *Member:* Association for Education in Journalism, Texas Association of College Teachers (publicity adviser to executive committee), University Film Producers Association.

WRITINGS: The Story of the U.S. Army Signal Corps, F. Watts, 1965; *Frank Luther Mott: Journalism Educator*, University of Missouri, 1968; *Cowles Guide to Careers and Professions*, Cowles, 1968. Contributor to military journals.

SIDELIGHTS: Marshall reads German and French.†

* * *

MARTELLARO, Joseph A. 1924-

PERSONAL: Surname is pronounced Mar-tel-*lar*-o; born July 20, 1924, in Rockford, Ill.; son of Vito and Mary (Ciaccio) Martellaro; married Loretta W. Kowalski, August 25, 1945; children: Joseph Michael, Charles, David. *Education:* University of Notre Dame, A.B., 1956, M.A., 1958, Ph.D., 1962. *Politics:* Independent. *Religion:* Roman Catholic. *Home:* 1702 Margaret Lane, DeKalb, Ill. 60115. *Office:* Department of Economics, Northern Illinois University, DeKalb, Ill. 60115.

CAREER: Indiana University, South Bend Campus, associate professor of economics and chairman of department, 1966-67; Northern Illinois University, DeKalb, professor of economics, 1967—, associate dean, and dean of graduate school, 1969-74. Fulbright professor to Argentina, 1965. *Military service:* U.S. Army Air Forces, 1943-44; U.S. Army Reserve, 1960—; current rank, major. *Member:* American Economic Association, Association for Comparative Economics. *Awards, honors:* Fulbright research grant to Italy, 1960-61; university research grants, Indiana University, 1966, Northern Illinois University, 1967.

WRITINGS: Economic Development in Southern Italy, 1950-1960, Catholic University of America Press, 1965; (contributor) *Perspectives for Teachers of Latin American Culture*, NDEA, 1970. Contributor to professional journals in United States and Argentina.

WORK IN PROGRESS: A book, *Non-economic Factors and the Italian Economy*.

SIDELIGHTS: Martellaro is proficient in Spanish and Italian.

* * *

MARTIN, John Rupert 1916-

PERSONAL: Born September 27, 1916, in Hamilton, Ontario, Canada; came to United States, 1941, naturalized, 1959; son of John Smith (an accountant) and Elizabeth (Hutchison) Martin; married Barbara Malcom, August 23, 1941; children: Hilary Jane. *Education:* McMaster University, B.A., 1938; Princeton University, M.F.A., 1941, Ph.D., 1947. *Home:* 51 Cleveland Lane, Princeton, N.J. 08540. *Office:* Princeton University, Princeton, N.J. 08540.

CAREER: University of Iowa, Iowa City, instructor in history of art, 1941-42; Princeton University, Princeton, N.J., 1947—, professor of art and archaeology, 1961-70, Marquand Professor, 1970—, chairman of department,

1973—. Princeton Junior Museum, president, 1962-64. *Military service:* Canadian Army, 1942-46; became major; mentioned in dispatches. *Member:* College Art Association of America, Renaissance Society of America, National Committee for the History of Art, Comite International d'Histoire de l'Art.

WRITINGS: The Illustration of the Heavenly Ladder of John Climacus, Princeton University Press, 1954; *The Portrait of John Milton at Princeton*, Princeton University Library, 1961; *The Farnese Gallery*, Princeton University Press, 1965; *Rubens' Ceiling Paintings for the Jesuit Church in Antwerp*, Arcade, 1968; *Rubens: The Antwerp Altarpieces: The Raising of the Cross, the Descent from the Cross*, Norton, 1969; *Rubens' Decorations for the Pompa Introitus Ferdinandi*, Arcade, 1972; (editor) *Rubens Before 1620*, Princeton University Press, 1972.

WORK IN PROGRESS: A book on Baroque art for Penguin.

SIDELIGHTS: His general interest in baroque painting is focused currently on the seminal figures of the early seventeenth century, such as Carracci, Caravaggio, and Rubens.

*   *   *

MARTIN, Michael L.   1932-

PERSONAL: Born February 3, 1932, in Cincinnati, Ohio; son of Thomas G. (a salesman) and Ruth (Quigley) Martin; married Jane Roland (a college professor), June 15, 1962; children: Timothy, Thomas. *Education:* U.S. Naval Academy, midshipman, 1950; Arizona State University, B.S., 1956; University of Arizona, M.A., 1958; Harvard University, Ph.D., 1962. *Religion:* None. *Home:* 389 Central St., Newton, Mass. 02166. *Office:* 232 Bay State Rd., Boston, Mass. 02115.

CAREER: University of Colorado, Boulder, assistant professor of philosophy, 1962-65; Boston University, Boston, Mass., assistant professor, 1965-69, associate professor of philosophy, 1969—. *Military service:* U.S. Marine Corps, 1948-50. *Member:* American Philosophical Association, Philosophy of Science Association.

WRITINGS: (Editor with Marguerite Foster) *Probability, Confirmation and Simplicity*, Odyssey, 1966; *Concepts of Science Education*, Scott, Foresman, 1972. Contributor to *Inquiry, Philosophy of Science*, and other professional journals.

WORK IN PROGRESS: Research in philosophical problems of social science.

*   *   *

MARTIN, Morgan   1921-

PERSONAL: Born April 19, 1921, in Hamilton, Ontario, Canada; married Mary Coverdale Folger, May 6, 1944; children: Susan, Sally, Nancy. *Education:* Queen's University, Kingston, Ontario, M.D. and C.M., 1944; Columbia University, M.Sc., 1960. *Address:* Box 508, Norwich, Conn. 06360.

CAREER: In general practice, Lockwood Clinic, Toronto, Ontario, 1946-47; Saskatchewan Hospitals at Weyburn and North Battleford, psychiatrist, 1947-52; director of Regina Mental Health Clinic, 1953-57, and of Munroe Wing, Regina General Hospital, 1957-59; University of Saskatchewan, Saskatoon, resident lecturer on faculty of medicine and in graduate school of nursing, 1956-59; Canadian Government, Department of National Health and Welfare, Ot-

tawa, Ontario, chief of Mental Health Division, 1960-66; Norwich Hospital, Norwich, Conn., superintendent, 1966—; Yale University School of Medicine, New Haven, Conn., lecturer, 1967—. Visiting lecturer at Regina College, 1957-59, Universite de Montreal, 1960-66, Queen's University, 1960-66, and Canadian Civil Defence College, 1960-66. Member of World Health Organization (WHO) Expert Committee on Mental Health. *Military service:* Royal Canadian Army, Medical Corps, 1943-46; became captain. *Member:* American Psychiatric Association, American College of Psychiatrists.

WRITINGS: The Mental Ward: A Personnel Guidebook, C. C Thomas, 1962.

*   *   *

MARTIN, Ronald E(dward)   1933-

PERSONAL: Born June 30, 1933, in Chicago, Ill.; son of Edward H. (a banker) and Lucille (Fisher) Martin; married Barbara K. Paterson, June 23, 1956; children: Katy, Christopher, Susan. *Education:* Carroll College, Waukesha, Wis., B.A., 1955; Boston University, A.M., 1957, Ph.D., 1963. *Home:* 234 West Main St., Newark, Del. 19711. *Office:* Department of English, University of Delaware, Newark, Del. 19711.

CAREER: Boston University, Boston, Mass., instructor in English, 1961-62; University of Delaware, Newark, assistant professor, 1962-67, associate professor of English, 1967—. *Member:* American Association of University Professors.

WRITINGS: The Fiction of Joseph Hergesheimer, University of Pennsylvania Press, 1965.

WORK IN PROGRESS: American Literature and the Universe of Force, a book about the effect on American literature, in the period 1880-1918, of philosophical views based on concepts from nineteenth-century physics.

*   *   *

MARTIN, Sylvia (Pass)   1913-

PERSONAL: Born July 25, 1913, in Chicago, Ill.; married Lawrence Martin (an author), November 1, 1937. *Education:* Northwestern University, B.S., 1934. *Politics:* Liberal. *Home:* 1864 Sherman Ave., Evanston, Ill. 60201. *Agent:* David M. Clay, 7 Peter Cooper Rd., New York, N.Y. 10010.

CAREER: Christian Century, Chicago, Ill., assistant editor, 1935-37; Society for Cultural Relations with Latin America, New York, N.Y., editor, 1937; full-time professional writer. Joint correspondent with husband in South America for *Chicago Times* (now *Sun-Times*), during 1940's; did free-lance editorial work for McGraw-Hill Book Co., Inc. and New American Library during the 1960's.

WRITINGS: You Meet Them in Mexico, Rutgers University Press, 1948; *Standard Guide to Mexico and the Caribbean*, Funk, 1954; *I, Madame Tussaud* (novel), Harper, 1956; (with husband, Lawrence Martin) *England: An Uncommon Guide*, McGraw, 1963; (with L. Martin) *Paris: An Uncommon Guide*, McGraw, 1963; (with L. Martin) *Switzerland: An Uncommon Guide*, McGraw, 1965; (with L. Martin) *Europe: The Grand Tour*, McGraw, 1967; (with L. Martin) *Enjoying Europe*, McGraw, 1975. Author of about 250 magazine articles, alone and in collaboration with her husband.

WORK IN PROGRESS: An historical novel.

MARTINS, Wilson 1921-

PERSONAL: Born March 3, 1921, in Sao Paulo, Brazil; son of Himelino and Raquel (Tomaselli) Martins; married Anna Schmidt, September 7, 1943. Education: University of Parana, law degree, 1943, Ph.D., 1952. Home: 1 Washington Square Village, New York, N.Y. 10012. Office: New York University, New York, N.Y. 10003.

CAREER: Estado de Sao Paulo (newspaper), Sao Paulo, Brazil, literary critic; New York University, New York, N.Y., professor, 1965—. Member: Hispania Society of America, American Association of Teachers of Spanish and Portuguese, Pi Delta Phi, Phi Lambda Beta. Awards, honors: Governador do Estado Prize (Sao Paulo), for A Critica Literaria no Brasil.

WRITINGS: Interpretacoes (literary criticism), Livraria Jose Olympio Editora, 1947; Introducao a Democracia Brasileira, Editora Globo, 1951; A Critica Literaria no Basil, Department of Culture (Sao Paulo), 1952; Un Brasil Diferente, Editora Anhembi, 1955; Codigo de Processo Penal, Editora Anhembi, 1956; A Palavra Escrita (history of the book, printing, and libraries), Editora Anhembi, 1957; A Literatura Brasileira, Volume VI, O Modernismo, Editora Cultrix, 1965; (with Seymour Mention) Teatro Brasileiro Contemporaneo, Appleton, 1966.

Contributor: (Author of preface) Dostoevski, Nietotchka Niezvanova, Livraria Jose Olympio Editora, 1947; Afranio Coutinho, editor, A Literatura no Brasil, Volume I, Editorial Sul-Americana, 1956; Joaquim de Montezuma de Carvalho, editor, Panorama das Literaturas das Americas, Municipio de Nova Lisboa, 1958; Bernice Slote, editor, Literature and Society, University of Nebraska Press, 1964.

Translator into Portuguese: Claude Levi-Strauss, Tristes Tropiques, Editora Anhembi, 1957; also translator of several volumes by Guy de Maupassant.

Contributor to The Theatre Annual, Western Reserve University Press, 1964, Enciclopedia Barsa, Diccionario de la Literatura Latinoamericana, Diccionario de Literatura Brasileira, and to journals in Brazil, Germany, Spain, and United States.

WORK IN PROGRESS: Pontos de Vista, a collection of his essays of literary criticism since 1939, expected to run to at least twenty volumes; an intellectual history of Brazil.

*   *   *

MARVIN, John T. 1906-
(Charles Richards)

PERSONAL: Born January 2, 1906, in Chicago, Ill.; son of Charles Richards (an insurance executive) and Valerie (Tilton) Marvin; married Bertha German, August 18, 1930; children: Valerie (Mrs. W. Stanley Walch). Education: Case Institute of Technology (now Case Western Reserve University), B.S., 1929, M.S. in Chem.Eng., 1935. Politics: Republican. Home: 3 Blythewood Rd., Doylestown, Pa. 18901.

CAREER: General Motors Corp., Dayton, Ohio, patent attorney, 1937-66; now retired. Judges all terriers at American Kennel Club shows throughout the United States. Member: West Highland White Terrier Club of America (past president), Dog Writers' Association of America (president, 1973—) American Fox Terrier Club (president, 1972—), Dayton Patent Law Association, Alpha Chi Sigma, Alpha Sigma Phi. Awards, honors: Honorable mention, Dog Writers' Association of America, for The Com-

plete Book of Dog Tales, 1963, and The Book of All Terriers, 1965; best article awards from Dog Writers' Association of America, 1966, 1973, and 1974; Gaines Award for dogdom's writer of the year, 1973.

WRITINGS: The Complete West Highland White Terrier, Howell Book, 1961, new edition, 1965, 3rd edition, 1971; The Complete Book of Dog Tales, Howell Book, 1961; The Book of All Terriers, Howell Book, 1964; The Book of the Scottish Terrier, Howell Book, 1967; The Complete Cairn Terrier, Howell Book, 1974. Under pseudonym Charles Richards, regular dog columnist, Dayton Daily News, 1946-66.

SIDELIGHTS: Marvin has traveled extensively in the United States and British Isles accumulating data on dogs, and has assembled an extensive cynological library.

*   *   *

MASON, Philip (Parker) 1927-

PERSONAL: Born April 28, 1927, in Salem, Mass.; son of Homer Philip and Mildred (Trask) Mason; married Henrietta Dow, June 16, 1951; children: Catherine, Susan, Steven, Jonathan, Christopher. Education: Boston University, B.A., 1950; University of Michigan, M.A., 1951, Ph.D., 1956. Religion: Unitarian Universalist. Home: 27 Maplefield Rd., Pleasant Ridge, Mich. 48069. Office: Wayne State University, Detroit, Mich. 48202.

CAREER: Michigan State Archives, Lansing, director, 1953-58; Wayne State University, Detroit, Mich., professor of history and university archivist, 1958—, director of archives of labor history and urban affairs, 1959—. Detroit Historical Society, trustee and historian, 1963—. Military service: U.S. Naval Reserve, 1945-46. Member: American Historical Association, Organization of American Historians, American Association for State and Local History, Society of American Archivists (executive secretary, 1963-68; president, 1970-71; fellow), Historical Society of Michigan (president, 1965-66), Prismatic Club.

WRITINGS: (Editor) Schoolcraft's Expedition to Lake Itasca: The Discovery of the Source of the Mississippi, Michigan State University Press, 1958; (with Paul J. Pentecost) From Bull Run to Appomattox: Michigan's Role in the Civil War, Wayne State University Press, 1961; (editor) Schoolcraft's Literary Voyager or Muzzeniengun, Michigan State University Press, 1962; (with Frank B. Woodford) Harper of Detroit: Origin and Growth of a Great Metropolitan Hospital, Wayne State University Press, 1964; Detroit, Fort Lernoult and the American Revolution, Wayne State University Press, 1964; A History of American Roads, Rand McNally, 1967; Prismatic of Detroit, Edwards Brothers, 1970. Editor, Detroit in Perspective.

*   *   *

MASSELINK, Ben 1919-
(George Toliver)

PERSONAL: Born November 13, 1919, in Grand Rapids, Mich.; son of Benjamin H. and Gertrude (Beyer) Masselink; married Jo Cassatt February 17, 1946 (divorced); married Dionyse Humphrey, August, 1969. Education: DePauw University, student, 1937-40. Politics: Democrat. Religion: Protestant. Home: 633 Radcliffe Ave., Pacific Palisades, Calif. 90272. Agent: Diarmuid Russell, Russell & Volkening, Inc., 551 Fifth Ave., New York, N.Y. 10017.

CAREER: Laborer and tile setter's helper before becoming

full-time writer. *Military service:* U.S. Marine Corps, 1941-45; served in Marshall Islands and Okinawa; became sergeant and combat correspondent. *Member:* Authors Guild of the Authors League of America, Writers Guild of America. *Awards, honors: TV Guide Award* for best show of year, 1964, for "Tyger, Tyger," on "Dr. Kildare" show.

WRITINGS: Partly Submerged, Methuen, 1957; *The Crackerjack Marines,* Little, Brown, 1959; *The Danger Islands,* Little, Brown, 1964; *The Deadliest Weapon,* Little, Brown, 1965; *Green,* Little, Brown, 1967. Television writer, including scripts for "Slattery's People," "Man's World," "Chrysler Theatre," "Dr. Kildare," "Marcus Welby, M.D.," "Barnaby Jones," "The Wonderful World of Disney," and "Nichols." Contributor of humorous articles to *Saturday Evening Post, Ladies' Home Journal, Collier's, Cosmopolitan,* and other popular magazines, and under pseudonym George Toliver, to *TV Guide.*

WORK IN PROGRESS: A travel book, *The Barefoot Book;* a novel, *The Story Tellers;* television and movie scripts.

AVOCATIONAL INTERESTS: Travel, people, and the sea.

*   *   *

MATHER, Kirtley F(letcher) 1888-

PERSONAL: Surname rhymes with "rather"; born February 13, 1888, in Chicago, Ill.; son of William Green (a railroad ticket agent) and Julia (King) Mather; married Marie Porter, June 12, 1912 (died September 17, 1971); children: Florence (Mrs. Sherman A. Wengerd), Julia (Mrs. Leroy G. Seils), Jean (Mrs. Dean W. Seibel). *Education:* Denison University, B.Sc., 1909; University of Chicago, Ph.D., 1915. *Politics:* Independent. *Religion:* Baptist. *Home:* 1044 Stanford Dr., N.E., Albuquerque, N.M. 87106.

CAREER: University of Arkansas, Fayetteville, instructor, 1911-12, assistant professor of geology, 1912-14; Queen's University at Kingston, Kingston, Ontario, Canada, associate professor of geology, 1915-17, professor of paleontology, 1917-18; Denison University, Granville, Ohio, professor of geology, 1918-24; Harvard University, Cambridge, Mass., associate professor of physiography, 1924-27, professor of geology, 1927-54, professor emeritus, 1954—. University of Chicago, fellow, 1914-15; Phi Beta Kappa visiting scholar, 1960-61; Danforth lecturer, 1961-62. U.S. Geological Survey, geologist, 1910-45; Richmond Levering and Co., field geologist in Bolivia, 1919-20; attended International Geological Congresses in England, Algeria, Mexico, Denmark, and India, between 1948-64. Educational Research Corp., president, 1946-53; Foundation for Integrative Education, president, 1946-69. Mcgraw-Hill, Inc., consulting editor, 1950-66; Scientific Book Club, Inc., chairman of editorial board, 1930-46; Nonfiction Book Club, judge, 1946-48. National Council of Young Men's Christian Associations, president, 1947-49. Civil Liberties Union of Massachusetts, chairman, 1946-49. Newton (Mass.) School Committee, member, 1927-34; Boston Center for Adult Education, president, 1930-36; Curry College, trustee, 1913—; Newton Community Forum, chairman, 1936-41. *Military service:* U.S. Army, Engineer Officers Reserve Corps, 1919-27; became captain.

MEMBER: American Association for the Advancement of Science (fellow; president, 1951), American Academy of Arts and Sciences (fellow; president, 1957-61), Geological Society of America (fellow), Royal Geographical Society

(fellow), American Association of Petroleum Geologists, American Geophysical Union, Oliver Wendell Holmes Association (president, 1962-70), Phi Beta Kappa, Sigma Xi. *Awards, honors:* Sc.D., Denison University, 1929, Colby College, 1936; Litt.D., Union College, 1942; L.H.D., Bates College, 1943; LL.D., Beloit College, 1949; D.Sc. of Oratory, Curry College, 1966. Abraham T. Alper Award of Civil Liberties Union of Massachusetts; Cullum Medal of American Geographical Society; Bradford Washburn Medal of Boston Museum of Science; Thomas Alva Edison Foundation award for best book on science for young people, 1964, for *The Earth Beneath Us.*

WRITINGS: Old Mother Earth, Harvard University Press, 1927; *Science in Search of God,* Holt, 1928; *Sons of the Earth,* Norton, 1931; (with Dorothy Hewitt) *Adult Education: A Dynamic for Democracy,* Appleton, 1937; (with Shirley L. Mason) *A Source Book in Geology,* McGraw, 1939, reprinted, Hafner, 1964, published as *A Source Book in Geology: 1400-1900,* Harvard University Press, 1970; *Enough and to Spare,* Harper, 1944; *Crusade for Life,* University of North Carolina Press, 1949; (contributor) Harlow Shapley, editor, *Science Ponders Religion,* Appleton, 1960; *The World in Which We Live,* Pilgrim Press, 1961; *The Earth Beneath Us,* Random House, 1964, revised edition, 1975; (contributor) Jerry R. Tompkins, editor, *D-Days in Dayton: Reflections on the Scopes Trial,* Louisiana State University Press, 1965; *Source Book in Geology: 1900-1950,* Harvard University Press, 1967. Editor of Appleton's "Earth Science" series, 1934-65. Contributor to *Atlantic Monthly, Forum,* and other popular and scientific periodicals. Editor, "Scientist's Bookshelf," *American Scientist,* 1945-54; member of book committee, Phi Beta Kappa's *Key Reporter,* 1950-75.

WORK IN PROGRESS: A "somewhat philosophical book," tentatively titled *The Permissive Universe.*

SIDELIGHTS: Mather was an expert witness for the defense in the Scopes evolution trial in Dayton, 1925. In addition to travels abroad for International Geological Congresses, he attended meetings of the World Alliance of Young Men's Christian Associations in Switzerland, Denmark, France, and Germany, 1948-57, and meetings of the World University Service in Turkey, England, India, and Netherlands, 1953-57.

*   *   *

MATHEW, Ray(mond Frank) 1929-

PERSONAL: Born April 14, 1929, in Sydney, Australia; son of Frank Leslie James (a laborer) and Lily Elizabeth Ann (Latta) Mathew. *Education:* Attended Sydney Teachers College, 1947-49. *Religion:* Atheist. *Home:* (permanent address) 75 Jessel House, Judd St., London W.C. 1, England; (temporary address) Via San Tommaso, Praiano, Salerno, Italy.

CAREER: Teacher in small schools in New South Wales, Australia, 1949-51; free-lance journalist in Australia, 1951-52; Commonwealth Scientific and Industrial Research Organization, Sydney, Australia, accounts officer, 1952-54; University of Sydney, Sydney, lecturer to Workers' Educational Association and tutor, during 1955-60; Arts Council of Great Britain, bursar for drama, 1960-61; has worked at interim jobs, including barman, language teacher, and typist, 1961—; professional writer. *Awards, honors:* Commonwealth Literary Fund grant for first two books of verse and first two collections of stories; Commonwealth literary fellowship, 1958.

WRITINGS: With Cypress Pine (verse), Lyre-Bird Writers, 1951; *Song and Dance* (verse), Lyre-Bird Writers, 1956; *A Bohemian Affair* (short stories), Angus & Robertson, 1961; *A Spring Song* (play), Queensland University Press, 1961; *South of the Equator* (verse), Angus & Robertson, 1961; *Miles Franklin* (criticism), Lansdowne Press, 1963; (with Mena Abdullah) *The Time of the Peacock* (stories), Angus & Robertson, 1965, Roy, 1968; *Charles Blackman's Painting*, Georgian House, 1965; *The Joys of Possession* (novel), Chapman & Hall, 1967; (with J. McKinney and S. Locke Elliot) *Khaki, Bush and Bigotry: Three Australian Plays*, University of Minnesota Press, 1968. Writer of plays produced in Australia, Scotland, and England. Works anthologized in Australia and England. Former contributor of book, theater, and art reviews to newspapers and literary journals in Australia; also contributor to *State, London Magazine*, and *Transatlantic Reveiw*, all England.

WORK IN PROGRESS: A play, tentatively titled "To Lie Alone," for Australian Elizabethan Theatre Trust.

SIDELIGHTS: Mathew told *CA:* "Visits to Paris, Italy, Greece have seemed important. Place is important in my work. Books that have influenced me most spectacularly (as a person, I'm not so sure as a writer) include works by Shaw, Austen, Forster, Chaucer, Tolstoy, Dostoevski, Chekov, Freud, Brigid Brophy's *Black Ship to Hell*, Rimbaud, Verlaine, Miles Franklin, Eve Langley, Shakespeare, Byron, Coleridge, and Joseph Furphy. I read French, German (vaguely), speak and read Italian."

BIOGRAPHICAL/CRITICAL SOURCES: Times Literary Supplement, March 9, 1967.†

* * *

MATHEWS, Donald G. 1932-

PERSONAL: Born April 15, 1932, in Caldwell, Idaho; son of Leo C. (a teacher) and Ruth (Baker) Mathews; married Jane Dehart (now a university professor), August 23, 1959. *Education:* College of Idaho, B.A., 1954; Yale University, B.D., 1957; Duke University, Ph.D., 1962. *Politics:* Independent. *Religion:* Calvinist. *Office:* Department of History, University of North Carolina, Chapel Hill, N.C. 27514.

CAREER: Duke University, Durham, N.C., instructor in history, 1961-62; Princeton University, Princeton N.J., instructor, 1962-65, assistant professor of history, 1965-68; University of North Carolina, Chapel Hill, associate professor, 1968-73, professor of history, 1973—. *Member:* American Historical Association, Organization of American Historians, Southern Historical Association.

WRITINGS: Slavery and Methodism: A Chapter in American Morality 1780-1840, Princeton University Press, 1965; (contributor) M. B. Duberman, editor, *The Antislavery Vanguard: New Essays on the Abolitionists*, Princeton University Press, 1965; (editor) *Agitation for Freedom: The Abolitionist Movement*, Wiley, 1971. Contributor to *Journal of American History, Journal of Southern History, American Quarterly, South Atlantic Quarterly, Mid-America*.

WORK IN PROGRESS: A book on religion and community in the South from the Great Awakening through Reconstruction; research for an analysis of the Southern clergy as a strategic elite, 1780-1880.

* * *

MATHIAS, Peter 1928-

PERSONAL: Born January 10, 1928; son of John Samuel and Marion (Love) Mathias; married Elizabeth Ann Blackmore, April 5, 1958; children: Samuel, Henry, Sophie. *Education:* Jesus College, Cambridge, B.A. and M.A., 1951; Harvard University, graduate study at Research Center in Entrepreneurial History, 1952-53. *Office:* All Souls College, Oxford University, Oxford, England.

CAREER: Cambridge University, Cambridge, England, research fellow of Jesus College, 1953-55, fellow and director of studies in history of Queen's College, 1955-68, tutor, 1957-65, assistant lecturer on history faculty, 1955-60, lecturer, 1960-68; Oxford University, Oxford, England, Chichele Professor of Economic History, and fellow of All Souls College, 1969—. Visiting professor at University of Toronto, 1961, School of Advanced Studies, Delhi, India, 1966, University of Pennsylvania, 1972; Virginia Gildersleeve Professor, Barnard College, 1972. Governor, Solihill School, 1966-72, Abbey School, 1969—. *Military service:* British Army, National Service, 1946-48. *Member:* Economic History Society (member of council; treasurer, 1967—), International Economic History Association (secretary, 1959-62; president, 1974—), Social Science Research Council (chairman of economic and social history committee, 1974—), Business Archives Council (chairman, 1967-72).

WRITINGS: The Brewing Industry in England, 1700-1830, Cambridge University Press, 1959; *English Trade Tokens: The Industrial Revolution Illustrated*, Abelard, 1962; *Retailing Revolution*, Longmans, Green, 1967; *The First Industrial Nation: An Economic History of Britain, 1700-1914*, Methuen, 1969, Scribner, 1970; (editor with A. W. Pearsall) *Shipping: A Survey of Historical Records*, David & Charles, 1971; (with Theodore C. Cardwell and Roy H. Campbell) *Business History*, 2nd edition, Historical Association (London), 1971; (editor and contributor) *Science and Society, 1600-1900*, Cambridge University Press, 1972. Contributor to *Economic History Review*. Assistant editor, *Economic History Review*, 1955-57; general editor, *Cambridge Economic History of Europe*, Cambridge University Press, and *Debates in Economic History*, Methuen.

WORK IN PROGRESS: An economic and social history of England in the eighteenth century, for Longman; research on the historical perspective of economic growth.

* * *

MAURER, David W. 1906-

PERSONAL: Born April 12, 1906, in Wellston, Ohio; son of Joseph C. (a cutter) and Erma (Warren) Maurer; married Barbara Starbuck (now a teacher), June 6, 1937; children: Joann. *Education:* Ohio State University, B.A., 1928, M.A., 1929, Ph.D., 1935; postdoctoral study at University of Michigan, 1937, and National University of Mexico, 1954. *Home:* 4124 Nachand Lane, Louisville, Ky. 40218.

CAREER: Golden Basin Mining Corp., Tinton, S.D., junior geologist, 1926-27; General Seafoods Corp., research at sea, 1929—; Ohio State University, Columbus, instructor, 1930-35; University of Louisville, Louisville, Ky., 1935-73, began as assistant professor, became professor of language and literature, professor emeritus, 1973—. Visiting Fulbright professor of linguistics, University of Muenster, 1955-56, and University of Rome, summer, 1956; visiting lecturer at several institutes in Germany, 1956. Joseph E. Seagram and Sons, Inc., Louisville, consultant to management, 1941-50; Southern Police Institute, Louisville, staff lecturer on narcotic drugs, 1953-63. *Member:* Linguistic Society of America, Modern Language

Association of America, American Studies Association, American Dialect Society (president, 1966-70), American Academy of Political and Social Science, American Association of University Professors.

WRITINGS: The Big Con: The American Confidence Man and the Confidence Game, Bobbs-Merrill, 1940, revised edition, New American Library, 1963; (with Victor Vogel) *Narcotics and Narcotic Addiction*, C. C Thomas, 1954, 4th edition, 1974; *Whiz-Mob: A Correlation of the Argot of Professional Pickpockets with Their Behavior Pattern*, University of Alabama Press for American Dialect Society, 1955, trade edition, College and University Press, 1964; (with Raven I. McDavid) *H. L. Mencken's The American Language, a One-Volume Abridgement and Modernization*, Knopf, 1964; *Kentucky Moonshine*, University Press of Kentucky, 1974; *The American Confidence Man*, C. C Thomas, 1974.

Author of a number of monographs on the argot of the racetrack, the moonshiner, the dice gambler, the prostitute, and other underworld and specialized groups; portions of his work on slang have been included in a dozen books by others, including *The American Thesaurus of Slang*, Crowell, 1942, Eric Partridge's *A Dictionary of the Underworld, British and American*, Macmillan, 1950, and *English as a Language*, Harcourt, 1961.

Writings include three television documentaries, "Fugue in High Octane," 1959, "Soup-Up," 1959, and "Squealyworm," 1960; several U.S. Public Health Service publications; over one hundred professional articles and papers published in America, Germany, and Italy; feature articles and book reviews in newspapers, magazines, and journals. Member of editorial board, American Dialect Society.

WORK IN PROGRESS: With Raven, I. McDavid, *The American Idiom*; an autobiographical book on the values encountered and the way of life discovered in exploring criminal sub-cultures in America, Latin America, and Europe; *Patterns of Professional Crime: A Study of the Culture Pattern of Several Well-Defined Sub-Cultures.*

* * *

MAYBURY-LEWIS, David H(enry) P(eter) 1929-

PERSONAL: Born May 5, 1929, in Hyderabad, Pakistan; son of Sydney Alan (an engineer) and Constance (Hambleton) Maybury-Lewis; married Elsebet Helga Henningsen, April 6, 1953; children: Biorn, Anthony, Jacqueline. *Education:* Attended King's School, Centerbury, England, 1942-47; Trinity Hall, Cambridge, B.A., 1952, M.A., 1956; Oxford University, M.A., 1956, D.Phil., 1960; University of Sao Paulo, M.Sc., 1956. *Home:* 30 Bowdoin St., Cambridge, Mass. *Office:* Department of Anthropology, Harvard University, Cambridge, Mass.

CAREER: University of Sao Paulo, Sao Paulo, Brazil, research fellow in anthropology, 1954-56; Horniman research fellow in Brazil and Great Britain, 1957-59; Harvard University, Cambridge, Mass., instructor, 1960-61, assistant professor, 1961-66, associate professor, 1966-69, professor of anthropology, 1969—, acting chairman of department, 1971, chairman of department, 1973—. Did field work with the Sherente of central Brazil, 1955-56, and with the Shavante of central Brazil, 1957-58, revisiting both areas 1962, 1963, 1964, with Elites of Pernambuco, Brazil, 1970-72. Consultant, Ford Foundation, Brazil, 1968—. *Military service:* British Army, West Yorkshire Regiment, 1947-49; became second lieutenant. *Member:* Royal Anthropological

Institute (fellow), Association of Social Anthropologists (fellow), American Anthropological Association (fellow), Latin American Studies Association (fellow).

WRITINGS: The Savage and the Innocent, World Publishing, 1965; *Akwe-Shavante Society*, Clarendon Press, 1966.

WORK IN PROGRESS: Structuralism, Social Theory, Relationship Systems; Indians of Central Brazil; and *Social Change and Development in Brazil.*

SIDELIGHTS: Maybury-Lewis told *CA:* "Study of languages and literature led me to an interest in the discovery and settlement of Latin America, thence to anthropology." He speaks French, German, Spanish, Russian, Danish, and the languages of the Shavante and Sherente Indians of Brazil. He reads Italian, Dutch, Norwegian, and Swedish.

Maybury-Lewis is president of Cultural Survival, a charitable foundation devoted to assisting small, relatively isolated societies threatened by the effects of economic development.

* * *

MAYHALL, Jane 1921-

PERSONAL: Born May 10, 1921, in Louisville, Ky.; daughter of Howard Wesley and Loula (Bennett) Mayhall; married Leslie Katz, 1940. *Education:* Attended Black Mountain College, three years, New School for Social Research, two years, Middlebury (Vt.) Music School, summer session, and Claremont (Calif.) College, summer session. *Home:* 50 Remsen St., Brooklyn, N.Y.

CAREER: Taught at New School for Social Research, New York, N.Y., one year; writer in residence at various times, at Yaddo Foundation and McDowell Colony; lecturer and novel consultant at Writers Workshop, Morehead State College, 1960, 1962. *Awards, honors:* Fletcher Pratt prose fellowship, Breadloaf School of English, 1958.

WRITINGS: Cousin to Human, Harcourt, 1960; *Ready for the Ha-Ha*, Eakins Press, 1966. Short stories included in *The Prize Stories, 1973: The O. Henry Awards*, Doubleday, 1973; *Bitches and Sad Ladies*, edited by Pat Rotter, Harper's Magazine Press, 1975. Contributor of articles, poems, and short stories to *Modern Language Quarterly, Antioch Review, Botteghe Oscure, Quarterly Review of Literature, Chelsea Review, Partisan Review, Nation*, and other periodicals. Author of verse drama, "Eclogue," produced by Poets' Company, 1954. Translator, with Otto Guth, of opera libretto, "Die Kluege," for San Francisco Opera Co.

WORK IN PROGRESS: A book on American women writers, from Colonial times to the present, biographical and critical for Macmillan; a book of feminist short stories.

AVOCATIONAL INTERESTS: Music, singing, and composition.

* * *

MAYHEW, David R(aymond) 1937-

PERSONAL: Born May 18, 1937, in Putnam, Conn.; son of Raymond W. and Jeanie (Nicholson) Mayhew. *Education:* Amherst College, B.A., 1958; Harvard University, Ph.D., 1964. *Home:* 123 York St., New Haven, Conn. 06511. *Office:* Department of Political Science, Yale University, New Haven, Conn. 06520.

CAREER: University of Massachusetts, Amherst, instructor, 1963-64, assistant professor of government, 1964-67;

Yale University, New Haven, Conn., assistant professor, 1968-72, associate professor of political science, 1972—. Congressional fellow, American Political Science Association, 1967-68. *Member:* American Political Science Association.

WRITINGS: Party Loyalty Among Congressmen: The Difference Between Democrats and Republicans, 1947-1962, Harvard University Press, 1966; *Congress: The Electoral Connection*, Yale University Press, 1974.

* * *

MAYO, William L. 1931-

PERSONAL: Born May 31, 1931. *Education:* University of Michigan, B.A., 1953, M.A., 1954, M.A., 1959, Ph.D., 1964. *Address:* (Permanent) P.O. Box 1, Ann Arbor, Mich. *Office:* Department of Education, Curry College, Milton, Mass. 02189.

CAREER: Curry College, Milton, Mass., professor and chairman, department of education, 1965—. *Member:* Association of American Geographers, Royal Geographical Society (fellow; U.S. representative), Royal Canadian Geographical Society.

WRITINGS: The Development and Status of Secondary School Geography in the United States and Canada, University Publishers, 1965.†

* * *

MAYSHARK, Cyrus 1926-

PERSONAL: Born August 3, 1926, in Atlantic City, N.J.; son of Casimir and Jessie Clark (Whitney) Mayshark; married Barbara Anne Fisher (a registered nurse), September 12, 1947; children: Gail, Pamela Mayshark Chambers, Lee, Linda, Laura. *Education:* Williams College, B.A., 1949; Boston University, M.Ed., 1952; Indiana University, H.S.D., 1954; Harvard University, M.S.Hyg., 1962. *Home:* 6 Belaire Ct., Champaign, Ill. 61820. *Office:* University of Illinois, Champaign, Ill.

CAREER: Young Men's Christian Association, Boston, Mass., physical director, 1949-52; National Foundation for Infantile Paralysis, state representative for Maine, New Hampshire, and Vermont, 1954-57; Oregon State University, Corvallis, assistant professor, 1957-61, associate professor of hygiene and health education, 1962-65; University of Tennessee, Knoxville, professor and chairman of health education, 1965-68, associate dean of College of Education, 1968-72; University of Texas, El Paso, dean of College of Education, 1972-74; University of Illinois, Champaign, dean of College of Physical Education, 1974—. Visiting summer professor at Colorado State College (now North Colorado State University), 1960, University of Southern California, 1964. National Commission on Community Health Services, process analyst, 1963-65; Oregon School Curriculum Development Committee, member, 1959-65. *Military service:* U.S. Army, Paratroops, 1944-46; became staff sergeant.

MEMBER: American School Health Association (fellow), American Association for Health, Physical Education and Recreation (fellow; executive council member, 1965-68; vice-president, 1969-70), American Public Health Association (fellow; vice-chairman of school health section, 1965-67), American Association for the Advancement of Science, American Association of Higher Education, Society of Public Health Educators, Phi Delta Kappa. *Awards, honors:* U.S. Office of Education research grant, 1966-67;

outstanding teacher and research award, University of Tennessee, 1969.

WRITINGS: The Corvallis, Oregon, School Health Program: A Case Study, privately printed, 1963; (with R. L. Covey) *School Health Service Administration, Eugene, Oregon: A Case Study*, Oregon State University Press, 1963; (contributor) *Synthesis of Research in Selected Areas of Health Instruction*, National Education Association, 1963; (with Leslie W. Irwin) *Health Education in Secondary Schools*, Mosby, 1964, 3rd edition with Roy A. Foster, 1972; (with Foster) *Methods in Health Education—A Workbook Using the Critical Incident Technique*, Mosby, 1966; (with Donald D. Shaw) *The Administration of School Health Programs: Its Theory and Practice*, Mosby, 1967; (with Robert Kirk and Robert Hornsby) *Personal Health in Ecologic Perspective*, Mosby, 1972. Co-author of test manual for Anderson and Langston's *Health Principles and Practice*, 3rd edition, Mosby, 1961. Weekly health columnist, *Corvallis Gazette Times*, 1957-59. Contributor of articles to journals. Editor, Oregon Public Health Association *Newsletter*, 1960-61; member of editorial board, Oregon Association for Health, Physical Education and Recreation, 1962-65.

WORK IN PROGRESS: Second edition of *Administration of School Health Programs*; fourth edition of *Health Education in Secondary Schools*.

* * *

MAZZEO, Joseph Anthony 1923-

PERSONAL: Surname is prounced Mat-*say*-o; born June 25, 1923, in New York, N.Y.; son of Joseph and Lia (Soraci) Mazzeo; married Lucy Welch, May 8, 1948. *Education:* Columbia University, A.B., 1946, A.M., 1947, Ph.D., 1950; University of Florence, graduate study, 1948-49. *Office:* Department of English, Columbia University, New York, N.Y. 10027.

CAREER: Hunter College, New York, N.Y., lecturer in English, 1947-48; Columbia University, New York, N.Y., instructor, 1949-53, assistant professor of English and comparative literature, 1953-55; Cornell University, Ithaca, N.Y., assistant professor, 1955-59, professor of English and Italian literature, 1959-60; Columbia University, professor of comparative literature, 1960—, Parr Professor of English and comparative literature, 1972—. *Military service:* U.S. Army, 1943-46; U.S. Army Reserve, became second lieutenant; received Bronze Star. *Member:* Modern Language Association of America, Comparative Literature Association, Renaissance Society of America. *Awards, honors:* American Council of Learned Societies fellow in Italy, 1948-49; American Philosophical Society grant, 1954; Guggenheim fellow, 1959; Gold Medal of Dante Society of Florence, 1959.

WRITINGS: Structure and Thought in the Paradiso, Cornell University Press, 1958; *Medieval Cultural Tradition in Dante's Comedy*, Cornell University Press, 1960; (editor) *Reason and the Imagination*, Columbia University Press, 1962; *Renaissance and 17th Century Studies*, Columbia University Press, 1964; *Renaissance and Revolution*, Pantheon, 1965; *The Design of Life: Major Themes in the Development of Biological Thought*, Pantheon, 1967; *Medieval Culture Tradition in Dante's Comedy*, Greenwood Press, 1968.

WORK IN PROGRESS: Essays in science and the Literary imagination; studies in the theory and practice of interpretation.

SIDELIGHTS: Joseph Anthony Mazzeo speaks French and Italian, reads Latin, Greek, and German. *Avocational interests:* Biology.

* * *

McARTHUR, Edwin Douglas 1907-

PERSONAL: Born September 24, 1907, in Denver, Colo.; son of William Wesley (a minister) and Anna Louise (Price) McArthur; married Blanche Victoria Pope, March 4, 1930. *Education:* Attended public schools in Denver, Colo.; studied at the Juilliard Foundation, and privately with Josef and Rosine Lhevinne. *Agent:* Harold Ober Associates, Inc., 40 East 49th St., New York, N.Y. 10017.

CAREER: St. Louis Municipal Theatre Association, St. Louis, Mo., musical director, 1945-67; Harrisburg Symphony Orchestra, Harrisburg, Pa., musical director and conductor, 1950-74; Saint Paul Opera Association, St. Paul, Minn., conductor, 1969—. Accompanist to Kirsten Flagstad, Elisabeth Rethberg, Gladys Swarthout, John Charles Thomas, Maria Jeritza, Ezio Pinza, and other singers; composer of songs, and the score of the musical play, "Rip Van Winkle." *Member:* Lotos Club and Dutch Treat Club (both New York). *Awards, honors:* D. Mus., Elizabethtown College, Elizabethtown, Pa; D. Mus., University of Denver.

WRITINGS: Flagstad: A Personal Memoir, Knopf, 1965.

WORK IN PROGRESS: Fifty Years of Life in Music.

AVOCATIONAL INTERESTS: Bridge, golf.

* * *

McBATH, James Harvey 1922-

PERSONAL: Born October 24, 1922, in Watertown, S.D.; son of Earl A. (a city official) and Edna (Harvey) McBath; married Jean Bloomquist, July 6, 1963. *Education:* Northwestern University, B.S., 1947, M.A., 1948, Ph.D., 1950; Institute of Historical Research, University of London, post doctoral work, 1952-53. *Religion:* Methodist. *Office:* Department of Speech Communication, University of Southern California, Los Angeles, Calif. 90007.

CAREER: Assistant professor of speech at University of New Mexico, Albuquerque, 1950-52, University of Iowa, Iowa City, 1953-54, and in University of Maryland Overseas Program in France, England, Germany, and Middle East, 1954-56; University of Southern California, Los Angeles, assistant professor, 1956-57, associate professor, 1957-63, professor of speech communication, 1963—, department chairman, 1965—, member of advisory committee for academic programmes abroad, 1973—. *Military service:* U.S. Army Air Forces, 1943-46; became sergeant. *Member:* Speech Communication Association, American Forensic Association (president, 1960-62), American Association of University Professors, Western Speech Association (president, 1968-69), Delta Sigma Rho-Tau Kappa Alpha (president, 1969-72).

WRITINGS: (With Milton Dickens) *Guidebook for Speech Practice*, Harcourt, 1961; (editor) *Argumentation and Debate*, Holt, 1963; (editor) *British Public Addresses, 1828-1960*, Houghton, 1971; (with Milton Dickens) *Guidebook for Speech Communication*, Harcourt, 1973; (editor) *A Study of New Directions for Forensic Education*, National Textbook Co., 1975. Editor, *Journal of the American Forensic Association*; associate editor, *Quarterly Journal of Speech.*

McBRIDE, Richard William 1928-

PERSONAL: Born May 8, 1928, in Washington, Ind.; son of John Graham and Marie (Jones) McBride; married Betty Joan Kostal, 1953; children: Sean David, Brennan Robert Shem. *Education:* Studied at Radio Drama Workshop, Milwaukee, Wis., Paducah Junior College, and Eastern Illinois University; Hastings College, Hastings, Neb., B.A., 1958. *Politics:* "Sometimes." *Religion:* "Life." *Home and office:* Old Dean Farm, Singleborough, Buckinghamshire, England.

CAREER: Announcer and scriptwriter for radio stations in Kentucky, Illinois, and Nebraska, 1948-58; Metro-Goldwyn-Mayer, San Francisco, Calif., file clerk, 1953-54; City Lights Books, San Francisco, business manager, 1966—; McBride Brothers & Bradley Ltd. (book distributors), Singleborough, Buckinghamshire, England, managing director, 1969—. Bookseller in San Francisco, 1952, and London, 1964. *Awards, honors:* Second prize, Maxwell Anderson verse play competition.

WRITINGS: Oranges (poetry), Bread and Wine, 1959; *Ballads of Blood* (poetry), Golden Mountain, c. 1960; *Lonely the Autumn Bird* (fiction), A. Swallow, 1963; *Memoirs of a Natural-Born Expatriate* (fiction), A. Swallow, 1966. Author of four plays produced in San Francisco little theaters; also author of column, "The Village Green," in *Hastings Daily Tribune*, 1973—. Contributor of poetry and fiction to little literary magazines.

* * *

McBRIEN, Richard P(eter) 1936-

PERSONAL: Born August 19, 1936, in Hartford, Conn.; son of Thomas Henry and Catherine (Botticelli) McBrien. *Education:* St. Thomas Seminary, Bloomfield, Conn., A.A., 1956; St. John Seminary, Brighton, Mass., B.A., 1958, M.A., 1962; Gregorian University, Rome, Italy, S.T.L., 1964, S.T.D., 1965. *Politics:* Independent. *Home:* 16 Fairmont Ave., Newton, Mass. 02158. *Office:* Department of Theology, Boston College, Chestnut Hill, Mass. 02167.

CAREER: Roman Catholic priest. Assistant pastor in West Haven, Conn., and Newman chaplain at Southern Connecticut State College, New Haven, 1962-63; Loyola University of Chicago, Rome Campus, Rome, Italy, lecturer in theology, 1965-65; Pope John XXIII National Seminary, Weston, Mass., member of theology faculty, 1965-74; Boston College, Chestnut Hill, Mass., professor of theology, 1970—. *Member:* Catholic Theological Society of America (president, 1973-74).

WRITINGS: The Church in the Thought of Bishop John Robinson, Westminster, 1966; *Do We Need the Church?*, Harper, 1969; *What Do We Really Believe?*, Pflaum, 1969; *Church: The Continuing Quest*, Newman, 1970; *Who Is a Catholic?*, Dimension, 1971; *For the Inquiring Catholic*, Dimension, 1973; *The Remaking of the Church*, Harper, 1973; *Has the Church Surrendered?*, Dimension, 1974. Writer of weekly theology column syndicated in the *Catholic Transcript*; contributor of essays to *Commonweal, America, Theological Studies*, and many other journals.

SIDELIGHTS: Richard McBrien reads Latin, French, German, Italian, and Spanish, and has some background knowledge of Hebrew and Greek.

* * *

McBURNEY, James H(oward) 1905-

PERSONAL: Born June 19, 1905, in Tyndall, S.D.; son of

William M. (a merchant) and Martha (Miller) McBurney; married Florence Beckwith, June 17, 1929 (died May, 1963); married Helen Mary Knauth, June, 1969; children: (first marriage) James William, Margaret Jean (Mrs. Robert Rardin), Martha Elizabeth. *Education:* Yankton College, A.B., 1925; University of South Dakota, M.A., 1929; University of Michigan, Ph.D., 1935; Columbia University, postdoctoral study, 1935-36. *Home:* 116 Meadowlark Dr., Tryon, N.C. 28782.

CAREER: High school teacher in Nebraska and Iowa, 1925-28; instructor in speech at University of South Dakota, Vermillion, 1928-29, University of Michigan, Ann Arbor, 1929-34; Columbia University, New York, N.Y., assistant professor of speech, 1936; Northwestern University, Evanston, Ill., associate professor, 1936-41, professor of speech, 1941-73, dean of School of Speech, 1942-73. Director and moderator of Mutual Broadcasting System radio forum, "Reviewing Stand," and of television forum, "Your Right to Say It," WGN-TV, Chicago, and WPIX-TV, New York. *Member:* Speech Association of America (president, 1949), Phi Beta Kappa, Delta Sigma Rho, Lambda Chi Alpha, University Club (Evanston). *Awards, honors:* Litt.D., Yankton College, 1962.

WRITINGS: (With J. M. O'Neill) *The Working Principles of Arguments,* Macmillan, 1932; (with Kenneth G. Hance) *The Principles and Methods of Discussion,* Harper, 1939, revised edition published as *Discussion in Human Affairs,* 1950; (with others) *The Foundations of Speech,* Prentice-Hall, 1941; (with Lew Sarett and W. T. Foster) *Speech* (high school course), Houghton, 1943; (with O'Neill and Glen E. Mills) *Argumentation and Debate: Techniques of a Free Society,* Macmillan, 1951, 2nd edition (with Mills), 1964; (with Ernest J. Wrage) *The Art of Good Speech,* Prentice-Hall, 1953; (with Wrage) *Guide to Good Speech,* Prentice-Hall, 1955, 4th edition, 1975.†

* * *

McCABE, Joseph E. 1912-

PERSONAL: Born April 23, 1912, in Bridgeville, Pa.; son of John S. and Rebecca (Fife) McCabe; married Margaret Welch, April 1, 1944; children: Jonathan Brandt, Alice. *Education:* Muskingum College, A.B., 1937; Ohio State University, M.A., 1940; Princeton Theological Seminary, B.Th., 1943, M.Th., 1947; University of Edinburgh, Ph.D., 1951. *Politics:* Republican. *Home:* 163 Thompson Dr. S.E., Cedar Rapids, Iowa 52403.

CAREER: Muskingum College, New Concord, Ohio, admissions counselor, 1938-39; ordained minister in United Presbyterian Church, 1943; minister in Lambertville, N.J., 1946-53; Princeton Theological Seminary, Princeton, N.J., critic of student preaching, 1951-56; Presbyterian Church of Chestnut Hill, Philadelphia, Pa., senior minister, 1953-58; Coe College, Cedar Rapids, Iowa, president, 1958-70, chancellor, 1970— . Member of national advisory panel for U.S. Air Force Reserve Officers Training Corps, of committee on admissions, College Entrance Examination Board, and of Fulbright Selection Committee, Iowa. Trustee of Princeton Theological Seminary, and Herbert Hoover Presidential Library. Member of board of directors, Cedar Rapids Chamber of Commerce. *Military service:* U.S. Naval Reserve, chaplain, 1943-46. *Member:* Presbyterian College Union (president, 1965-66), Independent Colleges of of Iowa (chairman of legislative committee). *Awards, honors:* D.D., Muskingum College, 1957; LL.D., Monmouth College, 1959; L.H.D., Waynesburg College, 1965, Litt.D., College of St. Thomas, 1966.

WRITINGS: The Power of God in a Parish Program, Westminster, 1959; *Service Book for Ministers,* McGraw, 1961; *Challenging Careers in the Church,* McGraw, 1965; *Your First Year at College,* Westminster Press, 1967; *Reason, Faith, and Love,* Parthenon Press, 1972; *Better Preaching, Better Pastoring,* Westminster Press, 1973. Also author of *Slander and Vindication,* 1974. Contributor to *Saturday Review* and to church publications.

* * *

McCALL, Daniel F(rancis) 1918-

PERSONAL: Born March 3, 1918, in Westfield, Mass.; son of Daniel and Margaret (Sweeny) McCall; married Martha Anton, May 12, 1946; children: Peter, Judith. *Education:* Boston University, B.A., 1949; Columbia University, Ph.D., 1955. *Office:* Department of Anthropology and History, Boston University, Boston, Mass. 02215.

CAREER: University of Liberia, Monrovia, professor of history and social sciences, 1953; Boston University, Boston, Mass., 1954—, began as research associate, African Research Program, became professor of anthropology and history, African Studies Center. Visiting lecturer, University College of Ghana, 1960-61. *Military service:* U.S. Coast Guard, 1941-46; received Commendation Medal. *Member:* American Anthropological Association, American Historical Association, American Society for Ethnohistory, African Studies Association, International African Institute. *Awards, honors:* Social Science Research Council fellow, 1952; Rockefeller Foundation grant, 1963-64.

WRITINGS: Africa in Time-Perspective, Oxford University Press, 1964; *A Report on African Materials and Activities in Some European Institutions* [Boston], 1967; (editor with Norman R. Bennett and Jeffrey Butler) *Eastern African History,* Praeger, 1969; (editor with Bennett and Butler) *Western African History,* Praeger, 1969; *Wolf Courts Girl: The Equivalence of Hunting and Mating in Bushman Thought* (booklet), Center for International Studies, Ohio University, 1970; (editor with Bennett) *Aspects of West African Islam,* African Studies Center, Boston University, 1971; (editor with Edna Bay) *African Images: Essays in African Iconology,* Holmes & Meier, 1974.

WORK IN PROGRESS: A history of Africa, not yet titled; a historical novel on West Africa.

SIDELIGHTS: McCall speaks Twi (West African), French, and some German; he reads French, Spanish, Italian, Portuguese, German, Dutch, and Spanish ("the latter two rather slightly"), and a little Russian.†

* * *

McCARTHY, Agnes 1933-

PERSONAL: Born June 20, 1933, in New York, N.Y.; daughter of Daniel Charles and Agnes (Blandford) McCarthy; married Harold L. Wise (an educational consultant), September 4, 1965; children: Daniel. *Education:* Catholic University of America, A.B., 1954; State University of New York, M.A., 1973. *Residence:* Woodstock, N.Y. *Agent:* McIntosh & Otis, Inc., 18 East 41st St., New York, N.Y. 10017.

CAREER: Elementary teacher in Casper, Wyo., 1956-58; Scholastic Magazines, New York, N.Y., coordinating editor, 1960-62; Harcourt, Brace & World, Inc., New York, N.Y., language text editor, 1962-64; American Education Publications, Middletown, Conn., professional materials editor, 1964-65; center for the study of Instruction, San Francisco, Calif., research associate, 1965-71; free-lance writer and editor of books for young people.

WRITINGS: Let'o Go to Vote, Putnam, 1961; *Let's Go to a Court*, Putnam, 1962; *Giant Animals of Long Ago*, Prentice-Hall, 1963; *Creatures of the Deep*, Prentice-Hall, 1963; *New York State: Its Land and People*, Doubleday, 1963; (with Lawrence Reddick) *Worth Fighting For: A Story of the Negro in the Civil War*, Zenith Books, 1965; *Room 10* (juvenile fiction), Doubleday, 1966; *The Impossibles* (juvenile fiction), Doubleday, 1968; (with M. Winslow and A. Djibo) *Expression: Black Americans*, Harcourt, 1971; *The Lost Truck* (juvenile fiction), Silver-Burdett, 1973; *Elementary Language Arts*, General Learning Corp., in press. Contributor of articles and short stories to elementary school publications.

Editor: *Language for Daily Use*, Book 5, Harcourt, 1965; *The Picture Story of Cape Cod*, Scrimshaw, 1965; *Around Cape Cod with Cap'n Goody*, Scrimshaw, 1965; *Cape Cod Seashore Life*, Scrimshaw, 1966.

WORK IN PROGRESS: Research on education for the future.

*   *   *

McCARTY, Clifford   1929-

PERSONAL: Born June 13, 1929, in Los Angeles, Calif.; son of Ernest Clifford and Florence (Anderson) McCarty; married Maxine Reich, July 21, 1955; children: Elizabeth Anne, Nora Ellen, John Henry. *Education:* California State College (now University), B.A., 1952. *Politics:* Democrat. *Home:* 3018 Manning Ave., Los Angeles, Calif., 90064. *Office:* Boulevard Bookshop, 10634 West Pico Blvd., Los Angeles, Calif. 90064.

CAREER: Pickwick Bookshop, Hollywood, Calif., salesman, 1953-57; Yellow Cab Co., Los Angeles, Calif., driver, 1958; Boulevard Bookshop, Los Angeles, Calif., owner and manager, 1958—.

WRITINGS: Film Composers in America: A Checklist of Their Work, John Valentine, 1953; (contributor) Frederic W. Grunfeld, editor, *Music and Recordings, 1955*, Oxford University Press, 1955; *Bogey: The Films of Humphrey Bogart*, Citadel, 1965; (contributor) William F. Nolan, *Dashiell Hammett: A Casebook*, McNally & Loftin, 1969; (with Tony Thomas and Rudy Behlmer) *The Films of Errol Flynn*, Citadel, 1969; *Published Screen plays: A Checklist*, Kent State University Press, 1971; (with Gene Reinggold) *The Films of Frank Sinatra*, Citadel, 1971; (contributor) Rudy Behlmer, editor, *Memo from David O. Selznick*, Viking, 1972; (contributor) Tony Thomas, *Music for the Movies*, A. S. Barnes, 1973. Contributor to *Films in Review, Screen Facts*, and other periodicals.

WORK IN PROGRESS: A revision and enlargement of *Film Composers in America.*

*   *   *

McCLEARY, Robert A(ltwig)   1923-

PERSONAL: Born January 9, 1923, in Dayton, Ohio; son of Harold (a machinist) and Cora Mae (Altwig) McCleary; married Nan S. Brown, February 4, 1945; children: Robert, Beverly, Susan. *Education:* Harvard University, B.A., 1944; Johns Hopkins University, M.D., 1947, Ph.D., 1951. *Home:* 5715 Kenwood Ave., Chicago, Ill. 60637. *Office:* Department of Psychology, University of Chicago, Chicago, Ill. 60637.

CAREER: Johns Hopkins University, Baltimore, Md., instructor in psychology, 1950-51; University of Michigan, Ann Arbor, assistant professor, 1953-57, associate professor, 1957-61; University of Chicago, Chicago, Ill., professor of psychology and physiology, 1961—. Consultant to U.S. Air Force, 1959—, and National Institutes of Health, 1961-66. *Military service:* U.S. Air Force, medical officer, 1951-53; became captain. *Member:* American Psychological Association, Psychonomic Society, Society of Experimental Psychologists. *Awards, honors:* U.S. Public Health Service fellow, 1954-55; National Institutes of Health fellow, 1956-57; Carnegie special research fellow at University of Oslo, 1957-58.

WRITINGS: (With R. Y. Moore) *Subcortical Mechanisms of Behavior*, Basic Books, 1965; (contributor) *Progress in Physiological Psychology*, Academic Press, 1966; (editor) *Genetic and Experimental Factors in Perception: Research and Commentary*, Scott, Foresman, 1970. Contributor of research articles to *Journal of Comparative and Physiological Psychology*, 1953—.

AVOCATIONAL INTERESTS: Science illustrating, amateur theatricals.†

*   *   *

McCONKEY, James (Rodney)   1921-

PERSONAL: Born September 2, 1921, in Lakewood, Ohio; son of Clayton Delano and Grace (Baird) McConkey; married Gladys Voorhees, 1944; children: Lawrence Clark, John Crispin, James Clayton. *Education:* Cleveland College, B.A., 1943; Western Reserve University (now Case Western Reserve University), M.A., 1946; State University of Iowa, Ph.D., 1953. *Address:* R.D. 1, Trumansburg, N.Y. *Office:* c/o Department of English, Cornell University, Ithaca, N.Y.

CAREER: Cleveland College, Cleveland, Ohio, teaching fellow, 1945-46; State University of Iowa, Iowa City, teaching assistant, 1949-50; Morehead State College, Morehead, Ky., began as assistant professor, became associate professor, 1950-56; Cornell University, Ithaca, N.Y., began as assistant professor, associate professor, 1956-62, professor of English, 1962—. Morehead Writer's Workshop, director, 1951-56; Antioch Seminar in Writing and Publishing, Yellow Springs, Ohio, director, 1957-60. *Wartime service:* U.S. Army Infantry, 1943-45; became corporal. *Member:* Modern Language Association, American Association of University Professors, Authors Guild, P.E.N., Book and Bowl Club.

WRITINGS: The Novels of E. M. Forster, Cornell University Press, 1957; (editor) *The Structure of Prose*, Harcourt, 1963; *Night Stand*, Cornell University Press, 1965; *Crossroads: An Autobiographical Novel*, Dutton, 1968; *A Journey to Sahalin* (novel), Coward, 1971. Editor, *Kentucky Writing, I and II*, Morehead State College, 1954, 1956. Contributor of stories and essays to *Atlantic, Western Review, Yale Review, New Yorker*, and other periodicals.

SIDELIGHTS: Reviewing *Crossroads*, Walter Sullivan writes "His aim is to show what it is to be a humanist, and he achieves a book of singular quality—one which is deeply moving and starkly honest, page after page."

*   *   *

McCORMICK, John O(wen)   1918-

PERSONAL: Born September 20, 1918, in Thief River Falls, Minn.; son of Owen C. and Antoinette (Smith)

McCormick; married Mairi Clare MacInnes (a poet, novelist, and editor), February 4, 1954; children: (prior marriage) Jonathan C.; (current marriage) Peter R., Antoinette, Fergus. *Education:* University of Minnesota, B.A. (magna cum laude), 1941; Harvard University, M.A., 1947, Ph.D., 1951. *Politics:* "Disgruntled socialist-democrat." *Religion:* Roman Catholic. *Home:* 158 Terhune Rd., Princeton, N.J. 08540. *Office:* Department of Comparative Literature, Livingston College, Rutgers University, New Brunswick, N.J.

CAREER: Salzburg Seminar in American Studies, Salzburg, Austria, lecturer and dean, 1951-52; Free University of Berlin, Berlin, Germany, lecturer, 1952-53; lecturer and free-lance writer in London, England, 1953-54; Free University of Berlin, professor and director of Amerika-Institut, 1954-59; Rutgers University, New Brunswick, N.J., professor of comparative literature, 1959—. Bruern fellow, University of Leeds, 1975-76. Editorial consultant to Capricorn Books (Macmillan), New York, 1964—. *Military service:* U.S. Naval Reserve, 1941-46; became lieutenant senior grade. *Member:* International Comparative Literature Association, Modern Language Association of America, Harvard Club (New York). *Awards, honors:* Longview Foundation award in nonfiction, 1961, for "The Frozen Country." published in *Kenyon Review*; Guggenheim fellowship, 1964-65.

WRITINGS: Catastrophe and Imagination: A Study of the Recent Novel in England and America, Longmans, Green, 1957; *Amerikanisch Lyrik der letzen funfzig Jahre*, Vandenhoeck & Ruprecht, 1957; *Der moderne amerikanische Roman*, Vandenhoeck & Ruprecht, 1960; (editor with wife, Mairi MacInnes, and joint author of linking passages) *Versions of Censorship* (anthology), Aldine, 1962; (with Mario Sevilla Mascarenas) *The Complete Aficionado*, World Publishing, 1966; *The Middle Distance: A Comparative History of American Imaginative Literature: 1919-1932,* Free Press, 1971; *Fiction as Knowledge*, Rutgers University Press, 1975.

Writer of various radio scripts for British Broadcasting Corp. and Sender Freies Berlin. Contributor of articles, reviews, and translations to journals, including *Kenyon Review, Commentary, Books and Bookmen* (London), *Poetry,* and *Libertinage* (Amsterdam).

WORK IN PROGRESS: A book on the relationship between nationalism and aesthetic judgment, completion expected in 1977.

* * *

McCORMICK, Scott, Jr. 1929-

PERSONAL: Born June 4, 1929, in Evanston, Ill.; son of Scott (a realtor) and Emma (Knuchell) McCormick; married Mary Helen McLeod, June 2, 1956; children: Jane Hoyt, Scott III, Donald Alexander. *Education:* Davis and Elkins College, B.A., 1953; Union Theological Seminary, Richmond, Va., B.D., 1956, Th.M., 1957, Th.D., 1959. *Home:* 1120 Pleasant St., Hastings, Neb. *Office:* Department of Religion, Hastings College, Hastings, Neb.

CAREER: Ordained minister of United Presbyterian Church in the U.S.A., 1956; minister in Radford, Va., 1958-65; Washington and Jefferson College, Washington, Pa., associate professor of religion, 1965-70; Hastings College, Hastings, Neb., associate professor of religion, 1970—; golf coach. Drive chairman of United Fund of Radford (Va.), 1960, chairman of board of directors, 1962-64; organizing chairman of Radford Council on Human Relations, 1963, educational chairman, 1964-65; member of in-

ternational study commissions, world Council of Churches, 1967-71; chairman Human Relations Commission of Washington, 1969-70; member of National Council of Churches' study commission on the eucharist, 1970-72. *Member:* Society of Biblical Literature.

WRITINGS: (Contributor) *The Unsilent South*, edited by D. W. Shriver, Jr., John Knox, 1965; *The Lord's Supper: A Biblical Interpretation*, Westminster, 1966; (contributor) *A New Song*, United Church Press, 1969. Compiler of index for *Interpretation*, Volumes I-X, 1947-56; contributor of articles to *Interpretation, Topic*, and devotional publications.

WORK IN PROGRESS: Baptism in the New Testament; preaching as an act of remembrance.

SIDELIGHTS: Scott McCormick, Jr. is competent in Greek, Hebrew, and German.

* * *

McCRACKEN, George E(nglert) 1904-

PERSONAL: Born February 6, 1904, in Dunmore, Pa.; son of Samuel (a banker) and Phebe (Englert) McCracken; married Emily Elizabeth Swettman, December 20, 1934; children: Samuel, Elizabeth Wrede. *Education:* Princeton University, A.B., 1926, A.M., 1932, Ph.D., 1933; Lafayette College, A.M., 1928; American Academy in Rome, F.A.A.R., 1931; postdoctoral study at University of Michigan, 1940, and Boston University, 1953. *Religion:* Presbyterian. *Home:* 1232 39th St., Des Moines, Iowa 50311.

CAREER: Lafayette College, Easton, Pa., instructor in Latin, 1926-29; Grove City College, Grove City Pa., instructor in Greek and German, 1933-34; Susquehanna University, Selinsgrove, Pa., assistant professor of Greek and Latin, 1934-35; Otterbein College, Westerville, Ohio, Flickinger Professor of Classics, 1935-46; Drake University, Des Moines, Iowa, associate professor, 1946-48, professor of classics, 1948-74, professor emeritus, 1974—. University of Texas, visiting professor, 1963-64. *Military service:* U.S. Army, Signal Corps, 1942-46; became captain. U.S. Army Reserve, 1946-62; retired with rank of lieutenant colonel. *Member:* American Society of Genealogists (fellow), New England Historic Genealogical Society, Iowa Foreign Language Association (past president), Iowa Genealogical Society, Genealogical Society of Pennsylvania, Harleian Society.

WRITINGS: A History of Ancient Tusculum, American Documentation Institute, 1938; (editor and translator) *Arnobius of Sicca Veneria*, two volumes, Newman, 1949; (editor and translator) *Early Medieval Theology*, Westminster, 1957; (editor and translator) St. Augustine, *City of God*, Volume I, Harvard University Press, 1957; (editor) *McFarland of Siam*, Vantage, 1958; *The Welcome Claimants, Proved, Disproved and Doubtful*, Genealogical Publishing, 1970; *The Commodores Kinsmen, A Study of the Bainbridge Family*, privately printed, 1975. Editor and publisher, *The American Genealogist*, 1966—.

SIDELIGHTS: George McCracken knows Latin, Greek, French, German, Italian and Spanish.

* * *

McCROSSON, Doris Ross 1923-

PERSONAL: Born February 13, 1923, in Berkeley, Calif.; daughter of John Thomas and Edith (Begg) McCrosson. *Education:* University of Pennsylvania, B.A., 1949, A.M., 1951, Ph.D., 1959. *Home:* Fayetteville, Pa.

CAREER: Worked in Yokohawa, Japan, 1952-53; University of Missouri, Columbia, instructor in English, 1954-56; Shippensburg State College, Shippensburg, Pa., assistant professor, 1958-60, associate professor, 1960-61, professor 1961-62; Wilson College, Chambersburg, Pa., associate professor of English, 1962—. Member of Equal Education Opportunity Task Force and consultant, Pennsylvania Department of Education, 1973; co-chairperson, Insurance Commissioner's Task Force on Women's Insurance Problems, 1973—. *Military service:* U.S. Navy, WAVES, 1943-45. *Member:* Modern·Language Association of American, National Council of Teachers of English, American Association of University Professors, National Association for the Advancement of Colored People.

WRITINGS: Walter de la Mare, Twayne, 1966.

WORK IN PROGRESS: Black Pennsylvania; Uncle, poems.

*   *   *

McCURDY, Harold Grier   1909-

PERSONAL: Born May 30, 1909, in Salisbury, N.C.; son of McKinnon Grier (a merchant) and Nellie (Curd) McCurdy; married Mary Burton Derrickson, September 15, 1937; children: John Derrickson, Ann Lewis. *Education:* Duke University, A.B., 1930, Ph.D., 1938. *Politics:* Democrat. *Religion:* Methodist. *Home:* Gooseneck Rd., Chapel Hill, N.C. 27514.

CAREER: Milligan College, Milligan College, Tenn., professor of psychology, 1938-41; Meredith College, Raleigh, N.C., associate professor, 1941-46, professor of psychology and philosophy, 1946-48; University of North Carolina, Chapel Hill, associate professor, 1948-55, professor, 1955-63, Kenan Professor of Psychology, 1963-71, professor emeritus, 1971—. *Member:* American Psychological Association, American Association for the Advancement of Science, Elisha Mitchell Scientific Society (president, 1962-63), Phi Beta Kappa, Sigma Xi.

WRITINGS: A Straw Flute (poems), Meredith College Press, 1946; *The Personality of Shakespeare,* Yale University Press, 1953; *The Personal World,* Harcourt, 1961; *Personality and Science,* Van Nostrand, 1965; (editor with Helen Follet) *Barbara, The Unconscious Autobiography of a Child Genius,* University of North Carolina Press, 1966; (contributor) Benjamin B. Wolman, *Historical Roots of Contemporary Psychology,* Harper, 1968; (contributor) Thomas A. Langford and William H. Poteat, editors, *Intellect and Hope: Essays in the Thought of Michael Polanyi,* Duke University Press, 1968; *The Chastening of Narcissus* (poems), Blair, 1970. Contributor to *International Encyclopedia of the Social Sciences,* and to journals in his field.

WORK IN PROGRESS: A book of poems, *Liliana and the Castle*; a manuscript on the application of mathematical analysis to literature, dreams, and human experience in general.

SIDELIGHTS: Harold McCurdy told *CA*: "Psychology has been for me a point of union, not entirely satisfactory, between science and poetry.... Think that science itself suffers when it sets itself resolutely against poetry, especially in psychology, and I am sure that our Western culture as a whole is endangered by the anti-poetry engendered by science. With my limited capacities I work toward a reconciliation." McCurdy can read French, German, Latin, and Greek.

McDERMOTT, Beatrice Schmulling

PERSONAL: Born in Hoboken, N.J.; daughter of Harry Louis (a city commissioner) Georgine (Alberts) Schmulling; married Cyril L. McDermott September 25, 1954 (deceased); married Russell S. Hume (a stockbroker), October 7, 1972. *Education:* College of New Rochelle, B.A.; Fordham University, LL.B., 1950. *Religion:* Roman Catholic. *Home:* 160 Henry St., Brooklyn, N.Y.

CAREER: Admitted to New York bar, 1951. Dwight, Harris, Koegel & Caskey, New York, N.Y., law librarian, 1937-42; Dewey, Ballantine, Bushby, Palmer & Wood, New York, N.Y., law librarian, 1942-73. American Red Cross, Hoboken, N.J. branch, in charge of prisoner of war division, 1943-45. *Member:* American Association of Law Libraries, Special Libraries Association, Association of Law Libraries of Upstate New York, Law Library Association of Greater New York (president, 1951-52) *Awards, honors:* Joseph L. Andrews Bibliographical Award, 1968, for *Government Regulation of Business, Including Antitrust.*

WRITINGS: (Member of editorial board) *Manual of Procedures for Private Law Libraries,* Rothman, for American Association of Law Libraries, 1962; (with Freada A. Coleman) *Government Regulation of Business, Including Antitrust,* Gale, 1966; (contributor) Richard Sloane, editor, *Recommended Law Books,* American Asoociation of Law Libraries, 1969.

*   *   *

McDERMOTT, Sister Maria Concepta   1913-

PERSONAL: Born April 1, 1913, in Dubuque, Iowa; daughter of John Charles and Mary Agnes (O'Connell) McDermott. *Education:* Attended Fordham University, 1932-35, Manhattan College, 1935-39, Dunbarton College, 1939-42; St. Mary's College, Notre Dame, Ind., B.A., 1943; Catholic University of America, M.A., 1948; University of Notre Dame, Ph.D., 1964. *Home and office:* St. Mary's College, Notre Dame, Ind. 46617.

CAREER: Roman Catholic nun of Holy Cross order (C.S.C.); teacher of French, English, and education at parochial schools in New York, N.Y., 1931-39, Washington, D.C., 1941-51, Danville, Ill., 1951-54; dean of studies at Catholic high schools in Hammond, Ind., 1955, Michigan City, Ind., 1955-58; St. Mary's College, Notre Dame, Ind., dean of women, 1958-61, dean of Graduate School, 1964-66, professor of education, 1966—. Participant in Carnegie Foundation-sponsored National Study of Catholic Education and in State of Indiana Project English; midwest regional representative of Glasser Institute of Reality Therapy. *Member:* National Catholic Education Association, National Education Association, History of Education Society, National Council of Teachers of French, National Council of Teachers of English, National Council of Secondary School Principals, National Council of Secondary School Supervisors, Council for Exceptional Children, Indiana State Teachers Association.

WRITINGS: The Making of a Sister-Teacher, University of Notre Dame Press, 1965. Contributor to educational journals. Editor, *Vineyard* (regional newspaper of educational activities of Holy Cross order).

WORK IN PROGRESS: Units in English for Gifted Students, grades 7-9; other writing on history of education.

McDONALD, William U(lma), Jr. 1927-

PERSONAL: Born June 10, 1927, in Meridian, Miss. Education: University of Alabama, B.A., 1947, M.A., 1949; Northwestern University, Ph.D., 1956. Office: University of Toledo, Toledo, Ohio 43606.

CAREER: Alabama Journal, Montgomery, reporter, 1947-48; Auburn University, Auburn, Ala., instructor in English, 1949-52; University of Toledo, Toledo, Ohio, instructor in English, 1955-57, assistant professor, 1957-61, associate professor, 1961-66, professor of English and associate chairman of department, 1966—, director of freshman English, 1968—. Member: Modern Language Association of America, National Council of Teachers of English (director, 1963-65), Conference on College Composition and Communication, Midwest Modern Language Association, English Association of Northwestern Ohio (executive secretary, 1962-63; president, 1963-64), Phi Beta Kappa, Phi Kappa Phi.

WRITINGS: (With James D. Barry) Language into Literature, Science Research Associates, 1965. Contributor to Encyclopedia of World Literature in the Twentieth Century, Romance Notes, Studies in Short Fiction, Comparative Literature, Composition and Communication, and other journals.

WORK IN PROGRESS: Bibliographic and textual studies of Eudora Welty's writings.

* * *

McDONNELL, Robert F. 1928-

PERSONAL: Born January 6, 1928, in Velva, N.D.; son of Joseph Patrick (a businessman) and Dora (Auerbach) McDonnell; married Joan Fortune, December 30, 1952; children: Margaret, Robert K., Patricia, Leigh, Aileen, Stephanie, Daniel, Nora. Education: St. John's University, Collegeville, Minn., B.A., 1951; University of Vienna, student, 1950-51; University of Minnesota, M.A., 1954, Ph.D., 1958. Politics: Democrat. Religion: Roman Catholic. Home: 612 Patricia Dr., San Luis Obispo, Calif. Office: California Polytechnic State University, San Luis Obispo, Calif.

CAREER: Iowa State University, Ames, instructor in English, 1952-53; Ohio University, Athens, instructor, 1957-59, assistant professor, 1959-64, associate professor of English, 1964-67, director of freshman English, 1959-62, director of undergraduate English, 1965-67; Western Washington State College, Bellingham, professor of English and chairman of department, 1967-75; California Polytechnic State University, San Luis Obispo, professor of English and head of department, 1975—. Director, University of Portland Institute of European Studies program in Salzburg, Austria, 1964-65; member of advisory council, Danforth graduate fellowship program, 1969-74; member of Washington State Commission for the Humanities, 1974-75. Military service: U.S. Army Air Forces, 1946-48. Member: Modern Language Association of America, Shakespeare Association of America, American Association of University Professors (president of Ohio University chapter, 1962-63; state council of Ohio, vice-president, 1963-64, president, 1964-65).

WRITINGS—Editor: (With William E. Morris) Modern America Through Foreign Eyes, Heath, 1959; (with Morris and Richard Lettis) Stephen Crane, The Red Badge of Courage: Text and Criticism, Harcourt, 1960; (with Morris) Form and Focus, Harcourt, 1961; (with Morris and

Lettis) Huck Finn and His Critics, Macmillan, 1962; (with G. B. Harrison) King Lear: Text Sources and Criticism, Harcourt, 1962; (with Morris) Form and Focus Three, Harcourt, in press. Contributor of articles and reviews to journals. Consulting editor, Concerning Poetry, 1968-75.

* * *

McELROY, John Alexander 1913-

PERSONAL: Born December 28, 1913, in Philadelphia, Pa.; son of Thomas Charles (an accountant) and Greta (Hanna) McElroy; married Mary Grace Shorter; children: Barbara, Ruth, Andra. Education: Dickinson College, Carlisle, Pa., A.B., 1935, D.D., 1951; Drew Theological Seminary, B.D., 1938; Temple University, S.T.M., 1947. Home: 11 Elm St., Newton, N.J.

CAREER: Ordained to Methodist ministry, 1938; pastor of churches in Philadelphia Annual Conference, 1938-58; pastor in East Orange, N.J., 1959-68; superintendent of Western District of Northern New Jersey Conference of the United Methodist Church, 1968-74; pastor in Newton, N.J., 1974—. Former trustee of Methodist Hospital, Philadelphia, Pa. Trustee, Drew University.

WRITINGS: Living With the Seven Words, Abingdon, 1961.

* * *

McELROY, Joseph 1930-

PERSONAL: Born August 21, 1930, in Brooklyn, N.Y.; son of Joseph Prince and Louise (Lawrence) McElroy; married Joan Leftwich (a designer), August 16, 1961; children: Hanna. Education: Williams College, B.A., 1951; Columbia University, M.A., 1952, Ph.D., 1961. Home: 121 Madison Ave., New York, N.Y. Agent: Georges Borchardt, 145 East 52nd St., New York, N.Y. 10022.

CAREER: Instructor or assistant professor with English department at University of New Hampshire, 1956-62; Queen's College of the City University of New York, Flushing, N.Y., professor of English, 1964—. Visiting professor at Johns Hopkins University. Awards, honors: Grants from Rockefeller Foundation, Ingram Merrill Foundation, and National Endowment for the Arts. Military service: U.S. Coast Guard, 1952-54.

WRITINGS—All novels: A Smuggler's Bible, Harcourt, 1966; Hind's Kidnap, Harper, 1969; Ancient History, Knopf, 1971, Lookout Cartridge, Knopf, 1974. Contributor to New Leader, Saturday Review, Art International, New American Review, and New York Times Book Review. Contributing editor, Tri-Quarterly.

WORK IN PROGRESS: Two novels, Plus, and Women and Men; a play, Marais.

BIOGRAPHICAL/CRITICAL SOURCES: Carolyn Riley, editor, Contemporary Literary Criticism, Volume V, Gale, 1976.

* * *

McEVOY, Harry K(irby) 1910-
(Kirby Mack)

PERSONAL: Born May 14, 1910, in Oak Park, Ill.; son of Harry K. and Louise (Cavey) McEvoy; married Marie Estelle Wright, September 25, 1943; children: Thomas, Stephen, Alan, Marcia. Education: Attended University of Illinois, 1928-31. Politics: Republican. Religion: Protestant. Home and office: 2155 Tremont Blvd., Grand Rapids, Mich. 49504.

CAREER: Salesman, 1939—; Tru-Balance Knife Co. (hand-crafted knives for hunting, throwing, and combat), Grand Rapids, Mich., owner, 1949—; *Military service:* U.S. Army Air Forces, 1942-45; became sergeant. *Member:* Company of Military Historians, Masons, Grand Valley Cap 'n' Ballers (Grand Rapids).

WRITINGS: Archery Today, Broadhead Publishing Co., 1937; (with Chas. V Gruzanski) *Knife Throwing as a Modern Sport,* C. C Thomas, 1965; *Knife Throwing: A Practical Guide,* Tuttle, 1973. Wrote archery adventure serial for *American Bowman-Review,* under pseudonym Kirby Mack, 1938-39. Contributor of articles to *Saga, Gunsport,* and other periodicals. Feature editor, *The Muzzle Loader,* 1974—.

AVOCATIONAL INTERESTS: Competitive rifle shooting (muzzle loaders), archery, knife throwing, fishing.

* * *

McFADDEN, Dorothy Loa 1902-

PERSONAL: Born June 11, 1902, in Frankfurt, Germany; daughter of Paul (a businessman) and Loa Brown (Kennan) Mausolff; married James Lyman McFadden (a manufacturer of equipment for chemists), May 12, 1923; children: James Alfred, Jean Loa (Mrs. William D. Arbus). *Politics:* Republican. *Religion:* Presbyterian.

CAREER: Junior Programs, Inc. (touring professional theater for children, playing coast to coast), New York, N.Y., president and executive director, 1936-43; WRGB-TV, Schenectady, N.Y., staff member and producer, 1944; *New York Times,* New York, N.Y., director of Boys' and Girls' Book Fairs, 1947-57; writer and lecturer on gardens and travel. *Member:* Listen-to-me Club of the Oranges, Scribblers (Morristown, N.J.), Morris-Photocolor Club (Morristown), Horticultural Society of New York, Garden Club of Mendham, Home Garden Club of Morristown.

WRITINGS: Lynn Decker, TV Apprentice, Dodd, 1953; *Growing Up in Puerto Rico,* Silver Burdett, 1958; *Which Way, Judy?,* Dodd, 1958; *History of Basking Ridge Presbyterian Church,* privately printed, 1962; *Touring the Gardens of Europe,* McKay, 1965; *Gardens of Europe: A Pictorial Tour,* A. S. Barnes, 1970. Articles have appeared in *House Beautiful, Popular Gardening, Flower Grower, Yachting, New York Times, New York Herald Tribune,* and other magazines and newspapers.

SIDELIGHTS: Dorothy McFadden told *CA* that her enthusiasms—travel, color photography, and gardens—dovetail with her husband's business, which takes them to Europe for several months every year. Out of these trips come articles, material for travel and garden lectures, and color slides. She speaks German fluently, some French and Spanish.

BIOGRAPHICAL/CRITICAL SOURCES: Morris County's Daily Record (Morristown, N.J.), May 21, 1965.†

* * *

McFADDEN, James A., Jr. 1913-

PERSONAL: Born September 25, 1913, in Philadelphia, Pa.; son of James A. and Elizabeth (Kelly) McFadden; wife deceased; children: Cheryl C. *Education:* University of Pennsylvania, B.S., 1935; New York University, M.S., 1949. *Home:* 151 Mount Lucas Rd., Princeton, N.J. *Office:* Aerospace Group, General Precision, Inc., 1150 McBride Ave., Little Falls, N.J.

CAREER: Certified public accountant, State of Pennsylvania. Robinson Clay Products Co., New York, N.Y., assistant sales manager, 1938-40; Switlik Parachute & Equipment Co., Trenton, N.J., assistant controller, 1940-42; Radio Corporation of America, Princeton, N.J., 1942-62, became administrative director; General Precision, Inc., Aerospace Group, Little Falls, N.J., assistant vice-president, finance, 1962—. *Member:* Controllers Institute of America (director), National Association of Accountants (vice-president), Delaware Accountants Association; Mercantile Literary Association and University Club (both Philadelphia); Nassau Club (Princeton, N.J.), Forsgate Country Club (Jamesburg, N.J.). *Awards, honors:* William L. Lybrand Literary Award of the National Association of Accountants, 1949, 1953, 1956, 1959; LL.D., Rider College, 1960.

WRITINGS: (With Clarence D. Tuska) *Accounting and Tax Aspects of Patents and Research,* Van Nostrand, 1960. Writer of articles for National Association of Accountants and other professional societies.†

* * *

McFARLAN, F. Warren 1937-

PERSONAL: Born October 18, 1937, in Boston Mass.; son of Ronald Lyman (a consultant) and Ethel (White) McFarlan; married second wife Karen Nelson, December 17, 1971; children: Andrew, Clarissa, Elizabeth. *Education:* Harvard University, A.B., 1959, M.B.A., 1961, D.B.A., 1965. *Home:* 37 Beatrice Circle, Belmont, Mass.

CAREER: Harvard University, Business School, Boston, Mass., assistant professor, 1964-69, associate professor, 1969-73, professor of business administration, 1973—. *Military service:* U.S. Army Reserve, 1961-67; became first lieutenant. *Member:* Institute of Management Sciences, American Accounting Association.

WRITINGS: (With John Dearden) *Management Information Systems,* Irwin, 1966; (with Dearden and William Zani) *Managing Computer Based Systems,* Irwin, 1971; (with James McKenney and John Seiler) *The Management Game,* Macmillan, 1971; (with Richard Nolan and David Norton) *Information Systems Administration,* Holt, 1973; (editor with Nolan) *Data Processing Manager's Handbook,* Irwin, 1975.

WORK IN PROGRESS: Management uses of computers; business games.

* * *

McGAHERN, John 1935-

PERSONAL: Born 1935, in Dublin, Ireland; son of Francis and Susan (McManus) McGahern. *Education:* Attended Presentation College, Carrick-on-Shannon, Ireland, and University College, Dublin. *Residence:* Leitrim, Ireland. *Address:* c/o Faber & Faber Ltd., 24 Russell Sq., London W.C. 1, England.

CAREER: Writer. O'Connor Professor of literature, Colgate University, 1969, 1972; British Northern Arts Fellow at University of Newcastle and University of Durham, 1974-76. *Awards, honors:* AE Memorial Award, 1962, for manuscript of *The Barracks;* Macaulay fellowship for prose fiction, 1964; Society of Authors' Award, 1967; British Arts Council Awards, 1968, 1970, 1973.

WRITINGS: The Barracks, Faber, 1963, Macmillan, 1964; *The Dark,* Faber, 1965, Knopf, 1966; *Nightlines,* Faber, 1970, Atlantic, 1971; *The Leavetaking,* Faber, 1974; Atlantic, 1975. Also author of radio play, "Sinclair," 1971, and television play, "Swallows," 1975.

SIDELIGHTS: McGahern's novel, *The Barracks*, was adapted into a two-act play, first produced at Olympia Theatre, Dublin, October 16, 1969.

BIOGRAPHICAL/CRITICAL SOURCES: Carolyn Riley, editor, *Contemporary Literary Criticism*, Volume V, Gale, 1976.

*   *   *

McGILL, Thomas E(merson)   1930-

PERSONAL: Born September 26, 1930, in Sharon, Pa.; son of Emerson Dickson and Margaret (McCallen) McGill; married Nancy Welch, June 14, 1955; children: Michael Howard, Steven Emerson. *Education:* Youngstown University, B.A., 1954; Princeton University, M.A., 1957, Ph.D., 1958; University of Edinburgh, postdoctoral study, 1964-65, 1969-70. *Home:* Green River Rd., Williamstown, Mass. 01267. *Office:* Psychology Department, Williams College, Williamstown, Mass.

CAREER: Williams College, Williamstown, Mass., instructor, 1958-59, assistant professor, 1960-65, associate professor of psychology, 1965-69, Hales professor of psychology, 1969—. U.S. Public Health Service, principal investigator of the behavior of inbred mice project, 1960—. *Member:* American Psychological Association, American Association for the Advancement of Science, Psychonomic Society, Behavior Genetics Association, Animal Behavior Society, Eastern Psychological Association, Sigma Xi. *Awards, honors:* National Academy of Science-National Research Council postdoctoral fellowship at University of Edinburgh, 1964-65.

WRITINGS: (Editor) *Readings in Animal Behavior*, Holt, 1965, 2nd edition, 1973.

WORK IN PROGRESS: Research leading to journal articles.

*   *   *

McGOLDRICK, Desmond Francis   1919-

PERSONAL: Born February 9, 1919, in Clones, County Monaghan, Ireland; son of Patrick (a building contractor) and Catherine (Fay) McGoldrick. *Education:* National University of Ireland, B.A. (honors), 1941; Holy Ghost Missionary College, Dublin, theological study. *Home:* 904 Dundas St., Woodstock, Ontario, Canada.

CAREER: Entered Roman Catholic order, Congregation of the Holy Ghost, 1936; missionary in Kenya, East Africa, 1946-54; member of Holy Ghost Fathers' mission band, preaching throughout Canada and United States, 1954—. Teacher of history, geography, English, and religion at various times and places, including Rockwell College in Ireland, Holy Ghost College in Mangu, East Africa, and St. Mary's School, Nairobi, Kenya.

WRITINGS: Fatima and Devotion to the Immaculate Heart of Mary, Catholic Book Crusade (Patna), 1947; *The Holy Year*, Rafika Yetu Press (Mombasa), 1950; "Duquesne Sister Formation" series, Duquesne University Press, Volume I: *The Martyrdom of Change*, 1961, Volume II: *Holy Restraint*, 1962, Volume III: *Independence Through Submission*, 1964, Volume IV: *Fostering Development*, 1965; *Living the Celibate Life: An Essay in the Higher Psychology of Faith*, Vantage, 1970.

SIDELIGHTS: McGoldrick told *CA* that he is "very inter-

ested in the 'vital stature' of the individual person. The art of living fascinates me. [I am] very critical of the modern psychological hogwash with which we are being saturated. . . . Sifting the meretricious from the true is my favorite delight." He is fluent in Kiswahili and Kikamba (Bantu languages), Gaelic, and reads Greek.†

*   *   *

McGOVERN, James   1923-

PERSONAL: Born December 3, 1923, in New York, N.Y.; son of James Charles and Anna (Leddy) McGovern; married Elizabeth Winslow, 1959; children: James, Elizabeth. *Education:* Harvard University, B.A., 1948. *Agent:* Oliver G. Swan, Julian Bach Literary Agency, Inc., 18 East 48th St., New York, N.Y. 10017.

CAREER: U.S. State Department, Berlin and Frankfurt, Germany, foreign service, 1949-54; Shell Chemical Co., New York, N.Y., worked in advertising department, 1954-57; Batten, Barton, Durstine, and Osborn, Inc., New York, N.Y., copywriter, 1957-59; McCann-Erickson, Inc., New York, N.Y., copywriter, 1959-61; Prentice-Hall, Inc., Trade Book Division, Englewood Cliffs, N.J., editor, 1961-63; Texaco, Inc., New York, N.Y., senior staff writer, 1972—. *Wartime service:* U.S. Army, 1942-46; became technician fifth class.

WRITINGS: Fraeulein, Crown, 1956; *No Ruined Castles*, Putnam, 1957; *The Berlin Couriers*, Abelard, 1960; (translator) Rolf Italiaander, *The New Leaders of Africa*, Prentice-Hall, 1961, *Crossbow and Overcast*, Morrow, 1964; *Martin Borman*, Morrow, 1968; *To the Yalu*, Morrow, 1972.

SIDELIGHTS: In 1953 James McGovern was selected to conduct an investigation into the whereabouts of Martin Borman. After checking out every shred of evidence about Borman's activities, he came to the conclusion that Borman had taken poison on the night of May 1, 1945, when trapped by Russian soldiers in Berlin.

*   *   *

McKELVEY, Blake F.   1903-

PERSONAL: Born June 10, 1903, in Centralia, Pa.; son of Ellis Elmer (a minister) and Eva (Faus) McKelvey; married Jean Trepp (a professor at Cornell University). *Education:* Syracuse University, A.B., 1925; Clark University, M.A., 1929; Harvard University, Ph.D., 1933. *Politics:* Democrat. *Religion:* Protestant. *Home:* 53 Aberthaw Rd., Rochester, N.Y. 14610.

CAREER: Haverhill High School, Haverhill, Mass., instructor in American history, 1926-28; Civilian Works Administration, Harrisburg, Pa., supervisor of local documentary survey, 1933-34; University of Chicago, Ill., researcher in history of Chicago project; *Encyclopaedia Britannica*, New York, N.Y., editorial assistant; Rochester Public Library, Rochester, N.Y., city historian, 1936-73. Chairman of Montgomery Neighborhood Center Board, 1948-53. *Member:* American Historical Association, Society of American Historians, Urban History Group (chairman, 1954-62), New York State Historical Association, Rochester Historical Society (secretary and editor, 1936-50), Genesee Country Historical Federation (secretary-treasurer, 1944-70), Fortnightly Club of Rochester. *Awards, honors:* Fellow, New York Historical Association, 1954, and Rochester Museum of Arts and Sciences, 1958; Rochester Annual Literary Award, 1963.

WRITINGS: American Prisons, University of Chicago Press, 1926; *Rochester: The Water Power City, 1812-1854*, Harvard University Press, 1945; *Rochester: The Flower City, 1855-1890*, Harvard University Press, 1949; *Rochester: The Quest for Quality, 1890-1925*, Harvard University Press, 1956; *Rochester: An Emerging Metropolis, 1925-1961*, Christopher Press, 1961; *The Urbanization of America 1860-1915*, Rutgers University Press, 1963; *The Emergence of Metropolitan America: 1915-1966*, Rutgers University Press, 1968; *The City in American History*, Allen & Unwin, 1969; *American Urbanization: A Comparative History*, Scott, Foresman, 1973; *Rochester on the Genesee: The Growth of a City*, Syracuse University Press, 1973. Editor, *Rochester History*, 1938—.

WORK IN PROGRESS: An updating of *American Prisons.*

* * *

McKENZIE, Robert T(relford) 1917-

PERSONAL: Born September 11, 1917, in Vancouver, British Columbia, Canada; son of William M. (a merchant) and Frances (Chapman) McKenzie. *Education:* University of British Columbia, B.A. (first class honors), 1937; University of London, Ph.D., 1954. *Office:* London School of Economics and Political Science, Houghton St., Aldwych, London W.C. 2, England.

CAREER: University of British Columbia, Vancouver, teacher, 1937-42; London School of Economics and Political Science, University of London, London, England, 1949—, professor of sociology (with special reference to politics), 1964—. Visiting lecturer on politics at Harvard University and Yale University, 1958-59. Regular broadcaster on current politics, British Broadcasting Corp. *Military service:* Canadian Army, 1943-46; became captain. *Member:* Royal Institute of International Affairs, Political Studies Association, British Sociological Association.

WRITINGS: British Political Parties, Heinemann, 1955, revised edition, St. Martin's, 1963; (with Allan Silver) *Angels in Marble: Working Class Conservatives in Urban England*, University of Chicago Press, 1968.

SIDELIGHTS: McKenzie's books have been translated into German, Spanish, and Japanese.

* * *

McKINNEY, Fred 1908-

PERSONAL: Born April 4, 1908, in Orleans Parish, La.; son of William Henry (a labor executive) and Clara Edna (Schneider) McKinney; married Margery Mulkern (an editor, University of Missouri Press), August 19, 1933; children: Megan Mary (Mrs. Robert W. Whitfield), Kent John, Molly (Mrs. Carliss Farmer), Doyne (Mrs. William S. McKenzie). *Education:* Tulane University of Louisiana, B.A., 1928, M.A., 1929; University of Chicago, Ph.D., 1931. *Politics:* Independent liberal Democrat. *Religion:* Episcopalian. *Home:* 710 Thilly Ave., Columbia, Mo. *Office:* 213 McAlester Hall, University of Missouri, Columbia, Mo.

CAREER: Diplomate, American Board of Examiners in Professional Psychology. Worked part-time for newspaper in New Orleans, La., 1923-29; John Marshall Law School, Chicago, Ill., instructor in psychology, 1930-31; University of Missouri, Columbia, instructor 1933-35, assistant professor, 1935-38, associate professor, 1939-44, professor of psychology, 1944—, chairman of department, 1945-55. U.S.

Office of Scientific Research and Development, civilian research associate, 1943-44; Stephens College, lecturer and consultant, 1956-57; University of Ankara and Middle East University, Ankara, Turkey, Fulbright professor, 1958-59. Missouri School of Religion, trustee, 1955-65.

MEMBER: American Psychological Association (division president, 1958-59), Midwestern Psychological Association (council, 1945-49), Missouri Psychological Association (president, 1948-49), Sigma Xi, Psi Chi (national president, 1932-34), Alpha Pi Zeta (president, 1949). *Awards, honors:* Ford Foundation grant, 1956; Distinguished Faculty Award, Alumni Association of University of Missouri, 1967.

WRITINGS: Psychology of Personal Adjustment, Wiley, 1940, 3rd edition, 1960; *You and Your Life*, Houghton, 1951; *Counseling for Personal Adjustment*, Houghton, 1959; *Understanding Personality: Cases in Counseling*, Houghton, 1965; (editor) *Psychology in Action*, Macmillan, 1967, 2nd edition, 1974.

Contributor: *Handbook for Child Guidance*, edited by E. Harms, Child Care Publications, 1947; *An Introduction to Clinical Psychology*, edited by L. A. Pennington and I. A. Berg, Ronald, 1948.

Producer of television kinescopes distributed by National Education Television, a television series for Stephens College, and a course in general psychology distributed by Great Plains Television Library. Contributor to professional journals. Associate editor, *Education and Psychological Measurement*, 1947-49, *Journal of Consulting Psychology, 1947-49.*

WORK IN PROGRESS: Research on self-concept.

AVOCATIONAL INTERESTS: Collector of American and British short story volumes.

* * *

McLAUGHLIN, Arthur Leo 1921-

PERSONAL: Born November 12, 1921, in Boston, Mass.; son of Arthur Leo, and Catherine (Fee) McLaughlin; married Edith D'Orlando, July 15, 1945; children: Kathleen Lenore, Janice Lee. *Education:* Attended Catholic school in Revere, Mass. *Religion:* Roman Catholic. *Home:* 2023 West 162nd St., Gardena, Calif. 90247.

CAREER: U.S. Post Office, Gardena, Calif., foreman of mails, 1958—. *Military service:* U.S. Army, Infantry, World War II; prisoner of war in Germany for twenty months; served in North Africa, Italy, France, and Germany.

WRITINGS: St. Vincent de Paul, Bruce, 1965.

WORK IN PROGRESS: Two books, *Enos Rudd* and *The Snows of Yester-Year.*

BIOGRAPHICAL/CRITICAL SOURCES: Wilson Library Bulletin, December, 1965.

* * *

McLEAN, Albert F(orbes), Jr. 1928-

PERSONAL: Surname is pronounced McLain; born July 2, 1928, in Boston, Mass.; son of Albert Forbes (a salesman) and Stella (Larsen) McLean; married Jean Mairs, July 29, 1952; children: Stuart, Cameron, Janet. *Education:* Williams College, A.B., 1951; Harvard University, M.A., 1953, Ph.D., 1960. *Religion:* Presbyterian. *Home:* 2333 Southwood Dr., Pittsburgh, Pa. 15241.

CAREER: Tufts University, Medford, Mass., instructor in English, 1956-60, assistant professor, 1960-61; Transylvania College, Lexington, Ky., associate professor of English, 1961-65, professor, 1965-67; Point Park College, Pittsburgh, Pa., professor of English, 1967—, dean of college, 1967-69, 1974—. Pemaquid Seminar (adult education), Damariscotta, Me., director, 1956-64. Lexington (Ky.) Committee on Religion and Human Rights, chairman of education subcommittee, 1965. *Member:* Modern Language Association of America, American Studies Association, American Association of University Professors (president of Transylvania chapter and of Kentucky conference), American Civil Liberties Union.

WRITINGS: William Cullen Bryant, Twayne, 1964; *American Vaudeville as Ritual*, University of Kentucky Press, 1965. Poetry included in *Best Poems of 1960* (Borestone Awards). Poems and articles published in *Theatre Survey, Yankee, Poetry Northwest, American Literature*, and *Beloit Poetry Journal.*

WORK IN PROGRESS: Research for a book on the New England Transcendental Movement.

* * *

McLEAN, Robert Colin 1927-

PERSONAL: Born September 3, 1927, in Chicago, Ill.; son of Alexander MacDonald and Ruth (Garrison) McLean; married Kathleen Rieman, February 28, 1952; children: Colin Garrison. *Education:* Indiana University, B.S., 1949, M.A., 1952; University of Edinburgh, graduate study, 1957-58; Washington University, St. Louis, Mo., Ph.D., 1960. *Politics:* Democrat. *Home:* North East 1005, Indiana St., Pullman, Wash.

CAREER: University of Rochester, Rochester, N.Y., instructor in English, 1958-61; Washington State University, Pullman, assistant professor, 1961-64, associate professor, 1964-69, professor of English, 1969—. *Military service:* U.S. Army, 1946-47. *Member:* Modern Language Association of America, American Studies Association, Philological Association of the Pacific Coast, Phi Beta Kappa.

WRITINGS: George Tucker: Moral Philosopher and Man of Letters, University of North Carolina Press, 1961. Contributor to *American Literature, Research Studies, Modern Language Quarterly, Papers on Language and Literature, North Carolina Historical Review*, and *Poe Studies.*

WORK IN PROGRESS: A study of Henry James's novels.

* * *

McLENDON, Jonathon C(ollins) 1919-

PERSONAL: Born November 6, 1919, in Lakeland, Fla.; son of Jonathon Collins (in railroad management) and Gladys D. (Turner) McLendon; married Lorraine C. Berry, October 31, 1942; children: Gladys Sue (Mrs. Gregory Masciana), Jonathon C. III, Robert Lee. *Education:* Attended Transylvania College (now University) 1936-38; University of Georgia, A.B., 1940; University of Minnesota, M.A., 1946, Ph.D., 1951. *Politics:* Independent Democrat. *Religion:* Christian. *Office:* University of Georgia, Athens, Ga. 30602.

CAREER: High school teacher of social studies and English in Moultrie, Ga., 1940-41, and Minneapolis, Minn., 1946-49; University of Alabama, University, assistant professor of secondary education, 1949-52; Duke University, Durham, N.C., assistant professor, 1952-54, associate professor of education, 1954-60; Northwestern University, School of Education, Evanston, Ill., associate professor of education, 1960-64, director of Social Studies Curriculum Study Center, 1964; Florida Atlantic University, Boca Raton, professor and coordinator of social science education, 1964-66; University of Georgia, Athens, professor, 1966-70, research professor of social studies education, 1970-74, chairman of department of social science, 1966-70. Summer teacher at University of Minnesota, Stanford University, University of Washington, and other universities. *Military service:* U.S. Army Air Forces, 1942-45; became technical sergeant (ground communications).

MEMBER: American Academy of Political and Social Science, American Educational Research Association, National Council for the Social Studies (former committee chairman), National Society for the Study of Education, American Association of University Professors, Horace Mann League, Social Science Education Consortium, Joint Council of Economic Development, Kappa Delta Pi, Phi Delta Kappa.

WRITINGS: (Contributor) T. Walter Walbank, editor, *Man's Story: World History in Its Geographic Setting*, Scott, Foresman, 1951, and revised editions; (contributor) *Living World History*, Scott, Foresman, 1958; *A Guide to Curriculum Study: Social Studies*, State Department of Public Instruction (Raleigh, N.C.), 1958; (with L. D. Haskew) *This is Teaching: An Introduction to Education in America*, Scott, Foresman, 1962, 3rd edition, 1968; *Improving the Educational Program in the Waycross City Schools*, Board of Education (Waycross, Ga.), 1963; *Social Studies in Secondary Education*, Macmillan, 1965; *Social Studies and the Disadvantaged*, National Center for Educational Communication, 1972.

Editor: (With L. D. Haskew) *Views on American Schooling: Introductory Readings on Education*, Scott, Foresman, 1961, 2nd edition, 1964; (with John R. Lee) *Readings on Elementary Social Studies*, Allyn & Bacon, 1965, 2nd edition (with Lee and William Joyce), 1970; *Social Foundations of Education: Current Readings from the Behavioral Sciences*, Macmillan, 1966; *Readings on Social Studies in Secondary Education*, Macmillan, 1966; *Guide to Reading for Social Studies Teachers*, National Council for the Social Studies, 1973. Writer of booklets and tests. Contributor of articles and reviews to professional journals. Editor, *Tarheel Social Studies Bulletin*, 1953-56, *Trends in Social Education*, 1965.

AVOCATIONAL INTERESTS: Bridge, swimming, and travel.

* * *

McMURRY, Robert N(oleman) 1901-

PERSONAL: Born December 19, 1901, in Chicago, Ill.; son of Oscar Lincoln (a teacher) and Sadie (Noleman) McMurry; married Doris Baird, October 3, 1936; married Katherine Stack Miller, April 29, 1966; children: (first marriage) Michael Baid, Saralou. *Education:* University of Chicago, Ph.B., 1925, M.S., 1932; University of Vienna, Ph.D., 1934. *Home:* 505 North Lake Shore Dr., Apt. 2608, Chicago, Ill. 60615. *Office:* 645 North Michigan Ave., Chicago, Ill. 60611.

CAREER: Diplomate, American Board of Examiners in Professional Psychology. Employed in Chicago, Ill., by Federal Electric Co., 1925-27, Yellow Cab Co., 1927-28, and Transit Mixers, Inc., 1928-31; Psychological Corp., area manager, Chicago, Ill., 1935-43; McMurry Co. (management consultants), Chicago, Ill., president, 1943—. Conductor of training conferences in Australia, New Zealand, India, England, Ireland, and Germany. *Member:* American Psychological Association (fellow), American Sociological Association, American Statistical. Association, American Marketing Association, Institute of Management Sciences, Chicago Psychoanalytic Society. *Awards, honors:* Carnegie Foundation fellowship, 1932-34.

WRITINGS: Handling Personality Adjustment in Industry, Harper, 1944; *Tested Techniques of Personnel Selection,* Darnell, 1955; *McMurry's Management Clinic,* Simon and Schuster, 1960; *How to Recruit, Select, and Place Salesmen,* Dartnell, 1964; *How to Build a Dynamic Sales Organization,* McGraw, 1966; *The Maverick Executive,* American Management Association, 1974. Contributor to *Nation's Business, Sales Management, Atlantic Monthly, Iron Age, Harvard Business Review, Michigan Business Review,* and other periodicals.

* * *

McNAIR, Kate

PERSONAL: Daughter of J. F. and Mabel (Harris) Mallory; married J. Dunlap McNair; children: E. Anthony, Susan Leslie. *Education:* Eastern Illinois University student, University of Illinois, B.S. *Politics:* Republican. *Religion:* Methodist. *Home:* 3400 Petty Rd., Muncie, Ind. *Agent:* Curtis Brown Ltd., 60 East 56th St., New York, N.Y. 10022.

MEMBER: National League of American Pen Women (chapter president, 1963-65). *Awards, honors:* Distinguished writing award in young adult category, University of Indiana, 1965.

WRITINGS: A Sense of Magic, Chilton, 1966; *A Book of Directions,* Chilton, 1970. Also author of play published by Dramatic Publishing. Contributor of short stories to *Ladies' Home Journal.*

* * *

McNAIRY, Philip F(rederick) 1911-

PERSONAL: Born March 19, 1911, in Lake City, Minn.; son of Harry Doughty and Clara (Moseman) McNairy; married Cary Elizabeth Fleming, November 19, 1935; children: Philip, Judith, Patricia. *Education:* Kenyon College, B.A., 1932; Bexley Hall Divinity School, B.D., 1934. *Home:* 1820 Knox Ave. So., Minneapolis, Minn. 55403. *Office:* Diocese of Minnesota, 309 Clifton Ave., Minneapolis, Minn. 55403.

CAREER: Ordained deacon in Episcopal Church, 1934; ordained priest, 1935. St. Andrew's Mission, Columbus, Ohio, vicar, 1934-35; St. Stephen's Church, Cincinnati, Ohio, rector, 1935-40; Christ Church, St. Paul, Minn., rector, 1940-50; St. Paul's Cathedral, Buffalo, N.Y., dean, 1950-58; diocese of Minnesota, Minneapolis, suffragen bishop, 1958-68, coadjutor, 1968-70, bishop of Minnesota, 1971—. *Member:* Governor's Human Rights Commission, Minnesota Council of Churches (member of board of directors), Minneapolis Council of Churches (member of board of directors), St. Paul Community Chest (honorary member of board of directors), Masonic Lodge, Minneapolis Club, Minikahda Club (Minneapolis), Minnesota Club (St. Paul). *Awards, honors:* D.D., Kenyon College, 1951, Seabury Western Seminary, 1970; L.L.D., Lake Erie College, 1962; S.T.D., St. John's College (Winnipeg), 1964.

WRITINGS: Family Story, Seabury, 1960; (contributor)

Kendig B. Cully, editor, *Confirmation Instruction: Its Rationale and Methods,* Seabury, 1961. Contributor to church periodicals.†

* * *

McNALLY, John 1914-

PERSONAL: Born January 13, 1914, in Bridgeport, Conn.; son of John and Margaret (Stepler) McNally. *Education:* Attended University of Chicago, 1940-42.

CAREER: Formerly newspaper feature writer; Famous Writers School, Westport, Conn., instructor, 1965. Freelance writer. *Military service:* U.S. Army, paratrooper, 1942-50, artillery officer, 1951; served in Europe and Korea. *Member:* Authors League of America.

WRITINGS: Dragon in Paradise (novel), Doubleday, 1963. Short stories have appeared in *True, Esquire,* and other magazines.

WORK IN PROGRESS: Aloha, a novel; research for a novel on the American theater from 1880 to the present.

SIDELIGHTS: McNally has lived in Japan, Thailand, and Hawaii.†

* * *

McNEILL, Robert B(lakely) 1915-

PERSONAL: Born May 21, 1915, in Birmingham, Ala.; son of Walter Patterson (in real estate) and Mary (McLeod) McNeill; married Jeanne Lancaster (a Job Corps counselor), August 25, 1944; children: Mary Janet, Frank, Walter. *Education:* Birmingham-Southern College, A.B., 1936; University of Alabama, graduate study, 1939; Union Theological Seminary, Richmond, Va., B.D., 1942; University of Kentucky, M.A., 1944; University of North Carolina, graduate study, 1950. *Politics:* Democrat. *Office:* Bream Memorial Presbyterian Church, 317 West Washington St., Charleston, W.Va. 25302.

CAREER: Linde Air Products, Birmingham, Ala., correspondent, 1937-39; ordained to ministry of Presbyterian Church in the U.S., 1942; minister with Bream Memorial Presbyterian Church, Charleston, W.Va. Member of Committee on Church and Society, General Assembly of the Presbyterian Church in the U.S.

WRITINGS: Prophet Speak Now, John Knox, 1961; *God Wills Us Free: The Ordeal of a Southern Minister,* Hill & Wang, 1965. Contributor to *Look.* Associate editor, *Presbyterian Outlook.*

BIOGRAPHICAL/CRITICAL SOURCES: Good Housekeeping, July, 1950.†

* * *

McNEIR, Waldo F(orest) 1908-

PERSONAL: Born September 13, 1908, in Houston, Tex.; son of Forest Waldemar and Stella (Frick) McNeir; married Corinne Crawford (a librarian), September 14, 1935; children: Clarence. *Education:* Rice University, B.A., 1929; University of North Carolina, M.A., 1932, Ph.D., 1940. *Politics:* Democrat. *Religion:* Methodist. *Home:* 490 West 26th Ave., Eugene, Ore. 97405. *Office:* Department of English, University of Oregon, Eugene, Ore. 97403.

CAREER: University of North Carolina, Chapel Hill, instructor in English, 1934-40; North Texas State University, Denton, assistant professor of English, 1940-42; University of Chicago, Chicago, Ill., assistant professor of English, 1946-49; Louisiana State University, Baton Rouge, assistant professor, 1949-53, associate professor, 1953-58, professor of English, 1958-61; University of Oregon, Eugene, professor of English, 1961—. Fulbright lecturer at University of Marburg, 1957, 1964, University of Muenster, 1968. *Military service:* U.S. Naval Reserve, active duty, 1942-46; now commander (retired); received four battle stars.

MEMBER: Modern Language Association of America (life member), Modern Humanities Research Association (life member), Mediaeval Academy of America, Renaissance Society of America, South-Central Modern Language Association (secretary-treasurer, 1951-54), South-Central Renaissance Conference (president, 1958-59), Philological Association of the Pacific Coast, Pacific Northwest Renaissance Conference, Malone Society, American Civil Liberties Union, Phi Beta Kappa.

WRITINGS: (With Henry W. Sams) *Problems in Reading and Writing*, Prentice-Hall, 1949, and *Teacher's Manual*, 1951; (with H. W. Sams) *New Problems in Reading and Writing*, Prentice-Hall, 1953, and *Teacher's Manual*, 1954; (contributor) *Studies in the English Renaissance Drama*, New York University Press, 1959; (contributor) *Festschrift fuer Walther Fischer*, Carl Winter, 1959; (with Foster Provost) *Annotated Bibliography of Edmund Spenser, 1937-1960*, Duquesne University Press, 1962, *The Merchant of Venice: An Outline-Guide to the Play*, Barnes & Noble, 1965; (contributor) *Essays on Shakespeare*, Pennsylvania State University Press, 1965; *William Shakespeare: The Merchant of Venice*, Barnes & Noble, 1967; (contributor) *Festschrift fuer Edgar Mertner*, Fink, 1969; (contributor) A. C. Hamilton, editor, *Essential Articles for the Study of Edmund Spencer*, Shoe String, 1972.

Editor: Forest W. McNeir, *Forest McNeir of Texas*, Naylor, 1956; John Earle Uhler, *Morley's Canzonets for Three Voices*, Louisiana State University Press, 1957; (with Leo B. Levy) *Studies in American Literature*, Louisiana State University Press, 1960; Lawrence A. Sasek, *The Literary Temper of the English Puritans*, Louisiana State University Press, 1961; Lili Rabel, *Khasi: A Language of Assam*, Louisiana State University Press, 1961; *Studies in Comparative Literature*, Louisiana State University Press, 1962; (and contributor) *Studies in English Renaissance Literature*, Louisiana State University Press, 1962; (with Hardin Craig) *Five Plays of Shakespeare*, Scott, Foresman, 1965; (with Thelma Greenfield; also contributor) *Pacific Coast Studies in Shakespeare*, University of Oregon Press, 1966.

Contributor to literary journals in United States and Europe.

SIDELIGHTS: McNeir speaks French, German, Spanish, and some Italian. *Avocational interests:* Salmon fishing in the Pacific Ocean.†

* * *

McPHEE, William N(orvell) 1921-

PERSONAL: Born March 7, 1921, in Denver, Colo.; son of J. Elmer and Sarah (Eddy) McPhee; married Miriam Emery (a teacher), October 4, 1944; children: Caroline W., John W., Sarah E. *Education:* Attended Yale University, 1940-41; Columbia University, Ph.D., 1958. *Politics:* Democrat. *Religion:* None. *Office:* Department of Sociology, University of Colorado, Boulder, Colo.

CAREER: Research Services, Inc., Denver, Colo., partner, 1945-51; Columbia University, New York, N.Y., research associate, Bureau of Applied Social Research, 1951-62, lecturer, 1958-62; University of Colorado, Boulder, pro-

fessor of sociology, 1962—. Member of board of directors, Research Services Inc., 1945—, and Simulmatics Corp., 1958—. *Military service:* U.S. Army, 1942-45.

WRITINGS: (With B. Berelson and P. F. Lazarsfeld) *Voting*, University of Chicago Press, 1954; (with W. Glaser) *Public Opinion and Congressional Elections*, Free Press of Glencoe, 1962; *Formal Theories of Mass Behavior*, Free Press of Glencoe, 1963.†

* * *

McPHERSON, Thomas Herdman 1925-

PERSONAL: Born July 30, 1925, in Dunedin, New Zealand; son of Hugh Paterson Bayne (a policeman) and Margaret (Herdman) McPherson; married Dilys Mary Price (an actress), June 29, 1957; children: Sian, Hugh Dylan, Catrin. *Education:* University of Otago, M.A., 1947; University College, Oxford, B. Phil., 1950. *Office:* Department of Philosophy, University College, Cardiff, Wales.

CAREER: University College of North Wales, Bangor, assistant lecturer, 1951-53, lecturer in philosophy, 1953-63; University College, Cardiff, Wales, senior lecturer, 1963-68, reader, 1968-71, professor of philosophy, 1971—. *Member:* Aristotelian Society, Mind Association.

WRITINGS: *The Philosophy of Religion*, Van Nostrand, 1965; *Political Obligation*, Humanities, 1967; *Social Philosophy*, Van Nostrand, 1970; *The Argument from Design*, Macmillan, 1972; *Philosophy and Religious Belief*, Hutchinson, 1974. Contributor of articles and reviews to professional journals.

WORK IN PROGRESS: Studies on social and political philosophy.

SIDELIGHTS: Thomas McPherson told *CA* he is " . . . not interested in philosophy as an ivory tower activity, but rather in its practical aspects—particularly, at the present time, in its relation to the social sciences."

* * *

McQUIGG, R. Bruce 1927-

PERSONAL: Born August 18, 1927, in Schaller, Iowa; son of F. Walter and Doris (Gould) McQuigg; married Joan Whalen, June 2, 1955; children: Susan, Paul. *Education:* Iowa State Teachers College (now University of Northern Iowa), B.A., 1948; University of Colorado, M.A., 1958, Ed.D., 1962. *Religion:* Methodist. *Home:* 3613 Park Lane, Bloomington, Ind. 47401. *Office:* Indiana University, Bloomington, Ind.

CAREER: Indiana University, Bloomington, assistant professor of education, 1960—. Associate director for secondary education, Ford Foundation five-year program in teacher education. *Military service:* U.S. Army, 1950-52; served in Far East; became sergeant first class. *Member:* National Education Association, Association for Supervision and Curriculum Development, American Association of University Professors, Phi Delta Kappa, University Club (president, 1966-67).

WRITINGS: (Editor with Frederick Smith) *Secondary Schools Today: Reading for Educators*, Houghton, 1965, 2nd edition, 1969; (editor with David Beggs III) *Partners in Conflict: America's Schools and Churches*, Indiana University Press, 1966; *Simulation: Focus on Decision Making*, Indiana University Press, 1970. Contributor to educational journals.†

McSHANE, Mark 1930-
(Marc Lovell)

PERSONAL: Born November 28, 1930, in Sydney, Australia; son of Mark (a merchant) and Albereda (Fowler) McShane; married Rosemarie Armstrong, October 5, 1963; children: Rebecca, Marcus Aurelius, Damon, Todd. *Education:* Attended Technical College, Blackpool, Lancashire, England. *Politics:* Liberal. *Religion:* Humanist. *Home:* La Cabaneta, Palma de Mallorca, Spain. *Agent:* Paul R. Reynolds, Inc., 599 Fifth Ave., New York, N.Y. 10017; Lady Diana Avebury, Strathmore Agency, Park Rd., St. John's Wood, London NW8, England.

CAREER: Professional writer.

WRITINGS: The Straight and Crooked, John Long, 1960; *The Passing of Evil,* Cassell, 1961; *Seance on a Wet Afternoon,* Cassell, 1961, published as *Seance,* Doubleday, 1962; *Untimely Ripped,* Cassell, 1962, Doubleday, 1963; *The Girl Nobody Knows,* Doubleday, 1965; *Night's Evil,* Doubleday, 1966; *The Crimson Madness of Little Doom,* Doubleday, 1966; *The Way to Nowhere,* R. Hale, 1967; *Ill Met by a Fish Shop on George Street,* Doubleday, 1968; *The Singular Case of the Multiple Dead,* Putnam, 1969; *The Man Who Left Well Enough,* McCall Publishing, 1970; *Seance For Two,* Doubleday, 1972; *The Othello Complex,* Gallimard, 1974; *The Headless Snowman,* Gallimard, 1974.

Under pseudonym Marc Lovell: *The Ghost of Megan,* Doubleday, 1968; *The Imitation Thieves,* Doubleday, 1971; *A Presence in the House,* Doubleday, 1972; *An Enquiry into the Existence of Vampires,* Doubleday, 1974.

WORK IN PROGRESS: "Books, books, books."

SIDELIGHTS: Mark McShane began writing "to prove to myself that even without previous experience I could produce something better than most of the garbage on the market. Result was accepted, path was clear.... Would like to lift the crime novel to a more respected level, above mere forgettable entertainment. Contiguous interests are in criminal psychology and psychic research. No longer care for travel after having lived in, up to the age of thirty, working backwards, Canada, Australia, England, the United States (four years), Canada, France, the United Kingdom, South Africa, British West Indies, the Argentine, New Zealand, Australia. Now firmly established in Majorca."

All the McShane novels have been published in France and Germany. *Seance on a Wet Afternoon* was made into a successful film, was runner-up for the Mystery Writers of America Edgar Allan Poe Award ("Edgar") in 1962 and runner-up for the Grand Prize of French Police Literature, 1963. Mel Chaitlin's adaptation of *The Passing of Evil* was filmed as "The Grasshopper," National General, 1968.

*   *   *

McWHIRTER, A(lan) Ross 1925-

PERSONAL: Born August 12, 1925, in London, England; son of William Allen (editor of *Daily Mail*) and Margaret (Williamson) McWhirter; married Rosemary J. Hamilton Grice, May 18, 1957; children: Ian Charles Hamilton, Andrew James Kennedy. *Education:* Attended Marlborough College, 1939-43; Trinity College, Oxford, B.A. and M.A., 1948. *Politics:* Conservative. *Religion:* Church of England. *Home:* 50 Village Rd., Enfield Middlesex, England. *Office:* McWhirter Twins Ltd., 2 Cecil Court, London Rd., Enfield, Middlesex, England.

CAREER: With his twin brother, Norris Dewar Mc-

Whirter, formed the British firm of McWhirter Twins Ltd., in London, 1950, a writing partnership that has produced the *Guinness Book of Records,* 1955—, and other compilations of facts and figures. *Athletics* (magazine), publisher, 1951-56; *Star,* London, staff sports writer, 1951-60; *Evening News,* London, staff sports writer, 1960-62; Dreghorn Publications Ltd., London, director, 1962—; Conservative candidate for Parliament for Edmonton constituency in 1964 general election (his twin also stood in the same election). Member of British Olympic and Empire Games Appeal Committees, 1964-72. *Military service:* Royal Navy, 1943-46. *Member:* Sports Writers Association (chairman, 1959), Vincents' Club (Oxford University; committee, 1964—), Achilles Club (Oxford and Cambridge; committee, 1952—).

WRITINGS: (With Norris D. McWhirter) *Get to Your Marks,* Kaye, 1950; (compiler with N. D. McWhirter) *Guinness Book of Records,* Guinness Superlatives, 1955, 21st edition, 1974, published as *Guinness Book of World Records,* Sterling, 1956, 5th edition, 1966; (compiler with N. D. McWhirter) *Dunlop Book of Facts,* Dreghorne Publications, 1964, 2nd edition, 1966; (editor) *Daily Book of Golden Discs,* McWhirter Twins, 1966; (with Sir Andrew Noble) *Centenary History of Oxford University Rugby Football Club,* Oxford University Rugby Football Club, 1969; (with U. A. Titley) *Centenary History of the Rugby Football Union,* Rugby Football Union, 1970. Weekly columnist, "World of Sport," in *Observer,* 1956-67.

WORK IN PROGRESS: A collection of the citations and biographical notes of winners of the George Cross for gallantry; a study of the breaches of constitutional law involved in Britain's entry into the common market. Continuing research for new editions of *Guinness Book of Records, Dunlop Book of Facts,* and *Daily Book of Golden Discs.*

SIDELIGHTS: The McWhirter twins' interest in what they call "useless information" began around the age of eight, when they began collecting reference books (now weighing in at four or five tons). After the war they set up a business supplying editors, writers, and newspapers with answers to queries, eventually undertook the *Guinness Book of Records,* which became Britain's best seller in nonfiction a few months after its initial appearance. The Guinness book, one quarter of which comprises sports records, now is published in American, French, Danish, Norwegian, Swedish, Japanese, Spanish, Finnish, German, Italian, Dutch, Czech, Portuguese and Serbo-Croatian editions, with total sales in an excess of twenty million.

A. Ross McWhirter ran for Oxford University in 1947-48, still is greatly interested in track as well as other field events, rugby football, and lawn tennis. He has traveled in about forty countries, mostly in connection with sports; is "pro United States and a detester of extreme right or left wing politics on scientific grounds."

BIOGRAPHICAL/CRITICAL SOURCES: Sports Illustrated, February 8, 1965 (an article by J. A. Maxtone Graham, condensed as "Last Word in Books," *Reader's Digest,* May, 1965).

*   *   *

McWILLIAMS, Margaret E. 1929-

PERSONAL: Born May 26, 1929, in Osage, Iowa; daughter of Alvin R. (a professor) and Mildred (Lane) Edgar; married Don A. McWilliams (now a physicist), September 20, 1953; children: Roger, Kathleen. *Education:*

Iowa State University of Science and Technology, B.S., 1951, M.S., 1953; Oregon State University, Ph.D., 1968. *Home:* 1916 North Gilbert, Fullerton, Calif. 92633. *Office:* California State University, 5151 State College Dr., Los Angeles, Calif. 90032.

CAREER: California State University, Los Angeles, assistant professor, 1961-66, associate professor of home economics, 1966-68, professorf home economics, and chairman of department, 1968—. *Member:* Institute of Food Technologists, American Home Economics Association, College Teachers of Food and Nutrition, American Association of University Professors, American Dietic Association, Phi Kappa Phi, Phi Upsilon Omicron, Omicron Nu, Iota Sigma Pi, Sigma Alpha Iota, Sigma Delta Epsilon.

WRITINGS: Food Fundamentals, Wiley, 1966, 2nd edition, 1974; *Nutrition for the Growing Years*, Wiley, 1967, 2nd edition, 1975; (with Lendal Kotschevar) *Understanding Food*, Wiley, 1969; (with Linda Davis) *Food for You*, Ginn, 1971; (with Frederick Stare) *Living Nutrition*, Wiley, 1973; *Meatless Cookbook*, Plycon, 1973; (with Stare) *Nutrition for Good Health*, Plycon, 1974. Also author of *Illustrated Guide to Food Preparation*, 2nd edition, Plycon, 1972. Assistant editor, *California Home Economist*.

* * *

MEAGHER, John C. 1935-

PERSONAL: Surname is pronounced *Mah*-her; born March 23, 1935, in St. Louis, Mo.; son of John Ford (a broker) and Eleanor (Ackerman) Meagher; married Sheila McMahon Cary, August 9, 1958; children: Mary, Kathleen, Margaret, Sean, Michael. *Education:* University of Notre Dame, B.A., 1956; Princeton University, M.A., 1958, Ph.D., 1962; University of London, Ph.D., 1961. *Religion:* Catholic. *Home:* 49 Williamson Rd., Toronto, Ontario, Canada. *Office:* St. Michael's College, Toronto M55 IJ4, Ontario, Canada.

CAREER: University of Notre Dame, Notre Dame, Ind., assistant professor of English, 1961-66; St. Michael's College, Toronto, Ontario, associate professor of English, 1966—, special lecturer in religious studies, 1970—. Director of Institute of Christian Thought, 1973—. *Member:* Malone Society, Canadian Association of University Teachers, American Academy of Religion, Society of Bibical Literature, Society for Religion in Higher Education, Association of Marshall Scholars and Alumni. *Awards, honors:* Woodrow Wilson fellowship, 1956; Danforth fellowship, 1956; Marshall scholarship for study at University of London, 1959; Cross Disciplinary fellowship for study at University of Paris and Institut Catholique, 1965.

WRITINGS: The Downfall of Robert Earl of Huntingdon, Malone Society, 1965; *Method and Meaning in Jonson's Masques*, University of Notre Dame Press, 1966; *The Gathering of the Ungifred*, Herder & Herder, 1972.

WORK IN PROGRESS: Tudor and Stuart entertainments; first-century theology; Renaissance drama (English).

* * *

MEECHAN, Hugh L(awrence) 1933-

PERSONAL: Born September 2, 1933, in Mossend, Scotland; son of Hugh (a steelworker) and Mary (McCaffrey) Meechan; married Ena Christie (a teacher), December 28,

1959; children: Catherine Grace, Hugh Thomas, Helen Louise. *Education:* University of Leicester, B.A. (honors), 1956, Certificate in Education, 1959. *Politics:* Variable. *Religion:* Roman Catholic. *Office:* Our Lady's Secondary School, Corby, Northamptonshire, England.

CAREER: Humphrey Perkins School, Barrow on Soar, Leicestershire, England, head of modern languages, 1959-64; Doncaster College of Education, Doncaster, England, lecturer in French, 1964-66; Pope John Memorial School, Corby, Northamptonshire, England, head of modern languages, 1966-70; Our Lady's Secondary School, Corby, headmaster, 1970—. *Military service:* British Army, Intelligence Corps, 1956-58; served as interpreter at headquarters of Allied Land Forces, Central Europe,; became sergeant.

WRITINGS: (With C. M. Walker) *Racontez-Moi*, Pergamon, 1966.

WORK IN PROGRESS: Research into audio-visual methods in secondary school language-teaching.

SIDELIGHTS: Fluent in French, has working knowledge of German and Spanish.

* * *

MEETH, Louis Richard 1934-

PERSONAL: Born April 7, 1934, in Ridgewood, N.J.; son of Louis H. (a school superintendent) and Melisse (Faulds) Meeth; married Sally Ann Bacon, August 1, 1964. *Education:* University of Florida, B.A., 1955; Union Theological Seminary, Richmond, Va., B.D., 1959; Union Theological Seminary, New York, N.Y., graduate study, 1959-61; Columbia University, Ed.D., 1964. *Office:* Department of Higher Education, 16 Foster Annex, State University of New York, Buffalo, N.Y. 14214.

CAREER: High school teacher of English, Largo, Fla., 1956; Boy's Reformatory of Virginia, part-time chaplain, 1956-59; Centerport Methodist Church, Centerport, N.Y., part-time minister of education, 1962-65; Columbia University, Teachers College, New York, N.Y., assistant to Earl J. McGrath at Institute of Higher Education, 1963-65; Baldwin-Wallace College, Berea, Ohio, assistant to the president, 1965-67; Park College, Parkville, Mo., academic dean, 1967-70; State University of New York, Buffalo, associate professor of higher education, 1970—. Part-time teacher of education at University of Missouri at Kansas City, 1967-70. Consultant to U.S. Office of Economic Opportunity, and schools, universities, and institutes. *Member:* American Association for Higher Education, Kappa Delta Pi, Phi Delta Kappa, Alpha Phi Omega. *Awards, honors:* D.H.L., Sterling College, 1973.

WRITINGS: (Assistant editor and contributor) *Cooperative Long-Range Planning for Liberal Arts Colleges*, Teachers College, Columbia University, 1964; *Faculty Selection and Retention in Protestant Colleges*, National Council of Churches, 1965; (contributor) *Higher Education: Some Newer Developments*, McGraw, 1965; (editor) *Selected Issues in Higher Education: An Annotated Bibliography*, Teachers College, Columbia University, 1965; (contributor) *Agony and Promise: Current Issues in Higher Education*, Josey-Bass, 1969; (editor with Harold Hodgkinson) *Power and Authority*, Josey-Bass, 1970; *Quality Education for Less Money*, Josey-Bass, 1974. Contributor to education and denominational journals.

* * *

MEGARGEE, Edwin I(nglee) 1937-

PERSONAL: Both g's in surname are pronounced as in

"beg"; born February 27, 1937, in Plainfield, N.J.; son of S. Edwin (an artist and author) and Jean (an editor; maiden name, Inglee) Megargee; married Ann Piemonte, August 1, 1959; children: Elyn Jean, Edwin I., Jr., Christopher John, Stephen Andrew. *Education:* Amherst College, B.A. (magna cum laude), 1958; University of California, Berkeley, Ph.D., 1964. *Politics:* Democrat. *Home:* 908 Lasswade, Tallahassee, Fla. 32303. *Office:* Psychology Department, Florida State University, Tallahassee, Fla.

CAREER: Alameda County (Calif.) Probation Department Guidance Clinic, clinical psychologist, 1961-64; University of Texas, Austin, assistant professor of psychology, 1964-67; Florida State University, Tallahassee, associate professor, 1967-70, professor of psychology, 1970—, Crime and Delinquency Specialty Program, area coordinator, 1973-74, director, 1972. Consultant to Hogg Foundation, 1964-68, U.S. Veteran's Administration, 1964-67 and 1974—, Federal Bureau of Prisons, 1967—, National Commission on the Causes and Prevention of Violence, 1968-69, U.S. Secret Service, 1969, and to other organizations and government agencies. *Member:* American Psychological Association (fellow), American Sociological Association (fellow), American Association of Correctional Psychologists (president, 1973-75), American Correctional Association (member of board of directors, 1973-75), Society for Personality Assessment (fellow), American Society of Criminology, International Society for Research on Aggression (fellow), Phi Beta Kappa, Sigma Xi, Delta Sigma Rho.

WRITINGS: (Editor) *Research in Clinical Assessment*, Harper, 1966; (with C. M. Rosenquist) *Delinquency in Three Cultures*, University of Texas Press, 1969; (editor with J. Hokanson) *The Dynamics of Aggression: Individual, Group, and International Analysis*, Harper, 1970; (contributor) C. D. Spiel-Berger, editor, *Current Topics in Clinic and Community Psychology*, Volume II, Academic Press, 1970; (contributor) J. E. Singer, editor, *The Control of Aggression and Violence: Cognitive and Physiological Factors*, Academic Press, 1971; (contributor) P. McReynolds, editor, *Advances in Psychological Assessment*, Volume II, Science and Behavior Books, 1971; *The California Psychological Inventory Handbook*, Jossey-Bass, 1972; *The Psychology of Violence and Aggression*, General Learning Corp., 1972; *Crime and Delinquency*, General Learning Corp., in press.

Editor of Federal Correctional Institution *Research Reports*, 1969—, and *Technical and Treatment Notes*, 1970—; associate editor, *Journal of Abnormal Child Psychology*, 1972—; consulting editor, *Journal of Personality Assessment*, 1969-73, *Journal of Criminal Law and Criminology*, 1970—; member of editorial board, "Community Mental Health Monograph Series," 1970-72, *Criminal Justice and Behavior*, 1970—.

AVOCATIONAL INTERESTS: Painting, sculpturing, hunting, fishing, archaeology.

* * *

MEGGERS, Betty J(ane) 1921-

PERSONAL: Born December 5, 1921, in Washington, D.C.; daughter of William Frederick (a physicist) and Edith (Raddant) Meggers; married Clifford Evans (a curator of archaeology), September 13, 1946. *Education:* University of Pennsylvania, A.B., 1943; University of Michigan, M.A., 1944; Columbia University, Ph.D., 1952. *Home:* 1227 30th St. N.W., Washington, D.C. 20007. *Office:* U.S. National Museum, Washington, D.C. 20560.

CAREER: American University, Washington, D.C., instructor in anthropology, 1950-51; Smithsonian Institution, Washington, D.C., research associate, 1954—. American Anthropological Association, Washington, D.C., executive secretary, 1959-61. Battelle Memorial Foundation, consultant. *Member:* American Anthropological Association (fellow), Society for American Archaeology (executive committee member, 1963-64), American Geographical Society, American Association for the Advancement of Science (committeeman-at-large member, 1966-73), Anthropological Society of Washington (vice-president, 1965-66; president, 1966-68), Phi Beta Kappa, Sigma Xi. *Awards, honors:* Washington Academy of Sciences Award for scientific achievement, 1956; Gold Medal of International Congress of Americanists for outstanding Americanist studies, 1966; Decoration of Merit, Government of Ecuador, 1966.

WRITINGS: (with husband, Clifford Evans) *Archaeological Investigations at the Mouth of the Amazon*, Smithsonian Institution, 1957; (with Clifford Evans) *Archeological Investigations in British Guiana*, Smithsonian Institution, 1960; (with Clifford Evans and Emilio Estrada) *Early Formative Period of Coastal Ecuador*, Smithsonian Institution, 1965; *Ecuador*, Praeger, 1966; (translator) Darcy Ribeiro, *The Civilizational Process*, Smithsonian Institution, 1968; *Amazonia*, Aldine, 1971; (with Geoffrey Ashe and others) *The Quest for America*, Pall Mall, 1971; *Prehistoric America*, Aldine, 1972; (editor with Edward S. Ayensu and W. Donald Duckworth, and contributor) *Tropical Forest Ecosystems in Africa and South America*, Smithsonian Institution, 1973; (contributor) Charles Wagley, editor, *Man and the Amazon*, University of Florida Press, 1974; (translator) Luis G. Lumbreras, *The People and Cultures of Ancient Peru*, Smithsonian Institution, 1974. Complier of "Current Research in Lowland South America" in *American Antiquity*. Assistant editor, Society for American Archaeology, 1954-70; editor of occasional publications of Anthropological Society of Washington.

WORK IN PROGRESS: Analysis of archaeological materials and preparation of monographs on field work conducted on coastal Ecuador, the upper Orinoco of Venezuela, Dominica (British West Indies), and Ponape (Caroline Islands); an introduction text on archeology for Aldine.

BIOGRAPHICAL/CRITICAL SOURCES: Lynn and Gray Poole, *Scientists Who Work Outdoors*, Dodd, 1963; *Times Literary Supplement*, April 27, 1967.

* * *

MEHDI, M(ohammed) T. 1928-

PERSONAL: Surname is pronounced *Meh-dee*; born January 6, 1928, in Baghdad, Iraq; son of Al-Haj M. and Zahra (Moeni) Mehdi; married Beverlee Turner (a teacher), June 20, 1953; children: Anisa, Janan, Laila. *Education:* University of California, Berkeley, B.A., 1953, M.A., 1954, Ph.D., 1961. *Office:* Action Committee on American-Arab Relations, 441 Lexington Ave., New York, N.Y. 10017.

CAREER: American Academy of Asian Studies, San Francisco, Calif., assistant professor, 1958-62; Action Committee on American-Arab Relations, New York, N.Y., secretary general, 1964—, executive editor, *Action* (newspaper), 1969—. *Member:* American Political Science Association, American Association for Legal and Political Philosophy. *Awards, honors:* Book of the Year award ($1,000), from Friends of Literature, University of Beirut, for *A Nation of Lions . . . Chained*.

WRITINGS: Constitutionalism—Western and Middle Eastern, New World Press, 1961; *The Question of Palestine*, Arab Information Center, 1962; *A Nation of Lions . . . Chained*, New World Press, 1963; (translator into Arabic) Hans Kelsen, *General Theory of Law and State*, University of Baghdad, 1967; *Peace in the Middle East*, New World Press, 1967. Writer of pamphlets and articles for professional journals.

WORK IN PROGRESS: Tomorrow and Beyond.

SIDELIGHTS: Mehdi writes: "I am an Arab who is interested in Thomas Jefferson and Alexander Hamilton. My interest in contemporary philosophy is within the field of logical empiricism. [I am] concerned with better American-Arab relations. Have coined the expression 'anti-Gentileism,' which refers to the prejudices of the Jews toward the Gentiles, much as the expression 'anti-Semitism' refers to the prejudices of the Gentiles toward the Jews."

* * *

MEIER, Richard L(ouis) 1920-

PERSONAL: Born May 16, 1920, in Kendallville, Ind.; son of Walter A. (a clerk and teacher) and Mary (Lottman) Meier; married Gitta Unger (in population-planning research), May 20, 1944; children: Karen, Andrea, Alan. *Education:* Attended Northern Illinois State Teachers College (now Northern Illinois University), 1936-39; University of Illinois, B.S., 1940; University of California, Los Angeles, M.A., 1942, Ph.D., 1944; University of Manchester, postdoctoral study, 1949-50. *Home:* 7 San Mateo Rd., Berkeley, Calif. 94707. *Office:* University of California, Berkeley, Calif. 94720.

CAREER: California Research Corp., research chemist, 1943-47; Federation of American Scientists, Washington, D.C., executive secretary, 1947-49; University of Chicago, Chicago, Ill., assitant professor, 1950-56; University of Michigan, Ann Arbor, research social scientist with Mental Health Research Institute, 1957—, associate professor in School of Natural Resources, 1960-65, professor of resources planning, 1965-67; University of California, Berkeley, professor of environmental design, 1967—. Visiting lecturer at Harvard University, 1959-60; visiting professor at Center of Ekistics, Athens, Greece, 1962.

MEMBER: American Chemical Society, American Sociological Association, American Geographical Society, Society for International Development, Federation of American Scientists, Society for General Systems Research (secretary-treasurer, 1957-69), Marine Technology Society, Regional Science Association. *Awards, honors:* Fulbright scholarship for study in England, 1949-50.

WRITINGS: Science and Economic Development, M.I.T. Press, 1956, 2nd edition, 1966; *Modern Science and the Human Fertility Problem*, Wiley, 1959; *A Communications Theory of Urban Growth*, M.I.T. Press, 1962; (with others) *Proposals for Human Resource Development in the Detroit Area*, University of Michigan, School of Natural Resources, 1964; *Developmental Planning*, McGraw, 1965; *Planning for an Urban World*, M.I.T. Press, 1974. Also author of urban planning studies for Center for Planning and Development Research, University of California, Berkeley.

WORK IN PROGRESS: A study of future directions for the development of cities in the world, emphasizing the design of "resource-conserving" urbanism that is simultaneously capable of modernizing itself and its region.

MEINTJES, Johannes 1923-

PERSONAL: Surname is pronounced Main-cheese; born May 19, 1923, in South Africa; son of Ernest Frederick (a farmer) and Valerie (Keyter) Meintjes; married Ronell Rossouw (now his secretary), March 25, 1960; children: Lynn (stepdaughter). *Education:* University of Capetown, B.A., 1943; studied art in London, Amsterdam, and Paris, 1946-47, 1958. *Home:* Grootzeekoegat, Molteno, Cape Provinces, South Africa. *Agent:* Blanche C. Gregory, 2 Tudor City Place, New York, N.Y. 10017. *Office:* Box 125, Molteno, Cape Province, South Africa.

CAREER: Author; professional painter, 1944—, work shown in one-man exhibitions in major cities of South Africa, and in group exhibitions nationally and abroad; Molteno, South Africa, librarian, 1967—. Lecturer in fine art, 1945, 1947-49; honorary curator, Molteno Museum, 1967—; member of the board of control, Burgersdorp Museum, 1973—. *Member:* South African P.E.N., South African Academy for Arts and Science. *Awards, honors:* Award as most original South African painter, 1949.

WRITINGS—In English: *Anton Anreith, Sculptor* (monograph), Juta, 1951; *Frontier Family*, Central News Agency, 1955; *Complex Canvas*, Afrikaanse Pers-Boekhandel, 1960; *Manor House*, Delacorte, 1964 (published in England as *The Silent Conspiracy*, Joseph, 1965); *Olive Schreiner: Portrait of a South African Woman*, Keartland, 1965; *De la Rey: Lion of the West*, Keartland, 1966; *Sword in the Sand*, Tafelberg, 1969; *President Steyn*, Nationale Boekhandel, 1969; *General Louis Botha*, Cassell, 1970; *Stormberg*, Nasionale Boekhandel, 1969; *Sandile*, Bulpin, 1971; *The Commandant-General*, Tafelberg, 1971; *The Voortrekkers*, Cassell, 1973; *President Paul Kruger*, Cassell, 1974.

In Afrikaans—*Maggie Laubser* (monograph), Hollands-Afrikaanse Uitgewersmaatskappy, 1944; *Kamerade* (short stories), Anreith, 1947; *Die Blanke Stilte* (play), Holloway, 1952; *Stormsvlei* (novel), Afrikaanes Pers-Boekhandel, 1955; *Die Soekendes* (play), Afrikaanse, Pers-Boekhandel, 1958; *Dagboek I* (diary), Bamboesberg, 1961; *Die Singende Reen* (novel), Bamboesberg, 1962; *Gister is Vandag* (novel), Afrikaanse Pers-Boekhandel, 1963; *Jeugjare* (autobiography), Bamboesberg, 1963; *Mallemeule* (novel), Afrikaanse Pers-Boekhandel, 1964; *Portrait of a South African Village* (monograph, bilingual edition), Bamboesberg, 1964; *Vader van sy Volk* (biography), Tafelberg, 1970; *Siem bam ba* (short stories and essays), Afrikaanse Pers, 1971; *Dagboek 2* (diary), Bamboesberg, 1972.

WORK IN PROGRESS: Sasol: The Realistic Miracle, a history of the South African Coal, Oil and Gas Corporation Ltd.

SIDELIGHTS: Meintjes is bilingual in English and Afrikaans. He prefers solitude—in the company of cats, lives in the country when possible, and once spent five years living in total isolation. *Avocational interests:* Reading, walking, collecting books (mainly Africana), and Cape Colonial furniture.

BIOGRAPHICAL/CRITICAL SOURCES: Pieter Marincowitz, *Meintjes—Lyrical Work* (monograph), Anreith Press, 1948; *Lantern*, March, 1963; Esme Berman, *Art and Artists of South Africa*, Balkema, 1970; *Panorama*, July, 1974.

* * *

MEISEL, John 1923-

PERSONAL: Born October 23, 1923, in Vienna, Austria;

son of Fryda (a businessman) and Ann (Heller) Meisel; married Murie Kelly (a designer), August 6, 1949. *Education:* University of Toronto, B.A., 1948, M.A., 1950; University of London, Ph.D., 1958. *Home:* 218 Albert St., Kingston, Ontario, Canada. *Office:* Queen's University, Kingston, Ontario, Canada.

CAREER: Queen's University, Kingston, Ontario, lecturer, 1951-53, assistant professor, 1953-60, associate professor, 1960-64, professor of political science, 1964-68, Hardy Professor of Political Science, 1968—, department head, 1965—. Research consultant, Royal Commission on Bilingualism and Biculturalism; member, Ontario Advisory Committee on Confederation.

WRITINGS: The Canadian General Election of 1957, University of Toronto Press, 1962; (editor) *Papers on the '62 Election*, University of Toronto Press, 1963; *Party Images in Canada*, Queens University, 1970; *Working Papers on Canadian Politics*, McGill-Queens University Press, 1972, enlarged edition, 1973. Contributor of articles to professional journals.

WORK IN PROGRESS: Research on Canadian party system and Canadian elections.

SIDELIGHTS: Meisel is competent in French, Czech, and German. *Avocational interests:* Bird watching, gardening, music, art, and tennis.†

*   *   *

MELAND, Bernard Eugene 1899-

PERSONAL: Born June 28, 1899, in Chicago, Ill.; son of Erik Bernhard (a cabinetmaker) and Elizabeth (Hansen) Meland; married Margaret Evans McClusky, August 6, 1926; children: Richard Dennis. *Education:* Park College, A.B., 1923; University of Illinois, graduate study, 1923-24; McCormick Theological Seminary, student, 1924-25; University of Chicago, B.D., 1928, Ph.D., 1929; University of Marburg, graduate study, 1928-29. *Politics:* Independent. *Home:* 6834 Oglesby Ave., Chicago, Ill. 60649. *Office:* Swift Hall, University of Chicago, Chicago, Ill. 60637.

CAREER: Ordained to Presbyterian ministry, 1928. Central College, Fayette, Mo., professor of religion and philosophy, 1929-36; Pomona College, Claremont, Calif., associate professor of religion, 1936-43, professor, 1943-45; University of Chicago, Chicago, Ill., professor of theology, 1945-64, visiting professor, 1965-68; visiting professor, Union Theological Seminary, 1968-69; Ottawa University, 1970. Barrows lecturer from University of Chicago in India and Burma, 1957-58, 1964-65. *Military service:* U.S. Army, 1918. *Member:* American Theological Society (president of Midwest division, 1960-61). *Awards, honors:* Alumni citation from Park College, 1954, honorary D.D., 1955; research grants for research at Cambridge University Library and British Museum, 1960, Huntington Library, 1962.

WRITINGS: Modern Man's Worship, Harper, 1934; (with Wieman) *American Philosophies of Religion*, Willett, Clark, 1936; *Write Your Own Ten Commandments*, Willett, Clark, 1938; *The Church and Adult Education*, American Association for Adult Education, 1939; *Seeds of Redemption*, Macmillan, 1947; *America's Spiritual Culture*, Harper, 1948; *The Reawakening of Christian Faith*, Macmillan, 1949; *Higher Education and the Human Spirit*, University of Chicago Press, 1953; *Faith and Culture*, Oxford University Press, 1953; *The Realities of Faith*, Oxford University Press, 1962; *The Secularization of Modern Cultures*, Oxford University Press, 1966; (editor

and contributor) *The Future of Empirical Theology*, University of Chicago Press, 1969.

Contributor: *Twentieth Century Encyclopedia of Religious Knowledge*, Volume II, Baker Book, 1955; Martin Marty and Dean G. Peerman, editors, *Handbook of Christian Theologians*, World Publishing, 1965; Philip Hefner, *The Scope of Faith*, Fortress Press, 1964; Philip Hefner, *The Scope of Grace*, Fortress Press, 1964; Robert W. Bretall, editor, *The Empirical Theology of Henry Nelson Wieman*, Macmillan, 1963.

Contributor to *Encyclopaedia Britannica* and of poems and articles to journals.

WORK IN PROGRESS: Research in the history of liberal theology and in religion and culture.

AVOCATIONAL INTERESTS: Music, poetry, architecture; carpentry and working with tools.

BIOGRAPHICAL/CRITICAL SOURCES: Christian Century, Volume LXXXI, Number 49, December 2, 1964; *Criterion* (publication of University of Chicago Divinity School), Volume III, Number 3, summer, 1964; *Quest* (publication of University of Chicago Divinity School), August, 1964; Harvey Arnold, *Near the Edge of Battle*, Divinity School Association, 1966.

*   *   *

MELARO, Constance L(oraine) 1929- (Monica Bruce)

PERSONAL: Surname is pronounced Me-*la*-ro; born November 15, 1929, on Oakmont, Pa.; daughter of John B. (a factory worker) and Rose (a beauty technician; maiden name, Toia) Melaro. *Education:* St. Mary's College, Notre Dame, Ind., B.A., 1951; Middlebury College, M.A., 1956; also attended Susquehanna University, Duquesne University, and University of Pittsburgh. *Politics:* Democrat. *Religion:* Roman Catholic.

CAREER: High school teacher in Ford City, Pa., 1951-52, Cheswick, Pa., 1952-54, Oakmont, Pa., 1954-61, Prince Georges County, Md., 1961-62, Howard County, Md., 1963-64; Dunbarton College of Holy Cross, Washington, D.C., assistant professor of French literature and language, beginning 1964. Visiting summer instructor in French at American University, 1964.

WRITINGS: Bitter Harvest: The Odyssey of a Teacher, Obolensky, 1965; (contributor) Martin Levin, editor, *The Bedside Phoenix Nest*, Ives Washburn, 1965; (contributor) *Writing: Unit Lessons in Composition*, Ginn, 1967. Contributor to *Saturday Review, Ingenue, Reader's Digest, Extension*, and other magazines.

SIDELIGHTS: Constance Melaro studied piano for fifteen years and has been a church organist (although having no formal training in organ) since early teens. She spoke Italian before learning English, but now her only foreign-language fluency is in French.

*   *   *

MELCHER, Robert Augustus 1910-

PERSONAL: Born March 5, 1910, in Ottumwa, Iowa; son of John Rudolph and Catherine (Grimmer) Melcher; married Anna Schmidt, July 13, 1935; children: Katherine Adelaide (Mrs. Jack Stuligross), Charlotte Anne (Mrs. John Leslie), Marian Schmidt. *Education:* Oberlin College, Mus.Sch.B., 1932, Ed.Mus.M., 1940; graduate study at Columbia University, 1940, Pius X School of Liturgical

Music, 1942, Juilliard School of Music, 1949, Accademia di Santa Cecilia 1962. *Politics:* Democrat. *Religion:* Roman Catholic. *Home:* 42 North Cedar St., Oberlin, Ohio 44074. *Office:* Conservatory of Music, Oberlin College, Oberlin, Ohio 44074.

CAREER: Teacher of violin and music theory at School of Fine Arts, Ottumwa, Iowa, 1932-33, Ohio Northern University, Ada, 1933-36; Oberlin College, Conservatory of Music, Oberlin, Ohio, instructor in school music, 1936-38, instructor in music theory, 1938-44, assistant professor, 1945-50; associate professor, 1951-57, professor of music theory, 1958—. Conductor of church choirs in Elyria, Ohio, 1941-43, Cleveland, Ohio, 1943-65. Lecturer on Gregorian chant. *Member:* American Association of University Professors, American Guild of Organists, Ohio Theory-Compostion Teachers Association (president, 1955-56), Pi Kappa Lambda, Oberlin City Club.

WRITINGS: (With Howard Murphy) *Music for Study*, Prentice-Hall, 1960, revised edition, with Willard Warch, 1973; (with Warch) *Music for Advanced Study*, Prentice-Hall, 1965; (with Warch) *Music for Keyboard Harmony*, Prentice-Hall, 1966 (with Warch) *Music For Score Reading*, Prentice-Hall, 1971.

* * *

MELDEN, A(braham) I(rving) 1910-

PERSONAL: Born February 9, 1910, in Montreal, Quebec, Canada; son of Max and Sadie (Milberg) Melden; married Regula Bernays, July 16, 1936; children: Jean, Regula. *Education:* University of California, Los Angeles, A.B., 1931; Brown University, A.M., 1932; University of California, Berkeley, Ph.D., 1938. *Home:* 1326 Hampshire Circle, Newport Beach, Calif. 92664. *Office:* Department of Philosophy, University of California, Irvine, Calif. 92650.

CAREER: University of California, Berkeley, instructor in philosophy, 1939-41; University of Washington, Seattle, assistant professor, 1946-50, associate professor, 1950-56, professor of philosophy, 1956-64; University of California, Irvine, professor of philosophy and chairman of department, 1964—. *Member:* American Philosophical Association (president, Pacific division, 1961-62), Council for Philosophical Studies, Phi Beta Kappa. *Awards, honors:* Ford Foundation fellow, 1955-56; Guggenheim Foundation fellow, 1961-62.

WRITINGS: Rights and Right Conduct, Basil Blackwell, 1959; (editor, and author of introduction) *Essays in Moral Philosophy*, University of Washington Press, 1959; *Free Action*, Routledge & Kegan Paul, 1961; (editor, and author of introduction) A. E. Murphy, *The Theory of Practical Reason*, Open Court, 1965; *Human Rights*, Wadsworth, 1970.

WORK IN PROGRESS: Editing and writing introduction for 3rd edition of *Ethical Theories*, for Prentice-Hall; writing *Moral Reasoning*.

* * *

MELENDY, H(oward) Brett 1924-

PERSONAL: Born May 3, 1924, in Eureka, Calif.; son of Howard Burton (an assessor) and Pearl (Brett) Melendy; married Marian Robinson, March 29, 1952; children: Brenda Dale, Darcie Brett, Lisa Marie. *Education:* Humboldt State College, student, 1942-45; Stanford University, A.B., 1946, M.A., 1948, Ph.D., 1952. *Politics:* Democrat.

Religion: Presbyterian. *Home:* 1519 Kamole St., Honolulu, Hawaii 96821. *Office:* Department of History, University of Hawaii, Honolulu, Hawaii 96822.

CAREER: High school teacher, Fresno, Calif., 1950-54; Fresno Junior College, Fresno, Calif., instructor, 1954-55; San Jose State College, San Jose, Calif., faculty member, 1955-70., chairman of history deparment, 1958-69, professor of history, 1961-70; University of Hawaii, Honolulu, professor of history, 1970—, vice-president for community colleges, 1970-73. College Entrance Examination Board, visiting representative of Council on College-Level Examinations, 1965-66. *Member:* American Historical Association, National Education Association, Masons. *Awards, honors:* American Philosophical Society grant, 1962 and 1974; American Council on Education fellowship, 1967-68.

WRITINGS: (With Benjamin F. Gilbert) *The Governors of California*, Talisman, 1965; *The Oriental Americans*, Twayne, 1972; (contributor) Roger Daniels and Spencer C. Olin, Jr., *Racism in California*, Macmillan, 1972. Contributor to *Encyclopaedia Britannica, Encyclopedia Americana*, and to historical journals.

WORK IN PROGRESS: Chinese in America and *Filipino, East Indian, and Korean Immigration to the United States*, for Twayne.

* * *

MELLOR, J(ohn) Leigh 1928-

PERSONAL: Born November 11, 1928, in London, England; son of Samuel Hall and Elizabeth (Murray) Mellor; married Mavis Yvonne Patricia Edwards, September 17, 1955; children: Corinne Elizabeth Timiane, Julian Felix Leigh. *Education:* University College, London, LL.B., 1951. *Politics:* Conservative. *Religion:* Anglican.

CAREER: Called to the bar, Inner Temple, London, England, 1952; practicing lawyer in London, England, 1952—. President, Hardwicke Society, 1953-54. *Military service:* Royal Air Force, 1946-48. *Member:* International Fiscal Association, 20-Ghost Club.

WRITINGS: Teach Yourself the Law, Universities Press, 1955, 3rd edition, 1966; *Income Tax*, Pitman, 1961. Contributor to *British Tax Review*.

AVOCATIONAL INTERESTS: Rolls-Royce cars, politics, and music.†

* * *

MELLOWN, Elgin W(endell, Jr.) 1931-

PERSONAL: Born December 29, 1931, in Selma, Ala.; son of Elgin W. (a school administrator) and Georgia (Clay) Mellown; married Muriel Jackson (an associate professor), June 22, 1957; children: Mary Ruth, Thomas Jackson. *Education:* Emory University, B.A., 1954; University of London, M.A., 1958, Ph.D., 1962. *Home:* 1004 Minerva Ave., Durham, N.C. *Office:* Department of English, Duke University, Durham, N.C.

CAREER: University of Alabama, University, instructor, 1958-60, assistant professor, 1962-65; Duke University, Durham, N.C., assistant professor, 1965-68, associate professor of English, 1968—. *Military service:* U.S. Army, 1954-56. *Member:* Modern Language Association of America.

WRITINGS: Bibliography of the Writings of Edwin Muir, University of Alabama Press, 1964, Supplement, 1971, 2nd revised edition, Vane, 1971; (with Peter Hoy) *A Checklist of Writings About Edwin Muir*, Whitston Press, 1971; *A Descriptive Catalogue of the Bibliographies of Twentieth-Century British Writers*, Whitston Press, 1972. Contributor of essays to scholarly journals.

WORK IN PROGRESS: Edwin Muir for Twayne's "English Authors" series.

* * *

MENDEL, Douglas H(eusted), Jr. 1921-

PERSONAL: Born October 18, 1921, in New York, N.Y.; son of Douglas Heusted (a banker) and Idalia (Collinson) Mendel. *Education:* Middlebury College, B.A. (magna cum laude), 1942; The University of Michigan, M.A., 1950, Ph.D., 1955. *Politics:* Liberal Republican. *Religion:* Presbyterian. *Home:* 3717 North Prospect, Shorewood, Wis. 53211.

CAREER: U.S. Military Government, South Korea, civilian adviser, 1946-47; University of California, Los Angeles, instructor, 1954-56, assistant professor of political science, 1956-61; Tunghai Christian University, Taichung, Formosa, Fulbright lecturer, 1961-62; University of Wisconsin, Milwaukee Campus, associate professor of political science, 1963—. Lecturer in Australia, 1962. Far East representative, Roper Public Opinion Research Center, Williams College; member of United States-Japan Trade Council. *Military service:* U.S. Navy, Naval Intelligence, 1943-46. *Member:* American Political Science Association, Association for Asian Studies, Foreign Policy Association, Midwest Conference of Political Scientists, Phi Beta Kappa. *Awards, honors:* Research grants 1957, 1962-63.

WRITINGS: The Japanese People and Foreign Policy, University of California Press, 1961; *The Politics of Formosan Nationalism*, University of California Press, 1970; *American Foreign Policy in a Polycentric World*, Dickenson, 1968, revised edition, 1974. Articles on Japan included in *Collier's Yearbook*, 1958-66; also contributor to *Asian Survey, Public Opinion Quarterly*, and other journals.

WORK IN PROGRESS: Contributing various book chapters on Taiwan, Chinese policy, and Japanese security; a journal article, "A Defense of Free China."

SIDELIGHTS: Mendel has spent a total of five years in post-war Japan (in ten trips), one year in Korea, one year in Formosa, and made four visits to western Europe.

* * *

MENDELSOHN, Everett 1931-

PERSONAL: Born October 28, 1931, in Yonkers, N.Y.; son of Morris H. and May (Albert) Mendelsohn; children: Daniel L., Sarah E., Joanna M. *Education:* Antioch College, A.B., 1953; Harvard University, Ph.D., 1960. *Office:* Harvard University, Holyoke Center 838, Cambridge, Mass. 02138.

CAREER: Harvard University, Cambridge, Mass., assistant professor, 1960-65, associate professor, 1965-69, professor of history of science, 1969—. Chairman of executive committee, American Friends Service Committee; trustee, Cambridge Friends School. *Member:* History of Science Society (council member), American Association for the Advancement of Science (fellow; council member, 1961-62), American Academy of Arts and Sciences (fellow).

WRITINGS: (Editor with I. B. Cohen and H. M. Jones) *Treasury of Scientific Prose*, Little, 1963; *Heat and Life*,

Harvard University Press, 1964; (editor) *Human Aspects of Biomedical Innovation*, Harvard University Press, 1971; (editor) *Science and Values*, Humanities, 1974. Editor, *Journal of the History of Biology*.

* * *

MENKUS, Belden 1931-

PERSONAL: Born May 6, 1931, in Sacramento, Calif.; son of Julian (a sales manager) and Ida (Dunnevitz) Menkus; married JoAnn Bozarth (a researcher), December 14, 1952; children: Neal, Belden, Jr., Donald, Juli Ann. *Education:* Attended Bob Jones University, 1949-51, Tennessee Temple College, 1952. *Politics:* Independent Democrat. *Religion:* Southern Baptist. *Home:* 7 Blauvelt Ave., Bergenfield, N.J. 07621.

CAREER: U.S. Air Force, records management technician at various locations, 1953-57; Southern Baptist Sunday School Board, Nashville, Tenn., records manager, 1957-62; Prentice-Hall, Inc., Englewood Cliffs, N.J., senior editor, 1962-64; Lybrand, Ross Bros. & Montgomery, New York, N.Y., consultant, 1964-65; Kennecott Copper Corp., New York, N.Y., senior management analyst, 1965-66; REA Express, New York, N.Y., director of administrative services, 1967-68; independent management consultant, 1968—. Member of faculty, New York University Management Institute, 1965-67, and U.S. Civil Defense Staff College, 1970—; judge of graphic arts competition, Printing Industries of America, 1974; member of Emmett Leahy Memorial Award Selection Committee, 1974.

MEMBER: Society of Professional Management Consultants, Society of Magazine Writers, Association for Systems Management, Society of American Archivists, National Microfilm Association, Association for State and Local History, American Records Management Association (regional vice-president, 1962-63), Near East Archaeological Society, National Conference of Christians and Jews, Interfaith Affairs Advisory Council, Conference on Faith and History, Association for the Development of Religious Information Systems, Business Forms Management Association, Conference on Jewish Social Studies, British Administrative Management Institute, British Microfilm Association, British Institute of Reprographic Technology, Evangelical Theological Society. *Awards, honors:* Silver Medallion from American Management Association, 1968, 1972; Distinguished Service Citation from National Microfilm Association, 1974.

WRITINGS: Meet the American Jew, Broadman, 1963; *Study Guide to Meet the American Jew*, Convention Press, 1966. Contributor to *Handbook of Modern Office Management and Administrative Services*, 1972, *Encyclopedia of Management*, 1973, *Dictionary of Christian Ethics*, 1974, and *Computer Security Handbook*, 1974. Contributor to professional and religious journals in United States and Canada. Editor, *Management Letter*, 1963-64, *Records Management Journal*, 1963-67, *Computer Security Letter*, 1974—; contributing editor, *Baptist Watchman-Examiner*, 1966-69, *Business Forms Reporter*, 1968, *Canadian Office Administrator*, 1968-70, *Business Graphics*, 1969-75, and *Administrative Management*, 1973—.

WORK IN PROGRESS: Forms Management Handbook; How to Detect and Prevent Computer Fraud; Microfilm Information Systems.

MENNINGER, Karl A. 1893-

PERSONAL: Born July 22, 1893, in Topeka, Kan.; son of Charles F. (a physician) and Flora V. (Knisely) Menninger; married Grace Gaines, September 9, 1916 (divorced, 1941); married Jeanetta Lyle (editor of *Bulletin of Menninger Clinic*), September 8, 1941; children: (first marriage) Julia (Mrs. A. H. Gottesman), Martha (Mrs. William Nichols), Robert Gaines; (second marriage) Rosemary Jeanetta Karla. *Education:* University of Wisconsin at Madison, A.B., 1914, B.S., 1915; Harvard Medical School, M.D. (cum laude), 1917. *Religion:* Presbyterian. *Home:* 1819 Westwood Circle, Topeka, Kan. *Office address:* Box 829, Topeka, Kan. 66601.

CAREER: The Menninger Foundation, Topeka, Kan., chief of staff, 1919—, chairman of board of trustees. Rotating internship, Kansas City General Hospital, 1917-1918; staff member, Stormont-Vail Hospital and St. Francis Hospital, Topeka, Kan., 1919—; assistant physician, Boston Psychopathic Hospital, 1918-20; assistant in neuropathology, Harvard Medical School, 1918-20; assistant in neurology, Tufts Medical School, 1919-20; manager, Winter Veterans Administration Hospital, Topeka, Kan., 1945-48; consultant in psychiatry to State of Illinois Department of Welfare, and Govenor of Illinois, 1953-54; dean, Menninger School of Psychiatry, Topeka, Kan., 1946—; clinical professor of psychiatry, University of Kansas Medical School, Kansas City, 1946-62; consultant, Office of Vocational Rehabilitation, Department of Health, Education, and Welfare, 1953-55; chairman of the board, The Menninger Foundation, 1954—; consultant, Bureau of Prisons, Department of Justice, 1956—. Trustee, Albert Deutsch Memorial Foundation, 1961, and Aspen Institute for Humanistic Studies, 1961-64.

MEMBER: Central Neuropsychiatric Association (secretary, 1922-32; president, 1932-33), American Orthopsychiatric Association (secretary, 1926-27; president, 1927-28), American Psychiatric Association (counselor, 1928-29, 1941-43), American Psychoanalytic Association (life member; president, 1941-43), American Association for Physical and Mental Rehabilitation, American League to Abolish Capital Punishment (vice-president), American Civil Liberties Union (vice-chairman of national committee), American Correctional Association, American Medical Association (fellow), American College of Physicians (life fellow), American Medical Writers Association (life member; 2nd vice-president, 1957-58; 1st vice-president, 1958-59), American Association for the Advancement of Science, World Medical Association for the Advancement of Science, World Medical Association, American Academy of Child Psychiatry.

AWARDS, HONORS: D.Sc., Washburn University, 1949; L.H.D., Park College, 1955; LL.D., Jefferson Medical College of Philadelphia, 1956; LL.D., Parsons College, 1960; LL.D., Kansas State University, 1962; L.H.D., Saint Benedict's College, 1963; D.Sc., University of Wisconsin, 1965; LL.D., Baker University, 1965; American Foundation of Religion and Psychiatry International Service award, 1968; L.H.D., Loyola University, 1972; L.L.D., Pepperdine University, 1974; L.H.D., DePaul University, 1974.

WRITINGS: The Human Mind, Knopf, 1930, 2nd edition, 1945; *Man Against Himself*, Harcourt, 1938; *Love Against Hate*, Harcourt, 1942; *A Guide to Psychiatric Books* (revised edition), Grune & Stratton, 1956, 3rd revised edition, 1972; *Theory of Psychoanalytic Technique*, Basic Books,

1958, revised edition with Philip Holzman, 1973; *A Psychiatrist's World*, Viking, 1959; *A Manual for Psychiatric Case Study* (revised edition), Grune & Stratton, 1962; *The Vital Balance*, Viking, 1963; *The Crime of Punishment*, Viking, 1968; *Sparks*, Crowell, 1973; *Whatever Became of Sin?*, Hawthorn, 1973. Editor-in-chief, *Bulletin of the Menninger Clinic*, 1936—; member of editorial board, *Archives of Criminal Psychodynamics*, *Psychoanalytic Quarterly*, *Excerpta Criminologica*, and *Academic Achievement*.

SIDELIGHTS: With his father, and brother William, Karl Menninger founded the famed Menninger clinic in 1919.

The importance of the clinic was noted in the citation of the Albert Lasker Group Award for 1955: "The Menninger Foundation and Clinic, headed by Drs. Karl and William Menninger, has provided a sustained and highly productive attack against mental disease for many years. Inspired by their father, Dr. Charles Frederick Menninger, these brothers have developed an outstanding institution which has served as an example for other mental disease hospitals.... The influence of the Menninger Foundation and Clinic in increasing professional and public interest in the care of the mentally ill cannot be measured, but it is indelibly recorded as a great service to mankind."

In his review of *The Vital Balance*, H. L. Moose wrote: "It is Menninger's basic position that all forms of mental illness are essentially the same in quality, differing quantatively.... [He] is not interested in finding specific causes. He thinks in vague terms." But F. J. Braceland added: "One need not agree with all that is said here to realize that this is an excellent and scholarly work, well documented and interestingly written."

BIOGRAPHICAL/CRITICAL SOURCES: New York Times, November 6, 1955; *Look*, September 30, 1958; Elizabeth L. Davis, *Fathers of America*, Revell, 1958; *Saturday Evening Post*, April 7, 1962, April 14, 1962, April 21, 1962, April 28, 1962; *Saturday Review*, January 25, 1964; *New York Times Book Review*, December 29, 1964; Caroline A. Chandler, *Famous Modern Men of Medicine*, Dodd, 1965.

* * *

MENZIES, Elizabeth G(rant) C(ranbrook) 1915-

PERSONAL: Born June 24, 1915, in Princeton, N.J.; daughter of Alan W. C. (a university professor) and Mary Isabella (Dickson) Menzies. *Education:* Educated at Miss Fine's School, Princeton, N.J., 1922-33, and privately. *Home:* 926 Kingston Rd., Princeton, N.J. 08540.

CAREER: Free-lance photographer; photographs exhibited at one-man show in Baltimore Museum of Art, and at three simultaneous showings at Princeton University, 1956. *Member:* Society of Architectural Historians, New Jersey Historical Society, Stony Brook-Millstone Watersheds Association. *Awards, honors:* New Jersey Tercentenary Medal; Award of Merit from American Association for State and Local History for *Princeton Architecture*, and Citation of Commendation for *Millstone Valley*; Author Award from New Jersey Association of Teachers of English for *Millstone Valley*.

WRITINGS: Before the Waters: The Upper Delaware Valley, Rutgers University Press, 1966; (with M. Gibbons and C. Greiff) *Princeton Architecture*, Princeton University Press, 1967; *Millstone Valley*, Rutgers University Press, 1969.

WORK IN PROGRESS: General Washington's Highway:

Route 27-206; Scotland and Early New Jersey; and a picture book, *The Seasons Where I Live.*

SIDELIGHTS: Ms. Menzies special interests embrace architectural history and geographical history in relation to the American heritage, and problems of conservation and preservation resulting from "progress."

* * *

MERLISS, Reuben 1915-

PERSONAL: Born March 20, 1915, in New York, N.Y.; son of Reuben and Shifrah (Mishkin) Merliss; children: Joshua, Matthew, Leslie. *Education:* Wayne State University, B.A., 1935, M.D., 1939. *Politics:* Democratic. *Religion:* Jewish. *Office:* 8820 Wilshire Blvd., Beverly Hills, Calif.

CAREER: Physician, specializing in practice of internal medicine, 1942—; private practice, Beverly Hills, Calif., 1945—; Loma Linda University, Medical School, Loma Linda, Calif., associate clinical professor of medicine, 1955—. *Member:* American Medical Association, American College of Physicians, American Occupational Medical Association (fellow). *Awards, honors:* Commonwealth Club of California Silver Medal, 1965, for *Year of the Death.*

WRITINGS: Year of the Death (novel), Doubleday, 1965; *Consider the Season* (novel), Doubleday, 1968.

* * *

MERRELL, James L(ee) 1930-

PERSONAL: Born October 24, 1930, in Indianapolis, Ind.; son of Mark W. (an insurance man) and Pauline (Tucker) Merrell; married Barbara Jeanne Burch, December 23, 1951; children: Deborah Lea, Cynthia Lynn, Stuart Allen. *Education:* Indiana University, A.B., 1952; Christian Theological Seminary, Indianapolis, Ind., B.D., 1956. *Home:* 5347 Warmwinds Ct., St. Louis, Mo. 63129. *Office address:* Christian Board of Publication, Box 179, St. Louis, Mo. 63166.

CAREER: Ordained minister of Christian Churches (Disciples of Christ), 1956; *World Call* (Christian Churches monthly magazine), Indianapolis, Ind., associate editor, 1956-66; Crestview Christian Church, Indianapolis, Ind., pastor, 1966-71; *World Call*, editor, 1971-73; *Disciple*, St. Louis, Mo., 1974—. *Member:* Associated Church Press, Religious Public Relations Council (vice-president of Indiana chapter), Christian Theological Seminary Alumni Association (president, 1966-68), Sigma Delta Chi. *Awards, honors:* Lit.D. from Culver-Stockton College, 1972.

WRITINGS: World Call—A Venture in Religious Journalism, World Call Publication Committee, 1956; *They Live Their Faith,* Bethany, 1965. Editorial consultant, *Indiana Christian.*

WORK IN PROGRESS: A book on national church leaders overseas.

* * *

MERRITT, Helen Henry 1920-

PERSONAL: Born June 15, 1920, in Norfolk, Va.; daughter of John Crockett (a government employee) and Mabel (Richards) Henry; married James W. Merritt (a university professor), January 22, 1946; children: Deborah. *Education:* University of Hawaii, student, 1938-40; Colby College, B.A., 1942; Rockford College, M.A., 1956;

Northern Illinois University, M.F.A., 1962; post-graduate work at Girton College, Cambridge, and Tokyo University of Fine Arts. *Politics:* Democrat. *Religion:* Unitarian Universalist. *Home:* 419 Garden Rd., DeKalb, Ill. 60115.

CAREER: Taught at Harvard Nursery School, Cambridge, Mass., 1946-47, DeKalb (Ill.) Public Schools, 1955-57; did studio teaching, 1947-55, 1958-62; Northern Illinois University, DeKalb, assistant professor, 1962-73, associate professor of art, 1973—. Free-lance artist in ceramic sculpture.

WRITINGS: Guiding Free Expression in Children's Art, Holt, 1964.

* * *

MERRITT, Miriam 1925-

PERSONAL: Born January 29, 1925, in Robstown, Tex.; daughter of Arthur (a farmer and rancher) and Anna Isabel (Schutze) Merritt. *Education:* University of Texas, B.J. 1946; graduate study at Columbia University, Stanford University, and University of Mexico Escuela de Verano. *Politics:* Democrat. *Religion:* Unitarian Universalist. *Residence:* Houston, Tex.

CAREER: Corpus Christi Caller-Times, Corpus Christi, Tex., reporter, 1946-48; secretary with Daniel Starch & Staff, New York, N.Y., 1948-49, and *Saturday Review,* New York, N.Y., 1949; *Texas Outlook* (magazine), Austin, editorial staff, 1951-52; free-lance writer, 1952—. Secretary and public relations work for political organization in Dallas, Tex., 1953-54, and for professional theater in Houston, Tex., 1964. Actor and director with Channing Players, Houston, Tex. *Member:* Authors Guild of the Authors League of America. *Awards, honors:* Creative writing fellowship to Stanford University, 1952-53; fiction award from Theta Sigma Phi for *By Lions, Eaten Gladly,* 1965.

WRITINGS: By Lions, Eaten Gladly (novel), Harcourt, 1965. Contributor of short stories to literary periodicals, including *Epoch, Southwest Review, Stanford Short Stories, New Campus Writing, University of Kansas City Review*; also contributor of book reviews to *Houston Post.*

WORK IN PROGRESS: a novel, untitled.

SIDELIGHTS: Competent in Spanish and German. *Avocational interests:* Arts, woodcarving.

* * *

MESKILL, Johanna Menzel 1930-
(Johanna Menzel)

PERSONAL: Born October 27, 1930, in Frankfurt am Main, Germany; daughter of Hans W. (a businessman) and Gertrude (von Holzhausen) Menzel; married John Meskill (a professor), September 7, 1965. *Education:* Attended University of Frankfurt, 1950-51; Rockford College, B.A., 1952; University of Chicago, M.A., 1953, Ph.D., 1957. *Office:* Department of History, Lehman College of the City University of New York, Bronx, N.Y. 10468.

CAREER: Vassar College, Poughkeepsie, N.Y., instructor, 1956-60, assistant professor, 1960-65, associate professor of history, 1965-68; Lehman College of the City University of New York, Bronx, N.Y., associate professor, 1968-72, professor of Chinese history, 1973—. Visiting associate professor, Columbia University, summer, 1966. *Member:* Association for Asian Studies, Society for Ch'ing Studies, Phi Beta Kappa. *Awards, honors:* Fellowship in Oriental studies, Columbia University, 1960-61; National Defense Education Act fellowships, 1961, 1964; Fulbright fellowship to Taiwan, 1962; American Council of Learned Societies-Social Science Research Council grant for research on Asia, 1964-65.

WRITINGS: (Editor under name Johanna Menzel) *The Chinese Civil Service: Career Open to Talent?*, Heath, 1963; *Hitler and Japan: The Hollow Alliance*, Atherton, 1966; (contributor) M. Freedman, editor, *Family and Kinship in Chinese Society*, Stanford University Press, 1970; (contributor) L. H. D. Gordon, editor, *Taiwan: Studies in Chinese Local History*, Columbia University Press, 1970; (with husband, John Meskill, and Ainslie T. Embree) *The Non-European World, 1500-1850*, Scott, Foresman, 1971. Contributor of articles and reviews to history journals.†

* * *

METCALF, Keyes DeWitt 1889-

PERSONAL: Born April 13, 1889, in Elyria, Ohio; son of Isaac Stevens (an engineer) and Harriet (Howes) Metcalf; married Martha Gerrish, June 16, 1914 (died, 1938); married Elinor Gregory, July 12, 1941; children: (first marriage) Margaret Gerrish (Mrs. Maxwell M. Small), William Gerrish. *Education:* Oberlin College, A.B., 1911; New York Public Library School, certificate, 1913; diploma, 1915. *Home and office:* 68 Fairmont St., Belmont, Mass. 02178.

CAREER: Oberlin College Library, Oberlin, Ohio, executive assistant, 1912, acting librarian, 1916-17; New York Public Library, New York, N.Y., chief of stacks, 1913-16, 1917-18, executive assistant, 1919-27, chief of reference department, 1928-37; Harvard University, Cambridge, Mass., director of University Library and librarian of Harvard College, 1937-55, professor of bibliography, 1945-55, librarian emeritus, 1955—. Adjunct professor, Rutgers University Library School, 1955-58; Fulbright lecturer in Australia, 1958-59. Consultant to more than four hundred libraries in United States; also has done consultantship work in Ireland, 1960, Japan, 1961, Australia, 1961-63, and in various countries of Southeast Asia, Africa, South and Central America, and Canada. Trustee of Radcliffe College, 1939-45, Massachusetts State Library, 1942-60, and Boston Athenaeum, 1960—.

MEMBER: American Academy of Arts and Sciences, American Library Association (president, 1942-43), Association of Research Libraries (executive secretary, 1938-42), American Antiquarian Society (member of council), Massachusetts Historical Society, Bibliographical Society of America, Bibliographical Society of London. *Awards, honors:* L.H.D., Yale University, 1946; LL.D., Harvard University, 1951, University of Toronto, 1954, Marquette University, 1958, Grinnell College, 1959, and St. Louis University, 1959; Litt.D., Brandeis University, 1959; other honorary degrees from Oberlin College, University of Notre Dame, Bowdoin College, Hamilton College, and Indiana State University; Knight of First Class (Norway); New York Public Library 50th Anniversary Award.

WRITINGS: (with John D. Russell and Andrew D. Osborn) *The Program of Instruction in Library Schools*, University of Illinois Press, 1943; (with Janet Doe, Thomas P. Fleming, and others) *The National Medical Library: Report of a Survey of the Army Medical Library*, American Library Association, 1944; (with Louis R. Wilson and Donald Coney) *A Report on Certain Problems of the Libraries and School of Library Service of Columbia University*, Columbia University Libraries, 1947; *Report on the Harvard University Library, A Study of Present and Prospective Problems*, Harvard University Library, 1955;

Planning Academic and Research Library Buildings, McGraw, 1965; *Planning the Academic Library: Metcalf and Ellsworth at York*, Oriel Press, 1971. Writer of reports on library surveys; contributor to professional journals.

* * *

MEYER, Alfred George 1920-

PERSONAL: Born February 5, 1920, in Germany; son of Gustav Nmi and Therese (Melchior) Meyer; married Eva R. Apel, 1946; children: Stefan G., Vera E. *Education:* Harvard University, A.M., 1946, Ph.D., 1950. *Home:* 4081 East Huron River Dr., Ann Arbor, Mich. 48104. *Office:* Department of Political Science, University of Michigan, Ann Arbor, Mich. 48104.

CAREER: Harvard University, Cambridge, Mass., 1949-53, began as research fellow and assistant to the director of the Russian Research Center, became assistant director; University of Washington, Seattle, acting assistant professor of political science and history, 1953-55; Columbia University, New York, N.Y., director of research program on the history of the Communist Party of the Soviet Union, 1955-57; Michigan State University, East Lansing, associate professor, 1957-60, professor of political science, 1960-66; University of Michigan, Ann Arbor, professor of political science, 1966—. Visiting professorships or lectureships for brief periods at Hunter College, University of Maine, Portland State University, and Free University of Berlin. *Military service:* U.S. Army, 1941-45; became first lieutenant; awarded Bronze Star.

WRITINGS: What You Should Know About Communism (pamphlet), Science Research Associates, 1953; (with Gustav Hilger) *The Incompatible Allies: A Memoir-History of German-Soviet Relations, 1918-1941*, Macmillan, 1953; *Marxism: The Unity of Theory and Practice*, Harvard University Press, 1954; *Leninism*, Harvard University Press, 1957; *Communism*, Random House, 1960, 2nd revised edition, 1963; *Marxism Since the Communist Manifesto* (pamphlet), Service Center for Teachers of History, 1961; *The Soviet Political System: An Interpretation*, Random House, 1965.

* * *

MEYER, D. Swing 1938-

PERSONAL: Born April 12, 1938, in New York, N.Y.; son of J. Edward, Jr. (a businessman) and Carolyn (Starring) Meyer; married Caroline Finlay, May 8, 1965. *Education:* Yale University, B.A., 1960. *Politics:* Republican. *Religion:* Episcopalian.

CAREER: Has worked as magazine subscription salesman, attendant to Billy Graham, and soup salesman; Ruder & Finn, Inc. (public relations), New York, N.Y., and Los Angeles, Calif., public relations counselor, 1964-65, senior associate, 1966—. Former public relations director, New York Young Republican Club.

WRITINGS: The Winning Candidate: How to Defeat Your Political Opponent, James Heineman, 1966.

BIOGRAPHICAL/CRITICAL SOURCES: King Features Syndicate, April 23-24, 1966.†

* * *

MEYER, Roy W(illard) 1925-

PERSONAL: Born January 20, 1925, in Zumbrota, Minn.; son of Fred (a farmer) and Anna (Nelson) Meyer; married

Betty L. Thomas, August 13, 1955; children: Annette Louise. *Education:* St. Olaf College, B.A., 1948; summer graduate study at University of Maine, 1947, University of Minnestoa, 1948; University of Iowa, M.A., 1949, Ph.D., 1957. *Politics:* Democrat. *Home:* 207 Ellis Ave., Mankoto, Minn. 56001. *Office:* Mankato State College, Mankato, Minn. 56001.

CAREER: Valley City State College, Valley City, N.D., instructor in English and history, 1950-57; Mankato State College, Mankato, Minn., assistant professor, 1957-65, associate professor, 1965-67, professor of English, 1967—. Fulbright lecturer, Australia, 1969. *Military service:* U.S. Army, 1944-46; served in Mediterranean and European theaters; became sergeant; received Army Commendation Ribbon. *Member:* American Studies Association, American Association of University Professors, Wilderness Society, Western Historical Association, Western Literature Association, Minnesota Historical Society. *Awards, honors:* Solon J. Buck Award, 1962, for article, "The Prairie Island Community," in *Minnesota History;* research grant, American Association for State and Local History, 1963; Western History Award, 1969, for article, "The Canadian Sioux," in *Minnesota History;* research grant, American Philosphical Society, 1973.

WRITINGS: The Middle Western Farm Novel in the Twentieth Century, University of Nebraska Press, 1965; *History of the Santee Sioux,* University of Nebraska Press, 1968; *A History of the Village Indians of the Upper Missouri,* University of Nebraska Press, 1975. Contributor to *American Scandinavian Review, National Parks Magazine, Journal of Popular Culture, American Studies, Western American Literature,* and regional history journals.

WORK IN PROGRESS: Contributions to *Bibliographic Guide to Midwestern Literature;* editing letters of Lewis H. Giarrard.

SIDELIGHTS: Long-standing interest in the American Indian, his history, and his present condition. Actively interested in environmental matters, especially state and national parks.

*   *   *

MEYERS, Joan Simpson   1927-

PERSONAL: Born September 20, 1927, in Boulder, Colo.; daughter of George Gaylord Simpson (a paleontologist and professor); children: Trina Anne Meyers, Peter Alexander Meyers. *Education:* University of Michigan, B.A.

CAREER: Partisan Review, New York, N.Y., staff member, 1960; Basic Books, Inc., New York, N.Y., editor, 1961-63; Columbia Broadcasting System-Columbia Records, New York, N.Y., literary editor, 1964-66.

WRITINGS: Poetry and a Libretto, A. Swallow, 1965; (with George Whitaker) *Dinosaur Hunt,* Harcourt, 1965; (editor) *John Fitzgerald Kennedy: As We Remember Him,* Atheneum, 1965.

WORK IN PROGRESS: A novel; poetry; nonfiction.†

*   *   *

MEYERS, Robert Rex   1923-

PERSONAL: Born August 7, 1923, in Okmulgee, Okla.; son of William Elmer and Albertine Gray (Martin) Meyers; married Billie Louise Bearden, July 30, 1948; children: Karen Kay, Robin Rex, Devon Dee. *Education:* Abilene

Christian College, B.A. (summa cum laude), 1948; University of Oklahoma, M.A., 1951; Washington University, St. Louis, Mo., Ph.D., 1957. *Office:* Department of English, Wichita State University, Wichita, Kan. 67208.

CAREER: Daily Free-Lance, Henryetta, Okla., editor, 1951-53; Harding College, Searcy, Ark., assistant professor, 1953-54, associate professor of English, 1957-60; Friends University, Wichita, Kan., associate professor, 1960-64, professor of English, 1964-67, chairman of Division of Humanities, 1960-67; Wichita State University, Wichita, Kan., professor of English, 1967—. Visiting summer professor at Stetson University, 1963, and United States International University, 1966. *Military service:* U.S. Army, 1943-46; served as instructor in army schools, and as radio and newspaper correspondent; became sergeant. *Member:* Modern Language Association of America, National Council of Teachers of English, Kansas Association of Teachers of English. *Awards, honors:* Awards for excellence in teaching from Harding College and Friends University.

WRITINGS: (Editor) *Voices of Concern,* Mission Press, 1966; *George Borrow,* Twayne, 1966. Contributor of articles and reviews to religious and scholarly journals, of reviews to *Dallas Times-Herald.* Member of editorial board, University of Kansas Press; editorial consultant, *Choice.*

WORK IN PROGRESS: A book on the Restoration Movement, a nineteenth-century religious phenomenon; monographs on folk etymology in the Midlands and several other subjects.

AVOCATIONAL INTERESTS: Scholarly biblical studies; collecting folk etymologies, Spoonerisms, euphemisms, and epitaphs.

*   *   *

MICHAEL, Paul Martin   1934-

PERSONAL: Born February 2, 1934, in Brooklyn, N.Y.; son of Nathan L. (an attorney) and Adele (Kurtin) Michael. *Education:* Vanderbilt University, B.A., 1955; also studied at Brooklyn Law School. *Home and office:* 342 East 67th St., New York, N.Y. 10021. *Agent:* John Starr, 240 West End Ave., New York, N.Y. 10023.

CAREER: Industrials Illustrated, New York, N.Y., producer and writer of television commercials and documentaries, 1958-59; *Frozen Food Age* and *Show Business,* New York, N.Y., managing editor, 1959-61; free-lance copywriter, 1961-62; Singer Features (syndicate), Buena Park, Calif., correspondent in Middle East, Israel, and Italy, 1962; Doubleday & Co. (publishers), Garden City, N.Y., began as copywriter, became copy chief in Book Club Division, 1962-63; *Book Reviews* (booksellers' guide to new books), New York, N.Y., editor and publisher, 1964—; Greystone Corp. (publishers), New York, N.Y., vice-president and creative director, 1966-71; Good News Publishing Co., New York, N.Y., executive vice-president, 1971-74; Marketing Dynamics, Inc., New York, N.Y., president, 1974—. *Military service:* U.S. Army, 1955-57.

WRITINGS: The Academy Awards: A Pictorial History, Bobbs-Merrill, 1964, 2nd edition, Crown, 1967; *Humphrey Bogart: The Man and His Films,* Bobbs-Merrill, 1965; *American Movies Reference Book,* Prentice-Hall, 1968; *The Emmy Awards: A Pictorial History,* Crown, 1969; *Professional Football's Greatest Games,* Prentice-Hall, 1970; *How to Make $30,000 A Year in a Mail Order Business of Your Own,* Vicount Press, 1971.

WORK IN PROGRESS: The Promise and the Performance, a research study of American political platforms.

* * *

MICHAELS, Sidney R(amon) 1927-

PERSONAL: Born August 17, 1927, in New York, N.Y.; son of Max (a theater manager) and Helen (Gould) Michaels; married Louisette Roser, November 29, 1956; children: Cotter Mark, Candia Bernaud. *Education:* Tufts University, B.A. (cum laude), 1949.

CAREER: Playwright. *Military service:* U.S. Coast Guard, 1945-46. *Member:* American Society of Composers, Authors and Publishers, Dramatists Guild, Writers Guild of America, West. *Awards, honors:* Glascock Poetry Prize, Mount Holyoke College, 1947; Ford Foundation Playwrights' Award for "The Plaster Bambino," 1959; LL.D., Tufts University, 1965.

WRITINGS—Plays, produced in year of publication, except as noted: *Tchin-Tchin* (two act comedy), Samuel French, 1962; *Dylan*, Random House, 1964; (book and lyrics) *Ben Franklin in Paris* (first produced in 1964), Random House, 1965.

Other dramas: "The Plaster Bambino"; television plays including "Richard Diamond," "Johnny Staccato," "The Deputy," and scripts for "G. E. Theatre," 1957-59; "Key Witness" (motion picture), Metro-Goldwyn-Mayer, 1959.

Plays included in anthologies, including *Best Plays of 1962-63*, Dodd, 1963 and *Best Plays of 1963-64*, Dodd, 1964.

WORK IN PROGRESS: A new play, "The Booties of Butternut Hill."

SIDELIGHTS: Each of Michaels' three Broadway hits, "Tchin-Tchin," "Dylan," and "Ben Franklin in Paris," ran for more than 200 performances and he became a success in what he calls "this wonderful crazy business." Michaels wrote: "Success is a writer who cannot sell a TV script to save his life, coming into New York, Labor Day, 1961, with $7 in the world, and a wife and child in California, and selling five options on five plans in five days and returning home with $8000 in advances."

In 1964 he was ready to comment on the merits of recognition as a successful Broadway playwright: 'Success is sweet. It's too easy to say that it is also bitter. Of course, sunlight produces a shadow. You demand more of yourself, you grow greedy for the oxygen of productions after such a long vacuum, you over-commit, you have to organize yourself ruthlessly to find time for your family, an external problem. But it seems to me a little ungrateful to complain. Whenever you reach the top of Mt. Everest you have to expect the wind will blow harder, it'll be colder and you'll even feel a little lonely—perhaps a little abominable like that forlorn snowman. With success, good things happen to you, are accumulated by you and surround you, but while they are good, those are only things—you still wake up every day just yourself."

Film rights for "Dylan" have been purchased by Columbia Pictures.

BIOGRAPHICAL/CRITICAL SOURCES: Show, October, 1964.†

* * *

MICKELSEN, Olaf 1912-

PERSONAL: Born July 29, 1912, in Perth Amboy, N.J.; son of Frederik and Marie (Nielsen) Mickelsen; married Edith Louise Nielsen, December 1, 1939 (died February 22, 1953); married Clarice Lewerenz, September 9, 1953; children: (first marriage) Elizabeth Karen (Mrs. T. W. Kurczynski), Margaret Louise (Mrs. D. A. Funk). *Education:* Rutgers, The State University (now Rutgers University), B.S., 1935; University of Wisconsin, M.S., 1937, Ph.D., 1939. *Home:* 4412 Tacoma Blvd., Okemos, Mich. 48864. *Office:* Michigan State University, East Lansing, Mich. 48823.

CAREER: University of Minnesota, Minneapolis, chemist in university hospitals, 1939-41, research associate, Laboratory of Physiology Hygiene, 1941-45, assistant professor, 1944-46, associate professor, 1946-48; U.S. Public Health Service, Washington, D.C., chemist, Nutrition Branch, 1948-51, chief of Laboratory of Nutrition and Endocrinology, National Institute of Arthritis and Metabolic Diseases, National Institutes of Health, Bethesda, Md., 1951-61; Michigan State University, East Lansing, professor of nutrition, with joint appointment to department of food and nutrition and department of biochemistry, 1962—. Consultant to nutrition study sections of National Institutes of Health and to commercial firms. *Member:* American Institute of Nutrition (secretary, 1963-66; president, 1973-74), American Chemical Society, Society for Experimental Biology and Medicine, American Society of Biological Chemists, American Academy of Nutrition, American Public Health Association, British Nutrition Society, Phi Beta Kappa, Phi Kappa Phi, Omicron Nu (honorary member), Sigma Xi.

WRITINGS: (With A. Keys, J. Brozek, A. Henschel, and H. L. Taylor) *The Biology of Human Starvation*, two volumes, University of Minnesota Press, 1950; *Nutrition Science and You*, Scholastic Book Services, 1964. Author or co-author of more than two hundred articles on biochemistry and nutrition. Associate editor, *Nutrition Reviews*, 1954—, *Journal of Nutrition*, 1960-63.

* * *

MICKS, Marianne H(offman) 1923-

PERSONAL: Born April 30, 1923, in Seneca Falls, N.Y.; daughter of Ransom Rathbone and Emma Louise (Hoffman) Micks. *Education:* Smith College, A.B., 1945; Columbia University, M.A., 1948; Church Divinity School of the Pacific, B.D., 1957; Yale University, Ph.D., 1960. *Religion:* Christian. *office:* Virginia Theological Seminary, Alexandria, Va. 22304.

CAREER: Prior to 1960, worked in university ministry with National Council of Episcopal Church at Smith College, Northampton, Mass., and University of California, Berkeley, Western College for Women, Oxford, Ohio, chairman of department of religion, 1960-66, dean and professor of religion, 1966-74; Virginia Theological Seminary, Alexandria, professor of Biblical and historical theology, 1974—. *Member:* Society of Biblical Literature, American Academy of Religion, Society for Religion in Higher Education, Phi Beta Kappa.

WRITINGS: Introduction to Theology, Seabury, 1964; *The Future Present: The Phenomenon of Christian Worship*, Seabury, 1970.

* * *

MIDGLEY, David A(lan) 1898-

PERSONAL: Born December 8, 1898, in Providence, R.I.; son of Henry Alec (a silversmith) and Clara (Upton)

Midgley; married Edith A. Singleton, April 11, 1927; children: Dorothy Ann (Mrs. J. Norman Wilkinson), David Alan, Jr. *Education:* Brown University, Ph.B., 1923; Harvard University, M.A., 1926. *Office:* Albany Academy, 46 Norwood Ave., Albany, N.Y. 12208.

CAREER: High school teacher of English, Amherst, Mass., 1924-25; Albany Academy, Albany, N.Y., head of history department, 1925-71. Russell Sage College, Albany Division, lecturer on history and government in evening classes, 1948-68. New York State Department of Education, consultant in preparation of history teaching material, 1954, 1964.

WRITINGS: How to Prepare for College Board: Achievement Tests in Social Studies, Barron's, 1964; *Social Studies: American History*, Barron's, 1965, 3rd edition, 1974; (with Nelson Close) *American History at a Glance*, Barrons, 1966, 3rd edition, 1974.

* * *

MIERNYK, William Henry 1918-

PERSONAL: Born January 8, 1918, in Durango, Colo.; son of Andrew Taber and Elizabeth (Sopko) Miernky; married Mary Lorraine Davis, October 1, 1942; children, Jan Andrew, Judith, Jeanne, James. *Education:* Fort Lewis Agricultural and Mechanical College (now Fort Lewis College), student, 1936-38; University of Colorado, B.A., 1946, M.A., 1947; Harvard University, M.A., 1952, Ph.D., 1953. *Politics:* Democrat. *Religion:* Roman Catholic. *Home:* 824 Price St., Morgantown, W.Va. 26505. *Office:* Regional Research Institute, West Virginia University, Morgantown, W.Va. 26506.

CAREER: University of Colorado, Boulder, instructor in economics, 1946-49; Northeastern University, Boston, Mass. 1950-62; began as assistant professor, professor of economics, 1956-62; University of Colorado, professor of economics, 1962-65; West Virginia University, Morgantown, Benedum Professor of economics and director of Regional Research Institute, 1965—. Visiting professor of economics at Massachusetts Institute of Technology, 1957-58, and Harvard University, 1969-70. Consultant to New England Telephone and Telegraph Co., 1955-62, and U.S. Senate Committee on Commerce, 1958-63; member of research subcommittee, National Manpower Advisory Committee, 1963-68. *Military service:* U.S. Army, 1940-45; became first sergeant. *Member:* American Economic Association, Industrial Relations Research Association, Regional Science Association.

WRITINGS: (With Arthur A. Bright, Jr. and others) *The Economic State of New England*, Yale University Press, 1954; *Inter-Industry Labor Mobility*, Northeastern University Press, 1955; *Depressed Industrial Areas* (monograph), National Planning Association, 1957; (with Manuel Zymelmen) *Inventories in the Textile Cycle* (monograph), U.S. Department of Commerce, 1961; *Trade Unions in the Age of Affluence*, Random House, 1962; *The Economics of Labor and Collective Bargaining*, Heath, 1965, revised edition, 1973; *The Elements of Input-Output Analysis*, Random House, 1965; (with others) *Impact of the Space Program on a Local Economy*, West Virginia University Press, 1967; (with others) *Simulating Regional Economic Development*, Heath, 1970; *Economics*, Random House, 1971; (with John T. Shears) *Air Pollution Abatement and Regional Economic Development*, Heath, 1974. Also writer of other monographs, as well as book reviews, chapters contributed to other books, and journal articles.

WORK IN PROGRESS: Development and application of regional and interregional input-output models.

* * *

MILLENDER, Dharathula H(ood) 1920-

PERSONAL: Born February 4, 1920, in Terre Haute, Ind.; daughter of Orestes (an electrical technician) and Daisy (a teacher; maiden name, Eslick) Hood; divorced; children: Naomi Estelle, Justine Faye. *Education:* Indiana State University, B.S., 1941, graduate work in library science; other graduate study in library science at Indiana University, Catholic University of America, and Purdue University. *Religion:* Lutheran. *Residence:* Gary, Ind. *Office:* Pulaski School, 1867 Georgia St., Gary, Ind.

CAREER: Teacher and school librarian in Trenton, S.C., 1941-42, and La Plata, Md., 1942-43; Library of Congress, Washington, D.C., reference assistant, 1943; Indiantown Gap (Pa.) Military Reservation, librarian, 1943-44; junior high school librarian in Baltimore, Md., 1952-60; Pulaski Junior High School, Gary, Ind., librarian, 1960—. Chairman of Negro History Week Observance, Gary, 1962-64, 1966, 1967. *Member:* American Federation of Teachers, National Association for the Advancement of Colored People (member, Negro Cultural Achievement Committee, 1967), Indiana School Library Association, Indiana State Teachers Association, Alpha Kappa Alpha.

WRITINGS: Crispus Attucks: Boy of Valor (juvenile), Bobbs-Merrill, 1965; *Yesterday in Gary: History of the Negro in Gary, 1906-1967*, [Gary, Ind.], 1967; *Real Negros, Honest Settings: Children's and Young People's Books About Negro Life and History*, American Federation of Teachers, 1967; *Martin Luther King, Jr.: Boy With a Dream*, Bobbs-Merrill, 1969; *Louis Armstrong: Young Music Maker*, Bobbs-Merrill, 1972. Writer of weekly column, "Yesterday in Gary," appearing in local newspaper; contributor and former editor, *Gary Crusader*. Contributor to *Education* and *Changing Education*.

WORK IN PROGRESS: The second volume of *Yesterday in Gary*; numerous short stories and articles.

BIOGRAPHICAL/CRITICAL SOURCES: Gary Post-Tribune, August 4, 1965.†

* * *

MILLER, Donald L(ane) 1918-

PERSONAL: Born May 14, 1918, in Pittsburgh, Pa.; son of Donald Edwin (an educator) and Arvilla (Lane) Miller; married Norma Reno (in public relations), February 2, 1951. *Education:* Kenyon College, A.B., 1940; graduate courses at University of Pittsburgh and University of Colorado. *Home:* 309 Green St., Alexandria, Va. 22314.

CAREER: Reporter for *Pittsburgh Sun-Telegraph*, Pittsburgh, Pa. 1940-42, and *Washington Post*, Washington, D.C. 1946; publicity writer, Westinghouse Electric Corp., 1947-51; Washington correspondent for *Tide* and *Billboard* (magazines), 1954-55; National Agriculture Chemical Association, Washington, D.C., director of information, 1955-58; Associated Public Relations Counselors, Washington, D.C., president, 1961—; Associated Senior Consultants, Inc., Washington, D.C., secretary, 1964—. Intercontinental Philatelic Corp., Washington, D.C., treasurer, 1966. National Captive Nations Committee, executive director; Friends of Free Asia, secretary. *Military service:* U.S. Naval Reserve, 1942-46, 1951-53; now lieutenant commander (retired). *Member:* Public Relations Society of

America, American Society of Association Executives, Phi Beta Kappa, National Press Club, Capitol Hill Club.

WRITINGS: Strategy for Conquest, Public Affairs, 1966; *The People Who Brought Us Liberty*, Braddock Publications, 1975. Columnist, "Along the Red Front," in *VFW Magazine*. Editor, "Free Asia Letter."

SIDELIGHTS: Miller has traveled extensively in free Asia; knows some French, Spanish, German, and Russian.

* * *

MILLER, Genevieve 1914-

PERSONAL: Born October 15, 1914, in Butler, Pa.; daughter of Charles Russell (a businessman) and Genevieve (Wolford) Miller. *Education:* Goucher College, A.B., 1935; Johns Hopkins University, M.A., 1939; Cornell University, Ph.D., 1955. *Home:* 2235 Overlook Rd., Cleveland Heights, Ohio 44106. *Office:* Cleveland Medical Library, 11000 Euclid Ave., Cleveland, Ohio 44106.

CAREER: Johns Hopkins University, Baltimore, Md., instructor in medical history, 1945-48; Cleveland Medical Library, Cleveland, Ohio, research associate in medical history, 1953-67, curator of Dittrick Museum, 1962-67, director, 1967—, Case Western Reserve University School of Medicine, Cleveland, Ohio, assistant professor 1953-67, associate professor of medical history, 1967—. National Institutes of Health, member of Study Section on the History of the Life Sciences, 1963-67; trustee of Goucher College, 1966-69. Fielding H. Garrison lecturer, 1973.

MEMBER: American Association for the History of Medicine (treasurer, 1942-43; council, 1960-63; secretary-treasurer, 1971—), History of Science Society (councilor, 1948-51), Society for the Advancement of Science, American Historical Association, International Society for the History of Medicine, Society of Architectural Historians, American Association of University Professors, American Association of Museums, Ohio Academy of Medical History (president, 1959), National Trust for Historic Preservation, Phi Beta Kappa. *Awards, honors:* William H. Welch Medal of American Association for the History of Medicine, 1962.

WRITINGS: William Beaumont's Formative Years: Two Early Notebooks 1811-1821, Henry Schuman, 1946; *The Adoption of Inoculation for Smallpox in England and France*, University of Pennsylvania Press, 1957; *Bibliography of the History of Medicine of the United States and Canada, 1939-60*, Johns Hopkins Press, 1964; *Bibliography of the Writings of Henry E. Sigerist*, McGill University Press, 1966. Articles on medical history include some on folk medicine and medical botany. Associate editor, *Bulletin of the History of Medicine*, 1944-48, acting editor, 1948, member of editorial advisory board, 1963—; member of editorial board, *Journal of the History of Medicine and Allied Sciences*, 1948-65; editor, *Bulletin of the Cleveland Medical Library*, 1954-72.

WORK IN PROGRESS: A study of American medical historiography.

SIDELIGHTS: Genevieve Miller is competent in French and German. *Avocational interests:* Trees, birds, archaeology, architectural history.

* * *

MILLER, Herbert E(lmer) 1914-

PERSONAL: Born August 11, 1914, in DeWitt, Iowa; son of Elmer Joseph and Marian (Briggs) Miller; married Lenore Snitkey, 1938; children: Barbara Ruth. *Education:* State University of Iowa (now University of Iowa), B.A., 1936, M.A., 1937; University of Minnesota, Ph.D., 1944. *Home:* 175 East Delaware, Chicago, Ill. 60611. *Office:* Arthur Anderson and Co., 69 West Washington, Chicago, Ill. 60602.

CAREER: Simpson College, Indianola, Iowa, instructor, 1937-38; University of Minnesota, Minneapolis, 1938-46, began as instructor, became assistant professor; University of Michigan, Ann Arbor, 1946-61, began as associate professor, became professor; Michigan State University, East Lansing, professor of accounting and finance, 1961-70; Arthur Anderson and Co., Chicago, Ill., partner, 1970—. Visiting professor at State University of Iowa (now University of Iowa), 1945, Stanford University, 1960, 1962, 1965, University of Hawaii, 1964, and Georgia State University, 1970. Worked at various times as staff accountant for Arthur Andersen & Co., Chicago, Ill., and Touche Ross, Bailey & Smart, Detroit, Mich. *Member:* American Institute of Certified Public Accountants, American Accounting Association (vice-president, 1958; president, 1965-66), Iowa Society of Certified Public Accountants, Illinois Society of Certified Public Accountants, Beta Gamma Sigma, Beta Alpha Psi, Acacia, Union League Club (Chicago). *Awards, honors:* Elijah Watt Sells Gold Medal Award, 1945; Paton Medal, 1946.

WRITINGS: (With Harry Anson Finney) *Principles of Accounting*, intermediate level, 4th edition, Prentice-Hall, 1951, 6th edition, 1965 (first three editions by Finney only); (contributing editor) *C.P.A. Review Manual*, Prentice-Hall, 1951, 3rd edition, 1966; (with Finney) *Principles of Accounting*, introductory level, 4th edition, 1953, 6th edition, 1963 (first three editions by Finney only); (with Finney) *The Accounting Process* (programmed adaptation of *Principles of Accounting*, introductory level), Prentice-Hall, 1963. Contributor of articles to *Journal of Accountancy, Accounting Review*, and other professional journals.

* * *

MILLER, Morris 1914-

PERSONAL: Born April 6, 1914, in Brooklyn, N.Y.; son of Samuel and Gussie (Zarut) Miller; married Selma Sarver (a school nurse-teacher); children: Susan (Mrs. Alan M. Hoffman), Amy (Mrs. Robert Cohen). *Education:* City College (now of the City University of New York), New York, B.B.A., 1934; New York University and City College (now of the City University of New York), New York, M.S., 1945; additional study at Hofstra University. *Home and office:* 5115 Dewey Pl., Sarasota, Fla. 33581.

CAREER: New York (N.Y.) public schools, teacher, 1934-50; Martin VanBuren High School, Queens Village, N.Y., supervisor of accounting department, 1950—. Baron and Miller (accountants), Valley Stream and Wantagh, N.Y., partner, 1951—. City College (now of the City University of New York), lecturer, 1945-72. *Member:* Eastern Business Teachers Association, Accounting Chairmen's Association of New York City (president, 1954), Association of High School Chairmen, Business Education Association of New York City. *Awards, honors:* Ph.D., University of Sarasota, 1973.

WRITINGS: (With Arthur Janis) *Fundamentals of Modern Bookkeeping, Workbook* I and II, and *Transparencies—First Year Bookkeeping*, Pitman, 1965; (with Janis) *Modern Bookkeeping and Accounting*, Pitman, 1973. Contributor to professional journals.

WORK IN PROGRESS: Developing instruction in data processing for high school business education students.

AVOCATIONAL INTERESTS: Photography.

* * *

MILLER, Paul Martin 1914-

PERSONAL: Born April 2, 1914, in Bainbridge, Pa.; son of Martin Z. and Rosa (Good) Miller; married Bertha Mumma, 1938; children: Rebecca (Mrs. Victor Fast), John, James, Rosemary. *Education:* Goshen College, A.B., 1949; Goshen Biblical Seminary, B.D., 1952; Southern Baptist Theological Seminary, Th.M., 1955, Th.D., 1961. *Home:* 1119 South Eighth St., Goshen, Ind. *Office:* Goshen Biblical Seminary, Goshen, Ind.

CAREER: Dairy farmer in Bainbridge, Pa., 1938-46; Mennonite pastor, Goshen, Ind., 1946-52; Mennonite bishop, Goshen, Ind., 1949—; professor of practical theology, Goshen Biblical Seminary, Goshen, Ind., 1952—. Director of research into patterns of the ministry, Association of East African Theological Colleges, 1966-68. *Member:* Association of Seminary Professors in Practical Fields, Christian Association for Psychological Studies, Association for Clinical Pastoral Education (acting Supervisor).

WRITINGS: Group Dynamics in Evangelism, Herald, 1958; *How God Heals*, Herald, 1960; *Servant of God's Servant*, Herald, 1964; *Equipping for Ministry in East Africa*, Herald, 1969.

* * *

MILLER, Richard (Connelly) 1925-

PERSONAL: Born September 17, 1925, in Cleveland, Ohio; son of Levi Lewis (a businessman) and Linda (Connelly) Miller; married Cora McCaughna, 1953; children: John, Lisa, Eric, Michael, Andrew, Kate. *Education:* Ohio State University, B.A., 1949; University of Paris, Certificat de Langue Francaise, 1951; Claremont Graduate School, M.A., 1956; University of California, Berkeley, Ph.D., 1961. *Politics:* Democrat. *Home:* 280 Grove Acre, Pacific Grove, Calif. 93950. *Agent:* Peter H. Matson, Harold Matson Co., Inc., 22 East 40th St., New York, N.Y. 10016. *Office:* San Francisco Art Institute, 800 Chestnut St., San Francisco, Calif. 94133.

CAREER: Merchant seaman, 1945-50; free-lance writer and photographer, 1950-53; College of the San Francisco Art Institute, San Francisco, Calif., faculty member, 1959—, currently teaching world history. Candidate for Democratic nomination to House of Representatives (12th Congressional District), 1964, 1966. Co-chairman, Monterey County Committee to End the War in Vietnam, 1965—. *Member:* American Historical Association. *Awards, honors:* Honorable mention, Joseph Henry Jackson Awards (literary awards administered by San Francisco Foundation), 1957.

WRITINGS: Amerloque (novel), Crown, 1966. Contributor to magazines and newspapers.

WORK IN PROGRESS: Nobody's Nazi: Bohemians and Hips, The Protoculture, Then and Now.

* * *

MILLER, S(eymour) M(ichael) 1922-

PERSONAL: Born November 21, 1922, in Philadelphia, Pa.; son of Morris S. and Lena (Landau) Miller; married Jean Baker (a physician), April 6, 1955; children: Jonathan,

Edward. *Education:* Brooklyn College (now of the State University of New York), B.A., 1943; Columbia University, M.A., 1945; Princeton University, A.M., 1946, Ph.D., 1951. *Home:* 105 Salisbury Rd., Brookline, Mass. 02146. *Office:* Sociology Department, Boston University, Boston, Mass. 02215.

CAREER: With National Bureau of Economic Research, 1945, and Federal Public Housing Administration, 1946-47; Rutgers University, New Brunswick, N.J., instructor in economics, 1947-49; Brooklyn College (now of the State University of New York), 1949-61, started as lecturer, became associate professor of sociology and anthropology; Syracuse University, Syracuse, N.Y., professor of sociology and research associate, Youth Development Center, 1961-66; New York University, New York, N.Y., visiting professor of education and sociology, 1966-72; Boston University, Boston, Mass., chairman of sociology department, 1973-76. Program advisor, Ford Foundation, 1966-68. *Member:* American Sociological Association, American Economic Association, Society for the Study of Social Problems, Industrial Relations Research Association. *Awards, honors:* Guggenheim fellow, 1972-73.

WRITINGS: (Co-author) *The Dynamics of the American Economy*, Knopf, 1956; (co-author) *Facts About Rockland County*, Volume I-II, Rockland County Mental Health Association, 1958; (co-author) *Theories of Terror*, University Group on Defence Policy (United Kingdom), 1962; (editor) *Max Weber: A Reader*, Crowell, 1963; (co-author) *The School Dropout Problem: Syracuse*, New York State Division of Youth, 1963; (co-author) *School Dropouts: A Commentary and Annotated Bibliography*, Youth Development Center, Syracuse University, 1964; (editor with Alvin W. Gouldner) *Applied Sociology: Opportunities and Problems*, Free Press of Glencoe, 1965; (with Frank Riessman) *Social Class and Social Policy*, Basic Books, 1968; (with Pamela Roby) *The Future of Inequality*, Basic Books, 1970; (editor with Bruno Stein) *Twenties and Social Policy*, Aldine, 1973.

Contributor: *Blue Collar World*, edited by Shostak and Gomberg, Prentice-Hall, 1964; *The New Sociology*, edited by Irving L. Horowitz, Oxford University Press, 1964; *Learning Together*, edited by Meyer Weinberg, Integrated Education Association, 1964; *The School Dropout*, edited by Daniel Schreiber, National Education Association, 1964; *Mental Health of the Poor*, edited by Riessman, Cohen, and Pearl, Free Press of Glencoe, 1964; *Perspectives on Urban Poverty*, edited by Shostak and Gomberg, Prentice-Hall, 1964; *Training Series for Social Agencies*, edited by Schasre and Wallach, Youth Studies Center, University of Southern California, 1965; *Poverty in America*, edited by Ferman, Kornbluh, and Haber, University of Michigan Press, 1965; *Poverty in Affluence*, edited by Will and Vatter, Harcourt, 1965; *Readings on Implications of Social Change*, Volume I, Schasre and Wallach, University of Southern California, 1965; *Readings in Social Agencies and Social Change*, Volume III, edited by Schasre and Wallach, University of Southern California, 1965; *Poverty as a Public Issue*, edited by Ben B. Seligman, Free Press of Glencoe, 1965; *Urban Education and Cultural Deprivation*, edited by C. W. Hunnicutt, Syracuse University Press, 1965; *Applied Sociology*, Gouldner and Miller, Free Press of Glencoe, 1965; *Class, Status, and Power*, revised edition, edited by Bendix and Lipset, Free Press of Glencoe, 1966; *Sociology in Action*, edited by A. B. Shostak, Dorsey, 1966; *Social Problems*, edited by Howard S. Becker, Wiley, 1966.

Author of report on "Comparative Social Mobility," published by UNESCO as entire issue of *Current Sociology*, 1960, and of script for "The Hard Way," distributed by National Educational Television, 1965. Contributor to proceedings of sociological conferences and about 150 articles to *New America, Trans-Action, British Journal of Sociology*, and various other journals in America and England.

* * *

MILLER, Wright (Watts) 1903-
(Mark North)

PERSONAL: Born January 17, 1903, in London, England; son of Wright (a building inspector) and Grace Edith (Watts) Miller; married Katharine Slater (an architect), September 22, 1942; children: Jonathan, Juliet, Susanna. *Education:* University College, London, B.A. (honors), 1923; University of Manchester, M.Ed., 1926. *Politics:* Labour. *Home:* 14 Cambridge Cottages, Kew Green, Surrey, England.

CAREER: Schoolmaster in England, 1923-27; senior lecturer in English at a teacher training college in London, England, 1927-41; British Broadcasting Corp., London, assistant to organizer of European Service, 1941-42; British Embassy in Moscow, attache, 1942-44; Central Office of Information, London editor of "British Ally"; Civil Service Commission, information officer, 1956-57; editor of *Anglia* (magazine for Soviet readers), 1960—. Chairman of finance committee, Hammersmith Borough Council, 1938-41. *Member:* Society of Authors, Institute of Professional Civil Servants, Great Britain-U.S.S.R. Association (committee member). *Awards, honors:* Member, Order of the British Empire, 1966.

WRITINGS: Books: An Introduction to Reading, Pitman, 1932; *The Young Traveller in Russia*, Phoenix House, 1958; *Russians as People*, Phoenix House, 1960, Dutton, 1961; *U.S.S.R.-Reader's Guide*, Cambridge University Press, 1961; *The U.S.S.R.*, Oxford University Press, 1963; *Russia—A Personal Anthology*, George Newnes, 1965; (contributor) *Russia and the Soviet Union—A Bibliographic Guide to Western-Language Publications*, University of Chicago Press, 1965; *Leningrad*, A. S. Barnes, 1970; *Who Are the Russians?: A History of the Russian People*, Taplinger, 1973. Author of pamphlets; contributor of reviews to *New Statesman, Guardian* and *International Affairs*.

SIDELIGHTS: Miller speaks French, German, Russian, and some Italian, Spanish, and Dutch. *Avocational interests:* Mountain walking, gardening, travel in less-frequented areas of Europe.†

* * *

MILLERSON, Geoffrey L. 1931-

PERSONAL: Born February 8, 1931, in England; son of Alfred Thomas and Ada Emily (Dance) Millerson; married Dianne Evans (a professional singer), March 26, 1965. *Education:* University of London, B.Sc., 1959, Ph.D., 1963. *Office:* Department of Sociology, University of Bristol, Bristol, England.

CAREER: London School of Economics and Political Science, London, England, senior research officer on juvenile delinquency, Survey Research Centre, 1962-66; University of Bristol, Bristol, England, lecturer in sociology, 1966—. *Military service:* British Army, Infantry, regimental instructor, 1953-55. *Member:* British Sociological Association, British Psychological Society.

WRITINGS: The Qualifying Associations: A Study in Professionalization, Humanities, 1964.

WORK IN PROGRESS: Further research into professions; with W. A. Belson and P. J. Didcott, a book on the development of technique for eliciting information about theft from juvenile males.

AVOCATIONAL INTERESTS: Music, painting, adult education.†

* * *

MILNE, Jean (Killgrove) 1920-

PERSONAL: Born October 5, 1920, in Los Angeles, Calif.; daughter of William T. (a musician) and Arvilla (Christensen) Killgrove; married Edmund A. Milne (a professor), May 30, 1954; children: Vicky, Marlene. *Education:* Pasadena City College, A.A., 1940; Occidental College, B.A., 1942; National University of Mexico, M.A., 1945; University of California, Los Angeles, graduate studies, 1947-48. *Politics:* Republican. *Religion:* Protestant. *Home:* 2 Shady Lane, Monterey, Calif. 93940.

CAREER: High school teacher in Tulare, Fowler, and Costa Mesa, Calif., 1943-47; U.S. Department of State, cultural relations work in San Jose, Costa Rica, 1948-51; high school teacher in Alhambra, Calif., 1951-54; Monterey (Calif.) public schools, teacher of Spanish and French, 1962—. *Member:* Phi Beta Kappa.

WRITINGS: Fiesta Time in Latin America, Ward Ritchie, 1965. Contributor of articles to *Travel* and *World Youth*; regular contributor to crossword puzzle magazines.

SIDELIGHTS: Jean Milne has traveled throughout Latin America and Europe. She speaks Spanish, French, and Italian. *Avocational interests:* Piano (performs as part of two-piano team).

* * *

MINGAY, G(ordon) E(dmund) 1923-

PERSONAL: Both syllables of surname are accented equally; born June 20, 1923, in Long Eaton, Derbyshire, England; son of William Edmund (a naval officer) and Florence (Tuckwood) Mingay; married Mavis Tippen, January 20, 1945. *Education:* University of Nottingham, B.A., 1952, Ph.D., 1958. *Office:* University of Kent at Canterbury, Canterbury, Kent, England.

CAREER: Woolwich Polytechnic, London, England, lecturer in economics, 1953-56; London School of Economics and Political Science, University of London, London, England, lecturer in economic history, 1957-65; University of Kent at Canterbury, Canterbury, Kent, England, reader in economic history, 1965-68, professor of agrarian history, 1968—. Visiting professor at University of Wisconsin, 1962-63, University of British Columbia, 1964, University of Montana, 1966, University of Nebraska, 1969, Western Washington State College, 1971, and University of Auckland, 1973. *Military service:* Royal Naval Volunteer Reserve, 1942-47; became lieutenant. *Member:* Economic History Society, Economic History Association, British Agricultural History Society, Agriculture History Society (United States).

WRITINGS: English Landed Society in the Eighteenth Century, Routledge & Kegan Paul, 1963; (with J. D. Chambers) *The Agricultural Revolution, 1750-1880*, Batsford, 1966; (author of introduction) Gonner, *Common Land and Inclosure*, 2nd edition, Cass & Co., 1966; (editor with E. L.

Jones) *Land, Labor and Population in the Industrial Revolution*, Edward Arnold, 1967; *Enclosure and the Small Farmer in the Age of the Industrial Revolution*, Macmillan, 1968; (with Philip S. Baghell) *Britain and America: A Study of Economic Change, 1850-1939*, Routledge, 1970; *Fifteen Years on: The B.E.T. Group, 1956-1971*, British Electric Traction Co., 1973; *The Gentry*, Penguin, 1975; *Arthur Young and his Times*, Macmillan, 1975; *Georgian London*, Batsford, 1975. Contributor to economic and agricultural history journals. Appointed editor, *The Agricultural History Review*, 1972—.

AVOCATIONAL INTERESTS: Adult education, opera.

*　　*　　*

MINTZ, Donald E(dward) 1932-

PERSONAL: Born July 19, 1932, in Queens, N.Y.; son of Irving and Pauline L. (Arenson) Mintz; children: Peter Graham, Hayley Ilana. *Education:* Columbia University, A.B., 1954, Ph.D., 1961. *Home:* 420 Riverside Dr., New York, N.Y. 10025. *Office:* City College of the City University of New York, New York, N.Y. 10031.

CAREER: Princeton University, Princeton, N.J., research associate, 1959-63; City College (now of the City University of New York), New York, N.Y., assistant professor, 1963-67, associate professor, 1967-74, professor of psychology, 1974—, chairman of department, 1971-74. Columbia University, lecturer, 1958-62. Educational Testing Service, consultant. *Military service:* U.S. Naval Reserve, 1954-70, with active duty, 1954-57; became lieutenant. *Member:* American Psychological Association, American Association for the Advancement of Science, Psychonomic Society, Eastern Psychological Association, New York Academy of Science, Phi Beta Kappa, Sigma Xi.

WRITINGS: (With Joseph M. Notterman) *Dynamics of Response*, Wiley, 1965. Contributor to *Science Journal of the Experimental Analysis of Behavior*, and *Psychonomic Science*.

*　　*　　*

MIRACLE, Marvin P(reston) 1933-

PERSONAL: Born January 31, 1933, in Grandfield, Okla. son of Howard Andrew (a farmer) and Clara Irene (Powell) Miracle; married Diane Schoening, August 18, 1962; children: Klara Irene, John Mills, Preston Thor. *Education:* Oklahoma State University, B.S., 1954; Stanford University, A.M. (agricultural economics research), 1956, A.M. (economics), 1957, Ph.D., 1963. *Home:* 3980 Plymouth Circle, Madison, Wis. 53705. *Office:* Department of Agricultural Economics, Agricultural Hall, University of Wisconsin, Madison, Wis. 53706.

CAREER: San Francisco State College (now University), San Francisco, Calif., instructor, 1961, assistant professor of economics, 1961-64; Stanford University, Stanford, Calif., research associate, Food Research Institute, 1961-62; University of Wisconsin, Madison, assistant professor 1964-66, associate professor, 1966-71, professor agricultural economics, 1971—. National Academy of Sciences-National Research Council Middle Africa Project, consultant, 1959; has done research in India, Brazil, Mexico, and ten African countries. *Military service:* U.S. Army, Intelligence, 1957; became first lieutenant. *Member:* American Economic Association. American Farm Economic Association, Econometric Society, African Studies Association. *Awards, honors:* Social Science Research Council grant,

1965; Agricultural Development Council grant, 1965; Ford Foundation grant, 1972-74.

WRITINGS: Traditional Agricultural Methods in the Congo Basin, Food Research Institute, Stanford University, 1964; *Maize in Tropical Africa*, University of Wisconsin Press, 1966; *Agriculture in the Congo Basin*, University of Wisconsin Press, 1967.

Contributor: Paul Bohannan and George Dalton, editors, *Markets in Africa*, Northwestern University Press, 1962; Martin S. Peterson and Donald K. Tressler, editors, *Food Technologies the World Over*, Volume II, Avi Publishing, 1965; Gabel and Bennett, editors, *Reconstructing African Culture History*, Boston University Press, 1967; D. A. Lury and Peter Robson, editors, *The Economy of Africa*, Allen & Unwin, 1969. Contributor to *Tropical Agriculture, Cahiers d'Etudes Africaines, Journal of African History*, and other professional journals.

WORK IN PROGRESS: Research on innovations in smallholder agriculture, Kenya.

SIDELIGHTS: Marvin Miracle speaks French, Portuguese, and Spanish.

*　　*　　*

MISHKIN, Paul J. 1927-

PERSONAL: Born January 1, 1927, in Trenton, N.J.; son of Mordecai Mark and Bella (Dworetsky) Mishkin; married Mildred B. Westover, January, 1975. *Education:* Columbia University, A.B., 1947, LL.B., 1950. *Home:* 1086 Miller Ave., Berkeley, Calif. 94708. *Office:* School of Law, University of California, Berkeley, Calif., 94720.

CAREER: Member of bar of state of New York and U.S. Supreme Court. University of Pennsylvania Law School, Philadelphia, instructor, 1950-52, assistant professor, 1952-54, associate professor, 1954-57, professor of law, 1957-73; University of California, Berkeley, professor, 1973—, Emanuel S. Heller Professor of Law, 1975—. Visiting professor at Haverford College, 1960-61; visiting summer professor at University of Michigan, 1961, University of Texas, 1964, 1972, and University of Colorado, 1975. Associate reporter, American Law Institute, Federal-State Jurisdiction Project, 1960-65. *Military service:* U.S. Navy, 1945-46. *Member:* American Academy of Arts and Sciences (fellow), American Law Institute, Phi Beta Kappa. *Awards, honors:* Fellow, Center for Advanced Study in the Behavioral Sciences, 1965; M.A., University of Pennsylvania, 1971.

WRITINGS: (With Clarence Morris) *On Law in Courts*, Foundation Press, 1965: (with P. Bator, D. Shapiro, and H. Wechsler) *Federal Courts and the Federal System*, 2nd edition, (Mishkin was not associated with first edition), Foundation Press, 1973. Contributor to law reviews and journals.

WORK IN PROGRESS: Studies on constitutional law, federal-state relations, and the judicial process.

*　　*　　*

MITCHELL, Kenneth R. 1930-

PERSONAL: Born June 7, 1930, in Cincinnati, Ohio; son of Ernest R. (an attorney) and Louise (Phillips) Mitchell; married Judith Bard, July 11, 1953; children: David, Susan, Catherine. *Education:* Princeton University, A.B., 1952; Princeton Theological Seminary, B.D., 1955; University of Chicago, Ph.D., 1965. *Residence:* Topeka, Kan. *Office:*

Division of Religion and Psychiatry, Menninger Foundation, Topeka, Kan.

CAREER: Clergyman of United Presbyterian Church in the U.S.A., 1955—; Vanderbilt University, Nashville, Tenn., assistant professor of theology and counseling, 1961-65, with concurrent appointments as assistant professor of human behavior, Medical School, and chaplain of university hospital; Menninger Foundation, Topeka, Kan., director for training, Division of Religion and Psychiatry, 1965-70, director of Division of Religion and Psychiatry, 1970—. Fulbright-Hays Senior lecturer, University of Nijmegen, 1972. *Member:* American Group Psychotherapy Association.

WRITINGS: Theological and Psychological Relationships in Multiple Staff Ministries, Westminster, 1966; *Hospital Chaplain*, Westminster, 1966; (contributor) William B. Oglesby, editor, *The New Shape of Pastoral Theology*, Abingdon, 1969; *Arbeitsfeld: Krankenhaus*, Vandenhoeck & Ruprecht, 1974. Contributor to pastoral journals.

WORK IN PROGRESS: Research on psychology of religious organizations, with emphasis on nature of ministerial leadership.

AVOCATIONAL INTERESTS: Music and comparative linguistics (both on a "strictly amateur, pleasure-for-myself basis").

* * *

MITCHELL, Yvonne 1925-

PERSONAL: Born July 7, 1925, in London, England; daughter of Bertie Joseph and Madge Mitchell; married Derek Monsey (a film critic and author), 1952; children: Cordelia. *Education:* Attended Battle Abbey and St. Paul's Schools, London, England. *Home:* Domaine du Plan-Sarain, La Roquette sur Siagne, A.M., France. *Agent:* David Higham, 76 Dean St., London W.1, England.

CAREER: Stage, screen, and television actress, 1939—. Made first appearance on stage at Rudolph Steiner Hall, London, England, as the child Estella in "Great Expectations," 1941; Basil C. Langton's travelling repertory company, played in "Arms and the Man," "Pygmalion," and other plays; made first appearance in West End of London, England, at Apollo Theatre as Teresa in "The Cradle Song," 1944; Oxford Playhouse, Oxford, England, played in several productions by Peter Ashmore, 1944-45; Bristol Old Vic repertory company, Bristol, England, played Viola in "Twelfth Night," and other roles, 1945-46; played in several productions for Old Vic repertory company and many independent productions, 1946-53; joined Shakespeare Memorial Theatre (now the Royal Shakespeare Theatre), Stratford-on-Avon, Warwickshire, England, played in "Merchant of Venice," "Richard III," "King Lear," and other plays, 1953-54; played in independent productions, 1954-60; directed husband's play. "Less Than Kind," Royal Court Theatre, London, England, 1958; made first appearance on Broadway at Billy Rose Theatre, New York, N.Y., as Rachel Apt in "The Wall," 1960; appeared in "Ivanov," opposite Sir John Gielgud, 1965, and as Virginia Woolf in "Bloomsbury," 1974. First appeared in films in "Queen of Spades," Stratford Pictures, 1949, other films include "Woman in a Dressing Gown," and "Trials of Oscar Wilde"; radio and television productions, 1952—, most recently appeared in B.B.C. television "Cheri." Arts Council of Great Britain, member of drama panel, 1962-65.

AWARDS, HONORS: Festival of Britain Prize (Arts Council Award) for best new play, 1950, for "Here Choose I" (published as *The Same Sky*); Television National Award, 1952-53; British Film Academy Award for best actress, 1954, for performance in "The Divided Heart"; International Film Festival (Berlin) Award for best actress, 1957, and Variety Club of Great Britain Award, 1957, both for performance in "Woman in a Dressing Gown."

WRITINGS: The Same Sky (play, originally titled "Here Choose I," produced at Duke of York's Theatre, London, 1951), Evans, 1953; *Actress* (novel), Routledge & Kegan Paul, 1957; *The Bedsitter* (novel), Barker, 1959; *Frame for Julian* (novel), Hutchinson, 1960, Morrow, 1961; *A Year in Time* (novel), Heinemann, 1964; *Cathy Away* (juvenile), Heinemann, 1964; *Cathy at Home* (juvenile), Heinemann, 1965; *The Family*, Heinemann, 1968; *Martha on Sunday*, Briggs & Bland, 1972; *But Wednesday Cried* (juvenile), R. Schlesinger, 1974; *God is Inexperienced*, Constable, 1974. Contributor of articles to daily and weekly journals in England.

WORK IN PROGRESS: A biography of Colette for Weidenfeld & Nicholson.

SIDELIGHTS: Miss Mitchell lists, as her favorite roles, Eliza in "Pygmalion," the Stepdaughter in "Six Characters in Search of an Author," and Nina in "The Seagull."

* * *

MIYAKAWA, T(etsuo) Scott 1906-

PERSONAL: Surname is pronounced Mee-yah-kah-wah; born November 23, 1906, in Los Angeles, Calif.; son of Yukio and Rin (Koybyashi) Miyakawa. *Education:* Cornell University, M.E., 1931; Columbia University, Ph.D., 1951. *Office:* Department of Sociology, Boston University, Boston, Mass. 02215.

CAREER: Research and public relations in international trade, New York, N.Y., 1931-41; Eastern representative of Japanese American Citizens League and liaison representative and consultant on relocation of West Coast evacuees, New York, N.Y., 1942-43; University of Missouri, Columbia, instructor in physics, 1943-44; University of Michigan, Ann Arbor, assistant to counselor in religious education, 1944-46; Boston University, Boston, Mass., 1946—, began as instructor, became professor of sociology. Doshisha University, Kyoto, Japan, Fulbright exchange professor, 1953-54; University of Massachusetts, Boston, visiting professor of sociology; Centre for Advanced Study and Training, Bandaragama, Ceylon, senior visitng faculty member, 1957-58; University of California, Los Angeles, director of Japanese American research project, 1962-68.

MEMBER: American Sociological Association, Association for Asian Studies, Society for the Scientific Study of Religion, American Association of University Professors, Japanese American Citizens League, Eastern Sociological Society. *Awards, honors:* Ford Foundation fellowship, 1951-52; special citation for leadership, Japanese American Citizens League.

WRITINGS: Protestants and Pioneers: Individualism and Conformity on the American Frontier, University of Chicago Press, 1964; (with Hilary Conroy) *East Across the Pacific: Historical and Sociological Studies of Japanese Immigration and Assimilation*, Clio Press, 1972. Contributor to journals.

WORK IN PROGRESS: Continuing interdisciplinary study of the history and acculturation of Japanese and Japanese Americans on the U.S. East Coast, publication of the report of this study expected in 1977.

SIDELIGHTS: Miyakawa's travels span much of Asia, and various countries in the Middle East and Europe.

* * *

MOLIN, Sven Eric 1929-

PERSONAL: Born May 12, 1929, in Rochester, N.Y.; son of Karl T. and Eunice (Bickford) Molin; married second wife, Barbara Hurt, June 26, 1969; children: (first marriage) Karl T. II, Peter Castle, John Bickford, Franklin Bache; (second marriage) Jason Eric. *Education:* Amherst College, B.A., 1950; Columbia University, M.A., 1951; University of Pennsylvania, Ph.D., 1956. *Home:* 6531 27th St. N., Arlington, Va. 22213. *Agent:* Collins-Knowlton-Wing, Inc., 24 East 38th St., New York, N.Y. 10016. *Office:* Department of English, George Mason University, Fairfax, Va. 22030.

CAREER: Randolph-Macon Woman's College, Lynchburg, Va., associate professor of English, 1958-71; George Mason University, Fairfax, Va., associate professor, 1971-74, professor of English, 1974—. *Member:* American Association of University Professors, Eighteenth Century Society.

WRITINGS: (With Robert Hogan) *Drama: The Major Genres,* Dodd, 1962.

* * *

MOLLENHOFF, Clark R(aymond) 1921-

PERSONAL: Born April 16, 1921, in Burnside, Iowa; son of Raymond Eldon (a salesman) and Margaret Genevieve (Clark) Mollenhoff; married Georgia Giles Osmundson, October 13, 1939; children: Gjore Jean, Jacquelin Sue (Mrs. Duane Montgomery), Clark Raymond, Jr. *Education:* Webster City Junior College, Webster City, Iowa, graduate, 1941; Drake University, LL.B., 1944. *Politics:* Independent. *Religion:* Roman Catholic. *Home:* 5704 32nd St. N.W., Washington D.C. *Office:* National Press Building, Washington, D.C. 20004.

CAREER: Des Moines Register and Tribune, Des Moines, Iowa, full-time police and municipal court reporter while studying law, 1941-44, county courthouse and statehouse reporter, 1946-49; admitted to Iowa Bar, 1944, Washington, D.C. Bar, and Bar of U.S. Supreme Court; Cowles Publications, Washington Bureau, Washington, D.C., reporter, writing for *Look,* and *Minneapolis Star and Tribune* 1950-69; special counsel to President Nixon, 1969-70; *Des Moines Register and Tribune,* chief of Washington Bureau, 1970—. Member, U.S. Advisory Commission on Information Policy, 1962-65. *Military service:* U.S. Navy, 1944-46; served in Pacific; became lieutenant junior grade.

MEMBER: American Bar Association, Iowa Bar Association National Press Club (governor, 1956-63; vice-president, 1964), Sigma Delta Chi. *Awards, honors:* Nieman fellowship at Harvard University, 1949-50; Sigma Delta Chi awards, 1952, 1954, 1958; Raymond Clapper Memorial Award and Heywood Broun Memorial Award, 1955; Distinguished Alumni Award, Drake University, 1956; Pulitzer Prize for national reporting, for inquiry into labor union racketeering, 1958; National Headliner Award for magazine article in *Atlantic Monthly,* 1960; Eisenhower exchange fellowship for study abroad, 1960-61; William Allen White Foundation Award for journalistic merit, 1964; Drew Pearson Award for investigative reporting, 1973, and

other awards from national organizations and universities. LL.D., Colby College, 1959, Simpson College, 1974; L.H.D., Cornell College, 1960; Litt.D., Drake University, 1961, and Iowa Wesleyan College, 1966.

WRITINGS: Washington Cover-Up, Doubleday, 1962; *Tentacles of Power,* World Publishing, 1965; *Despoilers of Democracy,* Doubleday, 1965; *The Pentagon,* Putnam, 1967; *George Romney: Mormon in Politics,* Meredith, 1968; *Strike Force,* Prentice-Hall, 1972. Contributor to a number of national magazines.

WORK IN PROGRESS: A book on 1969-70 experience in White House.

SIDELIGHTS: Most of Mollenhoff's kudos have resulted from investigative reporting; he broke the story of Wolf I. Ladejinsky's dismissal from a Department of Agriculture post in 1954 (Ladejinsky, dismissed for security reasons, was eventually cleared), and later spurred a Congressional investigation of labor unions and labor leaders, including Dave Beck and James Hoffa. His first three books deal with some of his probes; they all contain considerable material of an autobiographical nature.

BIOGRAPHICAL/CRITICAL SOURCES: John Hohenberg, *The Pulitzer Prize Story,* Columbia University Press, 1959; Hohenberg, *The New Front Page,* Columbia University Press, 1966; *New York Times Book Review,* March 19, 1967; *New Republic,* April 8, 1967.

* * *

MONTALE, Eugenio 1896-

PERSONAL: Born October 12, 1896, in Genoa, Italy; son of Domenico and Giuseppina (Ricci) Montale; married Drusilla (generally known as Mosca) Tanzi (died, 1963). *Education:* Attended schools in Genoa, Italy. *Home:* Via Bigli, 15, Milan, Italy.

CAREER: Studied to be singer but abandoned the possibility of a successful career as a baritone in favor of literature; in 1922 he helped found the literary journal, *Primo Tempo,* and, for the eight issues it lasted, was one of the major contributors; joined the editorial staff of Bemporad, an Italian publishing house, 1927-28; director of the Gabinetto Vieusseux Library in Florence, 1928-38'(he was forced to leave this post for political reasons); contributor to a number of literary journals, poetry critic for *La Fiera Letteraria,* and journalist, during the period 1938-48; literary editor and later music critic for the *Corriere della Sera,* 1948—. *Military service:* Italian Army, infantry officer, 1915-18. *Awards, honors:* Antico Fattore poetry prize, 1932, for *Casa dei doganieri;* Premio Manzotto, 1956, for *La Bufera e altro;* Feltrinelli prize, 1963-64; honorary degrees from University of Milan, University of Rome, Cambridge University, and Barel University; named Senator of the Republic.

WRITINGS—Poetry: *Ossi di Seppia,* Gobetti (Turin), 1925; *La casa dei doganieri e altre poesie,* Antico Fattore (Florence), 1932; *Le Occasioni,* Einaudi (Turin), 1939, 9th edition, Mondadori, 1970; *Finisterre,* Quaderni di Lugano (Lugano), 1943; *La bufera e altro,* Neri Pozza (Venice), 1956, 6th edition, Mondadori, 1972; *Poems,* translated by Edwin Morgan, printed in the School of Art, University of Reading (Reading, England), 1959; *Robert Lowell: Poesie di Montale* (bilingual edition with English adaptations by Lowell), Lanterna (Bologna), 1960; *Satura* (informally published collection of five poems), [Verona], 1963, English translation by Donald Sheehan and David Keller, published as *Satura: Five Poems*, Francesco Press, 1969; *Poesie: Poems*, translated by George Kay, Edinburgh University Press, 1964, published as *Selected Poems of Eugenio Montale*, Penguin, 1969; *Selected Poems*, bilingual edition by various translators, introduced by Glauco Cambon, New Directions, 1965; *Provisional Conclusions: A Selection of the Poetry of Eugenio Montale, 1920-1970*, translated by Edith Farnsworth, Regnery, 1970; *Trentadue variazioni*, G. Lucini, 1973; *Diario del '71 e del '72*, Mondadori, 1973.

Prose: *La solitudine dell'artista*, Associazione Italiana per la liberta della cultura (Rome), 1952; *La farfalla di Dinard*, [Venice] 1956, expanded edition, Mondadori, 1960, English translation by G. Singh, published as *The Butterfly of Dinard*, London Magazine Editions, 1970, University Press of Kentucky, 1971; *Accordi e pastelli*, Scheiwiller (Milan), 1963; *Lettere: Eugenio Montale—Italo Svevo* (includes Montale's critical essays on Svevo), De Donato (Bari), 1966; *Auto da fe*, Il Saggiatore (Milan), 1966; *Fuori di casa*, R. Riccardi, (Milan), 1969; *La poesia non esiste*, All'insegna del pesce d'oro, 1971; *Nel nostro tempo*, Rizzoli (Milan), 1972.

Translator into Italian: Melville, *La storia di Billy Budd*, [Milan], 1942; O'Neill, *Strano Interludio*, Edizione Teatro dell Universita (Rome), 1943; *Quaderno di traduzioni* (translations of Shakespeare, T. S. Eliot, Gerard Manley Hopkins, and others), Edizione della Meridiana, 1948; Shakespeare, *Amleto, principe di Danimarca*, Cederna (Milan), 1949; *Troilo e Cressida, Opera in tre atti* (translation of Christopher Hassall's libretto), Carisch (Milan), 1956; Steinbeck, *Al dio sconosciuto*, [Milan], 1954; Angus Wilson, *La cicuta e dopo*, [Milan], 1956; *Jorge Guillen: Tradotto da Eugenio Montale*, All'insegna del Pesce d'Oro (Milan), 1958; Corneille, *Il Cid*, Turin, 1961.

Collected works: "Poesie," Mondadori (Milan), in three volumes: *Poesie I. Ossi di Seppia*, 1948; *Poesie II. Le Occasioni*, 1949; *Poesie III. La Bufera e Altro*, 1957 (bilingual Italian-French edition published by Gallimard, 1966).

Contributor: Mario Praz, editor, *Teatro* (translations of Shakespeare's "The Comedy of Errors," "The Winter's Tale," and "Timon of Athens"), [Milan], 1942; A. Obertello, editor, *Teatro Elisabettiano* (translation of Marlowe's "Doctor Faustus"), [Milan], 1951; E. F. Accorocca, editor, *Ritratti su misura*, Socalizio del libro (Venice), 1960; Gianandrea Gavazzeni, editor, *I nemici della musica*, All'insegna del Pesce d'Oro, (Milan), 1965.

Contributor to anthologies: *Antologia popolare di poetica del Novecento*, edited by V. Masselli and G. A. Cibotto, Vallecchi, 1955; *Antologia poetica della Resistenza Italiana*, edited by E. F. Accrocca and V. Volpini, Landi (Arezzo), 1955; *La giovane poesia (Saggio e Repertorio)*, edited by Enrico Falqui, Colombo (Rome), 1956; *The Promised Land and other Poems: An Anthology of Four Contemporary Poets* (bilingual edition), edited by Sergi Pacifici, Vanni, 1957; *Poesia italiana del dopoguerra*, edited by Salvatore Quasimodo, Schwarz, 1958; *Dal Carducci ai Contemporanei: Antologia della lirica moderna*, edited by G. Getto and F. Portinari, Zanichelli (Bologna), 1958; *The Penguin Book of Italian Verse* (bilingual edition), edited by George Kay, Penguin, 1958; *Poesia italiana contemporanea*, edited by Giacinto Spagnoletti, Guanda (Parma), 1959; *La lirica del Novecento*, edited by Luciano Anceschi and Sergio Antonielli, Vallecchi, 1961; *Modern European Poetry*, edited by Willis Barnstone, Bantam, 1966.

Also contributor of numerous essays, critical pieces, and other articles and reviews to many literary journals, magazines, and newspapers, such as *Solaria* (Florence), *Letteratura* (Florence), *Botteghe Oscure* (Rome), *Gazzetta del Popolo* (Turin), and to several foreign publications.

SIDELIGHTS: Luciano Rebay has observed that "for Montale the aim of poetry is always to express something beyond the power of words to convey." "I obeyed a need of musical expression," explains Montale in "Intentions: An Imaginary Interview." "I wanted my words to be more fitting than those of the other poets I had known. Fitting what? I seemed to live under a glass bell and still I felt I was near something essential. A thin veil, hardly a thread, separated me from the final *quid*. Absolute expression would mean the tearing of that veil, of that thread: an explosion, or else the end of the delusion of the words as representation. But this was an unattainable end." Montale feels that he cannot penetrate the mystery of the world, nor fathom its absurdities, but his poetry is, nevertheless, intimately concerned with the struggle of the individual to survive, and to understand the suffering of life. He belongs, writes Glauco Cambon, "to the great Western tradition which, with Proust, Joyce, Eliot and Faulkner, has explored the paradoxes of time, existence, finitude and memory."

Montale found his poetic symbols in the reality surrounding him, and, in particular, in the rugged, tormented Ligurian landscape which he had known as a child. He evokes in many of his poems the unbearable heat and the relentless aridity of these harsh regions. His language becomes strident, rocky, and scabrous like the landscape itself. The very title of his first book *Ossi de Seppia* ("Cuttlefish Bones"), hints, remarked Mario Praz, "at the dry, desolate purity of his early inspiration: white cuttlefish bones stranded on the margin of the beach, where the sea casts up all its drift and wreckage."

In an analysis of Montale's use of language Cambon writes: "Montale transposed sound onto an inner level, varying rhyme with dissonance, shifting it into the body of the line, where it will exercise a more secret charm, and often seeking in alliteration a sound-unity for the content—a unity to be reconstructed from within, by valuing syllable and consonant to the extent of making them the vertebrae of a poetical organism. Like T. S. Eliot, to whom he has often been compared, Montale has a highly individual and memorable diction. Both poets, notes Irma Brandeis, "use prose rhythms as a basis for poetic structure," and both have had their poetry labeled "intellectual," and "complex." Eliot was, in fact, one of the first in the English-speaking world to recognize the merits of Montale's poetry and, similarly, Montale introduced Eliot to Italian readers. But Montale's art is more personal and passionate and his "world view," notes Willis Barnstone, "now seen arching from negativism to a kind of exalted resignation, holds without Eliot's visible stanchions of faith."

Much of Montale's poetry is overshadowed by a brooding pessimism. At the age of thirty he had written in a letter to his friend Italo Svevo: "I am a tree seared by the sirocco before time, and all that I could give—stifled cries and starts—is in *Ossi di Seppia*...." In a poem from this collection, "Meriggiare pallido e assorto" ("To rest at noon, pale and absorbed"), a stone wall glittering with broken glass becomes an image for the nature of existence, indicative of the despair which reverberates through the lines, and consonant with Montale's view of life as a lonely and bewildering journey. Another underlying theme in the poet's work is his conception of time as an inexorable and pitiless force to which, as exemplified in the poem "Arsenio," man is implacably chained. Montale believes that it is from his isolation, from what he terms his "disharmony with reality," that he can best attempt to communicate with the world. He has asserted that "even tomorrow, the most important voices will be those of the artists who, through their voice of isolated people, will let the world hear an echo of the fatal isolation of every one of us. In this sense, only those who are isolated speak."

There is, however, another side to Montale's poetry. In such poems as "I limoni" ("The Lemon Trees"), and "L'Anguilla" ("The Eel"), he emerges, says Rebay, as "the poet of colors and light and landscapes, the poet who has written some of the most striking love poems in modern Western literature." "The Eel" is a paean to the exuberant forces of life. Written in a thirty-line sentence, it is full of a vital energy, resounding, comments Praz, like a "proud hymn of confidence and joy." And Cambon has called "Dora Markus" "one of the most poignant love elegies of all time."

Montale's output as a poet is small, but as a critic and essayist he has been considerably more prolific. In reviewing *Auto da fe* (1966), a collection of Montale's essays and articles, G. Singh writes: "Montale's views on topics of vital interest are important not merely as being those of the greatest living poet of Italy, but also as a commentary on our *Zeitgeist* by one of the subtlest and most sensitive minds of the century, but one who has himself shaped and influenced that *Zeitgeist*—at least so far as Italy is concerned." Some of Montale's best prose is contained in *La Farfalla di Dinard*. *Lettere* consists of letters exchanged between the novelist Italo Svevo and Montale, together with several of the latter's essays on Svevo, whom he knew and greatly admired. In a recent interview Montale is reported to have said that if he had written novels he would have followed the example of Svevo. Singh remarks that in *Farfalla di Dinard*, which is Montale's nearest approach to a novel, there was already something rather Svevian in the psychological handling of the themes and in the style of the prose. It is, however, undoubtedly as a poet that Montale will best be remembered, and, as Rebay wrote, those who read his poems "may well experience the impact of one of the most compelling voices of our century."

BIOGRAPHICAL/CRITICAL SOURCES: Raoul Lunardi, *Eugenio Montale e la nouva poesia*, [Padua], 1948; *Nuovi Argomenti*, Number 26, 1950; Francesco Flora, *Scrittori italiani contemporanei*, Nistri-Lischi, 1952; Titta G. Rosa, *La poesia italiana del Novecento*, Maia, 1953; Oreste Macri, *Caratteri e figure della poesia italiana contemporanea*, Vallecchi, 1956; *Paragone*, Number 80, 1956; *Sewanee Review*, winter, 1958; *Italian Quarterly*, winter, 1959; *Italica*, XXXVII, 1960; Stanley Burnshaw, editor, *The Poem Itself*, Holt, 1960; Sergio Pacifici, *A Guide to Contemporary Italian Literature*, Meridian, 1962; Ettore Bonora, *Poesia di Montale*, Lauri (Turin), 1964; Silvio Ramat, *Montale: La cultura e il tempo*, Vallecchi, 1965; Willis Barnstone, editor, *Modern European Poetry*, Bantam, 1966; *New York Times Book Review*, November 20, 1966; *Books Abroad*, winter, 1967.

* * *

MONTEIRO, George 1932-

PERSONAL: Born May 23, 1932, in Cumberland, R.I.; son of Frank J. and Augusta (Temudo) Monteiro; married Lois Ann Hodgins (an assistant professor of community

medicine, Brown University), August 14, 1958; children: Katherine, Stephen, Emily. *Education:* Brown University, A.B., 1954, Ph.D., 1964; Columbia University, A.M., 1956. *Home:* Barnes Rd., Burrillville, R.I. *Office:* Department of English, Brown University, Providence, R.I. 02912.

CAREER: Brown University, Providence, R.I., instructor, 1961-65, assistant professor, 1965-68, associate professor, 1968-72, professor of American literature, 1972—, assistant to the dean for freshman, 1965-66. Fulbright lecturer in American Literature, Universidade de Sao Paulo (Brazil), 1969-71; co-chairman, American civilization, 1971-73. *Member:* Modern Language Association of America, American Folklore Society, Biographical Society of America.

WRITINGS: Henry James and John Hay: The Record of a Friendship, Brown University Press, 1965; (editor) *Poems by Emily Dickinson (1890-1896),* Scholars' Facsimiles and Reprints, 1967; (contributor) Jac Tharpe, editor, *Frost: Centennial Essays,* University of Mississippi Press, 1974. Contributor to *American Literature, Journal of American Folklore, Victorian Poetry,* and other journals.

WORK IN PROGRESS: A critical study of Stephen Crane's fiction; a study on Henry James and Henry Adams.

* * *

MOODY, Dale 1915-

PERSONAL: Born January 27, 1915, near Stamford, Tex.; son of Claude Sylvester and Mattie Ellen (Fuller) Moody; married Mildred French, June 12, 1939; children: Sue Ellen, Linda Marie, Marcia Ann, John Dale. *Education:* Baylor University, student, 1933-36, B.A. (with highest honors), 1941; Dallas Theological Seminary, student, 1936-37; Southern Baptist Theological Seminary, Th.M., 1942, Th.D., 1947; also studied at Columbia University, 1944-45, and at University of Basel, University of Zurich, 1948, University of Heidelberg, 1957-58; Oxford University, D.Phil., 1965. *Office:* Southern Baptist Theological Seminary, Louisville, Ky.

CAREER: Ordained Baptist minister, 1932; pastor in Texas, Indiana, and Kentucky, 1932-44, 1945-46; Southern Baptist Theological Seminary, Louisville, Ky., professor of theology, 1945—., John Emerson Brown Professor of Systematic Theology, 1954—. University of Heidelberg, faculty fellow, 1957-58; Regent's Park College, Oxford University, visiting fellow, 1961-63. Baptist World Alliance, member of Commission on the Church, 1948—; World Council of Churches, member of Faith and Order Commission, 1961—. Speaker in twenty-six countries. *Member:* Society for Religion in Higher Education (fellow). *Awards, honors:* Citation for civilian service, U.S. Air Force, 1954.

WRITINGS: (Contributor) *What Is the Church,* Broadman, 1958; (contributor) *The Theology of Emil Brunner,* Macmillan, 1962; *Christ and the Church,* Eerdmans, 1963; *The Hope of Glory,* Eerdmans, 1964; (contributor) *The Teacher's Yoke,* Baylor University Press, 1964; *Baptism: Foundation of Christian Unity,* Westminster, 1968; *Spirit of the Living God,* Westminster, 1968; (contributor) *The Concept of the Believer's Church,* Herald Press, 1969; *Romans,* Broadman, 1970; *The Letters of John,* Ward, 1970. Contributor to *Interpreter's Dictionary of the Bible,* and to *Library of Living Theology;* also contributor to periodicals.

MOODY, R. Bruce 1933-

PERSONAL: Born September 22, 1933, in New York, N.Y.; married Deborah Sullivan, July 19, 1960; children: Amanda Sidonie. *Education:* Attended Yale University, 1952; Columbia University, B.A., 1958; Hunter College, of the City University of New York, M.A., 1970; City University of New York, graduate study. *Home:* 233 West 13th St., New York, N.Y. 10011.

CAREER: Writer; teacher. *Awards, honors:* H. C. Bunner Prize.

WRITINGS: The Decline and Fall of Daphne Finn, Coward, 1966; (contributor) Richard Goldstone, editor, *Contexts of the Drama,* McGraw, 1968. Contributor to *New Yorker, Botteghe Oscure, National Review, Show, Look, Works,* and *Greenwich News.*

WORK IN PROGRESS: Fear, Anger, Pain, a study of primal feeling in literature; *The Disciplines,* a study of EST, Mind Control, TM, Arica; *The Chieftain,* a screenplay; *Golden Comedy,* a novel; *Revenge,* a book of short stories.

SIDELIGHTS: The Mugar Memorial Library of Boston University maintains the R. Bruce Moody Collection.

* * *

MOON, Douglas Mark 1937-

PERSONAL: Born September 10, 1937, in Fulda, Minn.; son of Harry Ernest (a paint manufacturer) and Geneva (Schueller) Moon; married Martha Ann Buck, May 5, 1964. *Education:* Student at University of Southern California, 1955-57, and California State College (now University), Long Beach, 1958-59; University of California, Berkeley, B.A., 1961, M.A., 1965, graduate study, 1965. *Home:* 2449 Dwight Way, Berkeley, Calif. 94704. *Agent:* Carl D. Brandt, 101 Park Ave., New York, N.Y. 10017.

WRITINGS: The King Diaries (novel), McGraw, 1967.

WORK IN PROGRESS: Harriet and Bethgamul, poetry; *Not Louder Shrieks,* a novel; writing a program for teaching English as a foreign language; research into the English stress system.

SIDELIGHTS: John J. Murray, speaking of *The King Diaries,* called the author "a new luna on the horizon," and added: "I thoroughly enjoyed his irreverent sallies. If he doesn't repeat himself, he should become a first-rate satirist. . . . [In this novel] he brilliantly satirizes the whole anonymous flock of fringe-lunatics who breed prolifically in the California preserve." The reviewer for the *Virginia Quarterly Review* said that in *The King Diaries* Moon exposed "a fatuous, unctuous, pious fraud representing himself to be rector of the Church of the Respectable Light in San Francisco, through the diaries of two eccentric, half-demented, rich, and obviously perverse creatures, mother and son, who are conveniently killed off by the author as a device to terminate his narrative." This reviewer does note, however, that Moon's novel "succeeds in one highly commendable respect, in that he exploits a fresh idea with some skill and deftness," though the reviewer believes that the book fails "simply because his material desiccates before his macabre yarn can be brought to a conclusion."

BIOGRAPHICAL/CRITICAL SOURCES: Best Sellers, March 15, 1967; *New York Times Book Review,* March 19, 1967; *Virginia Quarterly Review,* summer, 1967.†

MOONEY, Eugene F. 1930-

PERSONAL: Born December 2, 1930, in Jackson, Miss.; son of Eugene French (a member of Arkansas State Police) and Gertrude (Johnson) Mooney; married Ruth L. Teague, July 8, 1955; children: Michael Eugene, James McMillin, Matthew Lesueur. *Education:* University of Arkansas, A.B., 1957, LL.B., 1958; Yale University, LL.M., 1963. *Politics:* Democrat. *Home:* 313 Colony Rd., Lexington, Ken. 40506.

CAREER: Attorney with McMillin, Teague & Coates, Little Rock, Ark., and deputy prosecuting attorney of Sixth Arkansas District, 1958-59; University of Arkansas School of Law, Fayetteville, assistant professor of law, 1959-63; University of Kentucky College of Law, Lexington, associate professor of law, 1963-66, professor of law, 1966—. Hearing officer, Kentucky Department of Insurance; member of Lexington Committee on Human Rights. *Military service:* U.S. Air Force, 1951-55; served in Korea; became sergeant. *Member:* International Law Association, American Association of University Professors, Arkansas Bar Association.

WRITINGS: Foreign Seizures: Sabbatino and the Act of State Doctrine, University Press of Kentucky, 1966; (compiler with Robert Marshall Viles) *Handbook on the Legal Rights of the Mississippi Poor,* [Louisville, Ky.], 1966. Contributor to law journals.

WORK IN PROGRESS: Research on state regulation of securities distribution.†

* * *

MOORE, John Richard, Jr. 1925-
(Dick Moore)

PERSONAL: Born September 12, 1925, in Los Angeles, Calif.; son of John Richard (a banker) and Nora Eileen (Orr) Moore; married Patricia Dempsey, December 14, 1949 (marriage dissolved, 1954); married Eleanor Donhowe Fitzpatrick, November 8, 1959; children: (first marriage) Kevin Michael; (second marriage) Stephen Douglas. *Education:* Attended California State College (now University), Los Angeles, 1946-47; studied at Actors' Laboratory, Los Angeles, one year, and privately with acting and voice teachers in Los Angeles and New York, five years. *Home:* 865 West End Ave., New York, N.Y. 10025. *Agent:* Harriet Kaplan, 667 Madison Ave., New York, N.Y. *Office:* Dick Moore and Associates, Inc., 124 East 40th St., New York, N.Y. 10016.

CAREER: Billed as Dickie Moore, made motion picture debut in "Beloved Rogue" at age of eleven months; co-star of "Our Gang" comedy series, 1930-32; other principal film credits include roles in "The Squaw Man," 1931, "Manhattan Parade," 1932, "Union Depot," 1932, "Fireman, Save My Child," 1932, "So Big," 1932, "Oliver Twist," 1933, "The Story of Louis Pasteur," 1935, "Peter Ibbetson," 1935, "The Life of Emile Zola," 1937, "Sergeant York," 1941, "Miss Annie Rooney," 1942, "Are These Our Children," 1942, "The Song of Bernadette," 1943, "Together Again," 1944, "The Eve of St. Mark," 1944, "The Boy and the Eagle" (which he produced), 1949, "Eight Iron Men," 1951, and "Member of the Wedding," 1952; principal theatre roles include Michael in "The Fourposter," 1954, Lachie in "The Hasty Heart," and his New York debut as Brother Martin Ladvenu in Siobhan McKenna's "Saint Joan," 1956. Director of the radio series, "Time and the Play," Los Angeles, 1942; acted on

Broadway and in summer stock, 1948-54; director and manager of Arena Theatre, Glen Falls, N.Y., 1954, and Cincinnati Summer Theatre, Cincinnati, Ohio, 1955; instructor in acting and the theatre at American Academy of Dramatic Art, New York, N.Y., 1957; public relations director for Actors' Equity Association and editor of *Equity* Magazine, 1957-63; creative director of Meetings and Shows Department, Communications Affiliates, Inc., New York, N.Y., 1963-65; senior associate, Hal Leyshon and Associates (public relations), New York, N.Y., 1965-66; president of Dick Moore and Associates, Inc., New York, N.Y., 1966—. Member of State Department Professional Theatre advisory panel for International Cultural Exchange Program, 1962—, of National Council on the Arts and Government, 1957—, and of drama advisory panel, School of Performing Arts. *Military service:* U.S. Army, staff correspondent for *Stars and Stripes*, served in Pacific Theater, 1944-46; became sergeant. *Member:* Actors' Equity Association, Screen Actors Guild, American Federation of Television and Radio Artists, American Newspaper Guild, The Players (New York). *Awards, honors:* His production of "The Boy and the Eagle" was nominated for an Academy Award (Oscar), 1949.

WRITINGS—Under name Dick Moore: *Opportunities in Acting: Stage, Motion Pictures, Television*, foreword by Ralph Bellamy, Universal Publishing, 1963; *The Relationship of Amateur to Professional in the American Theatre*, Rockefeller Foundation, 1963. Author of television play, "The Jewel Box," produced for Matinee Theatre by National Broadcasting Co., 1958.

AVOCATIONAL INTERESTS: Fishing and falconry.†

* * *

MOORE, Virginia Dryden 1911-

PERSONAL: Born January 19, 1911, in Snow Hill, Md.; daughter of Putnam Warren (a businessman) and Mary Virginia (Shockley) Dryden; married William Thomas Moore, December 5, 1931. *Education:* Attended Salisbury State College, 1928-30; Johns Hopkins University, B.S., 1948; University of Maryland, M.Ed., 1950. *Politics:* Democrat. *Religion:* Methodist. *Home:* 503 West Forest View Rd., Linthicum Heights, Md. 21090. *Office:* Board of Education of Anne Arundel County, Green St., Annapolis, Md. 21404.

CAREER: Anne Arundel County Board of Education, Annapolis, Md., teacher, 1930-46, principal, 1943-46, supervisor of elementary schools, 1946-72; free-lance writer, 1972—. Visiting lecturer, summer and evening school, University of Maryland, 1953-64. Public lecturer and consultant at professional conferences and inservice education workshops.

MEMBER: International Reading Association (co-chairman, member of council aids committee, 1966-67), Association for Supervision and Curriculum Development (treasurer of Maryland branch, 1957-59), National Education Association, American Association for Health, Physical Education and Recreation, Maryland State Teachers Association, Maryland Corrective-Remedial Reading Association (president, 1963-64), Anne Arundel County Reading Council (president, 1963-64), Anne Arundel County Retired Teachers Association (vice-president, 1974—) Greater Washington Area Reading Council (chairman of constitution and by-laws committee, 1965-66), Women's Eastern Shore Society of Maryland (member of board of governors, 1974—), Delta Kappa Gamma, Pi Lambda Theta.

WRITINGS: (With James H. Humphrey and Warren Johnson) *Elementary School Health Education*, Harper, 1962; (with J. H. Humphrey) "Read and Play" series, Garrard, 1962; (with Will J. Massey) *Helping High School Students to Read Better*, Holt, 1965; (with Oliver E. Byrd, Elizabeth A. Neilson, and others) "Laidlaw Health Series," Grades 1-8, Laidlaw, 1974.

AVOCATIONAL INTERESTS: Reading, music, travel.

* * *

MOREY, Roy D. 1937-

PERSONAL: Born July 16, 1937, in Reno, Nev.; son of Douglas E. and Lucretia (Jacquot) Morey; married Delores Haaland, August 23, 1959; children: Diana Lynn, Carolyn Sue. *Education:* Northern Arizona University, B.A., 1959; University of Arizona, M.A., 1961, Ph.D., 1964. *Home:* 4628 Edgefield Road, Bethesda, Md. 20014.

CAREER: National Center for Education in Politics fellow and legislative assistant to Governor Paul J. Fannin of Arizona, 1961; American Political Science Association congressional fellow, Washington, D.C., 1964-65; Denison University, Granville, Ohio, assistant professor of government, and chairman of department of political science, 1965-71; White House Domestic Council, Washington, D.C., staff assistant to the President, 1971-73; U.S. Department of State, Washington, D.C., deputy assistant secretary, 1973—. Visiting assistant professor, Arizona State University, University of Arizona, Ohio State University. Visiting professor, Waseda University (Tokyo), and director, Great Lakes Colleges Association Japan Study Program. *Member:* American Political Science Association, American Association of University Professors, Midwest Political Science Association. Pi Sigma Alpha.

WRITINGS: *Politics and Legislation: The Office of Governor of Arizona*, University of Arizona Press, 1965; (editor with E. E. Walker and others) *Readings in American Public Opinion*, American Book Co., 1968. Contributor to *American Political Science Review, Western Political Quarterly, Social Science Quarterly*, and other political and social science journals.

WORK IN PROGRESS: A case study of the 1965 elementary and secondary education law (federal aid).

* * *

MORGAN, Charles, Jr. 1930-

PERSONAL: Born March 11, 1930, in Cincinnati, Ohio; son of Charles (manager of a life insurance firm) and Ethel (Mitchell) Morgan; married Camille Walpole, September 5, 1953; children: Charles Morgan III. *Education:* University of Alabama, B.S., 1953, LL.B., 1955. *Politics:* Democrat. *Religion:* Episcopalian. *Home:* 604 Independence Ave. S.E., Washington, D.C. *Agent:* Gerard McCauley, Inc., 551 Fifth Ave., New York, N.Y. 10017. *Office:* American Civil Liberties Union, 410 First St. S.E., Washington, D.C.

CAREER: Admitted to bar, Alabama, 1955, District of Columbia, 1972; University of Alabama, University, instructor in American economics, 1954-55; attorney in private practice, Birmingham, Ala., 1955-63; special counsel for National Association for the Advancement of Colored People Legal Defense and Educational Fund, 1963-64; American Association of University Professors, Washington, D.C., assistant counsel, 1964; American Civil Liberties Union, director of southern regional office, Atlanta,

Ga., 1964-72, director of Washington office, Washington, D.C., 1972—. Attorney in civil rights and civil liberties cases in the South, prior to American Civil Liberties Union post. National committeeman of Young Democrats of Alabama, 1951-55, and National Democratic Party of Alabama, 1968-69; chairman of speakers campaign of National Democratic Party, 1960. Member of board of directors of Alabama Association for Mental Health, 1958-63; president of Jefferson County Heart Foundation, 1963; trustee of Alabama Heart Association; member of Jefferson County Advisory Committee on Schools. *Member:* Phi Alpha Delta, Delta Tau Delta (president of chapter, 1951-52; vice-president of southern region, 1962-63; former member of national board of governors). *Awards, honors:* First honorary fellow, University of Pennsylvania Law School, 1964.

WRITINGS: A Time to Speak, Harper, 1964; (contributor) *Southern Justice* (anthology), Pantheon, 1965; *Playing Around*, Little, Brown, 1974. Contributor of articles to *Look, New York Herald Tribune*, and *New South*.

BIOGRAPHICAL/CRITICAL SOURCES: Reporter, February 10, 1966.

* * *

MORGAN, Chester A(lan) 1914-

PERSONAL: Born January 16, 1914, in Olds, Iowa; son of Herbert Luther and Edna (Sandall) Morgan; married Ferne Irene Hadley, 1937; children: Marsha Lee. *Education:* State University of Iowa (now University of Iowa), B.A., 1936, M.A., 1945, Ph.D., 1951. *Religion:* Methodist Episcopalian. *Home:* 834 seventh Ave., Iowa City, Iowa. *Office:* University of Iowa, 657 Phillips Hall, Iowa City, Iowa.

CAREER: Van Meter High School, Van Meter, Iowa, teacher of economics, 1936; London Mills High School, London Mills, Ill., teacher of economics, 1936-37; Mt. Pleasant High School, Mt. Pleasant, Iowa, teacher, 1937-43, principal, 1943-46; Simpson College, Indianola, Iowa, associate professor of economics, 1946-47, head of department of economics, 1947-52; State University of Iowa (now University of Iowa), Iowa City, assistant professor, 1952-57, associate professor and head of department of labor and management, 1957-64, professor of labor economics, 1961—, director of economics graduate program, 1964-66, chairman of department of economics, 1965-69. *Member:* American Economic Association, Industrial Relations Research Association, American Association of University Professors, Order of Artus (local president, 1957-58), Delta Sigma Pi, Lambda Chi Alpha, Beta Gamma Sigma.

WRITINGS: Labor Economics, Dorsey, 1962, 3rd revised edition, 1970. Contributor to *American People's Encyclopedia* and to professional journals. Also author of two monographs for the Center for Labor and Management, University of Iowa.

AVOCATIONAL INTERESTS: Travel, reading.

* * *

MORGAN, Daniel C(roxton), Jr. 1931-

PERSONAL: Born September 30, 1931, in Webster, Tex.; son of Daniel Croxton and Grace (Carmichael) Morgan; married Mary Lillian Blasingame, October 21, 1956; children: Robert Kenneth, Rebecca Ann. *Education:* University of Texas, B.B.A., 1953, M.A., 1955; University of Wisconsin, Ph.D., 1962. *Politics:* "Democrat officially,

preferably leftist independent." *Home:* 3204 Harris Park, Austin, Tex. 78705. *Office:* Department of Economics, University of Texas, Austin, Tex. 78712.

CAREER: Dow Chemical Co., Freeport, Tex., assistant superintendent of transportation, 1955-56; University of Wisconsin, Madison, assistant economist, 1957-59; University of Tennessee, Knoxville, assistant professor of economics, 1959-60; University of Texas, Austin, assistant professor, 1961-64, associate professor of economics, 1964—. *Military service:* U.S. Army Reserve, 1955-64, active duty, 1956; became captain. *Member:* American Economic Association, National Tax Association, Economic History Association, American Association of University Professors, Association for Evolutionary Economics, Southwestern Social Science Association, American Civil Liberties Union, Texas Association of College Teachers. *Awards, honors:* Ford Foundation fellowship, 1960-61.

WRITINGS: Retail Sales Tax: An Appraisal of New Issues, University of Wisconsin Press, 1964; *Financing Higher Education in Texas: Needs and Methods*, Institute of Public Affairs, University of Texas, 1965; (with Francis Gregory Hayden) *Elementary and Secondary Education Aid: Toward an Optional Program for the State Government of Texas*, Institute of Public Affairs, University of Texas, 1970.

WORK IN PROGRESS: Poverty and Income Distribution Problems in the United States (tentative title).†

* * *

MORGAN, Donald G(rant) 1911-

PERSONAL: Born June 7, 1911, in Chicago, Ill.; son of Elisha (a businessman and farmer) and Mary (Aull) Morgan; married Margaret Prince (an adoption caseworker), August 29, 1942; children: Julie (Mrs. J. William Schopf), Edward P., Margaret G. (Mrs. James B. Cross), Christopher. *Education:* Cornell University, A.B., 1933; Geneva School of International Studies, graduate study, 1937; Harvard University, Ed.M., 1938, A.M., 1939, Ph.D., 1942. *Religion:* Episcopalian. *Home:* 12 Staton Ave., South Hadley, Mass. 01075.

CAREER: Trinity College, Hartford, Conn., instructor, 1939-43; Mount Holyoke College, South Hadley, Mass., instructor, 1943-46, assistant professor, 1946-49, associate professor, 1949-55, professor of political science, 1955—, chairman of department, 1950-56. Smith College, visiting lecturer, 1946-47. South Hadley Town Meeting, elected member, 1957—. *Member:* American Political Science Association, American Association of University Professors, American Civil Liberties Union, Phi Beta Kappa, Phi Kappa Phi. *Awards, honors:* Research grants from Social Science Research Council, 1948-49, 1958-59, 1960-62, from American Philosophical Society, 1958-59, 1960, 1964-65, and Walter E. Meyer Research Institute of Law, 1964-65.

WRITINGS: Justice William Johnson, The First Dissenter, University of South Carolina Press, 1954; (contributor) W. M. Jones, editor, *Chief Justice John Marshall: A Reappraisal*, Cornell University Press, 1956; (contributor) Konvitz and Rossiter, editors, *Aspects of Liberty*, Cornell University Press, 1958; *Congress and the Constitution: A Study of Responsibility*, Belknap Press, 1966. Contributor to *William and Mary Quarterly* and law reviews.

WORK IN PROGRESS: A book on the nature and importance of constitutional government for the age of technology; political satire, perhaps in the form of plays.

SIDELIGHTS: Morgan told *CA:* "My knowlege of French is mediocre, and of German, worse." *Avocational interests:* Gardening, music, swimming, hiking.

* * *

MORGAN, Frederick 1922-

PERSONAL: Born April 25, 1922, in New York, N.Y.; son of John W. (a manufacturer) and Marion (Burt) Morgan; married Constance Canfield, 1942; married second wife, Rose Fillmore, August 19, 1957; married third wife, Paula Deitz, November 30, 1969; children: (first marriage) Evelyn, Gaylen, John (deceased) Seth, Veronica, George Frederick, III. *Education:* Princeton University, A.B. (magna cum laude), 1943. *Politics:* Democrat. *Residence:* New York, N.Y. *Office:* Hudson Review, 65 East 55th St., New York, N.Y. 10022.

CAREER: Hudson Review, New York, N.Y., founder, 1948, editor, 1948—. Chairman of advisory council to department of Romance languages, Princeton University. *Military service:* U.S. Army, 1943-45. *Member:* P.E.N., Century Association. *Awards, honors:* National Book Award nomination, 1972, for *A Book of Change.*

WRITINGS: (Editor) *The Hudson Review Anthology,* Random House, 1961; (editor) *The Modern Image,* Norton, 1965; *A Book of Change* (poems), Scribner, 1972.

* * *

MORGAN, Roger P(earce) 1932-

PERSONAL: Born March 3, 1932, in Burton, England; son of Donald Emlyn (a school principal) and Esther (Pearce) Morgan; married Annie-Francoise Combes (a university teacher); children: Caroline, Mark, Patrick, Benedict. *Education:* Cambridge University, B.A., 1953, M.A., 1957, Ph.D., 1959; graduate study at University of Paris, 1953-54, University of Hamburg, 1955. *Politics:* Labour. *Office:* School of European Studies, University of Sussex, Falmer, Brighton, England.

CAREER: University of London, London, England, tutor in social studies, 1957-59; University College of Wales, Aberystwyth, lecturer in international politics, 1959-63; University of Sussex, Brighton, England, lecturer in history and international relations, 1963—. Visiting professor of public law and government at Columbia University; research associate at Center for International affairs, Harvard University, 1965-66. Lecturer to adult education groups, American student groups visiting Europe, and for university extension courses. *Member:* Political Studies Association, Royal Institute for International Affairs, Institute for Strategic Studies, Association of University Teachers.

WRITINGS: The German Social Democrats and the First International: 1864-1872, Cambridge University Press, 1965; *Modern Germany,* Hamish Hamilton, 1966; (with James L. Henderson and others) *Since 1945: Aspects of Contemporary World History,* Methuen, 1966; (editor) *Germany 1870-1970: A Hundred Years of Turmoil,* Macdonald & Co., 1970; (editor with Karl Kaiser) *Britain and West Germany: Changing Societies and the Future of Foreign Policy,* Oxford University Press for the Royal Institute of International Affairs, 1971; *Western European Politics since 1945: The Shaping of the European Community,* Batsford, 1972; (editor) *Study of International Affairs: Essays in Honour of Kenneth Younger,* Oxford University Press, 1972; *High Politics, Low Politics: Toward a Foreign*

Policy for Western Europe, Sage, 1973. Also author of articles and book reviews on political science, recent history, and world affairs.

WORK IN PROGRESS: United States Relations With West Germany Since 1945.

SIDELIGHTS: Morgan has traveled in most of western Europe and the United States. He is fluent in French and German. *Avocational interests:* Music (amateur violinist).†

* * *

MORGAN, Theodore 1910-

PERSONAL: Born May 31, 1910, in Middletown, Ohio; son of Ben (a farmer) and Anna Louella (Knecht) Morgan; married Catharine Moomaw, June 30, 1943; children: Stephanie, Marian, Laura. *Education:* Ohio State University, A.B., 1930, A.M., 1931; Harvard University, M.A., 1940, Ph.D., 1941. *Religion:* Unitarian. *Home:* 3534 Topping Rd., Madison, Wis. 53705. *Office:* Department of Economics, University of Wisconsin, Madison, Wis. 53706.

CAREER: Harvard University, Cambridge, Mass., instructor and tutor in economics, 1940-41, 1942-47; Randolph-Macon Woman's College, Lynchburg, Va., assistant professor of economics, 1941-42; University of Wisconsin, Madison, associate professor, 1947-55, professor of economics, 1955—. Economic adviser to government of Ceylon, 1951-52, and to the Ministry of Economic Affairs of government of Thailand; deputy governor, Central Bank of Ceylon, Colombo, 1952-53. Consultant to World Bank, 1962-63, Ford Foundation, 1956, 1964-65. Member of senior staff, U.S. Council of Economic Advisers, 1964-65. *Member:* American Economic Association (chairman of policy board on summer institutes, 1957-63), Royal Economic Society (England), American Association of University Professors, Malayan Economic Society, Phi Beta Kappa.

WRITINGS: Development of the Hawaiian Economy, Harvard University Press, 1949; *Income and Employment,* Prentice-Hall, 1947, 2nd edition, 1952; *Introduction to Economics,* Prentice-Hall, 1951, 2nd edition, 1956; (coauthor) *Readings in Economic Development,* Wadsworth, 1963; (editor with Nyle Spoelstra) *Economic Interdependence in Southeast Asia,* University of Wisconsin Press, 1969; (editor with G. W. Betz) *Economic Development: Readings in Theory and Practice,* Wadsworth, 1970; (coeditor) *Exchange Rate Policy in Southeast Asia,* Heath-Lexington, 1973; *Economic Development: Concept and Strategy,* Harper, 1974. Contributor to economic journals.

WORK IN PROGRESS: Exchange Depreciation in Less-Developed Countries, 1971-73.

SIDELIGHTS: Morgan has done research and acted as an adviser in Asia and Africa.

* * *

MORLAN, Robert L(oren) 1920-

PERSONAL: Born May 25, 1920, in Madison, Ohio; son of Howard E. (a painting contractor) and Maude (Holmden) Morlan; married Anne Matthews, March 8, 1944; children: Shirley Anne, Janet Carol, Larry Howard, Susan Kay. *Education:* Denison University, B.A., 1942; University of Minnesota, M.A., 1947, Ph.D., 1949. *Politics:* Democrat. *Religion:* Baptist. *Home:* 1313 East Colton Ave., Redlands, Calif. 92373. *Office:* University of Redlands, Redlands, Calif. 92373.

CAREER: University of Minnesota, Minneapolis, instructor in political science, 1948-49; University of Redlands, Redlands, Calif., assistant professor, 1949-52, associate professor, 1952-56, professor of government, 1956—. Fulbright lecturer, University of Amsterdam, 1956-57; visiting professor (part-time), University of California, Riverside, 1958, 1964, 1965, 1967; Smith-Mundt Professor, College of Europe, 1959-60; visiting research scholar and professor, University of Leiden, 1972-73. Lecturer at University of Oslo, 1956, and International Institute of Social Studies, The Hague, 1957, 1960; lecturer for Radio Free Europe, 1960-61. Commissioner, California State Scholarship Commission, 1961-69; consultant to U.S. Department of Agriculture, 1967; president, Riverside and San Bernardino Counties Council of Churches, 1969-71. City councilman, Redlands, 1954-56, vice-mayor, 1956; president of Citrus Belt Division, League of California Cities, 1955-56. Military service: U.S. Army Air Forces, 1942-46.

MEMBER: American Political Science Association, American Association of University Professors, United Nations Association, World Federalists U.S.A., National Municipal League, Western Political Science Association (president, 1967-68), Southern California Political Science Association (president, 1955-56, 1962-63), Phi Beta Kappa, Omicron Delta Kappa (western states deputy, member of general council, 1954—), Tau Kappa Alpha. Awards, honors: National Distinguished Service Award, Omicron Delta Kappa, 1970; Denison University Alumni distinguished achievement citation, 1972.

WRITINGS: Intergovernmental Relations in Education, University of Minnesota Press, 1950; Capitol, Courthouse and City Hall, Houghton, 1954, 4th edition, 1972; Political Prairie Fire: The Nonpartisan League, 1915-1922, University of Minnesota Press, 1955; (with others) The Fifty States and Their Local Governments, Knopf, 1967; (with Leroy Hardy) Politics in California, Dickenson, 1968; American Government: Policy and Process, Houghton, 1971, 2nd edition, 1975; Gemeentepolitik in Debat: Oppvattingen van Burgers en Bestuurders, Samsom, 1974. Writer of pamphlets on the California ballot and public policy issues; contributor of about twenty-five articles on government and education to journals.

SIDELIGHTS: Morlan reads French, German, and Dutch.

* * *

MORRIS, Donald R. 1924-

PERSONAL: Born November 11, 1924; married Sylvia Stallings (a book reviewer), 1953 (divorced, 1973); children: four. Education: U.S. Naval Academy, B.S., 1948. Residence: Houston, Tex. Agent: Russell & Volkening, Inc., 551 Fifth Ave., Room 1517, New York, N.Y. 10017.

CAREER: U.S. Navy, 1942-60; U.S. Naval Reserve, 1960-72, retired as lieutenant commander; Houston Post, Houston, Tex., foreign news analyst and columnist, 1972—. Worked for Central Intelligence Agency, Washington, D.C., 1956-72. Member: Mensa, Aircraft Owners and Pilots Association.

WRITINGS: China Station (fiction), Farrar, Straus, 1951; Warm Bodies (fiction), Simon & Schuster, 1957; The Washing of the Spears (nonfiction), Simon & Schuster, 1965; (contributor) The Horizon Book of the British Empire, American Heritage, 1973. Contributor to Encyclopaedia Britannica. Contributor of articles to Argosy, True, Atlantic Monthly, Cornhill, and U.S. Naval Institute Proceedings.

MORRIS, Jackson E(dgar) 1918-

PERSONAL: Born March 22, 1918, in Hoquiam, Wash.; son of Oliver Sidney and Bess (Gibson) Morris; married Frances Markwell, June 15, 1952; children: Jennifer Delia, Jill Elaine. Education: Pomona College, B.A., 1940; Harvard University, M.A., 1941. Home: 4415 Pepperwood Ave., Long Beach, Calif. 90808.

CAREER: Pomona College, Claremont, Calif., instructor in astronomy, 1946-47; ill, 1947-51; North American Aviation, Downey, Calif., research engineer, 1952-62, senior flight test engineer, 1962-71. University of California, Los Angeles, instructor in scientific writing, 1956-66. Military service: U.S. Navy, 1942-45; U.S. Naval Reserve, became lieutenant junior grade. Member: Phi Beta Kappa.

WRITINGS: Principles of Scientific and Technical Writing, McGraw, 1966; (contributor) H. B. Maynard, editor, Industrial Engineering Handbook, McGraw, 1971. Occasional contributor of poetry on scientific themes to New Yorker and other publications. Contributor of articles to Astronautical Sciences Review, Yale Scientific, and other scientific journals.

WORK IN PROGRESS: Application of set theory to grammar.

* * *

MORRIS, William 1913-

PERSONAL: Born April 13, 1913, in Boston, Mass.; son of Charles Hyndman (an attorney) and Elizabeth Margaret (Hanna) Morris; married Jane Frazer, August 7, 1939; married Mary Elizabeth Davis (a writer), February 8, 1947; children: Ann Elizabeth (Mrs. Paul Downie), Susan McLeod, John Boyd, William Frazer, Mary Elizabeth, Evan Nathanael. Education: Harvard University, A.B., 1935. Politics: Independent Democrat. Religion: Episcopalian. Home: 355 Sound Beach Ave., Old Greenwich, Conn.

CAREER: Newman School, Lakewood, N.J., instructor in English and Latin, 1935-37; G. & C. Merriam Co., Springfield, Mass., college department staff, 1937-43; Grosset & Dunlap, Inc., New York, N.Y., managing editor, 1945-47, executive editor, 1947-53, editor-in-chief, 1953-60; Grolier, Inc., New York, N.Y. executive editor, International Encyclopedia, 1960-62, Grolier Universal Encyclopedia, 1962-64; American Heritage Publishing Co., New York, N.Y., editor-in-chief, American Heritage Dictionary, 1964—; Grosset & Dunlap, Inc., New York, editor-in-chief of Xerox Family Education Services, 1971—. Consulting editor for Funk & Wagnalls New Standard Dictionary, international edition, 1954-58, and New College Standard Dictionary, 1958-60. Military service: U.S. Maritime Service, 1943-45; served in various combat areas as communications officer; became lieutenant junior grade.

MEMBER: National Council of Teachers of English, Modern Language Association of America, American Library Association, Society for General Semantics; Dutch Treat Club (president), Society of Salurians, Overseas Press Club, Coffee House, and Harvard Club (all New York); Old Greenwich Boat Club.

WRITINGS: (Editor) Words: The New Dictionary, Grosset, 1947, revised edition with Charles P. Chadsey and Harold Wentworth, published as The Grosset Webster Dictionary, 1953, new edition, 1966; (editor) Concise Biographical Dictionary, Grosset, 1949; (editor with wife, Mary Morris) The Concise Dictionary of Famous Men and Women, revised edition, Grosset, 1951; It's Easy to In-

crease Your Vocabulary, Harper, 1957, revised edition, Penguin, 1975; (with Mary Morris) *The Word Game Book*, Harper, 1959, revised edition, Penguin, 1975; (with Mary Morris) *Dictionary of Word and Phrase Origins*, Harper, Volume I, 1962, Volume II, 1967, Volume III, 1971; *The William Morris Self-Enrichment Vocabulary Program*, Grolier, 1965; *Your Heritage of Words: How to Increase Your Vocabulary Instantly*, Dell, 1970; (editor and author of introduction) Harriet Wittels and Joan Greisman, *The Young People's Thesaurus,* Ward, Lock, 1973; (editor with Doris Duenewald) *Xerox Intermediate Dictionary*, Grosset, 1973; (editor) *The Weekly Reader Beginning Dictionary*, new edition, Grosset, 1974; (with Mary Morris) *Harper Dictionary of Contemporary Usage*, Harper, 1975.

Editor of "Berlitz Self-Teacher Language Books," 1949-53. Writer of column, "William Morris on Words," for Bell-McClure Syndicate, 1954-68; author, with Mary Morris, of column, "Words, Wit and Wisdom," for United Feature Syndicate, 1968—. Contributor to magazines, including *Saturday Review*, *Esquire*, *Changing Times*, and *Today's Living*.

* * *

MORRIS, William T(homas) 1928-

PERSONAL: Born November 12, 1928, in Concord, N.H.; son of William Clement and Ruth (Robinson) Morris; married Miriam Lemp, November 18, 1950; children: Cynthia Cristine, William Robert, Anne Marie. *Education:* Massachusetts Institute of Technology, S.B., 1950; Ohio State University, M.Sc., 1953, Ph.D., 1956. *Home:* 2333 Brandon Rd., Columbus, Ohio 43221. *Office:* Department of Industrial and Systems Engineering, Ohio State University, 190 West 19th Ave., Columbus, Ohio 43210.

CAREER: American Brake Shoe Co., New York, N.Y., employed in commercial research department, 1950-51; Ohio State University, Columbus, 1954—, now professor of industrial engineering, and chairman of department. Visiting lecturer at University of North Carolina, Purdue University, Industrial College of the Armed Forces, General Motors Institute, California Polytechnic Institute, Pennsylvania State University, and other universities. Consultant to National Cash Register Co., General Motors Corp., and other corporations and institutions. *Military service:* U.S. Army Air Forces, research and development officer, Wright-Patterson Air Force Base, 1951-54.

MEMBER: American Institute of Industrial Engineers, Operations Research Society of America, Institute of Management Sciences, Academy of Management, American Association for the Advancement of Science, American Society for Engineering Education, Sigma Xi, Tau Beta Pi, Alpha Pi Mu. *Awards, honors: Management Science in Action* was chosen as one of five outstanding books of 1963 by Academy of Management and McKinsey Foundation; Robert M. Critchfield Award for meritorious service, 1964, 1972; Ohio State University Alumni Award for distinguished teaching, 1965; Charles E. MacQuigg Award for teaching excellence, 1967; Raymond Q. Armington Award for meritorious service, 1967; Ronald W. Thompson Award for meritorious achievement, 1968.

WRITINGS: The Rationalization of Industrial Decision Processes, Ohio State University Studies, 1957; *Engineering Economy—The Analysis of Management Decisions*, Irwin, 1960, revised edition published as *The Analysis of Management Decisions*, Irwin, 1964; (contributor) Bass and others, editors, *Mathematical Models and*

Methods in Marketing, Irwin, 1961; *Analysis for Materials Handling Management*, Irwin, 1962; (contributor) Arthur Lesser, Jr., editor, *Applications of Economic Evaluation in Industry*, American Society for Engineering Education, 1962; *Management Science in Action*, Irwin, 1963.

(Contributor) Arthur Lesser, Jr., editor, *Decision-Making Criteria for Capital Expenditures*, American Society for Engineering Education, 1966; *The Capacity Decision System*, Irwin, 1967; *Decentralization in Management Systems*, Ohio State University Press, 1967; (contributor) E. Ralph Sims, Jr., editor, *The Planning and Management of the Material Flow Function*, Industrial Education Institute, 1968; *Management Science: A Bayesian Introduction*, Prentice-Hall, 1968; (contributor) A. Rappoport, editor, *Information for Decision Making*, Prentice-Hall, 1969; (with Harold Bierman and others) *Management Decision Making*, Pan Books, 1969.

(Contributor) Ralph M. Stogdill, editor, *The Process of Model-Building in the Behavioral Sciences*, Ohio State University Press, 1970; (contributor) *Modern Aspects of Management: Selected Readings*, Society of Manufacturing Engineers, 1970; (contributor) H. Aly and D. M. Albantino, editors, *Models in Financial Management*, Holden-Day, 1971; *Management for Action*, Reston Publishing, 1972; *How to Get Rich Slowly, But Almost Surely*, Reston Publishing, 1973. Contributor of articles to professional journals. Member of editorial board, *American Institute of Industrial Engineers Journal*, and *The Engineering Economist*.

* * *

MORRIS, Willie 1934-

PERSONAL: Born November 29, 1934, in Jackson, Miss.; son of Henry Rae (a bookkeeper) and Marian (Willie) Morris; married Celia Buchan, August 30, 1958; children: David Rae. *Education:* University of Texas, B.A., 1956; Oxford University, B.A., 1959, M.A., 1963. *Politics:* Independent. *Address:* Box 702, Bridgehampton, N.Y. 11937. *Agent:* Sterling Lord, 660 Madison Ave., New York, N.Y. 10019.

CAREER: Texas Observer, Austin, editor-in-chief, 1960-62; *Harper's*, New York, N.Y., editor, 1963-65, executive editor, 1966-67, editor-in-chief, 1967-71. *Member:* Phi Beta Kappa, Phi Eta Sigma, Sigma Delta Chi. *Awards, honors:* Rhodes scholarship, 1956; Houghton-Mifflin literary fellowship in nonfiction for work on memoirs.

WRITINGS: (Editor and author of foreword) *The South Today: 100 Years after Appomattox*, Harper, 1965; *North Toward Home* (memoirs), Houghton, 1967; *Yazoo* (nonfiction), Harper, 1971; *Good Old Boy* (juvenile), Harper, 1971; *The Last of the Southern Girls* (novel), Knopf, 1973. Contributor of stories and articles to *Nation, Harper's, New Yorker, Commentary, New Republic, Dissent, New York Times Magazine,* and *Texas Quarterly.*

BIOGRAPHICAL/CRITICAL SOURCES: Texas Observer, November 16, 1962; Willie Morris, *North Toward Home*, Houghton, 1967; *Newsweek*, March 15, 1971; *Christian Science Monitor*, March 25, 1971; *Antioch Review*, Spring, 1971; Larry L. King, *The Old Man and Lesser Mortals*, Viking, 1974.

* * *

MORRISSETTE, Bruce A(rcher) 1911-

PERSONAL: Born April 26, 1911, in Richmond, Va.; son

of James Archer (a designer) and Mary (Bell) Morrissette; married Dorothy Behrens, October 12, 1940; children: James. *Education:* University of Richmond, A.B., 1931; University of Clermont-Ferrand, Docteur d'Universite, 1933; Johns Hopkins University, Ph.D., 1938. *Home:* 5825 Dorchester, Chicago, Ill. 60637. *Office:* Department of Romance Languages, University of Chicago, 1050 East 59 St., Chicago, Ill. 60637.

CAREER: Johns Hopkins University, Baltimore, Md., instructor, 1934-38; Washington University, St. Louis, Mo., assistant professor, 1938-46, associate professor, 1946-56, professor of Romance languages, 1956-62; University of Chicago, Chicago, Ill., professor of French literature, 1962—, chairman of department of Romance languages and literature, 1973—, Sunny Distinguished Service Professor, 1974—. Visiting professor, University of Wisconsin, University of Illinois, and University of California at Los Angeles; Fulbright lecturer, University of Western Australia, 1969. *Member:* Modern Language Association of America (member of executive council, 1963-66), American Association of Teachers of French, Societe des Professeurs Francais en Amerique, Association Internationale d'Etudes Francais, Amis de Cerisy, Phi Beta Kappa. *Awards, honors:* Chevalier, Palmes Academique (France).

WRITINGS: L'Esthetique symboliste, Bussac, 1933; *The Life and Works of Mlle. Desjardins*, Washington University Press, 1947; *The Great Rimbaud Forgery*, Washington University Press, 1956; *Les Romans de Robbe-Grillet*, Editions de Minuit, 1963, revised editions, 1967, 1971; *Alain Robbe-Grillet*, Columbia University Press, 1965; *The Novels of Robbe-Grillet*, Cornell University Press, 1975. Contributor to *Evergreen, Critique, Symposium*, and other professional journals.

WORK IN PROGRESS: Preparing lecture series for universities in the U.S. and abroad.

SIDELIGHTS: Morrissette told *CA* that as a youth he was torn between literary and scientific interests. He chose literature because of a love for Baudelaire and Rimbaud. His scientific bent has been satisfied as a hobby, as he has published a dozen articles on electronics. Morrissette is currently interested in the relationship between film and literature. *Avocational interests:* Music and electronics.

* * *

MORS, Wallace P. 1911-

PERSONAL: Born August 25, 1911, in Chicago, Ill.; son of Albert J. (a secretary) and Christine (Webber) Mors; married Marjorie L. Becker, December 22, 1934. *Education:* University of Chicago, Ph.B., 1932, A.M., 1937, Ph.D., 1942; University of Illinois, C.P.A. *Religion:* Unitarian Universalist. *Home:* 22 Jefferson Rd., Wellesley, Mass. 02181. *Office:* Division of Finance, Babson College, Babson Park, Mass. 02157.

CAREER: Federal Reserve Bank of Chicago, Chicago, Ill., finance economist, 1946-48; Babson College, Babson Park, Mass., professor of finance and chairman of department, 1948-51; Western Reserve University (now Case Western Reserve University), Cleveland, Ohio, director of Bureau of Business Research, 1951-52; Babson College, professor of finance and chairman of department, 1952—, dean of faculty, 1960-62. Member of research staff, National Bureau of Economic Research, 1960-65. *Member:* American Economic Association, American Finance Association (vice-president, 1956), American Association of University Professors.

WRITINGS: Consumer Credit Theories, University of Chicago Press, 1944; *Consumer Credit Facts for You*, Western Reserve University Press, 1958; *Small Loan Laws in the United States*, Western Reserve University Press, 1961; *Consumer Credit Finance Changes: Rate Information and Quotation*, Columbia University Press, 1965. Contributor of articles to *Journal of Consumer Affairs, Insurance Law Journal, Journal of Business*, and other professional publications.†

* * *

MORSE, A. Reynolds, 1914-

PERSONAL: Born October 20, 1914, in Denver, Colo.; son of Bradish P. and Anna Reynolds (Garrey) Morse; married Eleanor Reese (secretary-treasurer IMS Co.) March 21, 1942; children: Brad G. *Education:* University of Colorado, B.A., 1938; Harvard University, M.B.A., 1939. *Politics:* Republican. *Religion:* Episcopalian. *Home:* 21709 Chagrin Blvd., Cleveland, Ohio 44122. *Office:* IMS Co., 24050 Commerce Park Rd., Cleveland, Ohio 44122.

CAREER: IMS Co., Cleveland, Ohio, president, 1949—. Art collector, owning world's largest single collection of Salvador Dali's works, and operator of Dali Museum (housed in wing of IMS building). Curator of Gearge Elbert Burr Collection, Denver Public Library. Member of economic development board, University of Colorado. *Member:* Phi Beta Kappa, Shaker Heights Country Club.

WRITINGS: The Works of M. P. Shiel, Fantasy Publishing, 1946; *Dali: A Study of His Life and Works*, New York Graphic Society, 1958; *Dali—1910-1965*, New York Graphic Society, 1965.

All privately printed by Reynolds Morse Foundation: *A New Introduction to Dali*, 1960; *Dali: A Collection and Panorama of His Art*, 1973, new edition, 1975; *Picasso and Dali: A Study in Their Similarities and Contrasts*, 1974; *Poetic Homage to Dali, Lorca, Ecuard, and James, Etc.*, 1974; *A Guide to Works by Salvador Dali in Public Museum Collections*, 1975. Contributor of article on Dali to *Art in America*. Also contributor of more than one hundred articles on plastics and plastics machinery to journals.

WORK IN PROGRESS: Continuing study of Dali.

* * *

MORSE, Grant W(esley) 1926-

PERSONAL: Born October 20, 1926, in Fredonia, N.Y.; son of Arthur Wesley and Anna (Mawhir) Morse; married Jocelyn Carlson (a registered nurse), December 29, 1956; children: Kendall Grant, Gail Evonne. *Education:* Ottawa University, Ottawa, Kan., B.A., 1951; Eastern Baptist Theological Seminary, B.D., 1954; State University of New York at Albany, M.S. in L.S., 1958. *Home:* 224 Gerland Rd., Rice Lake, Wis. 54868.

CAREER: Baptist clergyman, 1954-57; head librarian at Findlay College, Findlay, Ohio, 1958-60, and Ottawa University, Ottawa, Kan., 1960-61; Carthage College, Carthage, Ill., assistant librarian, 1961-62; Grove City College, Grove City, Pa., head librarian, 1962-64; Wagner College, Staten Island, N.Y., head librarian, 1964-66; University of Wisconsin Center, Barron County, Rice Lake, Wis., head librarian, 1966—. *Military service:* U.S. Army, Signal Corps, 1945-47; became sergeant. *Member:* American Association of University Professors, Association of University of Wisconsin Faculties.

WRITINGS: The Concise Guide to Library Research,

Washington Square, 1966, 2nd revised edition, Fleet Academic Editions, 1975. *Filing Rules: A Three-way Divided Catalog,* Linnet Books, 1971; *A Complete Guide to Organizing and Documenting Research Papers,* Fleet Academic Editions, 1974.

WORK IN PROGRESS: Testing library use.

AVOCATIONAL INTERESTS: Sports, Magic (amateur magician), wood-working, drawing cartoons, photography.

* * *

MORTON, Lena Beatrice 1901-

PERSONAL: Born June 15, 1901, in Flat Creek, Ky.; daughter of William (a grocer) and Susie (Stewart) Morton. *Education:* University of Cincinnati, A.B., 1922, A.M., 1925; Western Reserve University (now Case Western Reserve University), Ph.D., 1947; postdoctoral study at University of New Hampshire, 1955, University of London, 1956, and Harvard University, 1959. *Home:* 3256 Beresford Ave., Cincinnati, Ohio 45206.

CAREER: Public school teacher in Cincinnati, Ohio, 1922-48; University of Cincinnati, Cincinnati, Ohio, cooperating teacher, 1927-35, 1940-42; Langston University, Langston, Okla., professor of English, 1948-50; Lane College, Jackson, Tenn., professor of English and academic dean 1950-55; Southern University, Baton Rouge, La., professor of English, 1955-62; Texas College, Tyler, professor of English and head of Division of Humanities, 1962-72. Visiting professor, East Texas State University, Commerce, Tex., 1970-72. *Member:* Modern Language Association of America, International Platform Association, American Association of University Professors, Ohioana Library Association, Ohio Poetry Society, Conference of College Teachers of English of Texas, Texas Poetry Society, Delta Sigma Theta.

WRITINGS: Farewell to the Public Schools—I'm Glad We Met, Meador Publishing Co., 1952; *Man Under Stress,* Philosophical Library, 1960; *My First Sixty Years,* Philosophical Library, 1965; *The Development of Negro Poetry in America* (monograph), Revisionist Press, 1975; (editor) *Matthew Arnold's Multiple Editions* (monograph), Revisionist Press, 1975; *The Influence of the Sea on English Poetry from the Anglo-Saxon Period to the Victorian Period,* Revisionist Press, 1975. Contributor to *American Mercury* and other periodicals.

* * *

MOSHER, Ralph Lamont 1928-

PERSONAL: Born June 4, 1928, in Pittsburgh, Pa.; son of John Inglis (a professor) and Olivia Elizabeth (Lamont) Mosher; married Jessica Cumming, December 22, 1955; children: Robin Elizabeth, Pamela Jane, Jessica Suzanne. *Education:* Acadia University, B.A. (honors), 1949, M.A., 1951, B.Ed., 1955; Harvard University, Ed.D., 1964. *Home:* 58 Nonantum St., Newton, Mass. 02158. *Office:* Department of Education, Boston University, Boston, Mass.

CAREER: World University Service of Canada, Toronto, Ontario, national secretary, 1952-54; vice-principal and guidance director at high school in Berwick, Nova Scotia, 1955-56; Nova Scotia Teachers College (now Nova Scotia Agricultural College), Truro, instructor in educational psychology and guidance, 1956-59; Harvard University, Graduate School of Education, Cambridge, Mass., assistant director of secondary school apprentice teaching, 1962-64,

instructor, 1964, assistant professor, 1964-69, associate professor of education, 1969-72; Boston University, Boston, Mass., professor of education, 1972—. Consultant to schools and educational institutes.

WRITINGS: (Editor with R. F. Carle and C. Kehas) *Guidance—An Examination,* Harcourt, 1965; (with Thomas Allen and John Whiteley) *Dimensions of Effective Counseling,* C. E. Merrill, 1968; (contributor) John Whiteley, editor, *Research in Counseling: Evaluation and Refocus,* C. E. Merrill, 1968; (with N. A. Sprinthall) *Studies of Adolescents in the Secondary School,* Harvard Graduate School of Education, 1969; (contributor) John Herbert and David P. Ausubel, editors, *Psychology in Teacher Preparation,* Ontario Institute for Studies in Education, 1969.

(Contributor) Ronald T. Hyman, editor, *Contemporary Thought on Teaching,* Prentice-Hall, 1971; (contributor) Herman J. Peters, editor, *Guidance: An Introduction, Selected Readings,* C. E. Merrill, 1972; (contributor) D. Purpel and Belanger, editors, *Curriculum and the Cultural Revolution,* McCutchan, 1972; (with Purpel) *Supervision of Teaching: The Reluctant Profession,* Houghton, 1972; *Adolescents and Their Education,* McCutchan, 1975. Contributor of articles to *Journal of Teacher Education, Journal of Counseling Psychology, The American Psychologist,* and other professional publications. Member of editorial board, *Harvard Educational Review,* 1960-62, *The Counseling Psychologist,* 1967—.

WORK IN PROGRESS: Research in three areas—adolescent motivation for learning, cognitive flexibility as a variable in teacher effectiveness, and supervision in teaching.

* * *

MOSKIN, J(ohn) Robert 1923-

PERSONAL: Born May 9, 1923, in New York, N.Y.; son of Morris (a merchant) and Irma (Rosenfeld) Moskin; married Doris Bloch, October 7, 1948; children: Mark Douglas, David Scott, Nancy Irma. *Education:* Harvard University, B.S., 1944; Columbia University, M.A., 1947. *Address:* 140 Fox Meadow Rd., Scarsdale, N.Y. 10583; and 945 Fifth Ave., New York, N.Y. 10021. *Agent:* Phyllis Jackson, International Famous Agency, Inc., 1301 Avenue of the Americas, New York, N.Y. 10020.

CAREER: Reporter for *Boston Post,* Boston, Mass., 1941-42, *Newark News,* Newark, N.J., 1947-48; *New York Star,* New York, N.Y., assistant to general manager, 1948-49; *Westport Town Crier,* Westport, Conn., editor, 1949; *Look,* New York, N.Y., articles editor, 1950-53; *Woman's Home Companion,* New York, N.Y., managing editor, 1953-56; *Collier's,* New York, N.Y., senior editor, 1956; *Look,* senior editor, 1956-66, foreign editor, 1966-71; *Saturday Review,* New York, N.Y., editor-at-large, 1972—; freelance writer, 1972—. Member of Dana Reed Prize Committee, Harvard University, 1947—. Member of nominating committee, Scarsdale School Board, 1960-64, 1968; trustee of Scarsdale Adult School, 1965-68, chairman, 1969-70. Member, national board of directors, Sex Information and Education Council of the United States, 1972—; member of advisory committee, International Exchange of Scholars, 1974—. *Military service:* U.S. Army, 1943-46; served in western Pacific; became technical sergeant.

MEMBER: American Historical Association, National Press Club, Overseas Press Club, Authors Guild of the Authors League of America, Sigma Delta Chi, Scarsdale Town Club (governor, 1966-68), Signet Society (Harvard),

Harvard Club (New York), The Lotos Club. *Awards, honors:* Benjamin Franklin Gold Medal for public service, *Woman's Home Companion*, 1955; Page One Award of Newspaper Guild of New York, 1965, for magazine reporting in *Look*; Sidney Hillman Foundation Award, 1965; National Headliner Award, 1967; Overseas Press Club Award, 1969; Overseas Press Club Citation, 1971.

WRITINGS: (With William Attwood and George Leonard) *The Decline of the American Male*, Random House, 1958; *Morality in America*, Random House, 1966; *Turncoat*, Prentice-Hall, 1968; (with Teddy Kollek) *Jerusalem*, Grossman, 1974. Contributor to a number of national magazines. Member of editorial advisory board, *Present Tense*, 1973—.

WORK IN PROGRESS: A history of the U.S. Marine Corps, for American Heritage; research interests include American history and foreign policy, freedom of the press, medicine, problems of contemporary society, and biographies.

* * *

MOSS, C(laude) Scott 1924-

PERSONAL: Born May 17, 1924, in Newark, N.J.; son of Claude Scott (a newspaper columnist) and Leone (Dieter) Moss; married Bette L. Witty, September 23, 1956; children: Joel, Julie, Kevin. *Education:* University of Wisconsin, B.S., 1948; University of Illinois, M.S., 1951, Ph.D., 1953. *Religion:* Protestant. *Home:* 3180 Glengary Rd., Santa Ynez, Calif. 93460. *Office:* Federal Correctional Institution, Lompoc, Calif. 93436.

CAREER: Diplomate in clinical psychology, American Board of Examiners in Professional Psychology, and diplomate in psychological hypnosis, American Board of Examiners in Psychological Hypnosis. Jefferson Barracks Veterans Administration Hospital, clinical psychologist, and Washington University, St. Louis, Mo., instructor, 1953-56; State Hospital, Fulton, Mo., chief psychologist, and University of Missouri, Columbia, associate professor, 1956-60; National Institutes of Mental Health, San Francisco, Calif., consultant in mental health, 1961-67; University of Illinois, Urbana, professor of psychology, 1967-70; Federal Correctional Institutional, Lompoc, Calif., coordinator of mental health, 1970—. *Military service:* U.S. Army Air Forces, 1942-46. *Member:* American Psychological Association (fellow), Society for Clinical and Experimental Hypnosis (fellow), American Society of Clinical Hypnosis (fellow), Society for Psychophysiological Study of Sleep, International Council of Psychologists (fellow), American Academy of Psychotherapists, American Public Health Association (fellow).

WRITINGS: Hypnosis in Perspective, Macmillan, 1965; *Hypnotic Investigation of Dreams*, Wiley, 1967; *Dreams, Images and Fantasy: A Semantic Differential Casebook*, University of Illinois Press, 1970; *Black Rover, Come Over*, University of Illinois Press, 1970; *Recovery with Aphasia: The Aftermath of My Stroke*, University of Illinois Press, 1973; *The Crumbling Walls: Treatment and Counseling of Prisoners*, University of Illinois Press, 1974.

Contributor: J. Gordon, editor, *Handbook on Clinical and Experimental Hypnosis*, Macmillan, 1966; R. J. Braun, editor, *Clinical Psychology in Transition*, World, 1966; O. Buros, editor, *The Mental Measurements Yearbook* (reviews), Rutgers University Press, 1966; L. E. Abt and B. R. Reiff, editors, *Progress in Clinical Psychology*, Grune, 1969; J. G. Snider and C. E. Osgood, *Semantic Differential*

Technique, Aldine Press, 1969; A. Katzenstein, editor, *Psychologische Aspekte der Hypnose in der slinischen Draxis*, Veb Bustav Fisher Verlag (East Berlin), 1970; L. Diamant, editor, *Case Studies in Psychopathology*, C. E. Merrill, 1970. Contributor of about eighty-five articles to professional journals.

WORK IN PROGRESS: Violence and Criminality.

SIDELIGHTS: Moss has traveled extensively in Eastern Europe, and elsewhere abroad. He is currently working as a research consultant on many mental health problems. Moss is fluent in German.

* * *

MOSTELLER, (Charles) Frederick 1916-

PERSONAL: Surname is pronounced *Moss*-teller; born December 24, 1916, in Clarksburg, W.Va.; son of William Roy (a road builder) and Helen (Kelley) Mosteller; married Virginia Gilroy, May 17, 1941; children: William Samuel, Gale Robin. *Education:* Carnegie Institute of Technology (now Carnegie-Mellon University), B.S., 1938, M.S., 1939; Princeton University, A.M., 1941, Ph.D., 1946. *Home:* 28 Pierce Rd., Belmont, Mass. 02178. *Office:* Harvard University, 1 Oxford St., Cambridge, Mass. 02138.

CAREER: Office of Public Opinion Research, Princeton, N.J., research associate, 1942-44; Princeton University, Princeton, N.J., instructor in department of mathematics, 1942-44, research mathematician with Statistical Research Group, 1944-45; Harvard University, Cambridge, Mass., lecturer in department of social relations, 1946-48, associate professor, 1948-51, professor of mathematical statistics, 1951—, chairman of department of statistics, 1957-71. Miller Research Professor, University of California, Berkeley, 1974-75. U.S. War Department, special consultant, Research Branch, 1942-43. Teacher of National Broadcasting Company's television course in probability and statistics, 1960-61.

MEMBER: American Academy of Arts and Sciences, American Philosophical Society, Institute of Mathematical Statistics (fellow; president, 1974-75), American Statistical Association (fellow; vice-president, 1963-65; president, 1967), American Association for the Advancement of Science (fellow), American Society for Quality Control (fellow), International Statistical Institute, American Mathematical Society, Mathematical Association of America, Psychometric Society (president, 1957-58), Biometric Society, Royal Statistical Society (research section), American Anthropological Association, American Sociological Association, Sociological Research Association, National Academy of Sciences, Institute of Medicine. *Awards, honors:* Fund for Advancement of Education fellow at University of Chicago, 1954-55; fellow, Center for Advanced Study in the Behavioral Sciences, Stanford, Calif., 1962-63; D.Sc. from University of Chicago, 1973, and Carnegie-Mellon University, 1974.

WRITINGS: (Co-author) *Gauging Public Opinion*, edited by Hadley Cantril, Princeton University Press, 1944; *Sampling Inspection*, McGraw, 1948; (with others) *The Pre-election Polls of 1948*, Social Science Research Council Bulletins, 1949; (with R. R. Bush) *Stochastic Models for Learning*, Wiley, 1955; (with R. E. K. Rourke and G. B. Thomas, Jr.) *Probability with Statistical Applications*, Addison-Wesley, 1961, revised edition, 1970; (with R. E. K. Rourke and G. B. Thomas) *Probability: A First Cause*, Addison-Wesley, 1962, revised edition, 1970; (with D. L. Wallace) *Inference and Disputed Authorship: The Federal-*

ist, Addison-Wesley, 1964; *Fifty Challenging Problems in Probability*, Addison-Wesley, 1965; (co-author) *The National Halothene Study*, National Academy of Sciences, 1969; (co-editor) *Statistics: A Guide to the Unknown*, Holden-Day, 1972; (co-author) *Statistics by Example*, Addison-Wesley, 1973; (with R. E. K. Rourke) *Sturdy Statistics*, Addison-Wesley, 1973. Contributor to journals, mainly articles on mathematical statistics and their application to industrial, social science, and medical problems.

* * *

MOSTOFSKY, David I(saac) 1931-

PERSONAL: Born September 19, 1931, in Boston, Mass.; son of Benjamin and Leah (Caplan) Mostofsky. *Education:* Yeshiva University, B.A., 1953; Boston University, M.A., 1957, Ph.D., 1960. *Home:* 48 Marshal St., Brookline, Mass. 02146. *Office:* Boston University, 64 Cummington St., Boston, Mass. 02215.

CAREER: Boston University, Boston, Mass., instructor, 1959-61, assistant professor, 1961-65, associate professor, 1965-70, professor of psychology, 1970—, associate chairman of department of psychology, 1971—. Research assistant in clinical neurophysology, Harvard Medical Center, 1970—. *Member:* International Society of Neuropsychology, American Psychological Association, American Association for Behavior Therapy, American Epilepsy Society, American Association for the Advancement of Science, Massachusetts Psychological Association, Sigma Xi.

WRITINGS: (Editor) *Stimulus Generalization*, Stanford University Press, 1965; *Contemporary Theory and Analysis*, Appleton, 1970; *Behavior Control and Modification of Physiological Activity*, Prentice-Hall, 1975.

WORK IN PROGRESS: *The Behavior of Fish and Other Aquatic Animals*; *Learning: The Study of Adaptive Change*; *Psychology: The Art and Science of Studying Behavior Rehabilitation and the Developmental Disabilities*.

* * *

MOUNTFORT, Guy 1905-

PERSONAL: Born December 4, 1905, in London, England; son of Arnold George (an artist) and Alice (Hughes) Mountfort; married Joan Hartley Pink, January 28, 1931; children: Penelope (Mrs. Andrew Gillespie), Carol (Mrs. Niels Jensen). *Education:* Attended schools in England and Sorbonne, University of Paris. *Politics:* Conservative. *Religion:* Church of England. *Home:* Plovers Meadow, Possingworth Park, Blackboys, Sussex, England.

CAREER: General Motors (Frigidaire), Paris, France, advertising manager, 1928-38; Proctor & Gamble, United Kingdom, advertising manager, 1946-47; Mather & Crowther Ltd., London, England, director, 1947-64, managing director, 1964-66. Ogilvy & Mather International, Inc., New York, N.Y., former director. International trustee, World Wildlife Fund; leader of seven scientific expeditions to Coto Donana, Bulgaria, Hungary, Jordan, and other countries. *Military service:* British Army, 1939-46; became lieutenant colonel. *Member:* British Ornithologists' Union (president, 1971-75), American Ornithologists' Union (associate), Zoological Society of London (scientific fellow). *Awards, honors:* Medal of Societe d'Acclimatation (France) for ornithological work; Zoological Society of London, Stamford Raffles Prize for contributions to natural history; member, Order of the British Empire, for services to ornithology.

WRITINGS: With Roger Iory Peterson and P.A.D. Hollom) *A Field Guide to the Birds of Europe*, Collins, 1954; *The Hawfinch*, Collins, 1957; *Wild Paradise*, Houghton, 1958 (published in England as *Portrait of a Wilderness*, Hutchinson, 1958); *Wild Danube*, Houghton, 1962 (published in England as *Portrait of a River*, Hutchinson, 1962); *Portrait of a Desert*, Houghton, 1965; *The Vanishing Jungle*, Collins, 1969; *The Tiger*, David & Charles, 1973; *So Small a World*, Hutchinson, 1974, Scribner, 1975. Contributor of articles to magazines and newspapers, mostly on wildlife subjects.

SIDELIGHTS: *A Field Guide to the Birds of Europe* has been published in thirteen languages.

* * *

MOYES, Patricia 1923-

PERSONAL: Born January 19, 1923, in Bray, Ireland; daughter of Ernst (a judge in Indian Civil Service) and Marion (Boyd) Pakenham-Walsh; married John Moyes (a photographer), 1951 (divorced, 1959); married John S. Haszard (an official of International Monetary Fund), October 13, 1962. *Education:* Attended Overstone School, Northamptonshire, England, 1934-39. *Politics:* Liberal (non-party). *Religion:* Church of England. *Home:* 1219 34th Street N.W., Washington, D.C. *Agent:* Curtis Brown Ltd., 1 Craven Hill, London W2, England; John Cushman Associates, 25 West 43rd St., New York, N.Y.

CAREER: Peter Ustinov Productions Ltd., London, England, secretary, 1947-53; *Vogue*, London, assistant editor, 1954-58. Author of mystery novels. *Military service:* British Women's Auxiliary Air Force, Radar Section, 1940-45; became flight officer. *Awards, honors:* Edgar Allan Poe Special Award from Mystery Writers of America, 1970, for *Many Deadly Returns*.

*WRITINGS—*All published by Holt, except as indicated: *Dead Men Don't Ski*, Rinehart, 1959; *Down Among the Dead Men*, 1961 (published in England as *The Sunken Sailor*, Collins, 1961); *Death on the Agenda*, 1962; *Murder a la Mode*, 1963; *Falling Star*, 1964; *Johnny Underground*, 1965; *Murder by 3's* (omnibus volume), 1965; *Murder Fantastical*, 1967; *Helter-Skelter* (juvenile), 1968; *Death and the Dutch Uncle*, 1968; *Many Deadly Returns*, 1970; *Seasons of Snows and Sins*, 1971; *The Curious Affair of the Third Dog*, 1973; *Black Widower*, 1975. Translator of play by Jean Anouilh. "Time Remembered," produced at Morosco Theatre, 1957; writer of film script, "School for Scoundrels." Also writer of short stories.

WORK IN PROGRESS: A new detective book.

SIDELIGHTS: Patricia Moyes is fluent in French, knows enough Dutch to get by in the shops, and has a smattering of Italian. Her books have been published in German, Swedish, Norwegian, Polish, Danish, Finnish, Dutch, Portuguese, Spanish, and Japanese translations, and in paperback reprints in both United States and England. *Avocational interests:* Skiing, sailing, good food and wine, travel.

* * *

MUELLER, Gustav Emil 1898-

PERSONAL: Born May 12, 1898, in Bern, Switzerland; son of Adolf Arthur and Therese (Schwarzenbach) Mueller; married Renee, July 16, 1925; children: Brigit Barth, Mereth Meade, Gustav Thomas. *Education:* University of Bern, B.A., 1917, M.A., 1921, Ph.D., 1924; University of Heidelberg, graduate study, 1923-24; additional study in London. *Home:* Dufourstrasse 15, Bern 3005, Switzerland.

CAREER: University of Oregon, Eugene, instructor, 1925-26, assistant professor of philosophy, 1926-31; University of Oklahoma, Norman, associate professor, 1931-36, professor of philosophy, 1936-55, research professor of philosophy, 1955-68, emeritus research professor, 1968—. Visiting professor, University of Bern, 1937-38. Public lecturer, and lecturer for learned societies. *Member:* American Philosophical Society, Society for Aesthetics, American Association of University Professors, Southwestern Philosophical Society (president). *Awards, honors:* Lucerne Prize (Switzerland), 1937; honorary professor, University of Buenos Aires.

WRITINGS—Philosophy in English: *Philosophy of Our Uncertainties*, University of Oklahoma Press, 1936; *What Plato Thinks*, Open Court, 1937; *Philosophy and the War*, Harlow, 1943; *The World as Spectacle*, Philosophical Library, 1944; *Philosophy of Literature*, Philosophical Library, 1948; *Education Limited*, University of Oklahoma Press, 1949; *Discourses on Religion*, Bookman Associates, 1951, 2nd edition, 1965; *Dialectic: A Way Into and Within Philosophy*, Bookman Associates, 1956; *The Interplay of Opposites: A Dialectical Ontology*, Bookman Associates, 1956; (translator and annotater) Hegel, *Encyclopedia of Philosophy*, Philosophical Library, 1959; *Plato: The Founder of Philosophy as Dialectic*, Philosophical Library, 1965; *Origins and Dimensions of Philosophy: Some Correlations*, Pageant, 1965; *Hegel: The Man, His Vision and His Work*, new version of the 1959 book published in German (see below), Pageant, 1975; *Hegel and the Crisis of Christianity*, University of Oklahoma Press, in press.

Philosophy in German: *Geschichtsphilosophische Grundbegriffe bei Marx*, Paul Haupt (Bern), 1924; *Amerikanische Philosophie*, Frommann (Stuttgart), 1936, 2nd enlarged edition, 1950; *Der Mensch im Sein*, Frommann, 1938; *Hegel uber Offenbarung, Kirche und Philosophie*, Reinhart (Munich), 1938; *Hegel uber Sittlichkeit und Geschichte*, Reinhart, 1939; *Hegel: Denkgeschichte eines Lebendigen*, Francke (Bern), 1959; *Dialektische Philosophie*, Francke, 1974.

Poetry in German: *Indien: Ein Zyklus in Arabesken*, Francke, 1925; *Sonette um Odysseus*, Francke, 1931; *Sinnbilder*, Francke, 1936; *Abseits*, Francke, 1946; *Indien, Drei Kreise*, Francke, 1948; *Querschnitt*, Universitaetsverlag Wagner (Innsbruck), 1964; *Nachlese*, Paul Schaffer (Bern), 1975.

Plays in German: *Parazelsus*, Francke, 1924; *Der Ruf in die Wuste*, Francke, 1931. Author of two trilogies of one-act plays in English, "Spirit and Flesh," performed, 1954, and "Appearance and Reality," performed, 1955.

About 150 articles have been published in *Ethics, Books Abroad, Monist, Journal of the History of Ideas, Scientific Monthly, Saturday Review,* and a number of other American, German, Swiss, and Indian journals.

SIDELIGHTS: Mueller is competent in French, Italian, Spanish, classical Greek, and Latin. *Avocational interests:* Classical guitar, chess.

* * *

MUELLER, M(ax) G(erhard) 1925-

PERSONAL: Born May 20, 1925, in Hamburg, Germany; son of Leopold (a businessman) and Marianne (Polack) Mueller. *Education:* University of London, B.Sc., 1949;

University of Illinois, M.A., 1951, Ph.D., 1960. *Office:* Department of Political Economy, University of Glasgow, Glasgow G12 8QQ, Scotland.

CAREER: Economist on Economic Advisory Staff to the Government of Israel, Jerusalem, 1954-55; Michigan State University, East Lansing, instructor, 1956-60, assistant professor of economics, 1960-62; University of California, Los Angeles, assistant professor of economics, 1962-66; University of Maryland, College Park, visiting lecturer, 1967-68; University of Glasgow, Glasgow, Scotland, lecturer, 1968-72, senior lecturer in political economy, 1972—. *Member:* American Economic Association, Royal Economic Society (England), Indian Economic Association.

WRITINGS: (Editor) *Readings in Macroeconomics,* Holt, 1966, 2nd edition, 1971.

WORK IN PROGRESS: Research on problems of economic development in underdeveloped countries.

* * *

MUELLER, Willard Fritz 1925-

PERSONAL: Born January 23, 1925, in Ortonville, Minn.; son of Fritz (a farmer) and Adele Mueller; married Shirley I. Liesch, June 26, 1948; children: Keith, Scott, Kay Marie. *Education:* University of Wisconsin, B.S., 1950, M.S., 1952; Vanderbilt University, Ph.D., 1955. *Religion:* Unitarian Universalist. *Home:* 2135 Chamberlain Ave., Madison, Wis. 53705. *Office:* Department of Economics, University of Wisconsin, Madison, Wis. 53706.

CAREER: University of California, Davis, assistant professor of economics, 1954-57; University of Wisconsin, Madison, 1957-61, professor of economics (on leave), 1961-64; U.S. House of Representatives, Washington, D.C., chief economist, Select Committee for Small Business, 1961; Federal Trade Commission, Bureau of Economics, Washington, D.C., chief economist and director, 1961-68; President's Cabinet Committee on Price Stability, executive director, 1968-69; University of Wisconsin, Madison, Vilas Research Professor of Agricultural Economics, 1969—, professor of law, 1969—. *Military service:* U.S. Navy, 1943-46. *Member:* American Economic Association, American Farm Economic Association, Association of Evolutionary Economics (president, 1974).

WRITINGS: (Co-author) *Changing Market Structure of Food Retailing,* University of Wisconsin Press, 1961; *Monopoly and Competition,* Random House, 1970. Writer of articles on industrial organization and anti-trust policy. Associate editor, *Journal of Farm Economics,* 1958-60.

* * *

MUKERJI, Kshitimohon 1920-

PERSONAL: Born June 15, 1920, in Calcutta, Bengal, India; son of Kamalkumar (a railway employee) and Amiya (Sircar) Mukerji; married Vatsala Patil (a professor of econometrics and statistics). *Education:* Attended Hare School and Presidency College, both Calcutta, India; Calcutta University, B.Com., 1941, M.A. Com., 1943, D.Phil., 1958. *Politics:* Socialism. *Religion:* Agnostic. *Home:* Professors Quarters, The Campus (Vidyanagar), Shivaji University, Kolhapur 3, India.

CAREER: Reserve Bank of India, staff officer in Bombay, India, and Delhi, India, 1949-54; Gokhale Institute of Politics and Economics, Poona, India, reader in national income and developmental planning, 1958-66; Shivaji University, Kolhapur, India, professor of economics and department head, 1967—. Organizer and research director for Samaj Prabodhan Sanstha (an independent institution, in Poona, dedicated to social and cultural renaissance). *Member:* Indian Society of Research in Income and Wealth, Indian Economic Association, Indian Society of Labour Economics (member of executive committee).

WRITINGS: (Co-author) *Agro Economic Balance: An Expository Survey of the Sirur Taluka*, Popular Prakashan, 1963; *Levels of Economic Activity and Public Expenditure in India: A Historical and Quantitative Study*, Asia Publishing House, 1965. Contributor of about thirty articles to journals.

WORK IN PROGRESS: Research on long period movements in real wages, and on regional variations in real wages.

SIDELIGHTS: Mukerji knows English and "a little German."†

* * *

MULLINS, Edward S(wift) 1922-

PERSONAL: Born February 25, 1922, in Sanford, Me.; son of Ernest Allen (a businessman) and Josephine (Swift) Mullins; married Mary Kilkenny (an artist), May 26, 1944; children: Sheila (Mrs. Arnold Farese), David, Paul, Nicholas. *Education:* New England School of Art, diploma, 1942; University of London, special courses in fine arts, 1951; Boston University, B.S., 1953. *Religion:* Roman Catholic. *Home:* 31 Green St., Milford, Conn. *Office:* 54 Broad St., Milford, Conn.

CAREER: Instructor in art at New England School of Art, Boston, Mass., 1947-54, and Milford (Conn.) High School, 1954-56; artist and planning director, Norcross Greeting Card Co., New York, N.Y., 1956-61; free-lance artist and writer, Milford, Conn., 1961-64; Norcross Greeting Card Co., artist, 1964-66; director of Milford School of Art and Gallery on the Green, both Milford, Conn., 1966—. *Military service:* U.S. Army, Signal Corps, 1942-45. *Member:* Milford Art League (past president). *Awards, honors:* Various prizes for oil paintings and water colors.

WRITINGS: Animal Limericks (juvenile; self-illustrated), Follett, 1966; *The Big Book of Limericks* (juvenile; self-illustrated), Platt & Munk, 1969. Poems have been included in *Poets of America*, Avon, 1940. Columnist, "Thinking Out Loud," in *Milford Citizen*, 1956-58.

WORK IN PROGRESS: A novel; a children's book.

AVOCATIONAL INTERESTS: Philosophy, world affairs, politics, theater, extrasensory perception (in all its forms), and gardening.

* * *

MUNK, Erika 1939-

PERSONAL: Born February 4, 1939, in New York, N.Y.; daughter of Edward T. (a copy editor) and Erika (Boenisch) Zusi; divorced. *Education:* Reed College, B.A., 1959. *Politics:* "Democratic socialist sometimes, otherwise mainly anti-political." *Religion:* None. *Home:* 2027 Royal St., New Orleans, La. 70116.

CAREER: New America, New York, N.Y., editorial assistant, 1961; editorial assistant, *Realist,* intermittantly, 1961-62; *Partisan Review*, New York, N.Y., assistant to editor, 1962-63; Tulane University of Louisiana, New Orleans, managing editor, *Tulane Drama Review*, beginning 1963. *Member:* Louisiana Civil Liberties Union (member of

board, 1965—), New Orleans Intermedia Seminar and Performing Group.

WRITINGS: (Editor) *Stanislavski and America: An Anthology from the Tulane Drama Review*, Hill & Wang, 1966, 1966, Fawcett, 1967; (editor) *Brecht*, Bantam, 1972. Contributor, sometimes under pseudonyms, to *New America, Tulane Drama Review, Fact*, and *New Orleans.*†

* * *

MUNROE, Elizabeth L(ee) 1900-
(Lisa Grenelle)

PERSONAL: Born January 22, 1900; daughter of William Morton and Elizabeth (Ernst) Grinnell; married Henry Livermore Abbott, April 25, 1920 (divorced July, 1931); married David Headley Munroe, June 31, 1933 (divorced); children: (first marriage) Mary Lee, William Henry Grafeton; (second marriage) Peter Lee. *Education:* Attended Columbia University, 1946. *Politics:* Liberal Republican. *Religion:* Unity. *Home and office:* 140 East 92nd St., New York, N.Y. 10028.

CAREER: Poet; writer of daily column syndicated by King Features, 1933-39; instructor in adult education programs in New York and New Jersey, beginning 1953; instructor in creative writing in Cooper Union, New York, N.Y., Chatham, N.J., and several other New Jersey towns, 1966—. Lecturer, Rochester Poetry Society, 1970; conductor of workshops in poetry and juvenile writing at Oglethorpe College, 1971. Air warden during World War II. *Member:* Poetry Society of America (member of executive board). *Awards, honors:* Gustav Davidson Memorial award of Poetry Society of America, 1972.

WRITINGS—Poetry; under pseudonym Lisa Grenelle: *This Day Is Ours*, Dierkes Press, 1946; *No Light Evaded*, Golden Quill, 1957; *Self Is the Stranger*, Golden Quill, 1963; *No Scheduled Flight*, Golden Quill, 1973. Work represented in anthologies, including *The Golden Year: The Poetry Society of America Anthology (1910-1960)*, edited by Melville Cane, John Farrar, and Louise Townsend Nicholl, Fine Editions Press, 1960, *Fire and Sleet and Candlelight*, edited by August William Derleth, Arkham House, 1961, and several others. Contributor to newspapers and periodicals, including *Prairie Schooner, Voices, Lyric, Saturday Evening Post, New York Herald Tribune*, and *New York Times*.

SIDELIGHTS: Elizabeth Munroe explains why she writes: "Like Rodin, when asked why he continued to sculpt . . . he said, 'Nothing else makes any sense,' I am dedicated to creating. Only through writing or lecturing do I have any sense of fulfillment. Without these efforts I become deeply depressed." *Avocational interests:* Traveling.

* * *

MURPHY, Paul L(loyd) 1923-

PERSONAL: Born September 5, 1923, in Caldwell, Idaho; son of Paul (a professor of classics) and Ruth (Weltner) Murphy; married Helen W. Chase, September 8, 1946; children: Patricia Anne, Karen Diane. *Education:* College of Idaho, B.A., 1947; University of California, Berkeley, M.A., 1948, Ph.D., 1953. *Politics:* Liberal. *Religion:* Protestant. *Home:* 2159 Folwell St., Falcon Heights, Minn. 55108. *Office:* 827 Social Science Tower, University of Minnesota, Minneapolis, Minn. 55455.

CAREER: Jazz pianist and flutist before settling on academic career; Colorado State University, Fort Collins, assistant professor of history, 1953; Ohio State University, Columbus, instructor in history, 1953-57; University of Minnesota, Minneapolis, associate professor, 1957-69, professor of American history and American Studies, 1970—. Visiting assistant professor, Northwestern University, 1958-59; research fellow, Harvard University, Center for the Study of History and Liberty in America, 1961-62; visiting summer professor at University of Colorado, 1961, and Stanford University, 1966; Fulbright lecturer, University of Lagos (Nigeria), 1971-72. Director of Minnesota Civil Liberties Union, 1966-69; member of state central committee, Minnesota Democratic-Farmer Labor Party, 1966-68. *Military service:* U.S. Army, 1943-46.

MEMBER: American Historical Association, American Association of University Professors (president of Twin Cities chapter, 1972-73), Authors Guild, American Society of Legal History, Organization of American Historians, American Studies Association (secretary, Minnesota-Dakotas affiliate, 1964-66), American Federation of Musicians, Phi Beta Kappa, Phi Alpha Theta. *Awards, honors:* Guggenheim fellowship, 1965-66; American Bar Association Gavel Award, 1973, for *The Meaning of Freedom of Speech.*

WRITINGS: (Co-author) *Liberty and Justice: A Historical Record of American Constitutional Development*, Knopf, 1958, 2nd edition, 1968; *The Constitution in Crisis Times, 1918-1969*, Harper, 1972; *The Meaning of Freedom of Speech*, Greenwood, 1972; *Political Parties in American History*, Putnam, 1974; *The Passaic Textile Strike*, Wadsworth, 1974.

Contributor: *America's Ten Greatest Presidents*, Rand McNally, 1961; *A Global History of Man*, Allyn & Bacon, 1962; *Readings in World History*, Allyn & Bacon, 1962; *Main Problems in American History*, Dorsey, 1964. Contributor to *Encyclopaedia Britannica, Encyclopedia Americana, Dictionary of American Biography, Dictionary of American History*, and to *Virginia Quarterly Review* and history journals. Member of board of editors, Wisconsin Historical Society Press, 1963-66.

WORK IN PROGRESS: Civil Liberties in World War I, for Norton; *United States Constitutional History*, for Knopf.

SIDELIGHTS: Murphy told *CA*, "As a hard core civil libertarian . . . [I] find chronic and ongoing need for a more sophisticated knowledge of constitutional rights, and while my students at times complain that my courses deal too largely with civil wrongs, I feel I am serving a type of educational need all too often not fully met." Murphy still plays jazz piano and the flute on occasion, especially in faculty musicals.

*   *   *

MURPHY, William Francis 1906-

PERSONAL: Born November 20, 1906, in Malden, Mass.; son of Thomas Francis (an electrical engineer) and Edith Louise (White) Murphy; married Ruth Hannah Markman (an M.D. and psychiatrist), December 23, 1950; children: Jean Louise, Stephen Dennis. *Education:* Brown University, A.B., 1931; Tufts University School of Medicine, M.D., 1935. *Politics:* Independent. *Religion:* Liberal Unitarian. *Home:* 1 Concord Rd., Lincoln, Mass. *Office:* 82 Marlborough St., Boston, Mass. 02116.

CAREER: St. Elizabeth's Hospital, Washington, D.C.,

junior medical officer, 1935-37; St. Vincent's Hospital, Jacksonville, Fla., resident, 1937-38; visiting physician to medical institutions in Boston, Mass., and instructor in neuropsychiatry at Tufts University School of Medicine, Boston, 1938-41; diplomate, American Board of Psychiatry, 1941; private practice of psychoanalysis in Boston, Mass., 1946—. Cushing Veterans Administration Hospital, chief of open ward section, 1946-52; Boston Veterans Administration Hospital, chief of open ward section, 1952-58, consultant, 1958—; McLean Hospital, attending psychiatrist, 1956-74, senior consultant, 1974—. Harvard University, instructor in psychiatry, 1946-55, clinical associate, 1955—; assistant professor of psychiatry, 1956—. Boston Psychoanalytic Institute, instructor in psychosomatic medicine, 1951-56, member of teaching faculty, 1956—; Boston University School of Medicine, assistant professor of psychiatry, 1953-55. U.S. Naval Hospital, Chelsea, consultant, 1946—. *Military service:* U.S. Navy, psychiatrist, 1941-46. U.S. Naval Reserve, 1946-54; became commander.

MEMBER: American Psychiatric Association, American Psychoanalytic Association, International Psychoanalytic Association, Society for Research in Psychiatry and Neurology, New England Psychiatric Association, Massachusetts Psychiatric Association, Boston Society of Neurology and Psychiatry, Boston Psychoanalytic Society and Institute.

WRITINGS: The Psychosomatic Concept in Psychoanalysis, edited by Felix Deutsch, International Universities, 1953; (with F. Deutsch) *The Clinical Interview*, two volumes, International Universities, 1955; *On the Mysterious Leap from the Mind to the Body*, International Universities, 1959; *The Tactics of Psychotherapy*, International Universities, 1965; *Psychotherapy of Pathological Narcisism*, International Universities, 1975. Contributor of articles to medical journals, and about thirty reviews to *Psychoanalytic Quarterly.*

AVOCATIONAL INTERESTS: Skiing, tennis, badminton, bicycle riding, amateur astronomy, radio, music (plays classical guitar).

*   *   *

MURRAY, (Jesse) George 1909-

PERSONAL: Born December 28, 1909, in St. Louis, Mo.; son of Peter George (a dairyman) and Emma M. (Marshall) Murray; married Virginia M. Suechting (a foreign aid economist), October 16, 1948; children: George Read, Peter George. *Education:* Chaminade College, (now of Honolulu), student, 1919-23. *Religion:* Roman Catholic. *Residence:* Eureka Springs, Ark. 72632. *Agent:* Max Siegel, 154 East Erie St., Chicago, Ill. 60611.

CAREER: Newspaperman with *Chicago Herald and Examiner,* 1933-37; also worked on *Toronto Star* and other newspapers; U.S. Embassy, Vienna, Austria, press attache, 1948-53; *Chicago American,* Chicago, Ill., newspaperman, 1954-72.

WRITINGS: (Editor) *New Horizons* (autobiography of Francis E. Townsend), Stewart, 1954; *The Madhouse on Madison Street,* Follett, 1965; *Honest Al Capone (and His Heirs),* Putnam, 1975. Author with David Peltz of "Off the Record," comedy produced on Broadway, 1941. Wrote five-volume "History of the Rehabilitation of Austria" while press attache in Vienna, published by U.S. Army.

MURRAY, Hallard T(homas), Jr. 1937-

PERSONAL: Born May 11, 1937, in Coco Solo, Canal Zone, Panama; son of Hallard Thomas and Marion (Bryce) Murray; married Jacquelyn Ann Smith (a teacher), August 26, 1962. Education: University of Arizona, B.A., 1959, M.S., 1962; graduate study at Purdue University. Politics: Democrat.

CAREER: Purdue University, Lafayette, Ind., instructor in biology, beginning 1962. Military service: U.S. Army Reserve, Chemical Corps, beginning 1960. Member: Phi Beta Kappa, Sigma Xi, Phi Kappa Phi.

WRITINGS: (With S. N. Postlethwait and J. Novak) An Integrated Experience Approach to Learning, Burgess, 1964; Study Problems in Plant Science, Burgess, 1965.

WORK IN PROGRESS: Research on morphogenesis in corn.†

* * *

MURRAY, Sister Mary Verona 1909-

PERSONAL: Born September 7, 1909, in Cuyahoga Falls, Ohio; daughter of William (a real estate broker) and Beulah (Marria) Murray. Education: Sisters College of Cleveland, B.S.E., 1945; St. John College, Cleveland, Ohio, M.A., 1951. Home: 110-130 221st Street, Queens, N.Y. 11429.

CAREER: Roman Catholic nun of the Sisters of the Holy Humility of Mary, entering the order, 1928; teacher at parochial grade schools and other Catholic institutions in Ohio, 1931-66, with exception of two-year period at Sioux Indian reservation, Porcupine, S.D.; remedial reading consultant at parochial schools of Canton, Ohio, under federal aid to education program, 1966-73. Currently working on a religious life movement in New York, N.Y. Lecturer and demonstrator at workshops on phonics reading linguistics, in a number of states. Participant, Georgetown University creative writing conferences, 1967—. Member: National Catholic Educational Association, Ohio Educational Association.

WRITINGS: Author or co-author of nine books in "Christian Child Reading Series," Reardon, Baer, 1958; (co-author) "First Fun in Phonics Series," five books and teachers' manuals, 1965; Saint of the Week, Bruce, 1966; (co-author) "Phonics—Linguistic Series" (public school edition), Modern Curriculum Press, 1970. Contributor of stories to Highlights for Children (magazine). Contributor of articles to Ohio Reading Teacher and American Education.

WORK IN PROGRESS: Revising "Christian Child Reading Series."

* * *

MURTAGH, John M(artin) 1911-

PERSONAL: Born February 26, 1911, in New York, N.Y.; son of Thomas P. (a fireman) and Mary K. (Mee) Murtagh; married Mary B. Maguire, October 26, 1947; children: Joan Marie Frankel, Thomas Peter, Maeve, John M., Jr. Education: City College (now City College of the City University of New York), A.B. (cum laude), 1931; Harvard University, LL.B., 1934. Religion: Roman Catholic. Home: 529 West 217th St., New York, N.Y. 10034. Agent: McIntosh, McKee & Dodds, Inc., 30 East 60th St., New York, N.Y. 10022.

CAREER: Admitted to New York bar, 1935; began practice as attorney with Evarts, Choate, Curtin & Leon, New York, N.Y., 1935-38; assistant Attorney General, state of

New York, 1938-41; special assistant to U.S. Attorney General, 1942; City of New York, commissioner of investigation, 1945-50, chief magistrate of magistrates' courts, 1950-60, chief justice of Court of Special Sessions, 1960-62, administrative judge of Criminal Court, 1962-66; State of New York, justice of Supreme Court, 1967—. Member of National Council on Alcoholism (chairman, 1967-69). Military service: U.S. Army Air Forces, 1942-46; became lieutenant colonel; now colonel (retired), U.S. Air Force Reserve. Member: American Bar Association, American Judicature Society, Guild of Catholic Lawyers, New York State Bar Association, New York County Lawyers Association, Association of the Bar of City of New York, Alumni Association of the City College of the City University of New York (president, 1967-69). Phi Beta Kappa. Awards, honors: LL.D., LeMoyne College, 1956.

WRITINGS: (With Sara Harris) Cast the First Stone, McGraw, 1957; (with Harris) Who Live in Shadow, McGraw, 1959. Contributor to Catholic Encyclopedia, Saturday Evening Post, Atlantic Monthly, and other magazines.

* * *

MUSCAT, Robert J. 1931-

PERSONAL: Born March 6, 1931, in New York, N.Y.; son of Lewis (a businessman) and Bess (a musician; maiden name, Ginsberg) Muscat; married Juliette Comparte, July 28, 1957; children: David Lewis, Joshua Ethan, Elysabeth Nicole. Education: Columbia University, B.A., 1952, M.S., 1953, M.A., 1956, Ph.D., 1964. Office: U.S. Agency for International Development, c/o American Embassy, Rio de Janeiro, Brazil.

CAREER: U.S. Agency for International Development, economist in Bangkok, Thailand, 1957-62; International Bank for Reconstruction and Development, Washington, D.C., seconded to government of Malaya to be undersecretary of the Treasury, 1963-65; U.S. Agency for International Development, economist in Rio de Janeiro, Brazil, 1965—. Military service: U.S. Army, Medical Corps, 1953-55. Member: American Economic Association, Society for International Development. Awards, honors: Kshatriya Mangku Negara, King's Birthday Honours List, Malaya, 1965.

WRITINGS: Development Strategy in Thailand: A Study of Economic Growth, Praeger, 1966; (with Alan D. Berg) The Nutrition Factor: Its Role in National Development, Brookings Institution, 1973.

SIDELIGHTS: Muscat speaks French and Portuguese. Avocational interests: Playing the piano.†

* * *

MUSOLF, Lloyd D(aryl) 1919-

PERSONAL: Surname is pronounced Mew-solf; born October 14, 1919, in Yale, S.D.; son of William Ferdinand and Emma Marie (Pautz) Musolf; married Dorothy Berdyne Peet, June 30, 1944; children: Stephanie, Michael, Laura. Education: Huron College, B.A., 1941; University of South Dakota, M.A., 1946; Johns Hopkins University, Ph.D., 1950. Politics: Democrat. Home: 500 Antioch Dr., Davis, Calif. 95616. Office: University of California, Davis, Calif. 95616.

CAREER: Vassar College, Poughkeepsie, N.Y., instructor, 1949-50, assistant professor, 1950-55, associate professor of political science, 1955-59; Michigan State University, East Lansing, associate professor and chief of MSU advisory group, Saigon, Vietnam, 1959-61, professor of political science, 1961-63; University of California, Davis, professor of political science and director, Institute of Governmental Affairs, 1963—. Visiting professor, University of Michigan, 1955-56, Johns Hopkins University, and University of Delaware. Consultant to New York State Commission on a Constitutional Convention, 1957-58, California State Personnel Board, 1963-65, United Nations Seminar on Public Enterprise, Geneva, 1966, and to United Nations Public Administration Division, 1968. Member of U.S. delegation to International Congress of Administrative Sciences, Paris, 1965. *Military service:* U.S. Navy, 1942-45; became lieutenant; received Presidential Unit Citation.

MEMBER: American Political Science Association, American Society for Public Administration (member of council, 1967-70), Conference of University Bureaus of Governmental Research (chairman, 1965-67), American Association of University Professors, National Association of Schools of Public Affairs and Administration (member of executive council, 1972-74), Council on Graduate Education for Public Administration, Western Political Science Association, Western Governmental Research Association (member of executive board, 1966-68), California Conference on Education for Public Administration, Pi Gamma Mu, Pi Sigma Alpha.

WRITINGS: Federal Examiners and the Conflict of Law and Administration, Johns Hopkins Press, 1953; *Public Ownership and Accountability: The Canadian Experience,* Harvard University Press, 1959; (editor with Samuel Krislov) *The Politics of Regulation,* Houghton, 1964; *Government and the Economy,* Scott, Foresman, 1965; (editor) *Communications Satellites in Political Orbit,* Chandler, 1968; (editor with Allan Kornberg) *Legislatures in Developmental Perspective,* Duke University Press, 1970; (with others) *American National Government: Policies and Politics,* Scott, Foresman, 1971; *Mixed Enterprise in a Developmental Perspective,* Heath, 1972; *Legislatures, Environmental Protection, and Developmental Goals: British Columbia and California,* Sage, 1974. Contributor to *Asian Survey* and political science and public administration journals.

WORK IN PROGRESS: Research into functions of weak legislatures and of the Malaysian Parliament.

* * *

MYERS, Arthur 1922-

PERSONAL: Born October 24, 1922, in Buffalo, N.Y.; son of Edward A. (a Western Union executive) and Isabelle (Baker) Myers. *Education:* Hobart College, B.A., 1942. *Home:* 429 Pomeroy Ave., Pittsfield, Mass. *Office:* 33 Eagle St., Pittsfield, Mass. 01201. *Agent:* Toni Mendez, Inc., 140 East 56th St., New York, N.Y. 10022.

CAREER: Rochester Times-Union, Rochester, N.Y., various editorial posts, 1948-53; *Washington Post,* Washington, D.C., assistant city editor, 1955-57; *Berkshire Eagle,* Pittsfield, Mass., feature writer, 1957-64; free-lance writer. *Military service:* U.S. Army, World War II. *Member:* Society of Magazine Writers, American Newspaper Guild, Kappa Sigma. *Awards, honors:* Three Associated Press awards for reporting.

WRITINGS: (With Jeffrey O'Connell) *Safety Last,* Random House, 1966; *Careers for the Seventies: Journalism,* Crowell-Collier, 1971; *Analysis: The Short Story,* Sol

III Publications, 1975. Contributor of about 100 stories and articles to magazines, including *Saturday Review, Ladies' Home Journal, Sports Illustrated, Collier's, Woman's Day, Pageant, Coronet.* Editor, *Berkshire Sampler.*

WORK IN PROGRESS: Novels; nonfiction books; plays; and magazine articles.

SIDELIGHTS: Myers is competent in French.

* * *

MYERS, Jacob M(artin) 1904-

PERSONAL: Born October 25, 1904, in York County, Pa.; son of Harvey Allen and Annie (Seiffert) Myers; married Mary Helen Kimmel, June 26, 1926; children: Helen Elizabeth Myers Bream. *Education:* Gettysburg College, A.B., 1927; Lutheran Theological Seminary, Gettysburg, Pa., B.D., 1930, ST.M., 1931; Temple University, S.T.D., 1937; Johns Hopkins University, Ph.D., 1946. *Politics:* Democrat. *Home:* 141 Seminary Ave., Gettysburg, Pa. 17325. *Office:* Lutheran Theological Seminary, Gettysburg, Pa. 17325.

CAREER: Ordained Lutheran minister, 1930; Grace Lutheran parish, Gettysburg, Pa., pastor, 1930-50; Lutheran Theological Seminary, Gettysburg, Pa., instructor in New Testament, 1937-40, instructor in Old Testament, 1940-42, professor of Old Testament, 1942—. Visiting professor, Pittsburgh Theological Seminary, 1965, and 1967. *Member:* American Academy of Religion, Society of Biblical Literature, American Oriental Society, British Society for Old Testament Study (associate). *Awards, honors:* Outstanding Educator of America, 1972, 1973.

WRITINGS: The Linguistic and Literary Form of the Book of Ruth, E. J. Brill, 1955; *The Layman's Bible Commentary,* Volume XIV, 1959; *The Anchor Bible,* Anchor Books, Volume I: *I Chronicles,* Volume II: *II Chronicles,* Volume III: *Ezra-Nehemiah,* 1965; *Invitation to the Old Testament,* Doubleday, 1966; *The World of the Restoration,* Prentice-Hall, 1968; *I and II Esdras,* Doubleday, 1974.

Contributor: *Old Testament Commentary,* Muhlenberg, 1948; *Interpreter's Bible,* Volume II, Abingdon, 1953; *The Lesson Commentary,* Muhlenberg, 1958; *The Holy Bible: The Berkeley Version in Modern English,* Zondervan, 1959; (and co-editor) *Biblical Studies in Memory of H. C. Alleman,* J. J. Augustin, 1960; (and editor with O. Reimherr and H. N. Bream) *Theological and Mission Studies in Memory of John Aberly,* Gettysburg Times, 1964; Hans Goedicke, editor, *Near Eastern Studies in Honor of William Foxwell Albright,* Johns Hopkins Press, 1971. Contributor to *Encyclopedia Judaica,* Macmillan, 1971. Also contributor of articles and reviews to Lutheran and other religious journals.

WORK IN PROGRESS: Patterns of Grace and Torah in the Bible.

SIDELIGHTS: Myers told *CA* that he was brought up on a farm and has always been interested in the relationship of nature to Old Testament stories. He has traveled extensively in the Near East, studied its history, and learned Hebrew, Greek, Latin, Akkadian as well as German and French. About his study Myers said, "[I] saw what I believe to be essential for today—the need to see our problems in society from a larger perspective than that of modern religion and sociology."

BIOGRAPHICAL/CRITICAL SOURCES: Wentz, *History of Gettysburg Seminary,* two volumes, Lutheran

Theological Seminary Press, 1964-65; H. N. Bream, R. D. Heim, and C. A. Moore, editors, *A Light Unto My Path: Essays in Honor of Jacob M. Myers*, Temple University Press, 1974.

* * *

MYERS, Rollo Hugh 1892-

PERSONAL: Born January 23, 1892, in Chislehurst, Kent, England; son of Ernest and Nora M. (Lodge) Myers; married third wife, Mary Coop, 1936; children: two sons. *Education:* Educated privately; Balliol College, Oxford, M.A., 1913. *Home:* 241 Residences de Villeneuve, Vence 06140, France.

CAREER: Times and *Daily Telegraph*, London, England, music correspondent in Paris, France, 1919-34; British Broadcasting Corp., London, England, staff of music department, 1935-44; music officer for British Council in Paris, 1945-46; secretariat for Organization for European Economic Cooperation in Paris, 1949-56. *Member:* Saville Club. *Awards, honors:* Officier d'Academie (France).

WRITINGS: (Translator) Jean Cocteau, *Cock and Harlequin*, Egoist Press, 1921; *Modern Music*, Kegan Paul, 1923; *Music in the Modern World*, E. J. Arnold, 1939; *Erik Satie*, Dobson, 1948, Dover, 1968; *Debussy*, Duckworth, 1948; (translator) Marc Pincherle, *An Illustrated History of Music*, Reynal, 1960, revised edition, Macmillan, 1962; (general editor) *Twentieth Century Music*, J. Calder, 1960, Orion Press, 1968, 2nd edition, J. Calder, 1968; *Ravel: Life and Works*, Duckworth, 1960, Yoseloff, 1961; (translator) Louis Pauwels, *The Dawn of Magic*, Gibbs & Phillips, 1963; (translator) Jacques Chailley, *40,000 Years of Music*, Farrar, Straus, 1965; (editor) Romain Rolland, *Richard Strauss and Romain Rolland*, University of California Press, 1968; *Emmanuel Chabrier and His Circle*, Dent, 1969; *Modern French Music: From Faure to Boulez*, Praeger, 1971 (published in England as *Modern French Music: Its Evolution and Cultural Background from 1900 to the Present Day*, Basil Blackwell, 1971). Contributor to *Grove's Dictionary of Music and Musicians, Encyclopedie de la Pleiade*, and *Encyclopaedia Britannica*; also contributor to music journals.

WORK IN PROGRESS: Debussy and His Literary Image, for David & Charles; translating Stefan Jarocinski's *Debussy: Impressionism and Symbolism*.

* * *

NADER, Laura 1930-

PERSONAL: Born September 30, 1930, in Winsted, Conn.; daughter of Nadra (a businessman) and Rose Bouziane Nader; married Norman Milleron (a physicist), September 1, 1962; children: Nadia, Tarek, Rania. *Education:* Wells College, B.A., 1952; Radcliffe College, Ph.D., 1961. *Office:* Department of Anthropology, University of California, Berkeley, Calif.

CAREER: University of California, Berkeley, 1960—, now associate professor of anthropology. *Member:* American Anthropological Association, Society of Women Geographers. *Awards, honors:* Center for Advanced Study in the Behavioral Sciences, fellowship 1963-64.

WRITINGS: Talea and Juquila: A Comparison of Zapotec Social Organization, University of California Press, 1964. Editor, and contributor to "Ethnography of Law," a special issue of *American Anthropologist*, 1965. Produced film, "To Make the Balance," 1966.

WORK IN PROGRESS: To Make the Balance: A study of Zapotec Law; and *No Access to Law*, a study of complaint management in the U.S.

* * *

NAGLER, Barney 1912-

PERSONAL: Born August 24, 1912, in New York, N.Y.; son of Harris and Kate (Snope) Nagler; married Betty Rosenberg, October 24, 1932; children: Robert. *Education:* Educated in New York, N.Y. *Home:* 209-19 28th Rd., Bayside, N.Y. 11360. *Agent:* Frances Goldin, 305 East 11th St., New York, N.Y. 10003.

CAREER: New York Post-Bronx Home News, New York, N.Y., sports writer, 1934-50; *New York Morning Telegraph*, New York, N.Y., columnist, 1950-72; *Daily Racing Form*, columnist, 1970—. Producer-writer, American Broadcasting Co. and National Broadcasting Co. *Member:* Baseball Writers Association of America, Boxing Writers Association (president, 1960-66), Writers Guild of America, American Newspaper Guild, National Turf Writers Association, New York Turf Writers Association.

WRITINGS: James Norris and the Decline of Boxing, Bobbs-Merrill 1964; *The American Horse*, Macmillan, 1966; *Brown Bomber: The Pilgrimage of Joe Louis*, World, 1972. Contributor to anthologies. Also author of monograph on boxing in Madison Square Garden.

WORK IN PROGRESS: A novel, as yet untitled, for Macmillan.

* * *

NAJDER, Zdzislaw 1930-

PERSONAL: Surname pronounced *Nye*-der; born October 31, 1930, in Warsaw, Poland; son of Franciszek Leon and Jozefa (Kowalska) Najder; married Halina Paschalska (a translator), July 23, 1965; children: (previous marriage) Krzysztof. *Education:* University of Warsaw, M.Phil., 1954; Oxford University, B.Litt., 1963. *Home:* Obozna 3/23, Warsaw, Poland.

CAREER: Polish Academy of Sciences, Warsaw, Poland, senior assistant, Institute of Literary Research, 1952-57; University of Warsaw, Warsaw, Poland, senior assistant, department of philosophy, 1958-59; Columbia University, New York, N.Y. and Yale University, New Haven, Conn., lecturer in Polish literature, 1966; University of California, Berkeley, lecturer in Polish literature, 1966-67; University of California, Davis, visiting associate professor of philosophy, 1967-68, Regents' professor, 1970-71; Northern Illinois University, DeKalb, visiting professor of English, 1971-72; Stanford University, Stanford, Calif., visiting scholar, 1974-75. *Member:* Polish Writers Union, P.E.N.

WRITINGS: (Editor) *Orzeszkowa, Sienkiewicz, Prus o literaturze*, Czytelnik (Warsaw), 1956; (editor) *Conrad's Polish Background*, Oxford University Press, 1964; *Nad Conradem*, Panstwowy Instytut Wydawniczy (Warsaw), 1965; (editor) *Listy*, Panstwowy Instytut Wydawniczy, 1968; *Wartosci i oceny*, Panstwowe Wydawnictwo Naukowe, 1971; (editor) Joseph Conrad, *Dziela*, twenty-seven volumes, Panstwowy Instytut Wydawniczy, 1972-74; *Values and Evaluations*, Clarendon, 1975.

WORK IN PROGRESS: A complete edition of Joseph Conrad's letters in collaboration with F. R. Karl for Stanford University Press; and *The Chivalric Ethos in Modern Literature*.

NALL, T(orney) Otto   1900-

PERSONAL: Born May 23, 1900, in Terre Haute, Ind.; son of Torney Otto (a printer) and Alta Mae (Stokes) Nall; married Frances Marie Mahaffie, February 2, 1929. Education: Hamline University, B.A., 1921; graduate study at University of Minnesota, 1921-22, Northwestern University, 1923-24; Garrett Theological Seminary, B.D., 1925. Politics: Independent. Home: 2509 Wynnewood Dr., Cleanwater, Fla. 33515.

CAREER: Ordained to ministry of Methodist Episcopal Church, 1924; Epworth Herald, Chicago, Ill., associate editor, 1926-35; Christian Advocate, representative of editorial board, Cincinnati, Ohio, 1935-39, editor of Northwestern and Central editions, Kansas City, Mo., 1939-40, managing editor, Chicago, 1940-48, and editor, 1948-60; Together, Chicago, associate editor 1956-60; bishop of the Methodist Church, in Minnesota, 1960-68, in Hong Kong and Taiwan, 1968-72. Member of executive committee of World Methodist Council, 1954-68. Correspondent for Religious News Service; summer teacher of journalism at Garrett Theological Seminary and Iliff School of Theology. Military service: U.S. Army, 1918.

MEMBER: Methodist Press Association (president, 1944-47), Associated Church Press (president, 1945-47), Torch Club, Lake Shore Club (Chicago), Minneapolis Club. Awards, honors: D.D., Garrett Theological Seminary, 1936, Hamline University, 1939; Litt.D., Adrian College, 1950; LL.D., Wesleyan University, 1951; St. George's Award for distinguished service to Methodist Church, 1963.

WRITINGS: Youth's Work in the New World, Association Press, 1936; New Occupations for Youth, Association Press, 1938; (editor) Vital Religion, Methodist Book Concern, 1938; Move on, Youth!, Friendship, 1940; Jobs for Today's Youth, Association Press, 1941; (editor) These Prophetic Voices, Methodist Publishing House, 1941; (editor) The World Methodist Conference Speaks to the World, Methodist Evangelistic Materials, 1941; (with Bert H. Davis) Young Christians at Work, Association Press, 1949; (with Davis) Making Good as Young Couples, Association Press, 1953; The Bible When You Need It Most, Association Press, 1957; (editor) By John Wesley, Association Press, 1963; (editor) Who Is the Parish Minister?, Abingdon, 1965; Forever Beginning, Minnesota Commission on Archives and History, 1973.

SIDELIGHTS: Nall has made eleven trips to Europe, most for meetings of the executive committee of the World Methodist Council; he studies Methodist missions in Africa, India, and Pakistan, and religious movements in China and southeast Asia.

*   *   *

NAMOVICZ, Gene Inyart   1927-
(Gene Inyart)

PERSONAL: Born July 11, 1927, in Olney, Ill.; daughter of Ernest William (a retailer) and Pauline (Martin) Inyart; married Stanley B. Namovicz, Jr. (now a personnel specialist), October 3, 1959; children: Susan, Catherine, Matthew, Daniel. Education: University of Michigan, B.A. (with distinction), 1949; Catholic University of America, M.S. in L.S., 1963. Religion: Roman Catholic. Home: 333 Lincoln Ave., Takoma Park, Md. 20012.

CAREER: Public Library of District of Columbia, Washington, D.C., children's librarian, 1950-53, chief of Schools Divison, 1953-57, chief of Extension Department, 1957-60. Member: American Library Association. Awards, honors: Franklin Watts Juvenile Fiction Award, 1959, for The Tent under the Spider Tree.

WRITINGS—All under name Gene Inyart: The Tent under the Spider Tree, F. Watts, 1959; (with E. H. Gross) Childrens Service in Public Libraries: Organization and Administration, American Library Association, 1963; Susan and Martin, F. Watts, 1965; Jenny, F. Watts, 1966; Orange October, F. Watts, 1968.

WORK IN PROGRESS: Rabbit Girl for Sea Cliff Press; Black Dark Night for J. Philip O'Hara, Inc.

*   *   *

NARASIMHAN, Chakravarthi V.   1915-

PERSONAL: Born May 21, 1915, in Srirangam, South India; married Janaki Chari, May 26, 1938; children: Hemalatha Murli, Kanakalatha Mukund. Education: Madras University, B.A. (honors), 1934; Oxford University, B.A. (honors), 1936, M.A. 1942. Religion: Hindu. Home: 300 East 33rd St., New York, N.Y. 10016. Office: United Nations, United Nations Plaza, New York, N.Y. 10017.

CAREER: Joined Indian Civil Service, 1936, serving with Madras cadre, 1937-42, and with secretariat of Madras Government, 1942-50; Indian Ministry of Food and Agriculture, deputy secretary, then joint secretary, 1950-53; Indian Ministry of Finance, joint secretary of Department of Economic Affairs, 1953-56; United Nations Economic Commission for Asia and Far East, Bangkok, executive secretary, 1956-59; United Nations, New York, N.Y., undersecretary for special political affairs, 1959-62, chef de cabinet, 1961-73, undersecretary for General Assembly affairs, 1962-67, undersecretary-general inter-agency affairs and coordination, 1973—. Awards, honors: LL.D., Williams College, Williamstown, Mass., 1960.

WRITINGS: The Mahabharatha, Columbia University Press, 1965.

*   *   *

NASH, Manning   1924-

PERSONAL: Born May 4, 1924, in Philadelphia, Pa.; son of Abraham and Molly (Sukonik) Nash; married June C. Bousley (a professor), September 19, 1951 (divorced, 1964); children: Eric, Laura. Education: Temple University, B.S. (honors), 1949; University of Chicago, M.A., 1952, Ph.D., 1955. Office: Department of Anthropology, University of Chicago, Chicago, Ill.

CAREER: University of California, Los Angeles, instructor in anthropology and sociology, 1955-56; University of Washington, Seattle, assistant professor of anthropology, 1956-57; University of Chicago, Chicago, Ill., associate professor, 1957-62, professor of anthropology, 1962—. Military service: U.S. Army, 1942-46. Member: American Anthropological Association (fellow). Awards, honors: National Science Foundation fellowship, 1960-61; 1968-71.

WRITINGS: Machine Age Maya, Free Press of Glencoe, 1958; The Golden Road to Modernity, Wiley, 1965; Primitive and Peasant Economic Systems, Chandler Publishing, 1966; (with others) Anthropological Studies in Theravada Buddhism, Yale University Press, 1966; Peasant Citizens, Ohio University Press, 1974. Editor, Economic Development and Cultural Change, 1960-64.

NASH, Paul 1924-

PERSONAL: Born September 2, 1924, in Newcastle on Tyne, England; son of William Arthur and Elsie (Forbes) Nash; married Anne Steere, June 29, 1957; children: Christopher Forbes, Jennifer Anne. *Education:* University of London, B.Sc., London School of Economics and Political Science, 1949, teaching diploma, Institute of Education, 1950, academic diploma in education, Institute of Education, 1952; University of Toronto, M.Ed., 1955; Harvard University, Ed.D., 1959. *Religion:* Society of Friends (Quaker). *Home:* 123 Park St., Newton, Mass. 02158. *Office:* Boston University, 246 Bay State Rd., Boston, Mass. 02215.

CAREER: Teacher in elementary and secondary schools in England, 1949-52; Lower Canada College, Montreal, Quebec, history teacher, 1952-55; Clark University, Worcester, Mass., assistant professor of education, 1957-59; McGill University, Montreal, assistant professor of education, 1959-62; Boston University, Boston, Mass., professor of history and philosophy of education, 1962—. Harvard University, visiting professor of education, 1963-64. Consulting editor in education for Random House, Inc., and Alfred A. Knopf, Inc., 1965-68; John Wiley & Sons, Inc., 1968—. University of Chile, Fulbright lecturer, 1971; University of California, professor-in-residence, 1971-72. *Military service:* Royal Air Force, pilot, 1942-46; served in Europe, Africa, and North America. *Member:* Philosophy of Education Society, History of Education Society (vice-president, 1966-67), Comparative Education Society, American Association of University Professors, American Civil Liberties Union, New England Philosophy of Education Society (vice-president, 1966-67).

WRITINGS: (Editor with A. M. Kazamias and Henry J. Perkinson) *The Educated Man: Studies in the History of Educational Thought,* Wiley, 1965; *Culture and the State: Matthew Arnold and Continental Education,* Teachers College, Columbia University, 1966; *Authority and Freedom in Education: An Introduction to the Philosophy of Education,* Wiley, 1966; *Models of Man: Explorations in the Western Educational Tradition,* Wiley, 1968; *History and Education: The Educational Uses of the Past,* Random House, 1970. Contributor to journals. Member of editorial board, *History of Education Quarterly.*

SIDELIGHTS: Nash is fluent in French and Italian.

* * *

NASH, Ralph (Lee) 1925-

PERSONAL: Born February 22, 1925, in Sullivan, Ind.; son of Cecil E. and F. F. (Raines) Nash; married Berta Sturman, December 17, 1949; children: Thomas, Richard. *Education:* Duke University, A.B., 1945, M.A., 1946; Harvard University, Ph.D., 1951. *Residence:* Huntington Woods, Mich. *Office:* Wayne State University, Detroit, Mich.

CAREER: University of Louisville, Louisville, Ky., instructor in English, 1948-50; Washington University, St. Louis, Mo., assistant professor of English, 1950-54; Wayne State University, Detroit, Mich., instructor, 1955-58, assistant professor, 1958-61, associate professor, 1961-65, professor of Renaissance literature, 1965—, assistant chairman, 1965-68, chairman, department of English, 1968-72. *Member:* Modern Language Association of America, American Association of Teachers of Italian, Renaissance Society of America, North Central Renaissance Society.

WRITINGS: (Contributor) *Studies in Honor of John Wilcox,* Wayne State University Press, 1958; (translator) Jacopo Sannazaro, *Arcadia and Piscatorial Eclogues,* Wayne State University Press, 1966. Contributor of articles and reviews on Renaissance literature and modern poetry to scholarly journals.

WORK IN PROGRESS: A prose translation of *Jerusalem Delivered.*

SIDELIGHTS: Nash reads Italian, French, German, Spanish, Latin, Greek.

* * *

NASH, Roderick 1939-

PERSONAL: Born January 7, 1939, in New York, N.Y.; son of Jay B. (a professor) and Emma (Frazier) Nash; married Sandra Jackson; children: two daughters. *Education:* Harvard University, A.B. (magna cum laude), 1960; University of Wisconsin, M.A., 1961, Ph.D., 1964. *Home:* 690 San Ysido Rd., Santa Barbara, Calif. *Office:* Department of History, University of California, Santa Barbara, Calif.

CAREER: Dartmouth College, Hanover, N.H., instructor, 1964-66; University of California, Santa Barbara, assistant professor, 1966-69, associate professor, 1969-74, professor of history, 1974—, chairman, department of environmental studies, 1970—. Hanover Conservation Council, secretary, 1965—. *Member:* American Historical Association, Organization of American Historians, American Studies Association, Sierra Club, Wilderness Society. *Awards, honors:* Second place, William P. Lyons Master's Essay Competition, conducted by Loyola University (Chicago), 1961.

WRITINGS: (Contributor) Edward N. Saveth, editor, *American History and the Social Sciences,* Macmillan, 1964; (with Merle Curti) *Philanthropy in the Shaping of American Higher Education,* Rutgers University Press, 1965; *Wilderness and the American Mind,* Yale University Press, 1967, revised edition, 1973; *The American Environment,* Addison-Wesley, 1968; *The Nervous Generation,* Rand-McNally, 1970; *The Call of the Wild,* Braziller, 1970; *Grand Canyon of the Living Colorado,* Ballantine, 1970; *Environment and Americans,* Holt; *From These Beginnings,* Harper, 1973. Contributor to *American Quarterly, Living Wilderness, Wisconsin Magazine of History, Journal of Negro History* and *Forest History.*

SIDELIGHTS: Nash was a professional fishing guide, and member of the Harvard varsity swimming team during his student days; has done extensive wilderness travel in northern Canada and western United States. *Avocational interests:* Tennis, squash, skiing, fishing, whitewater boating and river running.

* * *

NATANSON, Maurice 1924-

PERSONAL: Born November 26, 1924, in New York, N.Y.; son of Charles (an actor) and Kate (Scheer) Natanson: married Lois Lichenstein, January 21, 1949; children: Charles, Nicholas, Kathy. *Education:* Lincoln Memorial University, A.B., 1945; New York University, M.A., 1948; University of Nebraska, Ph.D., 1950; New School for Social Research, D.S.Sc. (summa cum laude), 1953. *Politics:* Democrat. *Religion:* Jewish. *Home:* 615 Escalona Dr., Santa Cruz, Calif. 95060. *Office:* Cowell College, University of California, Santa Cruz, Calif.

CAREER: University of Nebraska, Lincoln, instructor, 1950-51; New School for Social Research, New York,

N.Y., lecturer in philosophy, Graduate Faculty, 1952-53; University of Houston, Houston, Tex., assistant professor, 1953-56, associate professor of philosophy, 1956-57; University of North Carolina, Chapel Hill, associate professor, 1957-62, professor of philosophy, 1962-65; University of California, Santa Cruz, professor of philosophy and fellow of Cowell College, 1965—. Pennsylvania State University, distinguished visiting professor, 1963; University of California, Berkeley, visiting professor, 1964-65; guest professor, University of Konstanz, 1974. *Member:* American Philosophical Association, International Phenomenological Society, Society for Phenomenology and Existential Philosophy. *Awards, honors:* American Council of Learned Societies scholar, 1951-53, fellow in Europe, 1961-62; University of California, senior faculty fellowship, 1967-68; National Endowment for the Humanites, senior fellow, 1971-72; National Book Award, 1974, for philosophy.

WRITINGS: A Critique of Jean-Paul Sartre's Ontology, University of Nebraska Press, 1951; *The Social Dynamics of George H. Mead,* Public Affairs, 1956; (contributor) *For Roman Ingarden,* Nijhoff, 1959; (contributor) *The Critical Matrix,* Georgetown University Press, 1961; (Contributor) *The World of Thomas Wolfe,* Scribner, 1962; *Literature, Philosophy, and the Social Sciences,* Nijhoff, 1962; (editor) Alfred Schutz, *The Problem of Social Reality,* Nijhoff, 1962; (editor) *Philosophy of the Social Sciences: A Reader,* Random, House, 1963; (contributor) *Psychiatrie der Gegenwart,* two volumes, Springer, 1963; (editor with Henry W. Johnstone, Jr.) *Philosophy, Rhetoric, and Argumentation,* Pennsylvania State University Press, 1965; (editor) *Essays in Phenomenology,* Nijhoff, 1966; (editor) *Psychiatry and Philosophy,* Springer, 1969; (editor) *Phenomenology and Social Reality,* Nijhoff, 1970; *The Journeying Self,* Addison-Wesley, 1970; *Edmund Husserl,* Northwestern University Press, 1973; (editor) *Phenomenology and the Social Sciences,* two volumes, Northwestern University Press, 1973; *Phenomenology, Role, and Reason,* C. C Thomas, 1974.

Contributor to philosophy and social science journals. Member of board of editors, *Philosophy and Phenomenological Research*; consulting editor, "Northwestern University Studies in Phenomenology and Existential Philosophy"; book review editor, *Man and World.*

WORK IN PROGRESS: Studies in the philosophy of death; two books for children, illustrated by Rosekrans-Hoffman.

*   *   *

NEFF, John C.   1913-

PERSONAL: Born October 31, 1913, in Cleveland, Ohio: son of Herman R. and Carrie J. Neff. *Education:* Keynon College, B.A. (cum laude), 1936; studied languages for three years at Berlitz Schools; during years in the military, completed course at Command and General Staff College, National War College, and Industrial College of the Armed Forces. *Home:* 120 East 75th St., New York, N.Y. 10021.

CAREER: Enlisted in U.S. Army as private, 1940, discharged as major, 1945, after serving as chief information officer with 83rd Infantry Division in Europe; free-lance writer, Cleveland, Ohio, 1945-48; U.S. Army Reserve, active duty with 77th Infantry Division (Reserve), New York, N.Y., 1949-62, retiring from post as division chief of staff with rank of colonel; Richardson Foundation, Inc., New York, N.Y., consultant, 1960-61, staff, 1962, as assistant to the president, 1962-63; National Strategy Informa-

tion Center, Inc., New York, N.Y., executive vice-president and treasurer, 1963-68; French and Polyclinic Medical School and Health Center, New York, N.Y., Secretary of long range planning committee, 1968-70, special projects officer, 1970-73. Freelance writer, 1973—.

MEMBER: Association of the United States Army (board of governors of Manhattan chapter), Reserve Officers Association (past president of Manhattan chapter), New York Society of Military and Naval Officers of the World Wars, Alpha Delta Phi, Army and Navy Club (Washington, D.C.), Ends of the Earth Club. *Awards, honors—*Military: Bronze Star with oak leaf cluster, World War II; Croix de Guerre with silver star and Legion of Honor, both for work with French Resistance Forces during the war and for his services later in organizing French reservists living in the metropolitan New York area; Army Commendation Medal, 1962.

WRITINGS: Maria (Novel), Ives Washburn, 1951; (co-editor) *American Strategy for the Nuclear Age,* Doubleday, 1960; (co-editor) *Peace and War in the Modern Age,* Doubleday, 1965; (editor) *A New Health Center for New York City,* privately printed, 1973. Writer of history of the 83rd Infantry Division European campaigns, and two radio plays for "Cavalcade of America." Short stories, articles and essays have appeared in *Collier's, Saturday Review, New Mexico Quarterly Review, Infantry Journal,* and other publications. Founder and editor of Kenyon monthly magazine, *Hika,* 1933-36.

SIDELIGHTS: Neff speaks French, Italian, German, and Spanish. Traveled in Europe and North America before and since the war. Traveled by freighter to Scandinavia in 1964 and took a 110 day trip around the world by freighter in 1965. He has since traveled in Europe and the Caribbean. *Avocational interest:* Book collector, with about four thousand classic, general, and reference volumes in his library.

*   *   *

NEGLEY, Glenn (Robert)   1907-

PERSONAL: Born November 5, 1907, in Indianapolis, Ind.; son of Homer Samuel Hanway (a building contractor) and Myrtle (Rhoades) Negley; married Julia Henderson, July 7, 1939. *Education:* Butler University, A.B., 1930, M.A., 1934; University of Chicago, Ph.D., 1939. *Politics:* Democrat. *Home:* 2132 Bedford Drive, Apt. 10, Yorktown, Durham, N.C. 27707. *Office:* Duke University, Durham, N.C.

CAREER: University of Oklahoma, Norman, instructor in philosophy, 1937-38; University of Illinois, Urbana, instructor, 1938-41, assistant professor, 1942-46; Duke University, Durham, N.C., professor of philosophy, 1946—, chairman of department, 1950-56. Visiting professor at University of Texas, University of Chicago, and San Jose State College; (now California State University, San Jose), staff observer, Administrative Staff College, Henley on Thames, England, 1960, 1966. *Military service:* U.S. Army Air Forces, 1942-46; became major. *Member:* American Philosophical Association, American Political Science Association, American Association of University Professors, Greenlands Association. *Awards, honors:* Rockefeller Foundation research fellow, 1946; Ford Foundation research fellow, 1953-54.

WRITINGS: The Organization of Knowledge, Prentice-Hall, 1942; (with T. V. Smith) *Democracy vs. Dictatorship,* National Council for Social Studies, 1943; (with J. M. Patrick) *The Quest for Utopia*, Henry Shuman, 1952, revised editions, 1962, 1971; *Political Authority and Moral Judgment*, Duke University Press, 1965; *A Bibliography of Utopian Works in Western Literature*, Friends of the Duke University Library, 1975.

Contributor: Albert Lepawsky, *Administration: The Art and Science of Organization and Management*, Knopf, 1949; Virgilius Ferm, editor, *A History of Philosophical Systems*, Philosophical Library, 1950; *Freedom and Authority in Our Time*, Conference on Science, Philosophy and Religion in Their Relation to the Democratic Way of Life, 1951; *Symbols and Values*, Conference on Science, Philosophy and Religion in Their Relation to the Democratic Way of Life, 1952; T. C. Denise and M. H. Williams, editors, *Retrospect and Prospect*, Syracuse University Press, 1956. Contributor to professional journals.

SIDELIGHTS: Responsible for Duke University Library "Utopia Collection" of some six hundred titles, assembled in the library's rare book room.

* * *

NEGUS, Kenneth George 1927-

PERSONAL: Born December 23, 1927, in Council Bluffs, Iowa; son of Calvin George and Madeline (Larsen) Negus; married Joan Rosenthal; children: Monica, Christopher, Jon. *Education:* Princeton University, B.A., 1952, M.A., 1954, Ph.D., 1957. *Politics:* Independent. *Religion:* Episcopalian. *Home:* 175 Harrison St., Princeton, N.J. 08540. *Office:* Rutgers University, 64 College Ave., New Brunswick, N.J. 08903.

CAREER: Instructor in German at Northwestern University, Evanston, Ill., 1955-57, Harvard University, Cambridge, Mass., 1957-59; Princeton University, Princeton, N.J., assistant professor of German, 1959-61; Rutgers University, New Brunswick, N.J., assistant professor, 1961-65, associate professor, 1965-66, professor of German, 1966—. *Military service:* U.S. Army, Signal Corps, 1946-50. *Member:* American Association of Teachers of German, Modern Language Association of America. *Awards, honors:* Fulbright fellow in Germany, 1954-55.

WRITINGS: E.T.A. Hoffmann's Other World, University of Pennsylvania Press, 1965; *H.J.C. von Grimmelshausen*, Twayne, 1974. Compiler of annual Romantic bibliography, German section, for *Modern Language Notes;* also contributor of articles and reviews on German literature to journals, and occasional technical articles to radio amateurs' periodicals.

WORK IN PROGRESS: Studies in seventeenth and nineteenth century German literature; astrology in literary symbolism.

SIDELIGHTS: Aside from German, Negus has some facility in Russian and reads most Western European languages and Latin.

AVOCATIONAL INTERESTS: Amateur radio, mnemonics, gardening, exotic cookery, and the occult.

* * *

NEIDER, Charles 1915-

PERSONAL: Surname rhymes with "rider"; born January 18, 1915, in Odessa, Russia; son of Calman and Olga (Hornstein) Neider; married Joan Muriel Merrick, August 5, 1952; children; Susan Muriel. *Education:* City College (now of the City University of New York), B.S., 1938.

Home: 24 Southern Way, Princeton, N.J. *Agent:* Curtis Brown Ltd., 60 East 56th St., New York, N.Y. 10022.

CAREER: Free-lance writer and editor, 1938—. *Awards, honors:* Residence fellowships at Yaddo Corp., Mac-Dowell Colony, and Huntington Hartford Foundation (seven times); grants from Chapelbrook Foundation, National Science Foundation, and Doherty Charitable Foundation.

WRITINGS: The Frozen Sea: A Study of Franz Kafka, Oxford University Press, 1948; *Kafka: His Mind and Art*, Routledge & Kegan Paul, 1949; *The White Citadel* (novel), Twayne, 1954; *The Authentic Death of Hendry Jones* (novel), Harper, 1956; *Family Album* (novel), Hamish Hamilton, 1962, published as *Naked Eye*, Horizon, 1964; *Susy: A Childhood* (biography), Horizon, 1966; *Mark Twain* (essays), Horizon, 1967; *Edge of the World: Ross Island, Antarctia*, Doubleday, 1974.

Editor: *The Stature of Thomas Mann* (anthology of commentary and criticism), New Directions, 1947; (and author of introduction) *Short Novels of the Masters*, Rinehart, 1948; *Great Short Stories From the World's Literature*, Rinehart, 1950, revised edition, 1972; (and author of introduction) *Great Shipwrecks and Castaways*, Harper, 1952; (and author of introduction) *The Fabulous Insects*, Harper, 1953; *Man Against Nature: Tales of Adventure and Exploration*, Harper, 1954; *Men of The High Calling* (short stories), Abingdon, 1954; (and author of introduction) Fanny Osbourne Stevenson (Mrs. Robert Louis) and Robert Louis Stevenson, *Our Samoan Adventure*, Harper, 1955; (and author of introduction) *Essays of the Masters*, Rinehart, 1956; (and author of introduction) *Complete Short Stories of Mark Twain*, Doubleday, 1957; *Man Against Woman: A Vade Mecum for the Weaker Sex and a Caution to Women*, Harper, 1957; (and author of introduction) Tolstoy, *Tales of Courage and Conflict*, Doubleday, 1958; (and author of introduction and notes) *The Great West*, Coward, 1958; (and author of introduction and notes) *The Autobiography of Mark Twain*, Harper, 1959; (and author of introduction) *The Complete Humorous Sketches and Tales of Mark Twain*, Doubleday, 1961; (and author of introduction and notes) *Mark Twain: Life As I Find It*, Doubleday, 1961; (and author of introduction and notes) *The Travels of Mark Twain*, Coward, 1961; (and author of introduction) *The Complete Essays of Mark Twain*, Doubleday, 1963; (and author of introduction) *The Complete Novels of Mark Twain*, Doubleday, 1963; (and author of introduction) Mark Twain, *The Adventures of Colonel Sellers*, Doubleday, (and author of introduction) *The Complete Travel Books of Mark Twain*, Doubleday, 1966; *The Complete Stories of Robert Louis Stevenson*, Doubleday, 1969; *Antarctica*, Random House, 1972; *The Complete Tales of Washington Irving*, Doubleday, 1975.

Author of introduction: Mark Twain, *Connecticut Yankee in King Arthur's Court*, Hill & Wang, 1960.

WORK IN PROGRESS: A novel with an authentic Antarctic setting.

* * *

NELSON, Lawrence Emerson 1893-

PERSONAL: Born July 25, 1893, in Clinton, Mo,; son of Thomas Lee (a lawyer) and Mary Ellen (Cowan) Nelson: married Rosalie Stamper, 1916; children: Beatric Marcella (Mrs. C. J. McLellan; deceased), Theron Francis, Thelma Yvonne (Mrs. Richard C. Sheere). *Education:* William Jewell College, A.B., 1915; University of Kansas, A.M.,

1921; Stanford University, Ph.D., 1930; attended summer sessions at University of Wisconsin, University of Minnesota, University of Missouri. *Religion:* Baptist. *Home:* 811 North University St., Redlands, Calif. *Office:* California Baptist College, 8432 Magnolia Ave., Riverside, Calif.

CAREER: Sioux Falls College, Sioux Falls, S.D., professor of English, 1918-25; University of Redlands, Redlands, Calif., professor of English, 1925-61, director of Division of Languages and Literature, 1942-52, director of graduate studies, 1942-46, 1952-58, dean of graduate studies, 1958-61; California Baptist College, Riverside, professor of English, 1961-70 chairman of Division of Humanities, 1961-65; director of Book of Life Museum, 1973——. Western Association of Schools and Colleges, chairman of accrediting committee, 1945-51; California State Board of Education, member of accrediting committee, 1960-64. *Member:* Writers Round Table (president, 1943-48), Round Table International (president, 1966-67), P.E.N. International, California Writers Guild (board; president, 1964-66).

WRITINGS: The Purple Feather (verse), privately printed, 1925; *Dreamer's Gold* (verse), privately printed, 1930; *Gypsy Scarlet* (verse), privately printed, 1936; *Our Roving Bible*, Abingdon, 1946; (with Walter Wallbank) *Studying Civilization*, two volumes, Scott, 1949; *Redlands: Biography of a College*, University of Redlands Press, 1958; *Only One Redlands*, Inland Printers, 1961; *Trademarks*, California Baptist College Press, 1965; *Ships Show Biblical Influence*, California Baptist College Press, 1966; *Rivers Show Biblical Influence*, California Baptist College Press, 1967; *Medicines Show Biblical Influence*, California Baptist College Press, 1968; (with Olie T. Brown) *It's a Great Day*, California Baptist College Press, 1970. Writer of articles and humor.

WORK IN PROGRESS: A series of monographs showing influence of the Bible on a wide range of interests, to supplement exhibits in the Book of Life Classroom Building at California Baptist College.

* * *

NELSON, Roy Paul 1923-

PERSONAL: Born June 17, 1923, in Portland, Ore.; son of Roy P. (a crane operator) and Esther F. Nelson; married Marie Helen Frazier, February 24, 1951; children: Chris Marie, Robin Rood, Tracy Joan, Bryan James. *Education:* Attended University of Southern California, 1943-44; University of Oregon, B.S., 1947, M.S., 1955; also studied at Art Center School, Los Angeles, Calif., 1947-48. *Politics:* Democrat. *Religion:* Protestant. *Office:* School of Journalism, University of Oregon, Eugene, Ore.

CAREER: McCann-Erickson, Portland, Ore., copywriter, 1947; United Press, reporter in Salt Lake City, Utah, 1948-49; American Forest Products Industries, Washington, D.C., assistant editorial director, 1949-53, district manager, San Francisco, Calif., 1954-55; University of Oregon, Eugene, 1955——, associate professor 1962-68, professor of journalism, 1968——. Graphic design consultant; free-lance cartoonist. *Military service:* U.S. Naval Reserve, 1944-47; became lieutenant junior grade.

WRITINGS: Fell's Guide to the Art of Cartooning, Fell, 1962; (with Byron Ferris) *Fell's Guide to Commercial Art*, Fell, 1966; *The Design of Advertising*, W. C. Brown, 1967; 2nd edition, 1973; (with John L. Hulteng) *The Fourth Estate*, Harper, 1971; *Publication Design*, W. C. Brown, 1972. Contributor of articles and reviews to journalism journals and general magazines.

WORK IN PROGRESS: The Life and Times of Homer Davenport; and *The Cartoonist's World.*

* * *

NETBOY, Anthony 1906-

PERSONAL: Born April 5, 1906, in Poland; came to U.S., 1909, naturalized citizen, 1930; son of Isaac (a merchant) and Ida (Perlman) Netboy; married Gladys Sheckett, September 5, 1931 (deceased); married Elizabeth B. Silsby, August 17, 1959; children: Nancy, Jane. *Education:* Northwestern University, B.Sc., 1926; Columbia University, M.A., 1928; Harvard University, graduate study, 1928-31. *Home address:* Box 420, Jacksonville, Ore. 07530.

CAREER: Free-lance writer and editor, 1937-42; U.S. government, writer in various federal agencies in Washington, D.C., 1942-52, and with Bonneville Power Administration, 1952-56; Portland State College (now University), Portland Continuation Center, Portland, Ore., associate professor of English, 1956-71. Director of Pacific Northwest Writers Institute, 1958, 1959, 1960, and 1966; executive secretary of Oregon State Legislature Interim Committee on Natural Resources, 1959-60. Centennial Award Lecturer, Atlantic Salmon Association, 1969; lecturer at British universities under Atlantic Salmon Trust, 1971. *Member:* British Salmon and Trout Association, Atlantic Salmon Association, National Audubon Society, American Fisheries Society, Sierra Club. *Awards, honors:* Conservation Foundation grant to study Atlantic salmon in Europe; International Atlantic Salmon Foundation grant to study salmon in Japan.

WRITINGS: (With James E. Gillespie) *Europe in Perspective*, Harcourt, 1942; (with Wayland J. Hayes) *The Small Community Looks Ahead*, Harcourt, 1947; (with Bernard Frank) *Water, Land and People*, Knopf, 1950; *Salmon of the Pacific Northwest*, Binfords, 1958; (editor) *The Pacific Northwest*, Doubleday, 1963; *The Atlantic Salmon: A Vanishing Species?*, Houghton, 1968; *The Salmon: Their Fight for Survival*, Houghton, 1973. Contributor to conservation, outdoor, and general magazines on environmental and ecological subjects, and articles on fisheries to British and French magazines. Editorial consultant, Oregon Fish Commission.

WORK IN PROGRESS: Two books, *Salmon: The World's Most Harassed Fishes*, and *The Tragedy of Industrial Man and His Coming End.*

* * *

NETTL, Bruno 1930-

PERSONAL: Born March 14, 1930, in Prague, Czechoslovakia; son of Paul (a musicologist) and Gertrud (Hutter) Nettl; married Wanda White, September 15, 1952; children: Rebecca, Gloria. *Education:* Inidana University, A.B., 1950, Ph.D., 1953; University of Michigan, M.A.L.S., 1960. *Home:* 1423 Cambridge Dr., Champaign, Ill. 61820. *Office:* School of Music, University of Illinois, Urbana, Ill. 61803.

CAREER: Wayne State University, Detroit, Mich., teacher of musicology and music librarian, 1953-64; University of Illinois, Urbana, associate professor of music, 1964-67, professor of music and anthropology, 1967——. University of Kiel, Kiel, Germany, visiting lecturer in musicology, 1956-58. *Member:* American Musicological Society (member of council, 1965——), Society for Ethnomusicology (member of executive board, 1959-61; president, 1969-71).

WRITINGS: North American Indian Musical Styles, American Folklore Society, 1954; *Music in Primitive Culture,* Harvard University Press, 1956; *Introduction to Folk Music in the United States,* Wayne State University Press, 1960; *Cheremis Musical Styles,* Indiana University Press, 1960; *Theory and Method in Ethnomusicology,* Free Press of Glencoe, 1964; *Folk and Traditional Music of the Western Continents,* Prentice-Hall, 1965, 2nd edition, 1972; *Daramad of Chaharaah: A Study of Persian Music,* Information Coordinators, 1972; (with Charles Hamm and Ronald Byrnside) *Contemporary Music and Music Cultures,* Prentice-Hall, 1974. Contributor to musicology and anthropology journals. Editor, *Ethnomusicology,* 1962-66; editor, *Yearbook,* of the International Folk Music Council, 1975—.

WORK IN PROGRESS: Research on American Indian music and music of Iran; community studies in traditional music cultures.

AVOCATIONAL INTERESTS: Low-stakes poker games.

* * *

NETZER, Lanore A. 1916-

PERSONAL: Born August 27, 1916, in Laona, Wis.; daughter of Henry N. and Julia (Niquette) Netzer. *Education:* Oconto County Normal School, diploma, 1935; Oshkosh State College, B.S., 1943; University of Wisconsin, M.S., 1948, Ph.D., 1951. *Home:* 3009 University Ave., #602, Madison, Wis. 53705. *Office:* Department of Educational Administration, University of Wisconsin, 1282 Education Science Bldg. I, 1025 West Johnson St., Madison, Wis. 53706.

CAREER: Teacher and teaching principal in Wisconsin public schools, 1935-46; instructor in Wisconsin State teacher's colleges, 1946-48, 1950-56; University of Wisconsin, associate professor of education, Milwaukee Campus, 1956-63, professor of educational administration, Madison Campus, 1963—. *Member:* Association for Supervision and Curriculum Development, National Education Association, American Educational Research Association, and Wisconsin branches of those organizations; American Association of School Administrators, American Association of Univeristy Professors, Association for Student Teaching, Phi Beta Sigma, Kappa Delta Pi, Pi Lambda Theta, Phi Delta Kappa.

WRITINGS: The Use of Industry Aids in Schools, Bruce, 1952; (with Glen G. Eye) *Supervision of Instruction: A Phase of Administration,* Harper, 1965, *Interdisciplinary Foundations of Supervision Administration,* Allyn & Bacon, 1970; (with Eye and others) *Education, Administration, and Change: The Redeployment of Resources,* Harper, 1970; *Strategies of Instructional Management,* Allyn & Bacon, 1975. Contributor to educational journals.

WORK IN PROGRESS: The Art of Using Supervision and Manual for Self-Directed Analysis: Early Teaching Experiences, with others, completion expected in 1976.

* * *

NEUGEBOREN, Jay 1938-

PERSONAL: Surname is pronounced New-ge-born; born May 30, 1938, in Brooklyn, N.Y.; son of David (a salesman) and Anne (a registered nurse; maiden name, Nassofer) Neugeboren; married Betsey Bendorf (a painter), June 7, 1964. *Education:* Columbia University, B.A., 1959; Indiana University, M.A., 1963. *Religion:* Jewish. *Home:*

252 River Dr., North Hadley, Me. 01035. *Agent:* Martha Winston, Curtis Brown Ltd., 60 East 56th St., New York, N.Y. 10022.

CAREER: General Motors Corp., Indianapolis, Ind., junior executive, 1960; Columbia University, New York, N.Y., preceptor in English, 1964-66; Stanford University, Stanford, Calif., lecturer in English, 1966—. *Member:* P.E.N., Phi Beta Kappa. *Awards, honors:* Fellowship in fiction to Bread Loaf Writers' Conference, 1966 Transatlantic Review Novella Award, 1967; National Endowment for Arts fellowship, 1972-73.

WRITINGS: Big Man (novel), Houghton, 1966; *Listen Ruben Fontanez* (novel), Houghton, 1968; *Corky's Brother* (stories), Farrar, Straus, 1969; *Parentheses: An Autobiographical Journey* (non-fiction), Dutton, 1970; *Sam's Legacy* (novel), Holt, 1974. Story included in *Best American Short Stories of 1965* and *Prize Stories: The O. Henry Awards,* 1968. Contributor of articles and stories to periodicals.

WORK IN PROGRESS: The Orphan's Tale, a novel publication by Holt expected in 1976.

* * *

NEVIN, Evelyn C. 1910-

PERSONAL: Born February 22, 1910, in Council Bluffs, Iowa; daughter of Benjamin Franklin and Nellie (Dorton) Cook; married John H. Nevin (deceased); married William B. Ferguson, April 9, 1954. *Education:* Attended Washington State University, 1929-33, and New York University, 1949. *Address:* Route 3, Box 1074, Rainier, Ore. 67048.

CAREER: Curtis Publishing Co., Philadelphia, Pa., associate editor of *Jack and Jill,* 1945-46; Westminster Press, Philadelphia, Pa., editor of *Stories* and *Trailblazer* (both children's publications), 1950-61; now free-lance writer. *Member:* Euradelphian Literary Society, Kappa Kappa Gamma.

WRITINGS: Lost Children of the Shoshones, Westminster, 1946; *Sign of the Anchor,* Westminster, 1947; *Underground Escape,* Westminster, 1949; *Captive of the Delawares,* Abingdon, 1952; *The River Spirit and the Mountain Demons,* Van Nostrand, 1965; *The Extraordinary Adventures of CheeChee McNerney,* Four Winds Press, 1971. Contributor to *Stories to Remember,* Lyons & Carnahan, 1951-53; contributor of short stories and serials to *Jack and Jill.*

SIDELIGHTS: Several of Mrs. Nevin's books have been translated into German.

* * *

NEVIUS, Blake (Reynolds) 1916-

PERSONAL: Born February 12, 1916, in Winona, Minn.; son of Blake Reynolds (an insurance man) and Helena (McLean) Nevius. *Education:* Antioch College, B.A., 1938; University of Chicago, M.A., 1941, Ph.D., 1947. *Politics:* Democrat. *Religion:* Episcopalian. *Home:* 4009 Woodcliff Rd., Sherman Oaks, Calif. 91403. *Office:* Department of English, University of California, Los Angeles, Calif. 90024.

CAREER: University of California, Los Angeles, 1947—, started as instructor, professor of English, 1961—. Fulbright lecturer in Germany, 1953-54. Advisor, West Humanities Center, National Endowment for Humanities,

1972. *Military service:* U.S. Army, Counter Intelligence Corps, 1942-45; became first lieutenant; received Bronze Star. *Member:* Modern Language Association of America, International Association of University Professors of English (treasurer, 1971-74), Philological Association of the Pacific Coast. *Awards, honors:* Guggenheim fellowship, 1962-63; Humanities Institute award, University of California, 1967, 1971.

WRITINGS: Edith Wharton: A Study of Her Fiction, University of California Press, 1953; *Robert Herrick: The Development of a Novelist,* University of California Press, 1962 (co-editor) *Dickens Centennial Essays,* University of California Press, 1971; (editor) Edith Wharton, *Ethan Frome,* Scribner, 1968; (editor) *The American Novel: Sinclair Lewis to the Present,* Appleton, 1970; (contributor) *Columbia Essays on Modern Writers,* Columbia University Press, 1970; *Ivy Compton-Burnett,* Columbia University Press, 1970; (contributor) *Studies Presented to Tauno Mustanoja, Neuphilol,* Mitt, 1972. *Nineteenth-Century Fiction,* editor, 1965-71, senior advisory editor, 1971—.

WORK IN PROGRESS: A monograph, *Cooper's Landscapes: An Essay on Romantic Art,* a study of the influence of the tradition of Italian and French landscape painting, theories of the picturesque, and landscape gardening on James Fenimore Cooper's settings.

SIDELIGHTS: Nevius is competent in French and German. *Avocational interests:* Gardening, back-packing, and trout fishing.†

* * *

NEWBY, I(dus) A. 1931-

PERSONAL: Born October 3, 1931, in Hawkinsville, Ga.; son of I. A. and Nomie Bell (Floyd) Newby. *Education:* Georgia Southern College, B.S., 1951; University of South Carolina, M.A., 1957; University of California, Los Angeles, Ph.D., 1962. *Politics:* Democrat. *Home:* 2533 Ala Wai Blvd., Honolulu, Hawaii 96815. *Office:* Department of History, University of Hawaii, Honolulu, Hawaii.

CAREER: Member of history faculty at Western Washington State College, Bellingham, 1962-63, and California State College (now University), Fullerton, 1963-66; University of Hawaii, Honolulu, associate professor, 1966-70, professor of history, 1970—. *Military service:* U.S. Air Force, 1951-55. *Member:* American Historical Association, Organization of American Historians, Southern Historical Association, Association for the Study of Negro Life and History.

WRITINGS: Jim Crow's Defense, Louisiana State University Press, 1965; *Challenge to the Court: Social Scientists and the Defense of Segregation, 1954-1966,* Louisiana State University Press, 1967, revised edition, 1969; (editor) *The Development of Segregationist Thought,* Dorsey, 1968; (compiler) *The Civil War and Reconstruction, 1850-1877,* Appleton, 1971; *Black Carolinians: A History of Blacks in South Carolina from 1895-1968,* University of South Carolina Press, 1973.†

* * *

NEWCOMB, Franc(es Lynette) J(ohnson) 1887-

PERSONAL: Born March 30, 1887, in Greenfield, Wis.; daughter of Frank Lewis (an architect) and Priscilla Taft (Woodard) Johnson; married Arthur J. Newcomb (an Indian trader), June 30, 1914 (deceased); children: Priscilla Ann (Mrs. William C. Thompson), Lynette Eloise (Mrs.

Joe Bertrem Wilson). *Education:* Attended public schools and teacher training school in Wisconsin. *Politics:* Independent. *Religion:* Episcopalian. *Home:* 1123 Las Lomas Rd., N.W., Albuquerque, N.M.

CAREER: Collector of Navajo sand-painting sketches and writer on Navajo lore. Lived for almost twenty-five years on the Navajo reservation in New Mexico, where her husband operated the Blue Mesa Trading Post; sketched five hundred Navajo sand paintings by memorizing the details on visits to ceremonial hogans (paper, pencil, and camera were banned), assembling the largest collection of sand paintings sketched by a single person. Leader in drive to establish Visiting Nursing Service in Albuquerque in the forties, and active in Indian welfare organizations. *Member:* American Folklore Society, P.E.O. Sisterhood, Albuquerque Woman's Club. *Awards, honors:* Woman of the Year, National League of American Pen Women, 1964.

WRITINGS: (With Gladys A. Reichard) *Sand-Paintings of the Shooting Chant,* J. J. Augustine (Berlin), 1937; *Navajo Omens and Taboos,* Rydal, 1940; (with Stanley Fishler and Mary Cabot Wheelwright) *A Study of Navajo Symbolism,* Cambridge University Press, 1956; *Hosteen Klah, Navajo Medicine Man and Sand-Painter,* University of Oklahoma Press, 1964; *Navajo Neighbors,* University of Oklahoma Press, 1966; *Navaho Folk Tales,* Museum of Navaho Ceremonial Art, 1967; *Navajo Bird Tales Told by Hosteen Clah Chee,* Theosophical Publishing House, 1970. Contributor of Navajo tales and articles on Indian life to periodicals.

WORK IN PROGRESS: Writing on Navajo medicinal herbs and magic medicines and on the history of Navajo rites.

SIDELIGHTS: Franc Newcomb's notes appear on the slipcase for the phonodisc of *Navajo Bird Tales* issued by Caedmon, 1972. Ms. Newcomb understands and speaks "fairly intelligible" Navajo.†

* * *

NEWCOMB, Wilburn Wendell 1935-

PERSONAL: Born July 1, 1935, in St. Louis, Mo.; son of Wilburn (an electrician) and Mary (Cutchin) Newcomb; married Ruth Moeller, February 5, 1956; children: Karen Ruth, Emily Rose, Suzanne. *Education:* Cincinnati Conservatory of Music, B.Mus. (honors), 1957; Indiana University, M.A., 1960; University of Goettingen, Ph.D. (magna cum laude), 1965. *Office:* Music Building, Pennsylvania State University, University Park, Pa. 16802.

CAREER: Tennessee Polytechnic Institute, Cookeville, assistant professor of German, 1962-63; Pennsylvania State University, University Park, assistant professor of German, 1963-65, assistant professor of musicology, 1965—. Lecturer in music history and instructor in recorder, adult education program, State College, Pa. *Member:* American Musicological Society, Deutsche Musikforschungs-Gesellschaft, International Musicological Society, Music Library Association, American Recorder Society, Lute Society of London, Pi Kappa Lambda, Delta Phi Alpha. *Awards, honors:* Fulbright award, 1960-62; German Government exchange award, 1964; research grant, Pennsylvania State University, 1965.

WRITINGS: (Contributor) *Musik in Geschichte und Gegenwart,* Baerenreiter Verlag, 1964; (editor and translator of German texts) *Renaissance Lieder,* Pennsylvania State University Press, 1964; (editor) William Barley, *Lute Music of Shakespeare's Time*, Pennsylvania State University Press, 1966; *Studien zur englischen Lautenpraxis im elisabethanischen Zeitalter* (Ph.D. dissertation), Baerenreiter Verlag, 1968. Translator of texts for Schwann Verlag's series, "Klangarchiv fuer Kirchenmusik." Associate editor, "Pennsylvania State Music Series."

AVOCATIONAL INTERESTS: Tennis.†

* * *

NEWMAN, Barclay M., Jr. 1931-

PERSONAL: Born February 22, 1931, in Princeton, W.Va.; son of Barclay M. (a biologist) and Lillie Mae (Whitman) Newman; married Jean Butler, May 30, 1953; children: Tina, Dana. *Education:* Union University, Jackson, Tenn., B.A., 1953; Southern Baptist Theological Seminary, B.D., 1956, Ph.D., 1960; also studied at Hebrew Union Jewish School of Religion, fall, 1958, Summer Institute of Linguistics, University of Oklahoma, 1960, and Hartford Seminary Foundation, fall, 1966. *Office:* American Bible Society, 1865 Broadway, New York, N.Y. 10023.

CAREER: Baptist clergyman. William Jewell College, Liberty, Mo., assistant professor of religion, 1960-63, associate professor of religion and Greek, 1963-66; American Bible Society, New York, N.Y., overseas translations consultant, 1966—. Member, Board of Trustees of Malaysia-Singapore Baptist Theological Seminary. *Member:* Society of Biblical Literature, Baptist Professors of Religion.

WRITINGS: The Meaning of the New Testament, Broadman, 1966; *Rediscovering the Book of Revelation*, Judson Press, 1968; *Concise Greek-English Dictionary*, United Bible Societies, 1971; (with Eugene A. Nida) *A Translator's Handbook on Acts*, United Bible Societies, 1972; (contributor) Claude A. Frazier, editor, *Should Preachers Play God?*, Independence Press, 1973; (with Nida) *A Translator's Handbook on Romans*, United Bible Societies, 1973; (contributor) *Commentary on Genesis*, Broadman Press, 1973; (with Nida) *A Translator's Handbook on the Gospel of John*, United Bible Societies, 1975. Contibutor to *New Testament Studies* (journal published by Cambridge University Press).

WORK IN PROGRESS: With Nida, *A Translator's Handbook on Matthew.*

SIDELIGHTS: Newman is competent in Greek, Hebrew, German; in a lesser degree, French, Latin, Arabic; studying Indonesian and Tagalog.

* * *

NEWMAN, Peter (Kenneth) 1928-

PERSONAL: Born October 5, 1928, in Mitcham, England; son of Charles Francis (a corn merchant) and Harriet (Newbold) Newman; married Genevieve Iris Turnac, April 4, 1953; children: Jean Ellen, John Lincoln, Kenneth Richard, Alan Peter.*Education:* University of London, B.Sc., 1949, M.Sc., 1951, D.Sc., 1962; Oxford University, postgraduate study, 1951-52. *Office:* Johns Hopkins University, Baltimore, Md.

CAREER: Stanford University, Stanford, Calif., research associate, 1952-53; Oxford University, Oxford, England, assistant research officer, Institute of Statistics, 1953-54; British Admiralty, Department of Operational Research, scientific officer, 1954-55; United Nations Technical Assistance Administration, Ceylon, economist, 1956-57; University of West Indies, Jamaica, senior lecturer in economics,

1957-61; University of Michigan, Ann Arbor, professor of economics, 1961-63; United Nations Technical Assistance Administration, East Africa, economic adviser, 1963-64; Robert Nathan Associates, Washington, D.C., senior associate, Costa Rica, 1965-66; Johns Hopkins University, Baltimore, Md., visiting lecturer, 1961, visiting professor of political economy, 1964-65, professor of political economy, 1966—. Consultant at various times to U.S., British, and Jamaican Governments. *Member:* Royal Economic Society, American Economic Association, Econometric Society.

WRITINGS: (With D. C. Hague) *Costs in Alternative Locations*, Cambridge University Press, 1952; *Studies in the Import Structure of Ceylon*, Government Printer (Ceylon), 1958; *British Guiana: Problems of Cohesion in an Immigrant Society*, Oxford University Press, 1964; *The Theory of Exchange*, Prentice-Hall, 1965; *Malaria Eradication and Population Growth*, School of Public Health, University of Michigan, 1965. Contributor of about thirty articles to economic and mathematics journals.

WORK IN PROGRESS: Allocation and Prices.

SIDELIGHTS: Newman speaks Spanish, French, some Italian.

* * *

NEWMAN, Philip L(ee) 1931-

PERSONAL: Born December 17, 1931, in Eugene, Ore.; son of Delmar J. and Loretta (Suver) Newman; married Jean-Ann McGee; children: Wendy, Renee, Charles. *Education:* University of Oregon, B.A., 1953; University of Washington, Seattle, M.A., 1957, Ph.D., 1962. *Office:* Department of Anthropology, University of California, Los Angeles, Calif. 90024.

CAREER: University of California, Los Angeles, assistant professor, 1961-65, associate professor of anthropology, 1965—. Ethnographic field work in highlands of New Guinea, 1959, 1964. *Military service:* U.S. Army, 1953-55. *Member:* American Anthropological Association. *Awards, honors:* Ogden Mills fellow, American Museum of Natural History, 1960.

WRITINGS: Knowing the Gururumba, Holt, 1965.†

* * *

NEWMARK, Leonard 1929-

PERSONAL: Born April 8, 1929, in Attica, Ind.; son of Max J. (a businessman) and Sophie (Glusker) Newmark; married Ruth Broessler, September 16, 1951; children: Katya, Mark. *Education:* University of Chicago, A.B., 1947; Indiana University,M.A., 1951, Ph.D., 1955. *Home:* 2643 St. Tropez, La Jolla, Calif.

CAREER: Ohio State University, Columbus, instructor in English, 1954-57, assistant professor, 1957-61, associate professor of linguistics, 1961-62; Indiana University, Bloomington, associate professor of linguistics, 1962-63; University of California, San Diego, professor of linguistics, 1963—, and chairman of department, 1963-72. University of Michigan, visiting associate professor, summer 1960. *Member:* Linguistic Society of America, Modern Language Association of America. *Awards, honors:* Grants from Social Science Research Council, 1951, 1953, American Philosophical Society, 1957, and National Science Foundation, 1963.

WRITINGS: (With I. Haznedari) *Spoken Albanian*,

[Bloomington], 1954; *Structural Grammar of Albanian*, Indiana University Research Center in Anthropology, Folklore, and Linguistics, 1957; (with M. Bloomfield) *A Linguistic Introduction to the History of English*, Knopf, 1963; (with J. Mintz and J. Lawson) *Using American English*, Harper, 1964.

WORK IN PROGRESS: Book on foreign language learning.

SIDELIGHTS: Newmark is competent in Dutch, French Albanian, and German. *Avocational interests:* Playing the recorder, chess.

* * *

NEWQUIST, Jerreld L. 1919-

PERSONAL: Born July 10, 1919, in Pendleton, Ore.; son of Oscar Peter and Martha (Guderian) Newquist; married Marie A. Stitt, June 27, 1941; children: Dianne, Shirley, Bonnie, Jerry, Randy, Ronnie. *Education:* Northwestern School of Commerce, Portland, Ore., graduate, 1939. *Religion:* Church of Jesus Christ of Latter-day Saints. *Home:* 3624 56th Ave. S.W., Seattle, Wash. 98116.

CAREER: Wagner Electric Corp., Portland, Ore., secretary, 1939-42; United Air Lines, Seattle, Wash., captain, 1945—. *Military service:* U.S. Army Air Forces, 1942-45; became major; received Air Medal with five clusters and Distinguished Flying Cross. *Member:* Air Line Pilots Association.

WRITINGS: Gospel Truth, Volume I, Zion Book Store (Salt Lake City), 1957, revised edition, Deseret, 1974, Volume II, Deseret, 1974; *Prophets, Principles and National Survival*, Publishers Press, 1964; (compiler) *An Enemy Hath Done This*, Parliament Publishers, 1969; (compiler) *God, Family, and Country*, Deseret, 1974. Articles in Mormon periodicals.

AVOCATIONAL INTERESTS: Political science, economics, religion, American history, golf, target shooting, camping, and hiking.

* * *

NG, Larry K. Y. 1940-

PERSONAL: Surname is pronounced Ing; born August 6, 1940, in Singapore; son of Khuan Seak (a goldsmith) and Poh Hiang (Tan) Ng. *Education:* Stanford University, A.B., 1961; Columbia University, M.D., 1965. *Religion:* Methodist. *Home:* 1627 21st St. N.W., Washington, D.C. *Office:* National Institutes of Health, 9000 Rockville Pike, Bethesda, Md. 20010.

CAREER: Mount Sinai Hospital, Los Angeles, Calif., intern, 1965-66; University of Pennsylvania, Philadelphia, resident in neurology, 1966-69; National Institutes of Health, Bethesda, Md., neurologist with National Institute of Mental Health, 1969-72, with National Institute on Drug Abuse, 1972—. *Member:* Society of Biological Psychiatry, World Academy of Art and Science, World-Man Fund (president), Phi Beta Kappa. *Awards, honors:* S. Weir Mitchell Award from American Academy of Neurology, 1971; A. E. Bennett Award, from Society of Biological Psychiatry, 1972; award for research in acupuncture from American Society of Chinese Medicine, 1975.

WRITINGS: (Associate editor) *The Population Crisis and Use of World Resources*, Indiana University Press, 1964; (editor) *The Population Crisis: Implications and Plans for Action*, Indiana University Press, 1965; (editor) *Alternatives to Violence: A Stimulus to Dialogue*, Time-Life, 1968.

NICHOL, John Thomas 1928-

PERSONAL: Surname originally Nykiel; born January 3, 1928, in Dorchester, Mass.; son of John (a minister) and Felixa (Kosmaciewski) Nykiel; married Dorothy Marie Jashinsky, August 30, 1952; children: Jonathan Mark, Jacqueline Carol. *Education:* Gordon College, A.B., 1949; Boston University, A.M., 1953, Ph.D., 1965; Harvard University, S.T.B., 1953, S.T.M., 1954. *Politics:* Independent. *Religion:* Protestant. *Home:* 17 Berry Wood Lane, Beverly, Mass. 01915. *Office:* Bentley College, Beaver and Forest Sts., Waltham, Mass. 02154.

CAREER: Precision Metal Products, Inc., Dorchester, Mass., director of sales and promotion, 1949-54; Gordon College, Wenham, Mass., associate professor, Division of Humanities, 1954-60; New England College of Pharmacy, associate professor of English and speech, 1960-62; Bentley College, Waltham, Mass, professor of history, 1962-1970, vice president for academic affairs and dean of faculties, 1971—. *Member:* American Historical Association, Organization of American Historians.

WRITINGS: Pentecostalism, Harper, 1966.

WORK IN PROGRESS: Business and Religion: The Great Divorce; History of Christianity in Poland, completion expected in 1976.

SIDELIGHTS: Nichol reads and speaks Polish; he reads French, German, Greek, and Latin. He is concerned with relating liberal education to professional educational programs and with "examining the problems that confront the religious person who must function in the world of business."

* * *

NICHOLLS, (C. G.) William 1921-

PERSONAL: Born October 10, 1921, in England; son of A. Charles (a barrister) and Kathleen (Thornton) Nicholls; married Hilary McCallum, July 15, 1950; children: Elizabeth H., Paul C. A., Felicity K. M. *Education:* St. John's College, Cambridge, B.A., 1947, M.A., 1949; studied at Wells Theological College, 1951-52. *Politics:* New Democratic Party. *Office:* Department of Religious Studies, University of British Columbia, Vancouver, British Columbia, Canada V0T 1WT.

CAREER: Priest of Anglican Church of Canada. World Student Christian Federation, Geneva, Switzerland, traveling secretary, 1949-51; chaplain to Anglican students, Edinburgh, Scotland, 1955-60; St. John's College, University of Manitoba, Winnipeg, associate professor of systematic theology, 1960-61; University of British Columbia, Vancouver, professor of religious studies, 1961—, head of department, 1964—. *Military service:* British Army, 1941-45; became captain. *Member:* Canadian Society for the Study of Religion, John Howard Society (Vancouver; member of board, 1964-66). *Awards, honors:* Norrisian Prize, Cambridge University, 1950, for manuscript of *Ecumenism and Catholicity*.

WRITINGS: Ecumenism and Catholicity, S.C.M. Press, 1952; *Revelation in Christ*, S.C.M. Press, 1958; *Jacob's Ladder: The Meaning of Worship*, Lutterworth, 1958; *Joining in Common Prayer*, British Council of Churches, c. 1964; (editor) *Conflicting Images of Man*, Seabury, 1966; *Systematic and Philosophical Theology*, Penguin, 1969; (with Ian Kent) *I AMness: The Discovery of the Self beyond the Ego*, Bobbs-Merrill, 1972. Editor-in-chief, *Studies in Religion*, University of Toronto Press, 1970-73. Columnist, *Saturday Night* (Toronto), 1963-72, and contributing editor, 1966-72.

WORK IN PROGRESS: Further work on self-discovery through religion and psychiatry; Christian mysticism in the context of psychiatry and world religion.

*   *   *

NICHTERN, Sol 1920-

PERSONAL: Born January 4, 1920, in New York, N.Y.; son of Morris B. and May (Goldman) Nichtern; married Claire Joseph (a theatrical producer), June 4, 1944 (divorced); children: Judith (Mrs. Harry Bird), David. *Education:* New York University, B.A., 1939; Chicago Medical School, M.D., 1943. *Home:* 61 West Ninth St., New York, N.Y. 10011.

CAREER: Private practice of medicine, 1946-64. West Nassau Mental Health Center, Nassau County, N.Y., psychiatric director, 1958-60; League School, New York, N.Y., psychiatric director, 1960-63; Hillside Hospital, New York, N.Y., director of department of child and adolescent psychiatry, 1964—. New York Council on Child Psychiatry, president, 1964-65. *Military service:* U.S. Army, World War II; became captain. *Member:* American Medical Association, American Psychiatric Association, American Orthopsychiatric Association, American Association for the Advancement of Science, New York State Medical Society. *Awards, honors:* Mental Health Service Award, American Psychiatric Association, 1965.

WRITINGS: (Contributor) *Clinical Studies in Culture Conflict*, Ronald, 1958; (contributor) *Child Psychiatry and the General Practitioner*, C. C Thomas, 1962; (with George T. Donahue) *Education and Rehabilitation of Childhood Schizophrenics*, [Elmont, N.Y.], 1963; (with Donahue) *Teaching the Troubled Child*, Free Press, 1965 (editor) *Mental Health Services for Adolescents*, Praeger, 1968; *Helping the Retarded Child*, Grosset, 1974. Contributor of chapters to three books, and more than a dozen articles to scientific journals.†

*   *   *

NIKELLY, Arthur G(eorge) 1927-

PERSONAL: Born April 7, 1927, in Evanston, Ill.; son of George and Mary (Kolettis) Nikelly. *Education:* Roosevelt University, B.A., 1954, M.A., 1955; University of Ottawa, Ottawa, Ontario, Ph.D., 1959. *Religion:* Greek Orthodox. *Office:* University of Illinois Health Service, 1109 South Lincoln Ave., Urbana, Ill. 61801.

CAREER: Jacksonville State Hospital, Jacksonville, Ill., staff psychologist, 1955-56; University of Illinois Health Service, Urbana, clinical psychologist, 1959—, assistant professor of health science, 1959-67, associate professor, 1967—. Peace Corps field assessment officer, summers, 1962-64. *Military service:* U.S. Army, 1950-52. *Member:* American Psychological Association, American Society of Adlerian Psychology, Illinois Psychological Association.

WRITINGS: Mental Health for Students: A Guide for Adjusting to College, C. C Thomas, 1966. Contributor of articles to psychiatric and health journals.

WORK IN PROGRESS: A book, tentatively titled *Achieving Competence and Self-fulfillment*, for Brooks, Cole.

NIMS, Charles F(rancis) 1906-

PERSONAL: Born October 18, 1906, in Norwalk, Ohio; son of Joel Benjamin (an accountant) and Grace (Wildman) Nims; married Myrtle Keillor, April 18, 1931. *Education:* Attended University of Toledo, 1924-25; Alma College, A.B., 1928; McCormick Theological Seminary, B.D., 1931; University of Chicago, Ph.D., 1937. *Home:* 5540 South Blackstone Ave., Chicago, Ill. 60637. *Office:* Oriental Institute, University of Chicago, Chicago, Ill. 60637.

CAREER: Ordained Presbyterian minister, 1931; University of Chicago, Chicago, Ill., research assistant, Oriental Institute, 1934-40; pastor in Eldorado, Ill., 1940-43; University of Chicago, research associate, Oriental Institute, 1946-67, associate professor, 1967-70, professor, 1970-72, professor emeritus, 1972—. Field director of Epigraphic Survey, Chicago House, Luxor, United Arab Republic, 1964-72. UNESCO-United Arab Republic Abu Simbel Project, consultant, 1956. *Military service:* U.S. Army, chaplain, 1943-46; became major. *Member:* American Oriental Society, Society of Biblical Literature, Egypt Exploration Society, American Schools of Oriental Research, American Research Center in Egypt, Foundation Egyptologique Reine Elisabeth, Military Chaplains Association of the U.S.A., Photographic Society of America.

WRITINGS: (Co-author) *Mereruka*, Volumes I-II, University of Chicago Press, 1938; (co-author) *Medinet Habu*, Volumes IV-VIII, University of Chicago Press, 1940-70; (co-author) *Reliefs and Inscriptions in Karnak*, Volume III, University of Chicago Press, 1954; *Thebes of the Pharaohs*, Stein & Day, 1965. Contributor to professional journals.

WORK IN PROGRESS: Further publications of the Epigraphic Survey; *The Tomb of Kheruef.*

*   *   *

NISSENSON, Hugh 1933-

PERSONAL: Born March 10, 1933, in New York, N.Y.; son of Charles Arthur (a manufacturer) and Harriette (Dolch) Nissenson; married Marilyn Claster (an educational film producer), November 10, 1962; children: Katherine. *Education:* Swarthmore College, B.A., 1955; *Politics:* Registered Democrat. *Religion:* Jewish. *Home:* 411 West End Ave., New York, N.Y. 10024.

CAREER: Full-time free-lance writer, 1958—. *Awards, honors:* Wallace Stegner literary fellow at Stanford University, 1961-62; Edward Lewis Wallant Memorial Award for fiction, 1965.

WRITINGS: A Pile of Stones (story collection), Scribner, 1965; *Notes from the Frontier* (nonfiction), Dial, 1968; *In the Reign of Peace* (story collection), Farrar, Straus, 1972. Stories included in anthologies. Stories and articles published in *The New Yorker, Harper's, Commentary, Holiday, Esquire, Playboy, London Magazine*, and other magazines.

WORK IN PROGRESS: A novel about the immigrant experience of a Jew in New York.

SIDELIGHTS: Nissenson's particular interest is in the relationship of the contemporary Jew to his people's past and to God. He has written of the implications of this relationship for Jews living in early twentieth-century Europe, modern Israel, and America.

BIOGRAPHICAL/CRITICAL SOURCES: Carolyn Riley, editor, *Contemporary Literary Criticism*, Volume IV, Gale, 1975.

NIXON, Allan 1918-

PERSONAL: Born August 17, 1918, in Boston, Mass.; son of Arthur A. and Mary (Hobbs) Nixon; married Marie Wilson (an actress), 1942 (divorced, 1951). *Education:* Attended Kent Hills Seminary, Kent Hills, Me., and University of Richmond. *Religion:* Protestant. *Residence:* Hollywood, Calif.

CAREER: Played professional football after college and wrestled professionally; did sports announcing in Richmond, Va., and free-lance features for *Richmond Times-Dispatch;* later, as a Powers' model was signed to movie contract by Metro-Goldwyn-Mayer, and worked briefly in films before World War II service; leg-man for Hollywood columnist Jimmy Fidler, and press agent, 1946-47; returned to acting as leading man for Mae West in national touring company of "Come on Up," 1947; played other stage leads with Nancy Kelly, Gladys George, Ann Dvorak, and with John Carradine in "Tobacco Road"; starred in twelve motion pictures in the 1950s, including "Pickup," Columbia Pictures, 1951; appeared in thirty-odd other films and a hundred or more television shows; full-time writer, 1962—. *Military service:* U.S. Army Air Forces, 1942-46; became sergeant.

WRITINGS: Blessed Are the Damned, Paperback Library, 1963; *Nobody Hides Forever,* Paperback Library, 1964, published as *Star,* 1968; *The Last of Vicky,* Paperback Library, 1966; *Actor,* Paperback Library, 1968; *Malibu Pickup,* Parliament, 1968; *Bitch Goddess,* Paperback Library, 1969; *Powerman,* Avon, 1972. Also author of *Get Garrity,* Parliament, *Go for Garrity* (original title, *Garrity Three*), Avon, *Gold and Glory Guy,* Avon, *Goodnight, Garrity,* Avon, and *Scavengers* (original title, *Any Ship, Any Ocean*), Avon. Regular contributor to *Private Pilot* and *Gun World;* contributor of articles and short stories to *Coronet, Knight,* and a number of "girlie" magazines.

WORK IN PROGRESS: The first of a contracted series of paperbacks, featuring a semi-private eye.

SIDELIGHTS: Allan Nixon writes: "Studios aided my decision to become a writer by failing to call me for acting jobs. The sands had run out in that department.... I'm doing what I should have done in the first place."

* * *

NJURURI, Ngumbu 1930-

PERSONAL: Born circa December, 1930, in Kenya, East Africa; son of Maiyani and Wahito Njururi; married Nataline Wakiuru (a student), January 29, 1966; children: Wahito Mary Florence. *Education:* Studied at Adams College, Natal, South Africa, 1953-54, Balham College, London, England, 1954-55, North Western Polytechnic, London, 1955-57; law student, Lincoln's Inn, London. *Politics:* "Worked for Kenyan freedom for many years." *Religion:* Roman Catholic. *Home:* Giathugu, Igana, Githi, Nyeri, Kenya, East Africa. *Office:* 25 Hertslet Rd., London, N. 7, England.

CAREER: Free-lance journalist and law student. Representative of Kenya African National Union in United Kingdom and Europe, 1961-63. *Member:* Kenyan Students Association in United Kingdom (former general secretary; vice-president).

WRITINGS: (Compiler) *Agikuyu Folk Tales,* Oxford University Press, 1966; (compiler) *Gikuyu Proverbs,* Macmillan, 1969. Also editor of *The Burning Spear: Selected Writings and Speeches of Jomo Kenyatta,* published by Secker & Warburg, and author of *Ndai cia Agikuyu* (title means "Agikuyu Riddles"), published by Longmans, Green. Contributor of short stories to magazines in Europe.

SIDELIGHTS: Njururi has been recording (in his books) the oral traditions of the Agikuyu tribe of Kenya—stories, songs, legends, and proverbs as he learned them from his elders, retold in English. He speaks Gikuyu (his mother tongue), Swahili, Kikamba, Zulu, and English, and a little German and Italian.†

* * *

NOBLE, J(ames) Kendrick, Jr. 1928-

PERSONAL: Born October 6, 1928, in New York, N.Y.; son of James Kendrick (a publisher) and Orrel Tennant (Baldwin) Noble; married Norma Jean Rowell, June 16, 1951; children: Anne Rowell, James Kendrick III. *Education:* Attended Princeton University, 1945-46; U.S. Naval Academy, B.S., 1950; New York University, M.B.A., 1961, doctoral studies, 1962-69. *Politics:* Republican. *Religion:* Protestant. *Home:* 45 Edgewood Lane, Bronxville, N.Y. 10708. *Office:* Auerbach, Pollak & Richardson, Inc., 1 New York Plaza, New York, N.Y. 10004.

CAREER: U.S. Navy, midshipman, 1946-50, regular officer, 1950-57, currently holding rank of captain in U.S. Naval Reserve; Noble and Noble, Publishers, Inc., New York, N.Y., assistant to president, 1957-60, director of special projects, 1960-62, executive vice-president and director, 1962-67; F. Eberstadt & Co., New York, N.Y., senior publishing analyst, 1966-69; Auerbach, Pollak & Richardson, Inc., New York, N.Y., vice-president, director, and senior publishing analyst, 1969—. Vice-president of Translation Publishing Co., Eastchester, N.Y., 1957-65, and Elbon Realty Corp., Yonkers, N.Y., 1959-65; director of Space and Science Train, Inc., 1962-63, MERIT, Inc., 1963-67, and Curriculum Information Center, 1971—. Vice-president of Bolton Gardens Community Association, 1959-61.

MEMBER: American Association for the Advancement of Science (fellow), American Textbook Publishers Institute. National Institute of Social Sciences, Naval Reserve Association (vice-president of New York chapter, 1969—), American Educational Research Association, American Association of School Administrators, New York Society of Security Analysts (director, 1975—), Institute of Chartered Financial Analysts, Printing and Publishing Industry Analysts Association (president, 1969-71), Kappa Delta Pi.

WRITINGS: (With Thomas A. Hamil) *Ploob,* Noble, 1949, revised edition, 1957; (editor) *The Years Between,* Noble, 1966; (contributor) Summer N. Levine, editor, *Financial Analysts Handbook,* Dow Jones-Irwin, 1975. Editor of textbooks published by Noble. Contributor to journals. Chairman of publications panel, education committee, American Rocket Society, 1958-62.

WORK IN PROGRESS: Research in the magazine, newspaper, and book publishing industries, publishing securities, educational marketing, instructional materials, learning theory, economics, and military history.

* * *

NOGEE, Joseph Lippman 1929-

PERSONAL: Born June 16, 1929, in Schenectady, N.Y.; son of Julius (a businessman) and Lena (Engel) Nogee; married Jo Nabors, December 17, 1960; children: Leah

Brooks, Jyle Engel. *Education:* Georgetown University, B.S.F.S., 1950; University of Chicago, M.A., 1951; Yale University, Ph.D., 1958. *Religion:* Jewish. *Office:* Department of Political Science, University of Houston, Houston, Tex. 77004.

CAREER: University of Houston, Houston, Tex., assistant professor, 1958-61, associate professor, 1961-66, professor of political science, 1966—, chairman of department of political science, 1966-68, director, Russian studies program, 1974—. Visiting associate professor, New York University, 1963-64; visiting professor, Vanderbilt University, 1969-70. Carnegie Endowment for International Peace, New York, N.Y., editorial assistant, summers of 1958, 1959, 1963, 1966. *Military service:* U.S. Army, 1952-54. *Member:* American Political Science Association, (member of council, 1968-70), American Association for the Advancement of Slavic Studies. *Awards, honors:* Research grants from Rockefeller Foundation and New York University, 1963-64.

WRITINGS: Soviet Policy toward International Control of Atomic Energy, University of Notre Dame Press, 1961; (with John W. Spanier) *The Politics of Disarmament: A Study in Soviet-American Gamesmanship,* Praeger, 1962; (editor) *Man, State and Society in the Soviet Union,* Praeger, 1973. Contributor to *The New International Yearbook: A Compendium of the World's Affairs,* Funk, 1963-65, and to *International Conciliation, Vital Issues, Orbis, Journal of Conflict Resolution,* and *Annals* of the American Academy of Political and Social Science.

WORK IN PROGRESS: Soviet Foreign Policy Since World War II, for Praeger.

* * *

NOLAN, Carroll A(nthony) 1906-

PERSONAL: Born March 15, 1906, in Sharon, Pa.; son of John J. (a postmaster) and Helen Irene (Madden) Nolan; married Helen M. Sterbutcel (a public school music teacher), December 21, 1937; children: Marcia Anne. *Education:* Grove City College, B.S., 1928; University of Pittsburgh, Ed.M., 1936; New York University, Ed.D., 1944. *Home:* 152 Brookside Lane, Fayetteville, N.Y. 13066.

CAREER: High school teacher, 1928-36; Ball State Teachers College (now University), Muncie, Ind., assistant professor of business education, 1937-42; Central Connecticut State College, New Britain, associate professor of business education, 1942-44; state of Delaware, Wilmington, supervisor of business education, 1944-48; Syracuse University, Syracuse, N.Y., associate professor, 1948-52, professor of business education, 1952-72, chairman of department, 1956-72, professor emeritus, 1972—. Summer staff, School of Retailing, New York, N.Y., 1945-47; consultant to business and industry. Member of team studying vocational education in northeast United States, 1965-66. *Member:* United Business Education Association, New York State Business Education Association, Sales and Marketing Club of Central New York, Delta Pi Epsilon, Phi Delta Kappa, Pi Omega Pi.

WRITINGS: (With Edward Rowse) *Fundamentals of Advertising,* South-Western Publishing, 1950; (with John W. Wingate) *Fundamentals of Selling,* South-Western Publishing, 1957, 10th edition, 1975; (with others) *Principles and Problems of Business Education,* 3rd edition, South-Western Publishing, 1967; (with Roman F. Warmke) *Marketing, Sales Promotion, and Advertising,* 8th edition published as *Marketing in Action,* 1974. Writer of narrative for

three films for high school business education, distributed by Coronet Films. Contributor to professional magazines.

* * *

NOLTINGK, B(ernard) E(dward) 1918-

PERSONAL: Surname rhymes with "bolting"; born March 4, 1918, in Torquay, England; son of L. B. (a merchant) and May (Dick) Notingk; married Daphne Williams, October 19, 1940; children: Janet, Christopher, Bridget. *Education:* King's College, University of London, B.Sc. (first class honors), 1937, Ph.D., 1940. *Politics:* Liberal party. *Religion:* United Reformed Church. *Home:* Windwhistle, Nutcombe Lane, Dorking, Surrey, England. *Office:* Central Electricity Research Laboratories, Leatherhead, Surrey, England.

CAREER: Research Engineer with Motor Industry Research Association, Brentford, England, 1941-47, Mullard Research Laboratories, Redhill, England, 1947-52, Mining Research Establishment, Isleworth, England, 1952-55, and Tube Investments Research Laboratories, Cambridge, England, 1955-60; Central Electricity Research Laboratories, Leatherhead, Surrey, England, research engineer and head of instrumentation section, 1960—. Lay preacher, Beekeeper. *Member:* Institute of Physics (fellow), Institution of Electrical Engineers (associate), Instrument Society of America (fellow), Royal Society of Arts (fellow).

WRITINGS: (Contributor) *Technical Aspects of Sound,* Volume II, Elsevier, 1957; *The Human Element in Research Management,* Elsevier, 1959; (contributor) *Handbuch der Physik,* Springer-Verlag, 1962; *The Art of Research—A Guide for the Graduate,* Elsevier, 1965. Contributor of articles on ultrasonics, instrumentation, and other technical subjects to journals.

* * *

NORMAN, Edward Robert 1938-

PERSONAL: Born November 22, 1938, in London, England; son of Ernest Edward (an accountant) and Yvonne (Bush) Norman. *Education:* Selwyn College, Cambridge, B.A., 1961, M.A. and Ph.D., 1964. *Home:* Peterhouse, Cambridge, England.

CAREER: Cambridge University, Cambridge, England, fellow in history, Selwyn College, 1961-64, fellow and assistant lecturer in history, Jesus College, 1964-72, dean of Peterhouse, 1972—.

WRITINGS: The Catholic Church and Ireland in the Age of Rebellion, 1859-1863, Longmans, Green, 1965; *The Catholic Church and Irish Politics in the Eighteen Sixties,* Dundalgan Press, 1965; *Anti-Catholicism in Victorian England,* Unwin, 1968; *The Conscience of the State in North America,* Cambridge University Press, 1968; (with F. K. S. St. Joseph) *The Early Development of Irish Society,* Cambridge University Press, 1969; *A History of Modern Ireland,* Allen Lane, 1971; *Church and Society in Modern England,* Clarendon, in press. Editor, *Cambridge Review,* 1963-64.

BIOGRAPHICAL/CRITICAL SOURCES: Month, London, England, April, 1965.

* * *

NORMAN, John 1912-

PERSONAL: Born July 20, 1912, in Syracuse, N.Y.; son of Ernest (a foreman) and Vina (Colozzi) Norman; married

Mary Lynott (a chemist), December 28, 1948; children: Eleanor, Anne, Sheila, Kathleen. *Education:* Syracuse University, B.A., 1935, M.A., 1938; Clark University, Worcester, Mass., Ph.D., 1942. *Politics:* Democrat. *Religion:* Roman Catholic. *Home:* 94 Cooper Rd., Ridgefield, Conn. *Office:* Department of History, Pace University, Westchester, Pleasantville, N.Y.

CAREER: Air Service Command, Rome, N.Y., supervisor of instructors, 1942-43; Syracuse University, Syracuse, N.Y., assistant professor of history and culture, 1943-44; Office of Strategic Services, field representative, 1944-45, attached to U.S. delegation to United Nations at San Francisco Conference, 1945; Carnegie Institute of Technology, Pittsburgh, assistant professor of history, 1946; Chatham College, Pittsburgh, Pa., associate professor of political science and chairman of department, 1946-49; U.S. Department of State, Washington, D.C., head of Italian Section, Office of Intelligence Research, 1949, historian, 1950-53; Fairfield University, Fairfield, Conn., associate professor, 1953-58, professor of history and government, 1958-66; Pace University, Westchester Campus, Pleasantville, N.Y., professor of history and government, 1966—. Member of Fairfield Board of Finance, 1959-61; chairman, Fairfield Charter Revision Committee, 1960-61, member of town committee, Ridgefield, Conn., 1972. State fact-finder, Connecticut Board of Arbitration and Mediation. *Military service:* National Guard, 1954-56; became sergeant.

MEMBER: American Political Science Association, American Historical Association, American Academy of Political and Social Science. *Awards, honors:* Fund for International Social and Economic Education research grant to study labor and politics in North Africa, 1960; Knighthood Medal in Order of Merit of the Republic (Italy); Outstanding Educator of America, 1971.

WRITINGS: (Contributor) *Essays in Honor of George H. Blakeslee*, Clark University Press, 1949; *Edward Gibbon Wakefield: A Political Reappraisal*, New Frontiers of Fairfield University, 1963; *Labor and Politics in Libya and Arab Africa*, Bookman Associates, 1965; *Adlai Stevenson's Wartime Report on Italy*, Pace College Press, 1972. Author of movie script for "Brother Ann," filmed in Greece. Contributor of articles on Italy and Austria to *Standard International Encyclopedia Year Book* and *World Scope Encyclopedia Year Book*; articles on Libya and Tunisia to *American Encyclopedia Annual*, also contributor to *Funk and Wagnalls Encyclopedia*, and to *Encyclopedia Americana*; contributor of articles and book reveiws to scholarly journals.

SIDELIGHTS: Norman speaks French and Italian, and has traveled in most of western Europe, large parts of North Africa, and throughout the United States. *Avocational interests:* Collecting paintings and records.

*   *   *

NORRIS, James Donald 1930-

PERSONAL: Born November 2, 1930, in Richmond, Mo.; son of Floyd and Gladys (Barger) Norris; married Nancy E. Hamilton, June 27, 1957; children: James Hamilton, Elizabeth Ann, Katherine Jane. *Education:* Attended Central Missouri State College (now University), 1948-50; University of Missouri, B.S., 1954, M.A., 1956, Ph.D., 1960. *Politics:* Democrat. *Office:* St. Louis Campus, University of Missouri, St. Louis, Mo.

CAREER: Hiram College, Hiram, Ohio, associate professor of history, 1960-64; University of Wisconsin, Madison, visiting associate professor of history, 1965-66; Uni-

versity of Missouri, St. Louis Campus, associate professor, 1966-68, professor of history, 1969—, chairman of department, 1970-72, director of university archives and manuscripts collection. Senior Fulbright lecturer, University of Ghana, 1972-73. *Military service:* U.S. Air Force, 1950-54. Missouri National Guard, 1956-60; became first lieutenant. *Member:* Organization of American Historians, Business History Society.

WRITINGS: Frontier Iron: The Maramec Iron Works 1826-1876, Wisconsin State Historical Society, 1965; *A Zn: A History of the American Zinc Company*, Wisconsin State Historical Society, 1968; (with A. Shaffer) *Politics and Patronage in the Gilded Age: The James A. Garfield-Charles Henry Correspondence*, Wisconsin Historical Society, 1970. Contributor to *Business History Review, Ohio History*, and *Business and Economic Review*.

WORK IN PROGRESS: A biography of R. G. Dun, completion expected in 1976; a dictionary of American mining history, completion expected in 1977; a study of the Morton family in American business and life, completion expected in 1978.

*   *   *

NORRIS, Richard A(lfred), Jr. 1930-

PERSONAL: Born March 18, 1930, in Washington, D.C.; son of Richard Alfred (a banker) and Alma (Schlosser) Norris. *Education:* Haverford College, B.A., 1952; Oxford University, B.A., 1954, M.A., 1959, D.Phil., 1961; General Theological Seminary, S.T.B., and S.T.M., 1957. *Politics:* Democrat. *Office:* General Theological Seminary, 175 Ninth Ave., New York, N.Y. 10011.

CAREER: Ordained Episcopal priest, 1955. General Theological Seminary, New York, N.Y., fellow and tutor, 1955-57; Divinity School of the Protestant Episcopal Church, Philadelphia, Pa., associate professor of church history, 1964-67, professor, 1967-70; University of Pennsylvania, Philadelphia, visiting lecturer in religious thought, 1965-70; General Theological Seminary, New York, N.Y., professor of dogmatic theology, 1970—. *Member:* American Theological Society, Phi Beta Kappa. *Awards, honors:* Rhodes scholarship, 1952-54, 1957-58; American Association of Theological Schools faculty fellowship, 1964.

WRITINGS: Manhood and Christ, Clarendon Press, 1963; *God and World in Early Christian Theology*, Seabury, 1965; (editor and contributor) *Lux in Lumine: Essays to Honor W. Norman Pittenger*, Seabury, 1966.

WORK IN PROGRESS: Research on the relationship between Greek scientific and philosophical ideas and early Christian theology; work on the history of Christian creeds and confessions.

*   *   *

NORTH, Robert Grady 1916-

PERSONAL: Born March 25, 1916, in Iowa City, Iowa; son of Grenville Paul (an attorney) and Vera (Grady) North. *Education:* St. Louis University, A.B., 1937, M.A., 1939; Pontifical Biblical Institute, Rome, Italy, S.S.D., 1954. *Politics:* Democrat. *Home and office:* Pontifical Biblical Institute, Via Pilotta 25, Rome, Italy 00187.

CAREER: Roman Catholic priest, member of Society of Jesus (Jesuits). Marquette University High School, Milwaukee, Wis., instructor in Greek, 1939-41; Pontifical Biblical Institute, Rome, Italy, professor of archaeology, 1951—, director of branch in Jerusalem, Israel, 1956-59; director of Ghassul archaeological excavation, Jericho,

Jordan, 1960-61; Marquette University, Milwaukee, professor of theology, 1961-69. Visiting professor of theology, St. Louis University, 1960-64, Canisius College and Corpus Christi College, Australia, and Bellarmine College, Philippines, 1963; visiting professor, Chonnam University and Daegun College, Korea, 1965-66, University of Windsor, Canada, and University of Michigan, 1973. *Member:* Catholic Biblical Association of America (vice-president, 1968-69), Society of Old Testament Studies, Society of Biblical Literature (executive board member, 1963-66), American Schools of Oriental Research, World Society for Jewish Studies, National Geographic Society. *Awards, honors:* Catholic Biblical Association of America scholar, 1945-51.

WRITINGS—All published by Pontifical Biblical Institute, except as indicated: *The General Who Rebuilt the Jesuits*, Bruce, 1944; *All-Stars of Christ*, Bruce, 1949; *Sociology of the Biblical Jubilee*, 1954; *Guide to Biblical Iran*, 1956; *Stratigraphia Palaestinae*, 1956; *Ghassul 1960 Excavation Report*, 1961; *Israel's Chronicle*, School of Divinity, St. Louis University, 1963; *Teilhard and the Creation of the Soul*, Bruce, 1967; *Archeo-Biblical Egypt*, 1967; *Chronistae Opus in Sua Scaena Postexsilica*, Biblico (Rome), 1967; *Les Fouilles dans la religion de Jericho*, 1967; (contributor) Raymond E. Brown and others, editors, *The Jerome Biblical Commentary*, Prentice-Hall, 1968; *Exegese pratique des petits prophetes postexiliens*, Biblico, 1969; *In Search of the Human Jesus*, Corpus Books, 1970; *Stratigraphia Geobiblica: Biblical Near East Archeology and Geography*, 3rd edition, Biblico, 1970. Also author of booklets, published by Pontifical Biblical Institute, to accompany slides on Biblical archaeology. Contributor to *Encyclopaedia Britannica*, *New Catholic Encyclopedia*, *Lexikon fuer Theologie und Kirche*, *Theologisches Woerterbuch zum Alten Testament*, *Theology Digest*, *Biblica*, *Catholic Biblical Quarterly*, *Orientalia*, *Journal of Biblical Literature*, and other periodicals.

WORK IN PROGRESS: Biblical guidebooks; a history of biblical scholarship.

SIDELIGHTS: North has participated in excavations in Lebanon, 1952, and Turkey and Iraq, 1955. He is competent in Italian, German, Hebrew, Spanish, Arabic, Polish, and Korean.

* * *

NOTTERMAN, Joseph M(elvin) 1923-

PERSONAL: Born January 14, 1923, in New York, N.Y.; son of Israel and Yetta (Schneiderman) Notterman; married Rebecca Feldsher (a pediatrician), August 10, 1947; children: Daniel A., Abby F. *Education:* Trenton State College, B.S., 1942; Columbia University, M.A., 1947, Ph.D., 1950; William Alanson White Institute of Psychiatry, special research student, 1950-52. *Home:* Feldsher Rd., Highstown, N.J. *Office:* Department of Psychology, Princeton University, Princeton, N.J. 08540.

CAREER: Columbia University, New York, N.Y., lecturer in psychology, 1948-60, research associate, 1951-54, senior psychologist, Electronics Research Laboratories, 1954-56; Princeton University, Princeton, N.J., assistant professor, 1956-59, associate professor, 1959-65, professor of psychology, 1965—, chairman of department, 1966-68. Regular consultant to Columbia University Electronics Research Laboratories, 1956—, and to International Telephone and Telegraph Laboratories, 1958-65; consultant to Office of the Surgeon-General, U.S. Department of Defense, 1964-69. American Psychological Association pro-

gram, visiting lecturer, 1961-62, visiting scientist, 1966-67, 1968-69. Member of East Windsor Municipal Authority, 1963—. *Military service:* U.S. Army, 1942-46; became first lieutenant.

MEMBER: American Psychological Association (fellow), American Association for the Advancement of Science (fellow), Academy of Psychoanalysis (scientific associate), Psychonomic Society, New York Academy of Sciences, Sigma Xi. *Awards, honors:* U.S. Public Health Service postdoctoral research fellow, 1950-52.

WRITINGS: (With D. E. Mintz) *Dynamics of Response*, Wiley, 1965; (contributor) T. Verhave, editor, *The Experimental Analysis of Behavior*, Appleton, 1966; *Behavior: A Systematic Approach*, Random House, 1970; (compiler) *Readings in Behavior*, Random House, 1970; *Laboratory Manual for Experiments in Behavior*, Random House, 1971. About forty articles and reviews, a number of the articles dealing with conditioned heart rate response and stress, have appeared in *Science*, *American Scientist*, and psychology journals. Editoral consultant, *Psychological Review*, *Journal for the Experimental Analysis of Behavior*, and *Journal of Comparative and Physiological Psychology*.

WORK IN PROGRESS: Perception of Dynamic Stimuli.†

* * *

NOVAK, Lorna 1927-

PERSONAL: Born April 27, 1927, in Amarillo, Tex.; daughter of James Lyle (an advertising man) and Lois (Tyson) McCormick; married Gordon Shaw Novak (owner of Novak Construction Co.), June 28, 1946; children: Gordon Shaw, Jr., Daniel McCormick, Kitty. *Education:* University of Texas, student, 1945-46.

WRITINGS: Does It Make Into a Bed? (novel), Doubleday, 1963; *How Amelia Secured the Tie That Binds with a Very Loose Knot* (novel), Doubleday, 1966. Writer of children's play, "Amorinda and the Caterpillar," and play adaptations, "Jack and the Beanstalk" and "Sleeping Beauty."

WORK IN PROGRESS: A novel.

AVOCATIONAL INTERESTS: Reading, gardening, horses, swimming, tennis, cooking, movies, and talking.†

* * *

NOVARR, David 1917-

PERSONAL: Born June 29, 1917, in Hartford, Conn.; son of Bennie (a merchant) and Minnie (Katz) Novarr; married Ruth Gordon, February 4, 1942; children: John, Frances. *Education:* Yale University, B.A., 1939, M.A., 1942, Ph.D., 1949. *Home:* 226 Valley Rd., Ithaca, N.Y. 14850. *Office:* Department of English, Cornell University, Ithaca, N.Y. 14850.

CAREER: Cornell University, Ithaca, N.Y., instructor, 1946-51, assistant professor, 1951-56, associate professor, 1956-63, professor of English, 1963—. *Military service:* U.S. Naval Reserve, 1942-45; became chief specialist, communications. *Member:* Modern Language Association of America, American Association of University Professors, Phi Beta Kappa. *Awards, honors:* Fellow, Fund for the Advancement of Education, 1951-52.

WRITINGS: The Making of Walton's "Lives", Cornell University Press, 1958; (editor) *Seventeenth-Century English Prose*, Knopf, 1967; (contributor) Peter A. Fiore, editor, *Just So Much Honor*, Pennsylvania State University

Press, 1972. Contributor to *English Studies, Modern Humanities Review*, and other journals in field. Member of editorial board for Folger Library edition of *The Works of Richard Hooker*.

WORK IN PROGRESS: The Lines of Life: The Recent History of Theory of Biography; and *John Donne: Texts and Context*.

* * *

NOYES, Kathryn Johnston 1930-

PERSONAL: Born October 3, 1930, in Boston, Mass.; daughter of Archibald Burtt (an engineer) and Margaret (Richard) Johnston; divorced; children: Michael, Susanna, Christopher, Drew. *Education:* Studied drama at Boston Conservatory. *Politics:* Independent. *Home:* 1106 Anderson, Durham, N.C. *Agent:* Littauer & Wilkinson, 500 Fifth Ave., New York, N.Y. 10036. *Office:* Learning Institute of North Carolina, Rougemont, N.C.

CAREER: Learning Institute of North Carolina (LINC), Rougemont, editorial director, 1965—. Literary and drama critic for several North Carolina newspapers. Member of Durham Council on Human Relations. *Member:* Authors Guild.

WRITINGS: Jacob's Ladder (novel), Bobbs-Merrill, 1965; *The South, The Law, and Me*, Red Clay, 1965. Editor, *LINC Quarterly* (educational review).

WORK IN PROGRESS: A novel about the depression years, tentatively titled, *From Time Memorial.*†

* * *

NUCERA, Marisa Lonette 1959-
(Marisa)

PERSONAL: Born November 1, 1959, in New York, N.Y.; daughter of Vincent Dominic (an artist) and Reisie (an artist and illustrator; maiden name Lonette) Nucera. *Home:* 41 Salisbury Ave., Stewart Manor, Long Island, N.Y.

WRITINGS—Under name Marisa: *One Day Means a Lot* (poems), Bobbs-Merrill, 1965.†

* * *

NUNAN, Desmond J. 1927-

PERSONAL: Born November 8, 1927, in New York, N.Y.; son of Peter Dominic (a teacher) and May (Breen) Nunan; married Gertrude V. Falini, December 26, 1953; children: Desmond, Christopher, Peter, Aidan, Julie. *Education:* Columbia University, B.A., 1950, M.A., 1951; University of Pennsylvania, Ed.D., 1969. *Home:* 2302 Fairview St., Allentown, Pa.

CAREER: High school teacher in Schwenksville, Pa., 1954-55; West Chester (Pa.) School District, junior high school teacher, 1955-63, curriculum director (for district), 1963-66; Allentown (Pa.) School District, assistant to superintendent, 1966—. *Military service:* U.S. Army Air Forces, Strategic Air Command, 1946-47; sergeant. *Member:* Association for Supervision and Curriculum Development, American Association of School Administrators. *Awards, honors:* National Science Foundation grant.

WRITINGS: (Editor) *The Junior High Schools Years—Growing Up: Problems and Pathways* (curriculum guide), Interstate, 1965; *Composition: Models and Exercises*, books for grades seven and eight, Harcourt, 1965,

2nd edition, 1970, consulting editor, book for grade nine, 1966, 2nd edition, 1970; *World Cultures: Two Units of Study*, Interstate, 1966.

* * *

NUTTALL, Kenneth 1907-

PERSONAL: Born July 14, 1907, in Whitworth, Lancashire, England; son of Walter (a headmaster) and Susannah (Hoyle) Nuttall; married Hilda Mary Addison, August 1, 1931; children: Jeffrey Addison, Anthony David. *Education:* City of Leeds Training College, Teacher's Certificate, 1927. *Home:* 23 Madeira Ave., Worthing, Sussex, BN11 2AT, England.

CAREER: Headmaster at Orcop School, Herefordshire, England, 1934-42, Ewyas Harold School, Herefordshire, 1942-44, Holmer School, Herefordshire, 1944-54, Hillside Primary School, Watford, Hertfordshire, England, 1954-67. Lecturer on drama at teachers' training schools. *Member:* National Book League.

WRITINGS: Your Book of Acting, Faber, 1957, revised edition, 1972; "Let's Act" series, five books (drama course for ages nine to eleven), Longmans, Green, 1959; *Play Production for Young People*, Faber, 1963; "Young Actors" series, three books (drama course for ages seven to eight), Longmans, Green, 1965; *Four Plays From History*, 1966; *Four Plays for Christmas*, Longmans, Green, 1966; (with John Graham, Malcolm Sayer and others) *Reading Routes*, Longman, 1974.

"Services We Use" series: *Letters by Post, Coal for the Fire, Water From the Tap, Savings From Waste, Gas for the Cooker, Waterways on Land, Road Accident, News for All, Fire!, Motorways, The Hospital, Ports and Harbours* (all published by Longmans, Green, 1964—).

WORK IN PROGRESS: The Secret of the Padlocked Door, an adventure story for children.

AVOCATIONAL INTERESTS: The theatre, music.

* * *

NWOGUGU, Edwin Ifeanyichukwu 1933-

PERSONAL: Born April 1, 1933, in Onitsha, Nigeria; son of Gabriel O. and Victoria (Ngwube) Nwogugu; married Grace N. Uzodike (a teacher), February 19, 1966. *Education:* University of Hull, LL.B. (honors), 1960; University of Manchester, Ph.D., 1963. *Office:* Law Faculty, University of Nigeria, Enugu Campus, Enugu, Nigeria.

CAREER: University of Lagos, Lagos, Nigeria, lecturer in law, 1963-65; University of Nigeria, Enugu Campus, lecturer in public international law and family law, 1965-73; senior lecturer, 1973—. Consultant to Foundation for the Establishment of an International Criminal Court; member, British Institute of International and Criminal Law. *Member:* American Society of International Law, Nigerian Society of International, International Law Association, Internation Bar Association, Nigerian Bar Association, Association of Nigerian Law Teachers. *Awards, honors:* Commonwealth scholar to United Kingdom.

WRITINGS: Legal Problems of Foreign Investment in Developing Countries, Manchester University Press, 1965; *Family Law in Nigeria*, Heinemann, 1974; *Oil and Gas Law in Nigeria*, Heinemann, 1975. Member of editorial board, *International and Comparative Earth Law Journal*.

WORK IN PROGRESS: Research on African international institutions; and on the legal effects of the Nigerian

Civil War on commercial transactions; a book on Africa and the Law of the Sea for Oceana.

* * *

OAKLEY, Helen (McKelvey) 1906-

PERSONAL: Born February 10, 1906, in New York, N.Y.; daughter of Ralph Huntington (an artist) and Helen (Fairchild) McKelvey; màrried Walter T. Oakley (a publisher), August 6, 1938; children: Valerie Thurston (Mrs. Charles R. Atherton, Jr.), Deborah Huntington (Mrs. Kenneth M. Bodner). *Education:* Bryn Mawr College, A.B., 1928. *Politics:* Republican. *Home:* 128 Park Ave., Manhasset, N.Y. 11030; and Shepherdstown, W.Va.

CAREER: Week-End Book Service, Inc., New York, N.Y., president and manager, 1929-41; Buckley Country Day School, Roslyn, N.Y., librarian; writer. Has done book condensation work for *Liberty* Magazine; paints, and has taught art at Vincent Smith School, Port Washington, N.Y., and an adult education class in creative writing, Manhasset, N.Y.; para-professional library assistant, Manhasset Junior High School. Trustee of Manhasset Public Library. *Member:* Authors Guild, Christopher Morley Knothole Association (president, 1971-75), Bryn Mawr Association of Long Island (founder-chairman), Manhasset Art Association.

WRITINGS: The Horse on the Hill (juvenile) Knopf, 1957; *The Ranch by the Sea* (juvenile) Knopf, 1958; *The Enchanter's Wheel* (juvenile) Norton, 1962; *Freedom's Daughter*, Norton, 1968; *Three Hours for Lunch: The Life and Times of Christopher Morley*, Watermill Publications, 1975.

WORK IN PROGRESS: ABCD, for Oxford University Press.

* * *

OATES, John F. 1934-

PERSONAL: Born August 7, 1934, in Holyoke, Mass.; son of William Adrian (a food broker) and Lilian (Woods) Oates; married Rosemary Walsh, June 27, 1957; children: Elizabeth, Emily, John, Jr., Sarah. *Education:* Yale University, B.A., 1956, M.A., 1958, Ph.D., 1960. *Home:* 2416 Alpine Rd., Durham, N.C. 27707. *Office:* Department of Classical Studies, Duke University, Durham, N.C.

CAREER: Yale University, New Haven, Conn., instructor, 1960-63, assistant professor of classics, 1963-67, fellow of Davenport College, 1961-67; Duke University, Durham, N.C., associate professor, 1967-71, professor of ancient history, and chairman of department of classical studies, 1971—. University of London, University College, London, England, research assistant in Greek, 1965-66. *Member:* American Philological Association, American Historical Association, American Society of Papyrologists (vice-president, 1971-73; director, 1973—), Association Internationale de Papyrologues, Elizabethan Club (New Haven), Phi Beta Kappa. *Awards, honors:* Fulbright fellowship, American School of Classical Studies in Athens, 1956-57; Morse faculty fellowship, Yale University, 1956-66; American Council of Learned Societies, fellowship, 1973-74.

WRITINGS: The Status Designation, "Yale Classical Studies," Volume 18, Yale University Press, 1963; (editor with C. B. Welles and A. E. Samuel) *The Papyri in the Beinecke Library at Yale*, Volume I, American Society of

Papyrologists, 1967. Contributor to *Bulletin*, of the American Society of Papyrologists.

WORK IN PROGRESS: A history of Roman Egypt; an editon of papyri in the Duke library.

* * *

O'BEIRNE, T(homas) H(ay) 1915-

PERSONAL: Surname rhymes with "stern"; born November 26, 1915, in Glasgow, Scotland; son of Andrew Thomson (a schoolmaster) and Marjorie Helen (Flett) O'Beirne; married Margaret Anne Latta Skilling, January 19, 1944; children: Judith Anne Flett, Ruth Margaret Skilling. *Education:* University of Glasgow, M.A. (first class honors in mathematics and physics), 1938. *Home:* 8 Rosslyn Ter., Glasgow G12 9NB, Scotland. *Office:* University of Glasgow, Glasgow, Scotland.

CAREER: Royal Naval Scientific Service, civilian employe in various locations in Great Britain, 1940-47; Ordnance Survey of Great Britain (geodesy, photogrammetry, cartography, geophysics), scientific adviser, 1947-49; Barr & Stroud Ltd. (scientific instruments and precision engineering), Glasgow, Scotland, chief mathematician, 1949-71; University of Glasgow, Glasgow, lecturer in computing department, 1971—. Lecturer to schools, universities, and professional groups; inventor of mathematical recreations. *Member:* Institute of Physics (fellow), British Mathematical Association, Mathematical Association of America, British Computer Society (former member of council), Institute of Mathematics and Its Applications (fellow), Edinburgh Mathematical Society, Glasgow Mathematical Association (former chairman). *Military service:* British Army, one day, 1944 ("by administrative muddle, before release to return to Royal Naval Scientific Service").

WRITINGS: (Translator from the German) R. Sprague, *Recreation in Mathematics*, Blackie & Son, 1963; *Puzzles and Parades*, Oxford University Press, 1965. Contributor of weekly series, "Puzzles and Paradoxes," to *New Scientist*, 1961-62; also contributor of reviews to periodicals. Member of editorial board, British Computer Society.

SIDELIGHTS: O'Beirne described himself to *CA* as a nationally-conscious Scot ("not withstanding my name"), whose mother's family has farmed the same land in Orkney for some five hundred years. He has presented some of his original mathematical puzzles on British and Dutch television programs, collects books on the lighter side of mathematics, and corresponds regularly with some like-minded people all over the world. *Avocational interests:* Music, drama, light verse, travel.†

* * *

O'BRIEN, Elmer 1911-

PERSONAL: Born November 30, 1911, in Everett, Mass.; son of Allan Daniel and Ethel (MacDonald) O'Brien. *Education:* Attended Boston College; University of Montreal, A.B., 1940; graduate study at Harvard University and Gregorian University (Rome); Catholic University of Louvain, S.T.D., 1950. *Politics:* Democrat. *Home and office:* Ignatius College, Guelph, Ontario, Canada. *Agent:* Curtis Brown Ltd., 60 East 56th St., New York, N.Y. 10022.

CAREER: Roman Catholic priest of Society of Jesus. Regis College, Toronto, Ontario, assistant professor of theology, 1951-60; Fordham University, Bronx, N.Y., visiting professor in Graduate School, 1952-53, 1954-58; Loyola College, Montreal, Quebec, professor of theology,

1962-66, research professor, 1966-73, founder and director of Contemporary Theology Institute, 1964-73; Ignatius College, Guelph, Ontario, writer in residence, 1973—. Institute of Judaeo-Christian Studies, editorial consultant, 1954—; Month Publications, London, England, theological consultant, 1961-62. *Member:* Patristic Academy of America, Catholic Biblical Association, American Academy of Religion, Society of Biblical Literature, American Theological Society.

WRITINGS: (Editor) "Christian Mystics" series, Scribner, Volume I: *The Mediaeval Mystics of England*, 1961, Volume II: *From Glory to Glory*, 1961; *The Essential Plotinus*, Mentor Books, 1964; *Varieties of Mystic Experience*, Holt, 1964; (editor) "Contemporary Theology," series, Herder & Herder, Volume I: *Theology in Transition*, 1965, Volume II: *The Convergence of Traditions*, 1967. Contributor to *Encyclopaedia Britannica*, and to *Commonweal, Cross Currents, The Month* (London), *Theological Studies, Thought* and other journals. Associate editor, *Way* (London), 1961—.

WORK IN PROGRESS: Writing four books, *The Life of the Liturgy, The Way to the Father, A Commentary on the Gospel of Mark,* and *I, Christian.*

* * *

O'BRIEN, James J. 1929-

PERSONAL: Born October 20, 1929, in Philadelphia, Pa; son of Sylvester J. (a doctor) and Emma (Filer) O'Brien; married Carmen Hiester, June 9, 1952; children: Jessica, Michael, David. *Education:* Cornell University, B.C.E., 1952; University of Houston, M.E., 1958. *Residence:* Levittown, Pa.

CAREER: Rohm & Haas, Bristol, Pa., and Houston, Tex., engineer, 1955-59; Radio Corp. of America, Moorestown, N.J., and Alaska, engineer, 1959-62; Meridian Engineering, Haddonfield, N.J., executive vice-president. *Military service:* U.S. Navy, Korean War; became lieutenant. *Member:* Society of CPM Consultants (director), Pennsylvania Society of Professional Engineers, Construction Specification Institute, American Society of Civil Engineers, American Institute of Industrial Engineers, Cornell Society of Engineers, Tau Beta Pi, Chi Epsilon.

WRITINGS: CPM in Construction Management, McGraw, 1965, 2nd edition, 1971; *Scheduling Handbook*, McGraw, 1969; *Management Information Systems*, Van Nostrand, 1970; *Management With Computers*, Van Nostrand, 1971. Contributor of twenty articles to professional journals, principally on Critical Path Method (CPM) planning Chapter on CPM in *Creative Cost Control*, American Institute of Architects, for McGraw.†

* * *

OBST, Frances Melanie

PERSONAL: Born in St. Paul, Minn.; daughter of Frank J. (a county treasurer) and Elsa M. (Redeker) Obst. *Education:* University of Minnesota, B.S., 1934, M.A., 1938; University of California, Los Angeles, Ed.D., 1955. *Religion:* Episcopalian. *Office:* Department of Education, University of California, 405 Hilgard, Los Angeles, Calif. 90024.

CAREER: University of Minnesota, Minneapolis, instructor, 1935-40; University of Wyoming, Laramie, assistant professor, 1941-44; University of Washington, Seattle, assistant professor, 1944-49; University of California, Los Angeles, associate professor of education, beginning 1949, head of folklore and mythology group. *Member:* American Home Economics Association, American Educational Research Association, American Vocational Association, California Home Economics Association.

WRITINGS: Art and Design in Home Living, Macmillan, 1963. Writer of study guide and color filmstrip, "Three Centuries of Historic Costumes." Contributor to education and antiques journals.

WORK IN PROGRESS: Research on Indonesian art.†

* * *

O'CALLAGHAN, Denis F(rancis) 1931-

PERSONAL: Surname is pronounced O'Callahan; born March 4, 1931, in County Cork, Ireland; son of John Denis (a farmer) and Mary (Sheehy) O'Callaghan. *Education:* St. Patrick's College, Maynooth, Ireland, B.A., 1952, D.D., 1958; Lateran University, Rome, Italy, D.C.L., 1962. *Home:* Meelin Newmarket, County Cork, Ireland. *Office:* St. Patrick's College, Maynooth, County Kildare, Ireland.

CAREER: Roman Catholic priest; St. Patrick's College, Maynooth, County Kildare, Ireland, professor of moral theology, 1958—. Maynooth Union Summer School, member of directing committee. *Member:* Irish Theological Association.

WRITINGS: Moral Principles of Fertility Control, Clonmore & Reynolds, 1962; (editor) *Sacraments*, M. H. Gill, 1965; (contributor) E. McDonagh, editor, *The Renewal of Moral Theology*, M. H. Gill, 1966; *Truth and Life*, M. H. Gill, 1968; *Penance: Sacrament of Reconciliation*, Chapman, 1975. Editor, *Irish Theological Quarterly*.

WORK IN PROGRESS: Further research, with view to publication, on topics of doctoral dissertations, "The Death and Resurrection with Christ in Baptism" and "The Binding Force of the Law Established on the Presumption of a General Danger."

SIDELIGHTS: O'Callaghan is competent in French, German and Italian.

* * *

OCHSENSCHLAGER, Edward L(loyd) 1932-

PERSONAL: Born April 5, 1932, in Aurora, Ill.; son of David William (vice-president of an auto supply company) and Melva (Robinson) Ochsenchlager. *Education:* Columbia University, B.S., 1954; New York University, M.A., 1961, studied at Fine Arts Institute, 1961-64. *Politics:* Independent. *Home:* Carmel Road, Cold Springs, N.Y. 10516. *Office:* Brooklyn College of the City University of New York, Bedford Ave., and Avenue H, Brooklyn, N.Y. 11210.

CAREER: Brooklyn College of the City University of New York, assistant professor 1962-68, associate professor of classics, 1968—, director, Archaeological Research Institute. New York University, assistant field director of Anatolian Research Project, Aphrodisias, Turkey, 1963-65, director of classical excavations at Thmuis for the Mendes Expedition, Mendes, Egypt, 1965—; American director of the Joint Yugoslav-American Excavations at Sirmiom, Yugoslavia; assistant to the field director of the Al-Hiba excavations in Iraq. Member of American Research Center in Egypt, Inc. and American Schools of Oriental Studies. *Member:* Archaeological Institute of America (member of executive committee), American Oriental Society, Classical Association of the Atlantic States, New York Classical Club, Explorers Club.

WRITINGS: The Egyptians in the Middle Kingdom, Coward, 1963; *Archaeology in American Colleges*, Archaeological Institute of America, 1967, 2nd edition (with Pamela E. Brown), 1970. Contributor to *Encyclopedia Americana* and *Living History of the World Yearbook*. Coeditor of *Sirmion Archaeological Investigations*. Editorial consultant, "Life Long Ago" series, Coward, 1963—.

WORK IN PROGRESS: Research on the Greeks and Romans in Egypt and their influence on the life of the Delta; research on Graeco-Roman mythology and religion in contact with the Egyptian.

SIDELIGHTS: Oshsenschlager speaks French, German, Italian, and Arabic.

* * *

OCHSNER, (Edward William) Alton 1896-

PERSONAL: Born May 4, 1896, in Kimball, S.D.; son of Edward Philip (a merchant) and Clara (Shontz) Ochsner; married Isabel Lockwood, September 13, 1923 (deceased); married Jane Kellogg, 1970; children: Alton, Jr., John, Mims, Isabel (Mrs. E. Allen Davis). *Education:* University of South Dakota, B.A., 1918; Washington University, St. Louis, Mo., M.D., 1920. *Religion:* Presbyterian. *Home:* 1347 Exposition Blvd., New Orleans, La. 70118. *Office:* Ochsner Clinic, 1514 Jefferson Hwy., New Orleans, La. 70121.

CAREER: Intern at Barnes Hospital, St. Louis, Mo., 1920-21, and surgical resident at Augustana Hospital, Chicago, Ill., 1921-22; exchange surgical resident at hospitals affiliated with University of Zurich, Zurich, Switzerland, 1922-23, and University of Frankfurt, Frankfurt am Main, Germany, 1923-24; visited European and American surgical clinics, 1924-25; private practice of surgery, Chicago, Ill., and instructor in surgery and surgical pathology at Northwestern University Medical School, Evanston, Ill., 1925-26; University of Wisconsin, Medical School, Madison, assistant professor of surgery, 1926-27; Tulane University of Louisiana, School of Medicine, New Orleans, professor of surgery, 1927-38, William Henderson Professor of Surgery, 1938-56, professor of clinical surgery, 1956-61, chairman of department of surgery, 1927-56, professor emeritus, 1961—; Ochsner Clinic and Ochsner Foundation Hospital, New Orleans, La., director of surgery, 1942—. Charity Hospital, New Orleans, La., senior visiting surgeon, 1927-61, consulting surgeon, 1961—; attending specialist in chest surgery, U.S. Public Health Service Hospital. Adviser to the surgeons general of the U.S. Army, Navy, and Public Health Service, World War II; consultant to Surgeon General, U.S. Air Force, 1959—, and National Health Foundation and Research Institute, 1964. Diplomate and founder member of American Board of Surgery and American Board of Thoracic Surgery. President of Alton Ochsner Medical Foundation, 1944-70, American Cancer Society, 1949-50, Cordell Hull Foundation for International Education, 1956—, Information Council of the Americas, 1962—, and International House of New Orleans, 1962. Trustee of National Society for Crippled Children and Adults, 1949-52, and Gulf South Research Institute, 1965-66. Director of National Airlines, Inc., 1962—, National Bank of Commerce in Jefferson Parish, 1962-66, International Trade Mart of New Orleans, 1963—.

MEMBER: Royal College of Surgeons (England; honorary fellow), Royal College of Surgeons (Ireland; honorary fel-

low), Societe Internationale de Chirurgie (president, 1962-63), American College of Surgeons (regent, 1935-52; president, 1951-52), American Association for Thoracic Surgery (president, 1947-48), Society for Vascular Surgery (president, 1947), International Cardiovascular Society (president, 1954-56), American Medical Association (president of surgical section, 1959-62), American Surgical Association, Society of Clinical Surgery, American Thoracic Society, American College of Chest Physicians, Interstate Postgraduate Medical Association of North America (president, 1955-56), Pan American Medical Association, Pan Pacific Surgical Association (president, 1961-63), American Geriatrics Society, American Medical Writers Association (fellow), American Medical Authors, Southern Medical Association, and other regional and state medical societies; Phi Beta Kappa, Sigma Xi, Alpha Omega Alpha, Omicron Delta Kappa, Kappa Delta Phi, Phi Delta Theta, New Orleans Country Club, Boston Club, Circumnavigators Club. Honorary member of more than forty medical societies in America and some fifteen countries of Latin America, Europe, and Japan.

AWARDS, HONORS: Orden al Merito (Ecuador), 1952; Order Vasco Nunez de Balboa (Panama), 1953; Citation of Merit, American College of Surgeons, 1954, for excellence of surgical films on separation of Siamese twins and on carcinoma of the stomach; Modern Medicine Award, 1955; Cruz Eloy Alfaro de Fundacion Internacional Eloy Alfaro (Panama), 1956; Rosewell Park Award, 1957; Mississippi Valley Medical Society Honor Award, 1958; Orden Rodolfo Robles (Guatemala), 1960; Golden Mike Award, Information Council of the Americas, 1963. Honorary degrees from University of South Dakota, 1936, Free University of Nicaragua, 1946, Brigham Young University, 1961, University of Madrid, 1962, University of Jacksonville, 1965, Tulane University of Louisiana, 1966. Citations and certificates from Government of El Salvador, and various states, cities, and organizations in United States.

WRITINGS: Varicose Veins, Mosby, 1938; *Smoking and Cancer: A Doctor's Report*, Messner, 1954; (editor with Michael E. DeBakey) *Christopher's Minor Surgery*, 5th edition, Saunders, 1955, 8th edition, 1959; *Smoking and Health*, Messner, 1959; *Smoking and Your Life*, Messner, 1964; *Smoking: Your Choice Between Life and Death*, Simon & Schuster, 1970. Contributor to numerous medical books and to *Britannica Book of the Year*, 1959-63. Contributor of more than 450 articles to medical journals.

Assistant editor, "Surgery of the Emergency" (World War II), Committee on Historical Records, National Research Council. Surgical editor, *The Cyclopedia of Medicine, Surgery and Specialities, Traumatic Medicine and Surgery for the Attorney*, and *Britannica Book of the Year*. Member of consulting and advisory board, *Funk and Wagnalls Encyclopedia*. Former editor, *Surgery and International Surgical Digest*; member of editorial board, *Cancer, Review of Surgery, General Practice Clinics, American Surgeon, Excerpta Medica* (international board), *Modern Medicine*, and *Academic Achievement*; member of advisory board, *Surgery of the Colon and Rectum, Journal of Cardiovascular Surgery, American Journal of Gastroenterology*, and *Medical Tribune*.

SIDELIGHTS: Ochsner was Rex of New Orleans Mardi Gras, 1948.

* * *

O'CONNELL, Maurice R. 1922-

PERSONAL: Born December 30, 1922, in County Tipperary, Ireland; son of Maurice Charles (an army officer) and Emily (O'Connell) O'Connell; married Elizabeth M. McCan, December 26, 1962. *Education:* University College, Dublin, B.A., 1952, M.A. (first class honors), 1954; University of Pennsylvania, Ph.D., 1962. *Politics:* Democrat. *Religion:* Roman Catholic. *Home:* 2400 Johnson Ave., Bronx, N.Y. 10463. *Office:* Department of History, Fordham University, Bronx, N.Y. 10458.

CAREER: With Bank of Ireland, 1941-53; University of Portland, Portland, Oregon, instructor, 1958-61, assistant professor of history, 1961-64; Fordham University, Bronx, N.Y., assistant professor, 1964-67, associate professor, 1967-73, professor of history, 1973—. *Member:* American Catholic Historical Society (chairman, nominations committee, 1964), American Irish Historical Society, American Committee for Irish Studies, Conference on British Studies, Irish Georgian Society (founding member), Irish Historical Society.

WRITINGS: Irish Politics and Social Conflict in the Age of the American Revolution, University of Pennsylvania Press, 1965; (editor) *The Correspondence of Daniel O'Connell,* Irish University Press, Volume I, 1973, Volume II, 1973, Volume III, 1974; (contributor) Harold E. Paglaro, editor, *Studies in Eighteenth Century Culture,* Volume V: *Thought,* University of Wisconsin Press, 1975. Also contributor to *Irish Historical Studies: Papers,* Dufour. Contributor of articles to *Irish Ecclesiastical Record, Irish History Review,* and *Duquesne Review.*

WORK IN PROGRESS: A study of British political radicalism, 1830-1846.

AVOCATIONAL INTERESTS: The history of architecture, particularly eighteenth-century domestic architecture.

* * *

O'CONNER, R(ay) L. 1928-

PERSONAL: Born November 5, 1928; son of Martin and Kathleen O'Conner; married May, 1954. *Education:* Studied at University of Wisconsin two years. *Politics:* "Open." *Religion:* Agnostic.

CAREER: Free-lance writer.

WRITINGS: Mexico After Dark, Macfadden, 1962; *The Bare Facts,* Macfadden, 1963; *The American Sex Revolution,* Brandon, 1965; *The G-Whiz String,* Brandon, 1966; *World of Sex,* Brandon, 1966. Contributor of about one hundred articles and stories to men's adventure and other magazines.

WORK IN PROGRESS: A study of the nation's correspondence clubs; a book, tentatively titled *Manifesto for Sex;* another book, *The Marriage Farce.†*

* * *

O'DONNELL, John A. 1916-

PERSONAL: Born October 29, 1916, in Jersey City, N.J.; son of John A. and Anna (Frank) O'Donnell; married Estelle Dillon, January 30, 1947; children: Kitty, John. *Education:* St. Peter's College, Jersey City, N.J., B.A., 1938; Fordham University, M.A., 1940; University of Kentucky, Ph.D., 1960. *Home:* 1842 Bellefonte Dr., Lexington, Ky. 40502. *Office:* Department of Sociology, University of Kentucky, Lexington, Ky. 40506.

CAREER: Social worker at U.S. Veterans Administration Hospital, Sheridan, Wyo., 1947-49, and Phoenix Mental Health Center, Phoenix, Ariz., 1949-51; U.S. Public

Health Service Hospital, Lexington, Ky., chief social worker, 1951-62; Addiction Research Center, Lexington, Ky., director of social science section, 1962-67; Clinical Research Center, Lexington, Ky., director of research sections, 1967-69; University of Kentucky, Lexington, professor of sociology, 1970—. *Military service:* U.S. Army, 1943-46; became captain. *Member:* American Sociological Association (fellow), Society for the Study of Social Problems, American Society of Criminology, Ohio Valley Sociological Society, Southern Sociological Society.

WRITINGS: (Editor with John C. Ball) *Narcotic Addiction,* Harper, 1966; *Narcotic Addicts in Kentucky,* U.S. Government Printing Office, 1969. Contributor to *Encyclopedia of Social Work* and professional journals.

WORK IN PROGRESS: Drug Use Among Young Men in the United States: A Nationwide Survey, completion expected in 1976.

* * *

O'DONNELL, John P. 1923-

PERSONAL: Born January 26, 1923, in Chicago, Ill.; son of Robert J. and Brigid (Garrity) O'Donnell. *Education:* St. Mary of the Lake Seminary, Mundelein, Ill., M.A., 1947, S.T.L., 1948; University of Notre Dame, M.A., 1957; Loyola University, Chicago, Ill., Ph.D., 1966. *Home:* 730 North Wabash Ave., Chicago, Ill. 60611. *Office:* Quigley Seminary, 103 East Chustnut St., Chicago, Ill. 60611.

CAREER: Roman Catholic priest; Quigley Preparatory Seminary North, Chicago, Ill., principal, 1961—; Holy Name Cathedral, Chicago, Ill., assistant pastor, 1961—. *Member:* National Catholic Education Association, National Catholic Theatre Conference, Illinois Association of Secondary Schools.

WRITINGS—Plays: *Shepherds on the Shelf,* Samuel French, 1961; *Haloes and Spotlights,* Samuel French, 1965. Drama critic, *New World,* 1959-63.

SIDELIGHTS: O'Donnell reads French, Latin, and Spanish.†

* * *

OFFNER, Eric D(elmonte) 1928-

PERSONAL: Born June 23, 1928, in Vienna, Austria; came to United States, 1941, naturalized, 1949; son of Sigmund G. (a businessman) and Kathe (Delmonte) Offner; married Julie Cousins, 1955 (died, 1959); married Barbara Shotton (a painter), June 4, 1961. *Education:* City College (now City College of the City University of New York), B.B.A., 1949; Cornell University, LL.B., 1952. *Religion:* Ethical Culture. *Home:* 5221 Arlington Ave., New York, N.Y., 10471. *Office:* 19 West 44th St., New York, N.Y. 10036.

CAREER: Admitted to bar of state of New York, 1952; Langner, Parry, Card & Langner, New York, N.Y., attorney, 1952-57; Haseltine, Lake & Waters (firm specialing in foreign patents and trademarks), New York, N.Y., partner, 1957—. President, Riverdale-Yonkers Society for Ethical Culture, 1964-67. Vice-president and member of board of directors, Riverdale Mental Health Clinic. *Member:* Association Internationale pour la Protection de la Propriete Industrielle, American Bar Association, U.S. Trademark Association, American Patent Law Association, New York Patent Law Association (member of board of governors), Bar Association of City of New York.

WRITINGS: International Trademark Protection, Fieldston Press, 1965. *Offner's International Trademark Service*, five volumes, Fieldston Press, 1970. Contributor to periodicals and to professional journals. Editor-in-chief, *Cornell Law Forum*, 1950-51; associate editor, *Bulletin of New York Patent Law Association*, 1961-66; member of editorial board, *Trademark Reporter*, 1961-64.

WORK IN PROGRESS: Articles.

AVOCATIONAL INTERESTS: Soccer, New Orleans jazz, and publishing.

*   *   *

OGATA, Sadako (Nakamura) 1927-

PERSONAL: Born September 16, 1927, in Tokyo, Japan; daughter of Toyoichi and Tsuneko (Yoshizawa) Nakamura; married Shijuro Ogata (a banker), January 21, 1961; children: Atsushi, Akiko. *Education:* University of the Sacred Heart, Tokyo, Japan, B.A., 1951; Georgetown University, M.A., 1953; Tokyo University, research student, 1953-56; University of California, Berkeley, Ph.D., 1963. *Religion:* Roman Catholic. *Home:* 1-1-16A-508 Meguro, Meguro-ku, Tokyo, Japan. *Office:* International Christian University, Mitaka, Tokyo, Japan.

CAREER: University of the Sacred Heart, Tokyo, Japan, lecturer in international relations, 1953-56; International Christian University, Tokyo, Japan, lecturer, 1965-73, associate professor of international relations and Japanese diplomatic and political history, 1974—. Member of Japanese delegation to the United Nations General Assembly, 1968, 1970, 1975. *Member:* Political Science Association and Association for American Studies (both Japan), Japan Association of International Relations.

WRITINGS: Defiance in Manchuria—The Making of Japanese Foreign Policy, 1931-32, University of California Press, 1964; *Manshu jihen to seisaku no keisei katei* (title means "Decision-Making Process of the Manchurian Affair Foreign Policy"), Hara Shobo, 1966; (contributor) Dorothy Borg and others, editors, *Pearl Harbor as History*, Columbia University Press, 1973.

WORK IN PROGRESS: A conference paper, to be published by University of California Press; research on the working security system in the Pacific, 1945-51; research on American-Japanese relations in the 1930's and on decision-making process of Japanese withdrawal from the League of Nations.

SIDELIGHTS: Sandako Ogata lived in England, 1962-64.

*   *   *

OGLETREE, Thomas W(arren) 1933-

PERSONAL: Born June 17, 1933, in Arab, Ala.; son of John Warren (an engineer) and Carrie (Brown) Ogletree; married Mary-Lynn Rimbey, May 26, 1973; children: (former marriage) Frank, Julia, Lauren. *Education:* Birmingham-Southern College, A.B., 1955; Garrett Theological Seminary, B.D., 1959; Vanderbilt University, Ph.D., 1963. *Politics:* Democrat. *Home address:* Station B, Box 1647, Nashville, Tenn. 37235. *Office:* Divinity School, Vanderbilt University, Nashville, Tenn. 37240.

CAREER: Ordained United Methodist minister, 1959; minister in Birmingham, Ala., 1952-55, Fort Atkinson, Wis., 1956-59; Vanderbilt University Divinity School, Nashville, Tenn., instructor in theology, 1961-62; Birmingham-Southern College, Birmingham, Ala., assistant professor of

philosophy and religion, 1963-65; Chicago Theological Seminary, Chicago, Ill., assistant professor, 1965-67, associate professor of constructive theology, 1967-70; Vanderbilt University Divinity School, Nashville, Tenn., associate professor, 1970-73, professor of theological ethics, 1973—.

WRITINGS: Christian Faith and History: A Critical Comparison of Ernst Troeltsch and Karl Barth, Abingdon, 1965; *The Death of God Controversy*, Abingdon, 1966; (editor, and author of introduction); *Openings for Marxist-Christian Dialogue*, Abingdon, 1968; (with Herbert Aptheker and Shepard Bliss) *From Hope to Liberation: Towards a Marxist-Christian Dialogue*, Fortress, 1974.

Work included in anthologies, *New Theology*, Numbers 6 and 8, edited by Marty Marty and Dean Peerman, Macmillan, 1967 and 1969. Contributor to *Encounter, Christian Advocate, Journal of Religion, Religion in Life*, and other publications. Editor, *Soundings: An Interdisciplinary Journal*, 1975—.

WORK IN PROGRESS: The Moral Agent: A Phenomenological Approach to Theological Ethics, completion expected in 1977.

*   *   *

O'HEARN, Peter J(oseph) T(homas) 1917.

PERSONAL: Born January 2, 1917, in Halifax, Nova Scotia, Canada; son of Walter Joseph Aloysius and Catherine (Mahony) O'Hearn; married Margaret Mary McCormick, September 8, 1944; children: Peter Kevin. *Education:* St. Mary's College, Halifax, Nova Scotia, B.A., 1937; Dalhousie University, teaching certificate, 1938, LL.B., 1947; McGill University, graduate study, 1938-39. *Religion:* Roman Catholic. *Home:* 6369 Berlin St., Halifax, Nova Scotia, Canada. *Office:* Court House, 1815 Upper Water St., Halifax, Nova Scotia, Canada.

CAREER: Fielding, O'Hearn & Vaughan (barristers and solicitors), Halifax, Nova Scotia, 1947-65, began as associate, became proprietor; Prosecuting Office, Halifax, Nova Scotia, assistant prosecuting officer, 1950-56, prosecuting officer, 1956-65; County Court, Halifax, Nova Scotia, judge, 1965—. Solicitor, Nova Scotia Barristers' Society, 1962-65; lecturer in criminal procedure, Dalhousie Law School. President of Nova Scotia division of Canadian Red Cross Society, 1956-58, Childrens Aid Society of Halifax, 1965-66. *Military service:* Canadian Army, Artillery, 1940-42; became lieutenant. *Member:* Canadian Bar Association, Archdiocesan Union of Holy Name Societies (president, 1958-60), Halifax Archdiocesan Ecumenical Commission (chairman, 1970-74).

WRITINGS: Peace, Order and Good Government: A New Constitution for Canada, Macmillan (Canada), 1964. Contributor to *Canadian Bar Review, Criminal Law Quarterly*.

WORK IN PROGRESS: Love, Law, and Liberty.

SIDELIGHTS: O'Hearn has some competence in Latin, French, German, and Gaelic, and knows a smattering of Greek. *Avocational interests:* Sociology, logic, mathematics, languages, theology.

*   *   *

OKIGBO, P(ius) N(wabufo) C. 1924-

PERSONAL: Born February 6, 1924, in Ojoto, Nigeria; son of James Okigbo; married Georgette Andrew, 1958; children: Pius, Uzo, Nwando, Nkiruka. *Education:* University of London, B.A. (honors), B.Sc., LL.B.; Oxford University, graduate study; Northwestern University, M.A. and Ph.D. *Home:* 3 Nike Ave., Enugu, Nigeria. *Office:* Cabinet Office, Lagos, Nigeria.

CAREER: Northwestern University, Evanston, Ill., lecturer in economics, 1955-57; Nuffield College, Oxford University, Oxford, England, postdoctoral research, 1957-58; government of Nigeria, economic adviser to Eastern Nigeria, 1958-62, ambassador to European Economic Community, 1963-66, economic adviser to federal government, Lagos, 1963-67; Skoup & Co. Ltd., Enugu, Nigeria, managing director, 1967—. *Member:* Nigerian Economic Society (president, 1964-65), American Economic Association, Royal Economic Society (England), Econometric Society (England).

WRITINGS: Nigerian National Accounts, 1950-57, Federal Ministry of Economic Development (Nigeria), 1962; *Nigerian Public Finance*, Northwestern University Press, 1965; *Africa and the Common Market*, Longmans, Green, 1967.

WORK IN PROGRESS: Growth and Structure of the Nigerian Economy.

* * *

OLAFSON, Frederick A(rlan) 1924-

PERSONAL: Born September 1, 1924, in Winnipeg, Manitoba, Canada; son of Kristinn (a clergyman) and Fredericka (Bjornson) Olafson; married Allie Lewis, June 20, 1952; children: Peter Niel, Christopher Arlan, Thomas Andrew. *Education:* Harvard University, B.A., 1947, M.A., 1948, Ph.D., 1951; Oxford University, postdoctoral study, 1951-52. *Home:* 6081 Arenida Chamnez, LaJolla, Calif. 92037. *Office:* Department of Philosophy, University of California at San Diego, LaJolla, Calif. 92037.

CAREER: Instructor at Princeton University, Princeton, N.J., 1950-51, Harvard University, Cambridge, Mass., 1952-54; Vassar College, Poughkeepsie, N.Y., assistant professor of philosophy, 1954-60; Johns Hopkins University, Baltimore, Md., associate professor of philosophy, 1960-64; Harvard University, professor of education and philosophy, Graduate School of Education, 1964-71; University of California at San Diego, LaJolla, professor of philosophy, 1971—, chairman of department, 1972—. Visiting professor, Stanford University, 1957. *Military service:* U.S. Naval Reserve, 1943-46; became lieutenant junior grade. *Member:* American Philosophical Association. *Awards, honors:* Fulbright scholar at Oxford University, 1951-52; Hodder fellow, Council of Humanities, 1960-61; Guggenheim fellowship, 1967-68.

WRITINGS: (Editor and author of introduction) *Society, Law and Morality*, Prentice-Hall, 1961; (editor and author of introduction) *Justice and Social Policy*, Prentice-Hall, 1961; *Principles and Persons: An Ethical Interpretation os Existentialism*, Johns Hopkins Press, 1967; *Ethics and Twentieth Century Thought*, Prentice-Hall, 1973. Contributor to professional journals.

* * *

OLFORD, Stephen F(rederick) 1918-

PERSONAL: Surname is pronounced Ol-*furd*; born March 29, 1918, in Kalene Hill, Northern Rhodesia; son of Frederick Ernest Samuel and Bessie Rhoden (Santmier) Olford; married Heather Brown, June 30, 1948; children: Jonathan McGregor, David Lindsay. *Education:* Educated privately

in Portuguese West Africa; St. Luke's College, Mildmay, London, England, diploma in theology, 1937; Missionary Training Colony, Upper Norwood, London, England, diploma, 1939. *Office:* Encounter Ministries, Inc., P.O. Box 1366, Holmes Beach, Fla. 33509.

CAREER: Army scripture reader with troops in Newport, South Wales, 1939-45; evangelist in England, Canada, and United States, 1945-53; minister of Baptist church in Richmond, Surrey, England, 1953-59; Calvary Baptist Church, New York, N.Y., minister, 1959-73, minister emeritus, 1973—. *Member:* Royal Geographical Society (fellow), Victoria Institute (London; fellow). *Awards, honors:* D.D., Wheaton College, Wheaton, Ill., 1966; D. Litt., Houghton College, 1966.

WRITINGS: Christianity and You, Eerdmans, 1958; *Successful Soul-Winning*, Moody, 1958, 2nd edition published as *The Secret of Soul-Winning*, 1963; *Heart-Cry for Revival*, Revell, 1962; (with Frank Lawes) *The Sanctity of Sex*, Revell, 1963; *The Living Word*, Moody, 1963; *I'll Take the High Road*, Zondervan, 1968; *The Tabernacle: Camping with God*, Loizeau Brothers, 1971; *The Grace of Giving*, Zonderran, 1972; *The Christian Message for Contemporary Man*, Word Books, 1973. Writer of booklets and contributor to Christian journals. Editor, *Encounter.*

SIDELIGHTS: Olford speaks Portuguese. *Avocational interests:* Golf, tennis, reading, photography, and listening to music.

BIOGRAPHICAL/CRITICAL SOURCES: Encounter, May, 1966.

* * *

OLIVER, William Irvin 1926-

PERSONAL: Born November 6, 1926, in Panama; son of William (a teacher) and Anna Oliver; married Barbara Marsh, 1950; children: Michael Conrad, Anna Ruth, Soren Albert. *Education:* Carnegie Institute of Technology (now Carnegie-Mellon University), B.F.A., 1950; Cornell University, M.A., 1955, Ph.D., 1959. *Politics:* "No fixed allegiance." *Religion:* None. *Home:* 2647 Piedmont, Berkeley, Calif. *Agent:* Bertha Klausner International Literary Agency, Inc., 130 East 40th St., New York, N.Y. 10016. *Office:* Department of Dramatic Art, University of California, Berkeley, Calif.

CAREER: Worked with private business firms in Fargo, N.D., 1950-53, and was concurrently director (with wife) of Fargo-Moorhead Community Theater; Cornell University, Ithaca, N.Y., business and publicity manager of University Theatre, 1953-58, instructor in drama, 1957-58; University of California, Berkeley, 1958—, began as assistant professor now professor of drama. Onteora Playhouse, Tannersville, N.Y., director, summers, 1955-56. Visiting professor, University of Chile, Santiago, 1966-67. *Military service:* U.S. Navy, 1945-46. *Member:* American Educational Theatre Association (chairman of aesthetics section), Phi Kappa Phi. *Awards, honors:* Dial Press Award for creative writing, 1949; Stanley Award of New York City Writers' Conference for play, "To Learn to Love," 1957; fine arts fellowship, University of California, Berkeley, 1965-66; Santiago Critics Award, for "Marat/Sade," as best production of year, 1966.

WRITINGS: (Contributor of play translation) *Don Juan in Dramatic Literature*, University of Nebraska Press, 1963; (editor with Travis Bogard) *Modern Drama: Essays in Criticism*, Oxford University Press, 1965; (contributor of translations) Robert Corrigan, editor, *Masterpieces of the Modern Spanish Theatre*, Collier, 1967; (contributor) *Literary Types and Themes*, Holt, 1970; *Voices of Change in the Spanish Theatre*, University of Texas Press, 1971; (contributor of play translation) *The Modern Stage in Latin America: Six Plays*, Dutton, 1971.

Plays produced: "The Stallion," Cornell University Theatre, 1955, and included in *Best Short Plays*, Beacon, 1957; "To Learn to Love," University of California, Berkeley, 1960; "The Antifarce of John and Leporello," University of California, Berkeley, 1963; "The Masques of Barbara Blomberg," Catawba College, 1971.

Translations produced: Fredrico Garcia Lorca, "Blood Wedding," Cornell University Theatre, 1955; Fredrico Garcia Lorca, "The Tragicomedy of Dona Rosita," New York, 1958, and included in *New World Writing*, Volume VIII; Sergio Vodonic, "Vina," Sausalito Little Theatre; Antonio Buero Vallejo, "The Dream Weaver," Case Western Reserve University, 1968; Griseldo Gambaro, "The Camp," Cornell University, 1970; Griseldo Gambaro, "The Siamese Twins," Southern Illinois University, 1972; Jose Manual Arce, "Scusemeplease," University of California, Berkeley, 1972; Enrique Buenaventura, "In the Right Hand of God the Father," Pan American University, 1972, and in New York at the Teatro Caras Nuevas, 1973; Emilio Carballido, "I Too Speak of the Rose," Occidental College, 1972. Also translator of numerous other plays from the Spanish. Member of editorial board, *Latin American Theatre Review*.

WORK IN PROGRESS: A play entitled, "The Dumbshows of the King," the third play of a trilogy; a book, *Rhetoric for the Theatre;* revisions of two earlier works for publication.

SIDELIGHTS: Oliver has directed more than thirty five plays in university theatres and summer stock.

* * *

OLSEN, John Edward 1925-
(Jack Olsen, Jonathan Rhoades)

PERSONAL: Born June 7, 1925, in Indianapolis, Ind.; son of Rudolph O. (a salesman) and Florence (Drecksage) Olsen. *Education:* University of Pennsylvania, student, 1945-46. *Agent:* Scott Meredith Literary Agency, 580 Fifth Ave., New York, N.Y. 10036. *Office:* Route 1, Box 720, Sequim, Wash. 98382.

CAREER: Reporter for *San Diego Union Tribune*, later for *San Diego Journal*, San Diego, Calif., 1947-50, *Washington Daily News*, Washington, D.C., 1950-51, *New Orleans Item*, New Orleans, La., 1952-53, and *Chicago Sun-Times*, Chicago, Ill., 1954-55; WMAL-TV, Washington, D.C., television news editor and broadcaster, 1950-51; *Time*, correspondent, 1956-58, chief of Midwest bureau, 1959; *Sports Illustrated*, New York, N.Y., senior editor, 1960-74. Author. *Military service:* U.S. Army, Office of Strategic Services, 1943-44. *Member:* Authors Guild of the Authors League of America, National Audubon Society. *Awards, honors:* National Headliner Award from Press Club of Atlantic City; Page One Award from Chicago Newspaper Guild; citations from University of Indiana and Columbia University.

WRITINGS—All under name Jack Olsen except where otherwise noted: *The Mad World of Bridge*, Holt, 1960; (under pseudonym Jonathan Rhoades) *Over the Fence Is Out*, Holt, 1961; *The Climb Up to Hell*, Harper, 1962;

(with Charles Goren) *Bridge Is My Game*, Doubleday, 1965; *Black Is Best: The Riddle of Cassius Clay*, Putnam, 1967; *Silence on Monte Sole*, Putnam, 1968; *The Black Athlete: A Shameful Story*, Time-Life, 1968; *Night of the Grizzlies*, Putnam, 1969; (with Fran Tarkenton) *Better Scramble than Lose*, Four Winds Press, 1969.

The Bridge at Chappaquiddick, Little, Brown, 1970; *Aphrodite: Desperate Mission*, Putnam, 1970; *Slaughter the Animals, Poison the Earth*, Simon & Schuster, 1971; *The Girls in the Office*, Simon & Schuster, 1972; *The Girls on the Campus*, Pocket Books, 1974; *Sweet Street*, Ballantine, 1974; *The Man with the Candy*, Simon & Schuster, 1974; *Alphabet Jackson*, Playboy Press, 1974; *Massy's Game*, Playboy Press, 1974.

Contributor of over 300 stories and articles to *Life*, *Reader's Digest*, *Fortune*, *This Week*, *Nouvelle Candide*, *Playboy*, *Daily Sketch* (London), and other periodicals. Contributor to anthologies.

SIDELIGHTS: Olsen once told *CA*: "I have spent 25 years telling it like it is." M. Stuart Madden said: "*Slaughter the Animals, Poison the Earth* is investigative reporting in the finest tradition of Upton Sinclair and Lincoln Steffens."

* * *

OLSTAD, Charles (Frederick) 1932-

PERSONAL: Born November 16, 1932, in New Ulm, Minn.; son of Porter Leonard Cornelius (a farmer) and Adelia (Schmiesing) Olstad; married Elizabeth Grace Simon, August 25, 1957; children: Carl Jay, Lois Helen, William Porter, Jan Frederick. *Education:* St. Olaf College, B.A., 1954; University of Iowa, M.A., 1956; University of Wisconsin, Ph.D., 1960. *Home:* 720 North Treat, Tucson, Ariz. 85716. *Office:* Department of Romance Languages, University of Arizona, Tucson, Ariz. 85721.

CAREER: University of Arizona, Tucson, assistant professor, 1960-66, associate professor, 1966-72, professor of Spanish, 1972—. Tucson Community School, chairman of board of directors, 1966-67. *Member:* Modern Language Association of America, American Association of Teachers of Spanish and Portuguese.

WRITINGS: (With Leo Barrow) *Creative Spanish*, Harper, 1965, revised edition, 1972; (with Barrow) *Aspectos de la literatura espanola*, Xerox College Publishing, 1972; (contributor) Paul Turner, editor, *Bilingualism in the Southwest*, University of Arizona Press, 1973; (contributor) David E. Pownall, editor, *Articles on Twentieth Century Literature: An Annotated Bibliography, 1955-1970*, seven volumes, Kraus-Thompson, 1973—. Contributor to *Hispania* and *Romance Notes*. Assistant editor, bibliography committee, *Twentieth Century Literature*.

SIDELIGHTS: Aside from Spanish, Olstad reads French, German, Italian, and Portuguese. *Avocational interests:* Short wave radio.

* * *

O'MEARA, Thomas A. 1935-

PERSONAL: Born May 15, 1935, in Des Moines, Iowa; son of Joseph M. (a salesman) and Frances C. (Rock) O'Meara. *Education:* Attended Loras College, 1953-55; Aquinas Institute of Philosophy, River Forest, Ill., M.A., 1959, Lic.Phil., 1959; Aquinas Institute of Theology, Dubuque, Iowa, M.A., 1963; University of Munich, Ph.D., 1967. *Home and office:* Aquinas Institute of Theology, Theological Faculties in Iowa, Dubuque, Iowa 52001.

CAREER: Ordained Roman Catholic priest, member of Dominican Order of Preachers, 1962. Aquinas Institute of Theology, Dubuque, Iowa, professor of systematic theology, 1966—. Visiting professor, Notre Dame University, Weston College School of Theology, Boston Theological Institute, and Seminary of S.S. Peter and Paul (Nigeria). Member of executive board, Catholic Committee on Urban Ministry.

WRITINGS: (With C. D. Weisser) *Paul Tillich in Catholic Thought*, Priory, 1964; *Mary in Protestant and Catholic Theology*, Sheed, 1966; (editor) *Rudolf Bultmann in Catholic Thought*, Herder & Herder, 1968; (editor) Thomas Aquinas, *Summa theologiae*, McGraw, 1968; *Holiness and Radicalism in Religious Life*, Herder & Herder, 1970; (editor) *Projections: Shaping An American Theology for the Future*, Doubleday, 1970; *Paul Tillich's Theology of God* Dubuque, 1971; *Loose in the World*, Paulist Press, 1974. Contributor of articles to *Harvard Theological Review, Theology Today*, and other periodicals.

* * *

O'NEILL, Barbara Powell 1929-

PERSONAL: Born April 25, 1929, in Dexter, Mo.; daughter of Clarence Albert (a lawyer) and Ethel (Mohrstadt) Powell; married Richard Winslow O'Neill (an author and editor), January 3, 1953 (divorced, February, 1966); children: Richard II, Susan Powell, Jennifer Anne, Julia Kay. *Education:* Wellesley College, B.A., 1950; graduate study at New York University and University of Bridgeport; Columbia University, M.A., 1967; also studied art at Silvermine College of Art, and privately, for six years. *Office:* Silvermine Guild of Artists, Silvermine Rd., New Canaan, Conn.

CAREER: Semiprofessional painter and photographer, doing watercolors, children's portraits, and press photography; writer. *Member:* Phi Beta Kappa, Sigma Xi.

WRITINGS: Careers for Women After Marriage and Children, Macmillan, 1965; (author with Richard Winslow O'Neill, and illustrator) *The Unhandy Man's Guide to Home Repairs*, Macmillan, 1966.†

* * *

O'NEILL, David P(atrick) 1918-

PERSONAL: Born June 9, 1918, in Wellington, New Zealand; son of Daniel (a clerk) and Ellen (Mulcahy) O'Neill. *Education:* Attended St. Patrick's College, Wellington, New Zealand, 1931-34; Holy Cross College, Mosgiel, New Zealand, seminarian, 1935-41; Victoria University of Wellington, Diploma in Social Science, 1951, and studies in Polynesian anthropology and Maori language and sociology; Boston University, Ph.D., 1970. *Home and office:* Holy Cross College, Mosgiel, New Zealand.

CAREER: Ordained Roman Catholic priest, 1941; did parish work, 1941-48; Catholic Social Services, Wellington, New Zealand, counselor, 1948-66, counseling consultant, 1966—; Holy Cross College, Mosgiel, New Zealand, professor of ethics and communications, 1972—. Lecturer in United States, 1961, 1973. *Member:* New Zealand Association of Social Workers.

WRITINGS—All published by Pflaum Press, except as indicated: *Priestly Celibacy and Maturity*, Sheed, 1965; *About Loving*, 1966; *The Priest in Crisis*, 1968; *The Sharing Community*, 1968; *The Way of Trusting*, 1969; *What Do You Say to a Child When You Meet a Flower,*

Abbey Press, 1972; *Christian Behavior*, 1973; *The Book of Rewi*, Seabury, 1975. Contributor to *Living Light* (educational monthly).

WORK IN PROGRESS: Study of value and attitude formation and change during adolescence; study of new techniques in personal and group counseling.

SIDELIGHTS: O'Neill reads French and Maori.

* * *

OPPENHEIMER, Harold L. 1919-

PERSONAL: Born November 22, 1919, in Kansas City, Mo.; son of Harold and Doris (Jones) Oppenheimer; married Sally Hamilton, February 19, 1944; children: Hamilton, Reed J., Harold Byrd, Eric. *Education:* Harvard University, graduated in anthropology, 1939. *Home:* 4810 McGee, Kansas City, Mo. *Office:* Oppenheimer Industries, Inc., 1808 Main, Kansas City, Mo. 64108.

CAREER: Harvard University, Cambridge, Mass., anthropologist in charge of expedition in Bolivia, 1939-41; president of Allied Motors and Baltimore Realty Co., both Kansas City, Mo., and operator of family farms, 1947-50, 1953-60; Atlas Acceptance Corp., The Armendaris Corp., and Oppenheimer Industries, Inc., Kansas City, Mo., chairman of board, 1953—. Starlight Theatre, Performing Arts Foundation, member of board of directors. *Military service:* U.S. Marine Corps, 1940-46, 1950-53; served in Pacific Theater, Alaska, and Korea; received Letter of Commendation, Presidential Unit Citation, and Bronze Star. U.S. Marine Corps Reserve, 1953; became brigadier general, 1968; received Legion of Merit Medal, 1972; retired, 1972. *Member:* Plymouth Dealer Association (president, 1947-50), Harvard Club of Kansas City, Harvard Club of New York, Mission Valley Hunt Club.

WRITINGS: Samoan Military Grammar, U.S. Marine Corps, 1943; *Cowboy Arithmetic*, Interstate, 1961, 3rd edition, 1971; *Cowboy Economics*, Interstate, 1965, 2nd edition, 1971; *March to the Sound of Drums*, Interstate, 1966; (with James Keast) *Cowboy Litigation*, Interstate, 1968, 2nd edition, 1972; *Land Speculation*, Interstate, 1972; *Cowboy Securities*, Interstate, 1974. Contributor of military articles to *Marine Corps Gazette, Leatherneck*, and *Military Review*. Also contributor of short stories and articles to *American Hereford Journal* and other trade magazines.

* * *

OPPENHEIMER, Max, Jr. 1917-

PERSONAL: Born July 27, 1917, in New York, N.Y.; son of Max and Louise (Pourfurst) Oppenheimer; married Christine Backus, October 14, 1942; children: Edmund M., Carolyn C. *Education:* University of Paris, Bachelor es Lettres (cum laude), 1935; New York University, B.A. (cum laude), 1941; University of California, Los Angeles, M.A., 1942; University of Southern California, Ph.D., 1947. *Religion:* Episcopalian. *Home address:* Box 309, Fredonia, N.Y. 14063. *Office:* Department of Languages, State University of New York, College at Fredonia, Fredonia, N.Y.

CAREER: Engaged in import-export business, New York, N.Y., and Paris, France, 1935-38; San Diego State College (now University), San Diego, Calif., instructor in French, German, and Spanish, 1947-49; Washington University, St. Louis, Mo., assistant professor of Romance languages, 1949-51; Central Intelligence Agency, intelligence officer (civilian), 1956-58, stationed in Germany, 1957-58; Florida

State University, Tallahassee, associate professor of Russian and German, 1958-61; University of Iowa, Iowa City, professor of Russian and chairman of department, 1961-67, State University of New York, College at Fredonia, professor and chairman of department of languages, 1967—. *Military service:* U.S. Army, 1942-46; received battlefield commission and Bronze Star. U.S. Army Reserve, Military Intelligence; served on active duty, 1951-56, with assignment in Germany, 1954-55; now lieutenant colonel.

MEMBER: Modern Language Association of America, American Association of Teachers of Slavic and East European Languages, American Translators Association, International Society for General Semantics, Midwest Modern Language Association, Reserve Officers Association, Phi Beta Kappa, Sigma Delta Pi, Pi Delta Phi (national president, 1946-51; honorary president, 1951—), Alpha Mu Gamma, Dobro Slovo, Elks. *Awards, honors:* Research grants from Florida State University Research Council, 1961, and from U.S. Office of Naval Research for translation of Russian book on hydraulics; State University of New York, faculty research fellowship, 1973.

WRITINGS: (Translator from the Russian with Michael Kasha) N. N. Semyonov, *Collective Interaction Processes in Polymers*, Institute of Molecular Biophysics, Florida State University, 1961; (translator from the Russian with Michael Kasha) A. S. Davydov, *Theory of Molecular Excitons*, McGraw, 1964; *A Basic Outline of Russian Grammar*, Lucas Brothers, 1962; (translator) A. A. Kostyukov, *Theory of Ship Waves and Wave Resistance*, Effective Communications (Iowa City), 1968; (contributor of translation) *Historical and Literary Perspectives: Essays and Studies in Honor of Albert D. Menut*, Coronado Press, 1973; (translator) Calderin, *The Fake Astrologer*, Coronado Press, 1975; (translator) Lope de Vega, *The Lady Simpleton*, Coronado Press, 1975. Contributor of many articles to *Slavic and East European Journal, Journal of Human Relations, Modern Language Notes, South Atlantic Bulletin*, and other language journals.

SIDELIGHTS: Oppenheimer has traveled in most of Europe and Great Britain and has visited the Scandinavian countries. In 1964 he traveled to Moscow, Leningrad, Prague, and Warsaw. He is completely fluent in Russian, Spanish, German and French. *Avocational interests:* Swimming, gymnastics, flying.

*   *   *

OREM, R(eginald) C(alvert) 1931-

PERSONAL: Born July 24, 1931, in Baltimore, Md.; son of Reginald (a newspaper editor) and Hazel (Robinson) Orem; married Edith Freund; children: John, Tom, Jessica. *Education:* University of Maryland, B.A., 1953, M.Ed., 1959. *Address:* Box 379, College Park, Md. 20740.

CAREER: Former public and private school teacher, director of guidance services at Fort George G. Meade Army Education Center, and administrator of District of Columbia Children Center; educational consultant, lecturer, and writer, 1965—. Member of National Advisory Council of the Reading Reform Foundation; honorary member, Optometric Extension Program Foundation. *Member:* Phi Kappa Phi. *Awards, honors:* Montessorian of the Year Award, 1972.

WRITINGS: (Editor) *A Montessori Handbook*, Putnam, 1965; (with William Amos) *Managing Student Behavior*, Warren H. Green, 1967; (editor) *Montessori for the Disadvantaged*, Putnam, 1967; (with George L. Stevens) *The*

Case for Early Reading, Warren H. Green, 1968; (editor) *Montessori and the Special Child*, Putnam, 1969; (editor with Kenneth Edelson) *Children's House Parent-Teacher Guide to Montessori*, Putnam, 1970; (with Stevens) *American Montessori Manual*, Mafex Associates, 1970; *Learning to See and Seeing to Learn*, Mafex Associates, 1971; (editor) *Montessori Today*, Putnam, 1971; *Montessori, Her Method and the Movement: What You Need to Know*, Putnam, 1974; *Developmental Vision for Lifelong Learning*, Mafex Associates, 1974. Contributor to journals and magazines, including *Ladies' Home Journal, Reading Teacher*, and *Nation's Business*.

WORK IN PROGRESS: A seventh Montessori book for Putnam.

*   *   *

ORENT, Norman B. 1920-

PERSONAL: Born October 19, 1920, in Brockton, Mass.; son of George Harry (a businessman) and Yetta (Eiferman) Orentlicher; married Dorothy Seidman, March 19, 1944; children: Jean, Rena. *Education:* Brown University, A.B., 1942; Harvard University, M.B.A., 1947. *Religion:* Jewish. *Residence:* Scarsdale, N.Y. *Office:* Jodere Corp., 39 Lincoln Rd., Scarsdale, N.Y. 10583.

CAREER: Westover Mills, Warwick, R.I., assistant to president, 1947-52; Verney Corp., Manchester, N.H., manager of Greige sales, 1952-54; Textron Corp., New York, N.Y., sales manager, 1954-55; Hamilton-Skotch Corp., New York, N.Y., vice-president and general manager, 1955-59, director, 1955—, president, 1959-70; Hampden Specialty Products Corp., New York, N.Y., president and director, 1959-70; Shott Chairs Corp., New York, N.Y., chairman of board, 1964-70; Jodere Corp., Scarsdale, N.Y., president, 1970—; Orent Enterprises, Scarsdale, N.Y., principal, 1970—. Director, Brooklyn chapter of American Red Cross; trustee, Union Savings Bank of New York. *Military service:* U.S. Army, Counter Intelligence, 1943-46; became first lieutenant; received Bronze Star. *Member:* Young Presidents Organization, World Business Council, Metropolitan Presidents Organization (president and director, 1974-75), Brown University Club, Harvard Business School Club of New York, Phi Beta Kappa.

WRITINGS: Your Future in Marketing, Rosen, 1966.

*   *   *

OSBORNE, (Reginald) Arthur 1906-

PERSONAL: Born September 25, 1906, in London, England; son of Owen John and Dulci Eden (Greville) Osborne; married Lucia Lipszyc; children: Catherine, Adam, Frania. *Education:* Christ Church, Oxford, B.A. (honors in modern history, later converted to M.A.), 1927. *Home and office:* Sri Ramanashram P.O., Tiruvannamalai, South India.

CAREER: Chulalongkorn University, Bangkok, Thailand, lecturer in English, 1937-45; Sri Ramanashram, Tiruvannamalai, South India, editor of *Mountain Path* (a quarterly), 1964—.

WRITINGS: Ramana Arunachala, Sri Ramanashram, 1952, 2nd edition, T. N. Venkataraman, 1958; *Ramana Maharshi and the Path of Self-Knowledge*, Rider & Co., 1954, S. Weiser, 1970; *The Incredible Sai Baba*, Orient Longmans, 1957, revised edition, Rider & Co. 1972; *Buddhism and Christianity in the Light of Hinduism*, Rider

& Co., 1959; (editor) *The Collected Works of Ramana Maharshi*, Sri Ramanashram, 1959, 3rd edition, 1968, S. Weiser, 1970; (editor) *The Teachings of Ramana Maharshi in His Own Worlds*, Sri Ramanashram, 1960; *The Question of Progress*, Bharatiya Vidya Bhavan, 1966.†

* * *

OSGOOD, Charles E(gerton) 1916-

PERSONAL: Born November 20, 1916, in Somerville, Mass.; son of Merrill White (a businessman) and Ruth (Egerton) Osgood; married Cynthia Thornton, June 27, 1939; children: Philip Thornton, Gail Ruth. *Education:* Dartmouth College, B.A., 1939; Yale University, Ph.D., 1945. *Politics:* Independent. *Religion:* "None." *Home:* 304 East Mumford Dr., Urbana, Ill. 61801. *Office:* University of Illinois, Urbana, Ill. 61801.

CAREER: University of Connecticut, Storrs, assistant professor of psychology, 1946-49; University of Illinois, Urbana, associate professor, 1949-52, professor of psychology, and communications, 1952—, director of Institute of Communications Research, 1957-65, and Center for Advanced Study, 1965—. Visiting professor, University of Hawaii, 1964-65. *Member:* American Psychological Association (president, 1962-63), Linguistic Society of America, American Academy of Arts and Sciences, National Academy of Science. *Awards, honors:* Guggenheim fellow, 1955; Center for Advanced Study in the Behavioral Sciences fellowship, 1958; award for distinguished contribution to psychology from American Psychological Association, 1961; D.Sc., Dartmouth College, 1962.

WRITINGS: Method and Theory in Experimental Psychology, Oxford University Press, 1953; (with Suci and Tannenbaum) *The Measurement of Meaning*, University of Illinois Press, 1957; *An Alternative to War or Surrender*, University of Illinois Press, 1962; *Perspective in Foreign Policy*, Pacific Books, 1966; (with May and Miron) *Cross-Cultural Universals of Affective Meaning*, University of Illinois Press, 1975; *Focus on Meaning*, three volumes, Mouton, In press.

WORK IN PROGRESS: Cross-cultural research on human semantic systems, and on communication and negotiation in international affairs.

* * *

OSTROWER, Alexander 1901-

PERSONAL: Born April 28, 1901, in Plock, Poland; son of Isaac Tobias and Sarah Rachel (Lask) Ostrower; married Karolina Finkelstein, March 28, 1926; children: Irene (Mrs. William A. Rosenthall). *Education:* University of Warsaw, Master of Laws, 1926; George Washington University, Master of Comparative Law, 1952. *Religion:* Jewish. *Home:* 4101 Cathedral Ave. N.W., Washington, D.C. 20016.

CAREER: Former member of bar, Warsaw, Poland; passed examination for judges in Poland, 1929, and held several court appointments in Warsaw during period, 1930-39; Xoslo Company (real estate and chain stores operation), Washington, D.C., counsel and general manager, from 1940 until retirement; concurrently did research and writing; now devoting time to research and writing on international law and foreign relations.

WRITINGS: Evening Moods, Herliah (Warsaw), 1922; *Language, Law, and Diplomacy: A Study of Linguistic Diversity in Official International Relations and International Law*, University of Pennsylvania Press, Volumes I and II, 1965, Volume III, 1975. Also author of *My Fight for Justice in the Courts of Poland: Reminiscences of a Lawyer*, 1975.

WORK IN PROGRESS: Research on U.S.-U.S.S.R. diplomatic efforts and motivations.

SIDELIGHTS: Ostrower is proficient in Latin, Hebrew, liturgical Aramaic, Russian, Polish, Czech, German, French, and Italian.

BIOGRAPHICAL/CRITICAL SOURCES: History of Plock, Publication Society (Buenos Aires), 1945; Sol Greenspan, *Jews of Plock*, Forward, 1960; *American Political Science Review*, December, 1965; *American Bar Association Journal*, May, 1966.

* * *

OSTWALD, Peter F. 1928-

PERSONAL: Born January 5, 1928, in Berlin, Germany; son of Eugene (a physician) and Kate (Ury) Ostwald; married Lise Deschamps, December 22, 1960; children: Chantal, David. *Education:* University of California, A.B., 1947, M.D., 1950; Cornell University, psychiatric residency training, 1951-55. *Home:* 60 Alton Ave., San Francisco, Calif. 94116. *Office:* University of California Medical Center, 401 Parnassus Ave., San Francisco, Calif. 94122.

CAREER: New York Hospital, Payne Whitney Clinic, New York, N.Y., resident, 1951-53, 1955-56; University of California School of Medicine, Langley Porter Neuropsychiatric Institute, San Francisco, Calif., senior resident, 1956-57, associate research psychiatrist, 1957-59, assistant professor, 1958-64, associate professor, 1964-70, professor of clinical psychiatry, 1970—, attending psychiatrist, 1958—; private practice as psychiatrist, San Francisco, Calif., 1958—; San Francisco Hospital, San Francisco, Calif., staff psychiatrist, 1963—. *Military service:* U.S. Army, Medical Corps, 1953-55; became captain. *Member:* American Psychiatric Association (fellow), American College of Psychiatrists (fellow), American Medical Association, American Association for the Advancement of Science, California Medical Association, San Francisco Medical Society.

WRITINGS: (Contributor) D. Barbara, editor, *Psychological and Psychiatric Aspects of Speech and Hearing*, C. C Thomas, 1960; (contributor) E. Schneider, editor, *Music Therapy 1960*, National Association of Music Therapists, 1960; *Soundmaking—The Acoustic Communication of Emotion*, C. C Thomas, 1963; (contributor) Hayes and Sebeok, editors, *Approaches to Semiotics*, Mouton & Co., 1964; (author of preface) Clyde L. Rousey and Alice Moriatry, *Diagnostic Implications of Speech Sounds: The Reflections of Developmental Conflict and Trauma*, C. C Thomas, 1965; *The Semantics of Human Sounds*, Mouton, 1973. Contributor of about thirty articles and fifty reviews to medical, mental hygiene, and psychiatric journals.

* * *

OSWALD, Ian 1929-

PERSONAL: Born August 4, 1929, in London, England; son of John S. L. and Lily (Hawkins) Oswald; married Joan Thomsett, August 8, 1951; children: Andrew John, Sally Elizabeth, Malcolm Leslie, James Ian. *Education:* Studied at University of Bristol; Cambridge University, B.A., 1950, B.Chir., 1953, M.B. and M.A., 1954, M.D., 1958; University of Edinburgh, D.Sc., 1963. *Politics:* Left-wing. *Religion:* Protestant. *Office:* Department of Psychiatry, School of Medicine, University of Edinburgh, Edinburgh, Scotland.

CAREER: Oxford University, Oxford, England, research fellow, Institute of Experimental Psychology, 1957-59; University of Edinburgh, Edinburgh, Scotland, lecturer, 1959-65, senior lecturer in psychiatry, 1965—. Visiting professor, University of Western Australia, 1965-67. *Military service:* Royal Air Force, medical officer, 1955. *Member:* Royal Society of Medicine (fellow), Royal Medico-Psychological Association, Experimental Psychology Society, Electroencephalography Society, Association for Psychophysiological Study of Sleep.

WRITINGS: Sleeping and Waking, Elsevier, 1962; *Sleep,* Penguin, 1965; *So Now You Know About Sleeping and Not Sleeping,* British Medical Association, 1970. Contributor to scientific journals.

WORK IN PROGRESS: A study of sleep.

SIDELIGHTS: Oswald told *CA* that he is interested in "modernising petty political systems that obstruct the provision of adequate medical care for all in a community."†

* * *

OSWALT, Wendell H(illman) 1927-

PERSONAL: Born July 26, 1927, in Youngstown, Ohio; son of E. J. (an engineer) and Sarah (Hillman) Oswalt; married Helen Louise Taylor, February 28, 1947; children: William M., Pamela K., Ivar. *Education:* University of Alaska, B.A., 1952; University of Arizona, Ph.D., 1959. *Office:* Department of Anthropology, University of California, Los Angeles, Calif.

CAREER: University of Alaska, College, research associate in anthropology, 1955-59; University of California, Los Angeles, assistant professor, 1959-65, associate professor, 1965-69, professor of anthropology, 1969—, chairman of department, 1972—. *Military service:* U.S. Coast Guard, 1945-46. *Member:* American Anthropological Association.

WRITINGS: Napaskiak: An Alaskan Eskimo Community, University of Arizona Press, 1963; *Mission of Change in Alaska,* Huntington Library, 1963; *This Land Was Theirs,* Wiley, 1966, 2nd edition, 1973; *Alaskan Eskimos,* Chandler, 1967; *Understanding Our Culture,* Holt, 1970; *Other People, Other Customs: Ethnography and its History,* Holt, 1972; *Habitat and Technology: The Evolution of Hunting,* Holt, 1973.

* * *

OTTLIK, Geza 1912-

PERSONAL: Given name sounds like *Gay-*zaw; born May 9, 1912, in Budapest, Hungary; son of Geza (a civil servant) and Elizabeth (Cs. Szabo) Ottlik; married Margaret Debreczeni, November 4, 1939. *Education:* Attended military high school and military academy in Hungary for seven years, and University of Budapest for five years. *Religion:* Calvinist. *Home:* Attila ut 45, Budapest 1, Hungary. *Agent:* Martonplay, Inc., 96 Fifth Ave., New York, N.Y. 10011; Hungarian Copyright Bureau, Budapest 5, Hungary.

CAREER: Literary adviser to Hungarian Radio Corp., Budapest, 1945-46; author and translator. *Member:* P.E.N. (secretary of Budapest center, 1946-57). *Awards, honors:* Received decoration, Munka Erdemrend, 1972.

WRITINGS: Hajnali haztetok (novella and short stories), Magveto, 1957; *Iskola a hataron* (novel), Magveto, 1959 translatiion published as *School at the Frontier,* Harcourt, 1966, revised edition, 1968; (editor) *Mai Amerikai Elbeszelok* (anthology), Europa, 1963; (editor) *Az Olomkristely* (an F. Scott Fitzgerald anthology), Europa, 1966; *Autobusz es Tguana* (anthology), Europa, 1968; *Minden Megvan* (stories) Magveto, 1969; (contributor) *Latogatoban,* Gondolat, 1971. Translations published in Hungarian include works of George Bernard Shaw, Charles Dickens, Ernest Hemingway, Eugene O'Neill, John Osborne, Evelyn Waugh, and other American, English, French, and German novelists and playwrights, 1949-66.

WORK IN PROGRESS: A volume of essays and criticism; a novel, tentatively titled *Buda,* publication by Magveto expected in 1976.

SIDELIGHTS: Despite the fact that he has translated extensively, Ottlik writes that he has "no command of any languages—excepting perhaps my own." Adds that his interests have been vocational, "for a novelist cannot afford to have other." *Avocational interests:* Mathematics, sports (track and field), competitive bridge (played in international matches in the 1930's), travel, people, cities ("no landscape; alas, no birds").

* * *

OWENDOFF, Robert S(cott) 1945-

PERSONAL: Born March 16, 1945, in Washington, D.C.; son of Robert Albert and Vauda (Paugh) Owendoff. *Education:* University of Virginia, student, 1963-64; U.S. Naval Academy, midshipman, 1964-68. *Home:* 11156 Byrd Dr., Fairfax, Va. *Office:* U.S.S. Thomaston (LSD-28), F.P.O., San Francisco, Calif. 96601.

CAREER: U.S. Navy, 1968—, with current rank of lieutenant; served as staff officer, Naval Oceanographic Office, Suitland, Md., 1968, main propulsion assistant, U.S.S. Page, Newport, R.I., 1969-70, engineer officer, U.S.S. San Marcos, Norfolk, Va., 1970-71, engineer officer, U.S.S. Thomaston, San Diego, Calif., 1971—, currently student at Naval Postgraduate School, Monterey, Calif. *Member:* Antiquarian Horological Society, Virginia Academy of Science. *Awards, honors:* Award for excellence in research, Virginia Academy of Science, 1960; award·from U.S. Army for new method of direction-finding in survival situations.

WRITINGS: Shadow-Tip Method for Direction, Arfax, 1962; *Better Ways of Pathfinding,* Stackpole, 1964; *Sun is Your Guide,* Government Printing Office, 1968. Contributor to *Field and Stream, Popular Science, Pilot, Griffith Observer, Infantry Journal,* and other periodicals.

* * *

OWENS, Rochelle 1936-

PERSONAL: Born April 2, 1936, in Brooklyn, N.Y.; daughter of Maxwell and Molly (Adler) Bass; married George Economou (a university professor), June 17, 1962. *Education:* Attended public schools in New York, N.Y., Herbert Berghof Studio, and New School for Social Research. *Politics:* "Variable." *Religion:* Jewish. *Home:* 606 West 116th St., No. 34, New York, N.Y. 10027. *Agent:* Elisabeth Marton, 96 Fifth Ave., New York, N.Y. 10011.

CAREER: Has held jobs at various times as clerk, typist, and telephone operator. Playwright, poet, and lecturer. *Member:* Dramatists Guild, New Dramatists Committee,

Actors Studio, Screen Writers Guild, New York Theatre Strategy (founding member), Women's Theatre Council (founding member). *Awards, honors:* Rockefeller grant for playwriting, 1965; Obie Award, 1967, for *Futz;* Yale School of Drama and American Broadcasting Corp. fellowship, 1968; Guggenheim fellowship, 1971.

WRITINGS—Poetry: *Not Be Essence That Cannot Be,* Trobar, 1961; (with others) LeRoi Jones, editor, *Four Young Lady Poets,* Totem-Corinth Press, 1962; *Salt and Core,* Black Sparrow Press, 1968; *I Am the Babe of Joseph Stalin's Daughter: Poems, 1961-1971,* Kulchur Press, 1972; *Poems from Joe's Garage,* limited edition, Wittenborn, 1973; *The Joe Eighty-Two Creation Poems,* Black Sparrow Press, 1974. Poetry represented in many anthologies, including *A Controversy of Poets,* edited by Paris Leary and Robert Kelly, Doubleday, 1965; *Technicians of the Sacred,* edited by Jerome Rothenberg, Doubleday, 1969; *Inside Outer Space,* edited by Robert Vas Dias, Anchor Books, 1970. Contributor of poetry to magazines and journals.

Plays: *Futz* (first produced in Minneapolis, Minn., at Tyrone Guthrie Theatre Workshop, 1965), Hawk's Well Press, 1962, revised edition published in *Futz and What Came After,* Random House, 1968 (also see below); "Istanboul," first produced in New York at Judson Poets Theatre, 1965; "The String Game," first produced in New York at Judson Poets Theatre, 1965; "Homo," first produced in Stockholm, 1966; produced, with "The Queen of Greece," in New York at Cafe LaMama, 1969; "Beclch," first produced in Philadelphia, Pa., at Theatre of the Living Arts, 1967; *Futz and What Came After* (contains "Futz," "The String Game," "Beclch," "Istanboul," and "Homo"), Random House, 1968; "The Queen of Greece," first produced, with "Homo," in New York at Cafe LaMama, 1969; (editor and contributor) *Spontaneous Combustion: Eight New American Plays,* Winter House, 1972; "The Karl Marx Play," first produced in New York at American Place Theatre, April 2, 1973. Also author of plays, "He Wants Shih!," 1969, and "Kontraption," 1970. Plays represented in many anthologies, including *New American Plays,* Volume II, edited by William M. Hoffman, Hill & Wang, 1968; *Best Short Plays,* edited by Stanley Richards, Chilton, 1971.

Founder with others of *Scripts/Performance* (magazine of theatre arts), 1971.

SIDELIGHTS: Charles Stein called Rochelle Owens' poetry collection, *Salt and Core,* "a strange collection for a 'Lady' poet—strange because the energy of the poetry is so phallic and sharply outward." He went on: "She is at her best when the cute side of her combines with the more violent and guttural.... Her attention is neither upon history nor myth, but she uses ancient persons or artifacts as opportunity for intense expressive display." Many of these qualities in her poetry carry over into Owens' dramatic work. She has said her playwrighting is an "organic evolution" from her poetry.

Lawrence Van Gelder said in a theatre review: "A naturalist who culls her specimens in the jungle of human degradation, Miss Owens works for the most part with primordial types, deformed in intellect or physique, who infect the planet with lingering coarseness, greed, racism, and war while lusting after the meretricious. Their distinguishing mode of expression—their primitive poetry—is the grunt, the moan, the obscene gesture, the gross insult or open brutality." Commenting on "Beclch," Clive Barnes noted "Where Miss Owens disappoints me is not in her

ideas—however raw and rough these may be on tender sensibilities—but in their execution. The play is badly written—or at least this production made it seem so, for it reads better than it was played here."

Other critics seem to agree on the difficulty of staging Rochelle Owens' work. Ross Welzsteon said of "Beclch": "In its obscene passions and raw arrogance and tortured probing of psychic wounds, the play may well be one of the most provocative and genius-tormented of the decade—but unfortunately the production is so inadequate I didn't even begin to think along these lines until I went home and read the script."

William Packard provided a possible answer: "Surely Rochelle Owens is doing something unique in the American theatre, writing plays that take place in the never-never land of unconscious allegory. She is exploring the archetypes of all our fantasies and projections, and in doing so she achieves extraordinary insights into how women see men. This is very difficult to portray effectively onstage. And now that I think back on the three plays by Rochelle Owens that I have seen produced, I have a disquieting sense that her work has not yet been fully explored in stage terms."

Expanding on the archetypal, Stanley Kauffmann explained: "She has taken a very low common denominator of life—human and/or animal—and with it has tried to shake us into element sensual reawakening—spurts of amoral pleasure, the smell of one's own feet (as in Joyce), the childlike abandon in the mud. 'Futz' is not a clarion call for a return to the sty, but its language and method invite us to a little black mass of pathos and disgust and cruelty which—with a bow to Artaud—hopes to investigate some things that were true about men before they became men."

In a slightly different vein Ross Wetzsteon proposed: "The genius of her work, in short, lies not in ideological commitments but in her access to the subconscious, and so her plays are not simple studies of the conflicts between our outer and inner selves (our motivations and behavior), but sublimely subtle examinations of the ways in which these two selves are inextricable (our nature itself)—and inextricable, furthermore, from the selves of others. By the very nature of her gifts, then, Miss Owens is unable to celebrate anything but life itself (certainly no complacent attacks on society's hypocrisy, certainly no advocacy of sentimental atavisms, the two most common misinterpretations of her work)—which makes her, not at all paradoxically (her characters, like people, always die, and her plays, ultimately, are about death) perhaps the most profoundly tragic playwright in the American theatre." Henry Hewes agrees: "Miss Owens is not the poet Jean Genet is. Nevertheless, the fact that she works with the same sense of subconscious totality commands our highest respect."

Rochelle Owens recorded "Primitive Rites and Songs" for Broadside Records and a movie version of *Futz* was released by Commonwealth United Productions in 1969. The Mugar Library of Boston University established the collection of Rochelle Owens' manuscripts and correspondence in 1969.

BIOGRAPHICAL/CRITICAL SOURCES: Village Voice, January 5, 1967, December 19, 1968; *Saturday Review,* January 7, 1967; *Poetry,* July 7, 1969.†

* * *

OZICK, Cynthia 1928-

PERSONAL: Born April 17, 1928, in New York, N.Y.;

daughter of William (a pharmacist) and Celia (Regelson) Ozick; married Bernard Hallote (a lawyer), September 7, 1952; children: Rachel Sarah. *Education:* New York University, B.A. (cum laude), 1949; Ohio State University, M.A., 1950. *Home:* 34 Soundview St., New Rochelle, N.Y. 10805. *Agent:* Theron Raines, Inc., 244 Madison Ave., New York, N.Y. 10016.

CAREER: New York University, New York, N.Y., instructor in English, 1964-65; full-time writer. Taught fiction workshop, Chautauqua Writers' Conference, July, 1966; Stolnitz Memorial Lecturer at Indiana University, 1972; member of fiction jury, National Book Award, 1972. *Member:* Phi Beta Kappa. *Awards, honors:* National Endowment for the Arts fellowship, 1968; B'nai B'rith Jewish Heritage Award, 1972; Edward Lewis Wallant Memorial Award, 1972; Jewish Book Council Award, 1972; nominated for National Book Award, 1972; American Academy of Arts Award for Literature, 1973; Hadassah Myrtle Wreath Award for Literature, 1974.

WRITINGS: Trust (novel), New American Library, 1966; *The Pagan Rabbi and Other Stories*, Knopf, 1971. Work represented in numerous anthologies, including *Best American Short Stories 1970*, edited by Martha Foley, Houghton, 1970; *A Treasury of Yiddish Poetry*, edited by Irving Howe and Eliezer Greenberg, Holt, 1972; *Best American Short Stories 1972*, edited by Foley, Houghton, 1972; *Prize Stories, 1974: The O. Henry Awards*, edited by William Abrahams, Doubleday, 1974. Contributor of poetry, articles, and translations to a variety of periodicals.

WORK IN PROGRESS: A collection of essays; a novel.

BIOGRAPHICAL/CRITICAL SOURCES: Carolyn Riley, editor, *Contemporary Literary Criticism,* Volume III, Gale, 1975.

*   *   *

OZMENT, Robert V. 1927-

PERSONAL: Born May 7, 1927, in Rome, Ga.; son of Lon V. (a state investigator) and Neba (McCool) Ozment; married Arah Jane Lingerfelt, May 6, 1944; children: Randall Robert, Richard Vince. *Education:* Attended Young Harris Junior College, 1944-46; Jacksonville State College, B.S., 1948; Emory University, B.D., 1951; attended Harvard University; Boston University, Ph.D., 1956. *Home:* 420 Terrell Mill Dr., Marietta, Ga. 30060.

CAREER: Ordained Methodist minister, 1951; minister in Lynn, Mass., 1951-55, Havana, Cuba, 1955-56, Oxford, Ga., 1956-57, Atlanta, Ga., 1957-65; First Methodist Church of Atlanta, Atlanta, Ga., pastor, 1966—.

WRITINGS: . . . but God Can, Revell, 1962; *Happy Is the Man*, Revell, 1963; *There's Always Hope*, Revell, 1964; *Putting Life Together Again*, Revell, 1965; *When Sorrow Comes*, Word Books, 1970. Columnist for thirteen daily and weekly newspapers; editor and publisher, *Light For Living* (monthly newspaper).

*   *   *

PADDOCK, John 1918-

PERSONAL: Born June 1, 1918, in Clinton, Iowa; son of J. Donald (a musician) and Marian (Gibbs) Paddock. *Education:* University of Illinois, student, intermittently, 1937-43; University of Southern California, B.A., 1951; Mexico City College (now University of the Americas), M.A., 1953; Stanford University, Ph.D., 1970. *Office:* Juarez 2, Mitla, Oaxaco, Mexico.

CAREER: Archeological research in Mexico, 1952—; University of the Americas, Mexico City, Mexico, member of faculty, 1953—, chairman of department of anthropology, 1957—. Visiting professor, San Francisco State College (now University), 1961. Technical adviser, Oaxaca Room, Museo Nacional de Antropologia; president of executive council, Museo Frissell de Arte Zapoteca Mitla, Oaxaca, Mexico. *Military service:* U.S. Army, World War II. *Member:* International Society for Research on Agression, Sociedad Mexicana de Antropologia, Society for American Archaeology.

WRITINGS: (Contributor) *Homenaje a Pablo Martinez del Rio*, Sociedad Mexicana de Antropologia, 1961; (editor and co-author) *Ancient Oaxaca*, Stanford University Press, 1966; (contributor) Robert Wauchope, editor, *The Indian Background of Latin American History*, Knopf, 1970. Faculty adviser and contributor, *Mesoamerican Notes*, 3-8 (publication of University of the Americas), 1953-66; Contributor of articles and translations to proceedings and professional journals; also contributor of about twenty reviews to professional journals and to *New York Times Book Review* and *Mexico City News*. Assistant editor for western Mesoamerica, *American Antiquity*; associate, *Current Anthropology*; editor, *Boletin de Estudios Oaxaquenos* (publication of Museo Frissell); member of editorial board, *Aggressive Behavior*.

WORK IN PROGRESS: A translation of Julio de la Fuente's *Yalalag*.

*   *   *

PADOVANO, Anthony T(homas) 1934-

PERSONAL: Born September 18, 1934, in Harrison, N.J.; son of Thomas Henry (a truck driver) and Mary Rose (Cierzo) Padovano. *Education:* Attended Darlington Seminary, 1954-56; Seton Hall University, A.B. (magna cum laude), 1956; Pontifical Gregorian University, S.T.B. (magna cum laude), 1958, S.T.L. (magna cum laude), 1960, S.T.D. (magna cum laude), 1962; St. Thomas Pontifical International University, Ph.L. (magna cum laude), 1962; New York University, M.A., 1971. *Address:* Ramapo College of New Jersey, Mahwah, N.J. 07430.

CAREER: Ordained Roman Catholic priest, 1959. Darlington Seminary, Darlington, N.J., professor of systematic theology, 1962-74; Ramapo College of New Jersey, Mahwah, professor of American literature, 1971—. Assistant chaplain, Medical Center, Jersey City, N.J., 1960; weekend assistant priest in Jersey City, N.J., 1962, Glen Rock, N.J., 1963-74; member of Newark, N.J. Archdiocesan Ecumenical Study Commission and Commission for Education of Clergy in Documents of Vatican II. Visiting professor at Villanova University, 1968, St. Mary's College, Notre Dame, Ind., 1969, University of St. Thomas, 1969, 1973, University of Wyoming, 1970, Barry College, 1971, Seattle University, 1972, 1973, 1974, University of San Francisco, 1973, Fordham University, 1973, 1974, Boston College, 1973, 1974, and Caldwell College, College of Racine, and College of St. Scholastica. *Member:* Catholic Theological Society of America, Mariological Society of America.

WRITINGS: (Editor) *Roman Echoes*, North American College (Rome), 1959; *The Cross of Christ: The Measure of the World*, Pontifical Gregorian University (Rome), 1962; (contributor) *The Episcopate and Christian Unity*, Graymoor Press, 1965; *The Estranged God: Modern Man's Search for Belief*, Sheed, 1966; *Who is Christ?*, Ave

Maria Press, 1967; *Belief in Human Life*, Paulist Press, 1969; *American Culture and the Quest for Christ*, Volume I, Sheed, 1970; *Dawn Without Darkness*, Paulist Press, 1971; *Free to Be Faithful*, Paulist Press, 1972; (contributor) John R. McCall, editor, *Dimensions in Religious Education*, CIM Consultants, Inc., 1973; *Eden and Easter*, Paulist/Newman Press, 1974. Regular feature writer, *National Catholic Reporter*, 1971—. Contributor to Marian Studies, Volume XVII, and to Catholic and Protestant magazines and other publications. Member of editorial board, *Advocate* (archdiocesan newspaper), 1966-73; member of editorial advisory board, *Schema XIII*, 1970.

SIDELIGHTS: Padovano is competent in French, Italian, Spanish, German, and Latin.

* * *

PAGE, Grover, Jr. 1918-
(K. K. McGinnis)

PERSONAL: Born May 28, 1918, in Nashville, Tenn.; son of Grover Cleveland (an editorial cartoonist) and Gertrude (Boland) Page. *Education:* Attended Haverford College, 1935-37; Columbia University, B.A., 1939, M.L.S., 1959; also studied at Chicago Academy of Fine Arts. *Home:* 1815 Casselbery Rd., Louisville, Ky. 20405.

CAREER: Newspaper reporter in New Orleans, La., 1939, and timekeeper and typist construction firm in Bedford, Ind., 1940; John S. Swift Co., Chicago, Ill., artist, 1948-50; Kent Lane (16 mm films), Louisville, Ky., art director, 1950-53; Fetter Printing Co., Louisville, Ky., artist, 1953-56; Queens Borough Public Library, New York, N.Y., trainee and librarian, 1957-59; Louisville Free Public Library, Louisville, Ky., reference librarian, 1959; Department of Libraries, Frankfort, Ky., regional director, 1960—. *Military Service:* U.S. Army, 38th Infantry Division, 1941-46; served in New Guinea and Philippines; became staff sergeant; received Bronze Star. *Member:* Kentucky Library Association, Friends of Kentucky Libraries. *Awards, honors:* Named Kentucky Librarian of the Year, 1964.

WRITINGS: The Brave Bookmobile, Seale, 1966.

WORK IN PROGRESS: More bookmobile stories for children; *Letters and Life of Aaron Burr*, with emphasis on his activities in Kentucky.

SIDELIGHTS: Page is competent in German, French, and Tagalog. *Avocational interests:* Music, art, Kentucky.†

* * *

PAGE, Martin 1938-
PERSONAL: Born June 30, 1938, in London, England; son of Basil Lloyd and Mary (Hacker) Page; married Jillian Vera Robertson. *Education:* Pembroke College, Cambridge, B.A. (honors). *Home:* 36 Margaretta Terrace, London S.W. 3, England. *Agent:* A. D. Peters, 10 Buckingham St., Adelphi, London W.C. 1, England; Harold Matson Co., Inc., 30 Rockefeller Plaza, New York, N.Y. 10020.

CAREER: Guardian, Manchester, England, reporter, 1960-62; *Daily Express*, London, England, foreign correspondent, then diplomatic correspondent, 1962-65, with two years in Moscow and war coverage in Algeria, Congo, Vietnam, Borneo, and India; free-lance writer, London, England, 1965—. *Member:* Cambridge University Union.

WRITINGS: (With David Berg) *The Day Khruschev Fell*,

Hawthorn, 1965; (with Berg) *Unpersoned*, Chapman & Hall, 1966; *The Company Savage: Life in the Corporate Jungle*, Cassell, 1972; *The Yam Factor, and other Insights into the Lives and Customs of The Executive Tribes of America*, Doubleday, 1972. Writer of television scripts. Contributor to *Atlantic Monthly, Vogue, Newsday*, and *Sunday Times* and *Times* (both London).

WORK IN PROGRESS: Research into British politics and monarchy during the crisis of 1936.

SIDELIGHTS: Page has traveled extensively in western Europe and Communist bloc countries, Africa, Middle East, Far East, and Australia.†

* * *

PAGE, Robert J(effress) 1922-
PERSONAL: Born November 18, 1922, in Oswego, N.Y.; son of Alanson S. (a paper manufacturer) and Virginia (Haskins) Page; married Elizabeth McKnown, November 21, 1947 (divorced, 1974); married Marilyle E. Sweit, 1974; children: Sharon Page Berg, Susan Page Tillett, Sarah W. *Education:* Hamilton College, A.B., 1944; Episcopal Theological School, S.T.B. (cum laude), 1947; Columbia University, Ph.D., 1955. *Politics:* Independent. *Home:* 2412 East Ave., Rochester, N.Y. 14610. *Office:* 1100 South Goodman St., Rochester, N.Y. 14620.

CAREER: Clergyman of The Protestant Episcopal Church, ordained, 1947; curate in Binghamton, N.Y., 1947-49; rector in Aurora, N.Y., 1949-52; Columbia University, New York, N.Y., assistant chaplain, 1953-55; Kenyon College, Bexley Hall, Gambier, Ohio, assistant professor, 1955-58, associate professor, 1958-61, professor of theology, 1961-68; Colgate Rochester/Berley Hall/Crozier Divinity Schools, Rochester, N.Y., professor of theology, 1968—. St. Augustine's College, Canterbury, England, visiting fellow, 1962-63; visiting professor, Graduate Theological Union, Berkeley, Calif., 1967, University of Rochester, 1970—. *Member:* American Theological Society, Academy of Religion and Mental Health.

WRITINGS: New Direction in Anglican Theology, Seabury, 1965. Contributor to theological periodicals.

* * *

PAGET, George Charles Henry Victor 1922-
(Marquess of Anglesey)

PERSONAL: Born October 8, 1922, in London, England; son of Charles, the 6th Marquess of Anglesey and Lady Victoria Marjorie Harriet (Manners) Paget; married Elizabeth Shirley Vaughan Morgan, 1948; children: Lady Henrietta, Earl of Uxbridge, Lady Sophia, Lord Rupert, Lady Amelia. *Education:* Attended Wixenford, Wokingham and Eton College. *Home:* Plas Newydd, Llanfairpwll, Anglesey, North Wales, United Kingdom.

CAREER: County Councillor for Anglesey, Anglesey, North Wales, 1951; Justice of the Peace for Anglesey, 1959; Deputy Lord Lieutenant of the Isle of Anglesey, 1960. National Museum of Wales, Cardiff, president, 1962-67; Welsh National Opera Company, Cardiff, Wales, director, 1959—. Welsh regional director, Nationwide Building Society. Freeman of the City of London. *Military service:* British Army Royal Horse Guards, 1941-46; became major. *Member:* Society of Antiquaries (fellow), Royal Cambrian Academy (honorary fellow), Society for Army Historical Research (council member), Redundant Churches Fund, National Trust, Historic Buildings Council for Wales,

Friends of Friendless Churches (president), Danilo Dolci Trust (Britain; treasurer), Anglesey Conservative Association (president), Royal Welsh Yacht Club (commodore).

WRITINGS—All under name Marquess of Anglesey: (Editor) *The Capel Letters, 1814-1817*, J. Cape, 1955; *One-Leg: The Life and Letters of the 1st Marquess of Anglesey, K.G., 1768-1854*, Morrow, 1961; (editor) *Sergeant Pearman's Memoirs*, J. Cape, 1969; (editor) *Little Hodge*, Cooper, 1971; *A History of the British Cavalry, 1816 to 1919*, Volume I: *1816 to 1850*, Cooper, 1973. Contributor of articles and book reviews to *Journal of Army Historical Research*, *History Today*, *Times Literary Supplement*, *Sunday Telegraph*, and other journals and newspapers.

WORK IN PROGRESS: The remaining three volumes of *A History of the British Cavalry, 1816 to 1919*, completion expected in 1977.

SIDELIGHTS: The Marquess of Anglesey has appeared at various times on British Broadcasting Corp. and instructional television programs. *Avocational interests:* Music, gardening.

*   *   *

PAISH, F(rank) W(alter) 1898-

PERSONAL: Surname rhymes with "creche"; born January 15, 1898, in Croydon, England; son of Sir George (an economist and journalist) and Emily Mary (Whitehead) Paish; married Beatrice Marie Eckhard, December 31, 1927; children: Elizabeth Mary (Mrs. Michael Thomson), Anthony George Conrad, Christopher Michael. *Education:* Trinity College, Cambridge, A.B., 1921, M.A., 1930. *Politics:* Liberal. *Home:* Shoreys, Ewhurst, Cranleigh, Surrey, England.

CAREER: Standard Bank of South Africa Ltd., employee in London, England, 1921-23, Cape Town, South Africa, 1923-32; London School of Economics and Political Science, London, England, lecturer, 1932-38, reader, 1938-41; British Ministry of Aircraft Production, London, England, deputy director, 1941-45; London School of Economics and Political Science, reader in economics, 1945-59, professor, 1949-65; now retired. Lloyds Bank, partime economic adviser, 1965-70. Economist, International Monetary Fund, Washington, D.C., 1951. *Military service:* British Army, Royal Field Artillery, 1916-69; became lieutenant; received Military Cross. *Member:* Royal Economic Society, British Association (section president, 1953), Association of University Teachers of Economics (chairman, 1950-65).

WRITINGS: (With G. L. Schwartz) *Insurance Funds and Their Investment*, P.S. King, 1934; *The Post-War Financial Problem*, Macmillan, 1949; *Business Finance*, Pitman, 1953; *Studies in an Inflationary Economy*, Macmillan, 1962; (editor) *Benham's Economics*, 7th edition, Pitman, 1964, 9th edition, with A. J. Culyer, 1973; (With Jossleyn Hennessey) *Policy for Incomes?*, Institute of Economic Affairs, 1964; *Long-Term and Short-Term Interest Rates in the United Kingdom*, Manchester University Press, 1966; *Rise and Fall of Incomes Policy*, Institute of Economic Affairs, 1969; *How the Economy Works, and Other Essays*, Macmillan, 1970. Contributor to professional journals. Editor, London and Cambridge Economic Service, 1947-51.

*   *   *

PALERMO, David Stuart 1929-

PERSONAL: Born August 21, 1929, in Norwood, Mass.; son of Alfonso Albert and Carolyn Mary (Pollock) Palermo; married Shirley Jean Bowen, 1952; children: Scott David, Craig Stuart, Lynn Elizabeth, Lisa Carolyn. *Education:* Lynchburg College, B.S., 1951; University of Massachusetts, M.A., 1953; University of Iowa, Ph.D., 1955. *Home:* 499 Sierra Lane, State College, Pa. *Office:* Department of Psychology, 441 Moore Building, Pennsylvania State University, University Park, Pa. 16802.

CAREER: Southern Illinois University, Carbondale, assistant professor of psychology, 1955-58; University of Minnesota, Minneapolis, assistant professor, Institute of Child Development, 1958-63; Pennsylvania State University, University Park, associate professor, 1963-66, professor of psychology, 1966—. *Member:* American Psychological Association (fellow), Society for Research in Child Development, Psychonomic Society, American Association for the Advancement of Science (fellow), American Association of University Professors, Midwestern Psychological Association, Eastern Psychological Association, Sigma Xi. *Awards, honors:* Grants from U.S. Public Health Service, 1960-65, National Science Foundation, 1963; Career Development Award, National Institute of Child Health and Human Development, 1965-70.

WRITINGS: (Contributor) Jerome M. Seidman, editor, *The Child: A Book of Readings*, Rinehart, 1958; (contributor) Morris L. Haimowitz and Natalie R. Haimowitz, editors, *Human Development: Selected Readings*, Crowell, 1960; (editor with L. P. Lipsitt) *Research Readings in Child Psychology*, Holt, 1963; (contributor) Lipsitt and C. C. Spiker, editors, *Advances in Child Development and Behavior*, Volume I, Academic Press, 1963; (with J. J. Jenkins) *Word Association Norms: Grade School through College*, University of Minnesota Press, 1964. Contributor to conference proceedings, and about sixty articles to professional journals. Member of editorial board, *Journal of Verbal Learning and Verbal Behavior*, 1964—; *Journal of Experimental Child Psychology*, member of editorial board, 1966—, editor, 1974—; editor, *Child Development Abstracts and Bibliography*, 1971-74.

*   *   *

PALISCA, Claude V. 1921-

PERSONAL: Born November 24, 1921, in Free City of Fiume (now Rijeka, Yugoslavia); became U.S. citizen; married Jane Pyne, June 12, 1960; children: Carl, Madeline. *Education:* Queens College (now Queens College of the City University of New York) B.A., 1943; Harvard University, M.A., 1948, Ph.D., 1954. *Home:* 68 Spring Rock Rd., Branford, Conn. 06405.

CAREER: University of Illinois, Urbana, instructor, 1953-54, assistant professor of music, 1954-59; Yale University, New Haven, Conn., associate professor, 1959-64, professor of the history of music, 1964—, chairman of department of music, 1969—. Research fellow, University of Illinois, 1957; senior fellow, National Endowment for the Humanities, 1972-73; visiting summer professor at University of California, Berkeley, 1955; visiting professor and senior fellow of Council of the Humanities, Princeton University, 1960; visiting summer lecturer at University of Michigan, 1962. President of American Council of the Arts for Education; chairman of music committee, Arts Council of Greater New Haven. *Military service:* U.S. Army Air Forces, 1943-46. *Member:* International Musicological Society (member of board of directors), American Musicological Society (vice-president), Society for Ethnomusicology,

Renaissance Society of America (member of council), American Association of University Professors, Harvard Club of Southern Connecticut. *Awards, honors:* Fulbright grant to Italy, 1950-52; Guggenheim fellowship, 1960-61.

WRITINGS: Girolamo Mei: Letters on Ancient and Modern Music to Vincenzo Galilei and Giovanni Bardi, American Institute of Musicology, 1960; (co-author) *Seventeenth Century Science and the Arts*, Princeton University Press, 1961; (co-author) *Musicology*, Prentice-Hall, 1963; *Baroque Music*, Prentice-Hall, 1968; (translator with Guy Marco) Zarlino, *The Art of Counterpoint*, Yale University Press, 1968. Contributor to music journals. Member of editorial board, *Ethnomusicology, Journal of American Musicology Society, Journal of Music Theory.*

* * *

PALMER, Frank R. 1922-

PERSONAL: Born April 9, 1922, in Westerleigh, Gloucestershire, England; son of George Samuel and Gertrude (Newman) Palmer; married Jean Moore, June 18, 1948; children: Peter Frank, Robert George, Jane Margaret, Andrew Mark, Ruth Elisabeth May. *Education:* New College, Oxford, M.A., 1948; Merton College, Oxford, graduate study, 1948-49. *Religion:* Church of England. *Office:* Department of Linguistic Science, University of Reading, Whiteknights, Reading, Berkshire, England.

CAREER: University of London, School of Oriental and African Studies, London, England, lecturer in linguistics, 1950-60; University of Wales, University College of North Wales, Bangor, professor of linquistics, 1960-65; University of Reading, Reading, Berkshire, England, professor of linguistics, 1965—. *Member:* Philogical Society, Linguistics Association of Great Britain, Societas Linguistica Europaea, Linguistic Society of America.

WRITINGS: The Morphology of the Tigre Noun, Oxford University Press, 1962; *A Linguistic Study of the English Verb*, Longmans, Green, 1965; (editor) *Selected Papers of J.R. Firth, 1951-58*, Longmans, Green, 1968; (editor) *Prosodic Analysis*, Oxford University Press, 1970; *Grammar*, Penguin, 1971; *The English Verb*, Lonman, 1974; *Semantics*, Cambridge University Press, 1975.

* * *

PALMER, Larry Garland 1938-

PERSONAL: Born November 13, 1938, in Warren, Ohio; son of Gerald L. (a minister) and Esther (Garland) Palmer. *Education:* Studied at Mozarteum in Salzburg, 1958-59; Oberlin College, Mus.B., 1960, University of Rochester, Mus.M., 1961, A.Mus.D., 1963; did research in Germany, summer, 1962, and studied in Holland, summers, 1964 and 1967; American Guild of Organists, choirmaster degree, 1966, A.A.G.O., 1967. *Politics:* Republican. *Religion:* Presbyterian. *Home:* 10125 Cromwell Dr., Dallas, Tex. *Office:* Meadows School of the Arts, Southern Methodist University, Dallas, Tex. 75275.

CAREER: St. Paul's College, Lawrenceville, Va., chairman of department of fine arts, 1963-65; Norfolk State College, Norfolk, Va., professor of music and director of college choir, 1965-70; Southern Methodist University, Dallas, Tex., associate professor of harpsichord and organ, 1970—. Concert organist, harpsichordist, and choral conductor; organist and choirmaster at St. Luke's Episcopal Church, Dallas. *Member:* American Guild of Organists, International Heinrich-Schuetz Society, International Harpsichord Society, Pi Kappa Lambda.

WRITINGS: (Contributor) T. Hoelty-Nickel, editor, *The Musical Heritage of the Church*, Volume VI, Concordia, 1963; *Hugo Distler and His Church Music*, Concordia, 1967. Translator into English, Hugo Distler's "A Little Advent Music", "I wish That I Were Going Home", "Christ, Who Alone Art Light of Day," "In the World You Have Fear," and "Sing With Joy, Glad Voices Lift," all choral compositions published by Concordian.

WORK IN PROGRESS: Further translations of the motets of Hugo Distler; a book on harpsichord repertoire in the twentieth century; a series of phonograph records for Musical Heritage Society.

* * *

PARES, Marion (Stapylton) 1914-
(Judith Campbell)

PERSONAL: Surname is pronounced "pairs"; born November 7, 1914, in West Farleigh, Kent, England; daughter of Walter John (a lieutenant commander, Royal Navy) and Dorothy (Chetwynd-Stapylton) Fletcher; married Humphrey Pares (a farmer and company director), June 5, 1937; children: Penelope Iris (Mrs. George Richard Spensley Simey), Susan Caroline (Mrs. John Gray), Theresa Judity (Mrs. William Papas), Frances Campbell (Mrs. Nigel Harland). *Education:* Educated at boarding school in England. *Politics:* "Traditionally Conservative—but interest lukewarm. Nor overfond of *any* politicians!" *Religion:* "Basically Church of England, but not great upholder of any man-made forms of religion." *Home and office:* Studfall Ridge, Lympne Hill, Hythe, Kent, England. *Agent:* Winant Towers Ltd., 14 Clifford's Inn, London E.C.4, England; and A. M. Heath, 40-42 William IV St., London W.C.2N 4DD, England. *U.S. Office:* Monica McCall, International Famous Agency, 1301 Avenue of the Americas, New York, N.Y. 10019.

CAREER: "Spent the years prior to marriage in the normal occupations and amusements for one of my day and age. Always said I 'would write,' but bar normal spate of adolescent poetry, did nothing about it. Wrote a lot during war years while husband abroad, but nothing published . . . until around 1958, when some very modest publishing began to push writing to the fore." Commentator for short films on the English countryside, Southern (Dover) Television.

WRITINGS—Under pseudonym Judith Campbell: *Four Ponies* (juvenile fiction), Muller, 1958; *Merrow Ponies* (juvenile fiction), Muller, 1960; *Family Pony* (nonfiction; illustrated with family photographs and drawings by daughter, Susan Caroline Pares), Lutterworth, 1961; *The Queen Rides* (nonfiction), Lutterworth, 1964, Viking, 1965; *Horses in the Sun* (nonfiction), M. Joseph, 1966, Sportshelf, 1969; *Police Horses*, David & Charles, 1967, A. S. Barnes, 1968; *Anne: Portrait of a Princess*, Cassell, 1969; *Pony Events*, Batsford, 1969; *The World of Horses*, Hamlyn, 1969; *The World of Ponies*, Hamlyn, 1970; *Horses and Ponies*, Grosset, 1971, enlarged edition, Hamlyn, 1972; *Elizabeth and Philip*, Regnery, 1972; *Princess Anne and Her Horses*, Brockhampton Press, 1972; *Family on Horseback*, Lutterworth, 1972; *The Champions*, Arthur Barker, 1973; *Royalty on Horseback*, Sidgwick & Jackson, 1974; *The Horseman's World*, Random House, 1975.

Wrote series of articles appearing at intervals on children's page of *Sunday Times* (London), 1960-63; monthly column on country life for *Daily Telegraph* (London), 1962-63; and monthly column on the countryside for *Look and Learn* (children's magazine), 1966.

WORK IN PROGRESS: A series of photographically-illustrated articles on Jordan; articles, and cutting of color film on Crete.

SIDELIGHTS: Brought up on a fruit farm, remote in the Kentish downs, Mrs. Pares has always lived in the country, with interests centered on farming, horses and ponies of the family variety, and wild flowers. The wanderings of four travel-minded daughters (one worked her way around the world; another spent a year in Crete) propelled her out of the countryside in 1965 to Jordon, where she studied King Hussein's stud of Arabian horses, those of the police force and Royal Guard, and camels of the Desert Patrol. *Horses in the Sun* resulted.

In researching *Horses in the Sun* and *The Queen Rides*, she was allowed to ride many of the horses. It was "a sometimes hilarious experience for someone who has spent her life riding rotund ponies belonging to our daughters." Research for *The Queen Rides* was done at the Royal Mews where Queen Elizabeth was "incredibly helpful and patient" in helping the author get what she wanted.

In the spring of 1966 Mrs. Pares and her husband went to Crete and the Pelopenese to do a film on village life and the flowers. In the fall they went to Iran for another film and material for *The World of Horses* and *The World of Ponies*. She has also researched material in Greece and France, often accompanied by her husband, and visited the United States in 1974 to gather information for *Horseman's World*. "If the films and books are successful," Mrs. Pares said, "we would like to make the ends of the earth the limits of our activity."

Mrs. Pares reported that she is "running a 'shoe-string' riding club . . . for local children with no other chance of riding. . . . They, under supervision, do all the work and provide me with a lot of reference!"

Her books have appeared in multiple translations, including Swedish, German, French, Italian, Danish, Dutch, and Norwigian.

* * *

PARIS, Bernard J. 1931-

PERSONAL: Born August 19, 1931, in Baltimore, Md.; son of Albert (a grocer) and Anna (Richmond) Paris; married Shirley Freedman, April 1, 1949; children: Susan Jean, Mark Eliot. *Education:* Towson State Teachers College (now Towson State College), student, 1948-49, 1951; Johns Hopkins University, A.B., 1952, Ph.D., 1959. *Home:* 2628 Rockwood Dr., East Lansing, Mich. 48823. *Office:* Department of English, Michigan State University, East Lansing, Mich. 48824.

CAREER: Lehigh University, Bethlehem, Pa., instructor in English, 1956-60; Michigan State University, East Lansing, assistant professor of English, 1960-64, associate professor, 1964-67, professor of English and comparative literature, 1967—. Visiting professor, Victorian Studies Centre of University of Leicester, 1972. *Member:* Modern Language Association of America. *Awards, honors:* National Endowment for the Humanities fellowship, 1969-70; Guggenheim fellowship, 1974-75.

WRITINGS: Experiments in Life: George Eliot's Quest for Values, Wayne State University Press, 1965; *A Psychological Approach to Fiction: Studies in Thakeray, Stendhal, George Eliot, Dostoevsky, and Conrad*, Indiana University Press, 1974. Contributor to professional journals.

WORK IN PROGRESS: Books on Jane Austen, on George Eliot, and on great characters in English and European fiction.

PARKER, Alfred Browning 1916-

PERSONAL: Born September 24, 1916, in Boston, Mass.; son of James Arden (a realtor) and Jewel Rae (Fry) Parker; married Martha Gifford, September 17, 1942 (divorced, 1956); married Jane Britt, June 13, 1959 (died July 29, 1971); children: (first marriage) Derek Browning, Gifford (Mrs. Robert Marshall), Robin Zachary, Jules Graham, Quentin Dart; (second marriage) Lebritia Browning. *Education:* University of Florida, B.S. in Architecture (with honor), 1939; Royal Academy, Stockholm, Sweden, graduate study, 1939. *Politics:* Democrat. *Religion:* Protestant. *Office:* 2921 Southwest 27th Ave., Miami, Fla. 33133.

CAREER: University of Florida, Gainesville, associate professor, College of Architecture, 1940-46; architect in private practice, Miami, Fla., 1946—; Flager Federal Savings & Loan Association, Miami, Fla., founding director and senior vice-president, 1956—. Director of Coconut Grove Bank, Sunshine State Bank, and other firms. Designer of *House Beautiful* Pacesetter Homes, 1954, 1959, and *Popular Mechanics* House of 1962. Member of Miami Building Board of Appeals, 1953—, and Miami River Advisory Committee; charter member, Coconut Grove Citizens Committee for Slum Clearance. *Military service:* U.S. Naval Reserve, 1942-46; became lieutenant senior grade. *Member:* American Institute of Architects (fellow; president of Florida South chapter 1949). *Awards, honors:* American Institute of Architects regional and state awards, anually, 1954-58, National Award of Merit and Excellence, 1959 and 1965.

WRITINGS: You and Architecture, Delacorte, 1965. Member of editorial board, *Florida Architecture*, 1954—.

WORK IN PROGRESS: Three books on architecture, drama, and contemporary life.

SIDELIGHTS: Parker speaks Spanish; he has traveled in Europe, Mexico, South America, and the Caribbean Islands, and spends part of every summer in Vermont. *Avocational interests:* Woodworking, masonry, photography, the theater, films, television, sailing, and farming.

* * *

PARMENTER, Ross 1912-

PERSONAL: Born May 30, 1912, in Toronto, Ontario, Canada; son of Reginald Holland (a lawyer) and Alice (Hargraft) Parmenter. *Education:* Trinity College, University of Toronto, B.A., 1933. *Home and office:* 320 East 42nd St., New York, N.Y. 10017; and Pension Suixa, Calzada Madero 113, Oaxaca, Mexico.

CAREER: New York Times, New York, N.Y., general reporter, 1934-40, music reviewer, 1940-55, music editor, 1955-64, columnist, "The World of Music," 1940-64; freelance writer, 1964—. *Military service:* U.S. Army Air Forces, Medical Corps, 1943-46.

WRITINGS: (Self-illustrated) *The Plant in My Window*, Crowell, 1949; (self-illustrated) *Week in Yanhuitlan*, University of New Mexico Press, 1964; *Explorer, Linguist and Ethnologist*, Southwest Museum (Los Angeles), 1966; (contributor) *Pioneers of American Anthropology*, University of Washington Press, 1966; *The Awakened Eye*, Wesleyan University Press, 1968. Also author of *A House for Buddha* and *Lawrence in Oaxaca*.

WORK IN PROGRESS: A full-length biography of Zelia Nuttall, an American archaeologist who worked in Mexico; study of Mexican codices.

SIDELIGHTS: Parmenter speaks Spanish and lives most of each year in Oaxaca, Mexico.

* * *

PARR, Michael 1927-

PERSONAL: Born April 14, 1927, in London, England; son of Stanley Albert (a company director) and Gladys (Hancock) Parr; married Mary Clarke, August 6, 1949; children: Michael David, Malcolm. *Education:* Left elementary school at 14; educated by tutors. *Politics:* "Left of centre." *Religion:* Christian. *Home:* 10 Clifford Ct., Scarborough, Ontario MIR 3L3, Canada.

CAREER: "After the Army, drifted and found myself doing various chores at the Savoy Hotel (electrician type); packing hairbrushes in Leyton; making fire alarms in Walthamstow; went on the dole once; worked for my father for a short while, but it didn't work out for a lot of peculiar reasons—the chief one being that I was pretty much of a dunderhead at office work and extremely uninterested in it. Took off to become a reporter in Hornsey, which somehow petered out before it even got off the ground. Married hereabouts and needed some money, so joined Charles Dickens' union—Association of Correctors of the Press (proofreaders)—and have been hard at it ever since. Now with Carswell Co. Ltd., Agincourt, Ontario. *Military service:* British Army, 1945-47.

WRITINGS: The Green Fig Tree (poems), St. Martin's, 1965. Contributor of poems to *Fiddlehead, Canadian Forum, Canadian Poetry, New York Times, Literary Review, Yale Review, New York Times Book Review,* and other publications.

WORK IN PROGRESS: New verse.

SIDELIGHTS: Parr told *CA:* "Comments indicative of my viewpoint on subjects I consider vital constitute the body of my poems—although at the moment I wouldn't care to think I am trying to be prophet/teacher/preacher/ or hot gospeler—just a maker of poems."

A *Virginia Quarterly Review* writer said: "Michael Parr . . . is a young poet who apparently looks to Dylan Thomas more than to any other modern figure for a model and an inspiration. His strengths are Thomas's strengths—energy, fresh rhythms, arresting rhymes, deep probings of the religious and amorous mind—and so, lamentably, are his weaknesses Thomas's—frivolous eccentricities, senseless contortions of syntax, and a disinclination to suppress clearly unsuccessful poems which contain a brilliant line or two. An unusually uneven collection, *The Green Fig Tree* neverthless contains some unusually fine poetry."

BIOGRAPHICAL/CRITICAL SOURCES: Canadian Forum, September, 1965; *Virginia Quarterly Review,* winter, 1966.

* * *

PASSONNEAU, Joseph Russell 1921-

PERSONAL: Born January 19, 1921, in Pullman, Wash.; son of Joseph and Amy (Anderson) Passonneau; married Janet Vivian (a biochemist), April 21, 1948; children: Christopher Neal, Rebecca Jane, Polly Nicole, Sarah Michele. *Education:* Harvard University, B.S., 1942, B.Arch., 1949; Massachusetts Institute of Technology, M.S. in Civil Engineering, 1949. *Politics:* Democrat. *Religion:* "None." *Home:* 3015 Q St. N.W., Washington, D.C. 20007.

CAREER: Holabird & Root & Burgee, junior designer, job

captain, and draftsman, 1949-50; Skidmore, Owings & Merrill, senior designer, 1950-52; Tennessee Valley Authority, chief of architectural design, 1952-54; Liberman & Passonneau, partner, 1954-55; private practice of architecture, St. Louis, Mo., 1955; Washington University, School of Architecture, St. Louis, Mo., design critic, 1955-56, acting dean, 1956-57, dean and professor of architecture, 1957-67; director of Crosstown Design Team, Chicago, Ill., 1967-70; private practice of architecture, 1970—. Visiting professor at Princeton University, Harvard University, Washington University, and University of Pennsylvania, 1970—. Engineering consultant on thin shell structures; member of advisory committee on overseas building program, U.S. State Department; first president, Landmarks Association of St. Louis; member, St. Louis City Plan Commission; member, President's Transportation Advisory Board. *Military service:* U.S. Navy, 1942-46; became lieutenant. *Member:* American Institute of Architects (fellow; past president of East Tennessee chapter), American Society of Civil Engineers. *Awards, honors:* Awards from *Progressive Architecture,* 1953, 1954; awards from Graham Foundation, and National Endowment for the Arts.

WRITINGS: (Contributor) Werner Hirsch, editor, *Urban Life and Form,* Holt, 1963; (with Richard Wurman) *Metropolitan Atlas: 20 American Cities,* M.I.T. Press, 1966; (contributor) Sam Warner, Jr., *Planning for a Nation of Cities,* M.I.T. Press, 1966; *Civic Design and Urban Transportation,* M.I.T. Press, 1976. Contributor to *Systems Analysis for Social Problems,* Operations Research Council, and *Handbook of Highway Engineering,* Van Nostrand.

* * *

PASTORE, Arthur R(alph), Jr. 1922-

PERSONAL: Surname is pronounced Pass-*taw*-ree; born April 22, 1922, in Brooklyn, N.Y.; son of Arthur Ralph (a businessman) and Elvira (Frasca) Pastore; married Evelyn Thomson (an author), 1951 (died, October 13, 1965). *Education:* Attended Union College and University, 1940-41; Yale University, B.A. (honors), 1947; Columbia University, M.S., 1948; University of Geneva, certificate, 1950; University of Maryland, M.A., 1972. *Politics:* Democrat. *Religion:* Roman Catholic. *Home:* 4700 Bradley Blvd., Chevy Chase, Md. 20015.

CAREER: Member of editorial staff of Fairchild Publications and copywriter with advertising agencies in earlier career; worked in Paris, France, as promotion director in Paris bureau of *Newsweek,* 1954-56, and staff writer, International News Service, 1956-57; Edward Gottlieb & Associates (public relations), New York, N.Y., director of magazine department, 1957-59; National Broadcasting Co., New York, N.Y., radio news writer-editor, 1959-61; New York (N.Y.) Commission on Human Rights, public relations director, 1961-62; New York (N.Y.) Housing Authority, assistant public relations director, 1962-63; Duquesne University, Pittsburgh, Pa., assistant professor of journalism, 1963-66; American University, Washington, D.C., visiting associate professor of journalism, beginning, 1966, State University of New York, Morrisville, assistant professor of journalism, 1973-75. Writer at various times for Voice of America, Radio Free Europe, and commercial stations; advertising and public relations consultant to J. Walter Thompson Co., Cities Service Corp., International Business Machines Corp., and other firms. *Military service:* U.S. Army, Medical Corps, 1943-46; served in Europe.

MEMBER: Society of American Travel Writers, National Press Club (Washington, D.C.), Pittsburgh Press Club, Disabled American Veterans, Sigma Delta Chi, Kappa Tau Alpha, Sigma Chi, Yale Club (New York).

WRITINGS: (With wife, Evelyn T. Pastore) *Where to Eat in Europe,* Crowell, 1954; (with Tania Gamez) *Mexico and Cuba on Your Own,* Garden City Books, 1954; (with Evelyn T. Pastore) *Fodor's Guide to Ireland,* McKay, 1956, and later editions; (contributor) *New York Herald Tribune Guide to France, Italy and Spain,* New York Herald Tribune, 1957; *Dynamite Under the Alps,* Coward, 1963. Writer, with Evelyn T. Pastore, of Greek section of *Worldmark Encyclopedia of Nations,* Harper, 1960, and Pennsylvania section of *Fodor's Guide to the USA,* McKay, 1966.

Free-lance contributor to magazines and newspapers, 1945—, with articles in *Travel, Today's Living, Nation's Business, This Week, Writer, Science Digest,* and other magazines, and in many of the country's major metropolitan newspapers.

WORK IN PROGRESS: A textbook on teaching by television methods; a novel; articles for magazines and newspapers.

SIDELIGHTS: Pastore spent eight years in Europe as a foreign correspondent and free-lance writer, has ranged throughout America, Canada, Mexico, the Near and Far East, and traveled in Africa, South America, and the Caribbean. He is competent in French, German, and Italian. *Avocational interests:* Music (especially opera and symphony), the theater, motion pictures, and acting in amateur productions.

* * *

PATINKIN, Don 1922-

PERSONAL: Born January 8, 1922, in Chicago, Ill.; son of Albert and Sadie (Brezinsky) Patinkin; married Dvorah Trossman, June, 1945; children: Naama, Aran, Ilana, Tmira. *Education:* Attended Central YMCA Junior College, Chicago, Ill., 1939-41; University of Chicago, B.A., 1943, Ph.D., 1947. *Religion:* Jewish. *Home:* 5 Chovevei Zion St. Jerusalem, Israel. *Office:* Hebrew University of Jerusalem, Jerusalem, Israel.

CAREER: Cowles Commission for Economic Research, Chicago, Ill., research associate, 1946-48; University of Chicago, Chicago, Ill., assistant professor of economics, 1947-48; University of Illinois, Urbana, associate professor of economics, 1948-49; Hebrew University of Jerusalem, Jerusalem, Israel, lecturer, 1949-52, associate professor, 1952-57, professor of economics, 1957—. Director of research, Maurice Falk Institute for Economic Research in Israel, 1956-72. *Member:* American Economic Association, Econometric Society (president, 1974), Israel Academy of Sciences and Humanities, American Academy of Arts and Sciences (honorary member), Royal Economic Society, Phi Beta Kappa, *Awards, honors:* Rothschild Prize for the sciences, 1959; Israel Prize for the social sciences, 1970.

WRITINGS: Money, Interest, and Prices, Harper, 1956, 2nd edition, 1965; *The Israel Economy: The First Decade,* Falk Project for Economic Research in Israel, 1959; *Studies in Monetary Economics,* Harper, 1972. Contributor to scientific journals.

WORK IN PROGRESS: Research on monetary aspects of development, the Israel economy, and the development of Keynesian monetary thought.

PATRICK, Douglas Arthur 1905-

PERSONAL: Born March 17, 1905, in Hamilton, Ontario, Canada; son of Arthur (a merchant) and Alberta (Yeager) Patrick; married Mary Powell (an editor), August 15, 1929; children: Robert John. *Education:* Studied at Hamilton Technical Art School, Sealey Art School, Miss Matice Art School, and Leonard Hutchinson Art Instruction. *Religion:* Anglican. *Home:* 1616 Applewood Rd., Mississauga, Ontario, Canada. *Office: Toronto Globe and Mail,* Toronto M5V 2S9, Ontario, Canada.

CAREER: Canadian Broadcasting Corp., Toronto, Ontario, script writer and conductor of "CBC Stamp Corner," 1950-71; *Globe and Mail,* Toronto, advertising representative, 1952-70, stamp editor, 1952—. Stamp editor, *Ottawa Journal, Hamilton Spectator, Calgary Herald, St. Catharines Standard,* and *Coin, Stamp, Antique News.* Honorary curator of philately, Royal Ontario Museum, 1962—; stamp cataloguer and arranger. *Member:* Royal Philatelic Society (fellow), Royal Philatelic Society of Canada (fellow), American Philatelic Congress (member of council), member of more than twenty philatelic societies and clubs.

WRITINGS: Stamp Collecting—The Most Interesting Hobby in the World, Ryerson, 1952; *Postage Stamps and Postal History of the United Nations,* Ryerson, 1956; *Canada Stamp Album,* Ryerson, 1959; *One Year of the Stamp Club,* Globe and Mail, 1960; *International Guide to Stamps and Stamp Collecting,* Dodd, 1962; *Canada's Postage Stamps,* McClelland & Stewart, 1964, second revised edition, 1975; *The Musson Stamp Dictionary,* Scott Publications, 1972 (published in England as *The Hodder Stamp Dictionary,* Hodder & Stroughton, 1973).

WORK IN PROGRESS: Flying Postmen, a history of airmail and aircraft from 1870 to 1970, for Musson Book.

SIDELIGHTS: Patrick's network program was unique in radio or television programming. His Stamp Club, publicized on Canadian Broadcasting Corp. Trans-Canada Service, has 64,000 members in 60 countries.

BIOGRAPHICAL/CRITICAL SOURCES: Time, January 14, 1966.

* * *

PATTERSON, Robert Leet 1893-

PERSONAL: Born August 16, 1893, in Leetsdale, Pa.; son of Thomas (a lawyer) and Harriet (Wilson) Patterson; married Clara Guthrie, January 15, 1938. *Education:* Hamilton College, B.A., 1917; Columbia University, M.A., 1922; Union Theological Seminary, New York, N.Y., B.D., 1922; University of London, Ph.D., 1933. *Politics:* Republican. *Home:* 40 Glenwood Dr., Greenwich, Conn. 06830.

CAREER: Johns Hopkins University, Baltimore, Md., lecturer in medieval philosophy, 1933-34; Duke University, Durham, N.C., 1945—, professor of philosophy, now professor emeritus. *Member:* American Philosophical Association, Medieval Academy of America, American Oriental Society, Aristotelian Society, Southern Society of Philosophy and Psychology, Southern Society of Philosophy.

WRITINGS: The Conception of God in the Philosophy of Aquinas, Allen & Unwin, 1933; *The Philosophy of William Ellery Channing,* Bookman Associates, 1952; *Irrationalism and Rationalism in Religion,* Duke University Press, 1954; *An Introduction to the Philosophy of Religion,* Holt, 1958; *Plato on Immortality,* Pennsylvania State University Press, 1965; *A Philosophy of Religion,* Duke University Press,

1970; *The Role of History in Religion*, Exposition Press, 1971.†

* * *

PATTERSON, Samuel C(harles) 1931-

PERSONAL: Born November 19, 1931, in Omaha, Neb.; son of Robert Foster (an academic dean) and Garnet Marie Patterson; married Suzanne Louise Dean, June 21, 1957; children: Polly Ann, Dean Foster, Grier Edmund. *Education:* University of South Dakota, B.A., 1953; University of Wisconsin, M.S., 1956, Ph.D., 1959. *Politics:* Democrat. *Religion:* Unitarian Universalist. *Home:* 431 South Summit St., Iowa City, Iowa 52240. *Office:* Department of Political Science, 305 Schaeffer Hall, University of Iowa, Iowa City, Iowa 52242.

CAREER: Oklahoma State University, Stillwater, assistant professor of political science, 1959-61; University of Iowa, Iowa City, assistant professor, 1961-64, associate professor, 1964-67, professor of political science, 1967—, chairman of department, 1974-77. Visiting lecturer, University of Wisconsin, summer, 1962; visiting professor, University of Oklahoma, 1968—, University of Essex, 1969-70. President, Iowa Conference of Political Scientists, 1969. *Military service:* U.S. Army, Infantry, 1953-55; became first lieutenant. *Member:* International Political Science Association, American Association for the Advancement of Science, American Political Science Association, Midwest Political Science Association, Phi Beta Kappa, Phi Kappa Phi. *Awards, honors:* Citizenship Clearing House postdoctoral fellowship, 1958-59; grants from Social Science Research Council, 1961, 1967, American Political Science Association, 1964-65, National Science Foundation, 1966; University of Iowa faculty summer research fellowship, 1967.

WRITINGS: (With Malcolm E. Jewell) *The Legislative Process in the United States*, Random House, 1966, 2nd edition, 1972; (editor) *American Legislative Behavior*, Van Nostrand, 1968; (editor) *Midwest Legislative Politics*, Institute of Public Affairs, University of Iowa, 1968; (editor with J. C. Wahlke) *Comparative Legislative Behavior: Frontiers of Research*, Wiley, 1972; (co-author) *Representatives and Represented*, Wiley, 1975.

Contributor: Donald G. Herzberg and Gerald M. Pomper, editors, *American Party Politics: Essays and Readings*, Holt, 1966; Frank Munger, editor, *American State Politics: Readings for Comparative Analysis*, Crowell, 1966; R. E. Crew, Jr., editor, *State Politics: Readings in Political Behavior*, Wadsworth, 1968; S. C. Patterson, editor, *American Legislative Behavior: A Reader*, Van Nostrand, 1968; Allan Kornberg and Lloyd Musolf, editors, *Legislatures in Developmental Perspective*, Duke University Press, 1970; William Crotty, editor, *Assassinations and the Political Order*, Harper, 1971; William E. Wright, *A Comparative Study of Party Organization*, Bobbs-Merrill, 1971; D. P. Sprengal, editor, *Comparative State Politics: A Reader*, Bobbs-Merrill, 1971; M. M. Reeves and P. N. Glendenning, compilers, *Controversies of State and Local Systems*, Allyn & Bacon, 1972; (with G. R. Boynton and R. D. Hedlund) Ada W. Finifter, editor, *Alienation and the Social System*, Wiley, 1972; S. K. Kirkpatrick and L. K. Pettit, editors, *The Social Psychology of Political Life*, Duxbury Press, 1972; (with Boynton and J. C. Wahlke) Kornberg, editor, *Legislatures in Comparative Perspective*, McKay, 1973; *Political Science and State and Local Government*, American Political Science Association, 1973;

Norman R. Luttbeg, editor, *Public Opinion and Public Policy*, revised edition, Dorsey, 1974.

Also author of monographs. Contributor to public opinion, business, and political science journals. Member of editorial board, *Midwest Journal of Political Science*, 1967-70; editor, *American Journal of Political Science*, 1970-73.

WORK IN PROGRESS: A book on comparative legislative behavior; a book on political leadership; a monograph on American state legislative politics.

* * *

PATTILLO, James W(ilson) 1937-

PERSONAL: Born April 17, 1937, in Robstown, Tex.; son of Reuben Terry (a grocer) and Ruby (Englert) Pattillo; married Susan Ann Tower, December 3, 1966; children: Kenneth, Teri. *Education:* St. Edward's University, B.S., 1958; Texas Technological College (now Texas Tech University), M.B.A., 1959; Louisiana State University, Ph.D., 1963. *Politics:* Independent. *Religion:* Roman Catholic. *Home:* 51199 Deer Path Dr., Granger, Ind. *Office:* University of Notre Dame, Notre Dame, Ind. 46556.

CAREER: University of Southern California, Los Angeles, assistant professor, 1962-65, associate professor of accounting, 1965-67; Louisiana State University, Baton Rouge, 1967-74, began as associate professor, became professor of accounting and director of graduate studies of College of Business Administration; University of Notre Dame, Notre Dame, Ind., Peat Marwick Mitchell Professor of Accounting, 1974—. Staff accountant, Ernst & Ernst, Los Angeles, 1963-67. Certified public accountant in Texas, 1962, California, 1967, Louisiana, 1968, Indiana, 1975. Certified management accountant, 1975. *Member:* American Institute of Certified Public Accountants, National Association of Accountants, American Accounting Association, Accounting Careers Council, Institute of Internal Auditors, Financial Executives Institute.

WRITINGS: Foundation of Financial Accounting, Louisiana State University Press, 1965; *A Guide to Accounting Instruction: Concepts and Practices*, American Accounting Association, 1968; (with Bruce Joplin) *Effective Accounting Reports*, Prentice-Hall, 1969. Contributor to professional journals.

WORK IN PROGRESS: A textbook, *Financial Accounting*.

* * *

PATTON, Kenneth L(eo) 1911-

PERSONAL: Born August 25, 1911, in Three Oaks, Mich.; son of Elias John (a decorator) and Martha Ellen (Bratt) Patton. *Education:* Eureka College, A.B. (magna cum laude), 1937; University of Chicago, M.A., 1939, B.D., 1940. *Politics:* Independent. *Home:* 391 Vesta Ct., Ridgewood, N.J.

CAREER: Minister of Unitarian Universalist Association; Madison Unitarian Society, Madison, Wis., minister, 1942-48; Charles Street Meeting House, Unitarian Universalist, Boston, Mass., minister, 1949—; Ridgewood, Unitarian Society, Ridgewood, N.J., minister, 1964—. Director, Institute for the Creative Arts for Liberal Religions.

WRITINGS: Hello Man, privately printed, 1945; *Strange Seed*, privately printed, 1946; *Beyond Doubt*, Beacon, 1946; *The Visitor* [and] *Hello Man*, Beacon, 1947; *Man's Hidden Search*, Meeting House Press, 1954; *Man Is the*

Meaning, Meeting House Press, 1956; (editor) *Readings for the Celebration of Life,* Meeting House Press, 1957; *Recognition,* Meeting House Press, 1960; *The Ground of Being,* Meeting House Press, 1962; *A Religion for One World,* Beacon, 1963; (contributor) *Hymns for the Celebration of Life,* Beacon, 1964; *This World My Home,* Beacon, 1966; *Services and Songs for the Celebration of Life,* Beacon, 1967; *The Sense of Life,* Meeting House Press, 1974.

*   *   *

PAUL, Gordon L. 1935-

PERSONAL: Born September 2, 1935, in Marshalltown, Iowa; son of Leon D. Paul and Ione (Hickman) Paul Perry; married Joan M. Wyatt, December 24, 1954; children: Dennis, Dana, Joni. *Education:* University of Iowa, B.A. (with honors), 1960; University of Illinois, M.A., 1962, Ph.D. (with distinction), 1964. *Home:* 1817 Maynard Dr., Champaign, Ill. 61820. *Office:* Psychological Clinic, University of Illinois, 51 East Gerty, Champaign, Ill. 61820.

CAREER: Certified psychologist, state of Illinois. U.S. Veterans Administration Hospital, Danville, Ill., social science analyst, 1962; University of Illinois Counseling Bureau, Urbana, counseling psychologist, 1963; U.S. Veterans Administration Hospital, Palo Alto, Calif., clinical psychologist, 1964-65; University of Illinois, assistant professor, 1965-67, associate professor, 1967-70, professor of psychology, 1970—. Supervising psychologist, Psychological Clinic, 1965—. Director, Clinical-Research Unit, Adolf Meyer Center, 1968—. Consultant to Mental Research Institute, 1964-65, Illinois Department of Mental Health, 1965-73, National Institute of Mental Health, 1967—. *Military service:* U.S. Navy, musician, 1954-58. *Member:* American Psychological Association, Midwestern Psychological Association, Phi Beta Kappa, Chi Gamma Iota. *Awards, honors:* American Institute for Research creative talent award in the field of development, counseling, and mental health, 1964, for research leading to book, *Insight vs. Desensitization in Psychotherapy.*

WRITINGS: Insight vs. Desensitization in Psychotherapy: An Experiment in Anxiety Reduction, Stanford University Press, 1966; (with D. Bernstein) *Anxiety and Clinical Problems,* General Learning Press, 1973. Contributor to books; also contributor to psychological and medical journals. Member of editorial boards of several journals. Contributor to psychological and medical journals, and to several books.

WORK IN PROGRESS: Research in innovation and evaluation of techniques for behavior modification, including hypnosis, psychotherapy, learning, and conditioning; two books, *Psychosocial Treatment of Chronic Mental Patients,* and *Observational Assessment Instrumentation for Institutional Research and Treatment.*

AVOCATIONAL INTERESTS: Music (formerly played in and led dance bands and orchestras), aviation (private pilot).

*   *   *

PAUL, Grace 1908-

PERSONAL: Born March 12, 1908, in Liberal, Kan.; daughter of David (a carpenter) and Myrtle Helen (Brewer) Paul. *Education:* Studied at University of Tulsa, night school, 1930-35, at Auburn University, 1948, and Columbia University, 1949-50. *Religion:* Presbyterian. *Home:* 705 North Main St., Temple, Tex. 76501.

CAREER: U.S. Government employee, 1942-71. Has worked as a claims examiner, 1958-71. Certified medical technologist (American Society of Clinical Pathologists). *Military service:* U.S. Army, Women's Army Corps (WAC), 1944-46. *Member:* Entomological Society of America, International Platform Association, Business and Professional Women's Club.

WRITINGS: Your Future in Medical Technology, Richards Rosen, 1962, revised edition, Arco, 1971; *A Short Course in Skilled Supervision* Dartnell, 1966; (contributor) *Environmental Engineers' Handbook,* Chilton, 1974; *Paramedical Careers,* Macrae, 1975. Contributor to trade and youth publications. Editor, *Kansas Scope* (publication of Kansas Society of Medical Technologists), 1954.

AVOCATIONAL INTERESTS: Volunteer work with underprivileged children and cultural, health, and recreational organizations.

*   *   *

PAULSEN, Wolfgang 1910-

PERSONAL: Born September 21, 1910, in Duesseldorf, Germany; came to United States in 1938; son of Hans (a physician) and Luise (Hunaeus) Paulsen; married Herta Schindler, June 18, 1938; children: Judith. *Education:* Studied at Universities of Tuebingen, Bonn, Berlin, Leipzig, and Berne, 1930-34; University of Berne, Ph.D., 1934. *Home:* 49 Maplewood Dr., Amherst, Mass. 01002. *Office:* Department of Germanic Languages, University of Massachusetts, Amherst, Mass. 01002.

CAREER: Assistant lecturer at University of Durham, Durham, England, 1935-37, and University of Reading, Reading, England, 1937-38; assistant professor of modern languages at Southwestern College, Memphis, Tenn., 1938-43, and of German at University of Iowa, Iowa City, 1943-47; Smith College, Northampton, Mass., associate professor of German, 1947-53; State University of New York at Albany, assistant professor of German, 1953; University of Connecticut, Storrs, professor of German, 1954-66; University of Massachusetts, Amherst, professor of German, 1966—, head of department of Germanic languages, 1966-71. *Member:* Modern Language Association of America, American Association of Teachers of German, American Association of University Professors, Schiller Gesellschaft, Internationale Vereinigung fuer germanische Sprache and Literaturwissenschaft.

WRITINGS: Expressionismus und Aktivismus, [Bern], 1935; (editor with Arno Schirokauer, and contributor) *Corona: Studies in Philology, In Celebration of the Eightieth Birthday of Samuel Singer,* Duke University Press, 1941; (with Fred L. Fehling) *Elementary German,* American Book Co., 1947, 2nd edition, 1957, 3rd edition (with Fehling, A. Reh, and S. Bauchinger), Van Nostrand, 1971; (editor with Fehling) *Vagabunden,* Holt, 1950; (editor) Werner Bergengruen, *Der spanische Rosenstock—Schneider und sein Obelisk,* Norton, 1957; *Georg Kaiser,* Max Niemeyer [Tuebingen], 1960; *"Die Ahnfrau": Zu Grillparzers frueher Dramatik,* Max Niemeyer, 1962; (editor and author of introduction and critical notes) Bonaventura, *Nachtwachen,* Reclam Verlag (Stuttgart), 1964; (editor) Franz Grillparzer, *Die Juedin von Toledo,* Reclam Verlag, 1966; (editor and contributor) *Amherster Kolloquien zur modernen deutschen Literatur,* seven volumes, Lothar Stiehm Verlag, 1967-75; (with S. J. Kapolowitt) *German Review Grammar,* Ronald, 1970; *Christoph Martin Wieland,* Francke Verlag (Bern), 1975. Also author of *Versuch ueber Rolf Bongs: Der Schriftsteller als Dichter*, Blaeschke Verlag (Darmstadt). Contributor of about thirty articles to journals in America, Germany, and England. Co-editor and regular contributor, *Universitas* and *Germanistik* (German periodicals); editor of "Franco-German Studies: A Current Bibliography," in *Bulletin of Bibliography*, 1948-57.

WORK IN PROGRESS: A book, *Eichendorff und sein Taugenichts.*

* * *

PAULSON, Ronald (Howard) 1930-

PERSONAL: Born May 27, 1930, in Bottineau, N.D.; son of Howard Clarence (a Boy Scout executive) and Ethel (Tvete) Paulson; married Barbara Appleton, May 25, 1957; children: Andrew Meredith, Melissa Katherine. *Education:* Yale University, B.A., 1952, M.A., 1956, Ph.D., 1958. *Home:* 819 West University Pkwy., Baltimore, Md. 21210. *Office:* Johns Hopkins University, Baltimore, Md. 21218.

CAREER: University of Illinois, Urbana, instructor, 1958-59, assistant professor, 1959-62, associate professor of English, 1962-63; Rice University, Houston, Tex., professor of English, 1963-67; Johns Hopkins University, Baltimore, Md., professor of English, 1967, Andrew W. Mellon Professor of the Humanities, 1973, chairman of English department, 1968. *Military service:* U.S. Army, Artillery, 1952-54; became first lieutenant. *Member:* Modern Language Association of America. *Awards, honors:* Guggenheim fellowship, 1965-66.

WRITINGS: Theme and Structure in Swift's "Tale of a Tub," Yale University Press, 1960; (editor) *Fielding: A Collection of Critical Essays*, Prentice-Hall, 1962; *Hogarth's Graphic Works*, Yale University Press, 1965, 2nd edition, 1970; (editor) *The Novelette*, Prentice-Hall, 1965; *The Fictions of Satire*, Johns Hopkins University Press, 1967; *Satire and the Novel in Eighteenth-Century England*, Yale University Press, 1967; (editor) *Henry Fielding: The Critical Heritage*, Routledge & Kegan Paul, 1969; (editor) *Satire: Modern Essays in Criticism*, Prentice-Hall, 1971; *Hogarth: His Life, Art, and Times*, Yale University Press, 1971; *Rowlandson: A New Interpretation*, Oxford University Press, 1972; *Emblem and Expressionism in English Art of the Eighteenth Century*, Thames & Hudson, 1975. Contributor to *English Literary History, Studies in English Literature.* Member of editorial board, *Eighteenth-Century Studies.*

* * *

PEACHEY, Laban 1927-

PERSONAL: Born April 6, 1927, in Springs, Pa.; son of Shem (a minister) and Salome (Bender) Peachey; married Helen Mumaw, June 13, 1955; children: Phyllis Ann, Lowell James, Byron Jay, Joyce Elaine. *Education:* Eastern Mennonite College, A.B., 1952; University of Virginia, M.Ed., 1958; George Washington University, D.Ed., 1963. *Religion:* Mennonite. *Office:* Hesston College, Hesston, Kan. 67062.

CAREER: Eastern Mennonite College, Harrisonburg, Va., dean of men, 1953-56, became instructor, 1954, professor of psychology, 1963-67, dean of students, 1957-65, registrar, 1960-62; Hesston College, Hesston, Kan., president, 1968—.' Visiting professor, Bridgewater College, summer, 1964. Research associate, Project on Student Development (supported by National Institute of Mental Health), 1965-

66. President, Harrisonburg-Rockingham Mental Health Association, 1963-64, Massanutten Mental Health Center Board, 1963-67; president of board of directors, Valley Mental Health Clinic, 1965. Member of executive committee, National Council of Independent Junior Colleges, 1972—; member of Board of Missions and Charities, 1970—. President, Hesston Chamber of Commerce, 1971-72. *Member:* American Psychological Association, American Academy of Political and Social Science, American Association of Community and Junior Colleges.

WRITINGS: Learning to Understand People, Herald, 1965.

WORK IN PROGRESS: A study of student personnel services in small colleges.

AVOCATIONAL INTERESTS: Nature, rural living.

* * *

PEARCE, Thomas Matthews 1902-

PERSONAL: Born May 22, 1902, in Covington, Ky.; son of Thomas Matthews (a dentist) and Josephine Calla (DeMoss) Pearce; married Helen Hendel Spang, April 10, 1941; children (stepdaughters) Carol Ancona Bair, Phyllis Ancona (Mrs. John C. Robinson). *Education:* University of Montana, B.A., 1923; University of Pittsburgh, M.A., 1925, Ph.D., 1930; graduate summer study at University of California, 1928, and University of Chicago, 1929. *Politics:* Democrat. *Religion:* Episcopalian. *Home:* 1712 Sigma Chi Rd., N.E., Albuquerque, N.M. 87106. *Office:* Bandelier Hall 102, University of New Mexico, Albuquerque, N.M. 87106.

CAREER: University of Pittsburgh, Pittsburgh, Pa., instructor in English, 1925-27; University of New Mexico, Albuquerque, assistant professor, 1927-29, associate professor, 1930-41, professor of English, 1941-64, professor emeritus, 1964—, head of department of English, 1940-51; full-time writer, 1964—. *Member:* College English Association (past vice-president), Modern Language Association of America, American Name Society (past president), American Folklore Society, American Dialect Society, American Association of University Professors, Phi Kappa Phi, Tau Kappa Alpha, Sigma Chi.

WRITINGS: (Editor with Telfair Hendon) *America in the Southwest* (anthology), University of New Mexico Press, 1933; *Christopher Marlowe: Figure of the Renaissance*, University of New Mexico Press, 1934; (with Jim "Lane" Cook) *Lane of the Llano*, Little, Brown, 1936; (with Mabel Major and Rebecca Smith) *Southwest Heritage: Literary History and Bibliography*, University of New Mexico Press, 1938, 3rd edition, 1972; *Cartoon Guide of New Mexico*, J. J. Augustin, 1939; *The Beloved House*, Caxton, 1940; *Democracy in Progress*, University of New Mexico Press, 1943; (editor with A. P. Thomason) *Southwesterners Write* (anthology), University of New Mexico Press, 1947; (editor with Major) *Signature of the Sun: Southwest Verse 1900-1950*, University of New Mexico Press, 1950; (editor with Ina S. Cassidy and Helen S. Pearce) *New Mexico Place Names: A Geographical Dictionary*, University of New Mexico Press, 1965; *Mary Hunter Austin*, Twayne, 1966; *Alice Corlin Henderson*, Steck, 1969; *Oliver La Farge*, Twayne, 1972; (editor with Alice Briley and Jeanne Bonnette) *Turquoise Land: Anthology of New Mexico Poetry*, Nortex Publications, 1974. Editor, *New Mexico Quarterly*, 1931-39; associate editor, *Western Folklore*, 1949—.

WORK IN PROGRESS: Research on the Mary Austin

Collection at the Huntington Library for a book entitled *Dear Friends and Friendly Foes: The Mary Austin Correspondence*, 1904-1934.

SIDELIGHTS: Pearce wrote: "My mother knew the English and Scottish ballads which were sung in her family, but she was also a professional vocalist, and I grew up in an atmosphere of concerts, symphony music and opera via the early record albums and an occasional visit of operatic companies to Cincinnati or Pittsburgh.... Despite terms in educational institutions and research hide-aways like the Henry E. Huntington or the Folger Shakespeare Library, I still find interesting the relics of folk poetry, song, architecture, design, ceramics, and art which mark America's past, whether English, Spanish, or Indian."

* * *

PEARSON, Jim Berry 1924-

PERSONAL: Born January 3, 1924, in Gilmer, Tex.; son of John Henry and Vera (Berry) Pearson; married June Louise Young, February 20, 1943 (deceased); married Mary F. Shields, 1972; children: (first marriage) Jim Berry, Jr., Terry Lee. *Education:* Attended Hardin Junior College, 1940-42; North Texas State College (now University), B.A., 1947, M.A., 1949; University of Texas, Ph.D., 1955. *Politics:* Democrat. *Religion:* Methodist. *Home:* 1003 Eagle Dr., Apt. 137, Denton, Tex. 76201.

CAREER: Midwestern University, Wichita Falls, Tex., professor of history, 1949-51, 1954-55; Arlington State College, Arlington, Tex., associate professor of social science, 1955-58; University of Texas, Austin, assistant professor, 1958-63, associate professor of history, 1963-71, professor of education, 1967-71, assistant dean, College of Arts and Sciences, 1962-66, assistant vice-president for academic affairs, 1970-71; North Texas State University, Denton, professor of education, 1971-73, professor of history, 1971—, associate vice-president of academic affairs, 1971-73, dean, College of Arts and Sciences, 1973—. Project director, Council of Chief State School Officers, 1966-68. Associate, Center for History of Education, 1968—. Chairman of program committee, Texas Council for the Social Studies. Member of executive board, Texas College and University American Bicentennial Committee, 1971—, Wesley Foundation; member of board of advisors, Educational Problems, Inc., Consultant, Education Testing Service, 1966, 1971-74, University of North Carolina, 1968, U.S. Office of Education. President, Austin-Travis County Heart Association, 1964. *Military service:* U.S. Army, 1943-46; became staff sargeant; received battle star.

MEMBER: Organization of American Historians, American Historical Association, Southwestern Social Science Association (chairman of American history program, 1972-74; chairman of history program, 1974), Texas Historical Association. *Awards, honors:* Outstanding Teacher Award, University of Texas Student Assembly, 1964; Distinguished Service Award, Council of Chief State School Officers, 1968; Theta Sigma Phi Award for *The Maxwell Land Grant*.

WRITINGS: The Maxwell Land Grant, University of Oklahoma Press, 1961; (editor with Edgar Fuller) *Education in the States*, National Education Association, Volume I: *Historical Developments*, 1969, Volume II: *National Development Since 1900*, 1969; (contributor) *Social Sciences*, Georgia State Department of Education, 1971; (with Ben Proctor and William Conroy) *Texas: The Land and Its People*, Hendrick-Long Publishing, 1972. Contributor of

articles and reviews to *American Historical Review, Canadian Journal of History, Social Science Quarterly, Southwestern Historical Quarterly, New Mexico Historical Review, Arizona and the West*.

SIDELIGHTS: Pearson has traveled to Mexico, Canada, Peru, India, China, and most of Europe. *Avocational interests:* Tennis, handball, bowling, fishing, bridge, and spectator sports.

* * *

PEEL, Bruce Braden 1916-

PERSONAL: Born November 11, 1916, in Ferland, Saskatchewan, Canada, son of William John (a farmer) and Alice (Switzer) Peel; married Margaret Fullerton, July 29, 1950; children: Brian, Alison. *Education:* University of Saskatchewan, B.A., 1944, M.A., 1946; University of Toronto, B.of L.S., 1946. *Politics:* New Democratic Party (Canadian). *Religion:* United Church of Canada. *Home:* 11047 83rd Ave., Edmonton, Alberta, Canada. *Office:* University of Alberta, Edmonton, Alberta, Canada.

CAREER: Schoolteacher in Saskatchewan, 1937-40, 1944-45; University of Saskatchewan, Saskatoon, Saskatchewan, Canadiana librarian, 1946-51; University of Alberta Library, Edmonton, Alberta, chief cataloger, 1951-54, assistant librarian, 1954-55, acting librarian, 1955-56, chief librarian, 1956—. *Member:* Canadian Library Association (president, 1969-70), Canadian Association of College and University Libraries (president, 1956-66), Bibliographical Society of Canada (president, 1971-73), Alberta Library Association (president, 1960-61), Historical Association of Alberta (former president). *Awards, honors:* Historical Society of Alberta merit award.

WRITINGS: (With Eric Knowles) *The Saskatoon Story, 1882-1952*, Mel East (Saskatoon), 1952; *Bibliography of the Prairie Provinces to 1953*, University of Toronto Press, 1956, 2nd edition, 1973; (editor) *Librarianship in Canada: 1946-1967*, Canadian Library Association, 1968; *Steamboats on the Saskatchewan*, Western Producer, 1972; *Early Printing in the Red River Settlement: 1859-1870*, Peguis Publishers, 1974; *The Rossville Mission Press*, Osiris Publishers, 1974. Author of pamphlet history of University of Alberta Library, 1965. Filmscripts include "Historic Saskatchewan: Mankota," produced by Saskatchewan Department of Education and Saskatchewan Archives, 1948, and "Steamboats on the Saskatchewan," television episode in "Our Western Heritage" series, 1963.

Contributor of annual review of events in Alberta to *Britannica Book of the Year*, 1962, 1963, other articles on historical topics to *Collier's Encyclopedia, Encyclopedia Americana*, and *Dictionary of Canadian Biography*; contributor to Canadian library and historical journals. Regular columnist, "Only Yesterday," *Saskatoon Star-Phoenix*, 1947-51, with about twenty articles reprinted in newspaper's special commemorative edition, 1952.

* * *

PEELOR, Harry N. 1922-

PERSONAL: Born June 30, 1922, in Indiana, Pa.; son of Harry and Beulah Peelor; married Ruth Lawson, October 8, 1946; children: Donna Francis, Judy Lynn, Harriet Sue, Lauren Lawson. *Education:* Attended Allegheny College and Bloomsburg State College; Indiana State College (now Indiana University of Pennsylvania), Indiana, Pa., B.S. in Ed., 1944; Yale University, B.D., 1946; University of

Pittsburgh, M.Ed., 1953, and studies toward Ph.D.. *Home:* 3300 Bethel Church Rd., Bethel Park, Pa. 15102. *Office:* 44 Highland Rd., Bethel Park, Pa. 15102.

CAREER: Methodist clergyman. Christ Methodist Church, Bethel Park, Pa., senior minister, 1949—. *Military service:* U.S. Naval Reserve, Chaplain Corps, 1943-48, 1950-52. *Awards, honors:* Honorary doctorate, Lycoming College, 1963.

WRITINGS: Angel with a Slingshot (sermons), Parthenon Press, 1961.

AVOCATIONAL INTERESTS: Raising show horses.†

*   *   *

PEET, William Bartlett   1915-
(Bill Peet)

PERSONAL: Surname altered to Peet about 1947, though not legally changed; born January 29, 1915, in Grandview, Ind.; son of Orion Hopkins (a salesman) and Emma (a teacher; maiden name, Thorpe) Peed; married Margaret Brunst, November 30, 1937; children: Bill, Jr., Stephen. *Education:* Attended John Herron Art Institute, 1933-36. *Home:* 11478 Laurelcrest Rd., Studio City, Calif. 91604.

CAREER: Worked briefly as an artist for greeting card company in the Middle West (left when assigned to draw roses and tulips for sympathy cards); went West and became sketch artist and continuity illustrator for motion picture industry, then screenwriter; author and illustrator of children's books. *Awards, honors:* Prizes for paintings at exhibits in Indianapolis and Chicago, 1934-37; John Herron Art Institute citation, 1958, as one of the outstanding students in the history of the school; *Box Office* (magazine) Blue Ribbon award, 1961, 1964, for best screenplay; Indiana University Writers' Conference award for most distinguished work in children's literature, 1966, for *Capyboppy*; Southern California Council on Literature for Children and Young People award, 1967, for *Farewell to Shady Glade*; named outstanding Hoosier author of children's literature, 1967.

WRITINGS—Under name Bill Peet; all self-illustrated; all published by Houghton, except as indicated: *Hubert's Hair-Raising Adventure*, 1959; *Huge Harold*, 1961; *Smokey*, 1962; *The Pinkish, Purplish, Bluish Egg*, 1963; *Ella*, 1964; *Randy's Dandy Lions*, 1964; *Chester the Worldly Pig*, 1965; *Kermit the Hermit*, 1965; *Farewell to Shady Glade*, 1966; *Capyboppy*, 1966; *Buford the Little Bighorn*, 1967; *Jennifer and Josephine*, 1967; *Fly Homer Fly*, 1969; *The Wing-ding-dilly*, 1970; *The Wump World (and Pollutus)*, 1970; *How Droofus the Dragon Lost His Head*, 1971; *The Caboose Who Got Loose*, 1971; *The Ant and the Elephant*, 1972; *Countdown to Christmas*, Golden Gate, 1972; *The Spooky Tail of Prewitt Peacock*, 1972; *Merle the High-Flying Squirrel*, 1974; *Cyrus the Unsinkable Sea Serpent*, 1975.

SIDELIGHTS: Peet's books have had multiple translations, including German, Dutch, Danish, Swedish, French, Japanese, and Afrikaans; fifteen of his books have issued in Braille.

*   *   *

PEIFER, Claude J(ohn)   1927-

PERSONAL: Surname rhymes with "cipher"; born September 20, 1927, in Lincoln, Ill.; son of John Henry and Armella (Meyer) Peifer. *Education:* St. John's University, Collegeville, Minn., A.B., 1949; Collegio di Sant' Anselmo, Rome, S.T.L., 1954; Pontificium Institutum Biblicum, Rome, S.S.L., 1956; Ecole Biblique et Archeologique Francaise, Jerusalem, Jordan, graduate study, 1956-57. *Home and office:* St. Bede Abbey, Peru, Ill. 61354.

CAREER: Roman Catholic monk and priest of Order of St. Benedict. St. Bede Abbey Seminary, Peru, Ill., professor of Sacred Scripture, 1957-69, novice master, 1968—. Summer instructor at St. Mary's College of California, 1962, Marquette University, 1963, and St. John's University, 1967-68, 1974. *Member:* Catholic Biblical Association, Society of Biblical Literature.

WRITINGS: First and Second Corinthians, Liturgical Press, 1960; *Monastic Spirituality*, Sheed, 1966; (contributor) M. Basil Pennington, editor, *Rule and Life: An Interdisciplinary Symposium*, Cistercian Publications, 1972; (contributor) Bernd Jaspert and Eugene Manning, editors, *Regulae Benedicti Studia: Annarium Internationale*, Volume I: *First International Congress on the Rule of St. Benedict*, Verlag Dr. H. A. Gerstenberg (Hildesheim), 1972. Contributor of articles and reviews to *Worship, American Benedictine Review, Catholic Biblical Quarterly, Sisters Today, Monastic Studies, Cistercian Studies*, and other journals. Associate editor, *Bible Today*.

WORK IN PROGRESS: Studies (when time permits) in the history and spirituality of monasticism and in Old and New Testament.

SIDELIGHTS: Peifer reads Latin, French, German, Spanish, and Italian, a smattering of classical Hebrew and Greek; and still less of Aramaic and Syriac.

*   *   *

PEJOVICH, Svetozar   1931-

PERSONAL: Born March 22, 1931, in Belgrade, Yugoslavia; U.S. citizen; son of Mitar (an accountant) and Zorka (Civrich) Paige (originally Pejovich); married Lilliana Davinich, May 25, 1958; children: Alexandra, Brenda, Philip. *Education:* University of Belgrade, LL.B., 1955; Georgetown University, Ph.D. (with honors), 1963. *Religion:* Eastern Orthodox. *Office:* Department of Economics, Ohio University, Athens, Ohio 45701.

CAREER: St. Mary's College, Winona, Minn., associate professor of economics, 1962-66; University of Dallas, Tex., associate professor of economics, 1966-67; Texas A&M University, College Station, member of faculty, 1967-70; Ohio University, Athens, professor of economics, 1970—. *Member:* American Economic Association, National Tax Association, Catholic Economic Association, Alpha Kappa Psi. *Awards, honors:* Ford Foundation fellowship; U.S. Department of Labor research grant; American Council of Learned Societies research grant.

WRITINGS: The Market-Planned Economy of Yugoslavia: A Schumpeterian Interpretation, University of Minnesota Press, 1966; (with Erik G. Furubotn) *The Economics of Property Rights*, Ballinger, 1973. Contributor to *National Tax Journal, Western Economic Journal, Social Order*, and other periodicals.

WORK IN PROGRESS: A textbook, *Towards a Theory of Comparative Economics*; research on the role of technical schools in improving the skill and earning power of labor in rural America.

SIDELIGHTS: Pejovich is competent in Slavic languages and German. *Avocational interests:* Chess.†

PELLA, Milton O(rville) 1914-

PERSONAL: Born February 13, 1914, in Wilmot, Wis.; son of Charles A. and Ida (Pagel) Pella; married Germaine M. Reich, December 8, 1944. *Education:* Milwaukee State Teachers College (now University of Wisconsin—Milwaukee), B.E., 1936; University of Wisconsin, M.S., 1940, Ph.D., 1948. *Religion:* Protestant. *Home:* 5518 Varsity Hill Dr., Madison, Wis. 53705. *Office:* Teacher Education Building, 225 North Mills St., University of Wisconsin, Madison, Wis. 53705.

CAREER: Teacher of science in Evansville, Wis., 1937-38; elementary teacher in Delavan, Wis., 1938-39; high school teacher of science in Madison, Wis., 1939-42, 1946-48; University of Wisconsin, Madison, assistant professor, 1948-52, associate professor, 1952-57, professor of science education, 1957—. Ford Foundation, science education consultant in Lebanon, Syria, Jordan, Turkey, Egypt, Costa Rica, Iran, and Iraq, at various periods, 1959—. *Military service:* U.S. Army, 1942-46; became technical sergeant; received Army Commendation Award. *Member:* American Association for the Advancement of Science (fellow), National Association for Research in Science Teaching (president, 1965), National Science Teachers Association, National Society for the Study of Education, Association for the Education of Teachers in Science, Central Association of Science and Mathematics Teachers (president, 1955), Wisconsin Education Association, Rotary, Masons.

WRITINGS: (With Aubrey G. Wood) *Physical Science for Progress*, Prentice-Hall, 1959, 3rd edition (sole author), 1970; (with Franklyn M. Branley and John Urban) *Science Horizons*, Volume I: *The World of Life*, Volume II: *The Physical World*, Ginn, 1965, 2nd edition, 1970. Contributor to education journals in several science fields.

WORK IN PROGRESS: Research on the teaching of science in kindergarten through twelfth grade, and on science teaching related to a philosophic structure of science; revising *Physical Science for Progress*.

*   *   *

PELLEGRINI, Angelo M. 1904-

PERSONAL: Born April 20, 1904, in Italy; son of Piacentino (a peasant) and Annunziata (Palidoni) Pellegrini; married Virginia Thompson, August 27, 1934; children: Angela (Mrs. Tom Owens), Toni (Mrs. Denis Lucey III), Brent. *Education:* University of Washington, Seattle, Ph.D., 1942. *Politics:* Democrat. *Home:* 5121 Northeast 75th St., Seattle, Wash. *Office:* Department of English, University of Washington, Seattle, Wash.

CAREER: University of Washington, Seattle, associate professor, 1951-58, professor of English, 1958—. *Awards, honors:* Guggenheim fellowship, 1949-50; Freedoms Foundation Award, 1951.

WRITINGS: The Unprejudiced Palate, Macmillan, 1948; *Immigrant's Return*, Macmillan, 1951; *Americans by Choice*, Macmillan, 1956; *Wine and the Good Life*, Knopf, 1965; *Washington: Profile of a State*, Coward, 1967; *The Food Lover's Garden*, Knopf, 1970. Contributor of essays to magazines and professional journals.

BIOGRAPHICAL/CRITICAL SOURCES: Donald Heiney, *America in Modern Italian Literature*, Rutgers University Press, 1964.

PELTIER, Leslie C(opus) 1900-

PERSONAL: Born January 2, 1900, in Delphos, Ohio; son of Stanley William and Resa (Copus) Peltier; married Dorotha Nihiser, November 25, 1933; children: Stanley, Gordon. *Education:* Attended high school in Delphos, Ohio. *Politics:* Republican. *Religion:* Methodist. *Home:* 327 South Bredeick St., Delphos, Ohio 45833.

CAREER: Delphos Bending Co., Delphos, Ohio, draftsman, cost accountant, designer, 1936—. Member, Delphos Chamber of Commerce. *Member:* International Astronomical Union, American Astronomical Society, American Association of Variable Star Observers (honorary member; vice-president, 1932), Amateur Astronomers Association (honorary member). *Awards, honors:* Ten Donohoe Comet medals, 1925-54; First Merit Award, American Association of Variable Star Observers, 1934; D.Sc., Bowling Green State University, 1947; Nova Medal, 1963; Ohioana Book Award, 1966; Blair Gold Medal, 1967.

WRITINGS: Starlight Nights, Harper, 1965; *Guideposts to the Stars*, Macmillan, 1972.

WORK IN PROGRESS: Research on variable stars, novae, and comets.

AVOCATIONAL INTERESTS: Mineralogy, photography, and nature study.

*   *   *

PENNY, Ruthanna (Merrick) 1914-

PERSONAL: Born July 20, 1914, in Ohio; married Harlan Penny, October, 1940. *Education:* Toledo State Hospital, R.N., 1939; San Francisco State College (now University), A.B., 1949; San Jose State College (now University), graduate study. *Home:* 258 North Newcomb St., Porterville, Calif. 93257.

CAREER: Registered nurse at hospitals in Ohio, Washington State, and California, 1939-74; Porterville State Hospital, Porterville, Calif., superintendent of nursing services, 1953-74. *Military service:* U.S. Army, Nurse Corps, 1945. *Member:* American Nurses Association, California State Employees Association.

WRITINGS: Practical Care of the Mentally Retarded and Mentally Ill, C. C Thomas, 1966; *Substitute Parents, or Training the Profoundly Retarded Patient for Return to the Community*, C. C Thomas, 1967.

*   *   *

PERILLO, Joseph M. 1933-

PERSONAL: Born January 2, 1933, in New York, N.Y.; son of Joseph (a travel agent) and Dora (Trojano) Perillo; married Barbara Mescher (an artist), January 26, 1963; children: Catherine, Joseph Paul. *Education:* Cornell University, A.B., 1953, LL.B., 1955; University of Florence, graduate study, 1960-62. *Religion:* Roman Catholic. *Home:* 106 Lexow Ave., Upper Nyack, N.Y. 10960. *Office:* School of Law, Fordham University, 140 West 62nd St., New York, N.Y. 10023.

CAREER: Private practice of law, New York, N.Y., 1957-60; Columbia University Project on International Procedure, New York, N.Y., associate, 1960-63; Fordham University, School of Law, New York, N.Y., associate professor of law, 1963—. Consultant New York Law Revision Commission, 1963-64. *Military service:* U.S. Navy, 1955-57. *Member:* American Foreign Law Association, Institute of Judicial Administration, Phi Beta Kappa, Order of Coif. *Awards, honors:* Fulbright scholar in Italy, 1960-62.

WRITINGS: (With Mauro Cappelletti) *Civil Procedure in Italy*, Nijhoff, 1965; (with Cappelletti and John Merryman) *The Italian Legal System*, Stanford University Press, 1967; (with John Calamari) *The Law of Contracts*, West Publishing, 1970.

* * *

PERISTIANY, John G(eorge) 1911-

PERSONAL: Born September 4, 1911, in Athens, Greece, son of George Theodore and Nitsa (Costopoulos) Peristiany; married Clio Ioannovich; children: Clio (Mrs. Christopher Addington), John. *Education:* Faculte de Droit, Paris, France, Licence en Droit, 1931, Doctorat en Droit, 1937; Oxford University, M.A. and D. Phil., 1938; London School of Economics and Political Science, postdoctoral study. *Home:* Kapsali 3, Athens 138, Greece. *Office:* United Nations Development Programme, 36, Amalia Avenue, Athens, Greece.

CAREER: Lecturer in social anthropology at University of London, London, England, and Cambridge University, Cambridge, England, 1946-49; Oxford University, Oxford, England, senior university lecturer, 1948-63, Sir James Fraser lecturer, 1954; Social Sciences Centre, Athens, Greece, UNESCO Professor of Sociology, 1960—. Sociologist to government of Kenya, 1947; visiting professor at University of Chicago, 1959. Field work in East Africa, Middle East, Greece, and Cyprus. *Member:* Royal Anthropological Institute of Great Britain and Ireland (past member, executive council), American Anthropological Association (foreign fellow), Association of Social Anthropologists (past member, executive council), Societe Francaise de Sociologie, Oxford Anthropological Society (past president).

WRITINGS: The Social Institutions of the Kipsigis, Routledge & Kegan Paul, 1939, 2nd edition, 1965; (author of introduction) Emile Durkheim, *Sociology and Philosophy*, Free Press, 1953; (editor and contributor) *Honor and Shame*, University of Chicago Press, 1966; (editor and contributor) *Contributions to Mediterranean Sociology*, Mouton & Co., 1968; (contributor) J. Beattie and G. Lienhardt, editors, *Essays in Social Anthropology*, Clarendon Press, 1974; (editor) *Mediterranean Kinship*, American Universities Field Staff (Rome), 1975; (editor and contributor) *Mediterranean Family Structures*, Cambridge University Press, 1976; *Further Studies in Honour and Shame*, University of Chicago Press, in press.

WORK IN PROGRESS: Editing and contributing to *Cypriot Studies in Urbanization*, completion expected in 1976, *Mediterranean Marriage Strategies and Marriage Presentations*, for 1976, *The Social Sciences and the Mediterranean*, for 1976, and *A Comparative Study of African Age-Sets*, for 1977.

* * *

PERKINS, Dwight Heald 1934-

PERSONAL: Born October 20, 1934, in Chicago, Ill.; son of Lawrence Bradford (an architect) and Margery (Blair) Perkins; married Julie Rate (a lawyer and editor), June 15, 1957; children: Lucy Fitch, Dwight Edward, Caleb Blair. *Education:* Cornell University, B.A., 1956; Harvard University, A.M., 1961, Ph.D., 1964. *Politics:* Democrat. *Religion:* Protestant. *Home:* 64 Pinehurst Rd., Belmont, Mass. 02178. *Office:* Department of Economics, Harvard University, Cambridge, Mass. 02138.

CAREER: Harvard University, Cambridge, Mass., 1963—, associate professor, 1966-69, professor of modern China studies and economics, 1969—, associate director of East Asian Research Center, 1973—. *Military service:* U.S. Naval Reserve, active duty, 1956-58; became lieutenant junior grade. *Member:* American Economic Association, Association for Asian Studies, Phi Beta Kappa. *Awards, honors:* Ford Foundation foreign area training fellowships, 1958-62; National Science Foundation Science faculty fellowship 1968-69.

WRITINGS: (With M. H. Halperin) *Communist China and Arms Control*, Praeger, 1965; *Market Control and Planning in Communist China*, Harvard University Press, 1966; *Agricultural Development in China, 1368-1968*, Aldine, 1969; (editor) *China's Modern Economy in Historical Perspective*, Stanford University Press, 1975. Contributor to journals. Editor: *Quarterly Journal of Economics, Review of Economics and Statistics*, and *The China Quarterly*.

WORK IN PROGRESS: An economic history of China.

SIDELIGHTS: Dwight Perkins lived in Hong Kong, and traveled in the Far East, 1961-62, Japan and Malaysia, 1968-69, and visited the People's Republic of China in 1974.

* * *

PERKINS, Michael 1942-

PERSONAL: Born November 3, 1942, in Lansing, Mich.; son of William and Virginia (Dávis) Perkins; married Renie McCune, June 20, 1960 (died, 1968); children: Leslie. *Education:* Ohio University, B.A., 1963; attended New School for Social Research and City College of New York (now City College of the City University of New York).

CAREER: Department of Welfare, New York, N.Y., case worker, 1963-66; Board of Education, New York, N.Y., corrective reading teacher, 1966—. Editor, Tompkins Square Press.

WRITINGS: The Blue Woman, and Other Poems, PN Press, 1966; *Blue Movie*, Essex House, 1968; *Queen of Heat*, Essex House, 1968; *Shorter Poems*, Croton Press, 1968; (with Harold M. Wit) *A Shovel is to Dig With* [and] *Shorter Poems* (the former by Wit, the latter by Perkins), Croton Press, 1968; *The Tour: Hell's Heated Vacancies*, Essex House, 1969; *Renie Perkins: The Life and Work of a Young Artist Who Died by her own Hand at the Age of Twenty-five*, Croton Press, 1969. Also author of *Third Street Poems*, published in New York, 1965. Contributor to *Loose Change One*, published by Half-Ass Press. Also contributor to *Wormwood Review* and *In New York*.†

* * *

PERKINSON, Henry J. 1930-

PERSONAL: Born November 27, 1930, in Philadelphia, Pa.; son of Thomas F. (a trolley motorman) and Helen (Kerner) Perkinson; married Audrey Wesley, March 28, 1953; children: Anthea, Aleta, Amelie, Ariel. *Education:* University of Pennsylvania, B.S., 1952; University of London, graduate student, 1954-55; Harvard University, M.Ed., 1956, Ed.D., 1959. *Home:* 3 Lindemann Ave., Closter, N.J. *Office:* School of Education, New York University, Washington Sq., New York, N.Y. 10003.

CAREER: Kent State University, Kent, Ohio, assistant professor of education, 1959-62; New York University, New York, N.Y., associate professor of educational history, 1962—. *Military service:* U.S. Army, 1952-54; became first lieutenant. *Member:* History of Education Society (president, 1970-71). *Awards, honors:* Italian government grant, 1958-59.

WRITINGS: (Editor with Paul Nash) *The Educated Man*, Wiley, 1965; *The Imperfect Panacea*, Random House, 1968; *The Possibilities of Error: An Approach to Education*, McKay, 1971. Editor, *History of Education Quarterly*, 1965—.†

* * *

PERL, Susan 1922-

PERSONAL: Born September 8, 1922, in Vienna, Austria; daughter of Norbert (an accountant) and Marie (Bargl) Perlman. *Education:* Attended state and art schools in Vienna, Austria. *Politics:* Democrat. *Religion:* "Metaphysic, New Thought." *Residence:* New York, N.Y.

CAREER: Advertising artist, and book and magazine illustrator. *Member:* Save a Cat Club, Greenwich Village Humane Society, Friends of Animals. *Awards, honors:* New York Art Directors Show awards; Palma d'Oro Award (for international cartoonists), Italy, 1965.

WRITINGS: (Self-Illustrated) *The Sex Life of the American Female*, Stein & Day, 1964.

Illustrator: A. A. Milne, *Once on a Time*, New York Graphic Society, circa 1962; Hubert I. Bermont, *Psychoanalysis is a Great Big Help!*, Stein & Day, 1963; Clement Moore, *The Night Before Christmas*, Dell, 1963; Sara Murphey, *Bing-Bang Pig*, Follett, 1964; Ruth S. Radlauer, *Stein, the Great Retriever*, Bobbs-Merrill, 1964; Norah Smaridge, *Watch Out!*, Abingdon, 1965; E. H. MacPherson, *The Wonderful Whistle*, Putnam, 1965.

Johanna Johnston, *The Story of the Barber of Seville*, Putnam, 1966; Bill Adler, editor, *Letters to Smokey the Bear*, Wonder Books, 1966; Norah Smaridge, *What a Silly Thing To Do*, Abingdon, 1967; Alice T. Gilbreath, *Beginning-To-Read Riddles and Jokes*, Follett, 1967; John Greenway, *Don't Talk to My Horse*, Silver Burdett, 1968; Harold S. Longman, *What's Behind the Word*, Coward, 1968; Herb Valen, *The Boy Who Could Enter Paintings*, Little, Brown, 1968; William Wise, *Sir Howard the Coward*, Putnam, 1968; Beth Goff, *Where is Daddy?*, Beacon Press, 1969; Dan Greenburg, *Jumbo the Boy and Arnold the Elephant*, Bobbs-Merrill, 1969; Susanne Kirtland, *Easy Answers to Hard Questions*, Grosset, 1969; Patrick McGivern, *The Ultimate Auto*, Putnam, 1969.

Barbara Klimowicz, *The Word-Birds of Davy McFifer*, Abingdon, 1970; Margaret Gabel, *Sparrows Don't Drop Candy Wrappers*, Dodd, 1971; Betty F. Horvath, *Small Paul and the Bully of Morgan Court*, Ginn, 1971; Marguerita Rudolph, *Sharp and Shiny*, McGraw, 1971; Solveig P. Russell, *Motherly Smith and Brother Bimbo*, Abingdon, 1971; Myra Scovel, *The Happiest Summer*, Harper, 1971; Martha L. Moffett, *A Flower Pot is Not a Hat*, Dutton, 1972; Norah Smaridge, *You Know Better Than That*, Abingdon, 1973; Leslie McGuire, *You: How Your Body Works*, Platt, 1974.

Creator of television commercial cartoons, "The Health-Tex Kids."

AVOCATIONAL INTERESTS: Children, animals (has five cats), travel, religion, metaphysics, and psychology.†

* * *

PERLMUTTER, Jerome H. 1924-

PERSONAL: Born October 17, 1924, in New York, N.Y.,

son of Morris and Rebecca (Shiffman) Perlmutter; married Evelyn Lea Friedman, September 19, 1948; children: Diane, Sandra, Bruce. *Education:* George Washington University, A.B. (cum laude), 1949; American University, M.A., 1957. *Home:* 513 East Indian Spring Dr., Silver Spring, Md.

CAREER: National Education Association, Washington, D.C., production editor of *NEA Journal*, and editor of *Journal of Health*, 1948-49; American Association for Health, Physical Education and Recreation, Washington, D.C., editor-in-chief, 1949-51; U.S. Department of Agriculture, Washington, D.C., writing and editorial posts, 1951-62, became chief editor, and secretary of Economic Publications Board; U.S. Department of State, Washington, D.C., chief of publishing and reproduction, 1962-72; National Endowment for the Arts, Washington, D.C., Federal Graphics coordinator, 1972—. Instructor in writing, U.S. Department of Agriculture Graduate School, 1954—, University of Maryland, 1966—. *Military service:* U.S. Navy, 1943-45

MEMBER: Federal Editors Association (vice-president, 1951), Phi Beta Kappa, Phi Eta Sigma, Sigma Delta Chi, B'nai B'rith. *Awards, honors:* U.S. Department of Agriculture Superior Service Award, 1959; Arthur S. Flemming Award, Junior Chamber of Commerce, 1963; U.S. Department of State Distinguished Service Award, 1963.

WRITINGS: A Practical Guide to Effective Writing, Random House, 1965. Writer of numerous government publications.

WORK IN PROGRESS: A book, *Style Guide on the English Language*.

* * *

PERRY, Stewart E(dmond) 1928-

PERSONAL: Born March 8, 1928, in Paris, France; son of U.S. citizens, John Edmond and Norma (Stewart) Perry; married Helen Swick (a social scientist), June 18, 1951. *Education:* Kenyon College, A.B. (with honors), 1947; graduate study at Georgetown University, 1947-48, and American University, 1953-57; Washington School of Psychiatry, Certificate in Applied Psychiatry, 1954; Harvard University, Ph.D., 1963. *Politics:* Independent/Democratic. *Home:* 10 Hilliard St., Cambridge, Mass. 02138. *Office:* Institute for New Enterprise Development, 385 Concord Ave., Belmont, Mass. 02178.

CAREER: Held clerical jobs, 1947-48; Washington School of Psychiatry, Washington, D.C., administrative assistant, 1948-50; National Institute of Mental Health, Bethesda, Md., social science analyst, 1953-58; Boston University, School of Medicine, Boston, Mass., research social scientist, 1958-60; University of California, School of Nursing, San Francisco, lecturer in sociology, 1963-66, associate research sociologist, and associate project director of Faculty Research Development Project, 1966-67; University of California, Berkeley, lecturer in sociology, 1965-67; Office of Economic Opportunity, Washington, D.C., research sociologist, 1967-69; Center for Community Economic Development, Cambridge, Mass., executive director, 1969-74; Institute for New Enterprise Development, Belmont, Mass., principal investigator, 1975—. Analyst for committee on disaster studies of National Academy of Sciences—National Research Council, 1954. *Military service:* U.S. Army, Medical Corps, 1950-52. *Member:* Society for Applied Anthropology, American Sociological Association, National League for Nursing, Pacific Sociological Association.

WRITINGS: (Editor with Alfred H. Stanton) *Personality and Political Crisis*, Free Press of Glencoe, 1951; (with Earle Silber and Donald A. Bloch) *The Child and His Family in Disaster*, National Academy of Sciences—National Research Council, 1956; (with wife, Helen S. Perry) *The Schoolhouse Disasters*, National Academy of Sciences—National Research Council, 1959; (contributor) James N. Rosenau, editor, *International Politics and Foreign Policy*, Free Press of Glencoe, 1961; *The Human Nature of Sciences; Researchers at Work in Psychiatry*, Free Press of Glencoe, 1966; (contributor) Irving Phillips, editor, *Prevention and Treatment of Mental Retardation*, Basic Books, 1966; (contributor) Claude S. Thomas and Bernard J. Bergen, editors, *Issues and Problems in Social Psychiatry*, C. C Thomas, 1966; (contributor) C. George Benello and Dimitrios Roussopoulos, editors, *The Case for Participatory Democracy*, Grossman, 1971; *Community Economic Development: A Strategy for Social Change*, Russell Sage Foundation, in press. Contributor of articles and reviews to psychiatry and social science journals.

WORK IN PROGRESS: Two books: *The Changing World of the Seaside Scavengers: A Garbage Workers' Cooperative*, and *Intellectual Behavior: Social Scientific Perspectives on Thought and Thinkers*.

* * *

PERSONS, Robert H(odge), Jr. 1922-

PERSONAL: Born September 13, 1922, in Dallas, Tex.; son of Robert H. (an engineer) and Vera (Horne) Persons; married Laura Gaisner (a teacher), June 3, 1949; children: Richard Fleet, Jill Diane. *Education:* University of Texas, B.A., 1946; Columbia University, M.A., 1950, Ph.D., 1957. *Home:* 16 Whitehouse Rd., White Plains, N.Y. 10607. *Office:* Department of Economics, University of Bridgeport, Bridgeport, Conn. 06602.

CAREER: Texas Technological College (now Texas Tech University), Lubbock, assistant professor of economics, 1949-52; Brooklyn College (now Brooklyn College of the City University of New York), Brooklyn, N.Y., instructor in economics, 1952-53; *Business Week*, New York, N.Y., assistant editor of "Business Outlook," 1953-56; National Industrial Conference Board, New York, N.Y., senior business analyst, 1956-59; *Investors Intelligence*, Larchmont, N.Y., chief editor, 1959-64; State University of New York at New Paltz, assistant professor of economics, 1964-65; University of Bridgeport, Bridgeport, Conn., associate professor, 1965-68, professor of economics, 1968—. Editor and writer for American Research Council, 1959—. *Military service:* U.S. Army Air Forces, 1942-45; became sergeant. *Member:* American Economic Association, American Statistical Association, Phi Beta Kappa, Phi Eta Sigma.

WRITINGS: *Life Insurance 1964*, American Research Council, 1964; *Airlines 1964*, American Research Council, 1964; (with others) *Mining Stocks of the World*, Investors' Press, 1964; *Life Insurance 1965*, American Research Council, 1965; *Handbook of Formula Plans in the Stock Market*, American Research Council, 1967; (editor) *Your Investments in Life Insurance Stocks*, 5th edition, American Research Council, 1969. Writer of regular monthly finance column for *Postgraduate Medicine*. Contributing editor, *Indicator Digest*, 1964—; editor, *Spotlight on Life Insurance Stocks*, a monthly report.†

PETER, James (Fletcher) 1919-

PERSONAL: Born August 8, 1919, in London, England; son of William Alexander (a master mariner) and Jane Corbetta (Fletcher) Peter; married Mary Eileen Jay, June 20, 1942; children Margaret, Ian, Lynnette, David. *Education:* University of Sydney, B.A., 1939, Dip. Ed. 1940, B.D., 1950; St. Andrew's Theological Hall, Sydney, Australia, additional study, 1946-48. *Home:* 46 Burra Rd., Artarmon, New South Wales, Australia. *Office:* Australian Broadcasting Commission, Sydney, Australia.

CAREER: Presbyterian minister; St. Andrew's Presbyterian Church, Maroubra, New South Wales, Australia, minister, 1948-51; Emmanuel College, University of Queensland, Brisbane, Australia, professor of theology, 1952-61; Australian Broadcasting Commission, Sydney, Australia, director of religious programs, 1961—. Chaplain, Citizens' Military Forces, 1950-74; preacher and lecturer in United States and Canada, 1954-55, 1958-59; First Presbyterian Church, Pasadena, Calif., summer preacher, 1964. Father and Son Welfare Movement, member of central council, 1954—, president of Queensland branch, 1954-61. *Military service:* Royal Australian Air Force, 1941-45; became flight lieutenant; mentioned in dispatches.

WRITINGS: *Principles of Religious Broadcasting*, Australian Broadcasting Commission, 1963; *Church Union in Australia*, Aldersgate Press, 1964; *Finding the Historical Jesus*, Collins, 1965. Contributor to theological journals. Associate editor, *Reformed Theological Review*.

* * *

PETER, Laurence J. 1919-

PERSONAL: Born September 16, 1919, in Vancouver, British Columbia, Canada; son of Victor (an actor) and Vincenta (Steves) Peter; married Irene Howe, February 25, 1967; children: John, Edward, Alice, Margaret. *Education:* University of British Columbia, courses annually, 1938-54; Western Washington State College, B.A., 1957, M.Ed., 1958; Washington State University, Ed.D., 1963. *Home:* 2332 Via Anacapa, Palos Verdes Estates, Calif. 90274.

CAREER: Teacher of industrial arts in British Columbia, 1941-47; Provincial Prison Department, Burnaby, British Columbia, instructor, 1947-48; Vancouver School Board, Vancouver, British Columbia, mental health coordinator and special counselor, 1948-64; University of British Columbia, Vancouver, assistant professor of education, 1964-66; University of Southern California, Los Angeles, associate professor, 1966-69, professor of education, 1969-70, director of Evelyn Frieden Center for Prescriptive Teaching, 1967-70; John Tracy Clinic, Los Angeles, Calif., professor in residence, 1970—. Psychologist, British Columbia Vocational Counselling Service, 1959; consultant to other British Columbia health and service organizations. Executive member, Vancouver Community Chest and Council, 1958-61; panel member of review board, Department of Health, Education and Welfare, 1969-70. *Member:* National Autistic Association, American Association of University Professors, Canadian Psychological Association, Canadian Mental Health Association, Canadian Association of University Teachers, P.E.N., American Federation of Television and Radio Artists, Northwest Writers Conference, Association for Retarded Children, British Columbia Teachers Association, Greater Los Angeles Big Brother Association (member of board), Phi Delta Kappa. *Awards, honors:* Phi Delta Kappa research award, University of Southern California, 1970.

WRITINGS: Prescription Teaching, McGraw, 1965; (with Raymond Hull) *The Peter Principle: Why Things Always Go Wrong* (*New York Times* and *Publisher's Weekly* best-seller list, 1969), Morrow, 1969; *The Peter Prescription and How to Make Things Go Right*, Morrow, 1972; *The Peter Plan: A Proposal for Survival*, Morrow, 1975; *Competencies for Teaching*, four volumes, Wadsworth, 1975. Contributor to *Education Panorama* (published in five languages), and other education journals.

SIDELIGHTS: Film rights for *The Peter Principle* have been purchased by comedian Alan King, June, 1969.

BIOGRAPHICAL/CRITICAL SOURCES: Canada Month, October, 1965; *Life*, July 18, 1969.

*   *   *

PETERS, Ken(neth Walter) 1929-

PERSONAL: Born May 17, 1929, in London, England; son of Walter Charles (a master joiner) and Doris (Connelly) Peters. *Education:* Attended St. Dunstan's College, Catford, England. *Home:* 4A Kings Rd., Biggin Hill, Kent, England. *Office:* Reditune Ltd., Cray Ave., Orpington, Kent, England.

CAREER: Worked for British Admiralty, London and Bath, England, 1951-59; editor of *Amateur Tape Recording* and *Popular Hi-Fi* (both magazines), London, England, 1959-64; publicity manager of Reditune Ltd., Orpington, Kent, England, 1964-67; *Hardware Review*, Surrey, England, editor, 1967—. Also editor of *Cassette. Military service:* Royal Air Force, 1947-49. *Member:* National Union of Journalists.

WRITINGS: Modern Tape Recording and Hi-Fi, Faber, 1963, 2nd edition, 1967; *Your Book of Tape Recording*, Faber, 1966.

WORK IN PROGRESS: Stamps and Invention and *Your Book on Inventing.*

AVOCATIONAL INTERESTS: Playing piano.†

*   *   *

PETERS, Victor 1915-

PERSONAL: Born July 27, 1915, in Petersdorf, Russia; son of Johann and Maria (Siemens) Peters; married Elizabeth Dyck (an assistant professor at University of Manitoba), June 27, 1942; children: Rosmarin, Karl. *Education:* University of Manitoba, B.A., 1952, M.A., 1958; University of Goettingen, Dr. Phil., 1960. *Politics:* Independent. *Religion:* Menonite. *Office:* Moorhead State College, Moorhead, Minn.

CAREER: Moorhead State College, Moorhead, Minn., professor of history, 1961—. Associate editor, Echo-Verlag. *Member:* American Historical Association, Canadian Historical Association, American Association of University Professors, Manitoba Historical and Scientific Society, Red River Historical Society. *Awards, honors:* Margaret McWilliams Medal, Manitoba Historical Society, 1966; Agassiz Plaque, 1967.

WRITINGS: Zwei Dokumente: Quellen zum Geschichtsstudium der Mennoniten in Russland, Echo-Verlag, 1965; *All Things Common: The Hutterian Way of Life*, University of Minnesota Press, 1965; *Nestor Makhno: The Life of an Anarchist*, Echo Books, 1970.

WORK IN PROGRESS: Research in agriculture in East Germany, and Foreign settlements in Tsarist Russia.

PETRIE, Charles (Alexander) 1895-

PERSONAL: Born September 28, 1895, in Liverpool, England; son of Sir Charles (first Baronet of Carrowcarden) and Hannah Lindsay (Hamilton) Petrie; married Ursula Gabrielle, 1920; married second wife, Jessie Cecilia Mason (formerly a member of the London County Council), February 24, 1926; children: (first marriage) Richard; (second marriage) Peter. *Education:* Educated privately and at Corpus Christi College, Oxford. *Politics:* Tory. *Religion:* Presbyterian. *Home:* 190 Coleherne Court, London S.W. 5, England. *Agent:* Curtis Brown Ltd., 60 East 56th St., New York, N.Y. 10022.

CAREER: Succeeded brother as third Baronet of Carrowcarden, 1929. Joined the staff of *Outlook*, London, England, shortly after the end of World War I and has been engaged in writing and lecturing, principally on historical topics, ever since; also editor, 1931—(serving as foreign editor of *English Review*, 1931-37, associate editor, and later editor of *Empire Review*, 1940-43, managing editor of *New English Review*, 1945-50, and editor of *Household Brigade*, 1945—. Official lecturer, H. M. Forces, 1940-45. *Military service:* Royal Artillery, 1915-59.

MEMBER: Royal Historical Society (fellow), Royal Spanish Academy of History (corresponding member), Military History Society of Ireland (president), Hispanic Society of America, Institucion Fernando el Catolico (corresponding member); Authors Club, Carlton Club, and Hurlingham Club (all London); University Club (Dublin). *Awards, honors:* Commander, Order of the British Empire, 1957; Knight Order of Civil Merit of Spain; Commander, Order of Isabel the Catholic (Spain); Commendatore, Order of the Crown of Italy; Commander, Order of George I of Greece; D. Phil. Universidad de Valladolid; D. Litt., National University of Ireland, 1971.

WRITINGS: The History of Government, Methuen, 1929 published as *The Story of Government*, Little, Brown, 1929; *George Canning*, Eyre & Spottiswoode, 1930, 2nd edition, 1946; *Mussolini*, Holme Press, 1931; *The Jacobite Movement*, Eyre & Spottiswoode, 1932 published as *The Stuart Pretenders*, Houghton, 1933, revised edition in two volumes, 1948-50, 3rd revised edition, 1959; *Monarchy*, Eyre & Spottiswoode, 1933; *The British Problem*, Nicholson & Watson, 1934; (author of Part II, with Louis Bertrand) *History of Spain*, Appleton, 1934; *Spain*, Arrowsmith, 1934; (editor) *Charles I, King of England: Letters, Speeches, and Proclamations*, Cassell, 1935; *The Four Georges*, Eyre & Spottiswoods, 1935, Houghton, 1936; *William Pitt*, Duckworth, 1935; *Walter Long and His Times*, Hutchinson, 1935; *Bolingbroke*, Collins, 1937; *Lords of the Inland Sea*, Dickson, 1937; *The Stuarts*, Eyre & Spottiswoode, 1937, 2nd edition, 1958; *The Chamberlain Tradition*, Frederick Stokes, 1938; *Louix XIV*, Butterworth, 1938; *The Life and Letters of the Right Hon. Sir Austen Chamberlain, K.G.C., M.P.*, two volumes, Cassell, 1939-40.

Joseph Chamberlain, Duckworth, 1940; *Twenty Years' Armistice and After: British Foreign Policy Since 1918*, Eyre & Spottiswoode, 1940; *When Britain Saved Europe*, Eyre & Spottiswoode, 1941; *Diplomatic History, 1713-1933*, Hollis & Carter, 1946, Macmillan, 1949; (translator) Paul Baudoin, *Private Diaries*, Eyre & Spottiswoode, 1948; *Earlier Diplomatic History, 1492-1713*, Macmillan, 1949; *Chapters of Life*, Eyre & Spottiswoode, 1950; (editor and author of introduction) F. Berwick, *The Duke of Berwick and His Son*, Eyre & Spottiswoode, 1951; *Monarchy in the*

Twentieth Century, Dakers, 1952; *The Marshal Duke of Berwick*, Eyre & Spottiswoode, 1953; *Lord Liverpool and His Times*, J. Barrie, 1954; *The Carlton Club*, Eyre & Spottiswoode, 1955; (editor) Jose Pla, *Gibraltar*, Hollis & Carter, 1955; *Wellington: A Reassessment*, J. Barrie, 1956; *Daniel O'Connor Sligo: His Family and His Times* (pamphlet), National University of Ireland, 1958; *The Powers Behind the Prime Ministers*, MacGibbon & Kee, 1958; *The Spanish Royal House*, Bles, 1958; *The Victorians*, Eyre & Spottiswoode, 1960; *The Modern British Monarchy*, Eyre & Spottiswoode, 1961; *King Alfonso XIII and His Age*, Chapman & Hall, 1963; *Philip II of Spain*, Norton, 1963; *The Edwardians*, Norton, 1965 (published in England as *The Scene of Edwardian Life*, Eyre & Spottiswoode, 1965); *Don John of Austria*, Norton, 1967; *The Great Tyrconnel*, Mercier Press, 1972; *A Historian Looks at His World*, Sidgwick & Jackson, 1972. Contributor to *Transactions of the Royal Historical Society* (London), 1931 and 1935.

AVOCATIONAL INTERESTS: "Anything and everything to do with Ireland and Spain."

* * *

PETTIT, Norman 1929-

PERSONAL: Born December 14, 1929, in Cambridge, Mass.; son of Horace (a medical doctor) and Millicent (Lewis) Pettit; married Beatrice Binger (a landscape architect), June 25, 1955. *Education:* Harvard University, A.B., 1954; Oxford University, B.A., 1956, M.A., 1959; Yale University, Ph.D., 1963. *Home:* 39 Martin St., Cambridge, Mass. *Office:* Department of English, Boston University, Boston, Mass.

CAREER: Hebrew University, Jerusalem, Israel, instructor, department of English, 1957-58; Massachusetts Institute of Technology, Cambridge, assistant professor, department of humanities, 1962-67; Brown University, Providence, R.I., assistant professor of English, 1967-68; Boston University, Boston, Mass., associate professor of English, 1968—. Cambridge (Mass.) Historic Districts Commission, adviser, 1964-67. *Military service:* U.S. Air Force, 1948-49. U.S. Air Force Reserve, 1949-62; became second lieutenant. *Member:* Colonial Society of Massachusetts (council member, 1966), Cambridge (Mass.) Historical Society (2nd vice-president, 1975), Pilgrim Society.

WRITINGS: The Heart Prepared: Grace and Conversion in Puritan Spiritual Life, Yale University Press, 1966; (with George H. Williams) *Thomas Hooker: Writings in England and Holland, 1626-1633*, Harvard Theological Studies, 1975. Contributor to journals.

WORK IN PROGRESS: Editing *Brainerd's Journal*, for Yale University Press edition of "The Works of Jonathan Edwards"; research on the Hebraic tradition in Puritan thought.

* * *

PFLIEGER, Elmer F. 1908-

PERSONAL: Surname is pronounced *Flee*-ger; born July 4, 1908, in Chicago, Ill.; son of Robert and Mary (Beyer) Pflieger; married Beata Wuggazer, June 14, 1934; children: Marilyn, Ronald. *Education:* Attended Concordia Teachers College, River Forest, Ill., 1926-29; Wayne State University, B.A., 1933, M.A. 1935, Ed.D., 1953. *Office:* Detroit Public Schools, 5057 Woodward Ave., Detroit, Mich. 48202.

CAREER: Teacher at Trinity Lutheran School, Utica,

Mich., 1929-35; principal in Royal Oak, Mich., 1935-36; (Mich.) public schools, teacher, 1936-46, evaluation director of Citizenship Education Study, 1946-50, supervisor of social studies, 1950-57, director of television teaching, 1957-62, divisional director of social studies, beginning 1963. Visiting professor of education at Wayne State University, University of California and Colorado State University. Staff member of Civic Education Project, National Council for the Social Studies, 1965-66; member of advisory board, Center for Information on America; chairman of board for higher education, Lutheran Church-Missouri Synod. *Member:* National Education Association, association for Supervision and Curriculum Development, National Council for the Social Studies (director, 1959-62), Michigan Council for Social Studies (president, 1956), Detroit Round Table of Christians and Jews, Detroit Economic Club, Phi Delta Kappa. *Awards, honors:* Valley Forge Teacher's Medal from Freedoms Foundation; Christus Primus Award.

WRITINGS: (With Grace Weston and Mildred Peters) *Democratic Citizenship and Development of Children*, Wayne University Press, 1949; (with Weston) *Emotional Adjustment: A Key to Good Citizenship*, Wayne University Press, 1953; (with Stanley Ellwood Dimond) *Our American Government*, Lippincott, 1957, 8th edition, 1971; (with others) *Using TV in the Classroom*, McGraw, 1961; (with Dimond) *Civics for Citizens*, Lippincott, 1965, revised edition, 1970; (with Donald Robinson, Harold Oyer, and Daniel Roselle) *Promising Practices in Civic Education*, National Council for Social Studies, 1967. Co-author of a number of educational pamphlets, and contributor to education journals.†

* * *

PHELPS, Robert 1922-

PERSONAL: Born November 16, 1922, in Elyria, Ohio; son of George and Eugenie (Wenger) Phelps; married Rosemarie Beck (a painter), September 14, 1945; children: Roger. *Education:* Attended Oberlin College, 1940-43, and University of Chicago, 1945. *Home:* 6 East Twelfth St., New York, N.Y. 10003. *Agent:* James Brown Associates, Inc., 22 East 60th St., New York, N.Y. 10022.

CAREER: Grove Press, Inc. (publishers), New York, N.Y., founder and editor, 1949-51; McDowell, Obolensky, Inc. (publishers), New York, N.Y., editor, 1957-60; George Braziller, Inc. (publishers), New York N.Y., editor, 1961-63, 1964; free-lance writer and editor. Director of creative writing workshops at New School for Social Research, 1966-75, and Columbia University, 1966-67; National Endowment for the Humanities, appointment to Manhattanville College, 1973-74. *Member:* P.E.N. *Awards, honors:* Rockefeller Foundation fellowship, 1970.

WRITINGS: Hereos and Orators (novel), McDowell, Obolensky, 1958; (edtior, and author of introduction) *Letters of James Agee to Father Flye*, Braziller, 1962; (compiler, and author of introduction) *The Breaking Up* (anthology), Braziller, 1965; (editor, and author of introduction) *Earthly Paradise: Colette's Autobiography Drawn from the Writings of Her Lifetime*, Farrar, Straus, 1966; (author of introduction) *Paris Diary of Ned Rorem*, Braziller, 1966; (editor with Peter Deane) *Literary Almanac, 1900-1950*, Farrar, Straus, 1968; *Professional Secrets*, Farrar, Straus, 1970; *The Silent Partner*, Farrar, Straus, 1975; *A Festival Life: Biographical Portrait of Marcel Jouhandeau*, Farrar, Straus, 1975. Writer of regular column for *Book Week*,

1963-64; contributor of articles and reviews to newspapers and magazines, including *New York Times, New York Herald Tribune, New Republic, Reporter, Life, Harper's Bazaar, Vogue*, and *Mademoiselle*.

BIOGRAPHICAL/CRITICAL SOURCES: Sewanee Review, spring, 1967.

*   *   *

PHIFER, Kenneth G.   1915-

PERSONAL: Born December 21, 1915, in Lewisburg, Tenn.; son of William Everette and Blanche (Wyatt) Phifer; married Mary Agnes Penney, June 17, 1941; children: Anne Penney, Lynn Cameron, William Riker. *Education:* Centre College of Kentucky, A.B., 1939; Louisville Presbyterian Theological Seminary, B.D., 1942; Vanderbilt University, M.A., 1944. *Politics:* Democrat. *Home:* 1644 State St., New Orleans, La. 70118. *Office:* St. Charles Avenue Presbyterian Church, 1545 State St., New Orleans, La. 70118.

CAREER: Presbyterian Church in the U.S., ordained minister, 1942; minister in Franklin, Tenn., 1942-45, Rock Hill, S.C., 1945-50, Alexandria, Va., 1950-59; Louisville Presbyterian Theological Seminary, Louisville, Ky., professor of homiletics, 1959-65; St. Charles Avenue Presbyterian Church, New Orleans, La., minister, 1965—. *Awards, honors:* D.D., Hampden-Sydney College, 1957; Litt.D., Centre College of Kentucky, 1961.

WRITINGS: A Star is Born, John Knox, 1952; *A Protestant Case for Liturgical Renewal*, Westminster, 1965; (contributor) Mary Virginia Robinson, editor, *Stories for Christmas*, John Knox, 1968; *Tales of Human Frailty and the Gentleness of God*, John Knox, 1974. Contributor to magazines and religious journals.

*   *   *

PHILLIPS, Dewi Zephaniah   1934-

PERSONAL: Born November 24, 1934, in Swansea, Wales; son of D. O. and A. F. (Davies) Phillips; married Margaret Monica Hanford; children: Aled Huw, Steffan John, Rhys David. *Education:* University College of Swansea, University of Wales, B.A. (first class honors in philosophy), 1956, M.A., 1958; St. Catherine's Society, Oxford, B.Litt., 1961. *Politics:* Welsh Nationalist. *Religion:* Congregationlist. *Home:* 45 Queen's Rd., Sketty, Swansea, Glamorganshire, Wales.

CAREER: University of St. Andrews, St. Andrews, Scotland, assistant lecturer in philosophy, 1961-62, lecturer, 1962-63; University of Wales, lecturer in philosophy at University College of North Wales, Bangor, 1962-65, at University College of Swansea, Swansea, Wales, 1965-67, senior lecturer, 1967-70, professor, 1971—. *Member:* Mind Association, Aristotelian Society, Welsh Philosophical Society.

WRITINGS: The Concept of Prayer, Schocken, 1965; (editor) *Religion and Understanding*, Macmillan, 1967; (editor) *Saith Ysgrif Ar Grefydd*, 1967; (editor) J. L. Stocks, *Morality and Purpose*, Routledge & Kegan Paul, 1969; (editor) *Studies in Ethics and the Philosophy of Religion*, Schocken, 1968-74; *Faith and Philosophical Enquiry*, Routledge & Kegan Paul, 1970, Schocken, 1971; *Death and Immortality*, St. Martin's, 1970; (with H.O. Mounce) *Moral Practices*, Schocken, 1970; (with Ilham Dilman) *Sense and Delusion*, Humanities Press, 1971; *Athronyddu Am Grefydd*, 1974.

Contributor: I. T. Ramsey, editor, *Christian Ethics and Contemporary Philosophy*, Collier, 1966; A. Godin, editor, *Du Cri a la Parole*, Editions De Lumen Vitae, 1967; Judith J. Thomson and Gerald Dworkin, editors, *Ethics*, Harper, 1968; J. E. Coenyn, editor, *Ysgrifau Beirnindol*, Volume IV, Gee & Sons, 1969; J. H. Gill, editor, *Philosophy Today*, Macmillan, 1969; W. D. Hudson, editor, *The Is/Ought Question*, Macmillan, 1969; B. Mitchell, editor, *The Philosophy of Religion*, Oxford University Press, 1971; *Problems of Moral Philosophy*, Dickenson, 1972. Contributor to proceedings of philosophy societies and to learned journals.

WORK IN PROGRESS: Philosophy and Religion: An Essay on Religion and Reductionism; essays for a collection, *Values and Limits*.

*   *   *

PHILLIPS, Robert (Schaeffer)   1938-

PERSONAL: Born February 2, 1938, in Milford, Del.; son of Thomas Allen and Katheryn Augusta (Schaeffer) Phillips; married Judith Anne Bloomingdale (a poet), June 16, 1962; children: Graham Van Buren. *Education:* Syracuse University, B.A., 1960, M.A., 1962. *Politics:* Republican. *Religion:* Episcopalian. *Home:* Cross River Rd., Katanak, N.Y. 10536. *Agent:* Blanche C. Gregory, Inc., 2 Tudor City Pl., New York, N.Y. 10017. *Office:* Grey Advertising, Inc., 777 Third Ave., New York, N.Y. 10017.

CAREER: Syracuse University, Syracuse, N.Y., assistant director of admissions, 1962-64; Benton & Bowles, Inc. (advertising), New York, N.Y., copywriter, 1964-67; McCann-Erickson, Inc. (advertising), New York, N.Y., senior writer, 1967-69; Grey Advertising, Inc., New York, N.Y., vice-president and creative supervisor, 1969—. *Member:* American P.E.N., Authors Guild, Authors League, National Book Critic's Circle.

WRITINGS: 8 & 8 (poems), J. J. Janos, 1960; *Inner Weather* (poetry), Golden Quill, 1966; *The Achievement of William Van O'Connor* (bibliography), Syracuse University Press, 1969; *The Land of Lost Content* (fiction), Vanguard Press, 1970; *Aspects of Alice: Lewis Carroll's Dreamchild* (criticism), Vanguard Press, 1971, revised edition, Penguin, 1974; (contributor) Aage Jorgensen, editor, *Isak Direson, Storyteller*, Akademisk Boghandel, 1972; *The Confessional Poets* (criticism), Southern Illinois University Press, 1973; (contributor) *Natives: An Anthology of Contemporary American Poetry*, edited by Ed Ochester, Quixote Press, 1973; (editor) *Moonstruck: An Anthology of Lunar Poetry*, Vanguard Press, 1974; (contributor) Robert K. Morris, editor, *Old Lines: New Forces*, Fairleigh Dickinson University Press, 1975; (contributor) Morris and Irving Malin, editors, *The Achievement of William Styron*, University of Georgia Press, 1975. Contributor of poetry, fiction, and essays to *New York Herald Tribune, New Mexico Quarterly, Western Humanities Review, Southwest Review, Voices, Renascence, Manhattan Review, Forum, Encounter, Poetry, Studies in Short Fiction, Saturday Review*, and other periodicals. Regular reviewer, *North American Review*, 1965-69. Book review editor, *Modern Poetry Studies*, 1971—.

WORK IN PROGRESS: William Goyan, a critical and biographical study, publication by Twayne expected in 1977; a third collection of poems; and a second collection of short stories.

SIDELIGHTS: "I have always written," writes Phillips. "When very young I composed 'books' and illustrated and bound them myself. These juvenilia were usually about stray horses and dogs. Subsequently the serious study of art and music helped liberate my imagination.

"Growing up in a small town has been the greatest influence upon my work. Most of my stories and poems are about provincial characters. Several critics have accused me of a preoccupation with 'the mean, the maimed, the foolish.' True. I am fascinated by the eccentric and the outrageous, especially characters whose 'inner weather' is turbulent. Any physical grotesqueries of my characters are usually symbolic representations of their mental conditions."

BIOGRAPHICAL/CRITICAL SOURCES: North American Review, November, 1966; *New York Times*, December 2, 1971; *Carleton Miscellany*, 1972-73; *Newday*, June 16, 1974.

* * *

PICK, Robert 1898-

PERSONAL: Born March 1, 1898, in Vienna, Austria; son of Anton and Ida (Bell) Pick; married Priscilla Kennaday, March 4, 1957. *Education:* Educated in Vienna, Austria. *Home:* 138 East 78th St., New York, N.Y.; and, Woodstock, N.Y. *Agent:* Sanford Jerome Greenburger, 595 Madison Ave., New York, N.Y. 10022.

CAREER: Professional writer. Editor, Alfred A. Knopf, Inc. *Member:* P.E.N. (member of executive board, 1946-64). *Awards, honors:* Guggenheim fellow, 1946.

WRITINGS: The Terhoven File (novel), Lippincott, 1944; *Guests of Don Lorenzo* (novel), Lippincott, 1950; (translator) Theodor Plievier, *World's Last Corner*, Appleton, 1951; (editor) *German Stories and Tales*, Knopf, 1954; *The Escape of Socrates* (novel), Knopf, 1954; (translator with James Stern) Hermann Kesten, *Casanova*, Harper, 1955; *Empress Maria Theresa* (biography), Harper, 1966; *The Last Days of Imperial Vienna*, Weidenfeld & Nicolson, 1975. Contributor to *Encyclopaedia Britannica*, and periodicals.

* * *

PICKELL, Charles N(orman) 1927-

PERSONAL: Surname is pronounced Pic-*kell*; born December 18, 1927, in Haddonfield, N.J.; son of William Norman (a salesman) and Ada (Kelley) Pickell; married second wife, Christina Frazer, March 11, 1972; children: Rachel Grace, Stuart Charles, Arthur John, Heather Lee, Luke Andrew. *Education:* Juniata College, B.A., 1949; Pittsburgh Theological Seminary, B.D., 1952, Th.M., 1957; additional study at Harvard University Divinity School, 1959-60, and Andover-Newton Theological School, 1961-62. *Home:* 237 Church St. N.E., Vienna, Va. 22180. *Office:* Vienna Presbyterian Church, P.O. Box 351, Vienna, Va. 22180.

CAREER: Ordained minister of United Presbyterian Church in the U.S.A., 1952. Pastor in Atlantic City, N.J., 1952-55, Monongahela, Pa., 1955-57, Newton, Mass., 1957-63; Wallace Memorial United Presbyterian Church, West Hyattsville, Md., pastor, 1963-70; Vienna Presbyterian Church, Vienna, Va., pastor, 1970—. Guest lecturer in practical theology at Gordon Divinity School, 1958-63. Trustee of Westminster College, New Wilmington, Pa., 1957-61; trustee of Gordon Divinity School, Wenham, Mass., 1959-70; trustee of Gordon College, Wenham, Mass., 1959—, chairman of academic affairs committee,

1966—. Moderator of Presbytery of Boston, 1959, and of Synod of New England, 1960; chairman of evangelism, Presbytery of Washington City, 1964-66, assistant stated clerk, 1969; incorporator, Gordon-Conwell Theological Seminary, South Hamilton, Mass., 1968-70. Member, National Capital Union Presbytery, 1972—. Chaplain, Fairfax County Fire and Rescue Services, 1973—; member of board of directors, Vienna Volunteer Fire Department, 1975—. *Member:* American Society of Church History, International Platform Association, World Future Society, Presbyterian Historical Society. *Awards, honors:* D.D., Sterling College, 1964; M.Div., Pittsburgh Theological Seminary, 1971.

WRITINGS: Preaching to Meet Men's Needs: The Meaning of the Acts for Preaching Today, Exposition, 1958; (editor and contributor) *Presbyterianism in New England: The Story of a Mission*, Synod of New England, 1962; *The Epistle to the Colossians*, Baker, 1965, 2nd edition, 1974; *Works Count Too!: Faith in Action in the Life of the Christian*, Zondervan, 1966; (contributor) Edward Viening, editor, *God's Minute*, Zondervan, 1970. Also author of *The Presbyterians*, 1972. Contributor to religious periodicals.

AVOCATIONAL INTERESTS: American history, particularly the Civil War period; legitimate theater, baseball, football, and golf.

* * *

PICKER, Martin 1929-

PERSONAL: Born April 3, 1929, in Chicago, Ill.; son of Louis (a merchant) and Ethel (Packer) Picker; married Ruth Gross (a teacher), June 21, 1956; children: Anne Theresa, Catherine Jeanne, John Martin. *Education:* University of Chicago, Ph.B., 1947, M.A., 1951; University of California, Berkeley, Ph.D., 1960. *Home:* 16 Barker Rd., Somerset, N.J. *Office:* Music Department, Rutgers University, New Brunswick, N.J.

CAREER: University of Illinois, School of Music, Urbana, instructor in music, 1959-61; Rutgers University, New Brunswick, N.J., assistant professor, 1961-65, associate professor 1965-68, professor of music, 1968—, chairman of department, 1973—. *Military service:* U.S. Army, 1953-54. *Member:* American Musicological Society, International Musicological Society, Renaissance Society of America, American Association of University Professors. *Awards, honors:* American Council of Learned Societies grant, 1962; Harvard University Center for Italian Renaissance Studies, fellow in Florence, 1966-67; National Endowment for the Humanities, fellow, 1972-73.

WRITINGS: The Chanson Albums of Marguerite of Austria, University of California Press, 1965; (with Martin Bernstein) *An Introduction to Music*, Prentice-Hall, 1966, 4th edition, 1972. Contributor to music journals. Editor-in-chief, *Journal of the American Musicological Society*, 1969-71.

WORK IN PROGRESS: An edition of Andrea Antico's *Motetti Novi* (1520), for University of Chicago Press; *Opera Omnia of Marbriano de Orto*, for American Institute of Musicology.

* * *

PIERCE, John Robinson 1910-
(J. J. Coupling)

PERSONAL: Born March 27, 1910, in Des Moines, Iowa;

son of John Starr and Harriett Anne (Robinson) Pierce; married Martha Peacock, November 5, 1938 (divorced March, 1964); married Ellen R. McKown, April 1, 1964; children: (first marriage) John Jeremy, Elizabeth Anne. *Education:* California Institute of Technology, B.S., 1933, M.S., 1934, Ph.D., 1936. *Home:* 931 Canon Dr., Pasadena, Calif. 91106. *Office:* California Institute of Technology, Pasadena, Calif. 91125.

CAREER: Bell Telephone Laboratories, Murray Hill, N.J., member of technical staff in New York, N.Y., 1936-46, and Murray Hill, 1946-52, director of electronics research, 1952-55, director of research electrical communications, 1955-58, director of research communications principles, 1958-62, executive director, Research-Communications Principles and Communications Systems Divisions, 1962-65, executive director, Research-Communications Sciences Division, 1965-71; California Institute of Technology, Pasadena, Calif., professor of engineering, 1971—. Trustee, Batelle Memorial Institute. Member of scientific advisory committee, American Newspaper Publishers Association; member of scientific advisory board, Gould, Inc.

MEMBER: American Physical Society (fellow), Acoustical Society of America (fellow), National Academy of Engineering, American Academy of Arts and Sciences (fellow), Institute of Electrical and Electronics Engineers (fellow), National Academy of Sciences, American Philosophical Society, Royal Academy of Sciences (Sweden). *Awards, honors:* Eta Kappa Nu Award for outstanding young electrical engineer, 1942; Morris Liebmann Memorial Prize of Institute of Radio Engineers, 1947; Stuart Ballantine medal, Franklin Institute, 1960; Edison medal, Institute of Electrical and Electronics Engineers, 1963; Valdemar Poulsen medal, Danish Academy of Technical Sciences, 1963; National Medal of Science, 1963; H. T. Cedergren medal, Royal Institute of Stockholm, 1964; D.Eng., Newark College of Engineering, 1961, Carnegie Institute of Technology, 1964; D.Sc., Northwestern University, 1961, Yale University, 1963, Polytechnic Institute of Brooklyn, 1963, Columbia University, 1965, University of Nevada, 1970; LL.D., University of Pennsylvania, 1974; D.El.Eng., University of Bologna, 1974.

WRITINGS: Theory and Design of Electronic Beams, Van Nostrand, 1949, 2nd edition, 1954; *Traveling Wave Tubes,* Van Nostrand, 1950; *Electrons, Waves and Messages,* Doubleday, 1956, revised and enlarged edition published as Volume I: *Electrons and Waves,* 1964, Volume II: *Quantum Electronics,* 1966, Volume III: *Waves and Messages,* 1967; (with E. E. David) *Man's World of Sound,* Doubleday, 1958; (with W. A. van Bergeijk and David) *Waves and the Ear,* Doubleday, 1960; *Symbols, Signals and Noise,* Harper, 1961; (with A. G. Tressler) *The Research State: A History of Science in New Jersey,* Van Nostrand, 1964; *Science, Art and Communication,* C. N. Potter, 1968; *Almost All about Waves,* M.I.T. Press, 1974. Also author of *The Beginnings of Satellite Communications,* 1968. Contributor to technical and scientific journals. Editor, *Proceedings of the IRE,* 1954-55. Author of science fiction stories published under pseudonym J. J. Coupling.

*   *   *

PILKINGTON, John, Jr.   1918-

PERSONAL: Born July 1, 1918, in Jacksonville, Fla.; son of John (an insurance man) and Adelia (Willis) Pilkington;

married Lillian Kirk (a manuscript editor), February 20, 1943; children: Charles Kirk. *Education:* Centre College of Kentucky, B.A., 1940; Johns Hopkins University, graduate study, 1940-41; Harvard University, M.A., 1947, Ph.D., 1952. *Politics:* Democrat. *Religion:* Presbyterian. *Address:* P.O. Box 173, University, Miss. *Office:* University of Mississippi, University, Miss.

CAREER: University of Mississippi, University, assistant professor, 1952-56, associate professor, 1956-60, professor of American literature, 1960—, associate dean of graduate school, 1970—. *Military service:* U.S. Navy, 1942-46; became lieutenant commander. *Member:* Modern Language Association of America, American Studies Association, South Central Modern Language Association, South Atlantic Modern Language Association, American Studies Association of the Lower Mississippi (secretary-treasurer).

WRITINGS: Francis Marion Crawford, Twayne, 1964; *Henry Blake Fuller,* Twayne, 1971. Also editor of *The Letters of Stark Young,* 1975. Editor, *Studies in English* (University of Mississippi).

WORK IN PROGRESS: A critical biography of Stark Young.

*   *   *

PINCKNEY, Catherine L(arkum)
(Cathey Pinckney)

PERSONAL: Born in New York, N.Y.; married Edward Robert Pinckney (a physician and writer), September 18, 1944; children: Cathey Lee. *Education:* New York University, A.B., 1946; Syracuse University, graduate study, 1946-47. *Address:* Box P, Beverly Hills, Calif. 90213.

CAREER: Full-time writer; consumer reporter. *Member:* Authors Guild of the Authors League of America, Writers Guild of America, West.

WRITINGS—Under name Cathey Pinckney: (With husband, Edward R. Pinckney) *Encyclopedia of Common Medical Illnesses,* Fawcett, 1962; (with E. R. Pinckney) *The Fallacy of Freud and Psychoanalysis,* Prentice-Hall, 1965; (with Irene Ryan) *Granny's Hillbilly Cookbook,* Prentice-Hall, 1966; (with E. R. Pinckney) *The Cholesterol Controversy,* Sherbourne Press, 1973. Writer, with Edward R. Pinckney, of two scripts for television's "Ben Casey Show," and of parts of motion pictures, "The Interns" and "The New Interns." Also author of *Blackguard Charlie* (screenplay), 1968. Author, with Edward R. Pinckney, of syndicated daily and Sunday newspaper column, "Mirror of Your Mind"; weekly book reviewer (especially of mystery novels) for King Features Syndicate; regular contributor of articles to *Medio & Consumer* (monthly magazine).

WORK IN PROGRESS: A Consumer's Guide to Common Medical Dilemmas.

*   *   *

PINCKNEY, Edward R(obert)   1924-

PERSONAL: Born November 16, 1924, in Boston, Mass.; married Catherine Larkum (a writer under name Cathey Pinckney), September 18, 1944; children: Cathey Lee. *Education:* University of Delaware, B.S., 1946; Syracuse College of Medicine, M.D., 1948; University of California, Berkeley, M.P.H., 1954; Blackstone College, LL.B., 1964. *Address:* Box P, Beverly Hills, Calif. 90213.

CAREER: Diplomate, American Board of Preventive Medicine. Intern, then chief resident in medicine, United

Hospital, Port Chester, N.Y., 1948-49; physician in private practice of medicine, 1949-62; full-time writer, 1962—. Panama Canal Health Department, medical officer, 1949-50, 1952-53; director of public health, Napa County, Calif., 1954-56. Lecturer at School of Public Health, University of California, Berkeley, 1955-56; associate professor of medicine, Northwestern University, 1958-61; associate clinical professor of medicine, Loma Linda University, 1959-62. *Military service:* U.S. Army, 1942-46. U.S. Navy, 1950-52; became lieutenant. *Member:* Authors League of America, Writers Guild of America (West), American College of Physicians (fellow), American Medical Authors (vice-president), National Association of Science Writers. *Awards, honors:* Honor award in medical journalism from American Medical Writers Association, for medical editing, 1960.

WRITINGS: You Can Prevent Illness, Lippincott, 1960; (with Phillip Lewin) *An Atlas of Foot Disorders in Children*, International Shoe Co., 1962; (with wife, Cathey Pinckney) *Encyclopedia of Common Medical Illnesses*, Fawcett, 1962; *How to Make the Most of Medicine*, Follett, 1963; (with Cathey Pinckney) *The Fallacy of Freud and Psychoanalysis*, Prentice-Hall, 1965; (with Cathey Pinckney) *The Cholesterol Controversy*, Sherbourne Press, 1973.

Author, with Cathey Pinckney, of two television scripts for "Ben Casey Show," and of parts of motion pictures, "The Interns" and "The New Interns." Author, with Cathey Pinckney, of syndicated daily and Sunday newspaper column, "Mirror of Your Mind." Contributor of medical articles to *Grolier International Encyclopedia;* regular contributor to *Blue Print for Health.* Chief medical editor of audiovisual postgraduate courses in medicine, distributed by Encyclopaedia Britannica Films, 1959-62; assistant editor, *Journal of the AMA*, 1956-60; editor, *New Physician*, 1957-64; associate editor, *Physician's Management*, 1959-61; executive editor, *Trauma*, 1960-64.

* * *

PING, Charles J. 1930-

PERSONAL: Born June 15, 1930, in Philadelphia, Pa.; son of C. J. and Mary (Marion) Ping; married Claire Oates, June 5, 1951; children: Andrew, Ann Shelton. *Education:* Southwestern at Memphis, A.B., 1951; Louisville Presbyterian Theological Seminary, B.D., 1954; Duke University, Ph.D., 1958. *Home:* 701 South Kinney St., Mt. Pleasant, Mich. 48858. *Office:* Office of the Provost, Central Michigan University, Mt. Pleasant, Mich. 48859.

CAREER: Presbyterian clergyman, ordained, 1954. Culver Military Academy, Culver, Ind., chaplain, 1954-55; Alma College, Alma, Mich., assistant professor, 1958-62, associate professor of philosophy and director of senior studies, 1962-66; Tusculum College, Greenville, Tenn., dean of faculty and professor of philosophy, 1966-71, vice-president and acting president, 1968-71; Central Michigan University, Mt. Pleasant, professor of philosophy and provost, 1971—. *Member:* American Philosophical Association.

WRITINGS: Man and the Modern World: The Examined Life, Alma College Press, 1963; *Meaningful Nonsense*, Westminster, 1966.

WORK IN PROGRESS: A book of readings, tentatively titled *A Free Man: An Introduction to the Liberal Arts*; two other books, tentatively titled *The Destiny of Man* and *The Genus of Christianity: A Study in Hegel's Philosophy of Religion.*†

PINSON, William M(eredith), Jr. 1934-

PERSONAL: Born August 3, 1934, in Fort Worth, Tex.; son of William M. (a businessman) and Ila (Jones) Pinson; married Bobbie Judd, June 4, 1955. *Education:* North Texas State University, B.A., 1955; University of Edinburgh, graduate student, 1956-57; Southwestern Baptist Seminary, B.D., 1959, Th.D., 1963. *Home:* 5333 Wooten, Fort Worth, Tex. 76133. *Office:* Southwestern Seminary, P.O. Box 22068, Fort Worth, Tex. 76122.

CAREER: Clergyman of Baptist Church; Christian Life Commission, Dallas, Tex., associate director, 1957-63; Southwestern Baptist Seminary, Fort Worth, Tex., professor of ethics, 1963—. *Member:* American Society of Christian Ethics. *Awards, honors:* Lilly Foundation scholarship, 1964; named one of the outstanding young men in America by U.S. Junior Chamber of Commerce, 1965.

WRITINGS: Ambassadors and Christian Citizenship, Brotherhood Commission, 1963; *How to Deal with Controversial Issues*, Broadman, 1966; *Resource Guide to Current Social Issues*, Broadman, 1968; *No Greater Challenge*, Convention Press, 1969; *Right or Wrong*, Broadman, 1971; (with Clyde Fant) *Twenty Centuries of Great Preaching*, thirteen volumes, Word Books, 1971; *A Program of Application for the Local Church*, Christian Life Commission, 1972; *Don't Blame the Game*, Word Books, 1972; *Contemporary Christian Trends*, Word Books, 1972; *The Local Church in Ministry*, Broadman, 1973; *The Five Worlds of Youth*, Convention Press, 1974.

Contributor: C. W. Scudder, editor, *Crisis in Morality*, Broadman, 1965; R. Coggins, editor, *The Gambling Menace*, Broadman, 1966; F. Valentine, editor, *Peace! Peace!*, Word Books, 1967.

WORK IN PROGRESS: Source book on biblical ethics; a book on decision making; an ethics text.

* * *

PINTOFF, Ernest 1931-

PERSONAL: Born December 15, 1931, in New York, N.Y.; son of Joseph and Sylvia (Kokol) Pintoff; separated; children: Jonathan, Gabriel. *Education:* Syracuse University, B.F.A., 1953; Michigan State University, M.A., 1955. *Residence:* New York, N.Y.

CAREER: Screen writer, director, producer, composer. *Awards, honors:* Academy of Motion Picture Arts and Sciences "Oscar", 1964, for "The Critic"; and winner of over fifteen film awards, including two British Academy Awards, Venice Film Festival Prize, San Francisco Film Festival First Prize.

WRITINGS: Always Help a Bird (Especially with a Broken Leg), Harper, 1965. Author of twelve screenplays, including "Harvey Middelman, Fireman" and "The Violinist," for Columbia Pictures, "The Wild, Wild East," for American Broadcasting Co. television.

SIDELIGHTS: Pintoff, a former jazz trumpeter, has composed seven film scores. He also has exhibited paintings in New York and Chicago.

* * *

PIPER, Henry Dan 1918-

PERSONAL: Born February 20, 1918, in Haskell, N.J.; son of Henry Anson and Blanche (Guy) Piper; married Roberta Bicknell, July 3, 1953; children: Andrew, Jonathan. *Education:* Princeton University, B.S., 1939; University of Pennsylvania, Ph.D., 1950. *Home:* Route 1, Murphysboro, Ill. 62966. *Office:* Department of English, Southern Illinois University, Carbondale, Ill.

CAREER: E. I. du Pont de Nemours & Co., Wilmington, Del., chemist, 1939-45; Columbia University, New York, N.Y., instructor in Graduate School of Philosophy, 1950-52; California Institute of Technology, Pasadena, assistant professor, 1952-56, associate professor of English, 1956-62; Southern Illinois University, Carbondale, dean of College of Arts and Sciences, 1962-66, professor of English, 1962—. Visiting Fulbright professor, France, 1953-54, England, 1967-68. U.S. State Department consultant in India, Pakistan, Afghanistan, and Bangladesh, 1974-75. *Military service:* U.S. Army, Corps of Engineers, 1947-48; assistant to director of Research Division of Manhattan Project. *Member:* American Studies Association, Modern Language Association of America. *Awards, honors:* Guggenheim fellow, 1957-58; American Council of Learned Societies grant, 1961-62.

WRITINGS: Guide to Technical Reporting, Holt, 1958; *American Literary Manuscripts,* University of Texas Press, 1960; (editor with J. K. Clark) *Dimensions in Drama,* Scribner, 1964; *F. Scott Fitzgerald,* Holt, 1965; (editor) Malcolm Cowley, *Look Back on Us: A Contemporary Chronicle of the 1930s,* Southern Illinois University Press, 1967; *Fitzgerald's "The Great Gatsby,"* Scribner, 1971; (editor) Cowley, *A Many Windowed House,* Southern Illinois University Press, 1972; (co-author) *Land Between the Rivers,* Southern Illinois University Press, 1973. Contributor to popular and scholarly journals.

WORK IN PROGRESS: Dick Whittington and the Middle-Class Mind: The Making of a Modern Myth.

*   *   *

PISTOLE, Elizabeth (Smith) 1920-

PERSONAL: Born February 4, 1920, in Halecenter, Tex.; daughter of Price C. and Sarah (Waller) Smith; married Hollis Sidney Pistole (a professor), February 14, 1941; children: Cynthia, Carole, David, John. *Education:* Anderson College, B.S., 1943; Ball State University, M.A., 1966. *Politics:* Republican. *Religion:* Protestant. *Home:* 616 Walnut, Anderson, Ind. 46012. *Office:* Anderson High School, Anderson, Ind.

CAREER: Anderson High School, Anderson, Ind., teacher of language arts and psychology, 1965—. *Member:* Sigma Tau Delta.

WRITINGS: (With husband, Hollis Pistole) *The Church in Thy House,* Warner, 1959; *Confidentially, Girls,* Warner, 1961; *Food and Fellowship* (cookbook), Warner, 1965.

*   *   *

PITCHER, Evelyn G(oodenough) 1915-
(Evelyn Goodenough)

PERSONAL: Born June 15, 1915, in Lansing, Ohio; daughter of Bert and Edna (Jackson) Wiltshire; married Erwin R. Goodenough, 1942 (divorced, 1962); married Robert B. Pitcher, August 6, 1962; children: (first marriage) Ursula W. (Mrs. Paul Levine), Daniel A. Goodenough. *Education:* Wilson College, Chambersburg, Pa., B.A., 1937; Yale University, M.A., 1939, Ph.D., 1956. *Politics:* Democrat. *Religion:* Unitarian Universalist. *Home:* 91 Somerset St., Belmont, Mass. 02178. *Office:* Eliot-Pearson Department of Child Study, Tufts University, Medford, Mass. 02155.

CAREER: Teacher at private and public schools and nursery schools in Pennsylvania and Connecticut, 1939-42, 1948-51; Gesell Institute of Child Development, New Haven, Conn., co-director of nursery school and pre-school examiner, 1951-59; New Haven College, New Haven, Conn., associate professor of early childhood education, 1956-57; Quinnipiac College, New Haven, Conn., lecturer in psychology, 1957-58; Tufts University, Medford, Mass., director of Eliot-Pearson School, 1959-64, professor and chairman of Eliot-Pearson department of child study, 1964—. Certified psychologist, state of Massachusetts. Unitarian Universalist Commission on Education and Liberal Religion, member, 1960-63; Massachusetts Mental Retardation Planning Project, member of task force on prevention. Consultant to U.S. Department of Health, Education, and Welfare, and to Children's Hospital Medical Center, Boston.

MEMBER: American Psychological Association, International Association of Women Psychologists, Society for Research in Child Development, American Association of University Professors, American Association of University Women, Massachusetts Psychological Association. *Awards, honors:* LL.D., New England College, 1962; research grants in field of child welfare, U.S. Department of Health, Education, and Welfare, 1962.

WRITINGS: (Under name Evelyn Goodenough, with Ilg, Ames, and Andersen) *Gesell Institute Party Book,* Harper, 1959; (with Ernst Prelinger) *Children Tell Stories: An Analysis of Fantasy,* International Universities, 1963; (with Louise B. Ames) *The Guidance Nursery School,* Harper, 1964, 2nd edition, 1974; (with Lasher, Feinburg, and Hammond) *Helping Young Children Learn,* C. E. Merrill, 1966; 2nd edition, revised, 1974. Contributor to *Atlantic Monthly* and education journals.

*   *   *

PITKIN, Thomas M(onroe) 1901-

PERSONAL: Born October 6, 1901, in Akron, Ohio. *Education:* University of Akron, B.A., 1926; Ohio State University, M.A., 1928, graduate study, 1929-30; Western Reserve University (now Case Western Reserve University), Ph.D., 1935. *Politics:* Democrat. *Religion:* None. *Home:* 115 West Tenth St., New York, N.Y. 10011.

CAREER: U.S. Government, Washington, D.C., historian, 1935-64. Historian with National Park Service, Department of the Interior, 1935-42, and Office of the Quartermaster General, War Department, 1942-44; leaflet writer in China Branch, Office of War Information, 1944-46; chief historian, Office of the Quartermaster General, Department of the Army, 1947-52; supervisor of historians, National Park Service, Department of the Interior, 1952-64. *Military service:* U.S. Army, 1917-19. U.S. Marine Corps, 1920-22, became sergeant. *Member:* American Historical Association, Organization of American Historians, Association for State and Local History, American Scenic and Historic Preservation Society (trustee), New York Historical Society, Ohio Historical Society.

WRITINGS: (With Charles E. Hatch) *Yorktown: Climax of the Revolution,* National Park Service, 1941; *Quartermaster Equipment for Special Forces,* Office of the Quartermaster General, 1944; (with Erna Risch) *Clothing the Soldier of World War II,* Office of the Quartermaster General, 1946; *Grant the Soldier,* Eastern National Park and Monument Association, 1965; *The Captain Departs: Ulysses S. Grant's Last Campaign,* Southern Illinois University Press, 1973. Writer of prospectus for the American Museum of Immigration, for National Park Service, 1955. Contributor to *Coronet, Antiques*, and *Mississippi Valley Historical Review*.

WORK IN PROGRESS: Keepers of the Gate: A History of Ellis Island.

* * *

PITRONE, Jean Maddern 1920-

PERSONAL: Born December 20, 1920, in Ishpeming, Mich.; daughter of William Courtney (a clerk) and Gladys (Beer) Maddern; married Anthony Peter Pitrone (a landscaper in civil service), October 26, 1940; children: Joseph, Jill, Anthony, Jr., Joyce, John, Janet, Julie, Jane, Cheryl. *Education:* Educated in public schools in Ishpeming, Mich. *Politics:* Democrat. *Religion:* Roman Catholic. *Home:* 8244 Riverview, Dearborn Heights, Mich. 48127.

CAREER: Teacher of piano, 1950, and church organist, 1955, both in Dearborn Heights, Mich.; teacher of magazine-writing in adult education classes, Dearborn, Mich., 1963. Staff member, annual writers' conference at Oakland University, 1962-65. *Member:* Women in Communications, Women's National Book Association, Detroit Women Writers. *Awards, honors:* First place award for juvenile literature, Friends of American Writers, 1970, for *Trailblazers*.

WRITINGS: The Great Black Robe, Daughters of St. Paul, 1964; *Trailblazer: Negro Nurse in the American Red Cross*, Harcourt, 1969; *The Touch of His Hand*, Alba, 1970; *Chavez: Man of the Migrants*, Alba, 1972. Monthly columnist in *Detroit Purchasor*; contributor of articles and short stories to newspapers and magazines, including *Extension, Columbia, Family Digest, Adult Teacher, Presbyterian Life, Catholic Digest*, and *Detroit News Sunday Magazine*. Editorial associate, *Writer's Digest*, 1967—.

WORK IN PROGRESS: The Dodges, an historical biography of the Horace and John Dodge Families.

* * *

PLATE, Robert 1918-

PERSONAL: Born July 31, 1918, in Brooklyn, N.Y.; son of Oscar H. and Loretta (Finnell) Plate. *Education:* Studied at Duke University, 1936-37, New York University, 1938-40. *Politics:* Democrat. *Home:* 71 Glasco Turnpike, Woodstock, N.Y. 1248.

CAREER: Free-lance writer, 1940-54; Scott Meredith Literary Agency, New York, N.Y., editor, 1954-55; full-time free-lance writer, 1955—.

WRITINGS: Palette and Tomahawk: The Story of George Catlin, McKay, 1962; *The Dinosaur Hunters: Cope and Marsh*, McKay, 1964; *Alexander Wilson: Wanderer in the Wilderness*, McKay, 1966; *Charles Wilson Peale: Son of Liberty, Father of Art and Science*, McKay, 1967; *John Singleton Copley: America's First Great Artist*, McKay, 1969; writer of television scripts and short stories.

WORK IN PROGRESS: Croquet, For Macmillan; a novel, *Work of National Importance*.

* * *

PLATT, John (Rader) 1918-

PERSONAL: Born June 29, 1918, in Jacksonville, Fla.; son of Louis Walter (a salesman) and Jennie (Sharp) Platt; married Ann Tammela, June 23, 1941 (deceased); children:

Terry, Christopher. *Education:* Northwestern University, B.S., 1936, M.S., 1937; University of Michigan, Ph.D., 1941. *Office:* Mental Health Research Institute, University of Michigan, 205 Washtenaw Place, Ann Arbor, Michigan 48104.

CAREER: University of Minnesota, Minneapolis, Rockefeller Foundation research fellow, 1941-43; Northwestern University, Evanston, Ill., instructor in physics, 1943-44; University of Chicago, Chicago, Ill., assistant professor, 1946-50, associate professor, 1950-57, professor of physics and biophysics, 1957-65; University of Michigan, Ann Arbor, professor of physics and biophysics, and associate director of Mental Health Research Institute, 1965—. Visiting lecturer and professor at University of London, University of Paris, Harvard University, Hebrew University, Massachusetts Institute of Technology, and Stanford University.

MEMBER: American Academy of Political and Social Science, Phi Beta Kappa, Sigma Xi, Phi Kappa Phi. *Awards, honors:* Guggenheim fellowship to King's College, University of London, 1952-53; National Association of Independent Schools Book Award, 1962, for *The Excitement of Science*; fellow, Center for Advanced Study in Behavioral Science, 1972-73.

WRITINGS: The Excitement of Science, Houghton, 1962; (editor) *Systematics of Electronic Spectra of Conjugated Molecules*, Wiley, 1964; (editor) *Free Electron Theory of Conjugated Molecules*, Wiley, 1964; (editor) *New Views of the Nature of Man*, University of Chicago Press, 1965; *The Step to Man*, Wiley, 1966; *Perception and Change*, University of Michigan Press, 1970. Contributor to scientific journals, and to popular magazines, including *Horizon, Harper's, Saturday Review, New Republic, Life International*.

WORK IN PROGRESS: A book, *On Social Transformation*.

BIOGRAPHICAL/CRITICAL SOURCES: A.A.U.W. Journal, May, 1966.

* * *

PLATT, Kin 1911-

PERSONAL: Born December 8, 1911, in New York, N.Y.; son of Daniel (a singer) and Etta (Hochberg) Platt; divorced; children: Christopher. *Agent:* Ruth Cantor, 120 West 42nd St., New York, N.Y. 10036.

CAREER: Cartoonist, painter and sculptor, and writer. New York Herald Tribune Syndicate, New York, N.Y., cartoonist (writer and illustrator) of comic strip, "Mr. and Mrs.," 1947-63, and "The Duke and the Duchess," 1950-54. Sometime theatrical caricaturist for New York newspapers, including *Village Voice*, and for *Los Angeles Times*. *Military service:* U.S. Army Air Force, Air Transport Command, 1943-46; served in China-Burma-India theater; received Bronze Star. *Member:* Writers Guild of America, Mystery Writers of America, National Cartoonist Society. *Awards, honors:* Mystery Writers of America "Edgar" award for juvenile mystery, 1967.

WRITINGS: The Blue Man (juvenile), Harper, 1961; *Big Max* (juvenile), Harper, 1965; *Sinbad and Me* (juvenile), Chilton, 1966; *The Boy Who Could Make Himself Disappear*, Chilton, 1968; *Mystery of the Witch Who Wouldn't*, Chilton, 1969; *The Pushbutton Butterfly*, Random House, 1970; *The Kissing Gourami*, Random House, 1970; *Hey, Dummy*, Chilton, 1971; *Dead As They Come*, Random House, 1972; *The Princess Stakes Murder*, Random House, 1973; *Chloris and the Creeps*, Chilton, 1973.

SIDELIGHTS: Platt told *CA* that he "would like to see less genteel supervised attitude toward books for children and more imaginative approaches welcomed. *Blue Man* was popular with children, not librarians, and lost the battle, for example." His novel, *The Boy Who Could Make Himself Disappear,* was adapted for a film entitled "Baxter," 1973.†

* * *

PLOTNICK, Alan R(alph) 1926-

PERSONAL: Born April 10, 1926, in Philadelphia, Pa.; son of Walter H. (an editorial director) and Rachel (Soffer) Plotnick; married Rosemary Alice Tracy, December 26, 1955; children: Alison Tracy, Ruth Alexandra. *Education:* Temple University, B.A., 1950; University of Pennsylvania, M.A., 1951, Ph.D., 1960. *Office:* Department of Economics, University of New Haven, West Haven, Conn. 06516.

CAREER: Instructor at Temple University, Philadelphia, Pa., 1955-56, and University of Maine, Orono, 1956-60; assistant professor at University of Rhode Island, Kingston, 1960-61, Drexel Institute of Technology, Philadelphia, Pa., 1961-62, and University of Alberta, Calgary, 1962-65; Southeastern Massachusetts Technological Institute, North Dartmouth, associate professor of economics, 1966-68; University of New Haven, West Haven, Conn., professor of economics, 1968—. *Military service:* U.S. Army, 1943-45. *Member:* American Association for the Advancement of Science, American Economic Association. *Awards, honors:* Canadian Social Science Research Council grant, 1965.

WRITINGS: Petroleum: Canadian Markets and U.S. Foreign Trade Policy, University of Washington Press, 1965. Contributor to *Canadian Business, Nation, Challenge, Oilweek* (Canada), and other journals.

* * *

POLE, J(ack) R(ichon) 1922-

PERSONAL: Born March 14, 1922, in London, England; son of Joseph (a playwright) and Phoebe (Rickards) Pole; married Marilyn Mitchell; children: Ilsa, Nicholas, Lucy. *Education:* Queen's College, Oxford, B.A., 1949; Princeton University, Ph.D., 1953; Cambridge University, M.A. (by incorporation), 1963. *Office:* Churchill College, Cambridge University, Cambridge CB3 0DS, England.

CAREER: Princeton University, Princeton, N.J., instructor in history, 1952-53; University College, University of London, London, England, lecturer in American history, 1953-63; Cambridge University, Cambridge, England, reader in American history and government, 1963—, fellow of Churchill College, 1963—, vice-master of Churchill College, 1975—. Visiting professor, University of California, Berkeley, 1960-61, University of Ghana, 1966; professorial lecturer, University of Chicago, 1969; Jefferson Memorial Lecturer, University of California, Berkeley, 1971; senate council member, Cambridge University, 1970-74; member of International Commission for the History of Parliamentary and Representative Institutions. *Military service:* British Army, 1941-46; became captain. *Member:* Royal Historical Society (fellow), Historical Society of Ghana (honorary fellow), Institute for Early American History and Culture (council member, 1973-76), British Association for American Studies, American Historical Association, Trojan Wanderers Cricket Club (co-founder). *Awards, honors:* Commonwealth Fund fellowship, 1956; Charles W.

Ramsdell Award of Southern Historical Association for article, "Representation and Authority in Virginia," in *Journal of Southern History,* 1959; Rockefeller research fellowship, 1960-61; Center for Advanced Study in Behavioral Sciences fellowship, 1969-70.

WRITINGS: Abraham Lincoln and the Working Classes of Britain, English-Speaking Union, 1959; *Abraham Lincoln,* Oxford University Press, 1964; *Abraham Lincoln and the American Commitment,* Cambridge University Press, 1966; *Political Representation in England and the Origins of the American Republic,* St. Martins, 1966; (editor) *The Advance of Democracy,* Harper, 1967; *The Seventeenth Century: The Origins of Legislative Power,* University of Virginia Press for Jamestown Foundation, 1969; *The Revolution in America, 1754-1788: Documents of the Internal Development of America During the Revolutionary Era,* Stanford University Press, 1971; (editor with Marvin Meyers) *The Meanings of American History,* Scott, Foresman, 1971; *Foundations of American Independence, 1763-1815,* Bobbs-Merrill, 1972; (editor) *Slavery, Secession, and Civil War,* Harrap, 1975; *The Decision for American Independence,* Lippincott, 1975.

General editor, "American Historical Documents" series, Harrap, 1975; member of editorial committee, "Cambridge Studies in the History and Theory of Politics" series, Cambridge University Press, 1964—. Contributor of numerous essays, articles, and reviews to journals. Member of editorial board, *Journal of American Studies,* 1967—.

WORK IN PROGRESS: The Idea of Equality in American History, 1740-1970.

AVOCATIONAL INTERESTS: History of ideas, race relations, cricket.

* * *

POLITI, Leo 1908-

PERSONAL: Born 1908, in Fresno, Calif.; married Helen Fontes. *Education:* Studied at National Art Institute, Monza, Italy, for six years.

CAREER: Politi's early years were spent in a circuitous route from California to a village in northern Italy, where his parents resettled when he was seven; returned to California in his early twenties; painted murals, carved primitive wooden figures, and was a sidewalk artist in Los Angeles; author and illustrator of children's books. *Awards, honors:* Caldecott Medal of American Library Association for best illustrated book of the year, 1950, for *Song of the Swallows;* Regina Medal of Catholic Library Association for continued distinguished contribution to children's literature, 1965.

*WRITINGS—*Author and illustrator, all published by Scribner, except as indicated: *Little Pancho,* Viking, 1938; *Pedro, the Angel of Olvera Street,* 1946; *Young Giotto,* Horn, 1947; *Juanita,* 1948; *Song of the Swallows,* 1949; *Little Leo,* 1951; *Mission Bell,* 1953; *Butterflies Come,* 1957; *Saint Francis and the Animals,* 1959; *Boat for Peppe,* 1960; *Moy Moy,* 1960; *All Things Bright and Beautiful,* 1962; *Lito and the Clown,* 1962; *Rosa,* 1963; *Bunker Hill, Los Angeles: Reminisences of Bygone Days,* Desert-Southwest, 1964; *Piccolo's Prank,* 1965; *Tales of the Los Angeles Parks,* Best-West Publications, 1966; *Mieko,* Golden Gate, 1969; *Emmet,* 1971; *The Nicest Gift,* 1973.

Illustrator: Ruth Sawyer, *The Least One,* Viking, 1941; Margarita Lopez, *Aquise Habla Espanol,* Heath, 1942; Helen Garrett, *Angelo the Naughty One,* Viking, 1944;

Frank Henius, *Stories from the Americas*, Scribner, 1944; Catherine Blanton, *The Three Miracles*, Day, 1946; Louis Perez, *El Coyote the Rebel*, Holt, 1947; Helen Rand Parish, *At the Palace Gates*, Viking, 1949; Margariet Lopez de Mestos and Esther Brown, *Vamos a Habla Espanol*, Heath, 1949; Ann Nolan Clark, *Magic Money*, Viking, 1950, and *Looking-for-Something*, Viking, 1952; Alice Dalgliesh, *The Columbus Story*, Scribner, 1955; Elizabeth Coatsworth, *The Noble Doll*, Viking, 1961.

SIDELIGHTS: Sister Mary Lucille McCreedy wrote: "Leo Politi has done more to break down prejudices existing for peoples with different cultural backgrounds than almost any other author-illustrator." In his Caldecott acceptance speech, Politi said that he tries to emphasize a "love for people, animals, birds, and flowers," and a "love for the simple, warm and earthy things."

Both *Pedro, the Angel of Olvera Street* and *Rosa* have been published in Spanish editions with vocabularies following the texts.

BIOGRAPHICAL/CRITICAL SOURCES: Horn Book, XXVI, July-August, 1950; May Hill Arbuthnot, *Children and Books*, 3rd edition, Scott, 1964; *Catholic Library World*, February, 1966.*†

*　　*　　*

POLLAK, Louis Heilprin 1922-

PERSONAL: Born December 7, 1922, in New York, N.Y.; son of Walter H. (a lawyer) and Marion (Heilprin) Pollak; married Katherine Weiss, July 25, 1952; children: Nancy, Elizabeth, Susan, Sarah, Deborah. *Education:* Harvard University, B.A. (magna cum laude), 1943; Yale University, LL.B., 1948. *Politics:* Democrat. *Religion:* Jewish. *Home:* 2225 Delancey Place, Philadelphia, Pa. 19103. *Office:* University of Pennsylvania Law School, 3400 Chestnut Street, Philadelphia, Pa. 19174.

CAREER: With U.S. Department of State, 1951-53; Yale University, New Haven, Conn., assistant professor, 1955-56, associate professor, 1956-61, professor of law, 1961-74; University of Pennsylvania, Philadelphia, professor of law, 1974—. Visiting lecturer, Howard University, 1953. Director of National Association for the Advancement of Colored People Legal Defense and Educational Fund, Inc. Former member, New Haven (Conn.) Board of Education. *Military service:* U.S. Army, 1943-46. *Member:* Association of American Law Schools, American Law Institute, American Bar Association, Connecticut Bar Association, Association of the Bar of City of New York, Phi Beta Kappa.

WRITINGS: The Constitution and the Supreme Court: A Documentary History, World Publishing, 1966. Contributor to law journals. Former editor-in-chief, *Yale Law Journal*.

*　　*　　*

POLLARD, Sidney 1925-

PERSONAL: Born April 21, 1925, in Vienna, Austria; son of Moses and Leontine (Katz) Pollak; married Eileen Andrews, August 13, 1949; children: Brian Joseph, David Hugh, Veronica Ruth. *Education:* London School of Economics and Political Science, London, B.Sc., 1948, Ph.D., 1950 *Home:* 523 Fulwood Rd., Sheffield 570 3QB, England. *Office:* 19/21 Northumberland Rd., Sheffield 570 2TN, England.

CAREER: University of Sheffield, Sheffield, England, Knoop fellow in economic history, 1950-52, lecturer, 1952-

60, senior lecturer, 1960-63, professor of economic history, 1963—. *Member:* Economic History Society (member of council); Society for the Study of Labour History (chairman, 1964-66; president, 1971—), National Liberal Club. *Awards, honors:* Thomas Newcomen Award in business history, 1967; for *The Genesis of Modern Management*.

WRITINGS: Three Centuries of Sheffield Steel, Marsh Brothers (Sheffield), 1954; *A History of Labour in Sheffield*, Liverpool University Press, 1959; *The Development of the British Economy, 1914-1950*, Edward Arnold, 1962, revised edition, 1967; *The Genesis of Modern Management*, Harvard University Press, 1965; (editor with C. Holmes) *Documents on European/Economic History*, three volumes, Edward Arnold, 1967-73; *The Idea of Progress*, Pitman, 1968; *European Economic Integration 1815-1970*, Thames & Hudson, 1974. Contributor to professional journals and to the British press. Editor, *Bulletin* of the Society for the Study of Labour History, 1960-71.

WORK IN PROGRESS: With D. W. Crossley, *Wealth of Britain, 1068-1960; Capital Formation in Britain, 1750-1850*.

AVOCATIONAL INTERESTS: The Co-operative Movement and cooperative education, music, walking, the cinema.

*　　*　　*

POLLEY, Robert L. 1933-

PERSONAL: Surname is pronounced to rhyme with "holly"; born April 18, 1933, in Marion, Ind.; son of Phillip William and Kathryn (Lutz) Polley; married Constance F. Safford, July 12, 1958. *Education:* University of Michigan, B.A., 1955; Northwestern University, M.S., 1959. *Politics:* Liberal. *Home:* 530 South Elm Grove Rd., Brookfield, Wis. *Office:* Country Beautiful Corp., 24198 West Bluemound, Waukesha, Wis.

CAREER: Saturday Evening Post, Philadelphia, Pa., editorial assistant, 1959-61; Country Beautiful Corp. (publishers of books and magazines), Waukesha, Wis., executive editor, 1961—, editorial vice-president, 1974—. *Military service:* U.S. Air Force, 1955-57; became first lieutenant. *Member:* Sigma Delta Chi.

WRITINGS: (Editor, and author of connective text) *America the Beautiful in the Words of John F. Kennedy*, Country Beautiful-Doubleday, 1964; (co-author and editor) *Circus!*, Country Beautiful-Hawthorn, 1964; (editor, and author of connective text and introduction) *Lincoln: His Words and His World*, Country Beautiful-Hawthorn, 1965; (editor) *Herbert Hoover's Challenge to America: His Life and Words*, Country Beautiful-Doubleday, 1965; (editor) *Man of Honor, Man of Peace: The Life and Words of Adlai Stevenson*, Country Beautiful-Putnam, 1965; (editor) *The Beauty of America in Great American Art*, Country Beautiful-Morrow, 1965; (editor, and author of introduction) *America the Beautiful in the Words of Henry Wadsworth Longfellow*, Country Beautiful-Morrow, 1966; (editor, and author of introduction) *America the Beautiful in the Words of Henry David Thoreau*, Country Beautiful-Morrow, 1966; (editor) *Great Art Treasures in America's Smaller Museums*, Putnam, 1967; (editor and author of introduction) *America's Historic Houses*, Putnam, 1967; (editor) *America's Folk Art*, Putnam, 1968.

WORK IN PROGRESS: Wind, Sky and Earth, an anthology of American Indian writings, oratories and tales.

SIDELIGHTS: Polley told *CA:* "I have traveled to 37

states, central and eastern Canada, Mexico, Australia, Philippines, Thailand, Japan, Hong Kong. I am primarily interested in history and art. In American history particularly, I believe the myths that have been presented as history must be replaced by reality. The violence and injustice that have played a prominent part in our past must be revealed. The contributions of radicals and other non-establishment figures must be given proper emphasis, also the contributions of non-whites. Thus in *America's Folk Art* the art of slaves and free blacks is given some attention."

* * *

POLOS, Nicholas C(hristopher) 1917-

PERSONAL: Born March 10, 1917, in Boston, Mass.; son of Christ and Constance (Angelos) Polos; married Ethel Francis Bach, September 1, 1937; children: Richard Arthur. *Education:* Pomona College, A.B. (honors), 1951; Harvard University, M.A., 1954; Claremont Graduate School and University Center, state junior college and general credentials, 1954; University of California, Berkeley, Ph.D., 1962. *Politics:* Republican. *Religion:* Presbyterian. *Home:* 3402 Duke Ave., Claremont, Calif. 91711.

CAREER: Claremont (Calif.) High School, teacher, 1954—, chairman of department of history and government, 1955-62. Mount San Antonio College, lecturer, 1955—; Claremont Graduate School and University Center, visiting lecturer, 1962; visiting summer lecturer at Queens College (now Queens College of the City University of New York), Flushing, N.Y., 1964-66, and University of Missouri, 1966. *Military service:* U.S. Navy, World War II and Korean War. *Member:* American Historical Association, Pacific Coast Historical Association, California Historical Society, California Social Science Association, Historical Society of Southern California, Southern California Social Science Association, Phi Beta Kappa. *Awards, honors:* Benjamin Franklin Gold Medal of Freedoms Foundation for articles, 1959, 1960, 1961, and Alexander Hamilton Gold Medal, 1960; teacher of the year award, University of California, Los Angeles, 1960.

WRITINGS: American Government in Action, W. C. Brown, 1964; *The Dynamics of Team Teaching,* W. C. Brown, 1965. Contributor of about thirty articles to *Branding Iron, Claremont Courier,* and education journals.

WORK IN PROGRESS: John Swett: The Giant of the Nineteenth Century, a biography of the Horace Mann of California; a biography of Victoria C. Woodhull, suffrage worker of the nineteenth century.

SIDELIGHTS: Nicholas Polos speaks Greek and Spanish, and reads French. *Avocational interests:* Horticulture, golf, travel.

* * *

POMEROY, Earl 1915-

PERSONAL: Born December 27, 1915, in Capitola, Calif.; son of Earl Spencer (a physician) and Hazel (Keesling) Pomeroy; married Mary C. Rentz, July 7, 1940; children: Susan M. (Mrs. R. E. Guilford), Peter R., James G., Caroline J. *Education:* San Jose State College (now University), B.A., 1936; University of California, Berkeley, M.A., 1937, Ph.D., 1940. *Religion:* Episcopalian. *Home:* 2475 Van Ness St., Eugene, Ore. 97403.

CAREER: University of Wisconsin, Madison, instructor in history, 1940-42; University of North Carolina, Chapel Hill, assistant professor of history, 1942-45; Ohio State

University, Columbus, assistant professor of history, 1945-49; University of Oregon, Eugene, associate professor, 1949-54, professor, 1954-61, Beekman Professor of History, 1961—, chairman of department, 1957-60, 1965-66. Visiting professor, Johns Hopkins University, Bologna Center, 1963-64, Stanford University, 1967. *Member:* American Historical Association, American Studies Association, Organization of American Historians, Oregon Historical Society. *Awards, honors:* Albert J. Beveridge Award of American Historical Association, 1942, for manuscript of *The Territories and the United States, 1861-1890*; Ford Foundation fellow, 1953-54; Guggenheim fellow, 1956-57, 1972; Fellow, National Endowment for the Humanities, 1968, and Center For Advanced Study in the Behavioral Sciences, 1974-75.

WRITINGS: The Territories and the United States, 1861-1890, University of Pennsylvania Press, for American Historical Association, 1947; *Pacific Outpost: Guam and Micronesia in American Policy,* Stanford University Press, 1951; *In Search of the Golden West: The Tourist in Western America,* Knopf, 1957; *The Pacific Slope: A History,* Knopf, 1965. Contributor of more than thirty articles to journals in his field.

WORK IN PROGRESS: Research on the West in the twentieth century.

* * *

POOL, Ithiel de Sola 1917-

PERSONAL: Born October 26, 1917, in New York, N.Y.; son of David de Sola (a rabbi) and Tamar (Hirshenson) Pool; married Jean Mackenzie (a psychologist), March 5, 1956; children: Jonathan, Jeremy, Adam. *Education:* University of Chicago, B.A., 1938, M.A., 1939, Ph.D., 1951. *Politics:* Democrat. *Religion:* Jewish. *Home:* 105 Irving St., Cambridge, Mass. 02138. *Office:* Center for International Studies, Massachusetts Institute of Technology, Cambridge, Mass. 02139.

CAREER: Hobart and William Smith Colleges, Geneva, N.Y., assistant professor, 1942-48, associate professor of political science, 1948-49, chairman of Division of Social Science, 1942-49; Stanford University, Stanford, Calif., research associate at Hoover Institution on War, Revolution, and Peace, 1949-53; Massachusetts Institute of Technology, Cambridge, associate professor, 1953-59, professor of political science, 1959—, chairman of department, 1959-61, 1965-69. Consultant to RAND Corp., 1951—. Visiting lecturer, Yale University, 1953-54. Member of scientific advisory board of U.S. Air Force, 1961-63, Defense Science Board, 1968-70, and Surgeon General's Committee on Television and Children's Behavior, 1970-71.

MEMBER: American Political Science Association, American Association for Public Opinion Research, American Sociological Association, Council on Foreign Relations, American Academy of Arts and Sciences (fellow), Cosmos Club (Washington, D.C.). *Awards, honors:* Center for Advanced Study in the Behavioral Sciences fellowship, 1957-58; Woodrow Wilson Award of American Political Science Association, 1964, for *American Business and Public Policy.*

WRITINGS: (With Nathan Leites) *Communist Propaganda in Reaction to Frustration,* Library of Congress, Experimental Division for the Study of Wartime Communications, Document No. 27, 1942; (with others) *Symbols of Internationalism,* Stanford University Press, 1951; *The Comparative Study of Symbols,* Stanford University Press,

1952; (with Robert North) *Kuomintang and Chinese Communist Elites*, Stanford University Press, 1952; (with others) *The "Prestige Papers,"* Stanford University Press, 1952; (with others) *Symbols of Democracy*, Stanford University Press, 1952; (with others) *Satellite Generals: A Study of Military Elites in the Soviet Sphere*, Stanford University Press, 1955; (editor) *Studies in Political Communication*, Princeton University, 1958; *Indian Images of America*, Center for International Studies, Massachusetts Institute of Technology, 1958; (editor) *Trends in Content Analysis*, University of Illinois Press, 1959.

(Editor with Raymond Bauer) *American Businessmen and International Trade Code Book and Data from a Study on Attitudes and Communications*, Free Press of Glencoe, 1960; *Communication and Values in Relation to War and Peace*, Institute for International Order, 1961; *Science and Public Policy*, Massachusetts Institute of Technology, 1961; (with Barbara Adler) *The Out-of-Classroom Audience of WGBH: A Study of Motivation in Viewing*, Center for International Studies, Massachusetts Institute of Technology, 1963; (with Wilbur Schramm and Jack Lyle) *People Look at Educational Television*, Stanford University Press, 1963; (with Raymond A. Bauer and Lewis A. Dexter) *American Business and Public Policy*, Atherton Press, 1963; (with Robert P. Abelson and Samuel Popkin) *Candidates, Issues and Strategies: A Computer Simulation of the 1960 Presidential Election*, Massachusetts Institute of Technology, 1964, revised edition, 1965; (editor) *Contemporary Political Science*, McGraw, 1967; *The Prestige Press*, MIT Press, 1969; (co-editor) *Handbook of Communication*, Rand-McNally, 1973; (editor) *Talking Back*, MIT Press, 1973.

Contributor: Bert Hoselitz, editor, *Industrialization and Society*, UNESCO, 1963; Wilbur Schramm, editor, *The Science of Human Communication*, Basic Books, 1963; Lucian W. Pye, editor, *Communications and Political Development*, Princeton University Press, 1963.

WORK IN PROGRESS: Research on the social effects of communication systems.

* * *

POPE, Richard Martin 1916-

PERSONAL: Born February 6, 1916, in Verona, Mo.; son of Martin T. (a minister) and Pearl (Swift) Pope; married Kathryn Holdridge, May 2, 1943; children: Susan, John, James. *Education:* Drury College, A.B., 1939; University of Chicago, B.D., 1942, Ph.D., 1955. *Politics:* Democrat. *Home:* 618 Wichita Dr., Lexington, Ky. 40503.

CAREER: Minister of the Christian Churches (Disciples of Christ), Drury College, Springfield, Mo., professor of Bible, religion, and philosophy, and dean of School of Religion, 1946-58; Lexington Theological Seminary, Lexington, Ky., professor of church history, 1958—. Member of Council of Christian Unity, Disciples of Christ. *Military service:* U.S. Army, chaplain, 1942-46. U.S. Army Reserve, 1946-75; became colonel. *Member:* American Society of Church History, Association of Disciples for Theological Discussion.

WRITINGS: The College of the Bible: A Brief History, College of the Bible Press, 1961; *The Church and its Culture*, Bethany, 1966; *The Man Who Responds*, Christian Board of Publication, 1969; *Our Changing and Changeless Faith*, Christian Board of Publication, 1974.

WORK IN PROGRESS: Studies on the church and the natural world.

PORTE, Joel (Miles) 1933-

PERSONAL: Born November 13, 1933, in Brooklyn, N.Y.; son of Jack and Frances (Derison) Porte; married Llana d'Ancona, June 17, 1962; children: Susanna Maria. *Education:* City College (now City College of the City University of New York), A.B. (magna cum laude), 1957; Harvard University, A.M., 1958, Ph.D., 1962. *Residence:* Cambridge, Mass. *Office:* Warren House, Harvard University, Cambridge, Mass. 02138.

CAREER: Harvard University, Cambridge, Mass., instructor, 1962-64, assistant professor, 1964-68, associate professor, 1968-69, professor of English and American literature, 1969—. Visiting lecturer, City College (now City College of the City University of New York), summer, 1958, and 1959.

WRITINGS: Emerson and Thoreau: Transcendentalists in Conflict, Wesleyan University Press, 1966; *The Romance in America: Studies in Cooper, Poe, Hawthorne, Melville and James*, Wesleyan University Press, 1969; (contributor) Harry Levin, editor, *Veins of Humor*, Harvard University Press, 1972; (contributor) Monroe Engel, editor, *Uses of Literature*, Harvard University Press, 1973; (contributor) Matthew Bruccoli, editor, *The Chief Glory of Every People*, Southern Illinois University Press, 1973; (contributor) Richard Thompson, editor, *The Gothic Imagination*, Washington State University Press, 1974. Contributor of articles and reviews to *New England Quarterly, Christian Science Monitor, New Leader*, and other periodicals and newspapers.

WORK IN PROGRESS: A study of Ralph Waldo Emerson, to be published by Oxford University Press.

* * *

PORTER, David T. 1928-

PERSONAL: Born September 15, 1928, in Buffalo, N.Y.; son of Roy Avery and Bertha (Thomas) Porter; married Lee Pedalino (an advertising consultant), August 5, 1957; children: Thomas Avery, David Lawrence, Stephen Francis. *Education:* Hamilton College, A.B., 1950; University of Rochester, Ph.D., 1963. *Home:* 106 West St., Amherst, Mass. 01002.

CAREER: Robert College, Istanbul, Turkey, instructor in English, 1953-55, chairman of lycee English, 1957-59; University of Massachusetts, Amherst, instructor, 1962-64, assistant professor, 1964-66, associate professor, 1966-72, professor of English, 1972—. University of Catania, Catania, Italy, senior Fulbright lecturer in American literature, 1966-67; visiting professor, University of Keele, England, 1970. *Military service:* U.S. Army, 1955-57.

WRITINGS: The Art of Emily Dickinson's Early Poetry, Harvard University Press, 1966. Contributor to literary reviews.

WORK IN PROGRESS: American Poetics: The Nineteenth-Century Background; Emerson's Aesthetics; Contemporary British Poetry.

BIOGRAPHICAL/CRITICAL SOURCES: Rocherster Alumni Review, cover story, spring, 1962.

* * *

PORTER, Joyce 1924-

PERSONAL: Born March 28, 1924, in England; daughter of Joshua and Bessie Evelyn (Earlam) Porter. *Education:* King's College, London, B.A. (honors), 1944. *Politics:*

"Unenthusiastic Conservative." *Religion:* None. *Home:* 68 Sand St., Longbridge Deverill, NR Warminster, Wiltshire, England. *Agent:* Curtis Brown Ltd., 1 Craven Hill, London WC2 3EW, England.

CAREER: Women's Royal Air Force (WRAF), flight officer, 1949-63; full-time writer, 1963—. *Member:* Mystery Writers of America, Crime Writers' Association.

WRITINGS: Dover One, Scribner, 1964; *Dover Two*, Scribner, 1965; *Dover Three*, J. Cape, 1965, Scribner, 1966; *Sour Cream with Everything*, Scribner, 1966; *Dover and the Unkindest Cut of All*, Scribner, 1967; *The Chinks in the Curtain*, J. Cape, 1967, Scribner, 1968; *Dover Goes to Pott*, Scribner, 1968; *Neither a Candle Nor a Pitchfork*, Weidenfeld & Nicolson, 1969, McCall Books, 1970; *Rather a Common Sort of Crime*, McCall Books, 1970; *Dover Strikes Again*, Weidenfeld & Nicolson, 1970, McKay, 1973; *Only with a Bargepole*, Weidenfeld & Nicolson, 1971, McKay, 1974; *A Meddler and Her Murder*, Weidenfeld & Nicolson, 1972, McKay, 1973; *It's Murder with Dover*, McKay, 1973. Also author of *The Package Included Murder*, 1975.

SIDELIGHTS: Ms. Porter told *CA:* "Began writing in order to be able to retire from Air Force. Continue writing because it is easier than work. Consider sole duty of my type of writer is to entertain." She speaks fluent Russian (learned in Air Force), and is especially interested in the uniforms and equipment of the Imperial Russian Army, and toured the Soviet Union by car in 1964. The first "Dover" book was published in nine European countries (besides England), and in Japan and Brazil; the later ones also have gone into translations.

*   *   *

POSTLETHWAIT, S(amuel) N(oel) 1918-

PERSONAL: Born April 16, 1918, in Willeysville, W. Va.; son of Frank and Etta Postlethwait; married Sara M. Cover, March 22, 1941; children: John, Robert. *Education:* Fairmont State College, A.B., 1940; University of West Virginia, M.S., 1947; University of Iowa, Ph.D., 1949. *Politics:* Democrat. *Religion:* Church of Christ. *Home:* 3180 Soldiers Home Rd., West Lafayette, Ind. 47906. *Office:* Biological Sciences, Purdue University, West Lafayette, Ind. 47907.

CAREER: Public school teacher in West Virginia, 1940-41; University of Iowa, Iowa City, instructor in botany and biology, 1948-49; Purdue University, West Lafayette, Ind., assistant professor, 1949-56, associate professor, 1956-63, professor of biology, 1963—. *Military service:* U.S. Naval Reserve, active duty, 1942-46; became lieutenant. *Member:* Botanical Society of America, American Association for the Advancement of Science, International Society of Plant Morphologists, American Society for Cell Biology, National Science Teachers Association, International Platform Association, International Society for Stereologoy, Indiana Academy of Science, New York Academy of Sciences, Torrey Botanical Club, Sigma Xi, Lambda Delta Lambda, Kappa Delta Pi, Omicron Delta Kappa. *Awards, honors:* National Science Foundation faculty fellowship, 1957-58.

WRITINGS: Workbook in Plant Science, Burgess, 1948; *Textbook of Intermediate Plant Science*, Burgess, 1950; *Plant Science—A Workbook with an Audio Program Approach*, Burgess, 1963, revised edition, 1966; *An Integrated Experience Approach to Learning with Emphasis on Independent Study*, Burgess, 1964; *The Audio Tutorial System*, Burgess, 1971.

POSVAR, Wesley W(entz) 1925-

PERSONAL: Born September 14, 1925, in Topeka, Kan.; son of Vladimir L. and Marie (Wentz) Posvar; married Mildred Miller (a solo artist in opera and concerts), April 30, 1950; children: Wesley William, Margot Marina, Lisa Christina. *Education:* U.S. Military Academy, B.S., 1946; Air Tactical School, graduate, 1947; Oxford University, B.A., 1951, M.A., 1954; Harvard University, M.P.A. and Ph.D., 1964. *Religion:* Episcopalian. *Office:* Office of the Chancellor, University of Pittsburgh, Pittsburgh, Pa. 15213.

CAREER: U.S. Army Air Forces and U.S. Air Force, 1946-67, with rank of colonel, 1960-67; Air Proving Ground, Fla., aircraft project officer and fighter test pilot, 1946-48; U.S. Military Academy, West Point, N.Y., 1951-54, began as instructor, became assistant professor, department of social sciences; U.S. Air Force Headquarters, Directorate of Plans, Washington, D.C., member of long-range objectives and programs group, 1954-57; U.S. Air Force Academy, Colorado Springs, Colo., professor and head of department of political science, 1957-67, chairman of Division of Social Sciences, 1960-62; University of Pittsburgh, Pittsburgh, Pa., chancellor, 1967—. Consultant to various government agencies. *Member:* Association of International Relations Clubs (member of advisory council), American Political Science Association, American Academy of Political and Social Science, International Studies Association (president, 1961-62), Institute for Strategic Studies, Operations Research Society of America, Association of American Rhodes Scholars, Western Political Science Association (member of executive council, 1958-60), Rocky Mountain Social Science Association (president, 1959-60), Rotary Club. *Awards, honors:* Rhodes Scholar at Oxford University, 1951-54; named one of ten outstanding young men of America, U.S. Chamber of Commerce, 1959; L.L.D., Carnegie-Mellon University, 1968, Temple University, 1970; L.H.D., Miami University, 1968.

WRITINGS: (With others) *American Defense Policy*, Johns Hopkins Press, 1965. Contributor to periodicals.†

*   *   *

POTOK, Chaim 1929-

PERSONAL: Given name pronounced *Hah*-yim; born February 17, 1929, in New York, N.Y.; son of Benjamin Max (a businessman) and Mollie (Friedman) Potok; married Adena Sarah Mosevitzky, June 8, 1958; children: Rena, Naama, Akiva. *Education:* Yeshiva University, B.A. (summa cum laude), 1950; Jewish Theological Seminary, M.H.L., 1954; University of Pennsylvania, Ph.D. (philosophy), 1965. *Residence:* Philadelphia, Pa.

CAREER: Ordained rabbi (Conservative), 1954. Jewish Theological Seminary, New York, N.Y., national director, Leaders Training Fellowship, 1954-55; Camp Ramah, Los Angeles, Calif., director, 1957-59; University of Judaism, Los Angeles, Calif., instructor, 1957-59; Har Zion Temple, Philadelphia, Pa., scholar-in-residence, 1959-63; Jewish Theological Seminary, member of faculty of Teachers' Institute, 1963-64; *Conservative Judaism*, New York, N.Y., managing editor, 1964-65; Jewish Publication Society, Philadelphia, Pa., editor, 1965-74, special projects editor, 1974—. *Military service:* U.S. Army, chaplain in Korea, 1956-57; became first lieutenant. *Member:* Rabbinical Assembly, P.E.N., Authors Guild. *Awards, honors:* Edward Lewis Wallant Award, for *The Chosen*; Atheneum Award, for *The Promise*.

WRITINGS—Novels: *The Chosen*, Simon & Schuster, 1967; *The Promise*, Knopf, 1969; *My Name Is Asher Lev*, Knopf, 1972; *In the Beginning*, Knopf, 1975. Contributor of short stories and articles to *Commentary, Reconstructionist, American Judaism, Saturday Review, New York Times Book Review*, and other periodicals.

WORK IN PROGRESS: A novel.

SIDELIGHTS: Potok, who decided to become a writer of fiction when he read Evelyn Waugh's *Brideshead Revisited* at the age of sixteen, wrote his first novel about the intricacies of two generations of Brooklyn Hasidists. Josh Greenfeld wrote "Happily, Chaim Potok has the ability to render the parochial as pure blessing, the mark of a true novelist: his details are hairline in quaint precision, but they reverberate with universal implications." Granville Hicks noted that Potok undertook the difficult task of making "good boys credible and interesting," and added: "It must have been even harder for Chaim Potok to bring to life a pair of good fathers, good in such different ways. But he succeeded, and the result is a fine, moving, gratifying book."

"This novel—whether or not it is a novel—," wrote Karl Shapiro, "is a deeply considered exegesis of modern Judaism. Formally, it should be ticketed as an allegory. The plot is simple and slight, though strong and graceful: the plot carries the deadly weight of the argument through seas almost too stormy for the mind to bear. The style has a *solo* quality, in the sense that Charles A. Lindbergh flew alone across the Atlantic, every second in peril of death. The style is beautifully quiet and gentle. One is amazed that so frail a structure can make it into port with such a freight of grief. It does so, heroically."

Potok has traveled to Japan, Hong Kong, and Israel. He knows Hebrew, French, German, and Spanish. He is interested in psychology, oil painting, and photography, and has a special interest in contemporary literature, with heavy emphasis on Hemingway, Mann, and Joyce. While he was a chaplain, he wrote an (unpublished) novel about the army during the Korean War.

The film rights to *The Chosen* were acquired by producers Willard Goodman and Charles Roth in 1972.

BIOGRAPHICAL/CRITICAL SOURCES: Publishers' Weekly, April 3, 1967; *Life*, April 21, 1967; *Time*, April 21, 1967; *Book Week*, April 23, 1967; *New York Times Book Review*, April, 1967, May, 1967; *Saturday Review*, April 29, 1967; *New Republic*, June 17, 1967; *Observer*, August 20, 1967; Carolyn Riley, editor, *Contemporary Literary Criticism*, Volume II, Gale, 1972.

* * *

PRABHAVANANDA, Swami 1893-

PERSONAL: Name originally Abani Ghosh; born December 26, 1893, in Vishnupur, India; came to United States in 1923; son of Kumud Bihari (a lawyer) and Jnanada (Sarkar) Ghosh. *Education:* Calcutta University, B.A., 1914. *Home and office:* 1946 Vedanta Pl., Hollywood, Calif. 90068.

CAREER: Joined Ramakrishna Order of India, 1914, ordained swami (monastic religious teacher), 1923; assistant leader of Vedanta Society (followers of a system of Hindu philosophy), San Francisco, Calif., 1923-25; founder and leader of Vedanta Society, Portland, Ore., 1925-29; founder, 1929, of Vedanta Society of Southern California, and senior minister of the group, which maintains a temple and monastic community in Hollywood, a temple and convent in Santa Barbara, and a monastery at Trabuco Canyon. President of a Calcutta and Madras session of Vivekananda centenary celebration in India, 1963-64.

WRITINGS: (Translator) *The Wisdom of God*, Putnam, 1943; (translator with Christopher Isherwood) *Shankara, Crest-Jewel of Discrimination*, Vedanta Press, 1947; *The Eternal Companion* (life and teachings of Swami Brahmananda), Vedanta Press, 1947; (translator with Christopher Isherwood, and author of commentary) *How to Know God* (Patanjali's *Yoga Aphorisms*), Vedanta Press, 1953; (translator with Christopher Isherwood) *Song of God: Bhagavad-Gita*, New American Library, 1954; (translator with Frederick Manchester) *The Upanishads*, New American Library, 1957; *The Spiritual Heritage of India*, Vedanta Press, 1963; (author of part-by-part commentary) *The Sermon on the Mount According to Vedanta*, Vedanta Press, 1964; (translator) *Narada's Way of Divine Love: The Bhakti Sutras*, Vedanta Press, 1971.

SIDELIGHTS: Swami Prabhavananda is fluent in Bengali and Sanskrit.

BIOGRAPHICAL/CRITICAL SOURCES: What Vedanta Means to Me, edited by John R. Yale, Doubleday, 1961; Christopher Isherwood, *An Approach to Vedanta*, Vedanta Press, 1963.

* * *

PREBBLE, Marjorie Mary Curtis 1912-
(Ann Compton, Denise Conway, Marjorie Curtis)

PERSONAL: Born March 14, 1912, in London, England; daughter of John William (a career officer in Royal Navy) and Florence (Wood) Prebble; married Charles Edward Scriven, December 2, 1939; children: Robin Charles, Penelope Jane. *Education:* Attended Lady Margaret Grammar School. *Religion:* Church of England.

CAREER: National Provincial Bank, London, England, clerk, 1929-43; owner of stationers and cards business, London, 1957—. Writer.

WRITINGS—Under pseudonym Ann Compton: *Harvest of Dreams*, Gresham, 1965; *A Ring for Your Finger*, Gresham, 1965.

Under pseudonym Denise Conway: *Sweet Surrender*, Gresham, 1966; *Coralita*, Gresham, 1967; *Duet to Happiness*, Gresham, 1967; *Love Finds a Way*, Gresham, 1968; *Assistant for Doctor Pritchard*, Gresham, 1970; *Nurse at Smoky River*, R. Hale, 1974; *A Kiss in Tangier*, R. Hale, 1974.

Under pseudonym Marjorie Curtis, all published by Gresham except as indicated: *Jewel of the North*, 1962; *The Pride of Love*, 1963; *Isle of Paradise*, 1963; *Hazard of Love*, 1963; *The Generous Lover*, R. Hale, 1963; *A Rose for Nurse Claire*, 1964; *Flower of the Jungle*, 1964; *The Lovely Imposter*, 1965; *Nurse in Distress*, 1966; *Shadow in Gold*, 1967; *Staff Nurse at Melford*, 1967; *Tropic Moon*, 1968; *Bid for Two Hearts*, 1968; *Mountains of the Moon*, 1969; *Lakeside Hospital*, 1969.

All published by R. Hale except as indicated: *Ace of Hearts*, Gresham, 1970; *Outdoor Girl*, Gresham, 1970; *Captive Heart*, Gresham, 1971; *Love from a Surgeon*, 1971; *Devil in Eden*, 1972; *Dr. Russell's New Recruit*, 1972; *Forbidden Garden*, 1973; *Dangerous Love*, 1973; *The Golden Lagoon*, 1973; *Bewildered Heart*, 1974; *Dew in the Morning*, 1975; *Love the Rebel*, 1975; *Doctor Intruder*, 1975; *Caribbean Moon*, 1975.

PREDMORE, Richard L. 1911-

PERSONAL: Born December 21, 1911, in Tottenville, N.Y.; son of Royal L. (a school principal) and Jennie (Trowbridge) Predmore; married Catherine Pennock, March 27, 1937; children: Michael, Richard, James. *Education:* Rutgers University, B.A., 1933, M.A., 1935; graduate study at University of Madrid, 1935-36, and Columbia University, 1936-37, 1941-42; Middlebury College, D.M.L., 1941. *Home:* Route 1, Box 379-P, Bahama, N.C. 27503. *Office:* Duke University, Durham, N.C. 27706.

CAREER: High school teacher of Spanish, Port Washington, N.Y., 1936-37; Rutgers University, New Brunswick, N.J., 1937-50, began as instructor, became associate professor of Romance languages, chairman of department, 1947-50; Duke University, Durham, N.C., professor of Romance languages, 1950—, secretary of the university, 1961-62, dean of Graduate School of Arts and Sciences, 1962-69, vice-provost, 1966-69. U.S. Office of Education, chief of Graduate Academic Programs Branch, Bureau of Higher Education (on leave from Duke University), 1966-67; member of Graduate Record Examination Board, 1969-73. *Member:* International Association of Hispanists, American Association of Teachers of Spanish and Portuguese, Modern Language Association of America, Phi Beta Kappa. *Awards, honors:* Fellow, Rockefeller Foundation, 1942-43, and Guggenheim Foundation, 1970-71.

WRITINGS: An Index to Don Quixote, Rutgers University Press, 1938; (editor) John L. Stephens, *Incidents of Travel in Central America, Chiapas, and Yucatan*, two volumes, Rutgers University Press, 1949, 2nd edition, 1956; *Topical Spanish Review Grammar*, Holt, 1954; *El Mundo de Quijote*, Insula (Madrid), 1958; *The World of Don Quixote*, Harvard University Press, 1967; *Cervantes*, Dodd, 1973. Also author of articles and reviews on Spanish language and literature.

WORK IN PROGRESS: Studies on twentieth-century Spanish writers, particularly a book on *Poeta en Nueva York* by Federico Garcia Lorca.

SIDELIGHTS: Richard Predmore has spent a total of almost three years in Spain, and traveled extensively in other parts of Europe, Mexico, and Central America. *Avocational interests:* Horseback riding, and hiking.

* * *

PRESSLY, Thomas J(ames) 1919-

PERSONAL: Born January 18, 1919, in Troy, Tenn.; son of James Wallace and Martha Belle (Bittich) Pressly; married Lillian Cameron, April 30, 1943; children: Thomas J., Stephanie Cameron. *Education:* Harvard University, A.B., 1940, A.M., 1941, Ph.D., 1950. *Religion:* Congregational. *Home:* 4545 East Laurel Dr. N.E., Seattle, Wash. 98105. *Office:* Department of History, University of Washington, Seattle, Wash. 98195.

CAREER: Princeton University, Princeton, N.J., instructor, 1946-49; University of Washington, Seattle, assistant professor, 1949-54, associate professor, 1954-60, professor of history, 1960—. Visiting professor at Princeton University, 1953-54, at Stanford University, summers, 1963, 1975, at State University of New York, Stony Brook, summers, 1967, 1968, 1969, at Johns Hopkins University, 1969-70. *Military service:* U.S. Army Air Forces, 1941-45. *Member:* American Historical Association, American Studies Association, Organization of American Historians, National Council for the Social Studies, Southern Historical Asso-

ciation. *Awards, honors:* Ford Foundation faculty fellowship, 1951-52; Center for Advanced Study in the Behavioral Sciences, fellow, 1955-56.

WRITINGS: Americans Interpret Their Civil War, Princeton University Press, 1954; (editor with William H. Scofield) *Farm Real Estate Values in the United States*, University of Washington Press, 1965; (compiler with others and contributor) *American Political Behavior: Historical Essays and Readings*, Harper, 1974.

WORK IN PROGRESS: A history of the idea of the "right of revolution" in the United States; a comparative reader, *After Slavery: Emancipation and Its Results in Nine Societies*.

* * *

PRICE, John Valdimir 1937-

PERSONAL: Born July 10, 1937, in Lamesa, Tex.; son of Noble Harold (a surgeon) and Asalie (Key) Price; married Sylvia Foster, December 20, 1958; children: Prescott, Valerie. *Education:* University of Texas, B.A., 1958, M.A., 1960, Ph.D., 1962. *Home:* 1001 North Third St., Lamesa, Tex. *Office:* University of Edinburgh, Edinburgh EH9 IRU, Scotland.

CAREER: University of California, Riverside, assistant professor of English, 1963-65; University of Edinburgh, Edinburgh, Scotland, lecturer in English literature, 1965—. *Member:* American Society for Eighteenth Century Studies, British Society for Eighteenth Century Studies (member of executive committee), Societe Francoise d'Etude du XVIIIe Siecle, Modern Language Association of America, Association of University Teachers (Great Britain).

WRITINGS: The Ironic Hume, University of Texas Press, 1965; *David Hume*, Twayne, 1967; (editor with E. C. Mossner) David Hume, *A Letter from a Gentleman to his Friend in Edinburgh*, University of Edinburgh Press, 1967; (editor) *Selected Poems of Alexander Robertson of Struah*, Tragara Press (Edinburgh), 1971; (editor) Tobias Smollett, *The Expedition of Humphry Clinker*, Edward Arnold, 1973; (editor) David Hume, *Dialogues Concerning Natural Religion*, Clarendon Press, 1976. Contributor to literary journals.

WORK IN PROGRESS: Editing David Hume's essays, publication by Clarendon Press expected in 1980; research in eighteenth century English literature, opera, and literary criticism.

* * *

PRICE, Martin 1920-

PERSONAL: Born January 29, 1920, in New York, N.Y.; married Mary Lee Parmer (an editor), May 4, 1941; children: Margaret Mattern, Peter Matthew. *Education:* City College (now City College of the City University of New York), B.A., 1938; University of Iowa, M.A., 1940; Yale University, Ph.D., 1950. *Home:* 86 Everit St., New Haven, Conn. *Office:* Department of English, Yale University, New Haven, Conn.

CAREER: Drake University, Des Moines, Iowa, instructor in English, 1941-42; Yale University, New Haven, Conn., instructor, 1948-51, assistant professor, 1952-58, associate professor, 1958-64, professor of English, beginning 1964. *Military service:* U.S. Army, 1944-45. *Awards, honors:* Guggenheim fellowship, 1957-58.

WRITINGS: Swift's Rhetorical Art, Yale University Press, 1953; (editor with Frank Brady) *English Prose and Poetry, 1660-1800*, Holt, 1961; *To the Palace of Wisdom: Studies in Order and Energy from Dryden to Blake*, Doubleday, 1964; (editor) Jonathan Swift, *Gulliver's Travels*, Bobbs-Merrill, 1964; (editor) *Selected Poetry of Alexander Pope*, New American Library, 1970.†

* * *

PRICE, Walter K(leber) 1924-

PERSONAL: Born April 13, 1924, in Lexington, Ky.; son of Walter Kleber and Fannie (Searcy) Price; married Edna Mae Parks (a teacher), June 14, 1953; children: Margaret Ann, Sarah Carolyn. *Education:* University of Kentucky, A.B., 1950; Southern Baptist Theological Seminary, Th.B., 1953. *Home:* 3444 Belvoir Dr., Lexington, Ky. 40502.

CAREER: Baptist minister; pastor in Fayette County, Ky., 1953-55, in Danville, Ky., 1955-57; Southern Baptist evangelist, 1957-61; Woodland Avenue Baptist Church, Lexington, Ky., pastor, 1961-74; evangelist and Bible Conference speaker.

WRITINGS: Revival in Romans, Zondervan, 1962; *Channels for Power*, Broadman, 1966, published as *The Holy Spirit: Channel of Power*; 1973; *Jesus' Prophetic Sermon*, Moody, 1972; *The Coming Antichrist*, Moody, 1973; *Next Year in Jerusalem*, Moody, 1974; *The City of the Great King*, Moody, 1975; *The Prophet Joel and the Day of the Lord*, Moody, in press.

WORK IN PROGRESS: Satan and Demons in Bible Prophecy.

* * *

PRIOR, Kenneth Francis William 1926-

PERSONAL: Born October 15, 1926, in London, England; son of Herbert James (a bank official) and Edith Maud (Brown) Prior; married Dorothy Margaret Stanborough, February 6, 1954; children: Hilary Ann, Richard Anthony Kenneth, Janet Alison. *Education:* Attended Imperial College of Science and Technology, London, 1943-45; Oak Hill College, Licentiate in Theology, 1948; University of Durham, B.A., 1949. *Home:* 82 Holmes Ave., Hove 4, Sussex, England.

CAREER: Clergyman, Church of England; curate in Barnet, Hertfordshire, 1949-52, and Eastbourne, Sussex, 1952-53; St. Paul's Church, Onslow Square, London, vicar, 1953-65; Bishop Hannington Memorial Church, Hove, Sussex, vicar, 1965-70; rector of Sevenoaks, Kent, 1970—.

WRITINGS: The Key to Christianity, Inter-Varsity Fellowship, 1959; *This Is the Way*, Evangelical Alliance, 1961; *Man's Greatest Problem*, Inter-Varsity Fellowship, 1962; *God and Mammon*, Hodder & Stoughton, 1965, Westminster, 1966; *The Way of Holiness*, Inter-Varsity Fellowship, 1967; *The Gospel in a Pagan Society*, Hodder & Stoughton, 1975. Regular contributor to *Church of England Newspaper* and occasional contributor to a number of other religious periodicals.

* * *

PRUDEN, (James) Wesley, Jr. 1935-

PERSONAL: Born December 18, 1935, in Jackson, Miss.; son of Wesley (a Baptist clergyman) and Anne (Wilder) Pruden; married Ann Rice Pulliam, 1960 (divorced, 1961). *Education:* Little Rock University, student, 1953-55. *Poli-*

tics: Democrat. *Religion:* Baptist. *Home:* 2070 Belmont Rd., N.W., Washington, D.C. *Office: National Observer*, 11501 Columbia Pike, Silver Spring, Md.

CAREER: Arkansas Gazette, Little Rock, assistant state editor, 1953-56; *Memphis Commercial Appeal*, Memphis, Tenn., reporter, 1956-63; *National Observer*, Silver Spring, Md., staff writer, 1963—. *Military service:* Arkansas Air National Guard, 1954-63. *Member:* Sigma Delta Chi.

WRITINGS: Vietnam: The War, National Observer Newsbooks, 1965.

WORK IN PROGRESS: A novel set in North Africa.

SIDELIGHTS: Pruden has traveled extensively in Southeast Asia, Australia, New Zealand, Mexico, Central America, Europe, and the Middle East on *National Observer* assignments.

* * *

PULLEN, John James 1913-

PERSONAL: Born December 17, 1913, in Amity, Me.; son of Orrin Willis (a farmer) and Grace Della (Reed) Pullen; married Jean A. DeLong, May 29, 1943. *Education:* Colby College, B.S., 1935. *Home:* 14 Great Hammock Rd., Old Saybrook, Conn. 06475.

CAREER: Daily Kennebec Journal, Kennebec, Me., reporter, 1935-36; Baker Advertising, Hartford, Conn., staff member, 1936-41; N. W. Ayer & Son, Inc., Philadelphia, Pa., staff member, 1948-65, executive director of copy department, 1958-63, vice-president, 1958-65. *Military service:* U.S. Army, Field Artillery, 1941-46; became captain. *Member:* Athenaeum of Philadelphia. *Awards, honors:* M.A., Colby College, 1958; D.Litt., Bowdoin College, 1958, Ricker College, 1960.

WRITINGS: The Twentieth Maine, Lippincott, 1957; *A Shower of Stars*, Lippincott, 1966; *Patriotism in America*, American Heritage Press, 1971; *The Transcendental Boiled Dinner*, Lippincott, 1972. Contributor to *Blair & Ketchum's Country Journal*.

* * *

PURDY, (Charles) Anthony 1932-

PERSONAL: Born July 25, 1932, in Portsmouth, England; son of John and Laurie (Naylor) Purdy; married Anne Mortimer; children: Simon, Suzanne, Jayne, Kim, Nicola, Emma. *Education:* Attended schools in Petersfield, Hampshire, England, and Steyning, Sussex, England. *Religion:* Church of England. *Home:* 9 Park Square Mews, Upper Harley St., London NW1, England.

CAREER: Professional writer.

WRITINGS: (With Wilfred Burchett) *Cosmonaut Yuri Gagarin, First Man in Space*, Gibbs & Phillips, 1961; (with Wilfred Burchett and Martin Caidin) *G. Titov, I Am Eagle*, Bobbs-Merrill, 1961; *Inside Monte Carlo*, World Distributors, 1963; (with Douglas Sutherland) *Burgess and Maclean*, Doubleday, 1963; (editor) *Churchill: A Pictorial Record*, Dell, 1965; *Royal Homes and Gardens*, Leslie Frewin, 1966.

WORK IN PROGRESS: H.M.S. Pickle, the story of the smallest ship at the battle of Trafalgar.

* * *

PUSTAY, John S(tephen) 1931-

PERSONAL: Born July 7, 1931, in Roebling, N.J.; son of

Stephen and Mary Pustay; married Lorraine Bago, July 4, 1954; children: Tanya, Melanie, Jean, John, Jr. *Education:* Attended Rutgers University, 1949-50; U.S. Naval Academy, B.S., 1954; San Francisco State College (now University), M.A., 1960; University of Denver, Ph.D., 1963. *Religion:* Roman Catholic.

CAREER: U.S. Navy, midshipman, 1950-54; U.S. Air Force, regular officer, 1954—; now major. Assigned to Intelligence Service, 1954-58, with overseas duty in Korea, Japan, Formosa, and Thailand; associate professor of political science at U.S. Air Force Academy, Colorado Springs, Colo., 1960-63, former assistant dean. Speaker and debater on regional radio and television. *Member:* International Studies Association (national treasurer, 1963; vice-president, 1964), U.S. Naval Institute, Western Political Science Association. *Awards, honors:* Armed Forces Commendation Medal, 1959; Air Force Commendation Medal, 1965.

WRITINGS: Counterinsurgency Warfare, Free Press of Glencoe, 1965. Contributor to *Proceedings* of Institute on World Affairs, 1962, 1963, 1965, and to *Military Review*.

SIDELIGHTS: Pustay has moderate fluency in Russian and Spanish.†

*   *   *

PYNCHON, Thomas 1937-

PERSONAL: Born May 8, 1937, in Glen Cove, Long Island, N.Y.; son of Thomas R. Pynchon (an industrial surveyor). *Education:* Cornell University, B.A., 1958. *Residence:* Currently living in California.

CAREER: Lived in Greenwich Village for one year after graduating from college; worked for Boeing Aircraft, Seattle, Wash., on a house organ; went to Mexico to finish his first novel; later moved to California. *Military service:* U.S. Navy, two years (interrupted his college studies). *Awards, honors:* William Faulkner novel award, 1963, for *V.*; Rosenthal Foundation Award National Institute of Arts and Letters, 1967, for *The Crying of Lot 49.*

WRITINGS: V. (novel; portions of Chapter 3 first appeared in another form as a short story, "Under the Rose," in *The Noble Savage*, number 3; another part was first published in *New World Writing*), Lippincott, 1963; *The Crying of Lot 49* (novel; sections first published as "The World [This One], the Flesh [Mrs. Oedipa Maas], and the Testament of Pierce Inverarity," in *Esquire*, December, 1965; another section in *Cavalier*), Lippincott, 1966; *Gravity's Rainbow* (novel), Viking, 1973. Also contributor to *Saturday Evening Post, Kenyon Review*, and *New World Writing.*

SIDELIGHTS: "Thomas Pynchon's gifts as a novelist are almost alarming," writes Erik Wensberg. "An impassioned comic writer, spendthrift of invention, he dwells in that romance with time which nourishes the born storyteller. And he commands the stranger power of enforcement: he can work upon his reader the very disorder and anxious exertions his fiction describes. His language throws off Joycean and Nabokovian scintillations—multiple meanings, cross-references and puns—which yet remain steadily, intelligently directed." Unfavorable critics consider his work a "lacklustre muddle," "a wearisome joke," "ludicrous," "cute Gothic," or "utterly dead."

Pynchon's theme, style, and characterizations are closely interrelated. Richard Poirier notes that "both novels are populated by self-mystified people running from the respon-

sibilities of love and compelled by phantoms, puzzles, the power of Things. No plot, political, novelistic, or personal, can issue from the circumstances of love, from the simple human needs, say, of a Rachel or an Oedipa, and Pynchon implicitly mocks this situation by the Byzantine complications of plots which do evolve from circumstances devoid of love." Pynchon's characters are obliquely delineated, reality and fantasy exist together, and bizarre humor is plentiful enough to leave "the imagination spent and the mind reeling," writes Arthur R. Gold.

His first novel, published when he was 26, is, according to George Plimpton, an example of modern picaresque, "brilliant and turbulent." The quest for the elusive V. animates one character among "the whole sick crew." Plimpton correctly assumed that the identity of V. would cause much speculation. He added: "What will be remembered, whether or not V. remains elusive, is Pynchon's remarkable ability—which includes a vigorous and imaginative style, a robust humor, a tremendous reservoir of information (one suspects that he could churn out a passable almanac in a fortnight's time) and, above all, a sense of how to use and balance these talents." Frederick J. Hoffman notes that "everything exists in brilliant profusion" in *V.* The plot "rivals Stendhal for dazzling intricacy and an outrageous use of coincidence," writes Gold. "Yet if we surrender to it we reap a very special kind of contemplative pleasure." The *Newsweek* reviewer wrote: "Pitched at the highest level of farce, at times, it seems, going too high for the human ear to hear, the novel is at once a frantic comedy, a tough puzzle, a spectacular cavalcade of Western life in the past 75 years, and a melancholy comment on the ways things are now (not that they ever were, on balance, any better)." The *Virginia Quarterly Review* called the novel "sprawling and desultory in concept, brilliant and otiose by turn, alternately sophisticated and naive," but added that it was "nevertheless arresting, bewildering, and entertaining, . . . literary refreshment of superior order."

Hoffmann, who considers *V.* to be "a very clever novel," also thinks that "one of its principal faults is that it makes fun of the reasons why it makes fun of everything else." Poirier, however, sees *V.* as "a designed indictment of its own comic elaborateness. . . . Pynchon's intricacies are meant to testify to the waste—a key word in *The Crying of Lot 49*—of imagination that first creates and is then enslaved by its own plottings, its machines, the products of its technology. . . . 'Plots' are an expression in Pynchon of the mad belief that *some* plot can ultimately take over the world, can ultimately control life to the point where it is manageably inanimate. . . . Nearly from the outset, the people of Pynchon's novels are the instruments of the 'plots' they help create. Their consequent dehumanization makes the prospect of an apocalypse and the destruction of self not a horror so much as the final ecstasy of power. . . . The process is part of daily news, and no other novelist predicts and records it with Pynchon's imaginative and stylistic grasp of contemporary materials."

The Crying of Lot 49 is a much shorter novel, which prompted Roger Shattuck to write that, "without the ocean of life that flooded the earlier book, lo! it is as if the tide had gone out. Yet low tide has its own attractions." The *Newsweek* reviewer noted: "In a way, *Lot 49* seems to be an outgrowth of *V.* . . . The world is the same—still impersonal but eventful, probably sinister, and freighted with menace and meaning for its citizens. The inhabitants of this world still are apprehensive and uneasy; they still scramble after understanding and collapse just short of achieving it.

But the seeker and the specific object of the search are quite different in *Lot 49*, simpler, clearer—and a lot funnier.'' Though it may be a simpler tale, ''the ironies are [still] intricate, the prose composed in styles varying from scholarly exposition to parodies of Jacobean tragedy to TV commercialese; but Mr. Pynchon does not lose control,'' writes Stephen Donadio. ''His primary observation remains central, and it is one which our current foreign policy only seems to confirm: that paranoia is the last sense of community left us.'' Wensberg believes that ''the book dreams upon America with a tenderness and elegiac sense of loss not present before in our specifically comic fiction.''

It has been said that Pynchon uses the techniques and virtues of other writers as a ''taking-off point.'' His assimilation of certain contemporaries, such as William Gaddis, is evident. Yet his work is very much an original expression. Poirier writes: ''Pynchon's technical virtuosity, his adaptations of the apocalyptic-satiric modes of Melville, Conrad, and Joyce, of Faulkner, Nathanael West, and Nabokov, the saturnalian inventiveness he shares with contemporaries like John Barth and Joseph Heller, his security with philosophical and psychological concepts, his anthropological intimacy with the off-beat—these evidences of extraordinary talent in the first novel continue to display themselves in the second. And the uses to which he puts them are very much the same.''

''Reading *Gravity's Rainbow*,'' writes W. T. Lhamon, Jr., in response to Pynchon's third novel, ''is a primary experience. I felt anguish about reading it alone, needed to touch the person next to me, as Pynchon urges throughout. I felt alone confronting a mysterious world without a sure explanation: felt humble then angry without an adequate culture to comprehend these fermenting codes. But with the review finished, and while reading it over, out my window I saw a large, beautifully clear rainbow. An omen. My feeling was right; our best fictions will always be about the need for more adequate fictions, about the construction of life's meaning from scratch. Like Joyce's *Ulysses*, this novel will surely go into the seminars all over the land. May it not be buried there. Academic minds can't possibly resist chasing its clues, nor should they. Yet if *Gravity's Rainbow* is read only around seminar tables to display one's gumshoe work in the stacks, the tragedy will be even greater than in the case of *Ulysses*, because *Gravity's Rainbow* comes cyclically out of people and people's culture and should return to Us and Ours, resonantly. It should not be routed into a 'no return' solitary confinement among the tastes of academe. Read this novel: it's one of the finest ever.''

Critical opinion is by no means in unanimous enthusiastic praise of the novel. David Thorburn observes bluntly that ''by page 400 even the committed reader must begin to feel that he has had enough; by page 600 one begins to understand that Pynchon cannot stop himself . . .,'' while Gerald Weales, in *The Hudson Review*, writes, ''If I am mistaken and if *Gravity's Rainbow* really is the masterpiece, the classic many reviewers have claimed it to be, then it is a fairly forgettable classic and one that I have little desire to re-read.'' The ambivalence about whether *Gravity's Rainbow* is or merely pretends to be a serious masterpiece must inhere in the novel itself, and Peter Ackroyd concedes, ''Thomas Pynchon has obviously taken great pains over the book, and presumably a great deal of his time. I salute his craftsmanship and dedication, and I only suggest that he fashioned it to more immediate and less apocalyptic ends. I had the comfortable feeling that there was a grand

symbolic design which I was continually missing, and if this is the case I blame Mr. Pynchon.''

That he does take pains to go to such great lengths causes Michael Wood to note that ''there is a whole region missing in Pynchon's fiction, the region of the suggested but not said, the shown but not expressed . . .'' It is precisely with such great length, however, that ''Pynchon may seem to be describing, even celebrating, the death of a culture,'' writes George Levine in *Partisan Review*. ''But his style and language are the signs of life, not death. In a passage which might be taken as a metaphor for his own writing, Pynchon gives us a characteristically vulgar and authentic boogie-woogie song called 'Sold on Suicide.' . . . *Gravity's Rainbow* is a defense against suicide, not a celebration of it. Nobody in it really dies. Nobody exhausts reality or even the possibilities of myths of unity. . . . Even Pynchon's style, as he knows, cannot exhaust everything in the suicidal catalogue, but the catalogue itself is a vital achievement. The style, denying and asserting connection, creating metaphors, being 'simply here,' becomes the real possibility of freedom. It challenges us to take the risk of letting ourselves loose from the destructive myths which support us, and to face, with Pynchonian confidence and authority, an irrational world of objects.''

If his characters are often encompassed by mystery, the same might be said of Pynchon. He is so shy of publicity that he has not allowed a photograph of himself to be publicly printed. He once turned down an offer to teach at Cornell, saying he was not good enough. He is a writer only, one whose concern for accuracy is profound. The *New York Times Book Review* reports: ''He is a tireless researcher and, caught in a minor error, suffers the humiliation of the damned. During the last stages of *V.* he kept one of his Village friends running to the library to look up data in the *World Almanac* of 1948. There was no copy of that in his part of Mexico, although there was privacy for a modest man.''

Richard Farina based an instrumental composition on *V.*

BIOGRAPHICAL / CRITICAL SOURCES—Books: Richard Kostelanetz, editor, *On Contemporary Literature*, Avon, 1964; Carolyn Riley, editor, *Contemporary Literary Criticism*, Gale, Volume II, 1974, Volume III, 1975; Joseph W. Slade, *Thomas Pynchon*, Warner Books, 1974.

Periodicals: *Newsweek*, April 1, 1963, May 2, 1966; *New York Times Book Review*, April 21, 1963, April 28, 1963, May 1, 1966, March 11, 1973; *New York Herald Tribune Books*, April 21, 1963; *Virginia Quarterly Review*, summer, 1963, autumn, 1970; *Commentary*, September, 1963, September, 1973; *New Statesman*, October 11, 1963, April 14, 1967; *Times Literary Supplement*, October 11, 1963; *Critique*, winter, 1963-64, No. 1, 1967, No. 2, 1972, No. 2, 1974; *Saturday Review*, April 30, 1966; *New Leader*, May 23, 1966; *New York Review of Books*, June 23, 1966, March 22, 1973; *Commonweal*, July 8, 1966; *Saturday Night*, August, 1966; *Partisan Review*, summer, 1966, No. 3, 1969, fall, 1973, No. 1, 1975; *Punch*, April 26, 1967; *Tri-Quarterly*, winter, 1967; *Nation*, September 25, 1967; *Chelsea Review*, December, 1969; *Yale Review*, summer, 1973; *Harper's*, March, 1975; *Twentieth Century Literature*, May, 1975.†

*   *   *

QUIGLEY, John 1927-

PERSONAL: Born September 30, 1927, in Scotland; son of John and Helen Quigley; married Elizabeth Kellock, November 27, 1952. *Education:* Attended schools in Glasgow, Scotland. *Home:* White Count, Killearn, Stirlingshire, Scotland. *Agent:* International Famous Agency, Ltd., Hanover St., London, England.

CAREER: Started in journalism at seventeen, with *Daily Record*, Glasgow, Scotland; feature writer with Beaverbrook Newspapers in Scotland, 1946-63, first for *Daily Express* and then the *Sunday Express*; when first book was published, left journalism to write more novels, and to look after the Scotch whisky business he founded under the trade name, Clanrana. *Military service:* Royal Navy, 1944-46.

WRITINGS—Novels: *To Remember With Tears*, Hutchinson, 1963; *The Bitter Lollipop*, Hutchinson, 1964; *The Secret Soldier*, New American Library, 1966; *The Golden Stream*, Collins, 1970; *The Last Checkpoint*, Coward, 1971; *King's Royal*, McCall Publishing, 1975.

WORK IN PROGRESS: A sequel to *King's Royal*, the saga of a whiskey dynasty.

SIDELIGHTS: John Quigley told *CA:* "Entry into the Scotch whisky business (as a provider rather than a consumer) resulted from my discovery of an ancient recipe for a Scotch liqueur said to have been first produced more than 200 years ago.... We have 5 cats, all of them ex-strays, and a dog."

The Bitter Lollipop was bought for filming by Bryan Forbes.

BIOGRAPHICAL/CRITICAL SOURCES: Weekly Scotsman, May 30, 1963, February 17, 1966.

*   *   *

QUIGLEY, Martin (P).   1913-

PERSONAL: Born June 9, 1913; son of Patrick J. and Petrea (Grafslund) Quigley; married Margaret Hertsgaard, September 30, 1939; children: Catherine M. *Education:* University of Minnesota, A.B., 1938. *Politics:* Independent. *Religion:* Lutheran. *Home:* 500 North and South Rd., St. Louis, Mo. 63130.

CAREER: Newspaperman in Midwest, working on *Kansas City Star, Minneapolis Tribune*, and other papers prior to World War II; member of public relations firms, New York, N.Y., 1945-52; director of information for Ford Foundation in Pasadena, Calif., and New York, N.Y., 1952-53; senior partner of Fleishman-Hillard, Inc. (public relations), St. Louis, Mo., 1953-68; editor, *The Midwest Motorist*, 1968—. Helped organize KETC, St. Louis educational television station, and served as general manager, 1954. *Military service:* U.S. Army Air Forces, 1943-45; duty with Twelfth Air Force in Mediterranean Theater; became staff sergeant; received Air Medal, Bronze Star, and five battle stars. *Member:* Society of Professional Journalists.

WRITINGS: A Tent on Corsica (novel), Lippincott, 1949; *The Secret Project of Sigurd O'Leary* (novel), Lippincott, 1959; (with Joe Garagiola) *Baseball is a Funny Game*, Lippincott, 1960; *Winners and Losers* (novel), Lippincott, 1961; *Today's Game* (novel), Viking, 1965; (with Kirby Higbe) *The High Hard One*, Viking, 1967. Wrote book for two musical comedies, "The Raspberry Queen," produced as a television special by Columbia Broadcasting System, 1953, and "Molly Darling," produced by St. Louis Municipal Opera, 1962. Book reviewer and contributor to magazines.

RABY, William L(ouis)   1927-

PERSONAL: Born July 16, 1927, in Chicago, Ill.; son of Gustave E. (a painter) and Helen (Burgess) Raby; married Norma Claire Schreiner, September 8, 1956; children: Burgess, Marianne. *Education:* Northwestern University, B.S., 1949; University of Illinois, C.P.A., 1950; University of Arizona, M.B.A., 1961, Ph.D., 1970. *Office:* 3303 North Central, Phoenix, Ariz. 85012.

CAREER: Swenson & Raby (certified public accountants), Rockford, Ill., partner, 1950-60; William L. Raby & Co. (certified public accountants), Tucson, Ariz., partner, 1961-69; Laventhon Dhorwath (certified public accountants), Phoenix, Ariz, partner, 1969—. Rockford College, Rockford, Ill., lecturer in accounting, 1954-55; University of Arizona, Tucson, lecturer in accounting, 1958-70, director of Tax Practitioners Institute, 1964—; Ohio University, Athens, associate professor of accounting, 1962-65. Member of Tax Court bar. *Military service:* U.S. Navy, 1942-45. *Member:* American Institute of Certified Public Accountants (member of executive committee, Federal tax division), American Accounting Association.

WRITINGS: The Income Tax and Business Decisions, Prentice-Hall, 1964, 3rd edition, 1974; *Building and Maintaining a Successful Tax Practice*, Prentice-Hall, 1964; (with Carl Riblet, Jr.) *The Reluctant Taxpayer*, Cowles, 1970; *Tax Practice Management*, American Institute of Certified Public Accountants, 1974. Contributor to professional journals. Member of editorial board, *Taxation for Accountants, The Tax Advisor*.

*   *   *

RAE, Hugh C(rauford)   1935-
(Robert Crawford)

PERSONAL: Born November 22, 1935, in Glasgow, Scotland; son of Robert Tennant (a carpenter) and Isobel (McNair) Rae; married Elizabeth Dunn, September 3, 1960; children: Gillian (daughter). *Education:* Attended secondary school, Glasgow, Scotland, 1940-51. *Politics:* Conservative. *Religion:* Presbyterian. *Agent:* Fraser & Dunlop Ltd., 91 Regent St., London W.1, England.

CAREER: Assistant to antiquarian bookseller, Glasgow, Scotland, 1952-65; full-time professional writer, 1965—. *Military service:* Royal Air Force, National Service, 1954-56. *Member:* P.E.N.

WRITINGS: Skinner, Viking, 1965; *Night Pillow*, Viking, 1967; *A Few Small Bones*, Blond, 1968; *The House at Balnesmoor*, Coward, 1969; *The Interview*, Coward, 1969; *The Saturday Epic*, Coward, 1970; *The Marksman*, Coward, 1971; *The Shooting Gallery*, Coward, 1972; *Rock Harvest*, Constable, 1973; *The Rookery*, St. Martin's, 1975.

Under pseudonym Robert Crawford: *Cockleburr*, Constable, 1969, Putnam, 1970; *The Shroud Society*, Putnam, 1969; *Kiss the Boss Goodbye*, Constable, 1970, Putnam, 1971; *Badger's Daughter*, Constable, 1971; *Whip Hand*, Constable, 1972.

Also writer of plays, television scripts, short stories, poems, and literary articles.

SIDELIGHTS: Rae wrote *CA:* "Compulsive writer.... No strong desire to travel. No foreign languages. No strong commitment to any specific cause through development of an 'innocent bystander' attitude. Boringly single-minded." *Avocational interests:* The cinema and theater, television, reading, sports (tennis and basketball).†

RALSTON, Alma
(Alma Smith Payne)

PERSONAL: Born In Oakland, Calif.; daughter of Robert Russell (a businessman) and Neva (Palmer) Smith; married James W. Chambers, October 10, 1924 (divorced, 1937); married Buford Burke Payne, September 26, 1947 (died 1959); married William Robertson Ralston, February 12, 1967 (died, 1969); children: (first marriage) Robert Warner Chambers, James W. Chambers, Jr.; step-children: Richard Montague Payne, Margaret Payne Ferris, William R. Ralston, Jr., Donald Ralston. *Education:* University of California, A.B., 1922, M.A., 1936. *Residence:* Walnut Creek, Calif. *Agent:* Curtis Brown Ltd., 60 East 56th St., New York, N.Y. 10022.

CAREER: California Department of Education, San Francisco, northern California supervisor of emergency education program nursery schools, 1936-40; Berkeley (Calif.) public schools, supervisor of nursery schools, parent education and child care centers, 1940-47; now full-time professional writer. Lecturer at University of California Extension, Berkeley, 1941-43; instructor in journalism and creative writing, Diabo Valley College, 1970—. Member of board of directors, California Heart Association; past president and member of board of directors, Alameda County Heart Association; president of Friends of California Libraries, 1966. *Member:* National League of American Pen Women (president of Piedmont Oakland branch, 1974—), Phi Beta Kappa, Theta Sigma Phi, California Writers Club (first vice-president). *Awards, honors:* Received California Heart Association bronze medallion, 1960, and silver medallions, 1964 and 1966, for nutrition work and for participation in the fight against heart disease.

WRITINGS—All under name Alma Smith Payne: (With Dorothy Callahan) *The Low Sodium Cook Book*, Little, Brown, 1953, 2nd revised edition published as *The Fat and Sodium Control Cookbook*, 1975; (with Callahan) *The Great Nutrition Puzzle*, Scribner, 1956; (with Callahan) *Young America's Cookbook*, Scribner, 1959; (with son, Robert Warner Chambers) *From Cell to Test Tube*, Scribner, 1960; *Discoverer of the Unseen World: Biography of Antoni van Leeuwenhoek*, World Publishing, 1966; *Partners in Science*, World Publishing, 1968; *Jinglebells and Pastry Shells*, World Publishing, 1968.

WORK IN PROGRESS: The *Herb/Wine Cookbook*, completion expected in 1976.

AVOCATIONAL INTERESTS: Grandchildren, the arts, travel, reading, and experimenting with foods.

* * *

RAMANUJAN, A(ttipat) K(rishnaswami) 1929-

PERSONAL: First two "a's" in surname are long vowels; born March 16, 1929, in Mysore, India; son of Attipat Asuri (a professor) and Seshammal Krishnaswami; married Molly Daniels, June 7, 1962; children: Krittika (daughter), Krishnaswami (son). *Education:* Mysore University, B.A. (honors), 1949, M.A., 1950; Deccan College, graduate diplomas, 1958, 1959; Indiana University, Ph.D., 1963. *Office:* South Asia Language and Area Center, University of Chicago, 1130 East 59th St., Chicago, Ill. 60637.

CAREER: Lecturer in English at colleges in India, 1950-57; at University of Baroda, Baroda, India, 1957-58; University of Chicago, Chicago, Ill., research associate in Tamil, 1961, assistant professor of linguistics (Tamil and Dravidian languages), 1962-65, associate professor, 1966-68, professor of linguistics and Dravidian studies, 1968—, academic director of Rotating Inter-University Summer School in Indian Studies, 1966. Visiting professor, University of Wisconsin, 1965, 1971, University of California at Berkeley, 1966, 1973, University of Michigan, 1970. *Member:* Linguistic Society of America, Association for Asian Studies, American Oriental Society, Linguistic Society of India, Chicago Linguistic Society. *Awards, honors:* Fulbright travel fellowship and Smith-Mundt fellowship for study in United States, 1959-60; faculty research fellowship, American Institute of Indian Studies, 1963-64; fellow, Indiana School of Letters, 1963; Fulbright-Hays fellowship, 1969; American Council of Learned Societies fellowship, 1973.

WRITINGS: Proverbs (in Kannada), Karnatak University, 1955; *Fifteen Tamil Poems*, Writer's Workshop (Calcutta), 1965; *The Striders* (poems), Oxford University Press, 1966; *The Interior Landscape* (translations of love poems from a classical Tamil anthology), Indiana University Press, 1967; (translator with Michael Garman and Rajeev Taranath) M. Gopalakrishna Adiga, *The Song of the Earth and Other Poems*, Writer's Workshop, 1968; *Relations*, Oxford University Press, 1972; *Speaking of Sira*, Penguin, 1973.

Also author of writings in Kannada which include essays, plays, poems, and translations. Poems in English have been published in Indian, British, and American periodicals. Contributor of articles to *Southern Folklore Quarterly*, *History of Religions*, and other journals.

WORK IN PROGRESS: A volume of poems; a book of translations from classical Tamil; a book of Indian folktales.

BIOGRAPHICAL/CRITICAL SOURCES: New York Times Book Review, November 20, 1966; *Poetry*, March, 1967.

* * *

RAMMELKAMP, Julian S(turtevant) 1917-

PERSONAL: Born August 4, 1917, in Jacksonville, Ill.; son of Charles Henry (a college president) and Jeannette (Capps) Rammelkamp; married Mabel Tippitt (an English teacher), February 25, 1942; children: David, Charles, Robert. *Education:* Illinois College, Jacksonville, A.B., 1939; Harvard University, M.A., 1947, Ph.D., 1961. *Politics:* Democrat. *Religion:* Protestant. *Home:* 416 Linden Ave., Albion, Mich. 49224. *Office:* Albion College, Albion, Mich. 49224.

CAREER: Albion College, Albion, Mich., member of department of history, 1954—. *Military service:* U.S. Army, Signal Corps, 1941-45; became sergeant. *Member:* American Historical Association, Organization of American Historians, Missouri Historical Society.

WRITINGS: Pulitzer's Post-Dispatch, 1878-1883, Princeton University Press, 1966. Contributor to history journals.

WORK IN PROGRESS: Further history of the *St. Louis Post-Dispatch*.

* * *

RAMS, Edwin M(arion) 1922-

PERSONAL: Born December 31, 1922, in Chicago, Ill.; son of Michael S. and Helen (Ptaszek) Rams; married Charlotte M. Maruda, April 7, 1951; children: Mary Joan, Margaret Ann, Thomas Edwin, Janet Lynn (deceased), Robert Michael. *Education:* Northern Illinois University,

B.S., 1944; University of Pennsylvania, graduate study, 1944-45; John Marshall Law School, LL.B., 1958, LL.M., 1959, Jur.D., 1965. *Religion:* Catholic. *Home:* 12112 Lerner Place, Bowie, Md. 20715. *Office:* Urban Research Associates, 1501 H St., N.W., Washington, D.C. 20005.

CAREER: Roosevelt University, Chicago, Ill., lecturer in real estate, 1952-53; Equitable Life Assurance Society of U.S., Columbus, Ohio, mortgage investment manager, 1953-56; self-employed real estate consultant in Columbus, Ohio, 1956-57; U.S. General Services Administration, Atlanta, Ga., regional appraiser, 1957-60; U.S. Urban Renewal Administration, Fort Worth, Tex., director of real estate disposition, 1960-64; Urban Research Associates (economic and real estate consultants), Washington, D.C., director, 1964—. Special lecturer in real estate for conferences and seminars at University of South Carolina, University of Georgia, and Texas Christian University. Consulting editor for business and professional books, Prentice-Hall, Inc., 1962—, and for Reston Publishing Co., 1974—. *Military service:* U.S. Navy, 1944-46.

MEMBER: American Institute of Real Estate Appraisers, Society of Residential Appraisers (president, Columbus chapter, 1957-58), American Society of Appraisers (past regional governor), American Right of Way Association (vice-president, Georgia chapter, 1956-57), Regional Science Association, Lambda Alpha (vice-president, 1963-65; international president, 1965—), Washington Society of Investment Analysts. *Awards, honors:* Arthur A. May award, American Institute of Real Estate Appraisers, 1966.

WRITINGS: (Contributor) *Appraisal Classics*, Society of Real Estate Appraisers, 1960; (reviser) G. L. Schmutz, *Condemnation Appraisal Handbook*, Prentice-Hall, 1963; *Principles of City Land Values*, Academy Publishing, 1964; *The Ideal City*, Bureau of Business and Economic Research, Georgia State College, 1964; *Means of Access and the Socio-Economic Structure of Urban Areas in the United States*, Academy Publishing, 1965; *Valuation for Eminent Domain*, Prentice-Hall, 1973; *Real Estate Appraising Handbook*, Prentice-Hall, 1975; *Analysis and Valuation of Retail Locations*, Reston Publishing, 1975. Contributor of some thirty articles to professional journals. Member of editorial board, *Georgia Builder Journal*, 1957-58. Contributor to *Appraisal and Valuation Manual*, American Society of Appraisers, 1959—.

* * *

RANDALL, Randolph C. 1900-

PERSONAL: Born June 10, 1900, in Arcadia, Ind.; son of Nathan Clarence and Bertha (Johnson) Randall; married Ellen Moore, October 15, 1932; children: Carol (Mrs. Ralph VanDeVeire), Robert Merritt, Katherine Ann. *Education:* Indiana University, A.B., 1922; Columbia University, A.M., 1926, Ph.D., 1955. *Religion:* Quaker. *Home:* 20231 South Lake Shore Blvd., Cleveland, Ohio 44123.

CAREER: Teacher at continuation school, Isabela, Puerto Rico, 1922-23; Centenary College, Shreveport, La., 1926-31, started as instructor, associate professor of English, 1929-31; Fenn College, Cleveland, Ohio, associate professor, 1931-34, professor of English, 1934-65, chairman of department, 1931-65; Cleveland State University, Cleveland, Ohio, professor of English and chairman of department, 1970. *Military service:* U.S. Army, 1918. *Member:* Modern Language Association of America, Northeastern Ohio College English Group (president, 1965-66). *Awards, honors:* Ohioana Book Award in biography, Ohioana Li-

brary Association, 1965, and Florence Roberts Head Award for literature, Columbus, Ohio, chapter of American Association of University Women, 1965, both for *James Hall, Spokesman of the New West.*

WRITINGS: James Hall, Spokesman of the New West, Ohio State University Press, 1964; (contributor) James Woodress, editor, *Essays Mostly on Periodical Publishing in America,* Duke University Press, 1973.

* * *

RAO, Hanumantha 1929-

PERSONAL: Born May 15, 1929, in Andhra, India; son of Srinivasa (an agriculturist) and Chandramma Rao; married Krishna Kumari, May 20, 1959. *Education:* Delhi University, Ph.D., 1962. *Home and office:* Institute of Economic Growth, Delhi 7, India.

CAREER: Institute of Economic Growth, Delhi, India, research and teaching fellow in economics, 1961—. University of Chicago, research fellow on problems of agricultural development in India, 1966.

WRITINGS: Agricultural Production Functions, Costs and Returns in India, Asia Publishing House, 1965; *Taxation of Agricultural Land in Andhra Pradesh,* Asia Publishing House, 1966; *Technological Change and the Distribution of Gains in Indian Agriculture,* Macmillan, 1975.

* * *

RAPKIN, Chester 1918-

PERSONAL: Born February 19, 1918, in New York, N.Y.; son of Robert and Minnie (Bogan) Rapkin; married Eva Samuel (a social worker), August 3, 1942; children: David, Naomi Ruth. *Education:* City College (now City College of the City University of New York), B.S., 1939; graduate study at The American University and George Washington University; Columbia University, Ph.D., 1953. *Politics:* Democrat. *Religion:* Jewish. *Home:* 473 West End Ave., New York, N.Y. 10024; and 26 The Western Way, Princeton, N.J. 08540. *Office:* School of Architecture and Urban Planning, Princeton, N.J. 08540.

CAREER: Federal Home Loan Bank Board, Washington, D.C., economist and statistician, 1941-46; National Housing Agency, Washington, D.C., credit and finance specialist, 1946-47; National Bureau of Economic Research, New York, N.Y., research economist, 1947-49; Columbia University, New York, N.Y., research associate of Institute for Urban Land Use and Housing Studies, 1949-55; University of Pennsylvania, Philadelphia, professor of city planning of department of city and regional planning, professor of finance of Wharton School of Finance and Commerce, and chairman of urban studies group of Institute for Environmental Studies, 1955-66; Columbia University, professor of urban planning, 1966-73; Princeton University, Princeton, N.J., professor of urban planning, 1973—. Staff director of President's Task Force on Urban Affairs, 1965-66; commissioner of New York City Planning Commission, 1969—. Consultant to U.N. Center for Housing, Building, and Planning, Israeli Ministry of Housing, State of Maryland, City of Melbourne, Australia, Office of the Mayor of Honolulu, Weizmann Institute of Science Libraries, Mortgage Guarantee Insurance Corporation, Bishop Estate of Honolulu, U.S. Bureau of the Census, University of Hawaii, University of Puerto Rico, Brookings Institution, to other government commissions and agencies, and to builders and architects. Member of board of directors, Citizens' Housing and Planning Council of New York.

MEMBER: American Economic Association, American Finance Association, American Institute of Planners (affiliate), American Real Estate and Urban Economics Association, American Statistical Association, American Sociological Society (fellow), International Federation of Housing and Planning, Inter-American Planning Society, National Association of Housing and Redevelopment Officials, National Association of Intergroup Relations Officials, Regional Science Association, Beta Gamma Sigma.

WRITINGS: (With Louis Winnick and David M. Blank) *Housing Market Analysis*, U.S. Government Printing Office, 1953; (with Robert B. Mitchell) *Urban Traffic: A Function of Land Use*, Columbia University Press, 1954; (with Ernest M. Fisher) *The Mutual Mortgage Insurance Fund*, Columbia University Press, 1956; *The Real Estate Market in an Urban Renewal Area*, New York City Planning Commission, 1959; (with William G. Grigsby) *Residential Renewal in the Urban Core*, University of Pennsylvania Press, 1959.

(With W. G. Grigsby) *The Demand for Housing in Eastwick*, University of Pennsylvania Press, 1960; (with W. G. Grigsby) *The Demand for Housing in Racially Mixed Areas*, University of California Press, 1960; (with others) *Industrial Renewal: Determining the Potential and Accelerating the Economy of the Utica Area*, New York State Division of Housing and Community Renewal, 1963; *The South Houston Industrial Area*, New York City Planning Commission, 1963; (with Grace Milgram and Paul L. Niebanck) *Population and Housing in New Haven, 1960-1980, a Section of the New Haven Community Renewal Program*, New Haven Redevelopment Agency, 1964; (with Paul L. Niebanck, Richard H. Broun, and John Pope) *Housing in the Greater Bridgeport Region, 1960-1980*, Greater Bridgeport Regional Planning Agency, 1965; (contributor) *Essays in Honor of Leo Grebler*, University of California Press, 1965; *Rental Housing Market in New York City: Two Decades of Rent Control*, New York City Rent and Rehabilitation Administration, 1967; *The Private Insurance of Home Mortgages*, University of Pennsylvania, 1967, revised edition, 1973.

Writer of about fifty other major reports, plans, and technical papers. Contributor to *Britannica Book of the Year*, 1952-58, *Encyclopaedia Britannica*, and of articles to professional journals.

WORK IN PROGRESS: *The Socio-Economic Problems of High Rise Residential Structures*, under a grant from Princeton University; another residential study, under a grant from U.S. National Bureau of Standards; other writings on urban planning, mortgage insurance, and the conversion of land from rural to urban use.

SIDELIGHTS: Rapkin is competent in French and German. *Avocational interests:* Fishing, mineralogy, travel.

* * *

RASPONI, Lanfranco 1914-

PERSONAL: Born December 11, 1914, in Florence, Italy; son of Nerino and Carolina (Montague) Rasponi. *Education:* University of California, B.A.; Columbia University, M.Sc. *Agent:* James Brown Associates, Inc., 22 East 60th St., New York, N.Y. 10022.

WRITINGS: *The International Nomads* (nonfiction), Putnam, 1966; *Golden Oases*, Putnam, 1967.

RATH, Patricia M(ink)

PERSONAL: Born in Chicago, Ill.; daughter of Dwight L. (an industrial sales executive) and Margaret (a psychiatric social worker; maiden name, Strom) Mink; married Melvin Eugene Rath (a certified public accountant), December 19, 1959; children: Eric. *Education:* Oberlin College, B.A.; Simmons College, M.S.; further study at Northwestern University. *Religion:* Protestant. *Home:* 1037 Cherry St., Winnetka, Ill. 60093.

CAREER: Carson Pirie Scott & Co., Chicago, Ill., executive trainee and assistant buyer, 1952-55; Joseph Magnin, San Francisco, Calif., assistant buyer, 1955; Springfield (Ill.) public schools, distributive education coordinator, 1956-58; Illinois State Board of Vocational Education, supervisor of business and distributive education in Springfield, 1958-60, in Chicago, Ill., 1960-65. *Member:* American Marketing Association, American Vocational Association, League of Women Voters, Illinois Foundation for Distributive Education. *Awards, honors:* Outstanding Service Award, Distributive Education Clubs of America, 1962.

WRITINGS: (With R. E. Mason) *Distributive Education Notebook for Occupational Growth*, Interstate, 1963; (with G. R. Tapp and Mason) *Case Studies in Marketing and Distribution*, Interstate, 1965; (contributor) Mason and P. G. Haines, *Cooperative Occupational Education*, Interstate, 1965; (with Mason) *Principles of Marketing and Distribution*, McGraw, 1968, 2nd edition (with Mason and H. L. Ross), 1974; (with Mason and Lloyd Phipps) *Applying for a Job*, Interstate, 1968; (with Mason and Phipps) *Succeeding on the Job*, Interstate, 1970; (with Mason and Phipps) *Supervising on the Job*, Interstate, 1972. Contributor to professional journals.

* * *

RATHE, Alex W(erner) 1912-

PERSONAL: Born January 21, 1912, in Berlin, Germany; son of Alex and Anne (Mathias) Rathe; married Kathleen Marjory Jones, November 1, 1947; children: Arthur Alan. *Education:* Charlottenburg Institute of Technology, Charlottenburg, Germany, B.S. in Electrical Engineering, 1933, M.Sc., 1935, D.Eng., 1936. *Home:* Bittersweet Lane, Mount Kisco, N.Y. 10549. *Office:* New York University, 100 Trinity Pl., New York, N.Y. 10006.

CAREER: Display Lighting Corp., New York, N.Y., industrial engineer, 1937-41; Jackson & Moreland (engineers), Boston, Mass., senior engineer, 1941-43; General Instrument Corp., Elizabeth, N.J., chief production engineer, 1943-44; Hudson American Corp., Ne York, N.Y., chief industrial engineer and assistant to vice-president, 1944-46; private practice as consulting engineer in management, 1946—, now in Mount Kisco, N.Y.; New York University, New York, N.Y., associate professor of management engineering, 1949-62, professor of management, Graduate School of Business Administration, 1962—. Visiting professor at Columbia University, 1961-62, University of Buenos Aires, summer, 1962. Distinguished lecturer, University of Southern California, 1971. Department of Defense, top management seminars, conference leader, 1966-68.

MEMBER: American Management Association (fellow; principal lecturer, 1952—), American Society of Mechanical Engineers (fellow), American Institute of Industrial Engineers (fellow; president, 1960-61), Engineers Joint Council (director, 1956-60), Council for International Progress in Management (director, 1963-70; president, 1969-70),

American Society for Engineering Education, International University Contact, Instituto para el Desarrollo de la Direccion de Empresa (honorary), Korean Federation of Executives (honorary), Thai Management Association (honorary), Association of Bolivian Business Executives (honorary), Argentine Engineering Council (honorary). *Awards, honors:* Certificates or citations for achievement from American Institute of Industrial Engineers, 1953, 1958, 1961, 1962, U.S. Army Command Management School, 1957, U.S. Army Logistics Management Center, 1959, Gantt Medal Board, 1962.

WRITINGS: How to Set Up Management Controls, Funk, 1948; (with Norbert Wiener and Luther Gulick) *Cybernetics and Society*, Executive Techniques, 1951; *Planning and Controlling*, American Management Association, 1954; *Planning and Review for Top Management*, American Management Association, 1954; (contributor) *Selected Speeches*, U.S. Army, 1958; (contributor) *Fifty Years' Progress Report in Management*, American Society of Mechanical Engineers, 1960; (contributor) *Management Control Systems*, edited by D. G. Malcolm and A. J. Rowe, Wiley, 1960; (editor) *Gantt on Management: Guidelines for Today's Executive*, American Management Association, 1961; (with Dhun Irani) *Scientists, Engineers and Managers: Partners in Space*, NASA, 1969; (with Frank M. Gryna, Jr.) *Company Practices in Industrial Engineering*, AMACOM, 1969. Contributor to professional journals.

* * *

RAY, D(avid) Michael 1935-

PERSONAL: Born December 25, 1935, in St. Austell, Cornwall, England; now Canadian citizen; son of Fred and Juliette (Gazard) Ray; married Marie Vincent, October 25, 1957; children: Jane, Jonathan. *Education:* University of Manchester, B.A. (honors in geography), 1956, Graduate Certificate in Education, 1957; University of Ottawa, M.A. (cum laude), 1961; University of Chicago, Ph.D., 1965. *Office:* Department of Geography, University of Ottawa, Ottawa, Ontario, Canada.

CAREER: Teacher with Montreal Catholic School Commission, Montreal, Quebec, 1957-58; University of Ottawa, Ottawa, Ontario, lecturer, 1958-61, assistant professor of geography, 1961-64; Spartan Air Services Ltd., Ottawa, Ontario, socio-economic geographer, 1965-67; University of Waterloo, Waterloo, Ontario, associate professor of geography, 1967-68; State University of New York at Buffalo, associate professor, 1968-71, professor of geography, 1971-73; University of Ottawa, Ottawa, Ontario, professor of geography, 1973—. Research associate, departments of geography and economics, Carleton University, Ottawa, 1966; consultant, Ministry of State and Urban Affairs of Canada, 1972—. *Member:* Canadian Association of Geographers, Association of American Geographers, Regional Science Association, American Association for the Advancement of Science.

WRITINGS: Market Potential and Economic Shadow: A Quantitative Analysis of Industrial Location in Southern Ontario, Department of Geography, University of Chicago, 1965; (contributor) R. M. Irving, editor, *Readings in Canadian Geography*, Holt, 1968, 2nd edition, 1972; (with others) *Trends, Issues and Possibilities for Urban Development*, Ontario Economic Council, 1970; *Dimensions of Canadian Regionalism*, Department of Energy, Mines, and Resources (Ottawa), 1971. Contributor to *Canadian Geographical Journal.*

WORK IN PROGRESS: "Urban Growth and the Concept of Economic Region," for *Urbanization in Canada*, edited by N. H. Lithwick and G. Paquet.†

* * *

READ, Leonard Edward 1898-

PERSONAL: Born September 26, 1898, in Hubbardston, Mich.; son of Orville Baker (a farmer) and Ada (Sturgis) Read; married Gladys Emily Cobb, July 15, 1920; children: Leonard Edward, James Baker. *Education:* Ferris Institute (now Ferris State College), graduate, 1917. *Politics:* Republican. *Religion:* Congregationalist. *Home:* Hillside, Irvington-on-Hudson, N.Y. *Office:* Foundation for Economic Education, Irvington-on-Hudson, N.Y.

CAREER: Ann Arbor Produce Co., Ann Arbor, Mich., president, 1919-25; Chamber of Commerce executive in Burlingame, Calif., 1927, Palo Alto, Calif., 1928; U.S. Chamber of Commerce, assistant manager, Western Division, Seattle, Wash, 1929-32, manager, 1932-39; Los Angeles Chamber of Commerce, Los Angeles, Calif., manager, 1939-45; National Industrial Conference Board, New York, N.Y., executive vice-president, 1945-46; Foundation for Economic Education, Inc., Irvington-on-Hudson, N.Y., president, 1946—. Lecturer and conductor of seminars throughout United States, and in South and Central America, Sweden, Canada, Japan, and other countries, covering about two million miles on the speaking circuit. *Military service:* U.S. Air Service, American Expeditionary Forces, 1917-19; survivor of torpedoed "Tuscania." *Member:* American Economic Association, Canadian Club of New York, St. Andrew's Golf Club. *Awards, honors:* Litt.D., Grove City College.

WRITINGS—all published by Foundation for Economic Education, except as indicated: *Romance of Reality*, Dodd, 1937; *Pattern for Revolt*, privately printed, 1945; *Students of Liberty*, 1950; *Outlook for Freedom*, 1951; *Government: An Ideal Concept*, 1954; *Why Not Try Freedom?*, Centro de Estudios sobre la Libertad, 1958; *Elements of Libertarian Leadership*, 1962; *Anything That's Peaceful*, 1964; *The Free Market and Its Enemy*, 1965; *Deeper Than You Think*, 1967; *Accent on the Right*, 1968; *The Coming Aristocracy*, 1969; *Let Freedom Reign*, 1969; *Talking to Myself*, 1970; *Then Truth Will Out*, 1971; *To Free or Freeze*, 1972; *Who's Listening?*, 1973; *Having My Way*, 1974.

* * *

RECHCIGL, Miloslav, Jr. 1930-

PERSONAL: Surname is pronounced "wrecks-eagle"; born July 30, 1930, in Mlada Boleslav, Czechoslovakia, came to U.S. in 1950, naturalized, 1955; son of Miloslav (a member of Czechoslovakian Parliament) and Marie (Rajtr) Rechcigl; married Eva Edwards, August 23, 1953; children: John Edward, Karen Marie. *Education:* Cornell University, B.S., 1954, M.N.S., 1955, Ph.D., 1958. *Home:* 1703 Mark Lane, Rockville, Md. 20852. *Office:* Agency for International Development, U.S. Department of State, Washington, D.C. 20523.

CAREER: Cornell University, Ithaca, N.Y., research associate in department of biochemistry, 1958; U.S. Public Health Service, National Cancer Institute, research fellow, 1958-60, senior investigator, laboratory of biochemistry, 1960-68, grants associate, 1968-69; Health Services and Mental Health Administration of the U.S. Department of Health, Education, and Welfare, assistant for nutrition and health to the director of Regional Medical Programs Service, 1969-70; U.S. Department of State, Agency for International Development, nutrition advisor, 1970—, executive secretary of grants council, 1970—, chief of grants division, 1971-73. Executive secretary of nutrition advisory committee of U.S. Health Services and Mental Health Administration, 1969-70; assistant director, Office of Research and Institutional Grants, 1973—. Member of council of National Cancer Institute Assembly of Scientists, 1963-65. Consultant to U.S. Department of Agriculture, 1969-70, U.S. Department of the Treasury, 1973—.

MEMBER: American Chemical Society, Society for Geochemistry and Health, American Institute of Chemists (fellow, member of council, 1972-74), American Society of Biological Chemists, International Society for Cell Biology, American Society for Cell Biology, American Institute of Biological Sciences, American Institute of Animal Science, Society for Developmental Biology, Society for Biological Rhythm, Federation of American Societies for Experimenal Biology, Society for Experimental Biology and Medicine, American Public Health Association, International Society for Research on Civilization Diseases and Vital Substances, International College of Applied Nutrition (fellow), American Institute of Nutrition, American Association for Cancer Research, American Association for the Advancement of Science (fellow), History of Science Society, New York Academy of Sciences, Washington Academy of Sciences (fellow), Society for International Development, Association for the Advancement of Slavic Studies, Czechoslovak Society of Arts and Science in America (co-founder; director at large, 1962—; vice-president, 1964—), Intercontinental Biographical Association (fellow), Sigma Xi, Phi Kappa Phi, Delta Tau Kappa, Cosmos Club (Washington, D.C.).

WRITINGS: Czechoslovakia and its Arts and Sciences: A Selective Bibliography in the Western European Languages, Mouton & Co., 1964; (with Zdenek Hruban) *Microbodies and Related Particles,* Academic Press, 1969.

Editor: *The Czechoslovak Contribution to World Culture,* Mouton & Co., 1964; *Czechoslovakia Past and Present,* Mouton & Co., Volume I: *Political, International, Social and Economic Aspects,* Volume II: *Essays on the Arts and Sciences,* 1968; (and contributor) *Enzyme Synthesis and Degradation in Mammalian Systems,* Karger, 1971; (and contributor) *Food, Nutrition, and Health,* Karger, 1973; *Man, Food, and Nutrition: Strategies and Technological Measures for Alleviating the World Food Problem,* CRC Press, 1973.

Contributor: A. A. Albanese, editor, *Newer Methods of Nutritional Biochemistry,* Academic Press, 1963; Catherine E. Forest Weber and George Weber, editors, *Advances in Enzyme Regulation,* Volume II, Pergamon, 1964; F. Homburger, editor, *Progress in Experimental Tumor Research,* Volume X, Karger, 1968; *Handbook of Biochemistry,* CRC Press, 1968, 2nd edition, 1970; Anthony San Pietro, editor, *Regulatory Mechanisms for Protein Synthesis in Mammalian Cells,* Academic Press, 1968; P. L. Horecky, editor, *East Central Europe: A Guide to Basic Publications,* University of Chicago Press, 1969.

Compiler of "Critical Bibliography of the History of Science and Its Cultural Influences" for *Isis* (quarterly of History of Science Society). Writer of research reports; contributor to more than fifteen journals, mainly scientific. Abstractor and translator, *Chemical Abstracts,* 1958—. Chaiman of publications committee, Czechoslovak Society

of Arts and Sciences in America, and editor of congress proceedings. Co-editor, *Journal of Interdisciplinary Cycle Research,* 1969—, member of editorial board, *The Journal of Applied Nutrition,* 1970—, member of editorial advisory board of American Biographical Institute, 1971—.

WORK IN PROGRESS: A treatise on comparative animal nutrition for Karger; a handbook of nutrition covering human, animal, plant, and microbial nutrition; and a bibliography of reviews relating to the world food problem, both for CRC Press.

BIOGRAPHICAL/CRITICAL SOURCES: The Czechoslovak Contribution to World Culture, Mouton & Co., 1964.

* * *

REDDAWAY, W(illiam) Brian 1913-
(Academic Investor)

PERSONAL: Born January 8, 1913, in Cambridge, England; son of William Fiddian (a lecturer at Cambridge University) and Kate (Sills) Reddaway; married Barbara Augusta Bennett, September 17, 1938; children: Peter B., Stewart F., Lawrence N., Jacqueline F. *Education:* King's College, Cambridge, B.A., 1934, M.A., 1938. *Religion:* Church of England. *Home:* 4 Adams Rd., Cambridge, England. *Office:* Economics Building, Cambridge University, Sidgwick Ave., Cambridge, England.

CAREER: University of Melbourne, Melbourne, Australia, research fellow in economics, 1936-37; Cambridge University, Cambridge, England, official fellow of Clare College, 1938—, university lecturer in economics, 1939-55, director of university department of applied economics, 1955-70, university reader in applied economics, 1957-65, professor of political economy, 1969—. Visiting lecturer, Economic Development Institute, 1966-67. Board of Trade (government), London, England, chief statistician, 1940-47. Economic advisor to Organization for European Economic Cooperation, Paris, France, 1951-52; visiting economist, Center for International Studies, New Delhi, India, 1959-60; member of international commission of experts, European Coal and Steel Community, 1953; member, Royal Commission on the Press, 1961-62, and National Board for Prices and Incomes, 1967-71. *Member:* Royal Economic Society, Royal Statistical Society. *Awards, honors:* Adam Smith Prize, Cambridge University, 1935, for *Russian Financial System.*

WRITINGS: Russian Financial System, Macmillan, 1935; *Economics of a Declining Population,* Allen & Unwin, 1939; (with C. F. Carter and Richard Stone) *Measurement of Production Movements,* Cambridge University Press, 1949; *Development of the Indian Economy,* Irwin, 1962; (contributor) LeKachman, editor, *Keynes: General Theory Reports of Three Decades,* St. Martin's, 1964; *Effects of United Kingdom Direct Investment Overseas,* Cambridge University Press, Volume I: *Interim Report,* 1967, Volume II: *Final Report,* 1968; *Effect of the Selective Employment Tax,* Cambridge University Press, 1973. Contributor to economic journals in England, Australia, India, Italy, Argentina, Pakistan, and France. Editor, *London and Cambridge Economic Bulletin,* 1949—.

WORK IN PROGRESS: Research in applied economics.

SIDELIGHTS: Reddaway's travels in more than fifty countries have intensified his interest in international understanding and efforts to raise the incomes of people in underdeveloped countries. He speaks French and German, and reads Spanish.

REED, John R(obert) 1938-

PERSONAL: Born January 24, 1938, in Duluth, Minn.; son of John Sam and Josephine (Zuponcic) Reed; married Ruth Yzenbaard. Education: University of Minnesota, Duluth, B.A., in Music and B.A. in English, 1959; University of Rochester, Ph.D., 1963. Home: 17320 Wildemere, Detroit, Mich. 48221. Office: Department of English, Wayne State University, Detroit, Mich. 48202.

CAREER: University of Cincinnati, Cincinnati, Ohio, instructor in English, 1962-64; University of Connecticut, Storrs, assistant professor of English, 1964-65; Wayne State University, Detroit, Mich., assistant professor, 1965-68, associate professor, 1968-71, professor of English, 1971—. Member: Modern Language Association of America. Awards, honors: Leverhulme fellowship to University of Warwick, 1966-67; Guggenheim fellowship, 1971; Wayne State University faculty grants.

WRITINGS: Old School Ties: The Public Schools in British Literature, Syracuse University Press, 1964; Perception and Design in Tennyson's "Idylls of the King," Ohio University Press, 1970; (contributor) Jerome Mazzaro, editor, Profile of Robert Lowell, C. E. Merrill, 1971; (contributor) Peter Lisca, editor, John Steinbeck, The Grapes of Wrath, Viking (critical edition), 1972; Hercules (poetry), Fiddlehead Poetry Books, 1973; Victorian Conventions, Ohio University Press, 1975. Contributor of articles to Western Humanities Review, Victorian Poetry, English Literary History, Nineteenth-Century Fiction, Dickens Studies Annual, and other periodicals, and poems to Sewanee Review, Poetry, Modern Poetry Studies, and other journals.

WORK IN PROGRESS: Research on the will in nineteenth-century English literature.

AVOCATIONAL INTERESTS: Writing poetry, music (plays trumpet), travel.

*   *   *

REESE, William Lewis 1921-

PERSONAL: Born February 15, 1921, in Jefferson City, Mo.; son of William Lewis (a minister) and Lillian (Fisher) Reese; married Louise Weeks (a librarian), June 11, 1945; children: Claudia, Patricia, William L. III. Education: Drury College, A.B., 1942; University of Chicago, B.D., 1945, Ph.D., 1947; Yale University, postdoctoral study, 1955-56. Religion: Unitarian Universalist. Home: Font Grove Road, Slingerlands, New York 12159. Office: Department of Philosophy, State University of New York, 1400 Washington Ave., Albany, N.Y. 12222.

CAREER: Drake University, Des Moines, Iowa, assistant professor, 1947-49, associate professor of philosophy, 1949-57, head of department, 1954-57; Grinnell College, Grinnell, Iowa, associate professor of philosophy, 1957-60; University of Delaware, Newark, professor of philosophy and chairman of department, 1960-67, H. Rodney Sharp Professor of Philosophy, 1965-68; State University of New York, Albany, professor of philosophy, 1967—, chairman of department, 1968—. Iowa State University, visiting professor, 1958; University of the Pacific, Tully Cleon Knoles lecturer, 1962. President and member of board of governors, Metaphilosophy Foundation, Inc. Member: Metaphysical Society of America (secretary-treasurer, 1962-65), American Philosphical Association, American Association of University Professors.

WRITINGS: (Contributor) Studies in C. S. Peirce, Har-

vard University Press, 1952; (with Charles Hartshorne) Philosophers Speak of God, University of Chicago Press, 1953; The Ascent from Below, Houghton, 1959; (general editor) Philosophy of Science, Volumes I-II, Interscience, 1963; (contributing editor) Philosophical Interrogations, Holt, 1964; (editor with Eugene Freeman) Process and Divinity: The Hartshorne Festschrift, Open Court, 1964; (contributor) Business and the Humanities: A Symposium, Humanities Center for Liberal Education, 1965; (general editor) Philosophy of Science, Springer-Verlag, 1967. Contributor to Saturday Review and to philosophical journals.

WORK IN PROGRESS: Additional volumes in philosophy and the philosophy of science.

SIDELIGHTS: Reese has some knowledge of French and Spanish.

*   *   *

REGALADO, Nancy Freeman 1935-

PERSONAL: Born June 8, 1935, in Boston, Mass.; daughter of Norman Easton (a surgeon) and Charlotte (Hume) Freeman; married Antonio Regalado (a professor of Spanish), August 27, 1960. Education: Smith College, junior year in France, 1955-56; Wellesley College, B.A., 1957; Yale University, Ph.D., 1966. Home: 100 Bleecker St., 7D, New York, N.Y. 10012. Office: Department of French, New York University, 19 University Place, New York, N.Y. 10003.

CAREER: Yale University, New Haven, Conn., assistant in instruction, 1958-62, acting instructor, 1962-65; Wesleyan University, Middletown, Conn., instructor, 1965-66, assistant professor of Romance languages, 1966-67. New York University, New York, associate professor of French. Member: Phi Beta Kappa.

WRITINGS: (With Michel Beaujour) RSVP Invitation a Ecrire, Harcourt, 1965; Poetic Patterns in Rutebeuf: A Study in Non-Courtly Poetic Modes of the Thirteenth Century, Yale University Press, 1970.

*   *   *

REGAN, Robert (Charles) 1930-

PERSONAL: Born March 13, 1930, in Indianapolis, Ind.; son of Francis Bernard (a salesman) and Alma (McBride) Regan; married Carole Bennett, July 23, 1960; children: Christopher, Amelia and Alison (twins). Education: Centenary College, B.A., 1951; Harvard University, M.A., 1952; University of California, Berkeley, Ph.D., 1965. Politics: Democrat. Religion: Episcopal. Home: 502 Merwyn Rd., Narberth, Pa. 19072. Office: Department of English, University of Pennsylvania, Philadelphia, Pa. 19174.

CAREER: Centenary College, Shreveport, La., instructor in English, 1956-57; University of Virginia, Charlottesville, assistant professor of English, 1963-67; University of Montpellier, France, Fulbright lecturer in English, 1967-68; University of Pennsylvania, Philadelphia, associate professor of English, 1968—. Military service: U.S. Naval Reserve, 1953-56, 1961-62; became lieutenant commander. Member: American Studies Association, Modern Language Association of America, American Association of University Professors.

WRITINGS: Unpromising Heroes: Mark Twain and His Characters, University of California Press, 1966; (editor) Poe: A Collection of Critical Essays, Prentice-Hall, 1967. Managing editor, American Quarterly, 1969-71.

WORK IN PROGRESS: Studies on nineteenth-century American poets and their audiences, hopefully leading to a book concentrating on Emily Dickinson, F. G. Tuckerman, and Jones Very; preparing an edition of Mark Twain's shorter travel writings, for publication by University of California Press, 1976.

* * *

REICHENBERGER, Arnold G(ottfried) 1903-

PERSONAL: Born March 2, 1903, in Karlsruhe, Germany, came to U.S. in 1939, naturalized citizen, 1946; son of Sigmund and Selma (Kahn) Reichenberger; married Nella-Lucretia Grigoropol, August 25, 1930. *Education:* Attended Universities of Heidelberg, Munich, and Berlin, 1921-25; University of Heidelberg, Dr. Phil. (classics), 1931; Ohio State University, Ph.D. (Romance languages), 1946. *Home:* 3521 Woodcrest Ave., Newtown Square, Pa. 19073. *Office:* 521 Williams Hall, University of Pennsylvania, Philadelphia, Pa. 19174.

CAREER: Teacher in state and private schools in Germany, 1926-33; University of Milan, Milan, Italy, reader in German, 1934-38; New School for Social Research, New York, N.Y., associate professor of modern languages, 1939-40; Capital University, Columbus, Ohio, instructor in German and philosophy, 1940-42; Ohio State University, Columbus, assistant instructor, later instructor, 1942-46; University of Pennsylvania, Philadelphia, 1946—, began as instructor, professor of Romance languages, 1961-73, professor emeritus, 1973—, chairman of department, 1965-67. Consultant to Hispanic Society of America, 1973-75.

MEMBER: International Association of Modern Language and Literature, Associacion Internacional de Hispanistas, American Association of Teachers of Spanish and Portuguese, Modern Language Association of America, American Association of Teachers of Italian, Modern Humanities Research Association, Renaissance Society of America, American Comparative Literature Association, American Association of University Professors, Hispanic Society of America. *Awards, honors:* Fulbright grant to University of Munich, 1960-61; American Council of Learned Societies grant, 1962; National Endowment for the Humanities senior fellowship, 1968-69.

WRITINGS: (Editor) Luis Velez de Guevara, *El Embuste Acreditado*, Universidad de Granada, 1956; (editor) Lope de Vega, *Carlos V en Francia*, University of Pennsylvania Press, 1962; (editor with Augusta E. Foley) Lope de Vega, *El primero Benavides*, University of Pennsylvania Press, 1973. Contributor to *Hispanic Review* and *Comparative Literature*. Co-editor, *Hispanic Review*, 1946-73, honorary editor, 1973—. Member of editorial board, *Criticism*, *Iberoromania*, and *Tamesis Books*.

WORK IN PROGRESS: A descriptive catalogue of the Dramatic Manuscripts, 1500-1750, in the library of the Hispanic Society of America.

SIDELIGHTS: Reichenberger is fluent, in varying degrees, in German, Spanish, Italian, French, Latin, and Greek.

* * *

REID, B(enjamin) L(awrence) 1918-

PERSONAL: Born May 3, 1918, in Louisville, Ky.; son of Isaac Errett (a minister) and Margaret (Lawrence) Reid; married Joan Davidson (a critic of literature and art), July 15, 1942; children: Jane Lawrence (Mrs. Michael A. Mc-

Anulty), Colin Way. *Education:* University of Louisville, A.B., 1943; Columbia University, A.M., 1951; University of Virginia, Ph.D., 1957. *Politics:* Democrat. *Religion:* Protestant. *Home:* 1 Greenwood Lane, South Hadley, Mass. *Office:* Mount Holyoke College, South Hadley, Mass.

CAREER: Instructor in English at Iowa State College (now University) of Science and Technology, Ames, 1946-48, and Smith College, Northampton, Mass., 1948-51; Sweet Briar College, Sweet Briar, Va., instructor, 1951-56, assistant professor of English, 1956-57; Mount Holyoke College, South Hadley, Mass., assistant professor, 1957-59, associate professor, 1959-63, professor, 1963-70, Andrew W. Mellon professor of English, 1970—. Amherst College, visiting professor, 1965-66. *Member:* Modern Language Association of America, American Association of University Professors. *Awards, honors:* Fulbright research grant to England, 1963-64; American Council of Learned Societies fellowship, 1966-67; Pulitzer Prize for biography, 1969, for *The Man from New York: John Quinn and his Friends*; D.H.L. from University of Louisville, 1970; National Endowment for the Humanites, senior fellowship, 1971-72.

WRITINGS: Art by Subtraction: A Dissenting Opinion of Gertrude Stein, University of Oklahoma Press, 1958; *William Butler Yeats: The Lyric of Tragedy*, University of Oklahoma Press, 1961; *The Man from New York: John Quinn and his Friends*, Oxford University Press, 1968; *The Long Boy and Others: Eighteenth Century Studies*, University of Georgia Press, 1969; *Tragic Occasions: Essays on Several Forms*, Kennikat, 1971. Contributor of essays to *Kenyon Review, Hudson Review, Yale Review*, and other literary journals; also contributor of a few short stories, verse, reviews, and a short experimental play to those and other journals. Contributing editor, *Massachusetts Review*; member of editorial board, *Sewanee Review*.

AVOCATIONAL INTERESTS: Old cars and old furniture, tennis, gardening, amateur carpentry.

* * *

REID, H. 1925-

PERSONAL: Born March 24, 1925, in Norfolk, Va.; son of Howard (a federal finance officer) and Kathleen (Stiff) Reid; married Virginia Ezell (a laboratory technologist), August 7, 1949. *Education:* Old Dominion College (now University), A.A., 1944; attended Elon College, 1944-45; College of William and Mary, B.A., 1946. *Politics:* Conservative. *Religion:* Episcopalian. *Office: Newport News Times-Herald*, Newport News, Va. 23607.

CAREER: On editorial staff of newspapers in Norfolk, Va., prior to 1950; Norfolk County (Va.) schools, director of public relations, 1950; *Newport News Times-Herald*, Newport News, Va., editor, 1951—. Free-lance cartoonist and photographer (steam railroads). *Awards, honors:* Virginia Press Association citation for feature, "Wreck of Old 97."

WRITINGS: The Virginian Railway, Kalmbach, 1961; *Extra South*, Starrucca, 1964; *Rails Through Dixie* (photographs by John Krause), Golden West, 1965; *Clinchfield's Old No. 5, Now No. 1 Attraction*, National Railway Historical Society, 1972. Contributor to more than fifteen books in steam railroad field, including those of Lucius Beebe and S. Kip Farrington. Regular contributor to railroad magazines and newspapers, 1941—, including *Trains, New York Times* and *Christian Science Monitor*; also has done popular music commentary for twenty-five years, specializing in big-name bands.

WORK IN PROGRESS: Norfolk and Western; assisting on several other hardcovers, including Michael Koch's *Shay Locomotive*.

SIDELIGHTS: H. Reid writes railroad history in narrative format, viewing history as day to day circumstances, with many days trivial.†

* * *

REID, Timothy E. H. 1936-
(Tim Reid)

PERSONAL: Born February 21, 1936, in Toronto, Ontario, Canada; son of Escott (a professor of political science) and Ruth (Herriot) Reid; married Julyan Fancott (a researcher in anthropology), October 8, 1963. *Education:* Trinity College, University of Toronto, B.A. (honors), 1959; Yale University, M.A., 1960; Christ Church, Oxford, B.Litt., 1966; additional summer study at University of Grenoble, 1955. *Politics:* Liberal. *Home:* 70 Belsize Dr., Toronto, Ontario, Canada. *Office:* Department of Economics, York University, Toronto, Ontario, Canada.

CAREER: Hamilton Tiger-Cat Football Club, Hamilton, Ontario, halfback, 1962; Canadian Institute on Public Affairs, Toronto, Ontario, executive secretary, 1962-63; University of Toronto, Toronto, Ontario, instructor in economics, 1963-64; York University, Toronto, Ontario, assistant in office of president and assistant secretary of board of governors, 1963-64, assistant to president, 1964-65, lecturer in economics, 1964—, coordinator of secondary school affairs, and secretary of the faculty of the graduate school, 1965-66. Liberal party candidate in Federal Riding of Danforth (Toronto), 1965.

MEMBER: Canadian Institute of International Affairs, Computer and Data Processing Society of Canada, Liberal Federation of Canada, Company of Young Canadians (interim council member), Canadian Atlantic Co-Ordinating Committee, Exchange for Political Ideas in Canada (treasurer), Policies for Political Action Group (steering committee member), International Teach-In Committee (faculty vice-chairman, 1965), Toronto and District Liberal Association (vice-president). *Awards, honors:* Rhodes scholar at Oxford University, 1960-62.

WRITINGS: (Editor) *Economic Planning in a Democratic Society*, University of Toronto Press, 1963; (editor) *Values in Conflict*, University of Toronto Press, 1963; (assistant in editing and publication) *Religion and the University*, University of Toronto Press, 1964; (contributor) John Fotheringham, editor, *Transition: Policies for Social Action*, McClelland & Stewart, 1966; (editor) *Contemporary Canada: Readings in Economics*, Holt, 1969; (under name Tim Reid; editor with wife, Julyan Reid) *Student Power and the Canadian Campus*, Peter Martin Associates, 1969. Contributor of articles and reviews to journals and newspapers. Member of editorial board, Policies for Political Action Group.

WORK IN PROGRESS: Postwar Economic Policy in Ontario; and *The Changing Role of Education and Leisure*.

AVOCATIONAL INTERESTS: Skiing, tennis, squash, swimming, walking.†

* * *

REIDY, John Patrick 1930-

PERSONAL: Born December 25, 1930, in Chicago, Ill.; son of Jeremiah James (a butcher) and Margaret (Kilty)

Reidy; married Mary Bridget Butterfield, June 30, 1962; children: Brigid Ann, Erin Elizabeth. *Education:* Loyola University, Chicago, Ill., B.S., 1953; Northwestern University, graduate study, 1958-60. *Politics:* Democrat. *Religion:* Roman Catholic.

CAREER: State of Illinois, Springfield, governor's speech writer, 1961-63, public information administrator and administrative assistant to the director, Department of Mental Health, 1963-66, supervisor of Division of Tourism, Chicago, 1966; self-employed as political campaign manager and free-lance writer, 1966—. *Military service:* U.S. Army, 1953-55.

WRITINGS: Zone Mental Health Centers: The Illinois Concept, C. C Thomas, 1964; *The True Story of John Fitzgerald Kennedy*, Children's Press, 1967; *John F. Kennedy*, Children's Press, 1967; (with Norman Richards) *Leonard Bernstein*, Children's Press, 1967.†

* * *

REIFF, Robert (Frank) 1918-

PERSONAL: Surname is pronounced Reef; born January 23, 1918, in Rochester, N.Y.; son of Charles Henry and Mabel (Doel) Reiff; married Helen Hayslette (a claims representative in Social Security office), February 8, 1925. *Education:* University of Rochester, A.B., 1941; Columbia University, Ph.D., 1961; studied art with Boardman Robinson and Hans Hofmann. *Politics:* Independent Democrat. *Religion:* Episcopalian. *Home:* 20 Gorham Lane, Middlebury, Vt. 05753. *Office:* Middlebury College, Middlebury, Vt. 05753.

CAREER: Muhlenburg College, Allentown, Pa., instructor, 1947-49; Oberlin College, Oberlin, Ohio, instructor, 1950-54; University of Chicago, Chicago, Ill., assistant professor, 1954-55; St. Cloud State College, St. Cloud, Minn., associate professor, 1955-57; Middlebury College, Middlebury, Vt., associate professor, 1956-73, professor of art history and chairman of department, 1973—. Professional painter, with one-man shows at Santa Barbara Museum of Art, De Young Museum, San Francisco, and Pasadena Art Institute, 1944, University of Virginia, Oberlin College, and Rochester Memorial Art Gallery; work shown in group exhibitions. Trustee of Sheldon Museum, Middlebury. *Military service:* U.S. Army Air Forces, 1942-46. *Member:* College Art Association, American Association of University Professors. *Awards, honors:* Belgian-American Educational Foundation traveling scholarship, 1952.

WRITINGS: Indian Miniatures: The Rajput Painters, Tuttle, 1959, republished in collection (other authors, William Lillys and Emil Esin), *Oriental Miniatures; Persian, Indian, Turkish*, Tuttle, 1965.

WORK IN PROGRESS: Compiling an anthology of the writings of architects on architecture; one hundred articles on modern subjects for a dictionary of art, edited by Bernard Myers for McGraw.

SIDELIGHTS: Reiff traveled in the Far East on leave from Middlebury College, 1966, and also has traveled extensively in Europe, Egypt, Turkey.

* * *

REISCHAUER, Edwin O(ldfather) 1910-

PERSONAL: Born October 15, 1910, in Tokyo, Japan; son of August Karl (a missionary) and Helen (Oldfather) Reischauer; married Adrienne Danton, 1935; married second wife, Haru Matsukata, February 4, 1956; children: (first marriage) Ann (Mrs. Steven Heinemann), Robert D., Joan. *Education:* Oberlin College, A.B., 1931; Harvard University, M.A., 1932, Ph.D., 1939; studied at University of Paris, 1933-35, at universities in Japan, 1935-37. *Religion:* Unitarian Universalist. *Home:* 863 Concord Ave., Belmont, Mass. *Office:* 1737 Cambridge St., Cambridge, Mass.

CAREER: Harvard University, Cambridge, Mass., instructor, 1938-42; in Washington, D.C., as senior research analyst, War Department, 1942-43, and chairman of Japan-Korea Secretariat and special assistant to director of Office of Far Eastern Affairs, Department of State, 1945-46; Harvard University, associate professor, 1946-50, professor of Far Eastern languages, 1950-61; director of Harvard-Yenching Institute, 1956-61; U.S. Ambassador to Japan, 1961-66; Harvard University, Cambridge, Mass., university professor, 1966—, chairman of board of Harvard-Yenching Institute, 1969—. *Military service:* U.S. Army, Military Intelligence, 1943-45; became lieutenant colonel; received Legion of Merit. *Member:* Association for Asian Studies (president, 1955-56), American Historical Association, Japan Society (Boston and New York), Phi Beta Kappa. *Awards, honors:* Honorary doctorates from Nihon University and Rikkyo University (both Japan), University of Maryland, Harvard University, University of Michigan, Yale University, Brandeis University, and Oberlin College; received Grand Cordon of the Rising Sun (Japan).

WRITINGS: (Compiler with Elisseeff and Yosihash) *Elementary Japanese for University Students*, two volumes, Harvard University Press, 1941, 2nd edition, 1943; (compiler with Elisseeff) *Selected Japanese Texts for University Students*, three volumes, Harvard University Press, 1942-47; (compiler with others) *Elementary Japanese for College Students*, Harvard University Press, 1944; *Japan, Past and Present*, Knopf, 1946, 3rd edition, 1964; *The United States and Japan*, Harvard University Press, 1950, 3rd edition, 1965; (editor and translator with Joseph Yamagiwai) *Translations for Early Japanese Literature*, Harvard University Press, 1951; (with others) *Japan and America Today* (symposium), Stanford University Press, 1953; *Wanted: An Asian Policy*, Knopf, 1955; (translator) Ennin, *Diary: The Record of a Pilgrimage to China in Search of the Law*, Ronald, 1955; *Ennin's Travels in T'ang China*, Ronald, 1955.

(With J. K. Fairbank) *East Asia: The Great Tradition*, Houghton, 1960; (with Fairbank and Craig) *East Asia: The Modern Transformation*, Houghton, 1965; *Beyond Vietnam: The United States and Asia*, Knopf, 1967; *Japan: The Story of a Nation*, Knopf, 1970, revised edition, 1974; (with Fairbank and Craig) *East Asia: Tradition and Transformation*, Houghton, 1973; *Toward the Twenty-First Century: Education for a Changing World*, Knopf, 1973.

*   *   *

REITAN, E(arl) A(aron)   1925-

PERSONAL: Surname is pronounced *Rye*-tan; born May 3, 1925, in Grove City, Minn.; son of Ernest A. (a banker) and Caren Helene (Jensen) Reitan; married Carol Anne Rylander, June 23, 1956; children: Julia, Thomas. *Education:* Concordia College, Moorhead, Minn., B.A., 1948; University of Illinois, M.A., 1950, Ph.D., 1954. *Politics:* Independent. *Religion:* Lutheran. *Home:* 403 Marian Ave., Normal, Ill. 61761.

CAREER: Pacific Lutheran University, Tacoma, Wash., assistant professor of history, 1951-52; Illinois State University, Normal 1954—, started as instructor, associate professor, 1958-65, professor of history, 1965—. Visiting professor, University of Illinois, 1966. *Military service:* U.S. Army, 1943-46. *Member:* American Historical Association, American Association of University Professors, British Historical Association, Conference on British Studies. *Awards, honors:* Eli Lilly fellow, 1963; Newberry Library fellow, 1966.

WRITINGS: (Editor) *George III: Tyrant or Constitutional Monarch?*, Heath, 1965. Contributor to *The Historical Journal*.

WORK IN PROGRESS: Economical reform in England, 1799-92.

*   *   *

REMAK, Henry H. H.   1916-

PERSONAL: Born July 27, 1916, in Berlin, Germany; son of John H. I. (an engineer) and Hedwig (Salz) Remak; came to United States, 1936, naturalized, 1943; married Ingrid Grunfeld, August 3, 1946; children: Roy Andrew, Steven Bruce, Renee June, Ronald Frank. *Education:* University of Bordeaux, Certificat d'Etudes Francaises, 1934; University of Montpellier, Licencie-es-Lettres, 1936; Indiana University, M.A., 1937; University of Chicago, Ph.D., 1947. *Politics:* Democrat. *Religion:* Jewish. *Home:* 1212 Maxwell Lane, Bloomington, Ind. 47403.

CAREER: Indiana University Extension Center, Indianapolis, lecturer in German and Spanish, 1939-43; U.S. Office of Censorship, San Juan, Puerto Rico, censor of foreign-language mail, 1943-44; Indiana University, Bloomington, instructor, 1946-48, assistant professor, 1948-55, associate professor, 1955-60, professor of German, 1960-64, professor of German and comparative literature, 1964—, acting chairman of department of comparative literature for four periods during 1954-63, acting chairman of department of German, 1962, chairman, west European studies, 1966-69, vice-chancellor and dean of faculty, 1969—. Visiting professor, Middlebury College, summers, 1958, 1960, and director of German summer school, 1967—; visiting professor, University of Wisconsin, summer, 1964. Fulbright professor at University of Lille, 1962-63, at University of Hamburg, 1967. *Military service:* U.S. Merchant Marine, 1944-46, serving in Pacific and Atlantic Theaters; became ensign.

MEMBER: American Association of Teachers of German (president of Indiana chapter), Modern Language Association of America (discussion group chairman, 1948, 1959, 1965), International Comparative Literature Association (member of executive council, 1964-67), International Association of University Professors and Lecturers (member of council), American Association of University Professors (member of national council; president of Indiana University chapter), Academie des Sciences, Beaux-Arts et Lettres (Marseille; corresponding member). *Awards, honors:* Herman F. Lieber Award for distinguished teaching, 1962; Guggenheim fellow, 1967-68; Litt.D., University of Lille, 1973.

WRITINGS: (Editor with E. D. Seeber) *Oeuvres de Charles-Michel Campion, Poete Marseillais du Dix-Huitieme Siecle*, Indiana University Press, 1945; (with Horst Frenz, N. P. Stallknecht, and others) *Comparative Literature: Method and Perspective*, Southern Illinois University Press, 1961; (with Helmut Rehder and others) *Symbolism in German Literature*, University of Texas Press, 1965. Contributor to *Business Horizons* and to language and literature journals in America, England, and Germany. *Yearbook of Comparative and General Literature*, associate editor (and contributor), 1961-65, editor, 1965—; *German Quarterly*, associate editor, 1958-62, review editor, 1961-62; member of editorial board, *PMLA*, 1966—; consulting editor in German, Blaisdell/Ginn Publishing Co., 1962—.

SIDELIGHTS: Aside from German, Remak also speaks, reads, and writes Spanish, and has reading competency in Dutch, Danish, Norwegian, Swedish, Italian, and Portuguese. *Avocational interests:* Covered bridges, passenger railroads, islands.†

* * *

REYNOLDS, Marie E. 1912-

PERSONAL: Born June 16, 1912, in Passaic, N.J.; daughter of Patrick A. and Mary (Tracey) Reynolds. *Education:* Syracuse University, B.S. and B.A., 1935; New York University, M.A., 1952, additional summer study, 1965, 1966. *Politics:* Republican. *Religion:* Roman Catholic. *Home:* 360 Main St., Johnson City, N.Y. 13790. *Office:* Johnson City Central School District, 666 Reynolds Rd., Johnson City, N.Y. 13790.

CAREER: Johnson City (N.Y.) Central School District, teacher, 1935-47, chairman of business education department, 1947-58, pupil personnel services administrator, 1958—. President, Broome County Committee on Alcoholism, 1969-70; charter secretary, Greater Triple Cities Multiple Sclerosis Society, 1965; member of board of directors, Broome County Social Planning Board, 1969—; director, Central New York School Study Council, 1972—. *Member:* National Education Association (life member), American Personnel and Guidance Association (life member), Administrative Management Society, New York State Teachers Association, Delta Kappa Gamma, Catholic Woman's Club of Binghamton (president), Altrusa. *Awards, honors:* Diamond Award Key, Administrative Management Society, 1966.

WRITINGS: (With E. K. Felter) *Basic Clerical Practice*, 2nd edition, Gregg Publishing Division, McGraw, 1959.

* * *

RHEIN, Francis Bayard 1915-

PERSONAL: Born January 5, 1915, in Philadelphia, Pa.; son of John H. W. (a physician) and Elizabeth (Kane) Rhein; married Jane Foster, September 12, 1942; children: Patricia Bayard, Elizabeth Kane, Peter Van Rensselear, Jane. *Education:* University of Virginia, B.S., 1942; Protestant Episcopal Theological Seminary in Virginia, M.Div., 1942.

CAREER: The Protestant Episcopal Church, ordained priest, 1942; Emmanuel Church, Harrisonburg, Va., rector, 1955-56; Madison College, Harrisonburg, Va., associate professor of Biblical literature and philosophy, 1956-65. *Military service:* U.S. Naval Reserve, chaplain, 1943-46. *Awards, honors:* S.T.M., Protestant Episcopal Seminary in Virginia, 1971.

WRITINGS: An Analytical Approach to the New Testament, M. G. Barron, 1965, revised edition published as *Understanding the New Testament*, 1974. *Barron's Simplified Approach to the New Testament*, M. G. Barron, 1967.

SIDELIGHTS: Rhein is competent in French and German.

RHODE, Robert B(artlett) 1916-

PERSONAL: Born October 24, 1916, in Ranchester, Wyo.; son of Oliver Guy and Ruth (Lewis) Rhode; married Katharine Fedrizzi, October 31, 1948; children: Loretta, Robert Gary. *Education:* University of Wyoming, B.A., 1938; University of Denver, M.A., 1952. *Home:* 2015 Grape Ave., Boulder, Colo. 80302. *Office:* University of Colorado, Boulder, Colo. 80302.

CAREER: Newspaperman in Sheridan, Wyo., 1939, Cheyenne, Wyo., 1939-42; *Rock Springs Rocket*, Rock Springs, Wyo., managing editor, 1946-48; University of Denver, Denver, Colo., assistant professor of journalism, 1948-53; University of Southern California, Los Angeles, assistant professor of journalism, 1953-55; University of Colorado, Boulder, assistant professor of journalism, 1955—. Part-time or summer employee of *Rocky Mountain News, Denver Post, Honolulu Advertiser*, and Station KLZ, Denver. Fulbright lecturer in Australia, 1961. *Military service:* U.S. Army, 1942-46; became captian. *Member:* Association for Education in Journalism, National Press Photographers Association, Colorado Press Photographers Association, Society of Professional Journalists.

WRITINGS: Press Photography: Reporting with a Camera, Macmillan, 1961; *Introduction to Photography*, Macmillan, 1965, 3rd edition, 1975.

WORK IN PROGRESS: Documentary still-photography; development of mining camp journalism in Colorado.

* * *

RHODES, Hari 1932-

PERSONAL: Born April 10, 1932, in Cincinnati, Ohio; stepson of Bob Carlos Bonner and son of Bessie (Nelson) Bonner; married Mimi Christil Kline; stepchildren: Mike Segura. *Education:* University of Cincinnati, attended Conservatory of Music. *Residence:* Los Angeles, Calif.

CAREER: Actor; member of cast of Columbia Broadcasting System weekly series, "Daktari," 1966-68; member of cast of National Broadcasting Company series, "The Bold Ones," 1969-71. Roles in various movies include "Satan Bug," 1965, "Mirage," 1965, "Taffy and the Jungle," 1965, "Blindfold," 1966, "Conquest of Planet of the Apes," 1972, "Detroit 9000," 1973. *Military service:* U.S. Marine Corps, 1947-52; became sergeant. *Member:* Montford Point Marines Association.

WRITINGS: A Chosen Few, Bantam, 1965. Also author of a book on black nationalism, *Harambee*, and a book about Hollywood, *Land of Odds*, both as yet unpublished.

AVOCATIONAL INTERESTS: Martial arts (judo and karate).

BIOGRAPHICAL/CRITICAL SOURCES: TV Guide, April 20, 1968.†

* * *

RHYS, J(ohn) Howard W(inslow) 1917-

PERSONAL: Born October 25, 1917, in Montreal, Quebec, Canada; son of John Gabriel (an accountant) and Maude (Stevens) Rhys; married Margaret Moore Taylor (a teacher), September 11, 1954. *Education:* McGill University, B.A., 1939; General Theological Seminary, New York, N.Y., S.T.B., 1944, S.T.M., 1949, Th.D., 1953. *Politics:* Democrat. *Home:* 3 Louisiana Circle, Sewanee, Tenn. 37375. *Office:* School of Theology, University of the South, Sewanee, Tenn.

CAREER: Episcopal clergyman. Assistant or vicar at churches in Montreal, Quebec, 1942-43, Black Mountain, N.C., 1944-48, Trenton, N.J., 1949-51; St. Paul's Parish, Washington, D.C., priest-in-charge, 1951-53; University of the South, School of Theology, Sewanee, Tenn., assistant professor, 1953-55, associate professor, 1955-62, professor of New Testament, 1962—. Also has taught college courses in archaeology, Greek comedy, Greek orators, and Greek tragedy. Member of board, School of Pastoral Care, Whitinsville, Mass. Member: Society of Biblical Literature, American Academy of Religion, American Association of University Professors. Awards, honors: American Association of Theological Schools research grant.

WRITINGS: The Epistle to the Romans, Macmillan, 1961. Contributor to Hastings' Dictionary of the Bible, new edition, Scribner, 1963. Author of scripts of Bible commentaries. Contributor of articles and reviews to periodicals.

WORK IN PROGRESS: Christian Ministry in the New Testament; a study of the Jewish Christians, a study of the theology of Christian work of healing.

SIDELIGHTS: Rhys speaks French, composes in classical Greek, reads Latin and German, and, laboriously, Hebrew. Avocational interests: Sailing, gardening.†

*   *   *

RICH, Elaine Sommers 1926-

PERSONAL: Born February 8, 1926, in Plevna, Ind.; daughter of Monroe and Effie (Horner) Sommers; married Ronald L. Rich (a chemistry professor), June 14, 1953; children: Jonathan, Andrew, Miriam, Mark. Education: Goshen College, B.A., 1947; Michigan State University, M.A., 1950. Religion: Mennonite. Address: House 348, International Christian University, 10-3 Osawa, 3 chome, Mitaka, Tokyo 181, Japan.

CAREER: Goshen College, Goshen, Ind., instructor in speech and English, 1947-49, 1950-53; Bethel College, North Newton, Kan., instructor in speech, 1966; International Christian University, Tokyo, Japan, lecturer, 1971—. Member: American Association of University Women, Women's International League for Peace and Freedom, World Poetry Society.

WRITINGS: (Editor) Breaking Bread Together, Herald, 1958; Hannah Elizabeth, Harper, 1964; Tomorrow, Tomorrow, Tomorrow, Herald, 1966. Contributor to Poet, Japan Christian Quarterly, and other periodicals.

WORK IN PROGRESS: A book with working title Black Hair.

*   *   *

RICHARDSON, Rupert Norval 1891-

PERSONAL: Born April 28, 1891, in Caddo, Tex.; son of Willis Baker (a stock farmer) and Nannie (Coon) Richardson; married Pauline Mayes (a teacher) December 28, 1915 (died April 28, 1965); children: Rupert N., Jr. Education: Simmons College (now Hardin-Simmons University), A.B., 1912; University of Chicago, Ph.B., 1914; University of Texas, M.A., 1922, Ph.D., 1928. Politics: Democrat. Religion: Baptist. Home: 2220 Simmons, Abilene, Tex. 79601. Office: Hardin-Simmons University, Abilene, Tex. 79601.

CAREER: Principal of high schools in Cisco and Sweetwater, Tex.,1915-17; Hardin-Simmons University, Abilene, Tex., professor of history, 1917—, vice-president of university, 1928-38, executive vice-president, 1938-40, acting president, 1943-45, president, 1945-53, president emeritus, 1953—. Visiting professor at University of Texas, 1931, 1940-41, and summers, and at University of Oklahoma, 1940. Military service: U.S. Army, 1918; became second lieutenant. Member: Organization of American Historians, Southwestern Social Science Association (president, 1937-38), Texas State Historical Association (president, 1969-70), West Texas Historical Association, Texas Philosophical Society (president, 1963-64), Lions International (president, Abilene club, 1935-36; district governor, 1938-39). Awards, honors: Award of Merit, American Association for State and Local History, 1951.

WRITINGS: The Comanche Barrier to South Plains Settlement, Arthur Clark, 1933; (with Carol Coke Rister) The Greater Southwest, Arthur Clark, 1934; Texas, the Lone Star State, Prentice-Hall, 1943, 2nd edition, 1958; Adventuring With a Purpose: Life Story of A. L. Wasson, Naylor, 1952; The Frontier of Northwest Texas, 1846-1876, Arthur Clark, 1963; Colonel House: The Texas Years, Hardin-Simmons University Press, 1964; Famous are Thy Halls: Hardin-Simmons University as I Have Seen It, Hardin-Simmons University Press, 1964; Caddo, Texas: The Biography of a Community, Hardin-Simmons University, 1966; Along Texas Old Forts Trail, Hardin-Simmons University, 1972. Editor, West Texas Historical Association Year Book, 1930—.

WORK IN PROGRESS: A revision of Famous are Thy Halls.

*   *   *

RICHIE, Donald (Steiner) 1924-

PERSONAL: Born April 17, 1924, in Lima, Ohio; son of Kent Hayes and Ona (Steiner) Richie; married Mary Evans (a writer), November, 1961 (divorced, 1965). Education: Attended Antioch College, 1942; Columbia University, B.S., 1953. Home: 802 Tsukiji Residence Tsukiji, 2-chome, 1-2 Chuo-Ku, Tokyo, Japan.

CAREER: Japan Times, Tokyo, film critic, 1955-68; Uni-Japan Film, Tokyo, adviser, 1961-68; New York Museum of Modern Art, New York, N.Y., curator of film, 1968-73; Zokeisha Publications, Tokyo, director, 1973—. Wartime service: U.S. Maritime Service, 1942-45. Member: P.E.N. (Tokyo). Awards, honors: Citation from Japanese government, 1963, 1970; citation from U.S. National Film Critics' Society, 1970.

WRITINGS: The Land and People of Japan, A. & C. Black, 1959; (with J. L. Anderson) The Japanese Film, Grove, 1959; The Japanese Movie: An Illustrated History, Kodansha (England), 1965; The Films of Akira Kurosawa, University of California Press, 1965; Companions of the Holiday, Weatherhill (Tokyo), 1968; George Stevens: An American Romantic, Museum of Modern Art, 1970; Japanese Cinema, Doubleday, 1971; The Inland Sea, Weatherhill, 1971; Ozu: The Man and His Films, University of California Press, 1974. Contributor to film journals.

WORK IN PROGRESS: The Cave of Amaterasu: Essays on Japanese Women, for Art Press; editing The Masters of Japanese Film.

SIDELIGHTS: Richie writes: "I consider biography and reportage to be the two major artistic forms, to be the most demanding and the most satisfying, and to be the most directly meaningful (they and not the novel) to our times." Avocational interests: Music (criticism and composition).

RICKETT, Harold William   1896-

PERSONAL: Born July 30, 1896, in Birmingham, England; came to United States, 1911, naturalized, 1917; son of Edmond William and Alys Maude (Hastilow) Rickett; children: Ann (Mrs. Thomas Wyatt Parker) *Education:* Attended Harvard University, 1913-15; University of Wisconsin, A.B., 1917, A.M., 1920, Ph.D., 1922.

CAREER: University of Wisconsin, Madison, instructor in botany, 1922-24; University of Missouri, Columbia, assistant professor, 1924-28, associate professor of botany, 1928-39; New York Botanical Garden, Bronx, N.Y., assistant bibliographer, 1939-42, bibliographer, 1942-60, senior curator of library, 1960-63, senior botanist in charge of wild flower books, 1963-73. Reed College, visiting professor, 1937-38. Delegate to International Botanical Congresses in Stockholm, Paris, Montreal. *Military service:* U.S. Army Reserve, Infantry, 1917-19; became second lieutenant. *Member:* Botanical Society of America, Phi Beta Kappa, Torrey Botanical Club. *Awards, honors:* National Science Foundation grant to Utrecht and London, 1958; Distinguished Service Awards from New York Botanical Garden, for wildflower books.

WRITINGS: (With William J. Robbins) *Botany: A Textbook for Colleges*, Van Nostrand, 1929, 3rd edition, 1939; (contributor of illustrations) *Flora of Columbia, Missouri*, University of Missouri, 1931; (with E. Naylor) *Instructions for Laboratory Work in General Botany*, Van Nostrand, 1935, 2nd edition, 1939; (editor) Kenneth K. MacKenzie, *North American Cariceae*, New York Botanical Garden, 1940; *The Green Earth: An Invitation to Botany*, Cattell, 1943, 2nd edition, Ronald, 1946; (with B. O. Dodge and P. P. Pirone) *Diseases and Pests of Ornamental Plants*, Cattell, 1943, 3rd edition, Ronald, 1960; *The Royal Botanical Expedition to New Spain*, Chronica Botanica, 1947; (editor and author of introduction) *Wild Flowers of America*, Crown, 1953; *Botany for Gardeners*, Macmillan, 1957; *The New Field Book of American Wild Flowers*, Putnam, 1963; *The Odyssey Book of American Wildflowers*, Odyssey, 1964.

Wild Flowers of the United States, McGraw, for New York Botanical Garden, Volume 1: *The Northeastern States*, 1966, Volume II: *The Southeastern States*, 1967, Volume III: *Texas*, 1969; Volume IV: *The Southwestern States*, 1970, Volume V: *The Northwestern States*, 1972, Volume VI: *The Central Mountains and Plains*, three parts, 1974, *Index*, 1975. Contributor to encyclopedias and periodicals. Sometime editor of *International Code of Botanical Nomenclature*; editor of various technical series.

SIDELIGHTS: Rickett has traveled frequently to Europe for study of botanical nomenclature. He reads French, German, Spanish, classical Latin, and Greek. *Avocational interests:* Bookbinding, hand weaving, photography, music.

*   *   *

RICKMAN, H(ans) P(eter)   1918-

PERSONAL: Born November 11, 1918, in Prague, Czechoslovakia; son of Ernst (a lawyer) and Grete (Wollin) Weisskopf; married Muriel Edith Taylor, May 5, 1947. *Education:* Educated in Czechoslovakia, 1924-38 (with one year at a university); University of London, B.A. (honors), 1941, M.A., 1948; New College, Oxford, D. Phil., 1943. *Home:* 18 Sheridan Gardens, Kenton, Middlesex, England. *Office:* Department of Social Sciences and Humanities, City University, London, England.

CAREER: University of Hull, Hull, England, staff tutor in philosophy and psychology, 1949-61; City University (formerly Northampton College of Advanced Technology), London, England, senior lecturer in philosophy, 1961-67, reader in philosophy, 1967—. *Military service:* British Army, intelligence and education posts, 1944-47. *Member:* Aristotelian Society, Royal Institute of Philosophy, British Sociological Assocation, Association of University Teachers.

WRITINGS: Meaning in History: Dilthey's Thought on History and Society, Allen & Unwin, 1961, published as *Pattern and Meaning in History*, Harper, 1962; *Preface to Philosophy*, Schenkman, 1964; *Living With Technology*, Zenith, 1966; *Understanding and the Human Studies*, Heinemann, 1967. Contributor to *Encyclopedia of Philosophy*, 1967; *Symposium Volume on VICO*, 1969. Also contributor of more than twenty articles to *Fortnightly, Hibbert Journal, German Life and Letters, British Journal of Sociology*, and other journals.

WORK IN PROGRESS: Living with Ideas.†

*   *   *

RIESS, Walter   1925-

PERSONAL: Born December 24, 1925, in Corunna, Ind.; son of Oswald (a Lutheran pastor) and Eleanor (koch) Riess; married Lois Marie Sattelmeier, August 7, 1951; children: Judy, Mary, Kathy. *Education:* Concordia College, Milwaukee, Wis., student, 1945; Concordia Seminary, St. Louis, Mo., B.D., 1954. *Home:* 12530 Elaine Dr., St. Louis, Mo. 63131.

CAREER: Ordained to Lutheran ministry, 1950; editor, *Detroit Lutheran*, 1951; minister in Ann Arbor, Mich., 1952; editor, "High School Discussion Guides," Lutheran Church, 1953-60; editor of *This Day* and *Spirit* (magazines), 1960-66.

*WRITINGS—*All published by Concordia: *Teen-Ager, Christ Is for You*, 1957; *Teen-Ager, the Bible Speaks to You*, 1959; *For You, Teen-Ager, In Love*, 1960; *Teen-Ager, Your Church Is for You*, 1961; *Teen-Ager, Christ's Love Will Make You Live*, 1962; *The Teen-Ager You're Dating*, 1964; *Prayers for a Time of Crisis*, 1966; *Before They Start to Leave*, 1967; *Christ's Love Will Make You Live*, 1973.†

*   *   *

RIGBY, Paul H(erbert)   1924-

PERSONAL: Born August 6, 1924, in Humboldt, Ariz.; son of John Herbert (a mining engineer) and Grace (Dailey) Rigby; married Dorothy Ann Sall, December 18, 1954; children: Peter Nathan, Mark Herbert. *Education:* University of Texas, B.B.A., 1945, M.B.A., 1948, Ph.D., 1952. *Home:* 131 Legion Lane, State College, Pa. 16801. *Office:* Pennsylvania State University, 801 Business Administration Bldg., University Park, Pa. 16802.

CAREER: U.S. Office of Price Stabilization, senior price economist, regional office, Seattle, Wash., 1951-52; University of Alabama, University, assistant professor of marketing and research associate of Bureau of Business Research, 1952-54; Georgia State College (now University), Atlanta, associate professor of economics and director of Bureau of Business and Economic Research, 1954-56; University of Houston, Houston, Tex., professor of economics and director of Center for Research in Business and Economics, 1956-62; University of Missouri, Columbia, associate professor of business and director of business studies,

1962-64; Pennsylvania State University, University Park, professor of business administration and director of Center for Research, 1964—. *Military service:* U.S. Army, 1945-46. *Member:* American Statistical Association, American Economic Association, Institute of Management Sciences, American Institute for Decision Sciences.

WRITINGS: (Contributor) *MANTRAP: Management Training Program*, University of Houston Press, 1963; *Conceptual Foundations of Business Research*, Wiley, 1965; (with O. MacKenzie and others) *Correspondence Instruction in the United States*, McGraw, 1968; *Models in Business Analysis*, C. E. Merrill, 1969. Contributor to journals. Editor, *Atlanta Economic Review*, 1954-56, *Business Review*, 1956-62.

WORK IN PROGRESS: Research in cost benefit, cost effectiveness analysis, and program evaluation; manuscript on analysis for managerial decision making.

SIDELIGHTS: Rigby speaks Spanish and lived in Mexico thirteen years.

* * *

RIGBY, T(homas) H(enry Richard) 1925-

PERSONAL: Born April 13, 1925, in Melbourne, Australia; son of Charles Edgar (a sportsman and laborer) and Mabel (Peglar) Rigby; married Norma Robertson; children: Richard William, Catherine Elizabeth. *Education:* University of Melbourne, B.A. (first class honors), 1950, M.A., 1951; University of London, Ph.D., 1954. *Politics:* Labor. *Religion:* Anglican. *Home:* 56 LaPerouse St., Manuka, Australian Capital Territory, Australia. *Office:* Institute of Advanced Studies, Australian National University, Canberra, Australia.

CAREER: Temporary public servant in Melbourne, Australia, 1942-43; temporary research officer, United Kingdom Foreign Office, 1953-54; Canberra University College, Canberra, Australia, senior lecturer, 1955-56; Unversity of London, London, England, senior research officer, 1956-57; United Kingdom Embassy, Moscow, U.S.S.R., second secretary, 1957-58; Australian National University, associate professor of Russian in School of General Studies, 1959-63, professorial fellow in political science at Institute of Advanced Studies, 1964—. *Military service:* Australian Army, 1943-46. *Member:* Australasian Institute of International Affairs, Australian Political Studies Association, Australian and New Zealand Sociological Association, Academy of the Social Sciences in Australia (fellow).

WRITINGS: (With L. A. Churchward) *Policy-Making in the U.S.S.R.*, Lansdowne Press, 1962; (editor with J. D. B. Miller) *The Disintegrating Monolith: Pluralist Trends in the Communist World*, Australian National University Press, 1965; (editor) *Stalin: A Book of Readings*, Prentice-Hall, 1966; *The Composition of the Soviet Communist Party, 1917-1967*, Princeton University Press, 1968; *The Stalin Dictatorship*, Sydney University Press, 1968. Contributor to political science journals.

WORK IN PROGRESS: *The Soviet Government Under Lenin.*

* * *

RIMMINGTON, Gerald T(horneycroft) 1930-

PERSONAL: Born March 18, 1930, in Leicester, England; son of Edward Thorneycroft (an engineer) and Mary (Eason) Rimmington; married Jean M. Chawner, April 5,

1952; children: David, Mark, Luke. *Education:* University of London, B.Sc., 1956, Ph.D., 1964; University of Leicester, M.A., 1959. *Religion:* Anglican. *Office:* Department of Education, Mount Allison University, Sackville, New Brunswick, Canada.

CAREER: Geography master at schools in Leicester, England, 1951-59; Union College, Sierra Leone, West Africa, lecturer in geography, 1959-60; Ministry of Education, Nyasaland (now Malawi), district education officer, 1961-63; Acadia University, Wolfville, Nova Scotia, associate professor of education, 1963-67; Brandon University, Brandon, Manitoba, associate professor of education, 1967-73; Mount Allison University, Sackville, New Brunswick, professor and head of department of education, 1973—. *Military service:* Royal Air Force, 1948-49. *Member:* Royal Geographical Society (fellow), Geographical Association, Canadian Association of Professors of Education, Society of Malawi (life fellow), Royal Society of Arts (life fellow). *Awards, honors:* M.Ed., University of Nottingham, 1972.

WRITINGS: (With J. G. Pike) *Malawi: A Geographical Study*, Oxford University Press, 1965; (with J. Connor, M. V. Marshall, and B. A. Robinson) *Yarmouth County Study: A Preliminary Socio-Economic Assessment*, Acadia University Institute, 1965; *The Resources of the Shubenacadie-Stewracke Area of Nova Scotia: A Socio-Economic Study*, Acadia University Institute, 1966; (with Lillian M. Logan) *Social Studies: A Creative Direction*, McGraw, 1969; (with Ronald D. Traill and Logan) *Teaching the Social Sciences*, McGraw, 1972. Contributor of articles on geographical and educational topics to journals in England and Canada.

* * *

RISJORD, Norman K. 1931-

PERSONAL: Born November 25, 1931, in Manitowoc, Wis.; son of Norman Edmund (an attorney) and Ireme F. (Kubista) Risjord; married Constance M. Winter, 1959; children: Mark, Eric. *Education:* College of William and Mary, A.B., 1953; Johns Hopkins University, graduate study, 1953-54; University of Virginia, M.A., 1957, Ph.D., 1960. *Home:* 5901 South Highlands, Madison, Wis.

CAREER: DePauw University, Greencastle, Ind., assistant professor of history, 1960-64; University of Wisconsin, Madison, 1964—, began as assistant professor, became professor of history. *Military service:* U.S. Army, 1954-56. *Member:* Phi Beta Kappa. *Awards, honors:* William H. Kiekhofer Prize for best teacher, University of Wisconsin, 1965.

WRITINGS: *The Old Republicans*, Columbia University Press, 1965; *Forging the American Republic, 1760-1815*, Addison-Wesley, 1973.

WORK IN PROGRESS: *Politics of the Chesapeake, 1782-1800.*

* * *

RISTOW, Walter W(illiam) 1908-

PERSONAL: Born April 20, 1908, in La Crosse, Wis.; son of Emil Frederick (a streetcar and bus operator) and Emilie (Herber) Ristow; married Helen F. Doerr (a kindergarten teacher), November 14, 1942; children: Walter Richard, William Whittlesey, Stephen Francis. *Education:* University of Wisconsin, B.A., 1931; Oberlin College, M.A., 1933; Clark University, Worcester, Mass., Ph.D., 1937. *Religion:* Presbyterian. *Home:* 6621 Claymore Court, McLean, Va. 22101.

CAREER: Eastern Washington State College, Cheney, instructor in geography, 1935-37; New York (N.Y.) Public Library, head of map room, later chief of Map Division, 1937-46; U.S. War Department, Military Intelligence, New York, N.Y., analyst and map specialist, 1942-45; Library of Congress, Washington, D.C., assistant chief of Map Division, 1946-64, associate chief of Geography and Map Division, 1965-68, chief of Geography and Map Division, 1968—. U.S. Board on Geographical Names, 1947-69, chairman, 1957-59. Member of board of trustees, Fairfax County, Va., Public Library, 1971—. *Member:* Association of American Geographers (secretary, 1948-50), National Council for Geographic Education, Special Libraries Association, American Association for the Advancement of Science, American Congress on Surveying and Mapping, Cosmos Club (Washington, D.C.).

WRITINGS: (With G. T. Renner and others) *Global Geography*, Crowell, 1944, revised edition, 1957; *Aviation Cartography*, 1956; (editor) Christopher Colles, *Roads of the U.S.A., 1789*, Harvard University Press, 1960; *A La Carte*, Library of Congress, 1972. Contributor to geography, cartography, bibliographic, and library journals.

WORK IN PROGRESS: A history of nineteenth-century map-making in America.

* * *

RITTER, Ed 1917-

PERSONAL: Born November 23, 1917, in Weldon, Iowa; son of Elias Edgar and Josephine (Crist) Ritter; married Helen Hall (a part-time writer), August 19, 1941; children: Gretchen Ritter McGarrigle, Brad, Susan. *Education:* Kansas Wesleyan University, B.A.; Stanford University, M.A. *Politics:* Democrat. *Religion:* Society of Friends (Quaker). *Office: Daily Independent*, Ninth and Main, Corona, Calif.

CAREER: Riverside County Schools, Riverside, Calif., director of publications, 1952-63; *Daily Independent*, Corona, Calif., managing editor, 1963—. Manager of Little League and Pony League baseball teams. *Member:* California Association of Secondary School Administrators.

WRITINGS: (With wife, Helen Ritter, and Stanley Spector) *Our Oriental Americans*, McGraw, 1965. Former columnist for *Riverside Press-Enterprise*; wrote "Out of my Mind" for *Daily Independent*. Contributor to magazines and education journals. Editor, *Riverside County Public Education Bulletin*, 1952—.†

* * *

RIVENBURGH, Viola K(leinke) 1897-

PERSONAL: Born March 15, 1897, in Albert Lea, Minn.; daughter of William Henry and Pauline P. (Murphy) Kleinke; married Bertram Gardenier Rivenburgh (an engineer), November 25, 1926; children: Charmian G. (Mrs. Thomas Dale Elliott). *Education:* Attended Northwest State Normal School, 1914-16, University of Wyoming, 1916-17; University of Nebraska, A.B., 1919; Columbia University, M.A., 1925; University of Washington, Seattle, postgraduate study. *Politics:* Democrat. *Religion:* Congregational. *Home:* 500 West Olympic Place, Seattle, Wash. 98119. *Office:* University of Washington, Seattle, Wash. 98105.

CAREER: Honolulu Business College, Honolulu, Hawaii, instructor in English, 1920-24; University of Hawaii, Honolulu, instructor in English, speech, and journalism, 1924-26;

University of Washington, Seattle, assistant professor of English, beginning, 1942. Honolulu City Planning and Organization Board, member, 1933-34. *Member:* American Association of University Women, American Association of University Professors, National League of American Pen Women (program chairman, Seattle branch, 1964-66, president, Seattle branch, 1968-70, state president, 1972-74), University of Washington Women's Faculty Club (secretary, 1960-61), Phi Beta Kappa, Gamma Phi Beta. *Awards, honors:* Gamma Phi Beta, Woman of the Year, 1973.

WRITINGS: Princess Kaiulani: A Fictional Historical Biography, Tongg Publishing, 1960; *Words at Work*, Bobbs-Merrill, 1965; *Monarchy to Annexation*, City and County of Honolulu, in press. Contributor of articles and poetry to *Alaska Weekly, Seattle Post-Intelligencer, Tacoma News Tribune, Nursing World*, and other publications.

WORK IN PROGRESS: Legends of Hawaii.

SIDELIGHTS: Mrs. Rivenburgh speaks French and German. Her book on Princess Kaiulani grew out of a short story she wrote that won the Matson Navigation Co. contest for a biography to be used in connection with the Princess Kaiulani Hotel on Waikiki Beach. *Avocational interests:* Painting, interior decorating.

* * *

RIVERS, Elias L(ynch) 1924-

PERSONAL: Born September 19, 1924, in Charleston, S.C.; son of Elias L. (a farmer) and Dorothy (Reid) Rivers; married Phyllis Pirl, March 17, 1945; married second wife, Georgina Sabat, September 19, 1969; children: (first marriage) Elias, Franklin, Cornelia. *Education:* Attended College of Charleston, 1941-43, Georgetown University, 1943-44; Yale University, B.A., 1948, M.A., 1950, Ph.D., 1952. *Politics:* Socialist. *Religion:* Episcopalian. *Office:* Johns Hopkins University, Baltimore, Md. 21218.

CAREER: Yale University, New Haven, Conn., instructor in Spanish, 1951-52; Dartmouth College, Hanover, N.H., 1952-62, started as instructor, professor of Spanish and head of department of Romance languages and literature, 1961-62; Ohio State University, Columbus, professor of Spanish, 1962-64; Johns Hopkins University, Baltimore, Md., professor of Spanish, 1964—. Asociacion Internacional de Hispanistas (UNESCO affiliate), secretary general, 1962—. *Military service:* U.S. Army, 1943-46; served in China-Burma-India Theater. *Member:* Modern Language Association of America, Phi Beta Kappa. *Awards, honors:* Howard fellowship, 1956-57; Guggenheim fellowship, 1959-60; M.S., Dartmouth College, 1962; Fulbright fellowship, 1964; National Endowment for the Humanities fellowships, 1967-68 and 1971-72.

WRITINGS: Francisco de Aldana, el divino Capitan, Diputacion Provincial (Badajoz, Spain), 1955; (editor) Francisco de Aldana, *Obras*, Espasa-Calpe (Madrid), 1958; (editor) *26 Spanish Poems*, Houghton, 1958; (editor) Garcilaso, *Obras completas*, Ohio State University Press, 1964; (editor) *Renaissance and Baroque Poetry of Spain*, Dell, 1966. Spanish editor, *Modern Language Notes*.

WORK IN PROGRESS: Variorium commentaries to works of Garcilaso, for Ohio State University Press; a study of oral and written traditions in Spanish literature.

SIDELIGHTS: Rivers is fluent in Spanish and has some competence in French, Italian, German, and Chinese.

Avocational interests: International cooperation in advanced Hispanic studies.

* * *

RIVERS, William L. 1925-

PERSONAL: Born March 17, 1925, in Gainesville, Fla.; son of Lucius B. and Minnie (Gable) Rivers; married Sarah Alford, February 4, 1949; children: Gail Ann, Marianne. *Education:* Louisiana State University, B.A., 1951, M.A., 1952; American University, Ph.D., 1960. *Home:* 665 Alvarado Row, Stanford, Calif. 94305. *Office:* Department of Communication, Stanford University, Stanford, Calif. 94305.

CAREER: Reporter or editorial writer on daily newspapers in Baton Rouge, La., 1950-52, 1954, and in Panama City, Fla., 1952-53; with Louisiana State University, Baton Rouge, 1953-54, University of Miami, Coral Gables, Fla., 1955-58, University of Texas, Austin, 1959-60, 1961-62; Stanford University, Stanford, Calif., professor of communication, 1962—, presently Paul C. Edwards Professor of Communication. Agency for International Development, researcher and consultant in East Africa, 1964. National Broadcasting Co., election analyst, 1960, 1962; Network Election Service, election manager and news analyst, 1964, 1966; Media and Consumer Foundation, member of board of directors, 1973—. Consultant to Education Program of the Ford Foundation, 1960, RAND Corporation, 1968-69, Twentieth Century Fund, 1969-70. *Military service:* U.S. Marine Corps, 1943-46.

MEMBER: American Political Science Association, Association for Education in Journalism, Authors League, National Press Club. *Awards, honors:* American Political Science Association congressional fellowship, 1954-55; North Atlantic Treaty Organization fellowship to Oxford Seminar on International Organizations, 1956, and fellowship to study the interplay of politics and press in western Europe, 1963; Ford Foundation mass media grant, 1958-59; distinguished research award, Sigma Delta Chi, 1966, for *The Opinionmakers*; Mellett Fund Award for press council experiments, 1967 and 1968.

WRITINGS: The Mass Media: Reporting, Writing, Editing, Harper, 1964; (with Theodore Peterson and Jay Jensen) *The Mass Media and Modern Society*, Holt, 1965, revised edition, 1971; *The Opinionmakers*, Beacon, 1965; (contributor) Bradley Greenberg and Edwin Parker, editors, *The Kennedy Assassination and the American Public*, Stanford University Press, 1965; *Finding Facts: A Research Manual*, Magazine Publishers Association, 1966; (with Wilbur Schramm) *Responsibility in Mass Communication*, Harper, 1969.

The Adversaries: Politics and the Press, Beacon, 1970; (with David M. Rubin) *A Region's Press: Anatomy of the Newspapers in the San Francisco Bay Area*, Institute of Governmental Studies, University of California, Berkeley, 1971; (with others) *Backtalk: Press Councils in America*, Canfield Press, 1972; *Free-Lancer and Staff Writer: Writing Articles for Magazines*, Wadsworth, 1972; (editor with Michael Nyhan) *Aspen Notebook on Government and the Media*, Praeger, 1973; (with William Slater) *Aspen Handbook on the Media: Research, Publications, Organizations*, Aspen Program on Communications and Society, 1973; (with Everette Dennis) *Other Voices: The New Journalism in America*, Canfield Press, 1974; *Writing: Craft and Art*, Prentice-Hall, 1975.

Florida correspondent, *Kiplinger Letters*, 1958; Wash-

ington correspondent, *Reporter*, 1960-61; columnist, *The Progressive Magazine*, Stanford, Calif., 1971—. Contributor of articles and reviews to *Harper's, Nation, New York Times Magazine, Editor and Publisher, Writer's Digest, Reader's Digest, National Observer, Saturday Review, Progressive, Columbia Journalism Review, Reporter*, and other magazines and newspapers.

WORK IN PROGRESS: Research and writing of book on government-media relationships.

SIDELIGHTS: Rivers told *CA:* "I believe very strongly that writing is both craft and art and that there comes a time when one who works hard enough at the craft may produce something artistic. I hope so."

* * *

RIVLIN, Harry N. 1904-

PERSONAL: Born December 30, 1904, in New York, N.Y.; son of Samuel (a businessman) and Jennie (Feldman) Rivlin; married Eugenie Graciany, August 23, 1928; children: Richard S., Paula (Mrs. Ivan Glickman). *Education:* City College (now City College of the City University of New York), B.S.S., 1924; Columbia University, M.A., 1926, Ph.D., 1930. *Home:* 205 West End Ave., New York, N.Y. 10023. *Office:* School of Education, Fordham University at Lincoln Center, New York, N.Y. 10023.

CAREER: New York (N.Y.) Board of Education, elementary and secondary school teacher of English, 1924-30; City College (now City College of the City University of New York), New York, N.Y., 1930-39, began as assistant professor, became associate professor of education; Queens College (now Queens College of the City University of New York), Flushing, N.Y., associate professor, 1939-47, professor of education and director of teacher education, 1947-57, chairman of department, 1939-57; The City University of New York, New York, N.Y., dean of teacher education, 1957-66; Fordham University, Bronx, N.Y., dean of School of Education, 1966-73, John Mosler Professor of Urban Education, 1973—, special assistant to the president, 1973—. Acting President, City College of the City University of New York, 1961-62. Summer lecturer at New York University, 1944-46; visiting professor at Columbia University, 1947, University of California, Berkeley, 1957. Director of test construction project for U.S. Army Specialized Training Division, 1943-44; member, National Commission on Teacher Education and Professional Standards, 1959-63; member of board of trustees, Center for Urban Education, 1965-71, and Bank Street College of Education, 1973—.

MEMBER: American Psychological Association (fellow; president of division of educational psychology, 1956-57), American Orthopsychiatric Association (fellow; president of New York regional division, 1949-50), National Society of College Teachers of Education (president of educational psychology section, 1952-54), American Association of Colleges for Teacher Education, American Educational Research Association, John Dewey Society (member of board of directors, 1964-66), Interstate Teacher Education Conference (president, 1953-54), New York Academy of Sciences, New York Academy of Public Education. *Awards, honors:* Townsend Harris Award of City College of the City University of New York, 1961; award for distinguished service to education, Newark State College, 1964; medal for educational leadership, Fordham University, 1973; George Johnson Award of Distinction, Catholic University of America, 1973.

WRITINGS: Functional Grammar, Teachers College, Columbia University, 1930, reprinted, AMS Press, 1972; *Educating for Adjustment*, Appleton, 1936; (editor) *Know Your Language*, Silver Burdett, 1941; (editor) *Encyclopedia of Modern Education*, Philosophical Library, 1943, reprinted, Kennikat, 1969; *Teaching Adolescents in Secondary Schools*, Appleton, 1948, 2nd edition, 1961; (with H. H. Remmers, E. I. Ryden, and David G. Ryans) *Growth, Teaching and Learning*, Harper, 1957; (senior editor) *The First Years in College—Preparing Students for a Successful College Career*, Little, Brown, 1965; (with Valda Robinson) *The Preparation of Urban Teachers: A Proposed Syllabus*, American Association of Colleges for Teacher Education, 1968; (editor with Sheldon Marcus) *Conflicts in Urban Education*, Basic Books, 1970; (editor with William R. Hazard and Madelon D. Stent) *Cultural Pluralism in Education: A Mandate for Change*, Appleton, 1973; (with Milton Gold) *Teachers for Multicultural Education*, Fordham University Press, 1975. Contributor to professional periodicals.

*   *   *

ROACH, Mary Ellen 1921-

PERSONAL: Born September 15, 1921, in Easton, Kan.; daughter of John Morgan (a postman) and Mary Jane (Mitchell) Roach. *Education:* University of Kansas, A.B., 1942; Iowa State University of Science and Technology, M.S., 1948; Michigan State University, Ph.D., 1960. *Home:* 406 North Segoe Rd., Madison, Wis. 53705. *Office:* 1270 Lincoln Dr., University of Wisconsin, Madison, Wis. 53706.

CAREER: High school teacher in Kansas, 1942-46; instructor in textiles and clothing at University of Connecticut, Storrs, 1948-53, University of Rhode Island, Kingston, 1953-54, Michigan State University, East Lansing, 1957-59; University of Wisconsin, School of Home Economics, Madison, assistant professor, 1960-63, associate professor, 1963-68, professor of textiles and clothing, 1968—. *Member:* American Home Economics Association, American Sociological Association, American Association of University Professors, Midwest Sociological Association, Costume Society of America, Costume Society of England, Association of College Professors of Textiles and Clothing, Wisconsin Academy of Arts, Letters and Science, Wisconsin Home Economics Association, Phi Beta Kappa, Pi Lambda Theta, Alpha Kappa Delta, Omicron Nu.

WRITINGS: (Co-editor and contributor) *Dress, Adornment, and the Social Order*, Wiley, 1965; (with J. B. Eicher) *The Visible Self: Perspectives on Dress*, Prentice-Hall, 1973; *Cultural and Social Psychological Aspects of Dress*, Prentice-Hall, in press. Contributor to *World Book Encyclopedia* and *Encyclopedia of Education*. Also contributor to *Home Economics Research Journal, Adolescence*, and *Journal of Home Economics*.

*   *   *

ROBBINS, J(ohn) Albert 1914-

PERSONAL: Born December 5, 1914, in Knoxville, Tenn.; son of John Albert and Pearl (Womack) Robbins; married Simone Bassett, July 8, 1950; children: Marise. *Education:* University of Florida, B.A., 1937, M.A., 1938; University of Pennsylvania, Ph.D., 1947. *Politics:* Democrat. *Religion:* Methodist. *Home:* 1011 South Hawthorne Dr., Bloomington, Ind. 47401. *Office:* Department of English, Indiana University, Bloomington, Ind. 47401.

CAREER: Duke University, Durham, N.C., instructor in English, 1946-50; Indiana University, Bloomington, assistant professor, 1950-55, associate professor, 1955-63, professor of English, 1963—. Fulbright lecturer on American literature in France, 1955-56. Visiting professor, University of North Carolina, summer, 1967. *Military service:* U.S. Naval Reserve, active duty, 1942-45; served in Pacific Theater; became lieutenant commander. *Member:* Modern Language Association of America.

WRITINGS: (With Joseph Jones and others) *American Literary Manuscripts: A Checklist of Holdings in Academic, Historical, and Public Libraries in the United States*, University of Texas Press, 1961, editor of revised edition, 1975; (editor, and author of introduction and notes) *EP to LU: Nine Letters Written to Louis Untermeyer by Ezra Pound*, Indiana University Press, 1963; (contributor) Irvin Ehrenpreis, editor, *American Poetry*, Edward Arnold, 1965; (contributor) James Woodress, editor, *American Literary Scholarship: An Annual*, Duke University Press, 1965-69; *Merrill Checklist of Edgar Allan Poe*, C. E. Merrill, 1969; (editor) *American Literary Scholarship: An Annual*, Duke University Press, 1970-74.

Author with David A. Randall of exhibition brochure for "Three Centuries of American Poetry," 1965. Member of editorial board, "Calendars of American Literary Manuscripts" series, Ohio State University Press. Contributor to quarterly bibliography, *American Literature*, 1952—; bibliographer, *PMLA* international bibliography, 1956-67; contributor to other bibliography, literature, library journals, and encyclopedias. Member of editorial advisory board, *ESQ: A Journal of the American Renaissance*.

*   *   *

ROBERTS, Charles Wesley 1916-

PERSONAL: Born December 19, 1916, in Huntington, W.Va.; son of Charles Wesley (a wholesale jeweler) and Elizabeth (Clack) Roberts; married Mary Stewart, November 10, 1945; children: Judith, Jill. *Education:* Attended Northwestern University, 1935-36; University of Minnesota, B.A., 1940. *Politics:* Independent. *Religion:* Episcopalian. *Home:* 8400 Fenway Rd., Bethesda, Md. 20034. *Office:* Washington Journalism Center, 2401 Virginia Ave. N.W., Washington, D.C. 20037.

CAREER: During school years did reporting for *Evanston News-Index*, Evanston, Ill., and *Minneapolis Journal*, Minneapolis, Minn.; reporter in Chicago, Ill., for City News Bureau, 1940-41, and *Chicago Tribune*, 1941; *Chicago Sun* and *Chicago Sun-Times*, Chicago, Ill., editorial staff, 1946-50, began as reporter, became assistant city editor; *Chicago Daily News*, Chicago, Ill., investigative reporter, 1950-51; *Newsweek*, Chicago bureau chief, 1951-53, editor of Periscope department in New York, N.Y., 1953-54, White House correspondent, Washington, D.C., 1954-69, assistant chief of Washington bureau, 1962-69, contributing editor, 1969-72; Washington Journalism Center, Washington, D.C., associate director, 1972—. *Military service:* U.S. Navy, 1941-45; became lieutenant; received Presidential Unit Citation with battle star, North Atlantic ribbon with two battle stars, European Theater ribbon with two battle stars.

MEMBER: National Press Club, Federal City Club (Washington, D.C.), Phi Delta Theta, Kenwood Country Club (Bethesda, Md.). *Awards, honors:* Page One Award of Chicago Newspaper Guild, 1951, for expose of Illinois harness race track scandal.

WRITINGS: LBJ's Inner Circle, Delacorte, 1965; *The Truth About the Assassination*, Grosset, 1967; (editor and author of introduction) *Has the President too Much Power?*, Harper's, 1974. Contributor to national magazines.

SIDELIGHTS: As White House correspondent Roberts covered three presidents—Eisenhower, Kennedy, and Johnson. During that time he flew more than 1,000,000 miles covering presidents on domestic and overseas jaunts to thirty-five countries.

* * *

ROBERTS, Vera Mowry 1918-

PERSONAL: Born October 21, 1918, in Pittsburgh, Pa.; daughter of Joseph E. (a painting contractor) and Emma (Steinmann) Mowry; married Parnell Roberts (an actor), January 4, 1951 (divorced, 1959); children: Christopher. *Education:* University of Pittsburgh, B.S., 1936, M.A., 1940, Ph.D., 1950. *Politics:* Republican. *Religion:* Christian. *Home:* Apartment W3D, 303 West 66th St., New York, N.Y. 10023.

CAREER: Pennsylvania State College (now University), district respresentative, 1941-43; George Washington University, Washington, D.C., assistant professor of English, 1946-54; Hunter College (now Hunter College of the City University of New York), instructor, 1955-61, assistant professor, 1962-65, associate professor, 1965-69; professor and head of department of theatre and cinema, 1969—. Co-founder of Arena Stage, Washington, D.C., and active in productions, 1950-54; also has done directing for Children's Theatre, Washington, D.C., and for various little theatre and summer stock companies. Drama consultant, Presbyterian Senior Services. *Military service:* U.S. Navy Women's Reserve (WAVES), 1943-46; became lieutenant senior grade. *Member:* American Educational Theatre Association (fellow; president, 1973), Speech Association of America, Phi Delta Gamma (national president, 1950-52). *Awards, honors:* Phi Delta Gamma National Achievement Award, 1966; Amoco National Award of Excellence for contributions to college theatre, 1974.

WRITINGS: On Stage: A History of Theatre, Harper, 1962, 2nd edition, 1974; *The Nature of Theatre*, Harper, 1972. Contributor to *Collier's Encyclopedia* and to speech and education journals. Member of national board of editors, Phi Delta Gamma, 1947-49.

* * *

ROBINS, Natalie S. 1938-

PERSONAL: Born June 20, 1938, in Bound Brook, N.J.; daughter of Louis and Mildred (Levy) Robins; married Christopher Charles Herbert Lehmann-Haupt (an editor of *The New York Times Book Review*), October 3, 1965. *Education:* Mary Washington College of the University of Virginia (now Mary Washington College), B.A., 1960.

CAREER: Writer. *Awards, honors:* Fellowship to Yaddo, 1964; citation from New Jersey Association of Teachers of English, for *My Father Spoke of His Riches.*

WRITINGS—Poetry: *Wild Lace*, A. Swallow, 1960; *My Father Spoke of His Riches*, A. Swallow, 1966; *The Peas Belong on Eye Level*, Swallow Press, 1971.

WORK IN PROGRESS: A novel.†

* * *

ROBINSON, David A. 1925-

PERSONAL: Born June 13, 1925, in San Marco, Calif.; son of Parker M. (an engineer) and Catherine (Adair) Robinson; married Elizabeth J. Harper, March 5, 1949 (divorced, 1972); children: Michele Ann, Karen Adair, David Scott. *Education:* Stanford University, B.S. (chemistry), 1947, M.A. (anthropology), 1957; University of Southern California, Ph.D., 1973. *Address:* P.O. Box 2451, Culver City, Calif. 90230. *Office:* Office of Admissions, University of Southern California, Los Angeles, Calif. 90007.

CAREER: Cerro de Pasco Corp., Lima, Peru, metallurgist, 1949-51; Stanford University, Palo Alto, Calif., research assistant, 1951-53; Pittsburgh Testing Laboratory, Lima, Peru, chemical engineer, 1953-64; American Studies Press, S.A., Lima, Peru, editor and publisher, 1964-67; University of Southern California, Los Angeles, assistant dean of admissions, foreign credentials, 1967—. *Military service:* U.S. Army, 1945-46. *Member:* American Geographical Society, American Anthropological Association, Society for International Development, Phi Alpha Theta.

WRITINGS: Peru in Four Dimensions, American Studies Press (Lima), 1964; (translator, editor, and author of introduction) Fernando Belaunde Terry, *Peru's Own Conquest*, American Studies Press (Lima), 1965.

WORK IN PROGRESS: Authorized biography of Fernando Belaunde Terry, president of Peru; English translations of Spanish-language books on Latin American history, politics, and geography.

SIDELIGHTS: Robinson writes: "During my more than ten years of living, working, and studying in Latin America, I came to feel that there was a great need for the publication of more books in English on that region, and my interest in this problem eventually became greater than my interest in chemical engineering. I founded American Studies Press primarily to publish English translations of basic works from or about all the South American countries, in order to make native points of view more readily available. The undertaking is not without its problems, you can be sure!" [The Press' first book, for example, is believed to be the first hard-cover book in English ever to be published in Peru, and was set and printed in a shop where no one spoke or read English. As a result, Robinson says, he turned into a printer of sorts himself.] "I am convinced, however, that it is one of the things which must be done if we are ever to understand each other."†

* * *

ROBINSON, Halbert B(enefiel) 1925-

PERSONAL: Born October 15, 1925, in Winslow, Ariz.; son of Halbert B. and Lois (Eastman) Robinson; married Nancy Lou Mayer, June 24, 1951; children: Christine Louise, Laura Ann, David Merrill, Elizabeth Mayer. *Education:* Attended Pomona College, 1946-49; Stanford University, A.B., 1951, M.A., 1953, Ph.D., 1957. *Home:* 5005 Northeast 45th St., Seattle, Wash. 98105. *Office:* Department of Psychology, University of Washington, Seattle, Wash. 98195.

CAREER: San Francisco State College (now San Francisco State University), San Francisco, Calif., instructor in psychology, 1957-59; University of North Carolina, Chapel Hill, assistant professor, 1959-61, associate professor, 1961-66, professor of psychology, 1966-69, acting chairman of department, 1963-64, director of developmental psychology program, 1964-69; University of Washington, Seattle, professor of psychology and director of developmental psychology laboratory, 1969—. Director of International Study Group for Early Child Care, 1968—. Consultant to Peace

Corps, Washington, D.C. *Military service:* U.S. Marine Corps, 1942-45. *Member:* American Psychological Association, Society for Research in Child Development, American Association for the Advancement of Science, Sigma Xi.

WRITINGS: (With wife, Nancy Mayer Robinson) *The Mentally Retarded Child: A Psychological Approach*, McGraw, 1965, 2nd edition, 1976; (with N. M. Robinson, M. Walins, U. Bronfenbrenner, and J. Richmond) *Early Child Care in the United States*, Gordon & Breach, 1973. Editor, with N. M. Robinson, of "International Monograph Series on Early Child Care," Gordon & Breach, 1972—. Contributor to *Child Development, Pediatrics*, and psychology journals.

* * *

ROBINSON, J(ohn) W(illiam) 1934-

PERSONAL: Born June 18, 1934, in London, England; son of William Walker and Mildred Florence (Enefer) Robinson; married Ann Gerike, October 20, 1959; children: David, Margaret, Catherine. *Education:* University College, Oxford, B.A., 1957, M.A., 1961; University of Glasgow, Ph.D., 1961. *Politics:* Liberal. *Office:* Department of English, University of Nebraska, Lincoln, Neb. 68508.

CAREER: University of Nebraska, Lincoln, assistant professor, 1961-64, associate professor, 1964-67, professor of English, 1967—, associate dean, 1969-72, chairman of department, 1972—. *Member:* Modern Language Association of America, American Society for Theatre Research, Society for Theatre Research (London), British Theatre Museum Association, American Association of University Professors, National Council of Teachers of English. *Awards, honors:* Library Association of the United Kingdom, Besterman Medal for bibliography, 1971; Outstanding Educator of America, 1971.

WRITINGS: (Editor of U.S. edition) "British Writers and Their Work," University of Nebraska Press by arrangement with British Council, Books 1-2, 1963, Books 3-6, 1964, Books 7-9, 1965, Books 10-13, 1966; (compiler with J. F. Arnott) *English Theatrical Literature 1559-1900: A Bibliography*, Society for Theatre Research (London), 1970; (editor) *Theatrical Street Ballads*, Society for Theatre Research, 1971. Contributor of articles on early English drama to scholarly journals in Britain and U.S.

WORK IN PROGRESS: A book on medieval drama.

SIDELIGHTS: The series on British writers, under the general editorship of Bonamy Dobree and T. O. Beachcroft, is to include essays on more than one hundred writers, with from two to six authors considered in each volume (Geoffrey Chaucer and Sir Thomas Malory are paired in Book 1). The essays by many different critics originally were issued separately in pamphlet form in England.

* * *

ROBINSON, James A(rthur) 1932-

PERSONAL: Born June 9, 1932, in Blackwell, Okla.; son of William L. (a banker) and Ethel (Hicks) Robinson; married Lucia Walton (an editor), December 11, 1965. *Education:* George Washington University, A.B., 1954; University of Oklahoma, M.A., 1955; Northwestern University, Ph.D., 1957. *Politics:* Democrat. *Religion:* Presbyterian. *Home:* 180 Dean Rd., Pensacola, Fla. *Office:* University of West Florida, Pensacola, Fla.

CAREER: Congressional fellow, American Political Sci-

ence Association, 1957-58; Northwestern University, Evanston, Ill., instructor, 1958-59, assistant professor, 1959-62, associate professor of political science, 1962-64; Ohio State University, Columbus, professor of political science, 1964-71; Macalester College, St. Paul, Minn., president, 1971-74; University of West Florida, Pensacola, Fla. 1974—. *Member:* American Political Science Association, American Association for the Advancement of Science, Cosmos Club (Washington, D.C.).

WRITINGS: (Co-author) *National and International Decision Making*, Institute for International Order, 1961; *Congress and Foreign Policy-Making*, Dorsey, 1962; *The House Rules Committee*, Bobbs-Merrill, 1964; (contributor) *Politics in the American States*, Little, Brown, 1965; *Political Science Annual: An International Review*, Bobbs-Merrill, 1966; *Congress: The First Branch*, American Enterprise Institute, 1966. General editor, "Handbooks for Research in Political Behavior," Northwestern University Press.

* * *

ROBINSON, James K(eith) 1916-

PERSONAL: Born July 24, 1916, in Waterman, Ill.; son of John B. (a farmer) and Ethyl (McCoy) Robinson; married Pamela Lyne, July 11, 1945; children: Christopher Lyne, Nicholas Keith. *Education:* University of Tennessee, B.A., 1938; Harvard University, M.A., 1940, Ph.D., 1949. *Home:* 847 Ludlow Ave., Cincinnati, Ohio 45220. *Office:* University of Cincinnati, Cincinnati, Ohio 45221.

CAREER: Northwestern University, Evanston, Ill., instructor, 1948-52, assistant professor of English, 1952-58; University of Cincinnati, Cincinnati, Ohio, associate professor, 1958-62, professor of English, 1962—, senior research associate in psychiatry, College of Medicine, 1960—, head of English department, 1966-70. Visiting professor, Harvard University, summer, 1963. *Military service:* U.S. Navy, 1942-46; became lieutenant commander. *Member:* Modern Language Association of America, College English Association, American Association of University Professors.

WRITINGS: (Editor with W. B. Rideout) *A College Book of Modern Verse*, Harper, 1958; (editor with Rideout) *A College Book of Modern Fiction*, Harper, 1961; (editor with G. W. Allen and Rideout) *American Poetry*, Harper, 1965; (editor) Thomas Hardy, *The Mayor of Casterbridge*, Norton, 1975. Contributor to *PMLA, Southern Review, Journal of Modern Literature*.

* * *

ROBOCK, Stefan H. 1915-

PERSONAL: Born July 31, 1915, in Redgranite, Wis.; son of Samuel and Elizabeth (Kushner) Robock; married Shirley Bernstein, June 17, 1946; children: Alan David, Jerry, Lisa. *Education:* University of Wisconsin, B.A., 1938; Harvard University, M.A., 1941, Ph.D., 1948. *Office:* Graduate School of Business, Columbia University, New York, N.Y. 10027.

CAREER: Economist or specialist with government agencies in Washington, D.C., 1940-42, 1946-47, and with U.S. Department of Justice, Boston, Mass., 1947-48; Tufts College (now University), Medford, Mass., instructor, 1948-49; Tennessee Valley Authority, Knoxville, chief economist, 1949-54; United Nations, economic development adviser to government of Brazil, 1954-56; Midwest Research

Institute, Kansas City, Mo., manager of Economics Division, 1956-58; Committee for Economic Development, New York, N.Y., deputy director of Area Development Division, 1958-60; Indiana University, Bloomington, professor of international business and director of international business program, 1960-67; Columbia University, New York, N.Y., professor of international business, 1967-69; Robert D. Calkins Professor of International Business, 1969—. Other United Nations assignments in Chile, Colombia, India, Venezuela, 1955-59, and in Bolivia, 1963; member of U.S. government economic missions to Liberia, 1961, and Nyasaland, 1963. Consultant at various periods to Ford Foundation, National Planning Association, Housing and Home Finance Agency, and government of Brazil. *Military service:* U.S. Navy, Air Intelligence, with duty in North Africa, Brazil, and Japan, 1942-46; became lieutenant senior grade.

MEMBER: American Economic Association, Society for International Development (council member, 1966), Regional Science Association, Phi Eta Sigma, Delta Sigma Rho, Phi Kappa Phi, Beta Gamma Sigma. *Awards, honors:* Honorary professor, University of Recife, Brazil, 1956; M.B.A., Escuela Superior de Tecnica Empresarial (Spain), 1974.

WRITINGS: (Co-author) *Coal and Metals in Japan's Economy*, U.S. Government Printing Office, 1946; (with Glenn E. McLaughlin) *Why Industry Moves South*, National Planning Association, 1949; *Nuclear Power and Economic Development in Brazil*, National Planning Association, 1957; (contributor) *Comparisons in Resource Management*, Johns Hopkins Press, 1961; *Brazil's Developing Northeast: A Study of Regional Planning and Foreign Aid*, Brookings Institution, 1963; (editor with Lee C. Nehrt) *Education in International Business*, Graduate School of Business, Indiana University, 1964; (contributor) *Planning Socio-Economic Change*, Agricultural Policy Institute, University of North Carolina, 1964; (editor with Leo Solomon) *International Development 1965*, Oceana, 1966; (contributor) *The Economic Impact of TVA*, University of Tennessee Press, 1967; (contributor) J. W. Markham and G. F. Papanek, editors, *Industrial Organization and Economic Development*, Houghton, 1970; (with Kenneth Simmonds) *International Business and Multinational Enterprises*, Irwin, 1973. Contributor to government reports, proceedings, and to *Business Horizons, Progressive, Saturday Review*, and other periodicals.

SIDELIGHTS: Robock is fluent in Portuguese.

*   *   *

RODER, Wolf   1932-

PERSONAL: Born October 9, 1932, in Schenectady, N.Y.; son of Hans and Elsa (von Kujawa) Roder; married Barbara Irwin, January 24, 1959; children: Cynthia Lynn, Brenda Joyce. *Education:* University of Chicago, B.A., 1954, M.A., 1956, Ph.D., 1965. *Religion:* Atheist. *Home:* 223 Woolper Ave., Cincinnati, Ohio 45220. *Office:* Department of Geography, University of Cincinnati, Cincinnati, Ohio 45221.

CAREER: Carl L. Gardner and Associates (planners), Chicago, Ill., planner, 1956-58; Elmhurst College, Elmhurst, Ill., instructor in geography, 1959-60; University of Cincinnati, Cincinnati, Ohio, assistant professor of geography, 1963-66; United Nations, Food and Agriculture Organization, socio-economist, 1966-67; University of Cincinnati, Cincinnati, associate professor, 1967-74, professor of

geography, 1974—. Ontario Department of Highways, consultant, 1965. *Military service:* U.S. Air Force, 1951-52. *Member:* Association of American Geographers, African Studies Association, Nigerian Geographical Society. *Awards, honors:* Ford Foundation foreign area fellowship for research in Rhodesia, 1960-63.

WRITINGS: The Sabi Valley Irrigation Projects, Department of Geography, University of Chicago, 1965; (editor) *Voices of Liberation in Southern Africa*, African Studies Association, 1972; (contributor) Akin L. Mabogunje, editor, *Kainji, A Nigerian Man-Made Lake*, Nigerian Institute for Social and Economic Research, 1973; (contributor) Gilbert F. White, editor, *National Hazard Research*, Oxford University Press, 1974.

SIDELIGHTS: Roder lived in Niger Valley, Nigeria, 1966-67. He is competent in German. *Avocational interests:* Photography.

*   *   *

RODGERS, William H.   1918-

PERSONAL: Born March 10, 1918, in Swissvale, Pa.; son of William Valley and Nellie (MacMunn) Rodgers; married Kathleen Bradley (a designer-artist), March 3, 1945. *Education:* "University of Pittsburgh dropout." *Politics:* "Liberal, if not radical, Republican." *Religion:* "Agnosticized Episcopal." *Home and office:* Arch Hill (town of Mount Pleasant), Briarcliff Manor, N.Y. 10510.

CAREER: Newspaperman from high school days to late 1940's, writing for *New York Herald Tribune, Philadelphia Inquirer*, and newspapers in Portland, Ore., and Johnstown and Pittsburgh, Pa.; free-lance writer. Editor of textbooks for Harcourt, Brace & World, Inc., and manuscript editor for other publishers on occasion; sometime development director (mainly public relations) for trade association; unsuccessful candidate for New York State Legislature, 1966. Actively associated with American Civil Liberties Union, Americans United for Separation of Church and State, and various other causes. *Wartime service:* U.S. Maritime Service, purser for three years, World War II.

WRITINGS: Hell and High Water (pictorial documentary), [Greensburg, Pa.], circa 1938; *Rockefeller's Follies: An Unauthorized View of Nelson A. Rockefeller*, Stein & Day, 1966; *Think: A Biography of the Watsons and IBM*, Stein & Day, 1969; *Brown-Out: The Power Crisis in America*, Stein & Day, 1972; *Corporate Country: A State Shaped to Suit Technology*, Rodale, 1973. Editorial consultant for Victor Bator's *Vietnam: Diplomatic Tragedy*, Oceana, 1965. Contributor to *Columbia Law Review* and other periodicals.

WORK IN PROGRESS: "Major work . . . not at liberty to disclose"; other research and writing on "technological, human and urban phenomena which are combining to revolutionize at best, degrade or destroy at worst, qualitative aspects of civilization."†

*   *   *

RODMAN, Hyman   1931-

PERSONAL: Born May 5, 1931, in Montreal, Quebec, Canada; son of Wolfe and Bertha (Cutler) Rodman; married Barbara Hilary Mahase, September 28, 1955; children: Kenneth, Derek, David, Gail. *Education:* McGill University, B.A., 1952, M.A., 1953; Harvard University, Ph.D., 1957. *Office:* Merrill-Palmer Institute, 71 East Ferry Ave., Detroit, Mich. 48202.

CAREER: Boston Children's Service Association, Boston, Mass., Russell Sage Foundation resident, 1957-59; Boston University, Boston, Mass., 1958-61, began as lecturer, became assistant professor of sociology; Merrill-Palmer Institute, Detroit, Mich., sociologist, 1961—. Detroit Co-ordinating Council on Human Relations, member of research committee, 1965-68. Bell lecturer, Vanier Institute of the Family, Canada, 1971. *Member:* American Sociological Association, Society for the Study of Social Problems (chairman of committee on marriage, family, and divorce, 1962-64), Canadian Sociology and Anthropology Association, National Council on Family Relations (member of board of directors, 1968-71), International Sociological Association, American Association for the Advancement of Science. *Awards, honors:* Research grants from U.S. Department of Health, Education, and Welfare agencies, 1962-75.

WRITINGS: (Editor) *Marriage, Family, and Society: A Reader,* Random House, 1965; *Teaching About Families,* Doyle, 1970; *Lower-Class Families,* Oxford University Press, 1971; (with Betty Sarvis) *The Abortion Controversy,* Columbia University Press, 1973, revised edition, 1974.

Contributor: Marvin B. Sussman, editor, *Sourcebook in Marriage and the Family,* 2nd edition, Houghton, 1963; Arthur B. Shostak and William Gomberg, editors, *Blue-Collar World,* Prentice-Hall, 1964; Alvin W. Gouldner and S. M. Miller, editors, *Applied Sociology: Opportunities and Problems,* Free Press of Glencoe, 1965; Shostak and Gomberg, editors, *New Perspectives on Poverty,* Prentice-Hall, 1965; Louis A. Ferman and others, editors, *Poverty in America,* University of Michigan Press, 1965. Contributor of about thirty-five articles to sociology journals. Consulting editor, *Merrill-Palmer Quarterly,* 1963—; *Social Problems,* editor, 1967-69, associate editor, 1969-74.

WORK IN PROGRESS: Research on family organization, values, the relationships between researchers and practitioners, and family policy issues.

* * *

RODRIGUEZ, Mario 1922-

PERSONAL: Born October 1, 1922, in Colusa, Calif.; son of Joseph and Amanda (Vallejo) Rodriguez; married Mildred P. Shepherd (a human nutritionist), September 3, 1943; children: Jacqueline (Mrs. Wayne Mattice). *Education:* University of California, Berkeley, A.B., 1946, M.A., 1948, Ph.D., 1952. *Politics:* Independent Democrat. *Religion:* Methodist. *Office:* Department of History, University of Southern California, University Park, Los Angeles, Calif. 90007.

CAREER: Tulane University of Louisiana, New Orleans, instructor in history, 1952-54; Yale University, New Haven, Conn., instructor, 1954-56, assistant professor of history, 1956-60; University of Arizona, Tucson, associate professor, 1960-62, professor of history, 1962-66; George Washington University, Washington, D.C., professor of Latin American history, 1966-72; University of Southern California, Los Angeles, professor of Latin American history, 1972—. Fulbright lecturer in Madrid, Spain, 1975-76. *Military service:* U.S. Army, 1942-45. *Member:* American Historical Association, Conference on Latin American History (general committee member, 1962-63). *Awards, honors:* James Alexander Robertson Prize of Conference on Latin American History, 1955, for article, "The Genesis of Economic Attitudes in the Rio de la Plata"; Morse fellowship from Yale University for research on Central America, 1958; Guggenheim fellowship in history, 1964-65.

WRITINGS: *A Palmerstonian Diplomat in Central America: Frederick Chatfield, Esquire,* University of Arizona Press, 1964; *Central America,* Prentice-Hall, 1965; *La Conspiracion de Belen en Nueva Perspectiva,* Centro Editorial Jose de Pineda Ibarra, 1965. Contributing editor, *Handbook of Latin American Studies,* University of Florida Press, annually, 1960—, doing introductory article, and reviews of historical items. Contributor of articles and more than thirty reviews to journals.

WORK IN PROGRESS: A book studying the impact of the Cadiz Constitution (1812) upon Central America; a book on Jose Francisco Barrundia (1787-1854); a book, *The Impact of the American Revolution Upon the Spanish World, 1776-1825.*

* * *

ROE, Anne 1904-

PERSONAL: Born August 20, 1904, in Denver, Colo.; daughter of Charles Edwin and Edna (Blake) Roe; married George Gaylord Simpson (a paleontologist), May 27, 1938. *Education:* University of Denver, B.A., 1923, M.A., 1925; Columbia University, Ph.D., 1933. *Politics:* Democrat. *Religion:* Atheist. *Home and office:* 5151 East Holmes St., Tucson, Ariz.

CAREER: Diplomate of American Board of Examiners in Professional Psychology. Consulting psychologist in private practice, 1936-38; Research Council for Problems of Alcohol, New York, N.Y., director of alcohol education study, 1941-42; Yale University, New Haven, Conn., research assistant and assistant professor in Laboratory of Applied Physiology, 1943-46; U.S. Veterans Administration, chief of clinical psychological research at Branch 2, New York, N.Y., 1946-47, chief of psychological training unit at Montrose Veterans Administration Hospital, Montrose, N.Y., 1955-57; New York University, New York, N.Y., adjunct professor of psychology, 1957-59; Harvard University, Graduate School of Education, Cambridge, Mass., lecturer of education and research associate, 1959-67, professor of education and director of Center for Research in Careers, 1963-67, professor emeritus, 1967—; University of Arizona, Tucson, lecturer in psychology, 1967—.

MEMBER: American Psychological Association (fellow; past division president), American Personnel and Guidance Association, National Vocational Guidance Association, Society for Vertebrate Paleontology, Arizona Psychological Association (past president). *Awards, honors:* Social Science Research Council grant, 1941-42; U.S. Public Health Service research grant, 1947-51; Guggenheim fellow, 1952-53; M.A., Harvard University, 1964; L.H.D., Lesley College, 1965; National Vocational Guidance Association, Lifetime Career Award, 1967; Richardson Creativity Award of the American Psychological Association, 1968; Clinical Division of the American Psychological Association Award for distinguished contribution to clinical psychology, 1972; Sc.D., Kenyon College, 1974.

WRITINGS: (With husband, George Gaylord Simpson) *Quantitative Zoology,* McGraw, 1939, 2nd edition (with Lewontin), Harcourt, 1960; *The Making of a Scientist,* Dodd, 1952; *The Psychology of Occupations,* Wiley, 1956; (editor with G. G. Simpson, and contributor) *Behavior and Evolution,* Yale University Press, 1958; (with Mary C. Sherwood) *Learning Experience Guides for Nursing Students,* Wiley, 1970.

Contributor: M. L. Reymert, editor, *Feelings and Emo-*

tions, McGraw, 1959; N. B. Henry, editor, *Rethinking Science Education*, 59th Yearbook of the National Society for the Study of Education, 1960; E. P. Torrance, editor, *Talent and Education*, University of Minnesota Press, 1961; P. C. Obler and H. A. Estrin, editors, *The New Scientist*, Doubleday, 1962; C. Taylor and F. Barron, editors, *Scientific Creativity*, Wiley, 1963; M. A. Coler, editor, *Essays on Creativity in the Sciences*, New York University Press, 1963; S. W. Washburn, editor, *Classification and Human Evolution*, Aldine, 1963; R. Ulich, editor, *Education and the Idea of Mankind*, Harcourt, 1964; K. Hill, editor, *The Management of Scientists*, Beacon, 1964; H. Borow, editor, *Man in a World of Work*, Houghton, 1964; W. D. Nunokawa, editor, *Human Values and Abnormal Behavior*, Scott Foresman, 1965; Walter B. Barbe, editor, *Psychology and Education of the Gifted*, Appleton, 1965; Eli Ginzberg, editor, *Theories and Scope*, Macmillan, 1966. Also contributor to professional journals.

SIDELIGHTS: Anne Roe has traveled throughout the world, accompanying husband on field trips.

* * *

ROGERS, William C(ecil) 1919-

PERSONAL: Born March 12, 1919, in Manhattan, Kan.; son of Charles E. (a professor) and Sadie (Burns) Rogers; married Mary Jane Anderson, August 31, 1941; children: Shelley, Faith, Mary Sarah. *Education:* University of Chicago, B.A., 1940, M.A. 1941, Ph.D., 1943. *Home:* 143 Orlin Ave., S.E., Minneapolis, Minn. 55414. *Office:* World Affairs Center, University of Minnesota, Minneapolis, Minn. 55455.

CAREER: Public Administration Clearing House, Chicago, Ill., assistant to director, 1943-47; University of Chicago, Chicago, Ill., lecturer in international relations, 1945-47; University of Virginia, Charlottesville, assistant professor and research associate in international administration, 1947-48; Western Reserve University (now Case Western Reserve University), Cleveland, Ohio, associate professor of political science, 1948-49; University of Minnesota, Minneapolis, director of World Affairs Center and Continuing Education in Public Policy, Continuing Education and Extension, 1949—. *Member:* American Political Science Association, Adult Education Association of the U.S.A. (past chairman, international relations section), National University Extension Association (secretary-treasurer, 1963-66).

WRITINGS: International Administration (annotated bibliography), Public Administration Service, 1945; *Community Education in World Affairs*, University of Minnesota Press, 1956; (contributor) *Handbook of Adult Education in the U.S.*, edited by M. S. Knowles, Adult Education Association of the U.S.A., 1960; *A Guide to Understanding World Affairs*, Oceana, 1966; *Global Dimensions in U.S. Education: The Community*, Center for War/Peace Studies, 1972.

Editor, "World Affairs Study Guide," for *Minneapolis Star*, annually, 1951-72. Contributor to *Dictionary of Political Science*, Philosophical Library, 1964. Also contributor of about seventy-five articles to thirty publications.

WORK IN PROGRESS: Public opinion and foreign policy.

SIDELIGHTS: Rogers told *CA* that he is a "founding father of Minnesota Jazz Sponsors, Inc.; plays the washboard and gut bucket, makes his own ale; owner of Funky Butt Press (hot type)."

ROGG, Sanford G. 1917-

PERSONAL: Born January 19, 1917, in New York, N.Y.; son of George Smith (in finance) and Nettie F. (Patterson) Rogg; married Marsha M. Melton, March 30, 1950; children: Diane D., George Matthew. *Education:* University of Edinburgh, B.A., 1938; University of Lausanne (Switzerland), M.D., 1942. *Office:* Medical Division, E. I. du Pont de Nemours & Co., Wilmington, Del.

CAREER: Diplomate, American Board of Psychiatry and Neurology. Resident at U.S. Veterans Administration and at Johns Hopkins Hospital, Baltimore, Md., 1948-50; Veterans Administration Hospital, Wilmington, Del., chief of neuropsychiatry, 1950-53; E. I. du Pont de Nemours & Co., Wilmington, Del., corporate psychiatrist with Medical Division, 1955—. With University of Pennsylvania School of Medicine, Philadelphia, 1950-55. *Military service:* U.S. Army, 1943-46; became major. *Member:* American Psychiatric Association (fellow), American Medical Association, American Academy of Occupational Medicine.

WRITINGS: (Contributor) *Modern Occupational Medicine*, 2nd edition, Lea & Febiger, 1960; (with C. A. D'Alonzo) *Emotions and the Job*, C. C Thomas, 1965. Contributor to medical journals.

* * *

ROGLER, Lloyd H(enry) 1930-

PERSONAL: Born July 21, 1930, in San Juan, Puerto Rico; son of Charles C. and Carmen (Canino) Rogler; children: Lynn, Lloyd. *Education:* University of Iowa, B.A., 1951, M.A., 1952, Ph.D., 1957. *Home:* 2575 Palisade Ave., Bronx, N.Y. 18463. *Office:* Fordham University, Bronx, N.Y. 10458.

CAREER: University of Iowa, Iowa City, instructor in sociology, 1955-57; University of Puerto Rico, Rio Piedras, assistant professor, School of Medicine and College of Social Sciences, 1957-58, consultant, 1958-60; Yale University, New Haven, Conn., lecturer, 1960-62, assistant professor, 1962-64, associate professor of sociology, 1964-68; Case Western Reserve University, Cleveland, Ohio, professor of sociology, 1968-74; Fordham University, Bronx, N.Y., Albert Schweitzer University Professor, 1974—. *Military service:* U.S. Army, 1952-54; became sergeant.

WRITINGS: (With August B. Hollingshead) *Trapped: Families and Schizophrenia*, Wiley, 1965; *Migrant in the City: The Life of a Puerto Rican Action Group*, Basic Books, 1972.

WORK IN PROGRESS: Study of the assimilation of the Puerto Rico migrant in the New York area.

* * *

ROJAS, Carlos 1928-

PERSONAL: Surname is pronounced Ro-has; born August 12, 1928, in Barcelona, Spain; son of Carlos Pinilla and Luisa (Vila) Rojas; married Eunice Mitcham, March, 1966. *Education:* University of Madrid, Ph.D., 1955. *Politics:* "A liberal and a pacifist." *Home:* 1344 Briarwood Dr. N.E., Atlanta, Ga. *Agent:* Carmen Balcells, 241 Urgel, Barcelona, Spain. *Office:* Department of Romance Languages, Emory University, Atlanta, Ga. 30322.

CAREER: Rollins College, Winter Park, Fla., assistant professor of Spanish, 1957-60; Emory University, Atlanta, Ga., assistant professor, 1960-63, associate professor, 1963-67, professor of Spanish, 1967—. *Awards, honors:* Premio

Ciudad de Barcelona for *El Asesino de Cesar*, 1959; Premio Navional de Literatura for *Auto de fe*, 1968; Premio Planeta for *Azana,* 1974.

WRITINGS—Novels: *De Barro y de Esperanza*, Editorial L. de Caralt, 1957; *El Futuro ha Comenzado*, Editorial A.H.R., 1958; *El Asesino de Cesar*, Editorial Planeta, 1959; *Las Llaves del Infierno*, Editorial L. de Caralt, 1962; *La Ternura del Hombre Invisible*, Editorial Plaza-Janes, 1963; *Adolfo Hitler Esta en Mi Casa*, Ediciones Rondas, 1965; *Dialogos Para Otra Espana*, Ediciones Ariel, 1966; *Auto de fe*, Ediciones Guadarrama, 1968; *Luis III, el Minotauro*, Ediciones Cuentatras, 1970; *Por que Perdimos la Guerra*, Ediciones Nauta, 1970; *Aguelarre*, Ediciones Nauta, 1970; *Diez Figuras ante la Guerra Civil*, Ediciones Nauta, 1973; *Azana*, Editorial Planeta, 1974.

Translator into Spanish: Paul Valery, *Le Cimitiere Marin*, Instituto Castellonese de Cultura, 1955; three books by Aldous Huxley, *Point Counterpoint, Those Barren Leaves,* and *Eyeless in Gaza*, Editorial Planeta, 1958; John Dos Passos, *Manhattan Transfer*, Editorial Planeta, 1958. Also wrote introductions to Spanish editions of the complete works of Huxley and Dos Passos, published by Editorial Planeta, 1958.

Editor: *De Cela a Castillo-Navarro*, Prentice-Hall, 1965; (with Thomas R. Hart) *La Espana Moderna Vista y Sentida Por Los Espanoles*, Prentice-Hall, 1966; *Maestros Americanos*, Editorial Planeta, 1967. Contributor to *Encyclopedia Espasa*. Short stories in English published in *Archon* and *Stylus*.

SIDELIGHTS: Rojas writes: "I am interested in fiction, history, literary and artistic criticism because I believe in words as the best means to an end which is always freedom." Rojas speaks English, French, Italian, and Catalan.

BIOGRAPHICAL/CRITICAL SOURCES: Sergio Vilar, *Arte y Libertad*, Las Americas, 1963.

*   *   *

ROLLIN, Roger Best   1930-

PERSONAL: Born February 12, 1930, in McKeesport, Pa.; son of John W. (a factory representative) and Hazel (Best) Rollin; married Marian Plants, December 19, 1952; children: Bruce Geoffrey, Lisa Ann. *Education:* Washington and Jefferson College, B.A., 1952; Yale University, M.A., 1957, Ph.D., 1960. *Politics:* Independent Democrat. *Religion:* Agnostic. *Home:* 1117 West Clay St., Lancaster, Pa. *Office:* Franklin and Marshall College, Lancaster, Pa.

CAREER: Franklin and Marshall College, Lancaster, Pa., instructor, 1959-60, assistant professor, 1960-65, associate professor, 1965-72, professor of English, 1972—. *Military service:* U.S. Army, 1952-55. *Member:* Modern Language Association of America, American Association of University Professors, College English Association, Pennsylvania College English Association, Popular Culture Association, American Civil Liberties Union, Phi Beta Kappa. *Awards, honors:* Faculty research grant, Franklin and Marshall College, 1965.

WRITINGS: Robert Herrick, Twayne, 1966; (editor) *Hero/Anti-Hero*, McGraw, 1973; (co-editor) *Herrick Studies*, University of Pittsburgh Press, 1975.

WORK IN PROGRESS: Works on Donne; works on popular culture.

SIDELIGHTS: Rollin is competent in French, German,

Russian, and Latin. *Avocational interests:* Aviation, military history, amateur acting.

*   *   *

ROMANO, Louis   1921-

PERSONAL: Born January 1, 1921, in Milwaukee, Wis.; son of Liborio and Mary Romano; married Shirley Mae Stevens, February 21, 1943; children: Jill Stevens (Mrs. Steven Styker), Pamela Ann. *Education:* Milwaukee State Teachers College (now University of Wisconsin, Milwaukee), B.S., 1943; University of Wisconsin, Madison, M.S., 1948, Ph.D., 1954. *Religion:* Methodist. *Home:* 4453 Manitou, Okemos, Mich. 48864.

CAREER: Shorewood (Wis.) public schools, teacher, 1944-54, assistant superintendent, 1954-64; Wilmette (Ill.) public schools, superintendent, 1964-66; Michigan State University, East Lansing, 1966—, began as associate professor, became professor of administration and higher education. *Military service:* U.S. Army Air Forces, World War II. *Member:* American Association of School Administrators, National Education Association (life), National Society for the Study of Education, Association for Supervision and Curriculum Development, Michigan Association of Middle School Educators, Rotary International, Phi Delta Kappa.

WRITINGS: A Guide to Successful Parent-Teacher Conferences, Franklin Publishers (Milwaukee), 1964; *Challenge of the Fives*, Franklin Publishers, 1965; (contributor) Richard P. Klahn, editor, *The Evaluation of Teacher Competency*, Franklin Publishers, 1965; (with N. Georgiady and J. Heald) *Selected Readings on General Supervision*, Macmillan, 1970; (with Georgiady, R. Featherstone, and A. Kloster) *Personnel Management: Selected Readings on Human Management*, MSS Corp., 1971; (with Georgiady and Heald) *The Middle School*, Nelson-Hall, 1973.

Texts with Nicholas Georgiady, all published by Follett: *Exploring Wisconsin*, 1957, revised edition, 1967; *Gertie the Duck*, 1958; *Our Country's Flag*, 1960; *Our National Anthem*, 1960; *This Is a Department Store*, 1960; *Tulita la Patita*, 1960; *Trudi la Cane*, 1960; *Anden Agda*, 1965; *Quack, die Entre*, 1965; *Anden Gertrude*, 1965.

With N. Georgiady, all published by Franklin Publishers: "Wisconsin State Indians" series, 1966; *Wisconsin Women, Badger Men, Wisconsin, Historical Sights*, and twenty other similarly titled books on Illinois, Michigan, Indiana, and Ohio, 1966; (and R. Green) "Famous Black Americans" series, 1969.

With N. Georgiady, all published by Franklin Publishers in 1974; "Know About" series: *Know About Stamps, . . . Money, . . . Highways, . . . Airports, . . . Shopping Centers, . . . Banks, . . . Motels, . . . Computers, . . . Skyscrapers, . . . Assembly Lines.*

WORK IN PROGRESS: Fifty-six texts on the signers of the Declaration of Independence.

*   *   *

RONALDSON, Agnes S.   1916-

PERSONAL: Born August 12, 1916, in New York, N.Y.; daughter of Robert Sinclair and Jessie (Sutherland) Ronaldson. *Education:* State University of New York, B.S., 1951; New York University, M.A., 1953; Columbia University, Ed.D., 1964.

CAREER: University of Florida, Gainesville, assistant

professor and director of Child Study Center, 1955-59; Berea College, Berea, Ky., associate professor of child development and family relations, 1961-65; Stout State University, Menomonie, Wis., dean of School of Home Economics, 1965—. Educational consultant, U.S. Government's Operation Head Start.

WRITINGS: The Spiritual Dimension of Personality, Westminster, 1965.†

* * *

ROOS, Hans Dietrich 1919-

PERSONAL: Born December 15, 1919, in Kunzelsau, Germany; son of Paul and Johanna (Staiger) Roos; married Ruth Otto. *Education:* Studied at Evangelical Theological Seminaries of Maulbronn and Blaubeuren, 1935-38, and University of Tuebingen, 1950-54. *Religion:* Evangelical. *Agent:* Prins & Prins, Amsterdam, Netherlands. *Office:* Historisches Seminar, Nikolausberger Weg 15, Goettingen, Germany.

CAREER: German National Defense Service, 1938-49, officer, 1940-49, and sometime prisoner of war; University of Tuebingen, Tuebingen, Germany, research associate at East Europe Institute, 1955-61; University of Goettingen, Goettingen, Germany, lecturer in medieval, modern, and East European history and director of department of history, 1962—. Member of Johann-Gottfried-Herder-Forschungsrat, Marburg, and Commission International pour l'Histoire des Assemblees d'Etats.

WRITINGS: Polen und Europa: Studien zur polnischen Aussenpolitik 1931-1939, I.C.B. Mohr, 1957, 2nd edition, 1965; (co-author) *Osteuropa-Handbuch, Band Polen*, Boehlau, 1959; *Geschichte der Polnischen Nation 1916-1960*, Kohlhammer, 1961, 2nd edition, 1964, translation by J. R. Foster published as *A History of Modern Poland*, Knopf, 1966.

WORK IN PROGRESS: A History of the Polish Republic, 966-1967; a book on the Polish nation and the idea of democracy in the age of partitions, 1764-1805.†

* * *

ROREM, Ned 1923-

PERSONAL: Born October 23, 1923, in Richmond, Ind.; son of Clarence R. (a medical economist) and Gladys (Miller) Rorem. *Education:* Attended Northwestern University, 1940-42, and Curtis Institute of Music, 1942-43; Juilliard School of Music, B.S., 1946, M.S., 1948. *Religion:* Society of Friends (Quaker). *Address:* c/o Boosey & Hawkes, 30 West 57th St., New York, N.Y. 10019.

CAREER: Composer. Wrote first songs at nine; produced more than three hundred songs during the 1940s, and had orchestral work, "Overture in C," performed by the New York Philharmonic, 1949; went abroad in 1949 and remained eight years (1949-57), composing his first extended works while living in France and Morocco; composer in residence, University of Buffalo, Buffalo, N.Y., 1959-61; composer in residence, University of Utah, Salt Lake City, 1965-67. Orchestral works include three symphonies, the first premiered in Vienna, 1951, the second commissioned by the La Jolla Orchestra, 1955, and the third premiered by Leonard Bernstein at Carnegie Hall, 1959. Compositions have been performed by Eugene Ormandy, Leopold Stokowski, Dimitri Mitropoulos, Paul Paray, Alfred Wallenstein, and Fritz Reiner.

MEMBER: American Society of Composers, Authors, and Performers. *Awards, honors:* Music Libraries Association award for the best published song of the year, 1948, for "The Lordly Hudson"; Gershwin Memorial Award, 1949, for "Overture in C"; Lili Boulanger Award, 1950; Fulbright fellowship for study with Honegger in Paris, 1951-52; Prix de Biarritz, 1951, for ballet, "Melos"; Eurydice Choral Award, 1954; Guggenheim fellowship, 1957; Ford Foundation grants.

WRITINGS: The Paris Diary of Ned Rorem, Braziller, 1966; *Music From Inside Out*, Braziller, 1967; (author of introduction) Jean Cocteau, *The Difficulty of Being*, Coward, 1967; *The New York Diary*, Braziller, 1967; *Music and People*, Braziller, 1968; *Critical Affairs: A Composer's Journal*, Braziller, 1970; *Pure Contraption*, Holt, 1973, new edition, 1974; *The Final Diary: 1961-1972*, Holt, 1974. Contributor to *New York Times Review of Books*.

Orchestral works: *First Symphony*, Southern Music Publishing Co., 1950; *Lento for Strings*, Southern Music Publishing Co., 1950; *Design for Orchestra*, Boosey & Hawkes, 1953; *Second Symphony*, Boosey & Hawkes, 1955; *Third Symphony*, Boosey & Hawkes, 1957; *Eagles*, Boosey & Hawkes, 1958; *Ideas*, Boosey & Hawkes, 1961; *Lions*, Boosey & Hawkes, 1963.

Operas: *A Childhood Miracle*, with libretto by Elliott Stein, Southern Music Publishing Co., 1952; (composer and librettist) *The Robbers*, Boosey & Hawkes, 1956; *The Anniversary* (incomplete), libretto by Jascha Kessler, Boosey & Hawkes, 1961; *Miss Julie*, libretto (based on the play by August Strindberg) by Kenward Elmslie, Boosey & Hawkes, 1964; *Bertha* (one-act), by Kenneth Koch, Boosey & Hawkes, 1973; *Fables* (five one-acts), poems by Jean de la Fontaine, translated by Marianne Moore, Boosey & Hawkes, 1974. Composer of unpublished opera, "Last Day," libretto by Jay Harrison, 1959.

Song cycles: *Flight for Heaven*, ten poems by Robert Herrick, Mercury, 1950; *Cycle of Holy Songs*, 4 psalms, Southern Music Publishing Co., 1951; *From an Unknown Past*, Southern Music Publishing Co., 1951; *Poems of Love and the Rain*, 17 songs on American poets, Boosey & Hawkes, 1963; *Hearing*, 7 poems by Kenneth Koch, Boosey & Hawkes, 1966; *Four Songs*, poems by Paul Goodman and Frank O'Hara, E. C. Schirmer, 1968; *Three Poems of Paul Goodman*, Boosey & Hawkes, 1968; *Three Poems of Demetrios Capetanakis*, Boosey & Hawkes, 1968; *Two Poems of Theodore Roethke*, Boosey & Hawkes, 1969; *Poems of Tennyson*, Boosey & Hawkes, 1969; *King Midas*, 10 poems by Howard Moss, Boosey & Hawkes, 1970; *Poems pour la Paix*, 6 poems in French, Boosey & Hawkes, 1970; *Five Poems of Walt Whitman*, Boosey & Hawkes, 1970; *Some Trees*, poems by John Ashbery, Boosey & Hawkes, 1970; *War Scenes*, poems by Walt Whitman, Boosey & Hawkes, 1971; *To a Young Girl*, 6 poems by W. B. Yeats, Boosey & Hawkes, 1972; *Love in a Life*, poems by Robert Browning, Boosey & Hawkes, 1972; *Jack l'eventreur*, poems by Marie Laure, Boosey & Hawkes, 1972; *Absalom*, poems by Paul Goodman, Boosey & Hawkes, 1972; *Canticles*, English settings of 7 liturgical songs, Boosey & Hawkes, 1972; *Little Prayers*, poems by Paul Goodman, Boosey & Hawkes, 1973; *The Last Poems of Wallace Stevens*, Boosey & Hawkes, 1974; *Ariel*, 5 poems by Sylvia Plath, Boosey & Hawkes, 1974.

Unpublished song cycles: "Penny Arcade," 6 poems by Harold Nourse, 1949; "Another Sleep," 3 prose-poems by Julien Green, 1951; "Eclogues," 6 poems by Fletcher, 1953; "Anacreontiche," 4 poems by Vitorelli, in Italian, 1954; "Two Poems of Plato," in Greek, 1964.

Compositions for piano: *First Sonata*, C. F. Peters, Inc., 1948; *Toccata*, C. F. Peters, 1948; *A Quiet Afternoon*, Southern Music Publishing Co., 1949; *Barcarolles*, C. F. Peters, 1949; *Second Sonata*, Pierre Noel, 1950; *Concerto No. 2*, Southern Music Publishing Co., 1950; *Sicilienne* (two pianos), Southern Music Publishing Co., 1950; *Third Sonata*, C. F. Peters, 1954; *Burlesque*, C. F. Peters, 1955; *Slow Waltz*, Composers Editions, 1958; *Piano Concerto in 6 Movements*, Boosey & Hawkes, 1970.

Chamber music: *Mountain Song*, Southern Music Publishing Co., 1948; *Violin Sonata*, C. F. Peters, 1949; *String Quartet No. 2*, Southern Music Publishing Co., 1950; *Lento for Strings*, Southern Music Publishing Co., 1950; *Sinfonia for 15 Wind Instruments*, C. F. Peters, 1957; *Pilgrims, for Strings*, Boosey & Hawkes, 1958; *Eleven Studies for Eleven Players*, Boosey & Hawkes, 1959; *Trio for Flute, Cello, and Piano*, C. F. Peters, 1960; *Ideas for Easy Orchestra*, Boosey & Hawkes, 1961; *Lovers* (narrative), Boosey & Hawkes, 1964. Composer of unpublished manuscript, "Concertina da Camera," 1946.

Other: *Mourning Scene* (for voice and string quartet), C. F. Peters, 1947; *Pastorale* (for organ), Southern Music Publishing Co., 1949; *Six Irish Poems* (for voice and orchestra), Southern Music Publishing Co., 1950; *Four Dialogues* (for two voices and two pianos), C. F. Peters, 1953-54; *Six Songs for High Voice and Orchestra*, Southern Music Publishing Co., 1954; *SUN* (for voice and orchestra), Boosey & Hawkes, 1966; *Truth in the Night Season* (for chorus and organ), Boosey & Hawkes, 1967; *Letters from Paris* (for chorus and small orchestra), extracts from Janet Flanner's Paris journal, Boosey & Hawkes, 1969; *A Sermon on Miracles* (for voice, chorus, strings, and/or piano), text by Paul Goodman, Boosey & Hawkes, 1970; *Water Music* (for violin, clarinet, and orchestra), Boosey & Hawkes, 1970; *Praises for the Nativity* (for 6 voices and organ), Boosey & Hawkes, 1971; *Miracles of Christmas* (for chorus and organ), text by Ruth Apprich Jacob, Boosey & Hawkes, 1971; *Gloria* (for two voices and piano), Boosey & Hawkes, 1972; *Canticle of the Lamb* (for chorus), Boosey & Hawkes, 1972; *Day Music* (for violin and piano), Boosey & Hawkes, 1973; *Nightmusic* (for violin and piano), Boosey & Hawkes, 1973; *In Time of Pestilence* (6 short madrigals), poems by Thomas Nashe, Boosey & Hawkes, 1974; *Missa Brevis* (for mixed chorus; Latin verses), Boosey & Hawkes, 1974; *Three Motets on Poems by Gerard Manley Hopkins* (for chorus and organ), Boosey & Hawkes, 1974.

Ballets: (With Marie Laure) "Melos," 1951; (with Jerome Robbins) "Ballet for Jerry," 1951; (with Jean Marais) "Dorian Gray," 1952; (with Valerie Betteis) "Early Voyagers," 1959, (with Norman Walker) "Eleven by Eleven," 1963, (with J. Marks) "Antics for Acrobats," 1964, (with M. Gordon) "Excursions," 1965, (with Glen Tetley) "Lovers," 1966 (preceding five works based on *Eleven Studies for Eleven Players*).

Theatrical works: (With Milton Robertson) "That We May Live," 1946; Charles Henri Ford, "At Noon Upon Two" (puppet show), 1947; (with John Myers) Boultenhouse, "Fire Boy" (puppet show), 1947; Kenward Elmslie, "The Ticklish Acrobat" (musical comedy), 1948; "The Pastry Shop" and "The Young Among Themselves" (two one-acts), produced off-Broadway at The Extension, New York, June 5, 1970. Composer of thirteen incidental music scores and about fifty published songs.

WORK IN PROGRESS: Planning to make a film with Susan Sontag.

SIDELIGHTS: Songs and orchestral music have been recorded for Odyssey, Desto, C.R.I., Westminster, Orion, and Columbia Records. Rorem himself is the pianist for "32 Songs by Ned Rorem" (Columbia Records) which includes many songs written during the 1940s, "a period of violent prolificacy," said Rorem. "In a single day I would sometimes spill out four or five songs, indiscriminately, some terrific, some terrible, but all based on good texts; for poetry was my first love." The cover design for the album was done by Jean Cocteau only a few days before his death.

Rorem told *Newsweek*: "I've set just about everything but the telephone book to music. I began to write for the voice because of a love of words." He wrote *Miss Julie* while in Morocco; "I loved Morocco," he told *Newsweek*. "Everything I've written began there. There were no diversions. The best influence for a composer is four walls. The light must come from inside. When it comes from outside the result is postcard music."

In speaking of his book, Rorem once told the *New York Times Book Review* that he regarded the diary as "the disorderly side of myself, the music as the orderly side." Gavin Lambert wrote: "*The Paris Diary of Ned Rorem . . .* is totally committed to self-revelation. As in a novel told in the first person, the 'I' provides a continuity of atmosphere and plot; the outside world seems to be viewed through a kaleidoscope, the writer's psyche through a magnifying lens. . . . The frame work . . . is the sentimental education of a young artist. The writing combines elegance, wryness and plain speaking. . . . Like many charmers, he is guilt ridden and unhappy, prone to drastic benders, romantically terrified of age and death. An early note establishes the link between sex and death, and since youth and beauty are the most desirable and evanescent things on earth, the moment must be seized and cherished. He wants a great love; but when it begins, he feels 'pleasant nausea.' Even though Julien Green remarks that anyone seen with Rorem, man, woman or child, would automatically be compromised (and Rorem is proud of this), the aftermath of drinking, lovemaking and success is always remorseful and lonely. Rorem, in fact, explores the familiar conflict between human needs and human nature in a series of sad, ecstatic ramifications."

Rorem told *CA* that he would most like to live "in a backward country which was once civilized, i.e. Greece or Morocco." He said that, for him, the summit of misery is a hangover and the end of love; his dream of happiness consists of "a vegetable garden, a lover, great fame, and health," but he adds that "happiness is stupid. Intelligent people are [infrequently] happy. . . . I don't believe in happiness (or dreams)." The greatest unhappiness for him would be anonymity. Rorem said that abjection in love is the fault for which he has the greatest tolerance, and that he most appreciates the quality of virility in a man, intelligence and culture in a woman. His favorite women are Marilyn Monroe, Billie Holiday, Martha Graham, and Monica Vitti. Among painters, he likes the Renaissance Italians "and the painting of most of my friends. But I don't *need* painting." His favorite musician is himself and he chooses "most of the French, few of the Germans" as his favorite prose authors and poets. He said that he has no heroes, either real-life or historical, "except movie stars." The occupation which he would most enjoy is "what I'm doing: writing music and words," and when asked what person he would most like to be, he replied: "Myself." He despises all military acts and admires reform that is pacifist and inter-racial. He says that he has all of the gifts of nature that he wants. He would like to die "in being devoured by a golden lion," and his present state of mind is "reasonably tranquil, for a change."

BIOGRAPHICAL/CRITICAL SOURCES—Books: Ned Rorem, The Paris Diary of Ned Rorem, Braziller, 1966; Ned Rorem, The New York Diary, Braziller, 1967; Ned Rorem, Critical Affairs: A Composer's Journal, Braziller, 1970; Ned Rorem, The Final Diary: 1961-1972, Holt, 1974. Periodicals: Newsweek, November 15, 1965; New York Times Book Review, July 10, 1966, July 24, 1966; Books, August, 1967; New York Times, November 9, 1969.†

* * *

ROSE, A(rthur) James 1927-

PERSONAL: Born July 7, 1927, in Takaka, New Zealand; son of Arthur Henry (a farmer) and Nita (Vaughan) Rose; married second wife, Glen Estelle Saleeba, November 19, 1964; children: Jane, Michael, Philippa, Charles; stepchildren: Simon, Benjamin. Education: Canterbury University College, B.A., 1948, M.A., 1949; University of London, graduate study, 1964-65. Office: Macquarie University, North Ryde, 2113, New South Wales, Australia.

CAREER: Canterbury University College, Christchurch, New Zealand, junior lecturer in geography, 1949-50; University of New England, Armidale, New South Wales, Australia, lecturer in geography, 1951-57; Australian National University, Canberra, Australian Capital Territory, senior lecturer in geography, 1957-65, reader, 1965-66; Macquarie University, Eastwood, New South Wales, Australia, professor of geography, 1966—. Visiting professor at University of British Columbia, 1963, and Western Washington State College, 1963-64. Member: New Zealand Geographical Society, Australian Institute of Geographers, American Geographical Society, Association of American Geographers. Awards, honors: Rockefeller Foundation fellow at University of London, 1964-65.

WRITINGS: Australia—How People Live, Educational Supply Association, 1959; Dilemmas Down Under, Van Nostrand, 1966; Patterns of Cities, Nelson, 1967. Contributor to professional journals.

WORK IN PROGRESS: Revision of Patterns of Cities.

* * *

ROSEN, Hjalmar 1922-

PERSONAL: Given name is pronounced Yawl-mar; born March 7, 1922, in Minneapolis, Minn.; son of Morris and Esther (Moe) Rosen; married Ruth Alice Hudson, April 17, 1954; children: Margot J., Holly Y. Education: University of Minnesota, B.A., 1943, M.A., 1944, Ph.D., 1951. Politics: Independent. Home: 18945 Parkside, Detroit, Mich. 48221. Office: Wayne State University, Detroit, Mich. 48202.

CAREER: University of Minnesota, Minneapolis, instructor in psychology, 1946-48; Amalgamated Clothing Workers of America, St. Paul, Minn., research and training director, 1948-51; University of Illinois, Urbana, 1951-62, started as assistant professor, became professor of psychology; Wayne State University, Detroit, Mich., professor of psychology, 1962—. Military service: U.S. Army, 1945-46; became staff sergeant. Member: American Psychological Association, American Sociological Association, Industrial Relations Research Association.

WRITINGS: (With wife, R. A. Hudson Rosen) The Union Member Speaks, Prentice-Hall, 1955; (with Ross Stagner) Psychology of Industrial Relations, Wadsworth, 1965.

WORK IN PROGRESS: Non-affective components of attitude; ipsative decision models for action research; motivation among managerial leadership.

SIDELIGHTS: Rosen lived in Mexico, 1957-58.

* * *

ROSENBAUM, Jean 1927-

PERSONAL: Born March 27, 1927, in Cottondale, Fla.; son of Isaac and Lena (Braxton) Rosenbaum; married Ruth Chaban, 1949; married second wife, Veryl Ellis (a poet), October 6, 1965; children: (first marriage) Aaron, Ethan; (second marriage) Marc. Education: Wayne State University, B.A. (cum laude), 1950, M.D., 1954; Detroit Psychoanalytic Institute, training as psychoanalyst, 1959-64. Politics: None. Religion: None. Address: Route 2, Box 115N, Durango, Colo. 81301. Office: 1341 Canyon Rd., Santa Fe, N.M. 87501.

CAREER: Physician in Detroit, Mich., 1954-65, and Santa Fe, N.M., 1965—; currently dividing his time between writing and his practice as a psychoanalyst. Wayne State University, Detroit, instructor in psychiatry at Detroit Receiving Hospital, 1956-63, assistant professor of humanities at Monteith College, 1963-64; Detroit House of Correction, Detroit, chief psychiatrist, 1957-58; St. John's College, Santa Fe, fencing master, 1965-67. Southwest Association for Psychanalysis, training analyst, 1965—. Member, Detroit Artists Workshop, 1964-65; chairman, Santa Fe Artists Workshop, chairman, 1965-66; gave biweekly readings of own poetry over WQRS-FM, Detroit, 1964-65, and conducted "American Poet Series" over KSNM-FM, Santa Fe, 1965. Military service: U.S. Naval Reserve, 1944-46. Member: American Academy of Psychoanalysis, American Psychiatric Association, New Mexico Psychoanalytic Association (president, 1965-72), Sigma Xi. Awards, honors: Wayne State University alumni research award, 1955; Max Thorek Award, Phi Lambda Kappa, 1955; research award, Michigan Society of Neurology and Psychiatry, 1960; sculpture award, Michigan Academy of Sciences, Arts, and Letters, 1961; Hart Crane Poetry Award from American Weave (journal), 1965.

WRITINGS: Love In a Dying World (poems), Dorrance, 1962; Only the Black at Heart (epoch poetry), American Poets Press, 1965; Arise Solomon (poetry), American Poets Press, 1965; (author of introduction) Marise Querlain, Women Without Men, Dell, 1965.

Becoming Yourself, St. Anthony Press, 1971; Practical Psychiatry: How to Use it in Daily Living, Parker, 1971; (with wife, Veryl Rosenbaum) The Psychiatrist's Cookbook, Sunstone Press, 1972; Is Your Volkswagen a Sex Symbol: What Your Lifestyle Reveals About You and Your Personality, Hawthorn, 1972; (with L. McAuliffe) What is Fear: An Introduction to Feelings, Prentice-Hall, 1972; (with V. Rosenbaum) Conquering Loneliness, Hawthorn, 1973; Mind Factor: How Your Emotions Affect Your Health, Prentice-Hall, 1973; (with V. Rosenbaum) Dental Psychology, Dental Economics Press, 1974; (with V. Rosenbaum) Lifemanship, Warner, 1974.

Author of three plays, "Cave of Shadows," 1963, "Ivy Leagued Heart," 1964, and "Only the Black at Heart," 1966, all initially produced by Concept East, Detroit. Contributor of over 300 articles to major magazines. Poetry has appeared in *Dust, Wormwood Review, Voices, Ole, Art and Artists, Poetmeat, Red Clay Reader, Fiddlehead, Bitteroot*, and other periodicals. Associate editor, *Voices*, 1962-65; editor, *American Poet*, 1964-70; editor, *Outcast* (poetry quarterly), 1966-70.

SIDELIGHTS: The Smithsonian Institution maintains a collection of Rosenbaums's papers relating to the artificial pacemaker which he invented in 1951. *Avocational interests:* Sculpturing and fencing.

* * *

ROSENBAUM, Maurice 1907-

PERSONAL: Born July 28, 1907, in Leeds, Yorkshire, England; son of Mark Bernard and Amelia (Taylor) Rosenbaum; married Eve Adelaide De Jongh, June 30, 1939; children: Sarah Lucy. *Education:* Attended University of Leeds and Sorbonne, University of Paris, awarded B.A. (with honors in modern languages), 1930. *Politics:* Socialist. *Religion:* "Jewish by birth but no religion practised." *Home:* Flat 2, 74 Elm Park Gardens, London S.W. 10, England.

CAREER—All London, England: Associated Press, desk editor, British section, 1939-45; *Daily Herald*, foreign subeditor, 1945-50; *News Chronicle*, foreign sub-editor, 1950-52; *Daily Telegraph*, foreign news sub-editor, features sub-editor, and deputy features editor, 1952-74; free-lance writer, 1974—.

WRITINGS: (Translator) Klaus Mehnert, *Anatomy of Soviet Man*, Weidenfeld & Nicolson, 1962; *London* (Junior Literary Guild selection), Rand McNally, 1963; *Traveller's Guide to Southern France*, Thornton Cox, 1975. Contributor to a wide range of periodicals, including *Lettres Nouvelles* (Paris).

WORK IN PROGRESS: Continuing research into nature, social significance, and impact of folk-song revival in Britain and America.

SIDELIGHTS: Rosenbaum is fluent in French, and has good working knowledge of German, Spanish, and Italian. He considers that the life of greatest fulfillment is that of the creative artist—"he [being] the only human being I envy."

* * *

ROSENBERGER, Homer Tope 1908-

PERSONAL: Born March 23, 1908, in Lansdale, Pa.; son of Daniel Hendricks and Jennie (Markley) Rosenberger; married Pauline Richards, July 14, 1934; children: Arley Jane (Mrs. Harry C. Furminger), Lucretia Hazel (Mrs. Patrick R. Myers). *Education:* Albright College, B.Sc., 1929; Cornell University, M.A., 1930, Ph.D., 1932. *Religion:* United Methodist. *Office:* 1307 New Hampshire Ave. N.W., Washington, D.C. 20036.

CAREER: High school teacher in Pennsylvania, 1930-31, and night school instructor, 1933-35; U.S. Office of Education, Washington, D.C., educational research and administration, 1935-42; U.S. Department of Justice, Washington, D.C., supervisor of training, Bureau of Prisons, 1942-57; U.S. Department of Commerce, Washington, D.C., chief of training, Bureau of Public Roads, 1957-65; private consultant on personnel training to government and other agencies, 1965—, including U.S. Department of Commerce, Agency for International Development, Pennsylvania Department of Highways, and United Hospitals of Newark (N.J.). Chairman of U.S. Training Officers Conference,

1949-50, 1955-57; organizer and moderator of Rose Hill Seminars, 1963—. Pennsylvania Historical and Museum Commission, 1972—. President, Bureau of Rehabilitation of the National Capital Area, 1958-61; chairman of Pennsylvania State Board of Private Correspondence Schools, 1972-73.

MEMBER: Pennsylvania Historical Association (president, 1967-69), Pennsylvania Historical Junto (founder; president, 1942-46, 1954-56), Columbia Historical Society (president, 1968—), Phi Delta Kappa, Pi Gamma Mu, Phi Alpha Theta, Alpha Pi Omega, Cosmos Club (Washington, D.C.). *Awards, honors:* LL.D., Albright College, 1955; Ford Foundation grant for personnel advisory project in Western Nigeria, 1963-64; citations from U.S. Training Officers Conference, 1957, Pennsylvania Historical Junto, 1957, 1967, and Bureau of Rehabilitation of the National Capitol Area, 1968.

WRITINGS: What Should We Expect of Education?, National Association of Secondary School Principals, 1956; *Letters from Africa*, American Peace Society, 1965; *The Pennsylvania Germans, 1891-1965* (75th anniversary volume), Pennsylvania German Society, 1966; *Adventures and Philosophy of a Pennsylvania Dutchman: An Autobiography in a Broad Setting*, Pennsylvania Heritage, 1971; *Man and Modern Society*, Pennsylvania Heritage, 1972; *Mountain Folks: Fragments of Central Pennsylvania Lore*, Annie Halenbake Ross Library, 1974. Also author of *The Philadelphia and Erie Railroad: Its Place in American Economic History*, 1974. Author of numerous training courses, tests, and filmstrips for U.S. government agencies. Historical articles include series for *Lock Haven Express*, Lock Haven, Pa.; also contributor to regional history journals, and education and prison administration journals. Chairman of publications committee, Pennsylvania Historical Association.

WORK IN PROGRESS: Grassroots Philosophy.

SIDELIGHTS: Rosenberger built and organized an extensive private collection of material on the history of Pennsylvania and the Pennsylvania Germans. His bibliographical record published by the Pennsylvania Historical Junto lists some 170 items (up to 1959), but he has never accepted money for writing. His bibliography is currently being updated by the Junto.

BIOGRAPHICAL/CRITICAL SOURCES: Homer Tope Rosenberger: A Bibliographical Record, Pennsylvania Historical Junto, 1958.

* * *

ROSENTHAL, Jules M. 1924-

PERSONAL: Born May 21, 1924, in Chicago, Ill.; son of Irving and Shulamite (Hurwitz) Rosenthal; married Margaret Gillison (a teacher), January 27, 1951; children: Marc, David. *Education:* Northern Illinois University, B.S., 1951, M.S., 1955. *Home:* 2101 Manor Green Dr., Madison, Wis. 53711. *Office:* University of Wisconsin, 1815 University Ave., Madison, Wis. 53706.

CAREER: Madison (Wis.) public schools, teacher of English, 1955-61, public relations posts, 1961-64; University of Wisconsin, Madison, audiovisual consultant, 1964—. Freelance photo-journalist, 1955—. *Military service:* U.S. Navy, World War II.

WRITINGS: Alice the Cat Who Was Hounded, Albert Whitman, 1966.

Illustrator: Charlotte Gibson, *Let's Take a Walk*, Advanced Learning Concepts, 1971; Charlotte Gibson, *My Feelings*, Advanced Learning Concepts, 1971. Weekly column on children's books, "A Child's World of Books," appears in daily newspapers throughout the Midwest.†

* * *

ROSEWELL, Paul Truman 1926-

PERSONAL: Born February 15, 1926, in Lincoln, Neb.; son of Emil Gotthard (a florist) and Leona (Corey) Rosewell; married Lucile Smith, December 22, 1952; children: Emily Ruth, Mark Nelson. *Education:* University of Nebraska, B.Sc., 1949, M.Ed., 1960, Ed.D., 1965. *Politics:* Democrat. *Religion:* Presbyterian. *Home:* 8517 Green Branch Dr., Waco, Tex. 76710. *Office:* School of Education, Baylor University, Waco, Tex. 76703.

CAREER: High school teacher in Nebraska, 1949-57; University of Nebraska, Lincoln, supervisor of English in laboratory school, 1957-60, assistant principal of laboratory school, 1961-65; McCook College, McCook, Neb., chairman of department of English, 1960-61; Hanover College, Hanover, Ind., assistant professor, 1965-67, associate professor of secondary education, 1967-68; MacMurray College, Jacksonville, Ill., associate professor of education and chairman of department, 1968-69; Iowa State University, Ames, associate professor of education, 1969-75; Baylor University, Waco, Tex., associate professor of education, 1976—. Television teacher, KUON-TV (University of Nebraska), 1961-62; consultant to National Council of Teachers of English, 1970. *Military service:* U.S. Army, 1944-46; became staff sergeant. *Member:* National Council of Teachers of English, National Society for the Study of Education, American Educational Studies Association, Association for Supervision and Curriculum Development, National Education Association, International Reading Association, Iowa Council on Reading, Phi Delta Kappa.

WRITINGS: (With Mary L. Mielenz) *Teaching Writing Skills*, University of Nebraska Press, 1952; (with M. Agnella Gunn, Thomas Devine, and David H. Russell) "Ginn Basic Reading Series," Ginn, 1965, 100 edition, 1967. Co-compiler of booklist, "Your Reading," issued by National Council of Teachers of English, 1966. Contributor to professional journals.

WORK IN PROGRESS: A book, *Preparing for Secondary School Teaching*; an essay for *Secondary School English Instruction in Historical Perspective: A Collection of Essays*.

* * *

ROSS, Eulalie Steinmetz 1910-
(Eulalie Steinmetz)

PERSONAL: Born January 19, 1910, in Cincinnati, Ohio; daughter of John William and Minnie (Hortsman) Steinmetz; married Albert Gallatin Ross, Jr., June 1, 1953 (deceased). *Education:* University of Cincinnati, A.B., 1942; Pratt Institute, B.L.S., 1943. *Home:* 1000 Magnolia Dr., Clearwater, Fla. 33516.

CAREER: New York (N.Y.) Public Library, supervisor of storytelling, 1945-53; Cincinnati (Ohio) Public Library, coordinator of work with children, 1955-63. University of Cincinnati, Cincinnati, Ohio, lecturer on children's literature, Extension Division, 1957-60; Simmons College, School of Library Science, Boston, Mass., summer lecturer on children's literature and storytelling, 1963-68. Visiting lecturer on storytelling at New York University, Temple

University, University of Minnesota, and elsewhere. *Member:* American Library Association (program chairman of Storytelling Festival, Miami Beach, Fla., 1956; member of council, 1959-62; member of board of children's services division, 1959-62), Florida Library Association, Phi Beta Kappa.

WRITINGS: (Under name Eulalie Steinmetz; compiler of bibliography) Marie L. Shedlock, *The Art of the Story-Teller*, 3rd edition, revised, Dover, 1951; (compiler) *The Buried Treasure*, Lippincott, 1958; (compiler) *The Lost Half Hour*, Harcourt, 1963; (compiler) *The Blue Rose*, Harcourt, 1966; *The Spirited Life: Bertha Mahoney Miller and Children's Books*, Horn Books, 1973. Contributor to *Horn Book, Top of the News, Library Journal*, and other library publications.

WORK IN PROGRESS: A children's book based on her own childhood in Ohio.

SIDELIGHTS: Giving folk plays with marionettes led her to library work and storytelling. She believes a good children's librarian is one who follows the last verse of Robert Frost's "Two Tramps in Mud Time," which reads in part: "But yield who will to their separation/My object in living is to unite/My avocation and my vocation/As my two eyes make one in sight. . . ."

* * *

ROSS, Frank E. 1925-

PERSONAL: Born January 16, 1925, in Chicago, Ill.; son of Frank E. (a school administrator) and Freda (Tonnette) Ross; divorced. *Education:* Northern Illinois University, B.S., 1950; DePaul University, M.A., 1956; Wayne State University, graduate study. *Office:* Department of English, Eastern Michigan University, Ypsilanti, Mich.

CAREER: Chicago (Ill.) public schools, teacher, 1950-51; National Council of Teachers of English, Champaign, Ill., business manager, 1951-54; *English Journal*, Chicago, Ill., assistant editor, 1951-54; Detroit (Mich.) public schools, teacher, 1954-60, supervisor of English, 1960-65; Oakland County Schools, Pontiac, Mich., director of English, 1965-66; Eastern Michigan University, Ypsilanti, associate professor of English, 1966—. Chairman, Detroit News Scholastic Awards, 1965-67. *Military service:* U.S. Army, Infantry, 1943-46; served in European theater; received Bronze Star, five battle stars, and Combat Infantryman's Badge. *Member:* National Council of Teachers of English (president, secondary section, 1964-66), Midwest English Conference (member of executive committee), North Central Association English Conference (member of executive committee), Michigan Council of Teachers of English.

WRITINGS: (Co-author) *The Students' Right to Read*, National Council of Teachers of English, 1963; (co-author) *Early Years of American Literature*, Macmillan, 1964; (co-author) *Growing Years of American Literature*, Macmillan, 1964; (co-author) *Contemporary Prose*, Macmillan, 1964; (co-author) *Success in Language*, Follett, 1965; (editor) *Camelot Reader*, Avon, 1966; *Transportation of Tomorrow*, Lothrop, 1968.

AVOCATIONAL INTERESTS: Geriatrics, urban renewal, and civil rights.†

* * *

ROSS, John A(ddison) 1919-

PERSONAL: Born October 17, 1919, in Stayner, Ontario, Canada; son of William George (a farmer) and Annie

(Craven) Ross; married Kathleen Cosens, June 30, 1943; children: Robin, Dawn, Martin, Karen. *Education:* University of Toronto, B.A., 1941, M.A., 1943, Ph.D., 1947; Knox College, Toronto, Ontario, B.D., 1944. *Home:* 1962 Acadia Rd., Vancouver, British Columbia, Canada.

CAREER: Ordained Presbyterian minister, 1944; pastor at Creemore, Ontario, 1944-49, and Woodbridge, Ontario, 1949-57; St. Andrew's Hall, Vancouver, British Columbia, dean of residence, 1957—. Chairman of Board of Christian Education, The Presbyterian Church in Canada, 1954-56.

WRITINGS: This We Believe, Abingdon, 1966. Author of series of articles, "My Thoughts on the Creed," for *Presbyterian Record*, 1963-65.

WORK IN PROGRESS: Three books, *Jesus and Socrates: The Principle of Polarity*; *Theology and Aesthetics: The Basis of Believing*, and *The Communication of Christianity*.

AVOCATIONAL INTERESTS: Geology (rock hound), marine biology, painting, and camping.†

* * *

ROSS, Murray George 1912-

PERSONAL: Born April 12, 1912, in Sydney, Nova Scotia, Canada; son of George and Catherine (MacKay) Ross; married Janet Lang (a physician), May 10, 1941; children: Susan, Robert Bruce. *Education:* Acadia University, B.A., 1936; University of Toronto, M.A., 1938; University of Chicago, graduate study, 1939; Columbia University, Ed.D., 1949. *Religion:* Protestant. *Home:* 75 Highland Crescent, Willowdale, Ontario, Canada. *Office:* York University, 2275 Bayview Ave., Toronto, Ontario, Canada.

CAREER: University of Toronto, Toronto, Ontario, associate professor, 1950-55, professor of sociology, 1955, executive assistant to the president, 1956-57, vice-president, 1957-60; York University, Toronto, Ontario, president, 1960-70, University Professor of social science, 1970-72, professor emeritus, 1972—. Canadian delegate Conference on North Atlantic Community, Bruges, Belgium, 1957. Member of board of directors of National Ballet School of Canada. Chairman of board of trustees, Ontario Historical Studies Series. Honorary director, Canadian National Exhibition. *Member:* American Academy of Political and Social Science, American Sociological Association (fellow), American Association for the Advancement of Science, Canadian Club (member of executive committee), Empire Club of Canada. *Awards, honors:* UNESCO fellowships for study in England, France, Israel, the Soviet Union and the People's Republic of China.

WRITINGS: (Editor) *Towards Professional Maturity*, Association Press, 1948; *Religious Beliefs of Youth*, Association Press, 1950; *The Y.M.C.A. in Canada*, Ryerson, 1951; *Community Organization: Theory and Principles*, Harper, 1955, 2nd edition, 1965; (with C. E. Hendry) *New Understandings of Leadership: A Survey and Application of Research*, Association Press, 1957; *Case Histories in Community Organization*, Harper, 1958; *The New University*, University of Toronto Press, 1961; (editor) *New Universities in the Modern World*, Macmillan (London), 1965. Author of pamphlets and articles. Member of editorial advisory committee, *The Quarterly of Canadian Studies*.

AVOCATIONAL INTERESTS: Music, tennis, bridge.

* * *

ROSS, Stanley R(obert) 1921-

PERSONAL: Born August 8, 1921, in New York, N.Y.; son of Max G. (a sales manager) and Ethel (Aks) Ross; married Leonore Jacobson (an artist), October 7, 1945; children: Steven David, Alicia Ellen, Janet Irene. *Education:* Queens College (now Queens College of the City University of New York), Flushing, N.Y., B.A., 1942; Columbia University, M.A., 1943, Ph.D., 1951. *Office:* Department of History, University of Texas, Austin, Tex.

CAREER: Instructor in history at Queens College (now Queens College of the City University of New York), Flushing, N.Y., 1946-47, Brooklyn College (now Brooklyn College of the City University of New York), Brooklyn, N.Y., 1947-48; University of Nebraska, Lincoln, instructor, 1948-51, assistant professor, 1951-57, associate professor, 1957-60, professor of history, 1960-62; State University of New York at Stony Brook, professor of history and chairman of department, 1962-66, acting dean of College of Arts and Sciences, 1963-66, dean of College of Arts and Sciences, 1966-68; University of Texas, Austin, professor of history, 1968—, director, Institute of Latin American Studies, 1971, Provost for Arts and Sciences, 1972—, vice president, 1973—. Visiting fellow, St. Anthony's College, Oxford, 1972-73. Suffolk County (N.Y.) Committee for School District Reorganization, vice-chairman, 1965. *Military service:* U.S. Army Air Forces, 1943-46; became first lieutenant. *Member:* American Historical Association, Conference on Latin American History, Pan American Institute of Geography and History (member of history commission), Organization of American Historians, American Association of University Professors. *Awards, honors:* U.S. Department of State traveling fellow, summers, 1947, 1948; Doherty Foundation fellow, 1952-53; research grants from University of Nebraska, 1955, 1960, Rockefeller Foundation, 1958-59, 1960-61.

WRITINGS: Francisco I. Madero, Apostle of Mexican Democracy, Columbia University Press, 1955; (co-editor) *Historia Documental de Mexico*, National University of Mexico, Volume I, 1964, Volume II, 1965; (editor) *Is the Mexican Revolution Dead?*, Knopf, 1965; (compiler) *Fuentes de la Historia Contemporanea de Mexico: Periodicos y Revistas*, two volumes, El Colegio de Mexico, 1965-66; (editor) *Latin American in Transition: Problems in Training and Research*, State University of New York Press, 1970; (editor) Paul Kennedy, *The Middle Beat*, Columbia University Teachers College Press, 1971; (editor with W. P. Glade) *Criticas constructivas del sistema politico mexicano*, Institute of Latin American Studies, 1973. Contributing editor, *Handbook of Latin American Studies*; member of editorial advisory board, *Americas*, 1956—, and *Hispanic American Historial Review*.

WORK IN PROGRESS: Studies on the diplomatic mission of Dwight Morrow in Mexico and on the Carranza phase of the Mexican Revolution.

* * *

ROSSIT, Edward A. 1921-

PERSONAL: Surname is pronounced *Ross*-it; born September 4, 1921, in New York, N.Y.; son of Edward (a machinist) and Doris (Reinhart) Rossit; married Nora E. Peterson, March 14, 1954; children: Jeffrey, Erik, Dawn, Randolph. *Education:* Attended City College (now City College of the City University of New York), 1940-43; New York University, B.A., 1947; Columbia University, graduate study, 1947-48. *Politics:* Republican. *Religion:* Lutheran. *Office:* 1007 North Rogers St., Olympia, Wash. 98502.

CAREER: New York Herald Tribune, New York, N.Y., reporter, 1940; U.S. Department of Defense, Military Government officer (civilian) in Germany, 1948-50; U.S. Department of State, Foreign Service staff officer in Germany, 1950-52; Federal Fence Co., Brentwood, N.Y., owner, 1952-60; E. A. Rossit & Associates (public relations), Seattle, Wash., president, 1960—. Engineer, Boeing Airplane Co., 1962-69; program manager, State of Washington Division of Vocational Rehabilitation, 1970—. Republican candidate for Secretary of State of Washington in 1964. Military service: U.S. Army Air Forces, 1942-46; received Air Medal with oak leaf cluster, two battle stars, and Presidential Unit Citation.

WRITINGS: Northwest Mountaineering, Caxton, 1965; Snow Camping and Mountaineering, Funk, 1970. Also writer of State Facilities Plan (reports), annually, 1971—. Contributor to Freeman, National Wildlife, Science Teacher, Journal of Rehabilitation, and V.F.W. Magazine.

* * *

ROSSNER, Judith (Perelman) 1935-

PERSONAL: Born March 1, 1935, in New York, N.Y.; daughter of Joseph George and Dorothy (Shapiro) Perelman; married Robert Rossner (a teacher and writer), June 13, 1954 (divorced); children: Jean, Daniel. Education: City College (now of the City University of New York), New York, N.Y., student, 1952-55. Residence: Croton-on-Hudson, N.Y. 10520. Agent: Wendy Weil, Julian Bach Agency, 3 East 48th St., New York, N.Y. 10017.

WRITINGS: To the Precipice, Morrow, 1966; Nine Months in the Life of an Old Maid, Dial, 1969; Any Minute I Can Split, McGraw, 1972; Looking for Mr. Goodbar, Simon & Schuster, 1975.

WORK IN PROGRESS: A novel.

* * *

ROSS WILLIAMSON, Hugh 1901-
(Ian Rossiter)

PERSONAL: Born January 2, 1901, in Romsey, Hampshire, England; son of Hugh (a Congregational minister) and Grace Winifred (Walker) Ross Williamson; married Margaret Joan Cox (an educator and television producer), November 3, 1941; children: Julia Nesbyth, Hugh. Education: University of London, B.A. (honours), 1922. Politics: None. Religion: Roman Catholic. Home: 193 Sussex Gardens, London W2, England. Agent: John Johnson, 51-54 Goschen Buildings, 12 Henrietta St., London WC2, England.

CAREER: Preparatory school master in Burgess Hill, Sussex, England, 1922-24; Yorkshire Post, Yorkshire, England, drama critic and assistant editor, 1925-30; The Bookman, London, England, editor, 1930-34; The Strand Magazine, London, acting editor, 1934-35; London General Press, London, director, 1935-42; clergyman of the Church of England, 1943-55; full-time professional writer and actor, 1955—. Member: Royal Society of Literature (fellow), Savage Club.

WRITINGS—Plays: Rose and Glove, Chatto & Windus, 1934; After the Event, Baker International Play Bureau, 1935; The Seven Deadly Virtues, In a Glass Darkly [and] Various Heavens (sequence), Constable, 1936; Cinderella's Grandchild, Baker International Play Bureau, 1936; Mr. Gladstone, Constable, 1937; Stories From History (10 plays for school), Duckworth, 1938; Paul, a Bondslave

(radio play), S.C.M. Press, 1945; Queen Elizabeth, Constable, 1947; Fool's Paradise, Evans, 1947.

"The Cardinal's Learning," in Best One-Act Plays of 1948-49, edited by J. W. Marriott, Harrap, 1950; "Conversation With a Ghost," in Best One-Act Plays of 1950-51, edited by J. W. Marriott, Harrap, 1950; "Gunpowder, Treason, and Plot," in Plays of the Year, edited by J. C. Trewin, Elek, 1951; "Diamond Cut Diamond," in Plays of the Year, edited by J. C. Trewin, Elek, 1952; His Eminence of England, Heinemann, 1953; "Heart of Bruce," in Plays of the Year, edited by J. C. Trewin, Elek, 1959; "Teresa of Avila," in Plays of the Year, edited by J. C. Trewin, Elek, 1961; Pavane for a Dead Infanta, Stourton Press, 1972.

Other writings: The Poetry of T. S. Eliot, Hodder & Stoughton, 1932; John Hampden, Hodder & Stoughton, 1933; King James I, Duckworth, 1935; Gods and Mortals in Love, Country Life, 1936; Who is for Liberty?, M. Joseph, 1939; George Villiers, First Duke of Buckingham, Duckworth, 1940; A.D. 33, Collins, 1941; Captain Thomas Schofield, Collins, 1942; Charles and Cromwell, Duckworth, 1946; The Arrow and the Sword, Faber, 1947, 2nd edition, 1955; The Story Without an End, Mowbray, 1947, 2nd edition, 1954; The Silver Bowl, M. Joseph, 1948, 2nd edition, New English Library, 1962; The Seven Christian Virtues, S.C.M. Press, 1949; Four Stuart Portraits, Evans, 1949.

The Gunpowder Plot, Faber, 1951; Sir Walter Raleigh, Faber, 1951; Jeremy Taylor, Dobson, 1952; Canterbury Cathedral, Country Life, 1953; The Ancient Capital: An Historian in Search of Winchester, Muller, 1953; The Children's Book of British Saints, Harrap, 1953; The Children's Book of French Saints, Harrap, 1954; Historical Whodunits, Phoenix, 1955, Macmillan, 1956; James, By the Grace of God, M. Joseph, 1955, Regnery, 1956; The Children's Book of Italian Saints, Harrap, 1955; The Great Prayer, Collins, 1955, Macmillan, 1956; The Church of England and "The Great Prayer," Catholic League, 1955; The Children's Book Spanish Saints, Harrap, 1956; The Walled Garden (autobiography), M. Joseph, 1956, Macmillan, 1957; The Day They Killed the King, Macmillan, 1957; Enigmas of History, Macmillan, 1957; The Beginning of the English Reformation, Sheed & Ward, 1957; The Sisters, M. Joseph, 1958, published as The Conspirators and the Crown, Hawthorn, 1959; The Children's Book of German Saints, Harrap, 1958; The Challenge of Bernadette, Newman, 1958.

Sixty Saints of Christendom (collection), Harrap, 1960, published as The Young People's Book of Saints, Hawthorn, 1960; A Wicked Pack of Cards, M. Joseph, 1961; The Day Shakespeare Died, M. Joseph, 1962; The Flowering Hawthorn, Hawthorn, 1962; Guy Fawkes, Collins, 1964; The Butt of Malmsey, M. Joseph, 1967; The Marriage Made in Blood, M. Joseph, 1968; A Matter of Martyrdom, M. Joseph, 1969; The Cardinal in Exile, M. Joseph, 1970; The Florentine Woman, St. Martin's, 1970; The Last of the Valois, St. Martin's, 1971; Paris is Worth a Mass, St. Martin's, 1971; Kind Kit, St. Martin's, 1972; The Modern Mass, Tan Books, 1972; The Great Betrayal, Tan Books, 1972; Catherine de Medici, Viking, 1973; Lorenzo the Magnificent, Putnam, 1974; Letter to Julia, Stourton Press, 1974,

Editor: Jack Waller, Wild Grows the Heather, Chappell, 1957; John Bunyan, Pilgrim's Work, Norton, 1959; (and author of introduction) William King, An Historical Account of the Heathen Gods and Heroes Necessary for the

Understanding of the Ancient Poets, Southern Illinois University Press, 1965.

Author of introduction: Reginald Scot, *The Discoverie of Witchcraft*, Southern Illinois University Press, 1964.

Unpublished plays: "Monsieur Moi" (produced and subsequently televised as "The Magnificent Egoist"), 1935; "Odds Beyond Arithmetic," 1947; "The Mime of Bernadette," 1958; "The Test of Truth," 1958; (with Ian Burford) "Quartet for Lovers," 1962; "The Prisoner of Longwood," 1964.

WORK IN PROGRESS: Series of novels on the sixteenth century.

SIDELIGHTS: Ross Williamson told *CA:* "In 1933 [I] entered politics at suggestion of [my] cousin, Sir John (later Lord) Simon, then Foreign Secretary. Later joined Labour Party and was prospective Labour candidate for East Dorset from 1937 to 1941 when [I] was officially expelled for [my] book *Who is for Liberty?* On becoming Anglican clergyman gave up political affiliations."

Ross Williamson uses the pseudonym Ian Rossiter only for acting.

BIOGRAPHICAL/CRITICAL SOURCES: The Walled Garden, M. Joseph, 1956, Macmillan, 1957.

* * *

ROTH, Robert J. 1920-

PERSONAL: Born November 28, 1920, in New Jersey; son of Leo V. and Margaret (Mascher) Roth. *Education:* Boston College, A.B., 1944; Fordham University, M.A., 1947, Ph.D., 1961. *Home and office:* Fordham University, Bronx, N.Y. 10458.

CAREER: Roman Catholic priest, member of Society of Jesus; Fordham University, Bronx, N.Y., instructor, 1953-57, assistant professor, 1957-64, associate professor, 1964-70, professor of philosophy, 1970—, vice-chairman of department, 1961-63, chairman of department, 1970-73, president of faculty senate, 1972-74, dean of Fordham College, 1974—. *Member:* American Philosophical Association, American Catholic Philosophical Association, Jesuit Philosophical Association.

WRITINGS: John Dewey and Self-Realization, Prentice-Hall, 1963; *American Religious Philosophy*, Harcourt, 1967; (editor) *God Knowable and Unknowable*, Fordham University Press, 1973; (editor) *Person and Community*, Fordham University Press, 1974. Contributor to *International Philosophical Quarterly, Thought, New Scholasticism, Humanist, Franciscan Studies, America*, and *Review for Religious*.

* * *

ROUSE, Parke (Shepherd), Jr. 1915-

PERSONAL: Born July 20, 1915, in Smithfield, Va.; son of Parke Shepherd and Pauline (Dashiell) Rouse; married Elizabeth Gayle, October 3, 1946; children: Elizabeth Marshall and Sarah Dashiell (twins), Parke Shepherd III. *Education:* Washington and Lee University, A.B., 1937. *Religion:* Episcopalian. *Home:* 14 Bayberry Lane, Williamsburg, Va. 23185.

CAREER: Richmond Times-Dispatch, Richmond, Va., editorial writer, 1946-48, Sunday editor, 1948-50; director of public relations, Virginia State Chamber of Commerce, Richmond, 1950-51, and Colonial Williamsburg, Inc., Williamsburg, Va., 1953-54; Jamestown Foundation, Williams-

burg, Va., executive director, 1954—. Member of alumni board of trustees, Washington and Lee University, 1957-58; director, Jamestown Glasshouse Foundation. Past president of Williamsburg Community Council and Williamsburg Chamber of Commerce; vice-president, Williamsburg Community Hospital; chairman of Williamsburg-James City County United Fund, 1964. *Military service:* U.S. Navy, 1942-46; served on communications and publications staff of Admiral Nimitz, Pacific Fleet; became lieutenant.

MEMBER: Sons of the Revolution, Society of Colonial Wars, Phi Beta Kappa, Omicron Delta Kappa, Sigma Delta Chi, Rotary Club (Williamsburg; past president), Golden Horseshoe Club. *Awards, honors:* First award in feature writing and editorial writing, Virginia Press Association, 1939-41; Meritorious Service Award, Virginia Travel Council, 1958; Freedoms Foundation Award, 1958.

WRITINGS: They Gave Us Freedom, Colonial Williamsburg, 1951; *The City That Turned Back Time*, Colonial Williamsburg, 1952; *Williamsburg in Color*, Colonial Williamsburg, 1954; *The Printer in 18th Century Williamsburg*, Colonial Williamsburg, 1955; *Jamestown, First English Colony*, American Heritage Publishing Co., 1965; *Virginia, The English Heritage in America*, Hastings, 1966; *Jamestown, and Jamestown Festival Park*, Jamestown Foundation, 1966. Contributor to *Saturday Evening Post, New York Times Magazine*, and other magazines and newspapers.

WORK IN PROGRESS: Virginia: A Pictorial History.

* * *

ROUX, Georges 1914-

PERSONAL: Surname is pronounced Rue; born November 16, 1914, in Salon, France; son of Fernand Edouard (an army officer) and Marie (Maumen) Roux; married Jocelyn D. Tonkin, June 10, 1950; children: (previous marriage) Serge, Michel; (present marriage) Isabelle, Martine. *Education:* Attended St. Joseph University, Beirut, Lebanon, 1928-33; University of Paris, M.D., 1941; also studied at Ecole du Louvre and Ecole des Hautes Etudes, Paris, 1947-50. *Religion:* Roman Catholic. *Home:* 4 rue de l'eglise, Paris 15, France. *Agent:* Curtis Brown Ltd., 13 King St., London W.C.2, England. *Office:* c/o Laboratories Glaxo, 43 rue vineuse, Paris 16, France.

CAREER: In private practice of medicine, Paris, France, 1943-50; Iraq Petroleum Co., medical officer in Qatar, Persian Gulf, 1950-52, in Basrah, Iraq, 1952-59; Glaxo Group Ltd., London, England, overseas medical adviser, 1960-66; Glaxo International Ltd., London, England, manager of medical division, 1966—. *Military service:* French Army, 1939-43; became second lieutenant. *Member:* British Medical Association.

WRITINGS: Ancient Iraq, Allen & Unwin, 1964. Contributor to *Revue d'Assyriologie, Sumer*, and *Bibliotheca Orientalis*.

WORK IN PROGRESS: Research in the history and culture of ancient Mesopotamia, particularly political and economic history, historical topography, religion; the Persian Gulf in antiquity.

SIDELIGHTS: Roux speaks English, French, German, and Arabic; has some knowledge of Latin, Akkadian, and Sumerian. *Avocational interests:* The arts, especially painting.

ROWE, John L. 1914-

PERSONAL: Born May 18, 1914, in Oconomowoc, Wis.; son of Alfred A. and Abbie (Erickson) Rowe. *Education:* Wisconsin State University-Whitewater, B.Ed., 1935, University of Iowa, M.A., 1939; Columbia University, professional diploma, 1944, Ed.D., 1946. *Politics:* Democrat. *Religion:* Roman Catholic. *Home:* 2515 Olson Dr., Grand Forks, N.D. 58201. *Office:* University of North Dakota, Grand Forks, N.D. 58201.

CAREER: Teacher in public and private schools of Wisconsin and Michigan; Boston University, Boston, Mass., associate professor of business education and head of department, 1945-48; Columbia University, Teachers College, New York, N.Y., associate professor of education, 1948-52; Northern Illinois University, De Kalb, professor of business education, 1952-55; University of North Dakota, Grand Forks, professor of business education, 1955-73, Chester Fritz Distinguished Professor of Business Education, 1973—, chairman of department, beginning 1955. Visiting professor, University of Puerto Rico, 1957; visiting summer professor at George Washington University, 1943, University of Florida, 1945, and Catholic University of America, 1955. Member of Governor's North Dakota Commission for Crippled Children, 1967-70, North Dakota Bicentennial Commission, 1968—, board of regents, Mary College.

MEMBER: National Business Education Association, National Association for Business Teacher Education (president, 1957-58), Catholic Business Education Association (president, Midwest branch, 1967—), American Vocational Association (vice-president, 1971—), American Association of University Professors, Newcomen Society in North America, Eastern Business Teachers Association, North Dakota Education Association, Delta Pi Epsilon, Gamma Theta Epsilon, Kappa Delta Pi, Phi Delta Kappa, Pi Omega Pi, Sigma Tau Delta.

WRITINGS—Co-author: *World Economic Geography*, South-Western Publishing, 1950; *Typewriting for Speed and Accuracy*, McGraw, 1952, 3rd edition published as *Typewriting Drills for Speed and Accuracy*, 1966; *Gregg Typing* (for high schools), beginning and advanced courses, McGraw, 1953, 5th edition published as *Typing 300*, Volume I, 1972, Volume II, 1973; *Typing Power Drills*, McGraw, 1956, revised edition, 1964; *Gregg Typewriting for Colleges*, McGraw, 1957, revised edition, 1963; *Gregg Typing for High Schools, Second Edition* (one-year course), McGraw, 1958, 3rd edition revised, 1964; *Gregg Typing 191*, McGraw, Volume I, 1962, Volume II, 1963, 2nd edition, 1967; *Typing 75*, three volumes, McGraw, 1972. Writer of film script for "Electric Typing Time," produced by RKO-Pathe and International Business Machines Corp., and more than one hundred articles dealing with teacher education. Editor, American Business Education *Yearbook*, 1956, 1957, and Eastern Business Teachers Association *Yearbook*, 1965; editor, National Association for Business Teacher Education quarterlies and bulletins, 1959-64.†

* * *

ROWE, Robert 1920-

PERSONAL: Born December 31, 1920, in Surbiton, Surrey, England; son of James Stewart and Anna Gray (Good) Rowe; married Barbara Elizabeth Hamilton Baynes, June, 1953; children: Madeleine E., Sebastian R. T., Rebecca C. *Education:* Cambridge University, M.A. (with honors),

1952; Southern College of Art, Museums Association Diploma. *Religion:* Roman Catholic. *Home:* Grove Lodge, Shadwell, Leeds 17, Yorkshire, England. *Office:* Leeds City Art Gallery and Temple, Newsam House, Leeds 15, Yorkshire, England.

CAREER: Birmingham Museum and Art Gallery, Birmingham, England, assistant keeper of art, 1950-56; Manchester City Art Galleries, Manchester, England, deputy director, 1956-58; Leeds City Art Gallery and Temple Newsam House, Leeds, England, director, 1958—. Extramural lecturer at University of Birmingham and University of Manchester, 1951-58; lecturer on Canadian tour sponsored by National Gallery of Canada, 1961. Governor of Leeds College of Art, 1961-68. Member of advisory council of Victoria and Albert Museum, 1969—. Member of art panel, Arts Council of Great Britain, 1959-62, 1973—, and of art treasurers committee, University of Leeds, 1961—. *Military service:* Royal Air Force, World War II. *Member:* Museums Association (fellow; member of council, 1963-66, 1970-73; president, 1973-74), Liveryman of Worshipful Company of Goldsmiths, Royal Society of Arts (fellow). *Awards, honors:* Commander, Order of the British Empire, 1969.

WRITINGS: Benozzo Gozzoli (educational monograph), Medici Society, 1956; *Pieter de Hooch* (educational monograph), Medici Society, 1958; *Adam Silver*, Faber, 1965. Contributor to educational and art periodicals.

WORK IN PROGRESS: Research on neo-classical movement in England, with special reference to silver.

* * *

ROZEBOOM, William W(arren) 1928-

PERSONAL: Surname is pronounced *Rose*-uh-bome; born February 29, 1928, in Ottumwa, Iowa; son of William Anthony (a high school teacher) and Cynthia (Pennings) Rozeboom; married Virginia Darline Munson, June 13, 1954; children: William Alan, Steven Lloyd, Cynthia Louise, Karl Eric, Mark Loren. *Education:* Attended Central College (now Central University of Iowa), 1945-47; University of Chicago, S.B., 1949, Ph.D., 1956. *Politics:* Liberal Republican. *Religion:* Atheist. *Office:* Department of Psychology, University of Alberta, Edmonton, Alberta, Canada.

CAREER: University of Minnesota, Minneapolis, National Science Foundation postdoctoral fellow, 1956-58; St. Olaf College, Northfield, Minn., 1958-61, began as instructor, became assistant professor of psychology; Wesleyan University, Middletown, Conn., assistant professor of psychology, 1961-64; University of Alberta, Edmonton, associate professor, 1964-68, professor of psychology, 1968—. *Military service:* U.S. Army, Medical Corps, 1950-52. *Member:* American Psychological Association, Canadian Psychological Association, Canadian Philosophical Association, British Society for the Philosophy of Science, Philosophy of Science Association, Society of Multivariate Experimental Psychology, Sigma Xi.

WRITINGS: Foundations of the Theory of Prediction, Dorsey, 1966; (editor with Joseph R. Royce, and contributor) *The Psychology of Knowing*, Gordon & Breach, 1972.

Contributor: H. Feigl and G. Maxwell, editors, *Current Issues in the Philosophy of Science*, Holt, 1961; *Minnesota Studies in the Philosophy of Science*, University of Minnesota Press, Volume III, edited by Feigl and Maxwell, 1962,

Volume IV, edited by M. Radner and S. Winokur, 1970; Joseph R. Royce, editor, *Toward Unification in Psychology*, Toronto University Press, 1970; E. F. Heerman and L. A. Braskamp, editors, *Readings in Statistics for Behavioral Sciences*, Prentice-Hall, 1970; D. E. Morrison and R. E. Henkel, editors, *Significance Tests in Behavioral Research*, Aldine, 1970; B. Lieberman, editor, *Contemporary Problems in Statistics*, Oxford University Press, 1970; P. Badia, A. Haber, and R. P. Runyon, editors, *Research Problems in Psychology*, Addison-Wesley, 1970; M. Roth and L. Galis, editors, *Knowing: Essays in the Analysis of Knowledge*, Random House, 1970; R. Buck and R. S. Cohen, editors, *Boston Studies in the Philosophy of Science*, Volume VIII, D. Reidel, 1971; J. A. Steger, editor, *Readings in Statistics*, Holt, 1971; S. R. Brown and D. J. Brenner, editors, *Science, Psychology and Communication: Essays Honoring William Stephenson*, Teachers College Press, 1972; R. M. Chisholm and R. J. Swartz, editors, *Empirical Knowledge*, Prentice-Hall, 1973; Royce, editor, *Multivariate Analysis and Psychological Theory*, Academic Press, 1973; E. Carterette and M. Friedman, editors, *Handbook of Perception*, Volume I, Academic Press, 1974; B. Freed, editor, *Forms of Representation*, D. Reidel, in press. Contributor to journals in his field.

WORK IN PROGRESS: A book, *The Theory of Data Analysis*; journal articles.

* * *

RUBIN, Eli Z(under) 1922-

PERSONAL: Born February 4, 1922, in Boston, Mass.; son of Jacob and Mabel (Cohn) Rubin; married Harriet Shurson, June 15, 1947; children: Christopher, Susan. *Education:* Harvard University, A.B., 1943; Boston University, M.A., 1947, Ph.D., 1951. *Home:* 618 North Rosedale, Grosse Pointe Woods, Mich. 48236. *Office:* Northeast Guidance Center, 17000 East Warren, Detroit, Mich. 48224.

CAREER: Massachusetts General Hospital, Boston, Mass., staff psychologist, 1949-51; Brown University, Providence, R.I., instructor in psychology, 1951-55; chief clinical psychologist at Bradley Home, Riverside, R.I., 1951-55, at Dayton Guidance Center and Receiving Hospital for Children, Dayton, Ohio, 1955-56; diplomate of American Board of Examiners in Professional Psychology, 1956; Lafayette Clinic, Detroit, Mich., chief psychologist, Children's Unit, 1956-60, director of rehabilitation and psychology, 1960-65, head of Division of Psychology, 1965-68, consultant, 1968—; Northeast Guidance Center, director, 1968—; Wayne State University, Detroit, Mich., adjunct assistant professor, 1956-61, adjunct associate professor, 1961-73, adjunct professor of psychology, 1973—. *Military service:* U.S. Army, 1943-46; became second lieutenant. *Member:* American Psychological Association, American Orthopsychiatric Association, Michigan Psychological Association.

WRITINGS: (With Clyde Simson and Marcus Betwee) *Emotionally Handicapped Children and the Elementary School*, Wayne State University Press, 1966; (with Lela Llorens) *Developing Ego Functions in Disturbed Children*, Wayne State University Press, 1967; (with Jean Braun and others) *Cognitive Perceptual Motor Dysfunction*, Wayne State University Press, 1972.

* * *

RUBLOWSKY, John M(artin) 1928-

PERSONAL: Born March 5, 1928, in Evansville, Pa.; son of Peter (a crane operator) and Frances (Ryzka) Rublowsky; married Ruth Kulin (a schoolteacher), March 19, 1949; children: Mia (Mrs. Howard Swerdloff), Stefan. *Education:* Attended Columbia University, 1946-49; studied violin with J. Thibaud, Paris, France, 1949-50; attended Manhattan School of Music, 1950-51. *Home:* 452 Fifth St., Brooklyn, N.Y. 11215.

CAREER: Violinist with St. Louis Symphony, 1951-55; *Brooklyn Heights Press*, Brooklyn, N.Y., and *The Village Voice*, New York, N.Y., columnist-writer, 1955-59; *Space World* (magazine), New York, N.Y., editor, 1959, 1963; full-time free-lance writer, 1963—. *Military service:* U.S. Navy, 1944-46. *Member:* Authors Guild, Anonymous Arts Recovery Society (co-founder), New York Cactus and Succulent Society (co-founder).

WRITINGS: Is Anybody Out There?, Walker & Co., 1962 (published in England as *Life on Other Worlds*, Constable, 1964); *Life and Death of the Sun*, Basic Books, 1964; *Light: Our Bridge to the Stars*, Basic Books, 1964; *Pop Art*, Basic Books, 1965; *Nature in the City*, Basic Books, 1967; *Popular Music*, Basic Books, 1967; *Music in America*, Macmillan, 1967; *After the Crash: America in the Great Depression*, Crowell-Collier, 1970; *Black Music in America*, Basic Books, 1971; *The Stoned Age: A History of Drugs in America*, Putnam, 1974.

WORK IN PROGRESS: A fairy tale for children, for Harper; research for a book on work attitudes in America from the earliest European settlements to the present.

* * *

RUBY, Robert Holmes 1921-

PERSONAL: Born April 23, 1921, in Mabton, Wash.; son of Henry Ward (a farmer) and Myrtle (Holmes) Ruby; married Lelia Jeanne Henderson, July 11, 1953; children: Edna Phyllis, Henry Ward, Mary Louise, Robert Henderson. *Education:* Whitworth College, B.A., 1942; Washington University, St. Louis, Mo., M.D., 1945. *Politics:* Republican. *Religion:* Presbyterian. *Home:* 4535 West Peninsula Drive, Moses Lake, Wash. 98837. *Office:* 1022 Ivy Street, Moses Lake, Wash. 98837.

CAREER: Physician and surgeon, practicing in Moses Lake, Wash. Chairman of board, Moses Lake Museum, 1958—, and Moses Lake Public Library, 1959-71. Member, Governor's Planning Committee, Governor's Conference on Libraries, 1967-69. *Military service:* U.S. Army, 1943-45. U.S. Army Air Forces, 1946-47; became captain. U.S. Public Health Service, 1953-54; became senior surgeon. *Member:* American Medical Association, Washington State Medical Society, Washington Library Association (director, 1971-73), Grant County Medical Society, Grant County Historical Society (member of board of directors, 1962—), Washington Library Trustees Association (president, 1967-69). *Awards, honors:* Northwest Author Award, 1966; Pacific Northwest Booksellers Award, 1966; Governor's Festival of Arts certificate, 1967, 1970.

WRITINGS: The Oglala Sioux, Vantage, 1955; (with John Brown) *Half Sun on the Columbia*, University of Oklahoma Press, 1965; (with Brown) *The Spokane Indians: Children of the Sun*, University of Oklahoma Press, 1970; (with Brown) *The Cayuse Indians: Imperial Tribesmen of Old Oregon*, University of Oklahoma Press, 1972; *Ferry Boats on the Columbia*, Superior, 1974. Contributor to magazines.†

RUDD, Margaret T(homas) 1907-

PERSONAL: Born December 15, 1907, in Ponce, Puerto Rico; daughter of Augustus Bartow (a minister) and May (Bagby) Rudd. *Education:* University of Richmond, B.A., 1929; Columbia University, M.A., 1937; summer courses at National University of Mexico, 1929, 1941, and Sorbonne, University of Paris, 1931. *Religion:* Baptist. *Home and office:* 2013 Franklin Ave., McLean, Va. 22101.

CAREER: Stuart Hall, Staunton, Va., teacher of Spanish and French, 1929-32; Blackstone Junior College, Blackstone, Va., dean, 1937-39, teacher of Spanish and French, 1937-41; Stephens College, Columbia, Mo., teacher of Spanish, 1941-43; University of Richmond, Westhampton College, Richmond, Va., assistant professor, 1943-46, associate professor of Spanish, 1948-63, chairman of department of modern foreign languages, 1955-63. Assistant professor of Spanish, College of William and Mary, Williamsburg, Va., 1967. Assistant director of Cultural Institute, U.S. State Department, Concepcion, Chile, 1945-46. *Member:* American Association of Teachers of Spanish and Portuguese, National League of America Pen Women, Altrusa International, World Poetry Society, Virginia Writers Club, Poetry Society of Virginia, Intercontinental. *Awards, honors:* Organization of American States grant for travel and research in Chile, 1963.

WRITINGS: (Co-author) *Nuestros vecinos mexicanos* (textbook), Ronald, 1945; *The Lone Heretic* (biography of Miguel de Unamuno), University of Texas Press, 1963; (contributor) *Moon Age Poets*, edited by Jaye Giammarino, Prairie Press Books, 1970; (contributor) *The Golden Anniversary Anthology*, edited by Bes B. Greshan, McClure Press, 1973; (co-author) *... And Three Small Fishes* (poems), McClure Press, 1974; *Gabriela Mistral: The Chilean Years*, University of New Mexico Press, 1975.

* * *

RUDER, William 1921-

PERSONAL: Born October 17, 1921, in New York, N.Y.; son of Jacob Loeb and Rose (Rosenberg) Ruder; married Helen Finn, September 21, 1945; children: Robin Ann, Abby, Brian, Michal Ellen, Eric. *Education:* City College (now City College of the City University of New York), B.S.S., 1941. *Home:* Beverly Rd., Rye, N.Y. *Office:* Ruder & Finn, Inc., 110 East 59th St., New York, N.Y. 10022.

CAREER: Samuel Goldwyn Productions, Hollywood, Calif., public relations staff, 1946-48; Ruder & Finn, Inc. (public relations), New York, N.Y., president, 1948—. U.S. Government, Washington, D.C., assistant secretary of commerce, 1961-62. Chairman of board, Manhattanville College; member of board of National Civil Service League, National Book League, and United Nations Association of the U.S.A.; member of New York Mayor's Committee in the Public Interest. *Military service:* U.S. Army Air Forces, 1941-46; became captain. *Member:* Public Relations Society of America, Chief Executives Forum, Atrium Club.

WRITINGS: (With Raymond Nathan) *The Businessman's Guide to Washington*, Prentice-Hall, 1964, revised edition, Macmillan, 1975.

AVOCATIONAL INTERESTS: Mosaics.

* * *

RUDOFSKY, Bernard 1905-

PERSONAL: Born April 13, 1905, in Austria; son of Bernard and Elisabeth (Primus) Rudofsky; married Berta Doctor, 1935. *Education:* Polytechnic University, Vienna, Austria, M.Arch. and Diplom-Ingenieur, 1928, Doctor Technicarum, 1931. *Residence:* New York, N.Y.

CAREER: Self-employed architect with offices in Italy and Brazil, 1932-41; Museum of Modern Art, New York, N.Y., beginning 1941, director of apparel research, 1944-45, guest director of exhibitions, 1944-45, 1956, 1960-65. Photographer. Chief architect of U.S. Government exhibits at Universal Exposition, Brussels, Belgium, 1957-58; visiting professor of art, Yale University, 1965-66. *Awards, honors:* Fulbright research scholarship at Waseda University, Tokyo, 1958-60; Rockefeller Foundation fellow, 1963; Guggenheim fellow, 1963-65.

WRITINGS: Are Clothes Modern?, Theobald, 1947; *Behind the Picture Window*, Oxford University Press, 1955; *Architecture Without Architects*, Museum of Modern Art, 1964; *The Kimono Mind*, Doubleday, 1965; *Streets for People: A Primer for Americans*, Doubleday, 1969; *The Unfashionable Human Body*, Doubleday, 1971. Editor of *Domus* (Milan), 1937-38; associate editor, *New Pencil Points* (now *Progressive Architecture*), 1943; editorial director, *Interiors*, 1946-49.†

* * *

RULAND, Vernon Joseph 1931-

PERSONAL: Born October 28, 1931, in Erie, Pa.; son of Vernon Joseph and Nell Marie (Driscoll) Ruland. *Education:* Bellarmine School of Theology (formerly West Baden College), Licentiate in Philosophy, 1957, Licentiate in Theology, 1964; Loyola University, Chicago, Ill., M.A., 1957; University of Chicago, Ph.D., 1967; University of Detroit, M.A., 1972. *Home:* Provincial Residence, 602 Boulevard Center Bldg., Cass at West Grand, Detroit, Mich.

CAREER: Roman Catholic priest, member of Society of Jesus (S.J.); St. Xavier High School, Cincinnati, Ohio, teacher of English, 1957-60; Jesuit School of Theology, Chicago, Ill., assistant professor of religious studies, 1968; University of Detroit, Detroit, Mich., associate professor of religious studies, 1969-74. Visiting professor, Carleton College, 1968, University of San Francisco, 1974-75.

WRITINGS: (Editor with Julian Maline) *Prose and Poetry of America*, Singer, 1965; *Horizons of Criticism: An Assessment of Religious Literary Premises*, American Library Association, 1975. Contributor to *Catholic Encyclopedia*; also contributor of articles and reviews to religious and learned journals.

SIDELIGHTS: Ruland told *CA:* "Theology in my opinion must be a theology of something—its major questions are posed by modern man's situation symbolized in his literature and elsewhere. I would like to integrate the roles of liturgical leader, pastoral psychotherapist, teacher, and scholar. My counseling, for example, has given me new experiential perspectives on Freud and Jung, whom I now use more resourcefully in literary criticism; in turn, I hope to bring to psychotherapy an informed sense of metaphor, of religious pseudonyms, and an eagerness to speculate on my experience". *Avocational interests:* Conversation and music.

* * *

RUMMEL, J(osiah) Francis 1911-

PERSONAL: Born June 16, 1911, in Lake Mills, Iowa; son of David Harry (a superintendent of schools) and Beulah

(Harris) Rummel; married Margaret Charrie Cooper, September 22, 1934; children: Richard Harris, Lawrence Dean. *Education:* State College of Iowa (now Iowa State University of Science and Technology), B.A., 1933; University of Iowa, M.A., 1947, Ph.D., 1950. *Politics:* Republican. *Religion:* Methodist. *Office:* University of Montana, Missoula, Mont. 59801.

CAREER: Elementary teacher in Cedar County, Iowa, 1930-31; Armour & Co., Mason City, Iowa, scale supervisor, 1934-42; high school principal, Cresco, Iowa, 1946-48; University of Oregon, Eugene, assistant professor, 1950-55, associate professor, 1955-61, professor of education, 1961-67, dean of graduate students, 1965-67; University of Montana, Missoula, professor of education and dean of School of Education, 1967—. International Co-operation Administration, specialist in education research and adviser to government of Egypt, 1955-56, technical assistant in teacher education program in Libya, 1956-57; Agency for International Development, director of program for development of teacher education in Cambodia, 1963. Consultant to Oregon State Department of Education, 1950-63, and Oregon State Board of Dental Examiners, 1952-55. *Military service:* U.S. Naval Reserve, Hospital Corps, 1942-45.

MEMBER: American Educational Research Association, National Council on Measurement in Education, National Society for the Study of Education, National Conference of Directors of State Testing Programs (chairman, 1961), Psychometric Society, American Association of University Professors, Phi Delta Kappa, Kappa Mu Epsilon.

WRITINGS: Know Your Pupils, Oregon State Department of Education, 1951; *An Introduction to Research Procedures in Education*, Harper, 1958, 2nd edition, 1964; (with H. H. Remmers and N. L. Gage) *A Practical Introduction to Measurement and Evaluation*, Harper, 1960, 2nd edition, 1966; (with W. C. Ballaine) *Research Methodology in Business*, Harper, 1964. Contributor to professional journals.

SIDELIGHTS: Rummel has traveled extensively in Europe and Asia. *Avocational interests:* Boating and fishing.

* * *

RUNYON, Charles W. 1928-
(Mark West)

PERSONAL: Born June 9, 1928, in Sheridan, Mo.; son of Monte Charles (a farmer and schoolteacher) and Nina (a schoolteacher; maiden name, West) Runyon; married Ruth Phillips (a student nurse), January 29, 1955; children: Charles W., Jr., Mark, Matthew. *Education:* Attended University of Missouri, 1947-50, 1953-54, Indiana University, 1950, and University of Munich, 1951-52. *Home:* Route 1, Box 220, Farmington, Mo. *Agent:* Richard Curtis, 1215 Fifth Ave., New York, N.Y. 10029.

CAREER: Former newspaper reporter in Columbia, Mo.; Sinclair Pipeline Co., Independence, Kan., editor, 1954-57; Standard Oil Co., Chicago, Ill., editor, 1957-60; free-lance writer, 1960—. *Military service:* U.S. Army, 1948-50, 1951-53. *Member:* Mystery Writers of America, Science Fiction Writers of America, St. Francois Writers Society. *Awards, honors:* Edgar Allan Poe Award from Mystery Writers of America, and best book of the year award from Missouri Writers Guild, both for *Power Kill.*

WRITINGS—All published by Gold Medal Books, except as indicated: *Death Cycle*, 1962; *Color Him Dead*, 1963; *The Prettiest Girl I Ever Killed*, 1965; *Bloody Jungle*, Ace

Books, 1966; *The Black Moth*, 1967; *No Place to Hide*, 1969; *Pig World*, Doubleday, 1971; *Ames Holbrook*, Curtis Books, 1972; *Power Kill*, 1972; *Soulmate*, Avon, 1974; *I, Weapon*, Doubleday, 1974.

Also author of *Dorian-Seven*, and *The Lonely Killer*; author of short story adapted for television production on "Alfred Hitchcock Presents." Contributor to *Stars and Stripes* and *Army Times*; contributor of short stories and novelettes to *Manhunt, Adam Year Book, Michael Shane, Fantastic, Super Science Fiction, Fantasy and Science Fiction*, and *Alfred Hitchcock's Mystery Magazine.*

WORK IN PROGRESS: Terror Treatment, and *Barrossan: The Gypsy King*, both for Pyramid Publications.

SIDELIGHTS: Death Cycle and *The Prettiest Girl I Ever Killed* have been made into motion pictures.

* * *

RUPPENTHAL, Karl M. 1917-

PERSONAL: Born October 5, 1917, in Russell, Kan.; son of John P. (a banker) and Viola (Whitaker) Ruppenthal; married Alice Autio (a librarian), May 30, 1942; children: Sara, Stephen, Brian. *Education:* University of Kansas, A.B., 1939, LL.B., 1941 (converted to J.D., 1968); University of California, Berkeley, M.B.A., 1950; Stanford University, Ph.D., 1959. *Home:* 3755 West 2nd Avenue, Vancouver, British Columbia, Canada.

CAREER: Admitted to practice, Kansas State Bar, 1941, and to Bars of District of Columbia and U.S. Supreme Court. Trans World Airlines, San Francisco, Calif., airline captain, 1942-68; Stanford University, Stanford, Calif., director of Transportation Management Program, 1957-70; University of Miami, Miami, Fla., Ryder professor of transportation, 1970; University of British Columbia, Vancouver, professor of transportation and director of Centre for Transportation Studies, 1971—. Director of Hazleton Laboratories, Karloid Corp., and Hazleton Nuclear Science Corp.; education consultant to Ethiopian Airlines. City councilman, Palo Alto, Calif., 1953-59. Director of research, Transportation Research Foundation, 1964. Executive vice-president, Canadian Transportation Research Forum. *Member:* American Economic Association, Industrial Relations Research Association, American Society of Traffic and Transportation, National Defense Transportation Association, Western Economic Association, Transportation Research Forum, American Judicature Society.

WRITINGS: The Air Lines Dispatcher in North America, Stanford University, 1962; *Issues in Transportation Economics*, C. E. Merrill, 1965; *Transportation Subsidies: Nature and Extent*, University of British Columbia Press, 1974.

Editor of "Transportation Series," Graduate School of Business, Stanford University: *Revolution in Transportation*, 1960; *Challenge to Transportation*, 1961; *Transportation Frontiers*, 1962; *New Dimensions in Business Logistics*, 1963; *Perspectives in Transportation*, 1963; *Developments in Business Logistics*, 1964; *Transportation Progress*, 1964; *Transportation and Tomorrow*, 1966; *Business Logistics in American Industry*, 1967. Contributing editor, *Oxford American Encyclopedia, Encyclopedia of Management*, and *Traffic and Distribution Management.*

WORK IN PROGRESS: Textbooks on airline management and business logistics; research on transportation and northern development, and a coordinated transportation system in Canada.

RUS, Vladimir 1931-

PERSONAL: Born December 9, 1931, in Czechoslovakia; son of Vaclav (a farmer) and Mary (Sedlacek) Rus; married Daphne Townsend, December 24, 1954; children: Todd, Kristina, Thomas. *Education:* University of South Carolina, A.B., 1952; New York University, M.A., 1954, Ph.D., 1963. *Home:* 82 Woodcock Lane, Levittown, N.Y. 11756.

CAREER: South Senior High School, Great Neck, Long Island, N.Y., teacher of German and Russian, 1957—.

WRITINGS: (Editor and translator) *Selections from Russian Poetry and Prose*, Harvey, 1965; (editor and translator) *Selections from German Poetry*, Harvey, 1966.†

* * *

RUSSELL, Claude Vivian 1919-

PERSONAL: Born December 9, 1919, in London, England; son of James Henry (an engineer) and Alice Claudine (Barrass) Russell. *Education:* University College, University of London, B.A. (honors), 1949; graduate teacher training, Institute of Education, University of London, 1950, Academic Diploma in Education, 1952. *Home:* 56 Village Rd., Enfield, Middlesex, England.

CAREER: Assistant master, The Grammar School, Hertford, England, 1951-58, Trinity School, Wood Green, London, England, 1958-59; Institute of Education, University of London, London, England, lecturer, 1960—. Associated Examining Board, member of modern languages advisory panel, and chairman of German subcommittee. *Military service:* British Army, Intelligence Service, 1940-45; became captain. *Member:* Association of University Teachers, Modern Languages Association (chairman of London branch, 1965-66), Delta Tau Kappa (honorary, University of Bridgeport chapter).

WRITINGS: (Contributor) *The Unusual Child*, edited by J. S. Roucek, Philosophical Library, 1962; (with P. L. Willig) *German Tests without Translation*, Pergamon, 1965; (editor and contributor) *Post O-level Studies in Modern Languages*, Pergamon, 1970. General editor, "Pergamon Oxford German Series." Assistant editor, *Yearbook of Education*, published jointly by Columbia University and University of London, 1960-61, and contributor to 1961, 1963, and 1964 editions; also contributor to learned journals.

WORK IN PROGRESS: Languages and Language Testing; research in modes and techniques of conducting public examinations in foreign languages in state secondary schools, and in methodology of foreign-language teaching.

SIDELIGHTS: Russell has traveled widely in Europe and has made special study of Danish and German educational systems. He is fluent in German and French.

* * *

RUSSELL, Franklin 1926-

PERSONAL: Born October 9, 1926, in Christchurch, Canterbury, New Zealand; son of Alexander Grant and Vida (McKay) Russell. *Education:* Educated in New Zealand at Nelson College and Victoria University of Wellington. *Politics:* None. *Religion:* None. *Home and office:* Swann's Way Out, Warsaw Rd., Frenchtown, N.J. 08825. *Agent:* John Cushman Associates, Inc., 24 East 38th St., New York, N.Y. 10016.

CAREER: Professional writer. *Awards, honors:* Guggenheim fellow, 1964-65; Canada Council fellowship, 1966.

WRITINGS: Watchers at the Pond, Knopf, 1961; *Argen the Gull*, Knopf, 1964; *The Frightened Hare* (juvenile), Holt, 1965; *Hawk in the Sky* (juvenile), Holt, 1965; *The Secret Islands*, Norton, 1966; *The Honeybees* (juvenile), Pantheon, 1966; *Searchers at the Gulf*, Norton, 1970; *The Atlantic Coast*, NSL (Canada), 1971; *Lotor the Raccoon* (juvenile), Scholastic, 1972; *Corvus the Crow* (juvenile), Scholastic, 1972; *Datra the Muskrat* (juvenile) Scholastic, 1973; *The Okefenoke Swamp*, Time-Life, 1973; *The Sea Has Wings*, Dutton, 1973; *Season on the Plain*, Reader's Digest Press, 1974.

WORK IN PROGRESS: Studies in animal behavior, the ocean, and history; juvenile books.

* * *

RUSSON, L(eslie) J(ohn) 1907-

PERSONAL: Born April 17, 1907, in London, England; son of John Henry (a teacher) and Minnie (Sedgwick) Russon; married Agatha Lipinski (a painter and writer), April 13, 1935. *Education:* St. Catharine's College, Cambridge, B.A., 1929, M.A., 1933. *Home:* 41 Hocombe Road, Chandler's Ford, Winchester, England.

CAREER: Assistant master of French and German at Holloway School, London, England, 1929-34, and Dulwich College, London, 1934-40; Winchester College, Winchester, England, assistant master of French and German, 1940-69, head of department of modern languages, 1953-67. Member of committee on modern languages, British Schools Council. *Member:* Modern Language Association of Great Britain, Royal Institute of Philosophy, Historical Association, Mind Association, British Society of Aesthetics.

WRITINGS—With wife, Agatha Russon, except as noted: (Sole author) *Spass Muss Sein*, Oxford University Press, 1939; (sole author) *Complete German Course for First Examinations*, Longmans, Green, 1948; *Simpler German Course for First Examinations*, Longmans, Green, 1955; *A First German Book*, Longmans, Green, 1959; *A Second German Book*, Longmans, Green, 1961; *A First German Reader*, Longmans, Green, 1963; *Advanced German Course*, Longmans, Green, 1965; *A Second German Reader*, Longmans, Green, 1966; *German Vocabulary in Context*, Longman, 1970. Contributor to *Modern Languages* and *Times Educational Supplement*.

WORK IN PROGRESS: Grammar of Contemporary German, for Longman.

SIDELIGHTS: Russon is fluent in German and French; he has working knowledge of Russian and Italian. *Avocational interests:* Philosophy, history, travel.

* * *

RUZIC, Neil P. 1930-

PERSONAL: Surname rhymes with "music"; born May 12, 1930, in Chicago, Ill.; son of Joseph F. (an oral surgeon) and Ida (Pierce) Ruzic; married Carol W. Kalsbeek, April 14, 1950; children: David Neil. *Education:* Attended Loyola University, Chicago, Ill., 1946-47; Northwestern University, B.S., 1950. *Politics:* Independent. *Office:* One IBM Plaza, Chicago, Ill. 60611.

CAREER: Former foreign correspondent in Central America, professional photographer, and building contractor; Armour Research Foundation (now Illinois Institute of Technology Research Institute), Chicago, Ill., director of publications, 1954-58; Industrial Research, Inc. (publishers of *Industrial Research* and other publications), Chicago, Ill., founder and president, 1958-72; Neil Ruzic & Co. (consultants to NASA), Chicago, Ill., founder and president, 1972—. *Military service:* U.S. Army, 1952-54. *Member:* Institute of Electrical and Electronics Engineers (senior member), American Vacuum Society, Sigma Delta Chi. *Awards, honors:* Three "best magazine" awards from Industrial Marketing Association, 1958-65.

WRITINGS: There's Adventure in Civil Engineering, Popular Mechanics, 1958; *There's Adventure in Meteorology,* Popular Mechanics, 1958; (editor) *Stimulus,* Industrial Research, 1960; *The Case for Going to the Moon,* Putnam, 1965; *Where the Winds Sleep,* Doubleday, 1970. Contributor of one hundred or more articles and short stories to technical, business, and science fiction magazines.

SIDELIGHTS: In 1967 Ruzic patented the "Ruzic Shield," the first U.S. patent to be granted for a device to be used exclusively on the moon. He is currently developing Little Stirrup Cay (Bahamas), as "Island for Science."

* * *

RYAN, Alvan Sherman 1912-

PERSONAL: Born May 2, 1912, in Needham Heights, Mass.; son of James Franklin (a carpenter and builder) and Rosina (Klauer) Ryan; married Pauline Louise Hillberg, June 26, 1937; children: David Barrett, Christina Marie. *Education:* University of Massachusetts, B.S. (cum laude), 1934; Harvard University, M.A., 1938; University of Iowa, Ph.D., 1940. *Home:* 224 Marlborough St., Boston, Mass.; (summer) Fiddler Hill Farm, R.F.D. 1, Brattleboro, Vt. *Office:* University of Massachusetts, Boston, Mass.

CAREER: University of Iowa, Iowa City, instructor in English, 1939-42; University of Notre Dame, Notre Dame, Ind., assistant professor of English, 1943-46; University of Massachusetts at Fort Devens (Army post), associate professor, 1946-47, professor of English, 1947-49; Marlboro College, Marlboro, Vt., professor of English, 1949-51; University of Notre Dame, associate professor, 1951-62, professor of English and head of department, 1962-65; University of Massachusetts, Boston Campus, professor of English, 1965—, chairman of Division of Humanities, 1965-67. University of the Saarland, senior Fulbright lecturer, 1961-62. Member of board of advisors, Marlboro College, 1972—.

MEMBER: Modern Language Association of America, College English Association (regional director, New England, 1949-50; chairman, national committee on doctoral studies and preparation for teaching, 1955-57), American Association of University Professors, American Tree Farm Association, Phi Kappa Phi, Lambda Chi Alpha. *Awards, honors:* Visiting fellow at Princeton University, 1955-56, under faculty fellowship from Fund for Advancement of Education; University of Massachusetts gold medal for professorial service, 1972.

WRITINGS: (Editor, and author of introduction and notes) *The Brownson Reader,* Kenedy, 1955.

Contributor: Yves R. Simon, editor, *La civilisation Americaine,* Desclee de Brouwer (Paris), 1950; Victor Yanitelli, editor, *A Newman Symposium,* Fordham University Press, 1952; Harold C. Gardiner, editor, *American Classics Reconsidered,* Scribner, 1958; *The Spirit of a Free Society* (festschrift for the 10th anniversary of the German Fulbright program), Quelle & Meyer (Heidelberg), 1962; (au-

thor of introduction) *Newman and Gladstone: The Vatican Decrees,* University of Notre Dame Press, 1962; (author of foreword) G. K. Chesterton, *The Victorian Age in Literature,* University of Notre Dame Press, 1963; Alfred Grommon, editor, *The Education of Teachers of English,* Appleton, for the National Council of Teachers of English, 1963; John V. Hagopian and Martin Dolch, editors, *Insight II: Analyses of Modern British Literature,* Hirschgraben-Verlag, 1964; J. L. Longley, Jr., editor, *Robert Penn Warren: A Collection of Critical Essays,* New York University Press, 1965; Lewis P. Simpson, compiler, *Profile of Robert Frost,* C. E. Merrill, 1971. Contributor of essays and reviews to *America, Thought, Mercure de France, Yale Review,* and other journals. Director of publications, Committee on International Relations, University of Notre Dame, 1957-61.

WORK IN PROGRESS: Studies in nineteenth-century American and English literature.

* * *

RYAN, Marleigh Grayer 1930-

PERSONAL: Born May 1, 1930, in New York, N.Y.; daughter of Harry (a lawyer) and Betty (Hurwick) Grayer; married Edward Ryan (a journalist), June, 1950. *Education:* New York University, B.A., 1950; Columbia University, M.A., 1956, Ph.D., 1965. *Home:* 403 Magowan Ave., Iowa City, Iowa 52240. *Office:* Department of East Asian Languages and Literature, University of Iowa, Iowa City, Iowa.

CAREER: Columbia University, New York, N.Y., assistant professor, 1961-70, associate professor of Japanese, 1970-72; University of Iowa, Iowa City, professor of Japanese and chairman of department of East Asian languages and literature, 1972—. Consultant in Japanese language teaching methods to Inter-University Center, Tokyo, Japan. *Member:* Modern Language Association of America, Association of Teachers of Japanese (secretary, 1962—), Association for Asian Studies. *Awards, honors:* Ford Foundation fellowship, 1958-60; Japan Foundation fellowship, 1973.

WRITINGS: (Junior author, with Herschel Webb) *Research in Japanese Sources: A Guide,* Columbia University Press, 1965; *Japan's First Modern Novel: Ukigumo of Futabatei Shimei,* Columbia University Press, 1967; *The Development of Realism in the Fiction of Tsubouchi Shoyo,* University of Washington Press, 1975. Editor, *Journal of the Association of Teachers of Japanese.*

* * *

RYF, Robert S. 1918-

PERSONAL: Surname rhymes with "life"; born August 12, 1918, in Berne, Ind.; son of Otto M. and Alice C. (Dutton) Ryf; married Elaine Abbitt, July 30, 1943; children: Steven, Susan. *Education:* Occidental College, A.B., 1939, M.A., 1953; Columbia University, Ph.D., 1956. *Home:* 5224 Maywood Ave., Los Angeles, Calif. 90041. *Office:* Department of English and Comparative Literature, Occidental College, Los Angeles, Calif. 90041.

CAREER: Columbia Broadcasting System, Los Angeles, Calif., writer, 1945-48; free-lance writer in Los Angeles, Calif., and New York, N.Y., 1948-53; Occidental College, Los Angeles, Calif., instructor in English, 1955-56, assistant professor, 1956-59, associate professor, 1959-63, professor of English and comparative literature, 1963-72, Arthur G. Coons Professor, 1972—, dean of students, 1961-65, chairman of department, 1965-67, dean of faculty and vice-president for academic affairs, 1967-72. *Military service:* U.S. Navy, 1940-45; served as lieutenant. *Member:* Modern Language Association of America, Phi Beta Kappa, Twilight Club (Pasadena). *Awards, honors:* Faculty award lecturer and Haynes summer fellow, 1959; Mosher resident grant, 1960.

WRITINGS: A New Approach to Joyce, University of California Press, 1962; *Henry Green*, Columbia University Press, 1967; *Joseph Conrad*, Columbia University Press, 1970.

* * *

SACHS, Marilyn (Stickle) 1927-

PERSONAL: Born December 18, 1927, in New York, N.Y.; daughter of Samuel and Anna (Smith) Stickle; married Morris Sachs (a marine microbiologist), January 26, 1947; children: Anne, Paul. *Education:* Hunter College (now Hunter College of the City University of New York), B.A., 1949; Columbia University, M.S. in L.S., 1953. *Politics:* "Changing constantly." *Religion:* Jewish. *Residence:* San Francisco, Calif.

CAREER: Brooklyn (N.Y.) Public Library, librarian, 1949-60; San Francisco (Calif.) Public Library, part-time children's librarian, 1962-67; writer of books for children.

WRITINGS—All published by Doubleday: *Amy Moves In*, 1964; *Laura's Luck*, 1965; *Amy and Laura*, 1966; *Veronica Ganz*, 1968; *Peter and Veronica*, 1969; *Marv*, 1970; *The Bear's House*, 1971; *The Truth About Mary Rose*, 1973; *A Pocket Full of Seeds*, 1973; *Matt's Mitt*, 1975.

AVOCATIONAL INTERESTS: Walking, reading, and good company.

* * *

SACKS, Sheldon 1930-

PERSONAL: Born February 20, 1930, in New York, N.Y.; son of Max (a corporation executive) and Pauline (Lindenbaum) Sacks; married Marjorie Hamilton (a lecturer and writer), May 10, 1952 (deceased); married Jean Karen Weber, June 2, 1967; children: (first marriage) Colin Hamilton, James Philip. *Education:* Northwestern University, B.S., 1952, M.A., 1953; University College, London, Fulbright scholar, 1955-56; University of Chicago, Ph.D., 1960. *Politics:* Democrat. *Religion:* Jewish. *Home:* 5765 Blackstone Ave., Chicago, Ill. 60637. *Office:* Department of English, University of Chicago, Chicago, Ill. 60637.

CAREER: University of Texas, Austin, instructor in English, 1956-58; University of California, Berkeley, instructor, 1958-60, assistant professor, 1960-65, associate professor of English, 1965-66; University of Chicago, Chicago, Ill., associate professor, 1966-67, professor of English and linguistics, 1967—. Visiting Fulbright lecturer in linguistics, University of Rome, 1961-62. Consultant to Educational Testing Service (college boards), 1963-64. *Member:* Modern Language Association of America, Linguistic Society of America, Midwest Modern Language Association. *Awards, honors:* E. Harris Harbison prize for gifted teaching, Danforth Foundation, 1970.

WRITINGS: Fiction and the Shape of Belief, University of California Press, 1964; (editor with Ralph Wilson Rader) *An Analytic Reader*, Little, Brown, 1964; (editor) R. S. Crane, *The Critical and Historical Principles of Literary History*, University of Chicago Press, 1972. Contributor of

articles to professional journals. Editor, *Critical Inquiry*, 1973—.

WORK IN PROGRESS: A Formal History of the English Novel.

* * *

SADDLEMYER, E(leanor) Ann 1932-

PERSONAL: Born November 28, 1932, in Prince Albert, Saskatchewan, Canada; daughter of Orrin Angus (a lawyer) and Elsie Sarah (Ellis) Saddlemyer. *Education:* University of Saskatchewan, B.A., 1953; graduate study (honors in English), 1953-55; Queen's University at Kingston, M.A., 1956; University of London, Ph.D., 1961. *Religion:* Protestant. *Office:* Department of English, Victoria College, University of Toronto, Toronto, Ontario, Canada.

CAREER: University of Victoria, Victoria, British Columbia, instructor, 1956-57, 1960-62, assistant professor, 1962-64, associate professor, 1964-68, professor of English, 1968-71; University of Toronto, professor of English, Victoria College, 1971—, director, Graduate Centre for Study of Drama, 1972—. Correspondent, Humanities Research of Canada, 1963-65; Berg Professor, New York University, 1975. *Member:* Modern Language Association of America, Association of Canadian University Teachers of English, Humanities Association of Canada, Society of Authors, Canadian Association of University Teachers, Canadian Association of Irish Studies, International Association for the Study of Anglo-Irish Literature (founding member; chairman, 1973—), Royal Irish Academy (committee member for Anglo-Irish manuscripts); Society for Theatre Research and Shaw Society (both England). *Awards, honors:* Canada Council short-term grant, 1962, 1963; Guggenheim fellowship, 1965-66; Canada Council research fellow, 1968.

WRITINGS: (Editor with Robin Skelton) *The World of W. B. Yeats*, University of Washington Press, 1965; *In Defense of Lady Gregory, Playwright*, Dolmen Press, 1966; (editor) J. M. Synge, *Collected Works*, volumes three and four: *Plays*, two volumes, Oxford University Press, 1968, published as *J. M. Synge: Plays*, 1969; (editor) *The Plays of Lady Gregory*, four volumes, Colin Smythe, 1970; (editor) *Letters to Molly: J. M. Synge to Maire O'Neill*, Harvard University Press, 1971; (compilor) *Some Letters of John M. Synge to Lady Gregory and W. B. Yeats*, Cuala Press, 1971.

Writer of lecture series for Canadian Broadcasting Corp. Contributor to *Irish Book, Anglo-Soviet Journal, Canadian Literature, Delhousie Review, Queen's Quarterly, Theatre Research* and other journals. Member of editorial board, *Yeats Studies, Irish University Review, Journal of Irish Literature, Modern Drama, English Studies in Canada, Canadian Theatre Review.*

WORK IN PROGRESS: The Collected Plays of J. M. Synge; Theatre Business: Management of Men; Letters of Lady Gregory, W. B. Yeats, and J. M. Synge; a study of modern comedy.

AVOCATIONAL INTERESTS: Contemporary theatre, music, and art; collecting books and prints of 1880-1915; the histories of the Irish and Canadian theatres.

* * *

SADIE, Stanley (John) 1930-

PERSONAL: Born October 30, 1930, in Wembley, Middlesex, England; son of David (a textile merchant) and Deborah (Simons) Sadie; married Adele Bloom, December 10, 1953; children: Graham Robert, Ursula Joan, Stephen Peter. *Education:* Cambridge University, B.A., 1953, Mus.B., 1953, M.A., 1957, and Ph.D., 1958. *Home:* 1 Carlisle Gardens, Harrow, Middlesex, England. *Office: Grove's Dictionary of Music and Musicians*, 44 Bedford Row, London WC1R 4JY, England.

CAREER: Trinity College of Music, London, England, lecturer, 1957-65; *Times*, London, England, music critic, 1964—; *Musical Times*, London, England, associate editor, 1966-67, editor, 1967—; *Grove's Dictionary of Music and Musicians*, London, England, editor, 1970—. Commentator on music for British Broadcasting Corp. *Military service:* Royal Air Force, 1948-49. *Member:* Royal Musical Association, Critics Circle (honorary secretary, music section, 1965-67; chairman, music section, 1967-70).

WRITINGS: Handel, J. Calder, 1962, Crowell, 1968; (with Arthur Jacobs) *Pan Book of Opera*, Pan Books, 1964, published in England as *The Opera Guide*, Hamish Hamilton, 1964, reissued in America as *Great Operas in Synopsis*, Crowell, 1966; *Mozart*, J. Calder, 1966, Grossman, 1970; *Beethoven*, Crowell, 1967; *Handel Concertos*, B.B.C., 1973. Contributor to *Gramophone, Musical Times, Opera*, and other musical publications.

WORK IN PROGRESS: Further studies on Mozart.

SIDELIGHTS: Travels as a music critic have taken Sadie to the United States and most European countries. *Avocational interests:* Reading, watching cricket.

*   *   *

SADIQ, Muhammad 1898-

PERSONAL: Born 1898, in Peshawar, West Pakistan; son of Muhammad Bakhsh; married Nur Fatimah; children: Ghalib Mustafa (son), Asifa (Mrs. Ashfaq Hasan). *Education:* Government College, Lahore, West Pakistan, M.A., 1924; Panjab University, Ph.D., 1939. *Home:* 292 Garden Town, Lahore, Pakistan.

CAREER: Islamia College, Lahore, West Pakistan, lecturer in English, 1924-26; joined government service as lecturer in English, 1926; Government College, Lahore, lecturer, 1940-47, professor of English, 1947-53, chairman of department of Urdu, 1948-53, chairman of department of English, 1950-53; Dyal Singh College, Lahore, dean of instruction, 1953-63, principal, 1963-65; Panjab University, Lahore, editor of Urdu section, "Literary History of Indo-Pakistan Muslims," 1965-66.

WRITINGS: Twentieth Century Urdu Literature, Padmaja Publications (Bombay), 1947; *A History of Urdu Literature*, Oxford University Press, 1964; *Muhammad Husain Azad: His Life and Works*, West-Pak Publishing, 1964; (editor) Muhammad Husain Azad, *Nairang-e-Khayal*, Majlis-e-Taraqqi-e-Adab (Lahore, Pakistan), 1972; *Ab-e-Hayat ki Himayat men aur Dusre Mazamin*, Majlis-e-Taraqqi-e-Adab, 1973; *Hafiz the Lyrist*, West-Pak Publishing, 1974; *Asar-e-Azad*, Majlis-e-Taraqqi-e-Adab, in press. Also author of *Sayyid Ahmad Khan*, published by Oxford University Press (Karachi) and contributor to *Literary History of Indo-Pakistan Muslims*, Sayyid Vaqar Azim, editor, Volume VII, 1971, S. F. Mahmud and Ibadat Brelvi, editors, Volume IX, 1972. Contributor of criticism to *Iqbal* (quarterly journal of Bazm-e-Iqbal).

WORK IN PROGRESS: Tarikh-e-Zaban-e-Urdu, a history of the Urdu language.

SAFIRE, William 1929-

PERSONAL: Born December 17, 1929; son of Oliver and Ida (Panish) Safire; married Helene B. Julius, December 16, 1962; children: Mark Lindsey, Annabel Victoria. *Education:* Attended Syracuse University, 1947-49. *Home:* 1085 Park Ave., New York, N.Y. 10028. *Agent:* Morton Janklow, 375 Park Ave., New York, N.Y. 10036. *Office: New York Times*, 1920 L St., Washington, D.C. 20036.

CAREER: Safire Public Relations, Inc., New York, N.Y., president, 1961-68; The White House, Washington, D.C., special assistant to the President, 1968-73; *New York Times*, Washington, D.C., columnist, 1973—.

MILITARY SERVICE: U.S. Army, 1952-54. *Member:* Public Relations Society of America, Newcomen Society in North America, Overseas Press Club (board of governors, 1957-59).

WRITINGS: The Relations Explosion, Macmillan, 1963; (with M. Loeb) *Plunging into Politics*, McKay, 1964; *The New Language of Politics*, Random House, 1968, revised edition, Macmillan, 1972; *Before the Fall*, Doubleday, 1975. Contributor to *Harvard Business Review, Cosmopolitan, Playboy, Esquire, Public Relations Journal, Redbook, Collier's*.

*   *   *

SAHAKIAN, William S(ahak) 1921-

PERSONAL: Surname is pronounced Sar-*hark*-ian; born October 7, 1921, in Boston, Mass.; son of Jacob and Anna (Pakchoian) Sahakian; married Mabel Marie Lewis (a professor of philosophy and psychology), 1945; children: James William, Richard Lewis, Barbara Jacquelyn, Paula Leslie. *Education:* Northeastern University, B.S., 1944; Boston University, M.Div., 1947, Ph.D., 1951; Harvard University, additional courses, 1948-55. *Politics:* Independent. *Home:* 135 Booth Rd., Dedham, Mass. 02026. *Office:* Suffolk University, 41 Temple St., Boston, Mass. 02114.

CAREER: Licensed psychologist, Commonwealth of Massachusetts. Suffolk University, Boston, Mass., 1946—, chairman of philosophy department, 1951—, professor, 1951—; Northeastern University, Boston, Mass., lecturer in philosophy and psychology, 1951—. Lecturer at Curry College, 1955-57, Lasell College, 1960-61, and of extension courses at Harvard University. Resident psychologist for Mendota Research Group, 1960-65; consultant to National Association on Standard Medical Vocabulary. *Member:* American Philosophical Association (fellow), New York Academy of Sciences, American Association for the Advancement of Science, Britannica Society Human Factors Society, Personalist Group, Association for Realistic Philosophy, New England Philosophy of Education Society, Massachusetts Psychological Association (fellow), Kappa Psi. *Awards, honors:* D.Sc., Curry College, 1956.

WRITINGS: Systems of Ethics and Value Theory, Philosophical Library, 1963; *Outline of Philosophers*, privately printed, 1963; (with wife, Mabel Lewis Sahakian) *Realms of Philosophy*, Schenkman, 1965, revised edition, 1974; *Philosophies of Religion*, Schenkman, 1965; *Psychology of Personality*, Rand McNally, 1965, revised edition, 1974; (with Mabel Lewis Sahakian) *Ideas of the Great Philosophers*, Barnes & Noble, 1966; *History of Psychology*, F. E. Peacock, 1968; *History of Philosophy*, Harper, 1968; *Philosophy*, Cliffs, 1968; *Psychotherapy and Counseling*, Rand McNally, 1969; *Psychopathology Today*, F. E. Peacock,

1970; *Psychology of Learning*, Rand McNally, 1970; *Social Psychology: Experimentation, Theory, and Research*, Intext Educational, 1972; *Systematic Social Psychology*, Chandler Publishing, 1974; *Ethics: Theories and Problems*, Harper, 1974; (with Mabel Lewis Sahakian) *Rousseau as Educator*, Twayne, 1974; (with Mabel Lewis Sahakian) *John Locke*, Twayne, 1975; *History and Systems of Psychology*, Wiley, 1975; (contributor) J. Fabry and R. Bulka, editors, *Aspects of Logotherapy*, Max Knight, in press; *Plato*, Twayne, in press.

Contributor to *International Encyclopedia of Neurology, Psychiatry, Psychoanalysis, and Psychology* and to *Encyclopaedia Britannica*. Contributor of book reviews to *Boston Globe* and of articles to psychology journals.

* * *

SALINGER, Pierre (Emil George) 1925-

PERSONAL: Born June 14, 1925, in San Francisco, Calif.; son of Herbert Edgar and Jehanne (Bietry) Salinger; married second wife, Nancy Brook Joy, June 28, 1957 (divorced); married Nicole Gillmann, June 18, 1965; children: (first marriage) Marc, Suzanne, Stephen; (third marriage) Gregory. *Education:* University of San Francisco, B.S., 1947. *Politics:* Democrat. *Agent:* Sterling Lord Agency, 660 Madison Ave., New York, N.Y., 10021. *Home:* 9101 Hazen Dr., Beverly Hills, Calif. 90211.

CAREER: San Francisco Chronicle, San Francisco, Calif., reporter, later night city editor, 1946-55; *Collier's* (magazine), New York, N.Y., West Coast editor and contributing editor, 1955-56; *House and Home* (magazine), New York, N.Y., assistant news editor, 1956-57; U.S. Senate Labor Rackets Committee, Washington, D.C., investigator, 1957-59; press secretary to Senator John F. Kennedy, 1959-60, to President Kennedy, 1961-63, and to President Lyndon B. Johnson, 1963-64; U.S. senator from California (appointed to fill vacancy), 1964; Continental Airlines, Los Angeles, Calif., vice-president for international affairs, 1965-68, also vice-president, deputy to the chairman of the board, and a director of subsidiary, Continental Air Services, Inc.; National General Corp. (theaters), Beverly Hills, Calif., vice-president, then consultant, 1965—; Fox Overseas Theatres, president, 1965—; Gramco Development Corporation, Los Angeles, Calif., president, 1968—. Gramco Ltd. (UK), department chairman, 1970-71; AMPROP, Inc., senior vice-president, 1969. Member of board of directors, National General Productions and California Museum of Science and Industry. Guest lecturer in journalism, Mills College, 1950-55. *Military service:* U.S. Naval Reserve, active duty, 1943-46; became lieutenant junior grade. *Member:* National Press Club (Washington, D.C.).

WRITINGS: (Editor with Sander Vanocur) *A Tribute to John F. Kennedy*, Encyclopaedia Britannica, 1964; *With Kennedy*, Doubleday, 1966; (editor with Edwin Guthman, Frank Mankiewicz, and John Seigenthaler) *An Honorable Profession: A Tribute to Robert F. Kennedy*, Doubleday, 1968; *On Instructions of My Government* (novel), Doubleday, 1971; *For the Eyes of the President Only*, Collins, 1971.

BIOGRAPHICAL/CRITICAL SOURCES: Roy Newquist, *Conversations*, Rand McNally, 1967; *New York Times*, June 3, 1971.†

SALISBURY, Frank B(oyer) 1926-

PERSONAL: Born August 3, 1926, in Provo, Utah; son of Frank M. (in insurance) and Catherine (Boyer) Salisbury; married Lois Marilyn Olson, September 1, 1949; children: Frank Clark, Stephen Scott, Michael James, Cynthia Kay, Phillip Boyer, Rebecca Lynn, Blake Charles. *Education:* University of Utah, B.S., 1951, M.A., 1952; California Institute of Technology, Ph.D., 1955. *Politics:* Republican. *Religion:* Church of Jesus Christ of Latter-day Saints. *Home:* 2020 Country Estates, North Logan, Utah 84321. *Office:* Plant Science Department UMC 48, Utah State University, Logan, Utah 84322.

CAREER: Pomona College, Claremont, Calif., assistant professor of botany, 1954-55; Colorado State University, Fort Collins, assistant professor and assistant botanist, Experiment Station, 1955-61, professor of plant physiology and plant physiologist, Experiment Station, 1955-61; Utah State University, Logan, professor of botany and of plant physiology, 1966—, head of plant science department, 1966-70. Colorado State University Research Foundation, trustee, 1959-62; member of biomedical programs, U.S. Atomic Energy Commission, 1973-74; consultant, Aerial Phenomena Research Organization. *Military service:* U.S. Army Air Forces, 1945. *Member:* American Association for the Advancement of Science (fellow), American Institute of Biological Sciences, American Society of Plant Physiologists, Ecological Society of America, Botanical Society of America, National Investigating Committee for Aerial Phenomena (member of board of directors), Utah Academy of Science, Arts, and Letters, Sigma Xi, Phi Kappa Phi. *Awards, honors:* National Science Foundation senior postdoctoral fellow in Tuebingen and Innsbruck, 1962-63.

WRITINGS: The Flowering Process, Pergamon, 1963; (with R. V. Parke) *Vascular Plants: Form and Function*, Wadsworth, 1964, 2nd edition, 1970; *Truth by Reason and by Revelation*, Deseret, 1965; (with Cleon Ross) *Plant Physiology*, Wadsworth, 1969; *The Biology of Flowering*, Natural History Press, 1971; (with William Jensen) *Botany: An Ecological Approach*, Wadsworth, 1972; *The Utah UFO Display: A Biologist's Report*, Devin-Adair, 1974. Author of technical, semi-popular, and popular articles on plant physiology, physiological ecology and space biology (especially the question of life on Mars), and unidentified flying objects; several articles have been published in German magazines. Member of editorial boards of *BioScience* and *Plant Physiology*.

WORK IN PROGRESS: What is Life?, a biology text for nonmajor students; *The Creation*, a discussion of scientific and religious concepts of creation; *Wilderness Questions*, an examination, set in Grand Teton National Park, of the important problems of interest to biologists and to mankind; *God, Science, and Reality*, a book attempting to point out that modern science can contribute much to our understanding of God; research on the physiology of flowering and on plants growing under extreme environmental conditions.

SIDELIGHTS: Salisbury is presently involved in "attempting to get the scientific community to consider the study of unidentified flying objects as a valid scientific pursuit." *Avocational interests:* Photography, mountaineering, drama, and sculpture.

SALKEVER, Louis R(omov)   1914-

PERSONAL: Born January 1, 1914, in Philadelphia, Pa.; son of Rea R. (a builder) and Eda (Spector) Salkever; married Edna Tiskowitz (an artist), June 26, 1936; children: Stephen Gregory, David Simeon. *Education:* University of Pennsylvania, B.A. (with major honors), 1936; American University, M.A., 1950; Cornell University, Ph.D., 1951. *Home:* 93 Jordan Blvd., Delmar, N.Y. 12054. *Office:* State University of New York at Albany, Albany, N.Y. 12203.

CAREER: Journalist in Pennsylvania, 1935, 1936-38; U.S. Government, Washington, D.C., economist, 1936-46; Sampson College, Sampson, N.Y., instructor, 1946-47, assistant professor of economics, 1947-49; Cornell University, Ithaca, N.Y., research associate, 1949-50; State University of New York College at New Paltz, assistant professor, 1950-53, associate professor, 1953-56, professor of economics, 1956-65; State University of New York at Albany, professor of economics and chairman of department, 1965-71, vice-president for research and dean of graduate studies, 1971—. Visiting lecturer at Hobart College, 1948-49, New York State School of Industrial and Labor Relations, 1951—, Syracuse University, 1961, Cornell University, 1963, Brown University, 1966, and other universities. Economic consultant to government departments, labor organizations, and industry, 1951—. Member of board of directors, New York State Council on Economic Education, 1958—, and State University of New York Research Foundation; executive director, Committee on Labor, Civil Service and Public Pensions of the New York State Constitutional Convention. *Military service:* U.S. Army, 1944-46.

MEMBER: American Economic Association, Industrial Relations Research Association, American Studies Association, Association for Higher Education, New York State Economics Association (president, 1965-66). *Awards, honors:* Ford Foundation faculty fellowships to Yale University, 1958, and Massachusetts Institute of Technology, 1961; L.H.D., Allen University, 1973.

WRITINGS: Personal Income in Philadelphia, City of Philadelphia, 1955; *Society, Economy and State: Essays in Economics and Public Policy*, New Paltz College Press, 1960; (with Helen Flynn) *Sub-Saharan Africa*, Curriculum Resources, 1963; *Toward a Wage Structure Theory: A Critique*, Humanities, 1964; (editor with J. Uppal) *Africa: Problems in Economic Development*, Fress Press, 1972; *Understanding the American Economy*, Holden-Day, in press. Contributor to professional journals.

*   *   *

SALMON, Margaret Belais   1921-

PERSONAL: Born March 16, 1921, in New York, N.Y.; daughter of Arnold and Hortense Belais; married Douglas A. Salmon (a chemical engineer), October 19, 1945; children: Robert, Betty Lynn, Donald. *Education:* University of California, Berkeley, B.S., 1941, graduate study, 1941-42; Duke University, Certificate of Hospital Dietetics, 1943; Columbia University, M.S., 1964, professional diploma, 1967. *Religion:* Unitarian Universalist. *Office address:* Salmon Consultants, Box 365, Harrington Park, N.J. 07640.

CAREER: Columbia-Presbyterian Medical Center, New York, N.Y., therapeutic dietitian, 1943-45, research dietitian, 1957-66; therapeutic and teaching dietitian at Englewood Hospital, Englewood, N.J., Hackensack Hospital, Hackensack, N.J., and Holy Name Hospital, Teaneck, N.J., 1954-66; St. Luke's Hospital Center, New York,

N.Y., administrative dietitian, 1966-70; Bronx-Lebanon Hospital Center, Bronx, N.Y., associate director, 1970-71; St. Joseph's Hospital and Medical Center, Paterson, N.J., chief therapeutic dietitian, 1971—. Salmon Consultants (nutrition consultants), Harrington Park, N.J., president, 1957—. Director of school lunch programs at Moriah Academy, Englewood, and Yavneh Academy, Paterson, 1962-66; extension lecturer at Rutgers University. *Member:* American Dietetic Association, New Jersey Dietetic Association (president, 1966-68), Kappa Delta Pi, Pi Lambda Theta, Omicron Nu.

WRITINGS: Food Facts for Teenagers, C. C Thomas, 1965; (editor) *Enjoying Your Restricted Diet*, C. C Thomas, 1972; (contributor) *Easy and Delicious Rice Flour Recipes*, C. C Thomas, 1973; (contributor) *Career Roles for Young Women*, C. C Thomas, 1974; (editor) *Physicians' Diet Handbook*, Harrington Press, 1975.

WORK IN PROGRESS: Continuing research on teenage nutrition.

AVOCATIONAL INTERESTS: Youth programs, especially international exchange programs.

*   *   *

SALMON, Wesley C(harles)   1925-

PERSONAL: Born August 9, 1925, in Detroit, Mich.; son of Wallis Samuel (an engineer) and Ruth (Springer) Salmon; married Nancy Pilson, November 26, 1949 (divorced, 1970); married Merrilee Hollenkamp Ashby, July 24, 1971; children: (first marriage) Victoria Anne. *Education:* Wayne State University, student, 1943-44; University of Chicago, M.A., 1947; University of California, Los Angeles, Ph.D., 1950. *Office:* Philosophy Department, University of Arizona, Tucson, Ariz. 85721.

CAREER: University of California, Los Angeles, instructor in philosophy, 1950-51; Washington State University, Pullman, instructor, 1951-53, assistant professor of philosophy, 1953-54; Northwestern University, Evanston, Ill., lecturer, 1954-55; Brown University, Providence, R.I., assistant professor, 1955-59, associate professor of philosophy, 1959-63; Indiana University, Bloomington, professor of the philosophy of science, 1963-67, Norwood Russell Hanson Professor of Philosophy of Science, 1967-73; University of Arizona, Tucson, professor of philosophy, 1973—. Visiting lecturer, University of Bristol, 1959; visiting professor, University of Minnesota Center for Philosophy of Science, 1963, University of Pittsburgh, 1968-69. *Member:* American Philosophical Association (member of executive committee of Western Division, 1969-71), Philosophy of Science Association (vice-president, 1968-70; president, 1971-72), International Union for the History and Philosophy of Science (chairman of U.S. national committee, 1967-68), Sigma Xi. *Awards, honors:* Fund for the Advancement of Science faculty fellow, 1953-54; M.A., Brown University, 1959.

WRITINGS: Logic, Prentice-Hall, 1963, 2nd edition, 1973; *The Foundations of Scientific Inference*, University of Pittsburgh Press, 1967; (editor) *Zeno's Paradoxes*, Bobbs-Merrill, 1970; (with others) *Statistical Explanation and Statistical Relevance*, University of Pittsburgh Press, 1971; *Space, Time, and Motion: A Philosophical Introduction*, Dickenson, 1975.

Contributor: Sidney Hook, editor, *Psychoanalysis, Scientific Method, and Philosophy*, New York University Press, 1959; Herbert Feigl and Grover Maxwell, editors, *Current*

Issues in the Philosophy of Science, Holt, 1961; Bernard H. Baumrin, editor, *Philosophy of Science: The Delaware Seminar II*, Wiley, 1963; Henry E. Kyburg, Jr. and Ernest Nagel, editors, *Induction: Some Current Issues*, Wesleyan University Press, 1963; Paul Feyerabend and Maxwell, editors, *Mind, Matter, and Method*, University of Minnesota Press, 1966; Robert G. Colodny, editor, *Mind and Cosmos*, University of Pittsburgh Press, 1966; Imre Lakatos, editor, *The Problem of Inductive Logic*, North-Holland Publishing, 1968; David L. Arm, editor, *Vistas in Science*, University of New Mexico Press, 1968; Nicholas Rescher, *Essays in Honor of Carl G. Hempel*, D. Reidel, 1969.

Roger H. Stuewer, editor, *Historical and Philosophical Perspectives of Science*, University of Minnesota Press, 1970; Joel Feinberg, editor, *Reason and Responsibility*, Dickenson, 2nd edition, 1971, 3rd edition, 1975 (Salmon not associated with 1st edition); George Nakhnikian, editor, *Bertrand Russell's Philosophy*, Duckworth, 1974; Maxwell and Robert M. Anderson, Jr., editors, *Induction, Probability, and Confirmation*, University of Minnesota Press, 1975; S. Koerner, editor, *Explanation*, Yale University Press, 1975.

Editor with Joel Feinberg of Prentice-Hall's "Contemporary Prospectives in Philosophy Series." Contributor to *Encyclopedia Americana* and to philosophy journals. Member of editorial board, *Journal of Philosophical Logic, Erkenntnis, American Philosophical Quarterly, Synthese,* and *Synthese Library*.

*   *   *

SALOT, Lorraine 1914-

PERSONAL: Born February 22, 1914, in Detroit, Mich.; daughter of Harry F. (a lawyer) and Mary (Duncan) Salot. *Education:* Michigan State University, B.A., 1936; Wayne State University, M.E., 1945, graduate study, 1945-61. *Home:* 20017 Steel Ave., Detroit, Mich. 48235.

CAREER: Public schools of Detroit, Mich., kindergarten teacher, 1942—, supervising teacher for student teachers, 1948—. *Member:* English-Speaking Union, Detroit Figure Skating Club, Delta Kappa Gamma, Kappa Kappa Gamma.

WRITINGS: (With Jerome Leavitt) *The Beginning Kindergarten Teacher*, Burgess, 1965. Author of children's stories about safety for Detroit public schools.

SIDELIGHTS: Lorraine Salot speaks French. She teaches conversational French to older children and a little French to her kindergarten children. *Avocational interests:* Travel, figure skating.

*   *   *

SAMACHSON, Joseph 1906-
(John Miller, William Morrison)

PERSONAL: Surname is pronounced *Sam*-ix-on; born October 13, 1906, in Trenton, N.J.; son of David Louis (a businessman) and Anna (Roshansky) Samachson; married Dorothy Mirkin (a pianist and writer), December 12, 1937; children: Michael, Miriam Samachson Berkley. *Education:* Rutgers University, B.S., 1926; Yale University, Ph.D., 1930. *Home:* 185 North Marion St., Oak Park, Ill. 60301.

CAREER: Research chemist with Atlantic Refining Co., 1930-33, and American Molasses Co., 1937-38; self-employed science writer, 1938-53; Brooklyn Jewish Hospital, Brooklyn, N.Y., biochemist, 1953-55; Montefiore Hospital, Bronx, N.Y., chief chemist, metabolic laboratory, 1955-61;

Hines Veterans Administration Hospital, Hines, Ill., chief chemist, metabolic research, 1961-73; University of Illinois, College of Medicine, Chicago, assistant professor of biochemistry, 1961-68; Loyola University, Chicago, Ill., Stritch College of Medicine, associate clinical professor, 1968-73. *Member:* American Chemical Society, American Association for the Advancement of Science, American Association of Clinical Chemists, New York Academy of Sciences.

WRITINGS—With wife, Dorothy Samachson: *Let's Meet the Theatre*, Abelard, 1954; *The Dramatic Story of the Theatre*, Abelard, 1955; *Gold Digging* (Junior Literary Guild selection), Rand McNally, 1960; *The Fabulous World of Opera* (Junior Literary Guild selection), Rand McNally, 1962; *Rome*, Rand McNally, 1964; *Masters of Music*, Doubleday, 1967; *The First Artists*, Doubleday, 1970; *The Russian Ballet and Three of Its Masterpieces*, Lothrop, 1971.

Sole author: (Under the pseudonym of John Miller) *Murder of a Professor*, Putnam, 1937; (under pseudonym William Morrison) *Mel Oliver and Space Rover on Mars*, Gnome Press, 1954; *The Armor Within Us: The Story of Bone*, Rand McNally, 1966. Author of many science fiction stories under pseudonym William Morrison; also writer of articles published in scientific journals, and of a number in general magazines. Translator of technical articles from the Russian and German.

SIDELIGHTS: Samachson has fair ("but now somewhat rusty") reading knowledge of French, German, Russian, and Italian.

*   *   *

SAMUEL, Irene 1915-

PERSONAL: Born May 14, 1915, in New York, N.Y.; daughter of Jacob and Lillie (Levine) Samuel. *Education:* Cornell University, B.A., 1935, M.A., 1936, Ph.D., 1940. *Home:* 17 West 67th St., New York, N.Y. 10023.

CAREER: Instructor in English at Bath Junior College, Bath, N.Y., 1936-37, and Rockford College, Rockford, Ill., 1937-38; Cornell University, Ithaca, N.Y., instructor in English, 1941; Queens College (now Queens College of the City University of New York) Flushing, N.Y., instructor in English, 1942-44; Hunter College of the City University of New York, New York, N.Y., instructor, 1944-48, assistant professor, 1949-61, associate professor, 1962-65, professor of English, 1965-71, professor emeritus, 1971—. Visiting scholar at Washington University, St. Louis, Mo., 1958-59, and at New York University, 1960-61; visiting professor, University of Western Ontario, summer, 1971, Emory University, spring, 1974; Andrew Mellon Visiting Professor, University of Pittsburgh, fall, 1972; Kenan Visiting Professor, University of North Carolina, spring, 1975. *Member:* Modern Language Association of America, Milton Society of America (vice-president, 1968; president, 1969; honorary scholar, 1972), Academy of Literary Studies, American Association of University Professors, Phi Beta Kappa. *Awards, honors:* Guggenheim fellowship, 1966-67; Huntington Library grant, 1971.

WRITINGS: *Plato and Milton*, Cornell University Press, 1947, 2nd edition, 1965; *Dante and Milton: "The Commedia" and "Paradise Lost,"* Cornell University Press, 1966; (contributor) Joseph Anthony Wittreich, Jr., editor, *Calm of Mind*, Press of Case Western Reserve University, 1972; (contributor) Balachandra Rajan, editor, *The Prison and the Pinnacle*, University of Toronto Press, 1973; (translator with Mariella Cavalchini) Torquato Tasso, *Discourses on the Heroic Poem*, Clarendon Press, 1973. Contributor of studies on Milton, Sidney, and Henry James to professional journals.

WORK IN PROGRESS: Writing on Milton's poetics and on Jonathan Swift.

SIDELIGHTS: Ms. Samuel has done research during several visits to Italy and England, visited Greece many times, and traveled in other western European countries and Mexico.

*   *   *

SANDERLIN, Owenita (Harrah) 1916-

PERSONAL: Born June 2, 1916, in Los Angeles, Calif.; daughter of Owen Melville (a physician and surgeon) and Marigold (Whitford) Harrah; married George William Sanderlin (a professor and writer), May 30, 1936; children: Frea Elizabeth (Mrs. Frank Sladek), Sheila Mary (Mrs. Rolland Buska), David George, John Owen (deceased). *Education:* The American University, B.A. (summa cum laude), 1937; graduate study at University of Maine, 1938, California State University, San Diego (now San Diego State University) and University of California, 1968-69. *Politics:* Democrat or independent. *Religion:* Roman Catholic. *Residence:* El Cajon, Calif.

CAREER: During student years worked as a restaurant cashier ("cashiered my way through college") and with a professional marionette company in Washington, D.C.; free-lance writer, 1938—; taught English part time at University of Maine, Orono, 1943 and 1947; head of speech and drama department, Academy of Our Lady of Peace, San Diego, Calif., 1961-62, 1963-68. *Member:* National Forensic League, National Association for Gifted Children, San Diego Tennis Patrons Association.

WRITINGS: Jeanie O'Brien (junior novel), F. Watts, 1965; *Johnny*, A. S. Barnes, 1968; *Creative Teaching*, A. S. Barnes, 1971; *Teaching Gifted Children*, A. S. Barnes, 1973. Monthly columnist in *Today's Family* and other religious periodicals, 1950-72; stories, plays, verse, and articles have appeared in a number of magazines, including *Parents' Magazine, Saturday Evening Post, Seventeen, Catholic Digest, Jack and Jill*, and *Catholic World*.

WORK IN PROGRESS: A novel about marriage and the family.

AVOCATIONAL INTERESTS: Playing tennis and working with local juniors (son, David, is a tennis pro).

*   *   *

SANDS, Leo G(eorge) 1912-
(Lee Craig, Jack Helmi)

PERSONAL: Born March 20, 1912, in Spokane, Wash.; son of Jacob Herman and Helmi (Laasanen) Sands; married Rhea Meuron, May 6, 1944; children: Lee Meuron, Craig Jacob. *Education:* Attended University of California, 1933-34, and Golden Gate College, 1935; took other specialized courses in electronics, writing, photography, French, and radar. *Home:* 250 East 73rd St., New York, N.Y. 10021. *Office:* 250 Park Ave., New York, N.Y. 10017.

CAREER: Engineer with U.S. War Department, Sacramento, Calif., 1942-44, and Curtiss-Wright Corp., Bloomfield, N.J., 1944-45; Bendix Corp., variously product sales manager, regional sales manager, and director of public relations and advertising in Baltimore, Kansas City, and Chi-

cago, 1945-51; Bogue Electric Manufacturing Co., Paterson, N.J., marketing director, 1951-53; RCA Corp., Camden, N.J., administrator, 1953-54; Sands Technology Corp., New York, N.Y., president, 1954—; free-lance writer. Santa Barbara (Calif.) Safety Council, vice-president and director, 1954-56. *Member:* Institute of Electrical and Electronics Engineers (senior member), Radio Club of America (fellow member).

WRITINGS: All published by Howard W. Sams, except as indicated: *Industrial Sound Systems*, 1958; *Guide to Mobile Radio*, Gernsback, 1958, revised edition, Chilton, 1967; *Marine Electronics Handbook*, 1959, 3rd revised edition, TAB Books, 1973.

(Under pseudonym Jack Helmi) *Two-Way Mobile Radio Handbook*, 1960, 2nd revised edition, 1964; *Class D Citizens Radio*, Ziff-Davis Publishing, 1960; *Fundamentals of Radio Control*, 1962; *ABCs of Radiotelephony*, 1962; *Commercial Sound Installer's Handbook*, 1962; *CB Radio Servicing Guide*, 1963, 3rd revised edition, 1974; *UHF Business Radio Handbook*, 1963; *Audel's Handbook of Commercial Sound Installations*, Audel, 1965; *Mobile and Marine Station License Manual*, 1965.

101 Questions and Answers About Transistors, 1966; *Having Fun in Electronics*, 1966; *Traffic Signal Control Systems*, Hayden Book Co., 1967; *Microwave Equipment Guide*, 1967; *Power Supplies for Electronics*, John F. Rider, 1967; (with Kenneth Dumas) *Microwave Systems Planning*, Hayden Book Co., 1967; *Electronics Handbook for the Electrician*, Chilton, 1967; *Rapid Radio Repair*, TAB Books, 1967; *VHF-FM Marine Radio*, Chilton, 1967; *Walkie-Talkie Handbook*, 1967; *101 Questions and Answers About CB Operations*, 1967, 2nd edition published as *Questions and Answers About CB Operations*, 1973; *Easy Way to Service Radio Receivers*, TAB Books, 1968; *Electronics Handbook for the Electrician*, Chilton, 1968; *101 Questions and Answers About Auto Tape Units*, 1968, 2nd edition published as *Questions and Answers About Auto Tape Units*, 1973; *101 Questions and Answers About Color TV*, 1968, 2nd edition published as *Questions and Answers About Color TV*, 1972; *101 Questions and Answers About Fixed Radiocommunications*, 1968; (with G. Geoffrey Tellet) *VHF-FM Marine Radio*, Chilton, 1968; *CBers' How-To Book*, Hayden Book Co., 1969; (with Fred Shunaman) *101 Questions and Answers About Hi-Fi and Stereo*, 1969; (with Kenneth Bourne) *101 Questions and Answers About Amateur Radio*, 1969; (with Lionel Rodgers) *Automobile Traffic Signal Control Systems*, Chilton, 1969.

CB Radio, A. S. Barnes, 1970; *Mobile-Radio Systems Planning*, 1970; *101 Questions and Answers About Transistor Circuits*, 1970; *101 Questions and Answers About Electricity*, 1971; (with Robert Burns) *Citizens Band Radio Service Manual*, TAB Books, 1971; *101 Questions and Answers About AM, FM, and SSB*, 1972; *Realistic Guide to Hi-Fi and Stereo*, Radio Shack, 1972; *Installing TV and FM Antennas*, TAB Books, 1973; *Mobile Radio Handbook*, TAB Books, 1974; *Electronic Security Systems*, Audel, 1974; *CB Radio Accessories*, 1974; *Encyclopedia Dictionary of Electronic Circuits*, Prentice-Hall, 1974; *Hi-Fi Accessories You Can Build*, TAB Books, 1974; *Auto Test Circuits You Can Build*, TAB Books, 1974; *Electronic Test Equipment You Can Build*, TAB Books, 1974; *Small Appliance Repair Guide*, two volumes, TAB Books, 1974; *Sound System Installers Handbook*, in press.

Writer of numerous texts for International Correspondence Schools, McGraw, RCA Institutes, CB Radio Repair

Course, Inc., and technical instruction books and sales manuals for U.S. Air Force, U.S. Navy, Hughes Aircraft Co., Bell Telephone Co,, and other firms; also has ghost-written books for industry, and edited trade journals. Articles (some sixteen hundred) have appeared in more than sixty popular and technical magazines, including *True, House Beautiful, Plant Engineering, Popular Electronics, Mechanix Illustrated, Motor Boating, Missiles & Space,* and *Communications.*

WORK IN PROGRESS: Several books under contract, on electronics, management, and communications.

* * *

SANFORD, Agnes (White) 1897-

PERSONAL: Born November 4, 1897, in Kashing, China; daughter of Hugh W. (a Presbyterian missionary) and Augusta (Graves) White; married Edgar L. Sanford (a clergyman), April 2, 1923 (deceased); children: Edgar L., Virginia T. (Mrs. Miles Clark), John A. *Education:* Attended Peace Institute (now Peace College), 1914-18; Agnes Scott College, special courses in literature, 1918-19. *Religion:* Episcopalian. *Address:* Box 946, Monrovia, Calif.

CAREER: Writer. Co-founder of School of Pastoral Care, Northborough, Mass., 1955. Lay lecturer on prayer and healing (sponsored only by the inviting churches), in United States, Canada, England, Australia, and New Zealand. *Awards, honors:* Lit.D., Peace College.

WRITINGS: The Healing Light, Macalester Park, 1946; *Oh, Watchman* (novel), Lippincott, 1951; *Lost Shepherd* (novel), Lippincott, 1953; *Let's Believe,* Harper, 1954; *A Pasture for Peterkin,* Macalester Park, 1957; *Behold Your God,* Macalester Park, 1958; *Dreams Are for Tomorrow* (novel), Lippincott, 1963; *The Second Mrs. Wu* (novel), Lippincott, 1965; *The Healing Gifts of the Spirit,* Lippincott, 1966; *The Rising River* (novel), Lippincott, 1968; *The Healing Power of the Bible,* Lippincott, 1969; *Twice Seven Words,* Logos International, 1971; *Sealed Orders,* Logos International, 1972; *Route One,* Logos International, 1975.

WORK IN PROGRESS: The Man, the Lamb and the Sticks, for children.

SIDELIGHTS: Mrs. Sanford is competent in Mandarin Chinese.

* * *

SANFORD, Terry 1917-

PERSONAL: Born August 20, 1917, in Laurinburg, N.C.; son of Cecil L. and Elizabeth (Martin) Sanford; married Margaret Rose Knight, July 4, 1942; children: Elizabeth Knight, James Terry. *Education:* University of North Carolina, A.B., 1939, J.D., 1946. *Politics:* Democrat. *Religion:* Methodist. *Home:* 1508 Pinecrest Rd., Durham, N.C. *Office:* Allen Bldg., Duke University, Durham, N.C.

CAREER: University of North Carolina, Chapel Hill, assistant director, Institute of Government, 1940-41, 1946-48; Federal Bureau of Investigation, special agent, 1941-42; admitted to North Carolina Bar, 1946; Sanford, Phillips, McCoy & Weaver (law firm), Fayetteville, N.C., partner, 1948-60; state senator, North Carolina, 1953; governor of North Carolina, 1961-65; Sanford, Cannon, Adams, and McCullough (law firm), Raleigh, N.C., partner, 1965—; Duke University, Durham, N.C., president, 1969—. Member of board of directors, Learning Institute of North Carolina; member, Carnegie Commission on Educational Television; member of board of trustees, Methodist Col-

lege, Fayetteville, and Howard University. *Military service:* U.S. Army, 1942-46; served with 517th Parachute Infantry Combat Team in Italy, France, Belgium, and Germany; became first lieutenant.

MEMBER: American Bar Association, American Judicature Society, American Academy of Political and Social Science, American Legion, Veterans of Foreign Wars of the U.S.A. *Awards, honors:* Honorary degrees from University of North Carolina at Chapel Hill, Wake Forest College (now University), Shaw University, Belmont Abbey College, Pfeiffer College, North Carolina State University, University of North Carolina at Greensboro, High Point College, Drew University, and Davidson College.

WRITINGS: But What About the People?, Harper, 1966; *Storm Over the States,* McGraw, 1967.

* * *

SANTAS, Joan Foster 1930-

PERSONAL: Born July 4, 1930, in Chicago, Ill.; daughter of Lee R. (a public school superintendent) and Olive (Eckert) Foster; married Gerasimos Santas (an associate professor of philosophy), April 25, 1953; children: Diane, Christopher. *Education:* Knox College, B.A., 1952; Cornell University, M.A., 1954, Ph.D., 1963. *Politics:* Democrat. *Office:* Department of English, California State College, Dominguez Hills, Calif. 90247

CAREER: Boston University, Boston, Mass., part-time staff member of English department, 1962-67; Northeastern University, Boston, Mass., assistant professor, 1967-68; Towson State College, Towson, Md., lecturer, 1968-71; California State College, Dominguez Hills, assistant professor of English, 1971—. Radcliffe Institute for Independent Study, Cambridge, Mass., part-time scholar, 1964-66. *Awards, honors: College Arts* poetry contest winner, 1967.

WRITINGS: Ellen Glasgow's American Dream, University Press of Virginia, 1965.

WORK IN PROGRESS: Short stories and poetry; a book on "the clash between ideal and real in late 19th- and 20th-century Southern society as seen in works of writers like Faulkner, Stark Young, Ellen Glasgow, Wolfe, . . ." for Louisiana State University Press; a book of poems for PTC Publishing.†

* * *

SANWAL, B(hairava) D(at) 1917-

PERSONAL: Born March 25, 1917, in Almora, Uttar Pradesh, India; son of Purnanand Sanwal (an engineer); married Hem Mangalik (a family planning leader), November 22, 1944; children: Harsh and Mukul (sons). *Education:* Allahabad University, B.Sc., 1936; University of London, B.A. (honors), 1938; Middle Temple, London, England, Barrister-at-Law, 1939. *Office:* Commissioner's Office, Lucknow, Uttar Pradesh, India.

CAREER: Permanent member, Indian Civil Service; city manager of Lucknow, Uttar Pradesh, 1948-53, of Kanpur, Uttar Pradesh, 1953-56; commissioner for local authorities, Uttar Pradesh, 1956-59; regional commissioner, Agra Division, 1959-63, Meerut Division, 1963-66; Uttar Pradesh region, agricultural production commissioner, 1970-72, chief secretary, 1973-75. Bharat Heavy Electricals, director. *Military service:* Territorial Army; became honorary major. *Member:* Uttar Pradesh Artists Association (treasurer), Mahabodhi Society of Uttarakhand (managing director),

Officers' Cooperative Housing Society of Dehra Dun (chairman).

WRITINGS: Nepal and the East India Company, Asia Publishing House, 1965; *Agra and Its Monuments*, Longmans Orient, 1966.

SIDELIGHTS: Sanwal speaks French, German, and Persian. *Avocational interests:* Treking in the Himalayas.

* * *

SAPORTA, Sol 1925-

PERSONAL: Born March 12, 1925, in New York, N.Y.; son of Ovadia and Rachel (Strugo) Saporta; married Raquel Andrade, April 14, 1952; children: Dave, Vic, Terri. *Education:* Brooklyn College (now Brooklyn College of the City University of New York), B.A., 1944; University of Illinois, M.A., 1952, Ph.D., 1955. *Office:* Department of Linguistics, University of Washington, Seattle, Wash. 98105.

CAREER: Indiana University, Bloomington, assistant professor of Spanish and linguistics, 1955-60; University of Washington, Seattle, professor of linguistics and chairman of department, 1960—. Condon Lecturer, state of Oregon, 1965. *Member:* Linguistic Society of America, Modern Language Association of America. *Awards, honors:* Fellow, Center for Advanced Study in the Behavioral Sciences, 1964-65.

WRITINGS: (With C. Osgood and T. Sebeok) *Psycholinguistics*, Indiana University Press, 1954; (with H. and R. Kahane) *Development of Verbal Categories in Child Language*, Indiana University Press, 1958; (with H. Contreras) *A Phonological Grammar of Spanish*, University of Washington Press, 1962.

WORK IN PROGRESS: Studies in psycholinguistics and sexist language.

* * *

SARICKS, Ambrose 1915-

PERSONAL: Born May 12, 1915, in Wilkes-Barre, Pa.; son of Ambrose and Barbara (Hauze) Saricks; married Reese Pyott, March 4, 1945; children: Christopher Lee, Alison Barbara. *Education:* Bucknell University, A.B., 1937, M.A., 1941; University of Wisconsin, Ph.D., 1950. *Home:* 2901 Santa Fe Lane, Lawrence, Kan. 66044. *Office:* Department of History, University of Kansas, Lawrence, Kan. 66044.

CAREER: High school teacher of social studies in Muncy, Pa., 1938-39; Liberty Mutual Insurance Co., Brooklyn, N.Y., salesman, 1939-40; Ohio State University, Columbus, instructor in history, 1947-50; University of Kansas, Lawrence, assistant professor, 1950-56, associate professor, 1956-62, professor of history, 1962-70, associate dean of graduate school, 1966-70; Wichita State University, Wichita, Kan., dean of graduate school, associate dean of faculties, and professor of history, 1970-72; University of Kansas, Lawrence, professor of history, 1972—, vice-chancellor for academic affairs, 1972-75. *Military service:* U.S. Army Air Forces, 1942-46; became sergeant.

MEMBER: American Historical Association, American Association of University Professors, Society for French Historical Studies, Kansas Association of Teachers of History (executive committee member, 1962-65), Kansas State Historical Society, Kiwanis Club. *Awards, honors:* Watkins Faculty fellowship, University of Kansas; Penrose

Fund grant, American Philosophical Society; Eleutherian Mills Historical Library fellowship.

WRITINGS: A Bibliography of the Frank E. Melvin Collection of Pamphlets of the French Revolution in the University of Kansas Libraries, two volumes, University of Kansas Libraries, 1960; *Pierre Samuel du Pont de Nemours*, University of Kansas Press, 1965. Contributor of articles and reviews to professional journals.

WORK IN PROGRESS: Editing manuscripts by and about the Marquis de Sade; research on dissident religious movements in eighteenth-century Europe.

SIDELIGHTS: Saricks reads French, German, and some Spanish.

* * *

SARMA, G. V. L. N. 1925-

PERSONAL: Born April 17, 1925, in Bhimavaram, India; son of Rama Rao and Sita (Mahalakshmi) Sarma; married Annapoorna, December 25, 1958; children: Jyothi, Maharaj Kumari, and Radha (daughters). *Education:* Government Arts College, B.Sc., 1943; Banaras Hindu University, M.A. (English), 1955, M.A. (Indian philosophy and religion), 1968; University of Leeds, Diploma in English Studies, 1960; Gauhati University, Ph.D., 1964. *Religion:* Hindu, Radhasoami faith. *Home:* Kasturi vari House, Marella vari St., Bhimavaram, Andhra Pradesh, India. *Office:* Regional Engineering College, Warangal 506004, India.

CAREER: Gauhati University, Assam, India, lecturer, 1955-61; Regional Engineering College, Warangal, Andhra Pradesh, India, assistant professor, 1961-65, professor of English, 1965—. *Awards, honors:* British Council scholar.

WRITINGS: English for Engineering Students, Asia Publishing House, 1964; *Aldous Huxley*, Kitab Mahal (Allahabad), 1966; (editor) *Seven Great Lives*, Visakhapatnam, 1971; (editor) *Great Social Reformers*, Triveni Publishers, 1974. Contributor to journals in his field. Editor, *Journal of English Studies* (Warangal), 1970—.

WORK IN PROGRESS: Three books, *A Book of English Verse*, *Technical Communication*, and *Modern English Stylistics*; also fiction reflecting the conscience and social forces operating in contemporary India.

* * *

SARNA, Nahum M(attathias) 1923-

PERSONAL: Born March 27, 1923, in London, England; came to United States in 1951, naturalized in 1959; son of Jacob J. (a bookseller) and Milly (Horonzick) Sarna; married Helen Horowitz, March 23, 1947; children: Jonathan, David. *Education:* University of London, B.A. (honors), 1944, M.A., 1946; Jews College, diploma, 1947; Dropsie College for Hebrew and Cognate Learning (now Dropsie University), Ph.D., 1955. *Religion:* Jewish. *Home:* 35 Everett St., Newton Centre, Mass. 02159.

CAREER: Lecturer at University College, University of London, 1946-49, and Gratz College, Philadelphia, Pa., 1951-57; Jewish Theological Seminary of America, New York, N.Y., librarian, 1957-63, associate professor of Bible, 1963-65; Brandeis University, Waltham, Mass., associate professor, 1965-67, Dora Golding Professor of Biblical Studies, 1967—, chairman of department of Near Eastern and Judaic Studies, 1969—. Visiting professor at Columbia University, 1964-65, Andover Newton Theological School, 1966-67, Dropsie College for Hebrew and Cognate Learning (now Dropsie University), 1967-68. Member of B'nai B'rith Advisory Board on Adult Jewish Education, 1967—; associate trustee, American Schools of Oriental Research, 1965-67; Boston Hebrew College, trustee, 1968—, member of executive committee, 1970—; member of academic advisory council, National Foundation for Jewish Culture, 1973—; consultant to Melton Research Center. *Member:* American Academy for Jewish Research (fellow), Association for Jewish Studies (honorary secretary-treasurer, 1972—), Biblical Colloquium (vice-president, 1971—), Royal Asiatic Society (fellow), World Jewish Bible Society, World Union of Jewish Studies, American Oriental Society, Israel Exploration Society, Palestine Exploration Society, Society of Biblical Literature. *Awards, honors:* Frank and Ethel S. Cohen award, 1967, for *Understanding Genesis*; American Council of Learned Societies senior fellowship, 1971-72.

WRITINGS: A Syllabus of Biblical History, College of Jewish Studies, 1953; (contributor) L. Schwartz, editor, *Study Guide to Great Ages and Ideas of the Jewish People*, Hadassah Education Department, 1958; *The Heritage of Biblical Israel*, Milton Research Center, 1964; *Understanding Genesis*, McGraw, 1966; (author of prolegomenon) M. Buttenwieser, *The Book of Psalms*, Ktav, 1969; (contributor) R. D. Barnett, editor, *The Sephardi Heritage*, Vallentine, Mitchell, 1971; (author of introduction) *Early Spanish Pentateuch Manuscript*, Makor, 1974.

Translator: S. Z. Shragal, *Vision and Realization*, [London], 1945; A. Barth, *The Mitzvoth—Their Aim and Purpose*, [Jerusalem], 1950; (with M. Greenberg and J. Greenfield) *A New Translation of the Book of Psalms*, Jewish Publication Society of America, 1973.

Contributor to *Encyclopedia International, Encyclopedia Migraith, Encyclopedia Hebraica, Encyclopedia Judaica*, and *Encyclopaedia Britannica*. Contributor of articles and reviews to journals. Editor and translator, Jewish Publication Society's Bible translation committee, 1965—; editor of Bible division, *Encyclopedia Judaica*, 1968-72; member of editorial board, *Journal of Biblical Literature*, 1973-75; general editor, *Bible Commentary*, 1974—.

WORK IN PROGRESS: A full-length *Commentary* to the Book of Psalms, in Hebrew and English.

SIDELIGHTS: Understanding Genesis was the first volume in "The Heritage of Biblical Israel," a series of books intended to make the Old Testament intelligible to students and adults without training in biblical studies. The series is a joint project of McGraw and Jewish Theological Seminary of America.

* * *

SARNER, Harvey 1934-

PERSONAL: Born February 13, 1934, in New York, N.Y.; son of Michael (a printer) and Lillian (Greenblatt) Sarner; married Lori Jelle, June 9, 1959; children: Kyra K., Surah S. *Education:* University of Minnesota, B.S.L., 1958, LL.B. (cum laude), 1959. *Home:* 17 North Wildwood Dr., Prospect Heights, Ill. *Office:* 211 East Chicago Ave., Chicago, Ill.

CAREER: Attorney in private practice in Chicago, Ill. Legal counsel, Federal Communications Commission, 1959-61, American Dental Association, 1961-71. *Military service:* U.S. Navy, 1951-55.

WRITINGS: Malpractice Avoidance, Year Book, 1963;

Dental Jurisprudence, Saunders, 1963; *Business Management of a Dental Practice*, Saunders, 1966; *Business Management of a Small Animal Practice*, Saunders, 1967; *Law for the Nurse*, Saunders, 1968; *Insurance for the Doctor*, Saunders, 1968. Contributor to dental and legal journals.

* * *

SARNOFF, Irving 1922-

PERSONAL: Born May 5, 1922, in Brooklyn, N.Y.; son of Nathan and Rose (Gelfand) Sarnoff; married Suzanne Fischbach (an artist, writer, and teacher), November 28, 1946; children: David, Sara. *Education:* Brooklyn College (now Brooklyn College of the City University of New York), B.A., 1946; University of Michigan, M.A., 1949, Ph.D., 1951. *Home:* 100 Bleecker St., New York, N.Y. 10012. *Office:* Department of Psychology, New York University, 21 Washington Pl., New York, N.Y. 10003.

CAREER: University of Michigan, Ann Arbor, research associate and extension service lecturer, 1951-54; University College, University of London, London, England, Fulbright advanced research scholar, 1954-55; Yale University, New Haven, Conn., assistant professor of psychology, 1955-60; Western Reserve University (now Case Western Reserve University), Cleveland, Ohio, professor of social work and psychology, 1960-62; New York University, New York, N.Y., professor of psychology, 1962—. Senior stipend, National Institute of Mental Health, 1968-69. *Military service:* U.S. Army, Signal Corps, 1943-46. *Member:* American Psychological Association.

WRITINGS: (Contributor) D. Katz and others, editors, *Public Opinion and Propaganda*, Dryden, 1954; *Personality Dynamics and Development*, Wiley, 1962; *Society with Tears*, Citadel, 1966; (contributor) R. Abelson and others, editors, *Theories of Cognitive Consistency: A Sourcebook*, Rand McNally, 1968; I. Katz and H. Silver, editors, *The University and Social Welfare*, Magnes Press, 1969; *Testing Freudian Concepts: An Experimental Social Approach*, Springer, 1971. Contributor of more than twenty-five articles and reviews to professional journals in America and England. Editorial advisor, *Encyclopaedia Britannica*, 1969—.

WORK IN PROGRESS: Several books on various aspects of the psychology of love.

BIOGRAPHICAL/CRITICAL SOURCES: Chester A. Insko, *Theories of Attitude Change*, Appleton, 1967.

* * *

SAVAS, E(manuel) S(tephen) 1931-

PERSONAL: Born June 8, 1931, in New York, N.Y.; son of John and Olga (Limbos) Savas; married Helen Andrew, December 25, 1955; children: Jonathan Andrew, Stephen Dean. *Education:* University of Chicago, B.A., 1951, B.S., 1953; Columbia University, M.A., 1956, Ph.D., 1960. *Politics:* Reform Democrat. *Religion:* Greek Orthodox. *Home:* 699 West 239 St., New York, N.Y. 10463. *Office:* Columbia University, New York, N.Y. 10027.

CAREER: International Business Machines Corp. (IBM), associate staff engineer, Yorktown Heights, N.Y., 1959-60, senior control systems specialist, New York, N.Y., 1961-65, manager of technical recruiting and placement, White Plains, N.Y., 1965-66, manager of urban systems, New York, N.Y., 1966-67; City of New York, N.Y., deputy city administrator, 1967-69, first deputy city administrator, 1970-72; Columbia University, New York, N.Y., professor of public systems management, 1973—. *Military service:* U.S. Army, Chemical Corps, 1953-55. *Member:* American Chemical Society, Institute of Management Sciences, Operations Research Society of America, Urban and Regional Information Systems Association, American Association for the Advancement of Science.

WRITINGS: Computer Control of Industrial Processes, McGraw, 1965. Contributor to public policy and urban management journals.

AVOCATIONAL INTERESTS: Public affairs, reading, traveling, skiing, squash.

*   *   *

SAWER, Geoffrey 1910-

PERSONAL: Surname rhymes with "door"; born December 21, 1910, in Maymyo, Burma; son of Edgar Geoffrey (a soldier) and Edith (Langman) Sawer; married Beatrice Mabel (a teacher), January 6, 1940 (died, 1969); married Nancy Martyr; children: (first marriage) Michael, Elizabeth. *Education:* University of Melbourne, LL.B., 1933, LL.M., 1934, B.A., 1950. *Home:* 90 Empire Circle, Deakin, Canberra, Australian Capital Territory, Australia.

CAREER: Attorney at law, 1933—; Australian National University, Canberra, Australian Capital Territory, research professor of law, 1950-74, pro-vice-chancellor, 1975—. Special magistrate, Australian Capital Territory. Visiting professor at New York University, at Max Planck Institute, Heidelberg, Germany, University of London, Oxford University, and Cambridge University. *Member:* Social Science Research Council, International Commission of Jurists, Victorian Bar Association, Society of Public Teachers of Law, Australian Law Schools Association, Australia Political Studies Association, Academy of Social Science (fellow; president, 1972-75).

WRITINGS: Australian Government Today, Cambridge University Press, 1947, 11th edition, 1974; *Guide to Australian Law for Journalists,* Cambridge University Press, 1947, 2nd edition, 1968; *Australian Constitutional Cases,* Law Book Co. of Australia, 1947, 3rd edition, 1964; *Australian Federal Politics and Law, 1901-1929,* Cambridge University Press, 1956; *Australian Federal Politics and Law, 1929-1949,* Cambridge University Press, 1962; *Law in Society,* Clarendon Press, 1966; *Australian Federalism in the Courts,* Melbourne University Press, 1967; *The Australian and the Law,* Pelican, 1968, 2nd edition, 1974; *Modern Federalism,* Pitman, 1969; *The Australian Constitution,* Australian Government Publishing Service, 1975. Member of board of editors, *Modern Law Review, Public Law* (London), and *University of Toronto Law Journal.*

WORK IN PROGRESS: 2nd edition of *Modern Federalism; The Ombudsman in Australia,* completion expected in 1977.

SIDELIGHTS: Sawer reads French and German.

*   *   *

SAWYER, Corinne Holt
(Corinne Holt Rickert)

PERSONAL: Born in Chisholm, Minn.; daughter of Grover Justine (an engineer) and Grace (Ueland) Holt; married Robert Rickert, September 2, 1946; married second husband, Hugh Alton Sawyer, Jr. (a sales representative), August 28, 1965. *Education:* University of Minnesota, B.A. (summa cum laude), 1945, M.A., 1947; University of Birmingham, Ph.D., 1954. *Religion:* Episcopalian. *Home:* 105 Hunnicutt Lane, Clemson, S.C.

CAREER: Station WCCO, Minneapolis, Minn., continuity director, 1945-46; University of Minnesota, Minneapolis, instructor in speech, 1946-47; University of Miami, Coral Gables, Fla., assistant professor of radio and television, 1947-51; University of Maryland Overseas, England, instructor in English, 1954-58; East Carolina College (now University), Greenville, N.C., director of broadcasting, 1958-66; WNCT-TV, Greenville, N.C., women's editor and writer, 1960-66, appearing in own household hints program, 1963-66; Clemson University, Clemson, S.C., assistant professor of English, 1966—. Sometime panelist, actress, and commercial announcer on radio and television. *Member:* Modern Language Association of America, National Collegiate Players, Southeastern Renaissance Society, South Atlantic Modern Language Association, Southern Humanities Conference, Mensa, Phi Beta Kappa, Alpha Epsilon Rho, Zeta Phi Eta.

WRITINGS: (Adapter with Frank M. Whiting) Mark Twain, *Huckleberry Finn,* Children's Theatre Press, 1946; *John Darrell: Minister and Exorcist,* University of Florida Press, 1962.

AVOCATIONAL INTERESTS: Duplicate bridge, French cookery.

*   *   *

SAWYER, Jesse O. 1918-

PERSONAL: Born February 9, 1918, in Earlville, Ill.; son of Jesse O. (a farmer) and Lila Ann (Ohme) Sawyer. *Education:* St. Olaf College, A.B., 1939; University of Wisconsin, graduate student, 1939-40; University of California, Berkeley, Ph.D., 1959. *Home:* 2555 Leimert Blvd., Oakland, Calif. 94602. *Office:* University of California, Berkeley, Calif.

CAREER: University of California, Berkeley, lecturer in speech, 1957-61, director of English program for foreign students, 1958-61, director of language laboratory, 1963—, lecturer in linguistics, 1964—. *Military service:* U.S. Navy, World War II and Korean War; became lieutenant commander. *Member:* Linguistic Society of America, Norwegian-American Historical Association, Sigma Xi. *Awards, honors:* Citation for distinguished teaching, University of California, Berkeley, 1962.

WRITINGS: (With Shirley K. Silver) *Conversations and Pronunciation Drills for Foreign Students of English,* California Book Co., 1959, revised edition, 1960; (with Ervin, Silver, and Aoki) *The Utility of Translation and Written Symbols during the First Thirty Hours of Language Study,* Department of Speech, University of California, 1962; *English-Wappo Vocabulary,* University of California Publications in Linguistics, 1965; (editor) *Studies in American Indian Languages,* University of California, 1971.

WORK IN PROGRESS: Continued work on Wappo and Yuki, California Indian languages; a collection of Minangkabau texts, a language of Sumatra.

*   *   *

SAYERS, Frances Clarke 1897-

PERSONAL: Born September 4, 1897, in Topeka, Kan.; daughter of Oscar Lincoln (a railroad official) and Mariam (Busby) Clarke; married Alfred H. P. Sayers, June 27, 1925 (deceased). *Education:* Attended University of Texas and Carnegie Institute of Technology (now Carnegie-Mellon University). *Politics:* Democrat. *Home and office:* 167 Fairview Rd., Ojai, Calif. 93023.

CAREER: New York Public Library, New York, N.Y., assistant in children's room, 1918-23, superintendent of work with children, 1941-52; University of California, Los Angeles, lecturer on children's literature, 1954-65; full-time writer, 1965—. *Member:* American Library Association, American Civil Liberties Union. *Awards, honors:* Joseph W. Lippincott Award for distinguished service in profession of librarianship, 1965; Clarence Day Award, 1966, for *Summoned by Books*; Southern California Children's Literature Award, 1969.

WRITINGS: Bluebonnets for Lucinda (juvenile), Viking, 1932; *Mr. Tidy-Paws* (juvenile), Viking, 1934; *Tag-Along Tooloo* (juvenile), 1941; *Sally Tait* (juvenile), Viking, 1948; *Ginny and Custard* (juvenile), Viking, 1951; (editor with Evelyn Sickels) *Anthology of Children's Literature*, 3rd edition, Houghton, 1958, 4th edition, 1970.

Summoned by Books: Essays and Speeches, edited by Marjeanne Blinn, Viking, 1965; *Children From Many Lands Illustrate Grimm's Fairy Tales*, American Federal Arts, 1967; (author of foreword) Kornei Chukovskii, *From Two to Five*, revised edition, University of California, Berkeley, 1968; (author of introduction) Jakob Grimm, *Grimm's Fairy Tales*, Follett, 1968; *Oscar Lincoln Busby Stokes*, Harcourt, 1970; *Anne Carroll More: A Biography*, Atheneum, 1972. Contributor of occasional articles to professional journals and magazines.

BIOGRAPHICAL/CRITICAL SOURCES: Horn Book, June, 1970.†

*   *   *

SAYLOR, J(ohn) Galen 1902-

PERSONAL: Born December 12, 1902, in Carleton, Neb.; son of John Oliver and Ella (Rothrock) Saylor; married Helen Smith, June 1, 1927; children: John Lowell, Sandra (Mrs. Jim McLean), Sherrill Kay (Mrs. Stephen Lahr). *Education:* McPherson College, A.B., 1922; Columbia University, M.A., 1934, Ph.D., 1941. *Religion:* Presbyterian. *Home:* 3344 South 29th St., Lincoln, Neb. 68502. *Office:* 104 Henzlik Hall, University of Nebraska, Lincoln, Neb. 68508.

CAREER: High school teacher of mathematics in Kansas, 1922-25; high school principal, Waverly, Neb., 1925-29; superintendent of schools, Waterloo, Neb., 1929-35; Nebraska State Education Association, Lincoln, director of research, 1936-38; University of Nebraska, Lincoln, professor of secondary education, 1940-71, professor emeritus, 1971—, chairman of department, 1949-68. Visiting professor at University of Maryland, 1959; Fulbright professor at University of Jyvaskyla, Finland, 1962-63; lecturer at Universities of Rome and Florence, 1963. Consultant on teacher education, Office of U.S. High Commissioner for Germany, 1950; U.S. Department of State representative at International Conference on Programmed Instruction and Teaching Machines, Berlin, 1963; trustee of Joint Council on Economic Education, 1964-67; delegate to world assembly of World Confederation of Organizations of the Teaching Profession, Seoul, Korea, 1966. Chairman of board of directors, *PTA Magazine*, 1961-64. Member at various times of Nebraska Governor's committees on safety, employment of the handicapped, beautification, and educational television. *Military service:* U.S. Naval Reserve, active duty, 1943-46; became lieutenant commander.

MEMBER: Association for Supervision and Curriculum Development (executive committee, 1964-67; president, 1965-66), National Association of Secondary School Princi-

pals, National Congress of Parents and Teachers (treasurer, 1960-63), National Education Association, Nebraska Congress of Parents and Teachers (president, 1953-56), Kiwanis Club (president of Lincoln chapter, 1942), Phi Delta Kappa. *Awards, honors:* LL.D., McPherson College, 1962; University of Nebraska distinguished teaching award (medal and $1,000), 1967.

WRITINGS: Factors Associated with Participation in Cooperative Curriculum Programs, Teachers College, Columbia University, 1941; (with others) *Junior College Studies*, University of Nebraska Press, 1948; (with William Alexander) *Secondary Education: Basic Principles and Practices*, Rinehart, 1950; (with others) *Better than Rating*, Association for Supervision and Curriculum Development, 1951; (with Alexander) *Curriculum Planning: Basic Principles and Practices*, Rinehart, 1954; (contributor) *La Educacion Secundaria en America*, Division of Education, Pan American Union, 1955; *Course Offerings, Subject Enrollments, Size, and Current Expenditures for Nebraska High Schools*, University of Nebraska Press, 1957; (with Alexander) *Modern Secondary Education*, Rinehart, 1959; (contributor) *Becoming an Educator*, edited by Van Cleve Morris, Houghton, 1963; (with Alexander) *Curriculum Planning for Modern Schools*, Holt, 1966; (with Alexander and E. Williams) *The High School: Today and Tomorrow*, Holt, 1971; (with Alexander) *Planning Curriculum for Schools*, Holt, 1974.

Contributor to *Encyclopedia of Educational Research, World Book Encyclopedia, Dictionary of Education, Book of Knowledge*, and to education journals. Special feature editor, *Educational Leadership*, 1947-49; editor of special issue, *Review of Educational Research*, June, 1957; chairman of publications committee, Association for Supervision and Curriculum Development, 1959-62.

WORK IN PROGRESS: Antecedents of Performance-Based Teacher Education.

AVOCATIONAL INTERESTS: Travel, photography.

*   *   *

SAYRES, William C(ortlandt) 1927-

PERSONAL: Born April 5, 1927, in Detroit, Mich.; son of Cortlandt W. (a teacher) and Doris (Abbott) Sayres; children: William Croneis, Jason Cortlandt, Nicole Jeananne. *Education:* Beloit College, A.B., 1949; Harvard University, M.A., 1951, Ph.D., 1953. *Residence:* Bogota, N.J. *Office:* Teachers College, Columbia University, New York, N.Y. 10027.

CAREER: National Science Foundation, postdoctoral fellow, 1953-54; Yale University, New Haven, Conn., instructor in anthropology and education, 1954-57; State University of New York, Albany, research associate in social sciences and education, 1957-63; Columbia University, Teachers College, New York, N.Y., associate professor and research associate, 1963—. *Military service:* U.S. Naval Reserve, 1945-46; became lieutenant junior grade. *Member:* American Anthropological Association, American Ethnological Society, Phi Beta Kappa, Sigma Xi, Omicron Delta Kappa, Beta Theta Pi.

WRITINGS: Sonotaw, Simon & Schuster, 1959; (editor with Edward T. Ladd, and contributor) *Social Aspects of Education: A Casebook*, Prentice-Hall, 1962; *Do Good*, Holt, 1966. About two hundred short stories, poems, articles, and reviews have appeared in professional and literary journals.

WORK IN PROGRESS: A novel; monograph; articles.

SCARBOROUGH, William Kauffman 1933-

PERSONAL: Born January 17, 1933, in Baltimore, Md.; son of James Blaine and Julia (Kauffman) Scarborough; married Patricia Estelle Carruthers, January 16, 1954; children: Catherine Lee, William Bradley. *Education:* University of North Carolina, A.B., 1954, Ph.D., 1962; Cornell University, M.A., 1957. *Politics:* Independent conservative. *Religion:* Presbyterian. *Home:* 1120 Estelle St., Hattlesburg, Miss. 39401.

CAREER: Millsaps College, Jackson, Miss., assistant professor of history, 1961-63; Northeast Louisiana State College (now Northeast Louisiana University), Monroe, assistant professor of history, 1963-64; University of Southern Mississippi, Hattiesburg, associate professor of history, 1964—. *Military service:* U.S. Naval Reserve, 1954-62; on active duty, 1954-56. *Member:* Organization of American Historians, American Historical Association, American Association of University Professors, Agricultural History Society, Southern Historical Association, Mississippi Historical Society, Phi Beta Kappa, Phi Eta Sigma, Phi Alpha Theta.

WRITINGS: The Overseer: Plantation Management in the Old South, Louisiana State University Press, 1966; (editor) *The Diary of Edmund Ruffin,* Louisiana State University Press, Volume I: *Toward Independence,* 1972, Volume II: *Ten Years of Hope,* in press; (contributor) Richard A. McLemore, editor, *A History of Mississippi,* University and College Press of Mississippi, 1973.

WORK IN PROGRESS: Final volume of Edmund Ruffin's diary, *A Dream Shattered*; research for a book, tentatively entitled *Planter Dynasties of the Old South.*

* * *

SCARRY, Patricia (Murphy) 1924-
(Patsy Scarry; pseudonym Liam Roy)

PERSONAL: Surname rhymes with "carry"; born September 9, 1924, in Vancouver, British Columbia, Canada; daughter of Laurence F. (an accountant) and Theresa (Mahann) Murphy); married Richard McClure Scarry (a writer and illustrator of children's books), September 7, 1949; children: Richard McClure II. *Education:* Attended Little Flower Academy, Vancouver, British Columbia. *Residence:* Lausanne, Switzerland.

CAREER: Canadian Broadcasting Corp., actress and radio writer in Vancouver and Toronto, 1942-1945; Young & Rubicam (advertising), New York, N.Y., radio and television writer, 1946-1949; Benton & Bowles (advertising), New York, N.Y., radio and television writer, 1950-51; author of children's books.

*WRITINGS—*All published by Golden Press, except as noted: (Under name Patsy Scarry) *Danny Beaver's Secret,* 1952; *Tiny Things,* 1952; *My Kitten,* Simon & Schuster, 1953; *My Teddy Bear,* 1953; *Pierre Bear,* 1954; *The Bunny Book,* 1955; *My Puppy,* Simon & Schuster, 1955; *My Snuggly Bunny,* 1956; *My Baby Brother,* Simon & Schuster, 1956; *Fun Around the World,* Silver Burdett, 1957; *Schools Around the World,* Silver Burdett, 1957; *My Pets,* 1958 (under name Patsy Scarry) *My Baby Sister,* 1958; (under name Patsy Scarry) *Histories d'ours,* Simon & Schuster, 1958; *My Pets: Three Stories About My Puppy, My Kitten, [and] My Snuggly Bunny,* 1959; *My Dolly and Me,* 1959.

Just for Fun, 1960; *Goodnight Little Bear,* 1961; *The Country Mouse and the City Mouse,* 1961; *Corky,* 1962;

The Wait for Me Kitten, 1962; *Tommy Visits the Dentist,* 1964; (with K. Jackson) *The Nursery Tale Book,* 1964; *Hop, Little Kangaroo,* 1965; *The Golden Story Book of River Bend,* 1969; *The Jeremy Mouse Book: Stories,* American Heritage Press, 1969.

The Sweet Smell of Christmas, 1970; *Little Richard,* American Heritage Press, 1970; *Little Richard and Prickles,* American Heritage Press, 1971; *Waggy and his Friends,* American Heritage Press, 1971; *More About Waggy,* McGraw, 1973.

AVOCATIONAL INTERESTS: Traveling, skiing, sailing.†

* * *

SCARRY, Richard (McClure) 1919-

PERSONAL: Surname rhymes with "carry"; born June 5, 1919, in Boston, Mass.; son of John James (proprietor of department stores) and Barbara (McClure) Scarry; married Patricia Murphy (a writer of children's books), September 7, 1949; children: Richard McClure II. *Education:* Boston Museum School of Fine Arts, student, 1938-41. *Residence:* Lausanne, Switzerland.

CAREER: Magazine and children's book illustrator, 1946—; writer. *Military service:* U.S. Army, 1941-46; served as art director, editor, writer, and illustrator, Morale Services Section, Allied Forces Headquarters, North African and Mediterranean theaters; became captain.

*WRITINGS—*All self-illustrated: *The Great Big Car and Truck Book,* Simon & Schuster, 1951; *Rabbit and His Friends,* Simon & Schuster, 1953; *Nursery Tales,* Simon & Schuster, 1958.

Tinker and Tanker, Garden City Books, 1960; *The Hickory Dickory Clock Book,* Doubleday, 1961; *Tinker and Tanker Out West,* Doubleday, 1961; *Tinker and Tanker and Their Space Ship,* Doubleday, 1961; *Tinker and Tanker and the Pirates,* Doubleday, 1961; *Tinker and Tanker, Knights of the Round Table,* Doubleday, 1963; *Tinker and Tanker in Africa,* Doubleday, 1963; *Best Word Book Ever,* Golden Press, 1963; *The Rooster Struts,* Golden Press, 1963, published as *The Golden Happy Book of Animals,* 1964 (published in England as *Animals,* Hamyln, 1963); *Polite Elephant,* Golden Press, 1964; *Feed the Hippo His ABC's,* Golden Press, 1964; *Busy, Busy World,* Golden Press, 1965; *Richard Scarry's Teeny Tiny Tales,* Golden Press, 1965; *The Santa Claus Book,* Golden Press, 1965; *The Bunny Book,* Golden Press, 1965.

Is This the House of Mistress Mouse?, Golden Press, 1966; *Storybook Dictionary,* Golden Press, 1966; *Planes,* Golden Press, 1967; *Trains,* Golden Press, 1967; *Boats,* Golden Press, 1967; *Cars,* Golden Press, 1967; *Richard Scarry's Egg in the Hole Book,* Golden Press, 1967; *What Animals Do,* Golden Press, 1968; *Best Storybook Ever,* Golden Press, 1968; *The Early Bird,* Random House, 1968; *What Do People Do All Day?,* Random House, 1968; *The Adventures of Tinker and Tanker* (contains *Tinker and Tanker, Tinker and Tanker Out West,* and *Tinker and Tanker and Their Space Ship*), Doubleday, 1968; *The Great Pie Robbery,* Random House, 1969; *The Supermarket Mystery,* Random House, 1969; *Richard Scarry's Great Big Schoolhouse,* Random House, 1969.

More Adventures of Tinker and Tanker (contains *Tinker and Tanker and the Pirates, Tinker and Tanker, Knights of the Round Table,* and *Tinker and Tanker in Africa*), Doubleday, 1971; *ABC Word Book,* Random House, 1971;

Richard Scarry's Best Stories Ever, Golden Press, 1971; *Richard Scarry's Fun With Words*, Golden Press, 1971; *Richard Scarry's Going Places*, Golden Press, 1971; *Richard Scarry's Great Big Air Book*, Random House, 1971; *Richard Scarry's Things to Know*, Golden Press, 1971; *Funniest Storybook Ever*, Random House, 1972; *Nicky Goes to the Doctor*, Golden Press, 1972; *Richard Scarry's Great Big Mystery Book* (contains *The Great Pie Robbery* and *The Supermarket Mystery*), Random House, 1972; *Hop Aboard, Here We Go*, Golden Press, 1972; *Babykins and His Family*, Golden Press, 1973; *Silly Stories*, Golden Press, 1973; *Richard Scarry's Find Your ABC's*, Random House, 1973; *Richard Scarry's Please and Thank You Book*, Random House, 1973; *Richard Scarry's Best Rainy Day Book Ever*, Random House, 1974; *Cars and Trucks and Things That Go*, Golden Press, 1974.

Editor and illustrator: Jean de La Fontaine, *Fables*, Doubleday, 1963.

Illustrator: Kathryn Jackson, *Let's Go Fishing*, Simon & Schuster, 1949; Jackson, *Mouse's House*, Simon & Schuster, 1949; Jackson, *Duck and His Friends*, Simon & Schuster, 1949; Jackson, *Brave Cowboy Bill*, Simon & Schuster, 1950; Jackson, *The Animals' Merry Christmas*, Simon & Schuster, 1950; Oliver O'Connor Barrett, *Little Benny Wanted a Pony*, Simon & Schuster, 1950; Patricia Scarry, *Danny Beaver's Secret*, Simon & Schuster, 1953; Leah Gale, *The Animals of Farmer Jones*, Simon & Schuster, 1953; Margaret Wise Brown, *Little Indian*, Simon & Schuster, 1954; Patricia Scarry, *Pierre Bear*, Golden Press, 1954; Jane Werner, *Smokey the Bear*, Simon & Schuster, 1955; Kathryn Jackson, *Golden Bedtime Book*, Simon & Schuster, 1955; Mary Maud Reed, *Mon petit dictionnaire geant*, Editions des deux coqs d'or, 1958.

Patricia Scarry, *Just for Fun*, Golden Press, 1960; *My Nursery Tale Book*, Golden Press, 1961; *Richard Scarry's Animal Mother Goose*, Golden Press, 1964; Barbara Shook Hazen, *Rudolph the Red-nosed Reindeer*, Golden Press, 1964; *The Golden Book of 365 Stories*, Golden Press, 1966; *I Am a Bunny*, Golden Press, 1966; *Richard Scarry's Best Mother Goose Ever*, Golden Press, 1970; *Richard Scarry's Mother Goose*, Golden Press, 1972.

Also illustrator of coloring activity books and children's foreign language dictionaries.

AVOCATIONAL INTERESTS: Skiing, sailing, traveling.

BIOGRAPHICAL/CRITICAL SOURCES: Young Readers Review, September, 1968; *New Yorker*, December 14, 1968; *Publishers Weekly*, October 29, 1969; Selma G. Lanes, *Down the Rabbit Hole*, Atheneum, 1971.†

* * *

SCHACHTER, Gustav 1926-

PERSONAL: Born May 27, 1926, in Botosani, Rumania; son of Herman and Gisella (Gropper) Schachter; married Francine Norma Lerner (a teacher and artist), February 25, 1958; children: Livia Rebecca, Levanto Gershon. *Education:* City College (now of the City University of New York), New York, N.Y., B.S., 1954; New York University, M.B.A., 1956, Ph.D., 1962. *Home:* 26 Egmont St., Brookline, Mass. 02146. *Office:* Northeastern University, Boston, Mass. 02115.

CAREER: United Nations, International Refugee Organization, Rome, Italy, administrative assistant, 1949-51; B & G, Inc. (food packers), New York, N.Y., production manager, 1951-59; City College (now of the City University of

New York), New York, N.Y., lecturer, 1960-62, instructor, 1962-64, assistant professor of economics, 1964-65; Northeastern University, Boston, Mass., assistant professor, 1965-66, associate professor, 1966-69, professor of economics, 1969—. Part-time visiting lecturer at Rutgers University, 1961-62, and Manhattan College, 1962-63. Principal investigator, National Science Foundation, 1970-72; Coordinator, Italian National Science Foundation, Rome, Italy, 1972-75. *Member:* American Economic Association, Society for International Development, Comparative Economics Association, National Planning Association, Regional Science Association, Economic History Association. *Awards, honors:* Italian government award; Fulbright travel grant; New York University Founders Day Award; Doctor of Science, Honoris Causa, Lowell Technological Institute.

WRITINGS: The Italian South: Mediterranean Economic Development, Random House, 1965; (with E. Dale) *The Economist Looks at Society*, Wiley, 1973. Contributor to business and economic journals. Associate editor, *International Reports*, 1961-62.

WORK IN PROGRESS: A textbook, *Inductive Economics*, completion expected in 1978.

SIDELIGHTS: Schachter has traveled for research in western Europe periodically since 1958. He is competent in Rumanian, Italian, French, German, and knows some Spanish and Hebrew.

BIOGRAPHICAL/CRITICAL SOURCES: Boston Sunday Herald, February 20, 1966; *International Economic Selections Bibliography*, March, 1966.

* * *

SCHAEFER, Jack Warner 1907-

PERSONAL: Born November 19, 1907, in Cleveland, Ohio; son of Carl Walter (a lawyer) and Minnie Luella (Hively) Schaefer; married Eugenia Hammond Ives, August 26, 1931 (divorced December, 1948); married Louise Wilhide Deans, June, 1949; children: (first marriage) Carl, Christopher, Susan, Jonathan; (stepchildren) Sharon, Stephani, Claudia. *Education:* Oberlin College, A.B., 1929; Columbia University, graduate study, 1929-30. *Home:* 1719 San Cristobel, Albuquerque, N.M. 87104. *Agent:* Harold Matson Co., Inc., 22 East 40th St., New York, N.Y. 10016.

CAREER: United Press, reporter and office man, 1930-31; Connecticut State Reformatory, assistant director of education, 1931-38; *New Haven Journal-Courier*, New Haven, Conn., associate editor, 1932-39, editor, 1939-42; *Baltimore Sun*, Baltimore, Md., editorial writer, 1942-44; *Norfolk Virginian-Pilot*, Norfolk, Va., associate editor, 1944-48; *Shoreliner*, editor, 1949; Lindsay Advertising Co., New Haven, Conn., associate, 1949; free-lance writer, 1949—. *Awards, honors: Old Ramon* was chosen as an American Library Association Notable book.

WRITINGS—All published by Houghton, except as indicated: *Shane*, 1949; *First Blood*, 1953; *The Big Range* (short stories), 1953; *The Canyon*, 1953; *The Pioneers* (short stories), 1954; *Company of Cowards*, 1957; *The Kean Land* (short stories), 1959; *Old Ramon*, 1960; *The Plainsmen*, 1963; *Monte Walsh*, 1963; *The Great Endurance Horse Race*, Stagecoach, 1963; *Stubby Pringle's Christmas*, 1964; *Heroes Without Glory: Some Goodmen of the Old West*, 1965; *Collected Stories*, 1966; *New Mexico*, Coward-McCann, 1967; *The Short Novels of Jack*

Schaefer, 1967; *Mavericks*, 1967; *An American Bestiary*, 1975.

(Editor) *Out West;* Houghton, 1955 (published in England as *Out West: A Western Omnibus,* Deutsch, 1959). Also author of screenplay, "Jinglebob," and special material on which the film "The Great Cowboy Race" is based. Contributor of short stories to magazines. Editor and publisher, *Theatre News*, 1935-40, *Movies*, 1939-41.

SIDELIGHTS: Shane was filmed by Paramount in 1953, and a film of *Monte Walsh* was produced in 1970.

* * *

SCHAKOVSKOY, (Princess) Zinaida 1908-
(Jacques Croise)

PERSONAL: Born August 30, 1906, in Moscow, Russia; daughter of Prince Alexis and Ann (von Kninen) Schakovskoy; married Sviatislay de Malewsky-Malevitch (a painter), November 21, 1926; *Education:* Attended American College for Girls, Turkey, 1921-23, Monastere de Berlaymont, Brussels, Belgium, 1923-25, and College de France, Paris, 1925-26. *Politics:* "I do not belong to any party, but I am anti-Marxist." *Religion:* Russian Orthodox. *Home:* 42, rue Laugier, Paris 75107, France.

CAREER: Writer, poet, contributor to Russian emigre journals, 1932—. Special correspondent for Belgian newspapers in Poland, Lithuania, Estonia and Latvia, 1937-38; literary critic for Belgian newspapers and reviews, 1937-40; Agence Francaise d'Information, London, England, editor, 1942-45; correspondent with Allied forces in Italy, Greece, Germany, and at Nuremberg Trials, 1945-47; Radio Television Francaise, Paris, France, head of cultural broadcasts in French and Russian, beginning 1955; *Rousskaya Mysl* (*La Pensee Russe;* Russian-language newspaper), Paris, France, editor-in-chief, 1968—. *Member:* Societaire des Gens de Lettres de France, Syndicate of Literary Critics, P.E.N. (all France). *Military service:* Army Red Cross, 1940; received Croix des Evades (Belgium) and Chevalier de la Legion d'Honneur (France). *Awards, honors:* Prix de Paris, 1949, for *Europe et Valerius;* Prix Therouanne de l'Academie Francaise, for *La Vie quotidienne a Moscou au XVII siecle*, 1964, and for *La Vie quotidenne a Saint-Petersbourg a l'epoque romantique;* named Officer des Arts et Lettres.

WRITINGS: Ouhod (poems in Russian), Polyglotte (Brussels), 1934; *Doroga* (poems in Russian), Polyglotte (Brussels), 1935; *Vie d'Alexandre Pouchkine*, Cite Chretienne (Brussels), 1937; *Hommage a Pouchkine* (anthology), Journal des Poetes (Brussels), 1937; *Insomnies* (poems), Journal des Poetes (Brussels), 1939; *Une Enfance* (autobiography), La Renaissance du Livre, 1939; *Ma Russie habille en USSR: Retour au pays natal*, Grasset, 1958, translation by Peter Wiles published as *The Privilege Was Mine: A Russian Princess Returns to the Soviet Union*, Putnam, 1959; *La Vie quotidienne a Moscou au XVII siecle*, Hachette, 1963; *The Fall of Eagles*, translation by J. Maxwell Browjohn, Harcourt, 1964 (published in England as *Precursors of Peter the Great*, J. Cape, 1964); *Tel est mon siecle* (memoires), Les Presses de la Cite, Volume I: *Lumieres et Ombres*, 1964, Volume II: *Une Maniere de vivre*, 1965, Volume III: *La Folle Clio*, 1966, Volume IV: *La Drole de paix*, 1967; *La vie quotidienne a Saint-Petersbourg a l'epoque romantique*, Hachette, 1966; *Pered Snom* (poems in Russian), La Pensee Russe, 1970. Contributor of poetry, articles, and criticism to literary journals in England and France.

Under pseudonym Jacques Croise; all novels: *Europe et Valerius*, Flammarion et Cie, 1949; *Sortie de secours*, Plon, 1953; *La Dialogue des aveugles*, Amiot-Dumont, 1955; *Jeu de massacres*, Grasset, 1956; (translator from Russian into French) Alexandre Grine, *Celle qui court sur les vagues*, Laffont, 1959.

WORK IN PROGRESS: Otrajenia (title means "Reflections"), literary memoirs, in Russian, on Russian emigrant authors writing between World Wars I and II.

SIDELIGHTS: Princess Schakovskoy has given numerous radio broadcasts and has made serveral television appearances in Paris and London. She has traveled extensively in Europe, United States, Canada, Mexico, and Africa. She is competent in English and Spanish, as well as Russian and French. *Avocational interests:* Reading, history, art, people, and animals (especially dogs).

* * *

SCHAUB, Marilyn McNamara 1928-
(Sister Marie Aquinas McNamara)

PERSONAL: Born March 24, 1928, in Chicago, Ill.; daughter of Bernard F. (a business executive) and Helen (Skehan) McNamara; married R. Thomas Schaub, 1969; children: one daughter. *Education:* Rosary College, A.B., 1953; University of Fribourg, Ph.D., 1957. *Home:* 25 McKelvey Ave., Pittsburgh, Pa. 15218. *Office:* Department of Theology, Duquesne University, Pittsburgh, Pa. 15219.

CAREER: Former professor of classical languages and New Testament at Rosary College, River Forest, Ill., beginning 1957; Duquesne University, Pittsburgh, Pa., associate professor of theology, 1973—. Honorary associate, American School of Oriental Research, 1966-67. *Member:* Archaeological Institute of America, American Philological Association, Catholic Biblical Association, Illinois Classical Conference.

WRITINGS—All under name Sister Marie Aquinas McNamara: (Translator) Ceslaus Spicq, *The Trinity and Our Moral Life According to St. Paul*, Newman Press, 1963; (translator with Sister Honoria Richter) Ceslaus Spicq, *Agape in the New Testament*, B. Herder, Volume I: *Agape in the Synoptic Gospels*, 1964, Volume II: *Agape in the Epistles of St. Paul, the Acts of the Apostles, and the Epistles of St. James, St. Peter and St. Jude*, 1965, Volume III: *Agape in the Gospel, Epistles and Apocalypse of St. John*, 1966; (translator) Ceslaus Spicq, *St. Paul and Christian Living*, M. H. Gill, 1964; *Friends and Friendship for Saint Augustine*, Alba, 1964.

* * *

SCHEFFLER, Harold W(alter) 1932-

PERSONAL: Born October 24, 1932, in St. Louis, Mo.; son of Walter and Dorothy (Briggs) Scheffler; married Elizabeth A. McKinny, July 6, 1956. *Education:* University of Missouri, B.A., 1956; University of Chicago, M.A., 1957, Ph.D., 1963. *Home:* 39 Birch Dr., New Haven, Conn.

CAREER: University of Connecticut, Storrs, instructor in anthropology, 1961-62; Bryn Mawr College, Bryn Mawr, Pa., lecturer in anthropology, 1962-63; Yale University, New Haven, Conn., assistant professor, 1963-67, associate professor, 1967-72, professor of anthropology, 1972—, chairman of department, 1974—. Research on field expeditions in British Solomon Islands and among Ojibwa Indians in United States and Canada. *Military service:* U.S. Army,

1954-55. *Member:* American Anthropological Association (fellow), Phi Beta Kappa, Sigma Xi (fellow). *Awards, honors:* Fulbright grant to Australian National University, 1960-61.

WRITINGS: Choiseul Island Social Structure, University of California Press, 1965; (with F. G. Lounsbury) *A Study in Structural Semantics: The Sirioro Kinship System,* Prentice-Hall, 1971. Contributor to professional journals.

WORK IN PROGRESS: Australian Systems of Kin Classification.

* * *

SCHEID, Francis J(ames) 1920-

PERSONAL: Surname rhymes with "ride"; born September 24, 1920, in Plymouth, Mass.; son of John J. (a dairyman) and Rose (Bergdoll) Scheid; married Barbara Paty, June 2, 1944; children: Betsy, Lisa, Sarah. *Education:* Boston University, B.S., 1942, M.A., 1943; Massachusetts Institute of Technology, Ph.D., 1948. *Home:* Elm St., Kingston, Mass. *Office:* Boston University, 270 Bay State Rd., Boston, Mass.

CAREER: Boston University, Boston, Mass., instructor, 1948-51, assistant professor, 1951-54, associate professor, 1954-59, professor of mathematics, 1960—, chairman of department, 1957—. University of Rangoon, Fulbright lecturer, 1961-62. Consultant to U.S. Air Force Cambridge Research Center, Massachusetts Institute of Technology Instrumentation Laboratory, and School Mathematics Study Group. Television and film lecturer for WGBH-TV; narrator for more than one hundred films on mathematical subjects; lecturer in Southeast Asia, Lebanon, and Switzerland, 1962. *Military service:* U.S. Naval Reserve, 1944-46; became ensign. *Member:* American Association for the Advancement of Science, The Institute of Management Sciences, Mathematical Association of America, Society for Industrial and Applied Mathematics, Association of Mathematics Teachers of New England.

WRITINGS: Elements of Finite Mathematics, Addison-Wesley, 1962; *Numerical Analysis,* McGraw, 1967; *Introduction to Computer Science,* McGraw, 1970. Author of monographs. Contributor of articles on mathematical subjects to journals and on golf handicapping and course rating to *Golf Digest.*

WORK IN PROGRESS: The Game of Numbers, an experimental treatment of arithmetic through calculus, designed for educational research.

* * *

SCHEINER, Seth M(ordecai) 1933-

PERSONAL: Born April 19, 1933, in New York, N.Y.; son of Elias (a bookkeeper) and Helen (Frankel) Scheiner; married Elayne Schachter, May 27, 1956; children: Jeffrey Owen, Adam David. *Education:* City College (now City College of the City University of New York), New York, N.Y., B.A., 1955; New York University, M.A., 1959, Ph.D., 1962. *Office:* Department of History, Rutgers University, New Brunswick, N.J. 08903.

CAREER: High school teacher of social studies in New York, N.Y., 1957-62; Temple University, Philadelphia, Pa., research historian with Center for Community Studies, 1962-64, assistant professor, 1964-66, associate professor of history, 1966-68; Rutgers University, New Brunswick, N.J., professor of history, 1968—. Consultant, Philadelphia Board of Education on Negro History, 1965-67. *Member:* American Historical Association, Organization of American Historians, Association for the Study of Negro Life and History, American Association of University Professors, Southern Historical Association, Pennsylvania Historical Association.

WRITINGS: Negro Mecca: A History of the Negro in New York City, 1865-1920, New York University Press, 1965; (editor) *Reconstruction: A Tragic Era?,* Holt, 1968; (contributor) W. G. Shade and R. C. Herrenkohl, editors, *Seven on Black,* Lippincott, 1969; (editor with Tilden G. Edelstein) *The Black Americans: Interpretive Readings,* Holt, 1971. Contributor to history journals. Editor, *Pennsylvania History,* 1967-68.

WORK IN PROGRESS: History of the social reform movement in Philadelphia, 1890-1917; *The Negro and the Red Scare, 1919-1921.†*

* * *

SCHEINFELD, Amram 1897-

PERSONAL: Born June 1, 1897, in Louisville, Ky.; son of Solomon Isaac (a rabbi) and Sanna Rachel (Sachs) Scheinfeld; married Dorothy Suratt (an assistant with a philanthropic foundation), November 21, 1951. *Education:* Between 1916-35 took various courses at University of Wisconsin, New York University, and New School for Social Research, and studied art at Art Students League, New York, N.Y.; also studied at the Academies De La Grande Chaumiere and Colarossi, Paris, France. *Politics:* Liberal ("Democrat or Republican"). *Religion:* Jewish. *Home:* 37 West 12th St., New York, N.Y. 10011. *Agent:* Paul R. Reynolds, Inc., 12 East 41 St., New York, N.Y. 10017.

CAREER: Variously reporter, feature writer, cartoonist, and department editor on newspapers in Milwaukee, Baltimore, and New York, 1915-25; writer for King Features and McNaught Syndicate, 1925-35; free-lance writer for magazines beginning, 1930; writer of column, "Looking into People," in *Cosmopolitan,* 1951-65; contributor to professional journals in fields of human genetics and psychology beginning, 1941; author and illustrator of books. Columbia University, New York, N.Y., former research associate at Institute of Psychological Research, Teachers College, and member of Seminar on Genetics and Evolution of Man beginning, 1958. Community Guidance Service, New York, vice-president of board of directors.

MEMBER: American Association for the Advancement of Science (fellow), American Sociological Association (fellow), Eugenics Society (England; fellow), New York Academy of Sciences (fellow), American Psychological Association, American Society of Human Genetics, National Association of Science Writers, National Council on Family Relations, P.E.N., Authors League, Society of Magazine Writers. *Awards, honors:* Saturday Review-Anisfield-Wolf award, 1966, for *Your Heredity and Environment.*

WRITINGS—All books self-illustrated: *You and Heredity,* Stokes-Lippincott, 1939; *Women and Men,* Harcourt, 1944; *Postscript to Wendy* (novel), Whittlesey House, 1948; *The New You and Heredity,* Lippincott, 1950; *The Human Heredity Handbook,* Lippincott, 1956 (revised edition published in England as *The Basic Facts of Human Heredity,* Pan Books, 1963), published as *Heredity in Humans,* Lippincott, 1972; *Why You Are You: The Fascinating Story of Human Heredity and Environment* (children's book), Abelard, 1959, revised edition, Association Press, 1970; *Your*

Heredity and Environment, Lippincott, 1965; *Twins and Supertwins*, Lippincott, 1967; (with Josef E. Garai) *Sex Differences in Mental and Behavioral Traits*, [Provincetown], 1968. Contributor to anthologies, encyclopedias, conference proceedings, professional journals, and magazines, with popular articles in *Collier's Reader's Digest, Saturday Evening Post, Esquire*, and *Ladies' Home Journal*.

WORK IN PROGRESS: Continuing research in human genetics and social sciences.

SIDELIGHTS: Amram Scheinfeld has a working knowledge of French and German; he has been a traveler in many countries of Europe, Central America, and Near East. *Avocational interests:* Drawing, cooking, and popular-song writing.†

* * *

SCHIFFHORST, Gerald J. 1940-

PERSONAL: Born October 13, 1940, in St. Louis, Mo.; son of Charles (a stationer) and Helen (Fleming) Schiffhorst. *Education:* St. Louis University, B.S., 1962, A.M., 1963; University of Illinois, graduate student, 1963-64; Washington University, St. Louis, Mo., Ph.D., 1973. *Home:* 200 St. Andrews Blvd., Winter Park, Fla. 32789. *Office:* Department of English, Florida Technological University, Orlando, Fla. 32816.

CAREER: University of Missouri, St. Louis, instructor in English, 1966-67; Florida Technological University, Orlando, Fla., assistant professor of English, 1970—. Visiting summer instructor, Iowa Wesleyan College. *Member:* Modern Language Association of America, Renaissance Society of America, Milton Society of America.

WRITINGS: A Simplified Approach to Theodore Dreiser's "An American Tragedy," Barron's, 1965. Contributor to journals.

WORK IN PROGRESS: Patience in the Renaissance: Some Prolegomena for the Study of an Idea and Its Iconography.

AVOCATIONAL INTERESTS: Travel, golf, music.

* * *

SCHIFFMAN, Joseph Harris 1914-

PERSONAL: Born June 13, 1914, in New York, N.Y.; son of Samuel (a house painter) and Minnie (Berger) Schiffman; married Elizabeth Selsbee, November 29, 1941; children: Jessica, Joshua. *Education:* Long Island University, B.A., 1937; Columbia University, M.A., 1947; New York University, Ph.D., 1951. *Home:* 551 South Hanover St., Carlisle, Pa. 17013. *Office:* English Department, Dickinson College, Carlisle, Pa. 17013.

CAREER: Long Island University, Brooklyn, N.Y., instructor, 1945-49, assistant professor, 1949-51, associate professor of English, 1951-58, coordinator of graduate program in American studies, 1956-58; Dickinson College, Carlisle, Pa., professor of English, 1958-68, James Hope Caldwell Professor of American Studies, 1968—, chairman of department, 1959-69. American Studies Research Center, India, founding director, 1964; University of Bordeaux, senior Fulbright professor, 1965-66; visiting professor at University of Pennsylvania Graduate School, summers, 1960 and 1967. *Military service:* U.S. Army, 1942-45; served in Europe. *Member:* Modern Language Association of America (head of American literature section, interna-

tional bibliography committee, 1961-64), American Studies Association (acting executive secretary, 1960), National Council of Teachers of English, Conference on College Composition and Communication (executive committee, 1960-62). *Awards, honors:* Lindback Foundation distinguished teaching award, 1962.

WRITINGS—Editor: Edward Bellamy, *Selected Writings on Religion and Society*, Bobbs-Merrill, 1955; Edward Bellamy, *Looking Backward*, Harper, 1959; Lindsay Swift, *Brook Farm*, Corinth Books, 1961; *Three Shorter Novels of Herman Melville*, Harper, 1962; Edward Bellamy, *The Duke of Stockbridge*, Harvard University Press, 1962. Contributor to *Cassell's Encyclopaedia* and to literary and historical journals. Acting editor, *American Quarterly*, 1960.

WORK IN PROGRESS: American Literature as Biography and Autobiography, completion expected in 1976.

SIDELIGHTS: Schiffman's chief foreign language is French.

* * *

SCHILLER, Barbara (Heyman) 1928-

PERSONAL: Born April 14, 1928, in Chicago, Ill.; daughter of Edward Devarco (a proofreader) and Sarah May (Brisk) Heyman; married Hillel Schiller (a filmmaker), December 27, 1952; children: Thomas Samuel. *Education:* Syracuse University, B.A., 1948. *Politics:* Democrat. *Religion:* Jewish. *Residence:* New York, N.Y.

CAREER: Doubleday & Co., Inc., New York, N.Y., assistant editor, 1951-54; Pocket Books, Inc., New York, N.Y., associate editor, 1954-57; free-lance writer, reviewer, and publishers' reader, 1957—.

WRITINGS: The White Rat's Tale, Holt, 1967.

Author of folktale adaptations: Sir Thomas Malory, *The Kitchen Knight*, Holt, 1965; *The Vinlanders' Saga*, Holt, 1966; *Audun and His Bear*, Holt, 1968; *Erec and Enid*, Dutton, 1970; *The Wandering Knight*, Dutton, 1971; *Hrafkel's Saga*, Seabury Press, 1972.†

* * *

SCHINAGL, Mary S(onora) 1914-

PERSONAL: Surname is pronounced Shi-*nah*-gl; born June 18, 1914, in Philadelphia, Pa.; daughter of Joseph S. and Mary S. (Weber) Schinagl. *Education:* Chestnut Hill College, B.A., 1941; University of Pennsylvania, M.A., 1946; Ph.D., 1962; Temple University, M.Ed., 1960; studied voice three years at Philadelphia Conservatory of Music, and three years with private tutor. *Home:* 1409 Webb St., Asbury Park, N.J. 07712. *Office:* Monmouth College, West Long Branch, N.J. 07764.

CAREER: Naval Air Material Center, Philadelphia, Pa., junior civil engineer, 1942-45; Office of Price Stabilization, Philadelphia, Pa., price economist, 1951-52; Frankford Arsenal, Philadelphia, Pa., management analyst, 1952-56; high school social science teacher in Mount Holly, N.J., 1956-58; junior high guidance counselor in Souderton, Pa., 1958-59; West Chester State College, West Chester, Pa., assistant dean of women, 1959-60; Overbrook High School, Lindenwold, N.J., acting guidance director, 1960-62; Monmouth College, West Long Branch, N.J., associate professor, 1962-67, professor of political science and business administration, 1967—. *Member:* International Personnel Management Association, American Management

Association, American Society of Public Administration, International Platform Association, American Political Science Association, American Academy of Political and Social Science, Academy of Political Science. *Awards, honors:* National Science Foundation award, 1965; Monmouth College research grants, 1969 and 1970.

WRITINGS: History of Efficiency Ratings in the Federal Government, Bookman Associates, 1966. Contributor to journals in her field.

WORK IN PROGRESS: Research on public administration, public personnel administration, and on the effects of the Reformation on American thought.†

* * *

SCHKADE, Lawrence L. 1930-

PERSONAL: Surname sounds like "scotty"; born July 31, 1930, in Port Arthur, Tex.; son of Henry W. and Henrietta (Leschber) Schkade; married Janette King, December 18, 1954; children: David, Paul. *Education:* Lamar State College of Technology (now Lamar University), B.B.A., 1956; Louisiana State University, M.B.A., 1957, Ph.D., 1961. *Religion:* Lutheran. *Home:* 6801 Roanoke Dr., Austin, Tex. 78723. *Office:* University of Texas, Arlington, Tex. 76010.

CAREER: Lamar State College of Technology (now Lamar University), Beaumont, Tex., assistant dean of men, 1957-59; University of Southern Louisiana, Lafayette, assistant professor of management, 1960-61; Louisiana State University, Baton Rouge, assistant professor of business statistics and management, 1961-63; University of Texas, Austin, associate professor of business statistics and management, 1963-66, associate professor of business statistics and computer science, 1966-67; North Texas State University, Denton, professor of business administration, 1967-69; University of Texas, Arlington, professor of business administration, 1969—. Statistical consultant, Dow Chemical Co., 1961-63. Professor of management, Escuela de Graduados en Administracion, Mexico, 1966-67. Consultant, LTV Aerospace Corp, 1967—. *Military service:* U.S. Air Force, 1948-52; became staff sergeant. *Member:* Operations Research Society of America, Southwestern Social Science Association (chairman of quantitative methods section, 1963-64). *Awards, honors:* Ford Foundation postdoctoral research fellow, 1963, 1965.

WRITINGS: (With R. H. Ryan and C. T. Clark) *From Farm to Factory,* Bureau of Business Research, University of Texas, 1963; (with Ryan and Clark) *An Economic Survey of Brackettville, Texas,* Bureau of Business Research, University of Texas, 1963; (with Ryan and Clark) *Hearne, Texas: An Economy at the Crossroads,* Bureau of Business Research, University of Texas, 1963; (with Ryan and Clark) *Bridge Into the Future: Eagle Pass, Tex.,* Bureau of Business Research, University of Texas, 1964; (with Ryan and Clark) *Patterns and Progress: Quanah, Texas,* Bureau of Business Research, University of Texas, 1964; (with C. A. Pieper and Clark) *Midland-Odessa: An Analysis of the Economic Base for Urban Development,* Bureau of Business Research, University of Texas, 1965; *Vectors and Matrices,* C. E. Merrill, 1967. Co-author of column, "Retail Trade," *Louisiana Business Review,* 1961-63. Associate editor, *Southwestern Social Science Quarterly.*

WORK IN PROGRESS: A textbook on business statistics.†

SCHLAIN, Bert H(oward) 1898-

PERSONAL: Born October 4, 1898, in Newark, N.J.; son of Abram (a salesman) and Sadye (Gutow) Schlain; married Lillian Kornbluth, December 8, 1920 (deceased); children: Abbott K., Charlotte (Mrs. Sherwin W. Corlin). *Education:* Rutgers University, B.Sc. (magna cum laude), 1920. *Politics:* Republican. *Religion:* Jewish. *Home:* 20628 Kensington Ct., Southfield, Mich. 48076.

CAREER: Salesman for Zenith Radio, 1924-30, and General Electric Co., 1930-37; Whitehead & Hoag Co., Newark, N.J., district manager in Detroit, Mich., 1934-37; self-employed manufacturers' representative, Detroit, Mich., 1937-43; Universal Match Corp., St. Louis, Mo., district sales manager, 1943-62, general sales manager, 1962-65; retired, 1965. *Member:* Sales/Marketing Executives of Detroit, Adcraft Club (Detroit), Phi Beta Kappa, Pi Sigma Epsilon (national director, 1961-67).

WRITINGS: Big League Salesmanship, Prentice-Hall, 1954; *The Professional Approach to Modern Salesmanship,* McGraw, 1966; *Brass Tacks Sales Management,* Dartnell Corp., 1971. Contributor to sales management and marketing journals.

SIDELIGHTS: Schlain speaks fair German and a smattering of French and Spanish. *Avocational interests:* Football, basketball, baseball, and track (once as participant, now as spectator), occasional golf, playing bridge, and reading.

* * *

SCHLENDER, William E(lmer) 1920-

PERSONAL: Born October 28, 1920, in Sawyer, Mich.; son of Gust A. and Marie (Zindler) Schlender; married Lela Ruth Pullen, June 9, 1956. *Education:* Valparaiso University, A.B., 1941; University of Denver, M.B.A., 1947; Ohio State University, Ph.D., 1955. *Religion:* Lutheran. *Home:* 12000 Edgewater Dr., Lakewood, Ohio 44107. *Office:* Euclid Ave. at East 24th St., Cleveland, Ohio 44115.

CAREER: U.S. Rubber Co., Mishawaka, Ind., industrial relations assistant, 1941-43, 1946; Bowling Green State University, Bowling Green, Ohio, assistant professor, 1947-50, associate professor of business administration, 1950-53; Ohio State University, Columbus, assistant professor, 1954-57, associate professor, 1957-61, professor of business organization, 1961-65, assistant dean of College of Commerce and Administration, 1959-62, associate dean, 1962-63; University of Texas, Austin, professor of management, 1965-68, department chairman, 1966-68; Cleveland State University, Cleveland, Ohio, dean of College of Business Administration, 1968—. Visiting professor, University of Denver, 1949, Columbia University, 1957-58. *Military service:* U.S. Army, 1943-45; became staff sergeant; received Bronze Star. *Member:* Academy of Management, American Management Association, Industrial Relations Research Association, Institute of Management Sciences, Southwest Social Science Association, Beta Gamma Sigma, Alpha Kappa Psi.

WRITINGS: (With M. J. Jucius) *Elements of Managerial Action,* Irwin, 1960, 3rd edition, 1973; (editor with W. G. Scott and A. C. Filley) *Management in Perspective: Selected Readings,* Houghton, 1965. Contributor to *Encyclopaedia Britannica Yearbook* and to professional journals.

WORK IN PROGRESS: Research on organizational structure of various business institutions and on leadership training.

SIDELIGHTS: Schlender has speaking and reading knowledge of German, reading knowledge of French.†

*   *   *

SCHLENKER, Elizabeth D. (Wallace) 1912-

PERSONAL: Born December 6, 1912, in Lebanon, Pa.; daughter of Edwin E. (a banker) and Maude (Dotter) Wallace; married Luther F. Schlenker (a minister), June 21, 1941 (deceased); children: Priscilla K. (Mrs. George G. Kinney), Christina E., Martha M., James W. *Education:* Moravian College, B.A., 1935; University of Michigan, M.A., 1939. *Office:* Board of Parish Education, The Lutheran Church in America, 2900 Queen Lane, Philadelphia, Pa. 19129.

CAREER: The Lutheran Church in America, Board of Parish Education, Philadelphia, Pa., assistant editor, beginning 1963.

WRITINGS: God's Ways in His World, Lutheran Church, 1965. Assistant editor of "Augsburg Uniform Series," Lutheran Church, and writer of curriculum materials for church schools.

SIDELIGHTS: Elizabeth Schlenker has "fair" competency in German and Classical Greek. *Avocational interests:* Bible study.†

*   *   *

SCHLESINGER, Benjamin 1928-

PERSONAL: Born July 20, 1928, in Berlin, Germany; son of Abraham (a businessman) and Esther (Trisker) Schlesinger; married Rachel Clara Aber, March 29, 1959; children: Peter, Leo, Esther, Michael. *Education:* Sir George Williams University, Montreal, Quebec, B.A., 1951; University of Toronto, M.S.W., 1953; Cornell University, Ph.D., 1961. *Religion:* Jewish. *Home:* 415 Roselawn Ave., Toronto, Ontario, Canada. *Office:* School of Social Work, University of Toronto, Toronto, Ontario M5S 1A1, Canada.

CAREER: Social worker for Jewish Immigrant Aid Society, Montreal, Quebec, 1947-51, and Children's Aid Society, Toronto, Ontario, 1953-56; Merrill-Palmer Institute, Detroit, Mich., intern in psychotherapy, 1956-57; Aloka World Assembly of Youth, Mysore, India, member of faculty, 1959-60; University of Toronto, Toronto, Ontario, assistant professor, 1960-64, associate professor of social work, 1965—. Visiting professor, University of the West Indies, Jamaica, 1967; visiting lecturer, University of Western Australia, 1971-72. *Member:* National Council on Family Relations (board member), Council on Social Work Education, Phi Delta Kappa.

WRITINGS: (Contributor) *Asian Cases*, Aloka Centre for Advanced Study and Training, 1960; (editor) *Multi-Problem Family: A Review and Annotated Bibliography*, University of Toronto Press, 1964, 3rd edition, 1970; (with Ray Godfrey) *Child Welfare Services: Winding Paths to Maturity*, Canadian Conference on Children, 1965; *Poverty in Canada and the United States: A Review and Annotated Bibliography*, University of Toronto Press, 1966; (with John Maxwell) *August Town Jamaica: A Community Study*, University of West Indies Institute of Social and Economic Research, 1966; *The One-Parent Family: Perspectives and Annotated Bibliography*, University of Toronto Press, 1969, 2nd edition, 1970; (editor) *The Jewish Family: A Survey and Annotated Bibliography*, University of Toronto Press, 1971; *The Family in Canada*, McGraw,

1973; (editor) *Family Planning in Canada: A Sourcebook*, University of Toronto Press, 1974. Contributor of sections to other books. Writer of talks published by Canadian Broadcasting Corp., and about one hundred articles published in professional journals in Canada and India, and in *Liberty, Chatelaine*, and *Toronto Globe and Mail*.

SIDELIGHTS: Schlesinger speaks French and German.

*   *   *

SCHMECK, Harold M(arshall), Jr. 1923-

PERSONAL: Born September 29, 1923, in Tonawanda, N.Y.; son of Harold Marshall (in advertising) and Dorothy (Arnold) Schmeck; married Lois Eleanor Gallo, March 12, 1950; children: Peter Chamberlain. *Education:* Cornell University, B.A., 1948; Harvard University, graduate study, 1953-54. *Religion:* Methodist. *Office:* New York *Times*, Washington Bureau, Washington, D.C.

CAREER: Cornell Alumni News (monthly), Ithaca, N.Y., assistant editor, 1948-49; newspaper reporter in Danville, Ill., 1949-50, Rochester, N.Y., 1950-57; *New York Times*, New York, N.Y., 1957—, began as science reporter, currently reporter for Washington Bureau. *Military service:* U.S. Army Air Forces, 1943-45; became first lieutenant. *Member:* National Association of Science Writers, Sons of the American Revolution, Sigma Delta Chi. *Awards, honors:* Nieman fellow at Harvard University, 1953-54.

WRITINGS: The Semi-Artificial Man, Walker & Co., 1965; *Immunology: The Many-Edged Sword*, Braziller, 1974. Contributor to general and specialized magazines; author of factual radio scripts.

SIDELIGHTS: Harold Schmeck traveled to Antarctica in 1961. *Avocational interests:* History, fiction, tennis, sailing, and skiing.†

*   *   *

SCHNALL, Maxine (Swartz) 1934-

PERSONAL: Born September 7, 1934, in Philadelphia, Pa.; daughter of Isadore Richard (a clothing manufacturer) and Clare (Salzmann) Swartz; married Nathan Schnall (an obstetrician and gynecologist), March 31, 1957; children: Ilene Sue, Rona Fay. *Education:* University of Pennsylvania, B.S. in Ed., 1956; Temple University, law student, 1959-60, 1974-75. *Religion:* Jewish. *Home:* 527 Davis Rd., Cheltenham, Pa. 19012.

CAREER: West Philadelphia High School, Philadelphia, Pa., teacher of English, 1957-59. Secretary, Rowland Park Civic Association; founder of wives self-help program. *Member:* Technion Society (education chairman, 1966), Phi Delta Epsilon (Philadelphia president, women's auxiliary, 1966—).

WRITINGS: My Husband, the Doctor, Fell, 1966; *The Broadbelters*, M. Evans, 1970. Contributor to *Contemporary Magazine, Pageant, Philadelphia Bulletin*.

*   *   *

SCHNECK, Jerome M. 1920-

PERSONAL: Born January 2, 1920, in New York, N.Y.; son of Maurice (a physician) and Rose (Weiss) Schneck; married Shirley R. Kaufman, July 24, 1943. *Education:* Cornell University, A.B., 1939; Long Island College of Medicine, M.D., 1943. *Home and office:* 26 West Ninth St., New York, N.Y. 10011.

CAREER: Diplomate of American Board of Psychiatry

and Neurology and of American Board of Clinical Hypnosis. Private practice as psychiatrist, New York, N.Y., 1947—; State University of New York Downstate Medical Center, Brooklyn, instructor, 1947-50, associate, 1950-53, assistant professor, 1955-58, clinical associate professor of psychiatry, 1958-70; Kings County Medical Center, Brooklyn, N.Y., associate visiting psychiatrist, 1959—. Visiting lecturer, New York Medical College, 1965; faculty member, American Institute of Psychotherapy and Psychoanalysis, 1970—. Consultant to Veterans Administration, 1947-48, and Council on Mental Health, American Medical Association, 1956-58. *Military service:* U.S. Army, 1945-47; became captain.

MEMBER: American Psychiatric Association (fellow), American Psychological Association (fellow), American Association for the Advancement of Science (fellow), Academy of Psychosomatic Medicine (fellow), American Society of Psychoanalytic Physicians (fellow), American Medical Authors (fellow), American Medical Writers' Association (fellow), International Society for Clinical and Experimental Hypnosis (fellow; U.S. representative on board, 1956—), American Medical Association, Association for the Advancement of Psychotherapy (charter member), Society for Clinical and Experimental Hypnosis (founder, 1949; president, 1949-56; fellow), American Academy of Psychotherapists (vice-president, 1956-58), American Board of Medical Hypnosis (president, 1958-60), Pan American Medical Association, New York Society for Medical History (executive committee, 1955-60). *Awards, honors:* Awards from Society for Clinical and Experimental Hypnosis include Award of Merit, 1955, Gold Medal Award for contribution to development of scientific hypnosis, 1958, and Best Book Award, 1965, for *The Principles and Practices of Hypnoanalysis*.

WRITINGS: (Editor) *Hypnotherapy and Hypnosis and Personality*, Grune, 1951; *Hypnosis in Modern Medicine*, C. C Thomas, 1953, 3rd edition, 1963; *Studies in Scientific Hypnosis*, Williams & Wilkins, 1954; *A History of Psychiatry*, C. C Thomas, 1960; *The Principles and Practices of Hypnoanalysis*, C. C Thomas, 1965.

Contributor: W. R. Dunton and S. Licht, editors, *Occupational Therapy, Principles and Practice*, C. C Thomas, 1950; L. M. LeCron, editor, *Experimental Hypnosis*, Macmillan, 1952; S. B. Wortis, M. Herman, and C. C. Hare, editors, *Psychiatric Treatment*, Williams & Wilkins, 1953; D. Brower and L. E. Abt, editor, *Progress in Clinical Psychology*, Grune, 1956; W. Wolff, editor, *Contemporary Psychotherapists Examine Themselves*, C. C Thomas, 1956; A. Burton, editor, *Case Studies in Counseling and Psychotherapy*, Prentice-Hall, 1959; M. V. Kline, editor, *The Nature of Hypnosis*, Institute for Research in Hypnosis, 1962; Kline, editor, *Clinical Correlations of Experimental Hypnosis*, C. C Thomas, 1963; *Current Psychiatric Therapies*, Grune, 1965.

Contributor of about 250 articles to journals. Associate editor, *International Journal of Clinical and Experimental Hypnosis*, 1953; contributing editor in psychiatry, *Psychosomatics*, beginning 1961; member of editorial board, *Voices, the Art and Science of Psychotherapy*, beginning 1965.

WORK IN PROGRESS: Further research and writing on psychiatry, psychoanalysis, and hypnosis; medical and psychiatric history and biography.†

SCHNEIDER, Stanley D(ale) 1921-

PERSONAL: Born October 15, 1921, in Massillon, Ohio; son of Orlando E. (a banker) and Odessa (Doughty) Schneider; married Marcella Degen (a librarian), August 24, 1945; children: Philip James, Carolyn Jean. *Education:* Capital University, A.B.; Evangelical Lutheran Theological Seminary, B.D.; further study at University of St. Andrews and Ecumenical Institute, Geneva, Switzerland. *Home:* 4464 Indian Rd., Toledo, Ohio 43615.

CAREER: Clergyman of the American Lutheran Church. Pastoral posts in Regina, Sasketchewan, 1945-47, Toledo, Ohio, 1947-49, Michigan City, Ind., 1949-54; Evangelical Lutheran Theological seminary, Columbus, Ohio, professor of homiletics and dean of students, 1954-75; St. Paul's Lutheran Church, Toledo, senior pastor, 1975—. Member of Commission on Evangelism, American Lutheran Church. *Member:* American Association of Theological Professors in the Practical Fields, Lutheran Society for Music, Worship, and the Arts, Catholic Homiletic Society (associate). *Awards, honors:* D.D., Capital University, 1964.

WRITINGS: As One Who Speaks for God, Augsburg, 1965; (editor with Fred W. Meuser) *Interpreting Luther's Legacy: Essays in Honor of Edward C. Fendt*, Augsburg, 1969. Conductor of "Question Box" column, appearing twice monthly in *Lutheran Standard*.

* * *

SCHNORE, Leo F(rancis) 1927-

PERSONAL: Born January 10, 1927, in Elyria, Ohio; son of Leo Francis and Mildred Elizabeth (Kraus) Schnore; married Elinor Carole Schick, September 9, 1950 (divorced, 1967); married Julie Rae Kraft, 1969 (divorced, 1972); children: (first marriage) Carol Elizabeth, Barbara Lee; (second marriage) Aaron. *Education:* Miami University, Oxford, Ohio, A.B. (cum laude), 1950; University of Michigan, M.A., 1951, Ph.D., 1954. *Politics:* Independent. *Home:* 3208 Bluff St., Madison, Wis. 53705. *Office:* Department of Sociology, 3220 Social Science Bldg., University of Wisconsin, Madison, Wis. 53706.

CAREER: Brown University, Providence, R.I., instructor in sociology, 1954-56; Michigan State University, East Lansing, assistant professor of sociology, 1956-57; University of California, Berkeley, assistant professor of sociology and biostatistics, 1957-59; University of Wisconsin, Madison, associate professor, 1959-61, professor of sociology, 1961—. Social Science Research Council, member of board of directors, 1964-67. *Military service:* U.S. Army, Paratroops, 1945-46; became staff sergeant. *Member:* American Sociological Association, Regional Science Association, Population Association of America (director), International Union for the Scientific Study of Population. *Awards, honors:* Auxiliary research award, Social Science Research Council; Guggenheim fellowship, 1974-75.

WRITINGS: The Urban Scene: Human Ecology and Demography, Free Press of Glencoe, 1965; (editor with Philip M. Hauser) *The Study of Urbanization*, Wiley, 1965; (editor with Henry Fagin) *Urban Research and Policy Planning*, Sage Publications, 1967; (editor) *Social Science and the City*, Praeger, 1967; *Class and Race in Cities and Suburbs*, Markham, 1972; (editor) *The New Urban History*, Princeton University Press, 1974. Contributor to professional journals.

WORK IN PROGRESS: A five-year program of research on ecological patterns in American cities.

AVOCATIONAL INTERESTS: Piano, acting, and baseball.

* * *

SCHOENBOHM, Wilko, B. 1913-

PERSONAL: Born April 28, 1913, in Denver, Iowa; son of Frederick Ernest (a minister) and Anna (Beyer) Schoenbohm; married Virginia Hymans (a speech coordinator); children: Siegfried, Herbert, Margret, Susan, Steven. *Education:* Wartburg College, B.A., 1933; studied at Universities of Berlin and Erlangen, 1933-35, and Wartburg Seminary, 1935-37; University of Iowa, M.A., 1952. *Politics:* Independent. *Religion:* Methodist. *Home:* 4311 Bassett Creek Dr., Golden Valley, Minn. *Office:* Courage Center, Golden Valley, Minn.

CAREER: Crippled Children's School, Jamestown, N.D., superintendent, 1938-48; University of Iowa, Iowa City, director of hospital school for handicapped children, 1948-52; Minneapolis Society for Crippled Children and Adults, Minneapolis, Minn., executive director, 1952—. Lecturer at University of Iowa, 1950-52, University of Wyoming, summers of 1950, 1951, University of Minnesota, 1953-56, and for Association for Crippled Children, Sao Paulo, Brazil, 1959-60. Trustee of National Society for Crippled Children, 1943-45; president of Minnesota Council for Special Education, 1953-54, 1961-62, and Minnesota Rehabilitation Association, 1965-66; member of Minnesota Commission for the Handicapped. *Member:* American Judicature Society, Rehabilitation International.

WRITINGS: Planning and Operating Facilities for Crippled Children, C. C Thomas, 1962. Contributor to professional journals and magazines.

WORK IN PROGRESS: A book on camping for the handicapped; a biography of Michael Dowling, handicapped Minnesota pioneer; *The Development of Courage Services* for the handicapped in Minnesota.

SIDELIGHTS: Schoenbohm speaks and writes fluent German and he has speaking and reading knowledge of Portuguese. *Avocational interests:* Conservation, international relations.

* * *

SCHOENFELD, David 1923-

PERSONAL: Born October 26, 1923, in New York, N.Y.; son of Harry (a restaurateur) and Anna (Blatt) Schoenfeld; married Madalynne Geller (a librarian), December 23, 1944. *Education:* Brooklyn College (now Brooklyn College of the City University of New York), B.A., 1945; University of Southern California, M.B.A., 1947. *Religion:* Jewish. *Home:* 21 Albemarle Rd., White Plains, N.Y. 10605. *Office:* J. C. Penney, 1301 Avenue of the Americas, New York, N.Y. 10019.

CAREER: Fleetwood Cleaners, Mount Vernon, N.Y., proprietor, 1947-62; Lincoln High School, Yonkers, N.Y., teacher of economics, beginning 1962; President's Committee on Consumer Interests, Washington, D.C., director for consumer education, 1967-69; Consumers Union of United States, Inc., director for educational services, 1969-74; J. C. Penney, New York, N.Y., manager of consumer relations, 1974—. Writer-consultant, New York State Education Department. *Military service:* U.S. Army, 1943-46; became technical sergeant. *Member:* National Council for Social Studies, Council on Consumer Information, Society of Consumer Affairs Professionals, Association for Con-

sumer Research, National Business Education Association, American Home Economics Association, American Council on Consumer Interests, Middle States Council for Social Studies, New York State Council on Economic Education, Hudson Valley Council on Economic Education, Jewish War Veterans. *Awards, honors:* Fellowship grant, New York State, 1963.

WRITINGS: (Editor with James E. Mendenhall) *Consumer Education in Lincoln High School,* Consumers Union, 1965; (with Arthur Natella) *The Consumer and His Dollars,* Oceana, 1966, 2nd edition, 1970; *Course Outline for Consumer Economics,* Oceana, 1966.

* * *

SCHOENWALD, Richard L. 1927-

PERSONAL: Born September 16, 1927, in Syracuse, N.Y.; son of Morris A. (a physician) and Sadye (Rakov) Schoenwald; married Audrey Stearns (a psychiatric social worker), September 2, 1957; children: Michael S., Jonathan M. *Education:* Syracuse University, A.B., 1947; Harvard University, A.M., 1948, Ph.D., 1952. *Office:* Department of History, Carnegie-Mellon University, Pittsburgh, Pa. 15213.

CAREER: Instructor in history at Bowdoin College, Brunswick, Me., 1953-54, and Wesleyan University, Middletown, Conn., 1954-56; Massachusetts Institute of Technology, Cambridge, instructor, 1956-59, assistant professor of history, 1959-64; Carnegie-Mellon University, Pittsburgh, Pa., associate professor, 1964-68, professor of history, 1968—. *Member:* American Historical Association, American Association of University Professors, Group for the Use of Psychology in History, Phi Beta Kappa.

WRITINGS: Freud: The Man and His Mind, Knopf, 1956; (editor) *Nineteenth-Century Thought: The Discovery of Change,* Prentice-Hall, 1965; (contributor) H. J. Dyos and M. Wolff, editors, *The Victorian City,* Routledge & Kegan Paul, 1973. Also writer of articles and reviews.

WORK IN PROGRESS: A biography of Herbert Spencer.

* * *

SCHON, Donald A(lan) 1930-

PERSONAL: Born September 30, 1930, in Boston, Mass.; son of Marcus D. H. (a lawyer) and Anne (Mason) Schon; married Nancy Quint (a sculptor), December 20, 1952; children: Ellen, Andrew, Elizabeth, Susan. *Education:* Yale University, B.A., 1947; Sorbonne, University of Paris, graduate study, 1949-50; Harvard University, M.A., 1952, Ph.D., 1955. *Politics:* Democrat. *Religion:* Jewish. *Home:* 291 Otis St., West Newton, Mass.

CAREER: University of California, Los Angeles, lecturer in philosophy, 1953; University of Kansas City (now University of Missouri at Kansas City), instructor, later assistant professor of philosophy, 1955-57; Arthur D. Little, Inc., Cambridge, Mass., founder of new product group in Research and Development Division, 1957-63; U.S. Department of Commerce, Washington, D.C., director of Office of Technical Services, 1963; National Bureau of Standards, Washington, D.C., director of Institute for Applied Technology, 1964-66; Organization for Social and Technical Innovation, Cambridge, Mass., president, beginning 1966. Research consultant; lecturer at universities and to professional groups and government organizations. *Military service:* U.S. Army, 1955-57. *Member:* American Philosophical Association, American Association of University

Professors, Phi Beta Kappa, Harvard Club (Boston). *Awards, honors:* First prize of Paris Conservatory, 1949; Woodrow Wilson fellowship, 1952.

WRITINGS: Displacement of Concepts, Tavistock Publications, 1963, published as *Invention and the Evolution of Ideas*, 1967; *Technology and Change*, Delacorte, 1967; *Beyond the Stable State*, Random House, 1971; (with Leonard J. Duhl) *Deliberate Social Change in the City*, Council of Planning Librarians (Monticello, Ill.), 1972; (with Chris Argyis) *Theory in Practice: Increasing Professional Effectiveness*, Jossey-Bass, 1974.†

* * *

SCHUMAN, Ben N. 1923-

PERSONAL: Born May 8, 1923, in Laurium, Mich.; son of Max (a businessman) and Esther (Blacher) Schuman; married Inge Mayer, December 31, 1945; children: Carolyn, Phillip. *Education:* University of Illinois, B.S., 1952, M.D., 1956. *Religion:* Jewish. *Home:* 6144 Rockridge N., Oakland, Calif. 94018.

CAREER: Psychiatrist. *Military service:* U.S. Army Air Forces, 1942-45. *Member:* American Medical Association, American Academy of General Practice, American Group Psychotherapy Society, Bay Psychiatric Society.

WRITINGS: The Human Skeleton, Atheneum, 1965; *The Human Eye*, Atheneum, 1968.

* * *

SCHUSKY, Ernest L(ester) 1931-

PERSONAL: Born October 13, 1931, in Portsmouth, Ohio; son of Ernest L. and Leona (Davis) Schusky; children: Read Eric, Mark Elliott. *Education:* Miami University, Oxford, Ohio, A.B., 1952; University of Chicago, M.A., 1957, Ph.D., 1960; postdoctoral study, London School of Economics, 1967. *Politics:* Democrat. *Religion:* None. *Home:* 412 Willowbrook, Collinsville, Ill. 62234. *Office:* Southern Illinois University, Edwardsville, Ill. 62025.

CAREER: South Dakota State College (now University), Brookings, instructor in sociology, 1958-60; Southern Illinois University, Edwardsville Campus, assistant professor, 1960-64, associate professor, 1964-69, professor of anthropology, 1969—. *Military service:* U.S. Army, 1953-54. *Member:* American Anthropological Association (fellow), Society for Applied Anthropology, American Ethnological Society, Central States Anthropological Society (president, 1974).

WRITINGS: A Manual for Analysis of Kinship, Holt, 1965; *The Right to Be Indian: Civil Rights Problems of American Indians*, Institute for Indian Studies (Vermillion, S.D.), 1965; (with T. Patrick Culbert) *Introducing Culture*, Prentice-Hall, 1967; *Variation in Kinship*, Holt, 1974; *Study in Cultural Anthropology*, Holt, 1975; *The Forgotten Sioux: An Ethnohistory of the Louis Brule Sioux Reservation*, Nelson-Hall, in press.

* * *

SCHUTZE, Gertrude 1917-

PERSONAL: Born June 5, 1917, in New York, N.Y.; daughter of John and Ann Maria (Kastner) Schutze. *Education:* Hunter College (now Hunter College of the City University of New York), B.S., 1939; Columbia University, M.S.L.S., 1949. *Home:* 7620 86th Ave., Woodhaven, N.Y. 11421.

CAREER: Research or technical librarian for Virginia-Carolina Chemical Corp., Carteret, N.J., 1940-43, Pennsylvania Salt Manufacturing Co., Philadelphia, Pa., 1944-46, and Bristol-Myers Co., Hillside, N.J., 1946-53; Grace Chemical R & D Corp., New York, N.Y., manager of information department, 1953-59; Standard & Poor's Corp., New York, N.Y., manager of information services, 1959-60; Union Carbide Research Institute, New York, N.Y., head of information services, 1960-63; consultant on library and information services, 1964-68; Ayerst Laboratories, New York, N.Y., manager of medical information service, 1969—. *Member:* American Documentation Institute, American Chemical Society (chemical literature division), Special Libraries Association, Medical Library Association.

WRITINGS: Bibliography of Guides to the Scientific-Technical-Medical Literature, privately printed, 1958, *Supplement, 1958-62*, 1963, *Supplement, 1963-65*, 1966; (contributor of annotated bibliography) C. Lewis, *Special Libraries: How to Plan and Equip Them*, Special Libraries Association, 1963; *Documentation Source Book*, Scarecrow, 1965; *Bibliography of Guides to the Social Science Literature*, privately printed, 1966; *Library and Information Science Source Book*, Scarecrow, 1972. Contributor to library and trade journals. Editor, *Documentation Digest*, 1948-59.

WORK IN PROGRESS: Supplement to *Library and Information Science Source Book*.

* * *

SCHWARTZ, Alfred 1922-

PERSONAL: Born January 8, 1922, in Chicago, Ill.; son of Isadore Schwartz; married Delle Weiss, August 26, 1945; children: Reid Mitchell, Karen Ruth. *Education:* Chicago Teachers College (now Chicago State University), B.E., 1944; University of Chicago, M.A., 1946, Ph.D., 1949. *Politics:* Independent Democrat. *Home:* 4044 Beaver Ave., Des Moines, Iowa 50310. *Office:* College of Education, Drake University, Des Moines, Iowa 50311.

CAREER: University of Chicago, Chicago, Ill., instructor in Laboratory School, 1947-50; Drake University, Des Moines, Iowa, associate professor of education, 1950-56; University of Delaware, Newark, associate professor of education, 1956-58; Drake University, dean of University College, 1958-64, dean of College of Education, 1964—. Chairman of Des Moines Community Action Organization, 1964-66; member of Iowa Governor's United Nations Committee and Governor's Commission for State and Local Governmental Relations. *Military service:* U.S. Army, 1944-45; received combat stars.

MEMBER: American Association for the Advancement of Science, American Association of School Administrators, American Educational Research Association, National Education Association, National Society for the Study of Education, Iowa State Education Association, Phi Delta Kappa. *Awards, honors:* Distinguished achievement award of Missouri Valley Adult Education Association, 1964; Des Moines Adult Education Advisory Council service award, 1966.

WRITINGS: (With Harlan L. Hagman) *Administration in Profile for School Executives*, Harper, 1955; (contributor) *Resource Ideas for Planning Classroom Programs*, State Department of Public Instruction (Iowa), 1955; (principal author) *Strengthening Human Values in the Iowa Public Schools*, State Department of Public Instruction, 1955;

(with Stuart Tiedeman and Donald G. Wallace) *Evaluating Student Progress in the Secondary Schools*, Longmans, Green, 1957; (contributor) *Dover Special School District*, University of Delaware Press, 1957; (contributor) *Partners in Education*, University of Pennsylvania Press, 1958; (with Willard Fox) *Managerial Guide for School Principals*, C. E. Merrill, 1965. Contributor to educational journals and newsletters.†

* * *

SCHWARTZ, David J., Jr. 1927-

PERSONAL: Born March 23, 1927, in Berne, Ind.; son of David J. (a farmer) and Flora (Sauder) Schwartz; children: David J. III. *Education:* University of Nebraska, B.S., 1948; Ohio State University, M.B.A., 1949, Ph.D., 1953. *Office:* Department of Business Administration, Georgia State University, Atlanta, Ga.

CAREER: Instructor at Mississippi State University, Starkville, 1949-51, and Ohio State University, Columbus, 1951-53; Wayne State University, Detroit, Mich., assistant professor of business, 1953-56; Georgia State University, Atlanta, professor of business administration, 1956—.

WRITINGS: The Magic of Thinking Big, Prentice-Hall, 1959; *The Magic of Psychic Power*, Prentice-Hall, 1965; (with Mauser) *American Business: An Introduction*, Harcourt, 1966, 3rd edition, 1972.

WORK IN PROGRESS: Concepts for Professional Management.

* * *

SCHWARTZ, Morris S. 1916-

PERSONAL: Born December 20, 1916, in Chicago, Ill.; son of Charles and Eva (Schneider) Schwartz; married Charlotte Green (a sociologist), March 23, 1951; children: Jonathan Eban, Robert David. *Education:* City College (now City College of the City University of New York), New York, N.Y., B.S.S., 1940; University of Chicago, M.A., 1946, Ph.D., 1951; Washington School of Psychiatry, Certificate in Applied Psychiatry for Sociologists, 1950. *Home:* 164 Gardner St., Brookline, Mass. 02146. *Office:* Department of Sociology, Brandeis University, Waltham, Mass. 02154.

CAREER: Washington School of Psychiatry, Washington, D.C., research sociologist, 1947-55; Joint Commission on Mental Illness and Health, Cambridge, Mass., director of task force on patterns of patient care, 1956-59; Brandeis University, Waltham, Mass., professor of sociology and human relations, 1959—. Consultant to various mental institutions throughout United States. *Member:* American Sociological Association (fellow).

WRITINGS: (With A. H. Stanton) *The Mental Hospital*, Basic Books, 1954; (with E. L. Shockley) *The Nurse and the Mental Patient*, Russell Sage, 1956; (with wife, C. G. Schwartz and others) *Social Approaches in Mental Patient Care*, Columbia University Press, 1964.†

* * *

SCHWEBEL, Milton 1914-

PERSONAL: Born May 11, 1914, in Troy, N.Y.; son of Frank (a merchant) and Sarah Schwebel; married Bernice Lois Davison (a teacher), September 3, 1939; children: Andrew, Robert. *Education:* Union College and University, A.B., 1934; New York College for Teachers (now

State University of New York at Albany), M.A., 1936; Columbia University, Ph.D., 1949, postdoctoral certificate in psychotherapy, 1958. *Home:* 1050 George St., New Brunswick, N.J. 08901. *Office:* Graduate School of Education, Rutgers University, 10 Seminary Pl., New Brunswick, N.J. 08903.

CAREER: Teacher in New York, 1936-39; National Youth Administration, White Plains, N.Y., counselor, 1939-41; employment counselor, New York State Employment Service, 1941-43; labor market analyst, War Manpower Commission, 1943; City College (now City College of the City University of New York), New York, N.Y., psychometrist, 1946; Mohawk College, Utica, N.Y., assistant professor of psychology and director of guidance, 1946-48, chairman of department, 1947-48; Champlain College, Plattsburg, N.Y., assistant professor of psychology, 1948-49; New York University, New York, N.Y., 1949-67, began as assistant professor, professor of education, 1958-67, chairman of department of guidance and personnel administration, 1964-66, associate dean of School of Education, 1965-67; Rutgers University, New Brunswick, N.J., professor of education, and dean of Graduate School of Education, 1967—. Diplomate, American Board of Examiners in Professional Psychology, 1951. Psychologist and lecturer at Postgraduate Center for Mental Health, Columbia University, 1958-61. Lecturer and consultant at Fordham University, University of Wisconsin, University of Oklahoma, and other institutions; visiting summer professor at University of Southern California, 1953, University of Hawaii, 1965. Trustee, National Committee on Employment of Youth, and National Child Labor Committee, 1967-73. *Military service:* U.S. Army, 1943-46; served in Europe; became sergeant.

MEMBER: American Psychological Association (fellow), American Orthopsychiatry Association (fellow), American Academy of Arts and Sciences, American Educational Research Association, Society for Psychological Study of Social Issues (fellow), American Personnel and Guidance Association (past president, New York chapter), National Committee on the Education of Migrant Children (chairman of advisory committee), American Association of University Professors, New York Academy of Science. *Awards, honors:* Fellowship, Postgraduate Center for Mental Health, Columbia University, 1954-56, Metropolitan Applied Research Council, 1970; grants from University Research Council, 1970-71, and U.S. Office of Education, 1970-72.

WRITINGS: Interests of Pharmacists, Columbia University Press, 1951; (with Ella Harris) *Health Counseling*, Chartwell, 1951; *Resistance to Learning*, Early Childhood Education Council, 1964; (editor) *Behavioral Science and Human Survival*, Science & Behavior Books, 1965; *Who Can Be Educated?*, Grove, 1968; (editor with Jane Raph) *Piaget in the Classroom*, Basic Books, 1973. Also author of film script, with wife, Bernice Schwebel, "Why Some Children Don't Learn," 1963. Contributor to professional journals.

Review editor, *American Journal of Orthopsychiatry*, 1963-71; member of editorial board, *Journal of Contemporary Psychotherapy*, 1960-72, *Journal of Counseling Psychology*, 1966—, *New York University Education Quarterly*, 1969-71, 1973—; member of editorial committee, *Journal of Social Issues*, 1965-70; member of editorial advisory board, *Change in Higher Education*, 1969—.†

SCHWEITZER, George K(eene) 1924-

PERSONAL: Born December 5, 1924, in Poplar Bluff, Mo.; son of Francis John (a banker) and Ruth E. (Keene) Schweitzer; married Verna Lee Pratt, June 4, 1948; children: Ruth A., Deborah K., Eric G. *Education:* Central College (now Central Methodist College), B.A., 1945, Sc.D., 1964; University of Illinois, M.S., 1946, Ph.D., 1948; Columbia University, M.A., 1959; New York University, Ph.D., 1964. *Religion:* Protestant. *Home:* 224 Golf Club Rd., Knoxville, Tenn. 37919. *Office:* Department of Chemistry, University of Tennessee, Knoxville, Tenn. 37916.

CAREER: University of Tennessee, Knoxville, assistant professor, 1948-52, associate professor, 1952-58; Columbia University, New York, N.Y., faculty research fellow, 1958-59; University of Tennessee, professor, 1960-69, Distinguished professor of chemistry, 1970—. Consultant to Monsanto, Procter & Gamble, American Cyanamid, Union Carbide, and other companies. *Member:* American Chemical Society, History of Science Society, Phi Beta Kappa, Sigma Xi. *Awards, honors:* Recipient of more than thirty endowed lectureships at American colleges and universities.

WRITINGS: Radioactive Tracer Techniques, Van Nostrand, 1950; *The Doctorate*, C. C Thomas, 1965. Contributor of more than one hundred research papers to scientific, philosophical, and religious journals.

WORK IN PROGRESS: Writing on the philosophy of science-and-religion, photoelectron spectroscopy, and history of science.

SIDELIGHTS: George Schweitzer is competent in German, French, Latin, Hebrew, and Greek.

* * *

SCHWEITZER, John C. 1934-

PERSONAL: Born December 17, 1934, in New York, N.Y.; son of Stanley S. and Gertrude (Loebl) Schweitzer; married Barbara Seplow (a teacher), June 14, 1956; children: Jeffrey, Carolyn. *Education:* Yale University, B.A., 1956, M.A., 1957. *Politics:* "Not active in any." *Religion:* "Not active in any." *Office:* Board of Education, Armonk, N.Y.

CAREER: Rye (N.Y.) Board of Education, teacher of English, 1957-67; Armonk (N.Y.) Board of Education, teacher of English, 1967—.

WRITINGS: (Editor) *A Variety of Short Plays*, Scribner, 1966; (editor with Marsden V. Dillenbech) *Seven Novellas*, Scribner, 1966; (editor, and author of notes) Ernest Hemingway, *A Farewell to Arms* (school edition), Scribner, 1967; (editor) *A Variety of Short Stories*, Scribner, 1968; (editor) *Discovering Short Stories*, Scribner, 1968. Chief editorial consultant and contributing author for Scribner's "Paperbacks for Schools."†

* * *

SCOFIELD, William H. 1915-

PERSONAL: Born November 7, 1915, in Groton, N.Y.; son of Charles H. (a county official) and Mary (Hildreth) Scofield; married Josephine Oakley, February 14, 1948; children: David C. *Education:* Cornell University, B.S., 1936; University of Illinois, M.S., 1941; University of Wisconsin, summer graduate study, 1941. *Home:* 3134 North Thomas St., Arlington, Va. 22207. *Office:* Economic Research Service, U.S. Department of Agriculture, Washington, D.C.

CAREER: U.S. Department of Agriculture, agricultural economist, Bureau of Agricultural Economics, Milwaukee, Wis., and Washington, D.C., 1939-51, in charge of Land Values Unit, 1948-51, research leader, Economic Research Service, Washington, D.C., 1951—. *Military service:* U.S. Army, 1942-45. *Member:* American Farm Economic Association, Association of Federal Appraisers, Western Farm Economic Association.

WRITINGS: (With T. J. Pressly) *Farm Real Estate Values in the U.S. by Counties, 1850-1959*, University of Washington Press, 1965. Senior author, "Farm Real Estate Market Developments," semiannually, 1951—. Also writer of professional articles, bulletins, and speeches.

WORK IN PROGRESS: Continuing research in structural changes in American agriculture, yielding articles and publications for U.S. Department of Agriculture.

* * *

SCOTT, Andrew M(acKay) 1922-

PERSONAL: Born November 27, 1922, in Pasadena, Calif.; son of Andrew MacKay and Ruth Stinson (Jarvis) Scott; married Anne Byrd Firor (a professor of history at Duke University), June 2, 1947; children: Rebecca, David, Donald. *Education:* Dartmouth College, A.B., 1946; Harvard University, M.A. and M.P.A., 1949, Ph.D., 1950. *Politics:* Democrat. *Home:* 1028 Highland Woods, Chapel Hill, N.C. *Office:* Department of Political Science, University of North Carolina, Chapel Hill, N.C.

CAREER: U.S. Central Intelligence Agency, Washington, D.C., staff, 1949-51; U.S. Mutual Security Agency, Washington, D.C., foreign affairs officer, 1951-53; assistant professor of political science at Dartmouth College, Hanover, N.H., 1953-54, and Haverford College, Haverford, Pa., 1954-58; University of North Carolina, Chapel Hill, 1958—, began as associate professor, professor of political science, 1966—. Fulbright lecturer, University of Bologna, Bologna, Italy, 1960-61. *Military service:* U.S. Navy, naval aviator, 1943-45; became lieutenant junior grade. *Member:* American Political Science Association, Southern Political Science Association.

WRITINGS: The Anatomy of Communism, Philosophical Library, 1951; *Political Thought in America*, Holt, 1959; (with Earle Wallace) *Politics: U.S.A.*, Macmillan, 1961, 4th edition, 1974; (editor with Raymond Dawson) *Readings in the Making of American Foreign Policy*, Macmillan, 1965; *The Revolution in Statecraft*, Random House, 1965; (with William A. and Trudi M. Lucas) *Simulation and National Development*, Wiley, 1966; (with Margaret Hunt) *Congress and Lobbies*, University of North Carolina Press, 1966; *The Functioning of the International Political System*, Macmillan, 1967; *Competition in American Politics: An Economic Model*, Holt, 1970; (with others) *Insurgency*, University of North Carolina Press, 1970; (with wife, Anne F. Scott) *One Half of the People: The Fight for Woman Suffrage*, Lippincott, 1974.

* * *

SCOTT, Cora Annett (Pipitone) 1931-
(Cora Annett)

PERSONAL: Born April 15, 1931, in Boston, Mass.; daughter of Salvatore (a tile contractor) and Concettina (Pepi) Pipitone; divorced; children: Clifford Duane Scott.

Education: Boston University, B.A., 1968; University of Massachusetts, M.S., 1973, Ph.D., 1974. *Religion:* Non-sectarian. *Home:* 47 Willow St., West Roxbury, Mass. 02132.

CAREER: Clinical psychologist, currently in psycho-therapy with adults and children. *Member:* American Psychological Association, Association for Research and Enlightenment.

WRITINGS—Under name Cora Annett: *The Dog Who Thought He Was a Boy*, Houghton, 1965; *Homerhenry*, Addison-Wesley, 1970; *When the Porcupine Moved In*, F. Watts, 1971; *How the Witch Got Alf*, F. Watts, 1975.

WORK IN PROGRESS: Book on meditation for creative living.

* * *

SCOTT, Ira O(scar), Jr. 1918-

PERSONAL: Born December 13, 1918, in Winfield, Kan.; married Rethel Richmond, 1964; children: Monyean, Christine. *Education:* University of Kansas, A.B., 1940, M.A. (political science), 1941; Harvard University, M.A. (economics), 1951, Ph.D., 1953. *Office:* Savings Bank Association-New York State, 200 Park Ave., New York, N.Y. 10017.

CAREER: Instructor at University of Kansas, Lawrence, 1947-49, and Harvard University, Cambridge, Mass., 1953-55; University of Minnesota, Minneapolis, assistant professor, 1955-56, associate professor of business administration, 1956-57; New York University, Graduate School of Business Administration, New York, N.Y., associate professor, 1957-58; Columbia University, Graduate School of Business Administration, New York, N.Y., associate professor, 1958-66; Arthur T. Roth Graduate School of Business Administration, professor of finance, and dean, 1966-70; Savings Banks Association, New York, N.Y., executive vice-president, 1970—. Consultant to Commission on Money and Credit, to House Banking and Currency Committee, and to Comptroller of the Currency. *Military service:* U.S. Army, 1942-46; became major. *Member:* American Economic Association, American Finance Association, National Association of Business Economists, American Association of University Professors, Phi Beta Kappa. *Awards, honors:* Grants from Merrill Foundation for the Advancement of Financial Knowledge and National Science Foundation; Guggenheim fellowship; Fulbright fellowships to Sweden and Italy.

WRITINGS: (Contributor) W. G. Campbell, editor, *Economics of Mobilization and War*, Irwin, 1952; (contributor) Friedrick and Galbraith, editors, *Public Policy*, Graduate School of Public Administration, Harvard University, 1954; (editor) *School District Organization*, Kansas Legislative Council, 1963; *Correspondent Relations: A Survey of Banker Opinion*, U.S. Government Printing Office, 1964; *Government Securities Market*, McGraw, 1965; *European Capital Markets*, National Publishing, 1968; *The Euro-Dollar Market and its Public Policy Implications*, U.S. Government Printing Office, 1970. Writer of government reports on banking matters; contributor of more than twenty articles to economic and banking journals in America and Europe.

WORK IN PROGRESS: A book, *Money and Credit.*†

* * *

SCOTT, Robert Haney 1927-

PERSONAL: Born September 18, 1927, in Garden City,

Kan.; son of Ira Oscar (a teacher) and Kathryn (Haney) Scott; married Joy Brewer, August 12, 1956; children: William, Ann, Sarah, Elizabeth. *Education:* University of Kansas, A.B., 1949, M.A., 1950; University of Nebraska, graduate study, 1951-53; Harvard University, M.A., 1956, Ph.D., 1961. *Politics:* Independent. *Religion:* Unitarian Universalist. *Home:* 4339 Northeast 45th, Seattle, Wash. 98105. *Office:* University of Washington, Seattle, Wash.

CAREER: Kansas State University, Manhattan, instructor in economics, 1957-61; University of Washington, Seattle, 1961—, professor of business economics, 1967—. *Military service:* U.S. Army Reserve, Military Intelligence, 1949-59; became first lieutenant. *Member:* American Economic Association. *Awards, honors:* Fulbright teaching award, 1966-67; Fulbright research award, 1973-74.

WRITINGS: Problems in National Income Analysis and Forecasting, Scott, Foresman, 1966, revised edition, 1972; *The Pricing System*, Holden-Day, 1973; (with William Pigott and Charles Henning) *Financial Markets and the Economy*, Prentice-Hall, 1975; (with E. J. Chambers and R. S. Smith) *National Income Analysis and Forecasting*, Scott, Foresman, 1975. Contributor of articles to *New Leader, National Review, London Economist, Western Farm Life*, and other professional journals.

WORK IN PROGRESS: Macroeconomic models for forecasting economic activity and for use in national policy formulation.

* * *

SCOTT, W(illiam) Richard 1932-

PERSONAL: Born December 18, 1932, in Parsons, Kan.; son of Charles Hoag and Hildegarde (Hewitt) Scott; married Joy Whitney, August 14, 1955; children: Jennifer Ann, Elliot Whitney, Sydney Brooke. *Education:* Attended Parsons Junior College, 1950-52; University of Kansas, A.B., 1954, M.A., 1955; University of Chicago, Ph.D., 1961. *Politics:* Democrat. *Religion:* Protestant. *Home:* 940 Lathrop Pl., Stanford, Calif. 94305. *Office:* Department of Sociology, Stanford University, Stanford, Calif. 94305.

CAREER: Stanford University, Stanford, Calif., 1960—, began as assistant professor, became professor of sociology. *Member:* American Sociological Association, Society for the Study of Social Problems, American Association of University Professors, Pacific Sociological Society. *Awards, honors:* Woodrow Wilson fellowship, 1954-55; Social Science Research Council fellowship, 1959; Ford Foundation faculty fellowship, 1966.

WRITINGS: (With Otis Dudley Duncan and others) *Metropolis and Region*, Johns Hopkins Press, 1960; (with Peter M. Blau) *Formal Organizations*, Chandler Publishing, 1962; (editor with Edmund H. Volkart) *Medical Care: Readings in the Sociology of Medical Institutions*, Wiley, 1966; (contributor) Howard M. Vollmer and Donald L. Mills, editors, *Professionalization*, Prentice-Hall, 1966; (editor) *Social Processes and Social Structures*, Holt, 1970; (with Sanford M. Dornbusch) *Evaluation and the Exercise of Authority*, Jossey-Bass, 1974. Also contributor to *Handbook of Modern Sociology*, Rand McNally, 1964, *Handbook of Organizations*, Rand McNally, 1965, and sociology journals. Associate editor, *Pacific Sociological Review*, 1964-67, *Administrative Science Quarterly*, 1965-68, *American Journal of Sociology*, 1965-71, and *Medical Care*, 1970-71.

SCUDDER, Rogers V(aughn)   1912-

PERSONAL: Born November 16, 1912, in St. Louis, Mo.; son of Rogers (a businessman) and Margaret (Price) Scudder. Education: Harvard University, A.B., 1934; New College, Oxford, Diploma in Classical Archaeology, 1955; University of Wisconsin, M.A., 1958. Politics: "More often Democrat than otherwise." Religion: Presbyterian. Home: Brooksville, Me.

CAREER: Brooks School, North Andover, Mass., teacher of Latin and Greek, 1936-66; St. John's School, Houston, Tex., teacher of Latin and Greek, 1966—. Wartime service: American Field Service, 1942-44. Member: American Philological Association, Archaeological Institute of America, Classical Association of New England, American Numismatic Society, Vergilian Society of America, Hellenic Society (England).

WRITINGS: (With Charles Jenney) Third Year Latin, Allyn & Bacon, 1963; (with Jenney) Fourth Year Latin, Allyn & Bacon, 1964; (with Eric C. Baade and Jenney) First Year Latin, Allyn & Bacon, 1970; (with Baade and Jenney) Second Year Latin, Allyn & Bacon, 1970. Editor, Vergilian Digest (now Vergilius), 1957-59.

WORK IN PROGRESS: Research in Roman history and archaeology, with a projected handbook for school and college classics courses in mind.

SIDELIGHTS: Scudder can "get along" in Italian and French. His travel and study in Italy has been focused on Roman imperial sites both in Italy itself and in North Africa and Asia Minor.†

*   *   *

SEALE, William   1939-

PERSONAL: Surname rhymes with "wheel"; born August 7, 1939, in Beaumont, Tex.; son of William (an independent oil operator) and Eugenia (Broocks) Seale; married Lucinda Lewis Smith, January 28, 1966. Education: Southwestern University, Georgetown, Tex., B.A., 1961; Duke University, M.A., 1962, Ph.D., 1965. Home and office: 805 Prince St., Alexandria, Va. 22314.

CAREER: Lamar State University, Beaumont, Tex., assistant professor of history, 1965-69; Historic Columbia Foundation, director, 1969-71; free lance writer, 1971-73; with National Park Service and White House Historical Association, 1973—. Awards, honors: Grants from National Endowment for the Humanities and the Victorian Society of America.

WRITINGS: Texas Riverman: The Life and Times of Captain Andrew Smyth, University of Texas Press, 1966; Sam Houston's Wife: A Biography of Margaret Lea Houston, University of Oklahoma Press, 1970; Texas in Our Time: A History of Texas in the Twentieth Century, Hendrick-Long Publishing, 1972; The Tasteful Interlude: American Interiors 1860-1917, Praeger, 1975; The Temples of Democracy, Harcourt, in press.

WORK IN PROGRESS: Development of a historical film for television on the history of the White House.

AVOCATIONAL INTERESTS: Historical restoration; study of 19th century American interiors.

*   *   *

SEARA VAZQUEZ, M(odesto)   1931-

PERSONAL: Born September 11, 1931, in Allariz, Spain; son of Aser (an industrialist) and Herculina (Vazquez Cal-

vino) Seara Pavon; married Rita Bertha Helene Michelmann de Seara, November 29, 1960. Education: Consejo Superior de Investigaciones Cientificas (Instituto Jaime Balmes), diploma in sociology, 1954; Sociedad Espanola de Estudios Internacionales y Coloniales, diploma in international politics, 1955; Universidad de Madrid, Bach. of Laws, 1955; University of Paris, Doctor of International Law, 1959. Home: Cerro dos Conejos 26, Mexico City, 21, Mexico. Office: Institute of Comparative Law, Universidad Nacional Autonoma de Mexico, Mexico City, 20, Mexico.

CAREER: Universidad Nacional Autonoma de Mexico, Mexico City, professor of international law in the National School of Political Sciences and the School of Laws, beginning 1961, research fellow in the Institute of Comparative Law, beginning 1961, professor of international organization in the National School of Political Sciences, beginning 1962, professor of international politics, beginning 1963, coordinator of Seminar on International Trade, 1964. Participated in Space Law Colloquium (London, 1959, Washington, 1961), International Congress on Comparative Law (Hamburg, 1962), and many other congresses on international law. Visiting professor at University of Utah, 1965-66, and University of Caracas, 1966; director of Seminar on World Order, University of Bogota, 1966. Member: Sociedad Espanola de Estudios Internacionales y Coloniales, Sociedad Astronomica de Espana y America, London Institute of World Affairs.

WRITINGS: The Functional Regulation of Extra-Atmospheric Space (English language), Springer Verlag, 1960; Introduction al derecho internacional cosmico, Universidad Nacional Autonoma de Mexico, 1961, published as Cosmic International Law, Wayne State University Press, 1965; Manual de derecho internacional publico, Pormaca, 1964, 2nd edition, 1967; Sintesis del derecho internacional publico, Universidad Nacional autonoma de mexico, 1965; Del Congreso de Viena a la paz de Versalles, Universidad Nacional Autonoma de Mexico, 1969; Paz y conflicto en la sociedad internacional: Articulos, Universidad Nacional Autonoma de Mexico, 1969; La politica exterior de Mexico: la practica de Mexico en la derecho internacional, Editorial Esfinge, 1969; La paz precaria: de Versalles a Danzig, Universidad Nacional Autonoma de Mexico, 1970; Derecho internacional publico, Editorial Porrua, 1971. Contributor of articles to Revista de Ciencias Politicas y Sociales (Mexico), II Diritto Aereo (Italy), Annuaire Francais de Droit International (France), and other professional journals.

WORK IN PROGRESS: Two books, Tratado general sobre la organizacion internacional and El derecho internacional publico segun la jursprudencia de la corte internacional de justicia.

SIDELIGHTS: Seara Vazquez speaks English, French, Portuguese, German, and Russian.

BIOGRAPHICAL/CRITICAL SOURCES: El Alcazar (Madrid), May 8, 1959, June 6, 1959; Le Figaro Litteraire, May 9, 1959; El Noticiero Universal (Barcelona), June 14, 1959; A B C (Madrid), June 25, 1959.†

*   *   *

SEARS, Paul Bigelow   1891-

PERSONAL: Born December 17, 1891, in Bucyrus, Ohio; son of Rufus Victor (a lawyer) and Sallie (Harris) Sears; married Marjorie McCutcheon, June 22, 1917; children: Paul McCutcheon, Catherine (Mrs. Arthur Frazer), Sallie

Harris. *Education:* Ohio Wesleyan University, B.S., 1913; University of Nebraska, M.A., 1915; University of Chicago, Ph.D., 1922. *Religion:* Episcopalian. *Home and office:* 17 Las Milpas, Taos, N.M. 87571.

CAREER: Ohio State University, Columbus, instructor in botany, 1915; University of Nebraska, Lincoln, assistant professor, 1919-25, associate professor of botany, 1925-27; University of Oklahoma, Norman, professor of botany and head of department, 1927-38; Oberlin College, Oberlin, Ohio, professor of botany and head of department, 1938-50; Yale University, New Haven, Conn., chairman of Conservation Program, 1950-60, professor emeritus of conservation, 1960—. Crawford County National Bank, director, 1945-62, honorary director, 1970—; member of National Science Board, 1958-64, of Plowshare Advisory Committee, Atomic Energy Commission, 1959-68; member of board, Pacific Tropical Botanical Garden, 1964-70. *Military service:* U.S. Army, 1917-18.

MEMBER: American Association for the Advancement of Science (president, 1956; chairman of commission on science education, 1963-65), Ecological Society of America (president, 1948), National Audubon Society (chairman of board, 1956-59; honorary president, 1970—), American Society of Naturalists (president, 1959). *Awards, honors:* Guggenheim fellowship, 1958; Richard Prentice Ettinger Medal for creative writing, 1963; eminent ecologist award of Ecological Society of America, 1965; Daly Medal, American Geographical Society, 1970; Alumni award, Ohio State University, 1971; Alumni award, University of Chicago, 1972; Browning Award, 1972; various conservation awards, including Garden Club of America and Louis Bromfield medals. Honorary D.Sc., Ohio Wesleyan University, 1937, Oberlin College, 1958; Litt.D., Marietta College, 1951; LL.D., University of Arkansas, 1957, University of Nebraska, 1957, Wayne State University, 1959.

WRITINGS: Deserts on the March, University of Oklahoma Press, 1935, 3rd revised edition, 1949; *This Is Our World*, University of Oklahoma Press, 1937, revised edition, 1971; *Who Are These Americans?*, Macmillan, 1939; *Life and Environment*, Bureau of Publications, Teachers College, Columbia University, 1939; (with I. James Quillen and P. R. Hanna) *This Useful World*, Scott, 1941; *Charles Darwin*, Scribner, 1950.

Where There Is Life, Dell, 1962 (published in England as *The Biology of the Living Landscape*, Allen & Unwin, 1964), published as *The Living Landscape*, Basic Books, 1966, new revised edition published as *Where There is Life: An Introduction to Ecology*, Dell, 1970; *Lands Beyond the Forest*, Prentice-Hall, 1969; (with Marion R. Becker and Frances J. Poetker) *Wild Wealth*, Bobbs-Merrill, 1971. Writer of articles of technical and general interest. Member of board of editors, *Daedalus*, 1957-69.

WORK IN PROGRESS: Studies and occasional articles on applied ecology.

* * *

SEARS, Robert R(ichardson) 1908-

PERSONAL: Born August 31, 1908, in Palo Alto, Calif.; son of Jesse Brundage and Stella (Richardson) Sears; married Pauline Snedden (a professor of child development), June 25, 1932; children: David O'Keefe, Nancy Louise (Mrs. Jonathan Barker). *Education:* Stanford University, A.B., 1929; Yale University, Ph.D., 1932. *Office:* Stanford University, Stanford, Calif. 94305.

CAREER: University of Illinois, Urbana, instructor in psychology, 1932-36; Yale University, New Haven, Conn., assistant professor of psychology, 1936-42; University of Iowa, Iowa City, professor of child psychology and director of Child Welfare Research Station, 1942-49; Harvard University, Cambridge, Mass., professor of education and child psychology, and director of Laboratory of Human Development, 1949-53; Stanford University, Stanford, Calif., professor of psychology and chairman of department, 1953-61, dean of School of Humanities and Sciences, 1961-70, trustee of Center for Advanced Study in the Behavioral Sciences. Consultant to National Institutes of Health and National Science Foundation; chairman of committee on child development, National Research Council, 1947-50; vice-chairman of board of directors, Social Science Research Council, 1950-53.

MEMBER: American Psychological Association (president, 1951), Society for Research in Child Development (president, 1973-75), Society of Experimental Psychologists, American Academy of Arts and Sciences, American Philosophical Society, Sigma Xi.

WRITINGS: (With J. Dollard, L. Doob, N. Miller, and O. Mowrer) *Frustration and Aggression*, Yale University Press, 1939; *Objective Studies of Psychoanalytic Concepts*, Social Science Research Council, 1943; (with E. Maccoby and H. Levin) *Patterns of Child Rearing*, Row, Peterson & Co., 1957; (with L. Rau and R. Alpert) *Identification and Child Rearing*, Stanford University Press, 1965; (editor with S. Feldman) *Seven Ages of Man*, William Kaufman, 1973. Writer of some fifty research and theoretical papers and monographs for psychological journals.

WORK IN PROGRESS: A psychobiographical study of Mark Twain.

* * *

SECHREST, Lee 1929-

PERSONAL: Surname is pronounced *Sea*-crest; born January 1, 1929, in Kansas City, Mo.; son of Wayne Burton (a decorator) and Lenarue (Madding) Sechrest; married Ruth Schnackenberg, August 14, 1949 (deceased); married Carol (Bell) DuBois, April 20, 1967; children: (first marriage) Sara, Stuart, Steven. *Education:* Attended Kansas State College of Pittsburgh, 1948-49; Ohio State Universiy, A.B., 1952, M.A., 1954, Ph.D., 1956. *Home:* 2921 Coldstream Dr., Tallahassee, Fla. 32303.

CAREER: Pennsylvania State University, University Park, assistant professor of psychology, 1956-58; Northwestern University, Evanston, Ill., assistant professor, 1958-63, associate professor, 1963-67, professor of psychology, 1967-73; Florida State University, Tallahassee, professor of psychology, 1973—. Member, advisory board for research and evaluation, Police Institute, 1973—. *Military service:* U.S. Marine Corps, 1946-48, 1950-51; became staff sergeant. *Member:* American Psychological Association, Phi Beta Kappa, Sigma Xi.

WRITINGS: (With A. P. Goldstein and K. Heller) *Psychotherapy and the Psychology of Behavior Change*, Wiley, 1966; (with E. Webb, D. T. Campbell, and R. J. Schwartz) *Unobtrusive Measures*, Rand McNally, 1966; (with J. Wallace) *Psychology and Human Problems*, C. E. Merrill, 1967; (with J. Cotton and B. C. Mathis) *Psychological Foundations of Education*, Academic Press, 1970; (with Wallace) *The Nature and Study of Psychology*, F. E. Peacock, 1973.

SEDGWICK, Alexander 1930-

PERSONAL: Born June 8, 1930, in Boston, Mass.; son of William Ellery and Sarah (Cabot) Sedgwick; married Charlene Mary Maute, June 24, 1961; children: Catherine Maria, Alexander Cameron. *Education:* Harvard University, B.A., 1952, Ph.D., 1963. *Politics:* Liberal Democrat. *Home:* 1409 Rugby Rd., Charlottesville, Va. 22903. *Office:* Department of History, University of Virginia, Charlottesville, Va. 22903.

CAREER: Dartmouth College, Hanover, N.H., instructor in history, 1962-63; University of Virginia, Charlottesville, assistant professor, 1963-66, associate professor, 1966-74, professor of history, 1974—. *Military service:* U.S. Army, 1952-54. *Member:* American Historical Association, Society for French Historical Studies, American Association of University Professors.

WRITINGS: The Ralliement in French Politics, 1890-98, Harvard University Press, 1965; *The Third Republic, 1870-1914*, Crowell, 1968.

WORK IN PROGRESS: Research on Jansenism as a force in French history.

*   *   *

SEGAL, Marilyn 1927-

PERSONAL: Born August 9, 1927, in Utica, N.Y.; daughter of Abraham L. (a financier) and Alice (Lyons) Mailman; children: Betty, Wendy, Richard, Patricia, Debra. *Education:* Wellesley College, B.A., 1948; McGill University, B.S., 1949; Nova University, Ph.D., 1969. *Politics:* Democrat. *Religion:* Jewish. *Home:* 700 Washington St., Hollywood, Fla. 33020.

CAREER: Social worker in Boston, Mass., 1959, 1969; The Pre-School, Hollywood, Fla., administrator, 1965-68; Nova University, Fort Lauderdale, Fla., director of University School, 1970-71, assistant professor of early childhood, 1971—, director of Institute of Early childhood and open education, 1971-72, chief investigator, School for Parents program, 1971-72. Member of board of trustees, University of Miami, 1969-71; member of board of governors, University School, 1969-72; chairman of education committee, Hollywood Chamber of Commerce, 1970-71.

WRITINGS: Run Away Little Girl, Random House, 1965; (contributor) *You Are Your Baby's First Teachers*, Nova University Press, 1973; *"Play and Learn" For Parents and Infants*, Nova University Press, 1974. Also writer of "To Reach a Child," television series for the Office of Child Development, 1973. Contributor to *Reader's Digest, Research in Education, Journal of Reading Behavior*, and *Inquiry*.

WORK IN PROGRESS: A teacher learning program for normal and handicapped pre-school children, STRIDE.

*   *   *

SEGLER, Franklin Morgan 1907-

PERSONAL: Born April 11, 1907, in Ardmore, Okla.; son of Samuel Matthew (a farmer) and Ada Pearl (Gabriel) Segler; married Fannie Mae McCord (an elementary teacher), June, 1935; children: Dana Franklin, Samuel Louis, Sylvia Annette. *Education:* Oklahoma Baptist University, B.A., 1930; Southwestern Baptist Theological Seminary, Th.M., 1938, Th.D., 1945; postdoctoral study at Union Theological Seminary, New York, N.Y., 1953, and Boston University, 1957-58. *Politics:* Democrat. *Home:* 30

Cliffside Dr., Fort Worth, Tex. *Office:* Southwestern Baptist Theological Seminary, Fort Worth, Tex. 76116.

CAREER: Baptist minister; assistant pastor in Duncan, Okla., 1931-32, and Oklahoma City, Okla., 1933-34; associate pastor in Ardmore, Okla., 1935, and Fort Worth, Tex., 1936-37; pastor in Henderson, Tex., 1938-40, Garland, Tex., 1940-45, and Alexandria, La., 1945-51; Southwestern Baptist Theological Seminary, Fort Worth, Tex., professor of theology, 1951-72; Broadway Baptist Church, Fortworth, Tex., minister of pastoral care, 1972—. Arab Baptist Seminary, Beirut, Lebanon, teacher for Baptist Foreign Mission Board during sabbatical year, 1964-65. *Member:* National Association of Biblical Instructors, Southern Baptist Association for Clinical Pastoral Education, Kiwanis Club. *Awards, honors:* American Association of Theological Schools Sealantic fellowship, 1957-58.

WRITINGS: A Theology of Church and Ministry, Broadman, 1960; (contributor) *Southwestern Sermons*, Broadman, 1960; (contributor) *J. Howard Williams*, Naylor, 1963; *The Christian Layman*, Broadman, 1964; *Christian Worship: Its Theology and Practice*, Broadman, 1967; *Broadman's Minister's Manual*, Broadman, 1968; *Your Emotions and Your Faith*, Broadman, 1970; *A Pailful of Stars*, Broadman, 1972; *Alive!—and Past Sixty-Five*, Broadman, 1975. Contributor to *Southern Baptist Encyclopedia*; writer of adult Sunday school lesson series; contributor to church periodicals and newspapers.

WORK IN PROGRESS: A Baptist Pastor's Manual.

*   *   *

SEIDEN, Morton Irving 1921-

PERSONAL: Born July 29, 1921, in New York, N.Y.; son of Harry and Sophie (Stern) Seiden. *Education:* New York University, B.S., 1943; Columbia University, M.A., 1944, Ph.D., 1952. *Office:* English Department, Boylan Hall, Brooklyn College of the City University of New York, Brooklyn, N.Y.

CAREER: Instructor in English at New York University, New York, N.Y., 1946-49, Smith College, Northampton, Mass., 1949-52, and Queens College (now Queen's College of the City University of New York), Flushing, N.Y., 1952-53; Brooklyn College of the City University of New York, Brooklyn, N.Y., instructor, 1952-62, assistant professor, 1963-67, associate professor, 1967-70, professor of English, 1970—. Lecturer in English at City College of the City University of New York, 1945, and Columbia University, 1948-49. Public lecturer on modern literature in Division of Adult Education, International Ladies' Garment Workers' Union, and to other groups and organizations. *Member:* Modern Language Association of America, Modern Humanities Research Association, English Institute, English Graduate Union of Columbia University. *Awards, honors:* Brooklyn College of the City University of New York award for teaching excellence, 1967.

WRITINGS: William Butler Yeats: The Poet As a Mythmaker, Michigan State University Press, 1962; *The Paradox of Hate: A Study in Ritual Murder*, Yoseloff, 1967. Contributor to *Accent, American Image, Canadian Slavic Studies, Western Humanities Review*, and other periodicals.

WORK IN PROGRESS: The Gordian Knot, a study of the Manichean heresy in the modern world; *The Sacred Quest*, essays on the philosophical and religious backgrounds of modern literature; *James Joyce's "Ulysses": A Theological Study*.

SIDELIGHTS: Seiden reads and speaks German and French.

* * *

SEILER, Robert E. 1925-

PERSONAL: Born October 12, 1925, in Fort Worth, Tex.; son of Ralph G. and Willie (Smith) Seiler; married Norma Allen, August 30, 1948; children: Suzanne, Robert, Glenn, Richard. *Education:* Texas Christian University, B.S., 1948, M.B.A., 1951; University of Alabama, Ph.D., 1953; University of Texas, postdoctoral study, 1963. *Office:* University of Houston, Houston, Tex.

CAREER: Lennox Furnace Co., Fort Worth, Tex., chief cost accountant, 1948-50; certified public accountant, Texas, 1950; Miami University, Oxford, Ohio, assistant professor of managerial accounting, 1953-55; University of Texas, Austin, associate professor of managerial accounting, 1955-65; Stanford University, International Division, Lima, Peru, professor of managerial accounting, 1965-67; University of Houston, Houston, Tex., professor of accounting, 1967—. *Military service:* U.S. Navy, Air Corps, pilot, 1943-46. *Member:* American Institute of Certified Public Accountants, American Accounting Association, International Association of Internal Auditors, Texas Society of Certified Public Accountants, Southwestern Social Science Association, Beta Alpha Psi, Beta Gamma Sigma. *Awards, honors:* Thurston Award of International Association of Internal Auditors for the outstanding publication in internal auditing, 1959; Ford Foundation Faculty fellowship for research in quantitative methodology, 1963.

WRITINGS: (With Robert L. Grinaker) *Auditing Practice Case*, Irwin, 1959; *Elementary Accounting: Theory, Technique, and Application*, C. E. Merrill, 1963, 2nd edition, 1968; *Improving the Effectiveness of Research and Development*, McGraw, 1965; *Principles of Accounting: A Managerial Approach*, C. E. Merrill, 1967, 2nd edition, 1975. Editor, *Education and Practice* and *Internal Auditor*, 1963-65.

SIDELIGHTS: Robert Seiler went to Lima in 1965 to help establish a new graduate school of business administration, Escuela de Administración de Negocios sara Graduados, the only one of its kind in South America. He is fluent in Spanish.

* * *

SELLERS, Charles Coleman 1903-

PERSONAL: Born March 16, 1903, in Overbrook, Pa.; son of Horace Wells (an architect) and Cora (Wells) Sellers; married Helen Earle Gilbert, October 6, 1932 (died February, 1951); married Barbara Stow Roberts, June 12, 1952; children: (first marriage) Horace Wells, Susan Pendleton. *Education:* Haverford College, B.A., 1925; Harvard University, M.A., 1926. *Politics:* Democrat. *Religion:* Episcopalian. *Home:* 161 West Louther St., Carlisle, Pa. 17013.

CAREER: In antiquarian book business, 1932-35; Wesleyan University Library, Middletown, Conn., bibliographical librarian, 1935-49; Dickinson College, Carlisle, Pa., member of library staff and teacher of American art, 1949-56, librarian, 1956-68. Writer and researcher, 1927—. Research associate, American Philosophical Society, 1947-51; librarian, Waldron Phoenix Belknap, Jr. Research Library of American Painting, Wintherthur, Del., 1956-59. *Member:* American Association of University Professors

(chapter president, 1961-62), College Art Association. *Awards, honors:* Litt.D., Temple University, 1957; Bancroft Prize, 1970, for *Charles Willson Peale*.

WRITINGS: Lorenzo Dow: Bearer of the Word, Minton, Balch, 1928; *Benedict Arnold: The Proud Warrior*, Minton, Balch, 1930; *Theophilus, the Battle-Axe*, privately printed, 1930; *Charles Willson Peale*, two volumes (first volume published as *The Artist of the Revolution: The Early Life of Charles Willson Peale*, 1939), American Philosophical Society, 1947; *Portraits and Miniatures by Charles Willson Peale*, American Philosophical Society, 1952, supplement published as *Charles Willson Peale with Patron and Populace*, 1969; (editor) Waldron Phoenix Belknap, *American Colonial Painting*, Belknap Press, 1959; *Benjamin Franklin in Portraiture*, Yale University Press, 1962; *Charles Willson Peale* (based on earlier publication with same title), Scribner, 1969; *Dickinson College: A History*, Wesleyan University Press, 1973. Contributor to *Britannica Encyclopedia of American Art*, and of articles, chiefly on art history, to periodicals.

WORK IN PROGRESS: History of Peale Museum.

* * *

SELLIN, Eric 1933-

PERSONAL: Surname is pronounced S'leen; born November 7, 1933, in Philadelphia, Pa.; son of Thorsten (a professor) and Amy (Anderson) Sellin; married Birgitta Sjoberg, January 25, 1958; children: Frederick, Christopher. *Education:* University of Pennsylvania, B.A., 1955, M.A., 1958, Ph.D., 1965. *Politics:* "Liberal in inclination." *Home:* 312 Kent Rd., Bala-Cynwyd, Pa. 19004. *Office:* Temple University, Philadelphia, Pa., 19122.

CAREER: University of Bordeaux, Bordeaux, France, lecturer in American literature, 1956-57; Clark University, Worcester, Mass., instructor in French, 1958-59; University of Pennsylvania, Philadelphia, lecturer in creative writing, 1960-62; Temple University, Philadelphia, Pa., instructor, 1962-65, assistant professor, 1965-67, associate professor, 1967-70, professor of French, 1970—, chairman of department of French and Italian, 1970-73. Fulbright-Hayes lecturer in American literature, University of Algiers, 1968-69. *Member:* American Association of Teachers of French, Modern Language Association of America, American Association for the Study of Dada and Surrealism (vice-president, 1970, 1972), American Association of University Professors, Phi Beta Kappa. *Awards, honors:* Burr Book Prize; Borestone Mountain Poetry Award; Cape Rock Poetry Award, 1971; National Endowment for the Humanities, senior fellowship, 1973-74.

WRITINGS: (Translator with C. Goll) Yvan Goll, *The Magic Circles*, Allen Press, 1962; *Night Voyage* (poems), Atlantis Editions, 1964; *The Dramatic Concepts of Antonin Artaud*, University of Chicago Press, 1968; *Trees at First Light* (poems), Killaly Press, 1973; *Tanker Poems*, Killaly Press, 1973; *Borne kilometrique* (poems), P. J. Oswald, 1973; *As-Shamsu* (broadsheet), Sceptre Press, 1973. Contributor of articles and poems to *Atlas, New York Times, Literary Review, Massachusetts Review, Solstice, Seed, New World Writing, The Fiddlehead, Cahiers du Sud, Chelsea*, and other journals. Editor, *Pennsylvania Literary Review*, 1954-55.

WORK IN PROGRESS: Sundry poems; research for books on Algerian literature of French expression; work on Camara Laye and Paul Valery.

SIDELIGHTS: Sellin told *CA*, "At times I find it difficult to distinguish vocation from vacation, so to speak, and what some might consider hobbies form a vital part of my esthetic and creative make-up. To take but one example: travel . . . [has] become for me almost an abstract (pure) poetic experience and almost all my poems composed in the last five or six years have been instigated by or deal with travel in Africa." *Avocational interests:* Reading, sports (especially officiating at soccer matches as a referee).

* * *

SENESI, Mauro 1931-

PERSONAL: Born October 10, 1931, in Volterra, Italy; son of Donato and Argia (Gonnelli) Senesi; children: Vauro. *Home:* Via dei Velluti 5, Florence, Italy.

CAREER: Full-time professional writer. *Awards, honors:* Eugene F. Saxton Memorial Trust Award (established by Harper & Brothers to assist writers of distinction), 1964-65, 1965-66.

WRITINGS: Longshadow and Nine Stories (novel), Regnery, 1965; *His Beard Grew on Only One Cheek*, Scribner, 1968; *Aspetta un po' che la bambina cresca* (novel), Ricci, 1974. Contributor to *Atlantic Monthly, Harper's, Cosmopolitan, Story, Short Story International, Modern Age, Texas Quarterly, Queen* (British), *She* (British), and other periodicals.

WORK IN PROGRESS: A children's novel, *The Venetian Elephant*; a novel, *But Then, Grandmother Is It?*; nonfiction, *Cinque anni della nostra vita.*

* * *

SENG, Peter J. 1922-

PERSONAL: Born March 30, 1922, in Milwaukee, Wis.; son of Frank G. (president of Industrial Oil Co.) and Lydia (Peters) Seng. *Education:* Marquette University, A.B., 1948; Harvard University, M.A., 1949, Ph.D., 1955. *Office:* Connecticut College, New London, Conn. 06320.

CAREER: Northwestern University, Evanston, Ill., instructor, 1952-55, assistant professor of English, 1956-59; Connecticut College, New London, Conn., assistant professor, 1959-65, associate professor, 1965-70, professor of English, 1970—. *Military service:* U.S. Army Air Forces, 1942-46. *Member:* National Council of Teachers of English, Modern Language Association of America, Renaissance Society, Malone Society. *Awards, honors:* Folger Library fellowship, 1957.

WRITINGS: (With C. F. Main) *Poems: Wadsworth Handbook and Anthology*, Wadsworth, 1961, 3rd edition, 1973; *The Vocal Songs in the Plays of Shakespeare*, Harvard University Press, 1967; *Plays: Wadsworth Handbook and Anthology*, Wadsworth, 1970.

* * *

SERIF, Med 1924-

PERSONAL: Surname is pronounced *Sair*-if; born April 5, 1924, in New York, N.Y.; son of Albert (a businessman) and Nora (Weinstein) Serif; married Marilyn Bloome, February 26, 1950; children: Michael Lawrence, Melissa Cara. *Education:* New York University, B.S., 1949, M.A., 1952. *Home:* 6 Ann Ct., Freeport, N.Y. 11520. *Office:* C.I.T. Financial Corp., 650 Madison Ave., New York, N.Y. 10022.

CAREER: Food Topics, New York, N.Y., associate edi-

tor, 1949-50; *LP-Gas Magazine*, New York, N.Y., editor, 1950-58; Cities Service Co. (petroleum), New York, N.Y., assistant manager of business research and education, 1958-62; Dunkin' Donuts (food franchiser), Quincy, Mass., assistant to executive vice-president, 1962-63; C.I.T. Financial Corp., New York, N.Y., communication services manager, 1963—. *Military service:* U.S. Army Air Forces, 1943-46; became sergeant. *Member:* Industrial Communication Council (secretary, 1966-73; vice-president, 1973-75), Public Relations Society of America, International Communication Association, National Council for Small Business Management Development (chairman of public relations, 1960—), New York Sales Executive club.

WRITINGS: How to Make More Money Selling Gas and Appliances, Moore Publishing, 1958; *How to Manage Yourself*, Fell, 1965; *Business Building Ideas for Franchises and Small Business*, Pilot, 1972. Also author of six books in Dun & Bradstreet business book series, and booklets for U.S. Small Business Administration. Contributor to more than one hundred journals.

WORK IN PROGRESS: Writing on programs to help independent businessmen and company executives improve their management and marketing abilities.

* * *

SETON, Anya

PERSONAL: Born in New York, N.Y.; daughter of Ernest Thompson (author-naturalist) and Grace (Gallatin) Seton; children: (first marriage) two; (second marriage) one. *Education:* Private tutors and courses at Oxford University, England. *Religion:* Episcopalian. *Home:* Binney Lane, Old Greenwich, Conn.

CAREER: Writer. *Member:* P.E.N., Author's League, Pen and Brush Club (honorary), National League of American Pen Women (pioneer branch).

WRITINGS: My Theodosia, Houghton, 1941; *Dragonwyck*, Houghton, 1944; *Turquoise*, Houghton, 1946; *Hearth and Eagle*, Houghton, 1948; *Foxfire*, Houghton, 1951; *Katherine*, Houghton, 1954; *Mistletoe and Sword: A Story of Roman Britain*, Doubleday, 1955; *Winthrop Woman*, Houghton, 1958; *Washington Irving*, Houghton, 1960; *Devil Water*, Houghton, 1962; *Avalon*, Houghton, 1965; *Green Darkness*, Houghton, 1973. Editorial board, *Writer's Magazine.*

SIDELIGHTS: Preferring to classify her novels as "biographical" rather than "historical," Miss Seton wrote in *Writer's Magazine*: "There is a difference. The standard costume piece or historical romance needs very little research. It is sufficient to pick a congenial period, then read a couple of books in order to properly clothe and feed the characters, who are invented by the author. And, since love and conflict are common to all humans in all ages, the historical background can be negligible. . . . I remember a historical novel about William the Conqueror whose author said ingenuously in the foreword, 'I know the Tower of London was not built at the time I said it was, but I needed the Tower for my plot. . . .' I have a passion for facts, for dates and for places. I love to recreate the past, and to do so with all the accuracy possible. This means an enormous amount of research, which is no hardship. I love it. . . . The actual writing, however, is another matter. That is just plain work, day in, day out, for a year or more. . . ."

An article that dealt with the heroine, Elizabeth, of *Winthrop Woman* is a good example of Miss Seton's exhaustive research. *Saturday Review* reported: "'For more than two years I studied over two hundred books, read and reread the five volumes of "Winthrop papers",' said Miss Seton. She spent hours poring over old manuscripts with a reading glass trying to decipher the ornate script . . . [and] returned to the scene of her heroine's youth, journeying twice to England, where she located the site of Elizabeth's father's apothecary shop, visited the Suffolk area where the Winthrops lived, and stood beneath Elizabeth's mulberry tree."

The daughter of Ernest Thompson Seton, co-founder of the Boy Scouts and a famous author-artist-naturalist, Miss Seton was more interested in medicine than writing in her earlier years. "I was thoroughly aware of the seamy side of the profession—the drudgery, the essential loneliness, and the tough hide needed to persevere through discouragement and misunderstandings," she told *Writer's Magazine*. "[When] the depression was in full swing," quoted the *New Yorker*, "I thought maybe I could make some money at home, so I began to write." This was in 1937.

All of her novels have been praised for their historical authenticity and readability. Geoffrey Bruun in the *New York Herald Tribune Book Review* called *Winthrop Woman* "a chronicle that stirs the senses and excites the imagination by its immediacy and intensity. In Elizabeth Fones Miss Seton has found a heroine worthy to stand beside the best in her gallery of interesting women." "The novel is noteworthy for its insights into the Puritan 'Bible Commonwealth,'" added Edmund Fuller in *Saturday Review*. "Miss Seton knows the courage, conviction and endurance that went into it, and nowhere does she mock or minimize. But she shows also its aspects of pitiless bigotry, its harsh and tragic distortion of Christianity. The author's portrayal of the persecution and expulsion of Anne Hutchinson is brilliantly executed."

R. C. Healy in *New York Herald Tribune Books* said of *Devil Water*: "Miss Seton's approach to historical fiction is brisk and strictly utilitarian, with no great fussing over subtlety or psychology. . . . Her sole purpose is to tell a rousing good tale plainly and simply and this she does admirably."

Discussing her travels and interests, Miss Seton told *CA*: "Extensive research on all my books necessitates much historical background and a large personal library. I was born British and have spent a quarter of my life in England. Much time in France." She speaks French, Italian, and Spanish and along with cooking, her other interests are "3M's—medicine, music and mysticism."

Dragonwyck, a Hudson River gothic, was a popular movie released by 20th Century-Fox in 1946. *Foxfire* was filmed by Universal in 1955. All her novels have been translated into several languages.

*   *   *

SETTEL, Gertrude S.
(Trudy S. Settel)

PERSONAL: Born March 15, 1919, in New York, N.Y.; married Irving Settel (a professor and writer), September 23, 1941; children: Kenneth, Joanne. *Education:* Hunter College (now Hunter College of the City University of New York), B.A., 1939. *Home:* 69-12 223rd St., Bayside, N.Y.

CAREER: Restaurant and travel editor, *Westbury Times*, 1959-73; Long Island dining editor for *Cue* magazine, 1974.

WRITINGS—Under name Trudy S. Settel: (With husband, Irving Settel) *The Best of Armstrong Circle Theatre*, Citadel, 1959; (editor) *The Wisdom of JFK*, Dutton, 1965; (editor) *The Faith of JFK*, Dutton, 1965; (editor) Dag Hammerskjold, *The Light and the Rock*, Dutton, 1965; *The Quotable Harry S. Truman*, Droke House, 1967; *The Faith of Billy Graham*, Droke House, 1968; (editor with Irving Settel) *Close to Home Auto Tours*, Hawthorn, 1973; (editor with Irving Settel) *Close to Home Auto Tours: Midwest*, Hawthorn, 1974.

*   *   *

SETTEL, Irving   1916-

PERSONAL: Born November 21, 1916, in New York, N.Y.; son of Joseph and Dora Settel; married Gertrude Schulman (a writer), September 23, 1941; children: Kenneth, Joanne. *Education:* Brooklyn College (now Brooklyn College of the City University of New York), B.A., 1951; New York University, M.S., 1955. *Home:* 69-12 223rd St., Bayside, N.Y. *Office:* Pace College, 41 Park Row, New York, N.Y.

CAREER: Pace College, New York, N.Y., 1946—, associate professor, 1960-65, professor of marketing, 1965—. Vice-president, Popular Library Publishers. Author, and writer for radio and television; creator of television network programs, "Who's the Boss?" and "Who Pays?"; co-producer of network program, "Where Have You Been?"; consultant in educational television.

WRITINGS: Effective Retail Advertising, Fairchild, 1950; *The Ad-Viser*, Hardware Age, 1952; (with Norman Glenn and others) *Television Advertising and Production Handbook*, Crowell, 1953; (editor) *Top TV Shows of the Year* (anthology), Hastings, 1955; (editor) *Best Television Humor of the Year*, Wyn, 1956; (editor) *Best TV Humor of 1957*, Ballantine, 1957; (editor) *Great TV Sermons*, Naylor, 1957; (editor) *How to Write Television Comedy*, Writer, Inc., 1958; *They Fell in Love*, Citadel, 1958; (with Bill Adler) *Congratulations, You're a Grandparent!*, Citadel, 1959; (with Adler) *Congratulations, You're Married!*, Citadel, 1959; (with Adler) *Congratulations, It's Your Birthday!*, Citadel, 1959; (with wife, Trudy S. Settel) *The Best of Armstrong Circle Theatre*, Citadel, 1959.

(Editor) *A Pictorial History of Radio*, Citadel, 1960, revised edition, Grosset, 1967; *The Lovers* (adaptation of film), Popular Library, 1960; *And God Created Woman* (adaptation), Popular Library, 1960; *Ecstacy* (adaptation), Popular Library, 1961.

(Compiler with Otto Kleppner) *Exploring Advertising*, Prentice-Hall, 1970; (editor with Trudy S. Settel) *Close to Home Auto Tours*, Hawthorn, 1973; (editor with Trudy S. Settel) *Close to Home Auto Tours: Midwest*, Hawthorn, 1974.

*   *   *

SEYMOUR, Digby G.   1923-

PERSONAL: Born November 25, 1923, in Knoxville, Tenn.; son of Charles Milne (a lawyer) and Flora Nell (Gloster) Seymour; married Lois Rasmussen, September 10, 1954; children: John, James, Thomas. *Education:* Student at University of Tennessee, 1941-43, and University of Kentucky, 1944; University of Wisconsin, B.S., 1946, M.D., 1948. *Politics:* Republican. *Religion:* Episcopalian. *Home:* 7119 Rockingham, Knoxville, Tenn.

CAREER: Diplomate of American Board of Anesthesiology. Physician, specializing in anesthesiology, Knoxville, Tennessee. Member of Tennessee Historical Commission. *Military service:* U.S. Army, 1943-46. U.S. Air Force, 1951-54; served in Korea as commanding officer of 51st Fighter Interceptor Medical Wing; received Bronze Star. *Member:* American Medical Association, American Society of Anesthesiologists, Tennessee Medical Association, Knoxville Academy of Medicine, Kappa Sigma, Nu Sigma Nu.

WRITINGS: Divided Loyalties: Fort Sanders and the Civil War in East Tennessee, University of Tennessee Press, 1963.

* * *

SHAFER, Boyd Carlisle 1907-

PERSONAL: Born May 8, 1907, in Crestline, Ohio; son of Boyd W. (a businessman) and Lillie (Carlisle) Shafer; married Carol Larsen (a writer), June 6, 1932; children: Kirstin (Mrs. Fred Moritz), Anders. *Education:* Miami University, Oxford, Ohio, B.A. (magna cum laude), 1929; University of Iowa, M.A., 1930, Ph.D., 1932; postdoctoral study in France, 1934, and at Columbia University, 1936-37. *Home:* 2815 East Hawthorne, Tucson, Ariz. 85716. *Office:* Department of History, University of Arizona, Tucson, Ariz. 85721.

CAREER: Professor and head of history and social science department at Stout Institute, 1932-42; University of Arkansas, Fayetteville, associate professor, 1947-51, professor of history, 1951-53, chairman of department, 1952-53; American Historical Association, Washington, D.C., executive secretary, and editor of *American Historical Review*, 1953-63; Macalester College, St. Paul, Minn., James Wallace Professor of History, 1963-72, chairman of department, 1965-71; University of Arizona, Tucson, professor of history, 1972—. *Military service:* U.S. Army Air Forces and War Department General Staff, 1943-46; became captain. *Member:* International Committee for Historical Sciences (vice-president, 1970-71, acting president, 1971-72), American Historical Association, Organization of American Historians, National Historical Publications Commission, Societe des Robespierristes, Southern Historical Association, Phi Beta Kappa, Phi Alpha Theta (president, 1972-73). *Awards, honors:* National Conference of Christians and Jews award for *Nationalism, Myth and Reality*, 1956; L.L.D. from Miami University, 1962; Troyer Steele Anderson Prize from American Historical Association, 1970; Ohioana Library Award, 1973.

WRITINGS: (With wife, Carol L. Shafer) *Life, Liberty and Pursuit of Bread*, Columbia University Press, 1940; *Nationalism: Myth and Reality*, Harcourt, 1955; *Nationalism: Interpreters and Interpretations*, Service Center for Teachers of History, 1959, 3rd edition published as *Nationalism: Interpretations and Interpreters*, 1966; (with Richard A. McLemore and Everett Augspurger) *1865 to the Present: A United States History for High School*, Laidlaw, 1966; (with McLemore and Augspurger) *United States History for High Schools*, Laidlaw, 1966, adaptation by Milton Finkelstein published as *A High School History of Modern America*, Laidlaw, 1966; (contributor and author of introduction) Michael Francois and others, editors, *Historical Study in the West*, Appleton, 1968; *Faces of Nationalism: New Realities and Old Myths*, Harcourt, 1972. Editor, "Age of European Expansion" series, University of Minnesota Press, and *American Historical Review*, 1953-63. Author of pamphlets; contributor to journals.

WORK IN PROGRESS: Studies of historiography, nationalism, and internationalism.

SHAFFER, Wilma L. 1916-

PERSONAL: Born June 30, 1916, in Warrensburg, Ill.; daughter of Jasper and Ethel (Thomas) Hatfield; married Bruce H. Shaffer (a service engineer), July 5, 1934; children: Janice J. (Mrs. Charles H. Smith), Lawrence Bruce, Roger Alan. *Education:* Attended University of Nebraska, 1953; University of Cincinnati, A.A., 1965, B.S., 1970. *Home:* 9984 Lake Park Dr., Cincinnati, Ohio 45231. *Office:* Standard Publishing, 8121 Hamilton Ave., Cincinnati, Ohio 45231.

CAREER: Standard Publishing, Cincinnati, Ohio, editor, 1957—, including editorship of *Christian Mother* (a quarterly). *Member:* Phi Kappa Epsilon.

WRITINGS—All published by Standard Publishing: *A Year of Junior Hi Programs*, 1958; *Devotions and Dialogs*, 1961; *Church Women at Work*, 1961; *Psalms and Programs*, 1964; *Proverbs and Programs*, 1972. Also author of *Lullaby Memories*, 1973, and *Baby Blossoms*, 1974. Writer of visual packets and quarterlies.

WORK IN PROGRESS: Problems and Pleasures, a book for young mothers; a devotional book for women.

* * *

SHAH, (Sayed) Idries 1924-

PERSONAL: Born June 16, 1924, in Simla, India; son of Ikbal (a professor) and Saira (Khanum) Ali-Shah; married Cynthia Kabraji; children: Saira, Safia, Tahir. *Education:* Privately educated. *Address:* c/o C. Hoare & Co., 37 Fleet St., London EC4P 4DG, England. *Agent:* Collins-Knowleton-Wing, Inc., 60 East 56th St., New York, N.Y. 10022; A. P. Watt & Son, 26/28 Bedford Row, London WC1R 4HL, England.

CAREER: International Press Agency Service, president, 1953-65; Institute for Cultural Research, London, England, director of studies, 1966—. Visiting professor, University of Geneva, Switzerland, 1972-73; professor (*Ad Honorem*), National University, La Plata, Argentina, 1974. Adviser to educational authorities in several countries, and to Heads of States. *Awards, honors:* Six first prizes, UNESCO International Book Year, 1972.

WRITINGS: Oriental Magic: Eastern Minority Beliefs, Rider, 1956, Dutton, 1973; *Destination Mecca*, Rider, 1957, 2nd edition, Octagon Press, 1969; *The Secret Lore of Magic: Documentation on European Minority Beliefs*, Hillary, 1957, Citadel, 1958; *The Sufis*, introduction by Robert Graves, Doubleday, 1964; *The Exploits of the Incomparable Mulla Nasrudin*, J. Cape, 1966, Simon & Schuster, 1967; *Special Problems in the Study of Sufi Ideas*, Institute for Cultural Research, 1966, 2nd edition, Octagon Press, 1971; *Tales of the Dervishes*, J. Cape, 1967, Dutton, 1971; *Caravan of Dreams*, Octagon Press, 1968, Penguin, 1972; *Reflections*, Zenith Books, 1968, 2nd edition, Octagon Press, 1969, Penguin, 1972; *The Way of the Sufi*, J. Cape, 1968, Dutton, 1969; *The Pleasantries of the Incredible Mulla Nasrudin*, J. Cape, 1968, Dutton, 1973; *The Book of the Book*, Octagon Press, 1969; *Wisdom of the Idiots*, Octagon Press, 1969, 2nd edition, 1970, Dutton, 1971; *The Dermis Probe*, J. Cape, 1970, Dutton, 1971; *Thinkers of the East*, Penguin, 1971; *The Magic Monastery*, Dutton, 1972; *The Subtleties of the Inimitable Mulla Nasrudin*, Dutton, 1973; *Graphic Sayings*, Kindersley & Skelton, 1973; *The Elephant in the Dark*, Octagon Press, 1974.

Other writings and productions: "The Dermis Probe" (film); "The Dreamwalkers" (color documentary on Shah), produced by British Broadcasting Corp. television, 1970; "Contentions" (film lecture series in animation); "Magnificent Idiot" (film based on the Mulla Nasrudin books), produced by Richard Williams. Editor of monographs published by Institute for Cultural Research. Contributor of short stories and articles on Middle East topics to journals and newspapers.

WORK IN PROGRESS: Learning How to Learn; Theory and Practice in Sufism.

SIDELIGHTS: Shah, known as The Sayed as his father was before him, claims descent from the Prophet Mohammed and the Emperors of Persia through the Caliph Musa al-Kasim. He writes: "Ancestry last verified in 1970 in internationally recognized documents issued by, *inter alia*, Mufti Zia al-Haqq and stamped by the Court and Islamic Doctors of Law. Titles of Emir, Sirdar, Badshah (sovereign), etc., verified and legally affirmed (latest instance, on death of father) 1970."

The film, "The Dermis Probe," was selected for showing at the London and New York film festivals. *Reflections* also was made into a film.

BIOGRAPHICAL/CRITICAL SOURCES: C. R. Fergusson, *Idries Shah: Reviews and Comments*, Key Press, 1973; L. F. Rushbrook, editor, *Sufi Studies: East and West*, Dutton, 1973; H. Ansair, *Books by Idries Shah*, Key Press, 1974; Seyyed N. Hosain, *Persian, Arabic, Turkish and Urbu Profiles of Idries Shah*, Key Press, 1974; L. Lewin, editor, *The Diffusion of Sufi Ideas in the West*, Dutton, 1975.

*   *   *

SHAH, Krishna B. 1938-

PERSONAL: Born May 10, 1938, in India; son of Bhogilal Maneklal (a businessman) and Shataben Shah; married Diane Hillman (a psychotherapist); children: Judson. *Education:* Yale University, LL.M., 1958; University of Iowa, M.A., 1960. *Religion:* Hindu. *Home:* 38 Walkeshwar House, Bombay 4, India. *Agent:* Shapro-Lichtman, 116 North Robertson Blvd., Los Angeles, Calif. 90049. *Office:* Muttontown Pictures, Inc., 450 Park Ave., New York, N.Y. 10020.

CAREER: Indian National Theatre, Bombay, artistic director, 1954-56; Durban Academy of Theatre Arts, Durban, South Africa, founder-director, 1962; playwright and director of plays produced in Bombay, New York, London, and South Africa. Productions directed include "Kadam Milake Ohalo," Bombay, 1957; "Sponono," New York, 1964; "Kindly Monkeys," London, 1965, and three Off-Broadway plays. Also director of films and television. *Awards, honors:* Best director of the year and best play of the year awards, State of Bombay, for "Kadam Milake Ohalo"; grant for film study at University of California, Los Angeles.

WRITINGS: (With Alan Paton) *Sponono* (a play based on Paton's *Tales from a Troubled Land*; first produced in Paris, 1964; produced in Chicago, Ill., 1966), Scribner, 1965. Also author of plays "Kadam Milake Ohalo"; "King of the Dark Chambers" (an adaptation of a Rabindranath Tagore work).

Screenplays: "Love and Karma"; "Jewel and the Lotus"; "Rivals"; "The Flower Child"; "The Wound"; "Island in Harlem" (based on a novel by M. Manrique); "April Morning."

Author of television scripts for "Man from U.N.C.L.E.,"

1966; "Maya," 1966; "Cimarron Strip," 1967; "The Flying Nun," 1968; "Judd for the Defense," 1968.

Contributor to magazines.

WORK IN PROGRESS: An original screenplay, "The Yaleman."

*   *   *

SHAPERE, Dudley 1928-

PERSONAL: Born May 27, 1928, in Harlingen, Tex.; son of Dudley (a surgeon) and Corinne (Pupkin) Shapere; married second wife Hannah Hardgrave, May 31, 1974; children: (first marriage) Alfred, Catharine. *Education:* Harvard University, B.A., 1949, M.A., 1955, Ph.D., 1957. *Home:* 1922 Maynard Dr., Champaign, Ill. 61820. *Office:* Department of Philosophy, University of Illinois, Urbana, Ill. 61801.

CAREER: Ohio State University, Columbus, instructor in philosophy, 1957-60; University of Chicago, Chicago, Ill., assistant professor, 1960-65, associate professor, 1965-67, professor of philosophy, 1967-72; University of Illinois, Urbana, professor of philosophy, 1972—, chairman of program in history and philosophy of science. Visiting professor at Rockefeller University, 1965-66, and Harvard University, 1968. National Science Foundation, member of advisory panel for history and philosophy of science, 1965-66, special consultant, history and philosophy of science program, 1966—; consultant, Commission on Undergraduate Education in Biological Sciences. *Military service:* U.S. Army, Infantry, 1950-52; became sergeant. *Member:* American Philosophical Association, American Association for the Advancement of Science (fellow), Philosophy of Science Society, History of Science Society. *Awards, honors:* Quantrell Award, 1968, for excellence in undergraduate education, University of Chicago.

WRITINGS: (Editor) *Philosophical Problems of Natural Science*, Macmillan, 1965; *Galileo: A Philosophical Study*, University of Chicago Press, 1974. Contributor to anthologies and philosophical journals.

AVOCATIONAL INTERESTS: Tennis, table tennis, chess.

*   *   *

SHAPIRO, Edward 1920-

PERSONAL: Born July 19, 1920, in Toledo, Ohio; son of Benjamin and Ida (Lafer) Shapiro. *Education:* University of Toledo, B.A., 1942; University of Michigan, graduate study, 1942; Ohio State University, M.A., 1945; Harvard University, M.A., 1947, Ph.D., 1950. *Home:* 2744 Farrington Rd., Toledo, Ohio 43606. *Office:* Department of Economics, University of Toledo, Toledo, Ohio 43606.

CAREER: U.S. Department of Commerce, Washington, D.C., economist, 1951; U.S. Office of Prize Stabilization, district economist, Detroit, Mich., 1952-53; Business Research Associates, Detroit, Mich., director of research, 1953-61; University of Detroit, Detroit, Mich., associate professor of economics, 1961-66; Wayne State University, Detroit, Mich., associate professor of economics, 1966-67; University of Toledo, Toledo, Ohio, professor of economics, 1967—. Visiting professor at California State University, Long Beach, 1970-71, and University of East Anglia, Norwich, England, 1975. *Military service:* U.S. Army, 1942-43; became sergeant. *Member:* American Economic Association.

WRITINGS: Macroeconomic Analysis, Harcourt, 1966, 3rd edition, 1974; (compiler) Macroeconomics: Selected Readings, Harcourt, 1970; (with B. L. Gensemer) Macroeconomics Analysis: A Student Workbook, Harcourt, 1970; Understanding Money, Harcourt, 1975. Contributor to Harvard Educational Review, Quarterly Review of Economics and Business, and other journals.†

* * *

SHAPIRO, Fred(eric) C(harles) 1931-

PERSONAL: Born February 3, 1931, in Washington, D.C.; son of Frederic E. and Ann (Spitzer) Shapiro; married Iris Hecht, December 24, 1959; children: Paul, Mary. Education: University of Missouri, A.B., 1952. Religion: Jewish. Home: 1177 East 14th St., Brooklyn, N.Y. 11230. Agent: John Cushman Associates, 25 West 43rd St., New York, N.Y. 10036. Office: New Yorker, 25 West 43rd St., New York, N.Y. 10036.

CAREER: Newspaper reporter and rewriteman for Portsmouth Star, Portsmouth, Va., 1954-55, Philadelphia Daily News, Philadelphia, Pa., 1955-57, Baltimore New-Post, Baltimore, Md., 1957-60, New York Journal American, New York, N.Y., 1960-63, and New York Herald Tribune, New York, N.Y., 1963-65; New Yorker, New York, N.Y., staff writer, 1965—. Military service: U.S. Army, 1953-54. Member: Newspaper Reporters Association of New York City, Overseas Press Club of America, Artist & Model Bohemian Club (Tokyo). Awards, honors: Robert F. Kennedy Journalism Award, 1970.

WRITINGS: (With James W. Sullivan) Race Riots, New York 1964, Crowell, 1964; Whitmore, Bobbs-Merrill, 1969.†

* * *

SHARP, John R. 1921-

PERSONAL: Born June 21, 1921, in Hull, Yorkshire, England; son of Alfred and Edith M. (Shepherdson) Sharp; married Grace A. Lightfoot, June 16, 1945; children: David J., Peter R. Education: Attended Hull Grammar School, 1932-37. Home: 8 Dale Bank, Oakdale, Harrogate, Yorkshire, England. Office: ICI Fibres, Hookstone Rd., Harrogate, Yorkshire, England.

CAREER: Worked in public libraries, Hull, Yorkshire, England, 1937-54; Short Brothers and Harland Ltd. (aircraft manufacturers), Belfast, Northern Ireland, technical librarian, 1954-58; Association of Special Libraries and Information Bureau (ASLIB), London, England, senior indexer, 1958-60; ICI Fibres Ltd., Pontypool, Monmouthshire, England, deputy librarian and information officer, beginning 1960; ICI Fibres, Harrogate, Yorkshire, England, librarian and information officer, 1972—. Military service: Royal Air Force, 1941-46. Member: Library Association (fellow); Institute of Information Scientists (fellow).

WRITINGS: (Contributor) Handbook of Special Librarianship, 4th edition, Association of Special Libraries and Information Bureau, 1975; Some Fundamentals of Information Retrieval, British Book (New York), 1965; Information Retrieval: Notes for Students, Deutsch, 1970. Contributor to Annual Review of Information Science and Technology of American Society for Information Science.

* * *

SHARPE, William D(onald) 1927-

PERSONAL: Born July 18, 1927, in Canton, Ohio; son of William D. (a professional engineer) and Nelly (Zembiec)

Sharpe. Education: University of Toronto, B.A., 1950; University of Buffalo (now State University of New York at Buffalo), M.A., 1953; Johns Hopkins University, M.D., 1958. Office: Cabrini Health Care Center, 227 East 19th St., New York, N.Y. 10003.

CAREER: Certified in clinical pathology and anatomic pathology, American Board of Pathology. New Jersey College of Medicine, Newark, associate clinical professor of pathology, 1963—. Curator, Pennsylvania Hospital Historical Library, Philadelphia, Pa. Military service: U.S. Naval Reserve, 1945-46. Member: American College of Clinical Pharmacology (fellow), College of American Pathologists (fellow), Mediaeval Academy of America, American Philological Association, College of Physicians of Philadelphia (fellow), New York Academy of Medicine (fellow).

WRITINGS: Isidore of Seville: The Medical Writings, American Philosophical Society, 1964; Medicine and the Ministry, Appleton, 1966. Contributor of scientific and historical articles and reviews to periodicals.

WORK IN PROGRESS: Research on chronic radium injury in human bone; further work in medical history, particularly post-classical Latin medicine in the Christian West down to the time of Salerno, and early American medicine, particularly around Philadelphia, down to about 1850; work on computer-compatible systematized medical nomenclatures.

SIDELIGHTS: William Sharpe is competent in classical and patristic/mediaeval Latin, classical Greek and French.

* * *

SHAVER, James P. 1933-

PERSONAL: Born October 19, 1933, in Wadena, Minn.; son of George C. (a county foreman) and Helen (Hubbell) Shaver; married Joyce G. Eroe, December 30, 1953 (divorced); children: Kim Evangeline, Jay Greville. Education: University of Washington, Seattle, B.A. (magna cum laude), 1955; Harvard University, A.M.T., 1957, Ed.D., 1961. Office: Utah State University, Logan, Utah 84322.

CAREER: Concord (Mass.) public schools, teacher and researcher, 1957-59; Harvard University, Cambridge, Mass., instructor and research associate, 1961-62; Utah State University, Logan, associate professor of education, 1962-64; Ohio State University, Columbus, associate professor of education and director of Social Studies Curriculum Center, 1964-65; Utah State University, Logan, associate professor, 1965, professor of educational research, and chairman of Bureau of Educational Research, 1966—. Visiting professor at University of Washington, Seattle, 1963, and Harvard University, 1964.

MEMBER: American Educational Research Association, National Council for Social Studies, Social Science Education Consortium (council), American Association of University Professors, Utah Education Association, Phi Beta Kappa, Phi Eta Sigma, Pi Sigma Alpha.

WRITINGS: (With Donald W. Oliver) Teaching Public Issues in the High School, Houghton, 1966; (with Harold Berlak) Democracy, Pluralism and the Social Studies: Readings and Commentary, Houghton, 1968; Values and Schooling: Perspectives for School People and Parents, Utah State University Press, 1972; (with Guy A. Larkins) Decision-Making in a Democracy, Houghton, 1973; (with Larkins) Instructor's Manual: The Analysis of Public Issues Program, Houghton, 1973; (with Larkins) The Police and Black America, Houghton, 1973; (with Larkins) Race

Riots in the Sixties, Houghton, 1973; (with Larkins and Donald E. Anctil) *Progress and the Environment: Water and Air Pollution*, Houghton, 1973; (with William Strong) *Values and the Teacher*, Wadsworth, 1975.

WORK IN PROGRESS: With Jedon Emenhiser, *Man and His Government: Making Community Decisions*.

* * *

SHAW, J(oseph) Thomas 1919-

PERSONAL: Born May 13, 1919, in Ashland City, Tenn.; son of George Washington and Ruby Mae (Pace) Shaw; married Betty Lee Ray, October 30, 1942; children: David Matthew, Joseph Thomas, Jr., James William. *Education:* University of Tennessee, A.B., 1940, M.A., 1941; Harvard University, M.A., 1947, Ph.D., 1950. *Home:* 4505 Mineral Point Rd., Madison, Wis. 53705.

CAREER: Indiana University, Bloomington, assistant professor, 1949-55, associate professor of Slavic languages, 1955-61; University of Wisconsin, Madison, professor of Slavic languages, 1961—, chairman of department, 1961-68, chairman of Division of the Humanities, 1964-65, 1973-74, associate dean, Graduate School, 1965-68. *Military service:* U.S. Naval Reserve, active duty, 1942-46, 1951-53; now captain. *Member:* Modern Language Association of America, American Association of Teachers of Slavic and East European Languages (member of executive committee, 1954-70, president, 1973, 1974), American Association of University Professors, Phi Kappa Phi.

WRITINGS: (Editor and translator) *The Letters of Alexander Pushkin*, University of Pennsylvania Press and Indiana University Press (joint publishers), 1963, revised edition, University of Wisconsin Press, 1967; *Pushkin's Rhymes: A Dictionary*, University of Wisconsin Press, 1974. Editor, *Slavic and East European Journal*, 1957-70.

WORK IN PROGRESS: *The Life and Works of Alexander Pushkin*; research in Russian literature (especially that of the first half of the nineteenth century).

* * *

SHAW, Ronald E. 1923-

PERSONAL: Born July 22, 1923, in Eden, N.Y.; son of Malin M. and Anne (Work) Shaw; married Judith Mortenson, December 19, 1961; children: Brian, Susan, Philip. *Education:* Carleton College, A.B., 1947; University of Rochester, Ph.D., 1954. *Home:* 206 Beechpoint Dr., Oxford, Ohio 45056. *Office:* Department of History, Miami University, Oxford, Ohio 45056.

CAREER: Wayne State University, Detroit, Mich., instructor in history, 1950-55; Miami University, Oxford, Ohio, assistant professor, 1955-61, associate professor, 1961-67, professor of history, 1967—. *Military service:* U.S. Army, 1943-46; became staff sergeant; received Bronze Star. *Member:* American Historical Association, Economic History Association, Organization of American Historians, Ohio Historical Society, Canal Society of New York State. *Awards, honors:* Prize Studies Award of Organization of American Historians, 1965, for manuscript of *Erie Water West*.

WRITINGS: Erie Water West: A History of the Erie Canal, 1792-1854, University of Kentucky Press, 1966. Contributor to historical journals.

WORK IN PROGRESS: Research into the history of the Canal Era in the United States, 1790-1860.

SHAW, Steven John 1918-

PERSONAL: Born November 16, 1918, in Hamilton, N.Y.; son of Constantine (a landscaper) and Agnes (Teller) Shaw; married Aracelis Governa (a professor of Spanish), June 8, 1952. *Education:* State University of New York, B.S., 1941; New York University, M.S., 1947, Ph.D., 1955. *Politics:* Democrat. *Religion:* Catholic. *Home:* 4832 Forest Ridge Lane, Columbia, S.C. 29208.

CAREER: Real Silk Hosiery Mills, Bridgeport, Conn., district manager, 1944-45; General Electric Co., York Wire Sales Division, New York, N.Y., sales manager, 1945-47; assistant professor of marketing at University of Miami, Miami, Fla., 1948-52, and University of Florida, Gainesville, 1954-57; University of South Carolina, Columbia, associate professor, 1957-60, professor of marketing and editor, *Southern Business Journal*, 1960—. *Member:* American Marketing Association, Southern Marketing Association (president, 1964), Pi Sigma Epsilon (founder of University of South Carolina branch), Sales and Marketing Executives Club.

WRITINGS: (With Joseph Thompson) *Salesmanship: Modern Viewpoints on Personal Communication*, Holt, 1960; (with C. McFerron Gittinger) *Marketing in Business Management*, Macmillan, 1963; *Marketing Management Strategy*, Prentice-Hall, 1972. Contributor to marketing journals.

WORK IN PROGRESS: Research in international marketing; national study of attitudes and opinions of state legislative bodies on consumerism.

AVOCATIONAL INTERESTS: Chess (Southern champion, 1957), travel, and golf.

* * *

SHEAHAN, John 1923-

PERSONAL: Born September 11, 1923, in Toledo, Ohio; son of Bernard William (an engineer) and Florence (Sheahan) Sheahan; married Denise Eugenie Morlino (a social worker); children: Yvette Marie, Bernard Eugene. *Education:* Stanford University, B.A., 1948; Harvard University, Ph.D., 1954. *Politics:* Democrat. *Home:* Lynde Lane, Williamstown, Mass. 01267. *Office:* Department of Economics, Williams College, Williamstown, Mass. 01267.

CAREER: U.S. Economic Cooperation Administration, economic analyst in Paris, France, 1951-54; Williams College, Williamstown, Mass., 1954—, professor of economics, 1966—. National research professor at Brookings Institution, 1959-60; visiting professor, El Colegio de Mexico, Mexico City, 1970-71. Economic adviser, Harvard University Development Advisory Service, Bogota, Colombia, 1963-65. *Military service:* U.S. Army, 1943-46; received Purple Heart. *Member:* American Economic Association.

WRITINGS: Promotion and Control of Industry in Postwar France, Harvard University Press, 1963; *The Wage-Price Guideposts*, Brookings Institution, 1967; *An Introduction to the French Economy*, C. E. Merrill, 1969. Contributor to professional journals in United States, Colombia, and France.

WORK IN PROGRESS: Research on public enterprise in Europe and in the developing countries.

SIDELIGHTS: John Sheahan is competent in French and Spanish.

SHEDD, Charlie W. 1915-

PERSONAL: Born August 8, 1915, in Cedar Rapids, Iowa; son of Francis H. (a clergyman) and Lelia Bell (Anderson) Shedd; married Martha Petersen, May 29, 1939; children: Philip Jack, Karen Marie (Mrs. Vincent Guarino), Paul Jim, Peter Jay, Timothy Vance. *Education:* Coe College, B.A., 1937; McCormick Theological Seminary, B.S., 1940; University of Chicago, divinity studies. *Politics:* Independent. *Home:* 6 Sleepy Oaks, Houston, Tex. 77024. *Office:* Memorial Drive Presbyterian Church, 11612 Memorial Dr,, Houston, Tex. 77024.

CAREER: Presbyterian clergyman; minister in LaSalle, Colo., 1941-42, Lexington, Neb., 1942-47, and Ponca City, Okla., 1947-55; Memorial Drive Presbyterian Church, Houston, Tex., minister, 1955—. Director of Bayou Manor, Hedgecroft Hospital, American Red Cross, and former director of Harris County Chapter of Commission on Alcoholism. *Member:* Fellowship of Christian Athletes, Association of Ministers of Greater Houston (president, 1960-61).

WRITINGS: Pray Your Weight Away, Lippincott, 1957; (with wife, Martha Shedd) *Word Focusing: A New Way to Pray*, Upper Room, 1961; *How to Develop a Tithing Church*, Abingdon, 1961; *Time for All Things*, Abingdon, 1962; *How to Develop a Praying Church*, Abingdon, 1964; *Pastoral Ministry of Church Officers*, John Knox, 1965; *Letters to Karen: On Keeping Love in Marriage*, Abingdon, 1965; *Letters to Philip: On How to Treat a Woman*, Doubleday, 1968; *The Stork Is Dead*, Word Books, 1968; *Promises to Peter: Building a Bridge From Parent to Child*, Word Books, 1970; *Is Your Family Turned On? Coping With the Drug Culture*, Word Books, 1971; *The Fat Is In Your Head: A Life Style to Keep It Off*, Word Books, 1972; *Where People Really Pray: The Exciting Church*, Word Books, 1974; *The Exciting Church: Where They Really Use the Bible*, Word Books, 1975; *Talk to Me*, Doubleday, 1975.†

* * *

SHEEHAN, James J(ohn) 1937-

PERSONAL: Born May 31, 1937, in San Francisco, Calif.; son of James B. (a businessman) and Sally (Walsh) Sheehan; married Elena Masharov (a teacher), June 12, 1960. *Education:* Stanford University, A.B., 1958; University of California, Berkeley, M.A., 1959, Ph.D., 1964. *Home:* 2802 Harrison St., Evanston, Ill. *Office:* Department of History, Northwestern University, Evanston, Ill.

CAREER: Stanford University, Stanford, Calif., instructor, 1962-64; Northwestern University, Evanston, Ill., assistant professor, 1964-67, associate professor, 1967-71, professor of history, 1971—. *Member:* American Historical Association.

WRITINGS: (Contributor) *Major Crises in Western Civilization*, Harcourt, 1965; *The Career of Lujo Brentano*, University of Chicago Press, 1966. Contributor of articles and reviews to journals.

WORK IN PROGRESS: Nineteenth-Century German Liberalism.

BIOGRAPHICAL/CRITICAL SOURCES: Times Literary Supplement, March 9, 1967.

* * *

SHEFFER, Isaiah 1935-

PERSONAL: Born December 30, 1935, in New York, N.Y.; son of Samuel B. (a businessman) and Esther (Scooler) Sheffer; married Ethel Shatunoff (an instructor at Barnard College), June 3, 1956; children: Susannah Esther. *Education:* Brooklyn College (now Brooklyn College of the City University of New York), B.A., 1956; University of Birmingham Shakespeare Institute, Stratford on Avon, England, fellow, 1956; Michigan State University, M.A., 1958. *Religion:* Jewish. *Home:* 194 Riverside Dr., New York, N.Y. 10025. *Office:* School of the Arts, Columbia University, New York, N.Y. 10027.

CAREER: Actor, producer, and director in the theater and in radio and television, 1958—. Station WBAI, New York, N.Y., drama critic, 1962—; Columbia University, New York, N.Y., instructor in theater arts, 1964—. *Member:* Actors Equity Association, American Federation of Television and Radio Artists, Society of Stage Directors and Choreographers. *Awards, honors:* Belgian-American Educational Foundation special fellowship, 1963; "Emmy" nomination, National Academy of Television Arts and Sciences, for National Broadcasting Co. television series which he wrote and produced, "The Road to the White House," 1965.

WRITINGS: (Translator and adapter from the works in Yiddish of Isaac L. Peretz) *The Theatre of Peretz*, Samuel French, 1964. Contributor to *Midstream*. Wrote screenplay and narration for "The Last Chapter," 1966, a documentary on 1,000 years of Polish Jewry.†

* * *

SHELBY, Carroll Hall 1923-

PERSONAL: Born January 11, 1923; son of Warren Hall and Eloise (Lawrence) Shelby; married Jeanne Fields, December, 1943; married Janet Bergquist, 1960; children: (first marriage) Sharon Anne Shelby Lavine, Michael Hall, Patrick Burke. *Education:* Attended public schools. *Religion:* Protestant.

CAREER: Automobile manufacturer. Co-owner of All American Racers, Inc., Santa Ana, Calif., and Terlingua Ranch in Texas; president of Carroll Shelby Enterprises, Garden Grove, Calif., and of School of High Performance Driving, Performance Design Associates, and Hi-Performance Motors, Inc., all Los Angeles, Calif. Member of board of directors, National Hot Rod Association. *Military service:* U.S. Army Air Forces, 1941-45; became second lieutenant. *Member:* United States Auto Club (life member), Sports Car Club of America (life member).

WRITINGS: (With John Bentley) *The Cobra Story*, Trident, 1965.†

* * *

SHELDON, Michael 1918-

PERSONAL: Born June 27, 1918, in London, England; emigrated to Canada, 1948; son of Charles Robert (a manufacturer) and Vera (Lion) Sheldon; married Marie-Claire Moisescu, August 1, 1940; children: Christopher, Sheila, Anthony. *Education:* Attended Sedbergh School, Yorkshire, England, 1931-35; Magdalen College, Oxford, B.A. and M.A., 1938. *Home:* 480 Grosvenor Ave., Montreal, Quebec, Canada. *Agent:* John Schaffner, 425 East 51st St., New York, N.Y. 10022. *Office:* Concordia University, 1420 Sherbrooke St. W., Montreal, Quebec, Canada.

CAREER: British Council, staff member in Rumania and Egypt, 1938-41; British Embassy, Brussels, Belgium, assistant press attache, 1945-47; British European Airways,

London, England, deputy press superintendent, 1947-48; Bank of Montreal, Montreal, Quebec, assistant to public relations manager, 1948-50; Bell Telephone Co. of Canada, Montreal, Quebec, supervisor of editorial services, 1950-62; Smith Kline & French (pharmaceutical firm), Montreal, Quebec, assistant to general manager, 1962-67; Bishop's University, Lennoxville, Quebec, assistant to principal, 1967-69; Concordia University, Montreal, Quebec, executive assistant to rector, 1969—. *Military service:* British Army, Intelligence Corps, 1941-45; became captain.

WRITINGS: The Gilded Rule, Hutchinson, 1963; *The Unmelting Pot*, Hutchinson, 1965; *The Personnel Man* (novel), McClelland & Stewart, 1967; *Death of a Leader*, R. Hale, 1971. Writer of television and radio scripts and translator of plays from the French for Canadian Broadcasting Corp.

* * *

SHELDON, William Denley 1915-

PERSONAL: Born October 21, 1915, in Swansea, Wales; brought to United States in 1923, naturalized in 1943; son of William Denley and Mary (Burke) Sheldon; married Rosalind Scharch, June 24, 1940; children: William Denley III, Mary Jane. *Education:* State University of New York College at Buffalo, B.S. in Ed., 1938; Syracuse University, M.S. in Ed., 1943, Ph.D., 1948; University of Chicago, graduate study, 1946. *Religion:* Unitarian Universalist. *Home:* 110 Scottholm Blvd., Syracuse, N.Y. 13210. *Office:* Syracuse University, Reading and Language Arts Center, 150 Marshall St., Syracuse, N.Y. 13210.

CAREER: Clerk, Buffalo, N.Y., 1933-34; public school principal, Clinton, N.Y., 1938-43; Syracuse University, Syracuse, N.Y., 1946—, began as instructor, became professor of education, 1957, director of reading center, 1948—. Educational consultant in Cambodia, 1957; consultant to General Electric Co., 1959—, Pitman Publishing Corp., 1962-63. President of Dewitt Number 11 School Board, 1958-59. *Military service:* U.S. Army, 1943-46; became staff sergeant. *Member:* International Reading Association (president, 1961-62), American Association of University Professors, National Education Association, National Conference on Research in English, National Council of Teachers of English, American Psychological Association, Phi Delta Kappa, Kappa Delta Pi, Sigma Upsilon, Sigma Chi Alpha, Syracuse Faculty Club, University Club (Syracuse). *Awards, honors:* Distinguished Alumni Award, State University of New York College at Buffalo, 1959.

WRITINGS: (With Lawrence Carillo) *Workbook in College Reading*, Syracuse University Press, c. 1955; (with L. S. Braam) *Reading for Dollars and Sense*, Syracuse University Press, 1958; (with Braam) *Reading Improvement for Men and Women in Industry*, Syracuse University Press, 1959; (with Braam) *Developing Efficient Reading*, Oxford University Press, 1959; *Influences Upon Reading Instruction in the United States*, Syracuse University School of Education, 1961; *Junior Science Book of Elephants*, Garrard, 1961; (compiler with others) *The Reading of Poetry*, Allyn & Bacon, 1963; (with others) *Picture Stories*, Allyn & Bacon, 1963; *The House Biter*, Holt, 1966; (with Donald R. Lashinger) *Effect of First Grade Instruction Using Basal Readers, Modified Linguistic Materials, and Linguistic Readers*, Syracuse University, 1966; (with Lashinger and Nancy J. Nichols) *Comparison of Three Methods of Teaching Reading in the Second Grade*, Syra-

cuse University, 1967. Senior author and compiler of "Sheldon Basic Reading Series," including readers, teacher's editions, and activity books, Allyn & Bacon, 1957-73; editor of "Breakthrough" series, Allyn & Bacon, 1969-73. Contributor to education journals.†

* * *

SHEPARD, Leslie (Alan) 1917-

PERSONAL: Born June 21, 1917, in West Ham, London, England; son of Robert William George and Annie Elizabeth (Williams) Shepard; married (wife deceased); children: one son, one daughter. *Education:* Attended elementary school at Harold Road, Upton Park, London, and Day Continuation School for Commercial Subjects, London, 1922-33. *Politics:* "Unpolitical, humanitarian." *Religion:* "No formal religious grading, but sympathetic to basic truths of many religions; usually class as Vedantist." *Home:* 1 Lakelands Close, Stillorgan, Blackrock, County Dublin, Irish Republic.

CAREER: Paul Rotha Productions Ltd., London, England, assistant organiser on bi-monthly newsreel for Ministry of Information, and scriptwriter, 1942-44; Data Film Productions Ltd., London, England, 1945-58, founder-member, assistant director on various industrial and educational films for Central Office of Information, and for industry, 1945-48, member of board of management, 1947, joint production manager-organiser on "Mining Review" (monthly news film), 1948-50, associate producer, 1950-57, scriptwriter, editor, director on other productions; Central Office of Information, London, England, production controlling officer, supervisor on documentary films and Public Service Television items for British Broadcasting Corp. and Independent Television, 1960-62; University Books, New York, N.Y., London editor, 1965-66; Gale Research Co., Detroit, Mich., editor and researcher, 1966—. Founder member, Standing Committee of Jews, Christians and Moslems. Active in ecumenical conferences. *Wartime service:* Served with Civil Defense stretcher party during World War II. *Member:* International Folk Music Council, Association of Cinematograph, Television and Allied Technicians, English Folk Dance and Song Society, British Institute of Recorded Sound, Private Libraries Association, British Society of Dowsers, College of Psychic Science, Fairy Investigation Society, Dracula Society.

WRITINGS: The Broadside Ballad: A Study in Origins and Meaning, Folklore Associates, 1962; *John Pitts, Ballad Printer of Seven Dials, London, 1765-1844, with a Short Account of His Predecessors in the Ballad & Chapbook Trade*, Singing Tree Press, 1969; *The History of Street Literature*, Singing Tree Press, 1973; (editor and reviser) H. T. Dave, *The Life and Philosophy of Shree Swaminaravan*, Allen & Unwin, 1974; (editor) Pandit Gopi Krishna, *Higher Consciousness*, Julian Press, 1974.

Author of forewords for more than seventy reprints, including the following; all published by University Books except as indicated: Rupert T. Gould, *Oddities*, 1965; Ralph Shirley, *The Mystery of the Human Double*, 1965; W. J. Kilner, *The Human Aura*, 1965; (postface to Volume II) Godfrey Higgins, *Anacalypsis*, 1965; A. E. (pseudonym of George William Russell), *The Candle of Vision*, 1965; G.R.S. Mead, *Apollonius of Tyana*, 1966; W. Y. Evans-Wentz, *The Fairy-Faith in Celtic Countries*, 1966; Nandor Fodor, *Encyclopedia of Psychic Science*, 1966; H. E. Rollins, *An Analytical Index to the Ballad Entries, 1557-1709, in the Registers of the Company of Stationers of London*,

Folklore Associates, 1967; S. Baring-Gould, *Curious Myths of the Middle Ages*, 1967; Charles Hindley, *Curiosities of Street Literature*, John Foreman, 1967; F. E. Willard and M. A. Livermore, *A Woman of the Century*, Gale, 1967; *The Works of William Hone*, Gale, 1967.

Recordings; all released by Folkways Records: (Compiler and author of booklet and notes) "Vox Humana: Experiments of Alfred Wolfsohn in Extension of Human Vocal Range"; (compiler and author of booklet and notes) "Yoga Vedanta: Documentary of Life in an Indian Ashram"; (author of booklet) "John Jacob Niles Sings". Contributor of articles to *Film and Television Technician, Books* (journals of National Book League), *New Society, Mountain Life and Work*, and to various folk music magazines.

WORK IN PROGRESS: Popular Broadside Ballads; books on yoga and on occultism; editing an English translation of the Hindu scripture *Vachanamrita,* and encyclopedias of allusions and of occultism.

SIDELIGHTS; In 1958 and 1959, Shepard studied Yoga and Hindu metaphysics in India, living in an old temple on the banks of the Ganges River in the foothills of the Himalayas. In 1959 he joined David Regan in his unsuccessful attempt to cross the Atlantic in a 28-foot cutter via the earliest sea route to America (the Viking route). During the voyage, Shepard acted as cinematographer, cook, and carpenter. Shepard owns a unique collection of broadside ballads "and related ephemera," and was an early populariser of the Kentucky Mountain dulcimer in Britain. In 1963 he presented a lecture, "John Jacob Niles, American Folk Singer," supplemented with recordings and broadcast by the British Broadcasting Corp. Third Programme.

*   *   *

SHERIDAN, Marion Campbell

PERSONAL: Born in New Haven, Conn.; daughter of Richard Moylan and Fannie J. (Campbell) Sheridan. *Education:* Columbia University, B.S.; Yale University, M.A., 1928, Ph.D., 1934. *Home:* Lake Shore, 1057 Whitney Ave., Hamden, Conn. 06517.

CAREER: Head of department of English at James Hillhouse High School, New Haven, Conn., 1930-61, director of pilot summer school, 1961-62; self-employed consultant in English, teaching, speaking, and writing, 1961—. Guest lecturer and discussion and conference leader at colleges and universities, 1930—. Examiner, College Entrance Examination Board, 1937-46; chairman of School and College Conference on English, 1944-46, archivist, 1962; chairman of World Heritage Film and Book Program, National Advisory Committee of Educators, 1962; member of Connecticut Service Council Steering Committee for WNHC-TV, Channel 8, 1963-66; liaison, A.A.U.W. and WTNH-TV, Channel 8, 1966—.

MEMBER: National Council of Teachers of English (president, 1949), American Association of University Women (president, Connecticut division, 1954-58; president, New Haven branch, 1963-65), English-Speaking Union of the United States (New York), New England Association of Teachers of English (president, 1935, 1952; life member), Connecticut Council of Teachers of English, New Haven Colony Historical Society (life member), Columbia Scholastic Press Advisers Association (life member). *Awards, honors:* Gold Key of Columbia Scholastic Press Association, 1949; National Council of Teachers of English citation, 1958, for outstanding contribution to teaching of English in secondary schools, grant, 1962-63; Yale University

Distinguished Teacher Award, 1962; Educational Press of America Award, 1973.

WRITINGS: (With W. Wilbur Hatfield and Laurence B. Goodrich) *Senior English Activities*, Book 3 and Workbook, American Book Co., 1939; (editor) William Saroyan, *The Human Comedy* (text edition), Harcourt, 1944; (contributor) Edward J. Gordon and Edward S. Noyes, editors, *Essays on the Teaching of English*, Appleton, 1960; (contributor) Robert C. Pooley, editor, *Perspectives on English*, Appleton, 1960; (with Harold H. Owen, Jr., Fred Marcus, and Ken Macrorie) *The Motion Picture and the Teaching of English*, Appleton, 1965; (contributor) *Educational Horizons*, Spring, 1972.

Collaborator with Thomas Clark Pollock and others in "Macmillan English Series," four books, for grades nine-twelve, Macmillan, 1955, 1961, 2nd revised edition, 1964. Chairman of advisory committee on "Writing," "STEP Tests," and "Dictionary Test," for Cooperative Test Division, Educational Testing Service. Contributor of articles and reviews to professional journals. Member of advisory editorial board for Scholastic Magazines, 1942-43.

WORK IN PROGRESS: A history of the teaching of reading in New Haven, Conn., 1938-1930.

SIDELIGHTS: Marion Sheridan has traveled around the world and in Europe and Australia as delegate to international conferences.

*   *   *

SHERIF, Carolyn W(ood)   1922-

PERSONAL: Born June 26, 1922, in Loogootee, Ind.; daughter of Lawrence Anselm (a teacher) and Bonny (Williams) Wood; married Muzafer Sherif (a social psychologist and author), December 29, 1945; children: Sue, Joan, Ann. *Education:* Purdue University, B.S., 1943; University of Iowa, M.A., 1944; University of Texas, Ph.D., 1961. *Home:* 507 Shannon Lane, State College, Pa. *Office:* Department of Psychology, Pennsylvania State University, University Park, Pa. 16801.

CAREER: Audience Research, Inc., Princeton, N.J., assistant to research director, 1944-45; private practice as psychologist, 1946-59; University of Oklahoma, Norman, research associate, Institute of Group Relations, 1959-66, adjunct assistant professor, Medical School, 1963, associate professor, 1963-64; Pennsylvania State University, University Park, visiting associate professor, 1965-66, associate professor, 1966-70, professor of psychology, 1970—. Visiting professor, Cornell University, 1969-70. *Member:* American Psychological Association, American Sociological Association, American Association for the Advancement of Science, Sigma Xi.

WRITINGS—With husband, Muzafer Sherif: *Groups in Harmony and Tension*, Harper, 1953; *An Outline of Social Psychology*, Harper, 1956; *Intergroup Conflict and Cooperation*, University of Oklahoma Press, 1961; *Reference Groups*, Harper, 1964; *Attitude and Attitude Change*, Saunders, 1965; (editor) *Problems of Youth*, Aldine, 1965; (editor) *Attitudes, Ego-Involvement and Change*, Wiley, 1967; *Social Psychology*, Harper, 1969; *Social and Personal Psychology*, Harper, 1975.

*   *   *

SHERMAN, Murray H(erbert)   1922-

PERSONAL: Born August 19, 1922, in New York, N.Y.; son of Harry (a retailer) and Gussie (Silverman) Sherman;

married Helene Zeeman (a college teacher), April 8, 1951. *Education:* Wayne State University, A.B., 1943; Columbia University, Ph.D., 1951. *Religion:* Hebrew. *Home and office:* 350 Central Park West, New York, N.Y. 10025.

CAREER: Clinical psychologist at Harlem Valley State Hospital, 1947-48, Bellevue Psychiatric Hospital, 1948-49, and Education Clinic, City College (now City College of the City University of New York), New York, N.Y., 1949-51; chief civilian psychologist at U.S. Naval Hospital, Camp LeJeune, N.C., 1951-53; psychologist for New York Magistrates Courts, 1954-57, Children's Court, 1957-62, and for Jewish Family Service, 1962-71; Roosevelt Hospital, New York, N.Y., director of family therapy, 1972-74; psychologist in private practice, New York, N.Y., 1950—. Lecturer at Hunter College, 1960-62, and Yeshiva University, 1960. *Military service:* U.S. Army, 1943-45; became staff sergeant; received Purple Heart. *Member:* American Psychological Association, National Psychological Association for Psychoanalysis, New York Society for Clinical Psychologists, New York State Psychological Association.

WRITINGS: (Editor) *A Rorschach Reader,* International Universities, 1960; (editor) *Psychoanalysis in America: Historical Perspectives,* C. C Thomas, 1966; (co-author) *Roles and Paradigms in Psychotherapy,* Grune, 1968. Editor, *Psychoanalytic Review.*

WORK IN PROGRESS: A biography of Theodor Reik.

*   *   *

SHERMAN, Theodore A(llison)   1901-

PERSONAL: Born December 1, 1901, in Schuyler, Neb.; son of Eugene Buren (an educator) and Maud (Shaw) Sherman; married Harriet Bliss, May, 1925 (deceased); married Eleanor Walker, January, 1948; children: Marian Alma (Mrs. Robert Mitchell). *Education:* Attended University of Idaho, 1920-23, M.A., 1933; Stanford University, B.A., 1924. *Home:* 834 North Grant, Moscow, Idaho.

CAREER: High school teacher and principal in Payette, Idaho, 1924-31; University of Idaho, Moscow, instructor, 1931-43, acting graduate manager, 1943-46, assistant professor, 1946-50, associate professor, 1950-55, professor of English, 1955-67. *Member:* Modern Language Association of America, National Council of Teachers of English.

WRITINGS: Modern Technical Writing, Prentice-Hall, 1955, 3rd edition, 1975.

*   *   *

SHIBUTANI, Tamotsu   1920-

PERSONAL: Born October 15, 1920, in Stockton, Calif.; son of Naonosuke (an insurance agent) and Taka (Aihara) Shibutani; married Tomika Harano, April 6, 1942 (divorced March 22, 1969). *Education:* Stockton Junior College, student, 1939-40; University of California, Berkeley, A.B., 1942; University of Chicago, A.M., 1944, Ph.D., 1948. *Politics:* Independent. *Home:* 136 Olive Mill Rd., Santa Barbara, Calif. 93108. *Office:* University of California, Santa Barbara, Calif. 93106.

CAREER: University of Chicago, Chicago, Ill., instructor in sociology, 1948-51; University of California, Berkeley, assistant professor of sociology, 1951-57; University of California, Santa Barbara, associate professor, 1962-66, professor of sociology, 1966—. *Military service:* U.S. Army, 1944-46. *Member:* American Sociological Association, American Association for the Advancement of Science.

WRITINGS: Society and Personality, Prentice-Hall, 1961; (with Kian M. Kwan) *Ethnic Stratification,* Macmillan, 1965; *Improvised News: A Sociological Study of Rumor,* Bobbs-Merrill, 1966; (editor) *Human Nature and Collective Behavior: Papers in Honor of Herbert Blumer,* Prentice-Hall, 1970. Contributor of articles and reviews to professional journals.

WORK IN PROGRESS: The Derelicts of Company K: A Chronicle of Demoralization and Anarchy; Sociology: The Study of Social Processes, completion expected in 1976; a sociological study of crowd phenomena.

*   *   *

SHIDLE, Norman G(lass)   1895-

PERSONAL: Surname is pronounced *Shy*-dle; born July 7, 1895, in Pittsburgh, Pa.; son of Harry Benton and Blanche (Glass) Shidle; married Ethelwyn Bower, 1919 (deceased); married Jan E. Meeter Howell, 1961. *Education:* Swarthmore College, A.B., 1917. *Politics:* Republican. *Residence:* Roxbury, Conn. 06783.

CAREER: Ronald Press, New York, N.Y., member of editorial staff, 1918-20; *Automotive Industries,* member of editorial staff, 1920-21, managing editor, 1921-24, editor, 1924-28; Chilton Co. (publishers), New York, N.Y., and Philadelphia, Pa., editor and member of board of directors, 1928-33; Society of Automotive Engineers, New York, N.Y., manager of publications and editor of *SAE Journal,* 1933-63; writer and consultant. Director of Lewis Corp., Woodbury, Conn.; trustee, Engineering Index, New York, N.Y. Seminar lecturer at University of Wisconsin, Purdue University, New York University, and other schools; counselor for New York Man Marketing Clinic and Brookfield (Conn.) Craft Center; chairman of board, Alumnae Advisory Center of New York; member of Swarthmore College Alumni Council. *Member:* American Business Writing Association, Society of Automotive Engineers, National Audubon Society, Overseas Press Club (New York), Phi Sigma Kappa. *Awards, honors:* LL.D., Occidental College, 1952.

WRITINGS: Finding Your Job, Ronald, 1921; (with T. A. Bissell) *Motor Vehicles and Their Engines,* Van Nostrand, 1941; *Getting Along with Others in Business,* B. C. Forbes & Sons, 1947; *Clear Writing for Easy Reading,* McGraw, 1951; *Instincts in Action,* Society of Automotive Engineers, 1961; *The Art of Successful Communication,* McGraw, 1965; *Formula for Harmonious Action,* Dorrance, 1971. Contributor to *Encyclopaedia Britannica, American People's Encyclopedia,* and *Grolier Encyclopedia;* contributor of several hundred articles to *Forbes' Magazine, McCall's,* and to industrial and technical magazines in the United States and Europe. Associate editor, *Journal of Business Communication;* member of editorial advisory board, Phi Sigma Kappa *Signet.*

WORK IN PROGRESS: Writing on trends and needs in engineering education, and on the individual in our collective economy.

*   *   *

SHILLINGLAW, Gordon   1925-

PERSONAL: Born July 26, 1925, in Albany, N.Y.; son of James McCombe (a prison inspector) and Margaret Blanche (Stephens) Shillinglaw; married Barbara Ann Cross, June 24, 1950; children: James McCombe II, Laura Cross. *Education:* Brown University, A.B. (magna cum laude), 1945; University of Rochester, M.S., 1948; Harvard University, Ph.D., 1952. *Office:* 621 Uris Hall, Columbia University, New York, N.Y. 10027.

CAREER: Hamilton College, Clinton, N.Y., assistant professor of economics, 1951-52; Joel Dean Associates, Yonkers, N.Y., consulting associate, 1952-55; Eliot-Pearson School, Medford, Mass., business manager and assistant treasurer, 1955-60; Massachusetts Institute of Technology, School of Industrial Management, Cambridge, assistant professor of industrial management, 1955-61; Columbia University, Graduate School of Business, New York, N.Y., associate professor, 1961-66, professor of accounting, 1966—. L'Institut pour l'Etude des Methodes de Direction de l'Enterprise, Lausanne, Switzerland, professor, 1964-65, 1967-69. Instructor in executive development programs at various universities. *Military service:* U.S. Navy, 1943-46. U.S. Naval Reserve, 1946-59; became lieutenant junior grade. *Member:* National Association of Accountants, American Accounting Association (vice-president, 1966-67), Financial Executives Institute, Phi Beta Kappa, Beta Gamma Sigma.

WRITINGS: Cost Accounting: Analysis and Control, Irwin, 1961, 3rd edition, 1972; (with Myron J. Gordon) *Accounting: A Management Approach,* 5th edition, Irwin, 1974.

Contributor: Robert I. Dickey, editor, *Accountants' Cost Handbook,* 2nd edition, Ronald, 1960; J. L. Dohr and others, editors, *Accounting and the Law: Cases and Materials,* 3rd edition, Foundation Press, 1964; Charles P. Bonini, Robert K. Jaedicke, and Harvey M. Wagner, editors, *Management Controls: New Directions in Basic Research,* McGraw, 1964; Morton Backer, editor, *Modern Accounting Theory,* 2nd edition, Prentice-Hall, 1966; Sidney Davidson, editor, *Handbook of Modern Accounting,* McGraw, 1970. Contributor of lesser sections to other books and to *Encyclopaedia Britannica*; author or co-author of American Management Association bulletins; contributor of about twenty-five articles and reviews to management and accounting journals.

WORK IN PROGRESS: A revision of *Cost Accounting: Analysis and Control*; research on international comparability of financial statements.

* * *

SHIRES, Henry M(illis) 1913-

PERSONAL: Born January 28, 1913, in Bernardsville, N.J.; son of Henry Herbert (a clergyman) and Mable (Millis) Shires; married Loie Judkins, June 29, 1941; children: Stephanie, Elizabeth, Henry. *Education:* Stanford University, B.A., 1934; Church Divinity School of the Pacific, B.D., 1937; Pacific School of Religion, Th.D., 1946; additional graduate study at Oxford University, 1951-52, American School of Oriental Research, Jerusalem, and in Florence, Italy. *Home:* 170 Brattle St., Cambridge, Mass. 02138. *Office:* Episcopal Divinity School, 99 Brattle St., Cambridge, Mass. 02138.

CAREER: Clergyman of Protestant Episcopal Church; rector of Episcopal church in San Leandro, Calif., 1940-42, in Alameda, Calif., 1942-51, in Los Altos, Calif., 1952-54; Episcopal Divinity School, Cambridge, Mass., assistant professor, 1954-57, professor of New Testament, 1957—. Church Divinity School of the Pacific, instructor, 1937-51. *Member:* American Society of Church History, Society of Biblical Literature, Alameda Kiwanis Club (president, 1950), Phi Beta Kappa. *Awards, honors:* D.D., Church Divinity School of the Pacific, 1963.

WRITINGS: The Eschatology of Paul, Westminster, 1966; *Finding the Old Testament in the New,* Westminster, 1974. Contributor to religious journals.

SIDELIGHTS: Henry Shires is competent in French.

* * *

SHIRK, Evelyn Urban 1918-

PERSONAL: Born September 12, 1918, in Flushing, Long Island, N.Y.; daughter of Amos Urban (a sales manager) and Mary Jane (Welchans) Shirk; married Justus Buchler (a professor of philosophy), February 20, 1943; children: Katherine Urban. *Education:* Wilson College, A.B. (cum laude), 1940; Columbia University, M.A., 1942, Ph.D., 1949. *Religion:* Ethical Culture Society. *Home:* 3 Homestead Ave., Garden City, Long Island, N.Y. *Office:* Department of Philosophy, Hofstra University, Hempstead, N.Y.

CAREER: Brooklyn College (now Brooklyn College of the City University of New York), Brooklyn, N.Y., instructor in philosophy, 1942-48; Hofstra University, Hempstead, N.Y., assistant professor, 1949-53, associate professor, 1953-63, professor of philosophy, 1963—. *Member:* American Philosophical Association, American Association of University Professors, American Association of University Women, Ethical Society of Long Island, Phi Beta Kappa.

WRITINGS: (Editor with husband, Justus Buchler and J. H. Randall, Jr.) *Readings in Philosophy,* Barnes & Noble, 1946; *Adventurous Idealism: The Philosophy of Alfred Lloyd,* University of Michigan Press, 1952; *The Ethical Dimension,* Appleton, 1963; (editor with Esther Kronovet) *In Pursuit of Awareness: The College Student in the Modern World,* Appleton, 1967. Contributor of articles and reviews to philosophy and education journals.

SIDELIGHTS: Evelyn Shirk told *CA*: "[I] rebuilt and restored an antique house in Lyndonville, Vt., where I spend my summers in writing, gardening, cooking, handcrafts, and all the things women like to do but for which I have no time during the academic year. I have won prizes at the Caledonia County Fair for jellies made out of things that grow wild."

* * *

SHIRK, George H(enry) 1913-

PERSONAL: Born May 1, 1913, in Oklahoma City, Okla.; son of John H. (an attorney) and Carrie (Hinderer) Shirk. *Education:* University of Oklahoma, A.B., 1934, LL.B., 1936. *Politics:* Democrat. *Religion:* Protestant. *Home:* 5201 Vernon Rd., Oklahoma City, Okla. 73111.

CAREER: Admitted to the Bar of Oklahoma State, 1936, and the Bar of U.S. Supreme Court, 1954; attorney at law, Oklahoma City, Okla., 1936—. Mayor of Oklahoma City, 1964-67. President of Oklahoma City Safety Council, 1959-62, Salvation Army Advisory Board 1972—, and Oklahoma City Appeals Review Board, 1973—. Member of executive committee, United Fund of Oklahoma City; member of Oklahoma Civil War Centennial Commission. *Military service:* U.S. Army, 1940-45; received Bronze Star, Legion of Merit, Legion of Honor, Croix de guerre avec palme. *Member:* Company of Military Collectors and Historians, Oklahoma Historical Society (president, 1958—), Oklahoma Philatelic Society (president, 1950), Phi Beta Kappa, Phi Delta Phi, Phi Delta Theta, Masons, Shrine, Bachelors Club of Oklahoma City (former president), Men's Dinner Club.

WRITINGS: (Editor with Muriel H. Wright) *The Rambler in Oklahoma* (Latrobe's tour with Washington Irving), Harlow Publishing, 1955; *Along the Washington Irving Trail in Oklahoma*, Oklahoma Historical Society, 1957; *Oklahoma Place Names*, University of Oklahoma Press, 1965, revised edition, 1974. Regular contributor to *Chronicles of Oklahoma*.

* * *

SHONTZ, Franklin C(urtis) 1926-

PERSONAL: Born December 9, 1926, in Cleveland, Ohio; son of Curtis Groner (in metallurgy) and Ida (Painter) Shontz; married Nancy Kimball, August 7, 1954; children: Jennifer, Sally, Kimball Curtis. *Education:* Western Reserve University (now Case Western Reserve University), B.S., 1950, M.A., 1953, Ph.D., 1955. *Religion:* Unitarian Universalist. *Home:* 514 Park Hill Ter., Lawrence, Kan. 66044. *Office:* University of Kansas, Lawrence, Kan.

CAREER: Western Reserve University (now Case Western Reserve University), Cleveland, Ohio, lecturer in psychology, 1953-60; Highland View Hospital, Cleveland, Ohio, chief psychologist, 1954-60; University of Kansas, Lawrence, 1960—, began as assistant professor, professor of psychology, 1966—. Consultant to Veterans Administration Center, Wadsworth, Kan., and Greater Kansas City Mental Health Foundation. *Military service:* U.S. Army, 1945-46. *Member:* American Psychological Association, American Association for the Advancement of Science, Midwestern Psychological Association, Phi Beta Kappa, Sigma Xi. *Awards, honors:* Research award of American Personnel and Guidance Association for research in rehabilitation, 1960.

WRITINGS: Research Methods in Personality, Appleton, 1965; *Perceptual and Cognitive Aspects of Body Experience*, Academic Press, 1969; (with W. Epstein) *Psychology in Progress*, Holt, 1971; *Psychological Aspects of Physical Illness and Health*, Macmillan, in press. Contributor to professional journals.

WORK IN PROGRESS: Research on rehabilitation of persons with physical disabilities, and on body perception and cognition.

* * *

SHOSTAK, Jerome 1913-

PERSONAL: Born June 24, 1913, in Brooklyn, N.Y.; son of Joseph (a salesman) and Sarah (Levine) Shostak; married Edna Schiff (a teacher), 1937. *Education:* City College (now City College of the City University of New York), New York, N.Y., B.A., 1933, M.S., 1934; New York University, guidance certification courses. *Politics:* Independent. *Religion:* Jewish. *Home and office:* 2810 Cedar Lane, Lake Luzerne, N.Y. 12846.

CAREER: New York (N.Y.) Board of Education, 1936—, high school teacher of English, later guidance counselor, and supervisor of guidance in District 27, Queens. *Member:* National Council of Teachers of English, American Personnel and Guidance Association.

WRITINGS: (Co-author) *High School Entrance*, Barron's, 1960; *English Achievements*, Barron's, 1962; "English Workshop Series," Oxford Book Co., 1964; "Learning Words Series," Oxford Book Co., 1964; (co-author) *Preparation for College Boards*, Pocket Books, 1965; *High School Entrance Examinations*, Barron's, 1966; (co-author) *Preparation for Civil Service Tests*, Bantam,

1967; *Concise Dictionary of Current American Usage*, Pocket Books, 1968; "Vocabulary Workshop Series," Sadlier, 1970; *Read, Write, React*, Sadlier, 1974.

WORK IN PROGRESS: Standard English Workbook for Sadlier.

* * *

SHUMWAY, Mary L. 1926-

PERSONAL: Born August 21, 1926, in Portage, Wis.; daughter of Oliver Arden (a carpenter) and Margaret (Tolleth) Shumway. *Education:* University of Chicago, A.B., 1957, also graduate study, 1956-57; San Francisco State College (now University), M.A., 1965; University of Denuer, Ph.D., 1971. *Office.* Department of English, University of Wisconsin, Stevens Point, Wis. 54481.

CAREER: George Williams College, Chicago, Ill., instructor in English and anthropology, 1957; San Francisco Art Institute College, San Francisco, Calif., instructor in English and social sciences, and dean of women, 1960-64; University of Wisconsin, Stevens Point, professor of English, 1965—. *Awards, honors:* Academy of American Poets prize, 1965, 1969; Robert Frost fellowship in poetry, 1969; MacDowell fellow, 1973, 1974.

WRITINGS: Song of the Archer, and Other Poems, Regnery, 1964; *Headlands*, Sono Nis, 1972; *Mindar and the Gandy Dancer*, Konglomerati Press, 1975. Work represented in many anthologies, including: *New Poetry Out of Wisconsin*, Stanton & Lee, 1969; *New Voices in American Poetry*, Winthrop, 1973; *Heartland II: Poets of the Midwest*, Northern Illinois University Press, 1975. Contributor to *Cimarron Review, Commonweal, Denver Quarterly*, and other journals.

* * *

SHUSTER, Albert H., Jr. 1917-

PERSONAL: Born May 7, 1917, in Philadelphia, Pa.; children: Patricia Anne, Doris Jean, Albert III. *Education:* Lynchburg College, B.A., 1943; George Peabody College for Teachers, M.A., 1946; University of Virginia, Ed.D., 1955. *Home:* Briarwood Dr., Athens, Ohio 45701.

CAREER: Ohio University, Athens, assistant professor, 1955-58, associate professor, 1958-63, professor of elementary education, 1963—, chairman of department, 1966—. *Member:* Phi Delta Kappa, Kappa Delta Pi.

WRITINGS: (With Wilson F. Wetzler) *Leadership in Elementary Administration and Supervision*, Houghton, 1958; (with Milton E. Ploghoft) *The Emerging Elementary Curriculum*, C. E. Merrill, 1963, revised edition, 1970; (with Ploghoft) *Social Science Education in the Elementary School*, C. E. Merrill, 1971, revised edition, 1975; (with Don Stewart) *The Principle and the Autonomous Elementary School*, C. E. Merrill, 1973.

* * *

SIDERS, Ellis L(eroy) 1920-

PERSONAL: Born December 4, 1920, in Delta, Iowa; son of Leo Joseph and Maud (Bowen) Siders; married Gertrude Litzenberg, May 28, 1942 (deceased); children: Barry Lee. *Education:* Simpson College, B.S., 1946; Stanford University, M.A., 1950. *Politics:* Independent. *Religion:* Protestant. *Home:* 23 Marques Place, San Ramon, Calif. 94583.

CAREER: General Motors Corp., Buick Motor Division, Flint, Mich., junior cost accountant, 1943-47; Coast Counties Gas & Electric Co., Santa Cruz, Calif., administrative assistant, 1947-49; Montgomery Ward & Co., Sacramento, Calif., store accountant, 1951-52; H. C. Shaw Co., Stockton, Calif., secretary and controller, 1952-54; Allis-Chalmers Manufacturing Co., Emeryville, Calif., farm equipment sales manager, 1954-58; Merritt College, Oakland, Calif., professor of business, 1958-68; Canal Zone College, Balboa, assistant professor, 1968-70; Merritt College, Oakland, Calif., professor of business, 1970—, and chairman of department of business and related occupations. *Military service:* U.S. Naval Reserve, 1944-46. *Member:* California Teachers Association, Faculty Association of the California Community Colleges, Pi Gamma Mu.

WRITINGS: Mathematics for Modern Business and Industry, Holt, 1964; *New College Arithmetic,* San Ramon Press, 1973. Contributor to *Western Farm Equipment.*

* * *

SIEGEL, Eli 1902-

PERSONAL: Born August 16, 1902, in Dvinsk, Latvia; brought to United States in 1905; son of Mendel and Sarah (Einhorn) Siegel; married Martha Baird (a writer), 1944. *Education:* Attended Baltimore City College, 1916-19. *Residence:* New York, N.Y. *Address:* c/o Definition Press, 141 Greene St., New York, N.Y. 10012.

CAREER: Associated with V. F. Calverton in founding of *Modern Quarterly,* 1923; columnist for *Baltimore American,* 1925; book reviewer for the *Literary Review of New York Evening Post,* 1926, and *Scribner's,* 1931-35; conductor of poetry readings at the Troubadour, Village Mill, Village Vanguard, and other New York City establishments, 1926-36; founder and teacher of Aesthetic Realism (defined as "the seeing of the world, art and self as explaining each other: each is the aesthetic oneness of opposites"), 1940—; author and poet. *Awards, honors:* Nation Poetry Prize, 1925, for "Hot Afternoons Have Been in Montana," the title poem of the collection which was nominated for the National Book Award in poetry, 1958.

WRITINGS: The Aesthetic Method in Self-Conflict, Definition Press, 1946; *Psychiatry, Economics, Aesthetics,* Definition Press, 1946; *Is Beauty the Making One of Opposites?* (broadside), Terrain Gallery, 1955; *Hot Afternoons Have Been in Montana: Poems,* Definition Press, 1957; *Williams' Poetry Talked About, and William Carlos Williams Present and Talking: 1952,* Terrain Gallery, 1964; *A Rosary of Evil,* Terrain Gallery, 1964; *Damned Welcome: Aesthetic Realism Maxims,* Terrain Gallery, 1964; *What's There—Lou Bernstein's Photographs,* Terrain Gallery, 1965; *James and the Children: A Consideration of Henry James's The Turn of the Screw,* Definition Press, 1968; *Hail, American Development* (poems), Definition Press, 1968; *Goodbye Profit System,* Definition Press, 1970; *The Williams-Siegel Documentary,* edited by Martha Baird, Definition Press, 1970; *Children's Guide to Parents and Other Matters,* Definition Press, 1971; *The Frances Sanders Lesson and Two Related Works,* Definition Press, 1974.

Work represented in many anthologies, including: *City in All Directions,* edited by Arnold Adoff, Macmillan, 1969; *Pith and Vinegar,* edited by William Cole, Simon & Schuster, 1969; *100 American Poems,* edited by Selden Rodman, New American Library, 1972; *Half Serious,* edited by William Cole, Eyre Methuen, 1973; *America: A Prophecy,* edited by Rothenberg and Quasha, Random House, 1973.

Other writings: A free verse translation of the Hebrew Kaddish, first published in *Commentary,* 1953; "Shakespeare's Hamlet: Revisited," 1963, performed in thirteen parts and also in a one-evening version for more than a year at the Terrain Gallery; poems, articles, and reviews in *Nation, New Republic, Hound & Horn, Harper's Bazaar, Poetry* (Chicago), *Times Literary Supplement* (London), *New Mexico Quarterly, New York Quarterly, Poor Old Tired Horse,* and other publications.

WORK IN PROGRESS: The Aesthetic Nature of the World.

SIDELIGHTS: William Carlos Williams believed that Siegel "belongs in the very first rank of our living artists," and credited him with important technical innovations in poetry. Siegel developed a theory of "Aesthetic Realism" (see also *CAREER*) which is, he says, "about how the having-to-do-withness or relation of people, is they, is themselves." His subject has always been experience. Another technical interest has been the writing of extremely short poems. His poem "One Question/I—/Why?" is reputedly the shortest poem ever written.

Howard Nemerov calls Siegel's manner "sometimes rhapsodic and repetitive, sometimes dry and quite funny." On the whole, however, Nemerov believes that the poems "mostly do not do their work, they are too easy, assume too much of what is to be demonstrated, and substitute too often the splendid intention for the thing made." Reviewing *Hail, American Development,* Kenneth Rexroth writes: "Odd he may be; naive he is not, and he is very far from being unlearned or devoid of insight into the works of the great dead.... His translations of Baudelaire and his commentaries on them rank him with the most understanding of the Baudelaire critics in any language."

BIOGRAPHICAL/CRITICAL SOURCES: Karl Shapiro, *In Defense of Ignorance,* Random House, 1960; Howard Nemerov, *Poetry and Fiction,* Rutgers University Press, 1963; *Poetry,* November, 1968; *New York Times Book Review,* March 23, 1969; *New Republic,* December 12, 1970.

* * *

SIEGEL, Jacob 1913-
(Jack Siegel)

PERSONAL: Born February 14, 1913, in New York, N.Y.; son of Reuben and Rose (Lippman) Siegel; married Fritzi Jokl (an opera director), January 31, 1942. *Education:* City College (now City College of the City University of New York), B.S.S., 1935. *Politics:* Independent. *Religion:* Jewish. *Home:* 240 West 75th St., New York, N.Y. *Agent:* Ben Kamsler, 8523 Sunset Blvd. W., Hollywood, Calif. 90069.

CAREER: Teacher, 1935-39; organization executive, 1945—, specifically, associate director of special projects, Jewish Theological Seminary, New York, N.Y., 1957-62, executive vice-president, Jewish Telegraphic Agency, New York, N.Y., 1963—. *Military service:* U.S. Army, Military Intelligence Service, 1943-45; received five campaign stars for service in European theater. *Member:* Authors League of America.

WRITINGS—Under name Jack Siegel: *Squeegee,* Horizon, 1965; *Dawn at Kahlenberg,* Pyramid Books, 1966; *The Ruby,* Pyramid Books, 1972. Also author of *The Groovy Genius.*

WORK IN PROGRESS: Three novels and two playscripts.

SIDELIGHTS: Jacob Siegel told *CA*: "[I] can't offer anything original on motivation; every writer comes to God in his own way. . . . [I] speak French and German and have traveled over a good part of the western world, also the eastern and Middle East. . . . I think a writer must know and identify with events as well as people."

* * *

SIKES, Herschel Moreland 1928-

PERSONAL: Born June 6, 1928, in Lake City, Fla.; son of Julian R. and Lamey (Witt) Sikes. *Education:* University of Florida, A.B. (cum laude), 1952; New York University, M.A., 1953, Ph.D. (with honors), 1957. *Politics:* Democrat. *Religion:* Protestant.

CAREER: New York University, New York, N.Y., instructor in English, 1954-57; Hunter College of the City University of New York, New York, N.Y., instructor, 1957-61, assistant professor, 1962-65, associate professor of English, 1965—. Fulbright professor, University of Zaragoza, Zaragoza, Spain, 1963-64. Lecturer on literary topics in Europe, Tunisia, and America. Consultant to Premier Books and Doubleday & Co., Inc. *Military service:* U.S. Army, 1946-48; became staff sergeant. *Member:* Modern Language Association of America, National Council of Teachers of English, Charles Lamb Society, Friends of the Library (New York University), Young Democrats, Sigma Tau Delta. *Awards, honors:* Research fellow, Newberry Library, 1960; George Shuster faculty research grant, 1961.

WRITINGS: (Contributor) *The Quest for Utopia*, Henry Schuman, 1951; *The Poetic Theory and Practice of Keats*, Iowa State University Press, 1959; *William Hone: Regency Patriot, Parodist, and Pamphleteer*, [Chicago], 1961; (editor) *The Hazlitt Sampler*, Premier Books, 1961. Author of other literary studies published by New York Public Library and Newberry Library. Contributor to *Collier's Encyclopedia* and *Modern Language Quarterly*. Associate editor, *Seventeenth-Century News*.

WORK IN PROGRESS: The Letters of William Hazlitt; a critical edition of Thomas De Quincy's *The Confessions of an English Opium Eater and Other Essays*; *Shelley and Spain*; *Florida Fiction*; and a book on the Romantic poets.

SIDELIGHTS: Sikes grew up "with books in a family of vivid story tellers (French, Spanish, German)." He collects travel books about Florida, his native state, and hopes someday to do a study of Jean Ribaut and the French in Florida.†

* * *

SILVA, Julio A(lberto) 1933-

PERSONAL: Born November 6, 1933, in Montevideo, Uruguay; son of Francisco (a colonel in the Uruguayan Army and mathematician) and Yolanda Silva. *Education:* University of Uruguay, B.Arch., 1957; Massachusetts Institute of Technology, M.Arch., 1962, postgraduate student, 1963-64. *Office:* Corporacion Venezolana de Guayana, Apartado 7000, Caracas, Venezuela.

CAREER: Cobas, Silva, Veira and Agrelo (engineering and architecture design and consulting), Montevideo, Uruguay, partner, 1956-59; Silva, Morixe, Peloche Associates (housing), Montevideo, Uruguay, partner, 1960-61; Carl Koch & Associates, Inc., Cambridge, Mass., architect, designer, 1962-63; Massachusetts Institute of Technology, Cambridge, research staff member working on low cost housing project for Inter-American Program in Civil Engi-

neering, 1963-64; Harvard University-Massachusetts Institute of Technology Joint Center for Urban Studies, Cambridge, Mass., housing adviser to Corporacion Venezolana de Guayana, Caracas, Venezuela, 1964—. United Nations Roster of International Experts, staff member, 1965—. Uruguayan delegate to Pan-American Congress of Architects, Buenos Aires, 1960, Washington, D.C., 1965.

WRITINGS: (With Albert G. H. Dietz and Marcia N. Koth) *Housing in Latin America*, M.I.T. Press, 1965. Author of research studies. Contributor to journals.

WORK IN PROGRESS: A manual for self-help housing construction.

SIDELIGHTS: Silva speaks, reads, and writes Spanish, English, Italian, French, and Portuguese.†

* * *

SILVERN, Leonard C. 1919-

PERSONAL: Born May 20, 1919, in New York, N.Y.; son of Ralph and Augusta (Thaler) Silvern; divorced; children: Ronald. *Education:* Long Island University, B.S., 1946; Columbia University, M.A., 1948, Ed.D., 1952. *Office:* Education and Training Consultants Co., 12121 Wilshire Blvd., Los Angeles, Calif. 90025.

CAREER: U.S. Department of the Navy, training supervisor and coordinator, New York, N.Y., 1939-44, 1946-49; State of New York, Division of Safety, Albany, training director, 1949-55; RAND Corp., resident engineering psychologist at Massachusetts Institute of Technology Lincoln Laboratory, Lexington, Mass., 1955-56; Hughes Aircraft Co., Culver City, Calif., director of education and training research laboratories, 1956-62; Northrop Corp., Hawthorne, Calif., senior scientist, 1962-64; Education and Training Consultants Co., Los Angeles, Calif., principal scientist, 1964-66, vice-president of behavioral systems, 1966-68, president of behavioral systems, 1968—. Adjunct professor at University of Southern California, 1957-65, and University of California, Los Angeles, 1962-69. Consultant, Headquarters, Air Training Command, Randolph Air Force Base, Tex. Licensed amateur radio operator, 1934—, now under call letters K6RXU. *Military service:* U.S. Navy, active duty, 1944-46; served in Pacific theater.

MEMBER: Institute of Electrical and Electronics Engineers (senior member), American Psychological Association, American Radio Relay League. *Awards, honors:* National Society for Programmed Instruction Citation, 1965, for publications on systems engineering of instructional systems.

WRITINGS: Workbook in Methods of Classroom Instruction, U.S. Department of Navy, 1948; *Guide to the State Fire Training Program*, Division of Safety, New York State, 1951; (with B. R. Townsend) *Guide to Fire Mobilization and Mutual Aid Plans in the State of New York*, Division of Safety, 1953; *Textbook in Methods of Instruction*, Hughes Aircraft Co., 1957, reissued as *Methods of Instruction*, Education and Training Consultants, 1962; (with H. S. Lynn) *Guide to Performance Testing*, Hughes Aircraft Co., 1957; *Fundamentals of Teaching Machine and Programmed Learning Systems*, three volumes and guide, Education and Training Consultants, 1964; *Analysis and Synthesis of a Typical Elementary School Instructional System: A Feasibility Study*, Education and Training Consultants, 1965; *Basic Analysis* (programmed course), Education and Training Consultants, 1965; *Administrative Factors Guide to Basic Analysis*, Education and Training

Consultants, 1965; *Systems Engineering of Education*, Education and Training Consultants, 1965; *Systems Engineering Applied to Training*, Gulf Publishing Co., 1972.

Also author of series "Systems Engineering of Education;" published by Education and Training Consultants: Volume I: *Systems Engineering of Learning—Public Education K-12: Analysis*, 1965, reissued as *The Evolution of Systems Thinking in Education*, 1971; Volume III: *Systems Analysis of Synthesis Applied to Occupational Instruction in Secondary Schools*, 1967; Volume IV: *Systems Analysis and Synthesis Applied Quantitatively to Create an Instructional System*, 1969; Volume VI: *Principles of Computer Assisted Instruction System*, 1970; Volume IX: *Anasynthesis of the Education and Training Supersystem*, 1970; Volume X: *Logos Language for Flowchart Modeling*, 1970; Volume XI: *Model for Producing a System*, 1970; Volume VII: *General Systems Model for Effective Curriculums*, 1971; Volume XIII: *Model for Producing Models*, 1971; Volume XII: *Systems Using Feedback*, 1971; Volume V: *Quantitative Concepts for Education Systems*, 1972; Volume XV: *Simulating a Real-Life Problem on the General System Model for Effective Curriculums*, 1972; Volume XVI: *Synthesis As a Process*, 1973; Volume XVII: *System Conceptualizations*, 1973; Volume XVIII: *Roles of Feedback and Feedforward During Simulation*, 1974.

Contributor: S. Margulies and L. D. Eigen, editors, *Applied Programed Instruction*, Wiley, 1962; R. Filep, editor, *Perspectives on Programing*, Macmillan, 1963; *Automated Education Handbook*, Automated Education Center, 1965; W. D. Orr, editor, *Conversational Computers*, Wiley, 1968; K. DeGreene, editor, *Systems Psychology*, McGraw, 1970; Carl Heyel, editor, *International Handbook of Automatic Data Processing*, McGraw, 1974. Also contributor to *Encyclopedia of Management*, and to technical, personnel, and education journals. Reviewer, *Computing Reviews*.

WORK IN PROGRESS: Spanish translations of *The Evolution of Systems Thinking in Education*, and *Systems Engineering Applied to Training*.

* * *

SIMINI, Joseph Peter 1921-

PERSONAL: Surname is pronounced See-*mee*-knee; born February 15, 1921, in Buffalo, N.Y.; son of Paul (a bakery owner) and Ida (Moro) Simini; married second wife, Marcelline T. McDermott, 1968; children: (first marriage) Paul. *Education:* St. Bonaventure University, B.S., 1940, B.B.A., 1949; University of California, Berkeley, M.B.A., 1957. *Politics:* Republican. *Religion:* Roman Catholic. *Home:* 11 Hopkins Alley, San Francisco, Calif. 94131. *Office:* University of San Francisco, 2130 Fulton St., San Francisco, Calif. 94117.

CAREER: Riveter and inspector in war plants, 1940-41; U.S. Navy Department, Bureau of Ordnance, senior inspector of optical material, Buffalo and Rochester, N.Y., 1942-44; Paul Simini Bakery, Buffalo, N.Y., manager, 1946-48; St. Bonaventure University, St. Bonaventure, N.Y., instructor in mathematics, 1948-49; auditor or accountant in San Francisco, Calif., with Di Giorgio Fruit Co., 1950-52, Keaton & Miller, 1952-53, Price Waterhouse & Co., 1953-1954; certified public accountant, state of California, 1954; R. L. Hanlin (certified public accountants), San Francisco, Calif., senior accountant, 1954-55; University of San Francisco, San Francisco, Calif., instructor, 1955-57, assistant professor, 1957-62, associate professor,

1962-66, professor of accounting, 1966—. California State Board of Accountancy, examiner, 1964-69. Holder of patent on trigonometric formula-finding device and inventor of word-building game. *Military service:* U.S. Naval Reserve, 1944-46; became ensign.

MEMBER: American Institute of Certified Public Accountants, American Accounting Association, National Association of Accountants, American Management Association, American Arbitration Association, American Association of University Professors, California Society of Certified Public Accountants, Delta Sigma Pi, Beta Gamma Sigma, Knights of Columbus. *Awards, honors:* Scouters' Key, Boy Scouts of America, 1960; Crown Zellerbach fellowship, 1968; outstanding teacher award from University of San Francisco College of Business, 1973; outstanding teacher award, University of San Francisco, 1975.

WRITINGS: (Co-author) *Principles of Accounting*, Pitman, 1959; *Accounting Made Simple*, Doubleday, 1966; *Accounting Essentials*, Wiley, 1972. Contributor to *Navy Civil Engineer* and accounting journals.

WORK IN PROGRESS: A cost accounting book for non-accountants and a book explaining how to make a million dollars in real estate.

SIDELIGHTS: Simini speaks, reads, and writes Italian. *Avocational interests:* Collecting stamps and swords.

* * *

SIMMONS, James W(illiam) 1936-

PERSONAL: Born April 20, 1936, in London, Ontario, Canada; son of James William (a carpenter) and Sara (Clark) Simmons; married Harriet Xanthakos, August 30, 1964. *Education:* University of Western Ontario, B.Sc., 1959; University of Chicago, M.A., 1962, Ph.D., 1964. *Politics:* New Democratic Party. *Religion:* Agnostic. *Office:* Department of Geography, University of Toronto, Toronto, Ontario, Canada.

CAREER: University of Western Ontario, London, assistant professor, 1963-66, associate professor of geography, 1966-67; University of Toronto, Toronto, Ontario, associate professor of geography, 1967—. Consultant to Metropolitan Toronto Urban Renewal Study, 1964-65. *Member:* Canadian Association of Geographers, Association of American Geographers, Canadian Political Science Association, Regional Science Association.

WRITINGS: The Changing Pattern of Retail Location, Department of Geography, University of Chicago, 1964; *Toronto's Changing Retail Complex*, Department of Geography, University of Chicago, 1966; *Flows in Urban Areas*, Department of Geography, University of Toronto, 1968; (with Robert Simmons) *Urban Canada*, Copp Clark, 1969; *Inter-provincial Interaction Patterns in Canada*, Department of Geography, University of Toronto, 1970; *Patterns of Interaction within Ontario and Quebec*, University of Toronto, Centre for Urban and Community Studies, 1970; *Net Migration Within Metropolitan Toronto*, University of Toronto, Centre for Urban and Community Studies, 1971; (Alan M. Baker) *Household Movement Patterns*, University of Toronto, Centre for Urban and Community Studies, 1972. Contributor to professional journals.†

* * *

SIMMS, Ruth P. 1937-

PERSONAL: Born June 21, 1937, in Savannah, Ga.;

daughter of Wendell Phillip (a storekeeper) and Ella (Jackson) Simms; married James Beclone Hamilton (a chemist), July 3, 1965. *Education:* Talladega College, B.A. (highest honors), 1958; Northwestern University, M.A., 1962, Ph.D., 1966.

CAREER: City Department of Urban Renewal, Savannah, Ga., relocation worker, 1959-60; Iowa State University of Science and Technology, Ames, assistant professor of sociology, 1965—. *Member:* American Sociological Association, Alpha Kappa Delta. *Awards, honors:* Grant from Center for Social Science Research, Northwestern University, for field work in Ghana, West Africa, 1963-64.

WRITINGS: Urbanization in West Africa: A Review of Current Literature, Northwestern University Press, 1965.

WORK IN PROGRESS: Writing and analyzing data from West Africa field research for future publication.†

* * *

SIMON, Matila 1908-

PERSONAL: Born October 11, 1908, in New York, N.Y. *Education:* Hunter College (now Hunter College of the City University of New York), B.A., 1928; Columbia University, M.A., 1929.

CAREER: New York (N.Y.) Board of Education, high school teacher of English, 1932-53; gave up teaching to become an art dealer, critic, and counselor in Europe, 1954-61, serving as art counsel for the Third and Fourth Biennials of American Art, Bordighera, Italy, 1954-57, and as European director of International Print Exchanges, Oregon State University, Corvallis, Ore., 1955-61; full-time writer and translator, New York, N.Y., 1961—. *Awards, honors:* Gold Medal, City of Bordighera, Italy, 1957; Palma d'Oro, International Festival of Humor, 1957.

WRITINGS: (Co-author) *Meisterwerke der Malerei*, Bertelsmann (West Germany), 1965; *Shorewood Art Reference Guide*, Shorewood, 1966, 3rd revised and enlarged edition, 1970; (translator into French) *Jacques Lipchitz*, Shorewood, 1966; *Be At Home in Europe*, Rand McNally, 1969; *The Battle of the Louvre: The Struggle to Save French Art in World War II*, Hawthorn, 1971. Has done translations and research for Time/Life Books, other translations from French and Italian, and translations into French; also writer of radio scripts in the 1940's, and compiler of art catalogues.

WORK IN PROGRESS: A Quick and Easy Guide to Antiques and *Basic Facts in the History of Music*, both for Collier; *Women Behind the Easel.*†

* * *

SIMON, Morton J. 1913-

PERSONAL: Born February 9, 1913, in Jersey City, N.J., married Carol M. Rosenheim, 1939; children: Morton J., Lawrence T. *Education:* Brown University, A.B., 1932; Harvard University, LL.B. (converted to J.D.), 1935. *Home:* 8108 Cadwalader Rd., Elkins Park, Pa. 19117. *Office:* 632 Fox Pavilion, Jenkintown, Pa. 19046.

CAREER: Admitted to Pennsylvania bar, 1935; attorney in private practice in Philadelphia, Pa., serving as counsel for advertising and marketing agencies and communication media. Instructor in legal problems of advertising and communications at Charles Morris Price School of Advertising and Journalism; adjunct lecturer in department of journalism at University of Pennsylvania, and department

of marketing, Temple University; member of advertising legal panels and clinics. *Military service:* U.S. Naval Reserve, active duty, 1942-46; became lieutenant. *Member:* League of Advertising Agencies, Eastern Industrial Advertisers, Television and Radio Advertising Club of Philadelphia; Poor Richard Club, Philmont Country Club, and Locust-Mid City Club (all Philadelphia).

WRITINGS: The Law for Advertising and Marketing, Norton, 1956; *Advertising Truth Book*, Advertising Federation of America, 1960; (contributor) *Advertising: Today/Yesterday/Tomorrow*, Printers' Ink, 1963; (contributor) *New Products Marketing*, Printers' Ink, 1964; *Public Relations Law*, Appleton, 1969; (contributor) Philip Lesly, editor, *Public Relations Handbook*, Prentice-Hall, 1971. Author of textbooks of advertising and marketing law for International Correspondence Schools, 1965. Contributor to advertising and communications periodicals; columnist, "Legal Report," *AIA Newsletter*, 1960-64.

* * *

SIMON, Walter G(old) 1924-

PERSONAL: Born July 11, 1924, in Lincoln, Neb.; son of Harry (a merchant) and Helen (Gold) Simon; married Sara Ipsen, June 21, 1952; married Brooke Williams, July 30, 1971; children: (first marriage) Jennifer Ann, Harry Willard; (second marriage) Mark. *Education:* University of Nebraska, A.B., 1950; University of Wisconsin, M.S., 1951, Ph.D., 1954. *Home:* 2255 Blueball, Boulder, Colo. *Office:* Department of History, University of Colorado, Boulder, Colo.

CAREER: State University of New York, Albany, assistant professor of modern European history, 1954-55; Massachusetts Institute of Technology, Cambridge, instructor in humanities, 1955-56; University of Colorado, Boulder, 1957—, began as assistant professor, became professor of early modern English history and English constitutional history, 1965, chairman of long range planning commission, 1970—. Member, Boulder Urban Renewal Study Commission, 1960-61; chairman, Boulder Human Relations Study Commission, 1961-62. *Military service:* U.S. Army, 1942-46. *Member:* Anglo-American History Association, American Historical Association, Conference on British Studies.

WRITINGS: The Restoration Episcopate, Bookman Associates, 1965. Contributor to journals in his field.

WORK IN PROGRESS: The Popish Plot; and *The Great Reform.*†

* * *

SIMONE, Albert Joseph 1935-

PERSONAL: Born December 16, 1935, in Boston, Mass.; son of Edward Alexander (a businessman) and Mary (DiGiovanni) Simone; married Carolie Menko, July 11, 1959; children: four. *Education:* Tufts University, B.A., 1957; Massachusetts Institute of Technology, Ph.D., 1962. *Religion:* Roman Catholic. *Office:* College of Business Administration, 155 Hanna, University of Cincinnati, Cincinnati, Ohio 45221.

CAREER: Lecturer in economics at Tufts University, Medford, Mass., and Boston University, Boston, Mass., 1958-59; Massachusetts Institute of Technology, Cambridge, instructor, 1959-60; Northeastern University, Boston, Mass., assistant professor of economics, 1960-62; Boston College, Chestnut Hill, Mass., associate professor of business administration, 1962-66, professor of quantitative methods, 1962-68; University of Cincinnati, Cincinnati, Ohio, professor of quantitative analysis and head of department, 1968-72, dean of College of Business Administration, 1972—. Economic consultant, U.S. Office of the Attorney General, 1966-68, State of Massachusetts, 1966-68. *Member:* Academy of Management, American Institute for Decision Sciences (vice-president of publications, 1969-71, for student liaison, 1969-71), American Institute of Industrial Engineers, Association for Computing Machinery, Institute of Management Sciences, American Economic Association, American Statistical Association, Econometric Society, Operations Research Society of America, Phi Beta Kappa.

WRITINGS: (With Robert H. Wessel) *Statistics as Applied to Business and Economics*, Holt, 1964, revised edition, 1965; (with Louis Osgood Kattsoff) *Finite Mathematics with Applications in the Social and Management Sciences*, McGraw, 1965; (with Kattsoff) *Foundations of Contemporary Mathematics with Applications in Social and Management Sciences*, McGraw, 1967; *Probability: An Introduction With Applications*, Allyn & Bacon, 1967. Advisory editor, Holt, Rinehart and Winston, Inc., 1965-70; editor, *Decision Science*, 1969-71.

WORK IN PROGRESS: Modern Mathematics; FORTRAN Programming in Business and Economics.†

*   *   *

SIMONS, David G(oodman) 1922-

PERSONAL: Born June 7, 1922, in Lancaster, Pa.; son of Samuel Shirk (a physician) and Rebecca (Goodman) Simons; married former wife, Vera Habrecht (an artist), June 12, 1959. *Education:* Franklin and Marshall College, B.S., 1943; Jefferson Medical College, M.D., 1946.

CAREER: Licensed to practice medicine in Pennsylvania, 1947; certified as flight surgeon, USAF School of Aerospace Medicine, 1950; diplomate, American Board of Preventive Medicine, 1955. Lancaster General Hospital, Lancaster, Pa., intern, 1947; U.S. Air Force, Medical Corps, regular officer, 1947-65, retiring as lieutenant colonel; U.S. Veterans Administration, Department of Medicine and Surgery, Washington, D.C., chief of research in physical medicine and rehabilitation, 1965—. Air Force assignments included project officer for monkey flights in V-2 rockets, 1948-49; chief of Space Biology Branch, Air Force Missile Development Center in New Mexico, 1953-59; chief of Department of Bioastronautics, Space Medicine Division, Brooks Air Force Base, Tex., 1959-61; and chief of Flight Medicine Branch at Brooks Air Force Base, 1962-65; also associate professor at Baylor University, College of Medicine. Consultant, Texas Institute for Rehabilitation and Research, 1965—. Inventor of anchor button.

MEMBER: American Medical Association, American Congress of Rehabilitation Medicine, Aerospace Medical Association (fellow), American Institute of Aeronautics and Astronautics (fellow; first chairman of human factors division, 1957-58; board of directors, 1959-61), American Astronautical Federation (fellow), Space Medicine Association, American College of Preventive Medicine (fellow), Society for Psychophysiological Research, Society of USAF Flight Surgeons, Institute of Electrical and Electronics Engineers, Association of Military Surgeons of the United States, New York Academy of Sciences.

AWARDS, HONORS—Military: Air Medal, 1952; Distinguished Flying Cross, 1957; Air Force Commendation Medal, 1965. Other awards: Arnold T. Tuttle Award,

Aerospace Medical Association, 1954 and 1957; honorary D.Sc., Franklin and Marshall College, 1957; Gold Medal Award, Federation Aeronautique Internationale, 1957; Prix Henry Delavaulx Medal, 1957; named one of ten outstanding young men in America, U.S. Junior Chamber of Commerce, 1958; Melbourne W. Boynton Award of American Astronautical Federation, 1958; Aerospace Medicine Honor Citation, American Medical Association, 1962; and other awards for high altitude balloon flights and studies of high altitude effects.

WRITINGS: (With D. Schanche) *Manhigh*, Doubleday, 1960.

Contributor: Kenneth F. Gantz, editor, *Man In Space*, Duell, Sloan & Pearce, 1959; O. Benson, editor, *The Physics and Medicine of the Atmosphere and Space*, Wiley, 1960; B. Flaherty, editor, *Psychophysiological Aspects of Space Flight*, Columbia University Press, 1961; P. Campbell, editor, *Medical and Biological Aspects of the Energies of Space*, Columbia University Press, 1961; O. Gauer, editor, *Gravitational Stress in Aerospace Medicine*, Little, Brown, 1961; N. Burns, editor, *Unusual Environments and Human Behavior*, Free Press of Glencoe, 1963; *Handbook of Physiology*, American Physiological Society, 1964. Contributor to *McGraw-Hill Encyclopedia of Science and Technology* and to journals.

WORK IN PROGRESS: Applying advanced aerospace medical developments to research for rehabilitation of veterans.

AVOCATIONAL INTERESTS: Deep sea fishing, travel, amateur radio.†

*   *   *

SIMONS, William Edward 1927-

PERSONAL: Born September 14, 1927, in Philadelphia, Pa.; son of Edward M. and Myrtle (Harman) Simons; married Sharon Arnold, November 24, 1951; children: Michael Edward, Eric William, Kendall Harman (daughter). *Education:* U.S. Naval Academy, B.S., 1950; Columbia University, M.A., 1954, Ed.D., 1959. *Religion:* Protestant. *Home:* 797 Salem Ave., Burlington, N.J. *Office:* RAND Corp., Santa Monica, Calif. 90406.

CAREER: U.S. Navy, enlisted service, 1945-46, midshipman, 1946-50; U.S. Air Force, regular officer, 1950—, with current rank of lieutenant colonel. Staff administrator of civilian institutions programs, Air Force Institute of Technology, Wright-Patterson Air Force Base, Ohio, 1954-56; assistant professor of history, U.S. Air Force Academy, Colorado Springs, Colo., 1956-62; long range planning staff officer, Headquarters, U.S. Air Force, Washington, D.C., 1962-66; U.S. Air Force research associate with RAND Corp., Santa Monica, Calif., 1966—. *Member:* Association for Asian Studies, Air Force Historical Foundation, American Military Institute, U.S. Naval Institute. *Awards, honors*—Military: Air Force Commendation Medal.

WRITINGS: Liberal Education in the Service Academies, Bureau of Publications, Teachers College, Columbia University, 1965; *Coercion in Vietnam?*, RAND Corporation, 1969; (with Alexander L. George) *The Limits of Coercive Diplomacy: Laos, Cuba, Vietnam*, Little, Brown, 1971. Contributor to RAND Corporation publications, *Proceedings*, of U.S. Naval Institute, *Air University Review*, and *Military Affairs*.

WORK IN PROGRESS: Research on U.S. national security policy, 1952-1966, gunboat diplomacy in China, 1900-1937, and the history of military education and theory.†

SIMPSON, E(rvin) P(eter) Y(oung) 1911-

PERSONAL: Born May 13, 1911, in Mangere, New Zealand; son of Thomas (a farmer) and Clara Glass (McEwen) Simpson; married Lillian Eileen Andrew, June 30, 1937; children: Donald McEwen, John Martin. *Education:* Studied at Auckland University College and Canterbury University College, 1925-32; New Sealand Baptist Theological College, Dip. Theol., 1936; University of New Zealand, B.A., 1947, M.A., 1948; Berkeley Baptist Divinity School, B.D., and M.Th., 1950, Th.D., 1952; Institute of Historical Research, London, postdoctoral study, 1958-59. *Office:* Department of History, Alderson-Broaddus College, Philippi, W.Va. 26416.

CAREER: Young Men's Christian Association, secretary in Auckland, New Zealand, 1929-30, and Christchurch, New Zealand, 1931-33; Baptist clergyman, 1936—, with pastorates in New Zealand, 1936-39, 1944-49, and in Oakland, Calif., 1949-51; Berkeley Baptist Divinity School, Berkeley, Calif., assistant professor, 1950-51, associate professor, 1951-55, professor of church history, 1955-67; Graduate Theological Union, Berkeley, Calif., professor of church history, 1962-67; Massey University, Palmerston North, New Zealand, senior lecturer in history, 1967-69; Alderson Broaddus College, Philippi, W.Va., professor of history, 1969—. Former member of two theological commissions, Baptist World Alliance; former member of board of directors, American Baptist Churches of Northern California. *Military service:* New Zealand Territorial Army Reserve, 1939-51, with active duty as chaplain, 1939-44; became major; received four decorations.

MEMBER: Historical Association (London), American Society of Church History (vice-president, Pacific Coast branch, 1956-67), Royal Anthropological Institute of Great Britain (fellow), Society of Antiquaries of Scotland (fellow), New Zealand Historical Society (foundation member), Knights Templar (grand prelate, California, 1957-58, 1964-65), and other Masonic bodies. *Awards, honors:* Fulbright fellowship, 1949 (first New Zealander to be nominated by University of New Zealand); U.S. Air Force citation, 1956, for outstanding service; faculty fellowship of American Association of Theological Schools, 1958-59.

WRITINGS: Primitive Maori Religion, 1937; *How Did The Church Get There?,* edited by A. A. Brash, Presbyterian Bookroom (Christchurch), 1948; *The History of the New Zealand Baptist Missionary Society,* 1949; *Ordination and Christian Unity,* Judson, 1966. Contributor of articles on anthropological topics and biblical and church history to journals. Consulting editor, *Foundations* (journal of American Baptist Historical Society).

WORK IN PROGRESS: Continuing research into family background (Scottish-Irish), to serve eventually as the basis for a historical work.

* * *

SIMPSON, Ida Harper 1928-

PERSONAL: Born June 9, 1928, in Pansey, Ala.; daughter of A. H. (a farmer) and Smithie (Croom) Harper; married Richard L. Simpson (a professor of sociology), July 11, 1955; children: Robert D. and Frank D. (twins). *Education:* University of Alabama, A.B., 1949, M.A., 1951; University of North Carolina, Ph.D., 1955. *Politics:* Democrat. *Religion:* Protestant. *Home:* 604 Brookview Rd., Chapel Hill, N.C. 27514. *Office:* Department of Sociology, Duke University, Durham, N.C. 27706.

CAREER: College of William and Mary, Williamsburg, Va., instructor in sociology, 1954-55; University of North Carolina, Chapel Hill, research associate, 1955-56; Pennsylvania State University, University Park, instructor, 1956-57; University of Illinois, Urbana, instructor, 1957-58; Duke University, Durham, N.C., assistant professor, 1958-63, research associate and lecturer, 1964-70, associate professor of sociology, 1971—. *Member:* American Sociological Society, Southern Sociological Society, League of Women Voters.

WRITINGS: (With Harry W. Martin) *Patterns of Psychiatric Nursing,* Institute for Research in Social Science, 1956; (with husband, Richard L. Simpson) *Social Organization and Behavior,* Wiley, 1964; (with John C. McKinney) *Social Aspects of Aging,* Duke University Press, 1966. Contributor to *Social Forces, Journal of Social Issues,* and other sociology journals.

WORK IN PROGRESS: A study of professionalization of student nurses.†

* * *

SIMPSON, Lewis P(earson) 1916-

PERSONAL: Born July 18, 1916, in Jacksboro, Tex.; son of John Pearson (a lawyer) and Grace (Sidebottom) Simpson; married Mary Elizabeth Ellis, July 14, 1941; children: Lewis David. *Education:* Attended North Texas State Agricultural College, 1933-35; University of Texas, B.A., 1938, M.A., 1939, Ph.D., 1948. *Religion:* Episcopal. *Home:* 965 Aberdeen Ave., Baton Rouge, La. 70808. *Office:* Department of English, Louisiana State University, Baton Rouge, La. 70803.

CAREER: University of Texas, Austin, tutor, 1941-42, instructor in English, 1944-45, 1946-48; Louisiana State University, Baton Rouge, assistant professor, 1948-53, associate professor, 1953-60, professor of English, 1960-71, William A. Read Professor of English Literature, 1971—. Lamar Memorial Lecturer, Mercer University, 1973. Consultant, National Endowment for the Humanities, 1970-74. *Member:* Modern Language Association of America, American Association of University Professors, American Studies Association, Organization of American Historians, Southern Historical Association, South Central Modern Language Association, Thoreau Society. *Awards, honors:* Guggenheim fellowship, 1954-55; Louisiana State University Foundation faculty fellowship, 1971-72.

WRITINGS: (Editor and author of introduction, notes, and bibliography) *The Federalist Literary Mind,* Louisiana State University Press, 1962; (author of introduction) Murry C. Falkner, *The Faulkners of Mississippi,* Louisiana State University Press, 1967; (editor and author of introduction) *Profile of Robert Frost,* C. E. Merrill, 1971; (editor and author of introduction) *The Poetry of Community: Essays on the Southern Sensibility of History and Literature,* School of Arts and Sciences, Georgia State University, 1972; (author of introduction) Donald Davidson, *Still Rebels, Still Yankees,* Louisiana State University Press, 1972; *The Man of Letters in New England and the South: Essays on the History of the Literary Vocation in America,* Louisiana State University Press, 1973; (author of foreword) John Tyree Fain and Thomas Daniel Young, *The Literary Correspondence of Donald Davidson and Allen Tate,* University of Georgia Press, 1974; *The Disposed Garden: Pastoral and History in Southern Literature,* University of Georgia Press, 1975; (editor and author of introduction) *The Possibilities of Order: Cleanth Brooks and His Work,* Louisiana State University Press, in press.

Contributor: Waldo McNeir and Leo B. Levy, editors, *Studies in American Literature*, Louisiana State University Press, 1960; Donald E. Stanford, editor, *Nine Essays in Modern Literature*, Louisiana State University Press, 1965; Thomas A. Kirby and W. J. Olive, editors, *Essays in Honor of Esmond Linworth Marilla*, Louisiana State University Press, 1970; Francis Lee Utley, Lynn Z. Bloom, and Arthur F. Kinney, editors, *Bear, Man, and God: Eight Approaches to William Faulkner's "The Bear,"* Random House, 1971; Eric W. Carlson and T. Lasley Dameron, editors, *Emerson's Relevance Today*, Transcendental, 1971; A. Owen Aldridge, *The Ibero-American Enlightenment*, University of Illinois Press, 1971; H. Ernest Lewald, editor, *The Cry of Home: Cultural Nationalism and the Modern Writer*, University of Tennessee Press, 1972; Louis D. Rubin, Jr., editor, *The Comic Imagination in American Literature*, Rutgers University Press, 1973; John Loos, editor, *Great Events in American History*, Salem Press, 1974.

General editor, "Library of Southern Civilization" series, 1969—. Contributor of articles and reviews to literature and history journals. Co-editor, *Southern Review*, 1963—; member of editorial board, *American Literature*, 1969-72.

* * *

SINCLAIR, Keith 1922-

PERSONAL: Born December 5, 1922, in Auckland, New Zealand; son of Ernest Duncan (a clerk) and Florence (Kennedy) Sinclair; married Mary Land, November 10, 1947; children: Mark L., Cameron L., Stephen K., Harry A. *Education:* University of Auckland, B.A., 1945, M.A., 1946, Ph.D., 1954. *Religion:* None. *Home:* 13 Mariposa Crescent, Birkenhead, Auckland, New Zealand. *Office:* University of Auckland, Auckland, New Zealand.

CAREER: University of Auckland, Auckland, New Zealand, lecturer, 1947-59, associate professor, 1959-63, professor of history, 1963—. *Military service:* New Zealand Army, 1941-44; became sergeant. Royal New Zealand Naval Volunteer Reserve, 1944-46; became sub-lieutenant. *Awards, honors:* Walter Frewen Lord Prize for Imperial History, Royal Commonwealth Society, 1951; Ernest Scott Prize for History, University of Melbourne, for *The Origins of the Maori Wars*, 1957, and *A History of New Zealand*, 1959; Hubert Church Award, P.E.N., 1965, for *William Pember Reeves*; F. P. Wilson Prize in New Zealand History, 1965, for *William Pember Reeves*; Litt.D., University of Auckland, 1969; Jessie McKay Award, P.E.N., 1973, for *The Firewheel Tree*.

WRITINGS: The Maori Land League, University of Auckland, 1950; *Songs for a Summer and Other Poems*, Pegasus Press, 1952; *Strangers or Beasts* (verse), Caxton, 1954; *The Origins of the Maori Wars*, New Zealand University Press, 1957, 2nd edition, 1961; *A History of New Zealand*, Harmondsworth, 1959, 2nd edition, Oxford University Press, 1961; (editor) John Eldon Gorst, *The Maori King*, new edition, Oxford University Press, 1959.

(With William F. Mandle) *Open Account: The Bank of New South Wales in New Zealand, 1861-1961*, Whitcombe & Tombs, 1961; (editor) *Distance Looks Our Way*, University of Auckland, 1961; (editor with Robert McDonald Chapman) *Studies of a Small Democracy*, Angus & Robertson, 1963; *A Time to Embrace* (verse), Paul's Book Arcade, 1963; (contributor) *The Future of New Zealand*, edited by Muriel F. Lloyd Prichard, Whitcombe & Tombs, 1964; *William Pember Reeves, New Zealand Fabian*, Oxford University Press, 1965.

The Firewheel Tree, Oxford University Press, 1973.

WORK IN PROGRESS: A biography of Sir Walter Nash.

* * *

SINGH, Harbans 1921-

PERSONAL: Born March 4, 1921, in Kotha Guru, District Bhatinda, Punjab, India; son of Ram Lal Uppal and Roop Kaur; married Kailash Kaur, March 23, 1944; children: Nripinder (son), Nikky (daughter). *Education:* Khalsa College, B.A. (honors in English), 1941, M.A., 1943. *Religion:* Sikh. *Home and office:* A1, Punjabi University, Patiala, Punjab, India.

CAREER: Khalsa College, Amritsar, Punjab, India, lecturer in English, 1943-44; Brijindra College, Faridkot, Punjab, head of department of English and dean of Arts Faculty, 1944-47; tutor to heir-apparent of Faridkot (Indian princely state), 1947-58; Government College, Muktsar, Punjab, principal, 1958-62; Punjabi University, Patiala, Punjab, registrar, 1962-67, chairman of the department of religious studies and dean of faculty of humanities and religious studies, 1970-73, professor of Sikh religion, 1973—.

WRITINGS: Maharaja Ranjit Singh (biography), Sikh Publishing House, 1952-53; *Aspects of Punjabi Literature*, Bawa Publishing House, 1961; *The Heritage of the Sikhs*, Asia Publishing House, 1964; *Higher Education in America*, Prentice-Hall (New Dehli), 1966; *Guru Gobind Singh*, Guru Gobind Singh Foundation (Chandigarh), 1966; *Guru Nanak and Origins of the Sikh Faith*, Asia Publishing House, 1969; *Bhai Vir Singh*, Indian Akademi of Letters (New Delhi), 1972; (with L. M. Joshi) *An Introduction to Indian Religions*, Punjabi University, 1973; (editor) *Approaches to the Study of Religion*, Punjabi University, 1973; (editor) *Perspectives on Guru Nanak*, Punjabi University, 1975; (editor) *Punjab Past and Present: Essays in Honor of Dr. Ganda Singh*, Punjabi University, in press.

WORK IN PROGRESS: Editing *Encyclopaedia of Sikhism* for publication by Punjabi University.

* * *

SINGH, Madanjeet 1924-

PERSONAL: Born April 16, 1924, in Benares, India; son of Dogar and Sumiter (Kaur) Singh; married Dhyanawati Sudjono, August 9, 1962; children: Mahendrajeet. *Education:* Government College, Lahore, India, B.Sc. (honors), 1949; Istituto Italiano per il Medio ed Estremo Oriente, diploma in Italian, 1951. *Religion:* Sikh.

CAREER: Indian Foreign Service, second secretary at Indian embassies in Rome, Italy, 1953-57, and Vientiane, Laos, 1957-59, first secretary in Stockholm, Sweden, 1960-63, undersecretary in Ministry of External Affairs, New Delhi, 1963-66, first secretary in India Embassy, Madrid, Spain, beginning 1966

WRITINGS: Indian Sculptures in Bronze and Stone, Institute of Middle and Far East (Rome, Italy), 1951; *India—Paintings from Ajanta Caves*, UNESCO (Paris), 1954; *Ajanta, Paintings of the Sacred and the Secular*, Macmillan, 1965; *Himalayan Art*, New York Graphic Society, 1968, revised small-format edition, Macmillan, 1971. Contributor to art journals in India and abroad.

SIDELIGHTS: Singh traveled extensively through India and surrounding mountain regions for material for *Himalayan Art*.†

SINGH, Nagendra 1914-

PERSONAL: Born March 18, 1914, in Dungarpur, Rajasthan, India; son of Maharawal Bijay Singh Ji Bahadur of Dungarpur and Rajmata Devendra Kunwer Saheba; married Rani Pushpa Kumari Devi. *Education:* Agra University, B.A., 1934; Cambridge University, B.A. (honors), 1936, M.A., 1941, LL.B., 1953, LL.M., 1955, LL.D., 1965; Trinity College, University of Dublin, B.Litt., 1954, LL.D., 1959; Bihar University, D.Litt., 1954; Calcutta University, D.Phil., 1957; Delhi University, D.C.L., 1964; University of Moscow, D.Sc., 1964 (all degrees after 1953 awarded on submission of dissertations or for published and unpublished works). *Home:* Bijaya Bhawan, Dungarpur, Rajasthan, India. *Office:* International Court of Justice, Peace Palace, The Hague, Netherlands, and 6 Akbar Road, New Delhi, India.

CAREER: Called to bar, Grays Inn, London, England, 1942; joined Indian Civil Service, 1938. Government of India, New Delhi, district magistrate and collector in Madhya Pradesh, 1938-46, member of the Constituent Assembly of India, 1947-48, regional commissioner in Eastern States, 1948, justice of the peace in Bombay, 1958, director-general of shipping, 1956-64, secretary to Ministry of Transport, 1956-65, special secretary to Ministry of Information and Broadcasting, 1964, secretary to President of India, 1966—, representative to United Nations General Assembly, 1966, 1969, 1971, constitutional adviser to Government of Bhutan, 1970, Supreme Appellate Authority, Prize Court of Law of India, 1972; International Court of Justice, The Hague, Netherlands, member and judge, 1973—. Leader of Indian delegations to international conferences, 1956—; president, Intergovernmental Maritime Consultive Organization Assembly, 1963-65; member of International Law Commission, 1966—, and Permanent Court of Arbitration, 1967—. Professor of maritime and international law, Madras University, 1965—; visiting professor at universities of Bombay, Delhi, Udaipur, and the Hague Academy of International Law. King Tribhuvan Professor of Human Rights, University of Nepal, Nehru Professor of International Cooperation, Graduate Institute of International Studies (Geneva), Sir Alladi Krishnaswami Aiyar Lecturer, Anahra University.

MEMBER: Institute of International Law (associate), Indian Society of International Law (president), Maritime Law Association of India (president), Law Institute of India (life member), Indian Institute of Public Administration (life member), India International Centre (life member). *Awards, honors:* Secretary of State for India's Prize under Home Department Notification, 1938; Langdon Medal of the Council of Legal Education (London), 1938; Cama Prize of St. John's College, Cambridge, 1938; elected Master of the Bench, Grays Inn, 1973.

WRITINGS: Termination of Membership of International Organisations, Stevens, 1958; *Nuclear Weapons and International Law,* Praeger, 1959; *Defence Mechanism of the Modern State,* Taplinger, 1963; *International Conventions of Merchant Shipping,* Stevens, 1963; (editor) *Essays in Maritime International Law and Organisation,* Andhra University Press, 1966; (with Raoul Colinvaux) *Shipowners,* Stevens, 1967; *The Theory of Force and Organization of Defence in Indian Constitutional History,* Asia Publishing, 1969; *Recent Trends in the Development of International Law,* S. Chand, 1969; *The Legal Regime of Merchant Shipping,* University of Bombay, 1969; *India and International Law,* S. Chand, 1969; *Human Rights and*

International Co-operation, S. Chand, 1969; *Achievements of UNCTAD-I and UNCTAD-II,* S. Chand, 1969; *Bhutan: A Kingdom in the Himalayas,* Thomson Press, 1972; *The Commercial Laws of India,* 1975.

*   *   *

SINHA, Sasadhar 1901-

PERSONAL: Born October 2, 1901, in Sylhet, Assam, India; son of Sasindra Chandra (a journalist) and Kumudini (Sen) Sinha; married Marthe Goldwyn (a schoolmistress and language specialist in London, England), August 6, 1938. *Education:* Calcutta University, B.A., 1924; London School of Economics and Political Science, B.Sc (honors), 1928, Ph.D., 1932; studied in Germany on scholarship, 1929-30. *Politics:* Indian National Congress. *Religion:* Hindu. *Home and office:* P 10, 124 Sukalyani, Kalyani, Nadia, West Bengal, India.

CAREER: Journalist and translator, and lecturer on current affairs and sociology for Workers' Educational Association and London County Council, London, England, 1932-45; owner of bookshop, The Bibliophile, adjacent to British Museum, London, England, 1936-42; editor, *Hindustan Standard,* Calcutta, India, 1945-47; director of Publications Division, Indian Ministry of Information and Broadcasting, New Delhi, 1947-56; Ford Foundation consultant to Ministry of Community Development, New Delhi, 1956-57. Life member of Visva-Bharati, Santiniketan, Bengal, India, and London School of Economics and Political Science.

WRITINGS: (Translator into English) *Rabindranath Tagore's Letters from Russia,* Visva-Bharati Press, 1960; *Social Thinking of Rabindranath Tagore,* Asia Publishing House, 1962; *Indian Independence in Perspective,* Asia Publishing House, 1964; *Aspects of Japan,* Asia Publishing House, 1968; *Asutosh Mookerjee,* Indian Ministry of Information and Broadcasting Publications Division (New Delhi), 1970; (translator) Saratchandra Chatterji, *The Drought and Other Stories,* Sahitya Akademi (New Delhi), 1970. Contributor to the press in England and India.

SIDELIGHTS: "Spent my childhood," Sinha wrote in an introduction to *Indian Independence in Perspective,* "in the exciting days of the Swadeshi movement (1905-10), in which my own family was deeply involved." His father refused to send him to a government school, and when the national school he attended was closed, young Sinha was enrolled in Rabindranath Tagore's School at Santiniketan, where he came to know Gandhi. In 1921, he quit his studies at Calcutta University to join Gandhi's noncooperation movement.

Much later, writing in London where he had gone in 1957 for quiet reading and writing on Indian affiars, Sinha took a more dispassionate view of Gandhi's role in Indian politics: "His real fatal weakness . . . lay in his minimal vision for India. It never became the full-blooded idea of a rounded life, as behooves a modern people. . . ."

Sinha completed his book on Tagore's approach to social problems and wrote *Indian Independence* after being invalided by a stroke in 1959 in London. He finished the Tagore work while convalescing in India; it had been intended for publication in the Tagore centenary year (1961), but appeared a year later. In London he had a second cerebral hemorrhage, which halted his writing. He returned to India, completed a second recovery and began writing again.†

SKALA, John J. 1923-

PERSONAL: Born January 26, 1923, in Canton, Ohio; son of John Y. (a tailor) and Pauline G. (Singer) Skala; married Dorothy Ann Bircher (a teacher), May 1, 1943; children: John J. III, James A., Timothy W., David F., Richard G., Pauline A., Caroline E., Mary Jane, Thomas R., Benedict V., Anina M., Theresa, Matthew F. Education: Forest City College, D.M.T., 1948; Northeastern College, Cleveland, Ohio, B.S., 1950; American Institute of Science, doctorate, 1952; studied at University of Illinois, Ohio University, Athens, and several Ohio colleges during period, 1952-62. Politics: Independent. Religion: Roman Catholic. Home and office: 1336 16th St. N.W., Canton, Ohio 44703.

CAREER: Onetime editorial assistant in a manufacturing firm, and newspaper reporter in Canton, Ohio; Forest City College, Cleveland, Ohio, lecturer in anatomy and physiology, 1953-55; Roman Catholic diocese of Youngstown, Youngstown, Ohio, teacher and guidance counselor, department of education, 1955-62; physical therapist in private practice, writer, and lecturer, 1962—. Director of Department of Physical Therapy and Rehabilitation at Molly Stark Hospital and Joseph T. Nist Geriatric Center, Canton, Ohio. Member: National Association of Physical Therapists, Canton Chamber of Commerce, Fraternal Order of Eagles (Canton Aerie, president, 1960; secretary, 1950—).

WRITINGS: Dad and His Teenagers, Daughters of St. Paul, 1960; The Marriage Maze, Daughters of St. Paul, 1965; Massage and Low Frequency Currents in Facial Therapy, Klicmann Publications, 1970; Text of Cosmetic Therapy and Its Basic Sciences, Klicmann Publications, 1971; Medical Massage and Manual Therapy Techniques, Klicmann Publications, 1972.

WORK IN PROGRESS: Church Crisis and the Layman.

* * *

SKARD, Sigmund 1903-

PERSONAL: Born July 31, 1903, in Kristiansand, Norway; son of Matias and Gyda (Christensen) Skard; married Ase Grude Koht (a university professor of psychology), January 5, 1933; children: Torild, Malfrid, Asmund, Halvdan, Anne. Education: University of Oslo, Magister artium, 1930, Dr. Philosophy, 1938. Home: Fjelivegen 2, Lysaker, Oslo, Norway.

CAREER: University of Oslo, Oslo, Norway, librarian, 1922-33, assistant professor of general literature, 1933-38; Royal Academy, Trondheim, Norway, librarian, 1938-46, on leave in Washington, D.C., as consultant to Library of Congress, 1941-43, and chief regional specialist, U.S. Office of War Information, 1943-45; University of Oslo, professor of American literature, 1946-73, founder and director of American Institute, 1948-73, president of International Summer School, 1958-68. Det Norske Samlaget, president, 1949-72. Member: Academies of Trondheim, Gothenburg and Oslo. Awards, honors: Doctorate, University of Pennsylvania, 1958, Free University of Berlin, 1967.

WRITINGS: Norsk Ordbok, Det Norske Samlaget, 1932; A. O. Vinje og antikken: Studier i norsk andshistorie, Det Norske Videnskaps-akademi, 1938; (with Halvdan Koht) The Voice of Norway, Columbia University Press, 1944; Boker om Norges kamp, Norwegian Embassy, Washington, D.C., 1945; Vestanfor havet (poetry), Gyldendal, 1946; Lang var (poetry), Gyldendal, 1946; The Use of Color in Literature, American Philosophical Society, 1946; Sola gar mot vest (poetry), Gyldendal, 1948; Amerikanske

problem, F. Bruns Forlag, 1949; Til Marcus Thranes idehistorie, Det Norske Videnskaps-akademi, 1949.

(Editor) Norsk litteraturvitenskap i det 20. arhundrede, Gyldendal, 1957; American Studies in Europe: Their Development and Present Organization, two volumes, University of Pennsylvania Press, 1958; The American Myth and the European Mind, University of Pennsylvania Press, 1959; Malstrid og massekultur, Det Norske Samlaget, 1963; Dad og dikt (essays), Det Norske Samlaget, 1963; Haustraun (poetry), Gyldendal, 1966; (editor) USA in Focus, Universitetsforlaget, 1966; (editor) Americana Norvegica: Norwegian Contributions to American Studies, three volumes, University of Pennsylvania Press, 1966-71; (editor with A.N.J. den Hollander) American Civilisation: An Introduction, Longmans, Green, 1968; Poppel ved flyplass (poetry), Gyldendal, 1970; Det levande ordet (biography of Matias Skard), Det Norske Samlaget, 1972; (editor with M. Saito) The American Image in the World (in Japanese), Nan'undo Publishing Co., 1972; Auga og hjarta (poetry), Gyldendal, 1973; Dikt i itval (poetry), Gyldendal, 1973; Andlet til andlet, Det Norske Samlaget, 1974; Ein arv til a goeyma, Det Norske Samlaget, 1974.

Translator: (From the English) Under nye stjerner (anthology of American poetry through three hundred years), Gyldendal, 1960; (from the Italian) Petrarch, Selected Sonnets, Det Norske Samlaget, 1962; (from medieval Latin) Vagantviser (poetry of the Goliards), Det Norske Samlaget, 1964, and several prose chronicles (Einhard, Notker Balbulus, Jordanis); (with H. Rytter) Dante, The Divine Comedy, Det Norske Samlaget, 1965; (from the French) Franske dikt (anthology of five poets), Det Norske Samlaget, 1967; (editor with Hartvig Kiran and Halldis Moren Vesaas) Framande dikt (a world anthology of poetry), Det Norske Samlaget, 1968.

Contributor of sections or chapters to books published in United States, France, Norway, Sweden, Denmark, and Japan, and to journals. Editor, Vinduet (literary quarterly), 1952-54; founding editor, "Newsletter" of the European Association for American Studies, 1955-57.

* * *

SKEDGELL, Marian (Castleman) 1921-

PERSONAL: Surname sounds like "schedule"; born February 22, 1921, in Chicago, Ill.; daughter of William (a printer) and Ann (Steinberg) Castleman; married Ralph Skedgell (a merchandising executive), November 9, 1946; children: John, Nicholas, Kristen. Education: University of Chicago, M.A., 1941. Agent: Lisel Eisenheimer, William Morris Agency, 1350 Avenue of the Americas, New York, N.Y. 10019.

CAREER: Editorial assistant, University of Chicago Press, Chicago, Ill., 1940-42, and Viking Press, New York, N.Y., 1943-47; Alfred A. Knopf, Inc. (publishers), New York, N.Y., copy editor, 1961-62; E. P. Dutton & Co. (publishers), New York, N.Y., production editor, 1962-64; freelance editor and writer, 1964—. Member: Authors League. Awards, honors: John Billings Fiske Poetry Prize for "The Return," 1941; Fund for the Republic Award for television script, "Boden's Grave," 1955.

WRITINGS: The Day of the Waxing Moon, Doubleday, 1965; (editor) Jean Ende and Clifford Earl, Buy It Right!, Dutton, 1974. Author of two plays, "Broken Record" and "The Game Preserve," of pageant, "On the Way," for Girl Scouts National Jamboree, 1956, and of television scripts. Contributor to Poetry, Dyn, Time, and New Leader.

WORK IN PROGRESS: A novel, *The Making of Mrs. Owens.*

AVOCATIONAL INTERESTS: Music, politics (as a spectator sport).†

* * *

SKINNER, Cornelia Otis 1901-

PERSONAL: Born May 30, 1901, in Chicago, Ill.; daughter of Otis (an actor) and Maud (an actress; maiden name Durbin) Skinner; married Alden S. Blodget, October 2, 1928 (deceased); children: Otis Skinner Blodget. *Education:* Attended Baldwin School, Bryn Mawr, and Sorbonne; studied for the stage with Societaires de Comedie Francaise and Theatre du Vieux Colombier, under Jacques Copeau. *Home:* 131 East 66th St., New York, N.Y. 10021.

CAREER: Actress, monologist, and writer. Made stage debut as Dona Sarasate in "Blood and Sand," Empire Theatre, 1921; other roles include Mrs. Ricketts in "Tweedles," Frazee Theatre, 1923, title role in "Candida," White Plains Playhouse, 1935, Angelica in "Love for Love," Hudson Theatre, 1941, Emily Hazen in "The Searching Wind," Fulton Theatre, 1944, Mrs. Erlynne in "Lady Windermere's fan," Cort Theatre, 1946, Lady Britomart in "Major Barbara," Martin Beck Theatre, 1956, Katherine Dougherty in "The Pleasure of His Company," Longacre Theatre, 1958, national company of "The Irregular Verb to Love," 1963-64; appeared in motion pictures, "Kismet," M-G-M, 1944, "The Uninvited," Paramount, 1944; appeared on Arthur Murray Show, NBC, 1957, narrator for "Debutante '62," NBC, 1962, and "The Littlest Angel," NBC, 1962; appeared in Marya Mannes' "They," NET, 1970; has toured in a one-woman presentation of short character sketches of her own authorship, 1925—. *Member:* Actors' Equity Association (second vice-president, 1941), Phi Beta Kappa (honorary member), Cosmopolitan Club, Colony Club. *Awards, honors:* D.F.A., Clark University; L.H.D., University of Pennsylvania; Doctor of Humanities degrees, St. Lawrence University, New York University, University of Rochester, and Temple University; other degrees from Mills College, Hofstra University, Tufts College; Barter Theatre Award, 1952, for outstanding acting on the Broadway Stage; Officier of the Academie Francaise, 1954.

WRITINGS: "Captain Fury" (play), produced in 1925; *Tiny Garments*, Farrar & Rinehart, 1932; *Excuse It, Please!*, Dodd, 1936; *Dithers and Jitters*, Dodd, 1938; *Soap Behind the Ears*, Dodd, 1941; (with Emily Kimbrough) *Our Hearts Were Young and Gay*, Dodd, 1942; *Popcorn*, Constable, 1943; *Family Circle* (autobiographical), Houghton, 1948 (published in England as *Happy Family*, Constable, 1950); *That's Me All Over: All the Favorite Absurdities from Dithers and Jitters, Soap Behind the Ears, and Excuse It, Please!, along with Tiny Garments*, Dodd, 1948; *Nuts in May*, Dodd, 1950; *Bottoms Up!*, Dodd, 1955; *The Ape in Me*, Houghton, 1959; *Elegant Wits and Grand Horizontals*, Houghton, 1962; *Madame Sarah*, Houghton, 1967.

Author of monologues, including "The Wives of Henry VII," "The Loves of Charles II," "The Empress Eugenie," and "Mansion of the Hudson." Also wrote a one-woman musical revue, "Paris '90." Contributor of articles and verse to *Harper's Bazaar, Vogue, New Yorker, Reader's Digest, Life* and *Theatre Art.*

SIDELIGHTS: In a review of *The Ape in Me*, L. K. Miller wrote: "True wit may take many forms, but among the essential ingredients are a sense of the ridiculous and the ability to make fun of oneself. Cornelia Otis Skinner has polished the latter to a fine sheen in her new collection of essays." Miss Skinner has often been the target of her own satire. In college, she wrote in *The Ape in Me*, "I was known as the Tall Girl of my set and the few callow youths who 'dated' me would hardly have been able to let linger a kiss on any feature much above my chin . . . even if I thrust it forward in the manner of an amorous heifer. . . . I recall a moment in Kyoto when, on entering the Ni-jo Palace, I all but scalped myself while walking through a low doorway." She has also been the victim of shaking hands. "For years I went to great lengths to conceal this detriment to my poise and charm. But now since modern psychiatry advises us to admit, if not actually to flaunt our disabilities with a 'Hey, look at my tic!' bravura, I might as well come clean and state that there are moments when I am no more capable of opening a softboiled egg than I am capable of performing a brain operation." A theatrical opening night is a strong inducement for an attack. "Maybe with luck, just after my entrance, I'll be struck down by a falling sandbag, or perhaps I'll be fortunate enough to expire in some less ludicrous fashion, a highly becoming heart attack, for instance. . . . During a . . . run of 'Major Barbara' it was solacing to find out that a seasoned veteran like Charles Laughton came successfully through an attack, and when one evening Eli Wallach went up in a line he knew backwards (and backwards was about the way he said it too) I felt better about the moment when I looked with a wild surmise at Glynis Johns who played my daughter Barbara and couldn't for the life of me think of her name."

In her humorous essays she is "particularly adept at treating the genteel moment of inadequacy or the small social dilemma," wrote H. B. Woodward. An example of this is her essay "Where to Look." "I am becoming more and more acutely sensitive," wrote Miss Skinner, "about those moments when one doesn't know where to look. . . . Fortunately such where-to-look situations do not arise with any frequency. One which does, however, is the elevator one. . . . The act of waiting for an elevator brings out a suspicious streak in people. You arrive before the closed landing door and push a button. Another person comes along and after a glance of mutual appraisal, you both look quickly away and continue to wait, thinking the while uncharitable thoughts of one another. The new arrival suspecting you of not having pushed the button and you wondering if the new arrival is going to be a mistrusting old meanie and go give the button a second shove; . . . an unspoken tension which is broken by one or the other of you walking over and doing just that. Then back to positions of waiting and the problem of where to look. . . . Hotels, of course, often supply framed reading matter, but you can study such items as 'Dance tonight in our Avocado Room to the Conga rhythms of Pepe Alvarez and Poncho Gauchos' just so long before you're taken for one of those retarded adults with a reading deficiency." In a speech to the American Gynecological Society in 1953 she noted: "For the nicely brought-up girl, there is something that is hard to reconcile with her genteel sensibilities about walking into the inner sanctum of a complete stranger, solemnly describing her symptoms and at the end of the recital hearing the stranger say 'Will you please go into the next room and take off everything except your shoes and stockings?' It wouldn't seem so bad if it weren't for that shoes and stockings clause! To my impressionable mind it has always smacked of the more erotic refinements of Berlin during its decadence."

Her latest book, _Madame Sarah_, deviated from Miss Skinner's usual fare and has become nearly as popular as her highly successful _Our Hearts Were Young and Gay_. "Cornelia Otis Skinner has written the life of Sarah Bernhardt as it must be written, with love and devotion," commented Andre Maurois. "Even her title 'Madame Sarah,' poses this nice problem as it should be posed: Sarah was not 'Bernhardt'; she was not Sarah Bernhardt; she was 'Madame,' like a queen, or 'the Great,' or 'the divine.' She was not an actress, but a Presence, an institution." Unfortunately, the non-Gaul does not share a Frenchman's infatuation with Madame Sarah and finds this devotion to the actress the flaw in Miss Skinner's biography. "Notable appreciations by contemporary French critics are generously strewn through Miss Skinner's biography," wrote Harold Clurman. "Most of them are ecstatic: they assure us that Bernhardt was an unforgettable phenomenon to those who attended her performances.... I nevertheless remain skeptical about most French criticism of acting: it tends to be effusively impressionistic, a kind of literary swoon adjusted to erotic and visceral reactions, rather than to ideas and scrupulous observation." The book, commented C. H. Simonds, "relies heavily on the actress's obviously romanticized memoirs and on adulatory volumes by her friends and relations. But should a dryasdust revisionist someday attempt to demolish the Bernhardt legend, he'll doubtless be dismissed as a surly spoil sport."

Our Hearts were Young and Gay was filmed by Paramount in 1944, and dramatized by Jean Kerr in 1946; a sequel, "Our Hearts Were Growing Up," was filmed by Paramount, 1946; _Family Circle_ was dramatized by Anne Martens, 1950; Alexander Cohen has taken an option on _Madame Sarah_ with the idea of making it into a musical, and the film rights were acquired by Walter Reade Organization.

BIOGRAPHICAL/CRITICAL SOURCES: Saturday Review, April 30, 1955; _Chicago Sunday Tribune_, September 20, 1959; _New York Times Book Review_, January 8, 1967; _Nation_, April 10, 1967; _National Review_, May 2, 1967.*

* * *

SKINNER, Knute (Rumsey) 1929-

PERSONAL: Born April 25, 1929, in St. Louis, Mo.; son of George Rumsey (a salesman) and Lidi (a civil servant; maiden name, Skjoldvig) Skinner; married Jean Pratt, November, 1953 (divorced, 1954); married Linda Kuhn, March 30, 1961; children: Francis, Dunstan, Morgan. _Education:_ Attended Culver-Stockton College, Canton, Mo., 1947-49; Colorado State College (now University of Northern Colorado), A.B., 1951; Middlebury College, M.A., 1954; State University of Iowa (now University of Iowa), Ph.D., 1958. _Home:_ 2600 Hampton Pl., Bellingham, Wash. 98225; and Killaspuglonane, Kilshanny, County Clare, Ireland (summer). _Office:_ English Department, Western Washington State College, Bellingham, Wash. 98225.

CAREER: Boise Senior High School, Boise, Idaho, teacher of English, 1951-54; State University of Iowa (now University of Iowa), Iowa City, instructor in English, 1955-56, 1957-58, 1960-61; Oklahoma College for Women, Chickasha, assistant professor of English, 1961-62; Western Washington State College, Bellingham, assistant professor, 1962-63, part-time lecturer in English, 1963-71, associate professor, 1971-73, professor of English, 1973—. Poetry editor, Southern Illinois University Press. Has given poetry readings at conferences, colleges, universities, and

high schools throughout the United States and Ireland. _Member:_ Poetry Society of America, American Committee for Irish Studies, Modern Language Association of America, Washington Poets Association. _Awards, honors:_ Huntington Hartford Foundation fellowship, 1961; National Endowment for the Arts fellowship in creative writing, 1975.

WRITINGS—Poetry: Stranger With a Watch, Golden Quill, 1965; _A Close Sky Over Killaspuglonane_, Dolmen Press (Dublin), 1968, Burton International, 1975; _In Dinosaur Country_, Pierian, 1969; _The Sorcerers: A Laotian Tale_, Goliards Press, 1972.

Work represented in many anthologies, including: _New Generation: Poetry Anthology_, Ann Arbor Review Books, 1971; _The Diamond Anthology_, edited by Charles Angoff, A. S. Barnes, 1971; _Our Only Hope is Humor: Some Public Poems_, Ashland Poetry Press, 1972; _Poetry: An Introduction Through Writing_, edited by Lewis Turco, Reston, 1973; _Messages: A Thematic Anthology of Poetry_, edited by X. J. Kennedy, Little, Brown, 1973.

Contributor of poems to many journals and periodicals, including _Prairie Schooner, Colorado Quarterly, New Republic, Shenandoah, Folio_, and _Chicago Review_; also contributor of stories and reviews to _Limbo, Quartet, Midwest, Irish Press, Northwest Review_, and _Hibernia_. Guest editor, _Pyramid_, Number 13, 1973.

WORK IN PROGRESS: Two books of poetry, _Hearing of the Hard Times_ and _The Flame Room_, completion of both expected in 1976.

SIDELIGHTS: Skinner, whose residence is divided between Bellingham, Washington, and rural Ireland, writes that the life in Ireland "exerts a strong influence on my work." He has recorded his poetry for the poetry rooms at Harvard, Leeds, Hull, and Durham Universities, for the British Council, and for radio stations in the United States and Ireland. His poetry is also the subject of an educational television film made at State University of New York College at Brockport. He has traveled in England, Denmark, France, Spain, Italy, Germany, Holland, Mexico, and Morocco.

* * *

SKIPPER, James K., Jr. 1934-

PERSONAL: Born September 14, 1934, in Columbus, Ohio; son of James K. (a college professor) and Dorothy (Levis) Skipper; married Joan Lois McCown, June 12, 1958; children: James K. III, John Fred. _Education:_ Northern Illinois University, B.S., 1956; Northwestern University, M.A., 1960, Ph.D., 1964. _Home:_ 2214 Thornridge Drive, Toledo, Ohio 43614. _Office:_ Department of Community Medicine, Medical College of Ohio at Toledo, P.O. Box 6190, Toledo, Ohio 43614.

CAREER: Research associate at Presbyterian-St. Luke's Hospital, Chicago, Ill., 1960-62, and Yale University, New Haven, Conn., 1963-65; Case Western Reserve University, Cleveland, Ohio, assistant professor, 1965-67, associate professor of sociology, 1967-71; University of Western Ontario, London, professor of sociology, 1970-72; Medical College of Ohio, Toledo, professor of community and family medicine, 1972—. Consultant to Cleveland Vocational Guidance and Rehabilitation Service, 1965-67, Case Western Reserve University Dental School, 1966-67, and Howard Advertising Agency, Inc., 1966-67; visiting professor, University of Hawaii, summer, 1968. _Military service:_

U.S. Army, active duty, 1957-58. U.S. Army Reserve, 1957-63; became sergeant first class.

WRITINGS: (Editor with Robert Leonard, and contributor) *Social Interaction and Patient Care*, Lippincott, 1965; (with Emily Mumford) *Sociology in Hospital Care*, Harper, 1967; (editor with Mark Lefton and Charles McCaghy, and contributor) *Approaches to Deviance: Theories, Concepts and Research Findings*, Appleton, 1968; (editor with Lefton and McCaghy) *On Their Own Behalf: Voices from the Margin*, Appleton, 1968, 2nd edition, 1973; (editor with Powhatan Wooldridge and Leonard) *Behavioral Science, Social Practice, and the Nursing Profession*, Press of Case Western Reserve Univerisyt, 1968; (editor with Wooldridge and Leonard) *Clinical Experiments for the Improvement of Patient Care*, Mosby, 1975. Contributor to health, education, and sociological periodicals in United States and Canada.

* * *

SKLANSKY, Morris Aaron 1919-

PERSONAL: Born December 7, 1919, in Dokscyze, Poland; son of Eli and Eska (Chernin) Sklansky, married Alice V. Reizen, 1946; children: Laura, Paul, Andrew. *Education:* Drew University, A.B., 1941; University of Louisville, M.D., 1945; Chicago Institute for Psychoanalysis, graduate study, 1949-55. *Home:* 800 Roslyn Pl., Evanston, Ill. 60201. *Office:* 180 North Michigan Ave., Chicago, Ill. 60601.

CAREER: Diplomate, American Board of Psychiatry and Neurology. U.S. Veterans Administration Hospital, Lexington, Ky., ward psychiatrist, 1946-48; Michael Reese Hospital, Chicago, Ill., resident psychiatrist, 1948-51, attending psychiatrist, 1951—; University of Illinois, Chicago, clinical assistant professor, 1951-63. Professorial lecturer in psychiatry and social science departments and clinical professor of psychiatry at University of Chicago; staff and training analyst at Chicago Institute for psychoanalysis. Member of board, Jewish Family Service. *Military service:* U.S. Army, 1942-48; became captain. *Member:* International Psychoanalytic Association. American Psychoanalytic Association, American Medical Association, Chicago Psychoanalytic Society (president, 1974-75).

WRITINGS: (With others) *Emotional Problems of Children: The Drop-Outs*, Free Press of Glencoe, 1962; *The High School Adolescent*, Association Press, 1970. Author of several scientific papers on psychotherapy and adolescence.

AVOCATIONAL INTERESTS: Literature, painting, archaeology, playing violin, and vacationing.

* * *

SKLARE, Arnold B(eryl) 1924-

PERSONAL: Born June 30, 1924, in Chicago, Ill.; son of Harry E. and Ida (Sogolow) Sklare. *Education:* University of Illinois, B.A., 1946, M.A., 1947; Sorbonne, University of Paris, Doctorat, 1949. *Home:* 31 Breeze Hill Rd., East Hampton, N.Y. 11937.

CAREER: Indiana University, Bloomington, instructor, 1949-50; University of Bridgeport, Bridgeport, Conn., assistant professor, 1950-53; Pace College (now University), New York, N.Y., adjunct associate professor, 1954-61; C. W. Post College of Long Island University, Greenvale, N.Y., associate professor of English, 1962-64; South-

hampton College of Long Island University, Southhampton, N.Y., professor of English, 1965—.

WRITINGS: (Editor with William Buckier) *Stories from Six Authors*, McGraw, first series, 1960, second series, 1966; *Creative Report Writing*, McGraw, 1964; (editor) *The Art of the Novella*, Macmillan, 1965; (with Buckler) *Essentials of Rhetoric*, Macmillan, 1966; *The Technician Writes*, Boyd & Fraser, 1971.

* * *

SLATER, Jerome N(orman) 1935-

PERSONAL: Born April 14, 1935, in New York, N.Y.; son of Max (a physician) and Frieda (Radack) Slater; married Judith Fairbank, June 1, 1962. *Education:* Alfred University, B.A., 1956; Yale University, M.A., 1958; Princeton University, Ph.D., 1965. *Home:* 134 Admiral Rd., Buffalo, N.Y. 14216. *Office:* Political Science Department, State University of New York, Buffalo, N.Y. 14226.

CAREER: Ohio State University, Columbus, assistant professor of political science, 1963-66; State University of New York, Buffalo, 1966—, started as assistant professor, became professor of political science. *Military service:* U.S. Naval Reserve, 1957-60; became lieutenant junior grade. *Member:* International Studies Association (treasurer, Midwest branch, 1964-65), American Political Science Association, American Association of University Professors.

WRITINGS: A Revaluation of Collective Security: The OAS in Action, Ohio State University Press, 1965; *The Organization of American States and United States Foreign Policy*, Ohio State University Press, 1967; *Intervention and Negotiation: The United States and the Dominican Revolution*, Harper, 1970. Contributor to *International Organization* and *Yale Review*.

* * *

SLAVSON, Samuel R(ichard) 1891-

PERSONAL: Born December 25, 1891, in Russia; came to United States, 1903, naturalized, 1913; son of Samuel Haim and Fanny (Tarsy) Slavson; married Cornelia Goldsmith, December, 1926; children: Robert M., Hertha Ann Slavson Klugman, Gerda L. Slavson Cooke. *Education:* Cooper Union, B.S., 1913; graduate study at City College (now City College of the City University of New York), and Columbia University. *Home:* 321 East 18th St., New York, N.Y. 10003.

CAREER: Curriculum consultant, Walden School, New York, N.Y., 1919-27; director of research in child psychology, Malting House School, Cambridge, England, 1927-29; consultant in group work and group psychotherapy to organizations and facilities in New York, New Jersey, and Connecticut, 1930—, with principal work at Madison House, New York, 1930-31, Young Men's Hebrew Association, New York, 1932-34, Jewish Board of Guardians, New York, 1934-56, Community Service Society, New York, 1946-51, Hudson Guild, New York, 1949-56, Children's Village, Dobbs Ferry, N.Y., 1957-62, Northshore Youth Consultation Service, Manhasset, N.Y., 1959-62, and currently at Brooklyn State Hospital and New York State Division for Youth. Lecturer at New York University, 1935-41, Yeshiva University, 1950-53; summer instructor at Springfield College, 1939, 1940. Co-president, International Congress on Group Psychotherapy, Zurich, 1957.

MEMBER: American Group Psychotherapy Association (founder; fellow; president, 1943-45; life member of board of directors), American Orthopsychiatric Association (fellow), International Council for Group Psychotherapy (founder), International Association for Social Psychiatry. *Awards, honors: Parent's Magazine* Award, 1939; Adolph Meyer Award in mental health, 1956; Wilfred C. Hulse Award, 1960.

WRITINGS: (With Robert K. Speer) *Science in the New Education*, Prentice-Hall, 1934; *Creative Group Education*, Association Press, 1937; *Character Education in a Democracy*, Association Press, 1939; *Introduction to Group Therapy*, Commonwealth Fund, 1942; *Recreation and Total Personality*, Association Press, 1946; (editor and contributor) *The Practice of Group Therapy*, International Universities, 1947.

Analytic Group Psychotherapy, Columbia University Press, 1950; *Child Psychotherapy*, Columbia University Press, 1952; *Re-Educating the Delinquent*, Harper, 1954; (editor) *The Fields of Group Psychotherapy*, International Universities, 1956; *Child-Centered Group Guidance of Parents*, International Universities, 1958; *A Textbook of Analytic Group Psychotherapy*, International Universities, 1964; *Reclaiming the Delinquent*, Free Press of Glencoe, 1965; *"Because I Live Here," Vita-Erg Therapy with Deteriorated Psychotic Women*, International Universities, 1970; (with Mortimer Schiffer) *Group Psychotherapies with Children: A Textbook*, International Universities, 1974.

Contributor: *Mothers' Encyclopedia*, Parents' Institute, 1942; D. C. Lewis and B. L. Pacella, editors, *Modern Trends in Child Psychiatry*, International Universities, 1945; Bernard Glueck, editor, *Current Psychiatric Treatment of Personality Disorders*, Grune, 1946; *The Caseworker in Psychotherapy*, Jewish Board of Guardians, 1946; Ernest Spiegel, editor, *Progress in Neuropsychiatry*, Grune, 1946; Ernest Harms, editor, *The Handbook of Child Guidance*, Child Care Publications, 1947; *Bulwarks Against Crime*, Yearbook of the National Probation and Parole Association, 1948; *Advances in the Understanding of the Offender*, Yearbook of the National Probation and Parole Association, 1950; Otto Polak, editor, *Social Science and Psychotherapy for Children*, Russell Sage Foundation, 1952; Dorothea Sullivan, editor, *Readings in Group Work*, Association Press, 1952; *The Fields of Group Psychotherapy*, International Universities, 1956; *Gruppen Psychotherapie*, Verlag Hans Huber (Bern, Switzerland), 1957; Eric Stern, editor, *Die Psychotherapie in der Gegenwart*, Volume II, Rascher Verlag (Zurich, Switzerland), 1958; Harold Greenwald, editor, *Great Cases in Psychoanalysis*, Ballantine, 1959; *Proceedings of the Second International Congress of Group Psychotherapy*, S. Karger Verlag (Basel, Switzerland), 1959; *Actuelle Fragen der Psychotherapie*, Volume II, S. Karger Verlag, 1960; *La Psychotherapie de groupe*, Presse Universitaires de France, 1971; *Psychoanalytishe Therapie in Gruppen*, Ernest Klett Verlag, 1971; Stefan de Sckill, editor, *The Challenge for group Psychotherapy*, International Universities, 1974.

Collaborator, *Psychiatric Dictionary*, 2nd edition. Contributor to periodicals. Editor, *The Group*, 1939-46; editor and founder, *International Journal of Group Psychotherapy*, 1951-60.

WORK IN PROGRESS: A volume of collected papers.

SIDELIGHTS: Five of his books have been translated into other languages, three into Japanese, with other translations in German, French, Italian, and Spanish.

BIOGRAPHICAL/CRITICAL SOURCES: Survey, Volume LXXXV, Number 2, 1949; *Courage is the Key*, edited by Alexander Klein, Twayne, 1953; *Family Health*, Volume IV, Number 3, 1972.

*   *   *

SLEDD, James Hinton 1914-

PERSONAL: Born December 5, 1914, in Atlanta, Ga.; son of Andrew (a professor) and Annie Florence (Candler) Sledd; married Joan Webb, July 16, 1939; children: Andrew, Robert, James, John, Ann. *Education:* Emory University, B.A., 1936; Oxford University, B.A., 1939; University of Texas, Ph.D., 1947. *Politics:* Democrat. *Religion:* Methodist. *Home:* 3704 Gilbert St., Austin, Tex. *Office:* Department of English, University of Texas, Austin, Tex. 78712.

CAREER: University of Chicago, Chicago, Ill., 1945-56, began as instructor, became associate professor of English; University of California, Berkeley, 1956-59, began as associate professor, became professor of English; Northwestern University, Evanston, Ill., professor of English, 1959-64; University of Texas, Austin, professor of English and linguistics, 1964—. *Member:* Modern Language Association of America, International Association of University Professors of English, National Council of Teachers of English, Linguistic Society, American Dialect Society. *Awards, honors:* Rhodes scholarship; Guggenheim fellowship.

WRITINGS: (With G. J. Kolb) *Dr. Johnson's Dictionary*, University of Chicago Press, 1955; *A Short Introduction to English Grammar*, Scott, Foresman, 1959; (with Wilma Ebbitt) *Dictionaries and That Dictionary*, Scott, Foresman, 1962; (with Harold Hungerford and Jay Robinson) *English Linguistics*, Scott, Foresman, 1970. Contributor of articles and reviews to professional journals.

WORK IN PROGRESS: Studies in medieval English literature, the history of the English language, English lexicography, English dialectology, and the teaching of English composition.

SIDELIGHTS: Sledd told *CA*: "So far, I've always been able to find somebody to pay me for doing what I like to do—i.e., reading, writing, teaching. If I could just find somebody to pay me for gardening, fishing, and hiking—."

*   *   *

SLESSER, Malcolm 1926-

PERSONAL: Born October 30, 1926, in Aberdeen, Scotland; son of William Duncan Vivian (in police work) and Alice Mary (McHardy) Slesser; married Janet Bond; children: Morag, Calum Vivian. *Education:* Attended Edinburgh Academy, 1930-43; University of Edinburgh, B.Sc. (first class honors), 1946, Ph.D., 1949. *Home:* Nether Glastry, Durblane Perthshire, Scotland. *Agent:* International Creative Management, 1301 Avenue of the Americas, New York, N.Y. 10019.

CAREER: Employed in chemical industry, 1943-56; University of Strathclyde, Glasgow, Scotland, lecturer in chemical engineering, 1956-66; University of Brazil, Rio de Janeiro, professor of chemical engineering, 1966-67. *Member:* Royal Geographical Society, Institution of Chemical Engineers (London), International P.E.N., Club Alpin Francais, Scottish Mountaineering Club (Edinburgh). *Awards, honors:* Polar Medal, 1955; Mungo Park Medal from Royal Scottish Geographical Society for explorations in northeast Greenland, 1962; Soviet Ministry of Sport Medal, 1963.

WRITINGS: Red Peak, Coward, 1964; *The Andes Are Prickly*, Gollancz, 1966; *Brazil: Land Without Limit*, Allen & Unwin, 1969, A. S. Barnes, 1970; *The Politics of Environment: Including a Guide to Scottish Thought and Action*, Allen & Unwin, 1972. Author of radio scripts for British Broadcasting Corp.

WORK IN PROGRESS: A novel set in Greenland; a system model for world political balance.

SIDELIGHTS: Mountaineering is a sideline that has sent Slesser up a total of twelve virgin peaks in Peru, Greenland, and Brazil. He has been on seven climbing expeditions since 1943, four of them to Greenland, and led expeditions in 1958, 1964, and 1966. During one thirteen-month period in Greenland, he spent three months on an ice cap. The Soviet medal came in recognition of his conquering the highest mountain in Soviet Asia, a 24,795-foot peak.

* * *

SLOAN, Irving J. 1924-

PERSONAL: Born November 14, 1924, in New York, N.Y.; son of Nathan (a businessman) and Ella (Klamka) Slomowitz; married Esther Gendleman (a medical researcher), May 30, 1955; children: Philip. *Education:* University of Wisconsin, B.A., 1946; Harvard University, LL.B., 1950; Yeshiva University, M.S., 1959. *Politics:* Democrat. *Religion:* Jewish. *Office:* Scarsdale Junior High School, Scarsdale, N.Y. 10583.

CAREER: Legal assistant in New York, N.Y., 1951-53; British Book Center, Inc., New York, N.Y., vice-president, 1954-56; IBM Corp., New York, N.Y., sales representative, 1956-58; Scarsdale (N.Y.) public schools, teacher of social studies, 1961—. Consultant to Educational Development Corp., *Reader's Digest* Educational Division, and Columbia University Institute of Civil Liberties Education and Research. *Member:* American Historical Society, American Political Science Association, National Council for Social Studies, Phi Kappa Delta. *Awards, honors:* American Federation of Teachers research grant. Educational Press Association award, 1968, for *The Negro in Modern American History Textbooks.*

WRITINGS: (Editor and compiler) *The American Negro: Fact Book and Chronology*, Oceana, 1965, 3rd edition published as *Blacks in America, 1492-1970: A Chronology and Fact Book*, 1971; *The Negro in Modern American History Textbooks*, American Federation of Teachers, 1966, 3rd edition, 1968; (editor) *Franklin Pierce, 1804-1869*, Oceana, 1968; (editor) *James Buchanan, 1791-1868*, Oceana, 1968; (editor) *Martin Van Buren, 1982-1862*, Oceana, 1969.

Our Violent Past: An American Chronicle, Random House, 1970; *The Treatment of Black Americans in Current Encyclopedias*, American Federation of Teachers, 1970; *Youth and the Law: Rights, Privleges and Obligations*, Oceana, 1970, 2nd edition, 1974; *Environment and the Law*, Oceana, 1971; (editor and compiler) *The Jews in America, 1621-1970: A Chronology and Fact Book*, Oceana, 1971; "Legislative Landmark Series", four volumes, Oceana, 1974-75. Contributor to *Saturday Review.*

* * *

SLONIM, Ruth 1918-

PERSONAL: Born January 30, 1918, in Chicago, Ill.; daughter of Sigmond M. (an attorney) and Lena E. Slonim. *Education:* Duluth State College (now University of Minnesota, Duluth), B.A. (with honors), 1938; University of

Minnesota, Minneapolis, M.A., 1942; graduate study at University of Minnesota and University of California, Berkeley. *Home:* Northeast 955 "C" St., Pullman, Wash. 99163. *Office:* Department of English, Washington State University, Pullman, Wash. 99163.

CAREER: Duluth State College (now University of Minnesota), Duluth, Minn., instructor in English and director of public relations, 1938-44; Central Washington State College, Ellensburg, assistant professor of English, 1944-46; Washington State University, Pullman, 1947—, began as instructor, professor of English, 1964—. Visiting professor at University of Puerto Rico, 1946-47, and School of Irish Studies, Dublin, 1970. Observer-member of U.S. delegation to sixth general conference of UNESCO, Paris, France, 1951. Representative of Washington State University to Northwest Poetry Circuit. *Member:* International Society for the Study of Anglo-Irish Literature, American Committee on Irish Studies, Oceanic Educational Foundation, Phi Kappa Phi (president, Washington State University chapter; member of editorial advisory board). *Awards, honors:* Award from Institute for Education by Radio, 1942, for guiding philosophy for major U.S. networks.

WRITINGS: London, Humphries, 1954; *San Francisco: "The City" in Verse*, Washington State University Press, 1965. Also author of address "Proems and Poems," published by Washington State University. Contributor of poems and critical essays to periodicals, including *Botteghe Oscure* (Rome), *Research Studies*, and *Irish University Review* (Dublin).

WORK IN PROGRESS: A volume of poetry.

SIDELIGHTS: Ruth Slonim was named Pullman woman of achievement in 1952, and outstanding faculty woman by students at Washington State University in 1965. Miss Slonim gave 21st Invited Address (highest honor conferred by Washington State University), "Proems and Poems," 1967.

* * *

SLONIMSKY, Nicolas 1894-

PERSONAL: Surname is pronounced Slo-*nim*-ski; born April 27, 1894, in St. Petersburg (now Leningrad), Russia; came to United States in 1923, naturalized in 1931; son of Leonid (an economist and political writer) and Faina (Vengerova) Slonimsky; married Dorothy Adlow (an art critic and lecturer), July 30, 1931 (died, 1964); children: Electra Slonimsky Yourke. *Education:* Studied at Conservatory of St. Petersburg, 1910-16, and University of St. Petersburg, 1912-16. *Politics:* Democrat. *Home:* 10808½ Wilshire Blvd., Los Angeles, Calif.

CAREER: Pianist, composer, teacher of music, and writer. Concert pianist, touring in southern and western Europe, 1921-23; instructor at Eastman School of Music, Rochester, N.Y., 1923-25, Boston Conservatory of Music, Boston, Mass., 1925-45; Harvard University, Cambridge, Mass., instructor in Slavic languages and literature, 1946-47; instructor or lecturer in music at Simmons College, 1948-49, Haverford College, Haverford, Pa., 1956-57, Peabody Conservatory, Baltimore, Md., 1956-57, University of California, Los Angeles, 1964-67. Conductor in New York, Boston, New York, Los Angeles, Berlin, Cuba, Paris, and Budapest, 1930-32, and on South American tours, 1938, 1941, 1942; traveled under auspices of State Department in Russia, Poland, Yugoslavia, Rumania, Bulgaria, Greece, Israel, 1962-63; composer of works for orchestra, piano, ballet, and voice, including "Studies in Black and White for

Piano,'' 1929, "My Toy Balloon" (performed at many children's concerts by New York Philharmonic and Boston Pops Orchestra), 1945, "Gravestones" (song cycle), 1945, "Yellowstone Park Suite" (for piano), 1950, "Suite for Cello and Piano," 1951, "Fifty Minitudes for Piano," 1973. *Member:* American Society of Composers, Authors and Publishers. *Awards, honors:* Award of Merit, National Association of American Composers and Conductors, 1960.

WRITINGS: Music Since 1900, Coleman-Ross, 1937, 4th expanded edition, Scribner, 1971; (contributor) David Ewen, editor, *The Book of Modern Composers*, Knopf, 1942, new edition, 1961; *Music of Latin America*, Crowell, 1945, 2nd edition, 1951, reprinted with new foreword, Da Capo, 1972; (editor-in-chief) Oscar Thompson, *International Cyclopedia of Music and Musicians*, 4th-8th editions, Dodd, 1946-59; *Road to Music* (collection of articles originally written for children's page of *Christian Science Monitor*; Book-of-the-Month Club alternate selection), Dodd, 1947, revised edition, 1965; *Thesaurus of Scales and Musical Patterns*, Coleman-Ross, 1947; *A Thing or Two About Music*, Allen, Towne & Heath, 1948, reprinted, Greenwood Press, 1972.

(Translator and editor) *Fifty Russian Art Songs from Glinka to Shostakovich*, Leeds Co., 1951; (translator from the Russian) A. Gretchaninoff, *My Life*, Coleman-Ross, 1952; (with David Ewen) *Fun with Musical Games and Quizzes*, Prentice-Hall, 1952; *Lexicon of Music Invective*, Coleman-Ross, 1953, 2nd edition, Scribner, 1965; (editor) *Baker's Biographical Dictionary of Musicians*, 5th edition, Schirmer, 1958, supplements, 1965, 1971.

Compiler of annual music surveys for *Britannica Book of the Year*, 1955-69, and member of editorial advisory board, *Encyclopaedia Britannica*, 1958—. Contributor to *Grove's Dictionary of Music and Musicians*, 5th edition, 1954, *Die Musik in Geschichte und Gegenwart*, 1960-67, and *Enciclopedia dello Spettacolo*, 1961-62. Contributor to *Boston Transcript*, 1927-41, *Christian Science Monitor*, 1936-63, *Musical Quarterly, Saturday Review*, and other publications. Columnist, *Etude*, 1950-57, *Bandwagon*, 1961-71, and *Medical Opinion and Review*, 1966-69. Associate editor, *New Music*, 1938-46.

WORK IN PROGRESS: Exposition of Music (history and theory of music); *Omnibus of Music* (collection of articles).

SIDELIGHTS: Slonimsky told *CA* that he has an intellectual curiosity about unexplored fields in musical biography. He has a general disregard for established viewpoints and prefers fresh examination and investigation. Slonimsky is fluent in French, Russian, Spanish, German, and Italian, with "an especial fondness for vulgar Latin." In 1956, he won $30,000 on a television quiz show. *Avocational interests:* "Everything except sports."

* * *

SLOVENKO, Ralph 1926-

PERSONAL: Born November 4, 1926; son of Samson (a realtor) and Chaia (Roitman) Slovenko. *Education:* Tulane University of Louisiana, B.E., 1948, LL.B., 1953, M.A., 1960, Ph.D., 1963; also studied in France as Fulbright scholar at University of Aix-Marseille and Sorbonne, University of Paris. *Religion:* Jewish. *Office:* School of Law, Wayne State University, Detroit, Mich.

CAREER: Louisiana Supreme Court, law clerk, 1953; Tulane University of Louisiana, New Orleans, professor of law, 1954-64, associate in psychiatry, School of Medicine, 1963-65; senior assistant district attorney, New Orleans, La., 1964-65; Menninger Foundation, Topeka, Kan., professor of law, 1965-67; University of Kansas, Lawrence, professor of law, 1965-67; Wayne State University, Detroit, Mich., professor of law, 1968—. *Member:* American Bar Association, American Orthopsychiatric Association, American Civil Liberties Union, Southern Society for Philosophy and Psychology, Louisiana Bar Association, Kansas Bar Association, New Orleans Bar Association, Omicron Delta Kappa.

WRITINGS: (Editor) *Civil Code of Louisiana and Ancillaries*, Claitor, 1961; (editor) *Symposium on LMRDA*, Claitor, 1961; (editor) *Symposium on Labor Relations Law*, Claitor, 1961; (editor) *Louisiana Civil Code, Ancillaries, and Code of Civil Procedure*, Claitor, 1961; *Louisiana Security Rights*, four volumes, Tulane University Press, 1962; *Mineral and Tidelands Law*, Claitor, 1963; (editor) *Oil and Gas Operations: Legal Considerations in the Tidelands and on Land*, Claitor, 1963; (editor) *Sexual Behavior and Law*, C. C Thomas, 1965; *Psychotherapy, Confidentiality, and Privileged Communication*, C. C Thomas, 1966; (editor) *Crime Law and Corrections*, C. C Thomas, 1966; (editor with James Knight) *Motivations in Play, Games and Sports*, C. C Thomas, 1967; *Handbook on Criminal Procedure*, Claitor, 1967; *Psychiatry and Law*, Little, Brown, 1973; *Tragicomedy in Court Opinions*, Claitor, 1973. Also editor of *American Lecture Series in Behavioral Science and Law*, C. C Thomas. Author of more than sixty articles in journals of law, psychiatry, and philosophy.

SIDELIGHTS: Ralph Slovenko is competent in Spanish, Yiddish, Russian, and French. *Avocational interests:* Sports, languages.

* * *

SMALLEY, Donald (Arthur) 1907-

PERSONAL: Born April 2, 1907, in North Manchester, Ind.; son of Charles Bert (a manufacturer) and Laura (Shankland) Smalley; married second wife, Barbara Jane Martin, 1952. *Education:* Indiana University, A.B. (summa cum laude), 1929, M.A., 1931; Harvard University, Ph.D., 1939. *Politics:* Independent. *Religion:* Episcopalian. *Home:* 1006 South Busey Ave., Urbana, Ill. 61801. *Office:* English Building 133, University of Illinois, Urbana, Ill. 61801.

CAREER: Indiana University, Bloomington, 1930-59, began as instructor, professor of English, 1951-59; University of Illinois, Urbana, professor of English literature, 1959—. Visiting summer professor at University of Minnesota, 1949, Harvard University, 1958. Supervisor of U.S. Naval Training School, Indiana University, 1942-44. *Member:* Modern Language Association of America, American Association of University Professors, Phi Beta Kappa.

WRITINGS: (Editor) Robert Browning, *Essay on Chatterton*, Harvard University Press, 1948; (editor, and author of introductory history of the writer's life in America) Frances Trollope, *Domestic Manners of the Americans*, Knopf, 1949; (editor with Bradford Booth) Anthony Trollope, *North America*, Knopf, 1951; (editor) *Poems of Robert Browning*, Houghton, 1956; (with others) *Victorian Fiction: A Guide to Research*, Harvard University Press, 1964; (editor) *Anthony Trollope: The Critical Heritage*, Routledge & Kegan Paul, 1969; (editor with Boyd Litzinger) *Browning: The Critical Heritage*, Routledge & Kegan Paul, 1970; (editor with others) *Works of Browning*, Ohio University

Press, Volume III, 1972, Volume V, 1974. Contributor to *Saturday Review* and to journals in his field.

SIDELIGHTS: Donald Smalley told *CA*: "[I was a] 'professional violinist' in my teens—i.e., earned a dollar a night for playing as one of two-piece orchestra (other being a pianist) at the local silent movie. I am a hi-fi addict, specializing in recorded Bach (including well over a 100 cantatas)."

* * *

SMELSER, Marshall 1912-

PERSONAL: Born February 4, 1912, in Joliet, Ill.; son of Albert Marion and Alma (Van Hook) Smelser; married Anna May Padberg, December 27, 1937; children: Mary Elizabeth, Mary Katherine. *Education:* Quincy College, A.B., 1935; Harvard University, A.M., 1942, Ph.D., 1948. *Religion:* Catholic. *Home:* 813 East Angela Blvd., South Bend, Ind. *Office:* Box 116, Notre Dame, Ind.

CAREER: College of St. Thomas, St. Paul, Minn., assistant professor, 1946-47; University of Notre Dame, Notre Dame, Ind., history faculty, 1947—, professor of history, 1957—, head of department, 1960-63. University of Chicago, Walgreen Lecturer, 1955; U.S. Naval Academy, Forrestal fellow, 1956-57. *Wartime service:* American Red Cross service with 95th Infantry Division, 1943-44, at National Headquarters, 1944-46. *Member:* Society of Indiana Pioneers. *Awards, honors:* Guggenheim fellow, 1963-64; President's Commencement Citation, 1972.

WRITINGS: American Colonial and Revolutionary History, Barnes & Noble, 1950; *The Campaign for the Sugar Islands, 1759*, University of North Carolina Press, 1955; *American History at a Glance*, Barnes & Noble, 1959; *The Congress Founds the Navy, 1787-1789*, University of Notre Dame Press, 1959; (with H. Kirwin) *Conceived in Liberty*, Doubleday, 1962; (co-author) *New Frontiers of Freedom*, Silver Burdett, 1965; *The Democratic Republic, 1801-1815*, Harper, 1969; *The Winning of Independence, 1774-1783*, F. Watts, 1972.

WORK IN PROGRESS: A life of Babe Ruth for Quadrangle Books.

* * *

SMELSER, Neil J(oseph) 1930-

PERSONAL: Born July 22, 1930, in Kahoka, Mo.; son of Joseph Nelson (a teacher) and Susie (Hess) Smelser; married Helen Margolis, July 10, 1954 (divorced, 1965); married Sharin Fately, December 20, 1967; children: (first marriage) Eric Jonathan, Tina Rachel, (second marriage) Joseph Neil, Sarah Joanne. *Education:* Harvard University, B.A. (summa cum laude), 1952, junior fellow of Society of Fellows, 1955-58, Ph.D., 1958; Oxford University, B.A. (first class honors), 1954, M.A., 1959; San Francisco Psychoanalytic Institute, graduate, 1971. *Home:* 8 Mosswood Rd., Berkeley, Calif. 94704. *Office:* Department of Sociology, 410 Barrows Hall, University of California, Berkeley, Calif. 94720.

CAREER: University of California, Berkeley, assistant professor, 1958-60, associate professor, 1960-62, professor, 1962-72, University Professor of Sociology, 1972—. Social Science Research Council, member of committee on economic growth, 1961-65, member of board of directors, 1968-73, chairman of board, 1971-73. *Member:* American Sociological Association (member of council, 1968-71, 1973-75; vice-president, 1971-73), American Association for the Advancement of Science, American Academy of Arts and Sciences (fellow), Pacific Sociological Association, Phi Beta Kappa. *Awards, honors:* Rhodes scholarship to Oxford University, 1952-54; faculty research fellow, Social Science Research Council, 1961-63, and auxiliary award of $4,000, 1962; research grants from National Science Foundation, 1965-66, and Ford Foundation, 1970-71; Guggenheim fellowship, 1973-74.

WRITINGS: (Junior author, with Talcott Parsons) *Economy and Society*, Free Press of Glencoe, 1956; *Social Change in the Industrial Revolution*, University of Chicago Press, 1959; (editor with Seymour M. Lipset) *Sociology: The Progress of a Decade*, Prentice-Hall, 1961; *Theory of Collective Behavior*, Free Press of Glencoe, 1963; (editor with brother, William T. Smelser, and co-author of introduction) *Personality and Social Systems*, Wiley, 1963, 2nd edition, 1970; *The Sociology of Economic Life* (college text), Prentice-Hall, 1963; (editor) *Readings on Economic Sociology*, Prentice-Hall, 1964; (editor with Lipset, and co-author of introductory chapter) *Social Structure, Mobility, and Economic Development*, Aldine, 1966; (editor) *Sociology*, Wiley, 1967, 2nd edition, 1973; *Essays in Sociological Explanation*, Prentice-Hall, 1968; *Sociological Theory: A Contemporary View*, General Learning Press, 1971; (editor with Gabriel Almond, and contributor) *Public Higher Education in California, 1950-70*, University of California Press, 1974.

Contributor: Wilbert E. Moore and Bert F. Hoselitz, editors, *Industrialization and Society*, Mouton & Co., 1963; Amitai and Eve Etzioni, editors, *Social Change: Sources, Patterns, and Consequences*, Basic Books, 1964; Milton L. Barron, *Contemporary Sociology: An Introductory Textbook of Readings*, Dodd, 1964; Alex Inkeles and Bernard Barber, editors, *Stability and Social Change*, Little, Brown, 1971; Ivan Vallier, editor, *Comparative Methods in Sociology*, University of California Press, 1971; Donald P. Warwick and Samuel Osherson, *Comparative Research Methods*, Prentice-Hall, 1973; David Riesman and Verne Stadtman, editors, *Academic Transformation*, McGraw, 1973; Talcott Parsons and Gerald Platt, *The American University*, Harvard University Press, 1973; Carl Kaysen, editor, *Content and Context: Essays on College Education*, 1973. Also contributor to *International Encyclopaedia of the Social Sciences*. Series editor in sociology, Prentice-Hall, 1966—. Advisory editor, *American Journal of Sociology*, 1960-62; editor, *American Sociological Review*, 1962-65.

WORK IN PROGRESS: Research on kinship structure and economic development; research on the methodology of comparative analysis.

* * *

SMIDT, Kristian 1916-

PERSONAL: Born 1916, in Sandefjord, Norway; son of Johannes and Jofrid (Grimstvedt) Smidt; married Aagot Karner, 1940 (marriage dissolved, 1973); married Anne Oulie-Hansen, 1973; children: (first marriage) Jon Kristian, Jofrid; (second marriage) Anne Katinka. *Education:* Larvik h. almenskole, Examen artium, 1933; University of Oslo, Cand. philol., 1939, Dr. philos., 1949; Princeton University, postdoctoral study, 1951-52. *Religion:* Lutheran. *Home:* S. Ytreber Ytrebergsgt 4, Tromsoe, Norway. *Office:* University of Tromsoe, Norway.

CAREER: Flekkefjord h. almenskole, Flekkefjord, Norway, lektor, 1940-45; University of Oslo, Oslo, Norway, instructor, 1945-52, associate professor, 1953-54, professor of English literature, 1955—. On leave from University of Oslo, serving as professor of English, University of Tromsoe, 1973—. *Member:* Norwegian Academy of Science and Letters, Norwegian Society of Authors, International Association of University Professors of English, New Society of Letters, Societas Johnsoniana (Oslo), Norwegian P.E.N. *Awards, honors:* Rockefeller fellowship for study of American literary criticism, 1951-52; Folger Shakespeare Library fellowship, 1960-61.

WRITINGS: Books and Men: A Short History of English and American Literature, J. W. Cappelens (Oslo), 1945, 8th edition, 1973; *Poetry and Belief in the Work of T. S. Eliot*, Norwegian Academy of Science and Letters, 1949, revised edition, Routledge & Kegan Paul, 1961; (editor with T. Sirevag and B. Sorensen) *Anglo-American Reader*, I-III, J. W. Cappelens, 1950-52; *James Joyce and the Cultic Use of Fiction*, Humanities, 1955, revised edition, 1959; *Iniurious [sic] Impostors and "Richard III,"* Humanities, 1964; (editor, and author of introduction) *Sonetter av William Shakespeare: Et utvalg av nordiske oversettelser med innledning* (title means "A Selection of Shakespeare's Sonnets in Scandinavian Translations"), Den norske bokklubben, 1964; *The Tragedy of King Richard the Third: Parallel Texts of the First Quarto and the First Folio*, Humanities, 1969; *Memorial Transmission and Quarto Copy in "Richard III,"* Humanities, 1970; (editor and author of introduction) *England forteller* (title means "England Narrates"), Den norske bokklubben, 1970; *Konstfuglen og nattergalen: Essays om diktning og kritikk* (title means "The Clockwork Bird and the Nightingale: Essays on Writing and Criticism"), Gyldendal Norsk Forlag, 1972; *The Importance of Recognition: Six Chapters on T. S. Eliot*, privately printed, 1973. Associate editor, *English Studies*, [Amsterdam], and *Shakespeare Translation*, [Tokyo].

* * *

SMITH, Alton E. 1917-

PERSONAL: Born June 16, 1917, in Cleveland, Ohio; wife's name, Mildred (a receptionist), married January 29, 1954. *Education:* Fenn College (now Cleveland State University), B.A., 1948; Western Reserve University (now Case Western Reserve University), graduate study, Evening Division, 1959-63. *Politics:* Republican. *Religion:* Presbyterian. *Home:* 4812 Anderson Rd., Cleveland, Ohio.

CAREER: Radelco Manufacturing Co., Cleveland, Ohio, purchasing agent, 1945-53; General Electric Co., Lamp Division, Cleveland, office manager, purchasing department, 1953-57; Electromark Corp., Cleveland, purchasing agent, 1957-66; Hupp Corp., Appliance Division, Cleveland, senior buyer, 1967-73, manager of purchasing, 1973—. *Military service:* U.S. Army, 1943-45. *Member:* National Writer's Club, Purchasing Agents Association of Cleveland.

WRITINGS: New Techniques for Creative Purchasing, Dartnell, 1966. Contributor of articles on procurement to purchasing and other business journals.

WORK IN PROGRESS: Potpourri of Creative Facts.

* * *

SMITH, D(avid) W(arner) 1932-

PERSONAL: Born November 14, 1932, in Loughborough, England; son of John Sidney (a farmer) and Ellen (Wootton) Smith; married Olaug Synnevag (formerly a li-

brarian), June 27, 1963; children: Ingrid Marie, Anne Catherine. *Education:* University of Leeds, B.A., 1954, Ph.D., 1961. *Politics:* "Left of centre." *Home:* 349 Manor Rd., Toronto, Ontario, Canada.

CAREER: Memorial University of Newfoundland, St. John's, assistant professor of French, 1960-63; University of Toronto, Victoria College, Toronto, Ontario, assistant professor, 1963-67, associate professor, 1967-71, professor of French, 1971—.

WRITINGS: Helvetius: A Study in Persecution, Clarendon Press, 1965; *Helvetius's Library*, Institute et musee Voltaire (Geneva), 1971.†

* * *

SMITH, Daniel M. 1922-

PERSONAL: Born July 12, 1922, in Sanford, N.C.; son of D. M. (a salesman) and Alma (Bruton) Smith; married Carolyn Aladeen Brown, January 11, 1946; children: Stephanie Ann, Daniel Bennett, Gregory Malloy. *Education:* University of California, Berkeley, A.B., 1949, M.A., 1950, Ph.D., 1954. *Home:* 315 Hopi Place, Boulder, Colo. *Office:* History Department, University of Colorado, Boulder, Colo.

CAREER: Stanford University, Stanford, Calif., instructor in history, 1953-57; University of Colorado, Boulder, assistant professor, 1957-60, associate professor, 1960-64, professor of history, 1964—, chairman of history department, 1968—; University of California, Berkeley, visiting instructor, summer, 1954; University of Oregon, Eugene, visiting professor, summer, 1965. *Military service:* U.S. Navy, 1942-46. *Member:* Organization of American Historians, American Historical Association, Phi Beta Kappa, Phi Alpha Theta.

WRITINGS: Robert Lansing and American Neutrality, 1914-1917, University of California Press, 1958; (editor) *Major Problems in American Diplomatic History*, Heath, 1964; *The Great Departure: United States and World War I, 1914-1920*, Wiley, 1965; (editor) *American Intervention, 1917*, Houghton, 1966; *The American Diplomatic Experience*, Houghton, 1972. Contributor of articles on U.S. diplomacy to American history journals.

WORK IN PROGRESS: Woodrow Wilson and the State Department, 1913-1921.

* * *

SMITH, Frank E(llis) 1918-

PERSONAL: Born February 21, 1918, in Sidon, Miss.; son of Frank Smith and Sadie (Ellis) Smith; married Helen Ashley McPhaul, December 15, 1945; children: Kathleen and Frederick (twins). *Education:* Sunflower Junior College, graduate, 1936; University of Mississippi, B.A., 1941; The American University, graduate study, 1946. *Politics:* Democrat. *Religion:* Methodist. *Home:* 5915 Huntview Dr., Jackson, Miss. 39206.

CAREER: Greenwood Morning Star, Greenwood, Miss., managing editor, 1946-47; Mississippi Legislature, Jackson, senator, 1948-50; U.S. House of Representatives, Washington, D.C., congressman representing Third District of Mississippi, 1950-62; Tennessee Valley Authority, Knoxville, director, 1962-72; Illinois Board of Higher Education, Springfield, associate director, 1974-75. Director, President Kennedy's Natural Resources Advisory Committee, 1960; sponsor, Atlantic Council of the United States; director, Southern Regional Council; visiting professor, Sangamon

State University, 1974-75. *Military service:* U.S. Army, 1942-46; served in Europe with Third Army; became major; received Bronze Star. *Member:* Beta Theta Pi. *Awards, honors:* Civil War Centennial Medallion.

WRITINGS: The Yazoo River, Holt, 1954; *Congressman from Mississippi*, Pantheon, 1964; *Look Away from Dixie*, Louisiana State University Press, 1965; *The Politics of Conservation*, Pantheon, 1966; *Mississippians All*, Pelican, 1968; *Land Between the Lakes*, University Press of Kentucky, 1971. General editor of Chelsea House's "Conservation in the United States: A Documentary History" series, five volumes; editor of two volumes, Van Nostrand's "Land and Water" series, 1971.

* * *

SMITH, J(ohn) Holland   1932-

PERSONAL: Born January 30, 1932, in Aylesbury, England; son of George Harry and Olive (Hitchman) Smith; married Margaret Gwen Evans, July 29, 1953. *Education:* Attended Exeter College, Oxford, 1952-55.

CAREER: Taught English privately in Germany, 1959-61, in England, 1962. Author and translator. *Member:* Society of Authors.

WRITINGS: (Translator from the French) Croegaert, *The Mass*, two volumes, Burns & Oates, 1959, 1960; *To Beg I Am Ashamed* (novel), Scepter Publishers, 1961; (translator from the German) Schmaus, *The Essence of Christianity*, Scepter Publishers, 1962; *Nine Days to Eternity* (novel), Chatto & Windus, 1963; (translator from the French) *Spiritual Autobiography of Charles de Foucauld*, Kenedy, 1964; *Understanding the Bible: A Guide for Catholics*, Nelson, 1965; (translator from the French) Dessauer, *Natural Meditation*, Kenedy, 1965; *The Great Schism, 1378*, Weybright & Talley, 1970; *Constantine the Great*, Scribner, 1971; *Francis of Assisi*, Scribner, 1972; *Joan of Arc*, Sidgwick & Jackson, 1973. Writes weekly column for *Maltese Observer*.

WORK IN PROGRESS: A socio-psychological and mythological study of the changing relationship between the individual and society lying behind our present Western civilization; a translation of Schmaus's *Wahrheit als Heilsbegegnung*, for Scepter; *Meditations on Loreto*, for Empire Press, Malta.

SIDELIGHTS: Smith once told *CA*: "Cultural and social history is a never-empty box of delights to me. I am both fascinated and repelled by the Mediterranean, its past and present, its glories and its squalor. Generally my chief interest is (inevitably) that of all writers.... learning to say what I have to say as well as I can."†

* * *

SMITH, Laura I(vory)   1902-

PERSONAL: Born September 28, 1902, in Dalrymple, Ontario, Canada; came to United States, 1923, naturalized citizen, 1966; daughter of George Washington and Agnes (Plewes) Ivory; married Gordon Hedderly Smith (a missionary), June 12, 1928; children: Douglas Hedderly, Leslie Gordon, Stanley Earl. *Education:* Toronto Bible College, graduate, 1924; studied at Moody Bible Institute, 1925, and Nyack Missionary College, 1928. *Permanent address:* United World Mission, Box 8000, St. Petersburg, Fla. 33738. *Current address:* 1427 Aldersgate Dr., Apartment L-2, Kissimmee, Fla. 32741.

CAREER: With husband, foreign missionary in Cambodia,

1929-34, in Vietnam, beginning, 1934. Studied French in Paris and Geneva, 1929, in preparation for work in Cambodia, 1929-34; later studied Raday and taught in that language in tribal Bible school in southern Vietnam; Bible school teacher (speaking Vietnamese) in Da Nang, Vietnam, beginning, 1956. Lecturer at Protestant churches of all denominations during furloughs in United States, Canada, England, Switzerland, and Holland.

WRITINGS: Gongs in the Night, Zondervan, 1943; *Light in the Jungle*, Moody, 1946; *Mawal, Jungle Boy of Viet Nam*, Moody, 1946; *Farther into the Night*, Zondervan, 1954; *Victory in Viet Nam*, Zondervan, 1964; *The Ten Dangerous Years*, Moody, in press.

SIDELIGHTS: From 1929 to 1955 under the Christian and Missionary Alliance, from 1958 to 1967 under the Worldwide Evangelization Crusade, and beginning 1967 under the United World Mission, Mrs. Smith and her husband have been training national preachers and establishing churches among the Vietnamese and the mountain tribespeople. They have also established two leprosariums and six orphanages and are now occupied with relief work among refugees.

* * *

SMITH, Louis M(ilde)   1929-

PERSONAL: Born December 24, 1929, in St. Louis, Mo.; son of Dudley R. (a physician) and Helen (Milde) Smith; married Marilyn Strong (a teacher), December 29, 1950; children: Cathy Helen, Curtis Louis. *Education:* Oberlin College, A.B., 1950; University of Minnesota, M.A., 1953, Ph.D., 1955. *Home:* 921 Lanyard, Kirkwood, Mo. *Office:* Graduate Institute of Education, Washington University, St. Louis, Mo.

CAREER: St. Paul (Minn.) public schools, psychologist, 1953-55; Washington University, St. Louis, Mo., assistant professor, 1955-61, associate professor, 1961-65, professor of education and psychology, 1965—. *Member:* American Psychological Association, American Educational Research Association, Society for Applied Anthropology, American Anthropological Association, American Association of University Professors.

WRITINGS: The Concurrent Validity of Six Personality and Adjustment Tests for Children, Psychological Monographs, 1958; (with B. B. Hudgins) *Educational Psychology*, Knopf, 1964; (with William Geoffrey) *The Complexities of an Urban Classroom*, Holt, 1967; (with Patricia Keith) *Anatomy of Educational Innovation*, Wiley, 1971; (contributor) *Four Evaluation Examples: Anthropological Economics, Narratives, and Portrayals*, Rand McNally, 1974.

AVOCATIONAL INTERESTS: Travel, camping, and fishing.

* * *

SMITH, Marion Hagens   1913-

PERSONAL: Born December 13, 1913, in Grand Rapids, Mich.; daughter of William W. and Adah (Rogers) Hagens; married Benjamin F. Smith (a retired mechanical engineer), February 19, 1937; children: Diana (Mrs. Arthur Curtis), Brian B. *Education:* Michigan State University, B.S., 1935. *Religion:* Protestant. *Home:* 8253 East Fulton Rd., Ada, Mich. 49301. *Office:* Fideler Co., 31 Ottawa Ave., Grand Rapids, Mich. 49502.

CAREER: Employed as laboratory chemist prior to World

War II; Fideler Co. (publishers), Grand Rapids, Mich., staff writer. *Member:* Phi Kappa Phi.

WRITINGS: (With Jerry E. Jennings) *The South*, Fideler, 1965; (with Carol S. Prescott) *Families Around the World*, Fideler, 1970; (with Prescott) *The Needs of Man*, Fideler, 1970; (with Prescott) *The Earth and Man*, Fideler, 1970.

* * *

SMITH, Richard A(ustin) 1911-

PERSONAL: Born December 3, 1911, in Clarksburg, W.Va.; son of Silas Morris (a businessman) and Mildred (Johnson) Smith; married Kathleen Knox, May 20, 1939; children: Richard, Jr., Roderick Sheldon. *Education:* Mercersburg Academy, student, 1927-31; Duke University, student, 1931-34. *Religion:* Episcopalian. *Home:* Cove Nook Farm, Noank, Conn.; and The Pilothouse, Noank, Conn. 06340.

CAREER: U.S. Department of Labor, Washington, D.C., writer of industrial and occupational analyses, 1934-38; International Business Machines Corp., New York, N.Y., staff writer, 1939, associate editor of *Think* (magazine), 1939-42; *Time*, New York, N.Y., financial writer, 1946; *Time, Life,* and *Fortune*, South Carolina correspondent, Charleston, 1946-48; *Time* and *Fortune*, economic correspondent, Washington, D.C., 1948-50; *Fortune*, New York, N.Y., associate editor, 1950-58, board of editors, 1958-66. Ferris Lecturer, Trinity College, Hartford, Conn., 1966. Editorial consultant, American Society of Tool and Manufacturing Engineers, 1966—. Trustee, Gunston School, Centerville, Md., 1962-70, Salem College, Salem, W.Va., 1963-69. *Military service:* U.S. Army, 1943-46; military correspondent in European theater, 1944-45. *Member:* Fiscal Correspondents Association, Phi Eta Sigma, Sigma Upsilon, National Press Club (Washington, D.C.), Manhasset Bay Yacht Club. *Awards, honors:* D.Litt., Salem College, 1955; Loeb Award, University of Connecticut, 1962, for distinguished writing (*Fortune* series on the electrical conspiracy).

WRITINGS: The Sun Dial (novel), Knopf, 1942; (co-author) *Why Do People Buy?*, McGraw, 1953; *Executive Life*, Doubleday, 1956; *The Art of Success*, Lippincott, 1956; *The Space Industry*, Prentice-Hall, 1962; *Corporations in Crisis*, Doubleday, 1962; *Reflections on Space*, U.S. Air Force Academy, 1964; (with others) *The Frontier States: Alaska, Hawaii*, Time/Life, 1968. Work anthologized in *One and Twenty*, Duke University Press, 1943. Author of seventy-five major articles for *Fortune* on people, corporations, states, industries, situations, and cities; contributor to other periodicals. Associate editor, *Dixie*, 1946-48; editor, Aviation Advisory Commission President's Report, 1971-72.

WORK IN PROGRESS: A novel about American business.

SIDELIGHTS: Smith's writings have been translated into a total of eight languages, including Arabic. He currently writes in the pilot house of a wrecked ship, removed to a site overlooking Fisher's Island Sound at Noank, Conn. Smith built a twenty-one foot cabin cruiser in his garage in 1953 and subsequently paid for half the cost of the boat by selling an article about a month's cruise to Lake Champlain to *Sports Illustrated*. *Avocational interests:* Glass and enamel work.†

SMITH, Wilbur M(oorehead) 1894-

PERSONAL: Born June 9, 1894, in Chicago, Ill.; son of Thomas S. and Sadie (Sanborn) Smith; married Mary Irene Ostrosky, August, 27, 1917; children: Thomas Sylvester (deceased). *Education:* Studied at Moody Bible Institute, 1913-14, College of Wooster, 1914-17; Dallas Theological Seminary, D.D., 1932. *Home and office:* 2490 Ridgeway Rd., San Marino, Calif. 91108.

CAREER: Ordained to Presbyterian ministry, 1922; pastor of churches in Baltimore, Md., 1922-27, Covington, Va., 1927-30, and Coatesville, Pa., 1930-37; Moody Bible Institute, Chicago, Ill., member of faculty, 1938-47; Fuller Theological Seminary, Pasadena, Calif., professor of English Bible, 1947-63; Trinity Evangelical Divinity School, Deerfield, Ill., professor of English Bible, 1963-67, professor emeritus, 1967—. *Member:* National Association of Biblical Instructors, American Society of Church History, Society of Biblical Literature, American Schools of Oriental Research (associate).

WRITINGS: The Bible: The Foundation of the American Republic (sermon), [Baltimore], 1923; *A List of Bibliographies of Theological and Biblical Literature Published in Great Britain and America, 1595-1931*, [Coatesville, Pa], 1931; *Select Notes on the International Sunday School Lessons*, 4 volumes, Wilde, 1934-37; *Time Periods of Prophecy*, American Bible Conference Association, 1935; *How to Study the Bible for the Enrichment of Our Spiritual Life*, 1936; *The Glorious Revival Under King Hezekiah*, Zondervan, 1937; *Profitable Bible Study*, Wilde, 1939, 2nd revised edition, 1963; *The Supernaturalness of Christ*, Wilde, 1940, new edition, Baker Book, 1974; *Glorious Deliverance by Resurrection*, The Bible Institute Colportage Association (Chicago), 1941; *The Gospel of Mark for Men in Service*, 1944; *Therefore Stand*, Wilde, 1945; *This Atomic Age and the Word of God*, Moody, 1945; *Annotated Bibliography of D. L. Moody*, Moody, 1948; *A Voice for God: The Life of Charles E. Fuller*, Wilde, 1949.

The Approaching World Crisis, 1950; *Chats from a Minister's Library*, 1950; *A Watchman on the Wall*, 1950; *Life of Will H. Houghton*, Eerdmans, 1951; *Egypt in Biblical Prophecy*, Wilde, 1960; *A Treasury of Books for Bible Study*, Wilde, 1960; *The Incomparable Book*, Beacon, 1961; (compiler) *Great Sermons on the Birth of Christ*, Wilde, 1963; (compiler) *Great Sermons on the Resurrection of Christ*, Wilde, 1964; (compiler) *Great Sermons on the Death of Christ*, Wilde, 1965; *Biblical Doctrine of Heaven*, Moody, 1968; *Best of D. L. Moody: Sixteen Sermons by the Great Evangelist*, Moody, 1971; *Before I Forget* (autobiography), Moody, 1971; *You Can Know the Future*, Regal Books, 1971; *The Minister in His Study*, Moody, 1973.

Editor of annual volume, *Peloubet's Select Notes on the International Sunday School Lessons*, 1935-70. Editor of "In the Study," *Moody Monthly*; contributing editor, *Christianity Today* and *Bibliotheca Sacra*.

* * *

SMITHDAS, Robert Joseph 1925-

PERSONAL: Born June 7, 1925, in Pittsburgh, Pa.; son of Joseph (a steel worker) and Anne (Mackevich) Smithdas. *Education:* Attended Western Pennsylvania School for the Blind and Perkins Institute for the Blind; St. John's University, Brooklyn, N.Y., B.A. (cum laude), 1950; New York University, M.A., 1953. *Politics:* Republican. *Religion:* Roman Catholic. *Home:* 225 First St., Mineola, N.Y.

11050. *Office:* National Center for Deaf-Blind Youths and Adults, 105 Fifth Ave., New Hyde Park, N.Y. 11040.

CAREER: Industrial Home for the Blind, Brooklyn N.Y., instructor, 1951-52, community relations work, 1952-63, acting director of services for the deaf and blind and community relations, 1963-65, associate director, 1966-71; National Center for Deaf-Blind Youths and Adults, director of community relations, 1971—. *Member:* Poetry Society of America, American Association of Workers for the Blind, Knights of Columbus. *Awards, honors:* New York State's Young Man of the Year, 1958; Poetry Society of America's Poet of the Year, 1960; Handicapped American of the Year, 1965, receiving trophy from Vice-President Humphrey; Governor's Award, New York State Committee on Employment of the Handicapped, 1965.

WRITINGS—All published by Industrial Home for the Blind, except as indicated: *My Heart Sings* (poems), 1953; *Christmas Bells and Other Poems*, 1954; *Christmas Vignette and Other Poems*, 1955; *Christmas Blessing and Other Poems*, 1956; *A Child's Christmas* (poems), 1957; *Life at My Fingertips* (autobiography), Doubleday, 1958; *City of the Heart* (poems), Taplinger, 1966. Contributor to *Vogue, Redbook*, and Catholic periodicals.

SIDELIGHTS: At the age of five, Smithdas suffered an attack of cerebro-spinal meningitis which left him blind and eighty percent deaf; within a few years he lost the remainder of his hearing. He is the first so handicapped person, since Helen Keller, to earn a bachelor's degree and the first to ever earn a master's degree. While at college he was a wrestler, and he is a Yankee fan, a poker player, and a deep-sea fisherman.

BIOGRAPHICAL/CRITICAL SOURCES: New York Daily News, April 29, 1966, July 20, 1966; *Washington Post*, April 29, 1966; *New York Times*, April 29, 1966.

* * *

SMYKAY, Edward Walter 1924-

PERSONAL: Born February 24, 1924, in South River, N.J.; son of Walter and Agnes (Bogucki) Smykay; married Ann Haenssler, 1947; children: Robert, Richard, Ronald, Anne Marie. *Education:* Rutgers University, B.S., 1948; University of Maine, M.S., 1952; University of Wisconsin, Ph.D., 1956. *Home:* 2327 Hamilton Rd., Okemos, Mich. *Office:* Michigan State University, Eppley Center, East Lansing, Mich. 48823.

CAREER: Marquette University, Milwaukee, Wis., instructor, later assistant professor of economics, 1953-56; Michigan State University, East Lansing, assistant professor of marketing and transportation, 1956—. Lecturer to marketing and economic associations in Japan, Canada, and United States. *Military service:* U.S. Army Air Forces, 1943-46; became second lieutenant. *Member:* American Economic Association, American Society of Traffic and Transportation, National Council of Physical Distribution Management (president, 1966-67), Associated Traffic Clubs of America (vice-president), Midwest Economics Association.

WRITINGS: (With Donald J. Bowersox and Frank H. Mossman) *Physical Distribution Management: Logistics Problems of the Firm*, Macmillan, 1961, revised edition (with Bowersox and Bernard J. LaLonde), 1968, 3rd edition (sole author), 1973; (editor) *Essays on Physical Distribution Management*, Traffic Service Corp., 1961; (with LaLonde) *Bibliography on Physical Distribution Management*, Mar-

keting Publications, 1967; (with LaLonde) *Physical Distribution: The New and Profitable Science of Business Logistics*, Dartnell, 1967; *Physical Distribution Management: Total Systems Route to New Profits*, [New York], 1967; (compiler with Bowersox and LaLonde) *Readings in Physical Distribution Management: The Logistics of Marketing*, Macmillan, 1969; (with Joan Breibart) *Introductory Marketing: A Programmed Approach*, Macmillan, 1971. Contributor to *Encyclopaedia Britannica*.

* * *

SNAVELY, Tipton Ray 1890-

PERSONAL: Born November 23, 1890, in Jonesville, Va.; son of William (a farmer) and Jennie (Graham) Snavely; married Nell Aldred, August 16, 1916 (died April 27, 1970); children: William Pennington. *Education:* Emory and Henry College, B.A., 1912; University of Virginia, M.A., 1915, Ph.D., 1919; Harvard University, A.M., 1918. *Politics:* Democrat. *Religion:* Methodist. *Home:* 1421 Gentry Lane, Charlottesville, Va. 22903. *Office:* Rouss Hall, University of Virginia, Charlottesville, Va. 22903.

CAREER: University of Virginia, Charlottesville, 1918—, professor of economics, 1924-61, chairman of department, 1923-56, professor emeritus, 1961—. Summer professor or lecturer at University of Southern California, University of Texas, and Harvard University. Director and vice-president, Citizens Bank and Trust Co., Charlottesville, 1937—. Member of various committees, Wage and Hour Division, U.S. Department of Labor, 1939-45; consultant, U.S. Bureau of Labor Statistics, 1940-44; chairman of Annual Assay Commission, U.S. Mint, 1940; chairman of Legislative Committee to Study Sales and Use Tax in Virginia, 1944-45. *Military service:* U.S. Army, 1917-18.

MEMBER: American Economic Association, International Institute of Public Finance, Royal Economic Society (England), Southern Economic Association (president, 1931-32), Phi Beta Kappa, Beta Gamma Sigma (president, 1936-39), Alpha Kappa Psi (grand counselor, 1923-31). *Awards, honors:* LL.D., Emory and Henry College, 1948; a chair endowed in his name, in Graduate School of Business Administration, University of Virginia, 1972.

WRITINGS: The Taxation of Negroes in Virginia, Michie Co., 1917; (with Duncan C. Hyde and Alvin B. Briscoe) *State Grants-in-Aid in Virginia*, Appleton, 1931; *The Fiscal System of Tennessee*, Tennessee State Planning Board, 1936; *George Tucker as Political Economist*, University Press of Virginia, 1964; *The Department of Economics at University of Virginia*, University Press of Virginia, 1967; *Origins of the Graduate School of Business Administration*, University Press of Virginia, 1975. Co-author of report of the Sales and Use Tax Commission, State of Virginia, 1945. Contributor to *Encyclopedia of Business* and to journals.

* * *

SNAVELY, William P(ennington) 1920-

PERSONAL: Born January 25, 1920, in Charlottesville, Va.; son of Tipton R. (a professor) and Nell (Aldred) Snavely; married Alice Pritchett, June 4, 1942; children: Nell Lee, William P., Jr., Elizabeth Tipton. *Education:* University of Virginia, B.A. (with honors), 1940, M.A., 1941, Ph.D., 1950; Harvard University, graduate study, 1946-47. *Politics:* Independent. *Religion:* Congregational. *Home:* 10807 Norman Ave., Fairfax, Va. 22030. *Office:* George Mason University, 4400 University Dr., Fairfax, Va. 22030.

CAREER: University of Connecticut, Storrs, instructor, 1947-50, assistant professor, 1950-55, associate professor, 1955-61, professor of economics, 1961-73, head of department, 1966-72; George Mason University, Fairfax, Va., professor of economics and chairman of department, 1973—. Ford Foundation economic consultant to Jordan Development Board, 1961-62, to Lebanese Ministry of Planning, 1964-65, and to graduate program in development administration, American University of Beirut, 1969-70; United Nations consultant to Jordan's National Planning Council, 1972. *Military service:* U.S. Army, 1942-45; became captain. *Member:* American Economic Association, American Finance Association, Southern Economic Association, Phi Beta Kappa, Phi Kappa Phi. *Awards, honors:* Ford Foundation fellowship, 1951-52; Foundation for Economic Education fellowship, 1952.

WRITINGS: (With W. Harrison Carter) *Intermediate Economic Analysis*, McGraw, 1961; *Theory of Economic Systems: Capitalism, Socialism, and Corporatism*, C. E. Merrill, 1969; (with M. T. Sadik) *Bahrain, Datar, and the United Arab Emirates*, Heath, 1972. Contributor to professional journals.

WORK IN PROGRESS: Research on the Swedish economy and on the economies of the Arabian Gulf States.

*   *   *

SNELLING, O(swald) F(rederick)   1916-
(Oswald Frederick)

PERSONAL: Born December 30, 1916, in London, England; son of Oswald Thomas and Caroline Eleanor (Skinner) Snelling; married Molly Sudeal (a registered nurse), December 12, 1964. *Education:* Attended Latymer School, Edmonton, London, 1929-33, and Hornsey School of Art, London, 1933-35. *Politics:* Left wing (no party affiliation). *Religion:* None. *Home:* 10 Roebuck House, 47 Bassett Rd., London W. 10, England. *Agent:* Georges Borchardt, 145 East 52 St., New York, N.Y. 10022.

CAREER: Cartoonist and commercial artist, London, England, 1936-39; later auctioneer of rare books and free-lance journalist. *Military service:* British Army, 1940-46. *Member:* Kensington Film Club (secretary, 1959-66), Bibliomites.

WRITINGS: *Double O Seven—James Bond: A Report*, Neville Spearman and Holland Press (joint publication), 1964; *A Bedside Book of Boxing*, Pelham Books, 1972. Contributor of articles on films, books, and sports to periodicals throughout the world, many of the articles ghosted for well-known personalities.

Under pseudonym Oswald Frederick: *White Hope*, Pendulum, 1947; *Battling Bruce*, Bertrand, 1948; *The Boys' Book of Boxing*, Bernard Henry, 1949.

SIDELIGHTS: *Double O Seven* has sold over a million copies and has been translated into many languages. Snelling says that he is gratified by the money that the humorously-critical study of the James Bond character has brought him ("since most of the other stuff never made me a penny").

*   *   *

SNYDER, Frank Gregory   1942-

PERSONAL: Born June 26, 1942, in Madison, Wis.; son of Frank George (a consulting geologist) and Margaret (Lundberg) Snyder. *Education:* Yale University, B.A., 1964; Institut d'Etudes Politiques, Paris, France, graduate study, 1964-65; Harvard University, law student, 1965—.

AWARDS, HONORS: Fulbright grant for study in France, 1964-65.

WRITINGS: *One-Party Government in Mali*, Yale University Press, 1965.

WORK IN PROGRESS: The Legal Profession and the Modernization of Law in French-Speaking West Africa.†

*   *   *

SNYDER, Gary   1930-

PERSONAL: Born May 8, 1930, in San Francisco, Calif.; son of Harold Alton and Lois (Willkie) Snyder; married Alison Gass, 1950 (divorced, 1951); married Joanne Kyger (a poet), 1960 (divorced, 1964); married Masa Uehara, August 6, 1967; children: Kai, Gen. *Education:* Reed College, B.A. (in anthropology and literature), 1951; attended Indiana University, 1951; University of California, Berkeley, graduate study in Oriental languages, 1953-56. *Politics:* Radical. *Religion:* Buddhist of the Mahayana-Vajrayana line. *Office:* 333 Sixth Ave., New York, N.Y. 10003.

CAREER: Poet. Spent most of his youth on his parents' farm north of Seattle, Wash.; in 1948 he shipped out from New York as a seaman; worked as logger and as a Forest Service trail crew member and forest lookout in Oregon, Washington, and California; in San Francisco, with Allen Ginsberg, Jack Kerouac, Philip Whalen, Michael McClure, and Philip Lamantia, helped to initiate and introduce to the public what developed into the "beat" movement in literature; worked at various jobs in San Francisco, including work for Kodak and as a burglar alarm installer; spent most of the period between 1956 and 1968 in Japan; prior to moving to Japan he worked as a wiper on an American Tanker with runs to the Persian Gulf and the South Pacific Islands; spent four months in 1961-62 in India, visiting temples and ashrams; since then he served one year (1964) as a member of the Department of English at the University of California, Berkeley, and participated in the Berkeley Poetry Conference, July, 1965; he has been living in the Sierra Nevada since 1970. *Awards, honors:* Scholarship to go to Japan, 1956, from First Zen Institute of America; National Academy of Arts and Letters poetry award, 1966; Bollingen Foundation grant, 1966-67; Frank O'Hara Prize, 1967; Levinson Prize, 1968; Guggenheim fellowship, 1968-69; Pulitzer Prize for poetry, 1974.

WRITINGS—All poetry, unless otherwise noted: *Riprap*, Orgin Press, 1959; *Myths & Texts*, Totem Press, 1960; *Riprap & Cold Mountain Poems* (the *Cold Mountain Poems* are Snyder's translations of poems by Han-Shan), Four Seasons Foundation, 1965; *Six Sections from Mountains and Rivers Without End*, Four Seasons Foundation, 1965; *A Range of Poems* (includes translations of the modern Japanese poet, Miyazawa Kenji), Fulcrum (London), 1966; *The Back Country*, New Directions, 1967; *Earth House Hold* (essays), New Directions, 1968; *Regarding Wave*, New Directions, 1970; *Turtle Island*, New Directions, 1974.

Work represented in numerous anthologies, including: *Contemporary American Poetry*, edited by Donald Hall, Penguin, 1962; *A New American Anthology*, edited by Walter Lowenfels, International Publications, 1964; *Poesia degli Ultima Americani*, edited by Fernando Pivano, Feltrinelli Editore (Milan), 1964; *12 Poets & 1 Painter*, edited by Donald M. Allen, Four Seasons Foundation, 1964; *A Controversy of Poets*, edited by Paris Leary and Robert Kelly, Doubleday, 1965; translations of Han-Shan in *Poems of the Late T'ang*, edited by A. C. Graham, Penguin, 1966.

Contributor to *Janus, Evergreen Review, Black Mountain Review, Yugen, Chicago Review, Jabberwock, San Francisco Review, Big Table, Poems from The Floating World, Origin, Kulchur, Journal for the Protection of All Beings, Nation, City Lights Journal, Yale Literary Magazine, Beloit Poetry Journal, Poetry,* and other publications.

WORK IN PROGRESS: A long poem, *Mountains and Rivers Without End,* begun in 1956, dramatically structured after a certain type of *No* play and titled after a Chinese sidewise scroll painting.

SIDELIGHTS: Snyder told *CA* that his axis is: paleolithic, energy-systems, Buddhist-Shamanist, 50,000-year humanist. The rhythms of his poems, he told Donald M. Allen, "follow the rhythm of the physical work I'm doing and life I'm leading at any given time—which makes music in my head which creates the line.... *Riprap* is really a class of poems I wrote under the influence of the geology of the Sierra Nevada and the daily trail-crew work of picking up and placing granite stones in tight cobble patterns on hard slab.... In part the line was influenced by the five- and seven-character line Chinese poems I'd been reading, which work like sharp blows on the mind.... *Myths and Texts* grew between 1952 and 1956. Its several rhythms are based on long days of quiet in lookout cabins; setting chokers for the Warm Springs Lumber Co.; and the songs and dances of Great Basin Indian tribes I used to hang around."

Though he himself is extremely knowledgeable, he is most tolerant of ignorance and appears to be least tolerant of cities—doesn't believe in them. "I think New York should be leveled and made into a buffalo pasture," he told *The Village Voice.* For *A Controversy of Poets* he wrote: "America five hundred years ago was clouds of birds, miles of bison, endless forests and grass and clear water. Today it is the tired ground of the world's dominant culture. Only Americans and a few western Europeans have lived with industry and the modern mass so long—the Africans and Chinese are fascinated children.... As poet I hold the most archaic values on earth. They go back to the Neolithic: the fertility of the soil, the magic of animals, the power-vision in solitude, the terrifying initiation and rebirth, the love and ecstasy of the dance, the common work of the tribe. A gas turbine or an electric motor is a finely-crafted flint knife in the hand. It is useful and full of wonder, but it is not our whole life." He also has said: "I feel that every landscape has its own demands, its own styles, its own mythologies and colors which, curiously enough, one discovers very clearly."

Snyder appears as the hero of Jack Kerouac's roman a clef, *Dharma Bums.* His own heroes are Mao Tse-tung, Yeats, D. H. Lawrence, and Crazy Horse, and his favorite heroine Naropa's wife, he told *CA*; his favorite fictional figures are Genji and the ladies in Tsao Hsueh-chin's *Dream of the Red Chamber.* Among poets he admires Tu Fu, Hafiz, Villon, Pound, Issa, Buson, Dharmakirti, Basho, Lawrence, Jeffers, Yeats, and Robert Duncan; among writers of prose, Charles Doughty, Sir Walter Raleigh, and Ssu-ma Ch'ien; he likes rhododendrons, sparrow-hawks, and the color turquoise.

Snyder is fluent in Japanese and reads Chinese.

BIOGRAPHICAL/CRITICAL SOURCES: Donald M. Allen, editor, *The New American Poetry,* Grove, 1960; *Prairie Schooner,* winter, 1960-61; Kenneth Rexroth, *Assays,* New Directions, 1961; Paris Leary and Robert Kelly, editors, *A Controversy of Poets,* Doubleday, 1965; David

Kherdian, *Gary Snyder,* Oyez (Berkeley), 1965; *New Statesman,* November 4, 1966; *Village Voice,* November 17, 1966; Carolyn Riley, editor, *Contemporary Literary Criticism,* Gale, Volume I, 1973, Volume II, 1974, Volume V, 1976.

* * *

SOLOMON, David J. 1925-

PERSONAL: Born December 26, 1925, in Santa Monica, Calif.; son of Llewellyn Morris ("a bootlegger and journalist") and Ida (Stieglitz) Solomon; married Martha Kephart, November 8, 1952; children: Kim and Lin (daughters). *Education:* New York University, B.A., 1951. *Politics:* "Utopian." *Home:* 39 Randolph Ave., London W.9, England.

CAREER: Free-lance editor. *Military service:* U.S. Army military intelligence, 1943-46; became sergeant.

WRITINGS: (Editor) *LSD, the Consciousness Expanding Drug,* Putnam, 1964; (editor) *The Marihuana Papers,* Bobbs-Merrill, 1966; (editor with George Andrews) *Drugs and Sexuality,* Panther Books, 1972; (editor with Andrews) *The Coca Leaf and Cocaine Papers,* Harcourt, 1975. Former editor, *Esquire, Metronome, Playboy.*

SIDELIGHTS: Solomon is a lay expert on psycho-active substances.

* * *

SOLT, Mary Ellen (Bottom) 1920-

PERSONAL: Born July 8, 1920, in Gilmore City, Iowa; daughter of Arthur (a minister) and Edith May (Littell) Bottom; married Leo Frank Solt (a professor of history), December 22, 1946; children: Catherine Anne, Susan Jane. *Education:* Iowa State Teachers College (now University of Northern Iowa), B.A., 1941; University of Iowa, M.A., 1948; Indiana University, School of Letters, graduate study, summers, 1957, 1958. *Home:* 836 Sheridan Rd., Bloomington, Ind. *Office:* Department of English, University of Indiana, Bloomington, Ind.

CAREER: Dinsdale High School, Dinsdale, Iowa, teacher of English, 1941-42; Hubbard High School, Hubbard, Iowa, teacher of English, 1942-44; Estherville High School, Estherville, Iowa, teacher of English, 1944-46; University High School, Iowa City, Iowa, teacher of English, 1946-48; Bentley School, New York, N.Y., teacher of English, 1949-52; writer, 1952—; Indiana University, Bloomington, associate professor of Comparative Literature, 1970—. Poet, critic, and lecturer. *Awards, honors:* Folio award for Prose, 1960, for article, "William Carlos Williams: Poems in the American Idiom," in *Folio,* winter, 1960.

WRITINGS: Flowers in Concrete (poems), Department of Fine Arts, Indiana University, 1966; (editor and author of introduction) *Concrete Poetry: A World View,* Indiana University Press, 1968. Contributor of articles to *Folio* and *Massachusetts Review*; contributor of poems to *Poor Old Tired Horse* (Scotland), *Labris* (Belgium), *Poetry, Chicago Review,* and other periodicals.

WORK IN PROGRESS: A second volume of "concrete" poems; *The Peoplemover: A Demonstration Poem,* for *West Coast Poetry Review*; and *William Carlos Williams: A Search for the American Idiom.*

* * *

SONTAG, Susan 1933-

PERSONAL: Born January 16, 1933, in New York, N.Y.;

married Philip Rieff (a professor of sociology), 1950 (divorced, 1958); children: David. *Education:* Attended University of California at Berkeley, 1948-49; University of Chicago, B.A., 1951; Harvard University, M.A. (English), 1954, M.A. (philosophy), 1955, Ph.D. candidate, 1955-57; St. Anne's College, Oxford, graduate study, 1957. *Address:* c/o Farrar, Straus & Giroux, 19 Union Sq. W., New York, N.Y. 10003.

CAREER: University of Connecticut, Storrs, instructor in English, 1953-54; *Commentary*, New York, N.Y., editor, 1959; lecturer in philosophy, City College (now City College of the City University of New York), New York, N.Y., and Sarah Lawrence College, Bronxville, N.Y., 1959-60; Columbia University, New York, N.Y., instructor in department of religion, 1960-64; Rutgers University, New Brunswick, N.J., writer-in-residence, 1964-65. Novelist; short-story writer; critic; essayist. Director of motion pictures "Duet for Cannibals," 1969, "Brother Carl," 1971, "Promised Lands," 1974. *Awards, honors:* Fellowships from American Association of University Women, 1957, Rockefeller Foundation, 1966, 1974, Guggenheim Memorial Foundation, 1966, 1975; George Polk Memorial Award, 1966, for contributions toward better appreciation of theatre, motion pictures, and literature.

WRITINGS—All published by Farrar, Straus, except as indicated: *The Benefactor* (novel), 1963; *Against Interpretation, and Other Essays*, 1966; *Death Kit* (novel), 1967; *Styles of Radical Will* (essays), 1969; *Trip to Hanoi*, 1969; (contributor) Douglas A. Hughes, editor, *Perspectives on Pornography*, St. Martin's, 1970; (author of introduction) Dugald Stermer, compiler, *The Art of Revolution*, McGraw, 1970; (author of introduction) E. M. Cioran, *The Temptation to Exist*, translated by Richard Howard, Quadrangle, 1970; *Duet for Cannibals* (screenplay), 1970; *Brother Carl* (screenplay), 1974; *On Photography* (essays), 1976; (editor and author of introduction) *Antonin Artaud: Selected Writings*, 1976. Also author of *Literature* (monograph), 1966. Contributor to *Great Ideas Today*, 1966; also contributor of short stories, reviews, essays, and articles to *Atlantic Monthly, American Review, Playboy, Partisan Review, Nation, Commentary, Harper's, New York Review of Books*, and other periodicals.

SIDELIGHTS: Discussing art in general, Susan Sontag told Joe David Bellamy: "I think nature imitates art more than art imitates nature, though we operate under the illusion that we are imitating nature. Artists are spokesmen of what in our sensibility is changing, and they choose among a number of possible different ways of rendering experience. I don't think there is one way of rendering experience which is correct. I believe in a plurality of experience. I don't believe there *is* such a thing as 'human experience.' There are different kinds of sensibility, different kinds of demands made on art, different self-conceptions of what the artist is... The artist is someone challenging accepted notions of experience or giving people *other* information about experience or other interpretations."

On writing in particular, she commented to Geoffrey Movius: "Writing is a mysterious activity. One has to be, at different stages of conception and execution, in a state of extreme alertness and consciousness and in a state of great naivete and ignorance. Although this is probably true of the practice of any art, it may be more true of writing because the writer—unlike the painter or composer—works in a medium that one employs all the time, throughout one's waking life."

She accounted for the lack of autobiographical material in her writing by explaining to Movius: "To write mainly about myself seems to me a rather indirect route to what I want to write about. Though my evolution as a writer has been toward more freedom with the 'I,' and more use of my private experience, I have never been convinced that my tastes, my fortunes and misfortunes, have any particularly exemplary character. My life is my capital, the capital of my imagination. I like to colonize... There is only so much revealing one can do. For every self-revelation, there has to be a self-concealment. A life-long commitment to writing involves a balancing of these incompatible needs. But I do think that the model of writing as self-expression is much too crude. If I thought that what I'm doing when I write is expressing myself, I'd junk my typewriter. It wouldn't be liveable-with. Writing is a much more complicated activity than that." "I have never been tempted to write about my own life," Susan Sontag explained to Bellamy. "Most writers consciously recount and transform their own experience. But the way in which I found freedom as a writer, and then as a film maker, was to invent... In the end, one does bring one's self to every character, but nothing I have written or related in film is autobiographical in the sense that it is an incident from my life."

Commenting on individual books, she related to Bellamy: "What interests me in each form is going beyond what I've done before. I think *Death Kit* is better than *The Benefactor* and that *Brother Carl* is better than *Duet for Cannibals*... Both *The Benefactor* and *Death Kit* were born as language in my head. I started to hear words in my head, a tone, a voice. A certain kind of language, a certain kind of rhythm, but words—I heard words and somebody talking...The two films ["Brother Carl" and "Duet for Cannibals"] were born as images. A film is not simply images. It is image and sound. But the first elements of the narrative I possessed were images. The dialogue seemed much less important."

Her interest in photography, she explained to Movius, is due to her belief that photography changes the world by "giving us an immense amount of experience that 'normally' is not our experience. And by making a selection of experience which is very tendentious, ideological." She related that she decided to write about photography because "I've had the experience of being obsessed by photographs. And because virtually all the important aesthetic, moral, and political problems—the question of 'modernity' itself and of 'modernist' taste—are played out in photography's relatively brief history."

BIOGRAPHICAL/CRITICAL SOURCES: New York Times Book Review, September 8, 1963, January 23, 1966; *New Republic*, September 21, 1963, February 19, 1966; *Book Week*, September 22, 1963; *Saturday Review*, February 12, 1966; *New York Review of Books*, June 9, 1966; *Books*, November, 1966; *Tri-Quarterly*, fall, 1966; *Atlantic Monthly,* September, 1966; *Detroit News*, January 15, 1967; *New Statesman*, March 24, 1967; *Time*, August 18, 1967; *New York Times*, August 18, 1967, October 3, 1969; *New Leader*, August 28, 1967; *Village Voice*, August 31, 1967; *Esquire*, July, 1968; Richard Gilman, *The Confusion of Realms*, Random House, 1970; *Vogue*, August 1, 1971; Carolyn Riley, editor, *Contemporary Literary Criticism*, Gale, Volume I, 1973, Volume II, 1974; Joe David Bellamy, editor, *The New Fiction: Interviews with Innovative American Writers*, University of Illinois Press, 1974; *Out*, April, 1974; *Boston Review*, Volume I, number 1, 1975; *Salmagundi*, Number 31, fall, 1975.

SOURKES, Theodore L(ionel) 1919-

PERSONAL: Born February 21, 1919, in Montreal, Quebec, Canada; son of Irving and Fannie (Golt) Sourkes; married Shena Rosenblatt (a physician), January 17, 1943; children: Barbara, Myra. *Education:* McGill University, B.Sc., 1939, M.Sc. (magna cum laude), 1946; Cornell University, Ph.D., 1948. *Home:* 4645 Montclair Ave., Montreal, Quebec, Canada.

CAREER: Chemist with industrial firms in Canada, 1942-45; Georgetown University Medical School, Washington, D.C., assistant professor of pharmacology, 1948-50; Merck Institute for Therapeutic Research, Rahway, N.J., research associate in department of enzyme chemistry, 1950-53; McGill University, Montreal, Quebec, senior research biochemist, Allan Memorial Institute of Psychiatry, 1953-65, director of Laboratory of Chemical Neurobiology, Allan Memorial Institute, 1965—, member of department of psychiatry, 1954—, professor of biochemistry, 1965—.

MEMBER: Canadian Biochemical Society, Canadian Physiological Society, Pharmacological Society of Canada, Canadian Society of Clinical Chemistry, American Society of Biological Chemists, American Society of Pharmacology and Experimental Therapeutics, Canadian Society for the Study of the History and Philosophy of Science, International Brain Research Organization, New York Academy of Sciences, Montreal Physiological Society (president, 1962-63), Montreal Biochemical Circle, Sigma Xi, Phi Kappa Phi. *Awards, honors:* Senior Fellowship award, Parkinson's Disease Foundation (New York), 1963-66.

WRITINGS: Biochemistry of Mental Disease, Harper, 1962; *Nobel Prize Winners in Medicine and Physiology, 1901-65* (revision and expansion of earlier work by L. G. Stevenson), Abelard, 1966. Associate editor, *Methods in Medical Research*, Volume IX. Member of editorial boards, *Journal of Neurochemistry, Pharmacology, Biochemistry and Behavior*, and *Canadian Journal of Biochemistry*. Contributor of over 200 scientific articles to professional journals.

*   *   *

SOUTHWELL, Eugene A. 1928-

PERSONAL: Born April 8, 1928, in San Diego, Calif.; son of Daniel and Nora (Valleroy) Southwell; married Gloria Powers, January 6, 1957; children: Kim, Kirk, William. *Education:* University of the Pacific, A.B., 1951, graduate study, 1951-52; University of Iowa, M.A. and Ph.D., 1961. *Home:* 314 Sheridan, Park Forest, Ill.

CAREER: Private practice as clinical psychologist, Olympia Fields, Ill. 1962—. Indiana University, Gary Campus, assistant professor, 1964-67, associate professor of psychology, 1967—, chairman of department, 1973—. Illinois Youth Commission, Joliet, psychological consultant, 1965-69; Calumet Region Planning Commission on Mental Health and Mental Retardation, executive secretary, 1966-69; Park Forest Health Council, chairman of mental health commission. *Military service:* U.S. Army Air Forces, 1947-49; became sergeant. *Member:* American Psychological Association. Council for the Advancement of the Psychological Professions and Sciences, Midwestern Psychological Association, Illinois Psychological Association, Indiana Psychological Association, Chicago Psychological Club, Sigma Xi.

WRITINGS: Personality: Theory and Research, Brooks-Cole, 1964, 2nd edition, 1971; *Abnormal Psychology:*

Theory and Research, Brooks-Cole, 1969. Contributor to psychology journals.

WORK IN PROGRESS: The Practice of Clinical Psychology.

SIDELIGHTS: Southwell is competent in French and German.

*   *   *

SOUTHWELL, Samuel B(eall) 1922-

PERSONAL: Born January 15, 1922, in Lockhart, Tex.; son of George T., Jr. and Lucile (Beall) Southwell; married Mary Jane Bamford; children: Michael Beall, Teresa Bamford. *Education:* University of Texas, B.J., 1947, M.A., 1949, Ph.D., 1956. *Politics:* Liberal. *Religion:* Roman Catholic. *Home:* 1217 West Main St., Houston, Tex. 77006. *Office:* University of Houston, Houston, Tex.

CAREER: Texas A&M University, College Station, 1949-59, became associate professor; U.S. Department of State, exchange officer at U.S. Embassy, Mexico City, Mexico, 1959-61, consul in Guadalajara, Mexico, 1961-65; University of Houston, Houston, Tex., associate professor, 1965-70, professor of English literature, 1970—, chairman of department, 1969-73. *Military service:* U.S. Navy, World War I; served in Pacific; became lieutenant junior grade. *Awards, honors:* Doctor Honoris Causa, Universidad Autonoma de Guadalajara, 1965.

WRITINGS: If All the Rebels Die (novel), Doubleday, 1966.

WORK IN PROGRESS: Browning's Quest for Eros: A Study of "Fifine at the Fair"; a second novel.

SIDELIGHTS: Southwell is fluent in Spanish.

*   *   *

SOUTHWORTH, Horton C. 1926-

PERSONAL: Born April 2, 1926, in Monroe, Mich.; son of Fred Osgood (a printer) and Bertha (Meier) Southworth; married Jannene McIntyre (a reading coordinator), April 20, 1971; children: Sue Ann, Nancy, James, Janet, Jaye, Brad, Alexandra. *Education:* Michigan State University, B.A., 1950, M.A., 1952, Ed.D., 1962. *Politics:* Democrat. *Religion:* Protestant. *Home:* 619 South Linden Ave., Pittsburgh, Pa. 15208. *Office:* 2805 Cathedral of Learning, School of Learning, School of Education, University of Pittsburgh, Pittsburgh, Pa. 15260.

CAREER: Elementary school principal in Bellevue, Mich., 1951-55, and Pontiac, Mich., 1955-59; Michigan State University, Macomb Teacher Education Center, Warren, instructor, 1959-63, assistant professor, 1963-64, associate professor of education, 1964-67; University of Pittsburgh, Pittsburgh, Pa., professor of elementary education, 1967—, head of department, 1967-73, chairperson of Division of Teacher Development, 1973—. Consultant to Association of American Schools in Mexico, 1964-66, American Academy for the Advancement of Science, 1968, and to U.S. Office of Education Model Dissemination Conferences, 1968-69; Lecturer and consultant to Education Association (London), 1969—. *Military service:* U.S. Naval Reserve, Anti-Submarine Warfare, 1944-46. *Member:* Association for Teacher Education, Association for Supervision and Curriculum Development, American Educational Research Association, Phi Delta Kappa.

WRITINGS: (Contributor) Hugo David, editor, *Handbook for Student Teachers*, W. C. Brown, 1964; (with

Robert W. Houston and Frank H. Blackington III) *Professional Growth Through Student Teaching,* C. E. Merrill, 1965. Contributor of articles to *Pennsylvania School Journal, Contemporary Education,* and other professional publications.

*   *   *

SOWERS, Robert (Watson) 1923-

PERSONAL: Surname rhymes with "flowers"; born January 7, 1923, in Milwaukee, Wis.; son of Ray V. (an educator) and Frances (Ellmaker) Sowers; married Theresa Obermayr. *Education:* Florida Southern College, student, 1941-43; New School for Social Research, B.A., 1948; Columbia University, M.A., 1950; Central School of Arts and Crafts, London, England, additional study, 1950-53.

CAREER: Designer of stained-glass windows. *Military service:* U.S. Army, 1943-46. *Member:* Foundation for Art, Religion and Culture. *Awards, honors:* Fulbright and Tiffany grants; Silver Medal (twice) of Architectural League of New York for stained glass windows in St. George's Church, Durham, N.H., and Holy Trinity Methodist Church, Danvers, Mass.; certificate of merit, Municipal Art Society of New York, for American Airlines terminal facade at Kennedy International Airport.

WRITINGS: The Lost Art: A Survey of 1000 Years of Stained Glass, Wittenborn, 1954; *Stained Glass: An Architectural Art,* Universe, 1965. Contributor to *New Catholic Encyclopedia.*

SIDELIGHTS: Sower's books have been published in England and Germany.†

*   *   *

SOWERS, Sidney Gerald, Jr. 1935-

PERSONAL: Born September 8, 1935, in Tacoma, Wash.; son of Sidney Gerald and Dorothy Margaret (Campbell) Sowers. *Education:* University of Puget Sound, A.B., 1957; San Francisco Theological Seminary, B.D., 1960; University of Basel, Th.D., 1964. *Politics:* Independent. *Home:* 331 South 41st Ave., West Richland, Wash. 99352. *Office:* Bethany United Presbyterian Church, West Richland, Wash.

CAREER: Ordained Presbyterian minister, 1963; pastor in Concrete, Wash., 1963-64; University of Tulsa, Tulsa, Okla., assistant professor, 1964-65; Knoxville College, Knoxville, Tenn., assistant professor of philosophy and religion, 1965-68; Macalester College, St. Paul, Minn., visiting associate professor of religion, 1968-70; pastor in Coulee City, Wash., 1970-74; Bethany United Presbyterian Church, West Richland, Wash., 1974—

WRITINGS: The Hermeneutics of Philo and Hebrews, John Knox, 1965; (contributor) *Oikonomia,* [Hamburg, Germany], 1967; (translator) Oscar Cullerman, *Salvation in History,* Harper, 1967. Contributor to *Theologische Zeitschrift.*

*   *   *

SPANN, Weldon O(ma) 1924-

PERSONAL: Born November 21, 1924, in North Little Rock, Ark.; son of Guy Simon (a truck driver) and Stella (Black) Spann. *Education:* Arkansas Polytechnic College, student, 1945-47; University of Arkansas, B.S. (chemistry), 1949. *Politics:* Independent. *Religion:* Methodist. *Home:* 1700 Marion, North Little Rock, Ark. 72114.

CAREER: Entered U.S. Navy at eighteen and served as aerial gunner and radio operator during World War II, spending twenty-seven months overseas, 1942-45; re-enlisted in Navy as aviation electronics technician, 1950-54, and spent sixteen months in the Pacific; joined Air Force as aircraft radio mechanic, 1954-58; has worked at various occupations ("stops along the way")—clerk in country grocery, service station attendant, house painter, chemist, television repairman, radio operator, and electronics technician; full-time writer ("with only an occasional break when my finances dwindled to zero"), beginning, 1963; currently owns an electronics repair business.

WRITINGS—All novels: *Outlaw Town,* Bouregy, 1965; *Return to Violence,* R. Hale, 1969; *Discharge to Danger,* R. Hale, 1969; *The Stink of Murder,* R. Hale, 1969; *Hunter for Hire,* R. Hale, 1970; *Wall of Jeopardy,* R. Hale, 1970; *Plunge into Peril,* R. Hale, 1970.

WORK IN PROGRESS: A novel, with working title, *Losers Throw Snake-eyes.*

SIDELIGHTS: Spann's books have been sold in France, Germany, Denmark, Spain, and Argentina. *Avocational interests:* Electronics (holds first class radio-telephone license from Federal Communications Commission), reading, hunting, and fishing.

*   *   *

SPENCER, Jean E(lizabeth) 1933-

PERSONAL: Born March 28, 1933, in Somerset, Pa.; daughter of James D. and Mabel S. (an associate professor) Spencer. *Education:* University of Maryland, B.A., 1955, M.A., 1961, Ph.D., 1966; University of Washington, Seattle, graduate study, 1955, 1957-1960. *Office:* Bureau of Governmental Research, University of Maryland, College Park, Md.

CAREER: University of Maryland, College Park, lecturer, 1962-66, assistant professor of political science, 1966—, Bureau of Governmental Research, research associate, 1962—. *Member:* American Political Science Association, National Municipal League, Phi Kappa Phi, Pi Sigma Alpha, Phi Delta Gamma.

WRITINGS: (With George A. Bell) *The Legislative Process in Maryland,* 2nd edition, Bureau of Governmental Research, University of Maryland, 1963; *Contemporary Local Government in Maryland,* Bureau of Governmental Research, University of Maryland, 1965.

WORK IN PROGRESS: A study of local and urban governmental development and change, tentative title, *Area and Process—Toward a Theory of Governmental Development and Change.*†

*   *   *

SPENCER, William 1922-

PERSONAL: Born June 1, 1922, in Erie, Pa.; son of Herbert Reynolds (a manufacturer) and Rachel (Davis) Spencer; married Martha Jane Brown, February 6, 1948; married Elizabeth Bouvier, May 18, 1969; children: (first marriage) Christopher, Meredith, Anne. *Education:* Princeton University, A.B., 1948; Duke University, A.M., 1950; American University, Ph.D., 1965. *Politics:* Democrat. *Religion:* United Church of Christ. *Home:* 1037 Betton Rd., Tallahassee, Fla. *Office:* Florida State University, Tallahassee, Fla. 32306.

CAREER: Middle East Journal, Washington, D.C., assistant editor, 1956-57; George Washington University, Washington, D.C., associate professor of political science, 1957-60; U.S. Office of Education, Washington, D.C., international programs specialist, 1960-62; UNESCO, Paris, France, chief of publications, 1962-64; American University, Washington, D.C., director of Institute of Non-Western Studies, 1965-68; Florida State University, Tallahassee, professor of Middle East history, 1968—. Consultant to Historical Evaluation and Research Organization and Special Operations Research Office; adviser to Government of Morocco (for UNESCO). *Military service:* U.S. Army, 1943-46; cryptanalyst in India; received Presidential Citation. *Member:* Middle East Studies Association, African Studies Association, Florida Heritage Foundation, Phi Kappa Phi, Pi Sigma Alpha. *Awards, honors:* Distinguished Service Award, U.S. Junior Chamber of Commerce, 1958; Carnegie fellowship; U.S. Office of Education Title V grant; Fulbright-Hays Award; Florida State University research grant.

WRITINGS: The Land and People of Turkey, Lippincott, 1958; *Political Evolution in the Middle East*, Lippincott, 1962; *The Land and People of Morocco*, Lippincott, 1965; *The Land and People of Tunisia*, Lippincott, 1967; *The Land and People of Algeria*, Lippincott, 1969; *Algiers in the Age of the Corsairs*, University of Oklahoma Press, 1975; *Story of North Africa*, McCormick-Mathers, 1975; (contributor) *The Ottoman Empire in the Nineteen Century*, Ohio State University Press, 1975. Contributor of articles to *World Book Encyclopedia* and to *Venture, Science and Technology, Washington Post*, and *New York Times*; regular contributor of book reviews to aforementioned newspapers, and to *Africa Report, American Historical Review*, and other journals.

WORK IN PROGRESS: Research for book on Mediterranean Africa.

SIDELIGHTS: Spencer has lived and traveled extensively in Europe and Middle East; he is fluent in French, with a reading knowledge of Spanish, Italian, and Turkish.

*   *   *

SPESHOCK, Phyllis (Nieboer)   1925-

PERSONAL: Born May 27, 1925, in Sparta, Mich.; daughter of James and Edith (Mutchler) Nieboer; married Edward J. Speshock (an employee of Teledyne Continental), April 10, 1944; children: Janis Elaine, Melissa Mary. *Education:* Calvin College, B.A., 1971. *Politics:* "Republican—generally speaking." *Religion:* Baptist. *Home:* 75 South Union, Sparta, Mich. 49345. *Agent:* Lenniger Literary Agency, 437 Fifth Ave., New York, N.Y. 10016.

CAREER: Substitute teacher, Sparta (Mich.), area schools; free-lance writer.

*WRITINGS—*All published by Zondervan: *First Love*, 1954; *Rise Up My Love*, 1956; *The Voice of My Beloved*, 1957; *The Upright Love*, 1959; *Hellbent for Election*, 1964. More than four hundred articles, short stories, and novelettes have been published in women's, family, confession, and juvenile magazines, and in trade and religious journals; some of those publications have been under undisclosed pseudonyms.

WORK IN PROGRESS: Short stories for magazines.

AVOCATIONAL INTERESTS: Antiquing, restoring and redecorating items found in resale shops.

SPIGEL, Irwin M(yron)   1926-

PERSONAL: Born January 2, 1926, in New York, N.Y.; son of Harold (an accountant) and Bertha (Pincus) Spigel; married Lois Sufrin, June 30, 1949; children: Steven, Gwynne-Ellen, Erik. *Education:* New York University, B.A., 1947; Temple University, M.A., 1959, Ph.D., 1962. *Office:* Department of Psychology, University of Toronto, Toronto, Ontario, Canada.

CAREER: University of Pittsburgh, School of Medicine, Pittsburgh, Pa., research psychologist in Psychiatric Institute, 1962-63; Temple University, Philadelphia, Pa., assistant professor of psychology, 1962-65; University of Toronto, Toronto, Ontario, associate professor of psychology, 1965—. *Member:* American Association for the Advancement of Science, Canadian Psychological Association.

WRITINGS: Reading in the Study of Visually Perceived Movement, Harper, 1965. Contributor to psychology journals.

WORK IN PROGRESS: Research in animal social behavior and human communication.

*   *   *

SPILHAUS, Athelstan (Frederick)   1911-

PERSONAL: Born November 25, 1911, in Rondeborsch, near Cape Town, South Africa; came to United States, 1931, naturalized, 1946; son of Karl Antonio (a merchant) and Nellie (Muir) Spilhaus; married Mary Atkins, 1935; married Gail T. Griffin, 1964; children: (first marriage) Athelstan F., Jr., Mary Muir, Eleanor, Margaret Ann, Karl Henry. *Education:* University of Cape Town, B.Sc., 1931, D.Sc., 1948; Massachusetts Institute of Technology, S.M., 1933. *Home address:* P.O. Box 1063, Middleburg, Va. 22117. *Office:* National Oceanic and Atmospheric Administration, U.S. Department of Commerce, Washington, D.C.

CAREER: Massachusetts Institute of Technology, Cambridge, research assistant, 1933-35; Woods Hole Oceanographic Institution, Woods Hole, Mass., research assistant, 1936-37, investigator in physical oceanography, 1938-60, associate, 1960—; New York University, New York, N.Y., assistant professor, 1937-38, associate professor, 1939-42, professor of meteorology, 1942-48, organizer, and chairman of department of meteorology, 1938-47; University of Minnesota, Institute of Technology, Minneapolis, dean, 1949-66, professor of physics, 1966-67; Franklin Institute, Philadelphia, Pa., president, 1967-69; president of Aqua International, Inc., 1969-70; Woodrow Wilson International Center for Scholars, Smithsonian Institution, Washington, D.C., fellow, 1971-74; National Oceanic and Atmospheric Administration of U.S. Department of Commerce, Washington, D.C., special assistant to the administrator, 1974—. Meteorological adviser, government of South Africa, 1947; member of various advisory committees, including U.S. Department of Interior, Department of Commerce, Army, and Air Force. Scientific director of weapons effects on two Nevada atomic tests, 1951; U.S. representative on executive board of UNESCO, 1954-58; member of U.S. National Committee for the International Geophysical Year, 1955-58; U.S. commissioner in charge of science exhibit, Seattle World's Fair, 1961-63; member, National Space Board, 1966-72.

Inventor of bathythermograph, Spilhaus space clock, and other oceanographic, aircraft, and meteorological instruments. Director of Pergamon Press and of several business firms. Scientific posts include committee on extent of air space, International Astronautical Federation, chairman of National Academy of Sciences-National Research Council committee on pollution and former chairman of committee on oceanography. Trustee of Science Service, Inc., International Oceanographic Foundation, Woods Hole Oceanographic Institution, Pacific Science Center Foundation; director of American Museum of Archaeology and North Star Research and Development Institute. *Military service:* Union of South Africa Defense Forces, assistant director of Technical Services, 1933-35; became lieutenant. U.S. Army Air Forces, 1943-46; became lieutenant colonel; received Legion of Merit.

MEMBER: Royal Meterological Society (fellow), American Institute of Aeronautics and Astronautics (fellow), American Association for the Advancement of Science (fellow; president, 1970; chairman of board of directors, 1971), Marine Technology Society (member of board of directors), Royal Society of South Africa, American Geophysical Union, American Meterorological Society, American Society of Limnology and Oceanography, American Society for Engineering Education, American Philosophical Society, Sigma Xi, Tau Beta Pi, Iota Alpha, Cosmos Club (Washington, D.C.).

AWARDS, HONORS: Exceptional Civilian Service Medal, U.S. Air Force, 1952; Patriotic Civilian Service Award, U.S. Army, 1959; Berzelius Medal, 1962; Proctor Prize of Scientific Research Society of America, 1968; D.Sc., Coe College, 1961, Rhode Island University, 1968, Hahnemann Medical College, 1968, Philadelphia College of Science, 1968, Hamilton College, 1970, Southeastern Massachusetts University, 1970, Durham University, 1970, University of South Carolina, 1971, Southwestern University at Memphis, 1972; L.L.D., from Nova University, 1970.

WRITINGS: (With James E. Miller) *Workbook in Meteorology,* McGraw, 1942; *Report on the Meteorological Services for the Union of South Africa,* Union of South Africa Government Printer, 1948; *Weathercraft,* Viking, 1951; (with W. E. K. Middleton) *Meteorological Instruments,* 3rd edition, revised, University of Toronto Press, 1953; (with Joseph J. George and others) *Weather is the Nation's Business,* U.S. Government Printing Office, 1953; *Satellite of the Sun,* Viking, 1958; *Turn to the Sea,* National Academy of Sciences, 1959, children's edition, Whitman Publishing Co., 1962; *The Ocean Laboratory,* Creative Educational Society, Inc., 1967; *Daring Experiments for Living,* Science Service, 1968.

Contributor: *The Nation Looks at Its Resources,* Resources for the Future, Inc., 1954; Morton Alperin and H. F. Gregory, editors, *Vistas in Aeronautics,* Volume II, Pergamon, 1959; M. Bailey and U. Leavell, editors, *A World to Discover,* American Book Co., 1963; Francois Leydet, editor, *Tomorrow's Wilderness,* Sierra Club, 1963; E. John Long, editor, *Ocean Sciences,* U.S. Naval Institute, 1964; *Our World in Peril: An Environment Review,* Fawcett, 1971; *The Restless Americans,* Xerox College Publishing, 1971.

Creator of illustrated strip on science, "Our New Age," published as Sunday feature in U.S. and several foreign newspapers, 1958-62, as daily feature in U.S. newspapers, 1962—. Contributor of more that two hundred articles to periodicals, mainly in engineering, geographic, and meteorological fields.

Chairman of American editorial board, Commonwealth and International Library of Science, Technology, and Engineering; chairman of scientific advisory committee, American Newspaper Publishers Association; member of honorary editorial board, *Underwater Yearbook;* member of advisory board, *Industrial Research, Oceanology* and *Planetary and Space Physics,* World Book Encyclopedia Science Service, and Industrial Research.

SIDELIGHTS: As a young scientist Spilhaus became internationally known for the bathythermograph, a device for measuring depth and temperature of ocean waters from a moving craft.

* * *

SPIRT, Diana L(ouise) 1925-
(Diana L. Lembo)

PERSONAL: Surname originally Lembo; born February 22, 1925, in Waterbury, Conn.; daughter of Louis and Thelma (Fava) Spirt; children: Stephen J. Lembo, Jarron L. Lembo, Deidre J. Lembo. *Education:* Cornell University, B.S., 1946; Long Island University, M.S., 1959, M.S. in L.S., 1961; New York University, Ph.D., 1970. *Home:* 17 Wayaawi Ave., Bayville, N.Y. 11709. *Office:* Graduate Library School, Long Island University, Greenvale, N.Y 11548.

CAREER: School librarian, Brookville, N.Y., 1958-65; Long Island University, Graduate Library School, Greenvale, N.Y., 1965—, began as associate professor, became professor of library science. Visiting professor, Dalhousie University, 1970, 1974, Kent State University, 1971. *Member:* American Library Association, Association for Educational Communications and Technology, New York Library Club, Nassau-Suffolk School Library Association (president, 1961), Pi Lambda Theta, Kappa Delta Pi. *Awards, honors:* New York Library Association award, 1962; New York University Founders Day Award, 1970.

WRITINGS—Under name Diana L. Lembo: (With Bishop, Copeland, and Eggers) *The Research Paper: A Manual for Planning, Organizing, Writing,* Kennikat, 1964; (with John Gillespie) *Junior Plots: A Book Talk Manual for Teachers and Librarians,* Bowker, 1967; (with Gillespie) *Introducing Books: A Guide for the Middle Grades,* Bowker, 1970. Also author, with Gillespie and Fokarelli, of "Library Learning Laboratory," 1970.

Under name Diana L. Spirt; all with John Gillespie: *Paperback Books for Young People,* American Library Association, 1972; *The Young Phenomenon,* American Library Association, 1972; *Creating a School Media Program,* Bowker, 1973. Contributor to library and education journals. Contributing editor, *Previews,* 1967—.

WORK IN PROGRESS: A manual for instruction in media.

* * *

SPLANE, Richard B. 1916-

PERSONAL: Born September 25, 1916, in Calgary, Alberta, Canada; son of Alfred W. and Clara (Allyn) Splane; married Verna Huffman (a teacher of nursing), February 22, 1971. *Education:* McMaster University, B.A., 1940; London School of Economics and Political Science, Certificate of Social Science and Administration, 1947; University of Toronto, M.A., 1948, M.S.W., 1951, D.S.W., 1961. *Home:* 1775 Allison Rd., Vancouver, British Columbia V6T 1S7, Canada.

CAREER: Teacher in rural Alberta, 1935-37; Children's Aid Society, Cornwall, Ontario, executive director, 1948-

50; Department of National Health and Welfare, Ottawa, Ontario, research economist, 1952-59, director of unemployment assistance, 1959-65, director-general, welfare assistance and services, 1965-70, assistant deputy minister of social allowances and social services, 1970-72; University of British Columbia, Vancouver, professor of social policy, 1972—. Canadian representative on board of United Nations Children's Fund (UNICEF) in New York, 1963, Bangkok, 1964; member of United Nations expert committee on Social Welfare Policy and Planning. Visiting professor, University of Alberta, 1972-73. *Military service:* Royal Canadian Air Force, 1942-46. *Member:* Canadian Association of Social Workers. *Awards, honors:* Publication award from Social Science Research Council of Canada, 1965, for *Social Welfare in Ontario 1791-1893*; Centennial Medal, 1967.

WRITINGS: Social Welfare in Ontario 1791-1893, University of Toronto Press, 1965.

WORK IN PROGRESS: Studies on the history of social welfare in Canada, and on the administration of social welfare in Canada.

* * *

SPODEK, Bernard 1931-

PERSONAL: Born September 17, 1931, in Brooklyn, N.Y.; son of David and Esther (Lebenbaum) Spodek; married Prudence Hoy, June 21, 1957; children: Esther Yinling, Jonathan Chou. *Education:* Brooklyn College (now of the City University of New York), New York, N.Y., B.A., 1952; Columbia University, M.A., 1955, Ed.D., 1962. *Home:* 1123 West Charles St., Champaign, Ill. 61820. *Office:* University of Illinois, Urbana, Ill. 61801.

CAREER: Beth Hayeled School, New York, N.Y., early childhood teacher, 1952-56; New York (N.Y.) public schools, elementary teacher, 1956-57; Brooklyn College (now of the City University of New York), Brooklyn, N.Y., laboratory school teacher, 1957-60; University of Wisconsin, Milwaukee Campus, assistant professor of elementary education, 1961-65; University of Illinois, Urbana, professor of early childhood education, 1965—. *Member:* Association for Childhood Education International, National Association for the Education of Young Children (secretary, 1964-68), Association for Supervision and Curriculum Development, American Educational Research Association, American Association of University Professors.

WRITINGS: (With Helen Robison) *New Directions in the Kindergarten*, Teachers College Press, 1965; (contributor) Georgianna Engstresn, editor, *Open Education*, National Association for the Education of Young Children, 1970; (contributor) Ira Gorden, editor, *Early Childhood Education*, National Society for the Study of Education, 1972; *Teaching in the Early Years*, Prentice-Hall, 1972; *Early Childhood Education*, Prentice-Hall, 1973; (with Herbert Walberg) *Studies in Open Education*, Agathon Press, 1974; (with Walberg) *Studies in Early Childhood Education*, National Society for the Study of Education, in press. Contributor to educational periodicals.

* * *

SPRAGUE, Rosemary

PERSONAL: Born in New York, N.Y.; daughter of Percy Carl (vice-president of M. A. Hanna Co., Cleveland, O.) and Nell Carethe (Andersen) Sprague. *Education:* Bryn Mawr College, A.B.; Western Reserve University (now Case Western Reserve University), M.A., Ph.D., 1959; additional study at Kenyon College, Oxford University, University of London, and Shakespeare Institute, Stratford on Avon, England. *Religion:* Episcopalian. *Home:* 2221 Tudor Dr., Cleveland Heights, Ohio 44106. *Office:* Department of English, Longwood College, Farmville, Va. 23901.

CAREER: Notre Dame College, South Euclid, Ohio, director of dramatics, 1947-50; lecturer in English at Fenn College (now Cleveland State University), Cleveland, Ohio, 1951-53, 1956-57, 1960-62, Western Reserve University (now Case Western Reserve University), Cleveland, 1953-54, 1957-59, and Cleveland Institute of Art, 1961-62; Longwood College, Farmville, Va., associate professor, 1962-65, professor of English, 1965-67, first Board of Visitors Distinguished Professor, 1967—. *Member:* American Association of University Professors, National Council of Teachers of English, Modern Language Association of America, Mediaeval Academy of America, Authors Guild, Poetry Society of America, American Library Association, National League of American Pen Women, American Association of University Women, College English Association, Daughters of the American Revolution, Colonial Dames, Daughters of Founders and Patriots, Victorian Society (England), Society for Theatre Research (London), New England Women, Mayflower Society, Theta Sigma Phi, Delta Kappa Gamma.

WRITINGS—Historical novels for young adults, except as indicated: *Northward to Albion*, Roy Publishers, 1947; *A Kingdom to Win*, Oxford University Press, 1953; *Heroes of the White Shield*, Oxford University Press, 1955; *Heir of Kiloran*, Oxford University Press, 1956; *Conquerors of Time*, Walck, 1957; *Dance for a Diamond Star*, Walck, 1959; *Fife and Fandango*, Walck, 1962; *The Jade Pagoda*, Walck, 1964; (editor) *Poems of Robert Browning*, Crowell, 1964; *Forever in Joy: A Biography of Robert Browning*, Chilton, 1965; *Red Lion and Gold Dragon: A Novel of the Norman Conquest*, Chilton, 1967; *George Eliot: A Biography*, Chilton, 1968; *Imaginary Gardens: A Study of Five American Poets*, Chilton, 1969. Contributor to journals, including *Theatre Annual*.

AVOCATIONAL INTERESTS: Piano, gardening, needlework, knitting, dancing, theater, gourmet cooking.†

* * *

SPYERS-DURAN, Peter 1932-

PERSONAL: Born January 26, 1932, in Budapest, Hungary; son of Alfred (a colonel) and Maria Balogh (Almassy) Spyers-Duran; married Jane F. Cumber, March 21, 1964; children: Kimberly, Hilary, Peter II. *Education:* University of Budapest, certificate, 1955; University of Chicago, M.A.L.S., 1960; Nova University, Ed. D., 1975. *Home:* 637 Southwest 14th St., Boca Raton, Fla. 33432. *Office:* Florida Atlantic University, Boca Raton, Fla. 33432.

CAREER: Chicago Public Library, Chicago, Ill., reference librarian, 1959-60; University of Wichita, Wichita, Kan., head of circulation department, 1960-62; American Library Association, Chicago, Ill., assistant executive secretary, 1962-63; University of Wisconsin, Milwaukee, assistant director of libraries and assistant professor, 1963-67, associate director of libraries and associate professor, 1967; Western Michigan University, Kalamazoo, associate professor, 1967-69, professor, 1969-70, director of libraries, 1967-70; Florida Atlantic University, Boca Raton, professor and director of libraries, 1970—, chairman of library science program, 1970—. *Member:* American Library Association (chairman of committees on retirement homes, on economic status, and on welfare and fringe benefits, 1966—), Southeastern Library Association, Florida Library Association, Florida Association of Public Junior Colleges.

WRITINGS: Moving Library Materials, University of Wisconsin-Milwaukee Library Associates, 1964, revised edition, American Library Association, 1965; *A Survey of Fringe Benefits Offered by Public Libraries in the United States*, American Library Association, 1966; *Basic Fringe Benefits for Public Libraries in the United States*, Libraries Unlimited, 1967; (contributor) Theodore Samore, editor, *Problems in Library Classification, Dewey 17 and Conversion*, University of Wisconsin, 1968; (editor) *Approval and Gathering Plans in Academic Libraries*, Western Michigan University, 1970; (editor) *Advances in Understanding Approval Plans in Academic Libraries*, Western Michigan University, 1970; (editor) *Advances in Understanding Approval Plans in Academic Libraries*, Western Michigan University, 1970; *Economics of Approval Plans*, Greenwood Press, 1972; (co-editor) *Management Problems in Serials Work*, Greenwood Press, 1973. Contributor of reviews and articles to professional journals, including *Wilson Library Bulletin, Incipit, Library Quarterly*, and *College Research Libraries*.

WORK IN PROGRESS: A Model Formula Budgeting System for Upper Division University Libraries.

AVOCATIONAL INTERESTS: Riding, tennis, swimming, the theater, music, deep-sea fishing, and boating.

* * *

SQUIER, Charles L(a Barge) 1931-

PERSONAL: Born April 28, 1931, in Milwaukee, Wis.; son of Theodore Louis (a physician) and Nina (La Barge) Squier; married Janice Stevenson, July 6, 1957; children: Alison Anne, Charles La Barge Stevenson. *Education:* Harvard University, A.B., 1953, A.M.T., 1957; University of Michigan, Ph.D., 1963. *Politics:* Democrat. *Office:* Department of English, University of Colorado, Boulder, Colo. 80302.

CAREER: University of Michigan, Ann Arbor, instructor in English, 1961-63; University of Colorado, Boulder, assistant professor, 1963-70, associate professor of English, 1970—. *Military service:* U.S. Army, 1953-55. *Member:* Shakespeare Association of America, Renaissance Society of America, American Federation of Teachers.

WRITINGS: (Editor with Robert M. Bender) *The Sonnet*, Washington Square, 1965; *A Study of the Works of Sir John Suckling*, Twayne , 1974. Contributor of poetry to *Snowy Egret, Midwest Quarterly, Ohio Review*, and *Open Places*.

* * *

STAFFORD, Kenneth R(ay) 1922-

PERSONAL: Born March 14, 1922, in Ryan, Okla.; son of William Henry and Dicie (Morrison) Stafford; married Lila Merle Kearns (an engineering technician), June 14, 1952. *Education:* University of Oklahoma, B.A., 1948, Ed.M., 1950, Ph.D., 1953. *Politics:* Democrat. *Home:* 8207 East Cholla Rd., Scottsdale, Ariz. *Office:* Arizona State University, Tempe, Ariz.

CAREER: University of Arkansas, Little Rock Campus, assistant professor of educational psychology, 1953-55; East Texas State College (now University), Commerce, instructor, 1955-56, assistant professor of educational psy-

chology, 1956-57; Arizona State University, Tempe, assistant professor, 1957-60, associate professor, 1960-66, professor of educational psychology, 1966—. Certified psychologist, state of Arizona; part-time private practice as psychologist, Phoenix, Ariz., and counselor to U.S. Veterans Administration, 1958-59. *Member:* American Psychological Association, American Educational Research Association, American Association for the Advancement of Science, American Association of University Professors, Western Psychological Association, Arizona Psychological Association, New York Academy of Sciences, Phi Delta Kappa, Kappa Delta Pi, Sigma Xi.

WRITINGS: (With S. Stansfield Sargent) *Basic Teachings of the Great Psychologists*, Doubleday, 1965. Contributor of more than twenty articles to professional journals.

WORK IN PROGRESS: Research on problem-solving as a function of language, under U.S. Office of Education grant; contribution to *Theories of Learning*, to be published by Dryden Press.

SIDELIGHTS: Stafford speaks German and French. *Avocational interests:* Horseback riding, dogs.

* * *

STAIB, Bjorn O. 1938-

PERSONAL: Born April 8, 1938, in Norway; son of Otto and Kari Staib. *Education:* Educated in Oslo, Norway, and London, England; University of Denver, finance major and candidate for degree in 1967. *Agent:* (Lectures) Martin A. Forrest, 80 Boylston St., Boston, Mass. 02116.

CAREER: Part-owner of manufacturing plant in Norway; participant in two man ski expedition across Greenland Ice Cap, 1962, and in expedition to North Pole sponsored by National Geographic Society, 1964. Public lecturer, narrating the film, "Man Against the Ice," which is based on these Arctic explorations. *Military service:* Norwegian Army, Infantry. *Member:* Explorers Club (New York), several Norwegian sports and business societies and clubs.

WRITINGS: Across Greenland in Nansen's Track, Allen & Unwin, 1963; *On Skis Toward the North Pole*, Doubleday, 1965. Contributor to European and American magazines, including *National Geographic*.

BIOGRAPHICAL/CRITICAL SOURCES: National Geographic, February, 1965.†

* * *

STANDON, Anna (Slater) 1929-

PERSONAL: Born September 19, 1929, in London, England; daughter of Montagu (a writer) and Enid (Mace) Slater; married Edward C. Standon (an artist and illustrator), June 8, 1957; children: Aaron, Simon. *Education:* Attended Burgess Hill School, 1944-47, and Camberwell School of Art, 1947-50. *Home:* 61 Talbot Rd., London N.6, England.

CAREER: Gregory Rowcliffe & Co. (solicitors), London, England, secretary, 1950-54; Berlitz School of Languages, English teacher in Paris, France, 1954-56, in London, England, 1956-57; temporary secretary in London, England, 1957-58; Shepherds Hill School, London, England, kindergarten teacher, 1961-63; free-lance writer, mainly for children, 1963—.

WRITINGS: The Singing Rhinoceros, Coward, 1963; *The Hippo Had Hiccups*, Coward, 1964; (with husband, Edward Standon) *A Flower for Ambrose*, Constable, 1964,

Delacorte, 1967; (with Edward Standon) *Three Little Cats,* constable, 1964, Delacorte, 1967; *The Tincan Tortoise,* Coward, 1965; (with Edward Standon) *Little Duck Lost,* Constable, 1965, Delacorte, 1966; (with Edward Standon) *Bridie the Bantam,* Dial, 1967; *A Penny Bell,* Harvey House, 1970. Author of television serials for children, "Magic Egg," 1963, and "In Search of a Unicorn," 1964.

SIDELIGHTS: Anna Standon speaks French, Italian, and Spanish. *Avocational interests:* Travel.†

* * *

STANSKY, Peter (David Lyman) 1932-

PERSONAL: Born January 18, 1932, in New York, N.Y.; son of Lyman (a lawyer) and Ruth (Macow) Stansky. *Education:* Yale University, B.A., 1953; King's College, Cambridge, B.A., 1955, M.A., 1959; Harvard University, Ph.D., 1961. *Office:* Department of History, Stanford University, Stanford, Calif. 94305. *Agent:* Margot Johnson Agency, 405 East 54th St., New York, N.Y. 10022.

CAREER: Harvard University, Cambridge, Mass., instructor, 1961-64, assistant professor of history, 1964-1968; Stanford University, Stanford, Calif., associate professor, 1968-74, professor, 1974-75, Frances and Charles Field Professor of History, 1975—. *Member:* American Historical Association, Conference of British Studies. *Awards, honors:* Guggenheim fellowship, 1966-67 and 1974-75.

WRITINGS: Ambitions and Strategies, Oxford University Press, 1964; (with William Abrahams) *Journey to the Frontier: Two Roads to the Spanish Civil War,* Little, Brown, 1966; (editor) *The Left and War,* Oxford University Press, 1969; (editor) *John Morley Nineteenth-Century Essays,* University of Chicago Press, 1970; (with Abrahams) *The Unknown Orwell,* Knopf, 1972; *England Since 1867,* Harcourt, 1973; (editor) *Churchill: A Profile,* Hill & Wang, 1973; (editor) *The Victorian Revolution,* F. Watts, 1973. Articles and reviews have appeared in *Victorian Studies, Partisan Review, History Today,* and other history journals.

* * *

STAPLETON, (Katharine) Laurence 1911-

PERSONAL: Born November 20, 1911, in Holyoke, Mass.; daughter of Richard Prout and Frances (Purtill) Stapleton. *Education:* Smith College, A.B., 1932; University of London, graduate study, 1932-33. *Politics:* Democrat. *Religion:* Nondenominational. *Home:* 229 North Roberts Rd., Bryn Mawr, Pa. 19010. *Office:* Department of English, Thomas Library, Bryn Mawr College, Bryn Mawr, Pa. 19010.

CAREER: Massachusetts Public Employment Service, registrar, 1933-34; Bryn Mawr College, Bryn Mawr, Pa., instructor, 1934-38, assistant professor, 1938-42, associate professor, 1942-48, professor of English and political theory, 1948-63, professor of English, 1963-64, Mary E. Garrett Professor of English, 1964—, chairman of department, 1954-65. Americans for Democratic Action, past member of national board of directors. *Member:* Modern Language Association of America, English Association (London), Renaissance Society of America, Phi Beta Kappa. *Awards, honors:* Guggenheim fellow, 1947-48; National Endowment for the Arts Creative Writing Fellowship, 1972-73.

WRITINGS: Justice and World Society, University of North Carolina Press, 1944; *The Design of Democracy,*

Oxford University Press, 1949; (editor) *H. D. Thoreau; A Writer's Journal,* Dover, 1960; *Yushin's Log and Other Poems,* A. S. Barnes, 1969; *The Elected Circle,* Princeton University Press, 1973. Contributor to *University of Toronto Quarterly, Studies in Philosophy, South Atlantic Quarterly, Philosophical Quarterly,* and other journals.

WORK IN PROGRESS: Critical studies.

* * *

STARBIRD, Kaye
(C. S. Jennison)

PERSONAL: Born at Fort Sill, Okla.; daughter of Alfred A. (a general, U.S. Army) and Ethel (Dodd) Starbird; married James Dalton (deceased); married N. E. Jennison (deceased); children: (first marriage) Kit (Mrs. Wayne Slawson), Beth (Mrs. Peter Snyder); (second marriage) Lee Jennison. *Education:* Attended University of Vermont, four years.

CAREER: Professional writer. *Awards, honors:* Bread Loaf Writers' Conference fellowship, 1961; MacDowell Colony fellowship, 1966-70, 72; Wurlitzer Foundation fellowship, 1967-68; Ella Cabot Lyman Trust grant, 1971; Ossabaw Island Project fellowship, 1971-73; Virginia Center for Creative Arts fellowship, 1971-73.

WRITINGS: Speaking of Cows (juvenile), Lippincott, 1960; *Don't Ever Cross a Crocodile* (juvenile), Lippincott, 1963; *A Snail's a Failure Socially* (juvenile), Lippincott, 1966; *The Pheasant on Route Seven* (juvenile), Lippincott, 1968; *Watch Out for the Mules,* Harcourt, 1968; *The Lion in the Lei Stand* (adult), Harcourt, 1970. Contributor of poetry to periodicals and anthologies. Also contributor, at times under name C. S. Jennison, of satirical verse, poems, essays, and short stories to magazines.

WORK IN PROGRESS: An adult novel, yet untitled.

* * *

STARR, Martin Kenneth 1927-

PERSONAL: Born May 21, 1927, in New York, N.Y.; son of Harry and Melanie (Krauss) Starr; married Mary Wright, April 5, 1955; children: Christopher, Loren M. *Education:* Massachusetts Institute of Technology, B.S., 1948; Columbia University, M.S., 1951, Ph.D., 1953. *Home:* 30 Fifth Ave., New York, N.Y. 10011.

CAREER: Columbia University, Graduate School of Business, New York, N.Y., associate professor, 1961-65, professor of management science, 1965—, vice-dean, 1974-75. Consultant in operations research, management science, and systems analysis, 1961—. *Military service:* U.S. Navy, 1945-47. *Member:* Institute for the Comparative Study of History, Philosophy, and the Sciences (England), American Association for the Advancement of Science, Institute of Management Sciences (president, 1974-75), Operations Research Society of America, Society for General Systems Research Association for Education in International Business, Systems and Procedures Association, Beta Gamma Sigma.

WRITINGS: (With David Miller) *Executive Decisions and Operations Research,* Prentice-Hall, 1960, 2nd edition, 1969; (with Miller) *Inventory Control: Theory and Practice,* Prentice-Hall, 1962; *Decision Theory and Produce Design,* Prentice-Hall, 1963; *Production Management: Systems and Synthesis,* Prentice-Hall, 1964, 2nd edition, 1972; (contributor) *Models, Measurement and Marketing,* sponsored by Market Research Council, Prentice-Hall, 1965; (editor)

Executive Readings in Management Science, Institute of Management Sciences and Macmillan, 1965; (with Miller) *The Structure of Human Decisions*, Prentice-Hall, 1967; (editor) *Management of Production*, Penguin, 1970; *System Management of Operations*, Prentice-Hall, 1971; *Management: A Modern Approach*, Harcourt, 1971.

Editor-in-chief, *Management Science: Application*, 1967-68 and 1969—, *Management Science: Theory*, 1969—; member of editorial board, *Journal of Operations Research Society of America*, 1960—, *Columbia Journal of World Business*, 1964-70, American Production and Inventory Control Society, 1968-70, *Behavioral Science*, 1970—, *Operational Research Quarterly*, 1970; member of publications committee, Society for general Systems Research, 1968—; member of editorial advisory board, *Design Methods Group Newsletter*, University of California, Berkley, 1968-70.

* * *

STARR, Wilmarth Holt 1913-

PERSONAL: Born April 27, 1913, in Charleston, W.Va.; son of Charles Holt and Jessie (Wilmarth) Starr; married Eva Jones, December 27, 1937; children: Judith Lake (Mrs. Charles J. McLaughlin III), Gail Wheaton (Mrs. Benjamin F. Blair, Jr.), Judson Wilmarth, Christopher Holt, Charles Holt. *Education:* Wesleyan University, Middletown, Conn., B.A., 1934; Johns Hopkins University, Ph.D., 1937. *Religion:* Protestant. *Home:* 6 Grace St., Old Greenwich, Conn. 06870. *Office:* New York University, Washington Square, New York, N.Y. 10003.

CAREER: University of Maine, Orono, instructor, 1937-41, assistant professor, 1941-44, associate professor and acting head of department of modern languages and classics, 1946-47, professor of Romance languages and head of department of foreign languages and classics, 1947-61; New York University, New York, N.Y., professor of Romance languages, 1961—, head of department of Romance and Slavic languages and literatures, 1961-65, head of department of Romance languages and literatures, 1965-70, director of New York University Abroad, 1971-75. U.S. Department of State, Mutual Security Agency, education and information office on technical and economic mission to Cambodia, Laos, and Vietnam, 1952-53; director of Foreign Language Proficiency Tests for Teachers and Advanced Students, Modern Language Association of America, 1959-65; member of advisory panel, Modern Language Materials Development Center, 1960—; member of National Council for Testing of English as a Foreign Language, 1961—; consultant, U.S. Office of Education Bureau of Research, 1965—; U.S. director, European and U.S. Joint Institutes in France and Germany, 1966-67; member of advisory board for research and graduate education, 1969-72. *Military service:* U.S. Naval Reserve, 1944-46; on staff of Seventh Fleet.

MEMBER: American Association of Teachers of French (vice-president of Maine chapter, 1950-52), Modern Language Association of America, Northeast Conference on Teaching of Foreign Languages (executive committee, 1959-63; board of directors and vice-chairman, 1963-64; chairman, 1964-65), U.S. Power Squadron, Sigma Nu, Phi Beta Kappa, Phi Kappa Phi. *Awards, honors:* Wesleyan University citation for outstanding achievement as teacher and scholar, 1964; Officier Palmes Academiques, 1970.

WRITINGS: (With Alfred G. Pellegrino and Casavant) *Functional French*, American Book Co., 1951; (with Pelle-

grino and Casavant) *Functional Spanish*, American Book Co., 1955; (with Pellegrino) *Spoken French and Grammar Review*, American Book Co., 1957; (with Pellegrino) *New Functional French*, American Book Co., 1959, 3rd edition with Pellegrino and Bernard Garniez, 1965; (editor) *Modern Foreign Languages and the Academically Talented*, National Education Association and Modern Language Association of America, 1960. Contributor to proceedings of conferences and to professional journals. Editor, *Maine Newsletter*, 1954-59.

SIDELIGHTS: Starr is competent in French, Spanish, Italian, German, and Chinese.†

* * *

STARRATT, Alfred B(yron) 1914-

PERSONAL: Born September 6, 1914, in Quincy, Mass.; son of Simon Peter and Lucy (Bishop) Starratt; married Anna Louise Mazur, June 2, 1937; children: Polly Anne (Mrs. William Lemire), Patricia Elizabeth (Mrs. Richard Hubbard), Penelope Louise. *Education:* Boston University, B.S. in Ed., 1939; Episcopal Theological School, Cambridge, Mass., B.D. (cum laude), 1942; Harvard University, Ph.D., 1952. *Home:* 16 Charlcote Pl., Baltimore, Md. 21218. *Office:* Emmanuel Church, 811 Cathedral St., Baltimore, Md. 21201.

CAREER: The Protestant Episcopal Church, minister, 1942—, with first appointment as rector in Lincoln, Mass., 1942-43; Huachung University, Wuchang, Hupeh, China, professor of religion, 1946-49; rector in Stockbridge, Mass., 1949-52; Kenyon College, Gambier, Ohio, professor of religion, 1952-55; Emmanuel Church, Baltimore, Md., rector, 1955—. Chairman of Division of Human Relations, Episcopal Diocese of Maryland. Member of board of directors, Episcopal Pacifist Fellowship, 1956—, of clergyman's advisory board, Planned Parenthood, 1952—, and of National Service Board for Religious Objectors, 1960—. Broadcasts two radio programs weekly in Baltimore.

WRITINGS: The Real God, Westminster, 1965. Contributor to *Expository Times* (England) and *Witness*. Former editor, *Central China Theological Review*.

WORK IN PROGRESS: A book on modern theology.

SIDELIGHTS: Starratt has some competence in French, German, Latin, Greek, Hebrew, and Aramaic. He was bilingual in Chinese and English at one time, but "haven't had much chance to use it [Chinese] for many years.†

* * *

STECKEL, William Reed 1915-

PERSONAL: Born February 11, 1915, in Doylestown, Pa.; son of William Eugene (a clergyman) and Mary (McNitt) Steckel; married Veva Haehl, July 2, 1941; children: William Burrel. *Education:* Harvard University, A.B., 1936, M.A., 1937; Stanford University, Ph.D., 1949. *Religion:* Presbyterian. *Home:* 2003 Hillside Dr., Laramie, Wyo. 82070. *Office:* Department of History, University of Wyoming, Laramie, Wyo. 82070.

CAREER: Private secretary to U.S. Minister to Denmark, 1937-38; instructor at Ohio Military Institute, Cincinnati, 1938-40, and Chadwick School, Rolling Hills, Calif., 1940-41; Stanford University, Stanford, Calif., instructor in history, 1947-49; University of Wyoming, Laramie, assistant professor, 1949-54, associate professor, 1954-58, professor of history, 1958—, director of American studies, 1954-56. University of Frankfurt, Frankfurt, Germany, Fulbright professor, 1956-57. Member of Laramie City Council, 1960-66; mayor of Laramie, 1963-64. Member of board of directors, Wyoming Association of Municipalities, 1962-64. *Military service:* U.S. Navy, 1942-46; became lieutenant senior grade.

MEMBER: American Historical Association (member of council, Pacific Coast branch, 1960-63), American Studies Association (national council, 1956-57; president, Rocky Mountain chapter, 1956-57), Organization of American Historians. *Awards, honors:* Annual prize for historical manuscript, Pacific Coast branch of American Historical Association, 1950.

WRITINGS: (Editor with De Conde and Rappaport) *Patterns in American History*, two volumes, Wadsworth, 1965, 3rd edition, 1973. Member of board of editors, Pacific Coast branch, American Historical Association, 1964-66.

WORK IN PROGRESS: A biography of Christopher Sauer, colonial American printer; research in the relations of British West Indies and continental English colonies in the eighteenth century.

* * *

STEDMAN, Murray S(alisbury), Jr. 1917-

PERSONAL: Born December 2, 1917, in Pittsburgh, Pa.; son of Murray Salisbury (a businessman) and Viola (Lanich) Stedman; married Susan Winter, January 3, 1943 (divorced, 1970); married Evelyn Dennys, 1970; children: Emily, Nancy. *Education:* Williams College, B.A., 1939; Columbia University, M.A., 1940, Ph.D., 1947. *Religion:* Presbyterian. *Home:* Alden Park Manor, 706-B, Philadelphia, Pa. 19144. *Office:* Department of Political Science, Temple University, Philadelphia, Pa. 19122.

CAREER: Columbia University, New York, N.Y., instructor in government, 1946-47; Brown University, Providence, R.I., assistant professor of political science, 1947-50; Swarthmore College, Swarthmore, Pa., associate professor of political science, 1950-57; United Presbyterian Church, New York, N.Y., director of information, 1957-60; National Council of Churches of Christ in the U.S.A., New York, N.Y., general director of interpretation, 1960-64; Trinity College, Hartford, Conn., professor of government and chairman of department, 1964-69; Temple University, Philadelphia, Pa., professor of political science, 1969—. UNESCO, political science specialist, Paris, France, 1953-54. *Military service:* U.S. Army, 1941-45; became captain. *Member:* American Political Science Association, American Academy of Political and Social Science, American Civil Liberties Union.

WRITINGS: Exporting Arms, King's Crown Press, 1947; (with Susan W. Stedman) *Discontent at the Polls*, Columbia University Press, 1950; (with John P. Roche) *Dynamics of Democratic Government*, McGraw, 1954; *Religion and Politics in America*, Harcourt, 1964; (with Eugene J. Meehan and Roche) *Dynamics of Modern Government*, McGraw, 1966; *Urban Politics*, Winthrop Publishing, 1972, 2nd edition, 1975. Contributor to political science and sociology journals.

* * *

STEESE, Peter B(echler) 1933-

PERSONAL: Born December 16, 1933, in Fillmore, N.Y.; son of Paul Alexander and Ruth (Zimmerman) Steese; married Marion Banks, December 22, 1956; children: Deborah Ann, Laura Lee. *Education:* Houghton College, B.A.,

1954; Western Reserve University (now Case Western Reserve University), M.A., 1958, Ph.D., 1963. *Religion:* Presbyterian. *Office:* Department of English, State University of New York College at Fredonia, Fredonia, N.Y. 14063.

CAREER: Pennsylvania State University, University Park, 1961-66, began as instructor, became assistant professor; Pennsylvania State University, McKeesport Campus, assistant professor of English and assistant director of Campus, 1966-67; State University of New York College at Fredonia, associate professor of English, 1967—. *Military service:* U.S. Army, 1954-56. *Member:* Modern Language Association of America, American Society for Eighteenth-Century Studies, Danforth Foundation (associate, 1971—).

WRITINGS: (Editor) *Ecclesiastes: A Casebook*, Allyn & Bacon, 1966; (with J. C. Rowlands) *The Rhetoric Reader*, Wiley, in press. Contributor to *Journal of Bible and Religion* and *Philological Quarterly*.

* * *

STEGEMAN, John F(oster) 1918-

PERSONAL: Surname is pronounced Stegg-e-man; born November 6, 1918, in Gulfport, Miss.; son of Herman James (an athletic director) and Dorothea (Washburne) Stegeman; married Janet Allais, March 20, 1942; children: Herman J., Paul A. (deceased), Ann A. *Education:* University of Georgia, B.S., 1940; Emory University School of Medicine, M.D., 1943. *Religion:* Protestant (non-member). *Home:* Greenbrier Rd., Athens, Ga. 30601.

CAREER: Diplomate, American Board of Internal Medicine. Physician in private practice of internal medicine, Athens, Ga.; chief of department of internal medicine at Athens General Hospital and St. Mary's Hospital, Athens, Ga., 1964—. American Field Service, founder of Athens chapter, chapter president, 1960-63, and treasurer, 1963-66. *Military service:* U.S. Army, Medical Corps, 1946-47; became captain. *Member:* American Medical Association, American College of Physicians (fellow), Alpha Omega Alpha.

WRITINGS: These Men She Gave, University of Georgia Press, 1964; *The Ghosts of Herty Field*, University of Georgia Press, 1966; (contributor) Claude A. Frazier, editor, *Faith Healing: Finger of God or Scientific Curiosity?*, T. Nelson, 1973. Contributor to medical journals, and contributor of articles about historic events to newspapers.

WORK IN PROGRESS: With wife, Janet Stegeman, *Caty of the Revolution*, a biography of Mrs. Nathaniel Greene.

SIDELIGHTS: Stegeman's books resulted from two long periods when he was incapacitated (for medical work) due to a ruptured disc.

* * *

STEIN, Leon 1910-

PERSONAL: Born September 18, 1910, in Chicago, Ill.; son of Harry and Rebecca (LaZar) Stein; married Anne Helman, October 30, 1937; children: Robert Edwin, Kenneth Erwin. *Education:* De Paul University, Mus.B., 1931, Mus.M., 1935, Ph.D., 1949; studied violin and composition privately, and orchestration and conducting under leaders of Chicago Symphony Orchestra. *Office:* School of Music, De Paul University, 25 East Jackson Blvd., Chicago, Ill. 60604.

CAREER: De Paul University School of Music, Chicago,

Ill., 1931—, started as instructor, professor and chairman of department of theory and composition and director of Graduate Division, School of Music, 1948—, founder-conductor of university's Chamber Orchestra, 1931—, dean of School of Music, 1966—. Conductor of Community Symphony Orchestra of Chicago, 1945—, Chicago Sinfonietta, 1955—; guest conductor in other U.S. cities and Canada. Composer of twenty-one works for orchestra, two one-act operas, two ballets, chamber music, and other music for piano, organ, and voice. *Military service:* U.S. Naval Reserve, active duty, 1944-45; became petty officer. *Member:* International Society for Contemporary Music (chairman of Chicago chapter, 1953-55), National Association of Schools of Music (examiner and consultant), American Composers Alliance, Music Educators National Conference. *Awards, honors:* Chicago Symphony Orchestra fellowship in conducting, 1937-40; American Composer's Commission Award for "Triptych on Three Poems of Walt Whitman," 1950; Midland Music Foundation Prize (co-winner of $1,000 award) for "Symphonic Movement," 1955.

WRITINGS: The Racial Thinking of Richard Wagner, Philosophical Library, 1950; (contributor) *Mid-Century,* Beechurst Press, 1957; *Structure and Style: The Study and Analysis of Musical Forms,* Summy, 1962; (editor) *Anthology of Musical Forms,* Summy, 1962. Musical works published by Leeds Publishing, Carl Fischer, American Composer's Alliance, Transcontinental Music Corp., Theodore Presser, Summy, and Dorn Publications. Contributor to *Journal of Musicology* and *Chicago Jewish Forum.* Composer of several works that have been recorded.

* * *

STEIN, Leon 1912-

PERSONAL: Born January 18, 1912, in Baltimore, Md.; son of Jacob (a tailor) and Freda Stein; married Miriam Spicehandler; children: Walter, Barbara. *Education:* City College (now of the City University of New York), New York, N.Y., Bachelor of Social Science, 1934. *Home:* 1142 East Fourth St., Brooklyn, N.Y. *Office:* 1710 Broadway, New York, N.Y.

CAREER: Justice (publication of International Ladies' Garment Workers' Union), New York, N.Y., managing editor, 1941-52, editor, 1952—. *Member:* International Labor Press Association (president, 1964-65), American Historical Association (member of board of editors of Labor History), Industrial Relations Research Association.

WRITINGS: ILGWU News-History, International Ladies' Garment Workers' Union, 1950; *Labor's Story,* Community Publishers, 1961; *The Triangle Fire,* Lippincott, 1962.

Editor: (And translator) *Education of Abraham Cahan,* Jewish Publication Society of America, 1969; *American Labor: From Conspiracy to Collective Bargaining,* 104 volumes, Arno, 1970; *American Women: Images and Realities,* forty-four volumes, Arno, 1972; *Big Business: Economic Power in a Free Society,* fifty-one volumes, Arno, 1973; *Women in America: From Colonial Times to the 20th Century,* fifty-nine volumes, Arno, 1974; *Politics and People: Ordeal of Self-Government in America,* fifty-eight volumes, Arno, 1974. Also editor of *Dictionary of American Biography,* three volumes, American Historical Review. Contributor to *Labor History.*

STEIN, M(eyer) L(ewis)

PERSONAL: Born in Escanaba, Mich.; son of Alexander (a merchant) and Fannie (Joseph) Stein; married Irene Noshlen, September 10, 1949; children: Andrea, Jeannine. *Educator:* University of Missouri, B.J., 1942; Wayne State University, graduate study, 1951; Stanford University, M.A., 1961. *Home:* 10011 Kaylor Ave., Los Alamitos, Calif. 90720.

CAREER: Royal Oak Daily Tribune, Royal Oak, Mich., reporter and telegraph editor, 1946-51; *San Francisco Examiner,* San Francisco, Calif., staff reporter and rewrite man, 1951-61; New York University, New York, N.Y., assistant professor, 1961-64, associate professor of journalism and chairman of department, 1965-74; California State University, Long Beach, chairman of journalism department, 1974—. *Military service:* U.S. Army, 1942-45; served in Italy; became sergeant. *Member:* Association for Education in Journalism, American Society of Journalism School Administrators, Society of Magazine Writers, Sigma Delta Chi, Kappa Tau Alpha.

WRITINGS: Your Career in Journalism, Messner, 1965; *Freedom of the Press—A Continuing Struggle,* Messner, 1966; *Write Clearly—Speak Effectively,* Simon & Schuster, 1967; *Under Fire: The Story of American War Correspondents,* Messner, 1968; *When Presidents Meet the Press,* Messner, 1969; *How to Write High School and College Papers,* Cornerstone Library, 1969; *Reporting Today: The Newswriter's Handbook,* Cornerstone Library, 1971. Contributor to business, technical, and general consumer magazines, and trade and journalism publications.

* * *

STEINER, Kurt 1912-

PERSONAL: Born June 10, 1912, in Vienna, Austria; came to United States in 1938; son of Jacob and Olga (Weil) Steiner; married Josepha Eisler, August 26, 1939. *Education:* University of Vienna, Dr. of Jurisprudence, 1935; Stanford University, Ph.D., 1955. *Home:* 832 Sonoma Ter., Stanford, Calif. 94305. *Office:* Stanford University, Stanford, Calif. 94305.

CAREER: Brauchbar (law office), Vienna, Austria, attorney, 1935-38; Berlitz Schools of Languages, director in Pittsburgh, Pa., and Cleveland, Ohio, 1940-43; Headquarters, Supreme Commander of the Allied Powers in Japan, Tokyo, prosecuting attorney and assistant to chief counsel, International Prosecution Section, 1948, chief of civil affairs and civil liberties branch, Legislative and Justice Division, 1949-51; Princeton University, Princeton, N.J., visiting research scholar, 1954-55; Stanford University, Stanford, Calif., assistant professor, 1955-58, associate professor, 1958-62, professor of political science, 1962—, director of Stanford in Germany, summer, 1961, director of Stanford Center for Japanese Studies, 1962. *Military service:* U.S. Army, 1944-48; served in Japan, 1946-48; became first lieutenant. *Member:* American Political Science Association, Association for Asian Studies, American Association of University Professors, Japanese-American Society for Legal Studies, International House of Japan.

WRITINGS: (Contributor) *Court and Constitution in Japan,* University of Washington Press, 1964; *Local Government in Japan,* Stanford University Press, 1965; (contributor) Robert E. Ward, editor, *Political Modernization in Japan,* Princeton University Press, 1968; *Politics in Austria,* Little, Brown, 1972.

WORK IN PROGRESS: Contribution to a symposium, *Political Opposition in Japan*.

SIDELIGHTS: Steiner speaks German and Japanese.

* * *

STEKLER, Herman O. 1932-

PERSONAL: Born November 4, 1932, in Vienna, Austria; naturalized U.S. citizen; son of Walter and Gisela Stekler. *Education:* Clark University, A.B., 1956; Massachusetts Institute of Technology, Ph.D., 1959. *Office:* State University of New York, Stony Brook, N.Y. 11790.

CAREER: University of California, Berkeley, assistant professor of business administration, 1959-66; Federal Reserve Board, Washington, D.C., economist, 1966-68; State University of New York, Stony Brook, professor of economics, 1968—. Visiting professor at Federal Reserve Board, Division of Research and Statistics, 1966-67. Consultant to Bank of America, 1962, and 1965-66. *Member:* Phi Beta Kappa. *Awards, honors:* Research grants from Small Business Administration, 1960-61, and from National Aeronautics and Space Administration, 1962-65.

WRITINGS: Profitability and Size of Firm, University of California Press, 1963; *The Structure and Performance of the Aerospace Industry*, University of California Press, 1965; *Economic Forecasting*, Praeger, 1970. Contributor of about thirty articles to professional journals.

* * *

STENDAHL, Krister 1921-

PERSONAL: Born April 21, 1921, in Stockholm, Sweden; came to United States in 1954; son of Olof (an engineer) and Sigrid (Ljungquist) Stendahl; married Brita Johnsson, September 7, 1946; children: John, Anna, Dan. *Education:* University of Uppsala, B.D., 1944, Teol. lic., 1949, Th.D., 1954; also studied at Cambridge University and in Paris, France. *Home:* 44 Francis Ave., Cambridge, Mass. 02138. *Office:* Harvard University Divinity School, Cambridge, Mass. 02138.

CAREER: Clergyman of Church of Sweden (Lutheran). Assistant priest in diocese of Stockholm, Sweden, 1944-46; University of Uppsala, Uppsala, Sweden, chaplain to students, 1948-50, instructor in New Testament and Old Testament exegesis, 1951-54; Harvard University, Divinity School, Cambridge, Mass., assistant professor, 1954-56, associate professor, 1956-58, John H. Morison Professor of New Testament Studies, 1958-63, Frothingham Professor of Biblical Studies, 1963-68, dean and John Lord O'Brian Professor, 1968—. *Member:* American Academy of Arts and Sciences (fellow), Studiorum Novi Testamenti Societas, Society for Religion in Higher Education, Society of Biblical Literature, Society Pro Fide Christianismo, Nathan Soederblom Saellskapet. *Awards, honors:* Guggenheim fellowship, 1959-60 and 1974-75; Litt.D., Upsala College, East Orange, N.J., 1963, Thiel College, 1966; A.M., Harvard University, 1956; D.D., Colby College, 1970, St. Olaf College, 1971, Whittier College, 1971; L.L.D., Susquehanna University, 1973.

WRITINGS: Bibelns Mening (title means "The Meaning of the Bible"), Svenska Kyrkens Diakonistyrelsens Bokforlag (Stockholm), 1952; *The School of St. Matthew and Its Use of the Old Testament*, Gleerups (Lund), 1954; (editor and contributor) *The Scrolls and the New Testament*, Harper, 1957; (editor and author of introduction) *Immortality and Resurrection: Four Essays* (Ingersoll lectures),

Macmillan, 1965; *The Bible and the Role of Women*, Fortress, 1966; (author of introduction) Leo Baeck, *The Pharisees and Other Essays*, Schocken, 1966; (author of foreword) Johannes Munck, *Christ and Israel: An Interpretation of Romans 9-11*, Fortress, 1967; (author of foreword) Merle Severy, editor, *Great Religions of the World*, National Geographic Society, 1971; (author of foreword) Anton Fridrichsen, *The Problem of Miracle in Primitive Christianity*, Augsburg, 1972; *Proclamation: Aids for Interpreting the Lessons of the Church Year*, Fortress, 1974.

Contributor to *Interpreter's Dictionary of the Bible, Encyclopaedia Britannica*, and of over 150 articles and reviews to theological journals in the United States and abroad.

* * *

STEPANCHEV, Stephen 1915-

PERSONAL: Surname is accented on second syllable; born January 30, 1915, in Yugoslavia; son of George (a farmer) and Olga (Dubrich) Stepanchev. *Education:* University of Chicago, A.B., 1937, M.A., 1938; New York University, Ph.D., 1950. *Home:* 140-60 Beech Ave., Flushing, N.Y. 11355.

CAREER: Purdue University, Lafayette, Ind., instructor in English, 1938-41; New York University, New York, N.Y., instructor in English, 1946-48; Queens College (now of the City University of New York). Flushing, N.Y., 1949—, professor of English, 1964—. *Military service:* U.S. Army, 1941-45; became first lieutenant; received Bronze Star. *Member:* Modern Language Association of America, English Graduate Association of New York University (former president), Phi Beta Kappa. *Awards, honors:* Society of Midland Authors Prize for group of poems published in *Poetry*, 1937.

WRITINGS—Poems: Three Priests in April, Contemporary Poetry, 1956; *American Poetry Since 1945: A Critical Survey*, Harper, 1965; *Spring in the Harbor*, Amity Press, 1967; *A Man Running in the Rain*, Black Sparrow Press, 1969; *The Mad Bomber*, Black Sparrow Press, 1972; *Mining the Darkness*, Black Sparrow Press, 1974. Poetry has appeared in *Nation, Sewanee Review, Saturday Review*, and other literary reviews, and in *New York Times*.

WORK IN PROGRESS: New poems.

* * *

STEPHENS, Alan 1925-

PERSONAL: Born December 19, 1925, in Greeley, Colo.; son of Alan Archer (a farmer) and Ellen (Meyers) Stephens; married Frances Jones, December 26, 1948; children: Alan, Daniel, Timothy. *Education:* University of Colorado, student, 1946-48; Colorado State College of Education (now University of Northern Colorado), student, 1948; University of Denver, A.B. and M.A., 1950; University of Missouri, Ph.D., 1954. *Politics:* Registered Democrat. *Religion:* None. *Home:* 326 Canon Dr., Santa Barbara, Calif. 93105.

CAREER: Arizona State University, Tempe, assistant professor of English, 1954-58; University of California, Santa Barbara, associate professor, 1959-67, professor of English, 1967—. *Military service:* U.S. Army Air Forces, 1943-45.

WRITINGS: The Sum, A. Swallow, 1958; (editor) Barnabe Googe, *Selected Poems*, A. Swallow, 1961; *Between Matter and Principle*, A. Swallow, 1963; *The Heat Lightning*, Bowdoin College Museum of Art, 1967; *Tree Medita-*

tion and Others, Swallow Press, 1970; *White River Poems*, Swallow Press, in press.

WORK IN PROGRESS: One collection of verse.

SIDELIGHTS: E. D. Blodgett, in his review of *Between Matter and Principle*, notes that "the accent in the title is on the word 'between.' It is this, in Stephens' poetry that obstructs criticism. He wishes the book to be a suspension of experience." Blodgett believes that, as a result, the book is somehow unresolved and that the reader is left looking forward to the next book, rather than reconsidering this one. "To the detriment of his poetry," writes Blodgett, "Stephens is intent upon removing chance from matter...." And although Blodgett believes that Stephens has not fully realized this intent, he does admire Stephens' "careful poetry." Blodgett adds: "Stephens enjoys the world as problem, as an object for science in the positivistic sense. Thus, matter is not quite flesh but a front or form; 'matter' is 'engrained and tough' where destiny and chance evolve in time and the imagination."

BIOGRAPHICAL/CRITICAL SOURCES: Minnesota Review, summer, 1964.

*   *   *

STEPHENSON, (William) Ralph (Ewing)   1910-

PERSONAL: Born September 3, 1910, in Dunedin, New Zealand; son of Ralph Stuart (a physician) and Annie Forsyth (Ewing) Stephenson; married Jane Hoover, February 5, 1940; children: David, Jonathan, Camilla. *Education:* University of Otago, M.A. (first class honors), 1932; additional study at Knox College, New Zealand, 1933-34, and London School of Economics and Political Science, London, 1935. *Politics:* Liberal. *Religion:* Presbyterian. *Home:* 55 Hambult Rd., London SW4, England.

CAREER: British Colonial Service, auditor in Hong Kong, 1936, principal auditor in the Seychelles, 1946-49, senior auditor in Ghana, Africa, 1950-52, director of audit in Sierra Leone, Africa, 1953-57; British Film Institute, London, England, administrative and finance officer, 1958—. *Military service:* Royal Naval Volunteer Reserve, Hong Kong Division, 1936-46; became lieutenant; prisoner of war, 1940-45. *Member:* Amateur Chamber Music Players, Royal Naval Volunteer Reserve Club.

WRITINGS: An Outline of Government Accounting, Crown Agents for Oversea Governments and Administration, 1958; *Body in My Arms* (crime novel), Gifford, 1963; *Darkest Death* (crime novel), Gifford, 1964; *Spies in Concert* (crime novel), Gifford, 1965; (with Jean Debrix) *The Cinema as Art*, Penguin, 1966; *Festival Death* (crime novel), Gifford, 1966; *Down Among the Dead Men* (crime novel), Gifford, 1966; *Animation in the Cinema*, A. S. Barnes, 1967; *The Animated Film*, A. S. Barnes, 1973; *5000 Miles in a Catamaran*, R. Hale, 1974; *Children in Films*, A. S. Barnes, 1975. Contributor to Encyclopaedia Britannica's *The Art of Motion Pictures*.

WORK IN PROGRESS: 8000 Miles in A Trimaran.

AVOCATIONAL INTERESTS: Sailing, crossword puzzles, piano.

*   *   *

STERN, Clarence A.   1913-

PERSONAL: Born January 6, 1913, in McClusky, N.D.; son of Adam M. (in real estate and insurance) and Minnie (Krieger) Stern; married Kathleen Gober, February 20,

1946. *Education:* Eastern Michigan University, A.B., 1934; Wayne State University, M.A., 1938; further study through LaSalle Extension University, 1947-49; University of Nebraska, Ph.D., 1958. *Home address:* P.O. Box 2294, Oshkosh, Wis. 54901. *Office:* History Department, University of Wisconsin, Oshkosh, Wis. 54901.

CAREER: Teacher in Michigan public schools, 1934-42, 1954-55; Lawrence Institute of Technology, Detroit, Mich., assistant professor of history, political science, and English, 1946-50; Wayne State College, Wayne, Neb., associate professor of history and political science, 1958-65; University of Wisconsin, Oshkosh, associate professor, department of history, 1965—. Member of faculty senate, University of Wisconsin, Oshkosh, 1971; honorary fellow of Harry S. Truman Institute of National and International Affairs. *Military service:* U.S. Army Air Forces, 1942-46; served in England and Germany. *Member:* Intercontinental Biographical Association (fellow), National Education Association, American Historical Association, American Political Science Association, American Association of University Professors (Nebraska conference secretary-treasurer, 1963-64; president of Wayne State College chapter, 1964-65), Organization of American Historians, American Civil Liberties Union, Wisconsin Civil Liberties Union (Academic Freedom Committee member), Phi Alpha Theta, Pi Gamma Mu, Kappa Delta Pi. *Awards, honors:* Ford Foundation grant, 1962; certificate of honor from Bicentennial Research Institute.

WRITINGS: Republican Heyday: Republicanism through the McKinley Years, Edwards Brothers, 1962; *Resurgent Republicanism: The Handiwork of Hanna*, Edwards Brothers, 1963; *Golden Republicanism: The Crusade for Hard Money*, Edwards Brothers, 1964; *Protectionist Republicanism: Republican Tariff Policy in the McKinley Period*, Edwards Brothers, 1971.

WORK IN PROGRESS: Pro-Trust Republicanism.

*   *   *

STERN, Madeleine B(ettina)   1912-

PERSONAL: Born July 1, 1912, in New York, N.Y.; daughter of Moses R. and Lillie (Mack) Stern. *Education:* Barnard College, A.B., 1932; Columbia University, M.A., 1933. *Religion:* Jewish. *Office:* Leona Rostenberg-Rare Books, 40 East 88th St., New York, N.Y. 10028.

CAREER: Teacher of English in high schools, New York, N.Y., 1934-43; writer, 1942—; partner, Leona Rostenberg—Rare Books, New York, N.Y., 1945—. *Member:* Antiquarian Booksellers Association of America, Modern Language Association of America, Authors League, Antiquarian Booksellers Association (England), Phi Beta Kappa. *Awards, honors:* Guggenheim fellowship, 1943-45.

WRITINGS: The Life of Margaret Fuller, Dutton, 1942; *Louisa May Alcott*, University of Oklahoma Press, 1950; *Purple Passage: The Life of Mrs. Frank Leslie*, University of Oklahoma Press, 1953, 2nd edition, 1971; *Imprints on History: Book Publishers and American Frontiers*, Indiana University Press, 1956; *We the Women: Career Firsts of 19th-Century America*, Schulte, 1963; *So Much in a Lifetime: The Story of Dr. Isabel Barrows*, Messner, 1964; *Queen of Publishers' Row: Mrs. Frank Leslie*, Messner, 1965; *The Pantarch: A Biography of Stephen Pearl Andrews*, University of Texas Press, 1968; *Heads and Headlines: The Phrenological Fowlers*, University of Oklahoma Press, 1971; (editor) *Women on the Move*, four volumes, DeGraaf, 1972; (with Leona Rostenberg) *Old and Rare:*

Thirty Years in the Book Business, Schram, 1974; (editor) *The Victoria Woodhull Reader*, M & S Press, 1974; (editor) *Louisa's Wonder Book: An Undiscovered Alcott Juvenile*, Central Michigan University, 1975; (editor) *Behind a Mask: The Unknown Thrillers of Louisa May Alcott*, Morrow, 1975. Contributor of articles on nineteenth-century American literature and Americana to scholarly journals.

SIDELIGHTS: As a rare book dealer, Stern specializes in sixteenth-, seventeenth-, and eighteenth-century volumes, published in French, Italian, Latin, and English; as a writer, she specializes in nineteenth-century American. Stern comments: "This dichotomy may lead to a split individuality, but it also leads to a very exciting life." Her books have been mentioned or used as a source in a number of other volumes, notably S. N. Behrman's *Portrait of Max*, Grace M. Mayer's *Once Upon a City*, John A. Garraty's *The Nature of Biography*, and John Tebbel's *A History of Book Publishing in the United States*.

*　　*　　*

STEVENS, Joseph C(harles) 1929-

PERSONAL: Born February 28, 1929, in Grand Rapids, Mich.; son of Joseph, Jr. (a business executive) and Anne (Ghysels) Stevens. *Education:* Calvin College, A.B., 1950; Michigan State University, M.A., 1953; Harvard University, Ph.D., 1957. *Religion:* Episcopalian. *Home:* 765 Jonathan Edwards College, Yale University, New Haven, Conn. *Office:* John B. Pierce Foundation, 290 Congress Ave., New Haven, Conn.

CAREER: Harvard University, Cambridge, Mass., instructor, 1957-60, assistant professor of psychology, 1961-66; Yale University, New Haven, Conn., research associate and lecturer, 1966—. *Member:* Psychonomic Society, Acoustical Society of America, Optical Society of America, American Association for the Advancement of Science, Society for Neuroscience, Eastern Psychological Association, Sigma Pi.

WRITINGS: (With R. J. Hernstein and G. S. Reynolds) *Laboratory Experiments in Psychology*, Holt, 1965. Contributor to psychology, acoustical, and optical journals.

*　　*　　*

STEVENS, Leonard A. 1920-

PERSONAL: Born November 7, 1920, in Lisbon, N.H.; son of Lawrence A. and Margaret (Healy) Stevens; married Carla McBride (a teacher of writing, New School of Social Research, N.Y.), December 18, 1954; children: Timothy, Brooke, Sara, April. *Education:* Attended St. Anselm's College; University of Iowa, B.A., 1947, M.A., 1949. *Politics:* Democrat. *Home:* Christian St., Bridgewater, Conn. *Office:* Box 38, New Milford, Conn. 06776.

CAREER: Full-time professional writer. Executive director, Housatonic Valley Association (Conn.), 1973-74; writer of booklets and newspapers and speaker of over 300 speeches, Citizens Committee for the Hoover Report (New York); news editor, Radio Station WSUI (Iowa City, Iowa), two years. Former chairman, Bridgewater Board of Education; chairman, Bridgewater Democratic Town Committee; member, Bridgewater Conservation Commission; delegate, Democratic National Convention, 1968, 1972. *Military service:* U.S. Army Air Forces, World War II; served in Guam with 20th Air Force; became captain.

WRITINGS: (With Ralph G. Nichols) *Are You Listening?*, McGraw, 1957; *Old Peppersass*, Dodd, 1959; *Jet*

Flight 808, Harper, 1962; *On Growing Older*, U.S. Government Printing Office, 1964; *The Ill-Spoken Word*, McGraw, 1966; *Trucks That Haul by Night*, Crowell, 1966; *The Elizabeth: Passage of a Queen*, Knopf, 1968; *North Atlantic Jet Flight*, Crowell, 1968; (with wife, Carla Stevens) *The Birth of Sunset's Kittens*, Young Scott Books, 1969; *How a Law is Made: The Story of a Bill against Air Pollution*, Crowell, 1970; *The Town That Launders Its Water*, Coward, 1971; *Explorers of the Brain*, Knopf, 1971; *Salute! The Case of the Bible vs. the Flag*, Coward, 1973; *Clean Water: Nature's Way to Stop Pollution*, Dutton, 1974; *Neurons: Building Blocks of the Brain*, Crowell, 1974. Contributor to magazines, including *Saturday Evening Post*, *Collier's*, *Reader's Digest*, *Nation*, *True*, *Think*, *Pageant*, *Coronet*, *Harvard Business Review*, *Look*, *Argosy*, *Catholic Digest*, *Nation's Business*, *Service*, and others.

*　　*　　*

STEWART, Lawrence H(oyle) 1922-

PERSONAL: Born October 5, 1922, in Cheoah, N.C.; married Shirley Meyer, 1946. *Education:* Western Carolina College (now Univeristy), B.A., 1943; Columbia University, M.A., 1948, Ed.D., 1950. *Home:* 1320 Grizzly Peak Blvd., Berkeley, Calif. *Office:* Department of Education, University of California, Berkeley, Calif. 94720.

CAREER: Columbia University, Teachers College, New York, N.Y., instructor in hygiene, 1949-50; George Peabody College for Teachers, Nashville, Tenn., assistant professor of educational psychology, 1950-54; University of California, Berkeley, 1954—, began as assistant professor, professor of education and counseling psychology, 1965—. *Military service:* U.S. Navy, 1943-45; became lieutenant. *Member:* American Psychological Association, American Personal and Guidance Association. *Awards, honors:* Distinguished Service Award, Western Carolina University, 1960; Fulbright Award, England, 1969-70.

WRITINGS: The Counselor and Society: A Cultural Approach, Houghton, 1965. Author of more than forty articles and monographs dealing with the measurement and guidance field.

WORK IN PROGRESS: Two research projects sponsored by U.S. Office of Education—"Characteristics of Students and Graduates of Occupation-Centered Curricula" and "Increasing the Academic Achievement of Culturally Disadvantaged Youth."

*　　*　　*

STEWART, Stanley N(ordahl) 1931-

PERSONAL: Born June 5, 1931, in Minneapolis, Minn.; son of Mark Hannah and Elvia (Probpst) Stewart; married Barbara Riviere, March, 1959; children: Bradford Scott, Duncan Heath. *Education:* University of California, Los Angeles, B.A., 1956, M.A., 1958, Ph.D., 1961. *Home:* 301 Massachusetts Ave., Riverside, Calif. *Office:* Department of English, University of California, Riverside, Calif. 92502.

CAREER: Space Technology Laboratories, El Segundo, Calif., part-time technical writer, 1960; University of California, Riverside, instructor, 1961-62, assistant professor, 1962-66, associate professor 1966-69, professor of English, 1969—. *Member:* Modern Language Association of America, Renaissance Society of America, Philological Association of the Pacific Coast, Renaissance Society of Southern

California, Augustan Reprint Society. *Awards, honors:* Senior fellowship, John Simon Guggenheim Memorial Foundation, 1971-72.

WRITINGS: (Editor) Anne Collins, *Divine Songs and Meditations (1653)*, Augustan Reprint Society, 1962; *The Enclosed Garden: The Tradition and the Image in Seventeenth-Century Poetry*, University of Wisconsin Press, 1966; *The Expanded Voice: The Art of Thomas Traherne*, Huntington Library, 1970. Writer of two plays produced by college companies. Contributor of short stories to little literary magazines, and critical articles to *Pacific Coast Studies in Shakespeare* and *Studies in English Literature*.

WORK IN PROGRESS: The Rhetoric of Annihilation in the Seventeenth Century, a book-length critical study; other writing on George Herbert, Andrew Marvell, and Carson McCullers; popular articles on bullfighting and the movies (his hobbies).

* * *

STILES, Ned B. 1932-

PERSONAL: Born August 7, 1932, in Mayslick, Ky.; son of Andrew Jackson (a farmer) and Frances (Berry) Stiles; married Lynn Shattuck; children: Michael P. *Education:* Miami University, Oxford, Ohio, A.B., 1953; University of Cincinnati, LL.B., 1958.

CAREER: Admitted to Ohio State Bar, 1958, and to New York State Bar, 1962. Securities and Exchange Commission, Washington, D.C., attorney, 1958-61; Cleary Gottlieb Steen and Hamilton, New York, N.Y., private practice, 1961—. *Military service:* U.S. Air Force, 1953-55; became captain. *Member:* Association of the Bar of the City of New York, New York County Lawyers Association.

WRITINGS: (With D. J. Baum) *The Silent Partners,* Syracuse University Press, 1965. Contributor of articles to *Corporate Practice Commentator* and *UCLA Law Review.*†

* * *

STINNETT, Tim Moore 1901-

PERSONAL: Born May 2, 1901, in Junction City, Ark.; married Mary Gantt, December 25, 1923; children: Thomas, Robert. *Education:* Henderson-Brown College (now Henderson State College), B.S., 1922; University of Arkansas, M.S., 1935; University of Texas, Ed.D., 1951. *Office:* National Education Association, 1201 16th St., N.W., Washington, D.C. 20036.

CAREER: Stamps (Ark.) public schools, high school teacher, 1923-37, principal, 1923-27, superintendent of schools, 1927-37; Arkansas State Department of Education, Little Rock, assistant state commissioner of education and director of teacher education and certification, 1937-45; Arkansas Education Association, Little Rock, executive secretary, 1945-47; National Education Association, Washington, D.C., associate secretary, National Commission on Teacher Education and Professional Standards, 1948-51, executive secretary, National Commission on Teacher Education and Professional Standards, 1951-61, assistant executive secretary for professional development and welfare, 1961-66. *Member:* National Education Association, Arkansas Education Association, Phi Delta Kappa. *Awards, honors:* Citation for distinguished service in public education, Classroom Teachers Association of New York State, 1962; distinguished honorary award of Henderson State College, 1963; honorary Dr. Pedagogy, Rhode Island College, 1963.

WRITINGS: (With Edgar B. Wesley and Crawford Greene) *Workbook in Problems in American Democracy*, Heath, 1933; *Exercise Manual in Problems of Government*, Health, 1934; (with Ruth Wood Gavian) *Exercise Manual to Accompany "Our Changing Social Order"* Heath, 1936; *The Teacher and Professional Organizations*, National Education Association, 1951; (with W. Earl Armstrong) *A Manual on Certification Requirements for School Personnel in the United States*, U.S. Office of Education, 1951, biennial editions by National Education Association, 1953-70; (with Albert J. Huggett) *Professional Problems of Teachers*, Macmillan, 1956, 3rd edition, 1968; (with G. K. Hodenfield) *The Education of Teachers: Conflict and Consensus*, Prentice-Hall, 1961; (with Ralph W. McDonald) *Journey to Now*, National Education Association, 1961; *The Profession of Teaching*, Center for Applied Research in Education, 1962; (with L. D. Haskew) *Teaching in American Schools—A Handbook for the Future Teacher*, Harcourt, 1962; (with W. O. Stanley) *Power and Professionalism in Teaching*, Indiana University, 1964; (with J. H. Kleinman and Martha L. Ware) *Professional Negotiation in Public Education*, Macmillan, 1966; *Turmoil in Teaching*, Macmillan, 1968; (with Clare B. Kennan) *All This and Tomorrow Too*, Arkansas Education Association, 1969; (editor) *The Teacher Dropout*, F. E. Peacock, 1970.

Contributor of sections to other books on education, and to yearbooks. Also contributor to *Encyclopedia of Educational Research, American People's Encyclopedia*, and to professional and general periodicals, including *Saturday Review*. Editor, *Journal of Teacher Education* and *TEPS Newsletter*, 1951-61.

* * *

STOCKWELL, Robert P(aul) 1925-

PERSONAL: Born June 12, 1925, in Oklahoma City, Okla.; son of Benjamin Paul (an engineer) and Ruth Anna (Cunningham) Stockwell; married Lucy Louisa Floyd (an editor), August 29, 1946; children: Paul Witten. *Education:* University of Virginia, B.A., 1946, M.A., 1949, Ph.D., 1952. *Home:* 4000 Hayvenhurst Ave., Encino, Calif. *Office:* Department of Linguistics, University of California, 405 Hilgard Ave., Los Angeles, Calif. 90024.

CAREER: Oklahoma City University, Oklahoma City, Okla., instructor in English, 1946-48; U.S. Department of State, Foreign Service Institute, Washington, D.C., instructor, 1952-53, assistant professor, 1953-55, associate professor of linguistics, 1955-56, chairman of Latin American languages and area program 1953-56; University of California, Los Angeles, assistant professor of English, 1956-58, associate professor, 1958-62, professor of linguistics, 1962—, chairman, Department of Linguistics, 1966—. University of the Philippines, visiting professor, 1959, 1960. *Military service:* U.S. Naval Reserve, 1943-45. *Member:* Linguistic Society of America (member of executive committee, 1965-67), Philological Society, Modern Language Association of America, Linguistic Association of Great Britain. *Awards, honors:* American Council of Learned Societies fellow, 1963-64; distinguished teaching awards, University of California, Los Angeles, Alumni Association and Graduate Studies Association, 1968.

WRITINGS: (With J. D. Bowen) *Sound Pattern of Spanish*, University of Chicago Press, 1960; (with Bowen) *The Sounds of English and Spanish*, University of Chicago Press, 1965; (with Bowen and J. W. Martin) *The Grammatical Structures of English and Spanish*, University of Chicago Press, 1965; (editor with R.S.K. Macaulay) *Linguistic Change and Generative Theory*, Indiana University Press, 1972; (with Paul Schachter and Barbara H. Parbee) *The Major Syntactic Structures of English*, Holt, 1973. Contributor to linguistics journals.

WORK IN PROGRESS: The Great English Vowel Shift; studies in English syntax and history of the English language.

AVOCATIONAL INTERESTS: Golf, music (flute and harpischord).

* * *

STOFFEL, Betty W. 1922-

PERSONAL: First syllable of surname rhymes with "scoff"; born October 19, 1922, in Richmond, Va.; daughter of William Carlyle (a minister) and Lura (Doyle) Williams; married Ernest Lee Stoffel (a Presbyterian minister), May 20, 1947; children: Bobby, Bee, Lee, Bonnie. *Education:* Agnes Scott College, B.A., 1944; Presbyterian School of Christian Education, M.A., 1947. *Politics:* Democrat. *Religion:* Presbyterian. *Home:* 4510 Ortega Blvd., Jacksonville, Fla. 32210.

MEMBER: National League of American Pen Women, North Carolina Poetry Society.

WRITINGS—Poetry: *Moments of Eternity,* John Knox, 1954; *Splendid Moments,* John Knox, 1965. Also writer of articles and devotionals.

WORK IN PROGRESS: A book of poems.

SIDELIGHTS: Betty Stoffel lived in Scotland one summer on husband's pastoral exchange, and visited India, Middle East, Greece and Rome while attending World Council of Churches meeting in 1961. She is a second cousin of writer Pearl Buck.

* * *

STOKES, Roy 1915-

PERSONAL: Born August 14, 1915, in Ipswich, England; son of Arthur Sheldrake (an engineer) and Daisy Maude (Bishop) Stokes; married Mona Jefferson, July, 1957; children: Jane, Catherine. *Education:* University of Nottingham, M.A. *Religion:* Church of England. *Home:* 101 Nanpantan Rd., Loughborough, England. *Office:* School of Librarianship, Loughborough College, Loughborough, England.

CAREER: Affiliated with Ipswich (East Suffolk, England) Public Library, 1933-38, and with Ilford (Essex, England) Public Library, 1938-46; Loughborough College, Loughborough, England, director of School of Librarianship, 1946—. Visiting professor of bibliography at University of Illinois, summers, 1952 and 1955, Syracuse University, summer, 1958, University of California, Los Angeles, summer, 1962, Simmons College, summers, 1965 and 1966, University of Pittsburgh, 1965-66. *Member:* Library Association (council member, 1950—), Bibliographical Society, Bibliographical Society of America, Cambridge Bibliographical Society, Bibliographical Society of University of Virginia.

WRITINGS: (Editor) A. Esdiale, *Student's Manual of Bibliography,* 4th edition, Barnes & Noble, 1967; *Bibliographical Control and Service,* London House, 1965; *The Function of Bibliography,* Deutsch, 1969, Academy Press, 1971. Contributor to library and bibliographical journals.†

STONE, Alan A(braham) 1929-

PERSONAL: Born August 14, 1929, in Boston, Mass.; son of Julius (a lawyer) and Betty (Pastan) Stone; married Sue Smart (a writer), June 15, 1952; children: Karen, Douglas, David. *Education:* Harvard University, A.B., 1950; Yale University, M.D., 1955. *Home:* 195 Brattle St., Cambridge, Mass. 02138. *Office:* Harvard Law School, Cambridge, Mass. 02138.

CAREER: Pediatric intern, Grace-New Haven Hospital, New Haven, Conn., 1955-56; McLean Hospital, Belmont, Mass., resident in psychiatry, 1956-58, associate psychiatrist, 1966-69; James Jackson Putnam Children's Center, National Institute of Mental Health fellow in child psychiatry, 1958-59; psychoanalytic training and practice, 1961—. Harvard University, Medical School, Cambridge, Mass., assistant professor, 1966-69, associate professor of psychiatry, 1969-72, visiting lecturer in psychiatry and psychoanalysis in Law School, 1968-69, professor of law and psychiatry in the faculty of law and the faculty of medicine, 1972—. Chairman, Task Force on Psychosurgery of the Department of Mental Health, Commonwealth of Massachusetts, 1974. *Military service:* U.S. Army, Medical Corps, 1959-61; became captain. *Member:* American Psychiatric Association (trustee, 1973—), group for the Advancement of Psychiatry (chairman, Committee on Psychiatry and Law, 1969-72), Massachusetts Medical Society, Massachusetts Society for Research in Psychiatry (secretary-treasurer, 1963-64; vice-president, 1964-65; president, 1965-66), Boston Psychoanalytic Society and Institute (president of candidates council, 1963-66).

WRITINGS: (With Gloria Onque) *Longitudinal Studies of Child Personality,* Harvard University Press, 1959; (with wife, Sue Smart Stone) *The Abnormal Personality Through Literature,* Prentice-Hall, 1966; *Mental Health and Law: A System in Transition,* National Institute of Mental Health, 1975. Contributor to *Archives of General Psychiatry* and *Psychosomatic Medicine.*

* * *

STONE, Albert Edward 1924-

PERSONAL: Born January 1, 1924, in New London, Conn.; son of Albert E. (a Navy officer) and Rebecca (Rollins) Stone; married Grace Woodbury, July 5, 1954; children: Albert Edward Jr., Rebecca Rollins. *Education:* Phillips Academy, Andover, student, 1940-52; Yale University, B.A., 1949, Ph.D., 1957; Columbia University, M.A., 1955. *Politics:* Democrat. *Religion:* Episcopalian. *Home:* 1052 Clifton R. N.E., Atlanta, Ga. 30307. *Office:* Department of English, Emory University, Atlanta, Ga. 30322.

CAREER: Casady School, Oklahoma City, Okla., instructor in English, 1949-52; Yale University, New Haven, Conn., instructor, 1955-59, assistant professor of English, 1959-62; Emory University, Atlanta, Ga., professor of English and chairman of department, 1962-68, professor of English and American Studies, 1968—. Member of advisory council, Danforth Foundation graduate fellowship program, 1965-68; Fulbright lecturer, Charles University, Prague, 1968-69. *Military service:* U.S. Army, Military Intelligence, 1943-46; served in Southwest Pacific; became master sergeant; received Purple Heart and Bronze Star. *Member:* Modern Language Association of America, American Studies Association, American Civil Liberties Union, Phi Beta Kappa, Elizabethan Club, Elihu Club. *Awards, honors:* Morse fellowship, Yale University, 1960-61; E. Harris Harbison Award for distinguished teaching, 1965-66.

WRITINGS—Under name Albert E. Stone, Jr.: *The Innocent Eye: Childhood in Mark Twain's Imagination*, Yale University Press, 1961; (editor) Crevecoeur, *Letters From an American Farmer*, New American Library, 1963; (editor) *Twentieth-Century Interpretations of the Ambassadors*, Prentice-Hall, 1969; (editor) Mark Twain, *Personal Recollections of Joan of Arc*, University of California Press, in press. Contributor to *American Heritage, American Literature, American Quarterly, Yale University Library Gazette, Genre, New England Quarterly, College Language Association Journal*, and other periodicals.

WORK IN PROGRESS: An edition of Twain's *A Tramp Abroad; The Recreated Self*, a study of autobiography in America.

* * *

STONE, Alfred R. 1926-

PERSONAL: Born February 11, 1926, in Marlin, Tex.; son of Ocie E. (a farmer) and Bertha (Burney) Stone; married Oleta Witcher, May 16, 1946; children: Deborah Ann, Pamela Gail, Karen Sue. *Education:* Attended college for three years. *Religion:* Baptist. *Office:* Box 4292, North Austin Station, Austin, Tex. 78751.

CAREER: Texas Department of Public Safety, Austin, training specialist, 1957-62, training officer, 1962—. Amateur Athetic Union, registration chairman of South Texas chapter, 1960. *Military service:* U.S. Marine Corps Reserve, 1943-46, 1950-51; became sergeant; received Purple Heart, U.S. Navy Unit Commendation, and Presidential Unit Citation. *Member:* National Safety Council, National Judo Black Belt Federation, Armed Forces Judo Association, American Society of Safety Engineers, Texas Safety Association, Texas Motor Transport Association, Texas Council of Safety Supervisors, Texas Police Association.

WRITINGS: Auto Dynamics, Steck, 1965; *Driver Assumptions*, Steck, 1969; *Caution: Driving Ahead* (textbook), Steck, 1973.

* * *

STONE, David U. 1927-

PERSONAL: Born February 4, 1927, in Santa Cruz, Calif.; son of Marshall Ernest (a realtor) and Grace Stone; married Iva Dell Frazier, July 20, 1946; children: Katherine, Russell, Susan. *Education:* Attended high school in Eugene, Ore. *Politics:* Independent. *Religion:* Protestant. *Home:* 236 Camino del Cerro, Los Gatos, Calif. 95030. *Office:* Stone Institute of Marketing and Management, 5297 Scotts Valley Drive, Scotts Valley, Calif. 95066.

CAREER: With Stone Real Estate Co., 1945-48; Broadway-Hale Department Stores, San Jose, Calif., manager, 1948-52; Carnation Milk Co., Oakland, Calif., sales supervisor, 1952-54; William Perry Co. (food brokers), San Francisco, Calif., sales supervisor, 1954-57; Stone and Schulte, Inc., Realtors, San Jose, Calif., general manager, 1957-66; Stone Institute of Marketing and Management, Scotts Valley, Calif., president, 1966—; consultant sales trainer, lecturer on sales training and communication techniques, 1966—. *Member:* National Association of Real Estate Boards, National Association of Home Builders, International Traders Club, Sales and Marketing Executives, California Real Estate Association (director), Home Builder's Sales Managers Club, San Jose Real Estate Board (secretary, 1966). *Awards, honors:* Sales Manager of the Year Award, National Association of Home Builders, 1960.

WRITINGS: How to Operate a Real Estate Trade-In Program, Prentice-Hall, 1962; *Real Estate Salesman's Training Manual,* Prentice-Hall, 1965; *Guaranteed Sales Plan for Realtors and Builders,* National Association of Home Builders, 1968; *How to Sell New Homes and Condominiums,* House & Home Press, 1975. Contributor to journals; co-author of California Real Estate Association publications; wrote and helped direct training film for National Association of Real Estate Boards, 1966. Also writer of real estate training manuals and cassette programs.

AVOCATIONAL INTERESTS: Public speaking, gardening, travel, painting.

* * *

STONE, James Champion 1916-

PERSONAL: Born January 15, 1916, in Cincinnati, Ohio; son of James Madison and Mabel (Champion) Stone; married Dorothy Brett, February 22, 1941; children: Mary, Ann, James. *Education:* University of Cincinnati, A.B., 1939, B.E., 1940, M.A., 1943; Stanford University, Ed.D., 1948. *Home:* Caballo Ranchero, Box 374, Diablo, Calif. *Office:* University of California, Berkeley, Calif. 94720.

CAREER: High school teacher in Cincinnati, Ohio, and owner and director of Wasaks Boy's Club, 1940-43; elementary teacher in Mountain View, Calif., 1946-47; Stanford University, Stanford, Calif., assistant professor of education, 1947-48; California State Department of Education, consultant on teacher education, 1948-52, specialist in teacher education, 1952-56; University of California, Berkeley, professor of education and director of teacher education, 1956—. Member of planning committee, White House Conference on Education; chairman of committee on accreditation, California State Board of Education. Consultant to Thomas Y. Crowell Co. and Ford Foundation. *Military service:* U.S. Army, 1945-46; became captain.

MEMBER: National Education Association, American Association of Land-Grant Colleges and State Universities (chairman), California Council on Education of Teachers (president), California Teachers Association (chairman, committee on teacher education).

WRITINGS: The Graduate Internship Program in Teacher Education—A Progress Report, University of California Press, 1959; *California's Commitment to Public Education,* Crowell, 1961; (with Clark N. Robinson) *The Graduate Internship Program in Teacher Education—The First Six Years,* University of California Press, 1965; (with Frederick W. Schneider) *The Foundations of Education—Commitment to Teaching,* Crowell, 1965, 2nd edition, 1971; (with F. W. Schneider) *Readings in the Foundation of Education—Commitment to Teaching,* Crowell, 1965, 2nd edition, 1971; *California Education Today,* Crowell, 1968; *How to Get Into College,* Dutton, 1968; *Breakthrough in Teacher Education,* Jossey-Bass, 1968; *Teachers for the Disadvantaged,* Jossey-Bass, 1969; *Teaching in the Inner City,* Crowell, 1970; *Portraits of the American University,* Jossey-Bass, 1971; *Teaching Multicultural Populations,* Van Nostrand, 1971.

AVOCATIONAL INTERESTS: Equitation, swimming and tennis.

* * *

STONEMAN, Elvyn Arthur 1919-

PERSONAL: Born November 5, 1919, in Lincoln, Neb.; son of Lewis Francis and Grace (Smith) Stoneman; married Edna Mae Friesen (now a teacher), May 6, 1940; children:

James Arthur, Jeanne Elizabeth, Judy Ann. *Education:* University of Nebraska, B.Sc., 1941, M.A., 1943; Clark University, Worcester, Mass., Ph.D., 1950. *Home:* 2613 Silverdale Ct., Wheaton, Md. 20906. *Office:* U.S. Department of State, 22nd and C, Washington, D.C.

CAREER: Member of geography faculty, Kansas City University (now University of Missouri at Kansas City), 1947-48, and Indiana University, Bloomington, 1948-51; U.S. government, Washington, D.C., geographer with Department of Defense, 1951-60, with Department of State, 1960—. *Military service:* U.S. Army, 1943-45. *Member:* Association of American Geographers.

WRITINGS: (Associate author with G. Etzel Pearcy) *World Political Geography,* 2nd edition, Crowell, 1957; (with Robert D. Hodgson) *The Changing Map of Africa,* Van Nostrand, 1963, 2nd edition, 1968; (with Pearcy) *A Handbook of New Nations,* Crowell, 1968.†

*   *   *

STOTLAND, Ezra 1924-

PERSONAL: Born June 9, 1924, in New York, N.Y.; son of Isaac (a furrier) and Rose (Chaiken) Stotland; married Patricia Joyce, July 12, 1963; children: Sheila Rose. *Education:* City College (now of the City University of New York), New York, N.Y., B.S.S.S., 1948; University of Michigan, M.A., 1949, Ph.D., 1953. *Office:* Society and Justice Program, University of Washington, Seattle, Wash.

CAREER: University of Michigan, Ann Arbor, research associte in psychology, 1953-57; University of Washington, Seattle, assistant professor, 1957-61, associate professor, 1961-65, professor of psychology, 1965—, director, society and justice program, 1971—. Consultant to U.S. Veterans Administration. *Military service:* U.S. Army, 1942-46; became sergeant. *Member:* American Civil Liberties Union, American Psychological Association, Society for the Psychological Study of Social Issues, Psychology-Law Association, Society and Law Association.

WRITINGS: (With A. L. Kobler) *End of Hope,* Free Press of Glencoe, 1964; (with Kobler) *Life and Death of a Mental Hospital,* University of Washington Press, 1965; *Psychology of Hope,* Jossey-Bass, 1969; (with S. Sherman and K. Shaver) *Empathy and Birth Order,* University of Nebraska Press, 1971; (with L. Canon) *Social Psychology: A Cognitive Approach,* Saunders, 1972.

*   *   *

STRANGE, Jack Roy 1921-

PERSONAL: Born February 13, 1921, in Dallas, Tex.; son of Anthony Lee (a farmer) and Katherine (Nebares) Strange; married Sallie Minter (a college teacher), April 18, 1947; children: Richard, Audrey. *Education:* Arlington State College, A.S., 1941; Southern Methodist University, B.A., 1943, M.A., 1947; Johns Hopkins University, Ph.D., 1950. *Home:* 3614 Lindenwood, Dallas, Tex. 75205. *Office:* Southern Methodist University, Dallas, Tex 75222.

CAREER: Southern Methodist University, Dallas, Tex., instructor in psychology, 1946-48; Johns Hopkins University, Baltimore, Md., instructor in psychology, 1948-50; Southern Methodist University, Dallas, Tex., assistant professor, 1950-53, associate professor, 1953-59, professor of psychology, 1959—, chairman of department, 1953-57, 1959-62, and 1967—. Visiting professor, San Francisco State College (now University), 1961; clinical professor, University of Texas Southwestern Medical School, 1967—.

Member of board of directors, Dallas Mental Health Association. *Military service:* U.S. Army, 1943-46; served as Japanese interpreter for Army Intelligence. *Member:* American Psychological Association, Southwestern Psychological Association, Texas Psychological Association (president, 1966-67), Dallas Psychological Association, Phi Beta Kappa, Sigma Xi, Psi Chi. *Awards, honors:* Danforth fellow, 1963-64.

WRITINGS: (With A. Q. Sartain) *Psychology: Understanding Human Behavior,* McGraw, 1958, *Abnormal Psychology: Understanding Behavior Disorders* (text with test booklet), McGraw, 1965; (with Ray Foster) *Readings in Physiological Psychology,* Wadsworth, 1966.

WORK IN PROGRESS: Abnormal Psychology: Case Histories, for McGraw; *Psychology: A History and Definition.*

AVOCATIONAL INTERESTS: Spending summers at cabin in Sangre de Cristo Mountains of New Mexico, trout-fishing, back-packing, and writing.†

*   *   *

STRATI, Saverio 1924-

PERSONAL: Born August 16, 1924, in Italy; son of Paolo (a mason) and Agatha (Romeo) Strati; married Hildegard Fleig, 1958; children: Giampaolo. *Home:* Via Leonardo da Vinci 8, Scandicci, Firenze, Italy.

CAREER: Professional writer. *Member:* Sindacato degli Serittori. *Awards, honors:* Charles Veillon International Prize (Lausanne), for *Tibi e Tascia;* Sila Prize, for *Gente in Viaggio.*

WRITINGS: La Marchesina, Mondadori (Milan), 1956; *La Teda,* Mondadori, 1957, translation published as *Terrarossa,* Abelard, 1957; *Tibi e Tascia,* Mondadori, 1959; *Mani vuote,* Mondadori, 1960, translation by Peter Moule published as *Empty Hands,* Abelard, 1964; *Avventura in citta,* Mondadori, 1962, translation by Angus Davidson published as *The Lights of Reggio,* J. Murray, 1962; *Il nodo,* Mondadori, 1965; *Gente in viaggio,* Mondadori, 1966; *Il codardo,* Bietti (Milan), 1970; *Noi lazzaroni,* Mondadori, 1972.†

*   *   *

STUART, Dabney 1937-

PERSONAL: Born November 4, 1937, in Richmond, Va.; son of Walker Dabney, Jr. and Martha (von Schilling) Stuart; married Martha Varney, August 14, 1965; children: Nathan von Schilling, Darren Wynne. *Education:* Davidson College, A.B., 1960; Harvard University, A.M., 1962. *Office:* Washington and Lee University, Lexington, Va. 24450.

CAREER: College of William and Mary, Williamsburg, Va., instructor in English, 1961-65; Washington and Lee University, Lexington, Va., instructor in English, 1965-66, assistant professor, 1966-69, associate professor, 1969-74, professor of English, 1974—. *Member:* Authors Guild of America, American Association of University Professors. *Awards, honors:* Dylan Thomas Award of Poetry Society of America for "The Two Lindens"; Howard Willett Research Prize for poetry manuscript; Borestone Mountain Awards, 1969 and 1974; National Endowment for the Humanities summer stipend, 1969; National Endowment for the Arts fellowship, 1974.

WRITINGS: The Diving Bell (poems), Knopf, 1966; *A*

Particular Place (poems), Knopf, 1969; *The Other Hand* (poems), Louisiana State University, 1974. Contributor of essays, reviews, and poetry to journals. Poetry editor, *Shenandoah*, 1966—.

WORK IN PROGRESS: Sovereign Power, a study of selected fiction by Vladimir Nabokov; two volumes of poems, *Round and Round* and *It's All in Your Mind*.

* * *

STUBBLEFIELD, Harold W. 1934-

PERSONAL: Born October 19, 1934, in Paducah, Ky.; son of Bobbie (a laundry operator) and Lorene (Fleming) Stubblefield; married Betty Hughes (an elementary teacher at time of marriage), February 4, 1961; children: Hugh Wayne. *Education:* Murray State College, B.A., 1955; Southern Baptist Theological Seminary, B.D., 1958, Th.M., 1960; Indiana University, Ed.D., 1973.

CAREER: Minister of Southern Baptist Convention; pastor in Lamasco, Ky., 1953-58; clinical pastoral intern at hospitals in Louisville and Lakeland, Ky., 1958, Institute of Religion, Houston, Tex., 1959-60; Western State Hospital, Hopkinsville, Ky., associate in chaplain's department, 1960; Clover Bottom Hospital and School (state school for mentally retarded), Donelson, Tenn., chaplain, beginning, 1960. *Member:* American Association on Mental Deficiency, American Protestant Hospital Association, Academy of Religion and Mental Health, Society for the Scientific Study of Religion, Southern Baptist Association for Clinical Pastoral Education.

WRITINGS: The Church's Ministry in Mental Retardation, Broadman, 1965. Contributor to religious, health, and education journals.

WORK IN PROGRESS: Exploring the Christian nurture of the mentally retarded and the relationship of religion in parental response to a retarded child.†

* * *

STYRON, Rose (Burgunder) 1928-

PERSONAL: Born April 4, 1928, in Baltimore, Md.; daughter of B. B. and Selma (Kann) Burgunder; married William Styron (a novelist), May 4, 1953; children: Susanna, Paola, Thomas, Alexandra. *Education:* Wellesley College, B.A., 1950; Johns Hopkins University, M.A., 1952. *Residence:* Roxbury, Conn.

CAREER: Poet, journalist, translator.

WRITINGS: From Summer to Summer (poetry), Viking, 1965; (contributor of translations) Olga Carlisle, editor, *Poets on Streetcorners: Portraits of Fifteen Russian Poets,* Random House, 1971; *Modern Russian Poetry,* Viking, 1972; *Thieves' Afternoon,* Viking, 1973. Contributor of poems to literary periodicals and of articles to *New York Review of Books, New Republic, Ms., Ramparts,* and other periodicals.

WORK IN PROGRESS: Amnesty International, Report on Torture: Chile, for Farrar, Straus.

* * *

SUBLETTE, Edith Blanche 1909-

PERSONAL: Born November 5, 1909, in Kansas City, Mo.; daughter of Warren Francis and Edith E. (Wallis) Sublette. *Education:* University of Missouri, B.S. in Ed., 1931, M.A., 1932; University of Iowa, Ph.D., 1938; postdoctoral study at University of Mexico, 1941, and University of the Andes, 1955. *Home:* 4625 Forest, Kansas City, Mo. 64110.

CAREER: Member of faculty of Clifton Junior College, Clifton, Tex., 1934-35, Hannibal Junior College, Hannibal, Mo., 1940-41, and Bethel College, North Newton, Kan., 1941-42; U.S. government, translator, San Antonio, Tex., 1942-43; Culver-Stockton College, Canton, Mo., head of language department, 1943-47; DePauw University, Greencastle, Ind., associate professor, 1947-54, professor of Romance languages, 1955-74. *Member:* American Association of Teachers of Spanish and Portuguese, Sigma Delta Pi, Phi Sigma Iota, Delta Kappa Gamma.

WRITINGS: (Editor) Palacio Valdes, *Marta y Maria* (textbook edition of novel), Odyssey, 1961; (editor) M. Mihura, *Carlota,* Odyssey, 1963; (editor) Alfonso Paso, *La Corbata,* Odyssey, 1966; (editor) Alfonso Paso, *Usted Puede Ser Un Asesino* (textbook edition), Bobbs-Merrill, 1974. Contributor to professional journals.

SIDELIGHTS: Edith Sublette has traveled extensively in South and Central America, West Indies, Europe.

* * *

SULLIVAN, Nancy 1929-

PERSONAL: Born July 3, 1929, in Newport, R.I.; daughter of Daniel and Helen (Murphy) Sullivan. *Education:* Hunter College (now Hunter College of the City University of New York), B.A., 1951; University of Rhode Island, M.A., 1953; University of Connecticut, Ph.D., 1963. *Office:* Department of English, Rhode Island College, Providence, R.I.

CAREER: Brown University, Providence, R.I., 1953-63, began as instructor, became assistant professor of English and assistant to the dean of Pembroke College; Rhode Island College, Providence, 1963—, began as associate professor, became professor of English. *Awards, honors:* First Annual Devins Memorial award, 1965, for *The History of the World as Pictures.*

WRITINGS: The History of the World as Pictures (poems), University of Missouri Press, 1965; *Perspective and the Poetic Process,* Mouton & Co., 1968; *Body English,* Hellcoal Press, 1972; (compiler with Jean Garrigue) *Love's Aspects: The World's Great Love Poems,* Doubleday, 1975; *Beyond Saying,* David Godine, 1975. Contributor of book reviews to *Providence Sunday Journal;* contributor of poems to *Accent, Beloit Poetry Journal, Carleton Miscellany, Massachusetts Review, Poetry Northwest, Quartet, Poetry, Quarterly Review of Literature, Ramparts, Saturday Review, Southern Review, Southwest Review, Transatlantic Review, Shenandoah,* and other periodicals.

BIOGRAPHICAL/CRITICAL SOURCES: A Controversy of Poets, edited by Paris Leary and Robert Kelly, Doubleday, 1965.

* * *

SUNDBERG, Trudy James 1925-

PERSONAL: Born February 28, 1925, in Woodsfield, Ohio; daughter of Philip Harley and Lillian (Kuban) James; married John Paul Sundberg (a commander, U.S. Navy), April 16, 1948; children: Kris, Jan, Lana, Dane. *Education:* Miami University, Oxford, Ohio, B.S. in B.A., 1946; University of Illinois, M.S. in Journalism, 1948; Western Washington State College, graduate study, 1964. *Politics:* Democrat. *Religion:* Unitarian Universalist. *Residence:* Oak Harbor, Wash.

CAREER: Shilito's Department Store, Cincinnati, Ohio, junior executive, 1947; University of Illinois, Urbana, instructor in rhetoric, 1948; junior high school teacher of English, Norfolk, Va., 1949-50; *Daily Review,* Hayward, Calif., women's editor and feature writer, 1959; *Whidbey News-Times,* Oak Harbor, Wash., feature writer and columnist, 1960; Oak Harbor Junior High School, Oak Harbor, Wash., teacher of physical education, 1961-63, of English and journalism, 1964—. Lecturer, 1960—. Conductor of charm school and physical fitness class. *Member:* National Education Association, Washington Education Association, League of Women Voters, Parent-Teacher Association, Phi Beta Kappa, Mortar Board, Delta Delta Delta, Washington Organization for Reading Development, Officers' Wives' Club. *Awards, honors:* "Lady of the month" award, *U.S. Lady* (magazine), February, 1958; two first awards for painting, Alameda Arts and Crafts Exhibit, 1960.

WRITINGS: Portrait of an Island, Whidbey Press, 1961; (with Robert Morrison) *Bank Correspondence Handbook,* Bankers, 1964. Play included in *The Human Nature of Playwriting,* edited by Samson Raphaelson, Macmillan, 1949. Regular contributor to *U.S. Lady,* 1960—; features published in *Minneapolis Star,* and other articles in *NEA Journal, Motive,* and *Daily Word.*

WORK IN PROGRESS: Serendipity, a book about family experiences while living in England when Commander Sundberg was at Royal Air Force Staff College; *Angels with Soiled Wings,* a collection of essays on her experiences while teaching retarded and handicapped children.

SIDELIGHTS: As a Navy wife, Mrs. Sundberg has lived in Hawaii, Japan, Europe, and in many sections of America.

BIOGRAPHICAL/CRITICAL SOURCES: U.S. Lady, February, 1958.†

*   *   *

SUNDERMAN, James F.   1919-

PERSONAL: Born July 20, 1919; son of Frank Sunderman; married Thelma A. Fentress, September 15, 1945; children: James F., Jr., William Blake, Michael J. *Education:* Capital University, B.A., 1941; University of Florida, M.A., 1949, additional study, 1950-51. *Religion:* Protestant. *Home:* 117 South Washington St., New Bremen, Ohio.

CAREER: Was a member of U.S. Army Air Forces; U.S. Air Force, 1951-75, was director of public affairs for NORAD, Ent Air Force Base, Colo.; retired as colonel. Served overseas in Southwest Pacific, Philippines, and Vietnam; decorations include Legion of Merit and Air Force Commendation Medal. *Member:* Air Force Association. *Awards, honors:* Arts and Letters Award of Air Force Association, for assisting in the creation of new literature on airpower and space.

WRITINGS—Editor: *Journey Into Wilderness,* University of Florida Press, 1953; *Early Air Pioneers,* F. Watts, 1959; *World War II in the Air: Pacific,* F. Watts, 1960; *World War II in the Air: Europe,* F. Watts, 1963; *Air Escape and Evasion,* F. Watts, 1964.

*   *   *

SWAIN, Dwight V(reeland)   1915-
(Clark South)

PERSONAL: Born November 17, 1915, in Rochester,

Mich.; son of John Edgar (a railroad telegrapher) and Florence (Vreeland) Swain; married Margaret Simpson (a musician and college teacher); married Joye Raechel Boulton, February 12, 1969; children: Thomas McCray. *Education:* University of Michigan, B.A., 1937; University of Oklahoma, M.A., 1954. *Politics:* Democrat. *Religion:* Methodist. *Home:* 1303 Garfield Ave., Norman, Okla, 73069. *Office:* School of Journalism, University of Oklahoma, Norman, Okla. 73069.

CAREER: Member of editorial staffs of daily and weekly newspapers in Michigan, Pennsylvania, California, and Oklahoma, and of *Flying* (magazine), 1937-41; full-time free-lance writer, 1942, 1946-48; part-time free-lance writer, 1934-41, 1948—; University of Oklahoma, Norman, script writer for Oklahoma Motion Picture Unit, 1949-65, professor of journalism, beginning 1952. Member of awards committee, National Cowboy Hall of Fame and Western Heritage Center, beginning 1960; member of national advisory board, Palmer Writers' School, beginning 1966; vice president, BHS Productions, Inc., 1961-71. *Military service:* U.S. Army, 1942-46. *Member:* American Medical Writers' Association, Science Fiction Writers of America, University Film Producers Association, American Association of University Professors.

WRITINGS: The Transposed Man, Ace Books, 1955; *Tricks and Techniques of the Selling Writer,* Doubleday, 1965, new edition published as *Techniques of the Selling Writer,* University of Oklahoma Press, 1974. Writer and co-producer of "Stark Fear" (film), 1963; writer of more than forty factual films for University of Oklahoma Motion Picture Unit and independent producers, and of radio scripts. Articles and fiction have appeared in national magazines of many types—ranging from *Amazing Stories* to *True, Giant Western* to *Labor Today,* and *Specialty Salesman* to *Writer's Digest,* with some stories in 1940's published under pseudonym, Clark South; also has written book reviews, pamphlets, and other materials.†

*   *   *

SWANSON, Roy Arthur   1925-

PERSONAL: Born April 7, 1925, in St. Paul, Minn.; son of Roy Benjamin (a mechanic) and Gertrude (Larson) Swanson; married Vivian Vitous, March 30, 1946; children: Lynn, Robin, Dyack, Dana. *Education:* University of Minnesota, B.A., 1948, B.S., 1949, M.A., 1951; University of Illinois, Ph.D., 1954. *Home:* 11618 North Bobolink Lane, Mequon, Wis. 53092. *Office:* University of Wisconsin, Milwaukee, Wis. 53201.

CAREER: Elementary school principal, St. Paul, Minn., 1949-51; University of Illinois, Urbana, instructor in education, 1952-53; Indiana University, Bloomington, instructor in classics, 1954-57; University of Minnesota, Minneapolis, assistant professor, 1957-61, associate professor, 1961-64, professor of classics and humanities and chairman of department of comparative literature, 1964-65; Macalester College, St. Paul, Minn., professor of English, 1965-67; University of Wisconsin, Milwaukee, professor of comparative literature and classics, 1967—. *Military service:* U.S. Army, 103rd Infantry Division, 1943-46; received Bronze Star. *Member:* American Philological Association, Modern Language Association of America, Society for the Advancement of Scandinavian Study, Phi Beta Kappa. *Awards, honors:* Fulbright scholarship to Rome, Italy, 1953; Lilly Foundation award for book research in Sweden, 1965-66.

WRITINGS: (Translator) Odi et Amo: The Complete Poetry of Catullus, Bobbs-Merrill, 1959; Heart of Reason: Introductory Essays in Modern-World Humanities, Denison, 1963; (translator) Pindar's Odes, Bobbs-Merrill, 1974. Contributor to Yearbook of Comparative and General Literature and to classical and other scholarly journals. Editor, Minnesota Review, 1963-67, Classical Journal, 1968-73.

WORK IN PROGRESS: A critical study of the works of Par Lagerkvist.

* * *

SWARTZ, Robert J(ason) 1936-

PERSONAL: Born February 15, 1936, in Boston, Mass.; son of Louis (a market manager) and Marian (Tapper) Swartz; married Christine Ivusic, May 28, 1961 (divorced); children: Alexander, Jennifer. Education: Harvard University, B.A., 1957, Ph.D., 1963. Office: Department of Philosophy, University of Massachusetts, Harbor Campus, Boston, Mass. 02125.

CAREER: University of Illinois, Urbana, instructor, 1963-65, assistant professor of philosophy 1965-67; Brown University, Providence, R.I., assistant professor, 1967-69, associate professor of philosophy, 1969-73; University of Massachusetts, Harbor Campus, Boston, professor of philosophy, 1973—, chairman of department, 1973—.

WRITINGS: (Editor and author of introduction) Perceiving, Sensing, and Knowing: A Book of Readings from Twentieth-Century Sources in the Philosophy of Perception, Anchor Books, 1965; (editor with Roderick M. Chisholm) Empirical Knowledge: Readings from Contemporary Sources, Prentice-Hall, 1973. Contributor of articles to Journal of Philosophy, Philosophical Studies, and other professional journals.†

* * *

SWEARENGEN, Thomas F. 1924-

PERSONAL: Born October 10, 1924, in Fort Worth, Tex.; son of Charles C. (with U.S. Marine Corps) and Mary B. (Younger) Swearengen; married Ruby Irene Proctor, March 13, 1948; children: Barbara Ann, Thomas F., Jr. Education: Attended Marine Corps schools at Quantico, Va., and ordnance schools. Politics: Independent. Religion: Methodist. Address: Marine Corps Air Station, Beaufort, South Carolina.

CAREER: U.S. Marine Corps, 1943—; current rank, chief warrant officer. Explosive ordnance disposal officer, assigned to disposal of unexploded ordnance, conventional high explosive, nuclear weapons, chemical and biological weapons; instructor in Marine Corps schools; researcher in foreign explosive ordnance. Member: National Rifle Association (life member), American Ordnance Association. Awards, honors—Military: Commendation medals, Presidential Unit Citation with two stars, Asiatic-Pacific Medal, Korean Medal, American Defense Medal, National Defense Medal, United Nations Medal, Korean Presidential Unit Citation.

WRITINGS: Tear Gas Munitions, C. C Thomas, 1966.

WORK IN PROGRESS: A revised and enlarged edition of Tear Gas Munitions; books on the combat shotgun and on machine pistols.

AVOCATIONAL INTERESTS: Firearms and ordnance history (worldwide), scuba diving (holds instructor's certificate).†

SWIDLER, Leonard 1929-

PERSONAL: Born January 6, 1929, in Sioux City, Iowa; son of Samuel A. and Josephine (Reed) Swidler; married Arlene Anderson; children: Carmel, Eva-Maria. Education: St. Norbert College, De Pere, Wis., B.A., 1950; Marquette University, M.A., 1955; University of Wisconsin, graduate study, 1955-57, Ph.D., 1961; University of Tuebingen, graduate study, 1957-58, S.T.L., 1959; University of Munich, graduate study, 1958-59. Religion: Roman Catholic. Office: Temple University, Philadelphia, Pa.

CAREER: Taught while studying at Milwaukee School of Engineering, Milwaukee, Wis., 1955, Edgewood College of the Sacred Heart, Madison, Wis., 1955-56, University of Wisconsin, 1956-57, University of Maryland in Europe, 1958-60; Duquesne University, Pittsburgh, Pa., assistant professor, 1960-63, associate professor of history, 1963-66, member of theology faculty, 1962-66; Temple University, Philadelphia, Pa., professor of religion, 1966—. Institute for Ecumenical and Cultural Research fellow, 1968-69; visiting professor, University of Tuebingen, 1972-73; lecturer at ecumenical conferences. Member: National Conference of Christians and Jews (executive board member of Pittsburgh chapter), Institute for Freedom in the Church, St. Joan's International Alliance.

WRITINGS: Dialogue for Reunion, Herder & Herder, 1962; (editor) Scripture and Ecumenism, Duquesne University Press, 1965; The Ecumenical Vanguard, Duquesne University Press, 1965; (with Marc H. Tanenbaum) Jewish-Christian Dialogues, National Council of Catholic Men and National Council of Catholic Women, 1966; (editor) Ecumenism: The Spirit and Worship, Duquesne University Press, 1967; (translator and author of introduction) Heinrich Fries, Bultmann, Earth, and Catholic Theology, Duquesne University Press, 1967; Freedom and the Church, Pflaum Press, 1969; (with Arlene Swidler) Bishops and People, Westminster Press, 1970; (translator with Swidler) Haye van der Meer, Women Priests in the Catholic Church, Temple University Press, 1973; (with Jan Kerkhofs) Isj and Isjah, Uitgeverij Patmos, 1973. Co-founder and editor, Journal of Ecumenical Studies.

WORK IN PROGRESS: Bloodwitness to Peace and Unity: The Life of May Joseph Metzger; The Status of Women in Formative Judaism; Jesus Was a Feminist.

* * *

SYDENHAM, Michael J(ohn) 1923-

PERSONAL: Born November 23, 1923, in London, England; son of John William (a businessman) and Winifred (Scoggins) Sydenham; married Jean Anderson Smillie, August 18, 1948; children: Anne Margaret, Jennifer Elizabeth. Education: University College, London, B.A. (honors in history), 1945; Westminster College of Education, Teaching Certificate, 1946; University of London, Ph.D., 1953.

CAREER: Ashville College, Harrogate, Yorkshire, England, assistant teacher, 1946-48; Chiswick College of Further Education, London, England, lecturer in history, 1948-56; Portsmouth College of Education, Portsmouth, England, principal lecturer in history, beginning, 1956; was reported, in 1975, to have immigrated to Canada. Visiting tutor in history, University of Southampton; visiting professor of history, Indiana University, 1967. Military service: British Home Guard; became quartermaster sergeant. Member: Royal Historical Society (fellow), Historical Association (chairman, Portsmouth branch, 1957-59, secretary, 1959-62).

WRITINGS: The Girondins, Athlone Press, 1961; *The French Revolution,* Putnam, 1965; *The First French Republic, 1792-1804,* University of California Press, 1974. Contributor to *History Today.*

AVOCATIONAL INTERESTS: Historical exhibitions, travel in France, rural life.†

* * *

SYKES, John 1918-

PERSONAL: Born July 31, 1918, in Bradford, Yorkshire, England; son of Charles (a knitting yarn manufacturer) and Amelia (Horner) Sykes; married Lilli Freuthal (head of a Montessori school), January 13, 1955; children: Joseph Noel, Daniel John. *Education:* Attended Bootham School, York, England, 1932-34, Bradford Technical College, Diploma in Textile Engineering, 1935. *Politics:* Independent radical. *Religion:* Society of Friends (Quaker).

CAREER: Charles Sykes & Co. Ltd. (yarn manufacturers), Bradford, Yorkshire, England, manager, 1937-39; full-time professional writer, 1945—. *Wartime service:* Society of Friends Ambulance Unit, 1939-45, serving in Finland, Greece, and Middle East; seconded to United Nations Relief and Rehabilitation Administration, 1944-45, as field director in Aegean area, Greece. *Member:* Society of Authors.

WRITINGS—Fiction, except as indicated: *The Levantine,* Laurie, 1952; *The Romantic Wife,* Laurie, 1953; *The Newcomer,* Hurst & Blackett, 1956; *A Japanese Family* (nonfiction), Wingate, 1957; *The Quakers* (nonfiction), Wingate, 1958, Lippincott, 1959; *The Ocean Crossing,* Hutchinson, 1958; *The Colonial,* Hutchinson, 1962, Coward, 1963; *Family in Peru* (nonfiction), Anthony Blond, 1963; *The Heat of Summer,* Hutchinson, 1964; *Caique: A Portrait of Greek Islanders* (nonfiction), Hutchinson, 1965; *The Couple,* Hutchinson, 1966; *Direction North: A View of Finland* (nonfiction), Chilton, 1967; *The Mountain Arabs: A Window on the Middle East* (nonfiction), Chilton, 1968; *Down into Egypt: A Revolution Observed* (nonfiction), Hutchinson, 1969; *A Summer in Turkey* (nonfiction), Hutchinson, 1970; *Portugal and Africa: The People and the War* (nonfiction), Hutchinson, 1971.

WORK IN PROGRESS: A novel, the subject a man at fifty.

SIDELIGHTS: Sykes has lived in fifteen countries, visited more than one hundred, and traveled twice around the world. He speaks French, Spanish, Italian, and Greek fluently, and is competent in German and Swedish. Interests include the mystical and religious, and social reform; collects contemporary paintings and sculpture; is an avid gardener and do-it-yourselfer.†

* * *

SYNAN, Edward A(loysius) 1918-

PERSONAL: Surname is pronounced *Sign*-on; born April 13, 1918, in Fall River, Mass.; son of Edward A. and Mary F. (McDermott) Synan. *Education:* Seton Hall College (now University), B.A., 1938; Catholic University of Louvain, graduate student, 1938-40; Catholic University of America, S.T.L., 1942; University of Toronto, M.A., 1950, Ph.D., 1952; Pontifical Institute of Mediaeval Studies, Toronto, M.S.L., 1951. *Home:* 59 Queen's Park, Toronto, Ontario M5S 2C4, Canada. *Office:* Pontifical Institute of

Mediaeval Studies, 59 Queen's Park, Toronto, Ontario M5S 2C4, Canada.

CAREER: Roman Catholic priest, ordained 1942; curate in Montclair, N.J., 1942-44; Seton Hall University, South Orange, N.J., professor of philosophy and chairman of department, 1952-59; University of Toronto, Toronto, Ontario, professor of philosophy, 1959—; Pontifical Institute of Mediaeval Studies, professor of philosophy, 1959—, president, 1973—. *Military service:* U.S. Army Air Forces, Chaplain Corps, captain, 1944-48. *Member:* Mediaeval Academy of America, American Catholic Philosophical Association, Catholic Theological Society of America, Renaissance Society of America. *Awards, honors:* LL.D., Seton Hall University, 1973.

WRITINGS: (Contributor) *Nine Mediaeval Thinkers,* Pontifical Institute of Mediaeval Studies, 1955; (contributor) *An Etienne Gilson Tribute,* Marquette University Press, 1959; *The Popes and the Jews in the Middle Ages,* Macmillan, 1965; *The Works of Richard of Campsall,* Volume I, Pontifical Institute of Mediaeval Studies, 1968; *The Fountain of Philosophy,* Pontifical Institute of Mediaeval Studies, 1972. Contributor to journals. Associate editor, *Bridge: A Yearbook of Judaeo-Christian Studies,* 1957-62.

WORK IN PROGRESS: Questions Deanima by Adam and Walter Burley; Volume II of *The Works of Richard of Campsall.*

* * *

SZASZ, Thomas (Stephen) 1920-

PERSONAL: Surname is pronounced Sass; born April 15, 1920, in Budapest, Hungary; son of Julius (a businessman) and Lily (Wellisch) Szasz; married Rosine Loshkajian, October 19, 1951 (divorced, 1970); children: Margot, Susan. *Education:* University of Cincinnati, A.B. (honors), 1941, M.D., 1944; Institute for Psychoanalysis, Chicago, Ill., certificate, 1950. *Home:* 116 Bradford Pkwy., Syracuse, N.Y. 13224. *Agent:* Elizabeth Otis, McIntosh & Otis, Inc., 18 East 41st St., New York, N.Y. 10017. *Office:* Upstate Medical Center, 750 East Adams St., Syracuse, N.Y. 13210.

CAREER: Diplomate, National Board of Medical Examiners, 1945, American Board of Psychiatry and Neurology, 1951; Boston City Hospital, Boston, Mass., intern, 1944-45; Cincinnati General Hospital, Cincinnati, Ohio, assistant resident, 1945-46, clinician, 1946; University of Chicago Clinics, Chicago, Ill., assistant resident in psychiatry, 1946-47; Institute for Psychoanalysis, Chicago, Ill., staff member, 1951-56; State University of New York, Upstate Medical Center, Syracuse, professor of psychiatry, 1956—; private practice of psychology and psychiatry in Chicago, Ill., 1949-54, Bethesda, Md., 1954-56, Syracuse, N.Y., 1956—. Member of board of directors, National Council on Crime and Delinquency; member of research advisory panel, Institute for the Study of Drug Addiction; member of national advisory committee, Living Libraries, Inc.; fellow, Postgraduate Center for Mental Health, 1962; visiting professor, University of Wisconsin, 1962, Marquette University, 1968; senior scholar, Eli Lilly Foundation, 1966—; Civil Liberties Carey Lecturer at Cornell University Law School, 1968; C. P. Snow Lecturer at Ithaca University, 1970; Root Tilden Lecturer at New York University School of Law, 1971.

MEMBER: International Psychoanalytic Association, American Psychiatric Association (fellow), American Psychoanalytic Association, American Humanist Association, American Association for the Abolition of Involuntary Mental Hospitalization (co-founder and chairman of board of directors). *Awards, honors:* Holmest-Munsterberg Award from International Academy of Forensic Psychology, 1969; Wisdom Award of Honor, 1970; Academy Prize from Institutum atque Academia Auctorum Internationalis, 1972; Humanist of the Year Award from American Humanist Association, 1973; Second Annual Independence Day Award for the Greatest Public Service Benefiting the Disadvantaged from American Institute for Public Service, 1974.

WRITINGS: Pain and Pleasure, Basic Books, 1957; *The Myth of Mental Illness*, Harper, 1961, revised edition, 1974; *Law, Liberty, and Psychiatry*, Macmillan, 1963; *The Ethics of Psychoanalysis*, Basic Books, 1965; *Psychiatric Justice*, Macmillan, 1965; *Ideology and Insanity*, Doubleday, 1970; *The Manufacture of Madness*, Harper, 1970; *The Second Sin*, Doubleday, 1973; (editor) *The Age of Madness*, Doubleday, 1973; *Ceremonial Chemistry*, Doubleday, 1974; *The Myth of Psychotherapy*, Doubleday, in press.

Contributor to professional journals and to popular publications, including *Harper's, New Republic*, and *New York Times*. Member of editorial board, *Contemporary Psychoanalysis, Journal of Humanistic Psychology, Humanist*, and *Journal of Drug Addiction*; member of board of consultants, *Psychoanalytic Review*; member of selection advisory board, *Tort and Medical Yearbook*; advisory editor, *Journal of Forensic Psychology*; consulting editor, *Science Digest*.

SIDELIGHTS: Szasz has, in effect, started a war on psychiatry as it is currently practiced in the United States. The basic argument of his book, *The Myth of Mental Illness*, is, according to Edwin M. Schur, "that both our uses of the term 'mental illness' and the activities of the psychiatric profession are often scientifically untenable and morally and socially indefensible...." Szasz believes that mental illness differs from organic illness, and he calls the former "problems of living." He believes psychiatrists have glossed over these differences and continue to treat mental disturbances as medical problems. They impose the definition "mentally ill" on a person instead of treating the illness as an objective fact. He further believes that anyone brought to trial for a criminal offense should be allowed to stand trial instead of, as sometimes happens, being submitted to a pretrial psychiatric examination and then being committed to a mental institution. In fact, he would have the plea of insanity abolished except in those rare cases when the defendant is, for example, in a catatonic stupor. Nor does he accept dangerousness to oneself as a legitimate basis for institutionalization. He writes: "In a free society, a person must have the right to injure or kill himself." As for dangerousness to others, Schur notes that Szasz expounds on those not incarcerated who are equally as dangerous to others, and cites drunken drivers as one example. Schur writes: "A person's 'dangerousness' becomes a matter for legitimate public control, Szasz argues, only when he actually commits a dangerous act. Then he can be dealt with in accordance with regular criminal law."

Other psychiatrists have called his work "reckless iconoclasm," "reprehensible," and "dangerous." Lawyers, including Arthur Goldberg, praise him. His sole concern, says Schur, is the protection of the individual. Szasz believes that "the poor need jobs and money, not psychoanalysis. The uneducated need knowledge and skills, not psy-

choanalysis." Though his arguments are often stated in their extreme forms, Schur believes that Szasz "quite probably ... has done more than any other man to alert the American public to the potential dangers of an excessively psychiatrized society."

BIOGRAPHICAL/CRITICAL SOURCES: New Republic, August 7, 1965; *New York Times Book Review*, August 22, 1965; *Atlantic*, June, 1966; *Toronto Daily Star*, June 20, 1966; *American Journal of Psychiatry*, April, 1969; *New Physician*, June, 1969; *Indiana Legal Forum*, fall, 1969; *Minnesota Mental Health Retardation Newsletter*, October, 1969; *Washington Post*, March 6, 1970; *New Scientist and Science Journal*, June 3, 1971; *New York Times Magazine*, October 3, 1971; *She*, February, 1972; *Human Behavior*, July/August, 1972; *World Medicine*, October 4, 1972; *Penthouse*, October, 1973.

* * *

SZEKELY, Endre 1922-

PERSONAL: Born September 9, 1922, in Budapest, Hungary; son of Istvan (a lawyer) and Elisabeth (Pinter) Szekely; married Frances Vivian Brown Finkelsen, January 6, 1961; children: John E. Finkelsen (stepson). *Education:* M. Kir Pazmany Peter Tudomany Egyetem, Ph.D., 1944; University of Queensland, Ph.D. (ad eundem statum) and M.A., 1955. *Home:* 67 Ronald Ave., Lane Core, Sydney, New South Wales, Australia. *Office:* Cumberland College of Health Sciences, Sydney, New South Wales, Australia.

CAREER: Ministry of Education (Culture), Budapest, Hungary, ministerial secretary, 1945-48; Department of Education, Hobart, Tasmania, Australia, teacher-librarian, 1950-53; Department of Mental Hygiene, Brisbane, Queensland, Australia, psychologist, 1954-60; Department of Public Health, Sydney, New South Wales, Australia, principal clinical psychologist, 1960-69; University of Newcastle, New South Wales, Australia, senior lecturer in psychology, 1969-74; Cumberland College of Health Sciences, Sydney, Australia, director of clinical studies, 1974. University of Queensland, part-time lecturer in psychology, 1957-60. *Member:* Australian Psychological Society, British Psychological Society (associate).

WRITINGS: Basic Analysis of Inner Psychological Functions, Cambridge University Press, 1965.

WORK IN PROGRESS: Research with a view to extending the theory and method of Basic Analysis for other books, in the fields of psychodynamics, psychobiology, and philosophical psychology; a project in psychodynamics.

SIDELIGHTS: Szekely speaks French, Hungarian, and German.

* * *

TAAFFE, James G. 1932-

PERSONAL: Surname rhymes with "safe"; born September 15, 1932, in Cincinnati, Ohio; son of Griffith C. Taaffe; married Donna Click, June 8, 1955; children: Patrick Michael, Lauren Kathleen. *Education:* Columbia University, B.A., 1954; Indiana University, M.A., 1956, Ph.D., 1960. *Home:* 2595 Norfolk Rd., Cleveland, Ohio 44106.

CAREER: Williams College, Williamstown, Mass., instructor in English, 1959-62; Vassar College, Poughkeepsie, N.Y., assistant professor of English, 1962-64; Case Western Reserve University, Cleveland, Ohio, 1964—, began as assistant professor, became professor of English, dean of graduate studies, and vice-president for undergraduate and graduate studies. *Member:* American Philosophical Society (fellow), Milton Society of America, Dante Society of America. *Awards, honors:* Newberry Library fellow, 1963; National Endowment for the Humanities fellowship, 1971.

WRITINGS: (Editor with Robert Wallace) *Poems on Poetry*, Dutton, 1965; (editor) Abraham Cowley, *Selected Poetry and Prose*, Appleton, 1970; (compiler with John Lincks) *Reading English Poetry*, Free Press, 1971; (editor with James H. Hanford) *A Milton Handbook*, 5th edition (Taaffe was not associated with earlier editions), Appleton, 1971; *A Student's Guide to Literary Terms*, World Publishing, 1971; *Abraham Cowley*, Twayne, 1972. Contributor to *Victorian Poetry, Modern Language Review*, and other journals.

WORK IN PROGRESS: Editing, *The Complete Works of Abraham Cowley*.

*   *   *

TABER, Robert

PERSONAL: Born in the United States. *Politics:* Anarchist. *Religion:* Anarchist. *Home:* 118 West 79th St., New York, N.Y.

CAREER: Merchant seaman, 1942-45. Was the only American among Fidel Castro's defending forces at Playa Giron.

WRITINGS: M26: Biography of a Revolution, Lyle Stuart, 1961; *The War of the Flea: A Study of Guerrilla Warfare Theory and Practise*, Lyle Stuart, 1965. Columnist, *The Independent*.

WORK IN PROGRESS: A book on the Black revolution in the United States; a study of Zen Buddhism as it applies to American life; a study of anarchism and revolution.

BIOGRAPHICAL/CRITICAL SOURCES: Book Week, November 7, 1965.†

*   *   *

TADLOCK, Max R. 1919-

PERSONAL: Born December 12, 1919, in Shawneetown, Ill.; son of Michael E. (a salesman) and Edith (Desper) Tadlock; married Marion Ruth Petrecca (a nurse), May 6, 1942; children: Maxa Ruth, Susanna Lee. *Education:* University of Toledo, A.B., 1948; Stanford University, M.A., 1950. *Office:* 127 Second St., Los Altos, Calif.

CAREER: Monterey Peninsula College, Monterey, Calif., dean of instruction, 1952-58, 1961-62, chairman of department of speech and drama, 1958-66; Tadlock Associates, Carmel, Calif., director of editorial services, 1964-66; Management & Economics Research Inc., Palo Alto, Calif., director of educational research, 1966-67; Tadlock Associates, Inc. (educational consultant firm), president, 1967—. *Military service:* U.S. Army, liaison pilot, 1941-46; became captain; received Air Medal and Distinguished Flying Cross.

WRITINGS: Correcting Your English, Houghton, 1965; (with Bass and others) *Politics and Teachers*, California Teachers Association, 1966; (with Fred Carvell) *It's Not Too Late*, Macmillan, 1971. Writer of standardized tests in speech and composition for U.S. Armed Forces Institute.

WORK IN PROGRESS: Managing the Educational Enterprise.

TAEUBER, Alma Ficks 1933-

PERSONAL: Surname is pronounced *Toy*-ber; born September 19, 1933, in Seattle, Wash.; daughter of George W. (a printer) and Alma (Beveridge) Ficks; married Karl E. Taeuber (a professor), March 17, 1960; children: Shawn Eric, Stacey Robin, Wendy Kim. *Education:* Washington State University, B.A., 1954; University of Chicago, M.A., 1960, Ph.D., 1962. *Home:* 1911 Vilas Ave., Madison, Wis. 53711. *Office:* Department of Sociology, University of Wisconsin, Madison, Wis. 53706.

CAREER: University of Chicago, Chicago, Ill., research associate in sociology, 1962-64; University of Wisconsin—Madison, research associate in sociology, 1965-66, research associate with Institute for Research on Poverty, 1966—. *Member:* Population Association of America, American Sociological Association.

WRITINGS: (With husband, Karl E. Taeuber) *Negroes in Cities*, Aldine, 1965. Contributor to professional journals. Deputy editor, *American Sociological Review*, 1966.

WORK IN PROGRESS: Research on occupational and industrial assimilation of Blacks; school segregation.

*   *   *

TAEUBER, Karl E(rnst) 1936-

PERSONAL: Surname is pronounced *Toy*-ber; born March 31, 1936, in Washington, D.C.; son of Conrad (a sociologist) and Irene (a demographer and sociologist; maiden name, Barnes) Taeuber; married Alma Ficks (a sociologist), March 17, 1960; children: Shawn, Stacy, Wendy. *Education:* Yale University, B.A., 1955; Harvard University, M.A., 1957, Ph.D., 1960; University of Chicago, graduate student, 1958-59. *Office:* Department of Sociology, University of Wisconsin, Madison, Wis. 53706.

CAREER: University of Chicago, Chicago, Ill., assistant professor of sociology and research associate of Population Research and Training Center, 1961-63; University of California, Berkeley, research associate in demography, 1963-64; University of Wisconsin, Madison, 1964—, began as assistant professor, became professor of sociology and fellow of Institute for Research on Poverty, chairman of department, 1970-73. Social Scientist, RAND Corp., 1969-70. *Military service:* U.S. Public Health Service Commissioned Corps, assistant scientist at National Cancer Institute, with rank of lieutenant, 1959-61. *Member:* Population Association of America, American Sociological Association, American Statistical Association.

WRITINGS: (With wife, Alma F. Taeuber) *Negroes in Cities*, Aldine, 1965; (with Leonard Chiazze, Jr. and William Haenszel) *Migration in the United States*, U.S. Government Printing Office, 1966. Contributor to *Scientific American, Social Problems*, and other sociological journals.

WORK IN PROGRESS: Studies of school segregation and updating studies of residential segregation.

*   *   *

TALBOT, Charlene Joy 1928-

PERSONAL: Born November 14, 1928, in Frankfort, Kan.; daughter of Charles Henry (a laborer) and Helen (Jillson) Talbot. *Education:* Kansas State College of Agriculture and Applied Science (now Kansas State University), B.S. in Journalism, 1950. *Home:* 21 Harrison St., New York, N.Y. 10013.

CAREER: After college wandered to New York, California, Mexico, and Europe, working as typist, secretary, waitress, and classified ad-taker; in 1958 found a cheap apartment in the market district of Manhattan, worked part-time as a secretary, began to write, and finally sold a children's story to a Sunday school paper. *Awards, honors:* Fellowship in juvenile literature to Bread Loaf Writers' Conference, 1966.

WRITINGS: *Tomas Takes Charge* (juvenile), Lothrop, 1966; *A Home With Aunt Florry* (juvenile), Atheneum, 1974. Stories have appeared in *Golden Magazine, Scholastic Newstime, Calling All Girls, Atlantic Advocate, Harvest Years,* and *American Restaurant.*

WORK IN PROGRESS: A romantic suspense novel, *Arsenal of Danger.*

SIDELIGHTS: Charlene Talbot said: "The wonderful thing about writing for children is that they're interested in everything. You can do all the things you wanted to do as a child, and then write about them as though you still were."

* * *

TALBOT, Ross B. 1919-

PERSONAL: Born November 3, 1919, in Long Point, Ill.; son of Ernest R. and Grace B. (Outram) Talbot; married Rena M. Hart, August 16, 1941; children: Mary Elizabeth, Nancy Lynn. *Education:* Illinois Wesleyan University, A.B., 1941; University of Chicago, A.M., 1949, Ph.D., 1953. *Politics:* Democratic party. *Religion:* Baptist. *Home:* 2117 Greenbriar Circle, Ames, Iowa 50010.

CAREER: University of North Dakota, Grand Forks, instructor, later assistant professor of political science, 1948-56; Columbia University, New York, N.Y., visiting assistant professor of political science, 1956-57; Iowa State University of Science and Technology, Ames, associate professor, 1956-62, professor of political science, 1962—. *Military service:* U.S. Army, 1941-46. U.S. Army Reserve, 1946-64; became lieutenant colonel. *Member:* American Political Science Association, American Association of University Professors (chapter president, 1963-64). *Awards, honors:* American Farm Economics Association award for best article published in *Journal of Farm Economics,* 1964; Fulbright fellowship to Belgium to study agricultural policies of European Economic Community, 1964-65.

WRITINGS: (With Don F. Hadwiger) *Pressures and Protests,* Chandler Publishing, 1965; *The Policy Process in American Agriculture,* Chandler Publishing, 1968.

* * *

TALLENT, Norman 1921-

PERSONAL: Born September 28, 1921, in Springfield, Mass.; son of Louis (a meat-cutter) and Sarah (Steinman) Tallent; married Shirley Rudman, January 23, 1949; children: Marc Andrew, Robert David, Anne Louise. *Education:* University of Illinois, B.S., 1946, M.S., 1947; Columbia University, M.A., 1949, Ph.D., 1954. *Religion:* Jewish. *Home:* 41 Hillside Rd., Northampton, Mass. 01060. *Office:* Veterans Administration Hospital, Northampton, Mass. 01060.

CAREER: Elgin State Hospital, Elgin, Ill., clinical psychologist, 1950-53; U.S. Veterans Administration Hospital, Hampton, Va., clinical psychologist, 1954-59; Veterans Administration Hospital, Northampton, Mass., clinical psychologist, 1959—. George Washington University Extension, Hampton, Va., instructor, 1955-59. *Military ser-*

vice: U.S. Army, 1943-45; received Purple Heart, Legion of Merit. *Member:* American Psychological Association (fellow), Society for Personality Assessment (fellow).

WRITINGS: *Clinical Psychological Consultation,* Prentice-Hall, 1963; *Psycological Perspectives on the Person,* Van Nostrand, 1967; *Prospettive psicologiche sulla Persona,* Ubaldini Editore, 1970; *Psychology: Understanding Ourselves and Others,* American Book Co., 1972; *Psychology Report Writing,* Prentice-Hall, 1975. Contributor to professional journals.

WORK IN PROGRESS: A book, *The Human Side of Sex,* and several professional papers on human sexuality.

* * *

TAMULAITIS, Vytas 1913-

PERSONAL: Given name is Victor in English; born January 17, 1913, in Sutkiskiai Village, Lithuania; son of Stasys (a farmer) and Barbara (Paukstys) Tamulaitis; married Maria Sinkevicius (an insurance clerk), December 25, 1938; children: Vida, Vytautas. *Education:* Attended University of Kaunas, law student, 1933-35, biology student, 1935-36, received government scholarship for further studies in France; War Academy, Kaunas, Lithuania, graduated as lieutenant, 1948. *Home:* 53 Ostend Ave., Toronto, Ontario, Canada.

CAREER: Lithuanian Army, instructor in war school, 1938-41; left Lithuania in 1944, lived in Germany, 1944-48, and migrated to Canada as laborer, 1948; now with Art Gallery of Ontario, Toronto. Author and translator. *Member:* Lithuanian-Canadian Writers' Association (vice-President, 1951-53), Lithuanian Writers' Association of the United States. *Awards, honors:* Lithuanian Red Cross prize for best children's book, 1935, for *Nimblefoot the Ant: Her Adventures;* prizes for short stories from the Lithunian-language newspapers, *Lietuviu Zodis* (West Germany), 1948, and *Draugas* (Chicago), 1954.

WRITINGS—All for children: *Skruzdelytes Greitutes Nuotykiai,* Vytis (Lithuania), 1935, translation published as *Nimblefoot the Ant: Her Adventures,* Manyland, 1965; *Kiskelio Uzrasai* (title means "The Rabbit's Memoirs"), Vytis, 1935; *Pauasaris Ateina* (title means "The Spring Is Coming"), Sakalas (Lithuania), 1937; *Vytuko Uzrasai* (title means "Vytukas' Journal"), Sakalas, 1937; *Naktis ant Nemuno* (title means "A Night on the Nemunas River"), Sakala, 1937; *Viena Karta* (title means "Once Upon A Time"), Sakalas, 1942; *Sugrizimas* (title means "The Return"), Patria (West Germany), 1948; *The Adventures of a Musician Cricket,* Parts 1-2, Immaculata Press, 1961. Co-translator from the French and German of two books published in Lithuania, 1937-38; translator of short stories into English, German, Estonian, Latvian, and Yugoslavian. Contributor to "Why & How Library," Field Enterprises, 1972. Editor of a cadet journal in Lithuania, 1938-40; assistant chief editor of youth journal, *Ziburelis,* 1940-44.

WORK IN PROGRESS: A story on the life of the bees.

SIDELIGHTS: Tamulaitis speaks German, Russian and English. *Avocational interests:* Beetles (has a collection started when he was twelve), wildlife, the sea, lakes, and boating.

* * *

TANNENBAUM, Arnold S(herwood) 1925-

PERSONAL: Born December 17, 1925, in Bayonne, N.J.; son of Benjamin (a merchant) and Rose (Wilder) Tannenbaum; married Ruth Gumpert, October 1, 1950; children: Carol, Peter, Michael, Rachel. *Education:* Purdue University, B.S.E.E., 1945; Syracuse University, Ph.D., 1954. *Home:* 2521 Newport Rd., Ann Arbor, Mich. *Office:* Survey Research Center, Institute for Social Research, P.O. Box 1248, University of Michigan, Ann Arbor, Mich. 48106.

CAREER: University of Michigan, Ann Arbor, staff of Survey Research Center, Institute for Social Research, 1949—, as research associate, 1956-58, and program director, 1958—, lecturer in department of psychology, 1962-63, associate professor, 1963-67, professor of psychology, 1967—. European productivity Agency, Paris, France, consultant, 1958-59. *Military service:* U.S. Naval Reserve, 1943-46; became ensign. *Member:* American Psychological Association, American Sociological Association, International University Contact for Management Education, Sigma Chi, Psi Chi.

WRITINGS: (With Robert L. Kahn) *Participation in Union Locals*, Row, Peterson & Co., 1958; (editor) *The Worker in the New Industrial Environment*, Foundation for Research on Human Behavior (Ann Arbor), 1962; (contributor) *Handbook of Organizations*, edited by J. March, Rand McNally, 1965; *Social Psychology of the Work Organization*, Wadsworth, 1966; *Control in Organizations*, McGraw-Hill, 1968; (with others) *Hierarchy in Organizations*, Jossey-Bass, 1974; (editor with others) *Organizational Behavior: Research and Issues*, Industrial Relations Research Association, 1974. Contributor to *International Encyclopedia of the Social Sciences* and to journals.

WORK IN PROGRESS: Editing a book of articles on social research in organizations.

*   *   *

TANNENBAUM, Edward R(obert)   1921-

PERSONAL: Born June 20, 1921, in Chicago, Ill.; son of Abraham and Esther (Kaplan) Tannenbaum. *Education:* University of Wisconsin, student, 1938-39; University of Chicago, A.B., 1942, Ph.D., 1950; University of Paris, graduate study, 1948-49. *Office:* New York University, 19 University Pl., New York, N.Y. 10003.

CAREER: Colorado State University, Fort Collins, instructor, later assistant professor of history, 1950-56; Rutgers University, Douglass College, New Brunswick, N.J., assistant professor of history, 1956-62; New York University, New York, N.Y., associate professor, 1962-65, professor of history, 1965—, director of graduate studies, 1972—. *Military service:* U.S. Army, 1943-46; received two Bronze Stars. *Member:* American Historical Association, Society for French Historical Studies, Society for Italian Historical Studies. *Awards, honors:* Ford faculty fellowship, 1955-56; American Philosophical Society research grant, 1967 and 1969; Howard R. Marraro Prize from American Historical Association, 1973, for *The Fascist Experience*; National Endowment for the Humanities senior fellowship, 1974-75.

WRITINGS: The New France, University of Chicago Press, 1961; *The Action Francaise*, Wiley, 1962; *European Civilization Since the Middle Ages*, Wiley, 1965; *The Fascist Experience: Italian Society and Culture, 1922-1945*, Basic Books, 1972; (editor) *A History of World Civilizations*, Wiley, 1973; (editor with Emiliana P. Noether) *Modern Italy: A Topical History Since 1861*, New York University Press, 1974.

WORK IN PROGRESS: European Culture and Society, 1890-1914.

*   *   *

TANNER, Daniel   1926-

PERSONAL: Born September 22, 1926, in New York, N.Y.; son of John (a businessman) and Lillian (Jupiter) Tanner; married Laurel Nan Jacobson (a professor at Temple University), July 11, 1948. *Education:* Michigan State University, B.S., 1949, M.S., 1952; Ohio State University, Ph.D., 1955. *Home:* 996 Village Dr. E., North Brunswick, N.J. 08902. *Office:* Rutgers University, New Brunswick, N.J. 08903.

CAREER: San Francisco State College (now University), San Francisco, Calif., assistant professor of education, 1955-60; Purdue University, Lafayette, Ind., associate professor of education, 1960-62; Northwestern University, Evanston, Ill., associate professor of education, 1962-64; City University of New York (now City College of the City University of New York), New York, N.Y., associate professor of educational research, 1964-66; University of Wisconsin, Milwaukee Campus, professor of curriculum, 1966-67; Rutgers University, Graduate School of Education, professor of education, 1967—, faculty research fellow, 1974-75. Visiting professorial scholar, University of London Institute of Education, 1974-75. Consultant, University of Texas Medical Center curriculum study, 1961-62, and Chicago school survey, 1963-64; consultant and examination assistant, Board of Examiners, New York City Board of Education, 1965-66; member of regional review panel, U.S. Office of Education college work-study program, 1965; consultant, American Telephone and Telegraph Co., 1970-71. Member of California State Personnel Board, 1957.

MEMBER: American Association for the Advancement of Science (fellow), American Educational Research Association, Association for Supervision and Curriculum Development, American Association of University Professors, Phi Delta Kappa, Phi Kappa Phi. *Awards, honors:* Service Award, Phi Delta Kappa, 1960.

WRITINGS: Schools for Youth: Change and Challenge in Secondary Education, Macmillan, 1965; *Developing the College Potential of Disadvantaged High School Youth* (monograph), Division of Teacher Education, City University of New York, 1966; *Secondary Curriculum: Theory and Development*, Macmillan, 1971; *Secondary Education: Perspectives and Prospects*, Macmillan, 1972; *Using Behavioral Objectives in the Classroom*, Macmillan, 1972; *Curriculum Development: Theory into Practice*, Macmillan, 1975. Contributor to anthologies; also contributor to *Atlantic Monthly* and to educational journals.

WORK IN PROGRESS: Models of Curriculum: Designing and Developing the Secondary School Curriculum.

AVOCATIONAL INTERESTS: Photography, golf.

BIOGRAPHICAL/CRITICAL SOURCES: New York Herald Tribune, July 14, 1958.

*   *   *

TANZER, Lester   1929-

PERSONAL: Born August 3, 1929, in New York, N.Y.; son of Charles and Clara (Ente) Tanzer; married Marlene Luckton, June 29, 1949; children: Stephen, Jeffrey, Andrew, David. *Education:* Columbia University, A.B., 1951, M.S., 1952; George Washington University, additional courses, 1965—. *Home:* 4859 North 30th St., Arlington, Va. 22207. *Agent:* John Cushman Associates, 25 West 43 St., New York, N.Y. 10036. *Office:* 2300 N St. N.W., Washington, D.C.

CAREER: Wall Street Journal, Washington, D.C., reporter, 1952-59; *Changing Times*, Washington, D.C., associate editor, 1959-64; *U.S. News & World Report*, Washington, D.C., associate executive editor, 1964—. *Member:* American Political Science Association, Sigma Delta Chi, National Press Club.

WRITINGS: (Editor) *The Kennedy Circle*, Robert B. Luce, 1961; (with Stefan Ilok) *Brotherhood of Silence*, Robert B. Luce, 1963; *Stretching Your Auto Dollar*, Kiplinger Washington Editors, 1964; *Ten Champions*, New Directions, 1965.

* * *

TARCHER, Martin 1921-

PERSONAL: Born March 1, 1921, in Brooklyn, N.Y.; son of Samuel and Sarah (Katz) Tarcher; married wife, Alyce B. (a physician), February 2, 1963. *Education:* University of Denver, B.S., 1948, M.A., 1950; Columbia University, Ed.D., 1958. *Home:* 36 Graystone Ter., San Francisco, Calif. 94114.

CAREER: University of Denver, Denver, Colo., acting director of creative graphics department, 1948-51; Institute for American Democracy, Inc., New York, N.Y., director, 1953-55; Adult Education Association of the U.S.A., Chicago, Ill. assistant director, 1956-57; Hewitt Associates (management consultants), consultants and communication specialist, 1957-58; Health and Welfare Council of Indianapolis and Marion County, Indianapolis, Ind., director of project on aging, 1958-60; University of California, Berkeley, extension head of leadership training center, 1960-63; Chabot College, Hayward, Calif., instructor, 1962-63; University of Hawaii, Honolulu professor of education and director of economic education, 1966-67; University of California, San Francisco Medical Center, chief consultant in social sciences, 1967—. Guest lecturer at other colleges and universities in America and England. Research writer for Italian Institute Community Centers, 1955, and Oxford University, 1963-64. Consultant to educational agencies. Chairman, Committee on Aging, Berkeley, Calif., 1961; field director, California Council of Economic Education, 1969-70. *Military service:* U.S. Marine Corps, 1941-45; became staff sergeant. *Member:* Adult Education Association of the U.S.A. (vice-president of Indiana State Council, 1957; chairman of section on aging, 1958-60), American Economic Association, Association for Evolutionary Economics, American Association of Higher Education.

WRITINGS: Leadership and the Power of Ideas, Harper, 1966; (contributor) Ralph Kaminsky, *The Economics of the City*, Joint Council on Economic Education, 1968. Filmstrips include "These Untrained Tongues" and "Out from Silence," Society for Visual Education, and "Tell Us, Kee Nez," Bureau of Indian Affairs; co-author or editor of other visual materials. Contributor of articles and reviews to adult education and communications journals.†

* * *

TATE, Merze

PERSONAL: Born in Blanchard, Mich.; daughter of Charles (a farmer and businessman) and Myrtle Katora (Lett) Tate. *Education:* Western Michigan University,

B.A., 1927; Columbia University, M.A., 1930; Oxford University, B.Litt., 1935; Radcliffe College, Ph.D., 1941. *Politics:* "Independent leanings toward Democratic party." *Religion:* Roman Catholic. *Home:* 1314 Perry St., N.E., Washington, D.C. 20017. *Office:* Department of History, Howard University, Washington, D.C. 20001.

CAREER: Barber-Scotia College, Concord, N.C., teacher of history and dean of women, 1935-36; Bennett College, Greensboro, N.C., head of Social Sciences Division, 1936-41; Morgan State College, Baltimore, Md., professor of political science, 1941-42; Howard University, Washington, D.C., professor of history, 1942—. Visiting summer professor at Wayne State University, 1953, and Western Michigan University, 1955. U.S. representative to UNESCO Seminar, 1948; Fulbright lecturer in India, 1950-51. Member of national board, Radcliffe College.

MEMBER: American Historical Association, American Association of University Women, International Platform Association, American Contract Bridge League, American Bridge Association, Phi Beta Kappa, Pi Gamma Mu, Alpha Kappa Alpha, Phi Delta Kappa (honorary), Radcliffe Club (Washington, D.C.; vice-president, 1960-63), Writers Club (Washington, D.C.), Howard University Women's Faculty Club. *Awards, honors:* Medal for distinguished professional service, Radcliffe College Alumnae Association, 1953; research grants from American Council of Learned Societies, 1959, *Washington Evening Star*, 1960, Rockefeller Foundation, 1961; James M. Nabrit, Jr. grant, 1962-63.

WRITINGS: The Disarmament Illusion—The Movement for a Limitation of Armaments to 1907, Macmillan, 1942; *The United States and Armaments*, Harvard University Press, 1948; *The United States and the Hawaiian Kingdom*, Yale University Press, 1965; *Hawaii: Reciprocity or Annexation*, Michigan State University Press, 1968; *Diplomacy in the Pacific*, History Department, Howard University, 1973.

WORK IN PROGRESS: Australia from the Tropics to the Pole; *New Zealand as a Pacific Power*; *Mineral Railways in Africa*; a biography of King Kamehameha IV of Hawaii.

SIDELIGHTS: Merze Tate is the first American Negro woman to matriculate at Oxford University and the first American Negro (man or woman) to receive a higher research degree there. She has done research in Hawaii, Fiji, New Zealand, Australia, Great Britain, France, West Germany, and Africa. *Avocational interests:* Photography, duplicate bridge, travel.

* * *

TAUBES, Frederic 1900-

PERSONAL: Born April 15, 1900, in Lwow, Poland; came to United States, 1930; son of Louis and Fanny (Taeni) Taubes; married Lili Jacobsen, May 25, 1923; children: Frank Alex. *Education:* Studied at Academy of Art, Vienna, 1916-18, Academy of Art, Munich, 1918-20, Bauhaus, Weimar, 1920-21, and in France and Italy. *Politics:* Conservative. *Religion:* "My own." *Home:* Haverstraw, N.Y.

CAREER: Painter, etcher, and lithographer, exhibiting at more than a hundred one-man shows, and in major museums and galleries throughout America, in Europe and Palestine; art educator and writer on art. Works owned by Metropolitan Museum of Art, San Francisco Museum, San Diego Fine Arts Gallery, William Rockhill Nelson Gallery of Art, High Museum of Atlanta, and some twenty other museums, universities, and corporations. Carnegie visiting professor and artist in residence at University of Illinois, 1940-41; visiting professor of art at Mills College, 1938, University of Hawaii, 1939, University of Wisconsin, 1945, University of Alberta, and Colorado State College; instructor at Cooper Union and Art Students' League; lecturer at other art schools in this country, London, and Edinburgh. Formulator of painting materials sold commercially as Taubes Varnishes and Copal Painting Media. *Member:* Royal Society of Arts (London; fellow).

WRITINGS: The Technique of Oil Painting, Dodd, 1941; *You Don't Know What You Like,* Dodd, 1942; *Studio Secrets,* Watson, 1943; *Oil Painting for the Beginner,* Watson, 1944; *The Amateur Painter's Handbook,* Dodd, 1947; *The Painters' Question and Answer Book,* Watson, 1948; *Anatomy of Genius,* Dodd, 1948; *Pictorial Composition and the Art of Drawing,* Dodd, 1949.

Paintings and Essays on Art, Dodd, 1950; *The Quickest Way to Paint Well,* Studio, 1950; *Better Frames for Your Pictures,* Studio, 1952; *New Essays on Art,* Watson, 1955; *Pen and Ink Drawing I,* Watson, 1956; *Pictorial Anatomy of the Human Body,* Studio, 1956; *The Art and Technique of Portrait Painting,* Dodd, 1957; *The Mastery of Oil Painting,* Viking, 1957; *The Quickest Way to Draw Well,* Studio, 1958; *Modern Art Sweet and Sour,* Watson, 1958.

The Art and Technique of Landscape Painting, Watson, 1960; *New Techniques in Painting,* Dodd, 1962; *Pen and Ink Drawing II,* Pitman, 1962; *Abracadabra and Modern Art,* Dodd, 1963; *Painting Techniques, Ancient and Modern,* Viking, 1963; *Oil Painting and Tempera,* Watson, 1965; *Taubes' Guide to Oil Painting,* Reinhold, 1965; *The Guide to the Great Art of Europe,* Reinhold, 1966; *Restoring and Preserving Antiques,* Watson-Guptill, 1969; *Antiques for the Amateur,* Watson-Guptill, 1970; *The Painters Dictionary of Arts and Crafts,* Watson-Guptill, 1972; *Guide to Value Judgements in Art,* C. N. Potter, in press.

American editor of *Artist* and conductor of "Ask Taubes" page in *Illustrator;* former contributing editor, *Encyclopaedia Britannica Yearbooks, American Artist,* and *Pacific Art Review;* contributor to other periodicals.

* * *

TAYLOR, Alastair M(acDonald) 1915-

PERSONAL: Born March 12, 1915, in Vancouver, British Columbia, Canada; son of James and Bertha E. (Redman) Taylor; married Mary E. Clements (a textbook writer), July 17, 1944; children: Angus, Graeme, Duncan. *Education:* University of Southern California, B.A., 1937, M.A., 1939; Columbia University, graduate study, 1941-42; Oxford University, D. Phil, 1955. *Home:* Cartwright's Point, Kingston, Ontario, Canada. *Office:* Queen's University, Kingston, Ontario, Canada.

CAREER: National Film Board, Ottawa, Ontario, writer and director of documentary films, 1942-44; United Nations Relief and Rehabilitation Administration Secretariat, Washington, D.C., special assistant, 1944-46; United Nations Secretariat, New York, N.Y., public information officer, with posts in Southeast Asia and Europe, 1946-52; University of Edinburgh, Edinburgh, Scotland, visiting professor of geography, 1959-60; Queen's University, Kingston, Ontario, associate professor, 1960-65, professor of political studies and geography, 1965—. Director of Ford Foundation project to examine role of Canada in international

peacekeeping and truce control, 1966; visiting professor, University of West Indies, 1967; member, faculty senate of Queens University, 1971-73, Social Science Research Council of Canada, 1972—; president, Canadian Center for Integrative Education, 1973—. *Member:* Canadian Political Science Association, Association of American Geographers, Canadian Association of Geographers, Canadian Institute of International Affairs, American Historical Association, Society for the History of Technology, American Academy of Political and Social Science, Phi Beta Kappa, Phi Kappa Phi. *Awards, honors:* Canadian Council fellowship, 1966-67.

WRITINGS: (With T. W. Wallbank) *Civilization: Past and Present,* two volumes, Scott, Foresman, 1942, one-volume revised edition, 1966, 4th edition, 1971; (with Wallbank) *The World in Turmoil, 1914-1944,* Scott, Foresman, 1944; *Indonesian Independence and the United Nations* (foreword by Lester B. Pearson), Cornell University Press, 1960; (with others) *The Development of Civilization: A Documentary History of Politics, Society and Thought,* Scott, Foresman, Volume I, 1961, Volume II, 1962; (with others) *Modern European Civilization: A Documentary History of Politics, Society, and Thought from the Renaissance to the Present,* Scott, Foresman, 1963; *For Canada: Both Swords and Ploughshares,* Canadian Institute of International Affairs, 1963; (with Wallbank) *Promise and Perils,* Scott, Foresman, 1966; *Imagination and the Growth of Science,* J. Murray, 1966; (with David Cox and J. L. Granatstein) *Peacekeeping: International Challenge and Canadian Response,* Canadian Institute of International Affairs, 1968; (with Wallbank) *Western Perspectives: A Concise History of Civilization,* Scott, Foresman, 1973. Contributor to *Sewanee Review, Occidente, International Journal,* and other periodicals.

WORK IN PROGRESS: A study for Edinburgh University Press on the impact of technology upon environments.

AVOCATIONAL INTERESTS: Golf, tennis.†

* * *

TAYLOR, Donald L(avor) 1916-

PERSONAL: Born November 5, 1916, in Ephraim, Utah; son of Lavor and Marguerite (Stevens) Taylor; married Martha Fitzgerald, December 30, 1943; children: Dianne, Susan, Lavar, Becky. *Education:* Snow Junior College, student, 1933-35; Utah State University, B.S., 1940, M.S., 1941; Duke University, Ph.D., 1945. *Home:* 6 Pine Lake Dr., Collinsville, Ill. 62234. *Office:* Southern Illinois University, Edwardsville, Ill. 62025.

CAREER: Member of faculty at Randolph-Macon Woman's College, Lynchburg, Va., 1943-46, and Macalester College, St. Paul, Minn., 1946-49; Colgate University, Hamilton, N.Y., associate professor of sociology, 1949-53; University of Pennsylvania, Philadelphia, instructor in family life, 1952-53; Salt Lake City (Utah) Board of Education, supervisor of community relations, 1953-59; Southern Illinois University, Edwardsville Campus, associate professor, 1959-63, professor of sociology, 1963—. In private practice of marriage counseling, Salt Lake City, Utah, 1953-59. *Member:* American Sociological Association, National Council on Family Relations, American Association of Marriage Counselors, American Association of Sex Educators and Counselors, American Association of University Professors, National School Public Relations Association, Midwest Sociological Society, Illinois Council on Family Relations.

WRITINGS: (With N. Himes) *Your Marriage*, Rinehart, 1955; (contributor) *Telling the School Story*, edited by Leslie W. Kindred, Prentice-Hall, 1960; *Marriage Counseling: New Dimensions in the Art of Helping People*, C. C Thomas, 1965; *Human Sexual Development*, F. A. Davis, 1970. Contributor to *Ingenue* and sociology and education journals.

WORK IN PROGRESS: Use of self-images in mate selection; democracy in German family systems.

SIDELIGHTS: Taylor speaks and reads German; he lived in Germany, 1965, to study the changing German family.

* * *

TAYLOR, John F(rank) A(dams) 1915-

PERSONAL: Born October 8, 1915, in Dallas, Tex.; son of Charles Bachman (a businessman) and Mary (Adams) Taylor; married Elizabeth Frost, August 12, 1939; children: Mary Elizabeth, Deborah Frost. *Education:* Princeton University, A.B., 1936, Ph.D., 1940. *Home:* 4539 Nakoma Dr., Okemos, Mich. 48864. *Office:* Department of Philosophy, Michigan State University, East Lansing, Mich.

CAREER: University of Pennsylvania, Philadelphia, instructor in philosophy, 1939-40; Columbia University, New York, N.Y., research in history of art, 1940-41; Princeton University, Princeton, N.J., fellow in art and archaeology, 1941-42; Michigan State University, East Lansing, professor of literature and fine arts and head of department, 1946-52, professor of philosophy, 1952—, Centennial Review lecturer, 1961, Provost lecturer, 1963. Woodrow Wilson National Fellowship Foundation, member of selection committee, 1962—. *Military service:* U.S. Naval Reserve, active duty, 1942-46; became lieutenant. *Member:* American Philosophical Association, American Association of University Professors, John Dewey Society, Phi Beta Kappa, Phi Kappa Phi. *Awards, honors:* Distinguished Faculty Award, Michigan State University, 1961; Guggenheim fellow, 1963-64; L.H.D., Lewis and Clark College, 1968.

WRITINGS: (Editor and major contributor) *An Introduction to Literature and the Fine Arts*, Michigan State University Press, 1950; *Design and Expression in the Visual Arts*, Dover, 1964; *The Masks of Society*, Appleton, 1966. Contributor to periodicals, including *Journal of Philosophy, Review of Metaphysics, Educational Forum, Saturday Review*, and *Harvard Business Review*.

* * *

TAYLOR, Kenneth N(athaniel) 1917-

PERSONAL: Born May 8, 1917, in Portland, Ore.; son of George N. (a minister) and Charlotte B. (Hoff) Taylor; married Margaret Louise West, September 13, 1940; children: Rebecca, John, Martha, Peter, Janet, Cynthia, Mark, Gretchen, Mary Lee, Alison. *Education:* Wheaton College, Wheaton, Ill., B.S., 1938; Dallas Theological Seminary, student, 1940-42; Northern Baptist Theological Seminary, Th.M., 1944. *Office:* Tyndale House Publishers, 336 Gundersen, Wheaton, Ill. 60187.

CARER: Moody Press, Chicago, Ill., director, Moody Literature Mission, 1947-63, director, Moody Press, 1948-61; Tyndale House Publishers, Wheaton, Ill., president, 1962—. Member of board of directors, Inter-Varsity Christian Fellowship, 1956-59. *Awards, honors:* Litt.D., Wheaton College, Wheaton, Ill., 1965.

WRITINGS—Adult; all published by Tyndale, except as noted: *Is Christianity Credible?*, Inter-Varsity, 1948; *Living Letters*, 1962; *Living Prophecies*, 1965; *Living Gospels*, 1966; *Living Psalms and Proverbs*, 1967; *Living Lessons of Life and Love*, 1968; *Living Books of Moses*, 1969; *Living History of Israel*, 1970; *The Living Bible*, 1971.

Juveniles; all published by Moody, except as noted: *Stories for the Children's Hour*, 1953; *Devotions for the Children's Hour*, 1954; *I See*, 1955, revised edition, 1958; *Bible in Pictures for Little Eyes to See*, 1956; *Lost on the Trail*, 1959; *Romans for the Children's Hour*, 1959; *Taylor's Bible Story Book*, Tyndale, 1970.

SIDELIGHTS: The Living Bible, a modern English paraphrase of the entire Bible, took Taylor fourteen years to complete and has sold over seven million copies.

* * *

TAYLOR, (Paul) Kent 1940-

PERSONAL: Born November 8, 1940, in New Castle, Pa.; son of Paul Douthitt (a salesman) and Goldie (McKee) Taylor; married Joan Czaban, October 5, 1963; children: Mark Shane. *Education:* Ohio Wesleyan University, B.A., 1962. *Politics:* "Independent radical." *Religion:* None. *Home:* 2176 Morrison Ave., Lakewood, Ohio 44107.

CAREER: Formerly research technician at Case Western Reserve University, Cleveland, Ohio; has worked as merchant seaman and longshoreman; St. Vincent Charity Hospital, Cleveland, Ohio, research technician, 1965—. *Member:* Psi Chi.

WRITINGS: Selected Poems, Renegade Press, 1963; *Aleatory Letters*, Renegade Press, 1964; (with d. a. levy) *Fortuitous Mother——*, Renegade Press, 1965; *Late Station* (poems), 7 Flowers Press, 1966; (with Carl Woideck and levy) *Three Poems by Cleveland Poets*, Seven Flowers Press, 1967; *Torn Birds* (poems), Black Rabbit Press, 1969; *Poems*, Black Rabbit Press, 1971; *Cleveland Dreams* (poems), Second Aeon Publications, c.1971. Author of chapbooks in "Polluted Lake Series" and "Ohio City Series," both 1965. Contributor to *Poetry Review* (Tampa), *Poetmeat, Free Lance input, kauri, Mother, Gooseberry, Marrahwanna Quarterly, Beginning, 15¢, Fine Arts, Radical Voice, Poetry Parade, Melody of the Muse, Silver Cesspool, Ole, Podium*, and other publications.

WORK IN PROGRESS: (With Douglass Blazek and John Cornillon) *Three Young Married Poets*, for Gooseberry.

SIDELIGHTS: Taylor wrote *CA:* "Travelled via hitch hiking sailing car. avid reader. music tastes run from serious to new thing in jazz. Frequently in demonstrations that i consider of vital important (civil rights others). try to create independent of various pressure. Major sidelight is being a full time *human* being."†

* * *

TAYLOR, Lester D(ean) 1938-

PERSONAL: Born March 8, 1938, in Toledo, Iowa; son of Samuel George (a farmer) and Willa (Brown) Taylor; married Carol Murdoch Austin, 1966; children: James Hendrick, Rebecca Susan. *Education:* University of Iowa, B.A., 1960; Harvard University, Ph.D., 1963. *Office:* University of Arizona, Department of Economics, Tucson, Ariz. 85721.

CAREER: Harvard University, Cambridge, Mass., instructor, 1963-64, assistant professor of economics, 1964-68; University of Michigan, Ann Arbor, associate professor of economics, 1969-74; University of Arizona, Tucson, professor of economics, 1974—. Staff economist, U.S. Council of Economic Advisers, Washington, D.C., 1964-65; research associate, National Bureau of Economic Research, 1972—. Consultant to President's Council of Economic Advisers, U.S. Department of Labor, U.S. Department of the Interior, Federal Energy Administration, and Oak Ridge National Laboratory. *Member:* Econometric Society, American Economic Association, Phi Beta Kappa.

WRITINGS: (With H. S. Houthakker) *Consumer Demand in the U.S.,* Harvard University Press, 1966, 2nd edition, 1970; (with Mary Lee Ingbar) *Hospital Costs in Massachusetts,* Harvard University Press, 1968; (with Thomas D. Wilson and Stephen J. Turnovsky) *Inflationary Process in North American Manufacturing,* Information Canada, 1973; *Probability and Mathematical Statistics,* Harper, 1974. Contributor to professional journals.

WORK IN PROGRESS: Residential Demand for Energy, completion expected in 1976; with Philip K. Verleger, *Demand for Automobiles and Gasoline,* completion expected in 1976.

AVOCATIONAL INTERESTS: Early Western Americana.

* * *

TAYLOR, Michael J. 1924-

PERSONAL: Born January 5, 1924, in Tacoma, Wash.; son of Ambrose and Florence Taylor. *Education:* Gonzaga University, B.A., 1947, Ph.L., 1948, M.A., 1949; Alma College, Los Gatos, Calif., S.T.L., 1955; Woodstock College, S.T.D., 1961. *Politics:* Democrat. *Home and office:* Seattle University, Seattle, Wash. 98122.

CAREER: Roman Catholic priest, member of Society of Jesus (Jesuits); Gonzaga University, Spokane, Wash., instructor in theology, 1956-59; Seattle University, Seattle, Wash., assistant professor, 1961-66, associate professor, 1967-72, professor of theology, 1973—. *Member:* Northwest Teachers of Religion, Liturgical Conference (Washington, D.C.). *Awards, honors:* Lilly postdoctoral fellowship in religion for ecumenical studies in Geneva, Switzerland, 1964-65.

WRITINGS: The Protestant Liturgical Renewal: A Catholic Viewpoint, Newman, 1963; (with R. P. Marshall) *Liturgy and Christian Unity,* Prentice-Hall, 1965; (contributor) *Living Room Dialogues,* edited by Greenspun and Norgren, Paulist Press, 1965; (editor) *Liturgical Renewal in the Christian Churches,* Helicon, 1967; (editor) *The Sacred and the Secular,* Prentice-Hall, 1968; (editor) *The Mystery of Sin and Forgiveness,* Alba, 1971; (editor) *Sex: Thoughts for Contemporary Christians,* Doubleday, 1972; (editor) *The Mystery of Suffering and Death,* Alba, 1973.

WORK IN PROGRESS: Editing a work of topical readings on St. Paul.

SIDELIGHTS: Taylor is involved in ecumenical activities in the Seattle area, including teaching Protestant Sunday school. He is competetent in French.

* * *

TAYLOR, Richard 1919-
(Diodorus Cronus)

PERSONAL: Born November 5, 1919, in Charlotte, Mich.; son of Floyd Clyde and Marie (Milbourn) Taylor; married Thelma Maxine Elworthy, January 14, 1955 (divorced, 1961); married Hylda Carpenter Higginson, January 26, 1961; children: (first marriage) Christopher, Randall. *Education:* University of Illinois, A.B., 1941; Oberlin College, A.M., 1947; Brown University, Ph.D., 1951. *Religion:* None. *Home:* Vinecliff, R.D. 1, Naples, N.Y. 14512.

CAREER: Brown University, Providence, R.I., 1951-63, professor of philosophy, 1958-59, William Herbert Perry Faunce Professor of Philosophy, 1959-63; Columbia University, New York, N.Y., professor of philosophy, 1963-65; University of Rochester, Rochester, N.Y., professor of philosophy, 1965—, chairman of department, 1966-70. Visiting professor at Swarthmore College, 1953, Ohio State University, 1959, 1963, Cornell University, 1961, Columbia University, 1962, Princeton University, 1963; Robert D. Campbell Professor of Philosophy, Wells College, 1968-69; R. Hawley Traux Professor of Philosophy, Hamilton College, 1971; Melvin Hill Professor of Humanities, Hobart and William Smith Colleges, 1973-74. *Military service:* U.S. Naval Reserve, 1942-46; became lieutenant. *Member:* American Philosophical Association, Metaphysical Society of America.

WRITINGS: (Editor and author of introduction) J. S. Mill, *Theism,* revised edition, Liberal Arts Press, 1957; (editor and author of introduction) *The Will to Live: Selected Essays of Arthur Schopenhauer,* Dolphin Books, 1961; *Metaphysics,* Prentice-Hall, 1963, revised edition, 1973; *Action and Purpose,* Prentice-Hall, 1966; *Good and Evil,* Macmillan, 1970; *With Heart and Mind,* St. Martin's Press, 1973; *Freedom, Anarchy and the Law,* Prentice-Hall, 1973.

Contributor: Sidney Hook, editor, *Determinism and Freedom,* New York University Press, 1958; Sidney Hook, editor, *Religious Experience and Truth,* New York University Press, 1961; S. Morgenbesser and J. Walsh, editors, *Free Will,* Prentice-Hall, 1962; D. J. O'Connor, editor, *A Critical History of Western Philosophy,* Collier-Macmillan (London), 1964; Sidney Hook, editor, *Law and Philosophy,* New York University Press, 1964; J. J. C. Smart, editor, *Problems of Space and Time,* Macmillan, 1964; (author of introduction) A. Plantinga, editor, *Essays on the Ontological Argument,* Doubleday, 1965; (author of introduction) Arthur Schopenhauer, *The Basis of Morality,* translated by E. F. J. Payne, Bobbs-Merrill, 1965; K. Lehrer, editor, *Freedom and Determinism,* Random House, 1966.

Contributor of more than fifty articles and a number of reviews to *Analysis, Monist, Mind,* and other philosophy journals, occasionally under pseudonym Diodorus Cronus.

* * *

TEETER, Karl V(an Duyn) 1929-

PERSONAL: Born March 2, 1929, in Berkeley, Calif.; son of Charles Edwin, Jr. (a professor) and Lura May (a professor; maiden name Shaffner) Teeter; married Anita Maria Bonacorsi (a teacher), August 25, 1951; children: Katharine Emilie, Judith Ann, Teresa Maria, Martha Elisabeth. *Education:* University of California, Berkeley, A.B. (with highest honors in Oriental languages), 1956, Ph.D., 1962. *Home:* 16½ Woodbridge St., Cambridge, Mass. 02140. *Office:* Holyoke Center 851, Cambridge, Mass. 02138.

CAREER: Harvard University, Cambridge, Mass., junior fellow, 1959-62, instructor, 1962-63, assistant professor, 1963-66, associate professor, 1966-69; professor of linguistics, 1969—. *Military service:* U.S. Army, 1946, 1951-54. *Member:* American Anthropological Association, Association of Teachers of Japanese, Linguistic Society of America, Linguistic Society of Japan, Linguistic Circle of New York, Phi Beta Kappa, Sigma Xi.

WRITINGS: The Wiyot Language, University of California Press, 1964. Contributor of articles and reviews to linguistic, Oriental, and anthropology journals.

WORK IN PROGRESS: Wiyot Lexicon, for University of California Press; *Malecite-Passamaquoddy Grammar,* for National Museum of Canada; *A New Introduction to the Study of Language,* for Harcourt; research in nature of linguistic change and language use in Algonquian languages, and in Japanese grammar.

SIDELIGHTS: Teeter speaks, reads, and writes Japanese and Italian; he reads Chinese, German, French, Spanish, Greek, Latin, Sanskrit, Thai, Old English, Old Norse.

* * *

TETLOW, Edwin 1905-

PERSONAL: Born May 19, 1905, in Timperley, Cheshire, England; son of William Chadwick (a company treasurer) and Mary (Entwistel) Tetlow; married Kathleen Whitworth Brown, September 14, 1932; children: Timothy Chadwick, Susan Edwina (Mrs. Ray Friend Bentley). *Education:* Educated in England at Altrincham School and University of Manchester. *Religion:* Church of England. *Home:* 120 East 79th St., New York, N.Y. 10021; Peterskill House, Alligerville, High Falls, N.Y. 12440.

CAREER: Daily Dispatch, Manchester, England, apprentice journalist, 1924-30; *Evening News,* London, England, member of staff, 1930-33; *Daily Mail,* London, England, home and foreign correspondent, 1933-39, war correspondent with Royal Navy, British Army, and U.S. Fifth Army, 1939-45; *Daily Telegraph,* London, England, Berlin correspondent, 1945-50, New York correspondent, 1950-65; free-lance writer and broadcaster, New York, N.Y., 1965—. *Member:* Foreign Press Association (executive committee member, 1960—; president, 1963-64). *Awards, honors:* Page One Award, Newspaper Guild, Kingston, N.Y., 1963.

WRITINGS: Eye on Cuba, Harcourt, 1966; *The United Nations: The First Twenty-Five Years,* P. Owen, 1970; *The Enigma of Hastings: An Embroidered Title,* St. Martin's, 1974. Articles have appeared in *New York Times, Economist, Saturday Review, New Republic, National Observer, Atlantic Monthly,* and other publications in America and Britain; reviewer for *Christian Science Monitor.*

WORK IN PROGRESS: A book, tentatively titled *America is a Foreign Country.*

SIDELIGHTS: Tetlow was on assignment in Havana when Castro took over the Cuban government in 1958, and Cuban affairs became his most important coverage for London's *Daily Telegraph* until he left the paper in 1965; he visited Cuba fourteen times in the interval, interviewed Castro, Guevara, and other leaders of the revolution many times, and has broadcast on Cuban developments for all the American networks and British Broadcasting Corp. His World War II coverage ranged from the Dunkirk evacuation to the occupation of Berlin. He was torpedoed once in the Mediterranean (but transferred from the doomed destroyer before it sank) and wounded by mortar fire at Cassino.†

* * *

THADEN, Edward Carl 1922-

PERSONAL: Born April 24, 1922, in Seattle, Wash.; son of Edward Carl J. (a merchant) and Astrid (Engvik) Thaden; married Marianna T. Forster, August 7, 1952. *Education:* University of Washington, Seattle, B.A., 1944; University of Zurich, graduate study, 1947-48; University of Paris, Ph.D., 1950. *Home:* 1515 Astor St., Chicago, Ill. 60610.

CAREER: Pennsylvania State University, University Park, instructor in history, 1952-55, assistant professor, 1955-58, associate professor, 1958-64, professor of Russian history, 1964-68; University of Illinois at Chicago Circle, professor of history, 1968—. Indiana University, visiting assistant professor, 1957; University of Marburg, visiting professor, 1965. *Military service:* U.S. Navy, 1943-46; became lieutenant junior grade. *Member:* American Historical Association, American Association for the Advancement of Slavic Studies, Phi Alpha Theta. *Awards, honors:* Fulbright research award to Finland, 1957-58, and to Germany, 1965-66; American Council of Learned Societies grant, 1963; Fulbright-Hayes research award to Finland, Germany, and Poland, 1968.

WRITINGS: Conservative Nationalism in Nineteenth-Century Russia, University of Washington Press, 1964; *Russia and the Balkan Alliance of 1912,* Pennsylvania State University Press, 1965; *Russia Since 1801: The Making of a New Society,* Wiley, 1971; (contributor) Anna Cienciala, *American Contributions to the Seventh International Congress of Slavists,* Volume III: *History,* Mouton & Co., 1973. Contributor of articles and reviews to historical journals here and abroad.

WORK IN PROGRESS: Nationality Policy in the Western Borderlands of the Russian Empire, 1830-1914; research on the rise of historicism in Russia.

* * *

THEIL, Henri 1924-

PERSONAL: Born October 31, 1924, in Amsterdam, Netherlands; son of Hendrik and Hermina (Siegmann) Theil; married Eleonore A. I. Goldschmidt, June 15, 1950. *Education:* University of Amsterdam, Ph.D., 1951. *Home:* 1345 East Park Place, Chicago, Ill. 60637. *Office:* Rosenwald Hall, University of Chicago, Chicago, Ill. 60637.

CAREER: Central Planning Bureau, The Hague, Netherlands, staff member, 1952-55; Netherlands School of Economics, Rotterdam, professor of econometrics and director of Econometric Institute, 1956-66; University of Chicago, Chicago, Ill., professor and director of Center for Mathematical Studies in Business and Economics, 1965—. Visiting professor at University of Chicago, 1955-56, Harvard University, 1960. *Member:* Econometric Society (fellow; president, 1961), International Statistical Institute, American Economic Association, American Academy of Arts and Sciences, Institute of Management Sciences. *Awards, honors:* LL.D., University of Chicago, 1964; doctor honoris causa, Free University of Brussels, 1974.

WRITINGS: Linear Aggregation of Economic Relations, North-Holland Publishing, 1954; *Economic Forecasts and Policy,* 2nd edition, North-Holland Publishing, 1961; *Optimal Decision Rules for Government and Industry,* American Elsevier, 1964; (with J.C.G. Boot and T. Kloek) *Voorspellen en beslissen,* Spectrum, 1964, published as *Operations Research and Quantitative Economics,* McGraw, 1965; *Applied Economic Forecasting,* American Elsevier, 1966; *Economics and Information Theory,* American Elsevier, 1967; *Principles of Econometrics,* Wiley, 1971; *Statistical Decomposition Analysis With Applications in the Social and Administrative Sciences,* American Elsevier, 1972.

THOMAS, Elizabeth Marshall 1931-

PERSONAL: Born September 13, 1931, in Boston, Mass.; daughter of Laurence K. and Loran (McLean) Marshall; married Stephen M. Thomas (a writer), January 24, 1956; children: Stephanie K., John R. *Education:* Attended Smith College, 1949-52; Radcliffe College, A.B., 1954. *Agent:* Marie Rodell, 141 East 55th St., New York, N.Y. 10022.

CAREER: Full-time professional writer. *Awards, honors:* *Mademoiselle* College Fiction Award, 1952; Guggenheim fellowship, 1962; Radcliffe Alumnae Award, 1966.

WRITINGS: The Harmless People, Knopf, 1959; *Warrior Herdsmen,* Knopf, 1965. Contributor to *New Yorker, New York Herald Tribune, American Scholar,* and *American Anthropologist.*

WORK IN PROGRESS: A book on Nigeria in collaboration with husband, Stephen M. Thomas.

SIDELIGHTS: Elizabeth Thomas has traveled in southwest Africa, Uganda, and Nigeria to gather material for books, and has also traveled in Europe and Morocco. *The Harmless People* has been published in England, France, Germany, Portugal, Denmark, and Norway.†

*   *   *

THOMAS, Norman C(arl) 1932-

PERSONAL: Born February 16, 1932, in Sioux Falls, S.D.; son of Russell (a college professor) and Helen (Matson) Thomas; married Marilyn L. Murphy, January 31, 1953; children: Robert, Margaret, Elizabeth, Anne. *Education:* University of Michigan, B.A., 1953; Princeton University, M.A., 1958, Ph.D., 1959. *Religion:* Protestant. *Home:* 510 Oliver Ct., Cincinnati, Ohio 45215. *Office:* Department of Political Science, University of Cincinnati, Cincinnati, Ohio 45221.

CAREER: University of Michigan, Ann Arbor, instructor, 1959-62, assistant professor, 1962-65, associate professor of political science, 1965-69. Duke University, Durham, N.C., professor of political science, 1969-71; University of Cincinnati, Cincinnati, Ohio, professor of political science and head of department, 1971—. *Military service:* U.S. Naval Reserve 1953-56; became lieutenant junior grade. *Member:* American Political Science Association, American Society for Public Administration. *Awards, honors:* Woodrow Wilson fellowship, 1956-57; Distinguished Service Award of University of Michigan Development Council, 1964.

WRITINGS: (With Karl A. Lamb) *Congress: Politics and Practice,* Random House, 1964; *Rule 9: Politics, Administration and Civil Rights,* Random House, 1966; *Education in National Politics,* McKay, 1975; (editor) *The Presidency in Contemporary Context,* Dodd, 1975. Contributor to political science, law, and parliamentary journals.

WORK IN PROGRESS: Research focused on policy-making by federal administrators, the American presidency, and the politics of education.

*   *   *

THOMAS, R(obert) Murray 1921-
   (Tom Roberts)

PERSONAL: Born July 28, 1921, in Cheyenne, Wyo.; son of Robert MacDonald (a civil engineer) and Elizabeth (Carson) Thomas; married Shirley Louise Moore (a psychologist), July 3, 1948; children: Robert G., K. Elizabeth.

Education: Colorado State College (now University of Northern Colorado), B.A., 1943, M.A., 1944; Stanford University, Ph.D., 1950. *Politics:* Democrat. *Religion:* Protestant. *Home:* 728 Calle de Los Amigos, Santa Barbara, Calif. 93105. *Office:* University of California, Santa Barbara, Calif.

CAREER: Mid-Pacific Institute, Honolulu, Hawaii, teacher of English, 1945-47; San Francisco State College (now University), San Francisco, Calif., instructor in psychology, 1949-50; State University of New York College at Brockport, professor of education and psychology, 1950-58; Padjadjaran University, Bandung, Indonesia, professor of education and psychology, 1958-61, 1964-65; University of California, Santa Barbara, professor of education, 1961-64, 1965—.

WRITINGS: Judging Student Progress, Longmans, Green, 1954, 2nd edition, McKay, 1960; (with Sherwin Swartout) *Integrated Teaching Materials,* McKay, 1960, 2nd edition, 1963; (under pseudonym Tom Roberts) *The Java Raids,* McKay, 1964; *Social Differences in the Classroom,* McKay; 1965; (with wife, Shirley M. Thomas) *Individual Differences in the Classroom,* McKay, 1965; *Aiding the Maladjusted Pupil,* McKay, 1967; (with Winarno Surachmad) *Penggunaan Statistik Dalam Jlmu Pengetahvan Sosial* (title means "Using statistics in Social Sciences"), Tarate, 1969; (with Dale Brubaker) *Decisions in Teaching Elementary Social Studies,* Wadsworth, 1971; (with Brubaker) *Curriculum Patterns in Elementary Social Studies,* Wadsworth, 1971; (with Brubaker) *Teaching Elementary Social Studies: Readings,* Wadsworth, 1972; *A Chronicle of Indonesian Higher Education,* Chopmen Enterprises (Singapore), 1973; *Indonesian Education: An Annotated Bibliography,* Graduate School of Education, University of California at Santa Barbara, 1973.

SIDELIGHTS: Thomas is competent in Indonesian and Spanish.

*   *   *

THOMAS, S(idney) Claudewell 1932-

PERSONAL: Born October 5, 1932, in New York, N.Y.; son of Humphrey Sidney and Frances E. (Collins) Thomas; married Carolyn P. Rozansky, September 6, 1958; children: Jeffrey Evan, Julie-Anne Elizabeth, Jessica Edith. *Education:* Columbia University, A.B., 1952; State University of New York Downstate Medical Center, M.D., 1956; Yale University, M.P.H., 1964. *Office:* Department of Psychiatry, College of Medicine and Dentistry of New Jersey, 100 Bergen St., Newark, N.J. 07103.

CAREER: Yale University, New Haven, Conn., instructor, 1963-65, assistant professor of public health sociology, and psychiatry, 1965-70, educational director of psychiatric emergency service, 1967-68, director of psychiatric emergency service, 1967-70, director of training program in social and community psychiatry, 1968-70; Connecticut Mental Health Center, New Haven, chief of emergency treatment service, 1966-67, director of Hill-West Haven Division, 1967-70, chief of community area service, 1967-68; National Institute of Mental Health, Rockville, Md., director of Division of Mental Health Service Programs, 1970-73; College of Medicine and Dentistry of New Jersey, Newark, professor of psychiatry and chairman of department, 1973—. Consultant psychiatrist, Connecticut Valley Hospital, 1962-68, Connecticut Division on Alcoholism, 1963-65; member of state and national health committees and councils. *Military service:* U.S. Air Force, Medical

Corps, psychiatrist, 1959-61; became captain. *Member:* American Psychiatric Association (fellow), American Association for the Advancement of Science, Royal Society of Health (fellow), American Public Health Association, American Sociological Association (associate member).

WRITINGS: (Editor with B. J. Bergen, and contributor) *Issues and Problems in Social Psychiatry*, C. C Thomas, 1966. Contributor to *Medical Times* and psychiatric journals.

WORK IN PROGRESS: A contribution to *Progress in Community Psychiatry*, edited by Bellak and Barton.

SIDELIGHTS: Thomas is competent is Spanish and German.

* * *

THOMAS, W(alter) Ian 1914-

PERSONAL: Born September 13, 1914, in London, England; son of Albert John (an architect) and Jane (Smith) Thomas; married Eveline Joan Gribbon (partner in husband's Christian fellowship work), November 12, 1941; children: Christopher Ian, Alexander Mark, Peter Cameron, Timothy Andrew. *Education:* Educated at Merchant Taylor's School, London, England, and University of London. *Office:* Capernwray Missionary Fellowship of Torchbearers, Capernwray Hall, Carnforth, Lancashire, England.

CAREER: Torchbearers Inc. (international young peoples' Christian fellowship organization), founder and director, with headquarters at Capernwray Hall, Carnforth, Lancashire, England, 1947-67; Capernway Missionary Fellowship, Carnforth, Lancashire, founder and central director, 1948-67; also director of conference grounds and Bible school in Germany, beginning, 1958, Austria, beginning, 1963, and New Zealand, beginning, 1966. Evangelist and Bible teacher in Britain, continental Europe, Canada, United States, Australia, Southeast Asia, Africa, and Saudi Arabia. *Military service:* British Army, Royal Fusiliers, reserve service, 1933—, with active duty, 1940-47; now major; received Distinguished Service Order.

WRITINGS: The Saving Life of Christ, Zondervan, 1961; *The Mystery of Godliness*, Zondervan, 1964; *If I Perish, I Perish*, Zondervan, 1966.†

* * *

THOMPSON, Edgar T(ristram) 1900-

PERSONAL: Born September 13, 1900, in Little Rock, S.C.; son of John Sanders and Annie (Smith) Thompson; married Alma Macy, June 15, 1929; children: Alma Lee (Mrs. Richard Schaffer). *Education:* University of South Carolina, A.B., 1922; University of Missouri, M.A., 1924; University of Chicago, Ph.D., 1932. *Home:* 138 Pinecrest Rd., Durham, N.C. *Office:* Duke University, Durham, N.C.

CAREER: High school teacher of history, Plant City, Fla., 1922-23; University of North Carolina, Chapel Hill, instructor in rural sociology, 1924-26; University of Texas, Austin, adjunct professor of sociology, 1927-28; Earlham College, Richmond, Ind., adjunct professor of sociology, and social science, 1928-29; YMCA College, Chicago, Ill., instructor, 1929-30; University of Washington, Seattle, assistant professor of sociology, 1930-31; University of Hawaii, Honolulu, research professor of sociology, 1932-35; Duke University, Durham, N.C., assistant professor, 1935-40, associate professor, 1940-46, professor of sociol-

ogy, 1946—, acting chairman of department, 1950-51, 1963-64, chairman of Center for Southern Studies, 1965—. Visiting professor at Northwestern University, 1951, University of Arizona, 1965. President of North Carolina Society for Crippled Children and Adults, 1959-61. *Member:* American Sociological Association, African Studies Association, Southern Sociological Society (president, 1961), Kappa Delta Pi. *Awards, honors:* First American Hugh le May fellow at Rhodes University, Republic of South Africa, 1956.

WRITINGS: Race Relations and the Race Problem, Duke University Press, 1939; (with wife, Alma Macy Thompson) *Race and Region*, University of North Carolina Press, 1949; *The Plantation: A Bibliography*, Pan American Union, 1957; (with Everett C. Hughes) *Race: Individual and Collective Behavior*, Free Press, 1965; (editor with John C. McKinney and contributor) *The South in Continuity and Change*, Duke University Press, 1965.

Contributor: D. K. Jackson, editor, *Essays in Honor of William K. Boyd*, Duke University Press, 1940; Charles S. Johnson, editor, *Education and Cultural Process*, University of Chicago Press, 1943; Howard W. Odum and Katherine Jocher, editors, *In Search of the Regional Balance in America*, University of North Carolina Press, 1945; Vera Rubin, editor, *Caribbean Studies*, Institute of Social and Economic Studies, University College of the West Indies, in association with Columbia University, 1957; *Plantation Systems in the New World*, Pan American Union, 1959; *Research into Factors Influencing Human Relations*, [Netherlands], 1959; J. Masuoka and Preston Valien, editors, *Race Relations: Theories and Problems*, University of North Carolina Press, 1961; (author of foreword) Lee M. Brooks and Alvin L. Bertrand, *History of the Southern Sociological Society*, University of Alabama Press, 1962; Allen Sindler, editor. *Change in the Contemporary South*, Duke University Press, 1963; Samuel S. Hill, Jr., editor, *Religion and the Solid South*, Abingdon, 1972. Contributor to journals, including *Social Forces* and *South African Outlook*.

WORK IN PROGRESS: A book of Thompson's collected papers, *Plantation Societies, Race Relations, the South*, for Duke University Press.

SIDELIGHTS: Thompson wrote, "I should like to contribute to a social science beyond dogma and ideolgy, one centering around the nature of human nature."

* * *

THOMPSON, Hildegard (Steerstedter) 1901-

PERSONAL: Born January 13, 1901, in DePauw, Ind.; daughter of Andrew and Ella (Thevenat) Steerstedter. *Education:* Indiana State Teachers College (now Indiana State University), student, 1924-27; University of Louisville, B.S.E., 1930. *Religion:* Catholic. *Residence:* Louisville, Ky.

CAREER: Teacher in Harrison County (Ind.) schools, 1921-30; Bureau of Education, Philippine Islands, teacher and textbook writer, 1931-36; U.S. Department of the Interior, Bureau of Indian Affairs, specialist in remedial reading, Oklahoma City, Okla., 1937-39, supervisor of education, Window Rock, Ariz., 1939-44, administrator of bilingual program for adult Navajo beginners, 1947-49, director of Navajo schools, 1949-52, chief of Bureau of Education, directing federal school system for all American Indians (including Alaska), 1952-65. Visiting instructor at various colleges and universities; consultant in Indian education at Northern Arizona University, 1966. Member of President's Committee on International Education, 1965.

MEMBER: American Academy of Political and Social Science, Council of Administrative Women, National Education Association (life member), Senior Citizens of America (charter member). *Awards, honors:* Certificate of Appreciation for service to Navajo Indians; Distinguished Service Award from U.S. Department of Interior.

WRITINGS: (With William Morgan and Robert Young) *Coyote Tales*, Bureau of Indian Affairs, 1949; *Getting to Know American Indians Today*, Coward, 1965; *Education for Cross·Cultural Enrichment*, Bureau of Indian Affairs, 1965; *A Survey of Problems of Indian College Students*, Bureau of Indian Affairs, 1966; *The Navajos Long Walk for Education: A History of Navajo Education*, Navajo Community College Press, 1975. Also author of "Navajo Life" series of readers for Bureau of Indian Affairs. Writer of lead articles and editor, *Indian Education*, 1952-65; contributor to other education journals.

WORK IN PROGRESS: Researching material for children's books on Indian life in the United States and Alaska.

SIDELIGHTS: Hildegard Thompson's major interest continues to be the improvement of educational opportunities for American Indians. She says the most exciting aspect of her career was the development of a bilingual program for non-English-speaking Navajo teen-agers that salvaged them from illiteracy and placed them in employment; over five thousand youths profited from this program, carried out between 1946 and 1960.

*   *   *

THOMPSON, Hunter S(tockton)   1939-
(Sebastian Owl)

PERSONAL: Born July 18, 1939, in Louisville, Ky.; son of Jack R. (an insurance agent) and Virginia (Ray) Thompson; married Sandra Dawn, May 19, 1963; children: Juan. *Education:* Attended public schools in Louisville, Ky. *Politics:* Anarchist. *Religion:* None. *Home:* Owl Farm, Woody Creek, Colo.

CAREER: New York Herald Tribune, New York, N.Y., Caribbean correspondent, 1959-60; *National Observer*, New York, N.Y., South American correspondent, 1961-63; national affairs editor, *Rolling Stone* (magazine), 1969-74. Free-lance writer, 1963—. *Military service:* U.S. Air Force, 1956-58. *Member:* Overseas Press Club, American Civil Liberties Union, National Rifle Association.

WRITINGS: Hell's Angels: A Strange and Terrible Saga, Random House, 1966; *Fear and Loathing in Las Vegas*, Random House, 1972; *Fear and Loathing on the Campaign Trail '72*, Straight Arrow Books, 1973. Contributor to *Esquire, New York Times Magazine, Nation, Reporter, Harper's*, and other publications.

WORK IN PROGRESS: Guts Ball, a novel based on Watergate.

SIDELIGHTS: In order to more accurately represent the Hell's Angels in his first book, Thompson spent a year riding and drinking with the California motorcycle gangs. Although he was finally stomped because the Angels demanded a share of the expected royalties from the book ("he barely escaped a rock that was meant to crush his head," notes *Newsweek*), "he does not weep for the Angels or romanticize them or glorify them," writes Elmer Bendiner. "Instead, he views them as creatures of an irre-

sponsible society, given their image by an irresponsible press, embodying the nation's puerile fantasy life." William Hogan explains that "Thompson sees the Angels as contemporary folk heroes whose romantic deliquency has a vast appeal in a nation of frightened dullards." Richard M. Elman asks: "If push comes to shove ... Mr. Thompson may end up as the poet laureate of the Angels, but who will take the trouble to keep track of his royalty statements? Who will bother to read his finely worked prose ecstasies?" But Elman concludes that *Hell's Angels* "is certainly the most informative, thorough, and vividly written account of this phenomenon yet to appear" and advises that Thompson "is a writer whose future career is worth watching."

Christopher Lehmann-Haupt described *Fear and Loathing in Las Vegas* as containing "a kind of mad, corrosive prose poetry that picks up where Norman Mailer's 'An American Dream' left off and explores what Tom Wolfe left out."

BIOGRAPHICAL/CRITICAL SOURCES: Saturday Review, February 18, 1967; *New Republic*, February 25, 1967; *New Yorker*, March 4, 1967; *New York Times Book Review*, March 5, 1967; *Newsweek*, March 6, 1967; *Nation*, April 3, 1967; *Commonweal*, April 7, 1967.

*   *   *

THOMPSON, Joan Berengild   1915-

PERSONAL: Born August 7, 1915, in Kingston, Ontario, Canada; daughter of Sydney Arthur (a British Army officer then stationed in Canada) and Beatrice Mary (Willcox) Thompson. *Education:* Royal College of Music, London, A.R.C.M., 1933; University of London, B.A., 1945, and B.Sc., 1951 (both external degrees); studied piano and voice privately. *Politics:* Liberal. *Religion:* Roman Catholic. *Home:* Leigh Cottage, London Rd., Datchet, Buckinghamshire, England.

CAREER: Training for an operatic career was interrupted by World War II; during the war years did Red Cross and Civil Defence work in the south of England; teacher of history at St. Bernards Convent Grammar School, Slough, Bucks, England, 1945—, head of department, 1950—, deputy headmistress, 1960, librarian of reference library.

WRITINGS: The Achievements of Western Civilization, Darton, Longman & Todd, 1964, Harper, 1965.

SIDELIGHTS: Joan Thompson speaks French and Italian and some Spanish and German. *Avocational interests:* Music and drama (has appeared in several Shakespearean roles with Windsor Theatre Guild, produced plays, and written music and songs).†

*   *   *

THOMPSON, William D.   1929-

PERSONAL: Born January 11, 1929, in Chicago, Ill.; son of Robert Ayre (a photoengraver) and Mary E. (McDowell) Thompson; married Jane Lynch Stanford, August 23, 1958 (died September 5, 1967); married Linda Stevenson, November 2, 1968; children: (first marriage) Tammy Lee, Kirk Stanford; (second marriage) Lisa, Rebecca, Gwyneth. *Education:* Wheaton College, Wheaton, Ill., A.B. (with honor), 1950; Northern Baptist Theological Seminary, B.D., 1954; Northwestern University, M.A., 1955, Ph.D., 1960. *Home:* 5829 Woodbine Ave., Philadelphia, Pa. 19131. *Office:* Eastern Baptist Theological Seminary, City and Lancaster Aves., Philadelphia, Pa. 19151.

CAREER: Clergyman of American Baptist Convention.

Wheaton College, Wheaton, Ill., speech instructor, 1952-55; pastor in Chicago's "back of the yards" district, 1956-59; Northern Baptist Seminary, Chicago, Ill., associate professor of speech, 1958-62; Eastern Baptist Theological Seminary, Philadelphia, Pa., professor of preaching, 1962. Consultant in preaching, St. Charles Seminary, Philadelphia, 1967-68. Member of council on theological education, American Baptist Convention. Interim pastor at several churches. *Member:* Speech Communication Association, American Academy of Homiletics (treasurer, 1967-71; president, 1973), Wheaton-Philadelphia Alumni Club (president, 1964-66). *Awards, honors:* American Association of Theological Schools faculty fellowship to Cambridge University, 1968-69.

WRITINGS: A Listener's Guide to Preaching, Abingdon, 1966; (with William Toohey) *Recent Homiletical Thought*, Abingdon, 1967; *The Congregation Shares in the Sermon*, Judson, 1967; (with Gordon Bennett) *Dialogue Preaching*, Judson, 1969. Contributor to *christian Century*, *Christian Home*, and *Speech Monographs*. Columnist for *Eternity*.

WORK IN PROGRESS: A basic textbook on homiletical theory.

* * *

THORMAN, Donald J. 1924-

PERSONAL: Born December 23, 1924, in Oak Park, Ill.; son of Harry and Adolphine (Levermann) Thorman; married Barbara Lisowski, February 22, 1952; children: Margaret, Judith, James, Elizabeth, David, Daniel, Damian. *Education:* DePaul University, B.A., 1949; Loyola University, Chicago, Ill., M.A., 1951; additional study at University of Fribourg, 1950, Fordham University, 1951, University of Notre Dame, 1956-57, University of Michigan and University of Chicago. *Religion:* Roman Catholic. *Home:* 5408 Baltimore, Kansas City, Mo. 64112. *Office: National Catholic Reporter*, P.O. Box 281, Kansas City, Mo. 64141.

CAREER: St. Jude Magazine (now *U.S. Catholic*), Chicago, Ill., managing editor, 1952-56; *Ave Maria* (magazine), Notre Dame, Ind., managing editor, 1956-62; Spiritual Life Institute of America, Sedona, Ariz., publisher and director, 1962-63; Catholic Communications Consultants, Chicago, Ill., owner, 1963-65; *National Catholic Reporter* Publishing Co., Kansas City, Mo., publisher, 1965—, editor of *National Catholic Reporter* (weekly newspaper), 1971—, president, 1975—. Loyola University, Chicago, Ill., part-time instructor, 1950-55; lecturer to laymen and clergy in United States and Canada. National Catholic Social Action Conference, president, 1958-60, member of board of directors; member of national advisory board of Family Life Bureau, National Catholic Welfare Conference, 1957-60; Catholic co-chairman of Kansas City area and member of national board of governors, National Conference of Christians and Jews; member of National Catholic Development Conference. *Military service:* U.S. Marine Corps, 1943-46; became sergeant.

MEMBER: Catholic Press Association (member of board of directors, 1958-61), American Catholic Sociological Society, Direct Mail/Marketing Association, American Marketing Association, American Management Association, International Transactional Analysis Association, Association of Couples for Marriage Enrichment, Advertising and Sales Executive Club (Kansas City), Overseas Press Club (New York City), Pi Gamma Mu, Alpha Sigma Nu.

WRITINGS: The Emerging Layman, Doubleday, 1962; (with Martin Work, John Cogley, and Daniel Callahan) *The Layman and the Council*, Templegate, 1964; (co-author) *New Directions in Religious Life*, University of Portland Press, 1965; *Christian Vision*, Doubleday, 1967; (contributor) W. J. Wilson, editor, *Demands for Christian Renewal*, Maryknoll, 1968; *American Catholics Face the Future*, Dimension Books, 1968; *Power to the People of God*, Paulist/Newman, 1970. Author of pamphlets. Contributor to *America, Critic, Christian Century, Catholic World, Sign, Writer's Digest, Social Order, Family Digest*, and other publications. Editor, *ACT* (Chirstian Family Movement monthly), 1955-64; member of editorial board, *American Catholic Scoiological Review*, 1951-55.

* * *

THORN, Richard S(emour) 1929-

PERSONAL: Born September 20, 1929, in New York, N.Y.; son of Benjamin (a jobber) and Ruth (Beyer) Thorn; married Regina Maria Ciezki, November 8, 1962; children: Eric Joseph, Clifford Gordon, Bettina Lairen. *Education:* Columbia University, A.B., 1951; University of Maryland, M.A., 1952; Yale University, Ph.D., 1958. *Home:* 1407 Beechwood Blvd., Pittsburgh, Pa. 15217. *Office:* University of Pittsburgh, Pittsburgh, Pa. 15260.

CAREER: Standard and Poore Corp., security analyst, 1951; International Monetary Fund, economist, 1957-62, representing the fund at various times at the European Economic Community, and participating in missions to Bolivia and Chile; Committee of Nine of the Alliance for Progress, economic consultant, 1962-63; City University of New York, New York, N.Y., associate professor, 1963; Inter-American Bank Mission to Bolivia, chief, 1964; University of Pittsburgh, Pittsburgh, Pa., professor of economics, 1965—. Visiting professor, University of Aix-Marseilles, 1973. Consultant, United Nations Center for Industrial Development, 1965; adviser to deputy prime minister of Iran. *Military service:* U.S. Coast Guard, 1952-55; became lieutenant. *Member:* American Economic Association, Econometric Society.

WRITINGS: (Editor) *Monetary Theory and Policy*, Random House, 1966; (editor) *Beyond the Revolution*, University of Pittsburgh Press, 1971; (with Stephen A. Kwitowski) *Business Mathematics*, Random House, 1971; (contributor) Balbir S. Sahni, editor, *Public Expenditure Analysis*, Rotterdam University Press, 1972; (contributor) Gustav Schachter and Edwin L. Dale, Jr., editors, *The Economist Looks at Society*, Xerox College Publishing, 1973; *Money and Banking*, Harper, 1975. Contributor to journals.

WORK IN PROGRESS: Research on public finance in developing countries.

* * *

THORNE, Bliss K(irby) 1916-

PERSONAL: Born March 6, 1916, in New York, N.Y.; son of Van Buren (a physician and writer) and May (Kirby) Thorne; married Edna Frances Mann, May 28, 1943; children: Keith Van Buren, Kirby Frances. *Education:* Phillips Exeter Academy, student, 1933-34; Dartmouth College, student, 1934-37. *Agent:* Gunther Stuhlmann, 65 Irving Pl., New York, N.Y. 10003.

CAREER: New York Times, New York, N.Y., reporter-columnist, 1940-55; Avco Corp., New York, N.Y., divisional public relations director, 1955-57; Henry Publications, New York, N.Y., executive editor, 1957-61; Arthur

Schmidt & Associates, New York, N.Y., public relations consultant, 1963; *Air Transport World,* New York, N.Y., editorial representative, beginning, 1964. Communications consultant to aviation firms. *Military service:* U.S. Army Air Forces, pilot, 1942-45; received Distinguished Flying Cross with cluster, Air Medal with cluster, two battle stars, Presidential Citation. *Member:* Aviation/Space Writers Association, Authors Guild, Wings Club, Silvermine Guild of Artists, Silurians, Sigma Delta Chi, Dartmouth Club of Western Connecticut, Lake Club (New Canaan, Conn.).

WRITINGS: The Hump: The Great Military Airlift of World War II, Lippincott, 1965. Contributor of articles to magazines.

WORK IN PROGRESS: Books on the space program and on airline safety; two novellas.

SIDELIGHTS: Thorne told *CA:* "As a very small boy I witnessed the famous flights from Roosevelt Field, Long Island—Lindbergh, Chamberlain, Earhart, and Acosta, and have been deeply involved in aviation and space ever since."†

* * *

THORSON, Thomas Landon 1934-

PERSONAL: Born January 30, 1934, in LaPorte, Ind.; son of George Edward (a laborer) and Marie (Volkert) Thorson; married Sondra Joan Simon; children: (previous marriage) Ingrid Marie, Carla Louise. *Education:* Indiana University, A.B. (honors), 1956, M.A., 1958; Princeton University, M.A., 1959, Ph.D., 1960. *Politics:* Democrat. *Religion:* Lutheran. *Office:* Department of Political Economy, University of Toronto, Toronto, Ontario, Canada.

CAREER: University of Wisconsin, Madison, instructor, 1960-61, assistant professor, 1961-63, associate professor of political science, 1963-66; University of Toronto, Toronto, Ontario, associate professor, 1966-70, professor of political science 1970—. Visiting professor, University of California, Berkeley, 1963; Rockefeller visiting professor, University of the Philippines, 1965-66. *Member:* American Political Science Association, American Association for Political and Legal Philosophy, American Association for the Advancement of Science. *Awards, honors:* William H. Kiekhofer Award for distinguished teaching, 1962; Guggenheim fellowship, 1962-63.

WRITINGS: The Logic of Democracy, Holt, 1962; (editor) *Plato: Totalitarian or Democrat?,* Prentice-Hall, 1963; *Biopolitics,* Holt, 1970. Contributor to professional journals.

WORK IN PROGRESS: Three Dogmas of Politics.

SIDELIGHTS: Walt Anderson called *Biopolitics,* "one of this century's most important works of political theory." In the book, Thorson recommends the use of evolutionary theories, developed by the biological sciences, in order to provide more complete models of political institutions.†

* * *

THORVALL, Kerstin 1925-

PERSONAL: Born August 12, 1925, in Eskilstuna, Sweden; daughter of Ake (a teacher) and Thora (Kristiansson) Thorvall; married Lars-Eric Falk, June 20, 1948, divorced, 1957; married Per Engstrom, May 11, 1961; children: (first marriage) Hans, Johan, Gunnar; (second marriage) Anders. *Education:* Attended Anders Beckman's School of Art, 1945-47. *Politics:* Liberal. *Religion:* Protestant. *Home:* Villa Bjorklunda, Ekero (Stockholm), Sweden.

CAREER: Free-lance author and journalist, illustrator, and fashion designer. *Member:* Swedish Society of Authors. *Awards, honors:* Award of honor of Bonnier's Youth-book Competition, 1960, for *Flicka i April.*

WRITINGS: (Interviewer) Gustav Jonsson, *Foerstaa mei saa foerstaar jag er,* Raben & Sjoegren (Stockholm), 1959; *Boken till dig,* Bonniers (Stockholm), 1959.

Flicka i April, Bonniers, 1960, translation by Annabelle Macmillan published as *Girl in April,* Harcourt, 1963; *Kvinnoglaedja: Med techningar av foerfattarinnan,* Geber (Stockholm), 1960; *Flicka i Paris,* Bonniers, 1962; *Flicka i verkligheten,* Bonniers, 1964; *Den nya kvinnan* (play; title means "The New Woman"; produced on Swedish television, 1965), Bonniers, 1965; *Portraett av ett mycket litet barn,* Raben & Sjoegren, 1965; *Jag vill dansa,* Norstedt (Stockholm), 1966; *Fula ord aer saa skoena,* Raben & Sjoegren, 1967; *Naer Gunnar ville spela ishockey,* Raben & Sjoegren, 1967; *Thomas: En vecka i maj,* Bonniers, 1967; *Det var inte meningen,* B. Wahlstroem (Stockholm), 1967; *Kvinnor och barn: Kaaserier,* Raben & Sjoegren, 1968; *Gunnar vill klippa haaret,* Raben & Sjoegren, 1968; *Gunnar goer maal,* [Stockholm], c. 1968, translation by Anne Parker published as *Gunnar Scores a Goal,* Harcourt, 1968; *"Vart ska du gaa?" "Ut,"* Bonniers, 1969.

Naemen Gunnar!, Raben & Sjoegren, 1970; *I min trotsaalder,* Askild & Kaernekull (Stockholm), 1971; *Foeljetong i skaert och svart,* Raben & Sjoegren, 1971; *Bad Words Feel So Good,* Anglo-American Center (Mullsjoe, Sweden), 1972; *Jag vet hur det kaenns,* Raben & Sjoegren, 1972; *I stallet for en pappa,* [Stockholm], c. 1973, translation by R. L. Mirro published as *And Leffe was Instead of a Dad,* Bradbury, 1974.

AVOCATIONAL INTERESTS: Jazz-ballet.†

* * *

THROCKMORTON, Peter 1928-

PERSONAL: Given name, Edgerton Alvord, legally changed to Peter; born July 30, 1928, in New York; son of Edgerton Alvord and Lucy Norton (Leonard) Throckmorton; married Joan Henley (a writer), June, 1964; children: Lucy Elizabeth, Paula. *Education:* Studied at University of Hawaii, 1951-54, University of the Americas, Mexico City, 1954, and Institute of Ethnology, University of Paris, 1954-55. *Home:* Odos Minos 16, Kastella Piraeus, Greece. *Agent:* McIntosh & Otis Inc., 18 East 41st St., New York, N.Y. 10017.

CAREER: Served as engineer on tankers, ran deep-sea fishing boats out of Honolulu, and conducted a diving and salvage business in the Hawaiian Islands, 1951-54; University of Pennsylvania Museum, Philadelphia, research associate, underwater archaeology programs, 1960-69; writer and photographer. Consultant on underwater archaeological methods to University of Chicago, Villa Guilia Museum, Hellenic Institute of Nautical Archaeology, and other institutions. Curator, National Maritime Historical Society. *Military service:* U.S. Army, Transportation Corps, 1948-51; served in Far East; became sergeant. *Member:* U.S. Naval Institute, American Society of Magazine Photographers, French Club (London), Ocean Cruising Club (Chichester). *Awards, honors:* D.M.H., Sea Research Institute, 1973.

WRITINGS: (With Henry Chapin) *Spiro of the Sponge Fleet,* Little, Brown, 1963; *The Lost Ships,* Atlantic-Little, Brown, 1964; (with others) *Surveying in Archaeology Un-*

derwater, Quaritch, 1969; *Shipwrecks and Archaeology: The Unharvested Sea*, Atlantic-Little, Brown, 1970. Writer-producer of one-hour television films on underwater archaeology, 1964, 1974-75; writer of other television scripts for American and British networks. Contributor of articles, mostly on underwater archaeology, to *Expedition, Greek Heritage, Archaeology, National Geographic, Journal of Nautical Archaeology, Atlantic Monthly, Argosy*, and other magazines and newspapers. Member of advisory board, *Triton*.

WORK IN PROGRESS: A popular book on underwater archaeology, for Little, Brown; a report on research done in Italy, 1964-65, 1967-68; a book on Greek Islands ships, in collaboration with Samual Barclay.

SIDELIGHTS: Throckmorton is fluent ("if ungrammatical") in modern Greek, Italian, Turkish, and French; he does research in German and Spanish and knows some Japanese and Tahitian. *Avocational interests:* Sailing, carpentry.

BIOGRAPHICAL/CRITICAL SOURCES: Herb Greer, *A Scattering of Dust*, Hutchinson, 1962; Arthur Clarke, *Treasure of the Great Reef*, Harper, 1964.

* * *

TIFFIN, Joseph 1905-

PERSONAL: Born July 4, 1905, in Falls City, Neb.; son of Joseph Henry (a salesman) and Maude (Nobles) Tiffin; married Mary Straight, May 18, 1927. *Education:* University of South Dakota, B.A., 1927; University of Iowa, M.A., 1928, Ph.D., 1930. *Politics:* Republican. *Home:* 221 Forest Hill Dr., West Lafayette, Ind. 47906.

CAREER: University of Iowa, Iowa City, assistant professor, 1931-35, associate professor of psychology and speech, 1935-37; Brooklyn College (now Brooklyn College of the City University of New York), Brooklyn, N.Y., director of Voice Science Laboratory, 1937-38; Purdue University, Lafayette, Ind., associate professor, 1938-40, professor of industrial psychology, 1940—. Consultant to several companies. *Member:* American Psychological Association (president, industrial division, 1959-60), Midwestern Psychological Association, Indiana Psychological Association, Phi Beta Kappa, Sigma Xi.

WRITINGS: (With George R. Thornton) *The Psychology of Normal People*, Heath, 1940; *Industrial Psychology*, Prentice-Hall, 1942, 6th edition, with Ernest J. McCormick, 1973. Contributor to psychology journals.

* * *

TILLY, Richard H(ugh) 1932-

PERSONAL: Born October 17, 1932, in Chicago, Ill.; son of Otto Charles (a salesman) and Naneth (Stott) Tilly; married Elisabeth Flach, May 31, 1960; children: Benjamin, Johanna, Eva, Stephanie. *Education:* University of Wisconsin, B.A., 1955, Ph.D., 1964. *Religion:* Protestant. *Home:* Kemperweg 3, Muenster, Germany.

CAREER: Yale University, New Haven, Conn., assistant professor, beginning 1966; currently at University of Muenster, professor of economic and social history. *Member:* Economic History Association. *Awards, honors:* Edwin Gay Prize of Economic History Association for manuscript of *Financial Institutions and Industrialization in the Rhineland, 1815-1870*.

WRITINGS: Financial Institutions and Industrialization

in the Rhineland, 1815-1870, University of Wisconsin Press, 1966; (with Charles and Louise Tilly) *The Rebellious Century*, Harvard University Press, 1975. Contributor to scholarly journals.

WORK IN PROGRESS: European, mainly German, economic history of the nineteenth century.

* * *

TIMKO, Michael 1925-

PERSONAL: Born August 16, 1925, in Garfield, N.J.; married Lois Joy Peltier (an artist and teacher), December 20, 1947; children: Nikki Lynn, Michael John, Christine Diane. *Education:* University of Missouri, B.J. and A.B., 1949, M.A., 1950; University of Wisconsin, Ph.D., 1956. *Home:* 52 Crescent Rd., Port Washington, N.Y. 11050.

CAREER: University of Missouri, Columbia, instructor in English, 1950-52; University of Illinois, Urbana, instructor, 1956-59, assistant professor of English, 1959-61; Queens College of the City University of New York, Flushing, N.Y., associate professor, 1961-66, professor of English, 1967—, chairman of department, 1970—. *Military service:* U.S. Navy, 1942-45. *Member:* Modern Language Association of America, American Society for Theatre Research, American Association of University Professors, Phi Beta Kappa.

WRITINGS: (Editor and author of introduction) H. G. Wells, *Hoopdriver's Holiday*, Purdue University, 1964; *Innocent Victorian: The Satiric Poetry of Arthur Hugh Clough*, Ohio University Press, 1966; *Arthur Hugh Clough: A Descriptive Catalogue*, New York Public Library, 1967; (contributor) Frederic E. Faverty, editor, *Victorian Poets: A Guide to Research*, revised edition, Harvard University Press, 1968; (editor) *Thirty-eight Short Stories: An Introductory Anthology*, Knopf, 1968. Member of editorial board, *Victorian Poetry*, and *Browning Institute Studies*. Contributor to *Criticism, English Studies, Victorian Poetry, New Literary History*, and other professional journals.

WORK IN PROGRESS: Editing a second anthology of short stories, for Knopf; a critical study of Victorian Literature.

* * *

TINSLEY, (John) Russell 1932-

PERSONAL: Born October 14, 1932, in Mason, Tex.; son of Oran D. and Dora (Passmore) Tinsley; married Marjorie Schott, April 19, 1955; children: Russell Reed, Cynthia Ann. *Education:* University of Texas, B.J., 1954. *Politics:* Democrat. *Religion:* Protestant. *Home:* 3200 Clawson Rd., Austin, Tex. 78704. *Agent:* Lenniger Literary Agency, 437 Fifth Ave., New York, N.Y. 10016. *Office: Austin American-Statesman*, Box 670, Austin, Tex. 78767.

CAREER: Outdoor columnist for *Austin American-Statesman*, Austin, 1956—, and hunting editor for *Archery World*; free-lance magazine writer. *Military service:* U.S. Air Force Reserve, active duty, 1954-55; became captain. *Member:* Outdoor Writers Association of America (former member of board), Texas Outdoor Writers Association (former member of board), Austin Woods and Waters Club. *Awards, honors:* Headliners Award for series of articles on surviving in the woods.

WRITINGS: Hunting the Whitetail Deer, Harper, 1965; *Shooter's Bible Taxidermy Guide*, Stoeger Arms Corp., 1967; *The Critters Come When Called*, Powell Press, 1967, revised edition, 1974; *Southern Living Camping Guide*, Oxmoor House, 1970; *Freshwater Fishing in Texas*, Cordovan Corp., 1973; *Bowhunting*, Stoeger Arms Corp., 1975. Contributor of more than eight hundred articles on outdoor recreation to magazines, including *Popular Mechanics, Outdoor Life*, and *Field and Stream*.

*   *   *

TITUS, Warren Irving 1921-

PERSONAL: Born July 17, 1921, in Deposit, N.Y.; son of Irving Roscoe (a dairyman) and Julia (Axtell) Titus; married Mary Cleveland (a school librarian), June 19, 1953; children: Mary Judith, John Warren, Janice Ann. *Education:* Rollins College, B.M., 1943; Columbia University, M.A., 1947; New York University, Ph.D., 1957. *Politics:* Democrat. *Religion:* Presbyterian. *Home:* 330 Lynn Dr., Nashville, Tenn. 37211. *Office:* George Peabody College, Nashville, Tenn. 37203.

CAREER: High school instructor in music, Cranford, N.J., 1948-49; George Peabody College for Teachers, Nashville, Tenn., 1949—, began as instructor, professor of English, 1954—. *Military service:* U.S. Army, Information-Education Branch, 1943-46. *Member:* American Studies Association, College English Association, Thoreau Society, South Atlantic Modern Language Association. *Awards, honors:* American Philosophical Society grant, 1964-65.

WRITINGS: Winston Churchill, Twayne, 1963; *John Fox, Jr.*, Twayne, 1971; (contributor) *Bibliographical Guide to Midwestern Literature*, Indiana University Press, in press. Contributor to historical and other learned journals.

WORK IN PROGRESS: A critical biography of Charles Dudley Warner, completion expected in 1976.

*   *   *

TJADER, Marguerite 1901-

PERSONAL: Surname is pronounced *Chay*-der; born November 24, 1901, in New York, N.Y.; daughter of Richard (an explorer and lecturer) and Margaret (Thorne) Tjader; divorced; children: Hilary Harris. *Education:* Attended Bryn Mawr College, 1920-21; Columbia University, A.B., 1925. *Politics:* Liberal Democrat. *Religion:* Roman Catholic. *Home:* Tokeneke Trail, Darien, Conn. 06820. *Agent:* Hellmut Meyer, 817 West End Ave., New York, N.Y.

CAREER: Direction (magazine of the arts), Darien, Conn., editor, 1937-45. Active in community, religious, and peace work. *Member:* Women's International League for Peace and Freedom, Fellowship of Reconciliation.

WRITINGS: Borealis (novel), Logos Press, 1930; *Theodore Dreiser: A New Dimension*, Silvermine, 1965; *Mother Elisabeth*, Herder & Herder, 1972; (editor) Theodore Dreiser, *Notes on Life*, Alabama University Press, 1974. Contributor of articles to *One World, New York Post, Twice a Year*, and other periodicals. Translator of articles from the French and German.

WORK IN PROGRESS: A book on Saint Brigitta of Sweden, with an analysis of her revelations.

SIDELIGHTS: Marguerite Tjader is competent in eight languages and has lived in Sweden, France, Switzerland, and Soviet Union.

TJERNAGEL, Neelak S(erawlook) 1906-

PERSONAL: Surname is pronounced *Chair*-nagel; born December 14, 1906, in Stanwood, Wash.; son of Henry M. and Anna (Brue) Tjernagel; married Ada Studholme, October 29, 1936; children: Anna Brue, Louise Young (Mrs. William Van Rooy), Allan Andreas. *Education:* Concordia College, St. Paul, Minn., diploma, 1929; Wisconsin Lutheran Seminary, C.T.M., 1933; Iowa State Teacher College (now University of Northern Iowa), B.A., 1947; State University of Iowa, M.A., 1949, Ph.D., 1955. *Home:* 0-60 Park Lawn Apts., Honeoye, N.Y. 14471.

CAREER: Lutheran minister in Iowa, 1933-47; Lutheran High School, Racine, Wis., principal, 1950-53; Concordia Teachers College, River Forest, Ill., professor of history, 1953-68. *Member:* American Historical Association, American Society for Reformation Research, American Society of Church History, Lutheran Academy for Scholarship, Lutheran Historical Conference.

WRITINGS: (Editor) *The Reformation Essays of Dr. Robert Barnes*, Concordia Publishing House (London), 1963; *The Reformation Era*, Concordia, 1965; *Henry VIII and the Lutherans*, Concordia, 1965; (with C. S. Meyer) *History of Western Christianity* (textbook), Concordia, 1971. Contributor to Lutheran periodicals: Editor-in-chief, *The Lutheran Sentinel*.

WORK IN PROGRESS: A biography of Robert Barnes; *Luther and the Saxon Princes*; and *The Lutheran Confessions: A Harmony and Resource Book*.

*   *   *

TOCH, Hans (Herbert) 1930-

PERSONAL: Born April 17, 1930, in Vienna, Austria. *Education:* Attended high school in Havana, Cuba; Brooklyn College (now Brooklyn college of the City University of New York), B.A. (summa cum laude), 1952; Princeton University, Ph.D., 1955. *Office:* School of Criminal Justice, State University of New York, Albany, N.Y. 12222.

CAREER: Michigan State University, East Lansing, instructor, 1957-58, assistant professor, 1958-61, associate professor, 1961-66, professor of psychology, 1966-68; State University of New York, School of Criminal Justice, Albany, professor of psychology, 1968—. *Military service:* U.S. Naval Reserve, active duty as enlisted man (morale researcher), 1955-57; reserve officer, 1957-66. *Member:* American Psychological Association (fellow). *Awards, honors:* Fulbright senior research fellowship.

WRITINGS: (Editor and contributor) *Legal and Criminal Psychology*, Holt, 1961; *The Social Psychology of Social Movements*, Bobbs-Merrill, 1965; (editor with H. C. Smith) *Social Perception*, Van Nostrand, 1968; *Violent Men: An Inquiry into the Psychology of Violence*, Aldine, 1969; (with others) *Agents of Change*, Schenkman, 1975; *Men in Crisis*, Aldine, in press. Author of column, "Ripples on Lake Success," *United Nations World*, 1949-50. Contributor of some fifty articles in communication, public opinion, criminology, psychology of religion, and experimental psychology to journals.

WORK IN PROGRESS: A monograph on police violence and prison violence for National Institutes of Mental Health; research on prison inmate psychological survival.

SIDELIGHTS: Toch wrote: "Have feeling that academic writing has became needlessly stilted and full of private language and obscurantisms.... Also feel that social science must deal with real life . . . and never view people as objects." He speaks Spanish and German, and a smattering of French.

* * *

TODD, Vivian Edmiston 1912-

PERSONAL: Born February 18, 1912, in Spokane, Wash.; daughter of Robert Lee (an attorney) and Sue (a nurse; maiden name, McCracken) Edmiston; married Leonard Chrisman Todd (a property manager), December 18, 1949; children: David Lee, Philip Campbell, Susan Mariko. *Education:* University of Idaho, B.S., 1931, M.S., 1932; University of Chicago, Ph.D., 1943. *Home:* 1873 Stearnlee Ave., Long Beach, Calif. 90815.

CAREER: Public school teacher, 1932-39; University of Chicago, Chicago, Ill., research assistant, department of education, 1939-41; Columbia University, Teachers College, New York, N.Y., research associate, 1941-42; Association of Colleges and Universities of New York State, Albany, consultant, 1942-44; New York State Department of Education, Albany, supervisor of research, 1944-46; Supreme Command of Allied Powers, Tokyo, Japan, curriculum specialist, 1946-49; private education specialist and consultant, 1949—, including consultant to California State University, 1962-63. Member of board of directors, Idaho Research Foundation. *Member:* Association for Childhood Education International, American Educational Research Association, National Association for the Education of Young People, National Education Association (life member), Sigma Xi, Pi Lambda Theta, Kappa Delta Pi. *Awards, honors:* Doctor of Pedagogy, University of Idaho, 1973.

WRITINGS: (Editor) *The American Way of Housekeeping*, Tuttle, 1951; (with Helen Heffernan) *The Kindergarten Teacher*, Heath, 1960; (with Heffernan) *The Years Before School*, Macmillan, 1964, 2nd edition, 1970; (with Heffernan) *Elementary Teacher's Guide to Working with Parents*, Parker Publishing, 1969; (with Georgennie H. Hunter) *The Aide in Early School Education*, Macmillan, 1973. Contributor to education periodicals.

WORK IN PROGRESS: Another book in early childhood education; instructional materials for teacher education.

* * *

TOLIVER, Raymond F. 1914-

PERSONAL: Born November 16, 1914, in Fort Collins, Colo.; son of Frances LeRoy (a merchant) and Hattie (Lowe) Toliver; married Jennie Sue Miller, April 28, 1935; children: Suzanne Toliver Kemp, Nancy Toliver Belknap, Janet Toliver Moskal. *Education:* Attended Colorado State University, 1933-37; U.S. Air Force Command and Staff School, graduate, 1948; Air War College, graduate, 1951. *Home:* 5286 Lindley Ave., Encino, Calif. 91316.

CAREER: U.S. Army Air Forces and U.S. Air Force, regular officer, 1938-40, 1942-65, retiring with rank of colonel; assignments included test pilot at Wright-Patterson Field, Ohio, 1942-44, bomber and fighter pilot stationed on Guam, 1944-45, and commander of 20th Tactical Fighter Wing, Essex, England, 1955-59. Pilot with Transcontinental & Western Airlines, 1940-41, and Royal Air Force Ferry Command, 1941-42; Lockheed Aircraft International, Burbank, Calif., export sales representative, 1965-74. *Member:* American Fighter Aces Association (historian), Society of Experimental Test Pilots, American Aviation Historical Society, Combat Pilots Association, and Quiet Birdmen.

WRITINGS—With Trevor J. Constable: *Fighter Aces*, Macmillan, 1965, revised edition, in press; *Horrido! Fighter Aces of the Luftwaffe*, Macmillan, 1968; *The Blond Knight of Germany*, Doubleday, 1970.

WORK IN PROGRESS: A novel on World War II pilots; a book on test pilots and one on Japanese flying aces.

SIDELIGHTS: Toliver writes: "Have flown just under 10,000 flying hours in more than 200 types of aircraft, foreign and domestic."

* * *

TOMASEK, Robert D(ennis) 1928-

PERSONAL: Born January 16, 1928, in Chicago, Ill.; son of Joseph A. (an engineer) and Louise Tomasek; married Ruth Vivian Waltershausen, November 28, 1953; children: Mary, Katherine, Sarah. *Education:* Grinnell College, B.A., 1950; Johns Hopkins University, graduate study, 1950-51; University of Michigan, M.A., 1955, Ph.D., 1957. *Politics:* Democrat. *Religion:* Episcopalian. *Home:* 2553 Jasu Dr., Lawrence, Kan. 66044. *Office:* Political Science Department, 414 Blake, University of Kansas, Lawrence, Kan. 66044.

CAREER: University of Kansas, Lawrence, assistant professor, 1957-63, associate professor, 1963-68, professor of political science, 1968—, director of university's junior year abroad group in Costa Rica, 1962. Visiting associate professor, University of Indiana, 1966-67. *Military service:* U.S. Army, 1951-53; served in Korea. *Member:* American Political Science Association, Pi Sigma Alpha. *Awards, honors:* University of Kansas research grant, 1958; Doherty grant for research in Chile on Chilean multiparty system, 1960-61.

WRITINGS: (Editor) *Latin American Politics: 24 Studies of the Contemporary Scene*, Anchor Books, 1966; (contributor) Kenneth Johnson and Ben Burnett, editors, *Latin American Politics* (textbook), Wadsworth, 1968, 2nd edition, 1970. Contributor to journals in his field, including *Political Science Quarterly*, *Midwest Journal of Political Science*, *Orbis*, and *Journal of Inter-American Studies*.

WORK IN PROGRESS: Research on the causes of the 1969 El Salvador-Honduras war and an evaluation of the Organization of American States in resolving the conflict; research on the exile activities in Latin America, and on conflict resolution in the hemisphere.

* * *

TOMPKINS, Dorothy (Campbell) 1908-

PERSONAL: Born July 9, 1908, in St. Paul, Minn.; daughter of Harry Arthur (a prosthetic dentist) and Alta (Hayes) Campbell; married John Barr Tompkins (a librarian), June 2, 1941. *Education:* University of California, Berkeley, A.B., 1929, M.A., 1937. *Home:* 909 Regal Rd., Berkeley, Calif. 94708.

CAREER: University of California, Institute of Governmental Studies (formerly Bureau of Public Administration), Berkeley, assistant, 1930-50, analyst, 1950-74. *Member:* American Society of Indexers, Museum Society of San Francisco. *Awards, honors:* Joseph Andrews Bibliographic Award from American Association of Law Libraries, 1971-72.

WRITINGS: *Materials for the Study of Federal Government*, Public Administration Service, 1948; *Sources for the Study of the Administration of Criminal Justice*, California

State Printer, 1949; *State Government and Administration: A Bibliography*, Public Administration Service, 1954; *The Supreme Court: A Bibliography*, Bureau of Public Information, University of California, 1959.

All published by Institute of Governmental Studies: *Water Plans for California*, 1961; *Conflict of Interest in the Federal Government: A Bibliography*, 1961; *The Offender: A Bibliography*, 1963; *Bail in the United States: A Bibliography*, 1964; *Probation Since World War II: A Bibliography*, 1964; *Juvenile Gangs and Street Groups: A Bibliography*, 1966; *Changes in Congress: Proposals to Change Congress—Term of Members of the House: A Bibliography*, 1966; *White Collar Crime: A Bibliography*, 1967; *Strikes by Public Employees and Professional Personnel*, 1967; *The Confession Issue: A Bibliography*, 1968; *Poverty in the United States During the Sixties: A Bibliography*, 1970; *Sentencing the Offender: A Bibliography*, 1971; *Research and Service: A Fifty Year Record, Bureau of Public Administration/Institute of Governmental Studies*, 1971; *The Prison and the Prisoner*, 1972; *Local Public Schools: How to Pay for Them?*, 1972; *Power from the Earth: Geothermal Power*, 1972; *Strip Mining for Coal*, 1973; *Court Organization and Administration: A Bibliography*, 1973; *Furlough from Prison*, 1973; *Selection of the Vice-President*, 1974.

Editor, *California Public Survey* (bimonthly), 1949-72; contributing editor, *Criminology*, 1966-73.

* * *

TOMPKINS, Jerry R(obert) 1931-

PERSONAL: Born July 4, 1931, in Dallas, Tex.; son of Robert Alva (a wholesale agent for an oil company) and Hazel (Chase) Tompkins; married Marcia Davis, June 11, 1955; children: Mary Elizabeth, Robert Dabney, Marcia Louisa, Thomas Chase. *Education:* Austin College, Sherman, Tex., B.A., 1951; Austin Presbyterian Theological Seminary, graduate, 1955. *Home:* 7107 Northeast Dr., Austin, Tex. 78723. *Office:* Austin Presbyterian Theological Seminary, 100 East 27th St., Austin, Tex. 78705.

CAREER: Ordained minister of Presbyterian church, 1955; pastor in Franklin, La., 1955-59; First Presbyterian Church, Monticello, Ark., pastor, 1959-68; Trinity Presbyterian Church, Midland, Tex., pastor, 1968-73; Austin Presbyterian Theological Seminary, Austin, Tex., vice-president, 1973—.

WRITINGS: (Editor, contributor, and author of preface) *D-Days at Dayton: Reflections on the Scopes Trial*, Louisiana State University Press, 1965; (editor, and author of introduction) *. . . And a Time to Laugh: Notes From the Pen of an Untamed Iconoclast*, Hurley Co., 1966.

SIDELIGHTS: Tompkins told *CA* he is particularly interested in "the nature of conflict—conflict between personalities and between philosophies. The Scopes Trial afforded an unusual range of study in both these areas. In the larger context I am concerned with how conflicts are resolved by compromise, by new synthesis, and by the impact of the mere passage of time, . . . that is, the winnowing effects of time on the history of an idea."

* * *

TOMS, Bernard 1931-

PERSONAL: Born September 22, 1931, in Newport, Wales; son of William (in aircraft construction) and Hilda-Mary (Hickey) Toms; married Veronica Mary Garrett (a secretary), November 17, 1953 (divorced); married Ann Gilfillan, July 3, 1973; children: (first marriage) Christopher Matthew Gerrard; (second marriage) Patrick Bernard, Connor James Francis. *Education:* Attended Abersychan Technical Institute in Wales, 1945-47, and Royal Air Force Apprentice School in England, 1947-49. *Politics:* None. *Home:* 20, Maryport St., Usk, Monmouthshire, England.

CAREER: Member of Metropolitan Police, London, England, 1951-60; full-time professional writer, 1962—.

WRITINGS: George Arbuthnott Jarrett (novel), Harcourt, 1965; *The Strange Affair* (novel), Constable, 1966.

SIDELIGHTS: The Strange Affair, Toms wrote, concerns "corruption and hardships in London Police." His consuming interest is in "humanity and in puzzling what it is; discrediting sciences, organizations, religions, beliefs, conventions; and TIME as a reality. The most vital subject is birth control. My future writing will be concerned with these things and I shall need to dispense with time in order to do it all."

The Strange Affair has been sold to Paramount Films, London.

* * *

TONEY, Anthony 1913-

PERSONAL: Born June 28, 1913, in Gloversville, N.Y.; son of Michael and Susan (Betor) Toney; married Edna Greenfield (a free-lance writer), April 8, 1947; children: Anita Karen, Adele Susan. *Education:* Syracuse University, B.F.A., 1934; studied in Paris at l'Academie de la Grande Chaumiere and l'Ecole Superieure des Beaux Arts, 1937-38; Teachers College, Columbia University, M.A., 1952, Ed.D., 1955. *Home:* 16 Hampton Pl., Katonah, N.Y. 10536.

CAREER: Painter associated with ACA Gallery, New York, N.Y., graphic artist and illustrator, and instructor in art. Work exhibited at one-man shows at ACA Gallery, 1949—, at Santa Barbara Museum, William Rockhill Nelson Gallery of Art, and elsewhere, and in group shows at Corcoran Gallery of Art, Carnegie Institute, Whitney Museum of American Art, Pennsylvania Academy, and at a number of university and art association exhibitions; paintings in collections of Whitney Museum, Berkshire Museum, University of Illinois, Ohio Wesleyan University, and private collections. Instructor in art at School for Advanced Study, 1934-36, Stevenson School, 1948-52, Hofstra College, 1953-55, New School for Social Research, 1953—. *Military service:* U.S. Army Air Forces, 1942-45; served in Southwest Pacific; received Distinguished Flying Cross with two oak leaf clusters and Air Medal with four oak leaf clusters.

MEMBER: Artists Equity Association, National Society of Mural Painters, Audubon Artists, Westchester Art Society. *Awards, honors:* Purchase prize, University of Illinois, 1950; first prize, Artists Equity Association Show, 1952; Grumbacher Award, 1954, Medal of Honor, 1966, and Pauline Mintz Memorial Award, 1974, from Audubon Artists; Emily Lowe Award, 1955; first prize, Mickewiecz Art Competition, 1956; purchase prize, Staten Island Museum, 1957; National Institute of Arts and Letters Award, 1968; National Academy Award, 1968.

WRITINGS: (Contributor of drawings with others) *The Tune of the Calliope* (poems and drawings of New York), Yoseloff, 1958; (editor) *150 Masterpieces of Drawing*, Dover, 1963; (author and illustrator) *Creative Painting and*

Drawing, Dover, 1966. Contributor to *Family Creative Workshop*.

* * *

TORCHIANA, Donald T(hornhill) 1923-

PERSONAL: Born October 22, 1923, in Swarthmore, Pa.; son of Paul John (a business executive) and Martha (Fitz-Gerald) Torchiana; married Margarida LeSueur (a pre-school teacher), 1952 (divorced, 1972); children: Katherine, David, William. *Education:* DePauw University, B.A., 1947; University of Iowa, M.A., 1949, Ph.D., 1953. *Home:* 1220 Hinman Ave., Evanston, Ill. *Office:* Northwestern University, Evanston, Ill.

CAREER: University of Iowa, Iowa City, instructor in English, 1952-53; Northwestern University, Evanston, Ill., instructor, 1953-58, assistant professor, 1958-63, associate professor, 1963-67, professor of English, 1967—. Fulbright lecturer at University College, Galway, Ireland, 1960-62, 1969-70. *Military service:* U.S. Army Air Forces, 8th Air Force, 1943-45; became captain; received Air Medal with three oak leaf clusters. *Member:* Modern Language Association of America, Irish Georgian Society, Phi Beta Kappa.

WRITINGS: W. B. Yeats and Georgian Ireland, Northwestern University Press, 1966.

BIOGRAPHICAL/CRITICAL SOURCES: New York Review of Books, April 6, 1967.

* * *

TRAGER, Frank N(ewton) 1905-

PERSONAL: Born October 9, 1905, in New York, N.Y.; son of Benjamin and Eda (Shapiro) Trager; married Helen Gilbson, 1936. *Education:* New York University, B.S., 1927, A.M., 1928, Ph.D., 1951. *Residence:* North Salem, N.Y. 10560. *Office:* Graduate School of Public Administration, New York University, Washington Sq., New York, N.Y. 10003.

CAREER: Johns Hopkins University, Baltimore, Md., instructor in philosophy, 1928-34; U.S. Government, Washington, D.C., civil servant 1934-36; program executive for private social agencies, New York, N.Y., 1938-43, 1945-51; Technical Cooperation Administration, director of U.S. aid program, Rangoon, Burma, 1951-53; New York University, New York, N.Y., administrator and research professor, 1953-58, professor of international affairs, 1958—. Visiting professor, Yale University, 1960-61; member of faculty, National War College, 1961-63; lecturer at U.S. Department of State Foreign Service Institute and Army, Army Air Forces, and Navy War colleges. Director of studies, National Strategy Information Center, 1966—. Consultant to RAND Corp., and Hudson Institute. Member, Foreign Policy Research Institute. *Military service:* U.S. Army Air Forces, 1943-45.

MEMBER: American Political Science Association, Association for Asian Studies (board member), Council on Foreign Relations, Asia Society, Royal Siam Society, Burma Research Society. *Awards, honors:* Research fellow at Center for International Studies, Massachusetts Institute of Technology, 1953-54; Carnegie fellow at Council on Foreign Relations, 1957-58; Air University award, 1966-69.

WRITINGS: Toward a Welfare State in Burma: Economic Reconstruction and Development, 1948-1954, Institute of Pacific Relations, 1954, revised edition published as *Building a Welfare State in Burma: 1948-1956*, 1958;

Burma: Land of Golden Pagodas, Foreign Policy Association, 1954; (editor and contributor) *Burma*, three volumes, Human Relations Area Files Press, 1956; (with Patricia Wohlgemuth and Lu-Yu Kiang) *Burma's Role in the United Nations: 1948-1955*, Institute of Pacific Relations, 1956; (editor) *Annotated Bibliography of Burma*, Human Relations Area Files Press, 1956, published as *Burma: A Selected and Annotated Bibliography*, 1973; (editor) *Japanese and Chinese Language Sources on Burma: An Annotated Bibliography*, Human Relations Area Files Press, 1957; (editor) *Area Handbook for Burma*, Human Relations Area Files Press, 1958; (editor and author of introduction) *Marxism in Southeast Asia: A Study of Four Countries*, Stanford University Press, 1959.

(Editor and compiler) *Furnivall of Burma: An Annotated Bibliography of the Works of John S. Furnivall*, Southeast Asia Studies, Yale University, 1963; *Burma: From Kingdom to Republic*, Praeger, 1966; *Why Viet Nam?*, Praeger, 1966; (editor) *Communist China, 1949-1969: A Twenty-Year Appraisal*, New York University Press, 1970; (editor and author of introduction) *Burma: Japanese Military Administration*, University of Pennsylvania Press, 1971; (editor with Philip S. Kronenberg) *National Security and American Society: Theory, Process, and Policy*, University Press of Kansas, 1973.

Contributor: Abshire and Allen, editors, *National Security: Political, Military and Economic Strategies in the Decade Ahead*, Praeger and Hoover Institution, 1963; Jeane J. Kirkpatrick, editor, *The Strategy of Deception*, Farrar, Straus, 1963; William Henderson, editor, *Southeast Asia: Problems of United States Policy*, M.I.T. Press, 1963; Robert K. Sakai, editor, *Studies on Asia, 1965*, University of Nebraska Press, 1965; Marvin E. Gettleman, editor, *Viet Nam: History, Documents, and Opinions on a Major World Crisis*, Fawcett, 1965. Contributor of about fifty articles, chiefly on Southeast Asia, to journals. Member of editorial board, *Orbis*.

* * *

TRAHEY, Jane 1923-
(Baba Erlanger)

PERSONAL: Born November 19, 1923, in Chicago, Ill.; daughter of David and Margaret (Hennessey) Trahey. *Education:* Mundelein College, B.A., 1943; University of Wisconsin, graduate study, 1945. *Home:* 180 East 79th St., New York, N.Y. 10021. *Agent:* Gloria Safier, Inc., 667 Madison Ave., New York, N.Y. *Office:* Trahey-Wolf Advertising, 919 3rd Ave., New York, N.Y. 10022.

CAREER: Carson, Pirie, Scott & Co. (department store), Chicago, Ill., copywriter, 1945-47; Neiman-Marcus (specialty store), Dallas, Tex., copywriter, advertising manager, and sales promotion director, 1947-58; Kayser-Roth (apparel manufacturer), New York, N.Y., director of advertising, 1955-57; Trahey-Wolf Advertising (advertising agency; formerly Trahey Advertising, Inc.), New York, N.Y., president, 1958—. *Member:* Fashion Group, Advertising Club, American Institute of Graphic Arts, Young Presidents Club. *Awards, honors: Good Housekeeping* Award; named Advertising Woman of the Year by American Advertising Federation, 1969.

WRITINGS: The Taste of Texas, Random House, 1955; (with Daren Pierce, under pseudonym Baba Erlanger) *The Compleat Martini Cookbook*, Random Thoughts, 1957; *Gin and Butter Diet*, Random Thoughts, 1960; *1000 Names and Where to Drop Them*, Random Thoughts, 1960; *The*

Magic Yarn, Random Thoughts, 1961; *Life With Mother Superior,* Farrar, Straus, 1962; (editor) *Harper's Bazaar: 100 Years of the American Female,* Random House, 1967; (with Pierce) *Son of the Martini Cookbook,* with drawings by Edward Gorey, Clovis Press, 1967; *Ring Round the Bathtub* (three-act play; first produced in Houston at The Alley Theater, 1970, produced on Broadway at Martin Beck Theatre, April 29, 1972), Samuel French, 1968; *Pecked to Death by Goslings,* Prentice-Hall, 1969.

SIDELIGHTS: Life With Mother Superior was made into the film, "The Trouble With Angels," Columbia Pictures Industries, 1966, and *Pecked to Death by Goslings* has been optioned for independent production.†

*   *   *

TREMAYNE, Ken(neth Eugene, Jr.)   1933-

PERSONAL: Born January 13, 1933, in Glendale, Calif.; son of Kenneth Eugene Tremayne (a businessman) and Emma Tremayne Graaf (nee Mueller); married Azuma Takahashi (a teacher of Japanese), November 15, 1964; children: Kenneth John. *Education:* Glendale College, A.A., 1952; California State College (now University) at Los Angeles, B.A., 1954; Tokyo School of Japanese Language, Japanese studies, 1958-59; University of California, Los Angeles, B.A. and graduate study, 1960-61. *Home:* 4087 Tropico Way, Los Angeles, Calif. 90065.

CAREER: Charles T. Tuttle Co. (publishers), Rutland, Vt., editor and book designer in Japanese branch, Tokyo, 1961-62, and promotion manager, 1962-66; advertising executive with Clinton E. Frank—West Coast, Los Angeles, Calif. Cartoonist and illustrator. *Military service:* U.S. Army, 1954-56. *Member:* Kappa Phi Sigma, Blue Key.

WRITINGS: (With Donn Draeger) *The Joke's on Judo,* Tuttle, 1965; (translator with John G. Milles and Toshie Takahama) Shintaro Ishihara, *Season of Violence,* Tuttle, 1966. Illustrator of *Tokyo Unzipped,* by Robert Dunham, Yuma Publishing, 1963.

SIDELIGHTS: Ken Tremayne speaks and writes Japanese.

*   *   *

TREVER, John C(ecil)   1915-

PERSONAL: Born November 26, 1915, in Milwaukee, Wis.; son of John Henry White (an attorney) and Hilda A. (Carpenter) Trever; married Elizabeth S. Burman, August 29, 1937; children: John Paul, James Edgar. *Education:* University of Southern California, A.B. (magna cum laude), 1937; Yale University, B.D., 1940, Ph.D., 1943. *Home:* 183 Fourth Ave., Berea, Ohio 44017. *Office:* Baldwin-Wallace College, Berea, Ohio 44017.

CAREER: Ordained Methodist minister, 1940; associate minister in Santa Monica, Calif., 1942-44; Drake University, College of Bible, Des Moines, Iowa, associate professor of Old Testament, 1944-47; International Council of Religious Education (now Division of Christian Education, National Council of Churches of Christ in the U.S.A.), Chicago, Ill., executive director of department of English Bible, 1948-53; Morris Harvey College, Charleston, W.Va., A. J. Humphreys Professor of Religion, 1953-59; Baldwin-Wallace College, Berea, Ohio, professor of religion, 1959—, founder of Dead Sea Scroll Research and Preservation Center, 1971. Delegate, Third Oxford Institute on Methodist Theology, 1965. *Member:* Society of Biblical Literature, American Academy of Religion, Amer-

ican Schools of Oriental Research, Phi Beta Kappa, Phi Kappa Phi. *Awards, honors:* Fellowship at American School of Oriental Research in Jerusalem, 1947-48; John F. Lewis Prize of American Philosophical Society, 1953, for article in society's *Proceedings.*

WRITINGS: (With Millar Burrows and William Brownlee) *The Dead Sea Scrolls of St. Mark's Monastery,* American Schools of Oriental Research, 1950; *Cradle of Our Faith,* Newsfoto, 1954; *The Untold Story of Qumran,* Revell, 1965; *Scrolls from Qumran Cave I,* Albright Institute of Archaeological Research and the Shrine of the Book (Jerusalem), 1972. Contributor of articles to *The Interpreter's Dictionary of the Bible, The Interpreter's Bible,* Volume 12, and *The Interpreter's One-Volume Commentary of the Bible.* Contributor to religious and other professional journals.

WORK IN PROGRESS: An Introduction to the Dead Sea Scrolls.

SIDELIGHTS: John Trever studied ancient Hebrew manuscripts in libraries of England and France, 1950, with further research in Israel and Jordan, 1958, 1962, 1966. Dr. Trever was the first American to see the Scrolls when he was asked to judge their antiquity. He was also chief photographer for "Et Tell" excavations in West Bank of Jordan, 1969. *Avocational Interests:* Color photography.

*   *   *

TREVINO, Elizabeth B(orton) de   1904-

PERSONAL: Born September 2, 1904, in Bakersfield, Calif.; daughter of Fred Ellsworth (a lawyer) and Carrie (Christensen) Borton; married Luis Trevino Gomez (a dealer in insurance and real estate), August 10, 1935; children: Luis Frederico, Enrique Ricardo. *Education:* Stanford University, B.A., 1925; studied violin at Boston Conservatory of Music. *Religion:* Roman Catholic. *Residence:* Cuernavaca, Mexico. *Agent:* McIntosh and Otis, 18 East 41st St., New York, N.Y. 10017.

CAREER: Formerly reviewer of performing arts for *Boston Herald,* Boston, Mass.; now professional writer and journalist. Honorary lecturer, American Institute for Foreign Trade. *Member:* Women in Communications, Hispanic Society, Pan American Round Tables, Altrusa Clubs, Phi Beta Kappa. *Awards, honors:* Honorary citizen of Texas; medal of Kansas City Woman's Organization; Newberry Medal, 1966, for *I, Juan de Pareja.*

WRITINGS: Pollyanna in Hollywood, L. C. Page, 1931; *Our Little Aztec Cousin,* L. C. Page, 1934; *Pollyanna's Castle in Mexico,* L. C. Page, 1934; *Our Little Ethiopian Cousin,* L. C. Page, 1935; *Pollyanna's Door to Happiness,* L. C. Page, 1936; *Pollyanna's Golden Horseshoe,* L. C. Page, 1939; *About Bellamy,* Harper, 1940; *Pollyanna and the Secret Mission,* L. C. Page, 1951; *My Heart Lies South* (memoirs), Crowell, 1953, reprinted, 1972; *A Carpet of Flowers,* Crowell, 1955; *Even As You Love* (novel), Crowell, 1957; *The Greek of Toledo* (novel), Crowell, 1959; *Where the Heart Is* (memoirs), Doubleday, 1962; *Nacar, the White Deer,* Farrar, Straus, 1963; *I, Juan de Pareja,* Farrar, Straus, 1965; *The Fourth Gift* (novel), Doubleday, 1966; *Casilda of the Rising Moon,* Farrar, Straus, 1967; *Turi's Poppa,* Farrar, Straus, 1968; *The House on Bitterness Street* (novel), 1970; *Here Is Mexico,* Farrar, Straus, 1970; *Beyond the Gates of Hercules,* Farrar, Straus, 1971; *The Music Within* (novel), Doubleday, 1973; *Juarez, Man of Law* (biography), Farrar, Straus, 1974.

WORK IN PROGRESS: The Hearthstone of My Heart (memoirs).

SIDELIGHTS: Mrs. Trevino is a violinist and plays with several chamber music groups.

* * *

TRIEM, Eve 1902-

PERSONAL: Born November 2, 1902, in New York, N.Y.; married Paul Ellsworth Triem (a medical writer), September 20, 1924; children: Yvonne Patricia (Mrs. Joseph Prete), Peter Dewey. Education: Attended University of California, Berkeley, 1920-24; studied classic Greek at University of Dubuque, 1954-55, and University of Washington, 1961. Politics: "Labeled, a Democrat; actually, a Citizen of the Universe." Religion: Episcopalian. Home: 911 Alder St., Apartment 790, Seattle, Wash. 98104.

CAREER: Poet; lecturer on poets; director of poetry workshops, YWCA, Seattle, 1962-64. Awards, honors: Award of the League to Support Poetry, 1946; award from National Institute of Arts and Letters, 1966; National Endowment on the Arts grant, 1968; Hart Crane and Alice Crane Memorial Fund prize, 1972.

WRITINGS: Parade of Doves (poetry), Dutton, 1946; Poems, A. Swallow, 1965; (translator) Heliodora: Translations from the Greek Anthology, Olivant, 1968; E. E. Cummings, University of Minnesota Press, 1969; Selected Poems, Olivant, in press. Contributor to The Poet (Scotland), Botteghe Oscure (Rome), Kavita (India), Seattle Magazine, and other publications.

WORK IN PROGRESS: A series of poems using the William Carlos Williams approach to the American language.

SIDELIGHTS: Mrs. Triem writes: "I have lived a difficult life but not like soldiers or ditch-diggers or engineers or war-correspondents. I have been cloistered within my marriage: perhaps the cloister within the cloister made me a poet. I am always grateful to anything, any incident, that kindles a poem. I envy, I wonder at, the creative ones who have acted in the phenomenal world: I too would have liked to canoe, to fish, to almost drown in waterfalls."

BIOGRAPHICAL/CRITICAL SOURCES: Poetry, May, 1966.

* * *

TROELSTRUP, Arch William 1901-

PERSONAL: Born December 22, 1901, in Belgrade, Minn.; son of John Frederick (a businessman) and Ann Troelstrup; married Ann Peterson (woman's page editor, Columbia Daily Tribune); children: William, Glenn, John, Susan Lee. Education: Macalester College, B.A., 1924; Columbia University, M.A., 1931. Politics: Democrat. Religion: Protestant. Home: 805 Edgewood, Columbia, Mo. 65201.

CAREER: Stephens College, Columbia, Mo., professor of family economics, 1942-69, chairman of Home and Family Division, 1956—. Lecturer and workshop director at other universities; lecturer in Japan at invitation of Minister of Trade and Industry, 1963; visiting professor, University of Missouri, 1970-72. Former member of consumer advisory committee, Federal Trade Commission; member of board of directors, Consumers Union of United States. Chairman of blood program, Boone County Red Cross, 1950-65. Member: American Council on Consumer Interests, American Association of University Professors, Kiwanis Club.

WRITINGS: Consumer Problems and Personal Finance, McGraw, 1952, 5th edition published as the Consumer in American Society: Personal and Family Finance, 1974; (with Jack L. Taylor) The Consumer in American Society: Additional Dimensions, McGraw, 1974. Contributor to education and consumer journals.

* * *

TSIEN, Tsuen-hsuin 1909-

PERSONAL: Born December 1, 1909, in Kiangsu, China; son of Wei-chen (a scholar) and Chuan-shih (Hsu) Tsien; married Wen-ching Hsu (a lecturer at University of Chicago), August 31, 1936; children: Ginger, Gloria, Mary (Mrs. Charles W. Hollenbeck). Education: University of Nanking, B.A., 1932; University of Chicago, M.A., 1952, Ph.D., 1957. Home: 1408 East Rochdale Pl., Chicago, Ill. 60615. Office: University of Chicago, Chicago, Ill. 60637.

CAREER: National Library of Peiping (Peking), chief of Shanghai office, Shanghai, China, and editor, 1937-47; University of Chicago, Chicago, Ill., professorial lecturer, 1949-58, associate professor, 1958-64, professor of Chinese literature, 1964—, curator of Far Eastern Library, 1949—. Visiting professor of Asian studies, University of Hawaii, summer, 1959. Chinese Student and Alumni Services, Inc., member of board of directors, 1958—, president, 1960-62; chairman, Committee on American Library Resources on the Far East, 1966-68. Member: American Oriental Society, Association for Asian Studies, American Library Association.

WRITINGS: Western Impact on China Through Translation, Department of Photographic Reproduction, University of Chicago, 1952; The Pre-Printing Records of China, Department of Photographic Reproduction, University of Chicago Library, 1957; Asian Studies in America, University of Hawaii, 1959; (with G. Raymond Nunn) Far Eastern Resources in American Libraries, 1959; Written on Bamboo and Silk: The Beginnings of Chinese Books and Inscriptions, University of Chicago Press, 1962; (editor with Howard W. Winger) Area Studies and the Library, University of Chicago Press, 1966; A History of the Book in Ancient China, Chinese University of Hong Kong Press, 1974. Contributor to Far Eastern Quarterly, Library Quarterly, Harvard Journal of Asiatic Studies, and other journals in America and China. Advisory editor, Tsing Hua Journal of Chinese Studies (New Haven and Taipei).

WORK IN PROGRESS: A History of Paper in China, a study of materials, techniques, and uses; A Manual of Chinese Bibliography, a study of the theory and technique of Chinese bibliographic methods, with an annotated list of Chinese bibliographies.

SIDELIGHTS: Tsuen-hsuin Tsien collects early printing and manuscripts from China, where, he points out, not only was block printing invented in the eighth century but movable type was used four hundred years before Gutenberg.

BIOGRAPHICAL/CRITICAL SOURCES: Library Quarterly, Volume XX, 1952, page 351, Volume XXIX, 1959, page 56, and Volume XXXV, 1965, page 385; Chicago Sun-Times Midwest Magazine, January 20, 1960; Hongkong Times, April 7, 1965.

* * *

TSUNEISHI, Warren M(ichio) 1921-

PERSONAL: Born July 4, 1921, in Monrovia, Calif.; son of Satoru and Sho (Murakami) Tsuneishi; married Betty

Takeuchi, November 16, 1948; children: David, Kenneth, Julia. *Education:* University of California, Berkeley, student, 1939-42; Syracuse University, B.A., 1943; Columbia University, M.A., 1948, M.S. in L.S., 1950; Yale University, Ph.D., 1960. *Home:* 5703 Maiden Lane, Bethesda, Md. 20034. *Office:* Orientalia Division, Library of Congress, Washington, D.C.

CAREER: Yale University Library, New Haven, Conn., curator of East Asia collections, 1950-57, 1961-66, lecturer in department of political science, 1964-65; Quinnipiac College, Hamden, Conn., assistant professor of government, 1965-66; Library of Congress, Washington, D.C., chief of Orientalia Division 1966—. *Military service:* U.S. Army, 1943-46; became technical sergeant; received Bronze Star. *Member:* American Library Association, Association for Asian Studies (executive group member, committee on American library resources on the Far East, 1964—).

WRITINGS: Japanese Political Style: An Introduction to the Government and Politics of Modern Japan, Harper, 1966; (editor with others) *Issues in Library Administration,* Columbia University Press, 1974. Contributor to *Journal of Asian Studies.* Editor of proceedings.

WORK IN PROGRESS: Research on Japanese party politics.

SIDELIGHTS: Tsuneishi reads Chinese, German, French, and Spanish.†

*   *   *

TUCKER, Edward L(lewellyn) 1921-

PERSONAL: Born November 19, 1921, in Crewe, Va.; son of Edward Llewellyn (a railway clerk) and Mary (Graham) Tucker. *Education:* Roanoke College, B.A. (with highest honors), 1946; Columbia University, M.A., 1947; University of Georgia, Ph.D., 1957. *Politics:* Democrat. *Religion:* Presbyterian. *Home:* College View Dr., Blacksburg, Va. 24060.

CAREER: Roanoke College, Salem, Va., instructor in English, 1949-54; University of Richmond, Richmond, Va., assistant professor of English, 1957-60; Virginia Polytechnic Institute and State University, Blacksburg, assistant professor, 1960-66, associate professor of English, 1966—. *Military service:* U.S. Army, 1943-46.

WRITINGS: Richard Henry Wilde: His Life and Selected Poems, University of Georgia Press, 1966; *Vocabulary Power,* Bantam, 1968. Contributor to southern literature and history journals.

WORK IN PROGRESS: Two books, *Richard Henry Wilde's Prose,* and *Kenneth Hari: Revival of the Portrait.*

*   *   *

TUCKER, Eva 1929-

PERSONAL: Born April 4, 1929, in Berlin, Germany; married John Tucker (a philosopher); children: Judith, Catherine, Sarah. *Education:* University of London, honours degree in German and English, 1954. *Religion:* None. *Home:* 63 Belsize Park Gardens, London N.W.3., England.

WRITINGS: Contact (novel), Calder & Boyars, 1966; *Drowning,* Calder & Boyars, 1969; (translator) Joseph Roth, *Radetzkymarch,* Overlook Press, 1974. *Radetzkymarch* was adapted for BBC radio, 1975. Contributor to *London Magazine, Vogue, Harpers, Studio International, European Judaism,* and *Times Literary Supplement.*

WORK IN PROGRESS: Crosscurrents (novel).

SIDELIGHTS: Mrs. Tucker is fluent in German and has reading knowledge of French. *Avocational interests:* Talking, walking, looking, listening.

*   *   *

TUCKER, Martin 1928-

PERSONAL: Born February 8, 1928, in Philadelphia, Pa.; son of Herman (an electrician) and Sarah (Goldberg) Tucker; married Joyce Hergenhan. *Education:* New York University, B.A., 1949, Ph.D., 1963; University of Arizona, M.A., 1954. *Home:* 35 High St., Armonk, N.Y. 10504. *Office:* Long Island University, Brooklyn, N.Y. 10012.

CAREER: Transradio Press, New York, N.Y., radio news writer, 1950-51; Associated Press, New York, N.Y., radio news writer, 1955; Long Island University, Brooklyn, N.Y., assistant professor, 1962-66, associate professor, 1966-68, professor of English, 1968—. Reader for Educational Testing Service, 1962-65; member of scholarship and admissions committee, British University Summer School Program; co-chairman of International Writers Conference, Long Island University, 1965; member of regional selection committee for Fulbright Awards, 1966—. *Member:* P.E.N. (member of executive board, 1974), New York University Graduate Alumni Association (president, 1968-74), Phi Beta Kappa. *Awards, honors:* Presidential Citation of Merit, 1973.

WRITINGS: (Editor with Ruth Z. Temple) *A Library of Literary Criticism: Modern British Literature,* Ungar, Volumes I, II, and III, 1966, Volume IV (with Rita Stein), 1974, Volume V (with John Ferres), 1975; (editor) *A Library of Literary Criticism by C. W. Moulton,* four-volume revised and abridged edition of original eight-volume work, Ungar, 1966; *Africa in Modern Literature,* Ungar, 1966; (contributor) *Vocabularies in Special Fields,* Funk, 1966; (editor with Temple) *A Bibliography of Modern British Literature,* Ungar, 1968; (author of introduction) James Ngugi, *Weep Not Child,* Macmillan, 1969; (editor) *The Critical Temper,* three volumes, Ungar, 1969; (general editor) *Twentieth-Century Criticism of English and American Literature,* three volumes, Ungar, 1971; (author of introduction) Olive Schreiner, *Undine,* Johnson Reprint, 1972; *Joseph Conrad,* Ungar, 1975.

Editor and consultant to "Belles-Lettres in English" series, Johnson Reprint; writer of sections on American and British literature for *Funk and Wagnalls International Yearbook,* 1961-66; contributor to numerous periodicals; editor, *Confrontation,* 1971—, *P.E.N. Newsletter,* 1973—.

*   *   *

TUCKER, (Arthur) Wilson 1914-
(Bob Tucker)

PERSONAL: Born November 23, 1914, in Deer Creek, Ill.; son of James Ira (a stage manager) and Marie (Ross) Tucker; married Fern Delores Brooks (a telephone supervisor), November 3, 1953; children: Judith (Mrs. David Mays), Robert, David R., Brian A., Wesley. *Education:* Attended high school in Normal, Ill. *Politics:* Independent. *Religion:* Independent. *Home:* 34 Greenbriar Dr., Jacksonville, Ill. 62650. *Agent:* Curtis Brown Ltd., 60 East 56th St., New York, N.Y. 10022.

CAREER: Motion picture projectionist at theaters in Bloomington-Normal, Ill., 1933-72; Illinois State University, Normal, stage electrician, 1972-74. Writer of science fiction and mystery novels; lecturer. Editor of house organs, Kane Advertising Agency, 1945. *Member:* Mystery Writers of America, Science Fiction Writers of America, Illinois Council of Motion Picture Projectionists (recording secretary, 1965-66) *Awards, honors:* Hugo Award, 1970.

WRITINGS: The Chinese Doll, Rinehart, 1946; *To Keep or Kill*, Rinehart, 1947; *The Dove*, Rinehart, 1948; *The Stalking Man*, Rinehart, 1949; *Red Herring*, Rinehart, 1951; *The City in the Sea*, Rinehart, 1951; *The Long Loud Silence*, Rinehart, 1952; *The Time Masters*, Rinehart, 1953, revised edition, Lancer Books, 1972; *Wild Talent*, Rinehart, 1954; (compiler) *The Science Fiction Subtreasury*, Rinehart, 1954; *Time Bomb*, Rinehart, 1955; *The Man in My Grave*, Rinehart, 1956; *Hired Target*, Ace Books, 1957; *The Lincoln Hunters*, Rinehart, 1958; *To the Tombaugh Station*, Ace Books, 1960; *Last Stop*, Doubleday, 1963; *A Procession of the Damned*, Doubleday, 1965; *The Warlock*, Doubleday, 1967; *The Year of the Quiet Sun*, Ace Books, 1970; *This Witch*, Doubleday, 1971; *Ice and Iron*, Doubleday, 1974, revised edition, Ballantine, 1975. Contributor of short stories to magazines, sometimes under the pseudonym Bob Tucker. Editor and publisher, *Science Fiction News Letter*, 1945-53.

WORK IN PROGRESS: A novel, *King Gilgamesh*, completion expected in 1976; *The Coming Ice Age* (nonfiction), 1977; *On the Trail of Gilgamesh* (nonfiction).

AVOCATIONAL INTERESTS: Astronomy and archeology (has based several novels on one or the other).

BIOGRAPHICAL/CRITICAL SOURCES: In Search of Wonder, Advent, 1956; *The Science Fiction Novel*, Advent, 1959.

* * *

TULL, Charles Joseph 1931-

PERSONAL: Born August 28, 1931, in Runnemede N.J.; son of John James (a chemist, bookkeeper, and politician) and Anna (Paull) Tull; married Mildred Mary Banker, August 22, 1953; children: Charles R., Robert F., Mary B., Richard G. and John P. (twins), Barbara C. *Education:* Creighton University, B.S., 1955; University of Notre Dame, M.A., 1957; Ph.D., 1962. *Politics:* Liberal Democrat. *Religion:* Roman Catholic. *Home:* 118 Wakewa Ave., South Bend, Ind. 46617. *Office:* History Department, Indiana University, South Bend, Ind. 46615.

CAREER: St. Vincent College, Latrobe, Pa., instructor in history, 1959-61; De Paul University, Chicago, Ill., assistant professor of history, 1961-65; University of Notre Dame, Notre Dame, Ind., visiting assistant professor of history, 1965-66; University of Indiana, South Bend, associate professor, 1966-71, professor of history, 1971—, chairman of department, 1968-70. Visiting assistant professor, University of Indiana, Bloomington, 1966; visiting associate professor, University of Notre Dame, 1967-68. *Military service:* U.S. Air Force, 1951-55; became staff sergeant. *Member:* American Historical Association, American Catholic Historical Association, American Association of University Professors, Organization of American Historians, Southern Historical Association, Western Historical Association.

WRITINGS: Father Coughlin and the New Deal, Syracuse University Press, 1965; *American History Since 1865*, Barnes & Noble, 1968; (with Robert Burns and others) *Episodes in American History*, Ginn, 1973. Contributor to *Encyclopedia Americana* and *New International Encyclo-*

pedia. Contributor of articles and reviews to journals in his field.

WORK IN PROGRESS: A biography of Edward Hurley, chairman of the War Shipping Board in World War I.

SIDELIGHTS: Tull reads French, German, and Latin; earned B.S. while in Air Force by serving night shift at Weather Central, Strategic Air Command Headquarters, Omaha, for more than three years, and attending university classes during the day.

* * *

TULLY, Andrew (Frederick, Jr.) 1914-

PERSONAL: Born October 24, 1914, in Southbridge, Mass.; son of Andrew Frederick (an insurance broker) and Amelia (Mason) Tully; married Mary Dani, April 15, 1939 (divorced); married Barbara Witchell, September 5, 1960 (divorced); married Mary Ellen Wood (a research analyst), December 19, 1964; children: (first marriage) Martha Hardy Brown, Mary Elizabeth Tully Sterling, Sheila Dani Hamilton, Andrew Frederick III, Mark Matthew; (third marriage) John Spaulding. *Education:* Educated at public schools in Southbridge, Mass. *Politics:* Independent. *Religion:* "Anti-administration Catholic." *Home:* 2104 48th St. N.W., Washington, D.C. 20007. *Agent:* Harold Matson Co., Inc., 22 East 40th St., New York, N.Y., 10016.

CAREER: Reporter in Southbridge, Mass., 1933-36, and Worcester, Mass., 1936-39; *Southbridge Press* (weekly), Southbridge, Mass., owner and publisher, 1939-43; *Boston Traveler*, Boston, Mass., war correspondent in Europe, 1943-45; *New York World Telegram*, New York, N.Y., reporter, 1945-47; Scripps-Howard Newspapers, Washington Bureau, Washington, D.C., columnist, 1948-61; Washington columnist for Bell-McClure Syndicate, New York, 1961-69; columnist for McNaught Syndicate, New York, 1969—; freelance writer. *Member:* White House Correspondents Association, National Press Club, Overseas Press Club, National City Club (Washington). *Awards, honors:* Ernie Pyle Award and Headliners Award, 1956, both for newspaper series on Soviet Union.

WRITINGS: Era of Elegance, Funk, 1947; *Treasury Agent*, Simon & Schuster, 1958; *A Race of Rebels*, Simon & Schuster, 1960; *When They Burned the White House*, Simon & Schuster, 1961; *CIA: The Inside Story*, Morrow, 1962; *Capitol Hill*, Simon & Schuster, 1962; *Berlin: Story of a Battle*, Simon & Schuster, 1963; *Supreme Court*, Simon & Schuster, 1963; (with Milton Britten) *Where Did Your Money Go?*, Simon & Schuster, 1964; *The FBI's Most Famous Cases*, Morrow, 1965; *The Time of the Hawk*, Morrow, 1967; *White Tie and Dagger*, Morrow, 1967; *The Super Spies*, Morrow, 1969; *The Secret War Against Dope*, Coward, 1973; *The Brahmin Arrangement*, Coward, 1974.

BIOGRAPHICAL/CRITICAL SOURCES: National Observer, February 27, 1967; *Best Sellers*, March 15, 1967; *Saturday Review,* September 27, 1969.

* * *

TUPPER, Margo (Browne) 1919-

PERSONAL: Born February 7, 1919, in Arcadia, Fla.; daughter of Perry Cornelius (a judge) and Lessie (Williams) Browne; married Richard Waring Tupper (acting director of public relations, American Automobile Association), May 15, 1942 (died January 16, 1970); children: Jan (Mrs. John Cogley), Richard Landon. *Education:* Attended Florida

State College (now University), 1934-38, and studied journalism at Stetson University, 1939-40. *Politics:* Democrat. *Religion:* Presbyterian. *Home:* 7919 Kentbury Dr., Bethesda, Md. 20014. *Agent:* McIntosh & Otis, Inc., 18 East 41st St., New York, N.Y. 10017.

CAREER: Lake County Advertiser, Leesburg, Fla., publisher and editor, 1939; *Belle Glade Herald*, Belle Glade, Fla., editor, 1939-40; International News Service, reporter, in Washington, D.C., 1941, 1942; editor and reporter for Associated Press during World War II, but didn't return to full-time writing until 1961; began again as writer and researcher for "David Brinkley's Journal" (television), and has since sold to a number of magazines, specializing in teenage problems and conservation subjects. Actress, with roles in Washington area little theater productions, in two documentary films, and in two motion pictures, "Houseboat" and "Advise and Consent." *Awards, honors: Belle Glade Herald*, under her editorship, won several Florida state press prizes, including first place for local news.

WRITINGS: No Place to Play, Chilton, 1966. Contributor of articles to *Parade, Suburbia Today, Redbook, National Wildlife, Catholic Digest*, and other magazines.

WORK IN PROGRESS: A book; magazine articles.

SIDELIGHTS: Margo Tupper spent two full years researching for *No Place to Play*, which was published simultaneously in Canada and United States. *Avocational interests:* Gardening.

*   *   *

TURNER, A(lmon) Richard 1932-

PERSONAL: Born July 28, 1932, in New Bedford, Mass.; son of Louis Alexander (a physicist) and Margaret (Mather) Turner; married Jane Beebe, June 25, 1955; children: Louis Hamilton, David Alexander. *Education:* Princeton University, A.B., 1955, M.F.A., 1958, Ph.D., 1959. *Politics:* Democrat. *Religion:* Unitarian Universalist. *Home:* 131 Laurel Rd., Princeton, N.J. 08540. *Office:* Princeton University, Princeton, N.J. 08540.

CAREER: University of Michigan, Ann Arbor, instructor, 1959-60; Princeton University, Princeton, N.J., assistant professor, 1960-65, associate professor, 1966, professor of art history, 1967—. Democratic county committeeman. *Member:* College Art Association, Renaissance Society of America.

WRITINGS: The Vision of Landscape in Renaissance Italy, Princeton University Press for Princeton University Department of Art and Archaeology, 1966. Contributor to art journals.

WORK IN PROGRESS: Study on religious art in fifteenth-century Italy.

BIOGRAPHICAL/CRITICAL SOURCES: Times Literary Supplement, March 30, 1967; *Virginia Quarterly Review,* spring, 1967.†

*   *   *

TURNER, Arthur C(ampbell) 1918-

PERSONAL: Born May 19, 1918, in Glasgow, Scotland; became U.S. citizen, 1958; son of Malcolm (a journalist) and Robina Arthur (Miller) Turner; married Anne Gordzialkowska (a social worker), January 21, 1950; children: Nadine (Mrs. M. J. O'Sullivan). *Education:* University of Glasgow, M.A. (first class honors), 1941; Queen's College, Oxford, B.A. (first class honors), 1943, M.A., 1947, B.Litt,

1948; University of California, Berkeley, Ph.D., 1951. *Home:* 1992 Rincon Ave., Riverside, Calif. 92506. *Office:* Political Science Department, University of California, Riverside, Calif. 92502.

CAREER: University of Glasgow, Glasgow, Scotland, lecturer in history, 1945-51; University of Toronto, Toronto, Ontario, special lecturer, 1951-52, assistant professor of history, 1952-53; University of California, Riverside, associate professor, 1953-58, professor of political science 1958—, chairman of department of social sciences, 1953-61, chairman of political science department, 1963-66. Visiting professor at University of California, 1950, 1966, 1971, and Claremount Graduate School, 1962-72. *Member:* American Political Science Association, American Historical Association, Southern California Political Science Association, Rotary International (vice-president, Riverside, 1961-62). *Awards, honors:* Blackwell Prize (literary), University of Aberdeen, 1943, 1951; Commonwealth Fund fellowship, 1948; Rockefeller Foundation research grant, 1959; Social Science Research Council travel grant, 1964.

WRITINGS: The Post-War House of Commons: How Should It be Elected?, Craig & Wilson, 1942; *Free Speech and Broadcasting*, Basil Blackwell, 1943; *Mr. Buchan, Writer: A Life of the First Lord Tweedsmuir*, S.C.M. Press, 1949; *Scottish Home Rule*, Basil Blackwell, 1952; *Bulwark of the West: Implications and Problems of NATO*, Ryerson, for Canadian Institute of International Affairs, 1953; *Towards European Integration*, Bureau of Current Affairs, Canadian Department of National Defense, 1953; *Pakistan: The Impossible Made Real*, Bureau of Current Affairs, Canadian Department of National Defense, 1957; (contributor) *Control of Foreign Relations in Modern Nations*, Norton, 1957; (editor with Leonard Freedman) *Tension Areas in World Affairs*, Wadsworth, 1964; *The Unique Partnership: Britain and the United States*, Bobbs-Merrill, 1972. Contributor to *Encyclopedia Americana, Current History*, and to professional journals.

*   *   *

TURNER, Robert Kean, Jr. 1926-

PERSONAL: Born November 30, 1926, in Richmond, Va.; son of Robert Kean and Eunice (Henderson) Turner; married Janet Bridges, August 21, 1948; children: Robert Kean III, Janet Gascoyne, William John Gascoyne. *Education:* Virginia Military Institute, B.A., 1947; University of Virginia, M.A., 1949, Ph.D., 1958. *Religion:* Episcopalian. *Home:* 2101 East Olive St., Milwaukee, Wis. 53211.

CAREER: Virginia Military Institute, Lexington, instructor, 1957-58, assistant professor of English, 1958-62; University of Wisconsin, Milwaukee, associate professor of English, 1963-65, professor of English, 1965—, chairman of department, 1967-70. *Military service:* U.S. Navy, 1944-46, U.S. Naval Reserve, 1946-68. *Member:* Modern Language Association of America, Bibliographical Society (London), Bibliographical Society of University of Virginia, Malone Society. *Awards, honors:* Grants-in-aid from American Council of Learned Societies, 1958, and Southern Fellowship Fund, 1960.

WRITINGS: (With John G. Barrett) *Letters of a New Market Cadet*, University of North Carolina Press, 1961; (editor) Francis Beaumont and John Fletcher, *A King and No King*, University of Nebraska Press, 1963; (editor) Thomas Heywood, *The Fair Maid of the West*, University of Nebraska Press, 1967; (editor with E. W. Williams) *Henry VI, Parts II and III*, Pelican, 1969; (editor) *Romeo and Juliet*, Scott, Foresman, 1970. Also contributing editor to *The Dramatic Works in the Beaumont and Fletcher Canon*, Cambridge University Press, 1966—. Contributor of twenty bibliographical and critical studies, principally on Elizabethan and Jacobean drama, to *The Library, Studies in Bibliography*, and other professional periodicals.

WORK IN PROGRESS: A variorum edition of Shakespeare's "A Winter's Tale," in collaboration with Cyrus Hoy.

*   *   *

TURNER, Wallace 1921-

PERSONAL: Born March 15, 1921, in Titusville, Fla.; son of C. H. and Inabelle (Wallace) Turner; married Pearl Burk (a teacher), June 12, 1943; children: Kathleen J. (Mrs. Michael Delay), Elizabeth A. *Education:* University of Missouri, B.J., 1943; Harvard University, Nieman fellow, 1958-59. *Home:* 1608 McDonald Way, Burlington, Calif. 94010. *Office:* Fox Plaza, San Francisco, Calif. 94102.

CAREER: Springfield News, Springfield, Mo., reporter, 1943; *Portland Oregonian*, Portland, Ore., reporter, 1943-59; KPTV, Portland, Ore., news director, 1960-61; U.S. Department of Health, Education, and Welfare, Washington, D.C., assistant to secretary, 1961-62; *New York Times*, San Francisco bureau, correspondent, 1962-70, bureau chief, 1970—. *Member:* National Press Club (Washington, D.C.), San Francisco Press Club, Sigma Delta Chi. *Awards, honors:* Heywood Broun Award of American Newspaper Guild, 1952, 1957; Pulitzer Prize in journalism, 1957, for articles on racketeering of Teamsters Union officials.

WRITINGS: Gamblers' Money: The New Force in American Life, Houghton, 1965; *The Mormon Establishment*, Houghton, 1966.†

*   *   *

TUSSING, A(ubrey) Dale 1935-

PERSONAL: Surname is pronounced *Too*-sing; born February 8, 1935, in Grants Pass, Ore.; son of Rex (a newspaper editor) and Carolyn (Johnson) Tussing; married Ann Katharine Underhill, June 18, 1955; children: Katharine Lee, Karel Michele (daughter), Aaron Trevor, Nicholas John. *Education:* San Francisco State College (now University), A.B., 1956; Syracuse University, Ph.D., 1964. *Politics:* Independent left-wing. *Office:* Department of Economics, Syracuse University, Syracuse, N.Y. 13210.

CAREER: Syracuse University, Syracuse, N.Y., instructor, 1962-64; Washington State University, Pullman, assistant professor, 1964-66; Syracuse University, assistant professor, 1966-71, associate professor of economics and associate director of Educational Policy Research Center, 1971—. Member of New York State college proficiency exam committee, 1967—. Democratic party, district committeeman. Syracuse Congress of Racial Equality, member of executive committee. *Member:* American Economic Association, American Finance Association, Congress of Racial Equality, Students for a Democratic Society.

WRITINGS: (With Melvin A. Eggers) *Economic Processes: The Level of Economic Activity*, Holt, 1965; (with Eggers) *The Composition of Economic Activity*, Holt, 1965; *Poverty in a Dual Economy*, St. Martin's, 1974. Contributor of articles and notes to finance and economic journals.

WORK IN PROGRESS: Research on bank failure and on interest rate stabilization.†

TUVESON, Ernest (Lee) 1915-

PERSONAL: Born September 5, 1915, in La Grande, Ore.; son of Siegfred and Dorothy (Kirvan) Tuveson. *Education:* Reed College, B.A., 1934; University of Washington, Seattle, M.A., 1941; Columbia University, Ph.D., 1949. *Home:* 2601 College Ave., Berkeley, Calif.

CAREER: Brown University, Providence, R.I., instructor in English, 1946-48; University of California, Berkeley, 1948—, began as lecturer, associate professor, 1955-60, professor of English literature, 1960—. *Member:* Modern Language Association of America, American Studies Association. *Awards, honors:* Guggenheim fellowship, 1951-52; Folger Shakespeare Library fellowship, 1956.

WRITINGS: Millennium and Utopia: A Study in the Background of the Idea of Progress, University of California Press, 1949; *The Imagination as a Means of Grace: Locke and the Aesthetics of Romanticism*, University of California Press, 1960; (editor) *Swift: A Collection of Critical Essays*, Prentice-Hall, 1963; *Redeemer Nation: The Idea of America's Millennial Role*, University of Chicago Press, 1968.

WORK IN PROGRESS: A study of the influence of hermetist ideas on English and American writers, eighteenth and nineteenth centuries.

*   *   *

TYLER, Leona E(lizabeth) 1906-

PERSONAL: Born May 10, 1906, in Chetek, Wis.; daughter of Leon M. (a painting contractor) and Bessie J. (Carver) Tyler. *Education:* University of Minnesota, B.S., 1925, M.S., 1939, Ph.D., 1941. *Politics:* Democrat. *Religion:* Liberal Protestant. *Home:* 3565 Glen Oak Dr., Eugene, Ore. 97405. *Office:* Department of Psychology, University of Oregon, Eugene, Ore. 97403.

CAREER: Diplomate in counseling, American Board of Examiners in Professional Psychology. High school teacher in Mountain Iron, Minn., and Muskegon Heights, Mich., 1935-38; University of Oregon, Eugene, instructor in psychology, 1940-42, assistant professor, 1942-47, associate professor, 1947-55, professor of psychology, 1955-71, dean of Graduate School, 1965-71. Visiting professor at University of California, Berkeley, 1957-58, and, University of Amsterdam, 1962-63. *Member:* American Psychological Association (fellow; president, 1972-73), Western Psychological Association (secretary, 1953-56; president, 1957-58), Oregon Psychological Association (president, 1953-54).

WRITINGS: The Psychology of Human Differences, Appleton, 1947, 3rd enlarged edition, 1965; *The Work of the Counselor*, Appleton, 1953, 3rd edition, 1969; (contributor) *Manual of Child Psychology*, Wiley, 1954; (with Florence Goodenough) *Developmental Psychology*, Appleton, 1959; (with Norman D. Sundberg) *Clinical Psychology: An Introduction to Research and Practice*, Appleton, 1962, revised edition (with Norman D. Sundberg and Julian Taplin) published as *Clinical Psychology: Expanding Horizons*, 1973; *Tests and Measurements*, Prentice-Hall, 1963, revised edition, 1971; (contributor) *Man in the World at Work*, Houghton, 1964; (contributor) *The Professional Preparation of Counseling Psychologists*, edited by A. S. Thompson and D. H. Super, Teachers College, Columbia University, 1964; (editor) *Intelligence: Some Recurring Issues*, Van Nostrand, 1969; *Individual Differences: Abilities and Motivational Directions*, Prentice-Hall, 1974.

Contributor to "Minnesota Studies in Student Personnel

Work," University of Minnesota Press, 1961; to *Proceedings* of the American Psychological Association; and about fifty articles to professional journals. Associate editor, *Journal of Counseling Psychology*, 1954-66; consulting editor, *Personnel and Guidance*, 1956-62.

WORK IN PROGRESS: Research on choice and values.

AVOCATIONAL INTERESTS: Playing piano.

*   *   *

UITTI, Karl David 1933-

PERSONAL: Born December 10, 1933, in Calumet, Mich.; son of Karl A. (a printer) and Joy G. (Weidelman) Uitti; married Maria E. Clark Alvarez (a librarian), January, 1953; children: Maria Elisabeth, Karl Gerard. *Education:* University of California, Berkeley, B.A. and M.A., 1952, Ph.D., 1959; University of Nancy, graduate study, 1952-53. *Politics:* Independent. *Religion:* Lutheran. *Home:* 125 Bayard Lane, Princeton, N.J. 08540. *Office:* Department of Romance Languages, Princeton University, Princeton, N.J. 08540.

CAREER: Princeton University, Princeton, N.J., instructor, 1959-61, assistant professor, 1961-65, associate professor, 1965-68, professor of Romance languages and literature, 1968—, preceptor, 1963—, chairman of department of Romance languages, 1973—. Visiting professor at University of Puerto Rico, summers, 1961, 1963, 1965, 1971, Queens College (now Queens College of the City University of New York), Flushing, N.Y., 1964, University of Pennsylvania, 1966, University of Washington, summer, 1967, University of Iowa, summer, 1968, Ecole Normale Superieure, spring, 1969, University of Warwick, winter, 1972, University of California, Los Angeles, summer, 1973. *Military service:* U.S. Army, 1954-56. *Member:* Modern Language Association of America, Linguistic Society of America, Societe des Professeurs Francais en Amerique, Medieval Academy, Dante Society, Comparative Literature Association, Phi Beta Kappa. *Awards, honors:* Guggenheim fellow, 1963-64.

WRITINGS: The Concept of Self in the Symbolist Novel, Mouton & Co., 1961; *La Passion litteraire de Remy de Gourmont*, P.U.F., 1962; *Linguistics and Literary Theory*, Prentice-Hall, 1969; *Story, Myth, and Celebration in Old French Narrative*, Princeton University Press, 1973. Contributor to professional journals. Assistant editor, *Romance Philology*, 1970—.

SIDELIGHTS: Uitti told *CA* that he is interested in the cultures of the Caribbean, especially of Puerto Rico. *Avocational interests:* Travel.†

*   *   *

ULANOFF, Stanley M(elvin) 1922-

PERSONAL: Surname is pronounced *You*-la-noff; born May 30, 1922, in Brooklyn, N.Y.; son of Samuel H. (a stockbroker) and Minnie (Druss) Ulanoff; married Bernice Mayer (an interior decorator), June 15, 1947; children: Roger, Amy, Lisa, Dory. *Education:* University of Iowa, B.A., 1943; Hofstra College (now University), M.B.A., 1955; New York University, Ph.D., 1968. *Office:* 17 The Serpentine, Roslyn, N.Y. 11576.

CAREER: Advertising account executive and copywriter for *New York Times*, 1946-49; marketing and public relations consultant to industry, and free-lance writer, 1951—; State University of New York, Stony Brook, assistant to the president, 1962-65; C. W. Post College of Long Island

University, Greenvale, N.Y., assistant professor of business administration, 1962-64; Kingsborough Community College of the City University of New York, Brooklyn, N.Y., associate professor of business, 1964-65; Bernard M. Baruch College of the City University of New York, New York, N.Y., associate professor of marketing, 1965—. Marketing consultant and researcher. *Military service:* U.S. Army, Infantry and Intelligence, 1943-46; served in Europe. U.S. Army Reserve, 1946—, lieutenant colonel, and training officer. *Member:* American College Public Relations Association, American Association of University Professors, Direct Mail Advertising Association (education committee), Military Government Association, Military Intelligence Reserve Society, Reserve Officers Association, Sigma Delta Chi.

WRITINGS: Illustrated Guide to U.S. Missiles and Rockets, Doubleday, 1959, revised edition, 1962; (editor) *Fighter Pilot*, Doubleday, 1962; *MATS—The Story of the Military Air Transport Service*, F. Watts, 1964; *Winged Warfare*, Doubleday, 1967; *Ace of Aces*, Doubleday, 1967; *Fighting Airman–The Way of the Eagle*, Doubleday, 1968. *Flying Fury*, Doubleday, 1968; *Wind in the Wires*, Doubleday, 1968; *Bombs Away*, Doubleday, 1969; *Illustrated History of World War I in the Air*, Arco, 1971; *Advertising Today*, Hastings House, 1975. Contributor of articles and reviews to *New York Times* and magazines.

SIDELIGHTS: Stanley Vlanoff speaks Spanish and French. *Avocational interests:* Travel, skiing, model-aircraft building, collecting military equipment and military miniatures.

*   *   *

ULLMANN, John E(manuel) 1923-

PERSONAL: Born December 25, 1923, in Vienna, Austria; came to United States, 1948, naturalized, 1954; son of Ernest and Anna (Honigsfeld) Ullmann; married Eva Gruenwald (an art teacher and university lecturer), August 30, 1953; children: James Ernest, Catherine Jenny. *Education:* University of London, B.Sc. in Engineering (honors), 1948; Columbia University, M.S., 1951, Ph.D., 1959. *Home:* 2518 Norwood Ave., North Bellmore, N.Y. 11712. *Office:* Hofstra University, Hempstead, N.Y. 11550.

CAREER: Plant engineer in England, 1941-48, with Worthington Corp., Harrison, N.J., 1948-50; assistant project engineer, Ford, Bacon & Davis, Inc., New York, N.Y., 1950-51, Bechtel Corp., New York, N.Y., 1951-53; licensed as professional engineer, New York State, 1953; Bulova Research & Development Laboratories, Inc., Woodside, N.Y., planning engineer, 1954-57; Columbia University, New York, N.Y., lecturer in industrial engineering, 1957-58; Stevens Institute of Technology, Hoboken, N.J., assistant professor of economics of engineering, 1958-61; Hofstra University, Hempstead, N.Y., professor of management, 1961—, chairman of department of management, marketing, and business statistics, 1961-73. Visiting summer professor, New York University, Graduate School of Business Administration, 1959. Consultant to public bodies and to industiral firms, 1953—. *Member:* New York Academy of Sciences.

WRITINGS: (Editor) *Conversion Prospects of the Defense Electronics Industry*, Hofstra University School of Business, 1965; (editor) *Innovation Policies of Selected Manufacturing Industries*, Hofstra University School of Business, Volume I, 1967, Volume II, 1974; (with S. E. Gluck) *Integrated Manufacturing*, Holt, 1969; (editor)

Waste Disposal Problems in Selected Industries, Hofstra University School of Business, 1969; *Civilian Markets for the Military Electronics Industry*, Praeger, 1971; *Quantitative Methods for Business Decisions*, McGraw, 1975.

Contributor: S. Melman, editor, *No Place to Hide*, Grove, 1962; *Passenger Car Design and Highway Safety*, Consumers Union, 1962; E. J. Henley and H. Kouts, editors, *Advances in Nuclear Science and Engineering*, Academic Press, 1962; S. Melman, editor, *A Strategy for American Security*, Lee Service, 1963; R. Gross and P. Osterman, editors. *The New Professionals*, Simon & Schuster, 1972. Author of monographs on glass manufacture and leather tannery prepared for International Cooperation Administration, 1959-60, and other monographs on community problems. Contributor of articles on industrial planning, national security, and product development to *Science, American Journal of Orthopsychiatry, War/Peace Report, Engineering Economist*, and other journals.

WORK IN PROGRESS: Editing *The Expensive Sprawl: Resource Use and the Growth of Suburbia.*

SIDELIGHTS: John Ullmann writes: "The titles of my writings, whether on peace, business, engineering, or economics, sound technical, but in all of them there is the common question: How can we survive with dignity, compassion and comfort and without despoiling the earth even more?"

*   *   *

ULLMANN, Leonard P(aul) 1930-

PERSONAL: Born May 28, 1930, in New York, N.Y.; son of Siegfried (an importer-exporter) and Irma (Lichtenstadter) Ullmann; married Rina Kalb, June 5, 1951 (divorced, 1972); children: Jeremy Michael, Nancy Leigh. *Education:* Lafayette College, A.B. (magna cum laude), 1951; Stanford University, A.M., 1953, Ph.D., 1955. *Home:* 2825 South King St., Honolulu, Hawaii 96814. *Office:* Psychology Department, University of Hawaii, Honolulu, Hawaii 96822.

CAREER: U.S. Veterans Administration, clinical psychology trainee, 1952-56; Veterans Administration Hospital, Palo Alto, Calif., coordinator of psychiatric evaluation project, 1956-63; San Jose State College (now University), San Jose, Calif., assistant professor of psychology, 1958-63; University of Illinois, Urbana, visiting associate professor, 1963, associate professor, 1964, professor of psychology, 1966-72; University of Hawaii, Honolulu, professor of psychology, 1972—. *Member:* American Psychological Association, American Association for the Advancement of Science, Society for Research in Child Development, Association for Advancement of Behavior Therapy, American Association of University Professors, Phi Beta Kappa, Sigma Xi.

WRITINGS: (With Leonard Krasner) *Research in Behavior Modification*, Holt, 1965; (with Krasner) *Case Studies in Behavior Modification*, Holt, 1965; *Institution and Outcome: A comparative Study of Psychiatric Hospitals*, Pergamon, 1967; (with Krasner) *A Psychological Approach to Abnormal Behavior*, Prentice-Hall, 1969, 2nd edition, 1975; (with Krasner) *Behavior Influence and Personality*, Holt, 1971. Contributor to psychology and medical journals.

WORK IN PROGRESS: Books on abnormal psychology and the psychology of behavior influence.

UNDERWOOD, John Weeden 1932-

PERSONAL: Born September 27, 1932; son of Weeden Benjamin (an electrical engineer) and Mary (Young) Underwood; married Mary Jane Callahan (a teacher in Los Angeles public schools), May 22, 1965. *Education:* Attended Glendale College and University of California, Los Angeles. *Politics:* Republican. *Home:* 2054 West Mountain, Glendale, Calif. 91201.

CAREER: Lightplane Review, Glendale, Calif., editor and publisher, 1959-62; Underwood, Collinge & Associates, Glendale, Calif., partner, 1962—; Clymer Publications, Los Angeles, Calif., editor, 1963-64; Heritage Press, North Hollywood, Calif., writer and editor, 1965—; full-time free-lance writer, 1966—. Acting technical editor, *Private Pilot* (magazine), 1965-67; correspondent for *Flight-International*, London, England, and *Flug-Revue*, Stuttgart, Germany. *Military service:* U.S. Army, pilot, 1953-56. *Member:* Aircraft Owners and Pilots Association, American Aviation Historical Society.

WRITINGS—All published by Heritage Press, except as noted: *Famous Racing Aircraft*, Clymer Publications, 1952; (with J. W. Caler) *Lightplane and Midget Racers*, Aero, 1956; *The World's Aircraft*, Aero, 1958; *Whatever Became of the Baby Austin?*, 1965; *The Stinsons*, 1968; *Acrobats in the Sky*, 1972; *Of Monocoupes and Men*, 1974; *The Vintage and Veteran Aircraft Guide*, 1974; *The Lightplane Since 1909*, 1975.

WORK IN PROGRESS: Biographies of G. M. Bellanca and Willy Messerschmitt; picture documentaries on air transportation, women in aerospace, high-speed aircraft for racing and research, and history of aviation in California; also working on children's books with his wife.

SIDELIGHTS: Underwood wrote: "Intensely interested in Latin America and in the history of transportation, mainly auto and air." He speaks Spanish.

*   *   *

UNGER, Hans 1915-

PERSONAL: Born August 8, 1915, in Germany; now British subject; son of Herrmann and Margarete Unger. *Education:* Attended grammar school in Berlin, Germany, and studied poster design in private studio, Berlin, 1934-35. *Home and office:* 15 Muswell Hill Rd., London N. 10, England.

CAREER: Left Germany for South Africa, 1936, and worked as free-lance commercial designer in Captown, 1936-39, 1945-48; free-lance graphic artist, mosaicist, and designer of stained glass windows, London, England, 1948—, probably most widely known for posters for London Transport. Recently completed three large scale mosaic murals in England and Wales. *Military service:* South African Army, Artillery, World War II; received Military Medal (Great Britain). Served in African campaigns; captured by Germans, 1942, and held prisoner of war in Italy, 1942-43; escaped via France to England, 1944. *Member:* Society of Industrial Artists and Designers (fellow). *Awards, honors:* Awards for poster designs.

WRITINGS: Practical Mosaics, Studio Publications (New York), 1965.

SIDELIGHTS: Hans Unger visited Uganda in 1958, made six-month cycling and sketching trip through Europe to Turkey, 1959, and has traveled extensively in Italy, Greece, Turkey, and Israel to study Byzantine and Roman mosaics. He is competent in German and Italian.

UNTERECKER, John 1922-

PERSONAL: First syllable of surname rhymes with "hunt"; born December 14, 1922, in Buffalo, N.Y.; son of John George (a confectioner) and Bertha (Ellinger) Unterecker; married Ann Apalian (a flutist and ethnomusicologist), February 28, 1952 (divorced, 1973). *Education:* Middlebury College, B.A., 1944; Columbia University, M.A., 1948, Ph.D., 1956. *Office:* Department of English, University of Hawaii, 1733 Donaghho Rd., Honolulu, Hawaii 96822.

CAREER: Radio Station WBNY, Buffalo, N.Y., announcer, 1944-45; U.S. Office of War Information, New York, N.Y., researcher, 1945-46; City College (now City College of the City University of New York), New York, N.Y., instructor in English, 1946-58; Columbia University, New York, N.Y., assistant professor, 1958-61, associate professor, 1961-66, professor of English, 1966-74; University of Hawaii, Honolulu, professor of English, 1974—. Visiting professor, University of Hawaii, 1969, University of Texas, 1974; lecturer, Yeats International Summer School, 1972-75. Part-time actor in radio, television, and the theater, 1942-54. Consultant and participant in poetry programs for commercial and educational radio and television, 1960—. *Member:* Modern Language Association of America, American Association of University Professors, American Committee for Irish Studies, American Gloxinia and Gesneriad Society, P.E.N., Writers Guild. *Awards, honors:* Grants from American Philosophical Society, 1962, American Council of Learned Societies, 1962, 1972, Council for Research in the Humanities, 1963; Guggenheim fellowship to Ireland and France, 1964-65; Yaddo fellowship, summer, 1969-72, 1974; National Book Award nomination, 1970, Van Amringe Award, 1970, Ohioana Book Award, 1971, all for *Voyager: A Life of Hart Crane.*

WRITINGS: A Reader's Guide to W. B. Yeats, Noonday, 1959; (editor and author of introduction) *Yeats: A Collection of Critical Essays,* Prentice-Hall, 1963; *Lawrence Durrell,* Columbia University Press, 1964; *The Dreaming Zoo* (juvenile), Walck, 1965; (editor and author of introduction) *Approaches to the Twentieth-Century Novel,* Crowell, 1965; (editor) *W. B. Yeats and Patrick McCartan: A Fenian Friendship,* Dolmen Press, 1967; *Voyager: A Life of Hart Crane,* Farrar, Strauss, 1969; *Dance Sequence* (poems), Kayak, 1975; (editor with Kathleen McGrory) *Yeats, Beckett and Joyce: A Modern Critical Spectrum,* Bucknell University Press, 1975. Editor, "Introductions to Modern American Poetry" series, Columbia University Press. Contributor to *Encyclopedia Americana Yearbook;* contributor of poems, essays, and reviews to *Shenandoah, Saturday Review, Sewanee Review, New York Times Book Review, New Leader, Yale Review, Poetry, Poetry Northwest, New Yorker, American Scholar,* and other journals.

WORK IN PROGRESS: Two books of poetry, *Stone,* for Dolmen Press, and *The Persons and the Objects in the Room;* a book on the plays of W. B. Yeats, for Dolmen Press; a book of photographs and interviews with members of the New York City Ballet, *Ballet Backstage.*

SIDELIGHTS: Critical discussion about *Voyager: A Life of Hart Crane* includes Alan Trachtenberg's assessment: "Unterecker bestows upon the poet a *presence* rare in literary biographies. . . . Unterecker's book is enormously valuable for its sensitive chronical of the conditions out of which Crane's poems emerged . . . its high virtue is that it shows the material, the contradictory 'I' out of which the lyric voice is made." Robert Emmet Long notes that the book "is an immense and powerful recreation of Crane's career, and the most considerable biography of a 20th-century literary figure since Richard Ellmann's 'James Joyce.'" Commentary on the amount of detail encompassed within the biography includes Brom Weber's belief that the "failure of this book . . . seems to be due to an excess of critical tact and a regrettable belief that the biographer's task is merely the accumulation and stringing-together of the verifiable details of another's life." Joel Conarroe, however, counters the charge that "the author has not been discriminating in his selection of material" with the assertion that "the research was painstaking and fruitful . . . the book still gives the illusion of telling all there is to tell, and then some. This in itself is hardly a flaw." Similarly, Conarroe believes that Unterecker has not "left largely uninterpreted the huge mass of information he has unearthed," but instead "lets the reader uncover for himself the various revealing patterns" and "interpret according to his own understanding."

Unterecker told *CA* that although he feels *Voyager: A Life of Hart Crane* is "a useful book in that it attempted both to present a full-length portrait of Hart Crane and to suggest something of the complex structure of any human personality," he considers his best work to be his poetry. He explained that he writes "to effect some sort of a communion—what Buber calls 'dialogue'—between myself and the reader." He believes that every poem "contains a privacy, but it's a privacy that can be shared." Though "not confessional," his own poetry, he feels, "draws on this privacy as a source for its energy and transmits to the reader a sense of shared intimacy; at its best, poetry of the sort that I write is—like the rest of my life—an ongoing love affair."

BIOGRAPHICAL/CRITICAL SOURCES: Voyages, Volume IV, winter, 1971.

* * *

UPTON, Anthony F. 1929-

PERSONAL: Born October 13, 1929, in Stockton Heath, England; son of Charles Alfred (a civil servant) and Sylvia (Macarthy) Upton; married Sirkka Pollanen, August 12, 1951; children: Nicholas, Timothy, Jeremy. *Education:* Queen's College, Oxford, B.A., 1951, M.A., 1955; Pembroke College, Cambridge, Diploma in Education, 1952; Duke University, A.M., 1953. *Politics:* Socialist. *Religion:* None. *Home:* 5 West Acres, St. Andrews, Fife, Scotland. *Office:* Department of Modern History, St. Salvator's College, St. Andrews, Scotland.

CAREER: University of Leeds, Leeds, England, assistant lecturer, 1953-56; University of St. Andrews, St. Andrews, Scotland, lecturer, 1956-66, senior lecturer, 1966-74, reader in modern history, 1974—. St. Andrews Labour party, chairman, 1964—. *Member:* Royal Historical Society (fellow).

WRITINGS: Sir Arthur Ingram: A Study in the Origins of an English Landed Family, Oxford University Press, 1961; *Finland in Crisis: A Study in Small-Power Politics,* Faber, 1964, Cornell University Press, 1965 (translator with wife, Sirkka Upton, of Finnish edition published as *Valirauha,* Kirjayhtyma, 1965); *The Communist Parties of Scandinavia and Finland,* Doubleday, 1973 (translator with Sirkka Upton of Finnish edition published as *Kommunismi Suomessa,* Kirjayhtyma, c. 1973); *Finland, 1939-40,* Davis Poynter, 1974. Contributor to periodicals.

WORK IN PROGRESS: A history of the Finnish Civil

War of 1918; further research on the origins of the seventeenth-century revolution in England.

SIDELIGHTS: Upton has working knowledge of Finnish, French, German, Russian, and Swedish.

* * *

URIS, Auren 1913-
(Auren Paul)

PERSONAL: Born November 18, 1913, in New York, N.Y.; son of Abraham (a builder) and Lena (Jacobson) Uris; married Bette Turner (a journalist), February 21, 1949; children: Mary, Victoria, Bettina, Daniel. *Education:* New School for Social Research, B.A., 1963. *Home:* 277 River Rd., Grandview, Nyack, N.Y. 10960. *Agent:* Mrs. Carolyn Willyoung Stagg, 15 East 48th St., New York, N.Y. 10017.

CAREER: Early work included owner-manager of custom molding shop and member of management staff of Plastics Division, Celanese Corp. of America; Research Institute of America, New York, N.Y., editor, 1947—. Lecturer on management, executive methods, and interpersonal relations in business. Wood sculptor, exhibiting at several one-man shows.

WRITINGS: Improved Foremanship, Macmillan, 1948; *Working with People*, Macmillan, 1949; *How to Be a Successful Leader*, McGraw, 1951, published as *Techniques of Leadership*, 1964; *Developing Your Executive Skills*, McGraw, 1955; *The Efficient Executive*, McGraw, 1957; *Discover Your Inner Self*, McGraw, 1959; *The Manager's Job*, Lincoln Extension Institute, 1962; *The Management Makers*, Macmillan, 1962; (under pseudonym Auren Paul) *The Love Machine* (fiction), Camerarts Publishing, 1962; *Mastery of People*, Prentice-Hall, 1964; *The Executive Job Market*, McGraw, 1965, published as *Action Guide for Job Seekers and Employees*, 1968; *Executive Breakthrough: Twenty-One Roads to the Top*, Doubleday, 1967; *Turn Your Job Into a Successful Career*, Simon & Schuster, 1967; *Keeping Young in Business*, McGraw, 1967; *Mastery of Management*, Dow Jones-Irwin, 1968; *Strategy of Success*, Macmillan, 1969; *The Executive Deskbook*, Van Nostrand, 1970; (with M. Noppel) *The Turned-On Executive: Building Your Skills for Management Revolution*, McGraw, 1970; *The Frustrated Titan: Emasculation of the Executive*, Van Nostrand, 1972; (with Jack Tarrant) *How to Win Your Boss's Love, Approval, and Job*, Van Nostrand, 1973; *Thank God It's Monday*, Crowell, 1974; *Memos for Managers*, Crowell, 1975; *Duns Book of Business Etiquette*, Crowell, in press. Author of weekly feature, "You and Your Job." Contributor to *Nation's Business, Coronet, Pageant, Chemical Engineering*, and other technical and business journals.

SIDELIGHTS: Several of Uris's books have been published in German, Japanese, Dutch, Arabic, and Portuguese editions. *Avocational interests:* Sailing, jewelry making and designing, oil painting.

* * *

USRY, Milton F. 1931-

PERSONAL: Born August 31, 1931, in Mineola, Tex.; son of Milton F. and Luciel (Weaver) Usry; married Dona White, November 25, 1951; children: Milton Wayne, Mark Lester. *Education:* Baylor University, B.B.A., 1952; University of Houston, M.B.A., 1959; University of Texas, Ph.D., 1964. *Religion:* Baptist. *Home:* 1015 West Knapp,

Stillwater, Okla. *Office:* College of Business Administration, Oklahoma State University, Stillwater, Okla.

CAREER: Shell Chemical Co., Houston, Tex., cost accountant, 1955-59; University of Houston, Houston, Tex., assistant professor of accounting, 1959-61; Oklahoma State University, Stillwater, 1961—, began as assistant professor, professor of accounting, 1965-72, regent's professor, 1972—. *Military service:* U.S. Army, 1952-54. *Member:* American Accounting Association, American Institute of Certified Public Accountants, National Association of Accountants, Oklahoma Society of Certified Public Accountants, Beta Gamma Sigma, Beta Alpha Psi.

WRITINGS: Capital Expenditure Planning and Control, Bureau of Business Research, University of Texas, 1966; (consulting editor) *Cost Accounting: Planning and Control*, South-Western Publishing, 1967.

* * *

VAIL, Robert William 1921-

PERSONAL: Born October 29, 1921, in Columbus, Ohio; son of Robert David (an artist) and Dorothy (Mosier) Vail; married Martha Henderson (a banker), April 7, 1939; children: William N., Veronica (Mrs. David Fish), David A., Ashley M., Victor, Lorelei, Hilary W. *Education:* Ohio State University, student, 1938-39. *Religion:* Protestant. *Home:* R.D. 1, Burton, Ohio 44021.

CAREER: Barnebey-Cheney Engineering Co., Columbus, Ohio, research chemist, 1941-44; Koppers Co., Petrolia, Pa., senior chemist, 1944-49; insurance agent in Butler, Pa., 1949-51; Carborundum Co., Niagara Falls, N.Y., research and development engineer, 1951-55; Allied Chemical Corp., New York, N.Y., in technical sales, 1955-60; U.S. Ceramic Tile Co., Canton, Ohio, research laboratory director, 1960-62; Ferro Corp., Cleveland, Ohio, technical sales engineer, 1962—. *Military service:* U.S. Naval Reserve, 1944. *Member:* American Chemical Society, Masonic Blue Lodge (member of chapter and council), Geauga Lyric Theater Guild.

WRITINGS: Teardrops Falling (poetry), Golden Quill, 1963. Contributor of articles to *Profitable Hobbies, Ford Times, Church Management;* contributor to poetry journals.

WORK IN PROGRESS: Two novels, *The Unwanted* and *Star Point; Flight into Tomorrow*, about the Ukrainian underground army; a book of poetry.

SIDELIGHTS: Vail speaks French, Spanish, and German. *Avocational interests:* Operating amateur radio station K8AQS; handball, magic, hypnotism, contesting, chess, acting and directing in little theater, fishing, hunting.†

* * *

VALENTINE, Foy (Dan) 1923-

PERSONAL: Born July 3, 1923, in Edgewood, Tex.; son of John Hardy and Josie Helen (Johnson) Valentine; married Mary Louise Valentine, May 6, 1947; children: Jean, Carol, Susan. *Education:* Baylor University, B.A., 1944; Southwestern Baptist Theological Seminary, Th.M., 1947, Th.D., 1949. *Politics:* Democrat. *Home:* 6354 Torrington Rd., Nashville, Tenn. 37205.

CAREER: Baptist clergyman, holding pastorate in Gonzales, Tex., 1950-53; Texas Baptist Christian Life Commission, director, 1953-60; Southern Baptist Convention,

Nashville, Tenn., executive secretary and treasurer of Christian Life Commission, 1960—. *Awards, honors:* D.D., William Jewell College, 1966; distinguished alumnus award from Southern Baptist Theological Seminary, 1970.

WRITINGS: (Editor) *Christian Faith in Action*, Broadman, 1956; *Believe and Behave*, Broadman, 1964; *Citizenship for Christians*, Broadman, 1965; *The Cross in the Marketplace*, Word Books, 1966; (editor) *Peace! Peace!*, Word Books, 1967; *Where the Action Is: Studies in James*, Word Books, 1969.

* * *

VALETT, Robert E. 1927-

PERSONAL: Born November 22, 1927, in Clinton, Iowa; son of Edward John (a pipefitter) and Myrtle (Petersen) Valett; married Shirley Bellman, July 8, 1950; children: Steven, Eric, Pamela, John, Lawrence. *Edcuation:* University of Iowa, student, 1946-48; George Williams College, B.S., 1949; University of Chicago, M.A., 1951; University of California, Los Angeles, Ed.D., 1957. *Politics:* Democrat. *Religion:* Unitarian Universalist. *Home:* 2617 West Bullard, Fresno, Calif. 93705.

CAREER: Orange Coast College, Costa Mesa, Calif., psychology instructor and counselor, 1955-58; Garden Grove (Calif.) elementary schools, coordinator of guidance and special education, 1958-63; Sacramento (Calif.) city schools, director of special education and school psychologist, 1963-70; California State University, Fresno, professor, 1970—. Visiting lecturer in clinical psychology, University of Canterbury, Christchurch, New Zealand, 1961-62. Consulting psychologist. *Military service:* U.S. Navy, 1945. *Member:* American Psychological Association, California State Psychological Association, California Association of School Psychologists and Psychometrists.

WRITINGS—All published by Fearon, except as noted: *The Practice of School Psychology: Professional Problems*, Wiley, 1963; *The Remediation of Learning Disabilities: A Handbook of Psychoeducational Resource Programs*, 1967, 2nd edition, 1974; *Programming Learning Disabilities*, 1969; *Modifying Children's Behavior: A Guide for Parents and Professionals*, 1969; *Prescriptions for Learning: A Parents' Guide to Remedial Home Training*, 1970; *Effective Teaching: A Guide to Diagnostic-Prescriptive Task Analysis*, 1970; *Sex and TLC*, 1973; *Learning Disabilities: Diagnostic-Prescriptive Instruments*, 1973; *Affective-Humanistic Education: Goals, Programs, and Learning Activities*, 1974; *The Psychoeducational Treatment of Hyperactive Children*, 1974; *Self-Actualization*, Argus Communications, 1974. Also author of clinical profile manuals, workbooks, and evaluation forms.

WORK IN PROGRESS: A series of twelve one-hour tape recordings for specific learning disabilities and humanistic education.

AVOCATIONAL INTERESTS: Furthering international goodwill through youth friendship tours; fishing, camping, tennis.

* * *

VALLEE, Jacques F. 1939-

PERSONAL: Born September 24, 1939, in Pontoise, France; married Janine Saley (engaged in psychological research), October 20, 1960; children: Larry Olivier. *Education:* Attended Sorbonne, University of Paris, 1957-59; University of Lille, Licence es Sciences and M.S., 1961.

CAREER: French Committee for Space Studies, Paris, France, research scientist, 1961-62; Thompson-Houston Co. (French branch), Paris, research engineer, 1962; University of Texas and McDonald Observatory, Austin, research associate, 1962-63; Mars Map Project (sponsored in part by General Dynamics/Astronautics), Texas computer consultant, 1962-65; Northwestern University, Technological Institute, Evanston, Ill., mathematician-analyst, beginning 1963. *Member:* American Mathematical Society, Alpha Pi Mu.

WRITINGS: Anatomy of a Phenomenon: Unidentified Objects in Space—A Scientific Appraisal, Regnery, 1965; (with wife, Janine Vallee) *Les Phenomenes insolites de l'espace: Le Dosier des mysterieux objets celestes,* La Table Ronde (Paris), 1966; (with Janine Vallee) *Challenge to Science: The UFO Enigma,* Regnery, 1966; *Passport to Magonia: From Folklore to Flying Saucers,* Regnery, 1969. Co-author of classified report on the Palmier G Antenna, 1962; contributor to *L'Astronomie.*

WORK IN PROGRESS: Research on the theory of self-optimizing and self-organizing systems and its application to the field of high-speed information retrieval.†

* * *

VANDE KIEFT, Ruth Marguerite 1925-

PERSONAL: Born September 12, 1925, in Holland, Mich.; daughter of John Martin (a clergyman) and Cornelia (Bogard) Vande Kieft. *Education:* Meredith College, B.A., 1946; University of Michigan, M.A., 1947, Ph.D., 1957; Oxford University, graduate study, 1953-54. *Politics:* Democrat. *Home:* 320 East 23rd St., New York, N.Y. 10010. *Office:* English Department, Queens College of the City University of New York, Flushing, N.Y. 11367.

CAREER: Calvin College, Grand Rapids, Mich., instructor in English, 1947-50; Wellesley College, Wellesley, Mass., instructor in English, 1956-59; Fairleigh Dickinson University, Madison, N.J., assistant professor of English, 1959-60; Queens College of the City University of New York, Flushing, N.Y., instructor, 1961-62, assistant professor, 1962-68, associate professor, professor of English, 1974—. *Member:* Modern Language Association of America, Society of Biblical Literature, Society for the Study of Southern Literature. *Awards, honors:* American Association of University Women fellowship, 1960-61; Yaddo fellowship, 1961.

WRITINGS: Eudora Welty, Twayne, 1962. Contributor of articles and reviews to *Sewanee Review, Nineteenth-Century Fiction, Georgia Review, College English, Southern Review,* and *Nation.* Abstractor.

WORK IN PROGRESS: A project involving literary analysis of the Bible; studies in Southern literature.

AVOCATIONAL INTERESTS: Music, photography.

* * *

van den HEUVEL, Albert H(endrik) 1932-

PERSONAL: Born March 24, 1932, in Utrecht, Netherlands: son of Hendrik (a civil servant) and Dirkje (Goudkuil) van den Heuvel; married Johanna Kramer, May 17, 1958; children: Hanna, Hendrik, Catherina. *Education:* Studied theology at State University of Utrecht, 1950-55, and Union Theological Seminary, New York, N.Y., 1956-57. *Politics:* Socialist. *Home:* Van Aerssenstraat 300, The Hague, Netherlands. *Office:* The Synod, Carngielaang, The Hague, Netherlands.

CAREER: National Council of Churches in the Netherlands, Utrecht, executive youth secretary, 1958-60; World Council of Churches, Youth Department, Geneva, Switzerland, assistant secretary, 1960-64, executive secretary, 1964-67, director of communications, 1967-72; Netherlands' Reformed Church, The Hague, general secretary, 1972—. Clergyman, Netherlands' Reformed Church.

WRITINGS: Gesprek over de Oecumene, Boekencentrum (The Hague), 1960; Aanbidding van de Status Quo, Dutch S.C.M. Press (Zeist), 1962; These Rebellious Powers, Friendship, 1965; (editor) The New Creation and the New Generation, Friendship, 1965; The Humiliation of the Church, Westminster, 1966; Meet the Man, Friendship, 1966; You Are Hiding God From Me, Fortress, 1967; Een nieuw Zendingstyd perk?, Kok (Kampen, Netherlands) 1972. Author of play, "Koning David."

WORK IN PROGRESS: Two books, one on the dialogue of world faiths and the other on modern church leadership.

SIDELIGHTS: These Rebelious Powers was translated into Spanish and Swedish, and You Are Hiding God From Me is being translated into German and Dutch. Van den Heuvel is competent in Dutch, English, German, and French. Avocational interests: Travel (has been on all continents), the theatre, sailing.

* * *

van der SMISSEN, Margaret Elisabeth 1927-
(Betty van der Smissen)

PERSONAL: Born December 27, 1927, in Great Bend, Kan.; daughter of Theodore Alwin (a minister) and Margaret (Dirks) van der Smissen. Education: University of Kansas, A.B., 1949, LL.B., 1952, J.D.; Indiana University, M.S., 1954, Re.D., 1955. Religion: Mennonite. Home: 235 Circle Dr., State College, Pa. 16801. Office: 257 Recreation Building, Pennsylvania State University, University Park, Pa. 16802.

CAREER: Ohio District Young Women's Christian Association (Y.W.C.A.), Columbus, program director, 1950-51; Manchester College, North Manchester, Ind., chairman of women's physical education, 1955-56; University of Iowa, Iowa City, 1956-65, associate professor, 1960-65; National Recreation Association, New York, N.Y., director of research, 1964-65; Pennsylvania State University, University Park, College of Health, Physical Education, and Recreation, associate professor, 1965-68, professor of recreation, 1968—, associate dean for graduate study and research, 1970-74.

WRITINGS: The Church Camp Program, Faith & Life, 1961; A Bibliography of Research Related to Recreation, privately printed, 1962; (with Helen Knierim) Fitness and Fun Through Recreational Sports and Games, Burgess, 1964; (with Oswald Goering) A Leader's Guide in Nature-oriented Activities, Iowa State University Press, 1965, 2nd edition, 1968; (with Dorothy V. Harris) Campcraft Series One, Instructor's Guide, Athletic Institute, 1965, and Campcraft Series Two, Athletic Institute, 1966; Legal Liability of Cities and Schools for Injuries Related to Recreation and Parks, W. H. Anderson, 1968; Evaluation and Self-Study of Public Recreation and Park Agencies, National Recreation and Park Association, 1972.

* * *

van HEYNINGEN, Christina 1900-
PERSONAL: Born July 16, 1900, in Fauresmith, Orange

Free State, South Africa; daughter of George Phillipus (a magistrate) and May (Higgs) van Heyningen. Education: University of Stellenbosch, M.A., 1922; Somerville College, Oxford, B.A. (honors in English), 1926. Politics: "Anti-nationalist (any kind of nationalism—black, white, Zionist, etc.)." Home: 148 Loop St., Pietermaritzburg, Natal, South Africa.

CAREER: Grey University College (now University of the Orange Free State), Bloemfontein, South Africa, senior lecturer in history of education, 1929; senior lecturer in English at University of Stellenbosch, Cape Province, South Africa, 1931-46, and University of the Witwatersrand, Johannesburg, Transvaal, South Africa, 1946-54; University of Natal, Pietermaritzburg, South Africa, senior lecturer, 1955-62, associate professor of English, 1962-65. Member: Education League (president), Blue Sash. Awards, honors: Hugh Le May fellowship to Rhodes University, 1952; D.Litt., University of Natal, 1963.

WRITINGS: (With A. W. van der Horst) A Practical Course in English, Maskew Miller, c.1934; (with van de Horst) English: Intelligent Reading and Good Writing, Maskew Miller, c.1936; This House Will Have to Do, H.A.U.M., 1946; "Clarissa," Poetry and Morals, Natal University Press, 1963; (editor) G. H. Durrant and others, On the Printed Page: Exercises in Literary Criticism, Maskew Miller, 1964; (with J. A. Berthoud) Uys Krige, Twayne, 1966; (editor) H. W. D. Manson, Plays, Verry, 1971; (with C. O. Gardner) H. W. D. Manson, Twayne, 1972. Contributor of essays on literature, painting, and education to scholarly periodicals. Editor of Theona (University of Natal), 1956-65.

WORK IN PROGRESS: Paradise Lost and Dr. Lewis, an analysis of Paradise Lost, answering Lewis's objections to it.

SIDELIGHTS: Christina van Heyningen is bilingual in English and Afrikaans, lecturing in both languages. She detests "scholarship," being inclined to think that "it is a great pity that literature was ever made a university subject, because . . . attention has been diverted from the actual works themselves to gossip and opinions about them."†

* * *

van KAAM, Adrian 1920-
PERSONAL: Born April 19, 1920, in The Hague, Netherlands; son of Charles L. van Kaam. Education: Studied philosophy and theology at Gemert, Netherlands, 1940-47, and psychology of personality and education at Hoogveld Institute, Nijmegen, Netherlands, 1950-51; Dutch Study Center, Gulemborg, M.O. in Educational Psychology, 1954; University of Chicago and Alfred Adler Institute, training in psychotherapy, 1956-57; Western Reserve University (now Case Western Reserve University), Ph.D., 1958. Office: Institute of Man, Duquesne University, Pittsburgh, Pa.

CAREER: Roman Catholic priest, member of Congregation of the Holy Ghost; psychological consultant to life schools for young adults in Netherlands, 1949-52; counselor in psychological observation center for juvenile delinquents, Veenendaal, Netherlands, 1952-54; Duquesne University, Pittsburgh, Pa., instructor, 1957; Brandeis University, Waltham, Mass., visiting professor of psychology, 1958-59; Duquesne University, assistant professor, 1959-60, associate professor, 1961-65, professor of psychology, 1965—, founder and director of Institute of Man, 1963—.

University of Heidelberg, visiting professor, summer, 1966. Lecturer at Universities of Heidelberg and Oslo, 1963; lecturer throughout United States with Institute of Man workshop, and on radio and television. Member of national advisory board, Religion in Education Foundation (nonsectarian). *Member:* Association of Existential Psychology and Psychiatry (council member, 1958—), American Psychological Association.

WRITINGS: De Jood Van Saverne (biography of Frances Libermann, Jewish-born founder of Congregation of the Holy Ghost), translation published as *Light to the Gentiles*, Duquesne University Press, 1959, new edition, Bruce, 1962; *The Third Force in European Psychology*, Psychosynthesis Research Foundation, 1960; *The Vocational Director and Counseling*, St. Paul Publications, 1962; *Religion and Personality*, Prentice-Hall, 1964; *Personality Fulfillment in the Spiritual Life*, Dimension, 1966; *Existential Foundations of Psychology*, Duquesne University Press, 1966; *The Art of Existential Counseling*, Dimension, 1966; *Religious Life in a Time of Transition*, Volume I: *Personality Fulfillment in Religious Life*, Dimemsion, 1967; (with Kathleen Healy) *The Demon and the Dove*, Duquesne University Press, 1967; *The Vowed Life*, Dimension, 1968; (co-author) *The Emergent Self*, Dimension, 1968, revised edition, 1968; (co-author) *The Participant Self*, Dimension, 1969; *On Being Involved*, Dimension, 1970; *On Being Yourself*, Dimension, 1972; *Envy and Originality*, Doubleday, 1972; *Spriituality and the Gentle Life*, Dimension, 1974; *In Search of Spiritual Identity*, Dimension, 1975.

Contributor: J. M. Lee and L. J. Putz, editors, *Seminary Education in a Time of Change*, Fides, 1965; K. T. Hargrove, editor, *Star and the Cross*, Bruce, 1966; Herbert C. Otto, editor, *Explorations in Human Potentialities*, C. C Thomas, 1966; D. S. Arbuckle, editor, *Counseling and Psychotherapy: An Overview*, McGraw, 1967.

Contributor to *International Encyclopedia of Psychiatry, Psychoanalysis, and Psychology,* and of more than thirty articles to scientific periodicals in Netherlands, 1952-54, and more recently to *Insight* and other journals in America; regular contributor to *Envoy*, 1964—. Editor of *Review of Existential Psychology and Psychiatry*, 1961—, and of *Humanitas* and *Envoy* (publications of Institute of Man, Duquesne University), 1965—; consulting editor, *Journal of Individual Psychology*, 1958—, and *Journal of Humanistic Psychology*, 1963—.

* * *

van ROOY, C(harles) A(ugust) 1923-

PERSONAL: Born January 15, 1923, in Bloemfontein, South Africa; son of Henri Charles and Elizabeth (Kling) van Rooy; married Maria E. W. Steyn, March 31, 1952; children: Hermanus Steyn, Charles Henri. *Education:* University of the Orange Free State, B.A., 1942, M.A., 1946, D.Litt., 1951; Corpus Christi College, Oxford, B.A. (honors), 1948, M.A., 1952; University of Leyden, research, 1960. *Home:* 408 Lynnwood Rd., Lynnwood, Pretoria, South Africa. *Office:* University of South Africa, P.O. Box 392, Pretoria, South Africa.

CAREER: University of the Orange Free State, Bloemfontein, South Africa, professor of Greek, 1957-65; University of South Africa, Pretoria, Transvaal, professor of classics, 1966—. *Member:* Classical Association of South Africa (secretary, 1961-62), South African Academy of Science and Arts, Afrikaans-German Cultural Union (chairman and member of national committee, 1966). *Awards, honors:* Rhodes scholarship for Orange Free State, 1946-48.

WRITINGS: Studies in Classical Satire and Related Literary Theory, E. J. Brill, 1965. Contributor of articles on classical subjects to journals.

WORK IN PROGRESS: A study of Latin satire and Greek satiric literature.

SIDELIGHTS: van Rooy has traveled widely in Europe, visiting West Germany at the invitation of Deutscher Akademischer Austauschdienst; he is fluent in Afrikaans, competent in Dutch and German, and has reading knowledge of French and Italian.†

* * *

van STRATEN, Florence W(ilhelmina) 1913-

PERSONAL: Born November 12, 1913, in Darien, Conn.; daughter of Jacques and Rosette (Roozeboom) van Straten. *Education:* New York University, B.S., 1933, M.A., 1937, Ph.D., 1939; Massachusetts Institute of Technology, certificate, 1943. *Religion:* Unitarian Universalist. *Home:* 5306 Ventnor Rd., Washington, D.C. 20016.

CAREER: New York University, New York, N.Y., instructor in chemistry, 1939-42; U.S. Navy, Naval Weather Service, Washington, D.C., head of Technical Requirements Branch, 1946-62. Consultant on atmospheric physics, 1962—. *Military service:* U.S. Naval Reserve, active duty, 1942-46; became commander. *Member:* American Meteorological Society, American Geophysical Union, Phi Beta Kappa, Sigma Xi. *Awards, honors:* Meritorious Civilian Service Award, U.S. Department of the Navy, 1958; Woman of the Year, Aerospace Medical Association, 1959; Alumnus of the Year, New York University, 1960.

WRITINGS: Weather or Not, Dodd, 1966. Writer of pamphlets and articles on atmosphere radioactive fallout and radar.

SIDELIGHTS: Florence van Straten is fluent in French and Dutch. *Avocational interests:* Music.

* * *

Van ZANDT, Roland 1918-

PERSONAL: Born December 22, 1918, in Plainfield, N.J.; son of Clarence (an industrial piping contractor) and Henrietta (Romberg) Van Zandt; married Leona Thompson, March 29, 1947; children: Caroline, Carla, Leona, Carter. *Education:* Rutgers University, B.A., 1940; Harvard University, graduate student, 1945-47; University of Minnesota, Ph.D., 1964. *Politics:* "Democrat in practice, Socialist in theory." *Home and office:* 173 Riverside Dr., New York, N.Y. 10024.

CAREER: Free-lance writer and historian. *Military service:* U.S. Army Air Forces, 1941-45; became first lieutenant; received Distinguished Flying Cross and Air Medal with three oak leaf clusters. *Member:* New York State Historical Association, New York Historical Society, Holland Society of New York, Greene County Historical Society.

WRITINGS: The Metaphysical Foundations of American History, Mouton & Co., 1959; *The Catskill Mountain House*, Rutgers University Press, 1966; *Wilson in the Promise Land* (play; first produced in Providence, R.I., December 9, 1969), Samuel French, 1970; (compiler) *Chronicles of the Hudson: Three Centuries of Travelers' Accounts*, Rutgers University Press, 1971. Contributor to *Rural Sociology* and regional history journals.

WORK IN PROGRESS: A book on the theory of American history for the general reader.

SIDELIGHTS: Van Zandt spends nine months of the year doing research and writing, and the other three months relaxing at his summer home in the heart of the Catskill State Forest Preserve. He believes in "continuous necessity of intellectual criticism and protest," voicing "complete sympathy with the most dissident groups. . . ." *Avocational interests:* Photography, playing piano.†

* * *

VARDAMAN, E. Jerry 1927-

PERSONAL: Born June 18, 1927, in Dallas, Tex.; son of Ephraim Jeremiah (a realtor) and Daisy (McCullough) Vardaman; married Alfalene Jolly, August 15, 1952; children: Carolyn, Celeste. *Education:* Baylor University, B.A., 1949, Ph.D., 1974; Southwestern Baptist Theological Seminary, B.D., 1952, Th.D., 1958; postdoctoral study at Pittsburgh Theological Seminary, 1959, Hebrew Union College (now Hebrew Union College—Jewish Institute of Religion), Jerusalem, Israel, 1963, Oxford University and University of London, 1966-67. *Home:* 31 Colonial Circle, Route 5, Starkville, Miss. 39759. *Office:* Cobb Institute of Archaeology, Mississippi State University, Box AR, State College, Miss. 39762.

CAREER: Ordained to Baptist ministry, 1948; Tarleton State College, Stephenville, Tex., professor of religion, 1952-55; Southwestern Baptist Theological Seminary, Fort Worth, Tex., instructor in biblical introduction and Old Testament, 1955-58; Southern Baptist Theological Seminary, Louisville, Ky., associate professor of biblical archaeology, 1958-72; Mississippi State University, State College, Miss., director of Cobb Institute of Archaeology, 1972—. Has worked on five different excavations in the Holy Land. *Military service:* U.S. Marine Corps, 1943-46; served in Pacific theater. *Member:* American Schools of Oriental Research, American Numismatic Society.

WRITINGS: (Editor) *The Teacher's Yoke; Studies in Memory of Henry Trantham*, Baylor University Press, 1964; *Archaeology and the Living Word*, Broadman, 1965. Contributor of articles and reviews to theology journals.

WORK IN PROGRESS: Paul in the Light of Archaeology; a corpus of all Herodian inscriptions.

* * *

VAS DIAS, Robert (Leonard Michael) 1931-

PERSONAL: Born January 19, 1931, in London, England; son of A. Arnold (a journalist) and Nini R. (Fuldauer) Vas Dias; married Susan McClintock (an actress), May 5, 1961; children: Jason Bartholomeu. *Education:* Grinnell College, B.A. (with honors), 1953; Columbia University, graduate study, 1959-61. *Address:* c/o The Poetry Society, 21 Earls Court Square, London S.W.5, England.

CAREER: Prentice-Hall, Inc., Englewood Cliffs, N.J., assistant editor, 1955-56; Allyn & Bacon, Inc., Englewood Cliffs, N.J., staff editor, 1956-57; free-lance editor with Prentice-Hall, Norton, Houghton Mifflin Co., Pantheon Books, Macmillan Co., Free Press, and Shorewood Publishing Co., 1957-65; Long Island University, Brooklyn, N.Y., instructor in English, 1964-66; New York University, American Language Institute, New York, N.Y., instructor in English, 1966-71; Thomas Jefferson College of the Grand Valley State Colleges, Allendale, Mich., tutor and poet-in-residence, 1971-74, director Thomas Jefferson College National Poetry Festival, 1971, 1973; Permanent Press, London, England, and New York, N.Y., editor and

publisher, 1973—. Director, Aspen Writers' Workshop, Aspen, Colo., 1964-67; member, New York Co-ordinating Council of Literary Magazines, 1975. *Military service:* U.S. Army, 1953-55. *Awards, honors:* New York State Creative Artists Program Service, fellowship, 1975.

WRITINGS: Ribbed Vision (poetry; with original lithographs by Jack Bosson), privately printed, 1963; *The Counted* (poetry), Caterpillar (New York), 1967; *Written in Orbit* (poetry), Pierrepont Press, 1970; (contributor) *The American Experience* (anthology) edited by H. Jaffe and J. Tytel, Harper, 1970; (editor) *Inside Outer Space* (anthology), Doubleday, 1970; *Speech Acts and Happenings* (poetry), Bobbs-Merrill, 1972; *The Life of Parts* (poetry), Perishable Press, 1972; *Making Faces* (poetry), Joe Di Maggio Press (London), 1975. Poems published in *Poetry, Chelsea, Choice, Sumac, Maps, Nation, Poetry Review, Stony Brook, Occidental Review, Colorado Quarterly*, and other literary reviews.

* * *

VASTA, Edward 1928-

PERSONAL: Born January 28, 1928, in Forest Park, Ill.; son of Joseph and Josephine (Malimaci) Vasta; married Geraldine Stocco, November 28, 1953; children: John Robert, Paula Lorraine, Joseph Edward, Catherine Ann, Barbara Josephine, Salvatore James. *Education:* University of Notre Dame, B.A., 1952; University of Florence, graduate study, 1952-53; University of Michigan, M.A., 1954; Stanford University, graduate study, 1954-58, Ph.D., 1963. *Religion:* Roman Catholic. *Home:* 52140 Harvest Dr., South Bend, Ind. 46637. *Office:* English Department, University of Notre Dame, Notre Dame, Ind. 46556.

CAREER: Stanford University, Stanford, Calif., acting instructor in English, 1956-58; University of Notre Dame, Notre Dame, Ind., instructor, 1958-61, assistant professor, 1961-66, associate professor, 1966-69; professor of English, 1969—, chairman of department, 1972—. *Military service:* U.S. Navy, 1946-48. *Member:* Modern Language Association of America, Mediaeval Academy of America, American Association of University Professors. *Awards, honors:* Fulbright scholarship to Italy, 1952-53; Danforth study grant, 1961-62.

WRITINGS: The Spiritual Basis of Piers Plowman, Mouton & Co., 1965; (editor) *Middle English Survey: Critical Essays*, University of Notre Dame Press, 1965; (editor) *Interpretations of Piers Plowman*, University of Notre Dame Press, 1968.

WORK IN PROGRESS: A critical study, *The Meaning and Structure of Piers Plowman*.

* * *

VAUGHAN, Alden T. 1929-

PERSONAL: Born January 23, 1929, in Providence, R.I.; son of Dana Prescott (an art educator) and Muriel (True) Vaughan; married Lauraine Freethy, June 1, 1956; children: Jeffrey Alden, Lynn Elizabeth. *Education:* Amherst College, B.A., 1950; Columbia University, M.A. (Teachers College), 1956, M.A., 1958, Ph.D., 1964. *Home:* 36 Ridge Road, Cos Cob, Conn. 06807. *Office:* 616 Fayerweather, Columbia University, New York, N.Y. 10027.

CAREER: Teacher of history, Tarrytown, N.Y., 1950-51, Mt. Vernon, N.Y., 1956-60; Columbia University, New York, N.Y., assistant professor, 1961-67, associate professor, 1967-69, professor of history, 1969—. *Military service:*

U.S. Naval Reserve, beginning, 1950; active duty, 1951-55; retired with rank of commander. *Member:* American Historical Association, Society of American Historians (secretary-treasurer, 1965-70), Organization of American Historians, American Association of University Professors, Colonial Society of Massachusetts. *Awards, honors:* Guggenheim fellowship, 1973-74; Charles Warren fellowship at Harvard University, 1974.

WRITINGS: New England Frontier: Puritans and Indians, 1620-1675, Little, Brown, 1965; (editor) *Chronicles of the American Revolution*, Grosset, 1965; (editor) *America Before the Revolution, 1725-1775*, Prentice-Hall, 1967; (contributor) S. Coben and L. Ratner, editors, *The Development of an American Culture*, Prentice-Hall, 1970; (contributor) J. Garraty and P. Gay, editors, *The Columbia History of the World*, Harper, 1972; (editor) *The Puritan Tradition in America, 1620-1730*, Harper, 1972; (with George A. Billias) *Perspectives on Early American History*, Harper, 1973; *American Genesis: Captain John Smith and the Founding of Virginia*, Little, Brown, 1975. Contributor to *Encyclopedia Americana* and to *William and Mary Quarterly, New England Quarterly*, and *American Heritage*. Managing editor, *Political Science Quarterly*, 1969-70.

WORK IN PROGRESS: Editing *New England Captivity Narratives* for Harvard University Press, completion expected in 1976; writing *Colonial America*, Volume I of *Oxford History of the United States*, completion expected in 1977; a book, *Indian-White Contact in British America*, completion expected in 1977.

*   *   *

VAUGHAN, Donald S(hores)   1921-

PERSONAL: Born October 17, 1921, in Cape Girardeau, Mo.; son of Arthur Winn (a teacher) and Harriett (Shores) Vaughan; married Sarah Auten (a commercial artist), November 3, 1945; children: Beverly Winn, Kenneth Auten. *Education:* Attended Southeast Missouri State College, 1939-41; Vanderbilt University, B.A., 1943; University of Alabama, M.A., 1947; Columbia University, Ph.D., 1967. *Politics:* Democrat. *Religion:* Methodist. *Address:* P.O. Box 72, University, Miss. 38677.

CAREER: University of Alabama, Tuscaloosa, instructor in political science, 1949-55, research assistant, 1950-51, assistant director of Montgomery Center, 1951-52, director of Gadsden Center, 1952-55; University of Mississippi, University, assistant professor, 1955-60, acting associate professor, 1960-67, professor of political science, 1967—, acting department chairman, 1968-69, department chairman, 1969—, assistant director for public administration research, 1957-62, assistant director of Bureau of Governmental Research, 1962-67, associate director, 1967-68, director, 1968—, faculty member of Highway Management Institute, 1967-73. Visiting lecturer, Southern Bell Telephone and Telegraph Co. Institute for Middle Management, 1959; advisor, Mississippi Commission on Efficiency and Economy, 1970; director, Study of Mound Bayou, Miss., 1972-73. *Military service:* U.S. Naval Reserve, 1942-63; retired as lieutenant. *Member:* American Political Science Association, American Society for Public Administration, Southern Political Science Association, Mississippi Political Science Association (president, 1972), Omicron Delta Kappa.

WRITINGS: (Editor with others) *A Directory of Mississippi Municipalities*, Bureau of Public Administration,

1957, 7th edition, Bureau of Governmental Research, University of Mississippi, 1970; (contributor) *Problems and Prospects in Public Management: A Digest of ASPA Regional Conferences—1956-57-58*, Bureau of Governmental Research, University of Mississippi, 1960; (co-author) *Yesterday's Constitution Today*, Bureau of Public Administration, University of Mississippi, 1960; (contributor) *Compendium on Legislative Apportionment*, 2nd edition, National Municipal League, 1962; (with Edward H. Hobbs) *A Manual of Mississippi Municipal Government*, Bureau of Governmental Research, University of Mississippi, 1962; (co-author) *Toward Improved Law Enforcement: A Comprehensive Plan for Mississippi Law Enforcement District III*, Bureau of Governmental Research, University of Mississippi, 1969; (co-author) *Mound Bayou: City in Transition*, Bureau of Governmental Research, University of Mississippi, 1973. Contributor to *Britannica Book of the Year*. Editor and contributor, *Public Administration Survey*, 1957-68.

WORK IN PROGRESS: Study of political science and public administration graduates, 1956-71.

AVOCATIONAL INTERESTS: Sports, radio, and woodworking.

*   *   *

VAYDA, Andrew P.   1931-

PERSONAL: Born December 7, 1931, in Hungary; became U.S. citizen; son of Sandor (a lawyer) and Zelma (Szentgyorgyi) Vayda; married Cherry Lowman, June 9, 1962; children: Andrea. *Education:* Columbia University, A.B., 1952, Ph.D., 1956. *Office:* Department of Human Ecology and Social Sciences, Cook College, Rutgers University, New Brunswick, N.J. 08903.

CAREER: Fulbright exchange scholar in New Zealand, 1954-55; Social Science Research Council postdoctoral research fellow, 1956-57; University of British Columbia, Vancouver, lecturer in anthropology, 1958-60; Columbia University, New York, N.Y., assistant professor, 1960-64, associate professor, 1964-68, professor of anthropology, 1968-72; Rutgers University, New Brunswick, N.J., professor of anthropology and ecology, 1972—. Anthropology and human ecology researcher in New Mexico, 1953, in South Pacific Islands, 1955, 1956-57, in New Guinea, 1962-63, 1966. National Science Foundation, panel member, 1961, 1962; Institute of War and Peace Studies, research associate, 1964-65; member of board of directors, Social Science Research Council, 1970-73; consultant to Man and the Biosphere program of UNESCO, 1974—. *Member:* American Anthropological Association (fellow), Phi Beta Kappa. *Awards, honors:* Research grants from American Museum of Natural History, California Academy of Sciences, American Academy of Arts and Sciences, American Council of Learned Societies, and National Science Foundation.

WRITINGS: Maori Warfare, Polynesian Society, 1960; (contributor) F. R. Fosberg, editor, *Man's Place in the Island Ecosystem*, Bernice P. Bishop Museum (Honolulu), 1963; (editor with Anthony Leeds) *Man, Culture, and Animals: The Role of Animals in Human Ecological Adjustments*, American Association for the Advancement of Science, 1965; (contributor) James A. Clifton, editor, *Introduction to Cultural Anthropology: Essays in the Scope and Methods of the Science of Man*, Houghton, 1968; (editor) *Peoples and Cultures of the Pacific: An Anthropological Reader*, Doubleday, 1968; (editor) *Environment and*

Cultural Behavior, Doubleday, 1969; *War in Ecological Perspective*, Plenum, in press. Contributor to *International Encyclopedia of the Social Sciences*; contributor of about forty articles and reviews to journals in the United States and abroad. Editor, *Human Ecology: An Interdisciplinary Journal*, 1971—.

WORK IN PROGRESS: Human Responses to Environmental Problems, possibly for Duxbury Press.

* * *

VECOLI, Rudolph J(ohn) 1927-

PERSONAL: Born March 2, 1927, in Wallingford, Conn.; son of Giovanni B. (a laborer) and Settima (Palmerini) Vecoli; married Jill Cherrington, June 27, 1959; children: Christopher, Lisa, Jeremy. *Education:* University of Connecticut, B.A., 1950; University of Pennsylvania, M.A., 1951; University of Wisconsin, Ph.D., 1963. *Office:* Department of History, University of Minnesota, Minneapolis, Minn.

CAREER: U.S. Department of State, Washington, D.C., foreign affairs officer, 1951-54; instructor in history at Ohio State University, Columbus, 1957-59, and Pennsylvania State University, State College, 1960-61; Rutgers University, New Brunswick, N.J., assistant professor of history, 1961-65; University of Illinois, Champaign, associate professor of history, 1965-67; University of Minnesota, Minneapolis, professor of history and director of Immigration History Research Center, 1967—. *Military service:* U.S. Navy, 1945-46. *Member:* American Historical Association, Organization of American Historians, American Association of University Professors, American Italian Historical Association (past president). *Awards, honors:* Social Science Research Council fellowship, 1959-60; Newberry Library fellowship, 1964; American-Scandinavian Foundation fellowship, 1970; American Philosophical Society grant, 1970; Fulbright-Hays senior research scholar in Italy, 1973-74; American Council of Learned Societies grant, 1974.

WRITINGS: The People of New Jersey, Van Nostrand, 1965; (contributor) Herbert J. Bass, editor, *The State of American History*, Quadrangle, 1970; (contributor) *The Reinterpretation of American History and Culture*, National Council for the Social Studies, 1973. Contributor to journals. Advisory editor of *International Migration Review* (formerly, *International Migration Digest*); member of editorial board, *Ethnicity*.

WORK IN PROGRESS: A history of the Italian-American labor and radical movements, completion expected in 1976.

SIDELIGHTS: Vecoli is competent in Italian and French. *Avocational interests:* Hiking, camping, boating, sports.

* * *

VEGLAHN, Nancy (Crary) 1937-

PERSONAL: Born July 17, 1937, in Sioux City, Iowa; daughter of Ralph William (a judge) and Margaret (Coleman) Crary; married L. Donald Veglahn (a Methodist minister), August 24, 1958; children: Daniel Wesley, Ruth Ann. *Education:* Morningside College, A.B. (summa cum laude), 1959. *Religion:* Methodist. *Home:* 303 17th Ave. S., Brookings, S.D. 57006.

CAREER: Yale University, Divinity School, New Haven, Conn., secretary to the associate dean, 1959-62. *Member:* Pi Kappa Delta, P.E.O. Sisterhood, Federated Women's Club, National League of American Penwomen.

WRITINGS: The Tiger's Tail, Harper, 1964; *The Spider of Brooklyn Heights*, Scribner, 1967; *Peter Cartwright*, Scribner, 1968; *South Dakota*, Coward, 1970; *The Buffalo King*, Scribner, 1971; *Follow the Golden Goose*, Addison-Wesley, 1971; *Getting to Know the Missouri River*, Coward, 1972; *The Vandals of Treason House* (Weekly Reader Book Club selection), Houghton, 1974; *Swimmers, Take Your Marks!*, Weekly Reader Book Club, in press.

* * *

VERMEULE, E(mily) D. T. 1928-

PERSONAL: Born August 11, 1928, in New York, N.Y.; daughter of Clinton Blake (an attorney) and Eleanor (Meneely) Townsend; married Cornelius C. Vermeule III (curator of classical art, Museum of Fine Arts, Boston), February 2, 1957; children: Emily Dickinson Blake, Cornelius Adrian Comstock. *Education:* Bryn Mawr College, B.A., 1950, Ph.D., 1956; advanced study at American School of Classical Studies, Athens, 1950-51, St. Anne's College, Oxford, 1953; Radcliffe College, M.A., 1954. *Politics:* Independent. *Religion:* Episcopalian. *Home:* 47 Coolidge Hill Rd., Cambridge, Mass. 02138. *Office:* Department of Classics, 319 Boylston Hall, Harvard University, Cambridge, Mass. 02138.

CAREER: Instructor in Greek at Bryn Mawr College, Bryn Mawr, Pa., 1956-57, and Wellesley College, Wellesley, Mass., 1957-58; Boston University, Boston, Mass., assistant professor of classics, 1958-62, associate professor of classics, 1962-65; Wellesley College, professor of art and Greek, 1965-70, chairman, art department, 1966-67; Harvard University, Cambridge, Mass., Samuel E. Zemurray and Doris Zemurray Stone-Radcliffe Professor, 1970—, director of Cyprus archaeological expedition, 1971—. *Member:* Archaeological Institute of America (vice-president of Boston chapter), American Philological Association, Classical Association (England), Society for Promotion of Hellenic Studies (England), American Oriental Society, Classical Association of New England. *Awards, honors:* Research fellow, Museum of Fine Arts, Boston; Fulbright fellowship, 1950-51; Guggenheim fellowship, 1964-65; American Association of Arts and Sciences fellowship, 1971; American Philosophical Society fellowship, 1972; honorary degrees from Bryn Mawr College, Rutgers University, University of Massachusetts, Smith College, and other colleges and universities.

WRITINGS: Greece in the Bronze Age, University of Chicago Press, 1964, 6th edition, 1974; (author of introduction) M. P. Nilsson, *Mycenaean Origins of Greek Mythology*, University of California Press, 1973; *Goetterkult*, Archaeologia Homerica, 1974. Translator of Euripides' *Electra*, published in *Complete Greek Tragedies V*, University of Chicago Press, 1959. Contributor to archeological, classical, and philological journals, and to *Poetry* and *New Yorker*.

WORK IN PROGRESS: Studies on the aesthetics of prehistoric Greek art, on Greek lyric poetry, on the relations of classical myth to art, and on expressions of Greek religious feeling.

SIDELIGHTS: Mrs. Vermeule has worked on archaeological excavations in Greece, Cyprus, and the Near East, and traveled extensively in Turkey and North Africa as well as in Greece and other European countries. She knows classical Greek, modern Greek, Latin, Turkish, French, and German. *Avocational interests:* Animal breeding and gardening.

VERNAM, Glenn R.   1896-

PERSONAL: Born 1896, in Pittsburg, Kan.; son of Eugene J. and Aurie V. (Buker) Vernam; married Irene M. Baker, April 2, 1917; children: three daughters and one son. *Residence:* Joseph, Ore. 97846.

CAREER: Starting at fifteen, worked all over the West as cowboy, long-line freight skinner, packer, stage driver, homesteader, and carpenter; now rancher and writer. *Member:* Western Writers of America, Masons. *Awards, honors:* Golden Saddleman award from Western Writers Association and Levi Strass Co., 1973, for *Man on Horseback.*

WRITINGS: Man on Horseback (non-fiction), Harper, 1965; *Indian Hater,* Doubleday, 1969; *Pioneer Breed,* Doubleday, 1972; *Redman in White Moccasins,* Doubleday, 1973; *The Talking Rifle,* Doubleday, 1973; *They Saddled the West* (non-fiction), Cornell Maritime, 1975. Work represented in anthologies, *Great Ghost Stories of the Old West,* Four Winds, 1968, and *Trails of the Iron Horse,* Doubleday, 1975. Contributor of 150 articles and short stories to magazines.

WORK IN PROGRESS: The Three Pillars of the Cow-Country, non-fiction, for Doubleday.

SIDELIGHTS: Vernam told *CA:* "I know most of the West first-hand, Canada to Mexico. I saw the tail end of the Old West and knew many of its incomparable characters." *Avocational interests:* Indian artifacts, history, horses, outdoors, painting and drawing, going places.

*   *   *

VERNAZZA, Marcelle Wynn   1909-

PERSONAL: Born March 10, 1909, in Somerset, Ky.; daughter of Ira (a painter) and Emeline Wynn; married Jerome A. Vernazza, June 1, 1932; children: J. Ben, Martha Elin. *Education:* Whitman Conservatory, diplomas in piano and in school music, 1930; San Francisco State College (now University), A.B., 1945; Mills College, M.A., 1951. *Home:* 2 Wood St., San Francisco, Calif. 94118.

CAREER: San Francisco State University, San Francisco, Calif., 1945—, Professor of Music Emeritus, 1974—. *Member:* International Society for Music Education, Music Educators National Conference, American Society of Composers, Authors and Publishers, National Association for Music Therapy, Music Teachers National Association, Society of Children's Book Writers, British Society of Music Therapy, California Association of Professional Music Teachers, Mu Phi Epsilon.

WRITINGS: Making and Playing Classroom Instruments, Fearon, 1959; (editor) *Basic Materials for Piano Students,* W. C. Brown, 1964, brailled edition, 1968, revised edition, 1972. Contributor of articles to *Music Educators Journal, American Music Teacher, The Triangle, Leka Nuhuo,* and other music periodicals.

*   *   *

VERNON, Walter N(ewton)   1907-

PERSONAL: Born March 24, 1907, in Verden, Okla.; son of Walter Newton (a minister) and Fannie (Dodd) Vernon; married Ruth Mason (a public school teacher), December 17, 1931; children: Walter N. III, Kathleen Frances (Mrs. Stanley P. Clark). *Education:* Southern Methodist University, B.A., 1928, B.D., 1931, M.A., 1934. *Politics:* Demo-

crat. *Home and office:* 4013 Dorcas Dr., Nashville, Tenn. 37215.

CAREER: Ordained to Methodist ministry, 1931; pastor in Dallas, Tex., 1931-38; The Methodist Church Board of Education, Editorial Division, Nashville, Tenn., administrative associate and editor, general publications, 1938-72. National Council of Churches, member of audio-visual team to Africa, 1953, delegate to World Convention on Christian Education, Tokyo, 1958, chairman of editors section, Division of Christian Education. *Member:* Western Writers of America (Nashville corral), North Texas United Methodist Conference (conference historian), Sigma Delta Chi. *Awards, honors:* D.Litt., West Virginia Wesleyan College, 1963.

WRITINGS: Methodist Profile, Methodist Publishing House, 1959; (compiler) *Living With Your Children,* Graded Press, 1961; *William Stevenson, Riding Preacher,* Southern Methodist University Press, 1964; *Methodism Moves Across North Texas,* North Texas Conference, 1967; *United Methodist Profile,* Graded Press, 1968; *Forever Building: The Life and Ministry of Paul E. Martin,* Southern Methodist University Press, 1973. Wrote words for hymn, "God of All, Who Art Our Father," published by Hymn Society of America, 1961. Contributor to newspapers and Methodist periodicals and to *Christian Century, Chronicles of Oklahoma, Tennessee Historical Quarterly, Arkansas Historical Quarterly,* and *East Texas Historical Journal.* Associate editor, *Encyclopedia of World Methodism,* 1974.

WORK IN PROGRESS: A brief history of Methodism among Indians of Oklahoma; compiling *Guidelines for Local Church Historians;* a history of Methodism in Arkansas.

*   *   *

VERONICA, Sister Mary   1924-

PERSONAL: Born May 7, 1924, in Philadelphia, Pa.; daughter of Henry and Clara (Datz) Kallfelz. *Education:* Trenton State College, B.S. in Ed., 1946; University of Pennsylvania, graduate study, 1947; Catholic University of America, M.A., 1960; Syracuse University, graduate study, 1963. *Home:* St. Anthony Motherhouse, 1024 Court St., Syracuse, N.Y. 13208.

CAREER: Roman Catholic nun of Order of St. Francis. Teacher at public schools in New Jersey, 1946-49; teacher at Catholic elementary and secondary schools in Syracuse, N.Y., 1950-51, 1960-61, 1963-66, Lorain, Ohio, 1951-59, and Mattydale, N.Y. 1961-63; Maria Regina College, Syracuse, N.Y., part-time instructor in geography, 1963—. Catholic University of America, summer instructor in geography, 1966, 1967. New York State Catholic Curriculum Committee, chairman of geography committee, 1966—. *Member:* Association of American Geographers, American Geographical Society, National Council for Geographic Education, National Council for the Social Studies, New York State Social Studies Council.

WRITINGS: Lands of the Western Hemisphere, Doubleday, 1960, revised edition, Webster Division, McGraw, 1963; (with Kenneth J. Bertrand) *Our Land in a World Setting,* Webster Division, McGraw, 1966.

WORK IN PROGRESS: A teachers' edition of *Our Land in A World Setting.†*

VERSACE, Marie Teresa Rios 1917-
(Tere Rios)

PERSONAL: Born November 9, 1917, in Brooklyn, N.Y.; daughter of Rafael (with government of Puerto Rico) and Marie (Dowd) Rios; married Humbert Joseph Versace (a retired colonel, U.S. Army), October 12, 1936; children: Humbert Roque, Stephen Vincent, Richard Patrick, John Michael, Teresa Dominique. *Education:* Attended schools in United States, Bermuda, and Puerto Rico; took writing courses at University of Pittsburgh, University of Wisconsin, and Johns Hopkins University. *Religion:* Roman Catholic. *Residence:* Black Earth, Wis. 53515.

CAREER: In the course of her travels as an Army wife, 1936-66, worked as an art museum assistant, hotel clerk, secretary in a cotton gin, bookkeeper, Gallup pollster, real estate saleswoman, postal clerk, and as volunteer with Red Cross and Civil Air Patrol; began writing after World War II "because people had such funny ideas about Puerto Ricans." *Member:* Writers Sodality of America, Wisconsin Regional Writers Association. *Awards, honors:* Honorable mention, *Atlantic Monthly*, for short story, "The Freedman," 1948; Doubleday prize for short story, "Los Carilargos," 1948.

*WRITINGS—*All under name Tere Rios: *An Angel Grows Up*, Duell, Sloan & Pearce, 1957; *Brother Angel*, Academy Library, 1963; *The Fifteenth Pelican*, Doubleday, 1965, published as *The Flying Nun*, 1965. Translator of short stories by Abelardo Diaz Alfaro. Contributor of short stories to magazines, and (formerly) occasional columns to *Southwest Louisiana Register*.

WORK IN PROGRESS: Free Country, a novel about American prisoners in Vietnam; *Quetzatl*, a novel about Latin-American mountain people; short stories and articles.

SIDELIGHTS: Marie Versace is fluent in Spanish, and speaks "survival" French and German. A weekly series, "The Flying Nun," Screen Gems-ABC-TV, is based on *The Fifteenth Pelican. Avocational interests:* Horses, flying, sailing, and eating out.

BIOGRAPHICAL/CRITICAL SOURCES: Catholic Review, February 28, 1964.†

* * *

VERWOERDT, Adriaan 1927-

PERSONAL: Born July 5, 1927, in Voorburg, Netherlands; came to United States in 1953, naturalized in 1958; son of Christopher and Juliana (Busch) Verwoerdt; married Dorothy Jean Taylor, October 9, 1965; children: Christopher. *Education:* Medical School of Amsterdam, M.D., 1952; University of North Carolina-Duke Psychoanalytic Institute, graduate, 1973. *Religion:* Episcopalian. *Office:* Duke University Medical Center, Durham, N.C.

CAREER: Touro Infirmary, New Orleans, La., intern, 1953-54; Duke University Medical Center, Durham, N.C., resident in psychiatry, 1954-55, 1958-60, instructor and fellow in psychiatric research, 1960, associate in psychiatry, 1962, assistant professor, 1963-67, associate professor, 1967-71, professor of psychiatry, 1971—, director of gero-psychiatry training program, 1966—. American Board of Psychiatry and Neurology, diplomate, 1962. Director, Psychiatric Residency Training Program, John Umstead Hospital, 1968—. *Military service:* U.S. Army, Medical Corps, psychiatrist, 1955-57; became captain. *Member:* American Medical Association, Pan American Medical Association (diplomate, 1972), American Psychiatric Association (fel-

low), Gerontological Society, American Psychosomatic Society, American Geriatrics Society, North Carolina Medical Society. *Awards, honors:* National Institute of Mental Health career teacher training award, 1964-66.

WRITINGS: Communication with the Fatally Ill, C. C Thomas, 1966. Contributor of about forty-five articles to medical journals.

WORK IN PROGRESS; Psychological coping with stress and crisis; attitudes toward death; patterns of sexual behavior in senescence; psychoanalysis; training in geropsychiatry.

SIDELIGHTS: Verwoerdt is competent in Dutch, French, German, Latin, Greek.

* * *

VIETS, Wallace T(rowbridge) 1919-

PERSONAL: Surname is pronounced Veets; born November 26, 1919; son of Raymond T. (an electrical engineer) and Hilda (Mix) Viets; married Evelyn Louise Cole (a teacher), June 3, 1944; children: Raymond, Robert, Wesley, Marian. *Education:* Yale University, B.A., 1941, B.D., 1944; Hartford Seminary Foundation, S.T.M., 1950; advanced theological study at Boston University, Union Theological Seminary, and Institute of Advanced Pastoral Studies, Bloomfield Hills, Mich. *Politics:* Independent voter. *Office:* The Methodist Church, 189 West Neck Rd., Huntington, Long Island, N.Y. 11743.

CAREER: Ordained deacon of The Methodist Church, 1943, elder, 1945; pastor in East Northport, N.Y., 1943-45, West Hartford, Conn., 1945-50, Albany, N.Y., 1950-57, Glens Falls, N.Y., 1957-60, and New Haven, Conn., 1960-66; Methodist Church of Huntington, Long Island, N.Y., pastor, 1966—. Yale University, New Haven, Conn., lecturer at Divinity School, 1960-66, fellow of Timothy Dwight College, 1960—. *Member:* Connecticut State Council of Churches, New York Conference of The Methodist Church, New Haven Council of Churches (vice-president, 1964—), Masons, Kiwanis Club, Yale Club, Yale Golf Club, Faculty Club.

WRITINGS: Seven Days That Changed the World, Abingdon, 1962; *My God, Why? And Other Questions From the Passion*, Abingdon, 1966. Contributor to *Christian Advocate*.

WORK IN PROGRESS: A book of Advent meditations and sermons on the Incarnation.

AVOCATIONAL INTERESTS: Drama and music (amateur acting and singing groups), travel (United States, Canada, South America, and Europe).

BIOGRAPHICAL/CRITICAL SOURCES: New Haven Journal Courier, January 4, 1966.†

* * *

VILLARD, Henry S(errano) 1900-

PERSONAL: Born March 30, 1900, in New York, N.Y.; son of Harold Garrison (a lawyer) and Mariquita (Serrano) Villard; married Tamara Gringutes, October 11, 1940; children: Dimitri Serrano, Sandra Darielle. *Education:* Harvard University, B.A. (cum laude), 1921; Magdalen College, Oxford, graduate study, 1922-23. *Home:* Chalet Les Sapins, 3780 Gstaad, Switzerland.

CAREER: Held various positions in teaching, journalism, and real estate, 1923-27. U.S. Foreign Service officer, 1928-61, serving on four continents and as ambassador to three countries; Washington Institute of Foreign Affairs. Washington, D.C., director of programs, 1963-65. Government posts included consul at Rio de Janeiro, 1935-36; secretary of U.S. Legation, Caracas, 1936-37; assistant chief of Division on Near Eastern Affairs, Department of State, 1940-44, chief of Division of African Affairs, 1944-46, and director of policy planning, 1947-48, 1951; counselor at Oslo, 1948-50; ambassador to Libya, 1952-54; deputy commandant for foreign affairs, National War College, 1955-57; special assistant to Undersecretary of State, 1957-58; U.S. representative at European headquarters of United Nations, Geneva, 1958-60; ambassador to Senegal and Mauritania 1960-61. Adviser to American delegation at three sessions of United Nations General Assembly. *Wartime service:* Ambulance driver with Italian Army, World War I. *Member:* Institute of Differing Civilizations (Brussels), Century Association (New York), Metropolitan Club and Cosmos Club (both Washington, D.C.).

WRITINGS: Libya, the New Arab Kingdom of North Africa, Cornell University Press, 1956; *Affairs at State,* Crowell, 1965; *Contact! The Story of the Early Birds,* Crowell, 1968. *The Great Road Races, 1894-1914,* Barker, 1972. Contributor to *Current History, Harper's, Nation, National Geographic, Foreign Service Journal,* and other periodicals.

WORK IN PROGRESS: Research on early history of aviation, and on American Red Cross ambulance service in Italy during World War II.

SIDELIGHTS: Villard is competent in French with less facility in German and Spanish.

*   *   *

VILLAREJO, Oscar M(ilton)   1909-

PERSONAL: Born May 3, 1909, in Milwaukee, Wis.; son of Oscar Felipe and Isabel (Gonzalez) Villarejo; married Mary Patricia Holan (a writer of children's books), March 28, 1945. *Education:* George Washington University, B.A., 1947, M.A., 1949; University of Birmingham, certificate of Shakespeare Institute, 1948; Columbia University, Ph.D., 1953. *Office:* U.S. Marine Corps, Command and Staff College, Education and Development Command, Quantico, Va. 22134.

CAREER: Instructor at George Washington University, Washington, D.C., 1947-49, and New Lincoln School, New York, N.Y., 1949-53; assistant professor of English at Nasson College, Springville, Me., 1954-55, and of English and Spanish at Texas Lutheran College, Seguin, 1955-56; Southern State College, Magnolia, Ark., associate professor of English and chairman of department, 1956-57; Memphis State University, Memphis, Tenn., assistant professor of English, 1957-59; Wisconsin State University—Stevens Point, associate professor of English, 1959-60; Glassboro State College, Glassboro, N.J., professor of English, 1960-64; Long Island University, C. W. Post Campus, Brookville, N.Y., associate professor of Spanish, 1964-66; Georgetown University, Washington, D.C., associate professor of Spanish, 1966-70; University of Maryland, College Park, associate professor of English and comparative literature, 1970-71; George Washington University, Washington, D.C., associate professor of English, 1971—; U.S. Marine Corps, Command and Staff College, Quantico, Va., professor of English, 1974—. Visiting scholar, Duke University, summers, 1957, 1959. *Military service:* U.S. Marine Corps, 1943-45; served as U.S. diplomatic courier on detached duty from Marine Corps in Europe, Africa, and Middle East, and South America.

WRITINGS: Dr. Kane's Voyage to the Polar Lands: A Narrative of the Second American Grinnell Arctic Exploring Expedition, University of Pennsylvania Press, 1965. Contributor of numerous articles in Spanish on Lope de Vega Carpio to *Segismundo, Hispanofila,* and *Revista de Filologia Espanola* (all Madrid); contributor of essay on Shakespeare to *Shakespeare Survey,* number 20, Cambridge University Press. Book reviewer, *Washington Star News,* 1973—.

WORK IN PROGRESS: Translation of *Diary of General Francisco de Paula Santander,* an associate of Simon de Bolivar; an article on Spanish influence on Elizabethan drama of England.

*   *   *

VITALE, Philip H.   1913-

PERSONAL: Born February 13, 1913, in Chicago, Ill.; son of Philip and Helen (Bonomo) Vitale; married Marguerite Jackman, August 14, 1947; children: Constance, Philip, Dennis. *Education:* Loyola University, Chicago, Ill., A.B., 1935, M.A., 1936, Ph.D., 1941; Chicago Teachers College (now Chicago State University), M.Ed., 1939. *Religion:* Roman Catholic. *Home:* Route 3, 150 Hawthorne Rd., Barrington, Ill. 60010. *Office:* DePaul University, 35 East Jackson Blvd., Chicago, Ill.

CAREER: Chicago City Junior College, Chicago, Ill., member of faculty, 1942-46; DePaul University, Chicago, Ill., assistant professor, 1946-48, associate professor, 1948-50, professor of English literature and chairman of English department, 1950—. *Member:* College English Association, Modern Humanities Research Association, Modern Language Association of America, American Association of University Professors.

WRITINGS: Questions in Literary Opinion, Auxiliary University Press, 1955; *Catholic Literary Opinion in the Nineteenth Century,* Academy Library Guild, 1956; *Catholic Literary Opinion in the Twentieth Century,* Auxiliary University Press, 1958; *An Outline Guide for English Majors,* Auxiliary University Press, 1960; *Catholic Critics,* two volumes, Auxiliary University Press, 1961, 1962; *Basic Tools of Research,* Barron's, 1963; *Questions and Problems in Bibliography and Research,* Auxiliary University Press, 1967; *Fielding: Tom Jones,* Barron's, 1967; *Bibliography: Historical and Bibliothecal,* Loyola University Press, 1971; *James: The Portrait of a Lady,* Barron's, 1973.

WORK IN PROGRESS: Scott: Ivanhoe, to be published by Barron's; *Pejoratives: Principles of Etymology and Semasiology.*

*   *   *

VIVANTE, Arturo   1923-

PERSONAL: Born October 17, 1923, in Rome, Italy; son of Leone (a philosopher) and Elena (a painter; maiden name, De Bosis) Vivante; married Nancy Bradish, April 19, 1958; children: Lucy, Lydia. *Education:* McGill University, B.A., 1945; University of Rome, M.D., 1949. *Politics:* Liberal. *Residence:* Wellfleet, Mass. *Agent:* A. Watkins, Inc., 77 Park Ave., New York, N.Y. 10016.

CAREER: Physician in practice of general medicine, Rome, Italy, 1950-58; now full-time writer. Writer in residence, University of North Carolina, 1968, Boston University, 1970, Purdue University, 1972-74. *Awards, honors:* Fulbright travel grant, 1952.

WRITINGS: Poesie, Ferrari (Venice), 1951; *A Goodly*

Babe (novel), Little, Brown, 1966; *The French Girls of Killini* (short stories), Little, Brown, 1967; *Doctor Giovanni* (novel), Little, Brown, 1969. Contributor of over fifty short stories to *New Yorker*, and others to *Guardian, Botteghe Oscure, Vogue, Southern Review, Cornhill, London Magazine*, and other periodicals.

WORK IN PROGRESS: Short stories; a novel, tentatively entitled *The Years Past*.

SIDELIGHTS: Arturo Vivante told *CA:* "My writing is mainly a study of life as I've known it. I write to know the mystery that even a small matter holds. Through my writing I have come on some of the calmest, clearest and brightest moments of my life."

BIOGRAPHICAL/CRITICAL SOURCES: John Barkham, Saturday Review Syndicate, May 28, 1966.

* * *

VOGEL, Helen Wolff 1918-

PERSONAL: Born February 27, 1918, in New York, N.Y.; daughter of Herbert Alfred (a lawyer) and Daisy (Kempner) Wolff; married John H. Vogel (a banker), December 20, 1947; children: Virginia, John, Jr., Thomas. *Education:* Columbia University, B.S., 1938, M.A., 1939. *Politics:* Democrat. *Religion:* Ethical Culture. *Home:* 18 Wynmor Rd., Scarsdale, N.Y.

CAREER: Teacher in adult education classes, New Rochelle, N.Y., Scarsdale, N.Y., and White Plains, N.Y. Former vice-president of Westchester Ethical Society.

WRITINGS: (With Mary Caruso) *Ocean Harvest*, Knopf, 1962; (with Martha E. Munzer) *Block by Block*, Knopf, 1973.

* * *

VOGT, Esther Loewen 1915-

PERSONAL: Surname is pronounced Vote; born November 19, 1915, in Collinsville, Okla.; daughter of Henry L. (a farmer and carpenter) and Agnes (Penner) Loewen; married Curt T. Vogt (a mechanic), May 24, 1942; children: Shirley Jean (Mrs. Danny Williams), Ranney Lee, Noami Ruth (Mrs. Lee Eitzen). *Education:* Tabor College, student, two years. *Politics:* Republican. *Religion:* Mennonite. *Home:* 502 East First, Hillsboro, Kan. 67063.

CAREER: Teacher in rural areas of Marion, Kan., 1939-40, and Hillsboro, Kan., 1940-42; part-time nurses' aide in a retirement center. Free-lance writer, 1955—. Young Women's Christian Association, Hillsboro, Kan., program chairman, 1961, 1964, 1965. *Member:* Kansas Authors Club (fourth district president, 1964-66), Mentor Study Club. *Awards, honors:* First prize in Native Kansas Sons and Daughters factual story contest, 1958; Tabor College Alumni Merit Award for outstanding service, 1974.

WRITINGS: Cry to the Wind, Zondervan, 1965; *The Sky is Falling*, Herald Press, 1968; *High Ground*, Herald Press, 1970; *Ann*, Herald Press, 1971; *Prairie Tales* (juvenile), Mennonite Brethren Publishing House, 1971; *I'll Walk Again* (biography), Herald Press, 1972. Writer of skits and short stories, with about three hundred stories sold, mostly to religious periodicals, 1955—.

SIDELIGHTS: Mrs. Vogt is fluent in German and Low German (Dutch).

* * *

VOLLMER, Howard M. 1928-

PERSONAL: Born March 18, 1928, in Los Angeles, Calif.; son of Norman L. (a telegrapher) and Celia (Mason) Vollmer; married; children: Daniel, Susan, Mason, Tina, Sandra. *Education:* Stanford University, B.A., 1950, M.A., 1951; University of California, Berkeley, Ph.D., 1958. *Politics:* Independent. *Religion:* Episcopalian. *Home:* 345 Cerrito Ave., Redwood City, Calif. 94061. *Office:* Bechtel Corporation, 50 Beale St., San Francisco, Calif. 94119.

CAREER: U.S. Army, Ordnance Corps, personnel research technician in Chambersburg, Pa., Rock Island, Ill., and Benicia, Calif., 1954-57; University of California, Institute of Industrial Relations, Berkeley, research sociologist, 1957-58; Stanford Research Institute, Menlo Park, Calif., senior sociologist, 1958-71; American University, Washington, D.C., chairman of sociology department, 1971-73; Bechtel Corp., San Francisco, Calif., management development program manager, 1973—. *Military service:* U.S. Army, 1951-54; became sergeant. *Member:* American Sociological Association (fellow).

WRITINGS: (With Leland H. Towle and Betty J. Maynard) *Development of a Radiation Safety Training Program for Industrial and Public Service Personnel*, U.S. Government Printing Office, 1960; (with Towle and Maynard) *Development of a Training Program for Radio-Isotope Workers in Industry*, U.S. Government Printing Office, 1960; *Employee Rights and the Employment Relationship*, University of California Press, 1960; *Applications of the Behavioral Sciences to Research Management: An Initial Study in the Office of Aerospace Research*, Stanford Research Institute, 1964; (with Todd R. La Porte, William C. Pedersen, and Phyllis A. Langton) *Adaptations of Scientists in Five Organizations: Methodology and Technical Appendix*, Stanford Research Institute, 1964; (editor) *The Fundamental Research Activity in a Technology-Dependent Organization*, Air Force Office of Scientific Research, 1965; *Work Activities and Attitudes of Scientists and Research Managers*, Stanford Research Institute, 1965; (editor with Donald L. Mills) *Professionalization*, Prentice-Hall, 1966; *Organization Design: Process and Concepts*, Stanford Research Institute, 1968; (with Philip Selznick and Philippe Nonet) *Law, Society, and Industrial Justice*, Russell Sage Foundation, 1969. Contributor to journals.

WORK IN PROGRESS: A book, *Going through Divorce*.

* * *

VON HILDEBRAND, Dietrich 1889-
(Peter Ott)

PERSONAL: Born October 12, 1889, in Florence, Italy; son of Adolf and Irene (Schaeuffelen) von Hildebrand; married Margarete Denk, May, 1912; married second wife, Alice Jourdain (a professor of philosophy), July 16, 1959; children: (first marriage) Franz. *Education:* Goettingen University, Ph.D., 1912. *Home:* 43 Calton Road, New Rochelle, N.Y. 10804. *Office:* c/o Fordham University, New York, N.Y.

CAREER: University of Munich, Munich, Germany, privatdozent, 1919-24, professor, 1924-33; University of Vienna, Vienna, Austria, professor, 1934-38 *Der christliche Staendestaat* (a Catholic anti-Nazi review), Vienna, Austria, founder and editor, 1933-38; Institut Catholique de Toulouse, Toulouse, France, professor, 1939-40; Fordham University, New York, N.Y., associate professor, 1941-49, professor, 1949-60, professor emeritus, 1960—. *Member:* German Pedagogical Institute (president of Munich branch), Katholische Akademiker Verband (member of the board), Mark Twain Association (honorary member). *Awards, honors:* Golden Award of the Catholic Writers' Guild, 1950.

WRITINGS: (Contributor) *Jahrbuch fuer Philosophie und phaenomenologische Forschung,* Max Niemeyer Verlag, Volume III, 1916, Volume V, 1921; (editor) *Der Geist des heiligen Franziskus und der dritte Orden* (title means "The Spirit of St. Francis and the Third Order"), Theatiner Verlag, 1921; *Reinheit und Jungfraeulichkeit* (Der Katholische Gedanke, No. 20), Oratoriums Verlag, 1927, published as *In Defense of Purity: An Analysis of the Catholic Ideals of Purity and Virginity,* Longmans, Green, 1931; *Die Ehe,* J. Mueller, 1929 (author's translation published as *Marriage,* Longmans, Green, 1942); *Metaphysik der Gemeinschaft: Untersuchungen ueber Wesen und Wert der Gemeinschaft* (title means "Metaphysics of Community: Inquiry into the Essence and Value of Community"), Haas und Grabherr, 1930, 2nd edition, Habbel, 1955; *Das Katholische Berufsethos* (title means "The Catholic Ethos of Professional Work"), Haas und Grabherr, 1931; *Zeitliches im Lichte des Ewigen* (essays, title means "Things Temporal in the Light of the Eternal"), Habbel, 1932; *Liturgie und Persoenlichkeit,* Anton Pustet 1933, 2nd edition, Styria, 1955 (author's translation published as *Liturgy and Personality,* edited and revised with Emmanuel Chapman, Longmans, Green, 1943, revised edition, Helicon Press, 1960); *Sittliche Grundhaltungen,* Matthias Gruenewald-Verlag, 1933 (English translation published as *Fundamental Moral Attitudes,* Longmans, Green, 1950); *Engelbert Dollfuss: Ein Katholischer Staatsmann* (title means "Engelbert Dollfuss: A Catholic Statesman"), Anton Pustet, 1934.

(First two editions under pseudonym Peter Ott) *Die Umgestaltung in Christus: Ueber christliche Grundhaltung,* Benziger, 1940, 4th edition, 1955, published as *Transformation in Christ: On the Christian Attitude of Mind,* Longmans, Green, 1948; (contributor) H. C. Gardiner, editor, *The Great Books: A Christian Appraisal,* Devin-Adair, Volume I, 1949, Volume II, 1950, Volume III, 1951; *Der Sinn philosophischen Fragens und Erkennens* (title means "The Meaning of Philosophical Inquiry and Knowledge"), Peter Hanstein Verlag, 1950; *Christian Ethics,* McKay, 1953; *The New Tower of Babel* (essays), Kenedy, 1953; *Die Menschheit am Scheideweg* (essays, title means "Humanity at the Crossroads"), Habbel, 1954; (with Alice Jourdain) *True Morality and its Counterfeits: A Critical Analysis of Existentialist Ethics,* McKay, 1955; (with Alice Jourdain) *Graven Images–Substitutes for True Morality: A Disentanglement of Morality from Mores,* McKay, 1957; *What Is Philosophy?,* Bruce, 1960; *Mozart, Beethoven, Schubert,* Habbel, 1962; *Not as the World Gives: St. Francis' Message to Laymen Today,* Franciscan Herald Press, 1963; (with wife, Alice Jourdain von Hildebrand) *The Art of Living,* Franciscan Herald Press, 1965; *Man and Woman,* Franciscan Herald Press, 1965; *The Sacred Heart: An Analysis of Human Divine Affectivity,* Helicon, 1965; *The Trojan Horse in the City of God,* Franciscan Herald Press, 1967; *Humanae Vitae: A Sign of Contradiction,* Franciscan Herald Press, 1968; *Celibacy: A Crisis of Faith,* Franciscan Herald Press, 1971; *Das Wesin der Liebe,* Kohlhammer, Habbil, 1971; *The Devastated Vineyard,* Franciscan Herald Press, 1974. Contributor of articles to theological, philosophical, sociological and general periodicals in Germany, France, and America.

WORK IN PROGRESS: Renewal or Apostasy, for Herder; *Die Liebe* (title means "Love"); and his memoirs.

SIDELIGHTS: Von Hildebrand has traveled extensively in Europe, the Near East, and North and South America. He Has lectured in 17 countries in four languages: German, English, French, and Italian. *Avocational interests:* Art and music.

BIOGRAPHICAL/CRITICAL SOURCES: Baldwin V. Schwarz, editor, *The Human Person and the World of Values: A Tribute to Dietrich von Hildebrand by his Friends in Philosophy,* Fordham University Press, 1960.

*   *   *

von MEHREN, Arthur T(aylor)   1922-

PERSONAL: Born August 10, 1922, in Albert Lea, Minn; son of Sigurd Anders (a civil engineer) and Eutalia Marion (Anderson) von Mehren; married Joan Elizabeth Moore, October 11, 1947; children: George Moore, Peter Anders, Philip Taylor. *Education:* Harvard University, B.S., 1942, LL.B., 1945, Ph.D., 1946; additional law study at University of Zurich, 1946-47, and University of Paris, 1948-49. *Home:* 68 Sparks St., Cambridge, Mass. 02138. *Office:* Harvard Law School, Cambridge, Mass. 02138.

CAREER: Law clerk to Chief Judge Calvert Magruder, U.S. Court of Appeals, Boston, Mass., 1945-46; Harvard University, Cambridge, Mass., assistant professor, 1946-53, professor of law, 1953—. U.S. Office of Military Government, Berlin, Germany, chief of Legislation Branch of Legal Division, 1947-48; University of Tokyo, Fulbright research professor, 1956-57; American Law Institute, Restatement Second, Contracts, advisor to the reporter, 1960—; Ford Foundation, consultant on legal education, New Delhi, India, 1962-63; Indian Law Institute, New Delhi, visiting professor, 1962-63; Delegation to the Hague Conference on Private International Law, member, 1966-68; Fulbright research professor, University of Rome, 1968-69; arbitrator in international arbitrations, 1970—.

MEMBER: American Association for the Comparative Study of Law (director), American Bar Association, American Foreign Law Association (past vice-president), American Association for Legal and Political Philosophy, American Arbitration Association, International · Academy of Comparative Law, International Law Association, Japanese American Society for Legal Studies (American Director), Phi Beta Kappa. *Awards, honors:* Guggenheim fellow, 1968-69.

WRITINGS: The Civil Law System: Cases and Materials for the Comparative Study of Law, Prentice-Hall, 1957, 2nd edition, Little, Brown, 1976; (editor with K. Nadelmann and J. Hazard) *Twentieth Century Comparative and Conflicts Law,* Sythoff (Leyden), 1961; (editor) *Law in Japan: The Legal Order in a Changing Society,* Harvard University Press, 1963; (with D. Trautman) *The Law of Multistate Problems: Cases and Materials on Conflict of Laws,* Little, Brown, 1965. Contributor to legal periodicals in the United States and abroad. Editor-in-chief, *Harvard Law Review,* 1944-45; member of board of editors, *American Journal of Comparative Law;* member of editorial committee, *International Encyclopedia of Comparative Law,* 1969—.

WORK IN PROGRESS: Editing with contributions, *Contracts in General: International Encyclopedia of Comparative Law,* Volume VII, to be published by Mohr and Mouton.

SIDELIGHTS: von Mehren speaks and reads French, German, and Italian.

von SCHMIDT, Eric 1931-

PERSONAL: Born May 28, 1931, in Bridgeport, Conn.; son of Harold (an illustrator) and Forest (Gilmore) von Schmidt; married Kuulei Kirn (a portrait artist); children: (previous marriage) Caitlin, Megan. *Education:* Studied at Farnsworth School of Art, 1950-51, and briefly at Art Students League, New York, N.Y., 1950. *Politics:* "Don't like them." *Religion:* "Self-taught." *Home:* 5201 Avenida del Mare, Sarasota, Fla.; San Miguel de Allende, Guanajuato, Mexico; (summer) Henniker, N.H.

CAREER: Graphic artist, covering "about everything" in the graphics field, 1950—, and with so many sidelines that he finds it hard to separate the vocations from the hobbies. Illustrator of over fifty children's books and twice as many record and book jackets. Songwriter and musician, turning out music and lyrics for more than thirty copyrighted songs; folksinger, appearing at New York Folk Festival in Carnegie Hall and Newport Folk Festival, 1965, 1968; recording artist for "The Folk Blues of Eric von Schmidt," Prestige Records, 1964, "Eric Sings von Schmidt," Prestige Records, 1965, "Who Knocked the Brains Out of the Sky," Smash/Mercury Records, 1969, and "Third Row, Second Right," Poppy Records, 1972; art director for Pathways of Sound (recordings for children), Cambridge, Mass., 1959-66. Ran own frame shop in Florida, 1955; taught painting, 1957; worked with disturbed children in Boston, Mass., 1958; began illustrating and then writing children's books in the 1960's. Formed Minglewood (a song publishing company affiliated with American Society of Composers, Authors and Publishers), 1970. *Military service:* U.S. Army, 1952-54; became sergeant. *Member:* American Society of Composers, Authors and Publishers, American Federation of Musicians, Authors Guild, Broadcast Music, Inc. *Awards, honors:* Fulbright scholarship to paint in Italy, 1955-56; other awards for painting and graphic art.

WRITINGS—All self-illustrated; juvenile: *Come For to Sing*, Houghton, 1963; *The Young Man Who Wouldn't Hoe Corn*, Houghton, 1964; *The Ballad of Bad Ben Bilge*, Houghton, 1965; *Mr. Chris and the Instant Animals*, Houghton, 1967; *Feeling Circus*, United Church Press, 1970, published (with teacher's guide by Hazel Schoonmaker and new introduction) as *Eric von Schmidt's Feeling Circus*, 1974. Adapted *The Ballad of Bad Ben Bilge* for a television pilot for Lilliputian Films.

WORK IN PROGRESS: More Children's books; a large painting (and possible book) on the Custer fight on the Little Big Horn; a musical play for children based on *The Young Man Who Wouldn't Hoe Corn*.

SIDELIGHTS: von Schmidt lived for a time on St. Vincent Island, British West Indies, and has traveled quite a bit in Europe and Asia. He has a deepening interest in the Plains Indians and the history of the West during the nineteenth-century.

BIOGRAPHICAL/CRITICAL SOURCES: St. Petersburg Times, April 17, 1966, December 17, 1972; *Tampa Tribune*, December 4, 1966; *The Boston Phoenix*, April 10, 1973.

*   *   *

VOS, Nelvin (LeRoy) 1932-

PERSONAL: Born July 11, 1932, in Edgerton, Minn.; son of Charley N. (a janitor) and Jeanette (Den Ouden) Vos; married Beverly Anne Drew, August 15, 1958; children: Christine Anne, Alicia Joan, David Drew. *Education:* Calvin College, A.B., 1954; University of Chicago, A.M., 1955, Ph.D., 1964. *Home address:* Box 15, Maxatawny, Pa. 19538. *Office:* Muhlenberg College, Allentown, Pa. 18104.

CAREER: Instructor in English and speech at Unity Christian High School, Hudsonville, Mich., 1955-57, and Calvin College, Grand Rapids, Mich., 1957-59; Trinity Christian College, Palos Heights, Ill., assistant professor of English, 1963-65; Muhlenberg College, Allentown, Pa., associate professor, 1965-70, professor of English, 1970—. Visiting professor at Lutheran School of Theology, Graduate School, summer, 1969, and Texas Tech University, summer, 1971. *Member:* Modern Language Association of America, National Council of Teachers of English, American Association of University Professors (chapter president, 1967-68), Conference on Christianity and Literature (secretary, 1965-67; president, 1968-70; member of board of directors, 1970-73), Society for the Arts, Religion, and Contemporary Culture, Association of Lutheran College Faculties, Omicron Delta Kappa. *Awards, honors:* Lindback Award for Distinguished Teaching, Mulhenberg College, 1967.

WRITINGS: The Drama of Comedy: Victim and Victor, John Knox, 1966; *For God's Sake, Laugh!*, John Knox, 1967; *Eugene Ionesco and Edward Albee: A Critical Essay*, Eerdmans, 1968; (co-editor) *Muhlenberg Essays*, Keller, 1968. Contributor to journals. Editor, "Newsletter" of Conference on Christianity and Literature, 1965-67; contributing editor, *The Reformed Journal*; drama editor, *For the Time Being*.

WORK IN PROGRESS: Studies on the theological understanding of contemporary drama.

SIDELIGHTS: Vos speaks and reads Dutch.

*   *   *

VOTAW, Dow 1920-

PERSONAL: Born August 18, 1920, in Boise, Idaho; son of Lorenzo D. (a teacher) and Gladys (Baker) Votaw; married Marian Moore, May 10, 1946; children: Ann Victoria, Beale. *Education:* Colorado College, Colorado Springs, B.A. (magna cum laude), 1941; Harvard University, M.B.A. (with distinction), 1943, LL.B., 1948. *Office:* 350 Barrows Hall, University of California, Berkeley, Calif. 94720.

CAREER: Admitted to California bar, 1948; private practice of law, San Francisco, Calif., 1948-57; University of California, Berkeley, 1948—, professor of business administration, 1959—. *Military service:* U.S. Naval Reserve, 1946-55; active duty, 1942-46; became lieutenant. *Member:* American Bar Association.

WRITINGS: Legal Aspects of Business Administration, Prentice-Hall, 1956, 3rd edition, 1969; *The Six-Legged Dog*, University of California Press, 1964; *Modern Corporations*, Prentice-Hall, 1965; (with S. P. Sethi) *The Corporate Dilemma*, Prentice-Hall, 1973. Also co-editor of series on economic institutions and social systems, Prentice-Hall, 1975—. Contributor to business, legal, and political journals.

WORK IN PROGRESS: A study of the "new populism"; a study of corporate directors.

SIDELIGHTS: Dow Votaw speaks Italian, and lived in Italy during 1955, 1961-62, and 1965. He has traveled and done research in other parts of Europe and in Japan. *Avocational interests:* Skiing and mountain climbing.

WADE, Richard Clement 1922-

PERSONAL: Born July 14, 1922, in Des Moines, Iowa; son of Clement Francis and Henrietta B. Wade; married second wife, Cynthia H. Whittaker, July 1, 1975. *Education:* University of Rochester, B.A., 1944, M.A., 1945; Harvard University, Ph.D., 1954. *Politics:* Democrat. *Home:* 20 Beekman Place, New York, N.Y. *Office:* City University of New York, Graduate Center, 33 West 42nd Street, New York, N.Y. 10036.

CAREER: University of Rochester, Rochester, N.Y., 1948-60, began as instructor, became professor of history; Washington University, St. Louis, Mo., professor of history, 1961-62; University of Chicago, Chicago, Ill., professor of American history, 1962-71; City University of New York, Graduate Center, New York, N.Y., Distinguished Professor of history, 1971—. Scholar-in-residence, Kansas City Historical Project, 1961; specialist in New Zealand and Australia, U.S. Department of State, 1966; Mary Bingham Visiting Professor of Humanities, University of Louisville, 1968-69; visiting professor, Emory University, 1969; Harmsworth Professor of American Institutions, Oxford University, 1974-75. *Member:* American Historical Association, Organization of American Historians, Urban History Group.

WRITINGS: The Urban Frontier: The Rise of Western Cities, Harvard University Press, 1959; *Slavery in the Cities: The South, 1820-1860,* Oxford University Press, 1964; *The Urban Frontier: Pioneer Life in Early Pittsburgh, Cincinnati, Lexington, Louisville and St. Louis,* University of Chicago Press, 1964; (editor) *The Negro in American Life,* Houghton, 1965, published as *Negroes in American Life: Selected Readings,* 1970; (with Louise Wade and Howard Wilder) *A History of the United States,* Houghton, 1966; (with Harold M. Mayer) *Chicago: The Growth of a Metropolis,* University of Chicago Press, 1969; (editor) *Cities in American Life,* Houghton, 1971; (editor) *The Growth of Urban America,* Arno, 1973; (editor) *The Growth of Metropolitan America,* Arno, 1974. Editor, Oxford University Press, "Urban Life in America" series, 1964—.

WORK IN PROGRESS: Concrete Roots: Cities in American Life.

* * *

WADIA, Maneck S. 1931-

PERSONAL: Born October 22, 1931, in Bombay, India; married Harriet F. Schilit, November 21, 1962; children: Sara, Mark. *Education:* St. Xavier College, B.A. (honors), 1952; Indiana University, M.A., 1955, Ph.D., 1957, M.B.A., 1958. *Home:* 1660 Luneta Dr., Del Mar, Calif. 92014.

CAREER: Indiana University, Bloomington, assistant professor of management, 1958-60; University of Pittsburgh, Administrative Science Center, Pittsburgh, Pa., Ford Foundation fellow, 1960-61; Stanford University, Stanford, Calif., assistant professor of business administration, 1961-65, research associate of International Center for the Advancement of Management Education, 1961-64; San Diego State College (now University), San Diego, Calif., associate professor, 1965-67, professor of management, 1967-71; currently president of Wadia Associates (management consultants), Del Mar, Calif. Consultant to government, business, educational, and armed forces organizations. *Member:* Society for Applied Anthropology (fellow), Society for Advancement of Management, Institute of Man-

agement Sciences, Academy of Management, Anthropological Society of Bombay, Indiana Academy of Science, Sigma Xi (associate member), Sigma Iota Epsilon (honorary member).

WRITINGS: (Contributor) *Readings in Organization and Management,* Holt, 1963; (contributor) *Educational Administration: Selected Readings,* Allyn & Bacon, 1965; (contributor) *Management and Organizational Behavior Theories,* Southwestern, 1965; *The Nature and Scope of Management,* Scott, Foresman, 1966; (co-author) *Marketing Management: Cases from Emerging Nations,* Addison-Wesley, 1966; (contributor) *International Marketing,* Wiley, 1967; (contributor) *Readings in Administration,* Appleton, 1967; *Management and the Behavioral Sciences,* Allyn & Bacon, 1968; *Multinational Business: Countries and Cases,* International Textbook, 1970. Contributor of more than twenty articles to professional journals.

WORK IN PROGRESS: Research in applied anthropology, organizational behavior, management and behavioral sciences.

* * *

WAINHOUSE, David Walter 1900-

PERSONAL: Born September 15, 1900, in Vilna, Lithuania; brought to United States in 1909, became U.S. citizen in 1923; son of Samuel (a shoe manufacturer) and Ida W. (Steinberg) Wainhouse; married Katharine Cohen (a landscape architect), August 5, 1925; children: Austryn, Jonathan (deceased). *Education:* Harvard University, A.B., 1923, A.M., 1926, LL.B., 1927; Oxford University, B.C.L., 1929. *Home:* 4301 Massachusetts Ave. N.W., Washington, D.C. 20016. *Office:* School of Advanced International Studies, Johns Hopkins University, 1740 Massachusetts Ave. N.W., Washington, D.C.

CAREER: Admitted to Maine bar, 1926, New York bar, 1934, and District of Columbia bar, 1948; assistant U.S. attorney for Southern District of New York, 1934-41; U.S. Department of State, 1946-62, deputy assistant Secretary of State, 1953-56, minister-counselor, U.S. Embassy, Vienna, Austria, 1956-62, consultant to U.S. Department of State, 1962—; Johns Hopkins School of Advanced International Studies, Washington, D.C., research associate, 1962-71. Fordham University, lecturer in political science, 1932-34; New York University, lecturer in public law, 1938-41; American University, professor of international law, 1963-64; Salzburg Seminar in American Studies, lecturer on American foreign policy, 1965; Austrian Diplomatic Academy, professorial lecturer, 1968-69. *Military service:* U.S. Army, staff officer, 1941-46; became colonel; received Legion of Merit. *Member:* Cosmos Club (Washington, D.C.), Harvard Club (Washington, D.C.). *Awards, honors:* Carl Schurz Memorial traveling fellowship, 1931.

WRITINGS: (Contributor) *American Foreign Relations,* Council on Foreign Relations, 1931; (with John Latane) *History of American Foreign Policy,* Doubleday, 1940; *Remnants of Empire,* Harper, 1965; (with others) *International Peace Observation,* Johns Hopkins Press, 1966; *Arms Control Agreements: Designs for Verification and Organization,* Johns Hopkins Press, 1968; *International Peacekeeping at the Crossroads,* Johns Hopkins Press, 1973.

AVOCATIONAL INTERESTS: Plays viola in string quartet.

WALDMAN, Eric 1914-

PERSONAL: Born September 21, 1914, in Vienna, Austria; came to United States, 1938, naturalized, 1943; son of Leo and Sophie (Blau) Waldman; married JoAnn Lowden, December 23, 1944; children: Heidi, Christopher. *Education:* University of Vienna, Ph.D., 1938; George Washington University, B.A. (with distinction), 1951, M.A., 1952, Ph.D., 1955. *Religion:* Roman Catholic. *Home:* 3616 Underhill Drive, N.W., Calgary, Alberta T2N 4G1, Canada. *Office:* Department of Political Science, University of Calgary, Calgary, Alberta T2N 1N4, Canada.

CAREER: Lecturer at George Washington University, Washington, D.C., and research analyst at Columbia University, New York, N.Y., 1952-55; Marquette University, Milwaukee, Wis., assistant professor, 1955-58, associate professor, 1958-62, professor of political science, 1962-66, director of Institute of German Affairs, 1957-66, chairman of department, 1958-62; University of Calgary, Calgary, Alberta, professor of political science, 1966—. Visiting professor, University of Marburg, 1965. Member of board, World Affairs Council of Milwaukee, 1957-61, 1964-66. Consultant, Research Analysis Corp., 1967-68. *Military service:* U.S. Army, Intelligence, 1942-49; became captain; received War Department citation. U.S. Army Reserve, 1949-66; retired as lieutenant colonel.

MEMBER: American Political Science Association, American Council on Germany, American Association of University Professors, United World Federalists (president, Milwaukee chapter, 1965-66), American Civil Liberties Union, Canadian Political Science Association, Canada Institute of International Affairs, Interuniversity Center for European Studies, Conference on European Problems, Conference on German Politics, Bund Freiheit der Wissenschaft, Western Political Science Association, Reserve Officers Association, Phi Beta Kappa, Pi Gamma Mu, Delta Phi Alpha, Knights of Malta. *Awards, honors:* German government research grants, 1958, 1964, 1965; North Atlantic Treaty Organization advanced research fellowship to Germany, 1960; Marquette University research grants, 1960-61, 1964-66; Fulbright senior research grant to Germany, 1961-62, and travel grant, 1965; German Federal Cross of Merit, 1966; Canada Council Grant, 1967-68, 1968-69, 1970-71, 1972; University of Calgary research grant, 1971-72, 1973-74, 1975; American Philosophical Society research grant, 1972.

WRITINGS: The Sparticist Uprising, Marquette University Press, 1958 (translation by the author published as *Spartakus: Der Aufstand von 1919 und die Krise der Deutschen Sozialistischen Bewegung,* Harald Boldt Verlag, 1967); *Soldat im Staat,* Harald Boldt Verlag, 1963, published as *The Goose Step is Verboten: The German Army Today,* Free Press of Glencoe, 1964; *Notstand und Demokratie,* Harald Boldt Verlag, 1968; *Die Sozialistische Einheitsparti Westberlin und die sowjetische Berlinpolitik,* Harald Boldt Verlag, 1972.

Contributor: J. S. Roucek, editor, *Contemporary Ideologies,* Philosophical Library, 1961; *Meet Germany,* Atlantic Bridge, 1963, 1966; J. Dunner, editor, *Dictionary of Political Science,* Philosophical Library, 1964; T. T. Hammond, editor, *Soviet Foreign Relations and World Communism,* Princeton University Press, 1965; Dunner, editor, *Handbook of World History,* Philosophical Library, 1967; R. N. Hunt, editor, *The Creation of the Weimar Republic,* Heath, 1969; *Yearbook on International Communist Affairs,* Hoover Institution, 1974, 1975. Also contributor of articles and reviews to *Monatshefte fuer Politik und Kultur, American Political Science Review, Social Science, Journal of Modern Languages, Canadian Journal of Political Science,* and other German, American and Canadian journals.

WORK IN PROGRESS: A history of the East German Socialist Unity Party.

SIDELIGHTS: Waldman is competent in French and German.

* * *

WALKER, Charles 1911-

PERSONAL: Born July 26, 1911, in Stafford, England; son of Charles (a railway worker) and Lucy (Stockton) Walker; married Dorice Elizabeth Jones, August 8, 1936; children: Anthony C., Audrey E. *Education:* University College of South Wales and Monmouthshire, Cardiff, Teaching Certificate, 1934. *Religion:* Church of England. *Home:* 1 Springfield Close, Crimplesham, Kings Lynn, Norfolk, England.

CAREER: Schoolmaster in England, 1934-71, as chemistry master at Manor Park Grammar School, Nuneaton, Warwickshire, England, 1950-71, and as deputy headmaster, 1951-71. *Military service:* Royal Army Ordnance Corps, 1941-46; became staff sergeant.

WRITINGS: Progress on Rails, Edward Arnold, 1964; *Progress on Roads,* Edward Arnold, 1965; *Progress with Energy,* Edward Arnold, 1966, St. Martin's, 1967; *Thomas Brassey: Railway Builder,* Muller, 1969; *Joseph Locke,* Shire Publications, 1975; *Master of Method or A Difficult and Dangerous Operation,* David & Charles, in press. Contributor to *Times Educational Supplement, The Teacher,* and *Popular Gardening.* Editor of *County Chronicle* (publication of Warwickshire County Teachers' Association) 1956-72.

WORK IN PROGRESS: Profitable Gardening with Polythene, completion expected in 1976 or 1977.

BIOGRAPHICAL/CRITICAL SOURCES: Coventry Evening Telegraph Year Book, September, 1965.

* * *

WALKER, Harold Blake 1904-

PERSONAL: Born May 7, 1904, in Denver, Colo.; son of Herbert Richards (a salesman) and Ethel Gertrude (Blake) Walker; married Mary Alice Corder, February 1, 1930; children: Herbert, Howard, Timothy. *Education:* University of Denver, A.B., 1926; Boston University, A.M., 1927; McCormick Theological Seminary, B.D., 1932; University of Chicago, graduate study, 1933-34. *Politics:* Independent. *Home and Office:* 425 Grove St., Evanston, Ill. 60201.

CAREER: Associated Press, Kansas City, Mo., writer, 1927-30; ordained to Presbyterian ministry, 1932; minister in Chicago, Ill., 1932-36, Utica, N.Y., 1936-42, Oklahoma City, Okla., 1942-47; First Presbyterian Church, Evanston, Ill., senior minister, 1947-70. President of board of directors, McCormick Theological Seminary; director of National Presbyterian Church, Washington, D.C., and Lake Forest College; member of Citizens Committee on Evanston Public Schools. *Member:* Presbyterian Council on Theological Education, Chicago Cleric, Phi Kappa Alpha, Masons. *Awards, honors:* D.D., Emporia College, 1944, Hamilton College, 1949, University of Denver, 1951; L.H.D., Lake Forest College, 1959, National College of

Education, 1970; Freedoms Foundation Award, 1950, 1955, for sermons; St.D., Northwestern University, 1970.

WRITINGS: Going God's Way, Presbyterian Board, 1947; *Ladder of Light*, Revell, 1947; *Upper Room on Main Street*, Harper, 1954; *Power to Manage Yourself*, Harper, 1955; (with wife, Mary Alice Walker) *Venture of Faith*, Harper, 1959; *Heart of the Christian Year*, Harper, 1961; *Faith in Times of Tension*, United Presbyterian Men, 1962; *Thoughts to Live By*, Dartnell, 1965; *To Conquer Loneliness*, Harper, 1966; *Memories to Live By*, Dartnell, 1967; *Inspirational Thoughts for Every Day*, Hawthorn, 1970. Contributor to religious journals. Columnist, Chicago Tribune-New York News Syndicate, 1954—, *Specialty Salesman*, 1954-64; director, *Presbyterian Tribune*, 1943-55.

*   *   *

WALKER, Kenneth Richard   1931-

PERSONAL: Born October 17, 1931, in Otley, Yorkshire, England; son of Arthur Bedford (a toolmaker) and Olive (Thornton) Walker; married June Abercrombie Collie (a physician); children: Neil George Arthur, Ruth Abercrombie. *Education:* University of Leeds, B.A., 1953; Oxford University, D.Phil, 1959. *Home:* 4 Harpenden Rd., St. Albans, Hertfordshire, England. *Office:* School of Oriental and African Studies, University of London, London W.C.1, England.

CAREER: University of Aberdeen, Aberdeen, Scotland, assistant lecturer in political economy, 1956-59; School of Oriental and African Studies, University of London, London, England, research fellow, 1959-61, lecturer, 1961-66, reader, 1966-72, professor of economics and head of department, 1972—.

WRITINGS: Planning in Chinese Agriculture: Socialisation and the Private Sector, 1956-1962, Aldine, 1965. Contributor to *China Quarterly* and economics journals in England and America.

WORK IN PROGRESS: Production and Distribution of Food Grains in China; for Cambridge University Press.

SIDELIGHTS: Walker reads modern Chinese. *Avocational interests:* Hills and mountains and walking; music, especially church choral music; golf, politics, gardening, birds.

*   *   *

WALKER, Marshall (John)   1912-

PERSONAL: Born January 23, 1912, in Bath, N.Y.; son of Marshall Houghton (a tobacconist) and Anna Mary (Faucett) Walker; married Georgianna Laura Robinson (a nutrition chemist), October 9, 1937; children: Robert Scofield, Dorothy Patricia (Mrs. Richard Harris). *Education:* Cornell University, B.Chem., 1933, A.M., 1936; Pennsylvania State University, Ph.D., 1950. *Home:* Star Route, Chaplin, Conn. 06235. *Office:* University of Connecticut, Storrs, Conn.

CAREER: E. I. duPont de Nemours, Parlin, N.J., assistant physicist, 1936-42; Allegany Ballistics Laboratory, Cumberland, Md., associate physicist, 1942-45; Massachusetts Institute of Technology, Cambridge, teaching fellow, 1945-46; Pennsylvania State University, University Park, research assistant, 1946-49; University of Connecticut, Storrs, assistant professor, 1949-58, associate professor, 1958-64, professor of physics and acting head of department, 1964—. Member, Eastford (Conn.) Board of Educa-

tion, 1965—. *Member:* American Physical Society, American Association of Physics Teachers, American Optical Society, American Association of University Professors, Connecticut Academy of Arts and Sciences, Sigma Xi, Sigma Pi Sigma.

WRITINGS: The Nature of Scientific Thought, Prentice-Hall, 1963.

*   *   *

WALKER, William H.   1913-

PERSONAL: Born December 20, 1913, in Bryan, Tex.; son of Claude Glenn (operator of a small business) and Sallie Bell (Higgs) Walker; married Erma Ethel Stevens, August 30, 1938; children: William, Stephen, Richard, Harold. *Education:* Wheaton College, Wheaton, Ill., B.A., 1935; Dallas Theological Seminary, Th.M., 1939. *Home:* 1014 De Soto Drive, Dalton, Ga. 30720.

CAREER: Clergyman of Independent Fundamental Churches of America; Central American Mission, missionary in El Salvador, Guatemala, 1942-49, general secretary, Dallas, Tex., 1951-59; Miami Bible College, Miami, Fla., academic dean, 1959-64, instructor in Bible and missions, 1965-68; Spanish Publications, Inc., Dalton, Ga., president, 1959—; Fellowship Bible Church, Dalton, Ga., pastor, 1972—.

WRITINGS: Will Russia Conquer the World?, Loizeaux, 1962; *Vocabulary Builder*, Spanish Publications, 1964; (editor) *Spanish Scofield Bible*, Spanish Publications, 1966; *Progressive Revelation*, Spanish Publications, 1971.

*   *   *

WALL, Patrick D(avid)   1925-

PERSONAL: Born April 5, 1925, in Nottingham, England; son of Thomas (an educator) and Ruth (Cresswell) Wall. *Education:* Oxford University, B.M., B.Ch., and M.A., 1948, D.M., 1960. *Office:* University College, University of London, Gower St., London WC1, England.

CAREER: Yale University School of Medicine, New Haven, Conn., instructor in physiology, 1948-50; University of Chicago, Chicago, Ill., assistant professor of anatomy, 1950-53; Harvard University, Cambridge, Mass., instructor in physiology, 1953-55; Massachusetts Institute of Technology, Cambridge, member of staff, Research Laboratory of Electronics, 1953-67, associate professor, 1957-58, professor of physiology, 1958-67; University of London, University College, London, England, professor and director of cerebral functions research group, 1967—.

WRITINGS: T.R.I.O., the Revolting Intellectual Organization, C. N. Potter, 1965. Editor, *Pain*, 1975—; member of editorial board, *Journal of Physiology, Experimental Neurology, Experimental Brain Research*.

*   *   *

WALLACH, Paul I.   1927-

PERSONAL: Born July 29, 1927, in Los Angeles, Calif.; son of Lewis J. and Ann (Krinitt) Wallach; divorced; children: Bruce John, Bret Richard, Robin Lianne, Adam Joseph. *Education:* University of California, Santa Barbara, B.A., 1951; California State College (now California State University), Los Angeles, M.A., 1956. *Politics:* Democrat. *Religion:* Jewish. *Home:* 2858 Carolina Ave., Redwood City, Calif. 94061.

CAREER: Teacher at U.S. Air Force dependant schools in

Europe, 1958-60; teacher of drafting and architecture in Los Angeles (Calif.) public schools, 1951-64, Sequoia Union High School District, 1964—. Instructor in architecture, Canada College, Redwood City, 1969—. *Military service:* U.S. Navy, 1945-46. *Member:* Epsilon Phi Tau.

WRITINGS: (With Hepler) *Architecture: Drafting and Design*, McGraw, 1965, 3rd edition, in press; (with Hepler) *Housing Today*, McGraw, 1965; (with Hepler) *Home Planning*, McGraw, 1966; *Study Guides for Architectural References*, Pierce Publishing Co., 1968; *Architectural Drafting Study Guides Workbook*, McGraw, 1972; *Metric Study Guide*, Pierce Publishing Co., 1975; *The Meter Reader*, Fearon, in press. Also author of *Machine Drafting and Blueprint Reading*. Creator of educational transparencies on drafting and architecture, and other study aids.

WORK IN PROGRESS: Architectural transparencies for the overhead projector; *Metric Drafting*.

AVOCATIONAL INTERESTS: Handball, tennis, and cycling.

* * *

WALLIS, George A. 1892-

PERSONAL: Born November 18, 1892, in Clarksville, Tex.; son of James Edmund and Edna A. (Kinard) Wallis; married Jessie L. Carpenter, November 19, 1919 (divorced, 1935); married Geneva M. Smith, November 16, 1936; children: (first marriage) Mrs. Earl O'Neal; (second marriage) Melba Wallis Tedford, Milton Alfred. *Education:* Attended Valparaiso University, 1916-17, University of Colorado, 1921-24, Arizona State University, 1934-36, B.A., 1949. *Politics:* Republican. *Religion:* Methodist. *Home and Office:* 4810 Key Road, Titusville, Fla. 32780. *Agent:* William H. Kelleher, 544 Westview Ave., Cliffside Park, N.J.

CAREER: Reporter in Amarillo, Tex., 1925-26, and editor of Nunn-Warren Newspapers, Texas, 1927-28; advertising manager of newspaper in Tucumcari, N.M., 1944-45; also has operated motels and resorts, and raised Angus cattle. Free-lance magazine writing, 1926—. *Military service:* New Mexico Infantry, 1916; took part in campaign against Pancho Villa. U.S. Army, prisoner of war escort, World War I.

WRITINGS: Cattle Kings of the Staked Plains, Sage Books, 1965; *J. P. Housman of Oregon*, Merchant's Press, 1966; *Unforgetable Men of the West*, Viking, 1974. Contributor to *Progressive Farmer, Scientific American, True West, Infantry, New Mexico Magazine, Mentor*, and others.

WORK IN PROGRESS: John Chisam—Cattle King of America; Exploring American Antiquity; This Was Fleury—This Was Verdun.

SIDELIGHTS: Cattle Kings of the Staked Plains was serialized in *True West*.

* * *

WALSH, John (Dixon) 1927-

PERSONAL: Born September 4, 1927, in Hornchurch, England; son of John Shaw (a minister) and Margaret (Dixon) Walsh; married Frances Innes, April 1, 1960; children: Rachel, James. *Education:* Magdalene College, Cambridge, B.A., 1951, Ph.D., 1956; University of Goettingen, postdoctoral student, 1956. *Office:* Jesus College, Oxford University, Oxford, England.

CAREER: Jesus College, Oxford University, Oxford, En-

gland, fellow and tutor, 1958—. *Military service:* British Army, 1946-48; became lieutenant.

WRITINGS: (Editor with G. V. Bennett) *Essays in Modern English Church History, in Memory of Norman Sykes*, Oxford University Press, 1966. Contributor to *New Cambridge Modern History*, Volume IX.

WORK IN PROGRESS: A book, *The Rise of Methodism.*

* * *

WALTER, Ingo 1940-

PERSONAL: Born April 11, 1940, in Kiel, Germany; son of Hellmuth (an executive) and Ingeborg (Moeller) Walter; married Jutta Ragnhild Dobernecker, June 28, 1963; children: Carsten Erik, Inga Maria. *Education:* Lehigh University, B.A. (summa cum laude), 1962, M.S., 1963; New York University, Ph.D., 1966. *Home:* 77 Club Road, Upper Montclair, N.J. 07043. *Office:* Graduate School of Business Administration, New York University, 100 Trinity Place, New York, N.Y. 10006.

CAREER: University of Missouri at St. Louis, assistant professor, 1965-67, associate professor of economics, 1967-70; New York University, New York, professor of economics and finance, and associate dean of Graduate School of Business Administration, 1970—. *Member:* American Economic Association, American Finance Association, Royal Economic Society, Phi Beta Kappa, Beta Gamma Sigma, Omicron Delta Epsilon (chapter founder and president, 1962-63).

WRITINGS: The Common Market: Economic Integration in Europe, Lippincott, 1965; (editor with F. B. Jensen) *International Economic Relations*, Ronald, 1966; *International Economics*, Ronald, 1966, 2nd edition, 1975; *State and Local Public Finance*, Ronald, 1969; *The European Common Market*, Praeger, 1969; *The United States and International Markets*, Heath-Lexington, 1972; *Readings in Macroeconomics*, McGraw, 1974; *International Economics of Pollution Control*, Macmillan, 1975; *Studies in International Environmental Economics*, Wiley, in press.

WORK IN PROGRESS: Research on international economics.

SIDELIGHTS: Walter speaks German, reads French.

* * *

WALTHER, Regis (Hills) 1917-

PERSONAL: Born November 24, 1917, in Chicago, Ill.; son of George Jacob (a nurseryman) and Margaret (Durmody) Walther; married Ferne Essene, August 14, 1939; children: Frances, Margaret, Linda; stepchildren: Richard. *Education:* University of California, Los Angeles, B.A., 1941; George Washington University, Ph.D., 1963. *Politics:* Democrat. *Home:* 1808 Collingwood Rd., Alexandria, Va. *Office:* Center for Behavioral Science and Social Research Group, George Washington University, Washington, D.C.

CAREER: U.S. Office of Price Administration, Washington, D.C., personnel officer, 1942-47; U.S. Department of State, Washington, D.C., medical administrator, 1948-56, personnel research officer, 1956-64; George Washington University, Washington D.C., director of Center for Behavioral Sciences and Social Research Group, 1964—, professorial lecturer in psychology research methods, 1960—, research professor of management science, 1971—. *Member:* American Psychological Association, American

Association for the Advancement of Science, Society for the Psychological Study of Social Issues, Sigma Xi.

WRITINGS: Psychological Dimension of Work, George Washington University Center for Behavioral Sciences, 1964; *Orientations and Behavioral Styles of Foreign Service Officers,* Carnegie Endowment for International Peace, 1965; *Socialization Principles and Work Styles of the Juvenile Court,* George Washington University Center for Behavioral Sciences, 1965; *Human Factors Related to Quality and Reliability of Unmanned Spacecraft Components,* George Washington University Center for Behavioral Sciences, 1965; (with Margaret L. Magnusson) *A Retrospective Study of the Effectiveness of Out-of-School Neighborhood Youth Corps Programs in Four Urban Sites,* George Washington University Social Research Group, 1967; *Job Adjustment and Health,* George Washington University Manpower Research Projects, 1968; *The Accelerated Learning Experiment: An Approach to the Remedial Education of Out-of-School Youth,* George Washington University Social Research Group, 1969.

The Measurement of Work Relevant Attitudes: A Report on the Development of a Measuring Instrument, George Washington University Manpower Research Projects, 1970; *A Study of Negro Male High School Dropouts Who Are Not Reached by Federal Work-Training Programs,* George Washington University Social Research Group, 1970; *A Study of the Effectiveness of Selected Out-of-School Neighborhood Youth Corps Programs,* George Washington University Social Research Group, 1971; *An Educational Model for Manpower Programs: A Manual of Recommended Practices,* George Washington University Manpower Research Projects, 1975; *A Longitudinal Study of Selected Out-of-School Neighborhood Youth Corps Programs—2 Programs in Four Cities,* George Washington University Manpower Research Projects, 1975.

*   *   *

WALTNER, Elma 1912-

PERSONAL: Born November 30, 1912, in Yankton, S.D.; daughter of Emil J. and Mary (Goering) Waltner. *Education:* Freeman Junior College, Freeman, S.D., student, 1926-28; Yankton College, A.B. (cum laude), 1930. *Religion:* General Conference Mennonite Church. *Home:* Bonnie Brook Pl., Hurley, S.D. 57036.

CAREER: Free-lance nonfiction writer since 1940's, teaming with brother, Willard Waltner, a photographer.

WRITINGS—All illustrated by Willard Waltner: *Carving Animal Caricatures,* McKnight & McKnight Publishers, 1951; *Wonders of Hobbycraft,* Lantern, 1962; *The New Hobbycraft Book,* Lantern, 1963; *Holiday Hobbycraft,* Lantern, 1964; *Hobbycraft Toys and Games,* Lantern, 1965; *Hobbycraft Around the World,* Lantern, 1966; *Hobbycraft for Juniors,* Lantern, 1967; *Year Round Hobbycraft,* Lantern, 1968; *A New Look at Old Crafts,* Lantern, 1971. Contributor of adult and juvenile articles to magazines, house organs, and trade journals.†

*   *   *

WALTON, George (H.) 1904-

PERSONAL: Born June 8, 1904, in Haddonfield, N.J.; son of Joseph (a woolen importer) and Addie (Austin) Walton, married Helen Scott Scammell, April 9, 1932; married Virginia Walton Hodges, June 7, 1975; children: Frank, Joseph. *Education:* University of Pennsylvania, B.S., 1927,

LL.B., 1930. *Religion:* Episcopalian. *Address:* P.O. Box 117, Cedar Key, Fla. 32625. *Agent:* John Cushman Associates, 25 West 43rd St. New York, N.Y. 10036.

CAREER: University of Pennsylvania, Philadelphia, instructor in political science, 1927-32; attorney in private practice, Camden, N.J., 1932-42; U.S. Army, 1942-45, with service in Mediterranean and European theaters, in ranks from captain to lieutenant colonel; private practice of law, Camden, N.J., 1946-57; U.S. Army, Washington, D.C., 1957-64, leaving service as colonel; full-time writer, 1964—. *Awards, honors*—Military: Legion of Merit, Bronze Star Medal and Commendation Ribbon with medal pendant.

WRITINGS: The Wasted Generation, Chilton, 1965; (with Robert H. Adelman) *The Devil's Brigade,* Chilton, 1966; (with John Terrell) *Faint the Trumpet Sounds,* McKay, 1966; *Let's End the Draft Mess,* McKay, 1967; (with Adleman) *Rome Fell Today,* Little, Brown, 1968; (with Adleman) *The Champagne Campaign,* Little, Brown, 1969; *Twelve Events that Changed Our World,* Cowles Book, 1970; *Sentinel of the Plains: Fort Leavenworth and the American West,* Prentice-Hall, 1973; *The Tarnished Shield: A Report on Today's Army,* Dodd, 1973; *Captain Madam,* Pyramid Publications, 1974.

WORK IN PROGRESS: Fearless and Free: The Story of the Seminole War.

SIDELIGHTS: The Devils' Brigade was made into a movie, produced by United Artists, 1968.

BIOGRAPHICAL/CRITICAL SOURCES: Book Week, April 30, 1967.

*   *   *

WALTZ, Jon R(ichard) 1929-

PERSONAL: Born October 11, 1929, in Delta, Ohio; son of Richard Rinehart (a banker) and Lenore (Tharp) Waltz. *Education:* College of Wooster, B.A., 1951; Yale University, LL.B., 1954. *Politics:* Independent. *Religion:* Presbyterian. *Home:* 3730 North Lake Shore Drive, Chicago, Ill. 60613. *Office:* School of Law, Northwestern University, 357 East Chicago Ave., Chicago, Ill. 60611.

CAREER: Practicing attorney, Chicago, Ill.; Northwestern University School of Law, Chicago, Ill., professor, 1964—. Lecturer on the workings of the adversary system of litigation and on American criminal justice. Member, Illinois Advisory committee, U.S. Commission on Civil Rights. *Military service:* U.S. Army, Judge Advocate General's Corps, 1955-58; became captain; received Commendation Medal. *Member:* Association of American Law Schools (chairman of committee on legal clinics), National Association of Defense Lawyers (member of advisory board), Association of the Bar of the Seventh Judicial Circuit, Chicago Bar Association, Phi Alpha Delta, Pi Sigma Alpha, Order of the Coif.

WRITINGS: (With John Kaplan) *The Trial of Jack Ruby,* Macmillan, 1965; (with D. W. Louisell and J. Kaplan) *Cases and Materials on Evidence,* Foundation Press, 1968, 2nd edition, 1972; (with D. W. Louisell and J. Kaplan) *Principles of Evidence and Proof,* Foundation Press, 1968, 2nd edition, 1972; (with Fred E. Inbau) *Medical Jurisprudence,* Macmillan, 1971; (contributor) Paul F. Rothstein, *The Federal Rules of Evidence: An Analysis,* Boardman, 1973; *Criminal Evidence,* Nelson Hall, 1975. Contributor to legal journals and book review media. Note and comment editor, *Yale Law Journal,* 1953-54. Member of advisory board, The Bracton Press, Inc.

WORK IN PROGRESS: With Walter W. Wadlington, *Problems of Law and Medicine.*

AVOCATIONAL INTERESTS: Collecting Oriental antiquities and antique furniture, Pekingese dogs.

* * *

WANAMAKER, A(llison) Temple 1918-

PERSONAL: Born July 16, 1918, in Seattle, Wash.; son of Allison Temple (a physician) and Mary Helen (Allmond) Wanamaker; married Sophia Wolkonsky, July 26, 1953; children: Peter, Natalie, Allison. *Education:* Stanford University, B.A., 1940.

CAREER: U.S. Department of State, Washington, D.C., foreign service officer, 1941—, serving in Barcelona, Spain, 1941-43, Bilbao, Spain, 1943-44, Ciudad Trujillo, Dominican Republic, 1946-47, Philippines, 1947-50, Tel Aviv, Israel, 1953-55, Nassau, Bahamas, 1956-58; assistant chief of Public Services Division, Department of State, Washington, D.C., 1958-59, director of Office of Public Services, 1960-62; consul in Cordoba, Argentina, 1964-65; public affairs officer, San Jose, Costa Rica, 1966—. *Military service:* U.S. Navy, 1944-46; became ensign. *Member:* Foreign Service Association, Phi Beta Kappa, Rotary Club of San Jose, Seattle Tennis Club.

WRITINGS: American Foreign Policy Today, preface by Dean Rusk, Bantam, 1964.

SIDELIGHTS: Wanamaker was wounded by machine gun bullets June 7, 1965, during an attempted assassination in Cordoba, Argentina.†

* * *

WARD, Don(ald G.) 1911-
(Powers Tracy)

PERSONAL: Born December 9, 1911, in Scipioville, N.Y.; son of Claude Mastin and Mae (Bishop) Ward; married Elizabeth Newton (a real estate broker), June 24, 1936; children: Michael, Grove, Kevin, Julie. *Education:* Syracuse University, A.B., 1935, Ph.D., 1941, law studies, 1943-45. *Politics:* Democrat. *Religion:* Unitarian Universalist. *Home:* 17 Hamilton Dr., Chappaqua, N.Y. 10514. *Office:* 151 East 50th St., New York, N.Y. 10022.

CAREER: State Teachers College (now State University of New York College) at Brockport, instructor in history and government, 1939-43; Syracuse University, Syracuse, N.Y., assistant director of U.S. Army Specialized Training Program, 1943-45; Western Publishing Co., Racine, Wis., and New York, N.Y., editor, 1945-55; free-lance editor and writer, 1955-58; New York State Department of Labor, New York, managing editor, 1958-59; free-lance editor and writer, 1959—. Executive secretary, Westchester Conference on County Development. *Member:* Westerners, New York Posse (sheriff, 1957-58), Phi Beta Kappa.

WRITINGS: (Editor) *Branded West,* Houghton, 1956; (editor) *Hoof Trails and Wagon Tracks,* Dodd, 1957; *Gunsmoke,* Ballantine, 1957; (editor) *Wild Streets,* Doubleday, 1958; (editor) *Bits of Silver,* Hastings, 1961; (with editors of American Heritage) *Cowboys and Cattle Country,* Meredith Press, 1961; (editor) *Great Short Novels of American West,* Collier, 1962; (editor with Milton Kline) *Favorite Stories of Hypnotism,* Dodd, 1965; (editor) *Pioneers West,* Dell, 1966; (editor) *Black Magic,* Dell, 1967; (compiler of index) *The Collected Catalogues of Dr. A.S.W. Rosenbach, 1904-1951,* Arno Press, 1968; (with Earl Hoyt) *Archery,* Athletic Institute, 1972; (with Edward Hamilton

Waldo) *Sturgeon's West,* Doubleday, 1973. Contributor of stories and reviews to magazines. Editor of *Brand Book* (New York Westerners), and *New York State Industrial Bulletin;* Americana editor for Hastings.

WORK IN PROGRESS: A book on Eastern woodland Indians; works on government in metropolitan regions of the United States, law enforcement in New York, and the district attorney's office and powers.

AVOCATIONAL INTERESTS: Travel in the American West, sports (especially baseball, football, tennis).†

* * *

WARD, Lynd (Kendall) 1905-

PERSONAL: Born June 26, 1905, in Chicago, Ill.; son of Harry F. (a minister and professor) and Daisy (Kendall) Ward; married May McNeer (a writer), June 11, 1926; children: Nanda Weedon, Robin Kendall (Mrs. Michael T. Savage). *Education:* Teachers College, Columbia University, B.S., 1926; National Academy for Graphic Arts, Leipzig, Germany, student, 1926-27. *Religion:* Methodist. *Home:* Lambs Lane, Cresskill, N.J. 07626.

CAREER: Illustrator and graphic artist, 1927—. Director, graphic arts division, Federal Art Project, New York, N.Y., 1937-39. Has exhibited wood engravings in most national print shows; prints are in permanent collections of the Library of Congress, Smithsonian Institution, Neward Museum, Metropolitan Museum, Victoria and Albert Museum, and others. *Member:* Society of American Graphic Artists (president, 1953-59), Society of Illustrators, National Academy of Design, P.E.N. *Awards, honors:* Zella de Milhau prize, 1947; Library of Congress award for wood engraving, 1948; National Academy of Design award, 1949; Caldecott Medal, 1953, for *The Biggest Bear;* Silver Medal of the Limited Editions Club, 1954; John Taylor Arms memorial award, 1962; Samuel F. B. Morse Medal, 1966; Rutgers Award, 1970; silver medallion from University of Southern Mississippi, 1973.

*WRITINGS—*All novels in woodcuts: *Gods' Man,* Cape & Smith, 1929, World, 1966; *Madman's Drum,* Cape & Smith, 1930; *Wild Pilgrimage,* Smith & Haas, 1932; *Prelude to a Million Years,* Equinox Press, 1933; *Song Without Words,* Random House, 1936; *Vertigo,* Random House, 1937; *Storyteller Without Words,* Abrams, 1974. Illustrator of more than 100 books. Contributor to *American Artist* and *Horn Book.*

Juveniles: *The Biggest Bear,* Houghton, 1952; *Nic of the Woods,* Houghton, 1965; *The Silver Pony,* Houghton, 1973.

BIOGRAPHICAL/CRITICAL SOURCES: Lee Bennett Hopkins, *Books are by People,* Citation Press, 1969.

* * *

WARD, Martha (Eads) 1921-

PERSONAL: Born July 21, 1921, in Quincy, Ill.; daughter of Oliver Thomas (manager of a plow company) and Gladys (Feagans) Eads; married Vincent P. Ward, February 3, 1951 (divorced). *Education:* Attended Knox College, 1938-40; University of Southern California, B.S., 1942; Pratt Institute, B.L.S., 1947; Quincy College, Teacher's Certificate, 1963. *Politics:* Republican. *Religion:* Protestant. *Home:* 2300 Hampshire St., Quincy, Ill. 62301. *Office:* Quincy Public Library, 526 Jersey, Quincy, Ill. 62301.

CAREER: U.S. Army Air Forces, civilian instructor in fuel, oil, and induction systems of fighter planes, 1943-44;

Quincy Public Library, Quincy, Ill., 1945—, chief librarian of children's department, 1948—. *Member:* American Library Association (recruitment representative, 1964-65), Illinois Library Association (chairman, children's librarians' section, 1953, 1965), Pi Beta Phi, University of Southern California Midwest Alumni Association (member of board of directors).

WRITINGS: (With Dorothy A. Marquardt) *Authors of Books for Young People*, Scarecrow, 1965; *Adlai Stevenson: Young Ambassador*, Bobbs-Merrill, 1967; *Ollie, Ollie, Oxen-Free*, Abingdon, 1969; (with D. A. Marquardt) *Illustrators of Books for Young People*, Scarecrow, 1971; *The Bug Man*, Abingdon, 1972.

AVOCATIONAL INTERESTS: Golf, travel, and staging puppet shows.

*   *   *

WARMKE, Roman F. 1929-

PERSONAL: Born November 23, 1929, in Easton, Minn.; married Dorothy Rose Emmer, 1952 (divorced 1974); children: Jonathan, James, Jerome, Julie Ann, Joseph, Matthew. *Education:* University of Minnesota, B.S., 1951, M.A., 1952, Ph.D., 1960. *Home:* Route 3, Box 178, Athens, Ohio 45701. *Office:* College of Business Administration, Ohio University, Athens, Ohio 45701.

CAREER: Austin Junior College, Austin, Minn., instructor in marketing and economics, 1952-54; Colorado State College (now University of Northern Colorado), Greeley, assistant professor, 1954-57, associate professor, 1957-61, professor of business and business education, 1961-62, director of Economic Education Center, 1962; University of Minnesota, Minneapolis, director of economic education, 1962-66; Ohio University, Athens, professor of economic education, 1966—, chairman of department, 1966-72, 1974—. National University of Mexico, visiting lecturer, 1960. Visiting professor and consultant to faculty of economics, Mara Institute of Technology (Malaysia), 1972-73. Executive director of Minnesota State Council on Economic Education, 1962-66; president, Ohio Council on Economic Education, 1966-72. *Member:* American Economic Association, National Council for Social Studies, National Business Education Association, Association for Supervision and Curriculum Development, American Educational Research Association, Midwest Economic Association, Delta Pi Epsilon, Phi Delta Kappa.

WRITINGS: (Contributor) *Die Deutsche Berufs—und Fachschule*, Rheininbessische Druckwerkstaette E. Dietl & Co., 1951; (contributor) *Business Education World*, Gregg Publishing Division, McGraw, 1957; *Supervision to Improve Instruction* (monograph), U.S. Office of Education, 1959; *Distributive Education Issues* (monograph), South-Western Publishing, 1961; (study director) *Study Guide for Selected Sixty-Session Series of the American Economy TV Films*, edited by Harlan M. Smith, Joint Council on Economic Education, 1964; (with Carroll A. Nolan) *Marketing, Sales Promotion and Advertising*, 7th edition, South-Western Publishing, 1965; (editor with Gerald Draager) *Selected Readings in Economic Education*, Ohio University, 1969.

(With W. Harmon Wilson) *Life on Paradise Island: Economic Life on an Imaginary Island*, Scott, Foresman, 1970; (with Wyllie, Wilson and Eyster) *Consumer Economic Problems*, 8th edition, South-Western Publishing, 1971; (with Wyllie and Sellers) *Consumer Decision Making*, South-Western Publishing, 1972; (with Chandriah Appa

Rao) *Economics*, Longman (Malaysia), 1974. Contributor to professional journals, trade journals, and house organs. Editor, American Vocational Association, 1959-65, and of special issue, *Business Education Forum*, 1965, 1966.

WORK IN PROGRESS: Introduction to Economics for Dickenson; a new edition of *Marketing, Sales Promotion, and Advertising* to be titled *Marketing in Action*; revised editions of *Consumer Economic Problems* and *Consumer Decision Making*.

*   *   *

WARREN, Austin 1899-

PERSONAL: Born July 4, 1899, in Waltham, Mass.; son of Edward Austin (a farmer) and Nellie M. (Anderson) Warren; married Antonia Degen (a medical doctor), September 5, 1946. *Education:* Wesleyan University, Middletown, Conn., B.A., 1920; Harvard University, M.A., 1922; Princeton University, Ph.D., 1926. *Politics:* Democrat. *Religion:* Episcopalian. *Home:* 90 Oriole Ave., Providence, R.I. 02906.

CAREER: Instructor in English at University of Kentucky, Lexington, 1920-21, and University of Minnesota, Minneapolis, 1922-24; Boston University, Boston, Mass., 1926-39, started as instructor, professor of English, 1934-39; University of Iowa, Iowa City, professor of English, 1939-48; University of Michigan, Ann Arbor, professor of English, 1948-68. St. Peter's School of Liberal and Humane Studies, Hebron, Conn., dean, summers, 1922-30. *Member:* Modern Language Association of America (executive council member, 1938-43), National Institute of Arts and Letters. *Awards, honors:* American Council of Learned Societies fellow, 1930-31; Rockefeller Foundation fellow, 1947-48, fellow, Kenyon School of English, 1948-50; Guggenheim fellow, 1950-51; senior fellow, School of Letters, Indiana University, 1950-65; Litt.D., Brown University, 1974.

WRITINGS: Alexander Pope as Critic, Princeton University Press, 1929; *The Elder Henry James*, Macmillan, 1934; *Richard Crashaw: A Study in Baroque Sensibility*, Louisiana State University Press, 1939; *Rage for Order*, University of Chicago Press, 1947; (with Rene Wellek) *Theory of Literature*, Harcourt, 1948; *New England Saints*, University of Michigan Press, 1956; *The New England Conscience*, University of Michigan Press, 1966; *Connections*, University of Michigan Press, 1970. Member of editorial boards, *New England Quarterly*, 1937-40, 1942-46, *American Literature*, 1940-42, and *Comparative Literature*, 1948-51; advisory editor, *Perspective*, and *Michigan Quarterly Review*.

WORK IN PROGRESS: An autobiography in several volumes, the first entitled, *Becoming What One Is*.

SIDELIGHTS: Most of Warren's writing is literary theory or literary criticism, with the literary criticism commonly on writers in whom religious or philosophical interest is coexistent with the literary. Theology, philosophy, and church history have always been his avocations; music, especially the organ, is a lifelong "serious recreation."

*   *   *

WASLEY, Robert S(echrist) 1918-

PERSONAL: Surname is pronounced *Wahz*-ley; born April 24, 1918; son of Bert (operator of electrical fixture company) and Gwendolyn (Hedgcock) Wasley; married Helen Bradford, December 27, 1958; children: Knox Bradford, James Hedgcock. *Education:* University of Denver, B.S., 1940; University of Colorado, M.S., 1941; Ohio State University, Ph.D., 1950. *Religion:* Presbyterian. *Home:* 3133 Fern Pl., Boulder, Colo. 80302. *Office:* School of Business, University of Colorado, Boulder, Colo. 80304.

CAREER: Ohio State University, Columbus, instructor, 1949-50; University of Colorado, School of Business, Boulder, 1941, 1946—, started as instructor in accounting, professor and head of Division of Accounting, 1959—, assistant to dean, 1955-56, acting dean, 1956-57, director of executive development program, 1958-63. University of Canterbury, Christchurch, New Zealand, visiting professor, 1966. *Military service:* U.S. Army, 1942-46. U.S. Army Reserve, 1946-65; became major. *Member:* National Associaton of Accountants (president, Denver chapter, 1957-58), American Accounting Association, Financial Executives Institute, Denver Estate Planning Council, Delta Sigma Pi, Beta Gamma Sigma, Rotary Club (Boulder). *Awards, honors:* Past President's Award for manuscripts, Denver chapter of National Association of Accountants, 1961, 1963.

WRITINGS: (With C. Orville Elliott) *Business Information Processing Systems*, Irwin, 1965, 4th edition, 1975. Regular contributor to *Accountants' Journal* (New Zealand).

AVOCATIONAL INTERESTS: Gardening, skiing.

* * *

WASSERSUG, Joseph D. 1912-
(Adam Bradford, M.D.)

PERSONAL: Born October 19, 1912, in Boston, Mass.; son of Jacob (in sales) and Dora (Blank) Wassersug; married Leona Alberts, November 3, 1940; children: Rona Jane (Mrs. Harold F. Goodman), Richard Joel, Robin Joan. *Education:* Harvard University, A.B. (cum laude), 1933; Boston University, graduate study, 1933-34; Tufts University, M.D. (cum laude), 1938. *Politics:* Republican. *Religion:* Jewish. *Home:* 8 Priscilla Lane, Quincy, Mass. 02169. *Office:* 22 Spear St., Quincy, Mass. 02169.

CAREER: Physician in private practice, specializing in internal medicine, Quincy, Mass., 1945—; Quincy Hospital, Quincy, Mass., physician, 1945—, currently senior physician; Boston City Hospital, Boston, Mass., assistant visiting physician, 1946-60. Also member of staff of Carney Hospital, Boston State Hospital, and Medfield State Hospital. Instructor in medicine at Tufts University Medical School, Boston, Mass., 1946-60. *Member:* American College of Chest Physicians (fellow), American Thoracic Society (fellow), American Medical Association, American Association for the Advancement of Science, American Heart Association, Massachusetts Medical Society, Alpha Omega Alpha.

WRITINGS: Your Rheumatism and Backaches, Wilfred Funk, 1945; *Your Coughs, Colds and Wheezes*, Wilfred Funk, 1947; *Hospital With a Heart*, Abelard, 1960; *Medicated Fables for Mice and Men*, Abelard, 1962; *Understanding Your Symptoms*, Abelard, 1964; *How to be Healthy and Happy after Sixty*, Abelard, 1966. Writer of medical column, "You're the Doctor," syndicated nationally by New York Herald Tribune Syndicate, 1960-63. Consulting editor, *Science Digest*. Contributor of about four hundred articles on health and science subjects to popular magazines, including *American Mercury, Science Digest, True Romances, True, Seventeen, Fantastic* (under pseudonym Adam Bradford, M.D.), and *Today's Health.*

WASSIL, Aly 1930-

PERSONAL: Born April 6, 1930, in Hyderabad, India; son of Mohammed Aly (a publisher and attorney) and Fatima (Khan) Fazil. *Education:* Attended Osmania University, 1944-47, Muslim University, 1948-49, and Massachusetts Institute of Technology, 1950-51; University of California, Los Angeles, B.A., 1954, graduate research, 1963-64. *Office:* Omniworld, Inc., 1642 North Sierra Bonita, Los Angeles, Calif. 90046.

CAREER: Lecturer in religion, philosophy, international affairs, and Asia, at schools, universities, and other groups, 1951—; script writer and actor in motion pictures and television, Hollywood, Calif., 1952—; editor and narrator in educational, religious and documentary films, 1952—; writer, 1957—; Omniworld (publishers), Los Angeles, Calif., president, 1965—. Model United Nations, director-general, 1954, member of committee, 1955—; World Authors, Lecturers, and Artists, Los Angeles, Calif., president, 1959—; International Fellowship of Christians, Moslems, and Jews, president, 1960—; United World Religions, founder and president, 1963—; United World Fellowship, founder and international president, 1964—.

MEMBER: International Platform Association (committee chairman; editor), International Cooperation Council (member of executive committee; editor), Conference on Science and Religion (member of board of directors; editor), Sufi International Order, Pi Kappa Delta. *Awards, honors:* Overseas state scholarship, Government of Hyderabad, 1950; Huntington Hartford fellowship, 1958; Great Seal of the State of California, conferred by Secretary of State, 1959.

WRITINGS: The Wisdom of Christ (selection of Book Club Guild and Religious Book Club), Harper, 1965; *Song of the Savior*, Omniworld, 1966, *The Rubaiyat of Modern Man*, United World Academy and Fellowship, 1967; *Dear Mr. President: An Open Letter to Richard Milhous Nixon*, Omniworld, 1972. Editor, *Platformer* (newsletter of International Platform Association), 1965—, *International Cooperation Directory* (annual of International Cooperation Council), 1966—. Contributor to *Reader's Digest, Time*, and other periodicals.

SIDELIGHTS: Wassil, founder of United World Fellowship, explained that the organization is based on the premise "that it is possible to be loyal to one's country without despising some other country; to love one's people and also to love all other people; to believe in one's religion while showing a genuine respect and profound understanding for other religions; to govern our personal, national, and international affairs by the purest truth, the highest wisdom, the greatest love, the brightest light, the boldest vision." *Avocational interests:* Travel, sports, dancing, music, chess, and intimate dinner parties.†

* * *

WATERMAN, Arthur E. 1926-

PERSONAL: Born March 18, 1926, in Niagara Falls, N.Y.; son of Verland E. and Ruth Louise (Dayton) Waterman: married Mary Margaret Laffer (a school librarian), August 23, 1948; children: Katherine Ann, Steven Paul, James Arthur, John Thomas, Richard Bird. *Education:* Allegheny College, A.B., 1949; University of Wisconsin, M.A., 1950, Ph.D., 1956. *Home:* 2720 Memorial Dr., S.E., Atlanta, Ga. 30317. *Office:* Georgia State University, Atlanta, Ga. 30303.

CAREER: University of Wisconsin, Madison, instructor, 1955-56; Central Michigan University, Mount Pleasant, assistant professor, 1956-60, associate professor of English, 1960-62; Georgia State University, Atlanta, professor of English, 1962—. Agnes Scott College, visiting lecturer, 1966. *Military service:* U.S. Naval Reserve, 1943-46; received Philippines Liberation Medal, five campaign stars. *Member:* Modern Language Association of America, American Association of University Professors, South Atlantic Modern Language Association.

WRITINGS: Flight and Search: Three Essays on the Modern American Novel, Georgia State College Press, 1965; *Susan Glaspell,* Twayne, 1966; *A Chronology of American Literary History,* C. E. Merrill, 1970. Contributor to *Critique, Modern Drama,* other journals in field of English and American literature.

WORK IN PROGRESS: Collection of essays on Conrad Aiken, with Douglas Robillard.

SIDELIGHTS: Waterman is competent in French and German. *Avocational interests:* Traveling and camping in United States, sailing.

* * *

WATSON, Richard L(yness), Jr. 1914-

PERSONAL: Born December 25, 1914, in Gill, Mass.; son of Richard Lyness (a teacher) and Alice (Vines) Watson; married Ruth Barker (a social worker), April 15, 1944; children: Richard Lyness III, James Barker, Patricia Alice. *Education:* Yale University, A.B., 1935, Ph.D., 1939. *Politics:* Democrat. *Religion:* Episcopalian. *Home:* 109 Pinecrest Rd., Durham, N.C. *Office:* 235 Allen, Duke University, Durham, N.C.

CAREER: Duke University; Durham, N.C., 1939—, started as instructor, professor of history, 1960—, chairman of department, 1960-67. Trustee, St. Augustine College, Raleigh, N.C., 1965-71. *Military service:* U.S. Army, Coast Artillery, 1941-43, Army Air Forces, 1943-46; became lieutenant colonel; received Army Commendation Ribbon with oak leaf cluster. *Member:* American Historical Association, American Association of University Professors, Organization of American Historians, American Civil Liberties Union, Southern Historical Association (member of executive council), Historical Society of North Carolina (president, 1973), North Carolina Literary and Historical Association (president, 1966). *Awards, honors:* R. D. W. Connor Award of North Carolina Literary and Historical Association, 1961 and 1965.

WRITINGS: (Editor, and author of introduction) *Bishop Cannon's Own Story,* Duke University Press, 1955; (editor with W. H. Cartwright) *Interpreting and Teaching American History,* American Council for the Social Studies, 1961; (editor, and author of introduction) *The United States in the Contemporary World, 1945-1962,* Free Press of Glencoe, 1965; (editor with Cartwright) *The Reinterpretation of American History and Culture,* American Council for the Social Studies, 1973; *The Development of National Power: The United States, 1900-1919,* Houghton, in press. Contributor to historical journals. Member of editorial board, *Mississippi Valley Historical Review,* 1958-61; *South Atlantic Quarterly,* 1967-73; associate editor, 1973—.

WORK IN PROGRESS: A biography, *The Political Career of F. M. Simmons.*

WAUGH, Alexander Raban 1898-
(Alec Waugh)

PERSONAL: Born July 8, 1898, in Hampstead, London, England; son of Arthur (editor and publisher, Chapman & Hall) and Catherine (Raban) Waugh; married Barbara Jacobs, 1919 (marriage annulled, 1923); married Joan Chirnside, 1932 (died, 1969); married Virginia Sorensen (an author), July 15, 1969; children: (second marriage) Andrew, Veronica Waugh Keeling, Peter. *Education:* Attended Sherborne School and Royal Military College, Sandhurst, England. *Address:* c/o A. D. Peters, 10 Buckingham St., Adelphi, W.C. 2, England.

CAREER: British Army, Dorset Regiment, 1917-19, served with British Expeditionary Forces in France, 1917-18, prisoner of war, 1918, transferred to Reserves, 1919, rejoined Dorset Regiment, 1939, with British Expeditionary Forces in France, 1940, staff captain, 1940, with Middle East Force, 1941, with intelligence staff in Lebanon and Baghdad, 1942-45, became major, 1944. Joined staff of Chapman & Hall (publishers), London, England, 1919, literary director, 1924-26. Lecturer in United States, 1931, 1960, and 1963. *Member:* Athenaeum, Beefsteak, Pratt's Savage (all England); Century, Coffee House (both New York).

WRITINGS: The Loom of Youth, Grant Richards, 1917, Doran, 1920; *Resentment* (poems), Grant Richards, 1918; *The Prisoners of Mainz,* Doran, 1919.

Pleasure, Grant Richards, 1921; *The Lonely Unicorn,* Grant Richards, 1922; *Roland Whately* (novel), Macmillan, 1922; *Public School Life,* Collins, 1922; *Card Castle* (novel), Grant Richards, 1924; *Myself When Young,* Brentano's, 1924; *Kept: A Story of Post-War London,* A. & C. Boni, 1925; *Love in These Days: A Modern Story,* Chapman & Hall, 1926, Doran, 1927; *On Doing What One Likes,* Cayme Press, 1926; *The Last Chukka,* Chapman & Hall, 1928; *Nor Many Waters,* Chapman & Hall, 1928; *Portrait of a Celibate,* Doubleday, Doran, 1929; *Three Score and Ten,* Chapman & Hall, 1929, Doubleday, Doran, 1930.

The Coloured Countries (travel), Chapman & Hall, 1930, published as *Hot Countries,* Farrar & Rinehart, 1939; *"Sir!" She Said,* Farrar & Rinehart, 1930; *Most Women* (travel), Farrar & Rinehart, 1931; *So Lovers Dream,* Cassell, 1931; *No Quarter,* Cassell, 1932; *Tropic Seed,* Farrar & Rinehart, 1932; *Thirteen Such Years,* Farrar & Rinehart, 1932; *That American Woman,* Farrar & Rinehart, 1932; *Wheels Within Wheels,* Cassell, 1933, published as *The Golden Ripple,* Farrar & Rinehart, 1933; *Leap Before You Look,* Farrar & Rinehart, 1933; *The Balliols,* Farrar & Rinehart, 1934; *Playing With Fire,* Benn, 1934; *Pages in Woman's Life* (stories), Cassell, 1934; *Jill Somerset,* Farrar & Rinehart, 1936; *Eight Short Stories,* Cassell, 1937; *Going Their Own Ways* (novel), Cassell, 1938, Farrar & Rinehart, 1939.

No Truce With Time, Farrar & Rinehart, 1941; *His Second War,* Cassell, 1944; *The Sunlit Caribbean,* Evans, 1948, published as *The Sugar Islands,* Farrar, Straus, 1949; *Unclouded Summer* (novel), Farrar, Straus, 1948.

The Lipton Story (history), Doubleday, 1950; *Where the Clock Strikes Twice,* Farrar, Straus, 1951 (published in England as *Where the Clock Chimes Twice,* Cassell, 1952); *Guy Renton,* Farrar, Straus, 1952; *Island in the Sun,* Farrar, Straus, 1955; *Merchants of Wine,* Cassell, 1957; *Love and the Caribbean,* Farrar, Straus, 1958; *In Praise of*

Wine, Cassell, 1959, published as *In Praise of Wine and Certain Noble Spirits*, Sloane Associates, 1959; *Fuel for the Flame*, Book Club (London), 1959, Farrar, Straus, 1960.

My Place in the Bazaar, Farrar, Straus, 1961; *The Early Years of Alec Waugh* (autobiography), Cassell, 1962, Farrar, Straus, 1963; *A Family of Islands*, Doubleday, 1964; *The Mule on the Minaret* (novel), Farrar, Straus, 1965; *My Brother Evelyn and Other Portraits*, Farrar, Straus, 1968; *Wines and Spirits*, Time-Life, 1968.

A Spy in the Family, Farrar, Straus, 1970; *Bangkok: The Story of a City*, Little, Brown, 1971; *The Fatal Gift*, Farrar, Straus, 1973; *A Year to Remember: A Reminiscence of 1931*, W. H. Allen, 1975.

SIDELIGHTS: Alec Waugh, older brother of the late Evelyn Waugh, considers himself "a very minor writer." His travel books, however, rank as some of the most lively and intelligent ever written. Phoebe Adams calls him "never profound, and never for one instant dull." Samuel Hynes, in a review of *My Place in the Bazaar*, writes: "He holds his audience's attention as a good storyteller should—by dealing with what is essential and perennial in human relations, and by making his settings, however romantic and strange, seem vividly real." Frederic Raphael says of *The Early Years of Alec Waugh*: "His real love is for action, not words.... His words are those of a magazine writer, clustering in cliches and compounded with unaffected facility. Such a writer is often at his best when describing events rather than inventing them. Autobiography suits Mr. Waugh perfectly."

Island in the Sun, probably his best-known work, was filmed in 1957; a story, "Circle of Deception" (included in *My Place in the Bazaar*), was filmed in 1961.

BIOGRAPHICAL/CRITICAL SOURCES: Newsweek, January 9, 1956; *New York Herald Tribune Book Review*, January 29, 1956; *New Yorker*, February 25, 1956; *New York Times Book Review*, July 24, 1960, May 28, 1961, October 6, 1963, November 14, 1965; *Atlantic*, August, 1961; *Time*, October 4, 1963, November 12, 1965; *Manchester Guardian*, January 21, 1965; *Spectator*, January 29, 1965; *Times Literary Supplement*, March 18, 1965; *Saturday Night*, April, 1965; *Saturday Review*, October 23, 1965; *Book Week*, October 24, 1965; *Books and Bookmen*, November, 1965; *National Observer*, November 1, 1965.

* * *

WEATHERBY, William J(ohn)

PERSONAL: Born in Heaton Moor, England; son of William (an artist) and Kathleen (Glancy) Weatherby. *Politics:* "democrat (with a small 'd')." *Religion:* Christian of no color." *Residence:* New York, N.Y. *Office:* Simon & Schuster, Inc., 630 Fifth Ave., New York, N.Y. 10020.

CAREER: Journalist in England and United States, and editor for Penguin Books, Inc., New York, N.Y.; Simon & Schuster, Inc., New York, N.Y., editor, 1972—.

WRITINGS: Breaking the Silence: The Negro Struggle in the U.S.A. (nonfiction), Penguin, 1965, published as *Love in the Shadows*, Stein & Day, 1966; *Out of Hiding* (fiction), Hart-Davis, 1966, Doubleday, 1967; (editor with Roi Ottley) *The Negro in New York* (nonfiction), New York Public Library and Oceana, 1967; *One of Our Priests is Missing* (novel), Doubleday, 1968.

Plays: "Breaking the Silence" (adaptation of own book), produced at Liverpool Playhouse, Winter, 1969. Book re-

viewer and essayist for *Times Literary Supplement* (London) and *Manchester Guardian*.

SIDELIGHTS: Weatherby has traveled around Europe and in America at various periods since 1956.

BIOGRAPHICAL/CRITICAL SOURCES: New York Times Book Review, March 5, 1967; *Best Sellers*, March 15, 1967.†

* * *

WEAVER, James H. 1933-

PERSONAL: Born July 26, 1933, in Prairie Grove, Ark.; son of Philip (a farmer) and Martha (Hill) Weaver; married Mary Ann Carver, May, 1961; children: Michael James, Eric Carver. *Education:* University of Arkansas, B.S.B.A., 1955; University of Oklahoma, Ph.D., 1963. *Politics:* Democrat. *Religion:* Unitarian Universalist. *Home:* 6423 Ridge Dr., Washington, D.C. 20016. *Office:* American University, Washington, D.C. 20016.

CAREER: American University, Washington, D.C., assistant professor, 1963-67, associate professor, 1967-69, professor of economics, 1969—, chairman of department, 1967—. Consultant to U.S. Department of Health, Education, and Welfare, 1963-64. *Military service:* U.S. Air Force, 1955-58; became first lieutenant. *Member:* American Economic Association, Southern Economic Association, Omicron Delta Kappa, Phi Eta Sigma, Beta Gamma Sigma.

WRITINGS: The International Development Association: A New Approach to Foreign Aid, Praeger, 1965; (editor with Gary R. Weaver) *The University and Revolution*, Prentice-Hall, 1969; (editor) *Modern Political Economy: Radical and Orthodox Views on Crucial Issues*, Allyn & Bacon, 1973.†

* * *

WEBB, Henry J(ameson) 1915-

PERSONAL: Born March 12, 1915, in Indianapolis, Ind.; son of Henry J. (a salesman) and Wilhelmina (Vehling) Webb; married Joyce Trost, September 6, 1947; children: Elaine, Margaret, Melissa, Rosemary. *Education:* New York University, B.S., 1937; University of Iowa, M.A., 1938, Ph.D., 1941. *Home:* 1408 East Ninth South St., Salt Lake City, Utah 84105.

CAREER: The Citadel, Charleston, S.C., assistant professor of English, 1941-42; University of Utah, Salt Lake City, instructor, 1940-41, assistant professor, then associate professor, 1945-57, professor of English, 1957—. *Military service:* U.S. Army, 1943-46; became master sergeant; received Bronze Star Medal with oak leaf cluster, and three battle stars for European campaigns. *Member:* American Association of University Professors, Western Historical Association, Utah Historical Society, Zeta Psi, Phi Kappa Phi.

WRITINGS: Elizabethan Military Science: The Books and the Practice, University of Wisconsin Press, 1965. Contributor to *Military Affairs* and professional journals in English and history.

WORK IN PROGRESS: A study of Elizabethan culture, military officers, and men.

AVOCATIONAL INTERESTS: Colorado river expeditions; covering desert trails by jeep and horse.

WEBB, Muriel S(chlosberg) 1913-

PERSONAL: Born May 29, 1913, in Brooklyn, N.Y.; daughter of Ira (an electrical engineer) and Harriett E. (Walker) Schlosberg; married Robert M. Webb (a social worker), July 9, 1934; children: Harriett Cordelia (Mrs. Hugh Wallace Reid III), Robert M., Jr. *Education:* Connecticut College for Women (now Connecticut College), B.A., 1933; Columbia University, graduate study, 1934-36. *Politics:* Democrat. *Religion:* Episcopalian. *Home:* 5 Mill Pond, Cos Cob, Conn. 06830. *Office:* Executive Council, National Episcopal Church, 815 Second Ave., New York, N.Y. 10017.

CAREER: Social worker in New York, N.Y., 1933-36, for Brooklyn (N.Y.) Bureau of Social Service, 1936-37; Episcopal Diocese of Long Island, Brooklyn, N.Y., executive secretary, department of Christian Social Relations, 1937-47; National Episcopal Church, Executive Council, Department of Christian Social Relations, New York, N.Y., assistant secretary, 1947-57, associate director, beginning 1957, currently director of section on experimental church services. President, Christian Social Welfare Associates, 1955-57; chairman of operating committee of immigration services, Church World Service, 1956; officer in Division of Overseas Ministry, National Council of Churches; member, National Conference on Social Welfare; member of board, Commission on Missionary Education. *Member:* National Association of Social Workers, Academy of Certified Social Workers.

WRITINGS: Social Ministry of the Local Church, National Council of Churches, 1955; (with husband, Robert Webb) *The Churches and Juvenile Delinquency,* Association Press, 1956; (with Robert Webb) *The Family in the United States,* Executive Council of Episcopal Church, 1958; (with Janette Harrington) *Who Cares?,* Friendship, 1961; (editor) *Wealth and Want in One World,* Friendship, 1966. Editor, *Christian Social Relations* (monthly publication), 1947—.†

* * *

WECHSLER, Henry 1932-

PERSONAL: Born August 16, 1932, in Warsaw, Poland; naturalized U.S. citizen; married Joan Goldstein, 1955; children: Stephen Bruce, Pamela Jane, Peter Thomas. *Education:* Washington and Jefferson College, A.B., 1953; Harvard University, M.A., 1955, Ph.D., 1957. *Office:* The Medical Foundation, 29 Commonwealth Ave., Boston, Mass. 02116.

CAREER: U.S. Public Health Service, research fellow in psychology, 1957-58; Clark University, Worcester, Mass., research associate and assistant professor, 1958-59; Massachusetts Mental Health Center, Boston, research social psychologist, 1959-62; Harvard University, Cambridge, Mass., research associate in psychology in department of psychiatry, Medical School, 1960-66, in department of epidemiology, School of Public Health, 1963-66, lecturer in social psychology in departments of health services administration and behaviorial sciences, School of Public Health, 1966—; The Medical Foundation, Inc., Boston, Mass., research director, 1965—. Lecturer in research, Simmons College, 1969—. *Member:* American Psychological Association (fellow), American Association for the Advancement of Science, American Sociological Association (fellow), American Public Health Association (fellow), Massachusetts Psychological Association (fellow), Massachusetts Public Health Association, Phi Beta Kappa.

WRITINGS: (Editor with G. Grosser and M. Greenblatt) *The Threat of Impending Disaster: Contributions to the Psychology of Stress,* M.I.T. Press, 1965; (editor with L. Solomon and B. M. Kramer) *Social Psychology and Mental Health,* Holt, 1970; (editor with J. H. Noble, Jr., M. E. LaMontagne, and M. A. Noble) *Emergency Medical Services: Selected Bibliography,* Behavioral Publications, 1974.

Contributor: *The Volunteer and the Psychiatric Patient,* American Psychiatric Association, 1959; M. Greenblatt, D. J. Levinson, and G. L. Klerman, editors, *Mental Patients in Transition,* C. C Thomas, 1961; Z. Votava, M. Horvath, and O. Vinar, editors, *Psychopharmacological Method,* Pergamon, 1963; J. H. Masserman, editor, *Current Psychiatric Therapies,* Volume IV, Grune, 1964; P. Solomon, editor, *Psychiatric Drugs,* Grune, 1966; B. K. Biddle and E. J. Thomas, editors, *Role Theory: Concepts and Research,* Wiley, 1966; H. Grunebaum, editor, *The Practice of Community Mental Health,* Little, Brown, 1970; S. Palmer and A. S. Linsky, editors, *Rebellion and Retreat: Readings in the Forms and Processes of Deviance,* C. E. Merrill, 1972; A. Shiloh and I. C. Selavan, editors, *Ethnic Groups of America: Their Morbidity, Mortality, and Behavior Disorders,* Volume I: *The Jews,* C. C Thomas, 1972. Contributor of over fifty articles to professional journals.

WORK IN PROGRESS: Handbook of Medical Specialties for Behavioral Publications; editing, with H. Z. Reinherz and D. D. Dobbin, *Social Work Research in the Human Services* for Behavioral Publications; editing, with G. F. Cahill, Jr., *Directions in Medical Research* for Harvard University Press.

* * *

WEDDA, John A. 1911-

PERSONAL: Born November 4, 1911, in Milwaukee, Wis.; son of John August (a publisher) and Euphrosyne (Wleklinski) Wedda; married Mary Elizabeth Davis, December 27, 1938; children: Bruce Cameron, Susan Marshall. *Education:* "No higher education." *Politics:* Democrat. *Home:* Lime Rock Rd., Salisbury, Conn. 06039.

CAREER: Designer and illustrator, Detroit, Mich., 1940-44; U.S. Office of War Information, London, England, chief of graphics, 1944-45; teacher of art at Pratt Institute, Brooklyn, N.Y., 1946, and Workshop School, New York, N.Y., 1948-49; *United Natioons World* (magazine), New York, N.Y., art director and member of editorial board, 1947-48; John P. Smith Co., Rochester, N.Y., creative director, 1949-50; U.S. Embassy, Tehran, Iran, publications officer, 1951-53; free-lance graphics designer and editorial consultant, 1953—. Member of board of directors, Opinions Unlimited. Selectman, town of Salisbury, 1963-69. *Awards, honors:* Awards for watercolors, Detroit Institute of Arts; American Institute of Graphic Arts award for brochure design.

WRITINGS—Self-illustrated: Sweet Land of Liberty, Fox, 1965; *New England Worships,* Random House, 1965; *But Not Forever* (poems) privately printed, 1968; *Gardens of the South,* Westover, 1971.

WORK IN PROGRESS: Tomorrow Became Yesterday Just Now.

SIDELIGHTS: Various assignments have taken him to Europe, Asia, Africa, and Central and South America. Wedda has "some ability" in French, Polish, and Farsi. *Avocational interests:* Golf, tennis, landscape design.

WEDDLE, Ferris 1922-

PERSONAL: Born January 10, 1922, in Leaday, Tex.; son of Hardy Lee (a farmer) and Frances Olive (Wood) Weddle. *Education:* Boise Junior College, A.A., 1949; University of Washington, Seattle, B.A., 1953. *Politics:* Democrat (liberal). *Religion:* No affiliation. *Residence:* Kamiah, Idaho, 83538.

CAREER: Free-lance writer in Idaho most of the time since 1947, working at intervals at sundry other occupations; did full-time newspaper writing (out of Boise, Idaho) for *Deseret News,* Salt Lake City Utah, 1950, public relations work for *Encyclopaedia Britannica,* Chicago, Ill., 1959-60, and helped manage an apartment in Chicago, 1963-64; also has farmed, been a sales clerk and a sawmill employee; principal writing has been for conservation magazines, 1963—, many of the articles illustrated with his own photographs. *Military service:* U.S. Army, Ordnance and Special Services, 1942-46; served in Europe. *Member:* Defenders of Wildlife, National Wildlife Federation, National Parks Association, Sierra Club.

WRITINGS: Blizzard Rescue (juvenile), F. Watts, 1959; *Blazing Mountain* (juvenile), F. Watts, 1961; *Wilderness Renegades* (juvenile), F. Watts, 1962; (contributor) Grace Jordan, editor, *Idaho Reader,* Syms-York, 1963; *Tall Like a Pine* (juvenile), Albert Whitman, 1974. Short stories have appeared in more than one hundred magazines and newspapers, most recently in *National Wildlife, Defenders of Wildlife,* and other conservation periodicals. Outdoors columnist for several Idaho newspapers, 1965—.

WORK IN PROGRESS: Two juvenile books, and research for a juvenile book on nongame and endangered wildlife.

SIDELIGHTS: Weddle told *CA:* "I think it was James Baldwin who wrote something to the effect 'We write because we are incomplete if we do not do so'—and perhaps that is a partial answer to the drudgery [of free-lance writing] and to the ever-present 'outsideness' all writers in isolated rural areas face. Over the next hill (and our Idaho hills are many and beautiful and still wild) there may be a moment of triumph, artistic and financial. Often, the latter outweighs the former in importance; it takes a hell of an effort to be concerned about 'art' when you may wonder where the next meal comes from! . . . I've lived in isolated rural areas by choice and inclination, although I have no illusions about the existence of the truly simple life."

* * *

WEDEEN, Shirley Ullman 1926-

PERSONAL: Born May 29, 1926, in New York, N.Y.; daughter of Hugo (an electrician) and Esther (Forschein) Ullman; married Peter Wedeen (a physician), January 13, 1952; children: Van, Glenn. *Education:* Brooklyn College (now Brooklyn College of the City University of New York), B.A. (cum laude), 1946; New York University, M.A., 1947, Ph.D., 1951. *Home:* 116 Buckingham Rd., Brooklyn, N.Y. 11226. *Office:* Brooklyn College of the City University of New York, Brooklyn, N.Y.

CAREER: Brooklyn College of the City University of New York, instructor, 1951-59, assistant professor, 1959-66, associate professor, 1966-71, professor of education, 1971—, assistant dean of students, 1966-68, curriculum coordinator, School of Education, 1971—, and counselor. Registered psychologist in state of New York. *Member:* International Reading Association, American Psychological Association,

College Reading Association, American Association of University Professors (secretary of Brooklyn College chapter, 1966-68), Women's Press Club, Kappa Delta Pi, Brooklyn College Alumni Association (member of executive board, 1963—).

WRITINGS: College Remedial Reader, Putnam, 1958, reissued as *College Reader,* 1960; *Advanced College Reader,* Putnam, 1963. Contributor of more than twenty-five articles to professional journals.

* * *

WEEKS, Constance Tomkinson 1915-
(Constance Tomkinson)

PERSONAL: Born June 22, 1915, in Canso, Nova Scotia, Canada; daughter of Harold (a minister) and Grace (Avard) Tomkinson; married Sir Hugh Weeks (an economist and bank chairman); children: Jane Avard. *Education:* Educated at schools in eastern Canada and United States; graduated from Yarmouth Academy, Nova Scotia, 1933, Neighborhood Playhouse (dramatic school), New York, N.Y., 1935. *Politics:* Conservative. *Religion:* Protestant. *Home:* 8 The Grove, Highgate Village, London N. 6, England. *Agent:* A. D. Peters, 10 Buckingham St., London W.C. 2; England; Diarmuid Russell, Russell & Volkening, Inc., 551 Fifth Ave., New York, N.Y. 10017.

CAREER: Dancer and actress in United States and Europe, 1936-39; British Ministry of Supply, New York, N.Y., temporary civil servant, 1940-44; Sadler's Wells Ballet, London, England, secretary, 1946-48; Old Vic Theatre, London, secretary to director, 1949-52. Writer. *Member:* Canadian Women's Club.

WRITINGS—Under name Constance Tomkinson: *Les Girls,* Little, Brown, 1956; *African Follies,* M. Joseph, 1959; *What a Performance!,* M. Joseph, 1962; *Dancing Attendance,* M. Joseph, 1965.

WORK IN PROGRESS: An autobiographical book with a theater background.

SIDELIGHTS: Lady Weeks told *CA* that she finds writing much harder than being a dancer or actress and "very lonely" for one trained to working in groups. Her books are written in a humorous vein ("you have to go in the direction in which what talent you have lies"), and nearly all include some phase of her travels about the world. *Les Girls* was serialized in the *Atlantic Monthly,* published as a book in four countries, and made into a movie (Metro-Goldwyn-Mayer, 1957). She speaks Italian, French, and German, "loves" children and animals (Airedales preferred among the latter), and swims for exercise.

* * *

WEGNER, Robert E. 1929-

PERSONAL: Born March 1, 1929, in Cleveland, Ohio; son of Ernst Robert (a teacher) and Esther (Strebelow) Wegner; married Phyllis Larimer (a teacher), January, 1950; children: Gregory, Julie, Mark. *Education:* Michigan State University, B.A., 1950; Western Reserve University (now Case Western Reserve University), M.A., 1951, Ph.D., 1959; University of Iowa, graduate study, 1952-53. *Home:* Rte. 1 Box 360, Vestaburg, Mich. 48891. *Office:* Alma College, Alma, Mich. 48801.

CAREER: Wilmington College, Wilmington, Ohio, assistant professor, 1955-57; Alma College, Alma, Mich., assistant professor, 1957-63, associate professor, 1963-68, professor of English, 1968—. *Member:* Mid-western Modern Language Association.

WRITINGS: The Poetry and Prose of E. E. Cummings, Harcourt, 1965; (contributor) Martha Foley and David Burnett, editors, *Best American Short Stories*, Mac-Gibbon, 1971; (contributor) R. F. Tracz and C. J. Howard, editors, *The Age of Anxiety*, Allyn & Bacon, 1972. Short stories, poems, and articles published in little literary magazines.

WORK IN PROGRESS: A series of three related novels.

AVOCATIONAL INTERESTS: American Indians, trout fishing.

* * *

WEINGART, L(aurence) O. 1931-

PERSONAL: Born May 28, 1931, in Cleveland, Ohio; son of Samuel Harry (a merchant) and Fay Ruth (Speert) Weingart. *Education:* Cornell University, B.A., 1952; graduate courses at New York University, 1952, 1955-59. *Politics:* "Unregistered Democrat." *Religion:* "Judaism, inactive." *Home:* 30-19 88th St., Flushing, N.Y. 11369.

CAREER: Cushing & Nevell, Inc., New York, N.Y., engineering writing, 1955-62; Norwich Design Corp., Norwich, N.Y., designer, 1962-63; Computer Usage Co., Inc., New York, N.Y., engineering writing, 1964—. Cornell Alumni Fund, assistant, 1964—. *Military service:* U.S. Army, Signal Corps, 1953-55. *Member:* Association for Computing Machinery, Systems and Procedures Association.

WRITINGS: (With Irving I. Solomon) *Management Uses of the Computer*, Harper, 1966. Columnist for Army newspaper, 1955.

WORK IN PROGRESS: Time-shared Computers, for International Business Machines Corp.; data communications in computer systems, potential course material and possible book.†

* * *

WEISER, Eric 1907-

PERSONAL: Born June 16, 1907, in Vienna, Austria; son of Julius and Ella (Back) Weiser; married Hanna Wolf, August 18, 1933; children: Frank Michael, Edgar Daniel. *Education:* University of Berlin, student, 1925-27; University of Leipzig, Doctorate of Law, 1929. *Religion:* Jewish. *Home:* 45 Avenue Gabriel Peri, 91330 Yerres, France. *Agent:* L. Dukas, Witikonerstrasse 98, Zurich, Switzerland.

CAREER: Agence France-Presse, Paris, France, editorial work, 1951-54; full-time professional writer on science subjects, 1954—. *Military service:* Israeli Army, 1948-49. *Member:* Kollegium der Medizinjournalisten (Munich; founder member).

WRITINGS: So entsteht der Mensch, Ullstein (Frankfurt), 1959, translation published as *Pregnancy: Conception and Heredity*, Blaisdell, 1965; *Wir wunschen uns ein Kind*, Hallwag (Bern), 1962; *Mein Kind und Ich*, Hallwag, 1964; *Die gewonnenen Jahre*, Econ, 1967; *Aelter werden-aktiv bleiben*, Mueller, 1970. Regular contributor of scientific reports to German newspapers.

WORK IN PROGRESS: Writing on genetics.

SIDELIGHTS: Weiser speaks English, German, and French. He is primarily interested in developing scientific subjects for the general reader, particularly in the fields of medicine and biology.

WEISS, Irving J. 1921-
(Robert Forio)

PERSONAL: Born September 11, 1921, in New York, N.Y.; son of Max and Rose (Kursh) Weiss; married Anne de la Vergne, December 14, 1949; children: Carla, Piera, Bruna, Hugh. *Education:* University of Michigan, A.B., 1942; Columbia University, A.M., 1948. *Home:* R.D. 2, Pine Bush, N.Y. 12566.

CAREER: Studied in Europe, 1949-54; American Dependents' School, Naples, Italy, teacher, 1952-53; Pennsylvania State University, University Park, instructor in English, 1955-57; *Funk and Wagnalls Standard Reference Work Encyclopedia*, humanities editor, 1957-60; Fashion Institute of Technology, New York, N.Y., instructor in English, 1960-64; New York State University at New Paltz, assistant professor, 1964-70, associate professor of English, 1970—, chairman of communication arts program. *Military service:* U.S. Army, Field Artillery, 1942-45; served in Europe; became battalion sergeant major.

WRITINGS: (Editor) *American Authors and Books, 1640 to the Present Day*, 2nd edition (Weiss was not associated with earlier edition), Crown, 1962, 3rd edition (with wife, Anne D. Weiss), 1972; (contributor) Raymond Rosenthal, editor, *McLuhan: Pro and Con*, Funk, 1968; (editor and translator) Malcolm de Chazal, *Plastic Sense*, Herder & Herder, 1971. Contributor of articles, stories, and poems to *Travel, Commentary, New Yorker, Catholic World, Contact, Chicago Review*, and other periodicals.

WORK IN PROGRESS: Collection of wall poems, visual verse, and conceptual verse.

AVOCATIONAL INTERESTS: Year-round sheet-compost vegetable gardening, blind television dialing.

* * *

WEISS, John 1927-

PERSONAL: Born March 31, 1927, in Detroit, Mich.; son of Karl E. (a tailor) and Mabel (Harper) Weiss; married Eva Gelfman, June 12, 1953 (divorced 1971); married Janice O'Hare (a political worker), March 9, 1972; children: (first marriage) Paul, Elizabeth. *Education:* Wayne State University, B.A., 1950; Columbia University, M.A., 1953, Ph.D., 1958. *Politics:* Democrat. *Home:* 2776 Webb Ave., Bronx, N.Y. 10468. *Office:* Department of History, Lehman College of the City University of New York, Bronx, N.Y. 10468.

CAREER: Wayne State University, Detroit, Mich., assistant professor, 1956-65, associate professor of European history, 1965-68; Lehman College of the City University of New York, Bronx, N.Y., professor of history, 1969—. Former head of Michigan Committee for McCarthy for President. *Military service:* U.S. Naval Reserve, 1944-46, became petty officer, 3rd class. *Member:* American Historical Association.

WRITINGS: Moses Hess, Utopian Socialist, Wayne State University Press, 1960; (editor) *Origins of Modern Consciousness*, Wayne State University Press, 1965; *The Facist Tradition*, Harper, 1967; (contributor) Hayden White, editor, *The Uses of History*, Wayne State University Press, 1968; (editor) *Nazis and Fascists in Europe*, Quadrangle, 1969; *The Ideology and Politics of Conservatism*, Thames & Hudson, in press. Contributor to scholarly journals. Editor, *Graduate Comment*, 1961-63; co-editor, *New University Thought*, 1962-66.

SIDELIGHTS: Weiss told *CA:* "My major interest is to

show the relationships between ideology and social and historical change. Plus, I am much interested in the wars and revolutions of the twentieth century."

* * *

WEISS, M(orton) Jerome 1926-
(M. Jerry Weiss)

PERSONAL: Born April 16, 1926, in Oxford, N.C.; son of Max I. (a merchant) and Fannie (Cohen) Weiss; married Helen Schwartzbard, October 21, 1950; children: Sharon, Frann, Eileen, Michael. *Education:* University of North Carolina, B.A., 1949; Columbia University, M.A., 1951, Ed.D., 1952. *Religion:* Jewish. *Home:* 131 Gordonhurst Ave., Upper Montclair, N.J. 07043. *Office:* Jersey City State College, 2039 Kennedy Blvd., Jersey City, N.J.

CAREER: High school teacher in Chase City, Va., 1949-50; New York (N.Y.) Board of Education, research assistant in Guidance Division, 1951-52; Rhodes Preparatory School, New York, N.Y., director of remedial reading, 1952-56; Defiance College, Defiance, Ohio, associate professor of English and director of reading improvement, 1956-58; Pennsylvania State University, University Park, assistant professor of secondary education, 1958-61; Jersey City State College, Jersey City, N.J., professor of English, reading and language arts, 1961—. University of Toledo, visiting professor, summer, 1957. Odyssey Press, Inc., educational adviser. *Military service:* U.S. Naval Reserve, 1944-46. *Member:* National Council of Teachers of English, College Reading Association (president, 1964-65), International Reading Association, American Personnel and Guidance Association.

WRITINGS: Guidance Through Drama, Whiteside, 1954; (co-author) *A Guide to Play Selection*, Appleton, 1958; (editor) *Reading in the Secondary Schools*, Odyssey, 1961; (editor) *An English Teacher's Reader*, Odyssey, 1962; (editor under name M. Jerry Weiss) *Man and War*, Dell, 1963; (editor) *Ten Short Plays*, Dell, 1963; (compiler with Theresa Oakes) *The Unfinished Journey*, McGraw, 1967; (editor under name M. Jerry Weiss) *Tales Out of School*, Dell, 1967; (compiler under name M. Jerry Weiss) *Kaleidoscope*, Cummings, 1970; (under name M. Jerry Weiss) *Man to Himself*, Cummings, 1970; (editor under name M. Jerry Weiss) *New Perspectives on Paperbacks*, College Reading Association, 1972. Contributor to professional journals.

WORK IN PROGRESS: Reading in Elementary School, for Odyssey; *Tales Out of School*, for Dell.

AVOCATIONAL INTERESTS: Theatre and records.†

* * *

WELLS, James M. 1917-

PERSONAL: Born November 4, 1917, in Charleston, W.Va. *Education:* Northwestern University, B.S., 1938; Columbia University, M.A., 1939. *Office:* Newberry Library, Chicago, Ill. 60610.

CAREER: West Virginia University, Morgantown, instructor in English, 1939-41; Columbia University, Columbia College, New York, N.Y., instructor in English, 1946-49; Newberry Library, Chicago, Ill., curator of Wing Foundation, 1951—, associate director of library, 1965—. *Military service:* U.S. Navy, 1942-46; became lieutenant. *Member:* Society of Typographic Arts (president, 1954), Renaissance English Text Society (secretary-treasurer, 1966—), Renaissance Society of America (member of council, 1965—), Modern Language Association of America,

Bibliographical Society of America, English-Speaking Union (director, Chicago branch), Modern Poetry Association (director), Bibliographical Society (London), American Institute of Graphic Arts, Caxton Club (Chicago; vice-president, 1966—), Grolier Club, Arts Club (Chicago). *Awards, honors:* American Council of Learned Societies fellow, 1941-42, 1949-51.

WRITINGS: Opera of Tagliente (1525), Newberry, 1953; *The Scholar Printers*, University of Chicago Press, 1964; (contributor) *Book Typography*, Benn, 1966. Contributor to *Encyclopaedia Britannica, World Book Encyclopedia, Dictionary of American Biography*, and other encyclopedias and journals. Editor, *Newberry Library Bulletin*.

WORK IN PROGRESS: Projects in calligraphy, bibliography, printing history, and book collecting.

SIDELIGHTS: Wells told *CA* that his work at Newberry Library involves dealing with the whole range of printing history in the Western Hemisphere, the history of writing and of libraries, and the buying of books in these fields, as well as in English literature. "It leaves a bit of time," he says, "for my own writing and other interests, with include gardening and politics."

* * *

WELLS, Leon W. 1925-

PERSONAL: Born March 10, 1925, in Lwow, Poland; son of Abraham Michael (a businessman) and Anna (Reis) Wells; married Frieda Weiss, October 14, 1955; children: Beth Ann, Alan, Julian. *Education:* Technical University, Munich, Germany, Ph.D., 1949; Lehigh University, postdoctoral study. *Religion:* Jewish. *Home:* 9 Ranch Lane, Closter, N.J. *Office:* Panopix Research, Inc., 100 East 42nd St., New York, N.Y. 10017.

CAREER: Courant Institute, New York University, New York, N.Y., did research in Graduate School of Mathematics and Mechanics, 1950-53; worked in research and development in field of applied optics and mechanisms, 1953-62; Panopix Research, Inc., New York, N.Y., director of research in field of optics, 1962—. *Awards, honors:* Industrial Motion Picture award, 1960.

WRITINGS: Brigada Smierci (title means "Death Brigade"), Historical Commission (Poland), 1946; *Mathematische Vorschule Fuer Ingenieure und Naturforscher*, Oldenburg, 1949; *The Janowska Road*, Macmillan, 1963. Contributor of articles and reviews to *Reconstructionist, New York Times*, and other publications.

SIDELIGHTS: Wells is a holder of patents on motion picture projecting systems.

* * *

WELSCH, Erwin Kurt 1935-

PERSONAL: Born April 17, 1935, in Philadelphia, Pa.; son of Frederick (a baker) and Anna (Schwarz) Welsch; married Carol Gessing, June 30, 1956; children: Carol Anne, Kurt. *Education:* University of Pennsylvania, B.F.A., 1958; Indiana University, M.A. (library science), 1961, M.A. (history), 1966, Ph.D., 1973. *Home:* 3211 Topping Rd., Madison, Wis. 53705.

CAREER: Indiana University Library, Bloomington, librarian for history, 1960-66; University of Wisconsin Memorial Library, Madison, social studies librarian, 1968—. *Member:* American Historical Association, Society for the Advancement of Scandinavian Studies.

WRITINGS: The Negro in the United States: A Research Guide, Indiana University Press, 1965; *French Libraries and Archives*, Council for European Studies, 1973; *German Libraries and Archives*, Council for European Studies, 1975. Compiler of "American Bibliography of Scandinavian Studies," 1972—. Contributor of articles to *Encyclopedia of Library and Information Science* and of reviews to *Library Journal*, and other periodicals. Section editor, *European Studies Newsletter*.

WORK IN PROGRESS: Bibliographic Introduction to Scandinavian History and Social Sciences, completion expected in 1976.

* * *

WELSH, David J(ohn) 1920-

PERSONAL: Born September 15, 1920, in London England; son of William (an importer) and Ada (Russell) Welsh. *Education:* University of London, B.A. (honors), 1958, Ph.D., 1966; University of Liverpool, M.A., 1962. *Home:* 16 J Tower Plaza, Ann Arbor, Mich. 48108. *Office:* Slavic Department, Modern Language Bldg. University of Michigan, Ann Arbor, Mich. 48104.

CAREER: British Embassy, Warsaw, Poland, interpreter, 1951-52; Royal Geographical Society, London, England, librarian, 1952-56; British Broadcasting Corp., London, England, language supervisor, 1956-58; International Library, Liverpool, England, director, 1958-61; University of Michigan, Ann Arbor, lecturer, 1961-62, assistant professor, 1964-65, associate professor, 1966-71, professor of Polish language and literature, 1971—. *Military service:* British Army, Intelligence, 1940-45. *Member:* American Association for the Advancement of Slavic Studies, American Association of Teachers of Slavic and Eastern European Languages, Polish Academy of Arts and Sciences (New York). *Awards, honors:* Jurzykowski Foundation Award, 1965, for best translation from the Polish; Polish Writers Union Award, 1971.

WRITINGS: (Translator) W. Odojewski, *Island of Salvation*, Harcourt, 1965; (translator) J. Andrzejewski, *Ashes and Diamonds*, Penguin, 1965; *Russian Comedy, 1765-1823*, Mouton & Co., 1966; *Adam Mickiewicz: A Study of the Poetry*, Twayne, 1966; *Ignacy Krasicki*, Twayne, 1969; (translator) B. Prus, *The Doll*, Twayne, 1972; *Jan Kochanowski*, Twayne, 1974. Contributor to *Intermurale, Polish Review, Slavonic and East European Review*, and other journals.

WORK IN PROGRESS: A study of Juliusz Slowacki for Twayne.

* * *

WELSH, George Schlager 1918-

PERSONAL: Born September 24, 1918, in Kingston, Pa.; son of George Schlager and Ethel MareA (Wells) Welsh; married L. Alice Mendenhall, June 14, 1946. *Education:* Attended University of Pennsylvania, 1936-38, Occidental College, 1938-39; University of Pennsylvania, B.A., 1940, graduate study, 1941-43; University of Minnesota, Ph.D., 1949. *Home:* 13 Friday Lane, Chapel Hill, N.C. 27514. *Office:* Department of Psychology, University of North Carolina, Chapel Hill, N.C. 27514.

CAREER: U.S. Veterans Administration, trainee in clinical psychology, Minneapolis, Minn., 1947-49, clinical psychologist in San Francisco, Calif., 1949, Oakland, Calif., 1950-53; University of North Carolina, Chapel Hill, asso-

ciate professor, 1953-61, professor of psychology in department of psychology, and clinical professor of psychology in department of psychiatry, 1961—, research professor at earlier periods, and 1959—. University of Florence, Fulbright professor at Istituto di Psicologia, 1956-57; University of California, Berkeley, visiting professor, 1958-59; University Center in Virginia, Inc., visiting scholar, 1972-73. Veterans Administration Training Program in Clinical Psychology, consultant, 1953—. *Military service:* U.S. Army, psychologist, 1943-46.

MEMBER: American Psychological Association (fellow), American Society for Aesthetics, British Society of Aesthetics, International Society for the Study of Symbols, Southeastern Psychological Association, Sigma Xi.

WRITINGS: (Editor with W. G. Dahlstrom, and contributor) *Basic Readings on the MMPI in Psychology and Medicine*, University of Minnesota Press, 1956; (with Dahlstrom) *An MMPI Handbook: A Guide to Use in Clinical Practice and Research*, University of Minnesota Press, Volume I, 1960, revised edition, 1972, Volume II, 1975; (with E. E. Baughman) *Personality: A Behavioral Science*, Prentice-Hall, 1962; *Creativity and Intelligence: A Personality Approach*, Institute for Research in Social Science, 1975. Writer of manual on the Welsh figure preference test, and of numerous articles in *Research Previews, Popular Government, Sciences de l'art, International Journal of Symbology*, and psychology journals.

* * *

WERNER, Hazen G. 1895-

PERSONAL: Born July 29, 1895, in Detroit, Mich; son of Samuel E. and Emma E. (Graff) Werner; married Catherine Stewart, May 22, 1924; children: Stewart Hazen, Joy Ann (Mrs. Wilfred Pollender). *Education:* Albion College, A.B., 1920; Columbia University, graduate study, 1921-23; Drew University, B.D., 1923. *Home:* 16 Walker Ave., Vergennes, Vt.

CAREER: Ordained elder of The Methodist Church, 1924; pastor in Detroit, Mich., 1924-31, Flint, Mich., 1931-34, Dayton, Ohio, 1934-45; Drew Theological Seminary, Madison, N.J., professor and chairman of practical theology, 1945-48; elected bishop of Methodist Church, 1948; resident bishop of Ohio Area, 1948-64; World Family Life Committee of Methodist Church, New York, N.Y., chairman, 1962-68, bishop assigned to Taiwan-Hong Kong Area and liaison bishop to Methodist Church in Korea, beginning 1964. Has traveled extensively in interest of missions, and held family life conferences on all continents; chairman of National Committee of Family Life of Methodist Church, 1948-62.

MEMBER: Academy of Religion and Mental Health, Alpha Tau Omega, Masons, Kiwanis. *Awards, honors:* D.D., Albion College, 1934, Ohio Wesleyan University, 1941; LL.D., Mount Union College, 1949, Ohio Northern University, 1949; and Miami University, Oxford, Ohio, 1960; S.T.D., Baldwin-Wallace College, 1957; Speaker of the Year Award in field of religion, Tau Kappa Alpha, 1959.

WRITINGS—All published by Abingdon: *And We Are Whole Again*, 1945; *Real Living Takes Time*, 1948; *Live with Your Emotions*, 1951; *Christian Family Living*, 1958; *No Saints Suddenly*, 1963; *Look at the Family Now*, 1970. Author of five pamphlets on religious subjects.

WEST, Elliot 1924-

PERSONAL: Born February 24, 1924, in Brooklyn, N.Y.; son of Harry Arthur (a vaudeville performer and theater manager) and Stella (Black) West; married Barbara Bergman, July 18, 1948; children: Jed, Diana. *Education:* Attended Erasmus Hall, 1937-41 ("dropout"). *Agent:* Harold Ober Associates, Inc., 40 East 49th St., New York, N.Y. 10017.

CAREER: Author. *Military service:* U.S. Army, rifleman, 1943-45; served in European theater; received Purple Heart. *Member:* Authors Guild, Writers Guild of America.

*WRITINGS—*Novels: *Man Running,* Little, Brown, 1959; *The Night Is a Time for Listening,* Random House, 1966; *These Lonely Victories,* Putnam, 1972; *Blaney,* Houghton, 1975. Also author of screenplay "The Fearmakers," United Artists, 1959.

SIDELIGHTS: Film rights to *The Night Is a Time for Listening* were sold to Universal.

* * *

WEST, G(eorge) Allen, Jr. 1915-

PERSONAL: Born May 3, 1915, in Coffee County, Ga.; son of George A. and Mary (Dukes) West; married Catherine Bugg, September 16, 1939; children: Janet Marie (Mrs. M. McCoy Dillard), George Allen III. *Education:* Stetson University, B.A., 1936; Southern Baptist Theological Seminary, Th.M., 1939, Th.D., 1942.

CAREER: Baptist minister. Woodmont Baptist Church, Nashville, Tenn., pastor, 1942—. Tennessee Baptist Convention, president; Baptist Hospital, Nashville, member of board. Member of Nashville Committee on Codes and Nashville Citizen's Safety Committee. *Member:* Palaver Club, Optimist Club.

WRITINGS: (Editor) *Christ for the World,* Broadman, 1963. Writer of Sunday school materials and training programs.

WORK IN PROGRESS: Research in biblical studies.

AVOCATIONAL INTERESTS: Photography.†

* * *

WESTBY-GIBSON, Dorothy Pauline 1920-

PERSONAL: Born January 26, 1920, in Philadelphia, Pa.; daughter of Ray Craig and Pauline Ida (Keller) Fenton; married Herbert Westby-Gibson (an educator), September 7, 1940. *Education:* Bucknell University, A.B., 1940; New School for Social Research, M.S.Sc., 1942; University of California, Berkeley, Ed.D., 1956. *Home:* 24 Addison St., San Francisco, Calif. 94131. *Office:* Department of Secondary Education, San Francisco State University, 1600 Holloway Ave., San Francisco, Calif. 94132.

CAREER: University of Washington, Seattle, associate director of Young Women's Christian Association (YWCA), 1942-45, part-time associate in sociology, 1944-45; Young Women's Christian Association, San Francisco, Calif., associate director of young adult department, 1945-50; San Francisco (Calif.) Unified School District, director of family life education service, Adult Education Division, 1950-58; San Francisco State University, San Francisco, assistant professor, 1958-61, associate professor, 1961-66, professor of education, 1966—, chairman of department of secondary education, 1969-70, 1972—. Visiting professor, University of the West Indies, summer, 1967, University of Maine, summer, 1968; visiting lecturer in education, Uni-

versity of Auckland, 1971. San Francisco Association for Mental Health, vice-president, 1964-66, board member-at-large, 1961—. Social group worker in New York, Seattle, and San Francisco. Consultant to U.S. Naval Command Schools, 1967, and California State Department of Public Health, 1969—. *Member:* American Sociological Association (fellow), National Association of Social Workers (charter member), American Educational Research Association, Adult Education Association, Pi Lambda Theta, Phi Delta Kappa.

WRITINGS: Social Perspectives on Education: The Society, the Student, the School, Wiley, 1965; (editor with Reed Brockbank) *Mental Health in a Changing Community,* Grune & Straton, 1965; *Grouping Students for Improved Instruction,* Prentice-Hall, 1966; *Social Foundations of Education: Current Issues and Research,* Free Press, 1967; *Inservice Education: Perspectives for Educators,* Far West Laboratory for Educational Research and Development, 1967; (editor) *Education in a Dymanic Society: A Contemporary Sourcebook,* Addison-Wesley, 1972; (contributor) Dwight W. Allen and Jeffrey C. Hecht, editors, *Controversies in Education,* Saunders, 1974. Contributor to *Guide and Workbook for the Professional Health Consultant to Extended Care Facilities,* 1969, and *Encyclopedia of Education,* 1971; also contributor to professional journals.

WORK IN PROGRESS: A book on adult education.

* * *

WESTLAKE, Donald E(dwin) 1933-
(Tucker Coe, Richard Stark)

PERSONAL: Born July 12, 1933, in New York, N.Y.; son of Albert Joseph (a salesman) and Lillian (Bounds) Westlake; married Nedra Henderson, August 10, 1957 (divorced, 1966); married Sandra Foley, April 9, 1967 (divorced, 1975); children: Sean Alan, Steven Albert. *Education:* Attended Champlain College and State University of New York at Binghamton. *Residence:* New Jersey. *Agent:* Henry Morrison, Inc., 58 West Tenth St., New York, N.Y. 10011.

CAREER: Worked at odd jobs prior to 1958 ("the same list as every other writer, except that I was never a short-order cook"); associate editor at literary agency, 1958-59; full-time professional writer, 1959—. *Military service:* U.S. Air Force, 1954-56 ("no awards, by mutual agreement"). *Awards, honors:* Edgar Allan Poe Award from Mystery Writers of America, 1967, for *God Save the Mark.*

WRITINGS: The Mercenaries, Random House, 1960; *Killing Time,* Random House, 1961; *361,* Random House, 1962; *Killy,* Random House, 1963; *Pity Him Afterwards,* Random House, 1964; *The Fugitive Pigeon,* Random House, 1965; *The Busy Body,* Random House, 1966; *The Spy in the Ointment,* Random House, 1966; *God Save the Mark,* Random House, 1967; *Philip,* Crowell, 1967; (compiler with Philip Klass) *Once Against the Law,* Macmillan, 1968; *Who Stole Sassi Manoon?,* Random House, 1968; *Somebody Owes Me Money,* Random House, 1969; *Up Your Banners,* Macmillan, 1969; *The Hot Rock,* Simon & Schuster, 1970; *Adios, Scheherazade,* Simon & Schuster, 1970; *I Gave at the Office,* Simon & Schuster, 1971; *Under an English Heaven,* Simon & Schuster, 1971; *Bank Shot,* Simon & Schuster, 1972; *Cops and Robbers,* M. Evans, 1972; (with Brain Garfield) *Gangway,* M. Evans, 1972; *Help I'm Being Held Prisoner,* M. Evans, 1974; *Jimmy the Kid,* M. Evans, 1974; *Two Much,* M. Evans, 1975; *A Travesty,* M. Evans, 1975.

Under pseudonym Tucker Coe: *Kinds of Love, Kinds of Death*, Random House, 1966; *Murder Among Children*, Random House, 1968; *Wax Apple*, Random House, 1970; *A Jade in Aries*, Random House, 1971; *Don't Lie to Me*, Random House, 1972.

Under pseudonym Richard Stark: *The Hunter*, Pocket Books, 1963; *The Man With the Getaway Face*, Pocket Books, 1963; *The Outfit*, Pocket Books, 1963; *The Mourner*, Pocket Books, 1963; *The Score*, Pocket Books, 1964; *The Jugger*, Pocket Books, 1965; *The Seventh*, Pocket Books, 1966; *The Handle*, Pocket Books, 1966; *The Rare Coin Score*, Gold Medal, 1967; *The Green Eagle Score*, Gold Medal, 1967; *The Damsel*, Macmillan, 1967; *The Dame*, Macmillan, 1967; *The Black Ice Score*, Gold Medal, 1968; *The Sour Lemon Score*, Gold Medal, 1969; *The Blackbird*, Macmillan, 1969; *Deadly Edge*, Random House, 1971; *Lemons Never Lie*, World Publishing Co., 1971; *Slayground*, Random House, 1971; *Plunder Squad*, Random House, 1972; *Butcher's Moon*, Random House, 1974; *The Steel Hit*, Berkley Publishing, 1975.

SIDELIGHTS: Anthony Boucher writes that, although Westlake is quite young, "already one can speak of his *oeuvre* in terms of Periods. In his First Period (1960-63), Westlake proved himself one of the ablest practitioners of the absolutely tough, hard-nosed novel of crime, with an acute insight into criminal thinking and an enviable ability to shock legitimately, without excess or bad taste. Then, after a one-book interlude (a psychological whodunit in 1964: Period 1-A), he entered on his present and glorious Second Period of criminous farce-comedies, as warm and funny as his early books were cold and frightening.... I'm sure that his Second Period will go down as one of the most entertaining episodes in suspense novel history."

Four of Westlake's novels have been filmed. Two written under his given name, *The Hot Rock*, released by Twentieth Century-Fox in 1972, and *The Busy Body*, Paramount, 1967, and two written under his pseudonym Richard Stark, "The Split," Metro-Goldwyn-Mayer, 1968, adapted from *The Seventh*, and "Point Blank," Metro-Goldwyn-Mayer, 1967, adapted from *The Hunter*.

BIOGRAPHICAL/CRITICAL SOURCES: New York Times Book Review, July 23, 1967; *Newsweek*, March 22, 1971.

* * *

WESTON, John (Harrison) 1932-

PERSONAL: Born May 17, 1932, in Prescott, Ariz; son of Omer Austin (a miner) and Eloine (Osment) Weston; married Catherine Jane Storms, February 6, 1954 (marriage dissolved); children: Tracy Cathlin, Jennifer Ann. *Education:* Arizona State University, B.A., 1954; University of Arizona, M.Ed., 1961; Yale University, graduate study, 1964-65. *Home:* 3413 Adina Dr., Los Angeles, Calif. 90068. *Agent:* Harold Matson Co., Inc., 22 East 40th St., New York, N.Y. 10016. *Office:* Department of English, California State University, Los Angeles, Calif. 90032.

CAREER: Teacher at public high schools in Needles, Calif., 1954-57, Yuma, Ariz., 1957-60, Tucson, Ariz., 1960-67; University of Arizona, Tucson, professor of English, 1967-71; California State University, Los Angeles, professor of English, 1971—. John Hay fellow in humanities at Williams College, summer, 1959, and Yale University, 1964-65; visiting writer-teacher, Indiana Writers Conference of University of Indiana, 1969; visiting lecturer in literature for young people, Drake University, 1971, 1972;

consultant to University of Oregon, 1966. Member of Southern California Council, Literature for Children. *Member:* College English Association, P.E.N., Society of Southwestern Writers. *Awards, honors:* Bread Loaf Writers Conference fellowship, 1966.

WRITINGS: Jolly (novel), McKay, 1965; *The Telling* (novel), McKay, 1966; *Hail Hero!* (novel), McKay, 1968; *Goat Songs* (novellas), Atheneum, 1971; *The Walled Parrot* (novel), McGraw, in press. Also author of short stories and travel features.

WORK IN PROGRESS: A book for young readers, *The Boy Who Sang the Birds*, for Scribner; a novel, *Tubalcain*; a book of prose-poetry; a collection of tales for children from California Indian myths and legends.

SIDELIGHTS: Weston told *CA*, "I am still working with Southwestern setting and point of view, and still look back often to Faulkner for inspiration." *Hail, Hero!* was made into a motion picture with the same title, National General Pictures, 1969. *Avocational interests:* Classical music, painting and collecting, international travel.

* * *

WHEELER, Helen Rippier

EDUCATION: Junior College of the Packer Collegiate Institute, A.A., 1946; Barnard College, B.A., 1950; Columbia University, M.S., 1951, Ed.D., 1964; University of Chicago, M.A., 1954. *Address:* Box 215, 7940 Jefferson Hwy., Baton Rouge, La. 70809.

CAREER: Hicksville Public Library, Hicksville, N.Y., library director, 1951-53; University of Chicago, Chicago, Ill., staff member of Laboratory School, and part-time foreign student adviser, 1953-55; teacher-librarian in a Chicago high school, 1955-56; Columbia University, Teachers College, New York, N.Y., staff member of Agnes Russell Center, 1956-58; City Colleges of Chicago, Chicago, library director and audio-visual coordinator, 1958-62; Columbia University, Latin American specialist, 1962-64; Drexel Institute of Technology (now Drexel University), Philadelphia, Pa., adjunct assistant professor, 1964-65; University of Hawaii, Honolulu, associate professor, 1965-66; Indiana State University, Terre Haute, associate professor, 1966-68; St. John's University, Jamaica, N.Y., associate professor, 1968-69; consultant and writer, 1969-71; Louisiana State University, Baton Rouge, associate professor, 1971-73; consultant and writer, 1973—. Member of staff, National Society for the Study of Education, 1953-55. *Member:* American Library Association, Association of College and Research Libraries, American Association of Community and Junior Colleges, American Association of University Professors, National Education Association, International House Association, American Association for Affirmative Action, Association of Feminist Consultants.

WRITINGS: (Contributor) Charles Trinkner, *Better Libraries Make Better Schools*, Shoe String, 1962; (contributor) Florence Lee, *Principles and Practices of Teaching in Secondary Schools*, McKay, 1964; *The Community College Library; A Plan for Action*, Shoe String, 1965; *A Basic Book Collection for the Community College Library*, Shoe String, 1968; *Womanhood Media*, Scarecrow, 1972, supplement, 1975. Contributor to social science periodicals.

SIDELIGHTS: Helen Wheeler is proficient in Spanish; she has traveled extensively.

WHEELER, Richard 1922-

PERSONAL: Born January 8, 1922, in Reading, Pa.; son of Clarence E. and Margaret (Wenrich) Wheeler. *Education:* Attended public school in Laureldale, Pa. *Politics:* Nonpartisan. *Home:* Route 1, Pine Grove, Pa. 17963. *Agent:* McIntosh & Otis, Inc., 18 East 41st St., New York, N.Y. 10017.

CAREER: Worked on a small weekly newspaper, now defunct, for several years after World War II; full-time professional writer, 1949—, doing light verse for magazines for about 15 years before switching to prose. *Military service:* U.S. Marines, 1942-45; received Purple Heart for wounds received on Iwo Jima. *Awards, honors:* Christopher Award, 1973, for *Voices of 1776.*

WRITINGS: The Bloody Battle for Suribachi, Crowell, 1965; *In Pirate Waters,* Crowell, 1969; *Voices of 1776,* Crowell, 1972; *Voices of the Civil War,* Crowell, in press. About eight hundred pieces of verse have appeared in thirty magazines, including one hundred twenty-five in *Saturday Evening Post.*

SIDELIGHTS: During the battle for Mount Suribach Wheeler's platoon lost forty-two of its original forty-six men; he wrote a long account of what actually had happened while recuperating in the hospital from his injuries, drew on it for his first magazine article, "The *First* Flag Raising on Iwo Jima," which appeared in *American Heritage,* June, 1964, as well as for his book. He says of his part in the battle, "I was a very scared marine surrounded by heroes."

BIOGRAPHICAL/CRITICAL SOURCES: Saturday Review, November 6, 1965.

*   *   *

WHEELER, Sessions S.

PERSONAL: Born near Fernley, Nev.; son of Lister L. (a rancher) and Lythia (Sessions) Wheeler; married Nevada Pedroli, April 24, 1948. *Education:* University of Nevada, B.S., 1934, M.S., 1935. *Religion:* Roman Catholic. *Home:* 25 Moore Lane, Reno, Nev. *Office:* Room 309, 1 East Liberty St., Reno, Nev.

CAREER: Biology instructor in Fernley, Nev., 1935-40; Reno High School, Reno, Nev., instructor in biology and chairman of science department, 1940-66; Nevada Fish and Game Commission, executive director (on leave from teaching), 1947-50; University of Nevada, Reno, assistant professor of conservation, summers, 1956—, lecturer in conservation, 1967—. Visiting Professor, University of Southern California, summer, 1961. Trustee of Max C. Fleischmann Foundation of Nevada, 1951—, Nevada State Museum, 1955-60; member of Nevada Indian Affairs Commission, 1965-68. *Awards, honors:* Nash Conservation Award, 1953; Nevada Federated Sportsmen Award, 1962; named outstanding biology teacher of Nevada, National Association of Biology Teachers, 1962; Distinguished Nevadan Award, University of Nevada, 1963; National Wildlife Federation—Sears, Roebuck Foundation Conservation Education Award, 1965; National Association of State Foresters, Smokey Bear Award, 1965.

WRITINGS: (Co-author) *Conservation and Nevada* (text), Nevada State Printer, 1949; (co-author) *Nevada Conservation Adventure* (text), Nevada State Printer, 1959; *Paiute* (historical novel), Caxton, 1965; *The Desert Lake: The Story of Nevada's Pyramid Lake,* Caxton, 1967; *The Nevada Desert,* Caxton, 1971. Author with W. O. Bay of

"Sage and Stream" (column), *Reno Evening Gazette,* 1941-50. Contributor of about thirty articles and stories to national and regional magazines.

WORK IN PROGRESS: Research in Nevada history and prehistory for a work on the Black Rock Desert.

*   *   *

WHEELIS, Allen B. 1915-

PERSONAL: Born October 23, 1915, in Marion, La.; son of Allen and Olive Minnie (Thompson) Wheelis; married Joyce Margaret Mitchell, November 20, 1937 (divorced, 1954); married Ilse Kaulbach (a psychiatrist and psychoanalyst), April 19, 1954; children: (first marriage) Mark Lewis, Victoria Lorelei (Mrs. Mark Jenkins); (second marriage) Joan. *Education:* University of Texas, A.B., 1937; Columbia University, M.D., 1943; New York Psychoanalytic Institute, graduate, 1952. *Home and Office:* 3731 Jackson St., San Francisco, Calif. 94118.

CAREER: Austen Riggs Center, Stockbridge, Mass., staff member, 1947-54; private practice of psychiatry and psychoanalysis, San Francisco, Calif., 1954—. *Military service:* U.S. Navy, 1943-46; became lieutenant senior grade. *Member:* American Psychiatric Association, American Psychoanalytic Association, American Medical Association, San Francisco Psychoanalytic Society.

WRITINGS: The Quest for Identity, Norton, 1958; *The Seeker,* Random House, 1960; *The Illusionless Man,* Norton, 1966; *The Desert* (novel), Basic Books, 1969; *The End of the Modern Age,* Basic Books, 1971; *The Moralist,* Basic Books, 1973; *How People Change,* Harper, 1973. Writer of scientific articles and short stories.

WORK IN PROGRESS: The Voyager; *On Not Knowing How to Live.*

*   *   *

WHICHER, John F. 1919-

PERSONAL: Born June 2, 1919, in New York, N.Y.; son of George F. (a professor) and Harriet (Fox) Whicher. *Education:* Amherst College, A.B., 1941; Columbia University, LL.B., 1947. *Politics:* Democrat. *Religion:* Episcopalian. *Office:* 292 Madison Ave., New York, N.Y. 10017.

CAREER: Admitted to bar, 1948; practicing attorney, New York, N.Y., 1948—. *Military service:* U.S. Army, 1942-46; became captain; received Commendation Ribbon and Philippines Liberation Medal with battle star. *Member:* American Bar Association (chairman of committee on government relations to copyrights, 1963-65), American Judicature Society, New York County Lawyers Association, Association of the Bar of the City of New York, Phi Beta Kappa, The Lambs.

WRITINGS: The Creative Arts and the Judicial Process, Federal Legal Publications, 1965. Contributor to *World Unfair Competition Law* (encyclopedia). Editor, *Bulletin of Copyright Society of the U.S.A.*†

*   *   *

WHITE, David Omar 1927-

PERSONAL: Born May 28, 1927, in Appleton, Wis.; son of Omar Washburn (a civil engineer) and Florence (Palmer) White; married Elizabeth Ann Arnold, April 19, 1957; children: Nathaniel Douglas, Amy Kirsten. *Education:* Attended Mount San Antonio College, 1946-47, Los Angeles Art Center School, 1947-48, Claremont Graduate School, 1948-50, and Columbia University, 1958-59.

CAREER: Artist; writer, mainly for children; illustrator. *Military service:* U.S. Naval Reserve, 1944-46. *Awards, honors:* Popular prize, Boston Arts Festival, 1962.

WRITINGS—Self-illustrated: *I Know a Giraffe*, Knopf, 1965; *Elizabeth's Shopping Spree*, Knopf, 1966; *The Boston Symphony Sketchbook*, privately printed, 1973.

Illustrator: Terry Berger, *Black Fairy Tales*, Atheneum, 1969; Bronson Potter, *Isfendiar and the Bears of Mazandaran*, Atheneum, 1969; Ken Denham, *My Learn to Fish Book*, Golden Press, 1971; Elizabeth Jamison Hodges, *A Song for Gilgamesh*, Atheneum, 1971; Adrienne Jones, *The Mural Master*, Houghton, 1974.

SIDELIGHTS: David White's comic strip "The Adventures of the White Rabbit," ran in *The Real Paper*, in Boston, 1968-74.

*   *   *

WHITE, Gillian Mary   1936-

PERSONAL: Born January 13, 1936, in Woodford, Essex, England; daughter of Albert George (a librarian) and Mabel (Bathurst) White. *Education:* King's College, London, LL.B. (first class honors), 1957, Ph.D., 1960. *Office:* Faculty of Law, University of Manchester, Manchester 13, England.

CAREER: Inland Revenue, Estate Duty Office, assistant examiner, 1954-57; called to the bar, Gray's Inn, 1960; Sweet & Maxwell Ltd. (publishers), London, England, editorial assistant, 1960-61; Cambridge University, Cambridge, England, research assistant to E. Lauterpacht of Trinity College, 1961-67, research fellow in international law, New Hall, 1963-67, director of studies in law, New Hall, 1964-67; University of Manchester, Manchester, England, lecturer in law, 1967-73, reader in law, 1973—. Research fellow, British Institute of International and Comparative Law. Lecturer at Syracuse, Columbia, Cornell, and New York Universities, 1965. *Member:* International Law Association, Society of Public Teachers of Law.

WRITINGS: Nationalization of Foreign Property, Stevens & Sons, 1961; *The Use of Experts by International Tribunals*, Syracuse University Press, 1965; (contributor) B. A. Wortley, editor, *An Introduction to the Law of the European Economic Community*, two volumes, Manchester University Press, 1972. Contributor to *International Law Reports*, Butterworth & Co., 1963—. Assistant editor, *British Practice in International Law* (published under auspices of International Law Fund and British Institute of International and Comparative Law), 1962—.

WORK IN PROGRESS: An essay; updating monograph of Sir Hersch Lauterpacht; work in collaboration with Sir Gerald Fitzmaurice.

SIDELIGHTS: White is competent in French and German. *Avocational interests:* British and European history, United Nations and European communities, music (classical), jazz (traditional), cookery.

*   *   *

WHITE, Minor   1908-

PERSONAL: Born July 9, 1908, in Minneapolis, Minn. *Education:* University of Minnesota, B.S., 1931; Columbia University, graduate study, 1945-46. *Home:* 203 Park Ave., Arlington, Mass. 02174.

CAREER: California School of Fine Arts, San Francisco, instructor in photography, 1946-52; George Eastman

House, Rochester, N.Y., editor of *Image*, 1953-55; Rochester Institute of Technology, Rochester, N.Y., lecturer in photography, 1955-64; Massachusetts Institute of Technology, Cambridge, professor of photography, 1965—. *Aperture* (photography quarterly), editor and president, 1952—. *Military service:* U.S. Army, 1942-45; became master sergeant.

WRITINGS: Zone System Manual, Morgan, 1961, 3rd edition, 1965, published as *New Zone System Manual*, 1974; *Mirrors, Messages, Manifestations* (photographs and text), Aperture, 1969; *The Expressive Photographer*, M.I.T. Press, in press; *Visualization Manual*, Morgan, in press. Contributor to photography and art magazines.

SIDELIGHTS: John Szarkowski wrote: "Of those photographers who reached their creative maturity after the Second War, none has been more influential than Minor White. Only three or four others of this generation have had a comparable impact on our sense of photography's potential: W. Eugene Smith, Harry Callahan, and Robert Frank are his contemporaries and peers. White's influence has depended not only on his own work as a photographer but on his service as teacher, critic, publisher, theoretician, proselytizer, and house mother for a large portion of the community of serious photographers. Indeed, White's omnipresence in the photographic world has made it easy to forget at times that he has remained first of all an artist: a photographer who has made some of the medium's most memorable pictures."

*   *   *

WHITE, Robert Lee   1928-

PERSONAL: Born May 3, 1928, in Louisville, Ky.; son of Zera J. and Anna (Simms) White; married Marilyn Porter, March 20, 1958; children: Lisa Anne, Michelle Theresa, Emily Jane. *Education:* University of Louisville, B.A., 1950; University of Minnesota, M.A., 1955, Ph.D., 1959. *Religion:* Roman Catholic. *Residence:* Toronto, Ontario, Canada.

CAREER: University of Kentucky, Lexington, instructor, 1959-62, assistant professor of American literature, 1962-67; York University, Toronto, Ontario, associate professor, 1967—. Fulbright lecturer in Finland, 1965-66, and 1972-73. *Military service:* U.S. Army, Corps of Engineers, 1950-52; became staff sergeant. *Member:* Modern Language Association of America, American Studies Association, American Society of Aesthetics. *Awards, honors:* Fulbright fellowship, 1955-56.

WRITINGS: John Peale Bishop, Twayne, 1966. Contributor to literary journals, including translations of Italian poetry. Editor, *Canadian Review of American Studies*.

WORK IN PROGRESS: An anthology of modern American poetry; studies in popular culture.

*   *   *

WHITE, Ruth M(argaret)   1914-

PERSONAL: Born September 7, 1914, in Ludlow, Ky.; daughter of Carl H. (a minister) and Mary (Irvin) White. *Education:* Ohio State University, B.S. in Ed., 1935; Western Reserve University (now Case Western Reserve University), B.S. in L.S., 1938; University of Chicago, A.M., 1963. *Religion:* Presbyterian. *Home:* 429 South Madison Ave., Pasadena, Calif. 91106. *Office:* Pasadena Public Library, 285 East Walnut St., Pasadena, Calif. 91101.

CAREER: High school teacher in Carnegie, Pa., 1935-37; school librarian in Providence, R.I., 1938-40, Columbus, Ohio, 1940-41, Toledo, Ohio, 1941-42, Cleveland, Ohio, 1942-43; Chapman Co., Milwaukee, Wis., assistant buyer, 1946-47; Chula Vista (Calif.) Public Library, librarian, 1947-51; U.S. Army, Special Services, staff librarian at Camp Tokyo, Tokyo, Japan, 1951-53; Chippewa Falls (Wis.) Public Library, librarian, 1954-55; Detroit (Mich.) Public Library, youth librarian, 1955-58; American Library Association, Chicago, Ill., assistant to executive secretary of Public Library Association, 1958-62, librarian, 1963-68, executive secretary of adult services and reference services divisions, 1968-70; Pasadena (Calif.) Public Library, coordinator of adult public services and assistant library director, 1971-74, coordinator of technical services, 1974—. Lecturer in librarianship, Northern Illinois University. *Military service:* U.S. Coast Guard, active duty, 1943-46; U.S. Coast Guard Reserve, 1946-74; became captain. *Member:* American Library Association, Special Libraries Association, Zonta International, California Library Association, Public Library Executives Association of Southern California, Friends of Huntington Library, Friends of Pacificulture Asia Museum, Beta Phi Mu, Pi Lambda Theta.

WRITINGS—All published by American Library Association: (Editor) *Plans for Six Public Library Buildings,* 1959; (editor) *Library Service to an Aging Population,* 1960; *Public Library Policies: General and Specific,* 1960, revised edition, 1970; *The School-Housed Public Library—A Survey,* 1963. Contributor to *Encyclopedia Americana.*

SIDELIGHTS: Ruth White holds commercial and instructor's licenses for single-engine land planes. *Avocational interests:* Travel.

* * *

WHITE, Stephanie F(rances) T(hirkell) 1942-

PERSONAL: Born October 1, 1942, in Hongood, Glamorganshire, Wales; daughter of John Sidney and Ruth P. (Gilbertson) Powell; married Roderick Douglas Thirkell White (an advertising executive), April 4, 1964. *Education:* Bedford College, London, B.A. (honors in sociology), 1963. *Office:* Tavistock Institute of Human Relations, 3 Devonshire St., London W. 1, England.

CAREER: Tavistock Institute of Human Relations, London, England, sociologist, 1963—.

WRITINGS: (With Everett E. Hagen) *Great Britain: The Quiet Revolution in Planning,* Syracuse University Press, 1966.

WORK IN PROGRESS: Studies of occupational choice and career patterns.†

* * *

WHITING, Robert L(ouis) 1918-

PERSONAL: Born February 25, 1918, in San Antonio, Tex.; son of Robert Elsworth (a merchant) and Nina L. (Guyton) Whiting; married Helen Sharon Smith, December 23, 1944; children: Robert Louis II, Sharon Carol, John Vance. *Education:* University of Texas, B.S., 1939, M.S., 1943. *Religion:* Christian. *Home:* 1031 Walton Dr., College Station, Tex. *Office:* Petroleum Engineering Department, Texas A&M University, College Station, Tex.

CAREER: Texas A&M University, College Station, 1946—, professor and head of department of petroleum engineering, 1949—. Owner of Whiting Industries and firm of Robert L. Whiting (consulting petroleum and natural gas

engineers). Director of Texas Petroleum Research Committee (independent agency), College Station, 1951-53, 1961—. *Member:* American Society for Engineering Education, Engineers Council for Professional Development, American Institute of Mining, Metallurgical and Petroleum Engineers, American Petroleum Institute, Society of Petroleum Engineers, American Association of University Professors.

WRITINGS: (With G. H. Fancher and J. H. Cretsinger) *Oil Resources of Texas,* Alexander Publishing, 1955; (with J. W. Amyx and D. M. Bass) *Petroleum Reservoir Engineering,* Volume I, McGraw, 1960.

WORK IN PROGRESS: Volume II of *Petroleum Reservoir Engineering;* and *Geothermal Resources of the World,* completion expected in 1976.

* * *

WHITMAN, Alden 1913-

PERSONAL: Born October 27, 1913, in New Albany, Nova Scotia, Canada; son of Frank S. (a teacher) and Mabel (Bloxsom) Whitman; married Joan McCracken (an editor), November 13, 1960; children: Pamela, Peter, Harriet, Daniel. *Education:* Harvard University, A.B., 1934. *Home:* Major's Path, Southampton, N.Y. 11968. *Office:* New York Times, New York, N.Y. 10036.

CAREER: *New York Herald Tribune,* New York, N.Y., copy editor, 1943-51; *New York Times,* New York, N.Y., reporter, 1951-65, chief obituary writer, 1965—. Columbia University, adjunct professor of journalism and consultant to Oral History Research Office; adviser to *Dictionary of American Biography. Member:* Century Club.

WRITINGS: *Early American Labor Parties,* International Publishers, 1944; *Portrait: Adlai E. Stevenson,* Harper, 1965; *The Obituary Book,* Stein & Day, 1971; (co-author) *The End of a Presidency,* Bantam Books, 1974. Contributor of book reviews to *New York Times, Los Angeles Times,* and other publications.

* * *

WHITMAN, Cedric H(ubbell) 1916-

PERSONAL: Born December 1, 1916, in Providence, R.I.; son of George Alfred and Muriel (Hubbell) Whitman; married Ruth A. Bashein, October 13, 1941 (divorced, 1958); married Anne Miller (in research and editorial work), June 7, 1959; children: (first marriage) Rachel Claudia, Leda Miriam. *Education:* Harvard University, A.B., 1943, Ph.D., 1947. *Home:* 3 Shady Hill Square, Cambridge, Mass. 02138. *Office:* Department of Classics, Harvard University, Cambridge, Mass.

CAREER: Harvard University, Cambridge, Mass., instructor, 1947-50, assistant professor, 1950-55, associate professor, 1955-59, professor, 1959-66, Francis R. Jones Professor of Classical Greek Literature, 1966-74, Eliot Professor of Greek Literature, 1974—, chairman of department of classics, 1960-66. *Military service:* U.S. Army, 1942. *Member:* American Philological Association, American Academy of Arts and Sciences, Archaeological Institute of America. *Awards, honors:* American Philological Association Award of Merit, 1952, for *Sophocles;* Christian Gauss Award of Phi Beta Kappa, 1958, for *Homer and the Heroic Tradition* (Gauss Award is for best book of literary scholarship published in United States); Guggenheim fellowship to Greece, 1961-62.

WRITINGS: *Orpheus and the Moon Craters* (poems),

Middlebury College Press, 1941; *Sophocles: A Study in Heroic Humanism*, Harvard University Press, 1951; *Homer and the Heroic Tradition*, Harvard University Press, 1958; *Aristophanes and the Comic Hero*, Harvard University Press, 1963; *Abelard* (narrative poem), Harvard University Press, 1965; *Euripides and the Full Circle of Myth*, Harvard University Press, 1974.

WORK IN PROGRESS: Commentary to Homer's *Iliad*.

SIDELIGHTS: Whitman's interests include modern Greek language and literature, an interest stimulated by trips to Greece in 1951, 1953, and a year's stay there in 1961-62.

*   *   *

WHITMAN, Edmund Spurr   1900-

PERSONAL: Born September 7, 1900, at Fort Meade, S.D.; son of Walter Monteith (a brigadier general, U.S. Army) and Nina (Edgerton) Whitman; married Sigrid Taillon, December 23, 1961; children: William Spurr, Wright Prescott. *Education:* Attended Williams College and Massachusetts Institute of Technology, 1917-18. *Politics:* Republican. *Religion:* Episcopalian. *Home and Office:* 1621 West Las Palmaritas, Phoenix, Ariz. 85021. ✎

CAREER: Entire business career, 1921-62, was with United Fruit Co.; began as time keeper on a tropical banana plantation; moved through tropical and domestic departments in agriculture, marketing, sales, advertising and public relations; vice-president for public relations, 1959-62. Free-lance writer during much of business career. Director, Caribbean Conservation Corp. Public relations consultant to Sperry Gyroscope Co., during World War II, and U.S. Department of the Interior, 1954; writing consultant to General Foods Corp., 1962—. *Member:* Pan American Society of the United States (past director), Business Council for International Understanding (past director), Royal Geographical Society (London; fellow), Explorers Club (New York).

WRITINGS: No Minor Vices, Albert & Charles Boni, 1931; *Guilty in the Tropics*, Sheridan, 1933; *Those Wild West Indies*, Sheridan, 1934; *Green Empire*, Street & Smith, 1935; (contributor) J. M. Bachelor and others, editors, *Current Thinking and Writing*, Appleton, 1964; *Revolt Against the Rain God*, McGraw, 1965; (with James Schmidt) *Plant Relocation*, American Management Association, 1966; *Little Pax*, Theosophical Publishing, 1972. Contributor of other articles and fiction to *American Mercury*, *Saturday Review*, *Reader's Digest*, and other magazines.

WORK IN PROGRESS: An adventure novel for teenagers about the Superstition Mountains, based on the legends and history of Arizona; and articles.

AVOCATIONAL INTERESTS: Archaeology of the Maya.

*   *   *

WHITMAN, Marina von Neumann   1935-

PERSONAL: Born March 6, 1935, in New York, N.Y.; daughter of John (a mathematician) and Mariette (Kovesi) von Neumann (mother now Mrs. Kuper); married Robert Freeman Whitman (a professor of English), June 23, 1956; children: Malcolm Russell, Laura Mariette. *Education:* Radcliffe College, B.A. (summa cum laude), 1956; Columbia University, M.A., 1959, Ph.D., 1962. *Office:* Department of Economics, University of Pittsburgh, Pittsburgh, Pa. 15260.

CAREER: Educational Testing Service, Princeton, N.J., administrative assistant, 1956-57; Pittsburgh (Pa.) Regional Planning Association, consultant, 1961, staff economist, Economic Study of the Pittsburgh Region (also sponsored by Center for Economic Studies), 1962; University of Pittsburgh, Pittsburgh, Pa., lecturer in economics, 1963, assistant professor of economics, 1963-66, associate professor, 1966-71, administrative officer of department, 1965; University of Pittsburgh, Pittsburgh, Pa., professor of economics, 1971-73, Distinguished Public Service Professor of Economics, 1973—. Council of Economic Advisers, senior staff economist, 1970-71, member, 1972-73; member of National Price Commission, 1971-72; member of private and governmental economic commissions; member of board of overseers of Harvard University and advisory council of economics department of Princeton University. *Member:* American Economic Association, Phi Beta Kappa.

WRITINGS: (Contributor) *Economic Study of the Pittsburgh Region*, University of Pittsburgh Press, 1963; *Government Risk-Sharing in Foreign Investment*, Princeton University Press, 1965. Contributor to "Princeton Studies in International Finance," and to economics journals. Member of editorial board, *American Economic Review* and *Foreign Policy*.

WORK IN PROGRESS: The future of the dollar in the international monetary system; domestic adjustment to exchange rate changes.

*   *   *

WHITTEN, Leslie H(unter)   1928-

PERSONAL: Born February 21, 1928, in Jacksonville, Fla.; son of Leslie Hunter (an electrical engineer) and Linnora (Harvey) Whitten; married Phyllis Webber, November 11, 1951; children: Leslie Hunter III, Andrew C., Daniel L. *Education:* Lehigh University, B.A. (magna cum laude), 1950. *Home:* 114 Eastmoor Dr., Silver Spring, Md. 20901. *Agent:* Curtis Brown Ltd., 60 East 56th St., New York, N.Y. 10022. *Office:* 1401 16th St. N.W., Washington, D.C. 20036.

CAREER: Radio Free Europe, news editor in Munich, Germany, 1952-55, news chief in New York, N.Y., 1955-57; International News Service, desk editor, Washington, D.C., 1957-58; United Press International, newsman, Columbia, S.C., 1958; *Washington Post*, Washington, D.C., reporter, 1958-62; Hearst Newspapers, Washington, D.C., reporter, 1963-66, assistant bureau chief, 1966-69, columnist, 1966—. Visiting associate professor, Lehigh University, 1968-70. *Military service:* U.S. Army, 1946-48; became staff sergeant. *Member:* American Civil Liberties Union. *Awards, honors:* Honorable mention, Washington Newspaper Guild Public Service Award, 1963; California Hospital Association News Award, 1965; Edgerton Award from American Civil Liberties Union, 1974.

WRITINGS: Progeny of the Adder (mystern novel), Doubleday, 1965; *Moon of the Wolf* (mystery novel), Doubleday, 1967; *Pinion, The Golden Eagle* (juvenile), Van Nostrand, 1968; (translator) Charles Baudelaire, *The Abyss*, The Smith, 1970; *F. Lee Bailey* (biography), Avon, 1971; *The Alchemist* (novel), Charterhouse Books, 1973.

WORK IN PROGRESS: A novel, publication by Doubleday; more translations from Baudelaire.

SIDELIGHTS: Whitten has traveled in the United States, Latin America, Europe, and Asia as a newsman.

WHITTEN, Mary Evelyn 1922-

PERSONAL: Born August 23, 1922, in Waskom, Tex.; daughter of Thomas Frank (an electrician) and Nellie (Huskey) Whitten. *Education:* East Texas State College (now University), B.A., 1947; University of Texas, M.A., 1949, Ph.D., 1956; additional study at University of Tennessee and University of Colorado. *Politics:* Independent. *Religion:* Roman Catholic. *Home:* 528 Headlee Lane, Denton, Tex. *Office:* North Texas State University, Denton, Tex.

CAREER: Central State College (now University), Edmond, Okla., supervisor of English, 1949-51; University of Tennessee, Knoxville, instructor in English, 1952-53; Central State College (now University), assistant professor of English, 1953-54; University of Texas, Austin, instructor in English, 1955-57; North Texas State University, Denton, professor of English, 1957—. *Member:* International Platform Association, National Council of Teachers of English, American Association of University Professors.

WRITINGS: (With John C. Hodges) *Harbrace College Handbook,* 5th edition, Harcourt, 1962, 7th edition, 1972; (with John Warriner and Joseph Blumenthal) *English Workshop: Grade 9,* Harcourt, 1964, published as *English Workshop,* 1970; (with J. Warriner) *English Grammar and Composition: Grade 9,* Harcourt, 1965, published as *English Grammer: Course Three,* 1973; *Creative Pattern Practice: A New Approach to Writing,* Harcourt, 1966, 2nd edition published as *Creative Pattern Practice,* 1975; *Decisions, Decisions: Style in Writing,* Harcourt, 1971; (with Alton C. Morris and others) *College English: The First Year,* Harcourt, 1973.

AVOCATIONAL INTERESTS: Deep-sea fishing.

*　　*　　*

WHITTEN, Norman E(arl), Jr. 1937-

PERSONAL: Born May 23, 1937, in Orange, N.J.; son of Norman E. (a professor) and Julia (Briggs) Whitten; married Dorothea Scott (a research associate), August 4, 1962. *Education:* Colgate University, A.B. (cum laude), 1959; University of North Carolina, M.A., 1961, Ph.D., 1964. *Politics:* "Usually Democrat." *Home:* 507 Harding Dr., Urbana, Ill. 61801. *Office:* Department of Anthropology, University of Illinois, Urbana, Ill. 61801.

CAREER: Tulane University and Universidad del Valle, Cali, Colombia, research associate, 1964-65; Washington University, St. Louis, Mo., assistant professor; 1965-68, associate professor of anthropology, 1968-70; University of Illinois, Urbana, associate professor, 1970-73, professor of anthropology, 1973—. Numerous trips for field work to central North Carolina, Ecuador, Colombia and Nova Scotia.

WRITINGS: Class, Kinship, and Power in an Ecuadorian Town: The Negroes of San Lorenzo, Stanford University Press, 1965; (editor with John F. Szwed) *Afro-American Anthropology: Contemporary Perspectives,* Free Press, 1970; *Black Frontiersmen: A South American Case,* Wiley, 1974; *Sacha Runa: Ethnicity and Adaptation of Ecuadorian Jungle Quichua,* University of Illinois Press, 1975. Contributor of over fifty articles and reviews to periodicals.

WORK IN PROGRESS: Preparing second book on jungle Quichua of eastern Ecuador; continuing field research on Black and Indian adaptation in lowland and highland South Africa.

WICKER, Brian 1929-

PERSONAL: Born March 24, 1929, in London, England; son of John Owen (a chartered surveyor) and Constance (Robinson) Wicker; married Teresa Clinton (a teacher), February 14, 1953; children: Mary, Philip, Lucy. *Education:* St. Edmund Hall, Oxford, B.A. (first class honors in English language and literature), 1952; University of Birmingham, M.A., 1960. *Politics:* Socialist. *Religion:* Roman Catholic. *Home:* 304 Vicarage Rd., Birmingham 14, England. *Office address:* P.O. Box 363, Department of Extramural Studies, University of Birmingham, Edgbaston, Birmingham 15, England.

CAREER: University of Birmingham, Birmingham, England, assistant secretary, university appointments board, 1956-60, staff tutor in department of extramural studies, 1960—. Visiting professor, Eastern Michigan University and Manhattanville College, 1968-69. *Military service:* British Army, instructor in Royal Educational Corps, 1947-49; became sergeant.

WRITINGS: Culture and Liturgy, Sheed (London), 1963; *God and Modern Philosophy,* Darton, Longman & Todd, 1964; *Work and the Christian Community,* Darton, Longman & Todd, 1964; *Culture and Theology,* Sheed, 1966; *First the Political Kindom,* Sheed, 1967; (editor) *From Culture to Revolution,* Sheed, 1968; (contributor) Stein and Gregor, editors, *The Prose for God,* Sheed, 1973; *The Story-Shaped World,* Notre Dame Press, in press. Writer of monthly column for *Guardian,* 1963-68; British correspondent for *Commonweal.* Contributor of articles to periodicals including *Essays in Criticism, New Blackfriars, Slant, Clergy Review, The Tablet, Encounter, Journal of Narrative Technique.*

*　　*　　*

WICKS, John H. 1936-

PERSONAL: Born April 4, 1936, in Minneapolis, Minn.; son of Walter (a sound technician) and Ruth (Jahn) Wicks. *Education:* University of South Dakota, B.A., 1957; University of Minnesota, graduate study, 1957-58; University of Illinois, M.A., 1961, Ph.D., 1962. *Office:* Department of Economics, University of Montana, Missoula, Mont. 59801.

CAREER: Augustana College, Sioux Falls, S.D., instructor in economics, 1957-58; assistant professor of economics at Western State College of Colorado, Gunnison, 1961-63, and Ohio State University, Columbus, 1963-64; University of Montana, Missoula, professor of economics, 1964—. Pitkin Publishing Co., Pitkin, Colo., officer, 1965—. *Military service:* U.S. Army Reserve, 1957-65; became captain. *Member:* American Economic Association, American Finance Association, National Tax Association, Western Economic Association, Western Finance Association, Rocky Mountain Social Sciences Association.

WRITINGS: (With Helen A. Cameron and Francis O. Woodard) *Cases in Public Finance,* Appleton, 1965; (with Woodard) *Program to Accompany Economics by John A. Guthrie and Robert F. Wallace,* Pitkin, 1965; *Alternative School Finance Programs for Montana,* Montana Legislative Council, 1972. Contributor to professional journals.

WORK IN PROGRESS: Research on state and local taxation.†

*　　*　　*

WICKS, Robert Stewart 1923-

PERSONAL: Born January 5, 1923, in Holyoke, Mass.;

son of Robert Russell (a minister) and Eleanor (Hall) Wicks; married Barbara Bruce, June 23, 1951; children: Sue Sarah, Robert Anthony Borden. *Education:* Princeton University, B.A., 1948; Union Theological Seminary, New York, N.Y., graduate study, 1953-54. *Politics:* Democrat. *Religion:* Presbyterian.

CAREER: Lawrenceville School (preparatory school), Lawrenceville, N.J., teacher, 1954—, chairman of department of religion. Guest preacher (lay) at secondary schools. *Military service:* U.S. Army, 1948-49.

WRITINGS: (Editor) *The Edge of Wisdom,* Scribner, 1964.

WORK IN PROGRESS: Developing a curriculum in the general area of religion that could be used in public schools.†

* * *

WIDGERY, Jan 1920-

PERSONAL: Given names were Jeanne-Anna; married surname is pronounced with soft "g"; born May 18, 1920, in Philadelphia, Pa.; daughter of Eugene Edmond (a chemist and author) and Carol (Messer) Ayres; married Rolande C. Widgery (an industry and government relations director for chemical company), March 29, 1948; children: Carolyn Gail, Catherine Darcy, Claudia Joan. *Education:* Chatham College, B.A., 1941; Radcliffe College, A.M., 1945. *Politics:* Independent. *Religion:* Protestant. *Home:* 2721 Oak Hill Dr., Allison Park, Pa. 15101. *Agent:* McIntosh & Otis, Inc., 18 East 41st St., New York, N.Y. 10017. *Office:* Winchester-Thurston School, 555 Morewood Ave., Pittsburgh, Pa. 15213.

CAREER: Chatham College, Pittsburgh, Pa., instructor in English, 1947-50; Ellis School, Pittsburgh, Pa., teacher of speech and director of drama, 1957-60; Winchester-Thurston School, Pittsburgh, Pa., chairman of department of English, 1960—.

WRITINGS: The Adversary (historical novel), Doubleday, 1966; *Trumpet at the Gates* (historical novel), Doubleday, 1970.

WORK IN PROGRESS: A contemporary novel, completion expected in 1976.

SIDELIGHTS: Mrs. Widgery told *CA:* "I write because of a strong need to communicate my convictions—convictions not about religion or politics or social conflict, but about interpersonal relationships, the paradox of human nature, the failure or achievement of understanding.... Admire such disparate writers as Dostoyevsky, James, Faulkner, Virginia Woolf, Robbe-Grillet, but neither would nor could imitate any of them." *Avocational interests:* Hiking, archery, and music (especially music of the seventeenth and eighteenth centuries).

BIOGRAPHICAL/CRITICAL SOURCES: Chatham Alumnae Recorder, spring, 1966; *Pittsburgh Post-Gazette,* May 9, 1966.

* * *

WIDMER, Eleanor (Rackow) 1925-

PERSONAL: Born January 4, 1925, in New York, N.Y.; daughter of Jack and Augusta (Rose) Rackow; married Kingsley Widmer (a literary critic), 1951; children: Matthew, Jonah. *Education:* Columbia University, M.A., 1947; University of Washington, Seattle, Ph.D., 1958. *Home:* 1575 Soledad Ave., La Jolla, Calif. 92037.

CAREER: Employed in Chicago, Ill., 1947-48; instructor in English at Portland State College (now Portland State University), Portland, Ore., 1955-56, at University of California, Extension Division, 1961-63; free-lance writer, 1966—; San Diego State University, San Diego, Calif., professor of literature, 1969—.

WRITINGS: (Editor with husband, Kingsley Widmer) *Literary Censorship,* Wadsworth, 1961; (editor with Kingsley Widmer) *Freedom and Culture: Literary Censorship in the 70's,* Wadsworth, 1970. Contributor of novella, "Mister Jack," to *Three: 1964,* Random House, 1964.

WORK IN PROGRESS: A novel, *Still Water;* an essay for *John Dos Passos in the 1930's,* edited by Warren French.†

* * *

WIENER, Solomon 1915-

PERSONAL: Born March 5, 1915, in New York, N.Y.; son of Morris David and Anna (Pinchuk) Wiener; married Gertrude Klings (an elementary school teacher), February 24, 1946; children: Marjorie Diane, Willa Kay. *Education:* Cornell University, B.S., 1936; New York University, M.P.A., 1946. *Religion:* Jewish. *Home:* 523 East 14th St., New York, N.Y. 10009. *Office:* Department of Personnel, City of New York, 220 Church St., New York, N.Y. 10013.

CAREER: Department of Personnel, City of New York, examining assistant, 1937-42, civil service examiner, 1946-55, assistant division chief, 1955-59, chief of administrative, medical, public health, and scientific examining division, 1959-67, assistant director of examinations, 1967-70, director of examinations, 1970-72, assistant personnel director for examinations, 1972—. Adult evening school teacher, 1949-60, and teacher-in-charge, 1960-67. *Military service:* U.S. Army Reserve, 1938-66; active duty, 1942-46, serving in Pacific Ocean area; became lieutenant colonel; received Bronze Star Medal. *Member:* American Society for Public Administration, International Personnel Management Association, Professional Association for Municipal Management (executive vice-president, 1969—), American Defense Preparedness Association, Reserve Officers Association of the United States.

WRITINGS: A Handy Book of Commonly Used American Idioms, Regents Publishing Co., 1958; *A Handy Guide to Irregular Verbs and the Use and Formation of Tenses,* Handy Book Press, 1959; *Questions and Answers in American Citizenship—An Americanization Manual and Naturalization Guide,* Regents Publishing Co., 1960; *Business Letter Writing,* Simon & Schuster, 1967. Contributor of articles to professional journals.

* * *

WIGGINS, James Wilhelm 1914-

PERSONAL: Born July 14, 1914, in Salisbury, N.C.; son of James Andrew (a minister) and Molly Louise (Wilhelm) Wiggins: married Kathryn Childers, June 14, 1938; children: Jack Wilhelm, Judy Ann. *Education:* Young Harris College, diploma, 1932; Georgia Southern College, B.S., 1934; Duke University, M.A., 1943, Ph.D., 1956; Emory University, graduate study, 1946-47. *Politics:* Republican. *Religion:* Presbyterian. *Home:* 245 Cart Dr., Spartanburg, S.C. 29302. *Office:* Converse College, Spartanburg, S.C.

CAREER: High school teacher in Georgia, 1934-42; Emory University, Atlanta, Ga., instructor, 1946-47, assistant professor, 1947-51, associate professor, 1951-59, professor of sociology, 1959-63, chairman of department of sociology and anthropology, 1952-60; Converse College, Spartanburg, S.C., professor of sociology and associate dean, 1963-73, Dana Distinguished Professor of Economics and Sociology, 1973—, head of Division of Social Science, 1971—. Consultant to American National Red Cross, American Medical Association, Mental Health Research Advisory Committee, American College of Hospital Administrators; trustee, Institute for Monetary Research; member, International Congress on Gerontology. Member of board of directors of Atlanta Citizens Crime Prevention Commission, 1948-52, of Atlanta Family Service Society, 1950-56. *Military service:* U.S. Army, 1942-46; received battle stars and Presidential Unit Citation. U.S. Army Reserve, 1946—; now lieutenant colonel.

MEMBER: American Association for the Advancement of Science (fellow), American Sociological Association (fellow), American Academy of Political and Social Science, Population Association of America, Reserve Officers Association, Military Government Association (chapter president, 1962), Intercollegiate Studies Institute, Philadelphia Society (president), Alpha Kappa Delta.

WRITINGS: (Editor with Helmut Schoeck, and contributor) *Foreign Aid Reexamined,* Public Affairs, 1958; (editor with Schoeck, and contributor) *Scientism and Values,* Van Nostrand, 1960; (co-editor and contributor) *Relativism and the Study of Man,* Van Nostrand, 1961; (co-editor and contributor) *Psychiatry and Responsibility,* Van Nostrand, 1962; (editor with Schoeck, and contributor) *The New Argument in Economics,* Van Nostrand, 1963; (editor with Schoeck, and contributor) *Central Planning and Neomercantilism,* Van Nostrand, 1964; (with Desmond P. Ellis) *Cooperation, Aggression and Learning in a Bi-Racial Classroom,* Department of Health, Education, and Welfare, 1968. Also editor of *Year Round Operation in Higher Education,* 1966. Contributor of articles and occasional reviews to *National Review, Wall Street Journal, University Bookman, California Medicine,* and other periodicals.

WORK IN PROGRESS: How Do They Know? (proposed title), a study of epistemology in the academic disciplines; a study of relationships between comfort index and divorce.†

* * *

WILHELM, James Jerome 1932-

PERSONAL: Born February 2, 1932, in Youngstown, Ohio; son of James J. and Ruth (Schreckengost) Wilhelm. *Education:* Yale University, B.A., 1954, Ph.D., 1961; University of Bologna, graduate study, 1954-55; Columbia University, M.A., 1958. *Home:* 30 East 38th St., 6C, New York, N.Y. 10016.

CAREER: Queens College of the City University of New York, Flushing, N.Y., assistant professor of English, 1961-65; Rutgers University, New Brunswick, N.J., professor of comparative literature, 1965—. *Member:* Modern Language Association of America, Mediaeval Academy of America, Elizabethan Club. *Awards, honors:* Fulbright fellowship, 1955-56.

WRITINGS: The Cruelest Month: Spring, Nature and Love in Classical and Medieval Lyrics, Yale University Press, 1965; *Seven Troubadours: The Creators of Modern Verse,* Pennsylvania State University Press, 1970; *Medieval Song: Anthology of Hymns and Lyrics,* Dutton, 1971; *Dante and Pound: The Epic of Judgment,* University of Maine Press, 1974; *The Later Cantos of Ezra Pound,* Mouton & Co., in press.

WILKERSON, Loree A. R(andleman) 1923-

PERSONAL: Born April 22, 1923, in Myrtle Point, Ore.; daughter of Claude A. (a logger) and Charlotte (Rickman) Randleman; married Thomas S. Wilkerson, Jr. (a retired Air Force officer, now teaching), October 10, 1946. *Education:* Oregon State University, student, 1940-41; University of Oregon, B.A., 1961; University of Florida, M.A., 1964, Ph.D. candidate, 1964—. *Politics:* Democrat.

CAREER: Production worker at Lockheed Aircraft, 1942-45; sheep and cattle ranch operator in Oregon, 1955-59. *Member:* American Political Science Association, Pi Sigma Alpha. *Awards, honors:* Rockefeller grant for research in Honduras and elsewhere in Central America, 1964-65.

WRITINGS: Fidel Castro's Political Programs from Reformism to Marxism-Leninism, University of Florida Press, 1965.

WORK IN PROGRESS: A study of the Liberal Party of Honduras.

SIDELIGHTS: Ms. Wilkerson is competent in Spanish. *Avocational interests:* Civilization of the Mayas and visiting Mayan ruins.†

* * *

WILKINS, Leslie T. 1915-

PERSONAL: Born March 8, 1915, in England; son of Henry John (a shoe factor) and Catharine (Hovey) Wilkins; married Barbara Lucy Swinstead (an assistant in a school for the handicapped), January 2, 1945; children: Arnold J., Cedric A., Janine C., Meriel C. *Education:* Attended City of London College and Hartley College. *Politics:* "Not yet known!" *Home:* 14 Brookwood Ave., Albany, N.Y. 12203. *Office:* State University of New York, Albany, N.Y. 12222.

CAREER: British Civil Service, statistician, 1945-56, deputy director of research, 1955-64; University of Strathclyde, Glasgow, Scotland, research director, 1964; United Nations, Technical Assistance Board, senior advisor of Asia and Far East Institute, Tokyo, 1964-66; University of California, Berkeley, professor of criminology, 1966-68, acting dean, 1968-69; State University of New York, School of Criminal Justice, Albany, professor and chairman of faculty, 1969—. *Military service:* Royal Air Force, 1940-45. *Member:* Royal Statistical Society (London; former chairman of general applications section), British Sociological Society, American Statistical Association, Incorporated Statistician. *Awards, honors:* Francis Wood Memorial Prize of Royal Statistical Society for the best social research using statistical methods, for *The Prevalence of Deafness.*

WRITINGS: The Prevalence of Deafness, H.M.S.O., 1948; *Adolescents in Britain,* H.M.S.O., 1950; (with H. Mannheim) *Prediction Methods in Relation to Borstal Training,* H.M.S.O., 1955; (with C. S. Scott) *Uses of Technical Literature,* H.M.S.O., 1959; *Social Deviance,* Prentice-Hall, 1964; *Effectiveness of Punishment,* Council of Europe, 1966; *Evaluation of Penal Measures,* Random House, 1969; (editor with Robert Carter) *Probation and Parole: Selected Readings,* Wiley, 1970.

Contributor: S. Glueck and E. Glueck, editors, *Social Maladjustment,* Knopf, 1960; A. T. Welford and others, editors, *Society: Problems and Methods of Study,* Routledge & Kegan Paul, 1961; N. B. Johnston and others, editors, *Sociology of Punishment and Correction,* Wiley, 1962; Marvin E. Wolfgang and others, editors, *Sociology of*

Crime and Delinquency, Wiley, 1962; L. E. Abt and B. F. Reiss, editors, *Progress in Clinical Psychology,* Volume VI, Grune, 1964; B. Rosenburg, editor, *Mass Society in Crisis,* Macmillan, 1965; Martin K. Starr, editor, *Executive Readings in Management Science,* Macmillan, 1965.

Author of more than twenty-five monographs and research reports published in England and United States. Contributor to *International Encyclopedia of the Social Sciences,* and some forty articles to criminology, psychology, and sociology journals here and abroad. Editor, *Howard Journal* (London); former co-editor, *Applied Statistics* and *Incorporated Statistician;* member of editorial board, *Excerpta Criminologica.*

WORK IN PROGRESS: Continuing research in connection with decision making in criminal justice, particularly regarding sentencing and parole.

SIDELIGHTS: Wilkins told *CA:* "Techniques of communication, particularly between scientist, laymen, and politicians must be improved if we are to hope for survival. Working towards this end is my hobby as well as part of my job . . ."

* * *

WILKINSON, Sylvia 1940-

PERSONAL: Born April 3, 1940, in Durham, N.C.; daughter of Thomas Noell (a building contractor) and Peggy (George) Wilkinson. *Education:* University of North Carolina at Greensboro, B.A., 1962; Hollins College, M.A., 1963; graduate study at Stanford University, 1965-66. *Address:* 109 Williams St., Chapel Hill, N.C. 27514.

CAREER: Asheville-Biltmore College (now University of North Carolina at Asheville), instructor in English, art, and drama, 1963-64; College of William and Mary, Williamsburg, Va., instructor in English, 1966-67; University of North Carolina at Chapel Hill, lecturer in English, 1967-70. Visiting writer, Creative Writing Learning Institute of North Carolina, 1968-69. Writer-in-residence at Hollins College, 1969, Richmond Humanities Center, 1972-74, Sweet Briar College, 1973-75. Participant in Poetry in the Schools program, 1972-74, and in various writer's workshops. *Member:* Authors League of America, Authors Guild, International Motor Sports Association, Sports Car Club of America, Sierra Club, Animal Protection Society, California Racing Association. *Awards, honors:* Eugene Saxton Memorial Trust Grant, 1964, for *Moss on the North Side;* Wallace Stegner creative writing fellowship, 1965-66; *Mademoiselle* Merit Award, 1966; Sir Walter Raleigh Award, 1968, for *A Killing Frost; Sports Car* magazine feature story award, 1972; National Endowment for the Arts creative writing fellowship, 1973-74.

WRITINGS: Moss on the North Side (novel), Houghton, 1966; *A Killing Frost* (novel), Houghton, 1967; *Cale* (novel), Houghton, 1970; *Change* (teaching handbook), LINC Press, 1971; (contributor) John Watson, editor, *Subject and Structure,* Little, Brown, 1972; *The Stainless Steel Carrot: An Auto Racing Odyssey,* Houghton, 1973. Also author of a play "ALF", first produced at Asheville-Biltmore College (now University of North Carolina at Asheville), with Miss Wilkinson in the leading role. Contributor to anthologies. Also contributor of articles and reviews to *Writer, Ingenue, Sports Car, Sports Illustrated, Southern Living, The American Scholar,* and other periodicals.

WORK IN PROGRESS: Sewer Lily (novel).

SIDELIGHTS: Miss Wilkinson told *CA:* "Writing is not a pleasant task for me. I find myself seeking for a thousand escapes from the hard chair in front of my typewriter—partly because it requires so much mental effort and no physical activity, tying me into a nervous knot like a ten-year-old in church." She also said that writing is a compulsion with her, "and I could not stop writing if I tried."

AVOCATIONAL INTERESTS: Sports car racing, tennis (was eastern North Carolina Women's tennis champion in 1959 and Durham champion for two years), horses, painting (has had several one-artist shows), acting, dancing, hiking, skiing, motorcycle riding.

BIOGRAPHICAL/CRITICAL SOURCES: Durham Sun, July 23, 1966.

* * *

WILL, Robert E(rwin) 1928-

PERSONAL: Born March 8, 1928, in Northfield, Minn.; son of Erwin E. (an entrepreneur) and Gena (Luedke) Will; married Barbara A. Couture (a sociologist), December 22, 1956; children: Jonathan, Jennifer, Leslie. *Education:* Carleton College, B.A., 1950; Yale University, M.A., 1951, Ph.D., 1965. *Politics:* Democrat. *Religion* Episcopalian. *Home:* 417 Union St., Northfield, Minn. 55057. *Office:* Department of Economics, Carleton College, Northfield, Minn. 55057.

CAREER: Yale University, New Haven, Conn., instructor in economics, 1951-54; University of Massachusetts, Amherst, instructor in economics, 1954-57; Carleton College, Northfield, Minn., assistant professor, 1957-65, associate professor, 1965-68, professor of economics, 1968-71, Williams Professor of Economics, 1971—, assistant dean, 1967-68, director of international studies, 1968-71, chairman of department of economics, 1971—. Lecturer, American Institute of Banking, 1956-57; visiting associate professor, University of Minnesota, 1965; John de Quedville Briggs Lecturer, St. Paul Academy, 1966-70; visiting faculty fellow, University of Sussex, 1970-71. Member of policy committee, United Shareowners of America, 1960—; member of advisory council, Minnesota Department of Manpower Services, 1966—; director, Community Electronics Corp. *Military service:* U.S. Naval Reserve, 1945—; currently lieutenant. *Member:* American Economic Association, Society for International Development, Industrial Relations Research Association, Association for Asian Studies, World Future Society, Economic History Association, American Association of University Professors, Phi Beta Kappa, Chactonbury Ring (Sussex, England). *Awards, honors:* Lilly Endowment grant, 1959-60; Ford Foundation fellowship, 1962-63; National Science Foundation fellowship, 1970-71.

WRITINGS: (Editor with H. G. Vatter) *Poverty in Affluence: The Political, Social, and Economic Dimensions of Poverty in the United States,* Harcourt, 1965, 2nd edition, 1970. Contributor to *Economic Impact, Contemporary Review, Choice, Books Abroad, Wisconsin Magazine of History, American Economic Review,* and other journals.

WORK IN PROGRESS: Economics of tourism, income and employment multiplier effects; inflation and private higher education.

* * *

WILLIAMS, Hugo 1942-

PERSONAL: Born February 20, 1942, in Windsor, Berkshire, England; son of Hugh (an actor and playwright) and

Margaret (Vyner) Williams; married Hermine Demoriane, October 9, 1965; children: Catherine Murphy. *Education:* Attended Eton College, 1955-60. *Home:* 3 Raleigh St., London N. 1, England. *Agent:* A. D. Peters, 10 Buckingham St., Adelphi, London W.C. 2, England. *Office: London Magazine,* 30 Thurloe Place, London S.W. 7, England.

CAREER: Alan Ross, Ltd. (publishers), London, England, assistant editor, including work on *London Magazine,* on and off, 1961—; worked briefly for *Weekend Telegraph;* poet and travel writer. *Awards, honors:* Eric Gregory Poetry Award, and Arts Council of Great Britain Poetry Award, both 1966.

WRITINGS: Symptoms of Loss (poems), Oxford University Press, 1965; *All the Time in the World* (travel), Alan Ross, 1966, Chilton, 1968; (editor and contributor) *London Magazine Poems,* Alan Ross, 1966; *Sugar Daddy* (poems), Oxford University Press, 1970. Poems included in anthology, *New Lines 2,* edited by Robert Conquest, Macmillan, 1963.

SIDELIGHTS: Williams told *CA* that he: "travelled in Asia for a year, more accidentally than geographically, it being the only way to Australia from Israel. Visited Israel, Egypt, Jordon, Saudi Arabia, Iran, Afghanistan, Pakistan, Kashmir, India, Nepal, Singapore, Thailand, Cambodia, Japan, Australia, Tahiti, Martinique."

A *Times Literary Supplement* reviewer wrote of *All the Time in the World:* "... One of the most refreshing things about Mr. Williams's book is its complete lack of pretentiousness.... What emerges is a young man who is fresh without being gauche, open but not soft-centered. Mr. Williams is also a very funny writer in a casual off-hand way, with a certain wry and economical ruthlessness."

About the development of Williams's poetry, an *Observer Review* writer said: "... *Symptoms of Loss* was precociously polished and worldly-wise, but unconvincing, full of elaborate artifice and tired Fifties mannerisms. At the end of the book, though, there were two poems ... which showed that this very young poet was beginning to discover a quite different voice, not borrowed or evasive but delicate, direct and gently shrewd, a voice for talking out of, not about, experience. It is this voice, its edges sharpened, and its scope extended, which appears in *Sugar Daddy.*"

AVOCATIONAL INTERESTS: Children, pop music, France (Williams speaks French), hitch-hiking, making scrapbooks, Old London, castles in Spain.

BIOGRAPHICAL/CRITICAL SOURCES: Poetry, November, 1966; *Times Literary Supplement,* March 9, 1967.†

* * *

WILLIAMS, Roger J(ohn) 1893-

PERSONAL: Born August 14, 1893, in Ootacumund, India; son of American citizens, Robert Runnels (a missionary) and Alice Evelyn (Mills) Williams; married Hazel Elizabeth Wood, August 1, 1916 (died, 1952); married Mabel Phyllis Hobson, May 9, 1953; children: (first marriage) Roger John, Janet Elizabeth, Arnold Eugene; (stepson) John Wallace Hobson. *Education:* University of Redlands, B.S., 1914; University of Chicago, M.S., 1918, Ph.D., 1919. *Religion:* Protestant. *Home:* 1604 Gaston Ave., Austin, Tex. *Office:* Clayton Foundation Biochemical Institute, University of Texas, Austin, Tex. 78712.

CAREER: Fleischmann Co., Chicago, Ill., research chemist, 1919-20; University of Oregon, Eugene, assistant pro-

fessor, 1920-21, associate professor, 1921-28, professor of chemistry, 1928-32; Oregon State College (now University) Corvallis, professor of chemistry, 1932-39; University of Texas, Austin, professor of chemistry, 1939-71, professor emeritus, 1971—, research professor, 1941-42, director of Clayton Foundation Biochemical Institute, 1941-63, consultant to Clayton Foundation Biochemical Institute, 1963—. Member of National Polio Board, 1951-53, of research and medical committee, National Multiple Sclerosis Society, of medical advisory board, Muscular Dystrophy Associations of America, of scientific advisory board, Southwest Foundation for Research and Education, of President's Advisory Panel on Heart Disease, 1972—.

MEMBER: International Academy of Preventive Medicine (first honorary president, 1972), American Association for the Advancement of Science (fellow), National Academy of Sciences, American Chemical Society (president, 1957), American Society of Biological Chemists, Biochemical Society of London (founding fellow), American Association for Cancer Research, Society for Experimental Biology and Medicine, American Association of University Professors, Texas Academy of Science (vice-president, 1948), New York Academy of Sciences, Philosophical Society of Texas, Texas State Teachers Association, Phi Beta Kappa, Sigma Xi, Phi Sigma, Alpha Chi Sigma, Phi Kappa Phi, Phi Lambda Upsilon, Pi Kappa Delta. *Awards, honors:* D.Sc., University of Redlands, 1934, Columbia University, 1942, and Oregon State University, 1956; Mead Johnson Award, American Institute of Nutrition, 1941; Chandler Medal, Columbia University, 1942; regional award, American Chemical Society, 1950.

WRITINGS: An Introduction to Organic Chemistry, Van Nostrand, 1927, 5th edition (with L. F. Hatch), 1948; (with R. Q. Brewster) *A Laboratory Manual of Organic Chemistry,* Van Nostrand, 1928, 4th edition, 1948; *An Introduction to Biochemistry,* Van Nostrand, 1931, 2nd edition (with E. Beerstecher), 1948; *A Textbook of Biochemistry,* Van Nostrand, 1938, 2nd edition, 1942; *What to Do About Vitamins,* University of Oklahoma Press, 1945; *The Human Frontier,* Harcourt, 1946; (with R. E. Eakin, E. Beerstecher, and W. Shive) *Biochemistry of the B Vitamins,* Reinhold, 1950; *Nutrition and Alcoholism,* University of Oklahoma Press, 1951; *Free and Unequal,* University of Texas Press, 1953; *Biochemical Individuality,* Wiley, 1956; *Alcoholism: The Nutritional Approach,* University of Texas Press, 1959; *Nutrition in a Nutshell,* Dolphin Books, 1962, hardcover edition, Doubleday, 1963.

You Are Extraordinary, Random House, 1967; (editor with E. M. Lansford) *Encyclopedia of Biochemistry,* Reinhold, 1967; *Nutrition Against Disease,* Pitman, 1971; *Physicians' Handbook of Nutritional Science,* C. C Thomas, 1974.

Contributor: E. A. Evans, editor, *The Biological Action of the Vitamins,* University of Chicago Press, 1942; R. S. Harris and K. Thimann, editors, *Vitamins and Hormones,* Academic Press, 1943; F. F. Nord and C. H. Werkman, editors, *Advances in Enzymology,* Interscience, 1943; M. G. Wohl, editor, *Dietotherapy: Clinical Application of Modern Nutrition,* Saunders, 1945; Felix Morley, editor, *Essays on Individuality,* University of Pennsylvania Press, 1958; Anthony A. Albanese, editor, *Protein and Amino Acid Nutrition,* Academic Press, 1959; M. Florkin and E. H. Stotz, editors, *Comprehensive Biochemistry,* Elsevier, 1963; C. A. Hampel and G. G. Hawley, editors, *Encyclopedia of Chemistry,* 3rd edition, Van Nostrand, 1973; D. Hawkins and L. Pauling, editors, *Orthomolecular Psy-*

chiatry, W. H. Freeman, 1973; F. Sargent II, editor, *Human Ecology*, North-Holland Publishing, 1974.

Author or co-author of a series of University of Texas Publications on vitamin and other nutrition studies, 1941-42. About two hundred articles have appeared in chemical and other scientific journals since 1919, and a few in legal, criminology, and health periodicals. Member of editorial board, *Archives of Biochemistry, 1946-60.*

WORK IN PROGRESS: A book on nutrition for teenagers; articles for scientific journals.

SIDELIGHTS: Williams is the discoverer of pantothenic acid. His other areas of research have included B vitamins in tissues (including malignant tissues), etiology of alcoholism, genetrophic disease, and propetology. Two of his books, *The Human Frontier* and *Biochemical Individuality*, have been translated for foreign publication. *Avocational interests:* Golf, fishing, travel (has traveled in Europe, Southeast Asia, and Africa).

BIOGRAPHICAL/CRITICAL SOURCES: Modern Medicine, Volume XXVI, number 1, January 1, 1958; *Science Digest*, Volume LIII, number 4, April, 1963.

* * *

WILLIAMS, Stanley W. 1917-

PERSONAL: Born October 31, 1917, in Augusta, Me.; son of Leon N. and Laura (White) Williams; married Patricia Cesmat, March 13, 1945; children: Anne, Katherine, Marilyn, Laurie. *Education:* Bates College, A.B., 1940; University of Southern California, M.S., 1946, Ed.D., 1949. *Politics:* Republican. *Religion:* Episcopalian. *Home:* 1640 Beacon Ave., Anaheim, Calif. 92802.

CAREER: Principal and teacher at secondary schools in Maine, 1940-43; Aroostook State Teachers College (now University of Maine), Presque Isle, instructor, 1946-47; California State College (now University), Los Angeles, assistant professor of education, 1949; Culver City (Calif.) public schools, junior high school principal, 1949-50, senior high school principal, 1950-52; California State University, Long Beach, professor of educational administration, 1952—. Summer lecturer at University of Rhode Island, 1957, University of Connecticut, 1958, and other universities. Western Association of Schools and Colleges, chairman of accreditation teams for California secondary schools. *Member:* National Education Association, Association of California School Administrators, Association of California State University Professors, Phi Delta Kappa.

WRITINGS: Educational Administration in Secondary Schools: Task and Challenge, Holt, 1964; *New Dimensions in Supervision*, Intext, 1972. Contributor to educational journals.

WORK IN PROGRESS: Emerging Designs for School Administration.

* * *

WILLIAMSON, Ellen Douglas
(Ellen Douglas)

PERSONAL: Born in Cedar Rapids, Iowa; daughter of George Bruce and Irene (Hazeltine) Douglas; married Gregory Williamson (a business executive), June 28, 1939; children: Margaret Douglas (Mrs. Nathaniel Litt). *Education:* Vassar College, B.A., 1927. *Politics:* Republican. *Religion:* Presbyterian. *Residence:* Princeton, N.J. *Agent:* Paul R. Reynolds, Inc., 599 Fifth Ave., New York, N.Y. 10017.

CAREER: Writer. Trustee of Coe College.

WRITINGS: (Under name Ellen Douglas) *Moon of Violence,* Bouregy, 1960; (under name Ellen Douglas) *Wall Street Made Easy,* Doubleday, 1965; *Spend Yourself Rich,* Doubleday, 1970.

WORK IN PROGRESS: A book, with tentative title *In Boston We Call It Ohio.*

* * *

WILLIAMSON, John Stewart 1908-
(Jack Williamson; pseudonym, Will Stewart)

PERSONAL: Born April 29, 1908, in Bisbee, Arizona Territory; son of Asa Lee (a rancher and teacher) and Lucy Betty (a onetime teacher; maiden name, Hunt) Williamson; married Blanche Slaten Harp (a merchant), August 15, 1947; children: (stepchildren) Keigm Harp, Adele Harp Lovorn. *Education:* Taught at home by parents until he was twelve, then attended high school in Richland, N.M.; studied at West Texas State College (now University), 1928-30, at University of New Mexico, 1932-33; Eastern New Mexico University, B.A. (summa cum laude) and M.A., 1957; University of Colorado, Ph.D., 1964. *Politics:* Democrat. *Religion:* Methodist. *Address:* Box 761, Portales, N.M. 88130. *Agent:* Scott Meredith Literary Agency, Inc., 580 Fifth Ave., New York, N.Y. 10036. *Office:* Eastern New Mexico University, Portales, N.M. 88130.

CAREER: Hooked by a tale he read in *Amazing Stories* in 1927, Jack Williamson began bombarding that magazine with fiction, sold his first piece in 1928, and wrote fantasies and science fiction full time for almost thirty years—with some digressions into college and university study, the Air Force, and a short stint of news work in Portales, N.M., 1947; creator of a comic strip, "Beyond Mars," run by the *New York Sunday News*, 1953-56; entered Eastern New Mexico University in 1953 to get a better background in the sciences, found academic life so much to his liking that teaching has become a primary career (still writes science fiction and teaches a course in it); taught English as an instructor at New Mexico Military Institute, Roswell, 1957-59, at University of Colorado, Boulder, 1960; associate professor of English at Eastern New Mexico University, Portales, 1960-69, professor, 1969—. *Military service:* U.S. Army Air Forces, 1942-45; became staff sergeant.

MEMBER: Science Fiction Writers of America, National Council of Teachers of English, Masons, Rotary.

WRITINGS—Under name Jack Williamson: *The Legion of Space*, Fantasy Press, 1947; *Darker Than You Think*, Fantasy Press, 1948; *The Humanoids*, Simon & Schuster, 1949.

The Green Girl, Avon, 1950; *The Cometeers*, Fantasy Press, 1950; *One Against the Legion*, Fantasy Press, 1950, reissued with novella *Nowhere Near*, Pyramid Books, 1967; *Dragon's Island*, Simon & Schuster, 1951; *The Legion of Time*, Fantasy Press, 1952; *After World's End*, Fantasy Press, 1952; (with Frederik Pohl) *Undersea Quest*, Gnome Press, 1954; *Dome Around America*, Ace Books, 1955; (with James E. Gunn) *Star Bridge*, Gnome Press, 1955; (with Pohl) *Undersea Fleet*, Gnome Press, 1956; (with Pohl) *Undersea City*, Gnome Press, 1958.

The Trial of Terra, Ace Books, 1962; *Golden Blood*, Lancer Books, 1964; (with Pohl) *The Reefs of Space*, Ballantine, 1964; (with Pohl) *Starchild*, Ballantine, 1965; *The Reign of Wizardry*, Lancer Books, 1965; *Bright New Universe*, Ace Books, 1967; (with Murray Leinster and John

Wyndham) *Three Stories*, Doubleday, 1967 (published in England as *A Sense of Wonder: Three Science Fiction Stories*, edited by Sam Moskowitz, Sidgwick & Jackson, 1967); *Trapped in Space*, Doubleday, 1968; *The Pandora Effect* (short stories), Ace Books, 1969; (with Pohl) *Rogue Star*, Ballantine, 1969.

(Contributor) Robert Silverberg, editor, *The Mirror of Infinity*, Harper, 1970; *People Machines* (short stories), Ace Books, 1971; *The Moon Children*, Putnam, 1972; *H. G. Wells: Critic of Progress*, Mirage Press, 1973; *Teaching Science Fiction* (booklet), privately printed, 1973; (contributor) Robin Scott Wilson, editor, *Those Who Can: A Science Fiction Reader*, New American Library, 1973; (with Pohl) *The Farthest Star*, Ballantine, 1975.

Under pseudonym Will Stewart, except as indicated: *Seetee Shock*, Simon & Schuster, 1950, reprinted under name Jack Williamson, Lancer Books, 1968; *Seetee Ship*, Gnome Press, 1951, reprinted under name Jack Williamson, Lancer Books, 1968.

Most of the science fiction magazines have carried his stories, with novels, novelettes, and short stories appearing in *Amazing Stories, Science Wonder Stories, Air Wonder Stories, Astounding Stories, Wonder Stories, Weird Tales, Astounding Science Fiction, Argosy*, and others.

WORK IN PROGRESS: Two books with Frederik Pohl, *Doomship*, and *Doomworld*, both for Ballantine; *The Early Williamson*, for Doubleday; *The Power of Blackness*, for Putnam; *Brother to Demons, Brother to Gods*.

SIDELIGHTS: Williamson's reputation as a science fiction writer had its grounding in 1928 when *Amazing Stories* carried a cover depicting a scene from his story, "The Metal Man." Thirteen of his first twenty-one published stories were spectacular enough to gain covers in early science fiction magazines, some running in a number of installments. *The Legion of Space* rocketed along in *Astounding Stories* for six issues in 1934 and became Williamson's first hardback publication many years later. In 1934 he began to drift away from fantasy toward scientific logic; in 1942 he suggested a series of stories on the engineering problems of making asteroids habitable, to the editor of *Astounding Science Fiction*. The resulting novelettes, originally published under the pseudonym Will Stewart, "have come to be considered the most outstanding exposition of the anti-matter ever written," explains Sam Moskowitz. Moskowitz credits Williamson with influencing several major trends in science-fiction writing and calls him "one of the most adaptable science-fiction writers alive."

Williamson says of his later union of two careers: "I am interested in science, particularly in the impact of scientific progress on human beings and human institutions; that's why I enjoy writing science fiction. I'm interested in young people and their problems in a world where progress moves at a dizzy rate; that's why I enjoy teaching." Williamson explained further: "Good science fiction is good literature, well worth academic attention. It fascinates young people, because they are going to be living in some of the alternative futures it tries to explore. Though a few skeptics aren't yet convinced, I think it can be more realistic than most 'realistic fiction' because it does accept and examine the fact that technology is changing our world. Creative teachers all across the country are using its appeal to interest and motivate students in many subjects, from physics and social science to religion and philosophy."

BIOGRAPHICAL/CRITICAL SOURCES: Amazing Stories, October, 1964; *Seekers of Tomorrow*, World Publishing, 1966.

WILLINGHAM, John R(obert) 1919-

PERSONAL: Born July 15, 1919, in Quinlan, Tex.; son of Joe Scott and Grace (Hurst) Willingham; married Yvonne Buster (an assistant press director), October 25, 1942; children: John Robert, Jr., Amy Frances. *Education:* Attended Southern Methodist University, 1936-38; East Texas State Teachers College (now East Texas State University), B.A., 1940; North Texas State Teachers College (now North Texas State University), B.S. in L.S., 1940, M.A., 1948; University of Oklahoma, Ph.D., 1953. *Politics:* Democrat. *Religion:* Episcopalian. *Home:* 2511 Yale Rd., Lawrence, Kan. 66044. *Office:* 3136 Wescoe Hall, University of Kansas, Lawrence, Kan. 66045.

CAREER: East Texas State Teachers College (now East Texas State University), Commerce, assistant librarian and instructor in library science, 1946-48; Southeastern State College, Durant, Okla., librarian and associate professor of library science, 1953-54; Centenary College of Louisiana, Shreveport, professor of English, 1954-61; University of Kansas, Lawrence, assistant professor, 1961-63, associate professor, 1963-66, professor of English, 1966—. Visiting assistant professor of English at Sam Houston State College (now University), 1950-51, and summer visiting professor, 1955-56; visiting professor, Bowling Green State University, 1967, University of Texas, 1968, University of Toledo, 1969. Textbook consultant to Allyn & Bacon, Inc., McGraw-Hill Book Co., Harper & Row Publishers, Inc., and Prentice-Hall, Inc. *Military service:* U.S. Army, 1942-46; became second lieutenant.

MEMBER: Modern Language Association of America, College English Association, American Association of University Professors, Kansas Association of Teachers of English.

WRITINGS: (With Wilfred Guerin, Earle Labor, and Lee Morgan) *A Handbook of Critical Approaches to Literature*, Harper, 1966; (with William R. Elkins and Jack Kendall) *Literary Reflections*, McGraw-Hill, 1967, 2nd edition, 1970; (with Guerin, Labor, and Morgan) *Mandala: Literature for Critical Analysis*, Harper, 1970. Contributor of articles and reviews to *Explicator, Nation, Kansas City Star*, and to literary and library journals. Associate editor, *South-Central MLA Bulletin*, 1956-60; acting editor, *Midcontinent American Studies Journal*, 1962, 1964.

WORK IN PROGRESS: A biography of Waldo Frank; the *Seven Arts* group.

* * *

WILLIS, John A(lvin) 1916-

PERSONAL: Born October 16, 1916, in Morristown, Tenn.; son of John Bradford (a pharmacist) and George Anne (Myers) Willis; married Claire Olivier (divorced, 1963). *Education:* Milligan College, B.A., 1938; University of Tennessee, M.A., 1941; graduate study at Indiana University and Harvard University. *Home:* 190 Riverside Dr., New York, N.Y. 10024.

CAREER: Actor for ten years, then teacher of English, speech, and drama for varying periods at University of Tennessee, Knoxville, National Academy of Dramatic Arts, New York, N.Y., and in New York (N.Y.) public schools; assistant editor of *Theatre World*, 1944-64, and *Screen World*, 1946-64 (both annual publications then edited by Daniel Blum); owner-editor of *Theatre World* and *Screen World*, 1964—, and *Dance World* (also published yearly), 1965—. *Military service:* U.S. Navy, 1941-45; became lieutenant. *Member:* Actors' Equity Association, New York Drama Desk, Alpha Psi Omega.

WRITINGS—Other publications; as assistant editor to Daniel Blum; *A Pictorial History of the American Theatre: 1900-1950*, Greenberg, 1950, revised edition, covering period between 1860 and 1960, Chilton, 1960, 2nd revised edition, Crown, 1970; *Great Stars of the American Stage*, Greenberg, 1952; *A Pictorial History of the Silent Screen*, Putnam, 1953; *A Pictorial History of the Talkies*, Greenberg, 1958; *A Pictorial History of Television*, Chilton, 1959; *A Pictorial Treasury of Opera in America*, Greenberg, 1960.

AVOCATIONAL INTERESTS: Collecting theater memorabilia.

* * *

WILSON, Carter 1941-

PERSONAL: Born December 27, 1941, in Washington, D.C.; son of George Wood (a lawyer) and Harriet (Fort) Wilson. *Education:* Harvard University, A.B., 1963; Syracuse University, M.A., 1965. *Residence:* Aptos, Calif. *Agent:* Candida Donadio and Associates, 111 West 57th St., New York, N.Y. 10019. *Office:* Kresge College, University of California, Santa Cruz, Santa Cruz, Calif. 95064.

CAREER: Stanford University, Palo Alto, Calif., lecturer in English, 1965-66; Harvard University, Cambridge, Mass., Briggs-Copeland Lecturer in English and General Education, 1966-69; Tufts University, Medford, Mass., lecturer, 1969-71, assistant professor of English and director of writing program, 1971-72; University of California, Santa Cruz, Calif., assistant professor, 1972-74, associate professor of community studies, 1974—.

WRITINGS: Crazy February: Death and Life in the Mayan Highlands of Mexico (novel), Lippincott, 1966, new edition, University of California Press, 1974; *I Have Fought the Good Fight* (novel), Lippincott, 1967; *On Firm Ice* (children's stories), Crowell, 1970; *A Green Tree and a Dry Tree* (novel), Macmillan, 1972; (contributor) Hennings Siverts, editor, *Drinking in the Mayan Highlands of Chiapas*, University of Bergen, 1973; (contributor) Edward Fishman, editor, *The Best From Fantasy and Science Fiction*, 19th edition, Doubleday, 1973. Also wrote film documentary, "Appeals to Santiago," 1968, released by Contemporary-McGraw Hill.

WORK IN PROGRESS: A memoir, *In Our Story So Far*; a feature screenplay, "Shadow Catcher," with Tim Hunter.

SIDELIGHTS: Wilson lived for a year among the Mayan Indians in the mountains of southern Mexico, the setting for his first novel which was called "anything but run-of-the-mill" in the *New York Times Book Review*. The reviewer found the characters of the Indians and Mexicans of the region "more subtly penetrated by Carter Wilson . . . than were the famous 'Children of Sanchez,' as tape-recorded by Oscar Lewis." Wilson speaks Spanish and a Mayan Indian dialect, Tzotzil.

BIOGRAPHICAL/CRITICAL SOURCES: New York Times Book Review, February 27, 1966.

* * *

WILSON, George W(ilton) 1928-

PERSONAL: Born February 15, 1928, in Winnipeg, Manitoba, Canada; son of Walter and Ida (Wilton) Wilson; mar-

ried Marie McKinney, September 6, 1952; children: Ronald Leslie, Douglas Scott, Suzanne Rita. *Education:* Carleton University, B. Comm., 1950; University of Kentucky, M.A., 1951; Cornell University, Ph.D., 1955. *Home:* 2335 Woodstock Pl., Bloomington, Ind. 47405. *Office:* Indiana University, Bloomington, Ind.

CAREER: Board of Transport Commissioners, Ottawa, Ontario, economist, 1951-52; Middlebury College, Middlebury, Vt., assistant professor of economics, 1955-57; Indiana University, Bloomington, assistant professor, 1957-59, associate professor of transportation, 1959-66, professor of economics, 1966—, chairman of department, 1966-70, dean of College of Arts and Sciences, 1970-73. Collaborator with Gunnar Myrdal in Sweden on study of South Asia economic development (sponsored by Twentieth Century Fund), 1961-62; director of study on transportation and economic development for Brookings Institution, 1964, and study on Canada's needs and resources for Twentieth Century Fund, 1964-65; member of President's Task Force on Transportation, 1964. *Member:* American Transportation Research Forum (vice-president for academic affairs; president, 1969), American Economic Association, Beta Gamma Sigma.

WRITINGS: (With others) *Mathematical Models and Methods in Marketing*, Irwin, 1961; *Essays on Some Unsettled Questions in the Economics of Transportation*, Bureau of Business Research, Indiana University, 1962; (with John Munro) *Road Transportation: History and Economics, Part I*, Bureau of Business Research, Indiana University, 1962; *An Introduction to Aggregative Economics, Part I*, Bureau of Business Research, Indiana University, 1962; (with John Spychalski and George M. Smerk) *Physical Distribution Management, Part I*, Bureau of Business Research, Indiana University, 1963; (contributor) *Essays in Transport Problems in the 1960's*, Bureau of Business Research, Indiana University, 1963; (editor) *Classics of Economic Theory*, Indiana University Press, 1964; (With Scott Gordon and Stanislaw Judlek) *Canada: An Appraisal of Its Needs and Resources*, Twentieth Century Fund, 1965; (with others) *The Impact of Highway Investment on Development*, Brookings Institution, 1966; *Growth and Change at Indiana University*, University Study Committee, 1966; (with others) *Report of the Tripartite Economic Survey of the Eastern Caribbean*, H.M.S.O., 1967; (with Gunnar Myrdal and others) *Asian Drama: An Inquiry Into the Poverty of Nations*, three volumes, Twentieth Century Fund, 1968; (with L. Darby) *Transportation on the Prairies*, Royal Commission on Consumer Problems and Inflation (Canada), 1968; (editor and contributor) *Essays in Economic Analysis and Policy*, Indiana University Press, 1970; (editor and contributor) *Technological Development and Economic Growth*, School of Business, Indiana University, 1971.

WORK IN PROGRESS: Transportation Needs and Economic Development in Indochina; Freight Rate Changes and the Future Development of Western Canada.

* * *

WILSON, Joyce M(uriel Judson)
(Joyce Stranger)

PERSONAL: Born in London, England; daughter of Ralph (an advertising manager) and Beryl Judson; married Kenneth Wilson (patents manager with Imperial Chemicals Industry), February 28, 1944; children: Andrew Bruce, Anne Patricia and Nicholas David (twins). *Education:*

University College, London, B.Sc., 1942. *Religion:* Church of England. *Agent:* Hughes Massie Ltd., 69 Great Russell St., London WCIB 3DH, England.

CAREER: Imperial Chemicals Industry, Manchester, England, research chemist, 1942-46. *Member:* Society of Authors, Society of Women Journalists and Writers, British Mammal Society, British Deer Society, Council for Wild Life, Institute of Journalists.

WRITINGS—All under pseudonym Joyce Stranger: *Wild Cat Island* (juvenile), Methuen, 1961; *Circus All Alone* (juvenile), Harrap, 1965; *The Running Foxes*, Hammond, Hammond, 1965, Viking, 1966; *Breed of Giants*, Hammond, Hammond, 1967; *Rex*, Harvill Press, 1967, Viking, 1968; *Jason* (juvenile), Dent, 1967; *Casey*, Harvill Press, 1968, published as *Born to Trouble*, Viking, 1969; *Rusty*, Harvill Press, 1969, published as *The Wind on the Dragon*, Viking, 1970; *The Honeywell Badger* (juvenile), Dent, 1969.

Zara, Harvill Press, 1970, Viking, 1971; *Chia: The Wildcat*, Harvill Press, 1971; *One for Sorrow*, Transworld Publishers, 1971; *Paddy Joe* (juvenile), Collins, 1972; *The Hare at Dark Hollow* (juvenile), Dent, 1972; (contributor) Noel Streatfeild, editor, *Summer Holiday Book*, Dent, 1972; *Lakeland Vet*, Harvill Press, 1972, Viking, 1973; (contributor) Noel Streatfeild, editor, *Christmas Holiday Book*, Dent, 1973; *Walk a Lonely Road*, Harvill Press, 1973; *Never Count Apples*, Harvill Press, 1974; *Trouble for Paddy Joe* (juvenile), Collins, 1974; *A Dog Called Gelert*, Dent, 1974; *The Secret Herds*, Dent, 1974; *Paddy Joe at Deep Hollow Farm* (juvenile), Collins, 1975; *Never Tell a Secret*, Harvill Press, 1975; *Joyce Stranger's Book of Hanak Animals*, Dent, in press; *The Fox at Drummer's Darkness*, Dent, in press; *Flash*, Harvill, in press.

Former writer of "The World About Us" column in *Annabel*. Contributor of short stories to *Woman's Journal*, *Womans' Own*, and other periodicals and of occasional articles to *Gamekeeper and Countryside*, *Dog World*, *Alsatian League Magazine*, and *Dog Training Weekly*.

WORK IN PROGRESS: Three books, one adult, one in the "Paddy Joe" series, and one for Dent.

SIDELIGHTS: The Honeywell Badger and *The Hare at Dark Hollow* were both adapted for television by British Broadcasting Corp. and *Jason* is to be filmed as an American television feature by Walt Disney Productions.

Joyce Wilson told *CA* she now owns two bluepoint Siamese cats, a Golden Retriever, and an Alsatian which had six pups in 1974. She is following up in the training and showing of four of the pups and occasionally teaches a dog training evening class.

*   *   *

WILSON, Lanford   1937-

PERSONAL: Born April 13, 1937, in Lebanon, Mo.; son of Ralph Eugene and Violetta (Tate) Wilson. *Education:* Attended Southwest Missouri State College, 1955-56, San Diego State College (now University), 1956-57, and University of Chicago, 1957-58. *Address:* Box 891, Sag Harbor, N.Y. 11963. *Agent:* Bridget Aschenberg, International Famous Agency, 1301 Avenue of the Americas, New York, N.Y. 10019.

CAREER: Playwright; director, actor, and designer for Caffe Cino and Cafe La Mama. Member of Actors Studio Playwrights Unit. *Awards, honors:* Rockefeller Foundation grant, 1966-67; Vernon Rice-Drama Desk Award, 1968, for

"The Rimers of Eldritch"; American Broadcasting Co.—Yale University fellowship, 1969; Guggenheim fellowship, 1972; nominated for "Emmy" award of National Academy of Television Arts and Sciences, 1972, for "The Migrants"; New York Drama Critics' Circle Award, Outer Circle Critics' Award, and "Obie" Award from *Village Voice*, all 1973, all for "The Hot l Baltimore"; "Obie" Award, 1975, for "The Mound Builders."

WRITINGS—Plays; published and produced: *Balm in Gilead and Other Plays* (includes: "Balm in Gilead," produced Off-Off Broadway at Cafe La Mama, 1965; "Ludlow Fair," produced Off-Off Broadway at Theatre East, 1966; "Home Free!," produced in New York, 1964, produced in London, 1968), Hill & Wang, 1965; *The Rimers of Eldritch and Other Plays* (includes: "Days Ahead," produced in New York, 1965; "This Is the Rill Speaking," produced under the title "Six from La Mama" Off-Broadway at Martinique Theatre, 1966; "The Madness of Lady Bright," produced Off-Broadway at Theatre East, 1966, produced in London, 1968, first published in *Eight Plays from Off-Off Broadway,* edited by Nick Orzel and Michael Smith, Bobbs-Merrill, 1966; "The Rimers of Eldritch," produced Off-Broadway at Cherry Lane Theatre, 1967; "Wandering," produced Off-Broadway at Cafe au Go Go, 1968), Hill & Wang, 1967; *The Gingham Dog* (produced in Washington, D.C. at Washington Theatre Club, 1968; produced on Broadway at Golden Theatre, 1969), Hill & Wang, 1969.

Lemon Sky (produced Off-Broadway at Playhouse Theatre, 1970), Dramatists Play Service, 1970; *The Sand Castle and Three Other Plays* (includes: "The Sand Castle," produced in New York at Cafe La Mama, 1965; "Sextet(Yes): A Play for Voices," produced in New York, 1971; "Wandering" (also see above); "Stoop: A Turn"), Dramatists Play Service, 1970; *Summer and Smoke* (adaptation of Tennessee Williams' book; produced in St. Paul, 1971; produced in New York, 1972), Belwin-Mills, 1972; *The Great Nebula in Orion and Three Other Plays* (includes: "The Great Nebula in Orion," produced in Manchester, 1970, produced Off-Off Broadway at Circle Theatre Co., 1971; "Ikke, Ikke, Nye, Nye, Nye," produced in New Haven, 1971; "The Family Continues," produced in New York, 1972; "Victory on Mrs. Dandywine's Island"), Dramatists Play Service, 1973; *The Hot l Baltimore* (produced Off-Off Broadway at Circle Theatre Co., 1973), Hill & Wang, 1973.

Plays; produced but not yet published: "So Long at the Fair," produced in New York at Caffe Cino, 1963; "No Trespassing," produced in New York, 1964; "Sex Is Between Two People," produced in New York, 1965; "Miss Williams," produced in New York, 1968; "Serenading Louie," produced in Washington, D.C. at Washington Theatre Club, 1970; "The Mound Builders," produced in New York, 1975.

Also author of screenplay "One Arm" (adaptation of Tennessee Williams's story), 1970; author, with Tennessee Williams, of film script, "The Migrants," for CBS-TV.

SIDELIGHTS: In his discussion of the Cafe La Mama production of "The Sand Castle," the *Village Voice* critic noted that "Wilson's strategy is to create a reality not only convincing but suffocating; he can then explode his emotions without fear of the foundations giving way.... The tone of the dialogue is light, the key actions are underplayed and muffled. But the stylized technique keeps reminding us that what we are watching is not random behavior but a play. The surface is only routinely ruffled, but the connotations are seething." The *Voice* reviewer praised not only "The Sand Castle," however. He saw this work as indicative of Wilson's considerable potential as a playwright.

Arthur Sainer commented in reference to "Lemon Sky": "Wilson is joyously, lavishly in love with his story, with the whole idea of theatre and its machinery ... the general theatrical style is a throwback to the early days of Williams and Miller, but Wilson is so infected with an enthusiasm for making the play happen that its whole texture is rendered as a continuously joyous quiver of discovery, each moment operates as a new act of discovery."

Discussing his working habits, Wilson said: "I've always worked in enormous spurts, sometimes for 20 hours at a stretch. When I'm writing well, it's like taking dictation, and the characters get way ahead of me. I wrote the first act of 'Lemon Sky' in one marathon session of 24 hours, and the last act of 'Gingham Dog' in eight hours."

Many of Wilson's plays have been produced on television, including "The Rimers of Eldritch," "The Sand Castle," "Wandering," and "The Mound Builders."

BIOGRAPHICAL/CRITICAL SOURCES: Village Voice, September 30, 1965.

*   *   *

WILSON, Robert N(eal)   1924-

PERSONAL: Born November 15, 1924, in Syracuse, N.Y.; son of Robert Marchant (a factory foreman) and May (Neal) Wilson; married Arleene E. Smith, August 21, 1948; married Joan Emery Wallace, August 1, 1973; children: Lynda, Deborah. *Education:* Attended Trinity Hall, Cambridge, 1945-46; Union College, Schenectady, N.Y., B.A., 1948; Harvard University, Ph.D., 1952. *Politics:* Democrat. *Religion:* Episcopalian. *Home:* 10 Fidelity Court Apartments, Carrboro, N.C. *Office:* University of North Carolina, Chapel Hill, N.C.

CAREER: Cornell University, Ithaca, N.Y., research associate, 1951-53; Social Science Research Council, Washington, D.C., member of staff, 1953-56; Center for Advanced Study in the Behavioral Sciences, Stanford, Calif., fellow, 1956-57; Harvard University, Cambridge, Mass., lecturer, 1957-60; Yale University, New Haven, Conn., associate professor of sociology, 1960-63; University of North Carolina, Chapel Hill, professor of sociology, 1963—. Consultant to National Institutes of Health and State Communities Aid Association. *Military service:* U.S. Army, 1943-46; received two battle stars for combat service in Europe. *Member:* American Sociological Association, Phi Beta Kappa. *Awards, honors:* Fulbright senior research scholar, Lund University, Sweden, 1975.

WRITINGS: (With Temple Burling and Edith M. Lentz) *The Give and Take in Hospitals,* Putnam, 1956; (editor with Alexander H. Leighton and John A. Clausen) *Explorations in Social Psychiatry,* Basic Books, 1957; *Man Made Plain,* Howard Allen, 1958; *The Arts in Society,* Prentice-Hall, 1964; *Coming Home: The Problem of After-Care,* Southern Regional Education Board, 1965; *Community Structure and Health Action,* Public Affairs Press, 1968; *The Sociology of Health,* Random House, 1970; *The Sociology and Psychology of Art,* General Learning Press, 1973. Contributor to *Journal of Aesthetics and Art Criticism, Psychiatry, Human Organization, Antioch Review,* and *American Image.*

WORK IN PROGRESS: Essays in the sociology of literature; studies in the sociology of planning.

AVOCATIONAL INTERESTS: Poetry, jazz, athletics.

WINAWER, Bonnie P. (Josephs)   1938-

PERSONAL: Born October 11, 1938, in Verona, N.J.; daughter of Paul and Helen (Joelson) Josephs. *Education:* Smith College, B.A., 1960; New York University, LL.B., 1966. *Residence:* New York, N.Y. *Office:* London, Buttenwieser, & Chalif, 575 Madison Ave., New York, N.Y. 10022.

CAREER: Cravath, Swaine & Moore, New York, N.Y., attorney, 1966-69; London, Buttenwieser, & Chalif, New York, N.Y., attorney, 1969—.

WRITINGS: (Editor) *The 40-Knot Sailboat,* Grosset, 1963; (with David Aaron) *Child's Play,* Harper, 1965; (contributor) Thomas I. Emerson and others, editors, *Political and Civil Rights in the United States,* 3rd edition, Little, Brown, 1967. Contributor to *New York Times, Motor Boating,* and *Ingenue.*

*   *   *

WINCHESTER, James H.   1917-

PERSONAL: Born June 27, 1917, in Midlothian, Tex.; son of James Hugh (a blacksmith) and Mary (Adams) Winchester; married Josephine Nowodzinski, February 14, 1948; children: Kenneth, Nancy. *Education:* Attended public schools in Manteca, Calif. *Politics:* Democrat. *Religion:* Protestant. *Home:* 15 Clark St., Pleasantville, N.Y. 10570.

CAREER: Newspaper reporter in Stockton, Calif., 1933-35, and for *New York Morning Telegraph,* New York, N.Y., 1935-38; public relations writer in New York, N.Y., for American Airlines, 1938-40, and Columbia Broadcasting System, 1940-42; reporter-writer for King Features Syndicate, New York, N.Y., 1946-61; free-lance writer for magazines, newspapers, radio, and television, Pleasantville, N.Y., 1961-67; *Reader's Digest,* Pleasantville, N.Y., staff writer, 1961—. *Military service:* U.S. Army Air Forces, 1942-45; became staff sergeant; received Army Commendation Medal and thirteen battle stars. *Member:* International Society of Aerospace Writers, National Association of Science Writers, American Society of Travel Writers (board member, 1962-65), Aviation/Space Writers Association, New York Travel Writers Association, Delta Sigma Chi, Overseas Press Club (New York). *Awards, honors:* Trans-World Airlines aviation writing award (eight times); aviation safety writing award (three times); Strebig Award from Aviation/Space Writers Association, 1967; Sigma Delta Chi—Deadline Club magazine writing award, 1974; Aviation/Space Writers Association magazine writing award, 1974.

WRITINGS: Wonders of Water, Putnam, 1964; *Hit Parade of Flying Stories,* Scholastic Book Services, 1965; *Hurricanes, Storms, Tornadoes,* Putnam, 1966. Writer of radio and television scripts; weekly columnist, "World Today," for King Features-Central Press; contributor of over 1000 articles to most leading magazines.

SIDELIGHTS: Winchester has covered and written stories from more than one hundred countries.

*   *   *

WINDER, R(ichard) Bayly   1920-

PERSONAL: Born September 11, 1920, in Greensboro, N.C.; son of Richard Bayly (in investment banking) and Julia (Purnell) Winder; married Viola Hitti, October 12, 1946; children: Bayly Philip. *Education:* Haverford College, A.B., 1946; Princeton University, A.M., 1947, Ph.D.,

1950. *Politics:* Democrat. *Religion:* Episcopalian. *Home:* 86 Castle Howard Ct., Princeton, N.J. 08540. *Office:* Office of the Dean, Faculty of Arts and Sciences, New York University, New York, N.Y. 10003.

CAREER: American University of Beirut, Beirut, Lebanon, member of staff, 1947-49; Princeton University, Princeton, N.J., instructor, 1950-52, assistant professor, 1952-57, associate professor of Oriental studies, 1957-66, director of overseas Arabic study program, 1961-66, assistant dean of the college, 1963-64; New York University, New York, N.Y., professor in the departments of history and Near Eastern languages and literatures, 1966—, Washington Square College, chairman of department of Near Eastern languages and literatures, 1966—, director of graduate program in Modern Near Eastern Studies, and Middle East Language and Area Center, 1966—, dean, 1968-71, dean of Faculty of Arts and Sciences, 1970—. Visiting summer professor at University of Michigan, 1951, University of Southern California, 1957, Harvard University, 1963, University of Utah, 1964, University of Pennsylvania, 1969. Member of board of directors and executive committee, American Field Service, 1961-68; member of advisory committee, Consultative Service on United States Undergraduate Study Abroad, 1962-65; member of national screening committee, Near East, Fulbright-Hays, 1963-67; Asia and Near East foreign area fellowship program, member, 1964-67, chairman, 1965-67; member of UNESCO Commission on Textbooks for Arab Refugees. Consultant to Ford Foundation in United Arab Republic, 1960-61, Time-Life Publishing Co., 1962, 1967, California-Texas Oil Co., and other organizations. Member of board of trustees, American University in Cairo, 1972—; treasurer of American Research Center in Egypt, 1972—. *Wartime service:* American Field Service, 1942-46; became first lieutenant; mentioned in dispatches (British); received theatre ribbons; awarded Purple Heart.

MEMBER: American Association of Teachers of Arabic (member of board of directors, 1967-70), American Middle East Rehabilitation (member of board of directors, 1968—), American Oriental Society, American Historical Association, Middle East Institute, Middle East Studies Association (member of board of directors, 1966-68; president, 1968-69), American Friends of the Middle East, Royal Asiatic Society (member of board of directors), Phi Beta Kappa. *Awards, honors:* Rockefeller Foundation fellow, 1947-49; Ford Foundation fellowship to Damascus, 1955-56; National Defense Education Act Center faculty award, 1964-65; Princeton University African travel grant, 1969.

WRITINGS: (With others) *A Glossary of Basic Arabic Grammatical, Poetic, and Linguistic Terms,* Department of Oriental Languages, Princeton University, 1952; (contributor) Richard Ettinghausen, editor, *A Selected and Annotated Bibliography of Books and Periodicals in Western Languages Dealing with the Near and Middle East, with Special Emphasis on Medieval and Modern Times* (with supplement), Middle East Institute, 1954; (translator) Constantine N. Zurayk, *The Meaning of the Disaster,* Khayat (Beirut), 1956; (with Farhat J. Ziadeh) *An Introduction to Modern Arabic,* Princeton University Press, 1957; (collaborator with Edward J. Jurji and Karl Saben Twitchell), *Saudi Arabia: With an Account of the Development of Its Natural Resources,* Princeton University Press, 3rd revised edition (Winder was not associated with earlier editions), 1958; (editor with James Kritzeck, and contributor) *The World of Islam: Studies in Honour of Philip K. Hitti,* St. Martin's, 1959, revised edition, 1960.

(Editor) *Current Problems in North Africa,* Princeton University Conference, 1960; *Saudi Arabia in the Nineteenth Century,* St. Martin's, 1965; (translator) Tewfik El Hakim, *Bird of the East,* Khayat, 1966; (contributor) L.A. Fallers, editor, *Immigrants and Associations,* Mouton & Co., 1967; (editor) *Near Eastern Round Table,* 1967-68, Near East Center and Center for International Studies, New York University, 1969. Contributor of articles to *Encyclopedia Americana,* and of more than twenty-five articles in English and Arabic to journals, including *Middle East Journal, Literature East and West,* and *Al-Kulliyah: Middle East Forum.*

WORK IN PROGRESS: Saudi Arabia in the Twentieth Century, completion expected in 1977.

SIDELIGHTS: In addition to Arabic, Winder is competent in French. *Avocational interests:* Choral singing, table tennis, and sailing.

* * *

WINFREY, Dorman H(ayward) 1924-

PERSONAL: Born September 4, 1924, in Henderson, Tex.; son of Luke Abel and Linnie (Fears) Winfrey; married Ruth Carolyn Byrd, June 12, 1954; children: Laura Madge, Jennifer Ruth. *Education:* University of Texas, B.A., 1950, M.A., 1951, Ph.D., 1962. *Religion:* Disciples of Christ. *Home:* 6503 Willamette Dr., Austin, Tex. 78723. *Office:* Texas State Library, Box 12927, Capitol Station, Austin, Tex. 78711.

CAREER: Texas State Historical Association, Austin, social science research associate, 1954-58; Texas State Library, Austin, state archivist, 1958-60; University of Texas, Austin, archivist, 1960-61; Texas State Library, director and librarian, 1962—. Chairman, Texas State Board of Library Examiners, 1962—; chairman, Texas State Records Preservation Advisory Committee, 1965—. *Military service:* U.S. Army, 1943-46; received two battle stars for European campaigns. *Member:* American Library Association, Society of American Archivists (fellow; president, 1971-72), Organization of American Historians, Texas Library Association, Texas State Historical Association (fellow), Texas Institute of Letters, Philosophical Society of Texas, Phi Alpha Theta, Pi Sigma Alpha. *Awards, honors:* American Association for State and Local History awards of merit for *A History of Rusk County, Texas,* 1961, and *Julien Sidney Devereux and His Monte Verdi Plantation,* 1964.

WRITINGS: Texas Indian Papers, three volumes, Texas State Library, 1959-60; *A History of Rusk County, Texas,* Texian, 1961; *Julien Sidney Devereux and His Monte Verdi Plantation,* Texian, 1964; (editor) *Indian Papers of Texas and the Southwest,* five volumes, Pemberton Press, 1966; *Arturo Toscanini in Texas: The 1950 NBC Symphony Orchestra Tour,* Encino Press, 1967; *Seventy-Five Years of Texas History: The Texas State Historical Association, 1897-1972,* Pemberton Press, 1974.

Contributor—All published by Texian, except as noted: *The Handbook of Texas,* two volumes, Texas State Historical Association, 1952; *Heroes of Texas,* 1964; *Six Missions of Texas,* 1965; *Frontier Forts of Texas,* 1966; *Battles of Texas,* 1967; *Six Flags of Texas,* 1968; *Rangers of Texas,* 1969; *Capitols of Texas,* 1970; *Indian Tribes of Texas,* 1971; *Women of Texas,* 1972; *Soldiers of Texas,* 1973.

Contributor to journals. Associate editor, *Junior Historian* (publication of Texas State Historical Association).

WORK IN PROGRESS: A book on Ashbel Smith.

WING, George Douglas   1921-

PERSONAL: Born May 17, 1921, in Middlesbrough, Yorkshire, England; son of Alan Douglas and Hilda (Lilly) Wing; married Joan Jamieson, December 22, 1945; children: Marjorie, Daphne. *Education:* University of Durham, B.A., 1941, M.A., 1947.

CAREER: British Council, lecturer in Teheran, Persia (now Iran), 1947-49; Achimota School, near Accra, Ghana, head of department of English, 1950-55; Royal Technical College, Nairobi, Kenya, dean of Arts Faculty, 1956-61; University College, University of East Africa, Nairobi, Kenya, dean of Arts Faculty, 1961-64, professor of English and head of department, beginning 1964. Member of council and senate of University of East Africa, beginning 1961. *Military service:* British Army, 1941-46; served in Africa and Italy; became major; received Military Cross, 1943.

WRITINGS: Hardy, Oliver & Boyd, 1963, Barnes & Noble, 1966; *Thomas Hardy,* Grove, 1963; *Old Tom* (a monograph on Hardy), Toucan Press (England), 1966; *Dickens,* Oliver & Boyd, 1969; *Old Tom and Young Tom: A Commentary on the Monographs,* Toucan Press, 1971. Contributor of articles on Hardy to journals.

WORK IN PROGRESS: A reassessment of Hardy's minor novels, titled, *Romance, Fantasy and Ingenuity;* research on nineteenth-century prose and poetry, and on African literature.†

*   *   *

WINGER, Howard W(oodrow)   1914-

PERSONAL: Born October 29, 1914, in Marion, Ind.; son of Joseph Pendleton (a farmer) and Amanda (Shoemaker) Winger; married Helen Gray, December 25, 1941; children: John, Michael, Philip, Elizabeth, Robert. *Education:* Manchester College, A.B., 1936; George Peabody College for Teachers, B.S. in L.S., 1945; University of Illinois, M.S., 1948, Ph.D., 1953. *Religion:* Protestant. *Home:* 121 Walnut, Park Forest, Ill. 60466. *Office:* University of Chicago, Chicago, Ill. 60637.

CAREER: High school teacher in Swayzee, Ind., 1936-37; Crowell Publishing Co., Springfield, Ohio, copywriter, 1937-38; high school librarian in Warren, Ind., 1940-42; University of Illinois, Urbana, library assistant, 1945-50; University of Wisconsin, Madison, assistant professor of library science, 1950-53; University of Chicago, Chicago, Ill., assistant professor, 1953-59, associate professor, 1959-68; professor of library science, 1968—, dean of students, 1953-56, dean of Graduate Library School, 1972—. Visiting summer lecturer, University of Wisconsin, 1959, University of California, 1963; consultant for libraries, *Encyclopedia Americana,* 1960-62; member of board of directors, Park Forest Public Library, 1955-61. *Military service:* U.S. Army, 1942-44. *Member:* American Library Association (council member, 1959), Association of American Library Schools (secretary-treasurer), Bibliographical Society (London), Bibliographical Society of the University of Virginia, Phi Beta Mu.

WRITINGS: (Editor and contributor) *Iron Curtains and Scholarship,* University of Chicago Press, 1959; (editor with Philip Ennis) *Seven Questions about the Profession of Librarianship,* University of Chicago Press, 1961; (editor with Leon Carnovsky) *The Medium-Sized Public Library,* University of Chicago Press, 1963; (editor with T. H. Tsien) *Area Studies and the Library,* University of Chicago

Press, 1966; (editor with Richard D. Smith) *Deterioration and Preservation of Library Materials,* University of Chicago Press, 1970. Managing editor, *Library Quarterly,* 1961-72.

*   *   *

WINKLER, Henry R(alph)   1916-

PERSONAL: Born October 27, 1916, in Waterbury, Conn.; son of Jacob and Ethel (Rieger) Winkler; married Clare Sapadin (an elementary teacher), August 18, 1940 (died January 7, 1972); children: Allan M., Karen J. *Education:* University of Cincinnati, A.B., 1938, A.M., 1940; University of Chicago, Ph.D., 1947. *Religion:* Jewish. *Home:* 335 North Fourth Ave., Highland Park, N.J. 08904. *Office:* Rutgers University, New Brunswick, N.J. 08901.

CAREER: University of Cincinnati, Cincinnati, Ohio, instructor in history, 1939-40; U.S. Office of War Information, information analyst, 1942-43; Roosevelt University, Chicago, Ill., assistant professor of history, 1946-47; Rutgers University, New Brunswick, N.J., assistant professor, 1947-52, associate professor, 1952-58, professor of history, 1958—, chairman of department, 1960-64, dean of faculty of liberal arts, 1967-68, vice-provost, 1968-70, vice-president for academic affairs, 1970-72, senior vice-president, 1972—. Visiting professor, London School of Economics and Political Science, 1953-54, Bryn Mawr College, 1959-60, Harvard University, summer, 1963, Columbia University; faculty member, John Hay Fellows Institute of Humanities, 1960-62. Chairman of European history committee, College Entrance Examination Board. Member, National Commission on the Humanities. Highland Park (N.J.) Board of Education, member, 1958-64, president, 1962-63. *Military service:* U.S. Navy, 1943-46; became lieutenant. *Member:* American Historical Association, Organization of American Historians (member of executive committee), National Humanities Faculty (member of board of directors; chairman, 1969—), American Council of Learned Societies, American Council on Education, Conference on British Studies, American Association of University Professors, Phi Beta Kappa, Tau Kappa Alpha. *Awards, honors:* Lindbach Foundation Award for distinguished teaching, 1963; Litt.D., Lehigh University, 1974.

WRITINGS: The League of Nations Movement in Great Britain, 1914-1919, Rutgers University Press, 1952, 2nd edition, Scarecrow, 1967; (editor with K. M. Setton) *Great Problems in European Civilization,* Prentice-Hall, 1954, 2nd edition, 1966; *Great Britain in the Twentieth Century,* American Historical Association, 1960, 2nd edition, 1966. Contributor of chapters to books, and of articles and book reviews to history and political science journals. Managing editor, *American Historical Review,* 1964-68.

WORK IN PROGRESS: A book, *National Power and Social Welfare: Great Britain in the Twentieth Century.*

*   *   *

WINN, Alison (Osborn), a pseudonym

PERSONAL: Born in England; married Ewart Wharmby (a publisher); children: David, Martin, Alison, Philip. *Home:* Cherry Burton, 3 Powys Ave., Leicester, England.

WRITINGS: Roundabout, Brockhampton Press, 1961; *Swings and Things,* Brockhampton Press, 1963, Rand McNally, 1965; *Helter Skelter,* Brockhampton Press, 1966; *A First Cinderella,* Brockhampton Press, 1966; (translator) Ulf Lofgrew, *The Magic Kite,* Brockhampton Press, 1973.

Also translator of *The Gunilla Wolde* and Ulf Lofgrew's *The Colour Trumpet*, both published by Brockhampton Press.

* * *

WINOLD, Allen 1929-

PERSONAL: Born May 29, 1929, in Cleveland, Ohio; son of Earl (a commercial artist) and Gladys (Riddell) Winold; married Helga Ulsamer (a concert cellist and teacher), December 17, 1963; children: Claire, Erika, Bettina, Hans Peter. *Education:* University of Cincinnati, B.M., 1951, M.M., 1952; Indiana University, Ph.D., 1963. *Politics:* Democrat. *Religion:* Quaker. *Home:* R.R. 12, Box 324, Bloomington, Ind. 47405. *Office:* School of Music, Indiana University, Bloomington, Ind. 47405.

CAREER: Assistant professor of music at Wilmington College, Wilmington, Ohio, and director of music therapy at Columbus State Hospital, Columbus, Ohio, 1952-54; Indiana University, School of Music, Bloomington, professor of music, 1956—. Former member, Cincinnati Symphony, North Carolina Symphony; guest professor, Vienna Academy, 1972-73; conductor of youth and professional orchestras in Canada and United States; violist in chamber music ensembles.

WRITINGS: Elements of Musical Understanding, Prentice-Hall, 1966; (with R. P. Delone) *Music Reading: An Ensemble Approach,* Addison-Westley, 1971; (with John Rehm) *Introduction to Music Theory,* Prentice-Hall, 1971; (contributor) *Aspects of Contemporary Music,* Prentice-Hall, 1975; (with William Christ and Delone) *Involvement with Music,* Harper, 1975; (with Ray Robinson) *The Choral Experience,* Carl Fisher, 1975. Former editor, *Your Musical Cue* (magazine of Indiana University School of Music).

WORK IN PROGRESS: Open Court Music Program for Open Court Publishing.

SIDELIGHTS: Winold is fluent in German.

* * *

WINTEROWD, W. Ross 1930-

PERSONAL: Born January 24, 1930, in Salt Lake City, Utah; son of Harold Ross and Henrietta (Fike) Winterowd; married Norma Graham, August 2, 1952; children: Geoffrey Ross, Anthony Gordon. *Education:* Utah State University, B.S., 1952; University of Vienna, graduate study, 1952-53; University of Utah, Ph.D., 1965. *Home:* 17551 San Roque Lane, Huntington Beach, Calif. 92647. *Office:* English Department, University of Southern California, Los Angeles, Calif. 90007.

CAREER: University of Utah, Salt Lake City, instructor in English, 1960-61; University of Montana, Missoula, assistant professor of English, 1962-66; University of Southern California, Los Angeles, associate professor, 1966-70, professor of English, 1970—. *Military service:* U.S. Army, 1953-55. *Member:* American Association of University Professors.

WRITINGS: Rhetoric and Writing, Allyn & Bacon, 1965; (with E. V. Stackpoole) *The Relevance of Rhetoric,* Allyn & Bacon, 1966; *Rhetoric: A Synthesis,* Holt, 1968; *The Contemporary Writer,* Harcourt, 1975; *Contemporary Rhetoric,* Harcourt, 1975.

WITHERS, Sara Cook 1924-

PERSONAL: Born June 30, 1924, in Birmingham, Ala.; daughter of James Kennedy (a bookkeeper) and Kate (Griffin) Cook; married Samuel Withers (a teacher of English), May 18, 1962; children: (previous marriage) Anne Henderson; (present marriage) Miranda. *Education:* Alabama College, A.B., 1945; University of North Carolina, M.A., 1947; additional study at The American University, 1953-54, Georgetown University, 1955, and University of Buffalo, summer, 1955. *Politics:* Democrat. *Religion:* Episcopalian. *Home:* 3609 T St. N.W., Washington, D.C. 20007. *Office:* Department of English, Gallaudet College, Kendall Green, Washington, D.C. 20002.

CAREER: The American University, Washington, D.C., instructor in English for foreigners, American Language Center, 1952-56; Gallaudet College, Washington, D.C., associate professor of English, 1957—. *Member:* National Council of Teachers of English, American Association of University Professors, Modern Language Association of America, American Association of University Women, American Instructors of the Deaf, South Atlantic Modern Language Association. *Awards, honors:* American Council of Learned Societies grant, 1956.

WRITINGS: (With Edith Crowell Trager) *Pronunciation Drills,* English Language Services, 1956; "American Language Course," Books 5-6, 9-10, English Language Services, 1960; (adapter) *Stories of the West,* Prentice-Hall, 1963; *A Key to Prepositions,* two books, Collier, 1964; *A Key to Verbs,* Collier, 1964; (editor) *A Key to Adjectives,* Collier, 1964; (adapter) Helen Keller, *The Story of My Life,* Collier, 1964; (with Bernard L. Greenberg) *Better English Usage,* Bobbs-Merrill, 1965; *The United Nations in Action: A Structured Reader,* Crowell, 1969. Contributor to journals.

WORK IN PROGRESS: An article on Edith Wharton.

SIDELIGHTS: Better English Usage is the first handbook of English written especially for the deaf.

* * *

WITTERMANS, Elizabeth (Pino)
(E. Pino)

PERSONAL: Born in Indonesia; daughter of Eduard and Cornelia (Johan) Pino; married Tamme Wittermans (a professor), September 19, 1951. *Education:* University of Indonesia, B.A., 1950; London School of Economics and Political Science, M.A., 1954; University of Leyden, Ph.D., 1964. *Office:* Department of Human Development, University of Hawaii at Manoa, Honolulu, Hawaii 96822.

CAREER: Social researcher on government-sponsored project, Netherlands, 1955-57; University of Hawaii, Honolulu, lecturer in Indonesian language, 1959-60; Punahou Academy, Honolulu, Hawaii, teacher of Asian history, 1962-63; University of Hawaii, East-West Center, language and area specialist in development of research translations, Institute of Advanced Projects, beginning 1963. *Member:* American Anthropological Association, Association for Asian Studies.

WRITINGS: (Under name E. Pino) *Bahasa Indonesia* (textbook for English-speaking students of Indonesian), two volumes, J. B. Wolters, 1950, 3rd edition, 1961; (under name E. Pino, with husband, T. Wittermans) *Kamus Inggeris* (English-Indonesian and Indonesian-English dictionary), two volumes, J. B. Wolters, 1954, 4th edition, 1966; *Inter-ethnic Relations in a Plural Society,* J. B. Wolters,

1964; (editor) *Doctor on Desima*, Sophia University, 1970; *Dictionary of Indonesian Abbreviations and Acronyms*, University of Hawaii, East-West Center, 1970. Writer of reviews for *American Anthropologist* and *Literature East and West.*†

*   *   *

WOELFL, Paul A(loysius)   1913-

PERSONAL: Born May 1, 1913, in Toledo, Ohio; son of Peter L. and Rose C. (Pauken) Woelfl. *Education:* Loyola University, Chicago, Ill., A.B., 1937, M.A., 1941; West Baden College, licentiate in Theology, 1945; St. Louis University, Ph.D., 1950. *Office:* Department of Political Science, John Carroll University, Cleveland, Ohio 44118.

CAREER: Roman Catholic priest, member of Society of Jesus; Loyola University, Chicago, Ill., assistant professor of political science and chairman of department, 1950-60; John Carroll University, Cleveland, Ohio, associate professor, 1960-63, professor of political science, 1963—, chairman of department, 1960—. *Member:* American Political Science Association, American Association of University Professors, Midwest Political Science Association.

WRITINGS: Politics and Jurisprudence, Loyola University Press (Chicago), 1966. Contributor of articles to *America, Detroit Law Journal*, and other professional journals. Assistant editor, *America*, 1961-62.

WORK IN PROGRESS: Contemporary domestic policies of the U.S.†

*   *   *

WOHL, Gerald   1934-

PERSONAL: Born August 9, 1934, in New York, N.Y.; son of Jack and Helen (Green) Wohl; married Sheila Goodman, June 14, 1959; children: Jeanne, Deborah, David. *Education:* City College (now of the City University of New York), New York, N.Y., B.B.A., 1956, M.B.A., 1961. *Religion:* Hebrew. *Home:* 211-10 18th Ave., Bayside, N.Y. 11360. *Office:* Pace College, 41 Park Row, New York, N.Y. 10038.

CAREER: Certified public accountant, state of New York, 1961. Public and private accountant, New York, N.Y., 1956—; Pace College, New York, N.Y., 1963—, began as associate professor, became professor of accounting. *Military service:* U.S. Army, 1953-54. *Member:* American Accounting Association, American Institute of Certified Public Accountants, New York State Society of Certified Public Accountants.

WRITINGS: (With Heinz Jauch) *The Computer—An Accounting Tool*, Irwin, 1965; (with Michael D'Angelico) *The Computer in Auditing: The Use of Test Data*, Irwin, 1966; *The Use of Generalized Packaged Programs*, Irwin, 1967; *Case Studies of Business Data Processing Systems*, Irwin, 1970.

*   *   *

WOLF, Eric R(obert)   1923-

PERSONAL: Born February 1, 1923, in Vienna, Austria; son of Arthur George (a textile converter) and Maria (Ossinovsky) Wolf; married Kathleen Bakeman (a social worker), September 24, 1943 (divorced, 1972); married Sydel Silverman (an anthropologist), March 18, 1972; children: John David, Daniel Jacob. *Education:* Queens College (now Queens College of the City University of New York), B.A., 1946; Columbia University, Ph.D., 1951. *Politics:* Independent. *Home:* Taxter Road, Elmsford, N.Y. 10523. *Office:* Department of Anthropology, Lehman College of the City University of New York, Bronx, N.Y. 10468.

CAREER: Doherty Foundation fellow in Mexico, 1951-52; University of Illinois, Urbana, assistant professor of anthropology, 1952-54, research associate, 1954-55; University of Virginia, Charlottesville, assistant professor of anthropology, 1955-58; Yale University, New Haven, Conn., assistant professor of anthropology, 1958-59; University of Chicago, Chicago, Ill., associate professor of anthropology, 1959-61; University of Michigan, Ann Arbor, professor of anthropology, 1961-71, and coordinator of Mediterranean study group; Lehman College of the City University of New York, Bronx, N.Y., Distinguished Professor of Anthropology, 1971—. Field work done in Mexico, Puerto Rico, and the Italian Alps. *Military service:* U.S. Army, Tenth Mountain Division, 1943-45; became technical sergeant; received Silver Star and Purple Heart. *Member:* American Anthropological Association (fellow), Royal Anthropological Society (fellow), American Ethnological Society. *Awards, honors:* Guggenheim fellowship, 1960-61; career development award, National Institute of Mental Health, 1965-70; National Endowment for the Humanities, senior fellowship, 1973-74.

WRITINGS: Sons of the Shaking Earth, University of Chicago Press, 1958; *Anthropology*, Prentice-Hall, 1964; *Peasants*, Prentice-Hall, 1966; *Peasant Wars of the Twentieth Century*, Harper, 1969; (with Edward C. Hansen) *The Human Condition in Latin America*, Oxford University Press, 1972; (with John W. Cole) *The Hidden Frontier*, Academic Press, 1974. Contributor to *American Anthropologist, Comparative Studies in History and Society, Revista Mexicana de Antropologia*, and other journals.

WORK IN PROGRESS: A study of the effects of Euro-American expansion; anthropological theory.

SIDELIGHTS: Wolf's major work is focused on peasantry. He considers the problem of how peasantry and the peasant world are to be integrated into modern industrial society to be the chief issue of our age.

*   *   *

WOLF, Karl E(verett)   1921-

PERSONAL: Born August 19, 1921, in Hartford, Conn.; son of Carl Fred and Anna (Voss) Wolf; married Lola Sue Stoner, August 1, 1948; children: Paula R., Gloria J., Glenn K. *Education:* U.S. Military Academy, B.S., 1943; University of Pennsylvania, LL.B., 1953; George Washington University, S.J.D., 1963. *Religion:* Protestant.

CAREER: U.S. Army, Infantry officer, 1943-50, Judge Advocate officer, 1953-63, retiring as lieutenant colonel; served in Korea, 1954, Okinawa, 1955; U.S. Military Academy, West Point, N.Y., assistant professor, 1956-59; assignments in Washington, D.C., as chief of Contract Law Branch, Judge Advocate General's Office, 1960-61, and Command Judge Advocate, Supply and Maintenance Command, 1962-63; Philco Corp., Philadelphia, Pa., associate counsel for government business, 1963—. Member of advisory board, Federal Contracts Report, Bureau of National Affairs. *Member:* American Bar Association, Federal Bar Association, National Tax Association. *Awards, honors*—Military: Silver Star, Bronze Star, Commendation Ribbon, Purple Heart, Croix de Guerre (Belgium).

WRITINGS: State Taxation of Government Contractors, Commerce Clearing House, 1964. Writer of several government publications on state and local taxes. Contributor to *Military Law Review* and *Tax Executive*.†

* * *

WOLF, William B. 1920-

PERSONAL: Born June 9, 1920, in Chicago, Ill.; son of Meyer and Mabel (Cohen) Wolf; married Anne Peters, December 22, 1951 (died August 4, 1968). *Education:* University of California, Berkeley, A.B., 1942; Northwestern University, M.B.A., 1945; University of Chicago, Ph.D., 1954. *Home:* 228 Renwick Dr., Ithaca, N.Y. 14850. *Office:* New York State School of Industrial and Labor Relations, Cornell University, Ithaca, N.Y.

CAREER: Union Asbestors & Rubber Co., Chicago, Ill., supervisor of industrial engineering, 1942-48; University of Chicago, Chicago, Ill., instructor in business administration, 1949-54; University of Washington, Seattle, associate professor of personnel and production, 1954-58; University of Southern California, Los Angeles, professor of management, 1958-69; Cornell University, New York State School of Industrial and Labor Relations, Ithaca, N.Y., professor of industrial relations, 1969—. Visiting professor at University of Hawaii, 1962, University of New South Wales, 1964, Hiroshima University, 1964. Consultant to business and government agencies.

MEMBER: Academy of Management (president, Western division, 1965, 1970-71), Society for Applied Anthropology, Industrial Relations Research Association, Society for International Development (president, Southern California chapter, 1968), American Sociological Association, American Arbitration Association, Laguna Beach Chamber Music Society (vice-president and director).

WRITINGS: Wage Incentives as a Managerial Tool, Columbia University Press, 1957; *Merit Rating as a Managerial Tool*, Bureau of Business Research, University of Washington, 1958; *The Management of Personnel*, Wadsworth, 1961; *Cases and Exercises in the Management of Personnel*, Wadsworth, 1962; (editor) *Management: Readings Toward a General Theory*, Wadsworth, 1964; *Conversations with Chester I. Barnard*, Cornell University, 1973; *The Basic Barnard*, Cornell University, 1974. Contributor of articles to periodicals.

WORK IN PROGRESS: Research into sensitivity training for group applications, and comparative administration as an approach to a general theory.

* * *

WOLFE, Winifred 1929-

PERSONAL: Born May 23, 1929, in Boston, Mass.; daughter of Philip Leonard (a decorator) and Esther (Emold) Wolfe; married Jack H. Gordun (a publisher), August 15, 1949; children: Douglas Wolfe Gordun. *Education:* Attended art schools in Boston, Mass. *Home and office:* 400 West End Ave., New York, N.Y. 10024. *Agent:* Audrey Wood, International Famous Agency, 1301 Avenue of the Americas, New York, N.Y. 10019.

CAREER: Staff writer for advertising agency before marriage; free-lance writer, 1950—, mostly as scripter for radio and television, 1950-60. *Member:* Dramatists Guild, Authors League, Writers Guild of America East, Academy of Television Art and Sciences.

WRITINGS: Ask Any Girl, (novel), Random House, 1958;

If a Man Answers (novel), Doubleday, 1961; *Never Step on a Rainbow* (novel), Harper, 1965. Head writer for television daytime series "As the World Turns." Other radio and television writing included scripts for "Theatre Guild" and "Alcoa Presents." Short stories and articles have appeared in *Redbook, Cosmopolitan, Saturday Evening Post, Good Housekeeping, Ladies' Home Journal*, and other national magazines and newspapers.

WORK IN PROGRESS: A novel and its play adaptation.

SIDELIGHTS: Both *Ask Any Girl* and *If a Man Answers* were made into films, the first produced by Metro-Goldwyn-Mayer, and the latter by Universal. *Never Step on a Rainbow* is presently under option for Broadway production. Her aim in writing: "To tell a good story, which would provide (hopefully) Food for thought as well as escape entertainment in any of three media: novels, theatre and film. Major road blocks: which of these three media to concentrate on, since all are of equal interest."

* * *

WOLFF, Maritta 1918-

PERSONAL: Born December 25, 1918, in Grass Lake, Mich.; daughter of Joseph and Ivy (Ellis) Wolff; married Leonard Stegman (in costume jewelry business), July 19, 1947; children: Hugh. *Education:* University of Michigan, B.A., 1940. *Politics:* Independent. *Home:* 282 Trino Way, Pacific Palisades, Calif. 90272.

CAREER: Author. *Awards, honors:* Avery and Jule Hopwood Award in fiction, University of Michigan, for *Whistle Stop*; special award, Metro-Goldwyn-Mayer Novel Contest, for *About Lyddy Thomas*.

WRITINGS—Novels, all published by Random House: *Whistle Stop*, 1941; *Night Shift*, 1942; *About Lyddy Thomas*, 1947; *Back of Town*, 1952; *The Big Nickelodeon*, 1956; *Buttonwood*, 1962.

WORK IN PROGRESS: Editing a just completed novel about modern marraige.

AVOCATIONAL INTERESTS: Music, motor racing, and collecting art nouveau bric-a-brac.

* * *

WOLFSON, Murray 1927-

PERSONAL: Born September 14, 1927, in New York, N.Y.; son of William and Bertha (Finklestein) Wolfson; married Betty A. Goessel (a music teacher), July 21, 1951; children: Paul, Susan, Deborah. *Education:* City College (now City College of the City University of New York), B.S. (cum laude), 1948; University of Wisconsin, M.S., 1951, Ph.D., 1964; additional study at Marquette University. *Religion:* Jewish. *Home:* 2707 Arnold Way, Corvallis, Ore. 97330. *Office:* Department of Economics, Oregon State University, Corvallis, Ore. 97331.

CAREER: High school teacher of mathematics, Montrose, Mich., 1959; Thornton Junior College, Harvey, Ill., teacher of economics, 1961; Oregon State University, Corvallis, professor of economics, 1963—. Visiting professor, Ahmadu Bello University, 1969-70, University of Canterbury, 1970, University of Durham, 1971-72, and University of Wisconsin. Consultant to Mineral Resources Division of U.S. Bureau of Mines. Counselor, B'nai B'rith Hillel Society. *Military service:* U.S. Navy, 1945-46. *Member:* American Economic Association, Western Economic Association, American Association of University professors,

Peace Science Association. *Awards, honors:* Kazanjian Award, Joint Council on Economic Education, 1970.

WRITINGS: A Reappraisal of Marxian Economics, Columbia University Press, 1966; *Films for Economic Education*, Oregon System of Higher Education, 1966; *Karl Marx*, Columbia University Press, 1971; (author of foreword) G. Sorenson, *The Effects of Income Changes on Labor Force Participation: A Theoretical Analysis*, Oregon State University Press, 1971; (contributor with A. C. Rayner) Michael Parkin, editor, *Essays in Modern Economics*, Longman, 1973; (with John Farrell) *The Prospects for Oregon-U.S.S.R. Trade in the Forest Products Machinery Industries*, Xerox Education Division, 1974; *Economics: Structure, Activities, Issues*, Methuen, in press. Also author, with Farrell, of *East-West Trade: The Oregon Interest*, 1973. Contributor of articles and book reviews to numerous professional journals, including *History of Political Economy, Nebraska Journal of Economics and Business, American Political Science Review, Journal of Economic Issues*, and *Australian Quarterly*.

WORK IN PROGRESS: Research on teaching economics by means of input-output, the demand for Black labor and growth, East-West trade, vector analysis and integrability of economic functions, the transformation problem, and the philosophical foundations of Marxian economics.

* * *

WOLPE, Joseph 1915-

PERSONAL: Born April 20, 1915, in Johannesburg, South Africa; son of Michael Salmon (a bookkeeper) and Sarah (Millner) Wolpe; married Stella Ettman, May 27, 1948; children: Allan, David. *Education:* University of the Witwatersrand, M.B., B.Ch., 1939, M.D., 1948. *Religion:* Jewish. *Office:* Temple University Medical School, Philadelphia, Pa.

CAREER: Consulting psychiatrist in Johannesburg, South Africa, 1948-59; University of the Witwatersrand, Johannesburg, South Africa, part-time lecturer in psychiatry, 1949-59; University of Virginia, Charlottesville, professor of psychiatry, 1960-65; Temple University, Philadelphia, Pa., professor of psychiatry, 1965—. *Military service:* South Africa Medical Corps, 1942-46; became captain. *Member:* American Psychiatric Association, American Psychological Association, American Psychopathological Association. *Awards, honors:* Fellow, Center for Advanced Study in the Behavioral Sciences, 1956-57; Mesmer Award, 1974.

WRITINGS: Psychotherapy by Reciprocal Inhibition, Stanford University Press, 1958; (editor with A. Salter and L. J. Reyna) *Conditioning Therapies: The Challenge in Psychotherapy*, Holt, 1964; *The Practice of Behavior Therapy*, Pergamon, 1969, 2nd edition, 1973; *Theme and Variations*, Pergamon, 1975.

Contributor: Arthur Burton, editor, *Case Studies in Counselling and Psychotherapy*, Prentice-Hall, 1959; A. J. Bachrach, editor, *Experimental Foundations of Clinical Psychology*, Basic Books, 1962; J. Scher, editor, *Theories of the Mind*, Macmillan, 1963; Alvin Mahrer, editor, *The Goals of Psychotherapy*, Thompson, 1965; C. Spielberger, editor, *Anxiety and Behavior*, Academic Press, 1966. Contributor to *International Encyclopedia of Social Sciences*, and more than one hundred articles to professional journals.

WOOD, Charles T(uttle) 1933-

PERSONAL: Born October 29, 1933, in St. Paul, Minn.; son of Harold Eaton (an investment banker) and Margaret (Frisbie) Wood; married Susan L. Danielson, July 9, 1955; children: Lucy Eaton, Timothy Walker, Martha Augusta, Mary Frisbie. *Education:* Harvard University, A.B., 1955, A.M., 1957, Ph.D., 1962. *Home:* 7 North Balch St., Hanover, N.H. 03755. *Agent:* Gerald F. McCauley, 551 Fifth Ave., New York, N.Y. 10017.

CAREER: Investment trader with Harold E. Wood & Co., St. Paul, Minn., 1955-56, and First Boston Corp., Boston, Mass., 1957; Harvard University, Cambridge, Mass., instructor in history, 1961-64; Dartmouth College, Hanover, N.H., assistant professor, 1964-67, associate professor, 1967-71, professor of history, 1971—. *Member:* American Historical Association, Mediaeval Academy of America, Conference on British Studies.

WRITINGS: The French Apanages and the Capetian Monarchy, 1224-1328, Harvard University Press, 1966; *Philip the Fair and Boniface VIII*, Holt, 1967; 2nd edition, 1971; *The Age of Chivalry: Manners and Morals 1000-1450*, Weidenfeld & Nicolson, 1970. Contributor to *Speculum, American Historical Review, History and Theory, French Historical Studies*, and *Tradito*.

WORK IN PROGRESS: A monograph on Richard III.

SIDELIGHTS: Wood is competent in French, Latin, and German.

* * *

WOOD, Harold A(rthur) 1921-

PERSONAL: Born June 1, 1921, in Balaclava, Jamaica, West Indies; son of Arthur Groves (a clergyman) and Alice (Henderson) Wood; married Rosemary Harrower, December 26, 1945; children: Christopher George James, Nigel Edward. *Education:* McMaster University, B.A., 1941, M.A., 1950; University of Toronto, Ph.D., 1958. *Religion:* United Church of Canada. *Office:* McMaster University, Hamilton, Ontario, Canada.

CAREER: College International, Cap Haitien, Haiti, headmaster, 1943-45; Manchester School, Mandeville, Jamaica, second master, 1945-47; Stony Brook School, Stony Brook, N.Y., instructor in modern languages, 1947-49; McMaster University, Hamilton, Ontario, instructor, 1950-56, assistant professor, 1956-60, associate professor, 1960-66, professor of geography, 1966—, department chairman, 1961—. Leader of survey parties for Canadian government in Newfoundland, northern Manitoba, and St. Lawrence Seaway area; field researcher in North, Central, and South America for Pan-American Union and Pan-American Institute of Geography and History. Member, City of Hamilton Urban Renewal Committee. *Member:* Pan-American Institute of Geography and History (president of regional geography committee, 1965—), Canadian Association of Geographers (councillor, 1960-62), Association of American Geographers, American Geographical Society, American Society of Photogrammetry.

WRITINGS: The United States and Latin America, Copp, 1962; *Northern Haiti: Land, Land Use and Settlement*, University of Toronto Press, 1963. Also editor of *Proceedings* of Interamerican Seminar on the Definition of Regions for Development Planning, 1967. Contributor to geographical and planning journals.

WORK IN PROGRESS: A text on geography of the West Indies, for University of London Press; compiling results of research on air photo interpretation of agricultural land use; study of land-use classification in the American tropics.†

* * *

WOODMAN, James Monroe 1931-
(Jim Woodman)

PERSONAL: Born June 24, 1931, in Evanston, Ill.; son of James (an advertising man) and Miriam (Jenkins) Woodman; married Margo Rose, April 18, 1957; children: Jim, Henry, Tanya. *Education:* University of New Mexico, B.A., 1957; University of Madrid, graduate diploma, 1958. *Home:* 8301 Hardee Rd., Miami, Fla. *Office address:* P.O. Box 543, Coconut Grove, Fla.

CAREER: Brazil Safaris & Tours Ltd., Rio de Janeiro, director, 1959—; Travel Advertising Agency, Inc., Miami, Fla., president, 1964—. Consultant to airlines, including APSA Peruvian Airlines and TAN Airlines. *Military service:* U.S. Marine Corps, combat correspondent, Korean War. *Member:* American Society of Travel Agents, Confederation of Tourist Organizations of Latin America, Society of American Travel Writers, and other travel industry associations.

WRITINGS—All under name Jim Woodman: *Key Biscayne,* Hurricane House, 1957, 3rd edition, 1962; *Air Travel Bargains,* Pocket Books, 1965, latest edition, *Air Travel Bargains Worldwide Guidebook,* 1973; *Discovering Yucatan,* Doubleday, 1966.

WORK IN PROGRESS: A novel.

SIDELIGHTS: Woodman travels about ten thousand air miles monthly on business. He speaks Spanish, Portuguese, Dutch, French, and German.†

* * *

WOODRING, Paul (Dean) 1907-

PERSONAL: Born July 16, 1907, in Delta, Ohio; son of Peter David and Ethel (Gormley) Woodring; married Jeannette McGraw, September 19, 1938. *Education:* Bowling Green State University, B.S. in Ed., 1930; Ohio State University, M.A., 1934, Ph.D., 1938. *Home:* 1512 Knox Ave., Bellingham, Wash. 98225. *Office:* Western Washington State College, Bellingham, Wash. 98225.

CAREER: Diplomate, American Board of Examiners in Professional Psychology. Criminal courts psychologist, Detroit, Mich., 1937-39; Western Washington State College, Bellingham, faculty member (with frequent and prolonged leaves of absence), 1939—, distinguished service professor, 1962—, interim president, 1964-65; *Saturday Review,* New York, N.Y., education editor, 1960-66, editor-at-large, 1966-70. Visiting professor at San Jose State University, Carleton College, and University of California, Berkeley; Spaulding Lecturer at Yale University and Bird Lecturer at Occidental College, 1958. Educational adviser, Ford Foundation, 1956-62. Consultant, Fund for Advancement of Education, 1956-62. *Military service:* U.S. Army, 1942-46; became lieutenant colonel.

MEMBER: American Psychological Association (fellow), American Association for the Advancement of Science, State Psychological Association of Washington (past president). *Awards, honors:* L.H.D., Kalamazoo College, 1959, Bowling Green University, 1965; Pd.D., Coe College, 1960; Litt.D., Ripon College, 1963; LL.D., University of Portland, 1966; School Bell Award, National Education Association, 1962, 1963; Educational Press Association

Award, 1963, 1964, 1966; Education Writers Association Award, 1964.

WRITINGS: Let's Talk Sense About Our Schools, McGraw, 1953; *A Fourth of a Nation,* McGraw, 1956; *New Directions in Teacher Education,* Fund for the Advancement of Education, 1956; (editor with John Scanlon) *American Education Today,* McGraw, 1963; *Introduction to American Education,* Harcourt, 1965; *The Higher Learning in America: A Reassessment,* McGraw, 1968; *Investment in Innovation,* Little, Brown, 1970. Editor, "Professional Education for Teachers" series, 1965. Author of "Woodring on Education" column in thirty-six newspapers, 1958-62.

WORK IN PROGRESS: A book on the new leisure class.

* * *

WOODS, Frederick 1932-
(Lawrence Ives)

PERSONAL: Born January 18, 1932, in Swindon Wilshire, England; son of Bertram Ernest Woods (a clergyman); married Elizabeth Anne Edwards, February 17, 1957 (marriage dissolved 1973); married Helen Noelle McArthur, February 14, 1974. *Education:* Attended Queen's College, Taunton, England, 1944-46, and Emanuel School, London, England, 1946-50. *Religion:* Church of England. *Home:* Austin House, Hospital St., Nantwich, Cheshire, England.

CAREER: World of Music (now-defunct periodical), England, editor, 1959-64; Performing Rights Society, London, England, assistant general manager, 1964-68; Aro Record Co., London, general manager and senior record producer, 1969-71; full-time writer, 1971—; owner-editor of *Folk Review* (magazine); producer of numerous recordings of classical, popular, and folk music and jazz. *Military service:* British Army, 1950-52. *Member:* Royal Society of Arts (fellow). *Awards, honors:* Prix de l'Accueil de Paris, 1950; National Audio Award for best record of the year, 1968, for "What Passing Bell, Wilfred Owen"; Knight of Mark Twain, 1974.

WRITINGS—Editor: *A Bibliography of the Works of Sir Winston Churchill,* Toronto University Press, 1963, 3rd edition, 1974; *Young Winston's Wars,* Viking, 1972; *Collected Centenary Edition of the Works of Sir Winston Churchill,* thirty-four volumes, Library of Imperial History (London), 1974-75; *Collected Essays of Sir Winston Churchill,* four volumes, Library of Imperial History, 1974-75; *The Making of Many Books: Churchill as Writer,* Library of Imperial History, 1975. Author of opera libretto based on *Treasure Island;* editor and producer of spoken word long-playing records, "What Passing Bell, Wilfred Owen," "Will It Be So Again," "D. H. Lawrence." Former regular columnist, *Audio Record Review;* occasional contributor to *Times Literary Supplement, Observer, Brio, Records and Recordings, Music,* and literary journals.

WORK IN PROGRESS: Editing Winston Churchill's writings.

SIDELIGHTS: Woods speaks French. He did most of the work on *A Bibliography of the Works of Sir Winston Churchill* while recovering from polio paralysis. *Avocational interests:* Book collecting; music, especially folk music; sports, especially cricket, rugby, pistol and rifle shooting.

* * *

WOODWARD, Robert H(anson) 1925-

PERSONAL: Born April 8, 1925, in Lapel, Ind.; son of

Herschel L. (a businessman) and Edith (Wiseman) Woodward; married Carol Loftis, January 7, 1949; children: William D., Lawrence R. *Education:* Attended University of Notre Dame, 1943; Indiana University, A.B., 1951, M.A., 1952, Ph.D., 1957. *Home:* San Jose, Calif. *Office:* Department of English, San Jose State University, San Jose, Calif. 95192.

CAREER: San Jose State University, San Jose, Calif., instructor, 1954-56, assistant professor, 1956-59, associate professor, 1959-62, professor of English, 1962—, chairman of department, 1962-66, associate dean, School of Humanities and the Arts, 1972-74, dean, 1974—. *Military service:* U.S. Army, Parachute Corps, 1943-46. *Member:* Modern Language Association of America, National Council of Teachers of English, John Steinbeck Society, Western Literature Association, Philological Association of Pacific Coast, English Council of California State Colleges (president, 1964-65), California Association of Teachers of English (executive board, 1964-65), New York Folklore Society, San Jose Museum of Art Association, San Jose Symphony Association, Phi Kappa Phi. *Awards, honors:* American Council of Learned Societies grant, 1962; research grants from Indiana University Foundation and San Jose State University Foundation.

WRITINGS: The Craft of Prose, Wadsworth, 1963, 3rd edition, 1972; (with Susan C. Hall) *Hawthorne to Hemingway*, Garrett, 1965; (with James J. Clark) *Success in America*, Wadsworth, 1966; (with Clark) *The Social Rebel in American Literature*, Odyssey, 1968; (editor with others) *Perspectives on American Literature*, Odyssey, 1968; (with Thomas F. O'Donnell and Stanton Garner) *Bibliography of Harold Frederic*, G. K. Hall, 1975; (with Garner and George Fortenberry) *Correspondence of Harold Frederic*, Texas Christian University Press, 1975; (with wife, Carol Woodward, and Frank Howell) *The Craft of Pottery*, Harper, 1975; *Jack London and the Amateur Press*, Wolf House Books, in press. Contributor of articles and verse to *American Literature, Author and Journalist, Folio, Mark Twain Quarterly, Simbolica, Sing Out!, Walt Whitman Review, Steinbeck Quarterly, Hemingway Notes, American Literary Realism, New York History, Collector's Weekly, Hobbies*, and other periodicals; also contributor of fiction to several magazines, mostly published under undisclosed pseudonym. Associate editor, *Folio*, 1953-54.

*   *   *

WOODY, Russell O(wen), Jr.   1934-

PERSONAL: Born July 19, 1934, in Lynchburg, Va.; son of Russell Owen (a building contractor) and Mary (Dawson) Woody; married Penelope Peggs, June 14, 1957; children: Luranah Maria, Leona Fletcher. *Education:* Wake Forest College (now Wake Forest University), student, 1953; University of Miami, Coral Gables, Fla., B.A., 1957; University of the Americas, M.F.A., 1960.

CAREER: Artist, and art teacher in public schools and privately. Paintings and graphics exhibited at one-man shows in Boston, Mexico City, Norfolk, Va., and Rockland, Me.; represented in group shows elsewhere. Lecturer at more than one hundred colleges and universities in United States and Canada, including University of California, University of Iowa, and University of Notre Dame. Consultant to Permanent Pigments, Inc., Norwood, Ohio, 1963—, and Binney and Smith, Inc., New York, N.Y., 1964—. *Military service:* U.S. Army, 1953-55; served in Korea.

WRITINGS: Painting with Synthetic Media (technical appendix by H. W. Levison), Reinhold, 1965; *Polymer Painting and Related Techniques*, Van Nostrand, 1969.†

*   *   *

WOOLGAR, (George) Jack   1894-

PERSONAL: Born May 4, 1894, in London, England; son of George John and Adelaide (Ritchin) Woolgar; married Florence Schweitzer, October 11, 1919; children: Kenneth James, Clifford Lloyd. *Education:* Attended business college four years; studied music at Wisconsin Conservatory of Music, and art privately. *Politics:* Republican. *Religion:* Protestant. *Home:* 222 East Indianola, Apt. 512, Phoenix, Ariz. 85012. *Agent:* Larry Sternig, 2407 North 44th St., Milwaukee, Wis. 53210.

CAREER: Full-time professional writer. General Electric Co., Hotpoint Division, Milwaukee, Wis., accountant, 1948-59; writer, mainly for magazines. *Military service:* Canadian Army, 1917-19. *Member:* Allied Authors (Milwaukee; secretary-treasurer, 1938-50), American Legion.

WRITINGS: Hot on Ice, Albert Whitman, 1965; *Mystery in the Desert*, Lantern Press, 1967; *Gold Mine Mystery*, Lantern Press, in press.

Short stories represented in many anthologies, including: *The Ghost Town Ghosts*, Lantern Press, 1963; *The Ghosts on Prospect Avenue*, Lantern Press, 1965; *Teen-age Detective Stories*, edited by A. L. Furman, Lantern Press, 1968; *Teen-age Secret Agents*, edited by Furman, Lantern Press, 1970. Author of 3 picture books, for Whitman Publishing. Contributor of more than 150 short stories and articles to magazines.

WORK IN PROGRESS: A book, *The Toothless Dinosaur*, for Albert Whitman.

SIDELIGHTS: Woolgar became interested in writing through a newspaper advertisement, and credits Somerset Maugham's *A Writer's Notebook* with helping him along the way. He speaks German and is competent in Latin (attended a classical high school). *Avocational interests:* Youth activities, particularly sports; golf, playing piano, cartooning.

*   *   *

WRIGHT, Andrew (Howell)   1923-

PERSONAL: Born June 28, 1923, in Columbus, Ohio; son of Francis Joseph (a lawyer) and Katharine (Timberman) Wright; married Virginia Banks, June 27, 1952; children: Matthew Leslie Francis, Emma Stanbery. *Education:* Harvard University, A.B., 1947; Ohio State University, M.A., 1948, Ph.D., 1951. *Politics:* Democrat. *Religion:* Episcopalian. *Home:* 7227 Olivetas Ave., La Jolla, Calif. 92037. *Office:* Department of Literature, University of California—San Diego, La Jolla, Calif. 92037.

CAREER: Ohio State University, Columbus, instructor, 1952-54, assistant professor, 1955-58, associate professor of English, 1958-63; University of California—San Diego, La Jolla, professor of English literature, 1963—, chairman of department, 1971-74. Fulbright senior research fellow, University of London, 1960-61. *Military service:* U.S. Army, Signal Corps, 1943-46; became second lieutenant. *Member:* Modern Humanities Research Association, Modern Language Association of America, Royal Society of Literature (fellow), P.E.N., Jane Austen Society, London Library. *Awards, honors:* Fulbright fellow at University of London, 1951-52; American Philosophical Society grants, 1956, 1958; American Council of Learned Societies grant, 1961; Guggenheim fellow, 1961-62, 1970-71.

WRITINGS: Jane Austen's Novels: A Study in Structure, Oxford University Press, 1953; *Joyce Cary: A Preface to His Novels*, Harper, 1958; (with Richard D. Altick) *Selective Bibliography for the Study of English and American Literature*, Macmillan, 1960, 4th edition, 1971; *Henry Fielding: Mask and Feast*, University of California Press, 1965; *Blake's "Job": A Commentary*, Clarendon Press, 1972. Consulting editor, *Eighteenth-Century Studies*, and *Nineteenth-Century Fiction*.

* * *

WRIGHT, R(obert) H(amilton) 1906-

PERSONAL: Born December 26, 1906, in Vancouver, British Columbia, Canada; son of Leslie Havelock (an insurance agent) and Clare DuPuy (Rogers) Wright; married Kathleen Joan Creer, September 9, 1931; children: R. L.D., I.G., Kathleen Jennifer. *Education:* University of British Columbia, B.A., 1928; McGill University, M.Sc., 1930, Ph.D., 1931. *Office:* 6822 Blenheim St., Vancouver, British Columbia, V6N 1R7; Canada.

CAREER: University of New Brunswick, Fredericton, 1931-46, began as assistant professor, became professor of physical chemistry; British Columbia Research Council, Vancouver, head of division of chemistry, 1946-62, head of olfactory response investigation, 1962-72. Holder of several U.S. and Canadian patents. *Member:* Chemical Institute (Canada; fellow), American Chemical Society, Entomological Society of America, Entomological Society of Canada.

WRITINGS: Manual of Laboratory Glass Blowing, Chemical Publishing Co., 1943; *The Science of Smell*, Basic Books, 1964; *Enjoy Training Your Family Dog*, J. J. Douglas, 1975. Contributor of about one hundred articles to *Nature* and to technical journals.

WORK IN PROGRESS: Studies in insect attraction and repulsion, infrared spectroscopy of perfumes, and substances that influence insect behavior.

* * *

WRIGHT, Robert Lee 1920-

PERSONAL: Born May 23, 1920, in Connersville, Ind.; son of Robert Lee and Grace (Beck) Wright; married Fern Georgia Satterlund, April 26, 1944; children: Rochelle Ann. *Education:* Defiance College, B.A., 1943; University of Minnesota, M.A., 1947; Harvard University, graduate study, summers, 1947-49; Columbia University, Ed.D., 1955; University of Stockholm, postdoctoral student, 1957-58. *Politics:* Democrat (liberal). *Home:* 274 Oakland Dr., East Lansing, Mich. 48823. *Office:* Department of American Thought and Language, Michigan State University, East Lansing, Mich. 48823.

CAREER: University of Minnesota, Minneapolis, instructor in English, 1946-48; Michigan State University, East Lansing, assistant professor of communication skills, 1948-51, 1954-57, associate professor, 1957-61, professor of American thought and language, 1961—, professor of comparative literature, 1962—. Instructor in English, Columbia University, Teachers College, New York, N.Y., 1953-54. *Military service:* U.S. Naval Reserve, active duty, 1943-46, 1951-53; became lieutenant commander. *Member:* National Council of Teachers of English, Society for Advancement of Scandinavian Study, Conference on College Composition and Communication, American Association of Univer-

sity Professors, Modern Language Association of America, American Scandinavian Foundation, Kappa Delta Pi, Phi Delta Kappa, Alpha Psi Omega. *Awards, honors:* Swedish Government fellow, 1957-58; Fulbright research scholar, 1962-63.

WRITINGS: Writing Without Rules, W. C. Brown, 1951, revised edition, 1955; (editor) *Swedish Emigrant Ballads*, University of Nebraska Press, 1965; (compiler with David Anderson) *The Dark and Tangled Path: Race in America*, Houghton, 1971. Contributor of articles and poetry to *Atlantic Monthly*, *American Swedish Monthly*, and education and literary journals; contributor to "Bibliographies of Research in the Teaching of English"; abstractor, *Abstracts of English Studies*.

WORK IN PROGRESS: Ballads and Songs of the Western Migration; and *The American Indian in World Literature*.

SIDELIGHTS: Wright is competent in French and Scandinavian languages.†

* * *

WU, Hsiu-Kwang 1935-

PERSONAL: Born December 14, 1935, in China; son of Kao Cheng and Edith (Huang) Wu; married Kathleen Johnson, August, 1968. *Education:* Princeton University, A.B., 1958; Wharton School of Finance and Commerce, M.B.A., 1960; University of Pennsylvania, Ph.D., 1963. *Religion:* Episcopal. *Home:* 27 Arcadia Dr., Tuscaloosa, Ala. 35401. *Office:* University of Alabama, University, Ala. 35486.

CAREER: Boston University, Boston, Mass., assistant professor, 1962-65, associate professor, 1965-68, professor of finance, 1968-72; University of Alabama, University, professor of finance, 1972—, Alabama Bankers Educational Foundation Banking Professor, 1973—, chairman of department of finance and economics, 1972—. Sloan Faculty Fellow, Massachusetts Institute of Technology, 1965-66; economic advisor to Office of Comptroller of Currency, U.S. Treasury, 1966-69; economic consultant, Institutional Investor Study, U.S. Securities and Exchange Commission, 1969-70; member of committee of examiners, Educational Testing Service, 1971—. *Member:* American Economic Association, American Statistical Association, Econometric Society, American Finance Association, Institute of Management Sciences. *Awards, honors:* Ford Foundation fellow, 1964, 1965.

WRITINGS: (Editor with A. J. Zakon) *Elements of Investments*, Holt, 1965, revised edition, 1972. Contributor to *Journal of Finance*, *Harvard Business Review*, and other professional journals.

WORK IN PROGRESS: Money and Capital Markets: Theory, Institutions and Public Policy.

* * *

WU, Yuan-li

EDUCATION: University of Berlin, language certificate, 1939; London School of Economics and Political Science, B.Sc., 1942, Ph.D., 1946. *Office:* Hoover Institution, Stanford, Calif.

CAREER: United Nations, member of Chinese delegation to Economic and Social Council, 1946, expert consultant, Economic Affairs Department, 1949-50; Stanford University, Stanford, Calif., lecturer in economics, 1952, coordinator of research, Human Relations Area Files Project,

1955-56; Marquette University, Milwaukee, Wis., associate professor of economics, 1956-58, professor and director of Institute for Asian Studies, 1958-60; Hoover Institution on War, Revolution, and Peace, Stanford, Calif., consultant, beginning 1960; University of San Francisco, San Francisco, Calif., professor of international economics, beginning 1960. Consultant, Stanford Research Institute, 1960-63, 1965. *Member:* American Economic Association, Association for Asian Studies, Royal Economic Society (fellow). *Awards, honors:* Social Science Research Council and American Council of Learned Societies research grant, 1961; Ford Foundation faculty research fellowship, 1961-62; Social Science Research Council research grant, 1962-63.

WRITINGS: Economic Warfare, Prentice-Hall, 1952; *An Economic Survey of Communist China,* Bookman Associates, 1956; *Economic Development and the Use of Energy Resources,* Praeger, 1963; *The Economy of Communist China: An Introduction,* Praeger, 1965; *The Steel Industry in Communist China,* Praeger, 1965; *Food and Agriculture in Communist China,* Praeger, 1966; (with H. C. Ling and Grace Hsiao Wu) *The Spatial Economy of Communist China: A Study on Industrial Location and Transportation,* Praeger, 1967; *As Peking Sees Us,* Hoover Institution Press, 1969; (with Robert B. Sheeks and others) *The Organization and Support of Scientific Research and Development in Mainland China,* Praeger, 1970; (editor) *China: A Handbook,* Praeger, 1973. Author of papers on Communist China for Hoover Institution and U.S. Army. Articles on China have appeared in *Current History, Orbis, Contemporary China,* and other journals.

WORK IN PROGRESS: Collaborating on *Mathematical Programming and the Theory of the Firm.*

SIDELIGHTS: Wu is competent in Chinese, Japanese, Russian, German, Italian, French, and English.†

*   *   *

WYCKOFF, James M. 1918-

PERSONAL: Born February 24, 1918, in New York, N.Y.; son of Clarence P. and Margaret (Macdona) Wyckoff; children: Angus M., Jenny M. *Education:* Educated at Bovee School, Choate School, and in schools of England, Switzerland, and France. *Home:* 128 East 91st St., New York, N.Y. 10028. *Agent:* Paul R. Reynolds, Inc., 12 East 41st St., New York, N.Y. 10017.

CAREER: Fawcett Publications, Inc., Greenwich, Conn., editor, 1957-66; Time-Life Books, New York, N.Y., editor, 1966-68. *Military service:* U.S. Army, 1942-46.

WRITINGS: The Middle of Time (novel), Tower Publications, 1961; *Kendall of the Coast Guard* (juvenile), Doubleday, 1961; *John Slaughter's Way* (biography), Doubleday, 1962; *Who Really Invented the Submarine* (juvenile), Putnam, 1964; *Lars* (western), Doubleday, 1965; *The Lost Continent of Atlantis* (juvenile), Putnam, 1968; *Wilhelm Reich: Life Force Explorer* (biography), Premier Press, 1973; *Franz Anton Mesmer* (biography), Prentice-Hall, 1975; *Slater's Book* (western), Doubleday, in press. Writer of twelve scripts for television, ten for radio. Contributor of more than twenty short stories to literary magazines in United States and England.

*   *   *

WYMAN, Walker D(eMarquis) 1907-

PERSONAL: Born December 7, 1907, in Danville, Ill.;

son of Austin Juvinall and Martha Ann (Condor) Wyman; married Helen Bryant, July 26, 1930; children: John Bryant, Walker D., Jr. *Education:* Illinois State Normal University (now Illinois State University), B.Ed., 1929; University of Iowa, M.A., 1931, Ph.D., 1935. *Politics:* Liberal. *Religion:* Protestant. *Home:* 415 Crescent St., River Falls, Wis. 55402. *Office:* Library 217, University of Wisconsin, River Falls, Wis. 55402.

CAREER: Wisconsin State College (now University of Wisconsin), River Falls, 1930-62, started as assistant professor, became professor of history, chairman of social science department, 1942-62, director of graduate studies, 1959-62; Wisconsin State University (now University of Wisconsin), Whitewater, president, 1962-67; University of Wisconsin, River Falls, Centennial Year Distinguished Professor of history, 1967—. Visiting professor at University of Minnesota, 1946, 1948, University of Maine, 1947, University of Wisconsin, 1954. Former member of city council, River Falls, Wis. *Member:* American Historical Association, National Council for the Social Studies, National Education Association, Organization of American Historians, Northwest Education Association (president, 1960-61), Wisconsin Historical Society (board of curators, 1955-61; vice-president, 1959-61). *Awards, honors:* Distinguished Alumni Award, Illinois State Normal University (now Illinois State University), 1958.

WRITINGS: The Wild Horse of the West, Caxton, 1945; *California Emigrant Letters,* Bookman Associates, 1952; *Nothing But Prairie and Sky,* University of Oklahoma Press, 1954; (with C. B. Kroeber) *The Frontier in Perspective,* University of Wisconsin Press, 1957.

(With Martin Ridge) *The American Adventure,* Lyons & Carnahan, 1964; (editor) *History of the Wisconsin State Universities,* River Falls University Press, 1968; *The Lumberjack Frontier,* University of Nebraska Press, 1969; *Mythical Creatures of the North Country,* River Falls University Press, 1969.

Frontier Woman, River Falls University Press, 1972; (with William L. Clark) *Charles Round Low Cloud: The Voice of the Winnebago,* River Falls University Press, 1972; *History of the Chippewa: The Life of the Great Lakes Woodland Tribe Over Three Centuries,* Ross & Haines, 1975; *Centennial History of the University of Wisconsin–River Falls,* River Falls University Press, 1975. Also author of pamphlet, *The Legend of Charley Glass,* with J. Hart, River Falls University Press, 1970. Contributor of about thirty articles to *American West, Nebraska Magazine of History,* and other journals.

WORK IN PROGRESS: Witching for Water, Precious Metals, and Oil.

SIDELIGHTS: Wyman writes: "My main thrust has been in the social history and lore of the common people, or Folk History as I choose to call it. My first interest was in the American frontier, then I moved into regional lore and history. An interest in Indians has come in recent times...." Wyman has been a daily diarist since 1930, writing about two hundred pages each year, with a total of seventy volumes at the present time.

*   *   *

WYNAR, Bohdan S(tephen) 1926-

PERSONAL: Born September 7, 1926, in Lviv, Ukraine; son of John O. and Euphrosina (Doryk) Wynar; married Christina L. Gehrt. *Education:* University of Munich,

Diplom-Volkswirt, 1949, Ph.D., 1950; University of Denver, M.A. in L.S., 1958. *Home:* 6008 South Lakeview, Littleton, Colo. 80120. *Office:* Libraries Unlimited, Inc., P.O. Box 263, Littleton, Colo. 80120.

CAREER: University of Denver, Denver, Colo., assistant to director of libraries, 1958-59, head of technical services, university libraries, 1959-62, associate professor of library science, 1962-66; State University of New York, College at Geneseo, professor of library science, and dean of School of Library Science, 1966-69; Libraries Unlimited, Littleton, Colo., president, 1969—. President of Denver branch, Ukrainian Congress Committee, 1964-66. *Member:* American Library Association, American Association for the Advancement of Slavic Studies, Ukrainian Academy of Arts and Sciences, Shevchenko Scientific Society (secretary of economics section, 1957—).

WRITINGS: Growth of Soviet Light Industry, New Pathway (Winnipeg), 1955; *Rozvytok Ukrain'skoi Lehkoi Promyslovosty*, Ukrainian Economic Commission, 1955; *Soviet Colonialism in Ukraine*, La Parole (Paris), 1957; (editor with H. W. Axford) *Inkynabula*, Graduate School of Librarianship, University of Denver, 1958; (director of preparation) *Manual for Catalog Department, Division of Technical Services*, University of Denver Library, Division of Technical Services, 1961; *Syllabus for Research Methods in Librarianship*, Graduate School of Librarianship, University of Denver, 1962; *Syllabus for Technical Processes in Libraries*, [Denver], 1962; *Introduction to Bibliography and Reference Books*, Graduate School of Librarianship, University of Denver, 1963, 4th edition, Libraries Unlimited, 1967; *Ukrainian Industry*, Shevchenko Scientific Society (Paris), 1964; (with Earl Tannenbaum) *Introduction to Cataloging and Classification*, Colorado Bibliographic Institute, 1964, 5th edition (sole author after 2nd edition), Libraries Unlimited, 1972; (editor) *Ukrains'ka Promyslovist*, Paris, 1964—; *Historiography of Economic Writings on Ukraine* [Munich], 1967; *Library Acquisitions*, Libraries Unlimited, 1968, 2nd edition, 1971; *Research Methods in Library Science*, Libraries Unlimited, 1971; *Reference Books in Paperback*, Libraries Unlimited, 1972. Also author of *Ekonomichnyi Kolonializm v Ukraini*, 1958, and *Materaly do Istorii Ekonomichnykh Doslidiv na Emigratsii*, 1965.

Editor of economics section of *Encyclopedia of Ukraine* (English and Ukrainian editions), University of Toronto Press, 1955—, *American Reference Books Annual*, Libraries Unlimited, 1970—; editor, "Studies in Librarianship," Graduate School of Librarianship, University of Denver, 1963-66, "Research Studies in Library Science," Libraries Unlimited, 1970—, *Rozbudova Derzhavy* (Ukrainian quarterly), 1953-57.

WORK IN PROGRESS: Editing, with J. Shera and G. Bobinsky, *Dictionary of American Library Biography*, completion expected 1976; *Social and Economic History of Ukraine*, three volumes, completion expected 1976-78; *Ukraine: A Retrospective Bibliographic Guide.*

SIDELIGHTS: Wynar is proficient in Russian, Polish, German, Czech, Latin, and Greek.

* * *

WYNNE-TYSON, (Timothy) Jon (Lyden) 1924-
(Michel Fourest, Jeremy Pitt)

PERSONAL: Born July 6, 1924, in Brockhurst, Hampshire, England; son of L. C. (a wing commander) and Esme (an author) Wynne-Tyson; married Joan Georgiana Stan-

ton, 1950; married Jennifer Mary Tyson, 1956; children: (first marriage) Caroline; (second marriage) Susan. *Education:* Educated in British private and public schools, including Brighton, Sussex, England. *Home:* Paddocks, Fontwell, Sussex, England. *Office:* Centaur Press Ltd., Fontwell, Sussex, England.

CAREER: Hutchinson & Co. (Publishers) Ltd., London, England, advertising manager, 1947-48; Williams & Norgate Ltd., London, England, literary adviser, 1949-51; Centaur Press Ltd. (Centaur Press and Linden Press), Fontwell, England, owner and managing director, 1954—. Publishers' reader and writer for periodicals in earlier years. *Member:* National Book League, Itchenor Sailing Club, Petworth House Tennis Court.

WRITINGS: Accommodation Wanted: A Short Guide to the "Bed Sitter", Putnam, 1951; *The Civilised Alternative: A Pattern for Protest*, Centaur Press, 1972; *Food for a Future: The Ecological Priority of a Humane Diet*, Davis-Poynter, 1975. Contributor to *Time and Tide, Spectator, New Statesman, Lady, Apollo, Chambers's Journal, John Bull, Country Life, Poetry Quarterly, Observer, Times Literary Supplement, Truth, Sunday Times, Poetry Review*, and other publications.

Under pseudonym Michel Fourest: *Behind the Smiling Moon*, Centaur Press, 1959.

Under pseudonym Jeremy Pitt: *Square Peg*, Centaur Press, 1961; *Don't Look and You'll Find Her*, Centaur Press, 1967.

Also author of *Grin and Bear It*, published by Centaur Press, but not attributed to Wynne-Tyson.

* * *

YAKOBSON, Helen B(ates) 1913-
(Helen L. Z. Bates)

PERSONAL: Born May 21, 1913, in St. Petersburg (now Leningrad), Russia; came to United States, 1938; naturalized U.S. citizen, 1941; daughter of Alexander (an orthopedic surgeon) and Zinaida (Volkov) James: married Abraham Bates, March 21, 1937 (divorced, 1950); married Sergius Yakobson (chief of Slavic and East European Division, Library of Congress), September 23, 1951; children: (first marriage) Natalie; (second marriage) Dennis. *Education:* University of Harbin, B.S. (law), 1934. *Politics:* Democrat. *Religion:* Greek Orthodox. *Home:* 3518 Porter St. N.W., Washington, D.C. 20016. *Office:* Department of Slavic Languages and Literatures, George Washington University, Washington, D.C. 20006.

CAREER: Tientsin Russian School, Tientsin, China, teacher of Russian language and literature, 1936-38; private tutor and researcher, 1938-46; U.S. Department of State, Washington, D.C., scriptwriter and announcer for Russian programs, 1947-50; George Washington University, Washington, D.C., lecturer, 1951-53, assistant professor, 1953-60, associate professor, 1960-64, professor of Russian, 1964—, executive officer of department of Slavic languages and literatures, 1953-60, chairman of department of Slavic and Oriental languages and literatures, 1960-69. Guest speaker, University of Sydney, 1960, University of Melbourne, 1960, New South Wales Department of Education, 1960, School of International Service, American University, 1961. Adviser, Russian Studies Center for Secondary Schools at Choate School, 1962—. Consultant, McGraw-Hill Book Co., 1959.

MEMBER: American Association of Teachers of Slavic

and East European Languages (president, 1961-63; first historian, 1966—), American Association for Advancement of Slavic Studies, National Slavic Honor Society (president, 1969-70), Modern Language Association of America, National Education Association (director of department of foreign languages), American Association of University Professors, Southern Slavic Conference (member of board of directors), Dobro Slovo (American vice-president), Mortar Board (honorary). *Awards, honors:* National Foreign Language Achievement Award, from National Federation of Modern Language Teachers Association, 1965; professor of the year award, George Washington University, 1966.

WRITINGS: (Under name Helen L. Z. Bates, with Andre von Gronicka) *Essentials of Russian: Reading, Conversation, Grammar,* Prentice-Hall, 1948, 4th edition, 1964; *TV Study Guide for Beginning Russian,* Educational Services, 1959; (under name Helen L. Z. Bates) *Beginners Book in Russian,* Educational Services, 1959; *A Guide to Conversational Russian,* George Washington University Book Store, 1960; *New Russian Reader,* George Washington University Bookstore, 1960; *Conversational Russian: An Intermediate Course,* Heath, 1965; (editor) *Russian Readings Past and Present: An Intermediate Reader,* Appleton, 1967.

WORK IN PROGRESS: A two-part structural approach to Russian for Prentice-Hall.†

* * *

YALEM, Ronald J(oseph) 1926-

PERSONAL: Born September 22, 1926, in St. Louis, Mo.; son of Arthur J. and Grace (S'Renco) Yalem; married Helen Dooley, June 3, 1950; children: Gary. *Education:* Washington University, St. Louis, Mo., A.B., 1950; American University, M.A., 1953, Ph.D., 1956. *Politics:* Democrat. *Office:* Department of Political Science, University of Alabama, University, Ala. 35486.

CAREER: University of Florida, Gainesville, instructor in political science, 1956-57; Berea College, Berea, Ky., assistant professor of political science, 1957-58; College of William and Mary, Norfolk, Va., associate professor of political science, 1959-64; University of Southern California, Los Angeles, visiting associate professor of international relations, 1964-66; University of Alabama, University, associate professor of political science, 1966—. Visiting assistant professor, University of Missouri, Columbia, 1959. *Military service:* U.S. Army, 1945-46. *Member:* American Political Science Association, International Studies Association, Pi Sigma Alpha. *Awards, honors:* Ford Foundation faculty fellow, 1957.

WRITINGS: Regionalism and World Order, Public Affairs Press, 1965. Contributor to professional journals. Member of editorial committee, *Background* (journal of International Studies Association), 1962-66.

WORK IN PROGRESS: International relations and international organization.

* * *

YAMAGUCHI, J(ohn) Tohr 1932-

PERSONAL: Born October 22, 1932, in Tokyo, Japan; son of Takatoshi (an orchestra conductor) and Toshiko (a professor; maiden name, Sakai) Yamaguchi; married Marianne Illenberger (an illustrator), September 10, 1960; children: Esme Turid. *Education:* Columbia University, B.S., 1960; Princeton University, Certificate in Advanced Studies in

Demography (C.A.D.), 1963; graduate study at Australian National University. *Politics:* "None." *Religion:* "None." *Office:* Department of Demography, Institute of Advanced Studies, Canberra, Australia.

CAREER: United Nations, New York, N.Y., associate social officer, 1963-66. *Member:* Population Association of America, International Union for the Scientific Study of Population.

WRITINGS: The Golden Crane: A Japanese Folktale, Holt, 1963; *Two Crabs and the Moonlight,* Holt, 1965.

SIDELIGHTS: Yamaguchi is fluent in English, with some knowledge of Spanish and German.†

* * *

YARN, David H(omer), Jr. 1920-

PERSONAL: Born July 7, 1920, in Atlanta, Ga.; son of David Homer (a clothing merchant) and Bessie H. (Herring) Yarn; married Marilyn Stevenson, August 27, 1946; children: Karen Louise, Steffani Ann, Rebecca Lee, Teresa Elaine, Jennifer Sue, Joanna Ruth. *Education:* Attended Georgia School of Technology (now Georgia Institute of Technology), 1938-39, and University of Georgia, Atlanta, 1943-45; Brigham Young University, B.A., 1946; Columbia University, M.A., 1949, Ed.D., 1958. *Home:* 933 East 500th South, Orem, Utah 84057.

CAREER: Brigham Young University, Provo, Utah, assistant professor, 1950-58, associate professor, 1958-59, professor of philosophy, 1959—, chairman of department of theology and philosophy, 1951-57, director of undergraduate studies in religion, 1958-59, dean of College of Religious Instruction, 1959-62, acting director of Institute of Mormon Studies, 1962-63, president of Eighth Stake, 1967-73. Church of Jesus Christ of Latter-day Saints, former missionary and high councilor, member of Sunday School General Board and bishop of Orem (Utah) 23rd ward. Member of general board, Young Men's Mutual Improvement Association. *Member:* Utah Academy of Science, Arts and Letters, University Archeological Society, Phi Kappa Phi, Phi Delta Kappa. *Awards, honors:* Maeser Associates award for teaching excellence, 1966.

WRITINGS: Faith in a Day of Unbelief, Deseret, 1960; *The Four Gospels as One,* Harper, 1961; *The Gospel: God, Man, and Truth,* Deseret, 1965; (editor with Edwin J. Butterworth) *Ernest L. Wilkinson, Earnestly Yours,* Deseret, 1971; (contributor) Charles Tate, editor, *To the Glory of God,* Brigham Young University Press, 1972; *Young Reuben: The Early Life of J. Reuben Clark, Jr.,* Brigham Young University Press, 1973.

* * *

YELLIN, Carol Lynn (Gilmer) 1920-

PERSONAL: Born March 3, 1920, in Clinton, Okla.; daughter of Thomas Prather (an electrical engineer) and Eulala (Rogers) Gilmer; married Thomas Heggen, August 6, 1942 (divorced April, 1946); married David Yellin (a professor), August 27, 1950; children: (second marriage) Charles Franklin, Thomas Gilmer, Douglas Simon, Emily Anne. *Education:* Northwestern University, B.S. (with honors), 1941, M.S.J. (cum laude), 1942. *Politics:* Democrat. *Religion:* Unitarian Universalist. *Home and office:* 4241 Park Ave., Memphis, Tenn. 38117.

CAREER: Reader's Digest, Pleasantville, N.Y., editorial assistant, 1942-44; *Coronet,* New York, N.Y., associate editor, 1946-49; *Reader's Digest,* associate editor, 1949-64, part-time editor for Special Projects Unit, Condensed Books, 1966—; editorial director, Memphis Multimedia Archival Project, 1970-74. Free-lance editorial consultant and writer. American Red Cross staff assistant in Hawaii and Saipan, World War II. *Member:* League of Women Voters, Women in Communications.

WRITINGS: (With Thomas L. Maynard and Neil Sullivan) *Bound for Freedom*, Little, Brown, 1965. Contributor to *Harper's, Redbook, Vogue, Coronet, Ms.*, and other magazines.

WORK IN PROGRESS: A book concerning International Women's Year, 1975.

* * *

YOCOM, Charles Frederick 1914-

PERSONAL: Born October 21, 1914, in Logan, Iowa; son of Fred Edward (a farmer and explosives expert) and Ida (Overman) Yocom; married Iris Graham, August 27, 1939; children: Barbara June Simmons, Nancy Lyn Kamph, Cynthia Iris Dowling. *Education:* Iowa State College of Agriculture and Mechanic Arts (now Iowa State University), B.S., 1939; Washington State University, M.S., 1942, Ph.D., 1949. *Politics:* Republican. *Religion:* Protestant. *Home:* 1666 Charles Ave., Arcata, Calif. 95521. *Office:* Humboldt State University, Arcata, Calif. 95521.

CAREER: Washington State Game Department, game biologist and head of Pullman Research Laboratory, 1942-47; Washington State University, Pullman, 1947-53, began as instructor, became assistant professor of game management; Humboldt State University, Arcata, Calif., associate professor, 1953-57, professor of wildlife management, 1958—, chairman of Division of Natural Resources, 1956-60. Has been consultant on wildlife problems to U.S. Fish and Wildlife Service, National Park Service, and U.S. Navy Pacific Missile Range; naturalist, Crater Lake National Park, summers, 1951-52; worked to get bighorn sheep reestablished at Lava Beds National Monument, California, summer, 1966; worked on waterfowl in the Yukon Flats, Tetlon area, and Copper River Valley in Alaska, summer, 1972; studied feral goats in Haleakala National Park, Maui, Hawaii, summer, 1973. *Military service:* U.S. Naval Reserve, active duty, 1944-46, serving in Pacific theater; now lieutenant commander, Allied Science Section of Medical Service Corps. *Member:* American Ornithologist Union, Wildlife Society, Cooper Ornithological Society, Pacific Northwest Bird and Mammal Society, California Academy of Science, Smithsonian Associates, Sigma Xi, Phi Kappa Phi.

WRITINGS: Waterfowl and Their Food Plants in Washington, University of Washington Press, 1951; (with G. E. Hudson) *A Distributional List of the Birds of Southeastern Washington*, Washington State University Research Studies, 1954; (with R. Dasmann) *The Pacific Coastal Wildlife Region, Its Common Wild Animals and Plants*, Naturegraph, 1957, revised edition, 1965; (with Vinson Brown and Aldene Starbuck) *The Wildlife of the Intermountain West, Its Common Wild Animals and Plants*, Naturegraph, 1958; (with William Baker, Earl Larrison, and Iain Baxter) *Wildlife of the Northern Rocky Mountains, including Common Wild Animals and Plants*, Naturegraph, 1961; *Shrubs of Crater Lake National Park*, Crater Lake Natural History Association, 1964; (with William Weber, Richard Beidleman, and Donald Malick) *Wildlife of the Southern Rocky Mountains*, Naturegraph, 1966, revised edition published as *Wildlife and Plants of the Southern Rocky Mountains*,

1969; (with James Harper, Joseph Harn, and Wallace Bentley) *The Status and Ecology of the Roosevelt Elk in California*, Wildlife Monographs, 1967; (with Brown) *Wildlife and Plants of the Cascades*, edited by Florence Musgrave, Naturegraph, 1971.

(Illustrator) William Weber, *Rocky Mountain Flora*, 3rd edition (Yocom was not associated with earlier editions), University of Colorado Press, 1967, 4th edition, 1972. Author of monographs and reports on wildlife studies made in the western United States, Alaska, and Hawaii. Contributor of 125 articles, the majority on birds and mammals, to *Murrelet, Audubon, Condor, Auk, Journal of Wildlife Management, California Fish and Game*, and other wildlife journals.

WORK IN PROGRESS: A book, *Status, Habits and distribution of Birds of Northwestern California*, with S. W. Harris; two more wildlife region books, with co-authors, for Naturegraph; a monograph on Canada geese along the Snake River.

SIDELIGHTS: In 1968, Yocom travelled to New Zealand and Australia, and 19 other countries in Asia and Europe.

* * *

YOUNG, Dallas M. 1914-

PERSONAL: Born January 15, 1914, in Christopher, Ill.; son of Arvel E. (a coal miner) and Jennie (Jordan) Young; married. *Education:* Southern Illinois University, B.Ed., 1936; University of Illinois, A.M., 1937, Ph.D., 1941. *Politics:* Democrat. *Religion:* Baptist. *Home:* University Circle Place, Suite 905, Cleveland, Ohio 44106. *Office:* Department of Organizational Administration, Case Western Reserve University, Cleveland, Ohio 44106.

CAREER: Jefferson City Junior College, Jefferson City, Mo., acting head of social studies department, 1941-42; War Labor Board, Kansas City, Mo., associate labor economist, later senior labor economist, 1942-45; Wage Stabilization Board, Chicago, Ill., assistant director, 1945; Northwestern University, Evanston, Ill., visiting lecturer in economics, 1945-46; Grinnell College, Grinnell, Iowa, associate professor of economics, 1946-48; Case Western Reserve University, Cleveland, Ohio, associate professor of economics, 1948-67, professor of labor relations, 1967—. President, Dallas M. Young & Associates, Inc. (personnel and labor relations consultants), Cleveland. Visiting lecturer, Illinois Institute of Technology, 1946; vice-chairman, Ohio-Kentucky Wage Stabilization Board, 1951-53; impartial umpire of labor disputes, Cleveland Transit System, 1956-61; member, National Defense Executive Reserve of U.S. Department of Labor, 1968-74; chairman, Cleveland Transit Board, 1968-70; consultant to Massachusetts Department of Public Welfare, 1970-71. *Member:* American Economic Association, Industrial Relations Research Association, Adult Education Association, National Academy of Arbitrators, American Association of University Professors.

WRITINGS: Understanding Labor Problems, McGraw, 1959; *Twentieth Century Experience in Urban Transit: A Study of the Cleveland System* (monograph), Western Reserve University Press, 1960. Contributor to *Journal* of the Illinois State Historical Society, *Monthly Labor Review* and *Western Reserve University Law Review*.

* * *

YOUNGER, R(onald) M(ichel) 1917-

PERSONAL: Born November 18, 1917, in Melbourne,

Australia; son of William and Mabel (Coombs) Younger; married Vera Irene Colenso, March 21, 1942; children: Peter Michel. *Education:* Attended Trinity Grammar School, Melbourne, Australia, 1924-35. *Office:* 2 Rockingham St., Kew, Victoria, Australia.

CAREER: Australian Department of Information, journalist in Canberra, 1942-45, in Melbourne, 1945-50; Australian News and Information Bureau, New York, N.Y., director, 1951-55, special writer, 1957-60; Victoria Promotion Committee, Melbourne, Australia, director, 1956-57; Special writer for Australian Information Service, 1957-61; North American-Australian Tourist Commission, San Francisco, Calif., manager, 1961-70. *Encyclopedia Americana,* New York, N.Y., advisory editor and contributor, 1957—, contributor to yearbook, 1959—. Free-lance writer.

WRITINGS: The Changing World of Australia, F. Watts, 1963; *Australia and the Australians,* Rigby, 1966; *Australia and the Australians: A New Concise History,* Humanities, 1970; *All the Best in Hawaii,* Dodd, 1972. Contributor of feature stories to magazines and newspapers in United States and Australia.

WORK IN PROGRESS: Politics of Australia; development of land and air transportation in Australia; history of the South Pacific.

SIDELIGHTS: Younger told *CA:* "My work has taken me into every corner of Australia; it has also brought me to the United States where I have held official positions developing cultural and general links between Australia and the United States.... Have researched and written about many major national projects, from immigration to the great hydroelectric and water conservation undertakings; but I see these in terms of people as much as in terms of planning."†

*   *   *

YU, George T(zuchiao) 1931-

PERSONAL: Born May 16, 1931, in London, England; son of Wangteh (an educator) and Ying (Ho) Yu; married Priscilla Chang, August 11, 1957; children: Anthony, Phillip. *Education:* University of California, Berkeley, A.B., 1954, M.A., 1957, Ph.D., 1961. *Home:* 6 Shuman Cir., Urbana, Ill. 61801. *Office:* Department of Political Science, University of Illinois, Urbana, Ill.

CAREER: University of North Carolina, Chapel Hill, assistant professor of political science, 1961-65; University of Illinois, Urbana, associate professor, 1965-70, professor of political science, 1970—. Visiting senior lecturer, University College, Nairobi, Kenya, spring, 1968. *Member:* American Political Science Association, Association for Asian Studies.

WRITINGS: (With Robert A. Scalopino) *The Chinese Anarchist Movement,* Center for Chinese Studies, University of California, 1961; *Party Politics in Republican China,* University of California Press, 1966; *China and Tanzania,* Center for Chinese Studies, University of California, 1970; (contributor) J. A. Cohen, editor, *The Dynamics of China's Foreign Relations,* Harvard University Press, 1970; (contributor) George W. Keeton and George Schwarzenberger, editors, *The Year Book of World Affairs, 1970,* Stevens & Sons, 1970; *China's African Policy,* Praeger, 1974; (contributor) James C. Hsiung, editor, *The Logic of Maoism: Critiques and Explication,* Praeger, 1974. Contributor to *Asian Survey, Race.*

WORK IN PROGRESS: Chinese Communism.

ZAKON, Alan J. 1935-

PERSONAL: Born December 26, 1935, in Brookline, Mass.; son of Edward and Lillian (Rubenstein) Zakon; married Susan Zaff, June 23, 1959; children: David, Shari. *Education:* Harvard University, A.B., 1957; Massachusetts Institute of Technology, S.M., 1959; University of California, Los Angeles, Ph.D., 1964. *Politics:* Independent. *Religion:* Jewish. *Home:* 459 Old Connecticut Path, Wayland, Mass. *Office:* Boston University, 685 Commonwealth Ave., Boston, Mass.

CAREER: Boston University, College of Business Administration, Boston, Mass., associate professor of finance, 1962—.

WRITINGS: (Editor with Hsiu-Kwang Wu) *Elements of Investments: Selected Readings,* Holt, 1965, 2nd edition, 1972. Contributor to marketing and business journals.

WORK IN PROGRESS: Research in behavioral aspects of common stock prices.†

*   *   *

ZAKUTA, Leo 1925-

PERSONAL: Born August 27, 1925, in Montreal, Quebec, Canada; son of Harry and Katie (Ain) Zakuta; married Annette Segal (a potter), September 4, 1956; children: Jamie, Silvie. *Education:* McGill University, B.A., 1946, M.A., 1948; University of Chicago, graduate study, 1948-50, Ph.D., 1961. *Home:* 44 Elm Ave., Toronto, Ontario, Canada. *Office:* Department of Sociology, University of Toronto, Toronto, Ontario, Canada.

CAREER: University of Manitoba, Winnipeg, lecturer in sociology, 1951-52; University of Toronto, Toronto, Ontario, lecturer, 1952-58, assistant professor, 1958-64, associate professor, 1964-67, professor of sociology, 1968—. *Member:* Canadian Sociological and Anthropological Association.

WRITINGS: A Protest Movement Becalmed: A Study of Change in the CCF, University of Toronto Press, 1964.†

*   *   *

ZALAMEA, Luis 1921-

PERSONAL: Born March 15, 1921, in Bogota, Colombia; son of Benito (a banker) and Margarita (Borda) Zalamea; married Natalia Goenaga, November 8, 1965; children: (previous marriages) Fernando, Pilar, Jorge. *Education:* Dartmouth College, B.A., 1942. *Politics:* Conservative. *Religion:* Roman Catholic ("non-practising"). *Home:* Avenida Caracas 51-53, Bogota, Colombia, South America. *Agent:* McIntosh, McKee & Dodds, Inc., 22 East 40th St., New York, N.Y. 10016. *Office:* Empresa Colombiana de Turismo, Calle 19 #6-68, Bogota, Columbia, South America.

CAREER: United Press International, New York, N.Y., reporter, 1942-43; Selecciones del Reader's Digest, New York, N.Y., translator-writer, 1943-44; McGraw-Hill World News, correspondent in Bogota, Colombia, 1944-47; United Nations Secretariat, New York, N.Y., information officer, 1948-62; Colombian delegation to United Nations, New York, N.Y., minister plenipotentiary, 1963; Empresa Columbiana de Turismo, Bogota, Colombia, managing director, 1964—. Chairman of standing executive committee, Inter-American Travel Congresses; executive secretary, Common Fund for Travel Promotion (six South American countries). *Member:* Authors Guild (United

States), American Society of Travel Agents, South American Travel Organization (vice-president).

WRITINGS: Requiem Neoyorquino y otros poemas, Botella al Mar (Buenos Aires) 1957; *Colombia: La Presencia permanente,* Impresos Modernos, 1960; *Germinacion del alba,* Editorial Cultura, 1961; *The Hour of Giving,* Houghton, 1965. Contributor to magazines in United States and Latin America.

WORK IN PROGRESS: A collection of three novellas, *Shattered Paradise;* another novel, *The Ravished Land.*†

* * *

ZALD, Mayer N(athan)   1931-

PERSONAL: Born June 17, 1931, in Detroit, Mich.; son of Harold and Ann (Levitt) Zald; married Joan Kadri, June 15, 1958; children: Ann, David, Harold. *Education:* Attended Wayne State University, 1949-51; University of Michigan, B.A., 1953, Ph.D., 1960; University of Hawaii, M.A., 1955. *Home:* 4128 Wallace Lane, Nashville, Tenn. 37215. *Office:* Department of Sociology and Anthropology, Vanderbilt University, Nashville, Tenn. 37235.

CAREER: University of Chicago, Chicago, Ill., instructor in sociology and psychology, 1960-61, assistant professor, 1961-64; Vanderbilt University, Nashville, Tenn., associate professor, 1964-1968, professor of sociology, 1968—, chairman of department, 1971-75. *Military service:* U.S. Army, 1955-56. *Member:* American Sociological Association, Society for the Study of Social Problems, American Association of University Professors, American Civil Liberties Union. *Awards, honors:* Career Development Award grants, National Institute of Mental Health, 1967-72.

WRITINGS: (Editor) *Social Welfare Institutions: A Sociological Reader,* Wiley, 1965; (editor) *Organizing for Community Welfare,* Quadrangle, 1967; *Organizational Change: The Political Economy of the YMCA,* University of Chicago Press, 1970; (editor) *Power in Organizations,* Vanderbilt University Press, 1970. Contributor to professional journals. Member of board of editors, *American Journal of Sociology,* 1960-74, associate editor, 1962-63; member of board of editors, *Social Problems,* 1965-68, *Journal of Health and Human Behavior,* 1967-70; and *Social Forces,* 1974—.

WORK IN PROGRESS: Social control of institutions.

* * *

ZALTMAN, Gerald   1938-

PERSONAL: Born July 9, 1938, in Boston, Mass.; son of Simon (in real estate) and Charlotte (Reine) Zaltman; married Jean Moodie, July 11, 1968; children: Jeffrey, Lindsay. *Education:* Bates College, A.B., 1960; University of Chicago, M.B.A., 1962; Johns Hopkins University, Ph.D., 1968. *Office:* School of Business, University of Pittsburgh, Pittsburgh, Pa. 15213.

CAREER: University of Alaska, College, instructor in marketing, 1962-64; Northwestern University, Evanston, Ill., assistant professor, 1968-71, associate professor of behavioral science, 1971-73, A. Montgomery Ward Professor of Marketing, 1973-75, professor of education, 1974-75, director of research, Graduate School of Management, 1971-75; University of Pittsburgh, Pittsburgh, Pa., Albert Wesley Frey Professor of Marketing, 1975—. Universidad del Valle, Cali, Columbia, professor of industrial administration, 1974—. *Member:* American Marketing Association, American Academy of Political and Social Science,

American Psychological Association, American Public Health Association, American Sociological Association, Association for Consumer Research (member of board of directors).

WRITINGS: Marketing: Contributions from the Behavioral Sciences, Harcourt, 1965; (editor with Philip Kotler and Ira Kaufman) *Creating Social Change,* Holt, 1972; (with Robert Duncan and Johnny Holbek) *Innovations and Organizations,* Wiley, 1973; (with Christian R. A. Rinson and Reinhard Angelman) *Metatheory and Consumer Research,* Holt, 1973; (with others) *Processes and Phenomena of Social Change,* Wiley, 1973; (with R. Schultz and P. C. Burger) *Cases in Marketing Research,* Dryden, 1975; (with Burger) *Marketing Research: Fundamentals and Dynamics,* Dryden, 1975; (with S. Levy) *Marketing, Society, and Conflict,* Prentice-Hall, 1975; (with Duncan) *Strategies for Planned Change,* Wiley Interscience, 1976; (with D. Florio and L. Sikorski) *Creating Educational Change,* Free Press, 1976; *Introduction to Consumer Behavior,* Wiley, in press; *Theory Construction in Marketing,* Wiley, in press. Contributor to journals in his field. Member of editorial board, *Journal of Business Research,* and *Simulation and Games;* editorial consultant, *Decision Sciences.*

SIDELIGHTS: In 1973 Zaltman traveled to Korea, Indonesia, Bangladesh, and the Philippines as a consultant to the U.S. Agency for International Development. He has also visited Central America several times to conduct research on nutrition in preventive medicine programs.

* * *

ZEBOUNI, Selma A(ssir)   1930-

PERSONAL: Born October 26, 1930, in Beirut, Lebanon; daughter of Joseph and Najia (Erzeroumi) Assir; married Nadim H. Zebouni (a college professor), July 28, 1955; children: Maria, Mia. *Education:* Faculte Francaise de Droit, Beirut, Lebanon, B.A. in Law, 1952; Sorbonne, University of Paris, Licence es-Lettres, 1955; Louisiana State University, Ph.D., 1963. *Home:* 264 Stanford Ave., Baton Rouge, La. 70808. *Office:* Department of Foreign Languages, Louisiana State University, Baton Rouge, La.

CAREER: Louisiana State University, Baton Rouge, 1963—, began as assistant professor, currently associate professor of French and comparative literature. *Member:* Modern Language Association of America, South Central Modern Language Association.

WRITINGS: Dryden, a Study in Heroic Characterization, Louisiana State University Press, 1965.

WORK IN PROGRESS: Moliere: Search for Identity in the Seventeenth Century.

SIDELIGHTS: Selma Zebouni has a native knowledge of French, Turkish, and Arabic, and an acquired knowledge of English and Italian.

* * *

ZERBE, Jerome   1904-

PERSONAL: Born July 24, 1904, in Euclid, Ohio; son of Jerome Brainard (president of Ohio & Pennsylvania Coal Co.) and Susan (Eichelberger) Zerbe. *Education:* Yale University, Ph.B., 1928; studied portrait painting in Paris, France, 1928-31. *Home:* 14 Sutton Pl. South, New York, N.Y. 10022.

CAREER: Art editor of *Parade* (a weekly), Cleveland,

Ohio, 1931-33; moved on to New York and invented a job for himself—the society photographer specializing in the personal candid camera; *Town and Country*, New York, N.Y., photographer, 1933—, society editor, 1949-74; feature writer for *Sunday Mirror*, 1945-58. Publicist in his early days in New York for the Rainbow Room and later, for another fashionable haunt, El Morocco; host at the Brazillian Pavillion at the New York World's Fair, 1939, and the Italian Pavillion, 1940 (departed when Italy declared war on France but hosted a party at his apartment for all the waiters and their wives to show personal friendliness); sometime columnist for *New York Journal American*; currently weekly columnist for *San Francisco Chronicle* and, in season, for *Palm Beach Illustrated*, 1967—. *Military service:* U.S. Naval Reserve, chief photographer's mate, 1942-45; served on Admiral Nimitz' staff in Honolulu and Guam, on Vice Admiral McCain's staff in the China Sea and off the Philippines, and aboard the "U.S.S. Essex" during the first Tokyo strike and Iwo Jima landings; landed on Okinawa and Japan with Marine forces; received Bronze Star, and Presidential Unit and Navy Unit citations.

WRITINGS: People on Parade (photo book; introduction by Lucius Beebe), Kemp, 1934; *El Morocco's Family Album* (photo book; introduction by Beebe), privately printed, 1937; *Les Pavillons* (photo book; text by Cyril Connolly), Macmillan, 1962; *The Art of Social Climbing*, Doubleday, 1965; *Happy Times*, Harcourt, 1973. Photographs have appeared in other books and in national magazines.

WORK IN PROGRESS: Another pavillon book, *Pavillons of Europe.*

SIDELIGHTS: Zerbe's first pavillon book was the result, he says, of "a long time dream of my youth to do a book on those enchanting little maisons de plaisance in and around Paris"; *The Art of Social Climbing* was done "not with tongue in my cheek, but in someone else's, as it was fun." He has never married, is devoted to his nieces and nephews, and entertains considerably. During the war he trained in Washington, D.C. ("ghastly place"), and then was sent to San Francisco ("sheer heaven, without a cent"). One of his favorite photographs is a candid shot he did of General Wainwright shortly after the landings in Japan.

* * *

ZIDEK, Anthony 1936-
(Tony Zidek)

PERSONAL: Born March 27, 1936, in Minneapolis, Minn.; son of Anton (a drycleaner) and Emma (Peterson) Zidek. *Education:* Attended high school and art school in Minnesota. *Residence:* Mineapolis, Minn.

CAREER: Prior to 1954 worked as fry cook, stock boy, and laborer in Minneapolis, Minn.; U.S. Civil Service, Minneapolis, Minn., postal clerk, 1958-59, illustrator, 1960—. Cartoonist and writer. *Military service:* U.S. Navy, 1954-58.

WRITINGS: (Under name Tony Zidek) *Choi Oi! The Lighter Side of Vietnam* (cartoons), Tuttle, 1965.†

* * *

ZIEROLD, Norman (John) 1927-

PERSONAL: Surname is pronounced *Zee*-rold; born July 26, 1927, in South Amana, Iowa; son of Elmer Henry (a singer) and Linn Elizabeth (Bendorf) Zierold. *Education:*

Harvard University, B.A., 1949; University of Iowa, M.A., 1951; also studied at Universities of Paris and Bordeaux. *Politics:* Liberal Democrat. *Religion:* Amana Church Society. *Residence:* South Amana, Iowa. *Agent:* Sterling Lord Agency, 660 Madison Ave., New York, N.Y. 10021.

CAREER: Kiosk (magazine), Paris, France, advertising salesman, 1952-53; Fairchild Publications, Inc., New York, N.Y., promotion writer, 1956; Brearley School, New York, N.Y., teacher, 1956-57; Crowell-Collier Press, New York, N.Y., editor, 1956-57; *Theatre Arts* (magazine), New York, N.Y., advertising manager, 1957-59, circulation director, 1959-60, associate publisher and editor-in-chief, 1960-62; *Show* (magazine), New York, N.Y., circulation manager, 1962-63; *Bravo!* (music magazine), New York, N.Y., advertising manager, 1963-64; free-lance writer, 1964—. *Military service:* U.S. Navy, 1945-46. *Member:* Historical Society of Pennsylvania, New York Historical Society, Friends of Columbia Library, Harvard Club (New York).

WRITINGS: The Child Stars, Coward, 1965; *Little Charley Ross: America's First Kidnapping for Ransom,* Little, Brown, 1967; *Three Sisters in Black,* Little, Brown, 1968; *Garbo,* Stein & Day, 1969; *The Moguls,* Coward, 1969 (published in England as *The Hollywood Tycoons,* Hamish Hamilton, 1969); (with James Wellman) *Chart Your Own Way to Career Happiness,* De Vorss, 1971; (with Wellman) *Chart Your Way to Financial Abundance,* De Vorss, 1972; *The Skyscraper Doom,* Lenox Hill, 1972; *Sex Goddesses of the Silent Screen,* Regnery, 1973. Contributor of articles to *Reader's Digest, Good Housekeeping, American Mercury, Kiwanis Magazine,* and *Popular Mechanics.*†

* * *

ZIETLOW, E(dward) R. 1932-

PERSONAL: First syllable of surname rhymes with "feet"; born August 13, 1932, in Presho, S.D.; son of Alvin Carl (a rancher) and Edith (Hemenway) Zietlow. *Education:* Dakota Wesleyan University, B.A., 1954; Boston University, M.A., 1959; University of Washington, Seattle, Ph.D., 1967. *Office:* University of Victoria, Victoria, British Columbia, Canada.

CAREER: University of Victoria, Victoria, British Columbia, assistant professor of English, 1965—. *Military service:* U.S. Army, 1954-57.

WRITINGS: These Same Hills, Knopf, 1960; *Heart of the Country,* Simon & Schuster, in press.

* * *

ZIMBARDO, Rose (Abdelnour) 1932-

PERSONAL: Born May 29, 1932; daughter of Albert J. (a clerk) and Angela (Lombardi) Abdelnour; married Philip Zimbardo (a professor of psychology), July 13, 1957; married Martin Stevens (a dean of humanities); children: (first marriage) Adam. *Education:* Brooklyn College (now Brooklyn College of the City University of New York), A.B., 1956; Yale University, M.A., 1957, Ph.D., 1960. *Home:* 7 Conscience Cir., Setauket, N.Y. 11733. *Office:* State University of New York, Stony Brook, N.Y.

CAREER: City College of the City University of New York, New York, N.Y., assistant professor of English, beginning 1960; now associate professor at State University of New York, Stony Brook.

WRITINGS: Wycherley's Drama: A Link in the Development of English Satire, Yale University Press, 1965; (editor with Neil D. Isaacs) *Tolkien and the Critics: Essays on J.R.R. Tolkien's The Lord and the Rings,* University of Notre Dame Press, 1968; (editor) *Twentieth Century Interpretations of Major Barbara,* Prentice-Hall, 1970. Contributor of articles to journals, including *Modern Drama* and *Shakespeare Quarterly.*

WORK IN PROGRESS: A book, *Shakespeare and the Structure of Comedy.*†

* * *

ZINSSER, William K. 1922-

PERSONAL: Surname is pronounced *Zin*-zer; born October 7, 1922, in New York, N.Y.; son of William H. and Joyce (Knowlton) Zinsser; married Caroline Fraser, October 10, 1954; children: Amy, John William. *Education:* Deerfield Academy, graduate, 1940; Princeton University, A.B., 1944. *Politics:* Democrat. *Religion:* Presbyterian. *Home and office:* 80 High St., New Haven, Conn. 06571.

CAREER: New York Herald Tribune, New York, N.Y., feature writer, 1946-49, drama editor, 1949-54, film critic, 1955-58, editorial writer, 1958-59; full-time free-lance writer, 1959—; Yale University, New Haven, Conn., member of English faculty, 1970—, master of Branford College, 1973—. Entertainment critic on "Sunday," National Broadcasting Co. television program, 1963-64. Member of board of governors, Brooklyn Museum, 1965-72; member of board of directors, Municipal Art Society of New York, 1964-70. *Military service:* U.S. Army, 1943-45; served in North Africa and Italy; became sergeant. *Member:* Century Association, Coffee House (both New York).

WRITINGS: Any Old Place With You, Simon and Schuster, 1957; *Seen Any Good Movies Lately?,* Doubleday, 1958; *Search and Research,* New York Public Library, 1961; *The City Dwellers,* Harper, 1962; (author with Howard Lindsay, Harry Golden, Walt Kelly, and John Updike) *Five Boyhoods,* Doubleday, 1962; *Weekend Guests,* Harper, 1963; *The Haircurl Papers,* Harper, 1964; *Pop Goes America,* Harper, 1966; *The Paradise Bit* (novel), Little, Brown, 1967; *The Lunacy Boom,* Harper, 1970; *On Writing Well,* Harper, in press.

Columnist for *Look,* 1967, *Life,* 1968-72. Contributor to magazines.

* * *

ZUBIN, Joseph 1900-

PERSONAL: Born October 9, 1900, in Raseiniai, Lithuania; came to United States, 1909; naturalized U.S. citizen, 1929; son of Jacob M. and Hannah (Brody) Zubin; married Winifred Anderson, October 12, 1934; children: Jonathan Arthur, David Anderson, Winifred Anne. *Education:* Attended Baltimore City College, 1917; Johns Hopkins University, A.B., 1921; Columbia University, Ph.D., 1932. *Home:* 190 Highwood Ave., Leonia, N.J. 07605. *Office:* Biometrics Research, New York State Department of Mental Hygiene, 722 West 168th St., New York, N.Y. 10032.

CAREER: City College (now City College of the City University of New York), New York, N.Y., instructor in educational psychology, 1934-36; National Committee on Mental Hygiene, assistant psychologist on mental hospital survey committee, 1936-38; New York State Psychiatric Institute and Hospital, New York, N.Y., associate re-

search psychologist, 1938-56; Columbia University, New York, N.Y., instructor, 1939-47, assistant professor, 1947-50, adjunct professor, 1950-56, professor of psychology, 1956-69, professor emeritus and special lecturer in psychiatry, 1969—. Diplomate from American Board of Examiners in Psychology, 1950; New York State Department of Mental Hygiene, New York, N.Y., principal research scientist in biometrics, 1956-60, chief of psychiatric research in biometrics, 1960—. Visiting professor, University of Wisconsin, summer, 1948, University of California, Los Angeles, summer, 1951, University of Hawaii, summer, 1961. Adjunct professor, Queens College of the City University of New York, 1969—; professorial lecturer in research, New York School of Psychiatry, 1971—. Consultant to U.S. Veterans Administration and National Institute of Mental Health. *Military service:* U.S. Public Health Service, sanitarian with rank of lieutenant commander, War Shipping Administration, 1944-45.

MEMBER: American Psychological Association (fellow), American Psychopathological Association (president, 1951-52), American College of Neuropsychopharmacology (president, 1971-72), American Association on Mental Deficiency (fellow), Association for Research in Nervous and Mental Disease, American Genetic Society, New York Academy of Medicine, New York Academy of Science, Psychometric Society, American Statistical Association, Harvey Society, Sigma Xi. *Awards, honors:* Paul H. Hoch Award from American Psychopathological Association, 1968; M.D., University of Lund, 1972; Stanley R. Dean Award from American College of Psychiatrists, 1974.

WRITINGS: Some Effects of Incentives: A Study of Individual Differences in Rivalry, Teachers College, Columbia University, 1932, reprinted, AMS Press, 1972; *Choosing a Life Work,* Union of American Hebrew Congregations, 1937; (with J. Thompson) *Sorting Tests in Relation to Drug Therapy in Schizophrenia,* New York State Psychiatric Institute, 1941; (with T. S. Lewinson) *Handwriting Analysis: A Series of Scales for Evaluating the Dynamic Aspects of Handwriting,* King's Crown Press, 1942; (with others) *Recent Advances in Diagnostic Psychological Testing,* C. C Thomas, 1950; (with Leonard D. Eron and Florence Schumer) *Experimental Approaches to Projective Techniques,* Wiley, 1965; (author of foreword) J. E. Cooper, R. E. Kendell, and others, *Psychiatric Diagnosis in New York and London: A Comparative Study of Mental Hospital Admissions,* Oxford University Press, 1972; (author of introduction) S. Fisher and Alfred M. Freedman, editors, *Opiate Addiction: Origins and Treatment,* Halsted, 1973; (author of foreword) R. Canero, N. Fox, and L. Shapiro, editors, *Strategic Intervention in Schizophrenia: Current Developments in Treatment,* Behavioral Publications, *1974.*

Editor: *Trends of Mental Disease,* King's Crown Press, 1945; (and contributor) *Field Studies in the Mental Disorders,* Grune, 1961; (with George A. Jervis) *Psychopathology of Mental Development,* Grune, 1967; (with Howard F. Hunt) *Comparative Psychopathology: Animal and Human,* Grune, 1967; (with Fritz A. Freyhan) *Social Psychiatry,* Grune, 1968; (with Charles Shagass, and contributor) *Neurobiological Aspects of Psychopathology,* Grune, 1969; (with Alfred M. Freedman) *The Psychopathology of Adolescence,* Grune, 1970; (with Freyhan) *Disorders of Mood,* Johns Hopkins Press, 1972; (with John Money, and author of foreword) *Contemporary Sexual Behavior: Critical Issues in the 1970's,* Johns Hopkins Press, 1973; (with Mitchell Kietzman and S. Sutton, and contributor) *Experi-*

mental Approaches to Psychopathology, Academic Press, 1975.

Editor with Paul H. Hoch, and contributor; all published by Grune: *Relation of Psychological Tests to Psychiatry*, 1952; *Current Problems in Psychiatric Diagnosis*, 1953; *Depression*, 1954; *Current Approaches to Psychoanalysis*, 1960; *Psychopathology of Aging*, 1961; *Comparative Epidemiology in the Mental Disorders*, 1961; *The Future of Psychiatry*, 1962: *The Evaluation of Psychiatric Treatment*, 1964; *Psychopathology of Perception*, 1965; *Psychopathology of Schizophrenia*, 1966.

Editor with Hoch; all published by Grune: *Psychosexual Development in Health and Disease*, 1949: *Anxiety*, 1950; *Psychiatry and the Law*, 1955; *Psychopathology of Childhood*, 1955; *Experimental Psychopathology*, 1957; *Psychopathology of Communication*, 1958; *Problems of Addiction and Habituation*, 1958; *Current Approaches to Psychoanalysis*, 1960.

Contributor: B. Glueck, editor, *Current Therapies of Personality*, Grune, 1946; T. G. Andrews, editor, *Methods of Psychology*, Wiley, 1948; F. A. Mettler, editor, *Selective Partial Ablations of the Frontal Cortex*, Hoeber Medical Division, Harper, 1949.

F. A. Mettler, editor, *Psycho-surgical Problems*, Blakiston Co., 1952; Nolan Lewis and others, editors, *Studies in Topectomy*, Grune, 1956; R. A. Patton, editor, *Current Trends in the Description and Analysis of Behavior*, University of Pittsburgh Press, 1958; *Psychopharmacology: Problems in Evaluation*, National Academy of Science-National Research Council, 1959; B. Pasamanick, editor, *Epidemiology of Mental Disorder*, American Association for the Advancement of Science, 1959.

J. H. Nodine and J. H. Moyes, editors, *Psychosomatic Medicine: The First Hahnemann Symposium*, Lea & Febiger, 1962; B. Wigdor, editor, *Recent Advances in the Study of Behavior Change*, McGill University Press, 1963; J. E. Birron and A. T. Welford, editors, *Behavior, Aging and the Nervous System*, C. C Thomas, 1964; O. Klineberg and R. Christie, editors, *Perspectives in Social Psychology*, Holt, 1965; Leonard D. Eron, editor, *The Classification of Behavioral Disorders*, Aldine, 1966; M. Katz, J. O. Cole, and W. E. Barton, editors, *The Role and Methodology of Classification in Psychiatry and Psychopathology*, U.S. Department of Health, Education, and Welfare, 1968; L. M. Roberts, N. Greenfield, and M. Miller, editors, *Comprehensive Mental Health: The Challenge of Evaluation*, University of Wisconsin Press, 1968; S. B. Sells, editor, *The Definition and Measurement of Mental Health*, U.S. Department of Health, Education, and Welfare, 1968.

W. O. Evans and N. S. Kline, editors, *Psychotropic Drugs in the Year 2,000: Use by Normal Humans*, C. C Thomas, 1971; M. A. Friedman, H. I. Kaplan, and B. J. Sadock, editors, *Comprehensive Textbook of Psychiatry*, 2nd edition (Zubin was not associated with earlier editions), Williams & Wilkins, 1974; A. Beck, H. Resnik, and D. Lettieri, editors, *The Prediction of Suicide*, Charles Press, 1974; Gene Usdin, editor, *An Overview of the Psychotherapies*, Drunner, 1975.

Contributor to *Annual Review of Psychology*, 1975. Writer of U.S. Public Health Service and other reports. Associate editor of *Comprehensive Psychiatry*, 1963—, *Journal of General Psychology*, 1964—, *Journal of Psychology*, 1964—, *Journal of Abnormal Psychology*, 1964-70, 1973—, *Journal of the Society of Biological Psychiatry*, 1972—.

WORK IN PROGRESS: A contribution to a book, *Treatment of Schizophrenia: Progress and Prospects*, edited by L. J. West and D. E. Flynn, for Grune.

*   *   *

ZUCKER, Dolores Mae Bolton (Dee Hill, Devra Hill)

PERSONAL: Born in Berkeley, Calif.; daughter of James John (a government employee) and Giovanna (Muzio) Bolton; married Irwin Zucker (president, Irwin Zucker Publicity); children: Lori Brana, Judi Michele, Shari Lynne. *Education:* Attended University of California, Berkeley, San Francisco State College (now University), and University of California, Los Angeles. *Politics:* Liberal. *Religion:* Open. *Home and office:* 714 North Crescent Dr., Beverly Hills, Calif. 90210.

CAREER: Holloway House Publishing Co., Hollywood, Calif., assistant editor, 1964-65; free-lance writer. *Member:* World Wildlife Fund, Hollywood Women's Press Club (secretary, 1963-64), Clean Air Program (Los Angeles).

WRITINGS—Under pseudonym Dee Hill: *Three to Make Merry*, Paperback Library, 1964; *My Name Is Leona Gage: Will Somebody Please Help Me*, Holloway House, 1965; *You Better Believe It*, Paperback Library, 1967; *The Maneater*, Avon, 1973. Writer of column for *Teen Screen*, 1961-64, *The Newspaper*, 1970-72. Critic for Southern California Publishing newspapers, writing on numerous subjects, including plays, movies, and concerts.

WORK IN PROGRESS: A book, *Preparation for Modern Marriage*, in collaboration with Lee Gladden and Vivianne Cervantes, for Dickenson; another book, *Bisexuality: A Natural Life Style*, with Cervantes. A television show, "On the Double"; film scripts, "Strangelove," and "Flash," with Sylvia Schneble.

*   *   *

ZUCKER, Norman L(ivingston)   1933-

PERSONAL: Born August 1, 1933, in New York, N.Y.; son of George M. and Beatrice (Livingston) Zucker; married Naomi J. Flink, June 25, 1961; children: Sara, George. *Education:* Rutgers University, B.A., 1954, M.A., 1956, Ph.D., 1960. *Office:* Department of Political Science, University of Rhode Island, Kingston, R.I.

CAREER: Northeastern University, Boston, Mass., instructor, 1960-61, assistant professor of political science, 1962; Tufts University, Boston, Mass., assistant professor of government, 1962-66; University of Rhode Island, Kingston, associate professor, 1966-69, professor of political science, 1969—. Editorial consultant to publishers. *Awards, honors:* Grants from American Philosophical Society, Wurzweiller Foundation, and University of Rhode Island.

WRITINGS: George W. Norris: Gentle Knight of American Democracy, University of Illinois Press, 1966; *The American Party Process: Comments and Readings*, Dodd, 1968; *The Coming Crisis in Israel: Private Faith and Public Policy*, M.I.T. Press, 1973. Contributor to professional journals.

WORK IN PROGRESS: A book on American politics; articles on Israeli politics.